P9-CBM-328

The Bedford INTRODUCTION TO LITERATURE

The Bedford INTRODUCTION TO LITERATURE

Second Edition

MICHAEL MEYER
University of Connecticut

BEDFORD BOOKS OF ST. MARTIN'S PRESS
BOSTON

For Bedford Books
Publisher: Charles H. Christensen
Associate Publisher: Joan E. Feinberg
Managing Editor: Elizabeth M. Schaaf
Developmental Editor: Karen S. Henry
Production Editor: Mary Lou Wilshaw
Copyeditor: Susan M. S. Brown
Text Design: Sandra Rigney, The Book Department, Inc.
Cover Design: Hannus Design Associates
Cover Art: The Picnic, 1901, by Maurice Brazil Prendergast. Graphite and watercolor on paper, 15⅝ x 22⅛ inches. The Carnegie Museum of Art, Pittsburgh; Gift of Mr. and Mrs. James H. Beal.

Library of Congress Catalog Card Number: 88–63044

Manufactured in the United States of America
4 3 2 1
f e d

For information, write: St. Martin's Press, Inc.
175 Fifth Avenue, New York, NY 10010

Editorial Offices: Bedford Books of St. Martin's Press
29 Winchester Street, Boston, MA 02116

ISBN: 0–312–02849–0

Acknowledgments

FICTION

A. L. Bader. "Nothing Happens in Modern Short Stories" from "The Structure of the Modern Short Story," *College English* 7 (November 1945). Copyright © 1945 by the National Council of Teachers of English. Reprinted by permission of the publisher.

Toni Cade Bambara. "The Lesson" from *Gorilla, My Love* by Toni Cade Bambara. Copyright © 1972 by Toni Cade Bambara. Reprinted by permission of Random House, Inc.

Warren Beck. "Sentimentality in Formula Fiction" from "Art and Formula in the Short Story," *College English* 5 (November 1943). Copyright © 1943 by the National Council of Teachers of English. Reprinted by permission of the publisher.

Mody C. Boatright. "A Typical Western Plot Formula" from "The Formula in Cowboy Fiction and Drama," *Western Folklore* 28 (April 1969). Reprinted by permission of the California Folklore Society.

Elizabeth Bowen. "The Writer's Roving Eye" from *Afterthoughts: Pieces on Writing* by Elizabeth Bowen. Reprinted by permission of Virago Press Ltd.

Edgar Rice Burroughs. Excerpt from *Tarzan of the Apes* by Edgar Rice Burroughs. Copyright © 1912 by Frank A. Munsey Company, used by permission of Edgar Rice Burroughs, Inc.

Raymond Carver. "Boxes" from the book *Where I'm Calling From,* copyright © 1988 by Raymond Carver. Used by permission of the Atlantic Monthly Press.

John Cheever. "Reunion." Copyright © 1962 by John Cheever. Reprinted from *The Stories of John Cheever* by permission of Alfred A. Knopf. "On Morals in Fiction" from "Interview with John Cheever" by Annette Grant in *Writers at Work: The Paris Review Interviews,* Fifth Series, edited by George Plimpton. Copyright © 1981 by The Paris Review, Inc. Reprinted by permission of Viking Penguin Inc.

Anton Chekhov. "The Lady With The Pet Dog" from *The Portable Chekhov,* edited by Avrahm Yarmolinsky. Copyright 1947 by The Viking Press, Inc. Copyright © The Viking Press, Inc., 1968. Copyright © renewed Avrahm Yarmolinsky 1975. Reprinted by permission of Viking Penguin, Inc. "On Morality in Fiction" excerpt from the letter from Anton Chekhov to Aleksey S. Suvorin in *Letters on the Short Story, the Drama and Other Literary Topics* by Anton Chekhov, translated by Constance Garnett and reprinted by A. P. Watt Ltd. on behalf of the Executors of the Estate of Constance Garnett.

Colette. "The Hand" from *The Collected Stories of Colette.* Translation copyright © 1957, 1966, 1983 by Farrar, Straus and Giroux, Inc. Reprinted by permission of Farrar, Straus and Giroux, Inc.

Frederick C. Crews. "A Psychological Reading of 'Young Goodman Brown' " from *The Sins of the Fathers: Hawthorne's Psychological Themes* by Frederick C. Crews. Copyright © 1966 by Frederick C. Crews. Reprinted by permission of Oxford University Press.

E. L. Doctorow. "The Importance of Fiction" from "Ultimate Discourse." Originally appeared in *Esquire* Magazine, August 1986. Reprinted by permission of the author.

Ralph Ellison. Chapter 1, "Battle Royal," copyright 1948 by Ralph Ellison. Reprinted from *Invisible Man* by Ralph Ellison, by permission of Random House, Inc.

Acknowledgments and copyrights are continued at the back of the book on pages 1859–1865, which constitute an extension of the copyright page.

Preface for Instructors

Like its predecessor, the second edition of *The Bedford Introduction to Literature* reflects the assumptions that understanding enhances the enjoyment of literature and that reading literature offers a valuable and unique means of apprehending life in its richness and diversity. The book also reflects the hope that the selections included will encourage students to become lifelong readers of imaginative literature. Designed to accommodate a variety of teaching styles, the collection of forty-five stories (seventeen of them new to the second edition), 390 poems (ninety of them new), and seventeen plays (six of them new) represents a wide range of periods, nationalities, and voices. Each selection has been carefully chosen for its appeal to students today and for its usefulness in demonstrating the effects, significance, and pleasures of literature.

Again, like its predecessor, the second edition of *The Bedford Introduction to Literature* is designed for the introductory course as it is taught today, which varies — from school to school and from instructor to instructor — more than ever before. Even the traditional course emphasizing the elements of literature and a broad range of works from the Western canon is changing in response to important developments in literary studies and, more generally, in higher education and in American society. The course is now viewed by many teachers as a rich opportunity to supplement classics of Western literature with the work of writers previously excluded from the traditional canon. Increasingly, it now also serves as an introduction to the discipline of literary study, a challenging development which brings to the undergraduate classroom important trends in literary theory and provocative new readings of both familiar and unfamiliar texts. Finally, and perhaps most often, the introduction to literature course is now also taught as a second course in composition in which the writing that students do is as important as the reading that they do. The second edition of *The Bedford Introduction to Literature* responds to these developments with distinctive features that address the needs of instructors who teach a traditional course but who are also interested in canonical issues, literary theory, and writing about literature.

Selected Major Authors Treated in Depth

The book includes for each genre a chapter focusing on two major figures. There are four stories each by Nathaniel Hawthorne and Flannery O'Connor, more than a dozen poems each by John Keats and Robert Frost, and two plays each by Sophocles and Shakespeare. Extensive introductions provide useful biographical and critical information about each of these important writers. In addition, a selection of "Perspectives" — excerpts from letters, journals, and critical commentaries — follows each writer's works to provide a context for discussion and writing.

Albums of Contemporary and World Literature

For each genre an album of contemporary selections offers some of the most interesting and lively stories, poems, and plays published in the last ten years, including works by Raymond Carver, Louise Erdrich, Fay Weldon, Amy Clampitt, Galway Kinnell, Sharon Olds, Caryl Churchill, August Wilson, and David Henry Hwang.

In addition, new albums of world literature in each genre section offer students a sampling of stories, poems, and plays from other cultures, including the work of Yukio Mishima (Japan), Anna Akhmatova (USSR), Claribel Alegria (Nicaragua), Li Ho (China), Federico García Lorca (Spain), Muhammad al-Maghut (Syria), and Wole Soyinka (Nigeria), among many others. Over half the stories, nearly a third of the poems, and a third of the plays in this edition are by women and minority writers and writers from other cultures.

In the second edition, "Connections" questions have been added to link the selections in the albums of contemporary and world literature to more traditional selections in the text. These questions provide engaging writing opportunities and provocative topics for class discussion. "Connections" questions also appear after a number of works in the chapters on the elements of fiction, poetry, and drama.

"Perspectives"

This popular feature of the first edition has been expanded in ways that make the second edition's "Perspectives" — journal notes, letters, classic and contemporary theoretical essays, interviews, and student responses — even more useful for class discussion and student writing. "Perspectives" are now included in four different places in the text: in the chapters treating major authors in depth; in a chapter-length collection at the end of each genre section; at the end of a new chapter on literary theory; and, finally, throughout the text's discussion chapters. Individual "Perspectives" in these chapters now follow the works to which they refer and, in many cases, discuss a literary work in terms of the element of literature for which it serves as an illustration.

Writing about Literature

The book's concern with helping students write about literature is pervasive. The chapters treating major figures in depth, the albums of contemporary and world literature, the "Connections" questions, and the "Perspectives" all offer intriguing writing opportunities. To provoke students' interest, sharpen their thinking, and help them improve their writing skills, the number and variety of writing assignments have been increased throughout the second edition. "Considerations" (questions and suggestions useful for class discussion or writing assignments) accompany virtually every selection in the discussion chapters and all the "Perspectives." In addition to the assignments, the expanded final section of the book offers a practical discussion of writing about literature, including advice about how to read a work closely, take notes, develop a topic into a thesis, and then revise and edit a paper into a final draft. Student examples illustrate the process and offer concrete models of the different types of papers usually assigned in an introductory course, including explication, analysis, and comparison-contrast. A detailed chapter on the literary research paper, with a student example, concludes the section.

Focus on Active and Critical Reading

To further encourage responsive reading and writing, new discussions of how to read imaginative literature have been added at the beginning of each genre section. They offer practical advice about the kinds of questions active readers ask themselves as they read. In addition, a new chapter, "Critical Strategies for Reading," deepens the introductory discussions of active reading by focusing on the different reading strategies employed by contemporary literary theorists. This chapter, which can be assigned at any point in the course, introduces students to eight major contemporary theoretical approaches — formalist, biographical, psychological, historical, sociological (including Marxist and feminist strategies), mythological, reader-response, and deconstructionist. In brief examples the approaches are applied in analyzing Kate Chopin's "The Story of an Hour," as well as other works, so that students will have a sense of how to use these strategies in their own read ing and writing. A selected bibliography for the approaches and a set of "Perspectives" by contemporary literary critics conclude this unique chapter.

Although the emphasis in this text is on critical reading and understanding rather than on critical terminology, terms such as *symbol, irony,* and *metaphor* are defined and illustrated to equip students with a basic working vocabulary for discussing and writing about literature. When first defined in the text, these terms appear in boldface type. An Index of Terms appears inside the back cover of the book for easy reference.

Connections between "Popular" and "Literary" Culture

As in the first edition, *The Bedford Introduction to Literature,* Second Edition, features introductions to each genre section that draw on carefully chosen examples from popular culture to explain the elements of the genre, inviting students to make connections between what they already know and what they will encounter in subsequent selections. The examples include excerpts from a romance novel and from *Tarzan of the Apes,* greeting card verse, and, new to the second edition, Tracy Chapman's "Fast Car" and scenes from the television drama *Cagney and Lacey.*

Resources for Teaching *The Bedford Introduction to Literature,* Second Edition

This thorough and practical instructor's manual discusses virtually every selection and suggests answers to the questions posed in the text, along with providing additional questions and writing assignments. The manual also offers questions and writing assignments for the selections in the collection chapter at the end of each genre section. It includes biographical information for authors whose backgrounds are not discussed in the text and offers selected bibliographies for authors treated in depth, as well as a bibliography of articles on teaching literature. Finally, the manual provides an annotated list of videos, films, and recordings related to the works of literature in the text.

Acknowledgments

For the first edition I benefited from the ideas, suggestions, and corrections of many careful readers who helped transform various stages of an evolving manuscript into a finished book. I am grateful to William Carroll, Boston University; Robert Connors, University of New Hampshire; Julia Epstein, Haverford College; Michael Holzman, University of Southern California; Joseph Kruppa, University of Texas, Austin; Donald McQuade, University of California, Berkeley; Shirley Morahan, Northeast Missouri State University; Anita Moss, University of North Carolina, Charlotte; Terry Myers, College of William and Mary; Edward Quinn, City College, CUNY; David Richter, Queens College; Mike Rose, University of California, Los Angeles; Richard Schotter, Queens College; Robert Wallace, Case Western Reserve University; Anne Williams, University of Georgia; and G. Jennifer Wilson, University of California, Los Angeles.

Many instructors who used the first edition of *The Bedford Introduction to Literature* responded to a questionnaire on the book. For their valuable comments and advice I am grateful to Katharyn Machan Aal, Ithaca College; Margaret L. Allison, Mesa Community College; Paul Benson, Mountain View College; Richard Benston, Bakersfield College; Jane Bradley, Virginia Polytechnic Institute and State University; Susan Breckenridge, Thiel College; Robin Calitri, Merced College; Ruth A. Cameron, Eastern Nazarene College; Steven R. Centola, Millersville University; Wendy Clein, University of Connecticut; Dianne Comiskey, University of Rhode Island; Emeric B. Deluca, Harrisburg Area Community College; George F. Edmonds, Catonsville Community College; Suzanne Edwards, The Citadel; David Elliott, Keystone

Junior College; Barbara L. Farley, Rutgers University; Roslyn R. Foy, University of Connecticut and Eastern Connecticut University; Rita K. Gollin, State University of New York, Geneseo; Drewey Wayne Gunn, Texas A & I University; Carolyn G. Hartnett, College of the Mainland; Keith Higginbotham, University of South Carolina; Carolyn Jewett, American River College; Carolyn T. Johnson, Montgomery County Community College; William Donald Jordan, Wright College; Patricia Cullen Ketchum, Butler County Community College; Karen A. Kildahl, South Dakota State University; G. T. Lenard, Stockton State College; John Lucarelli, Carlow College; Bruce J. Mann, Oakland University; John J. McKenna, University of Nebraska; Pamela A. Marks, University of Rhode Island; Ken Miller, American River College; Lee Nicholson, Modesto Junior College; Anna Paveglio, Merced College; Joseph Popson, Macon College; Charlotte Ravaioli, Keystone Junior College; Kathleen Reuter, Wake Forest University; Walter Gary Rice, Dundalk Community College; Jeremy Richard, University of Connecticut; Richard Robinson, Jr., Erie Community College; Susan Scheller, Sacramento City College; John D. Smith, University of the Pacific; Robert I. Strozier, Armstrong State College; Debra Sutton, St. Louis University; Gordon Taylor, Yuba College; Vivian Thomlinson, Cameron University; Sharon Thompson, Wilmington College; Dean Ward, Calvin College; Linda Wendler, Northwestern College; and Carolyn A. Wood, Santa Fe Community College.

I am also indebted to those who cheerfully answered questions and generously provided miscellaneous bits of information. What might have seemed to them like inconsequential conversations turned out to be important leads. Among these friends and colleagues are Raymond Anselment, Regina Barreca, Ann Charters, Irving Cummings, William Curtin, Herbert Goldstone, Lee Jacobus, Greta Little, William Moynihan, Joel Myerson, J. D. O'Hara, William Sheidley, Milton Stern, and Kenneth Wilson.

I am especially grateful for what I have learned from my students as I have taught them. I am also indebted to Ellen Darion, Christine Francis, Constance Mayer, J. Michael O'Neill, Anne Phillips, John Repp, and Dawn Skorczewski for their work on the instructor's manual.

At Bedford Books, my debts once again require more time to acknowledge than the deadline allows. Charles H. Christensen and Joan Feinberg initiated this project and launched it with their intelligence, energy, and sound advice. Karen Henry tirelessly steered both editions through rough as well as becalmed moments; her work was as first-rate as it was essential. The difficult tasks of production were skillfully managed by Mary Lou Wilshaw and Elizabeth Schaaf. I also thank Linda Belamarich and Lori Chong for their assistance with these tasks. Susan M. S. Brown provided careful copyediting, Noel Gilmore did meticulous proofreading, and Virginia Creeden deftly arranged the permissions. And all the people at Bedford Books — including Michael Eads, Jennifer Gordon, Ellen Kuhl, and Terri Walton — were more patient than I deserved.

Brief Contents

Contents

22. A Collection of Poems 742

31. Perspectives on Drama 1756

32. Critical Strategies for Reading 1777

WRITING ABOUT LITERATURE 1809

33. Reading and Writing 1811

INTRODUCTION

Reading Imaginative Literature

THE NATURE OF LITERATURE

Literature does not lend itself to a single tidy definition, because the making of it over the centuries has been as complex, unwieldy, and natural as life itself. Is literature everything that is written, from ancient prayers to graffiti? Does it include songs and stories that were not written down until many years after they were recited? Does literature include the television scripts from *The Cosby Show* as well as Shakespeare's *King Lear?* Is literature only that which has permanent value and continues to move people? Must literature be true or beautiful or moral? Should it be socially useful?

Although these kinds of questions are not conclusively answered in this book, they are implicitly raised by the stories, poems, and plays included here. No definition of literature, particularly a brief one, is likely to satisfy everyone, because definitions tend to weaken and require qualification when confronted by the uniqueness of individual works. In this context it is worth recalling Herman Melville's humorous use of a definition of a whale in *Moby-Dick*. In the course of the novel Melville presents his imaginative and symbolic whale as inscrutable, but he begins with a quotation from Georges Cuvier, a French naturalist who defines a whale in his nineteenth-century study *The Animal Kingdom* this way: "The whale is a mammiferous animal without hind feet." Cuvier's description is technically correct, of course, but there is little wisdom in it. Melville understood that the reality of the whale (which he describes as the "ungraspable phantom of life") cannot be caught by isolated facts. If the full meaning of the whale is to be understood, it must be sought on the open sea of experience, where the whale itself is, rather than in exclusionary definitions. Facts and definitions are helpful; however, they do not always reveal the whole truth.

Despite Melville's reminder that a definition can be too limiting and even comical, it is useful for our purposes to describe literature as a fiction consisting of carefully arranged words designed to stir the imagination. Stories, poems, and plays are fictional. They are made up — imagined — even when based upon actual historic events. Such imaginative writing differs from other kinds of writing because its purpose is not primarily to transmit facts or ideas. Imaginative literature is a source more of pleasure than of information, and we read it for basically the same reasons we listen to music or view a dance: enjoyment, delight, and satisfaction. Like other art forms, imaginative literature offers pleasure and usually attempts to convey a perspective, mood, feeling, or experience. Writers transform the facts the world provides — people, places, and objects — into experiences that suggest meanings.

Consider, for example, the difference between the following factual description of a snake and a poem on the same subject. Here is *Webster's Ninth New Collegiate Dictionary* definition:

> any of numerous limbless scaled reptiles (suborder Serpentes or Ophidia) with a long tapering body and with salivary glands often modified to produce venom which is injected through grooved or tubular fangs.

Contrast this matter-of-fact definition with Emily Dickinson's poetic evocation of a snake in "A narrow Fellow in the Grass":

A narrow Fellow in the Grass
Occasionally rides —
You may have met Him — did you not
His notice sudden is —

The Grass divides as with a Comb —
A spotted shaft is seen —
And then it closes at your feet
And opens further on —

He likes a Boggy Acre
A floor too cool for Corn —
Yet when a Boy, and Barefoot —
I more than once at Noon
Have passed, I thought, a Whip lash
Unbraiding in the Sun
When stooping to secure it
It wrinkled, and was gone —

Several of Nature's People
I know, and they know me —
I feel for them a transport
Of cordiality —

But never met this Fellow
Attended, or alone
Without a tighter breathing
And Zero at the Bone —

The dictionary provides a succinct, anatomical description of what a snake is, while Dickinson's poem suggests what a snake can mean. The definition offers facts; the poem offers an experience. The dictionary would probably allow someone who had never seen a snake to sketch one with reasonable accuracy. The poem also provides some vivid subjective descriptions — for example, the snake dividing the grass "as with a Comb" — yet it offers more than a picture of serpentine movements. The poem conveys the ambivalence many people have about snakes — the kind of feeling, for example, so evident on the faces of visitors viewing the snakes at a zoo. In the poem there is both a fascination with and a horror of what might be called snakehood; this combination of feelings has been coiled in most of us since Adam and Eve.

That "narrow Fellow" so cordially introduced by way of a riddle (the word *snake* is never used in the poem) is, by the final stanza, revealed as a snake in the grass. In between, Dickinson uses language expressively to convey her meaning. For instance, in the line "His notice sudden is," listen to the *s*-sound in each word and note how the verb *is* unexpectedly appears at the end, making the snake's hissing presence all the more "sudden." And anyone who has ever been surprised by a snake knows the "tighter breathing/And Zero at the Bone" that Dickinson evokes so successfully by the rhythm of her word choices and line breaks. Perhaps even more significant, Dickinson's poem allows those who have never encountered a snake to imagine such an experience.

A good deal more could be said about the numbing fear that undercuts the affection for nature at the beginning of this poem, but the point here is that imaginative literature gives us not so much the full, factual proportions of the world as some of its experiences and meanings. Instead of defining the world, literature encourages us to try it out in our imaginations.

THE VALUE OF LITERATURE

Mark Twain once shrewdly observed that a person who chooses not to read has no advantage over a person who is unable to read. In industrialized societies today, however, the question is not who reads, because nearly everyone can and does, but what is read. Why should anyone spend precious time with literature when there is so much reading material available that provides useful information about everything from the daily news to personal computers? Why should a literary artist's imagination compete for attention that could be spent on the firm realities that constitute everyday life? In fact, national best-seller lists much less often include collections of stories, poems, or plays than they do cookbooks and, not surprisingly, diet books. Although such fare may be filling, it doesn't stay with you. Most people have other appetites too.

Certainly one of the most important values of literature is that it nourishes our emotional lives. An effective literary work may seem to speak directly to us, especially if we are ripe for it. The inner life that good writers reveal in their characters often gives us glimpses of some portion of ourselves. We can be moved to laugh, cry, tremble, dream, ponder, shriek, or rage with a character by simply turning a page instead of turning our lives upside down. Although the experience itself is imagined, the emotion is real. That's why the final chapters of a good adventure novel can make a reader's heart race as much as a 100-yard dash or why the repressed love of Hester Prynne in *The Scarlet Letter* by Nathaniel Hawthorne is painful to a sympathetic reader. Human emotions speak a universal language regardless of when or where a work was written.

In addition to appealing to our emotions, literature broadens our perspectives on the world. Most of the people we meet are pretty much like ourselves, and what we can see of the world even in a lifetime is astonishingly limited. Literature allows us to move beyond the inevitable boundaries of our own lives and culture because it introduces us to people different from ourselves, places remote from our neighborhoods, and times other than our own. Reading makes us more aware of life's possibilities as well as its subtleties and ambiguities. Put simply, people who read literature experience more life and have a keener sense of a common human identity than those who do not. It is true, of course, that many people go through life without reading imaginative literature, but that is a loss rather than a gain. They may find themselves troubled by the same kinds of questions that reveal Daisy Buchanan's restless, vague discontentment in F. Scott Fitzgerald's *The Great Gatsby:* "What'll we do with ourselves this afternoon?" cried Daisy, "and the day after that, and the next thirty years?"

Sometimes students mistakenly associate literature more with school than with life. Accustomed to reading it in order to write a paper or pass an examination, students may perceive such reading as a chore instead of a pleasurable opportunity, something considerably less important than studying for the "practical" courses that prepare them for a career. The study of literature, however, is also practical, because it engages you in the kinds of problem solving important in a variety of fields, from philosophy to science and technology. The interpretation of literary texts requires you to deal with uncertainties, value judgments, and emotions; these are unavoidable aspects of life.

People who make the most significant contributions to their professions — whether in business, engineering, teaching, or some other area — tend to be challenged rather than threatened by multiple possibilities. Instead of retreating to the way things have always been done, they bring freshness and creativity to their work. F. Scott Fitzgerald once astutely described the "test of a first-rate intelligence" as "the ability to hold two opposed ideas in the mind at the same time, and still retain the ability to function." People with such intelligence know how to read situations, shape questions, interpret details, and evaluate competing points of view. Equipped with a healthy respect for facts, they also understand the value of pursuing hunches and exercising their imaginations. Reading literature encourages a suppleness of mind that is helpful in any discipline or work.

Once the requirements for your degree are completed, what ultimately matters are not the courses listed on your transcript but the sensibilities and habits of mind that you bring to your work, friends, family, and, indeed, the rest of your life. A healthy economy changes and grows with the times; people do too if they are prepared for more than simply filling a job description. The range and variety of life that literature affords can help you to interpret your own experiences and the world in which you live.

To discover the insights that literature reveals requires careful reading and sensitivity. One of the purposes of a college introduction to literature is to cultivate the analytic skills necessary for reading well. Class discussions often help establish a dialogue with a work that perhaps otherwise would not speak to you. Analytic skills can also be developed by writing about what you read. Writing is an effective means of clarifying your responses and ideas, because it requires you to account for the author's use of language as well as your own. This book is based on two premises: that reading literature is pleasurable, and that the more sensitively a work is read and understood by thinking, talking, or writing about it the more pleasurable the experience of it is.

Understanding its basic elements — such as point of view, symbol, theme, tone, irony, and so on — is a prerequisite to an informed appreciation of literature. This kind of understanding allows you to perceive more in a literary work in much the same way that a spectator at a tennis match sees more if he or she understands the rules and conventions of the game. But literature is not simply a spectator sport. The analytic skills that open up literature also have their uses when you watch a television program or film, and, more important, when you attempt to sort out the significance of the people, places, and events that constitute your own life. Literature enhances and sharpens your perceptions. What could be more lastingly practical as well as satisfying?

FICTION

1. Reading Fiction

READING FICTION RESPONSIVELY

Reading a literary work responsively can be an intensely demanding activity. Henry David Thoreau — about as intense and demanding a reader and writer as they come — insists that "books must be read as deliberately and reservedly as they were written." Thoreau is right about the necessity for a conscious, sustained involvement with a literary work. Imaginative literature does demand more from us than, say, browsing through *People* magazine in a dentist's waiting room, but Thoreau makes the process sound a little more daunting than it really is. For when we respond to the demands of responsive reading, our efforts are usually rewarded with pleasure as well as understanding. Careful, deliberate reading — the kind that engages a reader's imagination as it calls forth the writer's — is a means of exploration that can take a reader outside whatever circumstance or experience previously defined his or her world. Just as we respond moment by moment to people and situations in our lives, we also respond to literary works as we read them, though we may not be fully aware of how we are affected at each point along the way. The more conscious we are of how and why we respond to works in particular ways, the more likely we are to be imaginatively engaged in our reading.

In a very real sense both the reader and the author create the literary work. How a reader responds to a story, poem, or play will help to determine its meaning. The author arranges the various elements that constitute his or her craft — elements you will be examining in subsequent chapters on plot, character, setting, point of view, symbolism, and so on — but the author cannot completely control the reader's response any more than a person can absolutely predict how a remark or action will be received by a stranger, friend, or even family member. Few authors *tell* readers how to respond. Our sympathy, anger, confusion, laughter, sadness, or whatever the feeling might be is left up to us to experience. Writers may have the talent to evoke such feelings, but they don't have the power and authority to enforce them. Because of the range of possible responses produced by imaginative literature, there is no single, correct, definitive response or interpretation. There can be readings that are wrongheaded or foolish, and some readings are better than others — that is, more responsive to a work's details and more persuasive — but that doesn't mean there is only one possible reading of a work (see p. 362 for Questions for Responsive Reading).

Experience tells us that different people respond differently to the same work. Consider, for example, how often you've heard Melville's *Moby-Dick* described as one of the greatest American novels. This, however, is how a reviewer in *New Monthly Magazine* described the book when it was published in 1851: it is "a huge dose of hyperbolical slang, maudlin sentimentalism and tragic-comic bubble and squeak." Melville surely did not intend or desire this response; but there it is, and neither was it a singular, isolated reaction. This reading — like any reading — was influenced by the values, assumptions, and expectations that the readers brought to the novel from both previous readings and life experiences. The reviewer's refusal to take the book seriously may have missed the boat from the perspective of many other readers of *Moby-Dick,* but it indicates that even "classics" (perhaps especially those kinds of works) can generate disparate readings.

Consider the following brief story by Kate Chopin, a writer whose fiction (like Melville's) sometimes met with indifference or hostility in her own time. As you read, keep track of your responses to the central character, Mrs. Mallard. Write down your feelings about her in a substantial paragraph when you finish the story. Think, for example, about how you respond to the emotions she expresses concerning news of her husband's death. What do you think of her feelings about marriage? Do you think you would react the way she does under similar circumstances?

KATE CHOPIN (1851–1904)

The Story of an Hour

1894

Knowing that Mrs. Mallard was afflicted with a heart trouble, great care was taken to break to her as gently as possible the news of her husband's death.

It was her sister Josephine who told her, in broken sentences; veiled hints that revealed in half concealing. Her husband's friend Richards was there, too, near her. It was he who had been in the newspaper office when intelligence of the railroad disaster was received, with Brently Mallard's name leading the list of "killed." He had only taken the time to assure himself of its truth by a second telegram, and had hastened to forestall any less careful, less tender friend in bearing the sad message.

She did not hear the story as many women have heard the same, with a paralyzed inability to accept its significance. She wept at once, with sudden, wild abandonment, in her sister's arms. When the storm of grief had spent itself she went away to her room alone. She would have no one follow her.

There stood, facing the open window, a comfortable, roomy armchair. Into this she sank, pressed down by a physical exhaustion that haunted her body and seemed to reach into her soul.

She could see in the open square before her house the tops of trees that 5
were all aquiver with the new spring life. The delicious breath of rain was in the air. In the street below a peddler was crying his wares. The notes of a distant song which some one was singing reached her faintly, and countless sparrows were twittering in the eaves.

There were patches of blue sky showing here and there through the clouds that had met and piled one above the other in the west facing her window.

She sat with her head thrown back upon the cushion of the chair, quite motionless, except when a sob came up into her throat and shook her, as a child who has cried itself to sleep continues to sob in its dreams.

She was young, with a fair, calm face, whose lines bespoke repression and even a certain strength. But now there was a dull stare in her eyes, whose gaze was fixed away off yonder on one of those patches of blue sky. It was not a glance of reflection, but rather indicated a suspension of intelligent thought.

There was something coming to her and she was waiting for it, fearfully. What was it? She did not know; it was too subtle and elusive to name. But she felt it, creeping out of the sky, reaching toward her through the sounds, the scents, the color that filled the air.

Now her bosom rose and fell tumultuously. She was beginning to recog- 10
nize this thing that was approaching to possess her, and she was striving to beat it back with her will — as powerless as her two white slender hands would have been.

When she abandoned herself a little whispered word escaped her slightly parted lips. She said it over and over under her breath: "free, free, free!" The vacant stare and the look of terror that had followed it went from her eyes. They stayed keen and bright. Her pulses beat fast, and the coursing blood warmed and relaxed every inch of her body.

She did not stop to ask if it were or were not a monstrous joy that held her. A clear and exalted perception enabled her to dismiss the suggestion as trivial.

She knew that she would weep again when she saw the kind, tender hands folded in death; the face that had never looked save with love upon her, fixed and gray and dead. But she saw beyond that bitter moment a long procession of years to come that would belong to her absolutely. And she opened and spread her arms out to them in welcome.

There would be no one to live for her during those coming years; she would live for herself. There would be no powerful will bending hers in that blind persistence with which men and women believe they have a right to impose a private will upon a fellow-creature. A kind intention or a cruel intention made the act seem no less a crime as she looked upon it in that brief moment of illumination.

And yet she had loved him — sometimes. Often she had not. What did it 15
matter! What could love, the unsolved mystery, count for in face of this posses-

sion of self-assertion which she suddenly recognized as the strongest impulse of her being!

"Free! Body and soul free!" she kept whispering.

Josephine was kneeling before the closed door with her lips to the keyhole, imploring for admission. "Louise, open the door! I beg; open the door — you will make yourself ill. What are you doing, Louise? For heaven's sake open the door."

"Go away. I am not making myself ill." No; she was drinking in a very elixir of life through that open window.

Her fancy was running riot along those days ahead of her. Spring days, and summer days, and all sorts of days that would be her own. She breathed a quick prayer that life might be long. It was only yesterday she had thought with a shudder that life might be long.

20 She arose at length and opened the door to her sister's importunities. There was a feverish triumph in her eyes, and she carried herself unwittingly like a goddess of Victory. She clasped her sister's waist, and together they descended the stairs. Richards stood waiting for them at the bottom.

Some one was opening the front door with a latchkey. It was Brently Mallard who entered, a little travel-stained, composedly carrying his gripsack and umbrella. He had been far from the scene of accident, and did not even know there had been one. He stood amazed at Josephine's piercing cry; at Richards' quick motion to screen him from the view of his wife.

But Richards was too late.

When the doctors came they said she had died of heart disease — of joy that kills.

Did you find Mrs. Mallard a sympathetic character? Some readers think that she is callous, selfish, and unnatural — even "monstrous" — because she ecstatically revels in her newly discovered sense of freedom so soon after learning of her husband's presumed death. Others read her as a victim of her inability to control her own life in a repressive, male-dominated society. Is it possible to hold both views simultaneously, or are they mutually exclusive? Are your views in any way influenced by your being male or female? Does your age affect your perception? What about your social and economic background? Does your nationality, race, or religion in any way shape your attitudes? Do you have particular views about the institution of marriage that inform your assessment of Mrs. Mallard's character? Have other reading experiences — perhaps a familiarity with some of Chopin's other stories — predisposed you one way or another to Mrs. Mallard?

Understanding potential influences might be useful in determining whether a particular response to Mrs. Mallard is based primarily on the story's details and their arrangement or on an overt or subtle bias that is brought to the story. If you unconsciously project your beliefs and assumptions onto a literary work, you run the risk of distorting it to accommodate your prejudice. Your feelings can be a reliable guide to interpretation, but you should be aware of what those feelings are based on.

Often specific questions about literary works cannot be answered definitively. For example, Chopin does not explain why Mrs. Mallard suffers a heart attack at the end of this story. Is the shock of seeing her "dead" husband simply too much for this woman "afflicted with a heart trouble"? Does she die of what the doctors call a "joy that kills" because she was so glad to see her husband? Is she so profoundly guilty about feeling "free" at her husband's expense that she has a heart attack? Is her death a kind of willed suicide in reaction to her loss of freedom? Your answers to these questions will depend on which details you emphasize in your interpretation of the story and the kinds of perspectives and values you bring to it. If, for example, you read the story from a feminist perspective, you would be likely to pay close attention to Chopin's comments about marriage in paragraph 14. Or if you read the story as an oblique attack on the insensitivity of physicians of the period, you might want to find out if Chopin wrote elsewhere about doctors (she did) and compare her comments with historic sources. (A number of "Critical Strategies for Reading," including feminist and historical approaches, appear in Chapter 32.)

Reading responsively makes you an active participant in the process of creating meaning in a literary work. The experience that you and the author create will most likely not be identical to another reader's encounter with the same work, but then that's true of nearly any experience you'll have, and it is part of the pleasure of reading. Indeed, talking and writing about literature is a way of sharing responses so that they can be enriched and deepened.

EXPLORATIONS AND FORMULAS

Each time we pick up a work of fiction, go to the theater, or turn on the television, we have a trace of the same magical expectation that can be heard in the voice of a child who begs, "Tell me a story." Human beings have enjoyed stories ever since they learned to speak. Whatever the motive for creating stories — even if simply to delight or instruct — the basic human impulse to tell and hear stories existed long before the development of written language. Myths about the origins of the world and legends about the heroic exploits of demigods were among the earliest forms of storytelling to develop into oral traditions, which were eventually written down. These narratives are the ancestors of the stories we read on the printed page today. Unlike the early listeners to ancient myths and legends, we read our stories silently, but the pleasure derived from the mysterious power of someone else's artfully arranged words remains largely the same. Every one of us likes a good story.

The stories that appear in anthologies for college students are generally chosen for their high literary quality. Such stories can affect us at the deepest emotional level, reveal new insights into ourselves or the world, and stretch us by exercising our imaginations. They warrant careful reading and close study to appreciate the art that has gone into creating them. The following chapters on plot, character, setting, and the other elements of literature are designed to provide the terms and concepts that can help you understand how a work of fiction achieves its effects and meanings. It is worth acknowledging, however, that many people buy and read fiction that is quite different from the stories usually anthologized in college texts. What about all those paperbacks with exciting, colorful covers near the cash registers in shopping malls and corner drugstores?

These books, known as ***formula fiction,*** are the adventure, western, detective, science-fiction, and romance novels that entertain millions of readers annually. What makes them so popular? What do their characters, plots, and themes offer readers that accounts for the tremendous sales of stories with titles like *Caves of Doom, Silent Scream, Colt .45,* and *Forbidden Ecstasy?* Many of the writers included in this book have enjoyed wide popularity and written best-sellers, but there are more readers of formula fiction than there are readers of Hemingway, Fitzgerald, or Faulkner, to name only a few. Formula novels do, of course, provide entertainment, but that makes them no different from serious stories, if entertainment means pleasure. Any of the stories in this or any other anthology can be read for pleasure.

Formula fiction, though, is usually characterized as escape literature. There are sensible reasons for this description. Adventure stories about soldiers of fortune are eagerly read by men who live pretty average lives doing ordinary jobs. Romance novels about attractive young women falling in love with tall, dark, handsome men are read mostly by women who dream themselves out of their familiar existences. The excitement, violence, and passion that such stories provide are a kind of reprieve from everyday experience.

And yet readers of serious fiction may also use it as a refuge, a liberation from monotony and boredom. Mark Twain's humorous stories have, for example, given countless hours of pleasurable relief to readers who would rather spend time in Twain's light and funny world than in their own. Others might prefer the terror of Edgar Allan Poe's fiction or the painful predicament of two lovers in a Joyce Carol Oates story.

Thus, to get at some of the differences between formula fiction and serious literature, it is necessary to go beyond the motives of the reader to the motives of the writer and the qualities of the work itself.

Unlike serious fiction, the books displayed next to the cash registers (and their short story equivalents on the magazine racks) are written with only one object: to be sold. They are aimed at specific consumer markets that can be counted on to buy them. This does not mean that all serious writers must live in cold garrets writing for audiences who have not yet discovered their work. No one writes to make a career of poverty. It does mean, however, that if a writer's primary purpose is to anticipate readers' generic expectations about when the next torrid love scene, bloody gunfight, or thrilling chase is due, there is little room to be original or to have something significant to say. There is little if any chance to explore seriously a character, idea, or incident if the major focus is not on the integrity of the work itself.

Although the specific elements of formula fiction differ depending on the type of story, some basic ingredients go into all westerns, mysteries, adventures, science fiction, and romances. From the very start, a reader can anticipate a happy ending for the central character, with whom he or she will identify. There may be suspense, but no matter what or how many the obstacles, complications, or near defeats, the hero or heroine succeeds and reaffirms the values and attitudes the reader brings to the story. Virtue triumphs; love conquers all; honesty is the best policy; and hard work guarantees success. Hence, the villains are corralled; the wedding vows are exchanged; the butler confesses; and gold is discovered at the last moment. The visual equivalents of such formula stories are readily available at movie theaters and in a variety of television series. Some are better than others, but all are relatively limited by the necessity to give audiences what will sell.

Although formula fiction may not offer many surprises, it provides pleasure to a wide variety of readers. College professors, for example, are just as likely to be charmed by formula stories as anyone else. Readers of serious fiction who revel in exploring more challenging imaginative worlds can also enjoy formulaic stories, which offer little more than an image of the world as a simple place in which our assumptions and desires are confirmed. The familiarity of a given formula is emotionally satisfying because we are secure in our expectations of it. We know at the start of a Sherlock Holmes story that the mystery will be solved by that famous detective's relentless scientific analysis of the clues, but we take pleasure in seeing how Holmes unravels the mystery before us. Similarly, we know that James Bond's wit, grace, charm, courage, and skill will ultimately prevail over the diabolic schemes of eccentric villains, but we volunteer for the mission anyway.

Perhaps that happens for the same reason that we climb aboard a roller coaster: no matter how steep and sharp the curves, we stay on a track that is both exciting and safe. Although excitement, adventure, mystery, and romance are major routes to escape in formula fiction, most of us make that trip only temporarily, for a little relaxation and fun. Momentary relief from our everyday concerns is as healthy and desirable as an occasional daydream or fantasy. Such reading is a form of play because we — like spectators of or participants in a game — experience a formula of excitement, tension, and then release that can fascinate us regardless of how many times the game is played.

Many publishers of formula fiction — such as romance, adventure, or detective stories — issue a set number of new novels each month. Readers can buy them in stores or subscribe to them through the mail. These same publishers send "tip sheets" upon request to authors who want to write for a particular series. The details of the formula differ from one series to another, but each tip sheet covers the basic elements that go into a story.

The following composite tip sheet summarizes the typical advice offered by publishers of romance novels. These are among the most popular titles published in the United States; it has been estimated that four out of every ten paperbacks sold are romance novels. The categories and the tone of the language in this composite tip sheet are derived from a number of publishers and provide a glimpse of how formula fiction is written and what the readers of romance novels are looking for in their escape literature.

A Composite of a Romance Tip Sheet

PLOT

The story focuses on the growing relationship between the heroine and hero. After a number of complications, they discover lasting love and make a permanent commitment to each other in marriage. The plot should move quickly. Background information about the heroine should be kept to a minimum. The hero should appear as early as possible (preferably in the first chapter and no later than the second), so that the hero's and heroine's feelings about each other are in the foreground as they cope with misperceptions that keep them apart until the final pages of the story. The more tension created by their uncertainty about each other's love, the greater the excitement and anticipation for the reader.

Love is the major interest. Do not inject murder, extortion, international intrigue, hijacking, horror, or supernatural elements into the plot. Controversial social issues and politics, if mentioned at all, should never be allowed a significant role. Once the heroine and hero meet, they should clearly be interested in each other, but that interest should be complicated by some kind of misunderstanding. He, for example, might find her too ambitious, an opportunist, cold, or flirtatious; or he might assume that she is attached to someone else. She might think he is haughty, snobbish, power hungry, indifferent, or contemptuous of her. The reader knows what they do not: that eventually these obstacles will be overcome. Interest is sustained by keeping the lovers apart until very near the end so that the reader will stay with the plot to see how they get together.

HEROINE

The heroine is a modern American woman between the ages of nineteen and twenty-eight who reflects today's concerns. The story is told in the third person from her point of view. She is attractive and nicely dressed but not glamorous; glitter and sophistication should be reserved for the other woman (the heroine's rival for the hero), who will compare unfavorably with the heroine's modesty. When the heroine does dress up, however, her beauty should be stunningly apparent. Her trim figure is appealing but not abundant; a petite healthy appearance is desirable. Both her looks and clothes should be generously detailed.

Her personality is spirited and independent without being pushy or stubborn, because she knows when to give in. Although sensitive, she doesn't cry every time she is confronted with a problem (though she might cry in private moments). Because she is on her own, away from parents (usually deceased) or other protective relationships, she is self-reliant as well as vulnerable. The story may begin with her on the verge of an important decision about her life. She is clearly competent but not entirely certain of her own qualities. She does not take her attractiveness for granted or realize how much the hero is drawn to her.

Common careers for the heroine include executive secretary, nurse, teacher, interior designer, assistant manager, department store buyer, travel agent, or struggling photographer (no menial work). Her job can be described in some detail and made exciting, but it must not dominate her life. Although she is smart, she is not intellectual or defined by her work. Often she meets the hero through work, but her major concerns center on love, marriage, home, and family. Typically (and ideally), she should be a virgin who is equally inexperienced with drugs, alcohol, or cigarettes. White wine is okay, but she never drinks alone. She may be troubled, frustrated, threatened, and momentarily thwarted in the course of the story, but she never totally gives in to despair or desperation. She has strengths that the hero recognizes and admires.

HERO

The hero should be about ten years older than the heroine and can be foreign or American. He needn't be handsome in a traditional sense, but he must be strongly masculine. Always tall and well built (not brawny or thick) and usually dark, he looks as terrific in a three-piece suit as he does in sports clothes. His clothes reflect good taste and an affluent life-style. Very successful professionally and financially, he is a man in charge of whatever work he's engaged in (financier, doctor, publisher, architect, business executive, airline pilot, artist, etc.). His wealth is manifested in his sophistication and experience.

His past may be slightly mysterious or shrouded by some painful moment (perhaps with a woman) that he doesn't want to discuss. Whatever the circumstance — his wife's death or divorce are common — it was not his fault. Avoid chronic problems such as alcoholism, drug addiction, or sexual dysfunctions. To others he may appear moody, angry, unpredictable, and explosively passionate, but the heroine eventually comes to realize his warm, tender side. He should be attractive not only as a lover but also as a potential husband and father.

SECONDARY CHARACTERS

Because the major interest is in how the heroine will eventually get together with the hero, the other characters are used to advance the action. There are three major types:

(1) *The Other Woman:* Her vices serve to accent the virtues of the heroine; immediately beneath her glamorous sophistication is a deceptive, selfish, mean-spirited, rapacious predator. She may seem to have the hero in her clutches, but she never wins him in the end.

(2) *The Other Man:* He usually falls into two types: (a) the decent sort who is there when the hero isn't around, and (b) the selfish sort who schemes rather than loves. Neither is a match for the hero's virtues.

(3) *Other Characters:* Like furniture, they fill in the background and are useful for positioning the hero and heroine. These characters are familiar types such as the hero's snobbish aunt, the heroine's troubled younger siblings, the loyal friend, or the office gossip. They should be realistic, but they must not be allowed to obscure the emphasis on the lovers. The hero may have children from a previous marriage, but they should rarely be seen or heard. It's usually simpler and better not to include them.

SETTING

The setting is always contemporary. Romantic, exciting places are best: New York City, London, Paris, Rio, the mountains, the ocean — wherever it is exotic and love's possibilities are the greatest. Marriage may take the heroine and hero to a pretty suburb or small town.

LOVE SCENES

The hero and heroine may make love before marriage. The choice will depend largely on the heroine's sensibilities and circumstances. She should reflect modern attitudes. If the lovers do engage in premarital sex, it should be made clear that neither is promiscuous, especially the heroine. Even if their relationship is consummated before marriage, their lovemaking should not occur until late in the story. There should be at least several passionate scenes, but complications, misunderstandings, and interruptions should keep the couple from actually making love until they have made a firm commitment to each other. Descriptions should appeal to the senses; however, detailed, graphic close-ups are unacceptable. Passion can be presented sensually but not clinically; the lovemaking should be seen through a soft romantic lens. Violence and any out of the way sexual acts should not even be hinted at. No coarse language.

WRITING

Avoid extremely complex sentences, very long paragraphs, and lengthy descriptions. Use concise, vivid details to create the heroine's world. Be sure to include full descriptions of the hero's and heroine's physical features and clothes. Allow the reader to experience the romantic mood surrounding the lovers. Show how the heroine feels; do not simply report her feelings. Dialogue should sound like ordinary conversation, and the overall writing should be contemporary English without slang, difficult foreign expressions, strange dialects, racial epithets, or obscenities ("hell," "damn," and a few other mild swears are all right).

LENGTH

55,000 to 65,000 words in ten to twelve chapters.

Considerations

1. Who is the intended audience for this type of romance? Try to describe the audience in detail: How does a romance novel provide escape for these readers?
2. Why is it best that the heroine be "attractive and nicely dressed but not glamorous"? Why do you think publishers advise writers to include detailed descriptions of her clothes? Do you find the heroine appealing? Why or why not?
3. Why should the hero be "about ten years older than the heroine"? If he is divorced, why is it significant that "it was not his fault"?
4. Why do you think the hero and heroine are kept apart by complications until the end of the story? Does the plot sound familiar to you or remind you of any other stories?
5. Why are restrictions placed on the love scenes?
6. Why are "extremely complex sentences, very long paragraphs, and lengthy descriptions" discouraged?
7. Given the expectations implied by the tip sheet, what is revealed about those likely to write formula fiction? Do you think it is possible to write creatively within the demands of the formula?
8. To what extent does the tip sheet describe the strategies used in popular television programs, such as *Dallas, Dynasty,* or afternoon soap operas? How do you account for the appeal of these shows?
9. Explain how the tip sheet confirms traditional views of male and female roles in society. Does it accommodate any broken traditions?
10. Write up a tip sheet for another kind of popular formula story, such as a western or a detective story, that you have observed in a novel, television show, or film. How is the plot patterned? How are the characters made familiar? How is the setting related to the story? What are the obligatory scenes? How is the overall style consistent? To get started, you might consider an Agatha Christie novel, an episode from a police series on television, or a *Rocky* film.
11. Try writing a scene for a formula romance, or read the excerpt from Edgar Rice Burroughs's *Tarzan of the Apes* (p. 40) and try an adventure scene.

A COMPARISON OF TWO STORIES

Each of the following contemporary pieces of fiction is about a woman who experiences deep sorrow. The first, from *A Secret Sorrow* by Karen Van Der Zee, is an excerpt from a romance by Harlequin Books, a major publisher of formula fiction that has sold well over a billion copies of its romance titles — enough for more than half the world's population. The second piece, Gail Godwin's "A Sorrowful Woman," is a complete short story that originally appeared in *Esquire;* it is not a formula story. Unlike *A Secret Sorrow,* Godwin's story does not have a standard plot pattern employing familiar character types that appear in a series of separate but similar works.

Read each selection carefully and look for evidence of formulaic writing in the chapters from *A Secret Sorrow.* Pay particular attention to the advice offered in the composite tip sheet on plotting and characterization. As you read Godwin's short story, think about how it is different from Van Der Zee's excerpt; note also any similarities. The questions that follow the stories should help you consider how the experiences of reading the two are different.

KAREN VAN DER ZEE (b. 1947)

This excerpt consists of the final two chapters of *A Secret Sorrow.* This is what has happened so far: The central character, Faye, is recuperating from the psychological effects of a serious car accident in which she received a permanent internal injury. After the accident, she quit her job and breaks her engagement to Greg. She moves into her brother Chuck's house and falls in love with Kai, a visiting Texan and good friend of her brother. At the end of Chapter 10, Kai insists upon knowing why she will not marry him and asks, "Who is Doctor Jaworski?"

From A Secret Sorrow 1981

CHAPTER ELEVEN

Faye could feel the blood drain from her face and for one horrifying moment she thought she was going to faint right in Kai's arms. The room tilted and everything swirled around in a wild madman's dance. She clutched at him for support, fighting for control, trying to focus at some point beyond his shoulder. Slowly, everything steadied.

"I . . . I don't know him," she murmured at last. "I. . . ."

He reached in the breast pocket of his shirt, took out a slip of paper, and held it out for her to see. One glance and Faye recognized it as the note from Doctor Martin with Doctor Jaworski's name scrawled on it, thickly underlined.

"How did you get that?" Her voice was a terrified whisper. She was still holding on, afraid she would fall if she let go.

"I found it on the floor in my bedroom. It must have fallen out of your 5
wallet along with everything else on Saturday morning."

Yes — oh God! Her legs were shaking so badly, she knew it was only his arms that kept her from falling.

"Who is Doctor Jaworski, Faye?" His voice was patiently persistent.

"I . . . he. . . ." Her voice broke. "Let me go, please let me go." She felt as if she were suffocating in his embrace and she struggled against him, feebly, but it was no use.

"He's a psychiatrist, isn't he?" His voice was gentle, very gentle, and she looked up at him in stunned surprise.

He knew, oh God, he knew. She closed her eyes, a helpless sense of inevitability engulfing her.

"You know," she whispered. "How do you know?"

"Simple. Two minutes on the phone to Chicago." He paused. "Doctor Martin — was he one of the doctors who treated you at the hospital?"

"Yes."

"Why did he give you Doctor Jaworski's name? Did he want you to make an appointment with him?"

"Yes." Despondency overtook her. There was no going back now. No escape from the truth. No escape from his arms. Resistance faded and she felt numbed and lifeless. It didn't matter any more. Nothing mattered.

"Did you?" Kai repeated.

"Did I what?"

"See him — Doctor Jaworski."

"No."

"Why did Doctor Martin want you to see a psychiatrist?"

"I. . . ." Faye swallowed miserably. "It's . . . it's therapy for grieving . . . mourning." She made a helpless gesture with her hand. "When people lose a . . . a wife, or husband for instance, they go through a more or less predictable pattern of emotions. . . ." She gave him a quick glance, then looked away. "Like denial, anger. . . ."

". . . depression, mourning, acceptance," Kai finished for her, and she looked back at him in surprise.

"Yes."

His mouth twisted in a little smile. "I'm not totally ignorant about subjects other than agronomy." There was a momentary pause as he scrutinized her face. "Why did you need that kind of therapy, Faye?"

And then it was back again, the resistance, the revolt against his probing questions. She stiffened in defense — her whole body growing rigid with instinctive rebellion.

"It's none of your business!"

"Oh, yes, it is. We're talking about our life together. Your life and mine."

She strained against him, hands pushing against his chest. "Let me go! Please let me go!" Panic changed into tears. She couldn't take his nearness any more, the feel of his hard body touching hers, the strength of him.

"No, Faye, no. You're going to tell me. Now. I'm not letting you go until you've told me everything. Everything, you hear?"

"I can't!" she sobbed. "I can't!"

"Faye," he said slowly, "you'll *have* to. You told me you love me, but you don't want to marry me. You have given me no satisfactory reasons, and I'll be damned if I'm going to accept your lack of explanations."

"You have no right to demand an explanation!"

"Oh, yes, I have. You're part of me, Faye. Part of my life."

"You talk as if you own me!" She was trembling, struggling to get away from him. She couldn't stand there, so close to him with all the pent-up despair inside her, the anger, the fear of what she knew not how to tell him.

His hands were warm and strong on her back, holding her steady. Then, with one hand, he tilted back her head and made her look at him. "You gave me your love — I own that," he said softly. "True loving involves commitment, vulnerability, trust. Don't you trust me, Faye?"

New tears ran silently down her cheeks. "If I told you," she blurted out, "you wouldn't . . . you wouldn't. . . ."

"I wouldn't *what?*"

"You wouldn't want me any more!" The words were wrenched from her in blind, agonizing grief. "You wouldn't *want* me any more!"

He shook his head incredulously. "What makes you think you can make that decision for me? Do you have so little trust in my love for you?"

Faye didn't answer, couldn't answer. Through a mist of tears he was nothing but a blur in front of her eyes.

"What is so terrible that you can't tell me?"

She shrank inwardly, as if shriveling away in pain. "Let me go," she whispered. "Please let me go and I'll tell you."

After a moment's hesitation Kai released her. Faye backed away from him, feeling like a terrified animal. She stood with her back against the wall, glad for the support, her whole body shaking. She took a deep breath and wiped her face dry with her hand.

"I'm afraid . . . afraid to marry you."

"Afraid?" He looked perplexed. "Afraid of what? Of me? Of marriage?"

Faye closed her eyes, taking another deep breath. "I can't be what you want me to be. We can't have the kind of life you want." She looked at him, standing only a few feet away, anguish tearing through her. "I'm so afraid . . . you'll be disappointed," she whispered.

"Oh God, Faye," he groaned, "I love you." He came toward her and panic surged through her as he held her against the wall, his hands reaching up to catch her face between them.

"Don't," she whispered. "Please, don't touch me." But it was no use. His mouth came down on hers and he kissed her with a hard, desperate passion.

"I love you," he said huskily. "I love you."

Faye wrenched her face free from his hands. "Don't touch me! Please don't touch me!" She was sobbing now, her words barely audible. Her knees gave way and her back slid down along the wall until she crumpled on to the floor, face in her hands.

Kai took a step backward and pulled her up. "Stand up, Faye. For God's sake stand up!" He held her against the wall and she looked at him, seeing every line in his dark face, the intense blue of his eyes, and knew that this was the moment, that there was no more waiting.

And Kai knew it too. His eyes held hers locked in unrelenting demand. "Why should I be disappointed, Faye? *Why?*"

Her heart was thundering in her ears and it seemed as if she couldn't breathe, as if she were going to drown.

"Because . . . because I can't give you children! Because I can't get pregnant! I can't have babies! That's why!" Her voice was an agonized cry, torn from the depths of her misery. She yanked down his arms that held her locked against the wall and moved away from him. And then she saw his face.

It was ashen, gray under his tan. He stared at her as if he had never seen her before.

"Oh my God, Faye. . . ." His voice was low and hoarse. "Why didn't you tell me, why. . . ."

Faye heard no more. She ran out the door, snatching her bag off the chair as she went by. The only thought in her mind was to get away — away from Kai and what was in his eyes.

She reached for Kai's spare set of car keys in her bag, doing it instinctively, knowing she couldn't walk home alone in the dark. How she managed to get the keys in the door lock and in the ignition she never knew. Somehow, she made it home.

The phone rang as Faye opened the front door and she heard Chuck answer it in the kitchen.

"She's just got in," he said into the mouthpiece, smiling at Faye as she came into view. He listened for a moment, nodded. "Okay, fine with me."

Faye turned and walked up the stairs, taking deep breaths to calm her shattered nerves. Kai hadn't wasted any time checking up on her. She didn't care what he was telling Chuck, but she wasn't going to stand there listening to a one-sided conversation. But only a second later Chuck was behind her on the stairs.

"Kai wanted to know whether you'd arrived safely."

"I did, thank you," she said levelly, her voice surprisingly steady.

"I take it you ran out and took off with his car?"

"Did he say that?"

"No. He was *worried* about you. He wanted to make sure you went home." He sounded impatient, and she couldn't blame him. She was making life unbearable for everyone around her. Everybody worried about her. Everybody loved her. Everything should be right. Only it wasn't.

"Well, I'm home now, and I'm going to bed. Good night."

"Good night, Faye."

Faye lay in bed without any hope of sleep. Mechanically she started to sort through her thoughts and emotions, preparing mentally for the next confrontation. There would be one, she didn't doubt it for a moment. But she needed time — time to clear her head, time to look at everything in a reasonable, unemotional way.

It was a temptation to run — get in the car and keep driving, but it would be a stupid thing to do. There was no place for her to go, and Kai would find her, no matter what. If there was one thing she knew about Kai it was his stubbornness and his persistence. She had to stick it out, right here, get it over with, deal with it. Only she didn't know how.

She lay listening to the stillness, just a few sounds here and there — the house creaking, a car somewhere in the distance, a dog barking. She had to think, but her mind refused to cooperate. She *had* to think, decide what to say to Kai the next time she saw him, but she couldn't think, she *couldn't think*.

And then, as she heard the door open in the silence, the quiet footsteps coming up the stairs, she knew it was too late, that time had run out.

Without even knocking he came into her room and walked over to the bed. She could feel the mattress sag as his weight came down on it. Her heart was pounding like a sledgehammer, and then his arms came around her and he drew her against him.

"Faye," he said quietly, "please marry me."

"No," she said thickly. "No." She could feel him stiffen against her and she released herself from his arms and slid off the bed. She switched on the light and stood near the window, far from the bed, far from Kai. "I don't expect you to play the gentleman, I don't expect you to throw out a life of dreams just for the sake of chivalry. You don't have to marry me, Kai." She barely recognized her own voice. It was like the cool calm sound of a stranger, unemotional, cold. "You don't have to marry me," she repeated levelly, giving him a steady look.

Her words were underlined by the silence that followed, a silence loaded with a strange, vibrating energy, a force in itself, filling the room.

Kai rose to his feet, slowly, and the face that looked at her was like that of a stranger, a dangerous, angry stranger. Never before had she seen him so angry, so full of hot, fuming fury.

"Shut up," he said in a low, tight voice. "Shut up and stop playing the martyr!"

The sound of his voice and the words he said shocked Faye into silence. She stared at him open-mouthed, and then a slow, burning anger arose inside her.

"How dare you! How. . . ."

He strode toward her and took her upper arms and shook her. "Shut up and listen to me! What the hell are you thinking? What the hell did you expect me to do when you told me? You throw me a bomb and then walk out on me! What did you expect my reaction to be? Was I supposed to stay cool and calm and tell you it didn't matter? Would you have married me then? Well, let me tell you something! It matters! It matters to me! I am not apologizing for my reaction!" He paused, breathing hard. "You know I always wanted children, but what in God's name makes you think you're the only one who has the right to feel bad about it? I have that right too, you hear! I love you, dammit, and I want to marry you, and if we can't have children I have all the right in the world to feel bad about it!"

He stopped talking. He was still breathing hard and he looked at her with stormy blue eyes. Faye felt paralyzed by his tirade and she stared at him, incapable of speech. She couldn't move, she couldn't think.

"Why do you think I want you for my wife?" he continued on a calmer note. "Because you're some kind of baby factory? What kind of man do you think I am? I love *you,* not your procreating ability. So we have a problem. Well, we'll learn to deal with it, one way or another."

There was another silence, and still Faye didn't speak, and she realized she was crying, soundlessly, tears slowly dripping down her cheeks. She was staring at his chest, blindly, not knowing what to think, not thinking at all.

He lifted her chin, gently. "Look at me, Faye."

She did, but his face was only a blur.

"Faye, we're in this together — you and I. Don't you see that? It's not just *your* problem, it's *ours.*"

"No," she whispered. "No!" She shook her head wildly. "You have a choice, don't you see that? You don't have to marry me. You could marry someone else and have children of your own."

"Oh, God, Faye," he groaned, "you're wrong. Don't you know? Don't you see? I *don't* have a choice. I never did have a choice, or a chance. Not since I met you and fell in love with you. I don't *want* anybody else, don't you understand that? I want you, only you."

She wanted to believe it, give in to him. Never before had she wanted 90
anything more desperately than she wanted to give in to him now. But she couldn't, she couldn't. . . . She closed her eyes, briefly, fighting for reason, common sense.

"Kai, I . . . I can't live all my life with your regret and your disappointment. Every time we see some pregnant woman, every time we're with somebody else's children I'll feel I've failed you! I. . . ." Her voice broke and new sobs came unchecked.

He held her very tightly until she calmed down and then he put her from him a little and gave her a dark, compelling look.

"It's not *my* regret, or *my* disappointment," he said with quiet emphasis. "It's *ours.* We're not talking about *you* or *me.* We're taking about *us.* I love you, and you love me, and that's the starting point, that comes first. From then on we're in it together."

Faye moved out of his arms, away from him, but her legs wouldn't carry her and she sank into a chair. She covered her face with her hands and tried desperately to stop the crying, to stop the tears from coming and coming as if they would never end.

"How . . . how can I ever believe it?" 95

"Because I'm asking you to," he said quietly. He knelt in front of her, took her hands away from her wet face. "Look at me, Faye. No other woman can give me what you can — yourself, your love, your warmth, your sense of humor. All the facets of your personality that make up the final you. I've known other women, Faye, but none of them have ever stirred in me any feelings that come close to what I feel for you. You're an original, remember? There's no replacement for an original. There are only copies, and I don't want a copy. To me you're special, and you'll have to believe it, take it on faith. That's what love is all about."

He was holding her hands in his, strong brown hands, and she was looking down on them, fighting with herself, fighting with everything inside her to believe what he was saying, to accept it, to give into it.

Leaning forward, Kai kissed her gently on the mouth and smiled. "It's all been too much too soon for you, hasn't it? You never really got a chance to get over the shock, and when I fell in love with you it only made things worse." He smiled ruefully and Faye was surprised at his insight.

"Yes," she said. "It all happened too fast."

"Bad timing. If only we could have met later, after you'd sorted it all out 100
in your mind, then it would never have been such a crisis."

She looked at him doubtfully. "It wouldn't have changed the facts."

"No, but it might have changed your perspective."

Would it have? she wondered. Could she ever feel confident and secure in her worth as a woman? Or was she at this moment too emotionally bruised to accept that possibility?

"I don't understand," he said, "why I never guessed what was wrong. Now that I know, it all seems so obvious." He looked at her thoughtfully. "Faye," he said gently, "I want you to tell me exactly what happened to you, what Doctor Martin told you."

She stared at him, surprised a little. A thought stirred in the back of her 105
mind. Greg. He had never even asked. The why and the what had not interested him. But Kai, he wanted to know. She swallowed nervously and began the story, slowly, word for word, everything Doctor Martin had said. And he listened, quietly, not interrupting. "So you see," she said at last, "we don't have to hope for any miracles either."

"We'll make our own miracles," he said, and smiled. "Come here," he said then, "kiss me."

She did, shyly almost, until he took over and lifted her up and carried her to the bed. He looked down on her, eyes thoughtful. "I won't pretend I understand your feelings about this, the feelings you have about yourself as a woman, but I'll try." He paused for a moment. "Faye," he said then, speaking with slow emphasis, "don't *ever,* not for a single moment, think that you're not good enough for me. You're the best there is, Faye, the very best."

His mouth sought hers and he kissed her with gentle reassurance at first, then with rising ardor. His hands moved over her body, touching her with sensual, intimate caresses.

"You're my woman, Faye, you're mine. . . ."

Her senses reeled. She could never love anyone like she loved him. No 110
one had ever evoked in her this depth of emotion. This was real, this was for ever. Kai wanted her as much as ever. No chivalry, this, no game of pretense, she was very sure of that. And when he lifted his face and looked at her, it was all there in his eyes and the wonder of it filled her with joy.

"Do you believe me now?" he whispered huskily. "Do you believe I love you and want you and need you?"

She nodded wordlessly, incapable of uttering a sound.

"And do you love me?"

Again she nodded, her eyes in his.

"Okay, then." In one smooth flowing movement he got to his feet. He 115
crossed to the closet, opened it and took out her suitcases. He put one on the end of the bed and began to pile her clothes in it, taking armfuls out of the closet.

Faye watched incredulously. "What are you doing?" she managed at last.

Kai kept on moving around, opening drawers, taking out her things, filling the suitcase until it could hold no more. "Get dressed. We're going home."

"Home . . . ?"

For a moment he stopped and he looked at her with a deep blue glitter in his eyes. "Yes, *home*— where you belong. With me, in my house, in my bed, in my arms."

"Oh, Kai," she said tremulously, smiling suddenly, "It's midnight!" 120

His eyes were very dark. "I've waited long enough, I'm not waiting any more. You're coming with me, now. And I'm not letting you out of my sight until we're safely married. I don't want you getting any crazy ideas about running off to save me from myself, or some such notion."

Her throat was dry. "Please, let's not rush into it! Let's think about it first!"

Calmly he zipped up the full suitcase, swung it off the bed, and put it near the door. "I'm not rushing into anything," he said levelly. "I've wanted to marry you for quite a while, remember?"

He crossed to the bed, sat down next to her, and put his arm around her.

"Faye, I wish you wouldn't worry so. I'm not going to change my mind. And I haven't shelved my hopes for a family, either." There was a brief silence. "When we're ready to have kids, we'll have them. We'll adopt them. There are orphanages the world over, full of children in need of love and care. We'll do whatever it takes. We'll get them, one way or another."

Faye searched his face, faint hope flickering deep inside her. 125

"Would you want that?"

"Why not?"

"I don't know, really. I thought you . . . it isn't the same."

"No," he said levelly, "it isn't. Adoption is a different process from pregnancy and birth, but the kids will be ours just the same and we'll love them no less."

"Yes," she said, "yes." And suddenly it seemed as if a light had been turned 130
on inside her, as if suddenly she could see again, a future with Kai, a future with children.

A bronzed hand lifted her face. "Look, Faye, I'll always be sorry. I'll always be sorry not to see you pregnant, not to see you with a big stomach knowing you're carrying my child, but I'll live."

Faye lowered her eyes and tears threatened again. With both his hands he cupped her face.

"Look at me, Faye. I want you to stop thinking of yourself as a machine with a defect. You're not a damaged piece of merchandise, you hear? You're a living, breathing human being, a warm-blooded female, and I love you."

Through a haze of tears she looked at him, giving a weak smile. "I love you too." She put her arms around him and he heaved an unsteady breath.

"Faye," he said huskily, "you're my first and only choice." 135

CHAPTER TWELVE

Kai and Faye had their family, two girls and a boy. They came to them one at a time, from faraway places, with small faces and large dark eyes full of fear. In their faces Faye could read the tragedies of war and death and poverty. They were hungry for love, hungry for nourishment and care. At night they woke in terror, screaming, their memories alive in sleep.

Time passed, and in the low white ranch house under the blue skies of Texas they flourished like the crops in the fields. They grew tall and straight and healthy and the fear in the dark eyes faded. Like their father they wore jeans and boots and large-brimmed hats, and they rode horses and played the guitar. They learned to speak English with a Southern twang.

One day Kai and Faye watched them as they played in the garden, and joy and gratitude overflowed in Faye's heart. Life was good and filled with love.

"They're all ours," she said. Even now after all these years she sometimes still couldn't believe it was really so.

Kai smiled at her. His eyes, still very blue, crinkled at the corners. "Yes, 140
and you're all mine."

"They don't even look like us," she said. "Not even a tiny little bit." No blondes, no redheads.

Taking her in his arms, Kai kissed her. "They're true originals, like their mother. I wouldn't want it any other way."

There was love in his embrace and love in his words and in her heart there was no room now for doubt, no room for sorrow.

Sometimes in the night he would reach for her and she would wake to his touch, his hands on her breast, her stomach, searching. In the warm darkness of their bed she could come to him and they would hold each other close and she knew he had been dreaming.

She knew the dream. She was walking away from him, calling out that she couldn't marry him, the words echoing all around. *"I can't marry you! I can't marry you!"* And Kai was standing there watching her go, terrified, unable to move, his legs frozen to the ground. He wanted to follow her, keep her from leaving, but his legs wouldn't move.

Kai had told her of the dream, of the panic that clutched at him as he watched her walk out of his life. And always he would wake and search for her in the big bed, and she knew of only one way to reassure him. And in the warm afterglow of lovemaking, their bodies close together, she knew that to him she was everything, to him she was the only woman, beautiful, complete, whole.

GAIL GODWIN (b. 1937)

A Sorrowful Woman 1971

Once upon a time there was a wife and mother one too many times

One winter evening she looked at them: the husband durable, receptive, gentle; the child a tender golden three. The sight of them made her so sad and sick she did not want to see them ever again.

She told the husband these thoughts. He was attuned to her; he understood such things. He said he understood. What would she like him to do? "If you could put the boy to bed and read him the story about the monkey who ate too many bananas, I would be grateful." "Of course," he said. "Why, that's a pleasure." And he sent her off to bed.

The next night it happened again. Putting the warm dishes away in the cupboard, she turned and saw the child's grey eyes approving her movements. In the next room was the man, his chin sunk in the open collar of his favorite wool shirt. He was dozing after her good supper. The shirt was the grey of the child's trusting gaze. She began yelping without tears, retching in between. The man woke in alarm and carried her in his arms to bed. The boy followed them up the stairs, saying, "It's all right, Mommy," but this made her scream. "Mommy is sick," the father said, "go wait for me in your room."

The husband undressed her, abandoning her only long enough to root beneath the eiderdown for her flannel gown. She stood naked except for her bra, which hung by one strap down the side of her body; she had not the impetus to shrug it off. She looked down at the right nipple, shriveled with chill, and thought, How absurd, a vertical bra. "If only there were instant sleep," she said, hiccuping, and the husband bundled her into the gown and went out and came back with a sleeping draught guaranteed swift. She was to drink a little glass of cognac followed by a big glass of dark liquid and afterwards there was just time to say Thank you and could you get him a clean pair of pajamas out of the laundry, it came back today.

5 The next day was Sunday and the husband brought her breakfast in bed and let her sleep until it grew dark again. He took the child for a walk, and when they returned, red-cheeked and boisterous, the father made supper. She heard them laughing in the kitchen. He brought her up a tray of buttered toast, celery sticks, and black bean soup. "I am the luckiest woman," she said, crying real tears. "Nonsense," he said. "You need a rest from us," and went to prepare the sleeping draught, find the child's pajamas, select the story for the night.

She got up on Monday and moved about the house till noon. The boy, delighted to have her back, pretended he was a vicious tiger and followed her from room to room, growling and scratching. Whenever she came close, he would growl and scratch at her. One of his sharp little claws ripped her flesh, just above the wrist, and together they paused to watch a thin red line materialize on the inside of her pale arm and spill over in little beads. "Go away," she said. She got herself upstairs and locked the door. She called the husband's office and said, "I've locked myself away from him. I'm afraid." The husband told her in his richest voice to lie down, take it easy, and he was already on the phone to call one of the baby-sitters they often employed. Shortly after, she heard the girl let herself in, heard the girl coaxing the frightened child to come and play.

After supper several nights later, she hit the child. She had known she was going to do it when the father would see. "I'm sorry," she said, collapsing on the floor. The weeping child had run to hide. "What has happened to me, I'm not myself anymore." The man picked her tenderly from the floor and looked at her with much concern. "Would it help if we got, you know, a girl in? We could fix the room downstairs. I want you to feel freer," he said, understanding these things. "We have the money for a girl. I want you to think about it."

And now the sleeping draught was a nightly thing, she did not have to ask. He went down to the kitchen to mix it, he set it nightly beside her bed. The little glass and the big one, amber and deep rich brown, the flannel gown and the eiderdown.

The man put out the word and found the perfect girl. She was young, dynamic, and not pretty. "Don't bother with the room, I'll fix it up myself." Laughing, she employed her thousand energies. She painted the room white, fed the child lunch, read edifying books, raced the boy to the mailbox, hung her own watercolors on the fresh-painted walls, made spinach soufflé, cleaned a spot from the mother's coat, made them all laugh, danced in stocking feet to music in the white room after reading the child to sleep. She knitted dresses for herself and played chess with the husband. She washed and set the mother's soft ash-blonde hair and gave her neck rubs, offered to.

10 The woman now spent her winter afternoons in the big bedroom. She made a fire in the hearth and put on slacks and an old sweater she had loved at school, and sat in the big chair and stared out the window at snow-ridden branches, or went away into long novels about other people moving through other winters.

The girl brought the child in twice a day, once in the later afternoon when he would tell of his day, all of it tumbling out quickly because there was not much time, and before he went to bed. Often now, the man took his wife to dinner. He made a courtship ceremony of it, inviting her beforehand so she could get used to the idea. They dressed and were beautiful together again and went out into the frosty night. Over candlelight he would say, "I think you are better, you know." "Perhaps I am," she would murmur. "You look . . . like a cloistered queen," he said once, his voice breaking curiously.

One afternoon the girl brought the child into the bedroom. "We've been out playing in the park. He found something he wants to give you, a surprise." The little boy approached her, smiling mysteriously. He placed his cupped hands in hers and left a live dry thing that spat brown juice in her palm and leapt away. She screamed and wrung her hands to be rid of the brown juice. "Oh, it was only a grasshopper," said the girl. Nimbly she crept to the edge of the curtain, did a quick knee bend, and reclaimed the creature, led the boy competently from the room.

"The girl upsets me," said the woman to her husband. He sat frowning on the side of the bed he had not entered for so long. "I'm sorry, but there it is." The husband stroked his creased brow and said he was sorry too. He really did not know what they would do without that treasure of a girl. "Why don't you stay here with me in bed," the woman said.

Next morning she fired the girl who cried and said, "I loved the little boy, what will become of him now?" But the mother turned away her face and the girl took down the watercolors from the walls, sheathed the records she had danced to, and went away.

"I don't know what we'll do. It's all my fault, I know. I'm such a burden, I know that."

"Let me think. I'll think of something." (Still understanding these things.)

"I know you will. You always do," she said.

With great care he rearranged his life. He got up hours early, did the shopping, cooked the breakfast, took the boy to nursery school. "We will manage," he said, "until you're better, however long that is." He did his work, collected the boy from the school, came home and made the supper, washed the dishes, got the child to bed. He managed everything. One evening, just as she was on the verge of swallowing her draught, there was a timid knock on her door. The little boy came in wearing his pajamas. "Daddy has fallen asleep on my bed and I can't get in. There's not room."

Very sedately she left her bed and went to the child's room. Things were much changed. Books were rearranged, toys. He'd done some new drawings. She came as a visitor to her son's room, wakened the father and helped him to bed. "Ah, he shouldn't have bothered you," said the man, leaning on his wife. "I've told him not to." He dropped into his own bed and fell asleep with a moan. Meticulously she undressed him. She folded and hung his clothes. She covered his body with the bedclothes. She flicked off the light that shone in his face.

The next day she moved her things into the girl's white room. She put her hairbrush on the dresser; she put a note pad and pen beside the bed. She stocked the little room with cigarettes, books, bread, and cheese. She didn't need much.

At first the husband was dismayed. But he was receptive to her needs. He understood these things. “Perhaps the best thing is for you to follow it through,” he said. “I want to be big enough to contain whatever you must do.”

All day long she stayed in the white room. She was a young queen, a virgin in a tower; she was the previous inhabitant, the girl with all the energies. She tried these personalities on like costumes, then discarded them. The room had a new view of streets she'd never seen that way before. The sun hit the room in late afternoon and she took to brushing her hair in the sun. One day she decided to write a poem. “Perhaps a sonnet.” She took up her pen and pad and began working from words that had lately lain in her mind. She had choices for the sonnet, ABAB or ABBA for a start. She pondered these possibilities until she tottered into a larger choice: she did not have to write a sonnet. Her poem could be six, eight, ten, thirteen lines, it could be any number of lines, and it did not even have to rhyme.

She put down the pen on top of the pad.

In the evenings, very briefly, she saw the two of them. They knocked on her door, a big knock and a little, and she would call Come in, and the husband would smile though he looked a bit tired, yet somehow this tiredness suited him. He would put her sleeping draught on the bedside table and say, “The boy and I have done all right today,” and the child would kiss her. One night she tasted for the first time the power of his baby spit.

“I don't think I can see him anymore,” she whispered sadly to the man. 25
And the husband turned away, but recovered admirably and said, “Of course, I see.”

So the husband came alone. “I have explained to the boy,” he said. “And we are doing fine. We are managing.” He squeezed his wife's pale arm and put the two glasses on her table. After he had gone, she sat looking at the arm.

“I'm afraid it's come to that,” she said. “Just push the notes under the door; I'll read them. And don't forget to leave the draught outside.”

The man sat for a long time with his head in his hands. Then he rose and went away from her. She heard him in the kitchen where he mixed the draught in batches now to last a week at a time, storing it in a corner of the cupboard. She heard him come back, leave the big glass and the little one outside on the floor.

Outside her window the snow was melting from the branches, there were more people on the streets. She brushed her hair a lot and seldom read anymore. She sat in her window and brushed her hair for hours, and saw a boy fall off his new bicycle again and again, a dog chasing a squirrel, an old woman peek slyly over her shoulder and then extract a parcel from a garbage can.

In the evening she read the notes they slipped under her door. The child 30
could not write, so he drew and sometimes painted his. The notes were painstaking at first; the man and boy offering the final strength of their day to her. But sometimes, when they seemed to have had a bad day, there were only hurried scrawls.

One night, when the husband's note had been extremely short, loving but short, and there had been nothing from the boy, she stole out of her room as she often did to get more supplies, but crept upstairs instead and stood outside their doors, listening to the regular breathing of the man and boy asleep. She hurried back to her room and drank the draught.

She woke earlier now. It was spring, there were birds. She listened for sounds of the man and the boy eating breakfast; she listened for the roar of the motor when they drove away. One beautiful noon, she went out to look at her kitchen in the daylight. Things were changed. He had bought some new dish towels. Had the old ones worn out? The canisters seemed closer to the sink. She got out flour, baking powder, salt, milk (he bought a different brand of butter), and baked a loaf of bread and left it cooling on the table.

The force of the two joyful notes slipped under her door that evening pressed her into the corner of the little room; she had hardly space to breathe. As soon as possible, she drank the draught.

Now the days were too short. She was always busy. She woke with the first bird. Worked till the sun set. No time for hair brushing. Her fingers raced the hours.

Finally, in the nick of time, it was finished one late afternoon. Her veins pumped and her forehead sparkled. She went to the cupboard, took what was hers, closed herself into the little white room and brushed her hair for a while.

The man and boy came home and found: five loaves of warm bread, a roast stuffed turkey, a glazed ham, three pies of different fillings, eight molds of the boy's favorite custard, two weeks' supply of fresh-laundered sheets and shirts and towels, two hand-knitted sweaters (both of the same gray color), a sheath of marvelous watercolor beasts accompanied by mad and fanciful stories nobody could ever make up again, and a tablet full of love sonnets addressed to the man. The house smelled redolently of renewal and spring. The man ran to the little room, could not contain himself to knock, flung back the door.

"Look, Mommy is sleeping," said the boy. "She's tired from doing all our things again." He dawdled in a stream of the last sun for that day and watched his father roll tenderly back her eyelids, lay his ear softly to her breast, test the delicate bones of her wrist. The father put down his face into her fresh-washed hair.

"Can we eat the turkey for supper?" the boy asked.

Considerations

1. Describe what you found appealing in each story. Can you point to passages in both that strike you as especially well written or interesting? Was there anything in either story that did not appeal to you? Why?
2. How do the two women's attitudes toward family life differ? How does that difference constitute the problem in each story?
3. How is the woman's problem in "A Sorrowful Woman" made more complex than Faye's in *A Secret Sorrow*? What is the purpose of the husband and child in Godwin's story?
4. How would you describe the theme, the central point and meaning, in each story?
5. To what extent might "A Sorrowful Woman" be regarded as an unromantic sequel to *A Secret Sorrow*?
6. Can both stories be read a second or third time and still be interesting? Why or why not?
7. Explain how you think a romance formula writer would end "A Sorrowful Woman," or write the ending yourself.
8. Contrast what marriage means in the two stories.
9. Discuss your feelings about the woman in "A Sorrowful Woman." How does she

remain a sympathetic character in spite of her refusal to be a traditional wife and mother? (It may take more than one reading of the story to see that Godwin does sympathize with her.)

10. The happy ending of *A Secret Sorrow* may seem like that of a fairy tale, but it is realistically presented, because there is nothing strange, mysterious, or fabulous that tests our ability to believe it could happen. In contrast, "A Sorrowful Woman" begins with an epigraph *("Once upon a time . . .")* that causes us to expect a fairy-tale ending, but that story is clearly a fairly tale gone wrong. Consider the two stories as fairy tales. How might "A Sorrowful Woman" be read as a dark version of "Sleeping Beauty"?
11. Read the section on feminist criticism in Chapter 32, "Critical Strategies for Reading." Based on that discussion, what do you think a feminist critic might have to say about these two stories?

PERSPECTIVE

KAY MUSSELL (b. 1943)

A Defense of Formula Romances 1984

Working from female experience in culture, romance writers — like other formulaic authors — construct stories with simple solutions to complex problems. Romances are adolescent dramas that mirror the infantilism of women in a patriarchal culture. No wonder, then, that popular fiction for women consistently portrays heroines in relationships — successful or unsuccessful, fulfilling or painful — with men. But as stories of coming of age, romances are sadly deficient, for their heroines rarely even aspire to autonomy or genuine maturity. The available options lead not to autonomous adulthood but to conventional states of being that lack an imaginative structure for continued adult growth. Too frequently, the most resonant story told by or about a woman remains a story with an inherently unsatisfying ending — so unsatisfying that the story must be told over and over, as if its value had been missed the first time around.

Assertions about the sacred nature of female lives do not ameliorate the inherent mindlessness and triviality of existence within constricted spheres. Cultural imperatives do not alleviate the frustration of having nothing original or important to do, nor do prescriptive beliefs hide from individual women the bitter knowledge of their restricted moral purpose. There is nothing easy about being a man, or indeed about living at all; but imaginatively, through fiction, men are confronted with important things to do and with important moral choices to make that may be denied, in fiction and in life, to women. Romances seem far more acquiescent to patriarchal norms than the writing of women who question the *status quo,* and yet they accurately reflect the circularity and hopelessness of women's attempts to find their identity in humanity rather than in men.

Those who accuse romances of perpetuating female subservience, passivity, and powerlessness forget the paucity of alternative modes for the portrayal of female aspiration. In condemning romances, they ignore the common circumstances of women as writers in a patriarchy and they denigrate the value of female experience in itself. In addition, some critics apparently assume that escape fantasies for women are more trivial and less valid than those for men. Certainly, many romances appear trivial and inauthentic from the perspective of a cultural establishment that trivializes and judges their writers, protagonists, plots, and readers without examining them seriously. Because the central issues of many women's lives may appear to lack resonance or ethical power, few literary works besides romances assert without equivocation that woman's sphere has significance and meaning. Romances are less failed narratives than narratives of failure, and the failure belongs less to writers and readers than to patriarchy's denial of women's right to explicate their own lives.

Romances reflect the culture's failure of imagination about women. Shunted aside as women are shunted aside, these stories flounder and repeat themselves in a never-ending cycle of female adolescent experience, for only in the adventure of being chosen by the man who will care for her can a romance heroine experience her moment of glory. Romances substitute for real choices — how life may be lived from beginning to end — a single choice about how a woman's early life brings her to the point of a single action — or decision — that will determine the course of her remaining years. The romance fantasy may be both trivial and insignificant in the world of art, but it is genuinely tragic in the real world where women must live.

The simplicities of romances, in the end, tell us as much about patriarchy as about their writers and readers. Denied admission to the world at large, some women construct among themselves, through romances, an alternative world imbued with a surface significance far beyond its capacity to fulfill its own promise. The sensation, emotion, and melodrama of romances reflect the incapacity of the formula, in itself, to be profound; but romances are no more unrealistic or degrading than the male formulas — the hard-boiled detective story, the spy story, the Western — that critics define as "valid escape fantasy." If romances — like other popular formulas — fail to be noble and uplifting, they have at least a kind of virtue as a survival tactic. Romance writers and readers seem to be saying to each other: "If we may not participate in the wider world, we will construct a drama in our own. We need not threaten patriarchy, for that in turn threatens us. We may acquiesce — or seem to — in definitions of self that fail to fulfill. But, at least, we can make something of the one story that is left for us to tell."

It is no wonder that romances represent a covert and closed circle of authors and readers, who constantly repeat the one clearly acceptable form of adventure for women. At least in the pages of a romance, women experience uncertainty, testing, questions, choice-making, responsibility for their actions, and rewards for virtuous behavior. If women cannot see beyond those pages, then it is the culture that has slammed the door, cutting off vision and aspiration because the price of change may seem too high. Although one cannot draw a direct parallel between literature and life, women in culture face this dilemma no less certainly than do heroines in fiction. Lacking arenas for action in real life, some women turn over and over again to a vicarious experience where a limited form of action may prove acceptable. The attempt to relive and remake significance through vicarious courtship may be pathetic, but no more so than a culture that relegates women as a group to a restricted sphere and confines them there for life. When critics denigrate the one formula of popular literature that tries to invest women's lives with significance, they deny simultaneously the value of woman's sphere.

From *Fantasy and Reconciliation: Contemporary Formulas of Women's Romance Fiction*

Considerations

1. How, according to Mussell, are romances a response to "patriarchal culture"? How do social, economic, and sexual pressures affect the kinds of stories told in formula romances?
2. Does the excerpt from the Harlequin romance, *A Secret Sorrow* (p. 22), reflect the "constricted" kind of life Mussell describes?
3. Why does Mussell defend romances? What function do they serve?
4. Consider Mussell's statement: "If romances — like other popular formulas — fail to be noble and uplifting, they have at least a kind of virtue as a survival tactic." Write an essay in which you agree or disagree with her assessment.

2. Plot

Created by a writer's imagination, a work of fiction need not be factual or historically accurate. Although actual people, places, and events may be included in fiction, what is primarily important are not facts so much as the writer's use of them. We can learn much about Russian life in the early part of the nineteenth century from Leo Tolstoy's *War and Peace,* but that historical information is incidental to Tolstoy's exploration of human nature. Tolstoy, like most successful writers, makes us accept as real the world in his novel no matter how foreign it may be to our own reality. One of the ways a writer achieves this acceptance and engagement — and one of a writer's few obligations — is to interest us in what is happening in the story. We are carried into the writer's fictional world by the plot.

Plot is the author's arrangement of incidents in a story. It is the organizing principle that controls the order of events. This structure is, in a sense, what remains after a writer edits out what is irrelevant to the story being told. We don't need to know, for example, what happens to Rip Van Winkle's faithful dog, Wolf, while his amiable master takes his twenty-year nap in the Catskill Mountains in order to be enchanted by Washington Irving's story of a henpecked husband. Instead, what is told takes on meaning as it is brought into focus by a skillful writer who selects and orders the events that constitute the story's plot.

Events can be presented in a variety of orders. A chronological arrangement begins with what happens first, then second, and so on, until the last incident is related. That is how "Rip Van Winkle" is told. The events in William Faulkner's "A Rose for Emily," however, are not arranged in chronological order because that would give away the story's surprise ending; instead, Faulkner moves back and forth between the past and present to provide information that leads up to the final startling moment (which won't be given away here either; the story begins on p. 47).

Some stories begin at the end and then lead up to why or how events worked out as they did. If you read the first paragraph of Yukio Mishima's "Patriotism" (p. 412), you'll find an example of this arrangement that will make it difficult for you to stop reading. Stories can also begin in the middle of things (the Latin term for this common plot strategy is ***in medias res***). In this kind of plot we enter the story on the verge of some important moment. John Updike's "A & P" (p. 407) begins with the narrator, a teenager working at a checkout counter in a supermarket, telling us: "In walks these three girls in nothing but bathing suits." Right away we are brought into the middle of a situation that will ultimately create the conflict in the story.

Another common strategy is the ***flashback,*** a device that informs us about events that happened before the opening scene of a work. Nearly all of Ralph Ellison's "Battle Royal" (p. 179) takes the form of a flashback as the narrator recounts how his identity as a black man was shaped by the circumstances that attended a high-school graduation speech he delivered twenty years earlier in a hotel ballroom before a gathering of the town's leading white citizens, most of whom were "quite tipsy." Whatever the plot arrangement, you should be aware of how the writer's conscious ordering of events affects your responses to the action.

EDGAR RICE BURROUGHS (1875–1950)

A great many stories share a standard plot pattern. The following excerpt from Edgar Rice Burroughs's novel *Tarzan of the Apes* provides a conventional plot pattern in which the ***character,*** an imagined person in the story, is confronted with a problem leading to a climatic struggle that is followed by a resolution of the problem. The elements of a conventional plot are easily recognizable to readers familiar with fast-paced, action-packed mysteries, spy thrillers, westerns, or adventure stories. These page-turners are carefully plotted so that the reader is swept up by the action. More serious writers sometimes use similar strategies, but they do so with greater subtlety and for some purpose that goes beyond providing a thrill a minute. The writer of serious fiction is usually less concerned with what happens next to the central character than with why it happens. In Burroughs's adventure story, however, the emphasis is clearly upon action. *Tarzan of the Apes* may add little or nothing to our understanding of life, but it is useful for delineating some important elements of plot. Moreover, it is great fun.

Burroughs's novel, published in 1914 and the first of a series of enormously popular Tarzan books and films, charts the growth to manhood of a child raised in the African jungle by great apes. (See Gore Vidal's discussion of the popularity of Tarzan books in "Perspectives on Fiction," p. 482.) Tarzan struggles to survive his primitive beginnings and to reconcile what he has learned in the jungle with his equally powerful instincts to be a civilized human being. One of the more exciting moments in Tarzan's development is his final confrontation with his old enemy, Terkoz, a huge tyrannical ape that has kidnapped Jane, a pretty nineteen-year-old from Baltimore, Maryland, who has accompanied her father on an expedition to the jungle.

In the chapter preceding this excerpt, Tarzan falls in love with Jane and writes this pointed, if not eloquent, note to her: "I am Tarzan of the Apes. I want you. I am yours. You are mine." Just as he finishes the note, he hears "the agonized screams of a woman" and rushes to their source to find Esmeralda, Jane's maid, hysterical with fear and grief. She reports that Jane, the fair and gentle embodiment of civilization in the story, has been carried off by a gorilla. Here is the first half of the next chapter, which illustrates how Burroughs plots the sequence of events so that the emphasis is on physical action.

From Tarzan of the Apes 1914

From the time Tarzan left the tribe of great anthropoids in which he had been raised, it was torn by continual strife and discord. Terkoz proved a cruel and capricious king, so that, one by one, many of the older and weaker apes, upon whom he was particularly prone to vent his brutish nature, took their families and sought the quiet and safety of the far interior.

But at last those who remained were driven to desperation by the continued truculence of Terkoz, and it so happened that one of them recalled the parting admonition of Tarzan:

"If you have a chief who is cruel, do not do as the other apes do, and attempt, any one of you, to pit yourself against him alone. But, instead, let two or three or four of you attack him together. Then, if you will do this, no chief will dare to be other than he should be, for four of you can kill any chief who may ever be over you."

And the ape who recalled this wise counsel repeated it to several of his fellows, so that when Terkoz returned to the tribe that day he found a warm reception awaiting him.

There were no formalities. As Terkoz reached the group, five huge, hairy beasts sprang upon him.

At heart he was an arrant coward, which is the way with bullies among apes as well as among men; so he did not remain to fight and die, but tore himself away from them as quickly as he could and fled into the sheltering boughs of the forest.

Two more attempts he made to rejoin the tribe, but on each occasion he was set upon and driven away. At last he gave it up, and turned, foaming with rage and hatred, into the jungle.

For several days he wandered aimlessly, nursing his spite and looking for some weak thing on which to vent his pent anger.

It was in this state of mind that the horrible, manlike beast, swinging from tree to tree, came suddenly upon two women in the jungle.

He was right above them when he discovered them. The first intimation Jane Porter had of his presence was when the great hairy body dropped to the earth beside her, and she saw the awful face and the snarling, hideous mouth thrust within a foot of her.

One piercing scream escaped her lips as the brute hand clutched her arm. Then she was dragged toward those awful fangs which yawned at her throat. But ere they touched that fair skin another mood claimed the anthropoid.

The tribe had kept his women. He must find others to replace them. This hairless white ape would be the first of his new household, and so he threw her roughly across his broad, hairy shoulders and leaped back into the trees, bearing Jane away.

Esmeralda's scream of terror had mingled once with that of Jane, and then, as was Esmeralda's manner under stress of emergency which required presence of mind, she swooned.

But Jane did not once lose consciousness. It is true that that awful face, pressing close to hers, and the stench of the foul breath beating upon her nostrils, paralyzed her with terror; but her brain was clear, and she comprehended all that transpired.

With what seemed to her marvelous rapidity the brute bore her through the forest, but still she did not cry out or struggle. The sudden advent of the ape had confused her to such an extent that she thought now that he was bearing her toward the beach.

For this reason she conserved her energies and her voice until she could see that they had approached near enough to the camp to attract the succor she craved.

She could not have known it, but she was being borne farther and farther into the impenetrable jungle.

The scream that had brought Clayton and the two older men stumbling through the undergrowth had led Tarzan of the Apes straight to where Esmeralda lay, but it was not Esmeralda in whom his interest centered, though pausing over her he saw that she was unhurt.

For a moment he scrutinized the ground below and the trees above, until the ape that was in him by virtue of training and environment, combined with the intelligence that was his by right of birth, told his wondrous woodcraft the whole story as plainly as though he had seen the thing happen with his own eyes.

And then he was gone again into the swaying trees, following the high-flung spoor which no other human eye could have detected, much less translated.

At boughs' ends, where the anthropoid swings from one tree to another, there is most to mark the trail, but least to point the direction of the quarry; for there the pressure is downward always, toward the small end of the branch, whether the ape be leaving or entering a tree. Nearer the center of the tree, where the signs of passage are fainter, the direction is plainly marked.

Here, on this branch, a caterpillar has been crushed by the fugitive's great foot, and Tarzan knows instinctively where that same foot would touch in the next stride. Here he looks to find a tiny particle of the demolished larva, ofttimes not more than a speck of moisture.

Again, a minute bit of bark has been upturned by the scraping hand, and the direction of the break indicates the direction of the passage. Or some great limb, or the stem of the tree itself has been brushed by the hairy body, and a tiny shred of hair tells him by the direction from which it is wedged beneath the bark that he is on the right trail.

Nor does he need to check his speed to catch these seemingly faint records of the fleeing beast.

To Tarzan they stand out boldly against all the myriad other scars and bruises and signs upon the leafy way. But strongest of all is the scent, for Tarzan is pursuing up the wind, and his trained nostrils are as sensitive as a hound's.

There are those who believe that the lower orders are specially endowed by nature with better olfactory nerves than man, but it is merely a matter of development.

Man's survival does not hinge so greatly upon the perfection of his senses. His power to reason has relieved them of many of their duties, and so they have, to some extent, atrophied, as have the muscles which move the ears and scalp, merely from disuse.

The muscles are there, about the ears and beneath the scalp, and so are the nerves which transmit sensations to the brain, but they are underdeveloped because they are not needed.

Not so with Tarzan of the Apes. From early infancy his survival had depended upon acuteness of eyesight, hearing, smell, touch, and taste far more than upon the more slowly developed organ of reason.

The least developed of all in Tarzan was the sense of taste, for he could eat luscious fruits, or raw flesh, long buried with almost equal appreciation; but in that he differed but slightly from more civilized epicures.

Almost silently the ape-man sped on in the track of Terkoz and his prey, but the sound of his approach reached the ears of the fleeing beast and spurred it on to greater speed.

Three miles were covered before Tarzan overtook them, and then Terkoz, seeing that further flight was futile, dropped to the ground in a small open glade, that he might turn and fight for his prize or be free to escape unhampered if he saw that the pursuer was more than a match for him.

He still grasped Jane in one great arm as Tarzan bounded like a leopard into the arena which nature had provided for this primeval-like battle.

When Terkoz saw that it was Tarzan who pursued him, he jumped to the conclusion that this was Tarzan's woman, since they were of the same kind—white and hairless—and so he rejoiced at this opportunity for double revenge upon his hated enemy.

To Jane the strange apparition of this godlike man was as wine to sick nerves.

From the description which Clayton and her father and Mr. Philander had given her, she knew that it must be the same wonderful creature who had saved them, and she saw in him only a protector and a friend.

But as Terkoz pushed her roughly aside to meet Tarzan's charge, and she saw the great proportions of the ape and the mighty muscles and the fierce fangs, her heart quailed. How could any vanquish such a mighty antagonist?

Like two charging bulls they came together, and like two wolves sought each other's throat. Against the long canines of the ape was pitted the thin blade of the man's knife.

Jane—her lithe, young form flattened against the trunk of a great tree, her hands tight pressed against her rising and falling bosom, and her eyes wide with mingled horror, fascination, fear, and admiration — watched the primordial ape battle with the primeval man for possession of a woman — for her.

As the great muscles of the man's back and shoulders knotted beneath the tension of his efforts, and the huge biceps and forearm held at bay those mighty tusks, the veil of centuries of civilization and culture were swept from the blurred vision of the Baltimore girl.

When the long knife drank deep a dozen times of Terkoz' heart's blood, and the great carcass rolled lifeless upon the ground, it was a primeval woman who sprang forward with outstretched arms toward the primeval man who had fought for her and won.

And Tarzan?

He did what no red-blooded man needs lessons in doing. He took his woman in his arms and smothered her upturned, panting lips with kisses.

For a moment Jane lay there with half-closed eyes. For a moment — the first in her young life — she knew the meaning of love.

But as suddenly as the veil had been withdrawn it dropped again, and an outraged conscience suffused her face with its scarlet mantle, and a mortified woman thrust Tarzan of the Apes from her and buried her face in her hands.

Tarzan had been surprised when he had found the girl he had learned to love after a vague and abstract manner a willing prisoner in his arms. Now he was surprised that she repulsed him.

He came close to her once more and took hold of her arm. She turned upon him like a tigress, striking his great breast with her tiny hands.

Tarzan could not understand it.

A moment ago, and it had been his intention to hasten Jane back to her people, but that little moment was lost now in the dim and distant past of things which were but can never be again, and with it the good intention had gone to join the impossible.

Since then Tarzan of the Apes had felt a warm, lithe form close pressed to his. Hot, sweet breath against his cheek and mouth had fanned a new flame to life within his breast, and perfect lips had clung to his in burning kisses that had seared a deep brand into his soul — a brand which marked a new Tarzan.

Again he laid his hand upon her arm. Again she repulsed him. And then Tarzan of the Apes did just what his first ancestor would have done.

He took his woman in his arms and carried her into the jungle.

This episode begins with ***exposition,*** the background information the reader needs to make sense of the situation in which the characters are placed. The first eight paragraphs let us know that Terkoz has been overthrown as leader of the ape tribe and that he is roaming the jungle "looking for some weak thing on which to vent his pent anger." This exposition is in the form of a flashback. (Recall that the previous chapter ended with Esmeralda's report of the kidnapping; now we will see what happened.)

Once this information supplies a context for the characters, the plot gains momentum with the ***rising action,*** a complication that intensifies the situation: Terkoz, looking for a victim, discovers the vulnerable Esmeralda and Jane. His first impulse is to kill Jane, but his "mood" changes when he remembers that he has no woman of his own after having been forced to leave the tribe (more exposition). Hence, there is a further complication in the rising action when he decides to carry her off. Just when it seems that the situation could not get any worse, it does. The reader is invited to shudder even more than if Terkoz had made a meal of Jane, because she may have to endure the "awful face," "foul breath," and lust of this beast.

At this point we are brought up to the action that ended the preceding chapter. Tarzan races to the rescue by unerringly following the trail from the place where Jane was kidnapped. He relentlessly tracks Terkoz. Unfortunately, Burroughs slows down the pursuit here by including several paragraphs that abstractly consider the evolutionary development of humans relying on reason more than on their senses for survival. This discussion offers a rationale for Tarzan's remarkable ability to track Jane, but it is an interruption in the chase.

When Tarzan finally catches up to Terkoz, the ***conflict*** of this episode fully emerges. Tarzan must save the woman he loves by defeating his longstanding enemy. For Terkoz seeks to achieve a "double revenge" by killing Tarzan and taking his woman. Terkoz's assumption that Jane is Tarzan's woman is a ***foreshadowing,*** a suggestion of what is yet to come. In this conflict Tarzan is the ***protagonist*** or ***hero,*** the central character who engages our interest and empathy. *Protagonist* is often a more useful term than hero or ***heroine,*** however, because the central character of a story can be despicable as well as heroic. In Edgar Allan Poe's "The Tell-Tale Heart," for example, the central character is a madman and murderer. Terkoz is the ***antagonist,*** the force that opposes the protagonist.

The battle between Tarzan and Terkoz creates ***suspense,*** because the reader is made anxious about what is going to happen. Burroughs makes certain that the reader will worry about the outcome by having Jane wonder, "How could any vanquish such a mighty antagonist?" If we are caught up in the moment, we watch the battle, as Jane does, with "mingled horror, fascination, fear, and admiration" to see what will happen next. The moment of greatest emotional tension, the ***climax,*** occurs when Tarzan kills Terkoz. Tarzan's victory is the ***resolution*** of the conflict, also known as the ***dénouement*** (a French word meaning the "untying of the knot"). This could have been the conclusion to the episode except that Jane and Tarzan simultaneously discover their "primeval" selves sexually drawn to each other. Burroughs resolves one conflict — the battle with Terkoz — but then immediately creates another — by raising the question of what a respectable professor's daughter from Baltimore is doing in the sweaty arms of a panting, half-naked man.

For a brief moment the cycle of conflict, suspense, and resolution begins again as Jane passionately kisses Tarzan; then her "outraged conscience" causes her to regain her sense of propriety and she pushes him away. Although Tarzan succeeds in the encounter with Terkoz, he is not successful with Jane. However, Burroughs creates suspense for a third time at the very end of the episode, when the "new Tarzan," having been transformed by this sexual awakening, "took his woman in his arms and carried her into the jungle." What will he do next? Despite the novel's implausibility (beginning with the premise that apes could raise a human child) and its heavy use of coincidences (not the least of which is Tarzan's donning a loincloth for the first time only four pages before he meets Jane), the story is difficult to put down. The plot swings us swiftly and smoothly from incident to incident, even if there is an occasional interruption, such as Burroughs's discussion of evolution, in the flow of the action.

Although this pattern of exposition, rising action, conflict, suspense, climax, and resolution provides a useful outline of many plots that emphasize physical action, a greater value of this pattern is that it helps us to see how innovative artists move beyond formula fiction by manipulating and changing the pattern for their own purposes. At the furthest extreme are those modern storytellers who reject traditional plotting techniques in favor of experimental approaches. Instead of including characters who wrestle with conflicts, experimental fiction frequently may concern the writer's own efforts to create a story. Rather than ordering experience, such writers disrupt it by insisting that meanings in fiction are as elusive — or nonexistent — as meanings in life; they are likely to reject both traditional values and traditional forms of writing. Most writers, however, use conflicts in their plots to reveal characters and convey meanings. The nature of those conflicts can help determine how important physical action is to the plot.

The primary conflict that Tarzan experiences in his battle with Terkoz is external. External conflict is popular in adventure stories because the protagonist's physical struggles with a formidable foe or the ever-present dangers of a dense jungle echoing wild screams provide plenty of excitement. External conflicts may place the protagonist in opposition to another individual, nature, or society. Tarzan's battle with societal values begins the moment he instinctively takes Jane in his arms to carry her off into the jungle. He will learn that an individual's conflict with society can be as frustrating as it is complex, which is why so many plots in serious fiction focus on this conflict. It can be seen, to cite only two examples, in a mysterious stranger's alienation from a materialistic culture in Herman Melville's "Bartleby, the Scrivener" (p. 80) and in a young black man's struggle with racism in Ralph Ellison's "Battle Royal" (p. 179).

Conflict may also be internal; in such a case some moral or psychological issue must be resolved within the protagonist. Inner conflicts frequently accompany external ones, as in Godwin's "A Sorrowful Woman" (p. 30). Godwin's story is quiet and almost uneventful compared with *Tarzan of the Apes.* The conflict, though puzzling, is more significant in "A Sorrowful Woman," because that story subtly explores some troubling issues that cannot be resolved simply by "huge biceps" or a "lithe, young form." The protagonist struggles with both internal and external forces. We are not told why she withdraws from her considerate husband and beautiful son. There is no exposition to explain why she is hopelessly "sad and sick" of them. There is no readily identifiable antagonist in her way, but there are several possibilities. Her antagonist is some part of herself that cannot find satisfaction in playing the roles of wife and mother, yet her husband and child also seem to bear some of the responsibility, as does the domestic environment that defines her.

Godwin creates questions for the reader rather than suspense. We are compelled to keep asking why the protagonist in her story is so unhappy instead of what is going to happen next. The story ends with her flurry of domestic activity and her death, but we do not feel as if we have come to a resolution. "A Sorrowful Woman" will not let us go because we keep coming back to what causes the protagonist's rejection of her role. Has she gone mad? Are the husband and child not what they seem to be? Is her domestic life stifling rather than nourishing? Does her family destroy rather than support her? Who or what is to blame? No one is able to rescue the sorrowful woman from her conflict, nor does the design of Godwin's plot relieve the reader of the questions the story raises. The meaning of the action is not self-evident as it is in *Tarzan of the Apes.* It must be drawn from a careful reading of the interrelated details and dialogues that constitute this story's action.

Although Burroughs makes enormous demands on Tarzan to survive the perils of the jungle, the author makes few demands on the reader. In part, that's why *Tarzan of the Apes* is so much fun: we sit back while Tarzan does all the work, struggling heroically through all the conflicts Burroughs planted along his jungle paths. Godwin's story, in contrast, illustrates that there are other kinds of plots, less dependent on action but equally full of conflict. This kind of reading is more demanding, but ultimately more satisfying, because as we confront conflicts in serious fiction we read not only absorbing stories but also ourselves. We are invited not to escape life but to look long and hard at it. Although serious fiction can be as diverting and pleasurable as most standard action-packed plots, serious fiction offers an additional important element: a perspective on experience that reflects rather than deflects life.

The following two stories, William Faulkner's "A Rose for Emily" and Grace Paley's "A Conversation with My Father," are remarkable for the different kinds of tension produced in each by a subtle use of plot.

WILLIAM FAULKNER (1897–1962)

Born into an old Mississippi family that had lost its influence and wealth during the Civil War, William Faulkner lived nearly all his life in the South writing about Yoknapatawpha County, an imagined Mississippi county similar to his home in Oxford. Among his novels based on this fictional location are *The Sound and the Fury* (1929), *As I Lay Dying* (1930), *Light in August*

(1932), and *Absalom, Absalom!* (1936). Although his writings are regional in their emphasis on local social history, his concerns are broader. In his 1950 acceptance speech for the Nobel Prize, he insisted that the "problems of the human heart in conflict with itself . . . alone can make good writing because only that is worth writing about, worth the agony and the sweat." This commitment is evident in his novels and in *The Collected Stories of William Faulkner* (1950). "A Rose for Emily," about the mysterious life of Emily Grierson, presents a personal conflict rooted in her southern identity. It also contains a grim surprise.

A Rose for Emily 1931

I

When Miss Emily Grierson died, our whole town went to her funeral: the men through a sort of respectful affection for a fallen monument, the women mostly out of curiosity to see the inside of her house, which no one save an old manservant — a combined gardener and cook — had seen in at least ten years.

It was a big, squarish frame house that had once been white, decorated with cupolas and spires and scrolled balconies in the heavily lightsome style of the seventies, set on what had once been our most select street. But garages and cotton gins had encroached and obliterated even the august names of that neighborhood; only Miss Emily's house was left, lifting its stubborn and coquettish decay above the cotton wagons and the gasoline pumps — an eyesore among eyesores. And now Miss Emily had gone to join the representatives of those august names where they lay in the cedar-bemused cemetery among the ranked and anonymous graves of Union and Confederate soldiers who fell at the battle of Jefferson.

Alive, Miss Emily had been a tradition, a duty, and a care; a sort of hereditary obligation upon the town, dating from that day in 1894 when Colonel Sartoris, the mayor — he who fathered the edict that no Negro woman should appear on the streets without an apron — remitted her taxes, the dispensation dating from the death of her father on into perpetuity. Not that Miss Emily would have accepted charity. Colonel Sartoris invented an involved tale to the effect that Miss Emily's father had loaned money to the town, which the town, as a matter of business, preferred this way of repaying. Only a man of Colonel Sartoris' generation and thought could have invented it, and only a woman could have believed it.

When the next generation, with its more modern ideas, became mayors and aldermen, this arrangement created some little dissatisfaction. On the first of the year they mailed her a tax notice. February came, and there was no reply. They wrote her a formal letter, asking her to call at the sheriff's office at her convenience. A week later the mayor wrote her himself, offering to call or to send his car for her, and received in reply a note on paper of an archaic shape, in a thin, flowing calligraphy in faded ink, to the effect that she no longer went out at all. The tax notice was also enclosed, without comment.

5 They called a special meeting of the Board of Aldermen. A deputation waited upon her, knocked at the door through which no visitor had passed since she ceased giving china-painting lessons eight or ten years earlier. They were admitted by the old Negro into a dim hall from which a stairway mounted into still more shadow. It smelled of dust and disuse — a close, dank smell. The Negro led them into the parlor. It was furnished in heavy, leather-covered furniture. When the Negro opened the blinds of one window, they could see that the leather was cracked; and when they sat down, a faint dust rose sluggishly about their thighs, spinning with slow motes in the single sun-ray. On a tarnished gilt easel before the fireplace stood a crayon portrait of Miss Emily's father.

They rose when she entered — a small, fat woman in black, with a thin gold chain descending to her waist and vanishing into her belt, leaning on an ebony cane with a tarnished gold head. Her skeleton was small and spare; perhaps that was why what would have been merely plumpness in another was obesity in her. She looked bloated, like a body long submerged in motionless water, and of that pallid hue. Her eyes, lost in the fatty ridges of her face, looked like two small pieces of coal pressed into a lump of dough as they moved from one face to another while the visitors stated their errand.

She did not ask them to sit. She just stood in the door and listened quietly until the spokesman came to a stumbling halt. Then they could hear the invisible watch ticking at the end of the gold chain.

Her voice was dry and cold. "I have no taxes in Jefferson. Colonel Sartoris explained it to me. Perhaps one of you can gain access to the city records and satisfy yourselves."

"But we have. We are the city authorities, Miss Emily. Didn't you get a notice from the sheriff, signed by him?"

10 "I received a paper, yes," Miss Emily said. "Perhaps he considers himself the sheriff . . . I have no taxes in Jefferson."

"But there is nothing on the books to show that, you see. We must go by the — "

"See Colonel Sartoris. I have no taxes in Jefferson."

"But, Miss Emily — "

"See Colonel Sartoris." (Colonel Sartoris had been dead almost ten years.) "I have no taxes in Jefferson. Tobe!" The Negro appeared. "Show these gentlemen out."

II

15 So she vanquished them, horse and foot, just as she had vanquished their fathers thirty years before about the smell. That was two years after her father's death and a short time after her sweetheart — the one we believed would marry her — had deserted her. After her father's death she went out very little; after her sweetheart went away, people hardly saw her at all. A few of the ladies had the temerity to call, but were not received, and the only sign of life about the place was the Negro man — a young man then — going in and out with a market basket.

"Just as if a man — any man — could keep a kitchen properly," the ladies said; so they were not surprised when the smell developed. It was another link between the gross, teeming world and the high and mighty Griersons.

A neighbor, a woman, complained to the mayor, Judge Stevens, eighty years old.

"But what will you have me do about it, madam?" he said.

"Why, send her word to stop it," the woman said. "Isn't there a law?"

20 "I'm sure that won't be necessary," Judge Stevens said. "It's probably just a snake or a rat that nigger of hers killed in the yard. I'll speak to him about it."

The next day he received two more complaints, one from a man who came in diffident deprecation. "We really must do something about it, Judge. I'd be the last one in the world to bother Miss Emily, but we've got to do something." That night the Board of Aldermen met — three graybeards and one younger man, a member of the rising generation.

"It's simple enough," he said. "Send her word to have her place cleaned up. Give her a certain time to do it in, and if she don't . . ."

"Dammit, sir," Judge Stevens said, "will you accuse a lady to her face of smelling bad?"

So the next night, after midnight, four men crossed Miss Emily's lawn and slunk about the house like burglars, sniffing along the base of the brickwork and at the cellar openings while one of them performed a regular sowing motion with his hand out of a sack slung from his shoulder. They broke open the cellar door and sprinkled lime there, and in all the outbuildings. As they recrossed the lawn, a window that had been dark was lighted and Miss Emily sat in it, the light behind her, and her upright torso motionless as that of an idol. They crept quietly across the lawn and into the shadow of the locusts that lined the street. After a week or two the smell went away.

25 That was when people had begun to feel really sorry for her. People in our town, remembering how old lady Wyatt, her great-aunt, had gone completely crazy at last, believed that the Griersons held themselves a little too high for what they really were. None of the young men were quite good enough for Miss Emily and such. We had long thought of them as a tableau, Miss Emily a slender figure in white in the background, her father a spraddled silhouette in the foreground, his back to her and clutching a horsewhip, the two of them framed by the back-flung front door. So when she got to be thirty and was still single, we were not pleased exactly, but vindicated; even with insanity in the family she wouldn't have turned down all of her chances if they had really materialized.

When her father died, it got about that the house was all that was left to her; and in a way, people were glad. At last they could pity Miss Emily. Being left alone, and a pauper, she had become humanized. Now she too would know the old thrill and the old despair of a penny more or less.

The day after his death all the ladies prepared to call at the house and offer condolence and aid, as is our custom. Miss Emily met them at the door, dressed as usual and with no trace of grief on her face. She told them that her father was not dead. She did that for three days, with the ministers calling on her, and the doctors, trying to persuade her to let them dispose of the body. Just as they were about to resort to law and force, she broke down, and they buried her father quickly.

We did not say she was crazy then. We believed she had to do that. We remembered all the young men her father had driven away, and we knew that with nothing left, she would have to cling to that which had robbed her, as people will.

III

She was sick for a long time. When we saw her again, her hair was cut short, making her look like a girl, with a vague resemblance to those angels in colored church windows — sort of tragic and serene.

30 The town had just let the contracts for paving the sidewalks, and in the summer after her father's death they began the work. The construction company came with niggers and mules and machinery, and a foreman named Homer Barron, a Yankee — a big, dark, ready man, with a big voice and eyes lighter than his face. The little boys would follow in groups to hear him cuss the niggers, and the niggers singing in time to the rise and fall of picks. Pretty soon he knew everybody in town. Whenever you heard a lot of laughing anywhere about the square, Homer Barron would be in the center of the group. Presently we began to see him and Miss Emily on Sunday afternoons driving in the yellow-wheeled buggy and the matched team of bays from the livery stable.

At first we were glad that Miss Emily would have an interest, because the ladies all said, "Of course a Grierson would not think seriously of a Northerner, a day laborer." But there were still others, older people, who said that even grief could not cause a real lady to forget *noblesse oblige*° — without calling it *noblesse oblige.* They just said, "Poor Emily. Her kinsfolk should come to her." She had some kin in Alabama; but years ago her father had fallen out with them over the estate of old lady Wyatt, the crazy woman, and there was no communication between the two families. They had not even been represented at the funeral.

And as soon as the old people said, "Poor Emily," the whispering began. "Do you suppose it's really so?" they said to one another. "Of course it is. What else could . . ." This behind their hands; rustling of craned silk and satin behind jalousies closed upon the sun of Sunday afternoon as the thin, swift clop-clop-clop of the matched team passed: "Poor Emily."

She carried her head high enough — even when we believed that she was fallen. It was as if she demanded more than ever the recognition of her dignity as the last Grierson; as if it had wanted that touch of earthiness to reaffirm her imperviousness. Like when she bought the rat poison, the arsenic. That was over a year after they had begun to say "Poor Emily," and while the two female cousins were visiting her.

"I want some poison," she said to the druggist. She was over thirty then, still a slight woman, though thinner than usual, with cold, haughty black eyes in a face the flesh of which was strained across the temples and about the eye-sockets as you imagine a lighthouse-keeper's face ought to look. "I want some poison," she said.

35 "Yes, Miss Emily. What kind? For rats and such? I'd recom— "

"I want the best you have. I don't care what kind."

The druggist named several. "They'll kill anything up to an elephant. But what you want is — "

"Arsenic," Miss Emily said. "Is that a good one?"

"Is . . . arsenic? Yes, ma'am. But what you want — "

noblesse oblige: The obligation of people of high social position.

"I want arsenic." 40

The druggist looked down at her. She looked back at him, erect, her face like a strained flag. "Why, of course," the druggist said. "If that's what you want. But the law requires you to tell what you are going to use it for."

Miss Emily just stared at him, her head tilted back in order to look him eye for eye, until he looked away and went and got the arsenic and wrapped it up. The Negro delivery boy brought her the package; the druggist didn't come back. When she opened the package at home there was written on the box, under the skull and bones: "For rats."

IV

So the next day we all said, "She will kill herself"; and we said it would be the best thing. When she had first begun to be seen with Homer Barron, we had said, "She will marry him." Then we said, "She will persuade him yet," because Homer himself had remarked — he liked men, and it was known that he drank with the younger men in the Elks' Club — that he was not a marrying man. Later we said, "Poor Emily" behind the jalousies as they passed on Sunday afternoon in the glittering buggy, Miss Emily with her head high and Homer Barron with his hat cocked and a cigar in his teeth, reins and whip in a yellow glove.

Then some of the ladies began to say that it was a disgrace to the town and a bad example to the young people. The men did not want to interfere, but at last the ladies forced the Baptist minister — Miss Emily's people were Episcopal — to call upon her. He would never divulge what happened during that interview, but he refused to go back again. The next Sunday they again drove about the streets, and the following day the minister's wife wrote to Miss Emily's relations in Alabama.

So she had blood-kin under her roof again and we sat back to watch de- 45
velopments. At first nothing happened. Then we were sure that they were to be married. We learned that Miss Emily had been to the jeweler's and ordered a man's toilet set in silver, with the letters H. B. on each piece. Two days later we learned that she had bought a complete outfit of men's clothing, including a nightshirt, and we said, "They are married." We were really glad. We were glad because the two female cousins were even more Grierson than Miss Emily had ever been.

So we were not surprised when Homer Barron — the streets had been finished some time since — was gone. We were a little disappointed that there was not a public blowing-off, but we believed that he had gone on to prepare for Miss Emily's coming, or to give her a chance to get rid of the cousins. (By that time it was a cabal, and we were all Miss Emily's allies to help circumvent the cousins.) Sure enough, after another week they departed. And, as we had expected all along, within three days Homer Barron was back in town. A neighbor saw the Negro man admit him at the kitchen door at dusk one evening.

And that was the last we saw of Homer Barron. And of Miss Emily for some time. The Negro man went in and out with the market basket, but the front door remained closed. Now and then we would see her at a window for a moment, as the men did that night when they sprinkled the lime, but for almost six months she did not appear on the streets. Then we knew that this was to be expected too; as if that quality of her father which had thwarted her woman's life so many times had been too virulent and too furious to die.

When we next saw Miss Emily, she had grown fat and her hair was turning gray. During the next few years it grew grayer and grayer until it attained an even pepper-and-salt iron-gray, when it ceased turning. Up to the day of her death at seventy-four it was still that vigorous iron-gray, like the hair of an active man.

From that time on her front door remained closed, save for a period of six or seven years, when she was about forty, during which she gave lessons in china-painting. She fitted up a studio in one of the downstairs rooms, where the daughters and granddaughters of Colonel Sartoris' contemporaries were sent to her with the same regularity and in the same spirit that they were sent to church on Sundays with a twenty-five-cent piece for the collection plate. Meanwhile her taxes had been remitted.

Then the newer generation became the backbone and the spirit of the 50
town, and the painting pupils grew up and fell away and did not send their children to her with boxes of color and tedious brushes and pictures cut from the ladies' magazines. The front door closed upon the last one and remained closed for good. When the town got free postal delivery, Miss Emily alone refused to let them fasten the metal numbers above her door and attach a mailbox to it. She would not listen to them.

Daily, monthly, yearly we watched the Negro grow grayer and more stooped, going in and out with the market basket. Each December we sent her a tax notice, which would be returned by the post office a week later, unclaimed. Now and then we would see her in one of the downstairs windows — she had evidently shut up the top floor of the house — like the carven torso of an idol in a niche, looking or not looking at us, we could never tell which. Thus she passed from generation to generation — dear, inescapable, impervious, tranquil, and perverse.

And so she died. Fell ill in the house filled with dust and shadows, with only a doddering Negro man to wait on her. We did not even know she was sick; we had long since given up trying to get information from the Negro. He talked to no one, probably not even to her, for his voice had grown harsh and rusty, as if from disuse.

She died in one of the downstairs rooms, in a heavy walnut bed with a curtain, her gray head propped on a pillow yellow and moldy with age and lack of sunlight.

V

The Negro met the first of the ladies at the front door and let them in, with their hushed, sibilant voices and their quick, curious glances, and then he disappeared. He walked right through the house and out the back and was not seen again.

The two female cousins came at once. They held the funeral on the second 55
day, with the town coming to look at Miss Emily beneath a mass of bought flowers, with the crayon face of her father musing profoundly above the bier

and the ladies sibilant and macabre; and the very old men — some in their brushed Confederate uniforms — on the porch and the lawn, talking of Miss Emily as if she had been a contemporary of theirs, believing that they had danced with her and courted her perhaps, confusing time with its mathematical progression, as the old do, to whom all the past is not a diminishing road but, instead, a huge meadow which no winter ever quite touches, divided from them now by the narrow bottle-neck of the most recent decade of years.

Already we knew that there was one room in that region above stairs which no one had seen in forty years, and which would have to be forced. They waited until Miss Emily was decently in the ground before they opened it.

The violence of breaking down the door seemed to fill this room with pervading dust. A thin, acrid pall as of the tomb seemed to lie everywhere upon this room decked and furnished as for a bridal: upon the valance curtains of faded rose color, upon the rose-shaded lights, upon the dressing table, upon the delicate array of crystal and the man's toilet things backed with tarnished silver, silver so tarnished that the monogram was obscured. Among them lay a collar and tie, as if they had just been removed, which, lifted, left upon the surface a pale crescent in the dust. Upon a chair hung the suit, carefully folded; beneath it the two mute shoes and the discarded socks.

The man himself lay in the bed.

For a long while we just stood there, looking down at the profound and fleshless grin. The body had apparently once lain in the attitude of an embrace, but now the long sleep that outlasts love, that conquers even the grimace of love, had cuckolded him. What was left of him, rotted beneath what was left of the nightshirt, had become inextricable from the bed in which he lay; and upon him and upon the pillow beside him lay that even coating of the patient and biding dust.

Then we noticed that in the second pillow was the indentation of a head. 60
One of us lifted something from it, and leaning forward, that faint and invisible dust dry and acrid in the nostrils, we saw a long strand of iron-gray hair.

Considerations

1. What is the effect of the final paragraph of the story? How does it contribute to your understanding of Emily? Why is it important that we get this information last rather than at the beginning of the story?
2. What details foreshadow the conclusion of the story? Did you anticipate the ending?
3. Contrast the order of events as they happen in the story with the order in which they are told. How does this plotting create interest and suspense?
4. Faulkner uses a number of gothic elements in this plot: the imposing decrepit house, the decayed corpse, and the mysterious secret horrors connected with Emily's life. How do these elements forward the plot and establish the atmosphere?
5. How does the information provided by the exposition indicate the nature of the conflict in the story? What does Emily's southern heritage contribute to the story?
6. Who or what is the antagonist of the story? Why is it significant that Homer Barron is a construction foreman and a northerner?
7. In what sense does the narrator's telling of the story serve as "A Rose for Emily"? Why do you think the narrator uses *we* rather than *I*?

8. Explain how Emily's reasons for murdering Homer are related to her personal history and to the way she handled previous conflicts.
9. Discuss how Faulkner's treatment of the North and South contributes to the meaning of the story.
10. Provide an alternative title and explain how the emphasis in your title is reflected in the story.
11. Describe how this story could be rewritten as a piece of formula fiction and comment on the differences between Faulkner's story and your imagined formulaic version.

Connections

1. Contrast Faulkner's ordering of events with Yukio Mishima's strategy in "Patriotism" (p. 412). How does each author's arrangement of incidents create different effects on the reader?
2. To what extent do concepts of honor and tradition influence the action in "A Rose for Emily" and "Patriotism"?
3. Compare and contrast Faulkner's and Mishima's uses of death as a means of resolving conflicts having to do with love.

PERSPECTIVE

WILLIAM FAULKNER (1897–1962)

On "A Rose for Emily" 1959

Q. What is the meaning of the title "A Rose for Emily"?

A. Oh, it's simply the poor woman had had no life at all. Her father had kept her more or less locked up and then she had a lover who was about to quit her, she had to murder him. It was just "A Rose for Emily"—that's all.

Q. . . . What ever inspired you to write this story?

A. That to me was another sad and tragic manifestation of man's condition in which he dreams and hopes, in which he is in conflict with himself or with his environment or with others. In this case there was the young girl with a young girl's normal aspirations to find love and then a husband and a family, who was brow-beaten and kept down by her father, a selfish man who didn't want her to leave home because he wanted a housekeeper, and it was a natural instinct of—repressed which—you can't repress it—you can mash it down but it comes up somewhere else and very likely in a tragic form, and that was simply another manifestation of man's injustice to man, of the poor tragic human being struggling with its own heart, with others, with its environment, for the simple things which all human beings want. In that case it was a young girl that just wanted to be loved and to love and to have a husband and a family.

Q. And that purely came from your imagination?

A. Well, the story did but the condition is there. It exists. I didn't invent that condition, I didn't invent the fact that young girls dream of someone to love and children and a home, but the story of what her own particular tragedy was was invented, yes. . . .

Q. Sir, it has been argued that "A Rose for Emily" is a criticism of the North, and others have argued saying that it is a criticism of the South. Now, could this story, shall we say, be more properly classified as a criticism of the times?

A. Now that I don't know, because I was simply trying to write about people. The writer uses environment — what he knows — and if there's a symbolism in which the lover represented the North and the woman who murdered him represents the South, I don't say that's not valid and not there, but it was no intention of the writer to say, Now let's see, I'm going to write a piece in which I will use a symbolism for the North and another symbol for the South, that he was simply writing about people, a story which he thought was tragic and true, because it came out of the human heart, the human aspiration, the human — the conflict of conscience with glands, with the Old Adam. It was a conflict not between North and the South so much as between, well you might say, God and Satan.

Q. Sir, just a little more on that thing. You say it's a conflict between God and Satan. Well, I don't quite understand what you mean. Who is — did one represent the ——

A. The conflict was in Miss Emily, that she knew that you do not murder people. She had been trained that you do not take a lover. You marry, you don't take a lover. She had broken all the laws of her tradition, her background, and she had finally broken the law of God too, which says you do not take human life. And she knew she was doing wrong, and that's why her own life was wrecked. Instead of murdering one lover, and then to go and take another and when she used him up to murder him, she was expiating her crime.

Q. Was the "Rose for Emily" an idea or a character? Just how did you go about it?

A. That came from a picture of the strand of hair on the pillow. It was a ghost story. Simply a picture of a strand of hair on the pillow in the abandoned house.

From Frederick Gwynn and Joseph Blotner, eds., *Faulkner in the University*

Considerations

1. Discuss whether you think Faulkner's explanation of the conflict between "God and Satan" limits or expands the meaning of the story for you.
2. In what sense is "A Rose for Emily" a "ghost story"?
3. Compare Faulkner's account of how he conceived "A Rose for Emily" with Flannery O'Connor's description of "Good Country People" (p. 302). To what extent are their attitudes about symbolism similar?

GRACE PALEY (b. 1922)

Born in New York, Grace Paley lived there most of her life. Having grown up in a family that spoke English, Russian, and Yiddish, she writes, as she puts it, "with an accent." Her stories are characterized by the humor, irony, and everyday concerns she heard spoken around her. Although she attended Hunter College and New York University, her education was shaped more by her family life and her active political role in protesting the Vietnam War and the nuclear arms race. Her three collections of short stories, *The Little Disturbances of Man* (1959), *Enormous Changes at the Last Minute* (1974), which includes the following story, and *Later the Same Day* (1985), have earned her a reputation as a compassionate writer whose tact and humor reveal the mysteries of daily life. "A Conversation with My Father" brings together two of her greatest concerns: family life and the writing of stories.

A Conversation with My Father 1972

My father is eighty-six years old and in bed. His heart, that bloody motor, is equally old and will not do certain jobs any more. It still floods his head with brainy light. But it won't let his legs carry the weight of his body around the house. Despite my metaphors, this muscle failure is not due to his old heart, he says, but to a potassium shortage. Sitting on one pillow, leaning on three, he offers last-minute advice and makes a request.

"I would like you to write a simple story just once more," he says, "the kind de Maupassant wrote, or Chekhov,° the kind you used to write. Just recognizable people and then write down what happened to them next."

I say, "Yes, why not? That's possible." I want to please him, though I don't remember writing that way. I *would* like to try to tell such a story, if he means the kind that begins: "There was a woman . . ." followed by plot, the absolute line between two points which I've always despised. Not for literary reasons, but because it takes all hope away. Everyone, real or invented, deserves the open destiny of life.

Finally I thought of a story that had been happening for a couple of years right across the street. I wrote it down, then read it aloud. "Pa," I said, "how about this? Do you mean something like this?"

> Once in my time there was a woman and she had a son. They lived nicely, in a small apartment in Manhattan. This boy at about fifteen became a junkie, which is not unusual in our neighborhood. In order to maintain her close friendship with him, she became a junkie too. She said it was part of the youth culture, with which she felt very much at home. After a while, for a number of reasons, the boy gave it all up and left the city and his mother in disgust. Hopeless and alone, she grieved. We all visit her.

"O.K., Pa, that's it," I said, "an unadorned and miserable tale." 5

"But that's not what I mean," my father said. "You misunderstood me on

de Maupassant: Guy de Maupassant (1850–1893), French novelist and short story writer known for his pared-down realism and exact observation of characters; *Chekhov:* Anton Chekhov (1860–1904), Russian playwright and short story writer known for his artistic technique and compassionate characterization (see p. 146).

purpose. You know there's a lot more to it. You know that. You left everything out. Turgenev° wouldn't do that. Chekhov wouldn't do that. There are in fact Russian writers you never heard of, you don't have an inkling of, as good as anyone, who can write a plain ordinary story, who would not leave out what you have left out. I object not to facts but to people sitting in trees talking senselessly, voices from who knows where. . . ."

"Forget that one, Pa, what have I left out now? In this one?"

"Her looks, for instance."

"Oh. Quite handsome, I think. Yes."

"Her hair?" 10

"Dark, with heavy braids, as though she were a girl or a foreigner."

"What were her parents like, her stock? That she became such a person. It's interesting, you know."

"From out of town. Professional people. The first to be divorced in their county. How's that? Enough?" I asked.

"With you, it's all a joke," he said. "What about the boy's father? Why didn't you mention him? Who was he? Or was the boy born out of wedlock?"

"Yes," I said. "He was born out of wedlock." 15

"For Godsakes, doesn't anyone in your stories get married? Doesn't anyone have the time to run down to City Hall before they jump into bed?"

"No," I said. "In real life, yes. But in my stories, no."

"Why do you answer me like that?"

"Oh, Pa, this is a simple story about a smart woman who came to N.Y.C. full of interest love trust excitement very up to date, and about her son, what a hard time she had in this world. Married or not, it's of small consequence."

"It is of great consequence," he said. 20

"O.K.," I said.

"O.K. O.K. yourself," he said, "but listen. I believe you that she's good-looking, but I don't think she was so smart."

"That's true," I said. "Actually that's the trouble with stories. People start out fantastic. You think they're extraordinary, but it turns out as the work goes along, they're just average with a good education. Sometimes the other way around, the person's a kind of dumb innocent, but he outwits you and you can't even think of an ending good enough."

"What do you do then?" he asked. He had been a doctor for a couple of decades and then an artist for a couple of decades and he's still interested in details, craft, technique.

"Well, you just have to let the story lie around till some agreement can be reached between you and the stubborn hero." 25

"Aren't you talking silly now?" he asked. "Start again," he said. "It so happens I'm not going out this evening. Tell the story again. See what you can do this time."

"O.K.," I said. "But it's not a five-minute job." Second attempt:

> Once across the street from us, there was a fine handsome woman, our neighbor. She had a son whom she loved because she'd known him since

Turgenev: Ivan Turgenev (1818–1883), Russian novelist and short story writer and, like de Maupassant and Chekhov, a realist.

birth (in helpless chubby infancy, and in the wrestling, hugging ages, seven to ten, as well as earlier and later). This boy, when he fell into the fist of adolescence, became a junkie. He was not a hopeless one. He was in fact hopeful, an ideologue and successful converter. With his busy brilliance, he wrote persuasive articles for his high-school newspaper. Seeking a wider audience, using important connections, he drummed into Lower Manhattan newsstand distribution a periodical called *Oh! Golden Horse!*

In order to keep him from feeling guilty (because guilt is the stony heart of nine tenths of all clinically diagnosed cancers in America today, she said), and because she had always believed in giving bad habits room at home where one could keep an eye on them, she too became a junkie. Her kitchen was famous for a while — a center for intellectual addicts who knew what they were doing. A few felt artistic like Coleridge° and others were scientific and revolutionary like Leary.° Although she was often high herself, certain good mothering reflexes remained, and she saw to it that there was lots of orange juice around and honey and milk and vitamin pills. However, she never cooked anything but chili, and that no more than once a week. She explained, when we talked to her, seriously, with neighborly concern, that it was her part in the youth culture and she would rather be with the young, it was an honor, than with her own generation.

One week, while nodding through an Antonioni film,° this boy was severely jabbed by the elbow of a stern and proselytizing girl, sitting beside him. She offered immediate apricots and nuts for his sugar level, spoke to him sharply, and took him home.

She had heard of him and his work and she herself published, edited, and wrote a competitive journal called *Man Does Live by Bread Alone.* In the organic heat of her continuous presence he could not help but become interested once more in his muscles, his arteries, and nerve connections. In fact he began to love them, treasure them, praise them with funny little songs in *Man Does Live. . . .*

the fingers of my flesh transcend
my transcendental soul
the tightness in my shoulders end
my teeth have made me whole

To the mouth of his head (that glory of will and determination) he brought hard apples, nuts, wheat germ, and soybean oil. He said to his old friends, From now on, I guess I'll keep my wits about me. I'm going on the natch. He said he was about to begin a spiritual deep-breathing journey. How about you too, Mom? he asked kindly.

His conversion was so radiant, splendid, that neighborhood kids his age began to say that he had never been a real addict at all, only a journalist along for the smell of the story. The mother tried several times to give up what had become without her son and his friends a lonely habit. This effort only brought it to supportable levels. The boy and his girl took their electronic mimeograph and moved to the bushy edge of another borough. They were

Coleridge: Samuel Taylor Coleridge (1771–1834), English Romantic poet, who was an opium addict.
Leary: Timothy Leary (b. 1920), former Harvard professor of psychology and early advocate of the use of LSD.
Antonioni: Michelangelo Antonioni (b. 1912), Italian film director whose works often portray the meaninglessness and alienation of contemporary life.

very strict. They said they would not see her again until she had been off drugs for sixty days.

At home alone in the evening, weeping, the mother read and reread the seven issues of *Oh! Golden Horse!* They seemed to her as truthful as ever. We often crossed the street to visit and console. But if we mentioned any of our children who were at college or in the hospital or dropouts at home, she would cry out, My baby! My baby! and burst into terrible, face-scarring, time-consuming tears. The End.

First my father was silent, then he said, "Number One: You have a nice sense of humor. Number Two: I see you can't tell a plain story. So don't waste time." Then he said sadly, "Number Three: I suppose that means she was alone, she was left like that, his mother. Alone. Probably sick?"

I said, "Yes."

"Poor woman. Poor girl, to be born in a time of fools, to live among fools. 30
The end. The end. You were right to put that down. The end."

I didn't want to argue, but I had to say, "Well, it is not necessarily the end, Pa."

"Yes," he said, "what a tragedy. The end of a person."

"No, Pa," I begged him. "It doesn't have to be. She's only about forty. She could be a hundred different things in this world as time goes on. A teacher or a social worker. An ex-junkie! Sometimes it's better than having a master's in education."

"Jokes," he said. "As a writer that's your main trouble. You don't want to recognize it. Tragedy! Plain tragedy! Historical tragedy! No hope. The end."

"Oh, Pa," I said. "She could change." 35

"In your own life, too, you have to look it in the face." He took a couple of nitroglycerin. "Turn to five," he said, pointing to the dial on the oxygen tank. He inserted the tubes into his nostrils and breathed deep. He closed his eyes and said, "No."

I had always promised the family to always let him have the last word when arguing, but in this case I had a different responsibility. That woman lives across the street. She's my knowledge and my invention. I'm sorry for her. I'm not going to leave her there in that house crying. (Actually neither would Life, which unlike me has no pity.)

Therefore: She did change. Of course her son never came home again. But right now, she's the receptionist in a storefront community clinic in the East Village. Most of the customers are young people, some old friends. The head doctor has said to her, "If we only had three people in this clinic with your experiences. . . ."

"The doctor said that?" My father took the oxygen tubes out of his nostrils and said, "Jokes. Jokes again."

"No, Pa, it could really happen that way, it's a funny world nowadays." 40

"No," he said. "Truth first. She will slide back. A person must have character. She does not."

"No, Pa," I said. "That's it. She's got a job. Forget it. She's in that storefront working."

"How long will it be?" he asked. "Tragedy! You too. When will you look it in the face?"

Considerations

1. How do the daughter and father in this story feel about each other? Describe their relationship.
2. Why do you think the father prefers the second version of the addicts' story to the first? What reservations does he express about the second version?
3. The father complains that "jokes" are his daughter's "main trouble" as a writer, but she insists that "it's a funny world nowadays." What kinds of stories does the father like? How do his preferences differ from his daughter's?
4. The action in this story consists largely of storytelling. How are the two versions of the daughter's story within the story related to her differences with her father?
5. Explain whether you think the main interest in this story is the relationship between the father and daughter or that between the mother and son. Whose story is it? What is the major conflict?
6. What do the father's age and physical condition have to do with his tastes in storytelling? What do you know about the daughter that helps explain her perspective on fiction?
7. How do the father's and daughter's attitudes toward fiction reveal their attitudes toward life?
8. What do you think the father means in the final paragraph? If you were to extend the story by having the daughter reply to his question, what would you have her say? Explain your response.
9. Explain whether your view of what constitutes a good story is closer to the father's or the daughter's perspective.

Connections

1. Given the father's preference for a "simple story" with "recognizable people and then . . . . what happened to them next," what do you imagine he would have to say about the plot of Faulkner's "A Rose for Emily" (p. 47)?
2. In "A Conversation with My Father" the narrator resists, in both theory and practice, her father's desire for a traditional story, one in which the "plot" develops a straightforward "absolute line between two points." Compare her views and methods of storytelling with those of the narrator in Tim O'Brien's "How to Tell a True War Story" (p. 454). How does the plot of each story — the artistic arrangement of incidents — reflect a vision of what each narrator takes to be "true" about life and the fictional representation of it?

3. Character

Character is essential to plot. Without characters Burroughs's *Tarzan of the Apes* would be a travelogue through the jungle and Faulkner's "A Rose for Emily" little more than a faded history of a sleepy town in the South. If stories were depopulated, the plots would disappear because stories and plots are interrelated. A dangerous jungle is important only because we care what effect it has on a character. Characters are influenced by events just as events are shaped by characters. Tarzan's physical strength is the result of his growing up in the jungle, and his strength, along with his inherited intelligence, allows him to be master there.

The methods by which a writer creates people in a story so that they seem actually to exist are called ***characterization.*** Huck Finn never lived, yet those who have read Mark Twain's novel about his adventures along the Mississippi River feel as if they know him. A good writer gives us the illusion that a character is real, but we should also remember that a character is not an actual person but instead has been created by the author. Though we might walk out of a room in which Huck Finn's Pap talks racist nonsense, we would not throw away the book in a similar fit of anger. This illusion of reality is the magic that allows us to move beyond the circumstances of our own lives into a writer's fictional world, where we can encounter everyone from royalty to paupers, murderers, lovers, cheaters, martyrs, artists, destroyers, and, nearly always, some part of ourselves. The life that a writer breathes into a character adds to our own experiences and enlarges our view of the world.

A character is usually but not always a person. In Jack London's *Call of the Wild,* the protagonist is a devoted sled dog; in Herman Melville's *Moby-Dick* the antagonist is an unfathomable whale. Perhaps the only possible qualification to be placed on character is that whatever it is — whether an animal or even an inanimate object, such as a robot — it must have some recognizable human qualities. The action of the plot interests us primarily because we care about what happens to people and what they do. We may identify with a character's desires and aspirations, or we may be disgusted by his or her viciousness and selfishness. To understand our response to a story, we should be able to recognize the methods of characterization the author uses.

CHARLES DICKENS (1812–1870)

Charles Dickens is well known for creating characters who have stepped off the pages of his fictions into the imaginations and memories of his readers. His characters are successful not because readers might have encountered such people in their own lives, but because his characterizations are vivid and convincing. He manages to make strange and eccentric people appear familiar. The following excerpt from *Hard Times* is the novel's entire first chapter. In it Dickens introduces and characterizes a school principal addressing a classroom full of children.

From *Hard Times* 1854

"Now, what I want is, Facts. Teach these boys and girls nothing but Facts. Facts alone are wanted in life. Plant nothing else, and root out everything else. You can only form the minds of reasoning animals upon Facts: nothing else will ever be of any service to them. This is the principle on which I bring up my own children, and this is the principle on which I bring up these children. Stick to Facts, sir!"

The scene was a plain, bare, monotonous vault of a schoolroom, and the speaker's square forefinger emphasized his observations by underscoring every sentence with a line on the schoolmaster's sleeve. The emphasis was helped by the speaker's square wall of a forehead, which had his eyebrows for its base, while his eyes found commodious cellarage in two dark caves, overshadowed by the wall. The emphasis was helped by the speaker's mouth, which was wide, thin, and hard set. The emphasis was helped by the speaker's voice, which was inflexible, dry, and dictatorial. The emphasis was helped by the speaker's hair, which bristled on the skirts of his bald head, a plantation of firs to keep the wind from its shining surface, all covered with knobs, like the crust of a plum pie, as if the head had scarcely warehouse-room for the hard facts stored inside. The speaker's obstinate carriage, square coat, square legs, square shoulders — nay, his very neckcloth, trained to take him by the throat with an unaccommodating grasp, like a stubborn fact, as it was — all helped the emphasis.

"In this life, we want nothing but Facts, sir; nothing but Facts!"

The speaker, and the schoolmaster, and the third grown person present, all backed a little, and swept with their eyes the inclined plane of little vessels then and there arranged in order, ready to have imperial gallons of facts poured into them until they were full to the brim.

Dickens withholds his character's name until the beginning of the second chapter; he calls this fact-bound educator Mr. Gradgrind. Authors sometimes put as much time and effort into naming their characters as parents invest in naming their children. Names can be used to indicate qualities that the writer associates with the characters. Mr. Gradgrind is precisely what his name suggests. The "schoolmaster" employed by Gradgrind is Mr. M'Choakumchild. Pronounce this name aloud and you have the essence of this teacher's educational philosophy. In Nathaniel Hawthorne's *Scarlet Letter,* Chillingworth is cold and relentless in his single-minded quest for revenge. The innocent and youthful protagonist in Herman Melville's *Billy Budd* is nipped in the bud by the evil Claggart, whose name simply sounds unpleasant.

Names are also used in films to suggest a character's nature. One example that is destined to be a classic is the infamous villain Darth Vader, whose name identifies his role as an invader allied with the dark and death. On the heroic side, it makes sense that Marion Morrison decided to change his box-office name to John Wayne in order to play tough, masculine roles because both the first and last of his chosen names are unambiguously male and to the point, while his given name is androgynous. There may also be some significance to the lack of a specific identity. In Godwin's "A Sorrowful Woman" (p. 30) the woman, man, boy, and girl are reduced to a set of domestic functions, and their not being named emphasizes their roles as opposed to their individual identities. Of course, not every name is suggestive of the qualities a character may embody, but it is frequently worth determining what is in a name.

The only way to tell whether a name reveals character is to look at the other information the author supplies about the character. We evaluate fictional characters in much the same way we understand people in our own lives. By piecing together bits of information, we create a context that allows us to interpret their behavior. We can predict, for instance, that an acquaintance who is a chronic complainer is not likely to have anything good to say about a roommate. We interpret words and actions in the light of what we already know about someone, and that is why keeping track of what characters say (and how they say it) along with what they do (and don't do) is important.

Authors reveal characters by other means too. Physical descriptions can indicate important inner qualities; disheveled clothing, a crafty smile, or a blush might communicate as much as or more than what a character says. Characters can also be revealed by the words and actions of others who respond to them. In literature, moreover, we have one great advantage that life cannot offer; a work of fiction can give us access to a person's thoughts. Although in Herman Melville's "Bartleby, the Scrivener" (p. 80) we learn about Bartleby primarily through descriptive details, words, actions, and his relationships with the other characters, Melville allows us to enter the lawyer's consciousness.

Authors have two major methods of presenting characters: ***showing*** and ***telling.*** Characters shown in dramatic situations reveal themselves indirectly by what they say and do. In the first paragraph of the excerpt from *Hard Times,* Dickens shows us some of Gradgrind's utilitarian educational principles by having him speak. We can infer the kind of person he is from his reference to boys and girls as "reasoning animals," but we are not told what to think of him until the second paragraph. It would be impossible to admire Gradgrind after reading the physical description of him and the school that he oversees. The adjectives in the second paragraph make the author's evaluation of Gradgrind's values and personality clear: everything about him is rigidly "square"; his mouth is "thin and hard set"; his voice is "inflexible, dry, and dictatorial"; and he presides over a "plain, bare, monotonous vault of a schoolroom." Dickens directly lets us know how to feel about Gradgrind, but he does so artistically. Instead of simply being presented with a statement that Gradgrind is destructively practical, we get a detailed and amusing description.

We can contrast Dickens's direct presentation in this paragraph with the indirect showing that Gail Godwin uses in "A Sorrowful Woman" (p. 30). Godwin avoids telling us how we should think about the characters. Their story includes little description and no evaluations or interpretations by the author. To determine the significance of the events, the reader must pay close attention to what the characters say and do. Like Godwin, many twentieth-century authors favor showing over telling, because showing allows readers to discover the meanings, which modern authors are often reluctant to impose on an audience for whom fixed meanings and values are not as strong as they once were. However, most writers continue to reveal characters by telling as well as showing when the technique suits their purposes — when, for example, a minor character must be sketched economically or when a long time has elapsed, causing changes in a major character. Telling and showing complement each other.

Characters can be convincing whether they are presented by telling or showing, provided their actions are ***motivated.*** There must be reasons for how they behave and what they say. If adequate motivation is offered, we can understand and find ***plausible*** their actions no matter how bizarre. In "A Rose for Emily" (p. 47), Faulkner makes Emily Grierson's intimacy with a corpse credible by preparing us with information about her father's death along with her inability to leave the past and live in the present. Emily turns out to be ***consistent.*** Although we are surprised by the ending of the story, the behavior it reveals is compatible with her temperament.

Some kinds of fiction consciously break away from our expectations of traditional realistic stories. Consistency, plausibility, and motivation are not very useful concepts for understanding and evaluating characterizations in modern ***absurdist literature,*** for instance, in which characters are often alienated from themselves and their environment in an irrational world. In this world there is no possibility for traditional heroic action; instead we find an ***antihero*** who has little control over events. Yossarian from Joseph

Heller's *Catch-22* is an example of a protagonist who is thwarted by the absurd terms on which life offers itself to many twentieth-century characters.

In most stories we expect characters to act plausibly and in ways consistent with their personalities, but that does not mean that characters cannot develop and change. A ***dynamic*** character undergoes some kind of change because of the action of the plot. Huck Finn's view of Jim, the runaway slave in Mark Twain's novel, develops during their experiences on the raft. Huck discovers Jim's humanity and, therefore, cannot betray him, because Huck no longer sees his companion as merely the property of a white owner. On the other hand, Huck's friend, Tom Sawyer, is a ***static*** character because he does not change. He remains interested only in high adventure, even at the risk of Jim's life. As static characters often do, Tom serves as a foil to Huck; his frivolous concerns are contrasted with Huck's serious development. A ***foil*** helps to reveal by contrast the distinctive qualities of another character.

The protagonist in a story is usually a dynamic character who experiences some conflict that makes an impact on his or her life. Less commonly, static characters can also be protagonists. Rip Van Winkle wakes up from his twenty-year sleep in Washington Irving's story to discover his family dramatically changed and his country no longer a British colony, but none of these important events has an impact on his character; he continues to be the same shiftless and idle man that he was before he fell asleep. The protagonist in Faulkner's "A Rose for Emily" is also a static character; indeed, she rejects all change. Our understanding of her changes, but she does not. Ordinarily, however, a plot contains one or two dynamic characters with any number of static characters in supporting roles. This is especially true of short stories, in which brevity limits the possibilities of character development.

The extent to which a character is developed is another means by which character can be analyzed. The novelist E. M. Forster coined the terms *flat* and *round* to distinguish degrees of character development. A ***flat character*** embodies one or two qualities, ideas, or traits that can be readily described in a brief summary. For instance, Mr. M'Choakumchild in Dickens's *Hard Times* stifles students instead of encouraging them to grow. Flat characters tend to be one-dimensional. They are readily accessible because their characteristics are few and simple; they are not created to be psychologically complex.

Some flat characters are immediately recognizable as ***stock characters.*** These stereotypes are particularly popular in formula fiction, television programs, and drive-in movies. Stock characters are types rather than individuals. The poor but dedicated writer falls in love with a hard-working understudy who gets nowhere because the corrupt producer favors his boozy, pampered mistress for the leading role. Characters such as these — the loyal servant, the mean stepfather, the henpecked husband, the dumb blonde, the sadistic army officer, the dotty grandmother — are prepackaged; they lack individuality because their authors have, in a sense, not imaginatively created them but simply summoned them from a warehouse of clichés and social prejudices. Stock characters can become fresh if a good writer makes them vivid, interesting, or memorable, but too often a writer's use of these stereotypes is simply weak characterization.

Round characters are more complex than flat or stock characters. Round characters have more depth and require more attention. They may surprise us or puzzle us. Although they are more fully developed, round characters are also more difficult to summarize, because we are aware of competing ideas, values, and possibilities in their lives. As a flat character, Huck Finn's alcoholic, bigoted father is clear to us; we know that Pap is the embodiment of racism and irrationality. But Huck is considerably less predictable, because he struggles with what Twain calls a "sound heart and a deformed conscience."

In making distinctions between flat and round characters, you must understand that an author's use of a flat character — even as a protagonist — does not necessarily represent an artistic flaw. Moreover, both flat and round characters can be either dynamic or static. Each plot can be made most effective by its own special kind of characterization. Terms such as *round* and *flat* are helpful tools to determine what we know about a character, but they should not be used as an infallible measurement for the quality of a story.

The next two stories — William Faulkner's "Barn Burning" and Herman Melville's "Bartleby, the Scrivener" — offer character studies worthy of close analysis. As you read them, notice the methods of characterization used to bring each to life.

WILLIAM FAULKNER (1897–1962)

A biographical note for William Faulkner appears on page 46, before his story "A Rose for Emily." In "Barn Burning" Faulkner portrays a young boy's love and revulsion for his father, a frightening man who lives by a "ferocious conviction in the rightness of his own actions."

Barn Burning

1939

The store in which the Justice of the Peace's court was sitting smelled of cheese. The boy, crouched on his nail keg at the back of the crowded room, knew he smelled cheese, and more: from where he sat he could see the ranked shelves close-packed with the solid, squat, dynamic shapes of tin cans whose labels his stomach read, not from the lettering which meant nothing to his mind but from the scarlet devils and the silver curve of fish — this, the cheese which he knew he smelled and the hermetic meat which his intestines believed he smelled coming in intermittent gusts momentary and brief between the other constant one, the smell and sense just a little of fear because mostly of despair and grief, the old fierce pull of blood. He could not see the table where the Justice sat and before which his father and his father's enemy (*our enemy* he thought in that despair; *ourn! mine and hisn both! He's my father!*) stood, but he could hear them, the two of them that is, because his father had said no word yet:

"But what proof have you, Mr. Harris?"

"I told you. The hog got into my corn. I caught it up and sent it back to him. He had no fence that would hold it. I told him so, warned him. The next time I put the hog in my pen. When he came to get it I gave him enough wire to patch up his pen. The next time I put the hog up and kept it. I rode down to his house and saw the wire I gave him still rolled on to the spool in his yard. I told him he could have the hog when he paid me a dollar pound fee. That evening a nigger came with the dollar and got the hog. He was a strange nigger. He said, 'He say to tell you wood and hay kin burn.' I said, 'What?' 'That whut he say to tell you,' the nigger said. 'Wood and hay kin burn.' That night my barn burned. I got the stock out but I lost the barn."

"Where is the nigger? Have you got him?"

"He was a strange nigger, I tell you. I don't know what became of him." 5

"But that's not proof. Don't you see that's not proof?"

"Get that boy up here. He knows." For a moment the boy thought too that the man meant his older brother until Harris said, "Not him. The little one. The boy," and, crouching, small for his age, small and wiry like his father, in patched and faded jeans even too small for him, with straight, uncombed, brown hair and eyes gray and wild as storm scud, he saw the men between himself and the table part and become a lane of grim faces, at the end of which he saw the Justice, a shabby, collarless, graying man in spectacles, beckoning him. He felt no floor under his bare feet; he seemed to walk beneath the palpable weight of the grim turning faces. His father, stiff in his black Sunday coat donned not for the trial but for the moving, did not even look at him. *He aims for me to lie,* he thought, again with that frantic grief and despair. *And I will have to do hit.*

"What's your name, boy?" the Justice said.

"Colonel Sartoris Snopes," the boy whispered.

"Hey?" the Justice said. "Talk louder. Colonel Sartoris? I reckon anybody 10
named for Colonel Sartoris in this country can't help but tell the truth, can they?" The boy said nothing. *Enemy! Enemy!* he thought; for a moment he could not even see, could not see that the Justice's face was kindly nor discern that his voice was troubled when he spoke to the man named Harris: "Do you want me to question this boy?" But he could hear, and during those subsequent long seconds while there was absolutely no sound in the crowded little room save that of quiet and intent breathing it was as if he had swung outward at the end of a grape vine, over a ravine, and at the top of the swing had been caught in a prolonged instant of mesmerized gravity, weightless in time.

"No!" Harris said violently, explosively. "Damnation! Send him out of here!" Now time, the fluid world, rushed beneath him again, the voices coming to him again through the smell of cheese and sealed meat, the fear and despair and the old grief of blood:

"This case is closed. I can't find against you, Snopes, but I can give you advice. Leave this country and don't come back to it."

His father spoke for the first time, his voice cold and harsh, level, without emphasis: "I aim to. I don't figure to stay in a country among people who . . ." he said something unprintable and vile, addressed to no one.

"That'll do," the Justice said. "Take your wagon and get out of this country before dark. Case dismissed."

His father turned, and he followed the stiff black coat, the wiry figure walking a little stiffly from where a Confederate provost's man's musket ball had taken him in the heel on a stolen horse thirty years ago, followed the two backs now, since his older brother had appeared from somewhere in the crowd, no taller than the father but thicker, chewing tobacco steadily, between the two lines of grim-faced men and out of the store and across the worn gallery and down the sagging steps and among the dogs and half-grown boys in the mild May dust, where as he passed a voice hissed:

"Barn burner!"

Again he could not see, whirling; there was a face in a red haze, moonlike, bigger than the full moon, the owner of it half again his size, he leaping in the red haze toward the face, feeling no blow, feeling no shock when his head struck the earth, scrabbling up and leaping again, feeling no blow this time either and tasting no blood, scrabbling up to see the other boy in full flight and himself already leaping into pursuit as his father's hand jerked him back, the harsh, cold voice speaking above him: "Go get in the wagon."

It stood in a grove of locusts and mulberries across the road. His two hulking sisters in their Sunday dresses and his mother and her sister in calico and sunbonnets were already in it, sitting on or among the sorry residue of the dozen and more movings which even the boy could remember — the battered stove, the broken beds and chairs, the clock inlaid with mother-of-pearl, which would not run, stopped at some fourteen minutes past two o'clock of a dead and forgotten day and time, which had been his mother's dowry. She was crying, though when she saw him she drew her sleeve across her face and began to descend from the wagon. "Get back," the father said.

"He's hurt. I got to get some water and wash his . . ."

"Get back in the wagon," his father said. He got in too, over the tail-gate. His father mounted to the seat where the older brother already sat and struck the gaunt mules two savage blows with the peeled willow, but without heat. It was not even sadistic; it was exactly that same quality which in later years would cause his descendants to over-run the engine before putting a motor car in motion, striking and reining back in the same movement. The wagon went on, the store with its quiet crowd of grimly watching men dropped behind; a curve in the road hid it. *Forever* he thought. *Maybe he's done satisfied now, now that he has* . . . stopping himself, not to say it aloud even to himself. His mother's hand touched his shoulder.

"Does hit hurt?" she said.

"Naw," he said. "Hit don't hurt. Lemme be."

"Can't you wipe some of the blood off before hit dries?"

"I'll wash to-night," he said. "Lemme be, I tell you."

25 The wagon went on. He did not know where they were going. None of them ever did or ever asked, because it was always somewhere, always a house of sorts waiting for them a day or two days or even three days away. Likely his father had already arranged to make a crop on another farm before he . . . Again he had to stop himself. He (the father) always did. There was something about his wolflike independence and even courage when the advantage was at least neutral which impressed strangers, as if they got from his latent ravening ferocity not so much a sense of dependability as a feeling that his ferocious conviction in the rightness of his own actions would be of advantage to all whose interest lay with his.

That night they camped, in a grove of oaks and beeches where a spring ran. The nights were still cool and they had a fire against it, of a rail lifed from a nearby fence and cut into lengths — a small fire, neat, niggard almost, a shrewd fire; such fires were his father's habit and custom always, even in freezing weather. Older, the boy might have remarked this and wondered why not a big one; why should not a man who had not only seen the waste and extravagance of war, but who had in his blood an inherent voracious prodigality with material not his own, have burned everything in sight? Then he might have gone a step farther and thought that that was the reason: that niggard blaze was the living fruit of nights passed during those four years in the woods hiding from all men, blue or gray, with his strings of horses (captured horses, he called them). And older still, he might have divined the true reason: that the element of fire spoke to some deep mainspring of his father's being, as the element of steel or of powder spoke to other men, as the one weapon for the preservation of integrity, else breath were not worth the breathing, and hence to be regarded with respect and used with discretion.

But he did not think this now and he had seen those same niggard blazes all his life. He merely ate his supper beside it and was already half asleep over his iron plate when his father called him, and once more he followed the stiff back, the stiff and ruthless limp, up the slope and on to the starlit road where, turning, he could see his father against the stars but without face or depth — a shape black, flat, and bloodless as though cut from tin in the iron folds of the frockcoat which had not been made for him, the voice harsh like tin and without heat like tin:

"You were fixing to tell them. You would have told him."

He didn't answer. His father struck him with the flat of his hand on the side of the head, hard but without heat, exactly as he had struck the two mules at the store, exactly as he would strike either of them with any stick in order to kill a horse fly, his voice still without heat or anger. "You're getting to be a man. You got to learn. You got to learn to stick to your own blood or you ain't going to have any blood to stick to you. Do you think either of them, any man there this morning, would? Don't you know all they wanted was a chance to get at me because they knew I had them beat? Eh?" Later, twenty years later, he was to tell himself, "If I had said they wanted only truth, justice, he would have hit me again." But now he said nothing. He was not crying. He just stood there. "Answer me," his father said.

30 "Yes," he whispered. His father turned.

"Get on to bed. We'll be there tomorrow."

Tomorrow they were there. In the early afternoon the wagon stopped before a paintless two-room house identical almost with the dozen others it had stopped before even in the boy's ten years, and again, as on the other dozen occasions, his mother and aunt got down and began to unload the wagon, although his two sisters and his father and brother had not moved.

"Likely hit ain't fitten for hawgs," one of the sisters said.

"Nevertheless, fit it will and you'll hog it and like it," his father said. "Get out of them chairs and help your Ma unload."

The two sisters got down, big, bovine, in a flutter of cheap ribbons; one of them drew from the jumbled wagon bed a battered lantern, the other a worn broom. His father handed the reins to the older son and began to climb stiffly over the wheel. "When they get unloaded, take the team to the barn and feed them." Then he said, and at first the boy thought he was still speaking to his brother. "Come with me."

"Me?" he said.

"Yes," his father said. "You."

"Abner," his mother said. His father paused and looked back — the harsh level stare beneath the shaggy, graying, irascible brows.

"I reckon I'll have a word with the man that aims to begin tomorrow owning me body and soul for the next eight months."

They went back up the road. A week ago — or before last night, that is — he would have asked where they were going, but not now. His father had struck him before last night but never before had he paused afterward to explain why; it was as if the blow and the following calm, outrageous voice still rang, repercussed, divulging nothing to him save the terrible handicap of being young, the light weight of his few years, just heavy enough to prevent his soaring free of the world as it seemed to be ordered but not heavy enough to keep him footed solid in it, to resist it and try to change the course of events.

Presently he could see the grove of oaks and cedars and the other flowering trees and shrubs where the house would be, though not the house yet. They walked beside a fence massed with honeysuckle and Cherokee roses and came to a gate swinging open between two brick pillars, and now, beyond a sweep of drive, he saw the house for the first time and at that instant he forgot his father and the terror and despair both, and even when he remembered his father again (who had not stopped) the terror and despair did not return. Because, for all the twelve movings, they had sojourned until now in a poor country, a land of small farms and fields and houses, and he had never seen a house like this before. *Hit's big as a courthouse* he thought quietly, with a surge of peace and joy whose reason he could not have thought into words, being too young for that: *They are safe from him. People whose lives are a part of this peace and dignity are beyond his touch, he no more to them than a buzzing wasp: capable of stinging for a little moment but that's all; the spell of this peace and dignity rendering even the barns and stable and cribs which belong to it impervious to the puny flames he might contrive . . .* this, the peace and joy, ebbing for an instant as he looked again at the stiff black back, the stiff and implacable limp of the figure which was not dwarfed by the house, for the reason that it had never looked big anywhere and which now, against the serene columned backdrop, had more than ever that impervious quality of something cut ruthlessly from tin, depthless, as though, sidewise to the sun, it would cast no shadow. Watching him, the boy remarked the absolutely undeviating course which his father held and saw the stiff foot come squarely down in a pile of fresh droppings where a horse had stood in the drive and which his father could have avoided by a simple change of stride. But it ebbed only for a moment, though he could not have thought this into words either, walking on in the spell of the house, which he could even want but without envy, without sorrow, certainly never with that ravening and jealous rage which unknown to him walked in the ironlike black coat before him: *Maybe he will feel it too. Maybe it will even change him now from what maybe he couldn't help but be.*

They crossed the portico. Now he could hear his father's stiff foot as it came down on the boards with clocklike finality, a sound out of all proportion to the displacement of the body it bore and which was not dwarfed either by the white door before it, as though it had attained to a sort of vicious and ravening minimum not to be dwarfed by anything — the flat, wide, black hat, the formal coat of broadcloth which had once been black but which had now that friction-glazed greenish cast of the bodies of old house flies, the lifted sleeve which was too large, the lifted hand like a curled claw. The door opened so promptly that the boy knew the Negro must have been watching them all the time, an old man with neat grizzled hair, in a linen jacket, who stood barring the door with his body, saying, "Wipe yo foots, white man, fo you come in here. Major ain't home nohow."

"Get out of my way, nigger," his father said, without heat too, flinging the door back and the Negro also and entering, his hat still on his head. And now the boy saw the prints of the stiff foot on the doorjamb and saw them appear on the pale rug behind the machinelike deliberation of the foot which seemed to bear (or transmit) twice the weight which the body compassed. The Negro was shouting "Miss Lula! Miss Lula!" somewhere behind them, then the boy, deluged as though by a warm wave by a suave turn of the carpeted stair and a pendant glitter of chandeliers and a mute gleam of gold frames, heard the swift feet and saw her too, a lady — perhaps he had never seen her like before either — in a gray, smooth gown with lace at the throat and an apron tied at the waist and the sleeves turned back, wiping cake or biscuit dough from her hands with a towel as she came up the hall, looking not at his father at all but at the tracks on the blond rug with an expression of incredulous amazement.

"I tried," the Negro cried. "I tole him to . . ."

"Will you please go away?" she said in a shaking voice. "Major de Spain is 45
not at home. Will you please go away?"

His father had not spoken again. He did not speak again. He did not even look at her. He just stood stiff in the center of the rug, in his hat, the shaggy iron-gray brows twitching slightly above the pebble-colored eyes as he appeared to examine the house with brief deliberation. Then with the same deliberation he turned; the boy watched him pivot on the good leg and saw the stiff foot drag round the arc of the turning, leaving a final long and fading smear. His father never looked at it, he never once looked down at the rug. The Negro held the door. It closed behind them, upon the hysteric and indistinguishable woman-wail. His father stopped at the top of the steps and scraped his boot clean on the edge of it. At the gate he stopped again. He stood for a moment, planted stiffly on the stiff foot, looking back at the house. "Pretty and white, ain't it?" he said. "That's sweat. Nigger sweat. Maybe it ain't white enought yet to suit him. Maybe he wants to mix some white sweat with it."

Two hours later the boy was chopping wood behind the house within which his mother and aunt and the two sisters (the mother and aunt, not the two girls, he knew that; even at this distance and muffled by walls the flat loud voices of the two girls emanated an incorrigible idle inertia) were setting up the stove to prepare a meal; when he heard the hooves and saw the linen-clad man on a fine sorrel mare, whom he recognized even before he saw the rolled rug in front of the Negro youth following on a fat bay carriage horse — a suffused, angry face vanishing, still at full gallop, beyond the corner of the house where his father and brother were sitting in the two tilted chairs; and a moment later, almost before he could have put the axe down, he heard the hooves again and watched the sorrel mare go back out of the yard, already galloping again. Then his father began to shout one of the sisters' names, who presently emerged backward from the kitchen door dragging the rolled rug along the ground by one end while the other sister walked behind it.

"If you ain't going to tote, go on and set up the wash pot," the first said.

"You, Sarty!" the second shouted. "Set up the wash pot!" His father appeared at the door, framed against that shabbiness, as he had been against that other bland perfection, impervious to either, the mother's anxious face at his shoulder.

"Go on," the father said. "Pick it up." The two sisters stopped, broad, le- 50
thargic; stooping, they presented an incredible expanse of pale cloth and a flutter of tawdry ribbons.

"If I thought enough of a rug to have to git hit all the way from France I wouldn't keep hit where folks coming in would have to tromp on hit," the first said. They raised the rug.

"Abner," the mother said. "Let me do it."

"You go back and git dinner," his father said. "I'll tend to this."

From the woodpile through the rest of the afternoon the boy watched them, the rug spread flat in the dust beside the bubbling wash pot, the two sisters stooping over it with that profound and lethargic reluctance, while the father stood over them in turn, implacable and grim, driving them though never raising his voice again. He could smell the harsh homemade lye they were using; he saw his mother come to the door once and look toward them with an expression not anxious now but very like despair; he saw his father turn, and he fell to with the axe and saw from the corner of his eye his father raise from the ground a flattish fragment of field stone and examine it and return to the pot, and this time his mother actually spoke: "Abner. Abner. Please don't. Please, Abner."

Then he was done too. It was dusk; the whippoorwills had already begun. 55
He could smell coffee from the room where they would presently eat the cold food remaining from the midafternoon meal, though when he entered the house he realized they were having coffee again probably because there was a fire on the hearth, before which the rug now lay spread over the backs of the two chairs. The tracks of his father's foot were gone. Where they had been were now long, water-cloudy scoriations resembling the sporadic course of a lilliputian mowing machine.

It still hung there while they ate the cold food and then went to bed, scattered without order or claim up and down the two rooms, his mother in one bed, where his father would later lie, the older brother in the other, himself, the aunt, and the two sisters on pallets on the floor. But his father was not in bed yet. The last thing the boy remembered was the depthless, harsh silhouette of the hat and coat bending over the rug and it seemed to him that he had not even closed his eyes when the silhouette was standing over him, the fire almost dead behind it, the stiff foot prodding him awake. "Catch up the mule," his father said.

When he returned with the mule his father was standing in the black door, the rolled rug over his shoulder. "Ain't you going to ride?" he said.

"No. Give me your foot."

He bent his knee into his father's hand, the wiry, surprising power flowed smoothly, rising, he rising with it, on to the mule's bare back (they had owned a saddle once; the boy could remember it though not when or where) and with the same effortlessness his father swung the rug up in front of him. Now in the starlight they retraced the afternoon's path, up the dusty road rife with honeysuckle, through the gate and up the black tunnel of the drive to the lightless house, where he sat on the mule and felt the rough warp of the rug drag across his thights and vanish.

"Don't you want me to help?" he whispered. His father did not answer and now he heard again that stiff foot striking the hollow portico with that wooden and clocklike deliberation, that outrageous overstatement of the weight it carried. The rug, hunched, not flung (the boy could tell that even in the darkness) from his father's shoulder struck the angle of wall and floor with a sound unbelievably loud, thunderous, then the foot again, unhurried and enormous; a light came on in the house and the boy sat, tense, breathing steadily and quietly and just a little fast, though the foot itself did not increase its beat at all, descending the steps now; now the boy could see him.

"Don't you want to ride now?" he whispered. "We kin both ride now," the light within the house altering now, flaring up and sinking. *He's coming down the stairs now,* he thought. He had already ridden the mule up beside the horse block; presently his father was up behind him and he doubled the reins over and slashed the mule across the neck, but before the animal could begin to trot the hard, thin arm came around him, the hard, knotted hand jerking the mule back to a walk.

In the first red rays of the sun they were in the lot, putting plow gear on the mules. This time the sorrel mare was in the lot before he heard it at all, the rider collarless and even bareheaded, trembling, speaking in a shaking voice as the woman in the house had done, his father merely looking up once before stooping again to the hame he was buckling, so that the man on the mare spoke to his stooping back:

"You must realize you have ruined that rug. Wasn't there anybody here, any of your women . . ." he ceased, shaking, the boy watching him, the older brother leaning now in the stable door, chewing, blinking slowly and steadily at nothing apparently. "It cost a hundred dollars. But you never had a hundred dollars. You never will. So I'm going to charge you twenty bushels of corn against your crop. I'll add it in your contract and when you come to the commissary you can sign it. That won't keep Mrs. de Spain quiet but maybe it will teach you to wipe your feet before you enter her house again."

Then he was gone. The boy looked at his father, who still had not spoken or even looked up again, who was now adjusting the logger-head in the hame.

65 "Pap," he said. His father looked at him — the inscrutable face, the shaggy brows beneath which the gray eyes glinted coldly. Suddenly the boy went toward him, fast, stopping as suddenly. "You done the best you could!" he cried. "If he wanted hit done different why didn't he wait and tell you how? He won't git no twenty bushels! He won't git none! We'll gether hit and hide hit! I kin watch . . ."

"Did you put the cutter back in that straight stock like I told you?"

"No, sir," he said.

"Then go do it."

That was Wednesday. During the rest of that week he worked steadily, at what was within his scope and some which was beyond it, with an industry that did not need to be driven nor even commanded twice; he had this from his mother, with the difference that some at least of what he did he liked to do, such as splitting wood with the half-size axe which his mother and aunt had earned, or saved money somehow, to present him with at Christmas. In company with the two older women (and on one afternoon, even one of the sisters), he built pens for the shoat and the cow which were part of his father's contract with the landlord, and one afternoon, his father being absent, gone somewhere on one of the mules, he went to the field.

70 They were running a middle buster now, his brother holding the plow straight while he handled the reins, and walking beside the straining mule, the rich black soil shearing cool and damp against his bare ankles, he thought *Maybe this is the end of it. Maybe even that twenty bushels that seems hard to have to pay for just a rug will be a cheap price for him to stop forever and always from being what he used to be;* thinking, dreaming now, so that his brother had to speak sharply to him to mind the mule: *Maybe he even won't collect the twenty bushels. Maybe it will all add up and balance and vanish — corn, rug, fire; the terror and grief; the being pulled two ways like between two teams of horses — gone, done with for ever and ever.*

Then it was Saturday; he looked up from beneath the mule he was harnessing and saw his father in the black coat and hat. "Not that," his father said. "The wagon gear." And then, two hours later, sitting in the wagon bed behind his father and brother on the seat, the wagon accomplished a final curve, and he saw the weathered paintless store with its tattered tobacco- and patent-medicine posters and the tethered wagons and saddle animals below the gallery. He mounted the gnawed steps behind his father and brother, and there again was the lane of quiet, watching faces for the three of them to walk through. He saw the man in spectacles sitting at the plank table and he did not need to be told this was a Justice of the Peace; he sent one glare of fierce, exultant, partisan defiance at the man in collar and cravat now, whom he had seen but twice before in his life, and that on a galloping horse, who now wore on his face an expression not of rage but of amazed unbelief which the boy could not have known was at the incredible circumstance of being sued by one of his own tenants, and came and stood against his father and cried at the Justice: "He ain't done it! He aint' burnt . . ."

"Go back to the wagon," his father said.

"Burnt?" the Justice said. "Do I understand this rug was burned too?"

"Does anybody here claim it was?" his father said. "Go back to the wagon." But he did not, he merely retreated to the rear of the room, crowded as that other had been, but not to sit down this time, instead, to stand pressing among the motionless bodies, listening to the voices:

"And you claim twenty bushels of corn is too high for the damage you did to the rug?"

"He brought the rug to me and said he wanted the tracks washed out of it. I washed the tracks out and took the rug back to him."

"But you didn't carry the rug back to him in the same condition it was in before you made the tracks on it."

His father did not answer, and now for perhaps half a minute there was no sound at all save that of breathing, the faint, steady suspiration of complete and intent listening.

"You decline to answer that, Mr. Snopes?" Again his father did not answer. "I'm going to find against you, Mr. Snopes. I'm going to find that you were responsible for the injury to Major de Spain's rug and hold you liable for it. But twenty bushels of corn seems a little high for a man in your circumstances to have to pay. Major de Spain claims it cost a hundred dollars. October corn will be worth about fifty cents. I figure that if Major de Spain can stand a ninety-five dollar loss on something he paid cash for, you can stand a five-dollar loss you haven't earned yet. I hold you in damages to Major de Spain to the amount of ten bushels of corn over and above your contract with him, to be paid to him out of your crop at gathering time. Court adjourned."

It had taken no time hardly, the morning was but half begun. He thought they would return home and perhaps back to the field, since they were late, far behind all other farmers. But instead his father passed on behind the wagon, merely indicating with his hand for the older brother to follow with it, and crossed the road toward the blacksmith shop opposite, pressing on after his father, overtaking him, speaking, whispering up at the harsh, calm face beneath the weathered hat: "He won't git no ten bushels neither. He won't git one. We'll . . ." until his father glanced for an instant down at him, the face absolutely calm, the grizzled eyebrows tangled above the cold eyes, the voice almost pleasant, almost gentle:

"You think so? Well, we'll wait till October anyway."

The matter of the wagon — the setting of a spoke or two and the tightening of the tires — did not take long either, the business of the tires accomplished by driving the wagon into the spring branch behind the shop and letting it stand there, the mules nuzzling into the water from time to time, and the boy on the seat with the idle reins, looking up the slope and through the sooty tunnel of the shed where the slow hammer rang and where his father sat on an upended cypress bolt, easily, either talking or listening, still sitting there when the boy brought the dripping wagon up out of the branch and halted it before the door.

"Take them on to the shade and hitch," his father said. He did so and returned. His father and the smith and a third man squatting on his heels inside the door were talking, about crops and animals; the boy, squatting too in the ammoniac dust and hoof-parings and scales of rust, heard his father tell a long and unhurried story out of the time before the birth of the older brother even when he had been a professional horsetrader. And then his father came up beside him where he stood before a tattered last year's circus poster on the other side of the store, gazing rapt and quiet at the scarlet horses, the incredible poisings and convolutions of tulle and tights and the painted leers of comedians, and said, "It's time to eat."

But not at home. Squatting beside his brother against the front wall, he watched his father emerge from the store and produce from a paper sack a segment of cheese and divide it carefully and deliberately into three with his pocket knife and produce crackers from the same sack. They all three squatted on the gallery and ate, slowly, without talking; then in the store again, they drank from a tin dipper tepid water smelling of the cedar bucket and of living beech trees. And still they did not go home. It was a horse lot this time, a tall rail fence upon and along which men stood and sat and out of which one by one horses were led, to be walked and trotted and then cantered back and forth along the road while the slow swapping and buying went on and the sun began to slant westward, they — the three of them — watching and listening, the older brother with his muddy eyes and his steady, inevitable tobacco, the father commenting now and then on certain of the animals, to no one in particular.

It was after sundown when they reached home. They ate supper by lamplight, then, sitting on the doorstep, the boy watched the night fully accomplish, listening to the whippoorwills and the frogs, when he heard his mother's voice: "Abner! No! No! Oh, God. Oh, God. Abner!" and he rose, whirled, and saw the altered light through the door where a candle stub now burned in a bottle neck on the table and his father, still in the hat and coat, at once formal and burlesque as though dressed carefully for some shabby and ceremonial violence, emptying the reservoir of the lamp back into the five-gallon kerosene can from which it had been filled, while the mother tugged at his arm until he shifted the lamp to the other hand and flung her back, not savagely or viciously, just hard, into the wall, her hands flung out against the wall for balance, her mouth open and in her face the same quality of hopeless despair as had been in her voice. Then his father saw him standing in the door.

"Go to the barn and get that can of oil we were oiling the wagon with," he said. The boy did not move. Then he could speak.

"What . . ." he cried. "What are you . . ."

"Go get that oil," his father said. "Go."

Then he was moving, running, outside the house, toward the stable: this the old habit, the old blood which he had not been permitted to choose for himself, which had been bequeathed him willy nilly and which had run for so long (and who knew where, battening on what of outrage and savagery and lust) before it came to him. *I could keep on,* he thought. *I could run on and on and never look back, never need to see his face again. Only I can't. I can't,* the rusted can in his hand now, the liquid sploshing in it as he ran back to the house and into it, into the sound of his mother's weeping in the next room, and handed the can to his father.

"Ain't you going to even send a nigger?" he cried. "At least you sent a nigger before!"

This time his father didn't strike him. The hand came even faster than the blow had, the same hand which had set the can on the table with almost excruciating care flashing from the can toward him too quick for him to follow it, gripping him by the back of his shirt and on to tiptoe before he had seen it quit the can, the face stooping at him in breathless and frozen ferocity, the cold, dead voice speaking over him to the older brother who leaned against the table, chewing with that steady, curious, sidewise motion of cows:

"Empty the can into the big one and go on. I'll catch up with you."

"Better tie him up to the bedpost," the brother said.

"Do like I told you," the father said. Then the boy was moving, his bunched shirt and the hard, bony hand between his shoulder-blades, his toes just touching the floor, across the room and into the other one, past the sisters sitting with spread heavy thighs in the two chairs over the cold hearth, and to where his mother and aunt sat side by side on the bed, the aunt's arms about his mother's shoulders.

"Hold him," the father said. The aunt made a startled movement. "Not you," the father said. "Lennie. Take hold of him. I want to see you do it." His mother took him by the wrist. "You'll hold him better than that. If he gets loose don't you know what he is going to do? He will go up yonder." He jerked his head toward the road. "Maybe I'd better tie him."

"I'll hold him," his mother whispered.

"See you do then." Then his father was gone, the stiff foot heavy and measured upon the boards, ceasing at last.

Then he began to struggle. His mother caught him in both arms, he jerking and wrenching at them. He would be stronger in the end, he knew that. But he had no time to wait for it. "Lemme go!" he cried. "I don't want to have to hit you!"

"Let him go!" the aunt said. "If he don't go, before God, I am going up there myself!"

"Don't you see I can't?" his mother cried. "Sarty! Sarty! No! No! Help me, Lizzie!"

Then he was free. His aunt grasped at him but it was too late. He whirled, running, his mother stumbled forward on to her knees behind him, crying to the nearer sister. "Catch him, Net! Catch him!" But that was too late too, the sister (the sisters were twins, born at the same time, yet either of them now gave the impression of being, encompassing as much living meat and volume and weight as any other two of the family) not yet having begun to rise from the chair, her head, face, alone merely turned, presenting to him in the flying instant an astonishing expanse of young female features untroubled by any surprise even, wearing only an expression of bovine interest. Then he was out of the room, out of the house, in the mild dust of the starlit road and the heavy rifeness of honeysuckle, the pale ribbon unspooling with terrific slowness under his running feet, reaching the gate at last and turning in, running, his heart and lungs drumming, on up the drive toward the lighted house, the lighted door. He did not knock, he burst in, sobbing for breath, incapable for the moment of speech; he saw the astonished face of the Negro in the linen jacket without knowing when the Negro had appeared.

"De Spain!" he cried, panted. "Where's . . ." then he saw the white man too emerging from a white door down the hall. "Barn!" he cried. "Barn!"

"What?" the white man said. "Barn?"

"Yes!" the boy cried. "Barn!"

"Catch him!" the white man shouted.

But it was too late this time too. The Negro grasped his shirt, but the entire sleeve, rotten with washing, carried away, and he was out that door too and in the drive again, and had actually never ceased to run even while he was screaming into the white man's face.

Behind him the white man was shouting, "My horse! Fetch my horse!" and he thought for an instant of cutting across the park and climbing the fence into the road, but he did not know the park nor how high the vine-massed fence might be and he dared not risk it. So he ran on down the drive, blood and breath roaring; presently he was in the road again though he could not see it. He could not hear either: the galloping mare was almost upon him before he heard her, and even then he held his course, as if the very urgency of his wild grief and need must in a moment more find him wings, waiting until the ultimate instant to hurl himself aside and into the weed-choked roadside ditch as the horse thundered past and on, for an instant in furious silhouette against the stars, the tranquil early summer night sky which, even before the shape of the horse and rider vanished, strained abruptly and violently upward: a long, swirling roar incredible and soundless, blotting the stars, and he springing up and into the road again, running again, knowing it was too late yet still running even after he heard the shot and, an instant later, two shots, pausing now without knowing he had ceased to run, crying "Pap! Pap!," running again before he knew he had begun to run, stumbling, tripping over something and scrabbling up again without ceasing to run, looking backward over his shoulder at the glare as he got up, running on among the invisible trees, panting, sobbing, "Father! Father!"

At midnight he was sitting on the crest of a hill. He did not know it was midnight and he did not know how far he had come. But there was no glare behind him now and he sat now, his back toward what he had called home for four days anyhow, his face toward the dark woods which he would enter when breath was strong again, small, shaking steadily in the chill darkness, hugging himself into the remainder of his thin, rotten shirt, the grief and despair now no longer terror and fear but just grief and despair. *Father. My father,* he thought. "He was brave!" he cried suddenly, aloud but not loud, no more than a whisper: "He was! He was in the war! He was in Colonel Sartoris' cav'ry!" not knowing that his father had gone to that war a private in the fine old European sense, wearing no uniform, admitting the authority of and giving fidelity to no man or army or flag, going to war as Malbrouck° himself did: for booty — it meant nothing and less than nothing to him if it were enemy booty or his own.

The slow constellations wheeled on. It would be dawn and then sun-up after a while and he would be hungry. But that would be tomorrow and now he was only cold, and walking would cure that. His breathing was easier now and he decided to get up and go on, and then he found that he had been asleep because he knew it was almost dawn, the night almost over. He could tell that from the whippoorwills. They were everywhere now among the dark trees below him, constant and inflectioned and ceaseless, so that, as the instant for giving over to the day birds drew nearer and nearer, there was no interval at all between them. He got up. He was a little stiff, but walking would cure that too as it would the cold, and soon there would be the sun. He went on down the

Malbrouck: John Churchill, duke of Marlborough (1650–1722), English military commander who led the armies of England and Holland in the War of Spanish Succession.

hill, toward the dark woods within which the liquid silver voices of the birds called unceasing — the rapid and urgent beating of the urgent and quiring heart of the late spring night. He did not look back.

Considerations

1. Explain why Sarty is a dynamic or a static character. Which term best describes his father? Why?
2. Who is the central character in this story? Explain your choice.
3. How are Sarty's emotions revealed in the story's opening paragraphs? What seems to be the function of the italicized passages there and elsewhere?
4. What do we learn from the story's exposition that helps us understand Abner's character? How does his behavior reveal his character? What do other people say about him?
5. How does Faulkner's physical description of Abner further our understanding of his personality?
6. Explain how the justice of the peace, Mr. Harris, and Major de Spain serve as foils to Abner. Discuss whether you think they are round or flat characters.
7. Who are the story's stock characters? What is their purpose?
8. Explain how the description of Major de Spain's house helps to frame the major conflicts that Sarty experiences in his efforts to remain loyal to his father.
9. Write an essay describing Sarty's attitudes toward his father as they develop and change throughout the story.
10. What do you think happens to Sarty's father and brother at the end of the story? How does your response to this question affect your reading of the last paragraph?
11. How does the language of the final paragraph suggest a kind of resolution to the conflicts Sarty has experienced?

Connections

1. Compare and contrast Faulkner's characterizations of Abner Snopes in this story and Miss Emily in "A Rose for Emily" (p. 47). How does the author generate sympathy for each character even though both are guilty of terrible crimes? Which character do you find more sympathetic? Explain why.
2. How does Abner Snopes's motivation for revenge compare with Fleur Pillager's in Louise Erdrich's "Fleur" (p. 444). How do the victims of each character's revenge differ and thereby help to shape the meanings of each story?
3. Read the section on mythological criticism in Chapter 32, "Critical Strategies for Reading." How do you think a mythological critic would make sense of Sarty Snopes and Fleur Pillager?

HERMAN MELVILLE (1819–1891)

Hoping to improve his distressed financial situation, Herman Melville left New York and went to sea as a young common sailor. He returned to become an uncommon writer. His experiences at sea became the basis for his early novels: *Typee* (1846), *Omoo* (1847), *Mardi* (1849), *Redburn* (1849), and *White-Jacket* (1850). Ironically, with the publication of his masterpiece,

Moby-Dick (1851), Melville lost the popular success he had enjoyed with his earlier books, because his readers were not ready for its philosophical complexity. Although he wrote more, Melville's works were read less and slipped into obscurity. His final short novel, *Billy Budd,* was not published until the 1920s, when critics rediscovered him. In "Bartleby, the Scrivener," Melville presents a quiet clerk in a law office whose baffling "passive resistance" disrupts the life of his employer, a man who attempts to make sense of Bartleby's refusal to behave reasonably.

Bartleby, the Scrivener 1853

A STORY OF WALL STREET

I am a rather elderly man. The nature of my avocations, for the last thirty years, has brought me into more than ordinary contact with what would seem an interesting and somewhat singular set of men, of whom, as yet, nothing, that I know of, has ever been written — I mean, the law-copyists, or scriveners. I have known very many of them, professionally and privately, and, if I pleased, could relate divers histories, at which good-natured gentlemen might smile, and sentimental souls might weep. But I waive the biographies of all other scriveners, for a few passages in the life of Bartleby, who was a scrivener, the strangest I ever saw, or heard of. While, of other law-copyists, I might write the complete life, of Bartleby nothing of that sort can be done. I believe that no materials exist, for a full and satisfactory biography of this man. It is an irreparable loss to literature. Bartleby was one of those beings of whom nothing is ascertainable, except from the original sources, and, in his case, those are very small. What my own astonished eyes saw of Bartleby, *that* is all I know of him, except, indeed, one vague report, which will appear in the sequel.

Ere introducing the scrivener, as he first appeared to me, it is fit I make some mention of myself, my *employés,* my business, my chambers, and general surroundings, because some such description is indispensable to an adequate understanding of the chief character about to be presented. Imprimis:° I am a man who, from his youth upwards, has been filled with a profound conviction that the easiest way of life is the best. Hence, though I belong to a profession proverbially energetic and nervous, even to turbulence, at times, yet nothing of that sort have I ever suffered to invade my peace. I am one of those unambitious lawyers who never address a jury, or in any way draw down public applause; but, in the cool tranquillity of a snug retreat, do a snug business among rich men's bonds, and mortgages, and title-deeds. All who know me, consider me an eminently *safe* man. The late John Jacob Astor,° a personage little given to poetic enthusiasm, had no hesitation in pronouncing my first grand point to be prudence; my next, method. I do not speak it in vanity, but simply record the fact, that I was not unemployed in my profession by the late John Jacob Astor; a

Imprimis: In the first place.
John Jacob Astor: (1763–1848) An enormously wealthy American capitalist.

name which, I admit, I love to repeat; for it hath a rounded and orbicular sound to it, and rings like unto bullion. I will freely add, that I was not insensible to the late John Jacob Astor's good opinion.

Some time prior to the period at which this little history begins, my avocations had been largely increased. The good old office, now extinct in the State of New York, of a Master in Chancery, had been conferred upon me. It was not a very arduous office, but very pleasantly remunerative. I seldom lose my temper; much more seldom indulge in dangerous indignation at wrongs and outrages; but I must be permitted to be rash here and declare, that I consider the sudden and violent abrogation of the office of Master in Chancery, by the new Constitution, as a —— premature act; inasmuch as I had counted upon a life-lease of the profits, whereas I only received those of a few short years. But this is by the way.

My chambers were up stairs, at No. — Wall Street. At one end, they looked upon the white wall of the interior of a spacious skylight shaft, penetrating the building from top to bottom.

This view might have been considered rather tame than otherwise, defi- 5
cient in what landscape painters call "life." But, if so, the view from the other end of my chambers offered, at least, a contrast, if nothing more. In that direction, my windows commanded an unobstructed view of a lofty brick wall, black by age and everlasting shade; which wall required no spyglass to bring out its lurking beauties, but, for the benefit of all near-sighted spectators, was pushed up to within ten feet of my window-panes. Owing to the great height of the surrounding buildings, and my chambers being on the second floor, the interval between this wall and mine not a little resembled a huge square cistern.

At the period just preceding the advent of Bartleby, I had two persons as copyists in my employment, and a promising lad as an office-boy. First, Turkey; second, Nippers; third, Ginger Nut. These may seem names, the like of which are not usually found in the Directory. In truth, they were nicknames, mutually conferred upon each other by my three clerks, and were deemed expressive of their respective persons or characters. Turkey was a short, pursy Englishman, of about my own age — that is, somewhere not far from sixty. In the morning, one might say, his face was of a fine florid hue, but after twelve o'clock, meridian — his dinner hour — it blazed like a grate full of Christmas coals; and continued blazing — but, as it were, with a gradual wane — till six o'clock, P.M., or thereabouts; after which, I saw no more of the proprietor of the face, which, gaining its meridian with the sun, seemed to set with it, to rise, culminate, and decline the following day, with the like regularity and undiminished glory. There are many singular coincidences I have known in the course of my life, not the least among which was the fact, that, exactly when Turkey displayed his fullest beams from his red and radiant countenance, just then, too, at that critical moment, began the daily period when I considered his business capacities as seriously disturbed for the remainder of the twenty-four hours. Not that he was absolutely idle, or averse to business then; far from it. The difficulty was, he was apt to be altogether too energetic. There was a strange, inflamed, flurried, flighty recklessness of activity about him. He would be incautious in dipping his pen into his inkstand. All his blots upon my documents were dropped there after twelve o'clock, meridian. Indeed, not only would he be reckless, and sadly given to making blots in the afternoon, but, some days, he went further, and was rather noisy. At such times, too, his face flamed with augmented blazonry, as if cannel coal had been heaped on anthracite. He made an unpleasant racket with his chair; spilled his sand-box; in mending his pens, impatiently split them all to pieces, and threw them on the floor in a sudden passion; stood up, and leaned over his table, boxing his papers about in a most indecorous manner, very sad to behold in an elderly man like him. Nevertheless, as he was in many ways a most valuable person to me, and all the time before twelve o'clock, meridian, was the quickest, steadiest creature, too, accomplishing a great deal of work in a style not easily to be matched — for these reasons, I was willing to overlook his eccentricities, though, indeed, occasionally, I remonstrated with him. I did this very gently, however, because, though the civilest, nay, the blandest and most reverential of men in the morning, yet, in the afternoon, he was disposed, upon provocation, to be slightly rash with his tongue — in fact, insolent. Now, valuing his morning services as I did, and resolved not to lose them — yet, at the same time, made uncomfortable by his inflamed ways after twelve o'clock — and being a man of peace, unwilling by my admonitions to call forth unseemly retorts from him, I took upon me, one Saturday noon (he was always worse on Saturdays) to hint to him, very kindly, that, perhaps, now that he was growing old, it might be well to abridge his labors; in short, he need not come to my chambers after twelve o'clock, but, dinner over, had best go home to his lodgings, and rest himself till tea-time. But no; he insisted upon his afternoon devotions. His countenance became intolerably fervid, as he oratorically assured me — gesticulating with a long ruler at the other end of the room — that if his services in the morning were useful, how indispensable, then, in the afternoon?

"With submission, sir," said Turkey, on this occasion, "I consider myself your right-hand man. In the morning I but marshal and deploy my columns; but in the afternoon I put myself at their head, and gallantly charge the foe, thus" — and he made a violent thrust with the ruler.

"But the blots, Turkey," intimated I.

"True; but, with submission, sir, behold these hairs! I am getting old. Surely, sir, a blot or two of a warm afternoon is not to be severely urged against gray hairs. Old age — even if it blot the page — is honorable. With submission, sir, we *both* are getting old."

This appeal to my fellow-feeling was hardly to be resisted. At all events, I 10
saw that go he would not. So, I made up my mind to let him stay, resolving, nevertheless, to see to it that, during the afternoon, he had to do with my less important papers.

Nippers, the second on my list, was a whiskered, sallow, and, upon the whole, rather piratical-looking young man, of about five-and-twenty. I always deemed him the victim of two evil powers — ambition and indigestion. The ambition was evinced by a certain impatience of the duties of a mere copyist, an unwarrantable usurpation of strictly professional affairs such as the original drawing up of legal documents. The indigestion seemed betokened in an occasional nervous testiness and grinning irritability, causing the teeth to audibly grind together over mistakes committed in copying; unnecessary maledictions, hissed, rather than spoken, in the heat of business; and especially by a continual discontent with the height of the table where he worked. Though of a very ingenious mechanical turn, Nippers could never get this table to suit him. He put chips under it, blocks of various sorts, bits of pasteboard, and at last went so far as to attempt an exquisite adjustment, by final pieces of folded blotting-paper. But no invention would answer. If, for the sake of easing his back, he brought the table-lid at a sharp angle well up towards his chin, and wrote there like a man using the steep roof of a Dutch house for his desk, then he declared that it stopped the circulation in his arms. If now he lowered the table to his waistbands, and stooped over it in writing, then there was a sore aching in his back. In short, the truth of the matter was, Nippers knew not what he wanted. Or, if he wanted anything, it was to be rid of a scrivener's table altogether. Among the manifestations of his diseased ambition was a fondness he had for receiving visits from certain ambiguous-looking fellows in seedy coats, whom he called his clients. Indeed, I was aware that not only was he, at times, considerable of a ward-politician, but he occasionally did a little business at the justices' courts, and was not unknown on the steps of the Tombs.° I have good reason to believe, however, that one individual who called upon him at my chambers, and who, with a grand air, he insisted was his client, was no other than a dun, and the alleged title-deed, a bill. But, with all his failings, and the annoyances he caused me, Nippers, like his compatriot Turkey, was a very useful man to me; wrote a neat, swift hand; and, when he chose, was not deficient in a gentlemanly sort of deportment. Added to this, he always dressed in a gentlemanly sort of way; and so, incidentally, reflected credit upon my chambers. Whereas, with respect to Turkey, I had much ado to keep him from being a reproach to me. His clothes were apt to look oily, a smell of eating-houses. He wore his pantaloons very loose and baggy in summer. His coats were execrable, his hat not to be handled. But while the hat was a thing of indifference to me, inasmuch as his natural civility and deference, as a dependent Englishman, always led him to doff it the moment he entered the room, yet his coat was another matter. Concerning his coats, I reasoned with him; but with no effect. The truth was, I suppose, that a man with so small an income could not afford to sport such a lustrous face and a lustrous coat at one and the same time. As Nippers once observed, Turkey's money went chiefly for red ink. One winter day, I presented Turkey with a highly respectable-looking coat of my own — a padded gray coat, of a most comfortable warmth, and which buttoned straight up from the knee to the neck. I thought Turkey would appreciate the favor, and abate his rashness and obstreperousness of afternoons. But no; I verily believe that buttoning himself up in so downy and blanket-like a coat had a pernicious effect upon him — upon the same principle that too much oats are bad for horses. In fact, precisely as a rash, restive horse is said to feel his oats, so Turkey felt his coat. It made him insolent. He was a man whom prosperity harmed.

Though, concerning the self-indulgent habits of Turkey, I had my own private surmises, yet, touching Nippers, I was well persuaded that, whatever might be his faults in other respects, he was, at least, a temperate young man. But indeed, nature herself seemed to have been his vintner, and, at his birth, charged him so thoroughly with an irritable, brandy-like disposition, that all subsequent potations were needless. When I consider how, amid the stillness of my chambers, Nippers would sometimes impatiently rise from his seat, and stooping

the Tombs: A jail in New York City.

over his table, spread his arms wide apart, seize the whole desk, and move it, and jerk it, with a grim, grinding motion on the floor, as if the table were a perverse voluntary agent, intent on thwarting and vexing him, I plainly perceive that, for Nippers, brandy-and-water were altogether superfluous.

It was fortunate for me that, owing to its peculiar cause — indigestion — the irritability and consequent nervousness of Nippers were mainly observable in the morning, while in the afternoon he was comparatively mild. So that, Turkey's paroxysms only coming on about twelve o'clock, I never had to do with their eccentricities at one time. Their fits relieved each other, like guards. When Nippers' was on, Turkey's was off; and *vice versa.* This was a good natural arrangement, under the circumstances.

Ginger Nut, the third on my list, was a lad, some twelve years old. His father was a carman, ambitious of seeing his son on the bench instead of a cart, before he died. So he sent him to my office, as student at law, errand-boy, cleaner, and sweeper, at the rate of one dollar a week. He had a little desk to himself, but he did not use it much. Upon inspection, the drawer exhibited a great array of the shells of various sorts of nuts. Indeed, to this quick-witted youth, the whole noble science of the law was contained in a nutshell. Not the least among the employments of Ginger Nut, as well as one which he dischaged with the most alacrity, was his duty as cake and apple purveyor for Turkey and Nippers. Copying lawpapers being proverbially a dry, husky sort of business, my two scriveners were fain to moisten their mouths very often with Spitzenbergs, to be had at the numerous stalls nigh the Custom House and Post Office. Also, they sent Ginger Nut very frequently for that peculiar cake — small, flat, round, and very spicy — after which he had been named by them. Of a cold morning, when business was but dull, Turkey would gobble up scores of these cakes, as if they were mere wafers — indeed, they sell them at the rate of six or eight for a penny — the scrape of his pen blending with the crunching of the crisp particles in his mouth. Of all the fiery afternoon blunders and flurried rashness of Turkey, was his once moistening a ginger-cake between his lips, and clapping it on to a mortgage, for a seal. I came within an ace of dismissing him then. But he mollified me by making an oriental bow, and saying —

"With submission, sir, it was generous of me to find you in stationery on 15
my own account."

Now my original business — that of a conveyancer and title hunter, and drawer-up of recondite documents of all sorts — was considerably increased by receiving the Master's office. There was now great work for scriveners. Not only must I push the clerks already with me, but I must have additional help.

In answer to my advertisement, a motionless young man one morning stood upon my office threshold, the door being open, for it was summer. I can see that figure now — pallidly neat, pitiably respectable, incurably forlorn! It was Bartleby.

After a few words touching his qualifications, I engaged him, glad to have among my corps of copyists a man of so singularly sedate an aspect, which I thought might operate beneficially upon the flighty temper of Turkey, and the fiery one of Nippers.

I should have stated before that ground-glass folding-doors divided my premises into two parts, one of which was occupied by my scriveners, the other by myself. According to my humor, I threw open these doors, or closed them.

I resolved to assign Bartleby a corner by the folding-doors, but on my side of them, so as to have this quiet man within easy call, in case any trifling thing was to be done. I placed his desk close up to a small side-window in that part of the room, a window which originally had afforded a lateral view of certain grimy brickyards and bricks, but which, owing to subsequent erections, commanded at present no view at all, though it gave some light. Within three feet of the panes was a wall, and the light came down from far above, between two lofty buildings, as from a very small opening in a dome. Still further to a satisfactory arrangement, I procured a high green folding screen, which might entirely isolate Bartleby from my sight, though not remove him from my voice. And thus, in a manner, privacy and society were conjoined.

At first, Bartleby did an extraordinary quantity of writing. As if long famish- 20
ing for something to copy, he seemed to gorge himself on my documents. There was no pause for digestion. He ran a day and night line, copying by sunlight and by candle-light. I should have been quite delighted with his application, had he been cheerfully industrious. But he wrote on silently, palely, mechanically.

It is, of course, an indispensable part of a scrivener's business to verify the accuracy of his copy, word by word. Where there are two or more scriveners in an office, they assist each other in this examination, one reading from the copy, the other holding the original. It is a very dull, wearisome, and lethargic affair. I can readily imagine that, to some sanguine temperaments, it would be altogether intolerable. For example, I cannot credit that the mettlesome poet, Byron, would have contentedly sat down with Bartleby to examine a law document of, say five hundred pages, closely written in a crimpy hand.

Now and then, in the haste of business, it had been my habit to assist in comparing some brief document myself, calling Turkey or Nippers for this purpose. One object I had, in placing Bartleby so handy to me behind the screen, was, to avail myself of his services on such trivial occasions. It was on the third day, I think, of his being with me, and before any necessity had arisen for having his own writing examined, that, being much hurried to complete a small affair I had in hand, I abruptly called to Bartleby. In my haste and natural expectancy of instant compliance, I sat with my head bent over the original on my desk, and my right hand sideways, and somewhat nervously extended with the copy, so that, immediately upon emerging from his retreat, Bartleby might snatch it and proceed to business without the least delay.

In this very attitude did I sit when I called to him, rapidly stating what it was I wanted him to do — namely, to examine a small paper with me. Imagine my surprise, nay, my consternation, when, without moving from his privacy, Bartleby, in a singularly mild, firm voice, replied, "I would prefer not to."

I sat awhile in perfect silence, rallying my stunned faculties. Immediately it occurred to me that my ears had deceived me, or Bartleby had entirely misunderstood my meaning. I repeated my request in the clearest tone I could assume; but in quite as clear a one came the previous reply, "I would prefer not to."

"Prefer not to," echoed I, rising in high excitement, and crossing the room 25
with a stride. "What do you mean? Are you moonstruck? I want you to help me compare this sheet here — take it," and I thrust it towards him.

"I would prefer not to," said he.

I looked at him steadfastly. His face was leanly composed; his gray eye dimly calm. Not a wrinkle of agitation rippled him. Had there been the least uneasiness, anger, impatience, or impertinence in his manner; in other words, had there been anything ordinarily human about him, doubtless I should have violently dismissed him from the premises. But as it was, I should have as soon thought of turning my pale plaster-of-paris bust of Cicero out of doors. I stood gazing at him awhile, as he went on with his own writing, and then reseated myself at my desk. This is very strange, thought I. What had one best do? But my business hurried me. I concluded to forget the matter for the present, reserving it for my future leisure. So, calling Nippers from the other room, the paper was speedily examined.

A few days after this, Bartleby concluded four lengthy documents, being quadruplicates of a week's testimony taken before me in my High Court of Chancery. It became necessary to examine them. It was an important suit, and great accuracy was imperative. Having all things arranged, I called Turkey, Nippers, and Ginger Nut, from the next room, meaning to place the four copies in the hands of my four clerks, while I should read from the original. Accordingly, Turkey, Nippers, and Ginger Nut had taken their seats in a row, each with his document in his hand, when I called to Bartleby to join this interesting group.

"Bartleby! quick, I am waiting."

I heard a slow scrape of his chair legs on the uncarpeted floor, and soon he appeared standing at the entrance of his hermitage.

"What is wanted?" said he, mildly.

"The copies, the copies," said I, hurriedly. "We are going to examine them. There" — and I held towards him the fourth quadruplicate.

"I would prefer not to," he said, and gently disappeared behind the screen.

For a few moments I was turned into a pillar of salt, standing at the head of my seated column of clerks. Recovering myself, I advanced towards the screen, and demanded the reason for such extraordinary conduct.

"*Why* do you refuse?"

"I would prefer not to."

With any other man I should have flown outright into a dreadful passion, scorned all further words, and thrust him ignominiously from my presence. But there was something about Bartleby that not only strangely disarmed me, but, in a wonderful manner, touched and disconcerted me. I began to reason with him.

"These are your own copies we are about to examine. It is labor saving to you, because one examination will answer for your four papers. It is common usage. Every copyist is bound to help examine his copy. Is it not so? Will you not speak? Answer!"

"I prefer not to," he replied in a flute-like tone. It seemed to me that, while I had been addressing him, he carefully revolved every statement that I made; fully comprehended the meaning; could not gainsay the irresistible conclusion; but, at the same time, some paramount consideration prevailed with him to reply as he did.

"You are decided, then, not to comply with my request — a request made according to common usage and common sense?"

He briefly gave me to understand, that on that point my judgment was sound. Yes: his decision was irreversible.

It is not seldom the case that, when a man is browbeaten in some unprecedented and violently unreasonable way, he begins to stagger in his own plainest faith. He begins, as it were, vaguely to surmise that, wonderful as it may be, all the justice and all the reason is on the other side. Accordingly, if any disinterested persons are present, he turns to them for some reinforcement for his own faltering mind.

"Turkey," said I, "what do you think of this? Am I not right?"

"With submission, sir," said Turkey, in his blandest tone, "I think that you are."

"Nippers," said I, "what do *you* think of it?"

"I think I should kick him out of the office."

(The reader of nice perceptions will have perceived that, it being morning, Turkey's answer is couched in polite and tranquil terms, but Nippers replies in ill-tempered ones. Or, to repeat a previous sentence, Nippers' ugly mood was on duty, and Turkey's off.)

"Ginger Nut," said I, willing to enlist the smallest suffrage in my behalf, "what do *you* think of it?"

"I think, sir, he's a little *luny,*" replied Ginger Nut, with a grin.

"You hear what they say," said I, turning towards the screen, "come forth and do your duty."

But he vouchsafed no reply. I pondered a moment in sore perplexity. But once more business hurried me. I determined again to postpone the consideration of this dilemma to my future leisure. With a little trouble we made out to examine the papers without Bartleby, though at every page or two Turkey deferentially dropped his opinion, that this proceeding was quite out of the common; while Nippers, twitching in his chair with a dyspeptic nervousness, ground out, between his set teeth, occasional hissing maledictions against the stubborn oaf behind the screen. And for his (Nippers') part, this was the first and the last time he would do another man's business without pay.

Meanwhile Bartleby sat in his hermitage, oblivious to everything but his own peculiar business there.

Some days passed, the scrivener being employed upon another lengthy work. His late remarkable conduct led me to regard his ways narrowly. I observed that he never went to dinner; indeed, that he never went anywhere. As yet I had never, of my personal knowledge, known him to be outside of my office. He was a perpetual sentry in the corner. At about eleven o'clock though, in the morning, I noticed that Ginger Nut would advance toward the opening in Bartleby's screen, as if silently beckoned thither by a gesture invisible to me where I sat. The boy would then leave the office, jingling a few pence, and reappear with a handful of ginger-nuts, which he delivered in the hermitage, receiving two of the cakes for his trouble.

He lives, then, on ginger-nuts, thought I; never eats a dinner, properly speaking; he must be a vegetarian, then, but no; he never eats even vegetables, he eats nothing but ginger-nuts. My mind then ran on in reveries concerning the probable effects upon the human constitution of living entirely on ginger-nuts. Ginger-nuts are so called, because they contain ginger as one of their peculiar constituents, and the final flavoring one. Now, what was ginger? A hot, spicy thing. Was Bartleby hot and spicy? Not at all. Ginger, then, had no effect upon Bartleby. Probably he preferred it should have none.

Nothing so aggravates an earnest person as a passive resistance. If the individual so resisted be of a not inhumane temper, and the resisting one perfectly harmless in his passivity, then, in the better moods of the former, he will endeavor charitably to construe to his imagination what proves impossible to be solved by his judgment. Even so, for the most part, I regarded Bartleby and his ways. Poor fellow! thought I, he means no mischief; it is plain he intends no insolence; his aspect sufficiently evinces that his eccentricities are involuntary. He is useful to me. I can get along with him. If I turn him away, the chances are he will fall in with some less indulgent employer, and then he will be rudely treated, and perhaps driven forth miserably to starve. Yes. Here I can cheaply purchase a delicious self-approval. To befriend Bartleby; to humor him in his strange wilfulness, will cost me little or nothing, while I lay up in my soul what will eventually prove a sweet morsel for my conscience. But this mood was not invariable with me. The passiveness of Bartleby sometimes irritated me. I felt strangely goaded on to encounter him in new opposition — to elicit some angry spark from him answerable to my own. But, indeed, I might as well have essayed to strike fire with my knuckles against a bit of Windsor soap. But one afternoon the evil impulse in me mastered me, and the following little scene ensued:

"Bartleby," said I, "when those papers are all copied, I will compare them with you."

"I would prefer not to."

"How? Surely you do not mean to persist in that mulish vagary?"

No answer.

I threw open the folding-doors nearby, and turning upon Turkey and Nippers, exclaimed:

"Bartleby a second time says, he won't examine his papers. What do you think of it, Turkey?"

It was afternoon, be it remembered. Turkey sat glowing like a brass boiler; his bald head steaming; his hands reeling among his blotted papers.

"Think of it?" roared Turkey. "I think I'll just step behind his screen, and black his eyes for him!"

So saying, Turkey rose to his feet and threw his arms into a pugilistic position. He was hurrying away to make good his promise, when I detained him, alarmed at the effect of incautiously rousing Turkey's combativeness after dinner.

"Sit down, Turkey," said I, "and hear what Nippers has to say. What do you think of it, Nippers? Would I not be justified in immediately dismissing Bartleby?"

"Excuse me, that is for you to decide, sir. I think his conduct quite unusual, and, indeed, unjust, as regards Turkey and myself. But it may only be a passing whim."

"Ah," exclaimed I, "you have strangely changed your mind, then — you speak very gently of him now."

"All beer," cried Turkey; "gentleness is effects of beer — Nippers and I dined together to-day. You see how gentle *I* am, sir. Shall I go and black his eyes?"

"You refer to Bartleby, I suppose. No, not to-day, Turkey," I replied; "pray, put up your fists."

I closed the doors, and again advanced towards Bartleby. I felt additional incentives tempting me to my fate. I burned to be rebelled against again. I remembered that Bartleby never left the office.

"Bartleby," said I, "Ginger Nut is away; just step around to the Post Office, won't you?" (it was but a three minutes' walk) "and see if there is anything for me."

"I would prefer not to."

"You *will* not?"

"I *prefer* not."

I staggered to my desk, and sat there in a deep study. My blind inveteracy returned. Was there any other thing in which I could procure myself to be ignominiously repulsed by this lean, penniless wight?—my hired clerk? What added thing is there, perfectly reasonable, that he will be sure to refuse to do?

"Bartleby!"

No answer.

"Bartleby," in a louder tone.

No answer.

"Bartleby," I roared.

Like a very ghost, agreeably to the laws of magical invocation, at the third summons, he appeared at the entrance of his hermitage.

"Go to the next room, and tell Nippers to come to me."

"I prefer not to," he respectfully and slowly said, and mildly disappeared.

"Very good, Bartleby," said I, in a quiet sort of serenely-severe self-possessed tone, intimating the unalterable purpose of some terrible retribution very close at hand. At the moment I half intended something of the kind. But upon the whole, as it was drawing towards my dinner-hour, I thought it best to put on my hat and walk home for the day, suffering much from perplexity and distress of mind.

Shall I acknowledge it? The conclusion of this whole business was, that it soon became a fixed fact of my chambers, that a pale young scrivener, by the name of Bartleby, had a desk there; that he copied for me at the usual rate of four cents a folio (one hundred words); but he was permanently exempt from examining the work done by him, that duty being transferred to Turkey and Nippers, out of compliment, doubtless, to their superior acuteness; moreover, said Bartleby was never, on any account, to be dispatched on the most trivial errand of any sort; and that even if entreated to take upon him such a matter, it was generally understood that he would "prefer not to"—in other words, that he would refuse point-blank.

As days passed on, I became considerably reconciled to Bartleby. His steadiness, his freedom from all dissipation, his incessant industry (except when he chose to throw himself into a standing revery behind his screen), his great stillness, his unalterableness of demeanor under all circumstances, made him a valuable acquisition. One prime thing was this—*he was always there*—first in the morning, continually through the day, and the last at night. I had a singular confidence in his honesty. I felt my most precious papers perfectly safe in his hands. Sometimes, to be sure, I could not, for the very soul of me, avoid falling into sudden spasmodic passions with him. For it was exceeding difficult to bear in mind all the time those strange peculiarities, privileges, and unheard-of exemptions, forming the tacit stipulations on Bartleby's part under which he remained in my office. Now and then, in the eagerness of dispatching pressing business, I would inadvertently summon Bartleby, in a short, rapid tone, to put his finger, say, on the incipient tie of a bit of red tape with which I was about compressing some papers. Of course, from behind the screen the usual answer, "I prefer not to," was sure to come; and then, how could a human creature, with the common infirmities of our nature, refrain from bitterly exclaiming upon such perverseness — such unreasonableness? However, every added repulse of this sort which I received only tended to lessen the probability of my repeating the inadvertence.

Here it must be said, that, according to the custom of most legal gentlemen occupying chambers in densely populated law buildings, there were several keys to my door. One was kept by a woman residing in the attic, which person weekly scrubbed and daily swept and dusted my apartments. Another was kept by Turkey for convenience sake. The third I sometimes carried in my own pocket. The fourth I knew not who had.

Now, one Sunday morning I happened to go to Trinity Church, to hear a celebrated preacher, and finding myself rather early on the ground I thought I would walk round to my chambers for a while. Luckily I had my key with me; but upon applying it to the lock, I found it resisted by something inserted from the inside. Quite surprised, I called out; when to my consternation a key was turned from within; and thrusting his lean visage at me, and holding the door ajar, the apparition of Bartleby appeared, in his shirt-sleeves, and otherwise in a strangely tattered *deshabille,* saying quietly that he was sorry, but he was deeply engaged just then, and — preferred not admitting me at present. In a brief word or two, he moreover added, that perhaps I had better walk round the block two or three times, and by that time he would probably have concluded his affairs.

Now, the utterly unsurmised appearance of Bartleby, tenanting my law-chambers of a Sunday morning, with his cadaverously gentlemanly *nonchalance,* yet withal firm and self-possessed, had such a strange effect upon me, that incontinently I slunk away from my own door, and did as desired. But not without sundry twinges of impotent rebellion against the mild effrontery of this unaccountable scrivener. Indeed, it was his wonderful mildness chiefly, which not only disarmed me, but unmanned me, as it were. For I consider that one, for the time, is sort of unmanned when he tranquilly permits his hired clerk to dictate to him, and order him away from his own premises. Furthermore, I was full of uneasiness as to what Bartleby could possibly be doing in my office in his shirt-sleeves, and in an otherwise dismantled condition of a Sunday morning. Was anything amiss going on? Nay, that was out of the question. It was not to be thought of for a moment that Bartleby was an immoral person. But what could he be doing there? — copying? Nay again, whatever might be his eccentricities, Bartleby was an eminently decorous person. He would be the last man to sit down to his desk in any state approaching to nudity. Besides, it was Sunday; and there was something about Bartleby that forbade the supposition that he would by any secular occupation violate the proprieties of the day.

Nevertheless, my mind was not pacified; and full of a restless curiosity, at 90
last I returned to the door. Without hindrance I inserted my key, opened it, and entered. Bartleby was not to be seen. I looked round anxiously, peeped behind his screen; but it was very plain that he was gone. Upon more closely examining the place, I surmised that for an indefinite period Bartleby must have ate, dressed, and slept in my office, and that too without plate, mirror, or bed. The cushioned

seat of a rickety old sofa in one corner bore the faint impress of a lean, reclining form. Rolled away under his desk, I found a blanket; under the empty grate, a blacking box and brush; on a chair, a tin basin, with soap and a ragged towel; in a newspaper a few crumbs of ginger-nuts and a morsel of cheese. Yes, thought I, it is evident enough that Bartleby has been making his home here, keeping bachelor's hall all by himself. Immediately then the thought came sweeping across me, what miserable friendlessness and loneliness are here revealed! His poverty is great; but his solitude, how horrible! Think of it. Of a Sunday, Wall Street is deserted as Petra;° and every night of every day it is an emptiness. This building, too, which of week-days hums with industry and life, at nightfall echoes with sheer vacancy, and all through Sunday is forlorn. And here Bartleby makes his home; sole spectator of a solitude which he has seen all populous — a sort of innocent and transformed Marius brooding among the ruins of Carthage?°

For the first time in my life a feeling of overpowering stinging melancholy seized me. Before, I had never experienced aught but a not unpleasing sadness. The bond of a common humanity now drew me irresistibly to gloom. A fraternal melancholy! For both I and Bartleby were sons of Adam. I remembered the bright silks and sparkling faces I had seen that day, in gala trim, swan-like sailing down the Mississippi of Broadway; and I contrasted them with the pallid copyist, and thought to myself, Ah, happiness courts the light, so we deem the world is gay; but misery hides aloof, so we deem that misery there is none. These sad fancyings — chimeras, doubtless, of a sick and silly brain — led on to other and more special thoughts, concerning the eccentricities of Bartleby. Presentiments of strange discoveries hovered round me. The scrivener's pale form appeared to me laid out, among uncaring strangers, in its shivering winding-sheet.

Suddenly I was attracted by Bartleby's closed desk, the key in open sight left in the lock.

I mean no mischief, seek the gratification of no heartless curiosity, thought I; besides, the desk is mine, and its contents, too, so I will make bold to look within. Everything was methodically arranged, the papers smoothly placed. The pigeon-holes were deep, and removing the files of documents, I groped into their recesses. Presently I felt something there, and dragged it out. It was an old bandanna handkerchief, heavy and knotted. I opened it, and saw it was a saving's bank.

I now recalled all the quiet mysteries which I had noted in the man. I remembered that he never spoke but to answer; that, though at intervals he had considerable time to himself, yet I had never seen him reading — no, not even a newspaper; that for long periods he would stand looking out, at his pale window behind the screen, upon the dead brick wall; I was quite sure he never visited any refectory or eating-house; while his pale face clearly indicated that he never drank beer like Turkey; or tea and coffee even, like other men; that he never went anywhere in particular that I could learn; never went out for a walk, unless, indeed, that was the case at present; that he had declined telling who he was, or whence he came, or whether he had any relatives in the world; that though so thin and pale, he never complained of ill-health. And more than

Petra: An ancient Arabian city abandoned for many centuries.
Marius: Gaius Marius (157–86 B.C.), an exiled Roman general who sought refuge in *Carthage,* a city destroyed by the Romans.

all, I remembered a certain unconscious air of pallid — how shall I call it? — of pallid haughtiness, say, or rather an austere reserve about him, which has positively awed me into my tame compliance with his eccentricities, when I had feared to ask him to do the slightest incidental thing for me, even though I might know, from his long-continued motionlessness, that behind his screen he must be standing in one of those dead-wall reveries of his.

Revolving all these things, and coupling them with the recently discovered fact, that he made my office his constant abiding place and home, and not forgetful of his morbid moodiness; revolving all these things, a prudential feeling began to steal over me. My first emotions had been those of pure melancholy and sincerest pity; but just in proportion as the forlornness of Bartleby grew and grew to my imagination, did that same melancholy merge into fear, that pity into repulsion. So true it is, and so terrible, too, that up to a certain point the thought or sight of misery enlists our best affections; but, in certain special cases, beyond that point it does not. They err who would assert that invariably this is owing to the inherent selfishness of the human heart. It rather proceeds from a certain hopelessness of remedying excessive and organic ill. To a sensitive being, pity is not seldom pain. And when at last it is perceived that such pity cannot lead to effectual succor, common sense bids the soul be rid of it. What I saw that morning persuaded me that the scrivener was the victim of innate and incurable disorder. I might give alms to his body; but his body did not pain him; it was his soul that suffered, and his soul I could not reach.

I did not accomplish the purpose of going to Trinity Church that morning. Somehow, the things I had seen disqualified me for the time from church-going. I walked homeward, thinking what I would do with Bartleby. Finally, I resolved upon this — I would put certain calm questions to him the next morning, touching his history, etc., and if he declined to answer them openly and unreservedly (and I supposed he would prefer not), then to give him a twenty dollar bill over and above whatever I might owe him, and tell him his services were no longer required; but that if in any other way I could assist him, I would be happy to do so, especially if he desired to return to his native place, wherever that might be, I would willingly help to defray the expenses. Moreover, if, after reaching home, he found himself at any time in want of aid, a letter from him would be sure of a reply.

The next morning came.

"Bartleby," said I, gently calling to him behind his screen.

No reply.

"Bartleby," said I, in a still gentler tone, "come here; I am not going to ask you to do anything you would prefer not to do — I simply wish to speak to you."

Upon this he noiselessly slid into view.

"Will you tell me, Bartleby, where you were born?"

"I would prefer not to."

"Will you tell me *anything* about yourself?"

"I would prefer not to."

"But what reasonable objection can you have to speak to me? I feel friendly towards you."

He did not look at me while I spoke, but kept his glance fixed upon my bust of Cicero, which, as I then sat, was directly behind me, some six inches above my head.

"What is your answer, Bartleby?" said I, after waiting a considerable time for a reply, during which his countenance remained immovable, only there was the faintest conceivable tremor of the white attenuated mouth.

"At present I prefer to give no answer," he said, and retired into his hermitage.

It was rather weak in me I confess, but his manner, on this occasion, net- 110
tled me. Not only did there seem to lurk in it a certain calm disdain, but his perverseness seemed ungrateful, considering the undeniable good usage and indulgence he had received from me.

Again I sat ruminating what I should do. Mortified as I was at his behavior, and resolved as I had been to dismiss him when I entered my office, nevertheless I strangely felt something superstitious knocking at my heart, and forbidding me to carry out my purpose, and denouncing me for a villain if I dared to breathe one bitter word against this forlornest of mankind. At last, familiarly drawing my chair behind his screen, I sat down and said: "Bartleby, never mind, then, about revealing your history; but let me entreat you, as a friend, to comply as far as may be with the usages of this office. Say now, you will help to examine papers tomorrow or next day: in short, say now, that in a day or two you will begin to be a little reasonable: — say so, Bartleby."

"At present I would prefer not to be a little reasonable," was his mildly cadaverous reply.

Just then the folding-doors opened, and Nippers approached. He seemed suffering from an unusually bad night's rest, induced by severer indigestion than common. He overhead those final words of Bartleby.

"*Prefer not,* eh?" gritted Nippers — "I'd *prefer* him, if I were you, sir," addressing me — "I'd *prefer* him; I'd give him preferences, the stubborn mule! What is it, sir, pray, that he *prefers* not to do now?"

Bartleby moved not a limb. 115

"Mr. Nippers," said I, "I'd prefer that you would withdraw for the present."

Somehow, of late, I had got into the way of involuntarily using this word "prefer" upon all sorts of not exactly suitable occasions. And I trembled to think that my contact with the scrivener had already and seriously affected me in a mental way. And what further and deeper aberration might it not yet produce? This apprehension had not been without efficacy in determining me to summary measures.

As Nippers, looking very sour and sulky, was departing, Turkey blandly and deferentially approached.

"With submission, sir," said he, "yesterday I was thinking about Bartleby here, and I think that if he would but prefer to take a quart of good ale every day, it would do much towards mending him, and enabling him to assist in examining his papers."

"So you have got the word, too," said I, slightly excited. 120

"With submission, what word, sir?" asked Turkey, respectfully crowding himself into the contracted space behind the screen, and by so doing, making me jostle the scrivener. "What word, sir?"

"I would prefer to be left alone here," said Bartleby, as if offended at being mobbed in his privacy.

"*That's* the word, Turkey," said I—"*that's* it."

"Oh, *prefer?* oh yes—queer word. I never use it myself. But, sir, as I was saying, if he would but prefer—"

"Turkey," interrupted I, "you will please withdraw."

"Oh certainly, sir, if you prefer that I should."

As he opened the folding-door to retire, Nippers at his desk caught a glimpse of me, and asked whether I would prefer to have a certain paper copied on blue paper or white. He did not in the least roguishly accent the word "prefer." It was plain that it involuntarily rolled from his tongue. I thought to myself, surely I must get rid of a demented man, who already has in some degree turned the tongues, if not the heads of myself and clerks. But I thought it prudent not to break the dismission at once.

The next day I noticed that Bartleby did nothing but stand at his window in his dead-wall revery. Upon asking him why he did not write, he said that he had decided upon doing no more writing.

"Why, how now? what next?" exclaimed I, "do no more writing?"

"No more."

"And what is the reason?"

"Do you not see the reason for yourself?" he indifferently replied.

I looked steadfastly at him, and perceived that his eyes looked dull and glazed. Instantly it occurred to me, that his unexampled diligence in copying by his dim window for the first few weeks of his stay with me might have temporarily impaired his vision.

I was touched. I said something in condolence with him. I hinted that of course he did wisely in abstaining from writing for a while; and urged him to embrace that opportunity of taking wholesome exercise in the open air. This, however, he did not do. A few days after this, my other clerks being absent, and being in a great hurry to dispatch certain letters by the mail, I thought that, having nothing else earthly to do, Bartleby would surely be less inflexible than usual, and carry these letters to the Post Office. But he blankly declined. So, much to my inconvenience, I went myself.

Still added days went by. Whether Bartleby's eyes improved or not, I could not say. To all appearance, I thought they did. But when I asked him if they did, he vouchsafed no answer. At all events, he would do no copying. At last, in replying to my urgings, he informed me that he had permanently given up copying.

"What!" exclaimed I; "suppose your eyes should get entirely well—better than ever before—would you not copy then?"

"I have given up copying," he answered, and slid aside.

He remained as ever, a fixture in my chamber. Nay—if that were possible—he became still more of a fixture than before. What was to be done? He would do nothing in the office; why should he stay there? In plain fact, he had now become a millstone to me, not only useless as a necklace, but afflictive to bear. Yet I was sorry for him. I speak less than truth when I say that, on his own account, he occasioned me uneasiness. If he would but have named a single relative or friend, I would instantly have written, and urged their taking the poor fellow away to some convenient retreat. But he seemed alone, absolutely alone in the universe. A bit of wreck in the mid-Atlantic. At length, necessities connected with my business tyrannized over all other considerations. Decently as I could, I told Bartleby that in six days' time he must unconditionally leave the office. I warned him to take measures, in the interval, for procuring some other abode. I offered to assist him in this endeavor, if he himself would but take the first step towards a removal. "And when you finally quit me, Bartleby," added I, "I shall see that you go not away entirely unprovided. Six days from this hour, remember."

At the expiration of that period, I peeped behind the screen, and lo! Bartleby was there.

140 I buttoned up my coat, balanced myself; advanced slowly towards him, touched his shoulder, and said, "The time has come; you must quit this place; I am sorry for you; here is money; but you must go."

"I would prefer not," he replied, with his back still towards me.

"You *must.*"

He remained silent.

Now I had an unbounded confidence in this man's common honesty. He had frequently restored to me sixpences and shillings carelessly dropped upon the floor, for I am apt to be very reckless in such shirt-button affairs. The proceeding, then, which followed will not be deemed extraordinary.

145 "Bartleby," said I, "I owe you twelve dollars on account; here are thirty-two, the odd twenty are yours — Will you take it?" and I handed the bills towards him.

But he made no motion.

"I will leave them here, then," putting them under a weight on the table. Then taking my hat and cane and going to the door, I tranquilly turned and added — "After you have removed your things from these offices, Bartleby, you will of course lock the door — since every one is now gone for the day but you — and if you please, slip your key underneath the mat, so that I may have it in the morning. I shall not see you again; so good-bye to you. If, hereafter, in your new place of abode, I can be of any service to you, do not fail to advise me by letter. Good-bye, Bartleby, and fare you well."

But he answered not a word; like the last column of some ruined temple, he remained standing mute and solitary in the middle of the otherwise deserted room.

As I walked home in a pensive mood, my vanity got the better of my pity. I could not but highly plume myself on my masterly management in getting rid of Bartleby. Masterly I call it, and such it must appear to any dispassionate thinker. The beauty of my procedure seemed to consist in its perfect quietness. There was no vulgar bullying, no bravado of any sort, no choleric hectoring, and striding to and fro across the apartment, jerking out vehement commands for Bartleby to bundle himself off with his beggarly traps. Nothing of the kind. Without loudly bidding Bartleby depart — as an inferior genius might have done — I *assumed* the ground that depart he must; and upon that assumption built all I had to say. The more I thought over my procedure, the more I was charmed with it. Nevertheless, next morning, upon awakening, I had my doubts — I had somehow slept off the fumes of vanity. One of the coolest and wisest hours a man has, is just after he awakes in the morning. My procedure seemed as sagacious as ever — but only in theory. How it would prove in practice — there was the rub. It was truly a beautiful thought to have assumed Bartleby's departure; but, after all, that assumption was simply my own, and none of Bartleby's. The great point was, not whether I had assumed that he would quit me, but whether he would prefer to do so. He was more a man of preferences than assumptions.

After breakfast, I walked down town, arguing the probabilities *pro* and *con*. 150
One moment I thought it would prove a miserable failure, and Bartleby would be found all alive at my office as usual; the next moment it seemed certain that I should find his chair empty. And so I kept veering about. At the corner of Broadway and Canal Street, I saw quite an excited group of people standing in earnest conversation.

"I'll take odds he doesn't," said a voice as I passed.

"Doesn't go? — done!" said I, "put up your money."

I was instinctively putting my hand in my pocket to produce my own, when I remembered that this was an election day. The words I had overheard bore no reference to Bartleby, but to the success or non-success of some candidate for the mayoralty. In my intent frame of mind, I had, as it were, imagined that all Broadway shared in my excitement, and were debating the same question with me. I passed on, very thankful that the uproar of the street screened my momentary absent-mindedness.

As I had intended, I was earlier than usual at my office door. I stood listening for a moment. All was still. He must be gone. I tried the knob. The door was locked. Yes, my procedure had worked to a charm; he indeed must be vanished. Yet a certain melancholy mixed with this: I was almost sorry for my brilliant success. I was fumbling under the door mat for the key, which Bartleby was to have left there for me, when accidentally my knee knocked against a panel, producing a summoning sound, and in response a voice came to me from within — "Not yet; I am occupied."

It was Bartleby. 155

I was thunderstruck. For an instant I stood like the man who, pipe in mouth, was killed one cloudless afternoon long ago in Virginia, by summer lightning; at his own warm open window he was killed, and remained leaning out there upon the dreamy afternoon, till some one touched him, when he fell.

"Not gone!" I murmured at last. But again obeying that wondrous ascendancy which the inscrutable scrivener had over me, and from which ascendancy, for all my chafing, I could not completely escape, I slowly went down stairs and out into the street, and while walking round the block, considered what I should next do in this unheard-of perplexity. Turn the man out by an actual thrusting I could not; to drive him away by calling him hard names would not do; calling in the police was an unpleasant idea; and yet, permit him to enjoy his cadaverous triumph over me — this, too, I could not think of. What was to be done? or, if nothing could be done, was there anything further that I could *assume* in the matter? Yes, as before I had prospectively assumed that Bartleby would depart, so now I might retrospectively assume that departed he was. In the legitimate carrying out of this assumption, I might enter my office in a great hurry, and pretending not to see Bartleby at all, walk straight against him as if he were air. Such a proceeding would in a singular degree have the appearance of a home-thrust. It was hardly possible that Bartleby could withstand such an application of the doctrine of assumption. But upon second thoughts the success of the plan seemed rather dubious. I resolved to argue the matter over with him again.

"Bartleby," said I, entering the office, with a quietly severe expression, "I am seriously displeased. I am pained, Bartleby. I had thought better of you. I had imagined you of such a gentlemanly organization, that in any delicate dilemma a slight hint would suffice — in short, an assumption. But it appears I am deceived. Why," I added, unaffectedly starting, "you have not even touched that money yet," pointing to it, just where I had left it the evening previous.

He answered nothing.

"Will you, or will you not, quit me?" I now demanded in a sudden passion, advancing close to him.

"I would prefer *not* to quit you," he replied, gently emphasizing the *not*.

"What earthly right have you to stay here? Do you pay any rent? Do you pay my taxes? Or is this property yours?"

He answered nothing.

"Are you ready to go on and write now? Are your eyes recovered? Could you copy a small paper for me this morning? or help examine a few lines? or step round to the Post Office? In a word, will you do anything at all, to give a coloring to your refusal to depart the premises?"

He silently retired into his hermitage.

I was now in such a state of nervous resentment that I thought it but prudent to check myself at present from further demonstrations. Bartleby and I were alone. I remembered the tragedy of the unfortunate Adams and the still more unfortunate Colt in the solitary office of the latter; and how poor Colt, being dreadfully incensed by Adams, and imprudently permitting himself to get wildly excited, was at unawares hurried into his fatal act — an act which certainly no man could possibly deplore more than the actor himself. Often it had occurred to me in my ponderings upon the subject that had that altercation taken place in the public street, or at a private residence, it would not have terminated as it did. It was the circumstance of being alone in a solitary office, up stairs, of a building entirely unhallowed by humanizing domestic associations — an uncarpeted office, doubtless, of a dusty, haggard sort of appearance — this it must have been, which greatly helped to enhance the irritable desperation of the hapless Colt.°

But when this old Adam of resentment rose in me and tempted me concerning Bartleby, I grappled him and threw him. How? Why, simply by recalling the divine injunction: "A new commandment give I unto you, that ye love one another." Yes, this it was that saved me. Aside from higher considerations, charity often operates as a vastly wise and prudent principle — a great safeguard to its possessor. Men have committed murder for jealousy's sake, and anger's sake, and hatred's sake, and selfishness' sake, and spiritual pride's sake; but no man, that ever I heard of, ever committed a diabolical murder for sweet charity's sake. Mere self-interest, then, if no better motive can be enlisted, should, especially with high-tempered men, prompt all beings to charity and philanthropy. At any rate, upon the occasion in question, I strove to drown my exasperated feelings towards the scrivener by benevolently construing his conduct. Poor fellow, poor fellow! thought I, he don't mean anything; and besides, he has seen hard times, and ought to be indulged.

I endeavored, also, immediately to occupy myself, and at the same time to comfort my despondency. I tried to fancy, that in the course of the morning, at

John C. Colt: Brother of the gun maker. Killed *Samuel Adams* during a quarrel in 1842, leading to a sensational court case. Colt committed suicide just before he was to be hanged.

such time as might prove agreeable to him, Bartleby, of his own free accord, would emerge from his hermitage and take up some decided line of march in the direction of the door. But no. Half-past twelve o'clock came; Turkey began to glow in the face, overturn his inkstand, and become generally obstreperous; Nippers abated down into quietude and courtesy; Ginger Nut munched his noon apple; and Bartleby remained standing at his window in one of his profoundest dead-wall reveries. Will it be credited? Ought I to acknowledge it? That afternoon I left the office without saying one further word to him.

Some days now passed, during which, at leisure intervals I looked a little into "Edwards on the Will," and "Priestley on Necessity."° Under the circumstances, those books induced a salutary feeling. Gradually I slid into the persuasion that these troubles of mine, touching the scrivener, had been all predestined from eternity, and Bartleby was billeted upon me for some mysterious purpose of an all-wise Providence, which it was not for a mere mortal like me to fathom. Yes, Bartleby, stay there behind your screen, thought I; I shall persecute you no more; you are harmless and noiseless as any of these old chairs; in short, I never feel so private as when I know you are here. At last I see it, I feel it; I penetrate to the predestined purpose of my life. I am content. Others may have loftier parts to enact; but my mission in this world, Bartleby, is to furnish you with office-room for such period as you may see fit to remain.

I believe that this wise and blessed frame of mind would have continued with me, had it not been for the unsolicited and uncharitable remarks obtruded upon me by my professional friends who visited the rooms. But thus it often is, that the constant friction of illiberal minds wears out at last the best resolves of the more generous. Though to be sure, when I reflected upon it, it was not strange that people entering my office should be struck by the peculiar aspect of the unaccountable Bartleby, and so be tempted to throw out some sinister observations concerning him. Sometimes an attorney, having business with me, and calling at my office, and finding no one but the scrivener there, would undertake to obtain some sort of precise information from him touching my whereabouts; but without heeding his idle talk, Bartleby would remain standing immovable in the middle of the room. So after contemplating him in that position for a time, the attorney would depart, no wiser than he came.

Also, when a reference was going on, and the room full of lawyers and witnesses, and business driving fast, some deeply-occupied legal gentleman present, seeing Bartleby wholly unemployed, would request him to run round to his (the legal gentleman's) office and fetch some papers for him. Thereupon, Bartleby would tranquilly decline, and yet remain idle as before. Then the lawyer would give a great stare, and turn to me. And what could I say? At last I was made aware that all through the circle of my professional acquaintance, a whisper of wonder was running round, having reference to the strange creature I kept at my office. This worried me very much. And as the idea came upon me of his possibly turning out a long-lived man, and keeping occupying my chambers, and denying my authority; and perplexing my visitors; and scandalizing my professional reputation; and casting a general gloom over the premises; keeping soul and body together to the last upon his savings (for doubtless he spent but

Jonathan Edwards, Freedom of the Will (1754), *Joseph Priestley,* Doctrine of Philosophical Necessity (1777): Argued that human beings do not have free will.

half a dime a day), and in the end perhaps outlive me, and claim possession of my office by right of his perpetual occupancy: as all these dark anticipations crowded upon me more and more, and my friends continually intruded their relentless remarks upon the apparition in my room; a great change was wrought in me. I resolved to gather all my faculties together, and forever rid me of this intolerable incubus.

Ere revolving any complicated project, however, adapted to this end, I first simply suggested to Bartleby the propriety of his permanent departure. In a calm and serious tone, I commended the idea to his careful and mature consideration. But, having taken three days to meditate upon it, he apprised me, that his original determination remained the same; in short, that he still preferred to abide with me.

What shall I do? I now said to myself, buttoning up my coat to the last button. What shall I do? what ought I to do? what does conscience say I *should* do with this man, or, rather, ghost. Rid myself of him, I must; go, he shall. But how? You will not thrust him, the poor, pale, passive mortal — you will not thrust such a helpless creature out of your door? you will not dishonor yourself by such cruelty? No, I will not, I cannot do that. Rather would I let him live and die here, and then mason up his remains in the wall. What, then, will you do? For all your coaxing, he will not budge. Bribes he leaves under your own paperweight on your table; in short, it is quite plain that he prefers to cling to you.

Then something severe, something unusual must be done. What! surely you will not have him collared by a constable, and commit his innocent pallor to the common jail? And upon what ground could you procure such a thing to be done? — a vagrant, is he? What! he a vagrant, a wanderer, who refuses to budge? It is because he will *not* be a vagrant, then, that you seek to count him *as* a vagrant. That is too absurd. No visible means of support: there I have him. Wrong again: for indubitably he *does* support himself, and that is the only unanswerable proof that any man can show of his possessing the means so to do. No more, then. Since he will not quit me, I must quit him. I will change my offices; I will move elsewhere, and give him fair notice, that if I find him on my new premises I will then proceed against him as a common trespasser.

Acting accordingly, next day I thus addressed him: "I find these chambers 175
too far from the City Hall; the air is unwholesome. In a word, I propose to remove my offices next week, and shall no longer require your services. I tell you this now, in order that you may seek another place."

He made no reply, and nothing more was said.

On the appointed day I engaged carts and men, proceeded to my chambers, and having but little furniture, everything was removed in a few hours. Throughout, the scrivener remained standing behind the screen, which I directed to be removed the last thing. It was withdrawn; and, being folded up like a huge folio, left him the motionless occupant of a naked room. I stood in the entry watching him a moment, while something from within me upbraided me.

I re-entered, with my hand in my pocket — and — and my heart in my mouth.

"Good-bye, Bartleby; I am going — good-bye, and God some way bless you; and take that," slipping something in his hand. But it dropped upon the floor, and then — strange to say — I tore myself from him whom I had so longed to be rid of.

Established in my new quarters, for a day or two I kept the door locked, 180
and started at every footfall in the passages. When I returned to my rooms, after any little absence, I would pause at the threshold for an instant, and attentively listen, ere applying my key. But these fears were needless. Bartleby never came nigh me.

I thought all was going well, when a perturbed-looking stranger visited me, inquiring whether I was the person who had recently occupied rooms at No. —Wall Street.

Full of forebodings, I replied that I was.

"Then, sir," said the stranger, who proved a lawyer, "you are responsible for the man you left there. He refuses to do any copying; he refuses to do anything; he says he prefers not to; and he refuses to quit the premises."

"I am very sorry, sir," said I, with assumed tranquillity, but an inward tremor, "but, really, the man you allude to is nothing to me — he is no relation or apprentice of mine, that you should hold me responsible for him."

"In mercy's name, who is he?" 185

"I certainly cannot inform you. I know nothing about him. Formerly I employed him as a copyist; but he has done nothing for me now for some time past."

"I shall settle him, then — good morning, sir."

Several days passed, and I heard nothing more; and, though I often felt a charitable prompting to call at the place and see poor Bartleby, yet a certain squeamishness, of I know not what, withheld me.

All is over with him, by this time, thought I, at last, when, through another week, no further intelligence reached me. But, coming to my room the day after, I found several persons waiting at my door in a high state of nervous excitement.

"That's the man — here he comes," cried the foremost one, whom I rec- 190
ognized as the lawyer who had previously called upon me alone.

"You must take him away, sir, at once," cried a portly person among them, advancing upon me, and whom I knew to be the landlord of No. —Wall Street. "These gentlemen, my tenants, cannot stand it any longer; Mr. B——," pointing to the lawyer, "has turned him out of his room, and he now persists in haunting the building generally, sitting upon the banisters of the stairs by day, and sleeping in the entry by night. Everybody is concerned; clients are leaving the offices; some fears are entertained of a mob; something you must do, and that without delay."

Aghast at this torrent, I fell back before it, and would fain have locked myself in my new quarters. In vain I persisted that Bartleby was nothing to me — no more than to any one else. In vain — I was the last person known to have anything to do with him, and they held me to the terrible account. Fearful, then, of being exposed in the papers (as one person present obscurely threatened), I considered the matter, and, at length, said, that if the lawyer would give me a confidential interview with the scrivener, in his (the lawyer's) own room, I would, that afternoon, strive my best to rid them of the nuisance they complained of.

Going up stairs to my old haunt, there was Bartleby silently sitting upon the banister at the landing.

"What are you doing here, Bartleby?" said I.

195 "Sitting upon the banister," he mildly replied.

I motioned him into the lawyer's room, who then left us.

"Bartleby," said I, "are you aware that you are the cause of great tribulation to me, by persisting in occupying the entry after being dismissed from the office?"

No answer.

"Now one of two things must take place. Either you must do something, or something must be done to you. Now what sort of business would you like to engage in? Would you like to re-engage in copying for some one?"

200 "No; I would prefer not to make any change."

"Would you like a clerkship in a dry-goods store?"

"There is too much confinement about that. No, I would not like a clerkship; but I am not particular."

"Too much confinement," I cried, "why, you keep yourself confined all the time!"

"I would prefer not to take a clerkship," he rejoined, as if to settle that little item at once.

205 "How would a bar-tender's business suit you? There is no trying of the eyesight in that."

"I would not like it at all; though, as I said before, I am not particular."

His unwonted wordiness inspirited me. I returned to the charge.

"Well, then, would you like to travel through the country collecting bills for the merchants? That would improve your health."

"No, I would prefer to be doing something else."

210 "How, then, would going as a companion to Europe, to entertain some young gentleman with your conversation—how would that suit you?"

"Not at all. It does not strike me that there is anything definite about that. I like to be stationary. But I am not particular."

"Stationary you shall be, then," I cried, now losing all patience, and, for the first time in all my exasperating connection with him, fairly flying into a passion. "If you do not go away from these premises before night, I shall feel bound—indeed, I *am* bound—to—to quit the premises myself!" I rather absurdly concluded, knowing not with what possible threat to try to frighten his immobility into compliance. Despairing of all further efforts, I was precipitately leaving him, when a final thought occurred to me—one which had not been wholly unindulged before.

"Bartleby," said I, in the kindest tone I could assume under such exciting circumstances, "will you go home with me now—not to my office, but my dwelling—and remain there till we can conclude upon some convenient arrangement for you at our leisure? Come, let us start now, right away."

"No: at present I would prefer not to make any change at all."

215 I answered nothing; but, effectually dodging every one by the suddenness and rapidity of my flight, rushed from the building, ran up Wall Street towards Broadway, and, jumping into the first omnibus, was soon removed from pursuit. As soon as tranquillity returned, I distinctly perceived that I had now done all that I possibly could, both in respect to the demands of the landlord and his tenants, and with regard to my own desire and sense of duty, to benefit Bartleby, and shield him from rude persecution. I now strove to be entirely care-free and quiescent; and my conscience justified me in the attempt; though, indeed, it was

not so successful as I could have wished. So fearful was I of being again hunted out by the incensed landlord and his exasperated tenants, that, surrendering my business to Nippers, for a few days, I drove about the upper part of the town and through the suburbs, in my rockaway; crossed over to Jersey City and Hoboken, and paid fugitive visits to Manhattanville and Astoria. In fact, I almost lived in my rockaway for the time.

When again I entered my office, lo, a note from the landlord lay upon the desk. I opened it with trembling hands. It informed me that the writer had sent to the police, and had Bartleby removed to the Tombs as a vagrant. Moreover, since I knew more about him than any one else, he wished me to appear at that place, and make a suitable statement of the facts. These tidings had a conflicting effect upon me. At first I was indignant; but, at last, almost approved. The landlord's energetic, summary disposition, had led him to adopt a procedure which I do not think I would have decided upon myself; and yet, as a last resort, under such peculiar circumstances, it seemed the only plan.

As I afterwards learned, the poor scrivener, when told that he must be conducted to the Tombs, offered not the slightest obstacle, but, in his pale, unmoving way, silently acquiesced.

Some of the compassionate and curious by-standers joined the party; and headed by one of the constables arm-in-arm with Bartleby, the silent procession filed its way through all the noise, and heat, and joy of the roaring thoroughfares at noon.

The same day I received the note, I went to the Tombs, or, to speak more properly, the Halls of Justice. Seeking the right officer, I stated the purpose of my call, and was informed that the individual I described was, indeed, within. I then assured the functionary that Bartleby was a perfectly honest man, and greatly to be compassionated, however unaccountably eccentric. I narrated all I knew, and closed by suggesting the idea of letting him remain in as indulgent confinement as possible, till something less harsh might be done — though, indeed, I hardly knew what. At all events, if nothing else could be decided upon, the almshouse must receive him. I then begged to have an interview.

Being under no disgraceful charge, and quite serene and harmless in all his ways, they had permitted him freely to wander about the prison, and, especially, in the inclosed grass-platted yards thereof. And so I found him there, standing all alone in the quietest of the yards, his face towards a high wall, while all around, from the narrow slits of the jail windows, I thought I saw peering out upon him the eyes of murderers and thieves.

"Bartleby!"

"I know you," he said, without looking round — "and I want nothing to say to you."

"It was not I that brought you here, Bartleby," said I, keenly pained at his implied suspicion. "And to you, this should not be so vile a place. Nothing reproachful attaches to you by being here. And see, it is not so sad a place as one might think. Look, there is the sky, and here is the grass."

"I know where I am," he replied, but would say nothing more, and so I left him.

As I entered the corridor again, a broad meat-like man, in an apron, accosted me, and, jerking his thumb over his shoulder, said — "Is that your friend?"

"Yes."

"Does he want to starve? If he does, let him live on the prison fare, that's all."

"Who are you?" asked I, not knowing what to make of such an unofficially speaking person in such a place.

"I am the grub-man. Such gentlemen as have friends here, hire me to provide them with something good to eat."

"Is this so?" said I, turning the turnkey.

He said it was.

"Well, then," said I, slipping some silver into the grub-man's hands (for so they called him), "I want you to give particular attention to my friend there; let him have the best dinner you can get. And you must be as polite to him as possible."

"Introduce me, will you?" said the grub-man, looking at me with an expression which seemed to say he was all impatience for an opportunity to give a specimen of his breeding.

Thinking it would prove of benefit to the scrivener, I acquiesced; and, asking the grub-man his name, went up with him to Bartleby.

"Bartleby, this is a friend; you will find him very useful to you."

"Your sarvant, sir, your sarvant," said the grub-man, making a low salutation behind his apron. "Hope you find it pleasant here, sir; nice grounds — cool apartments — hope you'll stay with us some time — try to make it agreeable. What will you have for dinner to-day?"

"I prefer not to dine to-day," said Bartleby, turning away. "It would disagree with me; I am unused to dinners." So saying, he slowly moved to the other side of the inclosure, and took up a position fronting the deadwall.

"How's this?" said the grub-man, addressing me with a stare of astonishment. "He's odd, ain't he?"

"I think he is a little deranged," said I, sadly.

"Deranged? deranged is it? Well, now, upon my word, I thought that friend of yourn was a gentleman forger; they are always pale and genteel-like, them forgers. I can't help pity 'em — can't help it, sir. Did you know Monroe Edwards?" he added, touchingly, and paused. Then, laying his hand piteously on my shoulder, sighed, "he died of consumption at Sing-Sing. So you weren't acquainted with Monroe?"

"No, I was never socially acquainted with any forgers. But I cannot stop longer. Look to my friend yonder. You will not lose by it. I will see you again."

Some few days after this, I again obtained admission to the Tombs, and went through the corridors in quest of Bartleby; but without finding him.

"I saw him coming from his cell not long ago," said a turnkey, "may be he's gone to loiter in the yards."

So I went in that direction.

"Are you looking for the silent man?" said another turnkey, passing me. "Yonder he lies — sleeping in the yard there. 'Tis not twenty minutes since I saw him lie down."

The yard was entirely quiet. It was not accessible to the common prisoners. The surrounding walls, of amazing thickness, kept off all sounds behind them. The Egyptian character of the masonry weighed upon me with its gloom. But a soft imprisoned turf grew under foot. The heart of the eternal pyramids, it seemed, wherein, by some strange magic, through the clefts, grass-seed, dropped by birds, had sprung.

Strangely huddled at the base of the wall, his knees drawn up, and lying on his side, his head touching the cold stones, I saw the wasted Bartleby. But nothing stirred. I paused; then went close up to him; stooped over, and saw that his dim eyes were open; otherwise he seemed profoundly sleeping. Something prompted me to touch him. I felt his hand, when a tingling shiver ran up my arm and down my spine to my feet.

The round face of the grub-man peered upon me now. "His dinner is ready. Won't he dine to-day, either? Or does he live without dining?"

"Lives without dining," said I, and closed the eyes.

"Eh! — He's asleep, ain't he?"

"With kings and counselors,"° murmured I.

There would seem little need for proceeding further in this history. Imagination will readily supply the meagre recital of poor Bartleby's interment. But, ere parting with the reader, let me say, that if this little narrative has sufficiently interested him, to awaken curiosity as to who Bartleby was, and what manner of life he led prior to the present narrator's making his acquaintance, I can only reply, that in such curiosity I fully share, but am wholly unable to gratify it. Yet here I hardly know whether I should divulge one little item of rumor, which came to my ear a few months after the scrivener's decease. Upon what basis it rested, I could never ascertain; and hence, how true it is I cannot now tell. But, inasmuch as this vague report has not been without a certain suggestive interest to me, however sad, it may prove the same with some others; and so I will briefly mention it. The report was this: that Bartleby had been a subordinate clerk in the Dead Letter Office at Washington, from which he had been suddenly removed by a change in the administration. When I think over this rumor, hardly can I express the emotions which seize me. Dead letters! does it not sound like dead men? Conceive a man by nature and misfortune prone to a pallid hopelessness, can any business seem more fitted to heighten it than that of continually handling these dead letters, and assorting them for the flames? For by the cart-load they are annually burned. Sometimes from out the folded paper the pale clerk takes a ring — the finger it was meant for, perhaps, moulders in the grave; a bank-note sent in swiftest charity — he whom it would relieve, nor eats nor hungers any more; pardon for those who died despairing; hope for those who died unhoping; good tidings for those who died stifled by unrelieved calamities. On errands of life, these letters speed to death.

Ah, Bartleby! Ah, humanity!

"With kings and counselors": From Job 3:13–14: "then had I been at rest, / With kings and counsellors of the earth, / which built desolate places for themselves."

Considerations

1. How does this description of Melville shed light on the central concerns of "Bartleby, the Scrivener"?
2. Which side does Hawthorne seem to be on — "belief" or "unbelief"? Why?
3. Compare Hawthorne's description with Melville's view of Hawthorne (p. 292). What attitudes about life do they share?

4. Describe Bartleby's physical characteristics. How is his physical description a foreshadowing of what happens to him?
5. How does Bartleby's "I would prefer not to" affect the routine of the lawyer and his employees?
6. What is the significance of the subtitle: "A Story of Wall Street"?
7. Who is the protagonist? Whose story is it?
8. Does the lawyer change during the story? Does Bartleby? Who is the antagonist?
9. What motivates Bartleby's behavior? Why do you think Melville withholds the information about the Dead Letter Office until the end of the story? Does this background adequately explain Bartleby?
10. Does Bartleby have any lasting impact on the lawyer?
11. Do you think Melville sympathizes more with Bartleby or with the lawyer?
12. Describe the lawyer's changing attitudes toward Bartleby.
13. Consider how this story could be regarded as a kind of protest with nonnegotiable demands.
14. Discuss the story's humor and how it affects your response to Bartleby.
15. Trace your emotional reaction to Bartleby as he is revealed in the story.

Connections

1. Compare Bartleby's withdrawal from life with that of the protagonist in Godwin's "A Sorrowful Woman" (p. 30). Why does each character choose death?
2. How is Melville's use of Bartleby's experience in the Dead Letter Office similar to Nathaniel Hawthorne's use of Brown's forest encounter with the devil in "Young Goodman Brown" (p. 258)? Why is each experience crucial to an understanding of what informs the behavior of these characters?
3. Discuss the significant parallels between "Bartleby, the Scrivener" and Franz Kafka's "A Hunger Artist" (p. 376), both stories about self-denial and isolation. Explain whether you think Bartleby's and the hunger artist's responses to their environments are similar or different.

PERSPECTIVE

NATHANIEL HAWTHORNE (1804–1864)

On Herman Melville's Philosophic Stance 1856

[Melville] stayed with us from Tuesday till Thursday; and, on the intervening day, we took a pretty long walk together, and sat down in a hollow among the sand hills (sheltering ourselves from the high, cool wind) and smoked a cigar. Melville, as he always does, began to reason of Providence and futurity, and of everything that lies beyond human ken, and informed me that he had "pretty much made up his mind to be annihilated"; but still he does not seem to rest in that anticipation; and, I think, will never rest until he gets hold of a definite belief. It is strange how he persists — and has persisted ever since I knew him, and probably long before — in wandering to-and-fro over these deserts, as dismal and monotonous as the sand hills amid which we were sitting. He can neither believe, nor be comfortable in his unbelief; and he is too honest and courageous not to try to do one or the other. If he were a religious man, he would be one of the most truly religious and reverential; he has a very high and noble nature, and better worth immortality than most of us.

From *The American Notebooks*

Considerations

1. How does this description of Melville shed light on the central concerns of "Bartleby, the Scrivener"?
2. Which side does Hawthorne seem to be on — "belief" or "unbelief"? Why?
3. Compare Hawthorne's description with Melville's view of Hawthorne (p. 292). What attitudes about life do they share?

4. Setting

Setting is the context in which the action of a story occurs. The major elements of setting are the time, place, and social environment that frame the characters. These elements establish the world in which the characters act. In most stories they also serve as more than backgrounds and furnishings. If we are sensitive to the contexts provided by setting, we are better able to understand the behavior of the characters and the significance of their actions. It may be tempting to read quickly through a writer's descriptions and ignore the details of the setting once a geographic location and a historic period are established. But if you read a story so impatiently, the significance of the setting may slip by you. That kind of reading is similar to traveling on interstate highways: a lot of ground gets covered but very little is seen along the way.

Settings can be used to evoke a mood or atmosphere that will prepare the reader for what is to come. In "Young Goodman Brown" (p. 258), Nathaniel Hawthorne has his pious protagonist leave his wife and village one night to keep an appointment in a New England forest near the site of the seventeenth-century witch trials. This is Hawthorne's description of Brown entering the forest:

> He had taken a dreary road, darkened by all the gloomiest trees of the forest, which barely stood aside to let the narrow path creep through, and closed immediately behind. It was all lonely as could be; and there is this peculiarity in such a solitude, that the traveler knows not who may be concealed by the innumerable trunks and the thick boughs overhead; so that with lonely footsteps he may yet be passing through an unseen multitude.

The atmosphere established in this descriptive setting is somber and threatening. Careful reading reveals that the forest is not simply the woods; it is a moral wilderness, where anything can happen.

If we ask why a writer chooses to include certain details in a work, then we are likely to make connections that relate the details to some larger purpose, such as the story's meaning. The final scene in Godwin's "A Sorrowful Woman" (p. 30) occurs in the spring, an ironic time for the action to be set because instead of rebirth for the protagonist there is only death. There is usually a reason for placing a story in a particular time or location. Katherine Mansfield has the protagonist in "Miss Brill" (p. 394) discover her loneliness and old age in a French vacation town, a lively atmosphere that serves as a cruel contrast to an elderly (and foreign) lady's painful realization.

Melville's "Bartleby, the Scrivener" (p. 80) takes on meaning as Bartleby's "dead-wall reveries" begin to reflect his shattered vision of life. He is surrounded by walls. A folding screen separates him from others in the office; he is isolated. The office window faces walls; there is no view to relieve the deadening work. Bartleby faces a wall at the prison where he dies; the final wall is death. As the subtitle indicates, this is "A Story of Wall Street." Unless the geographic location or the physical details of a story are used merely as necessary props, they frequently shed light on character and action. All offices have walls, but Melville transforms the walls into an antagonist that represents the limitations Bartleby sees and feels all around him but does not speak of.

Time, location, and the physical features of a setting can all be relevant to the overall purpose of a story. So too is the social environment in which the characters are developed. In Faulkner's "A Rose for Emily" (p. 47) the changes in her southern town serve as a foil for Emily's tenacious hold on a lost past. She is regarded as a "fallen monument," as old-fashioned and peculiar as the "stubborn and coquettish decay" of her house. Neither she nor her house fits into the modern changes that are paving and transforming the town. Without the social context, this story would be mostly an account of a bizarre murder rather than an exploration of the conflicts Faulkner associated with the changing South. Setting enlarges the meaning of Emily's actions.

Some settings have traditional associations that are closely related to the action of a story. Adventure and romance, for example, flourish in the fertile soil of most exotic settings: the film version of Isak Dinesen's novel *Out of Africa* is a lush visual demonstration of how a jungle setting can play a significant role in generating the audience's expectations of love and excitement.

Sometimes, writers reverse traditional expectations. When a tranquil garden is the scene for a horrendously bloody murder, we are as much taken by surprise as the victim is. In John Updike's "A & P" (p. 407) there seems to be little possibility for heroic action in so mundane a place as a supermarket, but the setting turns out to be appropriate for the important, unexpected decision the protagonist makes about life. Traditional associations are also disrupted in "A Sorrowful Woman" (p. 30), in which Godwin disassociates home from the safety, security, and comfort usually connected with it by presenting the protagonist's home as a deadly trap. By drawing on traditional associations, a writer can fulfill or disrupt a reader's expectations about a setting in order to complement the elements of the story.

Not every story uses setting as a means of revealing mood, idea, meaning, or characters' actions. Some stories have no particularly significant setting. It is entirely possible to envision a story in which two characters speak to each other about a conflict between them and little or no mention is made of the time or place they inhabit. If, however, a shift in setting would make a serious difference to our understanding of a story, then the setting is probably an important element in the work. Consider how different "Bartleby, the Scrivener" (p. 80) would be if it were set in a relaxed, pleasant, sunny town in the South rather than in the grinding, limiting, materialism of Wall Street. Bartleby's withdrawal from life would be less comprehensible and meaningful in such a setting. The setting is integral to that story.

The following two stories — Eudora Welty's "Livvie" and Ernest Hemingway's "Soldier's Home" — include settings that serve to shape their meanings.

EUDORA WELTY (b. 1909)

Eudora Welty has spent almost her entire life in Jackson, Mississippi, where she was born in 1909. She began her undergraduate education at Mississippi State College for Women and then graduated from the University of Wisconsin in 1929. After studying advertising at the Columbia University School of Business, she returned to the South for a variety of jobs and to write fiction. Since the 1930s she has published short stories; many of these were brought together in *The Collected Stories of Eudora Welty* (1980). She has also published a number of novels, including *The Optimist's Daughter,* which was awarded the Pulitzer Prize in 1972. Her collection of essays and reviews, *The Eye of the Story* (1977), and *One Writer's Beginnings* (1984) offer insights into her responses to other writers' work as well as her own. Welty's stories are solidly grounded in Mississippi soil. "Livvie" appeared originally in *The Wide Net and Other Stories* (1943), a collection based on the history and geography of the Natchez Trace, an early nineteenth-century road that followed an old Indian trail from Natchez, Mississippi, to Nashville, Tennessee. Like so much of Welty's fiction, "Livvie" focuses on the protagonist's mysterious inner life, which is revealed by the suggestive details of Livvie's outer life.

Livvie 1943

Solomon carried Livvie twenty-one miles away from her home when he married her. He carried her away up on the Old Natchez Trace into the deep country to live in his house. She was sixteen — only a girl, then. Once people said he thought nobody would ever come along there. He told her himself that it had been a long time, and a day she did not know about, since that road was a traveled road with *people* coming and going. He was good to her, but he kept her in the house. She had not thought that she could not get back. Where she came from, people said an old man did not want anybody in the world to ever find his wife, for fear they would steal her back from him. Solomon asked her before he took her, would she be happy? — very dignified, for he was a colored man that owned his land and had it written down in the courthouse; and she said, "Yes, sir," since he was an old man and she was young and just listened and answered. He asked her, if she was choosing winter, would she pine for spring, and she said, "No indeed." Whatever she said, always, was because he was an old man . . . while nine years went by. All the time, he got older, and he got so old he gave out. At last he slept the whole day in bed, and she was young still.

It was a nice house, inside and outside both. In the first place, it had three rooms. The front room was papered in holly paper, with green palmettos from the swamp spaced at careful intervals over the walls. There was fresh newspaper cut with fancy borders on the mantel-shelf, on which were propped photographs of old or very young men printed in faint yellow — Solomon's people. Solomon had a houseful of furniture. There was a double settee, a tall scrolled rocker and an organ in the front room, all around a three-legged table with a pink marble top, on which was set a lamp with three gold feet, besides a jelly glass with pretty hen feathers in it. Behind the front room, the other room had the bright iron bed with the polished knobs like a throne, in which Solomon slept all day. There were snow-white curtains of wiry lace at the window, and a lace bedspread belonged on the bed. But what old Solomon slept so sound under was a big feather-stitched piece-quilt in the pattern "Trip Around the World," which had twenty-one different colors, four hundred and forty pieces, and a thousand yards of thread, and that was what Solomon's mother made in her life and old age. There was a table holding the Bible, and a trunk with a key. On the wall were two calendars, and a diploma from somewhere in Solomon's family, and under that, Livvie's one possession was nailed, a picture of the little white baby of the family she worked for, back in Natchez before she was married. Going through that room and on to the kitchen, there was a big wood stove and a big round table always with a wet top and with the knives and forks in one jelly glass and the spoons in another, and a cut-glass vinegar bottle between, and going out from those, many shallow dishes of pickled peaches, fig preserves, watermelon pickles and blackberry jam always sitting there. The churn sat in the sun, the doors of the safe were always both shut, and there were four baited mousetraps in the kitchen, one in every corner.

The outside of Solomon's house looked nice. It was not painted, but across the porch was an even balance. On each side there was one easy chair with high springs, looking out, and a fern basket hanging over it from the ceiling, and a dishpan of zinnia seedlings growing at its foot on the floor. By the door was a plow-wheel, just a pretty iron circle, nailed up on one wall, and a square mirror on the other, a turquoise-blue comb stuck up in the frame, with the wash stand beneath it. On the door was a wooden knob with a pearl in the end, and Solomon's black hat hung on that, if he was in the house.

Out front was a clean dirt yard with every vestige of grass patiently uprooted and the ground scarred in deep whorls from the strike of Livvie's broom. Rose bushes with tiny blood-red roses blooming every month grew in threes on either side of the steps. On one side was a peach tree, on the other a pomegranate. Then coming around up the path from the deep cut of the Natchez Trace below was a line of bare crape-myrtle trees with every branch of them ending in a colored bottle, green or blue. There was no word that fell from Solomon's lips to say what they were for, but Livvie knew that there could be a spell put in trees, and she was familiar from the time she was born with the way bottle trees kept evil spirits from coming into the house — by luring them inside the colored bottles, where they cannot get out again. Solomon had made the bottle trees with his own hands over the nine years, in labor amounting to about a tree a year, and without a sign that he had any uneasiness in his heart, for he took as much pride in his precautions against spirits coming in the house as he took in the house, and sometimes in the sun the bottle trees looked prettier than the house did.

5 It was a nice house. It was in a place where the days would go by and surprise anyone that they were over. The lamplight and the firelight would shine out the door after dark, over the still and breathing country, lighting the roses and the bottle trees, and all was quiet there.

But there was nobody, nobody at all, not even a white person. And if there had been anybody, Solomon would not have let Livvie look at them, just as he would not let her look at a field hand, or a field hand look at her. There was no house near, except for the cabins of the tenants that were forbidden to her, and there was no house as far as she had been, stealing away down the still, deep Trace. She felt as if she waded a river when she went, for the dead leaves on the ground reached as high as her knees, and when she was all scratched and bleeding she said it was not like a road that went anywhere. One day, climbing up the high bank, she had found a graveyard without a church, with ribbon-grass growing about the foot of an angel (she had climbed up because she thought she saw angel wings), and in the sun, trees shining like burning flames through the great caterpillar nets which enclosed them. Scarey thistles stood looking like the prophets in the Bible in Solomon's house. Indian paint brushes grew over her head, and the mourning dove made the only sound in the world. Oh, for a stirring of the leaves, and a breaking of the nets! But not by a ghost, prayed Livvie, jumping down the bank. After Solomon took to his bed, she never went out, except one more time.

Livvie knew she made a nice girl to wait on anybody. She fixed things to eat on a tray like a surprise. She could keep from singing when she ironed, and to sit by a bed and fan away the flies, she could be so still she could not hear herself breathe. She could clean up the house and never drop a thing, and wash the dishes without a sound, and she would step outside to churn, for churning sounded too sad to her, like sobbing, and if it made her homesick and not Solomon, she did not think of that.

But Solomon scarcely opened his eyes to see her, and scarcely tasted his food. He was not sick or paralyzed or in any pain that he mentioned, but he was surely wearing out in the body, and no matter what nice hot thing Livvie would bring him to taste, he would only look at it now, as if he were past seeing how he could add anything more to himself. Before she could beg him, he would go fast asleep. She could not surprise him any more, if he would not taste, and she was afraid that he was never in the world going to taste another thing she brought him — and so how could he last?

But one morning it was breakfast time and she cooked his eggs and grits, carried them in on a tray, and called his name. He was sound asleep. He lay in a dignified way with his watch beside him, on his back in the middle of the bed. One hand drew the quilt up high, though it was the first day of spring. Through the white lace curtains a little puffy wind was blowing as if it came from round cheeks. All night the frogs had sung out in the swamp, like a commotion in the room, and he had not stirred, though she lay wide awake and saying "Shh, frogs!" for fear he would mind them.

He looked as if he would like to sleep a little longer, and so she put back the tray and waited. When she tiptoed and stayed so quiet, she surrounded herself with a little reverie, and sometimes it seemed to her when she was so stealthy that the quiet she kept was for a sleeping baby, and that she had a baby and was its mother. When she stood at Solomon's bed and looked down at him, she would be thinking, "He sleeps so well," and she would hate to wake him up. And in some other way, too, she was afraid to wake him up because even in his sleep he seemed to be such a strict man.

Of course, nailed to the wall over the bed — only she would forget who it was — there was a picture of him when he was young. Then he had a fan of hair over his forehead like a king's crown. Now his hair lay down on his head, the spring had gone out of it. Solomon had a lightish face, with eyebrows scattered but rugged, the way privet grows, strong eyes, with second sight, a strict mouth, and a little gold smile. This was the way he looked in his clothes, but in bed in the daytime he looked a different and smaller man, even when he was wide awake, and holding the Bible. He looked like somebody kin to himself. And then sometimes when he lay in sleep and she stood fanning the flies away, and the light came in, his face was like new, so smooth and clear that it was like a glass of jelly held to the window, and she could almost look through his forehead and see what he thought.

She fanned him and at length he opened his eyes and spoke her name, but he would not taste the nice eggs she had kept warm under a pan.

Back in the kitchen she ate heartily, his breakfast and hers, and looked out the open door at what went on. The whole day, and the whole night before, she had felt the stir of spring close to her. It was as present in the house as a young man would be. The moon was in the last quarter and outside they were turning the sod and planting peas and beans. Up and down the red fields, over which smoke from the brush-burning hung showing like a little skirt of sky, a white horse and a white mule pulled the plow. At intervals hoarse shouts came through the air and roused her as if she dozed neglectfully in the shade, and they were telling her, "Jump up!" She could see how over each ribbon of field were moving men and girls, on foot and mounted on mules, with hats set on their heads and bright with tall hoes and forks as if they carried streamers on them and were going to some place on a journey — and how as if at a signal now and then they would all start at once shouting, hollering, cajoling, calling and answering back, running, being leaped on and breaking away, flinging to earth with a shout and lying motionless in the trance of twelve o'clock. The old women came out of the cabins and brought them the food they had ready for them, and then all worked together, spread evenly out. The little children came too, like a bouncing stream overflowing the fields, and set upon the men, the women, the dogs, the rushing birds, and the wave-like rows of earth, their little voices almost too high to be heard. In the middle distance like some white and gold towers were the haystacks, with black cows coming around to eat their edges. High above everything, the wheel of fields, house, and cabins, and the deep road surrounding like a moat to keep them in, was the turning sky, blue with long, far-flung white mare's-tail clouds, serene and still as high flames. And sound asleep while all this went around him that was his, Solomon was like a little still spot in the middle.

Even in the house the earth was sweet to breathe. Solomon had never let Livvie go any farther than the chicken house and the well. But what if she would walk now into the heart of the fields and take a hoe and work until she fell stretched out and drenched with her efforts, like other girls, and laid her cheek against the laid-open earth, and shamed the old man with her humbleness and delight? To shame him! A cruel wish could come in uninvited and so fast while she looked out the back door. She washed the dishes and scrubbed the table. She could hear the cries of the little lambs. Her mother, that she had not seen since her wedding day, had said one time, "I rather a man be anything, than a woman be mean."

15 So all morning she kept tasting the chicken broth on the stove, and when it was right she poured off a nice cupful. She carried it in to Solomon, and there he lay having a dream. Now what did he dream about? For she saw him sigh gently as if not to disturb some whole thing he held round in his mind, like a fresh egg. So even an old man dreamed about something pretty. Did he dream of her, while his eyes were shut and sunken, and his small hand with the wedding ring curled close in sleep around the quilt? He might be dreaming of what time it was, for even through his sleep he kept track of it like a clock, and knew how much of it went by, and waked up knowing where the hands were even before he consulted the silver watch that he never let go. He would sleep with the watch in his palm, and even holding it to his cheek like a child that loves a plaything. Or he might dream of journeys and travels on a steamboat to Natchez. Yet she thought he dreamed of her; but even while she scrutinized him, the rods of the foot of the bed seemed to rise up like a rail fence between them, and she could see that people never could be sure of anything as long as one of them was asleep and the other awake. To look at him dreaming of her when he might be going to die frightened her a little, as if he might carry her with him that way, and she wanted to run out of the room. She took hold of the bed and held on, and Solomon opened his eyes and called her name, but he did not want anything. He would not taste the good broth.

Just a little after that, as she was taking up the ashes in the front room for the last time in the year, she heard a sound. It was somebody coming. She pulled the curtains together and looked through the slit.

Coming up the path under the bottle trees was a white lady. At first she looked young, but then she looked old. Marvelous to see, a little car stood steaming like a kettle out in the field-track — it had come without a road.

Livvie stood listening to the long, repeated knockings at the door, and after a while she opened it just a little. The lady came in through the crack, though she was more than middle-sized and wore a big hat.

"My name is Miss Baby Marie," she said.

Livvie gazed respectfully at the lady and at the little suitcase she was holding close to her by the handle until the proper moment. The lady's eyes were running over the room, from palmetto to palmetto, but she was saying, "I live at home . . . out from Natchez . . . and get out and show these pretty cosmetic things to the white people and the colored people both . . . all around . . . years and years. . . . Both shades of powder and rouge . . . It's the kind of work a girl can do and not go clear 'way from home. . . ." And the harder she looked, the more she talked. Suddenly she turned up her nose and said, "It is not Christian or sanitary to put feathers in a vase," and then she took a gold key out of the front of her dress and began unlocking the locks on her suitcase. Her face drew the light, the way it was covered with intense white and red, with a little patty-cake of white between the wrinkles by her upper lip. Little red tassels of hair bobbed under the rusty wires of her picture-hat, as with an air of triumph and secrecy she now drew open her little suitcase and brought out bottle after bottle and jar after jar, which she put down on the table, the mantel-piece, the settee, and the organ.

"Did you ever see so many cosmetics in your life?" cried Miss Baby Marie.

"No'm" Livvie tried to say, but the cat had her tongue.

"Have you ever applied cosmetics?" asked Miss Baby Marie next.

"No'm," Livvie tried to say.

"Then look!" she said, and pulling out the last thing of all, "Try this!" she said. And in her hand was unclenched a golden lipstick which popped open like magic. A fragrance came out of it like incense, and Livvie cried out suddenly, "Chinaberry flowers!"

Her hand took the lipstick, and in an instant she was carried away in the air through the spring, and looking down with a half-drowsy smile from a purple cloud she saw from above a chinaberry tree, dark and smooth and neatly leaved, neat as a guinea hen in the dooryard, and there was her home that she had left. On one side of the tree was her mama holding up her heavy apron, and she could see it was loaded with ripe figs, and on the other side was her papa holding a fish-pole over the pond, and she could see it transparently, the little clear fishes swimming up to the brim.

"Oh, no, not chinaberry flowers — secret ingredients," said Miss Baby Marie. "My cosmetics have secret ingredients — not chinaberry flowers."

"It's purple," Livvie breathed, and Miss Baby Marie said, "Use it freely. Rub it on."

Livvie tiptoed out to the wash stand on the front porch and before the mirror put the paint on her mouth. In the wavery surface her face danced before her like a flame. Miss Baby Marie followed her out, took a look at what she had done, and said, "That's it."

Livvie tried to say "Thank you" without moving her parted lips where the paint lay so new.

By now Miss Baby Marie stood behind Livvie and looked in the mirror over her shoulder, twisting up the tassels of her hair. "The lipstick I can let you have for only two dollars," she said, close to her neck.

"Lady, but I don't have no money, never did have," said Livvie.

"Oh, but you don't pay the first time. I make another trip, that's the way I do. I come back again — later."

"Oh," said Livvie, pretending she understood everything so as to please the lady.

"But if you don't take it now, this may be the last time I'll call at your 35
house," said Miss Baby Marie sharply. "It's far away from anywhere, I'll tell you that. You don't live close to anywhere."

"Yes'm. My husband, he keep the *money,*" said Livvie, trembling. "He is strict as he can be. He don't know *you* walk in here — Miss Baby Marie!"

"Where is he?"

"Right now, he in yonder sound asleep, an old man. I wouldn't ever ask him for anything."

Miss Baby Marie took back the lipstick and packed it up. She gathered up the jars for both black and white and got them all inside the suitcase, with the same little fuss of triumph with which she had brought them out. She started away.

"Good-bye," she said, making herself look grand from the back, but at the 40
last minute she turned around in the door. Her old hat wobbled as she whispered, "Let me see your husband."

Livvie obediently went on tiptoe and opened the door to the other room. Miss Baby Marie came behind her and rose on her toes and looked in.

"My, what a little tiny old, old man!" she whispered, clasping her hands and shaking her head over them. "What a beautiful quilt! What a tiny old, old man!"

"He can sleep like that all day," whispered Livvie proudly.

They looked at him awhile so fast asleep, and then all at once they looked at each other. Somehow that was as if they had a secret, for he had never stirred. Livvie then politely, but all at once, closed the door.

"Well! I'd certainly like to leave you with a lipstick!" said Miss Baby Marie 45
vivaciously. She smiled in the door.

"Lady, but I told you I don't have no money, and never did have."

"And never will?" In the air and all around, like a bright halo around the white lady's nodding head, it was a true spring day.

"Would you take eggs, lady?" asked Livvie softly.

"No, I have plenty of eggs — plenty," said Miss Baby Marie.

"I still don't have no money," said Livvie, and Miss Baby Marie took her 50
suitcase and went on somewhere else.

Livvie stood watching her go, and all the time she felt her heart beating in her left side. She touched the place with her hand. It seemed as if her heart beat and her whole face flamed from the pulsing color of her lips. She went to sit by Solomon and when he opened his eyes he could not see a change in her. "He's fixin' to die," she said inside. That was the secret. That was when she went out of the house for a little breath of air.

She went down the path and down the Natchez Trace a way, and she did not know how far she had gone, but it was not far, when she saw a sight. It was a man, looking like a vision — she standing on one side of the Old Natchez Trace and he standing on the other.

As soon as this man caught sight of her, he began to look himself over.

Starting at the bottom with his pointed shoes, he began to look up, lifting his peg-top pants the higher to see fully his bright socks. His coat long and wide and leaf-green he opened like doors to see his high-up tawny pants and his pants he smoothed downward from the points of his collar, and he wore a luminous baby-pink satin shirt. At the end, he reached gently above his wide platter-shaped round hat, the color of a plum, and one finger touched at the feather, emerald green, blowing in the spring winds.

No matter how she looked, she could never look so fine as he did, and she was not sorry for that, she was pleased.

He took three jumps, one down and two up, and was by her side.

"My name is Cash," he said.

He had a guinea pig in his pocket. They began to walk along. She stared on and on at him, as if he were doing some daring spectacular thing, instead of just walking beside her. It was not simply the city way he was dressed that made her look at him and see hope in its insolence looking back. It was not only the way he moved along kicking the flowers as if he could break through everything in the way and destroy anything in the world, that made her eyes grow bright. It might be, if he had not appeared *that day* she would never have looked so closely at him, but the time people come makes a difference.

They walked through the still leaves of the Natchez Trace, the light and the shade falling through trees about them, the white irises shining like candles on the banks and the new ferns shining like green stars up in the oak branches. They came out at Solomon's house, bottle trees and all. Livvie stopped and hung her head.

Cash began whistling a little tune. She did not know what it was, but she had heard it before from a distance, and she had a revelation. Cash was a field hand. He was a transformed field hand. Cash belonged to Solomon. But he had stepped out of his overalls into this. There in front of Solomon's house he laughed. He had a round head, a round face, all of him was young, and he flung his head up, rolled it against the mare's-tail sky in his round hat, and he could laugh just to see Solomon's house sitting there. Livvie looked at it, and there was Solomon's black hat hanging on the peg on the front door, the blackest thing in the world.

"I been to Natchez," Cash said, wagging his head around against the sky. "*I* taken a trip, I ready for Easter!"

How was it possible to look so fine before the harvest? Cash must have stolen the money, stolen it from Solomon. He stood in the path and lifted his spread hand high and brought it down again and again in his laughter. He kicked up his heels. A little chill went through her. It was as if Cash was bringing that strong hand down to beat a drum or to rain blows upon a man, such an abandon and menace were in his laugh. Frowning, she went closer to him and his swinging arm drew her in at once and the fright was crushed from her body, as a little match-flame might be smothered out by what it lighted. She gathered the folds of his coat behind him and fastened her red lips to his mouth, and she was dazzled at herself then, the way he had been dazzled at himself to begin with.

In that instant she felt something that could not be told — that Solomon's death was at hand, that he was the same to her as if he were dead now. She cried out, and uttering little cries turned and ran for the house.

At once Cash was coming, following after, he was running behind her. He came close, and half-way up the path he laughed and passed her. He even picked up a stone and sailed it into the bottle trees. She put her hands over her head, and sounds clattered through the bottle trees like cries of outrage. Cash stamped and plunged zigzag up the front steps and in at the door.

When she got there, he had stuck his hands in his pockets and was turning slowly about in the front room. The little guinea pig peeped out. Around Cash, the pinned-up palmettos looked as if a lazy green monkey had walked up and down and around the walls leaving green prints of his hands and feet.

She got through the room and his hands were still in his pockets, and she 65
fell upon the closed door to the other room and pushed it open. She ran to Solomon's bed, calling "Solomon! Solomon!" The little shape of the old man never moved at all, wrapped under the quilt as if it were winter still.

"Solomon!" She pulled the quilt away, but there was another one under that, and she fell on her knees beside him. He made no sound except a sigh, and then she could hear in the silence the light springy steps of Cash walking and walking in the front room, and the ticking of Solomon's silver watch, which came from the bed. Old Solomon was far away in his sleep, his face looked small, relentless, and devout, as if he were walking somewhere where she could imagine the snow falling.

Then there was a noise like a hoof pawing the floor, and the door gave a creak, and Cash appeared beside her. When she looked up, Cash's face was so black it was bright, and so bright and bare of pity that it looked sweet to her. She stood up and held up her head. Cash was so powerful that his presence gave her strength even when she did not need any.

Under their eyes Solomon slept. People's faces tell of things and places not known to the one who looks at them while they sleep, and while Solomon slept under the eyes of Livvie and Cash his face told them like a mythical story that all his life he had built, little scrap by little scrap, respect. A beetle could not have been more laborious or more ingenious in the task of its destiny. When Solomon was young, as he was in his picture overhead, it was the infinite thing with him, and he could see no end to the respect he would contrive and keep in a house. He had built a lonely house, the way he would make a cage, but it grew to be the same with him as a great monumental pyramid and sometimes in his absorption of getting it erected he was like the builder-slaves of Egypt who forgot or never knew the origin and meaning of the thing to which they gave all the strength of their bodies and used up all their days. Livvie and Cash could see that as a man might rest from a life-labor he lay in his bed, and they could hear how, wrapped in his quilt, he sighed to himself comfortably in sleep, while in his dreams he might have been an ant, a beetle, a bird, an Egyptian, assembling and carrying on his back and building with his hands, or he might have been an old man of India or a swaddled baby, about to smile and brush all away.

Then without warning old Solomon's eyes flew wide open under the hedge-like brows. He was wide awake.

And instantly Cash raised his quick arm. A radiant sweat stood on his tem- 70
ples. But he did not bring his arm down — it stayed in the air, as if something might have taken hold.

It was not Livvie — she did not move. As if something said "Wait," she stood waiting. Even while her eyes burned under motionless lids, her lips parted in a stiff grimace, and with her arms stiff at her sides she stood above the prone old man and the panting young one, erect and apart.

Movement when it came came in Solomon's face. It was an old and strict face, a frail face, but behind it, like a covered light, came an animation that could play hide and seek, that would dart and escape, had always escaped. The mystery flickered in him, and invited from his eyes. It was that very mystery that Cash with his quick arm would have to strike, and that Livvie could not weep for. But Cash only stood holding his arm in the air, when the gentlest flick of his great strength, almost a puff of his breath, would have been enough, if he had known how to give it, to send the old man over the obstruction that kept him away from death.

"Young ones can't wait," said Solomon.

Livvie shuddered violently, and then in a gush of tears she stooped for a glass of water and handed it to him, but he did not see her.

75 "So here come the young man Livvie wait for. Was no prevention. No prevention. Now I lay eyes on young man and it come to be somebody I know all the time, and been knowing since he were born in a cotton patch, and watched grow up year to year, Cash McCord, growed to size, growed up to come in my house in the end — ragged and barefoot."

Solomon gave a cough of distaste. Then he shut his eyes vigorously, and his lips began to move like a chanter's.

"When Livvie married, her husband were already somebody. He had paid great cost for his land. He spread sycamore leaves over the ground from wagon to door, day he brought her home, so her foot would not have to touch ground. He carried her through his door. Then he growed old and could not lift her, and she were still young."

Livvie's sobs followed his words like a soft melody repeating each thing as he stated it. His lips moved for a little without sound, or she cried too fervently, and unheard he might have been telling his whole life, and then he said, "God forgive Solomon for sins great and small. God forgive Solomon for carrying away too young girl for wife and keeping her away from her people and from all the young people would clamor for her back."

Then he lifted up his right hand toward Livvie where she stood by the bed and offered her his silver watch. He dangled it before her eyes, and she hushed crying; her tears stopped. For a moment the watch could be heard ticking as it always did, precisely in his proud hand. She lifted it away. Then he took hold of the quilt; then he was dead.

.

80 Livvie left Solomon dead and went out of the room. Stealthily, nearly without noise, Cash went beside her. He was like a shadow, but his shiny shoes moved over the floor in spangles, and the green downy feather shone like a light in his hat. As they reached the front room, he seized her deftly as a long black cat and dragged her hanging by the waist round and round him, while he turned in a circle, his face bent down to hers. The first moment, she kept one arm and its hand stiff and still, the one that held Solomon's watch. Then the fingers softly let go, all of her was limp, and the watch fell somewhere on the

floor. It ticked away in the still room, and all at once there began outside the full song of a bird.

They moved around and around the room and into the brightness of the open door, then he stopped and shook her once. She rested in silence in his trembling arms, unprotesting as a bird on a nest. Outside the redbirds were flying and criss-crossing, the sun was in all the bottles on the prisoned trees, and the young peach was shining in the middle of them with the bursting light of spring.

Considerations

1. Describe Solomon's temperament. How does he live his life? What details about his house and yard reveal his character?
2. How do Livvie's attitudes and actions concerning the way she and Solomon live serve to characterize her?
3. What is Miss Baby Marie's function in the story? How is the lipstick she attempts to sell related to the plot?
4. Explain how Cash is a foil to Solomon.
5. What is the significance of Livvie's name? Do the names of the other three characters suggest any meanings?
6. What is the central conflict? How is it resolved?
7. Why do you think Welty sets the story at the beginning of spring? How are conventional associations with spring used to enhance the story's meaning?
8. How is Solomon's watch used symbolically? Why does he give Livvie the watch just before he dies? Explain the significance of her letting it drop to the floor. What other objects and actions are used to convey meanings in the story?
9. Choose a richly detailed paragraph and write an explication that relates the paragraph's details to the rest of the story.
10. Explore how time is an important element in the conflicts in "Livvie."

Connections

1. Discuss the significance of the settings in "Livvie" and Faulkner's "A Rose for Emily" (p. 47). Explain how the South is used as a means of characterizing the protagonist in each story.
2. How is the meaning of "home" essential to the meanings of "Livvie" and Ernest Hemingway's "Soldier's Home" (p. 121)?
3. Write an essay on the significance for the protagonists of the deaths of their husbands in "Livvie" and Chopin's "The Story of an Hour" (p. 12).

PERSPECTIVE

EUDORA WELTY (b. 1909)

Place in Fiction 1956

I think the sense of place is as essential in good and honest writing as a logical mind; surely they are somewhere related. It is by knowing where you stand that you grow able to judge where you are. Place absorbs our earliest notice and attention, it bestows on us our original awarness; and our critical powers spring up from the study of it and the growth of experience inside it. It perseveres in bringing us back to earth when we fly too high. It never really stops informing us, for it is forever astir, alive, changing, reflecting, like the mind of man itself. One place comprehended can make us understand other places better. Sense of place gives equilibrium; extended, it is sense of direction too. Carried off we might be in spirit, and should be, when we are reading or writing something good; but it is the sense of place going with us still that is the ball of golden thread to carry us there and back in every sense of the word to bring us home. . . .

Should the writer, then, write about home? It is both natural and sensible that the place where we have our roots should become the setting, the first and primary proving ground, of our fiction. Location, however, is not simply to be used by the writer — it is to be discovered, as each [story] itself, in the act of writing, is discovery. Discovery does not imply that the place is new, only that we are. Place is as old as the hills. Kilroy at least has been there, and left his name.° Discovery, not being a matter of writing our name on a wall, but of seeing what that wall is, and what is over it, is a matter of vision.

One can no more say, "To write stay home," than one can say, "To write leave home." It is the writing that makes its own rules and conditions for each person. And though place is home, it is for the writer writing simply *locus*. It is where the particular story he writes can be pinned down, the circle it can spin through and keep the state of grace, so that for the story's duration the rest of the world suspends its claim upon it and lies low as the story in peaceful extension, the *locus* fading off into the blue.

Naturally, it is the very breath of life, whether one writes a word of fiction or not, to go out and see what is to be seen of the world. For the artist to be unwilling to move, mentally or spiritually or physically, out of the familiar is a sign that spiritual timidity or poverty or decay has come upon him; for what is familiar will then have turned into all that is tyrannical.

One can only say: writers must always write best of what they know, and sometimes they do it by staying where they know it. But not for safety's sake. Although it is in the words of a witch — or all the more because of that — a comment of Hecate's in [Shakespeare's] *Macbeth* is worth our heed: "Security/is mortal's chiefest enemy." In fact, when we think in terms of the spirit, which are the terms of writing, is there a conception more stupefying than that of security? Yet writing of what you know has nothing to do with security: what is more dangerous? How can you go out on a limb if you do not know your own tree? No art ever came out of not risking your neck. And risk — experiment — is a considerable part of the joy of doing, which is the lone, simple reason all writers of serious fiction are willing to work as hard as they do.

From "Place in Fiction" in *South Atlantic Quarterly*

Kilroy . . . : a reference to the statement "Kilroy was here," which was written wherever Americans were during World War II.

Considerations

1. Why is a sense of place a sign of "good and honest writing" for Welty?
2. According to Welty, why should a writer avoid writing "for safety's sake"? Why is risk an important ingredient in fiction writing?
3. Explain how Solomon's "sense of place" is related to the conflict in "Livvie."

ERNEST HEMINGWAY (1899–1961)

In 1918, a year after graduating from high school in Oak Park, Illinois, Ernest Hemingway volunteered as an ambulance driver in World War I. At the Italian front, he was seriously wounded. This experience haunted him and many of the characters in his short stories and novels. *In Our Time* (1925) is a collection of short stories, including "Soldier's Home," that reflect some of Hemingway's own attempts to readjust to life back home after the war. *The Sun Also Rises* (1926), *A Farewell to Arms* (1929), and *For Whom the Bell Tolls* (1940) are also about war and its impact on people's lives. Hemingway courted violence all his life in war, the bullring, the boxing ring, and big game hunting. When he was sixty-two years old and terminally ill with cancer, he committed suicide by shooting himself with a shotgun. "Soldier's Home" takes place in a small town in Oklahoma; the war, however, is never distant from the protagonist's mind as he struggles to come home again.

Soldier's Home 1925

Krebs went to the war from a Methodist college in Kansas. There is a picture which shows him among his fraternity brothers, all of them wearing exactly the same height and style collar. He enlisted in the Marines in 1917 and did not return to the United States until the second division returned from the Rhine in the summer of 1919.

There is a picture which shows him on the Rhine with two German girls and another corporal. Krebs and the corporal look too big for their uniforms. The German girls are not beautiful. The Rhine does not show in the picture.

By the time Krebs returned to his home town in Oklahoma the greeting of heroes was over. He came back much too late. The men from the town who had been drafted had all been welcomed elaborately on their return. There had been a great deal of hysteria. Now the reaction had set in. People seemed to think it was rather ridiculous for Krebs to be getting back so late, years after the war was over.

At first Krebs, who had been at Belleau Wood, Soissons, the Champagne,

St. Mihiel, and in the Argonne° did not want to talk about the war at all. Later he felt the need to talk but no one wanted to hear about it. His town had heard too many atrocity stories to be thrilled by actualities. Krebs found that to be listened to at all he had to lie, and after he had done this twice he, too, had a reaction against the war and against talking about it. A distaste for everything that had happened to him in the war set in because of the lies he had told. All of the times that had been able to make him feel cool and clear inside himself when he thought of them; the times so long back when he had done the one thing, the only thing for a man to do, easily and naturally, when he might have done something else, now lost their cool, valuable quality and then were lost themselves.

5 His lies were quite unimportant lies and consisted in attributing to himself things other men had seen, done, or heard of, and stating as facts certain apocryphal incidents familiar to all soldiers. Even his lies were not sensational at the pool room. His acquaintances, who had heard detailed accounts of German women found chained to machine guns in the Argonne forest and who could not comprehend, or were barred by their patriotism from interest in, any German machine gunners who were not chained, were not thrilled by his stories.

Krebs acquired the nausea in regard to experience that is the result of untruth or exaggeration, and when he occasionally met another man who had really been a soldier and they talked a few minutes in the dressing room at a dance he fell into the easy pose of the old soldier among other soldiers: that he had been badly, sickeningly frightened all the time. In this way he lost everything.

During this time, it was late summer, he was sleeping late in bed, getting up to walk down town to the library to get a book, eating lunch at home, reading on the front porch until he became bored, and then walking down through the town to spend the hottest hours of the day in the cool dark of the pool room. He loved to play pool.

In the evening he practiced on his clarinet, strolled down town, read, and went to bed. He was still a hero to his two young sisters. His mother would have given him breakfast in bed if he had wanted it. She often came in when he was in bed and asked him to tell her about the war, but her attention always wandered. His father was noncommittal.

Before Krebs went away to the war he had never been allowed to drive the family motor car. His father was in the real estate business and always wanted the car to be at his command when he required it to take clients out into the country to show them a piece of farm property. The car always stood outside the First National Bank building where his father had an office on the second floor. Now, after the war, it was still the same car.

10 Nothing was changed in the town except that the young girls had grown up. But they lived in such a complicated world of already defined alliances and shifting feuds that Krebs did not feel the energy or the courage to break into it. He liked to look at them, though. There were so many good-looking young girls. Most of them had their hair cut short. When he went away only little girls wore their hair like that or girls that were fast. They all wore sweaters and shirt

Belleau Wood . . . : Sites of battles in World War I in which American troops were instrumental in pushing back the Germans.

waists with round Dutch collars. It was a pattern. He liked to look at them from the front porch as they walked on the other side of the street. He liked to watch them walking under the shade of the trees. He liked the round Dutch collars above their sweaters. He liked their silk stockings and flat shoes. He liked their bobbed hair and the way they walked.

When he was in town their appeal to him was not very strong. He did not like them when he saw them in the Greek's ice cream parlor. He did not want them themselves really. They were too complicated. There was something else. Vaguely he wanted a girl but he did not want to have to work to get her. He would have liked to have a girl but he did not want to have to spend a long time getting her. He did not want to get into the intrigue and the politics. He did not want to have to do any courting. He did not want to tell any more lies. It wasn't worth it.

He did not want any consequences. He did not want any consequences ever again. He wanted to live along without consequences. Besides he did not really need a girl. The army had taught him that. It was all right to pose as though you had to have a girl. Nearly everybody did that. But it wasn't true. You did not need a girl. That was the funny thing. First a fellow boasted how girls mean nothing to him, that he never thought of them, that they could not touch him. Then a fellow boasted that he could not get along without girls, that he had to have them all the time, that he could not go to sleep without them.

That was all a lie. It was all a lie both ways. You did not need a girl unless you thought about them. He learned that in the army. Then sooner or later you always got one. When you were really ripe for a girl you always got one. You did not have to think about it. Sooner or later it would come. He had learned that in the army.

Now he would have liked a girl if she had come to him and not wanted to talk. But here at home it was all too complicated. He knew he could never get through it all again. It was not worth the trouble. That was the thing about French girls and German girls. There was not all this talking. You couldn't talk much and you did not need to talk. It was simple and you were friends. He thought about France and then he began to think about Germany. On the whole had had liked Germany better. He did not want to leave Germany. He did not want to come home. Still, he had come home. He sat on the front porch.

He liked the girls that were walking along the other side of the street. He 15
liked the look of them much better than the French girls or the German girls. But the world they were in was not the world he was in. He would like to have one of them. But it was not worth it. They were such a nice pattern. He liked the pattern. It was exciting. But he would not go through all the talking. He did not want one badly enough. He liked to look at them all, though. It was not worth it. Not now when things were getting good again.

He sat there on the porch reading a book on the war. It was a history and he was reading about all the engagements he had been in. It was the most interesting reading he had ever done. He wished there were more maps. He looked forward with a good feeling to reading all the really good histories when they would come out with good detail maps. Now he was really learning about the war. He had been a good soldier. That made a difference.

One morning after he had been home about a month his mother came into his bedroom and sat on the bed. She smoothed her apron.

"I had a talk with your father last night, Harold," she said, "and he is willing for you to take the car out in the evenings."

"Yeah?" said Krebs, who was not fully awake. "Take the car out? Yeah?"

"Yes. Your father has felt for some time that you should be able to take the car out in the evenings whenever you wished but we only talked it over last night."

"I'll bet you made him," Krebs said.

"No. It was your father's suggestion that we talk the matter over."

"Yeah. I'll bet you made him," Krebs sat up in bed.

"Will you come down to breakfast, Harold?" his mother said.

"As soon as I get my clothes on," Krebs said.

His mother went out of the room and he could hear her frying something downstairs while he washed, shaved, and dressed to go down into the dining-room for breakfast. While he was eating breakfast his sister brought in the mail.

"Well, Hare," she said. "You old sleepyhead. What do you ever get up for?"

Krebs looked at her. He liked her. She was his best sister.

"Have you got the paper?" he asked.

She handed him the Kansas City *Star* and he shucked off its brown wrapper and opened it to the sporting page. He folded the *Star* open and propped it against the water pitcher with his cereal dish to steady it, so he could read while he ate.

"Harold," his mother stood in the kitchen doorway, "Harold, please don't muss up the paper. Your father can't read his *Star* if it's been mussed."

"I won't muss it," Krebs said.

His sister sat down at the table and watched him while he read.

"We're playing indoor over at school this afternoon," she said. "I'm going to pitch."

"Good," said Krebs. "How's the old wing?"

"I can pitch better than lots of the boys. I tell them all you taught me. The other girls aren't much good."

"Yeah?" said Krebs.

"I tell them all you're my beau. Aren't you my beau, Hare?"

"You bet."

"Couldn't your brother really be your beau just because he's your brother?"

"I don't know."

"Sure you know. Couldn't you be my beau, Hare, if I was old enough and if you wanted to?"

"Sure. You're my girl now."

"Am I really your girl?"

"Sure."

"Do you love me?"

"Uh, huh."

"Will you love me always?"

"Sure."

"Will you come over and watch me play indoor?"

"Maybe."

"Aw, Hare, you don't love me. If you loved me, you'd want to come over and watch me play indoor."

Krebs's mother came into the dining-room from the kitchen. She carried a plate with two fried eggs and some crisp bacon on it and a plate of buckwheat cakes.

"You run along, Helen," she said. "I want to talk to Harold."

She put the eggs and bacon down in front of him and brought in a jug of maple syrup for the buckwheat cakes. Then she sat down across the table from Krebs.

"I wish you'd put down the paper a minute, Harold," she said.

Krebs took down the paper and folded it.

"Have you decided what you are going to do yet, Harold?" his mother said, taking off her glasses.

"No," said Krebs.

"Don't you think it's about time?" His mother did not say this in a mean way. She seemed worried.

"I hadn't thought about it," Krebs said.

"God has some work for everyone to do," his mother said. "There can be no idle hands in His Kingdom."

"I'm not in His Kingdom," Krebs said.

"We are all of us in His Kingdom."

Krebs felt embarrassed and resentful as always.

"I've worried about you so much, Harold," his mother went on. "I know the temptations you must have been exposed to. I know how weak men are. I know what your own dear grandfather, my own father, told us about the Civil War and I have prayed for you. I pray for you all day long, Harold."

Krebs looked at the bacon fat hardening on his plate.

"Your father is worried, too," his mother went on. "He thinks you have lost your ambition, that you haven't got a definite aim in life. Charley Simmons, who is just your age, has a good job and is going to be married. The boys are all settling down; they're all determined to get somewhere; you can see that boys like Charley Simmons are on their way to being really a credit to the community."

Krebs said nothing.

"Don't look that way, Harold," his mother said. "You know we love you and I want to tell you for your own good how matters stand. Your father does not want to hamper your freedom. He thinks you should be allowed to drive the car. If you want to take some of the nice girls out riding with you, we are only too pleased. We want you to enjoy yourself. But you are going to have to settle down to work, Harold. Your father doesn't care what you start in at. All work is honorable as he says. But you've got to make a start at something. He asked me to speak to you this morning and then you can stop in and see him at his office."

"Is that all?" Krebs said.

"Yes. Don't you love your mother, dear boy?"

"No," Krebs said.

His mother looked at him across the table. Her eyes were shiny. She started crying.

"I don't love anybody," Krebs said.

It wasn't any good. He couldn't tell her, he couldn't make her see it. It was silly to have said it. He had only hurt her. He went over and took hold of her arm. She was crying with her head in her hands.

"I didn't mean it," he said. "I was just angry at something. I didn't mean I didn't love you."

His mother went on crying. Krebs put his arm on her shoulder.

"Can't you believe me, mother?"

His mother shook her head.

"Please, please, mother. Please believe me."

"All right," his mother said chokily. She looked up at him. "I believe you, Harold."

Krebs kissed her hair. She put her face up to him.

"I'm your mother," she said. "I held you next to my heart when you were a tiny baby."

Krebs felt sick and vaguely nauseated.

"I know, Mummy," he said. "I'll try and be a good boy for you."

"Would you kneel and pray with me, Harold?" his mother asked.

They knelt down beside the dining-room table and Krebs's mother prayed.

"Now, you pray, Harold," she said.

"I can't," Krebs said.

"Try, Harold."

"I can't."

"Do you want me to pray for you?"

"Yes."

So his mother prayed for him and then they stood up and Krebs kissed his mother and went out of the house. He had tried so to keep his life from being complicated. Still, none of it had touched him. He had felt sorry for his mother and she had made him lie. He would go to Kansas City and get a job and she would feel all right about it. There would be one more scene maybe before he got away. He would not go down to his father's office. He would miss that one. He wanted his life to go smoothly. It had just gotten going that way. Well, that was all over now, anyway. He would go over to the schoolyard and watch Helen play indoor baseball.

Considerations

1. What does the photograph of Krebs, the corporal, and the German girls reveal?
2. Belleau Wood, Soissons, the Champagne, St. Mihiel, and the Argonne were the sites of fierce and bloody fighting. What effect have these battles had on Krebs? Why do you think he won't talk about them to the people at home?
3. Why does Krebs avoid complications and consequences? How has the war changed his attitudes toward work and women? How is his hometown different from Germany and France? What is the conflict in the story?
4. Why do you think Hemingway refers to the protagonist as Krebs rather than Harold? What is the significance of his sister calling him "Hare"?
5. Describe Krebs's home. How does Hemingway use the reader's traditional associations with home in this story? What is there about the routine at home that alienates Krebs? Why does the war seem more real to him?
6. How does Krebs's mother embody the community values? What does Krebs think of those values?
7. Why can't Krebs pray with his mother?
8. What is the resolution to Krebs's conflict?
9. Comment on the appropriateness of the story's title.

10. Explain how Krebs's war experiences are present throughout the story even though we get no details about them.
11. Perhaps, after having been away from home for a time, you have returned to find yourself feeling alienated from your family or friends. Describe your experience. What caused the change?

Connections

1. Contrast the attitudes toward patriotism implicit in this story with those in Yukio Mishima's "Patriotism" (p. 412). How do the stories' settings help to account for the differences between them?
2. How might Krebs's rejection of his community's values be related to Sammy's relationship to his supermarket job in John Updike's "A & P" (p. 407)? What details does Updike use to make the setting in "A & P" a comic, though nonetheless serious, version of Krebs's hometown?
3. Explain how the violent details that Tim O'Brien uses to establish the setting in "How to Tell a True War Story" (p. 454) can be considered representative of the kinds of horrors that haunt Krebs after he returns home.

5. Point of View

Because one of the pleasures of reading fiction consists of seeing the world through someone else's eyes, it is easy to overlook the eyes that control our view of the plot, characters, and setting. ***Point of view*** refers to who tells us the story and how it is told. What we know and how we feel about the events in a story are shaped by the author's choice of a point of view. The teller of a story, the ***narrator,*** inevitably affects our understanding of the characters' actions by filtering what is told through his or her own perspective. The narrator should not be confused with the author who has created the narrative voice, because the two are usually distinct (more on this point later).

If the narrative voice is changed, the story will change. Consider, for example, how different "Bartleby, the Scrivener" (p. 80) would be if Melville had chosen to tell the story from Bartleby's point of view instead of the lawyer's. With Bartleby as narrator, much of the mystery concerning his behavior would be lost. The peculiar force of his saying "I would prefer not to" would be lessened amid all the other things he would have to say as narrator. Moreover, the lawyer's reaction — puzzled, upset, outraged, and finally sympathetic to Bartleby — would be lost too. It would be entirely possible, of course, to write a story from Bartleby's point of view, but it would not be the story Melville wrote.

The possible ways of telling a story are many, and more than one point of view can be worked into a single story. However, the various points of view that storytellers draw upon can be conveniently grouped into two broad categories: (1) the third-person narrator, and (2) the first-person narrator. The third-person narrator uses *he, she,* or *they* to tell the story and does not participate in the action. The first-person narrator uses *I* and is a major or minor participant in the action. A second-person narrator, *you,* is possible but rarely used because of the awkwardness in thrusting the reader into the story, as in "You are minding your own business on a park bench when a drunk steps out of the bushes and demands your lunch bag."

Let's look now at the most important and most often used variations within first- and third-person narrations.

THIRD-PERSON NARRATOR (nonparticipant)

1. Omniscient (the narrator takes us inside the character[s])
2. Limited omniscient (the narrator takes us inside one or two characters)
3. Objective (the narrator is outside the characters)

FIRST-PERSON NARRATOR (participant)

1. Major character
2. Minor character

No type of third-person narrator appears as a character in a story. The ***omniscient narrator*** is all-knowing. From this point of view, the narrator can move from place to place and pass back and forth through time, slipping into and out of characters as no human being possibly could in real life. This narrator can report the characters' thoughts and feelings as well as what they say and do. In the excerpt from *Tarzan of the Apes* (p. 40), Burroughs's narrator tells us about events concerning Terkoz in another part of the jungle that long preceded the battle between Terkoz and Tarzan. We also learn Tarzan's and Jane's inner thoughts and emotions during the episode. And Burroughs's narrator describes Terkoz as "an arrant coward" and a bully, thereby evaluating the character for the reader. This kind of intrusion is called ***editorial omniscience***. In contrast, narration that allows characters' actions and thoughts to speak for themselves is known as ***neutral omniscience***. Most modern writers use neutral omniscience so that readers can reach their own conclusions.

The ***limited omniscient*** narrator is much more confined than the omniscient narrator. With limited omniscience the author very often restricts the narrator to the single perspective of either a major or a minor character. Sometimes a narrator can see into more than one character, particularly in a longer work that focuses, for example, on two characters alternately from one chapter to the next. Short stories, however, frequently are restricted by length to a single character's point of view. The way people, places, and events appear to that character is the way they appear to the reader. The reader has access to the thoughts and feelings of the characters revealed by the narrator, but neither the reader nor the character has access to the inner lives of any of the other characters in the story. The events in Katherine Mansfield's "Miss Brill" (p. 394) are viewed entirely through the protagonist's eyes; we see a French vacation town as an elderly woman does. Miss Brill represents the central consciousness of the story. She unifies the story by being present through all the action. We are not told of anything that happens away from the character because the narration is based on her perception of things.

The most intense use of a central consciousness in narration can be seen in the ***stream of consciousness technique*** developed by modern writers such as James Joyce, Virginia Woolf, and William Faulkner. This technique takes a reader inside a character's mind to reveal perceptions, thoughts, and feelings on a conscious or unconscious level. A stream of consciousness suggests the flow of thought as well as its content; hence, complete sentences may give way to fragments as the character's mind makes rapid associations free of conventional logic or transitions.

The following passage is from Joyce's *Ulysses,* a novel famous for its extended use of this technique. In this paragraph the narrator describes a funeral.

> Coffin now. Got here before us, dead as he is. Horse looking round at it with his plume skeowways [askew]. Dull eye: collar tight on his neck, pressing on a bloodvessel or something. Do they know what they cart out of here every day? Must be twenty or thirty funerals every day. Then Mount Jerome for the protestants. Funerals all over the world everywhere every minute. Shovelling them under by the cartload doublequick. Thousands every hour. Too many in the world.

The narrator's thoughts range from specific observations to speculations about death. Joyce creates the illusion that we are reading the narrator's thoughts as they occur. The stream of consciousness technique provides an intimate perspective on a character's thoughts.

In contrast, the ***objective point of view*** employs a narrator who does not see into the mind of any character. From this detached and impersonal perspective, the narrator reports action and dialogue without telling us directly what characters feel and think. We observe the characters in much the same way we would perceive events in a film or play: we supply the meanings; no analysis or interpretation is provided by a narrator. This point of view places a heavy premium on dialogue, actions, and details to reveal character.

In Hemingway's "Soldier's Home" (p. 121), a limited omniscient narration is the predominant point of view. Krebs's thoughts and reaction to being home from the war are made available to the reader by the narrator, who tells us that Krebs "felt embarrassed and resentful" or "sick and vaguely nauseated" by the small-town life he has reentered. Occasionally, however, Hemingway uses an objective point of view when he dramatizes particularly tense moments between Krebs and his mother. In the following excerpt, Hemingway's narrator shows us Krebs's feelings instead of telling us what they are. Krebs's response to his mother's concerns is presented without comment. The external details of the scene reveal his inner feelings.

> "I've worried about you so much, Harold," his mother went on. "I know the temptations you must have been exposed to. I know how weak men are. I know what your own dear grandfather, my own father, told us

about the Civil War and I have prayed for you. I pray for you all day long, Harold."

Krebs looked at the bacon fat hardening on his plate.

"Your father is worried, too," his mother went on. "He thinks you have lost your ambition, that you haven't got a definite aim in life. Charley Simmons, who is just your age, has a good job and is going to be married. The boys are all settling down; they're all determined to get somewhere; you can see that boys like Charley Simmons are on their way to being really a credit to the community."

Krebs said nothing.

"Don't look that way, Harold. . . ."

When Krebs looks at the bacon fat we can see him cooling and hardening too. Hemingway did not describe the expression on Krebs's face, yet we know it is a look that disturbed his mother as she "went on" about what she thinks she knows. Krebs and his mother are clearly tense and upset; the details, action, and dialogue reveal that without the narrator telling the reader how each character feels.

With a ***first-person narrator,*** the *I* presents the point of view of only one character's consciousness. The reader is restricted to the perceptions, thoughts, and feelings of that single character. This is Melville's technique with the lawyer in "Bartleby, the Scrivener" (p. 80). Everything learned about the characters, action, and plot comes from the unnamed lawyer. Bartleby remains a mystery because we are limited to what the lawyer knows and reports. The lawyer cannot explain what Bartleby means because he does not entirely know himself. Melville's use of the first person encourages us to identify with the lawyer's confused reaction to Bartleby so that we pay attention not only to the scrivener but also to the lawyer's response to him. We are as perplexed as the lawyer and share his effort to make sense of Bartleby.

The lawyer is a major character in Melville's story; indeed, many readers take him to be the protagonist. A first-person narrator can, however, also be a minor character (imagine how different the story would be if it were told by, say, Ginger Nut or by an observer who has little or nothing to do with the action). Faulkner uses an observer in "A Rose for Emily" (p. 54). His *we,* though plural and representative of the town's view of Emily, is nonetheless a first-person narrator.

One of the primary reasons for identifying the point of view in a story is to determine where the author stands in relation to the story. Behind the narrative voice of any story is the author, manipulating events and providing or withholding information. It is a mistake to assume that the narrative voice of a story is the author. The narrator, whether a first-person participant or a third-person nonparticipant, is a creation of the writer. A narrator's perceptions may be accepted, rejected, or modified by an author, depending on how the narrative voice is articulated.

Faulkner seems to have shared the fascination, sympathy, and horror of the narrator in "A Rose for Emily," but Melville must not be so readily identified with the lawyer in "Bartleby, the Scrivener." The lawyer's description of himself as "an eminently *safe* man," convinced "that the easiest way of life is the best," raises the question of how well equipped he is to fathom Bartleby's protest. To make sense of Bartleby, it is also necessary to understand the lawyer's point of view. Until the conclusion of the story, this *"safe* man" is too self-serving, defensive, and obtuse to comprehend the despair embodied in Bartleby and the deadening meaninglessness of Wall Street life.

The lawyer is an ***unreliable narrator,*** whose interpretation of events is different from the author's. We cannot entirely accept the lawyer's assessment of Bartleby because we see that the lawyer's perceptions are not totally to be trusted. Melville does not expect us, for example, to agree with the lawyer's suggestion that the solution to Bartleby's situation might be to "entertain some young gentleman with your conversation" on a trip to Europe. Given Bartleby's awful silences, this absurd suggestion reveals the lawyer's superficial understanding. The lawyer's perceptions frequently do not coincide with those Melville expects his readers to share. Hence, the lawyer's unreliability preserves Bartleby's mysterious nature while revealing the lawyer's sensibilities. The point of view is artistically appropriate for Melville's purposes, because the eyes through which we perceive the plot, characters, and setting are also the subject of the story.

Narrators can be unreliable for a variety of reasons: they might lack self-knowledge, like Melville's lawyer, or they might be innocent and inexperienced, like Ralph Ellison's young narrator in "Battle Royal" (p. 178). Youthful innocence frequently characterizes a ***naive narrator*** such as Mark Twain's Huck Finn or Holden Caufield, J. D. Salinger's twentieth-century version of Huck in *The Catcher in the Rye.* These narrators lack the sophistication to interpret accurately what they see; they are unreliable because the reader must go beyond their understanding of events to comprehend the situations described. Huck and Holden describe their respective social environments, but the reader, with more experience, supplies the critical perspective that each boy lacks. In "Battle Royal" that perspective is supplemented by Ellison dividing the narration between the young man who experiences events and the mature man who reflects back on those events.

Few generalizations can be made about the advantages or disadvantages of using a specific point of view. What can be said with confidence, however, is that writers choose a point of view to achieve particular effects, because point of view determines what we know about the characters and events in a story. We should, therefore, be aware of who is telling the story and whether the narrator sees things clearly and reliably.

The next three works warrant a careful examination of their points of view. In Alice Munro's "How I Met My Husband," a married woman recounts her experiences as an innocent fifteen-year-old living away from home for the first time. In Anton Chekhov's and Joyce Carol Oates's versions of "The Lady with the Pet Dog," we are presented with similar stories told from two different perspectives that make for intriguing comparisons and contrasts.

ALICE MUNRO (b. 1931)

Born in Wingham, Ontario, Alice Munro was raised on a fox farm and attended the University of Western Ontario. Her prize-winning fiction typically focuses on the subtle complexities that constitute the lives of the small-town Canadians she knows so well. Her stories are especially recognized for evoking the emotional intensity of female characters who long to belong to a community and who also need to stand apart from it. Her collections of stories include *Dance of the Happy Shades* (1968), *Lives of Girls and Women* (1971), *Something I've Been Meaning to Tell You* (1974), *The Beggar Maid* (1979), and *The Progress of Love* (1986). In the following story the narrator explains how in meeting her husband she was also introduced to an important realization about herself.

How I Met My Husband 1974

We heard the plane come over at noon, roaring through the radio news, and we were sure it was going to hit the house, so we all ran out into the yard. We saw it come over the treetops, all red and silver, the first close-up plane I ever saw. Mrs. Peebles screamed.

"Crash landing," their little boy said. Joey was his name.

"It's okay," said Dr. Peebles. "He knows what he's doing." Dr. Peebles was only an animal doctor, but had a calming way of talking, like any doctor.

This was my first job — working for Dr. and Mrs. Peebles, who had bought an old house out on the Fifth Line, about five miles out of town. It was just when the trend was starting of town people buying up old farms, not to work them but to live on them.

We watched the plane land across the road, where the fairgrounds used to 5
be. It did make a good landing field, nice and level for the old race track, and the barns and display sheds torn down now for scrap lumber so there was nothing in the way. Even the old grandstand bays had burned.

"All right," said Mrs. Peebles, snappy as she always was when she got over her nerves. "Let's go back in the house. Let's not stand here gawking like a set of farmers."

She didn't say that to hurt my feelings. It never occurred to her.

I was just setting the dessert down when Loretta Bird arrived, out of breath, at the screen door.

"I thought it was going to crash into the house and kill youse all!"

She lived on the next place and the Peebleses thought she was a countrywoman, they didn't know the difference. She and her husband didn't farm, he worked on the roads and had a bad name for drinking. They had seven children and couldn't get credit at the HiWay Grocery. The Peebleses made her welcome, not knowing any better, as I say, and offered her dessert.

Dessert was never anything to write home about, at their place. A dish of Jell-O or sliced bananas or fruit out of a tin. "Have a house without a pie, be ashamed until you die," my mother used to say, but Mrs. Peebles operated differently.

Loretta Bird saw me getting the can of peaches.

"Oh, never mind," she said. "I haven't got the right kind of a stomach to trust what comes out of those tins, I can only eat home canning."

I could have slapped her. I bet she never put down fruit in her life.

"I know what he's landed here for," she said. "He's got permission to use the fairgrounds and take people up for rides. It costs a dollar. It's the same fellow who was over at Palmerston last week and was up the lakeshore before that. I wouldn't go up, if you paid me."

"I'd jump at the chance," Dr. Peebles said. "I'd like to see this neighborhood from the air."

Mrs. Peebles said she would just as soon see it from the ground. Joey said he wanted to go and Heather did, too. Joey was nine and Heather was seven.

"Would you, Edie?" Heather said.

I said I didn't know. I was scared, but I never admitted that, especially in front of children I was taking care of.

"People are going to be coming out here in their cars raising dust and trampling your property, if I was you I would complain," Loretta said. She hooked her legs around the chair rung and I knew we were in for a lengthy visit. After Dr. Peebles went back to his office or out on his next call and Mrs. Peebles went for her nap, she would hang around me while I was trying to do the dishes. She would pass remarks about the Peebleses in their own house.

"She wouldn't find time to lay down in the middle of the day, if she had seven kids like I got."

She asked me did they fight and did they keep things in the dresser drawer not to have babies with. She said it was a sin if they did. I pretended I didn't know what she was talking about.

I was fifteen and away from home for the first time. My parents had made the effort and sent me to high school for a year, but I didn't like it. I was shy of strangers and the work was hard, they didn't make it nice for you or explain the way they do now. At the end of the year the averages were published in the paper, and mine came out at the very bottom, 37 percent. My father said that's enough and I didn't blame him. The last thing I wanted, anyway, was to go on and end up teaching school. It happened the very day the paper came out with my disgrace in it, Dr. Peebles was staying at our place for dinner, having just helped one of our cows have twins, and he said I looked smart to him and his wife was looking for a girl to help. He said she felt tied down, with the two children, out in the country. I guess she would, my mother said, being polite, though I could tell from her face she was wondering what on earth it would be like to have only two children and no barn work, and then to be complaining.

When I went home I would describe to them the work I had to do, and it made everybody laugh. Mrs. Peebles had an automatic washer and dryer, the first I ever saw. I have had those in my own home for such a long time now it's hard to remember how much of a miracle it was to me, not having to struggle with the wringer and hang up and haul down. Let alone not having to heat water. Then there was practically no baking. Mrs. Peebles said she couldn't make pie crust, the most amazing thing I ever heard a woman admit. I could, of course, and I could make light biscuits and a white cake and dark cake, but they didn't want it, she said they watched their figures. The only thing I didn't like about working there, in fact, was feeling half hungry a lot of the time. I used to bring back a box of doughnuts made out at home, and hide them under my bed. The children found out, and I didn't mind sharing, but I thought I better bind them to secrecy.

The day after the plane landed Mrs. Peebles put both children in the car and drove over to Chesley, to get their hair cut. There was a good woman then at Chesley for doing hair. She got hers done at the same place, Mrs. Peebles did, and that meant they would be gone a good while. She had to pick a day Dr. Peebles wasn't going out into the country, she didn't have her own car. Cars were still in short supply then, after the war.

I loved being left in the house alone, to do my work at leisure. The kitchen was all white and bright yellow, with fluorescent lights. That was before they ever thought of making the appliances all different colors and doing the cupboards like dark old wood and hiding the lighting. I loved light. I loved the double sink. So would anybody new-come from washing dishes in a dishpan with a rag-plugged hole on an oilcloth-covered table by light of a coal-oil lamp. I kept everything shining.

The bathroom too. I had a bath in there once a week. They wouldn't have minded if I took one oftener, but to me it seemed like asking too much, or maybe risking making it less wonderful. The basin and the tub and the toilet were all pink, and there were glass doors with flamingoes painted on them, to shut off the tub. The light had a rosy cast and the mat sank under your feet like snow, except that it was warm. The mirror was three-way. With the mirror all steamed up and the air like a perfume cloud, from things I was allowed to use, I stood up on the side of the tub and admired myself naked, from three directions. Sometimes I thought about the way we lived out at home and the way we lived here and how one way was so hard to imagine when you were living the other way. But I thought it was still a lot easier, living the way we lived at home, to picture something like this, the painted flamingoes and the warmth and the soft mat, than it was anybody knowing only things like this to picture how it was the other way. And why was that?

I was through my jobs in no time, and had the vegetables peeled for supper and sitting in cold water besides. Then I went into Mrs. Peebles' bedroom. I had been in there plenty of times, cleaning, and I always took a good look in her closet, at the clothes she had hanging there. I wouldn't have looked in her drawers, but a closet is open to anybody. That's a lie. I would have looked in drawers, but I would have felt worse doing it and been more scared she could tell.

Some clothes in her closet she wore all the time, I was quite familiar with them. Others she never put on, they were pushed to the back. I was disappointed to see no wedding dress. But there was one long dress I could just see the skirt of, and I was hungering to see the rest. Now I took note of where it hung and lifted it out. It was satin, a lovely weight on my arm, light bluish-green in color, almost silvery. It had a fitted, pointed waist and a full skirt and an off-the-shoulder fold hiding the little sleeves.

Next thing was easy. I got out of my own things and slipped it on. I was slimmer at fifteen than anybody would believe who knows me now and the fit was beautiful. I didn't, of course, have a strapless bra on, which was what it needed, I just had to slide my straps down my arms under the material. Then I tried pinning up my hair, to get the effect. One thing led to another. I put on rouge and lipstick and eyebrow pencil from her dresser. The heat of the day and the weight of the satin and all the excitement made me thirsty, and I went out to the kitchen, got-up as I was, to get a glass of ginger ale with ice cubes from the refrigerator. The Peebleses drank ginger ale, or fruit drinks, all day, like water, and I was getting so I did too. Also there was no limit on ice cubes, which I was so fond of I would even put them in a glass of milk.

I turned from putting the ice tray back and saw a man watching me through the screen. It was the luckiest thing in the world I didn't spill the ginger ale down the front of me then and there.

"I never meant to scare you. I knocked but you were getting the ice out, you didn't hear me."

I couldn't see what he looked like, he was dark the way somebody is pressed up against a screen door with the bright daylight behind them. I only knew he wasn't from around here.

"I'm from the plane over there. My name is Chris Watters and what I was wondering was if I could use that pump."

There was a pump in the yard. That was the way the people used to get their water. Now I noticed he was carrying a pail.

"You're welcome," I said. "I can get it from the tap and save you pumping." I guess I wanted him to know we had piped water, didn't pump ourselves.

"I don't mind the exercise." He didn't move, though, and finally he said, "Were you going to a dance?"

Seeing a stranger there had made me entirely forget how I was dressed.

"Or is that the way ladies around here generally get dressed up in the afternoon?"

I didn't know how to joke back then. I was too embarrassed.

"You live here? Are you the lady of the house?"

"I'm the hired girl."

Some people change when they find that out, their whole way of looking at you and speaking to you changes, but his didn't.

"Well, I just wanted to tell you you look very nice. I was so surprised when I looked in the door and saw you. Just because you looked so nice and beautiful."

I wasn't even old enough then to realize how out of the common it is, for a man to say something like that to a woman, or somebody he is treating like a woman. For a man to say a word like *beautiful.* I wasn't old enough to realize or to say anything back, or in fact to do anything but wish he would go away. Not that I didn't like him, but just that it upset me so, having him look at me, and me trying to think of something to say.

He must have understood. He said good-bye, and thanked me, and went and started filling his pail from the pump. I stood behind the Venetian blinds in the dining room, watching him. When he had gone, I went into the bedroom and took the dress off and put it back in the same place. I dressed in my own clothes and took my hair down and washed my face, wiping it on Kleenex, which I threw in the wastebasket.

The Peebleses asked me what kind of man he was. Young, middle-aged, short, tall? I couldn't say.

"Good-looking?" Dr. Peebles teased me.

I couldn't think a thing but that he would be coming to get his water again, he would be talking to Dr. or Mrs. Peebles, making friends with them, and he would mention seeing me that first afternoon, dressed up. Why not mention it? He would think it was funny. And no idea of the trouble it would get me into.

After supper the Peebleses drove into town to go to a movie. She wanted to go somewhere with her hair fresh done. I sat in my bright kitchen wondering what to do, knowing I would never sleep. Mrs. Peebles might not fire me, when she found out, but it would give her a different feeling about me altogether. This was the first place I ever worked but I really had picked up things about the way people feel when you are working for them. They like to think you aren't curious. Not just that you aren't dishonest, that isn't enough. They like to feel you don't notice things, that you don't think or wonder about anything but what they liked to eat and how they liked things ironed, and so on. I don't mean they weren't kind to me, because they were. They had me eat my meals with them (to tell the truth I expected to, I didn't know there were families who don't) and sometimes they took me along in the car. But all the same.

I went up and checked on the children being asleep and then I went out. I had to do it. I crossed the road and went in the old fairgrounds gate. The plane looked unnatural sitting there, and shining with the moon. Off at the far side of the fairgrounds, where the bush was taking over, I saw his tent.

He was sitting outside it smoking a cigarette. He saw me coming.

"Hello, were you looking for a plane ride? I don't start taking people up till tomorrow." Then he looked again and said, "Oh, it's you. I didn't know you without your long dress on."

My heart was knocking away, my tongue was dried up. I had to say something. But I couldn't. My throat was closed and I was like a deaf-and-dumb.

"Did you want to ride? Sit down. Have a cigarette."

I couldn't even shake my head to say no, so he gave me one.

"Put it in your mouth or I can't light it. It's a good thing I'm used to shy ladies."

I did. It wasn't the first time I had smoked a cigarette, actually. My girl friend out home, Muriel Lowe, used to steal them from her brother.

"Look at your hand shaking. Did you just want to have a chat, or what?"

In one burst I said, "I wisht you wouldn't say anything about that dress."

"What dress? Oh, the long dress."

"It's Mrs. Peebles'."

"Whose? Oh, the lady you work for? Is that it? She wasn't home so you got dressed up in her dress, eh? You got dressed up and played queen. I don't blame you. You're not smoking the cigarette right. Don't just puff. Draw it in.

Did anybody ever show you how to inhale? Are you scared I'll tell on you? Is that it?"

I was so ashamed at having to ask him to connive this way I couldn't nod. I just looked at him and he saw *yes.*

"Well I won't. I won't in the slightest way mention it or embarrass you. I give you my word of honor."

Then he changed the subject, to help me out, seeing I couldn't even thank him.

"What do you think of this sign?"

It was a board sign lying practically at my feet.

SEE THE WORLD FROM THE SKY. ADULTS $1.00, CHILDREN 50¢. QUALIFIED PILOT.

"My old sign was getting pretty beat up, I thought I'd make a new one. That's what I've been doing with my time today."

The lettering wasn't all that handsome, I thought. I could have done a better one in half an hour.

"I'm not an expert at sign making."

"It's very good," I said.

"I don't need it for publicity, word of mouth is usually enough. I turned away two carloads tonight. I felt like taking it easy. I didn't tell them ladies were dropping in to visit me."

Now I remembered the children and I was scared again, in case one of them had waked up and called me and I wasn't there.

"Do you have to go so soon?"

I remembered some manners. "Thank you for the cigarette."

"Don't forget. You have my word of honor."

I tore off across the fairgrounds, scared I'd see the car heading home from town. My sense of time was mixed up, I didn't know how long I'd been out of the house. But it was all right, it wasn't late, the children were asleep. I got in bed myself and lay thinking what a lucky end to the day, after all, and among things to be grateful for I could be grateful Loretta Bird hadn't been the one who caught me.

The yard and borders didn't get trampled, it wasn't as bad as that. All the same it seemed very public, around the house. The sign was on the fairgrounds gate. People came mostly after supper but a good many in the afternoon, too. The Bird children all came without fifty cents between them and hung on the gate. We got used to the excitement of the plane coming in and taking off, it wasn't excitement anymore. I never went over, after that one time, but would see him when he came to get his water. I would be out on the steps doing sitting-down work, like preparing vegetables, if I could.

"Why don't you come over? I'll take you up in my plane."

"I'm saving my money," I said, because I couldn't think of anything else.

"For what? For getting married?"

I shook my head.

"I'll take you up for free if you come sometime when it's slack. I thought you would come, and have another cigarette."

I made a face to hush him, because you never could tell when the children would be sneaking around the porch, or Mrs. Peebles herself listening in the house. Sometimes she came out and had a conversation with him. He told her things he hadn't bothered to tell me. But then I hadn't thought to ask. He told her he had been in the war, that was where he learned to fly a plane, and now he couldn't settle down to ordinary life, this was what he liked. She said she couldn't imagine anybody liking such a thing. Though sometimes, she said, she was almost bored enough to try anything herself, she wasn't brought up to living in the country. It's all my husband's idea, she said. This was news to me.

"Maybe you ought to give flying lessons," she said.

"Would you take them?"

She just laughed.

Sunday was a busy flying day in spite of it being preached against from two 90
pulpits. We were all sitting out watching. Joey and Heather were over on the fence with the Bird kids. Their father had said they could go, after their mother saying all week they couldn't.

A car came down the road past the parked cars and pulled up right in the drive. It was Loretta Bird who got out, all importance, and on the driver's side another woman got out, more sedately. She was wearing sunglasses.

"This is a lady looking for the man that flies the plane," Loretta Bird said. "I heard her inquire in the hotel coffee shop where I was having a Coke and I brought her out."

"I'm sorry to bother you," the lady said. "I'm Alice Kelling, Mr. Watters' fiancée."

This Alice Kelling had on a pair of brown and white checked slacks and a yellow top. Her bust looked to me rather low and bumpy. She had a worried face. Her hair had had a permanent, but had grown out, and she wore a yellow band to keep it off her face. Nothing in the least pretty or even young-looking about her. But you could tell from how she talked she was from the city, or educated, or both.

Dr. Peebles stood up and introduced himself and his wife and me and 95
asked her to be seated.

"He's up in the air right now, but you're welcome to sit and wait. He gets his water here and he hasn't been yet. He'll probably take his break about five."

"That is him, then?" said Alice Kelling, wrinkling and straining at the sky.

"He's not in the habit of running out on you, taking a different name?" Dr. Peebles laughed. He was the one, not his wife, to offer iced tea. Then she sent me into the kitchen to fix it. She smiled. She was wearing sunglasses too.

"He never mentioned his fiancée," she said.

I loved fixing iced tea with lots of ice and slices of lemon in tall glasses. I 100
ought to have mentioned before, Dr. Peebles was an abstainer, at least around the house, or I wouldn't have been allowed to take the place. I had to fix a glass for Loretta Bird too, though it galled me, and when I went out she had settled in my lawn chair, leaving me the steps.

"I knew you was a nurse when I first heard you in that coffee shop."

"How would you know a thing like that?"

"I get my hunches about people. Was that how you met him, nursing?"

"Chris? Well yes. Yes, it was."

"Oh, were you overseas?" said Mrs. Peebles. 105

"No, it was before he went overseas. I nursed him when he was stationed at Centralia and had a ruptured appendix. We got engaged and then he went overseas. My, this is refreshing, after a long drive."

"He'll be glad to see you," Dr. Peebles said. "It's a rackety kind of life, isn't it, not staying one place long enough to really make friends."

"Youse've had a long engagement," Loretta Bird said.

Alice Kelling passed that over. "I was going to get a room at the hotel, but when I was offered directions I came on out. Do you think I could phone them?"

"No need," Dr. Peebles said. "You're five miles away from him if you stay at the hotel. Here, you're right across the road. Stay with us. We've got rooms on rooms, look at this big house."

Asking people to stay, just like that, is certainly a country thing, and maybe seemed natural to him now, but not to Mrs. Peebles, from the way she said, oh yes, we have plenty of room. Or to Alice Kelling, who kept protesting, but let herself be worn down. I got the feeling it was a temptation to her, to be that close. I was trying for a look at her ring. Her nails were painted red, her fingers were freckled and wrinkled. It was a tiny stone. Muriel Lowe's cousin had one twice as big.

Chris came to get his water, late in the afternoon just as Dr. Peebles had predicted. He must have recognized the car from a way off. He came smiling.

"Here I am chasing after you to see what you're up to," called Alice Kelling. She got up and went to meet him and they kissed, just touched, in front of us.

"You're going to spend a lot on gas that way," Chris said.

Dr. Peebles invited Chris to stay for supper, since he had already put up the sign that said: NO MORE RIDES TILL 7 P.M. Mrs. Peebles wanted it served in the yard, in spite of the bugs. One thing strange to anybody from the country is this eating outside. I had made a potato salad earlier and she had made a jellied salad, that was one thing she could do, so it was just a matter of getting those out, and some sliced meat and cucumbers and fresh leaf lettuce. Loretta Bird hung around for some time saying, "Oh, well, I guess I better get home to those yappers," and, "It's so nice just sitting here, I sure hate to get up," but nobody invited her, I was relieved to see, and finally she had to go.

That night after rides were finished Alice Kelling and Chris went off somewhere in her car. I lay awake till they got back. When I saw the car lights sweep my ceiling I got up to look down on them through the slats of my blind. I don't know what I thought I was going to see. Muriel Lowe and I used to sleep on her front veranda and watch her sister and her sister's boy friend saying good night. Afterward we couldn't get to sleep, for longing for somebody to kiss us and rub up against us and we would talk about suppose you were out in a boat with a boy and he wouldn't bring you in to shore unless you did it, or what if somebody got you trapped in a barn, you would have to, wouldn't you, it wouldn't be your fault. Muriel said her two girl cousins used to try with a toilet paper roll that one of them was a boy. We wouldn't do anything like that; just lay and wondered.

All that happened was that Chris got out of the car on one side and she got out on the other and they walked off separately — him toward the fairgrounds and her toward the house. I got back in bed and imagined about me coming home with him, not like that.

Next morning Alice Kelling got up late and I fixed a grapefruit for her the way I had learned and Mrs. Peebles sat down with her to visit and have another cup of coffee. Mrs. Peebles seemed pleased enough now, having company. Alice Kelling said she guessed she better get used to putting in a day just watching Chris take off and come down, and Mrs. Peebles said she didn't know if she should suggest it because Alice Kelling was the one with the car, but the lake was only twenty-five miles away and what a good day for a picnic.

Alice Kelling took her up on the idea and by eleven o'clock they were in the car, with Joey and Heather and a sandwich lunch I had made. The only thing was that Chris hadn't come down, and she wanted to tell him where they were going.

"Edie'll go over and tell him," Mrs. Peebles said. "There's no problem."

Alice Kelling wrinkled her face and agreed.

"Be sure and tell him we'll be back by five!"

I didn't see that he would be concerned about knowing this right away, and I thought of him eating whatever he ate over there, alone, cooking on his camp stove, so I got to work and mixed up a crumb cake and baked it, in between the other work I had to do; then, when it was a bit cooled, wrapped it in a tea towel. I didn't do anything to myself but take off my apron and comb my hair. I would like to have put some makeup on, but I was too afraid it would remind him of the way he first saw me, and that would humiliate me all over again.

He had come and put another sign on the gate: NO RIDES THIS P.M. APOLOGIES. I worried that he wasn't feeling well. No sign of him outside and the tent flap was down. I knocked on the pole.

"Come in," he said, in a voice that would just as soon have said *Stay out.*

I lifted the flap.

"Oh, it's you. I'm sorry. I didn't know it was you."

He had been just sitting on the side of the bed, smoking. Why not at least sit and smoke in the fresh air?

"I brought a cake and hope you're not sick," I said.

"Why would I be sick? Oh — that sign. That's all right. I'm just tired of talking to people. I don't mean you. Have a seat." He pinned back the tent flap. "Get some fresh air in here."

I sat on the edge of the bed, there was no place else. It was one of those fold-up cots, really: I remembered and gave him his fiancée's message.

He ate some of the cake. "Good."

"Put the rest away for when you're hungry later."

"I'll tell you a secret. I won't be around here much longer."

"Are you getting married?"

"Ha ha. What time did you say they'd be back?"

"Five o'clock."

"Well, by that time, this place will have seen the last of me. A plane can get further than a car." He unwrapped the cake and ate another piece of it, absent-mindedly.

"Now you'll be thirsty."

"There's some water in the pail."

"It won't be very cold. I could bring some fresh. I could bring some ice from the refrigerator."

"No," he said. "I don't want you to go. I want a nice long time of saying good-bye to you."

He put the cake away carefully and sat beside me and started those little kisses, so soft, I can't ever let myself think about them, such kindness in his face and lovely kisses, all over my eyelids and neck and ears, all over, then me kissing back as well as I could (I had only kissed a boy on a dare before, and kissed my own arms for practice) and we lay back on the cot and pressed together, just gently, and he did some other things, not bad things or not in a bad way. It was lovely in the tent, that smell of grass and hot tent cloth with the sun beating down on it, and he said, "I wouldn't do you any harm for the world." Once, when he had rolled on top of me and we were sort of rocking together on the cot, he said softly, "Oh, no," and freed himself and jumped up and got the water pail. He splashed some of it on his neck and face, and the little bit left, on me lying there.

"That's to cool us off, miss."

When we said good-bye I wasn't at all sad, because he held my face and said, "I'm going to write you a letter. I'll tell you where I am and maybe you can come and see me. Would you like that? Okay then. You wait." I was really glad I think to get away from him, it was like he was piling presents on me I couldn't get the pleasure of till I considered them alone.

No consternation at first about the plane being gone. They thought he had taken somebody up, and I didn't enlighten them. Dr. Peebles had phoned he had to go to the country, so there was just us having supper, and then Loretta Bird thrusting her head in the door and saying, "I see he's took off."

"What?" said Alice Kelling, and pushed back her chair.

"The kids come and told me this afternoon he was taking down his tent. Did he think he'd run through all the business there was around here? He didn't take off without letting you know, did he?"

"He'll send me word," Alice Kelling said. "He'll probably phone tonight. He's terribly restless, since the war."

"Edie, he didn't mention to you, did he?" Mrs. Peebles said. "When you took over the message?"

"Yes," I said. So far so true.

"Well why didn't you say?" All of them were looking at me. "Did he say where he was going?"

"He said he might try Bayfield," I said. What made me tell such a lie? I didn't intend it.

"Bayfield, how far is that?" said Alice Kelling.

Mrs. Peebles said, "Thirty, thirty-five miles."

"That's not far. Oh, well, that's really not far at all. It's on the lake, isn't it?"

You'd think I'd be ashamed of myself, setting her on the wrong track. I did it to give him more time, whatever time he needed. I lied for him, and also, I have to admit, for me. Women should stick together and not do things like that. I see that now, but didn't then. I never thought of myself as being in any way like her, or coming to the same troubles, ever.

She hadn't taken her eyes off me. I thought she suspected my lie.

"When did he mention this to you?"

"Earlier."

"When you were over at the plane?"

"Yes."

"You must've stayed and had a chat." She smiled at me, not a nice smile. "You must've stayed and had a little visit with him."

"I took a cake," I said, thinking that telling some truth would spare me telling the rest.

"We didn't have a cake," said Mrs. Peebles rather sharply.

"I baked one."

Alice Kelling said, "That was very friendly of you."

"Did you get permission," said Loretta Bird. "You never know what these girls'll do next," she said. "It's not they mean harm so much, as they're ignorant."

"The cake is neither here nor there," Mrs. Peebles broke in. "Edie, I wasn't aware you knew Chris that well."

I didn't know what to say.

"I'm not surprised," Alice Kelling said in a high voice. "I knew by the look of her as soon as I saw her. We get them at the hospital all the time." She looked hard at me with her stretched smile. "Having their babies. We have to put them in a special ward because of their diseases. Little country tramps. Fourteen and fifteen years old. You should see the babies they have, too."

"There was a bad woman here in town had a baby that pus was running out of its eyes," Loretta Bird put in.

"Wait a minute," said Mrs. Peebles. "What is this talk? Edie. What about you and Mr. Watters? Were you intimate with him?"

"Yes," I said. I was thinking of us lying on the cot and kissing, wasn't that intimate? And I would never deny it.

They were all one minute quiet, even Loretta Bird.

"Well," said Mrs. Peebles. "I am surprised. I think I need a cigarette. This is the first of any such tendencies I've seen in her," she said, speaking to Alice Kelling, but Alice Kelling was looking at me.

"Loose little bitch." Tears ran down her face. "Loose little bitch, aren't you? I knew as soon as I saw you. Men despise girls like you. He just made use of you and went off, you know that, don't you? Girls like you are just nothing, they're just public conveniences, just filthy little rags!"

"Oh, now," said Mrs. Peebles.

"Filthy," Alice Kelling sobbed. "Filthy little rags!"

"Don't get yourself upset," Loretta Bird said. She was swollen up with pleasure at being in on this scene. "Men are all the same."

"Edie, I'm very surprised," Mrs. Peebles said. "I thought your parents were so strict. You don't want to have a baby, do you?"

I'm still ashamed of what happened next. I lost control, just like a six-year-old, I started howling. "You don't get a baby from just doing that!"

"You see. Some of them are that ignorant," Loretta Bird said.

But Mrs. Peebles jumped up and caught my arms and shook me.

"Calm down. Don't get hysterical. Calm down. Stop crying. Listen to me. Listen. I'm wondering, if you know what being intimate means. Now tell me. What did you think it meant?"

"Kissing," I howled.

She let go. "Oh, Edie. Stop it. Don't be silly. It's all right. It's all a misunderstanding. Being intimate means a lot more than that. Oh, I *wondered.*"

"She's trying to cover up, now," said Alice Kelling. "Yes. She's not so stupid. She sees she got herself in trouble."

"I believe her," Mrs. Peebles said. "This is an awful scene."

"Well there is one way to find out," said Alice Kelling, getting up. "After all, I am a nurse."

Mrs. Peebles drew a breath and said, "No. No. Go to your room, Edie. And stop that noise. This is too disgusting."

I heard the car start in a little while. I tried to stop crying, pulling back each wave as it started over me. Finally I succeeded, and lay heaving on the bed.

Mrs. Peebles came and stood in the doorway.

"She's gone," she said. "That Bird woman too. Of course, you know you should never have gone near that man and that is the cause of all this trouble. I have a headache. As soon as you can, go and wash your face in cold water and get at the dishes and we will not say any more about this."

Nor we didn't. I didn't figure out till years later the extent of what I had been saved from. Mrs. Peebles was not very friendly to me afterward, but she was fair. Not very friendly is the wrong way of describing what she was. She had never been very friendly. It was just that now she had to see me all the time and it got on her nerves, a little.

As for me, I put it all out of my mind like a bad dream and concentrated on waiting for my letter. The mail came every day except Sunday, between one-thirty and two in the afternoon, a good time for me because Mrs. Peebles was always having her nap. I would get the kitchen all cleaned and then go up to the mailbox and sit in the grass, waiting. I was perfectly happy, waiting, I forgot all about Alice Kelling and her misery and awful talk and Mrs. Peebles and her chilliness and the embarrassment of whether she had told Dr. Peebles and the face of Loretta Bird, getting her fill of other people's troubles. I was always smiling when the mailman got there, and continued smiling even after he gave me the mail and I saw today wasn't the day. The mailman was a Carmichael. I knew by his face because there are a lot of Carmichaels living out by us and so many of them have a sort of sticking-out top lip. So I asked his name (he was a young man, shy, but good-humored, anybody could ask him anything) and then I said, "I knew by your face!" He was pleased by that and always glad to see me and got a little less shy. "You've got the smile I've been waiting on all day!" he used to holler out the car window.

It never crossed my mind for a long time a letter might not come. I believed in it coming just like I believed the sun would rise in the morning. I just put off my hope from day to day, and there was the goldenrod out around the mailbox and the children gone back to school, and the leaves turning, and I was wearing a sweater when I went to wait. One day walking back with the hydro bill stuck in my hand, that was all, looking across at the fairgrounds with the full-blown milkweed and dark teasels, so much like fall, it just struck me: *No letter was ever going to come.* It was an impossible idea to get used to. No, not impossible. If I thought about Chris's face when he said he was going to write to me, it was impossible, but if I forgot that and thought about the actual tin mailbox, empty, it was plain and true. I kept on going to meet the mail, but my heart was heavy now like a lump of lead. I only smiled because I thought of the mailman counting on it, and he didn't have an easy life, with the winter driving ahead.

Till it came to me one day there were women doing this with their lives, all over. There were women just waiting and waiting by mailboxes for one letter or another. I imagined me making this journey day after day and year after year, and my hair starting to go gray, and I thought, I was never made to go on like that. So I stopped meeting the mail. If there were women all through life waiting, and women busy and not waiting, I knew which I had to be. Even though there might be things the second kind of women have to pass up and never know about, it still is better.

I was surprised when the mailman phoned the Peebleses' place in the evening and asked for me. He said he missed me. He asked if I would like to go to Goderich, where some well-known movie was on, I forget now what. So I said yes, and I went out with him for two years and he asked me to marry him, and we were engaged a year more while I got my things together, and then we did marry. He always tells the children the story of how I went after him by sitting by the mailbox every day, and naturally I laugh and let him, because I like for people to think what pleases them and makes them happy.

Considerations

1. Characterize Edie. Although she is not a good student, she has many other qualities. What are they?
2. Describe the point of view used in the story. When does Edie sound more like a fifteen-year-old than like a married woman?
3. How does the married Edie differ from the girl she was at age fifteen? What attitudes and values reveal these differences? What is the effect of Munro's use of these two voices?
4. How does the story's point of view help to establish the mood of the setting?
5. How would this story be changed if it were told from Mrs. Peebles's point of view?
6. Explain why the use of an editorial omniscient point of view in this story would be inappropriate.
7. How do the women — Mrs. Peebles, Loretta Bird, and Alice Kelling — help to reveal Edie's character? How does Edie's perspective on life differ from theirs?
8. How do Chris Watters and Carmichael compare as potential husbands? What attracts Edie to them?
9. What does Edie learn about men in the story? Consider whether she made the right choice in marrying Carmichael.
10. Reread the story's next to last paragraph. What does Edie learn about herself here?
11. Discuss the appropriateness of the story's title. Do you consider it misleading or accurate? Invent an alternative title that captures the central meaning of the story for you.

Connections

1. Compare Munro's use of point of view with Ralph Ellison's strategies in "Battle Royal" (p. 179).
2. How does the use of point of view in Munro's story and Toni Cade Bambara's "The Lesson" (p. 364) help to create protagonists who seem especially real and human?

ANTON CHEKHOV (1860–1904)

Born in a small town in Russia, Anton Chekhov gave up the career his medical degree prepared him for in order to devote himself to writing. His concentration on realistic detail in the hundreds of short stories he published has had an important influence on fiction writing. Modern drama has also been strengthened by his plays, among them these classics: *The Seagull* (1896), *Uncle Vanya* (1899), *The Three Sisters* (1901), and *The Cherry Orchard* (1904). Chekhov was a close observer of people in ordinary situations who struggle to live their lives as best they can. They are not very often completely successful. Chekhov's compassion, however, makes their failures less significant than their humanity. In "The Lady with the Pet Dog," love is at the heart of a struggle that begins in Yalta, a resort town on the Black Sea.

The Lady with the Pet Dog 1899

TRANSLATED BY AVRAHM YARMOLINSKY

I

A new person, it was said, had appeared on the esplanade: a lady with a pet dog. Dmitry Dmitrich Gurov, who had spent a fortnight at Yalta and had got used to the place, had also begun to take an interest in new arrivals. As he sat in Vernet's confectionery shop, he saw, walking on the esplanade, a fair-haired young woman of medium height, wearing a beret; a white Pomeranian was trotting behind her.

And afterwards he met her in the public garden and in the square several times a day. She walked alone, always wearing the same beret and always with the white dog; no one knew who she was and everyone called her simply "the lady with the pet dog."

"If she is here alone without husband or friends," Gurov reflected, "it wouldn't be a bad thing to make her acquaintance."

He was under forty, but he already had a daughter twelve years old, and two sons at school. They had found a wife for him when he was very young, a student in his second year, and by now she seemed half as old again as he. She was a tall, erect woman with dark eyebrows, stately and dignified and, as she said of herself, intellectual. She read a great deal, used simplified spelling in her letters, called her husband, not Dmitry, but Dimitry, while he privately considered her of limited intelligence, narrow-minded, dowdy, was afraid of her, and did not like to be at home. He had begun being unfaithful to her long ago—had been unfaithful to her often and, probably for that reason, almost always spoke ill of women, and when they were talked of in his presence used to call them "the inferior race."

It seemed to him that he had been sufficiently tutored by bitter experience 5 to call them what he pleased, and yet he could not have lived without "the inferior race" for two days together. In the company of men he was bored and ill at ease, he was chilly and uncommunicative with them; but when he was among women he felt free, and knew what to speak to them about and how to comport himself; and even to be silent with them was no strain on him. In his appearance, in his character, in his whole makeup there was something attractive and elusive that disposed women in his favor and allured them. He knew that, and some force seemed to draw him to them, too.

Oft-repeated and really bitter experience had taught him long ago that with decent people — particularly Moscow people — who are irresolute and slow to move, every affair which at first seems a light and charming adventure inevitably grows into a whole problem of extreme complexity, and in the end a painful situation is created. But at every new meeting with an interesting woman this lesson of experience seemed to slip from his memory, and he was eager for life, and everything seemed so simple and diverting.

One evening while he was dining in the public garden the lady in the beret walked up without haste to take the next table. Her expression, her gait, her dress, and the way she did her hair told him that she belonged to the upper class, that she was married, that she was in Yalta for the first time and alone, and that she was bored there. The stories told of the immorality in Yalta are to a great extent untrue; he despised them, and knew that such stories were made up for the most part by persons who would have been glad to sin themselves if they had had the chance; but when the lady sat down at the next table three paces from him, he recalled these stories of easy conquests, of trips to the mountains, and the tempting thought of swift, fleeting liaison, a romance with an unknown woman of whose very name he was ignorant suddenly took hold of him.

He beckoned invitingly to the Pomeranian, and when the dog approached him, shook his finger at it. The Pomeranian growled; Gurov threatened it again.

The lady glanced at him and at once dropped her eyes.

"He doesn't bite," she said and blushed. 10

"May I give him a bone?" he asked; and when she nodded he inquired affably, "Have you been in Yalta long?"

"About five days."

"And I am dragging out the second week here."

There was a short silence.

"Time passes quickly, and yet it is so dull here!" she said, not looking at 15
him.

"It's only the fashion to say it's dull here. A provincial will live in Belyov or Zhizdra and not be bored, but when he comes here it's 'Oh, the dullness! Oh, the dust!' One would think he came from Granada."

She laughed. Then both continued eating in silence, like strangers, but after dinner they walked together and there sprang up between them the light banter of people who are free and contented, to whom it does not matter where they go or what they talk about. They walked and talked of the strange light on the sea: the water was a soft, warm, lilac color, and there was a golden band of moonlight upon it. They talked of how sultry it was after a hot day. Gurov told her that he was a native of Moscow, that he had studied languages and literature at the university, but had a post in a bank; that at one time he had trained to become an opera singer but had given it up, that he owned two houses in Moscow. And he learned from her that she had grown up in Petersburg, but had lived in S—— since her marriage two years previously, that she was going to stay in Yalta for about another month, and that her husband, who needed a rest, too, might perhaps come to fetch her. She was not certain whether her husband was a member of a Government Board or served on a Zemstvo Council,° and this amused her. And Gurov learned too that her name was Anna Sergeyevna.

Afterwards in his room at the hotel he thought about her — and was certain that he would meet her the next day. It was bound to happen. Getting into bed he recalled that she had been a schoolgirl only recently, doing lessons like his own daughter; he thought how much timidity and angularity there was still in her laugh and her manner of talking with a stranger. It must have been the first time in her life that she was alone in a setting in which she was followed, looked at, and spoken to for one secret purpose alone, which she could hardly fail to guess. He thought of her slim, delicate throat, her lovely gray eyes.

"There's something pathetic about her, though," he thought, and dropped off.

II

20 A week had passed since they had struck up an acquaintance. It was a holiday. It was close indoors, while in the street the wind whirled the dust about and blew people's hats off. One was thirsty all day, and Gurov often went into the restaurant and offered Anna Sergeyevna a soft drink or ice cream. One did not know what to do with oneself.

In the evening when the wind had abated they went out on the pier to watch the steamer come in. There were a great many people walking about the dock; they had come to welcome someone and they were carrying bunches of flowers. And two peculiarities of a festive Yalta crowd stood out: the elderly ladies were dressed like young ones and there were many generals.

Owing to the choppy sea, the steamer arrived late, after sunset, and it was a long time tacking about before it put in at the pier. Anna Sergeyevna peered at the steamer and the passengers through her lorgnette as though looking for acquaintances, and whenever she turned to Gurov her eyes were shining. She talked a great deal and asked questions jerkily, forgetting the next moment what she had asked; then she lost her lorgnette in the crush.

The festive crowd began to disperse; it was now too dark to see people's faces; there was no wind any more, but Gurov and Anna Sergeyevna still stood as though waiting to see someone else come off the steamer. Anna Sergeyevna was silent now, and sniffed her flowers without looking at Gurov.

"The weather has improved this evening," he said. "Where shall we go now? Shall we drive somewhere?"

25 She did not reply.

Then he looked at her intently, and suddenly embraced her and kissed her

Zemstvo Council: A district council.

on the lips, and the moist fragrance of her flowers enveloped him; and at once he looked round him anxiously, wondering if anyone had seen them.

"Let us go to your place," he said softly. And they walked off together rapidly.

The air in her room was close and there was the smell of the perfume she had bought at the Japanese shop. Looking at her, Gurov thought: "What encounters life offers!" From the past he preserved the memory of carefree, good-natured women whom love made gay and who were grateful to him for the happiness he gave them, however brief it might be; and of women like his wife who loved without sincerity, with too many words, affectedly, hysterically, with an expression that it was not love or passion that engaged them but something more significant; and of two or three others, very beautiful, frigid women, across whose faces would suddenly flit a rapacious expression — an obstinate desire to take from life more than it could give, and these were women no longer young, capricious, unreflecting, domineering, unintelligent, and when Gurov grew cold to them their beauty aroused his hatred, and the lace on their lingerie seemed to him to resemble scales.

But here there was the timidity, the angularity of inexperienced youth, a feeling of awkwardness; and there was a sense of embarrassment, as though someone had suddenly knocked at the door. Anna Sergeyevna, "the lady with the pet dog," treated what had happened in a peculiar way, very seriously, as though it were her fall — so it seemed, and this was odd and inappropriate. Her features drooped and faded, and her long hair hung down sadly on either side of her face; she grew pensive and her dejected pose was that of a Magdalene in a picture by an old master.

"It's not right," she said. "You don't respect me now, you first of all."

There was a watermelon on the table. Gurov cut himself a slice and began eating it without haste. They were silent for at least half an hour.

There was something touching about Anna Sergeyevna; she had the purity of a well-bred, naive woman who has seen little of life. The single candle burning on the table barely illumined her face, yet it was clear that she was unhappy.

"Why should I stop respecting you, darling?" asked Gurov. "You don't know what you're saying."

"God forgive me," she said, and her eyes filled with tears. "It's terrible."

"It's as though you were trying to exonerate yourself."

"How can I exonerate myself? No. I am a bad, low woman; I despise myself and I have no thought of exonerating myself. It's not my husband but myself I have deceived. And not only just now; I have been deceiving myself for a long time. My husband may be a good, honest man, but he is a flunkey! I don't know what he does, what his work is, but I know he is a flunkey! I was twenty when I married him. I was tormented by curiosity; I wanted something better. 'There must be a different sort of life,' I said to myself. I wanted to live! To live, to live! Curiosity kept eating at me — you don't understand it, but I swear to God I could no longer control myself; something was going on in me: I could not be held back. I told my husband I was ill, and came here. And here I have been walking about as though in a daze, as though I were mad; and now I have become a vulgar, vile woman whom anyone may despise."

Gurov was already bored with her; he was irritated by her naive tone, by her repentance, so unexpected and so out of place; but for the tears in her eyes he might have thought she was joking or play-acting.

"I don't understand, my dear," he said softly. "What do you want?"

She hid her face on his breast and pressed close to him.

"Believe me, believe me, I beg you," she said, "I love honesty and purity, and sin is loathsome to me; I don't know what I'm doing. Simple people say, 'The Evil One has led me astray.' And I may say of myself now that the Evil One has led me astray."

"Quiet, quiet," he murmured.

He looked into her fixed, frightened eyes, kissed her, spoke to her softly and affectionately, and by degrees she calmed down, and her gaiety returned; both began laughing.

Afterwards when they went out there was not a soul on the esplanade. The town with its cypresses looked quite dead, but the sea was still sounding as it broke upon the beach; a single launch was rocking on the waves and on it a lantern was blinking sleepily.

They found a cab and drove to Oreanda.

"I found out your surname in the hall just now: it was written on the board — von Dideritz," said Gurov. "Is your husband German?"

"No; I believe his grandfather was German, but he is Greek Orthodox himself."

At Oreanda they sat on a bench not far from the church, looked down at the sea, and were silent. Yalta was barely visible through the morning mist; white clouds rested motionlessly on the mountaintops. The leaves did not stir on the trees, cicadas twanged, and the monotonous muffled sound of the sea that rose from below spoke of the peace, the eternal sleep awaiting us. So it rumbled below when there was no Yalta, no Oreanda here; so it rumbles now, and it will rumble as indifferently and as hollowly when we are no more. And in this constancy, in this complete indifference to the life and death of each of us, there lies, perhaps, a pledge of our eternal salvation, of the unceasing advance of life upon earth, of unceasing movement towards perfection. Sitting beside a young woman who in the dawn seemed so lovely, Gurov, soothed and spellbound by these magical surroundings — the sea, the mountains, the clouds, the wide sky — thought how everything is really beautiful in this world when one reflects: everything except what we think or do ourselves when we forget the higher aims of life and our own human dignity.

A man strolled up to them — probably a guard — looked at them and walked away. And this detail, too, seemed so mysterious and beautiful. They saw a steamer arrive from Feodosia, its lights extinguished in the glow of dawn.

"There is dew on the grass," said Anna Sergeyevna, after a silence.

"Yes, it's time to go home."

They returned to the city.

Then they met every day at twelve o'clock on the esplanade, lunched and dined together, took walks, admired the sea. She complained that she slept badly, that she had palpitations, asked the same questions, troubled now by jealousy and now by the fear that he did not respect her sufficiently. And often in the square or the public garden, when there was no one near them, he suddenly drew her to him and kissed her passionately. Complete idleness, these kisses in broad daylight exchanged furtively in dread of someone's seeing them, the heat, the smell of the sea, and the continual flitting before his eyes of idle, well-dressed, well-fed people, worked a complete change in him; he kept telling Anna Sergeyevna how beautiful she was, how seductive, was urgently passionate; he would not move a step away from her, while she was often pensive and continually pressed him to confess that he did not respect her, did not love her in the least, and saw in her nothing but a common woman. Almost every evening rather late they drove somewhere out of town, to Oreanda or to the waterfall; and the excursion was always a success, the scenery invariably impressed them as beautiful and magnificent.

They were expecting her husband, but a letter came from him saying that he had eye-trouble, and begging his wife to return home as soon as possible. Anna Sergeyevna made haste to go.

"It's a good thing I am leaving," she said to Gurov. "It's the hand of Fate!"

She took a carriage to the railway station, and he went with her. They were 55
driving the whole day. When she had taken her place in the express, and when the second bell had rung, she said, "Let me look at you once more — let me look at you again. Like this."

She was not crying but was so sad that she seemed ill, and her face was quivering.

"I shall be thinking of you — remembering you," she said. "God bless you; be happy. Don't remember evil against me. We are parting forever — it has to be, for we ought never to have met. Well, God bless you."

The train moved off rapidly, its lights soon vanished, and a minute later there was no sound of it, as though everything had conspired to end as quickly as possible that sweet trance, that madness. Left alone on the platform, and gazing into the dark distance, Gurov listened to the twang of the grasshoppers and the hum of the telegraph wires, feeling as though he had just waked up. And he reflected, musing, that there had now been another episode or adventure in his life, and it, too, was at an end, and nothing was left of it but a memory. He was moved, sad, and slightly remorseful: this young woman whom he would never meet again had not been happy with him; he had been warm and affectionate with her, but yet in his manner, his tone, and his caresses there had been a shade of light irony, the slightly coarse arrogance of a happy male who was, besides, almost twice her age. She had constantly called him kind, exceptional, high-minded; obviously he had seemed to her different from what he really was, so he had involuntarily deceived her.

Here at the station there was already a scent of autumn in the air; it was a chilly evening.

"It is time for me to go north, too," thought Gurov as he left the platform. 60
"High time!"

III

At home in Moscow the winter routine was already established: the stoves were heated, and in the morning it was still dark when the children were having breakfast and getting ready for school, and the nurse would light the lamp for a short time. There were frosts already. When the first snow falls, on the first day the sleighs are out, it is pleasant to see the white earth, the white roofs; one draws easy, delicious breaths, and the season brings back the days of one's youth. The old limes and birches, white with hoar-frost, have a good-natured look; they are closer to one's heart than cypresses and palms, and near them one no longer wants to think of mountains and the sea.

Gurov, a native of Moscow, arrived there on a fine frosty day, and when he put on his fur coat and warm gloves and took a walk along Petrovka, and when on Saturday night he heard the bells ringing, his recent trip and the places he had visited lost all charm for him. Little by little he became immersed in Moscow life, greedily read three newspapers a day, and declared that he did not read the Moscow papers on principle. He already felt a longing for restaurants, clubs, formal dinners, anniversary celebrations, and it flattered him to entertain distinguished lawyers and actors, and to play cards with a professor at the physicians' club. He could eat a whole portion of meat stewed with pickled cabbage and served in a pan, Moscow style.

A month or so would pass and the image of Anna Sergeyevna, it seemed to him, would become misty in his memory, and only from time to time he would dream of her with her touching smile as he dreamed of others. But more than a month went by, winter came into its own, and everything was still clear in his memory as though he had parted from Anna Sergeyevna only yesterday. And his memories glowed more and more vividly. When in the evening stillness the voices of his children preparing their lessons reached his study, or when he listened to a song or to an organ playing in a restaurant, or when the storm howled in the chimney, suddenly everything would rise up in his memory: what had happened on the pier and the early morning with the mist on the mountains, and the steamer coming from Feodosia, and the kisses. He would pace about his room a long time, remembering and smiling; then his memories passed into reveries, and in his imagination the past would mingle with what was to come. He did not dream of Anna Sergeyevna, but she followed him about everywhere and watched him. When he shut his eyes he saw her before him as though she were there in the flesh; and she seemed to him lovelier, younger, tenderer than she had been, and he imagined himself a finer man than he had been in Yalta. Of evenings she peered out at him from the bookcase, from the fireplace, from the corner — he heard her breathing, the caressing rustle of her clothes. In the street he followed the women with his eyes, looking for someone who resembled her.

Already he was tormented by a strong desire to share his memories with someone. But in his home it was impossible to talk of his love, and he had no one to talk to outside; certainly he could not confide in his tenants or in anyone at the bank. And what was there to talk about? He hadn't loved her then, had he? Had there been anything beautiful, poetical, edifying, or simply interesting in his relations with Anna Sergeyevna? And he was forced to talk vaguely of love, of women, and no one guessed what he meant; only his wife would twitch her black eyebrows and say, "The part of a philanderer does not suit you at all, Dimitry."

One evening, coming out of the physicians' club with an official with whom 65
he had been playing cards, he could not resist saying:

"If you only knew what a fascinating woman I became acquainted with at Yalta!"

The official got into his sledge and was driving away, but turned suddenly and shouted: "Dmitry Dmitrich!"

"What is it?"

"You were right this evening: the sturgeon was a bit high."

These words, so commonplace, for some reason moved Gurov to indignation, and struck him as degrading and unclean. What savage manners, what mugs! What stupid nights, what dull, humdrum days! Frenzied gambling, gluttony, drunkenness, continual talk always about the same things! Futile pursuits and conversations always about the same topics take up the better part of one's time, the better part of one's strength, and in the end there is left a life clipped and wingless, an absurd mess, and there is no escaping or getting away from it— just as though one were in a madhouse or a prison.

Gurov, boiling with indignation, did not sleep all night. And he had a headache all the next day. And the following nights too he slept badly; he sat up in bed, thinking, or paced up and down his room. He was fed up with his children, fed up with the bank; he had no desire to go anywhere or to talk of anything.

In December during the holidays he prepared to take a trip and told his wife he was going to Petersburg to do what he could for a young friend—and he set off for S—— What for? He did not know, himself. He wanted to see Anna Sergeyevna and talk with her, to arrange a rendezvous if possible.

He arrived at S—— in the morning, and at the hotel took the best room, in which the floor was covered with gray army cloth, and on the table there was an inkstand, gray with dust and topped by a figure on horseback, its hat in its raised hand and its head broken off. The porter gave him the necessary information: von Dideritz lived in a house of his own on Staro-Goncharnaya Street, not far from the hotel: he was rich and lived well and kept his own horses; everyone in the town knew him. The porter pronounced the name: "Dridiritz."

Without haste Gurov made his way to Staro-Goncharnaya Street and found the house. Directly opposite the house stretched a long gray fence studded with nails.

"A fence like that would make one run away," thought Gurov, looking now at the fence, now at the windows of the house.

He reflected: this was a holiday, and the husband was apt to be at home. And in any case, it would be tactless to go into the house and disturb her. If he were to send her a note, it might fall into her husband's hands, and that might spoil everything. The best thing was to rely on chance. And he kept walking up and down the street and along the fence, waiting for the chance. He saw a beggar go in at the gate and heard the dogs attack him; then an hour later he heard a piano, and the sound came to him faintly and indistinctly. Probably it was Anna Sergeyevna playing. The front door opened suddenly, and an old woman came out, followed by the familiar white Pomeranian. Gurov was on the point of calling to the dog, but his heart began beating violently, and in his excitement he could not remember the Pomeranian's name.

He kept walking up and down, and hated the gray fence more and more, and by now he thought irritably that Anna Sergeyevna had forgotten him, and was perhaps already diverting herself with another man, and that that was very natural in a young woman who from morning till night had to look at that damn fence. He went back to his hotel room and sat on the couch for a long while, not knowing what to do, then he had dinner and a long nap.

"How stupid and annoying all this is!" he thought when he woke and looked at the dark windows: it was already evening. "Here I've had a good sleep for some reason. What am I going to do at night?"

He sat on the bed, which was covered with a cheap gray blanket of the kind seen in hospitals, and he twitted himself in his vexation:

"So there's your lady with the pet dog. There's your adventure. A nice place to cool your heels in."

That morning at the station a playbill in large letters had caught his eye. *The Geisha* was to be given for the first time. He thought of this and drove to the theater.

"It's quite possible that she goes to first nights," he thought.

The theater was full. As in all provincial theaters, there was a haze above the chandelier, the gallery was noisy and restless; in the front row, before the beginning of the performance the local dandies were standing with their hands clasped behind their backs; in the Governor's box the Governor's daughter, wearing a boa, occupied the front seat, while the Governor himself hid modestly behind the portiere and only his hands were visible; the curtain swayed; the orchestra was a long time tuning up. While the audience were coming in and taking their seats, Gurov scanned the faces eagerly.

Anna Sergeyevna, too, came in. She sat down in the third row, and when Gurov looked at her his heart contracted, and he understood clearly that in the whole world there was no human being so near, so precious, and so important to him; she, this little, undistinguished woman, lost in a provincial crowd, with a vulgar lorgnette in her hand, filled his whole life now, was his sorrow and his joy, the only happiness that he now desired for himself, and to the sounds of the bad orchestra, of the miserable local violins, he thought how lovely she was. He thought and dreamed.

A young man with small side-whiskers, very tall and stooped, came in with Anna Sergeyevna and sat down beside her; he nodded his head at every step and seemed to be bowing continually. Probably this was the husband whom at Yalta, in an access of bitter feeling, she had called a flunkey. And there really was in his lanky figure, his side-whiskers, his small bald patch, something of a flunkey's retiring manner; his smile was mawkish, and in his buttonhole there was an academic badge like a waiter's number.

During the first intermission the husband went out to have a smoke; she remained in her seat. Gurov, who was also sitting in the orchestra, went up to her and said in a shaky voice, with a forced smile:

"Good evening!"

She glanced at him and turned pale, then looked at him again in horror, unable to believe her eyes, and gripped the fan and the lorgnette tightly together in her hands, evidently trying to keep herself from fainting. Both were silent. She was sitting, he was standing, frightened by her distress and not daring to take a seat beside her. The violins and the flute that were being tuned up sang out. He suddenly felt frightened: it seemed as if all the people in the boxes were looking at them. She got up and went hurriedly to the exit; he followed her, and both of them walked blindly along the corridors and up and down stairs, and figures in the uniforms prescribed for magistrates, teachers, and officials of the Department of Crown Lands, all wearing badges, flitted before their eyes, as did also ladies, and fur coats on hangers; they were conscious of drafts and the smell of stale tobacco. And Gurov, whose heart was beating violently, thought:

"Oh, Lord! Why are these people here and this orchestra!"

90 And at that instant he suddenly recalled how when he had seen Anna Sergeyevna off at the station he had said to himself that all was over between them and that they would never meet again. But how distant the end still was!

On the narrow, gloomy staircase over which it said "To the Amphitheatre," she stopped.

"How you frightened me!" she said, breathing hard, still pale and stunned. "Oh, how you frightened me! I am barely alive. Why did you come? Why?"

"But do understand, Anna, do understand — " he said hurriedly, under his breath. "I implore you, do understand — "

She looked at him with fear, with entreaty, with love; she looked at him intently, to keep his features more distinctly in her memory.

95 "I suffer so," she went on, not listening to him. "All this time I have been thinking of nothing but you; I live only by the thought of you. And I wanted to forget, to forget; but why, oh, why have you come?"

On the landing above them two high school boys were looking down and smoking, but it was all the same to Gurov; he drew Anna Sergeyevna to him and began kissing her face and her hands.

"What are you doing, what are you doing!" she was saying in horror, pushing him away. "We have lost our senses. Go away today; go away at once — I conjure you by all that is sacred, I implore you — People are coming this way!"

Someone was walking up the stairs.

"You must leave," Anna Sergeyevna went on in a whisper. "Do you hear, Dmitry Dmitrich? I will come and see you in Moscow. I have never been happy; I am unhappy now, and I never, never shall be happy, never! So don't make me suffer still more! I swear I'll come to Moscow. But now let us part. My dear, good, precious one, let us part!"

100 She pressed his hand and walked rapidly downstairs, turning to look round at him, and from her eyes he could see that she really was unhappy. Gurov stood for a while, listening, then when all grew quiet, he found his coat and left the theater.

IV

And Anna Sergeyevna began coming to see him in Moscow. Once every two or three months she left S——, telling her husband that she was going to consult a doctor about a woman's ailment from which she was suffering — and her husband did and did not believe her. When she arrived in Moscow she would stop at the Slavyansky Bazar Hotel, and at once send a man in a red cap to Gurov. Gurov came to see her, and no one in Moscow knew of it.

Once he was going to see her in this way on a winter morning (the messenger had come the evening before and not found him in). With him walked his daughter, whom he wanted to take to school: it was on the way. Snow was coming down in big wet flakes.

"It's three degrees above zero,° and yet it's snowing," Gurov was saying to his daughter. "But this temperature prevails only on the surface of the earth; in the upper layers of the atmosphere there is quite a different temperature."

"And why doesn't it thunder in winter, papa?"

He explained that, too. He talked, thinking all the while that he was on his way to a rendezvous, and no living soul knew of it, and probably no one would ever know. He had two lives: an open one, seen and known by all who needed to know it, full of conventional truth and conventional falsehood, exactly like the lives of his friends and acquaintances; and another life that went on in secret. And through some strange, perhaps accidental, combination of circumstances, everything that was of interest and importance to him, everything that was essential to him, everything about which he felt sincerely and did not deceive himself, everything that constituted the core of his life, was going on concealed from others; while all that was false, the shell in which he hid to cover the truth — his work at the bank, for instance, his discussions at the club, his references to the "inferior race," his appearances at anniversary celebrations with his wife — all that went on in the open. Judging others by himself, he did not believe what he saw, and always fancied that every man led his real, most interesting life under cover of secrecy as under cover of night. The personal life of every individual is based on secrecy, and perhaps it is partly for that reason that civilized man is so nervously anxious that personal privacy should be respected.

Having taken his daughter to school, Gurov went on to the Slavyansky Bazar Hotel. He took off his fur coat in the lobby, went upstairs, and knocked gently at the door. Anna Sergeyevna, wearing his favorite gray dress, exhausted by the journey and by waiting, had been expecting him since the previous evening. She was pale, and looked at him without a smile, and he had hardly entered when she flung herself on his breast. Their kiss was a long, lingering one, as though they had not seen one another for two years.

"Well, darling, how are you getting on there?" he asked. "What news?"

"Wait; I'll tell you in a moment — I can't speak."

She could not speak; she was crying. She turned away from him, and pressed her handkerchief to her eyes.

"Let her have her cry; meanwhile I'll sit down," he thought, and he seated himself in an armchair.

Then he rang and ordered tea, and while he was having his tea she remained standing at the window with her back to him. She was crying out of sheer agitation, in the sorrowful consciousness that their life was so sad; that they could only see each other in secret and had to hide from people like thieves! Was it not a broken life?

"Come, stop now, dear!" he said.

It was plain to him that this love of theirs would not be over soon, that the end of it was not in sight. Anna Sergeyevna was growing more and more attached to him. She adored him, and it was unthinkable to tell her that their love was bound to come to an end some day; besides, she would not have believed it!

three degrees above zero: On the Celsius scale; about thirty-eight degrees Fahrenheit.

He went up to her and took her by the shoulders, to fondle her and say something diverting, and at that moment he caught sight of himself in the mirror.

His hair was already beginning to turn gray. And it seemed odd to him that he had grown so much older in the last few years, and lost his looks. The shoulders on which his hands rested were warm and heaving. He felt compassion for this life, still so warm and lovely, but probably already about to begin to fade and wither like his own. Why did she love him so much? He always seemed to women different from what he was, and they loved in him not himself, but the man whom their imagination created and whom they had been eagerly seeking all their lives; and afterwards, when they saw their mistake, they loved him nevertheless. And not one of them had been happy with him. In the past he had met women, come together with them, parted from them, but he had never once loved; it was anything you please, but not love. And only now when his head was gray he had fallen in love, really, truly — for the first time in his life.

Anna Sergeyevna and he loved each other as people do who are very close and intimate, like man and wife, like tender friends; it seemed to them that Fate itself had meant them for one another, and they could not understand why he had a wife and she a husband; and it was as though they were a pair of migratory birds, male and female, caught and forced to live in different cages. They forgave each other what they were ashamed of in their past, they forgave everything in the present, and felt that this love of theirs had altered them both.

Formerly in moments of sadness he had soothed himself with whatever logical arguments came into his head, but now he no longer cared for logic; he felt profound compassion, he wanted to be sincere and tender.

"Give it up now, my darling," he said. "You've had your cry; that's enough. Let us have a talk now, we'll think up something."

Then they spent a long time taking counsel together, they talked of how to avoid the necessity for secrecy, for deception, for living in different cities, and not seeing one another for long stretches of time. How could they free themselves from these intolerable fetters?

"How? How?" he asked, clutching his head. "How?"

And it seemed as though in a little while the solution would be found, and then a new and glorious life would begin; and it was clear to both of them that the end was still far off, and that what was to be most complicated and difficult for them was only just beginning.

Considerations

1. Why is it significant that the setting of this story is a resort town? How does the vacation atmosphere affect the action?
2. What does Gurov's view of women reveal about him? Why does he regard them as an "inferior race"?
3. What do we learn about Gurov's wife and Anna's husband? Why do you think Chekhov includes this exposition? How does it affect our view of the lovers?
4. When and why do Gurov's feelings about Anna begin to change? Is he really in love with her?
5. Who or what is the antagonist in this story? What is the nature of the conflict?

6. What is the effect of Gurov being the central consciousness? How would the story be different if it were told from Anna's perspective?
7. Why do you think Chekhov does not report what ultimately becomes of the lovers? Is there a resolution to the conflict? Is the ending of the story effective?
8. Discuss the validity of Gurov's belief that people lead their real lives in private rather than in public: "The personal life of every individual is based on secrecy, and perhaps it is partly for that reason that civilized man is so nervously anxious that personal privacy should be respected."
9. Describe your response to Gurov in Parts I and II, and discuss how your judgment of him changes in the last two parts of the story.
10. Based on your understanding of the characterizations of Gurov and Anna, consider the final paragraph of the story and summarize what you think will happen to them.
11. Consider the following assessment of the story: "No excuses can be made for the lovers' adulterous affair. They behave selfishly and irresponsibly. They are immoral — and so is the story." Explain what you think Chekhov's response to this view would be, given his treatment of the lovers.

PERSPECTIVE

ANTON CHEKHOV (1860–1904)

On Morality in Fiction 1890

You abuse me for objectivity, calling it indifference to good and evil, lack of ideals and ideas, and so on. You would have me, when I describe horse-thieves, say: "Stealing horses is an evil." But that has been known for ages without my saying so. Let the jury judge them; it's my job simply to show what sort of people they are. I write: You are dealing with horse-thieves, so let me tell you that they are not beggars but well-fed people, that they are people of a special cult, and that horse-stealing is not simply theft but a passion. Of course it would be pleasant to combine art with a sermon, but for me personally it is extremely difficult and almost impossible, owing to the conditions of technique. You see, to depict horse-thieves in seven hundred lines I must all the time speak and think in their tone and feel in their spirit, otherwise, if I introduce subjectivity, the image becomes blurred and the story will not be as compact as all short stories ought to be. When I write, I reckon entirely upon the reader to add for himself the subjective elements that are lacking in the story.

From a letter to Aleksey S. Suvorin in *Letters on the Short Story, the Drama, and Other Literary Topics by Anton Chekhov*

Considerations

1. Why does Chekhov reject sermonizing in his fiction?
2. How does his "objectivity" affect your reading of "The Lady with the Pet Dog"?
3. Compare and contrast Chekhov's views with Thomas Jefferson's belief that fiction should offer "sound morality" (p. 470).

JOYCE CAROL OATES (b. 1938)

Raised in New York, Joyce Carol Oates earned degrees at Syracuse University and the University of Wisconsin. Both the range and volume of her writing are extensive. A writer of novels, plays, short stories, poetry, and literary criticism, she has published some forty books. Oates has described the subject matter of her fiction as "real people in a real society," but her method of expression ranges from the realistic to the experimental. Her more recent novels include *them* (1969), *Do with Me What You Will* (1973), *Childwold* (1976), *Bellefleur* (1980), *A Bloodsmoor Romance* (1982), *Marya: A Life* (1986), and *You Must Remember This* (1987). Among her collections of short stories are *Raven's Wing* (1986) and *Marriages and Infidelities* (1972), which includes "The Lady with the Pet Dog." This story is her modern version of the Chekhov story of the same name, this time told from the woman's perspective.

The Lady with the Pet Dog 1972

I

Strangers parted as if to make way for him.

There he stood. He was there in the aisle, a few yards away, watching her.

She leaned forward at once in her seat, her hand jerked up to her face as if to ward off a blow — but then the crowd in the aisle hid him, he was gone. She pressed both hands against her cheeks. He was not here, she had imagined him.

"My God," she whispered.

She was alone. Her husband had gone out to the foyer to make a telephone 5
call; it was intermission at the concert, a Thursday evening.

Now she saw him again, clearly. He was standing there. He was staring at her. Her blood rocked in her body, draining out of her head . . . she was going to faint . . . They stared at each other. They gave no sign of recognition. Only when he took a step forward did she shake her head *no — no — keep away.* It was not possible.

When her husband returned, she was staring at the place in the aisle where her lover had been standing. Her husband leaned forward to interrupt that stare.

"What's wrong?" he said. "Are you sick?"

Panic rose in her in long shuddering waves. She tried to get to her feet, panicked at the thought of fainting here, and her husband took hold of her. She stood like an aged woman, clutching the seat before her.

At home he helped her up the stairs and she lay down. Her head was like 10
a large piece of crockery that had to be held still, it was so heavy. She was still panicked. She felt it in the shallows of her face, behind her knees, in the pit of her stomach. It sickened her, it made her think of mucus, of something thick

and gray congested inside her, stuck to her, that was herself and yet not herself — a poison.

She lay with her knees drawn up toward her chest, her eyes hotly open, while her husband spoke to her. She imagined that other man saying, *Why did you run away from me?* Her husband was saying other words. She tried to listen to them. He was going to call the doctor, he said, and she tried to sit up. "No, I'm all right now," she said quickly. The panic was like lead inside her, so thickly congested. How slow love was to drain out of her, how fluid and sticky it was inside her head!

Her husband believed her. No doctor. No threat. Grateful, she drew her husband down to her. They embraced, not comfortably. For years now they had not been comfortable together, in their intimacy and at a distance, and now they struggled gently as if the paces of this dance were too rigorous for them. It was something they might have known once, but had now outgrown. The panic in her thickened at this double betrayal: she drew her husband to her, she caressed him wildly, she shut her eyes to think about that other man.

A crowd of men and women parting, unexpectedly, and there he stood — there he stood — she kept seeing him, and yet her vision blotched at the memory. It had been finished between them, six months before, but he had come out here . . . and she had escaped him, now she was lying in her husband's arms, in his embrace, her face pressed against his. It was a kind of sleep, this love-making. She felt herself falling asleep, her body falling from her. Her eyes shut.

"I love you," her husband said fiercely, angrily.

She shut her eyes and thought of that other man, as if betraying him would give her life a center.

"Did I hurt you? Are you — ?" Her husband whispered.

Always this hot flashing of shame between them, the shame of her husband's near failure, the clumsiness of his love —

"You didn't hurt me," she said.

II

They had said good-by six months before. He drove her from Nantucket, where they had met, to Albany, New York, where she visited her sister. The hours of intimacy in the car had sealed something between them, a vow of silence and impersonality: she recalled the movement of the highways, the passing of other cars, the natural rhythms of the day hypnotizing her toward sleep while he drove. She trusted him, she could sleep in his presence. Yet she could not really fall asleep in spite of her exhaustion, and she kept jerking awake, frightened, to discover that nothing had changed — still the stranger who was driving her to Albany, still the highway, the sky, the antiseptic odor of the rented car, the sense of a rhythm behind the rhythm of the air that might unleash itself at any second. Everywhere on this highway, at this moment, there were men and women driving together, bonded together — what did that mean, to be together? What did it mean to enter into a bond with another person?

No, she did not really trust him; she did not really trust men. He would glance at her with his small cautious smile and she felt a declaration of shame between them.

Shame.

In her head she rehearsed conversations. She said bitterly, "You'll be relieved when we get to Albany. Relieved to get rid of me." They had spent so many days talking, confessing too much, driven to a pitch of childish excitement, laughing together on the beach, breaking into that pose of laughter that seems to eradicate the soul, so many days of this that the silence of the trip was like the silence of a hospital — all these surface noises, these rattles and hums, but an interior silence, a befuddlement. She said to him in her imagination, "One of us should die." Then she leaned over to touch him. She caressed the back of his neck. She said, aloud, "Would you like me to drive for a while?"

They stopped at a picnic area where other cars were stopped — couples, families — and walked together, smiling at their good luck. He put his arm around her shoulders and she sensed how they were in a posture together, a man and a woman forming a posture, a figure, that someone might sketch and show to them. She said slowly, "I don't want to go back. . . ."

Silence. She looked up at him. His face was heavy with her words, as if she had pulled at his skin with her fingers. Children ran nearby and distracted him — yes, he was a father too, his children ran like that, they tugged at his skin with their light, busy fingers.

"Are you so unhappy?" he said.

"I'm not unhappy, back there. I'm nothing. There's nothing to me," she said.

They stared at each other. The sensation between them was intense, exhausting. She thought that this man was her savior, that he had come to her at a time in her life when her life demanded completion, an end, a permanent fixing of all that was troubled and shifting and deadly. And yet it was absurd to think this. No person could save another. So she drew back from him and released him.

A few hours later they stopped at a gas station in a small city. She went to the women's rest room, having to ask the attendant for a key, and when she came back her eye jumped nervously onto the rented car — why? did she think he might have driven off without her? — onto the man, her friend, standing in conversation with the young attendant. Her friend was as old as her husband, over forty, with lanky, sloping shoulders, a full body, his hair thick, a dark, burnished brown, a festive color that made her eye twitch a little — and his hands were always moving, always those rapid conversational circles, going nowhere, gestures that were at once a little aggressive and apologetic.

She put her hand on his arm, a claim. He turned to her and smiled and she felt that she loved him, that everything in her life had forced her to this moment and that she had no choice about it.

They sat in the car for two hours, in Albany, in the parking lot of a Howard Johnson's restaurant, talking, trying to figure out their past. There was no future. They concentrated on the past, the several days behind them, lit up with a hot, dazzling August sun, like explosions that already belonged to other people, to strangers. Her face was faintly reflected in the green-tinted curve of the windshield, but she could not have recognized that face. She began to cry; she told herself: *I am not here, this will pass, this is nothing.* Still, she could not stop crying. The muscles of her face were springy, like a child's, unpredictable muscles. He stroked her arms, her shoulders, trying to comfort her. "This is so hard . . . this is impossible . . ." he said. She felt panic for the world outside this car, all that was not herself and this man, and at the same time she understood that she was free of him, as people are free of other people, she would leave him soon, safely, and within a few days he would have fallen into the past, the impersonal past. . . .

"I'm so ashamed of myself!" she said finally.

She returned to her husband and saw that another woman, a shadow-woman, had taken her place — noiseless and convincing, like a dancer performing certain difficult steps. Her husband folded her in his arms and talked to her of his own loneliness, his worries about his business, his health, his mother, kept tranquilized and mute in a nursing home, and her spirit detached itself from her and drifted about the rooms of the large house she lived in with her husband, a shadow-woman delicate and imprecise. There was no boundary to her, no edge. Alone, she took hot baths and sat exhausted in the steaming water, wondering at her perpetual exhaustion. All that winter she noticed the limp, languid weight of her arms, her veins bulging slightly with the pressure of her extreme weariness. *This is fate,* she thought, to be here and not there, to be one person and not another, a certain man's wife and not the wife of another man. The long, slow pain of this certainty rose in her, but it never became clear, it was baffling and imprecise. She could not be serious about it; she kept congratulating herself on her own good luck, to have escaped so easily, to have freed herself. So much love had gone into the first several years of her marriage that there wasn't much left, now, for another man. . . . She was certain of that. But the bath water made her dizzy, all that perpetual heat, and one day in January she drew a razor blade lightly across the inside of her arm, near the elbow, to see what would happen.

Afterward she wrapped a small towel around it, to stop the bleeding. The towel soaked through. She wrapped a bath towel around that and walked through the empty rooms of her home, lightheaded, hardly aware of the stubborn seeping of blood. There was no boundary to her in this house, no precise limit. She could flow out like her own blood and come to no end.

She sat for a while on a blue love seat, her mind empty. Her husband telephoned her when he would be staying late at the plant. He talked to her always about his plans, his problems, his business friends, his future. It was obvious that he had a future. As he spoke she nodded to encourage him, and her heartbeat quickened with the memory of her own, personal shame, the shame of this man's particular, private wife. One evening at dinner he leaned forward and put his head in his arms and fell asleep, like a child. She sat at the table with him for a while, watching him. His hair had gone gray, almost white, at the temples — no one would guess that he was so quick, so careful a man, still fairly young about the eyes. She put her hand on his head, lightly, as if to prove to herself that he was real. He slept, exhausted.

One evening they went to a concert and she looked up to see her lover 35
there, in the crowded aisle, in this city, watching her. He was standing there, with his overcoat on, watching her. She went cold. That morning the telephone

had rung while her husband was still home, and she had heard him answer it, heard him hang up — it must have been a wrong number — and when the telephone rang again, at 9:30, she had been afraid to answer it. She had left home to be out of the range of that ringing, but now, in this public place, in this busy auditorium, she found herself staring at that man, unable to make any sign to him, any gesture of recognition. . . .

He would have come to her but she shook her head. *No. Stay away.*

Her husband helped her out of the row of seats, saying, "Excuse us, please. Excuse us," so that strangers got to their feet, quickly, alarmed, to let them pass. Was that woman about to faint? What was wrong?

At home she felt the blood drain slowly back into her head. Her husband embraced her hips, pressing his face against her, in that silence that belonged to the earliest days of their marriage. She thought, *He will drive it out of me.* He made love to her and she was back in the auditorium again, sitting alone, now that the concert was over. The stage was empty; the heavy velvet curtains had not been drawn; the musicians' chairs were empty, everything was silent and expectant; in the aisle her lover stood and smiled at her — Her husband was impatient. He was apart from her, working on her, operating on her; and then, stricken, he whispered, "Did I hurt you?"

The telephone rang the next morning. Dully, sluggishly, she answered it. She recognized his voice at once — that "Anna?" with its lifting of the second syllable, questioning and apologetic and making its claim — "Yes, what do you want?" she said.

"Just to see you. Please — "

"I can't."

"Anna, I'm sorry, I didn't mean to upset you — "

"I can't see you."

"Just for a few minutes — I have to talk to you — "

"But why, why now? Why now?" she said.

She heard her voice rising, but she could not stop it. He began to talk again, drowning her out. She remembered his rapid conversation. She remembered his gestures, the witty energetic circling of his hands.

"Please don't hang up!" he cried.

"I can't — I don't want to go through it again — "

"I'm not going to hurt you. Just tell me how you are."

"Everything is the same."

"Everything is the same with me."

She looked up at the ceiling, shyly. "Your wife? Your children?"

"The same."

"Your son?"

"He's fine — "

"I'm so glad to hear that. I — "

"Is it still the same with you, your marriage? Tell me what you feel. What are you thinking?"

"I don't know. . . ."

She remembered his intense, eager words, the movement of his hands, that impatient precise fixing of the air by his hands, the jabbing of his fingers.

"Do you love me?" he said.

She could not answer.

"I'll come over to see you," he said.

"No," she said.

What will come next, what will happen?

Flesh hardening on his body, aging. Shrinking. He will grow old, but not soft like her husband. They are two different types: he is nervous, lean, energetic, wise. She will grow thinner, as the tension radiates out from her backbone, wearing down her flesh. Her collarbones will jut out of her skin. Her husband, caressing her in their bed, will discover that she is another woman — she is not there with him — instead she is rising in an elevator in a downtown hotel, carrying a book as a prop, or walking quickly away from that hotel, her head bent and filled with secrets. Love, what to do with it? . . . Useless as moths' wings, as moths' fluttering. . . . She feels the flutterings of silky, crazy wings in her chest.

He flew out to visit her every several weeks, staying at a different hotel each time. He telephoned her, and she drove down to park in an underground garage at the very center of the city.

She lay in his arms while her husband talked to her, miles away, one body fading into another. He will grow old, his body will change, she thought, pressing her cheek against the back of one of these men. If it was her lover, they were in a hotel room: always the propped-up little booklet describing the hotel's many services, with color photographs of its cocktail lounge and dining room and coffee shop. Grow old, leave me, die, go back to your neurotic wife and your sad, ordinary children, she thought, but still her eyes closed gratefully against his skin and she felt how complete their silence was, how they had come to rest in each other.

"Tell me about your life here. The people who love you," he said, as he always did.

One afternoon they lay together for four hours. It was her birthday and she was intoxicated with her good fortune, this prize of the afternoon, this man in her arms! She was a little giddy, she talked too much. She told him about her parents, about her husband. . . . "They were all people I believed in, but it turned out wrong. Now, I believe in you. . . ." He laughed as if shocked by her words. She did not understand. Then she understood. "But I believe truly in you. I can't think of myself without you," she said. . . . He spoke of his wife, her ambitions, her intelligence, her use of the children against him, her use of his younger son's blindness, all of his words gentle and hypnotic and convincing in the late afternoon peace of this hotel room . . . and she felt the terror of laughter, threatening laughter. Their words, like their bodies, were aging.

She dressed quickly in the bathroom, drawing her long hair up around the back of her head, fixing it as always, anxious that everything be the same. Her face was slightly raw, from his face. The rubbing of his skin. Her eyes were too bright, wearily bright. Her hair was blond but not so blond as it had been that summer in the white Nantucket air.

She ran water and splashed it on her face. She blinked at the water. Blind. Drowning. She thought with satisfaction that soon, soon, he would be back home, in that house on Long Island she had never seen, with that woman she had never seen, sitting on the edge of another bed, putting on his shoes. She wanted nothing except to be free of him. Why not be free? *Oh,* she thought suddenly, *I will follow you back and kill you. You and her and the little boy. What is there to stop me?*

She left him. Everyone on the street pitied her, that look of absolute zero.

III

A man and a child, approaching her. The sharp acrid smell of fish. The crashing of waves. Anna pretended not to notice the father with his son — there was something strange about them. That frank, silent intimacy, too gentle, the man's bare feet in the water and the boy a few feet away, leaning away from his father. He was about nine years old and still his father held his hand.

A small yipping dog, a golden dog, bounded near them.

Anna turned shyly back to her reading; she did not want to have to speak to these neighbors. She saw the man's shadow falling over her legs, then over the pages of her book, and she had the idea that he wanted to see what she was reading. The dog nuzzled her; the man called him away.

She watched them walk down the beach. She was relieved that the man had not spoken to her.

She saw them in town later that day, the two of them brown-haired and patient, now wearing sandals, walking with that same look of care. The man's white shorts were soiled and a little baggy. His pullover shirt was a faded green. His face was broad, the cheekbones wide, spaced widely apart, the eyes stark in their sockets, as if they fastened onto objects for no reason, ponderous and edgy. The little boy's face was pale and sharp; his lips were perpetually parted.

Anna realized that the child was blind.

The next morning, early, she caught sight of them again. For some reason she went to the back door of her cottage. She faced the sea breeze eagerly. Her heart hammered. . . . She had been here, in her family's old house, for three days, alone, bitterly satisfied at being alone, and now it was a puzzle to her how her soul strained to fly outward, to meet with another person. She watched the man with his son, his cautious, rather stooped shoulders above the child's small shoulders.

The man was carrying something, it looked like a notebook. He sat on the sand, not far from Anna's spot of the day before, and the dog rushed up to them. The child approached the edge of the ocean, timidly. He moved in short jerky steps, his legs stiff. The dog ran around him. Anna heard the child crying out a word that sounded like "Ty" — it must have been the dog's name — and then the man joined in, his voice heavy and firm.

"Ty — "

Anna tied her hair back with a yellow scarf and went down to the beach.

The man glanced around at her. He smiled. She stared past him at the waves. To talk to him or not to talk — she had the freedom of that choice. For a moment she felt that she had made a mistake, that the child and the dog would not protect her, that behind this man's ordinary, friendly face there was a certain arrogant maleness — then she relented, she smiled shyly.

"A nice house you've got there," the man said.

She nodded her thanks.

The man pushed his sunglasses up on his forehead. Yes, she recognized the eyes of the day before — intelligent and nervous, the sockets pale, untanned.

"Is that your telephone ringing?" he said.

She did not bother to listen. "It's a wrong number," she said.

Her husband calling: she had left home for a few days, to be alone.

But the man, settling himself on the sand, seemed to misinterpret this. He smiled in surprise, one corner of his mouth higher than the other. He said nothing. Anna wondered: *What is he thinking?* The dog was leaping about her, panting against her legs, and she laughed in embarrassment. She bent to pet it, grateful for its busyness. "Don't let him jump up on you," the man said. "He's a nuisance."

The dog was a small golden retriever, a young dog. The blind child, standing now in the water, turned to call the dog to him. His voice was shrill and impatient.

"Our house is the third one down — the white one," the man said.

She turned, startled. "Oh, did you buy it from Dr. Patrick? Did he die?"

"Yes, finally. . . ."

Her eyes wandered nervously over the child and the dog. She felt the nervous beat of her heart out to the very tips of her fingers, the fleshy tips of her fingers: little hearts were there, pulsing. *What is he thinking?* The man had opened his notebook. He had a piece of charcoal and he began to sketch something.

Anna looked down at him. She saw the top of his head, his thick brown hair, the freckles on his shoulders, the quick, deft movement of his hand. Upside down, Anna herself being drawn. She smiled in surprise.

"Let me draw you. Sit down," he said.

She knelt awkwardly a few yards away. He turned the page of the sketch pad. The dog ran to her and she sat, straightening out her skirt beneath her, flinching from the dog's tongue. "Ty!" cried the child. Anna sat, and slowly the pleasure of the moment began to glow in her; her skin flushed with gratitude.

She sat there for nearly an hour. The man did not talk much. Back and forth the dog bounded, shaking itself. The child came to sit near them, in silence. Anna felt that she was drifting into a kind of trance while the man sketched her, half a dozen rapid sketches, the surface of her face given up to him. "Where are you from?" the man asked.

"Ohio. My husband lives in Ohio."

She wore no wedding band.

"Your wife — " Anna began.

"Yes?"

"Is she here?"

"Not right now."

She was silent, ashamed. She had asked an improper question. But the man did not seem to notice. He continued drawing her, bent over the sketch pad. When Anna said she had to go, he showed her the drawings — one after another of her, Anna, recognizably Anna, a woman in her early thirties, her hair smooth and flat across the top of her head, tied behind by a scarf. "Take the one you like best," he said, and she picked one of her with the dog in her lap, sitting very straight, her brows and eyes clearly defined, her lips girlishly pursed, the dog and her dress suggested by a few quick irregular lines.

"Lady with pet dog," the man said.

She spent the rest of that day reading, nearer her cottage. It was not really a cottage — it was a two-story house, large and ungainly and weathered. It was mixed up in her mind with her family, her own childhood, and she glanced up from her book, perplexed, as if waiting for one of her parents or her sister to come up to her. Then she thought of that man, the man with the blind child, the man with the dog, and she could not concentrate on her reading. Someone — probably her father — had marked a passage that must be important, but she kept reading and rereading it: *We try to discover in things, endeared to us on that account, the spiritual glamour which we ourselves have cast upon them; we are disillusioned, and learn that they are in themselves barren and devoid of the charm that they owed, in our minds, to the association of certain ideas. . . .*

She thought again of the man on the beach. She lay the book aside and thought of him: his eyes, his aloneness, his drawings of her.

110 They began seeing each other after that. He came to her front door in the evening, without the child; he drove her into town for dinner. She was shy and extremely pleased. The darkness of the expensive restaurant released her; she heard herself chatter; she leaned forward and seemed to be offering her face up to him, listening to him. He talked about his work on a Long Island newspaper and she seemed to be listening to him, as she stared at his face, arranging her own face into the expression she had seen in that charcoal drawing. Did he see her like that, then? — girlish and withdrawn and patrician? She felt the weight of his interest in her, a force that fell upon her like a blow. A repeated blow. Of course he was married, he had children — of course she was married, permanently married. This flight from her husband was not important. She had left him before, to be alone, it was not important. Everything in her was slender and delicate and not important.

They walked for hours after dinner, looking at the other strollers, the weekend visitors, the tourists, the couples like themselves. Surely they were mistaken for a couple, a married couple. *This is the hour in which everything is decided,* Anna thought. They had both had several drinks and they talked a great deal. Anna found herself saying too much, stopping and starting giddily. She put her hand to her forehead, feeling faint.

"It's from the sun — you've had too much sun — " he said.

At the door to her cottage, on the front porch, she heard herself asking him if he would like to come in. She allowed him to lead her inside, to close the door. *This is not important,* she thought clearly, *he doesn't mean it, he doesn't love me, nothing will come of it.* She was frightened, yet it seemed to her necessary to give in; she had to leave Nantucket with that act completed, an act of adultery, an accomplishment she would take back to Ohio and to her marriage.

Later, incredibly, she heard herself asking: "Do you . . . do you love me?"

115 "You're so beautiful!" he said, amazed.

She felt this beauty, shy and glowing and centered in her eyes. He stared at her. In this large, drafty house, alone together, they were like accomplices, conspirators. She could not think: how old was she? which year was this? They had done something unforgivable together, and the knowledge of it was tugging at their faces. A cloud seemed to pass over her. She felt herself smiling shrilly.

Afterward, a peculiar raspiness, a dryness of breath. He was silent. She felt a strange, idle fear, a sense of the danger outside this room and this old comfortable bed — a danger that would not recognize her as the lady in that drawing, the lady with the pet dog. There was nothing to say to this man, this stranger. She felt the beauty draining out of her face, her eyes fading.

"I've got to be alone," she told him.

He left, and she understood that she would not see him again. She stood by the window of the room, watching the ocean. A sense of shame overpowered her: it was smeared everywhere on her body, the smell of it, the richness of it. She tried to recall him, and his face was confused in her memory: she would have to shout to him across a jumbled space, she would have to wave her arms wildly. *You love me! You must love me!* But she knew he did not love her, and she did not love him; he was a man who drew everything up into himself, like all men, walking away, free to walk away, free to have his own thoughts, free to envision her body, all the secrets of her body. . . . And she lay down again in the bed, feeling how heavy this body had become, her insides heavy with shame, the very backs of her eyelids coated with shame.

"This is the end of one part of my life," she thought. 120

But in the morning the telephone rang. She answered it. It was her lover: they talked brightly and happily. She could hear the eagerness in his voice, the love in his voice, that same still, sad amazement — she understood how simple life was, there were no problems.

They spent most of their time on the beach, with the child and the dog. He joked and was serious at the same time. He said, once, "You have defined my soul for me," and she laughed to hide her alarm. In a few days it was time for her to leave. He got a sitter for the boy and took the ferry with her to the mainland, then rented a car to drive her up to Albany. She kept thinking: *Now something will happen. It will come to an end.* But most of the drive was silent and hypnotic. She wanted him to joke with her, to say again that she had defined his soul for him, but he drove fast, he was serious, she distrusted the hawkish look of his profile — she did not know him at all. At a gas station she splashed her face with cold water. Alone in the grubby little rest room, shaky and very much alone. In such places are women totally alone with their bodies. The body grows heavier, more evil, in such silence. . . . On the beach everything had been noisy with sunlight and gulls and waves; here, as if run to earth, everything was cramped and silent and dead.

She went outside, squinting. There he was, talking with the station attendant. She could not think as she returned to him whether she wanted to live or not.

She stayed in Albany for a few days, then flew home to her husband. He met her at the airport, near the luggage counter, where her three pieces of pale-brown luggage were brought to him on a conveyer belt, to be claimed by him. He kissed her on the cheek. They shook hands, a little embarrassed. She had come home again.

"How will I live out the rest of my life?" she wondered. 125

In January her lover spied on her: she glanced up and saw him, in a public place, in the DeRoy Symphony Hall. She was paralyzed with fear. She nearly fainted. In this faint she felt her husband's body, loving her, working its love upon her, and she shut her eyes harder to keep out the certainty of his love — sometimes he failed at loving her, sometimes he succeeded, it had nothing to do with her or her pity or her ten years of love for him, it had nothing to do with a woman at all. It was a private act accomplished by a man, a husband, or a lover, in communion with his own soul, his manhood.

Her husband was forty-two years old now, growing slowly into middle age, getting heavier, softer. Her lover was about the same age, narrower in the shoulders, with a full, solid chest, yet lean, nervous. She thought, in her paralysis, of men and how they love freely and eagerly so long as their bodies are capable of love, love for a woman; and then, as love fades in their bodies, it fades from their souls and they become immune and immortal and ready to die.

Her husband was a little rough with her, as if impatient with himself. "I love you," he said fiercely, angrily. And then, ashamed, he said, "Did I hurt you? . . ."

"You didn't hurt me," she said.

Her voice was too shrill for their embrace. 130

While he was in the bathroom she went to her closet and took out that drawing of the summer before. There she was, on the beach at Nantucket, a lady with a pet dog, her eyes large and defined, the dog in her lap hardly more than a few snarls, a few coarse soft lines of charcoal . . . her dress smeared, her arms oddly limp . . . her hands not well drawn at all. . . . She tried to think: did she love the man who had drawn this? did he love her? The fever in her husband's body had touched her and driven her temperature up, and now she stared at the drawing with a kind of lust, fearful of seeing an ugly soul in that woman's face, fearful of seeing the face suddenly through her lover's eyes. She breathed quickly and harshly, staring at the drawing.

And so, the next day, she went to him at his hotel. She wept, pressing against him, demanding of him, "What do you want? Why are you here? Why don't you let me alone?" He told her that he wanted nothing. He expected nothing. He would not cause trouble.

"I want to talk about last August," he said.

"Don't — " she said.

She was hypotized by his gesturing hands, his nervousness, his obvious 135
agitation. He kept saying, "I understand. I'm making no claims upon you."

They became lovers again.

He called room service for something to drink and they sat side by side on his bed, looking through a copy of *The New Yorker,* laughing at the cartoons. It was so peaceful in this room, so complete. They were on a holiday. It was a secret holiday. Four-thirty in the afternoon, on a Friday, an ordinary Friday: a secret holiday.

"I won't bother you again," he said.

He flew back to see her again in March, and in late April. He telephoned her from his hotel — a different hotel each time — and she came down to him at once. She rose to him in various elevators, she knocked on the doors of various rooms, she stepped into his embrace, breathless and guilty and already angry with him, pleading with him. One morning in May, when he telephoned, she pressed her forehead against the doorframe and could not speak. He kept saying, "What's wrong? Can't you talk? Aren't you alone?" She felt that she was going insane. Her head would burst. Why, why did he love her, why did he pursue her? Why did he want her to die?

She went to him in the hotel room. A familiar room: had they been here before? "Everything is repeating itself. Everything is stuck," she said. He framed her face in his hands and said that she looked thinner — was she sick? — what was wrong? She shook herself free. He, her lover, looked about the same. There was a small, angry pimple on his neck. He stared at her, eagerly and suspiciously. Did she bring bad news?

"So you love me? You love me?" she asked.

"Why are you so angry?"

"I want to be free of you. The two of us free of each other."

"That isn't true — you don't want that — "

He embraced her. She was wild with that old, familiar passion for him, her body clinging to his, her arms not strong enough to hold him. Ah, what despair! — what bitter hatred she felt! — she needed this man for her salvation, he was all she had to live for, and yet she could not believe in him. He embraced her thighs, her hips, kissing her, pressing his warm face against her, and yet she could not believe in him, not really. She needed him in order to live, but he was not worth her love, he was not worth her dying. . . . She promised herself this: when she got back home, when she was alone, she would draw the razor more deeply across her arm.

The telephone rang and he answered it: a wrong number.

"Jesus," he said.

They lay together, still. She imagined their posture like this, the two of them one figure, one substance; and outside this room and this bed there was a universe of disjointed, separate things, blank things, that had nothing to do with them. She would not be Anna out there, the lady in the drawing. He would not be her lover.

"I love you so much . . ." She whispered.

"Please don't cry! We have only a few hours, please. . . ."

It was absurd, their clinging together like this. She saw them as a single figure in a drawing, their arms and legs entwined, their heads pressing mutely together. Helpless substance, so heavy and warm and doomed. It was absurd that any human being should be so important to another human being. She wanted to laugh: a laugh might free them both.

She could not laugh.

Sometime later he said, as if they had been arguing, "Look. It's you. You're the one who doesn't want to get married. You lie to me — "

"Lie to you?"

"You love me but you won't marry me, because you want something left over — Something not finished — All your life you can attribute your misery to me, to our not being married — you are using me — "

"Stop it! You'll make me hate you!" she cried.

"You can say to yourself that you're miserable because of *me.* We will never be married, you will never be happy, neither one of us will ever be happy — "

"I don't want to hear this!" she said.

She pressed her hands flatly against her face.

She went to the bathroom to get dressed. She washed her face and part of her body, quickly. The fever was in her, in the pit of her belly. She would rush home and strike a razor across the inside of her arm and free that pressure, that fever.

The impatient bulging of the veins: an ordeal over.

The demand of the telephone's ringing: that ordeal over.

The nuisance of getting the car and driving home in all that five o'clock traffic: an ordeal too much for a woman.

The movement of this stranger's body in hers: over, finished.

Now, dressed, a little calmer, they held hands and talked. They had to talk swiftly, to get all their news in: he did not trust the people who worked for him, he had faith in no one, his wife had moved to a textbook publishing company and was doing well, she had inherited a Ben Shahn painting from her father and wanted to "touch it up a little" — she was crazy! — his blind son was at another school, doing fairly well, in fact his children were all doing fairly well in spite of the stupid mistake of their parents' marriage — and what about her? what about her life? She told him in a rush the one thing he wanted to hear: that she lived with her husband lovelessly, the two of them polite strangers, sharing a bed, lying side by side in the night in that bed, bodies out of which souls had fled. There was no longer even any shame between them.

"And what about me? Do you feel shame with me still?" he asked.

She did not answer. She moved away from him and prepared to leave.

Then, a minute later, she happened to catch sight of his reflection in the bureau mirror — he was glancing down at himself, checking himself mechanically, impersonally, preparing also to leave. He too would leave this room: he too was headed somewhere else.

She stared at him. It seemed to her that in this instant he was breaking from her, the image of her lover fell free of her, breaking from her . . . and she realized that he existed in a dimension quite apart from her, a mysterious being. And suddenly, joyfully, she felt a miraculous calm. This man was her husband, truly — they were truly married, here in this room — they had been married haphazardly and accidentally for a long time. In another part of the city she had another husband, a "husband," but she had not betrayed that man, not really. This man, whom she loved above any other person in the world, above even her own self-pitying sorrow and her own life, was her truest lover, her destiny. And she did not hate him, she did not hate herself any longer; she did not wish to die; she was flooded with a strange certainty, a sense of gratitude, of pure selfless energy. It was obvious to her that she had, all along, been behaving correctly; out of instinct.

What triumph, to love like this in any room, anywhere, risking even the craziest of accidents!

"Why are you so happy? What's wrong?" he asked, startled. He stared at her. She felt the abrupt concentration in him, the focusing of his vision on her, almost a bitterness in his face, as if he feared her. What, was it beginning all over again? Their love beginning again, in spite of them? "How can you look so happy?" he asked. "We don't have any right to it. Is it because . . . ?"

"Yes," she said.

Considerations

1. How would this story be different if it were told only in chronological order as it is in Part III? What do Parts I and II contribute to the details and information provided in Part III?
2. Why are Anna and her lover drawn to each other? What do we learn about their spouses that helps explain their attraction? Are there any other explanations?
3. Why is Anna so unhappy after the affair on Nantucket begins? Why does she think of suicide?
4. What is Anna's attitude toward men? Does it change during the story?
5. What details in the story make the narration particularly convincing from a woman's perspective? How might a man tell the story differently?
6. "What triumph, to love like this in any room, anywhere, risking even the craziest of accidents!" Explain this reflection of Anna's (at the end of Part III) and relate it to her character.
7. How does Oates's arrangement of incidents validate Anna's feeling that "everything is repeating itself. Everything is stuck"?
8. Consider whether Anna reaches any kind of resolution to her problems by the end of the story. Is she merely "repeating" herself, or do you think she develops?
9. At the end of the first paragraph of Part II, Oates has Anna ask herself the question "What did it mean to enter into a bond with another person?" Write an essay explaining how the story answers that question.

Connections

1. What similarities in setting, plot, and character are there between Oates's version and Chekhov's story? Are there any significant differences?
2. Is it necessary to be familiar with Chekhov's story to appreciate Oates's? What's the point of retelling the story?
3. Describe how a familiarity with Chekhov's story affected your reading and expectations of Oates's version. Choose one version of the story and write an essay explaining why you prefer it over the other.

6. Symbolism

A ***symbol*** is a person, object, or event that suggests more than its literal meaning. This basic definition is simple enough, but the use of symbol in literature makes some students slightly nervous because they tend to regard it as a booby trap, a hidden device that can go off during a seemingly harmless class discussion. "I didn't see that when I was reading the story" is a frequently heard comment. This sort of surprise and recognition is both natural and common. Most readers go through a story for the first time getting their bearings, figuring out what is happening to whom and so on. Patterns and significant details often require a second or third reading before they become evident — before a symbol sheds light on a story. Then the details of a work may suddenly fit together and its meaning may be reinforced, clarified, or enlarged by the symbol. Symbolic meanings are usually embedded in the texture of a story, but they are not "hidden"; instead, they are carefully placed. Reading between the lines (where there is only space) is unnecessary. What is needed is a careful consideration of the elements of the story, a sensitivity to its language, and some common sense.

Common sense is a good place to begin. Symbols appear all around us; anything can be given symbolic significance. Without symbols our lives would be curiously stark and vacant. Awareness of a writer's use of symbols is not all that different from the kinds of perceptions and interpretations that allow us to make sense of our daily lives. We know, for example, that a ring used in a wedding is more than just a piece of jewelry because it suggests the unity and intimacy of a closed circle. The bride's gown may be white because we associate innocence and purity with that color. Or consider the meaning of a small alligator sewn on a shirt or some other article of clothing. What started out as a company trademark has gathered around it a range of meanings suggesting everything from quality and money to preppiness and silliness. The ring, the white gown, and the alligator trademark are symbolic because each has meanings that go beyond its specific qualities and functions.

Symbols such as these that are widely recognized by a society or culture are called ***conventional symbols.*** The Christian cross, the Star of David, a swastika, or a nation's flag all have meanings understood by large groups of people. Certain kinds of experiences also have traditional meanings in Western cultures. Winter, the setting sun, and the color black suggest death, while spring, the rising sun, and the color green evoke images of youth and new beginnings. (It is worth noting, however, that individual cultures sometimes have their own conventions; some Oriental countries associate white rather than black with death and mourning. And obviously the alligator trademark would mean nothing to anyone totally unfamiliar with American culture.) These broadly shared symbolic meanings are second nature to us.

Writers use conventional symbols to reinforce meanings. Kate Chopin, for example, emphasizes the spring setting in "The Story of an Hour" (p. 12) as a way of suggesting the renewed sense of life that Ms. Mallard feels when she thinks herself free from her husband.

A ***literary symbol*** can include traditional, conventional, or public meanings, but it may also be established internally by the total context of the work in which it appears. In "Soldier's Home" (p. 121), Hemingway does not use Krebs's family home as a conventional symbol of safety, comfort, and refuge from the war. Instead, Krebs's home becomes symbolic of provincial, erroneous presuppositions compounded by blind innocence, sentimentality, and smug middle-class respectability. The symbolic meaning of his home reveals that Krebs no longer shares his family's and town's view of the world. Their notions of love, the value of a respectable job, and a belief in God seem to him petty, complicated, and meaningless. The significance of Krebs's home is determined by the events within the story, which reverse and subvert the traditional associations readers might bring to it. Krebs's interactions with his family and the people in town reveal what home has come to mean to him.

A literary symbol can be a setting, character, action, object, name, or anything else in a work that maintains its literal significance while suggesting other meanings. Symbols cannot be restricted to a single meaning; they are suggestive rather than definitive. Their evocation of multiple meanings allows a writer to say more with less. Symbols are economical devices for evoking complex ideas without having to resort to painstaking explanations that would make a story more like an essay than an experience. The many walls in Melville's "Bartleby, the Scrivener" (p. 80) cannot be reduced to one idea. They have multiple meanings that unify the story. The walls are symbols of the deadening, dehumanizing, restrictive repetitiveness of the office routine, as well as of the confining, materialistic sensibilities of Wall Street. They suggest whatever limits and thwarts human aspirations, including death itself. We don't know precisely what shatters Bartleby's will to live, but the walls in the story, through their symbolic suggestiveness, indicate the nature of the limitations that cause the scrivener to slip into hopelessness and his "dead-wall reveries."

When a character, object, or incident indicates a single, fixed meaning, the writer is using ***allegory*** rather than symbol. Unlike with symbols, which have literal functions as well as multiple meanings, the primary focus in allegory is on the abstract idea called forth by the concrete object. John Bunyan's *Pilgrim's Progress,* published during the seventeenth century, is a classic example of allegory, because the characters, action, and setting have no existence beyond their abstract meanings. Bunyan's purpose is to teach his readers the exemplary way to salvation and heaven. The protagonist, named Christian, flees the City of Destruction in search of the Celestial City. Along the way he encounters characters who either help or hinder his spiritual journey. Among them are Mr. Worldly Wiseman, Faithful, Prudence, Piety, and a host of others named after the virtues or vices they display. These characters, places, and actions exist solely to illustrate religious doctrine. Allegory tends to be definitive rather than suggestive. It drives meaning into a corner and keeps it there. Most modern writers prefer the exploratory nature of symbol to the reductive nature of pure allegory.

Stories often include symbols that you may or may not perceive on a first reading. Their subtle use is a sign of a writer's skill in weaving symbols into the fabric of the characters' lives. Symbols may sometimes escape you, but that is probably better than finding symbols where only literal meanings are intended. Allow the text to help you determine if a symbolic reading is appropriate. Once you are clear about what literally happens, read carefully and notice the placement of details that are emphasized. The pervasive references to time in Faulkner's "A Rose for Emily" (p. 47) and the many kinds of walls that appear throughout "Bartleby, the Scrivener" call attention to themselves and warrant symbolic readings. A symbol, however, need not be repeated to have an important purpose in a story. In Welty's "Livvie" (p. 109), the simple application of lipstick helps to reinforce symbolically Livvie's eventual movement away from the repressive Solomon to the compelling freedom associated with Cash.

By keeping track of the total context of the story, you should be able to decide if your reading is reasonable and consistent with the other facts; plenty of lemons in literature yield no symbolic meaning even if they are squeezed. Be sensitive to the meanings that the author associates with people, places, objects, and actions. You may not associate home with provincial innocence as Hemingway does in "Soldier's Home," but a close reading of the story will permit you to see how and why he constructs that symbolic meaning. If you treat stories like people — with tact and care — they ordinarily are accessible and enjoyable.

The next three stories — Colette's "The Hand," Ralph Ellison's "Battle Royal," and Katherine Anne Porter's "The Grave" — rely on symbols to convey meanings that go far beyond the specific incidents described in their plots.

COLETTE (1873–1954)

Born in Burgundy, France, Sidonie Gabrielle Colette lived a long and remarkably diverse life. At various points during her career she supported herself as a novelist, music-hall performer, and journalist. Her professional life and three marriages helped to shape her keen insights into modern love and women's lives. She is regarded as a significant feminist voice in the twentieth century, and her reputation is firmly fixed by her having been the first woman admitted to the Goncourt Academy and by the continued popularity of her work among readers internationally. Her best-known works include *Mitsou, or, How Girls Grow Wise* (1919), *Chéri* (1920), *Claudine's House* (1922), and *Gigi* (1944). "The Hand" signals a telling moment in the life of a young bride.

The Hand 1924

He had fallen asleep on his young wife's shoulder, and she proudly bore the weight of the man's head, blond, ruddy-complexioned, eyes closed. He had slipped his big arm under the small of her slim, adolescent back, and his strong hand lay on the sheet next to the young woman's right elbow. She smiled to see the man's hand emerging there, all by itself and far away from its owner. Then she let her eyes wander over the half-lit room. A veiled conch shed a light across the bed the color of periwinkle.

"Too happy to sleep," she thought.

Too excited also, and often surprised by her new state. It had been only two weeks since she had begun to live the scandalous life of a newlywed who tastes the joys of living with someone unknown and with whom she is in love. To meet a handsome, blond young man, recently widowed, good at tennis and rowing, to marry him a month later: her conjugal adventure had been little more than a kidnapping. So that whenever she lay awake beside her husband, like tonight, she still kept her eyes closed for a long time, then opened them again in order to savor, with astonishment, the blue of the brand-new curtains, instead of the apricot-pink through which the first light of day filtered into the room where she had slept as a little girl.

A quiver ran through the sleeping body lying next to her, and she tightened her left arm around her husband's neck with the charming authority exercised by weak creatures. He did not wake up.

"His eyelashes are so long," she said to herself. 5

To herself she also praised his mouth, full and likable, his skin the color of pink brick, and even his forehead, neither noble nor broad, but still smooth and unwrinkled.

Her husband's right hand, lying beside her, quivered in turn, and beneath the curve of her back she felt the right arm, on which her whole weight was resting, come to life.

"I'm so heavy . . . I wish I could get up and turn the light off. But he's sleeping so well . . ."

The arm twisted again, feebly, and she arched her back to make herself lighter.

"It's as if I were lying on some animal," she thought. 10

She turned her head a little on the pillow and looked at the hand lying there next to her.

"It's so big! It really is bigger than my whole head."

The light, flowing out from under the edge of a parasol of bluish crystal, spilled up against the hand, and made every contour of the skin apparent, exaggerating the powerful knuckles and the veins engorged by the pressure on the arm. A few red hairs, at the base of the fingers, all curved in the same direction, like ears of wheat in the wind, and the flat nails, whose ridges the nail buffer had not smoothed out, gleamed, coated with pink varnish.

"I'll tell him not to varnish his nails," thought the young wife. "Varnish and pink polish don't go with a hand so . . . a hand that's so . . ."

An electric jolt ran through the hand and spared the young woman from 15
having to find the right adjective. The thumb stiffened itself out, horribly long and spatulate, and pressed tightly against the index finger, so that the hand suddenly took on a vile, apelike appearance.

"Oh!" whispered the young woman, as though faced with something slightly indecent.

The sound of a passing car pierced the silence with a shrillness that seemed luminous. The sleeping man did not wake, but the hand, offended, reared back and tensed up in the shape of a crab and waited, ready for battle. The screeching sound died down and the hand, relaxing gradually, lowered its claws, and became a pliant beast, awkwardly bent, shaken by faint jerks which resembled some sort of agony. The flat, cruel nail of the overlong thumb glistened. A curve in the little finger, which the young woman had never noticed, appeared, and the wallowing hand revealed its fleshy palm like a red belly.

"And I've kissed that hand! . . . How horrible! Haven't I ever looked at it?"

The hand, disturbed by a bad dream, appeared to respond to this startling discovery, this disgust. It regrouped its forces, opened wide, and splayed its tendons, lumps, and red fur like battle dress, then slowly drawing itself in again, grabbed a fistful of the sheet, dug into it with its curved fingers, and squeezed, squeezed with the methodical pleasure of a strangler.

"Oh!" cried the young woman. 20

The hand disappeared and a moment later the big arm, relieved of its burden, became a protective belt, a warm bulwark against all the terrors of night. But the next morning, when it was time for breakfast in bed — hot chocolate and toast — she saw the hand again, with its red hair and red skin, and the ghastly thumb curving out over the handle of a knife.

"Do you want this slice, darling? I'll butter it for you."

She shuddered and felt her skin crawl on the back of her arms and down her back.

"Oh, no . . . no . . ."

Then she concealed her fear, bravely subdued herself, and, beginning her 25
life of duplicity, of resignation, and of a lowly, delicate diplomacy, she leaned over and humbly kissed the monstrous hand.

Considerations

1. How well did the young woman know her husband before she married him? What attracted her to him?
2. How does the wife regard the hand at the very beginning of the story? At what point does she begin to change her attitude?
3. Explain how the wife's description of the hand affects your own response to it. What prompts her "Oh!" in paragraphs 16 and 20? What do you suppose the wife is thinking at these moments?
4. What powerful feelings does the hand evoke in the wife? How do her descriptions of the hand suggest symbolic readings of it?
5. Describe the conflict in the story. Explain whether there is a resolution to this conflict.
6. Do you think the story is more about the husband or about the wife? Who is the central character? Explain your choice. Consider also whether the characters are static or dynamic.
7. Why do you think the narrator mentions that the husband was "recently widowed"?
8. How significant is the setting of the story?
9. Why do you think the wife kisses her husband's hand in the final paragraph? Write an essay explaining how the kiss symbolizes the nature of their relationship.
10. Describe the point of view in the story. Why do you suppose Colette doesn't use a first-person perspective that would reveal more intimately the wife's perceptions and concerns?

Connections

1. In "The Birthmark" (p. 268) Nathaniel Hawthorne also uses a hand for symbolic purposes. Compare the meanings he associates with the hand in his story with Colette's. How does each writer invest meanings in a central symbol? What are the significant similarities and differences in meanings? Write an essay explaining why you find one story more effective than the other.
2. Compare the use of settings in "The Hand" and in John Updike's "A & P" (p. 407). To what extent does each story attach meaning to its setting?
3. How might Godwin's "A Sorrowful Woman" (p. 30) be read as a kind of sequel to "The Hand"?

RALPH ELLISON (b. 1914)

Born in Oklahoma and educated at the Tuskegee Institute in Alabama, where he studied music, Ralph Ellison gained his reputation as a writer on the strength of his only published novel, *Invisible Man* (1952). He has also published some scattered short stories and two collections of essays, *Shadow and Act* (1964) and *Going to the Territory* (1986). Although his writing has not been extensive, it is important because Ellison writes about race relations in the context of universal human concerns. *Invisible Man* is the story of a young black man who moves from the South to the North and discovers what it means to be black in America. "Battle Royal," published in 1947 as a short story, became the first chapter of *Invisible Man.* It concerns the beginning of the protagonist's long struggle for an adult identity in a world made corrupt by racial prejudice.

Battle Royal 1947

It goes a long way back, some twenty years. All my life I had been looking for something, and everywhere I turned someone tried to tell me what it was. I accepted their answers too, though they were often in contradiction and even self-contradictory. I was naïve. I was looking for myself and asking everyone except myself questions which I, and only I, could answer. It took me a long time and much painful boomeranging of my expectations to achieve a realization everyone else appears to have been born with: That I am nobody but myself. But first I had to discover that I am an invisible man!

And yet I am no freak of nature, nor of history. I was in the cards, other things having been equal (or unequal) eighty-five years ago. I am not ashamed of my grandparents for having been slaves. I am only ashamed of myself for having at one time been ashamed. About eighty-five years ago they were told that they were free, united with others of our country in everything pertaining to the common good, and, in everything social, separate like the fingers of the hand. And they believed it. They exulted in it. They stayed in their place, worked hard, and brought up my father to do the same. But my grandfather is the one. He was an odd old guy, my grandfather, and I am told I take after him. It was he who caused the trouble. On his deathbed he called my father to him and said, "Son, after I'm gone I want you to keep up the good fight. I never told you, but our life is a war and I have been a traitor all my born days, a spy in the enemy's country ever since I give up my gun back in the Reconstruction. Live with your head in the lion's mouth. I want you to overcome 'em with yeses, undermine 'em with grins, agree 'em to death and destruction, let 'em swoller you till they vomit or bust wide open." They thought the old man had gone out of his mind. He had been the meekest of men. The younger children were rushed from the room, the shades drawn and the flame of the lamp turned so low that it sputtered on the wick like the old man's breathing. "Learn it to the younguns," he whispered fiercely; then he died.

But my folks were more alarmed over his last words than over his dying. It was as though he had not died at all, his words caused so much anxiety. I was warned emphatically to forget what he had said and, indeed, this is the first time it has been mentioned outside the family circle. It had a tremendous effect upon me, however. I could never be sure of what he meant. Grandfather had been a quiet old man who never made any trouble, yet on his deathbed he had called himself a traitor and a spy, and he had spoken of his meekness as a dangerous activity. It became a constant puzzle which lay unanswered in the back of my mind. And whenever things went well for me I remembered my grandfather and felt guilty and uncomfortable. It was as though I was carrying out his advice in spite of myself. And to make it worse, everyone loved me for it. I was praised by the most lily-white men of the town. I was considered an example of desirable conduct — just as my grandfather had been. And what puzzled me was that the old man had defined it as *treachery*. When I was praised for my conduct I felt a guilt that in some way I was doing something that was really against the wishes of the white folks, that if they had understood they would have desired me to act just the opposite, that I should have been sulky and mean, and that that really would have been what they wanted, even though they were fooled and thought they wanted me to act as I did. It made me afraid that some day they would look upon me as a traitor and I would be lost. Still I was more afraid to act any other way because they didn't like that at all. The old man's words were like a curse. On my graduation day I delivered an oration in which I showed that humility was the secret, indeed, the very essence of progress. (Not that I believed this — how could I, remembering my grandfather? — I only believed that it worked.) It was a great success. Everyone praised me and I was invited to give the speech at a gathering of the town's leading white citizens. It was a triumph for our whole community.

It was in the main ballroom of the leading hotel. When I got there I discovered that it was on the occasion of a smoker, and I was told that since I was to be there anyway I might as well take part in the battle royal to be fought by some of my schoolmates as part of the entertainment. The battle royal came first.

5 All of the town's big shots were there in their tuxedoes, wolfing down the buffet foods, drinking beer and whiskey and smoking black cigars. It was a large room with a high ceiling. Chairs were arranged in neat rows around three sides of a portable boxing ring. The fourth side was clear, revealing a gleaming space of polished floor. I had some misgivings over the battle royal, by the way. Not from a distaste for fighting, but because I didn't care too much for the other fellows who were to take part. They were tough guys who seemed to have no grandfather's curse worrying their minds. No one could mistake their toughness. And besides, I suspected that fighting a battle royal might detract from the dignity of my speech. In those pre-invisible days I visualized myself as a potential Booker T. Washington. But the other fellows didn't care too much for me either, and there were nine of them. I felt superior to them in my way, and I didn't like the manner in which we were all crowded together into the servants' elevator. Nor did they like my being there. In fact, as the warmly lighted floors flashed past the elevator we had words over the fact that I, by taking part in the fight, had knocked one of their friends out of a night's work.

We were led out of the elevator through a rococo hall into an anteroom and told to get into our fighting togs. Each of us was issued a pair of boxing gloves and ushered out into the big mirrored hall, which we entered looking cautiously about us and whispering, lest we might accidentally be heard above the noise of the room. It was foggy with cigar smoke. And already the whiskey was taking effect. I was shocked to see some of the most important men of the town quite tipsy. They were all there — bankers, lawyers, judges, doctors, fire chiefs, teachers, merchants. Even one of the more fashionable pastors. Something we could not see was going on up front. A clarinet was vibrating sensuously and the men were standing up and moving eagerly forward. We were a small tight group, clustered together, our bare upper bodies touching and shining with anticipatory sweat; while up front the big shots were becoming increasingly excited over something we still could not see. Suddenly I heard the school superintendent, who had told me to come, yell, "Bring up the shines, gentlemen! Bring up the little shines!"

We were rushed up to the front of the ballroom, where it smelled even more strongly of tobacco and whiskey. Then we were pushed into place. I almost wet my pants. A sea of faces, some hostile, some amused, ringed around us, and in the center, facing us, stood a magnificent blonde — stark naked. There was dead silence. I felt a blast of cold air chill me. I tried to back away, but they were behind me and around me. Some of the boys stood with lowered heads, trembling. I felt a wave of irrational guilt and fear. My teeth chattered, my skin turned to goose flesh, my knees knocked. Yet I was strongly attracted and looked in spite of myself. Had the price of looking been blindness, I would have looked. The hair was yellow like that of a circus kewpie doll, the face heavily powdered and rouged, as though to form an abstract mask, the eyes hollow and smeared a cool blue, the color of a baboon's butt. I felt a desire to spit upon her as my eyes brushed slowly over her body. Her breasts were firm and round as the domes of East Indian temples, and I stood so close as to see the fine skin texture and beads of pearly perspiration glistening like dew around the pink and erected buds of her nipples. I wanted at one and the same time to run from the room, to sink through the floor, or go to her and cover her from my eyes and the eyes of the others with my body; to feel the soft thighs, to caress her and destroy her, to love her and murder her, to hide from her, and yet to stroke where below the small American flag tattooed upon her belly her thighs formed a capital V. I had a notion that of all in the room she saw only me with her impersonal eyes.

And then she began to dance, a slow sensuous movement; the smoke of a hundred cigars clinging to her like the thinnest of veils. She seemed like a fair bird-girl girdled in veils calling to me from the angry surface of some gray and threatening sea. I was transported. Then I became aware of the clarinet playing and the big shots yelling at us. Some threatened us if we looked and others if we did not. On my right I saw one boy faint. And now a man grabbed a silver pitcher from a table and stepped close as he dashed ice water upon him and stood him up and forced two of us to support him as his head hung and moans issued from his thick bluish lips. Another boy began to plead to go home. He was the largest of the group, wearing dark red fighting trunks much too small to conceal the erection which projected from him as though in answer to the insinuating low-registered moaning of the clarinet. He tried to hide himself with his boxing gloves.

And all the while the blonde continued dancing, smiling faintly at the big shots who watched her with fascination, and faintly smiling at our fear. I noticed a certain merchant who followed her hungrily, his lips loose and drooling. He was a large man who wore diamond studs in a shirtfront which swelled with the ample paunch underneath, and each time the blonde swayed her undulating hips he ran his hand through the thin hair of his bald head and, with his arms upheld, his posture clumsy like that of an intoxicated panda, wound his belly in a slow and obscene grind. This creature was completely hypnotized. The music had quickened. As the dancer flung herself about with a detached expression on her face, the men began reaching out to touch her. I could see their beefy fingers sink into the soft flesh. Some of the others tried to stop them as she began to move around the floor in graceful circles, as they gave chase, slipping and sliding over the polished floor. It was mad. Chairs went crashing, drinks were spilt, as they ran laughing and howling after her. They caught her just as she reached a door, raised her from the floor, and tossed her as college boys are tossed at a hazing, and above her red, fixed-smiling lips I saw the terror and disgust in her eyes, almost like my own terror and that which I saw in some of the other boys. As I watched, they tossed her twice and her soft breasts seemed to flatten against the air and her legs flung wildly as she spun. Some of the more sober ones helped her to escape. And I started off the floor, heading for the anteroom with the rest of the boys.

Some were still crying in hysteria. But as we tried to leave we were stopped 10
and ordered to get into the ring. There was nothing to do but what we were told. All ten of us climbed under the ropes and allowed ourselves to be blindfolded with broad bands of white cloth. One of the men seemed to feel a bit sympathetic and tried to cheer us up as we stood with our backs against the ropes. Some of us tried to grin. "See that boy over there?" one of the men said. "I want you to run across at the bell and give it to him right in the belly. If you don't get him, I'm going to get you. I don't like his looks." Each of us was told the same. The blindfolds were put on. Yet even then I had been going over my speech. In my mind each word was as bright as flame. I felt the cloth pressed into place, and frowned so that it would be loosened when I relaxed.

But now I felt a sudden fit of blind terror. I was unused to darkness. It was as though I had suddenly found myself in a dark room filled with poisonous cottonmouths. I could hear the bleary voices yelling insistently for the battle royal to begin.

"Get going in there!"

"Let me at that big nigger!"

I strained to pick up the school superintendent's voice, as though to squeeze some security out of that slightly more familiar sound.

"Let me at those black sonsabitches!" someone yelled. 15

"No, Jackson, no!" another voice yelled. "Here, somebody, help me hold Jack."

"I want to get at that ginger-colored nigger. Tear him limb from limb," the first voice yelled.

I stood against the ropes trembling. For in those days I was what they called ginger-colored, and he sounded as though he might crunch me between his teeth like a crisp ginger cookie.

Quite a struggle was going on. Chairs were being kicked about and I could hear voices grunting as with a terrific effort. I wanted to see, to see more desperately than ever before. But the blindfold was tight as a thick skin-puckering scab and when I raised my gloved hands to push the layers of white aside a voice yelled, "Oh, no you don't, black bastard! Leave that alone!"

"Ring the bell before Jackson kills him a coon!" someone boomed in the 20
sudden silence. And I heard the bell clang and the sound of the feet scuffling forward.

A glove smacked against my head. I pivoted, striking out stiffly as someone went past, and felt the jar ripple along the length of my arm to my shoulder. Then it seemed as though all nine of the boys had turned upon me at once. Blows pounded me from all sides while I struck out as best I could. So many blows landed upon me that I wondered if I were not the only blindfolded fighter in the ring, or if the man called Jackson hadn't succeeded in getting me after all.

Blindfolded, I could no longer control my motions. I had no dignity. I stumbled about like a baby or a drunken man. The smoke had become thicker and with each new blow it seemed to sear and further restrict my lungs. My saliva became like hot bitter glue. A glove connected with my head, filling my mouth with warm blood. It was everywhere. I could not tell if the moisture I felt upon my body was sweat or blood. A blow landed hard against the nape of my neck. I felt myself going over, my head hitting the floor. Streaks of blue light filled the black world behind the blindfold. I lay prone, pretending that I was knocked out, but felt myself seized by hands and yanked to my feet. "Get going, black boy! Mix it up!" My arms were like lead, my head smarting from blows. I managed to feel my way to the ropes and held on, trying to catch my breath. A glove landed in my mid-section and I went over again, feeling as though the smoke had become a knife jabbed into my guts. Pushed this way and that by the legs milling around me, I finally pulled erect and discovered that I could see the black, sweat-washed forms weaving in the smoky-blue atmosphere like drunken dancers weaving to the rapid drumlike thuds of blows.

Everyone fought hysterically. It was complete anarchy. Everybody fought everybody else. No group fought together for long. Two, three, four, fought one, then turned to fight each other, were themselves attacked. Blows landed below the belt and in the kidney, with the gloves open as well as closed, and with my eye partly opened now there was not so much terror. I moved carefully, avoiding blows, although not too many to attract attention, fighting from group to group. The boys groped about like blind, cautious crabs crouching to protect their mid-sections, their heads pulled in short against their shoulders, their arms stretched nervously before them, with their fists testing the smoke-filled air like the knobbed feelers of hypersensitive snails. In one corner I glimpsed a boy violently punching the air and heard him scream in pain as he smashed his hand against a ring post. For a second I saw him bent over holding his hand, then going down as a blow caught his unprotected head. I played one group against the other, slipping in and throwing a punch then stepping out of range while pushing the others into the melee to take the blows blindly aimed at me. The smoke was agonizing and there were no rounds, no bells at three minute intervals to relieve our exhaustion. The room spun round me, a swirl of lights, smoke, sweating bodies surrounded by tense white faces. I bled from both nose and mouth, the blood spattering upon my chest.

The men kept yelling, "Slug him, black boy! Knock his guts out!"

"Uppercut him! Kill him! Kill that big boy!" 25

Taking a fake fall, I saw a boy going down heavily beside me as though we were felled by a single blow, saw a sneaker-clad foot shoot into his groin as the two who had knocked him down stumbled upon him. I rolled out of range, feeling a twinge of nausea.

The harder we fought the more threatening the men became. And yet, I had begun to worry about my speech again. How would it go? Would they recognize my ability? What would they give me?

I was fighting automatically when suddenly I noticed that one after another of the boys was leaving the ring. I was surprised, filled with panic, as though I had been left alone with an unknown danger. Then I understood. The boys had arranged it among themselves. It was the custom for the two men left in the ring to slug it out for the winner's prize. I discovered this too late. When the bell sounded two men in tuxedoes leaped into the ring and removed the blindfold. I found myself facing Tatlock, the biggest of the gang. I felt sick at my stomach. Hardly had the bell stopped ringing in my ears than it clanged again and I saw him moving swiftly toward me. Thinking of nothing else to do I hit him smash on the nose. He kept coming, bringing the rank sharp violence of stale sweat. His face was a black blank of a face, only his eyes alive — with hate of me and aglow with a feverish terror from what had happened to us all. I became anxious. I wanted to deliver my speech and he came at me as though he meant to beat it out of me. I smashed him again and again, taking his blows as they came. Then on a sudden impulse I struck him lightly and as we clinched, I whispered, "Fake like I knocked you out, you can have the prize."

"I'll break your behind," he whispered hoarsely.

"For *them?*" 30

"For *me,* sonofabitch!"

They were yelling for us to break it up and Tatlock spun me half around with a blow, and as a joggled camera sweeps in a reeling scene, I saw the howling red faces crouching tense beneath the cloud of blue-gray smoke. For a moment the world wavered, unraveled, flowed, then my head cleared and Tatlock bounced before me. That fluttering shadow before my eyes was his jabbing left hand. Then falling forward, my head against his damp shoulder, I whispered,

"I'll make it five dollars more."

"Go to hell!"

But his muscles relaxed a trifle beneath my pressure and I breathed, "Seven?" 35

"Give it to your ma," he said, ripping me beneath the heart.

And while I still held him I butted him and moved away. I felt myself bombarded with punches. I fought back with hopeless desperation. I wanted to deliver my speech more than anything else in the world, because I felt that only these men could judge truly my ability, and now this stupid clown was ruining my chances. I began fighting carefully now, moving in to punch him and out again with my greater speed. A lucky blow to his chin and I had him going too — until I heard a loud voice yell, "I got my money on the big boy."

Hearing this, I almost dropped my guard. I was confused: Should I try to win against the voice out there? Would not this go against my speech, and was not this a moment for humility, for nonresistance? A blow to my head as I danced about sent my right eye popping like a jack-in-the-box and settled my dilemma. The room went red as I fell. It was a dream fall, my body languid and fastidious as to where to land, until the floor became impatient and smashed up to meet me. A moment later I came to. An hypnotic voice said FIVE emphatically. And I lay there, hazily watching a dark red spot of my own blood shaping itself into a butterfly, glistening and soaking into the soiled gray world of the canvas.

When the voice drawled TEN I was lifted up and dragged to a chair. I sat dazed. My eye pained and swelled with each throb of my pounding heart and I wondered if now I would be allowed to speak. I was wringing wet, my mouth still bleeding. We were grouped along the wall now. The other boys ignored me as they congratulated Tatlock and speculated as to how much they would be paid. One boy whimpered over his smashed hand. Looking up front, I saw attendants in white jackets rolling the portable ring away and placing a small square rug in the vacant space surrounded by chairs. Perhaps, I thought, I will stand on the rug to deliver my speech.

Then the M.C. called to us, "Come on up here boys and get your money." We ran forward to where the men laughed and talked in their chairs, waiting. Everyone seemed friendly now.

"There it is on the rug," the man said. I saw the rug covered with coins of all dimensions and a few crumpled bills. But what excited me, scattered here and there, were the gold pieces.

"Boys, it's all yours," the man said. "You get all you grab."

"That's right, Sambo," a blond man said, winking at me confidentially.

I trembled with excitement, forgetting my pain. I would get the gold and the bills, I thought. I would use both hands. I would throw my body against the boys nearest me to block them from the gold.

"Get down around the rug now," the man commanded, "and don't anyone touch it until I give the signal."

"This ought to be good," I heard.

As told, we got around the square rug on our knees. Slowly the man raised his freckled hand as we followed it upward with our eyes.

I heard, "These niggers look like they're about to pray!"

Then, "Ready," the man said. "Go!"

I lunged for a yellow coin lying on the blue design of the carpet, touching it and sending a surprised shriek to join those rising around me. I tried frantically to remove my hand but could not let go. A hot, violent force tore through my body, shaking me like a wet rat. The rug was electrified. The hair bristled up on my head as I shook myself free. My muscles jumped, my nerves jangled, writhed. But I saw that this was not stopping the other boys. Laughing in fear and embarrassment, some were holding back and scooping up the coins knocked off by the painful contortions of the others. The men roared above us as we struggled.

"Pick it up, goddamnit, pick it up!" someone called like a bass-voiced parrot. "Go on, get it!"

I crawled rapidly around the floor, picking up the coins, trying to avoid the coppers and to get greenbacks and the gold. Ignoring the shock by laughing, as I brushed the coins off quickly, I discovered that I could contain the electricity — a contradiction, but it works. Then the men began to push us onto the rug. Laughing embarrassedly, we struggled out of their hands and kept after the coins. We were all wet and slippery and hard to hold. Suddenly I saw a boy lifted into the air, glistening with sweat like a circus seal, and dropped, his wet back landing flush upon the charged rug, heard him yell and saw him literally dance upon his back, his elbows beating a frenzied tattoo upon the floor, his muscles twitching like the flesh of a horse stung by many flies. When he finally rolled off, his face was gray and no one stopped him when he ran from the floor amid booming laughter.

"Get the money," the M.C. called. "That's good hard American cash!"

And we snatched and grabbed, snatched and grabbed. I was careful not to come too close to the rug now, and when I felt the hot whiskey breath descend upon me like a cloud of foul air I reached out and grabbed the leg of a chair. It was occupied and I held on desperately.

"Leggo, nigger! Leggo!" 55

The huge face wavered down to mine as he tried to push me free. But my body was slippery and he was too drunk. It was Mr. Colcord, who owned a chain of movie houses and "entertainment palaces." Each time he grabbed me I slipped out of his hands. It became a real struggle. I feared the rug more than I did the drunk, so I held on, surprising myself for a moment by trying to topple *him* upon the rug. It was such an enormous idea that I found myself actually carrying it out. I tried not to be obvious, yet when I grabbed his leg, trying to tumble him out of the chair, he raised up roaring with laughter, and, looking at me with soberness dead in the eye, kicked me viciously in the chest. The chair leg flew out of my hand and I felt myself going and rolled. It was as though I had rolled through a bed of hot coals. It seemed a whole century would pass before I would roll free, a century in which I was seared through the deepest levels of my body to the fearful breath within me and the breath seared and heated to the point of explosion. It'll all be over in a flash, I thought as I rolled clear. It'll all be over in a flash.

But not yet, the men on the other side were waiting, red faces swollen as though from apoplexy as they bent forward in their chairs. Seeing their fingers coming toward me I rolled away as a fumbled football rolls off the receiver's fingertips, back into the coals. That time I luckily sent the rug sliding out of place and heard the coins ringing against the floor and the boys scuffling to pick them up and the M.C. calling, "All right, boys, that's all. Go get dressed and get your money."

I was limp as a dish rag. My back felt as though it had been beaten with wires.

When we had dressed the M.C. came in and gave us each five dollars, except Tatlock, who got ten for being last in the ring. Then he told us to leave. I was not to get a chance to deliver my speech, I thought. I was going out into the dim alley in despair when I was stopped and told to go back. I returned to the ballroom, where the men were pushing back their chairs and gathering in groups to talk.

The M.C. knocked on a table for quiet. "Gentlemen," he said, "we almost 60
forgot an important part of the program. A most serious part, gentlemen. This boy was brought here to deliver a speech which he made at his graduation yesterday . . ."

"Bravo!"

"I'm told that he is the smartest boy we've got out there in Greenwood. I'm told that he knows more big words than a pocket-sized dictionary."

Much applause and laughter.

"So now, gentlemen, I want you to give him your attention."

There was still laughter as I faced them, my mouth dry, my eye throbbing. 65
I began slowly, but evidently my throat was tense, because they began shouting, "Louder! Louder!"

"We of the younger generation extol the wisdom of that great leader and educator," I shouted, "who first spoke these flaming words of wisdom: 'A ship lost at sea for many days suddenly sighted a friendly vessel. From the mast of the unfortunate vessel was seen a signal: "Water, water; we die of thirst!" The answer from the friendly vessel came back: "Cast down your bucket where you are." The captain of the distressed vessel, at last heeding the injunction, cast down his bucket, and it came up full of fresh sparkling water from the mouth of the Amazon River.' And like him I say, and in his words, 'To those of my race who depend upon bettering their condition in a foreign land, or who underestimate the importance of cultivating friendly relations with the Southern white man, who is his next-door neighbor, I would say: "Cast down your bucket where you are" — cast it down in making friends in every manly way of the people of all races by whom we are surrounded . . .' "

I spoke automatically and with such fervor that I did not realize that the men were still talking and laughing until my dry mouth, filling up with blood from the cut, almost strangled me. I coughed, wanting to stop and go to one of the tall brass, sand-filled spittoons to relieve myself, but a few of the men, especially the superintendent, were listening and I was afraid. So I gulped it down, blood, saliva, and all, and continued. (What powers of endurance I had during those days! What enthusiasm! What a belief in the rightness of things!) I spoke even louder in spite of the pain. But still they talked and still they laughed, as though deaf with cotton in dirty ears. So I spoke with greater emotional emphasis. I closed my ears and swallowed blood until I was nauseated. The speech seemed a hundred times as long as before, but I could not leave out a single word. All had to be said, each memorized nuance considered, rendered. Nor was that all. Whenever I uttered a word of three or more syllables a group of voices would yell for me to repeat it. I used the phrase "social responsibility" and they yelled:

"What's that word you say, boy?"

"Social responsibility," I said.

"What?"

"Social . . ."

"Louder."

". . . responsibility."

"More!"

"Respon — "

"Repeat!"

" — sibility."

The room filled with the uproar of laughter until, no doubt, distracted by having to gulp down my blood, I made a mistake and yelled a phrase I had often seen denounced in newspaper editorials, heard debated in private.

"Social . . ."

"What?" they yelled.

". . . equality — "

The laughter hung smokelike in the sudden stillness. I opened my eyes, puzzled. Sounds of displeasure filled the room. The M.C. rushed forward. They shouted hostile phrases at me. But I did not understand.

A small dry mustached man in the front row blared out, "Say that slowly, son!"

"What, sir?"

"What you just said!"

"Social responsibility, sir," I said.

"You weren't being smart, were you, boy?" he said, not unkindly.

"No, sir!"

"You sure that about 'equality' was a mistake?"

"Oh, yes, sir," I said. "I was swallowing blood." 90

"Well, you had better speak more slowly so we can understand. We mean to do right by you, but you've got to know your place at all times. All right, now, go on with your speech."

I was afraid. I wanted to leave but I wanted also to speak and I was afraid they'd snatch me down.

"Thank you, sir," I said, beginning where I had left off, and having them ignore me as before.

Yet when I finished there was a thunderous applause. I was surprised to see the superintendent come forth with a package wrapped in white tissue paper, and, gesturing for quiet, address the men.

"Gentlemen, you see that I did not overpraise this boy. He makes a good 95 speech and some day he'll lead his people in the proper paths. And I don't have to tell you that that is important in these days and times. This is a good, smart boy, and so to encourage him in the right direction, in the name of the Board of Education I wish to present him a prize in the form of this . . ."

He paused, removing the tissue paper and revealing a gleaming calfskin brief case.

". . . in the form of this first-class article from Shad Whitmore's shop."

"Boy," he said, addressing me, "take this prize and keep it well. Consider it a badge of office. Prize it. Keep developing as you are and some day it will be filled with important papers that will help shape the destiny of your people."

I was so moved that I could hardly express my thanks. A rope of bloody saliva forming a shape like an undiscovered continent drooled upon the leather and I wiped it quickly away. I felt an importance that I had never dreamed.

"Open it and see what's inside," I was told. 100

My fingers a-tremble, I complied, smelling the fresh leather and finding an official-looking document inside. It was a scholarship to the state college for Negroes. My eyes filled with tears and I ran awkwardly off the floor.

I was overjoyed; I did not even mind when I discovered that the gold pieces I had scrambled for were brass pocket tokens advertising a certain make of automobile.

When I reached home everyone was excited. Next day the neighbors came to congratulate me. I even felt safe from grandfather, whose deathbed curse usually spoiled my triumphs. I stood beneath his photograph with my brief case in hand and smiled triumphantly into his stolid black peasant's face. It was a face that fascinated me. The eyes seemed to follow everywhere I went.

That night I dreamed I was at a circus with him and that he refused to laugh at the clowns no matter what they did. Then later he told me to open my brief case and read what was inside and I did, finding an official envelope stamped with the state seal; and inside the envelope I found another and another, endlessly, and I thought I would fall of weariness. "Them's years," he said. "Now open that one." And I did and in it I found an engraved document containing a short message in letters of gold. "Read it," my grandfather said. "Out loud!"

"To Whom It May Concern," I intoned. "Keep This Nigger-Boy Running." 105

I awoke with the old man's laughter ringing in my ears.

(It was a dream I was to remember and dream again for many years after. But at that time I had no insight into its meaning. First I had to attend college.)

Considerations

1. How does the first paragraph of the story sum up the conflict that the narrator confronts? In what sense is he "invisible"?
2. Why do his grandfather's last words cause so much anxiety in the family? What does his grandfather mean when he says, "I want you to overcome 'em with yeses, undermine 'em with grins, agree 'em to death"?
3. What is the symbolic significance of the naked blonde? What details reveal that she represents more than a sexual tease in the story?
4. How does the battle in the boxing ring and the scramble for money afterward suggest the kind of control whites have over blacks in the story?
5. Why is it significant that the town is named Greenwood and that the briefcase award comes from Shad Whitmore's shop? Can you find any other details that serve to reinforce the meaning of the story?
6. What is the narrator's perspective as an educated adult telling the story, in contrast to his assumptions and beliefs as a recent high-school graduate? How is this contrast especially evident in the speech before the "leading white citizens" of the town?
7. How can the dream at the end of the story be related to the major incidents that precede it?
8. Discuss how the young black man's expectations are similar to what has come to be known as the American dream, that assumes that ambition, hard work, perseverance, intelligence, and virtue always lead to success.
9. Given the grandfather's advice, explain how "meekness" can be a "dangerous activity" and a weapon against oppression.
10. Imagine the story as told from a third-person point of view. How would this change the story? Do you think the story would be more or less effective told from a third-person point of view? Explain your answer.

Connections

1. Compare and contrast Ellison's view of the South with Faulkner's in "A Rose for Emily" (p. 47).
2. Write an essay comparing and contrasting "Battle Royal" and James Joyce's "Araby" (p. 372) as symbolic stories that focus on their respective protagonists' illusions and disillusions about life.
3. Compare and contrast this story with M. Carl Holman's poem "Mr. Z" (p. 796).

PERSPECTIVE

RALPH ELLISON (b. 1914)

On Fiction as an Oblique Process 1974

[John] Hersey [Interviewer]: Do you have in mind an image of some actualized reader to whom you are communicating as you write?

Ellison: There is no *specific* person there, but there is a sort of ideal reader, or informed persona, who has some immediate sense of the material that I'm working with. Beyond that there is my sense of the rhetorical levers within American society, and these attach to all kinds of experiences and values. I don't want to be a behaviorist here, but I'm referring to the systems of values, the beliefs and customs and sense of the past, and that hope for the future, which have evolved through the history of the republic. These do provide a medium of communication.

For instance, the old underdog pattern. It turns up in many guises, and it allows the writer to communicate with the public over and beyond whatever the immediate issues of his fiction happen to be. That is, deep down we believe in the underdog, even though we give him hell; and this provides a rhetoric through which the writer can communicate with a reader beyond any questions of their disagreements over class values, race, or anything else. But the writer must be aware that that is what is there. On the other hand, I do not think he can manipulate his readers too directly; it must be an oblique process, if for no other reason than that to do it too directly throws you into propaganda, as against that brooding, questioning stance that is necessary for fiction.

From "A Talk with Ralph Ellison" in *Ralph Ellison: A Collection of Essays*

Considerations

1. What "rhetorical levers" does Ellison pull in "Battle Royal" to "provide a medium of communication" with his readers? What values do you think Ellison attributes to his readers?
2. How does Ellison's use of symbols in "Battle Royal" contribute to the "oblique process" he says is "necessary for fiction"?
3. Explain how "the old underdog pattern" functions in "Battle Royal" and how it affects your response to the narrator.

KATHERINE ANNE PORTER (1890–1980)

Born in Indian Creek, Texas, Katherine Anne Porter was raised by her grandmother and subsequently ran away from a convent school at the age of sixteen. At various points in her life she made a living as a journalist and teacher as well as a stage and film performer. Her extensive travels, six husbands, and many acknowledged lovers provided much of the material about human relations that makes its way into her fiction. Her collections of stories include *Flowering Judas* (1930), *The Leaning Tower* (1944), and *Collected Stories* (1965), which was awarded both the Pulitzer Prize and the National Book Award. Her novels include *Pale Horse, Pale Rider: Three Short Novels* (1939) and *Ship of Fools* (1962). "The Grave" describes a childhood experience filled with subtle, lasting significances.

The Grave 1944

The grandfather, dead for more than thirty years, had been twice disturbed in his long repose by the constancy and possessiveness of his widow. She removed his bones first to Louisiana and then to Texas as if she had set out to find her own burial place, knowing well she would never return to the places she had left. In Texas she set up a small cemetery in a corner of her first farm, and as the family connection grew, and oddments of relations came over from Kentucky to settle, it contained at last about twenty graves. After the grandmother's death, part of her land was to be sold for the benefit of certain of her children, and the cemetery happened to lie in the part set aside for sale. It was necessary to take up the bodies and bury them again in the family plot in the big new public cemetery, where the grandmother had been buried. At last her husband was to lie beside her for eternity, as she had planned.

The family cemetery had been a pleasant small neglected garden of tangled rose bushes and ragged cedar trees and cypress, the simple flat stones rising out of uncropped sweet-smelling wild grass. The graves were lying open and empty one burning day when Miranda and her brother Paul, who often went together to hunt rabbits and doves, propped their twenty-two Winchester rifles carefully against the rail fence, climbed over, and explored among the graves. She was nine years old and he was twelve.

They peered into the pits all shaped alike with such purposeful accuracy, and looking at each other with pleased adventurous eyes, they said in solemn tones: "These were graves!" trying by words to shape a special, suitable emotion in their minds, but they felt nothing except an agreeable thrill of wonder: they were seeing a new sight, doing something they had not done before. In them both there was also a small disappointment at the entire commonplaceness of the actual spectacle. Even if it had once contained a coffin for years upon years, when the coffin was gone a grave was just a hole in the ground. Miranda leaped into the pit that had held her grandfather's bones. Scratching around aimlessly and pleasurably as any young animal, she scooped up a lump of earth and weighed it in her palm. It had a pleasantly sweet, corrupt smell, being mixed with cedar needles and small leaves, and as the crumbs fell apart, she saw a silver dove no larger than a hazel nut, with spread wings and a neat fan-shaped tail. The breast had a deep round hollow in it. Turning it up to the fierce sunlight, she saw that the inside of the hollow was cut in little whorls. She scrambled out, over the pile of loose earth that had fallen back into one end of the grave, calling to Paul that she had found something, he must guess what. . . . His head appeared smiling over the rim of another grave. He waved a closed hand at her. "I've got something too!" They ran to compare treasures, making a game of it, so many guesses each, all wrong, and a final showdown with opened palms. Paul had found a thin wide gold ring carved with intricate flowers and leaves. Miranda was smitten at sight of the ring and wished to have it. Paul seemed more impressed by the dove. They made a trade, with some little bickering. After he had got the dove in his hand, Paul said, "Don't you know what this is? This is a screw head for a *coffin!* . . . I'll bet nobody else in the world has one like this!"

Miranda glanced at it without covetousness. She had the gold ring on her thumb; it fitted perfectly. "Maybe we ought to go now," she said, "maybe one of the niggers'll see us and tell somebody." They knew the land had been sold, the cemetery was no longer theirs, and they felt like trespassers. They climbed back over the fence, slung their rifles loosely under their arms — they had been shooting at targets with various kinds of firearms since they were seven years old — and set out to look for the rabbits and doves or whatever small game might happen along. On these expeditions Miranda always followed at Paul's heels along the path, obeying instructions about handling her gun when going through fences; learning how to stand it up properly so it would not slip and fire unexpectedly; how to wait her time for a shot and not just bang away in the air without looking, spoiling shots for Paul, who really could hit things if given a chance. Now and then, in her excitement at seeing birds whizz up suddenly before her face, or a rabbit leap across her very toes, she lost her head, and almost without sighting she flung her rifle up and pulled the trigger. She hardly ever hit any sort of mark. She had no proper sense of hunting at all. Her brother would be often completely disgusted with her. "You don't care whether you get your bird or not," he said. "That's no way to hunt." Miranda could not understand his indignation. She had seen him smash his hat and yell with fury when he had missed his aim. "What I like about shooting," said Miranda, with exasperating inconsequence, "is pulling the trigger and hearing the noise."

"Then by golly," said Paul, "whyn't you go back to the range and shoot at 5
bulls-eyes?"

"I'd just as soon," said Miranda, "only like this, we walk around more."

"Well, you just stay behind and stop spoiling my shots," said Paul, who, when he made a kill, wanted to be certain he had made it. Miranda, who alone brought down a bird once in twenty rounds, always claimed as her own any game they got when they fired at the same moment. It was tiresome and unfair and her brother was sick of it.

"Now, the first dove we see, or the first rabbit, is mine," he told her. "And the next will be yours. Remember that and don't get smarty."

"What about snakes?" asked Miranda idly. "Can I have the first snake?"

Waving her thumb gently and watching her gold ring glitter, Miranda lost 10
interest in shooting. She was wearing her summer roughing outfit: dark blue overalls, a light blue shirt, a hired-man's straw hat, and thick brown sandals. Her brother had the same outfit except his was a sober hickorynut color. Ordinarily Miranda preferred her overalls to any other dress, though it was making rather a scandal in the countryside, for the year was 1903, and in the back country the law of female decorum had teeth in it. Her father had been criticized for letting his girls dress like boys and go careering around astride barebacked horses. Big sister Maria, the really independent and fearless one, in spite of her rather affected ways, rode at a dead run with only a rope knotted around her horse's nose. It was said the motherless family was running down, with the grandmother no longer there to hold it together. It was known that she had discriminated against her son Harry in her will, and that he was in straits about money. Some of his old neighbors reflected with vicious satisfaction that now he would probably not be so stiffnecked, nor have any more high-stepping horses either. Miranda knew this, though she could not say how. She had met along the road

old women of the kind who smoked corn-cob pipes, who had treated her grandmother with most sincere respect. They slanted their gummy old eyes side-ways at the granddaughter and said, "Ain't you ashamed of yoself, Missy? It's against the Scriptures to dress like that. Whut yo Pappy thinkin about?" Miranda, with her powerful social sense, which was like a fine set of antennae radiating from every pore of her skin, would feel ashamed because she knew well it was rude and ill-bred to shock anybody, even bad-tempered old crones, though she had faith in her father's judgment and was perfectly comfortable in the clothes. Her father said, "They're just what you need, and they'll save your dresses for school. . . ." This sounded quite simple and natural to her. She had been brought up in rigorous economy. Wastefulness was vulgar. It was also a sin. These were truths; she had heard them repeated many times and never once disputed.

Now the ring, shining with the serene purity of fine gold on her rather grubby thumb, turned her feelings against her overalls and sockless feet, toes sticking through the thick brown leather straps. She wanted to go back to the farmhouse, take a good cold bath, dust herself with plenty of Maria's violet talcum powder — provided Maria was not present to object, of course — put on the thinnest, most becoming dress she owned, with a big sash, and sit in a wicker chair under the trees. . . . These things were not all she wanted, of course; she had vague stirrings of desire for luxury and a grand way of living which could not take precise form in her imagination but were founded on family legend of past wealth and leisure. These immediate comforts were what she could have, and she wanted them at once. She lagged rather far behind Paul, and once she thought of just turning back without a word and going home. She stopped, thinking that Paul would never do that to her, and so she would have to tell him. When a rabbit leaped, she let Paul have it without dispute. He killed it with one shot.

When she came up with him, he was already kneeling, examining the wound, the rabbit trailing from his hands. "Right through the head," he said complacently, as if he had aimed for it. He took out his sharp, competent bowie knife and started to skin the body. He did it very cleanly and quickly. Uncle Jimbilly knew how to prepare the skins so that Miranda always had fur coats for her dolls, for though she never cared much for her dolls she liked seeing them in fur coats. The children knelt facing each other over the dead animal. Miranda watched admiringly while her brother stripped the skin away as if he were taking off a glove. The flayed flesh emerged dark scarlet, sleek, firm; Miranda with thumb and finger felt the long fine muscles with the silvery flat strips binding them to the joints. Brother lifted the oddly bloated belly. "Look," he said, in a low amazed voice. "It was going to have young ones."

Very carefully he slit the thin flesh from the center ribs to the flanks, and a scarlet bag appeared. He slit again and pulled the bag open, and there lay a bundle of tiny rabbits, each wrapped in a thin scarlet veil. The brother pulled these off and there they were, dark gray, their sleek wet down lying in minute even ripples, like a baby's head just washed, their unbelievably small delicate ears folded close, their little blind faces almost featureless.

Miranda said, "Oh, I want to *see,*" under her breath. She looked and looked — excited but not frightened, for she was accustomed to the sight of animals killed in hunting — filled with pity and astonishment and a kind of shocked delight in the wonderful little creatures for their own sakes, they were so pretty. She touched one of them ever so carefully, "Ah, there's blood running over them," she said and began to tremble without knowing why. Yet she wanted most deeply to see and to know. Having seen, she felt at once as if she had known all along. The very memory of her former ignorance faded, she had always known just this. No one had ever told her anything outright, she had been rather unobservant of the animal life around her because she was so accustomed to animals. They seemed simply disorderly and unaccountably rude in their habits, but altogether natural and not very interesting. Her brother had spoken as if he had known about everything all along. He may have seen all this before. He had never said a word to her, but she knew now a part at least of what he knew. She understood a little of the secret, formless intuitions in her own mind and body, which had been clearing up, taking form, so gradually and so steadily she had not realized that she was learning what she had to know. Paul said cautiously, as if he were talking about something forbidden: "They were just about to be born." His voice dropped on the last word. "I know," said Miranda, "like kittens. I know, like babies." She was quietly and terribly agitated, standing again with her rifle under her arm, looking down at the bloody heap. "I don't want the skin," she said, "I won't have it." Paul buried the young rabbits again in their mother's body, wrapped the skin around her, carried her to a clump of sage bushes, and hid her away. He came out again at once and said to Miranda, with an eager friendliness, a confidential tone quite unusual in him, as if he were taking her into an important secret on equal terms: "Listen now. Now you listen to me, and don't ever forget. Don't you ever tell a living soul that you saw this. Don't tell a soul. Don't tell Dad because I'll get into trouble. He'll say I'm leading you into things you ought not to do. He's always saying that. So now don't you go and forget and blab out sometime the way you're always doing. . . . Now, that's secret. Don't you tell."

Miranda never told, she did not even wish to tell anybody. She thought 15
about the whole worrisome affair with confused unhappiness for a few days. Then it sank quietly into her mind and was heaped over by accumulated thousands of impressions, for nearly twenty years. One day she was picking her path among the puddles and crushed refuse of a market street in a strange city of a strange country, when without warning, plain and clear in its true colors as if she looked through a frame upon a scene that had not stirred nor changed since the moment it happened, the episode of that far-off day leaped from its burial place before her mind's eye. She was so reasonlessly horrified she halted suddenly staring, the scene before her eyes dimmed for the vision back of them. An Indian vendor had held up before her a tray of dyed sugar sweets, in the shapes of all kinds of small creatures: birds, baby chicks, baby rabbits, lambs, baby pigs. They were in gay colors and smelled of vanilla, maybe. . . . It was a very hot day and the smell in the market, with its piles of raw flesh and wilting flowers, was like the mingled sweetness and corruption she had smelled that other day in the empty cemetery at home: the day she had remembered always until now vaguely as the time she and her brother had found treasure in the opened graves. Instantly upon this thought the dreadful vision faded, and she saw clearly her brother, whose childhood face she had forgotten, standing again

in the blazing sunshine, again twelve years old, a pleased sober smile in his eyes, turning the silver dove over and over in his hands.

Considerations

1. Why do you think the story opens in a cemetery? Is it possible to answer this question before reading the entire story?
2. What do Miranda and Paul find in the graves? Why do they trade "treasures"?
3. Why do you suppose Porter provides background information about the "back country" where "the law of female decorum had teeth in it"? What is Miranda's relationship to this social environment?
4. What is Miranda's response to the dead, pregnant rabbit? What emotions does she experience?
5. Concerning the rabbit, what is it that Miranda "felt at once as if she had known all along"?
6. Why do you think it is appropriate that Miranda asks Paul if she can "have the first snake" before the incident with the rabbit?
7. How do the gold ring, the unborn rabbits, and the information about how Miranda dresses relate to one another? How does a careful consideration of the meaning of each help to shed light on the rest?
8. What is Paul's function in the story? Why does he want to keep everything secret?
9. How is Miranda's memory jarred in the story's final paragraph? What is it that causes her to remember the childhood episode almost twenty years earlier?
10. What does Miranda discover about life and herself on this day of hunting with her brother?
11. Write an essay that connects and explains the "mingled sweetness and corruption" of the principal symbols in the story — the grave, the dove, the ring, and the rabbits.

Connections

1. Read the description "What Is an Initiation Story?" by Mordecai Marcus (p. 481). Compare "The Grave" with Ellison's "Battle Royal" (p. 179), Toni Cade Bambara's "The Lesson" (p. 364), or James Joyce's "Araby" (p. 372), as initiation stories.
2. Write an essay that speculates on how the protagonists in "The Grave" and Colette's "The Hand" (p. 176) are affected by the realizations they come to.

7. Theme

Theme is the central idea or meaning of a story. It provides a unifying point around which the plot, characters, setting, point of view, symbols, and other elements of a story are organized. In some works the theme is explicitly stated. Nathaniel Hawthorne's "Wakefield," for example, begins with the author telling the reader that the point of his story is "done up neatly, and condensed into the final sentence." Most modern writers, however, present their themes implicitly (as Hawthorne does in the majority of his stories), so determining the underlying meaning of a work often requires more effort than it does from the reader of "Wakefield." One reason for the difficulty is that the theme is fused into the elements of the story, and these must be carefully examined in relation to one another as well as to the work as a whole. But then that's the value of determining the theme, for it requires a close analysis of all the elements of a work. This close reading often results in sharper insights into this overlooked character or that seemingly unrelated incident. Accounting for the details and seeing how they fit together result in greater understanding of the story. Such familiarity creates pleasure in much the same way that a musical piece heard more than once becomes a rich experience rather than simply a repetitive one.

Themes are not always easy to express, but some principles can aid you in articulating the central meaning of a work. First distinguish between the theme of a story and its subject. They are not equivalents. Many stories share identical subjects, such as fate, death, innocence, youth, loneliness, racial prejudice, and disillusionment. Yet each story usually makes its own statement about the subject and expresses some view of life. Hemingway's "Soldier's Home" (p. 121) and Faulkner's "Barn Burning" (p. 66) both describe young men who are unhappy at home and decide that they must leave, but the meaning of each story is quite different. A thematic generalization about "Soldier's Home" could be something like this: "The brutal experience of war can alienate a person from those who are innocent of war's actualities — even family and friends." The theme of Faulkner's story could be stated this way: "No matter how much one might love one's father, there comes a time when family loyalties must be left behind in order to be true to one's self."

These two statements of theme do not definitively sum up each story — there is no single, absolute way of expressing a work's theme — but they do describe a central idea in each. Furthermore, the emphasis in each of these themes could be modified or expanded, because interpretations of interesting, complex works are always subject to revision. People have different responses to life, and so it is hardly surprising that responses to literature are not identical. A consideration of theme usually expands the possibilities for meaning rather than reducing them to categories such as "right" or "wrong."

Although readers may differ in their interpretations of a story, that does not mean that *any* interpretation is valid. If we were to assert that the soldier's dissatisfactions in Hemingway's story could be readily eliminated by his settling down to marriage and a decent job (his mother's solution), we would have missed Hemingway's purposes in writing the story; we would have failed to see how Krebs's war experiences have caused him to reexamine the assumptions and beliefs that previously nurtured him but now seem unreal to him. We would have to ignore much in the story in order to arrive at such a reading. To be valid, the statement of the theme should be responsive to the details of the story. It must be based on evidence within the story rather than solely on experiences, attitudes, or values the reader brings to the work — such as personally knowing a war veteran who successfully adjusted to civilian life after getting a good job and marrying. Familiarity with the subject matter of a story can certainly be an aid to interpretation, but it should not get in the way of seeing the author's perspective.

Sometimes readers too hastily conclude that a story's theme always consists of a moral, some kind of lesson that is dramatized by the various elements of the work. There are stories that do this — "Wakefield," for example. Here are Hawthorne's final sentences in his story about a middle-aged man who drops out of life for twenty years:

> He has left us much food for thought, a portion of which shall lend its wisdom to a moral, and be shaped into a figure. Amid the seeming confusion of our mysterious world, individuals are so nicely adjusted to a system, and systems to one another and to a whole, that, by stepping aside for a moment, a man exposes himself to a fearful risk of losing his place forever. Like Wakefield, he may become, as it were, the Outcast of the Universe.

Most stories, however, do not include such direct caveats about the conduct of life. A tendency to look for a lesson in a story can produce a reductive and inaccurate formulation of its theme. Consider the damage done to Colette's "The Hand" (p. 176) if its theme is described as this: "Adolescents are too young to cope with the responsibilities of marriage."

Colette's focus in this story is on the young woman's response to her husband's powerful sexuality and dominance rather than on her inability to be a good wife.

In fact, a good many stories go beyond traditional moral values to explore human behavior instead of condemning or endorsing it. Chekhov's treatment of the adulterous affair between Gurov and Anna in "The Lady with the Pet Dog" (p. 146) portrays a love that is valuable and true despite the conventional moral codes it violates. That is not to say that the reader must agree with Chekhov's attitude that such love has a validity of its own. We are obligated to see that Chekhov is sympathetic to the lovers, but that does not necessitate our approval. All that is required is our willingness to explore with the author the issues set before us. The themes we encounter in literature may challenge as well as reassure us.

Determining the theme of a story can be a difficult task, because all the story's elements may contribute to its central idea. Indeed, you may discover that finding the theme is more challenging than coming to grips with the author's values as they are revealed in the story. There is no precise formula that can take you to the center of a story's meaning and help you to articulate it. However, several strategies are practical and useful once you have read the story. Apply these pointers during a second or third reading.

1. Pay attention to the title of the story; it will often provide a lead to a major symbol (Faulkner's "Barn Burning," p. 66) or focus on the subject around which the theme develops (Godwin's "A Sorrowful Woman," p. 30).
2. Look for details in the story that have potential for symbolic meanings. Careful consideration of names, places, objects, minor characters, and incidents can lead you to the central meaning — for example, think of the stripper in Ellison's "Battle Royal" (p. 179). Be especially attentive to elements you did not understand on the first reading.
3. Decide if the protagonist changes or develops some important insight as a result of the action. Carefully examine any generalizations the protagonist or narrator makes about the events in the story.
4. When you formulate the theme of the story in your own words, write it down in a complete sentence or two that make some point about the subject matter. Revenge may be the subject of a story, but its theme should make a statement about revenge: "Instead of providing satisfaction, revenge defeats the best in one's self" is one possibility.
5. Be certain that your expression of the theme is a generalized statement rather than a specific description of particular people, places, and incidents in the story. Contrast the preceding statement of a theme on revenge with this too-specific one: "In Nathaniel Hawthorne's *The Scarlet Letter,* Roger Chillingworth loses his humanity owing to his single-minded attempts to punish Arthur Dimmesdale for having an

affair with Chillingworth's wife, Hester." Hawthorne's theme is not restricted to a single fictional character named Chillingworth but to anyone whose life is ruined by revenge. Be certain that your statement of theme does not focus on only part of the story. The theme just cited for *The Scarlet Letter,* for example, relegates Hester to the status of a minor character. What it says about Chillingworth is true, but the statement is incomplete as a generalization about the novel.

6. Be wary of using clichés as a way of stating theme. They tend to short-circuit ideas instead of generating them. It may be tempting to resort to something like "Love conquers all" as a statement of the theme of Chekhov's "The Lady with the Pet Dog" (p. 146); however, even the slightest second thought reveals how much more ambiguous the ending of that story is.
7. Be aware that some stories emphasize theme less than others. Stories that have as their major purpose adventure, humor, mystery, or terror may have little or no theme. In Edgar Allan Poe's "The Pit and the Pendulum" (p. 398), the protagonist is not used to condemn torture; instead, he becomes a sensitive gauge to measure the pain and horror he endures at the hands of his captors.

What is most valuable about articulating the theme of a work is not a brief summary statement but the process by which the theme is determined. Ultimately, the theme is expressed by the story itself and is inseparable from the experience of reading the story. Tim O'Brien's explanation about "How to Tell a True War Story" (p. 454) is probably true of most kinds of stories: "In a true war story, if there's a moral [or theme] at all, it's like the thread that makes the cloth. You can't tease it out. You can't extract the meaning without unraveling the deeper meaning." Describing the theme should not be a way to consume a story, to be done with it. It is a means of clarifying our thinking about what we've read and probably felt intuitively.

Stephen Crane's "The Bride Comes to Yellow Sky" and Joseph Conrad's "An Outpost of Progress" are two stories whose respective themes emerge from the authors' skillful use of plot, character, setting, and symbol.

STEPHEN CRANE (1871–1900)

Born in Newark, New Jersey, Stephen Crane attended Lafayette College and Syracuse University and then worked as a free-lance journalist in New York City. He wrote newspaper pieces, short stories, poems, and novels for his entire, brief adult life. His first book, *Maggie: A Girl of the Streets* (1893), is a story about New York slum life and prostitution. His most famous novel, *The Red Badge of Courage* (1895), gives readers a vivid, convincing recreation of Civil War battles, even though Crane had never been to war. However, Crane was personally familiar with the American West, where he traveled as a reporter. "The Bride Comes to Yellow Sky" includes some of the ingredients of a typical popular western — a confrontation between a marshal and a drunk who shoots up the town — but the story's theme is less predictable and more serious than the plot seems to suggest.

The Bride Comes to Yellow Sky 1898

I

The great Pullman was whirling onward with such dignity of motion that a glance from the window seemed simply to prove that the plains of Texas were pouring eastward. Vast flats of green grass, dull-hued spaces of mesquit and cactus, little groups of frame houses, woods of light and tender trees, all were sweeping into the east, sweeping over the horizon, a precipice.

A newly married pair had boarded this coach at San Antonio. The man's face was reddened from many days in the wind and sun, and a direct result of his new black clothes was that his brick-colored hands were constantly performing in a most conscious fashion. From time to time he looked down respectfully at his attire. He sat with a hand on each knee, like a man waiting in a barber's shop. The glances he devoted to other passengers were furtive and shy.

The bride was not pretty, nor was she very young. She wore a dress of blue cashmere, with small reservations of velvet here and there, and with steel buttons abounding. She continually twisted her head to regard her puff sleeves, very stiff, straight, and high. They embarrassed her. It was quite apparent that she had cooked, and that she expected to cook, dutifully. The blushes caused by the careless scrutiny of some passengers as she had entered the car were strange to see upon this plain, under-class countenance, which was drawn in placid, almost emotionless lines.

They were evidently very happy. "Ever been in a parlor-car before?" he asked, smiling with delight.

"No," she answered; "I never was. It's fine, ain't it?" 5

"Great! And then after a while we'll go forward to the diner, and get a big lay-out. Finest meal in the world. Charge a dollar."

"Oh, do they?" cried the bride. "Charge a dollar? Why, that's too much — for us — ain't it, Jack?"

"Not this trip, anyhow," he answered bravely. "We're going to go the whole thing."

Later he explained to her about the trains. "You see, it's a thousand miles from one end of Texas to the other; and this train runs right across it, and never stops but four times." He had the pride of an owner. He pointed out to her the dazzling fittings of the coach; and in truth her eyes opened wider as she contemplated the sea-green figured velvet, the shining brass, silver, and glass, the wood that gleamed as darkly brilliant as the surface of a pool of oil. At one end a bronze figure sturdily held a support for a separated chamber, and at convenient places on the ceiling were frescos in olive and silver.

To the minds of the pair, their surroundings reflected the glory of their 10
marriage that morning in San Antonio; this was the environment of their new estate; and the man's face in particular beamed with an elation that made him appear ridiculous to the negro porter. This individual at times surveyed them from afar with an amused and superior grin. On other occasions he bullied them with skill in ways that did not make it exactly plain to them that they were being bullied. He subtly used all the manners of the most unconquerable kind of snobbery. He oppressed them; but of this oppression they had small knowledge, and they speedily forgot that infrequently a number of travellers covered them with stares of derisive enjoyment. Historically there was supposed to be something infinitely humorous in their situation.

"We are due in Yellow Sky at 3:42," he said, looking tenderly into her eyes.

"Oh, are we?" she said, as if she had not been aware of it. To evince surprise at her husband's statement was part of her wifely amiability. She took from a pocket a little silver watch; and as she held it before her, and stared at it with a frown of attention, the new husband's face shone.

"I bought it in San Anton' from a friend of mine," he told her gleefully.

"It's seventeen minutes past twelve," she said, looking up at him with a kind of shy and clumsy coquetry. A passenger, noting this play, grew excessively sardonic, and winked at himself in one of the numerous mirrors.

At last they went to the dining-car. Two rows of negro waiters, in glowing 15
white suits, surveyed their entrance with the interest, and also the equanimity, of men who had been forewarned. The pair fell to the lot of a waiter who happened to feel pleasure in steering them through their meal. He viewed them with the manner of a fatherly pilot, his countenance radiant with benevolence. The patronage, entwined with the ordinary deference, was not plain to them. And yet, as they returned to their coach, they showed in their faces a sense of escape.

To the left, miles down a long purple slope, was a little ribbon of mist where moved the keening Rio Grande. The train was approaching it at an angle, and the apex was Yellow Sky. Presently it was apparent that, as the distance from Yellow Sky grew shorter, the husband became commensurately restless. His brick-red hands were more insistent in their prominence. Occasionally he was even rather absent-minded and far-away when the bride leaned forward and addressed him.

As a matter of truth, Jack Potter was beginning to find the shadow of a deed weigh upon him like a leaden slab. He, the town marshal of Yellow Sky, a man known, liked, and feared in his corner, a prominent person, had gone to San Antonio to meet a girl he believed he loved, and there, after the usual prayers, had actually induced her to marry him, without consulting Yellow Sky for any part of the transaction. He was now bringing his bride before an innocent and unsuspecting community.

Of course people in Yellow Sky married as it pleased them in accordance with a general custom; but such was Potter's thought of his duty to his friends, or of their idea of his duty, or of an unspoken form which does not control men in these matters, that he felt he was heinous. He had committed an extraordinary crime. Face to face with this girl in San Antonio, and spurred by his sharp impulse, he had gone headlong over all the social hedges. At San Antonio he was like a man hidden in the dark. A knife to sever any friendly duty, any form, was easy to his hand in that remote city. But the hour of Yellow Sky — the hour of daylight — was approaching.

He knew full well that his marriage was an important thing to his town. It could only be exceeded by the burning of the new hotel. His friends could not forgive him. Frequently he had reflected on the advisability of telling them by telegraph, but a new cowardice had been upon him. He feared to do it. And now the train was hurrying him toward a scene of amazement, glee, and reproach. He glanced out of the window at the line of haze swinging slowly in toward the train.

Yellow Sky had a kind of brass band, which played painfully, to the delight 20
of the populace. He laughed without heart as he thought of it. If the citizens could dream of his prospective arrival with his bride, they would parade the band at the station and escort them, amid cheers and laughing congratulations, to his adobe home.

He resolved that he would use all the devices of speed and plainscraft in making the journey from the station to his house. Once within that safe citadel, he could issue some sort of vocal bulletin, and then not go among the citizens until they had time to wear off a little of their enthusiasm.

The bride looked anxiously at him. "What's worrying you, Jack?"

He laughed again. "I'm not worrying, girl; I'm only thinking of Yellow Sky."

She flushed in comprehension.

A sense of mutual guilt invaded their minds and developed a finer tender- 25
ness. They looked at each other with eyes softly aglow. But Potter often laughed the same nervous laugh; the flush upon the bride's face seemed quite permanent.

The traitor to the feelings of Yellow Sky narrowly watched the speeding landscape. "We're nearly there," he said.

Presently the porter came and announced the proximity of Potter's home. He held a brush in his hand, and, with all his airy superiority gone, he brushed Potter's new clothes as the latter slowly turned this way and that way. Potter fumbled out a coin and gave it to the porter, as he had seen others do. It was a heavy and muscle-bound business, as that of a man shoeing his first horse.

The porter took their bag, and as the train began to slow they moved forward to the hooded platform of the car. Presently the two engines and their long string of coaches rushed into the station of Yellow Sky.

"They have to take water here," said Potter, from a constricted throat and in mournful cadence, as one announcing death. Before the train stopped his eye had swept the length of the platform, and he was glad and astonished to see there was none upon it but the station-agent, who, with a slightly hurried and anxious air, was walking toward the water-tanks. When the train had halted, the porter alighted first, and placed in position a little temporary step.

"Come on, girl," said Potter, hoarsely. As he helped her down they each 30
laughed on a false note. He took the bag from the negro, and bade his wife cling to his arm. As they slunk rapidly away, his hang-dog glance perceived that they were unloading the two trunks, and also that the station-agent, far ahead near the baggage-car, had turned and was running toward him, making gestures. He laughed, and groaned as he laughed, when he noted the first effect of his marital bliss upon Yellow Sky. He gripped his wife's arm firmly to his side, and they fled. Behind them the porter stood, chuckling fatuously.

II

The California express on the Southern Railway was due at Yellow Sky in twenty-one minutes. There were six men at the bar of the Weary Gentleman saloon. One was a drummer who talked a great deal and rapidly; three were Texans who did not care to talk at that time; and two were Mexican sheep-herders, who did not talk as a general practice in the Weary Gentleman saloon. The barkeeper's dog lay on the board walk that crossed in front of the door. His head was on his paws, and he glanced drowsily here and there with the constant vigilance of a dog that is kicked on occasion. Across the sandy street were some vivid green grass-plots, so wonderful in appearance, amid the sands that burned near them in a blazing sun, that they caused a doubt in the mind. They exactly resembled the grass mats used to represent lawns on the stage. At the cooler end of the railway station, a man without a coat sat in a tilted chair and smoked his pipe. The fresh-cut bank of the Rio Grande circled near the town, and there could be seen beyond it a great plum-colored plain of mesquit.

Save for the busy drummer and his companions in the saloon, Yellow Sky was dozing. The new-comer leaned gracefully upon the bar, and recited many tales with the confidence of a bard who has come upon a new field.

"—and at the moment that the old man fell downstairs with the bureau in his arms, the old woman was coming up with two scuttles of coal, and of course—"

The drummer's tale was interrupted by a young man who suddenly appeared in the open door. He cried: "Scratchy Wilson's drunk, and has turned loose with both hands." The two Mexicans at once set down their glasses and faded out of the rear entrance of the saloon.

The drummer, innocent and jocular, answered: "All right, old man. S'pose he has? Come in and have a drink, anyhow."

But the information had made such an obvious cleft in every skull in the room that the drummer was obliged to see its importance. All had become instantly solemn. "Say," said he, mystified, "what is this?" His three companions made the introductory gesture of eloquent speech; but the young man at the door forestalled them.

"It means, my friend," he answered, as he came into the saloon, "that for the next two hours this town won't be a health resort."

The barkeeper went to the door, and locked and barred it; reaching out of the window, he pulled in heavy wooden shutters, and barred them. Immediately a solemn, chapel-like gloom was upon the place. The drummer was looking from one to another.

"But, say," he cried, "what is this, anyhow? You don't mean there is going to be a gun-fight?"

"Don't know whether there'll be a fight or not," answered one man, grimly; "but there'll be some shootin'—some good shootin'."

The young man who had warned them waved his hand. "Oh, there'll be a fight fast enough, if any one wants it. Anybody can get a fight out there in the street. There's a fight just waiting."

The drummer seemed to be swayed between the interest of a foreigner and a perception of personal danger.

"What did you say his name was?" he asked.

"Scratchy Wilson," they answered in chorus.

"And will he kill anybody? What are you going to do? Does this happen often? Does he rampage around like this once a week or so? Can he break in that door?"

"No; he can't break down that door," replied the barkeeper. "He's tried it three times. But when he comes you'd better lay down on the floor, stranger. He's dead sure to shoot at it, and a bullet may come through."

Thereafter the drummer kept a strict eye upon the door. The time had not yet called for him to hug the floor, but, as a minor precaution, he sidled near the wall. "Will he kill anybody?" he said again.

The men laughed low and scornfully at the question.

"He's out to shoot, and he's out for trouble. Don't see any good in experimentin' with him."

"But what do you do in a case like this? What do you do?"

A man responded: "Why, he and Jack Potter — "

"But," in chorus the other men interrupted, "Jack Potter's in San Anton'."

"Well, who is he? What's he got to do with it?"

"Oh, he's the town marshal. He goes out and fights Scratchy when he gets on one of these tears."

"Wow!" said the drummer, mopping his brow. "Nice job he's got."

The voices had toned away to mere whisperings. The drummer wished to ask further questions, which were born of an increasing anxiety and bewilderment; but when he attempted them, the men merely looked at him in irritation and motioned him to remain silent. A tense waiting hush was upon them. In the deep shadows of the room their eyes shone as they listened for sounds from the street. One man made three gestures at the barkeeper; and the latter, moving like a ghost, handed him a glass and a bottle. The man poured a full glass of whisky, and set down the bottle noiselessly. He gulped the whisky in a swallow, and turned again toward the door in immovable silence. The drummer saw that the barkeeper, without a sound, had taken a Winchester from beneath the bar. Later he saw this individual beckoning to him, so he tiptoed across the room.

"You better come with me back of the bar."

"No thanks," said the drummer, perspiring; "I'd rather be where I can make a break for the back door."

Whereupon the man of bottles made a kindly but peremptory gesture. The drummer obeyed it, and, finding himself seated on a box with his head below the level of the bar, balm was laid upon his soul at sight of various zinc and copper fittings that bore a resemblance to armor-plate. The barkeeper took a seat comfortably upon an adjacent box.

"You see," he whispered, "this here Scratchy Wilson is a wonder with a gun — a perfect wonder; and when he goes on the war-trail, we hunt our holes — naturally. He's about the last one of the old gang that used to hang out along the river here. He's a terror when he's drunk. When he's sober he's all right — kind of simple — wouldn't hurt a fly — nicest fellow in town. But when he's drunk — whoo!"

There were periods of stillness. "I wish Jack Potter was back from San Anton'," said the barkeeper. "He shot Wilson up once — in the leg — and he would sail in and pull out the kinks in this thing."

Presently they heard from a distance the sound of a shot, followed by three wild yowls. It instantly removed a bond from the men in the darkened saloon. There was a shuffling of feet. They looked at each other. "Here he comes," they said.

III

A man in a maroon-colored flannel shirt, which had been purchased for purposes of decoration, and made principally by some Jewish women on the East Side of New York, rounded a corner and walked into the middle of the main street of Yellow Sky. In either hand the man held a long, heavy, blue-black revolver. Often he yelled, and these cries rang through a semblance of a deserted village, shrilly flying over the roofs in a volume that seemed to have no relation to the ordinary vocal strength of a man. It was as if the surrounding stillness formed the arch of a tomb over him. These cries of ferocious challenge rang against walls of silence. And his boots had red tops with gilded imprints, of the kind beloved in winter by little sledding boys on the hillsides of New England.

The man's face flamed in a rage begot of whisky. His eyes, rolling, and yet keen for ambush, hunted the still doorways and windows. He walked with the creeping movement of the midnight cat. As it occurred to him, he roared menacing information. The long revolvers in his hands were as easy as straws; they were removed with an electric swiftness. The little fingers of each hand played sometimes in a musician's way. Plain from the low collar of the shirt, the cords of his neck straightened and sank, straightened and sank, as passion moved him. The only sounds were his terrible invitations. The calm adobes preserved their demeanor at the passing of this small thing in the middle of the street.

There was no offer of fight — no offer of fight. The man called to the sky. 65
There were no attractions. He bellowed and fumed and swayed his revolvers here and everywhere.

The dog of the barkeeper of the Weary Gentleman saloon had not appreciated the advance of events. He yet lay dozing in front of his master's door. At sight of the dog, the man paused and raised his revolver humorously. At sight of the man, the dog sprang up and walked diagonally away, with a sullen head, and growling. The man yelled, and the dog broke into a gallop. As it was about to enter the alley, there was a loud noise, a whistling, and something spat the ground directly before it. The dog screamed, and, wheeling in terror, galloped headlong in a new direction. Again there was a noise, a whistling, and sand was kicked viciously before it. Fear-stricken, the dog turned and flurried like an animal in a pen. The man stood laughing, his weapons at his hips.

Ultimately the man was attracted by the closed door of the Weary Gentleman saloon. He went to it and, hammering with a revolver, demanded drink.

The door remaining imperturbable, he picked a bit of paper from the walk, and nailed it to the framework with a knife. He then turned his back contemptuously upon this popular resort and, walking to the opposite side of the street and spinning there on his heel quickly and lithely, fired at the bit of paper. He missed it by a half inch. He swore at himself, and went away. Later he comfortably fusilladed the windows of his most intimate friend. The man was playing with this town; it was a toy for him.

But still there was no offer of fight. The name of Jack Potter, his ancient antagonist, entered his mind, and he concluded that it would be a glad thing if he should go to Potter's house, and by bombardment induce him to come out and fight. He moved in the direction of his desire, chanting Apache scalp-music.

When he arrived at it, Potter's house presented the same still front as had 70 the other adobes. Taking up a strategic position, the man howled a challenge. But this house regarded him as might a great stone god. It gave no sign. After a decent wait, the man howled further challenges, mingling with them wonderful epithets.

Presently there came the spectacle of a man churning himself into deepest rage over the immobility of a house. He fumed at it as the winter wind attacks a prairie cabin in the North. To the distance there should have gone the sound of a tumult like the fighting of two hundred Mexicans. As necessity bade him, he paused for breath or to reload his revolvers.

IV

Potter and his bride walked sheepishly and with speed. Sometimes they laughed together shamefacedly and low.

"Next corner, dear," he said finally.

They put forth the efforts of a pair walking bowed against a strong wind. Potter was about to raise a finger to point the first appearance of the new home when, as they circled the corner, they came face to face with a man in a maroon-colored shirt, who was feverishly pushing cartridges into a large revolver. Upon the instant the man dropped his revolver to the ground and, like lightning, whipped another from its holster. The second weapon was aimed at the bridegroom's chest.

There was a silence. Potter's mouth seemed to be merely a grave for his 75 tongue. He exhibited an instinct to at once loosen his arm from the woman's grip, and he dropped the bag to the sand. As for the bride, her face had gone as yellow as old cloth. She was a slave to hideous rites, gazing at the apparitional snake.

The two men faced each other at a distance of three paces. He of the revolver smiled with a new and quiet ferocity.

"Tried to sneak up on me," he said. "Tried to sneak up on me!" His eyes grew more baleful. As Potter made a slight movement, the man thrust his revolver venomously forward. "No, don't you do it, Jack Potter. Don't you move a finger toward a gun just yet. Don't you move an eyelash. The time has come for me to settle with you and I'm goin' to do it my own way, and loaf along with no interferin'. So if you don't want a gun bent on you, just mind what I tell you."

Potter looked at his enemy. "I ain't got a gun on me, Scratchy," he said. "Honest, I ain't." He was stiffening and steadying, but yet somewhere at the back of his mind a vision of the Pullman floated: the sea-green figured velvet, the shining brass, silver, and glass, the wood that gleamed as darkly brilliant as the surface of a pool of oil — all the glory of marriage, the environment of the new estate. "You know I fight when it comes to fighting, Scratchy Wilson; but I ain't got a gun on me. You'll have to do all the shootin' yourself."

His enemy's face went livid. He stepped forward, and lashed his weapon to and fro before Potter's chest. "Don't you tell me you ain't got no gun on you, you whelp. Don't tell me no lie like that. There ain't a man in Texas ever seen you without no gun. Don't take me for no kid." His eyes blazed with light, and his throat worked like a pump.

"I ain't takin' you for no kid," answered Potter. His heels had not moved 80
an inch backward. "I'm takin' you for a damn fool. I tell you I ain't got a gun, and I ain't. If you're goin' to shoot me up, you better begin now; you'll never get a chance like this again."

So much enforced reasoning had told on Wilson's rage; he was calmer. "If you ain't got a gun, why ain't you got a gun?" he sneered. "Been to Sunday-school?"

"I ain't got a gun because I've just come from San Anton' with my wife. I'm married," said Potter. "And if I'd thought there was going to be any galoots like you prowling around when I brought my wife home, I'd had a gun, and don't you forget it."

"Married!" said Scratchy, not at all comprehending.

"Yes, married. I'm married," said Potter, distinctly.

"Married?" said Scratchy. Seemingly for the first time, he saw the drooping, 85
drowning woman at the other man's side. "No!" he said. He was like a creature allowed a glimpse of another world. He moved a pace backward, and his arm, with the revolver, dropped to his side. "Is this the lady?" he asked.

"Yes; this is the lady," answered Potter.

There was another period of silence.

"Well," said Wilson at last, slowly, "I s'pose it's all off now."

"It's all off if you say so, Scratchy. You know I didn't make the trouble." Potter lifted his valise.

"Well, I 'low it's off, Jack," said Wilson. He was looking at the ground. 90
"Married!" He was not a student of chivalry; it was merely that in the presence of this foreign condition he was a simple child of the earlier plains. He picked up his starboard revolver, and, placing both weapons in their holsters, he went away. His feet made funnel-shaped tracks in the heavy sand.

Considerations

1. What is the nature of the conflict Marshal Potter feels on the train in Part I? Why does he feel like a "traitor" bringing a bride home to Yellow Sky?
2. What is the function of the "drummer," the traveling salesman, in Part II?
3. How do Mrs. Potter and Scratchy Wilson serve as foils for each other? What does each represent in the story?
4. What is the significance of the setting?
5. How does Crane create suspense about what will happen when Marshal Potter meets Scratchy Wilson? Is suspense the major point of the story?
6. Is Scratchy Wilson too drunk, comical, and ineffective to be a sympathetic character? What is the meaning of his conceding that "I s'pose it's all off now" at the end of Part IV? Is he a dynamic or a static character?

7. How do the title and first paragraph suggest the theme of the story? How does the theme differ from those of typical western stories you have read or seen?
8. What details seem to support the story's theme? Consider, for example, the descriptions of the bride's clothes and Scratchy Wilson's shirt and boots.
9. Explain why the heroes in western stories are rarely married and why Crane's use of marriage is central to his theme.
10. Compare and contrast the setting, characters, action, and theme in this story with the same elements in another western you have read or seen.

Connections

1. Although Scratchy Wilson and Katherine Mansfield's "Miss Brill" (p. 394) are radically different kinds of people, they share a painful recognition at the end of their stories. What does each of them learn? Discuss whether you think what each of them learns is of equal importance in changing his or her life.
2. Write an essay explaining why you agree or disagree with Eudora Welty's assessment of these two stories in "On the Plots of 'The Bride Comes to Yellow Sky' and 'Miss Brill' " (p. 475).

JOSEPH CONRAD (1857–1924)

Born Josef Teodor Konrad Korzeniowski in Poland, Joseph Conrad was orphaned at twelve and subsequently went to sea, traveling to Africa, South America, and the Far East. He became a captain of British merchant ships, but by the age of thirty he began writing in English fiction that incorporated many of the insights and adventures he experienced at sea. Conrad's powerful use of English is remarkable — especially so given that it was not his native language. His fiction has earned him a reputation as one of this century's greatest writers. His exotic stories take his readers on journeys into profound realms of human experience. Among his most famous novels are *Lord Jim* (1900), *Nostromo* (1904), *The Secret Agent* (1907), and *Victory* (1915). His shorter works include *Youth* (1902), and *Heart of Darkness* (1902), *Typhoon and Other Stories* (1903), and *The Secret Sharer* (1912). In "An Outpost of Progress" Conrad explores the vulnerability of "civilized" assumptions in the wilderness.

An Outpost of Progress 1898

I

There were two white men in charge of the trading station. Kayerts, the chief, was short and fat; Carlier, the assistant, was tall, with a large head and a very broad trunk perched upon a long pair of thin legs. The third man on the staff was a Sierra Leone nigger, who maintained that his name was Henry Price. However, for some reason or other, the natives down the river had given him the name of Makola, and it stuck to him through all his wanderings about the country. He spoke English and French with a warbling accent, wrote a beautiful hand, understood bookkeeping, and cherished in his innermost heart the worship of evil spirits. His wife was a negress from Loanda, very large and very noisy. Three children rolled about in sunshine before the door of his low, shedlike dwelling. Makola, taciturn and impenetrable, despised the two white men. He had charge of a small clay storehouse with a dried-grass roof, and pretended to keep a correct account of beads, cotton cloth, red kerchiefs, brass wire, and other trade goods it contained. Besides the storehouse and Makola's hut, there was only one large building in the cleared ground of the station. It was built neatly of reeds, with a veranda on all the four sides. There were three rooms in it. The one in the middle was the living room, and had two rough tables and a few stools in it. The other two were the bedrooms for the white men. Each had a bedstead and a mosquito net for all furniture. The plank floor was littered with the belongings of the white men; open half-empty boxes, torn wearing apparel, old boots; all the things dirty, and all the things broken, that accumulate mysteriously round untidy men. There was also another dwelling place some distance away from the buildings. In it, under a tall cross much out of the perpendicular, slept the man who had seen the beginning of all this; who had planned and had watched the construction of this outpost of progress. He had been, at home, an unsuccessful painter who, weary of pursuing fame on an empty stomach, had gone out there through high protections. He had been the first chief of that station. Makola had watched the energetic artist die of fever in the just finished house with his usual kind of "I told you so" indifference. Then, for a time, he dwelt alone with his family, his account books, and the Evil Spirit that rules the lands under the equator. He got on very well with his god. Perhaps he had propitiated him by a promise of more white men to play with, by and by. At any rate the director of the Great Trading Company, coming up in a steamer that resembled an enormous sardine box with a flat-roofed shed erected on it, found the station in good order, and Makola as usual quietly diligent. The director had the cross put up over the first agent's grave, and appointed Kayerts to the post. Carlier was told off as second in charge. The director was a man ruthless and efficient, who at times, but very imperceptibly, indulged in grim humor. He made a speech to Kayerts and Carlier, pointing out to them the promising aspect of their station. The nearest trading post was about three hundred miles away. It was an exceptional opportunity for them to distinguish themselves and to earn percentages on the trade. This appointment was a favor done to beginners. Kayerts was moved almost to tears by his director's kindness. He would, he said, by doing his best, try to justify the flattering confidence, etc., etc. Kayerts had been in the Administration of the Telegraphs, and knew how to express himself correctly. Carlier, an ex-noncommissioned officer of cavalry in an army guaranteed from harm by several European powers, was less impressed. If there were commissions to get, so much the better; and, trailing a sulky glance over the river, the forests, the impenetrable bush that seemed to cut off the station from the rest of the world, he muttered between his teeth. "We shall see, very soon."

Next day, some bales of cotton goods and a few cases of provisions having been thrown on shore, the sardine-box steamer went off, not to return for another six months. On the deck the director touched his cap to the two agents, who stood on the bank waving their hats, and turning to an old servant of the Company on his passage to headquarters, said, "Look at those two imbeciles. They must be mad at home to send me such specimens. I told those fellows to plant a vegetable garden, build new storehouses and fences, and construct a landing stage. I bet nothing will be done! They won't know how to begin. I always thought the station on this river useless, and they just fit the station!"

"They will form themselves there," said the old stager with a quiet smile.

"At any rate, I am rid of them for six months," retorted the director.

The two men watched the steamer round the bend, then, ascending arm 5
in arm the slope of the bank, returned to the station. They had been in this vast and dark country only a very short time, and as yet always in the midst of other white men, under the eye and guidance of their superiors. And now, dull as they were to the subtle influences of surroundings, they felt themselves very much alone, when suddenly left unassisted to face the wilderness; a wilderness rendered more strange, more incomprehensible by the mysterious glimpses of the vigorous life it contained. They were two perfectly insignificant and incapable individuals, whose existence is only rendered possible through the high organization of civilized crowds. Few men realize that their life, the very essence of their character, their capabilities and their audacities, are only the expression of their belief in the safety of their surroundings. The courage, the composure, the confidence; the emotions and principles; every great and every insignificant thought belongs not to the individual but to the crowd: to the crowd that believes blindly in the irresistible force of its institutions and of its morals, in the power of its police and of its opinion. But the contact with pure unmitigated savagery, with primitive nature and primitive man, brings sudden and profound trouble into the heart. To the sentiment of being alone of one's kind, to the clear perception of the loneliness of one's thoughts, of one's sensations — to the negation of the habitual, which is safe, there is added the affirmation of the unusual, which is dangerous; a suggestion of things vague, uncontrollable, and repulsive, whose discomposing intrusion excites the imagination and tries the civilized nerves of the foolish and the wise alike.

Kayerts and Carlier walked arm in arm, drawing close to one another as children do in the dark; and they had the same, not altogether unpleasant, sense of danger which one half suspects to be imaginary. They chatted persistently in familiar tones. "Our station is prettily situated," said one. The other assented with enthusiasm, enlarging volubly on the beauties of the situation. Then they passed near the grave. "Poor devil!" said Kayerts. "He died of fever, didn't he?" muttered Carlier, stopping short. "Why," retorted Kayerts, with indignation, "I've been told that the fellow exposed himself recklessly to the sun. The climate here, everybody says, is not at all worse than at home, as long as you keep out of the sun. Do you hear that, Carlier? I am chief here, and my orders are that you should not expose yourself to the sun!" He assumed his superiority jocularly, but his meaning was serious. The idea that he would, perhaps, have to bury Carlier and remain alone, gave him an inward shiver. He felt suddenly that this Carlier was more precious to him here, in the center of Africa, than a brother could be anywhere else. Carlier, entering into the spirit of the thing, made a military salute and answered in a brisk tone, "Your orders shall be attended to, chief!" Then he burst out laughing, slapped Kayerts on the back and shouted, "We shall let life run easily here! Just sit still and gather in the ivory those savages will bring. This country has its good points, after all!" They both laughed loudly while Carlier thought: "That poor Kayerts; he is so fat and unhealthy. It would be awful if I had to bury him here. He is a man I respect." . . . Before they reached the veranda of their house they called one another "my dear fellow."

The first day they were very active, pottering about with hammers and nails and red calico, to put up curtains, make their house habitable and pretty; resolved to settle down comfortably to their new life. For them an impossible task. To grapple effectually with even purely material problems requires more serenity of mind and more lofty courage than people generally imagine. No two beings could have been more unfitted for such a struggle. Society, not from any tenderness, but because of its strange needs, had taken care of those two men, forbidding them all independent thought, all initiative, all departure from routine; and forbidding it under pain of death. They could only live on condition of being machines. And now, released from the fostering care of men with pens behind the ears, or of men with gold lace on the sleeves, they were like those life-long prisoners who, liberated after many years, do not know what use to make of their freedom. They did not know what use to make of their faculties, being both, through want of practice, incapable of independent thought.

At the end of two months Kayerts often would say, "If it was not for my Melie, you wouldn't catch me here." Melie was his daughter. He had thrown up his post in the Administration of the Telegraphs, though he had been for seventeen years perfectly happy there, to earn a dowry for his girl. His wife was dead, and the child was being brought up by his sisters. He regretted the streets, the pavements, the cafés, his friends of many years; all the things he used to see, day after day; all the thoughts suggested by familiar things — the thoughts effortless, monotonous, and soothing of a Government clerk; he regretted all the gossip, the small enmities, the mild venom, and the little jokes of Government offices. "If I had had a decent brother-in-law," Carlier would remark, "a fellow with a heart, I would not be here." He had left the army and had made himself so obnoxious to his family by his laziness and impudence, that an exasperated brother-in-law had made superhuman efforts to procure him an appointment in the Company as a second-class agent. Having not a penny in the world he was compelled to accept this means of livelihood as soon as it became quite clear to him that there was nothing more to squeeze out of his relations. He, like Kayerts, regretted his old life. He regretted the clink of saber and spurs on a fine afternoon, the barrack-room witticisms, the girls of garrison towns; but, besides, he had also a sense of grievance. He was evidently a much ill-used man. This made him moody, at times. But the two men got on well together in the fellowship of their stupidity and laziness. Together they did nothing, absolutely nothing, and enjoyed the sense of the idleness for which they were paid. And in time they came to feel something resembling affection for one another.

They lived like blind men in a large room, aware only of what came in contact with them (and of that only imperfectly), but unable to see the general aspect of things. The river, the forest, all the great land throbbing with life, were like a great emptiness. Even the brilliant sunshine disclosed nothing intelligible. Things appeared and disappeared before their eyes in an unconnected and aimless kind of way. The river seemed to come from nowhere and flow nowhither. It flowed through a void. Out of that void, at times, came canoes, and men with spears in their hands would suddenly crowd the yard of the station. They were naked, glossy black, ornamented with snowy shells and glistening brass wire, perfect of limb. They made an uncouth babbling noise when they spoke, moved in a stately manner, and sent quick, wild glances out of their startled, never-resting eyes. Those warriors would squat in long rows, four or more deep, before the veranda, while their chiefs bargained for hours with Makola over an elephant tusk. Kayerts sat on his chair and looked down on the proceedings, understanding nothing. He stared at them with his round blue eyes, called out to Carlier, "Here, look! look at that fellow there — and that other one, to the left. Did you ever see such a face? Oh, the funny brute!"

Carlier, smoking native tobacco in a short wooden pipe, would swagger up 10
twirling his mustaches, and surveying the warriors with haughty indulgence, would say:

"Fine animals. Brought any bone? Yes? It's not any too soon. Look at the muscles of that fellow — third from the end. I wouldn't care to get a punch on the nose from him. Fine arms, but legs no good below the knee. Couldn't make cavalry men of them." And after glancing down complacently at his own shanks, he always concluded. "Pah! Don't they stink! You, Makola! Take that herd over to the fetish" (the storehouse was in every station called the fetish, perhaps because of the spirit of civilization it contained) "and give them up some of the rubbish you keep there. I'd rather see it full of bone than full of rags."

Kayerts approved.

"Yes, yes! Go and finish that palaver over there, Mr. Makola. I will come round when you are ready, to weigh the tusk. We must be careful." Then turning to his companion: "This is the tribe that lives down the river; they are rather aromatic. I remember, they had been once before here. D'ye hear that row? What a fellow has got to put up with in this dog of a country! My head is split."

Such profitable visits were rare. For days the two pioneers of trade and progress would look on their empty courtyard in the vibrating brilliance of vertical sunshine. Below the high bank, the silent river flowed on glittering and steady. On the sands in the middle of the stream, hippos and alligators sunned themselves side by side. And stretching away in all directions, surrounding the insignificant cleared spot of the trading post, immense forests, hiding fateful complications of fantastic life, lay in the eloquent silence of mute greatness. The two men understood nothing, cared for nothing but for the passage of days that separated them from the steamer's return. Their predecessor had left some torn books. They took up these wrecks of novels, and, as they had never read anything of the kind before, they were surprised and amused. Then during long days there were interminable and silly discussions about plots and personages. In the center of Africa they made acquaintance of Richelieu and of d'Artagnan, of Hawk's Eye and of Father Goriot,° and of many other people. All these imaginary personages became subjects for gossip as if they had been living friends.

Richelieu and . . . d'Artagnan: Historic and fictional characters respectively in Alexandre Dumas's novel *The Three Musketeers* (1844); *Hawk's Eye:* Natty Bumppo, the protagonist of James Fenimore Cooper's Leatherstocking Tales (1823–1841); *Father Goriot:* the protagonist of *Père Goriot* (1834), by Honoré de Balzac.

They discounted their virtues, suspected their motives, decried their successes; were scandalized at their duplicity or were doubtful about their courage. The accounts of crimes filled them with indignation, while tender or pathetic passages moved them deeply. Carlier cleared his throat and said in a soldierly voice, "What nonsense!" Kayerts, his round eyes suffused with tears, his fat cheeks quivering, rubbed his bald head, and declared, "This is a splendid book. I had no idea there were such clever fellows in the world." They also found some old copies of a home paper. That print discussed what it was pleased to call "Our Colonial Expansion" in high-flown language. It spoke much of the rights and duties of civilization, of the sacredness of the civilizing work, and extolled the merits of those who went about bringing light, and faith and commerce to the dark places of the earth. Carlier and Kayerts read, wondered, and began to think better of themselves. Carlier said one evening, waving his hand about, "In a hundred years, there will be perhaps a town here. Quays, and warehouses, and barracks, and — and — billiard rooms. Civilization, my boy, and virtue — and all. And then, chaps will read that two good fellows, Kayerts and Carlier, were the first civilized men to live in this very spot!" Kayerts nodded, "Yes, it is a consolation to think of that." They seemed to forget their dead predecessor; but, early one day, Carlier went out and replanted the cross firmly. "It used to make me squint whenever I walked that way," he explained to Kayerts over the morning coffee. "It made me squint, leaning over so much. So I just planted it upright. And solid, I promise you! I suspended myself with both hands to the crosspiece. Not a move. Oh, I did that properly."

15 At times Gobila came to see them. Gobila was the chief of the neighboring villages. He was a gray-headed savage, thin and black, with a white cloth round his loins and a mangy panther skin hanging over his back. He came up with long strides of his skeleton legs, swinging a staff as tall as himself, and, entering the common room of the station, would squat on his heels to the left of the door. There he sat, watching Kayerts, and now and then making a speech which the other did not understand. Kayerts, without interrupting his occupation, would from time to time say in a friendly manner: "How goes it, you old image?" and they would smile at one another. The two whites had a liking for that old and incomprehensible creature, and called him Father Gobila. Gobila's manner was paternal, and he seemed really to love all white men. They all appeared to him very young, indistinguishably alike (except for stature), and he knew that they were all brothers, and also immortal. The death of the artist, who was the first white man whom he knew intimately, did not disturb this belief, because he was firmly convinced that the white stranger had pretended to die and got himself buried for some mysterious purpose of his own, into which it was useless to inquire. Perhaps it was his way of going home to his own country? At any rate, these were his brothers, and he transferred his absurd affection to them. They returned it in a way. Carlier slapped him on the back, and recklessly struck off matches for his amusement. Kayerts was already ready to let him have a sniff at the ammonia bottle. In short, they behaved just like that other white creature that had hidden itself in a hole in the ground. Gobila considered them attentively. Perhaps they were the same being with the other — or one of them was. He couldn't decide — clear up that mystery; but he remained always very friendly. In consequence of that friendship the women of Gobila's village walked in single file through the reedy grass, bringing every morning to the station, fowls,

and sweet potatoes, and palm wine, and sometimes a goat. The Company never provisions the stations fully, and the agents required those local supplies to live. They had them through the good will of Gobila, and lived well. Now and then one of them had a bout of fever, and the other nursed him with gentle devotion. They did not think much of it. It left them weaker, and their appearance changed for the worse. Carlier was hollow-eyed and irritable. Kayerts showed a drawn, flabby face above the rotundity of his stomach, which gave him a weird aspect. But being constantly together, they did not notice the change that took place gradually in their appearance, and also in their dispositions.

Five months passed in that way.

Then, one morning, as Kayerts and Carlier, lounging in their chairs under the veranda, talked about the approaching visit of the steamer, a knot of armed men came out of the forest and advanced towards the station. They were strangers to that part of the country. They were tall, slight, draped classically from neck to heel in blue fringed cloths, and carried percussion muskets over their bare right shoulders. Makola showed signs of excitement, and ran out of the storehouse (where he spent all his days) to meet these visitors. They came into the courtyard and looked about them with steady, scornful glances. Their leader, a powerful and determined-looking Negro with bloodshot eyes, stood in front of the veranda and made a long speech. He gesticulated much, and ceased very suddenly.

There was something in his intonation, in the sounds of the long sentences he used, that startled the two whites. It was like a reminiscence of something not exactly familiar, and yet resembling the speech of civilized men. It sounded like one of those impossible languages which sometimes we hear in our dreams.

"What lingo is that?" said the amazed Carlier. "In the first moment I fancied the fellow was going to speak French. Anyway, it is a different kind of gibberish to what we ever heard."

"Yes," replied Kayerts. "Hey, Makola, what does he say? Where do they come from? Who are they?"

But Makola, who seemed to be standing on hot bricks, answered hurriedly, "I don't know. They come from very far. Perhaps Mrs. Price will understand. They are perhaps bad men."

The leader, after waiting for a while, said something sharply to Makola, who shook his head. Then the man, after looking round, noticed Makola's hut and walked over there. The next moment Mrs. Makola was heard speaking with great volubility. The other strangers — they were six in all — strolled about with an air of ease, put their heads through the door of the storeroom, congregated round the grave, pointed understandingly at the cross, and generally made themselves at home.

"I don't like those chaps — and, I say, Kayerts, they must be from the coast; they've got firearms," observed the sagacious Carlier.

Kayerts also did not like those chaps. They both, for the first time, became aware that they lived in conditions where the unusual may be dangerous, and that there was no power on earth outside of themselves to stand between them and the unusual. They became uneasy, went in and loaded their revolvers. Kayerts said, "We must order Makola to tell them to go away before dark."

The strangers left in the afternoon, after eating a meal prepared for them by Mrs. Makola. The immense woman was excited, and talked much with the visitors. She rattled away shrilly, pointing here and there at the forests and at the river. Makola sat apart and watched. At times he got up and whispered to his wife. He accompanied the strangers across the ravine at the back of the station-ground, and returned slowly looking very thoughtful. When questioned by the white men he was very strange, seemed not to understand, seemed to have forgotten French — seemed to have forgotten how to speak altogether. Kayerts and Carlier agreed that the nigger had had too much palm wine.

There was some talk about keeping a watch in turn, but in the evening everything seemed so quiet and peaceful that they retired as usual. All night they were disturbed by a lot of drumming in the villages. A deep, rapid roll near by would be followed by another far off — then all ceased. Soon short appeals would rattle out here and there, then all mingle together, increase, become vigorous and sustained, would spread out over the forest, roll through the night, unbroken and ceaseless, near and far, as if the whole land had been one immense drum booming out steadily an appeal to heaven. And through the deep and tremendous noise sudden yells that resembled snatches of songs from a madhouse darted shrill and high in discordant jets of sound which seemed to rush far above the earth and drive all peace from under the stars.

Carlier and Kayerts slept badly. They both thought they had heard shots fired during the night — but they could not agree as to the direction. In the morning Makola was gone somewhere. He returned about noon with one of yesterday's strangers, and eluded all Kayerts's attempts to close with him: had become deaf apparently. Kayerts wondered. Carlier, who had been fishing off the bank, came back and remarked while he showed his catch, "The niggers seem to be in a deuce of a stir; I wonder what's up. I saw about fifteen canoes cross the river during the two hours I was there fishing." Kayerts, worried, said, "Isn't this Makola very queer today?" Carlier advised, "Keep all our men together in case of some trouble."

II

There were ten station men who had been left by the Director. Those fellows, having engaged themselves to the Company for six months (without having any idea of a month in particular and only a very faint notion of time in general), had been serving the cause of progress for upwards of two years. Belonging to a tribe from a very distant part of the land of darkness and sorrow, they did not run away, naturally supposing that as wandering strangers they would be killed by the inhabitants of the country; in which they were right. They lived in straw huts on the slope of a ravine overgrown with reedy grass, just behind the station buildings. They were not happy, regretting the festive incantations, the sorceries, the human sacrifices of their own land; where they also had parents, brothers, sisters, admired chiefs, respected magicians, loved friends, and other ties supposed generally to be human. Besides, the rice rations served out by the Company did not agree with them, being a food unknown to their land, and to which they could not get used. Consequently they were unhealthy and miserable. Had they been of any other tribe they would have made up their minds to die — for nothing is easier to certain savages than suicide —

and so have escaped from the puzzling difficulties of existence. But belonging, as they did, to a warlike tribe with filed teeth, they had more grit, and went on stupidly living through disease and sorrow. They did very little work, and had lost their splendid physique. Carlier and Kayerts doctored them assiduously without being able to bring them back into condition again. They were mustered every morning and told off to different tasks — grass cutting, fence-building, tree-felling, etc., etc., which no power on earth could induce them to execute efficiently. The two whites had practically very little control over them.

In the afternoon Makola came over to the big house and found Kayerts watching three heavy columns of smoke rising above the forests. "What is that?" asked Kayerts. "Some villages burn," answered Makola, who seemed to have regained his wits. Then he said abruptly: "We have got very little ivory; bad six months' trading. Do you like get a little more ivory?"

"Yes," said Kayerts, eagerly. He thought of percentages which were low.

"Those men who came yesterday are traders from Loanda who have got more ivory than they can carry home. Shall I buy? I know their camp."

"Certainly," said Kayerts. "What are those traders?"

"Bad fellows," said Makola, indifferently. "They fight with people, and catch women and children. They are bad men, and got guns. There is a great disturbance in the country. Do you want ivory?"

"Yes," said Kayerts. Makola said nothing for a while. Then: "Those workmen of ours are no good at all," he muttered, looking round. "Station in very bad order, sir. Director will growl. Better get a fine lot of ivory, then he say nothing."

"I can't help it; the men won't work," said Kayerts. "When will you get that ivory?"

"Very soon," said Makola. "Perhaps tonight. You leave it to me, and keep indoors, sir. I think you had better give some palm wine to our men to make a dance this evening. Enjoy themselves. Work better tomorrow. There's plenty palm wine — gone a little sour."

Kayerts said "yes," and Makola, with his own hands, carried big calabashes to the door of his hut. They stood there till the evening, and Mrs. Makola looked into every one. The men got them at sunset. When Kayerts and Carlier retired, a big bonfire was flaring before the men's huts. They could hear their shouts and drumming. Some men from Gobila's village had joined the station hands, and the entertainment was a great success.

In the middle of the night, Carlier waking suddenly, heard a man shout loudly; then a shot was fired. Only one. Carlier ran out and met Kayerts on the veranda. They were both startled. As they went across the yard to call Makola, they saw shadows moving in the night. One of them cried, "Don't shoot! It's me, Price." Then Makola appeared close to them. "Go back, go back, please," he urged, "you spoil all." "There are strange men about," said Carlier. "Never mind; I know," said Makola. Then he whispered, "All right. Bring ivory. Say nothing! I know my business." The two white men reluctantly went back to the house, but did not sleep. They heard footsteps, whispers, some groans. It seemed as if a lot of men came in, dumped heavy things on the ground, squabbled a long time, then went away. They lay on their hard beds and thought: "This Makola is invaluable." In the morning Carlier came out, very sleepy, and pulled at the cord of the big bell. The station hands mustered every morning to the sound of the bell. That morning nobody came. Kayerts turned out also, yawning. Across the yard they saw Makola come out of his hut, a tin basin of soapy water in his hand. Makola, a civilized nigger, was very neat in his person. He threw the soapsuds skillfully over a wretched little yellow cur he had, then turning his face to the agent's house, he shouted from the distance, "All the men gone last night!"

They heard him plainly, but in their surprise they both yelled out together: "What!" Then they stared at one another. "We are in a proper fix now," growled Carlier. "It's incredible!" muttered Kayerts. "I will go to the huts and see," said Carlier, striding off. Makola coming up found Kayerts standing alone.

"I can hardly believe it," said Kayerts, tearfully. "We took care of them as if they had been our children."

"They went with the coast people," said Makola after a moment of hesitation.

"What do I care with whom they went — the ungrateful brutes!" exclaimed the other. Then with sudden suspicion, and looking hard at Makola, he added: "What do you know about it?"

Makola moved his shoulders, looking down on the ground. "What do I know? I think only. Will you come and look at the ivory I've got there? It is a fine lot. You never saw such."

He moved towards the store. Kayerts followed him mechanically, thinking about the incredible desertion of the men. On the ground before the door of the fetish lay six splendid tusks.

"What did you give for it?" asked Kayerts, after surveying the lot with satisfaction.

"No regular trade," said Makola. "They brought the ivory and gave it to me. I told them to take what they most wanted in the station. It is a beautiful lot. No station can show such tusks. Those traders wanted carriers badly, and our men were no good here. No trade, no entry in books; all correct."

Kayerts nearly burst with indignation. "Why!" he shouted, "I believe you have sold our men for these tusks!" Makola stood impassive and silent. "I — I — will — I," stuttered Kayerts. "You fiend!" he yelled out.

"I did the best for you and the Company," said Makola, imperturbably. "Why you shout so much? Look at this tusk."

"I dismiss you! I will report you — I won't look at the tusk. I forbid you to touch them. I order you to throw them into the river. You — you!"

"You very red, Mr. Kayerts. If you are so irritable in the sun, you will get fever and die — like the first chief!" pronounced Makola impressively.

They stood still, contemplating one another with intense eyes, as if they had been looking with effort across immense distances. Kayerts shivered. Makola had meant no more than he said, but his words seemed to Kayerts full of ominous menace! He turned sharply and went away to the house. Makola retired into the bosom of his family; and the tusks, left lying before the store, looked very large and valuable in the sunshine.

Carlier came back on the veranda. "They're all gone, hey?" asked Kayerts from the far end of the common room in a muffled voice. "You did not find anybody?"

"Oh, yes," said Carlier, "I found one of Gobila's people lying dead before the huts — shot through the body. We heard that shot last night."

Kayerts came out quickly. He found his companion staring grimly over the yard at the tusks, away by the store. They both sat in silence for a while. Then Kayerts related his conversation with Makola. Carlier said nothing. At the midday meal they ate very little. They hardly exchanged a word that day. A great silence seemed to lie heavily over the station and press on their lips. Makola did not open the store; he spent the day playing with his children. He lay full-length on a mat outside his door, and the youngsters sat on his chest and clambered all over him. It was a touching picture. Mrs. Makola was busy cooking all day as usual. The white men made a somewhat better meal in the evening. Afterwards, Carlier smoking his pipe strolled over to the store; he stood for a long time over the tusks, touched one or two with his foot, even tried to lift the largest one by its small end. He came back to his chief, who had not stirred from the veranda, threw himself in the chair and said:

"I can see it! They were pounced upon while they slept heavily after drinking all the palm wine you've allowed Makola to give them. A put-up job! See? The worst is, some of Gobila's people were there, and got carried off too, no doubt. The least drunk woke up, and got shot for his sobriety. This is a funny country. What will you do now?"

"We can't touch it, of course," said Kayerts.

"Of course not," assented Carlier.

"Slavery is an awful thing," stammered out Kayerts in an unsteady voice.

"Frightful — the sufferings," grunted Carlier with conviction.

They believed their words. Everybody shows a respectful deference to certain sounds that he and his fellows can make. But about feelings people really know nothing. We talk with indignation or enthusiasm; we talk about oppression, cruelty, crime, devotion, self-sacrifice, virtue, and we know nothing real beyond the words. Nobody knows what suffering or sacrifice mean — except, perhaps the victims of the mysterious purpose of these illusions.

Next morning they saw Makola very busy setting up in the yard the big scales used for weighing ivory. By and by Carlier said: "What's that filthy scoundrel up to?" and lounged out into the yard. Kayerts followed. They stood watching. Makola took no notice. When the balance was swung true, he tried to lift a tusk into the scale. It was too heavy. He looked up helplessly without a word, and for a minute they stood round that balance as mute and still as three statues. Suddenly Carlier said: "Catch hold of the other end, Makola — you beast!" and together they swung the tusk up. Kayerts trembled in every limb. He muttered, "I say! O! I say!" and putting his hand in his pocket found there a dirty bit of paper and the stump of a pencil. He turned his back on the others, as if about to do something tricky, and noted stealthily the weights which Carlier shouted out to him with unnecessary loudness. When all was over Makola whispered to himself: "The sun's very strong here for the tusks." Carlier said to Kayerts in a careless tone: "I say, chief, I might just as well give him a lift with this lot into the store."

As they were going back to the house Kayerts observed with a sigh: "It had to be done." And Carlier said: "It's deplorable, but, the men being Company's men the ivory is Company's ivory. We must look after it." "I will report to the Director, of course," said Kayerts. "Of course; let him decide," approved Carlier.

At midday they made a hearty meal. Kayerts sighed from time to time.

Whenever they mentioned Makola's name they always added to it an opprobrious epithet. It eased their conscience. Makola gave himself a half-holiday, and bathed his children in the river. No one from Gobila's villages came near the station that day. No one came the next day, and the next, nor for a whole week. Gobila's people might have been dead and buried for any sign of life they gave. But they were only mourning for those they had lost by the witchcraft of white men, who had brought wicked people into their country. The wicked people were gone, but fear remained. Fear always remains. A man may destroy everything within himself, love and hate and belief, and even doubt; but as long as he clings to life he cannot destroy fear: the fear, subtle, indestructible, and terrible, that pervades his being; that tinges his thoughts; that lurks in his heart; that watches on his lips the struggle of his last breath. In his fear, the mild old Gobila offered extra human sacrifices to all the Evil Spirits that had taken possession of his white friends. His heart was heavy. Some warriors spoke about burning and killing, but the cautious old savage dissuaded them. Who could foresee the woe those mysterious creatures, if irritated, might bring? They should be left alone. Perhaps in time they would disappear into the earth as the first one had disappeared. His people must keep away from them, and hope for the best.

Kayerts and Carlier did not disappear, but remained above on this earth, that, somehow, they fancied had become bigger and very empty. It was not the absolute and dumb solitude of the post that impressed them so much as an inarticulate feeling that something from within them was gone, something that worked for their safety, and had kept the wilderness from interfering with their hearts. The images of home; the memory of people like them, of men that thought and felt as they used to think and feel, receded into distances made indistinct by the glare of unclouded sunshine. And out of the great silence of the surrounding wilderness, its very hopelessness and savagery seemed to approach them nearer, to draw them gently, to look upon them, to envelop them with a solicitude irresistible, familiar, and disgusting.

65 Days lengthened into weeks, then into months. Gobila's people drummed and yelled to every new moon, as of yore, but kept away from the station. Makola and Carlier tried once in a canoe to open communications, but were received with a shower of arrows, and had to fly back to the station for dear life. That attempt set the country up and down the river into an uproar that could be very distinctly heard for days. The steamer was late. At first they spoke of delay jauntily, then anxiously, then gloomily. The matter was becoming serious. Stores were running short. Carlier cast his lines off the bank, but the river was low, and the fish kept out in the stream. They dared not stroll far away from the station to shoot. Moreover, there was no game in the impenetrable forest. Once Carlier shot a hippo in the river. They had no boat to secure it, and it sank. When it floated up it drifted away, and Gobila's people secured the carcass. It was the occasion for a national holiday, but Carlier had a fit of rage over it and talked about the necessity of exterminating all the niggers before the country could be made habitable. Kayerts mooned about silently; spent hours looking at the portrait of his Melie. It represented a little girl with long bleached tresses and a rather sour face. His legs were much swollen, and he could hardly walk. Carlier, undermined by fever, could not swagger any more, but kept tot-

tering about, still with a devil-may-care air, as became a man who remembered his crack regiment. He had become hoarse, sarcastic, and inclined to say unpleasant things. He called it "being frank with you." They had long ago reckoned their percentages on trade, including in them that last deal of "this infamous Makola." They had also concluded not to say anything about it. Kayerts hesitated at first — was afraid of the Director.

"He has seen worse things done on the quiet," maintained Carlier, with a hoarse laugh. "Trust him! He won't thank you if you blab. He is no better than you or me. Who will talk if we hold our tongues? There is nobody here."

That was the root of the trouble! There was nobody there; and being left there alone with their weakness, they became daily more like a pair of accomplices than like a couple of devoted friends. They had heard nothing from home for eight months. Every evening they said, "Tomorrow we shall see the steamer." But one of the Company's steamers had been wrecked, and the Director was busy with the other, relieving very distant and important stations on the main river. He thought that the useless station, and the useless men, could wait. Meantime Kayerts and Carlier lived on rice boiled without salt, and cursed the Company, all Africa, and the day they were born. One must have lived on such diet to discover what ghastly trouble the necessity of swallowing one's food may become. There was literally nothing else in the station but rice and coffee; they drank the coffee without sugar. The last fifteen lumps Kayerts had solemnly locked away in his box, together with a half-bottle of cognac, "in case of sickness," he explained. Carlier approved. "When one is sick," he said, "any little extra like that is cheering."

They waited. Rank grass began to sprout over the courtyard. The bell never rang now. Days passed, silent, exasperating, and slow. When the two men spoke, they snarled; and their silences were bitter, as if tinged by the bitterness of their thoughts.

One day after a lunch of boiled rice, Carlier put down his cup untasted, and said: "Hang it all! Let's have a decent cup of coffee for once. Bring out that sugar, Kayerts!"

"For the sick," muttered Kayerts, without looking up.

"For the sick," mocked Carlier. "Bosh! . . . Well! I am sick."

"You are no more sick than I am, and I go without," said Kayerts in a peaceful tone.

"Come! Out with that sugar, you stingy old slave dealer."

Kayerts looked up quickly. Carlier was smiling with marked insolence. And suddenly it seemed to Kayerts that he had never seen that man before. Who was he? He knew nothing about him. What was he capable of? There was a surprising flash of violent emotion within him, as if in the presence of something undreamt-of, dangerous, and final. But he managed to pronounce with composure:

"That joke is in very bad taste. Don't repeat it."

"Joke!" said Carlier, hitching himself forward on his seat. "I am hungry — I am sick — I don't joke! I hate hypocrites. You are a hypocrite. You are a slave dealer. I am a slave dealer. There's nothing but slave dealers in this cursed country. I mean to have sugar in my coffee today, anyhow!"

"I forbid you to speak to me in that way," said Kayerts with a fair show of resolution.

"You! — What?" shouted Carlier, jumping up.

Kayerts stood up also. "I am your chief," he began, trying to master the shakiness of his voice.

"What?" yelled the other. "Who's chief? There's no chief here. There's nothing 80
here: there's nothing but you and I. Fetch the sugar — you pot-bellied ass."

"Hold your tongue. Go out of this room," screamed Kayerts. "I dismiss you — you scoundrel!"

Carlier swung a stool. All at once he looked dangerously in earnest. "You flabby, good-for-nothing civilian — take that!" he howled.

Kayerts dropped under the table, and the stool struck the grass inner wall of the room. Then, as Carlier was trying to upset the table, Kayerts in desperation made a blind rush, head low, like a cornered pig would do, and overturning his friend, bolted along the veranda, and into his room. He locked the door, snatched his revolver, and stood panting. In less than a minute Carlier was kicking at the door furiously, howling, "If you don't bring out that sugar, I will shoot you at sight, like a dog. Now then — one — two — three. You won't? I will show you who's the master."

Kayerts thought the door would fall in, and scrambled through the square hole that served for a window in his room. There was then the whole breadth of the house between them. But the other was apparently not strong enough to break in the door, and Kayerts heard him running round. Then he also began to run laboriously on his swollen legs. He ran as quickly as he could, grasping the revolver, and unable yet to understand what was happening to him. He saw in succession Makola's house, the store, the river, the ravine, and the low bushes; and he saw all those things again as he ran for the second time round the house. Then again they flashed past him. That morning he could not have walked a yard without a groan.

And now he ran. He ran fast enough to keep out of sight of the other man. 85

Then as, weak and desperate, he thought, "Before I finish the next round I shall die," he heard the other man stumble heavily, then stop. He stopped also. He had the back and Carlier the front of the house, as before. He heard him drop into a chair cursing, and suddenly his own legs gave way, and he slid down into a sitting posture with his back to the wall. His mouth was as dry as a cinder, and his face was wet with perspiration — and tears. What was it all about? He thought it must be a horrible illusion; he thought he was dreaming; he thought he was going mad! After a while he collected his senses. What did they quarrel about? That sugar! How absurd! He would give it to him — didn't want it himself. And he began scrambling to his feet with a sudden feeling of security. But before he had fairly stood upright, a common-sense reflection occurred to him and drove him back into despair. He thought: "If I give way now to that brute of a soldier, he will begin this horror again tomorrow — and the day after — every day — raise other pretensions, trample on me, torture me, make me his slave — and I will be lost! Lost! The steamer may not come for days — may never come." He shook so that he had to sit down on the floor again. He shivered forlornly. He felt he could not, would not move any more. He was completely distracted by the sudden perception that the position was without issue — that death and life had in a moment become equally difficult and terrible.

All at once he heard the other push his chair back; and he leaped to his feet with extreme facility. He listened and got confused. Must run again! Right or left? He heard footsteps. He darted to the left, grasping his revolver, and at the very same instant, as it seemed to him, they came into violent collision. Both shouted with surprise. A loud explosion took place between them; a roar of red fire, thick smoke; and Kayerts deafened and blinded, rushed back thinking: "I am hit — it's all over." He expected the other to come round — to gloat over his agony. He caught hold of an upright of the roof — "All over!" Then he heard a crashing fall on the other side of the house, as if somebody had tumbled headlong over a chair — then silence. Nothing more happened. He did not die. Only his shoulder felt as if it had been badly wrenched, and he had lost his revolver. He was disarmed and helpless! He waited for his fate. The other man made no sound. It was a strategem. He was stalking him now! Along what side? Perhaps he was taking aim this very minute!

After a few moments of an agony frightful and absurd, he decided to go and meet his doom. He was prepared for every surrender. He turned the corner, steadying himself with one hand on the wall; made a few paces, and nearly swooned. He had seen on the floor, protruding past the other corner, a pair of turned-up feet. A pair of white naked feet in red slippers. He felt deadly sick, and stood for a time in profound darkness. Then Makola appeared before him, saying quietly: "Come along, Mr. Kayerts. He is dead." He burst into tears of gratitude; a loud, sobbing fit of crying. After a time he found himself sitting in a chair and looking at Carlier, who lay stretched on his back. Makola was kneeling over the body.

"Is this your revolver?" asked Makola, getting up.

"Yes," said Kayerts; then he added very quickly. "He ran after me to shoot me — you saw!"

"Yes, I saw," said Makola. "There is only one revolver; where's his?"

"Don't know," whispered Kayerts in a voice that had become suddenly very faint.

"I will go and look for it," said the other, gently. He made the round along the veranda, while Kayerts sat still and looked at the corpse. Makola came back empty-handed, stood in deep thought, then stepped quietly into the dead man's room, and came out directly with a revolver, which he held up before Kayerts. Kayerts shut his eyes. Everything was going round. He found life more terrible and difficult than death. He had shot an unarmed man.

After meditating for a while, Makola said softly, pointing at the dead man who lay there with his right eye blown out:

"He died of fever." Kayerts looked at him with a stony stare. "Yes," repeated Makola, thoughtfully, stepping over the corpse, "I think he died of fever. Bury him tomorrow."

And he went away slowly to his expectant wife, leaving the two white men alone on the veranda.

Night came, and Kayerts sat unmoving on his chair. He sat quiet as if he had taken a dose of opium. The violence of the emotions he had passed through produced a feeling of exhausted serenity. He had plumbed in one short afternoon the depths of horror and despair, and now found repose in the conviction that life had no more secrets for him: neither had death! He sat by the corpse thinking; thinking very actively, thinking very new thoughts. He seemed to have broken loose from himself altogether. His old thoughts, convictions, likes and dislikes, things he respected and things he abhorred, appeared in their true light at last! Appeared contemptible and childish, false and ridiculous. He reveled in his new wisdom while he sat by the man he had killed. He argued with himself about all things under heaven with that kind of wrong-headed lucidity which may be observed in some lunatics. Incidentally he reflected that the fellow dead there had been a noxious beast anyway; that men died every day in thousands; perhaps in hundreds of thousands — who could tell? — and that in the number, that one death could not possibly make any difference; couldn't have any importance, at least to a thinking creature. He, Kayerts, was a thinking creature. He had been all his life, till that moment, a believer in a lot of nonsense like the rest of mankind — who are fools; but now he thought! He knew! He was at peace; he was familiar with the highest wisdom! Then he tried to imagine himself dead, and Carlier sitting in his chair watching him; and his attempt met with such unexpected success, that in a very few moments he became not at all sure who was dead and who was alive. This extraordinary achievement of his fancy startled him, however, and by a clever and timely effort of mind he saved himself just in time from becoming Carlier. His heart thumped, and he felt hot all over at the thought of that danger. Carlier! What a beastly thing! To compose his now disturbed nerves — and no wonder! — he tried to whistle a little. Then, suddenly, he fell asleep, or thought he had slept; but at any rate there was a fog, and somebody had whistled in the fog.

He stood up. The day had come, and a heavy mist had descended upon the land: the mist penetrating, enveloping, and silent; the morning mist of tropical lands; the mist that clings and kills; the mist white and deadly, immaculate and poisonous. He stood up, saw the body, and threw his arms above his head with a cry like that of a man who, waking from a trance, finds himself immured forever in a tomb. *"Help! . . . My God!"*

A shriek inhuman, vibrating and sudden, pierced like a sharp dart the white shroud of that land of sorrow. Three short, impatient screeches followed, and then for a time, the fog-wreaths rolled on, undisturbed, through a formidable silence. Then many more shrieks, rapid and piercing, like the yells of some exasperated and ruthless creature, rent the air. Progress was calling to Kayerts from the river. Progress and civilization and all the virtues. Society was calling to its accomplished child to come, to be taken care of, to be instructed, to be judged, to be condemned; it called him to return to that rubbish heap from which he had wandered away, so that justice could be done.

Kayerts heard and understood. He stumbled out of the veranda, leaving the other man quite alone for the first time since they had been thrown there together. He groped his way through the fog, calling in his ignorance upon the invisible heaven to undo its work. Makola flitted by in the mist, shouting as he ran:

"Steamer! Steamer! They can't see. They whistle for the station. I go ring 100
the bell. Go down to the landing, sir. I ring."

He disappeared. Kayerts stood still. He looked upwards; the fog low over his head. He looked round like a man who has lost his way; and he saw a dark smudge, a cross-shaped stain, upon the shifting purity of the mist. As he began to stumble towards it, the station bell rang in a tumultuous peal its answer to the impatient clamor of the steamer.

The Managing Director of the Great Civilizing Company (since we know that civilization follows trade) landed first, and incontinently lost sight of the steamer. The fog down by the river was exceedingly dense; above, at the station, the bell rang unceasing and brazen.

The Director shouted loudly to the steamer:

"There is nobody down to meet us; there may be something wrong, though they are ringing. You had better come, too!"

And he began to toil up the steep bank. The captain and the engine-driver 105
of the boat followed behind. As they scrambled up the fog thinned, and they could see their Director a good way ahead. Suddenly they saw him start forward, calling to them over his shoulder: "Run! Run to the house! I've found one of them. Run, look for the other!"

He found one of them! And even he, the man of varied and startling experience, was somewhat discomposed by the manner of this finding. He stood and fumbled in his pocket (for a knife) while he faced Kayerts, who was hanging by a leather strap from the cross. He had evidently climbed the grave, which was high and narrow, and after tying the end of the strap to the arm, had swung himself off. His toes were only a couple of inches above the ground; his arms hung stiffly down; he seemed to be standing rigidly at attention, but with one purple cheek playfully posed on the shoulder. And, irreverently, he was putting out a swollen tongue at his Managing Director.

Considerations

1. How does Conrad characterize Makola as a type of person who is likely to survive most anything?
2. In what senses are Kayerts and Carlier "untidy men"?
3. How do Kayerts and Carlier first react to each other as they assume the duties of their situation? What gradually changes their dispositions?
4. How does society render Kayerts and Carlier "incapable of independent thought"?
5. How do Kayerts and Carlier regard the natives? What assumptions do they make about themselves and the natives as human beings?
6. Why do you think Conrad ends Part I at the point when the mysterious armed men appear at the station? What is the emotional effect of this arrangement of events?
7. Why do the ten natives who work for the station continue to live debased lives there? What has contact with white civilization done to them? What finally happens to them?
8. How are Kayerts and Carlier affected by their isolation after Gobila's people shun them and they lose their station men?
9. Why does Kayerts shoot Carlier? How does he try to rationalize this action?
10. How does the presence of the managing director of the Great Civilizing Company in the story's final paragraphs help to suggest the theme of the story?
11. Consider the following passage: "The contact with pure unmitigated savagery, with primitive nature and primitive man, brings sudden and profound trouble into the heart" (paragraph 5). How does this passage reflect the story's title and theme?

Connections

1. Compare and contrast the meaning of civilization in "An Outpost of Progress" and in Crane's "The Bride Comes to Yellow Sky" (p. 200).

2. How does Conrad's view of progress compare with Crane's presentation of it?
3. Write an essay in which you discuss the comic treatment of progress and civilization in Conrad's and Crane's stories.

PERSPECTIVE

JOSEPH CONRAD (1857–1924)

Fiction's Appeal to the Senses 1898

Fiction — if it at all aspires to be art — appeals to temperament. And in truth it must be, like painting, like music, like all art, the appeal of one temperament to all the other innumerable temperaments whose subtle and resistless power endows passing events with their true meaning, and creates the moral, the emotional atmosphere of the place and time. Such an appeal to be effective must be an impression conveyed through the senses; and, in fact, it cannot be made in any other way, because temperament, whether individual or collective, is not amenable to persuasion. All art, therefore, appeals primarily to the senses, and the artistic aim when expressing itself in written words must also make its appeal through the senses, if its high desire is to reach the secret spring of responsive emotions. It must strenuously aspire to the plasticity of sculpture, to the color of painting, and to the magic suggestiveness of music — which is the art of arts. And it is only through complete, unswerving devotion to the perfect blending of form and substance; it is only through an unremitting never-discouraged care for the shape and ring of sentences that an approach can be made to plasticity, to color; and the light of magic suggestiveness may be brought to play for an evanescent instant over the commonplace surface of words: of the old, old words, worn thin, defaced by ages of careless usage.

The sincere endeavor to accomplish that creative task, to go as far on that road as his strength will carry him, to go undeterred by faltering, weariness, or reproach, is the only valid justification for the worker in prose. And if his conscience is clear, his answer to those who, in the fullness of a wisdom which looks for immediate profit, demand specifically to be edified, consoled, amused; who demand to be promptly improved, or encouraged, or frightened, or shocked, or charmed, must run thus: — My task which I am trying to achieve is, by the power of the written word, to make you hear, to make you feel — it is, before all, to make you *see*. That — and no more, and it is everything. If I succeed, you shall find there according to your deserts: encouragement, consolation, fear, charm — all you demand and, perhaps, also that glimpse of truth for which you have forgotten to ask.

From Preface, *The Nigger of the "Narcissus"*

Considerations

1. According to Conrad, why must fiction appeal to the senses? Explain how Conrad achieves this appeal in "An Outpost of Progress."
2. What do you think Conrad means when he writes that he wants "to make you *see*"?

3. Conrad also hopes to provide his reader with "that glimpse of truth for which you have forgotten to ask." Explain whether the theme you discover in "An Outpost of Progress" offers such a truth.

THOMAS McCORMACK (b. 1932)

On the Problem of Teaching Theme 1988

Let's start calmly: Samples of the way "theme" is taught should be sent to Atlanta so the Centers for Disease Control can get on it; the NIH° should be called in, and a "Just Say No to 'Theme'" campaign should be promulgated among the youth of America. . . .

In flat: the way "theme" is currently taught is actively harmful.

I seriously pursue this crusade here, albeit in condensed, almost outline, form, because I believe that what's being done in classrooms stunts, and even kills, the ability and appetite of many of the best students. This deprives our globe of much talent that would otherwise find itself in writing, teaching, [and] reading. . . .

Their teaching of "theme" is harmful because of what it leads *to,* and what it leads *away from.*

In the student's mood and attitude, it leads to confusion, discouragement, and alienation.

In his knowledge it leads to error about what authors are trying to do, and about what is cherishable in fiction generally, and stories and novels individually.

It leads the student away from enjoyment, sanguine expectation, and trust in literature. It actually *reduces* the possibility of his focusing where the reward is.

It does this by forcibly thrusting on the student a concept that is fuzzy, arbitrary, trivializing, irrelevant, distracting, and ultimately deadening. . . .

The goal of getting the reader to pay closer attention is a good one. The assumption of the professors is that, by compelling the student to crawl back over the narrative in the effort to ensure that all the "major details" are "accounted for" by the theme, one forces the student to focus on each scene, each character, every element in the book. But . . . because during this crawl his focus is kept on the thin, flat, ideational plane, he's likely to miss the essential lovable things, like a chemist analyzing the molecular structure of different ice creams. It calls to mind the old days when history teachers figured that they'd do the job by compelling students to memorize a thousand names and dates.

But at least the chemist and historian inculcate some facts that may ultimately have some narrow use. The English professor in the end abandons that claim. He knows that themes like "People deceive themselves" and "Jealousy exacts a terrible cost" are indefensibly meager payoffs.

Never, despite their brief, abortive invocation of "significance", *do [the text-*

NIH: National Institutes of Health.

books] show any correlation whatever between the quality of theme and the quality of the story. . . .

But if there is no such correlation, if — as the textbook writers frequently admit — trite themes can beget great art, and great themes can beget trite art, and no theme at all can beget Poe, then the student has the right to ask: What earthly use is this vivisecting hunt for theme?

There must be ten thousand stories that, to a professor, would yield the theme "People deceive themselves." Ninety-nine percent of those stories are justifiably forgotten. But if theme is the significance of the story, why aren't all these stories equally significant? Because the professors are wrong in their teaching: The significance, the purpose, the meaning, the reason for being of a story does *not* lie in its "theme" but in something else.

Now, having dismissed theme as an end and also as a pedogogic means, it would seem meet for me to suggest an alternative technique. The technique should serve to get the student to pay the closer attention I approve of, but also to ensure that the focus is brought to bear where the true reward is.

The approach I'd recommend is based on . . . an intuition of an effect-wanted — followed by imagination's conjuring of narrative to produce that effect, and then by sensibility's judgments on those conjurings. This maintains that the aim of the artist is to produce an effect on the reader's head, heart, or gut.

[M]y own experience [is] that the most rewarding critics for me, over the years, have been those who often do no more than *point.* When Cowley° says to me, just go back and read the list of people who attended Gatsby's party, just savor how Fitzgerald describes them, it'll be worth it — he does me a profound service. If a great appreciator like Cowley tells me it will be worth it, just for itself, and not because it's necessary as step #7 in the derivation of an abstract generality, the very freedom from ulterior function enhances vision. To see the true color of the painting, do not wear glasses tinted with other intent. . . .

But then I must back down a bit and concede this teaching can't be done solely with the index finger.

What I recommend, then, is approaching the work of fiction with a program of questions devised to focus the reader on the effect achieved, and how the author achieved it.

For example, each character has a certain impact on us, the readers. To clarify how that impact is achieved, certainly notice what he says and does, what we're told about him; even ask crafty questions: What does he want or promise? What does he do to get it? What result does he cause? Why do we like or dislike him?

Move on to circuitry: How does he braid or conflict with others in the cast?

Then, really to clarify the appreciation of effects on us, and how the author is causing them, the gifted instructor, as rare teachers through the ages have when they were not fouled in the lines of theme, might bid his most gifted students to ask: *How would the story and our response be different if such-and-such were different?*

The instructor might help students to imagine a character different, or missing

Cowley: Malcolm Cowley (1898–1989), American writer, editor, poet, and critic.

entirely. What happens to the circuitry? Imagine what would be the story-effect of a new character: Hamlet's sister.

Examine each scene. First ask: Do we like it? Then ask: Why? The answer to this question always takes the form, ultimately, of simply pointing at things and taking a stand: I love this sentence; I love what she says, what he does; I think this description is great.

Sometimes crafty, gridlike questions about the scene help us push below the general pleasure to the specific credit in the narrative. How does the scene reveal or change character, circuitry, or circumstance? Are things different at the end of the scene from how they were at the beginning? How much of the vital feeling stems from this advancement, from our observation that something is really *going on,* things are *happening?* Always the aim is to notice the effect on us, the readers, as we contemplate each element of the narrative. . . . (How different would we feel if this tease, hint, threat, possibility were never introduced?)

From *The Fiction Editor, the Novel, and the Novelist*

Considerations

1. According to McCormack, what does abstracting and generalizing about the theme do to a reader's response to a story?
2. How does McCormack's advice compare with Conrad's ideas about fiction's appeal to the senses (see p. 225)?
3. Pick up McCormack's suggestion and imagine a new character for either "The Bride Comes to Yellow Sky" or "An Outpost of Progress" and explain how the imagined character affects the story.
4. To what extent does McCormack's advice correspond with the reading strategies offered by reader response critics (see Ch. 32)? Describe any significant differences.

8. Style, Tone, and Irony

STYLE

Style is a concept that everyone understands on some level because in its broadest sense it refers to the particular way in which anything is made or done. Style is everywhere around us. The world is saturated with styles in cars, clothing, buildings, teaching, dancing, music, politics — in anything that reflects a distinctive manner of expression or design. Consider, for example, how a tune sung by the Beatles differs from the same tune performed by a string orchestra. There's no mistaking the two styles.

Authors also have different characteristic styles. ***Style*** refers to the distinctive manner in which a writer arranges words to achieve particular effects. That arrangement includes individual word choices and matters such as the length of sentences, their structure, tone, and the use of irony.

Diction refers to a writer's choice of words. Because different words evoke different associations in a reader's mind, the writer's choice of words is crucial in controlling a reader's response. The diction must be appropriate for the characters and the situations in which the author places them. Consider how inappropriate it would have been if Melville had had Bartleby respond to the lawyer's requests with "Hell no!" instead of "I would prefer not to." The word *prefer* and the tentativeness of *would* help reinforce the scrivener's mildness, his dignity, and even his seeming reasonableness — all of which frustrate the lawyer's efforts to get rid of him. Bartleby, despite his passivity, seems to be in control of the situation. If he were to shout "Hell no!" he would appear angry, aggressive, desperate, and too informal, none of which would fit with his solemn, conscious decision to die. Melville makes the lawyer the desperate party by carefully choosing Bartleby's words.

Sentence structure is another element of a writer's style. Hemingway's terse, economical sentences are frequently noted and readily perceived. Here are the concluding sentences of Hemingway's "Soldier's Home" (p. 121), in which Krebs decides to leave home:

> He had tried so to keep his life from being complicated. Still, none of it had touched him. He had felt sorry for his mother and she had made him lie. He would go to Kansas City and get a job and she would feel all right about it. There would be one more scene maybe before he got away. He would not go down to his father's office. He would miss that one. He wanted his life to go smoothly. It had just gotten going that way. Well, that was all over now, anyway. He would go over to the schoolyard and watch Helen play indoor baseball.

Hemingway expresses Krebs's thought the way Krebs thinks. The style avoids any "complicated" sentence structures. Seven of the eleven sentences begin with the word *He.* There are no abstractions or qualifications. We feel as if we are listening not only to *what* Krebs thinks but to *how* he thinks. The style reflects his firm determination to make, one step at a time, a clean, unobstructed break from his family and the entangling complications they would impose on him.

Contrast this straightforward style with Vladimir Nabokov's description of a woman in his short story "The Vane Sisters." The sophisticated narrator teaches French literature at a women's college and is as observant as he is icily critical of the woman he describes in this passage.

> Her fingernails were gaudily painted, but badly bitten and not clean. Her lovers were a silent young photographer with a sudden laugh and two older men, brothers, who owned a small printing establishment across the street. I wondered at their tastes whenever I glimpsed, with a secret shudder, the higgledy-piggledy striation of black hairs that showed all along her pale shins through the nylon of her stockings with the scientific distinctness of a preparation flattened under glass; or when I felt, at her every movement, the dullish, stalish, not particularly conspicuous but all-pervading and depressing emanation that her seldom bathed flesh spread from under weary perfumes and creams.

This portrait — etched with a razor blade — is restrained but devastating. The woman's fingernails are "gaudily painted." She has no taste in men either. One of her lovers is "silent" except for a "sudden laugh," a telling detail that suggests a strikingly odd personality. Her other lovers, the two brothers (!), run a "small" business. We are invited to "shudder" along with the narrator as he vividly describes the "striation of black hairs" on her legs; we see the woman as if she were displayed under a microscope, an appropriate perspective given the narrator's close inspection. His scrutiny is relentless, and its object smells as awful as it looks (notice the difference in the language between this blunt description and the narrator's elegant distaste). He finds the woman "depressing" because the weight of her unpleasantness oppresses him.

The narrator reveals nearly as much about himself as about the woman, but Nabokov leaves the reader with the task of assessing the narrator's fastidious reactions. The formal style of this description is appropriately that of an educated, highly critical, close observer of life who knows how to convey the "dullish, stalish" essence of this woman. But, you might ask, what about the curious informality of *higgledy-piggledy?* Does that fit the formal professorial voice? Given Nabokov's well-known fascination with wit and, more important, the narrator's obvious relish for verbally slicing this woman into a slide specimen, the term is revealed as appropriately chosen once the reader sees the subtle, if brutal, pun on *piggledy.*

Hemingway's and Nabokov's uses of language are very different, yet each style successfully fuses what is said with how it is said. We could write summaries of both passages, but our summaries, owing to their styles, would not have the same effect as the originals. And that makes all the difference.

TONE

Style reveals ***tone,*** the author's implicit attitude toward the people, places, and events in a story. When we speak, tone is conveyed by our voice inflections, our wink of an eye, or some other gesture. A professor who says "You're going to fail the next exam" may be indicating concern, frustration, sympathy, alarm, humor, or indifference, depending on the tone of voice. In a literary work that spoken voice is unavailable; instead we must rely on the context in which a statement appears to interpret it correctly.

In Conrad's "An Outpost of Progress" (p. 208), for example, we read at the beginning of Part II that "there were ten station men who had been left by the Director. Those fellows, having engaged themselves to the Company for six months (without having any idea of a month in particular and only a very faint notion of time in general), *had been serving the cause of progress for upwards of two years*" (italics added). The italicized words, taken out of context, might be read as a serious laudatory assessment of their work, but placed in the larger context of Conrad's contempt for the corrupt colonial system imposed on the natives and the bankrupt values these ten workers have been reduced to, these words represent a scathing indictment of "the cause of progress." Moreover, their tone causes a rereading of the meaning of their "faint notion of time," since the station men can have, finally, nothing to do with "progress" at all. They serve instead their own degradation.

If we are sensitive to tone, we can get behind a character and see him or her from the author's perspective. In Melville's "Bartleby, the Scrivener" (p. 80) everything is told from the lawyer's point of view, but the tone of his remarks often separates him from the author's values and attitudes. When the lawyer characterizes himself at the beginning of the story, his use of language effectively allows us to see Melville disapproving of what the lawyer takes pride in.

> The late John Jacob Astor, a personage little given to poetic enthusiasm, had no hesitation in pronouncing my first grand point to be prudence; my next, method. I do not speak it in vanity.

But, of course, he is vain and a name-dropper as well. He likes the "rounded and orbicular sound" of Astor's name, because it "rings like unto bullion." Tone, here, helps to characterize the lawyer. Melville doesn't tell us that the lawyer is status conscious and materialistic; instead, we discover that through the tone. This stylistic technique is frequently an important element for interpreting a story. An insensitivity to tone can lead a reader astray in determining the theme of a work. Regardless of who is speaking in a story, it is wise to listen for the author's voice too.

IRONY

One of the enduring themes in literature is that things are not always what they seem to be. What we see — or think we see — is not always what we get. The unexpected complexity that often surprises us in life — what Herman Melville in *Moby-Dick* called the "universal thump" — is fertile ground for writers of imaginative literature. They cultivate that ground through the use of ***irony,*** a device that reveals a reality different from what appears to be true.

Verbal irony consists of a person saying one thing but meaning the opposite. If a student driver smashes into a parked car and the angry instructor turns to say "You sure did well today," the statement is an example of verbal irony. What is meant is not what is said. Verbal irony that is calculated to hurt someone by false praise is commonly known as ***sarcasm.*** In literature, however, verbal irony is usually not so openly aggressive; instead, it is more subtle and restrained though no less intense.

In Conrad's "An Outpost of Progress" (p. 208) the narrator describes "The Managing Director of the Great Civilizing Company" stepping ashore from a steamer into the African jungle. After noting the Director's full title, an irony in itself given the story's refusal to equate civilization with progress, the narrator adds parenthetically: "(since we know that civilization follows trade)." Tone is important here because the verbal irony indicates the narrator's conviction of just how corrupt an influence "civilization" can be in the jungle.

Situational irony exists when there is an incongruity between what is expected to happen and what actually happens. For instance, at the climactic showdown between Marshal Potter and Scratchy Wilson in Crane's "The Bride Comes to Yellow Sky" (p. 200), there are no gunshots, only talk — and what subdues Wilson is not Potter's strength and heroism but the fact that the marshal is now married. In Conrad's "An Outpost of Progress," the two representatives of civilization at the company station are the source of chaos and death in the wilderness they seek to tame. To take one more example, the protagonist in Godwin's "A Sorrowful Woman" (p. 30) seems, by traditional societal standards, to have all that a wife and mother could desire in a family, but, given her needs, that turns out not to be enough to sustain even her life, let alone her happiness. In each of these instances the ironic situation creates a distinction between appearances and realities and brings the reader closer to the central meaning of the story.

Another form of irony occurs when an author allows the reader to know more about a situation than a character knows. ***Dramatic irony*** creates a discrepancy between what a character believes or says and what the reader understands to be true. A chilling example of this can be found in "An Outpost of Progress" when Carlier, the station assistant, has a fit of frustration and rage over the dangers of living in the African wilderness. He raves "about the necessity of exterminating all the niggers before the country could be made habitable." The reader, however, understands that Carlier's remark makes him, rather than the natives, the true source of savagery. Dramatic irony can be an effective way for an author to have a character unwittingly reveal himself or herself.

As you read Gabriel García Márquez's "A Very Old Man with Enormous Wings," Tillie Olsen's "I Stand Here Ironing," and Mark Twain's "The Story of the Bad Little Boy," pay attention to the authors' artful use of style, tone, and irony to convey meanings.

GABRIEL GARCÍA MÁRQUEZ (b. 1928)

Born in Aracataca, Colombia, Gabriel García Márquez worked for many years as a journalist, film critic, and screenwriter. His fiction is characterized by a compelling combination of magic and realism that results in a mystical lyricism that is nonetheless grounded in common experience. His first book was *Leaf Storm and Other Stories* (1955), which includes "A Very Old Man with Enormous Wings." *One Hundred Years of Solitude* (1967) is generally regarded as his masterpiece. Other novels include *The Autumn of the Patriarch* (1976), *Chronicle of a Death Foretold* (1982), and *Love in the Time of Cholera* (1988). His stories are gathered in *The Collected Stories of Gabriel García Márquez* (1984). In 1982 he was awarded the Nobel Prize for literature. In "A Very Old Man with Enormous Wings" a stranger mystifies a community by his enigmatic presence.

A Very Old Man with Enormous Wings 1955

TRANSLATED BY GREGORY RABASSA

On the third day of rain they had killed so many crabs inside the house that Pelayo had to cross his drenched courtyard and throw them into the sea, because the newborn child had a temperature all night and they thought it was due to the stench. The world had been sad since Tuesday. Sea and sky were a single ash-gray thing and the sands of the beach, which on March nights glimmered like powdered light, had become a stew of mud and rotten shellfish. The light was so weak at noon that when Pelayo was coming back to the house after throwing away the crabs, it was hard for him to see what it was that was moving and groaning in the rear of the courtyard. He had to go very close to see that it was an old man, a very old man, lying face down in the mud, who, in spite of his tremendous efforts, couldn't get up, impeded by his enormous wings.

Frightened by that nightmare, Pelayo ran to get Elisenda, his wife, who was putting compresses on the sick child, and he took her to the rear of the courtyard. They both looked at the fallen body with mute stupor. He was dressed like a ragpicker. There were only a few faded hairs left on his bald skull and very few teeth in his mouth, and his pitiful condition of a drenched great-grandfather had taken away any sense of grandeur he might have had. His huge buzzard wings, dirty and half-plucked, were forever entangled in the mud. They looked at him so long and so closely that Pelayo and Elisenda very soon overcame their surprise and in the end found him familiar. Then they dared speak to him, and he answered in an incomprehensible dialect with a strong sailor's voice. That was how they skipped over the inconvenience of the wings and quite intelligently concluded that he was a lonely castaway from some foreign ship wrecked by the storm. And yet, they called in a neighbor woman who knew everything about life and death to see him, and all she needed was one look to show them their mistake.

"He's an angel," she told them. "He must have been coming for the child, but the poor fellow is so old that the rain knocked him down."

On the following day everyone knew that a flesh-and-blood angel was held captive in Pelayo's house. Against the judgment of the wise neighbor woman, for whom angels in those times were the fugitive survivors of a celestial conspiracy, they did not have the heart to club him to death. Pelayo watched over him all afternoon from the kitchen, armed with his bailiff's club, and before going to bed he dragged him out of the mud and locked him up with the hens in the wire chicken coop. In the middle of the night, when the rain stopped, Pelayo and Elisenda were still killing crabs. A short time afterward the child woke up without a fever and with a desire to eat. Then they felt magnanimous and decided to put the angel on a raft with fresh water and provisions for three days and leave him to his fate on the high seas. But when they went out into the courtyard with the first light of dawn, they found the whole neighborhood in front of the chicken coop having fun with the angel, without the slightest reverence, tossing him things to eat through the openings in the wire as if he weren't a supernatural creature but a circus animal.

Father Gonzaga arrived before seven o'clock, alarmed at the strange news. 5
By that time onlookers less frivolous than those at dawn had already arrived and they were making all kinds of conjectures concerning the captive's future. The simplest among them thought that he should be named mayor of the world. Others of sterner mind felt that he should be promoted to the rank of five-star general in order to win all wars. Some visionaries hoped that he could be put to stud in order to implant on earth a race of winged wise men who could take charge of the universe. But Father Gonzaga, before becoming a priest, had been a robust woodcutter. Standing by the wire, he reviewed his catechism in an instant and asked them to open the door so that he could take a close look at that pitiful man who looked more like a huge decrepit hen among the fascinated chickens. He was lying in a corner drying his open wings in the sunlight among the fruit peels and breakfast leftovers that the early risers had thrown him. Alien to the impertinences of the world, he only lifted his antiquarian eyes and murmured something in his dialect when Father Gonzaga went into the chicken coop and said good morning to him in Latin. The parish priest had his first suspicion of an impostor when he saw that he did not understand the language of God or know how to greet His ministers. Then he noticed that seen close up he was much too human: he had an unbearable smell of the outdoors, the back side of his wings were strewn with parasites and his main feathers had been mistreated by terrestrial winds, and nothing about him measured up to the proud dignity of angels. Then he came out of the chicken coop and in a brief sermon warned the curious against the risks of being ingenuous. He reminded them that the devil had the bad habit of making use of carnival tricks in order to confuse the unwary. He argued that if wings were not the essential element in determining the difference between a hawk and an airplane, they were even less so in the recognition of angels. Nevertheless, he promised to write a letter to his bishop so that the latter would write to his primate so that the latter would write to the Supreme Pontiff in order to get the final verdict from the highest courts.

His prudence fell on sterile hearts. The news of the captive angel spread with such rapidity that after a few hours the courtyard had the bustle of a marketplace and they had to call in troops with fixed bayonets to disperse the mob that was about to knock the house down. Elisenda, her spine all twisted from sweeping up so much marketplace trash, then got the idea of fencing in the yard and charging five cents admission to see the angel.

The curious came from far away. A traveling carnival arrived with a flying acrobat who buzzed over the crowd several times, but no one paid any attention to him because his wings were not those of an angel but, rather, those of a sidereal° bat. The most unfortunate invalids on earth came in search of health: a poor woman who since childhood had been counting her heartbeats and had run out of numbers; a Portuguese man who couldn't sleep because the noise of the stars disturbed him; a sleepwalker who got up at night to undo the things he had done while awake; and many others with less serious ailments. In the midst of that shipwreck disorder that made the earth tremble, Pelayo and Eli-

sidereal: Coming from the stars.

senda were happy with fatigue, for in less than a week they had crammed their rooms with money and the line of pilgrims waiting their turn to enter still reached beyond the horizon.

The angel was the only one who took no part in his own act. He spent his time trying to get comfortable in his borrowed nest, befuddled by the hellish heat of the oil lamps and sacramental candles that had been placed along the wire. At first they tried to make him eat some mothballs, which, according to the wisdom of the wise neighbor woman, were the food prescribed for angels. But he turned them down, just as he turned down the papal lunches that the penitents brought him, and they never found out whether it was because he was an angel or because he was an old man that in the end ate nothing but eggplant mush. His only supernatural virtue seemed to be patience. Especially during the first days, when the hens pecked at him, searching for the stellar parasites that proliferated in his wings, and the cripples pulled out feathers to touch their defective parts with, and even the most merciful threw stones at him, trying to get him to rise so they could see him standing. The only time they succeeded in arousing him was when they burned his side with an iron for branding steers, for he had been motionless for so many hours that they thought he was dead. He awoke with a start, ranting in his hermetic language and with tears in his eyes, and he flapped his wings a couple of times, which brought on a whirlwind of chicken dung and lunar dust and a gale of panic that did not seem to be of this world. Although many thought that his reaction had been one not of rage but of pain, from then on they were careful not to annoy him, because the majority understood that his passivity was not that of a hero taking his ease but that of a cataclysm in repose.

Father Gonzaga held back the crowd's frivolity with formulas of maidservant inspiration while awaiting the arrival of a final judgment on the nature of the captive. But the mail from Rome showed no sense of urgency. They spent their time finding out if the prisoner had a navel, if his dialect had any connection with Aramaic, how many times he could fit on the head of a pin,° or whether he wasn't just a Norwegian with wings. Those meager letters might have come and gone until the end of time if a providential event had not put an end to the priest's tribulations

It so happened that during those days, among so many other carnival at- 10
tractions, there arrived in town the traveling show of the woman who had been changed into a spider for having disobeyed her parents. The admission to see her was not only less than the admission to see the angel, but people were permitted to ask her all manner of questions about her absurd state and to examine her up and down so that no one would ever doubt the truth of her horror. She was a frightful tarantula the size of a ram and with the head of a sad maiden. What was most heart-rending, however, was not her outlandish shape but the sincere affliction with which she recounted the details of her misfortune. While still practically a child she had sneaked out of her parents' house to go to a dance, and while she was coming back through the woods after having danced all night without permission, a fearful thunderclap rent the sky in two and through the crack came the lightning bolt of brimstone that

fit on the head of a pin: An allusion to the medieval theological debate over how many angels could fit on the head of a pin.

changed her into a spider. Her only nourishment came from the meatballs that charitable souls chose to toss into her mouth. A spectacle like that, full of so much human truth and with such a fearful lesson, was bound to defeat without even trying that of a haughty angel who scarcely deigned to look at mortals. Besides, the few miracles attributed to the angel showed a certain mental disorder, like the blind man who didn't recover his sight but grew three new teeth, or the paralytic who didn't get to walk but almost won the lottery, and the leper whose sores sprouted sunflowers. Those consolation miracles, which were more like mocking fun, had already ruined the angel's reputation when the woman who had been changed into a spider finally crushed him completely. That was how Father Gonzaga was cured forever of his insomnia and Pelayo's courtyard went back to being as empty as during the time it had rained for three days and crabs walked through the bedrooms.

The owners of the house had no reason to lament. With the money they saved they built a two-story mansion with balconies and gardens and high netting so that crabs wouldn't get in during the winter, and with iron bars on the windows so that angels wouldn't get in. Pelayo also set up a rabbit warren close to town and gave up his job as bailiff for good, and Elisenda bought some satin pumps with high heels and many dresses of iridescent silk, the kind worn on Sunday by the most desirable women in those times. The chicken coop was the only thing that didn't receive any attention. If they washed it down with Creolin° and burned tears of myrrh inside it every so often, it was not in homage to the angel but to drive away the dungheap stench that still hung everywhere like a ghost and was turning the new house into an old one. At first, when the child learned to walk, they were careful that he not get too close to the chicken coop. But then they began to lose their fears and got used to the smell, and before the child got his second teeth he'd gone inside the chicken coop to play, where the wires were falling apart. The angel was no less standoffish with him than with other mortals, but he tolerated the most ingenious infamies with the patience of a dog who had no illusions. They both came down with chicken pox at the same time. The doctor who took care of the child couldn't resist the temptation to listen to the angel's heart, and he found so much whistling in the heart and so many sounds in his kidneys that it seemed impossible for him to be alive. What surprised him most, however, was the logic of his wings. They seemed so natural on that completely human organism that he couldn't understand why other men didn't have them too.

When the child began school it had been some time since the sun and rain had caused the collapse of the chicken coop. The angel went dragging himself about here and there like a stray dying man. They would drive him out of the bedroom with a broom and a moment later find him in the kitchen. He seemed to be in so many places at the same time that they grew to think that he'd been duplicated, that he was reproducing himself all through the house, and the exasperated and unhinged Elisenda shouted that it was awful living in that hell full of angels. He could scarcely eat and his antiquarian eyes had also become so foggy that he went about bumping into posts. All he had left were the bare cannulae° of his last feathers. Pelayo threw a blanket over him and extended

Creolin: Trade name for a cleaning product.
cannulae: The tubular pieces by which feathers are attached to a body.

him the charity of letting him sleep in the shed, and only then did they notice that he had a temperature at night, and was delirious with the tongue twisters of an old Norwegian. That was one of the few times they became alarmed, for they thought he was going to die and not even the wise neighbor woman had been able to tell them what to do with dead angels.

And yet he not only survived his worst winter, but seemed improved with the first sunny days. He remained motionless for several days in the farthest corner of the courtyard, where no one would see him, and at the beginning of December some large, stiff feathers began to grow on his wings, the feathers of a scarecrow, which looked more like another misfortune of decrepitude. But he must have known the reason for those changes, for he was quite careful that no one should notice them, that no one should hear the sea chanteys that he sometimes sang under the stars. One morning Elisenda was cutting some bunches of onions for lunch when a wind that seemed to come from the high seas blew into the kitchen. Then she went to the window and caught the angel in his first attempts at flight. They were so clumsy that his fingernails opened a furrow in the vegetable patch and he was on the point of knocking the shed down with the ungainly flapping that slipped on the light and couldn't get a grip on the air. But he did manage to gain altitude. Elisenda let out a sigh of relief, for herself and for him, when she saw him pass over the last houses, holding himself up in some way with the risky flapping of a senile vulture. She kept watching him even when she was through cutting the onions and she kept on watching until it was no longer possible for her to see him, because then he was no longer an annoyance in her life but an imaginary dot on the horizon of the sea.

Considerations

1. What is the impact of the story's first sentence and the last phrase of the first paragraph? How do they affect your expectations about the rest of the story?
2. In what sort of world is the story set?
3. Pelayo and Elisenda are described as looking at the old man "so long and so closely" that "very soon [they] overcame their surprise and in the end found him familiar." To what extent is your experience as a reader similar to their response to the old man? How does the author's style contribute to this creating of familiarity?
4. Characterize Pelayo and Elisenda. Are they merely crass exploiters?
5. What is Father Gonzaga's assessment of the angel? How do the crowds of people who pay admission to see the angel regard the old man?
6. How does the presence of the spider woman affect the angel's reputation as a curiosity? Why does the crowd prefer one over the other?
7. How does the angel manage to leave? Why does he do so?
8. How successfully have people in the town defined the angel? How do you explain him?
9. Locate instances of humor in the story. What kind of tone is established by the humor?

Connections

1. Compare García Márquez's mysterious angel and Melville's inscrutable Bartleby, the scrivener (p. 80). How is each made to seem like a plausible character despite his bizarre qualities?

2. Consider the public's reactions to the angel and to Franz Kafka's hunger artist (p. 376). Write an essay that explores what each of these extraordinary characters reveals about his public.
3. Compare García Márquez's angel with Kafka's hunger artist. How might the experiences of each character be read as a commentary on the decline of religion in the modern world?

TILLIE OLSEN (b. 1913)

Born in Omaha, Nebraska, Tillie Olsen lived through the struggles of working-class poverty that she described in her first novel, *Yonnondio,* begun in the early 1930s but not published until 1974. Her writing all but ended in the mid-1930s as she raised four children while working full-time, first in a factory and then as a secretary. During the 1950s she began writing again and published four stories in *Tell Me a Riddle* (1961), from which "I Stand Here Ironing" is excerpted. *Silences* (1978) is a collection of essays on the difficulties writers, particularly women, have in continuing to remain creative and productive. "I Stand Here Ironing," written during the early 1950s, concerns a mother who reflects on raising her oldest daughter.

I Stand Here Ironing 1961

I stand here ironing, and what you asked me moves tormented back and forth with the iron.

"I wish you would manage the time to come in and talk with me about your daughter. I'm sure you can help me understand her. She's a youngster who needs help and whom I'm deeply interested in helping."

"Who needs help." . . . Even if I came, what good would it do? You think because I am her mother I have a key, or that in some way you could use me as a key? She has lived for nineteen years. There is all that life that has happened outside of me, beyond me.

And when is there time to remember, to sift, to weigh, to estimate, to total? I will start and there will be an interruption and I will have to gather it all together again. Or I will become engulfed with all I did or did not do, with what should have been and what cannot be helped.

She was a beautiful baby. The first and only one of our five that was beau- 5
tiful at birth. You do not guess how new and uneasy her tenancy in her now-loveliness. You did not know her all those years she was thought homely, or see her poring over her baby pictures, making me tell her over and over how beautiful she had been — and would be, I would tell her — and was not, to the seeing eye. But the seeing eyes were few or nonexistent. Including mine.

I nursed her. They feel that's important nowadays. I nursed all the children, but with her, with all the fierce rigidity of first motherhood, I did like the books then said. Though her cries battered me to trembling and my breasts ached with swollenness, I waited till the clock decreed.

Why do I put that first? I do not even know if it matters, or if it explains anything.

She was a beautiful baby. She blew shining bubbles of sound. She loved motion, loved light, loved color and music and textures. She would lie on the floor in her blue overalls patting the surface so hard in ecstasy her hands and feet would blur. She was a miracle to me, but when she was eight months old I had to leave her daytimes with the woman downstairs to whom she was no miracle at all, for I worked or looked for work and for Emily's father, who "could no longer endure" (he wrote in his good-bye note) "sharing want with us."

I was nineteen. It was the pre-relief, pre-WPA world of the depression. I would start running as soon as I got off the streetcar, running up the stairs, the place smelling sour, and awake or asleep to startle awake, when she saw me she would break into a clogged weeping that could not be comforted, a weeping I can hear yet.

After a while I found a job hashing at night so I could be with her days, 10
and it was better. But it came to where I had to bring her to his family and leave her.

It took a long time to raise the money for her fare back. Then she got chicken pox and I had to wait longer. When she finally came, I hardly knew her, walking quick and nervous like her father, looking like her father, thin, and dressed in a shoddy red that yellowed her skin and glared at the pockmarks. All the baby loveliness gone.

She was two. Old enough for nursery school they said, and I did not know then what I know now — the fatigue of the long day, and the lacerations of group life in the kinds of nurseries that are only parking places for children.

Except that it would have made no difference if I had known. It was the only place there was. It was the only way we could be together, the only way I could hold a job.

And even without knowing, I knew. I knew the teacher that was evil because all these years it has curdled into my memory, the little boy hunched in the corner, her rasp, "why aren't you outside, because Alvin hits you? that's no reason, go out, scaredy." I knew Emily hated it even if she did not clutch and implore "don't go Mommy" like the other children, mornings.

She always had a reason why we should stay home. Momma, you look sick. 15
Momma, I feel sick. Momma, the teachers aren't here today, they're sick. Momma, we can't go, there was a fire there last night. Momma, it's a holiday today, no school, they told me.

But never a direct protest, never rebellion. I think of our others in their three-, four-year-oldness — the explosions, tempers, the denunciations, the demands — and I feel suddenly ill. I put the iron down. What in me demanded that goodness in her? And what was the cost, the cost to her of such goodness?

The old man living in the back once said in his gentle way: "You should smile at Emily more when you look at her." What *was* in my face when I looked at her? I loved her. There were all the acts of love.

It was only with the others I remembered what he said, and it was the face of joy, and not of care or tightness or worry I turned to them — too late for

Emily. She does not smile easily, let alone almost always as her brothers and sisters do. Her face is closed and sombre, but when she wants, how fluid. You must have seen it in her pantomimes, you spoke of her rare gift for comedy on the stage that rouses laughter out of the audience so dear they applaud and applaud and do not want to let her go.

Where does it come from, that comedy? There was none of it in her when she came back to me that second time, after I had to send her away again. She had a new daddy now to learn to love, and I think perhaps it was a better time.

Except when we left her alone nights, telling ourselves she was old enough. 20

"Can't you go some other time, Mommy, like tomorrow?" she would ask. "Will it be just a little while you'll be gone? Do you promise?"

The time we came back, the front door open, the clock on the floor in the hall. She rigid awake. "It wasn't just a little while. I didn't cry. Three times I called you, just three times, and then I ran downstairs to open the door so you could come faster. The clock talked loud. I threw it away, it scared me what it talked."

She said the clock talked loud again that night I went to the hospital to have Susan. She was delirious with the fever that comes before red measles, but she was fully conscious all the week I was gone and the week after we were home when she could not come near the new baby or me.

She did not get well. She stayed skeleton thin, not wanting to eat, and night after night she had nightmares. She would call for me, and I would rouse from exhaustion to sleepily call back: "You're all right, darling, go to sleep, it's just a dream," and if she still called, in a sterner voice, "now to go sleep, Emily, there's nothing to hurt you." Twice, only twice, when I had to get up for Susan anyhow, I went in to sit with her.

Now when it is too late (as if she would let me hold and comfort her like 25
I do the others) I get up and go to her at once at her moan or restless stirring. "Are you awake, Emily? Can I get you something?" And the answer is always the same: "No, I'm all right, go back to sleep, Mother."

They persuaded me at the clinic to send her away to a convalescent home in the country where "she can have the kind of food and care you can't manage for her, and you'll be free to concentrate on the new baby." They still send children to that place. I see pictures on the society page of sleek young women planning affairs to raise money for it, or dancing at the affairs, or decorating Easter eggs or filling Christmas stockings for the children.

They never have a picture of the children so I do not know if the girls still wear those gigantic red bows and the ravaged looks on the every other Sunday when parents can come to visit "unless otherwise notified"—as we were notified the first six weeks.

Oh it is a handsome place, green lawns and tall trees and fluted flower beds. High up on the balconies of each cottage the children stand, the girls in their red bows and white dresses, the boys in white suits and giant red ties. The parents stand below shrieking up to be heard and the children shriek down to be heard, and between them the invisible wall "Not To Be Contaminated by Parental Germs or Physical Affection."

There was a tiny girl who always stood hand in hand with Emily. Her parents never came. One visit she was gone. "They moved her to Rose Cottage" Emily shouted in explanation. "They don't like you to love anybody here."

She wrote once a week, the labored writing of a seven-year-old. "I am fine. How is the baby. If I write my leter nicly I will have a star. Love." There never was a star. We wrote every other day, letters she could never hold or keep but only hear read — once. "We simply do not have room for children to keep any personal possessions," they patiently explained when we pieced one Sunday's shrieking together to plead how much it would mean to Emily, who loved so to keep things, to be allowed to keep her letters and cards. 30

Each visit she looked frailer. "She isn't eating," they told us.

(They had runny eggs for breakfast or mush with lumps, Emily said later, I'd hold it in my mouth and not swallow. Nothing ever tasted good, just when they had chicken.)

It took us eight months to get her released home, and only the fact that she gained back so little of her seven lost pounds convinced the social worker.

I used to try to hold and love her after she came back, but her body would stay stiff, and after a while she'd push away. She ate little. Food sickened her, and I think much of life too. Oh she had physical lightness and brightness, twinkling by on skates, bouncing like a ball up and down up and down over the jump rope, skimming over the hill; but these were momentary.

She fretted about her appearance, thin and dark and foreign-looking at a time when every little girl was supposed to look or thought she should look a chubby blonde replica of Shirley Temple. The doorbell sometimes rang for her, but no one seemed to come and play in the house or be a best friend. Maybe because we moved so much. 35

There was a boy she loved painfully through two school semesters. Months later she told me how she had taken pennies from my purse to buy him candy. "Licorice was his favorite and I brought him some every day, but he still liked Jennifer better'n me. Why, Mommy?" The kind of question for which there is no answer.

School was a worry to her. She was not glib or quick in a world where glibness and quickness were easily confused with ability to learn. To her overworked and exasperated teachers she was an overconscientious "slow learner" who kept trying to catch up and was absent entirely too often.

I let her be absent, though sometimes the illness was imaginary. How different from my now-strictness about attendance with the others. I wasn't working. We had a new baby, I was home anyhow. Sometimes, after Susan grew old enough, I would keep her home from school, too, to have them all together.

Mostly Emily had asthma, and her breathing, harsh and labored, would fill the house with a curiously tranquil sound. I would bring the two old dresser mirrors and her boxes of collections to her bed. She would select beads and single earrings, bottle tops and shells, dried flowers and pebbles, old postcards and scraps, all sorts of oddments; then she and Susan would play Kingdom, setting up landscapes and furniture, peopling them with action.

Those were the only times of peaceful companionship between her and Susan. I have edged away from it, that poisonous feeling between them, that terrible balancing of hurts and needs I had to do between the two, and did so badly, those earlier years. 40

Oh there are conflicts between the others too, each one human, needing, demanding, hurting, taking — but only between Emily and Susan, no, Emily toward Susan that corroding resentment. It seems so obvious on the surface, yet it is not obvious. Susan, the second child, Susan, golden- and curly-haired and chubby, quick and articulate and assured, everything in appearance and manner Emily was not; Susan, not able to resist Emily's precious things, losing or sometimes clumsily breaking them; Susan telling jokes and riddles to company for applause while Emily sat silent (to say to me later: that was *my* riddle, Mother, I told it to Susan); Susan, who for all the five years' difference in age was just a year behind Emily in developing physically.

I am glad for that slow physical development that widened the difference between her and her contemporaries, though she suffered over it. She was too vulnerable for that terrible world of youthful competition, of preening and parading, of constant measuring of yourself against every other, of envy, "If I had that copper hair," "If I had that skin. . . ." She tormented herself enough about not looking like the others, there was enough of the unsureness, the having to be conscious of words before you speak, the constant caring—what are they thinking of me? without having it all magnified by the merciless physical drives.

Ronnie is calling. He is wet and I change him. It is rare there is such a cry now. That time of motherhood is almost behind me when the ear is not one's own but must always be racked and listening for the child cry, the child call. We sit for a while and I hold him, looking out over the city spread in charcoal with its soft aisles of light. *"Shoogily,"* he breathes and curls closer. I carry him back to bed, asleep. *Shoogily.* A funny word, a family word, inherited from Emily, invented by her to say: *comfort.*

In this and other ways she leaves her seal, I say aloud. And startle at my saying it. What do I mean? What did I start to gather together, to try and make coherent? I was at the terrible, growing years. War years. I do not remember them well. I was working, there were four smaller ones now, there was not time for her. She had to help be a mother, and housekeeper, and shopper. She had to set her seal. Mornings of crisis and near hysteria trying to get lunches packed, hair combed, coats and shoes found, everyone to school or Child Care on time, the baby ready for transportation. And always the paper scribbled on by a smaller one, the book looked at by Susan then mislaid, the homework not done. Running out to that huge school where she was one, she was lost, she was a drop; suffering over the unpreparedness, stammering and unsure in her classes.

There was so little time left at night after the kids were bedded down. She 45
would struggle over books, always eating (it was in those years she developed her enormous appetite that is legendary in our family) and I would be ironing, or preparing food for the next day, or writing V-mail to Bill, or tending the baby. Sometimes, to make me laugh, or out of her despair, she would imitate happenings or types at school.

I think I said once: "Why don't you do something like this in the school amateur show?" One morning she phoned me at work, hardly understandable through the weeping: "Mother, I did it. I won, I won; they gave me first prize; they clapped and clapped and wouldn't let me go."

Now suddenly she was Somebody, and as imprisoned in her difference as she had been in anonymity.

She began to be asked to perform at other high schools, even in colleges, then at city and statewide affairs. The first one we went to, I only recognized her that first moment when thin, shy, she almost drowned herself into the curtains. Then: Was this Emily? The control, the command, the convulsing and deadly clowning, the spell, then the roaring, stamping audience, unwilling to let this rare and precious laughter out of their lives.

Afterwards: You ought to do something about her with a gift like that — but without money or knowing how, what does one do? We have left it all to her, and the gift has as often eddied inside, clogged and clotted, as been used and growing.

She is coming. She runs up the stairs two at a time with her light graceful step, and I know she is happy tonight. Whatever it was that occasioned your call did not happen today.

"Aren't you ever going to finish the ironing, Mother? Whistler painted his mother in a rocker. I'd have to paint mine standing over an ironing board." This is one of her communicative nights and she tells me everything and nothing as she fixes herself a plate of food out of the icebox.

She is so lovely. Why did you want me to come in at all? Why were you concerned? She will find her way.

She starts up the stairs to bed. "Don't get me up with the rest in the morning." "But I thought you were having midterms." "Oh, those," she comes back in, kisses me, and says quite lightly, "in a couple of years when we'll all be atom-dead they won't matter a bit."

She has said it before. She *believes* it. But because I have been dredging the past, and all that compounds a human being is so heavy and meaningful in me, I cannot endure it tonight.

I will never total it all. I will never come in to say: She was a child seldom smiled at. Her father left me before she was a year old. I had to work her first six years when there was work, or I sent her home and to his relatives. There were years she had care she hated. She was dark and thin and foreign-looking in a world where the prestige went to blondeness and curly hair and dimples, she was slow where glibness was prized. She was a child of anxious, not proud, love. We were poor and could not afford for her the soil of easy growth. I was a young mother, I was a distracted mother. There were other children pushing up, demanding. Her younger sister seemed all that she was not. There were years she did not want me to touch her. She kept too much in herself, her life was such she had to keep too much in herself. My wisdom came too late. She has much to her and probably little will come of it. She is a child of her age, of depression, of war, of fear.

Let her be. So all that is in her will not bloom — but in how many does it? There is still enough left to live by. Only help her to know — help make it so there is cause for her to know — that she is more than this dress on the ironing board, helpless before the iron.

Considerations

1. Who is speaking in the second paragraph of this story? Is it possible to be specific?
2. Is this story primarily about the mother or about Emily? What does the point of view reveal?
3. How and why has the mother treated Emily differently from the other children?
4. What sort of mother is the narrator? Does your view of her change as you learn more about her?
5. What is the author's attitude toward the mother?

6. Why is it ironic that Emily is a talented comedienne?
7. Does the mother's ironing have any symbolic significance?
8. How is the summary in the next to last paragraph different in style and tone from the rest of the mother's account of Emily? What is the effect of this paragraph on your understanding of the mother's relationship with Emily?
9. Comment on Emily's reason for not worrying about her midterm exams: "in a couple of years when we'll all be atom-dead they won't matter a bit."
10. Describe what the mother's account of her daughter's experience reveals to her about her own life.

Connections

1. Contrast the narrator in this story with the mother in Godwin's "A Sorrowful Woman" (p. 30).
2. Contrast the tone of the mother's narration in this story with that of the teenager Sammy in John Updike's "A & P" (p. 407). How does each author achieve a convincing voice for the first-person narrator?

MARK TWAIN (1835–1910)

Mark Twain is the pen name of Samuel Langhorne Clemens, who was born and raised in Missouri. His formal education ended in his teens, after which he wrote for newspapers, worked on a Mississippi River steamboat, and traveled to Nevada and California once the Civil War began. Along the way he developed a shrewd eye for the people and places that provided his literary education, and he acquired a strong popular reputation for his earthy humor, wit, and insights. His novels have become part of the American literary landscape; they include *The Adventures of Tom Sawyer* (1876), *The Prince and the Pauper* (1882), *The Adventures of Huckleberry Finn* (1884), and *A Connecticut Yankee in King Arthur's Court* (1889). His short stories are collected in *The Complete Stories of Mark Twain* (1957). Some of his later works, such as *The Mysterious Stranger* (published posthumously in 1916), are bitterly pessimistic about the nature of human beings, but he is most remembered for the kind of satiric humor that reminds people that making distinctions between virtue and vice can be a tricky business. In "The Story of the Bad Little Boy" Twain offers his version of a Sunday-school lesson.

The Story of the Bad Little Boy 1865

Once there was a bad little boy whose name was Jim — though, if you will notice, you will find that bad little boys are nearly always called James in your Sunday-school books. It was strange, but still it was true, that this one was called Jim.

He didn't have any sick mother, either — a sick mother who was pious and had the consumption, and would be glad to lie down in the grave and be at rest but for the strong love she bore her boy, and the anxiety she felt that the world might be harsh and cold toward him when she was gone. Most bad boys in the Sunday books are named James, and have sick mothers, who teach them to say, "Now, I lay me down," etc., and sing them to sleep with sweet, plaintive voices, and then kiss them good night, and kneel down by the bedside and weep. But it was different with this fellow. He was named Jim, and there wasn't anything the matter with his mother — no consumption, nor anything of that kind. She was rather stout than otherwise, and she was not pious; moreover, she was not anxious on Jim's account. She said if he were to break his neck it wouldn't be much loss. She always spanked Jim to sleep, and she never kissed him good night; on the contrary, she boxed his ears when she was ready to leave him.

Once this little bad boy stole the key of the pantry, and slipped in there and helped himself to some jam, and filled up the vessel with tar, so that his mother would never know the difference; but all at once a terrible feeling didn't come over him, and something didn't seem to whisper to him, "Is it right to disobey my mother? Isn't it sinful to do this? Where do bad little boys go who gobble up their good kind mother's jam?" and then he didn't kneel down all alone and promise never to be wicked any more, and rise up with a light, happy heart, and go and tell his mother all about it, and beg her forgiveness, and be blessed by her with tears of pride and thankfulness in her eyes. No; that is the way with all other bad boys in the books; but it happened otherwise with this Jim, strangely enough. He ate that jam, and said it was bully, in his sinful, vulgar way; and he put in the tar, and said that was bully also, and laughed, and observed "that the old woman would get up and snort" when she found it out; and when she did find it out, he denied knowing anything about it, and she whipped him severely, and he did the crying himself. Everything about this boy was curious — everything turned out differently with him from the way it does to the bad Jameses in the books.

Once he climbed up in Farmer Acorn's apple tree to steal apples, and the limb didn't break, and he didn't fall and break his arm, and get torn by the farmer's great dog, and then languish on a sickbed for weeks, and repent and become good. Oh, no; he stole as many apples as he wanted and came down all right; and he was all ready for the dog, too, and knocked him endways with a brick when he came to tear him. It was very strange — nothing like it ever happened in those mild little books with marbled backs, and with pictures in them of men with swallow-tailed coats and bell-crowned hats, and pantaloons that are short in the legs, and women with the waists of their dresses under their arms, and no hoops on. Nothing like it in any of the Sunday-school books.

Once he stole the teacher's penknife, and, when he was afraid it would be 5
found out and he would get whipped, he slipped it into George Wilson's cap — poor Widow Wilson's son, the moral boy, the good little boy of the village, who always obeyed his mother, and never told an untruth, and was fond of his lessons, and infatuated with Sunday school. And when the knife dropped from the cap, and poor George hung his head and blushed, as if in conscious guilt, and the grieved teacher charged the theft upon him, and was just in the very act of

bringing the switch down upon his trembling shoulders, a white-haired, improbable justice of the peace did not suddenly appear in their midst, and strike an attitude and say, "Spare this noble boy — there stands the cowering culprit! I was passing the school door at recess, and, unseen myself, I saw the theft committed!" And then Jim didn't get whaled, and the venerable justice didn't read the tearful school a homily, and take George by the hand and say such a boy deserved to be exalted, and then tell him to come and make his home with him, and sweep out the office, and make fires, and run errands, and chop wood, and study law, and help his wife do household labors, and have all the balance of the time to play, and get forty cents a month, and be happy. No; it would have happened that way in the books, but it didn't happen that way to Jim. No meddling old clam of a justice dropped in to make trouble, and so the model boy George got thrashed, and Jim was glad of it because, you know, Jim hated moral boys. Jim said he was "down on them milksops." Such was the coarse language of this bad, neglected boy.

But the strangest thing that ever happened to Jim was the time he went boating on Sunday, and didn't get drowned, and that other time that he got caught out in the storm when he was fishing on Sunday, and didn't get struck by lightning. Why, you might look, and look, all through the Sunday-school books from now till next Christmas, and you would never come across anything like this. Oh, no; you would find that all the bad boys who go boating on Sunday invariably get drowned; and all the bad boys who get caught out in storms when they are fishing on Sunday infallibly get struck by lightning. Boats with bad boys in them always upset on Sunday, and it always storms when bad boys go fishing on the Sabbath. How this Jim ever escaped is a mystery to me.

This Jim bore a charmed life — that must have been the way of it. Nothing could hurt him. He even gave the elephant in the menagerie a plug of tobacco, and the elephant didn't knock the top of his head off with his trunk. He browsed around the cupboard after essence of peppermint, and didn't make a mistake and drink *aqua fortis.*° He stole his father's gun and went hunting on the Sabbath, and didn't shoot three or four of his fingers off. He struck his little sister on the temple with his fist when he was angry, and she didn't linger in pain through long summer days, and die with sweet words of forgiveness upon her lips that redoubled the anguish of his breaking heart. No; she got over it. He ran off and went to sea at last, and didn't come back and find himself sad and alone in the world, his loved ones sleeping in the quiet churchyard, and the vine-embowered home of his boyhood tumbled down and gone to decay. Ah, no; he came home as drunk as a piper, and got into the station-house the first thing.

And he grew up and married, and raised a large family, and brained them all with an ax one night, and got wealthy by all manner of cheating and rascality; and now he is the infernalest wickedest scoundrel in his native village, and is universally respected, and belongs to the legislature.

So you see there never was a bad James in the Sunday-school books that had such a streak of luck as this sinful Jim with the charmed life.

aqua fortis: Nitric acid.

Considerations

1. What is the story's central irony?
2. Which sentences are particularly effective in imitating the style of Sunday-school books? Which sentences are clearly Twain's style? What is the effect of having both styles side by side?
3. How does George Wilson serve as a foil for Jim? Is Twain sympathetic to George? Why or why not?
4. How does the story's tone reveal Twain's attitude toward Jim? Can you find any examples of verbal irony?
5. How does the magnitude of Jim's "sins" grow in the story? What do you think is his greatest sin? Which perversity does Twain think is the greatest?
6. Is there a serious point to the humor here? What is the theme of the story?
7. It might be tempting to sum up this story with something like "Nice guys finish last." Discuss the adequacy of this as a statement of theme.
8. Characterize the tone of voice that tells the story. Is it indignant, amused, cynical, bitter, disinterested, or what?

Connections

1. Contrast Jim's fate with that of the central character in Ellison's "Battle Royal" (p. 179).
2. Write an essay explaining the extent to which this story and Crane's "The Bride Comes to Yellow Sky" (p. 200) are dependent on a reader being familiar with the formulaic qualities of Sunday-school stories or traditional western stories.
3. How might Edwin Arlington Robinson's poem "Richard Cory" (p. 586) be regarded as an ironic inversion of "The Story of the Bad Little Boy"?

PERSPECTIVE

MARK TWAIN (1835–1910)

The Art of Authorship 1890

Your inquiry has set me thinking, but, so far, my thought fails to materialize. I mean that, upon consideration, I am not sure that I have methods in composition. I do suppose I have — I suppose I must have — but they somehow refuse to take shape in my mind; their details refuse to separate and submit to classification and description; they remain a jumble — visible, like the fragments of glass when you look in at the wrong end of a kaleidoscope, but still a jumble. If I could turn the whole thing around and look in at the other end, why then the figures would flash into form out of the chaos, and I shouldn't have any more trouble. But my head isn't right for that today, apparently. It might have been, maybe, if I had slept last night.

However, let us try guessing. Let us guess that whenever we read a sentence and like it, we unconsciously store it away in our model-chamber; and it goes with a myriad of its fellows to the building, brick, by brick, of the eventual edifice which we call our style. And let us guess that whenever we run across other forms — bricks — whose color, or some other defect, offends us, we unconsciously reject these, and so one never finds them in our edifice.

If I have subjected myself to any training processes, and no doubt I have, it must have been in this unconscious or half-conscious fashion. I think it unlikely that deliberate and consciously methodical training is usual with the craft. I think it likely that the training most in use is of this unconscious sort, and is guided and governed and made by-and-by unconsciously systematic, by an automatically-working taste — a taste which selects and rejects without asking you for any help, and patiently and steadily improves itself without troubling you to approve or applaud. Yes, and likely enough when the structure is at last pretty well up, and attracts attention, YOU feel complimented, whereas you didn't build it, and didn't even consciously superintend.

Yes; one notices, for instance, that long, involved sentences confuse him, and that he is obliged to re-read them to get the sense. Unconsciously, then, he rejects that brick. Unconsciously he accustoms himself to writing short sentences as a rule. At times he may indulge himself with a long one, but he will make sure that there are no folds in it, no vaguenesses, no parenthetical interruptions of its view as a whole; when he is done with it, it won't be a sea-serpent, with half its arches under the water, it will be a torchlight procession.

Well, also he will notice in the course of time, as his reading goes on, that the difference between the almost right word and the right word is really a large matter — 'tis the difference between the lightning-bug and the lightning. After that, of course, that exceedingly important brick, the exact word — however, this is running into an essay, and I beg pardon. So I seemed to have arrived at this: doubtless I have methods, but they begot themselves, in which case I am only their proprietor, not their father.

From *The Art of Authorship*

Considerations

1. This response to a letter describes Twain's methods of composition. Why does he "think it unlikely that deliberate and consciously methodical training is usual with the craft"? How does this compare with your own views on writing?
2. Does "The Story of the Bad Little Boy" reflect the heavy emphasis on individual words ("the difference between the almost right word and the right word") that Twain notes in this essay? Why or why not?
3. Write an essay that describes your own writing style and explains how you developed it. Is your method of composition similar to or different from Twain's?

9. A Study of Two Authors: Nathaniel Hawthorne and Flannery O'Connor

This chapter includes a number of short stories by Nathaniel Hawthorne and Flannery O'Connor in order to provide an opportunity to study two major fiction writers in some depth. Getting to know an author's work is similar to developing a friendship with someone: the more encounters, the more intimate the relationship becomes. Familiarity with a writer's concerns and methods in one story can help to illuminate another story. As we become accustomed to someone's voice — a friend's or a writer's — we become attuned to nuances in tone and meaning.

The nuances in Hawthorne's and O'Connor's fiction warrant close analysis. Each of the following works is a unique and absorbing story that rewards additional readings. Although neither grouping is wholly representative of the writer's work, each offers enough stories to suggest some of the techniques and concerns that characterize their work. Each grouping provides a useful context for reading individual stories. Moreover, the works of both Hawthorne and O'Connor invite comparisons and contrasts in their styles and themes. Following each set of stories are some brief commentaries by and about Hawthorne and O'Connor that establish additional contexts for understanding their fiction.

NATHANIEL HAWTHORNE

Nathaniel Hawthorne (1804–1864) once described himself as "the obscurest man of letters in America." During the early years of his career, this self-assessment was mostly accurate, but the publication of *The Scarlet Letter* in 1850 marked the beginning of Hawthorne's reputation as a major American writer. His novels and short stories have entertained and challenged generations of readers; they have wide appeal because they can be read on many levels. Hawthorne skillfully creates an atmosphere of complexity and ambiguity that makes it difficult to reduce his stories to a simple view of life. The moral and psychological issues that he examines through the conflicts his characters experience are often intricate and mysterious. Readers are frequently made to feel that in exploring Hawthorne's characters they are also encountering some part of themselves.

Hawthorne achieved success as a writer only after a steady and intense struggle. His personal history was hardly conducive to producing a professional writer. Born in Salem, Massachusetts, Hawthorne came from a Puritan family of declining fortunes that prided itself on an energetic pursuit of practical matters such as law and commerce. He never knew his father, a sea captain who died in Dutch Guiana when Hawthorne was only four years old, but he did have a strong imaginative sense of an early ancestor, who as a Puritan judge persecuted Quakers, and of a later ancestor, who was a judge during the Salem witchcraft trials. His forebears seemed to haunt Hawthorne, so that in some ways he felt more involved in the past than in the present.

In "The Custom-House," the introduction to *The Scarlet Letter,* Hawthorne considers himself in relation to his severe Puritan ancestors.

> No aim, that I have ever cherished, would they recognize as laudable; no success of mine . . . would they deem otherwise than worthless, if not positively disgraceful. "What is he?" murmurs one gray shadow of my forefathers to the other. "A writer of story-books! What kind of a business in life, — what mode of glorifying God, or being serviceable to mankind in his day and generation, — may that be? Why, the degenerate fellow might as well have been a fiddler!" Such are the compliments bandied between my great-grandsires and myself, across the gulf of time! And yet, let them scorn me as they will, strong traits of their nature have intertwined with mine.

Hawthorne's sense of what his forebears might think of his work caused him to worry that the utilitarian world was more real and important than his imaginative creations. This issue became a recurring theme in his work.

Despite the Puritan strain in Hawthorne's sensibilities and his own deep suspicion that a literary vocation was not serious or productive work, Hawthorne was determined to become a writer. He found encouragement at Bowdoin College in Maine and graduated in 1825 with a class that included the poet Henry Wadsworth Longfellow and Franklin Pierce, who would be elected president of the United States in the early 1850s. After graduation Hawthorne returned to his mother's house in Salem, where for the next twelve years he read New England history as well as writers such as John Milton, William Shakespeare, and John Bunyan. During this time he lived a relatively withdrawn life devoted to developing his literary art. Hawthorne wrote and revised stories as he sought a style that would express his creative energies. Many of these early efforts were destroyed when they did not meet his high standards. His first novel, *Fanshawe,* was published anonymously in 1828; it concerns a solitary young man who fails to realize his potential and dies young. Hawthorne very nearly succeeded in reclaiming and destroying all the published copies of this work. It was not attributed to the author until after his death; not even his wife was aware that he had written it. The stories eventually published as *Twice-Told Tales* (1837) represent work that was carefully revised and survived Hawthorne's critical judgments.

Writing did not provide an adequate income, so like nearly all nineteenth-century American writers, Hawthorne had to take on other employment. He worked in the Boston Custom House from 1839 through 1840 to save money to marry Sophia Peabody, but he lost that politically appointed job when administrations changed. In 1841 he lived at Brook Farm, a utopian community founded by idealists who hoped to combine manual labor with art and philosophy. Finding that monotonous physical labor left little time for thinking and writing, Hawthorne departed after seven months. The experience failed to improve his financial situation, but it did eventually serve as the basis for a novel, *The Blithedale Romance* (1852).

Married in the summer of 1842, Hawthorne and his wife moved to the Old Manse in Concord, Massachusetts, where their neighbors included Ralph Waldo Emerson, Henry David Thoreau, Amos Bronson Alcott, and other writers and thinkers who contributed to the lively literary environment of that small town. Although Hawthorne was on friendly terms with these men, his skepticism concerning human nature prevented him from sharing either their optimism or their faith in radical reform of individuals or society. Hawthorne's view of life was chastened by a sense of what he called in "Wakefield" the "iron tissue of necessity." His sensibilities were more akin to Herman Melville's. When Melville and Hawthorne met while Hawthorne was living in the Berkshires of western Massachusetts, they responded to each other intensely. Melville admired the "power of blackness" he discovered in Hawthorne's writings and dedicated *Moby-Dick* to him.

During the several years he lived in the Old Manse, Hawthorne published a second collection of *Twice-Told Tales* (1842) and additional stories in *Mosses from an Old Manse* (1846). To keep afloat financially, he worked in the Salem Custom House from 1846 until 1849, when he again lost his job through a change in administrations. This time, however, he discovered that by leaving the oppressive materialism of the Custom House he found more energy to write: "So little adapted is the atmosphere of a Custom House to the delicate harvest of fancy and sensibility, that, had I remained there through ten Presidencies yet to come, I doubt whether the tale of 'The Scarlet Letter' would ever have been brought before the public. My imagination was a tarnished mirror" there. Free of the Custom House, Hawthorne was at the height of his creativity and productivity during the early 1850s. In addition to *The Scarlet Letter* and *The Blithedale Romance,* he wrote *The House of the Seven Gables* (1851); *The Snow-Image and Other Twice-Told Tales* (1852); a campaign biography of his Bowdoin classmate, *The Life of Franklin Pierce* (1852); and two collections of stories for children, *A Wonder Book* (1852) and *Tanglewood Tales* (1853).

Hawthorne's financial situation improved during the final decade of his life. In 1853 his friend President Pierce appointed him to the U.S. consulship in Liverpool, where he remained for the next four years. Following a tour of Europe from 1858 to 1860, Hawthorne and his family returned to Concord, and he published *The Marble Faun* (1860), his final completed work of fiction. He died while traveling through New Hampshire with ex-President Pierce.

Hawthorne's stories are unlike the melodramatic but usually optimistic fiction published in many magazines contemporary to him. Instead of cheerfully confirming public values and attitudes, his work tends to be dark and brooding. Modern readers remain responsive to Hawthorne's work — despite the fact that his nineteenth-century style takes some getting used to — because his psychological themes are as fascinating as they are disturbing. The range of his themes is not broad, but their treatment is remarkable for its insights.

Hawthorne wrote about individuals who suffer from inner conflicts caused by sin, pride, untested innocence, hidden guilt, perverse secrecy, cold intellectuality, and isolation. His characters are often consumed by their own passions, whether those passions are motivated by an obsession with goodness or evil. He looks inside his characters and reveals to us that portion of their hearts, minds, and souls which they keep from the world and even from themselves. This emphasis accounts for the private, interior, and sometimes gloomy atmosphere in Hawthorne's works. His stories rarely end on a happy note, because the questions his characters raise are almost never completely answered. Rather than positing solutions to the problems and issues his characters encounter, Hawthorne leaves us with ambiguities suggesting that experience cannot always be fully understood and controlled. Beneath the surface appearances in his stories lurk ironies and shifting meanings that point to many complex truths instead of a single simple moral.

The following four Hawthorne stories provide an opportunity to study this writer in some depth. These stories are not intended to be entirely representative of the 120 or so that Hawthorne wrote, but they do offer some sense of the range of his techniques and themes. Hawthorne's fictional world of mysterious incidents and sometimes bizarre characters increases in meaning the more his stories are read in the context of one another.

The Wives of the Dead **1832**

The following story, the simple and domestic incidents of which may be deemed scarcely worth relating, after such a lapse of time, awakened some degree of interest, a hundred years ago, in a principal seaport of the Bay Province. The rainy twilight of an autumn day; a parlor on the second floor of a small house, plainly furnished, as beseemed the middling circumstances of its inhabitants, yet decorated with little curiosities from beyond the sea, and a few delicate specimens of Indian manufacture,—these are the only particulars to be premised in regard to scene and season. Two young and comely women sat together by the fireside, nursing their mutual and peculiar sorrows. They were the recent brides of two brothers, a sailor and a landsman, and two successive days had brought tidings of the death of each, by the chances of Canadian warfare, and the tempestuous Atlantic. The universal sympathy excited by this bereavement, drew numerous condoling guests to the habitation of the widowed sisters. Several, among whom was the minister, had remained till the verge of evening; when one by one, whispering many comfortable passages of Scripture, that were answered by more abundant tears, they took their leave and departed to their own happier homes. The mourners, though not insensible to the kindness of their friends, had yearned to be left alone. United, as they had been, by the relationship of the living, and now more closely so by that of the dead, each felt as if whatever consolation her grief admitted, were to be found in the bosom of the other. They joined their hearts, and wept together silently. But after an hour of such indulgence, one of the sisters, all of whose emotions were influenced by her mild, quiet, yet not feeble character, began to recollect the precepts of resignation and endurance, which piety had taught her, when she did not think to need them. Her misfortune, besides, as earliest known, should earliest cease to interfere with her regular course of duties; accordingly, having placed the table before the fire, and arranged a frugal meal, she took the hand of her companion.

"Come, dearest sister; you have eaten not a morsel to-day," she said. "Arise, I pray you, and let us ask a blessing on that which is provided for us."

Her sister-in-law was of a lively and irritable temperament, and the first pangs of her sorrow had been expressed by shrieks and passionate lamentation. She now shrunk from Mary's words, like a wounded sufferer from a hand that revives the throb.

"There is no blessing left for me, neither will I ask it," cried Margaret, with a fresh burst of tears. "Would it were His will that I might never taste food more."

Yet she trembled at these rebellious expressions, almost as soon as they 5
were uttered, and, by degrees, Mary succeeded in bringing her sister's mind nearer to the situation of her own. Time went on, and their usual hour of repose arrived. The brothers and their brides, entering the married state with no more than the slender means which then sanctioned such a step, had confederated themselves in one household, with equal rights to the parlor, and claiming exclusive privileges in two sleeping rooms contiguous to it. Thither the widowed ones retired after heaping ashes upon the dying embers of their fire, and placing a lighted lamp upon the hearth. The doors of both chambers were left open, so that a part of the interior of each, and the beds with their unclosed curtains, were reciprocally visible. Sleep did not steal upon the sisters at one and the same time. Mary experienced the effect often consequent upon grief quietly borne, and soon sunk into temporary forgetfulness, while Margaret became more disturbed and feverish, in proportion as the night advanced with its deepest and stillest hours. She lay listening to the drops of rain, that came down in monotonous succession, unswayed by a breath of wind; and a nervous impulse continually caused her to lift her head from the pillow, and gaze into

Mary's chamber and the intermediate apartment. The cold light of the lamp threw the shadows of the furniture up against the wall, stamping them immovably there, except when they were shaken by a sudden flicker of the flame. Two vacant arm-chairs were in their old positions on opposite sides of the hearth, where the brothers had been wont to sit in young and laughing dignity, as heads of families; two humbler seats were near them, the true thrones of that little empire, where Mary and herself had exercised in love, a power that love had won. The cheerful radiance of the fire had shone upon the happy circle, and the dead glimmer of the lamp might have befitted their reunion now. While Margaret groaned in bitterness, she heard a knock at the street-door.

"How would my heart have leapt at that sound but yesterday!" thought she, remembering the anxiety with which she had long awaited tidings from her husband. "I care not for it now; let them begone, for I will not arise."

But even while a sort of childish fretfulness made her thus resolve, she was breathing hurriedly, and straining her ears to catch a repetition of the summons. It is difficult to be convinced of the death of one whom we have deemed another self. The knocking was now renewed in slow and regular strokes, apparently given with the soft end of a doubled fist, and was accompanied by words, faintly heard through several thicknesses of wall. Margaret looked to her sister's chamber, and beheld her still lying in the depths of sleep. She arose, placed her foot upon the floor, and slightly arrayed herself, trembling between fear and eagerness as she did so.

"Heaven help me!" sighed she. "I have nothing left to fear, and methinks I am ten times more a coward than ever."

Seizing the lamp from the hearth, she hastened to the window that overlooked the street-door. It was a lattice, turning upon hinges; and having thrown it back, she stretched her head a little way into the moist atmosphere. A lantern was reddening the front of the house, and melting its light in the neighboring puddles, while a deluge of darkness overwhelmed every other object. As the window grated on its hinges, a man in a broad brimmed hat and blanket-coat, stepped from under the shelter of the projecting story, and looked upward to discover whom his application had aroused. Margaret knew him as a friendly innkeeper of the town.

"What would you have, Goodman Parker?" cried the widow. 10

"Lack-a-day, is it you, Mistress Margaret?" replied the innkeeper. "I was afraid it might be your sister Mary; for I hate to see a young woman in trouble, when I haven't a word of comfort to whisper her."

"For Heaven's sake, what news do you bring?" screamed Margaret.

"Why, there has been an express through the town within this half hour," said Goodman Parker, "traveling from the eastern jurisdiction with letters from the governor and council. He tarried at my house to refresh himself with a drop and a morsel, and I asked him what tidings on the frontiers. He tells me we had the better in the skirmish you wot of, and that thirteen men reported slain are well and sound, and your husband among them. Besides, he is appointed of the escort to bring the captivated Frenchers and Indians home to the province jail. I judged you wouldn't mind being broke of your rest, and so I stept over to tell you. Good night."

So saying, the honest man departed; and his lantern gleamed along the street, bringing to view indistinct shapes of things, and the fragments of a world, like order glimmering through chaos, or memory roaming over the past. But Margaret stayed not to watch these picturesque effects. Joy flashed in her heart, and lighted it up at once, and breathless, and with winged steps, she flew to the bedside of her sister. She paused, however, at the door of the chamber, while a thought of pain broke in upon her.

"Poor Mary!" she said to herself. "Shall I waken her, to feel her sorrow sharpened by my happiness? No; I will keep it within my own bosom till the morrow."

She approached the bed to discover if Mary's sleep were peaceful. Her face was turned partly inward to the pillow, and had been hidden there to weep; but a look of motionless contentment was now visible upon it, as if her heart, like a deep lake, had grown calm because its dead had sunk down so far within. Happy is it, and strange, that the lighter sorrows are those from which dreams are chiefly fabricated. Margaret shrunk from disturbing her sister-in-law, and felt as if her own better fortune, had rendered her involuntarily unfaithful, and as if altered and diminished affection must be the consequence of the disclosure she had to make. With a sudden step, she turned away. But joy could not long be repressed, even by circumstances that would have excited heavy grief at another moment. Her mind was thronged with delightful thoughts, till sleep stole on and transformed them to visions, more delightful and more wild, like the breath of winter, (but what a cold comparison!) working fantastic tracery upon a window.

When the night was far advanced, Mary awoke with a sudden start. A vivid dream had latterly involved her in its unreal life, of which, however, she could only remember that it had been broken in upon at the most interesting point. For a little time, slumber hung about her like a morning mist, hindering her from perceiving the distinct outline of her situation. She listened with imperfect consciousness to two or three volleys of a rapid and eager knocking; and first she deemed the noise a matter of course, like the breath she drew; next, it appeared a thing in which she had no concern; and lastly, she became aware that it was a summons necessary to be obeyed. At the same moment, the pang of recollection darted into her mind; the pall of sleep was thrown back from the face of grief: the dim light of the chamber, and the objects therein revealed, had retained all her suspended ideas, and restored them as soon as she unclosed her eyes. Again, there was a quick peal upon the street-door. Fearing that her sister would also be disturbed, Mary wrapped herself in a cloak and hood, took the lamp from the hearth, and hastened to the window. By some accident, it had been left unhasped, and yielded easily to her hand.

"Who's there?" asked Mary, trembling as she looked forth.

The storm was over, and the moon was up; it shone upon broken clouds above, and below upon houses black with moisture, and upon little lakes of the fallen rain, curling into silver beneath the quick enchantment of a breeze. A young man in a sailor's dress, wet as if he had come out of the depths of the sea, stood alone under the window. Mary recognized him as one whose livelihood was gained by short voyages along the coast; nor did she forget, that, previous to her marriage, he had been an unsuccessful wooer of her own.

"What do you seek here, Stephen?" said she.

"Cheer up, Mary, for I seek to comfort you," answered the rejected lover. "You must know I got home not ten minutes ago, and the first thing my good mother told me was the news about your husband. So, without saying a word to the old woman, I clapt on my hat, and ran out of the house. I couldn't have slept a wink before speaking to you, Mary, for the sake of old times."

"Stephen, I thought better of you!" exclaimed the widow, with gushing tears, and preparing to close the lattice; for she was no whit inclined to imitate the first wife of Zadig.°

"But stop, and hear my story out," cried the young sailor. "I tell you we spoke a brig yesterday afternoon, bound in from Old England. And who do you think I saw standing on deck, well and hearty, only a bit thinner than he was five months ago?"

Mary leaned from the window, but could not speak.

"Why, it was your husband himself," continued the generous seaman. "He and three others saved themselves on a spar, when the *Blessing* turned bottom upwards. The brig will beat into the bay by daylight, with this wind, and you'll see him here tomorrow. There's the comfort I bring you, Mary, and so good night."

He hurried away, while Mary watched him with a doubt of waking reality, that seemed stronger or weaker as he alternately entered the shade of the houses, or emerged into the broad streaks of moonlight. Gradually, however, a blessed flood of conviction swelled into her heart, in strength enough to overwhelm her, had its increase been more abrupt. Her first impulse was to rouse her sister-in-law, and communicate the new-born gladness. She opened the chamber-door, which had been closed in the course of the night, though not latched, advanced to the bedside, and was about to lay her hand upon the slumberer's shoulder. But then she remembered that Margaret would awake to thoughts of death and woe, rendered not the less bitter by their contrast with her own felicity. She suffered the rays of the lamp to fall upon the unconscious form of the bereaved one. Margaret lay in unquiet sleep, and the drapery was displaced around her; her young cheek was rosy-tinted, and her lips half opened in a vivid smile; an expression of joy, debarred its passage by her sealed eyelids, struggled forth like incense from the whole countenance.

"My poor sister! you will waken too soon from that happy dream," thought Mary.

Before retiring, she set down the lamp and endeavored to arrange the bedclothes, so that the chill air might not do harm to the feverish slumberer. But her hand trembled against Margaret's neck, a tear also fell upon her cheek, and she suddenly awoke.

Zadig: The hero and title of a novel by the French writer Voltaire (François-Marie Arouet; 1694–1778).

Considerations

1. Describe the tone of the first paragraph. How does the tone set up expectations about what is to come in the story?
2. Why do the young women prefer to be together instead of with other mourners? What is the significance of the setting?
3. How are Mary and Margaret different from each other in temperament? How does each react to the death of her husband?

4. Why does Margaret feel that news of her husband being alive will change her relationship with Mary?
5. How does Hawthorne balance the incidents affecting Mary and Margaret throughout the story? Does the story remain balanced?
6. Who awakens at the end? Identify the "she" in the final sentence, and explain the reasons for your identification.
7. Consider the story's title. How are we to understand its meaning?
8. What is the nature of the relationship between the husbands and wives in this story?
9. What do you think is the story's theme?
10. Given that the story focuses on dreams, does it have any psychological interest? How might this story be read from a psychoanalytic perspective (see Ch. 32 for a brief discussion of the reading strategies associated with this critical approach).

Connections

1. Contrast Hawthorne's treatment of husband-wife relationships in this story with Colette's in "The Hand" (p. 176).
2. Compare the plot of this story with that of Chopin's "The Story of an Hour" (p. 12). What are the significant similarities and differences between the two? Which story seems more complex to you? Explain why.
3. Why do the style and theme of Chopin's story seem more modern than those of Hawthorne's? Go beyond the dates of composition and explain the differences in an essay.

Young Goodman Brown 1835

Young Goodman Brown came forth at sunset into the street at Salem village; but put his head back, after crossing the threshold, to exchange a parting kiss with his young wife. And Faith, as the wife was aptly named, thrust her own pretty head into the street, letting the wind play with the pink ribbons of her cap while she called to Goodman Brown.

"Dearest heart," whispered she, softly and rather sadly, when her lips were close to his ear, "prithee put off your journey until sunrise and sleep in your own bed tonight. A lone woman is troubled with such dreams and such thoughts that she's afeared of herself sometimes. Pray tarry with me this night, dear husband, of all nights in the year."

"My love and my Faith," replied young Goodman Brown, "of all nights in the year, this one night must I tarry away from thee. My journey, as thou callest it, forth and back again, must needs be done 'twixt now and sunrise. What, my sweet, pretty wife, dost thou doubt me already, and we but three months married?"

"Then God bless you!" said Faith, with the pink ribbons; "and may you find all well when you come back."

"Amen!" cried Goodman Brown. "Say thy prayers, dear Faith, and go to 5
bed at dusk, and no harm will come to thee."

So they parted; and the young man pursued his way until, being about to turn the corner by the meeting-house, he looked back and saw the head of Faith still peeping after him with a melancholy air, in spite of her pink ribbons.

"Poor little Faith!" thought he, for his heart smote him. "What a wretch am I to leave her on such an errand! She talks of dreams, too. Methought as she spoke there was trouble in her face, as if a dream had warned her what work is to be done tonight. But no, no; 't would kill her to think it. Well, she's a blessed angel on earth; and after this one night I'll cling to her skirts and follow her to heaven."

With this excellent resolve for the future, Goodman Brown felt himself justified in making more haste on his present evil purpose. He had taken a dreary road, darkened by all the gloomiest trees of the forest, which barely stood aside to let the narrow path creep through, and closed immediately behind. It was all as lonely as could be; and there is this peculiarity in such a solitude, that the traveler knows not who may be concealed by the innumerable trunks and the thick boughs overhead; so that with lonely footsteps he may yet be passing through an unseen multitude.

"There may be a devilish Indian behind every tree," said Goodman Brown to himself; and he glanced fearfully behind him as he added, "What if the devil himself should be at my very elbow!"

His head being turned back, he passed a crook of the road, and, looking 10
forward again, beheld the figure of a man, in grave and decent attire, seated at the foot of an old tree. He arose at Goodman Brown's approach and walked onward side by side with him.

"You are late, Goodman Brown," said he. "The clock of the Old South was striking as I came through Boston, and that is full fifteen minutes agone."

"Faith kept me back a while," replied the young man, with a tremor in his voice, caused by the sudden appearance of his companion, though not wholly unexpected.

It was now deep dusk in the forest, and deepest in that part of it where these two were journeying. As nearly as could be discerned, the second traveler was about fifty years old, apparently in the same rank of life as Goodman Brown, and bearing a considerable resemblance to him, though perhaps more in expression than features. Still they might have been taken for father and son. And yet, though the elder person was as simply clad as the younger, and as simple in manner too, he had an indescribable air of one who knew the world, and who would not have felt abashed at the governor's dinner table or in King William's court, were it possible that his affairs should call him thither. But the only thing about him that could be fixed upon as remarkable was his staff, which bore the likeness of a great black snake, so curiously wrought that it might almost be seen to twist and wriggle itself like a living serpent. This, of course, must have been an ocular deception, assisted by the uncertain light.

"Come, Goodman Brown," cried his fellow-traveler, "this is a dull pace for the beginning of a journey. Take my staff, if you are so soon weary."

"Friend," said the other, exchanging his slow pace for a full stop, "having 15
kept covenant by meeting thee here, it is my purpose now to return whence I came. I have scruples touching the matter thou wot'st of."

"Sayest thou so?" replied he of the serpent, smiling apart. "Let us walk on, nevertheless, reasoning as we go; and if I convince thee not thou shalt turn back. We are but a little way in the forest yet."

"Too far! too far!" exclaimed the goodman, unconsciously resuming his walk. "My father never went into the woods on such an errand, nor his father before him. We have been a race of honest men and good Christians since the days of the martyrs; and shall I be the first of the name of Brown that ever took this path and kept" —

"Such company, thou wouldst say," observed the elder person, interpreting his pause. "Well said, Goodman Brown! I have been as well acquainted with your family as with ever a one among the Puritans; and that's no trifle to say. I helped your grandfather, the constable, when he lashed the Quaker woman so smartly through the streets of Salem; and it was I that brought your father a pitch-pine knot, kindled at my own hearth, to set fire to an Indian village, in King Philip's war. They were my good friends, both; and many a pleasant walk have we had along this path, and returned merrily after midnight. I would fain be friends with you for their sake."

"If it be as thou sayest," replied Goodman Brown, "I marvel they never spoke of these matters; or, verily, I marvel not, seeing that the least rumor of the sort would have driven them from New England. We are a people of prayer, and good works to boot, and abide no such wickedness."

"Wickedness or not," said the traveler with the twisted staff, "I have a very general acquaintance here in New England. The deacons of many a church have drunk the communion wine with me; the selectmen of divers towns make me their chairman; and a majority of the Great and General Court are firm supporters of my interest. The governor and I, too — But these are state secrets."

"Can this be so?" cried Goodman Brown, with a stare of amazement at his undisturbed companion. "Howbeit, I have nothing to do with the governor and council; they have their own ways, and are no rule for a simple husbandman like me. But, were I to go on with thee, how should I meet the eye of that good old man, our minister, at Salem village? Oh, his voice would make me tremble both Sabbath day and lecture day."

Thus far the elder traveler had listened with due gravity; but now burst into a fit of irrepressible mirth, shaking himself so violently that his snakelike staff actually seemed to wriggle in sympathy.

"Ha! ha! ha!" shouted he again and again; then composing himself, "Well, go on, Goodman Brown, go on; but, prithee, don't kill me with laughing."

"Well, then, to end the matter at once," said Goodman Brown, considerably nettled, "there is my wife, Faith. It would break her dear little heart; and I'd rather break my own."

"Nay, if that be the case," answered the other, "e'en go thy ways, Goodman Brown. I would not for twenty old women like the one hobbling before us that Faith should come to any harm."

As he spoke he pointed his staff at a female figure on the path, in whom Goodman Brown recognized a very pious and exemplary dame, who had taught him his catechism in youth, and was still his moral and spiritual adviser, jointly with the minister and Deacon Gookin.

"A marvel, truly that Goody Cloyse should be so far in the wilderness at nightfall," said he. "But with your leave, friend, I shall take a cut through the woods until we have left this Christian woman behind. Being a stranger to you, she might ask whom I was consorting with and whither I was going."

"Be it so," said his fellow-traveler. "Betake you to the woods, and let me keep the path."

Accordingly the young man turned aside, but took care to watch his companion, who advanced softly along the road until he had come within a staff's length of the old dame. She, meanwhile, was making the best of her way, with singular speed for so aged a woman, and mumbling some indistinct words — a prayer, doubtless — as she went. The traveler put forth his staff and touched her withered neck with what seemed the serpent's tail.

"The devil!" screamed the pious old lady.

"Then Goody Cloyse knows her old friend?" observed the traveler, confronting her and leaning on his writhing stick.

"Ah, forsooth, and is it your worship indeed?" cried the good dame. "Yea, truly is it, and in the very image of my old gossip, Goodman Brown, the grandfather of the silly fellow that now is. But — would your worship believe it? — my broomstick hath strangely disappeared, stolen, as I suspect, by that unhanged witch, Goody Cory, and that, too, when I was all anointed with the juice of smallage, and cinquefoil, and wolfsbane" —

"Mingled with fine wheat and the fat of a newborn babe," said the shape of old Goodman Brown.

"Ah, your worship knows the recipe," cried the old lady, cackling aloud. "So, as I was saying, being all ready for the meeting, and no horse to ride on, I made up my mind to foot it; for they tell me there is a nice young man to be taken into communion tonight. But now your good worship will lend me your arm, and we shall be there in a twinkling."

"That can hardly be," answered her friend. "I may not spare you my arm, Goody Cloyse; but here is my staff, if you will."

So saying, he threw it down at her feet, where, perhaps, it assumed life, being one of the rods which its owner had formerly lent to the Egyptian magi. Of this fact, however, Goodman Brown could not take cognizance. He had cast up his eyes in astonishment, and, looking down again, beheld neither Goody Cloyse nor the serpentine staff, but his fellow-traveler alone, who waited for him as calmly as if nothing had happened.

"That old woman taught me my catechism," said the young man; and there was a world of meaning in this simple comment.

They continued to walk onward, while the elder traveler exhorted his companion to make good speed and persevere in the path, discoursing so aptly that his arguments seemed rather to spring up in the bosom of his auditor than to be suggested by himself. As they went, he plucked a branch of maple to serve for a walking stick, and began to strip it of the twigs and little boughs, which were wet with evening dew. The moment his fingers touched them they became strangely withered and dried up as with a week's sunshine. Thus the pair proceeded, at a good free pace, until suddenly, in a gloomy hollow of the road, Goodman Brown sat himself down on the stump of a tree and refused to go any farther.

"Friend," he said, stubbornly, "my mind is made up. Not another step will I budge on this errand. What if a wretched old woman do choose to go to the devil when I thought she was going to heaven: is that any reason why I should quit my dear Faith and go after her?"

"You will think better of this by and by," said his acquaintance, composedly. "Sit here and rest yourself a while; and when you feel like moving again, there is my staff to help you along."

Without more words, he threw his companion the maple stick, and was as speedily out of sight as if he had vanished into the deepening gloom. The young man sat a few moments by the roadside, applauding himself greatly, and thinking with how clear a conscience he should meet the minister in his morning walk, nor shrink from the eye of good old Deacon Gookin. And what calm sleep would be his that very night, which was to have been spent so wickedly, but so purely and sweetly now, in the arms of Faith! Amidst these pleasant and praiseworthy meditations, Goodman Brown heard the tramp of horses along the road, and deemed it advisable to conceal himself within the verge of the forest, conscious of the guilty purpose that had brought him thither, though now so happily turned from it.

On came the hoof trams and the voices of the riders, two grave old voices, conversing soberly as they drew near. These mingled sounds appeared to pass along the road, within a few yards of the young man's hiding-place; but, owing doubtless to the depth of the gloom at that particular spot, neither the travelers nor their steeds were visible. Though their figures brushed the small boughs by the wayside, it could not be seen that they intercepted, even for a moment, the faint gleam from the strip of bright sky athwart which they must have passed. Goodman Brown alternately crouched and stood on tiptoe, pulling aside the branches and thrusting forth his head as far as he durst without discerning so much as a shadow. It vexed him the more, because he could have sworn, were such a thing possible, that he recognized the voices of the minister and Deacon Gookin, jogging along quietly, as they were wont to do, when bound to some ordination or ecclesiastical council. While yet within hearing, one of the riders stopped to pluck a switch.

"Of the two, reverend sir," said the voice like the deacon's, "I had rather miss an ordination dinner than tonight's meeting. They tell me that some of our community are to be here from Falmouth and beyond, and others from Connecticut and Rhode Island, besides several of the Indian powwows, who, after their fashion, know almost as much deviltry as the best of us. Moreover, there is a goodly young woman to be taken into communion."

"Mighty well, Deacon Gookin!" replied the solemn old tones of the minister. "Spur up, or we shall be late. Nothing can be done, you know, until I get on the ground."

The hoofs clattered again; and the voices, talking so strangely in the empty air, passed on through the forest, where no church had ever been gathered or solitary Christian prayed. Whither, then, could these holy men be journeying so deep into the heathen wilderness? Young Goodman Brown caught hold of a tree for support, being ready to sink down on the ground, faint and overburdened with the heavy sickness of his heart. He looked up to the sky, doubting whether there really was a heaven above him. Yet there was the blue arch, and the stars brightening in it.

"With heaven above and Faith below, I will yet stand firm against the devil!" cried Goodman Brown.

While he still gazed upward into the deep arch of the firmament and had lifted his hands to pray, a cloud, though no wind was stirring, hurried across the zenith and hid the brightening stars. The blue sky was still visible, except directly overhead, where this black mass of cloud was sweeping swiftly northward. Aloft in the air, as if from the depths of the cloud, came a confused and doubtful sound of voices. Once the listener fancied that he could distinguish the accents of townspeople of his own, men and women, both pious and ungodly, many of whom he had met at the communion table, and had seen others rioting at the tavern. The next moment, so indistinct were the sounds, he doubted whether he had heard aught but the murmur of the old forest, whispering without a wind. Then came a stronger swell of those familiar tones, heard daily in the sunshine at Salem village, but never until now from a cloud of night. There was one voice, of a young woman, uttering lamentations, yet with an uncertain sorrow, and entreating for some favor, which, perhaps, it would grieve her to obtain; and all the unseen multitude, both saints and sinners, seemed to encourage her onward.

"Faith!" shouted Goodman Brown, in a voice of agony and desperation; and the echoes of the forest mocked him, crying, "Faith! Faith!" as if bewildered wretches were seeking her all through the wilderness.

The cry of grief, rage, and terror was yet piercing the night, when the unhappy husband held his breath for a response. There was a scream, drowned immediately in a louder murmur of voices, fading into far-off laughter, as the dark cloud swept away, leaving the clear and silent sky above Goodman Brown. But something fluttered lightly down through the air and caught on the branch of a tree. The young man seized it, and beheld a pink ribbon.

"My Faith is gone!" cried he after one stupefied moment. "There is no 50
good on earth; and sin is but a name. Come, devil; for to thee is this world given."

And, maddened with despair, so that he laughed loud and long, did Goodman Brown grasp his staff and set forth again, at such a rate that he seemed to fly along the forest path rather than to walk or run. The road grew wilder and drearier and more faintly traced, and vanished at length, leaving him in the heart of the dark wilderness, still rushing onward with the instinct that guides mortal man to evil. The whole forest was peopled with frightful sounds — the creaking of the trees, the howling of wild beasts, and the yell of Indians; while sometimes the wind tolled like a distant church bell, and sometimes gave a broad roar around the traveler, as if all Nature were laughing him to scorn. But he was himself the chief horror of the scene, and shrank not from its other horrors.

"Ha! ha! ha!" roared Goodman Brown when the wind laughed at him. "Let us hear which will laugh loudest. Think not to frighten me with your deviltry. Come witch, come wizard, come Indian powwow, come devil himself, and here comes Goodman Brown. You may as well fear him as he fear you."

In truth, all through the haunted forest there could be nothing more frightful than the figure of Goodman Brown. On he flew among the black pines, brandishing his staff with frenzied gestures, now giving vent to an inspiration of horrid blasphemy, and now shouting forth such laughter as set all the echoes of the forest laughing like demons around him. The fiend in his own shape is less hideous than when he rages in the breast of man. Thus sped the demoniac on his course, until, quivering among the trees, he saw a red light before him, as when the felled trunks and branches of a clearing have been set on fire, and throw up their lurid blaze against the sky, at the hour of midnight. He paused, in a lull of the tempest that had driven him onward, and heard the swell of what seemed a hymn, rolling solemnly from a distance with the weight of many voices. He knew the tune; it was a familiar one in the choir of the village meeting-house. The verse died heavily away, and was lengthened by a chorus, not of human voices, but of all the sounds of the benighted wilderness pealing in awful harmony together. Goodman Brown cried out, and his cry was lost to his own ear by its unison with the cry of the desert.

In the interval of silence he stole forward until the light glared full upon his eyes. At one extremity of an open space, hemmed in by the dark wall of the forest, arose a rock, bearing some rude, natural resemblance either to an altar or a pulpit, and surrounded by four blazing pines, their tops aflame, their stems untouched, like candles at an evening meeting. The mass of foliage that had overgrown the summit of the rock was all on fire, blazing high into the night and fitfully illuminating the whole field. Each pendent twig and leafy festoon was in a blaze. As the red light arose and fell, a numerous congregation alternately shone forth, then disappeared in shadow, and again grew, as it were, out of the darkness, peopling the heart of the solitary woods at once.

"A grave and dark-clad company," quoth Goodman Brown.

In truth they were such. Among them, quivering to and fro between gloom and splendor, appeared faces that would be seen next day at the council board of the province, and others which, Sabbath after Sabbath, looked devoutly heavenward, and benignantly over the crowded pews, from the holiest pulpits in the land. Some affirm that the lady of the governor was there. At least there were high dames well known to her, and wives of honored husbands, and widows, a great multitude, and ancient maidens, all of excellent repute, and fair young girls, who trembled lest their mothers should espy them. Either the sudden gleams of light flashing over the obscure field bedazzled Goodman Brown, or he recognized a score of the church members of Salem village famous for their especial sanctity. Good old Deacon Gookin had arrived, and waited at the skirts of that venerable saint, his revered pastor. But, irreverently consorting with these grave, reputable, and pious people, these elders of the church, these chaste dames and dewy virgins, there were men of dissolute lives and women of spotted fame, wretches given over to all mean and filthy vice, and suspected even of horrid crimes. It was strange to see that the good shrank not from the wicked, nor were the sinners abashed by the saints. Scattered also among their pale-faced enemies were the Indian priests, or powwows, who had often scared their native forest with more hideous incantations than any known to English witchcraft.

"But where is Faith?" thought Goodman Brown; and, as hope came into his heart, he trembled.

Another verse of the hymn arose, a slow and mournful strain, such as the pious love, but joined to words which expressed all that our nature can conceive of sin, and darkly hinted at far more. Unfathomable to mere mortals is the lore of fiends. Verse after verse was sung; and still the chorus of the desert swelled between like the deepest tone of a mighty organ; and with the final peal of that dreadful anthem there came a sound, as if the roaring wind, the rushing streams, the howling beasts, and every other voice of the unconcerted wilderness were mingling and according with the voice of guilty man in homage to the prince of all. The four blazing pines threw up a loftier flame, and obscurely discovered shapes and visages of horror on the smoke wreaths above the impious assembly. At the same moment the fire on the rock shot redly forth and formed a glowing arch above its base, where now appeared a figure. With reverence be it spoken, the figure bore no slight similitude, both in garb and manner, to some grave divine of the New England churches.

"Bring forth the converts!" cried a voice that echoed through the field and rolled into the forest.

60 At the word, Goodman Brown stepped forth from the shadow of the trees and approached the congregation, with whom he felt a loathful brotherhood by the sympathy of all that was wicked in his heart. He could have well-nigh sworn that the shape of his own dead father beckoned him to advance, looking downward from a smoke wreath, while a woman, with dim features of despair, threw out her hand to warn him back. Was it his mother? But he had no power to retreat one step, nor to resist, even in thought, when the minister and good old Deacon Gookin seized his arms and led him to the blazing rock. Thither came also the slender form of a veiled female, led between Goody Cloyse, that pious teacher of the catechism, and Martha Carrier, who had received the devil's promise to be queen of hell. A rampant hag was she. And there stood the proselytes beneath the canopy of fire.

"Welcome, my children," said the dark figure, "to the communion of your race. Ye have found thus young your nature and your destiny. My children, look behind you!"

They turned; and flashing forth, as it were, in a sheet of flame, the fiend worshipers were seen; the smile of welcome gleamed darkly on every visage.

"There," resumed the sable form, "are all whom ye have reverenced from youth. Ye deemed them holier than yourselves and shrank from your own sin, contrasting it with their lives of righteousness and prayerful aspirations heavenward. Yet here are they all in my worshiping assembly. This night it shall be granted you to know their secret deeds: how hoary-bearded elders of the church have whispered wanton words to the young maids of their households; how many a woman, eager for widows' weeds, has given her husband a drink at bedtime and let him sleep his last sleep in her bosom; how beardless youths have made haste to inherit their fathers' wealth; and how fair damsels — blush not, sweet ones — have dug little graves in the garden, and bidden me, the sole guest, to an infant's funeral. By the sympathy of your human hearts for sin ye shall scent out all the places — whether in church, bedchamber, street, field, or forest — where crime has been committed, and shall exult to behold the whole earth one stain of guilt, one mighty blood spot. Far more than this. It shall be yours to penetrate, in every bosom, the deep mystery of sin, the fountain of all wicked arts, and which inexhaustibly supplies more evil impulses than human power — than my power at its utmost — can make manifest in deeds. And now, my children, look upon each other."

They did so; and, by the blaze of the hell-kindled torches, the wretched man beheld his Faith, and the wife her husband, trembling before that unhallowed altar.

65 "Lo, there ye stand, my children," said the figure, in a deep and solemn

tone, almost sad with its despairing awfulness, as if his once angelic nature could yet mourn for our miserable race. "Depending upon one another's hearts, ye had still hoped that virtue were not all a dream. Now are ye undeceived. Evil is the nature of mankind. Evil must be your only happiness. Welcome again, my children, to the communion of your race."

"Welcome," repeated the fiend worshipers; in one cry of despair and triumph.

And there they stood, the only pair, as it seemed, who were yet hesitating on the verge of wickedness in this dark world. A basin was hollowed, naturally, in the rock. Did it contain water, reddened by the lurid light? or was it blood? or, perchance, a liquid flame? Herein did the shape of evil dip his hand and prepare to lay the mark of baptism upon their foreheads, that they might be partakers of the mystery of sin, more conscious of the secret guilt of others, both in deed and thought, than they could now be of their own. The husband cast one look at his pale wife, and Faith at him. What polluted wretches would the next glance show them to each other, shuddering alike at what they disclosed and what they saw!

"Faith! Faith!" cried the husband, "look up to heaven, and resist the wicked one."

Whether Faith obeyed he knew not. Hardly had he spoken when he found himself amid calm night and solitude, listening to a roar of the wind which died heavily away through the forest. He staggered against the rock, and felt it chill and damp; while a hanging twig, that had been all on fire, besprinkled his cheek with the coldest dew.

The next morning young Goodman Brown came slowly into the street of Salem village, staring around him like a bewildered man. The good old minister was taking a walk along the graveyard to get an appetite for breakfast and meditate his sermon, and bestowed a blessing, as he passed, on Goodman Brown. He shrank from the venerable saint as if to avoid an anathema. Old Deacon Gookin was at domestic worship, and the holy words of his prayer were heard through the open window. "What God doth the wizard pray to?" quoth Goodman Brown. Goody Cloyse, that excellent old Christian, stood in the early sunshine at her own lattice, catechizing a little girl who had brought her a pint of morning's milk. Goodman Brown snatched away the child as from the grasp of the fiend himself. Turning the corner by the meeting-house, he spied the head of Faith, with the pink ribbons, gazing anxiously forth, and bursting into such joy at sight of him that she skipped along the street and almost kissed her husband before the whole village. But Goodman Brown looked sternly and sadly into her face, and passed on without a greeting.

Had Goodman Brown fallen asleep in the forest and only dreamed a wild dream of a witch-meeting?

Be it so if you will; but, alas! it was a dream of evil omen for young Goodman Brown. A stern, a sad, a darkly meditative, a distrustful, if not a desperate man did he become from the night of that fearful dream. On the Sabbath day, when the congregation were singing a holy psalm, he could not listen because an anthem of sin rushed loudly upon his ear and drowned all the blessed strain. When the minister spoke from the pulpit with power and fervid eloquence, and, with his hand on the open Bible, of the sacred truths of our religion, and of saintlike lives and triumphant deaths, and of future bliss or misery unutterable, then did Goodman Brown turn pale, dreading lest the roof should thunder down upon the gray blasphemer and his hearers. Often, awaking suddenly at midnight, he shrank from the bosom of Faith; and at morning or eventide, when the family knelt down at prayer, he scowled and muttered to himself, and gazed sternly at his wife, and turned away. And when he had lived long, and was borne to his grave a hoary corpse, followed by Faith, an aged woman, and children and grandchildren, a goodly procession, besides neighbors not a few, they carved no hopeful verse upon his tombstone, for his dying hour was gloom.

Considerations

1. What is the significance of Young Goodman Brown's name?
2. What is the symbolic value of the forest in this story? How are the descriptions of the forest contrasted with those of Salem village?
3. Characterize Young Goodman Brown at the beginning of the story. Why does he go into the forest? What does he mean when he says "Faith kept me back a while"?
4. What function do Faith's ribbons have in the story?
5. What foreshadows Young Goodman Brown's meeting with his "fellow-traveler"? Who is he? How do we know that Brown is keeping an appointment with a supernatural being?
6. The narrator describes the fellow-traveler's staff wriggling like a snake, but then says, "This, of course, must have been an ocular deception, assisted by the uncertain light." What is the effect of this and other instances of ambiguity in the story?
7. What does Young Goodman Brown discover in the forest? What does he come to think of his ancestors, the church and state, Goody Cloyse, and even his wife?
8. Is Salem populated by hypocrites who cover hideous crimes with a veneer of piety and respectability? Do Faith and the other characters Brown sees when he returns from the forest appear corrupt to you?
9. Near the end of the story the narrator asks, "Had Goodman Brown fallen asleep in the forest and only dreamed a wild dream of a witch-meeting?" Was it a dream or did the meeting actually happen? How does the answer to this question affect your reading of the story? Write an essay giving an answer to the narrator's question.
10. How is Young Goodman Brown changed by his experience in the forest? Does the narrator endorse Brown's unwillingness to trust anyone?
11. Discuss this story as an inward, psychological journey in which Young Goodman Brown discovers the power of blackness in himself but refuses to acknowledge that dimension of his personality.
12. Consider the story as a criticism of the village's hypocrisy.
13. Explain why it is difficult to summarize "Young Goodman Brown" with a tidy moral.

Connections

1. Compare and contrast Young Goodman Brown's reasons for withdrawal with those of Melville's Bartleby, the scrivener (p. 80). Do you find yourself more sympathetic with one character over the other? Explain.
2. To what extent is Hawthorne's use of dreams crucial in this story and in "The Wives of the Dead"? Explain how Hawthorne uses dreams as a means to complicate our view of his characters.

3. What does Young Goodman Brown's pursuit of sin have in common with Aylmer's quest for perfection in "The Birthmark" (below)? How do these pursuits reveal the characters' personalities and shed light on the theme of each story?

The Birthmark

1843

In the latter part of the last century there lived a man of science, an eminent proficient in every branch of natural philosophy, who not long before our story opens had made experience of a spiritual affinity more attractive than any chemical one. He had left his laboratory to the care of an assistant, cleared his fine countenance from the furnace smoke, washed the stain of acids from his fingers, and persuaded a beautiful woman to become his wife. In those days when the comparatively recent discovery of electricity and other kindred mysteries of Nature seemed to open paths into the region of miracle, it was not unusual for the love of science to rival the love of woman in its depth and absorbing energy. The higher intellect, the imagination, the spirit, and even the heart might all find their congenial ailment in pursuits which, as some of their ardent votaries believed, would ascend from one step of powerful intelligence to another, until the philosopher should lay his hand on the secret of creative force and perhaps make new worlds for himself. We know not whether Aylmer possessed this degree of faith in man's ultimate control over Nature. He had devoted himself, however, too unreservedly to scientific studies ever to be weaned from them by any second passion. His love for his young wife might prove the stronger of the two; but it could only be by intertwining itself with his love of science, and uniting the strength of the latter to his own.

Such a union accordingly took place, and was attended with truly remarkable consequences and a deeply impressive moral. One day, very soon after their marriage, Aylmer sat gazing at his wife with a trouble in his countenance that grew stronger until he spoke.

"Georgiana," said he, "has it never occurred to you that the mark upon your cheek might be removed?"

"No, indeed," said she, smiling; but perceiving the seriousness of his manner, she blushed deeply. "To tell you the truth it has been so often called a charm that I was simple enough to imagine it might be so."

5 "Ah, upon another face perhaps it might," replied her husband; "but never on yours. No, dearest Georgiana, you came so nearly perfect from the hand of Nature that this slightest possible defect, which we hesitate whether to term a defect or a beauty, shocks me, as being the visible mark of earthly imperfection."

"Shocks you, my husband!" cried Georgiana, deeply hurt; at first reddening with momentary anger, but then bursting into tears. "Then why did you take me from my mother's side? You cannot love what shocks you!"

To explain this conversation it must be mentioned that in the center of Georgiana's left cheek there was a singular mark, deeply interwoven, as it were, with the texture and substance of her face. In the usual state of her complexion — a healthy though delicate bloom — the mark wore a tint of deeper crimson, which imperfectly defined its shape amid the surrounding rosiness. When she blushed it gradually became more indistinct, and finally vanished amid the triumphant rush of blood that bathed the whole cheek with its brilliant glow. But if any shifting motion caused her to turn pale, there was the mark again, a crimson stain upon the snow, in what Aylmer sometimes deemed an almost fearful distinctness. Its shape bore not a little similarity to the human hand, though of the smallest pygmy size. Georgiana's lovers were wont to say that some fairy at her birth hour had laid her tiny hand upon the infant's cheek, and left this impress there in token of the magic endowments that were to give her such sway over all hearts. Many a desperate swain would have risked life for the privilege of pressing his lips to the mysterious hand. It must not be concealed, however, that the impression wrought by this fairy sign manual varied exceedingly, according to the difference of temperament in the beholders. Some fastidious persons — but they were exclusively of her own sex — affirmed that the bloody hand, as they chose to call it, quite destroyed the effect of Georgiana's beauty, and rendered her countenance even hideous. But it would be as reasonable to say that one of those small blue stains which sometimes occur in the purest statuary marble would convert the Eve of Powers to a monster. Masculine observers, if the birthmark did not heighten their admiration, contented themselves with wishing it away, that the world might possess one living specimen of ideal loveliness without the semblance of a flaw. After his marriage, — for he thought little or nothing of the matter before, — Aylmer discovered that this was the case with himself.

Had she been less beautiful, — if Envy's self could have found aught else to sneer at, — he might have felt his affection heightened by the prettiness of this mimic hand, now vaguely portrayed, now lost, now stealing forth again and glimmering to and fro with every pulse of emotion that throbbed within her heart; but seeing her otherwise so perfect, he found this one defect grow more and more intolerable with every moment of their united lives. It was the fatal flaw of humanity which Nature, in one shape or another, stamps ineffaceably on all her productions, either to imply that they are temporary and finite, or that their perfection must be wrought by toil and pain. The crimson hand expressed the ineludible gripe in which mortality clutches the highest and purest of earthly mold, degrading them into kindred with the lowest, and even with the very brutes, like whom their visible frames return to dust. In this manner, selecting it as the symbol of his wife's liability to sin, sorrow, decay, and death, Aylmer's somber imagination was not long in rendering the birthmark a frightful object, causing him more trouble and horror than ever Georgiana's beauty, whether of soul or sense, had given him delight.

At all the seasons which should have been their happiest, he invariably and without intending it, nay, in spite of a purpose to the contrary, reverted to this one disastrous topic. Trifling as it at first appeared, it so connected itself with innumerable trains of thought and modes of feeling that it became the central point of all. With the morning twilight Aylmer opened his eyes upon his wife's face and recognized the symbol of imperfection; and when they sat together at the evening hearth his eyes wandered stealthily to her cheek, and beheld, flickering with the blaze of the wood fire, the spectral hand that wrote mortality where he would fain have worshiped. Georgiana soon learned to shudder at his gaze. It needed but a glance with the peculiar expression that his face often wore to change the roses of her cheek into a deathlike paleness, amid which the crimson hand was brought strongly out, like a bas-relief of ruby on the whitest marble.

Late one night when the lights were growing dim, so as hardly to betray the stain on the poor wife's cheek, she herself, for the first time, voluntarily took up the subject.

"Do you remember, my dear Aylmer," said she, with a feeble attempt at a smile, "have you any recollection of a dream last night about this odious hand?"

"None! none whatever!" replied Aylmer, starting; but then he added, in a dry, cold tone, affected for the sake of concealing the real depth of his emotion, "I might well dream of it; for before I fell asleep it had taken a pretty firm hold of my fancy."

"And you did dream of it?" continued Georgiana hastily, for she dreaded lest a gush of tears should interrupt what she had to say. "A terrible dream! I wonder that you can forget it. Is it possible to forget this one expression?—'It is in her heart now; we must have it out!' Reflect, my husband; for by all means I would have you recall that dream."

The mind is in a sad state when Sleep, the all-involving, cannot confine her specters within the dim region of her sway, but suffers them to break forth, affrighting this actual life with secrets that perchance belong to a deeper one. Aylmer now remembered his dream. He had fancied himself with his servant Aminadab, attempting an operation for the removal of the birthmark; but the deeper went the knife, the deeper sank the hand, until at length its tiny grasp appeared to have caught hold of Georgiana's heart; whence, however, her husband was inexorably resolved to cut or wrench it away.

When the dream had shaped itself perfectly in his memory, Aylmer sat in his wife's presence with a guilty feeling. Truth often finds its way to the mind close muffled in robes of sleep, and then speaks with uncompromising directness of matters in regard to which we practice an unconscious self-deception during our waking moments. Until now he had not been aware of the tyrannizing influence acquired by one idea over his mind, and of the lengths which he might find in his heart to go for the sake of giving himself peace.

"Aylmer," resumed Georgiana solemnly, "I know not what may be the cost to both of us to rid me of this fatal birthmark. Perhaps its removal may cause cureless deformity; or it may be the stain goes as deep as life itself. Again: do we know that there is a possibility, on any terms, of unclasping the firm gripe of this little hand which was laid upon me before I came into the world?"

"Dearest Georgiana, I have spent much thought upon the subject," hastily interrupted Aylmer. "I am convinced of the perfect practicability of its removal."

"If there be the remotest possibility of it," continued Georgiana, "let the attempt be made at whatever risk. Danger is nothing to me; for life, while this hateful mark makes me the object of your horror and disgust,—life is a burden which I would fling down with joy. Either remove this dreadful hand, or take my wretched life! You have deep science. All the world bears witness of it. You have achieved great wonders. Cannot you remove this little, little mark, which I cover with the tips of two small fingers? Is this beyond your power, for the sake of your own peace, and to save your poor wife from madness?"

"Noblest, dearest, tenderest wife," cried Aylmer rapturously, "doubt not my power. I have already given this matter the deepest thought—thought which might almost have enlightened me to create a being less perfect than yourself. Georgiana, you have led me deeper than ever into the heart of science. I feel myself fully competent to render this dear cheek as faultless as its fellow; and then, most beloved, what will be my triumph when I shall have corrected what Nature left imperfect in her fairest work! Even Pygmalion, when his sculptured woman assumed life, felt not greater ecstasy than mine will be."

"It is resolved, then," said Georgiana, faintly smiling. "And, Aylmer, spare 20
me not, though you should find the birthmark take refuge in my heart at last."

Her husband tenderly kissed her cheek — her right cheek — not that which bore the impress of the crimson hand.

The next day Aylmer apprised his wife of a plan that he had formed whereby he might have opportunity for the intense thought and constant watchfulness which the proposed operation would require; while Georgiana, likewise, would enjoy the perfect repose essential to its success. They were to seclude themselves in the extensive apartments occupied by Aylmer as a laboratory, and where, during his toilsome youth, he had made discoveries in the elemental powers of Nature that had roused the admiration of all the learned societies in Europe. Seated calmly in this laboratory, the pale philosopher had investigated the secrets of the highest cloud region and of the profoundest mines; he had satisfied himself of the causes that kindled and kept alive the fires of the volcano; and had explained the mystery of fountains, and how it is that they gush forth, some so bright and pure, and others with such rich medicinal virtues, from the dark bosom of the earth. Here, too, at an earlier period, he had studied the wonders of the human frame, and attempted to fathom the very process by which Nature assimilates all her precious influences from earth and air, and from the spiritual world, to create and foster man, her masterpiece. The latter pursuit, however, Aylmer had long laid aside in unwilling recognition of the truth — against which all seekers sooner or later stumble — that our great creative Mother, while she amuses us with apparently working in the broadest sunshine, is yet severely careful to keep her own secrets, and, in spite of her pretended openness, shows us nothing but results. She permits us, indeed, to mar, but seldom to mend, and, like a jealous patentee, on no account to make. Now, however, Aylmer resumed these half-forgotten investigations, — not, of course, with such hopes or wishes as first suggested them, but because they involved much physiological truth and lay in the path of his proposed scheme for the treatment of Georgiana.

As he led her over the threshold of the laboratory, Georgiana was cold and tremulous. Aylmer looked cheerfully into her face, with intent to reassure her, but was so startled with the intense glow of the birthmark upon the whiteness of her cheek that he could not restrain a strong convulsive shudder. His wife fainted.

"Aminadab! Aminadab!" shouted Aylmer, stamping violently on the floor.

Forthwith there issued from an inner apartment a man of low stature, but 25
bulk frame, with shaggy hair hanging about his visage, which was grimed with the vapors of the furnace. This personage had been Aylmer's underworker during his whole scientific career, and was admirably fitted for that office by his great mechanical readiness, and the skill with which, while incapable of comprehending a single principle, he executed all the details of his master's experiments. With his vast strength, his shaggy hair, his smoky aspect, and the indescribable earthiness that encrusted him, he seemed to represent man's physical

nature; while Aylmer's slender figure, and pale, intellectual face, were no less apt a type of the spiritual element.

"Throw open the door of the boudoir, Aminadab," said Aylmer, "and burn a pastille."

"Yes, master," answered Aminadab, looking intently at the lifeless form of Georgiana; and then he muttered to himself, "If she were my wife, I'd never part with that birthmark."

When Georgiana recovered consciousness she found herself breathing an atmosphere of penetrating fragrance, the gentle potency of which had recalled her from her deathlike faintness. The scene around her looked like enchantment. Aylmer had converted those smoky, dingy, somber rooms, where he had spent his brightest years in recondite pursuits, into a series of beautiful apartments not unfit to be the secluded abode of a lovely woman. The walls were hung with gorgeous curtains, which imparted the combination of grandeur and grace that no other species of adornment can achieve; and as they fell from the ceiling to the floor, their rich and ponderous folds, concealing all angles and straight lines, appeared to shut in the scene from infinite space. For aught Georgiana knew, it might be a pavilion among the clouds. And Aylmer, excluding the sunshine, which would have interfered with his chemical processes, had supplied its place with perfumed lamps, emitting flames of various hue, but all uniting in a soft, empurpled radiance. He now knelt by his wife's side, watching her earnestly, but without alarm; for he was confident in his science, and felt that he could draw a magic circle round her within which no evil might intrude.

"Where am I? Ah, I remember," said Georgiana faintly; and she placed her hand over her cheek to hide the terrible mark from her husband's eyes.

"Fear not, dearest!" exclaimed he. "Do not shrink from me! Believe me, Georgiana, I even rejoice in this single imperfection, since it will be such a rapture to remove it."

"Oh, spare me!" sadly replied his wife. "Pray do not look at it again. I never can forget that convulsive shudder."

In order to soothe Georgiana, and, as it were, to release her mind from the burden of actual things, Aylmer now put in practice some of the light and playful secrets which science had taught him among its profounder lore. Airy figures, absolutely bodiless ideas, and forms of unsubstantial beauty came and danced before her, imprinting their momentary footsteps on beams of light. Though she had some indistinct idea of the method of these optical phenomena, still the illusion was almost perfect enough to warrant the belief that her husband possessed sway over the spiritual world. Then again, when she felt a wish to look forth from her seclusion, immediately, as if her thoughts were answered, the procession of external existence flitted across a screen. The scenery and the figures of actual life were perfectly represented, but with that bewitching, yet indescribable difference which always makes a picture, an image, or a shadow so much more attractive than the original. When wearied of this, Aylmer bade her cast her eyes upon a vessel containing a quantity of earth. She did so, with little interest at first; but was soon startled to perceive the germ of a plant shooting upward from the soil. Then came the slender stalk; the leaves gradually unfolded themselves; and amid them was a perfect and lovely flower.

"It is magical!" cried Georgiana. "I dare not touch it."

"Nay, pluck it," answered Aylmer: "pluck it, and inhale its brief perfume while you may. The flower will wither in a few moments and leave nothing save its brown seed vessels; but thence may be perpetuated a race as ephemeral as itself."

But Georgiana had no sooner touched the flower than the whole plant 35
suffered a blight, its leaves turning coal-black as if by the agency of fire.

"There was too powerful a stimulus," said Aylmer thoughtfully.

To make up for this abortive experiment, he proposed to take her portrait by a scientific process of his own invention. It was to be effected by rays of light striking upon a polished plate of metal. Georgiana assented; but, on looking at the result, was affrighted to find the features of the portrait blurred and indefinable; while the minute figure of a hand appeared where the cheek should have been. Aylmer snatched the metallic plate and threw it into a jar of corrosive acid.

Soon, however, he forgot these mortifying failures. In the intervals of study and chemical experiment he came to her flushed and exhausted, but seemed invigorated by her presence, and spoke in glowing language of the resources of his art. He gave a history of the long dynasty of the alchemists, who spent so many ages in quest of the universal solvent by which the golden principle might be elicited from all things vile and base. Aylmer appeared to believe that, by the plainest scientific logic, it was altogether within the limits of possibility to discover this long-sought medium; "but," he added, "a philosopher who should go deep enough to acquire the power would attain too lofty a wisdom to stoop to the exercise of it." Not less singular were his opinions in regard to the elixir vitae. He more than intimated that it was at his option to concoct a liquid that should prolong life for years, perhaps interminably; but that it would produce a discord in Nature which all the world, and chiefly the quaffer of the immortal nostrum, would find cause to curse.

"Aylmer, are you in earnest?" asked Georgiana, looking at him with amazement and fear. "It is terrible to possess such power, or even to dream of possessing it."

"Oh, do not tremble, my love," said her husband. "I would not wrong 40
either you or myself by working such inharmonious effects upon our lives; but I would have you consider how trifling, in comparison, is the skill requisite to remove this little hand."

At the mention of the birthmark, Georgiana, as usual, shrank as if a red-hot iron had touched her cheek.

Again Aylmer applied himself to his labors. She could hear his voice in the distant furnace-room giving directions to Aminadab, whose harsh, uncouth, misshapen tones were audible in response, more like the grunt or growl of a brute than human speech. After hours of absence, Aylmer reappeared and proposed that she should now examine his cabinet of chemical products and natural treasures of the earth. Among the former he showed her a small vial, in which, he remarked, was contained a gentle yet most powerful fragrance, capable of impregnating all the breezes that blow across a kingdom. They were of inestimable value, the contents of that little vial; and, as he said so, he threw some of the perfume into the air and filled the room with piercing and invigorating delight.

"And what is this?" asked Georgiana, pointing to a small crystal globe containing a gold-colored liquid. "It is so beautiful to the eye that I could imagine it the elixir of life."

"In one sense it is," replied Aylmer; "or rather, the elixir of immortality. It is the most precious poison that ever was concocted in this world. By its aid I could apportion the lifetime of any mortal at whom you might point your finger. The strength of the dose would determine whether he were to linger out years, or drop dead in the midst of a breath. No king on his guarded throne could keep his life if I, in my private station, should deem that the welfare of millions justified me in depriving him of it."

"Why do you keep such a terrific drug?" inquired Georgiana in horror. 45

"Do not mistrust me, dearest," said her husband, smiling; "its virtuous potency is yet greater than its harmful one. But see! here is a powerful cosmetic. With a few drops of this in a vase of water, freckles may be washed away as easily as the hands are cleansed. A stronger infusion would take the blood out of the cheek, and leave the rosiest beauty a pale ghost."

"Is it with this lotion that you intend to bathe my cheek?" asked Georgiana, anxiously.

"Oh, no," hastily replied her husband; "this is merely superficial. Your case demands a remedy that shall go deeper."

In his interviews with Georgiana, Aylmer generally made minute inquiries as to her sensations and whether the confinement of the rooms and the temperature of the atmosphere agreed with her. These questions had such a particular drift that Georgiana began to conjecture that she was already subjected to certain physical influences, either breathed in with the fragrant air or taken with her food. She fancied likewise, but it might be altogether fancy, that there was a stirring up of her system — a strange, indefinite sensation creeping through her veins, and tingling, half painfully, half pleasurably, at her heart. Still, whenever she dared to look into the mirror, there she beheld herself pale as a white rose and with the crimson birthmark stamped upon her cheek. Not even Aylmer now hated it so much as she.

To dispel the tedium of the hours which her husband found it necessary 50
to devote to the processes of combination and analysis, Georgiana turned over the volumes of his scientific library. In many dark old tomes she met with chapters full of romance and poetry. They were the works of the philosophers of the middle ages, such as Albertus Magnus, Cornelius Agrippa, Paracelsus, and the famous friar who created the prophetic Brazen Head. All these antique naturalists stood in advance of their centuries, yet were imbued with some of their credulity, and therefore were believed, and perhaps imagined themselves to have acquired from the investigation of Nature a power above Nature, and from physics a sway over the spiritual world. Hardly less curious and imaginative were the early volumes of the Transactions of the Royal Society, in which the members, knowing little of the limits of natural possibility, were continually recording wonders or proposing methods whereby wonders might be wrought.

But to Georgiana the most engrossing volume was a large folio from her husband's own hand, in which he had recorded every experiment of his scientific career, its original aim, the methods adopted for its development, and its final success or failure, with the circumstances to which either event was attributable. The book, in truth, was both the history and emblem of his ardent, ambitious, imaginative, yet practical and laborious life. He handled physical details as if there were nothing beyond them; yet spiritualized them all, and redeemed himself from materialism by his strong and eager aspiration towards the infinite. In his grasp the veriest clod of earth assumed a soul. Georgiana, as she read, reverenced Aylmer and loved him more profoundly than ever, but with a less entire dependence on his judgment than heretofore. Much as he had accomplished, she could not but observe that his most splendid successes were almost invariably failures, if compared with the ideal at which he aimed. His brightest diamonds were the merest pebbles, and felt to be so by himself, in comparison with the inestimable gems which lay hidden beyond his reach. The volume, rich with achievements that had won renown for its author, was yet as melancholy a record as ever mortal hand had penned. It was the sad confession and continual exemplification of the shortcomings of the composite man, the spirit burdened with clay and working in matter, and of the despair that assails the higher nature at finding itself so miserably thwarted by the earthly part. Perhaps every man of genius in whatever sphere might recognize the image of his own experience in Aylmer's journal.

So deeply did these reflections affect Georgiana that she laid her face upon the open volume and burst into tears. In this situation she was found by her husband.

"It is dangerous to read in a sorcerer's books," said he with a smile, though his countenance was uneasy and displeased. "Georgiana, there are pages in that volume which I can scarcely glance over and keep my senses. Take heed lest it prove as detrimental to you."

"It has made me worship you more than ever," said she.

"Ah, wait for this one success," rejoined he, "then worship me if you will. 55
I shall deem myself hardly unworthy of it. But come, I have sought you for the luxury of your voice. Sing to me, dearest."

So she poured out the liquid music of her voice to quench the thirst of his spirit. He then took his leave with a boyish exuberance of gaiety, assuring her that her seclusion would endure but a little longer, and that the result was already certain. Scarcely had he departed when Georgiana felt irresistibly impelled to follow him. She had forgotten to inform Aylmer of a symptom which for two or three hours past had begun to excite her attention. It was a sensation in the fatal birthmark, not painful, but which induced a restlessness throughout her system. Hastening after her husband, she intruded for the first time into the laboratory.

The first thing that struck her eye was the furnace, that hot and feverish worker, with the intense glow of its fire, which by the quantities of soot clustered above it seemed to have been burning for ages. There was a distilling apparatus in full operation. Around the room were retorts, tubes, cylinders, crucibles, and other apparatus of chemical research. An electrical machine stood ready for immediate use. The atmosphere felt oppressively close, and was tainted with gaseous odors which had been tormented forth by the processes of science. The severe and homely simplicity of the apartment, with its naked walls and brick pavement, looked strange, accustomed as Georgiana had become to the fantastic elegance of her boudoir. But what chiefly, indeed almost solely, drew her attention, was the aspect of Aylmer himself.

He was pale as death, anxious and absorbed, and hung over the furnace as if it depended upon his utmost watchfulness whether the liquid which it was distilling should be the draught of immortal happiness or misery. How different from the sanguine and joyous mien that he had assumed for Georgiana's encouragement!

"Carefully now, Aminadab; carefully, thou human machine; carefully, thou man of clay!" muttered Aylmer, more to himself than his assistant. "Now, if there be a thought too much or too little, it is all over."

"Ho! ho!" mumbled Aminadab. "Look, master! look!"

Aylmer raised his eyes hastily, and at first reddened, then grew paler than ever, on beholding Georgiana. He rushed towards her and seized her arm with a gripe that left the print of his fingers upon it.

"Why do you come hither? Have you no trust in your husband?" cried he impetuously. "Would you throw the blight of that fatal birthmark over my labors? It is not well done. Go, prying woman, go!"

"Nay, Aylmer," said Georgiana with the firmness of which she possessed no stinted endowment, "it is not you that have a right to complain. You mistrust your wife; you have concealed the anxiety with which you watch the development of this experiment. Think not so unworthily of me, my husband. Tell me all the risk we run, and fear not that I shall shrink; for my share in it is far less than your own."

"No, no, Georgiana!" said Aylmer impatiently; "it must not be."

"I submit," replied she calmly. "And, Aylmer, I shall quaff whatever draught you bring me; but it will be on the same principle that would induce me to take a dose of poison if offered by your hand."

"My noble wife," said Aylmer, deeply moved, "I knew not the height and depth of your nature until now. Nothing shall be concealed. Know, then, that this crimson hand, superficial as it seems, has clutched its grasp into your being with a strength of which I had no previous conception. I have already administered agents powerful enough to do aught except to change your entire physical system. Only one thing remains to be tried. If that fail us we are ruined."

"Why did you hesitate to tell me this?" asked she.

"Because, Georgiana," said Aylmer in a low voice, "there is danger."

"Danger? There is but one danger — that this horrible stigma shall be left upon my cheek!" cried Georgiana. "Remove it, remove it, whatever be the cost, or we shall both go mad!"

"Heaven knows your words are too true," said Aylmer sadly. "And now, dearest, return to your boudoir. In a little while all will be tested."

He conducted her back and took leave of her with a solemn tenderness which spoke far more than his words how much was now at stake. After his departure Georgiana became rapt in musings. She considered the character of Aylmer, and did it completer justice than at any previous moment. Her heart exulted, while it trembled, at his honorable love — so pure and lofty that it would accept nothing less than perfection nor miserably make itself contented with an earthlier nature than he had dreamed of. She felt how much more precious was such a sentiment than that meaner kind which would have borne with the imperfection for her sake, and have been guilty of treason to holy love by degrading its perfect idea to the level of the actual; and with her whole spirit she prayed that, for a single moment, she might satisfy his highest and deepest conception. Longer than one moment she well knew it could not be; for his spirit was ever on the march, ever ascending, and each instant required something that was beyond the scope of the instant before.

The sound of her husband's footsteps aroused her. He bore a crystal goblet containing a liquor colorless as water, but bright enough to be the draught of immortality. Aylmer was pale; but it seemed rather the consequence of a highly wrought state of mind and tension of spirit than of fear or doubt.

"The concoction of the draught has been perfect," said he, in answer to Georgiana's look. "Unless all my science have deceived me, it cannot fail."

"Save on your account, my dearest Aylmer," observed his wife, "I might wish to put off this birthmark of mortality by relinquishing mortality itself in preference to any other mode. Life is but a sad possession to those who have attained precisely the degree of moral advancement at which I stand. Were I weaker and blinder it might be happiness. Were I stronger, it might be endured hopefully. But, being what I find myself, methinks I am of all mortals the most fit to die."

"You are fit for heaven without tasting death!" replied her husband. "But why do we speak of dying? The draught cannot fail. Behold its effect upon this plant."

On the window seat there stood a geranium diseased with yellow blotches, which had overspread all its leaves. Aylmer poured a small quantity of the liquid upon the soil in which it grew. In a little time, when the roots of the plant had taken up the moisture, the unsightly blotches began to be extinguished in a living verdure.

"There needed no proof," said Georgiana quietly. "Give me the goblet. I joyfully stake all upon your word."

"Drink, then, thou lofty creature!" exclaimed Aylmer, with fervid admiration. "There is no taint of imperfection on thy spirit. Thy sensible frame, too, shall soon be all perfect."

She quaffed the liquid and returned the goblet to his hand.

"It is grateful," said she, with a placid smile. "Methinks it is like water from a heavenly fountain; for it contains I know not what of unobtrusive fragrance and deliciousness. It allays a feverish thirst that had parched me for many days. Now, dearest, let me sleep. My earthly senses are closing over my spirit like the leaves around the heart of a rose at sunset."

She spoke the last words with a gentle reluctance, as if it required almost more energy than she could command to pronounce the faint and lingering syllables. Scarcely had they loitered through her lips ere she was lost in slumber. Aylmer sat by her side, watching her aspect with the emotions proper to a man the whole value of whose existence was involved in the process now to be tested. Mingled with this mood, however, was the philosophic investigation characteristic of the man of science. Not the minutest symptom escaped him. A heightened flush of the cheek, a slight irregularity of breath, a quiver of the eyelid, a hardly perceptible tremor through the frame,—such were the details which, as the moments passed, he wrote down in his folio volume. Intense thought had set its stamp upon every previous page of that volume, but the thoughts of years were all concentrated upon the last.

While thus employed, he failed not to gaze often at the fatal hand, and not without a shudder. Yet once, by a strange and unaccountable impulse, he pressed it with his lips. His spirit recoiled, however, in the very act; and Georgiana, out of the midst of her deep sleep, moved uneasily and murmured as if in remonstrance. Again Aylmer resumed his watch. Nor was it without avail. The crimson hand, which at first had been strongly visible upon the marble paleness of Georgiana's cheek, now grew more faintly outlined. She remained not less pale than ever; but the birthmark, with every breath that came and went, lost somewhat of its former distinctness. Its presence had been awful; its departure was more awful still. Watch the stain of the rainbow fading out of the sky, and you will know how that mysterious symbol passed away.

"By Heaven! it is well-nigh gone!" said Aylmer to himself, in almost irrepressible ecstasy. "I can scarcely trace it now. Success! success! And now it is like the faintest rose color. The lightest flush of blood across her cheek would overcome it. But she is so pale!"

He drew aside the window curtain and suffered the light of natural day to fall into the room and rest upon her cheek. At the same time he heard a gross, hoarse chuckle, which he had long known as his servant Aminadab's expression of delight.

"Ah, clod! ah, earthly mass!" cried Aylmer, laughing in a sort of frenzy, "you have served me well! Matter and spirit — earth and heaven — have both done their part in this! Laugh, thing of the senses! You have earned the right to laugh."

These exclamations broke Georgiana's sleep. She slowly unclosed her eyes and gazed into the mirror which her husband had arranged for that purpose. A faint smile flitted over her lips when she recognized how barely perceptible was now that crimson hand which had once blazed forth with such disastrous brilliancy as to scare away all their happiness. But then her eyes sought Aylmer's face with a trouble and anxiety that he could by no means account for.

"My poor Aylmer!" murmured she.

"Poor? Nay, richest, happiest, most favored!" exclaimed he. "My peerless bride, it is successful! You are perfect!"

"My poor Aylmer," she repeated, with a more than human tenderness, "you have aimed loftily; you have done nobly. Do not repent that with so high and pure a feeling, you have rejected the best the earth could offer. Aylmer, dearest Aylmer, I am dying!"

Alas! it was too true! The fatal hand had grappled with the mystery of life, and was the bond by which an angelic spirit kept itself in union with a mortal frame. As the last crimson tint of the birthmark — that sole token of human imperfection — faded from her cheek, the parting breath of the now perfect woman passed into the atmosphere, and her soul, lingering a moment near her husband, took its heavenward flight. Then a hoarse, chuckling laugh was heard again! Thus ever does the gross fatality of earth exult in its invariable triumph over the immortal essence which, in this dim sphere of half development, demands the completeness of a higher state. Yet, had Aylmer reached a profounder wisdom, he need not thus have flung away the happiness which would have woven his mortal life of the selfsame texture with the celestial. The momentary circumstance was too strong for him; he failed to look beyond the shadowy scope of time, and, living once for all in eternity, to find the perfect future in the present.

Considerations

1. Is Aylmer evil? Is he simply a stock version of a mad scientist? In what sense might he be regarded as an idealist?
2. What does the birthmark symbolize? How does Aylmer's view of it differ from the other perspectives provided in the story? What is the significance of its hand-like shape?
3. Does Aylmer love Georgiana? Why does she allow him to risk her life to remove the birthmark?
4. In what sense can Aylmer be characterized as guilty of the sin of pride?
5. How is Aminadab a foil for Aylmer?
6. What is the significance of the descriptions of Aylmer's laboratory?
7. What do Aylmer's other experiments reveal about the nature of his work? How do they constitute foreshadowings of what will happen to Georgiana?
8. What is the theme of the story? What point is made about what it means to be a human being?
9. Despite the risks to Georgiana, Aylmer conducts his experiments in the hope and expectation of achieving a higher good. He devotes his life to science and yet he is an egotist. Explain.
10. Write an essay exploring this story as an early version of our modern obsession with physical perfection.
11. Discuss the extent to which Georgiana is responsible for her own death.

Connections

1. Compare Aylmer's unwillingness to accept things as they are with Young Goodman Brown's refusal to be a part of a community he regards as fallen.
2. Consider the devotion Georgiana expresses toward Aylmer along with Reiko's commitment to her soldier-husband in Yukio Mishima's "Patriotism" (p. 412). How might a feminist critic (see the brief discussion concerning this type of approach in Ch. 32) assess these relationships? Do Georgiana and Reiko have more or less in common as devoted, self-sacrificing wives?
3. What similarities do you see in Aylmer's growing feelings about the "crimson hand" on Georgiana's cheek and the young wife's feelings about her husband's hand in Colette's "The Hand" (p. 176)? How do Aylmer and the young wife cope with these feelings? How do you account for the differences between them?

The Minister's Black Veil 1836

A PARABLE°

The sexton stood in the porch of Milford meeting-house, pulling lustily at the bell-rope. The old people of the village came stooping along the street. Children, with bright faces, tript merrily beside their parents, or mimicked a

Another clergyman in New England, Mr. Joseph Moody, of York, Maine, who died about eighty years since, made himself remarkable by the same eccentricity that is here related of the Reverend Mr. Hooper. In his case, however, the symbol had a different import. In early life he had accidentally killed a beloved friend; and from that day till the hour of his own death, he hid his face from men. [Hawthorne's note.]

graver gait, in the conscious dignity of their Sunday clothes. Spruce bachelors looked sidelong at the pretty maidens, and fancied that the Sabbath sunshine made them prettier than on weekdays. When the throng had mostly streamed into the porch, the sexton began to toll the bell, keeping his eye on the Reverend Mr. Hooper's door. The first glimpse of the clergyman's figure was the signal for the bell to cease its summons.

"But what has good Parson Hooper got upon his face?" cried the sexton in astonishment.

All within hearing immediately turned about, and beheld the semblance of Mr. Hooper, pacing slowly his meditative way towards the meeting-house. With one accord they started, expressing more wonder than if some strange minister were coming to dust the cushions of Mr. Hooper's pulpit.

"Are you sure it is our parson?" inquired Goodman Gray of the sexton.

"Of a certainty it is good Mr. Hooper," replied the sexton. "He was to have 5
exchanged pulpits with Parson Shute of Westbury; but Parson Shute sent to excuse himself yesterday, being to preach a funeral sermon."

The cause of so much amazement may appear sufficiently slight. Mr. Hooper, a gentlemanly person of about thirty, though still a bachelor, was dressed with due clerical neatness, as if a careful wife had starched his band, and brushed the weekly dust from his Sunday's garb. There was but one thing remarkable in his appearance. Swathed about his forehead, and hanging down over his face, so low as to be shaken by his breath, Mr. Hooper had on a black veil. On a nearer view, it seemed to consist of two folds of crape, which entirely concealed his features, except the mouth and chin, but probably did not intercept his sight, farther than to give a darkened aspect to all living and inanimate things. With this gloomy shade before him, good Mr. Hooper walked onward, at a slow and quiet pace, stooping somewhat and looking on the ground, as is customary with abstracted men, yet nodding kindly to those of his parishioners who still waited on the meeting-house steps. But so wonder-struck were they, that his greeting hardly met with a return.

"I can't really feel as if good Mr. Hooper's face was behind that piece of crape," said the sexton.

"I don't like it," muttered an old woman, as she hobbled into the meeting-house. "He has changed himself into something awful, only by hiding his face."

"Our parson has gone mad!" cried Goodman Gray, following him across the threshold.

A rumor of some unaccountable phenomenon had preceded Mr. Hooper 10
into the meeting-house, and set all the congregation astir. Few could refrain from twisting their heads towards the door; many stood upright, and turned directly about; while several little boys clambered upon the seats, and came down again with a terrible racket. There was a general bustle, a rustling of the women's gowns and shuffling of the men's feet, greatly at variance with that hushed repose which should attend the entrance of the minister. But Mr. Hooper appeared not to notice the perturbation of his people. He entered with an almost noiseless step, bent his head mildly to the pews on each side, and bowed as he passed his oldest parishioner, a white-haired great-grandsire, who occupied an arm-chair in the center of the aisle. It was strange to observe, how slowly this venerable man became conscious of something singular in the appearance of his pastor. He seemed not fully to partake of the prevailing wonder,

till Mr. Hooper had ascended the stairs, and showed himself in the pulpit, face to face with his congregation, except for the black veil. That mysterious emblem was never once withdrawn. It shook with his measured breath as he gave out the psalm; it threw its obscurity between him and the holy page, as he read the Scriptures; and while he prayed, the veil lay heavily on his uplifted countenance. Did he seek to hide it from the dread Being whom he was addressing?

Such was the effect of this simple piece of crape, that more than one woman of delicate nerves was forced to leave the meeting-house. Yet perhaps the pale-faced congregation was almost as fearful a sight to the minister, as his black veil to them.

Mr. Hooper had the reputation of a good preacher, but not an energetic one: he strove to win his people heavenward, by mild persuasive influences, rather than to drive them thither, by the thunders of the Word. The sermon which he now delivered, was marked by the same characteristics of style and manner, as the general series of his pulpit oratory. But there was something, either in the sentiment of the discourse itself, or in the imagination of the auditors, which made it greatly the most powerful effort that they had ever heard from their pastor's lips. It was tinged, rather more darkly than usual, with the gentle gloom of Mr. Hooper's temperament. The subject had reference to secret sin, and those sad mysteries which we hide from our nearest and dearest, and would fain conceal from our own consciousness, even forgetting that the Omniscient can detect them. A subtle power was breathed into his words. Each member of the congregation, the most innocent girl, and the man of hardened breast, felt as if the preacher had crept upon them, behind his awful veil, and discovered their hoarded iniquity of deed or thought. Many spread their clasped hands on their bosoms. There was nothing terrible in what Mr. Hooper said; at least, no violence; and yet, with every tremor of his melancholy voice, the hearers quaked. An unsought pathos came hand in hand with awe. So sensible were the audience of some unwonted attribute in their minister, that they longed for a breath of wind to blow aside the veil, almost believing that a stranger's visage would be discovered, though the form, gesture, and voice were those of Mr. Hooper.

At the close of the services, the people hurried out with indecorous confusion, eager to communicate their pent-up amazement, and conscious of lighter spirits, the moment they lost sight of the black veil. Some gathered in little circles, huddled closely together, with their mouths all whispering in the center; some went homeward alone, wrapt in silent meditation; some talked loudly, and profaned the Sabbath-day with ostentatious laughter. A few shook their sagacious heads, intimating that they could penetrate the mystery; while one or two affirmed that there was no mystery at all, but only that Mr. Hooper's eyes were so weakened by the midnight lamp, as to require a shade. After a brief interval, forth came good Mr. Hooper also, in the rear of his flock. Turning his veiled face from one group to another, he paid due reverence to the hoary heads, saluted the middle-aged with kind dignity, as their friend and spiritual guide, greeted the young with mingled authority and love, and laid his hands on the little children's heads to bless them. Such was always his custom on the Sabbath-day. Strange and bewildered looks repaid him for his courtesy. None, as on former occasions, aspired to the honor of walking by their pastor's side. Old Squire Saunders, doubtless by an accidental lapse of memory, neglected to invite Mr. Hooper to his table, where the good clergyman had been wont to bless the food, almost every Sunday since his settlement. He returned, therefore, to the parsonage, and, at the moment of closing the door, was observed to look back upon the people, all of whom had their eyes fixed upon the minister. A sad smile gleamed faintly from beneath the black veil, and flickered about his mouth, glimmering as he disappeared.

"How strange," said a lady, "that a simple black veil, such as any woman might wear on her bonnet, should become such a terrible thing on Mr. Hooper's face!"

"Something must surely be amiss with Mr. Hooper's intellects," observed her husband, the physician of the village. "But the strangest part of the affair is the effect of this vagary, even on a sober-minded man like myself. The black veil, though it covers only our pastor's face, throws its influence over his whole person, and makes him ghost-like from head to foot. Do you not feel it so?"

"Truly do I," replied the lady; "and I would not be alone with him for the world. I wonder he is not afraid to be alone with himself!"

"Men sometimes are so," said her husband.

That afternoon service was attended with similar circumstances. At its conclusion, the bell tolled for the funeral of a young lady. The relatives and friends were assembled in the house, and the more distant acquaintances stood about the door, speaking of the good qualities of the deceased, when their talk was interrupted by the appearance of Mr. Hooper, still covered with his black veil. It was now an appropriate emblem. The clergyman stepped into the room where the corpse was laid, and bent over the coffin, to take a last farewell of his deceased parishioner. As he stooped, the veil hung straight down from his forehead, so that, if her eye-lids had not been closed for ever, the dead maiden might have seen his face. Could Mr. Hooper be fearful of her glance, that he so hastily caught back the black veil? A person, who watched the interview between the dead and living, scrupled not to affirm, that, at the instant when the clergyman's features were disclosed, the corpse had slightly shuddered, rustling the shroud and muslin cap, though the countenance retained the composure of death. A superstitious old woman was the only witness of this prodigy. From the coffin, Mr. Hooper passed into the chamber of the mourners, and thence to the head of the staircase, to make the funeral prayer. It was a tender and heart-dissolving prayer, full of sorrow, yet so imbued with celestial hopes, that the music of a heavenly harp, swept by the fingers of the dead, seemed faintly to be heard among the saddest accents of the minister. The people trembled, though they but darkly understood him, when he prayed that they, and himself, and all of mortal race, might be ready, as he trusted this young maiden had been, for the dreadful hour that should snatch the veil from their faces. The bearers went heavily forth, and the mourners followed, saddening all the street, with the dead before them, and Mr. Hooper in his black veil behind.

"Why do you look back?" said one in the procession to his partner.

"I had a fancy," replied she, "that the minister and the maiden's spirit were walking hand in hand."

"And so had I, at the same moment," said the other.

That night, the handsomest couple in Milford village were to be joined in wedlock. Though reckoned a melancholy man, Mr. Hooper had a placid cheerfulness for such occasions, which often excited a sympathetic smile, where livelier merriment would have been thrown away. There was no quality of his disposition which made him more beloved than this. The company at the wedding awaited his arrival with impatience, trusting that the strange awe, which had gathered over him throughout the day, would now be dispelled. But such was not the result. When Mr. Hooper came, the first thing that their eyes rested on was the same horrible black veil, which had added deeper gloom to the funeral, and could portend nothing but evil to the wedding. Such was its immediate effect on the guests, that a cloud seemed to have rolled duskily from beneath the black crape, and dimmed the light of the candles. The bridal pair stood up before the minister. But the bride's cold fingers quivered in the tremulous hand of the bridegroom, and her death-like paleness caused a whisper, that the maiden who had been buried a few hours before, was come from her grave to be married. If ever another wedding were so dismal, it was that famous one, where they tolled the wedding-knell. After performing the ceremony, Mr. Hooper raised a glass of wine to his lips, wishing happiness to the new-married couple, in a strain of mild pleasantry that ought to have brightened the features of the guests, like a cheerful gleam from the hearth. At that instant, catching a glimpse of his figure in the looking-glass, the black veil involved his own spirit in the horror with which it overwhelmed all others. His frame shuddered—his lips grew white—he spilt the untasted wine upon the carpet—and rushed forth into the darkness. For the Earth, too, had on her Black Veil.

The next day, the whole village of Milford talked of little else than Parson Hooper's black veil. That, and the mystery concealed behind it, supplied a topic for discussion between acquaintances meeting in the street, and good women gossiping at their open windows. It was the first item of news that the tavern-keeper told to his guests. The children babbled of it on their way to school. One imitative little imp covered his face with an old black handkerchief, thereby so affrighting his playmates, that the panic seized himself, and he well nigh lost his wits by his own waggery.

It was remarkable, that, of all the busy-bodies and impertinent people in the parish, not one ventured to put the plain question to Mr. Hooper, wherefore he did this thing. Hitherto, whenever there appeared the slightest call for such interference, he had never lacked advisers, nor shown himself averse to be guided by their judgment. If he erred at all, it was by so painful a degree of self-distrust, that even the mildest censure would lead him to consider an indifferent action as a crime. Yet, though so well acquainted with this amiable weakness, no individual among his parishioners chose to make the black veil a subject of friendly remonstrance. There was a feeling of dread, neither plainly confessed nor carefully concealed, which caused each to shift the responsibility upon another, till at length it was found expedient to send a deputation of the church, in order to deal with Mr. Hooper about the mystery, before it should grow into a scandal. Never did an embassy so ill discharge its duties. The minister received them with friendly courtesy, but became silent, after they were seated, leaving to his visitors the whole burthen of introducing their important business. The topic, it might be supposed, was obvious enough. There was the black veil, swathed round Mr. Hooper's forehead, and concealing every feature above his placid mouth, on which, at times, they could perceive the glimmering of a melancholy smile. But that piece of crape, to their imagination, seemed to hang down before his heart, the symbol of a fearful secret between him and them. Were the veil but cast aside, they might speak freely of it, but not till then. Thus they sat a considerable time, speechless, confused, and shrinking uneasily from Mr. Hooper's eye, which they felt to be fixed upon them with an invisible glance. Finally, the deputies returned abashed to their constituents, pronouncing the matter too weighty to be handled, except by a council of the churches, if, indeed, it might not require a general synod.

But there was one person in the village, unappalled by the awe with which the black veil had impressed all beside herself. When the deputies returned without an explanation, or even venturing to demand one, she, with the calm energy of her character, determined to chase away the strange cloud that appeared to be settling round Mr. Hooper, every moment more darkly than before. As his plighted wife, it should be her privilege to know what the black veil concealed. At the minister's first visit, therefore, she entered upon the subject, with a direct simplicity, which made the task easier both for him and her. After he had seated himself, she fixed her eyes steadfastly upon the veil, but could discern nothing of the dreadful gloom that had so overawed the multitude: it was but a double fold of crape, hanging down from his forehead to his mouth, and slightly stirring with his breath.

"No," said she aloud, and smiling, "there is nothing terrible in this piece of crape, except that it hides a face which I am always glad to look upon. Come, good sir, let the sun shine from behind the cloud. First lay aside your black veil: then tell me why you put it on."

Mr. Hooper's smile glimmered faintly.

"There is an hour to come," said he, "when all of us shall cast aside our veils. Take it not amiss, beloved friend, if I wear this piece of crape till then."

"Your words are a mystery too," returned the young lady. "Take away the veil for them, at least."

"Elizabeth, I will," said he, "so far as my vow may suffer me. Know, then, this veil is a type and a symbol, and I am bound to wear it ever, both in light and darkness, in solitude and before the gaze of multitudes, and as with strangers, so with my familiar friends. No mortal eye will see it withdrawn. This dismal shade must separate me from the world: even you, Elizabeth, can never come behind it!"

"What grievous affliction hath befallen you," she earnestly inquired, "that you should thus darken your eyes for ever?"

"If it be a sign of mourning," replied Mr. Hooper, "I, perhaps, like most other mortals, have sorrows dark enough to be typified by a black veil."

"But what if the world will not believe that it is the type of an innocent sorrow?" urged Elizabeth. "Beloved and respected as you are, there may be whispers, that you hide your face under the consciousness of secret sin. For the sake of your holy office, do away this scandal!"

The color rose into her cheeks, as she intimated the nature of the rumors that were already abroad in the village. But Mr. Hooper's mildness did not forsake him. He even smiled again — that same sad smile, which always appeared like a faint glimmering of light, proceeding from the obscurity beneath the veil.

"If I hide my face for sorrow, there is cause enough," he merely replied; "and if I cover it for secret sin, what mortal might not do the same?"

And with this gentle, but unconquerable obstinacy, did he resist all her entreaties. At length Elizabeth sat silent. For a few moments she appeared lost in thought, considering, probably, what new methods might be tried, to withdraw her lover from so dark a fantasy, which, if it had no other meaning, was perhaps a symptom of mental disease. Though of a firmer character than his own, the tears rolled down her cheeks. But, in an instant, as it were, a new feeling took the place of sorrow: her eyes were fixed insensibly on the black veil, when, like a sudden twilight in the air, its terrors fell around her. She arose, and stood trembling before him.

"And do you feel it then at last?" said he mournfully.

She made no reply, but covered her eyes with her hand, and turned to leave the room. He rushed forward and caught her arm.

"Have patience with me, Elizabeth!" cried he passionately. "Do not desert me, though this veil must be between us here on earth. Be mine, and hereafter there shall be no veil over my face, no darkness between our souls! It is but a mortal veil — it is not for eternity! Oh! you know not how lonely I am, and how frightened to be alone behind my black veil. Do not leave me in this miserable obscurity for ever!"

"Lift the veil but once, and look me in the face," said she.

"Never! It cannot be!" replied Mr. Hooper.

"Then, farewell!" said Elizabeth.

She withdrew her arm from his grasp, and slowly departed, pausing at the door, to give one long, shuddering gaze, that seemed almost to penetrate the mystery of the black veil. But, even amid his grief, Mr. Hooper smiled to think that only a material emblem had separated him from happiness, though the horrors which it shadowed forth, must be drawn darkly between the fondest of lovers.

From that time no attempts were made to remove Mr. Hooper's black veil, or, by a direct appeal, to discover the secret which it was supposed to hide. By persons who claimed a superiority to popular prejudice, it was reckoned merely an eccentric whim, such as often mingles with the sober actions of men otherwise rational, and tinges them all with its own semblance of insanity. But with the multitude, good Mr. Hooper was irreparably a bugbear. He could not walk the streets with any peace of mind, so conscious was he that the gentle and timid would turn aside to avoid him, and that others would make it a point of hardihood to throw themselves in his way. The impertinence of the latter class compelled him to give up his customary walk, at sunset, to the burial ground, for when he leaned pensively over the gate, there would always be faces behind the grave-stones, peeping at his black veil. A fable went the rounds that the stare of the dead people drove him thence. It grieved him, to the very depth of his kind heart, to observe how the children fled from his approach, breaking up their merriest sports, while his melancholy figure was yet afar off. Their instinctive dread caused him to feel, more strongly than aught else, that a preternatural horror was interwoven with the threads of the black crape. In truth, his own antipathy to the veil was known to be so great, that he never willingly passed before a mirror, nor stooped to drink at a still fountain, lest, in its peaceful bosom, he should be affrighted by himself. This was what gave plausibility to the whispers, that Mr. Hooper's conscience tortured him for some great crime, too horrible to be entirely concealed, or otherwise than so obscurely intimated.

Thus, from beneath the black veil, there rolled a cloud into the sunshine, an ambiguity of sin or sorrow, which enveloped the poor minister, so that love or sympathy could never reach him. It was said, that ghost and fiend consorted with him there. With self-shudderings and outward terrors, he walked continually in its shadow, groping darkly within his own soul, or gazing through a medium that saddened the whole world. Even the lawless wind, it was believed, respected his dreadful secret, and never blew aside the veil. But still good Mr. Hooper sadly smiled, at the pale visages of the worldly throng as he passed by.

Among all its bad influences, the black veil had the one desirable effect, of 45
making its wearer a very efficient clergyman. By the aid of his mysterious emblem — for there was no other apparent cause — he became a man of awful power, over souls that were in agony for sin. His converts always regarded him with a dread peculiar to themselves, affirming, though but figuratively, that, before he brought them to celestial light, they had been with him behind the black veil. Its gloom, indeed, enabled him to sympathize with all dark affections. Dying sinners cried aloud for Mr. Hooper, and would not yield their breath till he appeared; though ever, as he stooped to whisper consolation, they shuddered at the veiled face so near their own. Such were the terrors of the black veil, even when Death had bared his visage! Strangers came long distances to attend service at his church, with the mere idle purpose of gazing at his figure, because it was forbidden them to behold his face. But many were made to quake ere they departed! Once, during Governor Belcher's administration, Mr. Hooper was appointed to preach the election sermon. Covered with his black veil, he stood before the chief magistrate, the council, and the representatives, and wrought so deep an impression, that the legislative measures of that year, were characterized by all the gloom and piety of our earliest ancestral sway.

In this manner Mr. Hooper spent a long life, irreproachable in outward act, yet shrouded in dismal suspicions; kind and loving, though unloved, and dimly feared; a man apart from men, shunned in their health and joy, but ever summoned to their aid in mortal anguish. As years wore on, shedding their snows above his sable veil, he acquired a name throughout the New-England churches, and they called him Father Hooper. Nearly all his parishioners, who were of mature age when he was settled, had been borne away by many a funeral: he had one congregation in the church, and a more crowded one in the churchyard; and having wrought so late into the evening, and done his work so well, it was now good Father Hooper's turn to rest.

Several persons were visible by the shaded candlelight, in the death-chamber of the old clergyman. Natural connections he had none. But there was the decorously grave, though unmoved physician, seeking only to mitigate the last pangs of the patient whom he could not save. There were the deacons, and other eminently pious members of his church. There, also, was the Reverend Mr. Clark, of Westbury, a young and zealous divine, who had ridden in haste to pray by the bedside of the expiring minister. There was the nurse, no hired handmaiden of death, but one whose calm affection had endured thus long, in secrecy, in solitude, amid the chill of age, and would not perish, even at the dying hour. Who, but Elizabeth! And there lay the hoary head of good Father Hooper upon the death-pillow, with the black veil still swarthed about his brow and reaching down over his face, so that each more difficult gasp of his faint breath caused it to stir. All through life that piece of crape had hung between him and the world: it had separated him from cheerful brotherhood and woman's love, and kept him in that saddest of all prisons, his own heart; and still it lay upon his face, as if to deepen the gloom of his darksome chamber, and shade him from the sunshine of eternity.

For some time previous, his mind had been confused, wavering doubtfully between the past and the present, and hovering forward, as it were, at intervals, into the indistinctness of the world to come. There had been feverish turns, which tossed him from side to side, and wore away what little strength he had. But in his most convulsive struggles, and in the wildest vagaries of his intellect, when no other thought retained its sober influence, he still showed an awful solicitude lest the black veil should slip aside. Even if his bewildered soul could have forgotten, there was a faithful woman at his pillow, who, with averted eyes, would have covered that aged face, which she had last beheld in the comeliness of manhood. At length the death-stricken old man lay quietly in the torpor of mental and bodily exhaustion, with an imperceptible pulse, and breath that grew fainter and fainter, except when a long, deep, and irregular inspiration seemed to prelude the flight of his spirit.

The minister of Westbury approached the bedside.

50 "Venerable Father Hooper," said he, "the moment of your release is at hand. Are you ready for the lifting of the veil, that shuts in time from eternity?"

Father Hooper at first replied merely by a feeble motion of his head; then, apprehensive, perhaps, that his meaning might be doubtful, he exerted himself to speak.

"Yea," said he, in faint accents, "my soul hath a patient weariness until that veil be lifted."

"And is it fitting," resumed the Reverend Mr. Clark, "that a man so given to prayer, of such a blameless example, holy in deed and thought, so far as mortal judgment may pronounce; is it fitting that a father in the church should leave a shadow on his memory, that may seem to blacken a life so pure? I pray you, my venerable brother, let not this thing be! Suffer us to be gladdened by your triumphant aspect, as you go to your reward. Before the veil of eternity be lifted, let me cast aside this black veil from your face!"

And thus speaking, the Reverend Mr. Clark bent forward to reveal the mystery of so many years. But, exerting a sudden energy, that made all the beholders stand aghast, Father Hooper snatched both his hands from beneath the bedclothes, and pressed them strongly on the black veil, resolute to struggle, if the minister of Westbury would contend with a dying man.

55 "Never!" cried the veiled clergyman. "On earth, never!"

"Dark old man!" exclaimed the affrighted minister, "with what horrible crime upon your soul are you now passing to the judgment?"

Father Hooper's breath heaved; it rattled in his throat; but, with a mighty effort, grasping forward with his hands, he caught hold of life, and held it back till he should speak. He even raised himself in bed; and there he sat, shivering with the arms of death around him, while the black veil hung down, awful, at that last moment, in the gathered terrors of a life-time. And yet the faint, sad smile, so often there, now seemed to glimmer from its obscurity, and linger on Father Hooper's lips.

"Why do you tremble at me alone?" cried he, turning his veiled face round the circle of pale spectators. "Tremble also at each other! Have men avoided me, and women shown no pity, and children screamed and fled, only for my black veil? What, but the mystery which it obscurely typifies, has made this piece of crape so awful? When the friend shows his inmost heart to his friend; the lover to his best-beloved; when man does not vainly shrink from the eye of his Creator, loathsomely treasuring up the secret of his sin; then deem me a monster, for the symbol beneath which I have lived, and die! I look around me, and, lo! on every visage a Black Veil!"

While his auditors shrank from one another, in mutual affright, Father Hooper fell back upon his pillow, a veiled corpse, with a faint smile lingering on the lips. Still veiled, they laid him in his coffin, and a veiled corpse they bore him to the grave. The grass of many years has sprung up and withered on that grave, the burial-stone is moss-grown, and good Mr. Hooper's face is dust; but awful is still the thought, that it moldered beneath the Black Veil!

Considerations

1. Describe the veil Hooper wears. How does it affect his vision?
2. Characterize the townspeople. How does the community react to the veil?
3. What is Hooper's explanation for why he wears the veil? Is he more or less effective as a minister because he wears it?
4. What is the one feature of Hooper's face that we see? What does that feature reveal about him?
5. Describe what happens at the funeral and wedding ceremonies at which Hooper officiates. How are the incidents at these events organized around the veil?
6. Why does Elizabeth think "it should be her privilege to know what the black veil concealed"? Why doesn't Hooper remove it at her request?
7. How does Elizabeth react to Hooper's refusal to take off the veil? Why is her response especially significant?
8. How do others in town explain why Hooper wears the veil? Do these explanations seem adequate to you? Why or why not?
9. Why is Hooper buried with the veil? Of what significance is it that grass "withered" on his grave?
10. Describe the story's point of view. How would a first-person narrative change the story dramatically?
11. Why do you think Hooper wears the veil? Explain whether you think Hooper was right or wrong to wear it.

Connections

1. How might this story be regarded as a sequel to "Young Goodman Brown"? How are the themes similar?
2. Explain how Faith in "Young Goodman Brown," Georgiana in "The Birthmark," and Elizabeth in "The Minister's Black Veil" are used to reveal the central male characters in each story. Describe the similarities that you see among these women characters.
3. Compare Hawthorne's use of symbol in "The Minister's Black Veil" and "The Birthmark." Write an essay explaining which symbol you think works more effectively to evoke the theme of its story.

PERSPECTIVES ON HAWTHORNE

Hawthorne on Solitude 1837

Dear Sir,

Not to burthen you with my correspondence, I have delayed a rejoinder to your very kind and cordial letter, until now. It gratifies me to find that you have occasionally felt an interest in my situation. . . . You would have been nearer the truth if you had pictured me as dwelling in an owl's nest; for mine is about as dismal; and, like the owl I seldom venture abroad till after dark. By some witchcraft or other — for I really cannot assign any reasonable why and wherefore — I have been carried apart from the main current of life, and find it impossible to get back again. Since we last met . . . I have secluded myself from society; and yet I never meant any such thing, nor dreamed what sort of life I was going to lead. I have made a captive of myself and put me into a dungeon, and now I cannot find the key to let myself out — and if the door were open, I should be almost afraid to come out. You tell me that you have met with troubles and changes. I know not what they may have been; but I can assure you that trouble is the next best thing to enjoyment, and that there is no fate in this world so horrible as to have no share in either its joys or sorrows. For the last ten years, I have not lived, but only dreamed about living. It may be true that there have been some unsubstantial pleasures here in the shade, which I should have missed in the sunshine, but you cannot conceive how utterly devoid of satisfaction all my retrospects are. I have laid up no treasure of pleasant remembrances, against old age; but there is some comfort in thinking that my future years can hardly fail to be more varied, and therefore more tolerable, than the past.

You give me more credit than I deserve, in supposing that I have led a studious life. I have, indeed, turned over a good many books, but in so desultory a way that it cannot be called study, nor has it left me the fruits of study. As to my literary efforts, I do not think much of them — neither is it worth while to be ashamed of them. They would have been better, I trust, if written under more favorable circumstances. I have had no external excitement — no consciousness that the public would like what I wrote, nor much hope nor a very passionate desire that they should do so. Nevertheless, having nothing else to be ambitious of, I have felt considerably interested in literature; and if my writings had made any decided impression, I should probably have been stimulated to greater exertions; but there has been no warmth of approbation, so that I have always written with benumbed fingers. I have another great difficulty, in the lack of materials; for I have seen so little of the world, that I have nothing but thin air to concoct my stories of, and it is not easy to give a lifelike semblance to such shadowy stuff. Sometimes, through a peep-hole, I have caught a glimpse of the real world; and the two or three articles, in which I have portrayed such glimpses, please me better than the others. I have now, or shall soon have, one sharp spur to exertion, which I lacked at an earlier period; for I see little prospect but that I must scribble for a living. But this troubles me much less than you would suppose. I can turn my pen to all sorts of drudgery, such as children's books, etc., and by and by, I shall get some editorship that will answer my purpose. Frank Pierce, who was with us at college, offered me his influence to obtain an office in the Exploring Expedition; but I believe that he was mistaken in supposing that a vacancy existed. If such a post were attainable, I should certainly accept it; for, though fixed so long to one spot, I have always had a desire to run around the world.

The copy of my Tales was sent to Mr. Owen's, the bookseller's in Cambridge. I am glad to find that you had read and liked some of the stories. To be sure, you could not well help flattering me a little; but I value your praise too highly not to have faith in its sincerity. When I last heard from the publisher — which was not very recently — the book was doing pretty well. Six or seven hundred copies had been sold. I suppose, however, these awful times have now stopped the sale.

I intend in a week or two to come out of my owl's nest, and not return to it till late in the summer — employing the interval in making a tour somewhere in New England. You, who have the dust of distant countries on your "sandal-shoon," cannot imagine how much enjoyment I shall have in this little excursion. Whenever I get abroad, I feel just as young as I did, ten years ago. What a letter I am inflicting on you! I trust you will answer it.

Yours sincerely,
Nath. Hawthorne.

From a letter to Henry Wadsworth Longfellow, June 4, 1837

Considerations

1. How does Hawthorne regard his solitude? How does he feel it has affected his life and writing?
2. Hawthorne explains to Longfellow, one of his Bowdoin classmates, that "there is no fate in this world so horrible as to have no share in either its joys or sorrows." Explain how this idea is worked into "Young Goodman Brown."
3. Does Hawthorne indicate any positive results for having lived in his "owl's nest"? Consider how "The Minister's Black Veil" and this letter shed light on each other.

EDGAR ALLAN POE (1809–1849)

On a Story's Single Effect 1842

Were we called upon however to designate that class of composition which, next to such a [lyric] poem as we have suggested, should best fulfill the demands of high genius — should offer it the most advantageous field of exertion — we should unhesitatingly speak of the prose tale, as Mr. Hawthorne has here exemplified it. We allude to the short prose narrative, requiring from a half-hour to one or two hours in its perusal. The ordinary novel is objectionable, from its length, for reasons already stated in substance. As it cannot be read at one sitting, it deprives itself, of course, of the immense force derivable from *totality.* Worldly interests intervening during the pauses of perusal, modify, annul, or counteract, in a greater or less degree, the impressions of the book.

But simple cessation in reading would, of itself, be sufficient to destroy the true unity. In the brief tale, however, the author is enabled to carry out the fulness of his intention, be it what it may. During the hour of perusal the soul of the reader is at the writer's control. There are no external or extrinsic influences — resulting from weariness or interruption.

A skilfull literary artist has constructed a tale. If wise, he has not fashioned his thoughts to accommodate his incidents; but having conceived, with deliberate care, a certain unique or single *effect* to be wrought out, he then invents such incidents — he then combines such events as may best aid him in establishing this preconceived effect. If his very initial sentence tend not to the outbringing of this effect, then he has failed in his first step. In the whole composition there should be no word written, of which the tendency, direct or indirect, is not to the one pre-established design. And by such means, with such care and skill, a picture is at length painted which leaves in the mind of him who contemplates it with a kindred art, a sense of the fullest satisfaction. The idea of the tale has been presented unblemished, because undisturbed; and this is an end unattainable by the novel. Undue brevity is just as exceptionable here as in the poem; but undue length is yet more to be avoided.

From a review of Nathaniel Hawthorne's *Twice-Told Tales*

Considerations

1. Why does Poe insist that a story should be read "at one sitting"?
2. Poe's description of how a story is most effectively composed stresses a writer's deliberate choices over inspiration and discovery. Contrast his emphasis on a step-by-step approach for achieving a particular effect with Flannery O'Connor's account of writing "Good Country People" (p. 302). Which account seems more convincing to you? Why?
3. Compare Poe's "The Pit and the Pendulum" (p. 398) with his prescriptions for writing a short story. Does he follow his own advice?

Hawthorne on the Power of the Writer's Imagination 1850

. . . Moonlight, in a familiar room, falling so white upon the carpet, and showing all its figures so distinctly — making every object so minutely visible, yet so unlike a morning or noontide visibility — is a medium the most suitable for a romance-writer° to get acquainted with his illusive guests. There is the little domestic scenery of the well-known apartment; the chairs, with each its separate individuality; the center-table, sustaining a work-basket, a volume or two, and an extinguished lamp; the sofa; the book-case; the picture on the wall —

romance-writer: Hawthorne distinguished romance writing from novel writing. In the preface to *The House of the Seven Gables* he writes: "The latter form of composition is presumed to aim at a very minute fidelity, not merely to the possible, but to the probable and ordinary course of man's experience. The former — while, as a work of art, it must rigidly subject itself to laws, and while it sins unpardonably so far as it may swerve aside from the truth of the human heart — has fairly a right to present that truth under circumstances, to a great extent, of the writer's own choosing or creation."

all these details, so completely seen, are so spiritualized by the unusual light, that they seem to lose their actual substance, and become things of intellect. Nothing is too small or too trifling to undergo this change, and acquire dignity thereby. A child's shoe; the doll, seated in her little wicker carriage; the hobby-horse — whatever, in a word, has been used or played with, during the day, is now invested with a quality of strangeness and remoteness, though still almost as vividly present as by daylight. Thus, therefore, the floor of our familiar room has become a neutral territory, somewhere between the real world and fairy-land, where the Actual and the Imaginary may meet, and each imbue itself with the nature of the other. Ghosts might enter here, without affrighting us. It would be too much in keeping with the scene to excite surprise, were we to look about us and discover a form, beloved, but gone hence, now sitting quietly in a streak of this magic moonshine, with an aspect that would make us doubt whether it had returned from afar, or had never once stirred from our fireside.

The somewhat dim coal-fire has an essential influence in producing the effect which I would describe. It throws its unobtrusive tinge throughout the room, with a faint ruddiness upon the walls and ceiling, and a reflected gleam from the polish of the furniture. This warmer light mingles itself with the cold spirituality of the moonbeams, and communicates, as it were, a heart and sensibilities of human tenderness to the forms which fancy summons up. It converts them from snow-images into men and women. Glancing at the looking-glass, we behold — deep within its haunted verge — the smouldering glow of the half-extinguished anthracite, the white moonbeams on the floor, and a repetition of all the gleam and shadow of the picture, with one remove farther from the actual, and nearer to the imaginative. Then, at such an hour, and with this scene before him, if a man, sitting all alone, cannot dream strange things, and make them look like truth, he need never try to write romances.

From *The Scarlet Letter*

Considerations

1. Explain how Hawthorne uses light as a means of invoking the transforming powers of the imagination.
2. How do Hawthorne's stories fulfill his definition of romance writing? Why can't they be regarded as realistic?
3. Choose one story and discuss it as an attempt to evoke "the truth of the human heart."

HERMAN MELVILLE (1819–1891)

On Nathaniel Hawthorne's Tragic Vision 1851

There is a certain tragic phase of humanity which, in our opinion, was never more powerfully embodied than by Hawthorne. We mean the tragicalness of human thought in its own unbiased, native, and profounder workings. We think that in no recorded mind has the intense feeling of the visable truth ever entered more deeply than into this man's. By visable truth, we mean the apprehension of the absolute condition of present things as they strike the eye of the man who fears them not, though they do their worst to him — the man who, like Russia or the British Empire, declares himself a sovereign nature (in himself) amid the powers of heaven, hell, and earth. He may perish; but so long as he exists he insists upon treating with all Powers upon an equal basis. If any of those other Powers choose to withold certain secrets, let them; that does not impair my sovereignty in myself; that does not make me tributary. And perhaps, after all, there is *no* secret. We incline to think that the Problem of the Universe is like the Freemason's° mighty secret, so terrible to all children. It turns out, at last, to consist in a triangle, a mallet, and an apron — nothing more! . . . There is the grand truth about Nathaniel Hawthorne. He says NO! in thunder; but the Devil himself cannot make him say *yes.* For all men who say *yes,* lie; and all men who say *no* — why, they are in the happy condition of judicious, unincumbered travellers in Europe; they cross the frontiers into Eternity with nothing but a carpet-bag — that is to say, the Ego. Whereas those *yes*-gentry, they travel with heaps of baggage, and, damn them! they will never get through the Custom House. What's the reason, Mr. Hawthorne, that in the last stages of metaphysics a fellow always falls to *swearing* so? I could rip an hour.

From a letter to Hawthorne, April 16(?), 1851

Freemason's: A member of the secret fraternity of Freemasonry.

Considerations

1. What qualities in Hawthorne does Melville admire?
2. Explain how these qualities are embodied in one of the Hawthorne stories.
3. How might Melville's lawyer in "Bartleby, the Scrivener" (p. 80) be characterized as one of "those *yes*-gentry"?

Hawthorne on His Short Stories 1851

[These stories] have the pale tint of flowers that blossomed in too retired a shade — the coolness of a meditative habit, which diffuses itself through the feeling and observation of every sketch. Instead of passion there is sentiment; and, even in what purport to be pictures of actual life, we have allegory, not always warmly dressed in its habilments of flesh and blood as to be taken into the reader's mind without a shiver. Whether from lack of power, or an unconquerable reserve, the Author's touches have often an effect of tameness; the merriest man can hardly contrive to laugh at his broadest humor; the tenderest woman, one would suppose, will hardly shed warm tears at his deepest pathos. The book, if you would see anything in it, requires to be read in the clear brown, twilight atmosphere in which it was written; if opened in the sunshine, it is apt to look exceedingly like a volume of blank pages.

From the preface to the 1851 edition of *Twice-Told Tales*

Considerations

1. How does Hawthorne characterize his stories? Does his assessment accurately describe the stories you've read?
2. Why is a "twilight atmosphere" more conducive to an appreciation of Hawthorne's art than "sunshine"?
3. Write a one-page description of Hawthorne's stories in which you generalize about his characteristic approach to one of these elements: plot, character, setting, symbol, theme, tone.

HYATT H. WAGGONER (b. 1913)
Hawthorne's Style 1962

If the first thing we should notice about Hawthorne is his "modernity," his immediate relevance to us and our concerns, the second thing, if we are to avoid the distortion of seeing in him only our own image, is the way in which he is *not* one of us. It has been said that he was an eighteenth-century gentleman living in the nineteenth century, and the remark has enough truth in it to be useful to us at this point.

His style, for instance, though at its best a wonderfully effective instrument for the expression of sensibility, is likely to strike us as not nearly so modern as Thoreau's.° It was slightly old-fashioned even when he wrote it. It is very deliberate, with measured rhythms, marked by formal decorum. It is a public style and, as we might say, a "rhetorical" one — though of course all styles are rhetorical in one sense or another. It often prefers the abstract or generalized to the concrete or specific word. Compared to what the writers of handbooks, under the influence of modernist literature, have taught us to prefer — the private, informal, concrete, colloquial, imagistic, — Hawthorne's style can only be called premodern.

From *Nathaniel Hawthorne*

Thoreau's: Henry David Thoreau (1817–1862), author of *Walden* and the equally famous essay "Civil Disobedience."

Considerations

1. In what ways can Hawthorne's fiction be seen as having an "immediate relevance to us and our concerns"? How do his themes continue to speak to us?
2. Choose a paragraph from a Hawthorne story that fits Waggoner's description of Hawthorne's characteristic style and contrast its style to a paragraph from Hemingway's "Soldier's Home" (p. 121), or John Updike's "A & P" (p. 407).
3. Take a paragraph from any twentieth-century story included in this anthology and try rewriting it in Hawthorne's style.

FREDERICK C. CREWS (b. 1933)

A Psychological Reading of "Young Goodman Brown" 1966

Hawthorne reminds us in various ways that Brown is facing embodiments of his own thoughts in the characters he meets in the forest. The Devil's inducements are spoken "so aptly that his arguments seemed rather to spring up in the bosom of his auditor than to be suggested by himself." The haunted forest is horrible to Brown, "but he was himself the chief horror of the scene . . . ," and he races toward the witches' sabbath screaming blasphemies and giving vent to demonic laughter. Hawthorne comments: "The fiend in his own shape is less hideous than when he rages in the breast of man." This makes it clear that the presumptive appearance of devils in the story is meant to refer to Brown's subjective thoughts. No wonder that when he arrives at the sabbath and sees the damned congregation, "he felt a loathful brotherhood [with them] by sympathy of all that was wicked in his heart." Under these conditions the appearance of Faith in this company can have no bearing on her actual virtue or lack of it; she is there because Brown's inner *Walpurgisnacht*° has reserved a special role for her.

What does the Devil offer Goodman Brown? There is no ambiguity here. Having assembled likenesses of all the figures of authority and holiness in Salem village and treated them as proselytes of hell, the Devil points them out to Brown and his fellow initiates:

> "There," resumed the sable form, "are all whom ye have reverenced from youth. Ye deemed them holier than yourselves, and shrank from your own sin, contrasting it with their lives of righteousness and prayerful aspirations heavenward. Yet here are they all in my worshipping assembly. This night it shall be granted you to know their secret deeds: how hoary-bearded elders of the church have whispered wanton words to the young maids of their households; how many a woman, eager for widows' weeds, has given her husband a drink at bedtime and let him sleep his last sleep in her bosom; how beardless youths have made haste to inherit their fathers' wealth; and how fair damsels — blush not, sweet ones — have dug little graves in the garden, and bidden me, the sole guest, to an infant's funeral. By the sympathy of your human hearts for sin ye shall scent out all the places — whether in church, bedchamber, street, field, or forest — where crime has been committed, and shall exult to behold the whole earth one stain of guilt, one mighty blood spot. Far more than this. It shall be yours to penetrate, in every bosom, the deep mystery of sin, the fountain of all wicked arts, and which inexhaustibly supplies more evil impulses than human power — than my power at its utmost — can make manifest in deeds."

Knowledge of sin, then, and most often of sexual sin, is the prize for which Goodman Brown seems tempted to barter his soul. In this version of the Faustian pact, the offered power is unrelated to any practical influence in the world; what Brown aspires to, if we can take this bargain as emanating from his own wishes, is an acme of voyeurism, a prurience so effective in its ferreting for scandal that it can uncover wicked thoughts before they have been enacted.

Walpurgisnacht: The night before May Day, on which witches and the devil were believed to gather and celebrate.

Thus Goodman Brown, a curiously preoccupied bridegroom, escapes from his wife's embraces to a vision of general nastiness. The accusation that Brown's Devil makes against all mankind, and then more pointedly against Faith, clearly issues from Brown's own horror of adulthood, his inability to accept the place of sexuality in married love. Brown remains the little boy who has heard rumors about the polluted pleasures of adults, and who wants to learn more about them despite or because of the fact that he finds them disgusting. His forest journey, in fact, amounts to a vicarious and lurid sexual adventure. . . .

Brown's fantasy-experience . . . follows the classic Oedipal pattern: resentment of paternal authority is conjoined with ambiguous sexual temptation. . . . Furthermore, the hero's attitude toward womankind is violently ambivalent. A general slur on women is implied when Brown sees that the forest sinners include virtually all the respectable women he has known, from the Governor's wife and her friends through "wives of honored husbands, and widows, a great multitude, and ancient maidens, all of excellent repute, and fair young girls, who trembled lest their mothers should espy them." The near-universality of this company reminds us of the two critical figures who are missing: Brown's mother and his wife. Yet Faith does arrive, only to disappear at the hideous moment of initiation — as if Brown were not able to stand a final confrontation of his suspicions about her. And he has been led to this moment by reflecting that the woman who taught him his catechism as a boy, Goody Cloyse, is a witch; this is to say that maternal authority is as questionable as paternal authority. Like Ilbrahim, however, Brown finally absolves his mother, but not his father. Just as he is about to join the congregation of sinners, "He could have well-nigh sworn that the shape of his own dead father beckoned him to advance, looking downward from a smoke wreath, while a woman, with dim features of despair, threw out her hand to warn him back. Was it his mother?"

The general pattern of "Young Goodman Brown" is that fathers are degraded to devils and mothers to witches (both attributions, of course, are confirmed in psychoanalysis). Yet the outcome of that pattern, as is always true of Hawthorne's plots, is not simple degradation but a perpetuated ambivalence. Brown lives out a long life with Faith and has children by her, but entertains continual suspicions about her virtue. In retrospect we can say that the source of his uncertainty has been discernible from the beginning — namely, his insistence upon seeing Faith more as an idealized mother than as a wife. She has been his "blessed angel on earth," and he has nurtured a transparently filial desire to "cling to her skirts and follow her to heaven." A bridegroom with such notions is well prepared for an appointment with the Devil.

Nothing can be gained from disputing whether Brown's forest experience was real or dreamed, for in either case it serves his private need to make lurid sexual complaints against mankind. Yet the richness of Hawthorne's irony is such that, when Brown turns to a Gulliver-like° misanthropy and spends the rest of his days shrinking from wife and neighbors, we cannot quite dismiss his attitude as unfounded. Like Gulliver's, his distinctly pathological abhorrence has come from a deeper initiation into human depravity than his normal townsmen will ever know. Who is to say that they are exempt from the fantasies that have

Gulliver-like: A reference to the title character of Jonathan Swift's *Gulliver's Travels* (1726), who travels to four fantasy realms and returns home disillusioned by humanity.

warped him? The only sure point is that by indulging those fantasies Brown *has* become different; at least one case of human foul-heartedness has been amply documented, and for all we know, Salem may be teeming with latent Goodman Browns. In examining his own mind, I imagine, Hawthorne found good reasons for thinking that this might be so.

From *The Sins of the Fathers: Hawthorne's Psychological Themes*

Considerations

1. How does Crews make a case for understanding Brown's experience in the forest as a projection of his own repressed thoughts? Is Crews's argument consistent with the other details of the story?
2. Explain whether you agree with Crews that "nothing can be gained from disputing whether Brown's forest experience was real or dreamed." How does a reader's stand on this issue affect interpretation of the story?
3. Write an essay indicating whether you find Crews's interpretation convincing.
4. Crews does not discuss "The Wives of the Dead" in his book, but, given his approach here, what do you think he would make of that story?

JUDITH FETTERLEY (b. 1938)

A Feminist Reading of "The Birthmark" 1978

It is testimony at once to Hawthorne's ambivalence, his seeking to cover with one hand what he uncovers with the other; and to the pervasive sexism of our culture that most readers would describe "The Birthmark" as a story of failure rather than as the success story it really is — the demonstration of how to murder your wife and get away with it. It is, of course, possible to read "The Birthmark" as a story of misguided idealism, a tale of the unhappy consequences of man's nevertheless worthy passion for perfecting and transcending nature; and this is the reading usually given it. This reading, however, ignores the significance of the form idealism takes in the story. It is not irrelevant that "The Birthmark" is about a man's desire to perfect his wife, nor is it accidental that the consequence of this idealism is the wife's death. In fact, "The Birthmark" provides a brilliant analysis of the sexual politics of idealization and a brilliant exposure of the mechanisms whereby hatred can be disguised as love, neurosis can be disguised as science, murder can be disguised as idealization, and success can be disguised as failure. Thus, Hawthorne's insistence in his story on the metaphor of disguise serves as both warning and clue to a feminist reading. . . .

One cannot imagine this story in reverse — that is, a woman's discovering an obsessive need to perfect her husband and deciding to perform experiments on him — nor can one imagine the story being about a man's conceiving such an obsession for another man. It is woman, and specifically woman as wife, who elicits the obsession with imperfection and the compulsion to achieve perfection, just as it is man, and specifically man as husband, who is thus obsessed and compelled. In addition, it is clear from the summary that the imagined perfection is purely physical. Aylmer is not concerned with the quality of Georgiana's character or with the state of her soul, for he considers her "fit for heaven without tasting death." Rather, he is absorbed in her physical appearance, and perfection for him is equivalent to physical beauty. Georgiana is an exemplum of woman as beautiful object, reduced to and defined by her body. . . . "The Birthmark" demonstrates the fact that the idealization of women has its source in a profound hostility toward women and that it is at once a disguise for this hostility and the fullest expression of it. . . .

. . . Unable to accept himself for what he is, Aylmer constructs a mythology of science and adopts the character of a scientist to disguise his true nature and to hide his real motives, from himself as well as others. As a consequence, he acquires a way of acting out these motives without in fact having to be aware of them. One might describe "The Birthmark" as an exposé of science because it demonstrates the ease with which science can be invoked to conceal highly subjective motives."The Birthmark" is an exposure of the realities that underlie the scientist's posture of objectivity and rationality and the claims of science to operate in an amoral and value-free world. Pale Aylmer, the intellectual scientist, is a mask for the brutish, earthy, soot-smeared Aminadab, just as the mythology of scientific research and objectivity finally masks murder, disguising Georgiana's death as just one more experiment that failed. . . .

The implicit feminism in "The Birthmark" is considerable. On one level the story is a study of sexual politics, of the powerlessness of women and of the psychology which results from that powerlessness. Hawthorne dramatizes the fact that woman's identity is a product of men's responses to her: "It must not be concealed, however, that the impression wrought by this fairy sign manual varied exceedingly, according to the difference of temperament in the beholders." To those who love Georgiana, her birthmark is evidence of her beauty; to those who envy or hate her, it is an object of disgust. It is Aylmer's repugnance for the birthmark that makes Georgiana blanch, thus causing the mark to emerge as a sharply-defined blemish against the whiteness of her cheek. Clearly, the birthmark takes on its character from the eye of the beholder. And just as clearly Georgiana's attitude toward her birthmark varies in response to different observers and definers. Her self-image derives from internalizing the attitudes toward her of the man or men around her. Since what surrounds Georgiana is an obsessional attraction expressed as a total revulsion, the result is not surprising: continual self-consciousness that leads to a pervasive sense of shame and a self-hatred that terminates in an utter readiness to be killed. "The Birthmark" demonstrates the consequences to women of being trapped in the laboratory of man's mind, the object of unrelenting scrutiny, examination, and experimentation.

From *The Resisting Reader: A Feminist Approach to American Fiction*

Considerations

1. In what sense does Fetterley regard "The Birthmark" as a "success story"? How does her feminist perspective inform this view?

2. Why do you think Fetterley argues that it is impossible to imagine reversing the male-female roles in this story?
3. How does Fetterley make a case for reading the story as an "exposé of science"? Explain why science is described as an essentially male activity.
4. Although Fetterley does not include "The Minister's Black Veil" in her discussion, might it not be argued that it too harbors an "implicit feminism"? Write an analysis of the Reverend Mr. Hooper from a feminist perspective.

FLANNERY O'CONNOR

When Flannery O'Connor (1925–1964) died of lupus before her fortieth birthday, her work was cruelly cut short. Nevertheless, she had completed two novels, *Wise Blood* (1952) and *The Violent Bear It Away* (1960), as well as thirty-one short stories. Despite her short life and relatively modest output, her work is regarded as among the most distinguished American fiction of the mid-twentieth century. Her two collections of short stories, *A Good Man Is Hard to Find* (1955) and *Everything That Rises Must Converge* (1965), were included in *The Complete Stories of Flannery O'Connor* (1971), which won the National Book Award.

O'Connor's fiction is related to living a spiritual life in a secular world. Although this major concern is worked into each of her stories, she takes a broad approach to spiritual issues by providing moral, social, and psychological contexts that offer a wealth of insights and passion that her readers have found both startling and absorbing. Her stories are challenging because her characters, who initially seem radically different from people we know, turn out to be, by the end of each story, somehow familiar — somehow connected to us.

O'Connor inhabited simultaneously two radically different worlds. The world she created in her stories is populated with bratty children, malcontents, incompetents, pious frauds, bewildered intellectuals, deformed cynics, rednecks, hucksters, racists, perverts, and murderers who experience dramatically intense moments that surprise and shock readers. Her personal life, however, was largely uneventful. She humorously acknowledged its quiet nature in 1958 when she claimed that "there won't be any biographies of me because, for only one reason, lives spent between the house and the chicken yard do not make exciting copy."

A broad outline of O'Connor's life may not offer very much "exciting copy," but it does provide clues about why she wrote such powerful fiction. The only child of Catholic parents, O'Connor was born in Savannah, Georgia, where she attended a parochial grammar school and high school. When she was thirteen, her father became ill with disseminated lupus, a rare, incurable blood disease, and had to abandon his real estate business. The family moved to Milledgeville in central Georgia, where her mother's family had lived for generations. Because there were no Catholic schools in Milledgeville, O'Connor attended a public high school. In 1942, the year after her father died of lupus, O'Connor graduated from high school and enrolled in Georgia State College for Women. There she wrote for the literary magazine until receiving her diploma in 1945. Her stories earned her a fellowship to the Writers' Workshop at the University of Iowa, and for two years she learned to write steadily and seriously. She sold her first story to *Accent* in 1946 and earned her master of fine arts degree in 1947. She wrote stories about life in the rural South, and this subject matter, along with her devout Catholic perspective, became central to her fiction.

With her formal education behind her, O'Connor was ready to begin her professional career at the age of twenty-two. Equipped with determination ("No one can convince me that I shouldn't rewrite as much as I do") and offered the opportunity to be around other practicing writers, she moved to New York, where she worked on her first novel, *Wise Blood.* In 1950, however, she was diagnosed as having lupus, and, returning to Georgia for treatment, she took up permanent residence on her mother's farm in Milledgeville. There she lived a severely restricted but productive life, writing stories and raising peacocks.

With the exception of O'Connor's early years in Iowa and New York and some short lecture trips to other states, she traveled little. Although she made a pilgrimage to Lourdes (apparently more for her mother's sake than for her own) and then to Rome for an audience with the pope, her life was centered in the South. Like those of William Faulkner and many other southern writers, O'Connor's stories evoke the rhythms of rural southern speech and manners in insulated settings where widely diverse characters mingle. Also like Faulkner, she created works whose meanings go beyond their settings. She did not want her fiction to be seen in the context of narrowly defined regionalism: she complained that "in almost every hamlet you'll find at least one old lady writing epics in Negro dialect and probably two or three old gentlemen who have impossible historical novels on the way." Refusing to be caricatured, she knew that "the woods are full of regional writers, and it is the great horror of every serious Southern writer that he will become one of them." O'Connor's stories are rooted in rural southern culture, but in a larger sense they are set within the psychological and spiritual landscapes of the human soul. This interior setting universalizes local materials in much the same way that Nathaniel Hawthorne's New England stories do. Indeed, O'Connor once described herself as "one of his descendants": "I feel more of a kinship with him than any other American."

O'Connor's deep spiritual convictions coincide with the traditional emphasis on religion in the South, where, she said, there is still the belief "that man has fallen and that he is only perfectible by God's grace, not by his own unaided efforts." Although O'Connor's Catholicism differs from the prevailing Protestant Fundamentalism of the South, the religious ethos so pervasive even in rural southern areas provided fertile ground for the spiritual crises her characters experience. In a posthumous collection of her articles, essays, and reviews aptly titled *Mystery and Manners* (1969), she summarized her basic religious convictions:

> I am no disbeliever in spiritual purpose and no vague believer. I see from the standpoint of Christian orthodoxy. This means that for me the meaning of life is centered in our Redemption by Christ and what I see in the world I see in its relation to that. I don't think that this is a position that can be taken halfway or one that is particularly easy in these times to make transparent in fiction.

O'Connor realized that she was writing against the grain of the readers who discovered her stories in the *Partisan Review, Sewanee Review, Mademoiselle,* or *Harper's Bazaar.* Many readers thought that Christian dogma would make her writing doctrinaire, but she insisted that the perspective of Christianity allowed her to interpret the details of life and guaranteed her "respect for [life's] mystery." O'Connor's stories contain no prepackaged prescriptions for living, no catechisms that lay out all the answers. Instead, her characters struggle with spiritual questions in bizarre, incongruous situations. Their lives are grotesque — even comic — precisely because they do not understand their own spiritual natures. Their actions are extreme and abnormal. O'Connor explains the reasons for this in *Mystery and Manners;* she says she sought to expose the "distortions" of "modern life" that appear "normal" to her audience. Hence, she used "violent means" to convey her vision to a "hostile audience." "When you can assume that your audience holds the same beliefs you do, you can relax a little and use more normal means of talking to it." But when the audience holds different values, "you have to make your vision apparent by shock — to the hard of hearing you shout, and for the almost-blind you draw large and startling figures." O'Connor's characters lose or find their soul-saving grace in painful, chaotic circumstances that bear little or no resemblance to the slow but sure progress to the Celestial City of repentant pilgrims in traditional religious stories.

Because her characters are powerful creations who live convincing, even if ugly, lives, O'Connor's religious beliefs never supersede her storytelling. One need not be either Christian or Catholic to appreciate her concerns about human failure and degradation and her artistic ability to render fictional lives that are alternately absurdly comic and tragic. The ironies that abound in her work leave plenty of room for readers of all persuasions. O'Connor's work is narrow in the sense that her concerns are emphatically spiritual, but her compassion and her belief in human possibilities — even among the most unlikely characters — afford her fictions a capacity for wonder that is exhilarating. Her precise, deft use of language always reveals more than it seems to tell.

Like Hawthorne's fiction, O'Connor's stories present complex experiences that cannot be tidily summarized; it takes the entire story to suggest the meanings. Read the following four stories for the pleasure of entering the remarkable world O'Connor creates. You're in for some surprises.

Besides the neutral expression that she wore when she was alone, Mrs. Freeman had two others, forward and reverse, that she used for all her human dealings. Her forward expression was steady and driving like the advance of a heavy truck. Her eyes never swerved to left or right but turned as the story turned as if they followed a yellow line down the center of it. She seldom used the other expression because it was not often necessary for her to retract a statement, but when she did, her face came to a complete stop, there was an almost imperceptible movement of her black eyes, during which they seemed to be receding, and then the observer would see that Mrs. Freeman, though she might stand there as real as several grain sacks thrown on top of each other, was no longer there in spirit. As for getting anything across to her when this was the case, Mrs. Hopewell had given it up. She might talk her head off. Mrs. Freeman could never be brought to admit herself wrong on any point. She would stand there and if she could be brought to say anything, it was something like, "Well, I wouldn't of said it was and I wouldn't of said it wasn't," or letting her gaze range over the top kitchen shelf where there was an assortment of dusty bottles, she might remark, "I see you ain't ate many of them figs you put up last summer."

They carried on their most important business in the kitchen at breakfast. Every morning Mrs. Hopewell got up at seven o'clock and lit her gas heater and Joy's. Joy was her daughter, a large blonde girl who had an artificial leg. Mrs. Hopewell thought of her as a child though she was thirty-two years old and highly educated. Joy would get up while her mother was eating and lumber into the bathroom and slam the door, and before long, Mrs. Freeman would arrive at the back door. Joy would hear her mother call, "Come on in," and then they would talk for a while in low voices that were indistinguishable in the bathroom. By the time Joy came in, they had usually finished the weather report and were on one or the other of Mrs. Freeman's daughters, Glynese or Carramae, Joy called them Glycerin and Caramel. Glynese, a redhead, was eighteen and had many admirers; Carramae, a blonde, was only fifteen but already married and pregnant. She could not keep anything on her stomach. Every morning Mrs. Freeman told Mrs. Hopewell how many times she had vomited since the last report.

Mrs. Hopewell liked to tell people that Glynese and Carramae were two of the finest girls she knew and that Mrs. Freeman was a *lady* and that she was never ashamed to take her anywhere or introduce her to anybody they might meet. Then she would tell how she had happened to hire the Freemans in the first place and how they were a godsend to her and how she had had them four years. The reason for her keeping them so long was that they were not trash. They were good country people. She had telephoned the man whose name they had given as a reference and he had told her that Mr. Freeman was a good farmer but that his wife was the nosiest woman ever to walk the earth. "She's got to be into everything," the man said. "If she don't get there before the dust settles, you can bet she's dead, that's all. She'll want to know all your business. I can stand him real good," he had said, "but me nor my wife neither could have stood that woman one more minute on this place." That had put Mrs. Hopewell off for a few days.

She had hired them in the end because there were no other applicants but she had made up her mind beforehand exactly how she would handle the woman. Since she was the type who had to be into everything, then, Mrs. Hopewell decided, she would not only let her be into everything, she would *see to it* that she was into everything — she would give her the responsibility of everything, she would put her in charge. Mrs. Hopewell had no bad qualities of her own but she was able to use other people's in such a constructive way that she never felt the lack. She had hired the Freemans and she had kept them four years.

Nothing is perfect. This was one of Mrs. Hopewell's favorite sayings. An- 5
other was: that is life! And still another, the most important, was: well, other people have their opinions too. She would make these statements, usually at the table, in a tone of gentle insistence as if no one held them but her, and the large hulking Joy, whose constant outrage had obliterated every expression from her face, would stare just a little to the side of her, her eyes icy blue, with the look of someone who has achieved blindness by an act of will and means to keep it.

When Mrs. Hopewell said to Mrs. Freeman that life was like that, Mrs. Freeman would say, "I always said so myself." Nothing had been arrived at by anyone that had not first been arrived at by her. She was quicker than Mr. Freeman. When Mrs. Hopewell said to her after they had been on the place a while, "You know, you're the wheel behind the wheel," and winked, Mrs. Freeman had said, "I know it. I've always been quick. It's some that are quicker than others."

"Everybody is different," Mrs. Hopewell said.

"Yes, most people is," Mrs. Freeman said.

"It takes all kinds to make the world."

"I always said it did myself." 10

The girl was used to this kind of dialogue for breakfast and more of it for dinner; sometimes they had it for supper too. When they had no guest they ate in the kitchen because that was easier. Mrs. Freeman always managed to arrive at some point during the meal and to watch them finish it. She would stand in the doorway if it were summer but in the winter she would stand with one elbow on top of the refrigerator and look down on them, or she would stand by the gas heater, lifting the back of her skirt slightly. Occasionally she would stand against the wall and roll her head from side to side. At no time was she in any hurry to leave. All this was very trying on Mrs. Hopewell but she was a woman of great patience. She realized that nothing is perfect and that in the Freemans she had good country people and that if, in this day and age, you get good country people, you had better hang onto them.

She had had plenty of experience with trash. Before the Freemans she had averaged one tenant family a year. The wives of these farmers were not the kind you would want to be around you for very long. Mrs. Hopewell, who had divorced her husband long ago, needed someone to walk over the fields with her; and when Joy had to be impressed for these services, her remarks were usually so ugly and her face so glum that Mrs. Hopewell would say, "If you can't come pleasantly, I don't want you at all," to which the girl, standing square and rigid-shouldered with her neck thrust slightly forward, would reply, "If you want me, here I am — LIKE I AM."

Mrs. Hopewell excused this attitude because of the leg (which had been shot off in a hunting accident when Joy was ten). It was hard for Mrs. Hopewell to realize that her child was thirty-two now and that for more than twenty years she had had only one leg. She thought of her still as a child because it tore her heart to think instead of the poor stout girl in her thirties who had never danced a step or had any *normal* good times. Her name was really Joy but as soon as she was twenty-one and away from home, she had had it legally changed. Mrs. Hopewell was certain that she had thought and thought until she had hit upon the ugliest name in any language. Then she had gone and had the beautiful name, Joy, changed without telling her mother until after she had done it. Her legal name was Hulga.

When Mrs. Hopewell thought the name, Hulga, she thought of the broad blank hull of a battleship. She would not use it. She continued to call her Joy to which the girl responded but in a purely mechanical way.

Hulga had learned to tolerate Mrs. Freeman who saved her from taking walks with her mother. Even Glynese and Carramae were useful when they occupied attention that might otherwise have been directed at her. At first she had thought she could not stand Mrs. Freeman for she had found that it was not possible to be rude to her. Mrs. Freeman would take on strange resentments and for days together she would be sullen but the source of her displeasure was always obscure; a direct attack, a positive leer, blatant ugliness to her face — these never touched her. And without warning one day, she began calling her Hulga.

She did not call her that in front of Mrs. Hopewell who would have been incensed but when she and the girl happened to be out of the house together, she would say something and add the name Hulga to the end of it, and the big spectacled Joy-Hulga would scowl and redden as if her privacy had been intruded upon. She considered the name her personal affair. She had arrived at it first purely on the basis of its ugly sound and then the full genius of its fitness had struck her. She had a vision of the name working like the ugly sweating Vulcan° who stayed in the furnace and to whom, presumably, the goddess had to come when called. She saw it as the name of her highest creative act. One of her major triumphs was that her mother had not been able to turn her dust into Joy, but the greater one was that she had been able to turn it herself into Hulga. However, Mrs. Freeman's relish for using the name only irritated her. It was as if Mrs. Freeman's beady steel-pointed eyes had penetrated far enough behind her face to reach some secret fact. Something about her seemed to fascinate Mrs. Freeman and then one day Hulga realized that it was the artificial leg. Mrs. Freeman had a special fondness for the details of secret infections, hidden deformities, assaults upon children. Of diseases, she preferred the lingering or incurable. Hulga had heard Mrs. Hopewell give her the details of the hunting accident, how the leg had been literally blasted off, how she had never lost consciousness. Mrs. Freeman could listen to it any time as if it had happened an hour ago.

Vulcan: Roman god of fire.

When Hulga stumped into the kitchen in the morning (she could walk without making the awful noise but she made it — Mrs. Hopewell was certain — because it was ugly-sounding), she glanced at them and did not speak. Mrs. Hopewell would be in her red kimono with her hair tied around her head in rags. She would be sitting at the table, finishing her breakfast and Mrs. Freeman would be hanging by her elbow outward from the refrigerator, looking down at the table. Hulga always put her eggs on the stove to boil and then stood over them with her arms folded, and Mrs. Hopewell would look at her — a kind of indirect gaze divided between her and Mrs. Freeman — and would think that if she would only keep herself up a little, she wouldn't be so bad looking. There was nothing wrong with her face that a pleasant expression wouldn't help. Mrs. Hopewell said that people who looked on the bright side of things would be beautiful even if they were not.

Whenever she looked at Joy this way, she could not help but feel that it would have been better if the child had not taken the Ph.D. It had certainly not brought her out any and now that she had it, there was no more excuse for her to go to school again. Mrs. Hopewell thought it was nice for girls to go to school to have a good time but Joy had "gone through." Anyhow, she would not have been strong enough to go again. The doctors had told Mrs. Hopewell that with the best of care, Joy might see forty-five. She had a weak heart. Joy had made it plain that if it had not been for this condition, she would be far from these red hills and good country people. She would be in a university lecturing to people who knew what she was talking about. And Mrs. Hopewell could very well picture her there, looking like a scarecrow and lecturing to more of the same. Here she went about all day in a six-year-old skirt and a yellow sweat shirt with a faded cowboy on a horse embossed on it. She thought this was funny; Mrs. Hopewell thought it was idiotic and showed simply that she was still a child. She was brilliant but she didn't have a grain of sense. It seemed to Mrs. Hopewell that every year she grew less like other people and more like herself — bloated, rude, and squint-eyed. And she said such strange things! To her own mother she had said — without warning, without excuse, standing up in the middle of a meal with her face purple and her mouth half full — "Woman! do you ever look inside? Do you ever look inside and see what you are *not?* God!" she had cried sinking down again and staring at her plate, "Malebranche° was right: we are not our own light. We are not our own light!" Mrs. Hopewell had no idea to this day what brought that on. She had only made the remark, hoping Joy would take it in, that a smile never hurt anyone.

The girl had taken the Ph.D. in philosophy and this left Mrs. Hopewell at a complete loss. You could say, "My daughter is a nurse," or "My daughter is a schoolteacher," or even, "My daughter is a chemical engineer." You could not say, "My daughter is a philosopher." That was something that had ended with the Greeks and Romans. All day Joy sat on her neck in a deep chair, reading. Sometimes she went for walks but she didn't like dogs or cats or birds or flowers or nature or nice young men. She looked at nice young men as if she could smell their stupidity.

One day Mrs. Hopewell had picked up one of the books the girl had just 20

Nicolas Malebranche: (1638–1715) French philosopher.

put down and opening it at random, she read, "Science, on the other hand, has to assert its soberness and seriousness afresh and declare that it is concerned solely with what-is. Nothing — how can it be for science anything but a horror and a phantasm? If science is right, then one thing stands firm: science wishes to know nothing of nothing. Such is after all the strictly scientific approach to Nothing. We know it by wishing to know nothing of Nothing." These words had been underlined with a blue pencil and they worked on Mrs. Hopewell like some evil incantation in gibberish. She shut the book quickly and went out of the room as if she were having a chill.

This morning when the girl came in, Mrs. Freeman was on Carramae. "She thrown up four times after supper," she said, "and was up twict in the night after three o'clock. Yesterday she didn't do nothing but ramble in the bureau drawer. All she did. Stand up there and see what she could run up on."

"She's got to eat," Mrs. Hopewell muttered, sipping her coffee, while she watched Joy's back at the stove. She was wondering what the child had said to the Bible salesman. She could not imagine what kind of a conversation she could possibly have had with him.

He was a tall gaunt hatless youth who had called yesterday to sell them a Bible. He had appeared at the door, carrying a large black suitcase that weighted him so heavily on one side that he had to brace himself against the door facing. He seemed on the point of collapse but he said in a cheerful voice, "Good morning, Mrs. Cedars!" and set the suitcase down on the mat. He was not a bad-looking young man though he had on a bright blue suit and yellow socks that were not pulled up far enough. He had prominent face bones and a streak of sticky-looking brown hair falling across his forehead.

"I'm Mrs. Hopewell," she said.

"Oh!" he said, pretending to look puzzled but with his eyes sparkling, "I 25
saw it said 'The Cedars' on the mailbox so I thought you was Mrs. Cedars!" and he burst out in a pleasant laugh. He picked up the satchel and under cover of a pant, he fell forward into her hall. It was rather as if the suitcase had moved first, jerking him after it. "Mrs. Hopewell!" he said and grabbed her hand. "I hope you are well!" and he laughed again and then all at once his face sobered completely. He paused and gave her a straight earnest look and said, "Lady, I've come to speak of serious things."

"Well, come in," she muttered, none too pleased because her dinner was almost ready. He came into the parlor and sat down on the edge of a straight chair and put the suitcase between his feet and glanced around the room as if he were sizing her up by it. Her silver gleamed on the two sideboards; she decided he had never been in a room as elegant as this.

"Mrs. Hopewell," he began, using her name in a way that sounded almost intimate, "I know you believe in Chrustian service."

"Well yes," she murmured.

"I know," he said and paused, looking very wise with his head cocked on one side, "that you're a good woman. Friends have told me."

Mrs. Hopewell never liked to be taken for a fool. "What are you selling?" 30
she asked.

"Bibles," the young man said and his eye raced around the room before he added, "I see you have no family Bible in your parlor, I see that is the one lack you got!"

Mrs. Hopewell could not say, "My daughter is an atheist and won't let me keep the Bible in the parlor." She said, stiffening slightly, "I keep my Bible by my bedside." This was not the truth. It was in the attic somewhere.

"Lady," he said, "the word of God ought to be in the parlor."

"Well, I think that's a matter of taste," she began. "I think . . ."

"Lady," he said, "for a Chrustian, the word of God ought to be in every 35
room in the house besides in his heart. I know you're a Chrustian because I can see it in every line of your face."

She stood up and said, "Well, young man, I don't want to buy a Bible and I smell my dinner burning."

He didn't get up. He began to twist his hands and looking down at them, he said softly. "Well lady, I'll tell you the truth — not many people want to buy one nowadays and besides, I know I'm real simple. I don't know how to say a thing but to say it. I'm just a country boy." He glanced up into her unfriendly face. "People like you don't like to fool with country people like me!"

"Why!" she cried, "good country people are the salt of the earth! Besides, we all have different ways of doing, it takes all kinds to make the world go 'round. That's life!"

"You said a mouthful," he said.

"Why, I think there aren't enough good people in the world!" she said, 40
stirred. "I think that's what's wrong with it!"

His face had brightened. "I didn't introduce myself," he said. "I'm Manley Pointer from out in the country around Willohobie, not even from a place, just from near a place."

"You wait a minute," she said. "I have to see about my dinner." She went out to the kitchen and found Joy standing near the door where she had been listening.

"Get rid of the salt of the earth," she said, "and let's eat."

Mrs. Hopewell gave her a pained look and turned the heat down under the vegetables. "*I* can't be rude to anybody," she murmured and went back into the parlor.

He had opened the suitcase and was sitting with a Bible on each knee. 45

"You might as well put those up," she told him. "I don't want one."

"I appreciate your honesty," he said. "You don't see any more real honest people unless you go way out in the country."

"I know," she said, "real genuine folks!" Through the crack in the door she heard a groan.

"I guess a lot of boys come telling you they're working their way through college," he said, "but I'm not going to tell you that. Somehow," he said, "I don't want to go to college. I want to devote my life to Chrustian service. See," he said, lowering his voice, "I got this heart condition. I may not live long. When you know it's something wrong with you and you may not live long, well then, lady . . ." He paused, with his mouth open, and stared at her.

He and Joy had the same condition! She knew that her eyes were filling 50
with tears but she collected herself quickly and murmured, "Won't you stay for dinner? We'd love to have you!" and was sorry the instant she heard herself say it.

"Yes mam," he said in an abashed voice, "I would sher love to do that!"

Joy had given him one look on being introduced to him and then throughout the meal had not glanced at him again. He had addressed several remarks to her, which she had pretended not to hear. Mrs. Hopewell could not understand deliberate rudeness, although she lived with it, and she felt she had always to overflow with hospitality to make up for Joy's lack of courtesy. She urged him to talk about himself and he did. He said he was the seventh child of twelve and that his father had been crushed under a tree when he himself was eight years old. He had been crushed very badly, in fact, almost cut in two and was practically not recognizable. His mother had got along the best she could by hard working and she had always seen that her children went to Sunday School and that they read the Bible every evening. He was now nineteen years old and he had been selling Bibles for four months. In that time he had sold seventy-seven Bibles and had the promise of two more sales. He wanted to become a missionary because he thought that was the way you could do most for people. "He who losest his life shall find it," he said simply and he was so sincere, so genuine and earnest that Mrs. Hopewell would not for the world have smiled. He prevented his peas from sliding onto the table by blocking them with a piece of bread which he later cleaned his plate with. She could see Joy observing sidewise how he handled his knife and fork and she saw too that every few minutes, the boy would dart a keen appraising glance at the girl as if he were trying to attract her attention.

After dinner Joy cleared the dishes off the table and disappeared and Mrs. Hopewell was left to talk with him. He told her again about his childhood and his father's accident and about various things that had happened to him. Every five minutes or so she would stifle a yawn. He sat for two hours until finally she told him she must go because she had an appointment in town. He packed his Bibles and thanked her and prepared to leave, but in the doorway he stopped and wrung her hand and said that not on any of his trips had he met a lady as nice as her and he asked if he could come again. She had said she would always be happy to see him.

Joy had been standing in the road, apparently looking at something in the distance, when he came down the steps toward her, bent to the side with his heavy valise. He stopped where she was standing and confronted her directly. Mrs. Hopewell could not hear what he said but she trembled to think what Joy would say to him. She could see that after a minute Joy said something and that then the boy began to speak again, making an excited gesture with his free hand. After a minute Joy said something else at which the boy began to speak once more. Then to her amazement, Mrs. Hopewell saw the two of them walk off together, toward the gate. Joy had walked all the way to the gate with him and Mrs. Hopewell could not imagine what they had said to each other, and she had not yet dared to ask.

Mrs. Freeman was insisting upon her attention. She had moved from the refrigerator to the heater so that Mrs. Hopewell had to turn and face her in order to seem to be listening. "Glynese gone out with Harvey Hill again last night," she said. "She had this sty."

"Hill," Mrs. Hopewell said absently, "is the one who works in the garage?"

"Nome, he's the one that goes to chiropracter school," Mrs. Freeman said. "She had this sty. Been had it two days. So she says when he brought her in the other night he says, 'Lemme get rid of that sty for you,' and she says, 'How?' and he says, 'You just lay yourself down acrost the seat of that car and I'll show you.'

So she done it and he popped her neck. Kept on a-popping it several times until she made him quit. This morning," Mrs. Freeman said, "she ain't got no sty. She ain't got no traces of a sty."

"I never heard of that before," Mrs. Hopewell said.

"He ast her to marry him before the Ordinary,"° Mrs. Freeman went on, "and she told him she wasn't going to be married in no *office*."

"Well, Glynese is a fine girl," Mrs. Hopewell said. "Glynese and Carramae 60
are both fine girls."

"Carramae said when her and Lyman was married Lyman said it sure felt sacred to him. She said he said he wouldn't take five hundred dollars for being married by a preacher."

"How much would he take?" the girl asked from the stove.

"He said he wouldn't take five hundred dollars," Mrs. Freeman repeated.

"Well we all have work to do," Mrs. Hopewell said.

"Lyman said it just felt more sacred to him," Mrs. Freeman said. "The doc- 65
tor wants Carramae to eat prunes. Says instead of medicine. Says them cramps is coming from pressure. You know where I think it is?"

"She'll be better in a few weeks," Mrs. Hopewell said.

"In the tube," Mrs. Freeman said. "Else she wouldn't be as sick as she is."

Hulga had cracked her two eggs into a saucer and was bringing them to the table along with a cup of coffee that she had filled too full. She sat down carefully and began to eat, meaning to keep Mrs. Freeman there by questions if for any reason she showed an inclination to leave. She could perceive her mother's eye on her. The first round-about question would be about the Bible salesman and she did not wish to bring it on. "How did he pop her neck?" she asked.

Mrs. Freeman went into a description of how he had popped her neck. She said he owned a '55 Mercury but that Glynese said she would rather marry a man with only a '36 Plymouth who would be married by a preacher. The girl asked what if he had a '32 Plymouth and Mrs. Freeman said what Glynese had said was a '36 Plymouth.

Mrs. Hopewell said there were not many girls with Glynese's common sense. 70
She said what she admired in those girls was their common sense. She said that reminded her that they had had a nice visitor yesterday, a young man selling Bibles. "Lord," she said, "he bored me to death but he was so sincere and genuine I couldn't be rude to him. He was just good country people, you know," she said, " — just the salt of the earth."

"I seen him walk up," Mrs. Freeman said, "and then later — I seen him walk off," and Hulga could feel the slight shift in her voice, the slight insinuation, that he had not walked off alone, had he? Her face remained expressionless but the color rose into her neck and she seemed to swallow it down with the next spoonful of egg. Mrs. Freeman was looking at her as if they had a secret together.

"Well, it takes all kinds of people to make the world go 'round," Mrs. Hopewell said. "It's very good we aren't all alike."

"Some people are more alike than others," Mrs. Freeman said.

Ordinary: Justice of the peace.

Hulga got up and stumped, with about twice the noise that was necessary, into her room and locked the door. She was to meet the Bible salesman at ten o'clock at the gate. She had thought about it half the night. She had started thinking of it as a great joke and then she had begun to see profound implications in it. She had lain in bed imagining dialogues for them that were insane on the surface but that reached below to depths that no Bible salesman would be aware of. Their conversation yesterday had been of this kind.

75 He had stopped in front of her and had simply stood there. His face was bony and sweaty and bright, with a little pointed nose in the center of it, and his look was different from what it had been at the dinner table. He was gazing at her with open curiosity, with fascination, like a child watching a new fantastic animal at the zoo, and he was breathing as if he had run a great distance to reach her. His gaze seemed somehow familiar but she could not think where she had been regarded with it before. For almost a minute he didn't say anything. Then on what seemed an insuck of breath, he whispered, "You ever ate a chicken that was two days old?"

The girl looked at him stonily. He might have just put this question up for consideration at the meeting of a philosophical association. "Yes," she presently replied as if she had considered it from all angles.

"It must have been mighty small!" he said triumphantly and shook all over with little nervous giggles, getting very red in the face, and subsiding finally into his gaze of complete admiration, while the girl's expression remained exactly the same.

"How old are you?" he asked softly.

She waited some time before she answered. Then in a flat voice she said, "Seventeen."

80 His smiles came in succession like waves breaking on the surface of a little lake. "I see you got a wooden leg," he said. "I think you're brave. I think you're real sweet."

The girl stood blank and solid and silent.

"Walk to the gate with me," he said. "You're a brave sweet little thing and I liked you the minute I seen you walk in the door."

Hulga began to move forward.

"What's your name?" he asked, smiling down on the top of her head.

85 "Hulga," she said.

"Hulga," he murmured, "Hulga. Hulga. I never heard of anybody name Hulga before. You're shy, aren't you, Hulga?" he asked.

She nodded, watching his large red hand on the handle of the giant valise.

"I like girls that wear glasses," he said. "I think a lot. I'm not like these people that a serious thought don't ever enter their heads. It's because I may die."

"I may die too," she said suddenly and looked up at him. His eyes were very small and brown, glittering feverishly.

90 "Listen," he said, "don't you think some people was meant to meet on account of what all they got in common and all? Like they both think serious thoughts and all?" He shifted the valise to his other hand so that the hand nearest her was free. He caught hold of her elbow and shook it a little. "I don't work on Saturday," he said. "I like to walk in the woods and see what Mother Nature is wearing. O'er the hills and far away. Pic-nics and things. Couldn't we

go on a pic-nic tomorrow? Say yes, Hulga," he said and gave her a dying look as if he felt his insides about to drop out of him. He had even seemed to sway slightly toward her.

During the night she had imagined that she seduced him. She imagined that the two of them walked on the place until they came to the storage barn beyond the two back fields and there, she imagined, that things came to such a pass that she very easily seduced him and that then, of course, she had to reckon with his remorse. True genius can get an idea across even to an inferior mind. She imagined that she took his remorse in hand and changed it into a deeper understanding of life. She took all his shame away and turned it into something useful.

She set off for the gate at exactly ten o'clock, escaping without drawing Mrs. Hopewell's attention. She didn't take anything to eat, forgetting that food is usually taken on a picnic. She wore a pair of slacks and a dirty white shirt, and as an afterthought, she had put some Vapex° on the collar of it since she did not own any perfume. When she reached the gate no one was there.

She looked up and down the empty highway and had the furious feeling that she had been tricked, that he had only meant to make her walk to the gate after the idea of him. Then suddenly he stood up, very tall, from behind a bush on the opposite embankment. Smiling, he lifted his hat which was new and wide-brimmed. He had not worn it yesterday and she wondered if he had bought it for the occasion. It was toast-colored with a red and white band around it and was slightly too large for him. He stepped from behind the bush still carrying the black valise. He had on the same suit and the same yellow socks sucked down in his shoes from walking. He crossed the highway and said, "I knew you'd come!"

The girl wondered acidly how he had known this. She pointed to the valise and asked, "Why did you bring your Bibles?"

He took her elbow, smiling down on her as if he could not stop. "You can 95
never tell when you'll need the word of God, Hulga," he said. She had a moment in which she doubted that this was actually happening and then they began to climb the embankment. They went down into the pasture toward the woods. The boy walked lightly by her side, bouncing on his toes. The valise did not seem to be heavy today; he even swung it. They crossed half the pasture without saying anything and then, putting his hand easily on the small of her back, he asked softly, "Where does your wooden leg join on?"

She turned an ugly red and glared at him and for an instant the boy looked abashed. "I didn't mean you no harm," he said. "I only meant you're so brave and all. I guess God takes care of you."

"No," she said, looking forward and walking fast, "I don't even believe in God."

At this he stopped and whistled. "No!" he exclaimed as if he were too astonished to say anything else.

She walked on and in a second he was bouncing at her side, fanning with his hat. "That's very unusual for a girl," he remarked, watching her out of the corner of his eye. When they reached the edge of the wood, he put his hand

Vapex: Trade name for a nasal spray.

on her back again and drew her against him without a word and kissed her heavily.

The kiss, which had more pressure than feeling behind it, produced that 100
extra surge of adrenaline in the girl that enables one to carry a packed trunk out of a burning house, but in her, the power went at once to the brain. Even before he released her, her mind, clear and detached and ironic anyway, was regarding him from a great distance, with amusement but with pity. She had never been kissed before and she was pleased to discover that it was an unexceptional experience and all a matter of the mind's control. Some people might enjoy drain water if they were told it was vodka. When the boy, looking expectant but uncertain, pushed her gently away, she turned and walked on, saying nothing as if such business, for her, were common enough.

He came along panting at her side, trying to help her when he saw a root that she might trip over. He caught and held back the long swaying blades of thorn vine until she had passed beyond them. She led the way and he came breathing heavily behind her. Then they came out on a sunlit hillside, sloping softly into another one a little smaller. Beyond, they could see the rusted top of the old barn where the extra hay was stored.

The hill was sprinkled with small pink weeds. "Then you ain't saved?" he asked suddenly, stopping.

The girl smiled. It was the first time she had smiled at him at all. "In my economy," she said, "I'm saved and you are damned but I told you I didn't believe in God."

Nothing seemed to destroy the boy's look of admiration. He gazed at her now as if the fantastic animal at the zoo had put its paw through the bars and given him a loving poke. She thought he looked as if he wanted to kiss her again and she walked on before he had the chance.

"Ain't there somewheres we can sit down sometime?" he murmured, his 105
voice softening toward the end of the sentence.

"In that barn," she said.

They made for it rapidly as if it might slide away like a train. It was a large two-story barn, cool and dark inside. The boy pointed up the ladder that led into the loft and said, "It's too bad we can't go up there."

"Why can't we?" she asked.

"Yer leg," he said reverently.

The girl gave him a contemptuous look and putting both hands on the 110
ladder, she climbed it while he stood below, apparently awestruck. She pulled herself expertly through the opening and then looked down at him and said, "Well, come on if you're coming," and he began to climb the ladder, awkwardly bringing the suitcase with him.

"We won't need the Bible," she observed.

"You never can tell," he said, panting. After he had got into the loft, he was a few seconds catching his breath. She had sat down in a pile of straw. A wide sheath of sunlight, filled with dust particles, slanted over her. She lay back against a bale, her face turned away, looking out the front opening of the barn where hay was thrown from a wagon into the loft. The two pink-speckled hillsides lay back against a dark ridge of woods. The sky was cloudless and cold blue. The boy dropped down by her side and put one arm under her and the other over her and began methodically kissing her face, making little noises like a fish. He did not remove his hat but it was pushed far enough back not to interfere. When her glasses got in his way, he took them off of her and slipped them into his pocket.

The girl at first did not return any of the kisses but presently she began to and after she had put several on his cheek, she reached his lips and remained there, kissing him again and again as if she were trying to draw all the breath out of him. His breath was clear and sweet like a child's and the kisses were sticky like a child's. He mumbled about loving her and about knowing when he first seen her that he loved her, but the mumbling was like the sleepy fretting of a child being put to sleep by his mother. Her mind, throughout this, never stopped or lost itself for a second to her feelings. "You ain't said you loved me none," he whispered finally, pulling back from her. "You got to say that."

She looked away from him off into the hollow sky and then down at a black ridge and then down farther into what appeared to be two green swelling lakes. She didn't realize he had taken her glasses but this landscape could not seem exceptional to her for she seldom paid any close attention to her surroundings.

"You got to say it," he repeated. "You got to say you love me." 115

She was always careful how she committed herself. "In a sense," she began, "if you use the word loosely, you might say that. But it's not a word I use. I don't have illusions. I'm one of those people who see *through* to nothing."

The boy was frowning. "You got to say it. I said it and you got to say it," he said.

The girl looked at him almost tenderly. "You poor baby," she murmured. "It's just as well you don't understand," and she pulled him by the neck, face-down, against her. "We are all damned," she said, "but some of us have taken off our blindfolds and see that there's nothing to see. It's a kind of salvation."

The boy's astonished eyes looked blankly through the ends of her hair. "Okay," he almost whined, "but do you love me or don'tcher?"

"Yes," she said and added, "in a sense. But I must tell you something. 120
There mustn't be anything dishonest between us." She lifted his head and looked him in the eye. "I am thirty years old," she said. "I have a number of degrees."

The boy's look was irritated but dogged. "I don't care," he said. "I don't care a thing about what all you done. I just want to know if you love me or don'tcher?" and he caught her to him and wildly planted her face with kisses until she said, "Yes, yes."

"Okay then," he said, letting her go. "Prove it."

She smiled, looking dreamily out on the shifty landscape. She had seduced him without even making up her mind to try. "How?" she asked, feeling that he should be delayed a little.

He leaned over and put his lips to her ear. "Show me where your wooden leg joins on," he whispered.

The girl uttered a sharp little cry and her face instantly drained of color. 125
The obscenity of the suggestion was not what shocked her. As a child she had sometimes been subject to feelings of shame but education had removed the last traces of that as a good surgeon scrapes for cancer; she would no more have felt it over what he was asking than she would have believed in his Bible.

But she was as sensitive about the artificial leg as a peacock about his tail. No one ever touched it but her. She took care of it as someone else would his soul, in private and almost with her own eyes turned away. "No," she said.

"I known it," he muttered, sitting up. "You're just playing me for a sucker."

"Oh no no!" she cried. "It joins on at the knee. Only at the knee. Why do you want to see it?"

The boy gave her a long penetrating look. "Because," he said, "it's what makes you different. You ain't like anybody else."

She sat staring at him. There was nothing about her face or her round freezing-blue eyes to indicate that this had moved her; but she felt as if her heart had stopped and left her mind to pump her blood. She decided that for the first time in her life she was face to face with real innocence. This boy, with an instinct that came from beyond wisdom, had touched the truth about her. When after a minute, she said in a hoarse high voice, "All right," it was like surrendering to him completely. It was like losing her own life and finding it again, miraculously, in his.

Very gently he began to roll the slack leg up. The artificial limb, in a white 130
sock and brown flat shoe, was bound in a heavy material like canvas and ended in an ugly jointure where it was attached to the stump. The boy's face and his voice were entirely reverent as he uncovered it and said, "Now show me how to take it off and on."

She took it off for him and put it back on again and then he took it off himself, handling it as tenderly as if it were a real one. "See!" he said with a delighted child's face. "Now I can do it myself!"

"Put it back on," she said. She was thinking that she would run away with him and that every night he would take the leg off and every morning put it back on again. "Put it back on," she said.

"Not yet," he murmured, setting it on its foot out of her reach. "Leave it off for a while. You got me instead."

She gave a little cry of alarm but he pushed her down and began to kiss her again. Without the leg she felt entirely dependent on him. Her brain seemed to have stopped thinking altogether and to be about some other function that it was not very good at. Different expressions raced back and forth over her face. Every now and then the boy, his eyes like two steel spikes, would glance behind him where the leg stood. Finally she pushed him off and said, "Put it back on me now."

"Wait," he said. He leaned the other way and pulled the valise toward him 135
and opened it. It had a pale blue spotted lining and there were only two Bibles in it. He took one of these out and opened the cover of it. It was hollow and contained a pocket flask of whiskey, a pack of cards, and a small blue box with printing on it. He laid these out in front of her one at a time in an evenly-spaced row, like one presenting offerings at the shrine of a goddess. He put the blue box in her hand. THIS PRODUCT TO BE USED ONLY FOR THE PREVENTION OF DISEASE, she read, and dropped it. The boy was unscrewing the top of the flask. He stopped and pointed, with a smile, to the deck of cards. It was not an ordinary deck but one with an obscene picture on the back of each card. "Take a swig," he said, offering her the bottle first. He held it in front of her, but like one mesmerized, she did not move.

Her voice when she spoke had an almost pleading sound. "Aren't you," she murmured, "aren't you just good country people?"

The boy cocked his head. He looked as if he were just beginning to understand that she might be trying to insult him. "Yeah," he said, curling his lip slightly, "but it ain't held me back none. I'm as good as you any day in the week."

"Give me my leg," she said.

He pushed it farther away with his foot. "Come on now, let's begin to have us a good time," he said coaxingly. "We ain't got to know one another good yet."

"Give me my leg!" she screamed and tried to lunge for it but he pushed 140
her down easily.

"What's the matter with you all of a sudden?" he asked, frowning as he screwed the top on the flask and put it quickly back inside the Bible. "You just a while ago said you didn't believe in nothing. I thought you was some girl!"

Her face was almost purple. "You're a Christian!" she hissed. "You're a fine Christian! You're just like them all — say one thing and do another. You're a perfect Christian, you're . . ."

The boy's mouth was set angrily. "I hope you don't think," he said in a lofty indignant tone, "that I believe in that crap! I may sell Bibles but I know which end is up and I wasn't born yesterday and I know where I'm going!"

"Give me my leg!" she screeched. He jumped up so quickly that she barely saw him sweep the cards and the blue box into the Bible and throw the Bible into his valise. She saw him grab the leg and then she saw it for an instant slanted forlornly across the inside of the suitcase with a Bible at either side of its opposite ends. He slammed the lid shut and snatched up the valise and swung it down the hole and then stepped through himself.

When all of him had passed but his head, he turned and regarded her with 145
a look that no longer had any admiration in it. "I've gotten a lot of interesting things," he said. "One time I got a woman's glass eye this way. And you needn't to think you'll catch me because Pointer ain't really my name. I use a different name at every house I call at and don't stay nowhere long. And I'll tell you another thing, Hulga," he said, using the name as if he didn't think much of it, "you ain't so smart. I been believing in nothing ever since I was born!" and then the toast-colored hat disappeared down the hole and the girl was left, sitting on the straw in the dusty sunlight. When she turned her churning face toward the opening, she saw his blue figure struggling successfully over the green speckled lake.

Mrs. Hopewell and Mrs. Freeman, who were in the back pasture, digging up onions, saw him emerge a little later from the woods and head across the meadow toward the highway. "Why, that looks like that nice dull young man that tried to sell me a Bible yesterday," Mrs. Hopewell said, squinting. "He must have been selling them to the Negroes back in there. He was so simple," she said, "but I guess the world would be better off if we were all that simple."

Mrs. Freeman's gaze drove forward and just touched him before he disappeared under the hill. Then she returned her attention to the evil-smelling onion shoot she was lifting from the ground. "Some can't be that simple," she said. "I know I never could."

Considerations

1. Why is it significant that Mrs. Hopewell's daughter has two names? How do the other characters' names serve to characterize them?
2. Why do you think Mrs. Freeman and Mrs. Hopewell are introduced before Hulga? What do they contribute to Hulga's story?
3. Identify the conflict in this story. How is it resolved?
4. Hulga and the Bible salesman play a series of jokes on each other. How are these deceptions related to the theme?
5. What is the effect of O'Connor's use of the phrase "good country people" throughout the story? Why is it an appropriate title?
6. The Bible salesman's final words to Hulga are "you ain't so smart. I been believing in nothing ever since I was born!" What religious values are expressed in the story?
7. After the Bible salesman leaves Hulga at the end of the story, O'Connor adds two more paragraphs concerning Mrs. Hopewell and Mrs. Freeman. What is the purpose of these final paragraphs?
8. Hulga's perspective on life is ironic, but she is also the subject of O'Connor's irony. Explain how O'Connor uses irony to reveal Hulga's character.
9. This story would be different if told from Hulga's point of view. Describe how the use of a limited omniscient narrator contributes to the story's effects.
10. Comment on Hulga's conviction that intelligence and education are incompatible with religious faith.

Connections

1. Compare the Bible salesman's function in this story with the role Mary Grace plays in "Revelation" (p. 327).
2. How do Mrs. Hopewell's assumptions about life compare with those of Krebs's mother in Hemingway's "Soldier's Home" (p. 121)? Explain how the conflict in each story is related to what the mothers come to represent in the eyes of the central characters.

Everything That Rises Must Converge 1961

Her doctor had told Julian's mother that she must lose twenty pounds on account of her blood pressure, so on Wednesday nights Julian had to take her downtown on the bus for a reducing class at the Y. The reducing class was designed for working girls over fifty, who weighed from 165 to 200 pounds. His mother was one of the slimmer ones, but she said ladies did not tell their age or weight. She would not ride the buses by herself at night since they had been integrated, and because the reducing class was one of her few pleasures, necessary for her health, and *free,* she said Julian could at least put himself out to take her, considering all she did for him. Julian did not like to consider all she did for him, but every Wednesday night he braced himself and took her.

She was almost ready to go, standing before the hall mirror, putting on her hat, while he, his hands behind him, appeared pinned to the door frame, waiting like Saint Sebastian° for the arrows to begin piercing him. The hat was new and had cost her seven dollars and a half. She kept saying, "Maybe I shouldn't have paid that for it. No, I shouldn't have. I'll take it off and return it tomorrow. I shouldn't have bought it."

Julian raised his eyes to heaven. "Yes, you should have bought it," he said. "Put it on and let's go." It was a hideous hat. A purple velvet flap came down on one side of it and stood up on the other; the rest of it was green and looked like a cushion with the stuffing out. He decided it was less comical than jaunty and pathetic. Everything that gave her pleasure was small and depressed him.

She lifted the hat one more time and set it down slowly on top of her head. Two wings of gray hair protruded on either side of her florid face, but her eyes, sky-blue, were as innocent and untouched by experience as they must have been when she was ten. Were it not that she was a widow who had struggled fiercely to feed and clothe and put him through school and who was supporting him still, "until he got on his feet," she might have been a little girl that he had to take to town.

"It's all right, it's all right," he said. "Let's go." He opened the door himself 5
and started down the walk to get her going. The sky was a dying violet and the houses stood out darkly against it, bulbous liver-colored monstrosities of a uniform ugliness though no two were alike. Since this had been a fashionable neighborhood forty years ago, his mother persisted in thinking they did well to have an apartment in it. Each house had a narrow collar of dirt around it in which sat, usually, a grubby child. Julian walked with his hands in his pockets, his head down and thrust forward and his eyes glazed with the determination to make himself completely numb during the time he would be sacrificed to her pleasure.

The door closed and he turned to find the dumpy figure, surmounted by the atrocious hat, coming toward him. "Well," she said, "you only live once and paying a little more for it, I at least won't meet myself coming and going."

"Some day I'll start making money," Julian said gloomily—he knew he never would—"and you can have one of those jokes whenever you take the fit." But first they would move. He visualized a place where the nearest neighbors would be three miles away on either side.

"I think you're doing fine," she said, drawing on her gloves. "You've only been out of school a year. Rome wasn't built in a day."

She was one of the few members of the Y reducing class who arrived in hat and gloves and who had a son who had been to college. "It takes time," she said, "and the world is in such a mess. This hat looked better on me than any of the others, though when she brought it out I said, 'Take that thing back. I wouldn't have it on my head,' and she said, 'Now wait till you see it on,' and when she put it on me, I said, 'We-ull,' and she said, 'If you ask me, that hat does something for you and you do something for the hat, and besides,' she said, 'with that hat, you won't meet yourself coming and going.' "

Julian thought he could have stood his lot better if she had been selfish, if 10
she had been an old hag who drank and screamed at him. He walked along,

Saint Sebastian: A Roman martyred for his Christian beliefs.

saturated in depression, as if in the midst of his martyrdom he had lost his faith. Catching sight of his long, hopeless, irritated face, she stopped suddenly with a grief-stricken look, and pulled back on his arm. "Wait on me," she said. "I'm going to return it. I was out of my head. I can pay the gas bill with the seven-fifty."

He caught her arm in a vicious grip. "You are not going to take it back," he said. "I like it."

"Well," she said, "I don't think I ought . . ."

"Shut up and enjoy it," he muttered, more depressed than ever.

"With the world in the mess it's in," she said, "it's a wonder we can enjoy anything. I tell you, the bottom rail is on the top."

Julian sighed.

"Of course," she said, "if you know who you are, you can go anywhere." She said this every time he took her to the reducing class. "Most of them in it are not our kind of people," she said, "but I can be gracious to anybody. I know who I am."

"They don't give a damn for your graciousness," Julian said savagely. "Knowing who you are is good for one generation only. You haven't the foggiest idea where you stand now or who you are."

She stopped and allowed her eyes to flash at him. "I most certainly do know who I am," she said, "and if you don't know who you are, I'm ashamed of you."

"Oh hell," Julian said.

"Your great-grandfather was a former governor of this state," she said. "Your grandfather was a prosperous landowner. Your grandmother was a Godhigh."

"Will you look around you," he said tensely, "and see where you are now?" and he swept his arm jerkily out to indicate the neighborhood, which the growing darkness at least made less dingy.

"You remain what you are," she said. "Your great-grandfather had a plantation and two hundred slaves."

"There are no more slaves," he said irritably.

"They were better off when they were," she said. He groaned to see that she was off on that topic. She rolled onto it every few days like a train on an open track. He knew every stop, every junction, every swamp along the way, and knew the exact point at which her conclusion would roll majestically into the station: "It's ridiculous. It's simply not realistic. They should rise, yes, but on their own side of the fence."

"Let's skip it," Julian said.

"The ones I feel sorry for," she said, "are the ones that are half white. They're tragic."

"Will you skip it?"

"Suppose we were half white. We would certainly have mixed feelings."

"I have mixed feelings now," he groaned.

"Well let's talk about something pleasant," she said. "I remember going to Grandpa's when I was a little girl. Then the house had double stairways that went up to what was really the second floor — all the cooking was done on the first. I used to like to stay down in the kitchen on account of the way the walls smelled. I would sit with my nose pressed against the plaster and take deep breaths. Actually the place belonged to the Godhighs but your grandfather Chestny paid the mortgage and saved it for them. They were in reduced circumstances," she said, "but reduced or not, they never forgot who they were."

"Doubtless that decayed mansion reminded them," Julian muttered. He never spoke of it without contempt or thought of it without longing. He had seen it once when he was a child before it had been sold. The double stairways had rotted and been torn down. Negroes were living in it. But it remained in his mind as his mother had known it. It appeared in his dreams regularly. He would stand on the wide porch, listening to the rustle of oak leaves, then wander through the high-ceilinged hall into the parlor that opened onto it and gaze at the worn rugs and faded draperies. It occurred to him that it was he, not she, who could have appreciated it. He preferred its threadbare elegance to anything he could name and it was because of it that all the neighborhoods they had lived in had been a torment to him — whereas she had hardly known the difference. She called her insensitivity "being adjustable."

"And I remember the old darky who was my nurse, Caroline. There was no better person in the world. I've always had a great respect for my colored friends," she said. "I'd do anything in the world for them and they'd . . ."

"Will you for God's sake get off that subject?" Julian said. When he got on a bus by himself, he made it a point to sit down beside a Negro, in reparation as it were for his mother's sins.

"You're mighty touchy tonight," she said. "Do you feel all right?"

"Yes I feel all right," he said. "Now lay off." 35

She pursed her lips. "Well, you certainly are in a vile humor," she observed. "I just won't speak to you at all."

They had reached the bus stop. There was no bus in sight and Julian, his hands still jammed in his pockets and his head thrust forward, scowled down the empty street. The frustration of having to wait on the bus as well as ride on it began to creep up his neck like a hot hand. The presence of his mother was borne in upon him as she gave a pained sigh. He looked at her bleakly. She was holding herself very erect under the preposterous hat, wearing it like a banner of her imaginary dignity. There was in him an evil urge to break her spirit. He suddenly unloosened his tie and pulled it off and put it in his pocket.

She stiffened. "Why must you look like *that* when you take me to town?" she said. "Why must you deliberately embarrass me?"

"If you'll never learn where you are," he said, "you can at least learn where I am."

"You look like a — thug," she said. 40

"Then I must be one," he murmured.

"I'll just go home," she said. "I will not bother you. If you can't do a little thing like that for me . . ."

Rolling his eyes upward, he put his tie back on. "Restored to my class," he muttered. He thrust his face toward her and hissed, "True culture is in the mind, the *mind,*" he said, and tapped his head, "the mind."

"It's in the heart," she said, "and in how you do things and how you do things is because of who you *are.*"

"Nobody in the damn bus cares who you are." 45

"I care who I am," she said icily.

The lighted bus appeared on top of the next hill and as it approached, they moved out into the street to meet it. He put his hand under her elbow and hoisted her up on the creaking step. She entered with a little smile, as if she were going into a drawing room where everyone had been waiting for her. While he put in the tokens, she sat down on one of the broad front seats for three which faced the aisle. A thin woman with protruding teeth and long yellow hair was sitting on the end of it. His mother moved up beside her and left the room for Julian beside herself. He sat down and looked at the floor across the aisle where a pair of thin feet in red and white canvas sandals were planted.

His mother immediately began a general conversation meant to attract anyone who felt like talking. "Can it get any hotter?" she said and removed from her purse a folding fan, black with a Japanese scene on it, which she began to flutter before her.

"I reckon it might could," the woman with the protruding teeth said, "but I know for a fact my apartment couldn't get no hotter."

"It must get the afternoon sun," his mother said. She sat forward and looked up and down the bus. It was half filled. Everybody was white. "I see we have the bus to ourselves," she said. Julian cringed.

"For a change," said the woman across the aisle, the owner of the red and white canvas sandals. "I come on one the other day and they were thick as fleas — up front and all through."

"The world is in a mess everywhere," his mother said. "I don't know how we've let it get in this fix."

"What gets my goat is all those boys from good families stealing automobile tires," the woman with the protruding teeth said. "I told my boy, I said you may not be rich but you been raised right and if I ever catch you in any such mess, they can send you on to the reformatory. Be exactly where you belong."

"Training tells," his mother said. "Is your boy in high school?"

"Ninth grade," the woman said.

"My son just finished college last year. He wants to write but he's selling typewriters until he gets started," his mother said.

The woman leaned forward and peered at Julian. He threw her such a malevolent look that she subsided against the seat. On the floor across the aisle there was an abandoned newspaper. He got up and got it and opened it out in front of him. His mother discreetly continued the conversation in a lower tone but the woman across the aisle said in a loud voice, "Well that's nice. Selling typewriters is close to writing. He can go right from one to the other."

"I tell him," his mother said, "that Rome wasn't built in a day."

Behind the newspaper Julian was withdrawing into the inner compartment of his mind where he spent most of his time. This was a kind of mental bubble in which he established himself when he could not bear to be a part of what was going on around him. From it he could see out and judge but in it he was safe from any kind of penetration from without. It was the only place where he felt free of the general idiocy of his fellows. His mother had never entered it but from it he could see her with absolute clarity.

The old lady was clever enough and he thought that if she had started from any of the right premises, more might have been expected of her. She lived according to the laws of her own fantasy world, outside of which he had never seen her set foot. The law of it was to sacrifice herself for him after she had first created the necessity to do so by making a mess of things. If he had permitted her sacrifices, it was only because her lack of foresight had made them necessary. All of her life had been a struggle to act like a Chestny without the Chestny goods, and to give him everything she thought a Chestny ought to have; but since, said she, it was fun to struggle, why complain? And when you had won, as she had won, what fun to look back on the hard times! He could not forgive her that she had enjoyed the struggle and that she thought *she* had won.

What she meant when she said she had won was that she had brought him up successfully and had sent him to college and that he had turned out so well — good looking (her teeth had gone unfilled so that his could be straightened), intelligent (he realized he was too intelligent to be a success), and with a future ahead of him (there was of course no future ahead of him). She excused his gloominess on the grounds that he was still growing up and his radical ideas on his lack of practical experience. She said he didn't yet know a thing about "life," that he hadn't even entered the real world — when already he was as disenchanted with it as a man of fifty.

The further irony of all this was that in spite of her, he had turned out so well. In spite of going to only a third-rate college, he had, on his own initiative, come out with a first-rate education; in spite of growing up dominated by a small mind, he had ended up with a large one; in spite of all her foolish views, he was free of prejudice and unafraid to face facts. Most miraculous of all, instead of being blinded by love for her as she was for him, he had cut himself emotionally free of her and could see her with complete objectivity. He was not dominated by his mother.

The bus stopped with a sudden jerk and shook him from his meditation. A woman from the back lurched forward with little steps and barely escaped falling in his newspaper as she righted herself. She got off and a large Negro got on. Julian kept his paper lowered to watch. It gave him a certain satisfaction to see injustice in daily operation. It confirmed his view that with a few exceptions there was no one worth knowing within a radius of three hundred miles. The Negro was well dressed and carried a briefcase. He looked around and then sat down on the other end of the seat where the woman with the red and white canvas sandals was sitting. He immediately unfolded a newspaper and obscured himself behind it. Julian's mother's elbow at once prodded insistently into his ribs. "Now you see why I won't ride on these buses by myself," she whispered.

The woman with the red and white canvas sandals had risen at the same time the Negro sat down and had gone further back in the bus and taken the seat of the woman who had got off. His mother leaned forward and cast her an approving look.

Julian rose, crossed the aisle, and sat down in the place of the woman with 65
the canvas sandals. From this position, he looked serenely across at his mother. Her face had turned an angry red. He stared at her, making his eyes the eyes of a stranger. He felt his tension suddenly lift as if he had openly declared war on her.

He would have liked to get in conversation with the Negro and to talk with him about art or politics or any subject that would be above the comprehension of those around them, but the man remained entrenched behind his paper. He was either ignoring the change of seating or had never noticed it. There was no way for Julian to convey his sympathy.

His mother kept her eyes fixed reproachfully on his face. The woman with the protruding teeth was looking at him avidly as if he were a type of monster new to her.

"Do you have a light?" he asked the Negro.

Without looking away from his paper, the man reached in his pocket and handed him a packet of matches.

70 "Thanks," Julian said. For a moment he held the matches foolishly. A NO SMOKING sign looked down upon him from over the door. This alone would not have deterred him; he had no cigarettes. He had quit smoking some months before because he could not afford it. "Sorry," he muttered and handed back the matches. The Negro lowered the paper and gave him an annoyed look. He took the matches and raised the paper again.

His mother continued to gaze at him but she did not take advantage of his momentary discomfort. Her eyes retained their battered look. Her face seemed to be unnaturally red, as if her blood pressure had risen. Julian allowed no glimmer of sympathy to show on his face. Having got the advantage, he wanted desperately to keep it and carry it through. He would have liked to teach her a lesson that would last her a while, but there seemed no way to continue the point. The Negro refused to come out from behind his paper.

Julian folded his arms and looked stolidly before him, facing her but as if he did not see her, as if he had ceased to recognize her existence. He visualized a scene in which, the bus having reached their stop, he would remain in his seat and when she said, "Aren't you going to get off?" he would look at her as at a stranger who had rashly addressed him. The corner they got off on was usually deserted, but it was well lighted and it would not hurt her to walk by herself the four blocks to the Y. He decided to wait until the time came and then decide whether or not he would let her get off by herself. He would have to be at the Y at ten to bring her back, but he could leave her wondering if he was going to show up. There was no reason for her to think she could always depend on him.

He retired again into the high-ceilinged room sparsely settled with large pieces of antique furniture. His soul expanded momentarily but then he became aware of his mother across from him and the vision shriveled. He studied her coldly. Her feet in little pumps dangled like a child's and did not quite reach the floor. She was training on him an exaggerated look of reproach. He felt completely detached from her. At that moment he could with pleasure have slapped her as he would have slapped a particularly obnoxious child in his charge.

He began to imagine various unlikely ways by which he could teach her a lesson. He might make friends with some distinguished Negro professor or lawyer and bring him home to spend the evening. He would be entirely justified but her blood pressure would rise to 300. He could not push her to the extent of making her have a stroke, and moreover, he had never been successful at making any Negro friends. He had tried to strike up an acquaintance on the bus with some of the better types, with ones that looked like professors or ministers or lawyers. One morning he had sat down next to a distinguished-looking dark brown man who had answered his questions with a sonorous solemnity but who had turned out to be an undertaker. Another day he had sat down beside a cigar-smoking Negro with a diamond ring on his finger, but after a few stilted pleasantries, the Negro had rung the buzzer and risen, slipping two lottery tickets into Julian's hand as he climbed over him to leave.

He imagined his mother lying desperately ill and his being able to secure 75
only a Negro doctor for her. He toyed with that idea for a few minutes and then dropped it for a momentary vision of himself participating as a sympathizer in a sit-in demonstration. This was possible but he did not linger with it. Instead, he approached the ultimate horror. He brought home a beautiful suspiciously Negroid woman. Prepare yourself, he said. There is nothing you can do about it. This is the woman I've chosen. She's intelligent, dignified, even good, and she's suffered and she hasn't thought it *fun*. Now persecute us, go ahead and persecute us. Drive her out of here, but remember, you're driving me too. His eyes were narrowed and through the indignation he had generated, he saw his mother across the aisle, purple-faced, shrunken to the dwarflike proportions of her moral nature, sitting like a mummy beneath the ridiculous banner of her hat.

He was tilted out of his fantasy again as the bus stopped. The door opened with a sucking hiss and out of the dark a large, gaily dressed, sullen-looking colored woman got on with a little boy. The child, who might have been four, had on a short plaid suit and a Tyrolean hat with a blue feather in it. Julian hoped that he would sit down beside him and that the woman would push in beside his mother. He could think of no better arrangement.

As she waited for her tokens, the woman was surveying the seating possibilities — he hoped with the idea of sitting where she was least wanted. There was something familiar-looking about her but Julian could not place what it was. She was a giant of a woman. Her face was set not only to meet opposition but to seek it out. The downward tilt of her large lower lip was like a warning sign: DON'T TAMPER WITH ME. Her bulging figure was encased in a green crepe dress and her feet overflowed in red shoes. She had on a hideous hat. A purple velvet flap came down on one side of it and stood up on the other; the rest of it was green and looked like a cushion with the stuffing out. She carried a mammoth red pocketbook that bulged throughout as if it were stuffed with rocks.

To Julian's disappointment, the little boy climbed up on the empty seat beside his mother. His mother lumped all children, black and white, into the common category, "cute," and she thought little Negroes were on the whole cuter than little white children. She smiled at the little boy as he climbed on the seat.

Meanwhile the woman was bearing down upon the empty seat beside Julian. To his annoyance, she squeezed herself into it. He saw his mother's face change as the woman settled herself next to him and he realized with satisfaction that this was more objectionable to her than it was to him. Her face seemed almost gray and there was a look of dull recognition in her eyes, as if suddenly she had sickened at some awful confrontation. Julian saw that it was because she and the woman had, in a sense, swapped sons. Though his mother would not realize the symbolic significance of this, she would feel it. His amusement showed plainly on his face.

The woman next to him muttered something unintelligible to herself. He 80
was conscious of a kind of bristling next to him, muted growling like that of an angry cat. He could not see anything but the red pocketbook upright on the bulging green thighs. He visualized the woman as she had stood waiting for her

tokens — the ponderous figure, rising from the red shoes upward over the solid hips, the mammoth bosom, the haughty face, to the green and purple hat.

His eyes widened.

The vision of the two hats, identical, broke upon him with the radiance of a brilliant sunrise. His face was suddenly lit with joy. He could not believe that Fate had thrust upon his mother such a lesson. He gave a loud chuckle so that she would look at him and see that he saw. She turned her eyes on him slowly. The blue in them seemed to have turned a bruised purple. For a moment he had an uncomfortable sense of her innocence, but it lasted only a second before principle rescued him. Justice entitled him to laugh. His grin hardened until it said to her as plainly as if he were saying aloud: Your punishment exactly fits your pettiness. This should teach you a permanent lesson.

Her eyes shifted to the woman. She seemed unable to bear looking at him and to find the woman preferable. He became conscious again of the bristling presence at his side. The woman was rumbling like a volcano about to become active. His mother's mouth began to twitch slightly at one corner. With a sinking heart, he saw incipient signs of recovery on her face and realized that this was going to strike her suddenly as funny and was going to be no lesson at all. She kept her eyes on the woman and an amused smile came over her face as if the woman were a monkey that had stolen her hat. The little Negro was looking up at her with large fascinated eyes. He had been trying to attract her attention for some time.

"Carver!" the woman said suddenly. "Come heah!"

When he saw that the spotlight was on him at last, Carver drew his feet up and turned himself toward Julian's mother and giggled.

"Carver!" the woman said. "You heah me? Come heah!"

Carver slid down from the seat but remained squatting with his back against the base of it, his head turned slyly around toward Julian's mother, who was smiling at him. The woman reached a hand across the aisle and snatched him to her. He righted himself and hung backwards on her knees, grinning at Julian's mother. "Isn't he cute?" Julian's mother said to the woman with the protruding teeth.

"I reckon he is," the woman said without conviction.

The Negress yanked him upright but he eased out of her grip and shot across the aisle and scrambled, giggling wildly, onto the seat beside his love.

"I think he likes me," Julian's mother said, and smiled at the woman. It was the smile she used when she was being particularly gracious to an inferior. Julian saw everything lost. The lesson had rolled off her like rain on a roof.

The woman stood up and yanked the little boy off the seat as if she were snatching him from contagion. Julian could feel the rage in her at having no weapon like his mother's smile. She gave the child a sharp slap across his leg. He howled once and then thrust his head into her stomach and kicked his feet against her shins. "Behave," she said vehemently.

The bus stopped and the Negro who had been reading the newspaper got off. The woman moved over and set the little boy down with a thump between herself and Julian. She held him firmly by the knee. In a moment he put his hands in front of his face and peeped at Julian's mother through his fingers.

"I see yoooooooo!" she said and put her hand in front of her face and peeped at him.

The woman slapped his hand down. "Quit yo' foolishness," she said, "before I knock the living Jesus out of you!"

Julian was thankful that the next stop was theirs. He reached up and pulled 95
the cord. The woman reached up and pulled it at the same time. Oh my God, he thought. He had the terrible intuition that when they got off the bus together, his mother would open her purse and give the little boy a nickel. The gesture would be as natural to her as breathing. The bus stopped and the woman got up and lunged to the front, dragging the child, who wished to stay on, after her. Julian and his mother got up and followed. As they neared the door, Julian tried to relieve her of her pocketbook.

"No," she murmured, "I want to give the little boy a nickel."

"No!" Julian hissed. "No!"

She smiled down at the child and opened her bag. The bus door opened and the woman picked him up by the arm and descended with him, hanging at her hip. Once in the street she set him down and shook him.

Julian's mother had to close her purse while she got down the bus step but as soon as her feet were on the ground, she opened it again and began to rummage inside. "I can't find but a penny," she whispered, "but it looks like a new one."

"Don't do it!" Julian said fiercely between his teeth. There was a streetlight 100
on the corner and she hurried to get under it so that she could better see into her pocketbook. The woman was heading off rapidly down the street with the child still hanging backward on her hand.

"Oh little boy!" Julian's mother called and took a few quick steps and caught up with them just beyond the lamppost. "Here's a bright new penny for you," and she held out the coin, which shone bronze in the dim light.

The huge woman turned and for a moment stood, her shoulders lifted and her face frozen with frustrated rage, and stared at Julian's mother. Then all at once she seemed to explode like a piece of machinery that had been given one ounce of pressure too much. Julian saw the black fist swing out with the red pocketbook. He shut his eyes and cringed as he heard the woman shout, "He don't take nobody's pennies!" When he opened his eyes, the woman was disappearing down the street with the little boy staring wide-eyed over her shoulder. Julian's mother was sitting on the sidewalk.

"I told you not to do that," Julian said angrily. "I told you not to do that!"

He stood over her for a minute, gritting his teeth. Her legs were stretched out in front of her and her hat was on her lap. He squatted down and looked her in the face. It was totally expressionless. "You got exactly what you deserved," he said. "Now get up."

He picked up her pocketbook and put what had fallen out back in it. He 105
picked the hat up off her lap. The penny caught his eye on the sidewalk and he picked that up and let it drop before her eyes into the purse. Then he stood up and leaned over and held his hands out to pull her up. She remained immobile. He sighed. Rising above them on either side were black apartment buildings, marked with irregular rectangles of light. At the end of the block a man came out of a door and walked off in the opposite direction. "All right," he said, "suppose somebody happens by and wants to know why you're sitting on the sidewalk?"

She took the hand and, breathing hard, pulled heavily up on it and then stood for a moment, swaying slightly as if the spots of light in the darkness were circling around her. Her eyes, shadowed and confused, finally settled on his face. He did not try to conceal his irritation. "I hope this teaches you a lesson," he said. She leaned forward and her eyes raked his face. She seemed trying to determine his identity. Then, as if she found nothing familiar about him, she started off with a headlong movement in the wrong direction.

"Aren't you going on to the Y?" he asked.

"Home," she muttered.

"Well, are we walking?"

For answer she kept going. Julian followed along, his hands behind him. 110
He saw no reason to let the lesson she had had go without backing it up with an explanation of its meaning. She might as well be made to understand what had happened to her. "Don't think that was just an uppity Negro woman," he said. "That was the whole colored race which will no longer take your condescending pennies. That was your black double. She can wear the same hat as you, and to be sure," he added gratuitously (because he thought it was funny), "it looked better on her than it did on you. What all this means," he said, "is that the old world is gone. The old manners are obsolete and your graciousness is not worth a damn." He thought bitterly of the house that had been lost for him. "You aren't who you think you are," he said.

She continued to plow ahead, paying no attention to him. Her hair had come undone on one side. She dropped her pocketbook and took no notice. He stooped and picked it up and handed it to her but she did not take it.

"You needn't act as if the world had come to an end," he said, "because it hasn't. From now on you've got to live in a new world and face a few realities for a change. Buck up," he said, "it won't kill you."

She was breathing fast.

"Let's wait on the bus," he said.

"Home," she said thickly. 115

"I hate to see you behave like this," he said. "Just like a child. I should be able to expect more of you." He decided to stop where he was and make her stop and wait for a bus. "I'm not going any farther," he said, stopping. "We're going on the bus."

She continued to go on as if she had not heard him. He took a few steps and caught her arm and stopped her. He looked into her face and caught his breath. He was looking into a face he had never seen before. "Tell Grandpa to come get me," she said.

He stared, stricken.

"Tell Caroline to come get me," she said.

Stunned, he let her go and she lurched forward again, walking as if one 120
leg were shorter than the other. A tide of darkness seemed to be sweeping her from him. "Mother!" he cried. "Darling, sweetheart, wait!" Crumpling, she fell to the pavement. He dashed forward and fell at her side, crying, "Mamma, Mamma!" He turned her over. Her face was fiercely distorted. One eye, large and staring, moved slightly to the left as if it had become unmoored. The other remained fixed on him, raked his face again, found nothing, and closed.

"Wait here, wait here!" he cried and jumped up and began to run for help toward a cluster of lights he saw in the distance ahead of him. "Help, help!" he shouted, but his voice was thin, scarcely a thread of sound. The lights drifted farther away the faster he ran and his feet moved numbly as if they carried him nowhere. The tide of darkness seemed to sweep him back to her, postponing from moment to moment his entry into the world of guilt and sorrow.

Considerations

1. What is the significance of the setting in this story? How does it shape the characters' attitudes and behavior?
2. Are Julian's perceptions of himself and his mother reliable? Why or why not?
3. What "lesson" does Julian want to teach his mother? Why does he treat her so badly?
4. What does the black woman's hat mean to Julian?
5. Why does the black woman knock down Julian's mother?
6. How is Julian's mother's affliction foreshadowed?
7. What does Julian discover about himself and his world at the end of the story?
8. How does the title help you to interpret the story? What rises and what converges?
9. Discuss the accuracy of the following description of Julian and his relationship to his mother: "In spite of growing up dominated by a small mind, he had ended up with a large one; in spite of all her foolish views, he was free of prejudice and unafraid to face facts. Most miraculous of all, instead of being blinded by love for her as she was for him, he had cut himself emotionally free of her and could see her with complete objectivity."
10. Explain how the story reflects social change in the South.
11. Compare and contrast the racial attitudes of Julian and the black woman.

Connections

1. Explain the similarities and differences between Julian's view of his mother and Hulga's view of hers in "Good Country People." Explain whether you think either of them changes his or her view.
2. Write an essay exploring the meaning of the mansion in this story and Miss Emily's house in Faulkner's "A Rose for Emily" (p. 47).
3. Choose a topic that you think Julian's mother and the narrator's mother in Raymond Carver's "Boxes" (p. 436) would have in common and write a dialogue of their conversation on that topic. Try to reveal something essential about each character through that dialogue.

Revelation

1964

The doctor's waiting room, which was very small, was almost full when the Turpins entered and Mrs. Turpin, who was very large, made it look even smaller by her presence. She stood looming at the head of the magazine table set in the center of it, a living demonstration that the room was inadequate and ridiculous. Her little bright black eyes took in all the patients as she sized up the seating situation. There was one vacant chair and a place on the sofa occupied by a blond child in a dirty blue romper who should have been told to move over and make room for the lady. He was five or six, but Mrs. Turpin saw at once that no one was going to tell him to move over. He was slumped down in the seat, his arms idle at his sides and his eyes idle in his head; his nose ran unchecked.

Mrs. Turpin put a firm hand on Claud's shoulder and said in a voice that included anyone who wanted to listen, "Claud, you sit in that chair there," and gave him a push down into the vacant one. Claud was florid and bald and sturdy, somewhat shorter than Mrs. Turpin, but he sat down as if he were accustomed to doing what she told him to.

Mrs. Turpin remained standing. The only man in the room besides Claud was a lean stringy old fellow with a rusty hand spread out on each knee, whose eyes were closed as if he were asleep or dead or pretending to be so as not to get up and offer her his seat. Her gaze settled agreeably on a well-dressed gray-haired lady whose eyes met hers and whose expression said: if that child belonged to me, he would have some manners and move over — there's plenty of room there for you and him too.

Claud looked up with a sigh and made as if to rise.

"Sit down," Mrs. Turpin said. "You know you're not supposed to stand on 5
that leg. He has an ulcer on his leg," she explained.

Claud lifted his foot onto the magazine table and rolled his trouser leg up to reveal a purple swelling on a plump marble-white calf.

"My!" the pleasant lady said. "How did you do that?"

"A cow kicked him," Mrs. Turpin said.

"Goodness!" said the lady.

Claud rolled his trouser leg down. 10

"Maybe the little boy would move over," the lady suggested, but the child did not stir.

"Somebody will be leaving in a minute," Mrs. Turpin said. She could not understand why a doctor — with as much money as they made charging five dollars a day to just stick their head in the hospital door and look at you — couldn't afford a decent-sized waiting room. This one was hardly bigger than a garage. The table was cluttered with limp-looking magazines and at one end of it there was a big green glass ash tray full of cigarette butts and cotton wads with little blood spots on them. If she had had anything to do with the running of the place, that would have been emptied every so often. There were no chairs against the wall at the head of the room. It had a rectangular-shaped panel in it that permitted a view of the office where the nurse came and went and the secretary listened to the radio. A plastic fern in a gold pot sat in the opening and trailed its fronds down almost to the floor. The radio was softly playing gospel music.

Just then the inner door opened and a nurse with the highest stack of yellow hair Mrs. Turpin had ever seen put her face in the crack and called for the next patient. The woman sitting beside Claud grasped the two arms of her chair and hoisted herself up; she pulled her dress free from her legs and lumbered through the door where the nurse had disappeared.

Mrs. Turpin eased into the vacant chair, which held her tight as a corset. "I wish I could reduce," she said, and rolled her eyes and gave a comic sigh.

"Oh, *you* aren't fat," the stylish lady said. 15

"Ooooo I am too," Mrs. Turpin said. "Claud he eats all he wants to and never weighs over one hundred and seventy-five pounds, but me I just look at something good to eat and I gain some weight," and her stomach and shoulders shook with laughter. "You can eat all you want to, can't you, Claud?" she asked, turning to him.

Claud only grinned.

"Well, as long as you have such a good disposition," the stylish lady said, "I don't think it makes a bit of difference what size you are. You just can't beat a good disposition."

Next to her was a fat girl of eighteen or nineteen, scowling into a thick blue book which Mrs. Turpin saw was entitled *Human Development.* The girl raised her head and directed her scowl at Mrs. Turpin as if she did not like her looks. She appeared annoyed that anyone should speak while she tried to read. The poor girl's face was blue with acne and Mrs. Turpin thought how pitiful it was to have a face like that at that age. She gave the girl a friendly smile but the girl only scowled the harder. Mrs. Turpin herself was fat but she had always had good skin, and though she was forty-seven years old, there was not a wrinkle in her face except around her eyes from laughing too much.

Next to the ugly girl was the child, still in exactly the same position, and 20
next to him was a thin leathery old woman in a cotton print dress. She and Claud had three sacks of chicken feed in their pump house that was in the same print. She had seen from the first that the child belonged with the old woman. She could tell by the way they sat — kind of vacant and white-trashy, as if they would sit there until Doomsday if nobody called and told them to get up. And at right angles but next to the well-dressed pleasant lady was a lank-faced woman who was certainly the child's mother. She had on a yellow sweat shirt and wine-colored slacks, both gritty-looking, and the rims of her lips were stained with snuff. Her dirty yellow hair was tied behind with a little piece of red paper ribbon. Worse than niggers any day, Mrs. Turpin thought.

The gospel hymn playing was, "When I looked up and He looked down," and Mrs. Turpin, who knew it, supplied the last line mentally, "And wona these days I know I'll we-eara crown."

Without appearing to, Mrs. Turpin always noticed people's feet. The well-dressed lady had on red and gray suede shoes to match her dress. Mrs. Turpin had on her good black patent leather pumps. The ugly girl had on Girl Scout shoes and heavy socks. The old woman had on tennis shoes and the white-trashy mother had on what appeared to be bedroom slippers, black straw with gold braid threaded through them — exactly what you would have expected her to have on.

Sometimes at night when she couldn't go to sleep, Mrs. Turpin would occupy herself with the question of who she would have chosen to be if she couldn't have been herself. If Jesus had said to her before he made her, "There's only two places available for you. You can either be a nigger or white-trash," what would she have said? "Please, Jesus, please," she would have said, "just let me wait until there's another place available," and he would have said, "No, you have to go right now and I have only those two places so make up your mind." She would have wiggled and squirmed and begged and pleaded but it would have been no use and finally she would have said, "All right, make me a nigger then — but that don't mean a trashy one." And he would have made her a neat clean respectable Negro woman, herself but black.

Next to the child's mother was a red-headed youngish woman, reading one of the magazines and working a piece of chewing gum, hell for leather, as Claud would say. Mrs. Turpin could not see the woman's feet. She was not white-trash, just common. Sometimes Mrs. Turpin occupied herself at night naming the classes of people. On the bottom of the heap were most colored people, not the kind she would have been if she had been one, but most of them; then next to them — not above, just away from — were the white-trash; then above them were the home-owners, and above them the home-and-land owners, to which she and Claud belonged. Above she and Claud were people with a lot of money and much bigger houses and much more land. But here the complexity of it would begin to bear in on her, for some of the people with a lot of money were common and ought to be below she and Claud and some of the people who had good blood had lost their money and had to rent and then there were colored people who owned their homes and land as well. There was a colored dentist in town who had two red Lincolns and a swimming pool and a farm with registered white-face cattle on it. Usually by the time she had fallen asleep all the classes of people were moiling and roiling around in her head, and she would dream they were all crammed in together in a box car, being ridden off to be put in a gas oven.

"That's a beautiful clock," she said and nodded to her right. It was a big 25
wall clock, the face encased in a brass sunburst.

"Yes, it's very pretty," the stylish lady said agreeably. "And right on the dot too," she added, glancing at her watch.

The ugly girl beside her cast an eye upward at the clock, smirked, then looked directly at Mrs. Turpin and smirked again. Then she returned her eyes to her book. She was obviously the lady's daughter because, although they didn't look anything alike as to disposition, they both had the same shape of face and the same blue eyes. On the lady they sparkled pleasantly but in the girl's seared face they appeared alternately to smolder and to blaze.

What if Jesus had said, "All right, you can be white-trash or a nigger or ugly"!

Mrs. Turpin felt an awful pity for the girl, though she thought it was one thing to be ugly and another to act ugly.

The woman with the snuff-stained lips turned around in her chair and 30
looked up at the clock. Then she turned back and appeared to look a little to the side of Mrs. Turpin. There was a cast in one of her eyes. "You want to know wher you can get you one of themther clocks?" she asked in a loud voice.

"No, I already have a nice clock," Mrs. Turpin said. Once somebody like her got a leg in the conversation, she would be all over it.

"You can get you one with green stamps," the woman said. "That's most likely wher he got hisn. Save you up enough, you can get you most anythang. I got me some joo'ry."

Ought to have got you a wash rag and some soap, Mrs. Turpin thought.

"I get contour sheets with mine," the pleasant lady said.

The daughter slammed her book shut. She looked straight in front of her, 35
directly through Mrs. Turpin and on through the yellow curtain and the plate glass window which made the wall behind her. The girl's eyes seemed lit all of a sudden with a peculiar light, an unnatural light like night road signs give. Mrs. Turpin turned her head to see if there was anything going on outside that she should see, but she could not see anything. Figures passing cast only a pale

shadow through the curtain. There was no reason the girl should single her out for her ugly looks.

"Miss Finley," the nurse said, cracking the door. The gum-chewing woman got up and passed in front of her and Claud and went into the office. She had on red high-heeled shoes.

Directly across the table, the ugly girl's eyes were fixed on Mrs. Turpin as if she had some very special reason for disliking her.

"This is wonderful weather, isn't it?" the girl's mother said.

"It's good weather for cotton if you can get the niggers to pick it," Mrs. Turpin said, "but niggers don't want to pick cotton any more. You can't get the white folks to pick it and now you can't get the niggers — because they got to be right up there with the white folks."

"They gonna *try* anyways," the white-trash woman said, leaning forward. 40

"Do you have one of the cotton-picking machines?" the pleasant lady asked.

"No," Mrs. Turpin said, "they leave half the cotton in the field. We don't have much cotton anyway. If you want to make it farming now, you have to have a little of everything. We got a couple of acres of cotton and a few hogs and chickens and just enough white-face that Claud can look after them himself."

"One thang I don't want," the white-trash woman said, wiping her mouth with the back of her hand. "Hogs. Nasty stinking things, a-gruntin and a-rootin all over the place."

Mrs. Turpin gave her the merest edge of her attention. "Our hogs are not dirty and they don't stink," she said. "They're cleaner than some children I've seen. Their feet never touch the ground. We have a pig parlor — that's where you raise them on concrete," she explained to the pleasant lady, "and Claud scoots them down with the hose every afternoon and washes off the floor." Cleaner by far than that child right there, she thought. Poor nasty little thing. He had not moved except to put the thumb of his dirty hand into his mouth.

The woman turned her face away from Mrs. Turpin. "I know I wouldn't 45
scoot down no hog with no hose," she said to the wall.

You wouldn't have no hog to scoot down, Mrs. Turpin said to herself.

"A-gruntin and a-rootin and a-groanin," the woman muttered.

"We got a little of everything," Mrs. Turpin said to the pleasant lady. "It's no use in having more than you can handle yourself with help like it is. We found enough niggers to pick our cotton this year but Claud he has to go after them and take them home again in the evening. They can't walk that half a mile. No they can't. I tell you," she said and laughed merrily, "I sure am tired of buttering up niggers, but you got to love em if you want em to work for you. When they come in the morning, I run out and I say, 'Hi yawl this morning?' and when Claud drives them off to the field I just wave to beat the band and they just wave back." And she waved her hand rapidly to illustrate.

"Like you read out of the same book," the lady said, showing she understood perfectly.

"Child, yes," Mrs. Turpin said. "And when they come in from the field, I 50
run out with a bucket of icewater. That's the way it's going to be from now on," she said. "You may as well face it."

"One thang I know," the white-trash woman said. "Two thangs I ain't going to do: love no niggers or scoot down no hog with no hose." And she let out a bark of contempt.

The look that Mrs. Turpin and the pleasant lady exchanged indicated they both understood that you had to *have* certain things before you could *know* certain things. But every time Mrs. Turpin exchanged a look with the lady, she was aware that the ugly girl's peculiar eyes were still on her, and she had trouble bringing her attention back to the conversation.

"When you got something," she said, "you got to look after it." And when you ain't got a thing but breath and britches, she added to herself, you can afford to come to town every morning and just sit on the Court House coping and spit.

A grotesque revolving shadow passed across the curtain behind her and was thrown palely on the opposite wall. Then a bicycle clattered down against the outside of the building. The door opened and a colored boy glided in with a tray from the drugstore. It had two large red and white paper cups on it with tops on them. He was a tall, very black boy in discolored white pants and a green nylon shirt. He was chewing gum slowly, as if to music. He set the tray down in the office opening next to the fern and stuck his head through to look for the secretary. She was not in there. He rested his arms on the ledge and waited, his narrow bottom stuck out, swaying to the left and right. He raised a hand over his head and scratched the base of his skull.

"You see that button there, boy?" Mrs. Turpin said. "You can punch that 55
and she'll come. She's probably in the back somewhere."

"Is that right?" the boy said agreeably, as if he had never seen the button before. He leaned to the right and put his finger on it. "She sometime out," he said and twisted around to face his audience, his elbows behind him on the counter. The nurse appeared and he twisted back again. She handed him a dollar and he rooted in his pocket and made the change and counted it out to her. She gave him fifteen cents for a tip and he went out with the empty tray. The heavy door swung to slowly and closed at length with the sound of suction. For a moment no one spoke.

"They ought to send all them niggers back to Africa," the white-trash woman said. "That's wher they come from in the first place."

"Oh, I couldn't do without my good colored friends," the pleasant lady said.

"There's a heap of things worse than a nigger," Mrs. Turpin agreed. "It's all kinds of them just like it's all kinds of us."

"Yes, and it takes all kinds to make the world go round," the lady said in 60
her musical voice.

As she said it, the raw-complexioned girl snapped her teeth together. Her lower lip turned downwards and inside out, revealing the pale pink inside of her mouth. After a second it rolled back up. It was the ugliest face Mrs. Turpin had ever seen anyone make and for a moment she was certain that the girl had made it at her. She was looking at her as if she had known and disliked her all her life — all of Mrs. Turpin's life, it seemed too, not just all the girl's life. Why, girl, I don't even know you, Mrs. Turpin said silently.

She forced her attention back to the discussion. "It wouldn't be practical to send them back to Africa," she said. "They wouldn't want to go. They got it too good here."

"Wouldn't be what they wanted—if I had anythang to do with it," the woman said.

"It wouldn't be a way in the world you could get all the niggers back over there," Mrs. Turpin said. "They'd be hiding out and lying down and turning sick on you and wailing and hollering and raring and pitching. It wouldn't be a way in the world to get them over there."

"They got over here," the trashy woman said. "Get back like they got over." 65

"It wasn't so many of them then," Mrs. Turpin explained.

The woman looked at Mrs. Turpin as if here was an idiot indeed but Mrs. Turpin was not bothered by the look, considering where it came from.

"Nooo," she said, "they're going to stay here where they can go to New York and marry white folks and improve their color. That's what they all want to do, every one of them, improve their color."

"You know what comes of that, don't you?" Claud asked.

"No, Claud, what?" Mrs. Turpin said. 70

Claud's eyes twinkled. "White-faced niggers," he said with never a smile.

Everybody in the office laughed except the white-trash and the ugly girl. The girl gripped the book in her lap with white fingers. The trashy woman looked around her from face to face as if she thought they were all idiots. The old woman in the feed sack dress continued to gaze expressionless across the floor at the high-top shoes of the man opposite her, the one who had been pretending to be asleep when the Turpins came in. He was laughing heartily, his hands still spread out on his knees. The child had fallen to the side and was lying now almost face down in the old woman's lap.

While they recovered from their laughter, the nasal chorus on the radio kept the room from silence.

"You go to blank blank
And I'll go to mine
But we'll all blank along
To-geth-ther,
And all along the blank
We'll hep eachother out
Smile-ling in any kind of
Weath-ther!"

Mrs. Turpin didn't catch every word but she caught enough to agree with the spirit of the song and it turned her thoughts sober. To help anybody out that needed it was her philosophy of life. She never spared herself when she found somebody in need, whether they were white or black, trash or decent. And of all she had to be thankful for, she was most thankful that this was so. If Jesus had said, "You can be high society and have all the money you want and be thin and svelte-like, but you can't be a good woman with it," she would have had to say, "Well don't make me that then. Make me a good woman and it don't matter what else, how fat or how ugly or how poor!" Her heart rose. He had not made her a nigger or white-trash or ugly! He had made her herself and given her a little of everything. Jesus, thank you! she said. Thank you thank you thank you! Whenever she counted her blessings she felt as buoyant as if she weighed one hundred and twenty-five pounds instead of one hundred and eighty.

"What's wrong with your little boy?" the pleasant lady asked the white- 75
trashy woman.

"He has a ulcer," the woman said proudly. "He ain't give me a minute's peace since he was born. Him and her are just alike," she said, nodding at the old woman, who was running her leathery fingers through the child's pale hair. "Look like I can't get nothing down them two but Co' Cola and candy."

That's all you try to get down em, Mrs. Turpin said to herself. Too lazy to light the fire. There was nothing you could tell her about people like them that she didn't know already. And it was not just that they didn't have anything. Because if you gave them everything, in two weeks it would all be broken or filthy or they would have chopped it up for lightwood. She knew all this from her own experience. Help them you must, but help them you couldn't.

All at once the ugly girl turned her lips inside out again. Her eyes fixed like two drills on Mrs. Turpin. This time there was no mistaking that there was something urgent behind them.

Girl, Mrs. Turpin exclaimed silently, I haven't done a thing to you! The girl might be confusing her with somebody else. There was no need to sit by and let herself be intimidated. "You must be in college," she said boldly, looking directly at the girl. "I see you reading a book there."

The girl continued to stare and pointedly did not answer. 80

Her mother blushed at this rudeness. "The lady asked you a question, Mary Grace," she said under her breath.

"I have ears," Mary Grace said.

The poor mother blushed again. "Mary Grace goes to Wellesley College," she explained. She twisted one of the buttons on her dress. "In Massachusetts," she added with a grimace. "And in the summer she just keeps right on studying. Just reads all the time, a real book worm. She's done real well at Wellesley; she's taking English and Math and History and Psychology and Social Studies," she rattled on, "and I think it's too much. I think she ought to get out and have fun."

The girl looked as if she would like to hurl them all through the plate glass window.

"Way up north," Mrs. Turpin murmured and thought, well, it hasn't done 85
much for her manners.

"I'd almost rather to have him sick," the white-trash woman said, wrenching the attention back to herself. "He's so mean when he ain't. Look like some children just take natural to meanness. It's some gets bad when they get sick but he was the opposite. Took sick and turned good. He don't give me no trouble now. It's me waitin to see the doctor," she said.

If I was going to send anybody back to Africa, Mrs. Turpin thought, it would be your kind, woman. "Yes, indeed," she said aloud, but looking up at the ceiling, "it's a heap of things worse than a nigger." And dirtier than a hog, she added to herself.

"I think people with bad dispositions are more to be pitied than anyone on earth," the pleasant lady said in a voice that was decidedly thin.

"I thank the Lord he has blessed me with a good one," Mrs. Turpin said. "The day has never dawned that I couldn't find something to laugh at."

"Not since she married me anyways," Claud said with a comical straight face. 90

Everybody laughed except the girl and the white-trash.

Mrs. Turpin's stomach shook. "He's such a caution," she said, "that I can't help but laugh at him."

The girl made a loud ugly noise through her teeth.

Her mother's mouth grew thin and tight. "I think the worst thing in the world," she said, "is an ungrateful person. To have everything and not appreciate it. I know a girl," she said, "who has parents who would give her anything, a little brother who loves her dearly, who is getting a good education, who wears the best clothes, but who can never say a kind word to anyone, who never smiles, who just criticizes and complains all day long."

"Is she too old to paddle?" Claud asked. 95

The girl's face was almost purple.

"Yes," the lady said, "I'm afraid there's nothing to do but leave her to her folly. Some day she'll wake up and it'll be too late."

"It never hurt anyone to smile," Mrs. Turpin said. "It just makes you feel better all over."

"Of course," the lady said sadly, "but there are just some people you can't tell anything to. They can't take criticism."

"If it's one thing I am," Mrs. Turpin said with feeling, "it's grateful. When I think who all I could have been besides myself and what all I got, a little of everything, and a good disposition besides, I just feel like shouting, 'Thank you, Jesus, for making everything the way it is!' It could have been different!" For one thing, somebody else could have got Claud. At the thought of this, she was flooded with gratitude and a terrible pang of joy ran through her. "Oh thank you, Jesus, Jesus, thank you!" she cried aloud. 100

The book struck her directly over her left eye. It struck almost at the same instant that she realized the girl was about to hurl it. Before she could utter a sound, the raw face came crashing across the table toward her, howling. The girl's fingers sank like clamps into the soft flesh of her neck. She heard the mother cry out and Claud shout, "Whoa!" There was an instant when she was certain that she was about to be in an earthquake.

All at once her vision narrowed and she saw everything as if it were happening in a small room far away, or as if she were looking at it through the wrong end of a telescope. Claud's face crumpled and fell out of sight. The nurse ran in, then out, then in again. Then the gangling figure of the doctor rushed out of the inner door. Magazines flew this way and that as the table turned over. The girl fell with a thud and Mrs. Turpin's vision suddenly reversed itself and she saw everything large instead of small. The eyes of the white-trashy woman were staring hugely at the floor. There the girl, held down on one side by the nurse and on the other by her mother, was wrenching and turning in their grasp. The doctor was kneeling astride her, trying to hold her arm down. He managed after a second to sink a long needle into it.

Mrs. Turpin felt entirely hollow except for her heart which swung from side to side as if it were agitated in a great empty drum of flesh.

"Somebody that's not busy call for the ambulance," the doctor said in the off-hand voice young doctors adopt for terrible occasions.

Mrs. Turpin could not have moved a finger. The old man who had been 105 sitting next to her skipped nimbly into the office and made the call, for the secretary still seemed to be gone.

"Claud!" Mrs. Turpin called.

He was not in his chair. She knew she must jump up and find him but she felt like some one trying to catch a train in a dream, when everything moves in slow motion and the faster you try to run the slower you go.

"Here I am," a suffocated voice, very unlike Claud's, said.

He was doubled up in the corner on the floor, pale as paper, holding his leg. She wanted to get up and go to him but she could not move. Instead, her gaze was drawn slowly downward to the churning face on the floor, which she could see over the doctor's shoulder.

The girl's eyes stopped rolling and focused on her. They seemed a much 110
lighter blue than before, as if a door that had been tightly closed behind them was now open to admit light and air.

Mrs. Turpin's head cleared and her power of motion returned. She leaned forward until she was looking directly into the fierce brilliant eyes. There was no doubt in her mind that the girl did know her, knew her in some intense and personal way, beyond time and place and condition. "What you got to say to me?" she asked hoarsely and held her breath, waiting, as for a revelation.

The girl raised her head. Her gaze locked with Mrs. Turpin's. "Go back to hell where you came from, you old wart hog," she whispered. Her voice was low but clear. Her eyes burned for a moment as if she saw with pleasure that her message had struck its target.

Mrs. Turpin sank back in her chair.

After a moment the girl's eyes closed and she turned her head wearily to the side.

The doctor rose and handed the nurse the empty syringe. He leaned over 115
and put both hands for a moment on the mother's shoulders, which were shaking. She was sitting on the floor, her lips pressed together, holding Mary Grace's hand in her lap. The girl's fingers were gripped like a baby's around her thumb. "Go on to the hospital," he said. "I'll call and make the arrangements."

"Now let's see that neck," he said in a jovial voice to Mrs. Turpin. He began to inspect her neck with his first two fingers. Two little moon-shaped lines like pink fish bones were indented over her windpipe. There was the beginning of an angry red swelling above her eye. His fingers passed over this also.

"Lea' me be," she said thickly and shook him off. "See about Claud. She kicked him."

"I'll see about him in a minute," he said and felt her pulse. He was a thin gray-haired man, given to pleasantries. "Go home and have yourself a vacation the rest of the day," he said and patted her on the shoulder.

Quit your pattin me, Mrs. Turpin growled to herself.

"And put an ice pack over that eye," he said. Then he went and squatted 120
down beside Claud and looked at his leg. After a moment he pulled him up and Claud limped after him into the office.

Until the ambulance came, the only sounds in the room were the tremulous moans of the girl's mother, who continued to sit on the floor. The white-trash woman did not take her eyes off the girl. Mrs. Turpin looked straight ahead at nothing. Presently the ambulance drew up, a long dark shadow, behind the curtain. The attendants came in and set the stretcher down beside the girl and lifted her expertly onto it and carried her out. The nurse helped the mother gather up her things. The shadow of the ambulance moved silently away and the nurse came back in the office.

"That ther girl is going to be a lunatic, ain't she?" the white-trash woman asked the nurse, but the nurse kept on to the back and never answered her.

"Yes, she's going to be a lunatic," the white-trash woman said to the rest of them.

"Po' critter," the old woman murmured. The child's face was still in her lap. His eyes looked idly out over her knees. He had not moved during the disturbance except to draw one leg up under him.

"I thank Gawd," the white-trash woman said fervently, "I ain't a lunatic." 125

Claud came limping out and the Turpins went home.

As their pick-up truck turned into their own dirt road and made the crest of the hill, Mrs. Turpin gripped the window ledge and looked out suspiciously. The land sloped gracefully down through a field dotted with lavender weeds and at the start of the rise their small yellow frame house, with its little flower beds spread out around it like a fancy apron, sat primly in its accustomed place between two giant hickory trees. She would not have been startled to see a burnt wound between two blackened chimneys.

Neither of them felt like eating so they put on their house clothes and lowered the shade in the bedroom and lay down, Claud with his leg on a pillow and herself with a damp washcloth over her eye. The instant she was flat on her back, the image of a razor-backed hog with warts on its face and horns coming out behind its ears snorted into her head. She moaned, a low quiet moan.

"I am not," she said tearfully, "a wart hog. From hell." But the denial had no force. The girl's eyes and her words, even the tone of her voice, low but clear, directed only to her, brooked no repudiation. She had been singled out for the message, though there was trash in the room to whom it might justly have been applied. The full force of this fact struck her only now. There was a woman there who was neglecting her own child but she had been overlooked. The message had been given to Ruby Turpin, a respectable, hard-working, church-going woman. The tears dried. Her eyes began to burn instead with wrath.

She rose on her elbow and the washcloth fell into her hand. Claud was 130
lying on his back, snoring. She wanted to tell him what the girl had said. At the same time, she did not wish to put the image of herself as a wart hog from hell into his mind.

"Hey, Claud," she muttered and pushed his shoulder.

Claud opened one pale baby blue eye.

She looked into it warily. He did not think about anything. He just went his way.

"Wha, whasit?" he said and closed the eye again.

"Nothing," she said. "Does your leg pain you?" 135

"Hurts like hell," Claud said.

"It'll quit terreckly," she said and lay back down. In a moment Claud was snoring again. For the rest of the afternoon they lay there. Claud slept. She scowled at the ceiling. Occasionally she raised her fist and made a small stabbing motion over her chest as if she was defending her innocence to invisible guests who were like the comforters of Job, reasonable-seeming but wrong.

About five-thirty Claud stirred. "Got to go after those niggers," he sighed, not moving.

She was looking straight up as if there were unintelligible handwriting on the ceiling. The protuberance over her eye had turned a greenish-blue. "Listen here," she said.

"What?" 140

"Kiss me."

Claud leaned over and kissed her loudly on the mouth. He pinched her side and their hands interlocked. Her expression of ferocious concentration did not change. Claud got up, groaning and growling, and limped off. She continued to study the ceiling.

She did not get up until she heard the pick-up truck coming back with the Negroes. Then she rose and thrust her feet in her brown oxfords, which she did not bother to lace, and stumped out onto the back porch and got her red plastic bucket. She emptied a tray of ice cubes into it and filled it half full of water and went out into the back yard. Every afternoon after Claud brought the hands in, one of the boys helped him put out hay and the rest waited in the back of the truck until he was ready to take them home. The truck was parked in the shade under one of the hickory trees.

"Hi yawl this morning?" Mrs. Turpin asked grimly, appearing with the bucket and the dipper. There were three women and a boy in the truck.

"Us doin nicely," the oldest woman said. "Hi you doin?" and her gaze 145
struck immediately on the dark lump on Mrs. Turpin's forehead. "You done fell down, ain't you?" she asked in a solicitous voice. The old woman was dark and almost toothless. She had on an old felt hat of Claud's set back on her head. The other two women were younger and lighter and they both had new bright green sunhats. One of them had hers on her head; the other had taken hers off and the boy was grinning beneath it.

Mrs. Turpin set the bucket down on the floor of the truck. "Yawl hep yourselves," she said. She looked around to make sure Claud had gone. "No, I didn't fall down," she said, folding her arms. "It was something worse than that."

"Ain't nothing bad happen to you!" the old woman said. She said it as if they all knew that Mrs. Turpin was protected in some special way by Divine Providence. "You just had you a little fall."

"We were in town at the doctor's office for where the cow kicked Mr. Turpin," Mrs. Turpin said in a flat tone that indicated they could leave off their foolishness. "And there was this girl there. A big fat girl with her face all broke out. I could look at that girl and tell she was peculiar but I couldn't tell how. And me and her mama was just talking and going along and all of a sudden WHAM! She throws this big book she was reading at me and . . ."

"Naw!" the old woman cried out.

"And then she jumps over the table and commences to choke me." 150

"Naw!" they all exclaimed, "naw!"

"Hi come she do that?" the old woman asked. "What ail her?"

Mrs. Turpin only glared in front of her.

"Somethin ail her," the old woman said.

"They carried her off in an ambulance," Mrs. Turpin continued, "but before 155
she went she was rolling on the floor and they were trying to hold her down

to give her a shot and she said something to me." She paused. "You know what she said to me?"

"What she say?" they asked.

"She said," Mrs. Turpin began, and stopped, her face very dark and heavy. The sun was getting whiter and whiter, blanching the sky overhead so that the leaves of the hickory tree were black in the face of it. She could not bring forth the words. "Something real ugly," she muttered.

"She sho shouldn't said nothin ugly to you," the old woman said. "You so sweet. You the sweetest lady I know."

"She pretty too," the one with the hat on said.

"And stout," the other one said. "I never knowed no sweeter white lady." 160

"That's the truth befo' Jesus," the old woman said. "Amen! You des as sweet and pretty as you can be."

Mrs. Turpin knew exactly how much Negro flattery was worth and it added to her rage. "She said," she began again and finished this time with a fierce rush of breath, "that I was an old wart hog from hell."

There was an astounded silence.

"Where she at?" the youngest woman cried in a piercing voice.

"Lemme see her. I'll kill her!" 165

"I'll kill her with you!" the other one cried.

"She b'long in the sylum," the old woman said emphatically. "You the sweetest white lady I know."

"She pretty too," the other two said. "Stout as she can be and sweet. Jesus satisfied with her!"

"Deed he is," the woman declared.

Idiots! Mrs. Turpin growled to herself. You could never say anything intel- 170
ligent to a nigger. You could talk at them but not with them. "Yawl ain't drunk your water," she said shortly. "Leave the bucket in the truck when you're finished with it. I got more to do than just stand around and pass the time of day," and she moved off and into the house.

She stood for a moment in the middle of the kitchen. The dark protuberance over her eye looked like a miniature tornado cloud which might any moment sweep across the horizon of her brow. Her lower lip protruded dangerously. She squared her massive shoulders. Then she marched into the front of the house and out the side door and started down the road to the pig parlor. She had the look of a woman going single-handed, weaponless, into battle.

The sun was deep yellow now like a harvest moon and was riding westward very fast over the far tree line as if it meant to reach the hogs before she did. The road was rutted and she kicked several good-sized stones out of her path as she strode along. The pig parlor was on a little knoll at the end of a lane that ran off from the side of the barn. It was a square of concrete as large as a small room, with a board fence about four feet high around it. The concrete floor sloped slightly so that the hog wash could drain off into a trench where it was carried to the field for fertilizer. Claud was standing on the outside, on the edge of the concrete, hanging onto the top board, hosing down the floor inside. The hose was connected to the faucet of a water trough nearby.

Mrs. Turpin climbed up beside him and glowered down at the hogs inside. There were seven long-snouted bristly shoats in it — tan with liver-colored spots —

and an old sow a few weeks off from farrowing. She was lying on her side grunting. The shoats were running about shaking themselves like idiot children, their little slit pig eyes searching the floor for anything left. She had read that pigs were the most intelligent animal. She doubted it. They were supposed to be smarter than dogs. There had even been a pig astronaut. He had performed his assignment perfectly but died of a heart attack afterwards because they left him in his electric suit, sitting upright throughout his examination when naturally a hog should be on all fours.

A-gruntin and a-rootin and a-groanin.

"Gimme that hose," she said, yanking it away from Claud. "Go on and carry them niggers home and then get off that leg."

"You look like you might have swallowed a mad dog," Claud observed, but he got down and limped off. He paid no attention to her humors.

Until he was out of earshot, Mrs. Turpin stood on the side of the pen, holding the hose and pointing the stream of water at the hind quarters of any shoat that looked as if it might try to lie down. When he had had time to get over the hill, she turned her head slightly and her wrathful eyes scanned the path. He was nowhere in sight. She turned back again and seemed to gather herself up. Her shoulders rose and she drew in her breath.

"What do you send me a message like that for?" she said in a low fierce voice, barely above a whisper but with the force of a shout in its concentrated fury. "How am I a hog and me both? How am I saved and from hell too?" Her free fist was knotted and with the other she gripped the hose, blindly pointing the stream of water in and out of the eye of the old sow whose outraged squeal she did not hear.

The pig parlor commanded a view of the back pasture where their twenty beef cows were gathered around the hay-bales Claud and the boy had put out. The freshly cut pasture sloped down to the highway. Across it was their cotton field and beyond that a dark green dusty wood which they owned as well. The sun was behind the wood, very red, looking over the paling of the trees like a farmer inspecting his own hogs.

"Why me?" she rumbled. "It's no trash around here, black or white, that I haven't given to. And break my back to the bone every day working. And do for the church."

She appeared to be the right size woman to command the arena before her. "How am I a hog?" she demanded. "Exactly how am I like them?" and she jabbed the stream of water at the shoats. "There was plenty of trash there. It didn't have to be me.

"If you like trash better, go get yourself some trash then," she railed. "You could have made me trash. Or a nigger. If trash is what you wanted why didn't you make me trash?" She shook her fist with the hose in it and a watery snake appeared momentarily in the air. "I could quit working and take it easy and be filthy," she growled. "Lounge about the sidewalks all day drinking root beer. Dip snuff and spit in every puddle and have it all over my face. I could be nasty.

"Or you could have made me a nigger. It's too late for me to be a nigger," she said with deep sarcasm, "but I could act like one. Lay down in the middle of the road and stop traffic. Roll on the ground."

In the deepening light everything was taking on a mysterious hue. The pasture was growing a peculiar glassy green and the streak of highway had turned lavender. She braced herself for a final assault and this time her voice rolled out over the pasture. "Go on," she yelled, "call me a hog! Call me a hog again. From hell. Call me a wart hog from hell. Put that bottom rail on top. There'll still be a top and bottom!"

A garbled echo returned to her. 185

A final surge of fury shook her and she roared, "Who do you think you are?"

The color of everything, field and crimson sky, burned for a moment with a transparent intensity. The question carried over the pasture and across the highway and the cotton field and returned to her clearly like an answer from beyond the wood.

She opened her mouth but no sound came out of it.

A tiny truck, Claud's, appeared on the highway, heading rapidly out of sight. Its gears scraped thinly. It looked like a child's toy. At any moment a bigger truck might smash into it and scatter Claud's and the niggers' brains all over the road.

Mrs. Turpin stood there, her gaze fixed on the highway, all her muscles 190
rigid, until in five or six minutes the truck reappeared, returning. She waited until it had had time to turn into their own road. Then like a monumental statue coming to life, she bent her head slowly and gazed, as if through the very heart of mystery, down into the pig parlor at the hogs. They had settled all in one corner around the old sow who was grunting softly. A red glow suffused them. They appeared to pant with a secret life.

Until the sun slipped finally behind the tree line, Mrs. Turpin remained there with her gaze bent to them as if she were absorbing some abysmal life-giving knowledge. At last she lifted her head. There was only a purple streak in the sky, cutting through a field of crimson and leading, like an extension of the highway, into the descending dusk. She raised her hands from the side of the pen in a gesture hieratic and profound. A visionary light settled in her eyes. She saw the streak as a vast swinging bridge extending upward from the earth through a field of living fire. Upon it a vast horde of souls were rumbling toward heaven. There were whole companies of white-trash, clean for the first time in their lives, and bands of black niggers in white robes, and battalions of freaks and lunatics shouting and clapping and leaping like frogs. And bringing up the end of the procession was a tribe of people whom she recognized at once as those who, like herself and Claud, had always had a little of everything and the God-given wit to use it right. She leaned forward to observe them closer. They were marching behind the others with great dignity, accountable as they had always been for good order and common sense and respectable behavior. They alone were on key. Yet she could see by their shocked and altered faces that even their virtues were being burned away. She lowered her hands and gripped the rail of the hog pen, her eyes small but fixed unblinkingly on what lay ahead. In a moment the vision faded but she remained where she was, immobile.

At length she got down and turned off the faucet and made her slow way on the darkening path to the house. In the woods around her the invisible cricket choruses had struck up, but what she heard were the voices of the souls climbing upward into the starry field and shouting hallelujah.

Considerations

1. Why is it appropriate that the two major settings for the action in this story are a doctor's waiting room and a "pig parlor"?
2. How does Mrs. Turpin's treatment of her husband help to characterize her?
3. Mrs. Turpin notices people's shoes. What does this and her thoughts about "classes of people" reveal about her? How does she see herself in relation to other people?
4. Why does Mary Grace attack Mrs. Turpin?
5. Why is it significant that the book Mary Grace reads is *Human Development?* What is the significance of her name?
6. What does the background music played on the radio contribute to the story?
7. To whom does Mrs. Turpin address this anguished question: "What do you send me a message [Mary Grace's whispered words telling her "Go back to hell where you came from, you old wart hog"] like that for?" Why is Mrs. Turpin so angry and bewildered?
8. What is the "abysmal life-giving knowledge" that Mrs. Turpin discovers in the next to the last paragraph? Why is it "abysmal"? How is it "life-giving"?
9. Does your attitude toward Mrs. Turpin change or remain the same during the story? Explain why.
10. Given the serious theme, consider whether the story's humor is appropriate.
11. When Mrs. Turpin returns home bruised, a hired black woman tells her that nothing really "bad" happened: "You just had you a little fall." Pay particular attention to the suggestive language of this sentence, and discuss its significance in relation to the rest of the story.

Connections

1. Compare and contrast Mary Grace with Hulga of "Good Country People."
2. Explain how "Revelation" could be used as a title for any of the O'Connor stories you have read.
3. Discuss Mrs. Turpin's prideful hypocrisy in connection with the colonialist assumptions expressed by Kayerts and Carlier in Conrad's "An Outpost of Progress" (p. 208). How do pride and personal illusions inform these characters' racial attitudes?
4. Explore the nature of the "revelation" in O'Connor's story and in Louise Erdrich's "Fleur" (p. 444).

A Good Man Is Hard to Find 1953

The dragon is by the side of the road, watching those who pass. Beware lest he devour you. We go to the Father of Souls, but it is necessary to pass by the dragon.

—St. Cyril of Jerusalem°

The grandmother didn't want to go to Florida. She wanted to visit some of her connections in east Tennessee and she was seizing at every chance to change Bailey's mind. Bailey was the son she lived with, her only boy. He was sitting

St. Cyril of Jerusalem: (315?–386) Roman Catholic ecclesiastic and bishop of Jerusalem.

on the edge of his chair at the table, bent over the orange sports section of the *Journal*. "Now look here, Bailey," she said, "see here, read this," and she stood with one hand on her thin hip and the other rattling the newspaper at his bald head. "Here this fellow that calls himself The Misfit is aloose from the Federal Pen and headed toward Florida and you read here what it says he did to these people. Just you read it. I wouldn't take my children in any direction with a criminal like that aloose in it. I couldn't answer to my conscience if I did."

Bailey didn't look up from his reading so she wheeled around then and faced the children's mother, a young woman in slacks, whose face was as broad and innocent as a cabbage and was tied around with a green headkerchief that had two points on the top like a rabbit's ears. She was sitting on the sofa, feeding the baby his apricots out of a jar. "The children have been to Florida before," the old lady said. "You all ought to take them somewhere else for a change so they would see different parts of the world and be broad. They never have been to east Tennessee."

The children's mother didn't seem to hear her but the eight-year-old boy, John Wesley, a stocky child with glasses, said, "If you don't want to go to Florida, why dontcha stay at home?" He and the little girl, June Star, were reading the funny papers on the floor.

"She wouldn't stay at home to be queen for a day," June Star said without raising her yellow head.

5 "Yes and what would you do if this fellow, The Misfit, caught you?" the grandmother asked.

"I'd smack his face," John Wesley said.

"She wouldn't stay at home for a million bucks," June Star said. "Afraid she'd miss something. She has to go everywhere we go."

"All right, Miss," the grandmother said. "Just remember that the next time you want me to curl your hair."

June Star said her hair was naturally curly.

10 The next morning the grandmother was the first one in the car, ready to go. She had her big black valise that looked like the head of a hippopotamus in one corner, and underneath it she was hiding a basket with Pitty Sing, the cat, in it. She didn't intend for the cat to be left alone in the house for three days because he would miss her too much and she was afraid he might brush against one of the gas burners and accidentally asphyxiate himself. Her son, Bailey, didn't like to arrive at a motel with a cat.

She sat in the middle of the back seat with John Wesley and June Star on either side of her. Bailey and the children's mother and the baby sat in front and they left Atlanta at eight forty-five with the mileage on the car at 55890. The grandmother wrote this down because she thought it would be interesting to say how many miles they had been when they got back. It took them twenty minutes to reach the outskirts of the city.

The old lady settled herself comfortably, removing her white cotton gloves and putting them up with her purse on the shelf in front of the back window. The children's mother still had on slacks and still had her head tied up in a green kerchief, but the grandmother had on a navy blue straw sailor hat with a bunch of white violets on the brim and a navy blue dress with a small white dot in the print. Her collars and cuffs were white organdy trimmed with lace and at her neckline she had pinned a purple spray of cloth violets containing a sachet.

In case of an accident, anyone seeing her dead on the highway would know at once that she was a lady.

She said she thought it was going to be a good day for driving, neither too hot nor too cold, and she cautioned Bailey that the speed limit was fifty-five miles an hour and that the patrolmen hid themselves behind billboards and small clumps of trees and sped out after you before you had a chance to slow down. She pointed out interesting details of the scenery: Stone Mountain; the blue granite that in some places came up to both sides of the highway; the brilliant red clay banks slightly streaked with purple; and the various crops that made rows of green lace-work on the ground. The trees were full of silver-white sunlight and the meanest of them sparkled. The children were reading comic magazines and their mother had gone back to sleep.

"Let's go through Georgia fast so we won't have to look at it much," John Wesley said.

15 "If I were a little boy," said the grandmother, "I wouldn't talk about my native state that way. Tennessee has the mountains and Georgia has the hills."

"Tennessee is just a hillbilly dumping ground," John Wesley said, "and Georgia is a lousy state too."

"You said it," June Star said.

"In my time," said the grandmother, folding her thin veined fingers, "children were more respectful of their native states and their parents and everything else. People did right then. Oh look at the cute little pickaninny!" she said and pointed to a Negro child standing in the door of a shack. "Wouldn't that make a picture, now?" she asked and they all turned and looked at the little Negro out of the back window. He waved.

"He didn't have any britches on," June Star said.

20 "He probably didn't have any," the grandmother explained. "Little niggers in the country don't have things like we do. If I could paint, I'd paint that picture," she said.

The children exchanged comic books.

The grandmother offered to hold the baby and the children's mother passed him over the front seat to her. She set him on her knee and bounced him and told him about the things they were passing. She rolled her eyes and screwed up her mouth and stuck her leathery thin face into his smooth bland one. Occasionally he gave her a faraway smile. They passed a large cotton field with five or six graves fenced in the middle of it, like a small island. "Look at the graveyard!" the grandmother said, pointing it out. "That was the old family burying ground. That belonged to the plantation."

"Where's the plantation?" John Wesley asked.

"Gone with the Wind," said the grandmother. "Ha. Ha."

25 When the children finished all the comic books they had brought, they opened the lunch and ate it. The grandmother ate a peanut butter sandwich and an olive and would not let the children throw the box and the paper napkins out the window. When there was nothing else to do they played a game by choosing a cloud and making the other two guess what shape it suggested. John Wesley took one the shape of a cow and June Star guessed a cow and John Wesley said, no, an automobile, and June Star said he didn't play fair, and they began to slap each other over the grandmother.

The grandmother said she would tell them a story if they would keep quiet.

When she told a story, she rolled her eyes and waved her head and was very dramatic. She said once when she was a maiden lady she had been courted by a Mr. Edgar Atkins Teagarden from Jasper, Georgia. She said he was a very good-looking man and a gentleman and that he brought her a watermelon every Saturday afternoon with his initials cut in it, E. A. T. Well, one Saturday, she said, Mr. Teagarden brought the watermelon and there was nobody at home and he left it on the front porch and returned in his buggy to Jasper, but she never got the watermelon, she said, because a niger boy ate it when he saw the initials, E. A. T.! This story tickled John Wesley's funny bone and he giggled and giggled but June Star didn't think it was any good. She said she wouldn't marry a man that just brought her a watermelon on Saturday. The grandmother said she would have done well to marry Mr. Teagarden because he was a gentleman and had bought Coca-Cola stock when it first came out and that he had died only a few years ago, a very wealthy man.

They stopped at The Tower for barbecued sandwiches. The Tower was a part stucco and part wood filling station and dance hall set in a clearing outside of Timothy. A fat man named Red Sammy Butts ran it and there were signs stuck here and there on the building and for miles up and down the highway saying, TRY RED SAMMY'S FAMOUS BARBECUE. NONE LIKE FAMOUS RED SAMMY'S! RED SAM! THE FAT BOY WITH THE HAPPY LAUGH. A VETERAN! RED SAMMY'S YOUR MAN!

Red Sammy was lying on the bare ground outside The Tower with his head under a truck while a gray monkey about a foot high, chained to a small chinaberry tree, chattered nearby. The monkey sprang back into the tree and got on the highest limb as soon as he saw the children jump out of the car and run toward him.

Inside, The Tower was a long dark room with a counter at one end and tables at the other and dancing space in the middle. They all sat down at a board table next to the nickelodeon and Red Sam's wife, a tall burnt-brown woman with hair and eyes lighter than her skin, came and took their order. The children's mother put a dime in the machine and played "The Tennessee Waltz," and the grandmother said that tune always made her want to dance. She asked Bailey if he would like to dance but he only glared at her. He didn't have a naturally sunny disposition like she did and trips made him nervous. The grandmother's brown eyes were very bright. She swayed her head from side to side and pretended she was dancing in her chair. June Star said play something she could tap to so the children's mother put in another dime and played a fast number and June Star stepped out onto the dance floor and did her tap routine.

"Ain't she cute?" Red Sam's wife said, leaning over the counter. "Would 30
you like to come be my little girl?"

"No I certainly wouldn't," June Star said. "I wouldn't live in a broken-down place like this for a million bucks!" and she ran back to the table.

"Ain't she cute?" the woman repeated, stretching her mouth politely.

"Aren't you ashamed?" hissed the grandmother.

Red Sam came in and told his wife to quit lounging on the counter and hurry up with these people's order. His khaki trousers reached just to his hip bones and his stomach hung over them like a sack of meal swaying under his shirt. He came over and sat down at a table nearby and let out a combination sigh and yodel. "You can't win," he said. "You can't win," and he wiped his sweating red face off with a gray handkerchief. "These days you don't know who to trust," he said. "Ain't that the truth?"

"People are certainly not nice like they used to be," said the grandmother. 35

"Two fellers come in here last week," Red Sammy said, "driving a Chrysler. It was a old beat-up car but it was a good one and these boys looked all right to me. Said they worked at the mill and you know I let them fellers charge the gas they bought? Now why did I do that?"

"Because you're a good man!" the grandmother said at once.

"Yes'm, I suppose so," Red Sam said as if he were struck with this answer.

His wife brought the orders, carrying the five plates all at once without a tray, two in each hand and one balanced on her arm. "It isn't a soul in this green world of God's that you can trust," she said. "And I don't count nobody out of that, not nobody," she repeated, looking at Red Sammy.

"Did you read about that criminal, The Misfit, that's escaped?" asked the 40
grandmother.

"I wouldn't be a bit surprised if he didn't attact this place right here," said the woman. "If he hears about it being here, I wouldn't be none surprised to see him. If he hears it's two cent in the cash register, I wouldn't be a tall surprised if he. . . ."

"That'll do," Red Sam said. "Go bring these people their Co'-Colas," and the woman went off to get the rest of the order.

"A good man is hard to find," Red Sammy said. "Everything is getting terrible. I remember the day you could go off and leave your screen door unlatched. Not no more."

He and the grandmother discussed better times. The old lady said that in her opinion Europe was entirely to blame for the way things were now. She said the way Europe acted you would think we were made of money and Red Sam said it was no use talking about it, she was exactly right. The children ran outside into the white sunlight and looked at the monkey in the lacy chinaberry tree. He was busy catching fleas on himself and biting each one carefully between his teeth as if it were a delicacy.

They drove off again into the hot afternoon. The grandmother took cat 45
naps and woke up every few minutes with her own snoring. Outside of Toombsboro she woke up and recalled an old plantation that she had visited in this neighborhood once when she was a young lady. She said the house had six white columns across the front and that there was an avenue of oaks leading up to it and two little wooden trellis arbors on either side in front where you sat down with your suitor after a stroll in the garden. She recalled exactly which road to turn off to get to it. She knew that Bailey would not be willing to lose any time looking at an old house, but the more she talked about it, the more she wanted to see it once again and find out if the little twin arbors were still standing. "There was a secret panel in this house," she said craftily, not telling the truth but wishing that she were, "and the story went that all the family silver was hidden in it when Sherman° came through but it was never found. . . ."

"Hey!" John Wesley said. "Let's go see it! We'll find it! We'll poke all the

Sherman: William Tecumseh Sherman (1820–1891), Union Army commander who led infamous marches through the South during the Civil War.

woodwork and find it! Who lives there? Where do you turn off at? Hey Pop, can't we turn off there?"

"We never have seen a house with a secret panel!" June Star shrieked. "Let's go to the house with the secret panel! Hey Pop, can't we go see the house with the secret panel!"

"It's not far from here, I know," the grandmother said. "It won't take over twenty minutes."

Bailey was looking straight ahead. His jaw was as rigid as a horseshoe. "No," he said.

50 The children began to yell and scream that they wanted to see the house with the secret panel. John Wesley kicked the back of the front seat and June Star hung over her mother's shoulder and whined desperately into her ear that they never had any fun even on their vacation, that they could never do what THEY wanted to do. The baby began to scream and John Wesley kicked the back of the seat so hard that his father could feel the blows in his kidney.

"All right!" he shouted and drew the car to a stop at the side of the road. "Will you all shut up? Will you all just shut up for one second? If you don't shut up, we won't go anywhere."

"It would be very educational for them," the grandmother murmured.

"All right," Bailey said, "but get this: this is the only time we're going to stop for anything like this. This is the one and only time."

"The dirt road that you have to turn down is about a mile back," the grandmother directed. "I marked it when we passed."

55 "A dirt road," Bailey groaned.

After they had turned around and were headed toward the dirt road, the grandmother recalled other points about the house, the beautiful glass over the front doorway and the candle-lamp in the hall. John Wesley said that the secret panel was probably in the fireplace.

"You can't go inside this house," Bailey said. "You don't know who lives there."

"While you all talk to the people in front, I'll run around behind and get in a window," John Wesley suggested.

"We'll all stay in the car," his mother said.

60 They turned onto the dirt road and the car raced roughly along in a swirl of pink dust. The grandmother recalled the times when there were no paved roads and thirty miles was a day's journey. The dirt road was hilly and there were sudden washes in it and sharp curves on dangerous embankments. All at once they would be on a hill, looking down over the blue tops of trees for miles around, then the next minute, they would be in a red depression with the dust-coated trees looking down on them.

"This place had better turn up in a minute," Bailey said, "or I'm going to turn around."

The road looked as if no one had travled on it for months.

"It's not much farther," the grandmother said and just as she said it, a horrible thought came to her. The thought was so embarrassing that she turned red in the face and her eyes dilated and her feet jumped up, upsetting her valise in the corner. The instant the valise moved, the newspaper top she had over the basket under it rose with a snarl and Pitty Sing, the cat, sprang onto Bailey's shoulder.

The children were thrown to the floor and their mother, clutching the baby, was thrown out the door onto the ground; the old lady was thrown into the front seat. The car turned over once and landed right-side-up in a gulch off the side of the road. Bailey remained in the driver's seat with the cat — gray-striped with a broad white face and an orange nose — clinging to his neck like a caterpillar.

As soon as the children saw they could move their arms and legs, they scrambled out of the car, shouting, "We've had an ACCIDENT!" The grandmother was curled up under the dashboard, hoping she was injured so that Bailey's wrath would not come down on her all at once. The horrible thought she had before the accident was that the house she had remembered so vividly was not in Georgia but in Tennessee.

Bailey removed the cat from his neck with both hands and flung it out the window against the side of a pine tree. Then he got out of the car and started looking for the children's mother. She was sitting against the side of the red gutted ditch, holding the screaming baby, but she only had a cut down her face and a broken shoulder. "We've had an ACCIDENT!" the children screamed in a frenzy of delight.

"But nobody's killed," June Star said with disappointment as the grandmother limped out of the car, her hat still pinned to her head but the broken front brim standing up at a jaunty angle and the violet spray hanging off the side. They all sat down in the ditch, except the children, to recover from the shock. They were all shaking.

"Maybe a car will come along," said the children's mother hoarsely.

"I believe I have injured an organ," said the grandmother, pressing her side, but no one answered her. Bailey's teeth were clattering. He had on a yellow sport shirt with bright blue parrots designed in it and his face was as yellow as the shirt. The grandmother decided that she would not mention that the house was in Tennessee.

The road was about ten feet above and they could see only the tops of the trees on the other side of it. Behind the ditch they were sitting in there were more woods, tall and dark and deep. In a few minutes they saw a car some distance away on top of a hill, coming slowly as if the occupants were watching them. The grandmother stood up and waved both arms dramatically to attract their attention. The car continued to come on slowly, disappeared around a bend and appeared again, moving even slower, on top of the hill they had gone over. It was a big black battered hearse-like automobile. There were three men in it.

It came to a stop just over them and for some minutes, the driver looked down with a steady expressionless gaze to where they were sitting, and didn't speak. Then he turned his head and muttered something to the other two and they got out. One was a fat boy in black trousers and a red sweat shirt with a silver stallion embossed on the front of it. He moved around on the right side of them and stood staring, his mouth partly open in a kind of loose grin. The other had on khaki pants and a blue striped coat and a gray hat pulled down very low, hiding most of his face. He came around slowly on the left side. Neither spoke.

The driver got out of the car and stood by the side of it, looking down at them. He was an older man than the other two. His hair was just beginning to gray and he wore silver-rimmed spectacles that gave him a scholarly look. He had a long creased face and didn't have on any shirt or undershirt. He had on blue jeans that were too tight for him and was holding a black hat and a gun. The two boys also had guns.

"We've had an ACCIDENT!" the children screamed.

The grandmother had the peculiar feeling that the bespectacled man was someone she knew. His face was as familiar to her as if she had known him all her life but she could not recall who he was. He moved away from the car and began to come down the embankment, placing his feet carefully so that he wouldn't slip. He had on tan and white shoes and no socks, and his ankles were red and thin. "Good afternoon," he said. "I see you all had you a little spill."

"We turned over twice!" said the grandmother.

"Oncet," he corrected. "We seen it happen. Try their car and see will it run, Hiram," he said quietly to the boy with the gray hat.

"What you got that gun for?" John Wesley asked. "Whatcha gonna do with that gun?"

"Lady," the man said to the children's mother, "would you mind calling them children to sit down by you? Children make me nervous. I want all you all to sit down right together there where you're at."

"What are you telling US what to do for?" June Star asked.

Behind them the line of woods gaped like a dark open mouth. "Come here," said their mother.

"Look here now," Bailey said suddenly, "we're in a predicament! We're in. . . ."

The grandmother shrieked. She scrambled to her feet and stood staring. "You're The Misfit!" she said. "I recognized you at once!"

"Yes'm," the man said, smiling slightly as if he were pleased in spite of himself to be known, "but it would have been better for all of you, lady, if you hadn't of reckernized me."

Bailey turned his head sharply and said something to his mother that shocked even the children. The old lady began to cry and The Misfit reddened.

"Lady," he said, "don't you get upset. Sometimes a man says things he don't mean. I don't reckon he meant to talk to you thataway."

"You wouldn't shoot a lady, would you?" the grandmother said and removed a clean handkerchief from her cuff and began to slap at her eyes with it.

The Misfit pointed the toe of his shoe into the ground and made a little hole and then covered it up again. "I would hate to have to," he said.

"Listen," the grandmother almost screamed, "I know you're a good man. You don't look a bit like you have common blood. I know you must come from nice people!"

"Yes mam," he said, "finest people in the world." When he smiled he showed a row of strong white teeth. "God never made a finer woman than my mother and my daddy's heart was pure gold," he said. The boy with the red sweat shirt had come around behind them and was standing with his gun at his hip. The Misfit squatted down on the ground. "Watch them children, Bobby Lee," he said. "You know they make me nervous." He looked at the six of them huddled together in front of him and he seemed to be embarrassed as if he couldn't think of anything to say. "Ain't a cloud in the sky," he remarked, looking up at it. "Don't see no sun but don't see no cloud neither."

“Yes, it’s a beautiful day,” said the grandmother. “Listen,” she said, “you 90
shouldn’t call yourself The Misfit because I know you’re a good man at heart. I can just look at you and tell.”

“Hush!” Bailey yelled. “Hush! Everybody shut up and let me handle this!” He was squatting in the position of a runner about to sprint forward but he didn’t move.

“I pre-chate that, lady,” The Misfit said and drew a little circle in the ground with the butt of his gun.

“It’ll take a half a hour to fix this here car,” Hiram called, looking over the raised hood of it.

“Well, first you and Bobby Lee get him and that little boy to step over yonder with you,” The Misfit said, pointing to Bailey and John Wesley. “The boys want to ast you something,” he said to Bailey. “Would you mind stepping back in them woods there with them?”

“Listen,” Bailey began, “we’re in a terrible predicament! Nobody realizes 95
what this is,” and his voice cracked. His eyes were as blue and intense as the parrots in his shirt and he remained perfectly still.

The grandmother reached up to adjust her hat brim as if she were going to the woods with him but it came off in her hand. She stood staring at it and after a second she let it fall to the ground. Hiram pulled Bailey up by the arm as if he were assisting an old man. John Wesley caught hold of his father’s hand and Bobby Lee followed. They went off toward the woods and just as they reached the dark edge, Bailey turned and supporting himself against a gray naked pine trunk, he shouted, “I’ll be back in a minute, Mamma, wait on me!”

“Come back this instant!” his mother shrilled but they all disappeared into the woods.

“Bailey Boy!” the grandmother called in a tragic voice but she found she was looking at The Misfit squatting on the ground in front of her. “I just know you’re a good man,” she said desperately. “You’re not a bit common!”

“Nome, I ain’t a good man,” The Misfit said after a second as if he had considered her statement carefully, “but I ain’t the worst in the world neither. My daddy said I was a different breed of dog from my brothers and sisters. ‘You know,’ Daddy said, ‘it’s some that can live their whole life out without asking about it and it’s others has to know why it is, and this boy is one of the latters. He’s going to be into everything!’ ” He put on his black hat and looked up suddenly and then away deep into the woods as if he were embarrassed again. “I’m sorry I don’t have on a shirt before you ladies,” he said, hunching his shoulders slightly. “We buried our clothes that we had on when we escaped and we’re just making do until we can get better. We borrowed these from some folks we met,” he explained.

“That’s perfectly all right,” the grandmother said. “Maybe Bailey has an 100
extra shirt in his suitcase.”

“I’ll look and see terrectly,” The Misfit said.

“Where are they taking him?” the children’s mother screamed.

“Daddy was a card himself,” The Misfit said. “You couldn’t put anything over on him. He never got in trouble with the Authorities though. Just had the knack of handling them.”

“You could be honest too if you’d only try,” said the grandmother. “Think how wonderful it would be to settle down and live a comfortable life and not have to think about somebody chasing you all the time."

The Misfit kept scratching in the ground with the butt of his gun as if he 105
were thinking about it. "Yes'm, somebody is always after you," he murmured.

The grandmother noticed how thin his shoulder blades were just behind his hat because she was standing up looking down on him. "Do you ever pray?" she asked.

He shook his head. All she saw was the black hat wiggle between his shoulder blades. "Nome," he said.

There was a pistol shot from the woods, followed closely by another. Then silence. The old lady's head jerked around. She could hear the wind move through the tree tops like a long satisfied insuck of breath. "Bailey Boy!" she called.

"I was a gospel singer for a while," The Misfit said. "I been most everything. Been in the arm service, both land and sea, at home and abroad, been twict married, been an undertaker, been with the railroads, plowed Mother Earth, been in a tornado, seen a man burnt alive oncet," and he looked up at the children's mother and the little girl who were sitting close together, their faces white and their eyes glassy; "I even seen a woman flogged," he said.

"Pray, pray," the grandmother began, "pray, pray. . . ." 110

"I never was a bad boy that I remember of," The Misfit said in an almost dreamy voice, "but somewheres along the line I done something wrong and got sent to the penitentiary. I was buried alive," and he looked up and held her attention to him by a steady stare.

"That's when you should have started to pray," she said. "What did you do to get sent to the penitentiary that first time?"

"Turn to the right, it was a wall," The Misfit said, looking up again at the cloudless sky. "Turn to the left, it was a wall. Look up it was a ceiling, look down it was a floor. I forget what I done, lady. I set there and set there, trying to remember what it was I done and I ain't recalled it to this day. Oncet in a while, I would think it was coming to me, but it never come."

"Maybe they put you in by mistake," the old lady said vaguely.

"Nome," he said. "It wasn't no mistake. They had the papers on me." 115

"You must have stolen something," she said.

The Misfit sneered slightly. "Nobody had nothing I wanted," he said. "It was a head-doctor at the penitentiary said what I had done was kill my daddy but I known that for a lie. My daddy died in nineteen ought nineteen of the epidemic flu and I never had a thing to do with it. He was buried in the Mount Hopewell Baptist churchyard and you can see for yourself."

"If you would pray," the old lady said, "Jesus would help you."

"That's right," The Misfit said.

"Well then, why don't you pray?" she asked trembling with delight sud- 120
denly.

"I don't want no hep," he said. "I'm doing all right by myself."

Bobby Lee and Hiram came ambling back from the woods. Bobby Lee was dragging a yellow shirt with bright blue parrots in it.

"Throw me that shirt, Bobby Lee," The Misfit said. The shirt came flying at him and landed on his shoulder and he put it on. The grandmother couldn't name what the shirt reminded her of. "No, lady," The Misfit said while he was buttoning it up, "I found out the crime don't matter. You can do one thing or you can do another, kill a man or take a tire off his car, because sooner or later you're going to forget what it was you done and just be punished for it."

The children's mother had begun to make heaving noises as if she couldn't get her breath. "Lady," he asked, "would you and that little girl like to step off yonder with Bobby Lee and Hiram and join your husband?"

"Yes, thank you," the mother said faintly. Her left arm dangled helplessly 125
and she was holding the baby, who had gone to sleep, in the other. "Hep that lady up, Hiram," The Misfit said as she struggled to climb out of the ditch, "and Bobby Lee, you hold onto that little girl's hand."

"I don't want to hold hands with him," June Star said. "He reminds me of a pig."

The fat boy blushed and laughed and caught her by the arm and pulled her off into the woods after Hiram and her mother.

Alone with The Misfit, the grandmother found that she had lost her voice. There was not a cloud in the sky nor any sun. There was nothing around her but woods. She wanted to tell him that he must pray. She opened and closed her mouth several times before anything came out. Finally she found herself saying, "Jesus, Jesus," meaning Jesus will help you, but the way she was saying it, it sounded as if she might be cursing.

"Yes'm," The Misfit said as if he agreed. "Jesus thown everything off balance. It was the same case with Him as with me except He hadn't committed any crime and they could prove I had committed one because they had the papers on me. Of course," he said, "they never shown me my papers. That's why I sign myself now. I said long ago, you get your signature and sign everything you do and keep a copy of it. Then you'll know what you done and you can hold up the crime to the punishment and see do they match and in the end you'll have something to prove you ain't been treated right. I call myself The Misfit," he said, "because I can't make what all I done wrong fit what all I gone through in punishment."

There was a piercing scream from the woods, followed closely by a pistol 130
report. "Does it seem right to you, lady, that one is punished a heap and another ain't punished at all?"

"Jesus!" the old lady cried. "You've got good blood! I know you wouldn't shoot a lady! I know you come from nice people! Pray! Jesus, you ought not to shoot a lady. I'll give you all the money I've got!"

"Lady," The Misfit said, looking beyond her far into the woods, "there never was a body that give the undertaker a tip."

There were two more pistol reports and the grandmother raised her head like a parched old turkey hen crying for water and called, "Bailey Boy, Bailey Boy!" as if her heart would break.

"Jesus was the only One that ever raised the dead," The Misfit continued, "and He shouldn't have done it. He thown everything off balance. If He did what He said, then it's nothing for you to do but throw away everything and follow Him, and if He didn't, then it's nothing for you to do but enjoy the few minutes you got left the best way you can — by killing somebody or burning down his house or doing some other meanness to him. No pleasure but meanness," he said and his voice had become almost a snarl.

"Maybe He didn't raise the dead," the old lady mumbled, not knowing 135 what she was saying and feeling so dizzy that she sank down in the ditch with her legs twisted under her.

"I wasn't there so I can't say He didn't," The Misfit said. "I wisht I had of been there," he said, hitting the ground with his fist. "It ain't right I wasn't there because if I had of been there I would of known. Listen lady," he said in a high voice, "if I had of been there I would of known and I wouldn't be like I am now." His voice seemed about to crack and the grandmother's head cleared for an instant. She saw the man's face twisted close to her own as if he were going to cry and she murmured, "Why you're one of my babies. You're one of my own children!" She reached out and touched him on the shoulder. The Misfit sprang back as if a snake had bitten him and shot her three times through the chest. Then he put his gun down on the ground and took off his glasses and began to clean them.

Hiram and Bobby Lee returned from the woods and stood over the ditch, looking down at the grandmother who half sat and half lay in a puddle of blood with her legs crossed under her like a child's and her face smiling up at the cloudless sky.

Without his glasses, The Misfit's eyes were red-rimmed and pale and defenseless-looking. "Take her off and throw her where you thrown the others," he said, picking up the cat that was rubbing itself against his leg.

"She was a talker, wasn't she?" Bobby Lee said, sliding down the ditch with a yodel.

"She would of been a good woman," The Misfit said, "if it had been somebody there to shoot her every minute of her life."

"Some fun!" Bobby Lee said.

"Shut up, Bobby Lee," The Misfit said. "It's no real pleasure in life."

Considerations

1. How do the grandmother's concerns about the trip to Florida foreshadow events in the story?
2. Describe the grandmother. How does O'Connor make her the central character?
3. How does O'Connor portray the family? What is comic about them? What qualities about them are we to take seriously? Do you think they are responsible for what happens to them? Does your attitude toward them remain constant during the course of the story?
4. What is Red Sammy's purpose in the story? Relate his view of life to the story's conflicts.
5. Characterize the Misfit. What makes him so? Can he be written off as simply insane? How does the grandmother respond to him?
6. Why does the Misfit say that "Jesus thown everything off balance"? What does religion have to do with the brutal action of this story?
7. What does the Misfit mean when he says about the grandmother "She would of been a good woman . . . if it had been somebody to shoot her every minute of her life"?
8. Describe the story's tone. Is it consistent? What is the effect of O'Connor's use of tone?
9. How is coincidence used to advance the plot? How do coincidences lead to ironies in the story?
10. Explain how the title points to the story's theme.

Connections

1. Compare and contrast the realistic detail and bizarre events in this story with García Márquez's use of the supernatural and realism in "A Very Old Man with Enormous Wings" (p. 234). What makes each story so difficult to interpret in contrast, say, to reading Hawthorne's "The Birthmark" (p. 268)?
2. How does this family compare with the Snopeses in Faulkner's "Barn Burning" (p. 66)? Which family do you find more sympathetic?
3. Consider the criminal behavior of the Misfit and Abner Snopes. What motivates each character? Explain the significant similarities and differences between them.

PERSPECTIVES ON O'CONNOR

O'Connor on Faith 1955

I write the way I do because (not though) I am a Catholic. This is a fact and nothing covers it like the bald statement. However, I am a Catholic peculiarly possessed of the modern consciousness, the thing Jung° describes as unhistorical, solitary and guilty. To possess this within the Church is to bear a burden, the necessary burden for the conscious Catholic. It's to feel the contemporary situation at the ultimate level. I think that the Church is the only thing that is going to make the terrible world we are coming to endurable; the only thing that makes the Church endurable is that it is somehow the body of Christ and that on this we are fed. It seems to be a fact that you suffer as much from the Church as for it but if you believe in the divinity of Christ, you have to cherish the world at the same time that you struggle to endure it. This may explain the lack of bitterness in the stories.

From a letter to "A," July 20, 1955 in *The Habit of Being*

Jung: Carl Jung (1875–1961), a Swiss psychiatrist.

Considerations

1. Consider how O'Connor's fiction expresses her belief that "you have to cherish the world at the same time that you struggle to endure it."
2. Do you agree that "bitterness" is absent from O'Connor's stories? Explain why or why not.

O'Connor on the Materials of Fiction 1969

The beginning of human knowledge is through the senses, and the fiction writer begins where human perception begins. He appeals through the senses, and you cannot appeal to the senses with abstractions. It is a good deal easier for most people to state an abstract idea than to describe and thus re-create some object that they actually see. But the world of the fiction writer is full of matter, and this is what the beginning fiction writers are very loath to create. They are concerned primarily with unfleshed ideas and emotions. They are apt to be reformers and to want to write because they are possessed not by a story but by the bare bones of some abstract notion. They are conscious of problems, not of people, of questions and issues, not of the texture of existence, of case histories and of everything that has a sociological smack, instead of with all those concrete details of life that make actual the mystery of our position on earth. . . .

One of the most common and saddest spectacles is that of a person of really fine sensibility and acute psychological perception trying to write fiction by using these [abstract] qualities alone. This type of writer will put down one intensely emotional or keenly perceptive sentence after the other, and the result will be complete dullness. The fact is that the materials of the fiction writer are the humblest. Fiction is about everything human and we are made out of dust, and if you scorn getting yourself dusty, then you shouldn't try to write fiction. It's not a grand enough job for you.

From "The Nature and Aim of Fiction" in *Mystery and Manners*

Considerations

1. Explain O'Connor's idea that "the materials of the fiction writer are the humblest" by reference to the materials and details of her stories.
2. Choose a substantial paragraph from an O'Connor story and describe how it "appeals through the senses."
3. Write an essay in which you agree or disagree with the following statement: Hawthorne's fiction is a good example of the kinds of mistakes that O'Connor attributes to a beginning fiction writer.

O'Connor on the Use of Exaggeration and Distortion 1969

When I write a novel in which the central action is a baptism, I am very well aware that for a majority of my readers, baptism is a meaningless rite, and so in my novel I have to see that this baptism carries enough awe and mystery to jar the reader into some kind of emotional recognition of its significance. To this end I have to bend the whole novel — its language, its structure, its action. I have to make the reader feel, in his bones if nowhere else, that something is going on here that counts. Distortion in this case is an instrument; exaggeration has a purpose, and the whole structure of the story or novel has been made what it is because of belief. This is not the kind of distortion that destroys; it is the kind that reveals, or should reveal.

From "Novelist and Believer" in *Mystery and Manners*

Considerations

1. It has been observed that in many of O'Connor's works the central action takes the form of some kind of "baptism" that initiates, tests, or purifies a character. Select a story that illustrates this generalization and explain how the conflict results in a kind of baptism.

2. O'Connor says that exaggeration and distortion reveal something in her stories. What is the effect of such exaggeration and distortion? Typically, what is revealed by it? Focus your comments on a single story to illustrate your points.
3. Do you think that O'Connor's stories have anything to offer a reader who has no religious faith? Explain why or why not.

O'Connor on Theme and Symbol 1969

When you can state the theme of a story, when you can separate it from the story itself, then you can be sure the story is not a very good one. The meaning of a story has to be embodied in it, has to be made concrete in it. A story is a way to say something that can't be said any other way, and it takes every word in the story to say what the meaning is. You tell a story because a statement would be inadequate. When anybody asks what a story is about, the only proper thing is to tell him to read the story. The meaning of fiction is not abstract meaning but experienced meaning, and the purpose of making statements about the meaning of a story is only to help you to experience that meaning more fully.

The peculiar problem of the short-story writer is how to make the action he describes reveal as much of the mystery of existence as possible. He has only a short space to do it in and he can't do it by statement. He has to do it by showing, not by saying, and by showing the concrete — so that his problem is really how to make the concrete work double time for him.

In good fiction, certain of the details will tend to accumulate meaning from the action of the story itself, and when this happens they become symbolic in the way they work. I once wrote a story called "Good Country People," in which a lady Ph.D. has her wooden leg stolen by a Bible salesman whom she has tried to seduce. Now I'll admit that, paraphrased in this way, the situation is simply a low joke. The average reader is pleased to observe anybody's wooden leg being stolen. But without ceasing to appeal to him and without making any statements of high intention, this story does manage to operate at another level of experience, by letting the wooden leg accumulate meaning. Early in the story, we're presented with the fact that the Ph.D. is spiritually as well as physically crippled. She believes in nothing but her own belief in nothing, and we perceive that there is a wooden part of her soul that corresponds to her wooden leg. Now of course this is never stated. The fiction writer states as little as possible. The reader makes this connection from things he is shown. He may not even know that he makes the connection, but the connection is there nevertheless and it has its effect on him. As the story goes on, the wooden leg continues to accumulate meaning. The reader learns how the girl feels about her leg, how her mother feels about it, and how the country woman on the place feels about it; and finally, by the time the Bible salesman comes along, the leg has accumulated so much meaning that it is, as the saying goes, loaded. And when the Bible salesman steals it, the reader realizes that he has taken away part of the girl's personality and has revealed her deeper affliction to her for the first time.

If you want to say that the wooden leg is a symbol, you can say that. But it is a wooden leg first, and as a wooden leg it is absolutely necessary to the story. It has its place on the literal level of the story, but it operates in depth as well as on the surface. It increases the story in every direction, and this is essentially the way a story escapes being short.

Now a little might be said about the way in which this happens. I wouldn't want you to think that in that story I sat down and said, "I am now going to write a story about a Ph.D. with a wooden leg, using the wooden leg as a symbol for another kind of affliction." I doubt myself if many writers know what they are going to do when they start out. When I started writing that story, I didn't know there was going to be a Ph.D. with a wooden leg in it. I merely found myself one morning writing a description of two women that I knew something about, and before I realized it, I had equipped one of them with a daughter with a wooden leg. As the story progressed, I brought in the Bible salesman, but I had no idea what I was going to do with him. I didn't know he was going to steal that wooden leg until ten or twelve lines before he did it, but when I found out that this was what was going to happen, I realized that it was inevitable. This is a story that produces a shock for the reader, and I think one reason for this is that it produced a shock for the writer.

Now despite the fact that this story came about in this seemingly mindless fashion, it is a story that almost no rewriting was done on. It is a story that was under control throughout the writing of it, and it might be asked how this kind of control comes about, since it is not entirely conscious.

From "Writing Short Stories" in *Mystery and Manners*

Considerations

1. Why is a "statement" inadequate to convey the meaning of a story?
2. O'Connor describes how the wooden leg "continues to accumulate meaning" in "Good Country People." Choose another story by O'Connor and explain how something specific and concrete is invested with symbolic meaning.

JOSEPHINE HENDIN (b. 1946)

On O'Connor's Refusal to "Do Pretty" 1970

There is, in the memory of one Milledgeville matron, the image of O'Connor at nineteen or twenty who, when invited to a wedding shower for an old family friend, remained standing, her back pressed against the wall, scowling at the group of women who had sat down to lunch. Neither the devil nor her mother could make her say yes to this fiercely gracious female society, but Flannery O'Connor could not say no even in a whisper. She could not refuse the invitation but she would not accept it either. She did not exactly "fuss" but neither did she "do pretty."

From *The World of Flannery O'Connor*

Considerations

1. How is O'Connor's personality revealed in this anecdote about her ambivalent response to society? Allow the description to be suggestive for you, and flesh out a brief portrait of her.
2. Consider how this personality makes itself apparent in any one of O'Connor's stories you have read. How does the anecdote help to characterize the narrator's voice in the story?
3. To what extent do you think biographical details such as this — assuming the Milledgeville matron's memory to be accurate — can shed light on a writer's works?

CLAIRE KAHANE (b. 1935)

The Function of Violence in O'Connor's Fiction 1974

From the moment the reader enters O'Connor's backwoods, he is poised on the edge of a pervasive violence. Characters barely contain their rage; images reflect a hostile nature; and even the Christ to whom the characters are ultimately driven is a threatening figure . . . full of the apocalyptic wrath of the Old Testament.

O'Connor's conscious purpose is evident enough . . . : to reveal the need for grace in a world grotesque without a transcendent context. "I have found that my subject in fiction is the action of grace in territory largely held by the devil," she wrote [in *Mystery and Manners*], and she was not vague about what the devil is: "an evil intelligence determined on its own supremacy." It would seem that for O'Connor, given the fact of original Sin, any intelligence determined on its own supremacy was intrinsically evil. For in each work, it is the impulse toward secular autonomy, the smug confidence that human nature is perfectible by its own efforts, that she sets out to destroy, through an act of violence so intense that the character is rendered helpless, a passive victim of a superior power. Again and again she creates a fiction in which a character attempts to live autonomously, to define himself and his values, only to be jarred back to what she calls "reality" — the recognition of helplessness in the face of contingency, and the need for absolute submission to the power of Christ.

From "Flannery O'Connor's Rage of Vision" in *American Literature*

Considerations

1. Choose an O'Connor story and explain how grace — the divine influence from God that redeems a person — is used in it to transform a character.
2. Which O'Connor characters can be accurately described as having an "evil intelligence determined on its own supremacy"? Choose one character and write an essay explaining how this description is central to the conflict of the story.
3. Compare an O'Connor story with one of Hawthorne's in which a character "attempts to live autonomously, to define himself and his values, only to be jarred back to . . . 'reality' — the recognition of helplessness in the face of contingency. . . ."

DOROTHY T. McFARLAND (b. 1938)

A Formalist Reading of "Revelation" 1976

Mrs. Turpin, the protagonist of "Revelation," is convinced of her own goodness. Mrs. Turpin is a good Christian woman who looks after the poor, works for the church, and thanks Jesus effusively for making her what she is — and not "a nigger or white trash or ugly." Mrs. Turpin's failure of charity, despite her works of charity, is obvious as she sums up the other patients in the doctor's waiting room in which the story opens. Sizing up a "stylish lady" as one of her own kind and striking up a conversation with her, Mrs. Turpin reveals, through her words and thoughts, her interior judgments on the others present. Her veiled racism and social snobbery, her cheerful complacency, and her unabashed pride in her good disposition are too much for the stylish lady's daughter, a fat, scowling girl who has obviously had to suffer much of the same sort of thing from her mother. The girl responds to Mrs. Turpin's remarks with ugly looks until finally, provoked beyond endurance, she flings a book at Mrs. Turpin's head and lunges at her throat. "Go back to hell where you came from, you old wart hog," the girl whispers to her fiercely.

Hog imagery has already been introduced in the conversation between Mrs. Turpin and the stylish lady. Mrs. Turpin mentioned the hogs she raises in a concrete-floored pig parlor. Responding to an unwelcome interruption by a "white-trash woman," who declares hogs to be "Nasty stinking things, a-gruntin and a-rootin all over the place," Mrs. Turpin coldly replied that her hogs are washed down every day with a hose and are "cleaner than some children I've seen." ("Cleaner by far than that child right there" [the "white-trash" woman's child], she added to herself.)

O'Connor uses hogs in this story (and elsewhere) as symbols of unredeemed human nature. As no amount of external cleanliness can fundamentally change hog nature, so no amount of external goodness can fundamentally change human nature, which, in O'Connor's view, is contaminated with evil — whether it be . . . consciously chosen evil . . . or the more subtle evil of pride and self-righteousness displayed by . . . Mrs. Turpin.

Evil seems a strong word to apply to a character like Mrs. Turpin, who, for all her pride and complacency, is surely not a "bad" woman. Yet O'Connor obviously felt that Mrs. Turpin's belief in her own goodness was, if anything, more of an obstacle to the salvation of her soul than an outright commitment to evil. Thomas Merton reflects on this paradox: "Truly the great problem is the salvation of those who, being good, think they have no further need to be saved and imagine their task is to make others 'good' like themselves."°

Mrs. Turpin is at first shocked and indignant at the injustice of what has happened to her. Why should she, a hard-working, respectable, church-going woman, be singled out for such a message when there was "trash in the room to whom it might justly have been applied"? At the same time, however, Mrs.

Thomas Merton: (1915–1968) American Roman Catholic monastic and writer; author of *Conjectures of a Guilty Bystander* (Garden City, NY: Doubleday, 1968), 170.

Turpin senses that the girl "knew her in some intense and personal way, beyond time and place and condition," and the message, unpleasant as it is, has for her the force of divine revelation.

After pondering the girl's words with increasing wrath and indignation all afternoon, Mrs. Turpin marches down to the pig parlor on her farm and contemplates her hogs. "What do you send me a message like that for?" she demands of God. "How am I a hog and me both? How am I saved and from hell too?" She rails at God with increasing sarcasm until, with a final surge of fury, she roars, "Who do you think you are?" An echo of her own words comes back to her, like an answer, out of the silence.

Who does she think she is? The imagery surrounding this scene suggests that Mrs. Turpin considers herself the equal of God. The sun, that perennial symbol of God in O'Connor's fiction, seems comically obedient to Mrs. Turpin's presumption, and hangs over the tree line in an attitude almost exactly imitative of her own position on the fence of the pig parlor: "The sun was behind the wood, very red, looking over the paling of trees like a farmer inspecting his own hogs." While this image embodies Mrs. Turpin's assumption of the equality between her and God, it also suggests that the true relation between them is that God is the farmer, the world is His farm, and Mrs. Turpin is one of the "hogs"—humanity—at which He is gazing. His gaze—His light, symbolically the infusion of His grace into the world—is transforming; in the light of the setting sun the pigs are suffused with a red glow, and appear to "pant with a secret life." Mrs. Turpin, too, is touched by this transforming light, and life flows into her. "Like a monumental statue coming to life," she bends her head and gazes, "as if through the very heart of mystery, down into the pig parlor at the hogs."

The mystery of humanity, as O'Connor saw it, is that it is rooted in earth, yet bathed in God's light that fills it with secret life, the life of grace that is in no way dependent on worthiness or on the scale of human values Mrs. Turpin cherishes. The irrelevance of social values in the sphere of grace is manifested in the vision that is given to her as she lifts her eyes from the pigs and gazes at the purple streak in the sky left like a trail by the setting sun:

> She saw the streak as a vast swinging bridge extending upward from the earth through a field of living fire. Upon it a vast horde of souls were rumbling toward heaven. There were whole companies of white-trash, clean for the first time in their lives, and bands of black niggers in white robes, and battalions of freaks and lunatics shouting and clapping and leaping like frogs. And bringing up the end of the procession was a tribe of people whom she recognized at once as those who, like herself and Claud [her husband], had always had a little of everything and the God-given wit to use it right. . . . They were marching behind the others with great dignity, accountable as they had always been for good order and common sense and respectable behavior. They alone were on key. Yet she could see by their shocked and altered faces that even their virtues were being burned away.

For her to rise, to follow even at the end of the heaven-bound procession, it is necessary for her virtues to be burned away, for her to see herself as not more worthy of God's grace than the Negroes and white trash and freaks and lunatics she habitually looks down upon. Good works, in O'Connor's view, do not redeem; they only prevent Mrs. Turpin from seeing that she shares in the poverty and limitation and evil proclivities common to all humanity. She is not capable of lifting herself out of this condition by her own efforts; indeed, her efforts to do so only compound evil by making her think herself superior to others and thus reinforcing social inequality, pride, and complacency. "Rising" comes about by grace, and by Mrs. Turpin's response of openness to it. Appropriately enough, the instrument of grace — the ugly girl who hurled a book at Mrs. Turpin's head and declared that lady's kinship with hogs and hell — is named Mary Grace.

From *Flannery O'Connor*

Considerations

1. According to McFarland, what is the symbolic meaning of the hogs in "Revelation"?
2. How does McFarland's discussion of the story's imagery support her reading of the hogs' significance? What other images support this view?
3. Extend McFarland's discussion by writing an analysis of the images associated with Mary Grace that explain her function in the story.

10. A Collection of Stories

The sixteen short stories in this chapter represent a broad variety of styles and themes. They are written by men and women from a number of countries whose lives collectively span from the nineteenth century to the present. The three stories in "An Album of World Literature," by writers from Japan, India, and Argentina, introduce themes and styles from traditions that might differ quite a bit from your own. The four stories in "An Album of Contemporary Stories" — each written within the past five years — offer a sustained opportunity to explore the fiction being produced today. Inevitably, you will find some of the following stories more appealing than others, but every one of them is worth a careful reading, the kind of reading rewarded by pleasure and understanding.

QUESTIONS FOR RESPONSIVE READING

The following questions can help you consider important elements of fiction that reveal your responses to a story's effects and meanings. The questions are general, so they will not always be relevant to a particular story. Many of them, however, should prove useful for thinking, talking, and writing about a work of fiction. If you are uncertain about the meaning of a term used in a question, consult the Index of Terms on the inside back cover of this book for the pages that discuss the term.

Plot

1. Does the plot conform to a formula? Is it like those of any other stories you have read? Did you find it predictable?
2. What is the source and nature of the conflict for the protagonist? Was your major interest in the story based on what happens next or on some other concern? What does the title reveal now that you've finished the story?
3. Is the story told chronologically? If not, in what order is it told, and what is the effect of that order on your response to the action?

4. What does the exposition reveal? Are flashbacks used? Did you see any foreshadowings? Where is the climax?
5. Is the conflict resolved at the end? Would you characterize the ending as happy, unhappy, or somewhere in between?
6. Is the plot unified? Is each incident somehow related to some other element in the story?

Character

7. Do you identify with the protagonist? Who (or what) is the antagonist?
8. Does your response to any characters change as you read? What do you think caused the change? Do any characters change and develop in the course of the story?
9. Are round, flat, or stock characters used? Is their behavior motivated and plausible?
10. How does the author reveal characters? Are they directly described or indirectly presented? Are the characters' names used to convey something about them?
11. What is the purpose of the minor characters? Are they individualized, or do they primarily represent ideas or attitudes?

Setting

12. Is the setting important in shaping your response? If it were changed, would your response to the story's action and meaning be significantly different?
13. Is the setting used symbolically? Are the time, place, and atmosphere related to the theme?
14. Is the setting used as an antagonist?

Point of View

15. Who tells the story? Is it a first-person or third-person narrator? Is it a major or minor character or one who does not participate in the action at all? How much does the narrator know? Does the point of view change at all in the course of the story?
16. Is the narrator reliable and objective? Does the narrator appear too innocent, emotional, or self-deluded to be trusted?
17. Does the author directly comment on the action?
18. If told from a different point of view, how would your response to the story change? Would anything be lost?

Symbolism

19. Did you notice any symbols in the story? Are they actions, characters, settings, objects, or words?
20. How do the symbols contribute to your understanding of the story?

Theme

21. Did you find a theme? If so, what is it?
22. Is the theme stated directly, or is it developed implicitly through the plot, characters, or some other element?
23. Is the theme a confirmation of your values, or does it challenge them?

Style, Tone, and Irony

24. Do you think the style is consistent and appropriate throughout the story? Do all the characters use the same kind of language, or did you hear different voices?
25. Would you describe the level of diction as formal or informal? Are the sentences short and simple, long and complex, or some combination?
26. How does the author's use of language contribute to the tone of the story? Did it seem, for example, intense, relaxed, sentimental, nostalgic, humorous, angry, sad, or remote?
27. Do you think the story is worth reading more than once? Does the author's use of language bear close scrutiny so that you feel and experience more with each reading?

TONI CADE BAMBARA (b. 1939)

The Lesson

1972

Back in the days when everyone was old and stupid or young and foolish and me and Sugar were the only ones just right, this lady moved on our block with nappy hair and proper speech and no makeup. And quite naturally we laughed at her, laughed the way we did at the junk man who went about his business like he was some big-time president and his sorry-ass horse his secretary. And we kinda hated her too, hated the way we did the winos who cluttered up our parks and pissed on our handball walls and stank up our hallways and stairs so you couldn't halfway play hide-and-seek without a goddamn gas mask. Miss Moore was her name. The only woman on the block with no first name. And she was black as hell, cept for her feet, which were fish-white and spooky. And she was always planning these boring-ass things for us to do, us being my cousin, mostly, who lived on the block cause we all moved North the same time and to the same apartment then spread out gradual to breathe. And our parents would yank our heads into some kinda shape and crisp up our clothes so we'd be presentable for travel with Miss Moore, who always looked like she was going to church, though she never did. Which is just one of the things the grownups talked about when they talked behind her back like a dog. But when she came calling with some sachet she'd sewed up or some gingerbread she'd made or some book, why then they'd all be too embarrassed to turn her down and we'd get handed over all spruced up. She'd been to college and said it was only right that she should take responsibility for the young ones' education, and she not even related by marriage or blood. So they'd go for it. Specially Aunt Gretchen. She was the main gofer in the family. You got some ole dumb shit foolishness you want somebody to go for, you send for Aunt Gretchen. She been screwed into the go-along for so long, it's a blood-deep natural thing with her. Which is how she got saddled with me and Sugar and Junior in the first place while our mothers were in a la-de-da apartment up the block having a good ole time.

So this one day Miss Moore rounds us all up at the mailbox and it's pure-dee hot and she's knockin herself out about arithmetic. And school suppose to let up in summer I heard, but she don't never let up. And the starch in my pinafore scratching the shit outta me and I'm really hating this nappy-head bitch and her goddamn college degree. I'd much rather go to the pool or to the show where it's cool. So me and Sugar leaning on the mailbox being surly, which is a Miss Moore word. And Flyboy checking out what everybody brought for lunch. And Fat Butt already wasting his peanut-butter-and-jelly sandwich like the pig he is. And Junebug punchin on Q.T.'s arm for potato chips. And Rosie Giraffe shifting from one hip to the other waiting for somebody to step on her foot or ask her if she from Georgia so she can kick ass, preferably Mercedes'. And Miss Moore asking us do we know what money is, like we a bunch of retards. I mean real money, she say, like it's only poker chips or monopoly papers we lay on the grocer. So right away I'm tired of this and say so. And would much rather snatch Sugar and go to the Sunset and terrorize the West Indian kids and take their hair ribbons and their money too. And Miss Moore files that remark away for next week's lesson on brotherhood, I can tell. And finally I say we oughta get to the subway cause it's cooler and besides we might meet some cute boys. Sugar done swiped her mama's lipstick, so we ready.

So we heading down the street and she's boring us silly about what things cost and what our parents make and how much goes for rent and how money ain't divided up right in this country. And then she gets to the part about we all poor and live in the slums, which I don't feature. And I'm ready to speak on that, but she steps out in the street and hails two cabs just like that. Then she hustles half the crew in with her and hands me a five-dollar bill and tells me to calculate 10 percent tip for the driver. And we're off. Me and Sugar and Junebug and Flyboy hangin out the window and hollering to everybody, putting lipstick on each other cause Flyboy a faggot anyway, and making farts with our sweaty armpits. But I'm mostly trying to figure how to spend this money. But they all fascinated with the meter ticking and Junebug starts laying bets as to how much it'll read when Flyboy can't hold his breath no more. Then Sugar lays bets as to how much it'll be when we get there. So I'm stuck. Don't nobody want to go for my plan, which is to jump out at the next light and run off to the first bar-b-que we can find. Then the driver tells us to get the hell out cause we there already. And the meter reads eighty-five cents. And I'm stalling to figure out the tip and Sugar say give him a dime. And I decide he don't need it bad as I do, so later for him. But then he tries to take off with Junebug foot still in the door so we talk about his mama something ferocious. Then we check out that we on Fifth Avenue and everybody dressed up in stockings. One lady in a fur coat, hot as it is. White folks crazy.

"This is the place," Miss Moore say, presenting it to us in the voice she uses at the museum. "Let's look in the windows before we go in."

"Can we steal?" Sugar asks very serious like she's getting the ground rules squared away before she plays. "I beg your pardon," say Miss Moore, and we fall out. So she leads us around the windows of the toy store and me and Sugar screamin, "This is mine, that's mine, I gotta have that, that was made for me, I was born for that," till Big Butt drowns us out.

"Hey, I'm goin to buy that there."

"That there? You don't even know what it is, stupid."

"I do so," he say punchin on Rosie Giraffe. "It's a microscope."

"Whatcha gonna do with a microscope, fool?"

"Look at things."

"Like what, Ronald?" ask Miss Moore. And Big Butt ain't got the first notion. So here go Miss Moore gabbing about the thousands of bacteria in a drop of water and the somethinorother in a speck of blood and the million and one living things in the air around us is invisible to the naked eye. And what she say that for? Junebug go to town on that "naked" and we rolling. Then Miss Moore ask what it cost. So we all jam into the window smudgin it up and the price tag say $300. So then she ask how long'd take for Big Butt and Junebug to save up their allowances. "Too long," I say. "Yeh," adds Sugar, "outgrown it by that time." And Miss Moore say no, you never outgrow learning instruments. "Why, even medical students and interns and," blah, blah, blah. And we ready to choke Big Butt for bringing it up in the first damn place.

"This here costs four hundred eighty dollars," says Rosie Giraffe. So we pile up all over her to see what she pointin out. My eyes tell me it's a chunk of glass cracked with something heavy, and different-color inks dripped into the splits, then the whole thing put into a oven or something. But for $480 it don't make sense.

"That's a paperweight made of semi-precious stones fused together under tremendous pressure," she explains slowly, with her hands doing the mining and all the factory work.

"So what's a paperweight?" asks Rosie Giraffe.

"To weigh paper with, dumbbell," say Flyboy, the wise man from the East.

"Not exactly," say Miss Moore, which is what she say when you warm or way off too. "It's to weigh paper down so it won't scatter and make your desk untidy." So right away me and Sugar curtsy to each other and then to Mercedes who is more the tidy type.

"We don't keep paper on top of the desk in my class," say Junebug, figuring Miss Moore crazy or lyin one.

"At home, then," she say. "Don't you have a calendar and pencil case and a blotter and a letter-opener on your desk at home where you do your homework?" And she know damn well what our homes look like cause she nosys around in them every chance she gets.

"I don't even have a desk," say Junebug. "Do we?"

"No. And I don't get no homework neither," says Big Butt.

"And I don't even have a home," say Flyboy like he do at school to keep the white folks off his back and sorry for him. Send this poor kid to camp posters, is his specialty.

"I do," says Mercedes. "I have a box of stationery on my desk and a picture of my cat. My godmother bought the stationery and the desk. There's a big rose on each sheet and the envelopes smell like roses."

"Who wants to know about your smelly-ass stationery," say Rosie Giraffe fore I can get my two cents in.

"It's important to have a work area all your own so that . . ."

"Will you look at this sailboat, please," say Flyboy, cuttin her off and pointin to the thing like it was his. So once again we tumble all over each other to gaze at this magnificent thing in the toy store which is just big enough to maybe sail two kittens across the pond if you strap them to the posts tight. We all start reciting the price tag like we in assembly. "Handcrafted sailboat of fiberglass at one thousand one hundred ninety-five dollars."

"Unbelievable," I hear myself say and am really stunned. I read it again for myself just in case the group recitation put me in a trance. Same thing. For some reason this pisses me off. We look at Miss Moore and she lookin at us, waiting for I dunno what.

"Who'd pay all that when you can buy a sailboat set for a quarter at Pop's, a tube of glue for a dime, and a ball of string for eight cents? It must have a motor and a whole lot else besides," I say. "My sailboat cost me about fifty cents."

"But will it take water?" say Mercedes with her smart ass.

"Took mine to Alley Pond Park once," say Flyboy. "String broke. Lost it. Pity."

"Sailed mine in Central Park and it keeled over and sank. Had to ask my father for another dollar."

"And you got the strap," laugh Big Butt. "The jerk didn't even have a string on it. My old man wailed on his behind."

Little Q.T. was staring hard at the sailboat and you could see he wanted it bad. But he too little and somebody'd just take it from him. So what the hell. "This boat for kids, Miss Moore?"

"Parents silly to buy something like that just to get all broke up," say Rosie Giraffe.

"That much money it should last forever," I figure.

"My father'd buy it for me if I wanted it."

"Your father, my ass," say Rosie Giraffe getting a chance to finally push Mercedes.

"Must be rich people shop here," say Q.T.

"You are a very bright boy," say Flyboy. "What was your first clue?" And he rap him on the head with the back of his knuckles, since Q.T. the only one he could get away with. Though Q.T. liable to come up behind you years later and get his licks in when you half expect it.

"What I want to know is," I says to Miss Moore though I never talk to her, I wouldn't give the bitch that satisfaction, "is how much a real boat costs? I figure a thousand'd get you a yacht any day."

"Why don't you check that out," she says, "and report back to the group?" Which really pains my ass. If you gonna mess up a perfectly good swim day least you could do is have some answers. "Let's go in," she say like she got something up her sleeve. Only she don't lead the way. So me and Sugar turn the corner to where the entrance is, but when we get there I kinda hang back. Not that I'm scared, what's there to be afraid of, just a toy store. But I feel funny, shame. But what I got to be shamed about? Got as much right to go in as anybody. But somehow I can't seem to get hold of the door, so I step away from Sugar to lead. But she hangs back too. And I look at her and she looks at me and this is ridiculous. I mean, damn, I have never ever been shy about doing nothing or going nowhere. But then Mercedes steps up and then Rosie Giraffe and Big Butt crowd in behind and shove, and next thing we all stuffed into the doorway with only Mercedes squeezing past us, smoothing out her jumper and walking right down the aisle. Then the rest of us tumble in like a glued-together jigsaw done all wrong. And people lookin at us. And it's like the time me and Sugar crashed into the Catholic church on a dare. But once we got in there and everything so hushed and holy and the candles and the bowin and the handkerchiefs on all the drooping heads, I just couldn't go through with the plan. Which was for me to run up to the altar and do a tap dance while Sugar played the nose flute and messed around in the holy water. And Sugar kept givin me the elbow. Then later teased me so bad I tied her up in the shower and turned it on and locked her in. And she'd be there till this day if Aunt Gretchen hadn't finally figured I was lyin about the boarder takin a shower.

Same thing in the store. We all walkin on tiptoe and hardly touchin the games and puzzles and things. And I watched Miss Moore who is steady watchin us like she waitin for a sign. Like Mama Drewery watches the sky and sniffs the air and takes note of just how much slant is in the bird formation. Then me and Sugar bump smack into each other, so busy gazing at the toys, specially the sailboat. But we don't laugh and go into our fat-lady bump-stomach routine. We just stare at that price tag. Then Sugar run a finger over the whole boat. And I'm jealous and want to hit her. Maybe not her, but I sure want to punch somebody in the mouth.

"Watcha bring us here for, Miss Moore?"

"You sound angry, Sylvia. Are you mad about something?" Givin me one of them grins like she tellin a grown-up joke that never turns out to be funny. And she's lookin very closely at me like maybe she planning to do my portrait from memory. I'm mad, but I won't giver her that satisfaction. So I slouch around the store bein very bored and say, "Let's go."

Me and Sugar at the back of the train watchin the tracks whizzin by large then small then getting gobbled up in the dark. I'm thinkin about this tricky toy I saw in the store. A clown that somersaults on a bar then does chin-ups just cause you yank lightly at his leg. Cost $35. I could see me askin my mother for a $35 birthday clown. "You wanna who that costs what?" she'd say, cocking her head to the side to get a better view of the hole in my head. Thirty-five dollars could buy new bunk beds for Junior and Gretchen's boy. Thirty-five dollars and the whole household could go visit Granddaddy Nelson in the country. Thirty-five dollars would pay for the rent and the piano bill too. Who are these people that spend that much for performing clowns and $1000 for toy sailboats? What kinda work they do and how they live and how come we ain't in on it? Where we are is who we are, Miss Moore always pointin out. But it don't necessarily have to be that way, she always adds then waits for somebody to say that poor people have to wake up and demand their share of the pie and don't none of us know what kind of pie she talking about in the first damn place. But she ain't so smart cause I still got her four dollars from the taxi and she sure ain't gettin it. Messin up my day with this shit. Sugar nudges me in my pocket and winks.

Miss Moore lines us up in front of the mailbox where we started from, seem like years ago, and I got a headache for thinkin so hard. And we lean all over each other so we can hold up under the draggy-ass lecture she always finishes us off with at the end before we thank her for borin us to tears. But she just looks at us like she readin tea leaves. Finally she say, "Well, what did you think of F. A. O. Schwarz?"

Rosie Giraffe mumbles, "White folks crazy."

"I'd like to go there again when I get my birthday money," says Mercedes, and we shove her out the pack so she has to lean on the mailbox by herself.

"I'd like a shower. Tiring day," say Flyboy.

Then Sugar surprises me by sayin, "You know, Miss Moore, I don't think all of us here put together eat in a year what that sailboat costs." And Miss Moore lights up like somebody goosed her. "And?" she say, urging Sugar on. Only I'm standin on her foot so she don't continue.

"Imagine for a minute what kind of society it is in which some people can spend on a toy what it would cost to feed a family of six or seven. What do you think?"

"I think," say Sugar pushing me off her feet like she never done before, cause I whip her ass in a minute, "that this is not much of a democracy if you ask me. Equal chance to pursue happiness means an equal crack at the dough, don't it?" Miss Moore is besides herself and I am disgusted with Sugar's treachery. So I stand on her foot one more time to see if she'll shove me. She shuts up, and Miss Moore looks at me, sorrowfully I'm thinkin. And somethin weird is goin on, I can feel it in my chest.

"Anybody else learn anything today?" lookin dead at me. I walk away and Sugar has to run to catch up and don't even seem to notice when I shrug her arm off my shoulder.

"Well, we got four dollars anyway," she says.

"Uh hunh."

"We could go to Hascombs and get half a chocolate layer and then go to the Sunset and still have plenty money for potato chips and ice cream sodas."

"Un hunh."

"Race you to Hascombs," she say.

We start down the block and she gets ahead which is O.K. by me cause I'm going to the West End and then over to the Drive to think this day through. She can run if she want to and even run faster. But ain't nobody gonna beat me at nuthin.

JOHN CHEEVER (1912–1982)

Reunion

1962

The last time I saw my father was in Grand Central Station. I was going from my grandmother's in the Adirondacks to a cottage on the Cape that my mother had rented, and I wrote my father that I would be in New York between trains for an hour and a half and asked if we could have lunch together. His secretary wrote to say that he would meet me at the information booth at noon, and at twelve o'clock sharp I saw him coming through the crowd. He was a stranger to me — my mother divorced him three years ago, and I hadn't been with him since — but as soon as I saw him I felt that he was my father, my flesh and blood, my future and my doom. I knew that when I was grown I would be something like him; I would have to plan my campaigns within his limitations. He was a big, good-looking man, and I was terribly happy to see him again. He struck me on the back and shook my hand. "Hi, Charlie," he said. "Hi, boy. I'd like to take you up to my club, but it's in the Sixties, and if you have to catch an early train I guess we'd better get something to eat around here." He put his arm around me, and I smelled my father the way my mother sniffs a rose. It was a rich compound of whiskey, after-shave lotion, shoe polish, woolens, and the rankness of a mature male. I hoped that someone would see us together. I wished that we could be photographed. I wanted some record of our having been together.

We went out of the station and up a side street to a restaurant. It was still early, and the place was empty. The bartender was quarreling with a delivery boy, and there was one very old waiter in a red coat down by the kitchen door. We sat down, and my father hailed the waiter in a loud voice. *"Kellner!"* he shouted. *"Garçon! Cameriere!*° *You!"* His boisterousness in the empty restaurant seemed out of place. "Could we have a little service here!" he shouted. "Chop-chop." Then he clapped his hands. This caught the waiter's attention, and he shuffled over to our table.

"Were you clapping your hands at me?" he asked.

"Calm down, calm down, *sommelier,"*° my father said. "If it isn't too much to ask of you — if it wouldn't be too much above and beyond the call of duty, we would like a couple of Beefeater Gibsons."

"I don't like to be clapped at," the waiter said. 5

"I should have brought my whistle," my father said. "I have a whistle that is audible only to the ears of old waiters. Now, take out your little pad and your little pencil and see if you can get this straight: two Beefeater Gibsons. Repeat after me: two Beefeater Gibsons."

"I think you'd better go somewhere else," the waiter said quietly.

"That," said my father, "is one of the most brilliant suggestions I have ever heard. Come on, Charlie, let's get the hell out of here."

I followed my father out of that restaurant into another. He was not so boisterous this time. Our drinks came, and he cross-questioned me about the baseball season. He then struck the edge of his empty glass with his knife and began shouting again. *"Garçon! Kellner! You!* Could we trouble you to bring us two more of the same."

"How old is the boy?" the waiter asked. 10

"That," my father said, "is none of your goddamned business."

"I'm sorry, sir," the waiter said, "but I won't serve the boy another drink."

"Well, I have some news for you," my father said. "I have some very interesting news for you. This doesn't happen to be the only restaurant in New York. They've opened another on the corner. Come on, Charlie."

Kellner! . . . Garçon! Cameriere!: German, French, and Italian respectively for "Waiter!"
sommelier: Wine waiter (French).

He paid the bill, and I followed him out of that restaurant into another. Here the waiters wore pink jackets like hunting coats, and there was a lot of horse tack on the walls. We sat down, and my father began to shout again. "Master of the hounds! Tallyhoo and all that sort of thing. We'd like a little something in the way of a stirrup cup. Namely, two Bibson Greefeaters."

"Two Bibson Greefeaters?" the waiter asked, smiling.

"You know damned well what I want," my father said angrily. "I want two Beefeater Gibsons, and make it snappy. Things have changed in jolly old England. So my friend the duke tells me. Let's see what England can produce in the way of a cocktail."

"This isn't England," the waiter said.

"Don't argue with me," my father said. "Just do as you're told."

"I just thought you might like to know where you are," the waiter said.

"If there is one thing I cannot tolerate," my father said, "it is an impudent domestic. Come on, Charlie."

The fourth place we went to was Italian. *"Buon giorno,"* my father said *"Per favore, possiamo avere due cocktail americani, forti, forti. Molto gin, poco vermut."*°

"I don't understand Italian," the waiter said.

"Oh, come off it," my father said. "You understand Italian, and you know damned well you do. *Vogliamo due cocktail americani. Subito."*°

The waiter left us and spoke with the captain, who came over to our table and said, "I'm sorry, sir, but this table is reserved."

"All right," my father said. "Get us another table."

"All the tables are reserved," the captain said.

"I get it," my father said. "You don't desire our patronage. Is that it? Well, the hell with you. *Vada all' inferno.*° Let's go, Charlie."

"I have to get my train," I said.

"I'm sorry, sonny," my father said. "I'm terribly sorry." He put his arm around me and pressed me against him. "I'll walk you back to the station. If there had only been time to go up to my club."

"That's all right, Daddy," I said.

"I'll get you a paper," he said. "I'll get you a paper to read on the train."

Then he went up to a newsstand and said, "Kind sir, will you be good enough to favor me with one of your goddamned, no-good, ten-cent afternoon papers?" The clerk turned away from him and stared at a magazine cover. "Is it asking too much, kind sir," my father said, "is it asking too much for you to sell me one of your disgusting specimens of yellow journalism?"

"I have to go, Daddy," I said. "It's late."

"Now, just wait a second, sonny," he said. "Just wait a second. I want to get a rise out of this chap."

"Goodbye, Daddy," I said, and I went down the stairs and got my train, and that was the last time I saw my father.

Buon giorno . . . Per favore . . . : Good morning . . . Please, may we have two American cocktails, strong ones. Much gin, little vermouth (Italian).
Vogliamo due cocktail . . . : We want two American cocktails. Immediately (Italian).
Vada all' inferno: Go to hell (Italian).

JAMES JOYCE (1882–1941)

Araby

1916

North Richmond Street, being blind, was a quiet street except at the hour when the Christian Brothers' School set the boys free. An uninhabited house of two stories stood at the blind end, detached from its neighbors in a square ground. The other houses of the street, conscious of decent lives within them, gazed at one another with brown imperturbable faces.

The former tenant of our house, a priest, had died in the back drawing-room. Air, musty from having long been enclosed, hung in all the rooms, and the waste room behind the kitchen was littered with old useless papers. Among these I found a few paper-covered books, the pages of which were curled and damp: *The Abbot,* by Walter Scott, *The Devout Communicant* and *The Memoirs of Vidocq.* I liked the last best because its leaves were yellow. The wild garden behind the house contained a central apple-tree and a few straggling bushes under one of which I found the late tenant's rusty bicycle-pump. He had been a very charitable priest; in his will he had left all his money to institutions and the furniture of his house to his sister.

When the short days of winter came dusk fell before we had well eaten our dinners. When we met in the street the houses had grown somber. The space of sky above us was the color of ever-changing violet and towards it the lamps of the street lifted their feeble lanterns. The cold air stung us and we played till our bodies glowed. Our shouts echoed in the silent street. The career of our play brought us through the dark muddy lanes behind the houses where we ran the gantlet of the rough tribes from the cottages, to the back doors of the dark dripping gardens where odors arose from the ashpits, to the dark odorous stables where a coachman smoothed and combed the horse or shook music from the buckled harness. When we returned to the street light from the kitchen windows had filled the areas. If my uncle was seen turning the corner we hid in the shadow until we had seen him safely housed. Or if Mangan's sister came out on the doorstep to call her brother in to his tea we watched her from our shadow peer up and down the street. We waited to see whether she would remain or go in and, if she remained, we left our shadow and walked up to Mangan's steps resignedly. She was waiting for us, her figure defined by the light from the half-opened door. Her brother always teased her before he obeyed and I stood by the railings looking at her. Her dress swung as she moved her body and the soft rope of her hair tossed from side to side.

Every morning I lay on the floor in the front parlor watching her door. The blind was pulled down within an inch of the sash so that I could not be seen. When she came out on the doorstep my heart leaped. I ran to the hall, seized my books, and followed her. I kept her brown figure always in my eye and, when we came near the point at which our ways diverged, I quickened my pace and passed her. This happened morning after morning. I had never spoken to her, except for a few casual words, and yet her name was like a summons to all my foolish blood.

Her image accompanied me even in places the most hostile to romance. 5
On Saturday evenings when my aunt went marketing I had to go to carry some of the parcels. We walked through the flaring streets, jostled by drunken men

and bargaining women, amid the curses of laborers, the shrill litanies of shop-boys who stood on guard by the barrels of pigs' cheeks, the nasal chanting of street-singers, who sang a *come-all-you* about O'Donovan Rossa,° or a ballad about the troubles in our native land. These noises converged in a single sensation of life for me: I imagined that I bore my chalice safely through the throng of foes. Her name sprang to my lips at moments in strange prayers and praises which I myself did not understand. My eyes were often full of tears (I could not tell why) and at times a flood from my heart seemed to pour itself out into my bosom. I thought little of the future. I did not know whether I would ever speak to her or not or, if I spoke to her, how I could tell her of my confused adoration. But my body was like a harp and her words and gestures were like fingers running upon the wires.

One evening I went into the back drawing-room in which the priest had died. It was a dark rainy evening and there was no sound in the house. Through one of the broken panes I heard the rain impinge upon the earth, the fine incessant needles of water playing in the sodden beds. Some distant lamp or lighted window gleamed below me. I was thankful that I could see so little. All my senses seemed to desire to veil themselves and, feeling that I was about to slip from them, I pressed the palms of my hands together until they trembled, murmuring: *O love! O love!* many times.

At last she spoke to me. When she addressed the first words to me I was so confused that I did not know what to answer. She asked me was I going to *Araby*. I forget whether I answered yes or no. It would be a splendid bazaar, she said; she would love to go.

—And why can't you? I asked.

While she spoke she turned a silver bracelet round and round her wrist. She could not go, she said, because there would be a retreat that week in her convent. Her brother and two other boys were fighting for their caps and I was alone at the railings. She held one of the spikes, bowing her head towards me. The light from the lamp opposite our door caught the white curve of her neck, lit up her hair that rested there, and, falling, lit up the hand upon the railing. It fell over one side of her dress and caught the white border of a petticoat, just visible as she stood at ease.

— It's well for you, she said. 10

— If I go, I said, I will bring you something.

What innumerable follies laid waste my waking and sleeping thoughts after that evening! I wished to annihilate the tedious intervening days. I chafed against the work of school. At night in my bedroom and by day in the classroom her image came between me and the page I strove to read. The syllables of the word *Araby* were called to me through the silence in which my soul luxuriated and cast an Eastern enchantment over me. I asked for leave to go to the bazaar on Saturday night. My aunt was surprised and hoped it was not some Freemason affair. I answered few questions in class. I watched my master's face pass from amiability to sternness; he hoped I was not beginning to idle. I could not call my wandering thoughts together. I had hardly any patience with the serious

O'Donovan Rossa: (1831–1915) One of the leaders of the Fenian Brotherhood, a secret society devoted to making Ireland free of British rule.

work of life which, now that it stood between me and my desire, seemed to me child's play, ugly monotonous child's play.

On Saturday morning I reminded my uncle that I wished to go to the bazaar in the evening. He was fussing at the hall-stand, looking for the hat-brush, and answered me curtly:

—Yes, boy, I know.

As he was in the hall I could not go into the front parlor and lie at the 15
window. I left the house in bad humor and walked slowly towards the school. The air was pitilessly raw and already my heart misgave me.

When I came home to dinner my uncle had not yet been home. Still it was early. I sat staring at the clock for some time and, when its ticking began to irritate me, I left the room. I mounted the staircase and gained the upper part of the house. The high cold empty gloomy rooms liberated me and I went from room to room singing. From the front window I saw my companions playing below in the street. Their cries reached me weakened and indistinct and, leaning my forehead against the cool glass, I looked over at the dark house where she lived. I may have stood there for an hour, seeing nothing but the brown-clad figure cast by my imagination, touched discreetly by the lamplight at the curved neck, at the hand upon the railings, and at the border below the dress.

When I came downstairs again I found Mrs. Mercer sitting at the fire. She was an old garrulous woman, a pawnbroker's widow, who collected used stamps for some pious purpose. I had to endure the gossip of the tea-table. The meal was prolonged beyond an hour and still my uncle did not come. Mrs. Mercer stood up to go: she was sorry she couldn't wait any longer, but it was after eight o'clock and she did not like to be out late, as the night air was bad for her. When she had gone I began to walk up and down the room, clenching my fists. My aunt said:

—I'm afraid you may put off your bazaar for this night of Our Lord.

At nine o'clock I heard my uncle's latchkey in the halldoor. I heard him talking to himself and heard the hall-stand rocking when it had received the weight of his overcoat. I could interpret these signs. When he was midway through his dinner I asked him to give me the money to go to the bazaar. He had forgotten.

—The people are in bed and after their first sleep now, he said. 20

I did not smile. My aunt said to him energetically:

—Can't you give him the money and let him go? You've kept him late enough as it is.

My uncle said he was very sorry he had forgotten. He said he believed in the old saying: *All work and no play makes Jack a dull boy.* He asked me where I was going and, when I had told him a second time he asked me did I know *The Arab's Farewell to His Steed.* When I left the kitchen he was about to recite the opening lines of the piece to my aunt.

I held a florin tightly in my hand as I strode down Buckingham Street towards the station. The sight of the streets thronged with buyers and glaring with gas recalled to me the purpose of my journey. I took my seat in a third-class carriage of a deserted train. After an intolerable delay the train moved out of the station slowly. It crept onward among ruinous houses and over the twinkling river. At Westland Row Station a crowd of people pressed to the carriage doors; but the porters moved them back saying it was a special train for the bazaar. I remained alone in the bare carriage. In a few minutes the train drew up beside an improvised wooden platform. I passed out on to the road and saw by the lighted dial of a clock that it was ten minutes to ten. In front of me was a large building which displayed the magical name.

I could not find any sixpenny entrance and, fearing that the bazaar would be closed, I passed in quickly through a turnstile, handing a shilling to a weary-looking man. I found myself in a big hall girdled at half its height by a gallery. Nearly all the stalls were closed and the greater part of the hall was in darkness. I recognized a silence like that which pervades a church after a service. I walked into the center of the bazaar timidly. A few people were gathered about the stalls which were still open. Before a curtain, over which the words *Café Chantant*° were written in colored lamps, two men were counting money on a salver. I listened to the fall of the coins.

Remembering with difficulty why I had come I went over to one of the stalls and examined porcelain vases and flowered tea-sets. At the door of the stall a young lady was talking and laughing with two young gentlemen. I remarked their English accents and listened vaguely to their conversation.

—O, I never said such a thing!

—O, but you did!

—O, but I didn't!

—Didn't she say that?

—Yes. I heard her.

—O, there's a . . . fib!

Observing me the young lady came over and asked me did I wish to buy anything. The tone of her voice was not encouraging; she seemed to have spoken to me out of a sense of duty. I looked humbly at the great jars that stood like eastern guards at either side of the dark entrance to the stall and murmured:

—No, thank you.

The young lady changed the position of one of the vases and went back to the two young men. They began to talk of the same subject. Once or twice the young lady glanced at me over her shoulder.

I lingered before her stall, though I knew my stay was useless, to make my interest in her wares seem the more real. Then I turned away slowly and walked down the middle of the bazaar. I allowed the two pennies to fall against the sixpence in my pocket. I heard a voice call from one end of the gallery that the light was out. The upper part of the hall was now completely dark.

Gazing into the darkness I saw myself as a creature driven and derided by vanity; and my eyes burned with anguish and anger.

Café Chantant: A combination coffeehouse and music hall.

FRANZ KAFKA (1883–1924)

A Hunger Artist

1924

TRANSLATED BY EDWIN AND WILLA MUIR

During these last decades the interest in professional fasting has markedly diminished. It used to pay very well to stage such great performances under one's own management, but today that is quite impossible. We live in a different world now. At one time the whole town took a lively interest in the hunger artist; from day to day of his fast the excitement mounted; everybody wanted to see him at least once a day; there were people who bought season tickets for the last few days and sat from morning till night in front of his small barred cage; even in the nighttime there were visiting hours, when the whole effect was heightened by torch flares; on fine days the cage was set out in the open air, and then it was the children's special treat to see the hunger artist; for their elders he was often just a joke that happened to be in fashion, but the children stood open-mouthed, holding each other's hands for greater security, marveling at him as he sat there pallid in black tights, with his ribs sticking out so prominently, not even on a seat but down among straw on the ground, sometimes giving a courteous nod, answering questions with a constrained smile, or perhaps stretching an arm through the bars so that one might feel how thin it was, and then again withdrawing deep into himself, paying no attention to anyone or anything, not even to the all-important striking of the clock that was the only piece of furniture in his cage, but merely staring into vacancy with half shut eyes, now and then taking a sip from a tiny glass of water to moisten his lips.

Besides casual onlookers there were also relays of permanent watchers selected by the public, usually butchers, strangely enough, and it was their task to watch the hunger artist day and night, three of them at a time, in case he should have some secret recourse to nourishment. This was nothing but a formality, instituted to reassure the masses, for the initiates knew well enough that during his fast the artist would never in any circumstances, not even under forcible compulsion, swallow the smallest morsel of food; the honor of his profession forbade it. Not every watcher, of course, was capable of understanding this; there were often groups of night watchers who were very lax in carrying out their duties and deliberately huddled together in a retired corner to play cards with great absorption, obviously intending to give the hunger artist the chance of a little refreshment, which they supposed he could draw from some private hoard. Nothing annoyed the artist more than such watchers; they made him miserable; they made his fast seem unendurable; sometimes he mastered his feebleness sufficiently to sing during their watch for as long as he could keep going, to show them how unjust their suspicions were. But that was of little use; they only wondered at his cleverness in being able to fill his mouth even while singing. Much more to his taste were the watchers who sat close up to the bars, who were not content with the dim night lighting of the hall but focused him in the full glare of the electric pocket torch given them by the impresario. The harsh light did not trouble him at all, in any case he could never sleep properly, and he could always drowse a little, whatever the light, at any hour, even when the hall was thronged with noisy onlookers. He was quite happy at the prospect of spending a sleepless night with such watchers; he was ready to exchange jokes with them, to tell them stories out of his nomadic life, anything at all to keep them awake and demonstrate to them again that he had no eatables in his cage and that he was fasting as not one of them could fast. But his happiest moment was when the morning came and an enormous breakfast was brought them, at his expense, on which they flung themselves with the keen appetite of healthy men after a weary night of wakefulness. Of course there were people who argued that this breakfast was an unfair attempt to bribe the watchers, but that was going rather too far, and when they were invited to take on a night's vigil without a breakfast, merely for the sake of the cause, they made themselves scarce, although they stuck stubbornly to their suspicions.

Such suspicions, anyhow, were a necessary accompaniment to the profession of fasting. No one could possibly watch the hunger artist continuously, day and night, and so no one could produce first-hand evidence that the fast had really been rigorous and continuous; only the artist himself could know that, he was therefore bound to be the sole completely satisfied spectator of his own fast. Yet for other reasons he was never satisfied; it was not perhaps mere fasting that had brought him to such skeleton thinness that many people had regretfully to keep away from his exhibitions, because the sight of him was too much for them, perhaps it was dissatisfaction with himself that had worn him down. For he alone knew, what no other initiate knew, how easy it was to fast. It was the easiest thing in the world. He made no secret of this, yet people did not believe him, at the best they set him down as modest; most of them, however, thought he was out for publicity or else was some kind of cheat who found it easy to fast because he had discovered a way of making it easy, and then had the impudence to admit the fact, more or less. He had to put up with all that, and in the course of time had got used to it, but his inner dissatisfaction always rankled, and never yet, after any term of fasting — this must be granted to his credit — had he left the cage of his own free will. The longest period of fasting was fixed by his impresario at forty days, beyond that term he was not allowed to go, not even in great cities, and there was good reason for it, too. Experience had proved that for about forty days the interest of the public could be stimulated by a steadily increasing pressure of advertisement, but after that the town began to lose interest, sympathetic support began notably to fall off; there were of course local variations as between one town and another or one country and another, but as a general rule forty days marked the limit. So on the fortieth day the flower bedecked cage was opened, enthusiastic spectators filled the hall, a military band played, two doctors entered the cage to measure the results of the fast, which were announced through a megaphone, and finally two young ladies appeared, blissful at having been selected for the honor, to help the hunger artist down the few steps leading to a small table on which was spread a carefully chosen invalid repast. And at this very moment the artist always turned stubborn. True, he would entrust his bony arms to the outstretched helping hands of the ladies bending over him, but stand up he would not. Why stop fasting at this particular moment, after forty days of it? He had held out for a long time, an illimitably long time; why stop now, when he was in his best fasting form, or rather, not yet quite in his best fasting form? Why should he be cheated of the fame he would get for fasting longer, for being not only the record hunger artist of all time, which presumably he was already, but for beating his own record by a performance beyond human imagination, since he felt that there were no limits to his capacity for fasting? His public pretended to admire him so much, why should it have so little patience with him; if he could endure fasting longer, why shouldn't the public endure it? Besides, he was tired, he was comfortable sitting in the straw, and now he was supposed to lift himself to his full height and go down to a meal the very thought of which gave him a nausea that only the presence of the ladies kept him from betraying, and even that with an effort. And he looked up into the eyes of the ladies who were apparently so friendly and in reality so cruel, and shook his head, which felt too heavy on its strengthless neck. But then there happened yet again what always happened. The impresario came forward, without a word — for the band made speech impossible — lifted his arms in the air above the artist, as if inviting Heaven to look down upon its creature here in the straw, this suffering martyr, which indeed he was, although in quite another sense; grasped him round the emaciated waist, with exaggerated caution, so that the frail condition he was in might be appreciated; and committed him to the care of the blenching ladies, not without secretly giving him a shaking so that his legs and body tottered and swayed. The artist now submitted completely; his head lolled on his breast as if it had landed there by chance; his body was hollowed out; his legs in a spasm of self-preservation clung close to each other at the knees, yet scraped on the ground as if it were not really solid ground, as if they were only trying to find solid ground; and the whole weight of his body, a feather-weight after all, relapsed onto one of the ladies, who, looking round for help and panting a little — this post of honor was not at all what she had expected it to be — first stretched her neck as far as she could to keep her face at least free from contact with the artist, when finding this impossible, and her more fortunate companion not coming to her aid but merely holding extended on her own trembling hand the little bunch of knucklebones that was the artist's, to the great delight of the spectators burst into tears and had to be replaced by an attendant who had long been stationed in readiness. Then came the food, a little of which the impresario managed to get between the artist's lips, while he sat in a kind of half-fainting trance, to the accompaniment of cheerful patter designed to distract the public's attention from the artist's condition; after that a toast was drunk to the public, supposedly prompted by a whisper from the artist in the impresario's ear; the band confirmed it with a mighty flourish, the spectators melted away, and no one had any cause to be dissatisfied with the proceedings, no one except the hunger artist himself, he only, as always.

So he lived for many years, with small regular intervals of recuperation, in visible glory, honored by the world, yet in spite of that troubled in spirit, and all the more troubled because no one would take his trouble seriously. What comfort could he possibly need? What more could he possibly wish for? And if some good-natured person, feeling sorry for him, tried to console him by pointing out that his melancholy was probably caused by fasting; it could happen, especially when he had been fasting for some time, that he reacted with an outburst of fury and to the general alarm began to shake the bars of his cage like a wild animal. Yet the impresario had a way of punishing these outbreaks which he rather enjoyed putting into operation. He would apologize publicly for the artist's behavior, which was only to be excused, he admitted, because of the irritability caused by fasting; a condition hardly to be understood by well-fed people; then by natural transition he went on to mention the artist's equally incomprehensible boast that he could fast for much longer than he was doing; he praised the high ambition, the good will, the great self-denial undoubtedly implicit in such a statement; and then quite simply countered it by bringing out photographs, which were also on sale to the public, showing the artist on the fortieth day of a fast lying in bed almost dead from exhaustion. This perversion of the truth, familiar to the artist though it was, always unnerved him afresh and proved too much for him. What was a consequence of the premature ending of his fast was here presented as the cause of it! To fight against this lack of understanding, against a whole world of nonunderstanding, was impossible. Time and again in good faith he stood by the bars listening to the impresario, but as soon as the photographs appeared he always let go and sank with a groan back on to his straw, and the reassured public could once more come close and gaze at him.

A few years later when the witnesses of such scenes called them to mind, 5
they often failed to understand themselves at all. For meanwhile the aforementioned change in public interest had set in; it seemed to happen almost overnight; there may have been profound causes for it, but who was going to bother about that; at any rate the pampered hunger artist suddenly found himself deserted one fine day by the amusement seekers, who were streaming past him to other more favored attractions. For the last time the impresario hurried him over half Europe to discover whether the old interest might still survive here and there; all in vain; everywhere, as if by secret agreement, a positive revulsion from professional fasting was in evidence. Of course it could not really have sprung up so suddenly as all that, and many premonitory symptoms which had not been sufficiently remarked or suppressed during the rush and glitter of success now came retrospectively to mind, but it was now too late to take any countermeasures. Fasting would surely come into fashion again at some future date, yet that was no comfort for those living in the present. What, then, was the hunger artist to do? He had been applauded by thousands in his time and could hardly come down to showing himself in a street booth at village fairs, and as for adopting another profession, he was not only too old for that but too frantically devoted to fasting. So he took leave of the impresario, his partner in an unparalleled career, and hired himself to a large circus; in order to spare his own feelings he avoided reading the conditions of his contract.

A large circus with its enormous traffic in replacing and recruiting men, animals, and apparatus can always find a use for people at any time, even for a hunger artist, provided of course that he does not ask too much, and in this particular case anyhow it was not only the artist who was taken on but his famous and long-known name as well, indeed considering the peculiar nature of his performance, which was not impaired by advancing age, it could not be objected that there was an artist past his prime, no longer at the height of his professional skill, seeking a refuge in some quiet corner of a circus; on the contrary, the hunger artist averred that he could fast as well as ever, which was entirely credible; he even alleged that if he were allowed to fast as he liked, and this was at once promised him without more ado, he could astound the world by establishing a record never yet achieved, a statement which certainly provoked a smile among the other professionals, since it left out of account the change in public opinion, which the hunger artist in his zeal conveniently forgot.

He had not, however, actually lost his sense of the real situation and took it as a matter of course that he and his cage should be stationed, not in the middle of the ring as a main attraction, but outside, near the animal cages, on a site that was after all easily accessible. Large and gaily painted placards made a frame for the cage and announced what was to be seen inside it. When the public came thronging out in the intervals to see the animals, they could hardly avoid passing the hunger artist's cage and stopping there for a moment; perhaps they might even have stayed longer had not those pressing behind them in the narrow gangway, who did not understand why they should be held up on their way toward the excitements of the menagerie, made it impossible for anyone to stand gazing quietly for any length of time. And that was the reason why the hunger artist, who had of course been looking forward to these visiting hours as the main achievement of his life, began instead to shrink from them. At first he could hardly wait for the intervals; it was exhilarating to watch the crowds come streaming his way, until only too soon — not even the most obstinate self-deception, clung to almost consciously, could hold out against the fact — the conviction was borne in upon him that these people, most of them, to judge from their actions, again and again, without exception, were all on their way to the menagerie. And the first sight of them from the distance remained the best. For when they reached his cage he was at once deafened by the storm of shouting and abuse that arose from the two contending factions, which renewed themselves continuously, of those who wanted to stop and stare at him — he soon began to dislike them more than the others — not out of real interest but only out of obstinate self-assertiveness, and those who wanted to go straight on to the animals. When the first great rush was past, the stragglers came along, and these, whom nothing could have prevented from stopping to look at him as long as they had breath, raced past with long strides, hardly even glancing at him, in their haste to get to the menagerie in time. And all too rarely did it happen that he had a stroke of luck, when some father of a family fetched up before him with his children, pointed a finger at the hunger artist, and explained at length what the phenomenon meant, telling stories of earlier years when he himself had watched similar but much more thrilling performances, and the children, still rather uncomprehending, since neither inside nor outside school had they been sufficiently prepared for this lesson — what did they care about fasting? — yet showed by the brightness of their intent eyes that new and better times might be coming. Perhaps, said the hunger artist to himself many a time, things would be a little better if his cage were set not quite so near the menagerie. That made it too easy for people to make their choice, to say nothing of what he suffered from the stench of the menagerie, the animals' restlessness by night, the carrying past of raw lumps of flesh for the beasts of prey, the roaring at feeding times, which depressed him continually. But he did not dare to lodge a complaint with the management; after all, he had the animals to thank for the troops of people who passed his cage, among whom there might always be one here and there to take an interest in him, and who could tell where they might seclude him if he called attention to his existence and thereby to the fact that, strictly speaking, he was only an impediment on the way to the menagerie.

A small impediment, to be sure, one that grew steadily less. People grew familiar with the strange idea that they could be expected, in times like these, to take an interest in a hunger artist, and with this familiarity the verdict went out against him. He might fast as much as he could, and he did so; but nothing could save him now, people passed him by. Just try to explain to anyone the art of fasting! Anyone who has no feeling for it cannot be made to understand it. The fine placards grew dirty and illegible, they were torn down; the little notice board telling the number of fast days achieved, which at first was changed carefully every day, had long stayed at the same figure, for after the first few weeks even this small task seemed pointless to the staff; and so the artist simply fasted on and on, as he had once dreamed of doing, and it was no trouble to him, just as he had always foretold, but no one counted the days, no one, not even the artist himself, knew what records he was already breaking, and his heart grew heavy. And when once in a time some leisurely passerby stopped, made merry over the old figure on the board, and spoke of swindling, that was in its way the stupidest lie ever invented by indifference and inborn malice, since it was not the hunger artist who was cheating; he was working honestly, but the world was cheating him of his reward.

Many more days went by, however, and that too came to an end. An overseer's eye fell on the cage one day and asked the attendants why this perfectly good cage should be left standing there unused with dirty straw inside it; nobody knew, until one man, helped out by the notice board, remembered about the hunger artist. They poked into the straw with sticks and found him in it. "Are you still fasting?" asked the overseer. "When on earth do you mean to stop?" "Forgive me, everybody," whispered the hunger artist; only the overseer, who had his ear to the bars, understood him. "Of course," said the overseer, and tapped his forehead with a finger to let the attendants know what state the man was in, "we forgive you." "I always wanted you to admire my fasting," said the hunger artist. "We do admire it," said the overseer, affably. "But you shouldn't admire it," said the hunger artist. "Well, then we don't admire it," said the overseer, "but why shouldn't we admire it?" "Because I have to fast, I can't help it," said the hunger artist. "What a fellow you are," said the overseer, "and why can't you help it?" "Because," said the hunger artist, lifting his head a little and speaking, with his lips pursed, as if for a kiss, right into the overseer's ear, so that no syllable might be lost, "because I couldn't find the food I liked. If I had found it, believe me, I should have made no fuss and stuffed myself like you or anyone else." These were his last words, but in his dimming eyes remained the firm though no longer proud persuasion that he was still continuing to fast.

"Well, clear this out now!" said the overseer, and they buried the hunger 10
artist, straw and all. Into the cage they put a young panther. Even the most insensitive felt it refreshing to see this wild creature leaping around the cage that had so long been dreary. The panther was all right. The food he liked was brought him without hesitation by the attendants; he seemed not even to miss his freedom; his noble body, furnished almost to the bursting point with all that it needed, seemed to carry freedom around with it too; somewhere in his jaws it seemed to lurk; and the joy of life streamed with such ardent passion from his throat that for the onlookers it was not easy to stand the shock of it. But they braced themselves, crowded round the cage, and did not want ever to move away.

JAMAICA KINCAID (b. 1949)

Girl

1978

Wash the white clothes on Monday and put them on the stone heap; wash the color clothes on Tuesday and put them on the clothesline to dry; don't walk barehead in the hot sun; cook pumpkin fritters in very hot sweet oil; soak your little cloths right after you take them off; when buying cotton to make yourself a nice blouse, be sure that it doesn't have gum on it, because that way it won't hold up well after a wash; soak salt fish overnight before you cook it; is it true that you sing benna° in Sunday school?; always eat your food in such a way that it won't turn someone else's stomach; on Sundays try to walk like a lady and not like the slut you are so bent on becoming; don't sing benna in Sunday school; you mustn't speak to wharf-rat boys, not even to give directions; don't eat fruits on the street — flies will follow you; *but I don't sing benna on Sundays at all and never in Sunday school;* this is how to sew on a button; this is how to make a buttonhole for the button you have just sewed on; this is how to hem a dress when you see the hem coming down and so to prevent yourself from looking like the slut I know you are so bent on becoming; this is how you iron your father's khaki shirt so that it doesn't have a crease; this is how you iron your father's khaki pants so that they don't have a crease; this is how you grow okra — far from the house, because okra tree harbors red ants; when you are growing dasheen, make sure it gets plenty of water or else it makes your throat itch when you are eating it; this is how you sweep a corner; this is how you sweep a whole house; this is how you sweep a yard; this is how you smile to someone you don't like too much; this is how you smile to someone you don't like at all; this is how you smile to someone you like completely; this is how you set a table for tea; this is how you set a table for dinner; this is how you set a table for dinner with an important guest; this is how you set a table for lunch; this is how you set a table for breakfast; this is how to behave in the presence of men who don't know you very well, and this way they won't recognize immediately the slut I have warned you against becoming; be sure to wash every day, even if it is with your own spit; don't squat down to play marbles — you are not a boy, you know; don't pick people's flowers — you might catch something; don't throw stones at blackbirds, because it might not be a blackbird at all; this is how to make a bread pudding; this is how to make doukona;° this is how to make pepper pot; this is how to make a good medicine for a cold; this is how to make a good medicine to throw away a child before it even becomes a child; this is how to catch a fish; this is how to throw back a fish you don't like, and that way something bad won't fall on you; this is how to bully a man; this is how a man bullies you; this is how to love a man, and if this doesn't work there are other ways, and if they don't work don't feel too bad about giving up; this is how to spit up in the air if you feel like it, and this is how to move quick so that it doesn't fall on you; this is how to make ends meet; always squeeze bread to make sure it's fresh; *but what if the baker won't let me*

benna: Calypso music.
doukona: A spicy plantain pudding.

feel the bread?; you mean to say that after all you are really going to be the kind of woman who the baker won't let near the bread?

D. H. LAWRENCE (1885–1930)

The Horse Dealer's Daughter 1922

"Well, Mabel, and what are you going to do with yourself?" asked Joe, with foolish flippancy. He felt quite safe himself. Without listening for an answer, he turned aside, worked a grain of tobacco to the tip of his tongue, and spat it out. He did not care about anything, since he felt safe himself.

The three brothers and the sister sat round the desolate breakfast-table, attempting some sort of desultory consultation. The morning's post had given the final tap to the family fortunes, and all was over. The dreary dining-room itself, with its heavy mahogany furniture, looked as if it were waiting to be done away with.

But the consultation amounted to nothing. There was a strange air of ineffectuality about the three men, as they sprawled at table, smoking and reflecting vaguely on their own condition. The girl was alone, a rather short, sullen-looking young woman of twenty-seven. She did not share the same life as her brothers. She would have been good-looking, save for the impressive fixity of her face, "bull-dog," as her brothers called it.

There was a confused tramping of horses' feet outside. The three men all sprawled round in their chairs to watch. Beyond the dark holly bushes that separated the strip of lawn from the high-road, they could see a cavalcade of shire horses swinging out of their own yard, being taken for exercise. This was the last time. These were the last horses that would go through their hands. The young men watched with critical, callous look. They were all frightened at the collapse of their lives, and the sense of disaster in which they were involved left them no inner freedom.

5 Yet they were three fine, well-set fellows enough. Joe, the eldest, was a man of thirty-three, broad and handsome in a hot, flushed way. His face was red, he twisted his black mustache over a thick finger, his eyes were shallow and restless. He had a sensual way of uncovering his teeth when he laughed, and his bearing was stupid. Now he watched the horses with a glazed look of helplessness in his eyes, a certain stupor of downfall.

The great draft-horses swung past. They were tied head to tail, four of them, and they heaved along to where a lane branched off from the high-road, planting their great hoofs floutingly in the fine black mud, swinging their great rounded haunches sumptuously, and trotting a few sudden steps as they were led into the lane, round the corner. Every movement showed a massive, slumbrous strength, and a stupidity which held them in subjection. The groom at the head looked back, jerking the leading rope. And the cavalcade moved out of sight up the lane, the tail of the last horse, bobbed up tight and stiff, held out taut from the swinging great haunches as they rocked behind the hedges in a motionlike sleep.

Joe watched with glazed hopeless eyes. The horses were almost like his own body to him. He felt he was done for now. Luckily he was engaged to a woman as old as himself, and therefore her father, who was steward of a neighboring estate, would provide him with a job. He would marry and go into harness. His life was over, he would be a subject animal now.

He turned uneasily aside, the retreating steps of the horses echoing in his ears. Then, with foolish restlessness, he reached for the scraps of bacon-rind from the plates, and making a faint whistling sound, flung them to the terrier that lay against the fender. He watched the dog swallow them, and waited till the creature looked into his eyes. Then a faint grin came on his face, and in a high, foolish voice he said:

"You won't get much more bacon, shall you, you little b——?"

The dog faintly and dismally wagged its tail, then lowered its haunches, circled round, and lay down again.

There was another helpless silence at the table. Joe sprawled uneasily in his seat, not willing to go till the family conclave was dissolved. Fred Henry, the second brother, was erect, clean-limbed, alert. He had watched the passing of the horses with more *sang-froid.*° If he was an animal, like Joe, he was an animal which controls, not one which is controlled. He was master of any horse, and he carried himself with a well-tempered air of mastery. But he was not master of the situations of life. He pushed his coarse brown mustache upwards, off his lip, and glanced irritably at his sister, who sat impassive and inscrutable.

"You'll go and stop with Lucy for a bit, shan't you?" he asked. The girl did not answer.

"I don't see what else you can do," persisted Fred Henry.

"Go as a skivvy,"° Joe interpolated laconically.

The girl did not move a muscle.

"If I was her, I should go in for training for a nurse," said Malcolm, the youngest of them all. He was the baby of the family, a young man of twenty-two, with a fresh, jaunty *museau.*°

But Mabel did not take any notice of him. They had talked at her and round her for so many years, that she hardly heard them at all.

The marble clock on the mantelpiece softly chimed the half-hour, the dog rose uneasily from the hearth-rug and looked at the party at the breakfast-table. But still they sat on in ineffectual conclave.

"Oh, all right," said Joe suddenly, apropos of nothing. "I'll get a move on."

He pushed back his chair, straddled his knees with a downward jerk, to get them free, in horsey fashion, and went to the fire. Still he did not go out of the room; he was curious to know what the others would do or say. He began to charge his pipe, looking down at the dog and saying in a high, affected voice:

"Going wi' me? Going wi' me are ter? Tha'rt goin' further than tha counts on just now, dost hear?"

The dog faintly wagged its tail, the man stuck out his jaw and covered his pipe with his hands, and puffed intently, losing himself in the tobacco, looking down all the while at the dog with an absent brown eye. The dog looked up at

sang-froid: Coolness, composure.
skivvy: Domestic worker.
museau: Slang for face.

him in mournful distrust. Joe stood with his knees stuck out, in real horsey fashion.

"Have you had a letter from Lucy?" Fred Henry asked of his sister.

"Last week," came the neutral reply.

"And what does she say?"

There was no answer.

"Does she *ask* you to go and stop there?" persisted Fred Henry.

"She says I can if I like."

"Well, then, you'd better. Tell her you'll come on Monday."

This was received in silence.

"That's what you'll do then, is it?" said Fred Henry, in some exasperation.

But she made no answer. There was a silence of futility and irritation in the room. Malcolm grinned fatuously.

"You'll have to make up your mind between now and next Wednesday," said Joe loudly, "or else find yourself lodgings on the curbstone."

The face of the young woman darkened, but she sat on immutable.

"Here's Jack Fergusson!" exclaimed Malcolm, who was looking aimlessly out of the window.

"Where?" exclaimed Joe loudly.

"Just gone past."

"Coming in?"

Malcolm craned his neck to see the gate.

"Yes," he said.

There was a silence. Mabel sat on like one condemned, at the head of the table. Then a whistle was heard from the kitchen. The dog got up and barked sharply. Joe opened the door and shouted:

"Come on."

After a moment a young man entered. He was muffled up in overcoat and a purple woolen scarf, and his tweed cap, which he did not remove, was pulled down on his head. He was of medium height, his face was rather long and pale, his eyes looked tired.

"Hello, Jack! Well, Jack!" exclaimed Malcolm and Joe. Fred Henry merely said: "Jack."

"What's doing?" asked the newcomer, evidently addressing Fred Henry.

"Same. We've got to be out by Wednesday. Got a cold?"

"I have — got it bad, too."

"Why don't you stop in?"

"*Me* stop in? When I can't stand on my legs, perhaps I shall have a chance." the young man spoke huskily. He had a slight Scotch accent.

"It's a knock-out, isn't it," said Joe, boisterously, "if a doctor goes round croaking with a cold. Looks bad for the patients, doesn't it?"

The young doctor looked at him slowly.

"Anything the matter with *you,* then?" he asked sarcastically.

"Not as I know of. Damn your eyes, hope not. Why?"

"I thought you were very concerned about the patients, wondered if you might be one yourself."

"Damn it, no, I've never been patient to no flaming doctor, and hope I never shall be," returned Joe.

At this point Mabel rose from the table, and they all seemed to become aware of her existence. She began putting the dishes together. The young doctor looked at her, but did not address her. He had not greeted her. She went out of the room with the tray, her face impassive and unchanged.

"When are you off then, all of you?" asked the doctor.

"I'm catching the eleven-forty," replied Malcolm. "Are you goin' down wi' th' trap,° Joe?"

"Yes, I've told you I'm going down wi' th' trap, haven't I?"

"We'd better be getting her in then. So long, Jack, if I don't see you before I go," said Malcolm, shaking hands.

He went out, followed by Joe, who seemed to have his tail between his legs.

"Well, this is the devil's own," exclaimed the doctor, when he was left alone with Fred Henry. "Going before Wednesday, are you?"

"That's the orders," replied the other.

"Where, to Northampton?"

"That's it."

"The devil!" exclaimed Fergusson, with quiet chagrin.

And there was silence between the two.

"All settled up, are you?" asked Fergusson.

"About."

There was another pause.

"Well, I shall miss yer, Freddy, boy," said the young doctor.

"And I shall miss thee, Jack," returned the other.

"Miss you like hell," mused the doctor.

Fred Henry turned aside. There was nothing to say. Mabel came in again, to finish clearing the table.

"What are *you* going to do, then, Miss Pervin?" asked Fergusson. "Going to your sister's, are you?"

Mabel looked at him with her steady, dangerous eyes, that always made him uncomfortable, unsettling his superficial ease.

"No," she said.

"Well, what in the name of fortune *are* you going to do? Say what you mean to do," cried Fred Henry, with futile intensity.

But she only averted her head, and continued her work. She folded the white table-cloth, and put on the chenille cloth.

"The sulkiest bitch that ever trod!" muttered her brother.

But she finished her task with perfectly impassive face, the young doctor watching her interestedly all the while. Then she went out.

Fred Henry stared after her, clenching his lips, his blue eyes fixing in sharp antagonism, as he made a grimace of sour exasperation.

"You could bray her into bits, and that's all you'd get out of her," he said, in a small, narrowed tone.

The doctor smiled faintly.

"What's she *going* to do, then?" he asked.

"Strike me if *I* know!" returned the other.

There was a pause. Then the doctor stirred.

trap: A light two-wheeled carriage.

"I'll be seeing you tonight, shall I?" he said to his friend.

"Ay — where's it to be? Are we going over to Jessdale?"

"I don't know. I've got such a cold on me. I'll come round to the 'Moon and Stars,' anyway."

"Let Lizzie and May miss their night for once, eh?"

"That's it — if I feel as I do now."

"All's one ——"

The two young men went through the passage and down to the back door together. The house was large, but it was servantless now, and desolate. At the back was a small bricked houseyard and beyond that a big square, graveled fine and red, and having stables on two sides. Sloping, dank, winter-dark fields stretched away on the open sides.

But the stables were empty. Joseph Pervin, the father of the family, had been a man of no education, who had become a fairly large horse dealer. The stables had been full of horses, there was a great turmoil and come-and-go of horses and of dealers and grooms. Then the kitchen was full of servants. But of late things had declined. The old man had married a second time, to retrieve his fortunes. Now he was dead and everything was gone to the dogs, there was nothing but debt and threatening.

For months, Mabel had been servantless in the big house, keeping the home together in penury for her ineffectual brothers. She had kept house for ten years. But previously it was with unstinted means. Then, however brutal and coarse everything was, the sense of money had kept her proud, confident. The men might be foul-mouthed, the women in the kitchen might have bad reputations, her brothers might have illegitimate children. But so long as there was money, the girl felt herself established, and brutally proud, reserved.

No company came to the house, save dealers and coarse men. Mabel had no associates of her own sex, after her sister went away. But she did not mind. She went regularly to church, she attended to her father. And she lived in the memory of her mother, who had died when she was fourteen, and whom she had loved. She had loved her father, too, in a different way, depending upon him, and feeling secure in him, until at the age of fifty-four he married again. And then she had set hard against him. Now he had died and left them all hopelessly in debt.

She had suffered badly during the period of poverty. Nothing, however, could shake the curious, sullen, animal pride that dominated each member of the family. Now, for Mabel, the end had come. Still she would not cast about her. She would follow her own way just the same. She would always hold the keys of her own situation. Mindless and persistent, she endured from day to day. Why should she think? Why should she answer anybody? It was enough that this was the end, and there was no way out. She need not pass any more darkly along the main street of the small town, avoiding every eye. She need not demean herself any more, going into the shops and buying the cheapest food. This was at an end. She thought of nobody, not even of herself. Mindless and persistent, she seemed in a sort of ecstasy to be coming nearer to her fulfillment, her own glorification, approaching her dead mother, who was glorified.

In the afternoon she took a little bag, with shears and sponge and a small scrubbing-brush, and went out. It was a gray, wintry day, with saddened, dark green fields and an atmosphere blackened by the smoke of foundries not far off. She went quickly, darkly along the causeway, heeding nobody, through the town to the churchyard.

100 There she always felt secure, as if no one could see her, although as a matter of fact she was exposed to the stare of everyone who passed along under the churchyard wall. Nevertheless, once under the shadow of the great looming church, among the graves, she felt immune from the world, reserved within the thick churchyard wall as in another country.

Carefully she clipped the grass from the grave, and arranged the pinky white, small chrysanthemums in the tin cross. When this was done, she took an empty jar from a neighboring grave, brought water, and carefully, most scrupulously sponged the marble headstone and the coping-stone.

It gave her sincere satisfaction to do this. She felt in immediate contact with the world of her mother. She took minute pains, went through the park in a state bordering on pure happiness, as if in performing this task she came into a subtle, intimate connection with her mother. For the life she followed here in the world was far less real than the world of death she inherited from her mother.

The doctor's house was just by the church. Fergusson, being a mere hired assistant, was slave to the countryside. As he hurried now to attend to the outpatients in the surgery, glancing across the graveyard with his quick eye, he saw the girl at her task at the grave. She seemed so intent and remote, it was like looking into another world. Some mystical element was touching in him. He slowed down as he walked, watching her as if spellbound.

She lifted her eyes, feeling him looking. Their eyes met. And each looked again at once, each feeling, in some way, found out by the other. He lifted his cap and passed on down the road. There remained distinct in his consciousness, like a vision, the memory of her face, lifted from the tombstone in the churchyard, and looking at him with slow, large, portentous eyes. It *was* portentous, her face. It seemed to mesmerize him. There was a heavy power in her eyes which laid hold of his whole being, as if he had drunk some powerful drug. He had been feeling weak and done before. Now the life came back into him, he felt delivered from his own fretted, daily self.

105 He finished his duties at the surgery as quickly as might be, hastily filling up the bottles of the waiting people with cheap drugs. Then, in perpetual haste, he set off again to visit several cases in another part of his round, before teatime. At all times he preferred to walk if he could, but particularly when he was not well. He fancied the motion restored him.

The afternoon was falling. It was gray, deadened, and wintry, with a slow, moist, heavy coldness sinking in and deadening all the faculties. But why should he think or notice? He hastily climbed the hill and turned across the dark green fields, following the black cinder-track. In the distance, across a shallow dip in the country, the small town was clustered like smoldering ash, a tower, a spire, a heap of low, raw, extinct houses. And on the nearest fringe of the town, sloping into the dip, was Oldmeadow, the Pervins' house. He could see the stables and the outbuildings distinctly, as they lay towards him on the slope. Well, he would not go there many more times! Another resource would be lost to him, another place gone: the only company he cared for in the alien, ugly little town he was losing. Nothing but work, drudgery, constant hastening from dwelling to dwelling among the colliers and the iron-workers. It wore him out, but at the same time he had a craving for it. It was a stimulant to him to be in the homes of the working people, moving, as it were, through the innermost body of their life. His nerves were excited and gratified. He could come so near, into the very lives of the rough, inarticulate, powerful emotional men and women: He grumbled, he said he hated the hellish hole. But as a matter of fact it excited him, the contact with the rough, strongly-feeling people was a stimulant applied direct to his nerves.

Below Oldmeadow, in the green, shallow, soddened hollow of fields, lay a square, deep pond. Roving across the landscape, the doctor's quick eye detected a figure in black passing through the gate of the field, down towards the pond. He looked again. It would be Mabel Pervin. His mind suddenly became alive and attentive.

Why was she going down there? He pulled up on the path on the slope above, and stood staring. He could just make sure of the small black figure moving in the hollow of the failing day. He seemed to see her in the midst of such obscurity, that he was like a clairvoyant, seeing rather with the mind's eye than with ordinary sight. Yet he could see her positively enough, whilst he kept his eye attentive. He felt, if he looked away from her, in the thick, ugly falling dusk, he would lose her altogether.

He followed her minutely as she moved, direct and intent, like something transmitted rather than stirring in voluntary activity, straight down from the field towards the pond. There she stood on the bank for a moment. She never raised her head. Then she waded slowly into the water.

110 He stood motionless as the small black figure walked slowly and deliberately towards the center of the pond, very slowly, gradually moving deeper into the motionless water, and still moving forward as the water got up to her breast. Then he could see her no more in the dusk of the dead afternoon.

"There!" he exclaimed. "Would you believe it?"

And he hastened straight down, running over the wet, soddened fields, pushing through the hedges, down into the depression of callous wintry obscurity. It took him several minutes to come to the pond. He stood on the bank, breathing heavily. He could see nothing. His eyes seemed to penetrate the dead water. Yes, perhaps that was the dark shadow of her black clothing beneath the surface of the water.

He slowly ventured into the pond. The bottom was deep, soft clay, he sank in, and the water clasped dead cold round his legs. As he stirred he could smell the cold, rotten clay that fouled up into the water. It was objectionable in his lungs. Still, repelled and yet not heeding, he moved deeper into the pond. The cold water rose over his thighs, over his loins, upon his abdomen. The lower part of his body was all sunk in the hideous cold element. And the bottom was so deeply soft and uncertain, he was afraid of pitching with his mouth underneath. He could not swim, and was afraid.

He crouched a little, spreading his hands under the water and moving them round, trying to feel for her. The dead cold pond swayed upon his chest. He moved again, a little deeper, and again, with his hands underneath, he felt all around under the water. And he touched her clothing. But it evaded his fingers. He made a desperate effort to grasp it.

115 And so doing he lost his balance and went under, horribly, suffocating in the foul earthy water, struggling madly for a few moments. At last, after what

seemed an eternity, he got his footing, rose again into the air, and looked around. He gasped, and knew he was in the world. Then he looked at the water. She had risen near him. He grasped her clothing, and drawing her nearer, turned to take his way to land again.

He went very slowly, carefully, absorbed in the slow progress. He rose higher, climbing out of the pond. The water was now only about his legs; he was thankful, full of relief to be out of the clutches of the pond. He lifted her and staggered on to the bank, out of the horror of wet, gray clay.

He laid her down on the bank. She was quite unconscious and running with water. He made the water come from her mouth, he worked to restore her. He did not have to work very long before he could feel the breathing begin again in her; she was breathing naturally. He worked a little longer. He could feel her live beneath his hands; she was coming back. He wiped her face, wrapped her in his overcoat, looked round into the dim, dark gray world, then lifted her and staggered down the bank and across the fields.

It seemed an unthinkably long way, and his burden so heavy he felt he would never get to the house. But at last he was in the stable-yard, and then in the house-yard. He opened the door and went into the house. In the kitchen he laid her down on the hearth-rug and called. The house was empty. But the fire was burning in the grate.

Then again he kneeled to attend to her. She was breathing regularly, her eyes were wide open and as if conscious, but there seemed something missing in her look. She was conscious in herself, but unconscious of her surroundings.

He ran upstairs, took blankets from a bed, and put them before the fire to warm. Then he removed her saturated, earthy-smelling clothing, rubbed her dry with a towel, and wrapped her naked in the blankets. Then he went into the dining-room, to look for spirits. There was a little whiskey. He drank a gulp himself, and put some into her mouth.

The effect was instantaneous. She looked full into his face, as if she had been seeing him for some time, and yet had only just become conscious of him.

"Dr. Fergusson?" she said.

"What?" he answered.

He was divesting himself of his coat, intending to find some dry clothing upstairs. He could not bear the smell of the dead, clayey water, and he was mortally afraid for his own health.

"What did I do?" she asked.

"Walked into the pond," he replied. He had begun to shudder like one sick, and could hardly attend to her. Her eyes remained full on him, he seemed to be going dark in his mind, looking back at her helplessly. The shuddering became quieter in him, his life came back to him, dark and unknowing, but strong again.

"Was I out of my mind?" she asked, while her eyes were fixed on him all the time.

"Maybe, for the moment," he replied. He felt quiet, because his strength had come back. The strange fretful strain had left him.

"Am I out of my mind now?" she asked.

"Are you?" he reflected a moment. "No," he answered truthfully, "I don't see that you are." He turned his face aside. He was afraid now, because he felt dazed, and felt dimly that her power was stronger than his, in this issue. And she continued to look at him fixedly all the time. "Can you tell me where I shall find some dry things to put on?" he asked.

"Did you dive into the pond for me?" she asked.

"No," he answered. "I walked in. But I went in overhead as well."

There was silence for a moment. He hesitated. He very much wanted to go upstairs to get into dry clothing. But there was another desire in him. And she seemed to hold him. His will seemed to have gone to sleep, and left him, standing there slack before her. But he felt warm inside himself. He did not shudder at all, though his clothes were sodden on him.

"Why did you?" she asked.

"Because I didn't want you to do such a foolish thing," he said. 135

"It wasn't foolish," she said, still gazing at him as she lay on the floor, with a sofa cushion under her head. "It was the right thing to do. *I* knew best, then."

"I'll go and shift these wet things," he said. But still he had not the power to move out of her presence, until she sent him. It was as if she had the life of his body in her hands, and he could not extricate himself. Or perhaps he did not want to.

Suddenly she sat up. Then she became aware of her own immediate condition. She felt the blankets about her, she knew her own limbs. For a moment it seemed as if her reason were going. She looked round, with wild eye, as if seeking something. He stood still with fear. She saw her clothing lying scattered.

"Who undressed me?" she asked, her eyes resting full and inevitable on his face.

"I did," he replied, "to bring you round." 140

For some moments she sat and gazed at him, awfully, her lips parted.

"Do you love me, then?" she asked.

He only stood and stared at her, fascinated. His soul seemed to melt.

She shuffled forward on her knees, and put her arms round him, round his legs, as he stood there, pressing her breasts against his knees and thighs, clutching him with strange, convulsive certainty, pressing his thighs against her, drawing him to her face, her throat, as she looked up at him with flaring, humble eyes of transfiguration, triumphant in first possession.

"You love me," she murmured, in strange transport, yearning and trium- 145
phant and confident. "You love me. I know you love me, I know."

And she was passionately kissing his knees, through the wet clothing, passionately and indiscriminately kissing his knees, his legs, as if unaware of everything.

He looked down at the tangled wet hair, the wild, bare, animal shoulders. He was amazed, bewildered, and afraid. He had never thought of loving her. He had never wanted to love her. When he rescued her and restored her, he was a doctor, and she was a patient. He had had no single personal thought of her. Nay, this introduction of the personal element was very distasteful to him, a violation of his professional honor. It was horrible to have her there embracing his knees. It was horrible. He revolted from it, violently. And yet — and yet — he had not the power to break away.

She looked at him again, with the same supplication of powerful love, and that same transcendent, frightening light of triumph. In view of the delicate flame which seemed to come from her face like a light, he was powerless. And yet he had never intended to love her. He had never intended. And something stubborn in him could not give way.

"You love me," she repeated, in a murmur of deep, rhapsodic assurance. "You love me."

Her hands were drawing him, drawing him down to her. He was afraid, even a little horrified. For he had, really, no intention of loving her. Yet her hands were drawing him towards her. He put out his hand quickly to steady himself, and grasped her bare shoulder. A flame seemed to burn the hand that grasped her soft shoulder. He had no intention of loving her: his whole will was against his yielding. It was horrible. And yet wonderful was the touch of her shoulders, beautiful the shining of her face. Was she perhaps mad? He had a horror of yielding to her. Yet something in him ached also.

He had been staring away at the door, away from her. But his hand remained on her shoulder. She had gone suddenly very still. He looked down at her. Her eyes were now wide with fear, with doubt, the light was dying from her face, a shadow of terrible grayness was returning. He could not bear the touch of her eyes' question upon him, and the look of death behind the question.

With an inward groan he gave way, and let his heart yield towards her. A sudden gentle smile came on his face. And her eyes, which never left his face, slowly, slowly filled with tears. He watched the strange water rise in her eyes, like some slow fountain coming up. And his heart seemed to burn and melt away in his breast.

He could not bear to look at her any more. He dropped on his knees and caught her head with his arms and pressed her face against his throat. She was very still. His heart, which seemed to have broken, was burning with a kind of agony in his breast. And he felt her slow, hot tears wetting his throat. But he could not move.

He felt the hot tears wet his neck and the hollows of his neck, and he remained motionless, suspended through one of man's eternities. Only now it had become indispensable to him to have her face pressed close to him; he could never let her go again. He could never let her head go away from the close clutch of his arm. He wanted to remain like that for ever, with his heart hurting him in a pain that was also life to him. Without knowing, he was looking down on her damp, soft brown hair.

Then, as it were suddenly, he smelt the horrid stagnant smell of that water. And at the same moment she drew away from him and looked at him. Her eyes were wistful and unfathomable. He was afraid of them, and he fell to kissing her, not knowing what he was doing. He wanted her eyes not to have that terrible, wistful, unfathomable look.

When she turned her face to him again, a faint delicate flush was glowing, and there was again dawning that terrible shining of joy in her eyes, which really terrified him, and yet which he now wanted to see, because he feared the look of doubt still more.

"You love me?" she said, rather faltering.

"Yes." The word cost him a painful effort. Not because it wasn't true. But because it was too newly true, the *saying* seemed to tear open again his newly-torn heart. And he hardly wanted it to be true, even now.

She lifted her face to him, and he bent forward and kissed her on the mouth, gently, with the one kiss that is an eternal pledge. And as he kissed her his heart strained again in his breast. He never intended to love her. But now it was over. He had crossed over the gulf to her, and all that he had left behind had shriveled and become void.

After the kiss, her eyes again slowly filled with tears. She sat still, away from 160
him, with her face drooped aside, and her hands folded in her lap. The tears fell very slowly. There was complete silence. He too sat there motionless and silent on the hearth-rug. The strange pain of his heart that was broken seemed to consume him. That he should love her? That this was love! That he should be ripped open in this way! Him, a doctor! How they would all jeer if they knew! It was agony to him to think they might know.

In the curious naked pain of the thought he looked again to her. She was still sitting there drooped into a muse. He saw a tear fall, and his heart flared hot. He saw for the first time that one of her shoulders was quite uncovered, one arm bare, he could see one of her small breasts; dimly, because it had become almost dark in the room.

"Why are you crying?" he asked, in an altered voice.

She looked up at him, and behind her tears the consciousness of her situation for the first time brought a dark look of shame to her eyes.

"I'm not crying, really," she said, watching him, half frightened.

He reached his hand, and softly closed it on her bare arm. 165

"I love you! I love you!" he said in a soft, low vibrating voice, unlike himself.

She shrank, and dropped her head. The soft, penetrating grip of his hand on her arm distressed her. She looked up at him.

"I want to go," she said. "I want to go and get you some dry things."

"Why?" he said. "I'm all right."

"But I want to go," she said. "And I want you to change your things." 170

He released her arm, and she wrapped herself in the blanket, looking at him rather frightened. And still she did not rise.

"Kiss me," she said wistfully.

He kissed her, but briefly, half in anger.

Then, after a second, she rose nervously, all mixed up in the blanket. He watched her in her confusion as she tried to extricate herself and wrap herself up so that she could walk. He watched her relentlessly, as she knew. And as she went, the blanket trailing, and as he saw a glimpse of her feet and her white leg, he tried to remember her as she was when he had wrapped her in the blanket. But then he didn't want to remember, because she had been nothing to him then, and his nature revolted from remembering her as she was when she was nothing to him.

A tumbling, muffled noise from within the dark house startled him. Then 175
he heard her voice: "There are clothes." He rose and went to the foot of the stairs, and gathered up the garments she had thrown down. Then he came back to the fire, to rub himself down and dress. He grinned at his own appearance when he had finished.

The fire was sinking, so he put on coal. The house was now quite dark, save for the light of a street-lamp that shone in faintly from beyond the holly trees. He lit the gas with matches he found on the mantelpiece. Then he emptied the pockets of his own clothes, and threw all his wet things in a heap into the scullery. After which he gathered up her sodden clothes, gently, and put them in a separate heap on the copper-top in the scullery.

It was six o'clock on the clock. His own watch had stopped. He ought to go back to the surgery. He waited, and still she did not come down. So he went to the foot of the stairs and called:

"I shall have to go."

Almost immediately he heard her coming down. She had on her best dress of black voile, and her hair was tidy, but still damp. She looked at him — and in spite of herself, smiled.

"I don't like you in those clothes," she said.

"Do I look a sight?" he answered.

They were shy of one another.

"I'll make you some tea," she said.

"No, I must go."

"Must you?" And she looked at him again with the wide, strained, doubtful eyes. And again, from the pain of his breast, he knew how he loved her. He went and bent to kiss her, gently, passionately, with his heart's painful kiss.

"And my hair smells so horrible," she murmured in distraction. "And I'm so awful, I'm so awful! Oh, no, I'm too awful." And she broke into bitter, heart-broken sobbing. "You can't want to love me, I'm horrible."

"Don't be silly, don't be silly," he said, trying to comfort her, kissing her, holding her in his arms. "I want you, I want to marry you, we're going to be married, quickly, quickly — tomorrow if I can."

But she only sobbed terribly, and cried:

"I feel awful. I feel awful. I feel I'm horrible to you."

"No, I want you, I want you," was all he answered, blindly, with that terrible intonation which frightened her almost more than her horror lest he should *not* want her.

KATHERINE MANSFIELD (1888–1923)

Miss Brill 1922

Although it was so brilliantly fine — the blue sky powdered with gold and great spots of light like white wine splashed over the Jardins Publiques — Miss Brill was glad that she had decided on her fur. The air was motionless, but when you opened your mouth there was just a faint chill, like a chill from a glass of iced water before you sip, and now and again a leaf came drifting — from nowhere, from the sky. Miss Brill put up her hand and touched her fur. Dear little thing! It was nice to feel it again. She had taken it out of its box that afternoon, shaken out the moth-powder, given it a good brush, and rubbed the life back into the dim little eyes. "What has been happening to me?" said the sad little eyes. Oh, how sweet it was to see them snap at her again from the red eiderdown! . . . But the nose, which was of some black composition, wasn't at all firm. It must have had a knock, somehow. Never mind — a little dab of black sealing-wax when the time came — when it was absolutely necessary. . . . Little rogue! Yes, she really felt like that about it. Little rogue biting its tail just by her left ear. She could have taken it off and laid it on her lap and stroked it. She felt a tingling in her hands and arms, but that came from walking, she supposed. And when she breathed, something light and sad — no, not sad, exactly — something gentle seemed to move in her bosom.

There were a number of people out this afternoon, far more than last Sunday. And the band sounded louder and gayer. That was because the Season had begun. For although the band played all the year round on Sundays, out of season it was never the same. It was like some one playing with only the family to listen; it didn't care how it played if there weren't any strangers present. Wasn't the conductor wearing a new coat, too? She was sure it was new. He scraped with his foot and flapped his arms like a rooster about to crow, and the bandsmen sitting in the green rotunda blew out their cheeks and glared at the music. Now there came a little "flutey" bit — very pretty! — a little chain of bright drops. She was sure it would be repeated. It was; she lifted her head and smiled.

Only two people shared her "special" seat: a fine old man in a velvet coat, his hands clasped over a huge carved walking-stick, and a big old woman, sitting upright, with a roll of knitting on her embroidered apron. They did not speak. This was disappointing, for Miss Brill always looked forward to the conversation. She had become really quite expert, she thought, at listening as though she didn't listen, at sitting in other people's lives just for a minute while they talked around her.

She glanced, sideways, at the old couple. Perhaps they would go soon. Last Sunday, too, hadn't been as interesting as usual. An Englishman and his wife, he wearing a dreadful Panama hat and she button boots. And she'd gone on the whole time about how she ought to wear spectacles; she knew she needed them; but that it was no good getting any; they'd be sure to break and they'd never keep on. And he'd been so patient. He'd suggested everything — gold rims, the kind that curved round your ears, little pads inside the bridge. No, nothing would please her. "They'll always be sliding down my nose!" Miss Brill had wanted to shake her.

The old people sat on the bench, still as statues. Never mind, there was 5
always the crowd to watch. To and fro, in front of the flower-beds and the band rotunda, the couples and groups paraded, stopped to talk, to greet, to buy a handful of flowers from the old beggar who had his tray fixed to the railings. Little children ran among them, swooping and laughing; little boys with big white silk bows under their chins, little girls, little French dolls, dressed up in velvet and lace. And sometimes a tiny staggerer came suddenly rocking into the open from under the trees, stopped, stared, as suddenly sat down "flop," until its small high-stepping mother, like a young hen, rushed scolding to its rescue. Other people sat on the benches and green chairs, but they were nearly always the same, Sunday after Sunday, and — Miss Brill had often noticed — there was something funny about nearly all of them. They were odd, silent, nearly all old, and from the way they stared they looked as though they'd just come from dark little rooms or even — even cupboards!

Behind the rotunda the slender trees with yellow leaves down drooping, and through them just a line of sea, and beyond the blue sky with gold-veined clouds.

Tum-tum-tum tiddle-um! tiddle-um! tum tiddley-um tum ta! blew the band.

Two young girls in red came by and two young soldiers in blue met them, and they laughed and paired and went off arm-in-arm. Two peasant women with funny straw hats passed, gravely, leading beautiful smoke-colored donkeys. A cold, pale nun hurried by. A beautiful woman came along and dropped her bunch of violets, and a little boy ran after to hand them to her, and she took them and threw them away as if they'd been poisoned. Dear me! Miss Brill didn't know whether to admire that or not! And now an ermine toque and a gentleman in grey met just in front of her. He was tall, stiff, dignified, and she was wearing the ermine toque she'd bought when her hair was yellow. Now everything, her hair, her face, even her eyes, was the same color as the shabby ermine, and her hand, in its cleaned glove, lifted to dab her lips, was a tiny yellowish paw. Oh, she was so pleased to see him — delighted! She rather thought they were going to meet that afternoon. She described where she'd been — everywhere, here, there, along by the sea. The day was so charming — didn't he agree? And wouldn't he, perhaps? . . . But he shook his head, lighted a cigarette, slowly breathed a great deep puff into her face, and, even while she was still talking and laughing, flicked the match away and walked on. The ermine toque was alone; she smiled more brightly than ever. But even the band seemed to know what she was feeling and played more softly, played tenderly, and the drum beat, "The Brute! The Brute!" over and over. What would she do? What was going to happen now? But as Miss Brill wondered, the ermine toque turned, raised her hand as though she'd seen some one else, much nicer, just over there, and pattered away. And the band changed again and played more quickly, more gaily than ever, and the old couple on Miss Brill's seat got up and marched away, and such a funny old man with long whiskers hobbled along in time to the music and was nearly knocked over by four girls walking abreast.

Oh, how fascinating it was! How she enjoyed it! How she loved sitting here, watching it all! It was like a play. It was exactly like a play. Who could believe the sky at the back wasn't painted? But it wasn't till a little brown dog trotted on solemn and then slowly trotted off, like a little "theatre" dog, a little dog that had been drugged, that Miss Brill discovered what it was that made it so exciting. They were all on the stage. They weren't only the audience, not only looking on; they were acting. Even she had a part and came every Sunday. No doubt somebody would have noticed if she hadn't been there; she was part of the performance after all. How strange she'd never thought of it like that before! And yet it explained why she made such a point of starting from home at just the same time each week — so as not to be late for the performance — and it also explained why she had quite a queer, shy feeling at telling her English pupils how she spent her Sunday afternoons. No wonder! Miss Brill nearly laughed out loud. She was on the stage. She thought of the old invalid gentleman to whom she read the newspaper four afternoons a week while he slept in the garden. She had got quite used to the frail head on the cotton pillow, the hollowed eyes, the open mouth, and the high pinched nose. If he'd been dead she mightn't have noticed for weeks; she wouldn't have minded. But suddenly he knew he was having the paper read to him by an actress! "An actress!" The old head lifted; two points of light quivered in the old eyes. "An actress — are ye?" And Miss Brill smoothed the newspaper as though it were the manuscript of her part and said gently: "Yes, I have been an actress for a long time."

The band had been having a rest. Now they started again. And what they 10
played was warm, sunny, yet there was just a faint chill — a something, what was it? — not sadness — no, not sadness — a something that made you want to sing. The tune lifted, lifted, the light shone; and it seemed to Miss Brill that in another moment all of them, all the whole company, would begin singing. The young ones, the laughing ones who were moving together, they would begin, and the men's voices, very resolute and brave, would join them. And then she too, she too, and the others on the benches — they would come in with a kind of accompaniment — something low, that scarcely rose or fell, something so beautiful — moving. . . . And Miss Brill's eyes filled with tears and she looked smiling at all the other members of the company. Yes, we understand, we understand, she thought — though what they understood she didn't know.

Just at that moment a boy and a girl came and sat down where the old couple had been. They were beautifully dressed; they were in love. The hero and heroine, of course, just arrived from his father's yacht. And still soundlessly singing, still with that trembling smile, Miss Brill prepared to listen.

"No, not now," said the girl. "Not here, I can't."

"But why? Because of that stupid old thing at the end there?" asked the boy. "Why does she come here at all — who wants her? Why doesn't she keep her silly old mug at home?"

"It's her fu-fur which is so funny," giggled the girl. "It's exactly like a fried whiting."

"Ah, be off with you!" said the boy in an angry whisper. Then: "Tell me, 15
ma petite chère ——"

"No, not here," said the girl. "Not *yet.*"

On her way home she usually bought a slice of honey-cake at the baker's. It was her Sunday treat. Sometimes there was an almond in her slice, sometimes not. It made a great difference. If there was an almond it was like carrying home a tiny present — a surprise — something that might very well not have been there. She hurried on the almond Sundays and struck the match for the kettle in quite a dashing way.

But today she passed the baker's by, climbed the stairs, went into the little dark room — her room like a cupboard — and sat down on the red eiderdown. She sat there for a long time. The box that the fur came out of was on the bed. She unclasped the necklet quickly; quickly, without looking, laid it inside. But when she put the lid on she thought she heard something crying.

EDGAR ALLAN POE (1809–1849)

The Pit and the Pendulum 1842

Impia tortorum longas hic turba furores
Sanguinis innocui, non satiata, aluit.
Sospite nunc patria, fracto nunc funeris antro,
Mors ubi dira fuit vita salusque patent.°

[Quatrain composed for the gates of a market to be erected upon the site of the Jacobin Club House at Paris.]

I was sick — sick unto death with that long agony; and when they at length unbound me, and I was permitted to sit, I felt that my senses were leaving me. The sentence — the dread sentence of death — was the last of distinct accentuation which reached my ears. After that, the sound of the inquisitorial voices seemed merged in one dreamy indeterminate hum. It conveyed to my soul the idea of *revolution* — perhaps from its association in fancy with the burr of a mill-wheel. This only for a brief period, for presently I heard no more. Yet, for a while, I saw — but with how terrible an exaggeration! I saw the lips of the black-robed judges. They appeared to me white — whiter than the sheet upon which I trace these words — and thin even to grotesqueness; thin with the intensity of their expression of firmness — of immovable resolution — of stern contempt of human torture. I saw that the decrees of what to me was Fate were still issuing from those lips. I saw them writhe with a deadly locution. I saw them fashion the syllables of my name; and I shuddered because no sound succeeded. I saw, too, for a few moments of delirious horror, the soft and nearly imperceptible waving of the sable draperies which enwrapped the walls of the apartment. And then my vision fell upon the seven tall candles upon the table. At first they wore the aspect of charity, and seemed white slender angels who would save me; but then, all at once, there came a most deadly nausea over my spirit, and I felt every fiber in my frame thrill as if I had touched the wire of a galvanic battery, while the angel forms became meaningless specters, with heads of flame, and I saw that from them there would be no help. And then there stole into my fancy, like a rich musical note, the thought of what sweet rest there must be in the grave. The thought came gently and stealthily, and it seemed long before it attained full appreciation; but just as my spirit came at length properly to feel and entertain it, the figures of the judges vanished, as if magically, from before me; the tall candles sank into nothingness; their flames went out utterly; the blackness of darkness supervened; all sensations appeared swallowed up in a mad rushing descent as of the soul into Hades. Then silence, and stillness, and night were the universe.

I had swooned; but still will not say that all of consciousness was lost. What of it there remained I will not attempt to define, or even to describe; yet all was not lost. In the deepest slumber — no! In delirium — no! In a swoon — no! In death — no! even in the grave all *is not* lost. Else there is no immortality for

Impia . . . patent: Here a wicked band of torturers long nourished their insatiable lust for innocent blood. Our homeland is safe now, their bloody dungeons destroyed, and where death once reigned, life and happiness now thrive.

man. Arousing from the most profound of slumbers, we break the gossamer web of *some* dream. Yet in a second afterward (so frail may that web have been) we remember not that we have dreamed. In the return to life from the swoon there are two stages: first, that of the sense of mental or spiritual; secondly, that of the sense of physical, existence. It seems probable that if, upon reaching the second stage, we could recall the impressions of the first, we should find these impressions eloquent in memories of the gulf beyond. And that gulf is — what? How at least shall we distinguish its shadows from those of the tomb? But if the impressions of what I have termed the first stage are not, at will, recalled, yet, after long interval, do they not come unbidden, while we marvel whence they come? He who has never swooned, is not he who finds strange palaces and wildly familiar faces in coals that glow; is not he who beholds floating in midair the sad visions that the many may not view; is not he who ponders over the perfume of some novel flower; is not he whose brain grows bewildered with the meaning of some musical cadence which has never before arrested his attention.

Amid frequent and thoughtful endeavors to remember, amid earnest struggles to regather some token of the state of seeming nothingness into which my soul had lapsed, there have been moments when I have dreamed of success; there have been brief, very brief periods when I have conjured up remembrances which the lucid reason of a later epoch assures me could have had reference only to that condition of seeming unconsciousness. These shadows of memory tell, indistinctly, of tall figures that lifted and bore me in silence down — down — still down — till a hideous dizziness oppressed me at the mere idea of the interminableness of the descent. They tell also of a vague horror at my heart, on account of that heart's unnatural stillness. Then comes a sense of sudden motionlessness throughout all things; as if those who bore me (a ghastly train!) had outrun, in their descent, the limits of the limitless, and paused from the wearisomeness of their toil. After this I call to mind flatness and dampness; and then all is *madness* — the madness of a memory which busies itself among forbidden things.

Very suddenly there came back to my soul motion and sound — the tumultuous motion of the heart, and, in my ears, the sound of its beating. Then a pause in which all is blank. Then again sound, and motion, and touch — a tingling sensation pervading my frame. Then the mere consciousness of existence, without thought — a condition which lasted long. Then, very suddenly, *thought,* and shuddering terror, and earnest endeavor to comprehend my true state. Then a strong desire to lapse into insensibility. Then a rushing revival of soul and a successful effort to move. And now a full memory of the trial, of the judges, of the sable draperies, of the sentence, of the sickness, of the swoon. Then entire forgetfulness of all that followed; of all that a later day and much earnestness of endeavor have enabled me vaguely to recall.

So far, I had not opened my eyes. I felt that I lay upon my back, unbound. 5
I reached out my hand, and it fell heavily upon something damp and hard. There I suffered it to remain for many minutes, while I strove to imagine where and *what* I could be. I longed, yet dared not, to employ my vision. I dreaded the first glance at objects around me. It was not that I feared to look upon things horrible, but that I grew aghast lest there should be *nothing* to see. At length, with a wild desperation at heart, I quickly unclosed my eyes. My worst thoughts,

then, were confirmed. The blackness of eternal night encompassed me. I struggled for breath. The intensity of the darkness seemed to oppress and stifle me. The atmosphere was intolerably close. I still lay quietly, and made effort to exercise my reason. I brought to mind the inquisitorial proceedings, and attempted from that point to deduce my real condition. The sentence had passed; and it appeared to me that a very long interval of time had since elapsed. Yet not for a moment did I suppose myself actually dead. Such a supposition, notwithstanding what we read in fiction, is altogether inconsistent with real existence; — but where and in what state was I? The condemned to death, I knew, perished usually at the *auto-da-fés,* and one of these had been held on the very night of the day of my trial. Had I been remanded to my dungeon, to await the next sacrifice, which would not take place for many months? This I at once saw could not be. Victims had been in immediate demand. Moreover, my dungeon as well as all the condemned cells at Toledo, had stone floors, and light was not altogether excluded.

A fearful idea now suddenly drove the blood in torrents upon my heart, and for a brief period I once more relapsed into insensibility. Upon recovering, I at once started to my feet, trembling convulsively in every fiber. I thrust my arms wildly above and around me in all directions. I felt nothing; yet dreaded to move a step, lest I should be impeded by the walls of a *tomb.* Perspiration burst from every pore, and stood in cold big beads upon my forehead. The agony of suspense grew at length intolerable, and I cautiously moved forward, with my arms extended, and my eyes straining from their sockets in the hope of catching some faint ray of light. I proceeded for many paces; but still all was blackness and vacancy. I breathed more freely. It seemed evident that mine was not, at least, the most hideous of fates.

And now, as I still continued to step cautiously onward, there came thronging upon my recollection a thousand vague rumors of the horrors of Toledo. Of the dungeons there had been strange things narrated — fables I had always deemed them — but yet strange, and too ghastly to repeat, save in a whisper. Was I left to perish of starvation in this subterranean world of darkness; or what fate, perhaps even more fearful, awaited me? That the result would be death, and a death of more than customary bitterness, I knew too well the character of my judges to doubt. The mode and the hour were all that occupied or distracted me.

My outstretched hands at length encountered some solid obstruction. It was a wall, seemingly of stone masonry — very smooth, slimy, and cold. I followed it up; stepping with all the careful distrust with which certain antique narratives had inspired me. This process, however, afforded me no means of ascertaining the dimensions of my dungeon, as I might make its circuit and return to the point whence I set out without being aware of the fact, so perfectly uniform seemed the wall. I therefore sought the knife which had been in my pocket when led into the inquisitorial chamber; but it was gone; my clothes had been exchanged for a wrapper of coarse serge. I had thought of forcing the blade in some minute crevice of the masonry, so as to identify my point of departure. The difficulty, nevertheless, was but trivial; although, in the disorder of my fancy, it seemed at first insuperable. I tore a part of the hem from the robe and placed the fragment at full length, and at right angles to the wall. In groping my way around the prison, I could not fail to encounter this rag upon completing the circuit. So, at least, I thought; but I had not counted upon the extent of the dungeon, or upon my own weakness. The ground was moist and slippery. I staggered onward for some time, when I stumbled and fell. My excessive fatigue induced me to remain prostrate; and sleep soon overtook me as I lay.

Upon awaking, and stretching forth an arm, I found beside me a loaf and a pitcher with water. I was too much exhausted to reflect upon this circumstance, but ate and drank with avidity. Shortly afterward, I resumed my tour around the prison, and with much toil, came at last upon the fragment of the serge. Up to the period when I fell, I had counted fifty-two paces, and, upon resuming my walk, I had counted forty-eight more — when I arrived at the rag. There were in all, then, a hundred paces; and, admitting two paces to the yard, I presumed the dungeon to be fifty yards in circuit. I had met, however, with many angles in the wall, and thus I could form no guess at the shape of the vault, for vault I could not help supposing it to be.

10 I had little object — certainly no hope — in these researches; but a vague curiosity prompted me to continue them. Quitting the wall, I resolved to cross the area of the enclosure. At first, I proceeded with extreme caution, for the floor, although seemingly of solid material, was treacherous with slime. At length, however, I took courage, and did not hesitate to step firmly — endeavoring to cross in as direct a line as possible. I had advanced some ten or twelve paces in this manner, when the remnant of the torn hem of my robe became entangled between my legs. I stepped on it, and fell violently on my face.

In the confusion attending my fall, I did not immediately apprehend a somewhat startling circumstance, which yet, in a few seconds afterward, and while I still lay prostrate, arrested my attention. It was this: my chin rested upon the floor of the prison, but my lips, and the upper portion of my head, although seemingly at a less elevation than the chin, touched nothing. At the same time, my forehead seemed bathed in a clammy vapor, and the peculiar smell of decayed fungus arose to my nostrils. I put forward my arm, and shuddered to find that I had fallen at the very brink of a circular pit, whose extent, of course, I had no means of ascertaining at the moment. Groping about the masonry just below the margin, I succeeded in dislodging a small fragment, and let it fall into the abyss. For many seconds I hearkened to its reverberations as it dashed against the sides of the chasm in its descent; at length, there was a sullen plunge into water, succeeded by loud echoes. At the same moment, there came a sound resembling the quick opening and as rapid closing of a door overhead, while a faint gleam of light flashed suddenly through the gloom, and as suddenly faded away.

I saw clearly the doom which had been prepared for me, and congratulated myself upon the timely accident by which I had escaped. Another step before my fall, and the world had seen me no more. And the death just avoided was of that very character which I had regarded as fabulous and frivolous in the tales respecting the Inquisition. To the victims of its tyranny, there was the choice of death with its direst physical agonies, or death with its most hideous moral horrors. I had been reserved for the latter. By long suffering my nerves had been unstrung, until I trembled at the sound of my own voice, and had become in every respect a fitting subject for the species of torture which awaited me.

Shaking in every limb, I groped my way back to the wall — resolving there to perish rather than risk the terrors of the wells, of which my imagination now pictured many in various positions about the dungeon. In other conditions of mind, I might have had courage to end my misery at once, by a plunge into one of these abysses; but now I was the veriest of cowards. Neither could I forget what I had read of these pits — that the *sudden* extinction of life formed no part of their most horrible plan.

Agitation of spirit kept me awake for many long hours, but at length I again slumbered. Upon arousing, I found by my side, as before, a loaf and a pitcher of water. A burning thirst consumed me, and I emptied the vessel at a draft. It must have been drugged — for scarcely had I drunk, before I became irresistibly drowsy. A deep sleep fell upon me — a sleep like that of death. How long it lasted, of course I know not; but when, once again, I unclosed my eyes, the objects around me were visible. By a wild, sulfurous luster, the origin of which I could not at first determine, I was enabled to see the extent and aspect of the prison.

In its size I had been greatly mistaken. The whole circuit of its walls did not exceed twenty-five yards. For some minutes this fact occasioned me a world of vain trouble; vain indeed — for what could be of less importance, under the terrible circumstances which environed me, than the mere dimensions of my dungeon? But my soul took a wild interest in trifles, and I busied myself in endeavors to account for the error I had committed in my measurement. The truth at length flashed upon me. In my first attempt at exploration I had counted fifty-two paces, up to the period when I fell: I must then have been within a pace or two of the fragment of serge; in fact, I had nearly performed the circuit of the vault. I then slept — and, upon awakening, I must have returned upon my steps — thus supposing the circuit nearly double what it actually was. My confusion of mind prevented me from observing that I began my tour with the wall to the left, and ended it with the wall to the right.

I had been deceived, too, in respect to the shape of the enclosure. In feeling my way I had found many angles, and thus deduced an idea of great irregularity; so potent is the effect of total darkness upon one arousing from lethargy or sleep! The angles were simply those of a few slight depressions, or niches, at odd intervals. The general shape of the prison was square. What I had taken for masonry seemed now to be iron, or some other metal, in huge plates, whose sutures or joints occasioned the depression. The entire surface of this metallic enclosure was rudely daubed in all the hideous and repulsive devices to which the charnel superstition of the monks has given rise. The figures of fiends in aspects of menace, with skeleton forms, and other more really fearful images, overspread and disfigured the walls. I observed that the outlines of these monstrosities were sufficiently distinct, but that the colors seemed faded and blurred, as if from the effects of a damp atmosphere. I now noticed the floor, too, which was of stone. In the center yawned the circular pit from whose jaws I had escaped; but it was the only one in the dungeon.

All this I saw indistinctly and by much effort — for my personal condition had been greatly changed during slumber. I now lay upon my back, and at full length, on a species of low framework of wood. To this I was securely bound by a long strap resembling a surcingle. It passed in many convolutions about my limbs and body, leaving at liberty only my head, and my left arm to such extent, that I could, by dint of much exertion, supply myself with food from an earthen dish which lay by my side on the floor. I saw, to my horror, that the pitcher had been removed. I say to my horror — for I was consumed with intolerable thirst. This thirst it appeared to be the design of my persecutors to stimulate — for the food in the dish was meat pungently seasoned.

Looking upward, I surveyed the ceiling of my prison. It was some thirty or forty feet overhead, and constructed much as the side walls. In one of its panels a very singular figure riveted my whole attention. It was the painted figure of Time as he is commonly represented, save that, in lieu of a scythe, he held what, at a casual glance, I supposed to be the pictured image of a huge pendulum, such as we see on antique clocks. There was something, however, in the appearance of this machine which caused me to regard it more attentively. While I gazed directly upward at it (for its position was immediately over my own) I fancied that I saw it in motion. In an instant afterward the fancy was confirmed. Its sweep was brief, and of course slow. I watched it for some minutes somewhat in fear, but more in wonder. Wearied at length with observing its dull movement, I turned my eyes upon the other objects in the cell.

A slight noise attracted my notice, and, looking to the floor, I saw several enormous rats traversing it. They had issued from the well which lay just within view to my right. Even then, while I gazed, they came up in troops, hurriedly, with ravenous eyes, allured by the scent of the meat. From this it required much effort and attention to scare them away.

It might have been half an hour, perhaps even an hour (for I could take but imperfect note of time), before I again cast my eyes upward. What I then saw confounded and amazed me. The sweep of the pendulum had increased in extent by nearly a yard. As a natural consequence its velocity was also much greater. But what mainly disturbed me was the idea that it had perceptibly *descended.* I now observed — with what horror it is needless to say — that its nether extremity was formed of a crescent of glittering steel, about a foot in length from horn to horn; the horns upward, and the under edge evidently as keen as that of a razor. Like a razor also, it seemed massy and heavy, tapering from the edge into a solid and broad structure above. It was appended to a weighty rod of brass, and the whole *hissed* as it swung through the air.

I could no longer doubt the doom prepared for me by monkish ingenuity in torture. My cognizance of the pit had become known to the inquisitorial agents — *the pit,* whose horrors had been destined for so bold a recusant as myself — *the pit,* typical of hell and regarded by rumor as the Ultima Thule° of all their punishments. The plunge into this pit I had avoided by the merest of accidents, and I knew that surprise, or entrapment into torment, formed an important portion of all the grotesquerie of these dungeon deaths. Having failed to fall, it was no part of the demon plan to hurl me into the abyss, and thus (there being no alternative) a different and a milder destruction awaited me. Milder! I half smiled in my agony as I thought of such application of such a term.

What boots it to tell of the long, long hours of horror more than mortal, during which I counted the rushing oscillations of the steel! Inch by inch — line by line — with a descent only appreciable at intervals that seemed ages — down

Ultima Thule: The farthest extreme.

and still down it came! Days passed — it might have been that many days passed — ere it swept so closely over me as to fan me with its acrid breath. The odor of the sharp steel forced itself into my nostrils. I prayed — I wearied heaven with my prayer for its more speedy descent. I grew frantically mad, and struggled to force myself upward against the sweep of the fearful scimitar. And then I fell suddenly calm, and lay smiling at the glittering death, as a child at some rare bauble.

There was another interval of utter insensibility; it was brief; for, upon again lapsing into life, there had been no perceptible descent in the pendulum. But it might have been long — for I knew there were demons who took note of my swoon, and who could have arrested the vibration at pleasure. Upon my recovery, too, I felt very — oh! inexpressibly — sick and weak, as if through long inanition. Even amid the agonies of that period, the human nature craved food. With painful effort I outstretched my left arm as far as my bonds permitted, and took possession of the small remnant which had been spared me by the rats. As I put a portion of it within my lips, there rushed to my mind a half-formed thought of joy — of hope. Yet what business had *I* with hope? It was, as I say, a half-formed thought — man has many such, which are never completed. I felt that it was of joy — of hope; but I felt also that it had perished in its formation. In vain I struggled to perfect — to regain it. Long suffering had nearly annihilated all my ordinary powers of mind. I was an imbecile — an idiot.

The vibration of the pendulum was at right angles to my length. I saw that the crescent was designed to cross the region of the heart. It would fray the serge of my robe — it would return and repeat its operations — again — and again. Notwithstanding its terrifically wide sweep (some thirty feet or more), and the hissing vigor of its descent, sufficient to sunder these very walls of iron, still the fraying of my robe would be all that, for several minutes, it would accomplish. And at this thought I paused. I dared not go further than this reflection. I dwelt upon it with a pertinacity of attention — as if, in so dwelling, I could arrest *here* the descent of the steel. I forced myself to ponder upon the sound of the crescent as it should pass across the garment — upon the peculiar thrilling sensation which the friction of cloth produces on the nerves. I pondered upon all this frivolity until my teeth were on edge.

Down — steadily down it crept. I took a frenzied pleasure in contrasting its downward with its lateral velocity. To the right — to the left — far and wide — with the shriek of a damned spirit! to my heart, with the stealthy pace of the tiger! I alternately laughed and howled, as the one or the other idea grew predominant.

Down — certainly, relentlessly down! It vibrated within three inches of my bosom! I struggled violently — furiously — to free my left arm. This was free only from the elbow to the hand. I could reach the latter, from the platter beside me, to my mouth, with great effort, but no farther. Could I have broken the fastenings above the elbow, I would have seized and attempted to arrest the pendulum. I might as well have attempted to arrest an avalanche!

Down — still unceasingly — still inevitably down! I gasped and struggled at each vibration. I shrunk convulsively at its every sweep. My eyes followed its outward or upward whirls with the eagerness of the most unmeaning despair; they closed themselves spasmodically at the descent, although death would have been a relief, oh, how unspeakable! Still I quivered in every nerve to think how slight a sinking of the machinery would precipitate that keen, glistening axe upon my bosom. It was *hope* that prompted the nerve to quiver — the frame to shrink. It was *hope* — the hope that triumphs on the rack — that whispers to the death-condemned even in the dungeons of the Inquisition.

I saw that some ten or twelve vibrations would bring the steel in actual contact with my robe — and with this observation there suddenly came over my spirit all the keen, collected calmness of despair. For the first time during many hours — or perhaps days — I *thought*. It now occurred to me, that the bandage, or surcingle, which enveloped me, was *unique*. I was tied by no separate cord. The first stroke of the razor-like crescent athwart any portion of the band would so detach it that it might be unwound from my person by means of my left hand. But how fearful, in that case, the proximity of the steel! The result of the slightest struggle, how deadly! Was it likely, moreover, that the minions of the torturer had not foreseen and provided for this possibility? Was it probable that the bandage crossed my bosom in the track of the pendulum? Dreading to find my faint and, as it seemed, my last hope frustrated, I so far elevated my head as to obtain a distinct view of my breast. The surcingle enveloped my limbs and body close in all directions — *save in the path of the destroying crescent.*

Scarcely had I dropped my head back into its original position, when there flashed upon my mind what I cannot better describe than as the unformed half of that idea of deliverance to which I have previously alluded, and of which a moiety only floated indeterminately through my brain when I raised food to my burning lips. The whole thought was now present — feeble, scarcely sane, scarcely definite — but still entire. I proceeded at once, with the nervous energy of despair, to attempt its execution.

30 For many hours the immediate vicinity of the low framework upon which I lay had been literally swarming with rats. They were wild, bold, ravenous — their red eyes glaring upon me as if they waited but for motionlessness on my part to make me their prey. "To what food," I thought, "have they been accustomed in the well?"

They had devoured, in spite of all my efforts to prevent them, all but a small remnant of the contents of the dish. I had fallen into an habitual seesaw or wave of the hand about the platter; and, at length, the unconscious uniformity of the movement deprived it of effect. In their voracity, the vermin frequently fastened their sharp fangs in my fingers. With the particles of the oily and spicy viand which now remained, I thoroughly rubbed the bandage wherever I could reach it; then, raising my hand from the floor, I lay breathlessly still.

At first, the ravenous animals were startled and terrified at the change — at the cessation of movement. They shrank alarmedly back; many sought the well. But this was only for a moment. I had not counted in vain upon their voracity. Observing that I remained without motion, one or two of the boldest leaped upon the framework, and smelt at the surcingle. This seemed the signal for a general rush. Forth from the well they hurried in fresh troops. They clung to the wood — they overran it, and leaped in hundreds upon my person. The measured movement of the pendulum disturbed them not at all. Avoiding its strokes, they busied themselves with the anointed bandage. They pressed — they swarmed upon me in ever accumulating heaps. They writhed upon my throat; their cold lips sought my own; I was half stifled by their thronging pressure; disgust, for which the world has no name, swelled my bosom, and chilled, with a heavy clamminess, my heart. Yet one minute, and I felt that the struggle would be over. Plainly I perceived the loosening of the bandage. I knew that in more than one place it must be already severed. With a more than human resolution I lay *still.*

Nor had I erred in my calculations — nor had I endured in vain. I at length felt that I was *free.* The surcingle hung in ribands from my body. But the stroke of the pendulum already pressed upon my bosom. It had divided the serge of the robe. It had cut through the linen beneath. Twice again it swung, and a sharp sense of pain shot through every nerve. But the moment of escape had arrived. At a wave of my hand my deliverers hurried tumultuously away. With a steady movement — cautious, sidelong, shrinking, and slow — I slid from the embrace of the bandage and beyond the reach of the scimitar. For the moment, at least, *I was free.*

Free! — and in the grasp of the Inquisition! I had scarcely stepped from my wooden bed of horror upon the stone floor of the prison, when the motion of the hellish machine ceased, and I beheld it drawn up, by some invisible force, through the ceiling. This was a lesson which I took desperately to heart. My every motion was undoubtedly watched. Free! — I had but escaped death in one form of agony, to be delivered unto worse than death in some other. With that thought I rolled my eyes nervously around on the barriers of iron that hemmed me in. Something unusual — some change which, at first, I could not appreciate distinctly — it was obvious, had taken place in the apartment. For many minutes of a dreamy and trembling abstraction, I busied myself in vain, unconnected conjecture. During this period, I became aware, for the first time, of the origin of the sulfurous light which illumined the cell. It proceeded from a fissure, about half an inch in width, extending entirely around the prison at the base of the walls, which thus appeared, and were completely separated from the floor. I endeavored, but of course in vain, to look through the aperture.

As I arose from the attempt, the mystery of the alteration in the chamber broke at once upon my understanding. I have observed that, although the outlines of the figures upon the walls were sufficiently distinct, yet the colors seemed blurred and indefinite. These colors had now assumed, and were momentarily assuming, a startling and most intense brilliancy, that gave to the spectral and fiendish portraitures an aspect that might have thrilled even firmer nerves than my own. Demon eyes, of a wild and ghastly vivacity, glared upon me in a thousand directions, where none had been visible before, and gleamed with the lurid luster of a fire that I could not force my imagination to regard as unreal.

Unreal! — Even while I breathed there came to my nostrils the breath of the vapor of heated iron! A suffocating odor pervaded the prison! A deeper glow settled each moment in the eyes that glared at my agonies! A richer tint of crimson diffused itself over the pictured horrors of blood. I panted! I gasped for breath! There could be no doubt of the design of my tormentors — oh! most unrelenting! oh! most demoniac of men! I shrank from the glowing metal to the center of the cell. Amid the thought of the fiery destruction that impended, the idea of the coolness of the well came over my soul like balm. I rushed to its deadly brink. I threw my straining vision below. The glare from the enkindled roof illumined its inmost recesses. Yet, for a wild moment, did my spirit refuse to comprehend the meaning of what I saw. At length it forced — it wrestled its way into my soul — it burned itself in upon my shuddering reason. Oh! for a voice to speak! — oh! horror! — oh! any horror but this! With a shriek, I rushed from the margin, and buried my face in my hands — weeping bitterly.

The heat rapidly increased, and once again I looked up, shuddering as with a fit of the ague. There had been a second change in the cell — and now the change was obviously in the *form*. As before, it was in vain that I at first endeavored to appreciate or understand what was taking place. But not long was I left in doubt. The Inquisitorial vengeance had been hurried by my twofold escape, and there was to be no more dallying with the King of Terrors. The room had been square. I saw that two of its iron angles were now acute — two, consequently, obtuse. The fearful difference quickly increased with a low rumbling or moaning sound. In an instant the apartment had shifted its form into that of a lozenge. But the alteration stopped not here — I neither hoped nor desired it to stop. I could have clasped the red walls to my bosom as a garment of eternal peace. "Death," I said, "any death but that of the pit!" Fool! might I not have known that *into the pit* it was the object of the burning iron to urge me? Could I resist its glow? or if even that, could I withstand its pressure? And now, flatter and flatter grew the lozenge, with a rapidity that left me no time for contemplation. Its center, and of course its greatest width, came just over the yawning gulf. I shrank back — but the closing walls pressed me resistlessly onward. At length for my seared and writhing body there was no longer an inch of foothold on the firm floor of the prison. I struggled no more, but the agony of my soul found vent in one loud, long, and final scream of despair. I felt that I tottered upon the brink — I averted my eyes —

There was a discordant hum of human voices! There was a loud blast as of many trumpets! There was a harsh grating as of a thousand thunders! The fiery walls rushed back! An outstretched arm caught my own as I fell, fainting, into the abyss. It was that of General Lasalle. The French army had entered Toledo. The Inquisition was in the hands of its enemies.

JOHN UPDIKE (b. 1932)

A & P 1961

In walks these three girls in nothing but bathing suits. I'm in the third checkout slot, with my back to the door, so I don't see them until they're over by the bread. The one that caught my eye first was the one in the plaid green two-piece. She was a chunky kid, with a good tan and a sweet broad soft-looking can with those two crescents of white just under it, where the sun never seems to hit, at the top of the backs of her legs. I stood there with my hand on a box of HiHo crackers trying to remember if I rang it up or not. I ring it up again and the customer starts giving me hell. She's one of these cash-register-watchers, a witch about fifty with rouge on her cheekbones and no eyebrows, and I know it made her day to trip me up. She'd been watching cash registers for fifty years and probably never seen a mistake before.

By the time I got her feathers smoothed and her goodies into a bag — she gives me a little snort in passing, if she'd been born at the right time they would have burned her over in Salem — by the time I get her on her way the girls had circled around the bread and were coming back, without a pushcart, back my way along the counters, in the aisle between the checkouts and the Special bins. They didn't even have shoes on. There was this chunky one, with the two-piece — it was bright green and the seams on the bra were still sharp and her belly was still pretty pale so I guessed she just got it (the suit) — there was this one, with one of those chubby berry-faces, the lips all bunched together under her nose, this one, and a tall one, with black hair that hadn't quite frizzed right, and one of these sunburns right across under the eyes, and a chin that was too long — you know, the kind of girl other girls think is very "striking" and "attractive" but never quite makes it, as they very well know, which is why they like her so much — and then the third one, that wasn't quite so tall. She was the queen. She kind of led them, the other two peeking around and making their shoulders round. She didn't look around, not this queen, she just walked straight on slowly, on these long white prima-donna legs. She came down a little hard on her heels, as if she didn't walk in her bare feet that much, putting down her heels and then letting the weight move along to her toes as if she was testing the floor with every step, putting a little deliberate extra action into it. You never know for sure how girls' minds work (do you really think it's a mind in there or just a little buzz like a bee in a glass jar?) but you got the idea she had talked the other two into coming in here with her, and now she was showing them how to do it, walk slow and hold yourself straight.

She had on a kind of dirty-pink — beige maybe, I don't know — bathing suit with a little nubble all over it and, what got me, the straps were down. They were off her shoulders looped loose around the cool tops of her arms, and I guess as a result the suit had slipped a little on her, so all around the top of the cloth there was this shining rim. If it hadn't been there you wouldn't have known there could have been anything whiter than those shoulders. With the straps pushed off, there was nothing between the top of the suit and the top of her head except just *her,* this clean bare plane of the top of her chest down from the shoulder bones like a dented sheet of metal tilted in the light. I mean, it was more than pretty.

She had sort of oaky hair that the sun and salt had bleached, done up in a bun that was unraveling, and a kind of prim face. Walking into the A & P with your straps down, I suppose it's the only kind of face you *can* have. She held her head so high her neck, coming up out of those white shoulders, looked kind of stretched, but I didn't mind. The longer her neck was, the more of her there was.

She must have felt in the corner of her eye me and over my shoulder 5
Stokesie in the second slot watching, but she didn't tip. Not this queen. She kept her eyes moving across the racks, and stopped, and turned so slow it made my stomach rub the inside of my apron, and buzzed to the other two, who kind of huddled against her for relief, and then they all three of them went up the cat-and-dog-food-breakfast-cereal-macaroni-rice-raisins-seasonings-spreads-spaghetti-soft-drinks-crackers-and-cookies aisle. From the third slot I look straight up this aisle to the meat counter, and I watched them all the way. The fat one with the tan sort of fumbled with the cookies, but on second thought she put the package back. The sheep pushing their carts down the aisle — the girls were walking against the usual traffic (not that we have one-way signs or anything) —

were pretty hilarious. You could see them, when Queenie's white shoulders dawned on them, kind of jerk, or hop, or hiccup, but their eyes snapped back to their own baskets and on they pushed. I bet you could set off dynamite in an A & P and the people would by and large keep reaching and checking oatmeal off their lists and muttering "Let me see, there was a third thing, began with A, asparagus, no, ah, yes, applesauce!" or whatever it is they do mutter. But there was no doubt, this jiggled them. A few houseslaves in pin curlers even looked around after pushing their carts past to make sure what they had seen was correct.

You know, it's one thing to have a girl in a bathing suit down on the beach, where what with the glare nobody can look at each other much anyway, and another thing in the cool of the A & P, under the fluorescent lights, against all those stacked packages, with her feet paddling along naked over our checkerboard green-and-cream rubber-tile floor.

"Oh Daddy," Stokesie said beside me. "I feel so faint."

"Darling," I said. "Hold me tight." Stokesie's married, with two babies chalked up on his fuselage already, but as far as I can tell that's the only difference. He's twenty-two, and I was nineteen this April.

"Is it done?" he asks, the responsible married man finding his voice. I forgot to say he thinks he's going to be manager some sunny day, maybe in 1990 when it's called the Great Alexandrov and Petrooshki Tea Company or something.

10 What he meant was, our town is five miles from a beach, with a big summer colony out on the Point, but we're right in the middle of town, and the women generally put on a shirt or shorts or something before they get out of the car into the street. And anyway these are usually women with six children and varicose veins mapping their legs and nobody, including them, could care less. As I say, we're right in the middle of town, and if you stand at our front doors you can see two banks and the Congregational church and the newspaper store and three real-estate offices and about twenty-seven old freeloaders tearing up Central Street because the sewer broke again. It's not as if we're on the Cape, we're north of Boston and there's people in this town haven't seen the ocean for twenty years.

The girls had reached the meat counter and were asking McMahon something. He pointed, they pointed, and they shuffled out of sight behind a pyramid of Diet Delight peaches. All that was left for us to see was old McMahon patting his mouth and looking after them sizing up their joints. Poor kids, I began to feel sorry for them, they couldn't help it.

Now here comes the sad part of the story, at least my family says it's sad, but I don't think it's so sad myself. The store's pretty empty, it being Thursday afternoon, so there was nothing much to do except lean on the register and wait for the girls to show up again. The whole store was like a pinball machine and I didn't know which tunnel they'd come out of. After a while they come around out of the far aisle, around the light bulbs, records at discount of the Caribbean Six or Tony Martin Sings or some such gunk you wonder they waste the wax on, sixpacks of candy bars, and plastic toys done up in cellophane that fall apart when a kid looks at them anyway. Around they come, Queenie still leading the way, and holding a little gray jar in her hands. Slots Three through Seven are unmanned and I could see her wondering between Stokes and me, but Stokesie with his usual luck draws an old party in baggy gray pants who stumbles up with four giant cans of pineapple juice (what do these bums *do* with all that pineapple juice? I've often asked myself). So the girls come to me. Queenie puts down the jar and I take it into my fingers icy cold. Kingfish Fancy Herring Snacks in Pure Sour Cream: 49¢. Now her hands are empty, not a ring or a bracelet, bare as God made them, and I wonder where the money's coming from. Still with that prim look she lifts a folded dollar bill out of the hollow at the center of her nubbled pink top. The jar went heavy in my hand. Really, I thought that was so cute.

Then everybody's luck begins to run out. Lengel comes in from haggling with a truck full of cabbages on the lot and is about to scuttle into that door marked MANAGER behind which he hides all day when the girls touch his eye. Lengel's pretty dreary, teaches Sunday school and the rest, but he doesn't miss that much. He comes over and says, "Girls, this isn't the beach."

Queenie blushes, though maybe it's just a brush of sunburn I was noticing for the first time, now that she was so close. "My mother asked me to pick up a jar of herring snacks." Her voice kind of startled me, the way voices do when you see the people first, coming out so flat and dumb yet kind of tony, too, the way it ticked over "pick up" and "snacks." All of a sudden I slid right down her voice into the living room. Her father and the other men were standing around in ice-cream coats and bow ties and the women were in sandals picking up herring snacks on toothpicks off a big glass plate and they were all holding drinks the color of water with olives and sprigs of mint in them. When my parents have somebody over they get lemonade and if it's a real racy affair Schlitz in tall glasses with "They'll Do It Every Time" cartoons stenciled on.

15 "That's all right," Lengel said. "But this isn't the beach." His repeating this struck me as funny, as if it had just occurred to him, and he had been thinking all these years the A & P was a great big dune and he was the head lifeguard. He didn't like my smiling — as I say he doesn't miss much — but he concentrates on giving the girls that sad Sunday-school-superintendent stare.

Queenie's blush is no sunburn now, and the plump one in plaid, that I liked better from the back — a really sweet can — pipes up, "We weren't doing any shopping. We just came in for the one thing."

"That makes no difference," Lengel tells her, and I could see from the way his eyes went that he hadn't noticed she was wearing a two-piece before. "We want you decently dressed when you come in here."

"We *are* decent," Queenie says suddenly, her lower lip pushing, getting sore now that she remembers her place, a place from which the crowd that runs the A & P must look pretty crummy. Fancy Herring Snacks flashed in her very blue eyes.

"Girls, I don't want to argue with you. After this come in here with your shoulders covered. It's our policy." He turns his back. That's policy for you. Policy is what the kingpins want. What the others want is juvenile delinquency.

20 All this while, the customers had been showing up with their carts but, you know, sheep, seeing a scene, they had all bunched up on Stokesie, who shook open a paper bag as gently as peeling a peach, not wanting to miss a word. I could feel in the silence everybody getting nervous, most of all Lengel, who asks me, "Sammy, have you rung up their purchase?"

I thought and said "No" but it wasn't about that I was thinking. I go through the punches, 4, 9, GROC. TOT — it's more complicated than you think, and after you do it often enough, it begins to make a little song, that you hear words to, in my case "Hello *(bing)* there, you *(gung)* hap-py *pee*-pul *(splat)!"* — the *splat* being the drawer flying out. I uncrease the bill, tenderly as you may imagine, it just having come from between the two smoothest scoops of vanilla I had ever known were there, and pass a half and a penny into her narrow pink palm, and nestle the herrings in a bag and twist its neck and hand it over, all the time thinking.

The girls, and who'd blame them, are in a hurry to get out, so I say "I quit" to Lengel quick enough for them to hear, hoping they'll stop and watch me, their unsuspected hero. They keep right on going, into the electric eye; the door flies open and they flicker across the lot to their car, Queenie and Plaid and Big Tall Goony-Goony (not that as raw material she was so bad), leaving me with Lengel and a kink in his eyebrow.

"Did you say something, Sammy?"

"I said I quit."

"I thought you did." 25

"You didn't have to embarrass them."

"It was they who were embarrassing us."

I started to say something that came out "Fiddle-de-doo." It's a saying of my grandmother's, and I know she would have been pleased.

"I don't think you know what you're saying," Lengel said.

"I know you don't," I said. "But I do." I pull the bow at the back of my 30
apron and start shrugging it off my shoulders. A couple customers that had been heading for my slot begin to knock against each other, like scared pigs in a chute.

Lengel sighs and begins to look very patient and old and gray. He's been a friend of my parents for years. "Sammy, you don't want to do this to your Mom and Dad," he tells me. It's true, I don't. But it seems to me that once you begin a gesture it's fatal not to go through with it. I fold the apron, "Sammy" stitched in red on the pocket, and put it on the counter, and drop the bow tie on top of it. The bow tie is theirs, if you've ever wondered. "You'll feel this for the rest of your life," Lengel says, and I know that's true, too, but remembering how he made the pretty girl blush makes me so scrunchy inside I punch the No Sale tab and the machine whirs "pee-pul" and the drawer splats out. One advantage to this scene taking place in summer, I can follow this up with a clean exit, there's no fumbling around getting your coat and galoshes, I just saunter into the electric eye in my white shirt that my mother ironed the night before, and the door heaves itself open, and outside the sunshine is skating around on the asphalt.

I look around for my girls, but they're gone, of course. There wasn't anybody but some young married screaming with her children about some candy they didn't get by the door of a powder-blue Falcon station wagon. Looking back in the big windows, over the bags of peat moss and aluminum lawn furniture stacked on the pavement, I could see Lengel in my place in the slot, checking the sheep through. His face was dark gray and his back stiff, as if he'd just had an injection of iron, and my stomach kind of fell as I felt how hard the world was going to be to me hereafter.

AN ALBUM OF WORLD LITERATURE

YUKIO MISHIMA (Japanese/1925–1970)

Patriotism

1966

TRANSLATED BY GEOFFREY W. SARGENT

I

On the twenty-eighth of February, 1936 (on the third day, that is, of the February 26 Incident),° Lieutenant Shinji Takeyama of the Konoe Transport Battalion — profoundly disturbed by the knowledge that his closest colleagues had been with the mutineers from the beginning, and indignant at the imminent prospect of Imperial troops attacking Imperial troops — took his officer's sword and ceremoniously disemboweled himself in the eight-mat room of his private residence in the sixth block of Aoba-chō, in Yotsuya Ward. His wife, Reiko, followed him, stabbing herself to death. The lieutenant's farewell note consisted of one sentence: "Long live the Imperial Forces." His wife's, after apologies for her unfilial conduct in thus preceding her parents to the grave, concluded: "The day which, for a soldier's wife, had to come, has come. . . ." The last moments of this heroic and dedicated couple were such as to make the gods themselves weep. The lieutenant's age, it should be noted, was thirty-one, his wife's twenty-three; and it was not half a year since the celebration of their marriage.

II

Those who saw the bride and bridegroom in the commemorative photograph — perhaps no less than those actually present at the lieutenant's wedding — had exclaimed in wonder at the bearing of this handsome couple. The lieutenant, majestic in military uniform, stood protectively beside his bride, his right hand resting upon his sword, his officer's cap held at his left side. His expression was severe, and his dark brows and wide-gazing eyes well conveyed the clear integrity of youth. For the beauty of the bride in her white over-robe no comparisons were adequate. In the eyes, round beneath soft brows, in the slender, finely shaped nose, and in the full lips, there was both sensuousness and refinement. One hand, emerging shyly from a sleeve of the over-robe, held a fan, and the tips of the fingers, clustering delicately, were like the bud of a moonflower.

After the suicide, people would take out this photograph and examine it, and sadly reflect that too often there was a curse on these seemingly flawless unions. Perhaps it was no more than imagination, but looking at the picture after the tragedy it almost seemed as if the two young people before the gold-

Incident: When right-wing officers killed several moderate officials in an effort to establish a more militant Japan.

lacquered screen were gazing, each with equal clarity, at the deaths which lay before them.

Thanks to the good offices of their go-between, Lieutenant General Ozeki, they had been able to set themselves up in a new home at Aoba-chō in Yotsuya. "New home" is perhaps misleading. It was an old three-room rented house backing onto a small garden. As neither the six- nor the four-and-a-half-mat room downstairs was favored by the sun, they used the upstairs eight-mat room as both bedroom and guest room. There was no maid, so Reiko was left alone to guard the house in her husband's absence.

The honeymoon trip was dispensed with on the grounds that these were 5
times of national emergency. The two of them had spent the first night of their marriage at this house. Before going to bed, Shinji, sitting erect on the floor with his sword laid before him, had bestowed upon his wife a soldierly lecture. A woman who had become the wife of a soldier should know and resolutely accept that her husband's death might come at any moment. It could be tomorrow. It could be the day after. But, no matter when it came — he asked — was she steadfast in her resolve to accept it? Reiko rose to her feet, pulled open a drawer of the cabinet, and took out what was the most prized of her new possessions, the dagger her mother had given her. Returning to her place, she laid the dagger without a word on the mat before her, just as her husband had laid his sword. A silent understanding was achieved at once, and the lieutenant never again sought to test his wife's resolve.

In the first few months of her marriage Reiko's beauty grew daily more radiant, shining serene like the moon after rain.

As both were possessed of young, vigorous bodies, their relationship was passionate. Nor was this merely a matter of the night. On more than one occasion, returning home straight from maneuvers, and begrudging even the time it took to remove his mud-splashed uniform, the lieutenant had pushed his wife to the floor almost as soon as he had entered the house. Reiko was equally ardent in her response. For a little more or a little less than a month, from the first night of their marriage Reiko knew happiness, and the lieutenant, seeing this, was happy too.

Reiko's body was white and pure, and her swelling breasts conveyed a firm and chaste refusal; but, upon consent, those breasts were lavish with their intimate, welcoming warmth. Even in bed these two were frighteningly and awesomely serious. In the very midst of wild, intoxicating passions, their hearts were sober and serious.

By day the lieutenant would think of his wife in the brief rest periods between training; and all day long, at home, Reiko would recall the image of her husband. Even when apart, however, they had only to look at the wedding photograph for their happiness to be once more confirmed. Reiko felt not the slightest surprise that a man who had been a complete stranger until a few months ago should now have become the sun about which her whole world revolved.

All these things had a moral basis, and were in accordance with the Edu- 10
cation Rescript's injunction that "husband and wife should be harmonious." Not once did Reiko contradict her husband, nor did the lieutenant ever find reason to scold his wife. On the god shelf below the stairway, alongside the tablet from

the Great Ise Shrine, were set photographs of their Imperial Majesties, and regularly every morning, before leaving for duty, the lieutenant would stand with his wife at this hallowed place and together they would bow their heads low. The offering water was renewed each morning, and the sacred sprig of *sasaki* was always green and fresh. Their lives were lived beneath the solemn protection of the gods and were filled with an intense happiness, which set every fiber in their bodies trembling.

III

Although Lord Privy Seal Saitō's house was in their neighborhood, neither of them heard any noise of gunfire on the morning of February 26. It was a bugle, sounding muster in the dim, snowy dawn, when the ten-minute tragedy had already ended, which first disrupted the lieutenant's slumbers. Leaping at once from his bed, and without speaking a word, the lieutenant donned his uniform, buckled on the sword held ready for him by his wife, and hurried swiftly out into the snow-covered streets of the still darkened morning. He did not return until the evening of the twenty-eighth.

Later, from the radio news, Reiko learned the full extent of this sudden eruption of violence. Her life throughout the subsequent two days was lived alone, in complete tranquillity, and behind locked doors.

In the lieutenant's face, as he hurried silently out into the snowy morning, Reiko had read the determination to die. If her husband did not return, her own decision was made: she too would die. Quietly she attended to the disposition of her personal possessions. She chose her sets of visiting kimonos as keepsakes for friends of her schooldays, and she wrote a name and address on the stiff paper wrapping in which each was folded. Constantly admonished by her husband never to think of the morrow, Reiko had not even kept a diary and was now denied the pleasure of assiduously rereading her record of the happiness of the past few months and consigning each page to the fire as she did so. Ranged across the top of the radio were a small china dog, a rabbit, a squirrel, a bear, and a fox. There were also a small vase and a water pitcher. These comprised Reiko's one and only collection. But it would hardly do, she imagined, to give such things as keepsakes. Nor again would it be quite proper to ask specifically for them to be included in the coffin. It seemed to Reiko, as these thoughts passed through her mind, that the expression on the small animals' faces grew even more lost and forlorn.

Reiko took the squirrel in her hand and looked at it. And then, her thoughts turning to a realm far beyond these childlike affections, she gazed up into the distance at the great sunlike principle which her husband embodied. She was ready, and happy, to be hurtled along to her destruction in that gleaming sun chariot—but now, for these few moments of solitude, she allowed herself to luxuriate in this innocent attachment to trifles. The time when she had genuinely loved these things, however, was long past. Now she merely loved the memory of having once loved them, and their place in her heart had been filled by more intense passions, by a more frenzied happiness. . . . For Reiko had never, even to herself, thought of those soaring joys of the flesh as a mere pleasure. The February cold, and the icy touch of the china squirrel, had numbed

Reiko's slender fingers; yet, even so, in her lower limbs, beneath the ordered repetition of the pattern which crossed the skirt of her trim *meisen* kimono, she could feel now, as she thought of the lieutenant's powerful arms reaching out toward her, a hot moistness of the flesh which defied the snows.

She was not in the least afraid of the death hovering in her mind. Waiting alone at home, Reiko firmly believed that everything her husband was feeling or thinking now, his anguish and distress, was leading her — just as surely as the power in his flesh — to a welcome death. She felt as if her body could melt away with ease and be transformed to the merest fraction of her husband's thought.

Listening to the frequent announcements on the radio, she heard the names of several of her husband's colleagues mentioned among those of the insurgents. This was news of death. She followed the developments closely, wondering anxiously, as the situation became daily more irrevocable, why no Imperial ordinance was sent down, and watching what had at first been taken as a movement to restore the nation's honor come gradually to be branded with the infamous name of mutiny. There was no communication from the regiment. At any moment, it seemed, fighting might commence in the city streets, where the remains of the snow still lay.

Toward sundown on the twenty-eighth Reiko was startled by a furious pounding on the front door. She hurried downstairs. As she pulled with fumbling fingers at the bolt, the shape dimly outlined beyond the frosted-glass panel made no sound, but she knew it was her husband. Reiko had never known the bolt on the sliding door to be so stiff. Still it resisted. The door just would not open.

In a moment, almost before she knew she had succeeded, the lieutenant was standing before her on the cement floor inside the porch, muffled in a khaki greatcoat, his top boots heavy with slush from the street. Closing the door behind him, he returned the bolt once more to its socket. With what significance, Reiko did not understand.

"Welcome home."

Reiko bowed deeply, but her husband made no response. As he had already unfastened his sword and was about to remove his greatcoat, Reiko moved around behind to assist. The coat, which was cold and damp and had lost the odor of horse dung it normally exuded when exposed to the sun, weighed heavily upon her arm. Draping it across a hanger, and cradling the sword and leather belt in her sleeves, she waited while her husband removed his top boots and then followed behind him into the "living room." This was the six-mat room downstairs.

Seen in the clear light from the lamp, her husband's face, covered with a heavy growth of bristle, was almost unrecognizably wasted and thin. The cheeks were hollow, their luster and resilience gone. In his normal good spirits he would have changed into old clothes as soon as he was home and have pressed her to get supper at once, but now he sat before the table still in his uniform, his head drooping dejectedly. Reiko refrained from asking whether she should prepare the supper.

After an interval the lieutenant spoke.

"I knew nothing. They hadn't asked me to join. Perhaps out of consideration, because I was newly married. Kanō, and Homma too, and Yamaguchi."

Reiko recalled momentarily the faces of high-spirited young officers, friends of her husband, who had come to the house occasionally as guests.

"There may be an Imperial ordinance sent down tomorrow. They'll be posted as rebels, I imagine. I shall be in command of a unit with orders to attack them. . . . I can't do it. It's impossible to do a thing like that."

He spoke again.

"They've taken me off guard duty, and I have permission to return home for one night. Tomorrow morning, without question, I must leave to join the attack. I can't do it, Reiko."

Reiko sat erect with lowered eyes. She understood clearly that her husband had spoken of his death. The lieutenant was resolved. Each word, being rooted in death, emerged sharply and with powerful significance against this dark, unmovable background. Although the lieutenant was speaking of his dilemma, already there was no room in his mind for vacillation.

However, there was a clarity, like the clarity of a stream fed from melting snows, in the silence which rested between them. Sitting in his own home after the long two-day ordeal, and looking across at the face of his beautiful wife, the lieutenant was for the first time experiencing true peace of mind. For he had at once known, though she said nothing, that his wife divined the resolve which lay beneath his words.

"Well, then . . ." The lieutenant's eyes opened wide. Despite his exhaustion they were strong and clear, and now for the first time they looked straight into the eyes of his wife. "Tonight I shall cut my stomach."

Reiko did not flinch.

Her round eyes showed tension, as taut as the clang of a bell.

"I am ready," she said. "I ask permission to accompany you."

The lieutenant felt almost mesmerized by the strength of those eyes. His words flowed swiftly and easily, like the utterances of a man in delirium, and it was beyond his understanding how permission in a matter of such weight could be expressed so casually.

"Good. We'll go together. But I want you as a witness, first, for my own suicide. Agreed?"

When this was said a sudden release of abundant happiness welled up in both their hearts. Reiko was deeply affected by the greatness of her husband's trust in her. It was vital for the lieutenant, whatever else might happen, that there should be no irregularity in his death. For that reason there had to be a witness. The fact that he had chosen his wife for this was the first mark of his trust. The second, and even greater mark, was that though he had pledged that they should die together he did not intend to kill his wife first—he had deferred her death to a time when he would no longer be there to verify it. If the lieutenant had been a suspicious husband, he would doubtless, as in the usual suicide pact, have chosen to kill his wife first.

When Reiko said, "I ask permission to accompany you," the lieutenant felt these words to be the final fruit of the education which he had himself given his wife, starting on the first night of their marriage, and which had schooled her, when the moment came, to say what had to be said without a shadow of hesitation. This flattered the lieutenant's opinion of himself as a self-reliant man. He was not so romantic or conceited as to imagine that the words were spoken spontaneously, out of love for her husband.

With happiness welling almost too abundantly in their hearts, they could not help smiling at each other. Reiko felt as if she had returned to her wedding night.

Before her eyes was neither pain nor death. She seemed to see only a free and limitless expanse opening out into vast distances.

"The water is hot. Will you take your bath now?"

"Ah yes, of course."

"And supper . . . ?"

The words were delivered in such level, domestic tones that the lieutenant came near to thinking, for the fraction of a second, that everything had been a hallucination.

"I don't think we'll need supper. But perhaps you could warm some sake?"

"As you wish."

As Reiko rose and took a *tanzen* gown from the cabinet for after the bath, she purposely directed her husband's attention to the opened drawer. The lieutenant rose, crossed to the cabinet, and looked inside. From the ordered array of paper wrappings he read, one by one, the addresses of the keepsakes. There was no grief in the lieutenant's response to this demonstration of heroic resolve. His heart was filled with tenderness. Like a husband who is proudly shown the childish purchases of a young wife, the lieutenant, overwhelmed by affection, lovingly embraced his wife from behind and implanted a kiss upon her neck.

Reiko felt the roughness of the lieutenant's unshaven skin against her neck. This sensation, more than being just a thing of this world, was for Reiko almost the world itself, but now — with the feeling that it was soon to be lost forever — it had freshness beyond all her experience. Each moment had its own vital strength, and the senses in every corner of her body were reawakened. Accepting her husband's caresses from behind, Reiko raised herself on the tips of her toes, letting the vitality seep through her entire body.

"First the bath, and then, after some sake . . . lay out the bedding upstairs, will you?"

The lieutenant whispered the words into his wife's ear. Reiko silently nodded.

Flinging off his uniform, the lieutenant went to the bath. To faint background noises of slopping water Reiko tended the charcoal brazier in the living room and began the preparations for warming the sake.

Taking the *tanzen,* a sash, and some underclothes, she went to the bathroom to ask how the water was. In the midst of a coiling cloud of steam the lieutenant was sitting cross-legged on the floor, shaving, and she could dimly discern the rippling movements of the muscles on his damp, powerful back as they responded to the movement of his arms.

There was nothing to suggest a time of any special significance. Reiko, going busily about her tasks, was preparing side dishes from odds and ends in stock. Her hands did not tremble. If anything, she managed even more efficiently and smoothly than usual. From time to time, it is true, there was a strange throbbing deep within her breast. Like distant lightning, it had a moment of sharp intensity and then vanished without trace. Apart from that, nothing was in any way out of the ordinary.

The lieutenant, shaving in the bathroom, felt his warmed body miraculously healed at last of the desperate tiredness of the days of indecision and filled — in spite of the death which lay ahead — with pleasurable anticipation. The sound of his wife going about her work came to him faintly. A healthy physical craving, submerged for two days, reasserted itself.

The lieutenant was confident there had been no impurity in that joy they had experienced when resolving upon death. They had both sensed at that moment — though not, of course, in any clear and conscious way — that those permissible pleasures which they shared in private were once more beneath the protection of Righteousness and Divine Power, and of a complete and unassailable morality. On looking into each other's eyes and discovering there an honorable death, they had felt themselves safe once more behind steel walls which none could destroy, encased in an impenetrable armor of Beauty and Truth. Thus, so far from seeing any inconsistency or conflict between the urges of his flesh and the sincerity of his patriotism, the lieutenant was even able to regard the two as parts of the same thing.

Thrusting his face close to the dark, cracked, misted wall mirror, the lieu- 55
tenant shaved himself with great care. This would be his death face. There must be no unsightly blemishes. The clean-shaven face gleamed once more with a youthful luster, seeming to brighten the darkness of the mirror. There was a certain elegance, he even felt, in the association of death with this radiantly healthy face.

Just as it looked now, this would become his death face! Already, in fact, it had half departed from the lieutenant's personal possession and had become the bust above a dead soldier's memorial. As an experiment he closed his eyes tight. Everything was wrapped in blackness, and he was no longer a living, seeing creature.

Returning from the bath, the traces of the shave glowing faintly blue beneath his smooth cheeks, he seated himself beside the now well-kindled charcoal brazier. Busy though Reiko was, he noticed, she had found time lightly to touch up her face. Her cheeks were gay and her lips moist. There was no shadow of sadness to be seen. Truly, the lieutenant felt, as he saw this mark of his young wife's passionate nature, he had chosen the wife he ought to have chosen.

As soon as the lieutenant had drained his sake cup he offered it to Reiko. Reiko had never before tasted sake, but she accepted without hesitation and sipped timidly.

"Come here," the lieutenant said.

Reiko moved to her husband's side and was embraced as she leaned back- 60
ward across his lap. Her breast was in violent commotion, as if sadness, joy, and the potent sake were mingling and reacting within her. The lieutenant looked down into his wife's face. It was the last face he would see in this world, the last face he would see of his wife. The lieutenant scrutinized the face minutely, with the eyes of a traveler bidding farewell to splendid vistas which he will never revisit. It was a face he could not tire of looking at — the features regular yet not cold, the lips lightly closed with a soft strength. The lieutenant kissed those lips, unthinkingly. And suddenly, though there was not the slightest distortion of the face into the unsightliness of sobbing, he noticed that tears were welling slowly from beneath the long lashes of the closed eyes and brimming over into the glistening stream.

When, a little later, the lieutenant urged that they should move to the upstairs bedroom, his wife replied that she would follow after taking a bath. Climbing the stairs alone to the bedroom, where the air was already warmed by the gas heater, the lieutenant lay down on the bedding with arms outstretched and legs apart. Even the time at which he lay waiting for his wife to join him was no later and no earlier than usual.

He folded his hands beneath his head and gazed at the dark boards of the ceiling in the dimness beyond the range of the standard lamp. Was it death he was now waiting for? Or a wild ecstasy of the senses? The two seemed to overlap, almost as if the object of this bodily desire was death itself. But, however that might be, it was certain that never before had the lieutenant tasted such total freedom.

There was the sound of a car outside the window. He could hear the screech of its tires skidding in the snow piled at the side of the street. The sound of its horn reechoed from nearby walls. . . . Listening to these noises he had the feeling that the house rose like a solitary island in the ocean of a society going as restlessly about its business as ever. All around, vastly and untidily, stretched the country for which he grieved. He was to give his life for it. But would that great country, with which he was prepared to remonstrate to the extent of destroying himself, take the slightest heed of his death? He did not know; and it did not matter. His was a battlefield without glory, a battlefield where none could display deeds of valor: it was the front line of the spirit.

Reiko's footsteps sounded on the stairway. The steep stairs in this old house creaked badly. There were fond memories in that creaking, and many a time, while waiting in bed, the lieutenant had listened to its welcome sound. At the thought that he would hear it no more he listened with intense concentration, striving for every corner of every moment of this precious time to be filled with the sound of those soft footfalls on the creaking stairway. The moments seemed transformed to jewels, sparkling with inner light.

Reiko wore a Nagoya sash about the waist of her *yukata,* but as the lieuten- 65
ant reached toward it, its redness sobered by the dimness of the light, Reiko's hand moved to his assistance and the sash fell away, slithering swiftly to the floor. As she stood before him, still in her *yukata,* the lieutenant inserted his hands through the side slits beneath each sleeve, intending to embrace her as she was; but at the touch of his finger tips upon the warm naked flesh, and as the armpits closed gently about his hands, his whole body was suddenly aflame.

In a few moments the two lay naked before the glowing gas heater.

Neither spoke the thought, but their hearts, their bodies, and their pounding breasts blazed with the knowledge that this was the very last time. It was as if the words "The Last Time" were spelled out, in invisible brushstrokes, across every inch of their bodies.

The lieutenant drew his wife close and kissed her vehemently. As their tongues explored each other's mouths, reaching out into the smooth, moist interior, they felt as if the still-unknown agonies of death had tempered their senses to the keenness of red-hot steel. The agonies they could not yet feel, the distant pains of death, had refined their awareness of pleasure.

"This is the last time I shall see your body," said the lieutenant. "Let me look at it closely." And, tilting the shade on the lampstand to one side, he directed the rays along the full length of Reiko's outstretched form.

Reiko lay still with her eyes closed. The light from the low lamp clearly 70
revealed the majestic sweep of her white flesh. The lieutenant, not without a

touch of egocentricity, rejoiced that he would never see this beauty crumble in death.

At his leisure, the lieutenant allowed the unforgettable spectacle to engrave itself upon his mind. With one hand he fondled the hair, with the other he softly stroked the magnificent face, implanting kisses here and there where his eyes lingered. The quiet coldness of the high, tapering forehead, the closed eyes with their long lashes beneath faintly etched brows, the set of the finely shaped nose, the gleam of teeth glimpsed between full, regular lips, the soft cheeks and the small, wise chin . . . these things conjured up in the lieutenant's mind the vision of a truly radiant death face, and again and again he pressed his lips tight against the white throat — where Reiko's own hand was soon to strike — and the throat reddened faintly beneath his kisses. Returning to the mouth he laid his lips against it with the gentlest of pressures, and moved them rhythmically over Reiko's with the light rolling motion of a small boat. If he closed his eyes, the world became a rocking cradle.

Wherever the lieutenant's eyes moved his lips faithfully followed. The high, swelling breasts, surmounted by nipples like the buds of a wild cherry, hardened as the lieutenant's lips closed about them. The arms flowed smoothly downward from each side of the breast, tapering toward the wrists, yet losing nothing of their roundness or symmetry, and at their tips were those delicate fingers which had held the fan at the wedding ceremony. One by one, as the lieutenant kissed them, the fingers withdrew behind their neighbor as if in shame. . . . The natural hollow curving between the bosom and the stomach carried in its lines a suggestion not only of softness but of resilient strength, and while it gave forewarning of the rich curves spreading outward from here to the hips it had, in itself, an appearance only of restraint and proper discipline. The whiteness and richness of the stomach and hips was like milk brimming in a great bowl, and the sharply shadowed dip of the navel could have been the fresh impress of a raindrop, fallen there that very moment. Where the shadows gathered more thickly, hair clustered, gentle and sensitive, and as the agitation mounted in the now no longer passive body there hung over this region a scent like the smoldering of fragrant blossoms, growing steadily more pervasive.

At length, in a tremendous voice, Reiko spoke.

"Show me. . . . Let me look too, for the last time."

Never before had he heard from his wife's lips so strong and unequivocal 75
a request. It was as if something which her modesty had wished to keep hidden to the end had suddenly burst its bonds of constraint. The lieutenant obediently lay back and surrendered himself to his wife. Lithely she raised her white, trembling body, and — burning with an innocent desire to return to her husband what he had done for her — placed two white fingers on the lieutenant's eyes, which gazed fixedly up at her, and gently stroked them shut.

Suddenly overwhelmed by tenderness, her cheeks flushed by a dizzying uprush of emotion, Reiko threw her arms about the lieutenant's close-cropped head. The bristly hairs rubbed painfully against her breast, the prominent nose was cold as it dug into her flesh, and his breath was hot. Relaxing her embrace, she gazed down at her husband's masculine face. The severe brows, the closed eyes, the splendid bridge of the nose, the shapely lips drawn firmly together . . . the blue, clean-shaven cheeks reflecting the light and gleaming smoothly. Reiko kissed each of these. She kissed the broad nape of the neck, the strong, erect shoulders, the powerful chest with its twin circles like shields and its russet nipples. In the armpits, deeply shadowed by the ample flesh of the shoulders and chest, a sweet and melancholy odor emanated from the growth of hair, and in the sweetness of this odor was contained, somehow, the essence of young death. The lieutenant's naked skin glowed like a field of barley, and everywhere the muscles showed in sharp relief, converging on the lower abdomen about the small, unassuming navel. Gazing at the youthful, firm stomach, modestly covered by a vigorous growth of hair, Reiko thought of it as it was soon to be, cruelly cut by the sword, and she laid her head upon it, sobbing in pity, and bathed it with kisses.

At the touch of his wife's tears upon his stomach the lieutenant felt ready to endure with courage the cruelest agonies of his suicide.

What ecstasies they experienced after these tender exchanges may well be imagined. The lieutenant raised himself and enfolded his wife in a powerful embrace, her body now limp with exhaustion after her grief and tears. Passionately they held their faces close, rubbing cheek against cheek. Reiko's body was trembling. Their breasts, moist with sweat, were tightly joined, and every inch of the young and beautiful bodies had become so much one with the other that it seemed impossible there should ever again be a separation. Reiko cried out. From the heights they plunged into the abyss, and from the abyss they took wing and soared once more to dizzying heights. The lieutenant panted like the regimental standard-bearer on a route march. . . . As one cycle ended, almost immediately a new wave of passion would be generated, and together — with no trace of fatigue — they would climb again in a single breathless movement to the very summit.

IV

When the lieutenant at last turned away, it was not from weariness. For one thing, he was anxious not to undermine the considerable strength he would need in carrying out his suicide. For another, he would have been sorry to mar the sweetness of these last memories by overindulgence.

Since the lieutenant had clearly desisted, Reiko too, with her usual compli- 80
ance, followed his example. The two lay naked on their backs, with fingers interlaced, staring fixedly at the dark ceiling. The room was warm from the heater, and even when the sweat had ceased to pour from their bodies they felt no cold. Outside, in the hushed night, the sounds of passing traffic had ceased. Even the noises of the trains and streetcars around Yotsuya station did not penetrate this far. After echoing through the region bounded by the moat, they were lost in the heavily wooded park fronting the broad driveway before Akasaka Palace. It was hard to believe in the tension gripping this whole quarter, where the two factions of the bitterly divided Imperial Army now confronted each other, poised for battle.

Savoring the warmth glowing within themselves, they lay still and recalled the ecstasies they had just known. Each moment of the experience was relived. They remembered the taste of kisses which had never wearied, the touch of naked flesh, episode after episode of dizzying bliss. But already, from the dark boards of the ceiling, the face of death was peering down. These joys had been final, and their bodies would never know them again. Not that joy of this intensity — and the same thought had occurred to them both — was ever likely to be reexperienced, even if they should live on to old age.

The feel of their fingers intertwined — this too would soon be lost. Even the wood-grain patterns they now gazed at on the dark ceiling boards would be taken from them. They could feel death edging in, nearer and nearer. There could be no hesitation now. They must have the courage to reach out to death themselves, and to seize it.

"Well, let's make our preparations," said the lieutenant. The note of determination in the words was unmistakable, but at the same time Reiko had never heard her husband's voice so warm and tender.

After they had risen, a variety of tasks awaited them.

The lieutenant, who had never once before helped with the bedding, now cheerfully slid back the door of the closet, lifted the mattress across the room by himself, and stowed it away inside.

Reiko turned off the gas heater and put away the lamp standard. During the lieutenant's absence she had arranged this room carefully, sweeping and dusting it to a fresh cleanness, and now — if one overlooked the rosewood table drawn into one corner — the eight-mat room gave all the appearance of a reception room ready to welcome an important guest.

"We've seen some drinking here, haven't we? With Kanō and Homma and Noguchi . . ."

"Yes, they were great drinkers, all of them."

"We'll be meeting them before long, in the other world. They'll tease us, I imagine, when they find I've brought you with me."

Descending the stairs, the lieutenant turned to look back into this calm, clean room, now brightly illuminated by the ceiling lamp. There floated across his mind the faces of the young officers who had drunk there, and laughed, and innocently bragged. He had never dreamed then that he would one day cut open his stomach in this room.

In the two rooms downstairs husband and wife busied themselves smoothly and serenely with their respective preparations. The lieutenant went to the toilet, and then to the bathroom to wash. Meanwhile Reiko folded away her husband's padded robe, placed his uniform tunic, his trousers, and a newly cut bleached loincloth in the bathroom, and set out sheets of paper on the living-room table for the farewell notes. Then she removed the lid from the writing box and began rubbing ink from the ink tablet. She had already decided upon the wording of her own note.

Reiko's fingers pressed hard upon the cold gilt letters of the ink tablet, and the water in the shallow well at once darkened, as if a black cloud had spread across it. She stopped thinking that this repeated action, this pressure from her fingers, this rise and fall of faint sound, was all and solely for death. It was a routine domestic task, a simple paring away of time until death should finally stand before her. But somehow, in the increasingly smooth motion of the tablet rubbing on the stone, and in the scent from the thickening ink, there was unspeakable darkness.

Neat in his uniform, which he now wore next to his skin, the lieutenant emerged from the bathroom. Without a word he seated himself at the table, bolt upright, took a brush in his hand, and stared undecidedly at the paper before him.

Reiko took a white silk kimono with her and entered the bathroom. When she reappeared in the living room, clad in the white kimono and with her face lightly made up, the farewell note lay completed on the table beneath the lamp. The thick black brushstrokes said simply:

95 "Long Live the Imperial Forces — Army Lieutenant Takeyama Shinji."

While Reiko sat opposite him writing her own note, the lieutenant gazed in silence, intensely serious, at the controlled movement of his wife's pale fingers as they manipulated the brush.

With their respective notes in their hands — the lieutenant's sword strapped to his side, Reiko's small dagger thrust into the sash of her white kimono — the two of them stood before the god shelf and silently prayed. Then they put out all the downstairs lights. As he mounted the stairs the lieutenant turned his head and gazed back at the striking, white-clad figure of his wife, climbing behind him, with lowered eyes, from the darkness beneath.

The farewell notes were laid side by side in the alcove of the upstairs room. They wondered whether they ought not to remove the hanging scroll, but since it had been written by their go-between, Lieutenant General Ozeki, and consisted, moreover, of two Chinese characters signifying "Sincerity," they left it where it was. Even if it were to become stained with splashes of blood, they felt that the lieutenant general would understand.

The lieutenant, sitting erect with his back to the alcove, laid his sword on the floor before him.

100 Reiko sat facing him, a mat's width away. With the rest of her so severely white the touch of rouge on her lips seemed remarkably seductive.

Across the dividing mat they gazed intently into each other's eyes. The lieutenant's sword lay before his knees. Seeing it, Reiko recalled their first night and was overwhelmed with sadness. The lieutenant spoke, in a hoarse voice:

"As I have no second to help me I shall cut deep. It may look unpleasant, but please do not panic. Death of any sort is a fearful thing to watch. You must not be discouraged by what you see. Is that all right?"

"Yes."

Reiko nodded deeply.

105 Looking at the slender white figure of his wife the lieutenant experienced a bizarre excitement. What he was about to perform was an act in his public capacity as a soldier, something he had never previously shown his wife. It called for a resolution equal to the courage to enter battle; it was a death of no less degree and quality than death in the front line. It was his conduct on the battlefield that he was now to display.

Momentarily the thought led the lieutenant to a strange fantasy. A lonely death on the battlefield, a death beneath the eyes of his beautiful wife . . . in the sensation that he was now to die in these two dimensions, realizing an impossible union of them both, there was sweetness beyond words. This must be the very pinnacle of good fortune, he thought. To have every moment of his death observed by those beautiful eyes — it was like being borne to death on a gentle, fragrant breeze. There was some special favor here. He did not understand precisely what it was, but it was a domain unknown to others: a dispensation granted to no one else had been permitted to himself. In the radiant, bridelike figure of his white-robed wife the lieutenant seemed to see a vision of all those things he had loved and for which he was to lay down his life — the Imperial Household, the Nation, the Army Flag. All these, no less than the wife who sat before him, were presences observing him closely with clear and never-faltering eyes.

Reiko too was gazing intently at her husband, so soon to die, and she thought that never in this world had she seen anything so beautiful. The lieutenant always looked well in uniform, but now, as he contemplated death with severe brows and firmly closed lips, he revealed what was perhaps masculine beauty at its most superb.

"It's time to go," the lieutenant said at last.

Reiko bent her body low to the mat in a deep bow. She could not raise her face. She did not wish to spoil her makeup with tears, but the tears could not be held back.

When at length she looked up she saw hazily through the tears that her 110
husband had wound a white bandage around the blade of his now unsheathed sword, leaving five or six inches of naked steel showing at the point.

Resting the sword in its cloth wrapping on the mat before him, the lieutenant rose from his knees, resettled himself cross-legged, and unfastened the hooks of his uniform collar. His eyes no longer saw his wife. Slowly, one by one, he undid the flat brass buttons. The dusky brown chest was revealed, and then the stomach. He unclasped his belt and undid the buttons of his trousers. The pure whiteness of the thickly coiled loincloth showed itself. The lieutenant pushed the cloth down with both hands, further to ease his stomach, and then reached for the white-bandaged blade of his sword. With his left hand he massaged his abdomen, glancing downward as he did so.

To reassure himself on the sharpness of his sword's cutting edge the lieutenant folded back the left trouser flap, exposing a little of his thigh, and lightly drew the blade across the skin. Blood welled up in the wound at once, and several streaks of red trickled downward, glistening in the strong light.

It was the first time Reiko had ever seen her husband's blood, and she felt a violent throbbing in her chest. She looked at her husband's face. The lieutenant was looking at the blood with calm appraisal. For a moment — though thinking at the same time that it was hollow comfort — Reiko experienced a sense of relief.

The lieutenant's eyes fixed his wife with an intense, hawklike stare. Moving the sword around to his front, he raised himself slightly on his hips and let the upper half of his body lean over the sword point. That he was mustering his whole strength was apparent from the angry tension of the uniform at his shoulders. The lieutenant aimed to strike deep into the left of his stomach. His sharp eye pierced the silence of the room.

Despite the effort he had himself put into the blow, the lieutenant had the 115
impression that someone else had struck the side of his stomach agonizingly with a thick rod of iron. For a second or so his head reeled and he had no idea what had happened. The five or six inches of naked point had vanished completely into his flesh, and the white bandage, gripped in his clenched fist, pressed directly against his stomach.

He returned to consciousness. The blade had certainly pierced the wall of the stomach, he thought. His breathing was difficult, his chest thumped violently, and in some far deep region, which he could hardly believe was a part of himself, a fearful and excruciating pain came welling up as if the ground had split open to disgorge a boiling stream of molten rock. The pain came suddenly nearer, with terrifying speed. The lieutenant bit his lower lip and stifled an instinctive moan.

Was this *seppuku?*—he was thinking. It was a sensation of utter chaos, as if the sky had fallen on his head and the world was reeling drunkenly. His will power and courage, which had seemed so robust before he made the incision, had now dwindled to something like a single hairlike thread of steel, and he was assailed by the uneasy feeling that he must advance along this thread, clinging to it with desperation. His clenched fist had grown moist. Looking down, he saw that both his hand and the cloth about the blade were drenched in blood. His loincloth too was dyed a deep red. It struck him as incredible that, amidst this terrible agony, things which could be seen could still be seen, and existing things existed still.

The moment the lieutenant thrust the sword into his left side and she saw the deathly pallor fall across his face, like an abruptly lowered curtain, Reiko had to struggle to prevent herself from rushing to his side. Whatever happened, she must watch. She must be a witness. That was the duty her husband had laid upon her. Opposite her, a mat's space away, she could clearly see her husband biting his lip to stifle the pain. The pain was there, with absolute certainty, before her eyes. And Reiko had no means of rescuing him from it.

The sweat glistened on her husband's forehead. The lieutenant closed his eyes, and then opened them again, as if experimenting. The eyes had lost their luster, and seemed innocent and empty like the eyes of a small animal.

The agony before Reiko's eyes burned as strong as the summer sun, utterly 120
remote from the grief which seemed to be tearing herself apart within. The pain grew steadily in stature, stretching upward. Reiko felt that her husband had already become a man in a separate world, a man whose whole being had been resolved into pain, a prisoner in a cage of pain where no hand could reach out to him. But Reiko felt no pain at all. Her grief was not pain. As she thought about this, Reiko began to feel as if someone had raised a cruel wall of glass high between herself and her husband.

Ever since her marriage her husband's existence had been her own existence, and every breath of his had been a breath drawn by herself. But now, while her husband's existence in pain was a vivid reality, Reiko could find in this grief of hers no certain proof at all of her own existence.

With only his right hand on the sword the lieutenant began to cut sideways across his stomach. But as the blade became entangled with the entrails it was pushed constantly outward by their soft resilience; and the lieutenant realized that it would be necessary, as he cut, to use both hands to keep the point pressed deep into his stomach. He pulled the blade across. It did not cut as easily as he had expected. He directed the strength of his whole body into his right hand and pulled again. There was a cut of three or four inches.

The pain spread slowly outward from the inner depths until the whole stomach reverberated. It was like the wild clanging of a bell. Or like a thousand bells which jangled simultaneously at every breath he breathed and every throb of his pulse, rocking his whole being. The lieutenant could no longer stop himself from moaning. But by now the blade had cut its way through to below the navel, and when he noticed this he felt a sense of satisfaction, and a renewal of courage.

The volume of blood had steadily increased, and now it spurted from the wound as if propelled by the beat of the pulse. The mat before the lieutenant was drenched red with splattered blood, and more blood overflowed onto it from pools which gathered in the folds of the lieutenant's khaki trousers. A spot, like a bird, came flying across to Reiko and settled on the lap of her white kimono.

By the time the lieutenant had at last drawn the sword across to the right 125
side of his stomach, the blade was already cutting shallow and had revealed its naked tip, slippery with blood and grease. But, suddenly stricken by a fit of vomiting, the lieutenant cried out hoarsely. The vomiting made the fierce pain fiercer still, and the stomach, which had thus far remained firm and compact, now abruptly heaved, opening wide its wound, and the entrails burst through, as if the wound too were vomiting. Seemingly ignorant of their master's suffering, the entrails gave an impression of robust health and almost disagreeable vitality as they slipped smoothly out and spilled over into the crotch. The lieutenant's head drooped, his shoulders heaved, his eyes opened to narrow slits, and a thin trickle of saliva dribbled from his mouth. The gold markings on his epaulets caught the light and glinted.

Blood was scattered everywhere. The lieutenant was soaked in it to his knees, and he sat now in a crumpled and listless posture, one hand on the floor. A raw smell filled the room. The lieutenant, his head drooping, retched repeatedly, and the movement showed vividly in his shoulders. The blade of the sword, now pushed back by the entrails and exposed to its tip, was still in the lieutenant's right hand.

It would be difficult to imagine a more heroic sight than that of the lieutenant at this moment, as he mustered his strength and flung back his head. The movement was performed with sudden violence, and the back of his head struck with a sharp crack against the alcove pillar. Reiko had been sitting until now with her face lowered, gazing in fascination at the tide of blood advancing toward her knees, but the sound took her by surprise and she looked up.

The lieutenant's face was not the face of a living man. The eyes were hollow, the skin parched, the once so lustrous cheeks and lips the color of dried mud. The right hand alone was moving. Laboriously gripping the sword, it hovered shakily in the air like the hand of a marionette and strove to direct the point at the base of the lieutenant's throat. Reiko watched her husband make this last, most heartrending, futile exertion. Glistening with blood and grease, the point was thrust at the throat again and again. And each time it missed its aim. The strength to guide it was no longer there. The straying point struck the collar and the collar badges. Although its hooks had been unfastened, the stiff military collar had closed together again and was protecting the throat.

Reiko could bear the sight no longer. She tried to go to her husband's help, but she could not stand. She moved through the blood on her knees, and her white skirts grew deep red. Moving to the rear of her husband, she helped no more than by loosening the collar. The quivering blade at last contacted the naked flesh of the throat. At that moment Reiko's impression was that she herself had propelled her husband forward; but that was not the case. It was a movement planned by the lieutenant himself, his last exertion of strength. Abruptly he threw his body at the blade, and the blade pierced his neck, emerging at the nape. There was a tremendous spurt of blood and the lieutenant lay still, cold blue-tinged steel protruding from his neck at the back.

V

Slowly, her socks slippery with blood, Reiko descended the stairway. The 130
upstairs room was now completely still.

Switching on the ground-floor lights, she checked the gas jet and the main gas plug and poured water over the smoldering, half-buried charcoal in the brazier. She stood before the upright mirror in the four-and-a-half mat room and held up her skirts. The bloodstains made it seem as if a bold, vivid pattern was printed across the lower half of her white kimono. When she sat down before the mirror, she was conscious of the dampness and coldness of her husband's blood in the region of her thighs, and she shivered. Then, for a long while, she lingered over her toilet preparations. She applied the rouge generously to her cheeks, and her lips too she painted heavily. This was no longer makeup to please her husband. It was makeup for the world which she would leave behind, and there was a touch of the magnificent and the spectacular in her brushwork. When she rose, the mat before the mirror was wet with blood. Reiko was not concerned about this.

Returning from the toilet, Reiko stood finally on the cement floor of the porchway. When her husband had bolted the door here last night it had been in preparation for death. For a while she stood immersed in the consideration of a simple problem. Should she now leave the bolt drawn? If she were to lock the door, it could be that the neighbors might not notice their suicide for several days. Reiko did not relish the thought of their two corpses putrefying before discovery. After all, it seemed, it would be best to leave it open. . . . She released the bolt, and also drew open the frosted-glass door a fraction. . . . At once a chill wind blew in. There was no sign of anyone in the midnight streets, and stars glittered ice-cold through the trees in the large house opposite.

Leaving the door as it was, Reiko mounted the stairs. She had walked here and there for some time and her socks were no longer slippery. About halfway up, her nostrils were already assailed by a peculiar smell.

The lieutenant was lying on his face in a sea of blood. The point protruding from his neck seemed to have grown even more prominent than before. Reiko walked heedlessly across the blood. Sitting beside the lieutenant's corpse, she stared intently at the face, which lay on one cheek on the mat. The eyes were opened wide, as if the lieutenant's attention had been attracted by something. She raised the head, folding it in her sleeve, wiped the blood from the lips, and bestowed a last kiss.

Then she rose and took from the closet a new white blanket and a waist 135
cord. To prevent any derangement of her skirts, she wrapped the blanket about her waist and bound it there firmly with the cord.

Reiko sat herself on a spot about one foot distant from the lieutenant's body. Drawing the dagger from her sash, she examined its dully gleaming blade intently, and held it to her tongue. The taste of the polished steel was slightly sweet.

Reiko did not linger. When she thought how the pain which had previously opened such a gulf between herself and her dying husband was now to become a part of her own experience, she saw before her only the joy of herself entering a realm her husband had already made his own. In her husband's agonized face there had been something inexplicable which she was seeing for the first time. Now she would solve that riddle. Reiko sensed that at last she too would be able to taste the true bitterness and sweetness of that great moral principle in which her husband believed. What had until now been tasted only faintly through her husband's example she was about to savor directly with her own tongue.

Reiko rested the point of the blade against the base of her throat. She thrust hard. The wound was only shallow. Her head blazed, and her hands shook uncontrollably. She gave the blade a strong pull sideways. A warm substance flooded into her mouth, and everything before her eyes reddened, in a vision of spouting blood. She gathered her strength and plunged the point of the blade deep into her throat.

Connections

1. Contrast Reiko's response to her husband's death in this story with Mrs. Mallard's in Chopin's "The Story of an Hour" (p. 12). How do the differences indicate different sensibilities in the culture of each story?
2. Compare and contrast Mishima's description of the couple's suicides with Tim O'Brien's descriptions of a soldier being blown up and a water buffalo being shot in "How to Tell a True War Story" (p. 454). How do these descriptions of violent actions support the theme of each story?
3. How does Reiko's suicide provide meaning to her life in contrast to Mabel's suicide attempt in Lawrence's "The Horse Dealer's Daughter" (p. 383)? How is human passion a central concern in both stories?

R. K. NARAYAN (Indian/b. 1906)

Trail of the Green Blazer

1981

The Green Blazer stood out prominently under the bright sun and blue sky. In all that jostling crowd one could not help noticing it. Villagers in shirts and turbans, townsmen in coats and caps, beggars bare-bodied and women in multicolored saris were thronging the narrow passage between the stalls and moving in great confused masses, but still the Green Blazer could not be missed. The jabber and babble of the marketplace was there, as people harangued, disputed prices, haggled, or greeted each other; over it all boomed the voice of a Bible-preacher, and when he paused for breath, from another corner the loudspeaker of a health van amplified on malaria and tuberculosis. Over and above it all the Green Blazer seemed to cry out an invitation. Raju could not ignore it. It was not in his nature to ignore such a persistent invitation. He kept himself half-aloof from the crowd; he could not afford to remain completely aloof or keep himself in it too conspicuously. Wherever he might be, he was harrowed by the fear of being spotted by a policeman; today he wore a loincloth and was bare-bodied, and had wound an enormous turban over his head, which overshadowed his face completely, and he hoped that he would be taken for a peasant from a village.

He sat on a stack of cast-off banana stalks beside a shop awning and watched the crowd. When he watched a crowd he did it with concentration. It was his professional occupation. Constitutionally he was an idler and had just the amount of energy to watch in a crowd and put his hand into another person's pocket. It was a gamble, of course. Sometimes he got nothing out of a venture, counting himself lucky if he came out with his fingers intact. Sometimes he picked up a fountain pen, and the "receiver" behind the Municipal Office would not offer even four annas for it, and there was always the danger of being traced through it. Raju promised himself that someday he would leave fountain pens alone; he wouldn't touch one even if it were presented to him on a plate; they were too much bother — inky, leaky, and next to worthless if one could believe what the receiver said about them. Watches were in the same category, too.

What Raju loved most was a nice, bulging purse. If he saw one he picked it up with the greatest deftness. He took the cash in it, flung it far away, and went home with the satisfaction that he had done his day's job well. He splashed a little water over his face and hair and tidied himself up before walking down the street again as a normal citizen. He bought sweets, books, and slates for his children, and occasionally a jacket piece for his wife, too. He was not always easy in mind about his wife. When he went home with too much cash, he had always to take care to hide it in an envelope and shove it under a roof tile. Otherwise she asked too many questions and made herself miserable. She liked to believe that he was reformed and earned the cash he showed her as commission; she never bothered to ask what the commissions were for: a commission seemed to her something absolute.

Raju jumped down from the banana stack and followed the Green Blazer, always keeping himself three steps behind. It was a nicely calculated distance, acquired by intuition and practice. The distance must not be so much as to obscure the movement of the other's hand to and from his purse, nor so close as to become a nuisance and create suspicion. It had to be finely balanced and calculated — the same sort of calculations as carry a *shikari*° through his tracking of game and see him safely home again. Only this hunter's task was more complicated. The hunter in the forest could count his day a success if he laid his quarry flat; but here one had to extract the heart out of the quarry without injuring it.

Raju waited patiently, pretending to be examining some rolls of rush mat, 5
while the Green Blazer spent a considerable length of time drinking a coconut at a nearby booth. It looked as though he would not move again at all. After sucking all the milk in the coconut, he seemed to wait interminably for the nut to be split and the soft white kernel scooped out with a knife. The sight of the

shikari: A professional hunter.

white kernel scooped and disappearing in the other's mouth made Raju, too, crave for it. But he suppressed the thought: it would be inept to be spending one's time drinking and eating while one was professionally occupied; the other might slip away and be lost forever. . . . Raju saw the other take out his black purse and start a debate with the coconut seller over the price of coconuts. He had a thick, sawing voice which disconcerted Raju. It sounded like the growl of a tiger, but what jungle-hardened hunter ever took a step back because a tiger's growl sent his heart racing involuntarily! The way the other haggled didn't appeal to Raju either; it showed a mean and petty temperament . . . too much fondness for money. Those were the narrow-minded troublemakers who made endless fuss when a purse was lost. . . . The Green Blazer moved after all. He stopped before a stall flying colored balloons. He bought a balloon after an endless argument with the shopman — a further demonstration of his meanness. He said, "This is for a motherless boy. I have promised it him. If it bursts or gets lost before I go home, he will cry all night, and I wouldn't like it at all."

Raju got his chance when the other passed through a narrow stile, where people were pressing four-thick in order to see a wax model of Mahatma Gandhi° reading a newspaper.

Fifteen minutes later Raju was examining the contents of the purse. He went away to a secluded spot, behind a disused well. Its crumbling parapet seemed to offer an ideal screen for his activities. The purse contained ten rupees in coins and twenty in currency notes and a few annas in nickel. Raju tucked the annas at his waist in his loincloth. "Must give them to some beggars," he reflected generously. There was a blind fellow yelling his life out at the entrance to the fair and nobody seemed to care. People seemed to have lost all sense of sympathy these days. The thirty rupees he bundled into a knot at the end of his turban and wrapped this again round his head. It would see him through the rest of the month. He could lead a clean life for at least a fortnight and take his wife and children to a picture.

Now the purse lay limp within the hollow of his hand. It was only left for him to fling it into the well and dust off his hand and then he might walk among princes with equal pride at heart. He peeped into the well. It had a little shallow water at the bottom. The purse might float, and a floating purse could cause the worst troubles on earth. He opened the flap of the purse in order to fill it up with pebbles before drowning it. Now, through the slit at its side, he saw a balloon folded and tucked away. "Oh, this he bought . . ." He remembered the other's talk about the motherless child. "What a fool to keep this in the purse," Raju reflected. "It is the carelessness of parents that makes young ones suffer," he ruminated angrily. For a moment he paused over a picture of the growling father returning home and the motherless one waiting at the door for the promised balloon, and this growling man feeling for his purse . . . and, oh! it was too painful!

Raju almost sobbed at the thought of the disappointed child — the motherless boy. There was no one to comfort him. Perhaps this ruffian would beat him if he cried too long. The Green Blazer did not look like one who knew the

Mahatma Gandhi: (1869–1948) Hindu spiritual leader and prime mover in India's struggle for independence.

language of children. Raju was filled with pity at the thought of the young child—perhaps of the same age as his second son. Suppose his wife were dead . . . (personally it might make things easier for him, he need not conceal his cash under the roof); he overcame this thought as an unworthy side issue. If his wife should die it would make him very sad indeed and tax all his ingenuity to keep his young ones quiet. . . . That motherless boy must have his balloon at any cost, Raju decided. But how? He peeped over the parapet across the intervening space at the far-off crowd. The balloon could not be handed back. The thing to do would be to put it back into the empty purse and slip it into the other's pocket.

The Green Blazer was watching the heckling that was going on as the 10
Bible-preacher warmed up to his subject. A semicircle was asking, "Where is your God?" There was a hubbub. Raju sidled up to the Green Blazer. The purse with the balloon (only) tucked into it was in his palm. He'd slip it back into the other's pocket.

Raju realized his mistake in a moment. The Green Blazer caught hold of his arm and cried, "Pickpocket!" The hecklers lost interest in the Bible and turned their attention to Raju, who tried to look appropriately outraged. He cried, "Let me go." The other, without giving a clue to what he proposed, shot out his arm and hit him on the cheek. It almost blinded him. For a fraction of a second Raju lost his awareness of where and even who he was. When the dark mist lifted and he was able to regain his vision, the first figure he noticed in the foreground was the Green Blazer, looming, as it seemed, over the whole landscape. His arms were raised ready to strike again. Raju cowered at the sight. He said, "I . . . I was trying to put back your purse." The other gritted his teeth in fiendish merriment and crushed the bones of his arm. The crowd roared with laughter and badgered him. Somebody hit him again on the head.

Even before the Magistrate Raju kept saying, "I was only trying to put back the purse." And everyone laughed. It became a stock joke in the police world. Raju's wife came to see him in jail and said, "You have brought shame on us," and wept.

Raju replied indignantly, "Why? I was only trying to put it back."

He served his term of eighteen months and came back into the world—not quite decided what he should do with himself. He told himself, "If ever I pick up something again, I shall make sure I don't have to put it back." For now he believed God had gifted the likes of him with only one-way deftness. Those fingers were not meant to put anything back.

Connections

1. Compare the lesson Raju learns in this story with the one Sylvia learns in Bambara's "The Lesson" (p. 364). Explain how each lesson suits the character's individual circumstances.
2. What is the effect of the author's referring to the pickpocket's victim as "the Green Blazer"? How is this effect similar to Conrad's treatment of the colonialists in "An Outpost of Progress" (p. 208)?
3. Explain how the final sentence sums up the "moral" of Raju's experience. How might this irony be compared with Twain's "The Story of the Bad Little Boy"

(p. 245)? Which character do you sympathize with more? Are there any significant similarities in Narayan's and Twain's views of society in these stories?

LILIANA HEKER (Argentinian/b. 1943)

The Stolen Party (1982)

As soon as she arrived she went straight to the kitchen to see if the monkey was there. It was: what a relief! She wouldn't have liked to admit that her mother had been right. *Monkeys at a birthday?* her mother had sneered. *Get away with you, believing any nonsense you're told!* She was cross, but not because of the monkey, the girl thought; it's just because of the party.

"I don't like you going," she told her. "It's a rich people's party."

"Rich people go to Heaven too," said the girl, who studied religion at school.

"Get away with Heaven," said the mother. "The problem with you, young lady, is that you like to fart higher than your ass."

The girl didn't approve of the way her mother spoke. She was barely nine, 5
and one of the best in her class.

"I'm going because I've been invited," she said. "And I've been invited because Luciana is my friend. So there."

"Ah yes, your friend," her mother grumbled. She paused. "Listen, Rosaura," she said at last. "That one's not your friend. You know what you are to them? The maid's daughter, that's what."

Rosaura blinked hard: she wasn't going to cry. Then she yelled: "Shut up! You know nothing about being friends!"

Every afternoon she used to go to Luciana's house and they would both finish their homework while Rosaura's mother did the cleaning. They had their tea in the kitchen and they told each other secrets. Rosaura loved everything in the big house, and she also loved the people who lived there.

"I'm going because it will be the most lovely party in the whole world, 10
Luciana told me it would. There will be a magician, and he will bring a monkey and everything."

The mother swung around to take a good look at her child, and pompously put her hands on her hips.

"Monkeys at a birthday?" she said. "Get away with you, believing any nonsense you're told!"

Rosaura was deeply offended. She thought it unfair of her mother to accuse other people of being liars simply because they were rich. Rosaura too wanted to be rich, of course. If one day she managed to live in a beautiful palace, would her mother stop loving her? She felt very sad. She wanted to go to that party more than anything else in the world.

"I'll die if I don't go," she whispered, almost without moving her lips.

And she wasn't sure whether she had been heard, but on the morning of 15
the party she discovered that her mother had starched her Christmas dress. And in the afternoon, after washing her hair, her mother rinsed it in apple vinegar so that it would be all nice and shiny. Before going out, Rosaura admired herself in the mirror, with her white dress and glossy hair, and thought she looked terribly pretty.

Señora Ines also seemed to notice. As soon as she saw her, she said:

"How lovely you look today, Rosaura."

Rosaura gave her starched skirt a slight toss with her hands and walked into the party with a firm step. She said hello to Luciana and asked about the monkey. Luciana put on a secretive look and whispered into Rosaura's ear: "He's in the kitchen. But don't tell anyone, because it's a surprise."

Rosaura wanted to make sure. Carefully she entered the kitchen and there she saw it: deep in thought, inside its cage. It looked so funny that the girl stood there for a while, watching it, and later, every so often, she would slip out of the party unseen and go and admire it. Rosaura was the only one allowed into the kitchen. Señora Ines had said: "You yes, but not the others, they're much too boisterous, they might break something." Rosaura had never broken anything. She even managed the jug of orange juice, carrying it from the kitchen into the dining room. She held it carefully and didn't spill a single drop. And Señora Ines had said: "Are you sure you can manage a jug as big as that?" Of course she could manage. She wasn't a butterfingers, like the others. Like the blonde girl with the bow in her hair. As soon as she saw Rosaura, the girl with the bow had said:

"And you? Who are you?"

"I'm a friend of Luciana," said Rosaura.

"No," said the girl with the bow, "you are not a friend of Luciana because I'm her cousin and I know all her friends. And I don't know you."

"So what," said Rosaura. "I come here every afternoon with my mother and we do our homework together."

"You and your mother do your homework together?" asked the girl, laughing.

"I and Luciana do our homework together," said Rosaura, very seriously.

The girl with the bow shrugged her shoulders.

"That's not being friends," she said. "Do you go to school together?"

"No."

"So where do you know her from?" said the girl, getting impatient.

Rosaura remembered her mother's words perfectly. She took a deep breath.

"I'm the daughter of the employee," she said.

Her mother had said very clearly: "If someone asks, you say you're the daughter of the employee; that's all." She also told her to add: "And proud of it." But Rosaura thought that never in her life would she dare say something of the sort.

"What employee?" said the girl with the bow. "Employee in a shop?"

"No," said Rosaura angrily. "My mother doesn't sell anything in any shop, so there."

"So how come she's an employee?" said the girl with the bow.

Just then Señora Ines arrived saying *shh shh,* and asked Rosaura if she wouldn't mind helping serve out the hotdogs, as she knew the house so much better than the others.

"See?" said Rosaura to the girl with the bow, and when no one was looking she kicked her in the shin.

Apart from the girl with the bow, all the others were delightful. The one she liked best was Luciana, with her golden birthday crown; and then the boys. Rosaura won the sack race, and nobody managed to catch her when they played tag. When they split into two teams to play charades, all the boys wanted her for their side. Rosaura felt she had never been so happy in all her life.

But the best was still to come. The best came after Luciana blew out the candles. First the cake. Señora Ines had asked her to help pass the cake around, and Rosaura had enjoyed the task immensely, because everyone called out to her, shouting "Me, me!" Rosaura remembered a story in which there was a queen who had the power of life or death over her subjects. She had always loved that, having the power of life or death. To Luciana and the boys she gave the largest pieces, and to the girl with the bow she gave a slice so thin one could see through it.

After the cake came the magician, tall and bony, with a fine red cape. A true magician: he could untie handkerchiefs by blowing on them and make a chain with links that had no openings. He could guess what cards were pulled out from a pack, and the monkey was his assistant. He called the monkey "partner." "Let's see here, partner," he would say, "turn over a card." And, "Don't run away, partner: time to work now."

The final trick was wonderful. One of the children had to hold the monkey in his arms and the magician said he would make him disappear.

"What, the boy?" they all shouted.

"No, the monkey!" shouted back the magician.

Rosaura thought that this was truly the most amusing party in the whole world.

The magician asked a small fat boy to come and help, but the small fat boy got frightened almost at once and dropped the monkey on the floor. The magician picked him up carefully, whispered something in his ear, and the monkey nodded almost as if he understood.

"You mustn't be so unmanly, my friend," the magician said to the fat boy.

"What's unmanly?" said the fat boy.

The magician turned around as if to look for spies.

"A sissy," said the magician. "Go sit down."

Then he stared at all the faces, one by one. Rosaura felt her heart tremble.

"You, with the Spanish eyes," said the magician. And everyone saw that he was pointing at her.

She wasn't afraid. Neither holding the monkey, nor when the magician made him vanish; not even when, at the end, the magician flung his red cape over Rosaura's head and uttered a few magic words . . . and the monkey reappeared, chattering happily, in her arms. The children clapped furiously. And before Rosaura returned to her seat, the magician said:

"Thank you very much, my little countess."

She was so pleased with the compliment that a while later, when her mother came to fetch her, that was the first thing she told her.

"I helped the magician and he said to me, 'Thank you very much, my little countess.' "

It was strange because up to then Rosaura had thought that she was angry with her mother. All along Rosaura had imagined that she would say to her: "See that the monkey wasn't a lie?" But instead she was so thrilled that she told her mother all about the wonderful magician.

Her mother tapped her on the head and said: "So now we're a countess!"

But one could see that she was beaming.

And now they both stood in the entrance, because a moment ago Señora Ines, smiling, had said: "Please wait here a second."

Her mother suddenly seemed worried.

"What is it?" she asked Rosaura.

What is what?" said Rosaura. "It's nothing; she just wants to get the presents for those who are leaving, see?"

She pointed at the fat boy and at a girl with pigtails who were also waiting there, next to their mothers. And she explained about the presents. She knew, because she had been watching those who left before her. When one of the girls was about to leave, Señora Ines would give her a bracelet. When a boy left, Señora Ines gave him a yo-yo. Rosaura preferred the yo-yo because it sparkled, but she didn't mention that to her mother. Her mother might have said: "So why don't you ask for one, you blockhead?" That's what her mother was like. Rosaura didn't feel like explaining that she'd be horribly ashamed to be the odd one out. Instead she said:

"I was the best-behaved at the party."

And she said no more because Señora Ines came out into the hall with two bags, one pink and one blue.

First she went up to the fat boy, gave him a yo-yo out of the blue bag, and the fat boy left with his mother. Then she went up to the girl and gave her a bracelet out of the pink bag, and the girl with the pigtails left as well.

Finally she came up to Rosaura and her mother. She had a big smile on her face and Rosaura liked that. Señora Ines looked down at her, then looked up at her mother, and then said something that made Rosaura proud:

"What a marvelous daughter you have, Herminia."

For an instant, Rosaura thought that she'd give her two presents: the bracelet and the yo-yo. Señora Ines bent down as if about to look for something. Rosaura also leaned forward, stretching out her arm. But she never completed the movement.

Señora Ines didn't look in the pink bag. Nor did she look in the blue bag. Instead she rummaged in her purse. In her hand appeared two bills.

"You really and truly earned this," she said handing them over. "Thank you for all your help, my pet."

Rosaura felt her arms stiffen, stick close to her body, and then she noticed her mother's hand on her shoulder. Instinctively she pressed herself against her mother's body. That was all. Except her eyes. Rosaura's eyes had a cold, clear look that fixed itself on Señora Ines's face.

Señora Ines, motionless, stood there with her hand outstretched. As if she didn't dare draw it back. As if the slightest change might shatter an infinitely delicate balance.

Connections

1. How is Señora Ines's ignorant generosity similar to the lawyer's in Melville's "Bartleby, the Scrivener" (p. 80)? How does these characters' status blind them to the real concerns of Rosaura and Bartleby?
2. How do "The Stolen Party" and Mansfield's "Miss Brill" (p. 394) lead up to shocking moments of self-discovery for the central character in each story?

3. Write an essay that compares Heker's treatment of the rich and poor with Narayan's in "Trail of the Green Blazer" (p. 428). How does each story offer a commentary on societal values?

AN ALBUM OF CONTEMPORARY STORIES

RAYMOND CARVER (1939–1988)

Boxes

1986

My mother is packed and ready to move. But Sunday afternoon, at the last minute, she calls and says for us to come eat with her. "My icebox is defrosting," she tells me. "I have to fry up this chicken before it rots." She says we should bring our own plates and some knives and forks. She's packed most of her dishes and kitchen things. "Come on and eat with me one last time," she says. "You and Jill."

I hang up the phone and stand at the window for a minute longer, wishing I could figure this thing out. But I can't. So finally I turn to Jill and say, "Let's go to my mother's for a goodbye meal."

Jill is at the table with a Sears catalog in front of her, trying to find us some curtains. But she's been listening. She makes a face. "Do we have to?" she says. She bends down the corner of a page and closes the catalog. She sighs. "God, we been over there to eat two or three times in this last month alone. Is she ever actually going to leave?"

Jill always says what's on her mind. She's thirty-five years old, wears her hair short, and grooms dogs for a living. Before she became a groomer, something she likes, she used to be a housewife and mother. Then all hell broke loose. Her two children were kidnapped by her first husband and taken to live in Australia. Her second husband, who drank, left her with a broken eardrum before he drove their car through a bridge into the Elwha River. He didn't have life insurance, not to mention property-damage insurance. Jill had to borrow money to bury him, and then — can you beat it? — she was presented with a bill for the bridge repair. Plus, she had her own medical bills. She can tell this story now. She's bounced back. But she has run out of patience with my mother. I've run out of patience, too. But I don't see my options.

"She's leaving day after tomorrow," I say. "Hey, Jill, don't do any favors. Do 5
you want to come with me or not?" I tell her it doesn't matter to me one way or the other. I'll say she has a migraine. It's not like I've never told a lie before.

"I'm coming," she says. And like that she gets up and goes into the bathroom, where she likes to pout.

We've been together since last August, about the time my mother picked to move up here to Longview from California. Jill tried to make the best of it. But my mother pulling into town just when we were trying to get our act together was nothing either of us had bargained for. Jill said it reminded her of the situation with her first husband's mother. "She's a clinger," Jill said. "You know what I mean? I thought I was going to suffocate."

It's fair to say that my mother sees Jill as an intruder. As far as she's concerned, Jill is just another girl in a series of girls who have appeared in my life since my wife left me. Someone, to her mind, likely to take away affection, attention, maybe even some money that might otherwise come to her. But someone deserving of respect? No way. I remember — how can I forget it? — she called my wife a whore before we were married, and then called her a whore fifteen years later, after she left me for someone else.

Jill and my mother act friendly enough when they find themselves together. They hug each other when they say hello or goodbye. They talk about shopping specials. But Jill dreads the time she has to spend in my mother's company. She claims my mother bums her out. She says my mother is negative about everything and everybody and ought to find an outlet, like other people in her age bracket. Crocheting, maybe, or card games at the Senior Citizens Center, or else going to church. Something, anyway, so that she'll leave us in peace. But my mother had her own way of solving things. She announced she was moving back to California. The hell with everything and everybody in this town. What a place to live! She wouldn't continue to live in this town if they gave her the place and six more like it.

10 Within a day or two of deciding to move, she'd packed her things into boxes. That was last January. Or maybe it was February. Anyway, last winter sometime. Now it's the end of June. Boxes have been sitting around inside her house for months. You have to walk around them or step over them to get from one room to another. This is no way for anyone's mother to live.

After a while, ten minutes or so, Jill comes out of the bathroom. I've found a roach and am trying to smoke that and drink a bottle of ginger ale while I watch one of the neighbors change the oil in his car. Jill doesn't look at me. Instead, she goes into the kitchen and puts some plates and utensils into a paper sack. But when she comes back through the living room I stand up, and we hug each other. Jill says, "It's okay." What's okay, I wonder. As far as I can see, nothing's okay. But she holds me and keeps patting my shoulder. I can smell the pet shampoo on her. She comes home from work wearing the stuff. It's everywhere. Even when we're in bed together. She gives me a final pat. Then we go out to the car and drive across town to my mother's.

I like where I live. I didn't when I first moved here. There was nothing to do at night, and I was lonely. Then I met Jill. Pretty soon, after a few weeks, she brought her things over and started living with me. We didn't set any long-term goals. We were happy and we had a life together. We told each other we'd finally got lucky. But my mother didn't have anything going in her life. So she wrote me and said she'd decided on moving here. I wrote her back and said I didn't think it was such a good idea. The weather's terrible in the winter, I said. They're building a prison a few miles from town, I told her. The place is bumper-to-bumper tourists all summer, I said. But she acted as if she never got my letters, and came anyway. Then, after she'd been in town a little less than a month, she told me she hated the place. She acted as if it were my fault she'd moved here and my fault she found everything so disagreeable. She started calling me up and telling me how crummy the place was. "Laying guilt trips," Jill called it. She told me the bus service was terrible and the drivers unfriendly. As for the people at the Senior Citizens — well, she didn't want to play casino. "They can go to hell," she said, "and take their card games with them." The clerks at the supermarket were surly, the guys in the service station didn't give a damn about her or her car. And she'd made up her mind about the man she rented from, Larry Hadlock. King Larry, she called him. "He thinks he's *superior* to everyone because he has some shacks for rent and a few dollars. I wish to God I'd never laid eyes on him."

It was too hot for her when she arrived, in August, and in September it started to rain. It rained almost every day for weeks. In October it turned cold. There was snow in November and December. But long before that she began to put the bad mouth on the place and the people to the extent that I didn't want to hear about it anymore, and I told her so finally. She cried, and I hugged her and thought that was the end of it. But a few days later she started in again, same stuff. Just before Christmas she called to see when I was coming by with her presents. She hadn't put up a tree and didn't intend to, she said. Then she said something else. She said if this weather didn't improve she was going to kill herself.

"Don't talk crazy," I said.

15 She said, "I mean it, honey. I don't want to see this place again except from my coffin. I hate this g.d. place. I don't know why I moved here. I wish I could just die and get it over with."

I remember hanging on to the phone and watching a man high up on a pole doing something to a power line. Snow whirled around his head. As I watched, he leaned out from the pole, supported only by his safety belt. Suppose he falls, I thought. I didn't have any idea what I was going to say next. I had to say something. But I was filled with unworthy feelings, thoughts no son should admit to. "You're my mother," I said finally. "What can I do to help?"

"Honey, you can't do anything," she said. "The time for doing anything has come and gone. It's too late to do anything. I wanted to like it here. I thought we'd go on picnics and take drives together. But none of that happened. You're always busy. You're off working, you and Jill. You're never at home. Or else if you are at home you have the phone off the hook all day. Anyway, I never see you," she said.

"That's not true," I said. And it wasn't. But she went on as if she hadn't heard me. Maybe she hadn't.

"Besides," she said, "this weather is killing me. It's too damned cold here. Why didn't you tell me this was the North Pole? If you had, I'd never have come. I want to go back to California, honey. I can get out and go places there. I don't know anywhere to go here. There are people back in California. I've got friends there who care what happens to me. Nobody gives a damn here. Well, I just pray I can get through to June. If I can make it that long, if I can last to June, I'm leaving this place forever. This is the worst place I've ever lived in."

20 What could I say? I didn't know what to say. I couldn't even say anything about the weather. Weather was a real sore point. We said goodbye and hung up.

Other people take vacations in the summer, but my mother moves. She started moving years ago, after my dad lost his job. When that happened, when he was laid off, they sold their home, as if this were what they should do, and went to where they thought things would be better. But things weren't any better there, either. They moved again. They kept on moving. They lived in rented houses, apartments, mobile homes, and motel units even. They kept moving, lightening their load with each move they made. A couple of times they landed in a town where I lived. They'd move in with my wife and me for a while and then they'd move on again. They were like migrating animals in this regard, except there was no pattern to their movement. They moved around for years, sometimes even leaving the state for what they thought would be greener pastures. But mostly they stayed in Northern California and did their moving there. Then my dad died, and I thought my mother would stop moving and stay in one place for a while. But she didn't. She kept moving. I suggested once that she go to a psychiatrist. I even said I'd pay for it. But she wouldn't hear of it. She packed and moved out of town instead. I was desperate about things or I wouldn't have said that about the psychiatrist.

She was always in the process of packing or else unpacking. Sometimes she'd move two or three times in the same year. She talked bitterly about the place she was leaving and optimistically about the place she was going to. Her mail got fouled up, her benefit checks went off somewhere else, and she spent hours writing letters, trying to get it all straightened out. Sometimes she'd move out of an apartment house, move to another one a few blocks away, and then, a month later, move back to the place she'd left, only to a different floor or a different side of the building. That's why when she moved here I rented a house for her and saw to it that it was furnished to her liking. "Moving around keeps her alive," Jill said. "It gives her something to do. She must get some kind of weird enjoyment out of it, I guess." But enjoyment or not, Jill thinks my mother must be losing her mind. I think so, too. But how do you tell your mother this? How do you deal with her if this is the case? Crazy doesn't stop her from planning and getting on with her next move.

She is waiting at the back door for us when we pull in. She's seventy years old, has gray hair, wears glasses with rhinestone frames, and has never been sick a day in her life. She hugs Jill, and then she hugs me. Her eyes are bright, as if she's been drinking. But she doesn't drink. She quit years ago, after my dad went on the wagon. We finish hugging and go inside. It's around five in the afternoon. I smell whatever it is drifting out of her kitchen and remember I haven't eaten since breakfast. My buzz has worn off.

"I'm starved," I say.

"Something smells good," Jill says. 25

"I hope it tastes good," my mother says. "I hope this chicken's done." She raises the lid on a fry pan and pushes a fork into a chicken breast. "If there's anything I can't stand, it's raw chicken. I think it's done. Why don't you sit down? Sit anyplace. I still can't regulate my stove. The burners heat up too fast. I don't like electric stoves and never have. Move that junk off the chair, Jill. I'm living here like a damned gypsy. But not for much longer, I hope." She sees me looking around for the ashtray. "Behind you," she says. "On the windowsill, honey. Before you sit down, why don't you pour us some of that Pepsi? You'll have to use these paper cups. I should have told you to bring some glasses. Is the Pepsi cold? I don't have any ice. This icebox won't keep anything cold. It isn't worth a damn. My ice cream turns to soup. It's the worst icebox I've ever had."

She forks the chicken onto a plate and puts the plate on the table along with beans and coleslaw and white bread. Then she looks to see if there is anything she's forgetting. Salt and pepper! "Sit down," she says.

We draw our chairs up to the table, and Jill takes the plates out of the sack and hands them around the table to us. "Where are you going to live when you go back?" she says. "Do you have a place lined up?"

My mother passes the chicken to Jill and says, "I wrote that lady I rented from before. She wrote back and said she had a nice first-floor place I could have. It's close to the bus stop and there's lots of stores in the area. There's a bank and a Safeway. It's the nicest place. I don't know why I left there." She says that and helps herself to some coleslaw.

"Why'd you leave then?" Jill says. "If it was so nice and all." She picks up 30
her drumstick, looks at it, and takes a bite of the meat.

"I'll tell you why. There was an old alcoholic woman who lived next door to me. She drank from morning to night. The walls were so thin I could hear her munching ice cubes all day. She had to use a walker to get around, but that still didn't stop her. I'd hear that walker *scrape, scrape* against the floor from morning to night. That and her icebox door closing." She shakes her head at all she had to put up with. "I had to get out of there. *Scrape, scrape* all day. I couldn't stand it. I just couldn't live like that. This time I told the manager I didn't want to be next to any alcoholics. And I didn't want anything on the second floor. The second floor looks out on the parking lot. Nothing to see from there." She waits for Jill to say something more. But Jill doesn't comment. My mother looks over at me.

I'm eating like a wolf and don't say anything, either. In any case, there's nothing more to say on the subject. I keep chewing and look over at the boxes stacked against the fridge. Then I help myself to more coleslaw.

Pretty soon I finish and push my chair back. Larry Hadlock pulls up in back of the house, next to my car, and takes a lawnmower out of his pickup. I watch him through the window behind the table. He doesn't look in our direction.

"What's he want?" my mother says and stops eating.

"He's going to cut your grass, it looks like," I say. 35

"It doesn't need cutting," she says. "He cut it last week. What's there for him to cut?"

"It's for the new tenant," Jill says. "Whoever that turns out to be."

My mother takes this in and then goes back to eating.

Larry Hadlock starts his mower and begins to cut the grass. I know him a little. He lowered the rent twenty-five a month when I told him it was my mother. He is a widower — a big fellow, mid-sixties. An unhappy man with a good sense of humor. His arms are covered with white hair, and white hair stands out from under his cap. He looks like a magazine illustration of a farmer. But he isn't a farmer. He is a retired construction worker who's saved a little money. For a while, in the beginning, I let myself imagine that he and my mother might take some meals together and become friends.

"There's the king," my mother says. "King Larry. Not everyone has as much 40
money as he does and can live in a big house and charge other people high rents. Well, I hope I never see his cheap old face again once I leave here. Eat the rest of this chicken," she says to me. But I shake my head and light a cigarette. Larry pushes his mower past the window.

"You won't have to look at it much longer," Jill says.

"I'm sure glad of that, Jill. But I know he won't give me my deposit back."

"How do you know that?" I say.

"I just know," she says. "I've had dealings with his kind before. They're out for all they can get."

Jill says, "It won't be long now and you won't have to have anything more to do with him."

"I'll be so glad."

"But it'll be somebody just like him," Jill says.

"I don't want to think that, Jill," my mother says.

She makes coffee while Jill clears the table. I rinse the cups. Then I pour coffee, and we step around a box marked "Knick-knacks" and take our cups into the living room.

Larry Hadlock is at the side of the house. Traffic moves slowly on the street out in front, and the sun has started down over the trees. I can hear the commotion the mower makes. Some crows leave the phone line and settle onto the newly cut grass in the front yard.

"I'm going to miss you, honey," my mother says. Then she says, "I'll miss you, too, Jill. I'm going to miss both of you."

Jill sips her coffee and nods. Then she says, "I hope you have a safe trip back and find the place you're looking for at the end of the road."

"When I get settled — and this is my last move, so help me — I hope you'll come and visit," my mother says. She looks at me and waits to be reassured.

"We will," I say. But even as I say it I know it isn't true. My life caved in on me down there, and I won't be going back.

"I wish you could have been happier here," Jill says. "I wish you'd been able to stick it out or something. You know what? Your son is worried sick about you."

"Jill," I say.

But she gives her head a little shake and goes on. "Sometimes he can't sleep over it. He wakes up sometimes in the night and says, 'I can't sleep. I'm thinking about my mother.' There," she says and looks at me. "I've said it. But it was on my mind."

"How do you think I must feel?" my mother says. Then she says, "Other women my age can be happy. Why can't I be like other women? All I want is a house and a town to live in that will make me happy. That isn't a crime, is it? I hope not. I hope I'm not asking too much out of life." She puts her cup on the floor next to her chair and waits for Jill to tell her she isn't asking for too much. But Jill doesn't say anything, and in a minute my mother begins to outline her plans to be happy.

After a time Jill lowers her eyes to her cup and has some more coffee. I can tell she's stopped listening. But my mother keeps talking anyway. The crows work their way through the grass in the front yard. I hear the mower howl and then thud as it picks up a clump of grass in the blade and comes to a stop. In a minute, after several tries, Larry gets it going again. The crows fly off, back to their wire. Jill picks at a fingernail. My mother is saying that the secondhand-furniture dealer is coming around the next morning to collect the things she isn't going to send on the bus or carry with her in the car. The table and chairs, TV, sofa, and bed are going with the dealer. But he's told her he doesn't have any use for the card table, so my mother is going to throw it out unless we want it.

"We'll take it," I say. Jill looks over. She starts to say something but changes her mind.

I will drive the boxes to the Greyhound station the next afternoon and start them on the way to California. My mother will spend the last night with us, as arranged. And then, early the next morning, two days from now, she'll be on her way.

She continues to talk. She talks on and on as she describes the trip she is about to make. She'll drive until four o'clock in the afternoon and then take a motel room for the night. She figures to make Eugene by dark. Eugene is a nice town — she stayed there once before, on the way up here. When she leaves the motel, she'll leave at sunrise and should, if God is looking out for her, be in California that afternoon. And God *is* looking out for her, she knows he is. How else explain her being kept around on the face of the earth? He has a plan for her. She's been praying a lot lately. She's been praying for me, too.

"Why are you praying for him?" Jill wants to know.

"Because I feel like it. Because he's my son," my mother says. "Is there anything the matter with that? Don't we all need praying for sometimes? Maybe some people don't. I don't know. What do I know anymore?" She brings a hand to her forehead and rearranges some hair that's come loose from a pin.

The mower sputters off, and pretty soon we see Larry go around the house pulling the hose. He sets the hose out and then goes slowly back around the house to turn the water on. The sprinkler begins to turn.

My mother starts listing the ways she imagines Larry has wronged her since she's been in the house. But now I'm not listening, either. I am thinking how she is about to go down the highway again, and nobody can reason with her or do anything to stop her. What can I do? I can't tie her up, or commit her, though it may come to that eventually. I worry for her, and she is a heartache to me. She is all the family I have left. I'm sorry she didn't like it here and wants to leave. But I'm never going back to California. And when that's clear to me I understand something else, too. I understand that after she leaves I'm probably never going to see her again.

I look over at my mother. She stops talking. Jill raises her eyes. Both of them look at me.

"What is it, honey?" my mother says.

"What's wrong?" Jill says.

I lean forward in the chair and cover my face with my hands. I sit like that for a minute, feeling bad and stupid for doing it. But I can't help it. And the woman who brought me into this life, and this other woman I picked up with less than a year ago, they exclaim together and rise and come over to where I sit with my head in my hands like a fool. I don't open my eyes. I listen to the sprinkler whipping the grass.

"What's wrong? What's the matter?" they say.

"It's okay," I say. And in a minute it is. I open my eyes and bring my head up. I reach for a cigarette.

"See what I mean?" Jill says. "You're driving him crazy. He's going crazy with worry over you." She is on one side of my chair, and my mother is on the other side. They could tear me apart in no time at all.

"I wish I could die and get out of everyone's way," my mother says quietly. "So help me Hannah, I can't take much more of this."

"How about some more coffee?" I say. "Maybe we ought to catch the news," 75
I say. "Then I guess Jill and I better head for home."

Two days later, early in the morning, I say goodbye to my mother for what may be the last time. I've let Jill sleep. It won't hurt if she's late to work for a change. The dogs can wait for their baths and trimmings and such. My mother holds my arm as I walk her down the steps to the driveway and open the car door for her. She is wearing white slacks and a white blouse and white sandals. Her hair is pulled back and tied with a scarf. That's white, too. It's going to be a nice day, and the sky is clear and already blue.

On the front seat of the car I see maps and a thermos of coffee. My mother looks at these things as if she can't recall having come outside with them just a few minutes ago. She turns to me then and says, "Let me hug you once more. Let me love your neck. I know I won't see you for a long time." She puts an arm around my neck, draws me to her, and then begins to cry. But she stops almost at once and steps back, pushing the heel of her hand against her eyes. "I said I wouldn't do that, and I won't. But let me get a last look at you anyway. I'll miss you, honey," she says. "I'm just going to have to live through this. I've already lived through things I didn't think were possible. But I'll live through this too, I guess." She gets into the car, starts it, and runs the engine for a minute. She rolls her window down.

"I'm going to miss you," I say. And I *am* going to miss her. She's my mother, after all, and why shouldn't I miss her? But, God forgive me, I'm glad, too, that it's finally time and that she is leaving.

"Goodbye," she says. "Tell Jill thanks for supper last night. Tell her I said goodbye."

"I will," I say. I stand there wanting to say something else. But I don't know 80
what. We keep looking at each other, trying to smile and reassure each other. Then something comes into her eyes, and I believe she is thinking about the highway and how far she is going to have to drive that day. She takes her eyes off me and looks down the road. Then she rolls her window up, puts the car into gear, and drives to the intersection, where she has to wait for the light to change. When I see she's made it into traffic and headed toward the highway, I go back in the house and drink some coffee. I feel sad for a while, and then the sadness goes away and I start thinking about other things.

A few nights later my mother calls to say she is in her new place. She is busy fixing it up, the way she does when she has a new place. She tells me I'll be happy to know she likes it just fine to be back in sunny California. But she says there's something in the air where she is living, maybe it's pollen, that is causing her to sneeze a lot. And the traffic is heavier than she remembers from before. She doesn't recall there being so much traffic in her neighborhood. Naturally, everyone still drives like crazy down there. "California drivers," she says. "What else can you expect?" She says it's hot for this time of the year. She doesn't think the air-conditioning unit in her apartment is working right. I tell her she should talk to the manager. "She's never around when you need her," my mother says. She hopes she hasn't made a mistake in moving back to California. She waits before she says anything else.

I'm standing at the window with the phone pressed to my ear, looking out at the lights from town and at the lighted houses closer by. Jill is at the table with the catalog, listening.

"Are you still there?" my mother asks. "I wish you'd say something."

I don't know why, but it's then I recall the affectionate name my dad used sometimes when he was talking nice to my mother — those times, that is, when he wasn't drunk. It was a long time ago, and I was a kid, but always, hearing it, I felt better, less afraid, more hopeful about the future. *"Dear,"* he'd say. He called her "dear" sometimes — a sweet name. "Dear," he'd say, "if you're going to the store, will you bring me some cigarettes?" Or, "Dear, is your cold any better?" "Dear, where is my coffee cup?"

85 The word issues from my lips before I can think what else I want to say to go along with it. "Dear." I say it again. I call her "dear." "Dear, try not to be afraid," I say. I tell my mother I love her and I'll write to her, yes. Then I say goodbye, and I hang up.

For a while I don't move from the window. I keep standing there, looking out at the lighted houses in our neighborhood. As I watch, a car turns off the road and pulls into a driveway. The porch light goes on. The door to the house opens and someone comes out on the porch and stands there waiting.

Jill turns the pages of her catalog, and then she stops turning them. "This is what we want," she says. "This is more like what I had in mind. Look at this, will you." But I don't look. I don't care five cents for curtains. "What is it you see out there, honey?" Jill says. "Tell me."

What's there to tell? The people over there embrace for a minute, and then they go inside the house together. They leave the light burning. Then they remember, and it goes out.

Connections

1. Compare the narrator's emotional distance from his mother with Julian's relationship to his mother in O'Connor's "Everything That Rises Must Converge" (p. 316). How does each character come to realize that despite his mother's cantankerous disposition he loves her?
2. Discuss the meaning of the title. How do "boxes" figure in the story and point to the theme? Compare Carver's strategy for using a suggestive title with O'Connor's in "Everything That Rises Must Converge." How does each title function in its story?
3. Compare and contrast the narrator's connection with Jill with the relationship between Anna and her lover in Oates's "The Lady with the Pet Dog" (p. 159). Describe the tensions that shape both couples' lives.

LOUISE ERDRICH (b. 1954)

Fleur

1986

The first time she drowned in the cold and glassy waters of Lake Turcot, Fleur Pillager was only a girl. Two men saw the boat tip, saw her struggle in the waves. They rowed over to the place she went down, and jumped in. When they dragged her over the gunwales, she was cold to the touch and stiff, so they slapped her face, shook her by the heels, worked her arms back and forth, and pounded her back until she coughed up lake water. She shivered all over like a dog, then took a breath. But it wasn't long afterward that those two men disappeared. The first wandered off, and the other, Jean Hat, got himself run over by a cart.

It went to show, my grandma said. It figured to her, all right. By saving Fleur Pillager, those two men had lost themselves.

The next time she fell in the lake, Fleur Pillager was twenty years old and no one touched her. She washed onshore, her skin a dull dead gray, but when George Many Women bent to look closer, he saw her chest move. Then her eyes spun open, sharp black riprock, and she looked at him. "You'll take my place," she hissed. Everybody scattered and left her there, so no one knows how she dragged herself home. Soon after that we noticed Many Women changed, grew afraid, wouldn't leave his house, and would not be forced to go near water. For his caution, he lived until the day that his sons brought him a new tin bathtub. Then the first time he used the tub he slipped, got knocked out, and breathed water while his wife stood in the other room frying breakfast.

Men stayed clear of Fleur Pillager after the second drowning. Even though she was good-looking, nobody dared to court her because it was clear that Misshepeshu, the waterman, the monster, wanted her for himself. He's a devil, that one, love-hungry with desire and maddened for the touch of young girls, the strong and daring especially, the ones like Fleur.

Our mothers warn us that we'll think he's handsome, for he appears with 5
green eyes, copper skin, a mouth tender as a child's. But if you fall into his arms, he sprouts horns, fangs, claws, fins. His feet are joined as one and his skin, brass scales, rings to the touch. You're fascinated, cannot move. He casts a shell necklace at your feet, weeps gleaming chips that harden into mica on your breasts. He holds you under. Then he takes the body of a lion or a fat brown worm. He's made of gold. He's made of beach moss. He's a thing of dry foam, a thing of death by drowning, the death a Chippewa cannot survive.

Unless you are Fleur Pillager. We all knew she couldn't swim. After the first time, we thought she'd never go back to Lake Turcot. We thought she'd keep to herself, live quiet, stop killing men off by drowning in the lake. After the first time, we thought she'd keep the good ways. But then, after the second drowning, we knew that we were dealing with something much more serious. She was haywire, out of control. She messed with evil, laughed at the old women's advice, and dressed like a man. She got herself into some half-forgotten medicine, studied ways we shouldn't talk about. Some say she kept the finger of a child in her pocket and a powder of unborn rabbits in a leather thong around her neck. She laid the heart of an owl on her tongue so she could see at night, and went out, hunting, not even in her own body. We know for sure because the next morning, in the snow or dust, we followed the tracks of her bare feet and saw where they changed, where the claws sprang out, the pad broadened and pressed into the dirt. By night we heard her chuffing cough, the bear cough. By day her silence and the wide grin she threw to bring down our guard made us frightened. Some thought that Fleur Pillager should be driven off the reservation, but not a single person who spoke like this had the nerve. And finally, when people were just about to get together and throw her out, she left on her own and didn't come back all summer. That's what this story is about.

During that summer, when she lived a few miles south in Argus, things happened. She almost destroyed that town.

When she got down to Argus in the year of 1920, it was just a small grid of six streets on either side of the railroad depot. There were two elevators, one central, the other a few miles west. Two stores competed for the trade of the three hundred citizens, and three churches quarreled with one another for their souls. There was a frame building for Lutherans, a heavy brick one for Episcopalians, and a long narrow shingled Catholic church. This last had a tall slender steeple, twice as high as any building or tree.

No doubt, across the low, flat wheat, watching from the road as she came near Argus on foot, Fleur saw that steeple rise, a shadow thin as a needle. Maybe in that raw space it drew her the way a lone tree draws lightning. Maybe, in the end, the Catholics are to blame. For if she hadn't seen that sign of pride, that slim prayer, that marker, maybe she would have kept walking.

But Fleur Pillager turned, and the first place she went once she came into 10
town was to the back door of the priest's residence attached to the landmark church. She didn't go there for a handout, although she got that, but to ask for work. She got that too, or the town got her. It's hard to tell which came out worse, her or the men or the town, although the upshot of it all was that Fleur lived.

The four men who worked at the butcher's had carved up about a thousand carcasses between them, maybe half of that steers and the other half pigs, sheep, and game animals like deer, elk, and bear. That's not even mentioning the chickens, which were beyond counting. Pete Kozka owned the place, and employed Lily Veddar, Tor Grunewald, and my stepfather, Dutch James, who had brought my mother down from the reservation the year before she disappointed him by dying. Dutch took me out of school to take her place. I kept house half the time and worked the other in the butcher shop, sweeping floors, putting sawdust down, running a hambone across the street to a customer's bean pot or a package of sausage to the corner. I was a good one to have around because until they needed me, I was invisible. I blended into the stained brown walls, a skinny, big-nosed girl with staring eyes. Because I could fade into a corner or squeeze beneath a shelf, I knew everything, what the men said when no one was around, and what they did to Fleur.

Kozka's Meats served farmers for a fifty-mile area, both to slaughter, for it had a stock pen and chute, and to cure the meat by smoking it or spicing it in sausage. The storage locker was a marvel, made of many thicknesses of brick, earth insulation, and Minnesota timber, lined inside with sawdust and vast blocks of ice cut from Lake Turcot, hauled down from home each winter by horse and sledge.

A ramshackle board building, part slaughterhouse, part store, was fixed to the low, thick square of the lockers. That's where Fleur worked. Kozka hired her for her strength. She could lift a haunch or carry a pole of sausages without stumbling, and she soon learned cutting from Pete's wife, a string-thin blonde who chain-smoked and handled the razor-sharp knives with nerveless precision, slicing close to her stained fingers. Fleur and Fritzie Kozka worked afternoons, wrapping their cuts in paper, and Fleur hauled the packages to the lockers. The meat was left outside the heavy oak doors that were only opened at 5:00 each afternoon, before the men ate supper.

Sometimes Dutch, Tor, and Lily ate at the lockers, and when they did I stayed too, cleaned floors, restoked the fires in the front smokehouses, while the men sat around the squat cast-iron stove spearing slats of herring onto hard-tack bread. They played long games of poker or cribbage on a board made from the planed end of a slat crate. They talked and I listened, although there wasn't much to hear since almost nothing ever happened in Argus. Tor was married, Dutch had lost my mother, and Lily read circulars. They mainly discussed about the auctions to come, equipment, or women.

Every so often, Pete Kozka came out front to make a whist, leaving Fritzie 15
to smoke cigarettes and fry raised doughnuts in the back room. He sat and played a few rounds but kept his thoughts to himself. Fritzie did not tolerate him talking behind her back, and the one book he read was the New Testament. If he said something, it concerned weather or a surplus of sheep stomachs, a ham that smoked green or the markets for corn and wheat. He had a good-luck talisman, the opal-white lens of a cow's eye. Playing cards, he rubbed it between his fingers. That soft sound and the slap of cards was about the only conversation.

Fleur finally gave them a subject.

Her cheeks were wide and flat, her hands large, chapped, muscular. Fleur's shoulders were broad as beams, her hips fishlike, slippery, narrow. An old green dress clung to her waist, worn thin where she sat. Her braids were thick like the tails of animals, and swung against her when she moved, deliberately, slowly in her work, held in and half-tamed, but only half. I could tell, but the others never saw. They never looked into her sly brown eyes or noticed her teeth, strong and curved and very white. Her legs were bare, and since she padded around in beadwork moccasins they never saw that her fifth toes were missing. They never knew she'd drowned. They were blinded, they were stupid, they only saw her in the flesh.

And yet it wasn't just that she was a Chippewa, or even that she was a woman, it wasn't that she was good-looking or even that she was alone that made their brains hum. It was how she played cards.

Women didn't usually play with men, so the evening that Fleur drew a chair up to the men's table without being so much as asked, there was a shock of surprise.

"What's this," said Lily. He was fat, with a snake's cold pale eyes and pre- 20
cious skin, smooth and lily-white, which is how he got his name. Lily had a dog, a stumpy mean little bull of a thing with a belly drum-tight from eating pork rinds. The dog liked to play cards just like Lily, and straddled his barrel thighs through games of stud, rum poker, vingt-un. The dog snapped at Fleur's arm that first night, but cringed back, its snarl frozen, when she took her place.

"I thought," she said, her voice soft and stroking, "you might deal me in."

There was a space between the heavy bin of spiced flour and the wall where I just fit. I hunkered down there, kept my eyes open, saw her black hair swing over the chair, her feet solid on the wood floor. I couldn't see up on the table where the cards slapped down, so after they were deep in their game I raised myself up in the shadows, and crouched on a sill of wood.

I watched Fleur's hands stack and ruffle, divide the cards, spill them to each player in a blur, rake them up and shuffle again. Tor, short and scrappy, shut one eye and squinted the other at Fleur. Dutch screwed his lips around a wet cigar.

"Gotta see a man," he mumbled, getting up to go out back to the privy. The others broke, put their cards down, and Fleur sat alone in the lamplight that glowed in a sheen across the push of her breasts. I watched her closely, then she paid me a beam of notice for the first time. She turned, looked straight at me, and grinned the white wolf grin a Pillager turns on its victims, except that she wasn't after me.

"Pauline there," she said, "how much money you got?"

We'd all been paid for the week that day. Eight cents was in my pocket.

"Stake me," she said, holding out her long fingers. I put the coins in her palm and then I melted back to nothing, part of the walls and tables. It was a long time before I understood that the men would not have seen me no matter what I did, how I moved. I wasn't anything like Fleur. My dress hung loose and my back was already curved, an old woman's. Work had roughened me, reading made my eyes sore, caring for my mother before she died had hardened my face. I was not much to look at, so they never saw me.

When the men came back and sat around the table, they had drawn together. They shot each other small glances, stuck their tongues in their cheeks, burst out laughing at odd moments, to rattle Fleur. But she never minded. They played their vingt-un, staying even as Fleur slowly gained. Those pennies I had given her drew nickels and attracted dimes until there was a small pile in front of her.

Then she hooked them with five-card draw, nothing wild. She dealt, discarded, drew, and then she sighed and her cards gave a little shiver. Tor's eye gleamed, and Dutch straightened in his seat.

"I'll pay to see that hand," said Lily Veddar.

Fleur showed, and she had nothing there, nothing at all.

Tor's thin smile cracked open, and he threw his hand in too.

"Well, we know one thing," he said, leaning back in his chair, "the squaw can't bluff."

With that I lowered myself into a mound of swept sawdust and slept. I woke up during the night, but none of them had moved yet, so I couldn't either. Still later, the men must have gone out again, or Fritzie come out to break the game, because I was lifted, soothed, cradled in a woman's arms and rocked so quiet that I kept my eyes shut while Fleur rolled me into a closet of grimy ledgers, oiled papers, balls of string, and thick files that fit beneath me like a mattress.

The game went on after work the next evening. I got my eight cents back five times over, and Fleur kept the rest of the dollar she'd won for a stake. This time they didn't play so late, but they played regular, and then kept going at it night after night. They played poker now, or variations, for one week straight, and each time Fleur won exactly one dollar, no more and no less, too consistent for luck.

By this time, Lily and the other men were so lit with suspense that they got Pete to join the game with them. They concentrated, the fat dog sitting tense in Lily Veddar's lap, Tor suspicious, Dutch stroking his huge square brow, Pete steady. It wasn't that Fleur won that hooked them in so, because she lost hands too. It was rather that she never had a freak hand or even anything above a straight. She only took on her low cards, which didn't sit right. By chance, Fleur should have gotten a full or flush by now. The irritating thing was she beat with pairs and never bluffed, because she couldn't, and still she ended up each night with exactly one dollar. Lily couldn't believe, first of all, that a woman could be smart enough to play cards, but even if she was, that she would then be stupid enough to cheat for a dollar a night. By day I watched him turn the problem over, his hard white face dull, small fingers probing at his knuckles, until he finally thought he had Fleur figured out as a bit-time player, caution her game. Raising the stakes would throw her.

More than anything now, he wanted Fleur to come away with something but a dollar. Two bits less or ten more, the sum didn't matter, just so he broke her streak.

Night after night she played, won her dollar, and left to stay in a place that just Fritzie and I knew about. Fleur bathed in the slaughtering tub, then slept in the unused brick smokehouse behind the lockers, a windowless place tarred on the inside with scorched fats. When I brushed against her skin I noticed that she smelled of the walls, rich and woody, slightly burnt. Since that night she put me in the closet I was no longer afraid of her, but followed her close, stayed with her, became her moving shadow that the men never noticed, the shadow that could have saved her.

August, the month that bears fruit, closed around the shop, and Pete and Fritzie left for Minnesota to escape the heat. Night by night, running, Fleur had won thirty dollars, and only Pete's presence had kept Lily at bay. But Pete was gone now, and one payday, with the heat so bad no one could move but Fleur, the men sat and played and waited while she finished work. The cards sweat, limp in their fingers, the table was slick with grease, and even the walls were warm to the touch. The air was motionless. Fleur was in the next room boiling heads.

Her green dress, drenched, wrapped her like a transparent sheet. A skin of 40
lakeweed. Black snarls of veining clung to her arms. Her braids were loose, half-unraveled, tied behind her neck in a thick loop. She stood in steam, turning skulls through a vat with a wooden paddle. When scraps boiled to the surface, she bent with a round tin sieve and scooped them out. She'd filled two dishpans.

"Ain't that enough now?" called Lily. "We're waiting." The stump of a dog trembled in his lap, alive with rage. It never smelled me or noticed me above Fleur's smoky skin. The air was heavy in my corner, and pressed me down. Fleur sat with them.

"Now what do you say?" Lily asked the dog. It barked. That was the signal for the real game to start.

"Let's up the ante," said Lily, who had been stalking this night all month. He had a roll of money in his pocket. Fleur had five bills in her dress. The men had each saved their full pay.

"Ante a dollar then," said Fleur, and pitched hers in. She lost, but they let her scrape along, cent by cent. And then she won some. She played unevenly, as if chance was all she had. She reeled them in. The game went on. The dog was stiff now, poised on Lily's knees, a ball of vicious muscle with its yellow eyes slit in concentration. It gave advice, seemed to sniff the lay of Fleur's cards, twitched and nudged. Fleur was up, then down, saved by a scratch. Tor dealt seven cards, three down. The pot grew, round by round, until it held all the money. Nobody folded. Then it all rode on one last card and they went silent. Fleur picked hers up and blew a long breath. The heat lowered like a bell. Her card shook, but she stayed in.

Lily smiled and took the dog's head tenderly between his palms.

"Say, Fatso," he said, crooning the words, "you reckon that girl's bluffing?"

The dog whined and Lily laughed. "Me too," he said, "let's show." He swept his bills and coins into the pot and then they turned their cards over.

Lily looked once, looked again, then he squeezed the dog up like a fist of dough and slammed it on the table.

Fleur threw her arms out and drew the money over, grinning that same wolf grin that she'd used on me, the grin that had them. She jammed the bills in her dress, scooped the coins up in waxed white paper that she tied with string.

"Let's go another round," said Lily, his voice choked with burrs. But Fleur opened her mouth and yawned, then walked out back to gather slops for the one big hog that was waiting in the stock pen to be killed.

The men sat still as rocks, their hands spread on the oiled wood table. Dutch had chewed his cigar to damp shreds, Tor's eye was dull. Lily's gaze was the only one to follow Fleur. I didn't move. I felt them gathering, saw my stepfather's veins, the ones in his forehead that stood out in anger. The dog had rolled off the table and curled in a knot below the counter, where none of the men could touch it.

Lily rose and stepped out back to the closet of ledgers where Pete kept his private stock. He brought back a bottle, uncorked and tipped it between his fingers. The lump in his throat moved, then he passed it on. They drank, quickly felt the whiskey's fire, and planned with their eyes things they couldn't say out loud.

When they left, I followed. I hid out back in the clutter of broken boards and chicken crates beside the stock pen, where they waited. Fleur could not be seen at first, and then the moon broke and showed her, slipping cautiously along the rough board chute with a bucket in her hand. Her hair fell, wild and coarse, to her waist, and her dress was a floating patch in the dark. She made a pig-calling sound, rang the tin pail lightly against the wood, froze suspiciously. But too late. In the sound of the ring Lily moved, fat and nimble, stepped right behind Fleur and put out his creamy hands. At his first touch, she whirled and doused him with the bucket of sour slops. He pushed her against the big fence and the package of coins split, went clinking and jumping, winked against the wood. Fleur rolled over once and vanished in the yard.

The moon fell behind a curtain of ragged clouds, and Lily followed into the dark muck. But he tripped, pitched over the huge flank of the pig, who lay mired to the snout, heavily snoring. I sprang out of the weeds and climbed the side of the pen, stuck like glue. I saw the sow rise to her neat, knobby knees, gain her balance, and sway, curious, as Lily stumbled forward. Fleur had backed into the angle of rough wood just beyond, and when Lily tried to jostle past, the sow tipped up on her hind legs and struck, quick and hard as a snake. She plunged her head into Lily's thick side and snatched a mouthful of his shirt. She grunted in pained surprise. He seemed to ponder, breathing deep. Then he launched his huge body in a swimmer's dive.

The sow screamed as his body smacked over hers. She rolled, striking out 55
with her knife-sharp hooves, and Lily gathered himself upon her, took her foot-long face by the ears and scraped her snout and cheeks against the trestles of the pen. He hurled the sow's tight skull against an iron post, but instead of knocking her dead, he merely woke her from her dream.

She reared, shrieked, drew him with her so that they posed standing upright. They bowed jerkily to each other, as if to begin. Then his arms swung and flailed. She sank her black fangs into his shoulder, clasping him, dancing him forward and backward through the pen. Their steps picked up pace, went wild. The two dipped as one, box-stepped, tripped each other. She ran her split foot through his hair. He grabbed her kinked tail. They went down and came up, the same shape and then the same color, until the men couldn't tell one from the other in that light and Fleur was able to launch herself over the gates, swing down, hit gravel.

The men saw, yelled, and chased her at a dead run to the smokehouse. And Lily too, once the sow gave up in disgust and freed him. That is where I should have gone to Fleur, saved her, thrown myself on Dutch. But I went stiff with fear and couldn't unlatch myself from the trestles or move at all. I closed my eyes and put my head in my arms, tried to hide, so there is nothing to describe but what I couldn't block out, Fleur's hoarse breath, so loud it filled me, her cry in the old language, and my name repeated over and over among the words.

The heat was still dense the next morning when I came back to work. Fleur was gone but the men were there, slack-faced, hung over. Lily was paler and softer than ever, as if his flesh had steamed on his bones. They smoked, took pulls off a bottle. It wasn't noon yet. I worked awhile, waiting shop and sharpening steel. But I was sick, I was smothered, I was sweating so hard that my hands slipped on the knives, and I wiped my fingers clean of the greasy touch of the customers' coins. Lily opened his mouth and roared once, not in anger. There was no meaning to the sound. His boxer dog, sprawled limp beside his foot, never lifted its head. Nor did the other men.

They didn't notice when I stepped outside, hoping for a clear breath. And then I forgot them because I knew that we were all balanced, ready to tip, to fly, to be crushed as soon as the weather broke. The sky was so low that I felt the weight of it like a yoke. Clouds hung down, witch teats, a tornado's green-brown cones, and as I watched one flicked out and became a delicate probing thumb. Even as I picked up my heels and ran back inside, the wind blew suddenly, cold, and then came rain.

Inside, the men had disappeared already and the whole place was trem- 60
bling as if a huge hand was pinched at the rafters, shaking it. I ran straight through, screaming for Dutch or for any of them, and then I stopped at the heavy doors of the lockers, where they had surely taken shelter. I stood there a moment. Everything went still. Then I heard a cry building in the wind, faint at

first, a whistle and then a shrill scream that tore through the walls and gathered around me, spoke plain so I understood that I should move, put my arms out, and slam down the great iron bar that fit across the hasp and lock.

Outside, the wind was stronger, like a hand held against me. I struggled forward. The bushes tossed, the awnings flapped off storefronts, the rails of porches rattled. The odd cloud became a fat snout that nosed along the earth and sniffled, jabbed, picked at things, sucked them up, blew them apart, rooted around as if it was following a certain scent, then stopped behind me at the butcher shop and bored down like a drill.

I went flying, landed somewhere in a ball. When I opened my eyes and looked, stranger things were happening.

A herd of cattle flew through the air like giant birds, dropping dung, their mouths opened in stunned bellows. A candle, still lighted, blew past, and tables, napkins, garden tools, a whole school of drifting eyeglasses, jackets on hangers, hams, a checkerboard, a lampshade, and at last the sow from behind the lockers, on the run, her hooves a blur, set free, swooping, diving, screaming as everything in Argus fell apart and got turned upside down, smashed and thoroughly wrecked.

Days passed before the town went looking for the men. They were bachelors, after all, except for Tor, whose wife had suffered a blow to the head that made her forgetful. Everyone was occupied with digging out, in high relief because even though the Catholic steeple had been torn off like a peaked cap and sent across five fields, those huddled in the cellar were unhurt. Walls had fallen, windows were demolished, but the stores were intact and so were the bankers and shop owners who had taken refuge in their safes or beneath their cash registers. It was a fair-minded disaster, no one could be said to have suffered much more than the next, at least not until Fritzie and Pete came home.

Of all the businesses in Argus, Kozka's Meats had suffered worst. The boards of the front building had been split to kindling, piled in a huge pyramid, and the shop equipment was blasted far and wide. Pete paced off the distance the iron bathtub had been flung — a hundred feet. The glass candy case went fifty, and landed without so much as a cracked pane. There were other surprises as well, for the back rooms where Fritzie and Pete lived were undisturbed. Fritzie said the dust still coated her china figures, and upon her kitchen table, in the ashtray, perched the last cigarette she'd put out in haste. She lit it up and finished it, looking through the window. From there, she could see the old smokehouse Fleur had slept in was crushed to a reddish sand and the stockpens were completely torn apart, the rails stacked helter-skelter. Fritzie asked for Fleur. People shrugged. Then she asked about the others and suddenly, the town understood that three men were missing.

There was a rally of help, a gathering of shovels and volunteers. We passed boards from hand to hand, stacked them, uncovered what lay beneath the pile of jagged splinters. The lockers, full of the meat that was Pete and Fritzie's investment, slowly came into sight, still intact. When enough room was made for a man to stand on the roof, there were calls, a general urge to hack through and see what lay below. But Fritzie shouted that she wouldn't allow it because the meat would spoil. And so the work continued, board by board, until at last the heavy oak doors of the freezer were revealed and people pressed to the entry. Everyone wanted to be the first, but since it was my stepfather lost, I was let go in when Pete and Fritzie wedged through into the sudden icy air.

Pete scraped a match on his boot, lit the lamp Fritzie held, and then the three of us stood still in its circle. Light glared off the skinned and hanging carcasses, the crates of wrapped sausages, the bright and cloudy blocks of lake ice, pure as winter. The cold bit into us, pleasant at first, then numbing. We must have stood there a couple of minutes before we saw the men, or more rightly, the humps of fur, the iced and shaggy hides they wore, the bearskins they had taken down and wrapped around themselves. We stepped closer and tilted the lantern beneath the flaps of fur into their faces. The dog was there, perched among them, heavy as a doorstop. The three had hunched around a barrel where the game was still laid out, and a dead lantern and an empty bottle, too. But they had thrown down their last hands and hunkered tight, clutching one another, knuckles raw from beating at the door they had also attacked with hooks. Frost stars gleamed off their eyelashes and the stubble of their beards. Their faces were set in concentration, mouths open as if to speak some careful thought, some agreement they'd come to in each other's arms.

Power travels in the bloodlines, handed out before birth. It comes down through the hands, which in the Pillagers are strong and knotted, big, spidery, and rough, with sensitive fingertips good at dealing cards. It comes through the eyes, too, belligerent, darkest brown, the eyes of those in the bear clan, impolite as they gaze directly at a person.

In my dreams, I look straight back at Fleur, at the men. I am no longer the watcher on the dark sill, the skinny girl.

The blood draws us back, as if it runs through a vein of earth. I've come 70
home and, except for talking to my cousins, live a quiet life. Fleur lives quiet too, down on Lake Turcot with her boat. Some say she's married to the waterman, Misshepeshu, or that she's living in shame with white men or windigos, or that she's killed them all. I'm about the only one here who ever goes to visit her. Last winter, I went to help out in her cabin when she bore the child, whose green eyes and skin the color of an old penny made more talk, as no one could decide if the child was mixed blood or what, fathered in a smokehouse, or by a man with brass scales, or by the lake. The girl is bold, smiling in her sleep, as if she knows what people wonder, as if she hears the old men talk, turning the story over. It comes up different every time and has no ending, no beginning. They get the middle wrong too. They only know that they don't know anything.

Connections

1. What is the significance of Fleur's last name, *Pillager?* How is her revenge similar to that of Abner Snopes in Faulkner's "Barn Burning" (p. 66)? Why is Fleur a more sympathetic character than Abner is?
2. Compare Erdrich's narrative strategy in "Fleur" with Faulkner's in "A Rose for Emily" (p. 47). How does each narrator present the central character in a similar positive light, despite the character's bizarre eccentricities?
3. Compare the use and purpose of magic and myth in "Fleur" and in García Márquez's "A Very Old Man with Enormous Wings" (p. 234).

TIM O'BRIEN (b. 1946)

How to Tell a True War Story 1987

This is true.

I had a buddy in Vietnam. His name was Bob Kiley, but everybody called him Rat.

A friend of his gets killed, so about a week later Rat sits down and writes a letter to the guy's sister. Rat tells her what a great brother she had, how strack° the guy was, a number one pal and comrade. A real soldier's soldier, Rat says. Then he tells a few stories to make the point, how her brother would always volunteer for stuff nobody else would volunteer for in a million years, dangerous stuff, like doing recon° or going out on these really badass night patrols. Stainless steel balls, Rat tells her. The guy was a little crazy, for sure, but crazy in a good way, a real daredevil, because he liked the challenge of it, he liked testing himself, just man against gook. A great, great guy, Rat says.

Anyway, it's a terrific letter, very personal and touching. Rat almost bawls writing it. He gets all teary telling about the good times they had together, how her brother made the war seem almost fun, always raising hell and lighting up villes° and bringing smoke to bear every which way. A great sense of humor, too. Like the time at this river when he went fishing with a whole damn crate of hand grenades. Probably the funniest thing in world history, Rat says, all that gore, about twenty zillion dead gook fish. Her brother, he had the right attitude. He knew how to have a good time. On Halloween, this real hot spooky night, the dude paints up his body all different colors and puts on this weird mask and goes out on ambush almost stark naked, just boots and balls and an M-16. A tremendous human being, Rat says. Pretty nutso sometimes, but you could trust him with your life.

And then the letter gets very sad and serious. Rat pours his heart out. He 5
says he loved the guy. He says the guy was his best friend in the world. They were like soul mates, he says, like twins or something, they had a whole lot in common. He tells the guy's sister he'll look her up when the war's over.

So what happens?

Rat mails the letter. He waits two months. The dumb cooze never writes back.

A true war story is never moral. It does not instruct, nor encourage virtue, nor suggest models of proper human behavior, nor restrain men from doing the things they have always done. If a story seems moral, do not believe it. If at the end of a war story you feel uplifted, or if you feel that some small bit of rectitude has been salvaged from the larger waste, then you have been made the victim of a very old and terrible lie. There is no rectitude whatsover. There is no virtue. As a first rule of thumb, therefore, you can tell a true war story by its absolute and uncompromising allegiance to obscenity and evil. Listen to Rat

strack: A strict military appearance.
doing recon: Reconnaissance, or exploratory survey of enemy territory.
villes: Villages.

Kiley. *Cooze,* he says. He does not say *bitch.* He certainly does not say *woman,* or *girl.* He says *cooze.* Then he spits and stares. He's nineteen years old — it's too much for him — so he looks at you with those big gentle killer eyes and says *cooze,* because his friend is dead, and because it's so incredibly sad and true: she never wrote back.

You can tell a true war story if it embarrasses you. If you don't care for obscenity, you don't care for the truth; if you don't care for the truth, watch how you vote. Send guys to war, they come home talking dirty.

Listen to Rat: "Jesus Christ, man, I write this beautiful fucking letter, I slave 10
over it, and what happens? The dumb cooze never writes back."

The dead guy's name was Curt Lemon. What happened was, we crossed a muddy river and marched west into the mountains, and on the third day we took a break along a trail junction in deep jungle. Right away, Lemon and Rat Kiley started goofing off. They didn't understand about the spookiness. They were kids; they just didn't know. A nature hike, they thought, not even a war, so they went off into the shade of some giant trees — quadruple canopy, no sunlight at all — and they were giggling and calling each other motherfucker and playing a silly game they'd invented. The game involved smoke grenades, which were harmless unless you did stupid things, and what they did was pull out the pin and stand a few feet apart and play catch under the shade of those huge trees. Whoever chickened out was a motherfucker. And if nobody chickened out, the grenade would make a light popping sound and they'd be covered with smoke and they'd laugh and dance around and then do it again.

It's all exactly true.

It happened nearly twenty years ago, but I still remember that trail junction and the giant trees and a soft dripping sound somewhere beyond the trees. I remember the smell of moss. Up in the canopy there were tiny white blossoms, but no sunlight at all, and I remember the shadows spreading out under the trees where Lemon and Rat Kiley were playing catch with smoke grenades. Mitchell Sanders sat flipping his yo-yo. Norman Bowker and Kiowa and Dave Jensen were dozing, or half-dozing, and all around us were those ragged green mountains.

Except for the laughter things were quiet.

At one point, I remember, Mitchell Sanders turned and looked at me, not 15
quite nodding, then after a while he rolled up his yo-yo and moved away.

It's hard to tell what happened next.

They were just goofing. There was a noise, I suppose, which must've been the detonator, so I glanced behind me and watched Lemon step from the shade into bright sunlight. His face was suddenly brown and shining. A handsome kid, really. Sharp gray eyes, lean and narrow-waisted, and when he died it was almost beautiful, the way the sunlight came around him and lifted him up and sucked him high into a tree full of moss and vines and white blossoms.

In any war story, but especially a true one, it's difficult to separate what happened from what seemed to happen. What seems to happen becomes its own happening and has to be told that way. The angles of vision are skewed. When a booby trap explodes, you close your eyes and duck and float outside yourself. When a guy dies, like Lemon, you look away and then look back for a moment and then look away again. The pictures get jumbled; you tend to miss a lot. And then afterward, when you go to tell about it, there is always that surreal seemingness, which makes the story seem untrue, but which in fact represents the hard and exact truth as it seemed.

In many cases a true war story cannot be believed. If you believe it, be skeptical. It's a question of credibility. Often the crazy stuff is true and the normal stuff isn't because the normal stuff is necessary to make you believe the truly incredible craziness.

In other cases you can't even tell a true war story. Sometimes it's just beyond telling.

I heard this one, for example, from Mitchell Sanders. It was near dusk and we were sitting at my foxhole along a wide, muddy river north of Quang Ngai. I remember how peaceful the twilight was. A deep pinkish red spilled out on the river, which moved without sound, and in the morning we would cross the river and march west into the mountains. The occasion was right for a good story.

"God's truth," Mitchell Sanders said. "A six-man patrol goes up into the mountains on a basic listening-post operation. The idea's to spend a week up there, just lie low and listen for enemy movement. They've got a radio along, so if they hear anything suspicious — anything — they're supposed to call in artillery or gunships, whatever it takes. Otherwise they keep strict field discipline. Absolute silence. They just listen."

He glanced at me to make sure I had the scenario. He was playing with his yo-yo, making it dance with short, tight little strokes of the wrist.

His face was blank in the dusk.

"We're talking hardass LP. These six guys, they don't say boo for a solid week. They don't got tongues. *All* ears."

"Right," I said.

"Understand me?"

"Invisible."

Sanders nodded.

"Affirm," he said. "Invisible. So what happens is, these guys get themselves deep in the bush, all camouflaged up, and they lie down and wait and that's all they do, nothing else, they lie there for seven straight days and just listen. And man, I'll tell you — it's spooky. This is mountains. You don't *know* spooky till you been there. Jungle, sort of, except it's way up in the clouds and there's always this fog — like rain, except it's not raining — everything's all wet and swirly and tangled up and you can't see jack, you can't find your own pecker to piss with. Like you don't even have a body. Serious spooky. You just go with the vapors — the fog sort of takes you in. . . . And the sounds, man. The sounds carry forever. You hear shit nobody should *ever* hear."

Sanders was quiet for a second, just working the yo-yo, then he smiled at me. "So, after a couple days the guys start hearing this real soft, kind of wacked-out music. Weird echoes and stuff. Like a radio or something, but it's not a radio, it's this strange gook music that comes right out of the rocks. Faraway, sort of, but right up close, too. They try to ignore it. But it's a listening post, right? So they listen. And every night they keep hearing this crazyass gook concert. All kinds of chimes and xylophones. I mean, this is wilderness — no way, it can't be real — but there it *is,* like the mountains are tuned in to Radio Fucking Hanoi. Naturally they get nervous. One guy sticks Juicy Fruit in his ears. Another guy almost flips. Thing is, though, they can't report music. They can't get on the horn and call back to base and say, 'Hey, listen, we need some firepower, we got to blow away this weirdo gook rock band.' They can't do that. It wouldn't go down. So they lie there in the fog and keep their mouths shut. And what makes it extra bad, see, is the poor dudes can't horse around like normal. Can't joke it away. Can't even talk to each other except maybe in whispers, all hush-hush, and that just revs up the willies. All they do is listen."

Again there was some silence as Mitchell Sanders looked out on the river. The dark was coming on hard now, and off to the west I could see the mountains rising in silhouette, all the mysteries and unknowns.

"This next part," Sanders said quietly, "you won't believe."

"Probably not," I said.

"You won't. And you know why?" 35

"Why?"

He gave me a tired smile. "Because it happened. Because every word is absolutely dead-on true."

Sanders made a little sound in his throat, like a sigh, as if to say he didn't care if I believed it or not. But he did care. He wanted me to believe, I could tell. He seemed sad, in a way.

"These six guys, they're pretty fried out by now, and one night they start hearing voices. Like at a cocktail party. That's what it sounds like, this big swank gook cocktail party somewhere out there in the fog. Music and chitchat and stuff. It's crazy, I know, but they hear the champagne corks. They hear the actual martini glasses. Real hoity-toity, all very civilized, except this isn't civilization. This is Nam.

"Anyway, the guys try to be cool. They just lie there and groove, but after 40
a while they start hearing — you won't believe this — they hear chamber music. They hear violins and shit. They hear this terrific mama-san soprano. Then after a while they hear gook opera and a glee club and the Haiphong Boys Choir and a barbershop quartet and all kinds of weird chanting and Buddha-Buddha stuff. The whole time, in the background, there's still that cocktail party going on. All these different voices. Not human voices, though. Because it's the mountains. Follow me? The rock — it's *talking.* And the fog, too, and the grass and the goddamn mongooses. Everything talks. The trees talk politics, the monkeys talk religion. The whole country. Vietnam, the place talks.

"The guys can't cope. They lose it. They get on the radio and report enemy movement — a whole army, they say — and they order up the firepower. They get arty° and gunships. They call in air strikes. And I'll tell you, they fuckin' crash that cocktail party. All night long, they just smoke those mountains. They make jungle juice. They blow away trees and glee clubs and whatever else there is to blow away. Scorch time. They walk napalm up and down the ridges. They bring in the Cobras and F-4s, they use Willie Peter and HE° and incendiaries. It's all fire. They make those mountains burn.

"Around dawn things finally get quiet. Like you never even *heard* quiet

arty: Artillery.
Willie Peter: White phosphorus, an incendiary substance; *HE:* High explosives.

before. One of those real thick, real misty days — just clouds and fog, they're off in this special zone — and the mountains are absolutely dead-flat silent. Like Brigadoon° — pure vapor, you know? Everything's all sucked up inside the fog. Not a single sound, except they still *hear* it.

"So they pack up and start humping. They head down the mountain, back to base camp, and when they get there they don't say diddly. They don't talk. Not a word, like they're deaf and dumb. Later on this fat bird colonel comes up and asks what the hell happened out there. What'd they hear? Why all the ordnance? The man's ragged out, he gets down tight on their case. I mean, they spent six trillion dollars on firepower, and this fatass colonel wants answers, he wants to know what the fuckin' story is.

"But the guys don't say zip. They just look at him for a while, sort of funnylike, sort of amazed, and the whole war is right there in that stare. It says everything you can't ever say. It says, man, you got *wax* in your ears. It says, poor bastard, you'll never know — wrong frequency — you don't *even* want to hear this. Then they salute the fucker and walk away, because certain stories you don't ever tell."

You can tell a true war story by the way it never seems to end. Not then, 45
not ever. Not when Mitchell Sanders stood up and moved off into the dark.

It all happened.

Even now I remember that yo-yo. In a way, I suppose, you had to be there, you had to hear it, but I could tell how desperately Sanders wanted me to believe him, his frustration at not quite getting the details right, not quite pinning down the final and definitive truth.

And I remember sitting at my foxhole that night, watching the shadows of Quang Ngai, thinking about the coming day and how we would cross the river and march west into the mountains, all the ways I might die, all the things I did not understand.

Late in the night Mitchell Sanders touched my shoulder.

"Just came to me," he whispered. "The moral, I mean. Nobody listens. 50
Nobody hears nothing. Like that fatass colonel. The politicians, all the civilian types, what they need is to go out on LP. The vapors, man. Trees and rocks — you got to *listen* to your enemy."

And then again, in the morning, Sanders came up to me. The platoon was preparing to move out, checking weapons, going through all the little rituals that preceded a day's march. Already the lead squad had crossed the river and was filing off toward the west.

"I got a confession to make," Sanders said. "Last night, man, I had to make up a few things."

"I know that."

"The glee club. There wasn't any glee club."

"Right." 55

"No opera."

"Forget it, I understand."

Brigadoon: A fictional village in Scotland that only appears once every one hundred years; subject of a popular American musical (1947).

"Yeah, but listen, it's still true. Those six guys, they heard wicked sound out there. They heard sound you just plain won't believe."

Sanders pulled on his rucksack, closed his eyes for a moment, then almost smiled at me.

I knew what was coming but I beat him to it. 60

"All right," I said, "what's the moral?"

"Forget it."

"No, go ahead."

For a long while he was quiet, looking away, and the silence kept stretching out until it was almost embarrassing. Then he shrugged and gave me a stare that lasted all day.

"Hear that quiet, man?" he said. "There's your moral." 65

In a true war story, if there's a moral at all, it's like the thread that makes the cloth. You can't tease it out. You can't extract the meaning without unraveling the deeper meaning. And in the end, really, there's nothing much to say about a true war story, except maybe "Oh."

True war stories do not generalize. They do not indulge in abstraction or analysis.

For example: War is hell. As a moral declaration the old truism seems perfectly true, and yet because it abstracts, because it generalizes, I can't believe it with my stomach. Nothing turns inside.

It comes down to gut instinct. A true war story, if truly told, makes the stomach believe.

This one does it for me. I've told it before — many times, many versions — 70
but here's what actually happened.

We crossed the river and marched west into the mountains. On the third day, Curt Lemon stepped on a booby-trapped 105 round. He was playing catch with Rat Kiley, laughing, and then he was dead. The trees were thick; it took nearly an hour to cut an LZ for the dustoff.°

Later, higher in the mountains, we came across a baby VC° water buffalo. What it was doing there I don't know — no farms or paddies — but we chased it down and got a rope around it and led it along to a deserted village where we set for the night. After supper Rat Kiley went over and stroked its nose.

He opened up a can of C rations, pork and beans, but the baby buffalo wasn't interested.

Rat shrugged.

He stepped back and shot it through the right front knee. The animal did 75
not make a sound. It went down hard, then got up again, and Rat took careful aim and shot off an ear. He shot it in the hindquarters and in the little hump at its back. He shot it twice in the flanks. It wasn't to kill; it was just to hurt. He put the rifle muzzle up against the mouth and shot the mouth away. Nobody said much. The whole platoon stood there watching, feeling all kinds of things, but there wasn't a great deal of pity for the baby water buffalo. Lemon was dead. Rat Kiley had lost his best friend in the world. Later in the week he would write

LZ: Landing zone; *dustoff:* Helicopter evacuation of a casualty.
VC: Vietcong (North Vietnamese).

a long personal letter to the guy's sister, who would not write back, but for now it was a question of pain. He shot off the tail. He shot away chunks of meat below the ribs. All around us there was the smell of smoke and filth, and deep greenery, and the evening was humid and very hot. Rat went to automatic. He shot randomly, almost casually, quick little spurts in the belly and butt. Then he reloaded, squatted down, and shot it in the left front knee. Again the animal fell hard and tried to get up, but this time it couldn't quite make it. It wobbled and went down sideways. Rat shot it in the nose. He bent forward and whispered something, as if talking to a pet, then he shot it in the throat. All the while the baby buffalo was silent, or almost silent, just a light bubbling sound where the nose had been. It lay very still. Nothing moved except the eyes, which were enormous, the pupils shiny black and dumb.

Rat Kiley was crying. He tried to say something, but then cradled his rifle and went off by himself.

The rest of us stood in a ragged circle around the baby buffalo. For a time no one spoke. We had witnessed something essential, something brand-new and profound, a piece of the world so startling there was not yet a name for it.

Somebody kicked the baby buffalo.

It was still alive, though just barely, just in the eyes.

"Amazing," Dave Jensen said. "My whole life, I never seen anything like it."

"Never?"

"Not hardly. Not once."

Kiowa and Mitchell Sanders picked up the baby buffalo. They hauled it across the open square, hoisted it up, and dumped it in the village well.

Afterward, we sat waiting for Rat to get himself together.

"Amazing," Dave Jensen kept saying.

"For sure."

"A new wrinkle. I never seen it before."

Mitchell Sanders took out his yo-yo.

"Well, that's Nam," he said. "Garden of Evil. Over here, man, every sin's real fresh and original."

How do you generalize?

War is hell, but that's not the half of it, because war is also mystery and terror and adventure and courage and discovery and holiness and pity and despair and longing and love. War is nasty; war is fun. War is thrilling; war is drudgery. War makes you a man; war makes you dead.

The truths are contradictory. It can be argued, for instance, that war is grotesque. But in truth war is also beauty. For all its horror, you can't help but gape at the awful majesty of combat. You stare out at tracer rounds unwinding through the dark like brilliant red ribbons. You crouch in ambush as a cool, impassive moon rises over the nighttime paddies. You admire the fluid symmetries of troops on the move, the harmonies of sound and shape and proportion, the great sheets of metal-fire streaming down from a gunship, the illumination rounds, the white phosphorous, the purply black glow of napalm, the rocket's red glare. It's not pretty, exactly. It's astonishing. It fills the eye. It commands you. You hate it, yes, but your eyes do not. Like a killer forest fire, like cancer under a microscope, any battle or bombing raid or artillery barrage has the aesthetic purity of absolute moral indifference — a powerful, implacable beauty — and a true war story will tell the truth about this, though the truth is ugly.

To generalize about war is like generalizing about peace. Almost everything is true. Almost nothing is true. At its core, perhaps, war is just another name for death, and yet any soldier will tell you, if he tells the truth, that proximity to death brings with it a corresponding proximity to life. After a fire fight, there is always the immense pleasure of aliveness. The trees are alive. The grass, the soil — everything. All around you things are purely living, and you among them, and the aliveness makes you tremble. You feel an intense, out-of-the-skin awareness of your living self — your truest self, the human being you want to be and then become by the force of wanting it. In the midst of evil you want to be a good man. You want decency. You want justice and courtesy and human concord, things you never knew you wanted. There is a kind of largeness to it; a kind of godliness. Though it's odd, you're never more alive than when you're almost dead. You recognize what's valuable. Freshly, as if for the first time, you love what's best in yourself and in the world, all that might be lost. At the hour of dusk you sit at your foxhole and look out on a wide river turning pinkish red, and at the mountains beyond, and although in the morning you must cross the river and go into the mountains and do terrible things and maybe die, even so, you find yourself studying the fine colors on the river, you feel wonder and awe at the setting of the sun, and you are filled with a hard, aching love for how the world could be and always should be, but now is not.

Mitchell Sanders was right. For the common soldier, at least, war has the feel — the spiritual texture — of a great ghostly fog, thick and permanent. There is no clarity. Everything swirls. The old rules are no longer binding, the old truths no longer true. Right spills over into wrong. Order blends into chaos, love into hate, ugliness into beauty, law into anarchy, civility into savagery. The vapors suck you in. You can't tell where you are, or why you're there, and the only certainty is absolute ambiguity.

In war you lose your sense of the definite, hence your sense of truth itself, 95
and therefore it's safe to say that in a true war story nothing much is ever very true.

Often in a true war story there is not even a point, or else the point doesn't hit you until twenty years later, in your sleep, and you wake up and shake your wife and start telling the story to her, except when you get to the end you've forgotten the point again. And then for a long time you lie there watching the story happen in your head. You listen to your wife's breathing. The war's over. You close your eyes. You smile and think, Christ, what's the *point?*

This one wakes me up.

In the mountains that day, I watched Lemon turn sideways. He laughed and said something to Rat Kiley. Then he took a peculiar half step, moving from shade into bright sunlight, and the booby-trapped 105 round blew him into a tree. The parts were just hanging there, so Norman Bowker and I were ordered to shinny up and peel him off. I remember the white bone of an arm. I remember pieces of skin and something wet and yellow that must've been the intestines. The gore was horrible, and stays with me, but what wakes me up twenty years later is Norman Bowker singing "Lemon Tree" as we threw down the parts.

You can tell a true war story by the questions you ask. Somebody tells a story, let's say, and afterward you ask, "Is it true?" and if the answer matters, you've got your answer.

For example, we've all heard this one. Four guys go down a trail. A grenade 100
sails out. One guy jumps on it and takes the blast and saves his three buddies.

Is it true?

The answer matters.

You'd feel cheated if it never happened. Without the grounding reality, it's just a trite bit of puffery, pure Hollywood, untrue in the way all such stories are untrue. Yet even if it did happen—and maybe it did, anything's possible—even then you know it can't be true, because a true war story does not depend upon that kind of truth. Happeningness is irrelevant. A thing may happen and be a total lie; another thing may not happen and be truer than the truth. For example: Four guys go down a trail. A grenade sails out. One guy jumps on it and takes the blast, but it's a killer grenade and everybody dies anyway. Before they die, though, one of the dead guys says, "The fuck you do *that* for?" and the jumper says, "Story of my life, man," and the other guy starts to smile but he's dead.

That's a true story that never happened.

Twenty years later, I can still see the sunlight on Lemon's face. I can see 105
him turning, looking back at Rat Kiley, then he laughed and took that curious half step from shade into sunlight, his face suddenly brown and shining, and when his foot touched down, in that instant, he must've thought it was the sunlight that was killing him. It was not the sunlight. It was a rigged 105 round. But if I could ever get the story right, how the sun seemed to gather around him and pick him up and lift him into a tree, if I could somehow recreate the fatal whiteness of that light, the quick glare, the obvious cause and effect, then you would believe the last thing Lemon believed, which for him must've been the final truth.

Now and then, when I tell this story, someone will come up to me afterward and say she liked it. It's always a woman. Usually it's an older woman of kindly temperament and humane politics. She'll explain that as a rule she hates war stories, she can't understand why people want to wallow in blood and gore. But this one she liked. Sometimes, even, there are little tears. What I should do, she'll say, is put it all behind me. Find new stories to tell.

I won't say it but I'll think it.

I'll picture Rat Kiley's face, his grief, and I'll think, *You dumb cooze.*

Because she wasn't listening.

It wasn't a war story. It was a love story. It was a ghost story. 110

But you can't say that. All you can do is tell it one more time, patiently, adding and subtracting, making up a few things to get at the real truth. No Mitchell Sanders, you tell her. No Lemon, no Rat Kiley. And it didn't happen in the mountains, it happened in this little village on the Batangan Peninsula, and it was raining like crazy, and one night a guy named Stink Harris woke up screaming with a leech on his tongue. You can tell a true war story if you just keep on telling it.

In the end, of course, a true war story is never about war. It's about the special way that dawn spreads out on a river when you know you must cross the river and march into the mountains and do things you are afraid to do. It's about love and memory. It's about sorrow. It's about sisters who never write back and people who never listen.

Connections

1. Imagine Krebs from Hemingway's "Soldier's Home" (p. 121) writing a letter home recommending "How to Tell a True War Story" to his parents. Write that letter from Krebs's point of view.
2. Compare and contrast the "sister" Rat Kiley writes to with Krebs's sister. What purpose does each sister serve?
3. How do the settings of O'Brien's story and Conrad's "An Outpost of Progress" (p. 208) evoke mystery, fear, and horror? Write an essay that points to specific descriptions and explains the function of the setting in each story.

FAY WELDON (b. 1933)

IND AFF 1988

OR OUT OF LOVE IN SARAJEVO

This is a sad story. It has to be. It rained in Sarajevo, and we had expected fine weather.

The rain filled up Sarajevo's pride, two footprints set into a pavement which mark the spot where the young assassin Princip stood to shoot the Archduke Franz Ferdinand and his wife. (Don't forget his wife: everyone forgets his wife, the archduchess.) That was in the summer of 1914. Sarajevo is a pretty town, Balkan style, mountain-rimmed. A broad, swift, shallow river runs through its center, carrying the mountain snow away, arched by many bridges. The one nearest the two footprints has been named the Princip Bridge. The young man is a hero in these parts. Not only does he bring in the tourists — look, look, the spot, the very spot! — but by his action, as everyone knows, he lit a spark which fired the timber which caused World War I which crumbled the Austro-Hungarian Empire, the crumbling of which made modern Yugoslavia possible. Forty million dead (or was it thirty?) but who cares? So long as he loved his country.

The river, they say, can run so shallow in the summer it's known derisively as "the wet road." Today, from what I could see through the sheets of falling rain, it seemed full enough. Yugoslavian streets are always busy — no one stays home if they can help it (thus can an indecent shortage of housing space create a sociable nation) and it seemed as if by common consent a shield of bobbing umbrellas had been erected two meters high to keep the rain off the streets. It just hadn't worked around Princip's corner.

"Come all this way," said Peter, who was a professor of classical history, "and you can't even see the footprints properly, just two undistinguished puddles." Ah, but I loved him. I shivered for his disappointment. He was supervising my thesis on varying concepts of morality and duty in the early Greek States as evidenced in their poetry and drama. I was dependent upon him for my academic future. He said I had a good mind but not a first-class mind and somehow I didn't take it as an insult. I had a feeling first-class minds weren't all that good in bed.

5 Sarajevo is in Bosnia, in the center of Yugoslavia, that grouping of unlikely states, that distillation of languages into the phonetic reasonableness of Serbo-Croatian. We'd sheltered from the rain in an ancient mosque in Serbian Belgrade; done the same in a monastery in Croatia; now we spent a wet couple of days in Sarajevo beneath other people's umbrellas. We planned to go on to Montenegro, on the coast, where the fish and the artists come from, to swim and lie in the sun, and recover from the exhaustion caused by the sexual and moral torments of the last year. It couldn't possibly go on raining forever. Could it? Satellite pictures showed black clouds swishing gently all over Europe, over the Balkans, into Asia — practically all the way from Moscow to London, in fact. It wasn't that Peter and myself were being singled out. No. It was raining on his wife, too, back in Cambridge.

Peter was trying to decide, as he had been for the past year, between his wife and myself as his permanent life partner. To this end we had gone away, off the beaten track, for a holiday; if not with his wife's blessing, at least with her knowledge. Were we really, truly suited? We had to be sure, you see, that this was more than just any old professor-student romance; that it was the Real Thing, because the longer the indecision went on the longer Mrs. Piper would be left dangling in uncertainty and distress. They had been married for twenty-four years; they had stopped loving each other a long time ago, of course — but there would be a fearful personal and practical upheaval entailed if he decided to leave permanently and shack up, as he put it, with me. Which I certainly wanted him to do. I loved him. And so far I was winning hands down. It didn't seem much of a contest at all, in fact. I'd been cool and thin and informed on the seat next to him in a Zagreb theater (Mrs. Piper was sweaty and only liked telly); was now eager and anxious for social and political instruction in Sarajevo (Mrs. Piper spat in the face of knowledge, he'd once told me); and planned to be lissome (and I thought topless but I hadn't quite decided: this might be the area where the age difference showed) while I splashed and shrieked like a bathing belle in the shallows of the Montenegrin coast. (Mrs. Piper was a swimming coach: I imagined she smelt permanently of chlorine.)

In fact so far as I could see, it was no contest at all between his wife and myself. But Peter liked to luxuriate in guilt and indecision. And I loved him with an inordinate affection.

Princip's prints are a meter apart, placed as a modern cop on a training shoot-out would place his feet — the left in front at a slight outward angle, the right behind, facing forward. There seemed great energy focused here. Both hands on the gun, run, stop, plant the feet, aim, fire! I could see the footprints well enough, in spite of Peter's complaint. They were clear enough to me.

We went to a restaurant for lunch, since it was too wet to do what we loved to do: that is, buy bread, cheese, sausage, wine, and go off somewhere in our hired car, into the woods or the hills, and picnic and make love. It was a private restaurant — Yugoslavia went over to a mixed capitalist-communist economy years back, so you get either the best or worst of both systems, depending on your mood — that is to say, we knew we would pay more but be given a choice. We chose the wild boar.

"Probably ordinary pork soaked in red cabbage water to darken it," said 10
Peter. He was not in a good mood.

Cucumber salad was served first.

"Everything in this country comes with cucumber salad," complained Peter. I noticed I had become used to his complaining. I supposed that when you had been married a little you simply wouldn't hear it. He was forty-six and I was twenty-five.

"They grow a lot of cucumber," I said.

"If they can grow cucumbers," Peter then asked, "why can't they grow *mange-tout?*"° It seemed a why-can't-they-eat-cake sort of argument to me, but not knowing enough about horticulture not to be outflanked if I debated the point, I moved the subject on to safer ground.

"I suppose Princip's action couldn't really have started World War I," I 15
remarked. "Otherwise, what a thing to have on your conscience! One little shot and the deaths of thirty million."

"Forty," he corrected me. Though how they reckon these things and get them right I can't imagine. "Of course he didn't start the war. That's just a simple tale to keep the children quiet. It takes more than an assassination to start a war. What happened was that the buildup of political and economic tensions in the Balkans was such that it had to find some release."

"So it was merely the shot that lit the spark that fired the timber that started the war, et cetera?"

"Quite," he said. "World War I would have had to have started sooner or later."

"A bit later or a bit sooner," I said, "might have made the difference of a million or so; if it was you on the battlefield in the mud and the rain you'd notice; exactly when they fired the starting-pistol; exactly when they blew the final whistle. Is that what they do when a war ends; blow a whistle? So that everyone just comes in from the trenches."

But he wasn't listening. He was parting the flesh of the soft collapsed or- 20
angey-red pepper which sat in the middle of his cucumber salad; he was carefully extracting the pips. His nan had once told him they could never be digested, would stick inside and do terrible damage. I loved him for his dexterity and patience with his knife and fork. I'd finished my salad yonks ago, pips and all. I was hungry. I wanted my wild boar.

Peter might be forty-six, but he was six foot two and grizzled and muscled with it, in a dark-eyed, intelligent, broad-jawed kind of way. I adored him. I loved to be seen with him. "Muscular academic, not weedy academic" as my

mange-tout: A sugar pea or bean (French).

younger sister Clare once said. "Muscular academic is just a generally superior human being: everything works well from the brain to the toes. Weedy academic is when there isn't enough vital energy in the person, and the brain drains all the strength from the other parts." Well, Clare should know. Clare is only twenty-three, but of the superior human variety kind herself, vividly pretty, bright and competent — somewhere behind a heavy curtain of vibrant red hair, which she only parts for effect. She had her first degree at twenty. Now she's married to a Harvard professor of economics seconded to the United Nations. She can even cook. I gave up competing yonks ago. Though she too is capable of self-deception. I would say her husband was definitely of the weedy academic rather than the muscular academic type. And they have to live in Brussels.

The archduke's chauffeur had lost his way, and was parked on the corner trying to recover his nerve when Princip came running out of a café, planted his feet, aimed, and fired. Princip was nineteen — too young to hang. But they sent him to prison for life and, since he had TB to begin with, he only lasted three years. He died in 1918, in an Austrian prison. Or perhaps it was more than TB: perhaps they gave him a hard time, not learning till later, when the Austro-Hungarian Empire collapsed, that he was a hero. Poor Princip, too young to die — like so many other millions. Dying for love of a country.

"I love you," I said to Peter, my living man, progenitor already of three children by his chlorinated, swimming-coach wife.

"How much do you love me?"

"Inordinately! I love you with inordinate affection." It was a joke between us. Ind Aff!

"Inordinate affection is a sin," he'd told me. "According to the Wesleyans. John Wesley° himself worried about it to such a degree he ended up abbreviating it in his diaries, Ind Aff. He maintained that what he felt for young Sophy, the eighteen-year-old in his congregation, was not Ind Aff, which bears the spirit away from God towards the flesh: he insisted that what he felt was a pure and spiritual, if passionate, concern for her soul."

Peter said now, as we waited for our wild boar, and he picked over his pepper, "Your Ind Aff is my wife's sorrow, that's the trouble." He wanted, I knew, one of the long half-wrangles, half soul-sharings that we could keep going for hours, and led to piercing pains in the heart which could only be made better in bed. But our bedroom at the Hotel Europa was small and dark and looked out into the well of the building — a punishment room if ever there was one. (Reception staff did sometimes take against us.) When Peter had tried to change it in his quasi-Serbo-Croatian, they'd shrugged their Bosnian shoulders and pretended not to understand, so we'd decided to put up with it. I did not fancy pushing hard single beds together — it seemed easier not to have the pain in the heart in the first place. "Look," I said, "this holiday is supposed to be just the two of us, not Mrs. Piper as well. Shall we talk about something else?"

Do not think that the archduke's chauffeur was merely careless, an inefficient chauffeur, when he took the wrong turning. He was, I imagine, in a state of shock, fright, and confusion. There had been two previous attempts on the

John Wesley: (1703–1791) English religious leader and founder of Methodism.

archduke's life since the cavalcade had entered town. The first was a bomb which got the car in front and killed its driver. The second was a shot fired by none other than young Princip, which had missed. Princip had vanished into the crowd and gone to sit down in a corner café and ordered coffee to calm his nerves. I expect his hand trembled at the best of times — he did have TB. (Not the best choice of assassin, but no doubt those who arrange these things have to make do with what they can get.) The archduke's chauffeur panicked, took the wrong road, realized what he'd done, and stopped to await rescue and instructions just outside the café where Princip sat drinking his coffee.

"What shall we talk about?" asked Peter, in even less of a good mood.

"The collapse of the Austro-Hungarian Empire?" I suggested. "How does 30
an empire collapse? Is there no money to pay the military or the police, so everyone goes home? Or what?" He liked to be asked questions.

"The Hungro-Austrarian Empire," said Peter to me, "didn't so much collapse as fail to exist any more. War destroys social organizations. The same thing happened after World War II. There being no organized bodies left between Moscow and London — and for London read Washington, then as now — it was left to these two to put in their own puppet governments. Yalta, 1944. It's taken the best part of forty-five years for nations of West and East Europe to remember who they are."

"Austro-Hungarian," I said, "not Hungro-Austrarian."

"I didn't say Hungro-Austrarian," he said.

"You did," I said.

"Didn't," he said. "What the hell are they doing about our wild boar? Are 35
they out in the hills shooting it?"

My sister Clare had been surprisingly understanding about Peter. When I worried about him being older, she pooh-poohed it; when I worried about him being married, she said, "Just go for it, sister. If you can unhinge a marriage, it's ripe for unhinging, it would happen sooner or later, it might as well be you. See a catch, go ahead and catch! Go for it!"

Princip saw the archduke's car parked outside, and went for it. Second chances are rare in life: they must be responded to. Except perhaps his second chance was missing in the first place? Should he have taken his cue from fate, and just sat and finished his coffee, and gone home to his mother? But what's a man to do when he loves his country? Fate delivered the archduke into his hands: how could he resist it? A parked car, a uniformed and medaled chest, the persecutor of his country — how could Princip not, believing God to be on his side, but see this as His intervention, push his coffee aside and leap to his feet?

Two waiters stood idly by and watched us waiting for our wild boar. One was young and handsome in a mountainous Bosnian way — flashing eyes, hooked nose, luxuriant black hair, sensuous mouth. He was about my age. He smiled. His teeth were even and white. I smiled back, and instead of the pain in the heart I'd become accustomed to as an erotic sensation, now felt, quite violently, an associated yet different pang which got my lower stomach. The true, the real pain of Ind Aff!

"Fancy him?" asked Peter.

"No," I said. "I just thought if I smiled the wild boar might come quicker." 40

The other waiter was older and gentler: his eyes were soft and kind. I thought he looked at me reproachfully. I could see why. In a world which for once, after centuries of savagery, was finally full of young men, unslaughtered, what was I doing with this man with thinning hair?

"What are you thinking of?" Professor Piper asked me. He liked to be in my head.

"How much I love you," I said automatically, and was finally aware how much I lied. "And about the archduke's assassination," I went on, to cover the kind of tremble in my head as I came to my senses, "and let's not forget his wife, she died too — how can you say World War I would have happened anyway. If Princip hadn't shot the archduke, something else, some undisclosed, unsuspected variable, might have come along and defused the whole political/military situation, and neither World War I nor II ever happened. We'll just never know, will we?"

I had my passport and my travelers' checks with me. (Peter felt it was less confusing if we each paid our own way.) I stood up, and took my raincoat from the peg.

"Where are you going?" he asked, startled.

"Home," I said. I kissed the top of his head, where it was balding. It smelt gently of chlorine, which may have come from thinking about his wife so much, but might merely have been that he'd taken a shower that morning. ("The water all over Yugoslavia, though safe to drink, is unusually chlorinated": Guide Book.) As I left to catch a taxi to the airport the younger of the two waiters emerged from the kitchen with two piled plates of roasted wild boar, potatoes duchesse, and stewed peppers. ("Yugoslavian diet is unusually rich in proteins and fats": Guide Book.) I could tell from the glisten of oil that the food was no longer hot, and I was not tempted to stay, hungry though I was. Thus fate — or was it Bosnian willfulness? — confirmed the wisdom of my intent.

And that was how I fell out of love with my professor, in Sarajevo, a city to which I am grateful to this day, though I never got to see very much of it, because of the rain.

It was a silly sad thing to do, in the first place, to confuse mere passing academic ambition with love: to try and outdo my sister Clare. (Professor Piper was spiteful, as it happened, and did his best to have my thesis refused, but I went to appeal, which he never thought I'd dare, and won. I had a first-class mind after all.) A silly sad episode, which I regret. As silly and sad as Princip, poor young man, with his feverish mind, his bright tubercular cheeks, and his inordinate affection for his country, pushing aside his cup of coffee, leaping to his feet, taking his gun in both hands, planting his feet, aiming, and firing — one, two, three shots — and starting World War I. The first one missed, the second got the wife (never forget the wife), and the third got the archduke and a whole generation, and their children, and their children's children, and on and on forever. If he'd just hung on a bit, there in Sarajevo, that June day, he might have come to his senses. People do, sometimes quite quickly.

Connections

1. Compare and contrast "IND AFF" and Oates's "The Lady with the Pet Dog" (p. 159) as love stories. Do you think that the stories end happily, or the way you would want them to end? Are the endings problematic?

2. Explain how Weldon's concept of "Ind Aff"—"inordinate affection"—can be used to make sense of the relationship between Georgiana and Aylmer in Hawthorne's "The Birthmark" (p. 268).
3. How does passion figure in "IND AFF" and in Lawrence's "The Horse Dealer's Daughter" (p. 383)? Explain how Weldon's and Lawrence's perspectives on passion suggest differing views of love and human relationships.

11. Perspectives on Fiction

This chapter offers a variety of observations about fiction and individual stories. Some of these comments by writers and critics are general, while others make references to particular works. The assessments are wide-ranging: consider, for example, the difference between Thomas Jefferson's warning that reading fiction can act as a "poison [that] infects the mind" and E. L. Doctorow's celebration of storytelling a century and a half later as an "instrument of survival" for humankind. The following perspectives include Eudora Welty on the plots of Stephen Crane's "The Bride Comes to Yellow Sky" and Katherine Mansfield's "Miss Brill," Ernest Hemingway on what every writer needs to be an effective artist, William Faulkner on the demands of writing short stories, and John Cheever on morality in fiction. These and other commentaries raise a number of issues related to fiction that should help to stimulate your reading, thinking, and writing.

THOMAS JEFFERSON (1743–1826)

On the Dangers of Reading Fiction 1818

A great obstacle to good education is the inordinate passion prevalent for novels, and the time lost in that reading which should be instructively employed. When this poison infects the mind, it destroys its tone and revolts it against wholesome reading. Reason and fact, plain and unadorned, are rejected. Nothing can engage attention unless dressed in all the figments of fancy, and nothing so bedecked comes amiss. The result is a bloated imagination, sickly judgment, and disgust towards all the real businesses of life. This mass of trash, however, is not without some distinction; some few modeling their narratives, although fictitious, on the incidents of real life, have been able to make them interesting and useful vehicles of a sound morality. . . . For a like reason, too, much poetry should not be indulged. Some is useful for forming style and taste. Pope, Dryden, Thompson, Shakespeare, and of the French, Molière, Racine, the Corneilles, may be read with pleasure and improvement.

Letter to Nathaniel Burwell, March 14, 1818, in *The Writings of Thomas Jefferson*

Considerations

1. Jefferson voices several common objections to fiction. What, according to him, are the changes associated with reading fiction? Are these concerns still expressed today? Why or why not? To what extent are Jefferson's arguments similar to twentieth-century objections to watching television?
2. Explain why you agree or disagree that works of fiction should serve as "useful vehicles of a sound morality."
3. Compare and contrast the values about art stated in this paragraph with those expressed in E. L. Doctorow's "The Importance of Fiction" (p. 486).

KATHERINE MANSFIELD (1888–1923)

On the Style of "Miss Brill" 1921

It's a very queer thing how *craft* comes into writing. I mean down to details. *Par example.* In *Miss Brill* I choose not only the length of every sentence, but even the sound of every sentence. I choose the rise and fall of every paragraph to fit her, and to fit her on that day at that very moment. After I'd written it I read it aloud — numbers of times — just as one would *play over* a musical composition — trying to get it nearer and nearer to the expression of Miss Brill — until it fitted her.

Don't think I'm vain about the little sketch. It's only the method I wanted to explain. I often wonder whether other writers do the same — If a thing has really come off it seems to me there mustn't be one single word out of place, or one word that could be taken out. That's how I AIM at writing. It will take some time to get anywhere near there.

From a letter to Richard Murry, January 17, 1921,
in *The Letters of Katherine Mansfield*

Considerations

1. How does the style of "Miss Brill" "fit" the character of the protagonist?
2. Choose any other story from this anthology and explain how its style is "fitted" to its protagonist.

F. SCOTT FITZGERALD (1896–1940)

On the Continuity of a Writer's Works 1933

I am thirty-six years old. For eighteen years, save for a short space during the war, writing has been my chief interest in life, and I am in every sense a professional.

Yet even now when, at the recurrent cry of "Baby needs shoes," I sit down facing my sharpened pencils and block of legal-sized paper, I have a feeling of utter helplessness. I may write my story in three days or, as is more frequently the case, it may be six weeks before I have assembled anything worthy to be sent out. I can open a volume from a criminal-law library and find a thousand plots. I can go into highway and byway, parlor and kitchen, and listen to personal revelations that, at the hands of other writers, might endure forever. But all that is nothing — not even enough for a false start. . . .

Mostly, we authors must repeat ourselves — that's the truth. We have two or three great and moving experiences in our lives — experiences so great and moving that it doesn't seem at the time that anyone else has been so caught up and pounded and dazzled and astonished and beaten and broken and rescued and illuminated and rewarded and humbled in just that way ever before.

Then we learn our trade, well or less well, and we tell our two or three stories — each time in a new disguise — maybe ten times, maybe a hundred, as long as people will listen.

If this were otherwise, one would have to confess to having no individuality at all. And each time I honestly believe that, because I have found a new background and a novel twist, I have really got away from the two or three fundamental tales I have to tell. But it is rather like Ed Wynn's famous anecdote about the painter of boats who was begged to paint some ancestors for a client. The bargain was arranged, but with the painter's final warning that the ancestors would all turn out to look like boats.

When I face the fact that all my stories are going to have a certain family resemblance, I am taking a step toward avoiding false starts. If a friend says he's got a story for me and launches into a tale of being robbed by Brazilian pirates in a swaying straw hut on the edge of a smoking volcano in the Andes, with his fiancée bound and gagged on the roof, I can well believe there were various human emotions involved; but having successfully avoided pirates, volcanoes, and fiancées who get themselves bound and gagged on roofs, I can't feel them. Whether it's something that happened twenty years ago or only yesterday, I must start out with an emotion — one that's close to me and that I can understand.

From "One Hundred False Starts" in *Afternoon of an Author*

Considerations

1. Why does Fitzgerald believe that it is inevitable for writers to repeat themselves?
2. Consider the stories in Chapter 9 by Nathaniel Hawthorne and Flannery O'Connor. To what extent do each of these writer's stories share "a certain family resemblance"?

WARREN BECK (b. 1918)

Sentimentality in Formula Fiction 1943

The problem of the formula short story is indeed insistent and complex. Numerous narratives describable in terms of formula do crowd into the popular magazines and produce the illusion, which commercial teachers of writing foster, that command of a pattern is the straight and easy road to success. However, it is not as simple as it looks, and that is because formula is not the basic factor in question, is not a first cause. The formula short story is essentially the short story of platitude — the fable founded on sentimental mottoes. This assertion is based in part on the perhaps unconsciously rendered testimony of a practitioner — a rising slick-paper-magazine author once heard discussing formula narratives with a group of neophytes, ostensibly to teach them how to write such stories. Their laboratory specimen was a quite profitably published story about a man who couldn't make farming pay and went to the city, where he got a job in a livery stable, only to be oppressed and abused by his boss. The ex-farmer's young son was chagrined by his father's servitude and was delighted when papa finally socked the boss on the nose, quit the job, and decided to go back to the land. In his exegesis of this tale the rising author told the amateurs that the formula was: man's struggle with nature. The plot was alleged to have the proper inflection — the struggle abandoned, and the struggle heroically resumed. All present seemed to think it a story with a happy ending. If they did, what fulcrum supported the lever of their formula? Beyond the concept of the struggle-with-nature-resumed, were they not resting on several seedy platitudes — such as that, if at first you don't succeed, you should try, try again, and moreover that no red-blooded American should ever let the boss push him around, and finally, that a return to nature is always wise and virtuous? None of those analysts questioned whether it was heroic or even good horse sense for the man to start all over again on the farm, where presumably the same old unfavorable conditions prevailed. No one asked whether what the man had to take from the boss wasn't less than what both he and his family would have to take if he failed again in agriculture. No one even asked whether he couldn't have found another job in town. Such questions would have raised a reprehensible doubt about the happiness of the ending. The point is that such apparent happiness as there was in the story (apart from the natural but fleeting gratification of poking the boss on the snoot) was founded on the crudest of sentimental illusions. This is not to reject heroism or any other virtue. The literary short story is not necessarily either cynical or despairing. Its writers would agree that we live by admiration, hope, and love; but they would inquire what is most admirable, what hopes are reasonable and potent, and how love can best fulfill and refine human nature; and they would remember that ill-advised devotion and expectation can produce not happiness but tragedy.

The formula short story, however, demands obvious action at any price, even that of superficiality. Vicissitude is the essence of formula fiction, as in the satirical recipe: "Boy meets girl, boy loses girl, boy gets girl." This may be more comprehensively stated in the lingo of the prize-fight broadcast: "He's up, he's down, he's up." To get a happy ending, you stop when the hero is up, presumably the winner. That's all there is to formula itself. But the formula does not tell the writer, or the reader either, which way is up. For this sense of direction the formula short story depends on a whole arsenal, an ever normal granary, of platitudes, held to be self-evident — to wit, that love will find a way, that mother knows best, that the police, the U.S. Cavalry, the handsome hero, and all other agencies of rescue and just retribution operate infallibly on a nick-of-time schedule, because it's darkest just before dawn, and of course love conquers all, and in no ambiguous sense.

The greatest distinction of the literary short story is in its protest against such a deceptive sentimentalizing of reality, its attempt to lay aside rose-colored glasses, its positive desire to see into things. Instructively, it may be noted of that formula story about the "struggle with nature" that its factual elements seem veracious. Such a man in such a predicament might have behaved thus, and his boy might have been glad that he did. Beneath the synopsis, however, lies the interpretation, dependent upon the author's understanding and ideals. . . . Really imaginative treatment might let the reader sense the boy's illusion as illusion, with its pathetic devotion to deceptive human hopes; it might reveal the father's essential incapacity and evasiveness without condemning him; it might carry through to the whole family's morning-after on the unpromising farm; it might imply how men's passions still set them against each other, driving the less privileged and less able into the barren edges of economic wilderness; it might even show the boy's realization that he must find a better way than his father's. These are hypotheses, however, not formulas. Theme is always original, springing from the affirmations of personal life. . . .

Between popular and literary fiction thus may be observed general differences of orientation. These cannot be embraced in a rule, however, for to some readers certain allegedly literary short stories will seem delusively sentimental or destructively morbid, whereas many a popular action-story, while elementary in substance, will be felt by all but cynics and sophisticates to adhere incontestably to common sense, good taste, and kindness. . . . One may choose for one's self, if one dares, to try to live as much as possible without sentimental illusion; but criticism has no call to deny the harried housewife, the tired businessman, the repressed office girl, or the bored assembly-line worker a literary aspirin against the headache of a particular life.

From "Art and Formula in the Short Story" in *College English*

Considerations

1. According to Beck, what distinguishes "literary fiction" from formula fiction? What does each offer a reader?
2. Do you think formula fiction and serious fiction are mutually exclusive? Is it possible to enjoy both kinds of writing?
3. Write a response to the following statement: "Formula fiction is a total waste of time. Mysteries, romances, adventures, westerns, and other kinds of formula stories are to reading what chewing gum is to eating." Choose a side and draw upon your own experiences as a reader.

A. L. BADER (b. 1902)

Nothing Happens in Modern Short Stories 1945

Any teacher who has ever confronted a class with representative modern short stories will remember the disappointment, the puzzled "so-what" attitude, of certain members of the group. "Nothing happens in some of these stories," "They just end," or "They're not real stories" are frequent criticisms. . . . Sometimes the phrase "Nothing happens" seems to mean that nothing significant happens, but in a great many cases it means that the modern short story is charged with a lack of narrative structure. Readers and critics accustomed to an older type of story are baffled by a newer type. They sense the underlying and unifying design of the one, but they find nothing equivalent to it in the other. Hence they maintain that the modern short story is plotless, static, fragmentary, amorphous — frequently a mere character sketch or vignette, or a mere reporting of a transient moment, or the capturing of a mood or nuance — everything, in fact, except a story.

From "The Structure of the Modern Story" in *College English*

Considerations

1. What is the basic objection to the "newer type" of short story? How does it differ from the "older type"?
2. Consider any one of the stories from the Album of Contemporary Stories (p. 436) as an example of the newer type. Does anything "happen" in the story? How does it differ from the excerpt from Edgar Rice Burroughs's *Tarzan of the Apes* (p. 40)?
3. Read a recent story published in *The New Yorker* or the *Atlantic* and compare its narrative structure with that of Hemingway's "Soldier's Home" (p. 121) or Ellison's "Battle Royal" (p. 179).

EUDORA WELTY (b. 1909)
On the Plots of "The Bride Comes to Yellow Sky" and "Miss Brill" 1949

Stephen Crane's "The Bride Comes to Yellow Sky" tells a story of situation; it is a playful story, using two situations, like counters.

Jack Potter, the town marshal of Yellow Sky, has gone to San Anton' and gotten married and is bringing his bride home in a Pullman — the whole errand to be a complete surprise to the town of Yellow Sky. "He knew full well that his marriage was an important thing to his town. It could only be exceeded by the burning of the new hotel."

And in Yellow Sky another situation is building up in matching tempo with the running wheels. A messenger appears in the door of the Weary Gentleman saloon crying "Scratchy Wilson's drunk and has turned loose with both hands." "Immediately a solemn, chapel-like gloom was upon the place. . . . 'Scratchy Wilson is a wonder with a gun, a perfect wonder, and when he goes on the war-trail, we hunt our holes — naturally.'" Scratchy enters town, pistols in both hands. His "cries of ferocious challenge rang against walls of silence. And his boots had red tops with gilded imprints, of the kind beloved in winter by little sledding boys on the hillsides of New England. . . . He walked with the creeping movement of the midnight cat. As it occurred to him, he roared menacing information. . . . The little fingers of each hand played sometimes in a musician's way. . . . The only sounds were his terrible invitations."

All this is delightful to us not only for itself but for its function of play, of assuring our anticipation; the more ferocious Scratchy is, the more we are charmed. Our sense of the fairness, the proportion of things is gratified when he "comfortably fusiladed the windows of his most intimate friend. The man was playing with this town; it was a toy for him." This plot of situation gives us a kind of kinetic pleasure; just as being on a seesaw is pleasant not only for where we are but for where the other person is.

The train arrives, Jack Potter and bride get off, and Jack's emotion-charged meeting with Yellow Sky is due; and Scratchy Wilson turns out to be its protagonist. They come face to face, and Potter, who says, "I ain't got a gun on me, Scratchy," takes only a minute to make up his mind to be shot on his wedding day.

"If you ain't got a gun, why ain't you got a gun?" Scratchy sneers at the marshal. And Potter says, "I ain't got a gun because I've just come from San Anton' with my wife. I'm married." "Married?" asks Scratchy — he has to ask it several times, uncomprehending. "Married?"

"Seemingly for the first time, he saw the drooping, drowning woman at the other man's side. 'No!' he said. He was like a creature allowed a glimpse of another world. . . . 'Is this the lady?'

" 'Yes; this is the lady,' answered Potter.

" 'Well,' said Wilson at last, slowly, 'I s'pose it's all off now.'

". . . He was not a student of chivalry; it was merely that in the presence of this foreign condition he was a simple child of the earlier plains. He picked up his starboard revolver, and, placing both weapons in their holsters, he went away. His feet made funnel-shaped tracks in the heavy sand."

So, in Crane's story, two situations, two forces, gather, meet — or rather are magnetized toward one another, almost — and collide. One is vanquished — the unexpected one — with neatness and absurdity, and the vanquished one exists; all equivalents of comedy.

In Katherine Mansfield's "Miss Brill," there are only one character and only one situation. The narrative is simple, Miss Brill's action consists nearly altogether in sitting down; she does nothing but go and sit in the park, return home, and sit on her bed in her little room. Yet considerably more of a story is attempted by this lesser to-do than Crane attempted in "Yellow Sky"; its plot is all implication.

"Miss Brill" is set on a stage of delight. "Although it was so brilliantly fine — the blue sky powdered with gold, and great spots of light like white wine splashed over the *Jardins Publiques* — Miss Brill was glad that she had decided on her fur. . . . [She] put up her hand and touched her fur. Dear little thing!" We see right off that for Miss Brill delight is a kind of coziness. She sits listening to the band, her Sunday habit, and "Now there came a little flutely bit — very pretty! — a little chain of bright drops. She was sure it would be repeated. It was; she lifted her head and smiled."

Miss Brill has confidence in her world — anticipation: what will happen next? Ah, but she knows. She's delighted but safe. She sees the others from her little perch, her distance — the gay ones and then those on benches: "Miss Brill had often noticed there was something funny about nearly all of *them.* They were odd, silent, nearly all old, and from the way they stared they looked as though they'd just come from dark little rooms or even — even cupboards!" For she hasn't identified herself at all.

The drama is slight in this story. There is no collision. Rather the forces meeting in the *Jardins Publiques* have, at the story's end, passed through each other and come out the other side; there has not been a collision, but a change — something much more significant. This is because, though there is one small situation going on, a very large and complex one is implied — the outside world, in fact.

One of the forces in the story is life itself, corresponding to the part of Scratchy Wilson, so to speak. Not violent life — life in the setting of a park on Sunday afternoon in Paris. All it usually does for Miss Brill is promenade stylishly while the band plays, form little tableaux, separate momently into minor, rather darker encounters, and keep in general motion with bright colors and light touches — there are no waving pistols at all, to storm and threaten.

Yet, being life, it does threaten. In what way, at last? Well, how much more deadly to Miss Brill than a flourished pistol is an overheard remark — about *her*. Miss Brill's vision — a vision of love — is brought abruptly face to face with another, ruder vision of love. The boy and girl in love sit down on her bench, but they cannot go on with what they have been saying because of her, though "still soundlessly singing, still with that trembling smile, Miss Brill prepared to listen.

" 'No, not now,' said the girl. 'Not here, I can't.'

" 'But why? Because of that stupid old thing at the end there? . . . Why does she come here at all — who wants her? Why doesn't she keep her silly old mug at home?'

" 'It's her fur which is so funny,' giggled the girl. 'It's exactly like a fried whiting.'

" 'Ah, be off with you!' said the boy in an angry whisper."

So Miss Brill, she who could spare even pity for this world, in her innocence — pity, the spectator's emotion — is defeated. She had allowed herself occasional glimpses of lives not too happy, here in the park, which had moved her to little flutters of sadness. But that too had been coziness — coziness, a remedy visitors seek to take the chill off a strange place with. She hadn't known it wasn't good enough. All through the story she has sat in her "special seat" — another little prop to endurance — and all unknown to her she sat in mortal danger. This is the story. The danger nears, a word is spoken, the blow falls — and Miss Brill retires, ridiculously easy to mow down, as the man with the pistols was easy to stare down in "Yellow Sky," for comedy's sake. But Miss Brill was from the first defenseless and on the losing side, and her defeat is the deeper for it, and one feels sure it is for ever.

From "The Reading and Writing of Short Stories" in the *Atlantic Monthly*

Considerations

1. What does Welty see as the essential difference between the plots of these two stories? Why does she describe Mansfield in "Miss Brill" as attempting "considerably more of a story" than "Yellow Sky"?
2. Write an essay that compares and contrasts the plots of Faulkner's "A Rose for Emily" (p. 47) and Poe's "The Pit and the Pendulum" (p. 398). Which is "considerably more of a story" in the sense that Welty uses this phrase? Do you agree with her assessment?

ELIZABETH BOWEN (1899–1973)

The Writer's Roving Eye 1952

The writer, unlike his nonwriting adult friend, has no predisposed outlook; he seldom observes deliberately. He sees what he did not intend to see; he remembers what does not seem wholly possible. Inattentive learner in the schoolroom of life, he keeps some faculty free to veer and wander. His is the roving eye.

By that roving eye is his subject found. The glance, at first only vaguely caught, goes on to concentrate, deepen; becomes the vision. Just what *has* he seen, and why should it mean so much? The one face standing out of the crowd, the figure in the distance crossing the street, the glare or shade significant on a building, the episode playing out at the next table, the image springing out of a phrase of talk, the disproportionate impact of some one phrase of poetry, the reverberation after a street accident or tiny subjective echo of a huge world event, the flare-up of visual memory or of sensuous memory for which can be traced no reason at all — why should this or that be of such importance as to bring all else to a momentous stop? Fate has worked, as in a falling in love — the writer, in fact, first knows he has found his subject by finding himself already obsessed by it. The outcome of obsession is, that he writes — rationalization begins with his search for language. He must (like the child who cannot keep silent) share, make known, communicate what he has seen, or knows. The urgency of what is real to him demands that it should be realized by other people.

From *Seven Winters and Afterthoughts*

Considerations

1. According to Bowen, how does a writer's response to the world differ from a nonwriter's?
2. Choose a story that strikes you as especially rich in observed details and analyze a paragraph or two for what those details reveal about a character, action, setting, symbol, or theme.

ERNEST HEMINGWAY (1899–1961)

On What Every Writer Needs 1954

The most essential gift for a good writer is a built-in, shock-proof, shit detector. This is the writer's radar and all great writers have had it.

From *Writers at Work: The Paris Review Interviews* (Second Series)

Considerations

1. Hemingway is typically forthright here, but it is tempting to dismiss his point as simply humorous. Take him seriously. What does he insist a good writer must be able to do?

2. How might Krebs in Hemingway's "Soldier's Home" (p. 121) be seen as having a similar kind of "shit detector" and "radar"?
3. Try writing a pithy, quotable statement that makes an observation about reading or writing.

VLADIMIR NABOKOV (1899–1977)

On How to Be a Good Reader c. 1955

In reading, one should notice and fondle details. There is nothing wrong about the moonshine of generalization when it comes *after* the sunny trifles of the book have been lovingly collected. If one begins with a ready-made generalization, one begins at the wrong end and travels away from the book before one has started to understand it. . . . We should always remember that the work of art is invariably the creation of a new world, so that the first thing we should do is to study that new world as closely as possible, approaching it as something brand new, having no obvious connection with the worlds we already know. When this new world has been closely studied, then and only then let us examine its links with other worlds, other branches of knowledge.

One evening at a remote provincial college through which I happened to be jogging on a protracted lecture tour, I suggested a little quiz — ten definitions of a reader, and from these ten the students had to choose four definitions that would combine to make a good reader. I have mislaid the list, but as far as I remember the definitions went something like this. Select four answers to the question what should a reader be to be a good reader:

1. The reader should belong to a book club.
2. The reader should identify himself or herself with the hero or heroine.
3. The reader should concentrate on the social-economic angle.
4. The reader should prefer a story with action and dialogue to one with none.
5. The reader should have seen the book in a movie.
6. The reader should be a budding author.
7. The reader should have imagination.
8. The reader should have memory.
9. The reader should have a dictionary.
10. The reader should have some artistic sense.

The students leaned heavily on emotional identification, action, and the social-economic or historical angle. Of course, as you have guessed, the good reader is one who has imagination, memory, a dictionary, and some artistic sense — which sense I propose to develop in myself and in others whenever I have the chance.

Incidentally, I use the word *reader* very loosely. Curiously enough, one cannot *read* a book: one can only reread it. A good reader, a major reader, an active and creative reader is a rereader. And I shall tell you why. When we read a book for the first time the very process of laboriously moving our eyes from left to right, line after line, page after page, this complicated physical work upon the book, the very process of learning in terms of space and time what the book is about, this stands between us and artistic appreciation. When we look at a painting we do not have to move our eyes in a special way even if, as in a book, the picture contains elements of depth and development. The element of time does not really enter in a first contact with a painting. In reading a book, we must have time to acquaint ourselves with it. We have no physical organ (as we have the eye in regard to a painting) that takes in the whole picture and then can enjoy its details. But at a second, or third, or fourth reading we do, in a sense, behave towards a book as we do towards a painting. However, let us not confuse the physical eye, that monstrous masterpiece of evolution, with the mind, an even more monstrous achievement. A book, no matter what it is — a work of fiction or a work of science (the boundary line between the two is not as clear as is generally believed) — a book of fiction appeals first of all to the mind. The mind, the brain, the top of the tingling spine, is, or should be, the only instrument used upon a book.

Now, this being so, we should ponder the question how does the mind work when the sullen reader is confronted by the sunny book. First, the sullen mood melts away, and for better or worse the reader enters into the spirit of the game. The effort to begin a book, especially if it is praised by people whom the young reader secretly deems to be too old-fashioned or too serious, this effort is often difficult to make; but once it is made, rewards are various and abundant. Since the master artist used his imagination in creating his book, it is natural and fair that the consumer of a book should use his imagination too.

There are, however, at least two varieties of imagination in the reader's case. So let us see which one of the two is the right one to use in reading a book. First, there is the comparatively lowly kind which turns for support to the simple emotions and is of a definitely personal nature. (There are various subvarieties here, in this first section of emotional reading.) A situation in a book is intensely felt because it reminds us of something that happened to us or to someone we know or knew. Or, again, a reader treasures a book mainly because it evokes a country, a landscape, a mode of living which he nostalgically recalls as part of his own past. Or, and this is the worst thing a reader can do, he identifies himself with a character in the book. This lowly variety is not the kind of imagination I would like readers to use.

So what is the authentic instrument to be used by the reader? It is impersonal imagination and artistic delight. What should be established, I think, is an artistic harmonious balance between the reader's mind and the author's mind. We ought to remain a little aloof and take pleasure in this aloofness while at the same time we keenly enjoy — passionately enjoy, enjoy with tears and shivers — the inner weave of a given masterpiece. To be quite objective in these matters is of course impossible. Everything that is worthwhile is to some extent subjective. For instance, you sitting there may be merely my dream, and I may be your nightmare. But what I mean is that the reader must know when and where to curb his imagination and this he does by trying to get clear the specific world the author places at his disposal. We must see things and hear things, we must visualize the rooms, the clothes, the manners of an author's people.

From "Good Readers and Good Writers"
in *Vladimir Nabokov: Lectures on Literature*

Considerations

1. Why do you think Nabokov insists on examining closely the details in a work? Do you agree with all the points he makes in his first paragraph?
2. Why does Nabokov reject each of the first six definitions of a good reader in his list? Why are "imagination, memory, a dictionary, and some artistic sense" important?
3. What would Nabokov think of attempts to speed-read fiction? Why?
4. Do you agree that "the worst thing a reader can do" is to identify with a character in a work of fiction? Why, or why not?

WILLIAM FAULKNER (1897–1962)

On the Demands of Writing Short Stories 1959

Q. Mr. Faulkner, you spoke about *The Sound and the Fury* as starting out to write a short story and it kept growing. Well now, do you think that it's easier to write a novel than a short story?

A. Yes sir. You can be more careless, you can put more trash in it and be excused for it. In a short story that's next to the poem, almost every word has got to be almost exactly right. In the novel you can be careless but in the short story you can't. I mean by that the good short stories like Chekhov wrote. That's why I rate that second — it's because it demands a nearer absolute exactitude. You have less room to be slovenly and careless. There's less room in it for trash. In poetry, of course, there's no room at all for trash. It's got to be absolutely impeccable, absolutely perfect.

From Frederick Gwynn and Joseph Blotner, eds., *Faulkner in the University*

Considerations

1. Why does short story writing place more demands on an author than novel writing? What does a short story have in common with poetry? Do you agree with Faulkner that a writer can afford to be more careless in a novel than in a short story or poem? Why or why not?
2. Which do you find more satisfying to read, a short story or a novel? Explain why.

MORDECAI MARCUS (b. 1925)

What Is an Initiation Story? 1960

An initiation story may be said to show its young protagonist experiencing a significant change of knowledge about the world or himself, or a change of character, or of both, and this change must point or lead him toward an adult world. It may or may not contain some form of ritual, but it should give some evidence that the change is at least likely to have permanent effects.

Initiation stories obviously center on a variety of experiences and the initiations vary in effect. It will be useful, therefore, to divide initiations into types according to their power and effect. First, some initiations lead only to the threshold of maturity and understanding but do not definitely cross it. Such stories emphasize the shocking effect of experience, and their protagonists tend to be distinctly young. Second, some initiations take their protagonists across a threshold of maturity and understanding but leave them enmeshed in a struggle for certainty. These initiations sometimes involve self-discovery. Third, the most decisive initiations carry their protagonists firmly into maturity and understanding, or at least show them decisively embarked toward maturity. These initiations usually center on self-discovery. For convenience, I will call these types tentative, uncompleted, and decisive initiations.

From "What Is an Initiation Story?" in *The Journal of Aesthetics and Art Criticism*

Considerations

1. For a work to be classified as an initiation story, why should it "give some evidence that the change [in the protagonist] is at least likely to have permanent effects"?
2. Marcus divides initiations into three broad types: tentative, uncompleted, and decisive. Explain how you would categorize the initiations in the following stories: Ellison's "Battle Royal" (p. 179), Hawthorne's "Young Goodman Brown" (p. 258), O'Connor's "Good Country People" (p. 302) and "Everything That Rises Must Converge" (p. 316), and Updike's "A & P" (p. 407).

GORE VIDAL (b. 1925)

The Popularity of the Tarzan Books 1963

Until recently I assumed that most people were like myself: daydreaming ceases when the real world becomes interesting and reasonably manageable. Now I am not so certain. Pondering the . . . success of Burroughs leads one to believe that a good many people find their lives so unsatisfactory that they go right on year after year telling themselves stories in which they are able to dominate their environment in a way that is not possible in this overorganized society. . . . His fellow daydreamers recognized a master. In 1914 he published his first book, *Tarzan of the Apes* (Rousseau's noble savage reborn in Africa), and history was made. To date the Tarzan books have sold over twenty-five million copies in fifty-six languages. There is hardly an American male of my generation who has not at one time or another tried to master the victory cry of the great ape as it once bellowed forth from the androgynous chest of Johnny Weismuller, while a thousand arms and legs were broken by attempts to swing from tree to tree in the backyards of the republic. Between 1914 and his death in 1950, Burroughs, the squire of Tarzana, California (a prophet honored by his own land), produced over sixty books, while enjoying the unique status of being the first American writer to be a corporation. Burroughs is said to have been a pleasant, unpretentious man who liked to ride and play golf. Not one to disturb his own unconscious with reality, he never set foot in Africa.

With a sense of recapturing childhood, I have just reread several Tarzan books. It is fascinating to see how much one recalls after a quarter century. At times the sense of *déjà vu* is overpowering. It is equally interesting to discover that one's memories of *Tarzan of the Apes* are mostly action scenes. The plot had slipped one's mind. It is a lot of plot, too. The beginning is worthy of Conrad. "I had this story from one who had no business to tell it to me, or to any other. I may credit the seductive influence of an old vintage upon the narrator for the beginning of it, and my own skeptical incredulity during the days that followed for the balance of the strange tale." It is 1888. The young Lord and Lady Greystoke are involved in a ship mutiny ("there was in the whole atmosphere of the craft that undefinable something which presages disaster"). They are put ashore on the west coast of Africa. They build a tree house. Here Burroughs is at his best. He tells you the size of the logs, the way to hang a door when you have no hinges, the problems of roofing. All his books are filled with interesting details on how things are made. The Greystokes have a child. They die. The "man-child" is taken up by Kala, a Great Ape, who brings him up as a member of her tribe of apes. Burroughs is a rather vague anthropologist. His apes have a language. They are carnivorous. They can, he suspects, mate with human beings. Tarzan grows up as an ape; he kills his first lion (with a full nelson); he teaches himself to read and write English by studying some books found in the cabin. The method he used, sad to say, is the currently fashionable "look-see." Though he can read and write, he cannot speak any language except that of the apes. He gets on well with the animal kingdom, with Tantor the elephant, Ska the vulture, Numa the lion (Kipling has added his grist to the Burroughs dream mill). Then white people arrive: Professor Archimedes Q. Porter and his daughter Jane. Also, a Frenchman named D'Arnot who teaches Tarzan to speak French, which is confusing. By coincidence, Jane's suitor is the current Lord Greystoke, who thinks the Greystoke baby is dead. Tarzan saves Jane from an ape. Then he puts on clothes and goes to Paris where he drinks absinthe. Next stop, America. In Wisconsin, he saves Jane Porter from a forest fire; then he nobly gives her up to Lord Greystoke, not revealing the fact that *he* is the real Lord Greystoke. Fortunately in the next volume, *The Return of Tarzan,* he marries Jane and they live happily ever after in Africa, raising a son John, who in turn grows up and has a son. Yet even as a grandfather, Tarzan continues to have adventures with people a foot high, with descendants of Atlantis, with the heirs of a Roman legion who think that Rome is still a success. All through these stories one gets the sense that one is daydreaming, too. Episode follows episode with no particular urgency. Tarzan is always knocked on the head and taken captive; he always escapes; there is always a beautiful princess or high priestess who loves him and assists him; there is always a loyal friend who fights beside him. . . . But no matter how difficult the adventure, Tarzan, clad only in a loincloth with no weapon save a knife (the style is contagious), wins against all odds and returns to his shadowy wife.

These books are clearly for men. I have yet to meet a woman who found Tarzan interesting: no identification, as they say in series land.

Though Burroughs is innocent of literature . . . he does have a gift very few writers of any kind possess: he can describe action vividly. I give away no trade secrets when I say that this is as difficult for a Tolstoi as it is for a Burroughs (even William). Because it is so hard, the draftier contemporary novelists usually prefer to tell their stories in the first person, which is simply writing dialogue. In character, as it were, the writer settles for an impression of what happened rather than creating the sense of a happening. Tarzan *in action* is excellent.

There is something basic in the appeal of the 1914 Tarzan which makes me think that he can still hold his own as a daydream figure, despite the sophisticated challenge for his two contemporary competitors, Ian Fleming and Mickey Spillane. For most adults, Tarzan (and John Carter of Mars) can hardly compete with the conspicuous consumer consumption of James Bond or the sickly violence of Mike Hammer, but for children and adolescents, the old appeal continues. All of us need the idea of a world alternative to this one. From Plato's Republic to Opar to Bondland, at every level, the human imagination has tried to imagine something better for itself than the existing society. Man left Eden when we got up off all fours, endowing most of his descendants with nostalgia as well as chronic backache. In its naïve way, the Tarzan legend returns us to that Eden where, free of clothes and the inhibitions of an oppressive society, a man can achieve in reverie his continuing need, which is, as William Faulkner put it in his high Confederate style, to prevail as well as endure. . . . The individual's desire to dominate his environment is not a desirable trait in a society which every day grows more and more confining. Since there are few legitimate releases for the average man, he must take to daydreaming. James Bond, Mike Hammer and Tarzan are all dream-selves, and the aim of each is to establish personal primacy in a world which in reality diminishes the individual. Among adults, increasing popularity of these lively inferior fictions strikes me as a most significant (and unbearably sad) phenomenon.

From "Tarzan Revisited" in *Esquire*

Considerations

1. What does Vidal see as the lasting appeal of the Tarzan books? Is this true of most popular literature?
2. Explain why you agree or disagree with Vidal's view that "these books are clearly for men" rather than for women.
3. Vidal praises Burroughs's writing when he says, "Tarzan *in action* is excellent." Do you think the excerpt from *Tarzan of the Apes* (p. 40) supports this view? Explain why or why not.

MODY C. BOATRIGHT (1896–1970)

A Typical Western Plot Formula 1969

The hero is going on in the even tenor of his way when something occurs, either in the community where he lives or in some place he happens to be, apparently by accident, that morally compels him to act in behalf of others. . . .

A. The hero encounters:

1. someone in distress — often a woman or child — in the desert without water, sick in an isolated cabin, or wounded.

2. a community being oppressed — the crooks are in control, or a cattle baron is running out the small ranchers and farmers.
3. a crime being planned — the bank is to be robbed, or the sheriff murdered.

B. The action involves sacrifice and risk on the part of the hero:
1. he may be a fugitive, and succor means surrender to the law.
2. he may be a traveler passing through who must abandon, at least temporarily, the important mission of his journey.
3. he may be a local resident who appears to be no match for his antagonist.

C. The hero is successful; this may involve:
1. the use of firearms, perhaps killing.
2. a battle of wits.
3. a show of overwhelming force (the cavalry arrives and declares marshall [sic] law).

From "The Formula in Cowboy Fiction and Drama" in *Western Folklore*

Considerations

1. Try writing an outline similar to Boatright's for some other form of popular fiction, such as a detective or adventure story. Or try writing an outline for a favorite television program that employs a formula.
2. How does Crane's "The Bride Comes to Yellow Sky" (p. 200) use elements of Boatright's formula? How is Crane's story significantly different from the formula?

JOHN CHEEVER (1912–1982)

On Morals in Fiction 1976

Interviewer: Do you think that fiction should give lessons?

Cheever: No. Fiction is meant to illuminate, to explode, to refresh. I don't think there's any consecutive moral philosophy in fiction beyond excellence. Acuteness of feeling and velocity have always seemed to me terribly important. People look for morals in fiction because there has always been a confusion between fiction and philosophy.

Interviewer: How do you know when a story is right? Does it hit you right the first time, or are you critical as you go along?

Cheever: I think there is a certain heft in fiction. For example, my latest story isn't right. I have to do the ending over again. It's a question, I guess, of trying to get it to correspond to a vision. There is a shape, a proportion, and one knows when something that happens is wrong.

Interviewer: By instinct?

Cheever: I suppose that anyone who has written for as long as I have, it's probably what you'd call instinct. When a line falls wrong, it simply isn't right.

From *Writers at Work: The Paris Review Interviews* (Fifth Series)

Considerations

1. How does Cheever distinguish between "instinct" and "philosophy"? Why does he object to people looking for "morals" in stories?
2. Is there a moral to be found in Cheever's "Reunion" (p. 369)?
3. How do you think Cheever would respond to Hawthorne's "The Birthmark" (p. 268)? Why?

JOHN UPDIKE (b. 1932)

Fiction's Subtlety

1985

Fiction is nothing less than the subtlest instrument for self-examination and self-display that mankind has invented yet. Psychology and X-rays bring up some portentous shadows, and demographics and stroboscopic photography do some fine breakdowns, but for the full *parfum* and effluvia of being human, for feathery ambiguity and rank facticity, for the air and iron, fire and spit of our daily mortal adventure there is nothing like fiction: it makes sociology look priggish, history problematical, the film media two-dimensional, and the *National Enquirer* as silly as last week's cereal box.

From "The Importance of Fiction" in *Esquire*

Considerations

1. How do you interpret Updike's assertion that fiction is the "subtlest instrument" for understanding what it means to be human? Explain why you agree or disagree.
2. Consider Updike's claim that fiction makes film seem "two-dimensional" by comparison. What, in your view, does literature do better than film? What does film achieve more effectively than literature?
3. Using Updike's "A & P" (p. 407) as the basis for your discussion, write an essay that explains why a sociological analysis of Sammy's character would necessarily leave out significant aspects of his personality as Updike presents him. Consider also what a sociological description might add to our understanding of him. Choose either the fictional or the sociological approach, and explain why it captures your interests more.

E. L. DOCTOROW (b. 1931)

The Importance of Fiction

1986

When I was a boy everyone in my family was a good storyteller, my mother and father, my brother, my aunts and uncles and grandparents; all of them were people to whom interesting things seemed to happen. The events they spoke of were of a daily, ordinary sort, but when narrated or acted out they took on great importance and excitement as I listened.

Of course, when you bring love to the person you are listening to, the story has to be interesting, and in one sense the task of a professional writer who publishes books is to overcome the terrible loss of not being someone the reader knows and loves.

But apart from that, the people whose stories I heard as a child must have had a very firm view of themselves in the world. They must have been strong enough as presences in their own minds to trust that people would listen to them when they spoke.

I know now that everyone in the world tells stories. Relatively few people are given to mathematics or physics, but narrative seems to be within everyone's grasp, perhaps because it comes of the nature of language itself.

The moment you have nouns and verbs and prepositions, the moment you have subjects and objects, you have stories.

For the longest time there would have been nothing but stories, and no sharper distinction between what was real and what was made up than between what was spoken and what was sung. Religious arousal and scientific discourse, simple urgent communication and poetry, all burned together in the intense perception of a metaphor — that, for instance, the sun was a god's chariot driven across the heavens.

Stories were as important to survival as a spear or a hoe. They were the memory of the knowledge of the dead. They gave counsel. They connected the visible to the invisible. They distributed the suffering so that it could be borne.

In our era, even as we separate the functions of language, knowing when we speak scientifically we are not speaking poetically, and when we speak theologically we are not speaking the way we do to each other in our houses, and even as our surveys demand statistics, and our courts demand evidence, and our hypotheses demand proof — our minds are still structured for storytelling.

What we call fiction is the ancient way of knowing, the total discourse that antedates all the special vocabularies of modern intelligence.

The professional writer of fiction is a conservative who cherishes the ultimate structures of the human mind. He cultivates within himself the universal disposition to think in terms of conflict and its resolution, and in terms of character undergoing events, and of the outcome of events being not at all sure, and therefore suspenseful — the whole thing done, moreover, from a confidence of narrative that is grounded in our brains as surely as the innate talent to construe the world grammatically.

The fiction writer, looking around him, understands the homage a modern up-to-date world of nonfiction specialists pays to his craft — even as it isolates him and tells him he is a liar. Newsweeklies present the events of the world as installments in a serial melodrama. Weather reports on television are constructed with exact attention to conflict (high-pressure areas clashing with lows), suspense (the climax of tomorrow's prediction coming after the commercial), and the consistency of voice (the personality of the weathercaster). The marketing and advertising of product-facts is unquestionably a fictional enterprise. As is every government's representations of its activities. And modern psychology, with its concepts of *sublimation, repression, identity crisis, complex,* and so on, proposes the interchangeable parts for the stories of all of us; in this sense it is the industrialization of storytelling.

But nothing is as good at fiction as fiction. It is the most ancient way of knowing but also the most modern, managing when it's done right to burn all the functions of language back together into powerful fused revelation. Because it is total discourse it is ultimate discourse. It excludes nothing. It will express from the depth and range of its sources truths that no sermon or experiment or news report can begin to apprehend. It will tell you without shame what people do with their bodies and think with their minds. It will deal evenhandedly with their microbes or their intuitions. It will know their nightmares and blinding moments of moral crisis. You will experience love, if it so chooses, or starvation or drowning or dropping through space or holding a hot pistol in your hand with the police pounding on the door. This is the way it is, it will say, this is what it feels like.

Fiction is democratic, it reasserts the authority of the single mind to make and remake the world. By its independence from all institutions, from the family to the government, and with no responsibility to defend their hypocrisy or murderousness, it is a valuable resource and instrument of survival.

Fiction gives counsel. It connects the present with the past, and the visible with the invisible. It distributes the suffering. It says we must compose ourselves in our stories in order to exist. It says if we don't do it, someone else will do it for us.

From "Ultimate Discourse" in *Esquire*

Considerations

1. What does Doctorow mean when he describes fiction as the "ultimate discourse"? What is the relationship of fiction to theology, history, and science? How is fiction an "ancient way of knowing"?
2. Why is fiction a "valuable resource and instrument of survival"? Explain why you agree or disagree with this assessment of storytelling.

KENT THOMPSON (b. 1936)

A Short Short Story: "Unreeling" 1988

Helen has left me and moved back to 1930. She is singing in a log-cabin Roadhouse out on old Highway 42. Almost nobody travels out that way anymore. She wears an ivory colored evening gown and has marcelled her hair. Her lover is the owner who sometimes gives ballroom-dancing exhibitions with her. The patrons are kids who stare in wonder — not, as Helen and her lover believe, at the grace of the old ballroom dances or the sweetness of the lachrymose songs — but at the audacity of the two of them, daring to live outside their allotted time. I sometimes go there and contribute to the decor by sitting at a table wearing a fedora. But I think I am slipping out of her memory, and will disappear as soon as I am forgotten.

From *Open Windows: Canadian Short Short Stories*

Considerations

1. This complete story appears in a collection of very brief stories known in Canada as "postcard fiction" or "quick fiction." Does it satisfy your sense of what a short story is? Explain.
2. Try applying the Questions for Responsive Reading (p. 362) to this story. Which questions seem most relevant to you? Do they make the story seem more or less of an achievement?
3. Write your own postcard story — one that attempts to offer an open window on some aspect of life.

URSULA K. LE GUIN (b. 1929)

On Conflict in Fiction 1987

From looking at manuals used in college writing courses, and from listening to participants in writing workshops, I gather that it is a generally received idea that a story is the relation of a conflict, that without conflict there is no plot, that narrative and conflict are inseparable.

Now, that something or other has to happen in a story, I agree (in very general, broad terms; there are, after all, excellent stories in which everything has happened, or is about to happen). But that what happens in a story can be defined as, limited to, conflict, I doubt. And that to assert the dependence of narrative on conflict is to uphold Social Darwinism in all its glory, I sadly suspect.

Existence as struggle, life as a battle, everything in terms of defeat and victory: Man versus Nature, Man versus Woman, Black versus White, Good versus Evil, God versus Devil — a sort of apartheid view of existence, and of literature. What a pitiful impoverishment of the complexity of both!

In E. M. Forster's famous definition (in *Aspects of the Novel*), this is a story:

> The King died and then the Queen died.

And this is a plot:

> The King died and then the Queen died of grief.

In that charming and extremely useful example, where is the "conflict"? Who is pitted against what? Who wins?

Is the first book of *Genesis* a story? Where is the "conflict"?

Has *War and Peace* a plot? Can that plot be in any useful or meaningful way reduced to "conflict," or a series of "conflicts"?

People are cross-grained, aggressive, and full of trouble, the storytellers tell us; people fight themselves and one another, and their stories are full of their struggles. But to say that that *is* the story is to use one aspect of existence, conflict, to include and submerge other aspects which it does not include and does not comprehend.

Romeo and Juliet is a story of the conflict between two families, and its plot involves the conflict of two individuals with those families. Is that all it involves? Isn't *Romeo and Juliet* about something else, and isn't it the something else that makes the otherwise trivial tale of a feud into a tragedy?

I for one will be glad when this gladiatorial view of fiction has run its course.

From *Dancing at the Edge of the World: Thoughts on Words, Women, Places*

Considerations

1. What do you think is Le Guin's major objection to discussions of fiction that insist "narrative and conflict are inseparable"? Explain why you agree or disagree with her.
2. In a brief essay try to answer Le Guin's questions about "The King died and then the Queen died of grief." Can you identify a conflict in this "plot"?
3. Consider how practitioners of the various "Critical Strategies for Reading" in Chapter 32 (formalist, biographical, psychological, historical, Marxist, feminist, mythological, reader-response, and deconstructionist) find different kinds of conflicts in stories. Choose a story in this anthology and describe how any three of these approaches emphasize different conflicts in the story. Which approach do you find most revealing and helpful for making sense of the story?

POETRY

12. Reading Poetry

READING POETRY RESPONSIVELY

Perhaps the best way to begin reading poetry responsively is not to allow yourself to be intimidated by it. Come to it, initially at least, the way you might listen to a song on the radio. You probably listen to a song several times before you hear it all, before you have a sense of how it works, where it's going, and how it gets there. You don't worry about analyzing a song when you listen to it, even though after repeated experiences with it you know and anticipate a favorite part and know, on some level, why it works for you. Give yourself a chance to respond to poetry. The hardest work has already been done by the poet, so all you need to do at the start is listen for the pleasure produced by the poet's arrangement of words.

Try reading the following poem aloud. Read it aloud before you read it silently. You may stumble once or twice, but you'll make sense of it if you pay attention to its punctuation and don't stop at the end of every line where there is no punctuation. The title gives you an initial sense of what the poem is about.

MARGE PIERCY (b. 1934)

The Secretary Chant 1973

My hips are a desk.
From my ears hang
chains of paper clips.
Rubber bands form my hair.
My breasts are wells of mimeograph ink.
My feet bear casters.
Buzz. Click.

My head is a badly organized file.
My head is a switchboard
where crossed lines crackle.
Press my fingers
and in my eyes appear
credit and debit.
Zing. Tinkle.
My navel is a reject button.
From my mouth issue canceled reams.
Swollen, heavy, rectangular
I am about to be delivered
of a baby
Xerox machine.
File me under W
because I wonce
was
a woman.

What is your response to this secretary's chant? The point is simple enough — she feels dehumanized by her office functions — but the pleasures are manifold. Piercy makes the speaker's voice sound mechanical by using short bursts of sound and by having her make repetitive, flat, matter-of-fact statements ("My breasts . . . My feet . . . My head . . . My navel"). "The Secretary Chant" makes a serious statement about how such women are reduced to functionaries. The point is made, however, with humor since we are asked to visualize the misappropriation of the secretary's body — her identity — as it is transformed into little more than a piece of office equipment, which seems to be breaking down in the final lines, when we learn that she "wonce/ was/ a woman." Is there the slightest hint of something subversive in this misspelling of "wonce"? Maybe so, but the humor is clear enough, particularly if you try to make a drawing of what this dehumanized secretary has become.

The next poem creates a different kind of mood. Think about the title, "Those Winter Sundays," before you begin reading the poem. What associations do you have with winter Sundays? What emotions does the phrase evoke in you?

ROBERT HAYDEN (1913–1980)

Those Winter Sundays **1962**

Sundays too my father got up early
and put his clothes on in the blueblack cold,
then with cracked hands that ached
from labor in the weekday weather made
banked fires blaze. No one ever thanked him.

I'd wake and hear the cold splintering, breaking,
When the rooms were warm, he'd call,
and slowly I would rise and dress,
fearing the chronic angers of that house,

Speaking indifferently to him,
who had driven out the cold
and polished my good shoes as well.
What did I know, what did I know
of love's austere and lonely offices?

Did the poem match the feelings you have about winter Sundays? Either way your response can be useful in reading the poem. For most of us Sundays are days at home; they might be cozy and pleasant experiences or they might be dull and depressing. Whatever they are, Sundays are more evocative than, say, Tuesdays. Hayden uses that response to call forth a sense of missed opportunity in the poem. The person who reflects on those winter Sundays didn't know until much later how much he had to thank his father for "love's austere and lonely offices." This is a poem about a cold past and a present reverence for his father — elements brought together by the phrase "Winter Sundays." *His* father? You may have noticed that the poem doesn't use a masculine pronoun; hence the voice could be a woman's. Does the sex of the voice make any difference to your reading? Would it make any difference about which details are included or what language is used?

What is most important about your initial readings of a poem is that you ask questions. If you read responsively, you'll find yourself asking all kinds of questions about the words, descriptions, sounds, and structures of a poem. The specifics of those questions will be generated by the particular poem. We don't, for example, ask how humor is achieved in "Those Winter Sundays" because there is none, but it is worth asking what kind of tone is established by the description of "the chronic angers of that house." The remaining chapters in this part will help you to formulate and answer questions about a variety of specific elements in poetry, such as speaker, image, metaphor, symbol, rhyme, and rhythm. For the moment, however, read the following poem several times and note your response at different points in the poem. Then write down a half dozen questions or so about what produces your response to the poem. In order to answer questions it's best to know first what the questions are, and that's what the rest of this chapter is about.

JOHN UPDIKE (b. 1932)

Dog's Death 1969

She must have been kicked unseen or brushed by a car.
Too young to know much, she was beginning to learn
To use the newspapers spread on the kitchen floor
And to win, wetting there, the words, "Good dog! Good dog!"

We thought her shy malaise was a shot reaction.
The autopsy disclosed a rupture in her liver.
As we teased her with play, blood was filling her skin
And her heart was learning to lie down forever.

Monday morning, as the children were noisily fed
And sent to school, she crawled beneath the youngest's bed.
We found her twisted and limp but still alive.
In the car to the vet's, on my lap, she tried

To bite my hand and died. I stroked her warm fur
And my wife called in a voice imperious with tears.
Though surrounded by love that would have upheld her,
Nevertheless she sank and, stiffening, disappeared.

Back home, we found that in the night her frame,
Drawing near to dissolution, had endured the shame
Of diarrhoea and had dragged across the floor
To a newspaper carelessly left there. *Good dog.*

Here's a simple question to get started with your own questions: What would its effect have been if Updike had titled the poem "Good Dog" instead of "Dog's Death"?

THE PLEASURE OF WORDS

The impulse to create and appreciate poetry is as basic to human experience as language itself. Although no one can point to the precise origins of poetry, it is one of the most ancient of the arts, because it has existed ever since human beings discovered pleasure in language. The tribal ceremonies of peoples without written language suggest evidence that the earliest primitive cultures incorporated rhythmic patterns of words into their rituals. These chants, very likely accompanied by the music of a simple beat and the dance of a measured step, expressed what people regarded as significant and memorable in their lives. They echoed the concerns of the chanters and the listeners by chronicling acts of bravery, fearsome foes, natural disasters, mysterious events, births, deaths, and whatever else brought people pain or pleasure, bewilderment or revelation. Later cultures, such as the ancient Greeks, made poetry an integral part of religion.

Thus, from its very beginnings, poetry has been associated with what has mattered most to people. These concerns — whether natural or supernatural — can, of course, be expressed without vivid images, rhythmic patterns, and pleasing sounds, but human beings have always sensed a magic in words that goes beyond rational, logical understanding. Poetry is not simply a method of communication; it is a unique kind of experience in itself.

What is special about poetry? What makes it valuable? Why should we read it? How is reading it different from reading prose? To begin with, poetry pervades our world in a variety of forms, ranging from advertising jingles to song lyrics. These may seem to be a long way from the chants heard around a primitive camp fire, but they serve some of the same purposes. Like poems printed in a magazine or book, primitive chants, catchy jingles, and popular songs attempt to stir the imagination through the carefully measured use of words.

Although reading poetry usually makes more demands than does the kind of reading used to skim a magazine or newspaper, the appreciation of poetry comes naturally enough to anyone who enjoys playing with words. Play is an important element of poetry. Consider, for example, how the following words appeal to the children who gleefully chant them in playgrounds.

> I scream, you scream
> We all scream
> For ice cream.

These lines are an exuberant evocation of the joy of ice cream. Indeed, chanting the words turns out to be as pleasurable as eating ice cream. In poetry, the expression of the idea is as important as the idea expressed.

But is "I scream . . ." poetry? Some poets and literary critics would say that it certainly is one kind of poem, because the children who chant it experience some of the pleasures of poetry in its measured beat and repeated sounds. However, other poets and critics would define poetry more narrowly and insist, for a variety of reasons (some of which are included among the definitions in Chapter 23), that this isn't true poetry but merely ***doggerel,*** a term used for lines whose subject matter is trite and whose rhythm and sounds are monotonously heavy-handed.

Although probably no one would argue that "I scream . . ." is a great poem, it does contain some poetic elements that appeal, at the very least, to children. Does that make it poetry? The answer depends on one's definition, but poetry has a way of breaking loose from definitions. Because there are nearly as many definitions of poetry as there are poets, Edwin Arlington Robinson's succinct observations are useful: "poetry has two outstanding characteristics. One is that it is undefinable. The other is that it is eventually unmistakable."

This comment places more emphasis on how a poem affects a reader than on how a poem is defined. By characterizing poetry as "undefinable,"

Robinson acknowledges that it can include many different purposes, subjects, emotions, styles, and forms. What effect does the following poem have on you?

WILLIAM HATHAWAY (b. 1944)

Oh, Oh 1982

My girl and I amble a country lane,
moo cows chomping daisies, our own
sweet saliva green with grass stems.
"Look, look," she says at the crossing,
"the choo-choo's light is on." And sure
enough, right smack dab in the middle
of maple dappled summer sunlight
is the lit headlight — so funny.
An arm waves to us from the black window.
We wave gaily to the arm. "When I hear
trains at night I dream of being president,"
I say dreamily. "And me first lady," she
says loyally. So when the last boxcars,
named after wonderful, faraway places,
and the caboose chuckle by we look
eagerly to the road ahead. And there,
poised and growling, are fifty Hell's Angels.

Hathaway's poem serves as a convenient reminder that poetry can be full of surprises. Even on a first reading there is no mistaking the emotional reversal created by the last few words of this poem. With the exception of the final line, the poem's language conjures up an idyllic picture of a young couple taking a pleasant walk down a country lane. Contented as "moo cows," they taste the sweetness of the grass, hear peaceful country sounds, and are dazzled by "dappled summer sunlight." Their future together seems to be all optimism as they anticipate "wonderful, faraway places" and the "road ahead." Full of confidence, this couple, like the reader, is unprepared for the shock to come. When we see those "fifty Hell's Angels," we are confronted with something like a bucket of cold water in the face.

But even though our expectations are abruptly and powerfully reversed, we are finally invited to view the entire episode from a safe distance — the distance provided by the delightful humor in this poem. After all, how seriously can we take a poem that is titled "Oh, Oh"? The poet has his way with us, but we are brought in on the joke too. The terror takes on comic proportions as the innocent couple is confronted by no fewer than *fifty* Hell's Angels. This is the kind of raucous overkill that informs a short animated film produced some years ago titled *Bambi Meets Godzilla:* you might not have seen it, but you know how it ends. The poem's good humor comes through when we realize how pathetically inadequate the response of "Oh, Oh" is to the circumstances.

As you can see, reading a description of what happens in a poem is not the same as experiencing a poem. The exuberance of "I scream . . ." and the surprise of Hathaway's "Oh, Oh" are in the hearing or reading rather than in the retelling. A ***paraphrase*** is a prose restatement of the central ideas of a poem in your own language. Consider the difference between the following poem and the paraphrase that follows it. What is missing from the paraphrase?

ROBERT FRANCIS (1901–1987)

Catch 1950

Two boys uncoached are tossing a poem together,
Overhand, underhand, backhand, sleight of hand, every hand,
Teasing with attitudes, latitudes, interludes, altitudes,
High, make him fly off the ground for it, low, make him stoop,
Make him scoop it up, make him as-almost-as-possible miss it,
Fast, let him sting from it, now, now fool him slowly,
Anything, everything tricky, risky, nonchalant,
Anything under the sun to outwit the prosy,
Over the tree and the long sweet cadence down,
Over his head, make him scramble to pick up the meaning,
And now, like a posy, a pretty one plump in his hands.

Paraphrase: A poet's relationship to a reader is similar to a game of catch. The poem, like a ball, should be pitched in a variety of ways to challenge and create interest. Boredom and predictability must be avoided if the game is to be engaging and satisfying.

A paraphrase can help us achieve a clearer understanding of a poem, but, unlike a poem, it misses all the sport and fun. It is the poem that "outwit[s] the prosy," because the poem serves as an example of what it suggests poetry should be. Moreover, the two players — the poet and the reader — are "uncoached." They know how the game is played, but their expectations do not preclude spontaneity and creativity or their ability to surprise and be surprised. The solid pleasure of the workout — of reading poetry — is the satisfaction derived from exercising your imagination and intellect.

That pleasure is worth emphasizing. Poetry uses language to move and delight even when it includes a cast of fifty Hell's Angels. The pleasure is in having the poem work its spell on us. For that to happen, it is best to relax and enjoy poetry rather than worrying about definitions of it. Pay attention to what the poet throws you. We read poems for emotional and intellectual discovery — to feel and experience something about the world and ourselves. The ideas in poetry — what can be paraphrased in prose — are important, but the real value of a poem consists in the words that work their magic by allowing us to feel, see, and be more than we were before. Perhaps the best way to approach a poem is similar to what Francis's "Catch" implies: expect to be surprised; stay on your toes; and concentrate on the delivery.

Write a paraphrase of this next poem. How does your prose statement differ from the effects produced by the language in the poem? Which descriptions seem particularly vivid?

CONRAD HILBERRY (b. 1928)

Tongue

1980

He did not mean to test the cold
or his own daring. He did it idly,
not thinking, as he might suck
a little solace from his thumb.

Alone at recess, watching three boys
wrestle in the snow, he touched
his tongue to the cyclone fence
and it froze. The cold clanged shut.

With his fingers, he pulled at the tongue
as if it were a leech, sucking
the blood of his leg. But the ice held.
In panic, he tore away his mistake,

tore loose his tongue, leaving skin
like patches of rust on the metal.
What could he do with the torn and swollen
tongue, with shame that tasted like blood?

In school, he hid his mouth behind
his hands. He swallowed. He swallowed.

As much as this poem is painfully vivid, it provides pleasure for a reader because it renders the boy's pain and shame so convincingly.

Poets often remind us that beauty can be found in unexpected places. What is it that Elizabeth Bishop finds so beautiful about the "battered" fish she describes in the following poem?

ELIZABETH BISHOP (1911–1979)

The Fish

1946

I caught a tremendous fish
and held him beside the boat
half out of water, with my hook
fast in a corner of his mouth.
He didn't fight.
He hadn't fought at all.
He hung a grunting weight,
battered and venerable
and homely. Here and there
his brown skin hung in strips
like ancient wall-paper,
and its pattern of darker brown
was like wall-paper:
shapes like full-blown roses
stained and lost through age.
He was speckled with barnacles,
fine rosettes of lime,
and infested
with tiny white sea-lice,
and underneath two or three
rags of green weed hung down.
While his gills were breathing in
the terrible oxygen
— the frightening gills,
fresh and crisp with blood,
that can cut so badly —
I thought of the coarse white flesh
packed in like feathers,
the big bones and the little bones,
the dramatic reds and blacks
of his shiny entrails,
and the pink swim-bladder
like a big peony.
I looked into his eyes
which were far larger than mine
but shallower, and yellowed,
the irises backed and packed
with tarnished tinfoil
seen through the lenses
of old scratched isinglass.
They shifted a little, but not
to return my stare.
— It was more like the tipping
of an object toward the light.
I admired his sullen face,

the mechanism of his jaw,
and then I saw
that from his lower lip
— if you could call it a lip —
grim, wet, and weapon-like,
hung five old pieces of fish-line,
or four and a wire leader
with the swivel still attached,
with all their five big hooks
grown firmly in his mouth.
A green line, frayed at the end
where he broke it, two heavier lines,
and a fine black thread
still crimped from the strain and snap
when it broke and he got away.
Like medals with their ribbons
frayed and wavering,
a five-haired beard of wisdom
trailing from his aching jaw.
I stared and stared
and victory filled up
the little rented boat,
from the pool of bilge
where oil had spread a rainbow
around the rusted engine
to the bailer rusted orange,
the sun-cracked thwarts,
the oarlocks on their strings,
the gunnels — until everything
was rainbow, rainbow, rainbow!
And I let the fish go.

Considerations

1. Which lines in this poem provide especially vivid details of the fish? What makes these descriptions effective?
2. How is the fish characterized? Is it simply a weak victim because it "didn't fight"?
3. Comment on lines 65–76. In what sense has "victory filled up" the boat, given that the speaker finally lets the fish go?

The speaker in Bishop's "The Fish" ends on a triumphantly joyful note. The ***speaker*** is the voice used by the author in the poem; like the narrator in a work of fiction, the speaker is often a created identity rather than the author's actual self. The two should not automatically be equated. Contrast the attitude toward life of the speaker in "The Fish" with that of the speaker in the following poem.

PHILIP LARKIN (1922–1985)

A Study of Reading Habits 1964

When getting my nose in a book
Cured most things short of school,
It was worth ruining my eyes
To know I could still keep cool,
And deal out the old right hook
To dirty dogs twice my size.

Later, with inch-thick specs,
Evil was just my lark:
Me and my cloak and fangs
Had ripping times in the dark.
The women I clubbed with sex!
I broke them up like meringues.

Don't read much now: the dude
Who lets the girl down before
The hero arrives, the chap
Who's yellow and keeps the store,
Seem far too familiar. Get stewed:
Books are a load of crap.

What the speaker sees and describes in "The Fish" is close if not identical to Bishop's own vision and voice. The joyful response to the fish is clearly shared by the speaker and the poet, between whom there is little or no distance. In "A Study of Reading Habits," however, Larkin distances himself from a speaker whose sensibilities he does not share. The poet — and many readers — might identify with the reading habits described by the speaker in the first twelve lines, but Larkin uses the last six lines to criticize the speaker's attitude toward life as well as reading. The speaker recalls in lines 1–6 how as a schoolboy he identified with the hero, whose virtuous strength always triumphed over "dirty dogs," and in lines 7–12 he recounts how his schoolboy fantasies were transformed by adolescence into a fascination with violence and sex. This description of early reading habits is pleasantly amusing, because most readers of popular fiction will probably recall having moved through similar stages, but at the end of the poem the speaker provides more information about himself than he intends to.

As an adult the speaker has lost interest in reading, because it is no longer an escape from his own disappointed life. Instead of identifying with heroes or villains, he finds himself identifying with minor characters who are irresponsible and cowardly. Reading is now a reminder of his failures, so he turns to alcohol. His solution, to "Get stewed," because "Books are a load of crap," is obviously self-destructive. The speaker is ultimately exposed by Larkin as someone who never grew beyond fantasies. Getting drunk is consistent with the speaker's immature reading habits. Unlike the speaker, the poet understands that life is often distorted by escapist fantasies, whether through a steady diet of popular fiction or through alcohol. The speaker in this poem, then, is not Larkin but a created identity whose voice is filled with disillusionment and delusion.

The problem with Larkin's speaker is that he misreads books as well as his own life. Reading means nothing to him unless it serves as an escape from himself. It is not surprising that Larkin has him read fiction rather than poetry, because poetry places an especially heavy emphasis upon language. Fiction, indeed any kind of writing, including essays and drama, relies upon carefully chosen and arranged words, but poetry does so to an even greater extent. Notice, for example, how Larkin's deft use of trite expressions and slang characterizes the speaker so that his language reveals nearly as much about his dreary life as what he says. Larkin's speaker would have no use for poetry.

What is "unmistakable" in poetry (to use Robinson's term again) is its intense, concentrated use of language — its emphasis on individual words to convey meanings, experiences, emotions, and effects. Poets never simply process words; they savor them. Words in poems frequently create their own tastes, textures, scents, sounds, and shapes. They often seem more sensuous than ordinary language, and readers usually sense that a word has been hefted before making its way into a poem. Although poems are crafted differently from the ways a painting, sculpture, or musical composition is created, in each form of art the creator delights in the medium. Poetry is carefully orchestrated so that the words work together as elements in a structure to sustain close, repeated readings. The words are chosen to interact with one another in order to create the maximum desired effect, whether the purpose is to capture a mood or feeling, create a vivid experience, express a point of view, narrate a story, or portray a character.

Here is a poem that looks quite different from most ***verse,*** a term used for lines composed in a measured rhythmical pattern, which are often, but not necessarily, rhymed.

ROBERT MORGAN (b. 1944)

Mountain Graveyard 1979

for the author of "Slow Owls"

Spore Prose

stone notes
slate tales
sacred cedars
heart earth
asleep please
hated death

Though unconventional in its appearance, this is unmistakably poetry because of its concentrated use of language. The poem demonstrates how serious play with words can lead to some remarkable discoveries. At first glance "Mountain Graveyard" may seem intimidating. What, after all, does this list of words add up to? How is it in any sense a poetic use of language? But if the words are examined closely, it is not difficult to see how they work. The wordplay here is literally in the form of a game. Morgan uses a series of ***anagrams*** (words made from the letters of other words, such as *read* and *dare*) to evoke feelings about death. "Mountain Graveyard" is one of several poems that Morgan has called "Spore Prose" (another anagram) because he finds in individual words the seeds of poetry. He wrote the poem in honor of the fiftieth birthday of another poet, Jonathan Williams, the author of "Slow Owls," whose title is also an anagram.

The title, "Mountain Graveyard," indicates the poem's setting, which is also the context in which the individual words in the poem interact to provide a larger meaning. Morgan's discovery of the words on the stones of a graveyard is more than just clever. The observations he makes among the silent graves go beyond the curious pleasure a reader experiences in finding the words *sacred cedars,* referring to evergreens common in cemeteries, to consist of the same letters. The surprise and delight of realizing the connection between heart and earth is tempered by the more sober recognition that everyone's story ultimately ends in the ground. The hope that the dead are merely asleep is expressed with a plea that is answered grimly by a hatred of death's finality.

Little is told in this poem. There is no way of knowing who is buried or who is looking at the graves, but the emotions of sadness, hope, and rage, are unmistakable — and are conveyed in fewer than half the words of this sentence. Morgan takes words that initially appear to be a dead, prosaic list and energizes their meanings through imaginative juxtapositions.

The following poem also involves a startling discovery about words. With the peculiar title "l(a," the poem cannot be read aloud, so there is no sound, but is there sense, a ***theme,*** a central idea or meaning, in the poem?

E. E. CUMMINGS (1894–1962)

l(a 1958

l(a

le
af
fa

ll

s)
one
l

iness

Considerations

1. Discuss the connection between what appears inside and outside the parentheses in this poem.
2. What does Cummings draw attention to by breaking up the words? How do this strategy and the poem's overall shape contribute to its theme?
3. Which seems more important in this poem — what is expressed, or the way it is expressed?

Although "Mountain Graveyard" and "l(a" do not resemble the kind of verse that readers might recognize immediately as poetry on a page, both are actually a very common type of poem, called the ***lyric,*** usually a brief poem that expresses the personal emotions and thoughts of a single speaker. Lyrics are often written in the first person but sometimes — as in "Spore Prose" and "l(a" — no speaker is specified. Lyrics present a subjective mood, emotion, or idea. Very often they are about love or death, but almost any subject or experience that evokes some intense emotional response can be found in lyrics. In addition to brevity and emotional intensity, lyrics are also frequently characterized by their musical qualities. The word *lyric* derives from the Greek word *lyre,* meaning a musical instrument that originally accompanied the singing of a lyric. Lyric poems can be organized in a variety of ways, such as the sonnet, elegy, and ode (see Chapter 19), but it is enough to point out here that lyrics are an extremely popular kind of poetry with writers and readers.

The following anonymous lyric was found in a sixteenth-century manuscript.

ANONYMOUS

Western Wind

c. 1500

Western wind, when wilt thou blow,
The small rain down can rain?
Christ, if my love were in my arms,
And I in my bed again!

This speaker's intense longing for his lover is characteristic of lyric poetry. He impatiently addresses the western wind that brings spring to England and could make it possible for him to be reunited with the woman he loves. We do not know the details of these lovers' lives, because this poem focuses on the speaker's emotion. We do not learn why the lovers are apart or if they will be together again. We don't even know if the speaker is a man. But those issues are not really important. The poetry gives us a feeling rather than a story.

A poem that tells a story is called a ***narrative poem.*** Narrative poetry may be short or very long. An ***epic,*** for example, is a long narrative poem on a serious subject chronicling heroic deeds and important events. Among the most famous epics are Homer's *Iliad* and *Odyssey,* the Old English *Beowulf,* Dante's *Divine Comedy,* and John Milton's *Paradise Lost.* More typically, however, narrative poems are considerably shorter, such as the following poem, which tells the story of a child's memory of her father.

REGINA BARRECA (b. 1957)

Nighttime Fires 1986

When I was five in Louisville
we drove to see nighttime fires. Piled seven of us,
all pajamas and running noses, into the Olds,
drove fast toward smoke. It was after my father
lost his job, so not getting up in the morning
gave him time: awake past midnight, he read old newspapers
with no news, tried crosswords until he split the pencil
between his teeth, mad. When he heard
the wolf whine of the siren, he woke my mother,
and she pushed and shoved
us all into waking. Once roused we longed for burnt wood
and a smell of flames high into the pines. My old man liked
driving to rich neighborhoods best, swearing in a good mood
as he followed fire engines that snaked like dragons
and split the silent streets. It was festival, carnival.

If there were a Cadillac or any car
in a curved driveway, my father smiled a smile
from a secret, brittle heart.
His face lit up in the heat given off by destruction
like something was being made, or was being set right.
I bent my head back to see where sparks
ate up the sky. My father who never held us
would take my hand and point to falling cinders that
covered the ground like snow, or, excited, show us
the swollen collapse of a staircase. My mother
watched my father, not the house. She was happy
only when we were ready to go, when it was finally over
and nothing else could burn.
Driving home, she would sleep in the front seat
as we huddled behind. I could see his quiet face in the
rearview mirror, eyes like hallways filled with smoke.

This narrative poem could have been a short story if the poet had wanted to say more about the "brittle heart" of this unemployed man whose daughter so vividly remembers the desperate pleasure he took in watching fire consume other people's property. Indeed, a reading of Faulkner's short story "Barn Burning" (p. 66) suggests how such a character can be further developed and how his child responds to him. The similarities between Faulkner's angry character and the poem's father, whose "eyes [are] like hallways filled with smoke," are coincidental, but the characters' sense of "something . . . being set right" by flames is worth comparing. Although we do not know everything about this man and his family, we have a much firmer sense of their story than we do of the story of the couple in "Western Wind."

Although narrative poetry is still written, short stories and novels have largely replaced the long narrative poem. Lyric poems tend to be the predominant type of poetry today. Regardless of whether a poem is a narrative or a lyric, however, the strategies for reading it are somewhat different from those for reading prose. Try these suggestions for approaching poetry.

SUGGESTIONS FOR APPROACHING POETRY

1. Assume that it will be necessary to read a poem more than once. Give yourself a chance to become familiar with what the poem has to offer. Like a piece of music, a poem becomes more pleasurable with each encounter.
2. Do pay attention to the title; it will often provide a helpful context for the poem and serve as an introduction to it. Larkin's "A Study of Reading Habits" is precisely what its title describes.
3. As you read the poem for the first time, avoid becoming entangled in words or lines that you don't understand. Instead, give yourself a chance to take in the entire poem before attempting to resolve problems encountered along the way.
4. On a second reading, identify any words or passages that you don't understand. Look up words you don't know; these might include names, places, historical and mythical references, or anything else that is unfamiliar to you.
5. Read the poem aloud (or perhaps have a friend read it to you). You'll probably discover that some puzzling passages suddenly fall into place when you hear them. You'll find that nothing helps, though, if the poem is read in an artificial, exaggerated manner. Read in as natural a voice as possible, with slight pauses at line breaks. Silent reading is preferable to imposing a te-tumpty-te-tum reading on a good poem.
6. Read the punctuation. Poems use punctuation marks — in addition to the space on the page — as signals for readers. Be especially

careful not to assume that the end of a line marks the end of a sentence, unless it is concluded by punctuation. Consider, for example, the opening lines of Hathaway's "Oh, Oh."

> My girl and I amble a country lane,
> moo cows chomping daisies, our own
> sweet saliva green with grass stems.

Line 2 makes little or no sense if a reader stops after "own." Keeping track of the subjects and verbs will help you find your way among the sentences.

7. Paraphrase the poem to determine whether you understand what happens in it. As you work through each line of the poem, a paraphrase will help you to see which words or passages need further attention.
8. Try to get a sense of who is speaking and what the setting or situation is. Don't assume that the speaker is the author; often it is a created character.
9. Assume that each element in the poem has a purpose. Try to explain how the elements of the poem work together.
10. Be generous. Be willing to entertain perspectives, values, experiences, and subjects that you might not agree with or approve. Even if you loathe baseball, you should be able to comprehend its imaginative use in Francis's "Catch."
11. Try developing a coherent approach to the poem that helps you to shape a discussion of the text. See Chapter 32, Critical Strategies for Reading (p. 1777), to review formalist, biographical, historical, psychological, feminist, and other possible critical approaches.
12. Don't expect to produce a definitive reading. Many poems do not resolve all the ideas, issues, or tensions in them, and so it is not always possible to drive their meaning into an absolute corner. Your reading will explore rather than define the poem. Poems are not trophies to be stuffed and mounted. They're usually more elusive. And don't be afraid that a close reading will damage the poem. Poems aren't hurt when we analyze them; instead, they come alive as we experience them and put into words what we discover through them.

A list of more specific questions employing the literary terms and concepts discussed in the following chapters begins on page 742. That list, like the suggestions just made, raises issues and questions that can help you to read just about any poem closely. These strategies should be a useful means for getting inside poems to understand how they work. Furthermore, because reading poetry inevitably increases sensitivity to language, you're likely to find yourself a better reader of words in any form — whether in a novel, a newspaper editorial, an advertisement, a political speech, or a conversation — after having studied poetry. In short, many of the reading skills that make poetry accessible also open up the world you inhabit.

You'll probably find some poems amusing or sad, some fierce or tender, and some fascinating or dull. You may find, too, some poems that will get inside you. Their kinds of insights — the poet's and yours — are what Emily Dickinson had in mind when she defined poetry this way: "If I read a book and it makes my whole body so cold no fire can ever warm me, I know that it is poetry. If I feel physically as if the top of my head were taken off, I know that it is poetry." Dickinson's response may be more intense than most — poetry was, after all, at the center of her life — but you too might find yourself moved by poems in unexpected ways. In any case, as Edwin Arlington Robinson knew, poetry is, to an alert and sensitive reader, "eventually unmistakable."

POETRY IN POPULAR FORMS

Before you try out these strategies for reading on a few more poems, it is worth acknowledging that the verse which enjoys the widest readership appears not in collections, magazines, or even anthologies for students, but in greeting cards. A significant amount of the personal daily mail delivered in the United States consists of greeting cards. That represents millions of lines of verse going by us on the street and in planes over our heads. These verses share some similarities with the poetry included in this anthology, but there are also important differences that indicate the need for reading serious poetry closely rather than casually.

The popularity of greeting cards is easy to explain: just as many of us have neither the time nor the talent to make gifts for birthdays, weddings, anniversaries, graduations, Valentine's Day, Mother's Day, and other holidays, we are unlikely to write personal messages when cards conveniently say them for us. Though impersonal, cards are efficient and convey an important message no matter what the occasion for them: I care. These greetings are rarely serious poetry; they are not written to be. Nevertheless, they demonstrate the impulse in our culture to generate and receive poetry.

In a handbook for greeting-card free-lancers, a writer and past editor of such verse began with this advice:

> Once you determine what you want to say — and in this regard it is best to stick to one basic idea — you must choose your words to do several things at the same time:
>
> 1. Your idea must be expressed as a complete idea; it must have a beginning, a middle, and an end.
> 2. There must be coherence in your verse. Every line must be linked logically and smoothly with its neighbors.

3. Your expressions, as stressed before, must be conversational. High-flown language rarely comes off successfully in greeting card writing.
4. You must write with emphasis — and something else: enthusiasm. It's necessary to create interest in that all-important first line. From that point on, writing your verse is a matter of developing your idea and bringing it to a peak of emphasis in the last line. Occasionally you will find that you have shot your wad too early in the verse, and whatever you say after that point sounds like an afterthought.
5. You must do all of the above and at the same time make everything come out right in the meter-and-rhyme department.[1]

This advice is followed by a list of approximately fifty of the most frequently used rhyme sounds accompanied by rhyming words, such as *love, of, above* for the sound *uv.* The point of these prescriptions is that the verse must be written so that it is immediately accessible — consumable — by both the buyer and the recipient. Writers of these cards are expected to avoid any complexity.

Compare the following greeting-card verse with the poem that comes after it. "Magic of Love," by Helen Farries, has been a longtime favorite in a major greeting-card company's "wedding line"; with different endings it has been used also in valentines and friendship cards.

HELEN FARRIES
Magic of Love

There's a wonderful gift that can give you a lift,
It's a blessing from heaven above!
It can comfort and bless, it can bring happiness —
It's the wonderful MAGIC OF LOVE!

Like a star in the night, it can keep your faith bright,
Like the sun, it can warm your hearts, too —
It's a gift you can give every day that you live,
And when given, it comes back to you!

When love lights the way, there is joy in the day
And all troubles are lighter to bear,
Love is gentle and kind, and through love you will find
There's an answer to your every prayer!

May it never depart from your two loving hearts,
May you treasure this gift from above —
You will find if you do, all your dreams will come true,
In the wonderful MAGIC OF LOVE!

[1]Chris Fitzgerald, "Conventional Verse: The Sentimental Favorite," *The Greeting Card Writer's Handbook,* ed. H. Joseph Chadwick (Cincinnati: Writer's Digest, 1975): 13, 17.

JOHN FREDERICK NIMS (b. 1913)

Love Poem

1947

My clumsiest dear, whose hands shipwreck vases,
At whose quick touch all glasses chip and ring,
Whose palms are bulls in china, burs in linen,
And have no cunning with any soft thing

Except all ill-at-ease fidgeting people:
The refugee uncertain at the door
You make at home; deftly you steady
The drunk clambering on his undulant floor.

Unpredictable dear, the taxi drivers' terror,
Shrinking from far headlights pale as a dime
Yet leaping before red apoplectic streetcars —
Misfit in any space. And never on time.

A wrench in clocks and the solar system. Only
With words and people and love you move at ease.
In traffic of wit expertly maneuver
And keep us, all devotion, at your knees.

Forgetting your coffee spreading on our flannel,
Your lipstick grinning on our coat,
So gaily in love's unbreakable heaven
Our souls on glory of spilt bourbon float.

Be with me, darling, early and late. Smash glasses —
I will study wry music for your sake.
For should your hands drop white and empty
All the toys of the world would break.

Considerations

1. Read these two works aloud. Characterize their differences.
2. To what extent does the advice to would-be greeting-card writers apply to each work?
3. Compare the two speakers. Which do you find more appealing? Why?
4. How does Nims's description of love differ from Farries's?

In contrast to poetry, which transfigures and expresses an emotion or experience through an original use of language, the verse in "Magic of Love" relies upon ***clichés,*** ideas or expressions that have become tired and trite from overuse, such as describing love as "a blessing from heaven above." Clichés anesthetize readers instead of alerting them to the possibility of fresh perceptions. They are used to draw out ***stock responses,*** predictable, conventional reactions to language, characters, symbols, or situations; God, heaven, the flag, motherhood, hearts, puppies, and peace are some often-used objects of stock responses. Advertisers manufacture careers from this sort of business.

Clichés and stock responses are two of the major ingredients of sentimentality in literature. ***Sentimentality*** exploits the reader by inducing emotional responses that exceed what the situation warrants. This pejorative term should not be confused with *sentiment,* which is synonymous with *emotion* or *feeling.* Sentimentality cons readers into falling for the mass murderer who is devoted to stray cats, and it requires that we not think twice about what we're feeling, because those tears shed for the little old lady, the rage aimed at the vicious enemy soldier, and the longing for the simple virtues of poverty might disappear under the slightest scrutiny. The experience of sentimentality is not unlike biting into a swirl of cotton candy; it's momentarily sweet but wholly insubstantial.

Clichés, stock responses, and sentimentality are generally the hallmarks of weak writing. Poetry — the kind that is unmistakable — achieves freshness, vitality, and genuine emotion that sharpen our perceptions of life.

Although the most widely read verse is found in greeting cards, the most widely *heard* poetry appears in song lyrics. Not all songs are poetic, but a good many share the same effects and qualities as poems. Consider these lyrics by Tracy Chapman.

TRACY CHAPMAN (b. 1964)

Fast Car 1987

You got a fast car
I want a ticket to anywhere
Maybe we make a deal
Maybe together we can get somewhere
Anyplace is better
Starting from zero got nothing to lose
Maybe we'll make something
But me myself I got nothing to prove

You got a fast car
And I got a plan to get us out of here
I been working at the convenience store
Managed to save just a little bit of money
We won't have to drive too far
Just 'cross the border and into the city
You and I can both get jobs
And finally see what it means to be living

You see my old man's got a problem
He live with the bottle that's the way it is
He says his body's too old for working

I say his body's too young to look like his
My mama went off and left him
She wanted more from life than he could give
I said somebody's got to take care of him
So I quit school and that's what I did

You got a fast car
But is it fast enough so we can fly away
We gotta make a decision
We leave tonight or live and die this way

I remember we were driving driving in your car
The speed so fast I felt like I was drunk
City lights lay out before us
And your arm felt nice wrapped 'round my shoulder
And I had a feeling that I belonged
And I had feeling I could be someone, be someone, be someone

You got a fast car
And we go cruising to entertain ourselves
You still ain't got a job
And I work in a market as a checkout girl
I know things will get better
You'll find work and I'll get promoted
We'll move out of the shelter
Buy a big house and live in the suburbs

You got a fast car
And I got a job that pays all our bills
You stay out drinking late at the bar
See more of your friends than you do of your kids
I'd always hoped for better
Thought maybe together you and me would find it
I got no plans I ain't going nowhere
So take your fast car and keep on driving

You got a fast car
But is it fast enough so you can fly away
You gotta make a decision
You leave tonight or live and die this way

Considerations

1. Characterize the speaker in this song lyric. What sort of life does she live? How does she want to change it?
2. What is the effect of the repetition of "You got a fast car"? Describe the man in the song. What does his "fast car" come to represent to the speaker?
3. Why isn't punctuation necessary to read these lyrics?
4. Explain whether you think this song can be accurately called a narrative poem.

PERSPECTIVE

ROBERT FRANCIS (1901–1987)

On "Hard" Poetry 1965

When Robert Frost said he liked poems hard he could scarcely have meant he liked them difficult. If he had meant difficult he would have said he didn't like them easy. What he said was that he didn't like them soft.

Poems can be soft in several ways. They can be soft in form (invertebrate). They can be soft in thought and feeling (sentimental). They can be soft with excess verbiage. Frost used to advise one to squeeze the water out of a poem. He liked poems dry. What is dry tends to be hard, and what is hard is always dry, except perhaps on the outside.

Yet though hardness here does not mean difficulty, some difficulty naturally goes with hardness. A hard poem may not be hard to read but is hard to write. Not too hard, preferably. Not so hard to write that there is no flow in the writer. But hard enough for the growing poem to meet with some healthy resistance. Frost often found this healthy resistance in a tight rhyme scheme and strict meter. There are other ways of getting good resistance, of course.

And in the reader too, a hard poem will bring some difficulty. Preferably not too much. Not enough difficulty to completely baffle him. Ideally a hard poem should not be too hard to make sense of, but hard to exhaust its meaning and its beauty.

"What I care about is the hardness of the poems. I don't like them soft, I want them to be little pebbles, but placed where they won't dislodge easily. And I'd like them to be little pebbles of precious stone — precious, or semiprecious" (interview with John Ciardi, *Saturday Review,* March 21, 1959).

Here is hard prose talking about hard poetry. Frost was never shrewder or more illuminating. Here, as well as in anything else he ever said, is his flavor.

What contemporary of his can you imagine saying this or anything like it?

In 1843 Emerson jotted in his journal: "Hard clouds and hard expressions, and hard manners, I love."

From *The Satirical Rogue on Poetry*

Considerations

1. What is the distinction between "hard" and "soft" poetry?
2. Given Francis's brief essay and his poem "Catch" (p. 499), write a review of Helen Farries's "Magic of Love" (p. 511) as you think Francis would.
3. Explain whether you would characterize Chapman's "Fast Car" as hard or soft.

TED KOOSER (b. 1939)

Selecting a Reader 1974

First, I would have her be beautiful,
and walking carefully up on my poetry
at the loneliest moment of an afternoon,
her hair still damp at the neck
from washing it. She should be wearing
a raincoat, an old one, dirty
from not having money enough for the cleaners.
She will take out her glasses, and there
in the bookstore, she will thumb
over my poems, then put the book back
up on its shelf. She will say to herself,
"For that kind of money, I can get
my raincoat cleaned." And she will.

Considerations

1. What do the descriptive details in this poem reveal about the kind of reader the poet desires?
2. Based on this description of the poet's desired reader, write a one-paragraph description of the poem's speaker. Try to include some imaginative details that suggest his personality.

MARY OLIVER (b. 1935)

The Black Snake 1979

When the black snake
flashed onto the morning road,
and the truck could not swerve —
death, that is how it happens.

Now he lies looped and useless
as an old bicycle tire.
I stop the car
and carry him into the bushes.

He is as cool and gleaming
as a braided whip, he is as beautiful and quiet
as a dead brother.
I leave him under the leaves

and drive on, thinking
about *death:* its suddenness,

its terrible weight,
its certain coming. Yet under

reason burns a brighter fire, which the bones
have always preferred.
It is the story of endless good fortune.
It says to oblivion: not me!

It is the light at the center of every cell.
It is what sent the snake coiling and flowing forward
happily all spring through the green leaves before
he came to the road.

Considerations

1. What is this poem's central idea? State its theme.
2. Why do you suppose Oliver chose to write about a black snake rather than, say, a squirrel?

Connections

1. William Stafford's "Traveling through the Dark" (p. 591) recounts a similar occurrence. Describe the speaker's voice in that poem and in this one. Write an essay explaining how the poems differ in theme.
2. Compare the descriptions of snakes in Oliver's poem and in Dickinson's "A narrow Fellow in the Grass" (p. 4). What responses do these descriptions create in you?

ANONYMOUS

Sir Patrick Spens

c. 13th century

The king sits in Dumferling toune,° — *town*
  Drinking the blude-reid° wine: — *blood-red*
"O whar will I get guid° sailor, — *good*
  To sail this ship of mine?"

Up and spake an eldern knicht,° — *elderly knight*
  Sat at the king's richt° knee: — *right*
"Sir Patrick Spens is the best sailor
  That sails upon the sea."

The king has written a braid° letter — *broad*
  And signed it wi' his hand,
And sent it to Sir Patrick Spens,
  Was walking on the sand.

The first line that Sir Patrick read,
  A loud lauch° lauched he; — *laugh*
The next line that Sir Patrick read,
  The tear blinded his ee.° — *eye*

"O wha° is this has done this deed, *who*
This il deed done to me,
To send me out this time o' the year,
To sail upon the sea?

"Make haste, make haste, my merry men all,
Our guid ship sails the morn."
"O say na sae,° my master dear, *not so*
For I fear a deadly storm.

"Late, late yestre'en I saw the new moon
Wi' the auld moon in her arm,
And I fear, I fear, my dear mastér,
That we will come to harm."

O our Scots nobles were richt laith° *loath*
To weet° their cork-heeled shoon,° *wet; shoes*
But lang owre a'° the play were played *before all*
Their hats they swam aboon.° *above*

O lang, lang, may their ladies sit,
Wi' their fans into their hand,
Or ere they see Sir Patrick Spens
Come sailing to the land.

O lang, lang, may the ladies stand
Wi' their gold kems° in their hair, *combs*
Waiting for their ain° dear lords, *own*
For they'll see them na mair.

Half o'er, half o'er to Aberdour
It's fifty fadom deep,
And there lies guid Sir Patrick Spens
Wi' the Scots lords at his feet.

Considerations

1. Contrast the characterization of the nobles at court with that of Sir Patrick Spens. How does the poem praise Sir Patrick while criticizing those at court? What causes the disaster?
2. There is no transition between scenes in lines 11–12. How is this shift similar to the technique used to change scenes in a film? How are the other scene changes indicated?
3. What is the effect of leaving out details of the shipwreck?
4. This narrative poem is a ballad that was originally sung or recited as part of an oral tradition. What accounts for its lasting appeal?
5. Write an essay supporting or challenging Sir Patrick's sense of duty.

JOHN DONNE (1572–1631)

The Sun Rising c. 1633

Busy old fool, unruly sun,
Why dost thou thus,
Through windows, and through curtains, call on us?
Must to thy motions lovers' seasons run?
Saucy pedantic wretch, go chide
Late schoolboys, and sour prentices,
Go tell court-huntsmen that the king will ride,
Call country ants° to harvest offices; *farm workers*
Love, all alike, no season knows, nor clime,
Nor hours, days, months, which are the rags of time.

Thy beams, so reverend and strong
Why shouldst thou think?
I could eclipse and cloud them with a wink,
But that I would not lose her sight so long:
If her eyes have not blinded thine,
Look, and tomorrow late, tell me
Whether both the Indias° of spice and mine *East and West Indies*
Be where thou left'st them, or lie here with me.
Ask for those kings whom thou saw'st yesterday,
And thou shalt hear, all here in one bed lay.

She is all states, and all princes I,
Nothing else is.
Princes do but play us; compared to this,
All honor's mimic, all wealth alchemy.
Thou, sun, art half as happy as we,
In that the world's contracted thus;
Thine age asks ease, and since thy duties be
To warm the world, that's done in warming us.
Shine here to us, and thou art every where;
This bed thy center° is, these walls thy sphere. *of orbit*

Considerations

1. What is the situation in this poem? Why is the speaker angry with the sun? What does he urge the sun to do in the first stanza?
2. What claims does the speaker make about the power of love in stanzas 2 and 3? What does he mean when he says, "Shine here to us, and thou art every where"?
3. Are any of the speaker's exaggerations in any sense true? How?

Connections

1. Compare this lyric poem with Richard Wilbur's "A Late Aubade" (p. 536). What similarities do you find in the ideas and emotions expressed in each?

NIKKI GIOVANNI (b. 1943)

Nikki-Rosa 1968

childhood remembrances are always a drag
if you're Black
you always remember things like living in Woodlawn
with no inside toilet
and if you become famous or something
they never talk about how happy you were to have your mother
all to yourself and
how good the water felt when you got your bath from one of those
big tubs that folk in chicago barbecue in
and somehow when you talk about home
it never gets across how much you
understood their feelings
as the whole family attended meetings about Hollydale
and even though you remember
your biographers never understand
your father's pain as he sells his stock
and another dream goes
and though you're poor it isn't poverty that
concerns you
and though they fought a lot
it isn't your father's drinking that makes any difference
but only that everybody is together and you
and your sister have happy birthdays and very good christmasses
and I really hope no white person ever has cause to write about me
because they never understand Black love is Black wealth and they'll
probably talk about my hard childhood and never understand that
all the while I was quite happy

Considerations

1. How does reading this poem aloud help to convey its meaning and characterize the speaker? How does the lack of punctuation contribute to our image of the speaker?
2. Is this poem addressed primarily to whites, blacks, or both? Why?
3. Does the speaker describe his or her childhood as positive or negative?
4. Is this a sentimental treatment of childhood memories? Why or why not?

Connections

1. Compare the feelings evoked by the "childhood remembrances" in Giovanni's poem with those in Barreca's "Nighttime Fires" (p. 507).
2. Write an essay contrasting the attitude toward the past expressed in "Nikki-Rosa" with the black man's attitude in M. Carl Holman's "Mr. Z" (p. 796).

EMILY DICKINSON (1830–1886)

To make a prairie it takes a clover and one bee

published 1896

To make a prairie it takes a clover and one bee,
One clover, and a bee,
And revery.
The revery alone will do,
If bees are few.

Considerations

1. How can "a clover and one bee" make a prairie?
2. What does "revery" mean in this poem? Why is revery especially important to a writer?

13. Word Choice, Word Order, and Tone

DICTION

Like all good writers, poets are keenly aware of ***diction,*** their choice of words. Poets, however, choose words especially carefully, because the words in poems call attention to themselves. Characters, actions, settings, and symbols may appear in a poem, but in the foreground, before all else, is the poem's language. Also, poems are usually briefer than other forms of writing. A few inappropriate words in a two-hundred-page novel (which would have about 100,000 words) create fewer problems than they would in a 100-word poem. Functioning in a compressed atmosphere, the words in a poem must convey meanings gracefully and economically. Readers therefore have to be alert to the ways in which those meanings are released.

Although poetic language is often more intensely charged than ordinary speech, the words used in poetry are not necessarily different from everyday speech. Inexperienced readers may sometimes assume that language must be high-flown and out of date to be included in a poem: instead of reading about a boy "enjoying a swim," they expect to read about a boy "disporting with pliant arm o'er a glassy wave." During the eighteenth century this kind of ***poetic diction*** — the use of elevated language over ordinary language — was highly valued in English poetry, but since the nineteenth century poets have generally overridden the distinctions that were once made between words used in everyday speech and those used in poetry. Today all levels of diction can be found in poetry.

A poet, like any writer, has several levels of diction from which to choose; they range from formal to middle to informal. ***Formal diction*** consists of a dignified, impersonal, and elevated use of language. Notice, for example, the formality of Thomas Hardy's description of the sunken luxury liner *Titanic* in this stanza from "The Convergence of the Twain" (the entire poem appears on p. 539):

In a solitude of the sea
Deep from human vanity,
And the Pride of Life that planned her, stilly couches she.

There is nothing casual or relaxed about these lines. Hardy's use of *stilly,* meaning "quietly" or "calmly," is purely literary; the word rarely, if ever, turns up in everyday English.

The language used in Richard Wilbur's "A Late Aubade"(p. 536) represents a less formal level of diction; the speaker uses a ***middle diction*** spoken by most educated people. Consider how Wilbur's speaker tells his lover what she might be doing instead of being with him.

You could be sitting now in a carrel
Turning some liver-spotted page,
Or rising in an elevator-cage
Toward Ladies' Apparel.

The speaker elegantly enumerates his lover's unattractive alternatives to being with him — reading old books in a library or shopping in a department store — but the wit of his description lessens its formality.

Informal diction is evident in Larkin's "A Study of Reading Habits" (p. 503). The speaker's account of his early reading is presented ***colloquially,*** in a conversational manner that in this instance includes slang expressions not used by the culture at large.

When getting my nose in a book
Cured most things short of school,
It was worth ruining my eyes
To know I could still keep cool,
And deal out the old right hook
To dirty dogs twice my size.

This level of diction is clearly not that of Hardy's or Wilbur's speakers.

Poets may also draw on another form of informal diction, called ***dialect.*** Dialects are spoken by definable groups of people from a particular geographic region, economic group, or social class. New England dialects are often heard in Robert Frost's poems, for example. Gwendolyn Brooks employs a black dialect in "We Real Cool" (p. 541) to characterize a group of pool players. Another form of diction related to particular groups is ***jargon,*** a category of language defined by a trade or profession. Sociologists, photographers, carpenters, baseball players, and dentists, for example, all use words that are specific to their fields. E. E. Cummings manages to get quite a lot of mileage out of automobile jargon in "she being Brand" (p. 527).

Many levels of diction are available to poets. The variety of diction to be found in poetry is enormous, and that is how it should be. No language is foreign to poetry, because it is possible to imagine any human voice as the speaker of a poem. When we say a poem is formal, informal, or somewhere in between, we are making a descriptive statement rather than an evaluative one. What matters in a poem is not only which words are used but how they are used.

DENOTATIONS AND CONNOTATIONS

One important way that the meaning of a word is communicated in a poem is through sound: snakes *hiss,* saws *buzz.* This and other matters related to sound are discussed in Chapter 17. Individual words also convey meanings through denotations and connotations. ***Denotations*** are the literal, dictionary meanings of a word. For example, *bird* denotes a feathered animal with wings (other denotations for the same word include a shuttlecock, an airplane, or an odd person), but in addition to its denotative meanings *bird* also carries ***connotations,*** associations and implications that go beyond a word's literal meanings. Connotations derive from how the word has been used and the associations people make with it. Therefore, the connotations of *bird* might include fragility, vulnerability, altitude, the sky, or freedom, depending on the context in which the word is used. Consider also how different the connotations are for the following types of birds: hawk, dove, penguin, pigeon, chicken, peacock, duck, crow, turkey, gull, owl, goose, coot, and vulture. These words have long been used to refer to types of people as well as birds. They are rich in connotative meanings.

Connotations derive their resonance from a person's experiences with a word. Those experiences may not always be the same, especially when the people having them are in different times and places. *Theater,* for instance, was once associated with depravity, disease, and sin, while today the word usually evokes some sense of high culture and perhaps visions of elegant opulence. In several ethnic communities in the United States many people would find *squid* appetizing, but elsewhere the word is likely to produce negative connotations. Readers must recognize, then, that words written in other times and places may have unexpected connotations. Annotations usually help in these matters, which is why it makes sense to pay attention to them when they are available.

Ordinarily, though, the language of poetry is accessible, even when the circumstances of the reader and the poet are different. Although connotative language may be used subtly, it mostly draws on associations experienced by many people. Poets rely on widely shared associations rather than the idiosyncratic response that an individual might have to a word. Someone who has received a severe burn from a fireplace accident may associate the word *hearth* with intense pain instead of home and family life, but that reader must not allow a personal experience to undermine the response the poet intends to evoke. Connotative meanings are usually public meanings.

Perhaps this can be seen most clearly in advertising, where language is also used primarily to convey moods and feelings rather than information. For instance, our recent efforts to get in shape have created a collective consciousness that advertisers have capitalized on successfully. Knowing that we want to be slender or lean or slim (not spare or scrawny and certainly not gaunt), advertisers have created a new word to describe beers, wines, sodas, cheeses, canned fruits, and other products that tend to overload what used to be called sweatclothes and sneakers. The word is *lite.* The assumed denotative meaning of *lite* is low in calories, but as close readers of ingredient labels know, some *lites* are heavier than regularly prepared products. There can be no doubt about the connotative meaning of *lite,* however. Whatever is *lite* cannot hurt you; less is more. Even the word is lighter than *light;* there is no unnecessary droopy *g* or plump *h*. *Lite* is a brilliantly manufactured use of connotation.

Connotative meanings are valuable to poets because they allow them to be economical and suggestive simultaneously. In this way emotions and attitudes are carefully woven into the texture of the poem's language. Read the following poem and pay close attention to the connotative meanings of its words.

RANDALL JARRELL (1914–1965)

The Death of the Ball Turret Gunner 1945

From my mother's sleep I fell into the State
And I hunched in its belly till my wet fur froze.
Six miles from earth, loosed from its dream of life,
I woke to black flack and the nightmare fighters.
When I died they washed me out of the turret with a hose.

The title of this poem establishes the setting and the speaker's situation. Like the setting of a short story, the setting of a poem is important when the time and place influence what happens. "The Death of the Ball Turret Gunner" is set in the midst of a war and, more specifically, in a ball turret — a Plexiglas sphere housing machine guns on the underside of a bomber. The speaker's situation obviously places him in extreme danger; indeed, his fate is announced in the title.

Although the poem is written in the first-person singular, its speaker is clearly not the poet. Jarrell employs a ***persona,*** a speaker created by the poet. In this poem the persona is a disembodied voice that makes the gunner's story all the more powerful. What is his story? A paraphrase might read something like this:

> After I was born, I grew up to find myself at war, cramped into the turret of a bomber's belly some 31,000 feet above the ground. Below me were

exploding shells from antiaircraft guns and attacking fighter planes. I was killed, but the bomber returned to base, where my remains were cleaned out of the turret so the next man could take my place.

This paraphrase is accurate, but its language is much less suggestive than the poem's. The first line of the poem has the speaker emerge from his "mother's sleep," the anesthetized sleep of her giving birth. The phrase also suggests the comfort, warmth, and security he knew as a child. This safety was left behind when he "fell," a verb that evokes the danger and involuntary movement associated with his subsequent "States" (*fell* also echoes, perhaps, the fall from innocence to experience related in the Bible).

Several dictionary definitions appear for the noun *state;* it can denote a territorial unit, the power and authority of a government, a person's social status, or a person's emotional or physical condition. The context provided by the rest of the poem makes clear that "State" has several denotative meanings here: Because it is capitalized it certainly refers to the violent world of a government at war, but it also refers to the gunner's vulnerable status as well as his physical and emotional condition. By having "State" carry more than one meaning, Jarrell has created an intentional ambiguity. ***Ambiguity*** allows for two or more simultaneous interpretations of a word, phrase, action, or situation, all of which can be supported by the context of a work. Through his ambiguous use of "State," Jarrell connects the horrors of war not just to bombers and gunners but to the governments that control them.

Related to this ambiguity is the connotative meaning of "State" in the poem. The context demands that the word be read with a negative charge. The word is not used with patriotic pride but to suggest an anonymous, impersonal "State" that kills rather than nurtures the life in its "belly." The state's "belly" is a bomber, and the gunner is "hunched" like a fetus in the cramped turret, where, in contrast to the warmth of his mother's womb, everything is frozen, even the "wet fur" of his flight jacket (newborn infants have wet fur too). The gunner is not just 31,000 feet from the ground but "six miles from earth." *Six miles* has roughly the same denotative meaning as 31,000 feet, but Jarrell knew that the connotative meaning of *six miles* makes the speaker's position seem even more remote and frightening.

When the gunner is born into the violent world of war, he finds himself waking up to a "nightmare" that is all too real. The poem's final line is grimly understated, but it hits the reader with the force of an exploding shell: what the State-bomber-turret gives birth to is a gruesome death that is merely one of an endless series. It may be tempting to reduce the theme of this poem to the idea that "war is hell"; but Jarrell's target is more specific. He implicates the "State," which routinely executes such violence, and he does so without preaching or hysterical denunciations. Instead, his use of language conveys his theme subtly and powerfully. Consider how this next poem uses connotative meanings to express its theme.

E. E. CUMMINGS (1894–1962)

she being Brand 1926

she being Brand

-new;and you
know consequently a
little stiff i was
careful of her and(having

thoroughly oiled the universal
joint tested my gas felt of
her radiator made sure her springs were O.

K.)i went right to it flooded-the-carburetor cranked her

up,slipped the
clutch(and then somehow got into reverse she
kicked what
the hell)next
minute i was back in neutral tried and

again slo-wly;bare,ly nudg. ing (my

lev-er Right-
oh and her gears being in
A 1 shape passed
from low through
second-in-to-high like
greasedlightning) just as we turned the corner of Divinity

avenue i touched the accelerator and give

her the juice,good

(it

was the first ride and believe i we was
happy to see how nice she acted right up to
the last minute coming back down by the Public
Gardens i slammed on

the
internalexpanding
&
externalcontracting
brakes Bothatonce and

brought allofher tremB
-ling
to a:dead.

stand-
;Still)

Considerations

1. How does Cummings's arrangement of the words on the page help you to read this poem aloud? What does the poem describe?
2. What ambiguities in language does the poem ride on? At what point were you first aware of these double meanings?
3. Explain why you think the poem is primarily serious or humorous.
4. Find some advertisements for convertibles or sports cars in magazines and read them closely. What similarities do you find in the use of connotative language in them and in Cummings's poem? Write a brief essay explaining how language is used to convey the theme of one of the advertisements and the poem.

WORD ORDER

Meanings in poems are conveyed not only by denotations and connotations but also by the poet's arrangement of words into phrases, clauses, and sentences to achieve particular effects. The ordering of words into meaningful verbal patterns is called ***syntax***. A poet can manipulate the syntax of a line to place emphasis on a word; this is especially apparent when a poet varies normal word order. In Dickinson's "A narrow Fellow in the Grass" (p. 4), for example, the speaker says about the snake that "His notice sudden is." Ordinarily, that would be expressed as "his notice is sudden." By placing the verb *is* unexpectedly at the end of the line, Dickinson creates the sense of surprise we feel when we suddenly come upon a snake. Dickinson's inversion of the standard word order also makes the final sound of the line a hissing *is*.

Cummings uses one long sentence in "she being Brand" to take the reader on a ride that begins with a false start but accelerates quickly before coming to a halt. The jargon creates an exuberantly humorous mood that is helped along by the poem's syntax. How do Cummings's ordering of words and sentence structure reinforce the meaning of the lines?

TONE

Tone is the writer's attitude toward the subject, the mood created by all the elements in the poem. Writing, like speech, may be characterized as serious or light, sad or happy, private or public, angry or affectionate, bitter or nostalgic, or any other attitudes and feelings that human beings experience. In Jarrell's "The Death of the Ball Turret Gunner," the tone is clearly serious; the voice in the poem even sounds dead. Listen again to the persona's final words: "When I died they washed me out of the turret with a hose." The brutal, restrained matter-of-factness of this line is effective because the reader is called on to supply the appropriate anger and despair, a strategy that makes those emotions all the more convincing.

This next work is a ***dramatic monologue,*** a type of poem in which a character — the speaker — addresses a silent audience in such a way as to reveal unintentionally some aspect of his or her temperament or personality. What tone is created by Aal's use of a persona?

KATHARYN MACHAN AAL (b. 1952)

Hazel Tells LaVerne 1976

last night
im cleanin out my
howard johnsons ladies room
when all of a sudden
up pops this frog
musta come from the sewer
swimmin aroun an tryin ta
climb up the sida the bowl
so i goes ta flushm down
but sohelpmegod he starts talkin
bout a golden ball
an how i can be a princess
me a princess
well my mouth drops
all the way to the floor
an he says
kiss me just kiss me
once on the nose
well i screams
ya little green pervert
an i hitsm with my mop
an has ta flush
the toilet down three times
me
a princess

Considerations

1. What do you imagine the situation and setting are for this poem?
2. What creates the poem's humor? How does Hazel's use of language reveal her personality? Is her treatment of the frog consistent with her character?
3. Although it has no punctuation, this poem is easy to follow. How does the arrangement of the lines organize Hazel's speech for clarity and emphasis?
4. What is the theme? Is it conveyed through denotative or connotative language?
5. Write what you think might be LaVerne's reply to Hazel. First, write LaVerne's response as a series of ordinary sentences, and then try editing and organizing them into poetic lines.

Connections

1. Although Robert Browning's "My Last Duchess" (p. 637) is a more complex poem than Aal's, both use dramatic monologues to reveal character. How are the strategies in each poem similar?

Describe the differences in tone in the following two poems by Emily Dickinson.

EMILY DICKINSON (1830–1886)

If I can stop one Heart from breaking

c. 1864

If I can stop one Heart from breaking
I shall not live in vain
If I can ease one Life the Aching
or cool one Pain

Or help one fainting Robin
Unto his Nest again
I shall not live in Vain.

EMILY DICKINSON (1830–1886)

If I shouldn't be alive

c. 1860

If I shouldn't be alive
When the Robins come,
Give the one in Red Cravat,
A Memorial crumb.

If I couldn't thank you,
Being fast asleep,
You will know I'm trying
With my Granite lip!

Considerations

1. "If I can stop one Heart from breaking" appeared in its entirety on a U.S. Postal Service commemorative envelope in honor of Dickinson. Nearly 1,800 of Dickinson's poems survive. Why do you think the Postal Service chose this one?
2. What is the speaker's concern in lines 1–4 of "If I shouldn't be alive"? What is the tone of these lines? Confident? Playful? Despairing? Calm? Angry? How does the description of the robin help you answer this question?
3. In "If I shouldn't be alive," what is the connotation of "Being fast asleep"? How does that help to control the tone of lines 5–7?
4. What is the effect in "If I shouldn't be alive" of the final line on your reading of the preceding lines? How do the connotative meanings of "Granite" change the

overall tone of the poem? If the final line were deleted, how would the theme of the poem change? Would it be more or less like that of the first poem?

5. Given the use of language, tone, and theme in "If I shouldn't be alive," is the Postal Service likely to reprint it on any future commemorative envelopes honoring Dickinson? Why or why not?

The dramatic difference in tone between these two Dickinson poems can also occur within the same poem when a mixed attitude is present. How do the speaker's attitude and tone change during the course of this next poem?

MAXINE KUMIN (b. 1925)

Woodchucks 1972

Gassing the woodchucks didn't turn out right.
The knockout bomb from the Feed and Grain Exchange
was featured as merciful, quick at the bone
and the case we had against them was airtight,
both exits shoehorned shut with puddingstone,°
but they had a sub-sub-basement out of range.

Next morning they turned up again, no worse
for the cyanide than we for our cigarettes
and state-store Scotch, all of us up to scratch.
They brought down the marigolds as a matter of course
and then took over the vegetable patch
nipping the broccoli shoots, beheading the carrots.

The food from our mouths, I said, righteously thrilling
to the feel of the .22, the bullets' neat noses.
I, a lapsed pacifist fallen from grace
puffed with Darwinian° pieties for killing,
now drew a bead on the littlest woodchuck's face.
He died down in the everbearing roses.

Ten minutes later I dropped the mother. She
flipflopped in the air and fell, her needle teeth
still hooked in a leaf of early Swiss chard.
Another baby next. O one-two-three
the murderer inside me rose up hard,
the hawkeye killer came on stage forthwith.

There's one chuck left. Old wily fellow, he keeps
me cocked and ready day after day after day.
All night I hunt his humped-up form. I dream
I sight along the barrel in my sleep.

5 *puddingstone:* Pebbles cemented together. 16 *Darwinian:* Charles Darwin (1809–1882), an English naturalist associated with the ideas of evolution and natural selection.

If only they'd all consented to die unseen
gassed underground the quiet Nazi way.

Considerations

1. How does the word *airtight* help create the tone of the first stanza?
2. How does the speaker's attitude toward the woodchucks change in the second stanza? How does that affect the tone in lines 13–24?
3. What competing emotions are present in the speaker's descriptions of the woodchucks' activities and the descriptions of killing them?
4. Given that "Gassing" begins the poem, why does the speaker withhold the description of the woodchucks being "gassed underground the quiet Nazi way" until the final line?
5. Explain how line 15 suggests, along with the final stanza, the theme of the poem.

DICTION AND TONE IN FOUR LOVE POEMS

The first three of these love poems share the same basic situation and theme: a male speaker addresses a female (in the first poem it is a type of female) urging that love should not be delayed because time is short. This theme is as familiar in poetry as it is in life. In Latin this tradition is known as ***carpe diem,*** for "seize the day." Notice how the poets' diction helps create a distinctive tone in each poem, even though the subject matter and central ideas are similar (though not identical) in all three.

ROBERT HERRICK (1591–1674)

To the Virgins, to Make Much of Time 1648

Gather ye rose-buds while ye may,
Old Time is still a-flying;
And this same flower that smiles today,
Tomorrow will be dying.

The glorious lamp of heaven, the sun,
The higher he's a-getting,
The sooner will his race be run,
And nearer he's to setting.

That age is best which is the first,
When youth and blood are warmer;
But being spent, the worse, and worst
Times still succeed the former.

Then be not coy, but use your time,
And while ye may, go marry;
For having lost but once your prime,
You may for ever tarry.

Considerations

1. Would there be any change in meaning if the title of this poem were "To Young Women, to Make Much of Time"? Do you think the poem can apply to young men too?
2. What do the virgins have in common with the flowers (lines 1–4) and the course of the day (5–8)?
3. How does the speaker develop his argument? What will happen to the virgins if they don't "marry"? Paraphrase the poem.
4. What is the tone of the speaker's advice?

This next poem was also written in the seventeenth century, but it includes some words that have changed in usage and meaning over the past three hundred years. The title of Marvell's "To His Coy Mistress" requires some explanation. *Mistress* does not refer to a married man's illicit lover but to a woman who is loved and courted — a sweetheart. Marvell uses *coy* to describe a woman who is reserved and shy rather than coquettish or flirtatious. Often such shifts in meanings over time are explained in the notes that accompany reprintings of poems. You should keep in mind, however, that it is helpful to have a reasonably thick dictionary available when you are reading poetry. The most thorough is the *Oxford English Dictionary (OED),* which provides histories of words. The *OED* is a multivolume leviathan, but there are other useful unabridged dictionaries as well as desk dictionaries.

Knowing its original meaning can also enrich your understanding of why a contemporary poet chooses a particular word. Elizabeth Bishop begins "The Fish" this way: "I caught a tremendous fish." We know immediately in this context that *tremendous* means very large. In addition, given that the speaker clearly admires the fish in the lines that follow, we might even understand *tremendous* in the colloquial sense of wonderful and extraordinary. But a dictionary gives us some further relevant insights. Because, by the end of the poem, we see the speaker thoroughly moved as a result of the encounter with the fish ("everything/was rainbow, rainbow, rainbow!"), the dictionary's additional information about the history of *tremendous* shows why it is the perfect adjective to introduce the fish. The word comes from the Latin *tremere* (to tremble) and therefore once meant "such as to make one tremble." That is precisely how the speaker is at the end of the poem: deeply affected and trembling. Knowing the origin of *tremendous* gives us the full heft of the poet's word choice.

Although some of the language in "To His Coy Mistress" requires annotations for the modern reader, this poem continues to serve as a powerful reminder that time is a formidable foe, even for lovers.

ANDREW MARVELL (1621–1678)

To His Coy Mistress 1681

Had we but world enough, and time,
This coyness, lady, were no crime.
We would sit down, and think which way
To walk, and pass our long love's day.
Thou by the Indian Ganges'° side
Shouldst rubies find; I by the tide
Of Humber° would complain.° I would *write love songs*
Love you ten years before the Flood,
And you should, if you please, refuse
Till the conversion of the Jews.
My vegetable love should grow°
Vaster than empires, and more slow;
An hundred years should go to praise
Thine eyes and on thy forehead gaze,
Two hundred to adore each breast,
But thirty thousand to the rest:
An age at least to every part,
And the last age should show your heart.
For, lady, you deserve this state,
Nor would I love at lower rate.
    But at my back I always hear
Time's wingèd chariot hurrying near;
And yonder all before us lie
Deserts of vast eternity.
Thy beauty shall no more be found,
Nor in thy marble vault shall sound
My echoing song; then worms shall try
That long preserved virginity,
And your quaint honor turn to dust,
And into ashes all my lust.
The grave's a fine and private place,
But none, I think, do there embrace.
    Now, therefore, while the youthful hue
Sits on thy skin like morning dew,
And while thy willing soul transpires° *breathes forth*
At every pore with instant fires,
Now let us sport us while we may,
And now, like amorous birds of prey,
Rather at once our time devour
Than languish in his slow-chapped° power. *slow-jawed*
Let us roll all our strength and all
Our sweetness up into one ball,

5 *Ganges:* A river in India sacred to the Hindus. 7 *Humber:* A river that flows through Marvell's native town, Hull. 11 *My vegetable love . . . :* A slow, unconscious growth.

And tear our pleasures with rough strife
Thorough° the iron gates of life. *through*
Thus, though we cannot make our sun
Stand still, yet we will make him run.

Considerations

1. This poem is divided into a three-part argument. Briefly summarize each section: if (lines 1–20), but (21–32), therefore (33–46).
2. What is the speaker's tone in lines 1–20? How much time would he spend adoring his mistress? Is he sincere? How does he expect his mistress to respond to these lines?
3. How does the speaker's tone change beginning with line 21? What is his view of time in lines 21–32? What does this description do to the lush and leisurely sense of time in lines 1–20? How do you think his mistress would react to lines 21–32?
4. In the final lines of Herrick's "To the Virgins, to Make Much of Time," the speaker urges the virgins to "go marry." What does Marvell's speaker urge in lines 33–46? How is the pace of these lines (notice the verbs) different from that of the first twenty lines of the poem?
5. This poem is sometimes read as a vigorous but simple celebration of flesh. Is there more to the theme than that?

PERSPECTIVE

BERNARD DUYFHUIZEN (b. 1953)

"To His Coy Mistress": On How a Female Might Respond 1988

Clearly a female reader of "To His Coy Mistress" might have trouble identifying with the poem's speaker; therefore, her first response would be to identify with the listener-in-the-poem, the eternally silent Coy Mistress. In such a reading she is likely to recognize that she has heard this kind of line before although maybe not with the same intensity and insistence. Moreover, she is likely to (re)experience the unsettling emotions that such an egoistic assault on her virginal autonomy would provoke. She will also see differently, even by contemporary standards, the plot beyond closure, the possible consequences — both physical and social — that the Mistress will encounter. Lastly, she is likely to be angered by this poem, by her marginalization in an argument that seeks to overpower the core of her being.

From "Textual Harassment of Marvell's Coy Mistress:
The Institutionalization of Masculine Criticism,"
College English, April 1988

Considerations

1. Explain whether you find convincing Duyfhuizen's description of a female's potential response to the poem. How does his description compare with your own response?

2. Characterize the silent mistress of the poem. How do you think the speaker treats her? What do his language and tone suggest about his relationship to her?
3. Does the fact that this description of a female response is written by a man make any difference in your assessment of it? Explain why or why not.

The third in this series of *carpe diem* poems is a twentieth-century work. The language of Wilbur's "A Late Aubade" is more immediately accessible than that of Marvell's "To His Coy Mistress"; a dictionary will quickly identify any words unfamiliar to a reader, including the allusion to Arnold Schoenberg, the composer, in line 11. An ***allusion*** is a brief reference to a person, place, thing, event, or idea in history or literature. Allusive words, like connotative words, are both suggestive and economical; poets use allusions to conjure up biblical authority, scenes from Shakespeare's plays, historic figures, wars, great love stories, and anything else that might serve to deepen and enrich their own work. The speaker in "A Late Aubade" makes an allusion that an ordinary dictionary won't explain. He tells his lover that "I need not rehearse/The rosebuds-theme of centuries of verse." True to his word, he says no more about this for her or the reader. The lines refer, of course, to the *carpe diem* theme as found familiarly in Herrick's "To the Virgins, to Make Much of Time." Wilbur assumes that his reader will understand the allusion.

Allusions imply reading and cultural experiences shared by the poet and reader. Literate audiences once had more in common than they do today because more people had similar economic, social, and educational backgrounds. But a judicious use of specialized dictionaries, encyclopedias, and other reference tools can help you decipher allusions that grow out of this body of experience. See page 1842 for a list of useful reference works for students of literature. As you read more, you'll be able to make connections based on your own experiences with literature. In a sense, allusions make available what other human beings have deemed worth remembering, and that is certainly an economical way of supplementing and enhancing your own experience.

Here is Wilbur's version of the *carpe diem* theme. What strikes you as particularly modern about it?

RICHARD WILBUR (b. 1921)

A Late Aubade 1968

You could be sitting now in a carrel
Turning some liver-spotted page,
Or rising in an elevator-cage
Toward Ladies' Apparel.

You could be planting a raucous bed
Of salvia, in rubber gloves,
Or lunching through a screed of someone's loves
With pitying head,

Or making some unhappy setter
Heel, or listening to a bleak
Lecture on Schoenberg's serial technique.
Isn't this better?

Think of all the time you are not
Wasting, and would not care to waste,
Such things, thank God, not being to your taste.
Think what a lot

Of time, by woman's reckoning,
You've saved, and so may spend on this,
You who had rather lie in bed and kiss
Than anything.

It's almost noon, you say? If so,
Time flies, and I need not rehearse
The rosebuds-theme of centuries of verse.
If you *must* go,

Wait for a while, then slip downstairs
And bring us up some chilled white wine,
And some blue cheese, and crackers, and some fine
Ruddy-skinned pears.

Considerations

1. An *aubade* is a song about lovers parting at dawn, but in this "late aubade," "It's almost noon." Is there another way of reading the adjective *late* in the title?
2. How does the speaker's diction characterize both him and his lover? What sort of lives do they live? What does the casual allusion to Herrick's poem reveal about them?
3. What is the effect of using "liver-spotted page," "elevator-cage," "raucous bed," "screed," "unhappy setter," and "bleak Lecture" to describe the woman's activities?

Connections

1. How does the man's argument in "A Late Aubade" differ from the speakers' in Herrick's and Marvell's poems? Which of the three arguments do you find most convincing?
2. Explain how the tone of each poem is suited to its theme.

This fourth love poem is by a woman. Listen to the speaker's voice. Does it sound different from the way the men speak in the previous three poems?

EDNA ST. VINCENT MILLAY (1892–1950)

Never May the Fruit Be Plucked 1923

Never, never may the fruit be plucked from the bough
And gathered into barrels.
He that would eat of love must eat it where it hangs.
Though the branches bend like reeds,
Though the ripe fruit splash in the grass or wrinkle on the tree,
He that would eat of love may bear away with him
Only what his belly can hold,
Nothing in the apron,
Nothing in the pockets.
Never, never may the fruit be gathered from the bough
And harvested in barrels.
The winter of love is a cellar of empty bins,
In an orchard soft with rot.

Considerations

1. Compare the meaning of the fruit in this poem with that of the rosebuds in Herrick's "To the Virgins, to Make Much of Time."
2. Explain the consequences of "eat[ing] of love" in lines 3–5.
3. Why can't love be gathered or harvested into barrels? Is this a *carpe diem* poem? Why or why not?
4. Explain why you think this poem is addressed to men, women, or both.
5. Discuss the tone of the final two lines. Do you think this poem is closer in tone to "To the Virgins, to Make Much of Time," Marvell's "To His Coy Mistress," or Wilbur's "A Late Aubade"? Why?

Connections

1. Write an essay comparing Millay's view of love with that of E. E. Cummings in "since feeling is first" (p. 769).
2. Discuss how the idea of passionate abandon is central to Millay's poem and Emily Dickinson's "Wild Nights — Wild Nights!" (p. 774). Consider whether the tones of these poems are similar or different.
3. Contrast the ideal of love presented by Millay with that offered by John Keats in "Ode on a Grecian Urn" (p. 698).

POEMS FOR FURTHER STUDY

THOMAS HARDY (1840–1928)

The Convergence of the Twain 1912

Lines on the Loss of the "Titanic"°

I

In a solitude of the sea
Deep from human vanity,
And the Pride of Life that planned her, stilly couches she.

II

Steel chambers, late the pyres
Of her salamandrine° fires,
Cold currents thrid,° and turn to rhythmic tidal lyres. *thread*

III

Over the mirrors meant
To glass the opulent
The sea-worm crawls — grotesque, slimed, dumb, indifferent.

IV

Jewels in joy designed
To ravish the sensuous mind
Lie lightless, all their sparkles bleared and black and blind.

V

Dim moon-eyed fishes near
Gaze at the gilded gear
And query: "What does this vaingloriousness down here?"

VI

Well: while was fashioning
This creature of cleaving wing,
The Immanent Will that stirs and urges everything

VII

Prepared a sinister mate
For her — so gaily great —
A Shape of Ice, for the time far and dissociate.

VIII

And as the smart ship grew
In stature, grace, and hue,
In shadowy silent distance grew the Iceberg too.

Titanic: A luxurious ocean liner reputed to be unsinkable, but it sank after hitting an iceberg on its maiden voyage in 1912. Only a third of the 2,200 passengers survived. 5 *salamandrine fires:* Salamanders were, according to legend, able to survive fire; hence, the ship's fires burned even though under water.

IX

Alien they seemed to be:
No mortal eye could see
The intimate welding of their later history,

X

Or sign that they were bent
By paths coincident
On being anon twin halves of one august event,

XI

Till the Spinner of the Years
Said "Now!" And each one hears,
And consummation comes, and jars two hemispheres.

Considerations

1. How do the words used to describe the ship in this poem reveal the speaker's attitude toward the *Titanic?*
2. The diction of the poem suggests that the *Titanic* and the iceberg participate in something like an arranged marriage. What specific words imply this?
3. Who or what causes the disaster? Does the speaker assign responsibility?

DAVID R. SLAVITT (b. 1935)

Titanic

1983

Who does not love the *Titanic?*
If they sold passage tomorrow for that same crossing,
who would not buy?

To go down . . . We all go down, mostly
alone. But with crowds of people, friends, servants,
well fed, with music, with lights! Ah!

And the world, shocked, mourns, as it ought to do
and almost never does. There will be the books and movies
to remind our grandchildren who we were
and how we died, and give them a good cry.

Not so bad, after all. The cold
water is anesthetic and very quick.
The cries on all sides must be a comfort.

We all go: only a few, first-class.

Considerations

1. What, according to the speaker in this poem, is so compelling about the *Titantic?*
2. Discuss the speaker's tone. Why would it be inaccurate to describe it as solemn and mournful?
3. What is the effect of the poem's final line? What emotions does it produce in you?

Connections

1. How does "Titanic" differ in its attitude toward opulence from "The Convergence of the Twain"?
2. Which poem is more emotionally satisfying to you? Explain why.
3. Compare the speakers' tones in "Titanic" and "The Convergence of the Twain."
4. Hardy wrote his poem in 1912, the year the *Titanic* went down, but Slavitt wrote his more than seventy years later. How do you think Slavitt's poem would have been received if it had been published in 1912? Write an essay explaining why you think what you do.

GWENDOLYN BROOKS (b. 1917)

We Real Cool 1960

The Pool Players.
Seven at the Golden Shovel.

We real cool. We
Left school. We

Lurk late. We
Strike straight. We

Sing sin. We
Thin gin. We

Jazz June. We
Die soon.

Considerations

1. How does the speech of the pool players in this poem help to characterize them? What is the effect of the pronouns coming at the ends of the lines? How would the poem sound if the pronouns came at the beginnings of lines?
2. What is the author's attitude toward the players? Is there a change in tone in the last line?
3. How is the pool hall's name related to the rest of the poem and its theme?

MARGE PIERCY (b. 1936)

A Work of Artifice 1973

The bonsai tree
in the attractive pot
could have grown eighty feet tall
on the side of a mountain
till split by lightning.
But a gardener

carefully pruned it.
It is nine inches high.
Every day as he
whittles back the branches
the gardener croons,
It is your nature
to be small and cozy,
domestic and weak;
how lucky, little tree,
to have a pot to grow in.
With living creatures
one must begin very early
to dwarf their growth:
the bound feet,
the crippled brain,
the hair in curlers,
the hands you
love to touch.

Considerations

1. What is a bonsai tree? How is it likened to a woman in this poem? At what point in the poem does the comparison become apparent?
2. What attitudes are revealed by the language of the gardener's song? Which words have especially strong connotative values?
3. The final two lines ("the hands you/love to touch") allude to a soap commercial. Explain the effect this allusion has on your understanding of the poem's theme.

Connections

1. Write an essay comparing the tone of this poem with that of Stevie Smith's "How Cruel Is the Story of Eve" (below).
2. How does Piercy's theme compare with Henrik Ibsen's treatment of domesticity in his play *A Doll's House* (p. 1321)?
3. Contrast the attitudes expressed about women in Piercy's poem with those in Mishima's short story "Patriotism" (p. 412). How do you account for the differences between the two?

STEVIE SMITH (1902–1971)

How Cruel Is the Story of Eve 1972

How cruel is the story of Eve
What responsibility
It has in history
For cruelty.

Touch, where the feeling is most vulnerable,
Unblameworthy — ah reckless — desiring children,

Touch there with a touch of pain?
Abominable.

Ah what cruelty,
In history
What misery.

Put up to barter
The tender feelings
Buy her a husband to rule her
Fool her to marry a master
She must or rue it
The Lord said it.

And man, poor man,
Is he fit to rule,
Pushed to it?
How can he carry it, the governance,
And not suffer for it
Insuffisance?° *incompetency*
He must make woman lower then
So he can be higher then.

Oh what cruelty,
In history what misery.

Soon woman grows cunning
Masks her wisdom,
How otherwise will he
Bring food and shelter, kill enemies?
If he did not feel superior
It would be worse for her
And for the tender children
Worse for them.

Oh what cruelty,
In history what misery
Of falsity.

It is only a legend
You say? But what
Is the meaning of the legend
If not
To give blame to women most
And most punishment?

This is the meaning of a legend that colors
All human thought; it is not found among animals.

How cruel is the story of Eve,
What responsibility it has
In history
For misery.

Yet there is this to be said still:
Life would be over long ago
If men and women had not loved each other
Naturally, naturally,
Forgetting their mythology
They would have died of it else
Long ago, long ago,
And all would be emptiness now
And silence.

Oh dread Nature, for your purpose,
To have made them love so.

Considerations

1. How does Smith use the story of Eve to chart a history of the way men and women have related to each other since the beginning of time?
2. Compare Smith's reading of Eve with the Bible's version of her story in Genesis. What is the essential point Smith makes about Eve's "legend"?
3. Which words are repeated in the poem? What is the effect of these repetitions?
4. Describe the speaker's voice. How does it produce the poem's overall tone?

JANE KENYON (b. 1947)

Thinking of Madame Bovary 1984

The first hot April day the granite step
was warm. Flies droned in the grass.
When a car went past they rose
in unison, then dropped back down. . . .

I saw that a yellow crocus bud had pierced
a dead oak leaf, then opened wide. How strong
its appetite for the luxury of the sun!
Everyone longs for love's tense joys and red delights.

And then I spied an ant
dragging a ragged, disembodied wing
up the warm brick walk. It must have been
the Methodist in me that leaned forward,
preceded by my shadow, to put a twig
just where the ant was struggling
with its own desire. . . .

Considerations

1. Identify Madame Bovary. Explain how the allusion to her is crucial to understanding this poem.

2. What is the effect of the syntax in lines 11–15? How does the word order help to convey the meaning of these lines?
3. What is the effect of the poem ending with ellipsis marks rather than a period?

Connections

1. Compare this poem's treatment of "love's tense joys and red delights" with the attitudes expressed about love in Marvell's "To His Coy Mistress" (p. 534) or Wilbur's "A Late Aubade" (p. 536).
2. Explain how the speaker's relationship to "desire" in this poem compares with the speaker's attitude in Millay's "Never May the Fruit Be Plucked" (p. 538).
3. Suppose the title of this poem was "Thinking of Mrs. Mallard," recalling the name of the protagonist in Chopin's "Story of an Hour" (p. 12). How would that allusion affect your understanding of the poem?

14. Images

POETRY'S APPEAL TO THE SENSES

A poet, to borrow a phrase from Henry James, is one of those on whom nothing is lost. Poets take in the world and give us impressions of what they experience through images. An ***image*** is language that addresses the senses. The most common images in poetry are visual; they provide verbal pictures of the poets' encounters — real or imagined — with the world. But poets also create images that appeal to our other senses. Wilbur arouses several senses when he has the speaker in "A Late Aubade" gently urge his lover to linger in bed with him instead of getting on with her daily routines and obligations.

> Wait for a while, then slip downstairs
> And bring us up some chilled white wine,
> And some blue cheese, and crackers, and some fine
> Ruddy-skinned pears.

These images are simultaneously tempting and satisfying. We don't have to literally touch that cold, clear glass of wine (or will it come in a green bottle beaded with moisture?) or smell the cheese or taste the crackers to appreciate this vivid blend of colors, textures, tastes, and fragrances.

Images give us the physical world to experience in our imaginations. Some poems, like the following one, are written to do just that; they make no comment about what they describe.

WILLIAM CARLOS WILLIAMS (1883–1963)

Poem 1934

As the cat
climbed over
the top of

the jamcloset
first the right
forefoot

carefully
then the hind
stepped down

into the pit of
the empty
flowerpot

This poem defies paraphrase because it is all an image of agile movement. No statement is made about the movement; the title, "Poem" — really no title — signals Williams's refusal to comment on the movements. To impose a meaning on the poem, we'd probably have to knock over the flowerpot.

We experience the image in Williams's "Poem" more clearly because of how the sentence is organized into lines and groups of lines, or stanzas. Consider how differently the sentence is read if it is arranged as prose.

> As the cat climbed over the top of the jamcloset, first the right forefoot carefully then the hind stepped down into the pit of the empty flowerpot.

The poem's line and stanza division transforms what is essentially an awkward prose sentence into a rhythmic verbal picture. Especially when the poem is read aloud, this line and stanza division allows us to feel the image we see. Even the lack of a period at the end suggests that the cat is only pausing.

Images frequently do more than offer only sensory impressions, however. They also convey emotions and moods, as in this lyric.

ADELAIDE CRAPSEY (1878–1914)

Triad 1913

These be
Three silent things:
The falling snow . . . the hour
Before the dawn . . . the mouth of one
Just dead.

The tone of this poem is clearly somber. The three visual images of silence move from cold winter to anticipated time to the mouth of death. Taken together there is nothing pleasant about these images. The chord struck by this triad produces anxiety. We are given more than just images of the world selected by the poet; we are also given her feelings about them.

What mood is established in this next poem's view of Civil War troops moving across a river?

WALT WHITMAN (1819–1892)

Cavalry Crossing a Ford

1865

A line in long array where they wind betwixt green islands,
They take a serpentine course, their arms flash in the sun — hark to the musical
  clank,
Behold the silvery river, in it the splashing horses loitering stop to drink,
Behold the brown-faced men, each group, each person, a picture, the negligent
  rest on the saddles,
Some emerge on the opposite bank, others are just entering the ford — while,
Scarlet and blue and snowy white,
The guidon flags flutter gaily in the wind.

Considerations

1. What effect do the colors and sounds have in establishing the mood of this poem?
2. How would the poem's mood have been changed if Whitman had used *look* or *see* instead of *behold*?
3. Where is the speaker as he observes this troop movement?
4. Does *serpentine* have an evil connotation in this poem? Explain your answer.

Whitman seems to capture momentarily all the troop's actions, and through carefully chosen, suggestive details — really very few — he succeeds in making "each group, each person, a picture." Specific details, even when few are provided, give us the impression that we see the entire picture; it is as if those are the details we would remember if we had viewed the scene ourselves. Notice too that the movement of the "line in long array" is emphasized by the continuous winding syntax of the poem's lengthy lines.

Poets choose details the way they choose the words to present those details: only telling ones will do. Consider the images Theodore Roethke uses in "Root Cellar."

THEODORE ROETHKE (1908–1963)

Root Cellar

1948

Nothing would sleep in that cellar, dank as a ditch,
Bulbs broke out of boxes hunting for chinks in the dark,
Shoots dangled and drooped,
Lolling obscenely from mildewed crates,
Hung down long yellow evil necks, like tropical snakes.
And what a congress of stinks!

Roots ripe as old bait,
Pulpy stems, rank, silo-rich,
Leaf-mold, manure, lime, piled against slippery planks.
Nothing would give up life:
Even the dirt kept breathing a small breath.

Considerations

1. What senses are engaged by the images in this poem? Is the poem simply a series of sensations, or do the detailed images make some kind of point about the root cellar?
2. What controls the choice of details in the poem? Why isn't there, for example, a rusty shovel leaning against a dirt wall or a worn gardener's glove atop one of the crates?
3. Look up *congress* in a dictionary for its denotative meanings. Explain why "congress of stinks" is especially appropriate given the nature of the rest of the poem's imagery.
4. What single line in the poem suggests a theme?

The tone of the images and mood of the speaker are consistent in Roethke's "Root Cellar." In Matthew Arnold's "Dover Beach," however, they shift as the theme is developed.

MATTHEW ARNOLD (1822–1888)

Dover Beach 1867

The sea is calm tonight.
The tide is full, the moon lies fair
Upon the straits; — on the French coast the light
Gleams and is gone; the cliffs of England stand,
Glimmering and vast, out in the tranquil bay.
Come to the window, sweet is the night-air!
Only, from the long line of spray
Where the sea meets the moon-blanched land,
Listen! you hear the grating roar
Of pebbles which the waves draw back, and fling,
At their return, up the high strand,
Begin, and cease, and then again begin,
With tremulous cadence slow, and bring
The eternal note of sadness in.

Sophocles long ago
Heard it on the Aegean, and it brought
Into his mind the turbid ebb and flow
Of human misery;° we

15–18 *Sophocles long ago . . .:* In *Antigone,* lines 557–66, Sophocles likens the disasters that beset the house of Oedipus to a "mounting tide."

Find also in the sound a thought,
Hearing it by this distant northern sea.

The Sea of Faith
Was once, too, at the full, and round earth's shore
Lay like the folds of a bright girdle furled.
But now I only hear
Its melancholy, long, withdrawing roar,
Retreating, to the breath
Of the night-wind, down the vast edges drear
And naked shingles° of the world. *pebble beaches*

Ah, love, let us be true
To one another! for the world, which seems
To lie before us like a land of dreams,
So various, so beautiful, so new,
Hath really neither joy, nor love, nor light,
Nor certitude, nor peace, nor help for pain;
And we are here as on a darkling plain
Swept with confused alarms of struggle and flight,
Where ignorant armies clash by night.

Considerations

1. Contrast the images in lines 4–8 and 9–13. How do they reveal the speaker's mood? To whom is he speaking?
2. What is the cause of the "sadness" in line 14? What is the speaker's response to the ebbing "Sea of Faith"? Is there anything to replace his sense of loss?
3. What details of the beach seem related to the ideas in the poem? How is the sea used differently in lines 1–14 and lines 21–28?
4. Describe the differences in tone between lines 1–8 and 35–37. What has caused the change?

Connections

1. Explain how the images in Wilfred Owen's "Dulce et Decorum Est" (p. 552) develop further the ideas and sentiments suggested by Arnold's final line concerning "ignorant armies clash[ing] by night."
2. Write an essay comparing Arnold's reflections on faith with Thomas Hardy's in "The Oxen" (p. 619).
3. Contrast Arnold's images with those of Anthony Hecht in his parody "The Dover Bitch" (p. 794). How do Hecht's images create a very different mood from that of "Dover Beach"?

H. D.
[HILDA DOOLITTLE] (1886–1961)

Heat 1916

O wind, rend open the heat,
cut apart the heat,
rend it to tatters.

Fruit cannot drop
through this thick air —
fruit cannot fall into heat
that presses up and blunts
the points of pears
and rounds the grapes.

Cut the heat —
plough through it,
turning it on either side
of your path.

Considerations

1. What physical properties are associated with heat in this poem?
2. Explain the effect of the description of fruit in lines 4–9.
3. Why is the image of the cutting plow especially effective in lines 10–13?

WILLIAM BLAKE (1757–1827)

London 1794

I wander through each chartered° street, *defined by law*
Near where the chartered Thames does flow,
And mark in every face I meet
Marks of weakness, marks of woe.

In every cry of every man,
In every Infant's cry of fear,
In every voice, in every ban,
The mind-forged manacles I hear.

How the Chimney-sweeper's cry
Every black'ning Church appalls;
And the hapless Soldier's sigh
Runs in blood down Palace walls.

But most through midnight streets I hear
How the youthful Harlot's curse

Blasts the new-born Infant's tear,
And blights with plagues the Marriage hearse.

Considerations

1. How do the visual images in this poem suggest a feeling of being trapped?
2. What is the predominant sound heard in the poem?
3. What is the meaning of line 8? What is the cause of the problems that the speaker sees and hears in London? Does the speaker suggest additional causes?
4. The image in lines 11–12 cannot be read literally. Comment on its effectiveness.
5. How does Blake's use of denotative and connotative language enrich this poem's meaning?
6. An earlier version of Blake's last stanza appeared this way:

   But most the midnight harlot's curse
   From every dismal street I hear,
   Weaves around the marriage hearse
   And blasts the new-born infant's tear.

   Examine carefully the differences between the two versions. How do Blake's revisions affect his picture of London life? Which version do you think is more effective? Why?

WILFRED OWEN (1893–1918)

Dulce et Decorum Est

1920

Bent double, like old beggars under sacks,
Knock-kneed, coughing like hags, we cursed through sludge,
Till on the haunting flares we turned our backs,
And towards our distant rest began to trudge.
Men marched asleep. Many had lost their boots,
But limped on, blood-shod. All went lame, all blind;
Drunk with fatigue; deaf even to the hoots
Of gas-shells dropping softly behind.

Gas! GAS! Quick, boys! — An ecstasy of fumbling,
Fitting the clumsy helmets just in time,
But someone still was yelling out and stumbling
And flound'ring like a man in fire or lime. —
Dim through the misty panes and thick green light,
As under a green sea, I saw him drowning.

In all my dreams before my helpless sight
He plunges at me, guttering, choking, drowning.

If in some smothering dreams, you too could pace
Behind the wagon that we flung him in,
And watch the white eyes writhing in his face,
His hanging face, like a devil's sick of sin,
If you could hear, at every jolt, the blood

Come gargling from the froth-corrupted lungs
Bitter as the cud
Of vile, incurable sores on innocent tongues, —
My friend, you would not tell with such high zest
To children ardent for some desperate glory,
The old lie: *Dulce et decorum est*
Pro patria mori.

Considerations

1. The Latin quotation in lines 27–28 is from Horace: "It is sweet and fitting to die for one's country." Owen served as a British soldier during World War I and was killed. Is this poem unpatriotic? What is its purpose?
2. Which images in the poem are most vivid? To which senses do they speak?
3. Describe the speaker's tone. What is his relationship to his audience?
4. How are the images of the soldiers in this poem different from the images that typically appear in recruiting posters?

ROBERT LOWELL (1917–1977)

Skunk Hour 1959

For Elizabeth Bishop

Nautilus Island's hermit
heiress still lives through winters in her Spartan cottage;
her sheep still graze above the sea.
Her son's a bishop. Her farmer
is first selectman in our village;
she's in her dotage.

Thirsting for
the hierarchic privacy
of Queen Victoria's century,
she buys up all
the eyesores facing her shore,
and lets them fall.

The season's ill —
we've lost our summer millionaire,
who seemed to leap from an L. L. Bean°
catalogue. His nine-knot yawl
was auctioned off to lobstermen.
A red fox stain covers Blue Hill.

And now our fairy
decorator brightens his shop for fall;
his fishnet's filled with orange cork,

15 *L. L. Bean:* A famous Maine mail-order store specializing in outdoor clothes and equipment.

orange, his cobbler's bench and awl;
there is no money in his work,
he'd rather marry.

One dark night,
my Tudor Ford climbed the hill's skull;
I watched for love-cars. Lights turned down,
they lay together, hull to hull,
where the graveyard shelves on the town. . . .
My mind's not right.

A car radio bleats,
"Love, O careless Love. . . ." I hear
my ill-spirit sob in each blood cell,
as if my hand were at its throat. . . .
I myself am hell;
nobody's here —

only skunks, that search
in the moonlight for a bite to eat.
They march on their soles up Main Street:
white stripes, moonstruck eyes' red fire
under the chalk-dry and spar spire
of the Trinitarian Church.

I stand on top
of our back steps and breathe the rich air —
a mother skunk with her column of kittens swills the garbage pail.
She jabs her wedge-head in a cup
of sour cream, drops her ostrich tail,
and will not scare.

Considerations

1. How does the speaker in this poem characterize life in this Maine coastal town? Which images suggest his attitude toward the town?
2. What is the significance of the title? How is it related to the description of the town?
3. Comment on lines 32–35. What is the speaker's state of mind? How is it reflected throughout the poem?
4. What is the effect of the skunks' appearance at the end of the poem? What does the speaker's attitude toward them reveal about the speaker?
5. Work up a series of a dozen or so images that capture your impressions of a town or city with which you are familiar. Then summarize in a few sentences the overall tone the images evoke.

MARGARET ATWOOD (b. 1939)

Dreams of the Animals 1970

Mostly the animals dream
of other animals   each
according to its kind

(though certain mice and small rodents
have nightmares of a huge pink
shape with five claws descending)

: moles dream of darkness and delicate
mole smells

frogs dream of green and golden
frogs
sparkling like wet suns
among the lilies

red and black
striped fish, their eyes open
have red and black striped
dreams   defense, attack, meaningful
patterns

birds dream of territories
enclosed by singing.

Sometimes the animals dream of evil
in the form of soap and metal
but mostly the animals dream
of other animals.

There are exceptions:

the silver fox in the roadside zoo
dreams of digging out
and of baby foxes, their necks bitten

the caged armadillo
near the train
station, which runs
all day in figure eights
its piglet feet pattering,
no longer dreams
but is insane when waking;

the iguana
in the petshop window on St. Catherine Street
crested, royal-eyed, ruling
its kingdom of water-dish and sawdust

dreams of sawdust.

Considerations

1. How do the images used in this poem to describe the dreams of the moles, frogs, fish, and birds help to characterize those animals?
2. Explain how the dreams of the fox, armadillo, and iguana are different from those of the animals described in lines 1–19.
3. Which image most effectively describes one of the animals in the poem for you? Write one page explaining why.
4. How does the poem say that animal dreams are like human dreams? What do you think the poem's theme is?

MARK STRAND (b. 1934)

Pot Roast

1980

I gaze upon the roast,
that is sliced and laid out
on my plate
and over it
I spoon the juices
of carrot and onion.
And for once I do not regret
the passage of time.

I sit by a window
that looks
on the soot-stained brick of buildings
and do not care that I see
no living thing — not a bird,
not a branch in bloom,
not a soul moving
in the rooms
behind the dark panes.
These days when there is little
to love or to praise
one could do worse
than yield
to the power of food.

So I bend
to inhale
the steam that rises
from my plate, and I think
of the first time
I tasted a roast
like this.

It was years ago
in Seabright,
Nova Scotia;

my mother leaned
over my dish and filled it
and when I finished
filled it again.
I remember the gravy,
its odor of garlic and celery,
and sopping it up
with pieces of bread.

And now
I taste it again.
The meat of memory
The meat of no change.
I raise my fork in praise,
and I eat.

Considerations

1. What is the speaker's mood in lines 9–22? What causes it?
2. What feelings are evoked by the images in lines 22–40?
3. What alternative titles would be appropriate for this poem? Why do you think Strand called it "Pot Roast"?

RICHMOND LATTIMORE (b. 1906)

The Crabs

1972

There was a bucket full of them. They spilled,
crawled, climbed, clawed: slowly tossed
and fell: precision made: cold iodine color of their own
world of sand and occasional brown weed, round stone
chilled clean in the chopping waters of their coast.
One fell out. The marine thing on the grass
tried to trundle off, barbarian and immaculate and to be killed
with his kin. We lit water: dumped the living mass
in: contemplated tomatoes and corn: and with the good cheer of civilized man,
cigarettes, that is, and cold beer, and chatter,
waited out and lived down the ten-foot-away clatter
of crabs as they died for us inside their boiling can.

Considerations

1. How is the reader's initial attitude toward the crabs in this poem controlled by references to them as "precision made," "marine thing[s]," and "barbarian"?
2. How do the later images of the crabs as a "living mass" and their "clatter" as they are boiled compete with the images of them in lines 1–8?
3. What is the effect of the images describing the humans? How do you feel about these people?

4. The diction of this poem is informal and chatty, but it conveys a dark theme. Do you think the level of diction is appropriate for the theme?
5. Write a short essay that develops some point about the "chatter" of "civilized man" and the "clatter" of the crabs.

SALLY CROFT (b. 1935)

Home-Baked Bread

1981

> Nothing gives a household a greater sense of stability and common comfort than the aroma of cooling bread. Begin, if you like, with a loaf of whole wheat, which requires neither sifting nor kneading, and go on from there to more cunning triumphs.
>
> *The Joy of Cooking*

What is it she is not saying?
Cunning triumphs. It rings
of insinuation. Step into my kitchen,
I have prepared a cunning triumph
for you. Spices and herbs
sealed in this porcelain jar,

a treasure of my great-aunt
who sat up past midnight
in her Massachusetts bedroom
when the moon was dark. Come,
rest your feet. I'll make
you tea with honey and slices

of warm bread spread with peach butter.
I picked the fruit this morning
still fresh with dew. The fragrance
is seductive? I hoped you would say that.
See how the heat rises
when the bread opens. Come,

we'll eat together, the small flakes
have scarcely any flavor. What cunning
triumphs we can discover in my upstairs room
where peach trees breathe their sweetness
beside the open window and
sun lies like honey on the floor.

Considerations

1. Why does the speaker in this poem seize upon the phrase "cunning triumphs" from *The Joy of Cooking* excerpt?
2. Distinguish between the voice we hear in lines 1–3 and the second voice in lines 3–24. Who is the "you" in the poem?
3. Why is "insinuation" an especially appropriate word choice in line 3?

4. How do the images in lines 20–24 bring together all the senses evoked in the preceding lines?
5. Write a paragraph that describes the sensuous (and perhaps sensual) qualities of a food you enjoy.

JOHN REPP (b. 1953)

Cursing the Hole in the Screen, Wondering at the Romance Some Find in Summer 1986

Interminable as a slug inching up
the mildewed wall of a chicken coop
left to fall down or be wrecked some
wrung-out night by boys marking the new
swell in their balls with ruin —
summer shambles on, its random tiny horrors
hatch, sting, copulate, die, all
in these rooms. Kitchen? Midges throng
to every orifice. Bathroom? Wasps lumber
down from the sill. Bedroom? Mosquitoes
sing like autistic children.
Run out
to the pond with no clothes on and bob
in the tepid wet, a hellish middle C
penetrating everything. And bellicose
frogs feasting in chorus so dissonant
it puts to shame all the postmodernist°
harumping of hoarse tubas and hubcaps
loved by believers in naturalism
and the culturally symptomatic.
Night wrings
its filthy washcloth as the first coil
of heat unwinds, the few dewdrops steam away,
here dust on the marigolds, there a cat sprawled
in the willow's crackling shade, no Artemis,°
no Mark Twain Mississippi River, no veranda,
just the *pop* of a billion eggs falling open.

17 *postmodernist:* A term that refers to the interest in contemporary arts in experimental forms. 25 *Artemis:* A Greek goddess of hunting, healing, and fertility.

Considerations

1. What feelings do you associate with summer? How does this poem make you feel about summer? Do the poem's images confirm or challenge your associations with summer?
2. Describe the poem's speaker. How does the voice of lines 1–8 compare with that of lines 15–20? What do the diction and allusions tell you about the speaker?

3. Comment on the appropriateness of the poem's title. Explain whether you think it is helpful or intrusive.
4. Select an image from the poem and expand on it by writing a brief essay developing further what the image mentions.

Connections

1. Explain which image of heat you find more effective, Repp's or H.D.'s in "Heat" (p. 551).
2. Compare the views of summer in Repp's poem and Louise Bogan's "Dark Summer" (p. 759).
3. Write a response to William Shakespeare's "Shall I compare thee to a summer's day?" (p. 647) from the point of view of Repp's speaker. Try to capture the speaker's vivid use of images.

PERSPECTIVE

T. E. HULME (1883–1917)

On the Differences between Poetry and Prose 1924

In prose as in algebra concrete things are embodied in signs or counters which are moved about according to rules, without being visualized at all in the process. There are in prose certain type situations and arrangements of words, which move as automatically into certain other arrangements as do functions in algebra. One only changes the *X*'s and the *Y*'s back into physical things at the end of the process. Poetry, in one aspect at any rate, may be considered as an effort to avoid this characteristic of prose. It is not a counter language, but a visual concrete one. It is a compromise for a language of intuition which would hand over sensations bodily. It always endeavors to arrest you, and to make you continuously see a physical thing, to prevent you gliding through an abstract process. It chooses fresh epithets and fresh metaphors, not so much because they are new, and we are tired of the old, but because the old cease to convey a physical thing and become abstract counters. A poet says a ship "coursed the seas" to get a physical image, instead of the counter word "sailed." Visual meanings can only be transferred by the new bowl of metaphor; prose is an old pot that lets them leak out. Images in verse are not mere decoration, but the very essence of an intuitive language. Verse is a pedestrian taking you over the ground, prose — a train which delivers you at a destination.

From "Romanticism and Classicism," in *Speculations,*
edited by Herbert Read

Considerations

1. What distinctions does Hulme make between poetry and prose? Which seems to be the most important difference?
2. Write an essay that discusses Hulme's claim that poetry "is a compromise for a language of intuition which would hand over sensations bodily."

15. Figures of Speech

Figures of speech are broadly defined as a way of saying one thing in terms of something else. An overeager funeral director might, for example, be described as a vulture. Although figures of speech are indirect, they are designed to clarify, not obscure, our understanding of what they describe. Poets frequently use them because, as Emily Dickinson said, the poet's work is to "Tell all the truth but tell it slant" in order to capture the reader's interest and imagination. But figures of speech are not limited to poetry. Hearing them, reading them, or using them is as natural as using language itself.

Suppose that in the middle of a class discussion concerning the economic causes of World War II your history instructor introduces a series of statistics by saying, "Let's get down to brass tacks." Would anyone be likely to expect a display of brass tacks for students to examine? Of course not. To interpret the statement literally would be to wholly misunderstand the instructor's point that the time has come for a close look at the economic circumstances leading to the war. A literal response transforms the statement into the sort of hilariously bizarre material often found in a sketch by Woody Allen.

The class does not look for brass tacks, because, to put it in a nutshell, they understand that the instructor is speaking figuratively. They would understand, too, that in the preceding sentence *in a nutshell* refers to brevity and conciseness rather than to the covering of a kernel of a nut. Figurative language makes its way into our everyday speech and writing as well as into literature because it is a means of achieving color, vividness, and intensity.

Consider the difference, for example, between these two statements.

Literal: The diner strongly expressed anger at the waiter.
Figurative: The diner reared from his table and roared at the waiter.

The second statement is more vivid because it creates a picture of ferocious anger by likening the diner to some kind of wild animal, such as a lion or tiger. By comparison, "strongly expressed anger" is neither especially strong nor especially expressive; it is flat. Not all figurative language avoids this kind of flatness, however. Figures of speech such as "getting down to brass tacks" and "in a nutshell" are clichés because they lack originality and freshness. Still, they suggest how these devices are commonly used to give language some color, even if that color is sometimes a bit faded.

There is nothing weak about William Shakespeare's use of figurative language in the following passage from *Macbeth.* Macbeth has just learned that his wife is dead, and he laments her loss as well as the course of his own life.

WILLIAM SHAKESPEARE (1564–1616)

From *Macbeth (Act V, Scene v)* (1605–06)

Tomorrow, and tomorrow, and tomorrow
Creeps in this petty pace from day to day
To the last syllable of recorded time;
And all our yesterdays have lighted fools
The way to dusty death. Out, out, brief candle!
Life's but a walking shadow, a poor player,
That struts and frets his hour upon the stage,
And then is heard no more. It is a tale
Told by an idiot, full of sound and fury,
Signifying nothing.

This passage might be summarized as "life has no meaning," but such a brief paraphrase does not take into account the figurative language that reveals the depth of Macbeth's despair and his view of the absolute meaninglessness of life. By comparing life to a "brief candle," Macbeth emphasizes the darkness and death that surround human beings. The light of life is too brief and unpredictable to be of any comfort. Indeed, life for Macbeth is a "walking shadow," futilely playing a role that is more farcical than dramatic, because life is, ultimately, a desperate story filled with pain and devoid of significance. What the figurative language provides, then, is the emotional force of Macbeth's assertion; his comparisons are disturbing because they are so apt.

The remainder of this chapter discusses some of the most important figures of speech used in poetry. A familiarity with them will help you to understand how poetry achieves its effects.

SIMILE AND METAPHOR

The two most common figures of speech are simile and metaphor. Both compare things that are ordinarily considered unlike each other. A ***simile*** makes an explicit comparison between two things by using words such as *like, as, than, appears,* or *seems:* "A sip of Mrs. Cook's coffee is like a punch in the stomach." The force of the simile is created by the differences between the two things compared. There would be no simile if the comparison was stated this way: "Mrs. Cook's coffee is as strong as the cafeteria's coffee." This is a literal comparison because Mrs. Cook's coffee is compared with something like it, another kind of coffee. Consider how simile is used in this poem.

MARGARET ATWOOD (b. 1939)

you fit into me 1971

you fit into me
like a hook into an eye

a fish hook
an open eye

If you blinked on a second reading, you got the point of this poem, because you recognized that the simile "like a hook into an eye" gives way to a play on words in the final two lines. There the hook and eye, no longer a pleasant domestic image of fitting closely together, become a literal, sharp fishhook and a human eye. The wordplay qualifies the simile and drastically alters the tone of this poem by creating a strong and unpleasant surprise.

A ***metaphor,*** like a simile, makes a comparison between two unlike things, but it does so implicitly, without words such as *like* or *as:* "Mrs. Cook's coffee is a punch in the stomach." Metaphor asserts the identity of dissimilar things. Macbeth tells us that life *is* a "brief candle," life *is* a "walking shadow," life *is* a "poor player," life *is* a "tale / Told by an idiot." Metaphor transforms people, places, objects, and ideas into whatever the poet imagines them to be, and if metaphors are effective, the reader's experience, understanding, and appreciation of what is described are enhanced. Metaphors are frequently more demanding than similes because they are not signaled by particular words. They are both subtle and powerful.

Here is a poem about presentiment, a foreboding that something terrible is about to happen.

EMILY DICKINSON (1830–1886)

Presentiment — is that long Shadow — on the lawn — c. 1863

Presentiment — is that long Shadow — on the lawn —
Indicative that Suns go down —

The notice to the startled Grass
That Darkness — is about to pass —

The metaphors in this poem define the abstraction *presentiment.* The sense of foreboding that Dickinson expresses is identified with a particular moment, the moment when darkness is just about to envelope an otherwise tranquil ordinary scene. The speaker projects that fear onto the "startled Grass" so that it seems any life must be frightened by the approaching "Shadow" and "Darkness" — two richly connotative words associated with death. The metaphors obliquely tell us ("tell it slant" was Dickinson's motto, remember) that presentiment is related to a fear of death, and, more important, the metaphors convey the feelings which attend that idea.

Some metaphors are more subtle than others, because their comparison of terms is less explicit. Notice the difference between the following two metaphors, both of which describe a shaggy derelict refusing to leave the warmth of a hotel lobby. "He was a mule standing his ground" is a quite explicit comparison. The man is a mule; X is Y. But this metaphor is much more covert: "He brayed his refusal to leave." This second version is an ***implied metaphor,*** because it does not explicitly identify the man with a mule. Instead, it hints at or alludes to the mule. Braying is associated with mules and is especially appropriate in this context because of those animals' reputation for stubbornness. Implied metaphors can slip by readers, but they offer the alert reader the energy and resonance of carefully chosen, highly concentrated language.

Some poets write extended comparisons in which part or all of the poem consists of a series of related metaphors or similes. Extended metaphors are more common than extended similes. In "Catch" (p. 499), Francis creates an ***extended metaphor*** that compares poetry to a game of catch. The entire poem is organized around this comparison, just as all of the elements in Cummings's "she being Brand" (p. 527) are clustered around the extended comparison of a car and a woman. Because these comparisons are at work throughout the entire poem, they are called ***controlling metaphors.*** Extended comparisons can serve as a poem's organizing principle; they are also a reminder that in good poems metaphor and simile are not merely decorative but inseparable from what is expressed.

Notice the controlling metaphor in this poem, written by a woman whose contemporaries identified her more as a wife and mother than as a poet. Bradstreet's first volume of poetry, *The Tenth Muse,* was published by her brother-in-law in 1650 without her prior knowledge.

ANNE BRADSTREET (c. 1612–1672)

The Author to Her Book 1678

Thou ill-formed offspring of my feeble brain,
Who after birth did'st by my side remain,
Till snatched from thence by friends, less wise than true,
Who thee abroad exposed to public view;
Made thee in rags, halting, to the press to trudge,
Where errors were not lessened, all may judge.
At thy return my blushing was not small,
My rambling brat (in print) should mother call;
I cast thee by as one unfit for light,
Thy visage was so irksome in my sight;
Yet being mine own, at length affection would
Thy blemishes amend, if so I could:
I washed thy face, but more defects I saw,
And rubbing off a spot, still made a flaw.
I stretched thy joints to make thee even feet,
Yet still thou run'st more hobbling than is meet;
In better dress to trim thee was my mind,
But nought save homespun cloth in the house I find.
In this array, 'mongst vulgars may'st thou roam;
In critics' hands beware thou dost not come;
And take thy way where yet thou are not known.
If for thy Father asked, say thou had'st none;
And for thy Mother, she alas is poor,
Which caused her thus to send thee out of door.

The extended metaphor likening her book to a child came naturally to Bradstreet and allowed her to regard her work both critically and affectionately. Her conception of the book as her child creates just the right tone of amusement, self-deprecation, and concern.

OTHER FIGURES

Perhaps the humblest figure of speech — if not one of the most familiar — is the pun. A ***pun*** is a play on words that relies on a word having more than one meaning or sounding like another word. For example, "A fad is in one era and out the other" is the sort of pun that produces obligatory groans. But most of us find pleasant and interesting surprises in puns. Here's one that has a slight edge to its humor.

EDMUND CONTI (b. 1929)

Pragmatist **1985**

Apocalypse soon
Coming our way
Ground zero at noon
Halve a nice day.

Grimly practical under the circumstances, the pragmatist divides the familiar cheerful cliché by half. As simple as this poem is, its tone is mixed because it makes us laugh and wince at the same time.

Puns can be used to achieve serious effects as well as humorous ones. Although we may have learned to underrate puns as figures of speech, it is a mistake to underestimate their power and the frequency with which they appear in poetry. A close examination, for example, of Henry Reed's "Naming of Parts" (p. 597), Robert Frost's "Design" (p. 725), or almost any lengthy passage from a Shakespeare play will confirm the value of puns.

Synecdoche is a figure of speech in which part of something is used to signify the whole: a neighbor is a "wagging tongue" (a gossip); a criminal is placed "behind bars" (in prison). Less typically, synecdoche refers to the whole used to signify the part: "Germany invaded Poland"; "Princeton won the fencing match." Clearly, certain individuals participated in these activities, not all of Germany or Princeton. Another related figure of speech is ***metonymy,*** in which something closely associated with a subject is substituted for it: "She preferred the silver screen [motion pictures] to reading." "At precisely ten o'clock the paper shufflers [office workers] stopped for coffee."

Synecdoche and metonymy may overlap and are therefore sometimes difficult to distinguish. Consider this description of a disapproving minister entering a noisy tavern: "As those pursed lips came through the swinging door, the atmosphere was suddenly soured." The pursed lips signal the presence of the minister and are therefore a synecdoche, but they additionally suggest an inhibiting sense of sin and guilt that makes the bar patrons feel uncomfortable. Hence, the pursed lips are also a metonymy, since they are in this context so closely connected with religion. Although the distinction between synecdoche and metonymy can be useful, when a figure of speech overlaps categories, it is usually labeled a metonymy.

Knowing the precise term for a figure of speech is, finally, less important than responding to its use in a poem. Consider how metonymy and synecdoche convey the tone and meaning of the following poem.

DYLAN THOMAS (1914–1953)

The Hand That Signed the Paper 1936

The hand that signed the paper felled a city;
Five sovereign fingers taxed the breath,
Doubled the globe of dead and halved a country;
These five kings did a king to death.

The mighty hand leads to a sloping shoulder,
The finger joints are cramped with chalk;
A goose's quill has put an end to murder
That put an end to talk.

The hand that signed the treaty bred a fever,
And famine grew, and locusts came;
Great is the hand that holds dominion over
Man by a scribbled name.

The five kings count the dead but do not soften
The crusted wound nor stroke the brow;
A hand rules pity as a hand rules heaven;
Hands have no tears to flow.

The "hand" in this poem is a synecdoche for a powerful ruler, because it is a part of someone used to signify the entire person. The "goose's quill" is a metonymy that also refers to the power associated with the ruler's hand. By using these figures of speech, Thomas depersonalizes and ultimately dehumanizes the ruler. The final synecdoche tells us that "Hands have no tears to flow." It makes us see the political power behind the hand as remote and inhuman. How is the meaning of the poem enlarged when the speaker says, "A hand rules pity as a hand rules heaven"?

One of the ways writers energize the abstractions, ideas, objects, and animals that constitute their created worlds is through ***personification,*** the attribution of human characteristics to nonhuman things: temptation pursues the innocent; trees scream in the raging wind; mice conspire in the cupboard. We are not explicitly told that these things are people; instead, we are invited to see that they behave like people. Perhaps it is human vanity that makes personification a frequently used figure of speech. Whatever the reason, personification, a form of metaphor that connects the nonhuman with the human, makes the world understandable in human terms. Consider this concise example from William Blake's *The Marriage of Heaven and Hell,* a long poem that takes delight in attacking conventional morality: "Prudence is a rich ugly old maid courted by Incapacity." By personifying prudence, Blake transforms what is usually considered a virtue into a comic figure hardly worth emulating.

Often related to personification is another rhetorical figure called ***apostrophe,*** an address either to someone who is absent and therefore cannot hear the speaker or to something nonhuman that cannot comprehend.

Apostrophe provides an opportunity for the speaker of a poem to think aloud, and often the thoughts expressed are in a formal tone. John Keats, for example, begins "Ode on a Grecian Urn" (p. 698) this way: "Thou still unravished bride of quietness." Apostrophe is frequently accompanied by intense emotion that is signaled by phrasing such as "O Life." In the right hands — such as Keats's — apostrophe can provide an intense and immediate voice in a poem, but when it is overdone or extravagant it can be ludicrous. Modern poets are more wary of apostrophe than their predecessors, because apostrophizing strikes many self-conscious twentieth-century sensibilities as too theatrical. Thus modern poets tend to avoid exaggerated situations in favor of less charged though equally meditative moments, as in this next poem, with its amusing, half-serious cosmic twist.

JANICE TOWNLEY MOORE (b. 1939)

To a Wasp

1984

You must have chortled
finding that tiny hole
in the kitchen screen. Right
into my cheese cake batter
you dived,
no chance to swim ashore,
no saving spoon,
the mixer whirring
your legs, wings, stinger,
churning you into such
delicious death.
Never mind the bright April day.
Did you not see
rising out of cumulus clouds
That fist aimed at both of us?

Moore's apostrophe "To a Wasp" is based on the simplest of domestic circumstances; there is almost nothing theatrical or exaggerated in the poem's tone until "That fist" in the last line, when exaggeration takes center stage. As a figure of speech exaggeration is known as ***overstatement*** or ***hyperbole*** and adds emphasis without intending to be literally true: "The teenage boy ate everything in the house." Notice how the speaker of Marvell's "To His Coy Mistress" (p. 534) exaggerates his devotion in the following overstatement.

> An hundred years should go to praise
> Thine eyes and on thy forehead gaze,
> Two hundred to adore each breast,
> But thirty thousand to the rest:

That comes to 30,500 years. What is expressed here is heightened emotion, not deception.

The speaker also uses the opposite figure of speech, ***understatement,*** which says less than is intended. In the next section he sums up why he cannot take 30,500 years to express his love.

The grave's a fine and private place,
But none, I think, do there embrace.

The speaker is correct, of course, but by deliberately understating — saying "I think" when he is actually certain — he makes his point that death will overtake their love all the more emphatic. Another powerful example of understatement appears in the final line of Jarrell's "Death of the Ball Turret Gunner" (p. 525), when the disembodied voice of the machine-gunner describes his death in a bomber: "When I died they washed me out of the turret with a hose."

Paradox is a statement that initially appears to be self-contradictory but that, on closer inspection, turns out to make sense: "The pen is mightier than the sword." In a fencing match, anyone would prefer the sword, but if the goal is to win the hearts and minds of people, the art of persuasion can be more compelling than swordplay. To resolve the paradox, it is necessary to discover the sense that underlies the statement. If we see that "pen" and "sword" are used as metonymies for writing and violence, then the paradox rings true. ***Oxymoron*** is a condensed form of paradox in which two contradictory words are used together. Combinations such as "sweet sorrow," "silent scream," "sad joy," and "cold fire" indicate the kinds of startling effects that oxymorons can produce. Paradox is useful in poetry because it arrests a reader's attention by its seemingly stubborn refusal to make sense, and once a reader has penetrated the paradox, it is difficult to resist a perception so well earned. Good paradoxes are knotty pleasures. Here is a simple but effective one.

MICHAEL CADNUM (b. 1949)

Cat Spy 1985

He closes both eyes
and watches.

Anyone familiar with feline behavior knows the truth of this apparent contradiction.

The following poems are rich in figurative language. As you read and study them, notice how their figures of speech vivify situations, clarify ideas, intensify emotions, and engage your imagination. Although the terms for the various figures discussed in this chapter are useful for labeling the particular devices used in poetry, they should not be allowed to get in the way of your response to a poem. Don't worry about rounding up examples of figurative language. First relax and let the figures work their effects on you. Use the terms as a means of taking you further into poetry, and they will serve your reading well.

POEMS FOR FURTHER STUDY

ERNEST SLYMAN (b. 1946)

Lightning Bugs

1988

In my backyard,
They burn peepholes in the night
And take snapshots of my house.

Considerations

1. Explain why the title is essential to this poem.
2. What makes the description of the lightning bugs effective? How do the second and third lines complement each other?
3. As Slyman has done, take a simple, common fact of nature and make it vivid by using a figure of speech to describe it.

SYLVIA PLATH (1932–1963)

Mirror

1963

I am silver and exact. I have no preconceptions.
Whatever I see I swallow immediately
Just as it is, unmisted by love or dislike.
I am not cruel, only truthful —
The eye of a little god, four-cornered.
Most of the time I meditate on the opposite wall.
It is pink, with speckles. I have looked at it so long
I think it is a part of my heart. But it flickers.
Faces and darkness separate us over and over.

Now I am a lake. A woman bends over me,
Searching my reaches for what she really is.
Then she turns to those liars, the candles or the moon.
I see her back, and reflect it faithfully.
She rewards me with tears and an agitation of hands.
I am important to her. She comes and goes.
Each morning it is her face that replaces the darkness.
In me she has drowned a young girl, and in me an old woman
Rises toward her day after day, like a terrible fish.

Considerations

1. What is the effect of the personification in this poem? How would our view of the aging woman be different if she, rather than the mirror, told her story?
2. What is the mythical allusion in "Now I am a lake" (line 10)?
3. In what sense can "candles or the moon" be regarded as "liars." Explain this metaphor.
4. Discuss the effectiveness of the simile in the final line of the poem.

EMILY DICKINSON (1830–1886)

The thought beneath so slight a film —

c. 1860

The thought beneath so slight a film —
Is more distinctly seen —
As laces just reveal the surge —
Or Mists — the Apennine.° *Italian mountain range*

Considerations

1. State the paradox in lines 1–2 of this poem. What might "film" refer to?
2. What do "laces" and "Mists" have in common? How do the similes in lines 3–4 resolve the paradox?

EMILY DICKINSON (1830–1886)

Portraits are to daily faces

c. 1860

Portraits are to daily faces
As an Evening West,
To a fine, pedantic sunshine —
In a satin Vest!

Considerations

1. How is the basic strategy of this poem similar to the following statement: "Doorknob is to door as button is to sweater"?
2. Identify the four metonymies in the poem. Pay close attention to their connotative meanings.
3. If you don't know the meaning of *pedantic,* look it up in a dictionary. How does its meaning affect your reading of the word *fine?*
4. How is the theme of this poem related to the central idea in "The thought beneath so slight a film — "?
5. Dickinson once described herself as a literary artist this way: "My business is circumference." Discuss how these two poems both explain and express this characterization of her poetry.

Connections

1. Compare Dickinson's view of poetry in these two poems with Francis's perspective in "Catch" (p. 499). What important similarities and differences do you find?
2. Write an essay describing Robert Frost's strategy in "Mending Wall" (p. 713) or "Birches" (p. 719) as the business of circumference.

WILLIAM WORDSWORTH (1770–1850)

London, 1802

1802

Milton!° thou should'st be living at this hour:
England hath need of thee: she is a fen
Of stagnant waters: altar, sword, and pen,
Fireside, the heroic wealth of hall and bower,
Have forfeited their ancient English dower
Of inward happiness. We are selfish men;
Oh! raise us up, return to us again;
And give us manners, virtue, freedom, power.
Thy soul was like a star, and dwelt apart:
Thou hadst a voice whose sound was like the sea:
Pure as the naked heavens, majestic, free,
So didst thou travel on life's common way,
In cheerful godliness; and yet thy heart
The lowliest duties on herself did lay.

1 *John Milton:* (1608–1674) Poet famous especially for his religious epic *Paradise Lost* and his defense of political freedom.

Considerations

1. Explain the metonymies in lines 3–6 of this poem. What is the speaker's assessment of England?
2. How would the effect of the poem be different if it were in the form of an address to Wordsworth's contemporaries rather than an apostrophe to Milton? What qualities does Wordsworth attribute to Milton by the use of figurative language?

ROBERT GRAVES (1895–1985)

Down, Wanton, Down!

1933

Down, wanton, down! Have you no shame
That at the whisper of Love's name,
Or Beauty's, presto! up you raise
Your angry head and stand at gaze?

Poor bombard-captain,° sworn to reach
The ravelin and effect a breach —°
Indifferent what you storm or why,
So be that in the breach you die!

Love may be blind, but Love at least
Knows what is man and what mere beast;
Or Beauty wayward, but requires
More delicacy from her squires.

Tell me, my witless, whose one boast
Could be your staunchness at the post,
When were you made a man of parts
To think fine and profess the arts?

Will many-gifted Beauty come
Bowing to your bald rule of thumb,
Or Love swear loyalty to your crown?
Be gone, have done! Down, wanton, down!

5 *bombard:* An early type of cannon that catapulted stones. 6 *ravelin:* A fortification system; *effect a breach:* Break through a fortified defense.

Considerations

1. Identify the wanton apostrophized by the speaker.
2. What is the wanton's attitude toward Beauty and Love? What is the speaker's attitude?
3. Explain the puns in this poem. Is there a serious theme beyond the obvious fun?

Connections

1. Compare Graves's use of language here with Cummings's in "she being Brand" (p. 527).

WALT WHITMAN (1819–1892)

A Noiseless Patient Spider

1868

A noiseless patient spider,
I mark'd where on a little promontory it stood isolated,
Mark'd how to explore the vacant vast surrounding,
It launch'd forth filament, filament, filament, out of itself,
Ever unreeling them, ever tirelessly speeding them.

And you O my soul where you stand,
Surrounded, detached, in measureless oceans of space,
Ceaselessly musing, venturing, throwing, seeking the spheres to connect them,
Till the bridge you will need be form'd, till the ductile anchor hold,
Till the gossamer thread you fling catch somewhere, O my soul.

Considerations

1. Spiders are not usually regarded as pleasant creatures. Why does the speaker in this poem liken his soul to one? What similarities are there in the poem between spider and soul? Are there any significant differences?
2. How do the images of space relate to the connections made between the speaker's soul and the spider?

Connections

1. Read the early version of a "Noiseless Patient Spider" printed below. Which version is more unified by its metaphors? Which do you prefer? Why? Write an essay about the change of focus from the early version to the final one.

WALT WHITMAN (1819–1892)

The Soul, reaching, throwing out for love c. 1862

The Soul, reaching, throwing out for love,
As the spider, from some little promontory, throwing out filament after filament, tirelessly out of itself, that one at least may catch and form a link, a bridge, a connection
O I saw one passing along, saying hardly a word — yet full of love I detected him, by certain signs
O eyes wishfully turning! O silent eyes!
For then I thought of you o'er the world,
O latent oceans, fathomless oceans of love!
O waiting oceans of love! yearning and fervid! and of you sweet souls perhaps in the future, delicious and long:
But Death, unknown on the earth — ungiven, dark here, unspoken, never born:
You fathomless latent souls of love — you pent and unknown oceans of love!

DYLAN THOMAS (1914–1953)

Do not go gentle into that good night 1952

Do not go gentle into that good night,
Old age should burn and rave at close of day;
Rage, rage against the dying of the light.

Though wise men at their end know dark is right,
Because their words had forked no lightning they
Do not go gentle into that good night.

Good men, the last wave by, crying how bright
Their frail deeds might have danced in a green bay,
Rage, rage against the dying of the light.

Wild men who caught and sang the sun in flight,
And learn, too late, they grieved it on its way,
Do not go gentle into that good night.

Grave men, near death, who see with blinding sight
Blind eyes could blaze like meteors and be gay,
Rage, rage against the dying of the light.

And you, my father, there on the sad height,
Curse, bless, me now with your fierce tears, I pray.
Do not go gentle into that good night.
Rage, rage against the dying of the light.

Considerations

1. Thomas's father was close to death when this poem was written. How does the tone contribute to the poem's theme?
2. How is "good" used in line 1?
3. Characterize the men who are "wise" (line 4), "Good" (7), "wild" (10), and "Grave" (13).
4. What do figures of speech contribute to this poem?

Connections

1. Write an essay comparing Thomas's treatment of death with John Donne's in "Death Be Not Proud" (p. 775).
2. In Thomas's poem we experience "rage against the dying of the light." Contrast this with the rage you find in Sylvia Plath's "Daddy" (p. 830). What produces the emotion in Plath's poem?

JOHN DONNE (1572–1631)

A Valediction: Forbidding Mourning (1611)

As virtuous men pass mildly away,
And whisper to their souls to go,
While some of their sad friends do say,
The breath goes now, and some say, no:

So let us melt, and make no noise,
No tear-floods, nor sigh-tempests move;
'Twere profanation of our joys
To tell the laity our love.

Moving of th' earth° brings harms and fears, *earthquakes*
Men reckon what it did and meant,
But trepidation of the spheres,°
Though greater far, is innocent.

11 *trepidation of the spheres:* According to Ptolemaic astronomy, the planets sometimes moved violently, like earthquakes, but these movements were not felt by people on earth.

Dull sublunary° lovers' love
(Whose soul is sense) cannot admit
Absence, because it doth remove
Those things which elemented° it. *composed*

But we by a love so much refined,
That ourselves know not what it is,
Inter-assured of the mind,
Care less, eyes, lips, and hands to miss.

Our two souls therefore, which are one,
Though I must go, endure not yet
A breach, but an expansion,
Like gold to airy thinness beat.

If they be two, they are two so
As stiff twin compasses are two;
Thy soul the fixed foot, makes no show
To move, but doth, if th' other do.

And though it in the center sit,
Yet when the other far doth roam,
It leans, and hearkens after it,
And grows erect, as that comes home.

Such wilt thou be to me, who must
Like th' other foot, obliquely run;
Thy firmness makes my circle just,°
And makes me end, where I begun.

13 *sublunary:* Under the moon; hence mortal and subject to change. 35 *circle just:* The circle is a traditional symbol of perfection.

Considerations

1. A valediction is a farewell. Donne wrote this poem for his wife before leaving on a trip to France. What kind of "mourning" is the speaker forbidding?
2. Explain how the simile in lines 1–4 is related to the couple in lines 5–8. Who is described as dying?
3. How does the speaker contrast the couple's love to "sublunary lovers' love" (line 13)?
4. Explain the similes in lines 24 and 25–36.

MAY SWENSON (b. 1927)
The Secret in the Cat 1964

I took my cat apart
to see what made him purr.
Like an electric clock
or like the snore

of a warming kettle,
something fizzed and sizzled in him.
Was he a soft car,
the engine bubbling sound?

Was there a wire beneath his fur,
or humming throttle?
I undid his throat.
Within was no stir.

I opened up his chest
as though it were a door:
no whisk or rattle there.
I lifted off his skull:

no hiss or murmur.
I halved his little belly
but found no gear,
no cause for static.

So I replaced his lid,
laced his little gut.
His heart into his vest I slid
and buttoned up his throat.

His tail rose to a rod
and beckoned to the air.
Some voltage made him vibrate
warmer than before.

Whiskers and a tail:
perhaps they caught
some radar code
emitted as a pip, a dot-and-dash

of woolen sound.
My cat a kind of tuning fork? —
amplifier? — telegraph? —
doing secret signal work?

His eyes elliptic tubes:
there's a message in his stare.
I stroke him
but cannot find the dial.

Considerations

1. What is the secret in the cat? Does the poem answer this question? Explain why or why not.
2. What kinds of things is the cat compared to? What do they have in common? Why are they appropriate comparisons?

Connections

1. Write an essay comparing Swenson's response to her cat with Updike's treatment in "Dog's Death" (p. 496). How does each writer manage to evoke what is essential about the nature of the animal described in the poem?

LINDA PASTAN (b. 1932)

Marks

1978

My husband gives me an A
for last night's supper,
an incomplete for my ironing,
a B plus in bed.
My son says I am average,
an average mother, but if
I put my mind to it
I could improve.
My daughter believes
in Pass/Fail and tells me
I pass. Wait 'til they learn
I'm dropping out.

Considerations

1. Explain the appropriateness of the controlling metaphor in this poem. How does it reveal the woman's relationship to her family?
2. Discuss the meaning of the title.
3. How does the last line serve as both the climax of the woman's story and the controlling metaphor of the poem?

Connections

1. Compare the tone of this poem with that of Godwin's short story "A Sorrowful Woman" (p. 30).

EMILY DICKINSON (1830–1886)

I know that He exists

c. 1862

I know that He exists.
Somewhere — in Silence —
He has hid his rare life
From our gross eyes.

'Tis an instant's play.
'Tis a fond Ambush —

Just to make Bliss
Earn her own surprise!
But — should the play
Prove piercing earnest —
Should the glee-glaze —
In Death's — stiff — stare —

Would not the fun
Look too expensive!
Would not the jest —
Have crawled too far!

Considerations

1. Identify the "He" in the first line of this poem.
2. What is the poem's controlling metaphor?
3. What does the speaker contemplate in lines 9–12?
4. How does the speaker's tone change from beginning to end? Where does it start to change?
5. Comment on the appropriateness of "crawled" (line 16). Is there an allusion here?

ELAINE MAGARRELL (b. 1928)

The Joy of Cooking 1988

I have prepared my sister's tongue,
scrubbed and skinned it,
trimmed the roots, small bones, and gristle.
Carved through the hump it slices thin and neat.
Best with horseradish
and economical — it probably will grow back.
Next time perhaps a creole sauce
or mold of aspic?

I will have my brother's heart,
which is firm and rather dry,
slow cooked. It resembles muscle
more than organ meat
and needs an apple-onion stuffing
to make it interesting at all.
Although beef heart serves six
my brother's heart barely feeds two.
I could also have it braised
and served in sour sauce.

Considerations

1. How are the tongue and heart used to characterize the sister and brother in this poem?
2. Describe the speaker's tone. What effect does the title have on your determining the tone?

Connections

1. Write an essay that explains how cooking becomes a way of talking about something else in this poem and in Croft's "Home-Baked Bread" (p. 558).

PERSPECTIVE

JOHN R. SEARLE (b. 1932)

Figuring Out Metaphors 1979

If you hear somebody say, "Sally is a block of ice," or, "Sam is a pig," you are likely to assume that the speaker does not mean what he says literally, but that he is speaking metaphorically. Furthermore, you are not likely to have very much trouble figuring out what he means. If he says, "Sally is a prime number between 17 and 23," or "Bill is a barn door," you might still assume he is speaking metaphorically, but it is much harder to figure out what he means. The existence of such utterances — utterances in which the speaker means metaphorically something different from what the sentence means literally — poses a series of questions for any theory of language and communication: What is metaphor, and how does it differ from both literal and other forms of figurative utterances? Why do we use expressions metaphorically instead of saying exactly and literally what we mean? How do metaphorical utterances work, that is, how is it possible for speakers to communicate to hearers when speaking metaphorically inasmuch as they do not say what they mean? And why do some metaphors work and others do not?

From *Expression and Meaning*

Considerations

1. Searle poses a series of important questions. Write an essay that explores one of these questions, basing your discussion on the poems in this chapter.
2. Try writing a brief poem that provides a context for the line "Sally is a prime number between 17 and 23" or the line "Bill is a barn door." Your task is to create a context so that either one of these metaphoric statements is as readily understandable as "Sally is a block of ice" or "Sam is a pig." Share your poem with your classmates and explain how the line generated the poem you built around it.

16. Symbol, Allegory, and Irony

SYMBOL

A ***symbol*** is something that represents something else. An object, person, place, event, or action can suggest more than its literal meaning. A handshake between two world leaders might be simply a greeting, but if it is done ceremoniously before cameras it could be a symbolic gesture signifying unity, issues resolved, and joint policies that will be followed. We live surrounded by symbols. When a seventy-thousand-dollar Mercedes-Benz comes roaring by in the fast lane, we get a quick glimpse of not only an expensive car but an entire life-style that suggests opulence, broad lawns, executive offices, and power. One of the reasons some buyers are willing to spend roughly the cost of five Chevrolets for a single Mercedes-Benz is that they are aware of the car's symbolic value. A symbol is a vehicle for two things at once: it functions as itself and it implies meanings beyond itself.

The meanings suggested by a symbol are determined by the context in which they appear. The Mercedes could symbolize very different things depending upon where it was parked. Would an American political candidate be likely to appear in a Detroit blue-collar neighborhood with such a car? Probably not. Although a candidate might be able to afford the car, it would be an inappropriate symbol for someone seeking votes from all the people. As a symbol, the German-built Mercedes would backfire if voters perceived it as representing an entity partially responsible for layoffs of automobile workers or, worse, as a sign of decadence and corruption. Similarly, a huge statue of Lenin conveys different meanings to residents of Moscow than it would to farmers in Prairie Center, Illinois. Because symbols depend on contexts for their meaning, literary artists provide those contexts so that the reader has enough information to determine the probable range of meanings suggested by a symbol.

In the following poem the speaker describes walking at night. How is the night used symbolically?

ROBERT FROST (1874–1963)

Acquainted with the Night 1928

I have been one acquainted with the night.
I have walked out in rain — and back in rain.
I have outwalked the furthest city light.

I have looked down the saddest city lane.
I have passed by the watchman on his beat
And dropped my eyes, unwilling to explain.

I have stood still and stopped the sound of feet
When far away an interrupted cry
Came over houses from another street,

But not to call me back or say good-by;
And further still at an unearthly height
One luminary clock against the sky

Proclaimed the time was neither wrong nor right.
I have been one acquainted with the night.

In approaching this or any poem, you should read for literal meanings first, and then allow the elements of the poem to invite you to symbolic readings, if they are appropriate. Here the somber tone suggests that the lines have symbolic meaning too. The flat matter-of-factness created by the repetition of "I have" (lines 1–5, 7, 14) understates the symbolic subject matter of the poem, which is, finally, more about the "night" located in the speaker's mind or soul than it is about walking away from a city and back again. The speaker is "acquainted with the night." The importance of this phrase is emphasized by Frost's title and by the fact that he begins and ends the poem with it. Poets frequently use this kind of repetition to alert readers to details that carry more than literal meanings.

The speaker in this poem has personal knowledge of the night but does not indicate specifically what the night means. To arrive at the potential meanings of the night in this context, it is necessary to look closely at its connotations, along with the images provided in the poem. The connotative meanings of night suggest, for example, darkness, death, and grief. By drawing upon these connotations, Frost uses a ***conventional symbol,*** something that is recognized by many people to represent certain ideas. Roses conventionally symbolize love or beauty; laurels, fame; spring, growth; the moon, romance. Poets often use conventional symbols to convey tone and meaning.

Frost uses the night as a conventional symbol, but he also develops it into a ***literary*** or ***contextual symbol,*** which goes beyond traditional, public meanings. A literary symbol cannot be summarized in a word or two. It tends to be as elusive as experience itself. The night cannot be reduced or equated with darkness or death or grief, but it evokes those associations and more. Frost took what perhaps initially appears to be an overworked, conventional symbol and prevented it from becoming a cliché by deepening and extending its meaning.

The images in "Acquainted with the Night" lead to the poem's symbolic meaning. Unwilling, and perhaps unable, to explain explicitly to the watchman (and to the reader) what the night means, the speaker nevertheless conveys feelings about it. The brief images of darkness, rain, sad city lanes, the necessity for guards, the eerie sound of a distressing cry coming over rooftops, and the "luminary clock against the sky" proclaiming "the time was neither wrong nor right" all help to create a sense of anxiety in this tight-lipped speaker. Although we cannot know what unnamed personal experiences have acquainted the speaker with the night, the images suggest that whatever the night means, it is somehow associated with insomnia, loneliness, isolation, coldness, darkness, death, fear, and a sense of alienation from humanity and even time. Daylight — ordinary daytime thoughts and life itself — seems remote and unavailable in this poem. The night is literally the period from sunset to sunrise, but, more important, it is an internal state of being felt by the speaker and revealed through the images.

Frost used symbols rather than an expository essay that would explain the conditions which cause these feelings, because most readers can provide their own list of sorrows and terrors that evoke similar emotions. Through symbol, the speaker's experience is compressed and simultaneously expanded by the personal darkness that each reader brings to the poem. The suggestive nature of symbols makes them valuable for poets and evocative for readers.

ALLEGORY

Unlike expansive, suggestive symbols, ***allegory*** is a narration or description usually restricted to a single meaning because its events, actions, characters, settings, and objects represent specific abstractions or ideas. Although the elements in an allegory may be interesting in themselves, the emphasis tends to be on what they ultimately mean. Characters may be given names such as Hope, Pride, Youth, and Charity; they have few if any personal qualities beyond their abstract meanings. These personifications are a form of extended metaphor, but their meanings are severely restricted. They are not symbols because, for instance, the meaning of a character named Charity is precisely that virtue.

There is little or no room for broad speculation and exploration in allegories. If Frost had written "Acquainted with the Night" as an allegory, he might have named his speaker Loneliness and had him leave the City of Despair to walk the Streets of Emptiness, where Crime, Poverty, Fear, and other characters would define the nature of city life. The literal elements in an allegory tend to be deemphasized in favor of the message. Symbols, however, function both literally and symbolically, so that "Acquainted with the Night" is about both a walk and a sense that something is terribly wrong.

Allegory especially lends itself to ***didactic poetry,*** which is designed to teach an ethical, moral, or religious lesson. Many stories, poems, and plays are concerned with values, but didactic literature is specifically created to convey a message. "Acquainted with the Night" does not impart advice or offer guidance. If the poem argued that city life is self-destructive or sinful, it would be didactic; instead, it is a lyric poem that expresses the emotions and thoughts of a single speaker.

Although allegory is often enlisted in didactic causes because it can so readily communicate abstract ideas through physical representations, not all allegories teach a lesson. Here is a poem describing a haunted palace while also establishing a consistent pattern that reveals another meaning.

EDGAR ALLAN POE (1809–1849)

The Haunted Palace 1839

I

In the greenest of our valleys,
By good angels tenanted,
Once a fair and stately palace —
Radiant palace — reared its head.
In the monarch Thought's dominion —
It stood there!
Never seraph spread a pinion
Over fabric half so fair.

II

Banners yellow, glorious, golden,
On its roof did float and flow;
(This — all this — was in the olden
Time long ago)
And every gentle air that dallied,
In that sweet day,
Along the ramparts plumed and pallid,
A winged odor went away.

III

Wanderers in that happy valley
Through two luminous windows saw
Spirits moving musically
To a lute's well-tunèd law,
Round about a throne, where sitting
(Porphyrogene!)° *born to purple, royal*
In state his glory well befitting,
The ruler of the realm was seen.

IV

And all with pearl and ruby glowing
    Was the fair palace door,
Through which came flowing, flowing, flowing
    And sparkling evermore,
A troop of Echoes whose sweet duty
    Was but to sing,
In voices of surpassing beauty,
    The wit and wisdom of their king.

V

But evil things, in robes of sorrow,
    Assailed the monarch's high estate;
(Ah, let us mourn, for never morrow
    Shall dawn upon him, desolate!)
And, round about his home, the glory
    That blushed and bloomed
Is but a dim-remembered story
    Of the old time entombed.

VI

And travelers now within that valley,
    Through the red-litten windows see
Vast forms that move fantastically
    To a discordant melody;
While, like a rapid ghastly river,
    Through the pale door,
A hideous throng rush out forever,
    And laugh — but smile no more.

On one level this poem describes how a once happy palace is desolated by "evil things." If the reader pays close attention to the diction, however, an allegorical meaning becomes apparent on a second reading. A systematic pattern develops in the choice of words used to describe the palace, so that it comes to stand for a human mind. The palace, banners, windows, door, echoes, and throng are equated with a person's head, hair, eyes, mouth, voice, and laughter. That mind, once harmoniously ordered, is overthrown by evil, haunting thoughts that lead to the mad laughter in the poem's final lines. Once the general pattern is seen, the rest of the details fall neatly into place to strengthen the parallels between the surface description of a palace and the allegorical representation of a disordered mind.

Modern writers generally prefer symbol over allegory because they tend to be more interested in opening up the potential meanings of an experience instead of transforming it into a closed pattern of meaning. Perhaps the major difference is that while allegory may delight a reader's imagination, symbol challenges and enriches it.

IRONY

Another important resource writers use to take readers beyond literal meanings is ***irony,*** a technique that reveals a discrepancy between what appears to be and what is actually true. Here is a classic example in which appearances give way to the underlying reality.

EDWIN ARLINGTON ROBINSON (1869–1935)

Richard Cory 1897

Whenever Richard Cory went down town,
We people on the pavement looked at him:
He was a gentleman from sole to crown,
Clean favored, and imperially slim.

And he was always quietly arrayed,
And he was always human when he talked;
But still he fluttered pulses when he said,
"Good-morning," and he glittered when he walked.

And he was rich — yes, richer than a king —
And admirably schooled in every grace:
In fine, we thought that he was everything
To make us wish that we were in his place.

So on we worked, and waited for the light,
And went without the meat, and cursed the bread;
And Richard Cory, one calm summer night,
Went home and put a bullet through his head.

Richard Cory seems to have it all. Those less fortunate, "the people on the pavement," regard him as well bred, handsome, tasteful, and richly endowed with both money and grace. Until the final line of the poem, the reader, like the speaker, is charmed by Cory's good fortune, so quietly expressed in his decent, easy manner. That final, shocking line, however, shatters the appearances of Cory's life and reveals him to have been a desperately unhappy man. While everyone else assumes that Cory represented "everything" to which they aspire, the reality is that he could escape his miserable life only as a suicide. This discrepancy between what appears to be true and what actually exists is known as ***situational irony:*** what happens is entirely different from what is expected. We are not told why Cory shoots himself; instead, the irony in the poem shocks us into the recognition that appearances do not always reflect realities.

Words are also sometimes intended to be taken at other than face value. ***Verbal irony*** is saying something different from what is meant. After reading "Richard Cory," to say "That rich gentleman sure was happy" is ironic. The tone of voice would indicate that just the opposite was meant; hence, verbal irony is usually easy to detect in spoken language. In literature, however, a reader can sometimes take literally what a writer intends ironically. The remedy for this kind of misreading is to pay close attention to the poem's context. There is no formula that can detect verbal irony, but contradictory actions and statements as well as the use of understatement and overstatement can often be signals that verbal irony is present.

Consider how verbal irony is used in this poem.

KENNETH FEARING (1902–1961)

AD

1938

Wanted: Men;
Millions of men are *wanted at once* in a big new field;
New, tremendous, thrilling, great.
If you've ever been a figure in the chamber of horrors,
If you've ever escaped from a psychiatric ward,
If you thrill at the thought of throwing poison into wells, have heavenly visions of people, by the thousands, dying in flames —

You are the very man we want
We mean business and our business is *you*
Wanted: A race of brand-new men.

Apply: Middle Europe;
No skill needed;
No ambition required; no brains wanted and no character allowed;

Take a permanent job in the coming profession
Wages: *Death.*

This poem was written as Nazi troops stormed across Europe at the start of World War II. The advertisement suggests on the surface that killing is just an ordinary job, but the speaker indicates through understatement that there is nothing ordinary about the "business" of this "coming profession." Fearing uses verbal irony to indicate how casually and mindlessly people are prepared to accept the horrors of war.

"AD" is a ***satire,*** an example of the literary art of ridiculing a folly or vice in an effort to expose or correct it. The object of satire is usually some human frailty; people, institutions, ideas, and things are all fair game for satirists. Fearing satirizes the insanity of a world mobilizing itself for war: his irony reveals the speaker's knowledge that there is nothing *"New, tremendous, thrilling,* [or] *great"* about going off to kill and be killed. The implication of the poem is that no one should respond to advertisements for war. The poem serves as a satiric corrective to those who would troop off armed with unrealistic expectations; wage war and the wages consist of death.

Dramatic irony is used when a writer allows a reader to know more about a situation than a character does. This creates a discrepancy between what a character says or thinks and what the reader knows to be true. Dramatic irony is often used to reveal character. In the following poem the speaker delivers a public speech that ironically tells us more about him than it does about the patriotic holiday he is commemorating.

E. E. CUMMINGS (1894–1962)

next to of course god america i 1926

"next to of course god america i
love you land of the pilgrims' and so forth oh
say can you see by the dawn's early my
country 'tis of centuries come and go
and are no more what of it we should worry
in every language even deafanddumb
thy sons acclaim your glorious name by gorry
by jingo by gee by gosh by gum
why talk of beauty what could be more beautiful than these heroic happy dead
who rushed like lions to the roaring slaughter
they did not stop to think they died instead
then shall the voice of liberty be mute?"

He spoke. And drank rapidly a glass of water

This verbal debauch of chauvinistic clichés (notice the run-on phrases and lines) reveals that the speaker's relationship to God and country is not, as he claims, one of love. His public address suggests a hearty mindlessness that leads to "roaring slaughter" rather than to reverence or patriotism. Cummings allows the reader to see through the speaker's words to their dangerous emptiness. What the speaker means and what Cummings means are entirely different. Like Fearing's "AD," this poem is a satire that invites the reader's laughter and contempt in order to deflate the benighted attitudes expressed in it.

When a writer uses God, destiny, or fate to dash the hopes and expectations of a character or humankind in general, it is called ***cosmic irony.*** In "The Convergence of the Twain" (p. 539), for example, Hardy describes how "The Immanent Will" brought together the *Titanic* and a deadly iceberg. Technology and pride are no match for "the Spinner of the Years." Here's a painfully terse version of cosmic irony.

STEPHEN CRANE (1871–1900)

A Man Said to the Universe 1899

A man said to the universe:
"Sir, I exist!"
"However," replied the universe,
"The fact has not created in me
A sense of obligation."

Unlike in "The Convergence of the Twain," there is the slightest bit of humor in Crane's poem, but the joke is on us.

Irony is an important technique that allows a writer to distinguish between appearances and realities. In situational irony a discrepancy exists between what we expect to happen and what actually happens; in verbal irony a discrepancy exists between what is said and what is meant; in dramatic irony a discrepancy exists between what a character believes and what the reader knows to be true; and in cosmic irony a discrepancy exists between what a character aspires to and what universal forces provide. With each of these forms of irony, we are invited to move beyond surface appearances and sentimental assumptions to see the complexity of experience. Irony is often used in literature to reveal a writer's perspective on matters that previously seemed settled.

POEMS FOR FURTHER STUDY

CONRAD HILBERRY (b. 1928)

The Frying Pan 1978

My mark is my confusion.
If I believe it, I am
another long-necked girl
with the same face.
I am emptiness reflected
in a looking glass, a head
kept by a collar and leash,
a round belly with something
knocking to get in.

But cross the handle
with a short stroke
and I am Venus, the old
beauty. I am both the egg

and the pan it cooks in,
the slow heat, the miraculous
sun rising.

Considerations

1. Discuss the meanings of the "mark" in the first stanza. Can you think of any potential readings of it not mentioned by the speaker?
2. How is the pan transformed into an entirely different kind of symbol in the second stanza? How do the images of lines 13–16 create powerful symbolic values?
3. Discuss the significance of the poem's title.
4. The speaker of this poem is a woman, but the author is a man. Write an essay explaining whether knowing this makes any difference in your appreciation or understanding of the poem.

WILLIAM BLAKE (1757–1827)

The Sick Rose 1794

O Rose, thou art sick!
The invisible worm
That flies in the night,
In the howling storm,

Has found out thy bed
Of crimson joy,
And his dark secret love
Does thy life destroy.

Considerations

1. How does the use of personification in this poem indicate that the speaker laments the fate of more than a rose?
2. Discuss some of the possible meanings of the rose. How does the description of the worm help to explain the rose?
3. Is this poem to be read allegorically or symbolically? Can it be read literally?

W. D. SNODGRASS (b. 1926)

Lobsters in the Window 1963

First, you think they are dead.
Then you are almost sure
One is beginning to stir.
Out of the crushed ice, slow
As the hands of a schoolroom clock,
He lifts his one great claw
And holds it over his head;
Now, he is trying to walk.

But like a run-down toy;
Like the backward crabs we boys
Splashed after in the creek,
Trapped in jars or a net,
And then took home to keep.
Overgrown, retarded, weak,
He is fumbling yet
From the deep chill of his sleep

As if, in a glacial thaw,
Some ancient thing might wake
Sore and cold and stiff
Struggling to raise one claw
Like a defiant fist;
Yet wavering, as if
Starting to swell and ache
With that thick peg in the wrist.

I should wave back, I guess.
But still in his permanent clench
He's fallen back with the mass
Heaped in their common trench
Who stir, but do not look out
Through the rainstreaming glass.
Hear what the newsboys shout,
Or see the raincoats pass.

Considerations

1. Discuss the effectiveness of the images used in this poem to describe the movements of the lobster.
2. What is the effect of the images of coldness?
3. What is the speaker's response to the lobster? What is your response to the speaker?
4. Which lines invite symbolic readings? What is the poem's theme?

Connections

1. Write an essay comparing how symbols are used to convey themes in "Lobsters in the Window," Richmond Lattimore's "The Crabs," (p. 557) and Anne Sexton's "Lobster" (p. 845).

WILLIAM STAFFORD (b. 1914)

Traveling through the Dark 1962

Traveling through the dark I found a deer
dead on the edge of the Wilson River road.
It is usually best to roll them into the canyon:
that road is narrow; to swerve might make more dead.

By glow of the tail-light I stumbled back of the car
and stood by the heap, a dóe, a recent killing;
she had stiffened already, almost cold.
I dragged her off; she was large in the belly.

My fingers touching her side brought me the reason —
her side was warm; her fawn lay there waiting,
alive, still, never to be born.
Beside that mountain road I hesitated.

The car aimed ahead its lowered parking lights;
under the hood purred the steady engine.
I stood in the glare of the warm exhaust turning red;
around our group I could hear the wilderness listen.

I thought hard for us all — my only swerving —
then pushed her over the edge into the river.

Considerations

1. Notice the description of the car in this poem: the "glow of the tail-light," the "lowered parking lights," and how the engine "purred." How do these and other details suggest symbolic meanings for the car and the "recent killing"?
2. Discuss the speaker's tone. Does the speaker seem, for example, tough, callous, kind, sentimental, confused, or confident?
3. What is the effect of the last stanza's having only two lines rather than the established four lines of the previous stanzas?
4. Discuss the appropriateness of this poem's title. In what sense has the speaker "thought hard for us all"? What are those thoughts?
5. Is this a didactic poem?

RICHARD EBERHART (b. 1904)

The Groundhog 1936

In June, amid the golden fields,
I saw a groundhog lying dead.
Dead lay he; my senses shook,
And mind outshot our naked frailty.
There lowly in the vigorous summer
His form began its senseless change,
And made my senses waver dim
Seeing nature ferocious in him.
Inspecting close his maggots' might
And seething caldron of his being,
Half with loathing, half with a strange love,
I poked him with an angry stick.
The fever arose, became a flame
And Vigor circumscribed the skies,
Immense energy in the sun,

And through my frame a sunless trembling.
My stick had done nor good nor harm.
Then stood I silent in the day
Watching the object, as before;
And kept my reverence for knowledge
Trying for control, to be still,
To quell the passion of the blood;
Until I had bent down on my knees
Praying for joy in the sight of decay.
And so I left; and I returned
In Autumn strict of eye, to see
The sap gone out of the groundhog,
But the bony sodden hulk remained.
But the year had lost its meaning,
And in intellectual chains
I lost both love and loathing,
Mured° up in the wall of wisdom. *walled*
Another summer took the fields again
Massive and burning, full of life,
But when I chanced upon the spot
There was only a little hair left,
And bones bleaching in the sunlight
Beautiful as architecture;
I watched them like a geometer,
And cut a walking stick from a birch.
It has been three years, now.
There is no sign of the groundhog.
I stood there in the whirling summer,
My hand capped a withered heart,
And thought of China and of Greece,
Of Alexander° in his tent;
Of Montaigne° in his tower,
Of Saint Theresa° in her wild lament.

46 *Alexander:* Alexander the Great (356–323 B.C.) Macedonian king famous for conquering much of the world. 47 *Montaigne:* Michel de Montaigne (1533–1592) French essayist who commented on human affairs. 48 *Saint Theresa:* Saint Theresa of Avila (1515–1582) A mystic who founded a religious order.

Considerations

1. The speaker in this poem makes several visits to view the groundhog. Describe his changing feelings about the dead animal. What does the groundhog mean to the speaker?
2. How are the final four lines related to the speaker's response to the groundhog?
3. Why is a groundhog — rather than, say, a raccoon — an especially appropriate animal for the thematic purposes of this poem?
4. Explain whether you think this is an optimistic or pessimistic poem. Or is it somewhere in between?

Connections

1. Both "The Groundhog" and Stafford's "Traveling through the Dark" (p. 591) have as their subjects the death of an animal. Discuss how that death affects the speaker in each poem.
2. Write an essay that compares the symbolic meanings of the images of decay in "The Groundhog" and Roethke's "Root Cellar." (p. 548).
3. Compare and contrast the views of nature presented in "The Groundhog," "Traveling through the Dark," and D. H. Lawrence's "Snake" (below). How does each poem represent an effort to understand the nature of nature? Which view of nature do you find most convincing? Why?

D. H. LAWRENCE (1885–1930)

Snake

1923

A snake came to my water-trough
On a hot, hot day, and I in pajamas for the heat,
To drink there.

In the deep, strange-scented shade of the great dark carob-tree
I came down the steps with my pitcher
And must wait, must stand and wait, for there he was at the trough before me.

He reached down from a fissure in the earth-wall in the gloom
And trailed his yellow-brown slackness soft-bellied down, over the edge of the
    stone trough
And rested his throat upon the stone bottom,
And where the water had dripped from the tap, in a small clearness,
He sipped with his straight mouth,
Softly drank through his straight gums, into his slack long body,
Silently.

Someone was before me at my water-trough,
And I, like a second comer, waiting.

He lifted his head from his drinking, as cattle do,
And looked at me vaguely, as drinking cattle do,
And flickered his two-forked tongue from his lips, and mused a moment,
And stooped and drank a little more,
Being earth-brown, earth-golden from the burning bowels of the earth
On the day of Sicilian July, with Etna° smoking. *a volcano*
The voice of my education said to me
He must be killed,
For in Sicily the black, black snakes are innocent, the gold are venomous.

And voices in me said, If you were a man
You would take a stick and break him now, and finish him off.

But must I confess how I liked him,
How glad I was he had come like a guest in quiet, to drink at my water-trough

And depart peaceful, pacified, and thankless,
Into the burning bowels of this earth?

Was it cowardice, that I dared not kill him?
Was it perversity, that I longed to talk to him?
Was it humility, to feel so honored?
I felt so honored.

And yet those voices:
If you were not afraid, you would kill him!

And truly I was afraid, I was most afraid,
But even so, honored still more
That he should seek my hospitality
From out the dark door of the secret earth.

He drank enough
And lifted his head, dreamily, as one who has drunken,
And flickered his tongue like a forked night on the air, so black,
Seeming to lick his lips,
And looked around like a god, unseeing, into the air,
And slowly turned his head,
And slowly, very slowly, as if thrice adream,
Proceeded to draw his slow length curving round
And climb again the broken bank of my wall-face.

And as he put his head into that dreadful hole,
And as he slowly drew up, snake-easing his shoulders, and entered farther,
A sort of horror, a sort of protest against his withdrawing into that horrid black
hole,
Deliberately going into the blackness, and slowly drawing himself after,
Overcame me now his back was turned.

I looked round, I put down my pitcher,
I picked up a clumsy log
And threw it at the water-trough with a clatter.

I think it did not hit him,
But suddenly that part of him that was left behind convulsed in undignified
haste.
Writhed like lightning, and was gone
Into the black hole, the earth-lipped fissure in the wall-front,
At which, in the intense still noon, I stared with fascination.

And immediately I regretted it.
I thought how paltry, how vulgar, what a mean act!
I despised myself and the voices of my accursed human education.

And I thought of the albatross,
And I wished he would come back, my snake.

For he seemed to me again like a king,
Like a king in exile, uncrowned in the underworld,
Now due to be crowned again.

And so, I missed my chance with one of the lords
Of life.
And I have something to expiate;
A pettiness.

Considerations

1. Do you think Lawrence uses the snake in this poem as a conventional symbol of evil, or does he go beyond the traditional meanings associated with snakes? Consider the images used to describe the snake.
2. What is the "voice of my education" (line 22)? What is the conflict the speaker feels about the snake?
3. Identify the allusion to the albatross (line 66).
4. Explain why the speaker wishes the snake would return (lines 67–70). Why do you think the snake is described as "one of the lords / Of life" (71–72)?

LOUISE BOGAN (1897–1970)

The Dragonfly 1961

You are made of almost nothing
But of enough
To be great eyes
And diaphanous double vans;
To be ceaseless movement,
Unending hunger
Grappling love.

Link between water and air,
Earth repels you.
Light touches you only to shift into iridescence
Upon your body and wings.
Twice-born, predator,
You split into the heat.
Swift beyond calculation or capture
You dart into the shadow
Which consumes you.

You rocket into the day.
But at last, when the wind flattens the grasses,
For you, the design and purpose stop.
And you fall
With the other husks of summer.

Considerations

1. Which of the poem's images most effectively captures the movement and nature of a dragonfly?
2. Describe how the poem's tone changes from the first to the third stanza.

3. Do you think it is possible to read this poem symbolically? What might Bogan be describing in addition to a dragonfly? Which words are especially suggestive of additional meanings?
4. How would the tone and meaning of the poem be different if it ended with line 19?

HENRY REED (1914–1986)

Naming of Parts

1946

Today we have naming of parts. Yesterday,
We had daily cleaning. And tomorrow morning,
We shall have what to do after firing. But today,
Today we have naming of parts. Japonica
Glistens like coral in all of the neighboring gardens,
And today we have naming of parts.

This is the lower sling swivel. And this
Is the upper sling swivel, whose use you will see,
When you are given your slings. And this is the piling swivel,
Which in your case you have not got. The branches
Hold in the gardens their silent, eloquent gestures,
Which in our case we have not got.

This is the safety-catch, which is always released
With an easy flick of the thumb. And please do not let me
See anyone using his finger. You can do it quite easy
If you have any strength in your thumb. The blossoms
Are fragile and motionless, never letting anyone see
Any of them using their finger.

And this you can see is the bolt. The purpose of this
Is to open the breech, as you see. We can slide it
Rapidly backwards and forwards: we call this
Easing the spring. And rapidly backwards and forwards
The early bees are assaulting and fumbling the flowers:
They call it easing the Spring.

They call it easing the Spring: it is perfectly easy
If you have any strength in your thumb: like the bolt,
And the breech, and the cocking-piece, and the point of balance,
Which in our case we have not got; and the almond-blossom
Silent in all of the gardens and the bees going backwards and forwards,
For today we have naming of parts.

Considerations

1. Characterize the two speakers in this poem. Identify the lines spoken by each. How do their respective lines differ in tone?

2. What is the effect of the last line of each stanza?
3. How do ambiguities and puns contribute to the poem's meaning?
4. What symbolic contrast is made between the rifle instruction and the gardens? How is this contrast ironic?

ROBERT BROWNING (1812–1889)

Soliloquy of the Spanish Cloister 1842

Gr-r-r — there go, my heart's abhorrence!
  Water your damned flower-pots, do!
If hate killed men, Brother Lawrence,
  God's blood, would not mine kill you!
What? your myrtle-bush wants trimming?
  Oh, that rose has prior claims —
Needs its leaden vase filled brimming?
  Hell dry you up with its flames!

At the meal we sit together;
  Salve tibi!° I must hear
Wise talk of the kind of weather,
  Sort of season, time of year:
Not a plenteous cork-crop: scarcely
  Dare we hope oak-galls, I doubt;
What's the Latin name for "parsley"?
  What's the Greek name for "swine's snout"?

° *Hail to thee!*

Whew! We'll have our platter burnished,
  Laid with care on our own shelf!
With a fire-new spoon we're furnished,
  And a goblet for ourself,
Rinsed like something sacrificial
  Ere 'tis fit to touch our chaps —
Marked with L. for our initial!
  (He-he! There his lily snaps!)

Saint, forsooth! While Brown Dolores
  Squats outside the Convent bank
With Sanchicha, telling stories,
  Steeping tresses in the tank,
Blue-black, lustrous, thick like horsehairs,
  — Can't I see his dead eye glow,
Bright as 'twere a Barbary corsair's?
  (That is, if he'd let it show!)

When he finishes refection,
  Knife and fork he never lays
Cross-wise, to my recollection,
  As I do, in Jesu's praise.

I the Trinity illustrate,
Drinking watered orange-pulp —
In three sips the Arian° frustrate;
While he drains his at one gulp!

Oh, those melons! if he's able
We're to have a feast; so nice!
One goes to the Abbot's table,
All of us get each a slice.
How go on your flowers? None double?
Not one fruit-sort can you spy?
Strange! — And I, too, at such trouble,
Keep them close-nipped on the sly!

There's a great text in Galatians,
Once you trip on it, entails
Twenty-nine distinct damnations,
One sure, if another fails;
If I trip him just a-dying,
Sure of heaven as sure can be,
Spin him round and send him flying
Off to hell, a Manichee?° *a heretic*

Or, my scrofulous French novel
On gray paper with blunt type!
Simply glance at it, you grovel
Hand and foot in Belial's° gripe; *the Devil*
If I double down its pages
At the woeful sixteenth print,
When he gathers his greengages,
Ope a sieve and slip it in't?

Or, there's Satan! — one might venture
Pledge one's soul to him, yet leave
Such a flaw in the indenture
As he'd miss till, past retrieve,
Blasted lay that rose-acacia
We're so proud of! *Hy, Zy, Hine. . . .*°
'St, there's Vespers! *Plena gratia*
Ave, Virgo!° Gr-r-r — you swine! *Hail, Virgin, full of grace*

39 *Arian:* A follower of Arius, a heretic who denied the doctrine of the Trinity. 70 *Hy, Zy, Hine:* Possibly an incantation to call forth the Devil.

Considerations

1. How does the speaker of this poem, a monk in a monastery, characterize Brother Lawrence? What kinds of vices does he attribute to Brother Lawrence?
2. Why does the speaker hate Brother Lawrence so intensely? What is ironic about this growling hatred?
3. What does the speaker reveal about himself as he describes his fellow brother?

WILLIAM BLAKE (1757–1827)

The Chimney Sweeper 1789

When my mother died I was very young,
And my father sold me while yet my tongue
Could scarcely cry " 'weep! 'weep! 'weep! 'weep!"
So your chimneys I sweep, and in soot I sleep.

There's little Tom Dacre, who cried when his head,
That curled like a lamb's back, was shaved: so I said
"Hush, Tom! never mind it, for when your head's bare
You know that the soot cannot spoil your white hair."

And so he was quiet, and that very night,
As Tom was a-sleeping, he had such a sight!
That thousands of sweepers, Dick, Joe, Ned, and Jack,
Were all of them locked up in coffins of black.

And by came an Angel who had a bright key,
And he opened the coffins and set them all free;
Then down a green plain leaping, laughing, they run,
And wash in a river, and shine in the sun.

Then naked and white, all their bags left behind,
They rise upon clouds and sport in the wind;
And the Angel told Tom, if he'd be a good boy,
He'd have God for his father, and never want joy.

And so Tom awoke; and we rose in the dark,
And got with our bags and our brushes to work.
Though the morning was cold, Tom was happy and warm;
So if all do their duty they need not fear harm.

Considerations

1. Characterize the speaker in this poem, and describe his tone. Is his tone the same as the poet's? Consider especially lines 7–8 and 24.
2. What is the symbolic value of the dream in lines 11–20?
3. Why is irony central to the meaning of this poem?
4. Discuss the validity of this statement: " 'The Chimney Sweeper' is a sentimental poem about a shameful eighteenth-century social problem; such a treatment of child abuse cannot be taken seriously."

EMILY DICKINSON (1830–1886)

Lightly stepped a yellow star date unknown

Lightly stepped a yellow star
To its lofty place —
Loosed the moon her silver hat

From her lustral Face —
All of Evening softly lit
As an Astral Hall —
Father, I observed to Heaven,
You are punctual.

Considerations

1. Given the description in lines 1–7, why does the last line of this poem come as a surprise? What sort of sentiment did you expect? How does the speaker disrupt that expectation?
2. Describe the speaker's relationship to the "Father." What tone does the speaker adopt? How does the personification of the star contribute to the tone?

Connections

1. Write an essay comparing the theme and techniques of Dickinson's poem with those of Gerard Manley Hopkins's "God's Grandeur" (p. 614).
2. Discuss the views of God offered by Dickinson in this poem and in "I know that He exists" (p. 578). How does the tone contribute to the ways God is presented in each poem?

PERSPECTIVE

EZRA POUND (1885–1972)

On Symbols 1912

I believe that the proper and perfect symbol is the natural object, that if a man use "symbols" he must so use them that their symbolic function does not obtrude; so that *a* sense, and the poetic quality of the passage, is not lost to those who do not understand the symbol as such, to whom, for instance a hawk is a hawk.

From "Prolegomena," *Poetry Review,* February 1912

Considerations

1. Discuss whether you agree with Pound that the "perfect symbol" is a "natural object" that does not insist on being read as a symbol.
2. Write an essay in which you discuss Bogan's "The Dragonfly" (p. 596) as an example of the "perfect symbol" Pound proposes.
3. Do you think the poems by Pound in this anthology (see the index) fit his requirements for the way a symbol should function in a poem? Explain why or why not.

17. Sounds

Poems yearn to be read aloud. Much of their energy, charm, and beauty comes to life only when they are heard. Poets choose and arrange words for their sounds as well as for their meanings. Most poetry is best read with your lips, teeth, and tongue, because they serve to articulate the effects that sound may have in a poem. When a voice is breathed into a good poem, there is pleasure in the reading, the saying, and the hearing.

LISTENING TO POETRY

The earliest poetry — before writing and painting — was chanted or sung. The rhythmic quality of such oral performances served two purposes: it helped the chanting bard remember the lines, and it entertained audiences with patterned sounds of language, which were sometimes accompanied by musical instruments. Poetry has always been closely related to music. Indeed, as the word suggests, lyric poetry evolved from songs. "Western Wind" (p. 506), an anonymous Middle English lyric, survived as song long before it was written down. Had Robert Frost lived in a nonliterate society, he probably would have sung some version — a very different version to be sure — of "Acquainted with the Night" (p. 582) instead of writing it down. Even though Frost creates a speaking rather than a singing voice, the speaker's anxious tone is distinctly heard in any careful reading of the poem.

Like lyrics, early narrative poems were originally part of an anonymous oral folk tradition. A ***ballad*** such as "Sir Patrick Spens" (p. 517) or "Bonny Barbara Allan" (p. 745) told a story that was sung from one generation to the next until it was finally transcribed. Since the eighteenth century, this narrative form (discussed on p. 507) has sometimes been imitated by poets who write ***literary ballads.*** John Keats's "La Belle Dame sans Merci" (p. 692) is, for example, a more complex and sophisticated nineteenth-century reflection of the original ballad traditions that developed in the fifteenth century and earlier. In considering poetry as sound, we should not forget that poetry traces its beginnings to song.

These next lines exemplify poetry's continuing relation to song. What poetic elements can you find in this well-known song?

LEONARD COHEN (b. 1934)

Suzanne

1966

Suzanne takes you down
to her place near the river,
you can hear the boats go by
you can stay the night beside her.
And you know that she's half crazy
but that's why you want to be there
and she feeds you tea and oranges
that come all the way from China.
Just when you mean to tell her
that you have no gifts to give her,
she gets you on her wave-length
and she lets the river answer
that you've always been her lover.
    And you want to travel with her,
    you want to travel blind
    and you know that she can trust you
    because you've touched her perfect body
    with your mind.

Jesus was a sailor
when he walked upon the water
and he spent a long time watching
from a lonely wooden tower
and when he knew for certain
only drowning men could see him
he said All men will be sailors then
until the sea shall free them,
but he himself was broken
long before the sky would open,
forsaken, almost human,
he sank beneath your wisdom like a stone.
    And you want to travel with him,
    you want to travel blind
    and you think maybe you'll trust him
    because he touched your perfect body
    with his mind.

Now Suzanne takes your hand
and she leads you to the river,

she is wearing rags and feathers
from Salvation Army counters,
and the sun pours down like honey
on our lady of the harbour,
and she shows you where to look
among the garbage and the flowers.
There are heroes in the seaweed,
there are children in the morning,
they are leaning out for love
and they will lean that way forever
while Suzanne holds the mirror.
    And you want to travel with her,
    you want to travel blind
    and you know that you can trust her
    because she's touched your perfect body
    with her mind.

Considerations

1. What parallels are drawn between Jesus and Suzanne in this song? What do the images reveal about each of them? Which images are used metaphorically?
2. Who is the "you" of the song?
3. What is indicated by the changing pronouns in lines 17–18, 34–35, and 51–52?
4. What is the tone of this song?
5. Choose a contemporary song that you especially like and examine the lyrics. Write an essay explaining whether or not you consider the lyrics poetic.

Of course reading Cohen's "Suzanne" is not the same as hearing it. Like the lyrics of a song, many poems must be heard — or at least read with listening eyes — before they can be fully understood and enjoyed. The sounds of words are a universal source of music for human beings. This has been so from ancient tribes to bards to the two-year-old child in a bakery gleefully chanting "Cuppitycake, cuppitycake!"

Listen to the sound of this poem as you read it aloud. How do the words provide, in a sense, their own musical accompaniment?

JOHN UPDIKE (b. 1932)

Player Piano 1958

My stick fingers click with a snicker
And, chuckling, they knuckle the keys;
Light-footed, my steel feelers flicker
And pluck from these keys melodies.

My paper can caper; abandon
Is broadcast by dint of my din,

And no man or band has a hand in
The tones I turn on from within.

At times I'm a jumble of rumbles,
At others I'm light like the moon,
But never my numb plunker fumbles,
Misstrums me, or tries a new tune.

The speaker in this poem is a piano that can play automatically by means of a mechanism that depresses keys in response to signals on a perforated roll. Notice how the speaker's voice approximates the sounds of a piano. In each stanza a predominant sound emerges from the carefully chosen words. How is the sound of each stanza tuned to its sense?

Like Updike's "Player Piano," this next poem is also primarily about sounds.

MAY SWENSON (b. 1919)

A Nosty Fright 1984

The roldengod and the soneyhuckle,
the sack eyed blusan and the wistle theed
are all tangled with the oison pivy,
the fallen nine peedles and the wumbleteed.

A mipchunk caught in a wobceb tried
to hip and skide in a dandy sune
but a stobler put up a EEP KOFF sign.
Then the unfucky lellow met a phytoon

and was sept out to swea. He difted for drays
till a hassgropper flying happened to spot
the boolish feast all debraggled and wet,
covered with snears and tot.

Loonmight shone through the winey poods
where rushmooms grew among risted twoots.
Back blats flew betreen the twees
and orned howls hounded their soots.

A kumkpin stood with tooked creeth
on the sindow will of a house
where a icked wold itch lived all alone
except for her stoombrick, a mitten and a kouse.

"Here we part," said hassgropper.
"Pere we hart," said mipchunk, too.
They purried away on opposite haths,
both scared of some "Bat!" or "Scoo!"

October was ending on a nosty fright
with scroans and greeches and chanking clains,
with oblins and gelfs, coaths and urses,
skinning grulls and stoodblains.

Will it ever be morning, Nofember virst,
skue bly and the snappy hun, our friend?
With light breaves of wall by the fayside?
I sope ho, so that this oem can pend.

At just the right moments Swenson transposes letters to create amusing sound effects and wild wordplays. Although there is a story lurking in "A Nosty Fright," any serious attempt to interpret its meaning is confronted with "a EEP KOFF sign." Instead, we are invited to enjoy the delicious sounds the poet has cooked up.

Few poems revel in sound so completely. More typically, the sounds of a poem contribute to its meaning rather than become its meaning. Consider how sound is used in this next poem.

EMILY DICKINSON (1830–1886)

A Bird came down the Walk — c. 1862

A Bird came down the Walk —
He did not know I saw —
He bit an Angleworm in halves
And ate the fellow, raw,

And then he drank a Dew
From a convenient Grass —
And then hopped sidewise to the Wall
To let a Beetle pass —

He glanced with rapid eyes
That hurried all around —
They looked like frightened Beads, I thought —
He stirred his Velvet Head

Like one in danger, Cautious,
I offered him a Crumb
And he unrolled his feathers
And rowed him softer home —

Than Oars divide the Ocean,
Too silver for a seam —
Or Butterflies, off Banks of Noon
Leap, plashless as they swim.

This description of a bird offers a close look at how differently a bird moves when it hops on the ground than when it flies in the air. On the ground the bird moves quickly, awkwardly, and irregularly as it plucks up a worm, washes it down with dew, and then hops aside to avoid a passing beetle. The speaker recounts the bird's rapid, abrupt actions from a somewhat superior, amused perspective. By describing the bird in human terms (as if, for example, it chose to eat the worm "raw"), the speaker is almost condescending. But when the attempt to offer a crumb fails and the frightened bird flies off, the speaker is left looking up instead of down at the bird.

With that shift in perspective the tone shifts from amusement to awe in response to the bird's graceful flight. The jerky movements of lines 1–13 give way to the smooth motion of lines 15–20. The pace of the first three stanzas is fast and discontinuous. We tend to pause at the end of each line, and this reinforces a sense of disconnected movements. In contrast, the final six lines are to be read as a single sentence in one flowing movement, lubricated by various sounds.

Read again the description of the bird flying away. Several *o*-sounds contribute to the image of the serene, expansive, confident flight, just as the *s*-sounds serve as smooth transitions from one line to the next.

unr*o*lled	*s*o*f*ter	t*oo*	hi*s*	Ocean	Bank*s*
r*o*wed	*O*ars	N*oo*n	feather*s*	*s*ilver	plashle*ss*
h*o*me	*O*r		*s*ofter	*s*eam	a*s*
*O*cean	*o*ff		Oar*s*	Butterflie*s*	*s*wim

This blending of sounds (notice how "Leap, plashless" brings together the *p*- and *l*-sounds without a ripple) helps convey the bird's smooth grace in the air. Like a feathered oar, the bird moves seamlessly in its element.

The repetition of sounds in poetry is similar to the function of the tones and melodies that are repeated, with variations, in music. Just as the patterned sounds in music unify a work, so do the words in poems, which have been carefully chosen for the combinations of sounds they create. These sounds are produced in a number of ways.

The most direct way in which the sound of a word suggests its meaning is through ***onomatopoeia,*** which is the use of a word that resembles the sound it denotes: *quack, buzz, rattle, bang, squeak, bowwow, burp, choo-choo, ding-a-ling, sizzle.* The sound and sense of these words are closely related, but they represent a very small percentage of the words available to us. Poets usually employ more subtle means for echoing meanings.

Onomatopoeia can consist of more than just single words. In its broadest meaning the term refers to lines or passages in which sounds help to convey meanings, as in these lines from Updike's "Player Piano."

My stick fingers click with a snicker
And, chuckling, they knuckle the keys.

The sharp crisp sounds of these two lines approximate the sounds of a piano; the syllables seem to "click" against one another. Contrast Updike's rendition with the following lines:

> My long fingers play with abandon
> And, laughing, they cover the keys.

The original version is more interesting and alive, because the sounds of the words are pleasurable and reinforce the meaning through a careful blending of consonants and vowels.

Alliteration is the repetition of the same consonant sounds at the beginnings of nearby words: "*d*escending *d*ew*d*rops"; "*l*uscious *l*emons." Sometimes the term is also used to describe the consonant sounds within words: "tres*p*asser's re*p*roach"; "we*dd*ed la*d*y." Alliteration is based on sound rather than spelling. "*K*ean" and "*c*ar" alliterate, but "*c*ar" does not alliterate with "*c*ite." Rarely is heavy-handed alliteration effective. Used too self-consciously, it can be distracting instead of strengthening meaning or emphasizing a relation between words. Consider the relentless *h*'s in this line: "Horrendous horrors haunted Helen's happiness." Those *h*'s certainly suggest that Helen is being pursued, but they have a more comic than serious effect because they are overdone.

Assonance is the repetition of the same vowel sound in nearby words: "asl*ee*p under a tr*ee*"; "t*i*me and t*i*de"; "h*au*nt" and "*aw*esome"; "*ea*ch *e*vening." Both alliteration and assonance help to establish relations among words in a line or a series of lines. Whether the effect is ***euphony*** — lines that are musically pleasant to the ear and smooth, like the final lines of Dickinson's "A Bird came down the Walk —" — or the effect is ***cacophony*** — lines that are discordant and difficult to pronounce, like the claim that "never my numb plunker fumbles" in Updike's "Player Piano" — the sounds of words in poetry can be as significant as the words' denotative or connotative meanings.

This next poem provides a feast of sounds. Read the poem aloud and try to determine the effects of its sounds.

GALWAY KINNELL (b. 1927)

Blackberry Eating 1980

I love to go out in late September
among the fat, overripe, icy, black blackberries
to eat blackberries for breakfast,
the stalks very prickly, a penalty
they earn for knowing the black art
of blackberry-making; and as I stand among them
lifting the stalks to my mouth, the ripest berries

fall almost unbidden to my tongue,
as words sometimes do, certain peculiar words
like *strengths* or *squinched,*
many-lettered, one-syllabled lumps,
which I squeeze, squinch open, and splurge well
in the silent, startled, icy, black language
of blackberry-eating in late September.

Considerations

1. Underline the alliteration and circle the assonance throughout this poem. What is the effect of these sounds?
2. How do lines 4–6 fit into the poem? What does this prickly image add to the poem?
3. Explain what you think the poem's theme is.
4. Write an essay that considers the speaker's love of blackberry eating along with the speaker's appetite for words. How are the two blended in the poem?

RHYME

Like alliteration and assonance, ***rhyme*** is a way of creating sound patterns. Rhyme, broadly defined, consists of two or more words or phrases that repeat the same sounds: *happy* and *snappy*. Rhyme words often have similar spellings, but that is not a requirement of rhyme; what matters is that the words sound alike: *vain* rhymes with *reign* as well as *rain.* Moreover, words may look alike but not rhyme at all. In ***eye rhyme*** the spellings are similar but the pronunciations are not, as with *bough* and *cough,* or *brow* and *blow.*

Not all poems employ rhyme. Many great poems have no rhymes, and many weak verses use rhyme as a substitute for poetry. These are especially apparent in commercial messages and greeting-card lines. At its worst, rhyme is merely a distracting decoration that can lead to dullness and predictability. But used skillfully, rhyme creates lines that are memorable and musical.

Here's a poem using rhyme that you might remember the next time you are in a restaurant.

RICHARD ARMOUR (1906–1989)

Going to Extremes 1954

Shake and shake
    The catsup bottle
None'll come —
    And then a lot'll.

The experience recounted in this poem is common enough, but the rhyme's humor is special. The final line clicks the poem shut, an effect that is often achieved by the use of rhyme. That click provides a sense of a satisfying and fulfilled form. Rhymes have a number of uses: they can emphasize words, direct a reader's attention to relations between words, and provide an overall structure for a poem.

Rhyme is used in the following poem to imitate the sound of cascading water.

ROBERT SOUTHEY (1774–1843)

The Cataract of Lodore 1820

"How does the water
Come down at Lodore?"
My little boy ask'd me
Thus, once on a time;
And moreover he task'd me
To tell him in rhyme.
Anon at the word,
There first came one daughter
And then came another,
To second and third
The request of their brother,
And to hear how the water
Comes down at Lodore,
With its rush and its roar,
As many a time
They had seen it before.
So I told them in rhyme,
For of rhymes I had store:
And 'twas in my vocation
For their recreation
That so I should sing;
Because I was Laureate
To them and the King.

From its sources which well
In the tarn on the fell;
From its fountains
In the mountains,
Its rills and its gills;
Through moss and through brake,
It runs and it creeps
For awhile, till it sleeps
In its own little lake.
And thence at departing,

Awakening and starting,
It runs through the reeds
And away it proceeds,
Through meadow and glade,
In sun and in shade,
And through the wood-shelter,
Among crags in its flurry,
Helter-skelter,
Hurry-scurry.
Here it comes sparkling,
And there it lies darkling;
Now smoking and frothing
Its tumult and wrath in,
Till in this rapid race
On which it is bent,
It reaches the place
Of its steep descent.

The cataract strong
Then plunges along,
Striking and raging
As if a war waging
Its caverns and rocks among:
Rising and leaping,
Sinking and creeping,
Swelling and sweeping,
Showering and springing,
Flying and flinging,
Writhing and ringing,
Eddying and whisking,
Spouting and frisking,
Turning and twisting,
Around and around
With endless rebound!
Smiting and fighting,
A sight to delight in;
Confounding, astounding,
Dizzying and deafening the ear with its sound.

Collecting, projecting,
Receding and speeding,
And shocking and rocking,
And darting and parting,
And threading and spreading,
And whizzing and hissing,
And dripping and skipping,
And hitting and splitting,
And shining and twining,
And rattling and battling,
And shaking and quaking,

And pouring and roaring,
And waving and raving,
And tossing and crossing,
And flowing and going,
And running and stunning,
And foaming and roaming,
And dinning and spinning,
And dropping and hopping,
And working and jerking,
And guggling and struggling,
And heaving and cleaving,
And moaning and groaning;
And glittering and frittering,
And gathering and feathering,
And whitening and brightening,
And quivering and shivering,
And hurrying and skurrying,
And thundering and floundering;

Dividing and gliding and sliding,
And falling and brawling and spawling,
And driving and riving and striving,
And sprinkling and twinkling and wrinkling,
And sounding and bounding and rounding,
And bubbling and troubling and doubling,
And grumbling and rumbling and tumbling,
And clattering and battering and shattering;
Retreating and beating and meeting and sheeting,
Delaying and straying and playing and spraying,
Advancing and prancing and glancing and dancing,
Recoiling, turmoiling and toiling and boiling,
And gleaming and streaming and steaming and beaming,
And rushing and flushing and brushing and gushing,
And flapping and rapping and clapping and slapping,
And curling and whirling and purling and twirling,
And thumping and plumping and bumping and jumping,
And dashing and flashing and splashing and clashing;
And so never ending, but always descending,
Sounds and motions forever and ever are blending,
All at once and all o'er, with a mighty uproar;
And this way the water comes down at Lodore.

This deluge of rhymes consists of "Sounds and motions forever and ever . . . blending" (line 119). The pace quickens as the water creeps from its mountain source and then descends in rushing cataracts. As the speed of the water increases, so do the number of rhymes, until they run in fours: "dashing and flashing and splashing and clashing." Most rhymes meander through poems instead of flooding them; nevertheless, Southey's use of rhyme suggests how sounds can flow with meanings. "The Cataract of Lodore" has been criticized, however, for overusing onomatopoeia. Some readers find the poem silly; others regard it as a brilliant example of sound effects. What do you think?

A variety of types of rhyme is available to poets. The most common form, ***end rhyme,*** comes at the ends of lines.

It runs through the reeds
  And away it proceeds,
Through meadow and glade,
  In sun and in shade.

Internal rhyme places at least one of the rhymed words within the line, as in "Dividing and gliding and sliding" or, more subtly, in the fourth and final words of "In mist or cloud, on mast or shroud."

The rhyming of single-syllable words such as *grade* and *shade* is known as ***masculine rhyme.***

Loveliest of trees, the cherry now
Is hung with bloom along the bough.
–A. E. Housman

Rhymes using words of more than one syllable are also called masculine when the same sound occurs in a final stressed syllable, as in *defend, contend; betray, away.* A ***feminine rhyme*** consists of a rhymed stressed syllable followed by one or more rhymed unstressed syllables, as in *butter, clutter; gratitude, attitude; quivering, shivering.*

Lord confound this surly sister,
Blight her brow and blotch and blister.
–John Millington Synge

All the examples so far have been ***exact rhymes,*** because they share the same stressed vowel sounds as well as any sounds that follow the vowel. In ***near rhyme*** (also called ***off rhyme, slant rhyme,*** and ***approximate rhyme***), the sounds are almost but not exactly alike. There are several kinds of near rhyme. One of the most common is ***consonance,*** an identical consonant sound preceded by a different vowel sound: *home, same; worth, breath; trophy, daffy.* Near rhyme can also be achieved by using different vowel sounds with identical consonant sounds: *sound, sand; kind, conned; fellow, fallow.* The dissonance of *blade* and *blood* in the following lines helps to reinforce their grim tone.

Let the boy try along this bayonet-blade
How cold steel is, and keen with hunger of blood.
–Wilfred Owen

Near rhymes greatly broaden the possibility for musical effects in English, a language that, compared with Spanish or Italian, contains few exact rhymes. Do not assume, however, that a near rhyme represents a failed attempt at exact rhyme. Near rhymes allow a musical subtlety and variety, and can avoid the sometimes overpowering jingling effects that exact rhymes may create.

These basic terms hardly exhaust the ways in which the sound in poems can be labeled and discussed, but the terms can help you to describe how poets manipulate sounds for effect. Read "God's Grandeur" (below) aloud and try to determine how the sounds of the lines contribute to their sense.

PERSPECTIVE

DAVID LENSON (b. 1945)

On the Contemporary Use of Rhyme 1988

One impediment to a respectable return to rhyme is the popular survival of "functional" verse; greeting cards, pedagogical and mnemonic devices ("Thirty days hath September"), nursery rhymes, advertising jingles, and of course song lyrics. Pentameters, irregular rhymes, and free verse aren't much use in song-writing, where the meter has to be governed by the time signature of the music.

Far from universities, there has been a revival of rhymed couplets in Rap music, in which, to the accompaniment of synthesizers, vocalists deliver lengthy first-person narratives in tetrameter. While most writing teachers would dismiss such lyrics as doggerel, the aim of the songs is really not so far from that of Alexander Pope: to use rhyme to sharpen social insight, in the hope that the world may be reordered.

From *The Chronicle of Higher Education,* February 24, 1988

Considerations

1. Read some contemporary song lyrics from a wide range of groups or vocalists. Is Lenson correct in his assessment that irregular rhyme is not much use in song-writing?
2. Examine the rhymed couplets of some rap music. Discuss whether they are used "to sharpen social insight." What is the effect of using rhymes in rap music?
3. What is your own response to rhymed poetry? Do you like yours with or without? What do you think informs your preference?

SOUND AND MEANING

GERARD MANLEY HOPKINS (1844–1889)

God's Grandeur 1877

The world is charged with the grandeur of God
  It will flame out, like shining from shook foil;° *shaken gold foil*
  It gathers to a greatness, like the ooze of oil

Crushed.° Why do men then now not reck his rod?°
Generations have trod, have trod, have trod;
And all is seared with trade; bleared, smeared with toil;
And wears man's smudge and shares man's smell: the soil
Is bare now, nor can foot feel, being shod.

And for all this, nature is never spent;
There lives the dearest freshness deep down things;
And though the last lights off the black West went
Oh, morning, at the brown brink eastward, springs —
Because the Holy Ghost over the bent
World broods with warm breast and with ah! bright wings.

4 *Crushed:* Olives crushed in their oil; *reck his rod:* Obey God.

The subject of this poem is announced in the title and the first line: "The world is charged with the grandeur of God." The poem is a celebration of the power and greatness of God's presence in the world, but the speaker is also perplexed and dismayed by people who refuse to recognize God's authority and grandeur as they are manifested in the creation. Instead of glorifying God, "men" have degraded the earth through meaningless toil and cut themselves off from the spiritual renewal inherent in the beauty of nature. The relentless demands of commerce and industry have blinded people to the earth's natural and spiritual resources. In spite of this abuse and insensitivity to God's grandeur, however, "nature is never spent"; the morning light that "springs" in the east redeems the "black West" of the night and is a sign that the spirit of the Holy Ghost is ever present in the world. This summary of the poem sketches some of the thematic significance of the lines, but it does not do justice to how they are organized around the use of sound. Hopkins's poem, unlike Southey's "The Cataracts of Lodore," employs sounds in a subtle and complex way.

In the opening line Hopkins uses alliteration — a device apparent in almost every line of the poem — to connect "Go*d*" to the "worl*d*," which is "charge*d*" with his "gran*d*eur." These consonants unify the line as well. The alliteration in lines 2–3 suggests a harmony in the creation: the *f*'s in "*f*lame" and "*f*oil," the *sh*'s in "*sh*ining" and "*sh*ook," the *g*'s in "*g*athers" and "*g*reatness," and the visual (not alliterative) similarities of "*oo*ze *o*f *o*il" emphasize a world that is held together by God's will.

That harmony is abruptly interrupted by the speaker's angry question in line 4: "Why do men then now not reck his rod?" The question is as painful to the speaker as it is difficult to pronounce. The arrangement of the alliteration ("*n*ow," "*n*ot"; "*r*eck," "*r*od"), the assonance ("n*o*t," "r*o*d"; "m*e*n," "th*e*n," "r*e*ck"), and the internal rhyme ("m*en*," "th*en*") contribute to the difficulty in saying the line, a difficulty associated with human behavior. That behavior is introduced in line 5 by the repetition of "have trod" to emphasize the repeated mistakes — sins — committed by human beings.

The tone is dirgelike because humanity persists in its mistaken path rather than progressing. The speaker's horror at humanity is evident in the cacophonous sounds of lines 6–8. Here the alliteration of "*sm*eared," "*sm*udge," and "*sm*ell" along with the internal rhymes of "*sear*ed," "bl*ear*ed," and "sm*ear*ed" echo the disgust with which the speaker views human's "toil" with the "soil," an end rhyme that calls attention to our mistaken equation of nature with production rather than with spirituality.

In contrast to this cacophony, the final six lines build toward the joyful recognition of the new possibilities that accompany the rising sun. This recognition leads to the euphonic description of the "H*o*ly Gh*o*st *o*ver" (notice the reassuring consistency of the assonance) the world. Traditionally represented as a dove, the Holy Ghost brings love and peace to the "*w*orld," and "*br*oods *w*ith *w*arm *br*east and *w*ith ah! *br*ight *w*ings." The effect of this alliteration is mellifluous: the sound bespeaks the harmony that prevails at the end of the poem resulting from the speaker's recognition that nature can "never [be] spent" because God loves and protects the world.

The sounds of "God's Grandeur" enhance the poem's theme; more can be said about its sounds, but it is enough to point out here that for this poem the sound strongly echoes the theme in nearly every line. Here are some more poems in which sound plays a significant role.

POEMS FOR FURTHER STUDY

LEWIS CARROLL [CHARLES LUTWIDGE DODGSON] (1832–1898)

Jabberwocky

1871

'Twas brillig, and the slithy toves
  Did gyre and gimble in the wabe:
All mimsy were the borogoves,
  And the mome raths outgrabe.

"Beware the Jabberwock, my son!
  The jaws that bite, the claws that catch!
Beware the Jubjub bird, and shun
  The frumious Bandersnatch!"

He took his vorpal sword in hand;
  Long time the manxome foe he sought—
So rested he by the Tumtum tree,
  And stood awhile in thought.

And, as in uffish thought he stood,
  The Jabberwock, with eyes of flame,
Came whiffling through the tulgey wood,
  And burbled as it came!

One, two! One, two! And through and through
The vorpal blade went snicker-snack!
He left it dead, and with its head
He went galumphing back.

"And hast thou slain the Jabberwock?
Come to my arms, my beamish boy!
O frabjous day! Callooh, Callay!"
He chortled in his joy.

'Twas brillig, and the slithy toves
Did gyre and gimble in the wabe:
All mimsy were the borogoves,
And the mome raths outgrabe.

Considerations

1. What happens in this poem? Does it have any meaning?
2. Not all the words used in this poem appear in dictionaries. In *Through the Looking Glass,* Humpty Dumpty explains to Alice that " 'slithy' means 'lithe and slimy.' 'Lithe' is the same as 'active.' You see it's like a portmanteau — there are two meanings packed up into one word." Are there any other portmanteau words in the poem?
3. Which words in the poem sound especially meaningful, even if they are devoid of any denotative meanings?

Connections

1. Compare Carroll's strategies for creating sound and meaning with those used by Swenson in "A Nosty Fright" (p. 605).
2. Write an essay comparing what Robert Francis has to say about the words of a poem in "Glass" (p. 912) with Carroll's use of words. Discuss whether you think the two poets more or less agree or disagree in their respective approaches to writing poetry.
3. Read Marcus's "What Is an Initiation Story?" (p. 481). Consider whether the theme of "Jabberwocky" can (and should) be discussed in terms of an initiation story.

JEAN TOOMER (1894–1967)

Reapers

1923

Black reapers with the sound of steel on stones
Are sharpening scythes. I see them place the hones
In their hip-pockets as a thing that's done,
And start their silent swinging, one by one.
Black horses drive a mower through the weeds,
And there, a field rat, startled, squealing bleeds,
His belly close to ground. I see the blade,
Blood-stained, continue cutting weeds and shade.

Considerations

1. Is this poem primarily about harvesting, or does it suggest something else? Are there any symbols?
2. What is the poem's tone?
3. The reapers' work is described alliteratively as "silent swinging." How are the alliteration and assonance of lines 1–2 and 6 related to their meaning?
4. Why is Toomer's version of line 6 more effective than this one: "And there a startled, squealing field rat bleeds"?

JOHN DONNE (1572–1631)

Song

1633

Go and catch a falling star
　　Get with child a mandrake root,°
Tell me where all past years are,
　　Or who cleft the Devil's foot,
Teach me to hear mermaids singing,
　　Or to keep off envy's stinging,
　　　　And find
　　　　What wind
Serves to advance an honest mind.

If thou be'st borne to strange sights,
　　Things invisible to see,
Ride ten thousand days and nights,
　　Till age snow white hairs on thee,
Thou, when thou return'st, wilt tell me
　　All strange wonders that befell thee,
　　　　And swear
　　　　Nowhere
Lives a woman true, and fair.

If thou findst one, let me know,
　　Such a pilgrimage were sweet —
　　Yet do not, I would not go,
　　Though at next door we might meet;
Though she were true, when you met her,
　　And last, till you write your letter,
　　　　Yet she
　　　　Will be
False, ere I come, to two or three.

2 *mandrake root:* This V-shaped root resembles the lower half of the human body.

Considerations

1. What is the speaker's tone in this poem? What is his view of a woman's love? What does the speaker's use of hyperbole reveal about his emotional state?

2. Do you think Donne wants the speaker's argument to be taken seriously? Is there any humor in the poem?
3. Most of these lines end with masculine rhymes. What other kinds of rhymes are used for end rhymes?

JUDY GRAHN (b. 1940)

She Who bears it

1972

She Who bears it
bear down, breathe
bear down, bear down, breathe
bear down, bear down, bear down, breathe

She Who lies down in the darkness and bears it
She Who lies down in the lightness and bears it
the labor of She Who carries and bears is the first labor

all over the world
the waters are breaking everywhere
everywhere the waters are breaking
the labor of She Who carries and bears
and raises and rears is the first labor,
there is no other first labor.

Considerations

1. How do the sounds of this poem contribute to its sense of urgency?
2. What is the effect of the repeated words and phrases? How is that repetition related to what happens in the poem?
3. What do you think is the meaning of the phrase "the first labor" in line 7? How does the phrase take on additional meanings in lines 12 and 13?

THOMAS HARDY (1840–1928)

The Oxen

1915

Christmas Eve, and twelve of the clock.
	"Now they are all on their knees,"
An elder said as we sat in a flock
	By the embers in hearthside ease.

We pictured the meek mild creatures where
	They dwelt in their strawy pen,
Nor did it occur to one of us there
	To doubt they were kneeling then.

So fair a fancy few would weave
	In these years! Yet, I feel,

If someone said on Christmas Eve,
    "Come; see the oxen kneel
"In the lonely barton° by yonder coomb° *farmyard; ravine*
    Our childhood used to know,"
I should go with him in the gloom,
    Hoping it might be so.

Considerations

1. Traditionally, European peasants believed that animals worship God on Christmas Eve. How does the speaker feel about this belief? What is the difference between the speaker's attitude as a child and, "In these years," as an adult?
2. The speaker seems to feel nostalgic about his lost childhood. Does he feel the loss of anything more than that?
3. How do the sounds in the final stanza reinforce the tone and theme of the poem?

ALEXANDER POPE (1688–1774)

From *An Essay on Criticism*

1711

    But most by numbers° judge a poet's song; *versification*
And smooth or rough, with them, is right or wrong;
In the bright muse though thousand charms conspire,
Her voice is all these tuneful fools admire;
Who haunt Parnassus° but to please their ear,
Not mend their minds; as some to church repair,
Not for the doctrine, but the music there.
These equal syllables alone require,
Though oft the ear the open vowels tire;
While expletives° their feeble aid do join;
And ten low words oft creep in one dull line;
While they ring round the same unvaried chimes,
With sure returns of still expected rhymes;
Where'er you find "the cooling western breeze,"
In the next line, it "whispers through the trees":
If crystal streams "with pleasing murmurs creep,"
The reader's threatened (not in vain) with "sleep":
Then, at the last and only couplet fraught
With some unmeaning thing they call a thought,
A needless Alexandrine° ends the song,
That, like a wounded snake, drags its slow length along.
Leave such to tune their own dull rhymes, and know
What's roundly smooth, or languishingly slow;
And praise the easy vigor of a line,

5 *Parnassus:* A Greek mountain sacred to the Muses. 10 *expletives:* Unnecessary words used to fill a line, as the *do* in this line. 20 *Alexandrine:* A twelve-syllable line, as line 21.

Where Denham's strength, and Waller's° sweetness join.
True ease in writing comes from art, not chance,
As those move easiest who have learned to dance.
'Tis not enough no harshness gives offense,
The sound must seem an echo to the sense:
Soft is the strain when Zephyr° gently blows, *the west wind*
And the smooth stream in smoother numbers flows;
But when loud surges lash the sounding shore,
The hoarse, rough verse should like the torrent roar:
When Ajax° strives some rock's vast weight to throw,
The line too labors, and the words move slow;
Not so, when swift Camilla° scours the plain,
Flies o'er th' unbending corn, and skims along the main.

25 *Denham's, Waller's:* Sir John Denham (1615–1669), Edmund Waller (1606–1687) were poets who used heroic couplets. 34 *Ajax:* A Greek warrior famous for his strength in the Trojan War. 36 *Camilla:* A goddess famous for her delicate speed.

Considerations

1. These lines make a case for sound as an important element in poetry. In them Pope describes some faults he finds in poems and illustrates those faults within the lines that describe them. How do lines 4, 9, 10, 11, and 21 illustrate what they describe?
2. What is the objection to the "expected rhymes" in lines 12–17? How do they differ from Pope's end rhymes?
3. Some lines discuss how to write successful poetry. How do lines 23, 24, 32–33, 35, and 36–37 illustrate what they describe?
4. Do you agree that in a good poem "The sound must [always] seem an echo to the sense"?

RICHARD WILBUR (b. 1921)

The Death of a Toad 1950

A toad the power mower caught,
Chewed and clipped of a leg, with a hobbling hop has got
To the garden verge, and sanctuaried him
Under the cineraria leaves, in the shade
Of the ashen heartshaped leaves, in a dim,
Low, and a final glade.

The rare original heartsblood goes,
Spends on the earthen hide, in the folds and wizenings, flows
In the gutters of the banked and staring eyes. He lies
As still as if he would return to stone,
And soundlessly attending, dies
Toward some deep monotone,

Toward misted and ebullient seas
And cooling shores, toward lost Amphibia's emperies° *empires*
Day dwindles, drowning, and at length is gone
In the wide and antique eyes, which still appear
To watch, across the castrate lawn,
The haggard daylight steer.

Considerations

1. Look up a description of "cineraria" (line 4), a common garden plant. Why is it a particularly appropriate plant in the context of this poem?
2. How does Wilbur's word choice affect his treatment of the poem's subject? What is the tone? What is the significance of the toad's death?
3. Explain the effect of the alliteration in lines 2 and 15.
4. How does Wilbur's use of end rhyme reinforce meaning?

JONATHAN GALASSI (b. 1949)

Our Wives

1982

One rainy night that year we saw our wives
talking together in a barroom mirror,
and as our glasses drained I saw our lives

being lived, and saw that time deceives:
for we had thought of living as the Future,
but here these lovely women were, our wives,

and we were happy. And yet who believes
that what he's living now *is* his adventure,
that the beer we're drinking is our lives?

Think of all the pain that memory leaves,
things we got through we're glad we don't see clearer.
Think of our existence without wives,

our years in England — none of it survives.
It's over, fallen leaves, forgotten weather.
There was a time we thought we'd make our lives

into History. But history thrives
without us: what it leaves us is the future,
a barroom mirror lit up with our wives —
our wives who suddenly became our lives.

Considerations

1. Describe the speaker's tone in this poem. Do you think he is content with his life?
2. How is the speaker's sense of time woven into the poem? How does it compare with your own sense of time?

3. Galassi once explained that this "poem began out of the suggestiveness of the rhyme *wives/lives,* and it tries to explore the real-life relationship between these terms" (*Ecstatic Occasions, Expedient Forms,* edited by David Lehman). How do the rhyming words contribute to that exploration in the poem?
4. Write an essay that responds to the question posed in lines 7–9: "who believes/ that what he's doing now *is* his adventure,/that the beer we're drinking is our lives?"

PAUL HUMPHREY (b. 1915)

Blow 1983

Her skirt was lofted by the gale;
When I, with gesture deft,
Essayed to stay her frisky sail
She luffed, and laughed, and left.

Considerations

1. Point out instances of alliteration and assonance in this poem, and explain how they contribute to its euphonic effects.
2. What is the poem's controlling metaphor? Why is it especially appropriate?
3. Explain the ambiguity of the title.

ROBERT FRANCIS (1901–1987)

The Pitcher 1953

His art is eccentricity, his aim
How not to hit the mark he seems to aim at,

His passion how to avoid the obvious,
His technique how to vary the avoidance.

The others throw to be comprehended. He
Throws to be a moment misunderstood.

Yet not too much. Not errant, arrant, wild,
But every seeming aberration willed.

Not to, yet still, still to communicate
Making the batter understand too late.

Considerations

1. Explain how each pair of lines in this poem describes the pitcher's art.
2. Consider how the poem itself works the way a good pitcher does. Which lines illustrate what they describe?
3. Comment on the effects of the poem's rhymes. How are the final two lines differ-

ent in their rhyme from the previous lines? How does sound echo sense in lines 9–10?

4. Write an essay that considers "The Pitcher" as an extended metaphor for talking about poetry. How well does the poem characterize strategies for writing poetry as well as pitching?
5. Write an essay that develops an extended comparison between writing or reading poetry and playing or watching another sport.

Connections

1. Compare this poem with Robert Wallace's "The Double-Play" (p. 862), another poem that explores the relation of baseball to poetry.
2. Write an essay comparing "The Pitcher" with Lawrence Ferlinghetti's "Constantly risking absurdity" (p. 784). Explain which poem you find to be a more telling comparison — Francis's description of a poet as a pitcher or Ferlinghetti's of a poet as a tightrope walker.

HELEN CHASIN (b. 1938)

The Word Plum

1968

The word *plum* is delicious

pout and push, luxury of
self-love, and savoring murmur

full in the mouth and falling
like fruit

taut skin
pierced, bitten, provoked into
juice, and tart flesh

question
and reply, lip and tongue
of pleasure.

Considerations

1. Underline the alliteration and circle the assonance throughout the poem. What is the effect of these repetitions?
2. Which sounds in the poem are like the sounds one makes while eating a plum?
3. Discuss the title. Explain whether you think this poem is more about the word *plum* or about the plum itself. Consider whether the two can be separated in the poem.

Connections

1. How is Kinnell's "Blackberry Eating" (p. 608) similar in technique to Chasin's poem? Try writing such a poem yourself: choose a food to describe that allows you to evoke its sensuousness in sounds.

18. Patterns of Rhythm

The rhythms of everyday life surround us in regularly recurring movements and sounds. As you read these words, your heart pulsates while somewhere else a clock ticks, a cradle rocks, a drum beats, a dancer sways, a foghorn blasts, a wave recedes, or a child skips. We may tend to overlook rhythm since it is so tightly woven into the fabric of our experience, but it is there nonetheless, one of the conditions of life. Rhythm is also one of the conditions of speech, because the voice alternately rises and falls as words are stressed or unstressed and as the pace quickens or slackens. In poetry ***rhythm*** refers to the recurrence of stressed and unstressed sounds. Depending upon how the sounds are arranged, this can result in a pace that is fast or slow, choppy or smooth.

SOME PRINCIPLES OF METER

Poets use rhythm to create pleasurable sound patterns and to reinforce meanings. "Rhythm," Edith Sitwell once observed, "might be described as, to the world of sound, what light is to the world of sight. It shapes and gives new meaning." Prose can use rhythm effectively too, but prose that does so tends to be more of an exception. The following exceptional lines are from a speech by Winston Churchill to the House of Commons after Allied forces lost a great battle to German forces at Dunkirk during World War II.

> We shall not flag or fail. We shall go on to the end. We shall fight in France, we shall fight on the seas and oceans, we shall fight with growing confidence and growing strength in the air, we shall defend our island, whatever the cost may be, we shall fight on the beaches, we shall fight on the landing grounds, we shall fight in the fields and in the streets, we shall fight in the hills; we shall never surrender.

The stressed repetition of "we shall" bespeaks the resolute singleness of purpose that Churchill had to convey to the British people if they were to win the war. Repetition is also one of the devices used in poetry to create rhythmic effects. In the following excerpt from "Song of the Open Road," Walt Whitman urges the pleasures of limitless freedom upon his reader.

> Allons!° the road is before us! *Let's go!*
> It is safe — I have tried it — my own feet have tried it well — be not detain'd!
> Let the paper remain on the desk unwritten, and the book on the shelf unopen'd!
> Let the tools remain in the workshop! Let the money remain unearn'd!
> Let the school stand! mind not the cry of the teacher!
> Let the preacher preach in his pulpit! Let the lawyer plead in the court, and the judge expound the law.
>
> Camerado,° I give you my hand! *friend*
> I give you my love more precious than money,
> I give you myself before preaching or law;
> Will you give me yourself? will you come travel with me?
> Shall we stick by each other as long as we live?

These rhythmic lines quickly move away from conventional values to the open road of shared experiences. Their recurring sounds are not created by rhyme or alliteration and assonance (see Chapter 17) but by the repetition of words and phrases.

Although the repetition of words and phrases can be an effective means of creating rhythm in poetry, the more typical method consists of patterns of accented or unaccented syllables. Words contain syllables that are either stressed or unstressed. A ***stress*** (or ***accent***) places more emphasis on one syllable than on another. We say "*syl*lable" not "syl*la*ble," "*em*phasis" not "em*pha*sis." We routinely stress syllables when we speak: "*Is* she con*tent* with the *con*tents of the *yel*low *pack*age?" To distinguish between two people we might say "Is *she* con*tent*. . . ." In this way stress can be used to emphasize a particular word in a sentence. Poets often arrange words so that the desired meaning is suggested by the rhythm; hence, emphasis is controlled by the poet rather than left entirely to the reader.

When a rhythmic pattern of stresses recurs in a poem, the result is ***meter***. ***Scansion*** consists of measuring the stresses in a line to determine its metrical pattern. Several methods can be used to mark lines. One widely used system employs ´ for a stressed syllable and ˘ for an unstressed syllable. In a sense, the stress mark represents the equivalent of tapping one's foot to a beat.

> Hickory, dickory, dock,
> The mouse ran up the clock.
> The clock struck one,
> And down he run,
> Hickory, dickory, dock.

In the first two lines and the final line of this familiar nursery rhyme we hear three stressed syllables. In lines 3 and 4, where the meter changes for variety, we hear just two stressed syllables. The combination of stresses provides the pleasure of the rhythm we hear.

To hear the rhythms of "Hickory, dickory, dock" does not require a formal study of meter. Nevertheless, an awareness of the basic kinds of meter that appear in English poetry can enhance your understanding of how a poem achieves its effects. Understanding the sound effects of a poem and having a vocabulary with which to discuss those effects can intensify your pleasure in poetry. Although the study of meter can be extremely technical, the terms used to describe the basic meters of English poetry are relatively easy to comprehend.

The ***foot*** is the metrical unit by which a line of poetry is measured. A foot usually consists of one stressed and one or two unstressed syllables. A vertical line is used to separate the feet: "The clock | struck one" consists of two feet. A foot of poetry can be arranged in a variety of patterns; here are five of the chief ones.

Foot	*Pattern*	*Example*
iamb	˘ ´	away
trochee	´ ˘	Lovely
anapest	˘ ˘ ´	understand
dactyl	´ ˘ ˘	desperate
spondee	´ ´	dead set

The most common lines in English poetry contain meters based on iambic feet. However, even lines that are predominantly iambic will often include variations to create particular effects. Other important patterns include trochaic, anapestic, and dactylic feet. The spondee is not a sustained meter but occurs for variety or emphasis.

Iambic

What kept | his eyes | from giv | ing back | the gaze

Trochaic

He was | louder | than the | preacher

Anapestic

I am called | to the front | of the room

Dactylic

Sing it all | merrily

These meters have different rhythms and can create different effects. Iambic and anapestic are known as ***rising meters*** because they move from unstressed to stressed sounds, while trochaic and dactylic are known as

falling meters. Anapests and dactyls tend to move more lightly and rapidly than iambs or trochees. Although no single kind of meter can be considered always better than another for a given subject, it is possible to determine whether the meter of a specific poem is appropriate for its subject. A serious poem about a tragic death would most likely not be well served by lilting rhythms. Keep in mind too that though one or another of these four basic meters might constitute the predominant rhythm of a poem, variations can occur within lines to change the pace or call attention to a particular word.

A ***line*** is measured by the number of feet it contains. Here, for example, is an iambic line with three feet: "Ĭf shé | shŏuld wríte | ă nóte." These are the names for line lengths.

monometer: one foot	pentameter: five feet
dimeter: two feet	hexameter: six feet
trimeter: three feet	heptameter: seven feet
tetrameter: four feet	octameter: eight feet

By combining the name of a line length with the name of a foot, we can describe the metrical qualities of a line concisely. Consider, for example, the pattern of feet and length of this line.

I didn't want the boy to hit the dog.

The iambic rhythm of this line falls into five feet; hence it is called ***iambic pentameter.*** Iambic is the most common pattern in English poetry because its rhythm appears so naturally in English speech and writing. Unrhymed iambic pentameter is called ***blank verse;*** Shakespeare's plays are built upon such lines.

Less common than the iamb, trochee, anapest, or dactyl is the ***spondee,*** a two-syllable foot in which both syllables are stressed (´ ´). Note the effect of the spondaic foot at the beginning of this line.

Déad sét | ăgáinst | thĕ plán | hĕ wént | ăwáy.

Spondees can slow a rhythm and provide variety and emphasis, particularly in iambic and trochaic lines.

The effects of these English meters are easily seen in the following lines by Samuel Taylor Coleridge, in which the rhythm of each line illustrates the meter described in it.

Trochee trips from long to short;
From long to long in solemn sort
Slow Spondee stalks; strong foot yet ill able
Ever to come up with Dactylic trisyllable.
Iambics march from short to long —
With a leap and a bound the swift Anapests throng.

The speed of a line is also affected by the number of pauses in it. A pause within a line is called a ***caesura*** and is indicated by a double vertical line (||). A caesura can occur anywhere within a line and need not be indicated by punctuation.

> Camerado, || I give you my hand!
> I give you my love || more precious than money.

A slight pause occurs within each of these lines and at its end. Both kinds of pauses contribute to the lines' rhythm.

When a line has a pause at its end, it is called an ***end-stopped line.*** Such pauses reflect normal speech patterns and are often marked by punctuation. A line that ends without a pause and continues into the next line for its meaning is called a ***run-on line.*** Running over from one line to another is also called ***enjambment.*** The first and eighth lines of the following poem are run-on lines; the rest are end-stopped.

WILLIAM WORDSWORTH (1770–1850)

My Heart Leaps Up 1807

My heart leaps up when I behold
  A rainbow in the sky:
So was it when my life began;
So is it now I am a man;
So be it when I shall grow old,
  Or let me die!
The child is father of the Man;
And I could wish my days to be
Bound each to each by natural piety.

Run-on lines have a different rhythm from end-stopped lines. Lines 3–4 and 8–9 are both iambic, but the effect of their rhythms is very different when we read these lines aloud. The enjambment of lines 8 and 9 reinforces their meaning; just as the "days" are bound together, so are the lines.

The rhythm of a poem can be affected by several devices: the kind and number of stresses within lines, the length of lines, and the kinds of pauses that appear within lines or at their ends. In addition, as we saw in Chapter 17, the sound of a poem is affected by alliteration, assonance, rhyme, and consonance. These sounds help to create rhythms by controlling our pronunciations, as in the following lines by Alexander Pope.

> Soft is the strain when Zephyr gently blows,
> And the smooth stream in smoother numbers flows;
> But when loud surges lash the sounding shore,
> The hoarse, rough verse should like the torrent roar.

These lines are effective because their rhythm and sound work with their meaning.

SUGGESTIONS FOR SCANNING A POEM

These suggestions should help you in talking about a poem's meter.

1. After reading the poem through, read it aloud and mark the stressed syllables in each line. Then mark the unstressed syllables.
2. From your markings, identify what kind of foot is dominant (iambic, trochaic, dactylic, or anapestic) and divide the lines into feet, keeping in mind that the vertical line marking a foot may come in the middle of a word as well as at its beginning or end.
3. Determine the number of feet in each line. Remember that there may be variations; some lines may be shorter or longer than the predominant meter. What is important is the overall pattern. Do not assume that variations represent the poet's inability to fulfill the overall pattern. Notice the effects of variations and whether they emphasize words and phrases or disrupt your expectation for some other purpose.
4. Listen for pauses within lines and mark the caesuras; many times there will be no punctuation to indicate them.
5. Recognize that scansion does not always yield a definitive measurement of a line. Even experienced readers may differ over the scansion of a given line. What is important is not a precise description of the line but an awareness of how a poem's rhythms contribute to its effects.

The following poem demonstrates how you can use an understanding of meter and rhythm to gain a greater appreciation for what a poem is saying.

WILLIAM BUTLER YEATS (1865–1939)

That the Night Come 1912

She lived | in storm | and strife,
Her soul | had such | desire
For what | proud death | may bring
That it | could not | endure
The com | mon good | of life,
But lived | as 'twere | a king
That packed | his mar | riage day
With ban | neret | and pennon,
Trumpet | and kett | ledrum,
And the | outrag | eous cannon,

To bun | dle time | away
That the | night come

Scansion reveals that the predominant meter here is iambic trimeter. Each line contains three stressed and unstressed syllables that form a regular, predictable rhythm through line 7. That rhythm is disrupted, however, when the speaker compares the woman's longing for what death brings to a king's eager anticipation of his wedding night. The king packs the day with noisy fanfares and celebrations to fill up time and distract himself. Unable to accept "The common good of life," the woman fills her days with "storm and strife." In a determined effort to "bundle time away," she, like the king, impatiently awaits the night.

Lines 8–10 break the regular pattern established in the first seven lines. The extra unstressed syllable in lines 8 and 10 along with the trochaic feet in lines 9 *(trumpet)* and 10 *(And the)* interrupt the basic iambic trimeter and parallel the woman's and the king's frenetic activity. These lines thus echo the inability of the woman and king to "endure" regular or normal time. The last line is the most irregular in the poem. The final two accented syllables sound like the deep resonant beats of a kettledrum or a cannon firing. The words "night come" dramatically remind us that what the woman anticipates is not a lover but the mysterious finality of death. The meter serves, then, in both its regularity and variations to reinforce the poem's meaning and tone.

The following poems are especially rich in their rhythms and sounds. As you read and study them, notice how patterns of rhythm and the sounds of words reinforce meanings and contribute to the poems' effects. And, perhaps most importantly, read the poems aloud so that you can hear them.

POEMS FOR FURTHER STUDY

A. E. HOUSMAN (1859–1936)
When I was one-and-twenty 1896

When I was one-and-twenty
    I heard a wise man say,
"Give crowns and pounds and guineas
    But not your heart away;
Give pearls away and rubies
    But keep your fancy free."
But I was one-and-twenty,
    No use to talk to me.

When I was one-and-twenty
    I heard him say again,

"The heart out of the bosom
    Was never given in vain;
'Tis paid with sighs a plenty
    And sold for endless rue."
And I am two-and-twenty,
    And oh, 'tis true, 'tis true.

Considerations

1. Scan this poem. What is the basic metrical pattern?
2. How do lines 1–8 parallel lines 9–16 in their use of rhyme and metaphor? Are there any significant differences between the stanzas?
3. What do you think has happened to change the speaker's attitude toward love?
4. Explain why you agree or disagree with the advice given by the "wise man."
5. What is the effect of the repetition in line 16?

ROBERT FRANCIS (1901–1987)

Excellence 1914

Excellence is millimeters and not miles.
From poor to good is great. From good to best is small.
From almost best to best sometimes not measurable.
The man who leaps the highest leaps perhaps an inch
Above the runner-up. How glorious that inch
And that split-second longer in the air before the fall.

Considerations

1. How does alliteration help to support the meaning of this poem's first line?
2. Francis does not use iambic pentameter, the most common metrical line in English. What does he use? Why is it a more appropriate choice?
3. What is the effect of the caesura in line 2?
4. Why is Francis's version of line 6 better than this one: "And that split-second in the air before the fall"?

ROBERT HERRICK (1591–1674)

Delight in Disorder 1648

A sweet disorder in the dress
Kindles in clothes a wantonness.
A lawn° about the shoulders thrown
Into a fine distraction;
An erring lace, which here and there

linen scarf

Enthralls the crimson stomacher,
A cuff neglectful, and thereby
Ribbons to flow confusedly;
A winning wave, deserving note,
In the tempestuous petticoat;
A careless shoestring, in whose tie
I see a wild civility;
Do more bewitch me than when art
Is too precise in every part.

Considerations

1. Why does the speaker in this poem value "disorder" so highly?
2. What is the principal rhythmic order of the poem? Is it "precise in every part"? How does the poem's organization relate to its theme?
3. Which words in the poem indicate disorder? Which words indicate the speaker's response to that disorder? What are the connotative meanings of each set of words? Why are they appropriate? What do they suggest about the woman and the speaker?
4. Write a short essay in which you agree or disagree with the speaker's views on dress.

BEN JONSON (1573–1637)

Still to Be Neat — 1609

Still° to be neat, still to be dressed, — *continually*
As you were going to a feast;
Still to be powdered, still perfumed;
Lady, it is to be presumed,
Though art's hid causes are not found,
All is not sweet, all is not sound.

Give me a look, give me a face
That makes simplicity a grace;
Robes loosely flowing, hair as free;
Such sweet neglect more taketh me
Then all th' adulteries of art.
They strike mine eyes, but not my heart.

Considerations

1. What are the speaker's reservations about the lady in the first stanza? What do you think "sweet" means in line 6?
2. What does the speaker want from the lady in the second stanza? How has the meaning of "sweet" shifted from line 6 to line 10? What other words in the poem are especially charged with connotative meanings?
3. How do the rhythms of Jonson's lines help to reinforce meanings? Pay particular attention to lines 6 and 12.

Connections

1. Write an essay comparing the themes of "Still to Be Neat" and Herrick's "Delight in Disorder." How do the speakers make similar points but from different perspectives?
2. How does the rhythm of "Still to Be Neat" compare with that of "Delight in Disorder"? Which do you find more effective? Explain why.

WILLIAM BLAKE (1757–1827)

The Lamb

1789

Little Lamb, who made thee?
Dost thou know who made thee?
Gave thee life, and bid thee feed
By the stream and o'er the mead;
Gave thee clothing of delight,
Softest clothing, wooly, bright;
Gave thee such a tender voice,
Making all the vales rejoice?
Little Lamb, who made thee?
Dost thou know who made thee?

Little Lamb, I'll tell thee,
Little Lamb, I'll tell thee:
He is callèd by thy name,
For he calls himself a Lamb.
He is meek, and he is mild;
He became a little child.
I a child, and thou a lamb,
We are callèd by his name.
Little Lamb, God bless thee!
Little Lamb, God bless thee!

Considerations

1. This poem is from Blake's *Songs of Innocence.* Describe its tone. How do the meter, rhyme, and repetition help to characterize the speaker's voice?
2. Why is it significant that the animal addressed by the speaker is a lamb? What symbolic value would be lost if the animal were, for example, a doe?
3. How does the second stanza answer the question raised in the first? What is the speaker's view of the creation?

WILLIAM BLAKE (1757–1827)

The Tyger

1794

Tyger! Tyger! burning bright
In the forests of the night,
What immortal hand or eye
Could frame thy fearful symmetry?

In what distant deeps or skies
Burnt the fire of thine eyes?
On what wings dare he aspire?
What the hand dare seize the fire?

And what shoulder, and what art,
Could twist the sinews of thy heart?
And when thy heart began to beat,
What dread hand? and what dread feet?

What the hammer? what the chain?
In what furnace was thy brain?
What the anvil? what dread grasp
Dare its deadly terrors clasp?

When the stars threw down their spears,
And watered heaven with their tears,
Did he smile his work to see?
Did he who made the Lamb make thee?

Tyger! Tyger! burning bright
In the forests of the night,
What immortal hand or eye
Dare frame thy fearful symmetry?

Considerations

1. This poem is from Blake's *Songs of Experience* and is often paired with "The Lamb." Describe the poem's tone. Is the speaker's voice the same here as in "The Lamb"? Which words are repeated, and how do they contribute to the tone?
2. What is revealed about the nature of the tiger by the words used to describe its creation? What do you think the tiger symbolizes?
3. Unlike in "The Lamb," more than one question is raised in "The Tyger." What are these questions? Are they answered?
4. Compare the rhythms in "The Lamb" and "The Tyger." Each basically uses a seven-syllable line, but the effects are very different. Why?
5. Using these two poems as the basis of your discussion, describe what distinguishes innocence from experience.

DOROTHY PARKER (1893–1967)

One Perfect Rose 1926

A single flow'r he sent me, since we met.
    All tenderly his messenger he chose;
Deep-hearted, pure, with scented dew still wet —
    One perfect rose.

I knew the language of the floweret;
    "My fragile leaves," it said, "his heart enclose."
Love long has taken for his amulet
    One perfect rose.

Why is it no one ever sent me yet
    One perfect limousine, do you suppose?
Ah no, it's always just my luck to get
    One perfect rose.

Considerations

1. Describe the tone of the first two stanzas. How do rhyme and meter help to establish the tone?
2. How does the meaning of "One perfect rose" in line 12 compare with the way you read it in lines 4 and 8?
3. Describe the speaker. What sort of woman is she? How do you respond to her?

ALFRED, LORD TENNYSON (1809–1892)

Break, Break, Break 1842

Break, break, break,
    On thy cold gray stones, O Sea!
And I would that my tongue could utter
    The thoughts that arise in me.

O, well for the fisherman's boy,
    That he shouts with his sister at play!
O, well for the sailor lad,
    That he sings in his boat on the bay!

And the stately ships go on
    To their haven under the hill;
But O for the touch of a vanished hand,
    And the sound of a voice that is still!

Break, break, break
    At the foot of thy crags, O Sea!
But the tender grace of a day that is dead
    Will never come back to me.

Considerations

1. How do lines 1 and 13 differ from the predominant meter of this poem? How do these two lines control the poem's tone?
2. What is the effect of the repetition? What does "break" refer to in addition to the waves?

THEODORE ROETHKE (1908–1963)

My Papa's Waltz

1948

The whiskey on your breath
Could make a small boy dizzy;
But I hung on like death:
Such waltzing was not easy.

We romped until the pans
Slid from the kitchen shelf;
My mother's countenance
Could not unfrown itself.

The hand that held my wrist
Was battered on one knuckle;
At every step you missed
My right ear scraped a buckle.

You beat time on my head
With a palm caked hard by dirt,
Then waltzed me off to bed
Still clinging to your shirt.

Considerations

1. What details characterize the father in this poem? How does the speaker's choice of words reveal his feeling about his father? Is the remembering speaker still a boy?
2. Characterize the rhythm of the poem. Does it move "like death," or is it more like a waltz? Is the rhythm regular throughout the poem? What is its effect?
3. Comment on the appropriateness of the title. Why do you suppose Roethke didn't use "My Father's Waltz"?

ROBERT BROWNING (1812–1889)

My Last Duchess

1842

Ferrara°

That's my last Duchess painted on the wall,
Looking as if she were alive. I call

Ferrara: In the sixteenth century, the duke of this Italian city arranged to marry a second time after the mysterious death of his very young first wife.

That piece a wonder, now: Frà Pandolf's° hands
Worked busily a day, and there she stands.
Will't please you sit and look at her? I said
"Frà Pandolf" by design, for never read
Strangers like you that pictured countenance,
The depth and passion of its earnest glance,
But to myself they turned (since none puts by
The curtain I have drawn for you, but I)
And seemed as they would ask me, if they durst,
How such a glance came there; so, not the first
Are you to turn and ask thus. Sir, 'twas not
Her husband's presence only, called that spot
Of joy into the Duchess' cheek: perhaps
Frà Pandolf chanced to say "Her mantle laps
Over my lady's wrist too much," or "Paint
Must never hope to reproduce the faint
Half-flush that dies along her throat": such stuff
Was courtesy, she thought, and cause enough
For calling up that spot of joy. She had
A heart — how shall I say? — too soon made glad,
Too easily impressed; she liked whate'er
She looked on, and her looks went everywhere.
Sir, 'twas all one! My favor at her breast,
The dropping of the daylight in the West,
The bough of cherries some officious fool
Broke in the orchard for her, the white mule
She rode with round the terrace — all and each
Would draw from her alike the approving speech,
Or blush, at least. She thanked men, — good! but thanked
Somehow — I know not how — as if she ranked
My gift of a nine-hundred-years-old name
With anybody's gift. Who'd stoop to blame
This sort of trifling? Even had you skill
In speech — which I have not — to make your will
Quite clear to such an one, and say, "Just this
Or that in you disgusts me; here you miss,
Or there exceed the mark" — and if she let
Herself be lessoned so, nor plainly set
Her wits to yours, forsooth, and made excuse,
— E'en then would be some stooping; and I choose
Never to stoop. Oh sir, she smiled, no doubt,
Whene'er I passed her; but who passed without
Much the same smile? This grew; I gave commands;
Then all smiles stopped together. There she stands
As if alive. Will't please you rise? We'll meet
The company below, then. I repeat,
The Count your master's known munificence

3 *Frà Pandolf:* A fictitious artist.

Is ample warrant that no just pretense
Of mine for dowry will be disallowed;
Though his fair daughter's self, as I avowed
At starting, is my object. Nay, we'll go
Together down, sir. Notice Neptune, though,
Taming a sea-horse, thought a rarity,
Which Claus of Innsbruck° cast in bronze for me!

56 *Claus of Innsbruck:* Also a fictitious artist.

Considerations

1. To whom is the duke addressing his remarks about the duchess in this poem? What is ironic about the situation?
2. Why was the duke unhappy with his first wife? What does this reveal about the duke? What does the poem's title suggest about his attitude toward women in general?
3. What seems to be the visitor's response (lines 54–55) to the duke's account of his first wife?
4. How regular is the rhythm in this poem? Although the lines are rhymed pairs, the rhymes do not call attention to themselves. Analyze how Browning's use of caesuras and run-on lines affects the rhythm of the poem.

EMILY DICKINSON (1830–1886)

Because I could not stop for Death c. 1863

Because I could not stop for Death —
He kindly stopped for me —
The Carriage held but just Ourselves —
And Immortality.

We slowly drove — He knew no haste
And I had put away
My labor and my leisure too,
For His Civility —

We passed the School, where Children strove
At Recess — in the Ring —
We passed the Fields of Gazing Grain —
We passed the Setting Sun —

Or rather — He passed Us —
The Dews drew quivering and chill —
For only Gossamer, my Gown —
My Tippet° — only Tulle — *shawl*

We paused before a House that seemed
A Swelling of the Ground —

The Roof was scarcely visible —
The Cornice — in the Ground —

Since then — 'tis Centuries — and yet
Feels shorter than the Day
I first surmised the Horses' Heads
Were toward Eternity —

Considerations

1. Why couldn't the speaker stop for death?
2. How is Death personified in this poem? How does the speaker respond to him? Why are they accompanied by Immortality?
3. What is the significance of the things they "passed" in the third stanza?
4. What is the "House" in lines 17–20?
5. Discuss the rhythm of the lines. How, for example, is the rhythm of line 14 related to its meaning?

Connections

1. Compare the tone of this poem with that of Dickinson's "I heard a Fly buzz — when I died —" (p. 773).
2. Write an essay comparing Dickinson's view of death in this poem and in "If I shouldn't be alive" (p. 530). Which poem is more powerful for you? Explain why.

RICHARD LOVELACE (1618–1658)

To Lucasta, Going to the Wars 1649

Tell me not, sweet, I am unkind
That from the nunnery
Of thy chaste breast and quiet mind,
To war and arms I fly.

True, a new mistress now I chase,
The first foe in the field;
And with a stronger faith embrace
A sword, a horse, a shield.

Yet this inconstancy is such
As you too shall adore;
I could not love thee, dear, so much,
Loved I not honor more.

Considerations

1. How and why does the language of this poem tend to minimize the usual distinctions made between love and war?
2. Which words convey a religious tone? What do they contribute to the soldier's explanation of going to war?

3. How does the paradox in the final two lines resolve the soldier's problem of leaving the woman he loves?
4. What is the poem's predominant meter? Compare your scansion of the poem with another student's. If there is variation in the two scansions, how do you explain this variation?

EDWARD HIRSCH (b. 1950)

Fast Break

1985

(In Memory of Dennis Turner, 1946–1984)

A hook shot kisses the rim and
hangs there, helplessly, but doesn't drop

and for once our gangly starting center
boxes out his man and times his jump

perfectly, gathering the orange leather
from the air like a cherished possession

and spinning around to throw a strike
to the outlet who is already shoveling

an underhand pass toward the other guard
scissoring past a flat-footed defender

who looks stunned and nailed to the floor
in the wrong direction, turning to catch sight

of a high, gliding dribble and a man
letting the play develop in front of him

in slow motion, almost exactly
like a coach's drawing on the blackboard,

both forwards racing down the court
the way that forwards should, fanning out

and filling the lanes in tandem, moving
together as brothers passing the ball

between them without a dribble, without
a single bounce hitting the hardwood

until the guard finally lunges out
and commits to the wrong man

while the power-forward explodes past them
in a fury, taking the ball into the air

by himself now and laying it gently
against the glass for a layup,

but losing his balance in the process,
inexplicably falling, hitting the floor
with a wild, headlong motion
for the game he loved like a country

and swiveling back to see an orange blur
floating perfectly through the net.

Considerations

1. Why are run-on lines especially appropriate for this poem? How do they affect its sound and sense? What is the effect of the poem being one long sentence? Do the lines have a regular meter?
2. In addition to describing accurately a fast break, this poem is a tribute to a dead friend. How are the two purposes related in the poem?
3. How might this poem — to borrow a phrase from Robert Frost — represent a "momentary stay against confusion"?

PERSPECTIVE

LOUISE BOGAN (1897–1970)

On Formal Poetry 1953

What is formal poetry? It is poetry written in form. And what is *form?* The elements of form, so far as poetry is concerned, are meter and rhyme. Are these elements merely mold and ornaments that have been impressed upon poetry from without? Are they indeed restrictions which blind and fetter language and the thought and emotion behind, under, within language in a repressive way? Are they arbitrary rules which have lost all validity since they have been broken to good purpose by "experimental poets," ancient and modern? Does the breaking up of form, or its total elimination, always result in an increase of power and of effect; and is any return to form a sort of relinquishment of freedom, or retreat to old fogeyism?

From *A Poet's Alphabet*

Considerations

1. Choose one of the questions Bogan raises and write an essay in response to it using two or three poems from this chapter to illustrate your answer.
2. Try writing a poem in meter and rhyme. Does the experience make your writing feel limited or not?

19. Poetic Forms

Poems come in a variety of shapes. Although the best poems always have their own unique qualities, many of them also conform to traditional patterns. Frequently the ***form*** of a poem — its overall structure or shape — follows an already established design. A poem that can be categorized by the patterns of its lines, meter, rhymes, and stanzas is considered a ***fixed form,*** because it follows a prescribed model such as a sonnet. However, poems written in a fixed form do not always fit models precisely; writers sometimes work variations on traditional forms to create innovative effects.

Not all poets are content with variations on traditional forms. Some prefer to create their own structures and shapes. Poems that do not conform to established patterns of meter, rhyme, and stanza are called ***free verse*** or ***open form*** poetry. (See Chapter 20 for further discussion of open forms.) This kind of poetry creates its own ordering principles through the careful arrangement of words and phrases in line lengths that embody rhythms appropriate to the meaning. Modern and contemporary poets in particular have learned to use the blank space on the page as a significant functional element [for a striking example see Cummings's "l(a," p. 505]. Good poetry of this kind is structured in ways that can be as demanding, interesting, and satisfying as fixed forms. Open and fixed forms represent different poetic styles, but they are identical in the sense that both use language in concentrated ways to convey meanings, experiences, emotions, and effects.

SOME COMMON POETIC FORMS

A familiarity with some of the most frequently used fixed forms of poetry is useful, because it allows for a better understanding of how a poem works. Classifying patterns allows us to talk about the effects of established rhythm and rhyme and recognize how significant variations from them affect the pace and meaning of the lines. An awareness of form also allows us to anticipate how a poem is likely to proceed. As we shall see, a sonnet creates a different set of expectations in a reader from those of, say, a limerick. A reader isn't likely to find in limericks the kind of serious themes that often make their way into sonnets. The discussion that follows identifies some of the important poetic forms frequently encountered in English poetry.

The shape of a fixed form poem is often determined by the way in which the lines are organized into stanzas. A ***stanza*** consists of a grouping of lines, set off by a space, which usually has a set pattern of meter and rhyme. This pattern is ordinarily repeated in other stanzas throughout the poem. What is usual is not obligatory, however; some poems may use a different pattern for each stanza, somewhat like paragraphs in prose.

Traditionally, though, stanzas do share a common ***rhyme scheme,*** the pattern of end rhymes. We can map out rhyme schemes by noting patterns of rhyme with small letters: the first rhyme sound is designated *a,* the second becomes *b,* the third *c,* and so on. Using this system, we can describe the rhyme scheme in the following poem this way: *aabb, ccdd, eeff.*

A. E. HOUSMAN (1859–1936)

Loveliest of trees, the cherry now 1896

Loveliest of trees, the cherry now *a*
Is hung with bloom along the bough, *a*
And stands about the woodland ride *b*
Wearing white for Eastertide. *b*

Now, of my threescore years and ten, *c*
Twenty will not come again, *c*
And take from seventy springs a score, *d*
It only leaves me fifty more. *d*

And since to look at things in bloom *e*
Fifty springs are little room, *e*
About the woodlands I will go *f*
To see the cherry hung with snow. *f*

Considerations

1. What is the speaker's attitude in this poem toward time and life?
2. Why is spring an appropriate season for the setting rather than, say, winter?
3. Paraphrase each stanza. How do the images in each reinforce the poem's themes?
4. Lines 1 and 12 are not intended to rhyme, but they are close. What is the effect of the near rhyme of "now" and "snow"? How does the rhyme enhance the theme?

Poets often create their own stanzaic patterns; hence there is an infinite number of kinds of stanzas. One way of talking about stanzaic forms is to describe a given stanza by how many lines it contains.

A ***couplet*** consists of two lines that usually rhyme and have the same meter; couplets are frequently not separated from each other by space on the page. A ***heroic couplet*** consists of rhymed iambic pentameter. Here is an example from Pope's "An Essay on Criticism."

One science only will one genius fit; *a*
So vast is art, so narrow human wit: *a*
Not only bounded to peculiar arts, *b*
But oft in those confined to single parts. *b*

A ***tercet*** is a three-line stanza. When all three lines rhyme they are called a ***triplet.*** Two triplets make up this captivating poem.

ROBERT HERRICK (1591–1674)

Upon Julia's Clothes

1648

Whenas in silks my Julia goes, *a*
Then, then, methinks, how sweetly flows *a*
That liquefaction of her clothes. *a*

Next, when I cast mine eyes, and see *b*
That brave vibration, each way free, *b*
O, how that glittering taketh me! *b*

Considerations

1. Underline the alliteration in this poem. What purpose does it serve?
2. Comment on the effect of the meter. How is it related to the speaker's description of Julia's clothes?
3. Look up the word *brave* in the *Oxford English Dictionary.* Which of its meanings are appropriate to describe Julia's movement? Some readers interpret lines 4–6 to mean that Julia has no clothes on. What do you think?

Connections

1. Compare the tone of this poem with that of Humphrey's "Blow" (p. 623). Are the situations and speakers similar? Is there any difference in tone between these two poems?

Terza rima consists of an interlocking three-line rhyme scheme: *aba, bcb, cdc, ded,* and so on. Dante's *The Divine Comedy* uses this pattern, as does Frost's "Acquainted with the Night" (p. 582) and Percy Bysshe Shelley's "Ode to the West Wind" (p. 656).

A ***quatrain,*** or four-line stanza, is the most common stanzaic form in the English language and can have various meters and rhyme schemes (if any). The most common rhyme schemes are *aabb, abba, aaba,* and *abcb.* This last pattern is especially characteristic of the popular ***ballad stanza,*** which consists of alternating eight- and six-syllable lines. Samuel Taylor Coleridge adopted this pattern in "The Rime of the Ancient Mariner"; here is one representative stanza.

All in a hot and copper sky
The bloody Sun, at noon,
Right up above the mast did stand,
No bigger than the Moon.

There are a number of longer stanzaic forms and the list of types of stanzas could be extended considerably, but knowing these three most basic patterns should prove helpful to you in talking about the form of a great many poems. In addition to stanzaic forms, there are fixed forms that characterize entire poems. Lyric poems can be, for example, sonnets, villanelles, sestinas, or epigrams.

Sonnet

The ***sonnet*** has been a popular literary form in English since the sixteenth century, when it was adopted from the Italian *sonnetto,* meaning "little song." A sonnet consists of fourteen lines, usually written in iambic pentameter. Because the sonnet has been such a favorite form, writers have experimented with many variations on its essential structure. Nevertheless, there are two basic types of sonnets: the Italian and the English.

The ***Italian sonnet*** (also known as the ***Petrarchan sonnet,*** from the fourteenth-century Italian poet Petrarch) divides into two parts. The first eight lines (the ***octave***) typically rhyme *abbaabba.* The final six lines (the ***sestet***) may vary; common patterns are *cdecde, cdcdcd,* and *cdccdc.* Very often the octave presents a situation, attitude, or problem that the sestet comments upon or resolves, as in John Keats's "On First Looking into Chapman's Homer" (p. 678).

This pattern is also used in the next sonnet, but notice that the thematic break between octave and sestet comes within line 9 rather than between lines 8 and 9. This unconventional break helps to reinforce the speaker's impatience with the conventional attitudes he describes.

WILLIAM WORDSWORTH (1770–1850)

The World Is Too Much with Us 1807

The world is too much with us; late and soon,
Getting and spending, we lay waste our powers;
Little we see in Nature that is ours;
We have given our hearts away, a sordid boon!
This Sea that bares her bosom to the moon;
The winds that will be howling at all hours,
And are up-gathered now like sleeping flowers;

For this, for everything, we are out of tune;
It moves us not. — Great God! I'd rather be
A Pagan suckled in a creed outworn;
So might I, standing on this pleasant lea,
Have glimpses that would make me less forlorn;
Have sight of Proteus rising from the sea;
Or hear old Triton blow his wreathèd horn.

Considerations

1. What is the speaker's complaint in this sonnet? How do the conditions described affect him?
2. Look up "Proteus" and "Triton." What do these mythological allusions contribute to the sonnet's tone?
3. What is the effect of the personification of the sea and wind in the octave?

Connections

1. Compare the theme of this sonnet with that of Hopkins's "God's Grandeur" (p. 614).
2. Write an essay that explores Amy Clampitt's "Nothing Stays Put" (p. 890) as a modern urban version of Wordsworth's poem.

The ***English sonnet,*** more commonly known as the ***Shakespearean sonnet,*** is organized into three quatrains and a couplet, which typically rhyme *abab cdcd efef gg.* This rhyme scheme is more suited to English poetry because English has fewer rhyming words than Italian. English sonnets, because of their four-part organization, also have more flexibility about where thematic breaks can occur. Frequently, however, the most pronounced break or turn comes with the concluding couplet.

In the following Shakespearean sonnet, the three quatrains compare the speaker's loved one to a summer's day and explain why she is even more lovely. The couplet bestows eternal beauty and love upon both the loved one and the sonnet.

WILLIAM SHAKESPEARE (1564–1616)

Shall I compare thee to a summer's day? 1609

Shall I compare thee to a summer's day?
Thou art more lovely and more temperate:
Rough winds do shake the darling buds of May,
And summer's lease hath all too short a date.
Sometime too hot the eye of heaven shines,
And often is his gold complexion dimmed;
And every fair from fair sometime declines,
By chance, or nature's changing course, untrimmed.

But thy eternal summer shall not fade,
Nor lose possession of that fair thou ow'st° *possesses*
Nor shall death brag thou wand'rest in his shade,
When in eternal lines to time thou grow'st.
    So long as men can breathe or eyes can see,
    So long lives this, and this gives life to thee.

Considerations

1. Why is the speaker's loved one more lovely than a summer's day? What qualities does he admire in her?
2. Describe the shift in tone and subject matter that begins in line 9.
3. What does the couplet say about the relation between art and love?
4. Which syllables are stressed in the final line? How do these syllables relate to the meaning of the line?

Sonnets have been the vehicles for all kinds of subjects, including love, death, politics, and cosmic questions. Although most sonnets tend to treat their subjects seriously, this fixed form does not mean a fixed expression; humor is also possible in it. Compare this next Shakespearean sonnet with "Shall I compare thee to a summer's day?" They are, finally, both love poems, but their tones are markedly different.

WILLIAM SHAKESPEARE (1564–1616)

My mistress' eyes are nothing like the sun 1609

My mistress' eyes are nothing like the sun;
Coral is far more red than her lips' red;
If snow be white, why then her breasts are dun;
If hairs be wires, black wires grow on her head.
I have seen roses damasked red and white,
But no such roses see I in her cheeks;
And in some perfumes is there more delight
Than in the breath that from my mistress reeks.
I love to hear her speak, yet well I know
That music hath a far more pleasing sound;
I grant I never saw a goddess go:
My mistress, when she walks, treads on the ground.
    And yet, by heaven, I think my love as rare
    As any she,° belied with false compare. *lady*

Considerations

1. What does "mistress" mean in this sonnet?
2. Write a description of the mistress based on the images used in the sonnet.
3. What sort of person is the speaker? Does he truly love the woman he describes?

4. In what sense are this sonnet and "Shall I compare thee" about poetry as well as love?

Villanelle

The ***villanelle*** is a fixed form consisting of nineteen lines of any length divided into six stanzas: five tercets and a concluding quatrain. The first and third lines of the initial tercet rhyme; these rhymes are repeated in each subsequent tercet *(aba)* and in the final two lines of the quatrain *(abaa)*. Moreover, line 1 appears in its entirety as lines 6, 12, and 18, while line 3 appears as lines 4, 15, and 19. This form may seem to risk monotony, but in competent hands a villanelle can create haunting echoes, as in Theodore Roethke's "The Waking" (below) and in Dylan Thomas's "Do not go gentle into that good night" (p. 574).

THEODORE ROETHKE (1908–1963)
The Waking

1953

I wake to sleep, and take my waking slow.
I feel my fate in what I cannot fear.
I learn by going where I have to go.

We think by feeling. What is there to know?
I hear my being dance from ear to ear.
I wake to sleep, and take my waking slow.

Of those so close beside me, which are you?
God bless the Ground! I shall walk softly there,
And learn by going where I have to go.

Light takes the Tree; but who can tell us how?
The lowly worm climbs up a winding stair;
I wake to sleep, and take my waking slow.

Great Nature has another thing to do
To you and me; so take the lively air,
And, lovely, learn by going where to go.

This shaking keeps me steady. I should know.
What falls away is always. And is near.
I wake to sleep, and take my waking slow.
I learn by going where I have to go.

Considerations

1. What do you think the speaker means when he says, "I wake to sleep"? Write a paraphrase of the poem.
2. What is the speaker's attitude toward life?
3. Discuss this villanelle's sound effects.

Connections

1. Compare Roethke's poem with Thomas's "Do not go gentle into that good night" (p. 574). Given that both are villanelles, how do you account for the very different effects achieved in each? Which do you prefer? Why?
2. Compare Roethke's assertion "We think by feeling" with E. E. Cummings's poem "since feeling is first" (p. 769). Consider how well the form of each poem expresses its point about feeling and thinking.

Sestina

Although the ***sestina*** usually does not rhyme, it is perhaps an even more demanding fixed form than the villanelle. A sestina consists of thirty-nine lines of any length divided into six six-line stanzas and a three-line concluding stanza called an ***envoy.*** The difficulty is in repeating the six words at the ends of the first stanza's lines at the ends of the lines in the other five six-line stanzas as well. Those words must also appear in the final three lines, where they often resonate important themes. The sestina originated in the Middle Ages, but contemporary poets continue to find it a fascinating and challenging form.

ELIZABETH BISHOP (1911–1979)

Sestina

1965

September rain falls on the house.
In the failing light, the old grandmother
sits in the kitchen with the child
beside the Little Marvel Stove,
reading the jokes from the almanac,
laughing and talking to hide her tears.

She thinks that her equinoctial tears
and the rain that beats on the roof of the house
were both foretold by the almanac,
but only known to a grandmother.
The iron kettle sings on the stove.
She cuts some bread and says to the child,

It's time for tea now; but the child
is watching the teakettle's small hard tears
dance like mad on the hot black stove,
the way the rain must dance on the house.
Tidying up, the old grandmother
hangs up the clever almanac

on its string. Birdlike, the almanac
hovers half open above the child,
hovers above the old grandmother

and her teacup full of dark brown tears.
She shivers and says she thinks the house
feels chilly, and puts more wood in the stove.

It was to be, says the Marvel Stove.
I know what I know, says the almanac.
With crayons the child draws a rigid house
and a winding pathway. Then the child
puts in a man with buttons like tears
and shows it proudly to the grandmother.

But secretly, while the grandmother
busies herself about the stove,
the little moons fall down like tears
from between the pages of the almanac
into the flower bed the child
has carefully placed in the front of the house.

Time to plant tears, says the almanac.
The grandmother sings to the marvelous stove
and the child draws another inscrutable house.

Considerations

1. Number the end words of the first stanza 1, 2, 3, 4, 5, and 6, and then use those numbers for the corresponding end words in the remaining five stanzas to see how the pattern of the line-end words is worked out in this sestina. Also locate the six end words in the envoy.
2. What happens in this sestina? Why is the grandmother "laughing and talking to hide her tears"?
3. Underline the images that seem especially vivid to you. What effects do they create? What is the tone of the sestina?
4. How are the six end words — "house," "grandmother," "child," "stove," "almanac," and "tears" — central to the sestina's meaning?
5. How is the almanac used symbolically? Does Bishop use any other symbols to convey meanings?
6. Write a brief essay explaining why you think a poet might derive pleasure from writing in a fixed form such as a villanelle or sestina. Can you think of similar activities outside the field of writing in which discipline and restraint give pleasure?

Epigram

An ***epigram*** is a brief, pointed, and witty poem. Although most rhyme and often are written in couplets, epigrams take no prescribed form. Instead, they are typically polished bits of compressed irony, satire, or paradox. Here is an epigram that defines itself.

SAMUEL TAYLOR COLERIDGE (1772–1834)

What Is an Epigram? 1802

What is an epigram? A dwarfish whole;
Its body brevity, and wit its soul.

These additional examples by A. R. Ammons, David McCord, Paul Ramsey, and Emily Dickinson satisfy Coleridge's definition.

A. R. AMMONS (b. 1926)

Coward 1975

Bravery runs in my family.

DAVID McCORD (b. 1897)

Epitaph on a Waiter

By and by
God caught his eye.

PAUL RAMSEY (b. 1924)

On Industrialism 1984

The Road to Hell is paved.

EMILY DICKINSON (1830–1886)

"Faith" is a fine invention c. 1860

"Faith" is a fine invention
When Gentlemen can *see* —
But *Microscopes* are prudent
In an Emergency.

Considerations

1. In what sense is each of these epigrams, as Coleridge puts it, a "dwarfish whole"?
2. Explain which of these epigrams, in addition to being witty, make a serious point?
3. Try writing a few epigrams that say something memorable about whatever you choose to focus upon.

Limerick

The ***limerick*** is always light and humorous. Its usual form consists of five predominantly anapestic lines rhyming *aabba;* lines 1, 2, and 5 contain three feet, while lines 3 and 4 contain two. Limericks have delighted everyone from schoolchildren to sophisticated adults, and they range in subject matter from the simply innocent and silly to the satiric or obscene. The sexual humor helps to explain why so many limericks are written anonymously. Here is one that is anonymous but more concerned with physics than physiology.

> There was a young lady named Bright,
> Who traveled much faster than light,
>   She started one day
>   In a relative way,
> And returned on the previous night.

This next one is a particularly clever definition of a limerick.

LAURENCE PERRINE (b. 1915)

The limerick's never averse 1982

The limerick's never averse
To expressing itself in a terse
    Economical style,
    And yet, all the while,
The limerick's *always* a verse.

Considerations

1. Scan Perrine's limerick. How do the lines measure up to the traditional fixed metrical pattern?
2. Try writing a limerick. Use the following basic pattern.

˘ ˘ ´   ˘ ˘ ´   ˘ ˘ ´
˘ ˘ ´   ˘ ˘ ´   ˘ ˘ ´
            ˘ ˘ ´   ˘ ˘ ´
            ˘ ˘ ´   ˘ ˘ ´
˘ ˘ ´   ˘ ˘ ´   ˘ ˘ ´

You might begin with a friend's name or the name of your school or town. Your instructor is, of course, fair game, too, provided your tact matches your wit.

Clerihew

The ***clerihew*** is another humorous fixed form that, although not as popular as the limerick, has enjoyed a modest reputation ever since Edmund Clerihew Bentley created it. The clerihew usually consists of four irregular lines rhyming *aabb* that comment on a famous person who is named in the first line. Here is an example of the form by the creator himself.

EDMUND CLERIHEW BENTLEY (1875–1956)
John Stuart Mill

John Stuart Mill
By a mighty effort of will
Overcame his natural bonhomie
And wrote *Principles of Political Economy.*

Haiku

Another brief fixed poetic form, borrowed from the Japanese, is the ***haiku.*** A haiku is usually described as consisting of seventeen syllables organized into three unrhymed lines of five, seven, and five syllables. Owing to language difference, however, English translations of haiku are often only approximated, because a Japanese haiku exists in time (Japanese syllables have duration). The number of syllables in our sense is not as significant as the duration. These poems typically present an intense emotion or vivid image of nature, which, in the Japanese, are also designed to lead to a spiritual insight.

MATSUO BASHŌ (1644–1694)
Under cherry trees

Under cherry trees
Soup, the salad, fish and all . . .
Seasoned with petals.

The implied metaphor in the next haiku offers a striking comparison between a piece of land jutting out into the water and a bull charging a matador.

RICHARD WILBUR (b. 1921)
Sleepless at Crown Point 1976

All night, this headland
Lunges into the rumpling
Capework of the wind.

ETHERIDGE KNIGHT (b. 1931)

Eastern Guard Tower 1968

Eastern guard tower
glints in sunset; convicts rest
like lizards on rocks.

Considerations

1. What different emotions do these three haiku evoke?
2. What differences and similarities are there between the effects of a haiku and those of an epigram?
3. Compose a haiku; try to make it as allusive and suggestive as possible.

Elegy

An elegy in classical Greek and Roman literature was written in alternating hexameter and pentameter lines. Since the seventeenth century, however, the term ***elegy*** has been used to describe a lyric poem written to commemorate someone who is dead. The word is also used to refer to a serious meditative poem produced to express the speaker's melancholy thoughts. Elegies no longer conform to a fixed pattern of lines and stanzas, but their characteristic subject is related to death and their tone is mournfully contemplative.

SEAMUS HEANEY (b. 1939)

Mid-term Break 1966

I sat all morning in the college sick bay
Counting bells knelling classes to a close.
At two o'clock our neighbors drove me home.

In the porch I met my father crying —
He had always taken funerals in his stride —
And Big Jim Evans saying it was a hard blow.

The baby cooed and laughed and rocked the pram
When I came in, and I was embarrassed
By old men standing up to shake my hand

And tell me they were "sorry for my trouble,"
Whispers informed strangers I was the eldest,
Away at school, as my mother held my hand

In hers and coughed out angry tearless sighs.
At ten o'clock the ambulance arrived
With the corpse, stanched and bandaged by the nurses.

Next morning I went up into the room. Snowdrops
And candles soothed the bedside; I saw him
For the first time in six weeks. Paler now,

Wearing a poppy bruise on his left temple,
He lay in the four foot box as in his cot.
No gaudy scars, the bumper knocked him clear.

A four foot box, a foot for every year.

Considerations

1. How do simple details contribute to the effects of this elegy?
2. Does this elegy use any kind of formal pattern for its structure? What is the effect of the last line standing by itself?
3. Another spelling for *stanched* (line 15) is *staunched.* Usage is about evenly divided between the two in the United States. What is the effect of Heaney choosing the former spelling rather than the latter?
4. Comment on the elegy's title.

Connections

1. Compare Heaney's elegy with A. E. Housman's "To an Athlete Dying Young" (p. 801). Which do you find more moving? Explain why.
2. Write an essay comparing this story of a boy's death with Updike's "Dog's Death" (p. 496). Do you think either of the poems is sentimental? Explain why or why not.

Ode

An *ode* is characterized by a serious topic and formal tone, but no prescribed formal pattern describes all odes. In some odes the pattern of each stanza is repeated throughout, while in others each stanza introduces a new pattern. Odes are lengthy lyrics that often include lofty emotions conveyed by a dignified style. Typical topics include truth, art, freedom, justice, and the meaning of life. Frequently such lyrics tend to be more public than private, and their speakers often employ apostrophe.

PERCY BYSSHE SHELLEY (1792–1822)

Ode to the West Wind 1820

I

O wild West Wind, thou breath of Autumn's being,
Thou, from whose unseen presence the leaves dead
Are driven, like ghosts from an enchanter fleeing,

Yellow, and black, and pale, and hectic red,
Pestilence-stricken multitudes: O thou,
Who chariotest to their dark wintry bed

The wingèd seeds, where they lie cold and low,
Each like a corpse within its grave, until
Thine azure sister of the Spring shall blow

Her clarion o'er the dreaming earth, and fill
(Driving sweet buds like flocks to feed in air)
With living hues and odors plain and hill:

Wild Spirit, which art moving everywhere;
Destroyer and preserver; hear, oh, hear!

II

Thou on whose stream, mid the steep sky's commotion,
Loose clouds like earth's decaying leaves are shed,
Shook from the tangled boughs of Heaven and Ocean,

Angels° of rain and lightning: there are spread *messengers*
On the blue surface of thine airy surge,
Like the bright hair uplifted from the head

Of some fierce Maenad,° even from the dim verge
Of the horizon to the zenith's height,
The locks of the approaching storm. Thou dirge

Of the dying year, to which this closing night
Will be the dome of a vast sepulcher,
Vaulted with all thy congregated might

Of vapors, from whose solid atmosphere
Black rain, and fire, and hail will burst: oh, hear!

III

Thou who didst waken from his summer dreams
The blue Mediterranean, where he lay,
Lulled by the coil of his crystálline streams,

Beside a pumice isle in Baiae's bay,°
And saw in sleep old palaces and towers
Quivering within the wave's intenser day,

All overgrown with azure moss and flowers
So sweet, the sense faints picturing them! Thou
For whose path the Atlantic's level powers

Cleave themselves into chasms, while far below
The sea-blooms and the oozy woods which wear
The sapless foliage of the ocean, know

Thy voice, and suddenly grow gray with fear,
And tremble and despoil themselves: oh, hear!

IV

If I were a dead leaf thou mightest bear;

21 *Maenad:* In Greek mythology a frenzied worshiper of Dionysus, god of wine and fertility.
32 *Baiae's bay:* A bay in the Mediterranean Sea.

If I were a swift cloud to fly with thee;
A wave to pant beneath thy power, and share

The impulse of thy strength, only less free
Than thou, O uncontrollable! If even
I were as in my boyhood, and could be

The comrade by thy wanderings over Heaven,
As then, when to outstrip thy skyey speed
Scarce seemed a vision; I would ne'er have striven

As thus with thee in prayer in my sore need.
Oh, lift me as a wave, a leaf, a cloud!
I fall upon the thorns of life! I bleed!

A heavy weight of hours has chained and bowed
One too like thee: tameless, and swift, and proud.

V

Make me thy lyre,° even as the forest is:
What if my leaves are falling like its own!
The tumult of thy mighty harmonies

Will take from both a deep, autumnal tone,
Sweet though in sadness. Be thou, Spirit fierce,
My spirit! Be thou me, impetuous one!

Drive my dead thoughts over the universe
Like withered leaves to quicken a new birth!
And, by the incantation of this verse,

Scatter, as from an unextinguished hearth
Ashes and sparks, my words among mankind!
Be through my lips to unawakened earth

The trumpet of a prophecy! O Wind,
If Winter comes, can Spring be far behind?

57 *Make me thy lyre:* Sound is produced on an Aeolian lyre, or wind harp, by wind blowing across its strings.

Considerations

1. Write a summary of each of this ode's five sections.
2. What is the speaker's situation? What is his "sore need"? What does the speaker ask of the wind in lines 57–70?
3. What does the wind signify in this ode? How is it used symbolically?
4. Determine the meter and rhyme of the first five stanzas. How do these elements contribute to the ode's movement? Is this pattern continued in the other four sections?

Picture Poem

By arranging lines into particular shapes, poets can sometimes organize typography into ***picture poems*** of what they describe. Here is an example.

GEORGE HERBERT (1593–1633)

Easter Wings

1633

Lord, who createdst man in wealth and store,
Though foolishly he lost the same,
Decaying more and more
Till he became
Most poor:
With thee
O let me rise
As larks, harmoniously,
And sing this day thy victories:
Then shall the fall further the flight in me.

My tender age in sorrow did begin:
And still with sicknesses and shame
Thou didst so punish sin,
That I became
Most thin.
With thee
Let me combine,
And feel this day thy victory;
For, if I imp my wing on thine,
Affliction shall advance the flight in me.

Considerations

1. How is the shape of the poem connected to its theme?
2. How is the content of each line related to its length?
3. Why is the speaker's situation compared to that of larks? How do the poem's images convey the idea of humanity's fall and resurrection?

Words have been arranged into all kinds of shapes, from apples to light bulbs. Notice how the shape of this next contemporary poem embodies its meaning.

MICHAEL McFEE (b. 1954)

In Medias Res° 1985

His waist
like the plot
thickens, wedding
pants now breathtaking,
belt no longer the cinch
it once was, belly's cambium
expanding to match each birthday,
his body a wad of anonymous tissue
swung in the same centrifuge of years
that separates a house from its foundation,
undermining sidewalks grim with joggers
and loose-filled graves and families
and stars collapsing on themselves,
no preservation society capable
of plugging entropy's dike,
under his zipper's sneer
a belly hibernation-
soft, ready for
the kill.

In Medias Res: A Latin term for a story that begins "in the middle of things."

Considerations

1. Explain how the title is related to this poem's shape.
2. Identify the puns. How do they work in the poem?
3. What is "cambium"? Why is the phrase "belly's cambium" especially appropriate?
4. What is the tone of this poem? Is it consistent throughout?

Parody

A ***parody*** is a humorous imitation of another, usually serious, work. It can take any fixed or open form because parodists imitate the tone, language, and shape of the original. While a parody may be teasingly close to a work's style, it typically deflates the subject matter to make the original seem absurd. Parody can be used as a kind of literary criticism to expose the defects in a work, but it is also very often an affectionate acknowledgment that a well-known work has become both institutionalized in our culture and fair game for some fun. Read Dickinson's "Because I could not stop for Death" (p. 639) and then study this parody.

ANDREA PATERSON

Because I Could Not Dump 1981

Because I could not Dump the Trash —
Joe kindly stopped for Me —
The Garbage Truck held but Ourselves —
And Bacterial Colonies —

We slowly drove — Joe smelled of Skunk —
Yet risking no delay
My hairdo and composure too,
Were quickly Fumed away —

We passed a School, where Dumpsters stood
Recycling — in the Rain —
We picked up Yields of Industry —
Dead Cats and Window Panes —

Or rather — Joe picked up —
Seeing maggot-lined cans — I recoiled —
When heir to smelly Legacies,
What sort of Woman — Spoils?

We paused before a Dump that seemed
A Swelling of the Ground —
The Soil was scarcely visible —
Joe dropped — his Booty — down.

Since then — 'tis a fortnight — yet
Seems shorter than the Day
I first set out the Old Fish Heads —
And hoped Joe'd come my Way —

Considerations

1. How close is Paterson's version to Dickinson's style?
2. Contrast the theme of each poem. What makes their pairing so humorous?

The following poem should sound familiar enough (remember the *carpe diem* poems in Chapter 13?), but De Vries's version includes some interesting twists that make it a distinctly contemporary work.

PETER DE VRIES (b. 1910)

To His Importunate Mistress 1986

Andrew Marvell Updated

Had we but world enough, and time,
My coyness, lady, were a crime,
But at my back I always hear
Time's wingèd chariot, striking fear
The hour is nigh when creditors
Will prove to be my predators.
As wages of our picaresque,
Bag lunches bolted at my desk
Must stand as fealty to you
For each expensive rendezvous.
Obeisance at your marble feet
Deserves the best-appointed suite,
And would have, lacked I not the pelf
To pleasure also thus myself;
But aptly sumptuous amorous scenes
Rule out the rake of modest means.

Since mistress presupposes wife,
It means a doubly costly life;
For fools by second passion fired
A second income is required,
The earning which consumes the hours
They'd hoped to spend in rented bowers.
To hostelries the worst of fates
That weekly raise their daily rates!
I gather, lady, from your scoffing
A bloke more solvent in the offing.
So revels thus to rivals go
For want of monetary flow.
How vexing that inconstant cash
The constant suitor must abash,
Who with excuses vainly pled
Must rue the undisheveled bed,
And that for paltry reasons given
His conscience may remain unriven.

Considerations

1. How is De Vries's use of the term *mistress* different from Marvell's (p. 534)? How does the speaker's complaint in this poem differ from that in "To His Coy Mistress"?
2. Explain how "picaresque" is used in line 7.
3. To what extent does this poem duplicate Marvell's style?
4. Choose a poet whose work you know reasonably well or would like to know better and determine what is characteristic about his or her style. Then choose a

poem to parody. It's probably best to attempt a short poem or a section of a long work. If you have difficulty selecting an author, you might consider Herrick, Blake, Keats, Dickinson, Whitman, or Frost, since a number of their works are included in this book.

Connections

1. Read Anthony Hecht's "Dover Bitch" (p. 794), a parody of Arnold's "Dover Beach" (p. 549). Write an essay comparing the effectiveness of Hecht's parody with that of Paterson's "Because I Could Not Dump" and De Vries's "To His Importunate Mistress." Which parody do you prefer? Explain why.

PERSPECTIVE

ROBERT MORGAN (b. 1944)

On the Shape of a Poem 1983

In the body of the poem, lineation is part flesh and part skeleton, as form is the towpath along which the burden of content, floating on the formless, is pulled. All language is both mental and sacramental, is not "real" but is the working of lip and tongue to subvert the "real." Poems empearl irritating facts until they become opalescent spheres of moment, not so much résumés of history as of human faculties working with pain. Every poem is necessarily a fragment empowered by its implicitness. We sing to charm the snake in our spines, to make it sway with the pulse of the world, balancing the weight of consciousness on the topmost vertebra.

From *Epoch,* Fall–Winter 1983

Considerations

1. Explain Morgan's metaphors for describing lineation and form in a poem. Why are these metaphors useful?
2. Choose one of the poems in this chapter that makes use of a particular form and explain how it is "a fragment empowered by its implicitness."

20. Open Form

Many poems, especially those written in the twentieth century, are composed of lines that cannot be scanned for a fixed or predominant meter. Moreover, very often these poems do not rhyme. Known as ***free verse*** (from the French, *vers libre*), such lines can derive their rhythmic qualities from the repetition of words, phrases, or grammatical structures; the arrangement of words on the printed page; or some other means. In recent years the term ***open form*** has been used in place of *free verse* to avoid the erroneous suggestion that this kind of poetry lacks all discipline and shape.

Although the following two poems do not use measurable meters, they do have rhythm.

E. E. CUMMINGS (1894–1962)

in Just- **1923**

in Just-
spring   when the world is mud-
luscious the little
lame balloonman

whistles   far   and wee

and eddieandbill come
running from marbles and
piracies and it's
spring

when the world is puddle-wonderful

the queer
old balloonman whistles
far   and   wee
and bettyandisbel come dancing

from hop-scotch and jump-rope and

it's
spring
and
    the
        goat-footed

balloonMan   whistles
far
and
wee

Considerations

1. What is the effect of this poem's arrangement of words and the use of space on the page?
2. What is the effect of Cummings combining the names "eddieandbill" and "bettyandisbel"?
3. The allusion in line 20 refers to Pan, a Greek god associated with nature. How does this allusion add to the meaning of the poem?

WALT WHITMAN (1819–1892)

From *I Sing the Body Electric* 1855

O my body! I dare not desert the likes of you in other men and women, nor the likes of the parts of you,
I believe the likes of you are to stand or fall with the likes of the soul, (and that they are the soul,)
I believe the likes of you shall stand or fall with my poems, and that they are my poems.
Man's, woman's, child's, youth's, wife's, husband's, mother's, father's, young man's, young woman's poems.
Head, neck, hair, ears, drop and tympan of the ears.
Eyes, eye-fringes, iris of the eye, eyebrows, and the waking or sleeping of the lids,
Mouth, tongue, lips, teeth, roof of the mouth, jaws, and the jaw-hinges,
Nose, nostrils of the nose, and the partition,
Cheeks, temples, forehead, chin, throat, back of the neck, neck-slue,
Strong shoulders, manly beard, scapula, hind-shoulders, and the ample side-round of the chest,
Upper-arm, armpit, elbow-socket, lower-arm, arm-sinews, arm-bones,
Wrist and wrist-joints, hand, palm, knuckles, thumb, forefinger, finger-joints, finger-nails,
Broad breast-front, curling hair of the breast, breast-bone, breast-side,
Ribs, belly, backbone, joints of the backbone,
Hips, hip-sockets, hip-strength, inward and outward round, man-balls, man-root,

Strong set of thighs, well carrying the trunk above,
Leg-fibers, knee, knee-pan, upper-leg, under-leg,
Ankles, instep, foot-ball, toes, toe-joints, the heel;
All attitudes, all the shapeliness, all the belongings of my or your body or of any one's body, male or female,
The lung-sponges, the stomach-sac, the bowels sweet and clean,
The brain in its folds inside the skull-frame,
Sympathies, heart-valves, palate-valves, sexuality, maternity,
Womanhood, and all that is a woman, and the man that comes from woman,
The womb, the teats, nipples, breast-milk, tears, laughter, weeping, love-looks, love-perturbations and risings,
The voice, articulation, language, whispering, shouting aloud,
Food, drink, pulse, digestion, sweat, sleep, walking, swimming,
Poise on the hips, leaping, reclining, embracing, arm-curving and tightening,
The continual changes of the flex of the mouth, and around the eyes,
The skin, the sunburnt shade, freckles, hair,
The curious sympathy one feels when feeling with the hand the naked meat of the body,
The circling rivers the breath, and breathing it in and out,
The beauty of the waist, and thence of the hips, and thence downward toward the knees,
The thin red jellies within you or within me, the bones and the marrow in the bones,
The exquisite realization of health;
O I say these are not the parts and poems of the body only, but of the soul,
O I say now these are the soul!

Considerations

1. What informs the speaker's attitude toward the human body in this poem?
2. Read the poem aloud. Is it simply a tedious enumeration of body parts, or do the lines achieve some kind of rhythmic cadence?

PERSPECTIVE

WALT WHITMAN (1819–1892)

On Rhyme and Meter

1855

The poetic quality is not marshaled in rhyme or uniformity or abstract addresses to things nor in melancholy complaints or good precepts, but is the life of these and much else and is in the soul. The profit of rhyme is that it drops seeds of a sweeter and more luxuriant rhyme, and of uniformity that it conveys itself into its own roots in the ground out of sight. The rhyme and uniformity of perfect poems show the free growth of metrical laws and bud from them as unnerringly and loosely as lilacs or roses on a bush, and take shapes as compact as the shapes of chestnuts and oranges and melons and pears, and shed the perfume impalpable to form. The fluency and ornaments of the finest poems or music or orations or recitations are not independent but dependent. All beauty comes from beautiful blood and a beautiful brain. If the greatnesses are in conjunction in a man or woman it is enough . . . the fact will prevail through the universe . . . but the gaggery and gilt of a million years will not prevail. Who troubles himself about his ornaments or fluency is lost.

From the preface to the 1855 edition of *Leaves of Grass*

Considerations

1. According to Whitman, what determines the shape of a poem?
2. Why does Whitman prefer open forms over fixed forms such as the sonnet?
3. Is Whitman's poetry devoid of any structure or shape? Choose one of his poems (listed in the index) to illustrate your answer.

Open form poetry is sometimes regarded as formless because it is unlike the strict fixed forms of a sonnet, villanelle, or sestina. But even though open form poems may not employ traditional meters and rhymes, they still rely on an intense use of language to establish rhythms and relations between meaning and form. Open form poems use the arrangement of words and phrases on the printed page, pauses, line lengths, and other means to create unique forms that express their particular meaning and tone.

Cummings's "in Just—" and the excerpt from Whitman's "I Sing the Body Electric" demonstrate how the white space on a page and rhythmic cadences can be aligned with meaning, but there is one kind of open form poetry that doesn't even look like poetry on a page. A ***prose poem*** is printed as prose and represents, perhaps, the most clear opposite of fixed forms. Here is a brief example.

GEORGE STARBUCK (b. 1931)

Japanese Fish 1985

Have you ever eaten a luchu? It's poisonous like fugu, but it's cheaper and you cook it yourself.

You cut it into little squares as fast as possible but without touching the poison-gland. But first, you get all the thrill you can out of the fact that you're going to do it. You sit around for hours with your closest friends, drinking and telling long nostalgicky stories. You make toasts. You pick up your knives and sing a little song entitled "We who are about to dice a luchu." And then you begin.

Considerations

1. What is the effect of this prose poem? Does it have a theme?
2. What, if anything, is poetic in this work?
3. Arrange the lines so that they look like poetry on a page. What determines where you break the lines?

Much of the poetry published today is written in open form; however, many poets continue to take pleasure in the requirements imposed by fixed forms. Some write both fixed form and open form poetry. Each kind offers rewards to careful readers as well. Here are several more open form poems that establish their own unique patterns.

WILLIAM CARLOS WILLIAMS (1883–1936)

The Red Wheelbarrow 1923

so much depends
upon

a red wheel
barrow

glazed with rain
water

beside the white
chickens.

Considerations

1. What is the effect of these images? Do they have a particular meaning? What "depends upon" the things mentioned in the poem?
2. Do these lines have any kind of rhythm?
3. How does this poem resemble a haiku? How is it different?

ALLEN GINSBERG (b. 1926)

A Supermarket in California 1956

What thoughts I have of you tonight, Walt Whitman, for I walked down the sidestreets under the trees with a headache self-conscious looking at the full moon.

In my hungry fatigue, and shopping for images, I went into the neon fruit supermarket, dreaming of your enumerations!°

What peaches and what penumbras! Whole families shopping at night! Aisles full of husbands! Wives in the avocados, babies in the tomatoes — and you, Garcia Lorca,° what were you doing down by the watermelons?

I saw you, Walt Whitman, childless, lonely old grubber, poking among the meats in the refrigerator and eyeing the grocery boys.

2 *enumerations:* See the "enumerations" (the catalog of details), a typical poetic device of Whitman's, in "I Sing the Body Electric" (p. 665). 3 *Garcia Lorca:* Federico García Lorca (1898–1936), a Spanish poet whose nonrealistic techniques Ginsberg admired. See his "Somnambule Ballad" (p. 880).

I heard you asking questions of each: Who killed the pork chops? What price bananas? Are you my Angel?
I wandered in and out of the brilliant stacks of cans following you, and followed in my imagination by the store detective.
We strode down the open corridors together in our solitary fancy tasting artichokes, possessing every frozen delicacy, and never passing the cashier.

Where are we going, Walt Whitman? The doors close in an hour. Which way does your beard point tonight?
(I touch your book and dream of our odyssey in the supermarket and feel absurd.)
Will we walk all night through solitary streets? The trees add shade to shade, lights out in the houses, we'll both be lonely.
Will we stroll dreaming of the lost America of love past blue automobiles in driveways, home to our silent cottage?
Ah, dear father, graybeard, lonely old courage-teacher, what America did you have when Charon quit poling his ferry and you got out on a smoking bank and stood watching the boat disappear on the black waters of Lethe?°

Berkeley 1955

12 *When Charon quit poling . . .* : In Greek mythology Charon ferries the dead into Hades. Lethe is one of the rivers in Hades and is associated with forgetfulness, because a drink from it causes the dead to forget those they have left behind.

Considerations

1. How is the setting used symbolically in this poem?
2. What kinds of thoughts does the speaker have about Whitman?
3. What does the speaker think about America? About himself?

Connections

1. How are Ginsberg's techniques similar to Whitman's in "I Sing the Body Electric" (p. 665)?
2. How is Ginsberg's America different from the description Whitman provides in "Song of the Open Road" (p. 626)? In what sense is Ginsberg "shopping for images"?
4. Write an essay contrasting the tone of this poem with that of "Song of the Open Road."

SYLVIA PLATH (1932–1963)

Elm

For Ruth Fainlight

I know the bottom, she says. I know it with my great tap root:
It is what you fear.
I do not fear it: I have been there.

Is it the sea you hear in me,
Its dissatisfactions?
Or the voice of nothing, that was your madness?

Love is a shadow.
How you lie and cry after it.
Listen: these are its hooves: it has gone off, like a horse.

All night I shall gallop thus, impetuously,
Till your head is a stone, your pillow a little turf,
Echoing, echoing.

Or shall I bring you the sound of poisons?
This is rain now, this big hush.
And this is the fruit of it: tin-white, like arsenic.

I have suffered the atrocity of sunsets.
Scorched to the root
My red filaments burn and stand, a hand of wires.

Now I break up in pieces that fly about like clubs.
A wind of such violence
Will tolerate no bystanding: I must shriek.

The moon, also, is merciless: she would drag me
Cruelly, being barren.
Her radiance scathes me. Or perhaps I have caught her.

I let her go. I let her go
Diminished and flat, as after radical surgery.
How your bad dreams possess and endow me.

I am inhabited by a cry.
Nightly it flaps out
Looking, with its hooks, for something to love.

I am terrified by this dark thing
That sleeps in me;
All day I feel its soft, feathery turnings, its malignity.

Clouds pass and disperse.
Are those the faces of love, those pale irretrievables?
Is it for such I agitate my heart?

I am incapable of more knowledge.
What is this, this face
So murderous in its strangle of branches?——

Its snaky acids kiss.
It petrifies the will. These are the isolate, slow faults
That kill, that kill, that kill.

Considerations

1. What is the speaker's situation in this poem?
2. Comment on the meaning of the title.

3. Discuss the poem's tone. How do the images, metaphors, and structure create the tone?
4. How do the sounds in the final stanza emphasize the tone and theme?

DENISE LEVERTOV (b. 1923)

O Taste and See 1962

The world is
not with us enough.
O taste and see

the subway Bible poster said,
meaning **The Lord**, meaning
if anything all that lives
to the imagination's tongue,

grief, mercy, language,
tangerine, weather, to
breathe them, bite,
savor, chew, swallow, transform

into our flesh our
deaths, crossing the street, plum, quince,
living in the orchard and being

hungry, and plucking
the fruit.

Considerations

1. How does the speaker in this poem want people to respond to the world?
2. Are lines 8–11 simply a list of random words? How do they relate to one another and to the poem's theme?
3. Why are the lines arranged in stanzas? Would the experience of reading the poem be any different if it were all one stanza?

Connections

1. Write a short essay comparing and contrasting this poem with Wordsworth's "The World Is Too Much with Us" (p. 646) in form and content.

CAROLYN FORCHÉ (b. 1950)

The Colonel May 1978

What you have heard is true. I was in his house. His wife carried
a tray of coffee and sugar. His daughter filed her nails, his son went
out for the night. There were daily papers, pet dogs, a pistol on the

cushion beside him. The moon swung bare on its black cord over the house. On the television was a cop show. It was in English. Broken bottles were embedded in the walls around the house to scoop the kneecaps from a man's legs or cut his hands to lace. On the windows there were gratings like those in liquor stores. We had dinner, rack of lamb, good wine, a gold bell was on the table for calling the maid. The maid brought green mangoes, salt, a type of bread. I was asked how I enjoyed the country. There was a brief commercial in Spanish. His wife took everything away. There was some talk then of how difficult it had become to govern. The parrot said hello on the terrace. The colonel told it to shut up, and pushed himself from the table. My friend said to me with his eyes: say nothing. The colonel returned with a sack used to bring groceries home. He spilled many human ears on the table. They were like dried peach halves. There is no other way to say this. He took one of them in his hands, shook it in our faces, dropped it into a water glass. It came alive there. I am tired of fooling around he said. As for the rights of anyone, tell your people they can go fuck themselves. He swept the ears to the floor with his arm and held the last of his wine in the air. Something for your poetry, no? he said. Some of the ears on the floor caught this scrap of his voice. Some of the ears on the floor were pressed to the ground.

Considerations

1. What kind of horror is described in this prose poem? Characterize the colonel.
2. What makes this prose poem not a typical prose passage? How is it organized differently?
3. What poetic elements can you find in it?
4. What is the tone of the final two sentences?

SHARON OLDS (b. 1942)

The Elder Sister 1983

When I look at my elder sister now
I think how she had to go first, down through the
birth canal, to force her way
head-first through the tiny channel,
the pressure of Mother's muscles on her brain,
the tight walls scraping her skin.
Her face is still narrow from it, the long
hollow cheeks of a Crusader on a tomb,
and her inky eyes have the look of someone who has
been in prison a long time and
knows they can send her back. I look at her
body and think how her breasts were the first to
rise, slowly, like swans on a pond.

By the time mine came along, they were just
two more birds on the flock, and when the hair
rose on the white mound of her flesh, like
threads of water out of the ground, it was the
first time, but when mine came
they knew about it. I used to think
only in terms of her harshness, sitting and
pissing on me in bed, but now I
see I had her before me always
like a shield. I look at her wrinkles, her clenched
jaws, her frown-lines — I see they are
the dents on my shield, the blows that did not reach me.
She protected me, not as a mother
protects a child, with love, but as a
hostage protects the one who makes her
escape as I made my escape, with my sister's
body held in front of me.

Considerations

1. Which images, similes, and metaphors in this poem seem especially effective to you? Explain why.
2. How does the speaker's attitude toward her sister develop and change in the course of the poem? Why does she think differently about her "now"?
3. Explain how lines 26–30 sum up what the younger sister now understands.
4. What effect does the arrangement of the lines have on your reading the poem?

Found Poem

This next poem is a ***found poem,*** an unintentional poem discovered in a nonpoetic context, such as a conversation, news story, or advertisement. Found poems are playful reminders that the words in poems are very often the language we use every day. Whether such found language should be regarded as a poem is an issue left for you to consider.

DONALD JUSTICE (b. 1925)

Order in the Streets 1969

(From instructions printed on a child's toy, Christmas 1968, as reported in the New York Times*)*

1. 2. 3.
Switch on.

Jeep rushes
to the scene
of riot

Jeep goes
in all directions
by mystery action.

Jeep stops periodically
to turn hood over

machine gun appears
with realistic
shooting noise.

After putting down riot,
jeep goes
back to the headquarters.

Considerations

1. What is the effect of arranging these instructions in lines? How are the language and meaning enhanced by this arrangment?
2. Look for phrases or sentences in ads, textbooks, labels, or directions — in anything that might inadvertently contain provocative material that would be revealed by arranging the words in lines. You may even discover some patterns of rhyme and rhythm. After arranging the lines, explain why you organized them as you did.

21. A Study of Two Poets: John Keats and Robert Frost

This chapter includes a number of poems by John Keats and Robert Frost in order to provide an opportunity to study two major poets in some depth. Neither selection is wholly representative of the poet's work, but each offers enough poems to suggest some of the techniques and concerns that characterize their writings. The poems within each group speak not only to readers but to one another. That's natural enough: the more familiar you are with a writer's work, the easier it is to perceive and enjoy the strategies and themes he or she employs.

JOHN KEATS

The stone marking the grave of John Keats (1795–1821) bears an epitaph composed by him shortly before his death: "Here lies one whose name was writ in water." This assessment of his own achievement and fame is informed by the disappointment and anguish that characterized much of his life, but the inscription does not — because it could not — take into account the remarkable reputation that posterity has bestowed on Keats's poetry. His name, as it turns out, is written not only in stone rather than water but also in the minds of readers who have come to appreciate his literary art.

Keats's literary career had barely started when he died at the age of twenty-five. He did not begin writing poetry until he was eighteen, and critics generally agree that this early verse was not very promising. In 1816, however, he wrote the first of his greatest poems, a sonnet entitled "On First Looking into Chapman's Homer"; as he turned twenty-one he was also turning into a genuine poet.

His first volume, *Poems,* appeared in 1817 and was largely ignored; it was followed the next year by *Endymion,* a single poem of more than 4,000 lines about a quest for ideal beauty and happiness. Keats's most productive year was 1819, when he wrote nearly all the poems that have earned him a reputation as a major poet. His third and final volume of poetry, *Lamia, Isabella, The Eve of St. Agnes, and Other Poems,* was published in 1820.

During the final year of his life Keats could not write poetry because of the tuberculosis that was overtaking him. He traveled to Rome with the hope of regaining his health but wrote to a friend that he had "an habitual feeling of my life having past, and that I am leading a posthumous existence." He knew his illness was fatal and died three months later, in February of 1821. Almost incredibly, Keats's life as a writer spanned little more than the time required by most undergraduates to earn a bachelor's degree; and, more important, within those few years he outgrew his early sentimental and derivative verse to emerge as a powerful poet.

Keats's literary life moved toward greatness as he matured, but his personal life presented a series of abrupt dislocations and unfulfilled expectations. As a young boy he was exposed to the frailty and unpredictability of life. His father, manager of a livery stable in London, was killed by falling off a horse when Keats was only eight years old, and when the poet was fourteen his mother died of tuberculosis. The next year Keats's guardian withdrew him from school and apprenticed him to a five-year course in medicine at a London hospital.

While he studied medicine, Keats pursued his interest in literary studies, and upon completion of his surgical training he gave up medicine for poetry, a decision influenced by several literary friends who encouraged his efforts to become a writer. In 1818, however, this decision was severely tested by two reviews of *Endymion* that were so brutal as to foster the legend that they were the cause of Keats's early death.

But it was tuberculosis that killed Keats and that had caused his brother's death in 1818. Keats faithfully nursed his brother and therefore had a long hard look at the disease of which he was beginning to show symptoms. During this year Keats also lost another brother, who emigrated to America. But despite all these blows, Keats's spirits were high when he fell in love with Fanny Brawne. Unfortunately, his commitment to poetry as well as his financial situation and health prohibited their marriage and made his passionate love agonizing until his death. Keats's brief life seems hopelessly sad — his letters especially convey the sense of a remarkable sensibility overcome by a "world of circumstances."

Keats took a great risk by rejecting a medical career, but his interests were elsewhere. Perhaps his choice of profession was foreshadowed by the flowers that he sketched in the margins of his anatomy notes. Keats seems always to have been more concerned with beauty in life. In a sense, beauty was life to him. In life's transient materiality he found a constant that transcends space, time, and matter. He described this perception in these famous euphonic lines from *Endymion*.

A thing of beauty is a joy for ever:
Its loveliness increases; it will never
Pass into nothingness; but still will keep
A bower quiet for us, and a sleep
Full of sweet dreams, and health, and quiet breathing.

Therefore, on every morrow, are we wreathing
A flowery band to bind us to the earth,
Spite of despondence, of the inhuman dearth
Of noble natures, of the gloomy days,
Of all the unhealthy and o'er-darkened ways
Made for our searching: yes, in spite of all,
Some shape of beauty moves away the pall
From our dark spirits.

Keats preferred a direct, spontaneous response to life over the logical, rational abstractions that informed the intellectual tenor of his times. Putting his faith in an imaginative rather than a scientific approach to existence, he believed that literary imagination requires what he called a "Negative Capability," the ability to be "in uncertainties, mysteries, doubts, without any irritable reaching after fact and reason." Keats believed that the poetic imagination can tolerate ambiguities, and though it might not have all the answers, it has a greater capacity for asking questions than the sort of mind that demands "fact and reason." Truth was infinitely complex and problematic for Keats, and he found that he could not create beauty without being alert to the ugliness of evil. His ideal of "Negative Capability" represented, however, a positive creative power for the poet, because it demanded an openness to and sympathy with the possibilities of life and thought.

Although Keats created an imaginative world in his poems, he did not abandon "fact." Indeed, one of the major characteristics of his poetry is his use of detailed sensuous description. He builds a world by invoking the reader's senses of touch, smell, taste, hearing, and seeing so that experience is richly savored. His imagery is detailed and strong. Using diction that is both precise and opulent, Keats creates images that are not unlike a holograph. His melodic lines give us more of experience than a flat objective description could possibly offer.

Sonnets, odes, and narrative poems are the three poetic forms on which Keats's reputation rests. The typical subjects of his poems are familiar ones; he writes about love, death, fame, failure, poetry, art, and nature. The common thread running through these subjects is his keen awareness that everything is subject to change. Sometimes Keats attempts to transcend this changing world by pursuing a visionary imagination, but at other points he comes to understand that an acceptance of the transient nature of existence can be a way to appreciate its beauty. This conflict leads him into a series of tensions in which he celebrates sensations but simultaneously expresses a sadness that they cannot last. For Keats, pleasure and pain, love and death, dream and reality are the breathing out and breathing in of poetic imagination. He does not resolve these conflicts so much as articulate them.

"On First Looking into Chapman's Homer" is a fitting introduction to Keats's poetry, because it is about his own sense of discovery. At the age of twenty-one, Keats was introduced by a friend to George Chapman's poetic

Elizabethan translation of Homer's *Iliad* and *Odyssey*. Before his reading in Chapman, Keats had known only eighteenth-century translations, which were stilted and pedestrian, but with Chapman's version he suddenly realized the power and energy of Homer's poetry. Immediately after reading Chapman, Keats spent the night writing the following sonnet.

On First Looking into Chapman's Homer 1816

Much have I traveled in the realms of gold,
    And many goodly states and kingdoms seen;
    Round many western islands have I been
Which bards in fealty to Apollo° hold.
Oft of one wide expanse had I been told
    That deep-browed Homer ruled as his demesne;
    Yet did I never breathe its pure serene° *atmosphere*
Till I heard Chapman speak out loud and bold:
Then felt I like some watcher of the skies
    When a new planet swims into his ken;
Or like stout Cortez° when with eagle eyes
    He stared at the Pacific — and all his men
Looked at each other with a wild surmise —
    Silent, upon a peak in Darien.

4 *Apollo:* Greek god of poetry. 11 *Cortez:* Vasco Núñez Balboa, not Hernando Cortés, was the first European to sight the Pacific from Darien, a peak in Panama.

This is one of those rare poems in which we can accurately identify the speaker with the poet. Even so, it is less a fragment of autobiography than an evocation of excitement and wonder. This sonnet is not only about Keats's discovery of Chapman's Homer, because that personal experience serves as a symbol for any discovery. One way to state the theme is to say that reading can be a source of imaginative discovery as significant as the discovery of a planet or ocean. To express this theme, Keats uses a controlling metaphor built around a comparison of reading with traveling and exploration, an especially apt metaphor given the many journeys that appear in Homer. Keats shapes this metaphor into an Italian sonnet, which is often enough a traditional form for love poetry to suggest Keats's own passion for poetry.

In the octave, the speaker tells us that he has "traveled in the realms of gold" and seen many "goodly states and kingdoms." Given the context of the rest of the poem, we know that the speaker is referring to his wide reading in the literature of Western civilization ("western islands"). The diction of the octave is formal and dignified ("goodly states," "bards in fealty," "demesne," "serene"), fitting the respectful, if dispassionate, assessment of what the speaker has experienced in his reading. A shift occurs, however, between the octave and sestet, when the speaker moves to the impact that reading Chapman's Homer has had on him. Images of exploration give way to images of discovery, and the tone changes from elevated description to intense feelings of wonder.

Two similes in the sestet convey the speaker's wonder. First, he compares his excitement to that of an astronomer, a purposeful "watcher of the skies" who suddenly sees a new planet through a telescope. That discovery of a new world is brought down to earth in the second simile, when the speaker likens himself to Cortés, who (Keats mistakenly believed) inadvertently discovered the Pacific Ocean. Although the second simile brings us down to earth, it soars even higher than the first in its effect. The discovery of the ocean is more startling because it comes as a complete surprise. Cortés had no idea that the Pacific Ocean would be on the other side of the mountains.

The speaker's excitement is also evident in the change of rhythm in the sestet. A calm and measured movement can be heard in the octave, but the sestet's lines are less regular. This deviation from the predominant iambic pentameter is accompanied by run-on lines and dashes that convey the speaker's heightened emotions, which reach a climax in the final line. Here the trochaic "Silent," along with the comma that follows it, slows down the line, preparing us for the concluding image of awe.

The final allusive image of "stout Cortez" (notice how the heavy accents on these syllables emphasize the explorer's power) is a visual representation of the emotional intensity experienced by the speaker. This also completes the speaker's imagining himself as an explorer. We leave both the speaker and the explorer contemplating the beginning of further explorations and discoveries in worlds previously not even imagined. The sense of awe and expectation created in this poem serves as an appropriate first encounter with Keats's poetry, because it evokes some of the remarkable discoveries that readers have made in these poems.

On the Grasshopper and the Cricket 1816

The poetry of earth is never dead:
When all the birds are faint with the hot sun,
And hide in cooling trees, a voice will run
From hedge to hedge about the new-mown mead;
That is the grasshopper's — he takes the lead
In summer luxury — he has never done
With his delights; for when tired out with fun
He rests at ease beneath some pleasant weed.
The poetry of earth is ceasing never:
On a lone winter evening, when the frost
Has wrought a silence, from the stove there shrills

The cricket's song, in warmth increasing ever,
And seems to one in drowsiness half lost,
The grasshopper's among some grassy hills.

Considerations

1. How are two seasons contrasted in the octave and sestet of this sonnet?
2. What does the speaker mean by "The poetry of earth"? What is the view of nature in the sonnet?
3. How does the imagery contribute to the sonnet's effect?

To One Who Has Been Long in City Pent 1816

To one who has been long in city pent,
  'Tis very sweet to look into the fair
  And open face of heaven, — to breathe a prayer
Full in the smile of the blue firmament.
Who is more happy, when, with heart's content,
  Fatigued he sinks into some pleasant lair
  Of wavy grass, and reads a debonair
And gentle tale of love and languishment?

Returning home at evening, with an ear
  Catching the notes of Philomel,° — an eye
Watching the sailing cloudlet's bright career,
  He mourns that day so soon has glided by:
E'en like the passage of an angel's tear
  That falls through the clear ether silently.

Philomel: A nightingale.

Considerations

1. Although the city is not described in the sonnet, how does Keats make you feel about it?
2. What values is the countryside associated with here? How does this sonnet's evocation of nature compare with that of "On the Grasshopper and the Cricket"?
3. Do you think this sonnet is more about a sense of loss or a celebration of nature?

On Seeing the Elgin Marbles° 1817

My spirit is too weak; mortality
  Weighs heavily on me like unwilling sleep,
  And each imagined pinnacle and steep

Elgin Marbles: The remains of ancient figures and friezes from the Athenian Parthenon, acquired by Lord Elgin for the British Museum.

Of godlike hardship tells me I must die
Like a sick eagle looking at the sky.
Yet 'tis a gentle luxury to weep,
That I have not the cloudy winds to keep
Fresh for the opening of the morning's eye.
Such dim-conceived glories of the brain
Bring round the heart an indescribable feud;
So do these wonders a most dizzy pain,
That mingles Grecian grandeur with the rude
Wasting of old Time — with a billowy main,
A sun, a shadow of a magnitude.

Considerations

1. Why is the speaker in this sonnet "weak"? What causes the "dizzy pain" he feels in line 11?
2. What is the relationship between time and art in this sonnet?

When I have fears that I may cease to be 1818

When I have fears that I may cease to be
Before my pen has gleaned my teeming brain,
Before high-piled books, in charactery,° *print*
Hold like rich garners the full ripened grain;
When I behold, upon the night's starred face,
Huge cloudy symbols of a high romance,
And think that I may never live to trace
Their shadows, with the magic hand of chance;
And when I feel, fair creature of an hour,
That I shall never look upon thee more,
Never have relish in the faery° power *magic*
Of unreflecting love; — then on the shore
Of the wide world I stand alone, and think
Till love and fame to nothingness do sink.

Considerations

1. Describe the speaker's fear in each of the three quatrains of this sonnet. Is there any kind of progression?
2. What impact does the fear of death have on "love and fame" in the concluding couplet?

The Eve of St. Agnes° 1819

I

St. Agnes' Eve — Ah, bitter chill it was!
The owl, for all his feathers, was a-cold;
The hare limped trembling through the frozen grass,
And silent was the flock in woolly fold:
Numb were the Beadsman's° fingers, while he told
His rosary, and while his frosted breath,
Like pious incense from a censer old,
Seemed taking flight for heaven, without a death,
Past the sweet Virgin's picture, while his prayer he saith.

II

His prayer he saith, this patient, holy man;
Then takes his lamp, and riseth from his knees,
And back returneth, meager, barefoot, wan,
Along the chapel aisle by slow degrees:
The sculptured dead, on each side, seem to freeze,
Imprisoned in black, purgatorial rails:
Knights, ladies, praying in dumb orat'ries,° *chapels*
He passeth by; and his weak spirit fails
To think how they may ache in icy hoods and mails.

III

Northward he turneth through a little door,
And scarce three steps, ere Music's golden tongue
Flattered to tears this aged man and poor;
But no — already had his deathbell rung:
The joys of all his life were said and sung:
His was harsh penance on St. Agnes' eve:
Another way he went, and soon among
Rough ashes sat he for his soul's reprieve,
And all night kept awake, for sinner's sake to grieve.

IV

That ancient Beadsman heard the prelude soft;
And so it chanced, for many a door was wide,
From hurry to and fro. Soon, up aloft,
The silver, snarling trumpets 'gan to chide:
The level chambers, ready with their pride,
Were glowing to receive a thousand guests:
The carvèd angels, ever eager-eyed,
Stared, where upon their heads the cornice rests,
With hair blown back, and wings put crosswise on their breasts.

Eve of St. Agnes: January 20, supposed to be the coldest night of the year. St. Agnes, martyred in the fourth century, is the patroness of virgins. According to folk legend, a girl who performed certain rituals on St. Agnes's Eve would have a vision of her future husband. 5 *Beadsman:* A person hired to pray for someone.

V

At length burst in the argent revelry,
With plume, tiara, and all rich array,
Numerous as shadows haunting faerily° *magically*
The brain, new stuffed, in youth, with triumphs gay
Of old romance. These let us wish away,
And turn, sole-thoughted, to one Lady there,
Whose heart had brooded, all that wintry day,
On love, and winged St. Agnes' saintly care,
As she had heard old dames full many times declare.

VI

They told her how, upon St. Agnes' Eve,
Young virgins might have visions of delight,
And soft adorings from their loves receive
Upon the honeyed middle of the night,
If ceremonies due they did aright;
As, supperless to bed they must retire,
And couch supine their beauties, lily white;
Nor look behind, nor sideways, but require
Of heaven with upward eyes for all that they desire.

VII

Full of this whim was thoughtful Madeline:
The music, yearning like a God in pain,
She scarcely heard: her maiden eyes divine,
Fixed on the floor, saw many a sweeping train
Pass by — she heeded not at all: in vain
Came many a tiptoe, amorous cavalier,
And back retired; not cooled by high disdain;
But she saw not: her heart was otherwhere:
She sighed for Agnes' dreams, the sweetest of the year.

VIII

She danced along with vague, regardless eyes,
Anxious her lips, her breathing quick and short:
The hallowed hour was near at hand: she sighs
Amid the timbrels, and the thronged resort
Of whisperers in anger, or in sport;
'Mid looks of love, defiance, hate, and scorn,
Hoodwinked with faery fancy: all amort,° *as if dead*
Save to St. Agnes and her lambs unshorn,
And all the bliss to be before tomorrow morn.

IX

So, purposing each moment to retire,
She lingered still. Meantime, across the moors,
Had come young Porphyro, with heart on fire
For Madeline. Beside the portal doors,
Buttressed from moonlight,° stands he, and implores *in shadows*
All saints to give him sight of Madeline,

But for one moment in the tedious hours,
That he might gaze and worship all unseen;
Perchance speak, kneel, touch, kiss — in sooth such things have been.

X

He ventures in: let no buzzed whisper tell:
All eyes be muffled, or a hundred swords
Will storm his heart, Love's fev'rous citadel:
For him, those chambers held barbarian hordes,
Hyena foeman, and hot-blooded lords,
Whose very dogs would execrations howl
Against his lineage: not one breast affords
Him any mercy, in that mansion foul,
Save one old beldame, weak in body and in soul.

XI

Ah, happy chance! the aged creature came,
Shuffling along with ivory-headed wand,
To where he stood, hid from the torch's flame,
Behind a broad hall-pillar, far beyond
The sound of merriment and chorus bland:° *soft*
He startled her; but soon she knew his face,
And grasped his fingers in her palsied hand,
Saying, "Mercy, Porphyro! hie thee from this place;
They are all here tonight, the whole bloodthirsty race!

XII

"Get hence! get hence! there's dwarfish Hildebrand;
He had a fever late, and in the fit
He cursed thee and thine, both house and land:
Then there's that old Lord Maurice, not a whit
More tame for his gray hairs — Alas me! flit!
Flit like a ghost away." — "Ah, Gossip° dear, *friend*
We're safe enough; here in this armchair sit,
And tell me how" — "Good Saints! not here, not here;
Follow me, child, or else these stones will be thy bier."

XIII

He followed through a lowly arched way,
Brushing the cobwebs with his lofty plume,
And as she muttered "Well-a — well-a-day!"
He found him in a little moonlight room,
Pale, latticed, chill, and silent as a tomb.
"Now tell me where is Madeline," said he,
"O tell me, Angela, by the holy loom
Which none but secret sisterhood may see,
When they St. Agnes' wool are weaving piously."

XIV

"St. Agnes! Ah! it is St. Agnes' Eve —
Yet men will murder upon holy days:

Thou must hold water in a witch's sieve,
And be liege-lord of all the Elves and Fays,
To venture so: it fills me with amaze
To see thee, Porphyro! — St. Agnes' Eve!
God's help! my lady fair the conjuror plays
This very night: good angels her deceive!
But let me laugh awhile, I've mickle° time to grieve." *much*

XV

Feebly she laugheth in the languid moon,
While Porphyro upon her face doth look,
Like puzzled urchin on an aged crone
Who keepeth closed a wondrous riddle-book,
As spectacled she sits in chimney nook.
But soon his eyes grew brilliant, when she told
His lady's purpose; and he scarce could brook° *hold back*
Tears, at the thought of those enchantments cold,
And Madeline asleep in lap of legends old.

XVI

Sudden a thought came like a full-blown rose,
Flushing his brow, and in his pained heart
Made purple riot: then doth he propose
A stratagem, that makes the beldame start:
"A cruel man and impious thou art:
Sweet lady, let her pray, and sleep, and dream
Alone with her good angels, far apart
From wicked men like thee. Go, go! — I deem
Thou canst not surely be the same that thou didst seem."

XVII

"I will not harm her, by all saints I swear,"
Quoth Porphyro: "O may I ne'er find grace
When my weak voice shall whisper its last prayer,
If one of her soft ringlets I displace,
Or look with ruffian passion in her face:
Good Angela, believe me by these tears;
Or I will, even in a moment's space,
Awake, with horrid shout, my foeman's ears,
And beard them, though they be more fanged than wolves and bears."

XVIII

"Ah! why wilt thou affright a feeble soul?
A poor, weak, palsy-stricken, churchyard thing,
Whose passing bell° may ere the midnight toll; *death knell*
Whose prayers for thee, each morn and evening,
Were never missed" — Thus plaining,° doth she bring *complaining*
A gentler speech from burning Porphyro;
So woeful, and of such deep sorrowing,
That Angela gives promise she will do
Whatever he shall wish, betide her weal or woe.

XIX

Which was, to lead him, in close secrecy,
Even to Madeline's chamber, and there hide
Him in a closet, of such privacy
That he might see her beauty unespied,
And win perhaps that night a peerless bride,
While legioned faeries paced the coverlet,
And pale enchantment held her sleepy-eyed.
Never on such a night have lovers met,
Since Merlin paid his Demon all the monstrous debt.°

XX

"It shall be as thou wishest," said the Dame:
"All cates° and dainties shall be stored there — *delicacies*
Quickly on this feast night: by the tambour frame
Her own lute thou wilt see: no time to spare,
For I am slow and feeble, and scarce dare
On such a catering trust my dizzy head.
Wait here, my child, with patience; kneel in prayer
The while: Ah! thou must needs the lady wed,
Or may I never leave my grave among the dead."

XXI

So saying, she hobbled off with busy fear.
The lover's endless minutes slowly passed;
The dame returned, and whispered in his ear
To follow her; with aged eyes aghast
From fright of dim espial. Safe at last,
Through many a dusky gallery, they gain
The maiden's chamber, silken, hushed, and chaste;
Where Porphyro took covert, pleased amain.° — *greatly*
His poor guide hurried back with agues in her brain.

XXII

Her falt'ring hand upon the balustrade,
Old Angela was feeling for the stair,
When Madeline, St. Agnes' charmed maid,
Rose, like a missioned spirit, unaware:
With silver taper's light, and pious care,
She turned, and down the aged gossip led
To a safe level matting. Now prepare,
Young Porphyro, for gazing on that bed;
She comes, she comes again, like ring-dove frayed° and fled. — *frightened*

XXIII

Out went the taper as she hurried in;
Its little smoke, in pallid moonshine, died:

171 *Since Merlin paid . . . :* Merlin, the great magician of Arthurian legend, was duped by a crafty woman who turned one of his spells against him, causing his death.

She closed the door, she panted, all akin
To spirits of the air, and visions wide:
No uttered syllable, or, woe betide!
But to her heart, her heart was voluble,
Paining with eloquence her balmy side;
As though a tongueless nightingale should swell
Her throat in vain, and die, heart-stifled, in her dell.

XXIV

A casement high and triple-arched there was,
All garlanded with carven imag'ries
Of fruits, and flowers and bunches of knotgrass,
And diamonded with panes of quaint device,
Innumerable of stains and splendid dyes,
As are the tiger-moth's deep-damasked wings;
And in the midst, 'mong thousand heraldries,
And twilight saints, and dim emblazonings,
A shielded scutcheon° blushed with blood of queens and kings. *coat of arms*

XXV

Full on this casement shone the wintry moon,
And threw warm gules on Madeline's fair breast,
As down she knelt for heaven's grace and boon;
Rose-bloom fell on her hands, together pressed,
And on her silver cross soft amethyst,
And on her hair a glory, like a saint:
She seemed a splendid angel, newly dressed,
Save wings, for heaven: — Porphyro grew faint:
She knelt, so pure a thing, so free from mortal taint.

XXVI

Anon his heart revives: her vespers done,
Of all its wreathed pearls her hair she frees;
Unclasps her warmed jewels one by one;
Loosens her fragrant bodice; by degrees
Her rich attire creeps rustling to her knees:
Half-hidden, like a mermaid in sea-weed,
Pensive awhile she dreams awake, and sees,
In fancy, fair St. Agnes in her bed,
But dares not look behind, or all the charm is fled.

XXVII

Soon, trembling in her soft and chilly nest,
In sort of wakeful swoon, perplexed she lay,
Until the poppied warmth of sleep oppressed
Her soothed limbs, and soul fatigued away;
Flown, like a thought, until the morrow-day;
Blissfully havened both from joy and pain;
Clasped like a missal where swart Paynims° pray; *dark-skinned pagans*
Blinded alike from sunshine and from rain,
As though a rose should shut, and be a bud again.

XXVIII

Stolen to this paradise, and so entranced,
Porphyro gazed upon her empty dress,
And listened to her breathing, if it chanced
To wake into a slumberous tenderness;
Which when he heard, that minute did he bless,
And breathed himself: then from the closet crept,
Noiseless as fear in a wide wilderness,
And over the hushed carpet, silent, stepped,
And tween the curtains peeped, where, lo! — how fast she slept.

XXIX

Then by the bedside, where the faded moon
Made a dim, silver twilight, soft he set
A table, and, half anguished, threw thereon
A cloth of woven crimson, gold, and jet —
O for some drowsy Morphean amulet!°
The boisterous, midnight, festive clarion,
The kettledrum, and far-heard clarinet,
Affray his ears, though but in dying tone —
The hall door shuts again, and all the noise is gone.

XXX

And still she slept an azure-lidded sleep,
In blanchèd linen, smooth, and lavendered,
While he from forth the closet brought a heap
Of candied apple, quince, and plum, and gourd;
With jellies soother° than the creamy curd, *sweeter*
And lucent syrups, tinct with cinnamon;
Manna and dates, in argosy transferred
From Fez; and spicèd dainties, every one,
From silken Samarcand to cedared Lebanon.

XXXI

These delicates he heaped with glowing hand
On golden dishes and in baskets bright
Of wreathèd silver: sumptuous they stand
In the retired quiet of the night,
Filling the chilly room with perfume light. —
"And now, my love, my seraph fair, awake!
Thou art my heaven, and I thine eremite:
Open thine eyes, for meek St. Agnes' sake,
Or I shall drowse beside thee, so my soul doth ache."

XXXII

Thus whispering, his warm, unnerved arm
Sank in her pillow. Shaded was her dream
By the dusk curtains: 'twas a midnight charm

257 *Morphean amulet:* A charm used to induce sleep.

Impossible to melt as icèd stream:
The lustrous salvers in the moonlight gleam;
Broad golden fringe upon the carpet lies:
It seemed he never, never could redeem
From such a stedfast spell his lady's eyes;
So mused awhile, entoiled in woofèd° phantasies. *woven*

XXXIII

Awakening up, he took her hollow lute —
Tumultuous — and, in chords that tenderest be,
He played an ancient ditty, long since mute,
In Provence called, "La belle dame sans mercy":
Close to her ear touching the melody;
Wherewith disturbed, she uttered a soft moan:
He ceased — she panted quick — and suddenly
Her blue affrayed eyes wide open shone:
Upon his knees he sank, pale as smooth-sculptured stone.

XXXIV

Her eyes were open, but she still beheld,
Now wide awake, the vision of her sleep:
There was a painful change, that nigh expelled
The blisses of her dream so pure and deep,
At which fair Madeline began to weep,
And moan forth witless words with many a sigh;
While still her gaze on Porphyro would keep,
Who knelt, with joined hands and piteous eye,
Fearing to move or speak, she looked so dreamingly.

XXXV

"Ah, Porphyro!" said she, "but even now
Thy voice was at sweet tremble in mine ear,
Made tunable with every sweetest vow;
And those sad eyes were spiritual and clear:
How changed thou art! how pallid, chill, and drear!
Give me that voice again, my Porphyro,
Those looks immortal, those complainings dear!
Oh leave me not in this eternal woe,
For if thou diest, my Love, I know not where to go."

XXXVI

Beyond a mortal man impassioned far
At these voluptuous accents, he arose,
Ethereal, flushed, and like a throbbing star
Seen mid the sapphire heaven's deep repose;
Into her dream he melted, as the rose
Blendeth its odor with the violet —
Solution sweet: meantime the frost-wind blows
Like Love's alarum pattering the sharp sleet
Against the windowpanes; St. Agnes' moon hath set.

XXXVII

'Tis dark: quick pattereth the flaw-blown° sleet: *gusting*
"This is no dream, my bride, my Madeline!"
'Tis dark: the iced gusts still rave and beat:
"No dream, alas! alas! and woe is mine!
Porphyro will leave me here to fade and pine. —
Cruel! what traitor could thee hither bring?
I curse not, for my heart is lost in thine,
Though thou forsakest a deceivèd thing; —
A dove forlorn and lost with sick unprunèd wing."

XXXVIII

"My Madeline! sweet dreamer! lovely bride!
Say, may I be for aye° thy vassal blest? *forever*
Thy beauty's shield, heart-shaped and vermeil dyed?
Ah, silver shrine, here will I take my rest
After so many hours of toil and quest,
A famished pilgrim — saved by miracle.
Though I have found, I will not rob thy nest
Saving of thy sweet self; if thou think'st well
To trust, fair Madeline, to no rude infidel.

XXXIX

"Hark! 'tis an elfin-storm from faery land,
Of haggard° seeming, but a boon indeed: *wild*
Arise — arise! the morning is at hand; —
The bloated wassailers will never heed: —
Let us away, my love, with happy speed;
There are no ears to hear, or eyes to see —
Drowned all in Rhenish and the sleepy mead:°
Awake! arise! my love, and fearless be,
For o'er the southern moors I have a home for thee."

XL

She hurried at his words, beset with fears,
For there were sleeping dragons all around,
At glaring watch, perhaps, with ready spears —
Down the wide stairs a darkling way they found. —
In all the house was heard no human sound.
A chain-drooped lamp was flickering by each door;
The arras, rich with horseman, hawk, and hound,
Fluttered in the besieging wind's uproar;
And the long carpets rose along the gusty floor.

XLI

They glide, like phantoms, into the wide hall;
Like phantoms, to the iron porch, they glide;
Where lay the Porter, in uneasy sprawl,
With a huge empty flaggon by his side:

349 *Rhenish:* Rhine wine; *mead:* A fermented drink made with honey.

The wakeful bloodhound rose, and shook his hide,
But his sagacious eye an inmate owns:
By one, and one, the bolts full easy slide: —
The chains lie silent on the footworn stones; —
The key turns, and the door upon its hinges groans.

XLII

And they are gone: ay, ages long ago
These lovers fled away into the storm.
That night the Baron dreamt of many a woe,
And all his warrior-guests, with shade and form
Of witch, and demon, and large coffin-worm,
Were long be-nightmared. Angela the old
Died palsy-twitched, with meager face deform;
The Beadsman, after thousand aves° told, *prayers*
For aye unsought for slept among his ashes cold.

Considerations

1. Summarize the story told in this poem.
2. What is the setting? Contrast the interior and exterior settings. How do the descriptions of the setting help establish the poem's mood?
3. What roles do the Beadsman, Angela, and the revelers play in the story?
4. Are Madeline and Porphyro individualized characters as well as recognizable types? How are they individuals, and how are they types?
5. What do the contrasting images of sensuality and spirituality contribute to the poem's meaning? How does Keats build on contrasts of youth and age, love and hate, opulence and austerity, life and death, and heaven and hell? Use specific examples to explain how these contrasts relate to one another and to the poem's theme.
6. What sound effects in the poem seem especially effective? Why?
7. Select a stanza and analyze it in terms of sound and meter.

Bright star! would I were steadfast as thou art — 1819

Bright star, would I were steadfast as thou art —
Not in lone splendor hung aloft the night
And watching, with eternal lids apart,
Like nature's patient, sleepless Eremite,
The moving waters at their priestlike task
Of pure ablution round earth's human shores,
Or gazing on the new soft fallen mask
Of snow upon the mountains and the moors —
No — yet still steadfast, still unchangeable,
Pillowed upon my fair love's ripening breast,
To feel forever its soft fall and swell,
Awake forever in a sweet unrest,
Still, still to hear her tender-taken breath,
And so live ever — or else swoon to death.

Considerations

1. What does the speaker in this sonnet admire about the star? What qualities of the star does he reject?
2. What kind of sonnet is this? How does its structure help to shape its meaning?
3. How do the sound effects, particularly assonance and consonance, contribute to the meaning?
4. How does Keats vary the iambic pentameter here? What is the effect of these variations?
5. Is the theme of this sonnet similar to or different from that of "To Autumn" (p. 701)?

Why did I laugh to-night? 1819

Why did I laugh to-night? No voice will tell:
  No God, no Demon of severe response,
Deigns to reply from Heaven or from Hell.
  Then to my human heart I turn at once.
Heart! Thou and I are here sad and alone;
  I say, why did I laugh? O mortal pain!
O Darkness! Darkness! ever must I moan,
  To question Heaven and Hell and Heart in vain.
Why did I laugh? I know this Being's lease,
  My fancy to its utmost blisses spreads;
Yet would I on this very midnight cease,
  And the world's gaudy ensigns see in shreds;
Verse, Fame, and Beauty are intense indeed,
But Death intenser — Death is Life's high meed.

Considerations

1. What is the speaker's answer to the question posed in this sonnet?
2. Describe the sonnet's tone.
3. Write an essay considering the idea that "Death is Life's high meed" as a characteristic Keatsian sentiment.

La Belle Dame sans Merci° 1819

O what can ail thee, knight-at-arms,
  Alone and palely loitering?
The sedge has withered from the lake,
  And no birds sing.

La Belle Dame sans Merci: This title is borrowed from a medieval poem and means "The Beautiful Lady without Mercy."

O what can ail thee, knight-at-arms,
So haggard and so woe-begone?
The squirrel's granary is full,
And the harvest's done.

I see a lily on thy brow,
With anguish moist and fever dew,
And on thy cheeks a fading rose
Fast withereth too.

I met a lady in the meads,
Full beautiful — a faery's child,
Her hair was long, her foot was light,
And her eyes were wild.

I made a garland for her head,
And bracelets too, and fragrant zone;° *belt*
She looked at me as she did love,
And made sweet moan.

I set her on my pacing steed,
And nothing else saw all day long,
For sidelong would she bend, and sing
A faery's song.

She found me roots of relish sweet,
And honey wild, and manna dew,
And sure in language strange she said,
"I love thee true."

She took me to her elfin grot,
And there she wept, and sighed full sore,
And there I shut her wild wild eyes
With kisses four.

And there she lullèd me asleep,
And there I dreamed — Ah! woe betide!
The latest° dream I ever dreamed *last*
On the cold hill side.

I saw pale kings and princes too,
Pale warriors, death-pale were they all;
They cried — "La Belle Dame sans Merci
Hath thee in thrall!"

I saw their starved lips in the gloam,
With horrid warning gapèd wide,
And I awoke and found me here,
On the cold hill's side.

And this is why I soujourn here,
Alone and palely loitering,
Though the sedge has withered from the lake,
And no birds sing.

Considerations

1. How do the first three stanzas of this ballad serve to characterize the knight who describes his experience with the lady?
2. The lady is a familiar character in literature, a "femme fatale." Characterize her. Have you encountered other versions of her in literature or film?
3. What is the effect of the shortened final line in each stanza of this ballad?

Ode to Psyche° **1819**

O Goddess! hear these tuneless numbers, wrung
By sweet enforcement and remembrance dear,
And pardon that thy secrets should be sung
Even into thine own soft-conchèd° ear; *soft like a shell*
Surely I dreamt today, or did I see
The winged Psyche with awakened eyes?
I wandered in a forest thoughtlessly,
And, on the sudden, fainting with surprise,
Saw two fair creatures, couched side by side
In deepest grass, beneath the whisp'ring roof
Of leaves and trembled blossoms, where there ran
A brooklet, scarce espied:

'Mid hushed, cool-rooted flowers, fragrant-eyed,
Blue, silver-white, and budded Tyrian,°
They lay calm-breathing on the bedded grass;
Their arms embraced, and their pinions° too; *wings*
Their lips touched not, but had not bade adieu,
As if disjoined by soft-handed slumber,
And ready still past kisses to outnumber
At tender eye-dawn of aurorean love:
The winged boy I knew;
But who wast thou, O happy, happy dove?
His Psyche true!

O latest born and loveliest vision far
Of all Olympus' faded hierarchy!°
Fairer than Phoebe's° sapphire-regioned star, *Diana, the moon*
Or Vesper;° amorous glowworm of the sky; *evening star*
Fairer than these, though temple thou hast none,
Nor altar heaped with flowers;
Nor virgin choir to make delicious moan
Upon the midnight hours;

Psyche: In Greek, *psyche* means soul or mind, but Psyche was not one of the original Greek gods. Apuleius, a second-century Latin author, told the story of Cupid's love for Psyche and their eventual immortality together. 14 *budded Tyrian:* Purple dye produced in ancient Tyre. 25 *Of all Olympus'* . . . : Psyche was not regarded as a goddess before Apuleius wrote of her.

No voice, no lute, no pipe, no incense sweet
From chain-swung censer teeming;
No shrine, no grove, no oracle, no heat
Of pale mouthed prophet dreaming.

O brightest! though too late for antique vows,
Too, too late for the fond believing lyre,
When holy were the haunted forest boughs,
Holy the air, the water, and the fire;
Yet even in these days so far retired
From happy pieties, thy lucent fans,° *translucent wings*
Fluttering among the faint Olympians,
I see, and sing, by my own eyes inspired.
So let me be thy choir, and make a moan
Upon the midnight hours;
Thy voice, thy lute, thy pipe, thy incense sweet
From swinged censer teeming;
Thy shrine, thy grove, thy oracle, thy heat
Of pale-mouthed prophet dreaming.

Yes, I will be thy priest, and build a fane
In some untrodden region of my mind,
Where branched thoughts, new grown with pleasant pain,
Instead of pines shall murmur in the wind:
Far, far around shall those dark-clustered trees
Fledge the wild-ridged mountains steep by steep;
And there by zephyrs, streams, and birds, and bees,
The moss-lain Dryads° shall be lulled to sleep; *wood nymphs*
And in the midst of this wide quietness
A rosy sanctuary will I dress
With the wreathed trellis of a working brain,
With buds, and bells, and stars without a name,
With all the gardener Fancy e'er could feign,
Who breeding flowers, will never breed the same:
And there shall be for thee all soft delight
That shadowy thought can win,
A bright torch, and a casement ope at night,
To let the warm Love° in! *Cupid*

Considerations

1. What does the ideal love of Psyche and Cupid represent to the speaker in this ode?
2. What does the speaker lament in lines 36–39? What kind of loss is experienced here?
3. How will the speaker be a "priest, and build a fane / In some untrodden region of my mind" (lines 50–51)?
4. In what sense might it be said that this ode is about poetic imagination?

Ode to a Nightingale 1819

I

My heart aches, and a drowsy numbness pains
My sense, as though of hemlock° I had drunk, *a poison*
Or emptied some dull opiate to the drains
One minute past, and Lethe-wards° had sunk:
'Tis not through envy of thy happy lot,
But being too happy in thine happiness —
That thou, light-wingèd Dryad° of the trees, *wood nymph*
In some melodious plot
Of beechen green, and shadows numberless,
Singest of summer in full-throated ease.

II

O, for a draught of vintage! that hath been
Cooled a long age in the deep-delvèd earth,
Tasting of Flora° and the country green, *goddess of flowers*
Dance, and Provençal song,° and sunburnt mirth!
O for a beaker full of the warm South,
Full of the true, the blushful Hippocrene,°
With beaded bubbles winking at the brim,
And purple-stainèd mouth;
That I might drink, and leave the world unseen,
And with thee fade away into the forest dim:

III

Fade far away, dissolve, and quite forget
What thou among the leaves hast never known,
The weariness, the fever, and the fret
Here, where men sit and hear each other groan;
Where palsy shakes a few, sad, last gray hairs,
Where youth grows pale, and specter-thin, and dies,
Where but to think is to be full of sorrow
And leaden-eyed despairs,
Where Beauty cannot keep her lustrous eyes;
Or new Love pine at them beyond tomorrow.

IV

Away! away! for I will fly to thee,
Not charioted by Bacchus and his pards,°
But on the viewless wings of Poesy,
Though the dull brain perplexes and retards:
Already with thee! tender is the night,
And haply the Queen-Moon is on her throne,
Clustered around by all her starry Fays;

4 *Lethe-wards:* Toward Lethe, the river of forgetfulness in the Hades of Greek mythology. 14 *Provençal song:* The medieval troubadours of Provence, France, were known for their singing. 16 *Hippocrene:* The fountain of the Muses in Greek mythology. 32 *Bacchus and his pards:* The Greek god of wine traveled in a chariot drawn by leopards.

But here there is no light,
Save what from heaven is with the breezes blown
Through verdurous glooms and winding mossy ways.

V

I cannot see what flowers are at my feet,
Nor what soft incense hangs upon the boughs,
But, in embalmèd° darkness, guess each sweet — *perfumed*
Wherewith the seasonable month endows
The grass, the thicket, and the fruit-tree wild;
White hawthorn, and the pastoral eglantine;
Fast fading violets covered up in leaves;
And mid-May's eldest child,
The coming musk-rose, full of dewy wine,
The murmurous haunt of flies on summer eves.

VI

Darkling° I listen; and for many a time — *in the dark*
I have been half in love with easeful Death,
Called him soft names in many a musèd rhyme,
To take into the air my quiet breath;
Now more than ever seems it rich to die,
To cease upon the midnight with no pain,
While thou art pouring forth thy soul abroad
In such an ecstasy!
Still wouldst thou sing, and I have ears in vain —
To thy high requiem become a sod.

VII

Thou wast not born for death, immortal Bird!
No hungry generations tread thee down;
The voice I hear this passing night was heard
In ancient days by emperor and clown:
Perhaps the selfsame song that found a path
Through the sad heart of Ruth,° when, sick for home,
She stood in tears amid the alien corn:
The same that oft-times hath
Charmed magic casements, opening on the foam
Of perilous seas, in faery lands forlorn.

VIII

Forlorn! the very word is like a bell
To toll me back from thee to my sole self!
Adieu! the fancy cannot cheat so well
As she is famed to do, deceiving elf.
Adieu! adieu! thy plaintive anthem fades
Past the near meadows, over the still stream,
Up the hill side; and now 'tis buried deep

66 *Ruth:* A young widow in the Bible (see the Book of Ruth).

In the next valley-glades:
Was it a vision, or a waking dream?
Fled is that music: — Do I wake or sleep?

Considerations

1. Why does the speaker in this ode want to leave his world for the nightingale's? What does the nightingale symbolize?
2. How does the speaker attempt to escape his world? Is he successful?
3. What changes the speaker's view of death at the end of stanza VI?
4. What does the allusion to Ruth (line 66) contribute to the ode's meaning?
5. In which lines is the imagery especially sensuous? How does this effect add to the conflict presented?
6. What calls the speaker back to himself at the end of stanza VII and the beginning of stanza VIII?
7. Choose a stanza and explain how sound is related to its meaning.
8. How regular is the stanza form of this ode?

Ode on a Grecian Urn 1819

I

Thou still unravished bride of quietness,
Thou foster-child of silence and slow time,
Sylvan° historian, who canst thus express
A flowery tale more sweetly than our rhyme:
What leaf-fringed legend haunts about thy shape
Of deities or mortals, or of both,
In Tempe or the dales of Arcady?°
What men or gods are these? What maidens loath?
What mad pursuit? What struggle to escape?
What pipes and timbrels? What wild ecstasy?

II

Heard melodies are sweet, but those unheard
Are sweeter; therefore, ye soft pipes, play on;
Not to the sensual ear, but, more endeared,
Pipe to the spirit ditties of no tone:
Fair youth, beneath the trees, thou canst not leave
Thy song, nor ever can those trees be bare;
Bold Lover, never, never canst thou kiss,
Though winning near the goal — yet, do not grieve;
She cannot fade, though thou hast not thy bliss,
For ever wilt thou love, and she be fair!

III

Ah, happy, happy boughs! that cannot shed
Your leaves, nor ever bid the Spring adieu;

3 *Sylvan:* Rustic. The urn is decorated with a forest scene. 7 *Tempe, Arcady:* Beautiful rural valleys in Greece.

And, happy melodist, unwearièd,
    For ever piping songs for ever new;
More happy love! more happy, happy love!
    For ever warm and still to be enjoyed,
        For ever panting, and for ever young;
All breathing human passion far above,
    That leaves a heart high-sorrowful and cloyed,
        A burning forehead, and a parching tongue.

IV

Who are these coming to the sacrifice?
    To what green altar, O mysterious priest,
Lead'st thou that heifer lowing at the skies,
    And all her silken flanks with garlands dressed?
What little town by river or sea shore,
    Or mountain-built with peaceful citadel,
        Is emptied of this folk, this pious morn?
And, little town, thy streets for evermore
    Will silent be; and not a soul to tell
        Why thou art desolate, can e'er return.

V

O attic° shape! Fair attitude! with brede°
    Of marble men and maidens overwrought,
With forest branches and the trodden weed;
    Thou, silent form, dost tease us out of thought
As doth eternity: Cold Pastoral!
    When old age shall this generation waste,
        Thou shalt remain, in midst of other woe
Than ours, a friend to man, to whom thou say'st,
    Beauty is truth, truth beauty — that is all
        Ye know on earth, and all ye need to know.

41 *Attic:* Possessing classic Athenian simplicity; *brede:* Design.

Considerations

1. What is the speaker's attitude toward the urn in this ode? Does his view develop or change?
2. How is the happiness in stanza III related to the assertion in lines 11–12 that "Heard melodies are sweet, but those unheard / Are sweeter"?
3. What is the difference between the world depicted on the urn and the speaker's world?
4. What do lines 49–50 suggest about the relation of art to life? Why is the urn described as a "Cold Pastoral" (line 45)?
5. Which world does the speaker seem to prefer, the urn's or his own?

Connections

1. Write an essay comparing the view of time in this ode with that in Marvell's "To His Coy Mistress" (p. 534).

2. Discuss the treatment and meaning of love in this ode and in Richard Wilbur's "Love Calls Us to the Things of This World" (p. 865).
3. Compare the tone and attitude toward life in this ode with those in Keats's "To Autumn" (p. 701).

Ode on Melancholy

1819

I

No, no! go not to Lethe,° neither twist
Wolfsbane,° tight-rooted, for its poisonous wine;
Nor suffer thy pale forehead to be kissed
By nightshade,° ruby grape of Proserpine;° *Queen of Hades*
Make not your rosary of yew-berries,°
Nor let the beetle, nor the death-moth be
Your mournful Psyche,° nor the downy owl
A partner in your sorrow's mysteries;
For shade to shade will come too drowsily,
And drown the wakeful anguish of the soul.

II

But when the melancholy fit shall fall
Sudden from heaven like a weeping cloud,
That fosters the droop-headed flowers all,
And hides the green hill in an April shroud;
Then glut thy sorrow on a morning rose,
Or on the rainbow of the salt sand-wave,
Or on the wealth of globed peonies;
Or if thy mistress some rich anger shows,
Imprison her soft hand, and let her rave,
And feed deep, deep upon her peerless eyes.

III

She dwells with Beauty — Beauty that must die;
And Joy, whose hand is ever at his lips
Bidding adieu; and aching Pleasure nigh,
Turning to Poison while the bee-mouth sips:
Aye, in the very temple of Delight
Veiled Melancholy has her sovereign shrine,
Though seen of none save him whose strenuous tongue
Can burst Joy's grape against his palate fine;
His soul shall taste the sadness of her might,
And be among her cloudy trophies hung.

1 *Lethe:* In Greek mythology, the river of forgetfulness, which the dead cross to enter Hades. 2 *Wolfsbane:* A poisonous plant. 4 *nightshade:* Also a poisonous plant. 5 *yew-berries:* Associated with death, as are the beetle, moth, and owl in this stanza. 6–7 *nor let the death-moth be. . . :* The soul was depicted as a butterfly in Greek mythology. *Psyche* means soul or mind in Greek.

Considerations

1. What is melancholy? According to the speaker of this ode (lines 27–30), what produces the most intense melancholy? Is it good or bad, a strength or a weakness, to suffer from melancholy?
2. What do the images in this ode reveal about the relation between beauty and time? Between pleasure and pain?
3. Is this a sentimental poem? Explain why or why not.

To Autumn **1819**

I

Season of mists and mellow fruitfulness,
    Close bosom-friend of the maturing sun;
Conspiring with him how to load and bless
    With fruit the vines that round the thatch-eves run;
To bend with apples the mossed cottage-trees,
    And fill all fruit with ripeness to the core;
        To swell the gourd, and plump the hazel shells
    With a sweet kernel; to set budding more,
And still more, later flowers for the bees,
Until they think warm days will never cease,
        For summer has o'er-brimmed their clammy cells.

II

Who hath not seen thee oft amid thy store?
    Sometimes whoever seeks abroad may find
Thee sitting careless on a granary floor,
    Thy hair soft-lifted by the winnowing wind;
Or on a half-reaped furrow sound asleep,
    Drowsed with the fume of poppies, while thy hook° *scythe*
        Spares the next swath and all its twinèd flowers:
And sometimes like a gleaner thou dost keep
    Steady thy laden head across a brook;
    Or by a cider-press, with patient look,
        Thou watchest the last oozings hours by hours.

III

Where are the songs of spring? Ay, where are they?
    Think not of them, thou hast thy music too, —
While barred clouds bloom the soft-dying day,
    And touch the stubble-plains with rosy hue;
Then in a wailful choir the small gnats mourn
    Among the river swallows,° borne aloft *willows*
        Or sinking as the light wind lives or dies;
And full-grown lambs loud bleat from hilly bourn;° *territory*
    Hedge-crickets sing; and now with treble soft
    The redbreast whistles from a garden-croft,
        And gathering swallows twitter in the skies.

Considerations

1. How is autumn personified in each stanza of this ode?
2. Which senses are most emphasized in each stanza?
3. How is the progression of time expressed in the ode?
4. How does the imagery convey tone? Which words have particularly strong connotative values?
5. What is the speaker's view of death?

Connections

1. Compare this poem's tone and its perspective on death with those of Robert Frost's "After Apple-Picking" (p. 718).
2. Write an essay comparing the significance of the images of "mellow fruitfulness" in "To Autumn" with that of the images of ripeness in Roethke's "Root Cellar" (p. 548). Explain how the images in each poem lead to very different feelings about the same phenomenon.

PERSPECTIVES ON KEATS

Keats on the Truth of the Imagination 1817

I am certain of nothing but of the holiness of the Heart's affections and the truth of Imagination — What the imagination seizes as Beauty must be truth — whether it existed before or not — for I have the same Idea of all our Passions as of Love they are all in their sublime, creative of essential Beauty. . . . The Imagination may be compared to Adam's dream° — he awoke and found it truth. I am the more zealous in this affair, because I have never yet been able to perceive how any thing can be known for truth by consequitive reasoning — and yet it must be — Can it be that even the greatest Philosopher ever ~~when~~° arrived at his goal without putting aside numerous objections — However it may be, O for a Life of Sensations rather than of Thoughts! It is "a Vision in the form of Youth" a Shadow of reality to come — and this consideration has further conv[i]nced me for it has come as auxiliary to another favorite Speculation of mine, that we shall enjoy ourselves here after by having what we called happiness on Earth repeated in a finer tone and so repeated — And yet such a fate can only befall those who delight in sensation rather than hunger as you do after Truth — Adam's dream will do here and seems to be a conviction that Imagination and its empyreal reflection is the same as human Life and its spiritual repetition. But as I was saying — The simple imaginative Mind may have its rewards in the repeti[ti]on of its own silent Working coming continually on the spirit with a fine suddenness — to compare great things with small — have you never by being surprised with an old Melody — in a delicious place — by a

Adam's dream: In John Milton's *Paradise Lost* (Book VIII, 460–90), Adam dreams of Eve's creation and wakes up to find that she exists. Excerpts from Keats's letters in this section are reprinted from Hyder E. Rollins's edition of *The Letters of John Keats* (Cambridge, Mass.: Harvard University Press, 1970), which reproduces the letters as Keats wrote them, including the crossed-out words. Rollins's comments are in brackets.

delicious voice, fe[l]t over again your very speculations and surmises at the time it first operated on your soul — do you not remember forming to yourself the singer's face more beautiful that [*for* than] it was possible and yet with the elevation of the Moment you did not think so — even then you were mounted on the Wings of Imagination so high — that the Prototype must be here after — that delicious face you will see — What a time! I am continually running away from the subject — sure this cannot be exactly the case with a complex Mind — one that is imaginative and at the same time careful of its fruits — who would exist partly on sensation partly on thought — to whom it is necessary that years should bring the philosophic Mind — such an one I consider your's and therefore it is necessary to your eternal Happiness that you not only ~~have~~ drink this old Wine of Heaven which I shall call the redigestion of our most ethereal Musings on Earth; but also increase in knowledge and know all things.

From a letter to Benjamin Bailey, November 22, 1817

Considerations

1. "O for a life of Sensations rather than of Thoughts!" What do you think Keats means by this? Is this an antiintellectual statement?
2. Consider this passage from a letter to a friend, C. W. Dilke (September 22, 1819), in which Keats "Talking of pleasure" writes, "this moment I was writing with one hand, and with the other holding to my mouth a Nectarine — good God how fine. It went down soft, slushy, oozy — all its delicious embonpoint [plumpness] melted down my throat like a beatified Strawberry." Why is "delight in sensation," as Keats puts it in his letter to Bailey, so important to Keats's view of life and poetry?
3. How does Keats's description of the relation between beauty and truth in this letter compare with what he says in "Ode on a Grecian Urn" (p. 698)?

Keats on Unobtrusive Poetry 1818

We hate poetry that has a palpable design upon us — and if we do not agree, seems to put its hand in its breeches pocket. Poetry should be great & unobtrusive, a thing which enters into one's soul, and does not startle it or amaze it with itself but with its subject. — How beautiful are the retired flowers! how would they lose their beauty were they to throng into the highway crying out, "admire me I am a violet! dote upon me I am a primrose!"

From a letter to J. H. Reynolds, February 3, 1818

Considerations

1. Does Keats's poetry have a "palpable design" upon the reader? How do you think Keats would regard didactic poetry such as the excerpt from Pope's "An Essay on Criticism" (p. 620)?
2. In another letter to Reynolds (on April 9, 1819), Keats wrote, "I never wrote one single Line of Poetry with the least Shadow of public thought." With reference to specific poems, explain why Keats's poetry is more personal than public and more concerned with feelings than teachings.

Keats on His Poetic Principles 1818

In Poetry I have a few Axioms, and you will see how far I am from their Centre. 1st I think Poetry should surprise by a fine excess and not by Singularity — it should strike the Reader as a wording of his own highest thoughts, and appear almost a Remembrance — 2nd Its touches of Beauty should never be half way therby making the reader breathless instead of content: the rise, the progress, the setting of imagery should like the Sun come natural natural too him — shine over him and set soberly although in magnificence leaving him in the Luxury of twilight — but it is easier to think what Poetry should be than to write it — and this leads me on to another axiom. That if Poetry comes not as naturally as the Leaves to a tree it had better not come at all.

From a Letter to John Taylor, February 27, 1818

Considerations

1. The phrase *fine excess* appears to be a contradiction in terms. How does Keats's poetry resolve this seeming contradiction?
2. Given that Keats wrote in fixed poetic forms, such as the sonnet and ode, in what sense can his poetry be regarded as coming "naturally as the Leaves to a tree"?
3. Based on your reading of Keats's poems, create another axiom that serves as a useful generalization about his poetry.

Keats on the Vale of Soul-Making 1819

The common cognomen of this world among the misguided and superstitious is "a vale of tears" from which we are to be redeemed by a certain arbitrary interposition of God and taken to Heaven — What a little circumscribe[d] straightened notion! Call the world if you Please "The vale of Soul-making" Then you will find out the use of the world (I am speaking now in the highest terms for human nature admitting it to be immortal which I will here take for granted for the purpose of showing a thought which has struck me concerning it) I say *"Soul making"* Soul as distinguished from an Intelligence — There may be intelligences or sparks of the divinity in millions — but they are not Souls ~~the~~ till they acquire identities, till each one is personally itself. I[n]telligences are atoms of perception — they know and they see and they are pure, in short they are God — how then are Souls to be made? How then are these sparks which are God to have identity given them — so as ever to possess a bliss peculiar to each ones individual existence? How, but by the medium of a world like this? This point I sincerely wish to consider because I think it a grander system of salvation than the chrysteain religion — or rather it is a system of Spirit-creation — This is effected by three grand materials acting the one upon the other for a series of years — These three Materials are the *Intelligence* — the *human heart* (as distinguished from intelligence or Mind) and the *World* or *Elemental space* suited for the proper action of *Mind and Heart* on each other for the purpose of forming the *Soul* or *Intelligence destined to possess the sense of Identity.* I can scarcely express what I but dimly perceive — and yet I think I perceive it — that you may judge the more clearly I will put it in the most homely form possible — I will call the *world* a School instituted for the purpose of teaching little children to read — I will call the *human heart* the *horn Book* used in that School — and I will call the *Child able to read, the Soul* made from that *school* and its *hornbook.* Do you not see how necessary a World of Pains and troubles is to school an Intelligence and make it a soul? A Place where the heart must feel and suffer in a thousand diverse ways! Not merely is the Heart a Hornbook, It is the Minds Bible, it is the Minds experience, it is the teat from which the Mind or intelligence sucks its identity — As various as the Lives of Men are — so various become their souls, and thus does God make individual beings, Souls, identical Souls of the sparks of his own essence — This appears to me a faint sketch of a system of Salvation which does not affront our reason and humanity.

From a letter to George and Georgiana Keats, February 14–May 3, 1819

Considerations

1. How does Keats's perception of pain and suffering contrast with what he takes to be the traditional Christian view that life is "a vale of tears" that tests the soul? How are "Souls to be made"?
2. How is Keats's emphasis on a "World of Pains and troubles . . . to school an Intelligence and make it a soul" demonstrated in his poetry? What is the function of pain and suffering in his poetry? How are they related to the process of *"Soul Making"?*
3. Research Keats's personal life, particularly his illness. How does the biographical information you have found shed light on the characteristic tone and subject matter of his poetry?

HAROLD BLOOM (b. 1930)

On "Bright star! would I were steadfast as thou art —" 1961

Bright Star, the best of Keats's sonnets, left by him unpublished, written on a blank page in Shakespeare's Poems, facing *A Lover's Complaint,* is a direct analogue to the ode *To Autumn,* for it also is a poem beyond argument, though not also calm in mind, for passion informs it throughout. The octet is one of the major expressions of Keats's humanism; the sestet one of the most piercing of his longings after the world of Beulah land, the breathing garden of repose beyond bounds. The unity of the poem is constituted by its total freedom from Keats's characteristic conflicts. The octet shares in the resolution of *To Autumn,* giving us an anagoge of poetic eternity, without contraries. The sestet, as a Beulah poem, is set in that state of being where, according to Blake, "all contraries are equally true."

The initial line is a prayer. The next seven lines *describe* the steadfastness of the star, after making it clear that Keats wants to be as steadfast as the star, but not in the star's way of steadfastness. The sestet describes Keats's mode of desired being, and finally declares for an eternity of this being, or an immediate swoon to death. This tight structure confines a remarkable contrast, between the state of Eden and the state of Beulah, Blake would have said, but Keats, by his own choice, clearly opts for the lower paradise as his own.

The Miltonic bright star is not God's hermit but nature's patient, sleepless eremite. Never sleeping, its "eternal lids apart," like Milton's Eyelids of the Morning, it watches:

> The moving waters at their priestlike task
> Of pure ablution round earth's human shores

"Human shores" is powerfully Blakean; the contrast here is between the star as motionless, solitary hermit, and the waters as moving, companionable priest, the one watching, the other cleansing man. We miss the force of this if we do not see it as humanistic, not Christian, in its religious emphasis. The oceans themselves, as a part of unfallen nature, perform their task of *pure* ablution, and the shores of earth are themselves *human.* That last is more than similitude, i.e., metaphor; it is identity, anagogical typology. As Blake saw the physical universe as having itself an ultimately human form, so here also Keats sees the shores of earth as being "men seen afar." As in *To Autumn,* nature alone is sufficient for purifying herself and ourselves, insofar as we can still be hers. Nature's own grace, akin to Keats's poetry, reveals the human countenance of earth:

> Or gazing on the new soft fallen mask
> Of snow upon the mountains and the moors—

The snow is a mask because it covers the human features of earth—that is, mountains and moors. Keats does not ask for himself the priestlike work of the moving waters. . . . Here, at the furthest reach of his poetry, he prays instead for the hermit star's eminence and function, to watch, benevolently, nature's work of humanizing herself. But in his own place; "not in lone splendour hung aloft the night," but in his own Gardens of Adonis, where, still steadfast, still unchangeable (though how, there, can he expect that?) he will be able:

> Pillow'd upon my fair love's ripening breast,
> To feel for ever its soft fall and swell,
> Awake for ever in a sweet unrest,
> Still, still to hear her tender-taken breath
> And so live ever—

Her breast would be forever ripening, never ripe; keeping its sleeping rhythm forever while Keats, awake forever in his sweet unrest, could hear always that recurrence of her breath. This poem can help explain Keats's life; his life cannot explain the poem. Alternatively, the poem can help explain certain contemporary psychological reductions of human desire, but *they* cannot explain *it.*

From *The Visionary Company: A Reading of English Romantic Poetry*

Considerations

1. Explain how Bloom distinguishes between the poem's octet and sestet.
2. How do Bloom's allusions to Blake and Milton help explain his points?

3. What attitudes concerning psychological criticism does Bloom reveal in his final comments? Explain whether you agree or not.

JACK STILLINGER (b. 1931)

On "The Eve of St. Agnes" 1961

The commonest response to *The Eve of St. Agnes* has been the celebration of its "heady and perfumed loveliness." The poem has been called "a monody of dreamy richness," "one long sensuous utterance," "an expression of lyrical emotion," "a great affirmation of love," "a great choral hymn," an expression of "unquestioning rapture," and many things else. Remarks like these tend to confirm one's uneasy feeling that what is sometimes called "the most perfect" of Keats's longer poems is a mere fairy-tale romance, unhappily short on meaning. For many readers, as for Douglas Bush, the poem is "no more than a romantic tapestry of unique richness of color"; one is "moved less by the experience of the characters than . . . by the incidental and innumerable beauties of descriptive phrase and rhythm."

To be sure, not all critics have merely praised Keats's pictures. After all, the poem opens on a note of "bitter chill," and progresses through images of cold and death before the action gets under way. When young Porphyro comes from across the moors to claim his bride, he enters a hostile castle, where Madeline's kinsmen will murder even upon holy days; and in the face of this danger he proceeds to Madeline's bedchamber. With the sexual consummation of their love, a storm comes up, and they must escape the castle, past "sleeping dragons," porter, and bloodhound, out into the night. The ending reverts to the opening notes of bitter chill and death: Madeline's kinsmen are benightmared, the old Beadsman and Madeline's nurse Angela are grotesquely dispatched into the next world. Some obvious contrasts are made in the poem: the lovers' youth and vitality are set against the old age and death associated with Angela and the Beadsman; the warmth and security of Madeline's chamber are contrasted with the coldness and hostility of the rest of the castle and the icy storm outside; the innocence and purity of young love are played off against the sensuousness of the revelers elsewhere in the castle; and so on. Through these contrasts, says one critic [R. H. Fogle], Keats created a tale of young love "not by forgetting what everyday existence is like, but by using the mean, sordid, and commonplace as a foundation upon which to build a high romance"; the result is no mere fairy tale, but a poem that "has a rounded fulness, a complexity and seriousness, a balance which remove it from the realm of mere magnificent tour de force."

From "The Hoodwinking of Madeline: Skepticism in 'The Eve of St. Agnes,' " *Studies in Philology,* 1961.

Considerations

1. What is it about "The Eve of St. Agnes" that has drawn praise for "Keats's pictures"? Identify and discuss several passages that seem especially beautiful in their "descriptive phrase and rhythm."

2. What other contrasts do you find paired in the poem besides the "obvious" one cited by Stillinger?
3. Discuss whether you agree or disagree with the claim that "The Eve of St. Agnes" is "a mere fairy-tale romance, unhappily short on meaning."

ROBERT FROST

Few poets have enjoyed the popular success that Robert Frost achieved during his lifetime (1874–1963), and no twentieth-century American poet has had his or her work as widely read and honored. Frost is as much associated with New England as the stone walls that help define its landscape; his reputation, however, transcends regional boundaries. Although he was named poet laureate of Vermont only two years before his death, he was for many years the nation's unofficial poet laureate. Frost collected honors the way some people pick up burrs on country walks. Among his awards were four Pulitzer Prizes, the Bollingen Prize, a Congressional Medal, and dozens of honorary degrees. Perhaps his most moving appearance was his recitation of "The Gift Outright" for millions of Americans at the inauguration of John F. Kennedy in 1961.

Frost's recognition as a poet is especially remarkable because his career as a writer did not attract any significant attention until he was nearly forty years old. He taught himself to write while he labored at odd jobs, taught school, or farmed.

Frost's early identity seems very remote from the New England soil. Although his parents were descended from generations of New Englanders, he was born in San Francisco and was named Robert Lee Frost after the Confederate general. After his father died in 1885, his mother moved the family back to Massachusetts to live with relatives. Frost graduated from high school sharing valedictorian honors with the classmate who would become his wife three years later. Between high school and marriage, he attended Dartmouth College for a few months and then taught. His teaching prompted him to enroll in Harvard in 1897, but after less than two years he withdrew without a degree (though Harvard would eventually award him an honorary doctorate in 1937, four years after Dartmouth conferred its honorary degree upon him). For the next decade, Frost read and wrote poems when he was not chicken farming or teaching. In 1912, he sold his farm and moved his family to England, where he hoped to find the audience that his poetry did not have in America.

Three years in England made it possible for Frost to return home as a poet. His first two volumes of poetry, *A Boy's Will* (1913) and *North of Boston* (1914), were published in England. During the next twenty years, honors and awards were conferred on collections such as *Mountain Interval* (1916), *New Hampshire* (1923), *West Running Brook* (1928), and *A Fur-*

ther Range (1936). These are the volumes on which most of Frost's popular and critical reputation rests. Later collections include *A Witness Tree* (1942), *A Masque of Reason* (1945), *Steeple Bush* (1947), *A Masque of Mercy* (1947), *Complete Poems* (1949), and *In the Clearing* (1962). In addition to publishing his works, Frost endeared himself to audiences throughout the country by presenting his poetry almost as conversations. He also taught at a number of schools, including Amherst College, the University of Michigan, Harvard University, Dartmouth College, and Middlebury College.

Frost's countless poetry readings generated wide audiences eager to claim him as their poet. The image he cultivated resembled closely what the public likes to think a poet should be. Frost was seen as a lovable, wise old man; his simple wisdom and cracker-barrel sayings appeared comforting and homey. From this Yankee rustic, audiences learned that "There's a lot yet that isn't understood" or "We love the things we love for what they are" or "Good fences make good neighbors."

In a sense, Frost packaged himself for public consumption. "I am . . . my own salesman," he said. When asked direct questions about the meanings of his poems, he often winked or scratched his head to give the impression that the customer was always right. To be sure, there is a simplicity in Frost's language, but that simplicity does not fully reflect the depth of the man, the complexity of his themes, or the richness of his art.

The folksy optimist behind the public lectern did not reveal his private troubles to his audiences, although he did address those problems at his writing desk. Frost suffered from professional jealousies, anger, and depression. His family life was especially painful. Three of his four children died: a son at the age of four, a daughter in her late twenties from tuberculosis, and another son who was a suicide. His marriage was filled with tension. Although Frost's work is landscaped with sunlight, snow, birches, birds, blueberries, and squirrels, it is important to recognize that he was also intimately "acquainted with the night," a phrase that serves as the haunting title of one of his poems (see p. 582).

As a corrective to Frost's popular reputation, one critic, Lionel Trilling, described the world Frost creates in his poems as a "terrifying universe," characterized by loneliness, anguish, frustration, doubts, disappointment, and despair (see p. 735 for an excerpt from this essay). To point this out is not to annihilate the pleasantness and even good-natured cheerfulness that can be enjoyed in Frost's poetry, but it is to say that Frost is not so one-dimensional as he is sometimes assumed to be. Frost's poetry requires readers who are alert and willing to penetrate the simplicity of its language to see the elusive and ambiguous meanings that lie below the surface.

Frost's treatment of nature helps to explain the various levels of meaning in his poetry. The familiar natural world his poems evoke is sharply detailed. We hear icy branches clicking against themselves, we see the snow-white trunks of birches, we feel the smarting pain of a twig lashing across a face. The aspects of the natural world Frost describes are designed to give pleasure, but they are also frequently calculated to provoke thought. His use of nature tends to be symbolic. Complex meanings are derived from simple facts, such as a spider killing a moth or a crow shaking some snow off a tree (see "Design," p. 725, and "Dust of Snow," p. 722). Although Frost's strategy is to talk about particular events and individual experiences, his poems evoke universal issues.

Frost's poetry has strong regional roots and is "versed in country things," but it flourishes in any receptive imagination because, in the final analysis, it is concerned with human beings. Frost's New England landscapes are the occasion rather than the ultimate focus of his poems. Like the rural voices he creates in his poems, Frost typically approaches his themes indirectly. He explained the reason for this in a talk titled "Education by Poetry."

> Poetry provides the one permissible way of saying one thing and meaning another. People say, "why don't you say what you mean?" We never do that, do we, being all of us too much poets. We like to talk in parables and in hints and in indirections — whether from diffidence or some other instinct.

The result is that the settings, characters, and situations that make up the subject matter of Frost's poems are vehicles for his perceptions about life.

In "Stopping by Woods on a Snowy Evening" (p. 723), for example, Frost uses the kind of familiar New England details that constitute his poetry for more than descriptive purposes. He shapes them into a meditation on the tension we sometimes feel between life's responsibilities and the "lovely, dark, and deep" attraction that death offers. When the speaker's horse "gives his harness bells a shake," we are reminded that we are confronting a universal theme as well as a quiet moment of natural beauty.

Among the major concerns that appear in Frost's poetry are the fragility of life, the consequences of rejecting or accepting the conditions of one's life, the passion of inconsolable grief, the difficulty of sustaining intimacy, the fear of loneliness and isolation, the inevitability of change, the tensions between the individual and society, and the place of tradition and custom.

Whatever theme is encountered in a poem by Frost, a reader is likely to agree with him that "the initial delight is in the surprise of remembering something I didn't know." To achieve that fresh sense of discovery, Frost allowed himself to follow his instincts; his poetry

> inclines to the impulse, it assumes direction with the first line laid down, it runs a course of lucky events, and ends in a clarification of life — not necessarily a great clarification, such as sects and cults are founded on, but in a momentary stay against confusion.

This description from "The Figure a Poem Makes" (see p. 732 for the complete essay), Frost's brief introduction to *Complete Poems,* may sound as if his poetry is formless and merely "lucky," but his poems tend to be more conventional than experimental: "The artist in me," as he put the matter in one of his poems, "cries out for design."

From Frost's perspective, "free verse is like playing tennis with the net down." He exercised his own freedom in meeting the challenges of rhyme and meter. His use of fixed forms such as couplets, tercets, quatrains, blank verse, and sonnets was not slavish, because he enjoyed working them into the natural English speech patterns — especially the rhythms, idioms, and tones of speakers living north of Boston — that give voice to his themes. Frost often liked to use "Stopping by Woods on a Snowy Evening" as an example of his graceful way of making conventions appear natural and inevitable. He explored "the old ways to be new."

Frost's eye for strong, telling details was matched by his ear for natural speech rhythms. His flexible use of what he called "iambic and loose iambic" enabled him to create moving lyric poems that reveal the personal thoughts of a speaker and dramatic poems that convincingly characterize people caught in intense emotional situations. The language in his poems appears to be little more than a transcription of casual and even rambling speech, but it is in actuality Frost's poetic creation, carefully crafted to reveal the joys and sorrows that are woven into people's daily lives. What is missing from Frost's poems is artificiality, not art. Consider this poem.

The Road Not Taken **1916**

Two roads diverged in a yellow wood,
And sorry I could not travel both
And be one traveler, long I stood
And looked down one as far as I could
To where it bent in the undergrowth;

Then took the other, as just as fair,
And having perhaps the better claim,
Because it was grassy and wanted wear;
Though as for that the passing there
Had worn them really about the same,

And both that morning equally lay
In leaves no step had trodden black.
Oh, I kept the first for another day!
Yet knowing how way leads on to way,
I doubted if I should ever come back.

I shall be telling this with a sigh
Somewhere ages and ages hence:
Two roads diverged in a wood, and I —
I took the one less traveled by,
And that has made all the difference.

This poem intrigues readers because it is at once so simple and so deeply resonant. Recalling a walk in the woods, the speaker describes how he came upon a fork in the road, which forced him to choose one path over another. Though "sorry" that he "could not travel both," he made a choice after carefully weighing his two options. This, essentially, is what happens in the poem; there is no other action. However, the incident is charged with symbolic significance by the speaker's reflections on the necessity and consequences of his decision.

The final stanza indicates that the choice concerns more than simply walking down a road, for the speaker says that his chosen path has affected his entire life — "that [it] has made all the difference." Frost draws on a familiar enough metaphor when he compares life to a journey, but he is also calling attention to a less commonly noted problem: despite our expectations, aspirations, appetites, hopes, and desires, we can't have it all. Making one choice precludes another. It is impossible to determine what particular decision the speaker refers to: perhaps he had to choose a college, a career, a spouse; perhaps he was confronted with mutually exclusive ideas, beliefs, or values. There is no way to know, because Frost wisely creates a symbolic choice and implicitly invites us to supply our own circumstances.

The speaker's reflections about his choice are as central to an understanding of the poem as the choice itself; indeed, they may be more central. He describes the road taken as "having perhaps the better claim, / Because it was grassy and wanted wear"; he prefers the "less traveled" path. This seems to be an expression of individualism, which would account for "the difference" his choice made in his life. But Frost complicates matters by having the speaker also acknowledge that there was no significant difference between the two roads: one was "just as fair" as the other; each was "worn . . . really about the same"; and "both that morning equally lay / In leaves no step had trodden black."

The speaker imagines that in the future, "ages and ages hence," he will recount his choice with "a sigh" that will satisfactorily explain the course of his life, but Frost seems to be having a little fun here by showing us how the speaker will embellish his past decision to make it appear more dramatic. What we hear is someone trying to convince himself that the choice he made significantly changed his life. When he recalls what happened in the "yellow wood," a color that gives a glow to that irretrievable moment when his life seemed to be on verge of a momentous change, he appears more concerned with the path he did not choose than with the one he took. Frost shrewdly titles the poem to suggest the speaker's sense of loss at not being able to "travel both" roads. When the speaker's reflections about his choice are examined, the poem reveals his nostalgia instead of affirming his decision to travel a self-reliant path in life.

The rhymed stanzas of "The Road Not Taken" follow a pattern established in the first five lines *(abaab)*. This rhyme scheme reflects, perhaps, the speaker's efforts to shape his life into a pleasing and coherent form. The natural speech rhythms Frost uses allow him to integrate the rhymes unobtrusively, but there is a slight shift in lines 19–20, when the speaker asserts self-consciously that the "less traveled" road — which we already know to be basically the same as the other road — "made all the difference." Unlike all the other rhymes in the poem, "difference" does not rhyme precisely with "hence." The emphasis that must be placed on "differ*ence*" to make it rhyme perfectly with "hence" may suggest that the speaker is trying just a little too hard to pattern his life on his earlier choice in the woods.

Perhaps the best way to begin reading Frost's poetry is to accept the invitation he placed at the beginning of many volumes of his poems. "The Pasture" means what it says of course; it is about taking care of some farm chores, but it is also a means of "saying one thing in terms of another."

The Pasture 1913

I'm going out to clean the pasture spring;
I'll only stop to rake the leaves away
(And wait to watch the water clear, I may):
I shan't be gone long. — You come too.

I'm going out to fetch the little calf
That's standing by the mother. It's so young
It totters when she licks it with her tongue.
I shan't be gone long. — You come too.

Here is a simple but irresistible songlike invitation to the pleasure of looking at the world through the eyes of a poet.

Mending Wall 1914

Something there is that doesn't love a wall,
That sends the frozen-ground-swell under it,
And spills the upper boulders in the sun;
And makes gaps even two can pass abreast.
The work of hunters is another thing:
I have come after them and made repair
Where they have left not one stone on a stone,
But they would have the rabbit out of hiding,
To please the yelping dogs. The gaps I mean,
No one has seen them made or heard them made,
But at spring mending-time we find them there.
I let my neighbor know beyond the hill;
And on a day we meet to walk the line
And set the wall between us once again.
We keep the wall between us as we go.
To each the boulders that have fallen to each.

And some are loaves and some so nearly balls
We have to use a spell to make them balance:
"Stay where you are until our backs are turned!"
We wear our fingers rough with handling them.
Oh, just another kind of outdoor game,
One on a side. It comes to little more:
There where it is we do not need the wall:
He is all pine and I am apple orchard.
My apple trees will never get across
And eat the cones under his pines, I tell him.
He only says, "Good fences make good neighbors."
Spring is the mischief in me, and I wonder
If I could put a notion in his head:
"*Why* do they make good neighbors? Isn't it
Where there are cows? But here there are no cows.
Before I built a wall I'd ask to know
What I was walling in or walling out,
And to whom I was like to give offense.
Something there is that doesn't love a wall,
That wants it down." I could say "Elves" to him,
But it's not elves exactly, and I'd rather
He said it for himself. I see him there
Bringing a stone grasped firmly by the top
In each hand, like an old-stone savage armed.
He moves in darkness as it seems to me,
Not of woods only and the shade of trees.
He will not go behind his father's saying,
And he likes having thought of it so well
He says again, "Good fences make good neighbors."

Considerations

1. How do the speaker and his neighbor in this poem differ in sensibilities? What is suggested about the neighbor in lines 41–42?
2. What might the "Something" be that "doesn't love a wall"? Why does the speaker remind his neighbor each spring that the wall needs to be repaired? Is it ironic that the *speaker* initiates the mending? Is there anything good about the wall?
3. The neighbor likes the saying "Good fences make good neighbors" so well that he repeats it. Does the speaker also say something twice? What else suggests that the speaker's attitude toward the wall is not necessarily Frost's?
4. Although the speaker's language is colloquial, what is poetic about the sounds and rhythms he uses?
5. This poem was first published in 1914; Frost read it to an audience when he visited Russia in 1962. What do these facts suggest about the symbolic value of "Mending Wall"?

Connections

1. How do you think the neighbor in this poem would respond to Dickinson's idea of imagination in "To make a prairie it takes a clover and one bee" (p. 521)?

2. What similarities and differences does the neighbor have with the people Frost describes in "Neither Out Far nor In Deep" (p. 726)?
3. Write an essay discussing the function of walls in this poem and in Melville's story "Bartleby, the Scrivener" (p. 80).

Home Burial

1914

He saw her from the bottom of the stairs
Before she saw him. She was starting down,
Looking back over her shoulder at some fear.
She took a doubtful step and then undid it
To raise herself and look again. He spoke
Advancing toward her: "What is it you see
From up there always — for I want to know."
She turned and sank upon her skirts at that,
And her face changed from terrified to dull.
He said to gain time: "What is it you see,"
Mounting until she cowered under him.
"I will find out now — you must tell me, dear."
She, in her place, refused him any help
With the least stiffening of her neck and silence.
She let him look, sure that he wouldn't see,
Blind creature; and awhile he didn't see.
But at last he murmured, "Oh," and again, "Oh."

"What is it — what?" she said.

"Just that I see."

"You don't," she challenged. "Tell me what it is."

"The wonder is I didn't see at once.
I never noticed it from here before.
I must be wonted to it — that's the reason.
The little graveyard where my people are!
So small the window frames the whole of it.
Not so much larger than a bedroom, is it?
There are three stones of slate and one of marble,
Broad-shouldered little slabs there in the sunlight
On the sidehill. We haven't to mind *those*.
But I understand: it is not the stones,
But the child's mound —"

"Don't, don't, don't, don't," she cried.

She withdrew, shrinking from beneath his arm
That rested on the banister, and slid downstairs;
And turned on him with such a daunting look,
He said twice over before he knew himself:
"Can't a man speak of his own child he's lost?"

"Not you! — Oh, where's my hat? Oh, I don't need it!
I must get out of here. I must get air.
I don't know rightly whether any man can."

"Amy! Don't go to someone else this time.
Listen to me. I won't come down the stairs."
He sat and fixed his chin between his fists.
"There's something I should like to ask you, dear."

"You don't know how to ask it."

"Help me, then."
Her fingers moved the latch for all reply.

"My words are nearly always an offense.
I don't know how to speak of anything
So as to please you. But I might be taught,
I should suppose. I can't say I see how.
A man must partly give up being a man
With women-folk. We could have some arrangement
By which I'd bind myself to keep hands off
Anything special you're a-mind to name.
Though I don't like such things 'twixt those that love.
Two that don't love can't live together without them.
But two that do can't live together with them."
She moved the latch a little. "Don't — don't go.
Don't carry it to someone else this time.
Tell me about it if it's something human.
Let me into your grief. I'm not so much
Unlike other folks as your standing there
Apart would make me out. Give me my chance.
I do think, though, you overdo it a little.
What was it brought you up to think it the thing
To take your mother-loss of a first child
So inconsolably — in the face of love.
You'd think his memory might be satisfied —"

"There you go sneering now!"

"I'm not, I'm not!
You make me angry. I'll come down to you.
God, what a woman! And it's come to this,
A man can't speak of his own child that's dead."

"You can't because you don't know how to speak.
If you had any feelings, you that dug
With your own hand — how could you? — his little grave;
I saw you from that very window there,
Making the gravel leap and leap in air,
Leap up, like that, like that, and land so lightly
And roll back down the mound beside the hole.
I thought, Who is that man? I didn't know you.
And I crept down the stairs and up the stairs

To look again, and still your spade kept lifting.
Then you came in. I heard your rumbling voice
Out in the kitchen, and I don't know why,
But I went near to see with my own eyes.
You could sit there with the stains on your shoes
Of the fresh earth from your own baby's grave
And talk about your everyday concerns.
You had stood the spade up against the wall
Outside there in the entry, for I saw it."

"I shall laugh the worst laugh I ever laughed.
I'm cursed. God, if I don't believe I'm cursed."

"I can repeat the very words you were saying.
"Three foggy mornings and one rainy day
Will rot the best birch fence a man can build."
Think of it, talk like that at such a time!
What had how long it takes a birch to rot
To do with what was in the darkened parlor.
You *couldn't* care! The nearest friends can go
With anyone to death, comes so far short
They might as well not try to go at all.
No, from the time when one is sick to death,
One is alone, and he dies more alone.
Friends make pretense of following to the grave.
But before one is in it, their minds are turned
And making the best of their way back to life
And living people, and things they understand.
But the world's evil. I won't have grief so
If I can change it. Oh, I won't, I won't!"

"There, you have said it all and you feel better.
You won't go now. You're crying. Close the door.
The heart's gone out of it: why keep it up.
Amy! There's someone coming down the road!"

"*You* — oh, you think the talk is all. I must go —
Somewhere out of this house. How can I make you —"

"If — you — do!" She was opening the door wider.
"Where do you mean to go? First tell me that.
I'll follow and bring you back by force. I *will!* —"

Considerations

1. How has the burial of the child within sight of the stairway window affected the relationship of the couple in this poem? Is the child's grave a symptom or a cause of the conflict between them?
2. Is the husband insensitive and indifferent to his wife's grief? Characterize the wife. Has Frost invited us to sympathize with one character more than with the other?
3. What is the effect of splitting the iambic pentameter pattern in lines 18–19, 31–32, 45–46, and 70–71?

4. Is the conflict resolved at the conclusion of the poem? Do you think the husband and wife will overcome their differences?

After Apple-Picking

1914

My long two-pointed ladder's sticking through a tree
Toward heaven still,
And there's a barrel that I didn't fill
Beside it, and there may be two or three
Apples I didn't pick upon some bough.
But I am done with apple-picking now.
Essence of winter sleep is on the night,
The scent of apples: I am drowsing off.
I cannot rub the strangeness from my sight
I got from looking through a pane of glass
I skimmed this morning from the drinking trough
And held against the world of hoary grass.
It melted, and I let it fall and break.
But I was well
Upon my way to sleep before it fell,
And I could tell
What form my dreaming was about to take.
Magnified apples appear and disappear,
Stem end and blossom end,
And every fleck of russet showing clear.
My instep arch not only keeps the ache,
It keeps the pressure of a ladder-round.
I feel the ladder sway as the boughs bend.
And I keep hearing from the cellar bin
The rumbling sound
Of load on load of apples coming in.
For I have had too much
Of apple-picking: I am overtired
Of the great harvest I myself desired.
There were ten thousand thousand fruit to touch,
Cherish in hand, lift down, and not let fall.
For all
That struck the earth,
No matter if not bruised or spiked with stubble,
Went surely to the cider-apple heap
As of no worth.
One can see what will trouble
This sleep of mine, whatever sleep it is.
Were he not gone,
The woodchuck could say whether it's like his
Long sleep, as I describe its coming on,
Or just some human sleep.

Considerations

1. How does this poem illustrate Frost's view that "Poetry provides the one permissible way of saying one thing and meaning another"? When do you first sense that the detailed description of apple picking is being used that way?
2. What comes after apple picking? What does the speaker worry about in the dream beginning in line 18?
3. Why do you suppose Frost uses apples rather than, say, pears or squash?

Birches 1916

When I see birches bend to left and right
Across the lines of straighter darker trees,
I like to think some boy's been swinging them.
But swinging doesn't bend them down to stay
As ice-storms do. Often you must have seen them
Loaded with ice a sunny winter morning
After a rain. They click upon themselves
As the breeze rises, and turn many-colored
As the stir cracks and crazes their enamel.
Soon the sun's warmth makes them shed crystal shells
Shattering and avalanching on the snow-crust —
Such heaps of broken glass to sweep away
You'd think the inner dome of heaven had fallen.
They are dragged to the withered bracken by the load,
And they seem not to break; though once they are bowed
So low for long, they never right themselves:
You may see their trunks arching in the woods
Years afterwards, trailing their leaves on the ground
Like girls on hands and knees that throw their hair
Before them over their heads to dry in the sun.
But I was going to say when Truth broke in
With all her matter-of-fact about the ice-storm,
I should prefer to have some boy bend them
As he went out and in to fetch the cows —
Some boy too far from town to learn baseball,
Whose only play was what he found himself,
Summer or winter, and could play alone.
One by one he subdued his father's trees
By riding them down over and over again
Until he took the stiffness out of them,
And not one but hung limp, not one was left
For him to conquer. He learned all there was
To learn about not launching out too soon
And so not carrying the tree away
Clear to the ground. He always kept his poise
To the top branches, climbing carefully

With the same pains you use to fill a cup
Up to the brim, and even above the brim.
Then he flung outward, feet first, with a swish,
Kicking his way down through the air to the ground.
So was I once myself a swinger of birches.
And so I dream of going back to be.
It's when I'm weary of considerations,
And life is too much like a pathless wood
Where your face burns and tickles with the cobwebs
Broken across it, and one eye is weeping
From a twig's having lashed across it open.
I'd like to get away from earth awhile
And then come back to it and begin over.
May no fate willfully misunderstand me
And half grant what I wish and snatch me away
Not to return. Earth's the right place for love:
I don't know where it's likely to go better.
I'd like to go by climbing a birch tree,
And climb black branches up a snow-white trunk,
Toward heaven, till the tree could bear no more,
But dipped its top and set me down again.
That would be good both going and coming back.
One could do worse than be a swinger of birches.

Considerations

1. Why does the speaker in this poem prefer the birches to have been bent by boys instead of ice storms?
2. What does the swinging of birches symbolize?
3. How is "earth" described in the poem? Why does the speaker choose it over "heaven"?
4. How might the effect of this poem be changed if it were written in heroic couplets instead of blank verse?

"Out, Out —"° 1916

The buzz-saw snarled and rattled in the yard
And made dust and dropped stove-length sticks of wood,
Sweet-scented stuff when the breeze drew across it.
And from there those that lifted eyes could count
Five mountain ranges one behind the other
Under the sunset far into Vermont.
And the saw snarled and rattled, snarled and rattled,
As it ran light, or had to bear a load.
And nothing happened: day was all but done.

"Out, Out —": From Act V, Scene v, of Shakespeare's *Macbeth.* The passage appears on page 562.

Call it a day, I wish they might have said
To please the boy by giving him the half hour
That a boy counts so much when saved from work.
His sister stood beside them in her apron
To tell them "Supper." At the word, the saw,
As if to prove saws knew what supper meant,
Leaped out at the boy's hand, or seemed to leap —
He must have given the hand. However it was,
Neither refused the meeting. But the hand!
The boy's first outcry was a rueful laugh,
As he swung toward them holding up the hand
Half in appeal, but half as if to keep
The life from spilling. Then the boy saw all —
Since he was old enough to know, big boy
Doing a man's work, though a child at heart —
He saw all spoiled. "Don't let him cut my hand off —
The doctor, when he comes. Don't let him, sister!"
So. But the hand was gone already.
The doctor put him in the dark of ether.
He lay and puffed his lips out with his breath.
And then — the watcher at his pulse took fright.
No one believed. They listened at his heart.
Little — less — nothing! — and that ended it.
No more to build on there. And they, since they
Were not the one dead, turned to their affairs.

Considerations

1. How does Frost's allusion to *Macbeth* contribute to the meaning of this poem? Does the speaker seem to agree with the view of life expressed in Macbeth's lines?
2. This narrative poem is about the accidental death of a Vermont boy. What is the purpose of the story? Some readers have argued that the final lines reveal the speaker's callousness and indifference. What do you think?

Connections

1. What are the similarities and differences in theme between this poem and Frost's "The Need of Being Versed in Country Things" (p. 723)?
2. Write an essay comparing how grief is handled by the boy's family in this poem and the couple in "Home Burial" (p. 715).
3. Compare the tone and theme of "Out, Out —" and those of Crane's "A Man Said to the Universe" (p. 589).

Fire and Ice

1923

Some say the world will end in fire,
Some say in ice.
From what I've tasted of desire
I hold with those who favor fire.
But if I had to perish twice,
I think I know enough of hate
To say that for destruction ice
Is also great
And would suffice.

Considerations

1. What theories about the end of the world are alluded to in lines 1 and 2?
2. What characteristics of human behavior does the speaker associate with fire and ice?
3. How does the speaker's use of understatement and rhyme affect the tone of this poem?

Dust of Snow

1923

The way a crow
Shook down on me
The dust of snow
From a hemlock tree

Has given my heart
A change of mood
And saved some part
Of a day I had rued.

Considerations

1. This poem describes a literal incident in which the speaker somehow feels better as a result of what the crow does in the first quatrain. Ordinarily, one might see that as yet another ingredient of a bad day, such as getting caught in the rain. Why does the speaker view the incident as positive?
2. Which words in the poem have connotative values that invite a symbolic reading of what is described?
3. Why do you suppose the poem is entitled "Dust of Snow" rather than "Change of Mood"?
4. What is the significance of this entire poem being only one sentence?

Stopping by Woods on a Snowy Evening 1923

Whose woods these are I think I know.
His house is in the village, though;
He will not see me stopping here
To watch his woods fill up with snow.

My little horse must think it queer
To stop without a farmhouse near
Between the woods and frozen lake
The darkest evening of the year.

He gives his harness bells a shake
To ask if there is some mistake.
The only other sound's the sweep
Of easy wind and downy flake.

The woods are lovely, dark, and deep,
But I have promises to keep,
And miles to go before I sleep,
And miles to go before I sleep.

Considerations

1. What is the significance of the setting in this poem? How is tone conveyed by the images?
2. What does the speaker find appealing about the woods? What is the purpose of the horse in the poem?
3. Although the last two lines are identical, they are not read at the same speed. Why the difference? What is achieved by the repetition?
4. What is the rhyme scheme of this poem? What is the effect of the rhyme in the final stanza?

The Need of Being Versed in Country Things 1923

The house had gone to bring again
To the midnight sky a sunset glow.
Now the chimney was all of the house that stood,
Like a pistil after the petals go.

The barn opposed across the way,
That would have joined the house in flame
Had it been the will of the wind, was left
To bear forsaken the place's name.

No more it opened with all one end
For teams that came by the stony road
To drum on the floor with scurrying hoofs
And brush the mow with the summer load.

The birds that came to it through the air
At broken windows flew out and in,
Their murmur more like the sigh we sigh
From too much dwelling on what has been.

Yet for them the lilac renewed its leaf,
And the aged elm, though touched with fire;
And the dry pump flung up an awkward arm;
And the fence post carried a strand of wire.

For them there was really nothing sad.
But though they rejoiced in the nest they kept,
One had to be versed in country things
Not to believe the phoebes wept.

Considerations

1. How does this poem explain its title? What does one need to know about "country things"? Why?
2. How do the imagery and figures of speech contribute to the mood of the poem?
3. Some readers argue that the speaker in this poem is sentimental. What do you think?

Once by the Pacific 1928

The shattered water made a misty din.
Great waves looked over others coming in,
And thought of doing something to the shore
That water never did to land before.
The clouds were low and hairy in the skies,
Like locks blown forward in the gleam of eyes.
You could not tell, and yet it looked as if
The shore was lucky in being backed by cliff,
The cliff in being backed by continent;
It looked as if a night of dark intent
Was coming, and not only a night, an age.
Someone had better be prepared for rage.
There would be more than ocean-water broken
Before God's last *Put out the Light* was spoken.

Considerations

1. In what sense is the title of this poem ironic?
2. How do the descriptions of the waves, clouds, and night convey the storm's appalling fierceness?
3. The final line alludes to God's command in Genesis "Let there be light." What does the allusion add to the poem?

Desert Places 1936

Snow falling and night falling fast, oh, fast
In a field I looked into going past,
And the ground almost covered smooth in snow,
But a few weeds and stubble showing last.

The woods around it have it — it is theirs.
All animals are smothered in their lairs.
I am too absent-spirited to count;
The loneliness includes me unawares.

And lonely as it is, that loneliness
Will be more lonely ere it will be less —
A blanker whiteness of benighted snow
With no expression, nothing to express.

They cannot scare me with their empty spaces
Between stars — on stars where no human race is.
I have it in me so much nearer home
To scare myself with my own desert places.

Considerations

1. What kind of desert places does the speaker in this poem describe?
2. How does the speaker view the snow? Is this the same perspective as the one in "Stopping by Woods on a Snowy Evening" (p. 723)?
3. Who are "They" in line 13? Why is it that the speaker cannot be scared by them?

Design 1936

I found a dimpled spider, fat and white,
On a white heal-all,° holding up a moth
Like a white piece of rigid satin cloth —
Assorted characters of death and blight
Mixed ready to begin the morning right,
Like the ingredients of a witches' broth —
A snow-drop spider, a flower like a froth,
And dead wings carried like a paper kite.

What had the flower to do with being white,
The wayside blue and innocent heal-all?
What brought the kindred spider to that height,
Then steered the white moth thither in the night?
What but design of darkness to appall? —
If design govern in a thing so small.

2 *heal-all:* A common flower, usually blue, once used for medicinal purposes.

Considerations

1. How does the division of the octave and sestet in this sonnet serve to organize the speaker's thoughts and feelings? What is the predominant rhyme? How does that rhyme relate to the poem's meaning?
2. Which words seem especially rich in connotative meanings? Explain how they function in the sonnet.
3. What kinds of speculations are raised in the final two lines? Consider the meaning of the title. Is there more than one way to read it?

Connections

1. What similarities and differences are there in tone and theme between this poem and "The Need of Being Versed in Country Things" (p. 723).
2. Compare the ironic tone of "Design" with the tone of Hathaway's "Oh, Oh" (p. 498). What would you have to change in Hathaway's poem to make it more like Frost's?
3. In an essay discuss Frost's view of God in this poem and Dickinson's perspective in "I know that He exists" (p. 578).
4. Compare "Design" with "In White," Frost's early version of it (p. 730).

Neither Out Far Nor In Deep

1936

The people along the sand
All turn and look one way.
They turn their back on the land.
They look at the sea all day.

As long as it takes to pass
A ship keeps raising its hull;
The wetter ground like glass
Reflects a standing gull.

The land may vary more;
But wherever the truth may be —
The water comes ashore,
And the people look at the sea.

They cannot look out far.
They cannot look in deep.
But when was that ever a bar
To any watch they keep?

Considerations

1. Frost built this poem around a simple observation that raises some questions. Why do people at the beach almost always face the ocean? What feelings and thoughts are evoked by looking at the ocean?
2. Notice how the verb *look* takes on added meaning as the poem progresses. What are the people looking for?

3. How does the final stanza extend the poem's significance?
4. Does the speaker identify with the people described, or does he ironically distance himself from them?

Provide, Provide 1936

The witch that came (the withered hag)
To wash the steps with pail and rag,
Was once the beauty Abishag,°

The picture pride of Hollywood.
Too many fall from great and good
For you to doubt the likelihood.

Die early and avoid the fate.
Or if predestined to die late,
Make up your mind to die in state.

Make the whole stock exchange your own!
If need be occupy a throne,
Where nobody can call *you* crone.

Some have relied on what they knew;
Others on being simply true.
What worked for them might work for you.

No memory of having starred
Atones for later disregard,
Or keeps the end from being hard.

Better to go down dignified
With boughten friendship at your side
Than none at all. Provide, provide!

3 *Abishag:* A beautiful young woman who comforted King David in his old age (1 Kings 1:1–4).

Considerations

1. Do you agree or disagree with the sentiments expressed in lines 19–21 of this poem?
2. Does the speaker offer serious advice or satirize the values described here? Is this poem didactic or ironic?
3. What is the effect of the rhymes? Is this much rhyme characteristic of Frost's work?

Departmental 1936

An ant on the tablecloth
Ran into a dormant moth

Of many times his size.
He showed not the least surprise.
His business wasn't with such.
He gave it scarcely a touch,
And was off on his duty run.
Yet if he encountered one
Of the hive's enquiry squad
Whose work is to find out God
And the nature of time and space,
He would put him onto the case.
Ants are a curious race;
One crossing with hurried tread
The body of one of their dead
Isn't given a moment's arrest —
Seems not even impressed.
But he no doubt reports to any
With whom he crosses antennae,
And they no doubt report
To the higher up at court.
Then word goes forth in Formic:°
"Death's come to Jerry McCormic,
Our selfless forager Jerry.
Will the special Janizary°
Whose office it is to bury
The dead of the commissary
Go bring him home to his people.
Lay him in state on a sepal.
Wrap him for shroud in a petal.
Embalm him with ichor of nettle.
This is the word of your Queen."
And presently on the scene
Appears a solemn mortician;
And taking formal position
With feelers calmly atwiddle,
Seizes the dead by the middle,
And heaving him high in air,
Carries him out of there.
No one stands round to stare.
It is nobody else's affair.

It couldn't be called ungentle.
But how thoroughly departmental.

22 *Formic:* Acid given off by ants. 25 *Janizary:* Turkish infantry troops.

Considerations

1. Why are ants an especially appropriate insect for the speaker's observations in this poem?

2. How does the speaker regard the "departmental" nature of ants? Discuss whether you think the speaker is concerned primarily about ants or about something else.
3. Consider to what extent this poem is both humorous and serious.

The Silken Tent 1942

She is as in a field a silken tent
At midday when a sunny summer breeze
Has dried the dew and all its ropes relent,
So that in guys° it gently sways at ease, *ropes that steady a tent*
And its supporting central cedar pole,
That is its pinnacle to heavenward
And signifies the sureness of the soul,
Seems to owe naught to any single cord,
But strictly held by none, is loosely bound
By countless silken ties of love and thought
To everything on earth the compass round,
And only by one's going slightly taut
In the capriciousness of summer air
Is of the slightest bondage made aware.

Considerations

1. What is being compared in this sonnet? How does the detail accurately describe both elements of the comparison?
2. How does the form of this one-sentence sonnet help to express its theme? Pay particular attention to the final three lines.
3. How do the sonnet's sounds contribute to its meaning?

The Gift Outright 1942

The land was ours before we were the land's.
She was our land more than a hundred years
Before we were her people. She was ours
In Massachusetts, in Virginia,
But we were England's, still colonials,
Possessing what we still were unpossessed by,
Possessed by what we now no more possessed.
Something we were withholding made us weak
Until we found out that it was ourselves
We were withholding from our land of living,
And forthwith found salvation in surrender.
Such as we were we gave ourselves outright

(The deed of gift was many deeds of war)
To the land vaguely realizing westward,
But still unstoried, artless, unenhanced,
Such as she was, such as she would become.

Considerations

1. Frost once described this poem as "a history of the United States in sixteen lines." Is it? What events in American history does the poem focus on? What does it leave out?
2. This poem is built on several paradoxes. How are the paradoxes in lines 1, 6, 7, and 11 resolved?

Connections

1. Compare and contrast the theme and tone of this poem with those of Cummings's "next to of course god america i" (p. 588).
2. Write an essay on Frost's view of America as well as the views offered by Allen Ginsberg in "America" (p. 785) and Claude McKay in "America" (p. 814).

PERSPECTIVES ON FROST

In White: Frost's Early Version of *Design* 1912

A dented spider like a snow drop white
On a white Heal-all, holding up a moth
Like a white piece of lifeless satin cloth —
Saw ever curious eye so strange a sight? —
Portent in little, assorted death and blight
Like the ingredients of a witches' broth? —
The beady spider, the flower like a froth,
And the moth carried like a paper kite.

What had that flower to do with being white,
The blue prunella every child's delight.
What brought the kindred spider to that height?
(Make we no thesis of the miller's° plight.) *miller moth*
What but design of darkness and of night?
Design, design! Do I use the word aright?

Considerations

1. Read "In White" and "Design" (p. 725) aloud. Which version sounds better to you? Why?
2. Compare these versions line for line, paying particular attention to word choice. List the differences, and try to explain why you think Frost revised the lines.
3. How does the change in titles reflect a shift in emphasis in the poem?

Frost on the Living Part of a Poem 1914

The living part of a poem is the intonation entangled somehow in the syntax, idiom, and meaning of a sentence. It is only there for those who have heard it previously in conversation. . . . It is the most volatile and at the same time important part of poetry. It goes and the language becomes dead language, the poetry dead poetry. With it go the accents, the stresses, the delays that are not the property of vowels and syllables but that are shifted at will with the sense. Vowels have length there is no denying. But the accent of sense supersedes all other accent, overrides it and sweeps it away. I will find you the word *come* variously used in various passages, a whole, half, third, fourth, fifth, and sixth note. It is as long as the sense makes it. When men no longer know the intonations on which we string our words they will fall back on what I may call the absolute length of our syllables, which is the length we would give them in passages that meant nothing. . . . I say you can't read a single good sentence with the salt in it unless you have previously heard it spoken. Neither can you with the help of all the characters and diacritical marks pronounce a single word unless you have previously heard it actually pronounced. Words exist in the mouth not books.

From a letter to Sidney Cox in *A Swinger of Birches: A Portrait of Robert Frost*

Considerations

1. Why does Frost place so much emphasis on hearing poetry spoken?
2. Choose a passage from "Home Burial" (p. 715) or "After Apple-Picking" (p. 718) and read it aloud. How does Frost's description of his emphasis on intonation help explain the effects he achieves in the passage you have selected?
3. Do you think it is true that all poetry must be heard? Do "Words exist in the mouth not books"?

AMY LOWELL (1874–1925)
On Frost's Realistic Technique 1915

I have said that Mr. Frost's work is almost photographic. The qualification was unnecessary, it is photographic. The pictures, the characters, are reproduced directly from life, they are burnt into his mind as though it were a sensitive plate. He gives out what has been put in unchanged by any personal mental process. His imagination is bounded by what he has seen, he is confined within the limits of his experience (or at least what might have been his experience) and bent all one way like the windblown trees of New England hillsides.

From a review of *North of Boston, The New Republic,* February 20, 1915

Considerations

1. Consider the "photographic" qualities of Frost's poetry by discussing particular passages that strike you as having been "reproduced directly from life."

2. Write an essay that supports or refutes Lowell's assertion that "He gives out what has been put in unchanged by any personal mental process."

Frost on the Figure a Poem Makes 1939

Abstraction is an old story with the philosophers, but it has been like a new toy in the hands of the artists of our day. Why can't we have any one quality of poetry we choose by itself? We can have in thought. Then it will go hard if we can't in practice. Our lives for it.

Granted no one but a humanist much cares how sound a poem is if it is only *a* sound. The sound is the gold in the ore. Then we will have the sound out alone and dispense with the inessential. We do till we make the discovery that the object in writing poetry is to make all poems sound as different as possible from each other, and the resources for that of vowels, consonants, punctuation, syntax, words, sentences, meter are not enough. We need the help of context — meaning — subject matter. That is the greatest help towards variety. All that can be done with words is soon told. So also with meters — particularly in our language where there are virtually but two, strict iambic and loose iambic. The ancients with many were still poor if they depended on meters for all tune. It is painful to watch our sprung-rhythmists straining at the point of omitting one short from a foot for relief from monotony. The possibilities for tune from the dramatic tones of meaning struck across the rigidity of a limited meter are endless. And we are back in poetry as merely one more art of having something to say, sound or unsound. Probably better if sound, because deeper and from wider experience.

Then there is this wildness whereof it is spoken. Granted again that it has an equal claim with sound to being a poem's better half. If it is a wild tune, it is a poem. Our problem then is, as modern abstractionists, to have the wildness pure; to be wild with nothing to be wild about. We bring up as aberrationists, giving way to undirected associations and kicking ourselves from one chance suggestion to another in all directions as of a hot afternoon in the life of a grasshopper. Theme alone can steady us down. Just as the first mystery was how a poem could have a tune in such a straightness as meter, so the second mystery is how a poem can have wildness and at the same time a subject that shall be fulfilled.

It should be of the pleasure of a poem itself to tell how it can. The figure a poem makes. It begins in delight and ends in wisdom. The figure is the same as for love. No one can really hold that the ecstasy should be static and stand still in one place. It begins in delight, it inclines to the impulse, it assumes direction with the first line laid down, it runs a course of lucky events, and ends in a clarification of life — not necessarily a great clarification, such as sects and cults are founded on, but in a momentary stay against confusion. It has denouement. It has an outcome that though unforeseen was predestined from the first image of the original mood — and indeed from the very mood. It is but a trick poem and no poem at all if the best of it was thought of first and saved for the last. It finds its own name as it goes and discovers the best waiting for it in some final phrase at once wise and sad — the happy-sad blend of the drinking song.

No tears in the writer, no tears in the reader. No surprise for the writer, no surprise for the reader. For me the initial delight is in the surprise of remembering something I didn't know I knew. I am in a place, in a situation, as if I had materialized from cloud or risen out of the ground. There is a glad recognition of the long lost and the rest follows. Step by step the wonder of unexpected supply keeps growing. The impressions most useful to my purpose seem always those I was unaware of and so made no note of at the time when taken, and the conclusion is come to that like giants we are always hurling experience ahead of us to pave the future with against the day when we may want to strike a line of purpose across it for somewhere. The line will have the more charm for not being mechanically straight. We enjoy the straight crookedness of a good walking stick. Modern instruments of precision are being used to make things crooked as if by eye and hand in the old days.

I tell how there may be a better wildness of logic than of inconsequence. But the logic is backward, in retrospect, after the act. It must be more felt than seen ahead like prophecy. It must be a revelation, or a series of revelations, as much for the poet as for the reader. For it to be that there must have been the greatest freedom of the material to move about in it and to establish relations in it regardless of time and space, previous relation, and everything but affinity. We prate of freedom. We call our schools free because we are not free to stay away from them till we are sixteen years of age. I have given up my democratic prejudices and now willingly set the lower classes free to be completely taken care of by the upper classes. Political freedom is nothing to me. I bestow it right and left. All I would keep for myself is the freedom of my material — the condition of body and mind now and then to summons aptly from the vast chaos of all I have lived through.

Scholars and artists thrown together are often annoyed at the puzzle of where they differ. Both work for knowledge; but I suspect they differ most importantly in the way their knowledge is come by. Scholars get theirs with conscientious thoroughness along projected lines of logic; poets theirs cavalierly and as it happens in and out of books. They stick to nothing deliberately, but let what will stick to them like burrs where they walk in the fields. No acquirement is on assignment, or even self-assignment. Knowledge of the second kind is much more available in the wild free ways of wit and art. A school boy may be defined as one who can tell you what he knows in the order in which he learned it. The artist must value himself as he snatches a thing from some previous order in time and space into a new order with not so much as a ligature clinging to it of the old place where it was organic.

More than once I should have lost my soul to radicalism if it had been the originality it was mistaken for by its young converts. Originality and initiative are what I ask for my country. For myself the originality need be no more than the freshness of a poem run in the way I have described: from delight to wisdom. The figure is the same as for love. Like a piece of ice on a hot stove the poem must ride on its own melting. A poem may be worked over once it is in being, but may not be worried into being. Its most precious quality will remain its having run itself and carried away the poet with it. Read it a hundred times: it will forever keep its freshness as a metal keeps its fragrance. It can never lose its sense of a meaning that once unfolded by surprise as it went.

From *Complete Poems of Robert Frost*

Considerations

1. Frost places a high premium on sound in his poetry, because it "is the gold in the ore." Choose one of Frost's poems in this book and explain the effects of its sounds and how they contribute to its meaning.
2. Discuss Frost's explanation of how his poems are written. In what sense is the process both spontaneous and "predestined"?
3. What do you think Frost means when he says he's given up his "democratic prejudices"? Why is "political freedom" nothing to him?
4. Write an essay that examines in more detail the ways scholars and artists "come by" knowledge.
5. Explain what you think Frost means when he writes that "Like a piece of ice on a hot stove the poem must ride on its own melting."

Frost on the Way to Read a Poem 1951

The way to read a poem in prose or verse is in the light of all the other poems ever written. We may begin anywhere. We *duff* into our first. We read that imperfectly (thoroughness with it would be fatal), but the better to read the second. We read the second the better to read the third, the third the better to read the fourth, the fourth the better to read the fifth, the fifth the better to read the first again, or the second if it so happens. For poems are not meant to be read in course any more than they are to be made a study of. I once made a resolve never to put any book to any use it wasn't intended for by its author. Improvement will not be a progression but a widening circulation. Our instinct is to settle down like a revolving dog and make ourselves at home among the poems, completely at our ease as to how they should be taken. The same people will be apt to take poems right as know how to take a hint when there is one and not to take a hint when none is intended. Theirs is the ultimate refinement.

From "Poetry and School," *Atlantic Monthly,* June 1951

Considerations

1. Given your own experience, how good is Frost's advice about reading in general and his poems in particular?
2. In what sense is a good reader like a "revolving dog" and a person who knows "how to take a hint"?
3. Frost elsewhere in this piece writes that "One of the dangers of college to anyone who wants to stay a human reader (that is to say a humanist) is that he will become a specialist and lose his sensitive fear of landing on the lovely too hard. (With beak and talon.)" Write an essay in response to this concern. Do you agree with Frost's distinction between a "human reader" and a "specialist"?

LIONEL TRILLING (1905–1975)

On Frost as a Terrifying Poet 1959

I have to say that my Frost — *my Frost:* what airs we give ourselves when once we believe that we have come into possession of a poet! — I have to say that my Frost is not the Frost I seem to perceive existing in the minds of so many of his admirers. He is not the Frost who confounds the characteristically modern practice of poetry by his notable democratic simplicity of utterance: on the contrary. He is not the Frost who controverts the bitter modern astonishment at the nature of human life: the opposite is so. He is not the Frost who reassures us by his affirmation of old virtues, simplicities, pieties, and ways of feeling: anything but. I will not go so far as to say that my Frost is not essentially an American poet at all: I believe that he is quite as American as everyone thinks he is, but not in the way that everyone thinks he is.

In the matter of the Americanism of American literature one of my chief guides is that very remarkable critic, D. H. Lawrence. Here are the opening sentences of Lawrence's great outrageous book about classic American literature. "We like to think of the old fashioned American classics as children's books. Just childishness on our part. The old American art speech contains an alien quality which belongs to the American continent and to nowhere else." And this unique alien quality, Lawrence goes on to say, the world has missed. "It is hard to hear a new voice," he says, "as hard as to listen to an unknown language. . . . Why? Out of fear. The world fears a new experience more than it fears anything. It can pigeonhole any idea. But it can't pigeonhole a real new experience. It can only dodge. The world is a great dodger, and the Americans the greatest. Because they dodge their own very selves." I should like to pick up a few more of Lawrence's sentences, feeling the freer to do so because they have an affinity to Mr. Frost's prose manner and substance: "An artist is usually a damned liar, but his art, if it be art, will tell you the truth of his day. And that is all that matters. Away with eternal truth. Truth lives from day to day. . . . The old American artists were hopeless liars. . . . Never trust the artist. Trust the tale. The proper function of the critic is to save the tale from the artist who created it. . . . Now listen to me, don't listen to him. He'll tell you the lie you expect, which is partly your fault for expecting it."

Now in point of fact Robert Frost is *not* a liar. I would not hesitate to say that he was if I thought he was. But no, he is not. In certain of his poems — I shall mention one or two in a moment — he makes it perfectly plain what he is doing; and if we are not aware of what he is doing in other of his poems, where he is not quite so plain, that is not his fault but our own. It is not from him that the tale needs to be saved.

I conceive that Robert Frost is doing in his poems what Lawrence says the great writers of the classic American tradition did. That enterprise of theirs was of an ultimate radicalism. It consisted, Lawrence says, of two things: a disintegration and sloughing off of the old consciousness, by which Lawrence means the old European consciousness, and the forming of a new consciousness underneath.

So radical a work, I need scarcely say, is not carried out by reassurance, nor by the affirmation of old virtues and pieties. It is carried out by the representation of the terrible actualities of life in a new way. I think of Robert Frost as a terrifying poet. Call him, if it makes things any easier, a tragic poet, but it might be useful every now and then to come out from under the shelter of that literary word. The universe that he conceives is a terrifying universe. Read the poem called "Design" and see if you sleep the better for it. Read "Neither Out Far nor In Deep," which often seems to me the most perfect poem of our time, and see if you are warmed by anything in it except the energy with which emptiness is perceived.

But the *people,* it will be objected, the *people* who inhabit this possibly terrifying universe! About them there is nothing that can terrify; surely the people in Mr. Frost's poems can only reassure us by their integrity and solidity. Perhaps so. But I cannot make the disjunction. It may well be that ultimately they reassure us in some sense, but first they terrify us, or should. We must not be misled about them by the curious tenderness with which they are represented, a tenderness which extends to a recognition of the tenderness which they themselves can often give. But when ever have people been so isolated, so lightning-blasted, so tried down and calcined by life, so reduced, each in his own way, to some last irreducible core of being. Talk of the disintegration and sloughing off of the old consciousness! The people of Robert Frost's poems have done that with a vengeance. Lawrence says that what the Americans refused to accept was "the post-Renaissance humanism of Europe," "the old European spontaneity," "the flowing easy humor of Europe" and that seems to me a good way to describe the people who inhabit Robert Frost's America. In the interests of what great other thing these people have made this rejection we cannot know for certain. But we can guess that it was in the interest of truth, of some truth of the self. This is what they all affirm by their humor (which is so *not* "the easy flowing humor of Europe"), by their irony, by their separateness and isolateness. They affirm *this* of themselves: that they are what they are, that this is their truth, and that if the truth be bare, as truth often is, it is far better than a lie. For me the process by which they arrive at that truth is always terrifying. The manifest America of Mr. Frost's poems may be pastoral; the actual America is tragic.

From "A Speech on Robert Frost: A Cultural Episode," *Partisan Review,* Summer 1959

Considerations

1. How does Trilling distinguish *"my Frost"* from other readers'?
2. Read the section on biographical criticism in Chapter 32 (p. 1781) and familiarize yourself with Frost's life. How does a knowledge of Frost's biography influence your reading of his poems?
3. Write an essay indicating whether you agree or disagree with Trilling's assessment of Frost "as a terrifying poet." Use evidence from the poems to support your view.

GALWAY KINNELL (b. 1927)

From *For Robert Frost*° 1965

I saw you once on the TV,
Unsteady at the lectern,
The flimsy white leaf
Of hair standing straight up
In the wind, among top hats,
Old farmer and son
Of worse winters than this,
Stopped in the first dazzle

Of the District of Columbia,
Suddenly having to pay
For the cheap onionskin,
The worn-out ribbon, the eyes
Wrecked from writing poems
For us — stopped,
Lonely before millions,
The paper jumping in your grip,

And as the Presidents
Also on the platform
Began flashing nervously

Their Presidential smiles
For the harmless old guy,
And poets watching on the TV
Started thinking, Well that's
The end of *that* tradition,

And the managers of the event
Said, Boys this is it,
This sonofabitch poet
Is gonna croak,
Putting the paper aside
You drew forth
From your great faithful heart
The poem.

This tribute to Frost recalls his reciting "The Gift Outright" at the inauguration of John F. Kennedy in 1961. Frost originally planned to read the poem but was prevented from doing so by the glaring sun.

Considerations

1. Describe the difference in attitude expressed by the "Presidents" (line 16), the "poets" (22), and the "managers" (25) and that expressed by Kinnell in this excerpt. Why does Kinnell include the others in the poem?
2. Frost is said here to represent "The end of *that* tradition." What kind of tradition does he represent?
3. Research Frost's reputation. Why was he so popular with the American public?

HERBERT R. COURSEN, JR. (b. 1932)

A Reading of "Stopping by Woods on a Snowy Evening" 1962

Much ink has spilled on many pages in exegesis of this little poem. Actually, critical jottings have only obscured what has lain beneath critical noses all these years. To say that the poem means merely that a man stops one night to observe a snowfall, or that the poem contrasts the mundane desire for creature comfort with the sweep of aesthetic appreciation, or that it renders worldly responsibilities paramount, or that it reveals the speaker's latent death-wish is to miss the point rather badly. Lacking has been that mind simple enough to see what is *really* there. . . .

The "darkest evening of the year" in New England is December 21st, a date near that on which the western world celebrates Christmas. It may be that December 21st *is* the date of the poem, or (and with poets this seems more likely) that this is the closest the poet can come to Christmas without giving it all away. Who has "promises to keep" at or near this date, and who must traverse much territory to fulfill these promises? Yes, and who but St. Nick would know the location of *each* home? Only he would know who had "just settled down for a long winter's nap" (the poem's third line — "He will not see me stopping here" — is clearly a veiled allusion) and would not be out inspecting his acreage this night. The unusual phrase "fill up with snow," in the poem's fourth line, is a transfer of Santa's occupational preoccupation to the countryside; he is mulling the filling of countless stockings hung above countless fireplaces by countless careful children. "Harness bells," of course, allude to "Sleighing Song," a popular Christmas tune of the time the poem was written in which the refrain "Jingle Bells! Jingle Bells!" appears; thus again are we put on the Christmas track. The "little horse," like the date is another attempt at poetic obfuscation. Although the "rein-reindeer" ambiguity has been eliminated from the poem's final version,[1] probably because too obvious, we may speculate that the animal is really a reindeer disguised as a horse by the poet's desire for obscurity, a desire which we must concede has been fulfilled up to now.

The animal is clearly concerned, like the faithful Rudolph — another possible allusion (post facto, hence unconscious) — lest his master fail to complete his mission. Seeing no farmhouse in the second quatrain, but pulling a load of presents, no wonder the little beast wonders! It takes him a full two quatrains to rouse his driver to remember all the empty stockings which hang ahead. And Santa does so reluctantly at that, poor soul, as he ponders the myriad farmhouses and villages which spread between him and his own "winter's nap." The modern St. Nick, lonely and overworked, tosses no "Happy Christmas to all and to all a good night!" into the precipitation. He merely shrugs his shoulders and resignedly plods away.

From "The Ghost of Christmas Past: 'Stopping by Woods on a Snowy Evening,'"
College English, December 1962

[1]The original draft contained the following line: "That bid me give the reins a shake" (Stageberg-Anderson, *Poetry as Experience* [New York, 1952], p. 457). [Coursen's note]

Considerations

1. Is this critical spoof at all credible? Does the interpretation hold any water? Is the evidence reasonable? Why or why not? Which of the poem's details are accounted for and which are ignored?
2. Choose a Frost poem and try writing a parodic interpretation of it.
3. What criteria do you use to distinguish between a sensible interpretation of a poem and an absurd one?

DONALD J. GREINER (b. 1940)

An Analysis of "After Apple-Picking" 1982

"After Apple-Picking" was first published in *North of Boston* (1914), and it is my nomination for Frost's greatest poem. In the letter to John Cournos (27 July 1914), Frost explains that "After Apple-Picking" is the only poem in his second book that "will intone." Although he does not elaborate, he means that the rest of the poems sound like human speech whereas "After Apple-Picking" is a lyrical meditation on the tension between a job well done and the uncertainties accompanying the end of something significant. Note that the first word in the title is "After." Frost's refusal to specify what has ended, other than apple picking, is one of the glories of the poem.

The other glories are the examples of technical brilliance. The rhymes alone are worth the reading. Every one of the forty-two lines is rhymed, but Frost eschews the tradition of rhyme scheme altogether. The result is a beautiful, even haunting, rendering of the natural progression of a person's meditation as he uneasily ponders the ambiguities which suddenly well up before him now that his job is done. Similarly, the brilliant use of irregular iambic pentameter . . . to suggest the uncertain balance between the poet figure's need to maintain form in the face of confusion and the threat to his effort cast in the form of truncated lines illustrates the union of technique and theme when Frost is at his best. Although the poem begins with its longest line, the iambic heptameter "My long two-pointed ladder's sticking through a tree," and includes a line as short as "For all," the meter invariably returns to the predominant rhythm of iambic pentameter as the meditator struggles to keep his balance in uncertainty as he has kept it on the ladder of his life.

Nuances of aspiration, satisfaction, completion, rest, and death echo throughout "After Apple-Picking" beginning with the title. Like the speaker, the reader never knows how far to pursue the mythical associations between apples and man's expulsion from Eden. If such associations are to be dismissed, then the speaker has safely and satisfactorily completed his task — whatever it literally is — of harvesting the "ten thousand thousand fruit." The phrase "after apple-picking" thus suggests rest. But the genius of the poem is that the speaker is never sure. If the associations between apples and Eden are not to be dismissed, then the poet figure has finished his life's work only to be confronted with an overwhelming uncertainty about what awaits him now. "After Apple-Picking" thus suggests death.

The imagery of hazy speculation is precise. The phrase "toward heaven" indicates the speaker's ultimate aspiration, and the line "Essence of winter sleep is on the night" reverberates with suggestions of termination and the question of rebirth. The point is that the poet figure needs answers to questions he will not pose, and he can only see as through a glass darkly:

I cannot rub the strangeness from my sight
I got from looking through a pane of glass
I skimmed this morning from the drinking trough. . . .

The woodchuck, so unthinkingly confident of rebirth from its winter hibernation, cannot help him. "After Apple-Picking" is a poem of encroaching fear because it is a poem of uncertainty. Although the religious connotations are never obtrusive, this great poem is another of Frost's explorations of what he considered to be man's greatest terror: that our best may not be good enough in Heaven's sight.

From "The Indispensable Robert Frost," in *Critical Essays on Robert Frost,* edited by Philip L. Gerber

Considerations

1. How far do you think "the mythical associations between apples and man's expulsion from Eden" should be pursued by readers of this poem?
2. Greiner cites several examples of the poem's "technical brilliance." What other examples can you find?
3. Write an essay that explores as the theme of the poem Greiner's idea "that our best may not be good enough in Heaven's sight."

BLANCHE FARLEY (b. 1937)

The Lover Not Taken 1984

Committed to one, she wanted both
And, mulling it over, long she stood,
Alone on the road, loath
To leave, wanting to hide in the undergrowth.
This new guy, smooth as a yellow wood

Really turned her on. She liked his hair,
His smile. But the other, Jack, had a claim
On her already and she had to admit, he did wear
Well. In fact, to be perfectly fair,
He understood her. His long, lithe frame

Beside hers in the evening tenderly lay.
Still, if this blond guy dropped by someday,
Couldn't way just lead on to way?
No. For if way led on and Jack
Found out, she doubted if he would ever come back.

Oh, she turned with a sigh.
Somewhere ages and ages hence,
She might be telling this. "And I —"
She would say, "stood faithfully by."
But by then who would know the difference?

With that in mind, she took the fast way home,
The road by the pond, and phoned the blond.

Considerations

1. Which Frost poem is the object of this parody?
2. Describe how the stylistic elements mirror Frost's poem.
3. Does this parody seem successful to you? Explain what makes a successful parody.
4. Choose a Frost poem — or a portion of one if it is long — and try writing a parody of it.

22. A Collection of Poems

QUESTIONS FOR RESPONSIVE READING

The following questions can help you respond to important elements that reveal a poem's effects and meanings. The questions are general, so not all of them will necessarily be relevant to a particular poem. Many, however, should prove useful for thinking, talking, and writing about each poem in this collection. If you are uncertain about the meaning of a term used in a question, consult the Index of Terms, which lists pages that discuss the terms and is located on the inside back cover.

Before addressing these questions, read the poem you are studying in its entirety. Don't worry about interpretation on a first reading; allow yourself the pleasure of enjoying whatever makes itself apparent to you. Then on subsequent readings, use the questions to understand and appreciate how the poem works.

1. Who is the speaker? Is it possible to determine the speaker's age, sex, sensibilities, level of awareness, and values?
2. Is the speaker addressing anyone in particular?
3. How do you respond to the speaker? favorably? negatively? What is the situation? Are there any special circumstances that inform what the speaker says?
4. Is there a specific setting of time and place?
5. Does reading the poem aloud help you to understand it?
6. Does a paraphrase reveal the basic purpose of the poem?
7. What does the title emphasize?
8. Is the theme presented directly or indirectly?
9. Do any allusions enrich the poem's meaning?
10. How does the diction reveal meaning? Are any words repeated? Do any carry evocative connotative meanings? Are there any puns or other forms of verbal wit?
11. Are figures of speech used? How does the figurative language contribute to the poem's vividness and meaning?

12. Do any objects, persons, places, events, or actions have allegorical or symbolic meanings? What other details in the poem support your interpretation?
13. Is irony used? Are there any examples of situational irony, verbal irony, or dramatic irony? Is understatement or paradox used?
14. What is the tone of the poem? Is the tone consistent?
15. Does the poem use onomatopoeia, assonance, consonance, or alliteration? How do these sounds affect you?
16. What sounds are repeated? If there are rhymes, what is their effect? Do they seem forced or natural? Is there a rhyme scheme? Do the rhymes contribute to the poem's meaning?
17. Do the lines have a regular meter? What is the predominant meter? Are there significant variations? Does the rhythm seem appropriate for the tone of the poem?
18. Does the poem's form — its overall structure — follow an established pattern? Do you think the form is a suitable vehicle for the poem's meaning and effects?
19. Is the language of the poem intense and concentrated? Do you think it warrants more than one or two close readings?
20. Did you enjoy the poem? What, specifically, pleased or displeased you about what was expressed and how it was expressed?

LEONARD ADAME (b. 1947)

Black and White 1977

"Rhodesia, sweaty
flank of the world . . ."
i read as quietly
as they lay: "guerillas,"
it went on,
"put here as a lesson . . ."

they lay like a catch
in the plaza sun,
still damp, the eyes
not yet clouded,
the African heat
raising the bellies . . .

"it is the way
of our generals
to count what is theirs,
what is done
in their name,"
the secretary announced . . .

from their circle
photographers stare
and snap at the dead men,
at the keyboard of rifles
above their heads,
at the small town
that leads to
the jungle's edge —
they snap and freeze
it all, store it
in the silent world
of black and white . . .

A. R. AMMONS (b. 1926)

Winter Saint 1972

In the summer I live so
close to my neighbor I
can hear him sweat:

all my forced bushes, leafy
and birdy, do not
prevent this:

his drawers wrenched
off his sticky butt
clutch my speech white:

his beery mouth wakes up
under my tongue: his
lawnmower wilts my cereal.

I do not like to hear him
wheeze over difficult weeds:
I don't like his squishy toes:

I'm for ice and shutters
and the miles and miles
winter clears between us.

MAYA ANGELOU (b. 1928)

Africa 1975

Thus she had lain
sugar cane sweet

deserts her hair
golden her feet
mountains her breasts
two Niles her tears
Thus she has lain
Black through the years.

Over the white seas
rime white and cold
brigands ungentled
icicle bold
took her young daughters
sold her strong sons
churched her with Jesus
bled her with guns.
Thus she has lain.

Now she is rising
remember her pain
remember the losses
her screams loud and vain
remember her riches
her history slain
now she is striding
although she had lain.

ANONYMOUS (traditional Scottish ballad)

Bonny Barbara Allan

It was in and about the Martinmas° time,
    When the green leaves were afalling,
That Sir John Graeme, in the West Country,
    Fell in love with Barbara Allan.

He sent his men down through the town,
    To the place where she was dwelling:
"O haste and come to my master dear,
    Gin° ye be Barbara Allan." *if*

O hooly,° hooly rose she up, *slowly*
    To the place where he was lying,
And when she drew the curtain by:
    "Young man, I think you're dying."

"O it's I'm sick, and very, very sick,
    And 'tis a' for Barbara Allan." —

1 *Martinmas:* St. Martin's Day, November 11.

"O the better for me ye's never be,
Tho your heart's blood were aspilling.

"O dinna ye mind,° young man," said she, *don't you remember*
"When ye was in the tavern adrinking,
That ye made the health° gae round and round, *toasts*
And slighted Barbara Allan?"

He turned his face unto the wall,
And death was with him dealing:
"Adieu, adieu, my dear friends all,
And be kind to Barbara Allan."

And slowly, slowly raise she up,
And slowly, slowly left him,
And sighing said she could not stay,
Since death of life had reft him.

She had not gane a mile but twa,
When she heard the dead-bell ringing,
And every jow° that the dead-bell geid, *stroke*
It cried, "Woe to Barbara Allan!"

"O mother, mother, make my bed!
O make it saft and narrow!
Since my love died for me today,
I'll die for him tomorrow."

ANONYMOUS (traditional Scottish ballad)

Edward

"Why dois your brand° sae° drap wi' bluid, *sword; so*
Edward, Edward?
Why dois your brand sae drap wi' bluid?
And why sae sad gang° yee, O?" *go*
"O, I hae killed my hauke sae guid,
Mither, mither,
O, I hae killed my hauke sae guid,
And I had nae mair bot hee, O."

"Your haukis bluid was nevir sae reid,
Edward, Edward,
Your haukis bluid was nevir sae reid,
My deir son I tell thee, O."
"O, I hae killed my reid-roan steid,
Mither, mither,
O, I hae killed my reid-roan steid,
That erst° was sae fair and frie,° O." *once; free*

"Your steid was auld, and ye hae gat mair,
Edward, Edward,

Your steid was auld, and ye hae gat mair,
Sum other dule° ye drie,° O." *grief; suffer*
"O, I hae killed my fadir deir,
Mither, mither,
O, I hae killed my fadir, deir,
Alas, and wae is mee, O!"

"And whatten penance wul ye drie for that,
Edward, Edward?
And whatten penance wul ye drie for that?
My deir son, now tell me, O."
"Ile set my feit in yonder boat,
Mither, mither,
Ile set my feit in yonder boat,
And Ile fare ovir the sea, O."

"And what wul ye doe wi' your towirs and your ha',° *hall*
Edward, Edward,
And what wul ye doe wi' your towirs and your ha',
That were sae fair to see, O?"
"Ile let thame stand tul they doun fa',° *fall*
Mither, mither,
Ile let thame stand tul they doun fa',
For here nevir mair maun° I bee, O." *must*

"And what wul ye leive to your bairns and your wife,
Edward, Edward?
And what wul ye leive to your bairns and your wife,
When ye gang ovir the sea, O?"
"The warldis° room, late° them beg thrae° life, *world's; let; through*
Mither, mither,
The warldis room, late them beg thrae life,
For thame nevir mair wul I see, O."

"And what wul ye leive to your ain mither deir,
Edward, Edward?
And what wul ye leive to your ain mither deir?
My deir son, now tell me, O."
"The curse of hell frae me sall ye beir,
Mither, mither,
The curse of hell frae me sall ye beir,
Sic° counseils ye gave to me, O." *such*

ANONYMOUS

Frankie and Johnny — 1800s

Frankie and Johnny were lovers,
Lordy, how they could love,

Swore to be true to each other,
    True as the stars up above,
        He was her man, but he done her wrong.

Frankie went down to the corner,
    To buy her a bucket of beer,
Frankie says "Mister Bartender,
    Has my lovin' Johnny been here?
        He is my man, but he's doing me wrong."

"I don't want to cause you no trouble
    Don't want to tell you no lie,
I saw your Johnny half-an-hour ago
    Making love to Nelly Bly.
        He is your man, but he's doing you wrong."

Frankie went down to the hotel
    Looked over the transom so high,
There she saw her lovin' Johnny
    Making love to Nelly Bly.
        He was her man; he was doing her wrong.

Frankie threw back her kimono,
    Pulled out her big forty-four;
Rooty-toot-toot: three times she shot
    Right through that hotel door,
        She shot her man, who was doing her wrong.

"Roll me over gently,
    Roll me over slow,
Roll me over on my right side,
    'Cause these bullets hurt me so,
        I was your man, but I done you wrong."

Bring all your rubber-tired hearses
    Bring all your rubber-tired hacks,
They're carrying poor Johnny to the burying ground
    And they ain't gonna bring him back,
        He was her man, but he done her wrong.

Frankie says to the sheriff,
    "What are they going to do?"
The sheriff he said to Frankie,
    "It's the 'lectric chair for you.
        He was your man, and he done you wrong."

"Put me in that dungeon,
    Put me in that cell,
Put me where the northeast wind
    Blows from the southeast corner of hell,
        I shot my man, 'cause he done me wrong."

ANONYMOUS

Scottsboro°

1936

Paper come out — done strewed de news
Seven po' chillun moan deat' house blues,
Seven po' chillun moanin' deat' house blues.
Seven nappy heads wit' big shiny eye
All boun' in jail and framed to die,
All boun' in jail and framed to die.

Messin' white woman — snake lyin' tale
Hang and burn and jail wit' no bail.
Dat hang and burn and jail wit' no bail.
Worse ol' crime in white folks' lan'
Black skin coverin' po' workin' man,
Black skin coverin' po' workin' man.

Judge and jury — all in de stan'
Lawd, biggety name for same lynchin' ban'
Lawd, biggety name for same lynchin' ban'.
White folks and nigger in great co't house
Like cat down cellar wit' nohole mouse.
Like cat down cellar wit' nohole mouse.

Scottsboro: This blues song refers to the 1931 arrest of nine black youths in Scottsboro, Alabama, who were charged with raping two white women. All nine were acquitted after several trials, but a few of them had already been sentenced to death when this song was written.

ANONYMOUS (traditional Scottish ballad)

The Twa Corbies°

As I was walking all alane,
I heard twa corbies making a mane;° — *lament*
The tane° unto the t' other say, — *one*
"Where sall we gang° and dine to-day?" — *shall we go*

"In behint yon auld fail dyke,° — *old turf wall*
I wot° there lies a new-slain knight; — *know*
And naebody kens that he lies there,
But his hawk, his hound, and lady fair.

"His hound is to the hunting gane,
His hawk, to fetch the wild-fowl hame,
His lady's ta'en another mate,
So we may mak our dinner sweet.

The Twa Corbies: The two ravens.

"Ye'll sit on his white hause-bane,° *neck bone*
And I'll pike out his bonny blue een.° *eyes*
Wi' ae° lock o' his gowden° hair *with one; golden*
We'll theek° our nest when it grows bare. *thatch*

"Mony a one for him makes mane,
But nane sall ken whare he is gane;
O'er his white banes, when they are bare,
The wind sall blaw for evermair."

JOHN ASHBERY (b. 1927)

Crazy Weather

It's this crazy weather we've been having:
Falling forward one minute, lying down the next
Among the loose grasses and soft, white, nameless flowers.
People have been making a garment out of it,
Stitching the white of lilacs together with lightning
At some anonymous crossroads. The sky calls
To the deaf earth. The proverbial disarray
Of morning corrects itself as you stand up.
You are wearing a text. The lines
Droop to your shoelaces and I shall never want or need
Any other literature than this poetry of mud
And ambitious reminiscences of times when it came easily
Through the then woods and ploughed fields and had
A simple unconscious dignity we can never hope to
Approximate now except in narrow ravines nobody
Will inspect where some late sample of the rare,
Uninteresting specimen might still be putting out shoots,
    for all we know.

MARGARET ATWOOD (b. 1939)

Spelling

1981

My daughter plays on the floor
with plastic letters,
red, blue & hard yellow,
learning how to spell.
spelling,
how to make spells

And I wonder how many women
denied themselves daughters,

closed themselves in rooms,
drew the curtains
so they could mainline words.

A child is not a poem,
a poem is not a child.
There is no either/or.
However.

I return to the story
of the woman caught in the war
& in labor, her thighs tied
together by the enemy
so she could not give birth.

Ancestress: the burning witch,
her mouth covered by leather
to strangle words.

A word after a word.
after a word is power.

At the point where language falls away
from the hot bones, at the point
where the rock breaks open and darkness
flows out of it like blood, at
the melting point of granite
when the bones know
they are hollow & the word
splits & doubles & speaks
the truth & the body
itself becomes a mouth.

This is a metaphor.

How do you learn to spell?
Blood, sky & the sun,
your own name first,
your first naming, your first name,
your first word.

W. H. AUDEN (1907–1973)

As I Walked Out One Evening 1940

As I walked out one evening,
    Walking down Bristol Street,

The crowds upon the pavement
Were fields of harvest wheat.

And down by the brimming river
I heard a lover sing
Under an arch of the railway:
"Love has no ending.

"I'll love you, dear, I'll love you
Till China and Africa meet,
And the river jumps over the mountain
And the salmon sing in the street,

"I'll love you till the ocean
Is folded and hung up to dry
And the seven stars go squawking
Like geese about the sky.

"The years shall run like rabbits,
For in my arms I hold
The Flower of the Ages,
And the first love of the world."

But all the clocks in the city
Began to whirr and chime:
"O let not Time deceive you,
You cannot conquer Time.

"In the burrows of the Nightmare
Where Justice naked is,
Time watches from the shadow
And coughs when you would kiss.

"In headaches and in worry
Vaguely life leaks away,
And Time will have his fancy
Tomorrow or today.

"Into many a green valley
Drifts the appalling snow;
Time breaks the threaded dances
And the diver's brilliant bow.

"O plunge your hands in water,
Plunge them in up to the wrist;
Stare, stare in the basin
And wonder what you've missed.

"The glacier knocks in the cupboard,
The desert sighs in the bed,
And the crack in the teacup opens
A lane to the land of the dead.

"Where the beggars raffle the banknotes
And the Giant is enchanting to Jack,

And the Lily-white Boy is a Roarer,
    And Jill goes down on her back.

"O look, look in the mirror,
    O look in your distress;
Life remains a blessing
    Although you cannot bless.

"O stand, stand at the window
    As the tears scald and start;
You shall love your crooked neighbor
    With your crooked heart."

It was late, late in the evening,
    The lovers they were gone;
The clocks had ceased their chiming,
    And the deep river ran on.

W. H. AUDEN (1907–1973)

Lay Your Sleeping Head, My Love

1940

Lay your sleeping head, my love,
Human on my faithless arm;
Time and fevers burn away
Individual beauty from

Thoughtful children, and the grave
Proves the child ephemeral:
But in my arms till break of day
Let the living creature lie,
Mortal, guilty, but to me
The entirely beautiful.

Soul and body have no bounds:
To lovers as they lie upon
Her tolerant enchanted slope
In their ordinary swoon,
Grave the vision Venus sends
Of supernatural sympathy,
Universal love and hope;
While an abstract insight wakes
Among the glaciers and the rocks
The hermit's sensual ecstasy.

Certainty, fidelity
On the stroke of midnight pass
Like vibrations of a bell,
And fashionable madmen raise
Their pedantic boring cry:

Every farthing of the cost,
All the dreaded cards foretell,
Shall be paid, but from this night
Not a whisper, not a thought,
Not a kiss nor look be lost.

Beauty, midnight, vision dies:
Let the winds of dawn that blow
Softly round your dreaming head
Such a day of sweetness show
Eye and knocking heart may bless,
Find the mortal world enough;
Noons of dryness see you fed
By the involuntary powers,
Nights of insult let you pass
Watched by every human love.

W. H. AUDEN (1907–1973)

Musée des Beaux Arts° 1938

About suffering they were never wrong,
The Old Masters: how well they understood
Its human position; how it takes place
While someone else is eating or opening a window or just walking dully
    along;
How, when the aged are reverently, passionately waiting
For the miraculous birth, there always must be
Children who did not specially want it to happen, skating
On a pond at the edge of the wood:
They never forgot
That even the dreadful martyrdom must run its course
Anyhow in a corner, some untidy spot
Where the dogs go on with their doggy life and the torturer's horse
Scratches its innocent behind on a tree.

In Brueghel's *Icarus,*° for instance: how everything turns away
Quite leisurely from the disaster; the plowman may
Have heard the splash, the forsaken cry,
But for him it was not an important failure; the sun shone
As it had to on the white legs disappearing into the green
Water; and the expensive delicate ship that must have seen
Something amazing, a boy falling out of the sky,
Had somewhere to get to and sailed calmly on.

Musée des Beaux Arts: Museum of Fine Arts, in Brussels. 14 *Brueghel's* Icarus: *Landscape with the Fall of Icarus,* painting by Pieter Brueghel the Elder (c. 1525–1569), in the Brussels Museum.

W. H. AUDEN (1907–1973)

The Unknown Citizen

1940

(To JS/07/M/378
This Marble Monument
Is Erected by the State)

He was found by the Bureau of Statistics to be
One against whom there was no official complaint,
And all the reports on his conduct agree
That, in the modern sense of an old-fashioned word, he was a saint,
For in everything he did he served the Greater Community.
Except for the War till the day he retired
He worked in a factory and never got fired,
But satisfied his employers, Fudge Motors Inc.
Yet he wasn't a scab or odd in his views,
For his Union reports that he paid his dues,
(Our report on his Union shows it was sound)
And our Social Psychology workers found
That he was popular with his mates and liked a drink.
The Press are convinced that he bought a paper every day
And that his reactions to advertisements were normal in every way.
Policies taken out in his name prove that he was fully insured,
And his Health-card shows he was once in hospital but left it cured.
Both Producers Research and High-Grade Living declare
He was fully sensible to the advantages of the Installment Plan
And had everything necessary to the Modern Man,
A phonograph, radio, a car and a frigidaire.
Our researchers into Public Opinion are content
That he held the proper opinions for the time of year;
When there was peace, he was for peace; when there was war, he went.
He was married and added five children to the population,
Which our Eugenist says was the right number for a parent of his
    generation,
And our teachers report that he never interfered with their education.
Was he free? Was he happy? The question is absurd:
Had anything been wrong, we should certainly have heard.

JOHN BERRYMAN (1914–1972)

Dream Song 14

1964

Life, friends, is boring. We must not say so.
After all, the sky flashes, the great sea yearns,
we ourselves flash and yearn,
and moreover my mother told me as a boy
(repeatingly) "Ever to confess you're bored
means you have no

Inner Resources." I conclude now I have no
inner resources, because I am heavy bored.
Peoples bore me,
literature bores me, especially great literature,
Henry bores me, with his plights & gripes
as bad as achilles,°

Who loves people and valiant art, which bores me.
And the tranquil hills, & gin, look like a drag
and somehow a dog
has taken itself & its tail considerably away
into mountains or sea or sky, leaving
behind: me, wag.

12 *achilles:* Greek hero who fought in the Trojan War.

ELIZABETH BISHOP (1911–1979)
Five Flights Up

Still dark.
The unknown bird sits on his usual branch.
The little dog next door barks in his sleep
inquiringly, just once.
Perhaps in his sleep, too, the bird inquires
once or twice, quavering.
Questions — if that is what they are —
answered directly, simply,
by day itself.

Enormous morning, ponderous, meticulous;
gray light streaking each bare branch,
each single twig, along one side,
making another tree, of glassy veins . . .
The bird still sits there. Now he seems to yawn.

The little black dog runs in his yard.
His owner's voice arises, stern,
"You ought to be ashamed!"
What has he done?
He bounces cheerfully up and down;
he rushes in circles in the fallen leaves.

Obviously, he has no sense of shame.
He and the bird know everything is answered,
all taken care of,
no need to ask again.
— Yesterday brought to today so lightly!
(A yesterday I find almost impossible to lift.)

ELIZABETH BISHOP (1911–1979)

One Art 1976

The art of losing isn't hard to master;
so many things seem filled with the intent
to be lost that their loss is no disaster.

Lose something every day. Accept the fluster
of lost door keys, the hour badly spent.
The art of losing isn't hard to master.

Then practice losing farther, losing faster:
places, and names, and where it was you meant
to travel. None of these will bring disaster.

I lost my mother's watch. And look! my last, or
next-to-last, of three loved houses went.
The art of losing isn't hard to master.

I lost two cities, lovely ones. And, vaster,
some realms I owned, two rivers, a continent.
I miss them, but it wasn't a disaster.

—Even losing you (the joking voice, a gesture
I love) I shan't have lied. It's evident
The art of losing's not too hard to master
though it may look like (*Write* it!) like disaster.

WILLIAM BLAKE (1757–1827)

The Garden of Love 1794

I went to the Garden of Love,
And saw what I never had seen:
A Chapel was built in the midst,
Where I used to play on the green.

And the gates of this Chapel were shut,
And "Thou shalt not" writ over the door;
So I turned to the Garden of Love
That so many sweet flowers bore;

And I saw it was filled with graves,
And tomb-stones where flowers should be;
And Priests in black gowns were walking their rounds,
And binding with briars my joys and desires.

WILLIAM BLAKE (1757–1827)

The Little Black Boy

1789

The Little Black Boy

My mother bore me in the southern wild,
And I am black, but O! my soul is white,
White as an angel is the English child:
But I am black as if bereav'd of light.

My mother tought me underneath a tree
And sitting down before the heat of day,
She took me on her lap and kiſsed me,
And pointing to the east began to say:

Look on the rising sun: there God does live
And gives his light and gives his heat away
And flowers and trees and beasts and men recieve
Comfort in morning joy in the noon day.

And we are put on earth a little space,
That we may learn to bear the beams of love,
And these black bodies and this sunburnt face
Is but a cloud and like a shady grove.

For when our souls have learn'd the heat to bear
The cloud will vanish we shall hear his voice.
Saying: come out from the grove my love & care,
And round my golden tent like lambs rejoice.

Thus did my mother say and kiſsed me,
And thus I say to little English boy;
When I from black and he from white cloud free,
And round the tent of God like lambs we joy:

Ill shade him from the heat till he can bear,
To lean in joy upon our fathers knee.
And then Ill stand and stroke his silver hair,
And be like him and he will then love me.

Illuminated printing: Blake etched his poems and designs in relief, with acid on copper. Each printed page was then colored by hand. The design and the text work together to express Blake's vision.

WILLIAM BLAKE (1757–1827)

A Poison Tree

1794

I was angry with my friend:
I told my wrath, my wrath did end.
I was angry with my foe:
I told it not, my wrath did grow.

And I water'd it in fears,
Night & morning with my tears;
And I sunnéd it with smiles,
And with soft deceitful wiles.

And it grew both day and night,
Till it bore an apple bright.
And my foe beheld it shine,
And he knew that it was mine,

And into my garden stole,
When the night had veild the pole;
In the morning glad I see
My foe outstretched beneath the tree.

ROBERT BLY (b. 1926)

Snowfall in the Afternoon 1962

I
The grass is half-covered with snow.
It was the sort of snowfall that starts in late afternoon,
And now the little houses of the grass are growing dark.

II
If I reached my hands down, near the earth,
I could take handfuls of darkness!
A darkness was always there, which we never noticed.

III
As the snow grows heavier, the cornstalks fade farther away,
And the barn moves nearer to the house.
The barn moves all alone in the growing storm.

IV
The barn is full of corn, and moving toward us now,
Like a hulk blown toward us in a storm at sea;
All the sailors on deck have been blind for many years.

LOUISE BOGAN (1897–1970)

Dark Summer 1929

Under the thunder-dark, the cicadas resound.
The storm in the sky mounts, but is not yet heard.
The shaft and the flash wait, but are not yet found.
The apples that hang and swell for the late comer,
The simple spell, the rite not for our word,
The kisses not for our mouths, — light the dark summer.

ANNE BRADSTREET (c. 1612–1672)

Before the Birth of One of Her Children 1678

All things within this fading world hath end,
Adversity doth still our joys attend;

No ties so strong, no friends so dear and sweet,
But with death's parting blow is sure to meet.
The sentence past is most irrevocable,
A common thing, yet oh, inevitable.
How soon, my Dear, death may my steps attend,
How soon't may be thy lot to lose thy friend,
We both are ignorant, yet love bids me
These farewell lines to recommend to thee,
That when that knot's untied that made us one,
I may seem thine, who in effect am none.
And if I see not half my days that's due,
What nature would, God grant to yours and you;
The many faults that well you know I have
Let be interred in my oblivious grave;
If any worth or virtue were in me,
Let that live freshly in thy memory
And when thou feel'st no grief, as I no harms,
Yet love thy dead, who long lay in thine arms,
And when thy loss shall be repaid with gains
Look to my little babes, my dear remains.
And if thou love thyself, or loved'st me,
These O protected from stepdame's° injury. *stepmother's*
And if chance to thine eyes shall bring this verse,
With some sad sighs honor my absent hearse;
And kiss this paper for thy love's dear sake,
Who with salt tears this last farewell did take.

RUPERT BROOKE (1887–1915)

The Soldier

1915

If I should die, think only this of me:
That there's some corner of a foreign field
That is for ever England. There shall be
In that rich earth a richer dust concealed;
A dust whom England bore, shaped, made aware,
Gave, once, her flowers to love, her ways to roam,
A body of England's, breathing English air,
Washed by the rivers, blest by suns of home.

And think, this heart, all evil shed away,
A pulse in the eternal mind, no less
Gives somewhere back the thoughts by England given;
Her sights and sounds; dreams happy as her day;
And laughter, learnt of friends; and gentleness,
In hearts at peace, under an English heaven.

GWENDOLYN BROOKS (b. 1917)

The Bean Eaters 1959

They eat beans mostly, this old yellow pair.
Dinner is a casual affair.
Plain chipware on a plain and creaking wood,
Tin flatware.

Two who are Mostly Good.
Two who have lived their day,
But keep on putting on their clothes
And putting things away.

And remembering . . .
Remembering, with twinklings and twinges,
As they lean over the beans in their rented back room
that is full of beads and receipts and dolls and cloths,
tobacco crumbs, vases and fringes.

GWENDOLYN BROOKS (b. 1917)

The Mother 1945

Abortions will not let you forget.
You remember the children you got that you did not get,
The damp small pulps with a little or with no hair,
The singers and workers that never handled the air.
You will never neglect or beat
Them, or silence or buy with a sweet.
You will never wind up the sucking-thumb
Or scuttle off ghosts that come.
You will never leave them, controlling your luscious sigh,
Return for a snack of them, with gobbling mother-eye.

I have heard in the voices of the wind the voices of my dim
killed children.
I have contracted. I have eased
My dim dears at the breasts they could never suck.
I have said, Sweets, if I sinned, if I seized
Your luck
And your lives from your unfinished reach,
If I stole your births and your names,
Your straight baby tears and your games,
Your stilted or lovely loves, your tumults, your marriages, aches,
and your deaths,
If I poisoned the beginnings of your breaths,
Believe that even in my deliberateness I was not deliberate.
Though why should I whine,

Whine that the crime was other than mine? —
Since anyhow you are dead.
Or rather, or instead,
You were never made.

But that too, I am afraid,
Is faulty: oh, what shall I say, how is the truth to be said?
You were born, you had body, you died.
It is just that you never giggled or planned or cried.

Believe me, I loved you all.
Believe me, I knew you, though faintly, and I loved, I loved you
All.

ROBERT BROWNING (1812–1889)

Meeting at Night

1845

The gray sea and the long black land;
And the yellow half-moon large and low;
And the startled little waves that leap
In fiery ringlets from their sleep,
As I gain the cove with pushing prow,
And quench its speed i' the slushy sand.

Then a mile of warm sea-scented beach;
Three fields to cross till a farm appears;
A tap at the pane, the quick sharp scratch
And blue spurt of a lighted match,
And a voice less loud, through its joys and fears,
Than the two hearts beating each to each!

ROBERT BROWNING (1812–1889)

Parting at Morning

1845

Round the cape of a sudden came the sea,
And the sun looked over the mountain's rim:
And straight was a path of gold for him,
And the need of a world of men for me.

ROBERT BURNS (1759–1796)

John Anderson My Jo

1790

John Anderson my jo,° John, *dear*
        When we were first acquent,

Your locks were like the raven,
Your bonnie brow was brent;° *smooth*
But now your brow is beld, John,
Your locks are like the snaw,
But blessings on your frosty pow,° *head*
John Anderson my jo!

John Anderson my jo, John,
We clamb the hill thegither,
And monie a cantie° day, John *happy*
We've had wi' ane anither:
Now we maun° totter down, John, *must*
And hand in hand we'll go,
And sleep thegither at the foot,
John Anderson my jo!

GEORGE GORDON, LORD BYRON (1788–1824)

She Walks in Beauty **1814**

FROM HEBREW MELODIES

I
She walks in Beauty, like the night
Of cloudless climes and starry skies;
And all that's best of dark and bright
Meet in her aspect and her eyes:
Thus mellowed to that tender light
Which Heaven to gaudy day denies.

II
One shade the more, one ray the less,
Had half impaired the nameless grace
Which waves in every raven tress,
Or softly lightens o'er her face;
Where thoughts serenely sweet express,
How pure, how dear their dwelling-place.

III
And on that cheek, and o'er that brow,
So soft, so calm, yet eloquent,
The smiles that win, the tints that glow,
But tell of days in goodness spent,
A mind at peace with all below,
A heart whose love is innocent!

THOMAS CAMPION (1567–1620)

There is a garden in her face

1617

There is a garden in her face
Where roses and white lilies grow;
A heav'nly paradise is that place
Wherein all pleasant fruits do flow.
There cherries grow which none may buy
Till "Cherry-ripe"° themselves do cry.

Those cherries fairly do enclose
Of orient pearl a double row,
Which when her lovely laughter shows,
They look like rose-buds filled with snow;
Yet them nor° peer nor prince can buy, *neither*
Till "Cherry-ripe" themselves do cry.

Her eyes like angels watch them still;
Her brows like bended bows do stand,
Threat'ning with piercing frowns to kill
All that attempt, with eye or hand
Those sacred cherries to come nigh
Till "Cherry-ripe" themselves do cry.

6 *"Cherry-ripe":* Street cry of London fruit peddlers.

LUCILLE CLIFTON (b. 1936)

For de Lawd

1969

people say they have a hard time
understanding how I
go on about my business
playing my Ray Charles
hollering at the kids —
seem like my Afro
cut off in some old image
would show I got a long memory
and I come from a line
of black and going on women
who got used to making it through murdered sons
and who grief kept on pushing
who fried chicken
ironed
swept off the back steps
who grief kept
for their still alive sons
for their sons coming

for their sons gone
just pushing
in the inner city
or
like we call it
home
we think a lot about uptown
and the silent nights
and the houses straight as
dead men
and the pastel lights
and we hang on to our no place
happy to be alive
and in the inner city
or
like we call it
home

SAMUEL TAYLOR COLERIDGE (1772–1834)

Kubla Khan: or, a Vision in a Dream° 1798

In Xanadu did Kubla Khan°
    A stately pleasure-dome decree:
Where Alph, the sacred river, ran
Through caverns measureless to man
    Down to a sunless sea.
So twice five miles of fertile ground
With walls and towers were girdled round:
And here were gardens bright with sinuous rills
Where blossomed many an incense-bearing tree;
And there were forests ancient as the hills,
Enfolding sunny spots of greenery.

But oh! that deep romantic chasm which slanted
Down the green hill athwart a cedarn cover!°
A savage place! as holy and enchanted
As e'er beneath a waning moon was haunted
By woman wailing for her demon-lover!
And from this chasm, with ceaseless turmoil seething,
As if this earth in fast thick pants were breathing,
A mighty fountain momently was forced,
Amid whose swift half-intermitted burst

Vision in a Dream: This poem came to Coleridge in an opium-induced dream, but he was interrupted while writing it down by a visitor. He was later unable to remember the rest of the poem. 1 *Kubla Khan:* The historical Kublai Khan (1216–1294, grandson of Genghis Khan) was the founder of the Mongol dynasty in China. 13 *athwart . . . cover:* Spanning a grove of cedar trees.

Huge fragments vaulted like rebounding hail,
Or chaffy grain beneath the thresher's flail:
And 'mid these dancing rocks at once and ever
It flung up momently the sacred river.
Five miles meandering with a mazy motion
Through wood and dale the sacred river ran,
Then reached the caverns measureless to man,
And sank in tumult to a lifeless ocean:
And 'mid this tumult Kubla heard from far
Ancestral voices prophesying war!

The shadow of the dome of pleasure
Floated midway on the waves;
Where was heard the mingled measure
From the fountain and the caves.
It was a miracle of rare device,
A sunny pleasure-dome with caves of ice!

A damsel with a dulcimer
In a vision once I saw:
It was an Abyssinian maid,
And on her dulcimer she played,
Singing of Mount Abora.
Could I revive within me
Her symphony and song,
To such a deep delight 'twould win me,
That with music loud and long,
I would build that dome in air,
That sunny dome! those caves of ice!
And all who heard should see them there,
And all should cry, Beware! Beware!
His flashing eyes, his floating hair!
Weave a circle round him thrice,
And close your eyes with holy dread,
For he on honey-dew hath fed,
And drunk the milk of Paradise.

COUNTEE CULLEN (1903–1946)

For a Lady I Know

1925

She even thinks that up in heaven
Her class lies late and snores,
While poor black cherubs rise at seven
To do celestial chores.

COUNTEE CULLEN (1903–1946)

Saturday's Child° 1925

Some are teethed on a silver spoon,
With the stars strung for a rattle;
I cut my teeth as the black raccoon——
For implements of battle.

Some are swaddled in silk and down,
And heralded by a star;
They swathed my limbs in a sackcloth gown
On a night that was black as tar.

For some, godfather and goddame
The opulent fairies be;
Dame Poverty gave me my name,
And Pain godfathered me.

For I was born on Saturday——
"Bad time for planting a seed,"
Was all my father had to say,
And, "One mouth more to feed."

Death cut the strings that gave me life,
And handed me to Sorrow,
The only kind of middle wife
My folks could beg or borrow.

Saturday's Child: Reference to the nursery rhyme: Monday's child is fair of face . . . / Saturday's child must work hard for a living. . . .

E. E. CUMMINGS (1894–1962)

anyone lived in a pretty how town 1940

anyone lived in a pretty how town
(with up so floating many bells down)
spring summer autumn winter
he sang his didn't he danced his did.

Women and men (both little and small)
cared for anyone not at all
they sowed their isn't they reaped their same
sun moon stars rain

children guessed (but only a few
and down they forgot as up they grew
autumn winter spring summer)
that noone loved him more by more

when by now and tree by leaf
she laughed his joy she cried his grief
bird by snow and stir by still
anyone's any was all to her

someones married their everyones
laughed their cryings and did their dance
(sleep wake hope and then) they
said their nevers they slept their dream

stars rain sun moon
(and only the snow can begin to explain
how children are apt to forget to remember
with up so floating many bells down)

one day anyone died i guess
(and noone stooped to kiss his face)
busy folk buried them side by side
little by little and was by was

all by all and deep by deep
and more by more they dream their sleep
noone and anyone earth by april
wish by spirit and if by yes.

Women and men (both dong and ding)
summer autumn winter spring
reaped their sowing and went their came
sun moon stars rain

E. E. CUMMINGS (1894–1962)

Buffalo Bill 's° 1923

Buffalo Bill 's
defunct
          who used to
          ride a watersmooth-silver
                                        stallion
and break onetwothreefourfive pigeonsjustlikethat
                                                        Jesus
he was a handsome man
                    and what i want to know is
how do you like your blueeyed boy
Mister Death

Buffalo Bill: William Frederick Cody (1846–1917). An American frontier scout and Indian killer turned international circus showman with his Wild West show, which employed Sitting Bull and Annie Oakley.

E. E. CUMMINGS (1894–1962)

my sweet old etcetera

1926

my sweet old etcetera
aunt lucy during the recent

war could and what
is more did tell you just
what everybody was fighting

for,
my sister

isabel created hundreds
(and
hundreds) of socks not to
mention shirts fleaproof earwarmers

etcetera wristers etcetera, my

mother hoped that

i would die etcetera
bravely of course my father used
to become hoarse talking about how it was
a privilege and if only he
could meanwhile my

self etcetera lay quietly
in the deep mud et

cetera
(dreaming,
et
  cetera, of
Your smile
eyes knees and of your Etcetera)

E. E. CUMMINGS (1894–1962)

since feeling is first

1926

since feeling is first
who pays any attention
to the syntax of things
will never wholly kiss you;

wholly to be a fool
while Spring is in the world

my blood approves,
and kisses are a better fate

than wisdom
lady i swear by all flowers. Don't cry
— the best gesture of my brain is less than
your eyelids' flutter which says

we are for each other:then
laugh, leaning back in my arms
for life's not a paragraph

And death i think is no parenthesis

JAMES DICKEY (b. 1923)

Cherrylog Road

1963

Off Highway 106
At Cherrylog Road I entered
The '34 Ford without wheels,
Smothered in kudzu,
With a seat pulled out to run
Corn whiskey down from the hills,

And then from the other side
Crept into an Essex
With a rumble seat of red leather
And then out again, aboard
A blue Chevrolet, releasing
The rust from its other color,

Reared up on three building blocks.
None had the same body heat;
I changed with them inward, toward
The weedy heart of the junkyard,
For I knew that Doris Holbrook
Would escape from her father at noon

And would come from the farm
To seek parts owned by the sun
Among the abandoned chassis,
Sitting in each in turn
As I did, leaning forward
As in a wild stock-car race

In the parking lot of the dead.
Time after time, I climbed in
And out the other side, like
An envoy or movie star
Met at the station by crickets.
A radiator cap raised its head,

Become a real toad or a kingsnake
As I neared the hub of the yard,
Passing through many states,
Many lives, to reach
Some grandmother's long Pierce-Arrow
Sending platters of blindness forth

From its nickel hubcaps
And spilling its tender upholstery
On sleepy roaches,
The glass panel in between
Lady and colored driver
Not all the way broken out,

The back-seat phone
Still on its hook.
I got in as though to exclaim,
"Let us go to the orphan asylum,
John; I have some old toys
For children who say their prayers."

I popped with sweat as I thought
I heard Doris Holbrook scrape
Like a mouse in the southern-state sun
That was eating the paint in blisters
From a hundred car tops and hoods.
She was tapping like code,

Loosening the screws,
Carrying off headlights,
Sparkplugs, bumpers,
Cracked mirrors and gear-knobs,
Getting ready, already,
To go back with something to show

Other than her lips' new trembling
I would hold to me soon, soon,
Where I sat in the ripped back seat
Talking over the interphone,
Praying for Doris Holbrook
To come from her father's farm

And to get back there
With no trace of me on her face
To be seen by her red-haired father
Who would change, in the squalling barn,
Her back's pale skin with a strop,
Then lay for me

In a bootlegger's roasting car
With a string-triggered 12-gauge shotgun
To blast the breath from the air.

Not cut by the jagged windshields,
Through the acres of wrecks she came
With a wrench in her hand,

Through dust where the blacksnake dies
Of boredom, and the beetle knows
The compost has no more life.
Someone outside would have seen
The oldest car's door inexplicably
Close from within:

I held her and held her and held her,
Convoyed at terrific speed
By the stalled, dreaming traffic around us,
So the blacksnake, stiff
With inaction, curved back
Into life, and hunted the mouse

With deadly overexcitement,
The beetles reclaimed their field
As we clung, glued together,
With the hooks of the seat springs
Working through to catch us red-handed
Amidst the gray breathless batting

That burst from the seat at our backs.
We left by separate doors
Into the changed, other bodies
Of cars, she down Cherrylog Road
And I to my motorcycle
Parked like the soul of the junkyard

Restored, a bicycle fleshed
With power, and tore off
Up Highway 106, continually
Drunk on the wind in my mouth,
Wringing the handlebar for speed,
Wild to be wreckage forever.

EMILY DICKINSON (1830–1886)

The Brain — is wider than the Sky — (c. 1862)

The Brain — is wider than the Sky —
For — put them side by side —
The one the other will contain
With ease — and You — beside —

The Brain is deeper than the sea —
For — hold them — Blue to Blue —

The one the other will absorb —
As Sponges — Buckets — do —

The Brain is just the weight of God —
For — Heft them — Pound for Pound —
And they will differ — if they do —
As Syllable from Sound —

EMILY DICKINSON (1830–1886)
I heard a Fly buzz — when I died —
c. 1862

I heard a Fly buzz — when I died —
The Stillness in the Room
Was like the Stillness in the Air —
Between the Heaves of Storm —

The Eyes around — had wrung them dry —
And Breaths were gathering firm
For that last Onset — when the King
Be witnessed — in the Room —

I willed my Keepsakes — Signed away
What portion of me be
Assignable — and then it was
There interposed a Fly —

With Blue — uncertain stumbling Buzz —
Between the light — and me —
And then the Windows failed — and then
I could not see to see —

EMILY DICKINSON (1830–1886)
It dropped so low — in my Regard —
c. 1863

It dropped so low — in my Regard —
I heard it hit the Ground —
And go to pieces on the Stones
At bottom of my Mind —

Yet blamed the Fate that flung it — *less*
Than I denounced Myself,
For entertaining Plated Wares
Upon My Silver Shelf —

EMILY DICKINSON (1830–1886)

Much Madness is divinest Sense — 1890

Much Madness is divinest Sense —
To a discerning Eye —
Much Sense — the starkest Madness —
'Tis the Majority
In this, as All, prevail —
Assent — and you are sane —
Demur — you're straightway dangerous —
And handled with a Chain —

EMILY DICKINSON (1830–1886)

Success is counted sweetest 1878

Success is counted sweetest
By those who ne'er succeed.
To comprehend a nectar
Requires sorest need.

Not one of all the purple Host
Who took the Flag today
Can tell the definition
So clear of Victory

As he defeated — dying —
On whose forbidden ear
The distant strains of triumph
Burst agonized and clear!

EMILY DICKINSON (1830–1886)

Wild Nights — Wild Nights! c. 1861

Wild Nights — Wild Nights!
Were I with thee
Wild Nights should be
Our luxury!

Futile — the Winds —
To a Heart in port —
Done with the Compass —
Done with the Chart!

Rowing in Eden —
Ah, the Sea!
Might I but moor — Tonight —
In Thee!

JOHN DONNE (1572–1631)

Batter My Heart

1610

Batter my heart, three-personed God; for You
As yet but knock, breathe, shine, and seek to mend;
That I may rise and stand, o'erthrow me, and bend
Your force, to break, blow, burn, and make me new.
I, like an usurped town, to another due,
Labor to admit You, but Oh, to no end!
Reason, Your viceroy in me, me should defend,
But is captived, and proves weak or untrue.
Yet dearly I love You, and would be loved fain.
But am betrothed unto Your enemy:
Divorce me, untie, or break that knot again,
Take me to You, imprison me, for I,
Except You enthrall me, never shall be free,
Nor ever chaste, except You ravish me.

JOHN DONNE (1572–1631)

Death Be Not Proud

1611

Death be not proud, though some have callèd thee
Mighty and dreadful, for thou art not so;
For those whom thou think'st thou dost overthrow
Die not, poor Death, nor yet canst thou kill me.
From rest and sleep, which but thy pictures° be, *images*
Much pleasure; then from thee much more must flow,
And soonest our best men with thee do go,
Rest of their bones, and soul's delivery° *deliverance*
Thou art slave to Fate, Chance, kings, and desperate men,
And dost with Poison, War, and Sickness dwell;
And poppy or charms can make us sleep as well,
And better than thy stroke; why swell'st° thou then? *swell with pride*
One short sleep past, we wake eternally
And death shall be no more; Death, thou shalt die.

JOHN DONNE (1572–1631)

The Flea

1633

Mark but this flea, and mark in this°
How little that which thou deny'st me is;

1 *mark in this:* Take note of the moral lesson in this object.

It sucked me first, and now sucks thee,
And in this flea our two bloods mingled be;
Thou know'st that this cannot be said
A sin, nor shame, nor loss of maidenhead,
    Yet this enjoys before it woo,
    And pampered swells with one blood made of two,
    And this, alas, is more than we would do.°

Oh stay, three lives in one flea spare,
Where we almost, yea more than, married are.
This flea is you and I, and this
Our marriage bed, and marriage temple is;
Though parents grudge, and you, we're met
And cloistered in these living walls of jet.
    Though use° make you apt to kill me, *habit*
    Let not to that, self-murder added be,
    And sacrilege, three sins in killing three.

Cruel and sudden, hast thou since
Purpled thy nail in blood of innocence?
Wherein could this flea guilty be,
Except in that drop which it sucked from thee?
Yet thou triumph'st, and say'st that thou
Find'st not thyself, nor me, the weaker now;
    'Tis true; then learn how false, fears be;
    Just so much honor, when thou yield'st to me,
    Will waste, as this flea's death took life from thee.

9 *more than we would do:* I.e., if we do not join our blood in conceiving a child.

JOHN DONNE (1572–1631)

The Good-Morrow

1633

    I wonder, by my troth, what thou and I
        Did, till we loved? were we not weaned till then?
    But sucked on country pleasures, childishly?
        Or snorted° we in the Seven Sleepers' den? *snored*
    'Twas so; but this,° all pleasures fancies be. *except for this*
    If ever any beauty I did see,
Which I desired, and got, 'twas but a dream of thee.

    And now good-morrow to our waking souls,
        Which watch not one another out of fear;
    For love, all love of other sights controls,
        And makes one little room an everywhere.

4 *Seven Sleepers' den:* According to Christian and Muslim tradition, seven Christians of Ephesus escaped Roman persecution by sleeping in a cave for nearly two centuries.

Let sea-discoverers to new worlds have gone,
Let maps to other, worlds on worlds have shown,°
Let us possess one world, each hath one, and is one.

My face in thine eye, thine in mine appears,°
And true plain hearts do in the faces rest;
Where can we find two better hemispheres,
Without sharp north, without declining west?
Whatever dies was not mixed equally,°
If our two loves be one, or, thou and I
Love so alike that none do slacken, none can die.

13 *Let . . . shown:* Let us concede that maps to others have shown worlds on worlds. 15 *My face . . . appears:* Our faces are reflected in each other's eyes. 19 *Whatever . . . equally:* Scholastic philosophers believed that death was the result of an imbalance in the body's elements.

JOHN DONNE (1572–1631)

Hymn to God My God, in My Sickness 1635

Since I am coming to that holy room
Where, with thy choir of saints for evermore,
I shall be made thy music, as I come
I tune the instrument here at the door,
And what I must do then, think now before.

Whilst my physicians by their love are grown
Cosmographers, and I their map, who lie
Flat on this bed, that by them may be shown
That this is my southwest discovery,
Per fretum febris,° by these straits to die, *through the strait of fever*

I joy that in these straits I see my west;
For though those currents yield return to none,
What shall my west hurt me? As west and east
In all flat maps (and I am one) are one,
So death doth touch the resurrectiön.

Is the Pacific Sea my home? Or are
The eastern riches? Is Jerusalem?
Anyan° and Magellan and Gibraltar, *Bering Strait*
All straits, and none but straits, are ways to them,
Whether where Japhet dwelt, or Cham, or Shem.°

We think that Paradise and Calvary,
Christ's cross and Adam's tree, stood in one place;

Japhet . . . Cham . . . Shem: The three sons of Noah, who after the flood became the progenitors of the northern, southern, and Semitic peoples respectively (see Gen. 9:18–27).

Look, Lord, and find both Adams met in me;
As the first Adam's sweat surrounds my face,
May the last Adam's blood my soul embrace.

So, in his purple wrapped receive me, Lord;
By these his thorns give me his other crown;
And as to others' souls I preached thy word,
Be this my text, my sermon to mine own:
Therefore that he may raise, the Lord throws down.

H. D.
[HILDA DOOLITTLE] (1886–1961)
Leda° 1919

Where the slow river
meets the tide,
a red swan lifts red wings
and darker beak,
and underneath the purple down
of his soft breast
uncurls his coral feet.

Through the deep purple
of the dying heat
of sun and mist,
the level ray of sun-beam
has caressed
the lily with dark breast,
and flecked with richer gold
its golden crest.

Where the slow lifting
of the tide,
floats into the river
and slowly drifts
among the reeds,
and lifts the yellow flags,
he floats
where tide and river meet.

Ah kingly kiss —
no more regret
nor old deep memories
to mar the bliss;

Leda: In Greek myth, Zeus in the form of a swan seduced Leda and fathered Helen of Troy and Clytemnestra.

where the low sedge is thick,
the gold day-lily
outspreads and rests
beneath soft fluttering
of red swan wings
and the warm quivering
of the red swan's breast.

MICHAEL DRAYTON (1563–1631)

Since There's No Help 1619

Since there's no help, come let us kiss and part;
Nay, I have done, you get no more of me,
And I am glad, yea glad with all my heart
That thus so cleanly I myself can free;
Shake hands for ever, cancel all our vows,
And when we meet at any time again,
Be it not seen in either of our brows
That we one jot of former love retain.
Now at the last gasp of Love's latest breath,
When, his pulse failing, Passion speechless lies,
When Faith is kneeling by his bed of death,
And Innocence is closing up his eyes,
    Now if thou wouldst, when all have given him over,
    From death to life thou mightst him yet recover.

T. S. ELIOT (1888–1965)

Journey of the Magi° 1927

"A cold coming we had of it,
Just the worst time of the year
For a journey, and such a long journey:
The ways deep and the weather sharp,
The very dead of winter."°
And the camels galled, sore-footed, refractory,
Lying down in the melting snow.
There were times we regretted

Journey of the Magi: In Christian lore, the journey made by Melchior, Caspar, and Balthazar, the three wise men who followed the star to Bethlehem (see Matt. 2:1–12). 1–5 *"A cold . . . winter":* Eliot borrows from part of a sermon delivered on Christmas Day in 1622 by Lancelot Andrewes.

The summer palaces on slopes, the terraces,
And the silken girls bringing sherbet.
Then the camel men cursing and grumbling
And running away, and wanting their liquor and women,
And the night-fires going out, and the lack of shelters,
And the cities hostile and the towns unfriendly
And the villages dirty and charging high prices:
A hard time we had of it.
At the end we preferred to travel all night,
Sleeping in snatches,
With the voices singing in our ears, saying
That this was all folly.

Then at dawn we came down to a temperate valley,
Wet, below the snow line, smelling of vegetation;
With a running stream and a water-mill beating the darkness,
And three trees° on the low sky,
And an old white horse° galloped away in the meadow.
Then we came to a tavern with vine-leaves over the lintel,
Six hands at an open door dicing for pieces of silver,°
And feet kicking the empty wine-skins.
But there was no information, and so we continued
And arrived at evening, not a moment too soon
Finding the place; it was (you may say) satisfactory.

All this was a long time ago, I remember,
And I would do it again, but set down
This set down
This: were we led all that way for
Birth or Death? There was a Birth, certainly,
We had evidence and no doubt. I had seen birth and death,
But had thought they were different; this Birth was
Hard and bitter agony for us, like Death, our death.
We returned to our places, these Kingdoms,
But no longer at ease here, in the old dispensation,
With an alien people clutching their gods.
I should be glad of another death.

24 *three trees:* Suggests the three crosses on Golgotha (Luke 23:32–33). 25 *old white horse:* Perhaps an allusion to one of the horses in Revelation (see Rev. 6:2 and 19:11–16). 27 *dicing for . . . silver:* Recalls the soldiers casting lots at the Crucifixion (Matt. 27:35) and Judas's betrayal of Christ for thirty pieces of silver (Matt. 26:14–16).

T. S. ELIOT (1888–1965)
The Love Song of J. Alfred Prufrock 1917

S'io credesse che mia risposta fosse
A persona che mai tornasse al mondo,
Questa fiamma staria senza piu scosse.
Ma perciocche giammai di questo fondo
Non torno vivo alcun, s'i'odo il vero,
Senza tema d'infamia ti rispondo.°

Let us go then, you and I,
When the evening is spread out against the sky
Like a patient etherized upon a table;
Let us go, through certain half-deserted streets,
The muttering retreats
Of restless nights in one-night cheap hotels
And sawdust restaurants with oyster-shells:
Streets that follow like a tedious argument
Of insidious intent
To lead you to an overwhelming question . . .
Oh, do not ask, "What is it?"
Let us go and make our visit.

In the room the women come and go
Talking of Michelangelo.

The yellow fog that rubs its back upon the window-panes,
The yellow smoke that rubs its muzzle on the window-panes
Licked its tongue into the corners of the evening,
Lingered upon the pools that stand in drains,
Let fall upon its back the soot that falls from chimneys,
Slipped by the terrace, made a sudden leap,
And seeing that it was a soft October night,
Curled once about the house, and fell asleep.

And indeed there will be time°
For the yellow smoke that slides along the street,
Rubbing its back upon the window-panes;
There will be time, there will be time
To prepare a face to meet the faces that you meet;
There will be time to murder and create,

Epigraph: *S'io credesse . . . rispondo:* Dante's *Inferno,* XXVII, 58–63. In the Eighth Chasm of the Inferno, Dante and Virgil meet Guido da Montefeltro, one of the False Counselors, who is punished by being enveloped in an eternal flame. When Dante asks Guido to tell his life story, the spirit replies: "If I thought that my answer were to one who might ever return to the world, this flame would shake no more; but since from this depth none ever returned alive, if what I hear is true, I answer you without fear of infamy." 23 *there will be time:* An allusion to Ecclesiastes 3:1–8: "To everything there is a season, and a time to every purpose under heaven. . . ."

And time for all the works and days° of hands
That lift and drop a question on your plate;
Time for you and time for me,
And time yet for a hundred indecisions,
And for a hundred visions and revisions,
Before the taking of a toast and tea.

In the room the women come and go
Talking of Michelangelo.

And indeed there will be time
To wonder, "Do I dare?" and, "Do I dare?"
Time to turn back and descend the stair,
With a bald spot in the middle of my hair —
(They will say: "How his hair is growing thin!")
My morning coat, my collar mounting firmly to the chin,
My necktie rich and modest, but asserted by a simple pin —
(They will say: "But how his arms and legs are thin!")
Do I dare
Disturb the universe?
In a minute there is time
For decisions and revisions which a minute will reverse.

For I have known them all already, known them all —
Have known the evenings, mornings, afternoons,
I have measured out my life with coffee spoons;
I know the voices dying with a dying fall
Beneath the music from a farther room.
So how should I presume?

And I have known the eyes already, known them all —
The eyes that fix you in a formulated phrase,
And when I am formulated, sprawling on a pin,
When I am pinned and wriggling on the wall,
Then how should I begin
To spit out all the butt-ends of my days and ways?
And how should I presume?

And I have known the arms already, known them all —
Arms that are braceleted and white and bare
(But in the lamplight, downed with light brown hair!)
Is it perfume from a dress
That makes me so digress?
Arms that lie along a table, or wrap about a shawl.
And should I then presume?
And how should I begin?

. . . . .

Shall I say, I have gone at dusk through narrow streets

29 *works and days:* Hesiod's eighth century B.C. poem *Works and Days* gave practical advice on how to conduct one's life in accordance with the seasons.

And watched the smoke that rises from the pipes
Of lonely men in shirt-sleeves, leaning out of windows? . . .

I should have been a pair of ragged claws
Scuttling across the floors of silent seas.

. . . . .

And the afternoon, the evening, sleeps so peacefully!
Smoothed by long fingers,
Asleep . . . tired . . . or it malingers,
Stretched on the floor, here beside you and me.
Should I, after tea and cakes and ices,
Have the strength to force the moment to its crisis?
But though I have wept and fasted, wept and prayed,
Though I have seen my head (grown slightly bald) brought in upon a platter,°
I am no prophet — and here's no great matter;
I have seen the moment of my greatness flicker,
And I have seen the eternal Footman hold my coat, and snicker,
And in short, I was afraid.

And would it have been worth it, after all,
After the cups, the marmalade, the tea,
Among the porcelain, among some talk of you and me,
Would it have been worth while,
To have bitten off the matter with a smile,
To have squeezed the universe into a ball°
To roll it toward some overwhelming question,
To say: "I am Lazarus,° come from the dead,
Come back to tell you all, I shall tell you all" —
If one, settling a pillow by her head,
Should say: "That is not what I meant at all.
That is not it, at all."

And would it have been worth it, after all,
Would it have been worth while,
After the sunsets and the dooryards and the sprinkled streets,
After the novels, after the teacups, after the skirts that trail along the floor —
And this, and so much more? —
It is impossible to say just what I mean!
But as if a magic lantern threw the nerves in patterns on a screen:
Would it have been worth while
If one, settling a pillow or throwing off a shawl,
And turning toward the window, should say:
"That is not it at all,
That is not what I meant, at all."

. . . . .

82 *head . . . upon a platter:* At Salome's request, Herod had John the Baptist decapitated and had the severed head delivered to her on a platter (see Matt. 14:1–12 and Mark 6:17–29). 92 *squeezed the universe into a ball:* See Marvell's "To His Coy Mistress" (p. 534), lines 41–42: "Let us roll all our strength and all / Our sweetness up into one ball." 94 *Lazarus:* The brother of Mary and Martha who was raised from the dead by Jesus (John 11:1–44). In Luke 16:19–31, a rich man asks that another Lazarus return from the dead to warn the living about their treatment of the poor.

No! I am not Prince Hamlet, nor was meant to be;
Am an attendant lord,° one that will do
To swell a progress,° start a scene or two, *state procession*
Advise the prince; no doubt, an easy tool,
Deferential, glad to be of use,
Politic, cautious, and meticulous;
Full of high sentence, but a bit obtuse;
At times, indeed, almost ridiculous —
Almost, at times, the Fool.

I grow old . . . I grow old . . .
I shall wear the bottoms of my trousers rolled.

Shall I part my hair behind? Do I dare to eat a peach?
I shall wear white flannel trousers, and walk upon the beach.
I have heard the mermaids singing, each to each.

I do not think that they will sing to me.

I have seen them riding seaward on the waves
Combing the white hair of the waves blown back
When the wind blows the water white and black.

We have lingered in the chambers of the sea
By sea-girls wreathed with seaweed red and brown
Till human voices wake us, and we drown.

112 *attendant lord:* Like Polonius in Shakespeare's *Hamlet.*

LAWRENCE FERLINGHETTI (b. 1919)

Constantly risking absurdity 1958

Constantly risking absurdity
and death
whenever he performs
above the heads
of his audience
the poet like an acrobat
climbs on rime
to a high wire of his own making
and balancing on eyebeams
above a sea of faces
paces his way
to the other side of day
performing *entrechats*°
and sleight-of-foot tricks

13 *entrechats:* Vertical leaps in ballet during which the feet are crossed a number of times.

and other high theatrics
and all without mistaking
any thing
for what it may not be
For he's the super realist
who must perforce perceive
taut truth
before the taking of each stance or step
in his supposed advance
toward that still higher perch
where Beauty stands and waits
with gravity
to start her death-defying leap
And he
a little charleychaplin man
who may or may not catch
her fair eternal form
spreadeagled in the empty air
of existence

ALLEN GINSBERG (b. 1926)

America

1956

America I've given you all and now I'm nothing.
America two dollars and twentyseven cents January 17, 1956.
I can't stand my own mind.
America when will we end the human war?
Go fuck yourself with your atom bomb.
I don't feel good don't bother me.
I won't write my poem till I'm in my right mind.
America when will you be angelic?
When will you take off your clothes?
When will you look at yourself through the grave?
When will you be worthy of your million Trotskyites?° *American communists*
America why are your libraries full of tears?
America when will you send your eggs to India?
I'm sick of your insane demands.
When can I go into the supermarket and buy what I need with my good looks?
America after all it is you and I who are perfect not the next world.
Your machinery is too much for me.
You made me want to be a saint.
There must be some other way to settle this argument.

Burroughs° is in Tangiers I don't think he'll come back it's sinister.
Are you being sinister or is this some form of practical joke?
I'm trying to come to the point.
I refuse to give up my obsession.
America stop pushing I know what I'm doing.
America the plum blossoms are falling.
I haven't read the newspapers for months, everyday somebody goes on trial
    for murder.
America I feel sentimental about the Wobblies.°
America I used to be a communist when I was a kid I'm not sorry.
I smoke marijuana every chance I get.
I sit in my house for days on end and stare at the roses in the closet.
When I go to Chinatown I get drunk and never get laid.
My mind is made up there's going to be trouble.
You should have seen me reading Marx.
My psychoanalyst thinks I'm perfectly right.
I won't say the Lord's Prayer.
I have mystical visions and cosmic vibrations.
America I still haven't told you what you did to Uncle Max after he came
    over from Russia.

I'm addressing you.
Are you going to let your emotional life be run by Time Magazine?
I'm obsessed by Time Magazine.
I read it every week.
Its cover stares at me every time I slink past the corner candystore.
I read it in the basement of the Berkeley Public Library.
It's always telling me about responsibility. Businessmen are serious. Movie
    producers are serious. Everybody's serious but me.
It occurs to me that I am America.
I am talking to myself again.

Asia is rising against me.
I haven't got a chinaman's chance.
I'd better consider my national resources.
My national resources consist of two joints of marijuana millions of genitals
    an unpublishable private literature that goes 1400 miles an hour and
    twentyfive-thousand mental institutions.
I say nothing about my prisons nor the millions of underprivileged who
    live in my flowerpots under the light of five hundred suns.
I have abolished the whorehouses of France, Tangiers is the next to go.
My ambition is to be President despite the fact that I'm a Catholic.

America how can I write a holy litany in your silly mood?
I will continue like Henry Ford my strophes are as individual as his auto-
        mobiles more so they're all different sexes.

20 *Burroughs:* William Burroughs (1914–1981), author of *Naked Lunch* (1959), who traveled to Tangiers to avoid prosecution on drug charges. 27 *Wobblies:* Members of the Industrial Workers of the World (I.W.W.), a militant labor organization.

America I will sell you strophes $2500 apiece $500 down on your old strophe
America free Tom Mooney°
America save the Spanish Loyalists°
America Sacco & Vanzetti° must not die
America I am the Scottsboro boys.°
America when I was seven momma took me to Communist Cell meetings they sold us garbanzos a handful per ticket a ticket costs a nickel and the speeches were free everybody was angelic and sentimental about the workers it was all so sincere you have no idea what a good thing the party was in 1835 Scott Nearing was a grand old man a real mensch Mother Bloor made me cry I once saw Israel Amter plain. Everybody must have been a spy.°
America you don't really want to go to war.
America it's them bad Russians.
Them Russians them Russians and them Chinamen. And them Russians.
The Russia wants to eat us alive. The Russia's power mad. She wants to take our cars from out our garages.
Her wants to grab Chicago. Her needs a Red Readers' Digest. Her wants our auto plants in Siberia. Him big bureaucracy running our filling stations.
That no good. Ugh. Him make Indians learn read. Him need big black niggers. Hah. Her make us all work sixteen hours a day. Help.
America this is quite serious.
America this is the impression I get from looking in the television set.
America is this correct?
I'd better get right down to the job.
It's true I don't want to join the Army or turn lathes in precision parts factories, I'm nearsighted and psychopathic anyway.
America I'm putting my queer shoulder to the wheel.

57 *Tom Mooney:* (1882–1942) A labor organizer convicted of setting off a bomb in a San Francisco crowd; many believed in his innocence. He was released from prison after serving more than twenty years. 58 *Spanish Loyalists:* Resistance fighters who opposed the fascist regime of Francisco Franco. 59 *Sacco & Vanzetti:* Nicola Sacco (1891–1927) and Bartolomeo Vanzetti (1888–1927), anarchists and labor agitators convicted of a payroll robbery and murder for which they were executed. They were widely viewed as victims and political martyrs rather than criminals. 60 *Scottsboro boys:* Another famous court case involving nine blacks falsely accused of raping two white girls in Scottsboro, Alabama. 61 *Everybody . . . spy:* Nearing, Bloor, and Amter were all associated with the Communist party.

NIKKI GIOVANNI (b. 1943)

Poetry

1975

poetry is motion graceful
as a fawn
gentle as a teardrop
strong like the eye
finding peace in a crowded room

we poets tend to think
our words are golden
though emotion speaks too
loudly to be defined
by silence

sometimes after midnight or just before
the dawn
we sit typewriter in hand
pulling loneliness around us
forgetting our lovers or children
who are sleeping
ignoring the weary wariness
of our own logic
to compose a poem
    no one understands it
it never says "love me" for poets are
beyond love
it never says "accept me" for poems seek not
acceptance but controversy
it only says "i am" and therefore
i concede that you are too

a poem is pure energy
horizontally contained
between the mind
of the poet and the ear of the reader
if it does not sing discard the ear
for poetry is song
if it does not delight discard
the heart for poetry is joy
if it does not inform then close
off the brain for it is dead
if it cannot heed the insistent message
that life is precious

which is all we poets
wrapped in our loneliness
are trying to say

DONALD HALL (b. 1928)

My Son, My Executioner 1955

My son, my executioner,
    I take you in my arms,
Quiet and small and just astir,
    And whom my body warms.

Sweet death, small son, our instrument
    Of immortality,
Your cries and hungers document
    Our bodily decay.

We twenty-five and twenty-two,
    Who seemed to live forever,
Observe enduring life in you
    And start to die together.

DONALD HALL (b. 1928)

To a Waterfowl

1974

Women with hats like the rear ends of pink ducks
applauded you, my poems.
These are the women whose husbands I meet on airplanes,
who close their briefcases and ask, "What are *you* in?"
I look in their eyes, I tell them I am in poetry,

and their eyes fill with anxiety, and with little tears.
"Oh, yeah?" they say, developing an interest in clouds.
"My wife, she likes that sort of thing? Hah-hah?"
I guess maybe I'd better watch my grammar, huh?"
I leave them in airports, watching their grammar,

and take a limousine to the Women's Goodness Club
where I drink Harvey's Bristol Cream with their wives,
and eat chicken salad with capers, with little tomato wedges
and I read them "The Erotic Crocodile," and "Eating You."
Ah, when I have concluded the disbursement of sonorities,

crooning, "High on thy thigh I cry, Hi!" — and so forth —
they spank their wide hands, they smile like Jell-O,
and they say, "Hah-hah? My goodness, Mr. Hall,
but you certainly do have an imagination, huh?"
"Thank you, indeed," I say; "it brings in the bacon."

But now, my poems, now I have returned to the motel,
returned to *l'éternel retour*° of the Holiday Inn, *endless sameness*
naked, lying on the bed, watching *Godzilla Sucks Mt. Fuji,*
addressing my poems, feeling superior, and drinking bourbon
from a flask disguised to look like a transistor radio.

Ah, my poems, it is true,
that with the deepest gratitude and most serene pleasure,
and with hints that I am a sexual Thomas Alva Edison,
and not without collecting an exorbitant fee,
I have accepted the approbation of feathers.

And what about you? You, laughing? You, in the bluejeans,
laughing at your mother who wears hats, and at your father
who rides airplanes with a briefcase watching his grammar?
Will you ever be old and dumb, like your creepy parents?
Not you, not you, not you, not you, not you, not you.

THOMAS HARDY (1840–1928)

Channel Firing°

April 1914

That night your great guns, unawares,
Shook all our coffins as we lay,
And broke the chancel window squares,°
We thought it was the Judgment-day°

And sat upright. While drearisome
Arose the howl of wakened hounds:
The mouse let fall the altar-crumb,°
The worms drew back into the mounds,

The glebe cow° drooled. Till God called, "No;
It's gunnery practice out at sea
Just as before you went below;
The world is as it used to be:

"All nations striving strong to make
Red war yet redder. Mad as hatters
They do no more for Christés sake
Than you who are helpless in such matters.

"That this is not the judgment-hour
For some of them's a blessed thing,
For if it were they'd have to scour
Hell's floor for so much threatening . . .

"Ha, ha. It will be warmer when
I blow the trumpet (if indeed
I ever do; for you are men,
And rest eternal sorely need)."

So down we lay again. "I wonder,
Will the world ever saner be,"
Said one, "than when He sent us under
In our indifferent century!"

Channel Firing: The navy practiced firing guns on the English Channel in the summer of 1914, just before World War I began. 3 *chancel window squares:* A church's altar window. 4 *Judgment-day:* In Christian tradition, the day the dead are awakened for judgment. 7 *altar-crumb:* Particle from the wafer used in the celebration of the Eucharist. 9 *glebe cow:* Parish cow pastured on church land.

And many a skeleton shook his head.
"Instead of preaching forty year,"
My neighbor Parson Thirdly said,
"I wish I had stuck to pipes and beer."

Again the guns disturbed the hour,
Roaring their readiness to avenge.
As far inland as Stourton Tower,°
And Camelot,° and starlit Stonehenge.°

35 *Stourton Tower:* Eighteenth-century commemoration of King Alfred's ninth-century victory over the Danes in Stourhead Park, Wiltshire. 36 *Camelot:* The legendary castle that housed King Arthur's court, probably located in Cornwall; *Stonehenge:* A circular formation of great stones or monoliths erected about 1800 B.C., associated with religious rituals and perhaps with astronomical calculations, and located on Salisbury Plain, Wiltshire.

THOMAS HARDY (1840–1928)

The Darkling Thrush

December 31, 1900

I leant upon a coppice gate
    When Frost was specter gray,
And Winter's dregs made desolate
    The weakening eye of day.
The tangled bine-stems scored the sky
    Like strings of broken lyres,
And all mankind that haunted nigh
    Had sought their household fires.

The land's sharp features seemed to be
    The Century's corpse outleant,
His crypt the cloudy canopy,
    The wind his death-lament.
The ancient pulse of germ and birth
    Was shrunken hard and dry,
And every spirit upon earth
    Seemed fervorless as I.

At once a voice arose among
    The bleak twigs overhead
In a full-hearted evensong
    Of joy illimited;
And aged thrush, frail, gaunt, and small,
    In blast-beruffled plume,
Had chosen thus to fling his soul
    Upon the growing gloom.

So little cause for carolings
    Of such ecstatic sound

Was written on terrestrial things
Afar or nigh around,
That I could think there trembled through
His happy good-night air
Some blessed Hope, whereof he knew
And I was unaware.

THOMAS HARDY (1840–1928)

Hap

1866

If but some vengeful god would call to me
From up the sky, and laugh: "Thou suffering thing,
Know that thy sorrow is my ecstasy,
That thy love's loss is my hate's profiting!"

Then would I bear it, clench myself, and die,
Steeled by the sense of ire unmerited;
Half-eased in that a Powerfuller than I
Had willed and meted me the tears I shed.

But not so. How arrives it joy lies slain,
And why unblooms the best hope ever sown?
— Crass Casualty obstructs the sun and rain,
And dicing Time for gladness casts a moan. . . .
These purblind Doomsters had as readily strown
Blisses about my pilgrimage as pain.

THOMAS HARDY (1840–1928)

The Man He Killed

1902

Had he and I but met
By some old ancient inn,
We should have sat us down to wet
Right many a nipperkin!° *half-pint cup*

But ranged as infantry,
And staring face to face,
I shot at him as he at me,
And killed him in his place.

I shot him dead because —
Because he was my foe,
Just so: my foe of course he was;
That's clear enough; although

He thought he'd 'list, perhaps,
Off-hand-like — just as I —

Was out of work — had sold his traps —
No other reason why.

Yes; quaint and curious war is!
You shoot a fellow down
You'd treat, if met where any bar is,
Or help to half-a-crown.

SEAMUS HEANEY (b. 1939)

Digging

1966

Between my finger and my thumb
The squat pen rests; snug as a gun.

Under my window, a clean rasping sound
When the spade sinks into gravelly ground:
My father, digging. I look down

Till his straining rump among the flowerbeds
Bends low, comes up twenty years away
Stooping in rhythm through potato drills
Where he was digging.

The coarse boot nestled on the lug, the shaft
Against the inside knee was levered firmly.
He rooted out tall tops, buried the bright edge deep
To scatter new potatoes that we picked
Loving their cool hardness in our hands.

By God, the old man could handle a spade.
Just like his old man.

My grandfather cut more turf in a day
Than any other man on Toner's bog.
Once I carried him milk in a bottle
Corked sloppily with paper. He straightened up
To drink it, then fell to right away

Nicking and slicing neatly, heaving sods
Over his shoulder, going down and down
For the good turf. Digging.

The cold smell of potato mould, the squelch and slap
Of soggy peat, the curt cuts of an edge
Through living roots awaken in my head.
But I've no spade to follow men like them.

Between my finger and my thumb
The squat pen rests.
I'll dig with it.

ANTHONY HECHT (b. 1923)

The Dover Bitch°

1968

A Criticism of Life

So there stood Matthew Arnold and this girl
With the cliffs of England crumbling away behind them,
And he said to her, "Try to be true to me,
And I'll do the same for you, for things are bad
All over, etc., etc."
Well now, I knew this girl. It's true she had read
Sophocles in a fairly good translation
And caught that bitter allusion to the sea,°
But all the time he was talking she had in mind
The notion of what his whiskers would feel like
On the back of her neck. She told me later on
That after a while she got to looking out
At the lights across the channel, and really felt sad,
Thinking of all the wine and enormous beds
And blandishments in French and the perfumes.
And then she got really angry. To have been brought
All the way down from London, and then be addressed
As a sort of mournful cosmic last resort
Is really tough on a girl, and she was pretty.
Anyway, she watched him pace the room
And finger his watch-chain and seem to sweat a bit,
And then she said one or two unprintable things.
But you mustn't judge her by that. What I mean to say is,
She's really all right. I still see her once in a while
And she always treats me right. We have a drink
And I give her a good time, and perhaps it's a year
Before I see her again, but there she is,
Running to fat, but dependable as they come.
And sometimes I bring her a bottle of *Nuit d'Amour*.

The Dover Bitch: A parody of Arnold's poem "Dover Beach" (see page 549). 8 *allusion to the sea:* Lines 9–18 in "Dover Beach" refer to Sophocles' *Antigone,* lines 583–591.

GEORGE HERBERT (1593–1633)

The Collar

1633

I struck the board° and cried, "No more; *table*
          I will abroad!
What? shall I ever sigh and pine?
My lines and life are free, free as the road,

Loose as the wind, as large as store.°
Shall I be still in suit?° *serving another*
Have I no harvest but a thorn
To let me blood, and not restore
What I have lost with cordial° fruit? *restorative*
Sure there was wine
Before my sighs did dry it; there was corn
Before my tears did drown it.
Is the year only lost to me?
Have I no bays° to crown it, *triumphal wreaths*
No flowers, no garlands gay? All blasted?
All wasted?
Not so, my heart; but there is fruit,
And thou hast hands.
Recover all thy sigh-blown age
On double pleasures: leave thy cold dispute
Of what is fit, and not. Forsake thy cage,
Thy rope of sands,
Which petty thoughts have made, and made to thee
Good cable, to enforce and draw,
And be thy law,
While thou didst wink and wouldst not see.
Away! take heed;
I will abroad.
Call in thy death's-head° there; tie up thy fears.
He that forbears
To suit and serve his need,
Deserves his load."
But as I raved and grew more fierce and wild
At every word,
Methought I heard one calling, *Child!*
And I replied, *My Lord.*

5 *store:* A storehouse or warehouse. 29 *death's-head:* A skull, reminder of mortality.

GEORGE HERBERT (1593–1633)

The Pulley

1633

When God at first made man,
Having a glass of blessings standing by —
Let us (said he) pour on him all we can;
Let the world's riches, which disperséd lie,
Contract into a span.

So strength first made a way,
Then beauty flowed, then wisdom, honor, pleasure:

When almost all was out, God made a stay,
Perceiving that, alone of all His treasure,
Rest in the bottom lay.

For if I should (said he)
Bestow this jewel also on My creature,
He would adore My gifts instead of Me,
And rest in Nature, not the God of Nature:
So both should losers be.

Yet let him keep the rest,
But keep them with repining restlessness;
Let him be rich and weary, that at least,
If goodness lead him not, yet weariness
May toss him to My breast.

M. CARL HOLMAN (1919–1988)

Mr. Z

1967

Taught early that his mother's skin was the sign of error,
He dressed and spoke the perfect part of honor;
Won scholarships, attended the best schools,
Disclaimed kinship with jazz and spirituals;
Chose prudent, raceless views for each situation,
Or when he could not cleanly skirt dissension,
Faced up to the dilemma, firmly seized
Whatever ground was Anglo-Saxonized.

In diet, too, his practice was exemplary:
Of pork in its profane forms he was wary;
Expert in vintage wines, sauces and salads,
His palate shrank from cornbread, yams and collards.

He was as careful whom he chose to kiss:
His bride had somewhere lost her Jewishness,
But kept her blue eyes; an Episcopalian
Prelate proclaimed them matched chameleon.
Choosing the right addresses, here, abroad,
They shunned those places where they might be barred;
Even less anxious to be asked to dine
Where hosts catered to kosher accent or exotic skin.

And so he climbed, unclogged by ethnic weights,
An airborne plant, flourishing without roots.
Not one false note was struck — until he died:
His subtly grieving widow could have flayed
The obit writers, ringing crude changes on a clumsy phrase:
"One of the most distinguished members of his race."

GERARD MANLEY HOPKINS (1844–1889)

Pied Beauty

1877

Glory be to God for dappled things —
For skies of couple-color as a brinded cow;
For rose-moles all in stipple upon trout that swim;
Fresh-firecoal chestnut-falls;° finches' wings; *fallen chestnut*
Landscape plotted and pieced — fold, fallow, and plow;
And all trades, their gear and tackle and trim.

All things counter, original, spare, strange;
Whatever is fickle, freckled (who knows how?)
With swift, slow; sweet, sour; adazzle, dim;
He fathers-forth whose beauty is past change:
Praise him.

GERARD MANLEY HOPKINS (1844–1889)

Spring and Fall

1880

To a Young Child

Márgarét áre you gríeving
Over Goldengrove unleaving?
Leáves, like the things of man, you
With your fresh thoughts care for, can you?
Áh! ás the heart grows older
It will come to such sights colder
By and by, nor spare a sigh
Though worlds of wanwood° leafmeal° lie;
And yet you wíll weep and know why.
Now no matter, child, the name:
Sórrow's spríngs áre the same.
Nor mouth had, no nor mind, expressed
What heart heard of, ghost° guessed: *soul*
It ís the blight man was born for,
it is Margaret you mourn for.

8 *wanwood:* Gloomy woods; *leafmeal:* Leaves broken up piecemeal.

GERARD MANLEY HOPKINS (1844–1889)

The Windhover° 1877

To Christ Our Lord

I caught this morning morning's minion,° king- *favorite*
    dom of daylight's dauphin, dapple-dawn-drawn Falcon, in his riding
    Of the rolling level underneath him steady air, and striding
High there, how he rung upon the rein of a wimpling wing
In his ecstasy! then off, off forth on swing,
    As a skate's heel sweeps smooth on a bow-bend: the hurl and gliding
    Rebuffed the big wind. My heart in hiding
Stirred for a bird, — the achieve of, the mastery of the thing!

Brute beauty and valour and act, oh, air, pride, plume, here
    Buckle!° AND the fire that breaks from thee then, a billion
Times told lovelier, more dangerous, O my chevalier!

    No wonder of it: shéer plód makes plough down sillion° *furrow*
Shine, and blue-bleak embers, ah my dear,
    Fall, gall themselves, and gash gold-vermilion.

The Windhover: "A name for the kestrel [a kind of small hawk], from its habit of hovering or hanging with its head to the wind" [OED]. 9 *Buckle:* To join, to equip for battle, to crumple.

A. E. HOUSMAN (1859–1936)

Eight O'Clock 1922

He stood, and heard the steeple
    Sprinkle the quarters on the morning town.
One, two, three, four, to market-place and people
    It tossed them down.

Strapped, noosed, nighing his hour,
    He stood and counted them and cursed his luck;
And then the clock collected in the tower
    Its strength, and struck.

A. E. HOUSMAN (1859–1936)

Is my team ploughing 1896

"Is my team ploughing,
    That I was used to drive
And hear the harness jingle
    When I was man alive?"

Ay, the horses trample,
    The harness jingles now;
No change though you lie under
    The land you used to plough.

"Is football playing
    Along the river shore,
With lads to chase the leather,
    Now I stand up no more?"

Ay, the ball is flying,
    The lads play heart and soul;
The goal stands up, the keeper
    Stands up to keep the goal.

"Is my girl happy,
    That I thought hard to leave,
And has she tired of weeping
    As she lies down at eve?"

Ay, she lies down lightly,
    She lies not down to weep:
Your girl is well contented.
    Be still, my lad, and sleep.

"Is my friend hearty,
    Now I am thin and pine,
And has he found to sleep in
    A better bed than mine?"

Yes, lad, I lie easy,
    I lie as lads would choose;
I cheer a dead man's sweetheart,
    Never ask me whose.

A. E. HOUSMAN (1859–1936)

Terence,° this is stupid stuff 1896

"Terence, this is stupid stuff:
You eat your victuals fast enough;
There can't be much amiss, 'tis clear,
To see the rate you drink your beer.
But oh, good Lord, the verse you make,
It gives a chap the belly-ache.
The cow, the old cow, she is dead;
It sleeps well, the hornéd head:
We poor lads, 'tis our turn now

Terence: Housman's name for himself.

To hear such tunes as killed the cow.
Pretty friendship 'tis to rhyme
Your friends to death before their time
Moping melancholy mad:
Come, pipe a tune to dance to, lad."

Why, if 'tis dancing you would be,
There's brisker pipes than poetry.
Say, for what were hop-yards meant,
Or why was Burton built on Trent?°
Oh many a peer of England brews
Livelier liquor than the Muse,
And malt does more than Milton can
To justify God's ways to man.°
Ale, man, ale's the stuff to drink
For fellows whom it hurts to think:
Look into the pewter pot
To see the world as the world's not.
And faith, 'tis pleasant till 'tis past:
The mischief is that 'twill not last.
Oh I have been to Ludlow fair
And left my necktie God knows where,
And carried halfway home, or near,
Pints and quarts of Ludlow beer:
Then the world seemed none so bad,
And I myself a sterling lad;
And down in lovely muck I've lain,
Happy till I woke again.
Then I saw the morning sky:
Heigho, the tale was all a lie;
The world, it was the old world yet,
I was I, my things were wet,
And nothing now remained to do
But begin the game anew.

Therefore, since the world has still
Much good, but much less good than ill,
And while the sun and moon endure
Luck's a chance, but trouble's sure,
I'd face it as a wise man would,
And train for ill and not for good.
'Tis true, the stuff I bring for sale
Is not so brisk a brew as ale:
Out of a stem that scored the hand
I wrung it in a weary land.
But take it: if the smack is sour,
The better for the embittered hour;

18 *Trent:* Burton-on-Trent, an English city famous for its breweries. 22 *To . . . man:* John Milton's (1608–1674) announced purpose in *Paradise Lost.*

It should do good to heart and head
When your soul is in my soul's stead;
And I will friend you, if I may,
In the dark and cloudy day.

There was a king reigned in the East:
There, when kings will sit to feast,
They get their fill before they think
With poisoned meat and poisoned drink.
He gathered all that springs to birth
From the many-venomed earth;
First a little, thence to more,
He sampled all her killing store;
And easy, smiling, seasoned sound,
Sate the king when healths° went round. *toasts*
They put arsenic in his meat
And stared aghast to watch him eat;
They poured strychnine in his cup
And shook to see him drink it up:
They shook, they stared as white's their shirt:
Them it was their poison hurt.
— I tell the tale that I heard told.
Mithridates,° he died old.

76 *Mithridates:* King of Pontus in the first century B.C., who took gradually increasing doses of poison in order to develop a tolerance for them.

A. E. HOUSMAN (1859–1936)

To an Athlete Dying Young 1896

The time you won your town the race
We chaired° you through the marketplace;
Man and boy stood cheering by,
And home we brought you shoulder-high.

Today, the road all runners come,
Shoulder-high we bring you home,
And set you at your threshold down,
Townsman of a stiller town.

Smart lad, to slip betimes away
From fields where glory does not stay,
And early though the laurel° grows
It withers quicker than the rose.

2 *chaired:* Carried on the shoulders in triumphal parade. 11 *laurel:* Flowering shrub traditionally used to fashion wreaths of honor.

Eyes the shady night has shut
Cannot see the record cut,
And silence sounds no worse than cheers
After earth has stopped the ears:

Now you will not swell the rout
Of lads that wore their honors out,
Runners whom renown outran
And the name died before the man.

So set, before its echoes fade,
The fleet foot on the sill of shade,
And hold to the low lintel up
The still-defended challenge-cup.

And round that early-laureled head
Will flock to gaze the strengthless dead,
And find unwithered on its curls
The garland briefer than a girl's.

LANGSTON HUGHES (1902–1967)

Ballad of the Landlord

1951

Landlord, landlord,
My roof has sprung a leak.
Don't you 'member I told you about it
Way last week?

Landlord, landlord,
These steps is broken down.
When you come up yourself
It's a wonder you don't fall down.

Ten Bucks you say I owe you?
Ten Bucks you say is due?
Well, that's Ten Bucks more'n I'll pay you
Till you fix this house up new.

What? You gonna get eviction orders?
You gonna cut off my heat?
You gonna take my furniture and
Throw it in the street?

Um-huh! You talking high and mighty.
Talk on — till you get through.
You ain't gonna be able to say a word
If I land my fist on you.

Police! Police!
Come and get this man!

He's trying to ruin the government
And overturn the land!

Copper's whistle!
Patrol bell!
Arrest.

Precinct Station.
Iron cell.
Headlines in press:

MAN THREATENS LANDLORD
TENANT HELD NO BAIL
JUDGE GIVES NEGRO 90 DAYS IN COUNTY JAIL

LANGSTON HUGHES (1902–1967)

Harlem (A Dream Deferred) 1951

What happens to a dream deferred?

Does it dry up
like a raisin in the sun?
Or fester like a sore —
And then run?
Does it stink like rotten meat?
Or crust and sugar over —
like a syrupy sweet?

Maybe it just sags
like a heavy load.

Or does it explode?

TED HUGHES (b. 1930)

The Thought-Fox 1957

I imagine this midnight moment's forest:
Something else is alive
Beside the clock's loneliness
And this blank page where my fingers move.

Through the window I see no star:
Something more near
Though deeper within darkness
Is entering the loneliness:

Cold, delicately as the dark snow,
A fox's nose touches twig, leaf;

Two eyes serve a movement, that now
And again now, and now, and now

Sets neat prints into the snow
Between trees, and warily a lame
Shadow lags by stump and in hollow
Of a body that is bold to come

Across clearings, an eye,
A widening deepening greenness,
Brilliantly, concentratedly,
Coming about its own business

Till, with sudden sharp hot stink of fox
It enters the dark hole of the head.
The window is starless still; the clock ticks
the page is printed.

RANDALL JARRELL (1914–1965)

The Woman at the Washington Zoo 1960

The saris go by me from the embassies.

Cloth from the moon. Cloth from another planet.
The look back at the leopard like the leopard.

And I. . . .
this print of mine, that has kept its color
Alive through so many cleanings; this dull null
Navy I wear to work, and wear from work, and so
To my bed, so to my grave, with no
Complaints, no comment: neither from my chief,
The Deputy Chief Assistant, nor his chief —
Only I complain. . . . this serviceable
Body that no sunlight dyes, no hand suffuses
But, dome-shadowed, withering among columns,
Wavy beneath fountains — small, far-off, shining
In the eyes of animals, these beings trapped
As I am trapped but not, themselves, the trap,
Aging, but without knowledge of their age,
Kept safe here, knowing not of death, for death —
Oh, bars of my own body, open, open!

The world goes by my cage and never sees me.
And there come not to me, as come to these,
The wild beasts, sparrows pecking the llamas' grain,
Pigeons settling on the bears' bread, buzzards
Tearing the meat the flies have clouded. . . .
Vulture,

When you come for the white rat that the foxes left,
Take off the red helmet of your head, the black
Wings that have shadowed me, and step to me as man:
The wild brother at whose feet the white wolves fawn,
To whose hand of power the great lioness
Stalks, purring. . . .
You know what I was,
You see what I am: change me, change me!

BEN JONSON (1573–1637)

Come, My Celia° 1606

Come, my Celia, let us prove,
While we can, the sports of love;
Time will not be ours forever:
He at length our good will sever.
Spend not, then, his gifts in vain;
Suns that set may rise again,
But if once we lose this light,
'Tis with us perpetual night.
Why should we defer our joys?
Fame and rumor are but toys.
Cannot we delude the eyes
Of a few poor household spies?
Or his easier ears beguile,
Thus removéd by our wile?
'Tis no sin love's fruits to steal,
But the sweet thefts to reveal;
To be taken, to be seen,
These have crimes accounted been.

Come, My Celia: This song from the play *Volpone* is sung by the villain, a would-be sorcerer. Some of the poem derives from Catullus.

X. J. KENNEDY (b. 1929)

In a Prominent Bar in Secaucus One Day 1961

*To the tune of "The Old Orange Flute" or
the tune of "Sweet Betsy from Pike"*

In a prominent bar in Secaucus one day
Rose a lady in skunk with a topheavy sway,
Raised a knobby red finger — all turned from their beer —
While with eyes bright as snowcrust she sang high and clear:

"Now who of you'd think from an eyeload of me
That I once was a lady as proud as could be?
Oh I'd never sit down by a tumbledown drunk
If it wasn't, my dears, for the high cost of junk.

"All the gents used to swear that the white of my calf
Beat the down of a swan by a length and a half.
In the kerchief of linen I caught to my nose
Ah, there never fell snot, but a little gold rose.

"I had seven gold teeth and a toothpick of gold,
My Virginia cheroot was a leaf of it rolled
And I'd light it each time with a thousand in cash —
Why the bums used to fight if I flicked them an ash.

"Once the toast of the Biltmore, the belle of the Taft,
I would drink bottle beer at the Drake, never draft,
And dine at the Astor° on Salisbury steak
With a clean tablecloth for each bite I did take.

"In a car like the Roxy° I'd roll to the track,
A steel-guitar trio, a bar in the back,
And the wheels made no noise, they turned over so fast,
Still it took you ten minutes to see me go past.

"When the horses bowed down to me that I might choose,
I bet on them all, for I hated to lose.
Now I'm saddled each night for my butter and eggs
And the broken threads race down the backs of my legs.

"Let you hold in mind, girls, that your beauty must pass
Like a lovely white clover that rusts with its grass.
Keep your bottoms off barstools and marry you young
Or be left — an old barrel with many a bung.

"For when time takes you out for a spin in his car
You'll be hard-pressed to stop him from going too far
And be left by the roadside, for all your good deeds,
Two toadstools for tits and a face full of weeds."

All the house raised a cheer, but the man at the bar
Made a phonecall and up pulled a red patrol car
And she blew us a kiss as they copped her away
From that prominent bar in Secaucus, N.J.

19 *Astor:* The Biltmore, Taft, Drake, and Astor were elegant hotels in New York City. 21 *Roxy:* A lush New York theater.

ETHERIDGE KNIGHT (b. 1931)

A Watts Mother Mourns While Boiling Beans

The blooming flower of my life is roaming
in the night, and I think surely
that never since he was born
have I been free from fright.
My boy is bold, and his blood
grows quickly hot/ even now
he could be crawling in the street
bleeding out his life, likely as not.
Come home, my bold and restless son. — Stop
my heart's yearning! But I must quit
this thinking — my husband is coming
and the beans are burning.

PHILIP LARKIN (1922–1985)

Church Going 1955

Once I am sure there's nothing going on
I step inside, letting the door thud shut.
Another church: matting, seats, and stone,
And little books; sprawlings of flowers, cut
For Sunday, brownish now; some brass and stuff
Up at the holy end; the small neat organ;
And a tense, musty, unignorable silence,
Brewed God knows how long. Hatless, I take off
My cycle-clips in awkward reverence,

Move forward, run my hand around the font.
From where I stand, the roof looks almost new —
Cleaned, or restored? Someone would know: I don't.
Mounting the lectern, I peruse a few
Hectoring° large-scale verses, and pronounce *intimidating*
"Here endeth" much more loudly than I'd meant.
The echoes snigger briefly. Back at the door
I sign the book, donate an Irish sixpence,
Reflect the place was not worth stopping for.

Yet stop I did: in fact I often do,
And always end much at a loss like this,
Wondering what to look for; wondering, too,
When churches fall completely out of use
What we shall turn them into, if we shall keep
A few cathedrals chronically on show,
Their parchment, plate and pyx in locked cases,

And let the rest rent-free to rain and sheep.
Shall we avoid them as unlucky places?

Or, after dark, will dubious women come
To make their children touch a particular stone;
Pick simples° for a cancer; or on some — *healing herbs*
Advised night see walking a dead one?
Power of some sort or other will go on
In games, in riddles, seemingly at random;
But superstition, like belief, must die,
And what remains when disbelief has gone?
Grass, weedy pavement, brambles, buttress, sky,

A shape less recognizable each week,
A purpose more obscure. I wonder who
Will be the last, the very last, to seek
This place for what it was; one of the crew
That tap and jot and know what rood-lofts° were?
Some ruin-bibber,° randy for antique,
Or Christmas-addict, counting on a whiff
Of gown-and-bands and organ-pipes and myrrh?
Or will he be my representative,

Bored, uninformed, knowing the ghostly silt
Dispersed, yet tending to this cross of ground
Through suburb scrub because it held unspilt
So long and equably what since is found
Only in separation — marriage, and birth,
And death, and thoughts of these — for whom was built
This special shell? For, though I've no idea
What this accoutered frowsty° barn is worth, — *musty*
It pleases me to stand in silence here;

A serious house on serious earth it is,
In whose blent air all our compulsions meet,
Are recognized, and robed as destinies.
And that much never can be obsolete,
Since someone will forever be surprising
A hunger in himself to be more serious,
And gravitating with it to this ground,
Which, he once heard, was proper to grow wise in,
If only that so many dead lie round.

41 *rood-lofts:* Galleries over the rood screen (screen bearing crucifixes) that separates the main body of the church from the choir. 42 *ruin-bibber:* Ruin-consumer; i.e., an avid collector of antiques.

PHILIP LARKIN (1922–1985)

Toads 1955

Why should I let the toad *work*
 Squat on my life?
Can't I use my wit as a pitchfork
 And drive the brute off?

Six days of the week it soils
 With its sickening poison —
Just for paying a few bills!
 That's out of proportion.

Lots of folk live on their wits:
 Lecturers, lispers,
Losels,° loblolly-men,° louts — *losers; clowns*
 They don't end as paupers;

Lots of folk live up lanes
 With fires in a bucket,
Eat windfalls and tinned sardines —
 They seem to like it.

Their nippers° have got bare feet, *children*
 Their unspeakable wives
Are skinny as whippets — and yet
 No one actually *starves.*

Ah, were I courageous enough
 To shout *Stuff your pension!*
But I know, all too well, that's the stuff
 That dreams are made on;

For something sufficiently toad-like
 Squats in me, too;
Its hunkers are heavy as hard luck,
 And cold as snow,

And will never allow me to blarney
 My way to getting
The fame and the girl and the money
 All at one sitting.

I don't say, one bodies the other
 One's spiritual truth;
But I do say it's hard to lose either,
 When you have both.

DENISE LEVERTOV (b. 1923)

The Ache of Marriage

1964

The ache of marriage:

thigh and tongue, beloved,
are heavy with it,
it throbs in the teeth

We look for communion
and are turned away, beloved,
each and each

It is leviathan and we
in its belly°
looking for joy, some joy
not to be known outside it

two by two in the ark of
the ache of it.

8–9 *It is leviathan . . . in its belly:* An allusion to the biblical prophet Jonah, who was swallowed by a great fish but cast up alive on shore three days later. See the Book of Jonah.

AUDRE LORDE (b. 1934)

Hanging Fire

1978

I am fourteen
and my skin has betrayed me
the boy I cannot live without
still sucks his thumb
in secret
how come my knees are
always so ashy
what if I die
before morning
and momma's in the bedroom
with the door closed.

I have to learn how to dance
in time for the next party
my room is too small for me
suppose I die before graduation
they will sing sad melodies
but finally
tell the truth about me
There is nothing I want to do
and too much

that has to be done
and momma's in the bedroom
with the door closed.

Nobody even stops to think
about my side of it
I should have been on Math Team
my marks were better than his
why do I have to be
the one
wearing braces
I have nothing to wear tomorrow
will I live long enough
to grow up
and momma's in the bedroom
with the door closed.

RICHARD LOVELACE (1618–1658)

To Amarantha, That She Would Dishevel Her Hair 1649

Amarantha sweet and fair,
Ah, braid no more that shining hair!
As my curious hand or eye
Hovering round thee, let it fly.

Let it fly as unconfined
As its calm ravisher, the wind,
Who hath left his darling, th' East,
To wanton o'er that spicy nest.

Every tress must be confessed
But neatly tangled at the best,
Like a clue° of golden thread, *ball*
Most excellently raveléd.

Do not then wind up that light
In ribands, and o'ercloud in night;
Like the sun in's early ray,
But shake your head and scatter day.

See, 'tis broke! Within this grove,
The bower and the walks of love,
Weary lie we down and rest
And fan each other's panting breast.

Here we'll strip and cool our fire
In cream below, in milk-baths higher;
And when all wells are drawn dry,
I'll drink a tear out of thine eye.

Which our very joys shall leave,
That sorrows thus we can deceive;
Or our very sorrows weep,
That joys so ripe so little keep.

ROBERT LOWELL (1917–1977)

Mr. Edwards and the Spider°

1946

I saw the spiders marching through the air,
Swimming from tree to tree that mildewed day
In latter August when the hay
Came creaking to the barn. But where
The wind is westerly,
Where gnarled November makes the spiders fly
Into the apparitions of the sky,
They purpose nothing but their ease and die
Urgently beating east to sunrise and the sea;

What are we in the hands of the great God?
It was in vain you set up thorn and briar
In battle array against the fire
And treason crackling in your blood;
For the wild thorns grow tame
And will do nothing to oppose the flame;
Your lacerations tell the losing game
You play against a sickness past your cure.
How will the hands be strong? How will the heart endure?

A very little thing, a little worm,
Or hourglass-blazoned spider, it is said,
Can kill a tiger. Will the dead
Hold up his mirror and affirm
To the four winds the smell
And flash of his authority? It's well
If God who holds you to the pit of hell,
Much as one holds a spider, will destroy,
Baffle and dissipate your soul. As a small boy

On Windsor Marsh, I saw the spider die
When thrown into the bowels of fierce fire:
There's no long struggle, no desire
To get up on its feet and fly —
It stretches out its feet

Mr. Edwards and the Spider: Jonathan Edwards (1703–1758), preacher and Puritan theologian, wrote an essay when he was a boy describing in precise detail the habits of balloon spiders. This poem quotes that essay, as well as Edwards's sermons "Sinners in the Hands of an Angry God" and "The Future Punishment of the Wicked."

And dies. This is the sinner's last retreat;
Yes, and no strength exerted on the heat
Then sinews the abolished will, when sick
And full of burning, it will whistle on a brick.

But who can plumb the sinking of that soul?
Josiah Hawley,° picture yourself cast
Into a brick-kiln where the blast
Fans your quick vitals to a coal —
If measured by a glass
How long would it seem burning! Let there pass
A minute, ten, ten trillion; but the blaze
Is infinite, eternal: this is death,
To die and know it. This is the Black Widow, death.

38 *Josiah Hawley:* A parishioner instrumental in getting Edwards dismissed from his pastorate in Northampton, Massachusetts.

ARCHIBALD MacLEISH (1892–1982)

You, Andrew Marvell 1930

And here face down beneath the sun
And here upon earth's noonward height
To feel the always coming on
The always rising of the night:

To feel creep up the curving east
The earthly chill of dusk and slow
Upon those under lands the vast
And ever-climbing shadow grow

And strange at Ecbatan the trees
Take leaf by leaf the evening strange
The flooding dark about their knees
The mountains over Persia change

And now at Kermanshah the gate
Dark empty and the withered grass
And through the twilight now the late
Few travelers in the westward pass

And Baghdad darken and the bridge
Across the silent river gone
And through Arabia the edge
Of evening widen and steal on

And deepen on Palmyra's street
The wheel rut in the ruined stone
And Lebanon fade out and Crete
High through the clouds and overblown

And over Sicily the air
Still flashing with the landward gulls
And loom and slowly disappear
The sails above the shadowy hulls

And Spain go under and the shore
Of Africa the gilded sand
And evening vanish and no more
The low pale light across that land

Nor now the long light on the sea:
And here face downward in the sun
To feel how swift how secretly
The shadow of the night comes on . . .

CLAUDE McKAY (1890–1948)

America

1922

Although she feeds me bread of bitterness,
And sinks into my throat her tiger's tooth,
Stealing my breath of life, I will confess
I love this cultured hell that tests my youth!
Her vigor flows like tides into my blood,
Giving me strength erect against her hate.
Her bigness sweeps my being like a flood.
Yet as a rebel fronts a king in state,
I stand within her walls with not a shred
Of terror, malice, not a word of jeer.
Darkly I gaze into the days ahead,
And see her might and granite wonders there,
Beneath the touch of Time's unerring hand,
Like priceless treasures sinking in the sand.

CHRISTOPHER MARLOWE (1564–1593)

The Passionate Shepherd to His Love

1599?

Come live with me and be my love,
And we will all the pleasures prove
That valleys, groves, hills, and fields,
Woods, or steepy mountain yields.

And we will sit upon the rocks,
Seeing the shepherds feed their flocks,
By shallow rivers to whose falls
Melodious birds sing madrigals.

And I will make thee beds of roses
And a thousand fragrant posies,
A cap of flowers, and a kirtle
Embroidered all with leaves of myrtle;

A gown made of the finest wool
Which from our pretty lambs we pull;
Fair lined slippers for the cold,
With buckles of the purest gold;

A belt of straw and ivy buds,
With coral clasps and amber studs:
And if these pleasures may thee move,
Come live with me, and be my love.

The shepherd swains shall dance and sing
For thy delight each May morning:
If these delights thy mind may move,
Then live with me and be my love.

ANDREW MARVELL (1621–1678)

The Definition of Love 1681

I
My Love is of a birth as rare
as 'tis for object strange and high:
It was begotten by despair
Upon Impossibility.

II
Magnanimous Despair alone
Could show me so divine a thing,
Where feeble Hope could ne'r have flown
But vainly flapt its Tinsel Wing.

III
And yet I quickly might arrive
Where my extended Soul is fixt,
But Fate does Iron wedges drive,
And alwaies crouds it self betwixt.

IV
For Fate with jealous Eye does see
Two perfect Loves; nor lets them close;
Their union would her ruine be,
And her Tyrannick pow'r depose.

V
And therefore her Decrees of Steel
Us as the distant Poles have plac'd,

(Though Loves whole World on us doth wheel)
Not by themselves to be embrac'd.

VI
Unless the giddy Heaven fall,
And Earth some new Convulsion tear;
And, us to joyn, the World should all
Be cramp'd into a *Planisphere.*°

VII
As Lines so Loves *oblique* may well
Themselves in every Angle greet:
But ours so truly *Paralel,*
Though infinite can never meet.

VIII
Therefore the Love which us doth bind,
But Fate so enviously debarrs,
Is the Conjunction of the Mind,
And Opposition of the Stars.

24 *Planisphere:* A map made by projecting the whole part of a sphere on a plane.

EDNA ST. VINCENT MILLAY (1892–1950)

I Too beneath Your Moon, Almighty Sex 1939

I too beneath your moon, almighty Sex,
Go forth at nightfall crying like a cat,
Leaving the lofty tower I laboured at
For birds to foul and boys and girls to vex
With tittering chalk; and you, and the long necks
Of neighbours sitting where their mothers sat
Are well aware of shadowy this and that
In me, that's neither noble nor complex.
Such as I am, however, I have brought
To what it is, this tower; it is my own;
Though it was reared To Beauty, it was wrought
From what I had to build with: honest bone
Is there, and anguish; pride; and burning thought;
And lust is there, and nights not spent alone.

EDNA ST. VINCENT MILLAY (1892–1950)

What Lips My Lips Have Kissed 1923

What lips my lips have kissed, and where, and why,
I have forgotten, and what arms have lain
Under my head till morning; but the rain

Is full of ghosts tonight, that tap and sigh
Upon the glass and listen for reply,
And in my heart there stirs a quiet pain
For unremembered lads that not again
Will turn to me at midnight with a cry.
Thus in the winter stands the lonely tree,
Nor knows what birds have vanished one by one,
Yet knows its boughs more silent than before:

I only know that summer sang in me
A little while, that in me sings no more.

JOHN MILTON (1608–1674)

Lycidas°

1637

In this monody° the author bewails a learned friend,° unfortunately drowned in his passage from Chester on the Irish Seas, 1637. And by occasion foretells the ruin of our corrupted clergy then in their height.

Yet once more, O ye laurels, and once more,
Ye myrtles brown, with ivy° never sere,
I come to pluck your berries harsh and crude,° *unripened*
And with forced fingers rude
Shatter your leaves before the mellowing year.
Bitter constraint and sad occasion dear
Compels me to disturb your season due;
For Lycidas is dead, dead ere his prime,
Young Lycidas, and hath not left his peer.
Who would not sing for Lycidas? He knew
Himself to sing, and build the lofty rhyme.
He must not float upon his wat'ry bier
Unwept, and welter to the parching wind,
Without the meed of some melodious tear.
   Begin, then, Sisters of the Sacred Well°
That from beneath the seat of Jove° doth spring,
Begin, and somewhat loudly sweep the string.
Hence with denial vain and coy excuse:
So may some gentle Muse
With lucky words favor my destined urn,
And, as he passes, turn,
And bid fair peace be to my sable shroud!

Lycidas: Conventional name for a young shepherd in pastoral poetry. *monody:* A song, usually a lament, sung by a single voice. *Learned friend:* Edward King, poet, scholar, and a candidate for the ministry, who had been with Milton at Cambridge University. 1–2 *laurels, . . . myrtles, . . . ivy:* Traditional materials for poetic garlands. 15 *Sisters of the Sacred Well:* The Muses, goddesses presiding over learning and the creative arts — sources of inspiration. 16 *Jove:* Jupiter, the supreme Roman god.

For we were nursed upon the self-same hill,
Fed the same flocks, by fountain, shade, and rill;
    Together both, ere the high lawns appeared
Under the opening eyelids of the Morn,
We drove a-field, and both together heard
What time the gray-fly winds her sultry horn,
Batt'ning our flocks with the fresh dews of night,
Oft till the star that rose at evening bright
Toward Heav'n's descent had sloped his westering wheel.
Meanwhile the rural ditties were not mute,
Tempered to the oaten flute,
Rough satyrs danced, and fauns with cloven heel
From the glad sound would not be absent long;
And old Damoetas° loved to hear our song.
    But, O the heavy change, now thou art gone,
Now thou art gone, and never must return!
Thee, Shepherd, thee the woods and desert caves,
With wild thyme and the gadding vine o'ergrown,
And all their echoes mourn.
The willows, and hazel copses green,
Shall now no more be seen
Fanning their joyous leaves to thy soft lays.
As killing as the canker to the rose,
Or taint-worm to the weanling herds that graze,
Or frost to flowers, that their gay wardrobe wear
When first the white thorn blows;
Such, Lycidas, thy loss to shepherd's ear.
    Where were ye, Nymphs, when the remorseless deep
Closed o'er the head of your loved Lycidas?
For neither were ye playing on the steep
Where your old bards, the famous Druids,° lie,
Nor on the shaggy top of Mona° high,
Nor yet where Deva° spreads her wizard stream.
Ay me! I fondly dream!
"Had ye been there" — for what could that have done?
What could the Muse herself that Orpheus° bore,
The Muse herself, for her enchanting son,
Whom universal Nature did lament,
When, by the rout that made the hideous roar,
His gory visage down the stream was sent,
Down the swift Hebrus to the Lesbian° shore?

36 *Damoetas:* Conventional pastoral name, perhaps referring to a Cambridge tutor. 53 *Druids:* Poet-priests in pagan Britain. 54 *Mona:* Anglesey, an island off the coast of Wales, was identified as the home of the Druids. 55 *Deva:* The River Dee, which flows between England and Wales. Its changes in course were supposed to foretell shifts in luck between the two countries. 58 *Orpheus:* Son of Apollo and Calliope, Orpheus owed his fame to his great musical talent. Beasts and even trees would follow him to hear him play the lyre and sing. 63 *Hebrus . . . Lesbian:* Thracian women who, maddened by Orpheus's love for his dead wife, Eurydice, tore him to pieces and threw his head and his lyre into the River Hebrus.

Alas! What boots it with uncessant care
To tend the homely, slighted shepherd's trade,
And strictly meditate the thankless Muse?
Where it not better done, as others use,
To sport with Amaryllis in the shade,
Or with the tangles of Neaera's hair?°
Fame is the spur that the clear spirit doth raise
(That last infirmity of noble mind)
To scorn delights and live laborious days;
But the fair guerdon° when we hope to find, *reward*
And think to burst out into sudden blaze,
Comes the blind Fury with th' abhorréd shears,
And slits the thin-spun life.° "But not the praise,"
Phoebus replied, and touched my trembling ears:°
"Fame is no plant that grows on mortal soil,
Nor in the glistering foil,°
Set off to the world, nor in broad rumor° lies, *reputation*
But lives and spreads aloft by those pure eyes
And perfect witness of all-judging Jove;
As he pronounces lastly on each deed,
Of so much fame in Heav'n expect thy meed."
O fountain Arethuse,° and thou honored flood,
Smooth-sliding Mincius,° crowned with vocal reeds,
That strain I heard was of a higher mood:
But now my oat° proceeds, *oaten pipe, hence song*
And listens to the Herald of the Sea,
That came in Neptune's plea.°
He asked the waves, and asked the felon winds,
What hard mishap hath doomed this gentle swain?
And questioned every gust of rugged wings
That blows from off each beakéd promontory:
They knew not of his story;
And sage Hippotades° their answer brings,
That not a blast was from his dungeon strayed:
The air was calm, and on the level brine
Sleek Panope° with all her sisters played.
It was that fatal and perfidious bark,
Built in th' eclipse, and rigged with curses dark,
That sunk so low that sacred head of thine.
Next, Camus,° reverend sire, went footing slow,

68–69 *Amaryllis . . . Neaera:* Pastoral names for shepherdesses. 75–76 *the blind Fury . . . life:* The Furies were avenging deities in Greek and Roman mythology. The Fates spun and finally cut the thread of life. 77 *Phoebus . . . ears:* Phoebus, or Apollo, the Greco-Roman god of the sun and of poetry, touches the poet's ears as if to say "Remember!" 79 *foil:* A thin piece of gold or silver set behind a gem to show it to best advantage. 85 *Arethuse:* A fountain in Sicily near the birthplace of Theocritus, the Greek pastoral poet. 86 *Mincius:* River near Virgil's birthplace in Italy. 89–90 *Herald . . . plea:* Triton, who carried the message that Neptune, Roman god of the sea, was innocent of Lycidas's death. 96 *Hippotades:* Aeolus, the Greek god of the winds. 99 *Panope:* One of the Nereids, or nymphs of the sea. 103 *Camus:* Spirit of the River Cam, representing Cambridge University.

His mantle hairy, and his bonnet sedge,
Inwrought with figures dim, and on the edge
Like to that sanguine flower° inscribed with woe.
"Ah! who hath reft," quoth he, "my dearest pledge?"
Last came, and last did go,
The pilot of the Galilean lake,
Two massy keys he bore of metals twain
(The golden opes, the iron shuts amain).
He shook his mitered locks,° and stern bespake: —
"How well could I have spared for thee, young swain,
Enow of such as for their bellies' sake,
Creep, and intrude, and climb into the fold!
Of other care they little reck'ning make
Than how to scramble at the shearers' feast,
And shove away the worthy bidden guest.
Blind mouths! that scarce themselves know how to hold
A sheep-hook,° or have learned aught else the least
That to the faithful herdsman's art belongs!
What recks it them? What need they? they are sped;° *prosperous*
And, when they list,° their lean and flashy songs *incline*
Grate on their scrannel° pipes of wretched straw; *unmelodious*
The hungry sheep look up, and are not fed,
But, swoll'n with wind and the rank mist they draw,
Rot inwardly, and foul contagion spread;
Besides what the grim wolf° with privy° paw *stealthy*
Daily devours apace, and nothing said;
But that two-handed engine at the door
Stands ready to smite once, and smite no more."°
    Return, Alpheus;° the dread voice is past
That shrunk thy streams; return, Sicilian Muse,°
And call the vales, and bid them hither cast
Their bells and flow'rets of a thousand hues.
Ye valleys low, where the mild whispers use
Of shades, and wanton winds, and gushing brooks,
On whose fresh lap the swart star sparely looks,°
Throw hither all your quaint enameled eyes,
That on the green turf suck the honied showers,
And purple all the ground with vernal flowers.

106 *sanguine flower:* The hyacinth, created from the blood of the youth Hyacinthus by Apollo, who marked the flower with the letters AIAI ("alas, alas") to signify his grief. 109–112 *pilot . . . locks:* St. Peter, who was a fisherman in Galilee, was promised the keys to the kingdom of heaven (Matt. 16:19). He wears the bishop's miter as the first head of the Church. 120 *sheep-hook:* Resembling a bishop's crozier. 128 *grim wolf:* Anti-Protestant forces. 130–131 *two-handed . . . more:* Possibly the two-handed sword of the Archangel Michael, or the punishing sword of the Word of God, seen as a thunderbolt. 132 *Alpheus:* A river god who, pursuing the nymph Arethusa to Sicily, dove under the sea and emerged on the island. Arethusa was turned into a fountain and mingled with Alpheus's waters. 133 *Sicilian Muse:* The one who inspired the Sicilian Theocritus. 138 *swart star sparely looks:* Sirius, the dog star, was thought to turn vegetation black when the star was at its zenith.

Bring the rathe° primrose that forsaken dies, *early*
The tufted crow-toe, and pale jessamine,
The white pink, and the pansy freaked with jet,
The glowing violet,
The musk-rose, and the well-attired woodbine,
With cowslips wan that hang the pensive head,
And every flower that sad embroidery wears;
Bid amaranthus all his beauty shed,
And daffadillies fill their cups with tears,
To strew the laureate hearse where Lycid lies.
For so, to interpose a little ease,
Let our frail thoughts dally with false surmise.°
Ay me! whilst thee the shores and sounding seas
Wash far away, where'er thy bones are hurled;
Whether beyond the stormy Hebrides,
Where thou, perhaps, under the whelming tide
Visit'st the bottom of the monstrous world;
Or whether thou, to our moist vows° denied, *prayers*
Sleep'st by the fable of Bellerus° old,
Where the great Vision of the guarded mount°
Looks toward Namancos and Bayona's hold:°
Look homeward, angel, now, and melt with ruth;° *pity*
And, O ye dolphins,° waft the hapless youth.
    Weep no more, woeful shepherds, weep no more,
For Lycidas, your sorrow, is not dead,
Sunk though he be beneath the wat'ry floor:
So sinks the day-star in the ocean bed
And yet anon repairs his drooping head,
And tricks° his beams, and with new-spangled ore° *dresses; gold*
Flames in the forehead of the morning sky:
So Lycidas sunk low, but mounted high,
Through the dear might of Him that walked the waves,
Where, other groves and other streams along,
With nectar pure his oozy locks he laves,
And hears the unexpressive nuptial song,°
In the blest kingdoms meek of Joy and Love.
There entertain him all the Saints above,
In solemn troops, and sweet societies,
That sing, and singing in their glory move,
And wipe the tears forever from his eyes.
Now, Lycidas, the shepherds weep no more;
Henceforth thou art the Genius° of the shore, *tutelary spirit*
In thy large recompense, and shalt be good

153 *false surmise:* The hope that Lycidas's body could be recovered. 160 *Bellerus:* Legendary giant supposedly buried at Land's End in Cornwall. 161 *guarded mount:* Michael's Mount at the tip of Land's End, guarded by the Archangel Michael. 162 *Namancos and Bayona's hold:* In northwestern Spain. 164 *dolphins:* According to Greek legend, dolphins carry the spirits of the dead to the Blessed Isles. 176 *nuptial song:* Perhaps the song sung at the "marriage supper of the Lamb" (Rev. 19:9).

To all that wander in that perilous flood.

Thus sang the uncouth° swain to th' oaks and rills, *unlettered*
While the still Morn went out with sandals gray;
He touched the tender stops of various quills,°
With eager thought warbling his Doric lay:° *pastoral poem*
And now the sun had stretched out all the hills,
And now was dropped into the western bay.
At last he rose, and twitched° his mantle blue: *put on*
Tomorrow to fresh woods and pastures new.

188 *quills:* Reeds of a Pan's pipe.

JOHN MILTON (1608–1674)

On the Late Massacre in Piedmont° 1655

Avenge, O Lord, thy slaughtered saints, whose bones
Lie scattered on the Alpine mountains cold;
Even them who kept thy truth so pure of old,
When all our fathers worshiped stocks and stones,°
Forget not: in thy book record their groans
Who were thy sheep, and in their ancient fold
Slain by the bloody Piedmontese, that rolled
Mother with infant down the rocks.° Their moans
The vales redoubled to the hills, and they
To heaven. Their martyred blood and ashes sow
O'er all the Italian fields, where still doth sway
The triple Tyrant;° that from these may grow
A hundredfold, who, having learnt thy way,
Early may fly the Babylonian woe.°

On the Late Massacre . . . : Milton's protest against the treatment of the Waldenses, members of a Puritan sect living in Piedmont, was not limited to this sonnet. It is thought that he wrote Cromwell's appeals to the duke of Savoy and to others to end the persecution. 4 *When . . . stones:* In Milton's Protestant view, English Catholics had worshipped their stone and wooden statues in the twelfth century, when the Waldensian sect was formed. 5–8 *in thy book . . . rocks:* On Easter Day, 1655, 1,700 members of the Waldensian sect were massacred in Piedmont by the duke of Savoy's forces. 12 *triple Tyrant:* The Pope, with his three-crowned tiara, has authority on earth and in Heaven and Hell. 14 *Babylonian woe:* The destruction of Babylon, symbol of vice and corruption, at the end of the world (see Rev. 17–18). Protestants interpreted the "Whore of Babylon" as the Roman Catholic Church.

JOHN MILTON (1608–1674)

When I consider how my light is spent 1655?

When I consider how my light is spent,°
Ere half my days in this dark world and wide,
And that one talent° which is death to hide
Lodged with me useless, though my soul more bent
To serve therewith my Maker, and present
My true account, lest He returning chide;
"Doth God exact day-labor, light denied?"
I fondly° ask. But Patience, to prevent *foolishly*
That murmur, soon replies, "God doth not need
Either man's work or His own gifts. Who best
Bear His mild yoke, they serve Him best. His state
Is kingly: thousands at His bidding speed,
And post o'er land and ocean without rest;
They also serve who only stand and wait."

1 *how my light is spent:* Milton had been totally blind since 1651. 3 *that one talent:* Refers to Jesus's parable of the talents (units of money), in which a servant entrusted with a talent buries it rather than invests it, and is punished upon his master's return (Matt. 25:14–30).

MARIANNE MOORE (1887–1972)

Poetry 1921

I, too, dislike it: there are things that are important beyond all this fiddle.
Reading it, however, with a perfect contempt for it, one discovers in it
after all, a place for the genuine.
Hands that can grasp, eyes
that can dilate, hair that can rise
if it must, these things are important not because a

high-sounding interpretation can be put upon them but because they are
useful. When they become so derivative as to become unintelligible,
the same thing may be said for all of us, that we
do not admire what
we cannot understand: the bat
holding on upside down or in quest of something to

eat, elephants pushing, a wild horse taking a roll, a tireless wolf under
a tree, the immovable critic twitching his skin like a horse that feels a
flea, the base-
ball fan, the statistician —
nor is it valid
to discriminate against "business documents and

school-books"; all these phenomena are important. One must make a distinction

however: when dragged into prominence by half poets, the result is not
poetry,
nor till the poets among us can be
"literalists of
the imagination" — above
insolence and triviality and can present

for inspection, "imaginary gardens with real toads in them," shall we have
it. In the meantime, if you demand on the one hand,
the raw material of poetry in
all its rawness and
that which is on the other hand
genuine, you are interested in poetry.

OGDEN NASH (1902–1971)

Very Like a Whale° 1934

One thing that literature would be greatly the better for
Would be a more restricted employment by authors of simile and metaphor.
Authors of all races, be they Greeks, Romans, Teutons or Celts,
Can't seem just to say that anything is the thing it is but have to go out of their way to say that it is like something else.
What does it mean when we are told
That the Assryian came down like a wolf on the fold?
In the first place, George Gordon Byron had had enough experience
To know that it probably wasn't just one Assyrian, it was a lot of Assyrians.°
However, as too many arguments are apt to induce apoplexy and thus hinder longevity,
We'll let it pass as one Assyrian for the sake of brevity.
Now then, this particular Assyrian, the one whose cohorts were gleaming in purple and gold,
Just what does the poet mean when he says he came down like a wolf on the fold?
In heaven and earth more than is dreamed of in our philosophy there are a great many things,
But I don't imagine that among them there is a wolf with purple and gold cohorts or purple and gold anythings.
No, no, Lord Byron, before I'll believe that this Assyrian was actually like a wolf I must have some kind of proof;
Did he run on all fours and did he have a hairy tail and a big red mouth and big white teeth and did he say Woof woof woof?

Very Like a Whale: Polonius's response to Hamlet's assertion that a cloud was shaped like a whale (III.ii). To humor the supposedly mad prince, Polonius will agree to anything at all. 8 *To . . . Assyrians:* A reference to Lord Byron's "The Destruction of Sennacherib," which recounts the event described in 2 Kings 19:35.

Frankly I think it very unlikely, and all you were entitled to say, at the very most,
Was that the Assyrian cohorts came down like a lot of Assyrian cohorts about to destroy the Hebrew host.
But that wasn't fancy enough for Lord Byron, oh dear me no, he had to invent a lot of figures of speech and then interpolate them,
With the result that whenever you mention Old Testament soldiers to people they say Oh yes, they're the ones that a lot of wolves dressed up in gold and purple ate them.
That's the kind of thing that's being done all the time by poets, from Homer to Tennyson;
They're always comparing ladies to lilies and veal to venison.
How about the man who wrote,
Her little feet stole in and out like mice beneath her petticoat?
Wouldn't anybody but a poet think twice
Before stating that his girl's feet were mice?
Then they always say things like that after a winter storm
The snow is a white blanket. Oh it is, is it, all right then, you sleep under a six-inch blanket of snow and I'll sleep under a half-inch blanket of unpoetical blanket material and we'll see which one keeps warm,
And after that maybe you'll begin to comprehend dimly
What I mean by too much metaphor and simile.

HOWARD NEMEROV (b. 1920)

Life Cycle of Common Man 1960

Roughly figured, this man of moderate habits,
This average consumer of the middle class,
Consumed in the course of his average life span
Just under half a million cigarettes,
Four thousand fifths of gin and about
A quarter as much vermouth; he drank
Maybe a hundred thousand cups of coffee,
And counting his parents' share it cost
Something like half a million dollars
To put him through life. How many beasts
Died to provide him with meat, belt and shoes
Cannot be certainly said.
                    But anyhow,
It is in this way that a man travels through time,
Leaving behind him a lengthening trail
Of empty bottles and bones, of broken shoes,
Frayed collars and worn out or outgrown
Diapers and dinnerjackets, silk ties and slickers.

Given the energy and security thus achieved,
He did . . . ? What? The usual things, of course,

The eating, dreaming, drinking and begetting,
And he worked for the money which was to pay
For the eating, et cetera, which were necessary
If he were to go on working for the money, et cetera,
But chiefly he talked. As the bottles and bones
Accumulated behind him, the words proceeded
Steadily from the front of his face as he
Advanced into the silence and made it verbal.
Who can tally the tale of his words? A lifetime
Would barely suffice for their repetition;
If you merely printed all his commas the result
Would be a very large volume, and the number of times
He said "thank you" or "very little sugar, please,"
Would stagger the imagination. There were also
Witticisms, platitudes, and statements beginning
"It seems to me" or "As I always say."

Consider the courage in all that, and behold the man
Walking into deep silence, with the ectoplastic
Cartoon's balloon of speech proceeding
Steadily out of the front of his face, the words
Borne along on the breath which is his spirit
Telling the numberless tale of his untold Word°
Which makes the world his apple, and forces him to eat.

42 *Word:* Logos, the controlling principle of the universe.

FRANK O'HARA (1926–1966)

Ave Maria° 1960

Mothers of America
let your kids go to the movies!
get them out of the house so they won't know what you're up to
it's true that fresh air is good for the body
but what about the soul
that grows in darkness, embossed by silvery images
and when you grow old as grow old you must
they won't hate you
they won't criticize you they won't know
they'll be in some glamorous country
they first saw on a Saturday afternoon or playing hookey

they may even be grateful to you
for their first sexual experience
which only cost you a quarter

Ave Maria: The Catholic prayer Hail Mary, here referred to ironically.

and didn't upset the peaceful home
they will know where candy bars come from
and gratuitous bags of popcorn
as gratuitous as leaving the movie before it's over
with a pleasant stranger whose apartment is in the Heaven on Earth Bldg
near the Williamsburg Bridge°
oh mothers you will have made the little tykes
so happy because if nobody does pick them up in the movies
they won't know the difference
and if somebody does it'll be sheer gravy
and they'll have been truly entertained either way
instead of hanging around the yard
or up in their room
hating you
prematurely since you won't have done anything horribly mean yet
except keeping them from the darker joys
it's unforgivable the latter
so don't blame me if you won't take this advice
and the family breaks up
and your children grow old and blind in front of a TV set
seeing
movies you wouldn't let them see when they were young

20 *Williamsburg Bridge:* Links lower Manhattan and Brooklyn, New York.

SIMON J. ORTIZ (b. 1941)
When It Was Taking Place 1977

This morning, the sun has risen
already to the midpoint of where
it will be at the center of the day.
The old man, Amado Quintana,
doesn't get up early anymore.
He still wakes early in the morning
but he can't see the clear things
in the dim light before the sun rises,
and he can't hear the clear sounds.
So he lies on his cot or he sits
in the wooden chair by the stove.
Sometimes he forgets he has not built
the fire in the stove and he wonders
why the weather has changed so early.

He is an old man.
The people in the village
call him Old Man Humped Back.
He has a hump on his back,

and the history about that
is he has lived a long time
and it has grown on him.

This morning at this moment,
Quintana is pointing to the river
below the hill on which he
and his grandson are standing.
He made his grandson help him
climb unto the hill and now
he is showing him the river
and the land before them.
The hill is not very high
and children climb it
to explore and look for things,
but from there you can see
the fields and the canals.

The old man cannot really see
those anymore; his eyes are cloudy
with a gray covering; the only thing
he can see is the sun when it is
at its brightest. Sometimes
he forgets, and he asks why
the weather has changed suddenly
and insists that it must be the times
and the people that are the cause.
But he can see in his mind,
and he tells his grandson,
"You can see that canal that runs
from that gathering of cottonwoods
and then turns to the south
by Faustin's field, that canal
was dug by the first people
who came down from the Old Place.
It was dug then."

He had been a child then,
and he played most of the time,
but he can remember his father
and the others with him.
They dug the canal from the river
to the east and turned to the south,
and then it was easier
as the ground was softer
and the water found its own way.
They had worked and it was good.
They had talked a lot, laughed,
and they got so wearied.
At the end of the day, the men

drug themselves home,
and Amado can remember carrying
his father's handmade shovel
in his hands, and they would be
greeted at their home by his mother.
She would say, "Amo, my partner
and my son, have you worked so hard,"
and she would grab them and hold them
strongly to her.
She would especially make a fuss
over Amado, who, at the time,
was their only child.
At that time, they lived in a low
windcarved cave with a wall of stones
along the front of it.

Amado Quintana can see that,
and he points it all out to his grandson,
and he wants him to see all those things,
and he tells the boy, "I was your age then
when it was taking place."

WILFRED OWEN (1893–1918)

Anthem for Doomed Youth 1917

What passing-bells for these who die as cattle?
Only the monstrous anger of the guns.
Only the stuttering rifles' rapid rattle
Can patter out their hasty orisons.
No mockeries now for them; no prayers nor bells,
Nor any voice of mourning save the choirs, —
The shrill, demented choirs of wailing shells;
And bugles calling for them from sad shires.
What candles may be held to speed them all?
Not in the hands of boys, but in their eyes
Shall shine the holy glimmers of good-byes.
The pallor of girls' brows shall be their pall;
Their flowers the tenderness of patient minds,
And each slow dusk a drawing-down of blinds.

SYLVIA PLATH (1932–1963)

Daddy

1962

You do not do, you do not do
Any more, black shoe
In which I have lived like a foot
For thirty years, poor and white,
Barely daring to breathe or Achoo.

Daddy, I have had to kill you.
You died before I had time——
Marble-heavy, a bag full of God,
Ghastly statue with one gray toe
Big as a Frisco seal

And a head in the freakish Atlantic
Where it pours bean green over blue
In the waters off beautiful Nauset.° *Cape Cod inlet*
I used to pray to recover you.
Ach, du.° *Oh, you*

In the German tongue, in the Polish Town°
Scraped flat by the roller
Of wars, wars, wars.
But the name of the town is common.
My Polack friend

Says there are a dozen or two.
So I never could tell where you
Put your foot, your root,
I never could talk to you.
The tongue stuck in my jaw.

It stuck in a barb wire snare.
Ich, ich, ich, ich,° *I, I, I, I*
I could hardly speak.
I thought every German was you.
And the language obscene

An engine, an engine
Chuffing me off like a Jew.
A Jew to Dachau, Auschwitz, Belsen.°
I began to talk like a Jew.
I think I may well be a Jew.

The snows of the Tyrol, the clear beer of Vienna
Are not very pure or true.
With my gypsy-ancestress and my weird luck

16 *Polish town:* Refers to Otto Plath's birthplace, Granbow. 33 *Dachau . . . Belsen:* Nazi death camps in World War II.

And my Taroc° pack and my Taroc pack
I may be a bit of a Jew.

I have always been scared of *you,*
With your Luftwaffe,° your gobbledygoo.
And your neat mustache
And your Aryan eye, bright blue.
Panzer-man, panzer-man,° O You —

Not God but a swastika
So black no sky could squeak through.
Every woman adores a Fascist,
The boot in the face, the brute
Brute heart of a brute like you.

You stand at the blackboard, daddy,
In the picture I have of you,
A cleft in your chin instead of your foot
But no less a devil for that, no not
Any less the black man who

Bit my pretty red heart in two.
I was ten when they buried you.
At twenty I tried to die
And get back, back, back to you.
I thought even the bones would do

But they pulled me out of the sack,
And they stuck me together with glue.
And then I knew what to do.
I made a model of you,
A man in black with a Meinkampf° look

And a love of the rack and the screw.
And I said I do, I do.
So daddy, I'm finally through.
The black telephone's off at the root,
The voices just can't worm through.

If I've killed one man, I've killed two ——
The vampire who said he was you
And drank my blood for a year,
Seven years, if you want to know.
Daddy, you can lie back now.

There's a stake in your fat black heart

39 *Taroc:* Or *Tarot,* a pack of cards used to tell fortunes. It is said to have originated among the early Jewish Cabalists, and to have been transmitted to European Gypsies during the Middle Ages. 42 *Luftwaffe:* World War II German air force. 45 *panzer-man:* A member of the panzer division of the German army in World War II, which used armored vehicles and was organized for rapid attack. 65 *Meinkampf:* An allusion to Hitler's autobiography *(My Struggle).*

And the villagers never like you.
They are dancing and stamping on you.
They always *knew* it was you.
Daddy, daddy, you bastard, I'm through.

SYLVIA PLATH (1932–1963)
Metaphors

1960

I'm a riddle in nine syllables,
An elephant, a ponderous house,
A melon strolling on two tendrils.
O red fruit, ivory, fine timbers!
This loaf's big with its yeasty rising.
Money's new-minted in this fat purse.
I'm a means, a stage, a cow in calf.
I've eaten a bag of green apples,
Boarded the train there's no getting off.

SYLVIA PLATH (1932–1963)
Morning Song

1961

Love set you going like a fat gold watch.
The midwife slapped your footsoles, and your bald cry
Took its place among the elements.

Our voices echo, magnifying your arrival. New statue.
In a drafty museum, your nakedness
Shadows our safety. We stand round blankly as walls.

I'm no more your mother
Than the cloud that distils a mirror to reflect its own slow
Effacement at the wind's hand.

All night your moth-breath
Flickers among the flat pink roses. I wake to listen:
A far sea moves in my ear.

One cry, and I stumble from bed, cow-heavy and floral
In my Victorian nightgown.
Your mouth opens clean as a cat's. The window square

Whitens and swallows its dull stars. And now you try
Your handful of notes;
The clear vowels rise like balloons.

EZRA POUND (1885–1972)

In a Station of the Metro° 1913

The apparition of these faces in the crowd;
Petals on a wet, black bough.

Metro: Undergound railroad in Paris.

EZRA POUND (1885–1972)

Portrait d'une Femme° 1912

Your mind and you are our Sargasso Sea,°
London has swept about you this score years
And bright ships left you this or that in fee:
Ideas, old gossip, oddments of all things,
Strange spars of knowledge and dimmed wares of price.
Great minds have sought you — lacking someone else.
You have been second always. Tragical?
No. You preferred it to the usual thing:
One dull man, dulling and uxorious,
One average mind — with one thought less, each year.
Oh, you are patient, I have seen you sit
Hours, where something might have floated up.
And now you pay one. Yes, you richly pay.
You are a person of some interest, one comes to you
And takes strange gain away:
Trophies fished up; some curious suggestion;
Fact that leads nowhere; and a tale or two,
Pregnant with mandrakes,° or with something else
That might prove useful and yet never proves,
That never fits a corner or shows use,
Or finds its hour upon the loom of days:
The tarnished, gaudy, wonderful old work;
Idols and ambergris and rare inlays,
These are your riches, your great store; and yet
For all this sea-hoard of deciduous things,
Strange woods half sodden, and new brighter stuff:
In the slow float of differing light and deep,
No! there is nothing! In the whole and all,
Nothing that's quite your own.
Yet this is you.

Portrait d'une Femme: Portrait of a woman. 1 *Sargasso Sea:* Part of the Atlantic Ocean east of the southern United States and north of the West Indies. It is very still and covered with sargassum, a large spreading seaweed. 18 *mandrakes:* A plant with a phallus-shaped root that, according to superstition, could conceive a child in a woman.

EZRA POUND (1885–1972)
The River-Merchant's Wife: A Letter° 1915

While my hair was still cut straight across my forehead
I played about the front gate, pulling flowers.
You came by on bamboo stilts, playing horse,
You walked about my seat, playing with blue plums.
And we went on living in the village of Chokan:
Two small people, without dislike or suspicion.
At fourteen I married My Lord you.
I never laughed, being bashful.
Lowering my head, I looked at the wall.
Called to, a thousand times, I never looked back.

At fifteen I stopped scowling,
I desired my dust to be mingled with yours
Forever and forever and forever.
Why should I climb the lookout?

At sixteen you departed,
You went into far Ku-to-yen, by the river of swirling eddies,
And you have been gone five months.
The monkeys make sorrowful noise overhead.

You dragged your feet when you went out.
By the gate now, the moss is grown, the different mosses,
Too deep to clear them away!
The leaves fall early this autumn, in wind.
The paired butterflies are already yellow with August
Over the grass in the West garden;
They hurt me. I grow older.
If you are coming down through the narrows of the river Kiang,
Please let me know before hand,
And I will come out to meet you
    As far as Cho-fu-sa.

The River-Merchant's Wife: A Letter: A free translation of a poem by Li Po (Chinese, 701–762).

SIR WALTER RALEIGH (1554–1618)
The Nymph's Reply to the Shepherd 1600

If all the world and love were young,
And truth in every shepherd's tongue,
These pretty pleasures might me move
To live with thee and be thy love.

Time drives the flocks from field to fold,
When rivers rage, and rocks grow cold,

And Philomel° becometh dumb;
The rest complain of cares to come.

The flowers do fade, and wanton fields
To wayward winter reckoning yields:
A honey tongue, a heart of gall,
Is fancy's spring, but sorrow's fall.

Thy gowns, thy shoes, thy beds of roses,
Thy cap, thy kirtle, and thy posies
Soon break, soon wither, soon forgotten;
In folly ripe, in reason rotten.

Thy belt of straw and ivy buds,
Thy coral clasps and amber studs,
All these in me no means can move
To come to thee and be thy love.

But could youth last, and love still breed,
Had joys no date, nor age no need,
Then these delights my mind might move
To live with thee and be thy love.

7 *Philomel:* In Greek mythology, a Greek princess who was changed to a nightingale.

DUDLEY RANDALL (b. 1914)

Ballad of Birmingham 1969

(On the bombing of a church in Birmingham, Alabama, 1963)

"Mother dear, may I go downtown
Instead of out to play,
And march the streets of Birmingham
In a Freedom March today?"

"No, baby, no, you may not go,
For the dogs are fierce and wild,
And clubs and hoses, guns and jails
Aren't good for a little child."

"But, mother, I won't be alone.
Other children will go with me,
And march the streets of Birmingham
To make our country free."

"No, baby, no, you may not go,
For I fear those guns will fire.
But you may go to church instead
And sing in the children's choir."

She has combed and brushed her night-dark hair,
And bathed rose petal sweet.

And drawn white gloves on her small brown hands,
And white shoes on her feet.

The mother smiled to know her child
Was in the sacred place,
But that smile was the last smile
To come upon her face.

For when she heard the explosion,
Her eyes grew wet and wild.
She raced through the streets of Birmingham
Calling for her child.

She clawed through bits of glass and brick,
Then lifted out a shoe.
"Oh, here's the shoe my baby wore,
But, baby, where are you?"

JOHN CROWE RANSOM (1888–1974)

Bells for John Whiteside's Daughter 1924

There was such speed in her little body,
And such lightness in her footfall,
It is no wonder her brown study°
Astonishes us all.

Her wars were bruited in our high window.
We looked among orchard trees and beyond
Where she took arms against her shadow,
Or harried unto the pond

The lazy geese, like a snow cloud
Dripping their snow on the green grass,
Tricking and stopping, sleepy and proud,
Who cried in goose, Alas,

For the tireless heart within the little
Lady with rod that made them rise
From their noon apple-dreams and scuttle
Goose-fashion under the skies!

But now go the bells, and we are ready,
In one house we are sternly stopped
To say we are vexed at her brown study,
Lying so primly propped.

3 *brown study:* A state of mental abstraction.

ADRIENNE RICH (b. 1929)

Diving into the Wreck

1972

First having read the book of myths,
and loaded the camera,
and checked the edge of the knife-blade,
I put on
the body-armor of black rubber
the absurd flippers
the grave and awkward mask.
I am having to do this
not like Cousteau° with his
assiduous team
aboard the sun-flooded schooner
but here alone.

There is a ladder.
The ladder is always there
hanging innocently
close to the side of the schooner.
We know what it is for,
we who have used it.
Otherwise
it's a piece of maritime floss
some sundry equipment.

I go down.
Rung after rung and still
the oxygen immerses me
the blue light
the clear atoms
of our human air.
I go down.
My flippers cripple me,
I crawl like an insect down the ladder
and there is no one
to tell me when the ocean
will begin.

First the air is blue and then
it is bluer and then green and then
black I am blacking out and yet
my mask is powerful
it pumps my blood with power
the sea is another story
the sea is not a question of power

9 *Cousteau:* Jacques-Yves Cousteau (b. 1910), French oceanographer who has made many popular documentary films of his underwater adventures.

I have to learn alone
to turn my body without force
in the deep element.

And now: it is easy to forget
what I came for
among so many who have always
lived here
swaying their crenellated fans
between the reefs
and besides
you breathe differently down here.

I came to explore the wreck.
The words are purposes.
The words are maps.
I came to see the damage that was done
and the treasures that prevail.
I stroke the beam of my lamp
slowly along the flank
of something more permanent
than fish or weed

the thing I came for:
the wreck and not the story of the wreck
the thing itself and not the myth
the drowned face always staring
toward the sun
the evidence of damage
worn by salt and sway into this threadbare beauty
the ribs of the disaster
curving their assertion
among the tentative haunters.

This is the place.
And I am here, the mermaid whose dark hair
streams black, the merman in his armored body
We circle silently
about the wreck
we dive into the hold.
I am she: I am he

whose drowned face sleeps with open eyes
whose breasts still bear the stress
whose silver, copper, vermeil cargo lies
obscurely inside barrels
half-wedged and left to rot
we are the half-destroyed instruments
that once held to a course
the water-eaten log
the fouled compass

We are, I am, you are
by cowardice or courage
the one who find our way
back to this scene
carrying a knife, a camera
a book of myths
in which
our names do not appear.

ADRIENNE RICH (b. 1929)

Living in Sin

1955

She had thought the studio would keep itself,
no dust upon the furniture of love.
Half heresy, to wish the taps less vocal,
the panes relieved of grime. A plate of pears,
a piano with a Persian shawl, a cat
stalking the picturesque amusing mouse
had risen at his urging.
Not that at five each separate stair would writhe
under the milkman's tramp; that morning light
so coldly would delineate the scraps
of last night's cheese and three sepulchral bottles;
that on the kitchen shelf among the saucers
a pair of beetle-eyes would fix her own —
envoy from some black village in the mouldings . . .
Meanwhile, he, with a yawn,
sounded a dozen notes upon the keyboard,
declared it out of tune, shrugged at the mirror,
rubbed at his beard, went out for cigarettes;
while she, jeered by the minor demons,
pulled back the sheets and made the bed and found
a towel to dust the table-top,
and let the coffee-pot boil over on the stove.
By evening she was back in love again,
though not so wholly but throughout the night
she woke sometimes to feel the daylight coming
like a relentless milkman up the stairs.

ADRIENNE RICH (b. 1929)

Rape

1972

There is a cop who is both prowler and father:
he comes from your block, grew up with your brothers,

had certain ideals.
You hardly know him in his boots and silver badge,
on horseback, one hand touching his gun.

You hardly know him but you have to get to know him:
he has access to machinery that could kill you.
He and his stallion clop like warlords among the trash,
his ideals stand in the air, a frozen cloud
from between his unsmiling lips.

And so, when the time comes, you have to turn to him,
the maniac's sperm still greasing your thighs,
your mind whirling like crazy. You have to confess
to him, you are guilty of the crime
of having been forced.

And you see his blue eyes, the blue eyes of all the family
whom you used to know, grow narrow and glisten,
his hand types out the details
and he wants them all
but the hysteria in your voice pleases him best.

You hardly know him but now he thinks he knows you:
he has taken down your worst moment
on a machine and filed it in a file.
He knows, or thinks he knows, how much you imagined;
he knows, or thinks he knows, what you secretly wanted.

He has access to machinery that could get you put away;
and if, in the sickening light of the precinct,
and if, in the sickening light of the precinct,
your details sound like a portrait of your confessor,
will you swallow, will you deny them, will you lie your way home?

EDWIN ARLINGTON ROBINSON (1869–1935)

Mr. Flood's Party 1921

Old Eben Flood, climbing alone one night
Over the hill between the town below
And the forsaken upland hermitage
That held as much as he should ever know
On earth again of home, paused warily.
The road was his and not a native near;
And Eben, having leisure, said aloud,
For no man else in Tilbury Town to hear:

"Well, Mr. Flood, we have the harvest moon
Again, and we may not have many more;

The bird is on the wing, the poet says,°
And you and I have said it here before.
Drink to the bird." He raised up to the light
The jug that he had gone so far to fill,
And answered huskily: "Well, Mr. Flood,
Since you propose it, I believe I will."

Alone, as if enduring to the end
A valiant armor of scarred hopes outworn,
He stood there in the middle of the road
Like Roland's ghost winding a silent horn.°
Below him, in the town among the trees,
Where friends of other days had honored him,
A phantom salutation of the dead
Rang thinly till old Eben's eyes were dim.

Then, as a mother lays her sleeping child
Down tenderly, fearing it may awake,
He set the jug down slowly at his feet
With trembling care, knowing that most things break;
And only when assured that on firm earth
It stood, as the uncertain lives of men
Assuredly did not, he paced away,
And with his hand extended paused again:

"Well, Mr. Flood, we have not met like this
In a long time; and many a change has come
To both of us, I fear, since last it was
We had a drop together. Welcome home!"
Convivially returning with himself,
Again he raised the jug up to the light;
And with an acquiescent quaver said:
"Well, Mr. Flood, if you insist, I might.

"Only a very little, Mr. Flood —
For auld lang syne. No more, sir; that will do."
So, for the time, apparently it did,
And Eben evidently thought so too;
For soon amid the silver loneliness
Of night he lifted up his voice and sang,
Secure, with only two moons listening,
Until the whole harmonious landscape rang —

"For auld lang syne." The weary throat gave out,
The last word wavered, and the song being done.
He raised again the jug regretfully
And shook his head, and was again alone.

11 *The bird . . . says:* Edward Fitzgerald says this of the "Bird of Time" in "The Rubáiyát of Omar Khayyám." 20 *Like Roland's . . . horn:* Roland, hero of French romance, blew his ivory horn to warn his allies of impending attack.

There was not much that was ahead of him,
And there was nothing in the town below —
Where strangers would have shut the many doors
That many friends had opened long ago.

EDWIN ARLINGTON ROBINSON (1869–1935)

New England 1920

Here where the wind is always north-north-east
And children learn to walk on frozen toes,
Wonder begets an envy of all those
Who boil elsewhere with such a lyric yeast
Of love that you will hear them at a feast
Where demons would appeal for some repose,
Still clamoring where the chalice overflows
And crying wildest who have drunk the least.

Passion is here a soilure of the wits,
We're told, and Love a cross for them to bear;
Joy shivers in the corner where she knits
And Conscience always has the rocking-chair,
Cheerful as when she tortured into fits
The first cat that was ever killed by Care.

THEODORE ROETHKE (1908–1963)

I Knew a Woman 1958

I knew a woman, lovely in her bones,
When small birds sighed, she would sigh back at them;
Ah, when she moved, she moved more ways than one:
The shapes a bright container can contain!
Of her choice virtues only gods should speak,
Or English poets who grew up on Greek
(I'd have them sing in chorus, cheek to cheek).

How well her wishes went! She stroked my chin,
She taught me Turn, and Counter-turn, and Stand;°
She taught me Touch, that undulant white skin;
I nibbled meekly from her proffered hand;
She was the sickle; I, poor I, the rake,
Coming behind her for her pretty sake
(But what prodigious mowing we did make).

9 *Turn . . . Stand:* Parts of a Pindaric ode.

Love likes a gander, and adores a goose:
Her full lips pursed, the errant note to seize;
She played it quick, she played it light and loose;
My eyes, they dazzled at her flowing knees;
Her several parts could keep a pure repose,
Or one hip quiver with a mobile nose
(She moved in circles, and those circles moved).

Let seed be grass, and grass turn into hay:
I'm martyr to a motion not my own;
What's freedom for? To know eternity.
I swear she cast a shadow white as stone.
But who would count eternity in days?
These old bones live to learn her wanton ways:
(I measure time by how a body sways).

CHRISTINA ROSSETTI (1830–1894)

Uphill 1861

Does the road wind uphill all the way?
    Yes, to the very end.
Will the day's journey take the whole long day?
    From morn to night, my friend.

But is there for the night a resting place?
    A roof for when the slow dark hours begin.
May not the darkness hide it from my face?
    You cannot miss that inn.

Shall I meet other wayfarers at night?
    Those who have gone before.
Then must I knock, or call when just in sight?
    They will not keep you standing at that door.

Shall I find comfort, travel-sore and weak?
    Of labor you shall find the sum.
Will there be beds for me and all who seek?
    Yea, beds for all who come.

DELMORE SCHWARTZ (1913–1966)

The True-Blue American 1959

Jeremiah Dickson was a true-blue American,
For he was a little boy who understood America, for he felt that he must
Think about *everything;* because that's *all* there is to think about,

Knowing immediately the intimacy of truth and comedy,
Knowing intuitively how a sense of humor was a necessity
For one and for all who live in America. Thus, natively, and
Naturally when on an April Sunday in an ice cream parlor Jeremiah
Was requested to choose between a chocolate sundae and a banana split
He answered unhesitatingly, having no need to think of it
Being a true-blue American, determined to continue as he began:
Rejecting the either-or of Kierkegaard,° and many another European;
Refusing to accept alternatives, refusing to believe the choice of between;
Rejecting selection; denying dilemma; electing absolute affirmation:
    knowing
        in his breast
            The infinite and the gold
            Of the endless frontier, the deathless West.

"Both: I will have them both!" declared this true-blue American
In Cambridge, Massachusetts, on an April Sunday, instructed
        By the great department stores, by the Five-and-Ten,
Taught by Christmas, by the circus, by the vulgarity and grandeur of
        Niagara Falls and the Grand Canyon,
Tutored by the grandeur, vulgarity, and infinite appetite gratified and
        Shining in the darkness, of the light
On Saturdays at the double bills of the moon pictures,
The consummation of the advertisements of the imagination of the light
Which is as it was — the infinite belief in infinite hope — of Columbus,
        Barnum, Edison, and Jeremiah Dickson.

11 *Kierkegaard:* Søren Kierkegaard (1813–1855), Danish publisher and theologian, one of whose works is titled *Either-Or.*

ANNE SEXTON (1928–1974)

The Kiss

1969

My mouth blooms like a cut.
I've been wronged all year, tedious
nights, nothing but rough elbows in them
and delicate boxes of Kleenex calling *crybaby*
crybaby, you fool!

Before today my body was useless,
Now it's tearing at its square corners.
It's tearing old Mary's garments off, knot by knot
and see — Now it's shot full of these electric bolts.
Zing! A resurrection!

Once it was a boat, quite wooden
and with no business, no salt water under it

and in need of some paint. It was no more
than a group of boards. But you hoisted her, rigged her.
She's been elected.

My nerves are turned on. I hear them like
musical instruments. Where there was silence
the drums, the strings are incurably playing. You did this.
Pure genius at work. Darling, the composer has stepped
into fire.

ANNE SEXTON (1928–1974)

Lobster 1976

A shoe with legs,
a stone dropped from heaven,
he does his mournful work alone,
he is like the old prospector for gold,
with secret dreams of God-heads and fish heads.
Until suddenly a cradle fastens round him
and he is trapped as the U.S.A. sleeps.
Somewhere far off a woman lights a cigarette;
somewhere far off a car goes over a bridge;
somewhere far off a bank is held up.
This is the world the lobster knows not of.
He is the old hunting dog of the sea
who in the morning will rise from it
and be undrowned
and they will take his perfect green body
and paint it red.

WILLIAM SHAKESPEARE (1564–1616)

Not marble, nor the gilded monuments 1609

Not marble, nor the gilded monuments
Of princes, shall outlive this powerful rhyme;
But you shall shine more bright in these conténts
Than unswept stone, besmeared with sluttish time.
When wasteful war shall statues overturn,
And broils root out the work of masonry,
Nor Mars his° sword nor war's quick fire shall burn *possessive of Mars*
The living record of your memory.

'Gainst death and all-oblivious enmity
Shall you pace forth; your praise shall still find room
Even in the eyes of all posterity
That wear this world out to the ending doom.
    So, till the judgment that yourself arise,
    You live in this, and dwell in lovers' eyes.

WILLIAM SHAKESPEARE (1564–1616)

Spring° c. 1595

When daisies pied and violets blue
    And ladysmocks all silver-white
And cuckoobuds of yellow hue
    Do paint the meadows with delight,
The cuckoo then, on every tree,
Mocks married men;° for thus sings he,
            Cuckoo;
Cuckoo, cuckoo: Oh word of fear,
Unpleasing to a married ear!

When shepherds pipe on oaten straws,
    And merry larks are plowmen's clocks,
When turtles tread,° and rooks, and daws,
    And maidens bleach their summer smocks,
The cuckoo then, on every tree,
Mocks married men; for thus sings he,
            Cuckoo;
Cuckoo, cuckoo: Oh word of fear,
Unpleasing to a married ear!

Spring: Song from *Love's Labour's Lost,* V. ii. 6 *Mocks married men:* By singing "cuckoo," which sounds like "cuckold." 12 *turtles tread:* Turtledoves copulate.

WILLIAM SHAKESPEARE (1564–1616)

That time of year thou mayst in me behold 1609

That time of year thou mayst in me behold
When yellow leaves, or none, or few, do hang
Upon those boughs which shake against the cold,
Bare ruined choirs, where late the sweet birds sang.
In me thou see'st the twilight of such day
As after sunset fadeth in the west;

Which by and by black night doth take away,
Death's second self,° that seals up all in rest. *sleep*
In me thou see'st the glowing of such fire,
That on the ashes of his youth doth lie,
As the deathbed whereon it must expire,
Consumed with that which it was nourished by.
  This thou perceiv'st, which makes thy love more strong,
  To love that well which thou must leave ere long.

WILLIAM SHAKESPEARE (1564–1616)

When, in disgrace with Fortune and men's eyes 1609

When, in disgrace with Fortune and men's eyes,
I all alone beweep my outcast state,
And trouble deaf heaven with my bootless cries,
And look upon myself and curse my fate,
Wishing me like to one more rich in hope,
Featured like him, like him with friends possessed,
Desiring this man's art, and that man's scope,
With what I most enjoy contented least,
Yet in these thoughts myself almost despising,
Haply I think on thee, and then my state,
Like to the lark at break of day arising
From sullen earth, sings hymns at heaven's gate;
  For thy sweet love remembered such wealth brings
  That then I scorn to change my state with kings.

WILLIAM SHAKESPEARE (1564–1616)

Winter° c. 1595

When icicles hang by the wall
  And Dick the shepherd blows his nail,°
And Tom bears logs into the hall,
  And milk comes frozen home in pail.
When blood is nipped and ways be foul,
Then nightly sings the staring owl,
      Tu-who;
Tu-whit, tu-who: a merry note,
While greasy Joan doth keel the pot.°

Winter: Song from *Love's Labour's Lost,* V. ii. 2 *blows his nail:* Blows on his hands for warmth. 9 *keel the pot:* Cool the contents of the pot by stirring.

When all aloud the wind doth blow,
    And coughing drowns the parson's saw,° *maxim*
And birds sit brooding in the snow,
    And Marian's nose looks red and raw,
When roasted crabs° hiss in the bowl, *crabapples*
Then nightly sings the staring owl,
                    Tu-who;
Tu-whit, tu-who: a merry note
While greasy Joan doth keel the pot.

PERCY BYSSHE SHELLEY (1792–1822)

Ozymandias° 1818

I met a traveler from an antique land
Who said: Two vast and trunkless legs of stone
Stand in the desert. . . . Near them, on the sand,
Half sunk, a shattered visage lies, whose frown,
And wrinkled lip, and sneer of cold command,
Tell that its sculptor well those passions read
Which yet survive, stamped on these lifeless things,
The hand that mocked them, and the heart that fed:
And on the pedestal these words appear:
"My name is Ozymandias, King of Kings:
Look on my works, ye Mighty, and despair!"
Nothing beside remains. Round the decay
Of that colossal wreck, boundless and bare
The lone and level sands stretch far away.

Ozymandias: Greek name for Ramses II, pharaoh of Egypt for sixty-seven years during the 13th century B.C. His colossal statue lies prostrate in the sands of Luxor. Napoleon's soldiers measured it (56 feet long, ear 3½ feet long, weight 1,000 tons). Its inscription, according to the Greek historian Diodorus Siculus, was "I am Ozymandias, King of Kings; if anyone wishes to know what I am and where I lie, let him surpass me in some of my exploits."

SIR PHILIP SIDNEY (1554–1586)

Loving in Truth, and Fain in Verse My Love to Show 1591

Loving in truth, and fain in verse my love to show,
That she, dear she, might take some pleasure of my pain,
Pleasure might cause her read, reading might make her know,
Knowledge might pity win, and pity grace obtain,
I sought fit words to pain the blackest face of woe,
Studying inventions fine, her wits to entertain,

Oft turning others' leaves, to see if thence would flow
Some fresh and fruitful showers upon my sunburnt brain.
But words came halting forth, wanting Invention's stay;
Invention, Nature's child, fled step-dame° Study's blows; *stepmother*
And others' feet still seemed but strangers in my way.
Thus great with child to speak, and helpless in my throes,
Biting my truant pen, beating myself for spite:
"Fool," said my Muse to me, "look in thy heart and write."

LESLIE MARMON SILKO (b. 1948)

Deer Song 1974

I

Storm winds carry snow
to the mountain stream
clotted white in silence,
pale blue streak under ice
to the sea.

The ice shatters into glassy
bone splinters that tear deep into
soft parts of the hoof.
Swimming away from the wolves
before dawn
        choking back salt water
        the streaming red froth tide.

II

It is necessary.
Reflections that blind
from a thousand feet of
gray schist
        snow-covered in dying winter sunlight.
The pain is numbed by the freezing,
        the depths of the night sky,
        the distance beyond pale stars.

III

Do not think that I do not love you
if I scream
        while I die.
Antler and thin black hoof
smashed against dark rock —
                the struggle is the ritual
shining teeth tangled in
        sinew and flesh.

IV
You see,
I will go with you,
Because you call softly
because you are my brother
and my sister

Because the mountain is
our mother.
I will go with you
because you love me
while I die.

W. D. SNODGRASS (b. 1926)

April Inventory

1959

The green catalpa tree has turned
All white; the cherry blooms once more.
In one whole year I haven't learned
A blessed thing they pay you for.
The blossoms snow down in my hair;
The trees and I will soon be bare.

The trees have more than I to spare.
The sleek, expensive girls I teach,
Younger and pinker every year,
Bloom gradually out of reach.
The pear tree lets its petals drop
Like dandruff on a tabletop.

The girls have grown so young by now
I have to nudge myself to stare.
This year they smile and mind me how
My teeth are falling with my hair.
In thirty years I may not get
Younger, shrewder, or out of debt.

The tenth time, just a year ago,
I made myself a little list
Of all the things I'd ought to know,
Then told my parents, analyst,
And everyone who's trusted me
I'd be substantial, presently.

I haven't read one book about
A book or memorized one plot.
Or found a mind I did not doubt.

I learned one date. And then forgot.
And one by one the solid scholars
Get the degrees, the jobs, the dollars.

And smile above their starchy collars.
I taught my classes Whitehead's° notions;
One lovely girl, a song of Mahler's.°
Lacking a source-book or promotions,
I showed one child the colors of
A luna moth and how to love.

I taught myself to name my name,
To bark back, loosen love and crying;
To ease my woman so she came,
To ease an old man who was dying.
I have not learned how often I
Can win, can love, but choose to die.

I have not learned there is a lie
Love shall be blonder, slimmer, younger;
That my equivocating eye
Loves only by my body's hunger;
That I have forces, true to feel,
Or that the lovely world is real.

While scholars speak authority
And wear their ulcers on their sleeves,
My eyes in spectacles shall see
These trees procure and spend their leaves.
There is a value underneath
The gold and silver in my teeth.

Though trees turn bare and girls turn wives,
We shall afford our costly seasons;
There is a gentleness survives
That will outspeak and has its reasons.
There is a loveliness exists,
Preserves us, not for specialists.

32 *Whitehead:* Alfred North Whitehead (1861–1947), English mathematician and philosopher.
33 *Mahler:* Gustav Mahler (1860–1911), Austrian Post-Romantic composer, known for his songs and symphonies.

GARY SNYDER (b. 1930)
After weeks of watching the roof leak

After weeks of watching the roof leak
              I fixed it tonight
by moving a single board

GARY SNYDER (b. 1930)

Hay for the Horses 1966

He had driven half the night
From far down San Joaquin
Through Mariposa, up the
Dangerous mountain roads,
And pulled in at eight a.m.
With his big truckload of hay
behind the barn.
With winch and ropes and hooks
We stacked the bales up clean
To splintery redwood rafters
High in the dark, flecks of alfalfa
Whirling through shingle-cracks of light,
Itch of haydust in the
sweaty shirt and shoes.
At lunchtime under black oak
Out in the hot corral,
— The old mare nosing lunchpails,
Grasshoppers crackling in the weeds —
"I'm sixty-eight" he said,
"I first bucked hay when I was seventeen.
I thought, that day I started,
I sure would hate to do this all my life.
And dammit, that's just what
I've gone and done."

WALLACE STEVENS (1879–1955)

Disillusionment of Ten O'Clock 1923

The houses are haunted
By white night-gowns.
None are green,
Or purple with green rings,
Or green with yellow rings,
Or yellow with blue rings.
None of them are strange,
With socks of lace
And beaded ceintures.° *belts*
People are not going
To dream of baboons and periwinkles.
Only, here and there, an old sailor,
Drunk and asleep in his boots,
Catches tigers
In red weather.

WALLACE STEVENS (1879–1955)

The Emperor of Ice-Cream 1923

Call the roller of big cigars,
The muscular one, and bid him whip
In kitchen cups concupiscent curds.°
Let the wenches dawdle in such dress
As they are used to wear, and let the boys
Bring flowers in last month's newspapers.
Let be be finale of seem.°
The only emperor is the emperor of ice-cream.

Take from the dresser of deal,
Lacking the three glass knobs, that sheet
On which she embroidered fantails once
And spread it so as to cover her face.
If her horny feet protrude, they come
To show how cold she is, and dumb.
Let the lamp affix its beam.
The only emperor is the emperor of ice-cream.

3 *concupiscent curds:* "The words 'concupiscent curds' have no genealogy; they are merely expressive: at least, I hope they are expressive. They express the concupiscence of life, but, by contrast with the things in relation in the poem, they express or accentuate life's destitution, and it is this that gives them something more than a cheap lustre" (Wallace Stevens, *Letters* [New York: Knopf, 1960], p. 500). 7 *Let . . . seem:* "The true sense of Let be be the finale of seem is let being become the conclusion or denouement of appearing to be: in short, ice cream is an absolute good. The poem is obviously not about ice cream, but about being as distinguished from seeming to be" (*Letters,* p. 341).

WALLACE STEVENS (1879–1955)

Sunday Morning 1915

I

Complacencies of the peignoir, and late
Coffee and oranges in a sunny chair,
And the green freedom of a cockatoo
Upon a rug mingle to dissipate
The holy hush of ancient sacrifice.
She dreams a little, and she feels the dark
Encroachment of that old catastrophe,° *the Crucifixion*
As a calm darkens among water-lights.
The pungent oranges and bright, green wings
Seem things in some procession of the dead,
Winding across wide water, without sound.
The day is like wide water, without sound,
Stilled for the passing of her dreaming feet

Over the seas, to silent Palestine,
Dominion of the blood and sepulcher.

II

Why should she give her bounty to the dead?
What is divinity if it can come
Only in silent shadows and in dreams?
Shall she not find in comforts of the sun,
In pungent fruit and bright, green wings, or else
In any balm or beauty of the earth,
Things to be cherished like the thought of heaven?
Divinity must live within herself:
Passions of rain, or moods in falling snow;
Grievings in loneliness, or unsubdued
Elations when the forest blooms; gusty
Emotions on wet roads on autumn nights;
All pleasures and all pains, remembering
The bough of summer and the winter branch.
These are the measures destined for her soul.

III

Jove° in the clouds had his inhuman birth.
No mother suckled him, no sweet land gave
Large-mannered motions to his mythy mind
He moved among us, as a muttering king,
Magnificent, would move among his hinds,° *peasant subjects*
Until our blood, commingling, virginal,
With heaven, brought such requital to desire
The very hinds discerned it, in a star,° *of Bethlehem*
Shall our blood fail? Or shall it come to be
The blood of paradise? And shall the earth
Seem all of paradise that we shall know?
The sky will be much friendlier then than now,
A part of labor and a part of pain,
And next in glory to enduring love,
Not this dividing and indifferent blue.

IV

She says, "I am content when wakened birds,
Before they fly, test the reality
Of misty fields, by their sweet questionings;
But when the birds are gone, and their warm fields
Return no more, where, then, is paradise?"
There is not any haunt of prophecy,
Nor any old chimera of the grave,
Neither the golden underground, nor isle
Melodious, where spirits gat° them home, *got*
Nor visionary south, nor cloudy palm

31 *Jove:* Jupiter, the supreme Roman god.

Remote on heaven's hill, that has endured
As April's green endures, or will endure
Like her remembrance of awakened birds,
Or her desire for June and evening, tipped
By the consummation of the swallow's wings.

V

She says, "But in contentment I still feel
The need of some imperishable bliss."
Death is the mother of beauty; hence from her,
Alone, shall come fulfillment to our dreams
And our desires. Although she strews the leaves
Of sure obliteration on our paths,
The path sick sorrow took, the many paths
Where triumph rang its brassy phrase, or love
Whispered a little out of tenderness,
She makes the willow shiver in the sun
For maidens who were wont to sit and gaze
Upon the grass, relinquished to their feet.
She causes boys to pile new plums and pears
On disregarded plate. The maidens taste
And stray impassioned in the littering leaves.

VI

Is there no change of death in paradise?
Does ripe fruit never fall? Or do the boughs
Hang always heavy in that perfect sky,
Unchanging, yet so like our perishing earth,
With rivers like our own that seek for seas
They never find, the same receding shores
That never touch with inarticulate pang?
Why set the pear upon those river-banks
Or spice the shores with odors of the plum?
Alas, that they should wear our colors there,
The silken weavings of our afternoons,
And pick the strings of our insipid lutes!
Death is the mother of beauty, mystical,
Within whose burning bosom we devise
Our earthly mothers waiting, sleeplessly.

VII

Supple and turbulent, a ring of men
Shall chant in orgy° on a summer morn *ritual revelry*
Their boisterous devotion to the sun,
Not as a god, but as a god might be,
Naked among them, like a savage source.
Their chant shall be a chant of paradise,
Out of their blood, returning to the sky;
And in their chant shall enter, voice by voice,
The windy lake wherein their lord delights,

The trees, like serafin,° and echoing hills,
That choir among themselves long afterward.
They shall know well the heavenly fellowship
Of men that perish and of summer morn.
And whence they came and whither they shall go
The dew upon their feet shall manifest.

VIII

She hears, upon that water without sound,
A voice that cries, "The tomb in Palestine
Is not the porch of spirits lingering.
It is the grave of Jesus, where he lay."
We live in an old chaos of the sun,
Or old dependency of day and night,
Or island solitude, unsponsored, free,
Of that wide water, inescapable.
Deer walk upon our mountains, and the quail
Whistle about us their spontaneous cries;
Sweet berries ripen in the wilderness;
And, in the isolation of the sky,
At evening, casual flocks of pigeons make
Ambiguous undulations as they sink,
Downward to darkness, on extended wings.

100 *serafin:* Seraphim, angels having three sets of wings; the highest of the nine orders of angels.

WALLACE STEVENS (1879–1955)

Thirteen Ways of Looking at a Blackbird 1923

I

Among twenty snowy mountains,
The only moving thing
Was the eye of the blackbird.

II

I was of three minds,
Like a tree
In which there are three blackbirds.

III

The blackbird whirled in the autumn winds.
It was a small part of the pantomime.

IV

A man and a woman
Are one.
A man and a woman and a blackbird
Are one.

V
I do not know which to prefer,
The beauty of inflections
Or the beauty of innuendoes,
The blackbird whistling
Or just after.

VI
Icicles filled the long window
With barbaric glass.
The shadow of the blackbird
Crossed it, to and fro.
The mood
Traced in the shadow
An indecipherable cause.

VII
O thin men of Haddam,° *a town in Connecticut*
Why do you imagine golden birds?
Do you not see how the blackbird
Walks around the feet
Of the women about you?

VIII
I know noble accents
And lucid, inescapable rhythms;
But I know, too,
That the blackbird is involved
In what I know.

IX
When the blackbird flew out of sight,
It marked the edge
Of one of many circles.

X
At the sight of blackbirds
Flying in a green light,
Even the bawds of euphony
Would cry out sharply.

XI
He rode over Connecticut
In a glass coach.
Once, a fear pierced him,
In that he mistook
The shadow of his equipage
For blackbirds.

XII
The river is moving.
The blackbird must be flying.

XIII
It was evening all afternoon.
It was snowing
And it was going to snow.
The blackbird sat
In the cedar-limbs.

ALFRED, LORD TENNYSON (1809–1892)

Crossing the Bar

1889

Sunset and evening star,
And one clear call for me!
And may there be no moaning of the bar
When I put out to sea.

But such a tide as moving seems asleep,
Too full for sound and foam,
When that which drew from out the boundless deep
Turns again home.

Twilight and evening bell,
And after that the dark!
And may there be no sadness of farewell
When I embark;

For though from out our bourne of Time and Place
The flood may bear me far,
I hope to see my Pilot face to face
When I have crossed the bar.

ALFRED, LORD TENNYSON (1809–1892)

Tears, Idle Tears

1847

Tears, idle tears, I know not what they mean,
Tears from the depth of some divine despair
Rise in the heart, and gather to the eyes,
In looking on the happy autumn-fields,
And thinking of the days that are no more.

Fresh as the first beam glittering on a sail,
That brings our friends up from the underworld
Sad as the last which reddens over one
That sinks with all we love below the verge;
So sad, so fresh, the days that are no more.

Ah, sad and strange as in dark summer dawns
The earliest pipe of half-awakened birds

To dying ears, when unto dying eyes
The casement slowly grows a glimmering square;
So sad, so strange, the days that are no more.

Dear as remembered kisses after death,
And sweet as those by hopeless fancy feigned
On lips that are for others; deep as love,
Deep as first love, and wild with all regret;
O Death in Life, the days that are no more!

ALFRED, LORD TENNYSON (1809–1892)

Ulysses°

1833

It little profits that an idle king,
By this still hearth, among these barren crags,
Matched with an agéd wife,° I mete and dole *Penelope*
Unequal laws unto a savage race,
That hoard, and sleep, and feed, and know not me.
I cannot rest from travel; I will drink
Life to the lees. All times I have enjoyed
Greatly, have suffered greatly, both with those
That loved me, and alone; on shore, and when
Through scudding drifts the rainy Hyades°
Vexed the dim sea. I am become a name;
For always roaming with a hungry heart
Much have I seen and known — cities of men
And manners, climates, councils, governments,
Myself not least, but honored of them all —
And drunk delight of battle with my peers,
Far on the ringing plains of windy Troy.
I am a part of all that I have met;
Yet all experience is an arch wherethrough
Gleams that untraveled world, whose margin fades
For ever and for ever when I move.
How dull it is to pause, to make an end,
To rust unburnished, not to shine in use!
As though to breathe were life. Life piled on life
Were all too little, and of one to me
Little remains; but every hour is saved
From that eternal silence, something more,
A bringer of new things; and vile it were
For some three suns to store and hoard myself,
And this gray spirit yearning in desire

Ulysses: Ulysses, the hero of Homer's epic poem the *Odyssey,* is presented by Dante in *The Inferno,* XXVI, as restless after his return to Ithaca, and eager for new adventures. 10 *Hyades:* Five stars in the constellation Taurus, supposed by the ancients to predict rain when they rose with the sun.

To follow knowledge like a sinking star,
Beyond the utmost bound of human thought.

This is my son, mine own Telemachus,
To whom I leave the scepter and the isle —
Well-loved of me, discerning to fulfill
This labor by slow prudence to make mild
A rugged people, and through soft degrees
Subdue them to the useful and the good.
Most blameless is he, centered in the sphere
Of common duties, decent not to fail
In offices of tenderness, and pay
Meet adoration to my household gods,
When I am gone. He works his work, I mine.

There lies the port; the vessel puffs her sail:
There gloom the dark, broad seas. My mariners,
Souls that have toiled, and wrought, and thought with me —
That ever with a frolic welcome took
The thunder and the sunshine, and opposed
Free hearts, free foreheads — you and I are old;
Old age hath yet his honor and his toil.
Death closes all; but something ere the end,
Some work of noble note, may yet be done,
Not unbecoming men that strove with Gods.
The lights begin to twinkle from the rocks;
The long day wanes; the slow moon climbs; the deep
Moans round with many voices. Come, my friends.
'Tis not too late to seek a newer world.
Push off, and sitting well in order smite
The sounding furrows; for my purpose holds
To sail beyond the sunset, and the baths
Of all the western stars, until I die.
It may be that the gulfs will wash us down;
It may be we shall touch the Happy Isles,°
And see the great Achilles,° whom we knew.
Though much is taken, much abides; and though
We are not now that strength which in old days
Moved earth and heaven, that which we are, we are:
One equal temper of heroic hearts,
Made weak by time and fate, but strong in will
To strive, to seek, to find, and not to yield.

63 *Happy Isles:* Elysium, the home after death of heroes and others favored by the gods. It was thought by the ancients to lie beyond the sunset in the uncharted Atlantic. 64 *Achilles:* The hero of Homer's *Iliad.*

DYLAN THOMAS (1914–1953)

Fern Hill

1946

Now as I was young and easy under the apple boughs
About the lilting house and happy as the grass was green,
The night above the dingle starry,
Time let me hail and climb
Golden in the heydays of his eyes,
And honored among wagons I was prince of the apple towns
And once below a time I lordly had the trees and leaves
Trail with daisies and barley
Down the rivers of the windfall light.

And as I was green and carefree, famous among the barns
About the happy yard and singing as the farm was home,
In the sun that is young once only,
Time let me play and be
Golden in the mercy of his means,
And green and golden I was huntsman and herdsman, the calves
Sang to my horn, the foxes on the hills barked clear and cold,
And the sabbath rang slowly
In the pebbles of the holy streams.

All the sun long it was running, it was lovely, the hay
Fields high as the house, the tunes from the chimneys, it was air
And playing, lovely and watery
And fire green as grass.
And nightly under the simple stars
As I rode to sleep the owls were bearing the farm away,
All the moon long I heard, blessed among stables, the nightjars
Flying with the ricks, and the horses
Flashing into the dark.

And then to awake, and the farm, like a wanderer white
With the dew, come back, the cock on his shoulder; it was all
Shining, it was Adam and maiden,
The sky gathered again
And the sun grew round that very day.
So it must have been after the birth of the simple light
In the first, spinning place, the spellbound horses walking warm
Out of the whinnying green stable
On to the fields of praise.

And honored among foxes and pheasants by the gay house
Under the new made clouds and happy as the heart was long,
In the sun born over and over,
I ran my heedless ways,
My wishes raced through the house-high hay
And nothing I cared, at my sky-blue trades, that time allows

In all his tuneful turning so few and such morning songs
    Before the children green and golden
        Follow him out of grace,

Nothing I cared, in the lamb white days, that time would take me
Up to the swallow-thronged loft by the shadow of my hand,
    In the moon that is always rising,
        Nor that riding to sleep
    I should hear him fly with the high fields
And wake to the farm forever fled from the childless land.
Oh as I was young and easy in the mercy of his means,
        Time held me green and dying
    Though I sang in my chains like the sea.

ROBERT WALLACE (b. 1932)

The Double-Play 1961

In his sea lit
distance, the pitcher winding
like a clock about to chime comes down with

the ball, hit
sharply, under the artificial
banks of arc-lights, bounds like a vanishing string

over the green
to the shortstop magically
scoops to his right whirling above his invisible

shadows
in the dust redirects
its flight to the running poised second baseman

pirouettes
leaping, above the slide, to throw
from mid-air, across the colored tightened interval,

to the leaning-
out first baseman ends the dance
drawing it disappearing into his long brown glove

stretches. What
is too swift for deception
is final, lost, among the loosened figures

jogging off the field
(the pitcher walks), casual
in the space where the poem has happened.

EDMUND WALLER (1606–1687)

Go, Lovely Rose 1645

Go, lovely rose,
Tell her that wastes her time and me
That now she knows,
When I resemble° her to thee, *compare*
How sweet and fair she seems to be.

Tell her that's young
And shuns to have her graces spied,
That hadst thou sprung
In deserts where no men abide,
Thou must have uncommended died.

Small is the worth
Of beauty from the light retired:
Bid her come forth,
Suffer herself to be desired,
And not blush so to be admired.

Then die, that she
The common fate of all things rare
May read in thee,
How small a part of time they share
That are so wondrous sweet and fair.

WALT WHITMAN (1819–1892)

The Dalliance of the Eagles 1880

Skirting the river road, (my forenoon walk, my rest,)
Skyward in air a sudden muffled sound, the dalliance of the eagles,
The rushing amorous contact high in space together,
The clinching interlocking claws, a living, fierce, gyrating wheel,
Four beating wings, two beaks, a swirling mass tight grappling,
In tumbling turning clustering loops, straight downward falling,
Till o'er the river poised, the twain yet one, a moment's lull,
A motionless still balance in the air, then parting, talons loosing,
Upward again on slow-firm pinions slanting, their separate diverse flight,
She hers, he his, pursuing.

WALT WHITMAN (1819–1892)

One's-self I Sing 1867

One's-self I sing, a simple separate person,
Yet utter the word Democratic, the word En-Masse.

Of physiology from top to toe I sing,
Not physiognomy alone nor brain alone is worthy for the Muse, I say the Form complete is worthier far,
The Female equally with the Male I sing.

Of Life immense in passion, pulse, and power,
Cheerful, for freest action formed under the laws divine,
The Modern Man I sing.

WALT WHITMAN (1819–1892)

There Was a Child Went Forth 1855

There was a child went forth every day,
And the first object he looked upon, that object he became,
And that object became part of him for the day or a certain part of the day,
Or for many years or stretching cycles of years.

The early lilacs became part of this child,
And grass and white and red morning-glories, and white and red clover, and the song of the phoebe-bird,
And the Third-month° lambs and the sow's pink-faint litter, and the mare's foal and the cow's calf,
And the noisy brood of the barnyard or by the mire of the pond-side,
And the fish suspending themselves so curiously below there, and the beautiful curious liquid,
And the water-plants with their graceful flat heads, all became part of him.

The field-sprouts of Fourth-month and Fifth-month became part of him,
Winter-grain sprouts and those of the light-yellow corn, and the esculent roots of the garden,
And the apple-trees covered with blossoms and the fruit afterward, and wood-berries, and the commonest weeds by the road,
And the old drunkard staggering home from the outhouse of the tavern whence he had lately risen,
And the schoolmistress that passed on her way to the school,
And the friendly boys that passed, and the quarrelsome boys,
And the tidy and fresh-cheeked girls, and the barefoot negro boy and girl,
And all the changes of city and country wherever he went.

7 *Third-month:* March; Whitman is following the Quaker practice of naming the months by their number in the year's sequence.

His own parents, he that had fathered him and she that had conceived him in her womb and birthed him,
They gave this child more of themselves than that,
They gave him afterward every day, they became part of him.

The mother at home quietly placing the dishes on the supper-table,
The mother with mild words, clean her cap and gown, a wholesome odor falling off her person and clothes as she walks by,
The father, strong, self-sufficient, manly, mean, angered, unjust,
The blow, the quick loud word, the tight bargain, the crafty lure,
The family usages, the language, the company, the furniture, the yearning and swelling heart,
Affection that will not be gainsayed, the sense of what is real, the thought if after all it should prove unreal,
The doubts of day-time and the doubts of night-time, the curious whether and how,
Whether that which appears so is so, or is it all flashes and specks?
Men and women crowding fast in the streets, if they are not flashes and specks what are they?
The streets themselves and the facades of houses, and goods in the windows,
Vehicles, teams, the heavy-planked wharves, the huge crossing at the ferries,
The village on the highland seen from afar at sunset, the river between,
Shadows, aureola and mist, the light falling on roofs and gables of white or brown two miles off,
The schooner near by sleepily dropping down the tide, the little boat slack-towed astern,
The hurrying tumbling waves, quick-broken crests, slapping,
The strata of colored clouds, the long bar of maroon-tint away solitary by itself, the spread of purity it lies motionless in,
The horizon's edge, the flying sea-crow, the fragrance of salt marsh and shore mud,
These became part of that child who went forth every day, and who now goes, and will always go forth every day.

RICHARD WILBUR (b. 1921)

Love Calls Us to the Things of This World° 1956

The eyes open to a cry of pulleys,°
And spirited from sleep, the astounded soul
Hangs for a moment bodiless and simple
As false dawn.
Outside the open window
The morning air is all awash with angels.

Love Calls Us . . . : From St. Augustine's *Commentary on the Psalms.* 1 *pulleys:* Grooved wheels at each end of a laundry line; clothes are hung on the line and advance as the line is moved.

Some are in bed-sheets, some are in blouses,
Some are in smocks: but truly there they are.
Now they are rising together in calm swells
Of halcyon feeling, filling whatever they wear
With the deep joy of their impersonal breathing;
Now they are flying in place, conveying
The terrible speed of their omnipresence, moving
And staying like white water; and now of a sudden
They swoon down into so rapt a quiet
That nobody seems to be there.
The soul shrinks

From all that it is about to remember,
From the punctual rape of every blesséd day,
And cries,
"Oh, let there be nothing on earth but laundry,
Nothing but rosy hands in the rising steam
And clear dances done in the sight of heaven."

Yet, as the sun acknowledges
With a warm look the world's hunks and colors,
The soul descends once more in bitter love
To accept the waking body, saying now
In a changed voice as the man yawns and rises,

"Bring them down from their ruddy gallows;
Let there be clean linen for the backs of thieves;
Let lovers go fresh and sweet to be undone,
And the heaviest nuns walk in a pure floating
Of dark habits,
keeping their difficult balance."

RICHARD WILBUR (b. 1921)

Praise in Summer

1947

Obscurely yet most surely called to praise,
As sometimes summer calls us all, I said
The hills are heavens full of branching ways
Where star-nosed moles fly overhead the dead;
I said the trees are mines in air, I said
See how the sparrow burrows in the sky!
And then I wondered why this mad *instead*
Perverts our praise to uncreation, why
Such savor's in this wrenching things awry.
Does sense so stale that it must needs derange
The world to know it? To a praiseful eye
Should it not be enough of fresh and strange
That trees grow green, and moles can course in clay,
And sparrows sweep the ceiling of our day?

RICHARD WILBUR (b. 1921)

A Simile for Her Smile 1950

Your smiling, or the hope, the thought of it,
Makes in my mind such pause and abrupt ease
As when the highway bridgegates fall,
Balking the hasty traffic, which must sit
On each side massed and staring, while
Deliberately the drawbridge starts to rise:

Then horns are hushed, the oilsmoke rarifies,
Above the idling motors one can tell
The packet's smooth approach, the slip,
Slip of the silken river past the sides,
The ringing of clear bells, the dip
And slow cascading of the paddle wheel.

WILLIAM CARLOS WILLIAMS (1883–1963)

The Dance 1944

In Breughel's great picture, The Kermess,°
the dancers go round, they go round and
around, the squeal and the blare and the
tweedle of bagpipes, a bugle and fiddles
tipping their bellies (round as the thick-
sided glasses whose wash they impound)
their hips and their bellies off balance
to turn them. Kicking and rolling about
the Fair Grounds, swinging their butts, those
shanks must be sound to bear up under such
rollicking measures, prance as they dance
in Breughel's great picture, The Kermess.

1 *Breughel . . . Kermess: The Kermess,* which represents the feast day of a local patron saint, was painted by Flemish painter Pieter Brueghel (or Breughel), the Elder, c. 1525–1569.

WILLIAM CARLOS WILLIAMS (1883–1963)

Spring and All 1923

By the road to the contagious hospital
under the surge of the blue
mottled clouds driven from the
northeast — a cold wind. Beyond, the
waste of broad, muddy fields
brown with dried weeds, standing and fallen

patches of standing water
and scattering of tall trees

All along the road the reddish
purplish, forked, upstanding, twiggy
stuff of bushes and small trees
with dead, brown leaves under them
leafless vines —

Lifeless in appearance, sluggish
dazed spring approaches —

They enter the new world naked,
cold, uncertain of all
save that they enter. All about them
the cold, familiar wind —

Now the grass, tomorrow
the stiff curl of wildcarrot leaf
One by one objects are defined —
It quickens: clarity, outline of leaf

But now the stark dignity of
entrance — Still, the profound change
has come upon them: rooted, they
grip down and begin to awaken

WILLIAM CARLOS WILLIAMS (1883–1963)

This Is Just to Say 1934

I have eaten
the plums
that were in
the icebox

and which
you were probably
saving
for breakfast

Forgive me
they were delicious
so sweet
and so cold

WILLIAM WORDSWORTH (1770–1850)

I Wandered Lonely as a Cloud 1807

I wandered lonely as a cloud
That floats on high o'er vales and hills,

When all at once I saw a crowd,
A host, of golden daffodils,
Beside the lake, beneath the trees,
Fluttering and dancing in the breeze.

Continuous as the stars that shine
And twinkle on the milky way,
They stretched in never-ending line
Along the margin of a bay;
Ten thousand saw I at a glance,
Tossing their heads in sprightly dance.

The waves beside them danced, but they
Outdid the sparkling waves in glee;
A poet could not but be gay,
In such a jocund company;
I gazed — and gazed — but little thought
What wealth the show to me had brought:

For oft, when on my couch I lie
In vacant or in pensive mood,
They flash upon that inward eye
Which is the bliss of solitude;
And then my heart with pleasure fills,
And dances with the daffodils.

WILLIAM WORDSWORTH (1770–1850)

She Dwelt among the Untrodden Ways 1800

She dwelt among the untrodden ways
  Beside the springs of Dove,°
A Maid whom there were none to praise
  And very few to love:

A violet by a mossy stone
  Half hidden from the eye!
— Fair as a star, when only one
  Is shining in the sky.

She lived unknown, and few could know
  When Lucy ceased to be;
But she is in her grave, and, oh,
  The difference to me!

2 *Dove:* A stream near Wordsworth's home in the Lake District of England.

WILLIAM WORDSWORTH (1770–1850)

A Slumber Did My Spirit Seal

1800

A slumber did my spirit seal;
    I had no human fears —
She seemed a thing that could not feel
    The touch of earthly years.

No motion has she now, no force;
    She neither hears nor sees;
Rolled round in earth's diurnal course.
    With rocks, and stones, and trees.

WILLIAM WORDSWORTH (1770–1850)

The Solitary Reaper°

1807

Behold her, single in the field,
Yon solitary Highland lass!
Reaping and singing by herself;
Stop here, or gently pass!
Alone she cuts and binds the grain,
And sings a melancholy strain;
O listen! for the vale profound
Is overflowing with the sound.

No nightingale did ever chaunt
More welcome notes to weary bands
Of travelers in some shady haunt
Among Arabian sands.
A voice so thrilling ne'er was heard
In springtime from the cuckoo-bird,
Breaking the silence of the seas
Among the farthest Hebrides.

Will no one tell me what she sings? —
Perhaps the plaintive numbers flow
For old, unhappy, far-off things,
And battles long ago.
Or is it some more humble lay,
Familiar matter of today?
Some natural sorrow, loss, or pain,
That has been, and may be again?

The Solitary Reaper: Dorothy Wordsworth (William's sister) writes that the poem was suggested by this sentence in Thomas Wilkinson's *Tour of Scotland:* "Passed a female who was reaping alone; she sung in Erse, as she bended over her sickle; the sweetest human voice I ever heard: her strains were tenderly melancholy, and felt delicious, long after they were heard no more."

Whate'er the theme, the maiden sang
As if her song could have no ending;
I saw her singing at her work,
And o'er the sickle bending —
I listened, motionless and still;
And, as I mounted up the hill,
The music in my heart I bore
Long after it was heard no more.

JAMES WRIGHT (1927–1980)

Lying in a Hammock at William Duffy's Farm in Pine Island, Minnesota 1961

Over my head, I see the bronze butterfly,
Asleep on the black trunk,
Blowing like a leaf in green shadow.
Down the ravine behind the empty house,
The cowbells follow one another
Into the distances of the afternoon.
To my right,
In a field of sunlight between two pines,
The droppings of last year's horses
Blaze up into golden stones.
I lean back, as the evening darkens and comes on.
A chicken hawk floats over, looking for home.
I have wasted my life.

SIR THOMAS WYATT (1503–1542)

They Flee from Me 1557

They flee from me that sometime did me seek
With naked foot stalking in my chamber.
I have seen them gentle, tame, and meek
That now are wild and do not remember
That sometime they put themselves in danger
To take bread at my hand; and now they range
Busily seeking with a continual change.

Thankèd be Fortune, it hath been otherwise
Twenty times better; but once in special,
In thin array after a pleasant guise,
When her loose gown from her shoulders did fall,
And she me caught in her arms long and small;° *narrow*

And therewithall sweetly did me kiss,
And softly said, "Dear heart, how like you this?"

It was no dream; I lay broad waking.
But all is turned thorough my gentleness
Into a strange fashion of forsaking;
And I have leave to go of her goodness,
And she also to use newfangleness.
But since that I so kindely° am served, *kindly (ironic)*
I fain would know what she hath deserved.

WILLIAM BUTLER YEATS (1865–1939)

Adam's Curse° 1903

We sat together at one summer's end,
That beautiful mild woman, your close friend,
And you and I, and talked of poetry.
I said, "A line will take us hours maybe;
Yet if it does not seem a moment's thought,
Our stitching and unstitching has been naught.
Better go down upon your marrow-bones
And scrub a kitchen pavement, or break stones
Like an old pauper, in all kinds of weather;
For to articulate sweet sounds together
Is to work harder than all these, and yet
Be thought an idler by the noisy set
Of bankers, schoolmasters, and clergymen
The martyrs call the world."

And thereupon
That beautiful mild woman for whose sake
There's many a one shall find out all heartache
On finding that her voice is sweet and low
Replied, "To be born woman is to know —
Although they do not talk of it at school —
That we must labor to be beautiful."

I said, "It's certain there is no fine thing
Since Adam's fall but needs much laboring.
There have been lovers who thought love should be
So much compounded of high courtesy
That they would sigh and quote with learned looks
Precedents out of beautiful old books;
Yet now it seems an idle trade enough."

Adam's Curse: After his fall from grace and eviction from Eden, Adam was cursed with hard work, pain, and death.

We sat grown quiet at the name of love;
We saw the last embers of daylight die,
And in the trembling blue-green of the sky
A moon, worn as if it had been a shell
Washed by time's waters as they rose and fell
About the stars and broke in days and years.

I had a thought for no one's but your ears:
That you were beautiful, and that I strove
To love you in the old high way of love;
That it had all seemed happy, and yet we'd grown
As weary-hearted as that hollow moon.

WILLIAM BUTLER YEATS (1865–1939)

Crazy Jane Talks with the Bishop 1933

I met the Bishop on the road
And much said he and I.
"Those breasts are flat and fallen now,
Those veins must soon be dry;
Live in a heavenly mansion,
Not in some foul sty."

"Fair and foul are near of kin,
And fair needs foul," I cried.
"My friends are gone, but that's a truth
Nor grave nor bed denied,
Learned in bodily lowliness
And in the heart's pride.

"A woman can be proud and stiff
When on love intent;
But Love has pitched his mansion in
The place of excrement;
For nothing can be sole or whole
That has not been rent."

WILLIAM BUTLER YEATS (1865–1939)

The Lake Isle of Innisfree° 1892

I will arise and go now, and go to Innisfree,
And a small cabin build there, of clay and wattles made:

The Lake Isle of Innisfree: An island in Lough (or Lake) Gill, in western Ireland.

Nine bean-rows will I have there, a hive for the honey-bee,
And live alone in the bee-loud glade.

And I shall have some peace there, for peace comes dropping slow,
Dropping from the veils of the morning to where the cricket sings;
There midnight's all a glimmer, and noon a purple glow,
And evening full of the linnet's wings.

I will arise and go now, for always night and day
I hear lake water lapping with low sounds by the shore:
While I stand on the roadway, or on the pavements grey,
I hear it in the deep heart's core.

WILLIAM BUTLER YEATS (1865–1939)

Leda and the Swan° 1924

A sudden blow: the great wings beating still
Above the staggering girl, her thighs caressed
By the dark webs, her nape caught in his bill,
He holds her helpless breast upon his breast.

How can those terrified vague fingers push
The feathered glory from her loosening thighs?
And how can body, laid in that white rush,
But feel the strange heart beating where it lies?

A shudder in the loins engenders there
The broken wall, the burning roof and tower
And Agamemnon dead.
Being so caught up,
So mastered by the brute blood of the air,
Did she put on his knowledge with his power
Before the indifferent beak could let her drop?

Leda and the Swan: In Greek myth, Zeus in the form of a swan seduced Leda and fathered Helen of Troy (whose abduction started the Trojan War) and Clytemnestra, Agamemnon's wife and murderer. Yeats thought of Zeus's appearance to Leda as a type of annunciation, like the angel appearing to Mary.

WILLIAM BUTLER YEATS (1865–1939)

Sailing to Byzantium° 1927

I

That is no country for old men.° The young
In one another's arms, birds in the trees
— Those dying generations — at their song,
The salmon-falls, the mackerel-crowded seas
Fish, flesh, or fowl, commend all summer long
Whatever is begotten, born and dies.
Caught in that sensual music all neglect
Monuments of unaging intellect.

II

An aged man is but a paltry thing,
A tattered coat upon a stick, unless
Soul clap its hands and sing, and louder sing
For every tatter in its mortal dress,
Nor is there singing school but studying
Monuments of its own magnificence;
And therefore I have sailed the seas and come
To the holy city of Byzantium.

III

O sages standing in God's holy fire
As in the gold mosaic of a wall,
Come from the holy fire, perne in a gyre,°
And be the singing-masters of my soul.
Consume my heart away; sick with desire
And fastened to a dying animal
It knows not what it is; and gather me
Into the artifice of eternity.

IV

Once out of nature I shall never take
My bodily form from any natural thing,
But such a form as Grecian goldsmiths make
Of hammered gold and gold enameling
To keep a drowsy Emperor awake;°
Or set upon a golden bough° to sing
To lords and ladies of Byzantium
Of what is past, or passing, or to come.

Byzantium: Old name for the modern city of Istanbul, capital of the Eastern Roman Empire, ancient artistic and intellectual center. Yeats uses Byzantium as a symbol for "artificial" (and therefore deathless) art and beauty, as opposed to the beauty of the natural world, which is bound to time and death. 1. *That . . . men:* Ireland, part of the time-bound world. 19 *perne in a gyre:* Bobbin making a spiral pattern. 27–29 *such . . . awake:* "I have read somewhere that in the Emperor's palace at Byzantium was a tree made of gold and silver, and artificial birds that sang" (Yeats's note). 30 *golden bough:* In Greek legend, Aeneas had to pluck a golden bough from a tree in order to descend into Hades. As soon as the bough was plucked, another grew in its place.

WILLIAM BUTLER YEATS (1865–1939)

The Second Coming° 1921

Turning and turning in the widening gyre°
The falcon cannot hear the falconer;
Things fall apart; the center cannot hold;
Mere anarchy is loosed upon the world,
The blood-dimmed tide is loosed, and everywhere
The ceremony of innocence is drowned;
The best lack all conviction, while the worst
Are full of passionate intensity.

Surely some revelation is at hand;
Surely the Second Coming is at hand.
The Second Coming! Hardly are those words out
When a vast image out of *Spiritus Mundi*° *Soul of the world*
Troubles my sight: somewhere in sands of the desert
A shape with lion body and the head of a man,
A gaze blank and pitiless as the sun,
Is moving its slow thighs, while all about it
Reel shadows of the indignant desert birds.
The darkness drops again; but now I know
That twenty centuries of stony sleep
Were vexed to nightmare by a rocking cradle,
And what rough beast, its hour come round at last,
Slouches towards Bethlehem to be born?

The Second Coming: According to Matthew 24:29–44, Christ will return to earth after a time of tribulation to reward the righteous and establish the Millennium of Heaven on earth. Yeats saw his troubled time as the end of the Christian era, and feared the portents of the new cycle. 1 *gyre:* Widening spiral of a falcon's flight, used by Yeats to describe the cycling of history.

AN ALBUM OF WORLD LITERATURE

ANNA AKHMATOVA (Russian/1889–1966)

Apparition 1919

TRANSLATED BY JUDITH HEMSCHEMEYER

The round, hanging lanterns,
Lit early, are squeaking,
Ever more festively, ever brighter,
The flying snowflakes glitter.

And, quickening their steady gait,
As if sensing some pursuit,
Through the softly falling snow
Under a dark blue net, the horses race.

And the gilded footman
Stands motionless behind the sleigh,
And the Tsar looks around strangely
With light, empty eyes.

Connections

1. How do the second and third stanzas lead up to the image of the Czar in the third stanza of this poem? How is Akhmatova's strategy in the third stanza similar to James Merrill's in "Casual Wear" (p. 901)?
2. How does Akhmatova's image of the Czar suggest an attitude toward his power? Compare this view of the Czar's power with Rita Dove's perspective on El General in "Parsley" (p. 892).

CLARIBEL ALEGRÍA (Salvadoran/b. 1924)

I Am Mirror

TRANSLATED BY ELECTA ARENAL AND MARSHA GABRIELA DREYER

Water sparkles
on my skin
and I don't feel it
water streams
down my back
I don't feel it
I rub myself with a towel
I pinch myself in the arm
I don't feel
frightened I look at myself in the mirror
she also pricks herself
I begin to get dressed
stumbling
from the corners
shouts like lightning bolts
tortured eyes
scurrying rats
and teeth shoot forth
although I feel nothing
I wander through the streets:
children with dirty faces
ask me for charity
child prostitutes
who are not yet fifteen
the streets are paved with pain
tanks that approach
raised bayonets
bodies that fall

weeping
finally I feel my arm
I am no longer a phantom
I hurt
therefore I exist
I return to watch the scene:
children who run
bleeding
women with panic
in their faces
this time it hurts me less
I pinch myself again
and already I feel nothing
I simply reflect
what happens at my side
the tanks
are not tanks
nor are the shouts
shouts
I am a blank mirror
that nothing penetrates
my surface
is hard
is brillliant
is polished
I became a mirror
and I am fleshless
scarcely preserving
a vague memory
of pain.

Connections

1. Compare the ways Alegria uses mirror images to reflect life in Nicaragua with Plath's concerns in "Mirror" (p. 570).
2. Write an essay comparing the speaker's voice in this poem and that in Blake's "London" (p. 551). How do the speakers evoke emotional responses to what they describe?

CHARLES BAUDELAIRE (French/1821–1867)

To the Reader 1857

TRANSLATED BY ROBERT LOWELL

Infatuation, sadism, lust, avarice
possess our souls and drain the body's force;

we spoonfeed our adorable remorse,
like whores or beggars nourishing their lice.

Our sins are mulish, our confessions lies;
we play to the grandstand with our promises,
we pray for tears to wash our filthiness,
importantly pissing hogwash through our styes.

The devil, watching by our sickbeds, hissed
old smut and folk-songs to our soul, until
the soft and precious metal of our will
boiled off in vapor for this scientist.

Each day his flattery makes us eat a toad,
and each step forward is a step to hell,
unmoved, though previous corpses and their smell
asphyxiate our progress on this road.

Like the poor lush who cannot satisfy,
we try to force our sex with counterfeits,
die drooling on the deliquescent tits,
mouthing the rotten orange we suck dry.

Gangs of demons are boozing in our brain —
ranked, swarming, like a million warrior-ants,
they drown and choke the cistern of our wants;
each time we breathe, we tear our lungs with pain.

If poison, arson, sex, narcotics, knives
have not yet ruined us and stitched their quick,
loud patterns on the canvas of our lives,
it is because our souls are still too sick.

Among the vermin, jackals, panthers, lice,
gorillas and tarantulas that suck
and snatch and scratch and defecate and fuck
in the disorderly circus of our vice,

there's one more ugly and abortive birth.
It makes no gestures, never beats its breast,
yet it would murder for a moment's rest,
and willingly annihilate the earth.

It's BOREDOM. Tears have glued its eyes together.
You know well, my Reader. This obscene
beast chain-smokes yawning for the guillotine —
you — hypocrite Reader — my double — my brother!

Connections

1. Imagine Baudelaire's "Reader" to be the speaker in Eliot's "The Love Song of J. Alfred Prufrock" (p. 781). How does Prufrock match Baudelaire's description? Written in 1857, does this poem still address readers in the 1990s? Explain why or why not.

2. Try rewriting two or three stanzas of this poem in free verse. Read Ginsberg's "America" (p. 785) to get you into one possible rhythm.
3. Compare Baudelaire's treatment of boredom with Berryman's in "Dream Song 14" (p. 755).

FEDERICO GARCÍA LORCA (Spanish/1899–1936)

Somnambule° Ballad

TRANSLATED BY STEPHEN SPENDER AND J. L. GILI

Green, how much I want you green.
Green wind. Green branches.
The ship upon the sea
and the horse in the mountain.
With the shadow on her waist
she dreams on her balcony,
green flesh, hair of green,
and eyes of cold silver.
Green, how much I want you green.
Beneath the gypsy moon,
all things look at her
but she cannot see them.

Green, how much I want you green.
Great stars of white frost
come with the fish of darkness
that opens the road of dawn.
The fig tree rubs the wind
with the sandpaper of its branches,
and the mountain, a filching cat,
bristles its bitter aloes.
But who will come? And from where?
She lingers on her balcony,
green flesh, hair of green,
dreaming of the bitter sea.

— Friend, I want to change
my horse for your house,
my saddle for your mirror,
my knife for your blanket.
Friend, I come bleeding,
from the passes of Cabra.
— If I could, young man,
this pact would be sealed.
But I am no more I,

Somnambule: Sleepwalker.

nor is my house now my house.
—Friend, I want to die
decently in my bed.
Of iron, if it be possible,
with sheets of fine holland.
Do you not see the wound I have
from my breast to my throat?
—Your white shirt bears
three hundred dark roses
Your pungent blood oozes
around your sash.
But I am no more I,
nor is my house now my house.
—Let me climb at least
up to the high balustrades:
let me come! Let me come!
up to the green balustrades.
Balustrades of the moon
where the water resounds.

Now the two friends go up
towards the high balustrades.
Leaving a trail of blood,
leaving a trail of tears.
Small lanterns of tin
were trembling on the roofs.
A thousand crystal tambourines
were piercing the dawn.

Green, how much I want you green,
green wind, green branches.
The two friends went up.
The long wind was leaving
in the mouth a strange taste
of gall, mint and sweet-basil.
Friend! Where is she, tell me,
where is your bitter girl?
How often she waited for you!
How often did she wait for you,
cool face, black hair,
on this green balcony!

Over the face of the cistern
the gypsy girl swayed.
Green flesh, hair of green,
with eyes of cold silver.
An icicle of the moon
suspends her above the water.
The night became as intimate
as a little square.
Drunken civil guards

were knocking at the door.
Green, how much I want you green.
Green wind. Green branches.
The ship upon the sea.
And the horse on the mountain.

Connections

1. What lines are repeated in this poem? What is the effect of these repetitions? Compare their effects with those in Southey's "The Cataract of Lodore" (p. 610).
2. Compare the theme and tone of this poem with those of Keats's "Ode on Melancholy" (p. 700).

LI HO (Chinese/791–817)

A Beautiful Girl Combs Her Hair

TRANSLATED BY DAVID YOUNG

Awake at dawn
she's dreaming
by cool silk curtains

fragrance of spilling hair
half sandalwood, half aloes

windlass creaking at the well
singing jade

the lotus blossom wakes, refreshed

her mirror
two phoenixes
a pool of autumn light

standing on the ivory bed
loosening her hair
watching the mirror

one long coil, aromatic silk
a cloud down to the floor

drop the jade comb — no sound

delicate fingers
pushing the coils into place
color of raven feathers

shining blue-black stuff
the jewelled comb will hardly hold it

spring wind makes me restless
her slovenly beauty upsets me

eighteen and her hair's so thick
she wears herself out fixing it!

she's finished now
the whole arrangement in place

in a cloud-patterned skirt
she walks with even steps
a wild goose on the sand

turns away without a word
where is she off to?

down the steps to break a spray of
    cherry blossoms

Connections

1. Compare the description of hair in this poem with that in Cathy Song's "The White Porch" (p. 904). What significant similarities do you find?
2. Write an essay that explores the differing portraits in this poem and in Roethke's "I Knew a Woman" (p. 842). Which portrait is more interesting to you? Explain why.

MUHAMMAD AL-MAGHUT (Syria/b. 1934)

Tourist 1987

TRANSLATED BY MAY JAYYUSI AND JOHN HEATH-STUBBS

My childhood is a long way off
My old age is a long way off
My country, my exile, a long way off.
Tourist!
Give me your binoculars
Perhaps I might glimpse a hand or a handkerchief
In this whole world
Waving at me
Take my photograph as I weep
Crouching in my tatters on the steps of the hotel
Write on the back of the picture
"This is a poet from the East."
Spread your handkerchief on the pavement
And sit beside me under this tender rain
Let me disclose to you a great secret:
"Go dismiss all your guides
Throw to the mud . . . to the fire
All the notes and impressions you've written
Any old peasant in this land

Can tell you with two verses from our sad *ʿAtāba*° songs
All the history of the East
As he rolls his cigarette in front of his tent."

20 *ʿAtāba:* A nostalgic, sad folk song frequently about separated lovers.

Connections

1. How does the treatment of the tourist here compare with that in James Merrill's description in "Casual Wear" (p. 901)? What do these tourists have in common?
2. In an essay compare the speaker's tone in this poem with that in Felix Mnthali's "The Stranglehold of English Lit." (p. 885). What produces the strong emotion in these speakers?

CZESLAW MILOSZ (Polish/b. 1911)

A Poor Christian Looks at the Ghetto 1943

TRANSLATED BY THE AUTHOR

Bees build around red liver,
Ants build around black bone.
It has begun: the tearing, the trampling on silks,
It has begun: the breaking of glass, wood, copper, nickel, silver, foam
Of gypsum, iron sheets, violin strings, trumpets, leaves, balls, crystals.
Poof! Phosphorescent fire from yellow walls
Engulfs animal and human hair.

Bees build around the honeycomb of lungs,
Ants build around white bone.
Torn is paper, rubber, linen, leather, flax,
Fiber, fabrics, cellulose, snakeskin, wire.
The roof and the wall collapse in flame and heat seizes the foundations.
Now there is only the earth, sandy, trodden down,
With one leafless tree.

Slowly, boring a tunnel, a guardian mole makes his way,
With a small red lamp fastened to his forehead.
He touches burned bodies, counts them, pushes on,
He distinguishes human ashes by their luminous vapor,
The ashes of each man by a different part of the spectrum.
Bees build around a red trace.
Ants build around the place left by my body.

I am afraid, so afraid of the guardian mole.
He has swollen eyelids, like a Patriarch
Who has sat much in the light of candles
Reading the great book of the species.
What will I tell him, I, a Jew of the New Testament,

Waiting two thousand years for the second coming of Jesus?
My broken body will deliver me to his sight
And he will count me among the helpers of death:
The uncircumcised.

Connections

1. To what extent is the historic context in this poem and in Michael Harper's "The Militance of a Photograph in the Passbook of a Bantu under Detention" (p. 895) crucial to understanding these poems?
2. Compare the voices in this poem and in Alegria's "I Am Mirror" (p. 877).

FELIX MNTHALI (Malaŵi/b. 1933)

The Stranglehold of English Lit. 1961

(For Molara Ogundipe-Leslie)

Those questions, sister,
those questions
            stand
            stab
            jab
        and gore
too close to the centre!

For if we had asked
why Jane Austen's people°
carouse all day
and do no work

would Europe in Africa
have stood
the test of time?
and would she still maul
the flower of our youth
in the south?
Would she?

Your elegance of deceit,
Jane Austen.
lulled the sons and daughters
of the dispossessed
into a calf-love

9 *Jane Austen's people:* Characters in books by Jane Austen (1775–1817), famous English novelist of country gentry life; her works include *Sense and Sensibility* (1811), *Pride and Prejudice* (1813), and *Mansfield Park* (1814).

with irony and satire
around imaginary people.

While history went on mocking
the victims of branding irons
and sugar-plantations
that made Jane Austen's people
wealthy beyond compare!

Eng. Lit., my sister,
was more than a cruel joke —
it was the heart
of alien conquest.

How could questions be asked
at Makerere and Ibadan,
Dakar and Ford Hare —
with Jane Austen
at the centre?
How could they be answered?

Connections

1. How important is it to know about the place names mentioned in lines 36–37 in order to understand this poem? Use the library to learn about how these places figured in European colonialism in Africa. Compare the significance of the historic context in this poem with that in Shinkichi Takahashi's "Explosion" (p. 889).
2. Write an essay comparing the uses of Jane Austen in this poem with *Madame Butterfly* in David Henry Hwang's play *M. Butterfly* (p. 1707). What values are associated with Austen and *Madame Butterfly* in these works?

PABLO NERUDA (Chilean/1904–1973)

Sweetness, Always 1958

TRANSLATED BY ALASTAIR REID

Why such harsh machinery?
Why, to write down the stuff
and people of every day,
must poems be dressed up in gold,
in old and fearful stone?

I want verses of felt or feather
which scarcely weigh, mild verses
with the intimacy of beds
where people have loved and dreamed.
I want poems stained
by hands and everydayness.

Verses of pastry which melt
into milk and sugar in the mouth,
air and water to drink,
the bites and kisses of love.
I long for eatable sonnets,
poems of honey and flour.

Vanity keeps prodding us
to lift ourselves skyward
or to make deep and useless
tunnels underground.
So we forget the joyous
love-needs of our bodies.
We forget about pastries.
We are not feeding the world.

In Madras a long time since,
I saw a sugary pyramid,
a tower of confectionery —
one level after another,
and in the construction, rubies,
and other blushing delights,
medieval and yellow.

Someone dirtied his hands
to cook up so much sweetness.

Brother poets from here
and there, from earth and sky,
from Medellín, from Veracruz,
Abyssinia, Antofagasta,
do you know the recipe for honeycombs?

Let's forget all about that stone.

Let your poetry fill up
the equinoctial pastry shop
our mouths long to devour —
all the children's mouths
and the poor adults' also.
Don't go on without seeing,
relishing, understanding
all these hearts of sugar.

Don't be afraid of sweetness.

With us or without us,
sweetness will go on living
and is infinitely alive,
forever being revived,
for it's in a man's mouth,
whether he's eating or singing,
that sweetness has its place.

Connections

1. Compare the view of life offered in this poem with that in Frost's "Provide, Provide" (p. 727).
2. Write an essay that discusses Kinnell's "Blackberry Eating" (p. 608) and Chasin's "The Word *Plum*" (p. 624) as the sort of "eatable" poetry the speaker calls for in this poem.

OCTAVIO PAZ (Mexican/b. 1914)

the Street

A long silent street.
I walk in blackness and I stumble and fall
and rise, and I walk blind, my feet
stepping on silent stones and dry leaves.
Someone behind me also stepping on stones, leaves:
if I slow down, he slows;
if I run, he runs. I turn: nobody.
Everything dark and doorless.
Turning and turning among these corners
which lead forever to the street
where nobody waits for, nobody follows me,
where I pursue a man who stumbles
and rises and says when he sees me: nobody.

Connections

1. How does the speaker's anxiety in this poem compare with that in Frost's "Acquainted with the Night" (p. 582)?
2. Write an essay comparing the tone of this poem and that of Wright's "Lying in a Hammock at William Duffy's Farm in Pine Island, Minnesota" (p. 871). Pay particular attention to how you read the final lines of each poem.

RAINER MARIA RILKE (German/1875–1926)

The Panther

1927

TRANSLATED BY STEPHEN MITCHELL

His vision, from the constantly passing bars,
has grown so weary that it cannot hold
anything else. It seems to him there are
a thousand bars; and behind the bars, no world.

As he paces in cramped circles, over and over,
the movement of his powerful soft strides
is like a ritual dance around a center
in which a mighty will stands paralyzed.

Only at times, the curtain of the pupils
lifts, quietly—. An image enters in,
rushes down through the tensed, arrested muscles,
plunges into the heart and is gone.

Connections

1. How is the panther's situation in this poem similar to that of the animals in Atwood's "Dreams of the Animals" (p. 555)? Try writing an Atwoodlike dream to complete the image Rilke mentions in lines 10–12.
2. Compare the way a sense of movement is achieved by the images and rhythms in this poem and in Dickinson's "A Bird came down the Walk—" (p. 606).

SAPPHO (Greek/c. 612–c. 580 B.C.)

With his venom

TRANSLATED BY MARY BARNARD

With his venom

Irresistible
and bittersweet

that loosener
of limbs, Love

reptile-like
strikes me down

Connections

1. How does your response to the images of love in this poem compare with the response evoked by the images in Cathy Song's "The White Porch" (p. 904)?
2. Discuss the attitudes toward love expressed by Sappho and by Millay in "I Too beneath Your Moon, Almighty Sex" (p. 816).

SHINKICHI TAKAHASHI (Japanese/b. 1901)

Explosion 1973

TRANSLATED BY LUCIEN STRYK AND TAKASHI IKEMOTO

I'm an unthinking dog,
a good-for-nothing cat,

a fog over gutter,
a blossom-swiping rain.

I close my eyes, breathe —
radioactive air! A billion years
and I'll be shrunk to half,
pollution strikes my marrow.

So what — I'll whoop at what
remains. Yet scant blood left,
reduced to emptiness by nuclear
fission, I'm running very fast.

Connections

1. Discuss the significance of the images of running in this poem and in Robert Phillips's "Running on Empty" (p. 902).
2. How does the "So what" of line 9 in this poem compare in tone with Neruda's "Sweetness, Always" (p. 886)?

AN ALBUM OF CONTEMPORARY POEMS

AMY CLAMPITT (b. 1923)

Nothing Stays Put 1989

The strange and wonderful are too much with us.
The protea of the antipodes — a great,
globed, blazing honeybee of a bloom —
for sale in the supermarket! We are in
our decadence, we are not entitled.
What have we done to deserve
all the produce of the tropics —
this fiery trove, the largesse of it
heaped up like cannonballs, these pineapples, bossed
and crested, standing like troops at attention,
these tiers, these balconies of green, festoons
grown sumptuous with stoop labor?

The exotic is everywhere, it comes to us
before there is a yen or a need for it. The green-
grocers, uptown and down, are from South Korea.
Orchids, opulence by the pailful, just slightly
fatigued by the plane trip from Hawaii, are
disposed on the sidewalks; alstroemerias, freesias
fattened a bit in translation from overseas; gladioli
likewise estranged from their piercing ancestral crimson;
as well as, less altered from the original blue cornflower
of the roadsides and railway embankments of Europe, these
bachelor's buttons. But it isn't the railway embankments
their featherweight wheels of cobalt remind me of — it's

a row of them among prim colonnades of cosmos,
snapdragon, nasturtium, bloodsilk red poppies
in my grandmother's garden; a prairie childhood,
the grassland shorn, overlaid with a grid,
unsealed, furrowed, harrowed, and sown with immigrant grasses,
their massive corduroy, their wavering feltings embroidered
here and there by the scarlet shoulder patch of cannas
on a courthouse lawn, by a love knot, a cross-stitch
of living matter, sown and tended by women,
nurturers everywhere of the strange and wonderful,
beneath whose hands what had been alien begins,
as it alters, to grow as though it were indigenous.

But at this remove what I think of as
strange and wonderful — strolling the side streets of Manhattan
on an April afternoon, seeing hybrid pear trees in blossom,
a tossing, vertiginous colonnade of foam up above —
is the white petalfall, the warm snowdrift
of the indigenous wild plum of my childhood.
Nothing stays put. The world is a wheel.
All that we know, that we're
made of, is motion.

Connections

1. Clampitt's opening line echoes Wordsworth's "The World Is Too Much with Us" (p. 646) and therefore invites comparison. How does Clampitt's theme relate to Wordsworth's? Are their complaints similar or different?
2. Write an essay comparing the speakers' tones in this poem and in Ginsberg's "A Supermarket in California" (p. 668). Explain whether Ginsberg's poem might also be aptly titled "Nothing Stays Put."

ROBERT CREELEY (b. 1926)

Fathers **1986**

Scattered, aslant
faded faces a column
a rise of the packed
peculiar place to a
modest height makes
a view of common lots
in winter then, a ground
of battered snow crusted
at the edges under
it all, there under
my fathers their
faded women, friends,
the family all echoed,

names trees more tangible
physical place more tangible
the air of this place the road
going past to Watertown
or down to my mother's
grave, my father's grave, not
now this resonance of
each other one was his, his
survival only, his curious
reticence, his dead state,
his emptiness, his acerbic
edge cuts the hands to
hold him, hold on, wants
the ground, *wants* this frozen ground.

Connections

1. Compare the speaker's tone in this poem with that in Hall's "My Son, My Executioner" (p. 788).
2. Write an essay comparing the structures of this poem and Thomas's "Do not go gentle into that good night" (p. 574). How does the form of each poem contribute to its effects?

RITA DOVE (b. 1952)

Parsley°

1983

I. THE CANE FIELDS

There is a parrot imitating spring
in the palace, its feathers parsley green.
Out of the swamp the cane appears

to haunt us, and we cut it down. El General
searches for a word; he is all the world
there is. Like a parrot imitating spring,

we lie down screaming as rain punches through
and we come up green. We cannot speak an R——
out of the swamp, the cane appears

and then the mountain we call in whispers *Katalina.*°
The children gnaw their teeth to arrowheads.
There is a parrot imitating spring.

Parsley: "On October 2, 1957, Rafael Trujillo (1891–1961), dictator of the Dominican Republic, ordered 20,000 blacks killed because they could not pronounce the letter *r* in *perejil,* the Spanish word for parsley" (Dove's note). 10 *Katalina:* Katarina (see line 8).

El General has found his word: *perejil.*
Who says it, lives. He laughs, teeth shining
out of the swamp. The cane appears

in our dreams, lashed by wind and streaming.
And we lie down. For every drop of blood
there is a parrot imitating spring.
Out of the swamp the cane appears.

II. THE PALACE

The word the general's chosen is parsley.
It is fall, when thoughts turn
to love and death; the general thinks
of his mother, how she died in the fall
and he planted her walking cane at the grave
and it flowered, each spring stolidly forming
four-star blossoms. The general

pulls on his boots, he stomps to
her room in the palace, the one without
curtains, the one with a parrot
in a brass ring. As he paces he wonders
Who can I kill today. And for a moment
the little knot of screams
is still. The parrot, who has traveled

all the way from Australia in an ivory
cage, is, coy as a widow, practising
spring. Ever since the morning
his mother collapsed in the kitchen
while baking skull-shaped candies
for the Day of the Dead,° the general
has hated sweets. He orders pastries
brought up for the bird; they arrive

dusted with sugar on a bed of lace.
The knot in his throat starts to twitch;
he sees his boots the first day in battle
splashed with mud and urine
as a soldier falls at his feet amazed—
how stupid he looked!—at the sound
of artillery. *I never thought it would sing*
the soldier said, and died. Now

the general sees the fields of sugar
cane, lashed by rain and streaming.
He sees his mother's smile, the teeth
gnawed to arrowheads. He hears

39 *Day of the Dead:* A Roman Catholic festival, also known as Corpus Christi ("Body of Christ").

the Haitians sing without R's
as they swing the great machetes:
Katalina, they sing, *Katalina,*

mi madle, mi amol en muelte.° God knows
his mother was no stupid woman; she
could roll an R like a queen. Even
a parrot can roll an R! In the bare room
the bright feathers arch in a parody
of greenery, as the last pale crumbs
disappear under the blackened tongue. Someone

calls out his name in a voice
so like his mother's, a startled tear
splashes the tip of his right boot.
My mother, my love in death.
The general remembers the tiny green sprigs
men of his village wore in their capes
to honor the birth of a son. He will
order many, this time, to be killed

for a single, beautiful word.

57 *mi . . . muelte:* A mispronunciation of *mi madre, mi amor en muerte,* "my mother, my love in death."

Connections

1. Write an essay comparing Dove's portrait of El General with Forché's portrait in "The Colonel" (p. 671). What kinds of values does each military man represent? Which man is more complex?
2. Compare the themes of this poem and Thomas's "The Hand That Signed the Paper" (p. 567). How is power depicted in each poem?

RUTH FAINLIGHT (b. 1931)

Flower Feet

1989

(Silk Shoes in the Whitworth Art Gallery, Manchester, England)

Real women's feet wore these objects
that look like toys or spectacle cases stitched
from bands of coral, jade, and apricot silk
embroidered with twined sprays of flowers.
Those hearts, tongues, crescents, and disks, leather
shapes an inch across, are the soles of shoes
no wider or longer than the span of my ankle.

If the feet had been cut off and the raw stumps
thrust inside the openings, surely
it could not hurt more than broken toes, twisted
back and bandaged tight. An old woman,
leaning on a cane outside her door
in a Chinese village, smiled to tell how
she fought and cried, how when she stood on points
of pain that gnawed like fire, nurse and mother
praised her tottering walk on flower feet.
Her friends nodded, glad the times had changed.
Otherwise, they would have crippled their daughters.

Connections

1. How is the speaker's perspective on tradition and custom in this poem similar to that in Frost's "Mending Wall" (p. 713)?
2. The final line of this poem is startling. Why? How is it similar in its strategy to James Merrill's "Casual Wear" (p. 901)?
3. Compare the view of change in this poem with that in Clampitt's "Nothing Stays Put" (p. 890).

MICHAEL HARPER (b. 1938)

The Militance of a Photograph in the Passbook of a Bantu° under Detention 1985

Peace is the active presence of Justice.

The wrinkles on the brown face
of the carrying case
conform to the buttocks,
on which the streaks of water
from a five-gallon can
dribble on the tailfront
of the borrowed shirt
he would wear if he could
drain the pus from his swaddling
bandages, striations of skin
tunneling into the photograph.

This is no simple mug shot
of a runaway boy in a training
film, Soweto's° pummeled wire,

Bantu: A name once used derogatorily for African blacks, who in South Africa were forced to carry identification cards. 14 *Soweto:* Site of a 1976 demonstration in which more than six hundred blacks were killed.

though the turrets of light
glisten in smoke, the soft
coal hooding his platform
entrance, dull and quiet.

His father's miner's shoes
stand in puddles of polish,
the black soot baked
into images of brittle torso,
an inferno of bullets laid
out in a letter bomb,
the frontispiece of one sergeant-
major blackening his mustache.

On the drive to Evaton
a blank pass away from Sharpeville
where the freehold morgans°
were bought by a black bishop
from Ontario, Canada, on a trek
northward from the Cape in 1908,
I speak to myself as the woman
riding in the backseat talks
of this day, her husband's
death, twenty-three years ago,
run over by an Afrikaner in the wrong
passing lane; the passbook on the shoulder
of the road leading to Evaton
is not the one I have in my hand,
and the photograph is not of my great-
grandfather, who set sail for Philadelphia
in the war year of 1916.
He did not want a reception, his letters
embarking on a platform at Queenstown
where his eloquence struck two Zulu warriors
pledged to die in the homelands
because they could not spin their own gold.

These threaded heads weigh down the ears
in design of the warrior, Shaka,°
indifferent to the ruthless offerings
over the dead bodies of his wives,
childless in his campaigns with the British,
who sits on the ships of the Indian Ocean
each kraal° shuddering near the borders;

her lips turn in profile
to the dust rising over a road
where his house once stood;

29 *morgans:* South African term for about two acres of land. 50 *Shaka:* A powerful Zulu chief who ruled from 1818 to 1828. 55 *kraal:* Village.

one could think of the women
carrying firewood as an etching
in remembrance to the silence,
commencing at Sharpeville,
but this is Evaton, where he would come
from across the galleyship of spears
turning in his robes to a bookmark;
it is a good book, the picture of words
in the gloss of a photograph,
the burned image of the man who wears
this image on the tongue of a child,
who might hold my hand
as we walk in late afternoon
into the predestined sun.

The press of wrinkles on the blanketed
voice of the man who took the train
from Johannesburg
is flattened in Cape Town,
and the history of this book
is on a trestle where Gandhi°
worshipped in Natal,
and the Zulu lullaby
I cannot sing in Bantu
is this song in the body
of a passbook
and the book passes
into a shirt
and the back that wears it.

78 *Gandhi:* Mahatma Gandhi (1869–1948), pacifistic demonstrator for Indian rights whose activism began in South Africa.

Connections

1. Discuss Harper's use of the photograph in this poem and Dove's use of the word *parsley* in her poem by that name (p. 892) as effective means of presenting these poems' respective themes.
2. Write an essay comparing the injustices described in this poem and those in Conrad's short story "An Outpost of Progress" (p. 208). How is racism depicted as being central to injustice in these works?
3. Harper's title for this poem is unusually long. Would Adame's title "Black and White" (p. 743) be better? Explain why or why not.

GALWAY KINNELL (b. 1927)

After Making Love We Hear Footsteps 1980

For I can snore like a bullhorn
or play loud music
or sit up talking with any reasonably sober Irishman
and Fergus will only sink deeper
into his dreamless sleep, which goes by all in one flash,
but let there be that heavy breathing
or a stifled come-cry anywhere in the house
and he will wrench himself awake
and make for it on the run — as now, we lie together,
after making love, quiet, touching along the length of our bodies,
familiar touch of the long-married,
and he appears — in his baseball pajamas, it happens,
the neck opening so small
he has to screw them on, which one day may make him wonder
about the mental capacity of baseball players —
and says, "Are you loving and snuggling? May I join?"
He flops down between us and hugs us and snuggles himself to sleep,
his face gleaming with satisfaction at being this very child.

In the half darkness we look at each other
and smile
and touch arms across his little, startlingly muscled body —
this one whom habit of memory propels to the ground of his making,
sleeper only the mortal sounds can sing awake,
this blessing love gives again into our arms.

Connections

1. Write an essay comparing the tone and theme of this poem and those of Plath's "Morning Song" (p. 832), paying particular attention to the treatment of the child in each poem.
2. Discuss how this poem helps to bring into focus the sense of loss Frost evokes in "Home Burial" (p. 715).

DENISE LEVERTOV (b. 1923)

Gathered at the River 1983

For Beatrice Hawley and John Jagel

As if the trees were not indifferent . . .

A breeze flutters the candles but the trees give off
a sense of listening, of hush.

The dust of August on their leaves.
But it grows dark. Their dark green
is something known about, not seen.

But summer twilight takes away
only color, not form. The tree-forms,
massive trunks and the great domed heads,
leaning in towards us, are visible,

a half-circle of attention.

They listen because the war
we speak of, the human war with ourselves,

the war against earth,
against nature,
is a war against them.

The words are spoken
of those who survived a while,
living shadowgraphs, eyes fixed forever
on witnessed horror,
who survived to give
testimony, that no-one
may plead ignorance.
Contra naturam.° The trees, *Against nature (Latin)*
the trees are not indifferent.

We intone together, *Never again,*

we stand in a circle,
singing, speaking, making vows,

remembering the dead
of Hiroshima,
of Nagasaki.

We are holding candles: we kneel to set them
afloat on the dark river
as they do
there in Hiroshima. We are invoking

saints and prophets,
heroes and heroines of justice and peace,
to be with us, to help us
stop the torment of our evil dreams . . .

Windthreatened flames bob on the current . . .

They don't get far from shore. But none capsizes
even in the swell of a boat's wake.

The waxy paper cups sheltering them
catch fire. But still the candles
sail their gold downstream.

And still the trees ponder our strange doings, as if
well aware that if we fail,
we fail for them:
if our resolves and prayers are weak and fail

there will be nothing left of their slow and innocent wisdom,

no roots,
no bole nor branch,

no memory
of shade,
of leaf,

no pollen.

Connections

1. In her comments on "Gathered at the River" (p. 920), Levertov affirms her "underlying belief in a great design, a potential harmony which can be violated or be sustained." How does Frost's "Design" (p. 725) comment on Levertov's beliefs? Explain whether you agree with Levertov or not.
2. Levertov also expresses a concern in her essay for the necessity of having "a sense of the sacredness of the earthly creation" and mentions that Gerard Manley Hopkins has always been one of her favorite poets. Write an essay comparing "Gathered at the River" and Hopkins's "God's Grandeur" (p. 614) or "Pied Beauty" (p. 797). What significant similarities do you find?

PETER MEINKE (b. 1932)

The ABC of Aerobics

1983

Air seeps through alleys and our diaphragms
balloon blackly with this mix of
carbon monoxide and the thousand corrosives a city
doles out free to its constituents;
everyone's jogging through Edgemont Park,
frightened by death and fatty tissue,
gasping at the maximal heart rate,
hoping to outlive all the others streaming
in the lanes like lemmings lurching toward their last
jump. I join in despair
knowing my arteries jammed with
lint and tobacco, lard and bourbon — my
medical history a noxious marsh:
newts and moles slink through the sodden veins,
owls hoot in the lungs' dark branches;
probably I shall keel off the john like
queer Uncle George and lie on the bathroom floor
raging about Shirley Clark, my true love in

seventh grade, God bless her wherever she lives
tied to that turkey who hugely
undervalues the beauty of her tiny earlobes, one
view of which (either one: they are both perfect)
would add years to my life and I could skip these
x-rays, turn in my insurance card, and trade
yoga and treadmills and jogging and zen and
zucchini for drinking and dreaming of her, breathing hard.

Connections

1. Write an essay comparing the way Sharon Olds connects sex and exercise in "Sex without Love" (p. 902) with Meinke's treatment here.
2. Compare the voices in this poem and in Kinnell's "After Making Love We Hear Footsteps" (p. 898). Which do you find more appealing? Why?

JAMES MERRILL (b. 1926)

Casual Wear 1984

Your average tourist: Fifty. 2.3
Times married. Dressed, this year, in Ferdi Plinthbower
Originals. Odds 1 to 9
Against her strolling past the Embassy

Today at noon. Your average terrorist:
Twenty-five. Celibate. No use for trends,
At least in clothing. Mark, though, where it ends.
People have come forth made of colored mist

Unsmiling on one hundred million screens
To tell of his prompt phone call to the station,
"Claiming responsibility" — devastation
Signed with a flourish, like the dead wife's jeans.

Connections

1. Compare the satire in this poem with that in Meinke's "The ABC of Aerobics." What is satirized in each poem? Which satire is more pointed from your perspective?
2. Write an essay comparing this poem's profiles of the "average tourist" and "terrorist" with either Auden's "The Unknown Citizen" (p. 755) or Nemerov's "Life Cycle of Common Man" (p. 825). How are these profiles made convincing?

SHARON OLDS (b. 1942)

Sex without Love

1984

How do they do it, the ones who make love
without love? Beautiful as dancers,
gliding over each other like ice skaters
over the ice, fingers hooked
inside each other's bodies, faces
red as steak, wine, wet as the
children at birth whose mothers are going to
give them away. How do they come to the
come to the   come to the   God   come to the
still waters, and not love
the one who came there with them, light
rising slowly as steam off their joined
skin? These are the true religious,
the purists, the pros, the ones who will not
accept a false Messiah, love the
priest instead of the God. They do not
mistake the lover for their own pleasure,
they are like great runners: they know they are alone
with the road surface, the cold, the wind,
the fit of their shoes, their over-all cardio-
vascular health — just factors, like the partner
in the bed, and not the truth, which is the
single body alone in the universe
against its own best time.

Connections

1. How does the treatment of sex and love in Olds's poem compare with that in E. E. Cummings's "she being Brand" (p. 527)?
2. Just as Olds describes sex without love, she implies a definition of love in this poem. Consider whether the lovers in Wilbur's "A Late Aubade" (p. 536) fall within Olds's definition.

ROBERT PHILLIPS (b. 1938)

Running on Empty

1981

As a teenager I would drive Father's
Chevrolet cross-county, given me

reluctantly: "Always keep the tank
half full, boy, half full, ya hear?"

The fuel gauge dipping, dipping
toward Empty, hitting Empty, then

— thrilling — 'way below Empty,
myself driving cross-county

mile after mile, faster and faster,
all night long, this crazy kid driving

the earth's rolling surface,
against all laws, defying chemistry,

rules, and time, riding on nothing
but fumes, pushing luck harder

than anyone pushed before, the wind
screaming past like the Furies° . . .

I stranded myself only once, a white
night with no gas station open, ninety miles

from nowhere. Panicked for a while,
at standstill, myself stalled.

At dawn the car and I both refilled. But,
Father, I am running on empty still.

16 *Furies:* In Greek mythology, deities who pursue and torment evildoers.

Connections

1. Discuss the metaphoric use of cars in this poem and in Chapman's song "Fast Car" (p. 513). Do you think Phillips's poem would make effective lyrics for a song? Why or why not?
2. In an essay explore the father-son relationships in this poem and in Cheever's short story "Reunion" (p. 369). How do these sons feel about their fathers?

ALBERTO RÍOS (b. 1952)

Seniors 1985

William cut a hole in his Levi's pocket
so he could flop himself out in class
behind the girls so the other guys
could see and shit what guts we all said.
All Konga wanted to do over and over
was the rubber band trick, but he showed
everyone how, so nobody wanted to see
anymore and one day he cried, just cried
until his parents took him away forever.
Maya had a Hotpoint refrigerator standing
in his living room, just for his family to show
anybody who came that they could afford it.

Me, I got a French kiss, finally, in the catholic
darkness, my tongue's farthest half vacationing

loudly in another mouth like a man in Bermudas,
and my body jumped against a flagstone wall,
I could feel it through her thin, almost
nonexistent body: I had, at that moment, that moment,
a hot girl on a summer night, the best of all
the things we tried to do. Well, she
let me kiss her, anyway, all over.

Or it was just a flagstone wall
with a flaw in the stone, an understanding cavity
for burning young men with smooth dreams —
the true circumstance is gone, the true
circumstances about us all then
are gone. But when I kissed her, all water,
she would close her eyes, and they into somewhere
would disappear. Whether she was there
or not, I remember her, clearly, and she moves
around the room, sometimes, until I sleep.

I have lain on the desert in watch
low in the back of a pick-up truck
for nothing in particular, for stars, for
the things behind stars, and nothing comes
more than the moment: always now, here in a truck,
the moment again to dream of making love and sweat,
this time to a woman, or even to all of them
in some allowable way, to those boys, then,
who couldn't cry, to the girls before they were
women, to friends, me on my back, the sky over me
pressing its simple weight into her body
on me, into the bodies of them all, on me.

Connections

1. Compare the treatment of sex in this poem with that in Olds's "Sex without Love" (p. 902).
2. Think about "Seniors" as a kind of love poem and compare the speaker's voice here with the one in Eliot's "The Love Song of J. Alfred Prufrock" (p. 781). How are these two voices used to evoke cultural contexts? Of what value is love in these cultures?

CATHY SONG (b. 1955)

The White Porch

1983

I wrap the blue towel
after washing,
around the damp
weight of hair, bulky

as a sleeping cat,
and sit out on the porch.
Still dripping water,
it'll be dry by supper,
by the time the dust
settles off your shoes,
though it's only five
past noon. Think
of the luxury: how to use
the afternoon like the stretch
of lawn spread before me.
There's the laundry,
sun-warm clothes at twilight,
and the mountain of beans
in my lap. Each one,
I'll break and snap
thoughtfully in half.

But there is this slow arousal.
The small buttons
of my cotton blouse
are pulling away from my body.
I feel the strain of threads,
the swollen magnolias
heavy as a flock of birds
in the tree. Already,
the orange sponge cake
is rising in the oven.
I know you'll say it makes
your mouth dry
and I'll watch you
drench your slice of it
in canned peaches
and lick the plate clean.

So much hair, my mother
used to say, grabbing
the thick braided rope
in her hands while we washed
the breakfast dishes, discussing
dresses and pastries.
My mind often elsewhere
as we did the morning chores together.
Sometimes, a few strands
would catch in her gold ring.
I worked hard then,
anticipating the hour
when I would let the rope down
at night, strips of sheets,
knotted and tied,

while she slept in tight blankets.
My hair, freshly washed
like a measure of wealth,
like a bridal veil.
Crouching in the grass,
you would wait for the signal,
for the movement of curtains
before releasing yourself
from the shadow of moths.
Cloth, hair and hands,
smuggling you in.

Connections

1. Compare the images used to describe the speaker's "slow arousal" in this poem with Croft's images in "Home-Baked Bread" (p. 558). What similarities do you see? What makes each description so effective?
2. Write an essay comparing images of sensuality in this poem and Li Ho's "A Beautiful Girl Combs Her Hair" (p. 882). Which poem seems more erotic to you? Why?

23. Perspectives on Poetry

A variety of observations about poetry is presented in this chapter. The pieces offer a wide range of topics related to reading and writing poetry. The perspectives include William Wordsworth on the nature of poetry, Matthew Arnold on classic and popular literature, Ezra Pound on free verse, William Stafford on how poems get written, and Denise Levertov on the background and form of one of her poems. In addition, there are poems about poetry by Walt Whitman, Archibald MacLeish, and Robert Francis. These relatively short pieces provide materials to explore some of the topics and issues that readers and writers of poetry have found perennially interesting and challenging.

WILLIAM WORDSWORTH (1770–1850)

On the Nature of Poets and Poetry 1802

Taking up the subject, then, upon general grounds, I ask what is meant by the word "poet"? What is a poet? To whom does he address himself? And what language is to be expected from him? He is a man speaking to men: a man, it is true, endued with more lively sensibility, more enthusiasm and tenderness, who has a greater knowledge of human nature, and a more comprehensive soul, than are supposed to be common among mankind; a man pleased with his own passions and volitions, and who rejoices more than other men in the spirit of life that is in him; delighting to contemplate similar volitions and passions as manifested in the goings-on of the universe, and habitually impelled to create them where he does not find them. To these qualities he has added a disposition to be affected more than other men by absent things as if they were present; an ability of conjuring up in himself passions, which are indeed far from being the same as those produced by real events, yet (especially in those parts of the general sympathy which are pleasing and delightful) do more nearly resemble the passions produced by real events, than anything which, from the motions of their own minds merely, other men are accustomed to feel in themselves; whence, and from practice, he has acquired a greater readiness and power in expressing what he thinks and feels, and especially those thoughts and feelings which, by his own choice, or from the structure of his own mind, arise in him without immediate external excitement. . . .

I have said that poetry is the spontaneous overflow of powerful feelings: it takes its origin from emotion recollected in tranquility: the emotion is contemplated till by a species of reaction the tranquility gradually disappears, and an emotion, kindred to that which was before the subject of contemplation, is gradually produced, and does itself actually exist in the mind. In this mood successful composition generally begins, and in a mood similar to this it is carried on; but the emotion, of whatever kind and in whatever degree, from various causes is qualified by various pleasures, so that in describing any passions whatsoever, which are voluntarily described, the mind will upon the whole be in a state of enjoyment. Now, if nature be thus cautious in preserving in a state of enjoyment a being thus employed, the poet ought to profit by the lesson thus held forth to him, and ought especially to take care, that whatever passions he communicates to his reader, those passions, if his reader's mind be sound and vigorous, should always be accompanied with an overbalance of pleasure. Now the music of harmonious metrical language, the sense of difficulty overcome, and the blind association of pleasure which has been previously received from works of rhyme or meter of the same or similar construction, an indistinct perception perpetually renewed of language closely resembling that of real life, and yet, in the circumstance of meter, differing from it so widely, all these imperceptibly make up a complex feeling of delight, which is of the most important use in tempering the painful feeling which will always be found intermingled with powerful descriptions of the deeper passions. This effect is always produced in pathetic and impassioned poetry; while, in lighter compositions, the ease and gracefulness with which the poet manages his numbers are themselves confessedly a principal source of the gratification of the reader. I might perhaps include all which it is *necessary* to say upon this subject by affirming, what few persons will deny, that, of two descriptions, either of passions, manners, or characters, each of them equally well executed, the one in prose and the other in verse, the verse will be read a hundred times where the prose is read once.

From *Preface to Lyrical Ballads, with Pastoral and Other Poems*

Considerations

1. Discuss Wordsworth's description of a poet's sensibility and "ability of conjuring up in himself passions." What characteristics do you associate with a poetic temperament?
2. Explain why a writer's emotions are (or are not) so much more important in poetry than in prose.
3. Given that Wordsworth describes poetry as "the spontaneous overflow of powerful feelings," why can't his poems be characterized as formless bursts of raw emotion? Consider, for example, "London, 1802" (p. 572), "My Heart Leaps Up" (p. 629), or "The World Is Too Much with Us" (p. 646) to illustrate your response.

WALT WHITMAN (1819–1892)

When I Heard the Learned Astronomer 1865

When I heard the learned astronomer,
When the proofs, the figures, were ranged in columns before me,
When I was shown the charts and diagrams, to add, divide, and measure them,
When I sitting heard the astronomer where he lectured with much applause in the lecture-room,
How soon unaccountable I became tired and sick,
Till rising and gliding out I wandered off by myself,
In the mystical moist night-air, and from time to time,
Looked up in perfect silence at the stars.

Considerations

1. How does this poem illustrate the differences between poetry and science?
2. Many people today — rightly or wrongly — continue to regard science and poetry as antithetical. What do you think of their view? Write an essay about the methods and purposes of science and poetry in which you explore the differences and/or similarities between them. Use specific poems as evidence for your argument.

PERCY BYSSHE SHELLEY (1792–1822)

On Poets as "Unacknowledged Legislators" 1821

The most unfailing herald, companion, and follower of the awakening of a great people to work a beneficial change in opinion or institution, is poetry. At such periods there is an accumulation of the power of communicating and receiving intense and impassioned conceptions respecting man and nature. The persons in whom this power resides, may often, as far as regards many portions of their nature, have little apparent correspondence with that spirit of good of which they are the ministers. But even whilst they deny and abjure, they are yet compelled to serve, the power which is seated upon the throne of their own soul. It is impossible to read the compositions of the most celebrated writers of the present day without being startled with the electric life which burns within their words. They measure the circumference and sound the depths of human nature with a comprehensive and all-penetrating spirit, and they are themselves perhaps the most sincerely astonished at its manifestations, for it is less their spirit than the spirit of the age. Poets are the hierophants° of an unapprehended inspiration, the mirrors of the gigantic shadows which futurity casts upon the present, the words which express what they understand not; the trumpets which sing to battle, and feel not what they inspire: the influence which is moved not, but moves. Poets are the unacknowledged legislators of the world.

From *A Defense of Poetry*

hierophants: Interpreters of sacred mysteries.

Considerations

1. What kinds of powers does Shelley attribute to poets?
2. Compare Shelley's view of the poet with Karl Shapiro's (p. 913).

MATTHEW ARNOLD (1822–1888)

On Classic and Popular Literature 1888

The benefit of being able clearly to feel and deeply to enjoy the best, the truly classic, in poetry, — is an end . . . of supreme importance. We are often told that an era is opening in which we are to see multitudes of a common sort of readers, and masses of a common sort of literature; that such readers do not want and could not relish anything better than such literature, and that to provide it is becoming a vast and profitable industry. Even if good literature entirely lost currency with the world, it would still be abundantly worth while to continue to enjoy it by oneself. But it never will lose currency with the world, in spite of momentary appearances; it never will lose supremacy. Currency and supremacy are insured to it, not indeed by the world's deliberate and conscious choice, but by something far deeper, — by the instinct of self-preservation in humanity.

From "The Study of Poetry"

Considerations

1. What, in your opinion, makes a work of literature "truly classic"?
2. What kinds of assumptions does Arnold implicitly make about readers of classics and the "multitudes of a common sort"? Do you agree with his categorizations and assessment of these two kinds of readers? Why or why not?
3. Take a stroll through your local bookstore to get a sense of the amount of space allocated to "classics," science fiction, romances, fantasy, mysteries, cookbooks, health books, and so on. Pay particular attention to the poetry section. Also, check to see what books are on the current best-seller lists (they're usually posted by the cash register). Then write a two-part report: in the first part write up your findings as you think Arnold would describe such a "vast and profitable industry"; in the second explain why you agree or disagree with Arnold's perspective.

EZRA POUND (1885–1972)

On Free Verse 1912

I think one should write vers libre [free verse] when one "must," that is to say, only when the "thing" builds up a rhythm more beautiful than that of set meters, or more real, more a part of the emotion of the "thing," more germane, intimate, interpretative than the measure of regular accentual verse; a rhythm which discontents one with set iambic or set anapestic.

From "Prolegomena," *Poetry Review*

Considerations

1. What implications are there in Pound's statement concerning the relation of a poem's form to its content?
2. Compare this view with Whitman's (p. 909).
3. Select a free verse poem from the text and apply Pound's criteria to it. How are the poem's lines arranged to "a part of the emotion of the 'thing' "?

ARCHIBALD MACLEISH (1892–1982)

Ars Poetica

1926

A poem should be palpable and mute
As a globed fruit,

Dumb
As old medallions to the thumb,

Silent as the sleeve-worn stone
Of casement ledges where the moss has grown —

A poem should be wordless
As the flight of birds.

A poem should be motionless in time
As the moon climbs,

Leaving, as the moon releases
Twig by twig the night-entangled trees,

Leaving, as the moon behind the winter leaves,
Memory by memory the mind —

A poem should be motionless in time
As the moon climbs.

A poem should be equal to:
Not true.

For all the history of grief
An empty doorway and a maple leaf.

For love
The leaning grasses and two lights above the sea —

A poem should not mean
But be.

Considerations

1. The Latin title of this poem is translated as "The Art of Poetry." What is MacLeish's view of good poetry? In what sense can a poem be "wordless"? How do lines 19–20 illustrate that?
2. Explain the final two lines. Does the poem contradict its own announced values?
3. How does MacLeish's attitude toward poetry compare with Robert Francis's view in "Glass" (p. 912)?

ROBERT FRANCIS (1901–1987)

Glass

1949

Words of a poem should be glass
But glass so simple-subtle its shape
Is nothing but the shape of what it holds.

A glass spun for itself is empty,
Brittle, at best Venetian trinket.
Embossed glass hides the poem or its absence

Words should be looked through, should be windows.
The best word were invisible.
The poem is the thing the poet thinks.

If the impossible were not
And if the glass, only the glass,
Could be removed, the poem would remain.

Considerations

1. How is the form of a poem ideally like glass, according to Francis? Why is that not an achievable ideal?
2. Compare what Francis has to say about the words of a poem with what Dylan Thomas says (p. 913). Although each approaches the topic from a different perspective, do you think they are in basic agreement or disagreement?

E. E. CUMMINGS (1894–1962)

On the Artist's Responsibility

1953

So far as I am concerned, poetry and every other art was and is and forever will be strictly and distinctly a question of individuality . . . poetry is being, not doing. If you wish to follow, even at a distance, the poet's calling (and here, as always, I speak from my own totally biased and entirely personal point of view) you've got to come out of the measurable doing universe into the immeasurable house of being. . . . Nobody else can be alive for you; nor can you be alive for anybody else. Toms can be Dicks and Dicks can be Harrys, but none of them can ever be you. There's the artist's responsibility; and the most awful responsibility on earth. If you can take it, take it — and be. If you can't, cheer up and go about other people's business; and do (or undo) till you drop.

From *i: Six Nonlectures*

Considerations

1. What does Cummings mean when he says "poetry is being, not doing"? How does this compare with MacLeish's view in "Ars Poetica" (p. 911)?
2. How is Cummings's insistence upon individuality reflected in the style of "1(a" (p. 505) and the theme of "next to course god america i" (p. 588)?

KARL SHAPIRO (b. 1913)

On the Poet's Vision 1960

The poet really does see the world differently, and everything in it. He does not deliberately go into training to sharpen his senses; he is a poet because his senses are naturally open and vitally sensitive. But what the poet sees with his always new vision is not what is "imaginary"; he sees what others have forgotten how to see. The poet is always inadvertently stripping away the veils and showing us his reality. Many poets, as we know, go mad because they cannot bear the worlds of illusion and falsehood in which most human beings spend their lives.

From *In Defense of Ignorance*

Considerations

1. Select a poem from this book that illustrates Shapiro's statement that poets see "what others have forgotten how to see." What "reality" does the poem offer that you had forgotten, overlooked, or hadn't previously apprehended?
2. Do you agree that "most human beings spend their lives" in "worlds of illusion and falsehood"? Why or why not?

DYLAN THOMAS (1914–1953)

On the Words in Poetry 1961

You want to know why and how I just began to write poetry. . . .

To answer . . . this question, I should say I wanted to write poetry in the beginning because I had fallen in love with words. The first poems I knew were nursery rhymes, and before I could read them for myself I had come to love just the words of them, the words alone. What the words stood for, symbolized, or meant, was of very secondary importance. What mattered was the *sound* of them as I heard them for the first time on the lips of the remote and incomprehensible grown-ups who seemed, for some reason, to be living in my world. And these words were, to me, as the notes of bells, the sounds of musical instruments, the noises of wind, sea, and rain, the rattle of milkcarts, the clopping of hooves on cobbles, the fingering of branches on a window pane, might be to someone, deaf from birth, who has miraculously found his hearing. I did not care what the words said, overmuch, not what happened to Jack and Jill and the Mother Goose rest of them; I cared for the shapes of sound that their names, and the words describing their actions, made in my ears; I cared for the colors the words cast on my eyes. I realize that I may be, as I think back all that way, romanticizing my reactions to the simple and beautiful words of those pure poems; but that is all I can honestly remember, however much time might have falsified my memory. I fell in love — that is the only expression I can think of — at once, and am still at the mercy of words, though sometimes now, knowing a little of their behavior very well, I think I can influence them slightly and have even learned to beat them now and then, which they appear to enjoy. I tumbled for words at once. And, when I began to read the nursery rhymes for myself, and, later, to read other verses and ballads, I knew that I had discovered the most important things, to me, that could be ever. There they were, seemingly lifeless, made only of black and white, but out of them, out of their own being, came love and terror and pity and pain and wonder and all the other vague abstractions that make our ephemeral lives dangerous, great, and bearable. Out of them came the gusts and grunts and hiccups and heehaws of the common fun of the earth; and though what the words meant was, in its own way, often deliciously funny enough, so much funnier seemed to me, at that almost forgotten time, the shape and shade and size and noise of the words as they hummed, strummed, jugged, and galloped along. That was the time of innocence; words burst upon me, unencumbered by trivial or portentous association; words were their springlike selves, fresh with Eden's dew, as they flew out of the air. They made their own original associations as they sprang and shone. The words, "Ride a cock-horse to Banbury Cross," were as haunting to me, who did not know then what a cock-horse was nor cared a damn where Banbury Cross might be, as, much later, were such lines as John Donne's, "Go and catch a falling star, Get with child a mandrake root," which also I could not understand when I first read them. And as I read more and more, and it was not all verse, by any means, my love for the real life of words increased until I knew that I must live *with* them and *in* them always. I knew, in fact, that I must be a writer of words, and nothing else. The first thing was to feel and know their sound and substance; what I was going to do with those words, what use I was going to make of them, what I was going to *say* through them, would come later. I knew I had to know them most intimately in all their forms and moods, their ups and downs, their chops and changes, their needs and demands. (Here, I am afraid, I am beginning to talk too vaguely. I do not like writing *about* words, because then I often use bad and wrong and stale and wooly words. What I like to do is treat words as a craftsman does his wood or stone or what-have-you, to hew, carve, mold, coil, polish, and plane them into patterns, sequences, sculptures, fugues of sound expressing some lyrical impulse, some spiritual doubt or conviction, some dimly-realized truth I must try to reach and realize.)

From *Early Prose Writings*

Considerations

1. Why does Thomas value nursery rhymes so highly? What nursery rhyme was your favorite as a child? Why were you enchanted by it?
2. Explain what you think Thomas would have to say about Carroll's "Jabberwocky" (p. 616) or Swenson's "A Nosty Fright" (p. 605).
3. Consider Thomas's comparison at the end of this passage, in which he likens a poet's work to a craftsman's. In what sense is making poetry similar to sculpting, painting, or composing music? What are some of the significant differences?

SYLVIA PLATH (1932–1963)

On "Headline Poetry" 1962

The issues of our time which preoccupy me at the moment are the incalculable genetic effects of fallout and a documentary article on the terrifying, mad, omnipotent marriage of big business and the military in America. . . . Does this influence the kind of poetry I write? Yes, but in a sidelong fashion. I am not gifted with the tongue of Jeremiah,° though I may be sleepless enough before my vision of the apocalypse. My poems do not turn out to be about Hiroshima, but about a child forming itself finger by finger in the dark. They are not about the terrors of mass extinction, but about the bleakness of the moon over a yew tree in a neighboring graveyard. Not about the testaments of tortured Algerians, but about the night thoughts of a tired surgeon.

In a sense, these poems are deflections. I do not think they are an escape. For me, the real issues of our time are the issues of every time — the hurt and wonder of loving; making in all its forms, children, loaves of bread, paintings, building; and the conservation of life of all people in all places, the jeopardizing of which no abstract doubletalk of "peace" or "implacable foes" can excuse.

I do not think a "headline poetry" would interest more people any more profoundly than the headlines. And unless the up-to-the-minute poem grows out of something closer to the bone than a general, shifting philanthropy and is, indeed, that unicorn-thing — a real poem — it is in danger of being screwed up as rapidly as the news sheet itself.

From "Context," *London Magazine,* February 1962

Jeremiah: (c. 650–585 B.C.) One of the greatest Old Testament prophets.

Considerations

1. Why does Plath refuse to write "headline poetry"? What kind of poetry does she prefer? Read the Plath poems included in this anthology (see the index) and discuss whether the issues they address "are the issues of every time."
2. Do you agree that the poetry Plath prefers is not "an escape" from contemporary issues? Explain why or why not.
3. Compare Plath's view of poetry with Audre Lorde's perspective (p. 918). Write an essay about the significant similarities and differences you find between the two.

WILLIAM STAFFORD (b. 1914)

On the Writing of Poetry 1970

A writer is not so much someone who has something to say as he is someone who has found a process that will bring about new things he would not have thought of if he had started to say them. That is, he does not draw on a reservoir; instead, he engages in an activity that brings to him a whole succession of unforeseen stories, poems, essays, plays, laws, philosophies, religions, or — but wait!

Back in school, from the first when I began to try to write things, I felt this richness. One thing would lead to another; the world would give and give. Now, after twenty years or so of trying, I live by that certain richness, an idea hard to pin, difficult to say, and perhaps offensive to some. For there are strange implications in it.

One implication is the importance of just plain receptivity. When I write, I like to have an interval before me when I am not likely to be interrupted. For me, this means usually the early morning, before others are awake. I get pen and paper, take a glance out of the window (often it is dark out there), and wait. It is like fishing. But I do not wait very long, for there is always a nibble — and this is where receptivity comes in. To get started I will accept anything that occurs to me. Something always occurs, of course, to any of us. We can't keep from thinking. Maybe I have to settle for an immediate impression: it's cold, or hot, or dark, or bright, or in between! Or — well, the possibilities are endless. If I put down something, that thing will help the next thing come, and I'm off. If I let the process go on, things will occur to me that were not at all in my mind when I started. These things, odd or trivial as they may be, are somehow connected. And if I let them string out, surprising things will happen.

If I let them string out. . . . Along with initial receptivity, then, there is another readiness: I must be willing to fail. If I am to keep on writing, I cannot bother to insist on high standards. I must get into action and not let anything stop me, or even slow me much. By "standards" I do not mean "correctness" — spelling, punctuation, and so on. These details become mechanical for anyone who writes for a while. I am thinking about such matters as social significance, positive values, consistency, etc. I resolutely disregard these. Something better, greater, is happening! I am following a process that leads so wildly and originally into new territory that no judgment can at the moment be made about values, significance, and so on. I am making something new, something that has not been judged before. Later others — and maybe I myself — will make judgments. Now, I am headlong to discover. Any distraction may harm the creating.

So, receptive, careless of failure, I spin out things on the page. And a wonderful freedom comes. If something occurs to me, it is all right to accept it. It has one justification: it occurs to me. No one else can guide me. I must follow my own weak, wandering, diffident impulses.

A strange bonus happens. At times, without my insisting on it, my writings become coherent; the successive elements that occur to me are clearly related. They lead by themselves to new connections. Sometimes the language, even the syllables that happen along, may start a trend. Sometimes the materials alert me to something waiting in my mind, ready for sustained attention. At such times, I allow myself to be eloquent, or intentional, or for great swoops (Treacherous! Not to be trusted!) reasonable. But I do not insist on any of that; for I know that back of my activity there will be the coherence of my self, and that indulgence of my impulses will bring recurrent patterns and meanings again.

This attitude toward the process of writing creatively suggests a problem for me, in terms of what others say. They talk about "skills" in writing. Without denying that I do have experience, wide reading, automatic orthodoxies and maneuvers of various kinds, I still must insist that I am often baffled about what "skill" has to do with the precious little area of confusion when I do not know what I am going to say and then I find out what I am going to say. That precious interval I am unable to bridge by skill. What can I witness about it? It remains mysterious, just as all of us must feel puzzled about how we are so inventive as to be able to talk along through complexities with our friends, not needing to plan what we are going to say, but never stalled for long in our confident forward progress. Skill? If so, it is the skill we all have, something we must have learned before the age of three or four.

A writer is one who has become accustomed to trusting that grace, or luck, or — skill.

Yet another attitude I find necessary: most of what I write, like most of what I say in casual conversation, will not amount to much. Even I will realize, and even at the time, that it is not negotiable. It will be like practice. In conversation I allow myself random remarks — in fact, as I recall, that is the way I learned to talk — so in writing I launch many expendable efforts. A result of this free way of writing is that I am not writing for others, mostly; they will not see the product at all unless the activity eventuates in something that later appears to be worthy. My guide is the self, and its adventuring in the language brings about communication.

This process-rather-than-substance view of writing invites a final, dual reflection:

1. Writers may not be special — sensitive or talented in any usual sense. They are simply engaged in sustained use of a language skill we all have. Their "creations" come about through confident reliance on stray impulses that will, with trust, find occasional patterns that are satisfying.

2. But writing itself is one of the great, free human activities. There is scope for individuality, and elation, and discovery, in writing. For the person who follows with trust and forgiveness what occurs to him, the world remains always ready and deep, an inexhaustible environment, with the combined vividness of an actuality and flexibility of a dream. Working back and forth between experience and thought, writers have more than space and time can offer. They have the whole unexplored realm of human vision.

"A Way of Writing," *Field*

Considerations

1. Why is "receptivity" important to Stafford's writing process? Explain whether you think his poem "Traveling through the Dark" (p. 591) illustrates this idea.
2. Explain Stafford's "process-rather-than-substance view of writing." Why is the process so important to him?
3. Stafford's remarks about writing are directed toward poetry. Do they strike you as useful for other kinds of writing too? Explain why or why not.

AUDRE LORDE (b. 1934)

Poems Are Not Luxuries 1977

For each of us as women, there is a dark place within where hidden and growing our true spirit rises, "Beautiful and tough as chestnut / Stanchions against our nightmare of weakness" and of impotence. These places of possibility within ourselves are dark because they are ancient and hidden; they have survived and grown strong through darkness. Within these deep places, each one of us holds an incredible reserve of creativity and power, storehouse of unexamined and unrecorded emotion and feeling. The woman's place of power within each of us is neither white nor surface; it is dark, it is ancient, and it is deep.

When we view living, in the european mode, only as a problem to be solved, we rely solely upon our ideas to make us free, for these were what the white fathers told us were precious. But as we become more in touch with our own ancient, black, noneuropean view of living as a situation to be experienced and interacted with, we learn more and more to cherish our feelings, to respect those hidden sources of our power from where true knowledge and therefore lasting action comes. At this point in time, I believe that women carry within ourselves the possibility for fusion of these two approaches as a keystone for survival, and we come closest to this combination in our poetry. I speak here of poetry as the revelation or distillation of experience, not the sterile word play that, too often, the white fathers distorted the word *poetry* to mean — in order to cover their desperate wish for imagination without insight.

For women, then, poetry is not a luxury. It is a vital necessity of our existence. It forms the quality of the light within which we predicate our hopes and dreams toward survival and change, first made into language, then into idea, then into more tangible action. Poetry is the way we help give name to the nameless so it can be thought. The farthest external horizons of our hopes and fears are cobbled by our poems, carved from the rock experiences of our daily lives.

As they become known and accepted to ourselves, our feelings, and the honest exploration of them, become sanctuaries and fortresses and spawning grounds for the most radical and daring of ideas, the house of difference so necessary to change and the conceptualization of any meaningful action. Right now, I could name at least ten ideas I would once have found intolerable or incomprehensible and frightening, except as they came after dreams and poems. This is not idle fantasy, but the true meaning of "It feels right to me." We can train ourselves to respect our feelings and to discipline (transpose) them into a language that catches those feelings so they can be shared. And where that language does not yet exist, it is our poetry which helps to fashion it. Poetry is not only dream or vision, it is the skeleton architecture of our lives.

From "Poems Are Not Luxuries," in *Claims for Poetry,*
edited by Donald Hall

Considerations

1. What distinctions does Lorde make between black culture and "european" culture? How does she describe their different approaches to poetry? Do you agree or disagree with Lorde's assessment?

2. According to Lorde, why can't poetry be regarded as a luxury?
3. Read Lorde's poem "Hanging Fire" (p. 810) and discuss whether you think it fulfills her description of what poetry can do.

MARK STRAND (b. 1934)

On the Audience for Poetry 1977

Interviewer: Are you disturbed by a sense of coterie in recent poetry, by the fact that the audience is so small and ingrown?

Strand: The impression is a little deceptive. The audience for poetry is actually growing bigger, and it constantly changes. A lot of people are interested in poetry for a while, then fall behind and lose interest and get intrigued by other things. But new people are always coming along. The smallness of the audience doesn't bother me. I don't believe poetry is for everyone any more than I believe roast pork is for everyone. Poetry is demanding. It takes a certain amount of getting used to, a period of initiation. Only those people who are willing to spend *time* with it really get anything out of it. No, the lack of audience doesn't bother me. Some poets have 100,000 readers, but I don't believe that many really read poetry. I think if I had that many readers I'd begin to feel that something was *wrong* in my poems.

From an interview by Richard Vine and Robert von Hallberg
in *Chicago Review,* Spring 1977

Considerations

1. What is your impression about the size of audiences for poetry? Are they growing larger or smaller? Explain why.
2. Write an essay in which you agree or disagree with Strand's statement "I don't believe poetry is for everyone any more than I believe roast pork is for everyone."
3. Do you think that if a poet is very popular, there might be something *"wrong"* with his or her poems? Explain why or why not.

GALWAY KINNELL (b. 1927)

The Female and Male Principles of Poetry 1989

If poetry could be divided into two parts, knowing and making, then I would give to knowing the name *the female principle,* and to making I would give the name *the male principle.* Another poet might reverse those names, because these things are myths that just accumulate and we can use them as flexibly as we want. In my own case, you see, I had an Irish mother who brooded and thought and meditated a lot on things and was very articulate. I thought of her as a knower; she really wanted to know. She'd always ask me really hard questions, "Do you really think there's a heaven?" and she would mean it. She wasn't trying to educate me, she wanted to know if there was a heaven. My father, on the other hand, was a maker, he was a carpenter. I spent many hours at his side making things that were solid, had good structure, that wouldn't fall apart, that would last forever.

When I'm writing and I'm doing that beam work and that kind of construction, I always feel that what I'm doing owes a lot to my father, but when I have these moments when I think I know something, which is the most essential thing in poetry, I think that my mother is talking through me. That's why it's worked out that way in my mythology. But I can see how it might be completely different for somebody else.

From "Being with Reality: An Interview with Galway Kinnell,"
Columbia Magazine

Considerations

1. Read Kinnell's "Blackberry Eating" (p. 608) and discuss the poem in terms of Kinnell's ideas about the female principle of knowing and the male principle of making. Can you see evidence of the two principles at work in this poem?
2. One can talk about these principles in relation to reading poetry as well as writing it. Choose three or four poems from Chapter 22 and decide which aspects of the poems you simply know (either by intuition or by a sudden apprehension) and which aspects you must work at to understand. Would you use Kinnell's distinction between female knowing and male making to describe your experience of the poems?

DENISE LEVERTOV (b. 1923)

On "Gathered at the River" 1985

This is the prose of it: Each year on August 6 (and sometimes on August 9 as well) some kind of memorial observance of the bombing of Hiroshima and Nagasaki is held in the Boston/Cambridge area, as in so many other locations. Some years this has consisted of a silent vigil held near Faneuil Hall and other monuments of the American Revolution. Participants stand in a circle facing outward to display signs explaining the theme of the vigil, or pace slowly round, sometimes accompanied by the drums and chanting of attendant Buddhist monks. People stay for varying periods — there may be a constant presence for three days and nights. In 1982 the poet Suzanne Belote (of the Catholic radical peace group Ailanthus) and some others created a variation on this event. Participants (with the usual age range — babes in arms to white-haired old men and women) came to the Cambridge Friends' Meeting House for a brief preparatory assembly, then filed out to receive a candle apiece — thick Jahrzeit candles nailed to pieces of wood and shielded by paper cups — and proceeded to walk in a hushed column along Memorial Drive, beside the Charles River. The sun was low; a long summer day was ending. When we got to the wide grassy area near the Lars Anderson Bridge, where our ceremony was to take place, it was twilight.

Shielding flickering flames from the evening breeze, we formed a large circle, into the center of which stepped successive readers of portions from the descriptions recorded (as in the book *Unforgettable Fire*) by survivors of the atomic bombings. A period of silence followed. And then "saints and prophets, heroes and heroines of justice and peace"—including Gandhi, Martin Luther King, A. J. Muste, Emma Goldman, Archbishop Romero, Eugene Debs, Pope John XXIII, Dorothy Day, Saint Francis of Assisi, Saint Thomas More, Prince Kropotkin, Ammon Hennacy, the Prophet Isaiah, and many others I can't remember—were invoked. A form of ritual—an ecumenical liturgy—had been devised for the occasion, and as each such name was uttered by some member of the circle, the rest responded with a phrase that said essentially, "Be with us, great spirits, in this time of great need." The persons conducting the continuum of the liturgy turned slowly as they read the survivors' testimony, or statements of dedication to the cause of peace, so that all could hear at least part of each passage: for we had no microphones, preferring to depend on the unaided human voice for an occasion which had a personal, intimate character for each participant rather than being a PR event. Some music was interspersed among the verbal antiphonies, and the human atmosphere was solemn, harmonious, truly dedicated: from within it I began to feel the strong presence of the trees which half encircled us. Cars passed along Memorial Drive—slowed as drivers craned to see what was happening—passed on. A few blinked their lights in a friendly way, guessing from the date, I suppose, why we were there.

While we earnestly committed—or recommitted—ourselves to do all in our power to prevent nuclear war from ever taking place, it was growing dark. In the soft summer darkness details stood out: hands cupping wicks, small children's gold-illumined faces gazing up in wonder at the crouch and leap of flames, adults' heads bent close to one another as they clustered in twos and threes to relight candles blown out. And now the first part of the ritual was over and it was time to set our candles afloat, as they are set on the river in Hiroshima each year, that river where many drowned in the vain attempt to escape the burning of their own flesh.

People scrambled and helped each other down the short slope of the riverbank to launch the little candle-boats. Oblivious, a motorboat or two sped upriver, and minutes after a big slow wave would reach the shore. The water was black; the candle-boats seemed so fragile, and so tenacious. And all the time the large plane trees (saved from a road-widening project years before, incidentally, by citizens who chained themselves to their trunks in protest), and the other trees and bushes near them, were intensely, watchfully present. I have been asked if I really believe trees can listen. I've always thought our scientific knowledge has made us very arrogant in our assumptions. Wiser and older individuals and cultures have believed other kinds of consciousness and feeling could and did exist alongside of ours; I see no reason to disagree. It is not that I don't know trees have no "gray matter." It is possible that there are other routes to sentience than those with which we consider ourselves familiar.

The form of the poem: The title came from the literal sense of our being gathered there on the shore of the Charles, and also with the cognizance of the Quaker sense of gathering—a *"gathered meeting"* being, to my understanding, one which has not merely acquired the full complement of those who are going to attend it but which has attained a certain level, or quality, of attunement. Then, too, I had a vague memory of the song or hymn from which James Wright took the title of one of his books, and which I presumed must refer to the river of Jordan — "one more river, one more river to cross," as another song says. And though the symbolism there is of heaven lying upon the far shore, yet there is also, in the implication of *lastness,* of a final ordeal, the clear sense of a catastrophic alternative to attaining that shore. (No doubt *Pilgrim's Progress* was in the back of my mind too.) The analogy is obviously not a very close one, since survival of life on earth is a more modest goal than eternal bliss. Yet, relative to the hell proposed by our twentieth-century compound of the ancient vices of greed and love of power with nuclear and other "advanced" technology, mere survival would be a kind of heaven — especially since survival is not a static condition but offers the opportunity, and therefore the hope, of positive change. (For if one hopes for the survival of life on earth, one must logically hope and *intend* also the reshaping of those forces and factors which, unchanged, will only continue to threaten annihilation by one means or another.)

The structure of the poem stems as directly as the title from my experience of the event. The first line stands alone because that perception of the trees as animate and not uninterested presences — witnesses — was the discrete first in a series of heightened perceptions, most of which came in clusters. The following two-line stanza expands the first, more tentative observation, and places the trees' air of attention in the context of a breeze (which does not seem to distract them) and of the fluttering candles, which are thus introduced right at the start. Looking more closely at the trees, I see their late-summer color, but then recognize I am no longer seeing it, for dusk is falling — literally, but also metaphorically. The next stanza notes the largeness (and implied gravity, in both senses) of the trees, which it is not too dark to see, then again in a single line reasserts with more assurance the focus of my own attention: the trees' attentiveness. Following that comes the recognition of why, and for what, they are listening. The Latin words introduced here (echoing Pound's use of them) express the idea that "sin" occurs when humans violate the well-being of their own species and other living things, denying the natural law, the interdependence of all. (That usury belongs in this category, as Pound reemphasized, is not irrelevant to the subject of this poem, recalling the economic underpinning of the arms race and of war itself.)

My underlying belief in a great design, a potential harmony which can be violated or be sustained, probably strikes some people as quaint; but I would be dishonest, as person and artist, if I disowned it. I don't at this stage of my life feel ready for a public discussion of my religious concepts: but I think it must be clear from my writings that I have never been an atheist, and that — given my background and the fact that all my life George Herbert, Henry Vaughan, Thomas Traherne, and Gerard Manley Hopkins have been on my "short list" of favorite poets — whatever degree of belief I might attain would have a Christian context. This in turn implies a concern with the osmosis of "faith and works" and a sense of the sacredness of the earthly creation. That sense, not exclusive to Christianity, and deeply experienced and expressed by, for instance, Native Americans, is linked for Christians to the mystery of the Incarnation. To violate ourselves and our world is to violate the Divine.

The trees' concern, proposed with a tentative "as if" at the beginning, and then as an impression they "give off," is now asserted unequivocally. Once more comes a single line, "We intone together, *Never again,*" focused on the purpose of our gathering; and the words "never again" bring together the thought of the Nazi Holocaust with that of the crime committed by the U.S. against Japanese civilians, a crime advocates of the arms race prepare to commit again on a scale vaster than that of any massacre in all of history. This association might carry with it, I would hope, the sense that those who vow to work for prevention of war also are dedicated to political, economic, and racial justice, and understand something of the connections between long-standing oppression, major and "minor" massacres, and the giant shadow of global war and annihilation.

The narration continues, up to the launching of the candle-boats; pauses — a pause indicated by the asterisk — as we hold our breath to watch them go; and continues as they "bob on the current" and, though close to shore, begin to move downstream. Like ourselves, they are few and pitifully small. But at least they don't sink. Like all candles lit for the dead or in prayer, they combine remembrance with aspiration.

Finally the poem returns its regard to the trees, with the feeling that they know what we know — a knowledge those lines state and which it would be silly to paraphrase. The single lines again center on the primary realizations. Indeed, I see that a kind of précis of the entire poem could be extracted by reading the isolated lines alone:

As if the trees were not indifferent . . .
. . . .
a half-circle of attention.
. . . .
We intone together, *Never again.*
. . . .
Windthreatened flames bob on the current . . .
. . . .
there will be nothing left of their slow and innocent wisdom,
. . . .
no pollen,

except that one absolutely essential bone would be missing from that skeleton: the "if" of "if we fail." The poem, like the ceremony it narrates, and which gives it its slow, serious *pace* and, I hope, tone, is about interconnection, about dread, and about hope; that word, *if,* is its core.

" 'Gathered at the River': Background and Form" in *Singular Voices: American Poetry Today,* edited by Stephen Berg (Levertov's essay was written in response to a request from Berg.)

Considerations

1. In this essay, Levertov describes why and how she wrote "Gathered at the River" (p. 898). Does her account of the memorial observance help you to appreciate the poem more? Why or why not? Is the background information to the poem ("the prose of it") essential for an understanding of it?
2. Why is the word *if* essential to the poem's meaning?

3. Does Levertov exhaust the possibilities for discussing the poem? What can you add to her comments?
4. Poets are usually extremely reluctant to comment on their own poetry. Why do you think they frequently refuse to talk about the background and form of their poems?

ALICE FULTON (b. 1952)

On the Validity of Free Verse 1987

Until recently, I believed that Pound (along with Blake and Whitman, among others) had managed to establish beyond all argument the value of *vers libre* as a poetic medium. I thought that questions concerning the validity of free verse could be filed along with such antique quarrels as "Is photography Art?" and "Is abstract art Art?" In the past few years, however, I've heard many people — professors, poets, readers — speak of free verse as a failed experiment. To these disgruntled souls, free verse apparently describes an amorphous prosaic spouting, distinguished chiefly by its neglect of meter or rhyme, pattern or plan. Perhaps the word *free* contributes to the misconception. It's easy to interpret *free* as "free from all constraints of form," which lead to "free-for-all." However, any poet struggling with the obdurate qualities of language can testify that the above connotations of "free" do not apply to verse.

Since it's impossible to write unaccented English, free verse has meter. Of course, rather than striving for regularity, the measure of free verse may change from line to line, just as the tempo of twentieth-century music may change from bar to bar. As for allegations about formlessness, it seems to me that only an irregular structure with no beginning or end could be described as formless. (If the structure were regular, we could deduce the whole from a part. If irregular and therefore unpredictable, we'd need to see the whole in order to grasp its shape.) By this definition, there are fairly few examples of formless phenomena: certain concepts of God or of the expanding universe come to mind. However, unlike the accidental forms of nature, free verse is characterized by the poet's conscious shaping of content and language: the poet's choices at each step of the creative process give rise to form. Rather than relying on regular meter or rhyme as a means of ordering, the structures of free verse may be based upon registers of diction, irregular meter, sound as analogue for content, syllabics, accentuals, the interplay of chance with chosen elements, theories of lineation, recurring words, or whatever design delights the imagination and intellect. I suspect that the relation between content and form can be important or arbitrary in both metered and free verse. In regard to conventional forms, it's often assumed that decisions concerning content follow decisions concerning form (the add-subject-and-stir approach). However, poets consciously choose different subjects for sonnets than for ballads, thus exemplifying the interdependency of content and form. The reverse assumption is made about free verse: that the subject supersedes or, at best, dictates the form. But this is not necessarily the case. The poet can decide to utilize a structural device, such as the ones suggested previously, and then proceed to devise the content.

When we read a sestina, the form is clearly discernible. This is partly because we've read so many sestinas (familiarity breeds recognition) and partly because it's easy to perceive a highly repetitive pattern. More complex designs, however, often appear to be random until scrutinized closely. Much of what we call free verse tries to create a structure suitable only to itself — a pattern that has never appeared before, perhaps. As in serious modern music or jazz, the repetitions, if they do exist, may be so widely spaced that it takes several readings to discern them. Or the poems' unifying elements may be new to the reader, who must become a creative and active participant in order to appreciate the overall scheme. This is not meant to be a dismissal of the time-honored poetic forms. I admire and enjoy poets who breathe new life into seemingly dead conventions or structures. And I'm intrigued by poetry that borrows its shape from the models around us: poems in the form of TV listings, letters, recipes, and so forth. But I also value the analysis required and the discovery inherent in reading work that invents a form peculiar to itself. I like the idea of varying the meter from line to line so that nuances of tone can find their rhythmic correlative (or antithesis).

From *Ecstatic Occasions, Expedient Forms,* edited by David Lehman

Considerations

1. How does Fulton defend free verse against "allegations about formlessness"?
2. Compare Fulton's comments on the relationship of a poem's form to its content with Whitman's views (p. 909).
3. Browse through Chapter 22 and choose a poem "that invents a form peculiar to itself." Now analyze that poem.

DRAMA

24. Reading Drama

READING DRAMA RESPONSIVELY

The publication of a short story, novel, or poem represents for most writers the final step in a long creative process that might have begun with an idea, issue, emotion, or question that demanded expression. ***Playwrights*** — writers who make plays — may begin a work in the same way as other writers, but rarely are they satisfied with only its publication, because most dramatic literature — what we call ***plays*** — is written to be performed by actors on a stage before an audience. Playwrights typically create a play keeping in mind not only readers but also actors, producers, directors, costumers, designers, technicians, and a theater full of other support staff who have a hand in presenting the play to a live audience.

Drama is literature equipped with arms, legs, tears, laughs, whispers, shouts, and gestures that are alive and immediate. Indeed, the word ***drama*** derives from the Greek word ***dran,*** meaning "to do" or "to perform." The text of many plays — the ***script*** — may come to life fully only when the written words are transformed into a performance. Although there are plays that do not invite production, they are relatively few. Such plays, written to be read rather than performed, are called ***closet dramas.*** In this kind of work (primarily associated with nineteenth-century English literature), literary art outweighs all other considerations. The majority of playwrights, however, view the written word as the beginning of a larger creation and hope that a producer will deem their scripts worthy of production.

Given that most playwrights intend their works to be performed, it might be argued that reading a play is a poor substitute for seeing it acted on a stage — perhaps something like reading a recipe without having access to the ingredients and a kitchen. This analogy is tempting, but it overlooks the literary dimensions of a script; the words we hear on a stage were written first. Read from a page, these words can feed an imagination in ways that a recipe cannot satisfy a hungry cook. We can fill in a play's missing faces, voices, actions, and settings in much the same way that we imagine these elements in a short story or novel. Like any play director, we are free to include as many ingredients as we have an appetite for.

This imaginative collaboration with the playwright creates a mental world that can be nearly as real and vivid as a live performance. Sometimes readers find that they prefer their own reading of a play to a director's interpretation. Shakespeare's Hamlet, for instance, has been presented as a whining son but you may read him as a strong prince. Rich plays often accommodate a wide range of imaginative responses to their texts. Reading, then, is an excellent way to appreciate and evaluate a production of a play. Moreover, reading is valuable in its own right, because it allows us to enter the playwright's created world even when a theatrical production is unavailable.

Reading a play, however, requires more creative imagining than sitting in an audience watching actors on a stage presenting lines and actions before you. As a reader you become the play's director; you construct an interpretation based on the playwright's use of language, development of character, arrangement of incidents, description of settings, and directions for staging. Keeping track of the playwright's handling of these elements will help you to organize your response to the play. You may experience suspense, fear, horror, sympathy, or humor, but whatever experience a play evokes, ask yourself why you respond to it as you do. You may discover that your assessment of Hamlet's character is different from someone else's, but whether you find him heroic, indecisive, neurotic, or a complex of competing qualities, you'll be better equipped to articulate your interpretation of him if you pay attention to your responses and ask yourself questions as you read. Consider, for example, how his reactions might be similar to or different from your own. How does his language reveal his character? Does his behavior seem justified? How would you play the role yourself? What actor do you think might best play the Hamlet that you have created in your imagination? Why would he or she (women have also played Hamlet onstage) fill the role best?

These kinds of questions (see Questions for Responsive Reading, p. 954) can help you to think and talk about your responses to a play. Happily, such questions needn't — and often can't — be fully answered as you read the play. Frequently you must experience the entire play before you can determine how its elements work together. That's why reading a play can be such a satisfying experience. You wouldn't think of asking a live actor onstage to repeat her lines because you didn't quite comprehend their significance, but you can certainly reread a page in a book. Rereading allows you to replay language, characters, and incidents carefully and thoroughly to your own satisfaction.

TRIFLES

In the following play, Susan Glaspell skillfully draws on many dramatic elements and creates an intense story that is as effective on the page as it is in the theater. Glaspell wrote *Trifles* in 1916 for the Provincetown Players on Cape Cod, in Massachusetts. Their performance of the work helped her develop a reputation as a writer sensitive to feminist issues. The year after *Trifles* was produced, Glaspell transformed the play into a short story titled "A Jury of Her Peers." (A passage from the story appears on p. 1758 for comparison.)

Glaspell's life in the Midwest provided her with the setting for *Trifles.* Born and raised in Davenport, Iowa, she graduated from Drake University in 1899 and then worked for a short time as a reporter on the *Des Moines News,* until her short stories were accepted in magazines such as *Harper's* and *Ladies' Home Journal.* Glaspell moved to the Northeast when she was in her early thirties to continue writing fiction and drama. She published some twenty plays, novels, and more than forty short stories. *Alison's House,* based on Emily Dickinson's life, earned her a Pulitzer prize for drama in 1931. *Trifles* and "A Jury of Her Peers" remain, however, Glaspell's best-known works.

Glaspell wrote *Trifles* to complete a bill that was to feature several one-act plays by Eugene O'Neill. In *The Road to the Temple* (1926) she recalls how the play came to her as she sat in the theater looking at a bare stage. First, "the stage became a kitchen. . . . Then the door at the back opened, and people all bundled up came in — two or three men. I wasn't sure which, but sure enough about the two women, who hung back, reluctant to enter that kitchen. When I was a newspaper reporter out in Iowa, I was sent down-state to do a murder trial, and I never forgot going to the kitchen of a woman who had been locked up in town."

Trifles is about a murder committed in a midwestern farmhouse, but the play goes beyond the kinds of questions raised by most whodunit stories. The murder is the occasion instead of the focus. The play's major concerns are the moral, social, and psychological aspects of the assumptions and perceptions of the men and women who search for the murderer's motive. Glaspell is finally more interested in the meaning of Mrs. Wright's life than in the details of Mr. Wright's death.

As you read the play keep track of your responses to the characters and note in the margin the moments when Glaspell reveals how men and women respond differently to the evidence before them. What do those moments suggest about the kinds of assumptions these men and women make about themselves and each other? How do their assumptions compare with your own?

SUSAN GLASPELL (1882–1948)

Trifles

1916

Characters

George Henderson, county attorney
Henry Peters, sheriff
Lewis Hale, a neighboring farmer
Mrs. Peters
Mrs. Hale

SCENE: *The kitchen in the now abandoned farmhouse of John Wright, a gloomy kitchen, and left without having been put in order — the walls covered with a faded wall paper. Down right is a door leading to the parlor. On the right wall above this door is a built-in kitchen cupboard with shelves in the upper portion and drawers below. In the rear wall at right, up two steps is a door opening onto stairs leading to the second floor. In the rear wall at left is a door to the shed and from there to the outside. Between these two doors is an old-fashioned black iron stove. Running along the left wall from the shed door is an old iron sink and sink shelf, in which is set a hand pump. Downstage of the sink is an uncurtained window. Near the window is an old wooden rocker. Center stage is an unpainted wooden kitchen table with straight chairs on either side. There is a small chair down right. Unwashed pans under the sink, a loaf of bread outside the breadbox, a dish towel on the table — other signs of incompleted work. At the rear the shed door opens and the Sheriff comes in followed by the County Attorney and Hale. The Sheriff and Hale are men in middle life, the County Attorney is a young man; all are much bundled up and go at once to the stove. They are followed by the two women — the Sheriff's wife, Mrs. Peters, first; she is a slight wiry woman, a thin nervous face. Mrs. Hale is larger and would ordinarily be called more comfortable looking, but she is disturbed now and looks fearfully about as she enters. The women have come in slowly, and stand close together near the door.*

County Attorney (at stove rubbing his hands): This feels good. Come up to the fire, ladies.

Mrs. Peters (after taking a step forward): I'm not — cold.

Sheriff (unbuttoning his overcoat and stepping away from the stove to right of table as if to mark the beginning of official business): Now, Mr. Hale, before we move things about, you explain to Mr. Henderson just what you saw when you came here yesterday morning.

County Attorney (crossing down to left of the table): By the way, has anything been moved? Are things just as you left them yesterday?

Sheriff (looking about): It's just about the same. When it dropped below zero last night I thought I'd better send Frank out this morning to make a fire for us — *(sits right of center table)* no use getting pneumonia with a big case on, but I told him not to touch anything except the stove — and you know Frank.

County Attorney: Somebody should have been left here yesterday.

Sheriff: Oh — yesterday. When I had to send Frank to Morris Center for that man who went crazy — I want you to know I had my hands full yesterday. I knew you could get back from Omaha by today and as long as I went over everything here myself ——

County Attorney: Well, Mr. Hale, tell just what happened when you came here yesterday morning.

Hale (crossing down to above table): Harry and I had started to town with a load of potatoes. We came along the road from my place and as I got here I said, "I'm going to see if I can't get John Wright to go in with me on a party telephone." I spoke to Wright about it once before and he put me off, saying folks talked too much anyway, and all he asked was peace and quiet — I guess you know about how much he talked himself; but I thought maybe if I went to the house and talked about it before his wife, though I said to Harry that I didn't know as what his wife wanted made much difference to John ——

County Attorney: Let's talk about that later, Mr. Hale. I do want to talk about that, but tell now just what happened when you got to the house.

Hale: I didn't hear or see anything; I knocked at the door, and still it was all quiet inside. I knew they must be up, it was past eight o'clock. So I knocked again, and I thought I heard somebody say, "Come in." I wasn't sure, I'm not sure yet, but I opened the door — this door *(indicating the door by which the two women are still standing)* and there in that rocker — *(pointing to it)* sat Mrs. Wright. *(They all look at the rocker down left.)*

County Attorney: What — was she doing?

Hale: She was rockin' back and forth. She had her apron in her hand and was kind of — pleating it.

County Attorney: And how did she — look?

Hale: Well, she looked queer.

County Attorney: How do you mean — queer?

Hale: Well, as if she didn't know what she was going to do next. And kind of done up.

County Attorney (takes out notebook and pencil and sits left of center table): How did she seem to feel about your coming?

Hale: Why, I don't think she minded — one way or other. She didn't pay much attention. I said, "How do, Mrs. Wright, it's cold, ain't it?" And she said, "Is it?" — and went on kind of pleating at her apron. Well, I was surprised; she didn't ask me to come up to the stove, or to set down, but just sat there, not even looking at me, so I said, "I want to see John." And then she — laughed. I guess you would call it a laugh. I thought of Harry and the team outside, so I said a little sharp: "Can't I see John?" "No," she says, kind o' dull like. "Ain't he home?" says I. "Yes," says she, "he's home." "Then why can't I see him?" I asked her, out of patience. " 'Cause he's dead," says she. *"Dead?"* says I. She just nodded her head, not getting a bit excited, but rockin' back and forth. "Why — where is he?" says I, not knowing what to say. She just pointed upstairs — like that. *(Himself pointing to the room above.)* I started for the stairs, with the idea of going up there. I walked from there to here — then I says, "Why, what did he die of?" "He died of a rope round his neck," says she, and just went on pleatin' at her apron. Well, I went out and called Harry. I thought I might — need help. We went upstairs and there he was lyin' ——

County Attorney: I think I'd rather have you go into that upstairs, where you can point it all out. Just go on now with the rest of the story.

Hale: Well, my first thought was to get that rope off. It looked . . . *(stops; his face twitches)* . . . but Harry, he went up to him, and he said, "No, he's dead all right, and we'd better not touch anything." So we went back downstairs. She was still sitting that same way. "Has anybody been notified?" I asked. "No," says she, unconcerned. "Who did this, Mrs. Wright?" said Harry. He said it businesslike — and she stopped pleatin' of her apron. "I don't know," she says. "You don't *know?"* says Harry. "No," says she. "Weren't you sleepin' in the bed with him?" says Harry. "Yes," says she, "but I was on the inside." "Somebody slipped a rope round his neck and strangled him and you didn't wake up?" says Harry. "I didn't wake up," she said after him. We must 'a' looked as if we didn't see how that could be, for after a minute she said, "I sleep sound." Harry was going to ask her more questions but I said maybe we ought to let her tell her story first to the coroner, or the sheriff, so Harry went fast as he could to Rivers' place, where there's a telephone.

County Attorney: And what did Mrs. Wright do when she knew that you had gone for the coroner?

Hale: She moved from the rocker to that chair over there *(pointing to a small chair in the down right corner)* and just sat there with her hands held together and looking down. I got a feeling that I ought to make some conversation, so I said I had come in to see if John wanted to put in a telephone, and at that she started to laugh, and then she stopped and looked at me — scared. *(The County Attorney, who has had his notebook out, makes a note.)* I dunno, maybe it wasn't scared. I wouldn't like to say it was. Soon Harry got back, and then Dr. Lloyd came and you, Mr. Peters, and so I guess that's all I know that you don't.

County Attorney (rising and looking around): I guess we'll go upstairs first — and then out to the barn and around there. *(To the Sheriff.)* You're convinced that there was nothing important here — nothing that would point to any motive?

Sheriff: Nothing here but kitchen things. *(The County Attorney, after again looking around the kitchen, opens the door of a cupboard closet in right wall. He brings a small chair from right — gets on it and looks on a shelf. Pulls his hand away, sticky.)*

County Attorney: Here's a nice mess. *(The women drew nearer up center.)*

Mrs. Peters (to the other woman): Oh, her fruit; it did freeze. *(To the Lawyer.)* She worried about that when it turned so cold. She said the fire'd go out and her jars would break.

Sheriff (rises): Well, can you beat the women! Held for murder and worryin' about her preserves.

County Attorney (getting down from chair): I guess before we're through she may have something more serious than preserves to worry about. *(Crosses down right center.)*

Hale: Well, women are used to worrying over trifles. *(The two women move a little closer together.)*

County Attorney (with the gallantry of a young politician): And yet, for all their worries, what would we do without the ladies? *(The women do not unbend. He goes below the center table to the sink, takes a dipperful of water from the pail, and pouring it into a basin, washes his hands. While he is doing this the Sheriff and Hale cross to cupboard, which they inspect. The County Attorney starts to wipe his hands on the roller towel, turns it for a cleaner place.)* Dirty towels! *(Kicks his foot against the pans under the sink.)* Not much of a housekeeper, would you say, ladies?

Mrs. Hale (stiffly): There's a great deal of work to be done on a farm.

County Attorney: To be sure. And yet *(with a little bow to her)* I know there are some Dickson County farmhouses which do not have such roller towels. *(He gives it a pull to expose its full length again.)*

Mrs. Hale: Those towels get dirty awful quick. Men's hands aren't always as clean as they might be.

County Attorney: Ah, loyal to your sex, I see. But you and Mrs. Wright were neighbors. I suppose you were friends, too.

Mrs. Hale (shaking her head): I've not seen much of her of late years. I've not been in this house — it's more than a year.

County Attorney (crossing to women up center): And why was that? You didn't like her?

Mrs. Hale: I liked her all well enough. Farmers' wives have their hands full, Mr. Henderson. And then ——

County Attorney: Yes ——?

Mrs. Hale (looking about): It never seemed a very cheerful place.

County Attorney: No — it's not cheerful. I shouldn't say she had the homemaking instinct.

Mrs. Hale: Well, I don't know as Wright had, either.

County Attorney: You mean that they didn't get on very well?

Mrs. Hale: No, I don't mean anything. But I don't think a place'd be any cheerfuller for John Wright's being in it.

County Attorney: I'd like to talk more of that a little later. I want to get the lay of things upstairs now. *(He goes past the women to up right where steps lead to a stair door.)*

Sheriff: I suppose anything Mrs. Peters does'll be all right. She was to take in some clothes for her, you know, and a few little things. We left in such a hurry yesterday.

County Attorney: Yes, but I would like to see what you take, Mrs. Peters, and keep an eye out for anything that might be of use to us.

Mrs. Peters: Yes, Mr. Henderson. *(The men leave by up right door to stairs. The women listen to the men's steps on the stairs, then look about the kitchen.)*

Mrs. Hale (crossing left to sink): I'd hate to have men coming into my kitchen, snooping around and criticizing. *(She arranges the pans under sink which the Lawyer had shoved out of place.)*

Mrs. Peters: Of course it's no more than their duty. *(Crosses to cupboard up right.)*

Mrs. Hale: Duty's all right, but I guess that deputy sheriff that came out to make the fire might have got a little of this on. *(Gives the roller towel a pull.)* Wish I'd thought of that sooner. Seems mean to talk about her for not having things slicked up when she had to come away in such a hurry. *(Crosses right to Mrs. Peters at cupboard.)*

Mrs. Peters (who has been looking through cupboard, lifts one end of towel that covers a pan): She had bread set. *(Stands still.)*

Mrs. Hale (eyes fixed on a loaf of bread beside the breadbox, which is on a low shelf of the cupboard): She was going to put this in there. *(Picks up loaf, abruptly drops it. In a manner of returning to familiar things.)* It's a shame about her fruit. I wonder if it's all gone. *(Gets up on the chair and looks.)* I think there's some here that's all right, Mrs. Peters. Yes — here; *(holding it toward the window)* this is cherries, too. *(Looking again.)* I declare I believe that's the only one. *(Gets down, jar in her hand. Goes to the sink and wipes it off on the outside.)* She'll feel awful bad after all her hard work in the hot weather. I remember the afternoon I put up my cherries last summer. *(She puts the jar on the big kitchen table, center of the room. With a sigh, is about to sit down in the rocking chair. Before she is seated realizes what chair it is; with a slow look at it, steps back. The chair which she has touched rocks back and forth. Mrs. Peters moves to center table and they both watch the chair rock for a moment or two.)*

Mrs. Peters (shaking off the mood which the empty rocking chair has evoked. Now in a businesslike manner she speaks): Well I must get those things from the front room closet. *(She goes to the door at the right but, after looking into the other room, steps back.)* You coming with me, Mrs. Hale? You could help me carry them. *(They go in the other room; reappear, Mrs. Peters carrying a dress, petticoat, and skirt, Mrs. Hale following with a pair of shoes.)* My, it's cold in there. *(She puts the clothes on the big table and hurries to the stove.)*

Mrs. Hale (right of center table examining the skirt): Wright was close. I think maybe that's why she kept so much to herself. She didn't even belong to the Ladies' Aid. I suppose she felt she couldn't do her part, and then you don't enjoy things when you feel shabby. I heard she used to wear pretty clothes and be lively, when she was Minnie Foster, one of the town girls singing in the choir. But that — oh, that was thirty years ago. This all you want to take in?

Mrs. Peters: She said she wanted an apron. Funny thing to want, for there isn't much to get you dirty in jail, goodness knows. But I suppose just to make her feel more natural. *(Crosses to cupboard.)* She said they was in the top drawer in this cupboard. Yes, here. And then her little shawl that always hung behind the door. *(Opens stair door and looks.)* Yes, here it is. *(Quickly shuts door leading upstairs.)*

Mrs. Hale (abruptly moving toward her): Mrs. Peters?

Mrs. Peters: Yes, Mrs. Hale? *(At up right door.)*

Mrs. Hale: Do you think she did it?

Mrs. Peters (in a frightened voice): Oh, I don't know.

Mrs. Hale: Well, I don't think she did. Asking for an apron and her little shawl. Worrying about her fruit.

Mrs. Peters (starts to speak, glances up, where footsteps are heard in the room above. In a low voice): Mr. Peters says it looks bad for her. Mr. Henderson is awful sarcastic in a speech and he'll make fun of her sayin' she didn't wake up.

Mrs. Hale: Well, I guess John Wright didn't wake when they was slipping that rope under his neck.

Mrs. Peters (crossing slowly to table and placing shawl and apron on table with other clothing): No, it's strange. It must have been done awful crafty and still. They say it was such a — funny way to kill a man, rigging it all up like that.

Mrs. Hale (crossing to left of Mrs. Peters at table): That's just what Mr. Hale said. There was a gun in the house. He says that's what he can't understand.

Mrs. Peters: Mr. Henderson said coming out that what was needed for the case was a motive; something to show anger, or — sudden feeling.

Mrs. Hale (who is standing by the table): Well, I don't see any signs of anger around here. *(She puts her hand on the dish towel, which lies on the table, stands looking down at table, one-half of which is clean, the other half messy.)* It's wiped to here. *(Makes a move as if to finish work, then turns and looks at loaf of bread outside the breadbox. Drops towel. In that voice of coming back to familiar things.)* Wonder how they are finding things upstairs. *(Crossing below table to down right.)* I hope she had it a little more red-up up there. You know, it seems kind of *sneaking.* Locking her up in town and then coming out here and trying to get her own house to turn against her!

Mrs. Peters: But, Mrs. Hale, the law is the law.

Mrs. Hale: I s'pose 'tis. *(Unbuttoning her coat.)* Better loosen up your things, Mrs. Peters. You won't feel them when you go out. *(Mrs. Peters takes off her fur tippet, goes to hang it on chair back left of table, stands looking at the work basket on floor near down left window.)*

Mrs. Peters: She was piecing a quilt. *(She brings the large sewing basket to the center table and they look at the bright pieces, Mrs. Hale above the table and Mrs. Peters left of it.)*

Mrs. Hale: It's a log cabin pattern. Pretty, isn't it? I wonder if she was goin' to quilt it or just knot it? *(Footsteps have been heard coming down the stairs. The Sheriff enters followed by Hale and the County Attorney.)*

Sheriff: They wonder if she was going to quilt it or just knot it! *(The men laugh, the women look abashed.)*

County Attorney (rubbing his hands over the stove): Frank's fire didn't do much up there, did it? Well, let's go out to the barn and get that cleared up. *(The men go outside by up left door.)*

Mrs. Hale (resentfully): I don't know as there's anything so strange, our takin' up our time with little things while we're waiting for them to get the evidence. *(She sits in chair right of table smoothing out a block with decision.)* I don't see as it's anything to laugh about.

Mrs. Peters (apologetically): Of course they've got awful important things on their minds. *(Pulls up a chair and joins Mrs. Hale at the left of the table.)*

Mrs. Hale (examining another block): Mrs. Peters, look at this one. Here, this is the one she was working on, and look at the sewing! All the rest of it has been so nice and even. And look at this! It's all over the place! Why, it looks as if she didn't know what she was about! *(After she has said this they look at each other, then start to glance back at the door. After an instant Mrs. Hale has pulled at a knot and ripped the sewing.)*

Mrs. Peters: Oh, what are you doing, Mrs. Hale?

Mrs. Hale (mildly): Just pulling out a stitch or two that's not sewed very good. *(Threading a needle.)* Bad sewing always made me fidgety.

Mrs. Peters (with a glance at door, nervously): I don't think we ought to touch things.

Mrs. Hale: I'll just finish up this end. *(Suddenly stopping and leaning forward.)* Mrs. Peters?

Mrs. Peters: Yes, Mrs. Hale?

Mrs. Hale: What do you suppose she was so nervous about?

Mrs. Peters: Oh — I don't know. I don't know as she was nervous. I sometimes sew awful queer when I'm just tired. *(Mrs. Hale starts to say something, looks at Mrs. Peters, then goes on sewing.)* Well, I must get these things wrapped up. They may be through sooner than we think. *(Putting apron and other things together.)* I wonder where I can find a piece of paper, and string. *(Rises.)*

Mrs. Hale: In that cupboard, maybe.

Mrs. Peters (crosses right looking in cupboard): Why, here's a bird-cage. *(Holds it up).* Did she have a bird, Mrs. Hale?

Mrs. Hale: Why, I don't know whether she did or not — I've not been here for so long. There was a man around last year selling canaries cheap, but I don't know as she took one; maybe she did. She used to sing real pretty herself.

Mrs. Peters (glancing around): Seems funny to think of a bird here. But she must have had one, or why would she have a cage? I wonder what happened to it?

Mrs. Hale: I s'pose maybe the cat got it.

Mrs. Peters: No, she didn't have a cat. She's got that feeling some people have about cats — being afraid of them. My cat got in her room and she was real upset and asked me to take it out.

Mrs. Hale: My sister Bessie was like that. Queer, ain't it?

Mrs. Peters (examining the cage): Why, look at this door. It's broke. One hinge is pulled apart. *(Takes a step down to Mrs. Hale's right.)*

Mrs. Hale (looking too): Looks as if someone must have been rough with it.

Mrs. Peters: Why, yes. *(She brings the cage forward and puts it on the table.)*

Mrs. Hale (glancing toward up left door): I wish if they're going to find any evidence they'd be about it. I don't like this place.

Mrs. Peters: But I'm awful glad you came with me, Mrs. Hale. It would be lonesome for me sitting here alone.

Mrs. Hale: It would, wouldn't it? *(Dropping her sewing.)* But I tell you what I do wish, Mrs. Peters. I wish I had come over sometimes when *she* was here. I — *(looking around the room)* — wish I had.

Mrs. Peters: But of course you were awful busy, Mrs. Hale — your house and your children.

Mrs. Hale (rises and crosses left): I could've come. I stayed away because it weren't cheerful — and that's why I ought to have come. I — *(looking out left window)* — I've never liked this place. Maybe because it's down in a hollow and you don't see the road. I dunno what it is, but it's a lonesome place and always was. I wish I had come over to see Minnie Foster sometimes. I can see now — *(Shakes her head.)*

Mrs. Peters (left of table and above it): Well, you mustn't reproach yourself, Mrs. Hale. Somehow we just don't see how it is with other folks until — something turns up.

Mrs. Hale: Not having children makes less work — but it makes a quiet house, and Wright out to work all day, and no company when he did come in. *(Turning from window.)* Did you know John Wright, Mrs. Peters?

Mrs. Peters: Not to know him; I've seen him in town. They say he was a good man.

Mrs. Hale: Yes — good; he didn't drink, and kept his word as well as most, I guess, and paid his debts. But he was a hard man, Mrs. Peters. Just to pass the time of day with him — *(Shivers.)* Like a raw wind that gets to the bone. *(Pauses, her eye falling on the cage.)* I should think she would 'a' wanted a bird. But what do you suppose went with it?

Mrs. Peters: I don't know, unless it got sick and died. *(She reaches over and swings the broken door, swings it again, both women watch it.)*

Mrs. Hale: You weren't raised round here, were you? *(Mrs. Peters shakes her head.)* You didn't know — her?

Mrs. Peters: Not till they brought her yesterday.

Mrs. Hale: She — come to think of it, she was kind of like a bird herself — real sweet and pretty, but kind of timid and — fluttery. How — she — did — change. *(Silence: then as if struck by a happy thought and relieved to get back to everyday things. Crosses right above Mrs. Peters to cupboard, replaces small chair used to stand on to its original place down right.)* Tell you what, Mrs. Peters, why don't you take the quilt in with you? It might take up her mind.

Mrs. Peters: Why, I think that's a real nice idea, Mrs. Hale. There couldn't possibly be any objection to it could there? Now, just what would I take? I wonder if her patches are in here — and her things. *(They look in the sewing basket.)*

Mrs. Hale (crosses to right of table): Here's some red. I expect this has got sewing things in it. *(Brings out a fancy box.)* What a pretty box. Looks like something somebody would give you. Maybe her scissors are in here. *(Opens box. Suddenly puts her hand to her nose.)* Why —— *(Mrs. Peters bends nearer, then turns her face away.)* There's something wrapped up in this piece of silk.

Mrs. Peters: Why, this isn't her scissors.

Mrs. Hale (lifting the silk): Oh, Mrs. Peters — it's —— *(Mrs. Peters bends closer.)*

Mrs. Peters: It's the bird.

Mrs. Hale: But, Mrs. Peters — look at it! Its neck! Look at its neck! It's all — other side *to.*

Mrs. Peters: Somebody — wrung — its — neck. *(Their eyes meet. A look of growing comprehension, of horror. Steps are heard outside. Mrs. Hale slips box under quilt pieces, and sinks into her chair. Enter Sheriff and County Attorney. Mrs. Peters steps down left and stands looking out of window.)*

County Attorney (as one turning from serious things to little pleasantries): Well, ladies, have you decided whether she was going to quilt it or knot it? *(Crosses to center above table.)*

Mrs. Peters: We think she was going to — knot it. *(Sheriff crosses to right of stove, lifts stove lid, and glances at fire, then stands warming hands at stove.)*

County Attorney: Well, that's interesting, I'm sure. *(Seeing the bird-cage.)* Has the bird flown?

Mrs. Hale (putting more quilt pieces over the box): We think the — cat got it.

County Attorney (preoccupied): Is there a cat? *(Mrs. Hale glances in a quick covert way at Mrs. Peters.)*

Mrs. Peters (turning from window takes a step in): Well, not *now.* They're superstitious, you know. They leave.

County Attorney (to Sheriff Peters, continuing an interrupted conversation): No sign at all of anyone having come from the outside. Their own rope. Now let's go up again and go over it piece by piece. *(They start upstairs.)* It would have to have been someone who knew just the —— *(Mrs. Peters sits down left of table. The two women sit there not looking at one another, but as if peering into something and at the same time holding back. When they talk now it is in the manner of feeling their way over strange ground, as if afraid of what they are saying, but as if they cannot help saying it.)*

Mrs. Hale (hesitatively and in hushed voice): She liked the bird. She was going to bury it in that pretty box.

Mrs. Peters (in a whisper): When I was a girl — my kitten — there was a boy took a hatchet, and before my eyes — and before I could get there —— *(Covers her face an instant.)* If they hadn't held me back I would have — *(catches herself, looks upstairs where steps are heard, falters weakly)* — hurt him.

Mrs. Hale (with a slow look around her): I wonder how it would seem never to have had any children around. *(Pause.)* No, Wright wouldn't like the bird — a thing that sang. She used to sing. He killed that, too.

Mrs. Peters (moving uneasily): We don't know who killed the bird.

Mrs. Hale: I knew John Wright.

Mrs. Peters: It was an awful thing was done in this house that night, Mrs. Hale. Killing a man while he slept, slipping a rope around his neck that choked the life out of him.

Mrs. Hale: His neck. Choked the life out of him. *(Her hand goes out and rests on the bird-cage.)*

Mrs. Peters (with rising voice): We don't know who killed him. We don't *know.*

Mrs. Hale (her own feeling not interrupted): If there'd been years and years of nothing, then a bird to sing to you, it would be awful — still, after the bird was still.

Mrs. Peters (something within her speaking): I know what stillness is. When we homesteaded in Dakota, and my first baby died — after he was two years old, and me with no other then ——

Mrs. Hale (moving): How soon do you suppose they'll be through looking for the evidence?

Mrs. Peters: I know what stillness is. *(Pulling herself back.)* The law has got to punish crime, Mrs. Hale.

Mrs. Hale (not as if answering that): I wish you'd seen Minnie Foster when she wore a white dress with blue ribbons and stood up there in the choir and sang. *(A look around the room.)* Oh, I *wish* I'd come over here once in a while! That was a crime! That was a crime! Who's going to punish that?

Mrs. Peters (looking upstairs): We mustn't — take on.

Mrs. Hale: I might have known she needed help! I know how things can be — for women. I tell you, it's queer, Mrs. Peters. We live close together and we live far apart. We all go through the same things — it's all just a different kind of the same thing. *(Brushes her eyes, noticing the jar of fruit, reaches out for it.)* If I was you I wouldn't tell her her fruit was gone. Tell her it *ain't.* Tell her it's all right. Take this in to prove it to her. She — she may never know whether it was broke or not.

Mrs. Peters (takes the jar, looks about for something to wrap it in; takes petticoat from the clothes brought from the other room, very nervously begins winding this around the jar. In a false voice): My, it's a good thing the men couldn't hear us. Wouldn't they just laugh! Getting all stirred up over a little thing like a—dead canary. As if that could have anything to do with—with—wouldn't they *laugh! (The men are heard coming downstairs.)*

Mrs. Hale (under her breath): Maybe they would—maybe they wouldn't.

County Attorney: No, Peters, it's all perfectly clear except a reason for doing it. But you know juries when it comes to women. If there was some definite thing. *(Crosses slowly to above table. Sheriff crosses down right. Mrs. Hale and Mrs. Peters remain seated at either side of table.)* Something to show—something to make a story about—a thing that would connect up with this strange way of doing it——*(The women's eyes meet for an instant. Enter Hale from outer door.)*

Hale (remaining by door): Well, I've got the team around. Pretty cold out there.

County Attorney: I'm going to stay awhile by myself. *(To the Sheriff.)* You can send Frank out for me, can't you? I want to go over everything. I'm not satisfied that we can't do better.

Sheriff: Do you want to see what Mrs. Peters is going to take in? *(The Lawyer picks up the apron, laughs.)*

County Attorney: Oh, I guess they're not very dangerous things the ladies have picked out. *(Moves a few things about, disturbing the quilt pieces which cover the box. Steps back.)* No, Mrs. Peters doesn't need supervising. For that matter a sheriff's wife is married to the law. Ever think of it that way, Mrs. Peters?

Mrs. Peters: Not—just that way.

Sheriff (chuckling): Married to the law. *(Moves to down right door to the other room.)* I just want you to come in here a minute, George. We ought to take a look at these windows.

County Attorney (scoffingly): Oh, windows!

Sheriff: We'll be right out, Mr. Hale. *(Hale goes outside. The Sheriff follows the County Attorney into the room. Then Mrs. Hale rises, hands tight together, looking intensely at Mrs. Peters, whose eyes make a slow turn, finally meeting Mrs. Hale's. A moment Mrs. Hale holds her, then her own eyes point the way to where the box is concealed. Suddenly Mrs. Peters throws back quilt pieces and tries to put the box in the bag she is carrying. It is too big. She opens box, starts to take bird out, cannot touch it, goes to pieces, stands there helpless. Sound of a knob turning in the other room. Mrs. Hale snatches the box and puts it in the pocket of her big coat. Enter County Attorney and Sheriff, who remains down right.)*

County Attorney (crosses to up left door facetiously): Well, Henry, at least we found out that she was not going to quilt it. She was going to—what is it you call it, ladies?

Mrs. Hale (standing center below table facing front, her hand against her pocket): We call it—knot it, Mr. Henderson.

Curtain.

Considerations

1. Describe the setting of this play. What kind of atmosphere is established by the details in the opening scene?
2. Where are Mrs. Hale and Mrs. Peters while Mr. Hale explains to the county attorney how the murder was discovered? How does their location suggest the relationship between the men and the women in the play?
3. What kind of person was Minnie Foster before she married? How do you think her marriage affected her?
4. Characterize John Wright. Why did his wife kill him?
5. Why do the men fail to see the clues that Mrs. Hale and Mrs. Peters discover?
6. What is the significance of the bird cage and the dead bird? Why do Mrs. Hale and Mrs. Peters respond so strongly to them? How do you respond?
7. Why don't Mrs. Hale and Mrs. Peters reveal the evidence they have uncovered? What would you have done?
8. How do the men's conversations and actions reveal their attitudes toward women?
9. Why do you think Glaspell allows us only to hear about Mr. and Mrs. Wright? What is the effect of their never appearing on stage?
10. Does your impression of Mrs. Wright change in the course of the play? If so, what changes it?
11. What is the significance of the play's last line, spoken by Mrs. Hale: "We call it — knot it, Mr. Henderson"? Explain what you think the tone of Mrs. Hale's voice is when she says this line. What is she feeling? What are you feeling?
12. Several times the characters say things that they don't mean, and this creates a discrepancy between what appears to be and what is actually true. Point to instances of irony in the play and explain how they contribute to its effects and meanings. (For discussions of irony elsewhere in this book, see the Index of Terms.)
13. Explain the significance of the play's title. Do you think *Trifles* or "A Jury of Her Peers," Glaspell's title for the short story version of the play, is more appropriate? Can you think of other titles that capture the play's central concerns?
14. If possible, find a copy of "A Jury of Her Peers" in the library (reprinted in *The Best Short Stories of 1917,* ed. E. J. O'Brien [Boston: Small, Maynard 1918], pp. 256–82), and write an essay that explores the differences between the play and the short story. (An alternative is to work with the excerpt in Chapter 31, p. 1758.)

Connections

1. Compare and contrast how Glaspell provides background information in *Trifles* with how Sophocles does so in *Oedipus the King* (p. 964).
2. Both Mrs. Wright and Shakespeare's Othello (p. 1166) murder their spouses. To what extent do you think they are responsible and guilty for these crimes?
3. Write an essay comparing the views of marriage in *Trifles* and in Chopin's short story "The Story of an Hour" (p. 12). What similarities do you find in the themes of these two works? Are there any significant differences between the works?

ELEMENTS OF DRAMA

Trifles is a ***one-act play;*** in other words, the entire play takes place in a single location and unfolds as one continuous action. As in a short story, the characters in a one-act play are presented economically, and the action is sharply focused. In contrast, full-length plays can include many characters as well as different settings in place and time. The main divisions of a full-length play are typically ***acts;*** their ends are indicated by lowering a curtain or turning up the houselights. Playwrights frequently employ acts to accommodate changes in time, setting, characters on stage, or mood. In many full-length plays, such as Shakespeare's *Hamlet,* acts are further divided into ***scenes;*** according to tradition a scene changes when the location of the action changes or a when a new character enters. Acts and scenes are ***conventions*** that are understood and accepted by audiences because they have come, through usage and time, to be recognized as familiar techniques. The major convention of a one-act play is that it typically consists of only a single scene; nevertheless, one-act plays contain many of the elements of drama that characterize their full-length counterparts.

One-act plays create their effects through compression. They especially lend themselves to modestly budgeted productions with limited stage facilities, such as those put on by little theater groups. However, the potential of a one-act play to move audiences and readers is not related to its length. As *Trifles* shows, one-acts represent a powerful form of dramatic literature.

The single location that comprises the ***setting*** for *Trifles* is described at the very beginning of the play; it establishes an atmosphere that will later influence our judgment of Mrs. Wright. The kitchen, "gloomy" and with walls "covered with a faded wall paper," is disordered, bare, and sparsely equipped with a stove, sink, and rocker — each of them "old" — an unpainted table, some chairs, three doors, and an uncurtained window. The only color mentioned is, appropriately, black. These details are just enough to allow us to imagine the stark, uninviting place where Mrs. Wright spent most of her time. Moreover, "signs of incompleted work," coupled with the presence of the sheriff and county attorney, create an immediate tension by suggesting that something is terribly wrong. Before a single word is spoken, ***suspense*** is created as the characters enter. This suspenseful situation causes an anxious uncertainty about what will happen next.

The setting is further developed through the use of ***exposition,*** a device that provides the necessary background information about the characters and their circumstances. For example, we immediately learn through ***dialogue*** — the verbal exchanges between characters — that Mr. Henderson, the county attorney, is just back from Omaha. This establishes the setting as somewhere in the Midwest, where winters can be brutally cold and barren. We also find out that John Wright has been murdered and that his wife has been arrested for the crime.

Even more important, Glaspell deftly characterizes the Wrights through exposition alone. Mr. Hale's conversation with Mr. Henderson explains how Mr. Wright's body was discovered, but it also reveals that Wright was a non-communicative man, who refused to share a "party telephone" and who did not consider "what his wife wanted." Later Mrs. Hale adds to this characterization when she tells Mrs. Peters that though Mr. Wright was an honest, good man who paid his bills and did not drink, he was a "hard man" and "Like a raw wind that gets to the bone." Mr. Hale's description of Mrs. Wright sitting in the kitchen dazed and disoriented gives us a picture of a shattered, exhausted woman. But it is Mrs. Hale who again offers further insights when she describes how Minnie Foster, a sweet, pretty, timid young woman who sang in the choir, was changed by her marriage to Mr. Wright and by her childless, isolated life on the farm.

This information about Mr. and Mrs. Wright is worked into the dialogue throughout the play in order to suggest the nature of the ***conflict*** or struggle between them, a motive, and, ultimately, a justification for the murder. In the hands of a skillful playwright, exposition is not merely a mechanical device, it can provide important information while simultaneously developing characterizations and moving the action forward.

The action is shaped by the ***plot,*** the author's arrangement of incidents in the play that gives the story a particular focus and emphasis. Plot involves more than simply what happens; it involves how and why things happen. Glaspell begins with a discussion of the murder. Why? She could have begun with the murder itself: the distraught Mrs. Wright looping the rope around her husband's neck. The moment would be dramatic and horribly vivid. We neither see the body nor hear very much about it. When Mr. Hale describes finding Mr. Wright's body, Glaspell has the county attorney cut him off by saying, "I think I'd rather have you go into that upstairs, where you can point it all out. Just go on now with the rest of the story." It is precisely the "rest of the story" that interests Glaspell. Her arrangement of incidents prevents us from sympathizing with Mr. Wright. We are, finally, invited to see Mrs. Wright instead of her husband as the victim.

Mr. Henderson's efforts to discover a motive for the murder appear initially to be the play's focus, but the real conflicts are explored in what seems to be a ***subplot,*** a secondary action that reinforces or contrasts with the main plot. The discussions between Mrs. Hale and Mrs. Peters and the tensions between the men and the women turn out to be the main plot because they address the issues that Glaspell chooses to explore. Those issues are not about murder but about marriage and how men and women relate to each other.

The ***protagonist*** of *Trifles,* the central character with whom we tend to identify, is Mrs. Hale. The ***antagonist,*** the character who is in some kind of opposition to the central character, is the county attorney, Mr. Henderson. These two characters embody the major conflicts presented in the play because each speaks for a different set of characters who represent disparate values. Mrs. Hale and Mr. Henderson are developed less individually than as representative types.

Mrs. Hale articulates a sensitivity to Mrs. Wright's miserable life as well as an awareness of how women are repressed in general by men; she also helps Mrs. Peters to arrive at a similar understanding. When Mrs. Hale defends Mrs. Wright's soiled towels from Mr. Henderson's criticism, Glaspell has her say more than the county attorney is capable of hearing. The ***stage directions,*** the playwright's instructions about how the actors are to move and behave, indicate that Mrs. Hale responds "stiffly" to Mr. Henderson's disparagements: "Men's hands aren't always as clean as they might be." Mrs. Hale eventually comes to see that the men are, in a sense, complicit because it was insensitivity like theirs that drove Mrs. Wright to murder.

Mr. Henderson, on the other hand, represents the law in a patriarchal, conventional society that blithely places a minimal value on the concerns of women. In his attempt to gather evidence against Mrs. Wright, he implicitly defends men's severe dominance over women. He also patronizes Mrs. Hale and Mrs. Peters. Like Sheriff Peters and Mr. Hale, he regards the women's world as nothing more than "kitchen things" and "trifles." Glaspell, however, patterns the plot so that the women see more about Mrs. Wright's motives than the men do and shows that the women have a deeper understanding of justice.

Many plays are plotted in what has come to be called a ***pyramidal pattern,*** because the plot is divided into three essential parts. Such plays begin with a ***rising action,*** in which complication creates conflict for the protagonist. The resulting tension builds to the second major division, known as the ***climax,*** when the action reaches a final ***crisis,*** a turning point that has a powerful effect on the protagonist. The third part consists of ***falling action;*** here the tensions are diminished in the ***resolution*** of the plot's conflicts and complications (the resolution is also referred to as the ***conclusion*** or ***denouement,*** a French word meaning "unknotting"). These divisions may occur at different times. There are many variations to this pattern. The terms are helpful for identifying various moments and movements within a given plot, but they are less useful if seen as a means of reducing dramatic art to a formula.

Because *Trifles* is a one-act play, this pyramidal pattern is less elaborately worked out than it might be in a full-length play, but the basic elements of the pattern can still be discerned. The complication consists mostly of Mrs. Hale's refusal to assign moral or legal guilt to Mrs. Wright's murder of her husband. Mrs. Hale is able to discover the motive in the domestic details that are beneath the men's consideration. The men fail to see the significance of the fruit jars, messy kitchen, and badly sewn quilt.

At first Mrs. Peters seems to voice the attitudes associated with the men. Unlike Mrs. Hale, who is "more comfortable looking," Mrs. Peters is "a slight wiry woman" with "a thin nervous face" who sounds like her husband, the sheriff, when she insists, "the law is the law." She also defends the men's patronizing attitudes, because "they've got awful important things on their minds." But Mrs. Peters is a ***foil*** — a character whose behavior and values contrast with the protagonist's — only up to a point. When the most telling clue is discovered, Mrs. Peters suddenly understands, along with Mrs. Hale, the motive for the killing. Mrs. Wright's caged life was no longer tolerable to her after her husband had killed the bird (which was the one bright spot in her life and which represents her early life as the young Minnie Foster). This revelation brings about the climax, when the two women must decide whether to tell the men what they have discovered. Both women empathize with Mrs. Wright as they confront this crisis, and their sense of common experience leads them to withhold the evidence.

This resolution ends the play's immediate conflicts and complications. Presumably, without a motive the county attorney will have difficulty prosecuting Mrs. Wright — at least to the fullest extent of the law. However, the larger issues related to the ***theme,*** the central idea or meaning of the play, are left unresolved. The men have both missed the clues and failed to perceive the suffering that acquits Mrs. Wright in the minds of the two women. The play ends with Mrs. Hale's ironic answer to Mr. Henderson's question about quilting. When she says "knot it," she gives him part of the evidence he needs to connect Mrs. Wright's quilting with the knot used to strangle her husband. Mrs. Hale knows — and we know — that Mr. Henderson will miss the clue she offers because he is blinded by his own self-importance and assumptions.

Though brief, *Trifles* is a masterful representation of dramatic elements working together to keep both audiences and readers absorbed in its characters and situations.

DRAMA IN POPULAR FORMS

Audiences for live performances of plays have been thinned by high ticket prices but perhaps even more significantly by the impact of motion pictures and television. Motion pictures, the original threat to live theater, have in turn been superseded by television (along with videocassettes), now the most popular form of entertainment in America. Television audiences are measured in the millions. Probably more people have seen a single weekly episode of a top-rated prime-time program such as *thirtysomething* in one evening than have viewed a live performance of *Hamlet* in nearly four hundred years.

Though most of us are seated more often before a television than before live actors, our limited experience with the theater presents relatively few obstacles to appreciation, because many of the basic elements of drama are similar whether the performance is on videotape or on a stage. Television has undoubtedly seduced audiences that otherwise might have been attracted to the theater, but television obviously satisfies some aspects of our desire for drama and can be seen as a potential introduction to live theater rather than as its irresistible rival.

Significant differences do, of course, exist between television and theater productions. Most obviously, television's special camera effects can capture phenomena such as earthquakes, raging fires, car chases, and space travel that cannot be realistically rendered on a live stage. The presentation of characters and the plotting of action are also handled differently owing to both the possibilities and limitations of television and the theater. Television's multiple camera angles and close-ups provide a degree of intimacy that cannot be duplicated by actors on stage, yet this intimacy does not achieve the immediacy that live actors create. On commercial television the plot must accommodate itself to breaks in the action so that advertisements can be aired at regular intervals. Beyond these and many other differences, however, there are enough important similarities that the experience of watching television shows can enhance our understanding of a theater production.

CAGNEY & LACEY

Cagney & Lacey was produced from 1982 to 1988. By 1985 this popular television show attracted a weekly audience of nearly 21 million viewers. Although this award-winning series has ceased production, reruns have preserved its popularity. An hour-long dramatic series, *Cagney & Lacey* presents two women detectives in the New York City Police Department; never before had a network prime-time drama featured two women in its leading roles. In addition to offering crimes that have to be solved and criminals who are inevitably caught, the show brings into focus the friendship of the two main characters — Chris Cagney, played by Sharon Gless, and Mary Beth Lacey, played by Tyne Daly. These partners are portrayed as women who work as detectives rather than as detectives who happen to be women.

Cagney and Lacey serve as foils for each other. Although they are both in their late thirties to early forties, Cagney is a single, ambitious woman whose brassy sexiness and hot-tempered confidence get her most of the show's wisecracking lines as well as most of her co-worker's anger. She is quick, impulsive, and sometimes arrogant. In contrast, Lacey is relatively calm, deliberate, and cautious. She is dedicated to her job, her marriage, and her two boys, but she is also tough and streetwise. Although her responses are more measured and considered than Cagney's, she is equally sensitive to the difficulties that women encounter in a traditionally all-male career path.

The uniqueness and popularity of this show were highlighted in the January 1987 issue of *Ms.* magazine, which named Gless and Daly "Women of the Year" for "transforming *Cagney & Lacey* from a pioneer to a classic, and for making friendship and partnership between women as natural on television as they are in real life."

In addition to emphasizing the friendship between these female partners, the show was also highly regarded because it went beyond most other police series, such as *Miami Vice,* in its treatment of social issues. Although *Cagney & Lacey* incorporated many of the typical elements of police drama —

crimes, villains, heroic actions, suspense, and so on — it also attempted to address some serious issues. Plots often included topics related to racism, sexism, alcoholism, pornography, illegal adoptions, working mothers, abandoned children, breast cancer, and other issues, especially those that affect women. Daly once described the show's aim in a *New York Times Magazine* interview (September 22, 1985): "If TV is fast food, like McDonald's, and you have to wrap it up and get it out once a week," she said, "then, on this menu of french fries and onion rings and double burgers we would like to be the green salad." She wanted the show to be "nourishing and interesting" as well as entertaining.

The following scene from *Cagney & Lacey* is a ***teaser*** — a brief vignette lasting only a couple of minutes before the opening credits of a television show — from a script titled "You Call This Plainclothes?" As short as it is, this teaser contains some of the same dramatic elements found in a play. Notice how quickly and efficiently the setting, characterizations, and plot are established.

BARBARA AVEDON, BARBARA CORDAY, AND BARNEY ROSENZWEIG

Cagney & Lacey 1982

"You Call this Plainclothes?"

Fade in.

Exterior seedy street — establishing shot — night

Camera picks out the swinging derriere of an obvious prostitute as she saunters down the street, past a bar, a porno theater, an adult bookstore to the mouth of an alley where another prostitute leans against the building. The first turns into camera as she speaks and we realize that it's Cagney . . . the prostitute leaning against the building is Lacey.

Cagney: Any action?

Lacey: You know, I think I'd welcome some. Anything to get off my feet; they're killing me.

Cagney: You mean you're not loving the lights, the glamour, the sweet song of the streets?

Lacey glares at her, says into her cleavage:

Lacey: What do ya say, guys? Let's call it a day.

They look toward end of block. An unwashed, unmarked van is parked at the curb.

Interior van — night

It is outfitted with all kinds of electronic equipment. Half-eaten sandwiches are everywhere, as are Styrofoam cups and cigarette butts. Isbecki and La Guardia look beat. Isbecki has a headset on, and La Guardia fools with the controls of the tape recorder while constantly checking the window through the blinds. Isbecki looks at his watch, then at La Guardia.

Isbecki: She wants to pack it in.
La Guardia: Couldn't be too soon for me.

Back to Cagney and Lacey. Shooting past them at the van. The van's lights go on, then off, then on, then off. They sigh in relief . . .

Cagney: Where's the car?
Lacey (patiently): In the next block . . . where we parked it.

They start through the alley as

Cagney: The John Detail . . . . That's the lowest.
Lacey: I could handle it, if it called for day work, but I haven't had dinner with my kids for two weeks . . . and I kind of miss the smell of lima beans in my hair.
Cagney: Lima beans are one thing, this crummy assignment is really cutting into my social—

They react to the sound of feet running down the iron fire escape steps into the alley.
Another angle. Vinnie Martorano, a tall, slim, thirty-year-old man, drops to the alley floor.

Vinnie: Hey girls . . . psst.

Cagney and Lacey quickly assume their tough hooker composure again.

Cagney: Yeah.

Vinnie keeps looking up toward the fire escape, nervously.

Vinnie: How'd you girls like to make a couple a clams . . . real fast and real easy.
Cagney: Forget it, buster, this girl's ready for a bath and a *single* bed. Come back tomorrow.

Vinnie, really nervous now, steps closer to the women, who make eye contact with each other. They're ready for trouble.

Vinnie (all business): Not that. *(Conspiratorially.)* I think I'm being tailed. *(Even closer; quieter.)* Narcs.

Cagney and Lacey react, impressed and innocent.

Lacey: Whew! No kiddin'.
Cagney: What's the score?

Vinnie pulls a small package out of his pocket.

Vinnie: I gotta make a drop at midnight and if I don't show up I'm outa business . . . *(Meaningfully.)* . . . permanently.

Cagney and Lacey look at each other.

Vinnie (continuing; pleadingly): Just drop this in the trash can in front of Nick's on the corner. When I ditch these guys I'll come back for it.

He takes some money out of his pocket and is about to peel off some bills. As he takes his eyes off the women, Cagney takes out her badge and Lacey takes out her gun. Cagney grabs the package as

Cagney: You're under arrest.
Vinnie (in shock): Police broads!

Lacey twists his arm behind his back and snaps the cuffs on him as we fade out.

Considerations

1. What is the effect of our first viewing Cagney from behind? Why would this visual strategy be especially effective for a weekly series?
2. Write a detailed description of the setting — the street and van — as you imagine them.
3. Explain how humor is worked into nearly every line of this teaser. What other emotions does the teaser evoke? Describe its overall tone.
4. How does the dialogue between Cagney and Lacey serve to characterize each of them?
5. *Cagney & Lacey* was aired on Monday evenings opposite *Monday Night Football.* Why do you think programmers scheduled the show for that slot in prime time?
6. View a rerun of a *Cagney & Lacey* episode. How does reading a teaser script compare with watching the show? Which do you prefer? Why?

Like those of many plays, the setting for this teaser is more suggestive than it is detailed. We're told it is a dark, "seedy street" that includes a bar, porno theater, adult bookstore, and alley, but none of these locations is described further. Even without seeing a set designer's version of the scene, we can readily create a mental picture of a sleazy, tawdry, and dangerous neighborhood. For *Cagney & Lacey,* a realistic set was used that replicated the details a viewer would observe in an actual street scene. If the scene were presented onstage, however, a set designer might use minimal sets and props, to suggest rather than duplicate a red-light district. The director of such a production would rely on the viewers' imaginations to supply the details of the setting.

Similarly, the stage directions are spare; little information is provided about how the characters are dressed or how they move. The details are left to the director or the reader. In sum, just because a stage is relatively bare doesn't mean that the audience has to perceive it that way. A combination of convincing dialogue and compelling acting can build a world. So can imaginative readers.

Though extremely brief, this teaser includes exposition to provide the necessary background about the characters and their circumstances. As Cagney and Lacey walk through the alley after they have decided to call it quits for the night, we learn through dialogue, for example, that Lacey has children and misses taking care of them as well as cooking; her domesticity is contrasted with Cagney's complaint that night assignments are cutting into her social life. These bits of information help to characterize the women beyond their decoy roles as prostitutes and allow an audience to place the partners' attitudes and comments in a larger context that will be useful for making sense of the rest of the script too.

The plot in this teaser shapes the conflicts to emphasize surprise. As in any good play, incidents are carefully arranged to achieve a particular effect. At the beginning of the script, for example, we are surprised (if we are regular viewers of the weekly series — or at least familiar with it) to discover that the "swinging derriere of an obvious prostitute" is Cagney. The scene could have begun by simply establishing that the two detectives are weary after having been unsuccessful in luring any "Johns" into their trap, but that would have been a slow start instead of the surprise with which the script hooks us. Rather than dramatizing background information, the scriptwriter arranges incidents to create a particular focus and effect while working in the necessary exposition through the characters' dialogue.

Again, consider how surprise is the intended effect of this teaser: We are surprised that the prostitutes are detectives. They are surprised that just as they're ready to "pack it in" their work has begun, they hear the "sound of feet running down the iron fire escape steps" (here's the complication of the pyramidal plot pattern discussed in "Elements of Drama," p. 942). This complication results in further surprise and tension when Vinnie, the antagonist, turns out to want not sex but help in eluding the police. This irony leads to an even bigger surprise for Vinnie when Cagney and Lacey arrest him at the climax of the teaser. The instantaneous resolution comes with Vinnie's recognition of "Police broads!" as the conclusion snaps shut along with the sound of the handcuffs closing around his wrists.

Although the script's seedy setting is threatening and the characters are unpredictable, the tension in the teaser is relieved by the comic surprises as well as dialogue, such as Lacey talking into her cleavage or saying she misses the smell of lima beans in her hair. The audience is left smiling even though the scene is built around prostitution, drug dealing, and potential violence. The main plot is resolved to everyone's satisfaction — the police get their man — while the subplot involving Cagney's and Lacey's dissatisfaction with being relegated to "the lowest" job — working the presumably victimless "John Detail" — is also resolved, because they are able to make an important drug arrest. Hence, the main plot and subplot connect and comment on each other.

The teasers that begin television shows are often unrelated to the stories that follow; they are typically used to engage audiences quickly so that they won't change the station. Moreover, when a show goes into syndication and reruns, teasers are frequently cut to allow for more commercials. In "You Call This Plainclothes?," however, the teaser provides a kind of preview of what the rest of the story is about.

In the main story Cagney and Lacey have to prove themselves yet again to their fellow male officers, because their drug arrest is written off as merely luck. They are reassigned to the "John Detail," but their job turns more serious when a series of prostitutes are brutally murdered and their role as decoys becomes deadly earnest. A further complication develops when Cagney wants to make a deal with Vinnie for leading them to the "top guy" dealing drugs, a criminal who is also a dangerous Mafia leader. Once again the criminals are caught — both the murderer and the drug dealer — but the arrests are made largely because of Cagney's ambition rather than Lacey's cautious approach. Cagney takes on the murderer herself and almost winds up his victim. The final scene at the police station, observed by male detectives, complicates the relationship between the partners but also ultimately makes it stronger.

Interior precinct corridor — day

As Isbecki and Petrie head down the hall, Lacey steams toward them. She looks at them with an unspoken question in her furious eyes.

Isbecki (with a nod of his head): She's in there.

Lacey keeps going. Camera pans her to the Detectives' Room, and she strides in and closes the door behind her.

Interior Detectives' Room — day

Lacey faces Cagney.

Cagney (somewhat embarrassed): Hiya.

Lacey (furious): That really stinks. You really don't know a damn thing about teamwork . . . or friendship, do you? You know what you are? You're macha!

Cagney (reaches out): Hey, Mary Beth . . .

Lacey (flinches away): No. If you got yourself killed last night, I'd have to live the rest of my life feeling like I let you down . . . like it was my fault.

Cagney: Listen, if I hadn't been there, some other woman would have gotten killed. Anyway, I was so upset about Vinnie I just had to find something to do.

Lacey: You've never had any trouble finding something to do before. Don't give me that crap, Chris. Somewhere in the back of your head you wanted to make that collar alone. Maybe we're two different cops. I want to do my job and I want to do it well, but to me it's a job. To you it's . . . a . . .

Cagney: I really have been pulling you pretty hard, haven't I?

Lacey: You want to be a star.

Cagney (a beat): Maybe I saw too many movies when I was a kid. You're right . . . down deep, what I've been pushing for is to be a star.

There's a long beat as they look at each other.

Cagney (continuing): You want my autograph?

They throw their arms around each other as the tension crumbles.

Lacey: I was so damn worried about you. Hearing it on the radio, even though I knew it was over, I just kept picturing you dead.

They stand apart and Lacey levels.

Lacey (continuing): I couldn't stand that. I love you. I need you in my life.

Cagney: I need you too, and I'll never pull any of that solo stuff on you again. Okay?

Lacey nods. They put their arms around each other. Samuels walks in.

Samuels: Hey, you two . . . none of that female crap in the precinct, huh? Whadda say?

As they simultaneously bombard him with paper clips and erasers, we fade out.

Although the teaser and the main story are filled with surprises and comic situations, there is a serious theme implicit in the action: these women detectives, albeit undervalued and stereotyped as "police broads" by criminals, their department, and perhaps even a portion of the show's audience, are nonetheless professional and competent when the going gets tough. That's probably what Tyne Daly had in mind when she said that for all the predictability of a formulaic police show, the menu that sums up *Cagney & Lacey* also offers a "green salad" of "nourishing and interesting" perspectives on two working women who have complicated lives as both partners and friends.

PERSPECTIVE

CARL SAUTTER (b. 1949)
On the Principles of Screenwriting

1988

[A] key principle of any form of screenwriting is that *a script is not linear.* An interesting TV movie or screenplay does not move from one obvious step to the next. Instead, a good script surprises us by skipping the boring steps we don't need to see and letting information come out where it is most interesting, not necessarily where it is most logical. This is a direct contradiction to the fundamentals of expository writing we all learned in Senior English: The lead paragraph introduces the most important information; each paragraph starts with a topic sentence, etc. Not in a screenplay. If the most important information is in the first scene of a movie, the movie has no plot. If each scene begins with a lead sentence, there's no reason to see the rest of the scene. The emphasis in expository writing is on making a point clearly. The emphasis in screenwriting is on making the point in the most interesting way possible.

All of which leads to [another] important basic of the screenwriting craft — *avoid anything that is OTN* ("On the nose"). This pejorative acronym is used widely (and excessively) by story editors, producers, and critics. OTN means that the writer has made an obvious choice. A plot twist may be OTN because it's exactly the twist the reader expected (which means it wasn't a twist at all). A character may be OTN because he or she is a cliché: the prostitute with the heart of gold, the villain with a missing finger, the smart-aleck maid. Dialogue may be OTN when characters say exactly what they are feeling or what they have learned. When a character is facing a gun and says "I've got to get out of here," *that's* OTN. When the crisis is resolved and the hero kisses the heroine and proclaims "I'm so happy," *that's* OTN. The audience should realize these feelings and lessons from the story they're seeing, not from what the characters say about themselves. To avoid being OTN, the writer must try to find subtle and surprising ways to advance the story and the characters. . . .

Finally, one of the hardest basic lessons to learn is that *screenwriting is visual writing.* It is always better to show something than to talk about it. The less characters talk about the plot, the better . . . the story should move through visuals — reactions from the characters, physical action, anything the audience can see. Surprisingly, the rule holds true even for radio drama, where there is no picture whatsoever. The best radio scripts create a picture of the story through dialogue and stage directions, allowing the listener to see what's happening even though there are no pictures. This is the gift of the great radio storytellers — Garrison Keillor, Orson Welles. We've never seen Lake Wobegon, but we all have a good idea what it looks like.

From *How to Sell Your Screenplay: The Real Rules of Film and Television*

Considerations

1. A successful screenwriter who includes among his credits award-winning scripts for *Moonlighting,* Sautter makes a crucial distinction between screenwriting and expository writing. Describe this distinction and explain why you agree or disagree with it.
2. Using the opening scene from *Cagney & Lacey* as a model, and keeping in mind Sautter's principles for screenwriting, try writing a teaser for one of the short stories or plays in this anthology.

QUESTIONS FOR RESPONSIVE READING

The remaining plays in this anthology are rich with possibilities for both reading and production. The questions in this section can help you consider important elements that reveal a play's effects and meanings. These questions are general and will not, therefore, always be relevant to a particular play. Many of them, however, should prove useful for thinking, talking, and writing about drama. If you are uncertain about the meaning of a term used in a question, consult the Index of Terms for pages that discuss the term. Some of these terms are defined in the fiction and poetry sections, because they are relevant for fiction and poetry as well as drama.

1. Did you enjoy the play? What, specifically, pleased or displeased you about what was expressed and how it was expressed?
2. What is the significance of the play's title? How does it suggest the author's overall emphasis?

3. What information do the stage directions provide about the characters, action, and setting? Are these directions primarily descriptive, or are they also interpretive?
4. How is the exposition presented? What does it reveal? How does the playwright's choice *not* to dramatize certain events on stage help to determine what the focus of the play is?
5. In what ways is the setting important? Would the play be altered significantly if the setting were changed?
6. Are foreshadowings used to suggest what is to come? Are flashbacks used to dramatize what has already happened?
7. What is the major conflict the protagonist faces? What complications constitute the rising action? Where is the climax? Is the conflict resolved?
8. Are one or more subplots used to qualify or complicate the main plot? Is the plot unified so that each incident somehow has a function that relates it to some other element in the play?
9. Does the author purposely avoid a pyramidal plot structure of rising action, climax, and falling action? Is the plot experimental? Is the plot logically and chronologically organized, or is it fantastical or absurd? What effects are produced by the plot? How does it reflect the author's view of life?
10. Who is the protagonist? Who (or what) is the antagonist?
11. By what means does the playwright reveal character? What do the characters' names, physical qualities, actions, and words convey about them? What do the characters reveal about each other?
12. What is the purpose of the minor characters? Are they individualized, or do they primarily represent ideas or attitudes? Are any character foils used?
13. Do the characters all use the same kind of language, or is their speech differentiated? Is it formal or informal? How do the characters' diction and manner of speaking serve to characterize them?
14. Does your response to the characters change in the course of the play? What causes the change?
15. Are words and images repeated in the play so that they take on special meanings? Which speeches seem particularly important? Why?
16. How does the playwright's use of language contribute to the tone of the play? Is the dialogue, for example, predominantly light, humorous, relaxed, sentimental, sad, angry, intense, or violent?
17. Are any symbols used in the play? Which actions, characters, settings, objects, or words convey more than their literal meanings?
18. Are any unfamiliar theatrical conventions used that present problems in understanding the play? How does knowing more about the nature of the theater from which the play originated help to resolve these problems?
19. Is the theme stated directly, or is it developed implicitly through

the plot, characters, or some other element? Does the theme confirm or challenge most people's values?

20. How does the play reflect the values of the society in which it is set and in which it was written?
21. How does the play reflect or challenge your own values?
22. Is there a recording, film, or videocassette of the play available in your library or media center? How does this version compare with your own reading?
23. How would you produce the play on a stage? Consider scenery, costumes, casting, and characterizations. What would you emphasize most in your production?

25. A Study of Sophocles

Sophocles lived a long, productive life (496?–406 B.C.) in Athens. During his life Athens became a dominant political and cultural power after the Persian Wars, but before he died Sophocles witnessed the decline of Athens as a result of the Peloponnesian Wars and the city's subsequent surrender to Sparta. He saw Athenian culture reach remarkable heights as well as collapse under enormous pressures.

Sophocles embodied much of the best of Athenian culture; he enjoyed success as a statesman, general, treasurer, priest, and, of course, prize-winning dramatist. Although surviving fragments indicate that he wrote over 120 plays, only a handful remain intact. Those that survive consist of the three plays he wrote about Oedipus and his children — *Oedipus the King, Oedipus at Colonus,* and *Antigone* — and four additional tragedies: *Philoctetes, Ajax, Maidens of Trachis,* and *Electra.*

His plays won numerous prizes at festival competitions because of his careful, subtle plotting and the sense of inevitability with which their action is charged. Moreover, his development of character is richly complex. Instead of relying on the extreme situations and exaggerated actions that earlier tragedians used, Sophocles created powerfully motivated characters who even today fascinate audiences with their psychological depth.

In addition to crafting sophisticated tragedies for the Greek theater, Sophocles introduced several important innovations to the stage. Most important, he broke the tradition of using only two actors; adding a third resulted in more complicated relationships and intricate dialogue among characters. As individual actors took more of the center stage, Sophocles reduced the role of the chorus (discussed on p. 958). This shift placed even more emphasis on the actors, although the chorus remained important as a means of commenting on the action and establishing its tone. Sophocles was also the first dramatist to write plays with specific actors in mind, a development that influenced many later playwrights, including Shakespeare. But without question Sophocles' greatest contribution to drama was

Oedipus the King, which, it has been argued, is the most influential drama ever written.

THEATRICAL CONVENTIONS OF GREEK DRAMA

More than twenty-four hundred years have passed since 430 B.C., when Sophocles' *Oedipus the King* was probably first produced on a Greek stage. We inhabit a vastly different planet than Sophocles' audience did, yet concerns about what it means to be human in a world that frequently runs counter to our desires and aspirations have remained relatively constant. The ancient Greeks continue to speak to us. But inexperienced readers or viewers may have some initial difficulty understanding the theatrical conventions used in classical Greek tragedies such as *Oedipus the King* and *Antigone.* If Sophocles were alive today, he would very likely need some sort of assistance with the conventions of an Arthur Miller play or a television production of *Cagney & Lacey*.

Classical Greek drama developed from religious festivals that paid homage to Dionysus, the god of wine and fertility. Most of the details of these festivals have been lost, but we do know that they included dancing and singing that celebrated legends about Dionysus. From these choral songs developed stories of both Dionysus and mortal culture-heroes. These heroes became the subject of playwrights whose works were produced in contests at the festivals. The Dionysian festivals lasted more than five hundred years, but relatively few of their plays have survived. Among the works of the three great writers of tragedy, only seven plays each by Sophocles and Aeschylus (525?–456 B.C.) and eighteen plays by Euripides (480?–406 B.C.) survive.

Plays were such important events in Greek society that they were partially funded by the state. The Greeks associated drama with religious and community values as well as entertainment. In a sense, their plays celebrate their civilization; in approving the plays, audiences applauded their own culture. The enormous popularity of the plays is indicated by the size of surviving amphitheaters. Although information about these theaters is sketchy, we do know that most of them shared a common form. They were built into hillsides with rising rows of seats accommodating more than fourteen thousand people. These seats partially encircled an ***orchestra*** or "dancing place," where the ***chorus*** of a dozen or so men chanted lines and danced.

Tradition credits the Greek poet Thespis with adding an actor who was separate from the choral singing and dancing of early performances. A second actor was subsequently included by Aeschylus and a third, as noted earlier, by Sophocles. These additions made possible the conflicts and complicated relationships that evolved into the dramatic art we know today. The two or three male actors who played all the roles appeared behind the orchestra in front of the ***skene,*** a stage building that served as dressing rooms. As Greek theater evolved, a wall of the skene came to be painted to suggest a palace or some other setting, and the roof was employed to indicate, for instance, a mountain location. Sometimes gods were lowered from the roof by mechanical devices to set matters right among the mortals below. This method of rescuing characters from complications beyond their abilities to resolve was known in Latin as ***deus ex machina*** ("god from the machine"), a term now used to describe any improbable means by which an author provides a too-easy resolution for a story.

Inevitably, the conventions of the Greek theaters affected how plays were presented. Few if any scene changes occurred, because the amphitheater stage was set primarily for one location. If an important event happened somewhere else, it was reported by a minor character, such as a messenger. The chorus also provided necessary background information. In *Oedipus the King* and *Antigone,* the choruses, acting as townspeople, also assess the characters' strengths and weaknesses, praising them for their virtues, chiding them for their rashness, and giving them advice. The reactions of the chorus provide a connection between the actors and audience because the chorus is at once a participant in and an observer of the action. In addition, the chorus helps structure the action by indicating changes in

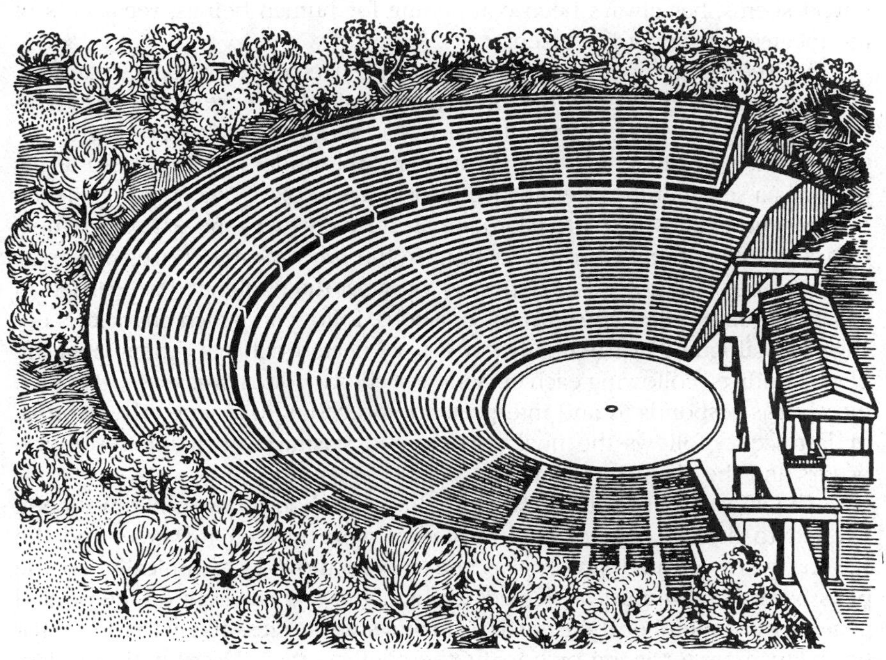

Based on scholarly sources, this drawing represents the features typical of classical Greek theater. (Drawing by Gerda Becker. From Kenneth Macgowan and David Melnitz, *The Living Stage,* © 1955 by Prentice-Hall, Inc.)

scene or mood. Thus the chorus could be used in a variety of ways to shape the audience's response to the play's action and characters.

Actors in classical Greek amphitheaters faced considerable challenges. An intimate relationship with the audience was impossible because many spectators would have been too far away to see a facial expression or subtle gesture. Indeed, some in the audience would have had difficulty even hearing the voices of individual actors. To compensate for these disadvantages, actors wore large masks that extravagantly expressed the major characters' emotions or identified the roles of minor characters. The masks also allowed the two or three actors in a performance to play all the characters without confusing the audience. Each mask was fitted so that the mouthpiece amplified the actor's voice. The actors were further equipped with padded costumes and elevated shoes ***(cothurni*** or ***buskins)*** that made them appear larger than life.

As a result of these adaptive conventions, Greek plays tend to emphasize words — formal, impassioned speeches — more than physical action. We are invited to ponder actions and events rather than to see all of them enacted. Although the stark simplicity of Greek theater does not offer an audience realistic detail, the classical tragedies that have survived present characters in dramatic situations that transcend theatrical conventions. Tragedy, it seems, has always been compelling for human beings, regardless of the theatrical forms it has taken.

A Greek tragedy is typically divided into five parts: prologue, parodos, episodia, stasimon, and exodus. In some translations these terms appear as headings, but in more recent translations, as those by Robert Fagles included here, the headings do not appear. Still, understanding these terms provides a sense of the overall rhythm of a Greek play. The opening speech or dialogue is known as the ***prologue*** and usually gives the exposition necessary to follow the subsequent action. In the ***parodos*** the chorus makes its first entrance and gives its perspective on what the audience has learned in the prologue. Several ***episodia,*** or episodes, follow, in which characters engage in dialogue that frequently consists of heated debates dramatizing the play's conflicts. Following each episode is a choral ode or ***stasimon,*** in which the chorus responds to and interprets the preceding dialogue. The ***exodus,*** or last scene, follows the final episode and stasimon; in it the resolution occurs and the characters leave the stage.

The effect of alternating dialogues and choral odes has sometimes been likened to that of opera. Greek tragedies were written in verse, and the stasima were chanted or sung as the chorus moved rhythmically, so the plays have a strong musical element that is not always apparent on the printed page. If we remember their musical qualities we are less likely to forget that no matter how terrifying or horrific the conflicts they describe, these plays are stately, measured, and dignified works that reflect a characteristic Greek sense of order and proportion.

TRAGEDY

Newspapers are filled with daily reports of "tragedies": a child is struck and crippled by a car; an airplane plunges into a suburban neighborhood; a volcano erupts and kills tens of thousands. These unexpected instances of suffering are commonly and accurately described as "tragic," but they are not tragedies in the literary sense of the term. A literary ***tragedy*** presents courageous individuals who confront powerful forces within or outside themselves with a dignity that reveals the breadth and depth of the human spirit in the face of failure, defeat, and even death.

Aristotle (384–322 B.C.), in his *Poetics,* defined *tragedy* on the basis of the plays contemporary to him. His definition has generated countless variations, qualifications, and interpretations, but we still derive our literary understanding of this term from Aristotle.

The protagonist of a Greek tragedy is someone regarded as extraordinary rather than typical: a great man or woman brought from happiness to agony. The character's stature is important because it makes his or her fall all the more terrifying. The protagonist also carries mythic significance for the audience. Oedipus and Antigone, for example, are not only human beings but legendary figures from a distant, revered past. Although the gods do not appear onstage in either *Oedipus the King* or *Antigone,* their power is ever-present as the characters invoke their help or attempt to defy them. In addition, Greek tragedy tends to be public rather than private. The fate of the community — the state — is often linked with that of the protagonist, as when Thebes suffers a plague as a result of Oedipus's mistaken actions.

The protagonists of classical Greek tragedies (and of those of Shakespeare) are often rulers of noble birth who represent the monarchical values of their periods, but in modern tragedies the protagonists are more likely to reflect democratic values that make it possible for anyone to be a suitable subject. What is finally important is not so much the protagonist's social stature as a greatness of character that steadfastly confronts suffering, whether it comes from supernatural, social, or psychological forces. Although Greek tragic heroes were aristocrats, the nobility of their characters was more significant than their inherited titles and privileges.

The protagonist's eminence and determination to complete some task or goal make him or her admirable in Greek tragedy, but that does not free the protagonist from what Aristotle described as "some error or frailty" that brings about his or her misfortune. The term Aristotle used for this weakness is ***hamartia.*** This word has frequently been interpreted to mean that the protagonist's fall is the result of an internal ***tragic flaw,*** such as an excess of pride, ambition, passion, or some other character trait that leads directly to disaster.

Sometimes, however, misfortunes are not the result of a character flaw but of misunderstood events that overtake and thwart the protagonist's best intentions. Thus, virtue can lead to tragedy too. *Hamartia* has also been interpreted to mean "wrong act" — a mistake based not on a personal failure but on circumstances outside the protagonist's personality and control. Many readers find that a combination of these two interpretations sheds the most light on the causes of the tragic protagonist's fall. Both internal and external forces can lead to downfall, because the protagonist's personality may determine crucial judgments that result in mistaken actions.

However the idea of tragic flaw is understood, it is best not to use it as a means of reducing the qualities of a complex character to an adjective or two that labels Oedipus as guilty of "overweening pride" (the Greek term for which is ***hubris*** or ***hybris***) or Antigone as "fated." The protagonists of tragedies require more careful characterization than a simplistic label can provide.

Whatever the causes of the tragic protagonist's downfall, he or she accepts responsibility for it. Hence, even in his or her encounter with failure (and possibly death) the tragic protagonist displays greatness of character. Perhaps it is the witnessing of this greatness, which seems both to accept and to transcend human limitations, that makes audiences feel relief rather than hopelessness at the end of a tragedy. Aristotle described this response as a ***catharsis,*** or purgation of the emotions of "pity and fear." We are faced with the protagonist's misfortune, which often seems out of proportion to his or her actions, and so we are likely to feel compassionate pity. Simultaneously, we may experience fear, because the failure of the protagonist, who is so great in stature and power, is a frightening reminder of our own vulnerabilities. Ultimately, however, both these negative emotions are purged, because the tragic protagonist's suffering is an affirmation of human values — even if they are not always triumphant — rather than a despairing denial of them.

Nevertheless, tragedies are disturbing. Instead of coming away with the reassurance of a happy ending, we must take solace in the insight produced by the hero's suffering. And just as our expectations are changed, so are the protagonist's. Artistotle described the moment in the plot when this change occurs as a ***reversal*** (peripeteia), the point when the hero's fortunes turn in an unexpected direction. He more specifically defined this term as meaning an action performed by a character that has the opposite of its intended effect. An example cited by Aristotle is the messenger's attempts to relieve Oedipus's anxieties about his relationship to his father and mother. Instead, the messenger reveals previously unknown information that eventually results in a ***recognition*** (*anagnorisis*); Oedipus discovers the terrible truth that he has killed his father and married his mother.

Tragedy is typically filled with ironies, because there are so many moments in the plot when what seems to be turns out to be radically different from what actually is. Because of this, a particular form of irony called ***dramatic irony*** is also known as ***tragic irony.*** In dramatic irony, the meaning of a character's words or actions is understood by the audience but not by the character. Audiences of Greek tragedy shared with the playwrights a knowledge of the stories on which many tragic plots were based. Consequently, they frequently were aware of what was going to happen before the characters were. When Oedipus declares that he will seek out the person responsible for the plague that ravishes his city, the audience already knows that the person Oedipus pursues is himself.

OEDIPUS THE KING

A familiarity with the Oedipus legend allows modern readers to appreciate the series of ironies that unfolds in Sophocles' *Oedipus the King.* In the opening scene, Oedipus appears with a "telltale limp." As an infant, he had been abandoned by his parents, Laius and Jocasta, the king and queen of Thebes, because a prophecy warned that their son would kill his father and marry his mother. They instructed a servant to leave him on a mountain to die. The infant's feet were pierced and pinned together, but he was not left on the mountain; instead the servant, out of pity, gave him to a shepherd, who in turn presented him to the king and queen of Corinth. They named him Oedipus (for "swollen foot") and raised him as their own son.

Upon reaching manhood, Oedipus learned from an oracle that he would kill his father and marry his mother; to avoid this horrendous fate, he left Corinth forever. In his travels, Oedipus found his way blocked by a chariot at a crossroads; in a fit of anger, he killed the servants and their passenger. That passenger, unknown to Oedipus, was his real father. In Thebes, Oedipus successfully answered the riddle of the Sphinx, a winged lion with a woman's head. The reward for defeating this dreaded monster was both the crown and the dead king's wife. Oedipus and Jocasta had four children and prospered. But when the play begins, Oedipus's rule is troubled by a plague that threatens to destroy Thebes, and he is determined to find the cause of the plague in order to save the city again.

Oedipus the King is widely recognized as the greatest of the surviving Greek tragedies. Numerous translations are available (Robert Fagles's recent highly regarded translations of *Oedipus the King* and *Antigone,* the choice here, are especially accessible to modern readers. For an excerpt from another version of *Oedipus the King,* see Perspectives on Sophocles, p. 1047). The play has absorbed readers for centuries because Oedipus's character — his intelligence, confidence, rashness, and suffering — represents powers and limitations that are both exhilarating and chastening. Although no reader or viewer is likely to identify with Oedipus' extreme circumstances, anyone can appreciate his heroic efforts to find the truth about himself. In that sense, he is one of us — at our best.

SOPHOCLES (496?–406 B.C.)

Oedipus the King c. 430 B.C.

TRANSLATED BY ROBERT FAGLES

Characters

Oedipus, King of Thebes
A Priest of Zeus
Creon, brother of Jocasta
A Chorus of Theban citizens and their *Leader*
Tiresias, a blind prophet
Jocasta, the queen, wife of Oedipus
A Messenger from Corinth
A Shepherd
A Messenger from inside the palace
Antigone, Ismene, daughters of Oedipus and Jocasta
Guards and attendants
Priests of Thebes

TIME AND SCENE: *The royal house of Thebes. Double doors dominate the facade; a stone altar stands at the center of the stage.*

Many years have passed since Oedipus solved the riddle of the Sphinx and ascended the throne of Thebes, and now a plague has struck the city. A procession of priests enters; suppliants, broken and despondent, they carry branches wound in wool and lay them on the altar.

The doors open. Guards assemble. Oedipus comes forward, majestic but for a telltale limp, and slowly views the condition of his people.

Oedipus: Oh my children, the new blood of ancient Thebes,
why are you here? Huddling at my altar,
praying before me, your branches wound in wool.°
Our city reeks with the smoke of burning incense,
rings with cries for the Healer and wailing for the dead.
I thought it wrong, my children, to hear the truth
from others, messengers. Here I am myself —
you all know me, the world knows my fame:
I am Oedipus.

Helping a Priest to his feet.

Speak up, old man. Your years,
your dignity — you should speak for the others.
Why here and kneeling, what preys upon you so?
Some sudden fear? some strong desire?
You can trust me; I am ready to help,
I'll do anything. I would be blind to misery
not to pity my people kneeling at my feet.
Priest: Oh Oedipus, king of the land, our greatest power!
You see us before you, men of all ages

3 *wool:* Wool was used in offerings to Apollo, god of poetry, sun, prophecy, and healing.

clinging to your altars. Here are boys,
still too weak to fly from the nest,
and here the old, bowed down with the years,
the holy ones — a priest of Zeus° myself — and here
the picked, unmarried men, the young hope of Thebes.
And all the rest, your great family gathers now,
branches wreathed, massing in the squares,
kneeling before the two temples of queen Athena°
or the river-shrine where the embers glow and die
and Apollo sees the future in the ashes.
Our city —
look around you, see with your own eyes —
our ship pitches wildly, cannot lift her head
from the depths, the red waves of death . . .
Thebes is dying. A blight on the fresh crops
and the rich pastures, cattle sicken and die,
and the women die in labor, children stillborn,
and the plague, the fiery god of fever hurls down
on the city, his lightning slashing through us —
raging plague in all its vengeance, devastating
the house of Cadmus!° And Black Death luxuriates
in the raw, wailing miseries of Thebes.

Now we pray to you. You cannot equal the gods,
your children know that, bending at your altar.
But we do rate you first of men,
both in the common crises of our lives
and face-to-face encounters with the gods.
You freed us from the Sphinx; you came to Thebes
and cut us loose from the bloody tribute we had paid
that harsh, brutal singer. We taught you nothing,
no skill, no extra knowledge, still you triumphed.
A god was with you, so they say, and we believe it —
you lifted up our lives.
So now again,
Oedipus, king, we bend to you, your power —
we implore you, all of us on our knees:
find us strength, rescue! Perhaps you've heard
the voice of a god or something from other men,
Oedipus . . . what do you know?
The man of experience — you see it every day —
his plans will work in a crisis, his first of all.

Act now — we beg you, best of men, raise up our city!
Act, defend yourself, your former glory!
Your country calls you savior now
for your zeal, your action years ago.

21 *Zeus:* The highest Olympian deity and father of Apollo. 25 *Athena:* Goddess of wisdom and protector of Greek cities. 37 *Cadmus:* The legendary founder of Thebes.

Never let us remember of your reign:
you helped us stand, only to fall once more.
Oh raise up our city, set us on our feet.
The omens were good that day you brought us joy —
be the same man today!
Rule our land, you know you have the power,
but rule a land of the living, not a wasteland.
Ship and towered city are nothing, stripped of men
alive within it, living all as one.

Oedipus:

My children,
I pity you. I see — how could I fail to see
what longings bring you here? Well I know
you are sick to death, all of you,
but sick as you are, not one is sick as I.
Your pain strikes each of you alone, each
in the confines of himself, no other. But my spirit
grieves for the city, for myself and all of you.
I wasn't asleep, dreaming. You haven't wakened me —
I've wept through the nights, you must know that,
groping, laboring over many paths of thought.
After a painful search I found one cure:
I acted at once. I sent Creon,
my wife's own brother, to Delphi — °
Apollo the Prophet's oracle — to learn
what I might do or say to save our city.

Today's the day. When I count the days gone by
it torments me . . . what is he doing?
Strange, he's late, he's gone too long.
But once he returns, then, then I'll be a traitor
if I do not do all the god makes clear.

Priest: Timely words. The men over there
are signaling — Creon's just arriving.

Oedipus:

Sighting Creon, then turning to the altar.

Lord Apollo,
let him come with a lucky word of rescue,
shining like his eyes!

Priest: Welcome news, I think — he's crowned, look,
and the laurel wreath is bright with berries.

Oedipus: We'll soon see. He's close enough to hear —

Enter Creon from the side; his face is shaded with a wreath.

Creon, prince, my kinsman, what do you bring us?
What message from the god?

Creon: Good news.

82 *Delphi:* The shrine where the oracle of Apollo held forth.

I tell you even the hardest things to bear,
if they should turn out well, all would be well.
Oedipus: Of course, but what were the god's *words?* There's no hope
and nothing to fear in what you've said so far.
Creon: If you want my report in the presence of these . . .

Pointing to the priests while drawing Oedipus toward the palace.

I'm ready now, or we might go inside.
Oedipus: Speak out,
speak to us all. I grieve for these, my people,
far more than I fear for my own life.
Creon: Very well,
I will tell you what I heard from the god.
Apollo commands us — he was quite clear —
"Drive the corruption from the land,
don't harbor it any longer, past all cure,
don't nurse it in your soil — root it out!"
Oedipus: How can we cleanse ourselves — what rites?
What's the source of the trouble?
Creon: Banish the man, or pay back blood with blood.
Murder sets the plague-storm on the city.
Oedipus: Whose murder?
Whose fate does Apollo bring to light?
Creon: Our leader,
my lord, was once a man named Laius,
before you came and put us straight on course.
Oedipus: I know —
or so I've heard. I never saw the man myself.
Creon: Well, he was killed, and Apollo commands us now —
he could not be more clear,
"Pay the killers back — whoever is responsible."
Oedipus: Where on earth are they? Where to find it now,
the trail of the ancient guilt so hard to trace?
Creon: "Here in Thebes," he said.
Whatever is sought for can be caught, you know,
whatever is neglected slips away.
Oedipus: But where,
in the palace, the fields or foreign soil,
where did Laius meet his bloody death?
Creon: He went to consult an oracle, he said,
and he set out and never came home again.
Oedipus: No messenger, no fellow-traveler saw what happened?
Someone to cross-examine?
Creon: No,
they were all killed but one. He escaped,
terrified, he could tell us nothing clearly,
nothing of what he saw — just one thing.
Oedipus: What's that?
One thing could hold the key to it all,

a small beginning gives us grounds for hope.
Creon: He said thieves attacked them — a whole band,
not single-handed, cut King Laius down.
Oedipus: A thief,
so daring, wild, he'd kill a king? Impossible,
unless conspirators paid him off in Thebes.
Creon: We suspected as much. But with Laius dead
no leader appeared to help us in our troubles.
Oedipus: Trouble? Your *king* was murdered — royal blood!
What stopped you from tracking down the killer
then and there?
Creon: The singing, riddling Sphinx.
She . . . persuaded us to let the mystery go
and concentrate on what lay at our feet.
Oedipus: No,
I'll start again — I'll bring it all to light myself!
Apollo is right, and so are you, Creon,
to turn our attention back to the murdered man.
Now you have *me* to fight for you, you'll see:
I am the land's avenger by all rights
and Apollo's champion too.
But not to assist some distant kinsman, no,
for my own sake I'll rid us of this corruption.
Whoever killed the king may decide to kill me too,
with the same violent hand — by avenging Laius
I defend myself.

To the priests.

Quickly, my children.
Up from the steps, take up your branches now.

To the guards.

One of you summon the city here before us,
tell them I'll do everything. God help us,
we will see our triumph — or our fall.

Oedipus and Creon enter the palace, followed by the guards.

Priest: Rise, my sons. The kindness we came for
Oedipus volunteers himself.
Apollo has sent his word, his oracle —
Come down, Apollo, save us, stop the plague.

The priests rise, remove their branches, and exit to the side. Enter a Chorus, the citizens of Thebes, who have not heard the news that Creon brings. They march around the altar, chanting.

Chorus: Zeus!
Great welcome voice of Zeus, what do you bring?
What word from the gold vaults of Delphi

comes to brilliant Thebes? I'm racked with terror —
terror shakes my heart
and I cry your wild cries, Apollo, Healer of Delos°
I worship you in dread . . . what now, what is your price?
some new sacrifice? some ancient rite from the past
come round again each spring? —
what will you bring to birth?
Tell me, child of golden Hope
warm voice that never dies!
You are the first I call, daughter of Zeus
deathless Athena — I call your sister Artemis,°
heart of the market place enthroned in glory,
guardian of our earth —
I call Apollo astride the thunderheads of heaven —
O triple shield against death, shine before me now!
If ever, once in the past, you stopped some ruin
launched against our walls
you hurled the flame of pain
far, far from Thebes — you gods
come now, come down once more!

No, no
the miseries numberless, grief on grief, no end —
too much to bear, we are all dying
O my people . . .
Thebes like a great army dying
and there is no sword of thought to save us, no
and the fruits of our famous earth, they will not ripen
no and the women cannot scream their pangs to birth —
screams for the Healer, children dead in the womb
and life on life goes down
you can watch them go
like seabirds winging west, outracing the day's fire
down the horizon, irresistibly
streaking on to the shores of Evening
Death
so many deaths, numberless deaths on deaths, no end —
Thebes is dying, look, her children
stripped of pity . . .
generations strewn on the ground
unburied, unwept, the dead spreading death
and the young wives and gray-haired mothers with them
cling to the altars, trailing in from all over the city —
Thebes, city of death, one long cortege
and the suffering rises

173 *Delos:* Apollo was born on this sacred island. 181 *Artemis:* Apollo's sister, goddess of hunting, the moon, and chastity.

wails for mercy rise
and the wild hymn for the Healer blazes out
clashing with our sobs our cries of mourning —
O golden daughter of god, send rescue
radiant as the kindness in your eyes!

Drive him back! — the fever, the god of death
that raging god of war
not armored in bronze, not shielded now, he burns me,
battle cries in the onslaught burning on —
O rout him from our borders!
Sail him, blast him out to the Sea-queen's chamber
the black Atlantic gulfs
or the northern harbor, death to all
where the Thracian surf comes crashing.
Now what the night spares he comes by day and kills —
the god of death.

O lord of the stormcloud,
you who twirl the lightning, Zeus, Father,
thunder Death to nothing!

Apollo, lord of the light, I beg you —
whip your longbow's golden cord
showering arrows on our enemies — shafts of power
champions strong before us rushing on!

Artemis, Huntress,
torches flaring over the eastern ridges —
ride Death down in pain!

God of the headdress gleaming gold, I cry to you —
your name and ours are one, Dionysus° —
come with your face aflame with wine
your raving women's cries°
your army on the march! Come with the lightning
come with torches blazing, eyes ablaze with glory!
Burn that god of death that all gods hate!

Oedipus enters from the palace to address the Chorus, as if addressing the entire city of Thebes.

Oedipus: You pray to the gods? Let me grant your prayers.
Come, listen to me — do what the plague demands:
you'll find relief and lift your head from the depths.

I will speak out now as a stranger to the story,
a stranger to the crime. If I'd been present then,
there would have been no mystery, no long hunt
without a clue in hand. So now, counted

239 *Dionysus:* God of fertility and wine. 241 *Your . . . cries:* Dionysus was attended by female celebrants.

a native Theban years after the murder,
to all of Thebes I make this proclamation:
if any one of you knows who murdered Laius,
the son of Labdacus, I order him to reveal
the whole truth to me. Nothing to fear,
even if he must denounce himself,
let him speak up
and so escape the brunt of the charge —
he will suffer no unbearable punishment,
nothing worse than exile, totally unharmed.

Oedipus pauses, waiting for a reply.

Next,
if anyone knows the murderer is a stranger,
a man from alien soil, come, speak up.
I will give him a handsome reward, and lay up
gratitude in my heart for him besides.

Silence again, no reply.

But if you keep silent, if anyone panicking,
trying to shield himself or friend or kin,
rejects my offer, then hear what I will do.
I order you, every citizen of the state
where I hold throne and power: banish this man —
whoever he may be — never shelter him, never
speak a word to him, never make him partner
to your prayers, your victims burned to the gods.
Never let the holy water touch his hands.
Drive him out, each of you, from every home.
He is the plague, the heart of our corruption,
as Apollo's oracle has revealed to me
just now. So I honor my obligations:
I fight for the god and for the murdered man.

Now my curse on the murderer. Whoever he is,
a lone man unknown in his crime
or one among many, let that man drag out
his life in agony, step by painful step —
I curse myself as well . . . if by any chance
he proves to be an intimate of our house,
here at my hearth, with my full knowledge,
may the curse I just called down on him strike me!

These are your orders: perform them to the last.
I command you, for my sake, for Apollo's, for this country
blasted root and branch by the angry heavens.
Even if god had never urged you on to act,
how could you leave the crime uncleansed so long?
A man so noble — your king, brought down in blood —
you should have searched. But I am the king now,

I hold the throne that he held then, possess his bed
and a wife who shares our seed . . . why, our seed
might be the same, children born of the same mother
might have created blood-bonds between us
if his hope of offspring hadn't met disaster —
but fate swooped at his head and cut him short.
So I will fight for him as if he were my father,
stop at nothing, search the world
to lay my hands on the man who shed his blood,
the son of Labdacus descended of Polydorus,
Cadmus of old and Agenor, founder of the line:
their power and mine are one.
Oh dear gods,
my curse on those who disobey these orders!
Let no crops grow out of the earth for them —
shrivel their women, kill their sons,
burn them to nothing in this plague
that hits us now, or something even worse.
But you, loyal men of Thebes who approve my actions,
may our champion, Justice, may all the gods
be with us, fight beside us to the end!

Leader: In the grip of your curse, my king, I swear
I'm not the murderer, cannot point him out.
As for the search, Apollo pressed it on us —
he should name the killer.

Oedipus: Quite right,
but to force the gods to act against their will —
no man has the power.

Leader: Then if I might mention
the next best thing . . .

Oedipus: The third best too —
don't hold back, say it.

Leader: I still believe . . .
Lord Tiresias sees with the eyes of Lord Apollo.
Anyone searching for the truth, my king,
might learn it from the prophet, clear as day.

Oedipus: I've not been slow with that. On Creon's cue
I sent the escorts, twice, within the hour.
I'm surprised he isn't here.

Leader: We need him —
without him we have nothing but old, useless rumors.

Oedipus: Which rumors? I'll search out every word.

Leader: Laius was killed, they say, by certain travelers.

Oedipus: I know — but no one can find the murderer.

Leader: If the man has a trace of fear in him
he won't stay silent long,
not with your curses ringing in his ears.

Oedipus: He didn't flinch at murder,
he'll never flinch at words.

Enter Tiresias, the blind prophet, led by a boy with escorts in attendance. He remains at a distance.

Leader: Here is the one who will convict him, look,
they bring him on at last, the seer, the man of god.
The truth lives inside him, him alone.
Oedipus: O Tiresias,
master of all the mysteries of our life,
all you teach and all you dare not tell,
signs in the heavens, signs that walk the earth!
Blind as you are, you can feel all the more
what sickness haunts our city. You, my lord,
are the one shield, the one savior we can find.

We asked Apollo — perhaps the messengers
haven't told you — he sent his answer back:
"Relief from the plague can only come one way.
Uncover the murderers of Laius,
put them to death or drive them into exile."
So I beg you, grudge us nothing now, no voice,
no message plucked from the birds, the embers
or the other mantic ways within your grasp.
Rescue yourself, your city, rescue me —
rescue everything infected by the dead.
We are in your hands. For a man to help others
with all his gifts and native strength:
that is the noblest work.
Tiresias: How terrible — to see the truth
when the truth is only pain to him who sees!
I knew it well, but I put it from my mind,
else I never would have come.
Oedipus: What's this? Why so grim, so dire?
Tiresias: Just send me home. You bear your burdens,
I'll bear mine. It's better that way,
please believe me.
Oedipus: Strange response — unlawful,
unfriendly too to the state that bred and raised you;
you're withholding the word of god.
Tiresias: I fail to see
that your own words are so well-timed.
I'd rather not have the same thing said of me . . .
Oedipus: For the love of god, don't turn away,
not if you know something. We beg you,
all of us on our knees.
Tiresias: None of you knows —
and I will never reveal my dreadful secrets,
not to say your own.
Oedipus: What? You know and you won't tell?
You're bent on betraying us, destroying Thebes?
Tiresias: I'd rather not cause pain for you or me.

So why this . . . useless interrogation?
You'll get nothing from me.
Oedipus: Nothing! You,
you scum of the earth, you'd enrage a heart of stone!
You won't talk? Nothing moves you?
Out with it, once and for all!
Tiresias: You criticize my temper . . . unaware
of the one *you* live with, you revile me.
Oedipus: Who could restrain his anger hearing you?
What outrage — you spurn the city!
Tiresias: What will come will come.
Even if I shroud it all in silence.
Oedipus: What will come? You're bound to *tell* me that.
Tiresias: I'll say no more. Do as you like, build your anger
to whatever pitch you please, rage your worst —
Oedipus: Oh I'll let loose, I have such fury in me —
now I see it all. You helped hatch the plot,
you did the work, yes, short of killing him
with your own hands — and given eyes I'd say
you did the killing single-handed!
Tiresias: Is that so!
I charge you, then, submit to that decree
you just laid down: from this day onward
speak to no one, not these citizens, not myself.
You are the curse, the corruption of the land!
Oedipus: You, shameless —
aren't you appalled to start up such a story?
You think you can get away with this?
Tiresias: I have already.
The truth with all its power lives inside me.
Oedipus: Who primed you for this? Not your prophet's trade.
Tiresias: You did, you forced me, twisted it out of me.
Oedipus: What? Say it again — I'll understand it better.
Tiresias: Didn't you understand, just now?
Or are you tempting me to talk?
Oedipus: No, I can't say I grasped your meaning.
Out with it, again!
Tiresias: I say you are the murderer you hunt.
Oedipus: That obscenity, twice — by god, you'll pay.
Tiresias: Shall I say more, so you can really rage?
Oedipus: Much as you want. Your words are nothing —
futile.
Tiresias: You cannot imagine . . . I tell you,
you and your loved ones live together in infamy,
you cannot see how far you've gone in guilt.
Oedipus: You think you can keep this up and never suffer?
Tiresias: Indeed, if the truth has any power.
Oedipus: It does
but not for you, old man. You've lost your power,

stone-blind, stone-deaf — senses, eyes blind as stone!
Tiresias: I pity you, flinging at me the very insults
each man here will fling at you so soon.
Oedipus: Blind,
lost in the night, endless night that nursed you!
You can't hurt me or anyone else who sees the light —
you can never touch me.
Tiresias: True, it is not your fate
to fall at my hands. Apollo is quite enough,
and he will take some pains to work this out.
Oedipus: Creon! Is this conspiracy his or yours?
Tiresias: Creon is not your downfall, no, you are your own.
Oedipus: O power —
wealth and empire, skill outstripping skill
in the heady rivalries of life,
what envy lurks inside you! Just for this,
the crown the city gave me — I never sought it,
they laid it in my hands — for this alone, Creon,
the soul of trust, my loyal friend from the start
steals against me . . . so hungry to overthrow me
he sets this wizard on me, this scheming quack,
this fortune-teller peddling lies, eyes peeled
for his own profit — seer blind in his craft!

Come here, you pious fraud. Tell me,
when did you ever prove yourself a prophet?
When the Sphinx, that chanting Fury kept her deathwatch here,
why silent then, not a word to set our people free?
There was a riddle, not for some passer-by to solve —
it cried out for a prophet. Where were you?
Did you rise to the crisis? Not a word,
you and your birds, your gods — nothing.
No, but I came by, Oedipus the ignorant,
I stopped the Sphinx! With no help from the birds,
the flight of my own intelligence hit the mark.

And this is the man you'd try to overthrow?
You think you'll stand by Creon when he's king?
You and the great mastermind —
you'll pay in tears, I promise you, for this,
this witch-hunt. If you didn't look so senile
the lash would teach you what your scheming means!
Leader: I'd suggest his words were spoken in anger,
Oedipus . . . yours too, and it isn't what we need.
The best solution to the oracle, the riddle
posed by god — we should look for that.
Tiresias: You are the king no doubt, but in one respect,
at least, I am your equal: the right to reply.
I claim that privilege too.
I am not your slave. I serve Apollo.

I don't need Creon to speak for me in public.
So,
you mock my blindness? Let me tell you this.
You with your precious eyes,
you're blind to the corruption of your life,
to the house you live in, those you live with —
who *are* your parents? Do you know? All unknowing
you are the scourge of your own flesh and blood,
the dead below the earth and the living here above,
and the double lash of your mother and your father's curse
will whip you from this land one day, their footfall
treading you down in terror, darkness shrouding
your eyes that now can see the light!
Soon, soon
you'll scream aloud — what haven won't reverberate?
What rock of Cithaeron° won't scream back in echo?
That day you learn the truth about your marriage,
the wedding-march that sang you into your halls,
the lusty voyage home to the fatal harbor!
And a load of other horrors you'd never dream
will level you with yourself and all your children.

There. Now smear us with insults — Creon, myself
and every word I've said. No man will ever
be rooted from the earth as brutally as you.

Oedipus: Enough! Such filth from him? Insufferable —
what, still alive? Get out —
faster, back where you came from — vanish!
Tiresias: I'd never have come if you hadn't called me here.
Oedipus: If I thought you'd blurt out such absurdities,
you'd have died waiting before I'd had you summoned.
Tiresias: Absurd, am I? To you, not to your parents:
the ones who bore you found me sane enough.
Oedipus: Parents — who? Wait . . . who is my father?
Tiresias: This day will bring your birth and your destruction.
Oedipus: Riddles — all you can say are riddles, murk and darkness.
Tiresias: Ah, but aren't you the best man alive at solving riddles?
Oedipus: Mock me for that, go on, and you'll reveal my greatness.
Tiresias: Your great good fortune, true, it was your ruin.
Oedipus: Not if I saved the city — what do I care?
Tiresias: Well then, I'll be going.

To his attendant.

Take me home, boy.
Oedipus: Yes, take him away. You're a nuisance here.
Out of the way, the irritation's gone.

Turning his back on Tiresias, moving toward the palace.

481 *Cithaeron:* The mountains where Oedipus was abandoned as an infant.

Tiresias: I will go,
once I have said what I came here to say.
I'll never shrink from the anger in your eyes —
you can't destroy me. Listen to me closely:
the man you've sought so long, proclaiming,
cursing up and down, the murderer of Laius —
he is here. A stranger,
you may think, who lives among you,
he soon will be revealed a native Theban
but he will take no joy in the revelation.
Blind who now has eyes, beggar who now is rich,
he will grope his way toward a foreign soil,
a stick tapping before him step by step.

Oedipus enters the palace.

Revealed at last, brother and father both
to the children he embraces, to his mother
son and husband both — he sowed the loins
his father sowed, he spilled his father's blood!

Go in and reflect on that, solve that.
And if you find I've lied
from this day onward call the prophet blind.

Tiresias and the boy exit to the side.

Chorus: Who —
who is the man the voice of god denounces
resounding out of the rocky gorge of Delphi?
The horror too dark to tell,
whose ruthless bloody hands have done the work?
His time has come to fly
to outrace the stallions of the storm
his feet a streak of speed —
Cased in armor, Apollo son of the Father
lunges on him, lightning-bolts afire!
And the grim unerring Furies°
closing for the kill.
Look,
the word of god has just come blazing
flashing off Parnassus'° snowy heights!
That man who left no trace —
after him, hunt him down with all our strength!
Now under bristling timber
up through rocks and caves he stalks
like the wild mountain bull —
cut off from men, each step an agony, frenzied, racing blind

536 *Furies:* Three spirits who avenged evildoers. 539 *Parnassus:* A mountain in Greece associated with Apollo.

but he cannot outrace the dread voices of Delphi
ringing out of the heart of Earth,
the dark wings beating around him shrieking doom
the doom that never dies, the terror —

The skilled prophet scans the birds and shatters me with terror!
I can't accept him, can't deny him, don't know what to say,
I'm lost, and the wings of dark foreboding beating —
I cannot see what's come, what's still to come . . .
and what could breed a blood feud between
Laius' house and the son of Polybus?°
I know of nothing, not in the past and not now,
no charge to bring against our king, no cause
to attack his fame that rings throughout Thebes —
not without proof — not for the ghost of Laius,
not to avenge a murder gone without a trace.

Zeus and Apollo know, they know, the great masters
of all the dark and depth of human life.
But whether a mere man can know the truth,
whether a seer can fathom more than I —
there is no test, no certain proof
though matching skill for skill
a man can outstrip a rival. No, not till I see
these charges proved will I side with his accusers.
We saw him then, when the she-hawk° swept against him,
saw with our own eyes his skill, his brilliant triumph —
there was the test — he was the joy of Thebes!
Never will I convict my king, never in my heart.

Enter Creon from the side.

Creon: My fellow-citizens, I hear King Oedipus
levels terrible charges at me. I had to come.
I resent it deeply. If, in the present crisis,
he thinks he suffers any abuse from me,
anything I've done or said that offers him
the slightest injury, why, I've no desire
to linger out this life, my reputation a shambles.
The damage I'd face from such an accusation
is nothing simple. No, there's nothing worse:
branded a traitor in the city, a traitor
to all of you and my good friends.
Leader: True,
but a slur might have been forced out of him,
by anger perhaps, not any firm conviction.
Creon: The charge was made in public, wasn't it?
I put the prophet up to spreading lies?

555 *Polybus:* The King of Corinth, who is thought to be Oedipus's father. 569 *she-hawk:* The Sphinx.

Leader: Such things were said . . .
I don't know with what intent, if any.
Creon: Was his glance steady, his mind right
when the charge was brought against me?
Leader: I really couldn't say. I never look
to judge the ones in power.

The doors open. Oedipus enters.

Wait,
here's Oedipus now.
Oedipus: You — here? You have the gall
to show your face before the palace gates?
You, plotting to kill me, kill the king —
I see it all, the marauding thief himself
scheming to steal my crown and power!
Tell me,
in god's name, what did you take me for,
coward or fool, when you spun out your plot?
Your treachery — you think I'd never detect it
creeping against me in the dark? Or sensing it,
not defend myself? Aren't you the fool,
you and your high adventure. Lacking numbers,
powerful friends, out for the big game of empire —
you need riches, armies to bring that quarry down!
Creon: Are you quite finished? It's your turn to listen
for just as long as you've . . . instructed me.
Hear me out, then judge me on the facts.
Oedipus: You've a wicked way with words, Creon,
but I'll be slow to learn — from you.
I find you a menace, a great burden to me.
Creon: Just one thing, hear me out in this.
Oedipus: Just one thing,
don't tell me you're not the enemy, the traitor.
Creon: Look, if you think crude, mindless stubbornness
such a gift, you've lost your sense of balance.
Oedipus: If you think you can abuse a kinsman,
then escape the penalty, you're insane.
Creon: Fair enough, I grant you. But this injury
you say I've done you, what is it?
Oedipus: Did you induce me, yes or no,
to send for that sanctimonious prophet?
Creon: I did. And I'd do the same again.
Oedipus: All right then, tell me, how long is it now
since Laius . . .
Creon: Laius — what did *he* do?
Oedipus: Vanished,
swept from sight, murdered in his tracks.
Creon: The count of the years would run you far back . . .
Oedipus: And that far back, was the prophet at his trade?

Creon: Skilled as he is today, and just as honored.
Oedipus: Did he ever refer to me then, at that time?
Creon: No,
never, at least, when I was in his presence.
Oedipus: But you did investigate the murder, didn't you?
Creon: We did our best, of course, discovered nothing.
Oedipus: But the great seer never accused me then — why not?
Creon: I don't know. And when I don't, *I* keep quiet.
Oedipus: You do know this, you'd tell it too —
if you had a shred of decency.
Creon: What?
If I know, I won't hold back.
Oedipus: Simply this:
if the two of you had never put heads together,
we'd never have heard about *my* killing Laius.
Creon: If that's what he says . . . well, you know best.
But now I have a right to learn from you
as you just learned from me.
Oedipus: Learn your fill,
you never will convict me of the murder.
Creon: Tell me, you're married to my sister, aren't you?
Oedipus: A genuine discovery — there's no denying that.
Creon: And you rule the land with her, with equal power?
Oedipus: She receives from me whatever she desires.
Creon: And I am the third, all of us are equals?
Oedipus: Yes, and it's there you show your stripes —
you betray a kinsman.
Creon: Not at all.
Not if you see things calmly, rationally,
as I do. Look at it this way first:
who in his right mind would rather rule
and live in anxiety than sleep in peace?
Particularly if he enjoys the same authority.
Not I, I'm not the man to yearn for kingship,
not with a king's power in my hands. Who would?
No one with any sense of self-control.
Now, as it is, you offer me all I need,
not a fear in the world. But if I wore the crown . . .
there'd be many painful duties to perform,
hardly to my taste.
How could kingship
please me more than influence, power
without a qualm? I'm not that deluded yet,
to reach for anything but privilege outright,
profit free and clear.
Now all men sing my praises, all salute me,
now all who request your favors curry mine.
I'm their best hope: success rests in me.
Why give up that, I ask you, and borrow trouble?

A man of sense, someone who sees things clearly
would never resort to treason.
No, I've no lust for conspiracy in me,
not could I ever suffer one who does.

Do you want proof? Go to Delphi yourself,
examine the oracle and see if I've reported
the message word-for-word. This too:
if you detect that I and the clairvoyant
have plotted anything in common, arrest me,
execute me. Not on the strength of one vote,
two in this case, mine as well as yours.
But don't convict me on sheer unverified surmise.

How wrong it is to take the good for bad,
purely at random, or take the bad for good.
But reject a friend, a kinsman? I would as soon
tear out the life within us, priceless life itself.
You'll learn this well, without fail, in time.
Time alone can bring the just man to light;
the criminal you can spot in one short day.

Leader: Good advice,
my lord, for anyone who wants to avoid disaster.
Those who jump to conclusions may be wrong.

Oedipus: When my enemy moves against me quickly,
plots in secret, I move quickly too, I must,
I plot and pay him back. Relax my guard a moment,
waiting his next move — he wins his objective,
I lose mine.

Creon: What do you want?
You want me banished?

Oedipus: No, I want you dead.

Creon: Just to show how ugly a grudge can . . .

Oedipus: So,
still stubborn? you don't think I'm serious?

Creon: I think you're insane.

Oedipus: Quite sane — in my behalf.

Creon: Not just as much in mine?

Oedipus: You — my mortal enemy?

Creon: What if you're wholly wrong?

Oedipus: No matter — I must rule.

Creon: Not if you rule unjustly.

Oedipus: Hear him, Thebes, my city!

Creon: My city too, not yours alone!

Leader: Please, my lords.

Enter Jocasta from the palace.

Look, Jocasta's coming,
and just in time too. With her help
you must put this fighting of yours to rest.

Jocasta: Have you no sense? Poor misguided men,
such shouting — why this public outburst?
Aren't you ashamed, with the land so sick,
to stir up private quarrels?

To Oedipus.

Into the palace now. And Creon, you go home.
Why make such a furor over nothing?
Creon: My sister, it's dreadful . . . Oedipus, your husband,
he's bent on a choice of punishments for me,
banishment from the fatherland or death.
Oedipus: Precisely. I caught him in the act, Jocasta,
plotting, about to stab me in the back.
Creon: Never — curse me, let me die and be damned
if I've done you any wrong you charge me with.
Jocasta: Oh god, believe it, Oedipus,
honor the solemn oath he swears to heaven.
Do it for me, for the sake of all your people.

The Chorus begins to chant.

Chorus: Believe it, be sensible
give way, my king, I beg you!
Oedipus: What do you want from me, concessions?
Chorus: Respect him — he's been no fool in the past
and now he's strong with the oath he swears to god.
Oedipus: You know what you're asking?
Chorus: I do.
Oedipus: Then out with it!
Chorus: The man's your friend, your kin, he's under oath —
don't cast him out, disgraced
branded with guilt on the strength of hearsay only.
Oedipus: Know full well, if that's what you want
you want me dead or banished from the land.
Chorus: Never —
no, by the blazing Sun, first god of the heavens!
Stripped of the gods, stripped of loved ones,
let me die by inches if that ever crossed my mind.
But the heart inside me sickens, dies as the land dies
and now on top of the old griefs you pile this,
your fury — both of you!
Oedipus: Then let him go,
even if it does lead to my ruin, my death
or my disgrace, driven from Thebes for life.
It's you, not him I pity — your words move me.
He, wherever he goes, my hate goes with him.
Creon: Look at you, sullen in yielding, brutal in your rage —
you'll go too far. It's perfect justice:
natures like yours are hardest on themselves.
Oedipus: Then leave me alone — get out!

Creon: I'm going.
You're wrong, so wrong. These men know I'm right.

Exit to the side. The Chorus turns to Jocasta.

Chorus: Why do you hesitate, my lady
why not help him in?
Jocasta: Tell me what's happened first.
Chorus: Loose, ignorant talk started dark suspicions
and a sense of injustice cut deeply too.
Jocasta: On both sides?
Chorus: Oh yes.
Jocasta: What did they say?
Chorus: Enough, please, enough! The land's so racked already
or so it seems to me . . .
End the trouble here, just where they left it.
Oedipus: You see what comes of your good intentions now?
And all because you tried to blunt my anger.
Chorus: My king,
I've said it once, I'll say it time and again —
I'd be insane, you know it,
senseless, ever to turn my back on you.
You who set our beloved land — storm-tossed, shattered —
straight on course. Now again, good helmsman,
steer us through the storm!

The Chorus draws away, leaving Oedipus and Jocasta side by side.

Jocasta: For the love of god,
Oedipus, tell me too, what is it?
Why this rage? You're so unbending.
Oedipus: I will tell you. I respect you, Jocasta,
much more than these . . .

Glancing at the Chorus.

Creon's to blame, Creon schemes against me.
Jocasta: Tell me clearly, how did the quarrel start?
Oedipus: He says *I* murdered Laius — I am guilty.
Jocasta: How does he know? Some secret knowledge
or simple hearsay?
Oedipus: Oh, he sent his prophet in
to do his dirty work. You know Creon,
Creon keeps his own lips clean.
Jocasta: A prophet?
Well then, free yourself of every charge!
Listen to me and learn some peace of mind:
no skill in the world,
nothing human can penetrate the future.
Here is proof, quick and to the point.
An oracle came to Laius one fine day
(I won't say from Apollo himself

but his underlings, his priests) and it said
that doom would strike him down at the hands of a son,
our son, to be born of our own flesh and blood. But Laius,
so the report goes at least, was killed by strangers,
thieves, at a place where three roads meet . . . my son —
he wasn't three days old and the boy's father
fastened his ankles, had a henchman fling him away
on a barren, trackless mountain.
There, you see?
Apollo brought neither thing to pass. My baby
no more murdered his father than Laius suffered —
his wildest fear — death at his own son's hands.
That's how the seers and their revelations
mapped out the future. Brush them from your mind.
Whatever the god needs and seeks
he'll bring to light himself, with ease.

Oedipus: Strange,
hearing you just now . . . my mind wandered,
my thoughts racing back and forth.

Jocasta: What do you mean? Why so anxious, startled?

Oedipus: I thought I heard you say that Laius
was cut down at a place where three roads meet.

Jocasta: That was the story. It hasn't died out yet.

Oedipus: Where did this thing happen? Be precise.

Jocasta: A place called Phocis, where two branching roads,
one from Daulia, one from Delphi,
come together — a crossroads.

Oedipus: When? How long ago?

Jocasta: The heralds no sooner reported Laius dead
than you appeared and they hailed you king of Thebes.

Oedipus: My god, my god — what have you planned to do to me?

Jocasta: What, Oedipus? What haunts you so?

Oedipus: Not yet.
Laius — how did he look? Describe him.
Had he reached his prime?

Jocasta: He was swarthy,
and the gray had just begun to streak his temples,
and his build . . . wasn't far from yours.

Oedipus: Oh no no,
I think I've just called down a dreadful curse
upon myself — I simply didn't know!

Jocasta: What are you saying? I shudder to look at you.

Oedipus: I have a terrible fear the blind seer can see.
I'll know in a moment. One thing more —

Jocasta: Anything,
afraid as I am — ask, I'll answer, all I can.

Oedipus: Did he go with a light or heavy escort,
several men-at-arms, like a lord, a king?

Jocasta: There were five in the party, a herald among them,
and a single wagon carrying Laius.
Oedipus: Ai —
now I can see it all, clear as day.
Who told you all this at the time, Jocasta?
Jocasta: A servant who reached home, the lone survivor.
Oedipus: So, could he still be in the palace — even now?
Jocasta: No indeed. Soon as he returned from the scene
and saw you on the throne with Laius dead and gone,
he knelt and clutched my hand, pleading with me
to send him into the hinterlands, to pasture,
far as possible, out of sight of Thebes.
I sent him away. Slave though he was,
he'd earned that favor — and much more.
Oedipus: Can we bring him back, quickly?
Jocasta: Easily. Why do you want him so?
Oedipus: I'm afraid,
Jocasta, I have said too much already.
That man — I've got to see him.
Jocasta: Then he'll come.
But even I have a right, I'd like to think,
to know what's torturing you, my lord.
Oedipus: And so you shall — I can hold nothing back from you,
now I've reached this pitch of dark foreboding.
Who means more to me than you? Tell me,
whom would I turn toward but you
as I go through all this?

My father was Polybus, king of Corinth.
My mother, a Dorian, Merope. And I was held
the prince of the realm among the people there,
till something struck me out of nowhere,
something strange . . . worth remarking perhaps,
hardly worth the anxiety I gave it.
Some man at a banquet who had drunk too much
shouted out — he was far gone, mind you —
that I am not my father's son. Fighting words!
I barely restrained myself that day
but early the next I went to mother and father,
questioned them closely, and they were enraged
at the accusation and the fool who let it fly.
So as for my parents I was satisfied,
but still this thing kept gnawing at me,
the slander spread — I had to make my move.
And so,
unknown to mother and father I set out for Delphi,
and the god Apollo spurned me, sent me away
denied the facts I came for,

but first he flashed before my eyes a future
great with pain, terror, disaster — I can hear him cry,
"You are fated to couple with your mother, you will bring
a breed of children into the light no man can bear to see —
you will kill your father, the one who gave you life!"
I heard all that and ran. I abandoned Corinth,
from that day on I gauged its landfall only
by the stars, running, always running
toward some place where I would never see
the shame of all those oracles come true.
And as I fled I reached that very spot
where the great king, you say, met his death.
Now, Jocasta, I will tell you all.
Making my way toward this triple crossroad
I began to see a herald, then a brace of colts
drawing a wagon, and mounted on the bench . . . a man,
just as you've described him, coming face-to-face,
and the one in the lead and the old man himself
were about to thrust me off the road — brute force —
and the one shouldering me aside, the driver,
I strike him in anger! — and the old man, watching me
coming up along his wheels — he brings down
his prod, two prongs straight at my head!
I paid him back with interest!
Short work, by god — with one blow of the staff
in this right hand I knock him out of his high seat,
roll him out of the wagon, sprawling headlong —
I killed them all — every mother's son!

Oh, but if there is any blood-tie
between Laius and this stranger . . .
what man alive more miserable than I?
More hated by the gods? *I* am the man
no alien, no citizen welcomes to his house,
law forbids it — not a word to me in public,
driven out of every hearth and home.
And all these curses I — no one but I
brought down these piling curses on myself!
And you, his wife, I've touched your body with these,
the hands that killed your husband cover you with blood.

Wasn't I born for torment? Look me in the eyes!
I am abomination — heart and soul!
I must be exiled, and even in exile
never see my parents, never set foot
on native earth again. Else I'm doomed
to couple with my mother and cut my father down . . .
Polybus who reared me, gave me life.

But why, why?

Wouldn't a man of judgment say — and wouldn't he be right —
some savage power has brought this down upon my head?

Oh no, not that, you pure and awesome gods,
never let me see that day! Let me slip
from the world of men, vanish without a trace
before I see myself stained with such corruption,
stained to the heart.

Leader: My lord, you fill our hearts with fear.
But at least until you question the witness,
do take hope.

Oedipus: Exactly. He is my last hope —
I'm waiting for the shepherd. He is crucial.

Jocasta: And once he appears, what then? Why so urgent?

Oedipus: I'll tell you. If it turns out that his story
matches yours, I've escaped the worst.

Jocasta: What did I say? What struck you so?

Oedipus: You said *thieves* —
he told you a whole band of them murdered Laius.
So, if he still holds to the same number,
I cannot be the killer. One can't equal many.
But if he refers to one man, one alone,
clearly the scales come down on me:
I am guilty.

Jocasta: Impossible. Trust me,
I told you precisely what he said,
and he can't retract it now;
the whole city heard it, not just I.
And even if he should vary his first report
by one man more or less, still, my lord,
he could never make the murder of Laius
truly fit the prophecy. Apollo was explicit:
my son was doomed to kill my husband . . . my son,
poor defenseless thing, he never had a chance
to kill his father. They destroyed him first.

So much for prophecy. It's neither here nor there.
From this day on, I wouldn't look right or left.

Oedipus: True, true. Still, that shepherd,
someone fetch him — now!

Jocasta: I'll send at once. But do let's go inside.
I'd never displease you, least of all in this.

Oedipus and Jocasta enter the palace.

Chorus: Destiny guide me always
Destiny find me filled with reverence
pure in word and deed.
Great laws tower above us, reared on high
born for the brilliant vault of heaven —

Olympian sky their only father,
nothing mortal, no man gave them birth,
their memory deathless, never lost in sleep:
within them lives a mighty god, the god does not grow old.

Pride breeds the tyrant
violent pride, gorging, crammed to bursting
with all that is overripe and rich with ruin —
clawing up to the heights, headlong pride
crashes down the abyss — sheer doom!
No footing helps, all foothold lost and gone,
But the healthy strife that makes the city strong —
I pray that god will never end that wrestling:
god, my champion, I will never let you go.

But if any man comes striding, high and mighty
in all he says and does,
no fear of justice, no reverence
for the temples of the gods —
let a rough doom tear him down,
repay his pride, breakneck, ruinous pride!
If he cannot reap his profits fairly
cannot restrain himself from outrage —
mad, laying hands on the holy things untouchable!

Can such a man, so desperate, still boast
he can save his life from the flashing bolts of god?
If all such violence goes with honor now
why join the sacred dance?

Never again will I go reverent to Delphi,
the inviolate heart of Earth
or Apollo's ancient oracle at Abae
or Olympia of the fires —
unless these prophecies all come true
for all mankind to point toward in wonder.
King of kings, if you deserve your titles
Zeus, remember, never forget!
You and your deathless, everlasting reign.

They are dying, the old oracles sent to Laius,
now our masters strike them off the rolls.
Nowhere Apollo's golden glory now —
the gods, the gods go down.

Enter Jocasta from the palace, carrying a suppliant's branch wound in wool.

Jocasta: Lords of the realm, it occurred to me,
just now, to visit the temples of the gods,
so I have my branch in hand and incense too.

Oedipus is beside himself. Racked with anguish,
no longer a man of sense, he won't admit

the latest prophecies are hollow as the old —
he's at the mercy of every passing voice
if the voice tells of terror.
I urge him gently, nothing seems to help,
so I turn to you, Apollo, you are nearest.

Placing her branch on the altar, while an old herdsman enters from the side, not the one just summoned by the king but an unexpected messenger from Corinth.

I come with prayers and offerings . . . I beg you,
cleanse us, set us free of defilement!
Look at us, passengers in the grip of fear,
watching the pilot of the vessel go to pieces.

Messenger:

Approaching Jocasta and the Chorus.

Strangers, please, I wonder if you could lead us
to the palace of the king . . . I think it's Oedipus.
Better, the man himself — you know where he is?

Leader: This is his palace, stranger. He's inside.
But here is his queen, his wife and mother
of his children.

Messenger: Blessings on you, noble queen,
queen of Oedipus crowned with all your family —
blessings on you always!

Jocasta: And the same to you, stranger, you deserve it . . .
such a greeting. But what have you come for?
Have you brought us news?

Messenger: Wonderful news —
for the house, my lady, for your husband too.

Jocasta: Really, what? Who sent you?

Messenger: Corinth.
I'll give you the message in a moment.
You'll be glad of it — how could you help it? —
though it costs a little sorrow in the bargain.

Jocasta: What can it be, with such a double edge?

Messenger: The people there, they want to make your Oedipus
king of Corinth, so they're saying now.

Jocasta: Why? Isn't old Polybus still in power?

Messenger: No more. Death has got him in the tomb.

Jocasta: What are you saying? Polybus, dead? — dead?

Messenger: If not,
if I'm not telling the truth, strike me dead too.

Jocasta:

To a servant.

Quickly, go to your master, tell him this!

You prophecies of the gods, where are you now?
This is the man that Oedipus feared for years,

he fled him, not to kill him — and now he's dead,
quite by chance, a normal, natural death,
not murdered by his son.

Oedipus:

Emerging from the palace.

Dearest,
what now? Why call me from the palace?

Jocasta:

Bringing the Messenger closer.

Listen to *him,* see for yourself what all
those awful prophecies of god have come to.

Oedipus: And who is he? What can he have for me?
Jocasta: He's from Corinth, he's come to tell you
your father is no more — Polybus — he's dead!

Oedipus:

Wheeling on the Messenger.

What? Let me have it from your lips.

Messenger: Well,
if that's what you want first, then here it is:
make no mistake, Polybus is dead and gone.
Oedipus: How — murder? sickness? — what? what killed him?
Messenger: A light tip of the scales can put old bones to rest.
Oedipus: Sickness then — poor man, it wore him down.
Messenger: That,
and the long count of years he'd measured out.
Oedipus: So!
Jocasta, why, why look to the Prophet's hearth,
the fires of the future? Why scan the birds
that scream above our heads? They winged me on
to the murder of my father, did they? That was my doom?
Well look, he's dead and buried, hidden under the earth,
and here I am in Thebes, I never put hand to sword —
unless some longing for me wasted him away,
then in a sense you'd say I caused his death.
But now, all those prophecies I feared — Polybus
packs them off to sleep with him in hell!
They're nothing, worthless.
Jocasta: There.
Didn't I tell you from the start?
Oedipus: So you did. I was lost in fear.
Jocasta: No more, sweep it from your mind forever.
Oedipus: But my mother's bed, surely I must fear —
Jocasta: Fear?
What should a man fear? It's all chance,
chance rules our lives. Not a man on earth
can see a day ahead, groping through the dark.

Better to live at random, best we can.
And as for this marriage with your mother —
have no fear. Many a man before you,
in his dreams, has shared his mother's bed.
Take such things for shadows, nothing at all —
Live, Oedipus,
as if there's no tomorrow!

Oedipus: Brave words,
and you'd persuade me if mother weren't alive.
But mother lives, so for all your reassurances
I live in fear, I must.

Jocasta: But your father's death,
that, at least, is a great blessing, joy to the eyes!

Oedipus: Great, I know . . . but I fear *her* — she's still alive.

Messenger: Wait, who is this woman, makes you so afraid?

Oedipus: Merope, old man. The wife of Polybus.

Messenger: The queen? What's there to fear in her?

Oedipus: A dreadful prophecy, stranger, sent by the gods.

Messenger: Tell me, could you? Unless it's forbidden
other ears to hear.

Oedipus: Not at all.
Apollo told me once — it is my fate —
I must make love with my own mother,
shed my father's blood with my own hands.
So for years I've given Corinth a wide berth,
and it's been my good fortune too. But still,
to see one's parents and look into their eyes
is the greatest joy I know.

Messenger: You're afraid of that?
That kept you out of Corinth?

Oedipus: My *father,* old man —
so I wouldn't kill my father.

Messenger: So that's it.
Well then, seeing I came with such good will, my king,
why don't I rid you of that old worry now?

Oedipus: What a rich reward you'd have for that.

Messenger: What do you think I came for, majesty?
So you'd come home and I'd be better off.

Oedipus: Never, I will never go near my parents.

Messenger: My boy, it's clear, you don't know what you're doing.

Oedipus: What do you mean, old man? For god's sake, explain.

Messenger: If you ran from *them,* always dodging home . . .

Oedipus: Always, terrified Apollo's oracle might come true —

Messenger: And you'd be covered with guilt, from both your parents.

Oedipus: That's right, old man, that fear is always with me.

Messenger: Don't you know? You've really nothing to fear.

Oedipus: But why? If I'm their son — Merope, Polybus?

Messenger: Polybus was nothing to you, that's why, not in blood.

Oedipus: What are you saying — Polybus was not my father?

Messenger: No more than I am. He and I are equals.
Oedipus: My father —
how can my father equal nothing? You're nothing to me!
Messenger: Neither was he, no more your father than I am.
Oedipus: Then why did he call me his son?
Messenger: You were a gift,
years ago — know for a fact he took you
from my hands.
Oedipus: No, from another's hands?
Then how could he love me so? He loved me, deeply . . .
Messenger: True, and his early years without a child
made him love you all the more.
Oedipus: And you, did you . . .
buy me? find me by accident?
Messenger: I stumbled on you,
down the woody flanks of Mount Cithaeron.
Oedipus: So close,
what were you doing here, just passing through?
Messenger: Watching over my flocks, grazing them on the slopes.
Oedipus: A herdsman, were you? A vagabond, scraping for wages?
Messenger: Your savior too, my son, in your worst hour.
Oedipus: Oh —
when you picked me up, was I in pain? What exactly?
Messenger: Your ankles . . . they tell the story. Look at them.
Oedipus: Why remind me of that, that old affliction?
Messenger: Your ankles were pinned together; I set you free.
Oedipus: That dreadful mark — I've had it from the cradle.
Messenger: And you got your name from that misfortune too,
the name's still with you.
Oedipus: Dear god, who did it? —
mother? father? Tell me.
Messenger: I don't know.
The one who gave you to me, he'd know more.
Oedipus: What? You took me from someone else?
You didn't find me yourself?
Messenger: No sir,
another shepherd passed you on to me.
Oedipus: Who? Do you know? Describe him.
Messenger: He called himself a servant of . . .
if I remember rightly — Laius.

Jocasta turns sharply.

Oedipus: The king of the land who ruled here long ago?
Messenger: That's the one. That herdsman was *his* man.
Oedipus: Is he still alive? Can I see him?
Messenger: They'd know best, the people of these parts.

Oedipus and the Messenger turn to the Chorus.

Oedipus: Does anyone know that herdsman,

the one he mentioned? Anyone seen him
in the fields, in town? Out with it!
The time has come to reveal this once for all.

Leader: I think he's the very shepherd you wanted to see,
a moment ago. But the queen, Jocasta,
she's the one to say.

Oedipus: Jocasta,
you remember the man we just sent for?
Is *that* the one he means?

Jocasta: That man . . .
why ask? Old shepherd, talk, empty nonsense,
don't give it another thought, don't even think —

Oedipus: What — give up now, with a clue like this?
Fail to solve the mystery of my birth?
Not for all the world!

Jocasta: Stop — in the name of god,
if you love your own life, call off this search!
My suffering is enough.

Oedipus: Courage!
Even if my mother turns out to be a slave,
and I a slave, three generations back,
you would not seem common.

Jocasta: Oh no,
listen to me, I beg you, don't do this.

Oedipus: Listen to you? No more. I must know it all,
see the truth at last.

Jocasta: No, please —
for your sake — I want the best for you!

Oedipus: Your best is more than I can bear.

Jocasta: You're doomed —
may you never fathom who you are!

Oedipus:

To a servant.

Hurry, fetch me the herdsman, now!
Leave her to glory in her royal birth.

Jocasta: Aieeeeee —
man of agony —
that is the only name I have for you,
that, no other — ever, ever, ever!

Flinging through the palace doors. A long, tense silence follows.

Leader: Where's she gone, Oedipus?
Rushing off, such wild grief . . .
I'm afraid that from this silence
something monstrous may come bursting forth.

Oedipus: Let it burst! Whatever will, whatever must!
I must know my birth, no matter how common
it may be — must see my origins face-to-face.

She perhaps, she with her woman's pride
may well be mortified by my birth,
but I, I count myself the son of Chance,
the great goddess, giver of all good things —
I'll never see myself disgraced. She is my mother!
And the moons have marked me out, my blood-brothers,
one moon on the wane, the next moon great with power.
That is my blood, my nature — I will never betray it,
never fail to search and learn my birth!

Chorus: Yes — if I am a true prophet
if I can grasp the truth,
by the boundless skies of Olympus,
at the full moon of tomorrow, Mount Cithaeron
you will know how Oedipus glories in you —
you, his birthplace, nurse, his mountain-mother!
And we will sing you, dancing out your praise —
you lift our monarch's heart!
Apollo, Apollo, god of the wild cry
may our dancing please you!
Oedipus —
son, dear child, who bore you?
Who of the nymphs who seem to live forever
mated with Pan,° the mountain-striding Father?
Who was your mother? who, some bride of Apollo
the god who loves the pastures spreading toward the sun?
Or was it Hermes, king of the lightning ridges?
Or Dionysus, lord of frenzy, lord of the barren peaks —
did he seize you in his hands, dearest of all his lucky finds? —
found by the nymphs, their warm eyes dancing, gift
to the lord who loves them dancing out his joy!

Oedipus strains to see a figure coming from the distance. Attended by palace guards, an old Shepherd enters slowly, reluctant to approach the king.

Oedipus: I never met the man, my friends . . . still,
if I had to guess, I'd say that's the shepherd,
the very one we've looked for all along.
Brothers in old age, two of a kind,
he and our guest here. At any rate
the ones who bring him in are my own men,
I recognize them.

Turning to the leader.

But you know more than I,
you should, you've seen the man before.

Leader: I know him, definitely. One of Laius' men,
a trusty shepherd, if there ever was one.

1207 *Pan:* God of shepherds, who was, like Hermes and Dionysus, associated with the wilderness.

Oedipus: You, I ask you first, stranger,
you from Corinth — is this the one you mean?
Messenger: You're looking at him. He's your man.
Oedipus:

To the Shepherd.

You, old man, come over here —
look at me. Answer all my questions.
Did you ever serve King Laius?
Shepherd: So I did . . .
a slave, not bought on the block though,
born and reared in the palace.
Oedipus: Your duties, your kind of work?
Shepherd: Herding the flocks, the better part of my life.
Oedipus: Where, mostly? Where did you do your grazing?
Shepherd: Well,
Cithaeron sometimes, or the foothills round about.
Oedipus: This man — you know him? ever see him there?
Shepherd:

Confused, glancing from the Messenger to the King.

Doing what — what man do you mean?
Oedipus:

Pointing to the Messenger.

This one here — ever have dealings with him?
Shepherd: Not so I could say, but give me a chance,
my memory's bad . . .
Messenger: No wonder he doesn't know me, master.
But let me refresh his memory for him.
I'm sure he recalls old times we had
on the slopes of Mount Cithaeron;
he and I, grazing our flocks, he with two
and I with one — we both struck up together,
three whole seasons, six months at a stretch
from spring to the rising of Arcturus° in the fall,
then with winter coming on I'd drive my herds
to my own pens, and back he'd go with his
to Laius' folds.

To the Shepherd.

Now that's how it was,
wasn't it — yes or no?
Shepherd: Yes, I suppose . . .
it's all so long ago.
Messenger: Come, tell me,

1249 *Arcturus:* A star whose rising marked the end of summer.

you gave me a child back then, a boy, remember?
A little fellow to rear, my very own.
Shepherd: What? Why rake up that again?
Messenger: Look, here he is, my fine old friend —
the same man who was just a baby then.
Shepherd: Damn you, shut your mouth — quiet!
Oedipus: Don't lash out at him, old man —
you need lashing more than he does.
Shepherd: Why,
master, majesty — what have I done wrong?
Oedipus: You won't answer his question about the boy.
Shepherd: He's talking nonsense, wasting his breath.
Oedipus: So, you won't talk willingly —
then you'll talk with pain.

The guards seize the Shepherd.

Shepherd: No, dear god, don't torture an old man!
Oedipus: Twist his arms back, quickly!
Shepherd: God help us, why? —
what more do you need to know?
Oedipus: Did you give him that child? He's asking.
Shepherd: I did . . . I wish to god I'd died that day.
Oedipus: You've got your wish if you don't tell the truth.
Shepherd: The more I tell, the worse the death I'll die.
Oedipus: Our friend here wants to stretch things out, does he?

Motioning to his men for torture.

Shepherd: No, no, I gave it to him — I just said so.
Oedipus: Where did you get it? Your house? Someone else's?
Shepherd: It wasn't mine, no, I got it from . . . someone.
Oedipus: Which one of them?

Looking at the citizens.

Whose house?
Shepherd: No —
god's sake, master, no more questions!
Oedipus: You're a dead man if I have to ask again.
Shepherd: Then — the child came from the house . . .
of Laius.
Oedipus: A slave? or born of his own blood?
Shepherd: Oh no,
I'm right at the edge, the horrible truth — I've got to say it!
Oedipus: And I'm at the edge of hearing horrors, yes, but I must hear!
Shepherd: All right! His son, they said it was — his son!
But the one inside, your wife,
she'd tell it best.
Oedipus: My wife —
she gave it to you?
Shepherd: Yes, yes, my king.

Oedipus: Why, what for?
Shepherd: To kill it.
Oedipus: Her own child,
how could she?
Shepherd: She was afraid —
frightening prophecies.
Oedipus: What?
Shepherd: They said —
he'd kill his parents.
Oedipus: But you gave him to this old man — why?
Shepherd: I pitied the little baby, master,
hoped he'd take him off to his own country,
far away, but he saved him for this, this fate.
If you are the man he says you are, believe me,
you were born for pain.
Oedipus: O god —
all come true, all burst to light!
O light — now let me look my last on you!
I stand revealed at last —
cursed in my birth, cursed in marriage,
cursed in the lives I cut down with these hands!

Rushing through the doors with a great cry. The Corinthian Messenger, the Shepherd, and attendants exit slowly to the side.

Chorus: O the generations of men
the dying generations — adding the total
of all your lives I find they come to nothing . . .
does there exist, is there a man on earth
who seizes more joy than just a dream, a vision?
And the vision no sooner dawns than dies
blazing into oblivion.

You are my great example, you, your life,
your destiny, Oedipus, man of misery —
I count no man blest.

You outranged all men!
Bending your bow to the breaking-point
you captured priceless glory, O dear god,
and the Sphinx came crashing down,
the virgin, claws hooked
like a bird of omen singing, shrieking death —
like a fortress reared in the face of death
you rose and saved our land.

From that day on we called you king
we crowned you with honors, Oedipus, towering over all —
mighty king of the seven gates of Thebes.

But now to hear your story — is there a man more agonized?
More wed to pain and frenzy? Not a man on earth,

the joy of your life ground down to nothing
O Oedipus, name for the ages —
one and the same wide harbor served you
son and father both
son and father came to rest in the same bridal chamber.
How, how could the furrows your father plowed
bear you, your agony, harrowing on
in silence O so long?

But now for all your power
Time, all-seeing Time has dragged you to the light,
judged your marriage monstrous from the start —
the son and the father tangling, both one —
O child of Laius, would to god
I'd never seen you, never never!
Now I weep like a man who wails the dead
and the dirge comes pouring forth with all my heart!
I tell you the truth, you gave me life
my breath leapt up in you
and now you bring down night upon my eyes.

Enter a Messenger from the palace.

Messenger: Men of Thebes, always the first in honor,
what horrors you will hear, what you will see,
what a heavy weight of sorrow you will shoulder . . .
if you are true to your birth, if you still have
some feeling for the royal house of Thebes.
I tell you neither the waters of the Danube
nor the Nile can wash this palace clean.
Such things it hides, it soon will bring to light —
terrible things, and none done blindly now,
all done with a will. The pains
we inflict upon ourselves hurt most of all.
Leader: God knows we have pains enough already.
What can you add to them?
Messenger: The queen is dead.
Leader: Poor lady — how?
Messenger: By her own hand. But you are spared the worst,
you never had to watch . . . I saw it all,
and with all the memory that's in me
you will learn what that poor woman suffered.

Once she'd broken in through the gates,
dashing past us, frantic, whipped to fury,
ripping her hair out with both hands —
straight to her rooms she rushed, flinging herself
across the bridal-bed, doors slamming behind her —
once inside, she wailed for Laius, dead so long,
remembering how she bore his child long ago,

the life that rose up to destroy him, leaving
its mother to mother living creatures
with the very son she'd borne.
Oh how she wept, mourning the marriage-bed
where she let loose that double brood — monsters —
husband by her husband, children by her child.
And then —
but how she died is more than I can say. Suddenly
Oedipus burst in, screaming, he stunned us so
we couldn't watch her agony to the end,
our eyes were fixed on him. Circling
like a maddened beast, stalking, here, there
crying out to us —
Give him a sword! His wife,
no wife, his mother, where can he find the mother earth
that cropped two crops at once, himself and all his children?
He was raging — one of the dark powers pointing the way,
none of us mortals crowding around him, no,
with a great shattering cry — someone, something leading him on —
he hurled at the twin doors and bending the bolts back
out of their sockets, crashed through the chamber.
And there we saw the woman hanging by the neck,
cradled high in a woven noose, spinning,
swinging back and forth. And when he saw her,
giving a low, wrenching sob that broke our hearts,
slipping the halter from her throat, he eased her down,
in a slow embrace he laid her down, poor thing . . .
then, what came next, what horror we beheld!

He rips off her brooches, the long gold pins
holding her robes — and lifting them high,
looking straight up into the points,
he digs them down the sockets of his eyes, crying, "You,
you'll see no more the pain I suffered, all the pain I caused!
Too long you looked on the ones you never should have seen,
blind to the ones you longed to see, to know! Blind
from this hour on! Blind in the darkness — blind!"
His voice like a dirge, rising, over and over
raising the pins, raking them down his eyes.
And at each stroke blood spurts from the roots,
splashing his beard, a swirl of it, nerves and clots —
black hail of blood pulsing, gushing down.

These are the griefs that burst upon them both,
coupling man and woman. The joy they had so lately,
the fortune of their old ancestral house
was deep joy indeed. Now, in this one day,
wailing, madness and doom, death, disgrace,
all the griefs in the world that you can name,
all are theirs forever.

Leader: Oh poor man, the misery —
has he any rest from pain now?

A voice within, in torment.

Messenger: He's shouting,
"Loose the bolts, someone, show me to all of Thebes!
My father's murderer, my mother's — "
No, I can't repeat it, it's unholy.
Now he'll tear himself from his native earth,
not linger, curse the house with his own curse.
But he needs strength, and a guide to lead him on.
This is sickness more than he can bear.

The palace doors open.

Look,
he'll show you himself. The great doors are opening —
you are about to see a sight, a horror
even his mortal enemy would pity.

Enter Oedipus, blinded, led by a boy. He stands at the palace steps, as if surveying his people once again.

Chorus: O the terror —
the suffering, for all the world to see,
the worst terror that ever met my eyes.
What madness swept over you? What god,
what dark power leapt beyond all bounds,
beyond belief, to crush your wretched life? —
godforsaken, cursed by the gods!
I pity you but I can't bear to look.
I've much to ask, so much to learn,
so much fascinates my eyes,
but you . . . I shudder at the sight.
Messenger: Oh, Ohhh —
the agony! I am agony —
where am I going? where on earth?
where does all this agony hurl me?
where's my voice? —
winging, swept away on a dark tide —
My destiny, my dark power, what a leap you made!
Chorus: To the depths of terror, too dark to hear, to see.
Oedipus: Dark, horror of darkness
my darkness, drowning, swirling around me
crashing wave on wave — unspeakable, irresistible
headwind, fatal harbor! Oh again,
the misery, all at once, over and over
the stabbing daggers, stab of memory
raking me insane.
Chorus: No wonder you suffer

twice over, the pain of your wounds,
the lasting grief of pain.
Oedipus: Dear friend, still here?
Standing by me, still with a care for me,
the blind man? Such compassion,
loyal to the last. Oh it's you,
I know you're here, dark as it is
I'd know you anywhere, your voice —
it's yours, clearly yours.
Chorus: Dreadful, what you've done . . .
how could you bear it, gouging out your eyes?
What superhuman power drove you on?
Oedipus: Apollo, friends, Apollo —
he ordained my agonies — these, my pains on pains!
But the hand that struck my eyes was mine,
mine alone — no one else —
I did it all myself!
What good were eyes to me?
Nothing I could see could bring me joy.
Chorus: No, no, exactly as you say.
Oedipus: What can I ever see?
What love, what call of the heart
can touch my ears with joy? Nothing, friends.
Take me away, far, far from Thebes,
quickly, cast me away, my friends —
this great murderous ruin, this man cursed to heaven,
the man the deathless gods hate most of all!
Chorus: Pitiful, you suffer so, you understand so much . . .
I wish you'd never known.
Oedipus: Die, die —
whoever he was that day in the wilds
who cut my ankles free of the ruthless pins,
he pulled me clear of death, he saved my life
for this, this kindness —
Curse him, kill him!
If I'd died then, I'd never have dragged myself,
my loved ones through such hell.
Chorus: Oh if only . . . would to god.
Oedipus: I'd never have come to this,
my father's murderer — never been branded
mother's husband, all men see me now! Now,
loathed by the gods, son of the mother I defiled
coupling in my father's bed, spawning lives in the loins
that spawned my wretched life. What grief can crown this grief?
It's mine alone, my destiny — I am Oedipus!
Chorus: How can I say you've chosen for the best?
Better to die than be alive and blind.
Oedipus: What I did was best — don't lecture me,
no more advice. I, with *my* eyes,

how could I look my father in the eyes
when I go down to death? Or mother, so abused . . .
I've done such things to the two of them,
crimes too huge for hanging.
                                        Worse yet,
the sight of my children, born as they were born,
how could I long to look into their eyes?
No, not with these eyes of mine, never.
Not this city either, her high towers,
the sacred glittering images of her gods —
I am misery! I, her best son, reared
as no other son of Thebes was ever reared,
I've stripped myself, I gave the command myself.
All men must cast away the great blasphemer,
the curse now brought to light by the gods,
the son of Laius — I, my father's son!

Now I've exposed my guilt, horrendous guilt,
could I train a level glance on you, my countrymen?
Impossible! No, if I could just block off my ears,
the springs of hearing, I would stop at nothing —
I'd wall up my loathsome body like a prison,
blind to the sound of life, not just the sight.
Oblivion — what a blessing . . .
for the mind to dwell a world away from pain.

O Cithaeron, why did you give me shelter?
Why didn't you take me, crush my life out on the spot?
I'd never have revealed my birth to all mankind.

O Polybus, Corinth, the old house of my fathers,
so I believed — what a handsome prince you raised —
under the skin, what sickness to the core.
Look at me! Born of outrage, outrage to the core.

O triple roads — it all comes back, the secret,
dark ravine, and the oaks closing in
where the three roads join . . .
You drank my father's blood, my own blood
spilled by my own hands — you still remember me?
What things you saw me do? Then I came here
and did them all once more!
                                        Marriages! O marriage,
you gave me birth, and once you brought me into the world
you brought my sperm rising back, springing to light
fathers, brothers, sons — one deadly breed —
brides, wives, mothers. The blackest things
a man can do, I have done them all!
                                                        No more —
it's wrong to name what's wrong to do. Quickly,
for the love of god, hide me somewhere,

kill me, hurl me into the sea
where you can never look on me again.

Beckoning to the Chorus as they shrink away.

Closer,
it's all right. Touch the man of sorrow.
Do. Don't be afraid. My troubles are mine
and I am the only man alive who can sustain them.

Enter Creon from the palace, attended by palace guards.

Leader: Put your requests to Creon. Here he is,
just when we need him. He'll have a plan, he'll act.
Now that he's the sole defense of the country
in your place.
Oedipus: Oh no, what can I say to him?
How can I ever hope to win his trust?
I wronged him so, just now, in every way.
You must see that — I was so wrong, so wrong.
Creon: I haven't come to mock you, Oedipus,
or to criticize your former failings.

Turning to the guards.

You there,
have you lost all respect for human feeling?
At least revere the Sun, the holy fire
that keeps us all alive. Never expose a thing
of guilt and holy dread so great it appalls
the earth, the rain from heaven, the light of day!
Get him into the halls — quickly as you can.
Piety demands no less. Kindred alone
should see a kinsman's shame. This is obscene.
Oedipus: Please, in god's name . . . you wipe my fears away,
coming so generously to me, the worst of men.
Do one thing more, for your sake, not mine.
Creon: What do you want? Why so insistent?
Oedipus: Drive me out of the land at once, far from sight,
where I can never hear a human voice.
Creon: I'd have done that already, I promise you.
First I wanted the god to clarify my duties.
Oedipus: The god? His command was clear, every word:
death for the father-killer, the curse —
he said destroy me!
Creon: So he did. Still, in such a crisis
it's better to ask precisely what to do.
Oedipus: You'd ask the oracle about a man like me?
Creon: By all means. And this time, I assume,
even you will obey the god's decrees.
Oedipus: I will,
I will. And you, I command you — I beg you . . .

the woman inside, bury her as you see fit.
It's the only decent thing,
to give your own the last rites. As for me,
never condemn the city of my fathers
to house my body, not while I'm alive, no,
let me live on the mountains, on Cithaeron,
my favorite haunt, I have made it famous.
Mother and father marked out that rock
to be my everlasting tomb — buried alive.
Let me die there, where they tried to kill me.
Oh but this I know: no sickness can destroy me,
nothing can. I would never have been saved
from death — I have been saved
for something great and terrible, something strange.
Well let my destiny come and take me on its way!

About my children, Creon, the boys at least,
don't burden yourself. They're men;
wherever they go, they'll find the means to live.
But my two daughters, my poor helpless girls,
clustering at our table, never without me
hovering near them . . . whatever I touched,
they always had their share. Take care of them,
I beg you. Wait, better — permit me, would you?
Just to touch them with my hands and take
our fill of tears. Please . . . my king.
Grant it, with all your noble heart.
If I could hold them, just once, I'd think
I had them with me, like the early days
when I could see their eyes.

Antigone and Ismene, two small children, are led in from the palace by a nurse.

What's that?
O god! Do I really hear you sobbing? —
my two children. Creon, you've pitied me?
Sent me my darling girls, my own flesh and blood!
Am I right?

Creon: Yes, it's my doing.
I know the joy they gave you all these years,
the joy you must feel now.

Oedipus: Bless you, Creon!
May god watch over you for this kindness,
better than he ever guarded me.
Children, where are you?
Here, come quickly —

Groping for Antigone and Ismene, who approach their father cautiously, then embrace him.

Come to these hands of mine,
your brother's hands, your own father's hands

that served his once bright eyes so well —
that made them blind. Seeing nothing, children,
knowing nothing, I became your father,
I fathered you in the soil that gave me life.

How I weep for you — I cannot see you now . . .
just thinking of all your days to come, the bitterness,
the life that rough mankind will thrust upon you.
Where are the public gatherings you can join,
the banquets of the clans? Home you'll come,
in tears, cut off from the sight of it all,
the brilliant rites unfinished.
And when you reach perfection, ripe for marriage,
who will he be, my dear ones? Risking all
to shoulder the curse that weighs down my parents,
yes and you too — that wounds us all together.
What more misery could you want?
Your father killed his father, sowed his mother,
one, one and the selfsame womb sprang you —
he cropped the very roots of his existence.

Such disgrace, and you must bear it all!
Who will marry you then? Not a man on earth.
Your doom is clear: you'll wither away to nothing,
single, without a child.

Turning to Creon.

Oh Creon,
you are the only father they have now . . .
we who brought them into the world
are gone, both gone at a stroke —
Don't let them go begging, abandoned,
women without men. Your own flesh and blood!
Never bring them down to the level of my pains.
Pity them. Look at them, so young, so vulnerable,
shorn of everything — you're their only hope.
Promise me, noble Creon, touch my hand.

Reaching toward Creon, who draws back.

You, little ones, if you were old enough
to understand, there is much I'd tell you.
Now, as it is, I'd have you say a prayer.
Pray for life, my children,
live where you are free to grow and season.
Pray god you find a better life than mine,
the father who begot you.

Creon: Enough.
You've wept enough. Into the palace now.

Oedipus: I must, but I find it very hard.

Creon: Time is the great healer, you will see.

Oedipus: I am going — you know on what condition?
Creon: Tell me. I'm listening.
Oedipus: Drive me out of Thebes, in exile.
Creon: Not I. Only the gods can give you that.
Oedipus: Surely the gods hate me so much —
Creon: You'll get your wish at once.
Oedipus: You consent?
Creon: I try to say what I mean; it's my habit.
Oedipus: Then take me away. It's time.
Creon: Come along, let go of the children.
Oedipus: No —
don't take them away from me, not now! No no no!

Clutching his daughters as the guards wrench them loose and take them through the palace doors.

Creon: Still the king, the master of all things?
No more: here your power ends.
None of your power follows you through life.

Exit Oedipus and Creon to the palace. The Chorus comes forward to address the audience directly.

Chorus: People of Thebes, my countrymen, look on Oedipus.
He solved the famous riddle with his brilliance,
he rose to power, a man beyond all power.
Who could behold his greatness without envy?
Now what a black sea of terror has overwhelmed him.
Now as we keep our watch and wait the final day,
count no man happy till he dies, free of pain at last.

Exit in procession.

Considerations

1. In the opening scene what does the priest's speech reveal about how Oedipus has been regarded as a ruler of Thebes?
2. What do Oedipus's confrontations with Tiresias and Creon indicate about his character?
3. Aristotle defined a tragic flaw as consisting of "error and frailties." What errors does Oedipus make? What are his frailties?
4. What causes Oedipus's downfall? Is he simply a pawn in a predetermined game played by the gods? Can he be regarded as responsible for the suffering and death in the play?
5. Locate instances of dramatic irony in the play. How do they serve as foreshadowings?
6. Describe the function of the Chorus. How does the Chorus's view of life and the gods differ from Jocasta's?
7. Trace the images of vision and blindness throughout the play. How are they related to the theme? Why does Oedipus blind himself instead of joining Jocasta in suicide?
8. "What goes on four feet in the morning, two at noon, and three in the evening?" This was the riddle posed by the Sphinx. Oedipus answered the question cor-

rectly: "Man," because babies crawl, adults walk erect, and in old age people use canes. How is this riddle related to the other questions Oedipus seeks to answer?

9. What is your assessment of Oedipus at the end of the play? Was he foolish? heroic? fated? To what extent can your emotions concerning him be described as "pity and fear"?
10. Is it possible for a twentieth-century reader to identify with Oedipus's plight? What philosophic issues does he confront?
11. *Oedipus complex* is a well-known term used in psychoanalysis. What does it mean? Does the concept offer any insights into the conflicts dramatized in the play?

Connections

1. Consider the endings of *Oedipus the King* and Shakespeare's *Hamlet* (p. 1065). What feelings do you have about these endings? Are they irredeemably unhappy? Is there anything that suggests hope for the future at the ends of these plays?
2. Sophocles does not include violence in his plays; any bloodshed occurs offstage. Compare and contrast the effects of this strategy with the use of violence in either *Hamlet* or *Othello* (p. 1166).
3. Write an essay explaining why *Oedipus the King* cannot be considered a realistic play in the way that Henrik Ibsen's *A Doll's House* (p. 1321) can be.

ANTIGONE

Antigone was actually written before Sophocles' other two plays about Oedipus and his family. *Oedipus the King* ends with Oedipus, the king of Thebes, blinding himself because he has unknowingly murdered his father and married his mother, Jocasta. Creon, his brother-in-law, becomes the ruler of Thebes and is entrusted with caring for Oedipus's two daughters, Antigone and Ismene. *Oedipus at Colonus* continues the story some twenty years later. Oedipus has been rejected by his two sons, Polynices and Eteocles, and wanders in exile, cared for by Antigone. Meanwhile, his sons struggle for power in Thebes. Polynices travels to Argos to gather a force to attack his brother as Oedipus arrives in Colonus, near Athens. There Oedipus curses his sons for their ruthless selfishness and predicts their violent deaths. Oedipus, however, dies in peace, with dignity, and bestows a blessing on Athens.

Antigone begins after the two brothers have killed each other in battle. The throne of Thebes subsequently returns to Creon, who decrees that Polynices was traitorous and therefore must not be buried. As the play opens, Antigone tells her sister that she will defy Creon's ruling, even though the penalty for disobedience is death.

Antigone's insistence on obeying the law of the gods instead of civil laws dramatizes a conflict that continues to move audiences and readers who ponder the relation of the individual's conscience to the demands of the state. One manifestation of this concern in the twentieth century is Jean

Anouilh's 1944 production of *Antigone* in Paris, when that city was occupied by German troops during World War II. Anouilh's Antigone reflects the French resistance movement, and his Creon is a representative of German authority who must preserve order in the face of unyielding opposition. (A brief excerpt of this play appears on p. 1051.) Sophocles' play — as does Anouilh's — presents an agonizing dilemma. Neither Antigone nor Creon is wholly virtuous or blameless, so the complexities they embody remain a moral and intellectual challenge.

SOPHOCLES (496?–406 B.C.)

Antigone

C. 441 B.C.

TRANSLATED BY ROBERT FAGLES

Characters

Antigone, daughter of Oedipus and Jocasta
Ismene, sister of Antigone
A Chorus of old Theban citizens and their *Leader*
Creon, king of Thebes, uncle of Antigone and Ismene
A Sentry
Haemon, son of Creon and Eurydice
Tiresias, a blind prophet
A Messenger
Eurydice, wife of Creon
Guards, attendants, and a boy

TIME AND SCENE. *The royal house of Thebes. It is still night, and the invading armies of Argos have just been driven from the city. Fighting on opposite sides, the sons of Oedipus, Eteocles and Polynices, have killed each other in combat. Their uncle, Creon, is now king of Thebes.*

Enter Antigone, slipping through the central doors of the palace. She motions to her sister, Ismene, who follows her cautiously toward an altar at the center of the stage.

Antigone: My own flesh and blood — dear sister, dear Ismene,
how many griefs our father Oedipus handed down!
Do you know one, I ask you, one grief
that Zeus° will not perfect for the two of us
while we still live and breathe? There's nothing,
no pain — our lives are pain — no private shame,
no public disgrace, nothing I haven't seen
in your griefs and mine. And now this:
an emergency decree, they say, the Commander
has just declared for all of Thebes.
What, haven't you heard? Don't you see?

4 *Zeus:* The highest Olympian deity.

The doom reserved for enemies
marches on the ones we love the most.

Ismene: Not I, I haven't heard a word, Antigone.
Nothing of loved ones,
no joy or pain has come my way, not since
the two of us were robbed of our two brothers,
both gone in a day, a double blow —
not since the armies of Argos vanished,
just this very night. I know nothing more,
whether our luck's improved or ruin's still to come.

Antigone: I thought so. That's why I brought you out here,
past the gates, so you could hear in private.

Ismene: What's the matter? Trouble, clearly . . .
you sound so dark, so grim.

Antigone: Why not? Our own brothers' burial!
Hasn't Creon graced one with all the rites,
disgraced the other? Eteocles, they say,
has been given full military honors,
rightly so — Creon's laid him in the earth
and he goes with glory down among the dead.
But the body of Polynices, who died miserably —
why, a city-wide proclamation, rumor has it,
forbids anyone to bury him, even mourn him.
He's to be left unwept, unburied, a lovely treasure
for birds that scan the field and feast to their heart's content.

Such, I hear, is the martial law our good Creon
lays down for you and me — yes, me, I tell you —
and he's coming here to alert the uninformed
in no uncertain terms,
and he won't treat the matter lightly. Whoever
disobeys in the least will die, his doom is sealed:
stoning to death inside the city walls!

There you have it. You'll soon show what you are,
worth your breeding, Ismene, or a coward —
for all your royal blood.

Ismene: My poor sister, if things have come to this,
who am I to make or mend them, tell me,
what good am I to you?

Antigone: Decide.
Will you share the labor, share the work?

Ismene: What work, what's the risk? What do you mean?

Antigone:

Raising her hands.

Will you lift up his body with these bare hands
and lower it with me?

Ismene: What? You'd bury him —
when a law forbids the city?

Antigone: Yes!
He is my brother and — deny it as you will —
your brother too.
No one will ever convict me for a traitor.
Ismene: So desperate, and Creon has expressly —
Antigone: No,
he has no right to keep me from my own.
Ismene: Oh my sister, think —
think how our own father died, hated,
his reputation in ruins, driven on
by the crimes he brought to light himself
to gouge out his eyes with his own hands —
then mother . . . his mother and wife, both in one,
mutilating her life in the twisted noose —
and last, our two brothers dead in a single day,
both shedding their own blood, poor suffering boys,
battling out their common destiny hand-to-hand.

Now look at the two of us, left so alone . . .
think what a death we'll die, the worst of all
if we violate the laws and override
the fixed decree of the throne, its power —
we must be sensible. Remember we are women,
we're not born to contend with men. Then too,
we're underlings, ruled by much stronger hands,
so we must submit in this, and things still worse.

I, for one, I'll beg the dead to forgive me —
I'm forced, I have no choice — I must obey
the ones who stand in power. Why rush to extremes?
It's madness, madness.
Antigone: I won't insist,
no, even if you should have a change of heart,
I'd never welcome you in the labor, not with me.
So, do as you like, whatever suits you best —
I'll bury him myself.
And even if I die in the act, that death will be a glory.
I'll lie with the one I love and loved by him —
an outrage sacred to the gods! I have longer
to please the dead than please the living here:
in the kingdom down below I'll lie forever.
Do as you like, dishonor the laws
the gods hold in honor.
Ismene: I'd do them no dishonor . . .
but defy the city? I have no strength for that.
Antigone: You have your excuses. I am on my way,
I'll raise a mound for him, for my dear brother.
Ismene: Oh Antigone, you're so rash — I'm so afraid for you!
Antigone: Don't fear for me. Set your own life in order.

Ismene: Then don't, at least, blurt this out to anyone.
Keep it a secret. I'll join you in that, I promise.
Antigone: Dear god, shout it from the rooftops. I'll hate you
all the more for silence — tell the world!
Ismene: So fiery — and it ought to chill your heart.
Antigone: I know I please where I must please the most.
Ismene: Yes, if you can, but you're in love with impossibility.
Antigone: Very well then, once my strength gives out
I will be done at last.
Ismene: You're wrong from the start,
you're off on a hopeless quest.
Antigone: If you say so, you will make me hate you,
and the hatred of the dead, by all rights,
will haunt you night and day.
But leave me to my own absurdity, leave me
to suffer this — dreadful thing. I'll suffer
nothing as great as death without glory.

Exit to the side.

Ismene: Then go if you must, but rest assured,
wild, irrational as you are, my sister,
you are truly dear to the ones who love you.

Withdrawing to the palace. Enter a Chorus, the old citizens of Thebes, chanting as the sun begins to rise.

Chorus: Glory! — great beam of sun, brightest of all
that ever rose on the seven gates of Thebes,
you burn through night at last!
Great eye of the golden day,
mounting the Dirce's° banks you throw him back —
the enemy out of Argos, the white shield, the man of bronze —
he's flying headlong now
the bridle of fate stampeding him with pain!

And he had driven against our borders,
launched by the warring claims of Polynices —
like an eagle screaming, winging havoc
over the land, wings of armor
shielded white as snow,
a huge army massing,
crested helmets bristling for assault.

He hovered above our roofs, his vast maw gaping
closing down around our seven gates,
his spears thirsting for the kill
but now he's gone, look,
before he could glut his jaws with Theban blood

121 *the Dirce:* A river near Thebes.

or the god of fire put our crown of towers to the torch.
He grappled the Dragon none can master — Thebes —
the clang of our arms like thunder at his back!

Zeus hates with a vengeance all bravado,
the mighty boasts of men. He watched them
coming on in a rising flood, the pride
of their golden armor ringing shrill —
and brandishing his lightning
blasted the fighter just at the goal,
rushing to shout his triumph from our walls.

Down from the heights he crashed, pounding down on the earth!
And a moment ago, blazing torch in hand —
mad for attack, ecstatic
he breathed his rage, the storm
of his fury hurling at our heads!
But now his high hopes have laid him low
and down the enemy ranks the iron god of war
deals his rewards, his stunning blows — Ares°
rapture of battle, our right arm in the crisis.

Seven captains marshaled at seven gates
seven against their equals, gave
their brazen trophies up to Zeus,
god of the breaking rout of battle,
all but two: those blood brothers,
one father, one mother — matched in rage,
spears matched for the twin conquest —
clashed and won the common prize of death.

But now for Victory! Glorious in the morning,
joy in her eyes to meet our joy
she is winging down to Thebes,
our fleets of chariots wheeling in her wake —
Now let us win oblivion from the wars,
thronging the temples of the gods
in singing, dancing choirs through the night!
Lord Dionysus,° god of the dance
that shakes the land of Thebes, now lead the way!

Enter Creon from the palace, attended by his guard.

But look, the king of the realm is coming,
Creon, the new man for the new day,
whatever the gods are sending now . . .
what new plan will he launch?
Why this, this special session?
Why this sudden call to the old men
summoned at one command?

154 *Ares:* God of war. 171 *Dionysus:* God of fertility and wine.

Creon: My countrymen,
the ship of state is safe. The gods who rocked her,
after a long, merciless pounding in the storm,
have righted her once more.
Out of the whole city
I have called you here alone. Well I know,
first, your undeviating respect
for the throne and royal power of King Laius.
Next, while Oedipus steered the land of Thebes,
and even after he died, your loyalty was unshakable,
you still stood by their children. Now then,
since the two sons are dead — two blows of fate
in the same day, cut down by each other's hands,
both killers, both brothers stained with blood —
as I am next in kin to the dead,
I now possess the throne and all its powers.

Of course you cannot know a man completely,
his character, his principles, sense of judgment,
not till he's shown his colors, ruling the people,
making laws. Experience, there's the test.
As I see it, whoever assumes the task,
the awesome task of setting the city's course,
and refuses to adopt the soundest policies
but fearing someone, keeps his lips locked tight,
he's utterly worthless. So I rate him now,
I always have. And whoever places a friend
above the good of his own country, he is nothing:
I have no use for him. Zeus my witness,
Zeus who sees all things, always —
I could never stand by silent, watching destruction
march against our city, putting safety to rout,
nor could I ever make that man a friend of mine
who menaces our country. Remember this:
our country *is* our safety.
Only while she voyages true on course
can we establish friendships, truer than blood itself.
Such are my standards. They make our city great.

Closely akin to them I have proclaimed,
just now, the following decree to our people
concerning the two sons of Oedipus.
Eteocles, who died fighting for Thebes,
excelling all in arms: he shall be buried,
crowned with a hero's honors, the cups we pour
to soak the earth and reach the famous dead.

But as for his blood brother, Polynices,
who returned from exile, home to his father-city
and the gods of his race, consumed with one desire —

to burn them roof to roots — who thirsted to drink
his kinsmen's blood and sell the rest to slavery:
that man — a proclamation has forbidden the city
to dignify him with burial, mourn him at all.
No, he must be left unburied, his corpse
carrion for the birds and dogs to tear,
an obscenity for the citizens to behold!

These are my principles. Never at my hands
will the traitor be honored above the patriot.
But whoever proves his loyalty to the state:
I'll prize that man in death as well as life.

Leader: If this is your pleasure, Creon, treating
our city's enemy and our friend this way . . .
The power is yours, I suppose, to enforce it
with the laws, both for the dead and all of us,
the living.

Creon: Follow my orders closely then,
be on your guard.

Leader: We're too old.
Lay that burden on younger shoulders.

Creon: No, no,
I don't mean the body — I've posted guards already.

Leader: What commands for us then? What other service?

Creon: See that you never side with those who break my orders.

Leader: Never. Only a fool could be in love with death.

Creon: Death is the price — you're right. But all too often
the mere hope of money has ruined many men.

A Sentry enters from the side.

Sentry: My lord,
I can't say I'm winded from running, or set out
with any spring in my legs either — no sir,
I was lost in thought, and it made me stop, often,
dead in my tracks, wheeling, turning back,
and all the time a voice inside me muttering,
"Idiot, why? You're going straight to your death."
Then muttering, "Stopped again, poor fool?
If somebody gets the news to Creon first,
what's to save your neck?"
And so,
mulling it over, on I trudged, dragging my feet,
you can make a short road take forever . . .
but at last, look, common sense won out,
I'm here, and I'm all yours,
and even though I come empty-handed
I'll tell my story just the same, because
I've come with a good grip on one hope,
what will come will come, whatever fate —

Creon: Come to the point!
What's wrong — why so afraid?
Sentry: First, myself, I've got to tell you,
I didn't do it, didn't see who did —
Be fair, don't take it out on me.
Creon: You're playing it safe, soldier,
barricading yourself from any trouble.
It's obvious, you've something strange to tell.
Sentry: Dangerous too, and danger makes you delay
for all you're worth.
Creon: Out with it — then dismiss!
Sentry: All right, here it comes. The body —
someone's just buried it, then run off . . .
sprinkled some dry dust on the flesh,
given it proper rites.
Creon: What?
What man alive would dare —
Sentry: I've no idea, I swear it.
There was no mark of a spade, no pickaxe there,
no earth turned up, the ground packed hard and dry,
unbroken, no tracks, no wheelruts, nothing,
the workman left no trace. Just at sunup
the first watch of the day points it out —
it was a wonder! We were stunned . . .
a terrific burden too, for all of us, listen:
you can't see the corpse, not that it's buried,
really, just a light cover of road-dust on it,
as if someone meant to lay the dead to rest
and keep from getting cursed.
Not a sign in sight that dogs or wild beasts
had worried the body, even torn the skin.

But what came next! Rough talk flew thick and fast,
guard grilling guard — we'd have come to blows
at last, nothing to stop it; each man for himself
and each the culprit, no one caught red-handed,
all of us pleading ignorance, dodging the charges,
ready to take up red-hot iron in our fists,
go through fire, swear oaths to the gods —
"I didn't do it, I had no hand in it either,
not in the plotting, not in the work itself!"

Finally, after all this wrangling came to nothing,
one man spoke out and made us stare at the ground,
hanging our heads in fear. No way to counter him,
no way to take his advice and come through
safe and sound. Here's what he said:
"Look, we've got to report the facts to Creon,
we can't keep this hidden." Well, that won out,
and the lot fell on me, condemned me,

unlucky as ever, I got the prize. So here I am,
against my will and yours too, well I know —
no one wants the man who brings bad news.

Leader: My king,
ever since he began I've been debating in my mind,
could this possibly be the work of the gods?

Creon: Stop —
before you make me choke with anger — the gods!
You, you're senile, must you be insane?
You say — why it's intolerable — say the gods
could have the slightest concern for that corpse?
Tell me, was it for meritorious service
they proceeded to bury him, prized him so? The hero
who came to burn their temples ringed with pillars,
their golden treasures — scorch their hallowed earth
and fling their laws to the winds.
Exactly when did you last see the gods
celebrating traitors? Inconceivable!

No, from the first there were certain citizens
who could hardly stand the spirit of my regime,
grumbling against me in the dark, heads together,
tossing wildly, never keeping their necks beneath
the yoke, loyally submitting to their king.
These are the instigators, I'm convinced —
they've perverted my own guard, bribed them
to do their work.
Money! Nothing worse
in our lives, so current, rampant, so corrupting.
Money — you demolish cities, root men from their homes,
you train and twist good minds and set them on
to the most atrocious schemes. No limit,
you make them adept at every kind of outrage,
every godless crime — money!
Everyone —
the whole crew bribed to commit this crime,
they've made one thing sure at least:
sooner or later they will pay the price.

Wheeling on the Sentry.

You —
I swear to Zeus as I still believe in Zeus,
if you don't find the man who buried that corpse,
the very man, and produce him before my eyes,
simple death won't be enough for you,
not till we string you up alive
and wring the immorality out of you.
Then you can steal the rest of your days,
better informed about where to make a killing.

You'll have learned, at last, it doesn't pay
to itch for rewards from every hand that beckons.
Filthy profits wreck most men, you'll see —
they'll never save your life.

Sentry: Please,
may I say a word or two, or just turn and go?

Creon: Can't you tell? Everything you say offends me.

Sentry: Where does it hurt you, in the ears or in the heart?

Creon: And who are you to pinpoint my displeasure?

Sentry: The culprit grates on your feelings,
I just annoy your ears.

Creon: Still talking?
You talk too much! A born nuisance —

Sentry: Maybe so,
but I never did this thing, so help me!

Creon: Yes you did —
what's more, you squandered your life for silver!

Sentry: Oh it's terrible when the one who does the judging
judges things all wrong.

Creon: Well now,
you just be clever about your judgments —
if you fail to produce the criminals for me,
you'll swear your dirty money brought you pain.

Turning sharply, reentering the palace.

Sentry: I hope he's found. Best thing by far.
But caught or not, that's in the lap of fortune;
I'll never come back, you've seen the last of me.
I'm saved, even now, and I never thought,
I never hoped —
dear gods, I owe you all my thanks!

Rushing out.

Chorus: Numberless wonders
terrible wonders walk the world but none the match for man —
that great wonder crossing the heaving gray sea,
driven on by the blasts of winter
on through breakers crashing left and right,
holds his steady course
and the oldest of the gods he wears away —
the Earth, the immortal, the inexhaustible —
as his plows go back and forth, year in, year out
with the breed of stallions turning up the furrows.

And the blithe, lightheaded race of birds he snares,
the tribes of savage beasts, the life that swarms the depths —
with one fling of his nets
woven and coiled tight, he takes them all,
man the skilled, the brilliant!

He conquers all, taming with his techniques
the prey that roams the cliffs and wild lairs,
training the stallion, clamping the yoke across
his shaggy neck, and the tireless mountain bull.

And speech and thought, quick as the wind
and the mood and mind for law that rules the city —
all these he has taught himself
and shelter from the arrows of the frost
when there's rough lodging under the cold clear sky
and the shafts of lashing rain —
ready, resourceful man!
Never without resources
never an impasse as he marches on the future —
only Death, from Death alone he will find no rescue
but from desperate plagues he has plotted his escapes.

Man the master, ingenious past all measure
past all dreams, the skills within his grasp —
he forges on, now to destruction
now again to greatness. When he weaves in
the laws of the land, and the justice of the gods
that binds his oaths together
he and his city rise high —
but the city casts out
that man who weds himself to inhumanity
thanks to reckless daring. Never share my hearth
never think my thoughts, whoever does such things.

Enter Antigone from the side, accompanied by the Sentry.

Here is a dark sign from the gods —
what to make of this? I know her,
how can I deny it? That young girl's Antigone!
Wretched, child of a wretched father,
Oedipus. Look, is it possible?
They bring you in like a prisoner —
why? did you break the king's laws?
Did they take you in some act of mad defiance?

Sentry: She's the one, she did it single-handed —
we caught her burying the body. Where's Creon?

Enter Creon from the palace.

Leader: Back again, just in time when you need him.
Creon: In time for what? What is it?
Sentry: My king,
there's nothing you can swear you'll never do —
second thoughts make liars of us all.
I could have sworn I wouldn't hurry back
(what with your threats, the buffeting I just took),

but a stroke of luck beyond our wildest hopes,
what a joy, there's nothing like it. So,
back I've come, breaking my oath, who cares?
I'm bringing in our prisoner — this young girl —
we took her giving the dead the last rites.
But no casting lots this time; this is *my* luck,
my prize, no one else's.
Now, my lord,
here she is. Take her, question her,
cross-examine her to your heart's content.
But set me free, it's only right —
I'm rid of this dreadful business once for all.

Creon: Prisoner! Her? You took her — where, doing what?

Sentry: Burying the man. That's the whole story.

Creon: What?
You mean what you say, you're telling me the truth?

Sentry: She's the one. With my own eyes I saw her
bury the body, just what you've forbidden.
There. Is that plain and clear?

Creon: What did you see? Did you catch her in the act?

Sentry: Here's what happened. We went back to our post,
those threats of yours breathing down our necks —
we brushed the corpse clean of the dust that covered it,
stripped it bare . . . it was slimy, going soft,
and we took to high ground, backs to the wind
so the stink of him couldn't hit us;
jostling, baiting each other to keep awake,
shouting back and forth — no napping on the job,
not this time. And so the hours dragged by
until the sun stood dead above our heads,
a huge white ball in the noon sky, beating,
blazing down, and then it happened —
suddenly, a whirlwind!
Twisting a great dust-storm up from the earth,
a black plague of the heavens, filling the plain,
ripping the leaves off every tree in sight,
choking the air and sky. We squinted hard
and took our whipping from the gods.

And after the storm passed — it seemed endless —
there, we saw the girl!
And she cried out a sharp, piercing cry,
like a bird come back to an empty nest,
peering into its bed, and all the babies gone . . .
Just so, when she sees the corpse bare
she bursts into a long, shattering wail
and calls down withering curses on the heads
of all who did the work. And she scoops up dry dust,
handfuls, quickly, and lifting a fine bronze urn,

lifting it high and pouring, she crowns the dead
with three full libations.

Soon as we saw
we rushed her, closed on the kill like hunters,
and she, she didn't flinch. We interrogated her,
charging her with offenses past and present —
she stood up to it all, denied nothing. I tell you,
it made me ache and laugh in the same breath.
It's pure joy to escape the worst yourself,
it hurts a man to bring down his friends.
But all that, I'm afraid, means less to me
than my own skin. That's the way I'm made.

Creon:

Wheeling on Antigone.

You,
with your eyes fixed on the ground — speak up.
Do you deny you did this, yes or no?

Antigone: I did it. I don't deny a thing.

Creon:

To the sentry.

You, get out, wherever you please —
you're clear of a very heavy charge.

He leaves; Creon turns back to Antigone.

You, tell me briefly, no long speeches —
were you aware a decree had forbidden this?

Antigone: Well aware. How could I avoid it? It was public.

Creon: And still you had the gall to break this law?

Antigone: Of course I did. It wasn't Zeus, not in the least,
who made this proclamation — not to me.
Nor did that Justice, dwelling with the gods
beneath the earth, ordain such laws for men.
Nor did I think your edict had such force
that you, a mere mortal, could override the gods,
the great unwritten, unshakable traditions.
They are alive, not just today or yesterday:
they live forever, from the first of time,
and no one knows when they first saw the light.

These laws — I was not about to break them,
not out of fear of some man's wounded pride,
and face the retribution of the gods.
Die I must, I've known it all my life —
how could I keep from knowing? — even without
your death-sentence ringing in my ears.
And if I am to die before my time
I consider that a gain. Who on earth,

alive in the midst of so much grief as I,
could fail to find his death a rich reward?
So for me, at least, to meet this doom of yours
is precious little pain. But if I had allowed
my own mother's son to rot, an unburied corpse —
that would have been an agony! This is nothing.
And if my present actions strike you as foolish,
let's just say I've been accused of folly
by a fool.

Leader: Like father like daughter,
passionate, wild . . .
she hasn't learned to bend before adversity.

Creon: No? Believe me, the stiffest stubborn wills
fall the hardest; the toughest iron,
tempered strong in the white-hot fire,
you'll see it crack and shatter first of all.
And I've known spirited horses you can break
with a light bit — proud, rebellious horses.
There's no room for pride, not in a slave,
not with the lord and master standing by.

This girl was an old hand at insolence
when she overrode the edicts we made public.
But once she'd done it — the insolence,
twice over — to glory in it, laughing,
mocking us to our face with what she'd done.
I'm not the man, not now: she is the man
if this victory goes to her and she goes free.

Never! Sister's child or closer in blood
than all my family clustered at my altar
worshiping Guardian Zeus — she'll never escape,
she and her blood sister, the most barbaric death.
Yes, I accuse her sister of an equal part
in scheming this, this burial.

To his attendants.

Bring her here!
I just saw her inside, hysterical, gone to pieces.
It never fails: the mind convicts itself
in advance, when scoundrels are up to no good,
plotting in the dark. Oh but I hate it more
when a traitor, caught red-handed,
tries to glorify his crimes.

Antigone: Creon, what more do you want
than my arrest and execution?

Creon: Nothing. Then I have it all.

Antigone: Then why delay? Your moralizing repels me,
every word you say — pray god it always will.
So naturally all I say repels you too.

Enough.
Give me glory! What greater glory could I win
than to give my own brother decent burial?
These citizens here would all agree,

To the Chorus.

they'd praise me too
if their lips weren't locked in fear.

Pointing to Creon.

Lucky tyrants — the perquisites of power!
Ruthless power to do and say whatever pleases *them.*
Creon: You alone, of all the people in Thebes,
see things that way.
Antigone: They see it just that way
but defer to you and keep their tongues in leash.
Creon: And you, aren't you ashamed to differ so from them?
So disloyal!
Antigone: Not ashamed for a moment,
not to honor my brother, my own flesh and blood.
Creon: Wasn't Eteocles a brother too — cut down, facing him?
Antigone: Brother, yes, by the same mother, the same father.
Creon: Then how can you render his enemy such honors,
such impieties in his eyes?
Antigone: He'll never testify to that,
Eteocles dead and buried.
Creon: He will —
if you honor the traitor just as much as him.
Antigone: But it was his brother, not some slave that died —
Creon: Ravaging our country! —
but Eteocles died fighting in our behalf.
Antigone: No matter — Death longs for the same rites for all.
Creon: Never the same for the patriot and the traitor.
Antigone: Who, Creon, who on earth can say the ones below
don't find this pure and uncorrupt?
Creon: Never. Once an enemy, never a friend,
not even after death.
Antigone: I was born to join in love, not hate —
that is my nature.
Creon: Go down below and love,
if love you must — love the dead! While I'm alive,
no woman is going to lord it over me.

Enter Ismene from the palace, under guard.

Chorus: Look,
Ismene's coming, weeping a sister's tears,
loving sister, under a cloud . . .
her face is flushed, her cheeks streaming.
Sorrow puts her lovely radiance in the dark.

Creon: You —
in my house, you viper, slinking undetected,
sucking my life-blood! I never knew
I was breeding twin disasters, the two of you
rising up against my throne. Come, tell me,
will you confess your part in the crime or not?
Answer me. Swear to me.

Ismene: I did it, yes —
if only she consents — I share the guilt,
the consequences too.

Antigone: No,
Justice will never suffer that — not you,
you were unwilling. I never brought you in.

Ismene: But now you face such dangers . . . I'm not ashamed
to sail through trouble with you,
make your troubles mine.

Antigone: Who did the work?
Let the dead and the god of death bear witness!
I've no love for a friend who loves in words alone.

Ismene: Oh no, my sister, don't reject me, please,
let me die beside you, consecrating
the dead together.

Antigone: Never share my dying,
don't lay claim to what you never touched.
My death will be enough.

Ismene: What do I care for life, cut off from you?

Antigone: Ask Creon. Your concern is all for him.

Ismene: Why abuse me so? It doesn't help you now.

Antigone: You're right —
if I mock you, I get no pleasure from it,
only pain.

Ismene: Tell me, dear one,
what can I do to help you, even now?

Antigone: Save yourself. I don't grudge you your survival.

Ismene: Oh no, no, denied my portion in your death?

Antigone: You chose to live, I chose to die.

Ismene: Not, at least,
without every kind of caution I could voice.

Antigone: Your wisdom appealed to one world — mine, another.

Ismene: But look, we're both guilty, both condemned to death.

Antigone: Courage! Live your life. I gave myself to death,
long ago, so I might serve the dead.

Creon: They're both mad, I tell you, the two of them.
One's just shown it, the other's been that way
since she was born.

Ismene: True, my king,
the sense we were born with cannot last forever . . .
commit cruelty on a person long enough
and the mind begins to go.

Creon: Yours did,
when you chose to commit your crimes with her.
Ismene: How can I live alone, without her?
Creon: Her?
Don't even mention her — she no longer exists.
Ismene: What? You'd kill your own son's bride?
Creon: Absolutely:
there are other fields for him to plow.
Ismene: Perhaps,
but never as true, as close a bond as theirs.
Creon: A worthless woman for my son? It repels me.
Ismene: Dearest Haemon, your father wrongs you so!
Creon: Enough, enough — you and your talk of marriage!
Ismene: Creon — you're really going to rob your son of Antigone?
Creon: Death will do it for me — break their marriage off.
Leader: So, it's settled then? Antigone must die?
Creon: Settled, yes — we both know that.

To the guards.

Stop wasting time. Take them in.
From now on they'll act like women.
Tie them up, no more running loose;
even the bravest will cut and run,
once they see Death coming for their lives.

The guards escort Antigone and Ismene into the palace. Creon remains while the old citizens form their chorus.

Chorus: Blest, they are the truly blest who all their lives
have never tasted devastation. For others, once
the gods have rocked a house to its foundations
the ruin will never cease, cresting on and on
from one generation on throughout the race —
like a great mounting tide
driven on by savage northern gales,
surging over the dead black depths
roiling up from the bottom dark heaves of sand
and the headlands, taking the storm's onslaught full-force,
roar, and the low moaning
echoes on and on
and now
as in ancient times I see the sorrows of the house,
the living heirs of the old ancestral kings,
piling on the sorrows of the dead
and one generation cannot free the next —
some god will bring them crashing down,
the race finds no release.
And now the light, the hope
springing up from the late last root
in the house of Oedipus, that hope's cut down in turn

by the long, bloody knife swung by the gods of death
by a senseless word
by fury at the heart.
Zeus,
yours is the power, Zeus, what man on earth
can override it, who can hold it back?
Power that neither Sleep, the all-ensnaring
no, nor the tireless months of heaven
can ever overmaster — young through all time,
mighty lord of power, you hold fast
the dazzling crystal mansions of Olympus.
And throughout the future, late and soon
as through the past, your law prevails:
no towering form of greatness
enters into the lives of mortals
free and clear of ruin.
True,
our dreams, our high hopes voyaging far and wide
bring sheer delight to many, to many others
delusion, blithe, mindless lusts
and the fraud steals on one slowly . . . unaware
till he trips and puts his foot into the fire.
He was a wise old man who coined
the famous saying: "Sooner or later
foul is fair, fair is foul
to the man the gods will ruin" —
He goes his way for a moment only
free of blinding ruin.

Enter Haemon from the palace.

Here's Haemon now, the last of all your sons.
Does he come in tears for his bride,
his doomed bride, Antigone —
bitter at being cheated of their marriage?
Creon: We'll soon know, better than seers could tell us.

Turning to Haemon.

Son, you've heard the final verdict on your bride?
Are you coming now, raving against your father?
Or do you love me, no matter what I do?
Haemon: Father, I'm your *son* . . . you in your wisdom
set my bearings for me — I obey you.
No marriage could ever mean more to me than you,
whatever good direction you may offer.
Creon: Fine, Haemon.
That's how you ought to feel within your heart,
subordinate to your father's will in every way.
That's what a man prays for: to produce good sons —

households full of them, dutiful and attentive,
so they can pay his enemy back with interest
and match the respect their father shows his friend.
But the man who rears a brood of useless children,
what has he brought into the world, I ask you?
Nothing but trouble for himself, and mockery
from his enemies laughing in his face.
Oh Haemon,
never lose your sense of judgment over a woman.
The warmth, the rush of pleasure, it all goes cold
in your arms, I warn you . . . a worthless woman
in your house, a misery in your bed.
What wound cuts deeper than a loved one
turned against you? Spit her out,
like a mortal enemy — let the girl go.
Let her find a husband down among the dead.

Imagine it: I caught her in naked rebellion,
the traitor, the only one in the whole city.
I'm not about to prove myself a liar,
not to my people, no, I'm going to kill her!
That's right — so let her cry for mercy, sing her hymns
to Zeus who defends all bonds of kindred blood.
Why, if I bring up my own kin to be rebels,
think what I'd suffer from the world at large.
Show me the man who rules his household well:
I'll show you someone fit to rule the state.
That good man, my son,
I have every confidence he and he alone
can give commands and take them too. Staunch
in the storm of spears he'll stand his ground,
a loyal, unflinching comrade at your side.

But whoever steps out of line, violates the laws
or presumes to hand out orders to his superiors,
he'll win no praise from me. But that man
the city places in authority, his orders
must be obeyed, large and small,
right and wrong.
Anarchy —
show me a greater crime in all the earth!
She, she destroys cities, rips up houses,
breaks the ranks of spearmen into headlong rout.
But the ones who last it out, the great mass of them
owe their lives to discipline. Therefore
we must defend the men who live by law,
never let some woman triumph over us.
Better to fall from power, if fall we must,
at the hands of a man — never be rated
inferior to a woman, never.

Leader: To us,
unless old age has robbed us of our wits,
you seem to say what you have to say with sense.

Haemon: Father, only the gods endow a man with reason,
the finest of all their gifts, a treasure.
Far be it from me — I haven't the skill,
and certainly no desire, to tell you when,
if ever, you make a slip in speech . . . though
someone else might have a good suggestion.

Of course it's not for you,
in the normal run of things, to watch
whatever men say or do, or find to criticize.
The man in the street, you know, dreads your glance,
he'd never say anything displeasing to your face.
But it's for me to catch the murmurs in the dark,
the way the city mourns for this young girl.
"No woman," they say, "ever deserved death less,
and such a brutal death for such a glorious action.
She, with her own dear brother lying in his blood —
she couldn't bear to leave him dead, unburied,
food for the wild dogs or wheeling vultures.
Death? She deserves a glowing crown of gold!"
So they say, and the rumor spreads in secret,
darkly . . .
I rejoice in your success, father —
nothing more precious to me in the world.
What medal of honor brighter to his children
than a father's growing glory? Or a child's
to his proud father? Now don't, please,
be quite so single-minded, self-involved,
or assume the world is wrong and you are right.
Whoever thinks that he alone possesses intelligence,
the gift of eloquence, he and no one else,
and character too . . . such men, I tell you,
spread them open — you will find them empty.

No,
it's no disgrace for a man, even a wise man,
to learn many things and not to be too rigid.
You've seen trees by a raging winter torrent,
how many sway with the flood and salvage every twig,
but not the stubborn — they're ripped out, roots and all.
Bend or break. The same when a man is sailing:
haul your sheets too taut, never give an inch,
you'll capsize, go the rest of the voyage
keel-up and the rowing-benches under.

Oh give way. Relax your anger — change!
I'm young, I know, but let me offer this:

it would be best by far, I admit,
if a man were born infallible, right by nature.
If not — and things don't often go that way,
it's best to learn from those with good advice.
Leader: You'd do well, my lord, if he's speaking to the point,
to learn from him,

Turning to Haemon.

and you, my boy, from him.
You both are talking sense.
Creon: So,
men our age, we're to be lectured, are we? —
schooled by a boy his age?
Haemon: Only in what is right. But if I seem young,
look less to my years and more to what I do.
Creon: Do? Is admiring rebels an achievement?
Haemon: I'd never suggest that you admire treason.
Creon: Oh? —
isn't that just the sickness that's attacked her?
Haemon: The whole city of Thebes denies it, to a man.
Creon: And is Thebes about to tell me how to rule?
Haemon: Now, you see? Who's talking like a child?
Creon: Am I to rule this land for others — or myself?
Haemon: It's no city at all, owned by one man alone.
Creon: What? The city *is* the king's — that's the law!
Haemon: What a splendid king you'd make of a desert island —
you and you alone.
Creon:

To the Chorus.

This boy, I do believe,
is fighting on her side, the woman's side.
Haemon: If you are a woman, yes;
my concern is all for you.
Creon: Why, you degenerate — bandying accusations,
threatening me with justice, your own father!
Haemon: I see my father offending justice — wrong.
Creon: Wrong?
To protect my royal rights?
Haemon: Protect your rights?
When you trample down the honors of the gods?
Creon: You, you soul of corruption, rotten through —
woman's accomplice!
Haemon: That may be,
but you'll never find me accomplice to a criminal.
Creon: That's what *she* is,
and every word you say is a blatant appeal for her —
Haemon: And you, and me, and the gods beneath the earth.
Creon: You'll never marry her, not while she's alive.

Haemon: Then she'll die . . . but her dea
Creon: What, brazen threats? You go too f
Haemon:
Combating your empty, mindless jud
Creon: You'll suffer for your sermons, y
Haemon: If you weren't my father, I'd s
Creon: Don't flatter me with Father — y
Haemon: You really expect to fling abu
and not receive the same?
Creon: Is
Now, by heaven, I promise you, y
taunting, insulting me! Bring her
that hateful — she'll die now, her
in front of his eyes, beside her g
Haemon: No, no, she will never die
don't delude yourself. And you will never
see me, never set eyes on my face again.
Rage your heart out, rage with friends
who can stand the sight of you.

Rushing out.

Leader: Gone, my king, in a burst of anger.
A temper young as his . . . hurt him once,
he may do something violent.
Creon: Let him do —
dream up something desperate, past all human limit!
Good riddance. Rest assured,
he'll never save those two young girls from death.
Leader: Both of them, you really intend to kill them both?
Creon: No, not her, the one whose hands are clean;
you're quite right.
Leader: But Antigone —
what sort of death do you have in mind for her?
Creon: I'll take her down some wild, desolate path
never trod by men, and wall her up alive
in a rocky vault, and set out short rations,
just a gesture of piety
to keep the entire city free of defilement.
There let her pray to the one god she worships:
Death — who knows? — may just reprieve her from death.
Or she may learn at last, better late than never,
what a waste of breath it is to worship Death.

Exit to the palace.

Chorus: Love, never conquered in battle
Love the plunderer laying waste the rich!
Love standing the night-watch
guarding a girl's soft cheek,
you range the seas, the shepherds' steadings off in the wilds —

ods can flee your onset,
or a day —
grip is driven mad.
Love
minds of the righteous into outrage,
to their ruin — you have ignited this,
d strife, father and son at war
and Love alone the victor —
glance of the bride triumphant, burning with desire!
oned in power, side-by-side with the mighty laws!
resistible Aphrodite,° never conquered —
Love, you mock us for your sport.

Antigone is brought from the palace under guard.

But now, even I'd rebel against the king,
I'd break all bounds when I see this —
I fill with tears, can't hold them back,
not any more . . . I see Antigone make her way
to the bridal vault where all are laid to rest.

Antigone: Look at me, men of my fatherland,
setting out on the last road
looking into the last light of day
the last I'll ever see . . .
the god of death who puts us all to bed
takes me down to the banks of Acheron° alive —
denied my part in the wedding-songs,
no wedding-song in the dusk has crowned my marriage —
I go to wed the lord of the dark waters.

Chorus: Not crowned with glory, crowned with a dirge,
you leave for the deep pit of the dead.
No withering illness laid you low,
no strokes of the sword — a law to yourself,
alone, no mortal like you, ever, you go down
to the halls of Death alive and breathing.

Antigone: But think of Niobe° — well I know her story —
think what a living death she died,
Tantalus' daughter, stranger queen from the east:
there on the mountain heights, growing stone
binding as ivy, slowly walled her round
and the rains will never cease, the legends say
the snows will never leave her . . .
wasting away, under her brows the tears
showering down her breasting ridge and slopes —
a rocky death like hers puts me to sleep.

893 *Aphrodite:* Goddess of love. 905 *Acheron:* A river in the underworld, to which the dead go. 915 *Niobe:* A queen of Thebes who was punished by the gods for her pride and was turned into stone.

Chorus: But she was a god, born of gods,
and we are only mortals born to die.
And yet, of course, it's a great thing
for a dying girl to hear, just hear
she shares a destiny equal to the gods,
during life and later, once she's dead.
Antigone: O you mock me!
Why, in the name of all my fathers' gods
why can't you wait till I am gone —
must you abuse me to my face?
O my city, all your fine rich sons!
And you, you springs of the Dirce,
holy grove of Thebes where the chariots gather,
you at least, you'll bear me witness, look,
unmourned by friends and forced by such crude laws
I go to my rockbound prison, strange new tomb —
always a stranger, O dear god,
I have no home on earth and none below,
not with the living, not with the breathless dead.
Chorus: You went too far, the last limits of daring —
smashing against the high throne of Justice!
Your life's in ruins, child — I wonder . . .
do you pay for your father's terrible ordeal?
Antigone: There — at last you've touched it, the worst pain
the worst anguish! Raking up the grief for father
three times over, for all the doom
that's struck us down, the brilliant house of Laius.
O mother, your marriage-bed
the coiling horrors, the coupling there —
you with your own son, my father — doomstruck mother!
Such, such were my parents, and I their wretched child.
I go to them now, cursed, unwed, to share their home —
I am a stranger! O dear brother, doomed
in your marriage — your marriage murders mine,
your dying drags me down to death alive!

Enter Creon.

Chorus: Reverence asks some reverence in return —
but attacks on power never go unchecked,
not by the man who holds the reins of power.
Your own blind will, your passion has destroyed you.
Antigone: No one to weep for me, my friends,
no wedding-song — they take me away
in all my pain . . . the road lies open, waiting.
Never again, the law forbids me to see
the sacred eye of day. I am agony!
No tears for the destiny that's mine,
no loved one mourns my death.

Chorus: Can't you see?
If a man could wail his own dirge *before* he dies,
he'd never finish.

To the guards.

Take her away, quickly!
Wall her up in the tomb, you have your orders.
Abandon her there, alone, and let her choose —
death or a buried life with a good roof for shelter.
As for myself, my hands are clean. This young girl —
dead or alive, she will be stripped of her rights,
her stranger's rights, here in the world above.

Antigone: O tomb, my bridal-bed — my house, my prison
cut in the hollow rock, my everlasting watch!
I'll soon be there, soon embrace my own,
the great growing family of our dead
Persephone° has received among her ghosts.
I,
the last of them all, the most reviled by far,
go down before my destined time's run out.
But still I go, cherishing one good hope:
my arrival may be dear to father,
dear to you, my mother,
dear to you, my loving brother, Eteocles —
When you died I washed you with my hands,
I dressed you all, I poured the cups
across your tombs. But now, Polynices,
because I laid your body out as well,
this, this is my reward. Nevertheless
I honored you — the decent will admit it —
well and wisely too.
Never, I tell you,
if I had been the mother of children
or if my husband died, exposed and rotting —
I'd never have taken this ordeal upon myself,
never defied our people's will. What law,
you ask, do I satisfy with what I say?
A husband dead, there might have been another.
A child by another too, if I had lost the first.
But mother and father both lost in the halls of Death,
no brother could ever spring to light again.

For this law alone I held you first in honor.
For this, Creon, the king, judges me a criminal
guilty of dreadful outrage, my dear brother!
And now he leads me off, a captive in his hands,
with no part in the bridal-song, the bridal-bed,

982 *Persephone:* Queen of the underworld.

denied all joy of marriage, raising children —
deserted so by loved ones, struck by fate,
I descend alive to the caverns of the dead.

What law of the mighty gods have I transgressed?
Why look to the heavens any more, tormented as I am?
Whom to call, what comrades now? Just think,
my reverence only brands me for irreverence!
Very well: if this is the pleasure of the gods,
once I suffer I will know that I was wrong.
But if these men are wrong, let them suffer
nothing worse than they mete out to me —
these masters of injustice!

Leader: Still the same rough winds, the wild passion
raging through the girl.

Creon:

To the guards.

Take her away.
You're wasting time — you'll pay for it too.

Antigone: Oh god, the voice of death. It's come, it's here.

Creon: True. Not a word of hope — your doom is sealed.

Antigone: Land of Thebes, city of all my fathers —
O you gods, the first gods of the race!
They drag me away, now, no more delay.
Look on me, you noble sons of Thebes —
the last of a great line of kings,
I alone, see what I suffer now
at the hands of what breed of men —
all for reverence, my reverence for the gods!

She leaves under guard; the Chorus gathers.

Chorus: Danaë, Danaë° —
even she endured a fate like yours,
in all her lovely strength she traded
the light of day for the bolted brazen vault —
buried within her tomb, her bridal-chamber,
wed to the yoke and broken.
But she was of glorious birth
my child, my child
and treasured the seed of Zeus within her womb,
the cloudburst streaming gold!
The power of fate is a wonder,
dark, terrible wonder —
neither wealth nor armies
towered walls nor ships

1035 *Danaë:* Locked in a cell by her father because it was prophesied that her son would kill him, but visited by Zeus in the form of a shower of gold. Their son was Perseus.

black hulls lashed by the salt
can save us from that force.

The yoke tamed him too
young Lycurgus° flaming in anger
king of Edonia, all for his mad taunts
Dionysus clamped him down, encased
in the chain-mail of rock
and there his rage
his terrible flowering rage burst —
sobbing, dying away . . . at last that madman
came to know his god —
the power he mocked, the power
he taunted in all his frenzy
trying to stamp out
the women strong with the god —
the torch, the raving sacred cries —
enraging the Muses° who adore the flute.

And far north where the Black Rocks
cut the sea in half
and murderous straits
split the coast of Thrace
a forbidding city stands
where once, hard by the walls
the savage Ares thrilled to watch
a king's new queen, a Fury rearing in rage
against his two royal sons —
her bloody hands, her dagger-shuttle
stabbing out their eyes — cursed, blinding wounds —
their eyes blind sockets screaming for revenge!

They wailed in agony, cries echoing cries
the princes doomed at birth . . .
and their mother doomed to chains,
walled off in a tomb of stone —
but she traced her own birth back
to a proud Athenian line and the high gods
and off in caverns half the world away,
born of the wild North Wind
she sprang on her father's gales,
racing stallions up the leaping cliffs —
child of the heavens. But even on her the Fates
the gray everlasting Fates rode hard
my child, my child.

Enter Tiresias, the blind prophet, led by a boy.

1052 *Lycurgus:* Punished by Dionysus because he would not worship him. 1065 *Muses:* Goddesses of the arts.

Tiresias: Lords of Thebes,
I and the boy have come together,
hand in hand. Two see with the eyes of one . . .
so the blind must go, with a guide to lead the way.
Creon: What is it, old Tiresias? What news now?
Tiresias: I will teach you. And you obey the seer.
Creon: I will,
I've never wavered from your advice before.
Tiresias: And so you kept the city straight on course.
Creon: I owe you a great deal, I swear to that.
Tiresias: Then reflect, my son: you are poised,
once more, on the razor-edge of fate.
Creon: What is it? I shudder to hear you.
Tiresias: You will learn
when you listen to the warnings of my craft.
As I sat on the ancient seat of augury,°
in the sanctuary where every bird I know
will hover at my hands — suddenly I heard it,
a strange voice in the wingbeats, unintelligible,
barbaric, a mad scream! Talons flashing, ripping,
they were killing each other — that much I knew —
the murderous fury whirring in those wings
made that much clear!
I was afraid,
I turned quickly, tested the burnt-sacrifice,
ignited the altar at all points — but no fire,
the god in the fire never blazed.
Not from those offerings . . . over the embers
slid a heavy ooze from the long thighbones,
smoking, sputtering out, and the bladder
puffed and burst — spraying gall into the air —
and the fat wrapping the bones slithered off
and left them glistening white. No fire!
The rites failed that might have blazed the future
with a sign. So I learned from the boy here;
he is my guide, as I am guide to others.
And it's you —
your high resolve that sets this plague on Thebes.
The public altars and sacred hearths are fouled,
one and all, by the birds and dogs with carrion
torn from the corpse, the doomstruck son of Oedipus!
And so the gods are deaf to our prayers, they spurn
the offerings in our hands, the flame of holy flesh.
No birds cry out an omen clear and true —
they're gorged with the murdered victim's blood and fat.
Take these things to heart, my son, I warn you.
All men make mistakes, it is only human.

1103 *seat of augury:* Where Tiresias looked for omens among birds.

But once the wrong is done, a man
can turn his back on folly, misfortune too,
if he tries to make amends, however low he's fallen,
and stops his bullnecked ways. Stubbornness
brands you for stupidity — pride is a crime.
No, yield to the dead!
Never stab the fighter when he's down.
Where's the glory, killing the dead twice over?

I mean you well. I give you sound advice.
It's best to learn from a good adviser
when he speaks for your own good:
it's pure gain.

Creon: Old man — all of you! So,
you shoot your arrows at my head like archers at the target —
I even have *him* loosed on me, this fortune-teller.
Oh his ilk has tried to sell me short
and ship me off for years. Well,
drive your bargains, traffic — much as you like —
in the gold of India, silver-gold of Sardis.
You'll never bury that body in the grave,
not even if Zeus's eagles rip the corpse
and wing their rotten pickings off to the throne of god!
Never, not even in fear of such defilement
will I tolerate his burial, that traitor.
Well I know, we can't defile the gods —
no mortal has the power.
No,
reverend old Tiresias, all men fall,
it's only human, but the wisest fall obscenely
when they glorify obscene advice with rhetoric —
all for their own gain.

Tiresias: Oh god, is there a man alive
who knows, who actually believes . . .

Creon: What now?
What earth-shattering truth are you about to utter?

Tiresias: . . . just how much a sense of judgment, wisdom
is the greatest gift we have?

Creon: Just as much, I'd say,
as a twisted mind is the worst affliction going.

Tiresias: You are the one who's sick, Creon, sick to death.

Creon: I am in no mood to trade insults with a seer.

Tiresias: You have already, calling my prophecies a lie.

Creon: Why not?
You and the whole breed of seers are mad for money!

Tiresias: And the whole race of tyrants lusts to rake it in.

Creon: This slander of yours —
are you aware you're speaking to the king?

Tiresias: Well aware. Who helped you save the city?

Creon: You —
you have your skills, old seer, but you lust for injustice!
Tiresias: You will drive me to utter the dreadful secret in my heart.
Creon: Spit it out! Just don't speak it out for profit.
Tiresias: Profit? No, not a bit of profit, not for you.
Creon: Know full well, you'll never buy off my resolve.
Tiresias: Then know this too, learn this by heart!
The chariot of the sun will not race through
so many circuits more, before you have surrendered
one born of your own loins, your own flesh and blood,
a corpse for corpses given in return, since you have thrust
to the world below a child sprung for the world above,
ruthlessly lodged a living soul within the grave —
then you've robbed the gods below the earth,
keeping a dead body here in the bright air,
unburied, unsung, unhallowed by the rites.

You, you have no business with the dead,
nor do the gods above — this is violence
you have forced upon the heavens.
And so the avengers, the dark destroyers late
but true to the mark, now lie in wait for you,
the Furies sent by the gods and the god of death
to strike you down with the pains that you perfected!

There. Reflect on that, tell me I've been bribed.
The day comes soon, no long test of time, not now,
that wakes the wails for men and women in your halls.
Great hatred rises against you —
cities in tumult, all whose mutilated sons
the dogs have graced with burial, or the wild beasts,
some wheeling crow that wings the ungodly stench of carrion
back to each city, each warrior's hearth and home.

These arrows for your heart! Since you've raked me
I loose them like an archer in my anger,
arrows deadly true. You'll never escape
their burning, searing force.

Motioning to his escort.

Come, boy, take me home.
So he can vent his rage on younger men,
and learn to keep a gentler tongue in his head
and better sense than what he carries now.

Exit to the side.

Leader: The old man's gone, my king —
terrible prophecies. Well I know,
since the hair on this old head went gray,
he's never lied to Thebes.

Creon: I know it myself — I'm shaken, torn.
It's a dreadful thing to yield . . . but resist now?
Lay my pride bare to the blows of ruin?
That's dreadful too.
Leader: But good advice,
Creon, take it now, you must.
Creon: What should I do? Tell me . . . I'll obey.
Leader: Go! Free the girl from the rockey vault
and raise a mound for the body you exposed.
Creon: That's your advice? You think I should give in?
Leader: Yes, my king, quickly. Disasters sent by the gods
cut short our follies in a flash.
Creon: Oh it's hard.
giving up the heart's desire . . . but I will do it —
no more fighting a losing battle with necessity.
Leader: Do it now, go, don't leave it to others.
Creon: Now — I'm on my way! Come, each of you,
take up axes, make for the high ground,
over there, quickly! I and my better judgment
have come round to this — I shackled her,
I'll set her free myself. I am afraid . . .
it's best to keep the established laws
to the very day we die.

Rushing out, followed by his entourage. The Chorus clusters around the altar.

Chorus: God of a hundred names!
Great Dionysus —
Son and glory of Semele! Pride of Thebes —
Child of Zeus whose thunder rocks the clouds —
Lord of the famous lands of evening —
King of the Mysteries!
King of Eleusis, Demeter's plain°
her breasting hills that welcome in the world —
Great Dionysus!
Bacchus,° living in Thebes
the mother-city of all your frenzied women —
Bacchus
living along the Ismenus'° rippling waters
standing over the field sown with the Dragon's teeth!

You — we have seen you through the flaring smoky fires,
your torches blazing over the twin peaks
where nymphs of the hallowed cave climb onward
fired with you, your sacred rage —
we have seen you at Castalia's running spring°

1243 *Demeter's plain:* The goddess of grain was worshiped at Eleusis, near Athens. 1245 *Bacchus:* Another name for Dionysus. 1247 *Ismenus:* A river near Thebes where the founders of the city were said to have sprung from a dragon's teeth. 1253 *Castalia's running spring:* The sacred spring of Apollo's oracle at Delphi.

and down from the heights of Nysa° crowned with ivy
the greening shore rioting vines and grapes
        down you come in your storm of wild women
                ecstatic, mystic cries —
                                Dionysus —
down to watch and ward the roads of Thebes!

First of all cities, Thebes you honor first
you and your mother, bride of the lightning —
come, Dionysus! now your people lie
in the iron grip of plague,
come in your racing, healing stride
                down Parnassus'° slopes
or across the moaning straits.
                        Lord of the dancing —
dance, dance the constellations breathing fire!
Great master of the voices of the night!
Child of Zeus, God's offspring, come, come forth!
Lord, king, dance with your nymphs, swirling, raving
arm-in-arm in frenzy through the night
    they dance you, Iacchus° —
                        Dance, Dionysus
giver of all good things!

Enter a Messenger from the side.

Messenger: Neighbors,
friends of the house of Cadmus° and the kings,
there's not a thing in this life of ours
I'd praise or blame as settled once for all.
Fortune lifts and Fortune fells the lucky
and unlucky every day. No prophet on earth
can tell a man his fate. Take Creon:
there was a man to rouse your envy once,
as I see it. He saved the realm from enemies;
taking power, he alone, the lord of the fatherland,
he set us true on course — flourished like a tree
with the noble line of sons he bred and reared . . .
and now it's lost, all gone.
                        Believe me,
when a man has squandered his true joys,
he's good as dead, I tell you, a living corpse.
Pile up riches in your house, as much as you like —
live like a king with a huge show of pomp,
but if real delight is missing from the lot,
I wouldn't give you a wisp of smoke for it,
not compared with joy.

1254 *Nysa:* A mountain where Dionysus was worshiped. 1264 *Parnassus:* A mountain in Greece that was sacred to Dionysus as well as other gods and goddesses. 1271 *Iacchus:* Dionysus. 1274 *Cadmus:* The legendary founder of Thebes.

Leader: What now?
What new grief do you bring the house of kings?
Messenger: Dead, dead — and the living are guilty of their death!
Leader: Who's the murderer? Who is dead? Tell us.
Messenger: Haemon's gone, his blood spilled by the very hand —
Leader: His father's or his own?
Messenger: His own . . .
raging mad with his father for the death —
Leader: Oh great seer,
you saw it all, you brought your word to birth!
Messenger: Those are the facts. Deal with them as you will.

As he turns to go, Eurydice enters from the palace.

Leader: Look, Eurydice. Poor woman, Creon's wife,
so close at hand. By chance perhaps,
unless she's heard the news about her son.
Eurydice: My countrymen,
all of you — I caught the sound of your words
as I was leaving to do my part,
to appeal to queen Athena° with my prayers.
I was just loosing the bolts, opening the doors,
when a voice filled with sorrow, family sorrow,
struck my ears, and I fell back, terrified,
into the women's arms — everything went black.
Tell me the news, again, whatever it is . . .
sorrow and I are hardly strangers;
I can bear the worst.
Messenger: I — dear lady,
I'll speak as an eye-witness. I was there.
And I won't pass over one word of the truth.
Why should I try to soothe you with a story,
only to prove a liar in a moment?
Truth is always best.
So,
I escorted your lord, I guided him
to the edge of the plain where the body lay,
Polynices, torn by the dogs and still unmourned.
And saying a prayer to Hecate of the Crossroads,
Pluto° too, to hold their anger and be kind,
we washed the dead in a bath of holy water
and plucking some fresh branches, gathering . . .
what was left of him, we burned them all together
and raised a high mound of native earth, and then
we turned and made for that rocky vault of hers,
the hollow, empty bed of the bride of Death.
And far off, one of us heard a voice,

1305 *Athena:* Goddess of wisdom and protector of Greek cities. 1321–22 *Hecate, Pluto:* Gods of the underworld.

a long wail rising, echoing
out of that unhallowed wedding-chamber;
he ran to alert the master and Creon pressed on,
closer — the strange, inscrutable cry came sharper,
throbbing around him now, and he let loose
a cry of his own, enough to wrench the heart,
"Oh god, am I the prophet now? going down
the darkest road I've ever gone? My son —
it's *his* dear voice, he greets me! Go, men,
closer, quickly! Go through the gap,
the rocks are dragged back —
right to the tomb's very mouth — and look,
see if it's Haemon's voice I think I hear,
or the gods have robbed me of my senses."
The king was shattered. We took his orders,
went and searched, and there in the deepest,
dark recesses of the tomb we found her . . .
hanged by the neck in a fine linen noose,
strangled in her veils — and the boy,
his arms flung around her waist,
clinging to her, wailing for his bride,
dead and down below, for his father's crimes
and the bed of his marriage blighted by misfortune.
When Creon saw him, he gave a deep sob,
he ran in, shouting, crying out to him,
"Oh my child — what have you done? what seized you,
what insanity? what disaster drove you mad?
Come out, my son! I beg you on my knees!"
But the boy gave him a wild burning glance,
spat in his face, not a word in reply,
he drew his sword — his father rushed out,
running as Haemon lunged and missed! —
and then, doomed, desperate with himself,
suddenly leaning his full weight on the blade,
he buried it in his body, halfway to the hilt.
And still in his senses, pouring his arms around her,
he embraced the girl and breathing hard,
released a quick rush of blood,
bright red on her cheek glistening white.
And there he lies, body enfolding body . . .
he has won his bride at last, poor boy,
not here but in the houses of the dead.

Creon shows the world that of all the ills
afflicting men the worst is lack of judgment.

Eurydice turns and reenters the palace.

Leader: What do you make of that? The lady's gone,
without a word, good or bad.

Messenger: I'm alarmed too
but here's my hope — faced with her son's death,
she finds it unbecoming to mourn in public.
Inside, under her roof, she'll set her women
to the task and wail the sorrow of the house.
She's too discreet. She won't do something rash.
Leader: I'm not so sure. To me, at least,
a long heavy silence promises danger,
just as much as a lot of empty outcries.
Messenger: We'll see if she's holding something back,
hiding some passion in her heart.
I'm going in. You may be right — who knows?
Even too much silence has its dangers.

Exit to the palace. Enter Creon from the side, escorted by attendants carrying Haemon's body on a bier.

Leader: The king himself! Coming toward us,
look, holding the boy's head in his hands.
Clear, damning proof, if it's right to say so —
proof of his own madness, no one else's,
no, his own blind wrongs.
Creon: Ohhh,
so senseless, so insane . . . my crimes,
my stubborn, deadly —
Look at us, the killer, the killed,
father and son, the same blood — the misery!
My plans, my mad fanatic heart,
my son, cut off so young!
Ai, dead, lost to the world,
not through your stupidity, no, my own.
Leader: Too late,
too late, you see what justice means.
Creon: Oh I've learned
through blood and tears! Then, it was then,
when the god came down and struck me — a great weight
shattering, driving me down that wild savage path,
ruining, trampling down my joy. Oh the agony,
the heartbreaking agonies of our lives.

Enter the Messenger from the palace.

Messenger: Master,
what a hoard of grief you have, and you'll have more.
The grief that lies to hand you've brought yourself —

Pointing to Haemon's body.

the rest, in the house, you'll see it all too soon.
Creon: What now? What's worse than this?
Messenger: The queen is dead.

The mother of this dead boy . . . mother to the end —
poor thing, her wounds are fresh.

Creon: No, no,
harbor of Death, so choked, so hard to cleanse! —
why me? why are you killing me?
Herald of pain, more words, more grief?
I died once, you kill me again and again!
What's the report, boy . . . some news for me?
My wife dead? O dear god!
Slaughter heaped on slaughter?

The doors open; the body of Eurydice is brought out on her bier.

Messenger: See for yourself:
now they bring her body from the palace.

Creon: Oh no,
another, a second loss to break the heart.
What next, what fate still waits for me?
I just held my son in my arms and now,
look, a new corpse rising before my eyes —
wretched, helpless mother — O my son!

Messenger: She stabbed herself at the altar,
then her eyes went dark, after she'd raised
a cry for the noble fate of Megareus,° the hero
killed in the first assault, then for Haemon,
then with her dying breath she called down
torments on your head — you killed her sons.

Creon: Oh the dread,
I shudder with dread! Why not kill me too? —
run me through with a good sharp sword?
Oh god, the misery, anguish —
I, I'm churning with it, going under.

Messenger: Yes, and the dead, the woman lying there,
piles the guilt of all their deaths on you.

Creon: How did she end her life, what bloody stroke?

Messenger: She drove home to the heart with her own hand,
once she learned her son was dead . . . that agony.

Creon: And the guilt is all mine —
can never be fixed on another man,
no escape for me. I killed you,
I, god help me, I admit it all!

To his attendants.

Take me away, quickly, out of sight.
I don't even exist — I'm no one. Nothing.

Leader: Good advice, if there's any good in suffering.
Quickest is best when troubles block the way.

1428 *Megareus:* A son of Creon and Eurydice; he died when Thebes was attacked.

Creon:

Kneeling in prayer.

Come, let it come! — that best of fates for me
that brings the final day, best fate of all.
Oh quickly, now —
so I never have to see another sunrise.

Leader: That will come when it comes;
we must deal with all that lies before us.
The future rests with the ones who tend the future.

Creon: That prayer — I poured my heart into that prayer!

Leader: No more prayers now. For mortal men
there is no escape from the doom we must endure.

Creon: Take me away, I beg you, out of sight.
A rash, indiscriminate fool!
I murdered you, my son, against my will —
you too, my wife . . .
Wailing wreck of a man,
whom to look to? where to lean for support?

Desperately turning from Haemon to Eurydice on their biers.

Whatever I touch goes wrong — once more
a crushing fate's come down upon my head.

The Messenger and attendants lead Creon into the palace.

Chorus: Wisdom is by far the greatest part of joy,
and reverence toward the gods must be safeguarded.
The mighty words of the proud are paid in full
with mighty blows of fate, and at long last
those blows will teach us wisdom.

The old citizens exit to the side.

Considerations

1. What are Creon's reasons for issuing the decree forbidding Polynices' burial? What are Antigone's reasons for rejecting Creon's order? Whose arguments are more convincing?
2. What is the Chorus's position on Creon's decree? Does the Chorus see the conflict between Antigone and Creon as simply a collision between two strong-willed individuals, or does it see a larger issue at stake?
3. Despite the title, it is sometimes argued that the protagonist of the play is Creon rather than Antigone, because he undergoes a significant change, while she has already died offstage. Whose story is it?
4. How does Ismene serve as a foil to Antigone? Does Ismene seem weak, or is she reasonable? Why does Antigone reject her sister's offer to martyr herself?
5. How does Haemon serve as a foil to Creon? Is Haemon's decision to commit suicide plausible?
6. What is Creon's attitute toward women? How does this affect his reaction to Antigone's disobedience to the state?
7. Who is responsible for what happens? Does Sophocles suggest that the tragedy

could have been avoided if Creon or Antigone had behaved differently? Do Creon and Antigone share any similar characteristics?

8. Describe what you think Sophocles' attitudes were concerning the competing claims for the authority of the state over the individual. Explain how those views are indicated in the play and whether you agree or disagree with them.
9. How might the emphasis of the play have been changed if Sophocles had included the scene in the tomb between Haemon and Antigone? Why do you think he left out such a potentially affecting scene?
10. If you were to stage this play in a contemporary setting, describe what kinds of sets you would use and how you would costume the players.

Connections

1. How is Creon's reaction to Haemon's and Tiresias's pleas that he rescind the decree similar to Oedipus's reaction to Creon and Tiresias in *Oedipus the King?*
2. What similarities and differences are there in Sophocles' characterization of Creon in *Antigone* and in *Oedipus the King?*
3. Consider this assessment of Antigone by the leader of the Chorus (lines 525–27):

   Like father like daughter,
   passionate, wild . . .
   she hasn't learned to bend before adversity.

   Does this accurately characterize Antigone? What similarities are there between Oedipus and his daughter? Could these lines also be used to describe Haemon and Ismene?
4. Imagine Antigone as one of the top girls at the dinner party in Caryl Churchill's *Top Girls* (p. 1603). Write a monologue for her that reveals her character.

PERSPECTIVES ON SOPHOCLES

ARISTOTLE (384–322 B.C.)

On Tragic Character c. 340 B.C.

Now since in the finest kind of tragedy the structure should be complex and not simple, and since it should also be a representation of terrible and piteous events (that being the special mark of this type of imitation), in the first place, it is evident that good men ought not to be shown passing from happiness to misfortune, for this does not inspire either pity or fear, but only revulsion; nor evil men rising from ill fortune to prosperity, for this is the most untragic plot of all — it lacks every requirement, in that it neither elicts human sympathy nor stirs pity or fear. And again, neither should an extremely wicked man be seen falling from prosperity into misfortune, for a plot so constructed might indeed call forth human sympathy, but would not excite pity or fear, since the first is felt for a person whose misfortune is undeserved and the second for someone like ourselves — pity for the man suffering undeservedly, fear for the man like ourselves — and hence neither pity nor fear would be aroused in this case. We are left with the man whose place is between these extremes. Such is the man who on the one hand is not pre-eminent in virtue and justice, and yet on the other hand does not fall into misfortune through vice or depravity, but falls because of some mistake; one among the number of the highly renowned and prosperous, such as Oedipus . . . and other famous men from families like [his].

It follows that the plot which achieves excellence will necessarily be single in outcome and not, as some say, double, and will consist in a change of fortune, not to prosperity from misfortune, but the opposite, from prosperity to misfortune, occasioned not by depravity, but by some great mistake on the part of one who is either such as I have described or better than this rather than worse. What actually has taken place has confirmed this; for though at first the poets accepted whatever myths came to hand, today the finest tragedies are founded upon the stories of only a few houses . . . and such . . . as have chanced to suffer terrible things or to do them. So then, tragedy having this construction is the finest kind of tragedy from an artistic point of view. And consequently those persons fall into the same error who bring it as a charge against Euripides° that this is what he does in his tragedies and that most of his plays have unhappy endings. For this is in fact the right procedure, as I have said; and the best proof is that on the stage and in the dramatic contests, plays of this kind seem the most tragic, provided they are successfully worked out, and Euripides, even if in everything else his management is faulty, seems at any rate to be the most tragic of the poets.

Second to this is the kind of plot that some persons place first, that which like the *Odyssey*° has a double structure and ends in opposite ways for the better characters and the worse. If it seems to be first, that is attributable to the weakness of the audience, since the poets only follow their lead and compose the kind of plays the spectators want. The pleasure it gives, however, is not that which comes from tragedy, but is rather the pleasure proper to comedy; for in comedy those who in the legend are the worst of enemies . . . end by leaving the scene as friends, and nobody is killed by anybody. . . .

With regard to the Characters there are four things to aim at. First and foremost is that the characters be good. The personages will have character if, as aforesaid, they reveal in speech or in action what their moral choices are, and a good character will be one whose choices are good. It is possible to portray goodness in every class of persons; a woman may be good and a slave may be good, though perhaps as a class women are inferior and slaves utterly base. The second requisite is to make the character appropriate. Thus it is possible to portray any character as manly, but inappropriate for a female character to be manly or formidable in the way I mean. Third is to make the characters lifelike, which is something different from making them good and appropriate as described above. Fourth is to make them consistent. Even if the person being imitated is inconsistent and this is what the character is supposed to be, he should nevertheless be portrayed as consistently inconsistent. . . .

In the characters and in the plot-construction alike, one must strive for that

Euripedes: Fifth century B.C. Greek playwright whose tragedies include *Electra, Medea,* and *Alcestis.*
Odyssey: The epic by the ancient Greek poet Homer that chronicles the voyage home from the Trojan War of Odysseus (also known as Ulysses).

which is either necessary or probable, so that whatever a character of any kind says or does may be the sort of thing such a character will inevitably or probably say or do and the events of the plot may follow one after another either inevitably or with probability. (Obviously, then, the *denouement* of the plot should arise from the plot itself and not be brought about "from the machine." . . . The machine is to be used for matters lying outside the drama, either antecedents of the action which a human being cannot know, or things subsequent to the action that have to be prophesied and announced; for we accept it that the gods see everything. Within the events of the plot itself, however, there should be nothing unreasonable, or if there is, it should be kept outside the play proper as is done in the *Oedipus* of Sophocles.)

Inasmuch as tragedy is an imitation of persons who are better than the average, the example of good portrait-painters should be followed. These, while reproducing the distinctive appearance of their subjects in a recognizable likeness, make them handsomer in the picture than they are in reality. Similarly the poet when he comes to imitate men who are irascible or easygoing or have other defects of character should depict them as such and yet as good men at the same time.

From *Poetics,* translated by James Hutton

Considerations

1. Why does Aristotle insist that both virtuous and depraved characters are unsuitable as tragic figures? What kind of person constitutes a tragic character according to him?
2. Aristotle argues that it is "inappropriate for a female character to be manly or formidable." Do you think Antigone fits this negative description? Does she seem "inferior" to the men in the play?
3. Aristotle says that characters should be "lifelike," but he also points out that characters should be made "handsomer . . . than they are in reality." Is this a contradiction? Explain why or why not.

SOPHOCLES (496?–406 B.C.)

Another Translation of a Scene from Oedipus the King

1920

Enter Oedipus, blind.

Chorus: O sight for all the world to see
Most terrible! O suffering
Of all mine eyes have seen most terrible!
Alas! What Fury came on thee?
What evil Spirit, from afar,
O Oedipus! O Wretched!
Leapt on thee, to destroy?

I cannot even Alas! look
Upon thy face, though much I have
To ask of thee, and much to hear,
Aye, and to see — I cannot!
Such terror is in thee!
Oedipus: Alas! O Wretched! Whither go
My steps? My voice? It seems to float
Far, far away from me.
Alas! Curse of my Life, how far
Thy leap hath carried thee!
Chorus: To sorrows none can bear to see or hear.
Oedipus: Ah! The cloud!
Visitor unspeakable! Darkness upon me horrible!
Unconquerable! Cloud that may not ever pass away!
Alas!
And yet again, alas! How deep they stab —
These throbbing pains, and all those memories.
Chorus: Where such afflictions are, I marvel not,
If soul and body made one doubled woe.
Oedipus: Ah! My friend!
Still remains thy friendship. Still thine is the help that comforts me,
And kindness, that can look upon these dreadful eyes unchanged.
Ah me!
My friend, I feel thy presence. Though mine eyes
Be darkened, yet I hear thy voice, and know.
Chorus: Oh, dreadful deed! How wert thou steeled to quench
Thy vision thus? What Spirit came on thee?
Oedipus: Apollo! 'Twas Apollo, friends,
Willed the evil, willed, and brought the agony to pass!
And yet the hand that struck was mine, mine only, wretched.
Why should I see, whose eyes
Had no more any good to look upon?
Chorus: 'Twas even as thou sayest.
Oedipus: Aye. For me . . . Nothing is left for sight.
Nor anything to love:
Nor shall the sound of greetings any more
Fall pleasant on my ear.
Away! Away! Out of the land, away!
Banishment, Banishment! Fatal am I, accursed,
And the hate on me, as on no man else, of the gods!
Chorus: Unhappy in thy fortune and the wit
That shows it thee. Would thou hadst never known.
Oedipus: A curse upon the hand that loosed
In the wilderness the cruel fetters of my feet,
Rescued me, gave me life! Ah! Cruel was his pity,
Since, had I died, so much
I had not harmed myself and all I love.
Chorus: Aye, even so 'twere better.
Oedipus: Aye, for life never had led me then

To shed my father's blood;
Men had not called me husband of the wife
That bore me in the womb.
But now — but now — Godless am I, the son
Born of impurity, mate of my father's bed,
And if worse there be, I am Oedipus! It is mine!

Chorus: In this I know not how to call thee wise,
For better wert thou dead than living — blind.

Oedipus: Nay, give me no more counsel. Bid me not
Believe my deed, thus done, is not well done.
I know 'tis well. When I had passed the grave,
How could those eyes have met my father's gaze,
Or my unhappy mother's — since on both
I have done wrongs beyond all other wrong?
Or live and see my children? — Children born
As they were born! What pleasure in that sight?
None for these eyes of mine, for ever, none.
Nor in the sight of Thebes, her castles, shrines
And images of the gods, whereof, alas!
I robbed myself — myself, I spoke that word,
I that she bred and nurtured, I her prince,
And bade her thrust the sinner out, the man
Proved of the gods polluted — Laïus' son.
When such a stain by my own evidence
Was on me, could I raise my eyes to them?
No! Had I means to stop my ears, and choke
The wells of sound, I had not held my hand,
But closed my body like a prison-house
To hearing as to sight. Sweet for the mind
To dwell withdrawn, where troubles could not come.
Cithaeron! Ah, why didst thou welcome me?
Why, when thou hadst me there, didst thou not kill,
Never to show the world myself — my birth!
O Polybus, and Corinth, and the home
Men called my father's ancient house, what sores
Festered beneath that beauty that ye reared,
Discovered now, sin out of sin begot.
O ye three roads, O secret mountain-glen,
Trees, and a pathway narrowed to the place
Where met the three, do you remember me?
I gave you blood to drink, my father's blood,
And so my own! Do you remember that?
The deed I wrought for you? Then, how I passed
Hither to other deeds?
O Marriage-bed
That gave me birth, and, having borne me, gave
Fresh children to your seed, and showed the world
Father, son, brother, mingled and confused,
Bride, mother, wife in one, and all the shame

Of deeds the foulest ever known to man.
No. Silence for a deed so ill to do
Is better. Therefore lead me hence, away!
To hide me or to kill. Or to the sea
Cast me, where you shall look on me no more.
Come! Deign to touch me, though I am a man
Accurséd. Yield! Fear nothing! Mine are woes
That no man else, but I alone, must bear.

Translated by J. T. Sheppard

Considerations

1. This excerpt from Sheppard's translation corresponds to lines 1433–1549 in Robert Fagles's translation (pp. 1000–1003). Examine both versions of the scene and describe the diction and tone of each. If you find one of the translations more effective than the other, indicate why.
2. Explain whether the different translations affect your understanding or interpretation of the scene.

MURIEL RUKEYSER (1913–1980)

On Oedipus the King

1973

MYTH

Long afterward, Oedipus, old and blinded, walked the
roads.   He smelled a familiar smell.   It was
the Sphinx.   Oedipus said, "I want to ask one question.
Why didn't I recognize my mother?"   "You gave the
wrong answer," said the Sphinx.   "But that was what
made everything possible," said Oedipus.   "No," she said.
"When I asked, What walks on four legs in the morning,
two at noon, and three in the evening, you answered,
Man.   You didn't say anything about woman."
"When you say Man," said Oedipus, "you include women
too. Everyone knows that."   She said, "That's what
you think."

Considerations

1. What elements of the Oedipus story does Rukeyser allude to in the poem?
2. To what does the title refer? How does the word *myth* carry more than one meaning?
3. This poem is amusing, but its ironic ending points to a serious theme. What is it? Does Sophocles' play address any of the issues raised in the poem?

JEAN ANOUILH (1910–1987)

A Scene from Antigone

1944

Creon: I shall save you yet. *(He goes below the table to the chair at end of table, takes off his coat, and places it on the chair.)* God knows, I have things enough to do today without wasting my time on an insect like you. There's plenty to do, I assure you, when you've just put down a revolution. But urgent things can wait. I am not going to let politics be the cause of your death. For it is a fact that this whole business is nothing but politics: the mournful shade of Polynices, the decomposing corpse, the sentimental weeping, and the hysteria that you mistake for heroism — nothing but politics.

Look here. I may not be soft, but I'm fastidious. I like things clean, shipshape, well scrubbed. Don't think that I am not just as offended as you are by the thought of that meat rotting in the sun. In the evening, when the breeze comes in off the sea, you can smell it in the palace, and it nauseates me. But I refuse even to shut my window. It's vile; and I can tell you what I wouldn't tell anybody else: it's stupid, monstrously stupid. But the people of Thebes have got to have their noses rubbed into it a little longer. My God! If it was up to me, I should have had them bury your brother long ago as a mere matter of public hygiene. I admit that what I am doing is childish. But if the featherheaded rabble I govern are to understand what's what, that stench has got to fill the town for a month!

Antigone (turns to him): You are a loathsome man!

Creon: I agree. My trade forces me to be. We could argue whether I ought or ought not to follow my trade; but once I take on the job, I must do it properly.

Antigone: Why do you do it at all?

Creon: My dear, I woke up one morning and found myself King of Thebes. God knows, there were other things I loved in life more than power.

Antigone: Then you should have said no.

Creon: Yes, I could have done that. Only, I felt that it would have been cowardly. I should have been like a workman who turns down a job that has to be done. So I said yes.

Antigone: So much the worse for you, then. I didn't say yes. I can say no to anything I think vile, and I don't have to count the cost. But because you said yes, all that you can do, for all your crown and your trappings, and your guards — all that you can do is to have me killed.

Creon: Listen to me.

Antigone: If I want to. I don't have to listen to you if I don't want to. You've said your *yes.* There is nothing more you can tell me that I don't know. You stand there, drinking in my words. *(She moves behind chair.)* Why is it that you don't call your guards? I'll tell you why. You want to hear me out to the end; that's why.

Creon: You amuse me.

Antigone: Oh, no, I don't. I frighten you. That is why you talk about saving me. Everything would be so much easier if you had a docile, tongue-tied little Antigone living in the palace. I'll tell you something, Uncle Creon: I'll give you back one of your own words. You are too fastidious to make a good tyrant. But you are going to have to put me to death today, and you know it. And that's what frightens you. God! Is there anything uglier than a frightened man!

Creon: Very well. I am afraid, then. Does that satisfy you? I am afraid that if you insist upon it, I shall have to have you killed. And I don't want to.

Antigone: I don't have to do things that I think are wrong. If it comes to that, you didn't really want to leave my brother's body unburied, did you? Say it! Admit that you didn't.

Creon: I have said it already.

Antigone: But you did it just the same. And now, though you don't want to do it, you are going to have me killed. And you call that being a king!

Creon: Yes, I call that being a king.

Antigone: Poor Creon! My nails are broken, my fingers are bleeding, my arms are covered with the welts left by the paws of your guards — but I am a queen!

Creon: Then why not have pity on me, and live? Isn't your brother's corpse, rotting there under my windows, payment enough for peace and order in Thebes? My son loves you. Don't make me add your life to the payment. I've paid enough.

Antigone: No, Creon! You said yes, and made yourself king. Now you will never stop paying.

Creon: But God in heaven! Won't you try to understand me! I'm trying hard enough to understand you! There had to be one man who said yes. Somebody had to agree to captain the ship. She had sprung a hundred leaks; she was loaded to the water line with crime, ignorance, poverty. The wheel was swinging with the wind. The crew refused to work and were looting the cargo. The officers were building a raft, ready to slip overboard and desert the ship. The mast was splitting, the wind was howling, the sails were beginning to rip. Every man jack on board was about to drown — and only because the only thing they thought of was their own skins and their cheap little day-to-day traffic. Was that a time, do you think, for playing with words like yes and no? Was that a time for a man to be weighing the pros and cons, wondering if he wasn't going to pay too dearly later on; if he wasn't going to lose his life, or his family, or his touch with other men? You grab the wheel, you right the ship in the face of a mountain of water. You shout an order, and if one man refuses to obey, you shoot straight into the mob. Into the mob, I say! The beast as nameless as the wave that crashes down upon your deck; as nameless as the whipping wind. The thing that drops when you shoot may be someone who poured you a drink the night before; but it has no name. And you, braced at the wheel, you have no name, either. Nothing has a name — except the ship, and the storm. *(A pause as he looks at her.)* Now do you understand?

Antigone: I am not here to understand. That's all very well for you. I am here to say no to you, and die.

Creon: It is easy to say no.

Antigone: Not always.

Creon: It is easy to say no. To say yes, you have to sweat and roll up your sleeves and plunge both hands into life up to the elbows. It is easy to say no, even if saying no means death. All you have to do is to sit still and wait. Wait to go on living; wait to be killed. That is the coward's part. *No* is one of your man-made words. Can you imagine a world in which trees say *no* to the sap? In which beasts say *no* to hunger or to propagation? Animals are good, simple, tough. They move in droves, nudging one another onwards, all traveling the same road. Some of them keel over, but the rest go on; and no matter how many may fall by the wayside, there are always those few left that go on bringing their young into the world, traveling the same road with the same obstinate will, unchanged from those who went before.

Antigone: Animals, eh, Creon! What a king you could be if only men were animals!

Translated by Lewis Galantière

Considerations

1. What are Creon's reasons for not burying Polynices? How does he defend his actions as a ruler?
2. In what sense is Antigone correct when she describes Creon as "too fastidious to make a good tyrant"?
3. Do you agree with Creon that Antigone takes "the coward's part" by saying no rather than yes? With which character do you sympathize more? How might Creon's position be related to the fact that France was occupied by German troops during World War II, when Anouilh wrote this play?
4. How does Anouilh's treatment of Creon compare with Sophocles'?

MAURICE SAGOFF

A Humorous Distillation of Antigone 1980

Tyrant Creon's stern advice is
"Do not bury Polynices!
Thebes' defenders had to squash him —
Now we'll let the buzzards nosh him!"
But Antigone, the brave,
Dared to dig her brother's grave:
"Man-made laws my soul defies —
Live by laws divine!" she cries.

Creon locks her up, the demon!
Though she's pledged to marry Haemon
(That's his son). Now comes a seer
Prophesying woes severe:
If her brother's not entombed
And she dies, then Haemon's doomed!

Creon seeing things go screwy,
Wilts, and tries to bang a U-ee,
But the Gods who drive the hearse
Seldom shove it in reverse . . .

Carnage follows, sure as Fate;
Here's the body-count to date —
1. Antigone 2. her brother
3. young Haemon 4. his mother
(If more bodies fail to fall,
It's because the cast is small).

Strung-out Creon takes the blame.
Exits, croaking "Rotten shame!"

From *Shrinklits: Seventy of the World's Towering Classics Cut Down to Size*

Considerations

1. Sagoff writes in his tongue-in-cheek introduction to *Shrinklits* that "inside every fat book is a skinny book trying to get out, struggling to cut through the mummylike wrappings of long-winded descriptions, superfluous characters, endless conversations, and turgid style." How successful is this poem in summarizing the plot of *Antigone?* What is left out of Sagoff's account?
2. Using Sagoff's version of *Antigone* as your inspiration, choose another play in the text and try writing a shrinklit that does it humorous justice.

26. A Study of William Shakespeare

Although relatively little is known about William Shakespeare's life, his writings reveal him to have been an extraordinary man. His vitality, compassion, and insights are evident in his broad range of characters, who have fascinated generations of audiences, and his powerful use of the English language, which has been celebrated since his death nearly four centuries ago. His contemporary Ben Jonson rightly claimed that "he was not of an age, but for all time!" Shakespeare's plays have been produced so often and his writings read so widely that quotations from them have woven their way into our everyday conversations. If you have ever experienced "fear and trembling" because there was "something in the wind" or discovered that it was "a foregone conclusion" that you would "make a virtue of necessity," then it wouldn't be quite accurate for you to say that Shakespeare "was Greek to me," because these phrases come, respectively, from his plays *Much Ado about Nothing, Comedy of Errors, Othello, The Two Gentlemen of Verona,* and *Julius Caesar.* Many more examples could be cited, but it is enough to say that Shakespeare's art endures. His words may give us only an oblique glimpse of his life, but they continue to give us back the experience of our own lives.

Shakespeare was born in Stratford-on-Avon on or about April 23, 1564. His father, an important citizen who held several town offices, married a woman from a prominent family; however, when their son was only a teenager, the family's financial situation became precarious. Shakespeare probably attended the Stratford grammar school, but no records of either his schooling or his early youth exist. As limited as his education was, it is clear that he was for his time a learned man. At the age of eighteen, he struck out on his own and married the twenty-six-year-old Anne Hathaway, who bore him a daughter in 1583 and twins, a boy and a girl, in 1585. Before he was twenty-one, Shakespeare had a wife and three children to support.

What his life was like for the next seven years is not known, but there is firm evidence that by 1592 he was in London enjoying some success as both an actor and a playwright. By 1594 he had also established himself as a poet with two lengthy poems, *Venus and Adonis* and *The Rape of Lucrece.* But it was in the theater that he made his living and his strongest reputation. He was well connected with a successful troupe first known as the Lord Chamberlain's Men; they built the famous Globe Theatre in 1599. Later this company, because of the patronage of King James, came to be known as the King's Men. Writing plays for this company throughout his career, Shakespeare also became one of its principal shareholders, an arrangement that allowed him to prosper in London as well as in his native Stratford, where in 1597 he bought a fine house called New Place. About 1611 he retired there with his family, although he continued writing plays. He died on April 23, 1616, and was buried at Holy Trinity Church in Stratford.

The documented details of Shakespeare's life provide barely enough information for a newspaper obituary. But if his activities remain largely unknown, his writings — among them thirty-seven plays and one hundred and fifty-four sonnets — more than compensate for that loss. Plenty of authors have produced more work, but no writer has created so much literature that has been so universally admired. Within twenty-five years Shakespeare's dramatic works included *Hamlet, Macbeth, King Lear, Othello, Julius Caesar, Richard III, 1 Henry IV, Romeo and Juliet, Love's Labour's Lost, A Midsummer Night's Dream, The Tempest, Twelfth Night,* and *Measure for Measure.* These plays represent a broad range of characters and actions conveyed in poetic language that reveals human nature as well as the author's genius.

SHAKESPEARE'S THEATER

Drama languished in Europe after the fall of Rome during the fifth and sixth centuries. From about A.D. 400 to 900 almost no record of dramatic productions exists except for those of minstrels and other entertainers, such as acrobats and jugglers, who traveled through the countryside. The Catholic church was instrumental in suppressing drama because the theater — represented by the excesses of Roman productions — was seen as subversive. No state-sponsored festivals brought people together in huge theaters the way they had in Greek and Roman times.

In the tenth century, however, the church helped revive theater by incorporating dialogues into the Mass as a means of dramatizing portions of the Gospels. These brief dialogues developed into more elaborate mystery plays, miracle plays, and morality plays, anonymous works that were created primarily to inculcate religious principles rather than to entertain. But these works also marked the reemergence of relatively large dramatic productions.

Mystery plays dramatize stories from the Bible, such as the Creation, the Fall of Adam and Eve, or the Crucifixion. The most highly regarded surviving example is *The Second Shepherd's Play* (c. 1400), which dramatizes

Christ's nativity. ***Miracle plays*** are based on the lives of saints. An extant play of the late fifteenth century, for example, is titled *Saint Mary Magdalene*. ***Morality plays*** present allegorical stories in which virtues and vices are personified to teach humanity how to achieve salvation. *Everyman* (c. 1500), the most famous example, has as its central conflict every person's struggle to avoid the sins that lead to Hell and practice the virtues that are rewarded in Heaven.

The clergy who performed these plays gave way to trade guilds that presented them outside the church on stages featuring scenery and costumed characters. The plays' didactic content was gradually abandoned in favor of broad humor and worldly concerns. Thus by the sixteenth century religious drama had been replaced largely by secular drama.

Because theatrical productions were no longer sponsored and financed by the church or trade guilds during Shakespeare's lifetime, playwrights had to figure out ways to draw audiences willing to pay for entertainment. This necessitated some simple but important changes. Somehow, people had to be prevented from seeing a production unless they paid. Hence an enclosed space with controlled access was created. In addition, the plays had to change frequently enough to keep audiences returning, and this resulted in more experienced actors and playwrights sensitive to their audiences' tastes and interests. Plays compelling enough to attract audiences had to employ powerful writing brought to life by convincing actors in entertaining productions. Shakespeare always wrote his dramas for the stage — for audiences who would see and hear his characters. The conventions of the theater for which he wrote are important, then, for appreciating and understanding his plays. Detailed information about Elizabethan theater (theater during the reign of Elizabeth I, from 1558 to 1603) is less than abundant, but historians have been able to piece together a good sense of what the theaters were like from sources such as drawings, building contracts, and stage directions.

Early performances of various kinds took place in the courtyards of inns and taverns. These secular entertainments attracted people of all classes. To the dismay of London officials, such gatherings were also settings for the illegal activities of brawlers, thieves, and prostitutes. To avoid licensing regulations, some theaters were constructed outside the city's limits. The Globe, for instance, built by the Lord Chamberlain's company with which Shakespeare was closely associated, was located on the south bank of the Thames River. Regardless of the play, an Elizabethan theatergoer was likely to have an exciting time. Playwrights understood the varied nature of their audiences, so the plays appealed to a broad range of sensibilities and tastes. Philosophy and poetry rubbed shoulders with violence and sexual jokes, and somehow all were made compatible.

Physically, Elizabethan theaters resembled the courtyards where they originated, but the theaters could accommodate more people — perhaps as many as twenty-five hundred. The exterior of a theater building was many-sided or round and enclosed a yard that was only partially roofed over, to

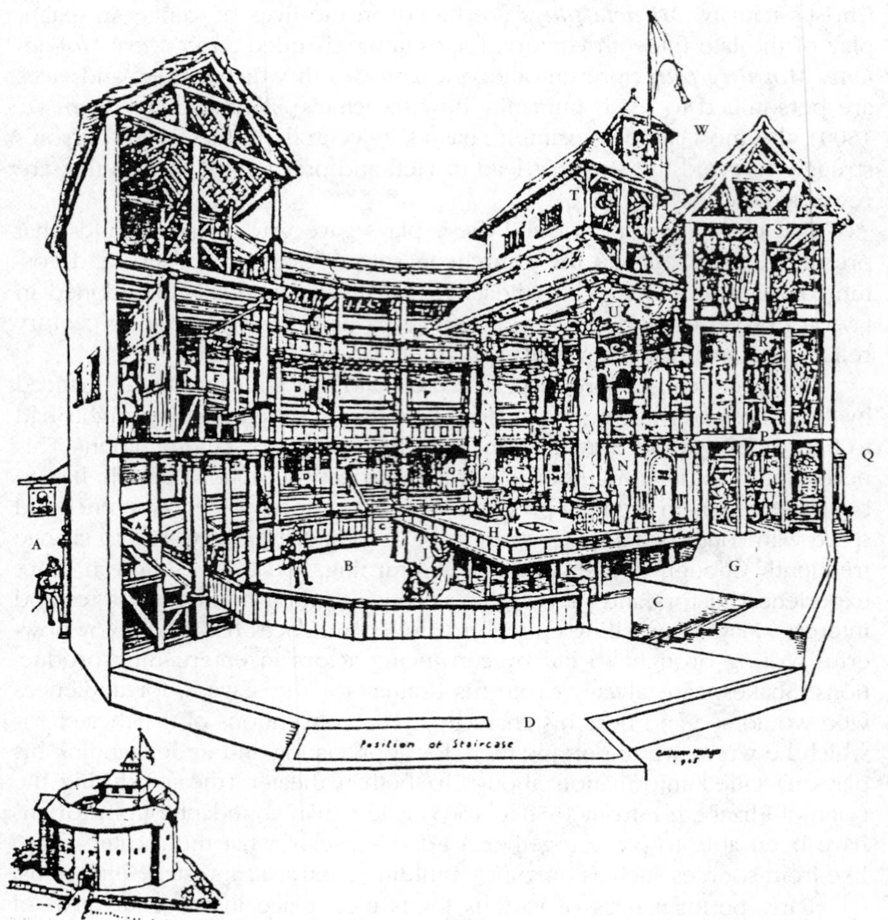

A Main entrance
B The Yard
C Entrances to lowest gallery
D Position of entrances to staircase and upper galleries
E Corridor serving the different sections of the middle gallery
F Middle gallery ("Twopenny Rooms")
G Position of "Gentlemen's Rooms" or "Lords Rooms"
H The stage
J The hanging being put up round the stage
K The "Hell" under the stage
L The stage trap leading down to the Hell
M Stage doors
N Curtained "place behind the stage"
O Gallery above the stage, used as required sometimes by musicians, sometimes by spectators, and often as part of the play
P Backstage area (the tiring-house)
Q Tiring-house door
R Dressing-rooms
S Wardrobe and storage
T The hut housing the machine for lowering enthroned gods, etc., to the stage
U The "Heavens"
W Hoisting the playhouse flag

A conjectural reconstruction of the Globe Theatre, 1599–1613. (Drawing by C. Walter Hodges from his *The Globe Restored.* Reprinted by permission of Oxford University Press.)

take advantage of natural light. The interior walls consisted of three galleries of seats looking onto a platform stage that extended from the rear wall. These seats were sheltered from the weather and more comfortable than the area in front of the stage, which was known as the *pit.* Here "groundlings" paid a penny to stand and watch the performance. Despite the large number of spectators, the theater created an intimate atmosphere because the audience closely surrounded the stage on three sides.

This arrangement produced two theatrical conventions: asides and soliloquies. An ***aside*** is a speech directed only to the audience. It makes the audience privy to a character's thoughts, allowing them to perceive ironies and intrigues that the other characters know nothing about. In a large performing space, such as a Greek amphitheater, asides would be unconvincing because they would have to be declaimed loudly to be heard, but they were well suited to Elizabethan theaters. A ***soliloquy*** is a speech delivered while an actor is alone on the stage; like an aside, it reveals a character's state of mind. Hamlet's "To be or not to be" speech is the most famous example of a soliloquy.

The Elizabethan platform stage was large enough — approximately 25 feet deep and 40 feet wide — to allow a wide variety of actions, ranging from festive banquets to bloody battles. Sections of the floor could be opened or removed to create, for instance, the gravediggers' scene in *Hamlet* or to allow characters to exit through trapdoors. At the rear of the platform an inner stage was covered by curtains that could be drawn to reveal an interior setting, such as a bedroom or tomb. The curtains were also a natural location for a character to hide in order to overhear conversations. On each side of the curtains were doors through which characters entered and exited. An upper stage could be used as a watchtower, a castle wall, or a balcony. Although most of the action occurred on the main platform stage, there were opportunities for fluid movements from one acting area to another, providing a variety of settings.

These settings were not, however, elaborately indicated by scenery or props. A scene might change when one group of characters left the stage and another entered. A table and some chairs could be carried on quickly to suggest a tavern. But the action was not interrupted for set changes. Instead, the characters' speeches often identify the location of a scene. (In modern editions of Shakespeare's plays, editors indicate in brackets the scene breaks, settings, and movements of actors not identified in the original manuscripts to help readers keep track of things.) Today's performances of the plays frequently use more elaborate settings and props. But Shakespeare's need to paint his scenery with words resulted in many poetic descriptions. Here is one of moonlight from *Merchant of Venice:*

> How sweet the moonlight sleeps upon this bank!
> Here will we sit and let the sounds of music
> Creep in our ears. Soft stillness and the night
> Become the touches of sweet harmony.

Although the settings were scant and the props mostly limited to what an actor carried onto the stage (a sword, a document, a shovel), Elizabethan costuming was an elaborate visual treat that identified the characters. Moreover, because women were not permitted to act in the theater, their roles were played by young boys dressed in female costumes. In addition, elaborate sound effects were used to create atmosphere. A flourish of trumpets might accompany the entrance of a king; small cannons might be heard during a battle; thunder might punctuate a storm. In short, Elizabethan theater was alive with sights and sounds, but at the center of the stage was the playwright's language; that's where the magic began.

THE RANGE OF SHAKESPEARE'S DRAMA: HISTORY, COMEDY, AND TRAGEDY

Shakespeare's plays fall into three basic categories: histories, comedies, and tragedies. Broadly speaking, a history play is any drama based on historical materials. In this sense, Shakespeare's *Antony and Cleopatra* and *Julius Caesar* would fit the definition, since they feature historical figures. More specifically, though, a ***history play*** is a British play based primarily on Raphael Holinshed's *Chronicles of England, Scotland, and Ireland* (1578). This account of British history was popular toward the end of the sixteenth century because of the patriotic pride that was produced by the British defeat of the Spanish Armada in 1588, and it was an important source for a series of plays Shakespeare wrote treating the reigns of British kings from Richard II to Henry VIII. The political subject matter of these plays both entertained audiences and instructed them in the virtues and vices involved in England's past efforts to overcome civil war and disorder. Ambition, deception, and treason were of more than historical interest. Shakespeare's audiences saw these plays about the fifteenth century as ways of sorting through the meanings of both the calamities of the past and the uncertainties of the present.

Although Shakespeare used Holinshed's *Chronicles* as a source, he did not hesitate to make changes for dramatic purposes. In *1 Henry IV,* for example, he ages Henry IV to contrast him with the youthful Prince Hal, and he makes Hotspur younger than he actually was to have him serve as a foil to the prince. The serious theme of Hal's growth into the kind of man who would make an ideal king is counterweighted by Shakespeare's comic creation of Falstaff, that good-humored "huge hill of flesh" filled with delightful contradictions. Falstaff had historic antecedents, but the true source of his identity is the imagination of Shakespeare, a writer who was, after all, a dramatist first.

Comedy is a strong element in *1 Henry IV,* but the play's overall tone is serious. Falstaff's riotous behavior ultimately gives way to the measured march of English history. While Shakespeare encourages us to laugh at some of the participants, we are not invited to laugh at the history of English monarchies. Comedy even appears in Shakespeare's tragedies, as in Hamlet's jests with the gravediggers, or in Emilia's biting remarks in *Othello.* This use of comedy is called ***comic relief,*** a humorous scene or incident that alleviates tension in an otherwise serious work. In many instances these moments enhance the thematic significance of the story in addition to providing laughter. When Hamlet jokes with the gravediggers we laugh, but something hauntingly serious about the humor also intensifies our more serious emotions.

A true comedy, however, lacks a tragedy's sense that some great disaster will finally descend on the protagonist. There are conflicts and obstacles that must be confronted, but in comedy the characters delight us by overcoming whatever initially thwarts them. We can laugh at their misfortunes because we are confident that everything will turn out fine in the end. Shakespearean comedy tends to follow this general principle; it begins with problems and ends with their resolution.

Shakespeare's comedies are called ***romantic comedies*** because they typically involve lovers whose hearts are set on each other but whose lives are complicated by disapproving parents, deceptions, jealousies, illusions, confused identities, disguises, or other misunderstandings. Conflicts are present, but they are more amusing than threatening. This lightness is apparent in some of the comedies' titles: the conflict in a play such as *A Midsummer Night's Dream* is, in a sense, *Much Ado about Nothing* — *As You Like It* in a comedy. Shakespeare orchestrates the problems and confusion that typify the initial plotting of a romantic comedy into harmonious wedding arrangements in the final scenes. In these comedies life is a celebration, a feast that always satisfies, because the generosity of the humor leaves us with a revived appetite for life's surprising possibilities. Discord and misunderstanding give way to concord and love. Marriage symbolizes a pledge that life itself is renewable, so we are left with a sense of new beginnings.

Although a celebration of life, comedy is also frequently used as a vehicle for criticizing human affairs. ***Satire*** casts a critical eye on vices and follies by holding them up to ridicule — usually to point out an absurdity so that it can be avoided or corrected. In *Twelfth Night* Malvolio is satirized for his priggishness and pomposity. He thinks himself better than almost everyone around him, but Shakespeare reveals him to be comic as well as pathetic. We come to understand what Malvolio will apparently never comprehend: that no one can take him as seriously as he takes himself. Polonius is subjected to a similar kind of scrutiny in *Hamlet.*

Malvolio's ambitious efforts to attract Olivia's affections are rendered absurd by Shakespeare's use of both high and low comedy. ***High comedy*** consists of verbal wit, while ***low comedy*** is generally associated with physical action and is less intellectual. Through puns and witty exchanges, Shakespeare's high comedy displays Malvolio's inconsistencies of character. His self-importance is deflated by low comedy. We are treated to a ***farce,*** a form of humor based on exaggerated, improbable incongruities, when the staid Malvolio is tricked into wearing bizarre clothing and behaving like a fool to win Olivia. Our laughter is Malvolio's pain, but though he has been "notoriously abus'd" and he vows in the final scene to be "reveng'd on the whole pack" of laughing conspirators who have tricked him, the play ends on a light note. Indeed, it concludes with a song, the last line of which reminds us of the predominant tone of the play as well as the nature of comedy: "And we'll strive to please you every day."

Tragedy, in contrast, does not promise peace and contentment. The basic characteristics of tragedy have already been outlined in the context of Greek drama (see Chapter 25). Like Greek tragic heroes, Shakespeare's protagonists are exceptional human beings whose stature makes their misfortune all the more dramatic. These characters pay a high price for their actions. Oedipus's search for the killer of Laius, Antigone's and Creon's refusal to compromise their principles, Hamlet's agonized conviction that "The time is out of joint," and Othello's willingness to doubt his wife's fidelity all lead to irreversible results. Comic plots are largely free of this sense of inevitability. Instead of the festive mood that prevails once the characters in a comedy recognize their true connection to each other, tragedy gives us dark reflections that emanate from suffering. The laughter of comedy is a shared experience, a recognition of human likeness, but suffering estranges tragic heroes from the world around them.

Some of the wrenching differences between comedy and tragedy can be experienced in *Othello*. Although this play is a tragedy, Shakespeare includes in its plot many of the ingredients associated with comedy. For a time it seems possible that Othello and Desdemona will overcome the complications of a disapproving father, along with the seemingly minor deceptions, awkward misperceptions, and tender illusions that hover around them. But in *Othello* marriage is not a sign of concord displacing discord; instead, love and marriage mark the beginning of the tragic action.

Another important difference between tragedy and comedy is the way characters are presented. The tragic protagonist is portrayed as a remarkable individual whose unique qualities compel us with their power and complexity. Macbeth is not simply a murderer nor is Othello merely a jealous husband. But despite their extreme passions, behavior, and even crimes, we identify with tragic heroes in ways that we do not with comic characters. We can laugh at pretentious fools, smug hypocrites, clumsy oafs, and thwarted lovers because we see them from a distance. They are amusing precisely because their problems are not ours; we recognize them as types instead of as ourselves (or so we think). No reader of *Twelfth Night* worries about Sir Toby Belch's excessive drinking; he is a cheerful "sot" whose passion for ale is cause for celebration rather than concern. Shakespeare's comedy is sometimes disturbing — Malvolio's character certainly is — but it is never devastating. Tragic heroes do confront devastation; they command our respect and compassion because they act in spite of terrifying risks. Their triumph is not measured by the attainment of what they seek but by the wisdom that defeat imposes on them.

A NOTE ON READING SHAKESPEARE

Readers who have had no previous experience with Shakespeare's language may find it initially daunting. They might well ask whether people ever talked the way, for example, Hamlet does in his most famous soliloquy:

> To be, or not to be: that is the question:
> Whether 'tis nobler in the mind to suffer
> The slings and arrows of outrageous fortune,
> Or to take arms against a sea of troubles,
> And by opposing end them?

People did not talk like this in Elizabethan times. Hamlet speaks poetry. Shakespeare might have had him say something like this: "The most important issue one must confront is whether the pain that life inevitably creates should be passively accepted or resisted." But Shakespeare chose poetry to reveal the depth and complexity of Hamlet's experience. This heightened language is used to clarify rather than obscure his characters' thoughts. Shakespeare has Hamlet, as well as many other characters, speak in prose too, but in general his plays are written in poetry. If you keep in mind that Shakespeare's dialogue is not typically intended to imitate everyday speech, it should be easier to understand that his language is more than simply a vehicle for expressing the action of the play.

Here are a few practical suggestions to enhance your understanding of and pleasure in reading Shakespeare's plays.

1. Keep track of the characters by referring to the *dramatis personae* (characters) listed and briefly described at the beginning of each play.
2. Remember that poetic language deserves to be read slowly and carefully. A difficult passage can sometimes be better understood if it's read aloud. Don't worry if every line isn't absolutely clear to you.
3. Pay attention to the annotations, which explain unfamiliar words, phrases, and allusions in the text. These can be distracting, but they are sometimes necessary to determine the basic meaning of a passage.
4. As you read each scene, try to imagine how it would be played on a stage.
5. If you find the reading especially difficult, try listening to a recording of the play. (Most college libraries have records and tapes of Shakespeare's plays.) Allowing professional actors to do the reading aloud for you can enrich your imaginative reconstruction of the action and

characters. Hearing a play can help you with subsequent readings of it.

6. After reading the play, view a film or videocassette recording of a performance. It is important to view the performance *after* your reading, though, so that your own mental re-creation of the play is not short-circuited by a director's production.

And finally, to quote Hamlet, "Be not too tame . . . let your own discretion be your tutor." Read Shakespeare's work as best you can; it warrants such careful attention not because the language and characters are difficult to understand, but because they offer so much to enjoy.

HAMLET, PRINCE OF DENMARK

Hamlet, the most famous play in English literature, continues to fascinate and challenge both readers and audiences. Interpretations of Hamlet's character and actions abound, because the play has produced so many intense and varied responses. No small indication of the tragedy's power is that actors long to play its title role.

A brief summary can suggest the movement of the plot but not the depth of Hamlet's character. After learning of his father's death, Prince Hamlet returns to the Danish court from his university studies to find Claudius, the dead king's brother, ruling Denmark and married to Hamlet's mother, Gertrude. Her remarriage within two months of his father's death has left Hamlet disillusioned, confused, and suspicious of Claudius. When his father's ghost appears before Hamlet to reveal that Claudius murdered the king, Hamlet is confronted with having to avenge his father's death.

Hamlet's efforts to carry out this obligation would have been a familiar kind of plot to Elizabethan audiences. ***Revenge tragedy*** was a well established type of drama that traced its antecedents to Greek and Roman plays, particularly through the Roman playwright, Seneca (c. 3 B.C.–A.D. 65) whose plays were translated and produced in English in the late sixteenth century. Shakespeare's audiences knew its conventions, particularly from Thomas Kyd's popular *Spanish Tragedy* (c. 1587). Basically, this type of play consists of a murder that has to be avenged by a relative of the victim. Typically, the victim's ghost appears to demand revenge, and invariably madness of some sort is worked into subsequent events, which ultimately result in the deaths of the murderer, the avenger, and a number of other characters. Crime, madness, ghostly anguish, poison, overheard conversations, conspiracies, and a final scene littered with corpses: *Hamlet* subscribes to the basic ingredients of the formula, but it also transcends the conventions of revenge tragedy because Hamlet contemplates not merely revenge but suicide and the meaning of life itself.

Hamlet must face not only a diseased social order but also conflicts within himself when his indecisiveness becomes as agonizing as the corruption surrounding him. However, Hamlet is also a forceful and attractive character. His intelligence is repeatedly revealed in his penetrating use of language; through images and metaphors he creates a perspective on his world that is at once satiric and profoundly painful. His astonishing and sometimes shocking wit is leveled at his mother, his beloved Ophelia, and Claudius as well as himself. Nothing escapes his critical eye and divided imagination. Hamlet, no less than the people around him, is perplexed by his alienation from life.

Hamlet's limitations as well as his virtues make him one of Shakespeare's most complex characters. His keen self-awareness is both agonizing and liberating. Although he struggles throughout the play with painful issues ranging from family loyalties to matters of state, he retains his dignity as a tragic hero, a hero whom generations of audiences have found compelling.

WILLIAM SHAKESPEARE (1564–1616)

Hamlet, Prince of Denmark — 1600

[Dramatis Personae

Claudius, King of Denmark
Hamlet, son to the late, and nephew to the present king
Polonius, lord chamberlain
Horatio, friend to Hamlet
Laertes, son to Polonius
Voltimand, *Cornelius*, *Rosencrantz*, *Guildenstern*, *Osric*, *A Gentleman* — courtiers
A Priest
Marcellus, *Bernardo* — officers
Francisco, a soldier
Reynaldo, servant to Polonius
Players
Two Clowns, grave-diggers
Fortinbras, Prince of Norway
A Captain
English Ambassadors
Gertrude, Queen of Denmark, and mother to *Hamlet*
Ophelia, daughter to Polonius
Lords, Ladies, Officers, Soldiers, Sailors, Messengers, and other Attendants
Ghost of Hamlet's Father

SCENE: *Denmark.]*

[ACT I

SCENE I. *Elsinore. A platform° before the castle.]*

Enter Bernardo and Francisco, two sentinels.

Bernardo: Who's there?
Francisco: Nay, answer me:° stand, and unfold yourself.
Bernardo: Long live the king!°
Francisco: Bernardo?
Bernardo: He.
Francisco: You come most carefully upon your hour.
Bernardo: 'Tis now struck twelve; get thee to bed, Francisco.
Francisco: For this relief much thanks: 'tis bitter cold,
And I am sick at heart.
Bernardo: Have you had quiet guard?
Francisco: Not a mouse stirring.
Bernardo: Well, good night.
If you do meet Horatio and Marcellus,
The rivals° of my watch, bid them make haste.

Enter Horatio and Marcellus.

Francisco: I think I hear them. Stand, ho! Who is there?
Horatio: Friends to this ground.
Marcellus: And liegemen to the Dane.
Francisco: Give you° good night.
Marcellus: O, farewell, honest soldier:
Who hath reliev'd you?
Francisco: Bernardo hath my place.
Give you good night. *Exit Francisco.*
Marcellus: Holla! Bernardo!
Bernardo: Say,
What, is Horatio there?
Horatio: A piece of him.
Bernardo: Welcome, Horatio: welcome, good Marcellus.
Marcellus: What, has this thing appear'd again to-night?
Bernardo: I have seen nothing.
Marcellus: Horatio says 'tis but our fantasy,
And will not let belief take hold of him
Touching this dreaded sight, twice seen of us:
Therefore I have entreated him along
With us to watch the minutes of this night;

ACT I. SCENE I. *platform:* A level space on the battlements of the royal castle at Elsinore, a Danish seaport; now Helsingör. 2 *me:* This is emphatic, since Francisco is the sentry. 3 *Long live the king:* Either a password or greeting; Horatio and Marcellus use a different one in line 15. 13 *rivals:* Partners. 16 *Give you:* God give you.

That if again this apparition come,
He may approve° our eyes and speak to it.
Horatio: Tush, tush, 'twill not appear.
Bernardo: Sit down awhile;
And let us once again assail your ears,
That are so fortified against our story
What we have two nights seen.
Horatio: Well, sit we down,
And let us hear Bernardo speak of this.
Bernardo: Last night of all,
When yond same star that's westward from the pole°
Had made his course t' illume that part of heaven
Where now it burns, Marcellus and myself,
The bell then beating one, —

Enter Ghost.

Marcellus: Peace, break thee off; look, where it comes again!
Bernardo: In the same figure, like the king that's dead.
Marcellus: Thou art a scholar;° speak to it, Horatio.
Bernardo: Looks 'a not like the king? mark it, Horatio.
Horatio: Most like: it harrows° me with fear and wonder.
Bernardo: It would be spoke to.°
Marcellus: Speak to it, Horatio.
Horatio: What art thou that usurp'st this time of night,
Together with that fair and warlike form
In which the majesty of buried Denmark°
Did sometimes march? by heaven I charge thee, speak!
Marcellus: It is offended.
Bernardo: See, it stalks away!
Horatio: Stay! speak, speak! I charge thee, speak! *Exit Ghost.*
Marcellus: 'Tis gone, and will not answer.
Bernardo: How now, Horatio! you tremble and look pale:
Is not this something more than fantasy?
What think you on 't?
Horatio: Before my God, I might not this believe
Without the sensible and true avouch
Of mine own eyes.
Marcellus: Is it not like the king?
Horatio: As thou art to thyself:
Such was the very armour he had on
When he the ambitious Norway combated;
So frown'd he once, when, in an angry parle,

29 *approve:* Corroborate. 36 *pole:* Polestar. 42 *scholar:* Exorcisms were performed in Latin, which Horatio as an educated man would be able to speak. 44 *harrows:* Lacerates the feelings. 45 *It . . . to:* A ghost could not speak until spoken to. 48 *buried Denmark:* the buried king of Denmark.

He smote° the sledded Polacks° on the ice.
'Tis strange.
Marcellus: Thus twice before, and jump° at this dead hour,
With martial stalk hath he gone by our watch.
Horatio: In what particular thought to work I know not;
But in the gross and scope° of my opinion,
This bodes some strange eruption to our state.
Marcellus: Good now,° sit down, and tell me, he that knows,
Why this same strict and most observant watch
So nightly toils° the subject° of the land,
And why such daily cast° of brazen cannon,
And foreign mart° for implements of war;
Why such impress° of shipwrights, whose sore task
Does not divide the Sunday from the week;
What might be toward, that this sweaty haste
Doth make the night joint-labourer with the day:
Who is't that can inform me?
Horatio: That can I;
At least, the whisper goes so. Our last king,
Whose image even but now appear'd to us,
Was, as you know, by Fortinbras of Norway,
Thereto prick'd on° by a most emulate° pride,
Dar'd to the combat; in which our valiant Hamlet —
For so this side of our known world esteem'd him —
Did slay this Fortinbras; who, by a seal'd compact,
Well ratified by law and heraldry,°
Did forfeit, with his life, all those his lands
Which he stood seiz'd° of, to the conqueror:
Against the which, a moiety competent°
Was gaged by our king; which had return'd
To the inheritance of Fortinbras,
Had he been vanquisher; as, by the same comart,°
And carriage° of the article design'd,
His fell to Hamlet. Now, sir, young Fortinbras,
Of unimproved° mettle hot and full,°
Hath in the skirts of Norway here and there
Shark'd up° a list of lawless resolutes,°
For food and diet,° to some enterprise
That hath a stomach in't; which is no other —
As it doth well appear unto our state —

63 *smote:* Defeated; *sledded Polacks:* Polanders using sledges. 65 *jump:* Exactly. 68 *gross and scope:* General drift. 70 *Good now:* An expression denoting entreaty or expostulation. 72 *toils:* Causes or makes to toil; *subject:* people, subjects. 73 *cast:* Casting, founding. 74 *mart:* Buying and selling, traffic. 75 *impress:* Impressment. 83 *prick'd on:* Incited; *emulate:* Rivaling. 87 *law and heraldry:* Heraldic law, governing combat. 89 *seiz'd:* Possessed. 90 *moiety competent:* Adequate or sufficient portion. 93 *comart:* Joint bargain. 94 *carriage:* Import, bearing. 96 *unimproved:* Not turned to account; *hot and full:* Full of fight. 98 *Shark'd up:* Got together in haphazard fashion; *resolutes:* Desperadoes. 99 *food and diet:* No pay but their keep.

But to recover of us, by strong hand
And terms compulsatory, those foresaid lands
So by his father lost: and this, I take it,
Is the main motive of our preparations,
The source of this our watch and the chief head
Of this post-haste and romage° in the land.
Bernardo: I think it be no other but e'en so:
Well may it sort° that this portentous figure
Comes armed through our watch; so like the king
That was and is the question of these wars.
Horatio: A mote° it is to trouble the mind's eye.
In the most high and palmy state° of Rome,
A little ere the mightiest Julius fell,
The graves stood tenantless and the sheeted dead
Did squeak and gibber in the Roman streets:
As stars with trains of fire° and dews of blood,
Disasters° in the sun; and the moist star°
Upon whose influence Neptune's empire° stands
Was sick almost to doomsday with eclipse:
And even the like precurse° of fear'd events,
As harbingers preceding still the fates
And prologue to the omen coming on,
Have heaven and earth together demonstrated
Unto our climatures and countrymen. —

Enter Ghost.

But soft, behold! lo, where it comes again!
I'll cross° it, though it blast me. Stay, illusion!
If thou hast any sound, or use of voice,
Speak to me! *It° spreads his arms.*
If there be any good thing to be done,
That may to thee do ease and grace to me,
Speak to me!
If thou art privy to thy country's fate,
Which, happily, foreknowing may avoid,
O, speak!
Or if thou hast uphoarded in thy life
Extorted treasure in the womb of earth,
For which, they say, you spirits oft walk in death, *The cock crows.*
Speak of it:° stay, and speak! Stop it, Marcellus.
Marcellus: Shall I strike at it with my partisan?°
Horatio: Do, if it will not stand.

107 *romage:* Bustle, commotion. 109 *sort:* Suit. 112 *mote:* Speck of dust. 113 *palmy state:* Triumphant sovereignty. 117 *stars . . . fire:* I.e., comets. 118 *Disasters:* Unfavorable aspects; *moist star:* The moon, governing tides. 119 *Neptune's empire:* The sea. 121 *precurse:* Heralding. 127 *cross:* Meet, face; thus bringing down the evil influence on the person who crosses it. 129 *It:* The Ghost, or perhaps Horatio. 133–139 *If . . . it:* Horatio recites the traditional reasons why ghosts might walk. 140 *partisan:* Long-handled spear with a blade having lateral projections.

Bernardo: 'Tis here!
Horatio: 'Tis here!
Marcellus: 'Tis gone! *[Exit Ghost.]*
We do it wrong, being so majestical,
To offer it the show of violence;
For it is, as the air, invulnerable,
And our vain blows malicious mockery.
Bernardo: It was about to speak, when the cock crew.°
Horatio: And then it started like a guilty thing
Upon a fearful summons. I have heard,
The cock, that is the trumpet to the morn,
Doth with his lofty and shrill-sounding throat
Awake the god of day; and, at his warning,
Whether in sea or fire, in earth or air,
Th' extravagant and erring° spirit hies
To his confine:° and of the truth herein
This present object made probation.°
Marcellus: It faded on the crowing of the cock.
Some say that ever 'gainst° that season comes
Wherein our Saviour's birth is celebrated,
The bird of dawning singeth all night long:
And then, they say, no spirit dare stir abroad;
The nights are wholesome; then no planets strike,°
No fairy takes, nor witch hath power to charm,
So hallow'd and so gracious° is that time.
Horatio: So have I heard and do in part believe it.
But, look, the morn, in russet mantle clad,
Walks o'er the dew of yon high eastward hill:
Break we our watch up; and by my advice,
Let us impart what we have seen to-night
Unto young Hamlet; for, upon my life,
This spirit, dumb to us, will speak to him.
Do you consent we shall acquaint him with it,
As needful in our loves, fitting our duty?
Marcellus: Let's do 't, I pray; and I this morning know
Where we shall find him most conveniently. *Exeunt.*

[SCENE II. *A room of state in the castle.]*

Flourish. Enter Claudius, King of Denmark, Gertrude the Queen, Councilors,

147 *cock crew:* According to traditional ghost lore, spirits returned to their confines at cockcrow. 154 *extravagant and erring:* Wandering. Both words mean the same thing. 155 *confine:* Place of confinement. 156 *probation:* Proof, trial. 158 *'gainst:* Just before. 162 *planets strike:* It was thought that planets were malignant and might strike travelers by night. 164 *gracious:* Full of goodness.

Polonius and his Son Laertes, Hamlet, cum aliis° [including Voltimand and Cornelius].

King: Though yet of Hamlet our dear brother's death
The memory be green, and that it us befitted
To bear our hearts in grief and our whole kingdom
To be contracted in one brow of woe,
Yet so far hath discretion fought with nature
That we with wisest sorrow think on him,
Together with remembrance of ourselves.
Therefore our sometime sister, now our queen,
Th' imperial jointress° to this warlike state,
Have we, as 'twere with a defeated joy, —
With an auspicious and a dropping eye,
With mirth in funeral and with dirge in marriage,
In equal scale weighing delight and dole, —
Taken to wife: nor have we herein barr'd
Your better wisdoms, which have freely gone
With this affair along. For all, our thanks.
Now follows, that° you know, young Fortinbras,
Holding a weak supposal° of our worth,
Or thinking by our late dear brother's death
Our state to be disjoint° and out of frame,°
Colleagued° with this dream of his advantage,°
He hath not fail'd to pester us with message,
Importing° the surrender of those lands
Lost by his father, with all bands of law,
To our most valiant brother. So much for him.
Now for ourself and for this time of meeting:
Thus much the business is: we have here writ
To Norway, uncle of young Fortinbras, —
Who, impotent and bed-rid, scarcely hears
Of this his nephew's purpose, — to suppress
His further gait° herein; in that the levies,
The lists and full proportions, are all made
Out of his subject:° and we here dispatch
You, good Cornelius, and you, Voltimand,
For bearers of this greeting to old Norway;
Giving to you no further personal power
To business with the king, more than the scope
Of these delated° articles allow.
Farewell, and let your haste commend your duty.

SCENE II. *cum aliis:* With others. 9 *jointress:* Woman possessed of a jointure, or, joint tenancy of an estate. 17 *that:* That which. 18 *weak supposal:* Low estimate. 20 *disjoint:* Distracted, out of joint; *frame:* Order. 21 *Colleagued:* added to; *dream . . . advantage:* Visionary hope of success. 23 *Importing:* Purporting, pertaining to. 31 *gait:* Proceeding. 33 *Out of his subject:* At the expense of Norway's subjects (collectively). 38 *delated:* Expressly stated.

Cornelius:
Voltimand: } In that and all things will we show our duty.
King: We doubt it nothing: heartily farewell.
[Exeunt Voltimand and Cornelius.]
And now, Laertes, what's the news with you?
You told us of some suit; what is't, Laertes?
You cannot speak of reason to the Dane,°
And lose your voice:° what wouldst thou beg, Laertes,
That shall not be my offer, not thy asking?
The head is not more native° to the heart,
The hand more instrumental° to the mouth,
Than is the throne of Denmark to thy father.
What wouldst thou have, Laertes?
Laertes: My dread lord,
Your leave and favour to return to France;
From whence though willingly I came to Denmark,
To show my duty in your coronation,
Yet now, I must confess, that duty done,
My thoughts and wishes bend again toward France
And bow them to your gracious leave and pardon.°
King: Have you your father's leave? What says Polonius?
Polonius: He hath, my lord, wrung from me my slow leave
By laboursome petition, and at last
Upon his will I seal'd my hard consent:
I do beseech you, give him leave to go.
King: Take thy fair hour, Laertes; time be thine,
And thy best graces spend it at thy will!
But now, my cousin° Hamlet, and my son, —
Hamlet [aside]: A little more than kin, and less than kind!°
King: How is it that the clouds still hang on you?
Hamlet: Not so, my lord; I am too much in the sun.°
Queen: Good Hamlet, cast thy nighted colour off,
And let thine eye look like a friend on Denmark.
Do not for ever with thy vailed lids
Seek for thy noble father in the dust:
Thou know'st 'tis common; all that lives must die,
Passing through nature to eternity.
Hamlet: Ay, madam, it is common.°
Queen: If it be,
Why seems it so particular with thee?

44 *the Dane:* Danish king. 45 *lose your voice:* Speak in vain. 47 *native:* Closely connected, related. 48 *instrumental:* Serviceable. 56 *leave and pardon:* Permission to depart. 64 *cousin:* Any kin not of the immediate family. 65 *A little . . . kind:* My relation to you has become more than kinship warrants; it has also become unnatural. 67 *I am . . . sun:* The senses seem to be: I am too much out of doors, I am too much in the sun of your grace (ironical), I am too much of a son to you. Possibly an allusion to the proverb "Out of heaven's blessing into the warm sun"; i.e., Hamlet is out of house and home in being deprived of the kingship. 74 *Ay . . . common:* It is common, but it hurts nevertheless; possibly a reference to the commonplace quality of the queen's remark.

Hamlet: Seems, madam! nay, it is; I know not "seems."
'Tis not alone my inky cloak, good mother,
Nor customary suits° of solemn black,
Nor windy suspiration° of forc'd breath,
No, nor the fruitful river in the eye,
Nor the dejected 'haviour of the visage,
Together with all forms, moods, shapes of grief,
That can denote me truly: these indeed seem,
For they are actions that a man might play:
But I have that within which passeth show;
These but the trappings and the suits of woe.
King: 'Tis sweet and commendable in your nature, Hamlet,
To give these mourning duties to your father:
But, you must know, your father lost a father;
That father lost, lost his, and the survivor bound
In filial obligation for some term
To do obsequious° sorrow: but to persever
In obstinate condolement° is a course
Of impious stubbornness; 'tis unmanly grief;
It shows a will most incorrect° to heaven,
A heart unfortified, a mind impatient,
An understanding simple and unschool'd:
For what we know must be and is as common
As any the most vulgar thing° to sense,
Why should we in our peevish opposition
Take it to heart? Fie! 'tis a fault to heaven,
A fault against the dead, a fault to nature,
To reason most absurd; whose common theme
Is death of fathers, and who still hath cried,
From the first corse till he that died to-day,
"This must be so." We pray you, throw to earth
This unprevailing° woe, and think of us
As of a father: for let the world take note,
You are the most immediate° to our throne;
And with no less nobility° of love
Than that which dearest father bears his son,
Do I impart° toward you. For your intent
In going back to school in Wittenberg,°
It is most retrograde° to our desire:
And we beseech you, bend you° to remain
Here, in the cheer and comfort of our eye,
Our chiefest courtier, cousin, and our son.

78 *customary suits:* Suits prescribed by custom for mourning. 79 *windy suspiration:* Heavy sighing. 92 *obsequious:* Dutiful. 93 *condolement:* Sorrowing. 95 *incorrect:* Untrained, uncorrected. 99 *vulgar thing:* Common experience. 107 *unprevailing:* Unavailing. 109 *most immediate:* Next in succession. 110 *nobility:* High degree. 112 *impart:* The object is apparently *love* (l. 110). 113 *Wittenberg:* Famous German university founded in 1502. 114 *retrograde:* Contrary. 115 *bend you:* Incline yourself; imperative.

Queen: Let not thy mother lose her prayers, Hamlet:
I pray thee, stay with us; go not to Wittenberg.
Hamlet: I shall in all my best obey you, madam.
King: Why, 'tis a loving and a fair reply:
Be as ourself in Denmark. Madam, come;
This gentle and unforc'd accord of Hamlet
Sits smiling to my heart: in grace whereof,
No jocund health that Denmark drinks to-day,
But the great cannon to the clouds shall tell,
And the king's rouse° the heaven shall bruit again,°
Re-speaking earthly thunder. Come away.
Flourish. Exeunt all but Hamlet.
Hamlet: O, that this too too sullied flesh would melt,
Thaw and resolve itself itself into a dew!
Or that the Everlasting had not fix'd
His canon 'gainst self-slaughter! O God! God!
How weary, stale, flat and unprofitable,
Seem to me all the uses of this world!
Fie on't! ah fie! 'tis an unweeded garden,
That grows to seed; things rank and gross in nature
Possess it merely.° That it should come to this!
But two months dead: nay, not so much, not two:
So excellent a king; that was, to this,
Hyperion° to a satyr; so loving to my mother
That he might not beteem° the winds of heaven
Visit her face too roughly. Heaven and earth!
Must I remember? why, she would hang on him,
As if increase of appetite had grown
By what it fed on: and yet, within a month —
Let me not think on't — Frailty, thy name is woman! —
A little month, or ere those shoes were old
With which she followed my poor father's body,
Like Niobe,° all tears: — why she, even she —
O God! a beast, that wants discourse of reason,°
Would have mourn'd longer — married with my uncle,
My father's brother, but no more like my father
Than I to Hercules: within a month:
Ere yet the salt of most unrighteous tears
Had left the flushing in her galled° eyes,
She married. O, most wicked speed, to post
With such dexterity° to incestuous sheets!
It is not nor it cannot come to good:
But break, my heart; for I must hold my tongue.

127 *rouse:* Draft of liquor; *bruit again:* Echo. 137 *merely:* Completely, entirely. 140 *Hyperion:* God of the sun in the older regime of ancient gods. 141 *beteem:* Allow. 149 *Niobe:* Tantalus's daughter, who boasted that she had more sons and daughters than Leto; for this Apollo and Artemis slew her children. She was turned into stone by Zeus on Mount Sipylus. 150 *discourse of reason:* Process or faculty of reason. 155 *galled:* Irritated. 157 *dexterity:* Facility.

Enter Horatio, Marcellus, and Bernardo.

Horatio: Hail to your lordship!
Hamlet: I am glad to see you well:
Horatio! — or I do forget myself.
Horatio: The same, my lord, and your poor servant ever.
Hamlet: Sir, my good friend; I'll change that name with you:°
And what make you from Wittenberg, Horatio?
Marcellus?
Marcellus: My good lord —
Hamlet: I am very glad to see you. Good even, sir.
But what, in faith, make you from Wittenberg?
Horatio: A truant disposition, good my lord.
Hamlet: I would not hear your enemy say so,
Nor shall you do my ear that violence,
To make it truster of your own report
Against yourself: I know you are no truant.
But what is your affair in Elsinore?
We'll teach you to drink deep ere you depart.
Horatio: My lord, I came to see your father's funeral.
Hamlet: I prithee, do not mock me, fellow-student;
I think it was to see my mother's wedding.
Horatio: Indeed, my lord, it follow'd hard° upon.
Hamlet: Thrift, thrift, Horatio! the funeral bak'd meats°
Did coldly furnish forth the marriage tables.
Would I had met my dearest° foe in heaven
Or ever I had seen that day, Horatio!
My father! — methinks I see my father.
Horatio: Where, my lord!
Hamlet: In my mind's eye, Horatio.
Horatio: I saw him once; 'a° was a goodly king.
Hamlet: 'A was a man, take him for all in all,
I shall not look upon his like again.
Horatio: My lord, I think I saw him yesternight.
Hamlet: Saw? who?
Horatio: My lord, the king your father.
Hamlet: The king my father!
Horatio: Season your admiration° for a while
With an attent ear, till I may deliver,
Upon the witness of these gentlemen,
This marvel to you.
Hamlet: For God's love, let me hear.
Horatio: Two nights together had these gentlemen,
Marcellus and Bernardo, on their watch,

163 *I'll . . . you:* I'll be your servant, you shall be my friend; also explained as "I'll exchange the name of friend with you." 179 *hard:* Close. 180 *bak'd meats:* Meat pies. 182 *dearest:* Direst. The adjective *dear* in Shakespeare has two different origins: O.E. *deore,* "beloved," and O.E. *deor,* "fierce." *Dearest* is the superlative of the second. 186 *'a:* He. 192 *Season your admiration:* Restrain your astonishment.

In the dead waste and middle of the night,
Been thus encount'red. A figure like your father,
Armed at point exactly, cap-a-pe,°
Appears before them, and with solemn march
Goes slow and stately by them: thrice he walk'd
By their oppress'd° and fear-surprised eyes,
Within his truncheon's° length; whilst they, distill'd°
Almost to jelly with the act° of fear,
Stand dumb and speak not to him. This to me
In dreadful secrecy impart they did;
And I with them the third night kept the watch:
Where, as they had deliver'd, both in time,
Form of the thing, each word made true and good,
The apparition comes: I knew your father;
These hands are not more like.

Hamlet: But where was this?

Marcellus: My lord, upon the platform where we watch'd.

Hamlet: Did you not speak to it?

Horatio: My lord, I did;
But answer made it none: yet once methought
It lifted up it° head and did address
Itself to motion, like as it would speak;
But even then the morning cock crew loud,
And at the sound it shrunk in haste away,
And vanish'd from our sight.

Hamlet: 'Tis very strange.

Horatio: As I do live, my honour'd lord, 'tis true;
And we did think it writ down in our duty
To let you know of it.

Hamlet: Indeed, indeed, sirs, but this troubles me.
Hold you the watch to-night?

Marcellus:
Bernardo: } We do, my lord.

Hamlet: Arm'd, say you?

Marcellus:
Bernardo: } Arm'd, my lord.

Hamlet: From top to toe?

Marcellus:
Bernardo: } My lord, from head to foot.

Hamlet: Then saw you not his face?

Horatio: O, yes, my lord; he wore his beaver° up.

Hamlet: What, look'd he frowningly?

Horatio: A countenance more in sorrow than in anger.

Hamlet: Pale or red?

Horatio: Nay, very pale.

Hamlet: And fix'd his eyes upon you?

200 *cap-a-pe:* From head to foot. 203 *oppress'd:* Distressed. 204 *truncheon:* Officer's staff; *distill'd:* Softened, weakened. 205 *act:* Action. 216 *it:* Its. 230 *beaver:* Visor on the helmet.

Horatio: Most constantly.
Hamlet: I would I had been there.
Horatio: It would have much amaz'd you.
Hamlet: Very like, very like. Stay'd it long?
Horatio: While one with moderate haste might tell a hundred.
Marcellus: }
Bernardo: } Longer, longer.
Horatio: Not when I saw't.
Hamlet: His beard was grizzled, — no?
Horatio: It was, as I have seen it in his life,
A sable° silver'd.
Hamlet: I will watch to-night;
Perchance 'twill walk again.
Horatio: I warr'nt it will.
Hamlet: If it assume my noble father's person,
I'll speak to it, though hell itself should gape
And bid me hold my peace. I pray you all,
If you have hitherto conceal'd this sight,
Let it be tenable in your silence still;
And whatsoever else shall hap to-night,
Give it an understanding, but no tongue:
I will requite your loves. So, fare you well:
Upon the platform, 'twixt eleven and twelve,
I'll visit you.
All: Our duty to your honour.
Hamlet: Your loves, as mine to you: farewell.

Exeunt [all but Hamlet].

My father's spirit in arms! all is not well;
I doubt° some foul play: would the night were come!
Till then sit still, my soul: foul deeds will rise,
Though all the earth o'erwhelm them, to men's eyes. *Exit.*

[SCENE III. *A room in Polonius's house.*]

Enter Laertes and Ophelia, his Sister.

Laertes: My necessaries are embark'd: farewell:
And, sister, as the winds give benefit
And convoy is assistant,° do not sleep,
But let me hear from you.
Ophelia: Do you doubt that?
Laertes: For Hamlet and the trifling of his favour,
Hold it a fashion° and a toy in blood,°
A violet in the youth of primy° nature,
Forward,° not permanent, sweet, not lasting,

242 *sable:* Black color. 256 *doubt:* Fear. SCENE III. 3 *convoy is assistant:* Means of conveyance are available. 6 *fashion:* Custom, prevailing usage; *toy in blood:* Passing amorous fancy. 7 *primy:* In its prime. 8 *Forward:* Precocious.

The perfume and suppliance of a minute;°
No more.

Ophelia: No more but so?

Laertes: Think it no more:
For nature, crescent,° does not grow alone
In thews° and bulk, but, as this temple° waxes,
The inward service of the mind and soul
Grows wide withal. Perhaps he loves you now,
And now no soil° nor cautel° doth besmirch
The virtue of his will: but you must fear,
His greatness weigh'd,° his will is not his own;
For he himself is subject to his birth:
He may not, as unvalued persons do,
Carve for himself; for on his choice depends
The safety and health of this whole state;
And therefore must his choice be circumscrib'd
Unto the voice and yielding° of that body
Whereof he is the head. Then if he says he loves you,
It fits your wisdom so far to believe it
As he in his particular act and place
May give his saying deed;° which is no further
Than the main voice of Denmark goes withal.
Then weigh what loss your honour may sustain,
If with too credent° ear you list his songs,
Or lose your heart, or your chaste treasure open
To his unmast'red° importunity.
Fear it, Ophelia, fear it, my dear sister,
And keep you in the rear of your affection,
Out of the shot and danger of desire.
The chariest° maid is prodigal enough,
If she unmask her beauty to the moon:
Virtue itself 'scapes not calumnious strokes:
The canker galls the infants of the spring,°
Too oft before their buttons° be disclos'd,°
And in the morn and liquid dew° of youth
Contagious blastments° are most imminent.
Be wary then; best safety lies in fear:
Youth to itself rebels, though none else near.

Ophelia: I shall the effect of this good lesson keep,
As watchman to my heart. But, good my brother,
Do not, as some ungracious° pastors do,
Show me the steep and thorny way to heaven;

9 *suppliance of a minute:* Diversion to fill up a minute. 11 *crescent:* Growing, waxing. 12 *thews:* Bodily strength; *temple:* Body. 15 *soil:* blemish; *cautel:* Crafty device. 17 *greatness weigh'd:* High position considered. 23 *voice and yielding:* Assent, approval. 27 *deed:* Effect. 30 *credent:* Credulous. 32 *unmast'red:* unrestrained. 36 *chariest:* Most scrupulously modest. 39 *The canker . . . spring:* The cankerworm destroys the young plants of spring. 40 *buttons:* buds; *disclos'd:* opened. 41 *liquid dew:* I.e., time when dew is fresh. 42 *blastments:* Blights. 47 *ungracious:* Graceless.

Whiles, like a puff'd° and reckless libertine,
Himself the primrose path of dalliance treads,
And recks° not his own rede.°

Enter Polonius.

Laertes: O, fear me not.
I stay too long: but here my father comes.
A double° blessing is a double grace;
Occasion° smiles upon a second leave.

Polonius: Yet here, Laertes? aboard, aboard, for shame!
The wind sits in the shoulder of your sail,
And you are stay'd for. There; my blessing with thee!
And these few precepts° in thy memory
Look thou character.° Give thy thoughts no tongue,
Nor any unproportion'd° thought his act.
Be thou familiar, but by no means vulgar.°
Those friends thou hast, and their adoption tried,
Grapple them to thy soul with hoops of steel;
But do not dull thy palm with entertainment
Of each new-hatch'd, unfledg'd° comrade. Beware
Of entrance to a quarrel, but being in,
Bear't that th' opposed may beware of thee.
Give every man thy ear, but few thy voice;
Take each man's censure, but reserve thy judgement.
Costly thy habit as thy purse can buy,
But not express'd in fancy;° rich, not gaudy;
For the apparel oft proclaims the man,
And they in France of the best rank and station
Are of a most select and generous chief in that.°
Neither a borrower nor a lender be;
For loan oft loses both itself and friend,
And borrowing dulleth edge of husbandry.°
This above all: to thine own self be true,
And it must follow, as the night the day,
Thou canst not then be false to any man.
Farewell: my blessing season° this in thee!

Laertes: Most humbly do I take my leave, my lord.

Polonius: The time invites you; go; your servants tend.

Laertes: Farewell, Ophelia; and remember well
What I have said to you.

Ophelia: 'Tis in my memory lock'd,
And you yourself shall keep the key of it.

Laertes: Farewell. *Exit Laertes.*

49 *puff'd:* Bloated. 51 *recks:* Heeds, *rede:* Counsel. 53 *double:* I.e., Laertes has already bade his father good-by. 54 *Occasion:* Opportunity. 58 *precepts:* Many parallels have been found to the series of maxims which follows, one of the closer being that in Lyly's *Euphues.* 59 *character:* Inscribe. 60 *unproportion'd:* Inordinate. 61 *vulgar:* Common. 65 *unfledg'd:* Immature. 71 *express'd in fancy:* Fantastical in design. 74 *Are . . . that: Chief* is usually taken as a substantive meaning "head," "eminence." 77 *husbandry:* Thrift. 81 *season:* Mature.

Polonius: What is 't, Ophelia, he hath said to you?
Ophelia: So please you, something touching the Lord Hamlet.
Polonius: Marry, well bethought:
'Tis told me, he hath very oft of late
Given private time to you; and you yourself
Have of your audience been most free and bounteous:
If it be so, as so't is put on° me,
And that in way of caution, I must tell you,
You do not understand yourself so clearly
As it behoves my daughter and your honour.
What is between you? give me up the truth.
Ophelia: He hath, my lord, of late made many tenders°
Of his affection to me.
Polonius: Affection! pooh! you speak like a green girl,
Unsifted° in such perilous circumstance.
Do you believe his tenders, as you call them?
Ophelia: I do not know, my lord, what I should think.
Polonius: Marry, I will teach you: think yourself a baby;
That you have ta'en these tenders° for true pay,
Which are not sterling.° Tender° yourself more dearly;
Or — not to crack the wind° of the poor phrase,
Running it thus — you'll tender me a fool.°
Ophelia: My lord, he hath importun'd me with love
In honourable fashion.
Polonius: Ay, fashion° you may call it; go to, go to.
Ophelia: And hath given countenance° to his speech, my lord,
With almost all the holy vows of heaven.
Polonius: Ay, springes° to catch woodcocks.° I do know,
When the blood burns, how prodigal the soul
Lends the tongue vows: these blazes, daughter,
Giving more light than heat, extinct in both,
Even in their promise, as it is a-making,
You must not take for fire. From this time
Be somewhat scanter of your maiden presence;
Set your entreatments° at a higher rate
Than a command to parley.° For Lord Hamlet,
Believe so much in him,° that he is young,
And with a larger tether may he walk
Than may be given you: in few,° Ophelia,
Do not believe his vows; for they are brokers;°
Not of that dye° which their investments° show,

94 *put on:* Impressed on. 99, 103 *tenders:* Offers. 102 *Unsifted:* Untried. 106 *tenders:* Promises to pay. 107 *sterling:* Legal currency; *Tender:* Hold. 108 *crack the wind:* I.e., run it until it is broken-winded. 109 *tender . . . fool:* Show me a fool (for a daughter). 112 *fashion:* Mere form, pretense. 113 *countenance:* Credit, support. 115 *springes:* Snares; *woodcocks:* Birds easily caught, type of stupidity. 122 *entreatments:* Conversations, interviews. 123 *command to parley:* Mere invitation to talk. 124 *so . . . him:* This much concerning him. 126 *in few:* Briefly. 127 *brokers:* Go-betweens, procurers. 128 *dye:* Color or sort; *investments:* Clothes.

But mere implorators° of unholy suits,
Breathing° like sanctified and pious bawds,
The better to beguile. This is for all:
I would not, in plain terms, from this time forth,
Have you so slander° any moment leisure,
As to give words or talk with the Lord Hamlet.
Look to 't, I charge you: come your ways.

Ophelia: I shall obey, my lord. *Exeunt.*

[SCENE IV. *The platform.*]

Enter Hamlet, Horatio, and Marcellus.

Hamlet: The air bites shrewdly; it is very cold.
Horatio: It is a nipping and an eager air.
Hamlet: What hour now?
Horatio: I think it lacks of twelve.
Marcellus: No, it is struck.
Horatio: Indeed? I heard it not: then it draws near the season
Wherein the spirit held his wont to walk.

A flourish of trumpets, and two pieces go off.

What does this mean, my lord?
Hamlet: The king doth wake° to-night and takes his rouse,°
Keeps wassail,° and the swagg'ring up-spring° reels;°
And, as he drains his draughts of Rhenish° down,
The kettle-drum and trumpet thus bray out
The triumph of his pledge.°
Horatio: Is it a custom?
Hamlet: Ay, marry, is 't:
But to my mind, though I am native here
And to the manner born,° it is a custom
More honour'd in the breach than the observance.
This heavy-headed revel east and west
Makes us traduc'd and tax'd of other nations:
They clepe° us drunkards, and with swinish phrase°
Soil our addition;° and indeed it takes
From our achievements, though perform'd at height,
The pith and marrow of our attribute.°
So, oft it chances in particular men,
That for some vicious mole of nature° in them,
As, in their birth — wherein they are not guilty,
Since nature cannot choose his origin —

129 *implorators of:* Solicitors of. 130 *Breathing:* Speaking. 133 *slander:* Bring disgrace or reproach upon. SCENE IV. 8 *wake:* Stay awake, hold revel; *rouse:* Carouse, drinking bout. 9 *wassail:* Carousal; *up-spring:* Last and wildest dance at German merry-makings. *reels:* Reels through. 10 *Rhenish:* Rhine wine. 12 *triumph . . . pledge:* His glorious achievement as a drinker. 15 *to . . . born:* Destined by birth to be subject to the custom in question. 19 *clepe:* Call; *with swinish phrase:* By calling us swine. 20 *addition:* Reputation. 22 *attribute:* Reputation. 24 *mole of nature:* Natural blemish in one's constitution.

By the o'ergrowth of some complexion,
Oft breaking down the pales° and forts of reason,
Or by some habit that too much o'er-leavens°
The form of plausive° manners, that these men,
Carrying, I say, the stamp of one defect,
Being nature's livery,° or fortune's star,° —
Their virtues else — be they as pure as grace,
As infinite as man may undergo —
Shall in the general censure take corruption
From that particular fault: the dram of eale°
Doth all the nobel substance of a doubt
To his own scandal.°

Enter Ghost.

Horatio: Look, my lord, it comes!
Hamlet: Angels and ministers of grace° defend us!
Be thou a spirit of health or goblin damn'd,
Bring with thee airs from heaven or blasts from hell,
Be thy intents wicked or charitable,
Thou com'st in such a questionable° shape
That I will speak to thee: I'll call thee Hamlet,
King, father, royal Dane: O, answer me!
Let me not burst in ignorance; but tell
Why thy canoniz'd° bones, hearsed° in death,
Have burst their cerements;° why the sepulchre,
Wherein we saw thee quietly interr'd,
Hath op'd his ponderous and marble jaws,
To cast thee up again. What may this mean,
That thou, dead corse, again in complete steel
Revisits thus the glimpses of the moon,°
Making night hideous; and we fools of nature°
So horridly to shake our disposition
With thoughts beyond the reaches of our souls?
Say, why is this? wherefore? what should we do?

[Ghost] beckons [Hamlet].

Horatio: It beckons you to go away with it,
As if it some impartment° did desire
To you alone.
Marcellus: Look, with what courteous action
It waves you to a more removed° ground:

28 *pales:* Palings (as of a fortification). 29 *o'er-leavens:* Induces a change throughout (as yeast works in bread). 30 *plausive:* Pleasing. 32 *nature's livery:* Endowment from nature; *fortune's star:* The position in which one is placed by fortune, a reference to astrology. The two phrases are aspects of the same thing. 36–38 *the dram . . . scandal:* A famous crux: *dram of eale* has had various interpretations, the preferred one being probably, "a dram of evil." 39 *ministers of grace:* Messengers of God. 43 *questionable:* Inviting question or conversation. 47 *canoniz'd:* Buried according to the canons of the church; *hearsed:* Coffined. 48 *cerements:* Grave-clothes. 53 *glimpses of the moon:* The earth by night. 54 *fools of nature:* Mere men, limited to natural knowledge. 59 *impartment:* Communication. 61 *removed:* Remote.

But do not go with it.
Horatio: No, by no means.
Hamlet: It will not speak; then I will follow it.
Horatio: Do not, my lord!
Hamlet: Why, what should be the fear?
I do not set my life at a pin's fee;
And for my soul, what can it do to that,
Being a thing immortal as itself?
It waves me forth again: I'll follow it.
Horatio: What if it tempt you toward the flood, my lord,
Or to the dreadful summit of the cliff
That beetles o'er° his base into the sea,
And there assume some other horrible form,
Which might deprive your sovereignty of reason°
And draw you into madness? think of it:
The very place puts toys of desperation,°
Without more motive, into every brain
That looks so many fathoms to the sea
And hears it roar beneath.
Hamlet: It waves me still.
Go on; I'll follow thee.
Marcellus: You shall not go, my lord.
Hamlet: Hold off your hands!
Horatio: Be rul'd; you shall not go.
Hamlet: My fate cries out,
And makes each petty artere° in this body
As hardy as the Nemean lion's° nerve.°
Still am I call'd. Unhand me, gentlemen.
By heaven, I'll make a ghost of him that lets° me!
I say, away! Go on; I'll follow thee. *Exeunt Ghost and Hamlet.*
Horatio: He waxes desperate with imagination.
Marcellus: Let's follow; 'tis not fit thus to obey him.
Horatio: Have after. To what issue° will this come?
Marcellus: Something is rotten in the state of Denmark.
Horatio: Heaven will direct it.°
Marcellus: Nay, let's follow him. *Exeunt.*

[SCENE V. *Another part of the platform.*]

Enter Ghost and Hamlet.

Hamlet: Whither wilt thou lead me? speak; I'll go no further.
Ghost: Mark me.

71 *beetles o'er:* Overhangs threateningly. 73 *deprive . . . reason:* Take away the sovereignty of your reason. It was thought that evil spirits would sometimes assume the form of departed spirits in order to work madness in a human creature. 75 *toys of desperation:* Freakish notions of suicide. 82 *artere:* Artery. 83 *Nemean lion's:* The Nemean lion was one of the monsters slain by Hercules; *nerve:* Sinew, tendon. The point is that the arteries which were carrying the spirits out into the body were functioning and were as stiff and hard as the sinews of the lion. 85 *lets:* Hinders. 89 *issue:* Outcome. 91 *it:* I.e., the outcome.

Hamlet: I will.
Ghost: My hour is almost come,
When I to sulphurous and tormenting flames
Must render up myself.
Hamlet: Alas, poor ghost!
Ghost: Pity me not, but lend thy serious hearing
To what I shall unfold.
Hamlet: Speak; I am bound to hear.
Ghost: So art thou to revenge, when thou shalt hear.
Hamlet: What?
Ghost: I am thy father's spirit,
Doom'd for a certain term to walk the night,
And for the day confin'd to fast° in fires,
Till the foul crimes done in my days of nature
Are burnt and purg'd away. But that I am forbid
To tell the secrets of my prison-house,
I could a tale unfold whose lightest word
Would harrow up thy soul, freeze thy young blood,
Make thy two eyes, like stars, start from their spheres,°
Thy knotted° and combined° locks to part
And each particular hair to stand an end,
Like quills upon the fretful porpentine:°
But this eternal blazon° must not be
To ears of flesh and blood. List, list, O, list!
If thou didst ever thy dear father love —
Hamlet: O God!
Ghost: Revenge his foul and most unnatural° murder.
Hamlet: Murder!
Ghost: Murder most foul, as in the best it is;
But this most foul, strange and unnatural.
Hamlet: Haste me to know't, that I, with wings as swift
As meditation or the thoughts of love,
May sweep to my revenge.
Ghost: I find thee apt;
And duller shouldst thou be than the fat weed°
That roots itself in ease on Lethe wharf,°
Wouldst thou not stir in this. Now, Hamlet, hear:
'Tis given out that, sleeping in my orchard,
A serpent stung me; so the whole ear of Denmark
Is by a forged process of my death
Rankly abus'd: but know, thou noble youth,
The serpent that did sting thy father's life

SCENE V. 12 *fast:* Probably, do without food. It has been sometimes taken in the sense of doing general penance. 18 *spheres:* Orbits. 19 *knotted:* Perhaps intricately arranged; *combined:* Tied, bound. 21 *porpentine:* Porcupine. 22 *eternal blazon:* Promulgation or proclamation of eternity, revelation of the hereafter. 26 *unnatural:* I.e., pertaining to fratricide. 33 *fat weed:* Many suggestions have been offered as to the particular plant intended, including asphodel; probably a general figure for plants growing along rotting wharves and piles. 34 *Lethe wharf:* Bank of the river of forgetfulness in Hades.

Now wears his crown.

Hamlet: O my prophetic soul!
My uncle!

Ghost: Ay, that incestuous, that adulterate° beast,
With witchcraft of his wit, with traitorous gifts, —
O wicked wit and gifts, that have the power
So to seduce! — won to his shameful lust
The will of my most seeming-virtuous queen:
O Hamlet, what a falling-off was there!
From me, whose love was of that dignity
That it went hand in hand even with the vow
I made to her in marriage, and to decline
Upon a wretch whose natural gifts were poor
To those of mine!
But virtue, as it never will be moved,
Though lewdness court it in a shape of heaven,
So lust, though to a radiant angel link'd,
Will sate itself in a celestial bed,
And prey on garbage.
But, soft! methinks I scent the morning air;
Brief let me be. Sleeping within my orchard,
My custom always of the afternoon,
Upon my secure° hour thy uncle stole,
With juice of cursed hebona° in a vial,
And in the porches of my ears did pour
The leperous° distilment; whose effect
Holds such an enmity with blood of man
That swift as quicksilver it courses through
The natural gates and alleys of the body,
And with a sudden vigour it doth posset°
And curd, like eager° droppings into milk,
The thin and wholesome blood: so did it mine;
And a most instant tetter bark'd about,
Most lazar-like,° with vile and loathsome crust,
All my smooth body.
Thus was I, sleeping, by a brother's hand
Of life, of crown, of queen, at once dispatch'd:°
Cut off even in the blossoms of my sin,
Unhous'led,° disappointed,° unanel'd,°
No reck'ning made, but sent to my account
With all my imperfections on my head:
O, horrible! O, horrible! most horrible!°

43 *adulterate:* Adulterous. 62 *secure:* Confident, unsuspicious. 63 *hebona:* Generally supposed to mean henbane, conjectured *hemlock; ebenus,* meaning "yew." 65 *leperous:* Causing leprosy. 69 *posset:* Coagulate, curdle. 70 *eager:* Sour, acid. 73 *lazar-like:* Leperlike. 76 *dispatch'd:* Suddenly bereft. 78 *Unhous'led:* Without having received the sacrament; *disappointed:* Unready, without equipment for the last journey; *unanel'd:* Without having received extreme unction. 81 *O . . . horrible:* Many editors give this line to Hamlet; Garrick and Sir Henry Irving spoke it in that part.

If thou hast nature in thee, bear it not;
Let not the royal bed of Denmark be
A couch for luxury° and damned incest.
But, howsomever thou pursues this act,
Taint not thy mind,° nor let thy soul contrive
Against thy mother aught: leave her to heaven
And to those thorns that in her bosom lodge,
To prick and sting her. Fare thee well at once!
The glow-worm shows the matin° to be near,
And 'gins to pale his uneffectual fire:°
Adieu, adieu, adieu! remember me. *[Exit.]*

Hamlet: O all you host of heaven! O earth! what else?
And shall I couple° hell? O, fie! Hold, hold, my heart;
And you, my sinews, grow not instant old,
But bear me stiffly up. Remember thee!
Ay, thou poor ghost, whiles memory holds a seat
In this distracted globe.° Remember thee!
Yea, from the table of my memory
I'll wipe away all trivial fond records,
All saws° of books, all forms, all pressures° past,
That youth and observation copied there;
And thy commandment all alone shall live
Within the book and volume of my brain,
Unmix'd with baser matter: yes, by heaven!
O most pernicious woman!
O villain, villain, smiling, damned villain!
My tables,°— meet it is I set it down,
That one may smile, and smile, and be a villain;
At least I am sure it may be so in Denmark: *[Writing.]*
So, uncle, there you are. Now to my word;°
It is "Adieu, adieu! remember me,"
I have sworn't.

Enter Horatio and Marcellus.

Horatio: My lord, my lord —
Marcellus: Lord Hamlet, —
Horatio: Heavens secure him!
Hamlet: So be it!
Marcellus: Hillo, ho, ho,° my lord!
Hamlet: Hillo, ho, ho, boy! come, bird, come.
Marcellus: How is't, my noble lord?
Horatio: What news, my lord?
Hamlet: O, wonderful!
Horatio: Good my lord, tell it.

84 *luxury:* Lechery. 86 *Taint . . . mind:* Probably, deprave not thy character, do nothing except in the pursuit of a natural revenge. 90 *matin:* Morning. 91 *uneffectual fire:* Cold light. 94 *couple:* Add. 98 *distracted globe:* Confused head. 101 *saws:* Wise sayings; *pressures:* Impressions stamped. 108 *tables:* Probably a small portable writing-tablet carried at the belt. 111 *word:* Watchword. 116 *Hillo, ho, ho:* A falconer's call to a hawk in air.

Hamlet: No; you will reveal it.
Horatio: Not I, my lord, by heaven.
Marcellus: Nor I, my lord.
Hamlet: How say you, then; would heart of man once think it?
But you'll be secret?
Horatio: / *Marcellus:* Ay, by heaven, my lord.
Hamlet: There's ne'er a villain dwelling in all Denmark
But he's an arrant° knave.
Horatio: There needs no ghost, my lord, come from the grave
To tell us this.
Hamlet: Why, right; you are in the right;
And so, without more circumstance at all,
I hold it fit that we shake hands and part:
You, as your business and desire shall point you;
For every man has business and desire,
Such as it is; and for my own poor part,
Look you, I'll go pray.
Horatio: These are but wild and whirling words, my lord.
Hamlet: I am sorry they offend you, heartily;
Yes, 'faith, heartily.
Horatio: There's no offence, my lord.
Hamlet: Yes, by Saint Patrick,° but there is, Horatio,
And much offence too. Touching this vision here,
It is an honest° ghost, that let me tell you:
For your desire to know what is between us,
O'ermaster 't as you may. And now, good friends,
As you are friends, scholars and soldiers,
Give me one poor request.
Horatio: What is 't, my lord? we will.
Hamlet: Never make known what you have seen to-night.
Horatio: / *Marcellus:* My lord, we will not.
Hamlet: Nay, but swear 't.
Horatio: In faith,
My lord, not I.
Marcellus: Nor I, my lord, in faith.
Hamlet: Upon my sword.°
Marcellus: We have sworn, my lord, already.
Hamlet: Indeed, upon my sword, indeed. *Ghost cries under the stage.*
Ghost: Swear.
Hamlet: Ah, ha, boy! say'st thou so? art thou there, truepenny?°
Come on — you hear this fellow in the cellarage —
Consent to swear.

125 *arrant:* Thoroughgoing. 137 *Saint Patrick:* St. Patrick was keeper of Purgatory and patron saint of all blunders and confusion. 139 *honest:* I.e., a real ghost and not an evil spirit. 147 *sword:* I.e., the hilt in the form of a cross. 150 *truepenny:* Good old boy, or the like.

Horatio: Propose the oath, my lord.
Hamlet: Never to speak of this that you have seen,
Swear by my sword.
Ghost [beneath]: Swear.
Hamlet: Hic et ubique?° then we'll shift our ground.
Come hither, gentlemen,
And lay your hands again upon my sword:
Swear by my sword,
Never to speak of this that you have heard.
Ghost [beneath]: Swear by his sword.
Hamlet: Well said, old mole! canst work i' th' earth so fast?
A worthy pioner!° Once more remove, good friends.
Horatio: O day and night, but this is wondrous strange!
Hamlet: And therefore as a stranger give it welcome.
There are more things in heaven and earth, Horatio,
Than are dreamt of in your philosophy.
But come;
Here, as before, never, so help you mercy,
How strange or odd soe'er I bear myself,
As I perchance hereafter shall think meet
To put an antic° disposition on,
That you, at such times seeing me, never shall,
With arms encumb'red° thus, or this head-shake,
Or by pronouncing of some doubtful phrase,
As "Well, well, we know," or "We could, an if we would,"
Or "If we list to speak," or "There be, an if they might,"
Or such ambiguous giving out,° to note°
That you know aught of me: this not to do,
So grace and mercy at your most need help you,
Swear.
Ghost [beneath]: Swear.
Hamlet: Rest, rest, perturbed spirit! *[They swear.]* So, gentlemen,
With all my love I do commend me to you:
And what so poor a man as Hamlet is
May do, t' express his love and friending° to you,
God willing, shall not lack. Let us go in together;
And still your fingers on your lips, I pray.
The time is out of joint: O cursed spite,
That ever I was born to set it right!
Nay, come, let's go together. *Exeunt.*

156 *Hic et ubique?:* Here and everywhere? 163 *pioner:* Digger, miner. 172 *antic:* Fantastic. 174 *encumb'red:* Folded or entwined. 178 *giving out:* Profession of knowledge; *to note:* To give a sign. 186 *friending:* Friendliness.

[ACT II

SCENE I. *A room in Polonius's house.*]

Enter old Polonius with his man [Reynaldo].

Polonius: Give him this money and these notes, Reynaldo.
Reynaldo: I will, my lord.
Polonius: You shall do marvellous wisely, good Reynaldo,
Before you visit him, to make inquire
Of his behaviour.
Reynaldo: My lord, I did intend it.
Polonius: Marry, well said; very well said. Look you, sir,
Inquire me first what Danskers° are in Paris;
And how, and who, what means, and where they keep,°
What company, at what expense; and finding
By this encompassment° and drift° of question
That they do know my son, come you more nearer
Than your particular demands will touch it:°
Take° you, as 'twere, some distant knowledge of him;
As thus, "I know his father and his friends,
And in part him": do you mark this, Reynaldo?
Reynaldo: Ay, very well, my lord.
Polonius: "And in part him; but" you may say "not well:
But, if 't be he I mean, he's very wild;
Addicted so and so": and there put on° him
What forgeries° you please; marry, none so rank
As may dishonour him; take heed of that;
But, sir, such wanton,° wild and usual slips
As are companions noted and most known
To youth and liberty.
Reynaldo: As gaming, my lord.
Polonius: Ay, or drinking, fencing,° swearing, quarrelling,
Drabbing;° you may go so far.
Reynaldo: My lord, that would dishonour him.
Polonius: 'Faith, no; as you may season it in the charge.
You must not put another scandal on him,
That he is open to incontinency;°
That's not my meaning: but breathe his faults so quaintly°
That they may seem the taints of liberty,°
The flash and outbreak of a fiery mind,

ACT II. SCENE I. 7 *Danskers:* Danke was a common variant for "Denmark"; hence "Dane." 8 *keep:* Dwell. 10 *encompassment:* Roundabout talking; *drift:* Gradual approach or course. 11–12 *come . . . it:* I.e., you will find out more this way than by asking pointed questions. 13 *Take:* Assume, pretend. 19 *put on:* Impute to. 20 *forgeries:* Invented tales. 22 *wanton:* Sportive, unrestrained. 25 *fencing:* Indicative of the ill repute of professional fencers and fencing schools in Elizabethan times. 26 *Drabbing:* Associating with immoral women. 30 *incontinency:* Habitual loose behavior. 31 *quaintly:* Delicately, ingeniously. 32 *taints of liberty:* Blemishes due to freedom.

A savageness in unreclaimed° blood,
Of general assault.°

Reynaldo: But, my good lord, —

Polonius: Wherefore should you do this?

Reynaldo: Ay, my lord,
I would know that.

Polonius: Marry, sir, here's my drift;
And, I believe, it is a fetch of wit:°
You laying these slight sullies on my son,
As'twere a thing a little soil'd i' th' working,
Mark you,
Your party in converse, him you would sound,
Having ever° seen in the prenominate° crimes
The youth you breathe of guilty, be assur'd
He closes with you in this consequence;°
"Good sir," or so, or "friend," or "gentleman,"
According to the phrase or the addition
Of man and country.

Reynaldo: Very good, my lord.

Polonius: And then, sir, does 'a this — 'a does — what was I about to say?
By the mass, I was about to say something: where did I leave?

Reynaldo: At "closes in the consequence," at "friend or so," and "gentleman."

Polonius: At "closes in the consequence," ay, marry;
He closes thus: "I know the gentleman;
I saw him yesterday, or t' other day,
Or then, or then; with such, or such; and, as you say,
There was 'a gaming; there o'ertook in 's rouse;°
There falling out at tennis": or perchance,
"I saw him enter such a house of sale,"
Videlicet,° a brothel, or so forth.
See you now;
Your bait of falsehood takes this carp of truth:
And thus do we of wisdom and of reach,°
With windlasses° and with assays of bias,°
By indirections° find directions° out:
So by my former lecture° and advice,
Shall you my son. You have me, have you not?

Reynaldo: My lord, I have.

Polonius: God bye ye;° fare ye well.

Reynaldo: Good my lord!

Polonius: Observe his inclination in yourself.°

34 *unreclaimed:* Untamed. 35 *general assault:* Tendency that assails all untrained youth. 38 *fetch of wit:* Clever trick. 43 *ever:* At any time; *prenominate:* Before-mentioned. 45 *closes . . . consequence:* Agrees with you in this conclusion. 57 *o'ertook in 's rouse:* Overcome by drink. 60 *Videlicet:* Namely. 63 *reach:* Capacity, ability. 64 *windlasses:* I.e., circuitous paths; *assays of bias:* Attempts that resemble the course of the bowl, which, being weighted on one side, has a curving motion. 65 *indirections:* Devious courses; *directions:* Straight courses, i.e., the truth. 66 *lecture:* Admonition. 68 *bye ye:* Be with you. 70 *Observe . . . yourself:* In your own person, not by spies; or conform your own conduct to his inclination; or test him by studying yourself.

Reynaldo: I shall, my lord.
Polonius: And let him ply his music.°
Reynaldo: Well, my lord.
Polonius: Farewell! *Exit Reynaldo.*

Enter Ophelia.

How now, Ophelia! what's the matter?
Ophelia: O, my lord, my lord, I have been so affrighted!
Polonius: With what, i' th' name of God?
Ophelia: My lord, as I was sewing in my closet,°
Lord Hamlet, with his doublet° all unbrac'd;°
No hat upon his head; his stockings foul'd,
Ungart'red, and down-gyved° to his ankle;
Pale as his shirt; his knees knocking each other;
And with a look so piteous in purport
As if he had been loosed out of hell
To speak of horrors, — he comes before me.
Polonius: Mad for thy love?
Ophelia: My lord, I do not know;
But truly, I do fear it.
Polonius: What said he?
Ophelia: He took me by the wrist and held me hard;
Then goes he to the length of all his arm;
And, with his other hand thus o'er his brow,
He falls to such perusal of my face
As 'a would draw it. Long stay'd he so;
At last, a little shaking of mine arm
And thrice his head thus waving up and down,
He rais'd a sigh so piteous and profound
As it did seem to shatter all his bulk°
And end his being: that done, he lets me go:
And, with his head over his shoulder turn'd,
He seem'd to find his way without his eyes;
For out o' doors he went without their helps,
And, to the last, bended their light on me.
Polonius: Come, go with me: I will go seek the king.
This is the very ecstasy of love,
Whose violent property° fordoes° itself
And leads the will to desperate undertakings
As oft as any passion under heaven
That does afflict our natures. I am sorry.
What, have you given him any hard words of late?
Ophelia: No, my good lord, but, as you did command,
I did repel his letters and denied
His access to me.

72 *ply his music:* Probably to be taken literally. 76 *closet:* Private chamber. 77 *doublet:* close-fitting coat; *unbrac'd:* Unfastened. 79 *down-gyved:* Fallen to the ankles (like gyves or fetters). 94 *bulk:* Body. 102 *property:* Nature; *fordoes:* Destroys.

Polonius: That hath made him mad.
I am sorry that with better heed and judgement
I had not quoted° him: I fear'd he did but trifle,
And meant to wrack thee; but, beshrew my jealousy!°
By heaven, it is as proper to our age
To cast beyond° ourselves in our opinions
As it is common for the younger sort
To lack discretion. Come, go we to the king:
This must be known; which, being kept close, might move
More grief to hide than hate to utter love.°
Come. *Exeunt.*

[SCENE II. *A room in the castle.*]

Flourish. Enter King and Queen, Rosencrantz, and Guildenstern [with others].

King: Welcome, dear Rosencrantz and Guildenstern!
Moreover that° we much did long to see you,
The need we have to use you did provoke
Our hasty sending. Something have you heard
Of Hamlet's transformation; so call it,
Sith° nor th' exterior nor the inward man
Resembles that it was. What it should be,
More than his father's death, that thus hath put him
So much from th' understanding of himself,
I cannot dream of: I entreat you both,
That, being of so young days° brought up with him,
And sith so neighbour'd to his youth and haviour,
That you vouchsafe your rest° here in our court
Some little time: so by your companies
To draw him on to pleasures, and to gather,
So much as from occasion you may glean,
Whether aught, to us unknown, afflicts him thus,
That, open'd, lies within our remedy.
Queen: Good gentlemen, he hath much talk'd of you;
And sure I am two men there are not living
To whom he more adheres. If it will please you
To show us so much gentry° and good will
As to expend your time with us awhile,
For the supply and profit° of our hope,
Your visitation shall receive such thanks
As fits a king's remembrance.
Rosencrantz: Both your majesties

111 *quoted:* Observed. 112 *beshrew my jealousy:* Curse my suspicions. 114 *cast beyond:* Overshoot, miscalculate. 117–118 *might . . . love:* I.e., I might cause more grief to others by hiding the knowledge of Hamlet's love to Ophelia than hatred to me and mine by telling of it. SCENE II. 2 *Moreover that:* Besides the fact that. 6 *Sith:* Since. 11 *of . . . days:* From such early youth. 13 *vouchsafe your rest:* Please to stay. 22 *gentry:* Courtesy. 24 *supply and profit:* Aid and successful outcome.

Might, by the sovereign power you have of us,
Put your dread pleasures more into command
Than to entreaty.

Guildenstern: But we both obey,
And here give up ourselves, in the full bent°
To lay our service freely at your feet,
To be commanded.

King: Thanks, Rosencrantz and gentle Guildenstern.

Queen: Thanks, Guildenstern and gentle Rosencrantz:
And I beseech you instantly to visit
My too much changed son. Go, some of you,
And bring these gentlemen where Hamlet is.

Guildenstern: Heavens make our presence and our practices
Pleasant and helpful to him!

Queen: Ay, amen!

Exeunt Rosencrantz and Guildenstern [with some Attendants].
Enter Polonius.

Polonius: Th' ambassadors from Norway, my good lord,
Are joyfully return'd.

King: Thou still hast been the father of good news.

Polonius: Have I, my lord? I assure my good liege,
I hold my duty, as I hold my soul,
Both to my God and to my gracious king:
And I do think, or else this brain of mine
Hunts not the trail of policy so sure
As it hath us'd to do, that I have found
The very cause of Hamlet's lunacy.

King: O, speak of that; that do I long to hear.

Polonius: Give first admittance to th' ambassadors;
My news shall be the fruit to that great feast.

King: Thyself do grace to them, and bring them in. *[Exit Polonius.]*
He tells me, my dear Gertrude, he hath found
The head and source of all your son's distemper.

Queen: I doubt° it is no other but the main;°
His father's death, and our o'erhasty marriage.

King: Well, we shall sift him.

Enter Ambassadors [Voltimand and Cornelius, with Polonius.]

Welcome, my good friends!
Say, Voltimand, what from our brother Norway?

Voltimand: Most fair return of greetings and desires.
Upon our first, he sent out to suppress
His nephew's levies; which to him appear'd
To be a preparation 'gainst the Polack;
But, better look'd into, he truly found
It was against your highness: whereat griev'd,

30 *in . . . bent:* To the utmost degree of our mental capacity. 56 *doubt:* Fear; *main:* Chief point, principal concern.

That so his sickness, age and impotence
Was falsely borne in hand,° sends out arrests
On Fortinbras; which he, in brief, obeys;
Receives rebuke from Norway, and in fine°
Makes vow before his uncle never more
To give th' assay° of arms against your majesty.
Whereon old Norway, overcome with joy,
Gives him three score thousand crowns in annual fee,
And his commission to employ those soldiers,
So levied as before, against the Polack:
With an entreaty, herein further shown, *[giving a paper.]*
That it might please you to give quiet pass
Through your dominions for this enterprise,
On such regards of safety and allowance°
As therein are set down.

King: It likes° us well;
And at our more consider'd° time we'll read,
Answer, and think upon this business.
Meantime we thank you for your well-took labour:
Go to your rest; at night we'll feast together:
Most welcome home! *Exeunt Ambassadors.*

Polonius: This business is well ended.
My liege, and madam, to expostulate
What majesty should be, what duty is,
Why day is day, night night, and time is time,
Were nothing but to waste night, day and time.
Therefore, since brevity is the soul of wit,°
And tediousness the limbs and outward flourishes,°
I will be brief: your noble son is mad:
Mad call I it; for, to define true madness
What is 't but to be nothing else but mad?
But let that go.

Queen: More matter, with less art.

Polonius: Madam, I swear I use no art at all.
That he is mad, 'tis true: 'tis true 'tis pity;
And pity 'tis 'tis true: a foolish figure;°
But farewell it, for I will use no art.
Mad let us grant him, then: and now remains
That we find out the cause of this effect,
Or rather say, the cause of this defect,
For this effect defective comes by cause:
Thus it remains, and the remainder thus.
Perpend.°
I have a daughter — have while she is mine —

67 *borne in hand:* Deluded. 69 *in fine:* In the end. 71 *assay:* Assault, trial (of arms). 79 *safety and allowance:* Pledges of safety to the country and terms of permission for the troops to pass. 80 *likes:* Pleases. 81 *consider'd:* Suitable for deliberation. 90 *wit:* Sound sense or judgment. 91 *flourishes:* Ostentation, embellishments. 98 *figure:* Figure of speech. 105 *Perpend:* Consider.

Who, in her duty and obedience, mark,
Hath given me this: now gather, and surmise. *[Reads the letter]* "To the celestial and my soul's idol, the most
beautified Ophelia," —
That's an ill phrase, a vile phrase; "beautified" is a vile phrase: but you shall hear. Thus: *[Reads.]*
"In her excellent white bosom, these, & c."

Queen: Came this from Hamlet to her?

Polonius: Good madam, stay awhile; I will be faithful.
[Reads.]

"Doubt thou the stars are fire;
Doubt that the sun doth move;
Doubt truth to be a liar;
But never doubt I love.

"O dear Ophelia, I am ill at these numbers;° I have not art to reckon° my groans: but that I love thee best, O most best, believe it. Adieu.

"Thine evermore, most dear lady, whilst this machine° is to him,
HAMLET."

This, in obedience, hath my daughter shown me,
And more above,° hath his solicitings,
As they fell out° by time, by means° and place,
All given to mine ear.

King: But how hath she
Receiv'd his love?

Polonius: What do you think of me?

King: As of a man faithful and honourable.

Polonius: I would fain prove so. But what might you think,
When I had seen this hot love on the wing —
As I perceiv'd it, I must tell you that,
Before my daughter told me — what might you,
Or my dear majesty your queen here, think,
If I had play'd the desk or table-book,°
Or given my heart a winking,° mute and dumb,
Or look'd upon this love with idle sight;
What might you think? No, I went round to work,
And my young mistress thus I did bespeak:°
"Lord Hamlet is a prince, out of thy star;°
This must not be": and then I prescripts gave her,
That she should lock herself from his resort,
Admit no messengers, receive no tokens.
Which done, she took the fruits of my advice;
And he, repelled — a short tale to make —
Fell into a sadness, then into a fast,

120 *ill . . . numbers:* Unskilled at writing verses. 121 *reckon:* Number metrically, scan. 123 *machine:* Bodily frame. 126 *more above:* Moreover. 127 *fell out:* Occurred; *means:* Opportunities (of access). 136 *play'd . . . table-book:* I.e., remained shut up, concealed this information. 137 *given . . . winking:* Given my heart a signal to keep silent. 140 *bespeak:* Address. 141 *out . . . star:* Above thee in position.

Thence to a watch,° thence into a weakness,
Thence to a lightness,° and, by this declension,°
Into the madness wherein now he raves,
And all we mourn for.

King: Do you think 'tis this?

Queen: It may be, very like.

Polonius: Hath there been such a time — I would fain know that —
That I have positively said " 'Tis so,"
When it prov'd otherwise?

King: Not that I know.

Polonius [pointing to his head and shoulder]: Take this from this, if this be otherwise:
If circumstances lead me, I will find
Where truth is hid, though it were hid indeed
Within the centre.°

King: How may we try it further?

Polonius: You know, sometimes he walks four hours together
Here in the lobby.

Queen: So he does indeed.

Polonius: At such a time I'll loose my daughter to him:
Be you and I behind an arras° then;
Mark the encounter: if he love her not
And be not from his reason fall'n thereon,°
Let me be no assistant for a state,
But keep a farm and carters.

King: We will try it.

Enter Hamlet [reading on a book].

Queen: But, look, where sadly the poor wretch comes reading.

Polonius: Away, I do beseech you both, away:

Exeunt King and Queen [with Attendants].

I'll board° him presently. O, give me leave.
How does my good Lord Hamlet?

Hamlet: Well, God-a-mercy.

Polonius: Do you know me, my lord?

Hamlet: Excellent well; you are a fishmonger.°

Polonius: Not I, my lord.

Hamlet: Then I would you were so honest a man.

Polonius: Honest, my lord!

Hamlet: Ay, sir; to be honest, as this world goes, is to be one man picked out of ten thousand.

Polonius: That's very true, my lord.

Hamlet: For if the sun breed maggots in a dead dog, being a good kissing carrion,° — Have you a daughter?

148 *watch:* State of sleeplessness. 149 *lightness:* Lightheadedness; *declension:* Decline, deterioration. 160 *centre:* Middle point of the earth. 164 *arras:* Hanging, tapestry. 166 *thereon:* On that account. 171 *board:* Accost. 175 *fishmonger:* An opprobrious expression meaning "bawd," "procurer." 183 *good kissing carrion:* I.e., a good piece of flesh for kissing (?).

Polonius: I have, my lord.

Hamlet: Let her not walk i' the sun:° conception° is a blessing: but as your daughter may conceive — Friend, look to 't.

Polonius [aside]: How say you by° that? Still harping on my daughter: yet he knew me not at first; 'a said I was a fishmonger: 'a is far gone, far gone: and truly in my youth I suffered much extremity for love; very near this. I'll speak to him again. What do you read, my lord?

Hamlet: Words, words, words.

Polonius: What is the matter,° my lord?

Hamlet: Between who?°

Polonius: I mean, the matter that you read, my lord.

Hamlet: Slanders, sir: for the satirical rogue says here that old men have grey beards, that their faces are wrinkled, their eyes purging° thick amber and plum-tree gum and that they have a plentiful lack of wit, together with most weak hams: all which, sir, though I most powerfully and potently believe, yet I hold it not honesty° to have it thus set down, for yourself, sir, should be old as I am, if like a crab you could go backward.

Polonius [aside]: Though this be madness, yet there is method in 't. — Will you walk out of the air, my lord?

Hamlet: Into my grave.

Polonius: Indeed, that's out of the air. *(Aside.)* How pregnant sometimes his replies are! a happiness° that often madness hits on, which reason and sanity could not so prosperously° be delivered of. I will leave him, and suddenly contrive the means of meeting between him and my daughter. — My honourable lord, I will most humbly take my leave of you.

Hamlet: You cannot, sir, take from me any thing that I will more willingly part withal: except my life, except my life, except my life.

Enter Guildenstern and Rosencrantz.

Polonius: Fare you well, my lord.

Hamlet: These tedious old fools!

Polonius: You go to seek the Lord Hamlet; there he is.

Rosencrantz [to Polonius]: God save you, sir! *[Exit Polonius.]*

Guildenstern: My honoured lord!

Rosencrantz: My most dear lord!

Hamlet: My excellent good friends! How dost thou, Guildenstern? Ah, Rosencrantz! Good lads, how do ye both?

Rosencrantz: As the indifferent° children of the earth.

Guildenstern: Happy, in that we are not over-happy;
On Fortune's cap we are not the very button.

Hamlet: Nor the soles of her shoe?

Rosencrantz: Neither, my lord.

185 *i' the sun:* In the sunshine of princely favors; *conception:* Quibble on "understanding" and "pregnancy." 187 *by:* Concerning. 192 *matter:* Substance. 193 *Between who:* Hamlet deliberately takes *matter* as meaning "basis of dispute"; modern usage demands *whom* instead of *who.* 196 *purging:* discharging. 199 *honesty:* Decency. 206 *happiness:* Felicity of expression. 207 *prosperously:* Successfully. 221 *indifferent:* Ordinary.

Hamlet: Then you live about her waist, or in the middle of her favours?

Guildenstern: 'Faith, her privates° we.

Hamlet: In the secret parts of Fortune? O, most true; she is a strumpet. What's the news?

Rosencrantz: None, my lord, but that the world's grown honest.

Hamlet: Then is doomsday near: but your news is not true. Let me question more in particular: what have you, my good friends, deserved at the hands of Fortune, that she sends you to prison hither?

Guildenstern: Prison, my lord!

Hamlet: Denmark's a prison.

Rosencrantz: Then is the world one.

Hamlet: A goodly one; in which there are many confines,° wards and dungeons, Denmark being one o' the worst.

Rosencrantz: We think not so, my lord.

Hamlet: Why, then, 'tis none to you; for there is nothing either good or bad, but thinking makes it so: to me it is a prison.

Rosencrantz: Why then, your ambition makes it one; 'tis too narrow for your mind.

Hamlet: O God, I could be bounded in a nutshell and count myself a king of infinite space, were it not that I have bad dreams.

Guildenstern: Which dreams indeed are ambition, for the very substance of the ambitious° is merely the shadow of a dream.

Hamlet: A dream itself is but a shadow.

Rosencrantz: Truly, and I hold ambition of so airy and light a quality that it is but a shadow's shadow.

Hamlet: Then are our beggars bodies, and our monarchs and outstretched heroes the beggars' shadows. Shall we to the court? for, by my fay,° I cannot reason.°

Rosencrantz:
Guildenstern: } We'll wait upon° you.

Hamlet: No such matter: I will not sort° you with the rest of my servants, for, to speak to you like an honest man, I am most dreadfully attended.° But, in the beaten way of friendship,° what make you at Elsinore?

Rosencrantz: To visit you, my lord: no other occasion.

Hamlet: Beggar that I am, I am ever poor in thanks; but I thank you: and sure, dear friends, my thanks are too dear a° halfpenny. Were you not sent for? Is it your own inclining? Is it a free visitation? Come, come, deal justly with me: come, come; nay, speak.

Guildenstern: What should we say, my lord?

Hamlet: Why, any thing, but to the purpose. You were sent for; and there is a kind of confession in your looks which your modesties have not craft enough to colour: I know the good king and queen have sent for you.

Rosencrantz: To what end, my lord?

227 *privates:* I.e., ordinary men (with sexual pun on *private parts*). 237 *confines:* Places of confinement. 246–247 *very . . . ambitious:* That seemingly most substantial thing which the ambitious pursue. 252 *fay:* Faith. 253 *reason:* Argue; *wait upon:* Accompany. 254 *sort:* Class. 255 *dreadfully attended:* Poorly provided with servants. 256 *in the . . . friendship:* As a matter of course among friends. 259 *a:* I.e., at a.

Hamlet: That you must teach me. But let me conjure° you, by the rights of our fellowship, by the consonancy of our youth,° by the obligation of our ever-preserved love, and by what more dear a better proposer° could charge you withal, be even and direct with me, whether you were sent for, or no?

Rosencrantz [aside to Guildenstern]: What say you?

Hamlet [aside]: Nay, then, I have an eye of you. — If you love me, hold not off.

Guildenstern: My lord, we were sent for.

Hamlet: I will tell you why; so shall my anticipation prevent your discovery,° and your secrecy to the king and queen moult no feather. I have of late — but wherefore I know not — lost all my mirth, forgone all custom of exercises; and indeed it goes so heavily with my disposition that this goodly frame, the earth, seems to me a sterile promontory, this most excellent canopy, the air, look you, this brave o'erhanging firmament, this majestical roof fretted° with golden fire, why, it appeareth nothing to me but a foul and pestilent congregation of vapours. What a piece of work is a man! how noble in reason! how infinite in faculties!° in form and moving how express° and admirable! in action how like an angel! in apprehension° how like a god! the beauty of the world! the paragon of animals! And yet, to me, what is this quintessence° of dust? man delights not me: no, nor woman neither, though by your smiling you seem to say so.

Rosencrantz: My lord, there was no such stuff in my thoughts.

Hamlet: Why did you laugh then, when I said "man delights not me"?

Rosencrantz: To think, my lord, if you delight not in man, what lenten° entertainment the players shall receive from you: we coted° them on the way; and hither are they coming, to offer you service.

Hamlet: He that plays the king shall be welcome; his majesty shall have tribute of me; the adventurous knight shall use his foil and target;° the lover shall not sigh gratis; the humorous man° shall end his part in peace; the clown shall make those laugh whose lungs are tickle o' the sere;° and the lady shall say her mind freely, or the blank verse shall halt for 't.° What players are they?

Rosencrantz: Even those you were wont to take delight in, the tragedians of the city.

Hamlet: How chances it they travel? their residence,° both in reputation and profit, was better both ways.

268 *conjure:* Adjure, entreat. 269 *consonancy of our youth:* The fact that we are of the same age. 270 *better proposer:* One more skillful in finding proposals. 278 *prevent your discovery:* Forestall your disclosure. 283 *fretted:* Adorned. 285 *faculties:* Capacity. 286 *express:* Well-framed (?), exact (?). 287 *apprehension:* Understanding. 288 *quintessence:* The fifth essence of ancient philosophy, supposed to be the substance of the heavenly bodies and to be latent in all things. 293 *lenten:* Meager. 294 *coted:* Overtook and passed beyond. 297 *foil and target:* Sword and shield. 298 *humorous man:* Actor who takes the part of the humor characters. 299–300 *tickle o' the sere:* Easy on the trigger. 300–301 *the lady . . . for 't:* The lady (fond of talking) shall have opportunity to talk, blank verse or no blank verse. 304 *residence:* Remaining in one place.

Rosencrantz: I think their inhibition° comes by the means of the late innovation.°

Hamlet: Do they hold the same estimation they did when I was in the city? are they so followed?

Rosencrantz: No, indeed, are they not.

Hamlet: How comes it? do they grow rusty?

Rosencrantz: Nay, their endeavour keeps in the wonted pace: but there is, sir, an aery° of children, little eyases,° that cry out on the top of question,° and are most tyrannically° clapped for 't: these are now the fashion, and so berattle° the common stages°—so they call them—that many wearing rapiers° are afraid of goose-quills° and dare scarce come thither.

Hamlet: What, are they children? who maintains 'em? how are they escoted?° Will they pursue the quality° no longer than they can sing?° will they not say afterwards, if they should grow themselves to common° players—as it is most like, if their means are no better—their writers do them wrong, to make them exclaim against their own succession?°

Rosencrantz: 'Faith, there has been much to do on both sides; and the nation holds it no sin to tarre° them to controversy: there was, for a while, no money bid for argument,° unless the poet and the player went to cuffs° in the question.°

Hamlet: Is't possible?

Guildenstern: O, there has been much throwing about of brains.

Hamlet: Do the boys carry it away?°

Rosencrantz: Ay, that they do, my lord; Hercules and his load° too.

Hamlet: It is not very strange; for my uncle is king of Denmark, and those that would make mows° at him while my father lived, give twenty, forty, fifty, a hundred ducats° a-piece for his picture in little.° 'Sblood, there is something in this more than natural, if philosophy could find it out.

A flourish [of trumpets within].

Guildenstern: There are the players.

Hamlet: Gentlemen, you are welcome to Elsinore. Your hands, come then: the appurtenance of welcome is fashion and ceremony: let me comply°

306 *inhibition:* Formal prohibition (from acting plays in the city or, possibly, at court). 307 *innovation:* The new fashion in satirical plays performed by boy actors in the "private" theaters. 311–331 *How . . . load too:* The passage is the famous one dealing with the War of the Theatres (1599–1602); namely, the rivalry between the children's companies and the adult actors. 313 *aery:* Nest; *eyases:* Young hawks. 313–314 *cry . . . question:* Speak in a high key dominating conversation; clamor forth the height of controversy; probably "excel" (cf. l. 459); perhaps intended to decry leaders of the dramatic profession. 314 *tyrannically:* Outrageously. 315 *berattle:* Berate; *common stages:* Public theaters. 316 *many wearing rapiers:* Many men of fashion, who were afraid to patronize the common players for fear of being satirized by the poets who wrote for the children; *goose-quills:* I.e., pens of satirists. 319 *escoted:* Maintained; *quality:* Acting profession; *no longer . . . sing:* I.e., until their voices change. 321 *common:* Regular, adult. 323 *succession:* future careers. 325 *tarre:* Set on (as dogs). 326 *argument:* Probably, plot for a play. 327 *went to cuffs:* Came to blows; *question:* Controversy. 330 *carry it away:* Win the day. 331 *Hercules . . . load:* Regarded as an allusion to the sign of the Globe Theatre, which was Hercules bearing the world on his shoulder. 333 *mows:* Grimaces. 334 *ducats:* Gold coins worth 9s. 4d; *in little:* In miniature. 338 *comply:* Observe the formalities of courtesy.

with you in this garb,° lest my extent° to the players, which, I tell you, must show fairly outwards, should more appear like entertainment than yours. You are welcome: but my uncle-father and aunt-mother are deceived.

Guildenstern: In what, my dear lord?

Hamlet: I am but mad north-north-west:° when the wind is southerly I know a hawk from a handsaw.°

Enter Polonius.

Polonius: Well be with you, gentlemen!

Hamlet: Hark you, Guildenstern; and you too: at each ear a hearer: that great baby you see there is not yet out of his swaddling-clouts.°

Rosencrantz: Happily he is the second time come to them; for they say an old man is twice a child.

Hamlet: I will prophesy he comes to tell me of the players; mark it. — You say right, sir: o' Monday morning;° 'twas then indeed.

Polonius: My lord, I have news to tell you.

Hamlet: My lord, I have news to tell you. When Roscius° was an actor in Rome, —

Polonius: The actors are come hither, my lord.

Hamlet: Buz, buz!°

Polonius: Upon my honour, —

Hamlet: Then came each actor on his ass, —

Polonius: The best actors in the world, either for tragedy, comedy, history, pastoral, pastoral-comical, historical-pastoral, tragical-historical, tragical-comical-historical-pastoral, scene individable,° or poem unlimited:° Seneca° cannot be too heavy, nor Plautus° too light. For the law of writ and the liberty,° these are the only men.

Hamlet: O Jephthah, judge of Israel,° what a treasure hadst thou!

Polonius: What a treasure had he, my lord?

Hamlet: Why,

"One fair daughter, and no more,
The which he loved passing well."

Polonius [aside]: Still on my daughter.

Hamlet: Am I not i' the right, old Jephthah?

Polonius: If you call me Jephthah, my lord, I have a daughter that I love passing° well.

Hamlet: Nay, that follows not.

Polonius: What follows, then, my lord?

339 *garb:* Manner; *extent:* Showing of kindness. 344 *I am . . . north-north-west:* I am only partly mad, i.e., in only one point of the compass. 345 *handsaw:* A proposed reading of *hernshaw* would mean "heron"; *handsaw* may be an early corruption of *hernshaw*. Another view regards *hawk* as the variant of *hack,* a tool of the pickax type, and *handsaw* as a saw operated by hand. 348 *swaddling-clouts:* Cloths in which to wrap a newborn baby. 352 *o' Monday morning:* Said to mislead Polonius. 354 *Roscius:* A famous Roman actor. 357 *Buz, buz:* An interjection used at Oxford to denote stale news. 362 *scene individable:* A play observing the unity of place; *poem unlimited:* A play disregarding the unities of time and place. 363 *Seneca:* Writer of Latin tragedies, model of early Elizabethan writers of tragedy; *Plautus:* Writer of Latin comedy. 363–364 *law . . . liberty:* Pieces written according to rules and without rules, i.e., "classical" and "romantic" dramas. 365 *Jephthah . . . Israel:* Jephthah had to sacrifice his daughter; see Judges 11. 373 *Passing:* surpassingly.

Hamlet: Why,

"As by lot, God wot,"
and then, you know,
"It came to pass, as most like° it was," —
the first row° of the pious chanson° will show you more; for look, where my abridgement comes.°

Enter the Players.

You are welcome, masters; welcome, all. I am glad to see thee well. Welcome, good friends. O, old friend! why, thy face is valanced° since I saw thee last: comest thou to beard me in Denmark? What, my young lady and mistress! By'r lady, your ladyship is nearer to heaven than when I saw you last, by the altitude of a chopine.° Pray God, your voice, like a piece of uncurrent° gold, be not cracked within the ring.° Masters, you are all welcome. We'll e'en to 't like French falconers, fly at any thing we see: we'll have a speech straight: come, give us a taste of your quality; come, a passionate speech.

First Player: What speech, my good lord?

Hamlet: I heard thee speak me a speech once, but it was never acted; or, if it was, not above once; for the play, I remember, pleased not the million; 'twas caviary to the general:° but it was — as I received it, and others, whose judgements in such matters cried in the top of° mine — an excellent play, well digested in the scenes, set down with as much modesty as cunning.° I remember, one said there were no sallets° in the lines to make the matter savoury, nor no matter in the phrase that might indict° the author of affectation; but called it an honest method, as wholesome as sweet, and by very much more handsome than fine.° One speech in 't I chiefly loved: 'twas Æneas' tale to Dido;° and thereabout of it especially, where he speaks of Priam's slaughter: if it live in your memory, begin at this line: let me see, let me see —
"The rugged Pyrrhus,° like th' Hyrcanian beast,°" —
'tis not so: — it begins with Pyrrhus: —
"The rugged Pyrrhus, he whose sable arms,
Black as his purpose, did the night resemble
When he lay couched in the ominous horse,°
Hath now this dread and black complexion smear'd
With heraldry more dismal; head to foot

378 *like:* Probable. 379 *row:* Stanza; *chanson:* Ballad. 380 *abridgement comes:* Opportunity comes for cutting short the conversation. 382 *valanced:* Fringed (with a beard). 385 *chopine:* Kind of shoe raised by the thickness of the heel; worn in Italy, particularly at Venice. 386 *uncurrent:* Not passable as lawful coinage; *cracked within the ring:* In the center of coins were rings enclosing the sovereign's head; if the coin was cracked within this ring, it was unfit for currency. 393 *caviary to the general:* Not relished by the multitude. 394 *cried in the top of:* Spoke with greater authority than. 396 *cunning:* Skill; *sallets:* Salads: here, spicy improprieties. 398 *indict:* Convict. 399 *as wholesome . . . fine:* Its beauty was not that of elaborate ornament, but that of order and proportion. 400 *Æneas' tale to Dido:* The lines recited by the player are imitated from Marlowe and Nashe's *Dido Queen of Carthage* (II. i. 214 ff.). They are written in such a way that the conventionality of the play within a play is raised above that of ordinary drama. 403 *Pyrrhus:* A Greek hero in the Trojan War; *Hyrcanian beast:* The tiger; see Virgil, *Aeneid,* IV. 266. 407 *ominous horse:* Trojan horse.

Now is he total gules;° horridly trick'd°
With blood of fathers, mothers, daughters, sons,
Bak'd and impasted° with the parching streets,
That lend a tyrannous and a damned light
To their lord's murder: roasted in wrath and fire,
And thus o'er-sized° with coagulate gore,
With eyes like carbuncles, the hellish Pyrrhus
Old grandsire Priam seeks."
So, proceed you.

Polonius: 'Fore God, my lord, well spoken, with good accent and good discretion.

First Player: "Anon he finds him
Striking too short at Greeks; his antique sword,
Rebellious to his arm, lies where it falls,
Repugnant° to command: unequal match'd,
Pyrrhus at Priam drives; in rage strikes wide;
But with the whiff and wind of his fell sword
Th' unnerved father falls. Then senseless Ilium,°
Seeming to feel this blow, with flaming top
Stoops to his base, and with a hideous crash
Takes prisoner Pyrrhus' ear: for, lo! his sword
Which was declining on the milky head
Of reverend Priam, seem'd i' th' air to stick:
So, as a painted tyrant,° Pyrrhus stood,
And like a neutral to his will and matter,°
Did nothing.
But, as we often see, against° some storm,
A silence in the heavens, the rack° stand still,
The bold winds speechless and the orb below
As hush as death, anon the dreadful thunder
Doth rend the region,° so, after Pyrrhus' pause,
Aroused vengeance sets him new a-work;
And never did the Cyclops' hammers fall
On Mars's armour forg'd for proof eterne°
With less remorse than Pyrrhus' bleeding sword
Now falls on Priam.
Out, out, thou strumpet, Fortune! All you gods,
In general synod,° take away her power;
Break all the spokes and fellies° from her wheel,
And bowl the round nave° down the hill of heaven,
As low as to the fiends!"

Polonius: This is too long.

410 *gules:* Red, a heraldic term; *trick'd:* Spotted, smeared. 412 *impasted:* Made into a paste. 415 *o'er-sized:* Covered as with size or glue. 423 *Repugnant:* Disobedient. 426 *Then senseless Ilium:* Insensate Troy. 432 *painted tyrant:* Tyrant in a picture. 433 *matter:* Task. 435 *against:* Before. 436 *rack:* Mass of clouds. 439 *region:* Assembly. 442 *proof eterne:* External resistance to assault. 446 *synod:* Assembly. 447 *fellies:* Pieces of wood forming the rim of a wheel. 448 *nave:* Hub.

Hamlet: It shall to the barber's, with your beard. Prithee, say on: he's for a jig° or a tale of bawdry,° or he sleeps: say on: come to Hecuba.°

First Player: "But who, ah woe! had seen the mobled° queen—"

Hamlet: "The mobled queen?"

Polonius: That's good; "mobled queen" is good.

First Player: "Run barefoot up and down, threat'ning the flames
With bisson rheum;° a clout° upon that head
Where late the diadem stood, and for a robe,
About her lank and all o'er-teemed° loins,
A blanket, in the alarm of fear caught up;
Who this had seen, with tongue in venom steep'd,
'Gainst Fortune's state would treason have pronounc'd:°
But if the gods themselves did see her then
When she saw Pyrrhus make malicious sport
In mincing with his sword her husband's limbs,
The instant burst of clamour that she made,
Unless things mortal move them not at all,
Would have made milch° the burning eyes of heaven,
And passion in the gods."

Polonius: Look, whe'r he has not turned° his colour and has tears in 's eyes. Prithee, no more.

Hamlet: 'Tis well; I'll have thee speak out the rest soon. Good my lord, will you see the players well bestowed? Do you hear, let them be well used; for they are the abstract° and brief chronicles of the time: after your death you were better have a bad epitaph than their ill report while you live.

Polonius: My lord, I will use them according to their desert.

Hamlet: God's bodykins,° man, much better: use every man after his desert, and who shall 'scape whipping? Use them after your own honour and dignity: the less they deserve, the more merit is in your bounty. Take them in.

Polonius: Come, sirs.

Hamlet: Follow him, friends: we'll hear a play tomorrow. *[Aside to First Player.]* Dost thou hear me, old friend; can you play the Murder of Gonzago?

First Player: Ay, my lord.

Hamlet: We'll ha 't to-morrow night. You could, for a need, study a speech of some dozen or sixteen lines,° which I would set down and insert in 't, could you not?

First Player: Ay, my lord.

452 *jig:* Comic performance given at the end or in an interval of a play; *bawdry:* Indecency; *Hecuba:* Wife of Priam, king of Troy. 453 *mobled:* Muffled. 457 *bisson rheum:* Blinding tears; *clout:* Piece of cloth. 459 *o'er-teemed:* Worn out with bearing children. 462 *pronounc'd:* Proclaimed. 468 *milch:* Moist with tears. 470 *turned:* Changed. 474 *abstract:* Summary account. 478 *bodykins:* Diminutive form of the oath "by God's body." 488 *dozen or sixteen lines:* Critics have amused themselves by trying to locate Hamlet's lines. Lucianus's speech III. ii. 226–231 is the best guess.

Hamlet: Very well. Follow that lord; and look you mock him not. — My good friends, I'll leave you till night: you are welcome to Elsinore.

Exeunt Polonius and Players.

Rosencrantz: Good my lord! *Exeunt [Rosencrantz and Guildenstern.]*

Hamlet: Ay, so, God bye to you. — Now I am alone.
O, what a rogue and peasant° slave am I!
Is it not monstrous that this player here,
But in a fiction, in a dream of passion,
Could force his soul so to his own conceit
That from her working all his visage wann'd,°
Tears in his eyes, distraction in 's aspect,
A broken voice, and his whole function suiting
With forms to his conceit?° and all for nothing!
For Hecuba!
What's Hecuba to him, or he to Hecuba,
That he should weep for her? What would he do,
Had he the motive and the cue for passion
That I have? He would drown the stage with tears
And cleave the general ear with horrid speech,
Make mad the guilty and appal the free,
Confound the ignorant, and amaze indeed
The very faculties of eyes and ears.
Yet I,
A dull and muddy-mettled° rascal, peak,°
Like John-a-dreams,° unpregnant of° my cause,
And can say nothing; no, not for a king.
Upon whose property° and most dear life
A damn'd defeat was made. Am I a coward?
Who calls me villain? breaks my pate across?
Plucks off my beard, and blows it in my face?
Tweaks me by the nose? gives me the lie i' th' throat,
As deep as to the lungs? who does me this?
Ha!
'Swounds, I should take it: for it cannot be
But I am pigeon-liver'd° and lack gall
To make oppression bitter, or ere this
I should have fatted all the region kites°
With this slave's offal: bloody, bawdy villain!
Remorseless, treacherous, lecherous, kindless° villain!
O, vengeance!
Why, what an ass am I! This is most brave,
That I, the son of a dear father murder'd,

495 *peasant:* Base. 499 *wann'd:* Grew pale. 501–502 *his whole . . . conceit:* His whole being responded with forms to suit his thought. 513 *muddy-mettled:* Dull-spirited; *peak:* Mope, pine. 514 *John-a-dreams:* An expression occurring elsewhere in Elizabethan literature to indicate a dreamer; *unpregnant of:* Not quickened by. 516 *property:* Proprietorship (of crown and life). 524 *pigeon-liver'd:* The pigeon was supposed to secrete no gall; if Hamlet, so he says, had had gall, he would have felt the bitterness of oppression, and avenged it. 526 *region kites:* Kites of the air. 528 *kindless:* Unnatural.

Prompted to my revenge by heaven and hell,
Must, like a whore, unpack my heart with words,
And fall a-cursing, like a very drab,°
A stallion!°
Fie upon 't! foh! About,° my brains! Hum, I have heard
That guilty creatures sitting at a play
Have by the very cunning of the scene
Been struck so to the soul that presently
They have proclaim'd their malefactions;
For murder, though it have no tongue, will speak
With most miraculous organ. I'll have these players
Play something like the murder of my father
Before mine uncle: I'll observe his looks:
I'll tent° him to the quick: if 'a do blench,°
I know my course. The spirit that I have seen
May be the devil:° and the devil hath power
T' assume a pleasing shape; yea, and perhaps
Out of my weakness and my melancholy,
As he is very potent with such spirits,°
Abuses me to damn me: I'll have grounds
More relative° than this:° the play's the thing
Wherein I'll catch the conscience of the king. *Exit.*

[ACT III

SCENE I. *A room in the castle.*]

Enter King, Queen, Polonius, Ophelia, Rosencrantz, Guildenstern, Lords.

King: And can you, by no drift of conference,°
Get from him why he puts on this confusion,
Grating so harshly all his days of quiet
With turbulent and dangerous lunacy?
Rosencrantz: He does confess he feels himself distracted;
But from what cause 'a will by no means speak.
Guildenstern: Nor do we find him forward° to be sounded,
But, with a crafty madness, keeps aloof,
When we would bring him on to some confession
Of his true state.
Queen: Did he receive you well?
Rosencrantz: Most like a gentleman.
Guildenstern: But with much forcing of his disposition.°

534 *drab:* Prostitute. 535 *stallion:* Prostitute (male or female). 536 *About:* About it, or turn thou right about. 545 *tent:* Probe; *blench:* Quail, flinch. 547 *May be the devil:* Hamlet's suspicion is properly grounded in the belief of the time. 550 *spirits:* Humors. 552 *relative:* Closely related, definite; *this:* I.e., the ghost's story. ACT III. SCENE I. 1 *drift of conference:* Device of conversation. 7 *forward:* Willing. 12 *forcing of his disposition:* I.e., against his will.

Rosencrantz: Niggard of question;° but, of our demands,
Most free in his reply.
Queen: Did you assay° him
To any pastime?
Rosencrantz: Madam, it so fell out, that certain players
We o'er-raught° on the way: of these we told him;
And there did seem in him a kind of joy
To hear of it: they are here about the court,
And, as I think, they have already order
This night to play before him.
Polonius: 'Tis most true:
And he beseech'd me to entreat your majesties
To hear and see the matter.
King: With all my heart; and it doth much content me
To hear him so inclin'd.
Good gentlemen, give him a further edge,°
And drive his purpose into these delights.
Rosencrantz: We shall, my lord. *Exeunt Rosencrantz and Guildenstern.*
King: Sweet Gertrude, leave us too;
For we have closely° sent for Hamlet hither,
That he, as 'twere by accident, may here
Affront° Ophelia:
Her father and myself, lawful espials,°
Will so bestow ourselves that, seeing, unseen,
We may of their encounter frankly judge,
And gather by him, as he is behav'd,
If 't be th' affliction of his love or no
That thus he suffers for.
Queen: I shall obey you.
And for your part, Ophelia, I do wish
That your good beauties be the happy cause
Of Hamlet's wildness:° so shall I hope your virtues
Will bring him to his wonted way again,
To both your honours.
Ophelia: Madam, I wish it may. *[Exit Queen.]*
Polonius: Ophelia, walk you here. Gracious,° so please you,
We will bestow ourselves. *[To Ophelia.]* Read on this book;
That show of such an exercise° may colour°
Your loneliness. We are oft to blame in this, —
'Tis too much prov'd — that with devotion's visage
And pious action we do sugar o'er
The devil himself.
King: *[aside]* O, 'tis too true!
How smart a lash that speech doth give my conscience!

13 *Niggard of question:* Sparing of conversation. 14 *assay:* Try to win. 17 *o'er-raught:* Overtook. 26 *edge:* Incitement. 29 *closely:* Secretly. 31 *Affront:* Confront. 32 *lawful espials:* Legitimate spies. 40 *wildness:* Madness. 43 *Gracious:* Your grace (addressed to the king). 45 *exercise:* Act of devotion (the book she reads is one of devotion); *colour:* Give a plausible appearance to.

The harlot's cheek, beautied with plast'ring art,
Is not more ugly to° the thing° that helps it
Than is my deed to my most painted word:
O heavy burthen!

Polonius: I hear him coming: let's withdraw, my lord.

[Exeunt King and Polonius.]

Enter Hamlet.

Hamlet: To be, or not to be: that is the question:
Whether 'tis nobler in the mind to suffer
The slings and arrows of outrageous fortune,
Or to take arms against a sea° of troubles,
And by opposing end them? To die: to sleep;
No more; and by a sleep to say we end
The heart-ache and the thousand natural shocks
That flesh is heir to, 'tis a consummation
Devoutly to be wish'd. To die, to sleep;
To sleep: perchance to dream: ay, there's the rub;
For in that sleep of death what dreams may come
When we have shuffled° off this mortal coil,°
Must give us pause: there's the respect°
That makes calamity of so long life;°
For who would bear the whips and scorns of time,°
Th' oppressor's wrong, the proud man's contumely,
The pangs of despis'd° love, the law's delay,
The insolence of office° and the spurns°
That patient merit of th' unworthy takes,
When he himself might his quietus° make
With a bare bodkin?° who would fardels° bear,
To grunt and sweat under a weary life,
But that the dread of something after death,
The undiscover'd country from whose bourn°
No traveller returns, puzzles the will
And makes us rather bear those ills we have
Than fly to others that we know not of?
Thus conscience° does make cowards of us all;
And thus the native hue° of resolution
Is sicklied o'er° with the pale cast° of thought,
And enterprises of great pitch° and moment°

52 *to:* Compared to; *thing:* I.e., the cosmetic. 59 *sea:* The mixed metaphor of this speech has often been commented on; A later emendation *siege* has sometimes been spoken on the stage. 67 *shuffled:* Sloughed, cast; *coil:* Usually means "turmoil"; here, possibly "body" (conceived of as wound about the soul like rope); *clay, soil, veil,* have been suggested as emendations. 68 *respect:* Consideration. 69 *of . . . life:* So long-lived. 70 *time:* The world. 72 *despis'd:* Rejected. 73 *office:* Office-holders; *spurns:* Insults. 75 *quietus:* Acquittance; here, death. 76 *bare bodkin:* Mere dagger; *bare* is sometimes understood as "unsheathed;" *fardels:* Burdens. 79 *bourn:* Boundary. 83 *conscience:* Probably, inhibition by the faculty of reason restraining the will from doing wrong. 84 *native hue:* Natural color; metaphor derived from the color of the face. 85 *sicklied o'er,* Given a sickly tinge; *cast:* Shade of color. 86 *pitch:* Height (as of a falcon's flight); *moment:* Importance.

With this regard° their currents° turn awry,
And lose the name of action — Soft you now!
The fair Ophelia! Nymph, in thy orisons°
Be all my sins remember'red.

Ophelia: Good my lord,
How does your honour for this many a day?

Hamlet: I humbly thank you; well, well, well.

Ophelia: My lord, I have remembrances of yours,
That I have longed long to re-deliver;
I pray you, now receive them.

Hamlet: No, not I;
I never gave you aught.

Ophelia: My honour'd lord, you know right well you did;
And, with them, words of so sweet breath compos'd
As made the things more rich: their perfume lost,
Take these again; for to the noble mind
Rich gifts wax poor when givers prove unkind.
There, my lord.

Hamlet: Ha, ha! are you honest?

Ophelia: My lord?

Hamlet: Are you fair?

Ophelia: What means your lordship?

Hamlet: That if you be honest and fair, your honesty° should admit no discourse to° your beauty.°

Ophelia: Could beauty, my lord, have better commerce° than with honesty?

Hamlet: Ay, truly; for the power of beauty will sooner transform honesty from what it is to a bawd than the force of honesty can translate beauty into his likeness: this was sometime a paradox, but now the time° gives it proof. I did love you once.

Ophelia: Indeed, my lord, you made me believe so.

Hamlet: You should not have believed me; for virtue cannot so inoculate° our old stock but we shall relish of it:° I loved you not.

Ophelia: I was the more deceived.

Hamlet: Get thee to a nunnery: why wouldst thou be a breeder of sinners? I am myself indifferent honest;° but yet I could accuse me of such things that it were better my mother had not borne me: I am very proud, revengeful, ambitious, with more offences at my beck° than I have thoughts to put them in, imagination to give them shape, or time to act them in. What should such fellows as I do crawling between earth and heaven? We are arrant knaves, all; believe none of us. Go thy ways to a nunnery. Where's your father?

Ophelia: At home, my lord.

87 *regard:* Respect, consideration; *currents:* Courses. 89 *orisons:* Prayers. 103–8 *are you . . . beauty: Honest* meaning "truthful" (l. 103) and "chaste" (l. 107), and *fair* meaning "just, honorable" (l. 105) and "beautiful" (l. 107) are not mere quibbles; the speech has the irony of a *double entendre.* 107 *your honesty:* Your chastity. 108 *discourse to:* Familiar intercourse with. 109 *commerce:* Intercourse. 112 *the time:* The present age. 115 *inoculate:* Graft (metaphorical). 116 *but . . . it:* i.e., That we do not still have about us a taste of the old stock; i.e., retain our sinfulness. 119 *indifferent honest:* Moderately virtuous. 121 *beck:* Command.

Hamlet: Let the doors be shut upon him, that he may play the fool no where but in 's own house. Farewell.

Ophelia: O, help him, you sweet heavens!

Hamlet: If thou dost marry, I'll give thee this plague for thy dowry: be thou as chaste as ice, as pure as snow, thou shalt not escape calumny. Get thee to a nunnery, go: farewell. Or, if thou wilt needs marry, marry a fool; for wise men know well enough what monsters° you make of them. To a nunnery, go, and quickly too. Farewell.

Ophelia: O heavenly powers, restore him!

Hamlet: I have heard of your° paintings too, well enough; God hath given you one face, and you make yourselves another: you jig,° you amble, and you lisp; you nick-name God's creatures, and make your wantonness your ignorance.° Go to, I'll no more on 't; it hath made me mad. I say, we will have no moe marriage: those that are married already, all but one,° shall live; the rest shall keep as they are. To a nunnery, go.

Exit.

Ophelia: O, what a noble mind is here o'er-thrown!
The courtier's, soldier's, scholar's, eye, tongue, sword;
Th' expectancy and rose° of the fair state,
The glass of fashion and the mould of form,°
Th' observ'd of all observers,° quite, quite down!
And I, of ladies most deject and wretched,
That suck'd the honey of his music vows,
Now see that noble and most sovereign reason,
Like sweet bells jangled, out of time and harsh;
That unmatch'd form and feature of blown° youth
Blasted with ecstasy:° O, woe is me,
T' have seen what I have seen, see what I see!

Enter King and Polonius.

King: Love! his affections do not that way tend;
Nor what he spake, though it lack'd form a little,
Was not like madness. There's something in his soul,
O'er which his melancholy sits on brood;
And I do doubt° the hatch and the disclose°
Will be some danger: which for to prevent,
I have in quick determination
Thus set it down: he shall with speed to England,
For the demand of our neglected tribute:
Haply the seas and countries different
With variable° objects shall expel
This something-settled° matter in his heart,

133 *monsters:* An allusion to the horns of a cuckold. 136 *your:* Indefinite use. 137 *jig:* Move with jerky motion; probably allusion to the *jig,* or song and dance, of the current stage. 138–139 *make . . . ignorance:* I.e., excuse your wantonness on the ground of your ignorance. 141 *one:* i.e., The king. 144 *expectancy and rose:* Source of hope. 145 *The glass . . . form:* The mirror of fashion and the pattern of courtly behavior. 146 *observ'd . . . observers:* I.e., the center of attention in the court. 151 *blown:* Blooming. 152 *ecstasy:* Madness. 158 *doubt:* Fear; *disclose:* Disclosure or revelation (by chipping of the shell). 164 *variable:* Various. 165 *something-settled:* Somewhat settled.

Whereon his brains still beating puts him thus
From fashion of himself.° What think you on 't?

Polonius: It shall do well: but yet do I believe
The origin and commencement of his grief
Sprung from neglected love. How now, Ophelia!
You need not tell us what Lord Hamlet said;
We heard it all. My lord, do as you please;
But, if you hold it fit, after the play
Let his queen mother all alone entreat him
To show his grief: let her be round° with him;
And I'll be plac'd, so please you, in the ear
Of all their conference. If she find him not,
To England send him, or confine him where
Your wisdom best shall think.

King: It shall be so:
Madness in great ones must not unwatch'd go. *Exeunt.*

[SCENE II. *A hall in the castle.*]

Enter Hamlet and three of the Players.

Hamlet: Speak the speech, I pray you, as I pronounced it to you, trippingly on the tongue: but if you mouth it, as many of your° players do, I had as lief the town-crier spoke my lines. Nor do not saw the air too much with your hand, thus, but use all gently; for in the very torrent, tempest, and, as I may say, whirlwind of your passion, you must acquire and beget a temperance that may give it smoothness. O, it offends me to the soul to hear a robustious° periwig-pated° fellow tear a passion to tatters, to very rags, to split the ears of the groundlings,° who for the most part are capable of° nothing but inexplicable° dumb-shows and noise: I would have such a fellow whipped for o'er-doing Termagant;° it out-herods Herod:° pray you, avoid it.

First Player: I warrant your honour.

Hamlet: Be not too tame neither, but let your own discretion be your tutor: suit the action to the word, the word to the action; with this special observance, that you o'er-step not the modesty of nature: for any thing so overdone is from the purpose of playing, whose end, both at the first and now, was and is, to hold, as 't were, the mirror up to nature; to show virtue her own feature, scorn her own image, and the very age and body of the time his form and pressure.° Now this overdone, or come tardy off,° though it make the unskilful laugh, cannot but make

167 *From . . . himself:* Out of his natural manner. 175 *round:* Blunt. SCENE II. 2 *your:* Indefinite use. 7 *robustious:* Violent, boisterous; *periwig-pated:* Wearing a wig. 8 *groundlings:* Those who stood in the yard of the theater. 9 *capable of:* Susceptible of being influenced by; *inexplicable:* Of no significance worth explaining. 10 *Termagant:* A god of the Saracens; a character in the St. Nicholas play, where one of his worshipers, leaving him in charge of goods, returns to find them stolen; whereupon he beats the god (or idol), which howls vociferously. 11 *Herod:* Herod of Jewry; a character in *The Slaughter of the Innocents* and other cycle plays. The part was played with great noise and fury. 19 *pressure:* Stamp, impressed character. 20 *come tardy off:* Inadequately done.

the judicious grieve; the censure of the which one° must in your allowance o'erweigh a whole theatre of others. O, there be players that I have seen play, and heard others praise, and that highly, not to speak it profanely, that, neither having the accent of Christians nor the gait of Christian, pagan, nor man, have so strutted and bellowed that I have thought some of nature's journeymen° had made men and not made them well, they imitated humanity so abominably.

First Player: I hope we have reformed that indifferently° with us, sir.

Hamlet: O, reform it altogether. And let those that play your clowns speak no more than is set down for them; for there be of° them that will themselves laugh, to set on some quantity of barren° spectators to laugh too; though, in the mean time, some necessary question of the play be then to be considered: that's villanous, and shows a most pitiful ambition in the fool that uses it. Go, make you ready.

[Exeunt Players.]

Enter Polonius, Guildenstern, and Rosencrantz.

How now, my lord! will the king hear this piece of work?

Polonius: And the queen too, and that presently.

Hamlet: Bid the players make haste. *[Exit Polonius.]*
Will you two help to hasten them?

Rosencrantz:
Guildenstern: } We will, my lord. *Exeunt they two.*

Hamlet: What ho! Horatio!

Enter Horatio.

Horatio: Here, sweet lord, at your service.
Hamlet: Horatio, thou art e'en as just° a man
As e'er my conversation cop'd withal.
Horatio: O, my dear lord, —
Hamlet: Nay, do not think I flatter;
For what advancement may I hope from thee
That no revenue hast but thy good spirits,
To feed and clothe thee? Why should the poor be flatter'd?
No, let the candied tongue lick absurd pomp,
And crook the pregnant° hinges of the knee
where thrift° may follow fawning. Dost thou hear?
Since my dear soul was mistress of her choice
And could of men distinguish her election,
S' hath seal'd thee for herself; for thou hast been
As one, in suff'ring all, that suffers nothing,
A man that fortune's buffets and rewards
Hast ta'en with equal thanks: and blest are those
Whose blood and judgement are so well commeddled,
That they are not a pipe for fortune's finger

21 *the censure . . . one:* The judgment of even one of whom. 26 *journeymen:* Laborers not yet masters in their trade. 28 *indifferently:* Fairly, tolerably. 30 *of:* i.e., Some among them. 31 *barren:* I.e., of wit. 41 *just:* Honest, honorable. 48 *pregnant:* Pliant. 49 *thrift:* profit.

To sound what stop° she please. Give me that man
That is not passion's slave, and I will wear him
In my heart's core, ay, in my heart of heart,
As I do thee. — Something too much of this. —
There is a play to-night before the king;
One scene of it comes near the circumstance
Which I have told thee of my father's death:
I prithee, when thou seest that act afoot,
Even with the very comment of thy soul°
Observe my uncle: if his occulted° guilt
Do not itself unkennel in one speech,
It is a damned° ghost that we have seen,
And my imaginations are as foul
As Vulcan's stithy.° Give him heedful note;
For I mine eyes will rivet to his face,
And after we will both our judgements join
In censure of his seeming.°

Horatio: Well, my lord:
If 'a steal aught the whilst this play is playing,
And 'scape detecting, I will pay the theft.

Enter trumpets and kettledrums, King, Queen, Polonius, Ophelia [Rosencrantz, Guildenstern, and others].

Hamlet: They are coming to the play; I must be idle:° Get you a place.

King: How fares our cousin Hamlet?

Hamlet: Excellent, i' faith; of the chameleon's dish:° I eat the air, promise-crammed: you cannot feed capons so.

King: I have nothing with° this answer, Hamlet; these words are not mine.°

Hamlet: No, nor mine now. *[To Polonius.]* My lord, you played once i' the university, you say?

Polonius: That did I, my lord; and was accounted a good actor.

Hamlet: What did you enact?

Polonius: I did enact Julius Cæsar: I was killed i' the Capitol; Brutus killed me.

Hamlet: It was a brute part of him to kill so capital a calf there. Be the players ready?

Rosencrantz: Ay, my lord; they stay upon your patience.

Queen: Come hither, my dear Hamlet, sit by me.

Hamlet: No, good mother, here's metal more attractive.

Polonius [to the king]: O, ho! do you mark that?

Hamlet: Lady, shall I lie in your lap?

[Lying down at Ophelia's feet.]

Ophelia: No, my lord.

58 *stop:* Hole in a wind instrument for controlling the sound. 66 *very . . . soul:* Inward and sagacious criticism. 67 *occulted:* Hidden. 69 *damned:* In league with Satan. 71 *stithy:* Smithy, place of *stiths* (anvils). 74 *censure . . . seeming:* Judgment of his appearance or behavior. 77 *idle:* Crazy, or not attending to anything serious. 79 *chameleon's dish:* Chameleons were supposed to feed on air. (Hamlet deliberately misinterprets the king's "fares" as "feeds.") 81 *have . . . with:* Make nothing of; *are not mine:* Do not respond to what I asked.

Hamlet: I mean, my head upon your lap?
Ophelia: Ay, my lord.
Hamlet: Do you think I meant country° matters?
Ophelia: I think nothing, my lord.
Hamlet: That's a fair thought to lie between maids' legs.
Ophelia: What is, my lord?
Hamlet: Nothing.
Ophelia: You are merry, my lord.
Hamlet: Who, I?
Ophelia: Ay, my lord.
Hamlet: O God, your only° jig-maker.° What should a man do but be merry? for, look you, how cheerfully my mother looks, and my father died within's two hours.
Ophelia: Nay, 'tis twice two months, my lord.
Hamlet: So long? Nay then, let the devil wear black, for I'll have a suit of sables.° O heavens! die two months ago, and not forgotten yet? Then there's hope a great man's memory may outlive his life half a year: but, by 'r lady, 'a must build churches, then; or else shall 'a suffer not thinking on,° with the hobbyhorse, whose epitaph is "For, O, for, O, the hobbyhorse is forgot."°

The trumpets sound. Dumb show follows.

Enter a King and a Queen [very lovingly]; the Queen embracing him, and he her. [She kneels, and makes show of protestation unto him.] He takes her up, and declines his head upon her neck: he lies him down upon a bank of flowers: she, seeing him asleep, leaves him. Anon comes in another man, takes off his crown, kisses it, pours poison in the sleeper's ears, and leaves him. The Queen returns; finds the King dead, makes passionate action. The Poisoner, with some three or four come in again, seem to condole with her. The dead body is carried away. The Poisoner wooes the Queen with gifts: she seems harsh awhile, but in the end accepts love. [Exeunt.]

Ophelia: What means this, my lord?
Hamlet: Marry, this is miching mallecho;° it means mischief.
Ophelia: Belike this show imports the argument of the play.

Enter Prologue.

Hamlet: We shall know by this fellow: the players cannot keep counsel; they'll tell all.
Ophelia: Will 'a tell us what this show meant?
Hamlet: Ay, or any show that you'll show him: be not you ashamed to show, he'll not shame to tell you what it means.
Ophelia: You are naught, you are naught:° I'll mark the play.
Prologue: For us, and for our tragedy,

98 *country:* With a bawdy pun. 106 *your only:* Only your; *jig-maker:* Composer of jigs (song and dance). 110–111 *suit of sables:* Garments trimmed with the fur of the sable, with a quibble on *sable* meaning "black." 113–114 *suffer . . . on:* Undergo oblivion. 114–115 *"For . . . forgot:"* Verse of a song occurring also in *Love's Labour's Lost,* III. i. 30. The hobbyhorse was a character in the Morris Dance. 117 *miching mallecho:* Sneaking mischief. 124 *naught:* Indecent.

Here stooping° to your clemency,
We beg your hearing patiently. *[Exit.]*
Hamlet: Is this a prologue, or the posy° of a ring?
Ophelia: 'Tis brief, my lord.
Hamlet: As woman's love.

Enter [two Players as] King and Queen.

Player King: Full thirty times hath Phoebus' cart gone round
Neptune's salt wash° and Tellus'° orbed ground,
And thirty dozen moons with borrowed° sheen
About the world have times twelve thirties been,
Since love our hearts and Hymen° did our hands
Unite commutual° in most sacred bands.
Player Queen: So many journeys may the sun and moon
Make us again count o'er ere love be done!
But, woe is me, you are so sick of late,
So far from cheer and from your former state,
That I distrust° you. Yet, though I distrust,
Discomfort you, my lord, it nothing must:
For women's fear and love holds quantity;°
In neither aught, or in extremity.
Now, what my love is, proof hath made you know;
And as my love is siz'd, my fear is so:
Where love is great, the littlest doubts are fear;
Where little fears grow great, great love grows there.
Player King: 'Faith, I must leave thee, love, and shortly too;
My operant° powers their functions leave° to do:
And thou shalt live in this fair world behind,
Honour'd, belov'd; and haply one as kind
For husband shalt thou —
Player Queen: O, confound the rest!
Such love must needs be treason in my breast:
In second husband let me be accurst!
None wed the second but who kill'd the first.
Hamlet (aside): Wormwood, wormwood.
Player Queen: The instances that second marriage move
Are base respects of thrift, but none of love:
A second time I kill my husband dead,
When second husband kisses me in bed.
Player King: I do believe you think what now you speak;
But what we do determine oft we break.
Purpose is but the slave to memory,
Of violent birth, but poor validity:
Which now, like fruit unripe, sticks on the tree;

126 *stooping:* Bowing. 128 *posy:* Motto. 132 *salt wash:* The sea; *Tellus:* Goddess of the earth *(orbed ground).* 133 *borrowed:* I.e., reflected. 135 *Hymen:* God of matrimony. 136 *commutual:* Mutually. 141 *distrust:* Am anxious about. 143 *holds quantity:* Keeps proportion between. 150 *operant:* Active; *leave:* Cease.

But fall, unshaken, when they mellow be.
Most necessary 'tis that we forget
To pay ourselves what to ourselves is debt:
What to ourselves in passion we propose,
The passion ending, doth the purpose lose.
The violence of either grief or joy
Their own enactures° with themselves destroy:
Where joy most revels, grief doth most lament;
Grief joys, joy grieves, on slender accident.
This world is not for aye,° nor 'tis not strange
That even our loves should with our fortunes change;
For 'tis a question left us yet to prove,
Whether love lead fortune, or else fortune love.
The great man down, you mark his favourite flies;
The poor advanc'd makes friends of enemies.
And hitherto doth love on fortune tend;
For who° not needs shall never lack a friend,
And who in want a hollow friend doth try,
Directly seasons° him his enemy.
But, orderly to end where I begun,
Our wills and fates do so contrary run
That our devices still are overthrown;
Our thoughts are ours, their ends° none of our own:
So think thou wilt no second husband wed;
But die thy thoughts when thy first lord is dead.

Player Queen: Nor earth to me give food, nor heaven light!
Sport and repose lock from me day and night!
To desperation turn my trust and hope!
An anchor's° cheer° in prison be my scope!
Each opposite° that blanks° the face of joy
Meet what I would have well and it destroy!
Both here and hence pursue me lasting strife,
If, once a widow, ever I be wife!

Hamlet: If she should break it now!

Player King: 'Tis deeply sworn. Sweet, leave me here awhile;
My spirits grow dull, and fain I would beguile
The tedious day with sleep. *[Sleeps.]*

Player Queen: Sleep rock thy brain;
And never come mischance between us twain! *Exit.*

Hamlet: Madam, how like you this play?

Queen: The lady doth protest too much, methinks.

Hamlet: O, but she'll keep her word.

King: Have you heard the argument? Is there no offence in 't?

Hamlet: No, no, they do but jest, poison in jest; no offence i' the world.

King: What do you call the play?

173 *enactures:* Fulfillments. 176 *aye:* Ever. 183 *who:* Whoever. 185 *seasons:* Matures, ripens. 189 *ends:* Results. 195 *An anchor's:* An anchorite's; *cheer:* Fare; sometimes printed as *chair.* 196 *opposite:* Adverse thing; *blanks:* Causes to *blanch* or grow pale.

Hamlet: The Mouse-trap. Marry, how? Tropically.° This play is the image of a murder done in Vienna: Gonzago° is the duke's name; his wife, Baptista: you shall see anon; 't is a knavish piece of work: but what o' that? your majesty and we that have free souls, it touches us not: let the galled jade° winch,° our withers° are unwrung.°

Enter Lucianus.

This is one Lucianus, nephew to the king.
Ophelia: You are as good as a chorus,° my lord.
Hamlet: I could interpret between you and your love, if I could see the puppets dallying.°
Ophelia: You are keen, my lord, you are keen.
Hamlet: It would cost you a groaning to take off my edge.
Ophelia: Still better, and worse.°
Hamlet: So you mistake° your husbands. Begin, murderer; pox,° leave thy damnable faces, and begin. Come: the croaking raven doth bellow for revenge.
Lucianus: Thoughts black, hands apt, drugs fit, and time agreeing;
Confederate° season, else no creature seeing;
Thou mixture rank, of midnight weeds collected,
With Hecate's° ban° thrice blasted, thrice infected,
Thy natural magic and dire property,
On wholesome life usurp immediately.

[Pours the poison into the sleeper's ears.]

Hamlet: 'A poisons him i' the garden for his estate. His name's Gonzago: the story is extant, and written in very choice Italian: you shall see anon how the murderer gets the love of Gonzago's wife.
Ophelia: The king rises.
Hamlet: What, frighted with false fire!°
Queen: How fares my lord?
Polonius: Give o'er the play.
King: Give me some light: away!
Polonius: Lights, lights, lights! *Exeunt all but Hamlet and Horatio.*
Hamlet: Why, let the strucken deer go weep,
The hart ungalled play;
For some must watch, while some must sleep:
Thus runs the world away.°

211 *Tropically:* Figuratively, *trapically* suggests a pun on *trap* in *Mouse-trap* (1. 211). 212 *Gonzago.* In 1538 Luigi Gonzago murdered the Duke of Urbano by pouring poisoned lotion in his ears. 215 *galled jade:* Horse whose hide is rubbed by saddle or harness; *winch:* Wince; *withers:* The part between the horse's shoulder blades; *unwrung:* Not wrung or twisted. 217 *chorus:* In many Elizabethan plays the action was explained by an actor known as the "chorus"; at a puppet show the actor who explained the action was known as an "interpreter," as indicated by the lines following. 219 *dallying:* With sexual suggestion, continued in *keen* (sexually aroused), *groaning* (i.e., in pregnancy), and *edge* (i.e., sexual desire or impetuosity). 222 *Still . . . worse:* More keen, less decorous. 223 *mistake:* Err in taking; *pox:* An imprecation. 227 *Confederate:* Conspiring (to assist the murderer). 229 *Hecate:* The goddess of witchcraft; *ban:* Curse. 236 *false fire:* Fireworks, or a blank discharge. 241–244 *Why . . . away:* Probably from an old ballad, with allusion to the popular belief that a wounded deer retires to weep and die. Cf. *As You Like It,* II. i. 66.

Would not this,° sir, and a forest of feathers° — if the rest of my fortunes turn Turk with° me — with two Provincial roses° on my razed° shoes, get me a fellowship in a cry° of players,° sir?

Horatio: Half a share.°

Hamlet: A whole one, I.
For thou dost know, O Damon dear,
This realm dismantled° was
Of Jove himself; and now reigns here
A very, very° — pajock.°

Horatio: You might have rhymed.

Hamlet: O good Horatio, I'll take the ghost's word for a thousand pound. Didst perceive?

Horatio: Very well, my lord.

Hamlet: Upon the talk of the poisoning?

Horatio: I did very well note him.

Hamlet: Ah, ha! Come, some music! come, the recorders!°
For if the king like not the comedy,
Why then, belike, he likes it not, perdy.°
Come, some music!

Enter Rosencrantz and Guildenstern.

Guildenstern: Good my lord, vouchsafe me a word with you.

Hamlet: Sir, a whole history.

Guildenstern: The king, sir, —

Hamlet: Ay, sir, what of him?

Guildenstern: Is in his retirement marvellous distempered.

Hamlet: With drink, sir?

Guildenstern: No, my lord, rather with choler.°

Hamlet: Your wisdom should show itself more richer to signify this to his doctor; for, for me to put him to his purgation would perhaps plunge him into far more choler.

Guildenstern: Good my lord, put your discourse into some frame° and start not so wildly from my affair.

Hamlet: I am tame, sir: pronounce.

Guildenstern: The queen, your mother, in most great affliction of spirit, hath sent me to you.

245 *this:* I.e., the play; *feathers:* Allusion to the plumes which Elizabethan actors were fond of wearing. 246 *turn Turk with:* Go back on; *two Provincial roses:* Rosettes of ribbon like the roses of Provins near Paris, or else the roses of Provence; *razed:* Cut, slashed (by way of ornament). 247 *fellowship . . . players:* Partnership in a theatrical company; *cry:* Pack (as of hounds). 248 *Half a share:* Allusion to the custom in dramatic companies of dividing the ownership into a number of shares among the householders. 250–253 *For . . . very:* Probably from an old ballad having to do with Damon and Pythias. 251 *dismantled:* Stripped, divested. 253 *pajock:* Peacock (a bird with a bad reputation). Possibly the word was *patchock,* diminutive of *patch,* clown. 260 *recorders:* Wind instruments of the flute kind. 262 *perdy:* Corruption of *par dieu.* 270 *choler:* Bilious disorder, with quibble on the sense "anger." 274 *frame:* Order.

Hamlet: You are welcome.

Guildenstern: Nay, good my lord, this courtesy is not of the right breed. If it shall please you to make me a wholesome° answer, I will do your mother's commandment; if not, your pardon and my return shall be the end of my business.

Hamlet: Sir, I cannot.

Guildenstern: What, my lord?

Hamlet: Make you a wholesome answer; my wit's diseased: but, sir, such answer as I can make, you shall command; or, rather, as you say, my mother: therefore no more, but to the matter:° my mother, you say, —

Rosencrantz: Then thus she says; your behaviour hath struck her into amazement and admiration.

Hamlet: O wonderful son, that can so 'stonish a mother! But is there no sequel at the heels of this mother's admiration? Impart.

Rosencrantz: She desires to speak with you in her closet, ere you go to bed.

Hamlet: We shall obey, were she ten times our mother. Have you any further trade with us?

Rosencrantz: My lord, you once did love me.

Hamlet: And do still, by these pickers and stealers.°

Rosencrantz: Good my lord, what is your cause of distemper? you do, surely, bar the door upon your own liberty, if you deny your griefs to your friend.

Hamlet: Sir, I lack advancement.

Rosencrantz: How can that be, when you have the voice° of the king himself for your succession in Denmark?

Hamlet: Ay, sir, but "While the grass grows,"° — the proverb is something musty.

Enter the Players with recorders.

O, the recorders! let me see one. To withdraw° with you: — why do you go about to recover the wind° of me, as if you would drive me into a toil?°

Guildenstern: O, my lord, if my duty be too bold, my love is too unmannerly.°

Hamlet: I do not well understand that. Will you play upon this pipe?

Guildenstern: My lord, I cannot.

Hamlet: I pray you.

Guildenstern: Believe me, I cannot.

Hamlet: I beseech you.

Guildenstern: I know no touch of it, my lord.

Hamlet: 'Tis as easy as lying: govern these ventages° with your fingers and

281 *wholesome:* Sensible. 288 *matter:* Matter in hand. 298 *pickers and stealers:* Hands, so called from the catechism "to keep my hands from picking and stealing." 303 *voice:* Support. 305 *"While . . . grows:"* The rest of the proverb is "the silly horse starves." Hamlet may be destroyed while he is waiting for the succession to the kingdom. 307 *withdraw:* Speak in private. 308 *recover the wind:* Get to the windward side; *toil:* Snare. 309–310 *if . . . unmannerly:* If I am using an unmannerly boldness, it is my love which occasions it. 317 *ventages:* Stops of the recorders.

thumb, give it breath with your mouth, and it will discourse most eloquent music. Look you, these are the stops.

Guildenstern: But these cannot I command to any utterance of harmony; I have not the skill.

Hamlet: Why, look you now, how unworthy a thing you make of me! You would play upon me; you would seem to know my stops; you would pluck out the heart of my mystery; you would sound me from my lowest note to the top of my compass:° and there is much music, excellent voice, in this little organ;° yet cannot you make it speak. 'Sblood, do you think I am easier to be played on than a pipe? Call me what instrument you will, though you can fret° me, you cannot play upon me.

Enter Polonius.

God bless you, sir!

Polonius: My lord, the queen would speak with you, and presently.

Hamlet: Do you see yonder cloud that 's almost in shape of a camel?

Polonius: By the mass, and 'tis like a camel, indeed.

Hamlet: Methinks it is like a weasel.

Polonius: It is backed like a weasel.

Hamlet: Or like a whale?

Polonius: Very like a whale.

Hamlet: Then I will come to my mother by and by. *[Aside.]* They fool me to the top of my bent.° — I will come by and by.°

Polonius: I will say so. *[Exit.]*

Hamlet: By and by is easily said.
Leave me, friends. *[Exeunt all but Hamlet.]*
'Tis now the very witching time° of night,
When churchyards yawn and hell itself breathes out
Contagion to this world: now could I drink hot blood,
And do such bitter business as the day
Would quake to look on. Soft! now to my mother.
O heart, lose not thy nature; let not ever
The soul of Nero° enter this firm bosom:
Let me be cruel, not unnatural:
I will speak daggers to her, but use none;
My tongue and soul in this be hypocrites;
How in my words somever she be shent,°
To give them seals° never, my soul, consent! *Exit.*

325 *compass:* Range of voice. 326 *organ:* Musical instrument, i.e., the pipe. 328 *fret:* Quibble on meaning "irritate" and the piece of wood, gut, or metal which regulates the fingering. 338 *top of my bent:* Limit of endurance, i.e., extent to which a bow may be bent; *by and by:* Immediately. 342 *witching time:* I.e., time when spells are cast. 348 *Nero:* Murderer of his mother, Agrippina. 352 *shent:* Rebuked. 353 *give them seals:* Confirm with deeds.

[SCENE III. *A room in the castle.*]

Enter King, Rosencrantz, and Guildenstern.

King: I like him not, nor stands it safe with us
To let his madness range. Therefore prepare you;
I your commission will forthwith dispatch,°
And he to England shall along with you:
The terms° of our estate° may not endure
Hazard so near us as doth hourly grow
Out of his brows.°
Guildenstern: We will ourselves provide:
Most holy and religious fear it is
To keep those many many bodies safe
That live and feed upon your majesty.
Rosencrantz: The single and peculiar° life is bound,
With all the strength and armour of the mind,
To keep itself from noyance;° but much more
That spirit upon whose weal depend and rest
The lives of many. The cess° of majesty
Dies not alone; but, like a gulf,° doth draw
What's near it with it: it is a massy wheel,
Fix'd on the summit of the highest mount,
To whose huge spokes ten thousand lesser things
Are mortis'd and adjoin'd; which, when it falls,
Each small annexment, petty consequence,
Attends° the boist'rous ruin. Never alone
Did the king sigh, but with a general groan.
King: Arm° you, I pray you, to this speedy voyage;
For we will fetters put about this fear,
Which now goes too free-footed.
Rosencrantz: We will haste us.
Exeunt Gentlemen [Rosencrantz and Guildenstern].

Enter Polonius.

Polonius: My lord, he's going to his mother's closet:
Behind the arras° I'll convey° myself,
To hear the process;° I'll warrant she'll tax him home:°
And, as you said, and wisely was it said,
'Tis meet that some more audience than a mother,
Since nature makes them partial, should o'erhear
The speech, of vantage.° Fare you well, my liege:
I'll call upon you ere you go to bed,
And tell you what I know.

SCENE III. 3 *dispatch:* Prepare. 5 *terms:* Condition, circumstances; *estate:* State. 7 *brows:* Effronteries. 11 *single and peculiar:* Individual and private. 13 *noyance:* Harm. 15 *cess:* Decease. 16 *gulf:* Whirlpool. 22 *Attends:* Participates in. 24 *Arm:* Prepare. 28 *arras:* Screen of tapestry placed around the walls of household apartments; *convey:* Implication of secrecy, *convey* was often used to mean "steal." 29 *process:* Proceedings; *tax him home:* Reprove him severely. 33 *of vantage:* From an advantageous place.

King. Thanks, dear my lord.

Exit [Polonius].

O, my offence is rank, it smells to heaven;
It hath the primal eldest curse° upon't,
A brother's murder. Pray can I not,
Though inclination be as sharp as will:°
My stronger guilt defeats my strong intent;
And, like a man to double business bound,
I stand in pause where I shall first begin,
And both neglect. What if this cursed hand
Were thicker than itself with brother's blood,
Is there not rain enough in the sweet heavens
To wash it white as snow? Whereto serves mercy
But to confront° the visage of offence?
And what's in prayer but this two-fold force,
To be forestalled° ere we come to fall,
Or pardon'd being down? Then I'll look up;
My fault is past. But, O, what form of prayer
Can serve my turn? "Forgive me my foul murder"?
That cannot be: since I am still possess'd
Of those effects for which I did the murder,
My crown, mine own ambition° and my queen.
May one be pardon'd and retain th' offence?°
In the corrupted currents° of this world
Offence's gilded hand° may shove by justice,
And oft 'tis seen the wicked prize° itself
Buys out the law: but 'tis not so above;
There is no shuffling,° there the action lies°
In his true nature; and we ourselves compell'd,
Even to the teeth and forehead° of our faults,
To give in evidence. What then? what rests?°
Try what repentance can: what can it not?
Yet what can it when one can not repent?
O wretched state! O bosom black as death!
O limed° soul, that, struggling to be free,
Art more engag'd!° Help, angels! Make assay!°
Bow, stubborn knees; and, heart with strings of steel,
Be soft as sinews of the new-born babe!
All may be well. *[He kneels.]*

Enter Hamlet.

37 *primal eldest curse:* The curse of Cain, the first to kill his brother. 39 *sharp as will:* I.e., his desire is as strong as his determination. 47 *confront:* Oppose directly. 49 *forestalled:* Prevented. 55 *ambition:* I.e., realization of ambition. 56 *offence:* Benefit accruing from offense. 57 *currents:* Courses. 58 *gilded hand:* Hand offering gold as a bribe. 59 *wicked prize:* Prize won by wickedness. 61 *shuffling:* Escape by trickery; *lies:* Is sustainable. 63 *teeth and forehead:* Very face. 64 *rests:* Remains. 68 *limed:* Caught as with birdlime. 69 *engag'd:* Embedded; *assay:* Trial.

Hamlet: Now might I do it pat,° now he is praying;
And now I'll do't. And so 'a goes to heaven;
And so am I reveng'd. That would be scann'd:°
A villain kills my father; and for that,
I, his sole son, do this same villain send
To heaven.
Why, this is hire and salary, not revenge.
'A took my father grossly, full of bread;°
With all his crimes broad blown,° as flush° as May;
And how his audit stands who knows save heaven?
But in our circumstance and course° of thought,
'Tis heavy with him: and am I then reveng'd,
To take him in the purging of his soul,
When he is fit and season'd for his passage?°
No!
Up, sword; and know thou a more horrid hent:°
When he is drunk asleep,° or in his rage,
Or in th' incestuous pleasure of his bed;
At game, a-swearing, or about some act
That has no relish of salvation in't;
Then trip him, that his heels may kick at heaven,
And that his soul may be as damn'd and black
As hell, whereto it goes. My mother stays:
This physic° but prolongs thy sickly days. *Exit.*
King: [Rising] My words fly up, my thoughts remain below:
Words without thoughts never to heaven go. *Exit.*

[SCENE IV. *The Queen's closet.*]

Enter [Queen] Gertrude and Polonius.

Polonius: 'A will come straight. Look you lay° home to him:
Tell him his pranks have been too broad° to bear with,
And that your grace hath screen'd and stood between
Much heat° and him. I'll sconce° me even here.
Pray you, be round° with him.
Hamlet (within): Mother, mother, mother!
Queen: I'll warrant you,
Fear me not: withdraw, I hear him coming.
[Polonius hides behind the arras.]

Enter Hamlet.

73 *pat:* Opportunely. 75 *would be scann'd:* Needs to be looked into. 80 *full of bread:* Enjoying his worldly pleasures (see Ezekiel 16:49). 81 *broad blown:* In full bloom; *flush:* Lusty. 83 *in . . . course:* As we see it in our mortal situation. 86 *fit . . . passage:* I.e., reconciled to heaven by forgiveness of his sins. 88 *hent:* Seizing; or more probably, occasion of seizure. 89 *drunk asleep:* In a drunken sleep. 96 *physic:* Purging (by prayer). SCENE IV. 1 *lay:* Thrust. 2 *broad:* Unrestrained. 4 *Much heat:* I.e., the king's anger; *sconce:* Hide. 5 *round:* Blunt.

Hamlet: Now, mother, what's the matter?
Queen: Hamlet, thou hast thy father much offended.
Hamlet: Mother, you have my father° much offended.
Queen: Come, come, you answer with an idle tongue.
Hamlet: Go, go, you question with a wicked tongue.
Queen: Why, how now, Hamlet!
Hamlet: What's the matter now?
Queen: Have you forgot me?
Hamlet: No, by the rood,° not so:
You are the queen, your husband's brother's wife;
And — would it were not so! — you are my mother.
Queen: Nay, then, I'll set those to you that can speak.
Hamlet: Come, come, and sit you down; you shall not budge;
You go not till I set you up a glass
Where you may see the inmost part of you.
Queen: What wilt thou do? thou wilt not murder me?
Help, help, ho!
Polonius [behind]: What, ho! help, help; help!
Hamlet [drawing]: How now! a rat? Dead, for a ducat, dead!
[Makes a pass through the arras.]
Polonius [behind]: O, I am slain! *[Falls and dies.]*
Queen: O me, what hast thou done?
Hamlet: Nay, I know not:
Is it the king?
Queen: O, what a rash and bloody deed is this!
Hamlet: A bloody deed! almost as bad, good mother,
As kill a king, and marry with his brother.
Queen: As kill a king!
Hamlet: Ay, lady, it was my word.
[Lifts up the arras and discovers Polonius.]
Thou wretched, rash, intruding fool, farewell!
I took thee for thy better: take thy fortune;
Thou find'st to be too busy is some danger.
Leave wringing of your hands: peace! sit you down,
And let me wring your heart; for so I shall,
If it be made of penetrable stuff,
If damned custom have not braz'd° it so
That it be proof and bulwark against sense.
Queen: What have I done, that thou dar'st wag thy tongue
In noise so rude against me?
Hamlet: Such an act
That blurs the grace and blush of modesty,
Calls virtue hypocrite, takes off the rose
From the fair forehead of an innocent love
And sets a blister° there, makes marriage-vows

9–10 *thy father, my father:* I.e., Claudius, the elder Hamlet. 14 *rood:* Cross. 38 *braz'd:* Brazened, hardened. 45 *sets a blister:* Brands as a harlot.

As false as dicers' oaths: O, such a deed
As from the body of contraction° plucks
The very soul, and sweet religion° makes
A rhapsody° of words: heaven's face does glow
O'er this solidity and compound mass
With heated visage, as against the doom
Is thought-sick at the act.°

Queen: Ay me, what act,
That roars so loud, and thunders in the index?°

Hamlet: Look here, upon this picture, and on this.
The counterfeit presentment° of two brothers.
See, what a grace was seated on this brow;
Hyperion's° curls; the front° of Jove himself;
An eye like Mars, to threaten and command;
A station° like the herald Mercury
New-lighted on a heaven-kissing hill;
A combination and a form indeed,
Where every god did seem to set his seal,
To give the world assurance° of a man:
This was your husband. Look you now, what follows:
Here is your husband; like a mildew'd ear,°
Blasting his wholesome brother. Have you eyes?
Could you on this fair mountain leave to feed,
And batten° on this moor?° Ha! have you eyes?
You cannot call it love; for at your age
The hey-day° in the blood is tame, it's humble,
And waits upon the judgement: and what judgement
Would step from this to this? Sense, sure, you have,
Else could you not have motion;° but sure, that sense
Is apoplex'd;° for madness would not err,
Nor sense to ecstasy was ne'er so thrall'd°
But it reserv'd some quantity of choice,°
To serve in such a difference. What devil was't
That thus hath cozen'd° you at hoodman-blind?°
Eyes without feeling, feeling without sight,
Ears without hands or eyes, smelling sans° all,
Or but a sickly part of one true sense

47 *contraction:* The marriage contract. 48 *religion:* Religious vows. 49 *rhapsody:* Senseless string. 49–52 *heaven's . . . act:* Heaven's face blushes to look down upon this world, compounded of the four elements, with hot face as though the day of doom were near, and thought-sick at the deed (i.e., Gertrude's marriage). 53 *index:* Prelude or preface. 55 *counterfeit presentment:* Portrayed representation. 57 *Hyperion:* The sun god; *front:* Brow. 59 *station:* Manner of standing. 63 *assurance:* Pledge, guarantee. 65 *mildew'd ear:* See Genesis 41:5–7. 68 *batten:* Grow fat; *moor:* Barren upland. 70 *hey-day:* State of excitement. 72–73 *Sense . . . motion:* Sense and motion are functions of the middle or sensible soul, the possession of sense being the basis of motion. 74 *apoplex'd:* Paralyzed. Mental derangement was thus of three sorts: apoplexy, ecstasy, and diabolic possession. 75 *thrall'd:* Enslaved. 76 *quantity of choice:* Fragment of the power to choose. 78 *cozen'd:* Tricked, cheated; *hoodman-blind:* Blindman's buff. 80 *sans:* Without.

Could not so mope.°
O shame! where is thy blush? Rebellious hell,
If thou canst mutine° in a matron's bones,
To flaming youth let virtue be as wax,
And melt in her own fire: proclaim no shame
When the compulsive ardour gives the charge,°
Since frost itself as actively doth burn
And reason pandars will.°

Queen: O Hamlet, speak no more:
Thou turn'st mine eyes into my very soul;
And there I see such black and grained° spots
As will not leave their tinct.

Hamlet: Nay, but to live
In the rank sweat of an enseamed° bed,
Stew'd in corruption, honeying and making love
Over the nasty sty, —

Queen: O, speak to me no more;
These words, like daggers, enter in mine ears;
No more, sweet Hamlet!

Hamlet: A murderer and a villain;
A slave that is not twentieth part the tithe
Of your precedent lord;° a vice of kings;°
A cutpurse of the empire and the rule,
That from a shelf the precious diadem stole,
And put it in his pocket!

Queen: No more!

Enter Ghost.

Hamlet: A king of shreds and patches,° —
Save me, and hover o'er me with your wings,
You heavenly guards! What would your gracious figure?

Queen: Alas, he's mad!

Hamlet: Do you not come your tardy son to chide,
That, laps'd in time and passion,° lets go by
Th' important° acting of your dread command?
O, say!

Ghost: Do not forget: this visitation
Is but to whet thy almost blunted purpose.
But, look, amazement° on thy mother sits:

82 *mope:* Be in a depressed, spirtless state, act aimlessly. 85 *mutine:* Mutiny, rebel. 87 *gives the charge:* Delivers the attack. 89 *reason pandars will:* The normal and proper situation was one in which reason guided the will in the direction of good; here, reason is perverted and leads in the direction of evil. 91 *grained:* Dyed in grain. 93 *enseamed:* Loaded with grease, greased. 99 *precedent lord:* I.e., the elder Hamlet; *vice of kings:* Buffoon of kings; a reference to the Vice, or clown, of the morality plays and interludes. 103 *shreds and patches:* I.e., motley, the traditional costume of the Vice. 108 *laps'd . . . passion:* Having suffered time to slip and passion to cool; also explained as "engrossed in casual events and lapsed into mere fruitless passion, so that he no longer entertains a rational purpose." 109 *important:* Urgent. 113 *amazement:* Frenzy, distraction.

O, step between her and her fighting soul:
Conceit in weakest bodies strongest works:
Speak to her, Hamlet.

Hamlet: How is it with you, lady?

Queen: Alas, how is 't with you,
That you do bend your eye on vacancy
And with th' incorporal° air do hold discourse?
Forth at your eyes your spirits wildly peep;
And, as the sleeping soldiers in th' alarm,
Your bedded° hair, like life in excrements,°
Start up, and stand an° end. O gentle son,
Upon the heat and flame of thy distemper
Sprinkle cool patience. Whereon do you look?

Hamlet: On him, on him! Look you, how pale he glares!
His form and cause conjoin'd,° preaching to stones,
Would make them capable. — Do not look upon me;
Lest with this piteous action you convert
My stern effects:° then what I have to do
Will want true colour;° tears perchance for blood.

Queen: To whom do you speak this?

Hamlet: Do you see nothing there?

Queen: Nothing at all; yet all that is I see.

Hamlet: Nor did you nothing hear?

Queen: No, nothing but ourselves.

Hamlet: Why, look you there! look, how it steals away!
My father, in his habit as he liv'd!
Look, where he goes, even now, out at the portal! *Exit Ghost.*

Queen: This is the very coinage of your brain:
This bodiless creation ecstasy
Is very cunning in.

Hamlet: Ecstasy!
My pulse, as yours, doth temperately keep time,
And makes as healthful music: it is not madness
That I have utt'red: bring me to the test,
And I the matter will re-word,° which madness
Would gambol° from. Mother, for love of grace,
Lay not that flattering unction° to your soul,
That not your trespass, but my madness speaks:
It will but skin and film the ulcerous place,
Whiles rank corruption, mining° all within,
Infects unseen. Confess yourself to heaven;

119 *incorporal:* Immaterial. 122 *bedded:* Laid in smooth layers; *excrements:* The hair was considered an excrement or voided part of the body. 123 *an:* On. 127 *conjoin'd:* United. 129–130 *convert . . . effects:* Divert me from my stern duty. For *effects,* possibly *affects* (affections of the mind). 131 *want true colour:* Lack good reason so that (with a play on the normal sense of *colour*) I shall shed tears instead of blood. 144 *re-word:* Repeat in words. 145 *gambol:* Skip away. 146 *unction:* Ointment used medicinally or as a rite; suggestion that forgiveness for sin may not be so easily achieved. 149 *mining:* Working under the surface.

Repent what's past; avoid what is to come;°
And do not spread the compost° on the weeds,
To make them ranker. Forgive me this my virtue;°
For in the fatness° of these pursy° times
Virtue itself of vice must pardon beg,
Yea, curb° and woo for leave to do him good.

Queen: O Hamlet, thou hast cleft my heart in twain.

Hamlet: O, throw away the worser part of it,
And live the purer with the other half.
Good night: but go not to my uncle's bed;
Assume a virtue, if you have it not.
That monster, custom, who all sense doth eat,
Of habits devil, is angel yet in this,
That to the use of actions fair and good
He likewise gives a frock or livery,
That aptly is put on. Refrain to-night,
And that shall lend a kind of easiness
To the next abstinence: the next more easy;
For use almost can change the stamp of nature,
And either . . . the devil, or throw him out°
With wondrous potency. Once more, good night:
And when you are desirous to be bless'd,°
I'll blessing beg of you. For this same lord, *[Pointing to Polonius.]*
I do repent: but heaven hath pleas'd it so,
To punish me with this and this with me,
That I must be their scourge and minister.
I will bestow him, and will answer well
The death I gave him. So, again, good night.
I must be cruel, only to be kind:
Thus bad begins and worse remains behind.
One word more, good lady.

Queen: What shall I do?

Hamlet: Not this, by no means, that I bid you do:
Let the bloat° king tempt you again to bed;
Pinch wanton on your cheek; call you his mouse;
And let him, for a pair of reechy° kisses,
Or paddling in your neck with his damn'd fingers,
Make you to ravel all this matter out,
That I essentially° am not in madness,
But mad in craft. 'Twere good you let him know;
For who, that's but a queen, fair, sober, wise,
Would from a paddock,° from a bat, a gib,°

151 *what is to come:* I.e., the sins of the future. 152 *compost:* Manure. 153 *this my virtue:* My virtuous talk in reproving you. 154 *fatness:* Grossness; *pursy:* Short-winded, corpulent. 156 *curb:* Bow, bend the knee. 170 Defective line usually emended by inserting *master* after *either.* 172 *be bless'd:* Become blessed, i.e., repentant. 183 *bloat:* Bloated. 185 *reechy:* Dirty, filthy. 188 *essentially:* In my essential nature. 191 *paddock:* Toad; *gib:* Tomcat.

Such dear concernings° hide? who would do so?
No, in despite of sense and secrecy,
Unpeg the basket on the house's top,
Let the birds fly, and, like the famous ape,°
To try conclusions,° in the basket creep,
And break your own neck down.

Queen: Be thou assur'd, if words be made of breath,
And breath of life, I have no life to breathe
What thou hast said to me.

Hamlet: I must to England; you know that?

Queen: Alack,
I had forgot: 'tis so concluded on.

Hamlet: There's letters seal'd: and my two schoolfellows,
Whom I will trust as I will adders fang'd,
They bear the mandate; they must sweep my way,°
And marshal me to knavery. Let it work;
For 'tis the sport to have the enginer°
Hoist° with his own petar:° and 't shall go hard
But I will delve one yard below their mines,
And blow them at the moon: O, 'tis most sweet,
When in one line two crafts° directly meet.
This man shall set me packing:°
I'll lug the guts into the neighbour room.
Mother, good night. Indeed this counsellor
Is now most still, most secret and most grave,
Who was in life a foolish prating knave.
Come, sir, to draw° toward an end with you.
Good night, mother.

Exeunt [severally; Hamlet dragging in Polonius.]

[ACT IV

SCENE I. *A room in the castle.*]

Enter King and Queen, with Rosencrantz and Guildenstern.

King: There's matter in these sighs, these profound heaves:
You must translate: 'tis fit we understand them.
Where is your son?

Queen: Bestow this place on us a little while.

192 *dear concernings:* Important affairs. 195 *the famous ape:* A letter from Sir John Suckling seems to supply other details of the story, otherwise not identified: "It is the story of the jackanapes and the partridges; thou starest after a beauty till it be lost to thee, then let'st out another, and starest after that till it is gone too." 196 *conclusions:* Experiments. 205 *sweep my way:* Clear my path. 207 *enginer:* Constructor of military works, or possibly, artilleryman. 208 *Hoist:* Blown up; *petar:* Defined as a small engine of war used to blow in a door or make a breach, and as a case filled with explosive materials. 211 *two crafts:* Two acts of guile, with quibble on the sense of "two ships." 212 *set me packing:* Set me to making schemes, and set me to lugging (him), and, also, send me off in a hurry. 217 *draw:* Come, with quibble on literal sense.

[Exeunt Rosencrantz and Guildenstern.]

Ah, mine own lord, what have I seen to-night!
King: What, Gertrude? How does Hamlet?
Queen: Mad as the sea and wind, when both contend
Which is the mightier: in his lawless fit,
Behind the arras hearing something stir,
Whips out his rapier, cries, "A rat, a rat!"
And, in this brainish° apprehension,° kills
The unseen good old man.
King: O heavy dead!
It had been so with us, had we been there:
His liberty is full of threats to all;
To you yourself, to us, to every one.
Alas, how shall this bloody deed be answer'd?
It will be laid to us, whose providence°
Should have kept short,° restrain'd and out of haunt,°
This mad young man: but so much was our love,
We would not understand what was most fit;
But, like the owner of a foul disease,
To keep it from divulging,° let it feed
Even on the pith of life. Where is he gone?
Queen: To draw apart the body he hath kill'd:
O'er whom his very madness, like some ore
Among a mineral° of metals base,
Shows itself pure; 'a weeps for what is done.
King: O Gertrude, come away!
The sun no sooner shall the mountains touch,
But we will ship him hence: and this vile deed
We must, with all our majesty and skill,
Both countenance and excuse. Ho, Guildenstern!

Enter Rosencrantz and Guildenstern.

Friends both, go join you with some further aid:
Hamlet in madness hath Polonius slain,
And from his mother's closet hath he dragg'd him:
Go seek him out; speak fair, and bring the body
Into the chapel. I pray you, haste in this.

[Exeunt Rosencrantz and Guildenstern.]

Come, Gertrude, we'll call up our wisest friends;
And let them know, both what we mean to do,
And what's untimely done . . .°
Whose whisper o'er the world's diameter,°
As level° as the cannon to his blank,°
Transports his pois'ned shot, may miss our name,

ACT IV. SCENE I. 11 *brainish:* Headstrong, passionate; *apprehension:* Conception, imagination. 17 *providence:* Foresight. 18 *short:* I.e., on a short tether; *out of haunt:* Secluded. 22 *divulging:* Becoming evident. 26 *mineral:* Mine. 40 Defective line; some editors add: *so, haply, slander;* others add: *for, haply, slander;* other conjectures. 41 *diameter:* Extent from side to side. 42 *level:* Straight; *blank:* White spot in the center of a target.

And hit the woundless° air. O, come away!
My soul is full of discord and dismay. *Exeunt.*

[SCENE II. *Another room in the castle.*]

Enter Hamlet.

Hamlet: Safely stowed.

Rosencrantz:
Guildenstern: (*within*) Hamlet! Lord Hamlet!

Hamlet: But soft, what noise? who calls on Hamlet? O, here they come.

Enter Rosencrantz and Guildenstern.

Rosencrantz: What have you done, my lord, with the dead body?
Hamlet: Compounded it with dust, whereto 'tis kin.
Rosencrantz: Tell us where 'tis, that we may take it thence
And bear it to the chapel.
Hamlet: Do not believe it.
Rosencrantz: Believe what?
Hamlet: That I can keep your counsel° and not mine own. Besides, to be demanded of a sponge! what replication° should be made by the son of a king?
Rosencrantz: Take you me for a sponge, my lord?
Hamlet: Ay, sir, that soaks up the king's countenance, his rewards, his authorities.° But such officers do the king best service in the end: he keeps them, like an ape an apple, in the corner of his jaw; first mouthed, to be last swallowed: when he needs what you have gleaned, it is but squeezing you, and, sponge, you shall be dry again.
Rosencrantz: I understand you not, my lord.
Hamlet: I am glad of it: a knavish speech sleeps in a foolish ear.
Rosencrantz: My lord, you must tell us where the body is, and go with us to the king.
Hamlet: The body is with the king, but the king is not with the body.° The king is a thing —
Guildenstern: A thing, my lord!
Hamlet: Of nothing: bring me to him. Hide fox, and all after.° *Exeunt.*

[SCENE III. *Another room in the castle.*]

Enter King, and two or three.

King: I have sent to seek him, and to find the body.
How dangerous is it that this man goes loose!

44 *woundless:* Invulnerable. SCENE II. 9 *keep your counsel:* Hamlet is aware of their treachery but says nothing about it. 10 *replication:* Reply. 14 *authorities:* Authoritative backing. 22 *The body . . . body:* There are many interpretations; possibly, "The body lies in death with the king, my father; but my father walks disembodied"; or "Claudius has the bodily possession of kingship, but kingliness, or justice of inheritance, is not with him." 25 *Hide . . . after:* An old signal cry in the game of hide-and-seek.

Yet must not we put the strong law on him:
He's lov'd of the distracted° multitude,
Who like not in their judgement, but their eyes;
And where 'tis so, th' offender's scourge° is weigh'd,°
But never the offence. To bear all smooth and even,
This sudden sending him away must seem
Deliberate pause:° diseases desperate grown
By desperate appliance are reliev'd,
Or not at all.

Enter Rosencrantz, [Guildenstern,] and all the rest.

How now! what hath befall'n?
Rosencrantz: Where the dead body is bestow'd, my lord,
We cannot get from him.
King: But where is he?
Rosencrantz: Without, my lord; guarded, to know your pleasure.
King: Bring him before us.
Rosencrantz: Ho! bring in the lord.

They enter [with Hamlet].

King: Now, Hamlet, where's Polonius?
Hamlet: At supper.
King: At supper! where?
Hamlet: Not where he eats, but where 'a is eaten: a certain convocation of politic° worms° are e'en at him. Your worm is your only emperor for diet: we fat all creatures else to fat us, and we fat ourselves for maggots: your fat king and your lean beggar is but variable service,° two dishes, but to one table: that's the end.
King: Alas, alas!
Hamlet: A man may fish with the worm that hath eat of a king, and eat of the fish that hath fed of that worm.
King: What dost thou mean by this?
Hamlet: Nothing but to show you how a king may go a progress° through the guts of a beggar.
King: Where is Polonius?
Hamlet: In heaven; send thither to see: if your messenger find him not there, seek him i' the other place yourself. But if indeed you find him not within this month, you shall nose him as you go up the stairs into the lobby.
King [to some Attendants]: Go seek him there.
Hamlet: 'A will stay till you come. *[Exeunt Attendants.]*
King: Hamlet, this deed, for thine especial safety, —
Which we do tender,° as we dearly grieve
For that which thou hast done, — must send thee hence
With fiery quickness: therefore prepare thyself;

SCENE III. 4 *distracted:* I.e., without power of forming logical judgments. 6 *scourge:* Punishment; *weigh'd:* Taken into consideration. 9 *Deliberate pause:* Considered action. 20–21 *convocation . . . worms:* Allusion to the Diet of Worms (1521); *politic:* Crafty. 23 *variable service:* A variety of dishes. 29 *progress:* Royal journey of state. 39 *tender:* Regard, hold dear.

The bark is ready, and the wind at help,
Th' associates tend, and everything is bent
For England.

Hamlet: For England!

King: Ay, Hamlet.

Hamlet: Good.

King: So is it, if thou knew'st our purposes.

Hamlet: I see a cherub° that sees them. But, come; for England! Farewell, dear mother.

King: Thy loving father, Hamlet.

Hamlet: My mother: father and mother is man and wife; man and wife is one flesh; and so, my mother. Come, for England! *Exit.*

King: Follow him at foot;° tempt him with speed aboard;
Delay it not; I'll have him hence to-night:
Away! for every thing is seal'd and done
That else leans on th' affair: pray you, make haste.
[Exeunt all but the King.]
And, England, if my love thou hold'st at aught —
As my great power thereof may give thee sense,
Since yet thy cicatrice° looks raw and red
After the Danish sword, and thy free awe°
Pays homage to us — thou mayst not coldly set
Our sovereign process; which imports at full,
By letters congruing to that effect,
The present death of Hamlet. Do it, England;
For like the hectic° in my blood he rages,
And thou must cure me: till I know 'tis done,
Howe'er my haps,° my joys were ne'er begun. *Exit.*

[SCENE IV. *A plain in Demark.*]

Enter Fortinbras with his Army over the stage.

Fortinbras: Go, captain, from me greet the Danish king;
Tell him that, by his license,° Fortinbras
Craves the conveyance° of a promis'd march
Over his kingdom. You know the rendezvous.
If that his majesty would aught with us,
We shall express our duty in his eye;°
And let him know so.

Captain: I will do't, my lord.

Fortinbras: Go softly° on. *[Exeunt all but Captain.]*

Enter Hamlet, Rosencrantz, [Guildenstern,] &c.

Hamlet: Good sir, whose powers are these?

46 *cherub:* Cherubim are angels of knowledge. 51 *at foot:* Close behind, at heel. 57 *cicatrice:* Scar. 58 *free awe:* Voluntary show of respect. 63 *hectic:* Fever. 65 *haps:* Fortunes. SCENE IV. 2 *license:* Leave. 3 *conveyance:* Escort, convoy. 6 *in his eye:* In his presence. 8 *softly:* Slowly.

Captain: They are of Norway, sir.
Hamlet: How purpos'd, sir, I pray you?
Captain: Against some part of Poland.
Hamlet: Who commands them, sir?
Captain: The nephew to old Norway, Fortinbras.
Hamlet: Goes it against the main° of Poland, sir,
Or for some frontier?
Captain: Truly to speak, and with no addition,
We go to gain a little patch of ground
That hath in it no profit but the name.
To pay five ducats, five, I would not farm it;°
Nor will it yield to Norway or the Pole
A ranker rate, should it be sold in fee.°
Hamlet: Why, then the Polack never will defend it.
Captain: Yes, it is already garrison'd.
Hamlet: Two thousand souls and twenty thousand ducats
Will not debate the question of this straw:°
This is th' imposthume° of much wealth and peace,
That inward breaks, and shows no cause without
Why the man dies. I humbly thank you, sir.
Captain: God be wi' you, sir. *[Exit.]*
Rosencrantz: Will 't please you go, my lord?
Hamlet: I'll be with you straight. Go a little before.
[Exeunt all except Hamlet.]

How all occasions° do inform against° me,
And spur my dull revenge! What is a man,
If his chief good and market of his time°
Be but to sleep and feed? a beast, no more.
Sure, he that made us with such large discourse,
Looking before and after, gave us not
That capability and god-like reason
To fust° in us unus'd. Now, whether it be
Bestial oblivion, or some craven scruple
Of thinking too precisely on th' event,
A thought which, quarter'd, hath but one part wisdom
And ever three parts coward, I do not know
Why yet I live to say "This thing 's to do";
Sith I have cause and will and strength and means
To do 't. Examples gross as earth exhort me:
Witness this army of such mass and charge
Led by a delicate and tender prince,
Whose spirit with divine ambition puff'd
Makes mouths at the invisible event,
Exposing what is mortal and unsure

15 *main:* Country itself. 20 *farm it:* Take a lease of it. 22 *fee:* Fee simple. 26 *debate . . . straw:* Settle this trifling matter. 27 *imposthume:* Purulent abscess or swelling. 32 *occasions:* Incidents, events; *inform against:* generally defined as "show," "betray" (i.e., his tardiness); more probably *inform* means "take shape," as in *Macbeth,* II. i. 48. 34 *market of his time:* The best use he makes of his time, or, that for which he sells his time. 39 *fust:* Grow moldy.

To all that fortune, death and danger dare,
Even for an egg-shell. Rightly to be great
Is not to stir without great argument,
But greatly to find quarrel in a straw
When honour's at the stake. How stand I then,
That have a father kill'd, a mother stain'd,
Excitements of° my reason and my blood,
And let all sleep? while, to my shame, I see
The imminent death of twenty thousand men,
That, for a fantasy and trick° of fame,
Go to their graves like beds, fight for a plot°
Whereon the numbers cannot try the cause,
Which is not tomb enough and continent
To hide the slain? O, from this time forth,
My thoughts be bloody, or be nothing worth! *Exit.*

[SCENE V. *Elsinore. A room in the castle.*]

Enter Horatio, [Queen] Gertrude, and a Gentleman.

Queen: I will not speak with her.
Gentleman: She is importunate, indeed distract:
Her mood will needs be pitied.
Queen: What would she have?
Gentleman: She speaks much of her father; says she hears
There's tricks° i' th' world; and hems, and beats her heart;°
Spurns enviously at straws;° speaks things in doubt,
That carry but half sense: her speech is nothing,
Yet the unshaped° use of it doth move
The hearers to collection;° they yawn° at it,
And botch° the words up fit to their own thoughts;
Which, as her winks, and nods, and gestures yield° them,
Indeed would make one think there might be thought,
Though nothing sure, yet much unhappily.°
Horatio: 'Twere good she were spoken with: for she may strew
Dangerous conjectures in ill-breeding minds.°
Queen: Let her come in. *[Exit Gentleman.]*
[Aside.] To my sick soul, as sin's true nature is,
Each toy seems prologue to some great amiss:°
So full of artless jealousy is guilt,
It spills itself in fearing to be spilt.°

Enter Ophelia [distracted].

58 *Excitements of:* Incentives to. 61 *trick:* Toy, trifle. 62 *plot:* I.e., of ground. SCENE V. 5 *tricks:* Deceptions; *heart:* I.e., breast. 6 *Spurns . . . straws:* Kicks spitefully at small objects in her path. 8 *unshaped:* Unformed, artless. 9 *collection:* Inference, a guess at some sort of meaning; *yawn:* Wonder. 10 *botch:* Patch. 11 *yield:* Deliver, bring forth (her words). 13 *much unhappily:* Expressive of much unhappiness. 15 *ill-breeding minds:* Minds bent on mischief. 18 *great amiss:* Calamity, disaster. 19–20 *So . . . spilt:* Guilt is so full of suspicion that it unskillfully betrays itself in fearing to be betrayed.

Ophelia: Where is the beauteous majesty of Denmark?
Queen: How now, Ophelia!
Ophelia (she sings): How should I your true love know
From another one?
By his cockle hat° and staff,
And his sandal shoon.°
Queen: Alas, sweet lady, what imports this song?
Ophelia: Say you? nay, pray you mark.
(Song) He is dead and gone, lady,
He is dead and gone;
At his head a grass-green turf,
At his heels a stone.
O, ho!
Queen: Nay, but, Ophelia —
Ophelia: Pray you, mark
[Sings.] White his shroud as the mountain snow, —

Enter King.

Queen: Alas, look here, my lord.
Ophelia (Song): Larded° all with flowers;
Which bewept to the grave did not go
With true-love showers.
King: How do you, pretty lady?
Ophelia: Well, God 'ild° you! They say the owl° was a baker's daughter. Lord, we know what we are, but know not what we may be. God be at your table!
King: Conceit upon her father.
Ophelia: Pray let's have no words of this; but when they ask you what it means, say you this:
(Song) To-morrow is Saint Valentine's day,
All in the morning bedtime,
And I a maid at your window,
To be your Valentine.°
Then up he rose, and donn'd his clothes,
And dupp'd° the chamber-door;
Let in the maid, that out a maid
Never departed more.
King: Pretty Ophelia!
Ophelia: Indeed, la, without an oath, I'll make an end on 't:
[Sings.] By Gis° and by Saint Charity,
Alack, and fie for shame!
Young men will do 't, if they come to 't;

25 *cockle hat:* Hat with cockleshell stuck in it as a sign that the wearer has been a pilgrim to the shrine of St. James of Compostella. The pilgrim's garb was a conventional disguise for lovers. 26 *shoon:* Shoes. 38 *Larded:* Decorated. 42 *God 'ild:* God yield or reward; *owl:* Reference to a monkish legend that a baker's daughter was turned into an owl for refusing bread to the Saviour. 51 *Valentine:* This song alludes to the belief that the first girl seen by a man on the morning of this day was his valentine or true love. 53 *dupp'd:* Opened. 58 *Gis:* Jesus.

By cock,° they are to blame.
Quoth she, before you tumbled me,
You promis'd me to wed.
So would I ha' done, by yonder sun,
An thou hadst not come to my bed.

King: How long hath she been thus?

Ophelia: I hope all will be well. We must be patient: but I cannot choose but weep, to think they would lay him i' the cold ground. My brother shall know of it: and so I thank you for your good counsel. Come, my coach! Good night, ladies; good night, sweet ladies; good night, good night. *[Exit.]*

King: Follow her close; give her good watch, I pray you. *[Exit Horatio.]*
O, this is the poison of deep grief; it springs
All from her father's death. O Gertrude, Gertrude,
When sorrows come, they come not single spies,
But in battalions. First, her father slain:
Next your son gone; and he most violent author
Of his own just remove: the people muddied,
Thick and unwholesome in their thoughts and whispers,
For good Polonius' death; and we have done but greenly,°
In hugger-mugger° to inter him: poor Ophelia
Divided from herself and her fair judgement,
Without the which we are pictures, or mere beasts:
Last, and as much containing as all these,
Her brother is in secret come from France;
Feeds on his wonder, keeps himself in clouds,°
And wants not buzzers° to infect his ear
With pestilent speeches of his father's death;
Wherein necessity, of matter beggar'd,°
Will nothing stick° our person to arraign
In ear and ear.° O my dear Gertrude, this,
Like to a murd'ring-piece,° in many places
Gives me superfluous death. *A noise within.*

Queen: Alack, what noise is this?

King: Where are my Switzers?° Let them guard the door.

Enter a Messenger.

What is the matter?

Messenger: Save yourself, my lord:
The ocean, overpeering° of his list,°
Eats not the flats with more impiteous haste
Than young Laertes, in a riotous head,
O'erbears your officers. The rabble call him lord;

61 *cock:* Perversion of "God" in oaths. 80 *greenly:* Foolishly. 81 *hugger-mugger:* Secret haste. 86 *in clouds:* Invisible. 87 *buzzers:* Gossipers. 89 *of matter beggar'd:* Unprovided with facts. 90 *nothing stick:* Not hesitate. 91 *In ear and ear:* In everybody's ears. 92 *murd'ring-piece:* Small cannon or mortar; suggestion of numerous missiles fired. 94 *Switzers:* Swiss guards, mercenaries. 96 *overpeering:* Overflowing; *list:* Shore.

And, as the world were now but to begin,
Antiquity forgot, custom not known,
The ratifiers and props of every word,°
They cry "Choose we: Laertes shall be king":
Caps, hands, and tongues, applaud it to the clouds:
"Laertes shall be king, Laertes king!" *A noise within.*

Queen: How cheerfully on the false trail they cry!
O, this is counter,° you false Danish dogs!

King: The doors are broke.

Enter Laertes with others.

Laertes: Where is this king? Sirs, stand you all without.

Danes: No, let's come in.

Laertes: I pray you, give me leave.

Danes: We will, we will. *[They retire without the door.]*

Laertes: I thank you: keep the door. O thou vile king,
Give me my father!

Queen: Calmly, good Laertes.

Laertes: That drop of blood that's calm proclaims me bastard,
Cries cuckold to my father, brands the harlot
Even here, between the chaste unsmirched brow
Of my true mother.

King: What is the cause, Laertes,
That thy rebellion looks so giant-like?
Let him go, Gertrude; do not fear our person:
There's such divinity doth hedge a king,
That treason can but peep to° what it would,°
Acts little of his will. Tell me, Laertes,
Why thou art thus incens'd. Let him go, Gertrude.
Speak, man.

Laertes: Where is my father?

King: Dead.

Queen: But not by him.

King: Let him demand his fill.

Laertes: How came he dead? I'll not be juggled with:
To hell, allegiance! vows, to the blackest devil!
Conscience and grace, to the profoundest pit!
I dare damnation. To this point I stand,
That both the worlds I give to negligence,°
Let come what comes; only I'll be reveng'd
Most throughly for my father.

King: Who shall stay you?

Laertes: My will,° not all the world's:
And for my means, I'll husband them so well,
They shall go far with little.

102 *word:* Promise. 107 *counter:* A hunting term meaning to follow the trail in a direction opposite to that which the game has taken. 121 *peep to:* I.e., look at from afar off; *would:* Wishes to do. 131 *give to negligence:* He despises both the here and the hereafter. 134 *My will:* He will not be stopped except by his own will.

King: Good Laertes,
If you desire to know the certainty
Of your dear father, is 't writ in your revenge,
That, swoopstake,° you will draw both friend and foe,
Winner and loser?
Laertes: None but his enemies.
King: Will you know them then?
Laertes: To his good friends thus wide I'll ope my arms;
And like the kind life-rend'ring pelican,°
Repast° them with my blood.
King: Why, now you speak
Like a good child and a true gentleman.
That I am guiltless of your father's death,
And am most sensibly in grief for it,
It shall as level to your judgement 'pear
As day does to your eye.

A noise within: "Let her come in."

Laertes: How now! what noise is that?

Enter Ophelia.

O heat,° dry up my brains! tears seven times salt,
Burn out the sense and virtue of mine eye!
By heaven, thy madness shall be paid with weight,
Till our scale turn the beam. O rose of May!
Dear maid, kind sister, sweet Ophelia!
O heavens! is 't possible, a young maid's wits
Should be as mortal as an old man's life?
Nature is fine in love, and where 'tis fine,
It sends some precious instance of itself
After the thing it loves.
Ophelia (Song): They bore him barefac'd on the bier;
Hey non nonny, nonny, hey nonny;
And in his grave rain'd many a tear: —
Fare you well, my dove!
Laertes: Hadst thou thy wits, and didst persuade revenge,
It could not move thus.
Ophelia [sings]: You must sing a-down a-down,
An you call him a-down-a.
O, how the wheel° becomes it! It is the false steward,°
that stole his master's daughter.
Laertes: This nothing's more than matter.
Ophelia: There 's rosemary,° that 's for remembrance; pray you, love, remember: and there is pansies,° that 's for thoughts.

139 *swoopstake:* Literally, drawing the whole stake at once, i.e., indiscriminately. 143 *pelican:* Reference to the belief that the pelican feeds its young with its own blood. 144 *Repast:* Feed. 151 *heat:* Probably the heat generated by the passion of grief. 169 *wheel:* Spinning wheel as accompaniment to the song refrain; *false steward:* The story is unknown. 172 *rosemary:* Used as a symbol of remembrance both at weddings and at funerals. 173 *pansies:* Emblems of love and courtship. Cf. French *pensées.*

Laertes: A document° in madness, thoughts and remembrance fitted.
Ophelia: There's fennel° for you, and columbines:° there's rue° for you; and here's some for me: we may call it herb of grace o' Sundays: O, you must wear your rue with a difference. There's a daisy:° I would give you some violets,° but they withered all when my father died: they say 'a made a good end, —
[Sings.] For bonny sweet Robin is all my joy.°
Laertes: Thought° and affliction, passion, hell itself,
She turns to favour and to prettiness.
Ophelia (Song): And will 'a not come again?°
And will 'a not come again?
No, no, he is dead:
Go to thy death-bed:
He never will come again.

His beard was as white as snow,
All flaxen was his poll:°
He is gone, he is gone,
And we cast away° moan:
God ha' mercy on his soul!
And of all Christian souls, I pray God. God be wi' you. *[Exit.]*
Laertes: Do you see this, O God?
King: Laertes, I must commune with your grief,
Or you deny me right.° Go but apart,
Make choice of whom your wisest friends you will,
And they shall hear and judge 'twixt you and me:
If by direct or by collateral° hand
They find us touch'd,° we will our kingdom give,
Our crown, our life, and all that we call ours,
To you in satisfaction; but if not,
Be you content to lend your patience to us,
And we shall jointly labour with your soul
To give it due content.
Laertes: Let this be so;
His means of death, his obscure funeral —
No trophy, sword, nor hatchment° o'er his bones,
No noble rite nor formal ostentation —
Cry to be heard, as 'twere from heaven to earth,
That I must call 't in question.
King: So you shall;

174 *document:* Piece of instruction or lesson. 175 *fennel:* Emblem of flattery; *columbines:* Emblem of unchastity (?) or ingratitude (?); *rue:* Emblem of repentance. It was usually mingled with holy water and then known as *herb of grace.* Ophelia is probably playing on the two meanings of *rue,* "repentant" and "even for ruth (pity)"; the former signification is for the queen, the latter for herself. 177 *daisy:* Emblem of dissembling, faithlessness. 178 *violets:* Emblems of faithfulness. 180 *For . . . joy:* Probably a line from a Robin Hood ballad. 181 *Thought:* Melancholy thought. 183 *And . . . again:* This song appeared in the songbooks as "The Merry Milkmaids' Dumps." 189 *poll:* Head. 191 *cast away:* Shipwrecked. 196 *right:* My rights. 199 *collateral:* Indirect. 200 *touch'd:* Implicated. 207 *hatchment:* Tablet displaying the armorial bearings of a deceased person.

And where th' offence is let the great axe fall.
I pray you, go with me. *Exeunt.*

[SCENE VI. *Another room in the castle.*]

Enter Horatio and others.

Horatio: What are they that would speak with me?
Gentleman: Sea-faring men, sir: they say they have letters for you.
Horatio: Let them come in. *[Exit Gentleman]*
I do not know from what part of the world
I should be greeted, if not from lord Hamlet.

Enter Sailors.

First Sailor: God bless you, sir.
Horatio: Let him bless thee too.
First Sailor: 'A shall sir, an 't please him. There's a letter for you, sir; it comes from the ambassador that was bound for England; if your name be Horatio, as I am let to know it is.
Horatio [Reads]: "Horatio, when thou shalt have overlooked this, give these fellows some means° to the king: they have letters for him. Ere we were two days old at sea, a pirate of very warlike appointment gave us chase. Finding ourselves too slow of sail, we put on a compelled valour, and in the grapple I boarded them: on the instant they got clear of our ship; so I alone became their prisoner. They have dealt with me like thieves of mercy:° but they knew what they did; I am to do a good turn for them. Let the king have the letters I have sent; and repair thou to me with as much speed as thou wouldest fly death. I have words to speak in thine ear will make thee dumb; yet are they much too light for the bore° of the matter. These good fellows will bring thee where I am. Rosencrantz and Guildenstern hold their course for England: of them I have much to tell thee. Farewell.
"He that thou knowest thine, HAMLET."
Come, I will give you way for these your letters;
And do 't the speedier, that you may direct me
To him from whom you brought them. *Exeunt.*

[SCENE VII. *Another room in the castle.*]

Enter King and Laertes.

King: Now must your conscience° my acquittance seal,
And you must put me in your heart for friend,
Sith you have heard, and with a knowing ear,
That he which hath your noble father slain
Pursued my life.
Laertes: It well appears: but tell me

SCENE VI. 12 *means:* Means of access. 17 *thieves of mercy:* Merciful thieves. 21 *bore:* Caliber, importance. SCENE VII. 1 *conscience:* Knowledge that this is true.

Why you proceeded not against these feats,
So criminal and so capital° in nature,
As by your safety, wisdom, all things else,
You mainly° were stirr'd up.

King: O, for two special reasons;
Which may to you, perhaps, seem much unsinew'd,°
But yet to me th' are strong. The queen his mother
Lives almost by his looks; and for myself —
My virtue or my plague, be it either which —
She's so conjunctive° to my life and soul,
That, as the star moves not but in his sphere,°
I could not but by her. The other motive,
Why to a public count° I might not go,
Is the great love the general gender° bear him;
Who, dipping all his faults in their affection,
Would, like the spring° that turneth wood to stone,
Convert his gyves° to graces; so that my arrows,
Too slightly timber'd° for so loud° a wind,
Would have reverted to my bow again,
And not where I had aim'd them.

Laertes: And so have I a noble father lost;
A sister driven into desp'rate terms,°
Whose worth, if praises may go back° again,
Stood challenger on mount° of all the age°
For her perfections: but my revenge will come.

King: Break not your sleeps for that: you must not think
That we are made of stuff so flat and dull
That we can let our beard be shook with danger
And think it pastime. You shortly shall hear more:
I lov'd your father, and we love ourself;
And that, I hope, will teach you to imagine —

Enter a Messenger with letters.

How now! what news?

Messenger: Letters, my lord, from Hamlet:
These to your majesty; this to the queen.°

King: From Hamlet! who brought them?

Messenger: Sailors, my lord, they say; I saw them not:
They were given me by Claudio;° he receiv'd them
Of him that brought them.

7 *capital:* Punishable by death. 9 *mainly:* Greatly. 10 *unsinew'd:* Weak. 14 *conjunctive:* Comformable (the next line suggesting planetary conjunction). 15 *sphere:* The hollow sphere in which, according to Ptolemaic astronomy, the planets were supposed to move. 17 *count:* Account, reckoning. 18 *general gender:* Common people. 20 *spring:* I.e., one heavily charged with lime. 21 *gyves:* Fetters; here, faults, or possibly, punishments inflicted (on him). 22 *slightly timber'd:* Light; *loud:* Strong. 26 *terms:* State, condition. 27 *go back:* I.e., to Ophelia's former virtues. 28 *on mount:* Set up on high, *mounted* (on horseback); *of all the age:* Qualifies *challenger* and not *mount.* 37 *to the queen:* One hears no more of the letter to the queen. 40 *Claudio:* This character does not appear in the play.

King: Laertes, you shall hear them.
Leave us. *[Exit Messenger.]*
[Reads.] "High and mighty, You shall know I am set naked° on your kingdom. To-morrow shall I beg leave to see your kingly eyes: when I shall, first asking your pardon thereunto, recount the occasion of my sudden and more strange return. "HAMLET."
What should this mean? Are all the rest come back?
Or is it some abuse, and no such thing?
Laertes: Know you the hand?
King: 'Tis Hamlet's character. "Naked!"
And in a postscript here, he says "alone."
Can you devise° me?
Laertes: I 'm lost in it, my lord. But let him come;
It warms the very sickness in my heart,
That I shall live and tell him to his teeth,
"Thus didst thou."
King: If it be so, Laertes —
As how should it be so? how otherwise?° —
Will you be rul'd by me?
Laertes: Ay, my lord;
So you will not o'errule me to a peace.
King: To thine own peace. If he be now return'd,
As checking at° his voyage, and that he means
No more to undertake it, I will work him
To an exploit, now ripe in my device,
Under the which he shall not choose but fall:
And for his death no wind of blame shall breathe,
But even his mother shall uncharge the practice°
And call it accident.
Laertes: My lord, I will be rul'd;
The rather, if you could devise it so
That I might be the organ.°
King: It falls right.
You have been talk'd of since your travel much,
And that in Hamlet's hearing, for a quality
Wherein, they say, you shine: your sum of parts
Did not together pluck such envy from him
As did that one, and that, in my regard,
Of the unworthiest siege.°
Laertes: What part is that, my lord?
King: A very riband in the cap of youth,
Yet needful too; for youth no less becomes

43 *naked:* Unprovided (with retinue). 51 *devise:* Explain to. 56 *As . . . otherwise?* How can this (Hamlet's return) be true? (yet) how otherwise than true (since we have the evidence of his letter)? Some editors read *How should it not be so,* etc., making the words refer to Laertes's desire to meet with Hamlet. 60 *checking at:* Used in falconry of a hawk's leaving the quarry to fly at a chance bird, turn aside. 65 *uncharge the practice:* Acquit the stratagem of being a plot. 68 *organ:* Agent, instrument. 74 *siege:* Rank.

The light and careless livery that it wears
That settled age his sables° and his weeds,
Importing health and graveness. Two months since,
Here was a gentleman of Normandy: —
I have seen myself, and serv'd against, the French,
And they can well° on horseback: but this gallant
Had witchcraft in 't; he grew unto his seat;
And to such wondrous doing brought his horse,
As had he been incorps'd and demi-natur'd°
With the brave beast: so far he topp'd° my thought,
That I, in forgery° of shapes and tricks,
Come short of what he did.
Laertes: A Norman was 't?
King: A Norman.
Laertes: Upon my life, Lamord.°
King: The very same.
Laertes: I know him well: he is the brooch indeed
And gem of all the nation.
King: He made confession° of you,
And gave you such a masterly report
For art and exercise° in your defence°
And for your rapier most especial,
That he cried out, 'twould be a sight indeed,
If one could match you: the scrimers° of their nation,
He swore, had neither motion, guard, nor eye,
If you oppos'd them. Sir, this report of his
Did Hamlet so envenom with his envy
That he could nothing do but wish and beg
Your sudden coming o'er, to play° with you.
Now, out of this, —
Laertes: What out of this, my lord?
King: Laertes, was your father dear to you?
Or are you like the painting of a sorrow,
A face without a heart?
Laertes: Why ask you this?
King: Not that I think you did not love your father;
But that I know love is begun by time;
And that I see, in passages of proof,°
Time qualifies the spark and fire of it.
There lives within the very flame of love
A kind of wick or snuff that will abate it;
And nothing is at a like goodness still;

78 *sables:* Rich garments. 82 *can well:* Are skilled. 85 *incorps'd and demi-natur'd:* Of one body and nearly of one nature (like the centaur). 86 *topp'd:* Surpassed. 87 *forgery:* Invention. 90 *Lamord:* This refers possibly to Pietro Monte, instructor to Louis XII's master of the horse. 93 *confession:* Grudging admission of superiority. 95 *art and exercise:* Skillful exercise; *defence:* Science of defense in sword practice. 98 *scrimers:* Fencers. 103 *play:* Fence. 110 *passages of proof:* Proved instances.

For goodness, growing to a plurisy,°
Dies in his own too much:° that we would do,
We should do when we would; for this "would" changes
And hath abatements° and delays as many
As there are tongues, are hands, are accidents;°
And then this "should" is like a spendthrift° sigh,
That hurts by easing. But, to the quick o' th' ulcer:° —
Hamlet comes back: what would you undertake,
To show yourself your father's son in deed
More than in words?

Laertes: To cut his throat i' th' church.

King: No place, indeed, should murder sanctuarize;°
Revenge should have no bounds. But, good Laertes,
Will you do this, keep close within your chamber.
Hamlet return'd shall know you are come home:
We'll put on those shall praise your excellence
And set a double varnish on the fame
The Frenchman gave you, bring you in fine together
And wager on your heads: he, being remiss,
Most generous and free from all contriving,
Will not peruse the foils; so that, with ease,
Or with a little shuffling, you may choose
A sword unbated,° and in a pass of practice°
Requite him for your father.

Laertes: I will do 't:
And, for that purpose, I'll anoint my sword.
I bought an unction of a mountebank,°
So mortal that, but dip a knife in it,
Where it draws blood no cataplasm° so rare,
Collected from all simples° that have virtue
Under the moon,° can save the thing from death
That is but scratch'd withal: I'll touch my point
With this contagion, that, if I gall° him slightly,
It may be death.

King: Let's further think of this;
Weigh what convenience both of time and means
May fit us to our shape:° if this should fail,
And that our drift look through our bad performance,°
'Twere better not assay'd: therefore this project
Should have a back or second, that might hold,

115 *plurisy:* Excess, plethora. 116 *in his own too much:* Of its own excess. 118 *abatements:* Diminutions. 119 *accidents:* Occurrences, incidents. 120 *spendthrift:* An allusion to the belief that each sigh cost the heart a drop of blood. 121 *quick o' th' ulcer:* Heart of the difficulty. 125 *sanctuarize:* Protect from punishment; allusion to the right of sanctuary with which certain religious places were invested. 136 *unbated:* Not blunted, having no button; *pass of practice:* Treacherous thrust. 139 *mountebank:* Quack doctor. 141 *cataplasm:* Plaster or poultice. 142 *simples:* Herbs. 143 *Under the moon:* I.e., when collected by moonlight to add to their medicinal value. 145 *gall:* Graze, wound. 148 *shape:* Part we propose to act. 149 *drift . . . performance:* Intention be disclosed by our bungling.

If this should blast in proof.° Soft! let me see:
We'll make a solemn wager on your cunnings:°
I ha 't:
When in your motion you are hot and dry —
As make your bouts more violent to that end —
And that he calls for drink, I'll have prepar'd him
A chalice° for the nonce, whereon but sipping,
If he by chance escape your venom'd stuck,°
Our purpose may hold there. But stay, what noise?

Enter Queen.

Queen: One woe doth tread upon another's heel,
So fast they follow: your sister's drown'd, Laertes.
Laertes: Drown'd! O, where?
Queen: There is a willow° grows askant° the brook,
That shows his hoar° leaves in the glassy stream;
There with fantastic garlands did she make
Of crow-flowers,° nettles, daisies, and long purples°
That liberal° shepherds give a grosser name,
But our cold maids do dead men's fingers call them:
There, on the pendent boughs her crownet° weeds
Clamb'ring to hang, an envious sliver° broke;
When down her weedy° trophies and herself
Fell in the weeping brook. Her clothes spread wide;
And, mermaid-like, awhile they bore her up:
Which time she chanted snatches of old lauds;°
As one incapable° of her own distress,
Or like a creature native and indued°
Upon that element: but long it could not be
Till that her garments, heavy with their drink,
Pull'd the poor wretch from her melodious lay
To muddy death.
Laertes: Alas, then, she is drown'd?
Queen: Drown'd, drown'd.
Laertes: Too much of water hast thou, poor Ophelia,
And therefore I forbid my tears: but yet
It is our trick;° nature her custom holds,
Let shame say what it will: when these are gone,
The woman will be out.° Adieu, my lord:
I have a speech of fire, that fain would blaze,
But that this folly drowns it. *Exit.*

152 *blast in proof:* Burst in the test (like a cannon). 153 *cunnings:* Skills. 158 *chalice:* Cup. 159 *stuck:* Thrust (from *stoccado*). 164 *willow:* For its significance of forsaken love; *askant:* Aslant. 165 *hoar:* White (i.e., on the underside). 167 *crow-flowers:* Buttercups; *long purples:* Early purple orchis. 168 *liberal:* Probably, free-spoken. 170 *crownet:* Coronet; made into a chaplet. 171 *sliver:* Branch. 172 *weedy:* I.e., of plants. 175 *lauds:* Hymns. 176 *incapable:* Lacking capacity to apprehend. 177 *indued:* Endowed with qualities fitting her for living in water. 185 *trick:* Way. 186–187 *when . . . out:* When my tears are all shed, the woman in me will be satisfied.

King: Let's follow, Gertrude:
How much I had to do to calm his rage!
Now fear I this will give it start again;
Therefore let 's follow. *Exeunt.*

[ACT V

SCENE I. *A churchyard.*]

Enter two Clowns° [with spades, &c.].

First Clown: Is she to be buried in Christian burial when she wilfully seeks her own salvation?

Second Clown: I tell thee she is; therefore make her grave straight:° the crowner° hath sat on her, and finds it Christian burial.

First Clown: How can that be, unless she drowned herself in her own defence?

Second Clown: Why, 'tis found so.

First Clown: It must be "se offendendo";° it cannot be else. For here lies the point: if I drown myself wittingly,° it argues an act: and an act hath three branches;° it is, to act, to do, and to perform: argal,° she drowned herself wittingly.

Second Clown: Nay, but hear you, goodman delver,° —

First Clown: Give me leave. Here lies the water; good: here stands the man; good: if the man go to this water, and drown himself, it is, will he, nill he, he goes, — mark you that; but if the water come to him and drown him, he drowns not himself: argal, he that is not guilty of his own death shortens not his own life.

Second Clown: But is this law?

First Clown: Ay, marry, is 't; crowner's quest° law.

Second Clown: Will you ha' the truth on 't? If this had not been a gentlewoman, she should have been buried out o' Christian burial.

First Clown: Why, there thou say'st:° and the more pity that great folk should have countenance° in this world to drown or hang themselves, more than their even° Christian. Come, my spade. There is no ancient gentlemen but gardeners, ditchers, and grave-makers: they hold up° Adam's profession.

Second Clown: Was he a gentleman?

First Clown: 'A was the first that ever bore arms.

Second Clown: Why, he had none.

First Clown: What, art a heathen? How dost thou understand the Scripture?

ACT V. SCENE I. *Clowns:* The word *clown* was used to denote peasants as well as humorous characters; here applied to the rustic type of clown. 3 *straight:* Straightway, immediately; some interpret "from east to west in a direct line, parallel with the church." 4 *crowner:* Coroner. 8 *"se offendendo:"* For *se defendendo,* term used in verdicts of justifiable homicide. 9 *wittingly:* Intentionally. 10 *three branches:* Parody of legal phraseology; *argal:* Corruption of *ergo,* therefore. 12 *delver:* Digger. 19 *quest:* Inquest. 22 *there thou say'st:* That's right. 23 *countenance:* Privilege. 24 *even:* Fellow. 25 *hold up:* Maintain, continue.

The Scripture says "Adam digged": could he dig without arms? I'll put another question to thee: if thou answerest me not to the purpose, confess thyself° —

Second Clown: Go to.°

First Clown: What is he that builds stronger than either the mason, the shipwright, or the carpenter?

Second Clown: The gallows-maker; for that frame outlives a thousand tenants.

First Clown: I like thy wit well, in good faith: the gallows does well; but how does it well? it does well to those that do ill: now thou dost ill to say the gallows is built stronger than the church: argal, the gallows may do well to thee. To 't again, come.

Second Clown: "Who builds stronger than a mason, a shipwright, or a carpenter?"

First Clown: Ay, tell me that, and unyoke.°

Second Clown: Marry, now I can tell.

First Clown: To 't.

Second Clown: Mass,° I cannot tell.

Enter Hamlet and Horatio [at a distance].

First Clown: Cudgel thy brains no more about it, for your dull ass will not mend his pace with beating; and, when you are asked this question next, say "a grave-maker": the houses he makes lasts till doomsday. Go, get thee in, and fetch me a stoup° of liquor.

[Exit Second Clown.] Song. [He digs.]

In youth, when I did love, did love,
Methought it was very sweet,
To contract — O — the time, for — a — my behove,°
O, methought, there — a — was nothing — a — meet.

Hamlet: Has this fellow no feeling of his business, that 'a sings at grave-making?

Horatio: Custom hath made it in him a property of easiness.°

Hamlet: 'Tis e'en so: the hand of little employment hath the daintier sense.

First Clown: (Song.) But age, with his stealing steps,
Hath claw'd me in his clutch,
And hath shipped me into the land
As if I had never been such. *[Throws up a skull.]*

Hamlet: That skull had a tongue in it, and could sing once: how the knave jowls° it to the ground, as if 'twere Cain's jaw-bone,° that did the first murder! This might be the pate of a politician,° which this ass now o'er-reaches;° one that would circumvent God, might it not?

Horatio: It might, my lord.

Hamlet: Or of a courtier; which could say "Good morrow, sweet lord! How

33 *confess thyself:* "And be hanged" completes the proverb. 34 *Go to:* Perhaps, "begin," or some other form of concession. 45 *unyoke:* After this great effort you may unharness the team of your wits. 48 *Mass:* By the Mass. 52 *stoup:* Two-quart measure. 55 *behove:* Benefit. 59 *property of easiness:* A peculiarity that now is easy. 66 *jowls:* Dashes; *Cain's jaw-bone:* Allusion to the old tradition that Cain slew Abel with the jawbone of an ass. 67 *politician:* Schemer, plotter; *o'er-reaches:* Quibble on the literal sense and the sense "circumvent."

dost thou, sweet lord?" This might be my lord such-a-one, that praised my lord such-a-one's horse, when he meant to beg it; might it not?

Horatio: Ay, my lord.

Hamlet: Why, e'en so: and now my Lady Worm's; chapless, and knocked about the mazzard with a sexton's spade: here's fine revolution, an we had the trick to see 't. Did these bones cost no more the breeding, but to play at loggats with 'em? mine ache to think on 't.

First Clown: (Song.) A pick-axe, and a spade, a spade,
For and a shrouding sheet:
O, a pit of clay for to be made
For such a guest is meet. *[Throws up another skull.]*

Hamlet: There 's another: why may not that be the skull of a lawyer? Where be his quiddities now, his quillities, his cases, his tenures, and his tricks? why does he suffer this mad knave now to knock him about the sconce with a dirty shovel, and will not tell him of his action of battery? Hum! This fellow might be in 's time a great buyer of land, with his statutes, his recognizances, his fines, his double vouchers, his recoveries: is this the fine of his fines, and the recovery of his recoveries, to have his fine pate full of fine dirt? will his vouchers vouch him no more of his purchases, and double ones too, than the length and breadth of a pair of indentures? The very conveyances of his lands will scarcely lie in this box; and must the inheritor himself have no more, ha?

Horatio: Not a jot more, my lord.

Hamlet: Is not parchment made of sheep-skins?

Horatio: Ay, my lord, and of calf-skins too.

Hamlet: They are sheep and calves which seek out assurance in that. I will speak to this fellow. Whose grave's this, sirrah?

First Clown: Mine, sir.
[Sings.] O, a pit of clay for to be made
For such a guest is meet.

Hamlet: I think it be thine, indeed; for thou liest in 't.

First Clown: You lie out on 't, sir, and therefore 't is not yours: for my part, I do not lie in 't, yet it is mine.

Hamlet: Thou dost lie in 't, to be in 't and say it is thine: 'tis for the dead, not for the quick; therefore thou liest.

First Clown: 'Tis a quick lie, sir; 'twill away again, from me to you.

Hamlet: What man dost thou dig it for?

First Clown: For no man, sir.

Hamlet: What woman, then?

First Clown: For none, neither.

74 *chapless:* Having no lower jaw. 75 *mazzard:* Head. 77 *loggats:* A game in which six sticks are thrown to lie as near as possible to a stake fixed in the ground, or block of wood on a floor. 79 *For and:* And moreover. 83 *quiddities:* Subtleties, quibbles; *quillities:* Verbal niceties, subtle distinctions; *tenures:* The holding of a piece of property or office or the conditions or period of such holding. 85 *sconce:* Head. 87 *statutes, recognizances:* Legal terms connected with the transfer of land; *vouchers:* Persons called on to warrant a tenant's title; *recoveries:* Process for transfer of entailed estate. 88 *fine:* The four uses of this word are as follows: (1) end, (2) legal process, (3) elegant, (4) small. 91 *indentures:* Conveyances or contracts. 92 *inheritor:* Possessor, owner. 95 *calfskins:* Parchments. 96 *assurance in that:* Safety in legal parchments.

Hamlet: Who is to be buried in 't?

First Clown: One that was a woman, sir; but, rest her soul, she's dead.

Hamlet: How absolute° the knave is! we must speak by the card,° or equivocation° will undo us. By the Lord, Horatio, these three years I have taken note of it; the age is grown so picked° that the toe of the peasant comes so near the heel of the courtier, he galls° his kibe.° How long hast thou been a grave-maker?

First Clown: Of all the day i' the year, I came to 't that day that our last king Hamlet overcame Fortinbras.

Hamlet: How long is that since?

First Clown: Cannot you tell that? every fool can tell that: it was the very day that young Hamlet was born; he that is mad, and sent into England.

Hamlet: Ay, marry, why was he sent into England?

First Clown: Why, because 'a was mad: 'a shall recover his wits there; or, if 'a do not, 'tis no great matter there.

Hamlet: Why?

First Clown: 'Twill not be seen in him there; there the men are as mad as he.

Hamlet: How came he mad?

First Clown: Very strangely, they say.

Hamlet: How strangely?

First Clown: Faith, e'en with losing his wits.

Hamlet: Upon what ground?

First Clown: Why, here in Denmark: I have been sexton here, man and boy, thirty years.°

Hamlet: How long will a man lie i' the earth ere he rot?

First Clown: Faith, if 'a be not rotten before 'a die — as we have many pocky° corses now-a-days, that will scarce hold the laying in — 'a will last you some eight year or nine year: a tanner will last you nine year.

Hamlet: Why he more than another?

First Clown: Why, sir, his hide is so tanned with his trade, that 'a will keep out water a great while; and your water is a sore decayer of your whoreson dead body. Here's a skull now hath lain you i' th' earth three and twenty years.

Hamlet: Whose was it?

First Clown: A whoreson mad fellow's it was: whose do you think it was?

Hamlet: Nay, I know not.

First Clown: A pestilence on him for a mad rogue! 'a poured a flagon of Rhenish on my head once. This same skull, sir, was Yorick's skull, the king's jester.

Hamlet: This?

First Clown: E'en that.

Hamlet: Let me see. *[Takes the skull.]* Alas, poor Yorick! I knew him, Horatio: a fellow of infinite jest, of most excellent fancy: he hath borne me

113 *absolute:* Positive, decided; *by the card:* With precision, i.e., by the mariner's card on which the points of the compass were marked; *equivocation:* Ambiguity in the use of terms. 115 *picked:* Refined, fastidious. 116 *galls:* Chafes; *kibe:* Chilblain. 135 *thirty years:* This statement with that in line 122 shows Hamlet's age to be thirty years. 138 *pocky:* Rotten, diseased.

on his back a thousand times; and now, how abhorred in my imagination it is! my gorge rises at it. Here hung those lips that I have kissed I know not how oft. Where be your gibes now? your gambols? your songs? your flashes of merriment, that were wont to set the table on a roar? Not one now, to mock your own grinning? quite chap-fallen? Now get you to my lady's chamber, and tell her, let her paint an inch thick, to this favour she must come; make her laugh at that. Prithee, Horatio, tell me one thing.

Horatio: What's that, my lord?

Hamlet: Dost thou think Alexander looked o' this fashion i' the earth?

Horatio: E'en so.

Hamlet: And smelt so? pah! *[Puts down the skull.]*

Horatio: E'en so, my lord.

Hamlet: To what base uses we may return, Horatio! Why may not imagination trace the noble dust of Alexander, till 'a find it stopping a bung-hole?

Horatio: 'Twere to consider too curiously,° to consider so.

Hamlet: No, faith, not a jot; but to follow him thither with modesty enough, and likelihood to lead it: as thus: Alexander died, Alexander was buried, Alexander returneth into dust; the dust is earth; of earth we make loam;° and why of that loam, whereto he was converted, might they not stop a beer-barrel?

Imperious° Cæsar, dead and turn'd to clay,
Might stop a hole to keep the wind away:
O, that that earth, which kept the world in awe,
Should patch a wall t'expel the winter's flaw!°

But soft! but soft awhile! here comes the king,

Enter King, Queen, Laertes, and the Corse of [Ophelia, in procession, with Priest, Lords, etc.].

The queen, the courtiers: who is this they follow?
And with such maimed rites? This doth betoken
The corse they follow did with desp'rate hand
Fordo° it° own life: 'twas of some estate.
Couch° we awhile, and mark. *[Retiring with Horatio.]*

Laertes: What ceremony else?

Hamlet: That is Laertes,
A very noble youth: mark.

Laertes: What ceremony else?

First Priest: Her obsequies have been as far enlarg'd°
As we have warranty: her death was doubtful;
And, but that great command o'ersways the order,
She should in ground unsanctified have lodg'd
Till the last trumpet; for charitable prayers,
Shards,° flints and pebbles should be thrown on her:

171 *curiously:* Minutely. 174 *loam:* Clay paste for brickmaking. 177 *Imperious:* Imperial. 180 *flaw:* Gust of wind. 185 *Fordo:* Destroy; *it:* Its. 186 *Couch:* Hide, lurk. 190 *enlarg'd:* Extended, referring to the fact that suicides are not given full burial rites. 195 *Shards:* Broken bits of pottery.

Yet here she is allow'd her virgin crants,°
Her maiden strewments° and the bringing home
Of bell and burial.°

Laertes: Must there no more be done?

First Priest: No more be done:
We should profane the service of the dead
To sing a requiem and such rest to her
As to peace-parted° souls.

Laertes: Lay her i' th' earth:
And from her fair and unpolluted flesh
May violets spring! I tell thee, churlish priest,
A minist'ring angel shall my sister be,
When thou liest howling.°

Hamlet: What, the fair Ophelia!

Queen: Sweets to the sweet: farewell!

[Scattering flowers.]

I hop'd thou shouldst have been my Hamlet's wife;
I thought thy bride-bed to have deck'd, sweet maid,
And not have strew'd thy grave.

Laertes: O, treble woe
Fall ten times treble on that cursed head,
Whose wicked deed thy most ingenious sense°
Depriv'd thee of! Hold off the earth awhile,
Till I have caught her once more in mine arms:

[Leaps into the grave.]

Now pile your dust upon the quick and dead,
Till of this flat a mountain you have made,
T' o'ertop old Pelion,° or the skyish head
Of blue Olympus.

Hamlet: *[Advancing]* What is he whose grief
Bears such an emphasis? whose phrase of sorrow
Conjures the wand'ring stars,° and makes them stand
Like wonder-wounded hearers? This is I,
Hamlet the Dane. *[Leaps into the grave.]*

Laertes: The devil take thy soul! *[Grappling with him.]*

Hamlet: Thou pray'st not well.
I prithee, take thy fingers from my throat;
For, though I am not splenitive° and rash,
Yet have I in me something dangerous,
Which let thy wisdom fear: hold off thy hand.

King: Pluck them asunder.

Queen: Hamlet, Hamlet!

196 *crants:* Garlands customarily hung upon the biers of unmarried women. 197 *strewments:* Traditional strewing of flowers. 197–198 *bringing . . . burial:* The laying to rest of the body, to the sound of the bell. 202 *peace-parted:* Allusion to the text "Lord, now lettest thou thy servant depart in peace." 206 *howling:* I.e., in hell. 212 *ingenious sense:* Mind endowed with finest qualities. 217 *Pelion:* Olympus, Pelion, and Ossa are mountains in the north of Thessaly. 220 *wand'ring stars:* Planets. 225 *splenitive:* Quick-tempered.

All: Gentlemen, —
Horatio: Good my lord, be quiet.

[The Attendants part them, and they come out of the grave.]

Hamlet: Why, I will fight with him upon this theme
Until my eyelids will no longer wag.°
Queen: O my son, what theme?
Hamlet: I lov'd Ophelia: forty thousand brothers
Could not, with all their quantity° of love,
Make up my sum. What wilt thou do for her?
King: O, he is mad, Laertes.
Queen: For love of God, forbear° him.
Hamlet: 'Swounds,° show me what thou 'lt do:
Woo't° weep? woo't fight? woo't fast? woo't tear thyself?
Woo't drink up eisel?° eat a crocodile?
I'll do 't. Dost thou come here to whine?
To outface me with leaping in her grave?
Be buried quick with her, and so will I:
And, if thou prate of mountains, let them throw
Millions of acres on us, till our ground,
Singeing his pate against the burning zone,°
Make Ossa like a wart! Nay, an thou 'lt mouth,
I'll rant as well as thou.
Queen: This is mere madness:
And thus awhile the fit will work on him;
Anon, as patient as the female dove.
When that her golden couplets° are disclos'd,
His silence will sit drooping.
Hamlet: Hear you, sir;
What is the reason that you use me thus?
I lov'd you ever: but it is no matter;
Let Hercules himself do what he may,
The cat will mew and dog will have his day.
King: I pray thee, good Horatio, wait upon him.

Exit Hamlet and Horatio.

[To Laertes.] Strengthen your patience in° our last night's speech;
We'll put the matter to the present push.°
Good Gertrude, set some watch over your son.
This grave shall have a living° monument:
An hour of quiet shortly shall we see;
Till then, in patience our proceeding be. *Exeunt.*

231 *wag:* Move (not used ludicrously). 234 *quantity:* Some suggest that the word is used in a deprecatory sense (little bits, fragments). 237 *forbear:* Leave alone. 238 *'Swounds:* Oath, "God's wounds." 239 *Woo 't:* Wilt thou. 240 *eisel:* Vinegar. Some editors have taken this to be the name of a river, such as the Yssel, the Weissel, and the Nile. 246 *burning zone:* Sun's orbit. 251 *golden couplets:* The pigeon lays two eggs; the young when hatched are covered with golden down. 258 *in:* By recalling. 259 *present push:* Immediate test. 261 *living:* Lasting; also refers (for Laertes's benefit) to the plot against Hamlet.

[SCENE II. *A hall in the castle.*]

Enter Hamlet and Horatio.

Hamlet: So much for this, sir: now shall you see the other;
You do remember all the circumstance?
Horatio: Remember it, my lord!
Hamlet: Sir, in my heart there was a kind of fighting,
That would not let me sleep: methought I lay
Worse than the mutines° in the bilboes.° Rashly,°
And prais'd be rashness for it, let us know,
Our indiscretion sometime serves us well,
When our deep plots do pall:° and that should learn us
There's a divinity that shapes our ends,
Rough-hew° them how we will, —
Horatio: That is most certain.
Hamlet: Up from my cabin,
My sea-gown° scarf'd about me, in the dark
Grop'd I to find out them; had my desire,
Finger'd° their packet, and in fine° withdrew
To mine own room again; making so bold,
My fears forgetting manners, to unseal
Their grand commission; where I found, Horatio, —
O royal knavery! — an exact command,
Larded° with many several sorts of reasons
Importing Denmark's health and England's too,
With, ho! such bugs° and goblins in my life,°
That, on the supervise,° no leisure bated,°
No, not to stay the grinding of the axe,
My head should be struck off.
Horatio: Is 't possible?
Hamlet: Here's the commission: read it at more leisure.
But wilt thou hear me how I did proceed?
Horatio: I beseech you.
Hamlet: Being thus be-netted round with villanies, —
Ere I could make a prologue to my brains,
They had begun the play° — I sat me down,
Devis'd a new commission, wrote it fair:
I once did hold it, as our statists° do,
A baseness to write fair° and labour'd much
How to forget that learning, but, sir, now

SCENE II. 6 *mutines:* Mutineers; *bilboes:* Shackles; *Rashly:* Goes with line 12. 9 *pall:* Fail. 11 *Rough-hew:* Shape roughly; it may mean "bungle." 13 *sea-gown:* "A sea-gown, or a coarse, high-collered, and short-sleeved gowne, reaching down to the mid-leg, and used most by seamen and saylors" (Cotgrave, quoted by Singer). 15 *Finger'd:* Pilfered, filched; *in fine:* Finally. 20 *Larded:* Enriched. 22 *such . . . life:* Such imaginary dangers if I were allowed to live; *bugs:* Bugbears. 23 *supervise:* Perusal; *leisure bated:* Delay allowed. 30–31 *prologue . . . play:* I.e., before I could begin to think, my mind had made its decision. 33 *statists:* Statesmen. 34 *fair:* In a clear hand.

It did me yeoman's° service: wilt thou know
Th' effect of what I wrote?
Horatio: Ay, good my lord.
Hamlet: An earnest conjuration from the king,
As England was his faithful tributary,
As love between them like the palm might flourish,
As peace should still her wheaten garland° wear
And stand a comma° 'tween their amities,
And many such-like 'As'es° of great charge,°
That, on the view and knowing of these contents,
Without debatement further, more or less,
He should the bearers put to sudden death,
Not shriving-time° allow'd.
Horatio: How was this seal'd?
Hamlet: Why, even in that was heaven ordinant.°
I had my father's signet in my purse,
Which was the model of that Danish seal;
Folded the writ up in the form of th' other,
Subscrib'd it, gave 't th' impression, plac'd it safely,
The changeling never known. Now, the next day
Was our sea-fight; and what to this was sequent°
Thou know'st already.
Horatio: So Guildenstern and Rosencrantz go to 't.
Hamlet: Why, man, they did make love to this employment;
They are not near my conscience; their defeat
Does by their own insinuation° grow:
'Tis dangerous when the baser nature comes
Between the pass° and fell incensed° points
Of mighty opposites.
Horatio: Why, what a king is this!
Hamlet: Does it not, think thee, stand° me now upon —
He that hath kill'd my king and whor'd my mother,
Popp'd in between th' election° and my hopes,
Thrown out his angle° for my proper life,
And with such coz'nage° — is 't not perfect conscience,
To quit° him with this arm? and is't not to be damn'd,
To let this canker° of our nature come
In further evil?
Horatio: It must be shortly known to him from England
What is the issue of the business there.
Hamlet: It will be short: the interim is mine;

36 *yeoman's:* I.e., faithful. 41 *wheaten garland:* Symbol of peace. 42 *comma:* Smallest break or separation. Here *amity* begins and *amity* ends the period, and *peace* stands between like a dependent clause. The comma indicates continuity, link. 43 *'As'es:* The "whereases" of a formal document, with play on the word *ass; charge:* Import, and burden. 47 *shriving-time:* Time for absolution. 48 *ordinant:* Directing. 54 *sequent:* Subsequent. 59 *insinuation:* Interference. 61 *pass:* Thrust; *fell incensed:* Fiercely angered. 63 *stand:* Become incumbent. 65 *election:* The Danish throne was filled by election. 66 *angle:* Fishing line. 67 *coz'nage:* Trickery. 68 *quit:* Repay. 69 *canker:* Ulcer, or possibly the worm which destroys buds and leaves.

And a man's life's no more than to say "One."
But I am very sorry, good Horatio,
That to Laertes I forgot myself;
For, by the image of my cause, I see
The portraiture of his: I'll court his favours:
But, sure, the bravery° of his grief did put me
Into a tow'ring passion.

Horatio: Peace! who comes here?

Enter a Courtier [Osric].

Osric: Your lordship is right welcome back to Denmark.

Hamlet: I humbly thank you, sir. *[To Horatio.]* Dost know this water-fly?°

Horatio: No, my good lord.

Hamlet: Thy state is the more gracious; for 'tis a vice to know him. He hath much land, and fertile: let a beast be lord of beasts,° and his crib shall stand at the king's mess:° 'tis a chough;° but, as I say, spacious in the possession of dirt.

Osric: Sweet lord, if your lordship were at leisure, I should impart a thing to you from his majesty.

Hamlet: I will receive it, sir, with all diligence of spirit. Put your bonnet to his right use; 'tis for the head.

Osric: I thank you lordship, it is very hot.

Hamlet: No, believe me, 'tis very cold; the wind is northerly.

Osric: It is indifferent° cold, my lord, indeed.

Hamlet: But yet methinks it is very sultry and hot for my complexion.

Osric: Exceedingly, my lord; it is very sultry,— as 'twere,— I cannot tell how. But, my lord, his majesty bade me signify to you that 'a has laid a great wager on your head: sir, this is the matter, —

Hamlet: I beseech you, remember° —

[Hamlet moves him to put on his hat.]

Osric: Nay, good my lord; for mine ease,° in good faith. Sir, here is newly come to court Laertes; believe me, an absolute gentleman, full of most excellent differences, of very soft° society and great showing:° indeed, to speak feelingly° of him, he is the card° or calendar of gentry,° for you shall find in him the continent of what part a gentleman would see.

Hamlet: Sir, his definement° suffers no perdition° in you; though, I know, to divide him inventorially° would dozy° the arithmetic of memory, and yet but yaw° neither, in respect of his quick sail. But, in the verity of

79 *bravery:* Bravado. 82 *water-fly:* Vain or busily idle person. 85 *lord of beasts:* Cf. Genesis 1:26, 28; *his crib . . . mess:* He shall eat at the king's table, i.e., be one of the group of persons (usually four) constituting a *mess* at a banquet. 86 *chough:* Probably, chattering jackdaw; also explained as *chuff,* provincial boor or churl. 94 *indifferent:* Somewhat. 99 *remember:* I.e., remember thy courtesy; conventional phrase for "Be covered." 100 *mine ease:* Conventional reply declining the invitation of "Remember thy courtesy." 102 *soft:* Gentle; *showing:* Distinguished appearance. 103 *feelingly:* With just perception; *card:* Chart, map; *gentry:* Good breeding. 105 *definement:* Definition; *perdition:* Loss, diminution. 106 *divide him inventorially:* I.e., enumerate his graces; *dozy:* Dizzy. 107 *yaw:* To move unsteadily (of a ship).

extolment, I take him to be a soul of great article;° and his infusion° of such dearth and rareness,° as, to make true diction of him, his semblable° is his mirror; and who else would trace° him, his umbrage,° nothing more.

Osric: Your lordship speaks most infallibly of him.

Hamlet: The concernancy,° sir? why do we wrap the gentleman in our more rawer breath?°

Osric: Sir?

Horatio [aside to Hamlet]: Is 't not possible to understand in another tongue?° You will do 't, sir, really.

Hamlet: What imports the nomination° of this gentleman?

Osric: Of Laertes?

Horatio [aside to Hamlet]: His purse is empty already; all 's golden words are spent.

Hamlet: Of him, sir.

Osric: I know you are not ignorant —

Hamlet: I would you did, sir; yet, in faith, if you did, it would not much approve° me. Well, sir?

Osric: You are not ignorant of what excellence Laertes is —

Hamlet: I dare not confess that, lest I should compare with him in excellence; but, to know a man well, were to know himself.°

Osric: I mean, sir, for his weapon; but in the imputation° laid on him by them, in his meed° he's unfellowed.

Hamlet: What's his weapon?

Osric: Rapier and dagger.

Hamlet: That's two of his weapons: but, well.

Osric: The king, sir, hath wagered with him six Barbary horses: against the which he has impawned,° as I take it, six French rapiers and poniards, with their assigns, as girdle, hangers,° and so: three of the carriages, in faith, are very dear to fancy,° very responsive° to the hilts, most delicate° carriages, and of very liberal conceit.°

Hamlet: What call you the carriages?

Horatio [aside to Hamlet]: I knew you must be edified by the margent° ere you had done.

Osric: The carriages, sir, are the hangers.

Hamlet: The phrase would be more german° to the matter, if we could carry cannon by our sides: I would it might be hangers till then. But, on: six Barbary horses against six French swords, their assigns, and three liberal-conceited carriages; that's the French bet against the Danish. Why is this "impawned," as you call it?

108 *article:* Moment or importance; *infusion:* Infused temperament, character imparted by nature. 109 *dearth and rareness:* Rarity. 110 *semblable:* True likeness; *trace:* Follow; *umbrage:* Shadow. 113 *concernancy:* Import. 114 *breath:* Speech. 116 *Is 't . . . tongue?:* I.e., can one converse with Osric only in this outlandish jargon? 118 *nomination:* Naming. 125 *approve:* Command. 128 *but . . . himself:* But to know a man as excellent were to know Laertes. 129 *imputation:* Reputation. 130 *meed:* Merit. 135 *he has impawned:* He has wagered. 136 *hangers:* Straps on the sword belt from which the sword hung. 137 *dear to fancy:* Fancifully made; *responsive:* Probably, well balanced, corresponding closely. 138 *delicate:* I.e., in workmanship; *liberal conceit:* Elaborate design. 140 *margent:* Margin of a book, place for explanatory notes. 143 *german:* Germain, appropriate.

Osric: The king, sir, hath laid, that in a dozen passes between yourself and him, he shall not exceed you three hits: he hath laid on twelve for nine; and it would come to immediate trial, if your lordship would vouchsafe the answer.

Hamlet: How if I answer "no"?

Osric: I mean, my lord, the opposition of your person in trial.

Hamlet: Sir, I will walk here in the hall: if it please his majesty, it is the breathing time° of day with me; let the foils be brought, the gentleman willing, and the king hold his purpose, I will win for him as I can; if not, I will gain nothing but my shame and the odd hits.

Osric: Shall I re-deliver you e'en so?

Hamlet: To this effect, sir; after what flourish your nature will.

Osric: I commend my duty to your lordship.

Hamlet: Yours, yours. *[Exit Osric.]* He does well to commend it himself; there are no tongues else for 's turn.

Horatio: This lapwing° runs away with the shell on his head.

Hamlet: 'A did comply, sir, with his dug,° before 'a sucked it. Thus has he — and many more of the same breed that I know the drossy° age dotes on — only got the tune° of the time and out of an habit of encounter;° a kind of yesty° collection, which carries them through and through the most fann'd and winnowed° opinions; and do but blow them to their trial, the bubbles are out.°

Enter a Lord.

Lord: My lord, his majesty commended him to you by young Osric, who brings back to him, that you attend him in the hall: he sends to know if your pleasure hold to play with Laertes, or that you will take longer time.

Hamlet: I am constant to my purposes; they follow the king's pleasure: if his fitness speaks, mine is ready; now or whensoever, provided I be so able as now.

Lord: The king and queen and all are coming down.

Hamlet: In happy time.°

Lord: The queen desires you to use some gentle entertainment to Laertes before you fall to play.

Hamlet: She well instructs me. *[Exit Lord.]*

Horatio: You will lose this wager, my lord.

Hamlet: I do not think so; since he went into France, I have been in continual practice; I shall win at the odds. But thou wouldst not think how ill all 's here about my heart: but it is no matter.

Horatio: Nay, good my lord, —

155 *breathing time:* Exercise period. 163 *lapwing:* Peewit; noted its wiliness in drawing a visitor away from its nest and its supposed habit of running about when newly hatched with its head in the shell; possibly an allusion to Osric's hat. 164 *did comply . . . dug:* Paid compliments to his mother's breast. 165 *drossy:* Frivolous. 166 *tune:* Temper, mood. 166–167 *habit of encounter:* Demeanor of social intercourse; *yesty:* Frothy. 168 *fann'd and winnowed:* Select and refined. 168–169 *blow . . . out:* I.e., put them to the test, and their ignorance is exposed. 178 *In happy time:* A phrase of courtesy.

Hamlet: It is but foolery; but it is such a kind of gain-giving,° as would perhaps trouble a woman.

Horatio: If your mind dislike any thing, obey it: I will forestal their repair hither, and say you are not fit.

Hamlet: Not a whit, we defy augury: there's a special providence in the fall of a sparrow. If it be now, 'tis not to come; if it be not to come, it will be now; if it be not now, yet it will come: the readiness is all:° since no man of aught he leaves knows, what is 't to leave betimes? Let be.

A table prepared. [Enter] Trumpets, Drums, and Officers with cushions; King, Queen, [Osric,] and all the State; foils, daggers, [and wine borne in;] and Laertes.

King: Come, Hamlet, come, and take this hand from me.

[The King puts Laertes's hand into Hamlet's.]

Hamlet: Give me your pardon, sir: I have done you wrong;
But pardon 't as you are a gentleman.
This presence° knows,
And you must needs have heard, how I am punish'd
With a sore distraction. What I have done,
That might your nature, honour and exception°
Roughly awake, I here proclaim was madness.
Was 't Hamlet wrong'd Laertes? Never Hamlet:
If Hamlet from himself be ta'en away,
And when he's not himself does wrong Laertes,
Then Hamlet does it not, Hamlet denies it.
Who does it, then? His madness: if 't be so,
Hamlet is of the faction that is wrong'd;
His madness is poor Hamlet's enemy.
Sir, in this audience,
Let my disclaiming from a purpos'd evil
Free me so far in your most generous thoughts,
That I have shot mine arrow o'er the house,
And hurt my brother.

Laertes: I am satisfied in nature,°
Whose motive, in this case, should stir me most
To my revenge: but in my terms of honour
I stand aloof; and will no reconcilement,
Till by some elder masters, of known honour,
I have a voice° and precedent of peace,
To keep my name ungor'd. But till that time,
I do receive your offer'd love like love,
And will not wrong it.

Hamlet: I embrace it freely;
And will this brother's wager frankly play.
Give us the foils. Come on.

187 *gain-giving:* Misgiving. 193 *all:* All that matters. 198 *presence:* Royal assembly. 201 *exception:* Disapproval. 214 *nature:* I.e., he is personally satisfied, but his honor must be satisfied by the rules of the code of honor. 219 *voice:* Authoritative pronouncement.

Laertes: Come, one for me.
Hamlet: I'll be your foil,° Laertes: in mine ignorance
Your skill shall, like a star i' th' darkest night,
Stick fiery off° indeed.
Laertes: You mock me, sir.
Hamlet: No, by this hand.
King: Give them the foils, young Osric. Cousin Hamlet,
You know the wager?
Hamlet: Very well, my lord;
Your grace has laid the odds o' th' weaker side.
King: I do not fear it; I have seen you both:
But since he is better'd, we have therefore odds.
Laertes: This is too heavy, let me see another.
Hamlet: This likes me well. These foils have all a length?

[They prepare to play.]

Osric: Ay, my good lord.
King: Set me the stoups of wine upon that table.
If Hamlet give the first or second hit,
Or quit in answer of the third exchange,
Let all the battlements their ordnance fire;
The king shall drink to Hamlet's better breath;
And in the cup an union° shall he throw,
Richer than that which four successive kings
In Denmark's crown have worn. Give me the cups;
And let the kettle° to the trumpet speak,
The trumpet to the cannoneer without,
The cannons to the heavens, the heavens to earth,
"Now the king drinks to Hamlet." Come begin:

Trumpets the while.

And you, the judges, bear a wary eye.
Hamlet: Come on, sir.
Laertes: Come, my lord. *[They play.]*
Hamlet: One.
Laertes: No.
Hamlet: Judgement.
Osric: A hit, a very palpable hit.

Drum, trumpets, and shot. Flourish. A piece goes off.

Laertes: Well; again.
King: Stay; give me drink. Hamlet, this pearl° is thine;
Here's to thy health. Give him the cup.
Hamlet: I'll play this bout first; set it by awhile.
Come. *[They play.]* Another hit; what say you?
Laertes: A touch, a touch, I do confess 't.
King: Our son shall win.

225 *foil:* Quibble on the two senses: "background which sets something off," and "blunted rapier for fencing." 227 *Stick fiery off:* Stand out brilliantly. 242 *union:* Pearl. 245 *kettle:* Kettledrum. 252 *pearl:* I.e., the poison.

Queen: He's fat,° and scant of breath.
Here, Hamlet, take my napkin, rub thy brows:
The queen carouses° to thy fortune, Hamlet.
Hamlet: Good madam!
King: Gertrude, do not drink.
Queen: I will, my lord; I pray you, pardon me. *[Drinks.]*
King [aside]: It is the poison'd cup: it is too late.
Hamlet: I dare not drink yet, madam; by and by.
Queen: Come, let me wipe thy face.
Laertes: My lord, I'll hit him now.
King: I do not think't.
Laertes: [aside]: And yet 'tis almost 'gainst my conscience.
Hamlet: Come, for the third, Laertes: you but dally;
I pray you, pass with your best violence;
I am afeard you make a wanton° of me.
Laertes: Say you so? come on. *[They play.]*
Osric: Nothing, neither way.
Laertes: Have at you now!

[Laertes wounds Hamlet; then, in scuffling, they change rapiers,° and Hamlet wounds Laertes.]

King: Part them; they are incens'd.
Hamlet: Nay, come again. *[The Queen falls.]*
Osric: Look to the queen there, ho!
Horatio: They bleed on both sides. How is it, my lord?
Osric: How is 't, Laertes?
Laertes: Why, as a woodcock° to mine own springe,° Osric;
I am justly kill'd with mine own treachery.
Hamlet: How does the queen?
King: She swounds° to see them bleed.
Queen: No, no, the drink, the drink, — O my dear Hamlet, —
The drink, the drink! I am poison'd. *[Dies.]*
Hamlet: O villany! Ho! let the door be lock'd:
Treachery! Seek it out. *[Laertes falls.]*
Laertes: It is here, Hamlet: Hamlet, thou art slain;
No med'cine in the world can do thee good;
In thee there is not half an hour of life;
The treacherous instrument is in thy hand,
Unbated° and envenom'd: the foul practice
Hath turn'd itself on me; lo, here I lie,
Never to rise again: thy mother's poison'd:

257 *fat:* Not physically fit, out of training. Some earlier editors speculated that the term applied to the corpulence of Richard Burbage, who originally played the part, but the allusion now appears unlikely. *Fat* may also suggest "sweaty." 259 *carouses:* Drinks a toast. 269 *wanton:* Spoiled child. 272 *in scuffling, they change rapiers:* According to a widespread stage tradition, Hamlet receives a scratch, realizes that Laertes's sword is unbated, and accordingly forces an exchange. 276 *woodcock:* As type of stupidity or as decoy; *springe:* Trap, snare. 278 *swounds:* Swoons. 287 *Unbated:* Not blunted with a button.

I can no more: the king, the king's to blame.

Hamlet: The point envenom'd too!
Then, venom, to thy work. *[Stabs the King.]*

All: Treason! treason!

King: O, yet defend me, friends; I am but hurt.

Hamlet: Here, thou incestuous, murd'rous, damned Dane,
Drink off this potion. Is thy union here?
Follow my mother. *[King dies.]*

Laertes: He is justly serv'd;
It is a poison temper'd° by himself.
Exchange forgiveness with me, noble Hamlet:
Mine and my father's death come not upon thee,
Nor thine on me! *[Dies.]*

Hamlet: Heaven make thee free of it! I follow thee.
I am dead, Horatio. Wretched queen, adieu!
You that look pale and tremble at this chance,
That are but mutes° or audience to this act,
Had I but time — as this fell sergeant,° Death,
Is strict in his arrest — O, I could tell you —
But let it be. Horatio, I am dead;
Thou livest; report me and my cause aright
To the unsatisfied.

Horatio: Never believe it:
I am more an antique Roman° than a Dane:
Here 's yet some liquor left.

Hamlet: As th' art a man,
Give me the cup: let go, by heaven, I'll ha 't.
O God! Horatio, what a wounded name,
Things standing thus unknown, shall live behind me!
If thou didst ever hold me in thy heart,
Absent thee from felicity awhile,
And in this harsh world draw thy breath in pain,
To tell my story. *A march afar off.*
What warlike noise is this?

Osric: Young Fortinbras, with conquest come from Poland,
To the ambassadors of England gives
This warlike volley.

Hamlet: O, I die, Horatio;
The potent poison quite o'er-crows° my spirit:
I cannot live to hear the news from England;
But I do prophesy th' election lights
On Fortinbras: he has my dying voice;
So tell him, with th' occurrents,° more and less,
Which have solicited.° The rest is silence. *[Dies.]*

Horatio: Now cracks a noble heart. Good night, sweet prince;

298 *temper'd:* Mixed. 305 *mutes:* Performers in a play who speak no words. 306 *sergeant:* Sheriff's officer. 311 *Roman:* It was the Roman custom to follow masters in death. 323 *o'er-crows:* Triumphs over. 327 *occurrents:* Events, incidents. 328 *solicited:* Moved, urged.

And flights of angels sing thee to thy rest!
Why does the drum come hither? *[March within.]*

Enter Fortinbras, with the [English] Ambassadors [and others].

Fortinbras: Where is this sight?
Horatio: What is it you would see?
If aught of woe or wonder, cease your search.
Fortinbras: This quarry° cries on havoc.° O proud Death,
What feast is toward in thine eternal cell,
That thou so many princes at a shot
So bloodily hast struck?
First Ambassador: The sight is dismal;
And our affairs from England come too late:
The ears are senseless that should give us hearing,
To tell him his commandment is fulfill'd,
That Rosencrantz and Guildenstern are dead:
Where should we have our thanks?
Horatio: Not from his mouth,°
Had it th' ability of life to thank you:
He never gave commandment for their death.
But since, so jump° upon this bloody question,°
You from the Polack wars, and you from England,
Are here arriv'd, give order that these bodies
High on a stage° be placed to the view;
And let me speak to th' yet unknowing world
How these things came about: so shall you hear
Of carnal, bloody, and unnatural acts,
Of accidental judgements, casual slaughters,
Of deaths put on by cunning and forc'd cause,
And, in this upshot, purposes mistook
Fall'n on th' inventors' heads: all this can I
Truly deliver.
Fortinbras: Let us haste to hear it,
And call the noblest to the audience.
For me, with sorrow I embrace my fortune:
I have some rights of memory° in this kingdom,
Which now to claim my vantage doth invite me.
Horatio: Of that I shall have also cause to speak,
And from his mouth whose voice will draw on more:°
But let this same be presently perform'd,
Even while men's minds are wild; lest more mischance,
On° plots and errors, happen.
Fortinbras: Let four captains
Bear Hamlet, like a soldier, to the stage;
For he was likely, had he been put on,

334 *quarry:* Heap of dead; *cries on havoc:* Proclaims a general slaughter. 342 *his mouth:* I.e., the king's. 345 *jump:* Precisely; *question:* Dispute. 348 *stage:* Platform. 359 *of memory:* Traditional, remembered. 362 *voice . . . more:* Vote will influence still others. 365 *On:* On account of, or possibly, on top of, in addition to.

To have prov'd most royal: and, for his passage,°
The soldiers' music and the rites of war
Speak loudly for him.
Take up the bodies: such a sight as this
Becomes the field,° but here shows much amiss.
Go, bid the soldiers shoot.

Exeunt [marching, bearing off the dead bodies; after which a peal of ordnance is shot off].

368 *passage:* Death. 372 *field:* I.e., of battle.

Considerations

1. Claudius urges Hamlet to leave behind his "obstinate condolement" and give up grieving for his dead father because it represents "impious stubbornness" (I.ii.93–94). Consider Claudius's advice in this speech (lines 87–117). Is it sensible? Why won't Hamlet heed this advice?
2. Are Polonius's admonitions to Laertes and Ophelia in Act I, Scene iii good advice? What does his advice suggest about life at court, given that he is the chief counselor to the king?
3. When the ghost tells Hamlet that Claudius murdered him, Hamlet cries out, "O my prophetic soul!" (I.v.41). Why? What does the ghost demand of Hamlet?
4. What is known about the kind of person Hamlet was before his father's death? Does he have the stature of a tragic hero such as Oedipus? How does news of the murder and his mother's remarriage affect his behavior and view of life? Is he mad, as Polonius assumes, or is he pretending to be mad? Is there a "method in 't" (II.ii.202)? What do we learn from Hamlet's soliloquies?
5. Why does Hamlet find avenging his father's death so difficult? Why doesn't he take decisive action as soon as he seems convinced of Claudius's guilt?
6. What is the purpose of the play within the play? How does it provide a commentary on the action of the larger play?
7. Is Ophelia connected in any way with the crime Hamlet seeks to avenge? Why is he so brutal to Ophelia in Act III, Scene i? Why does she go mad?
8. Does Hamlet think Gertrude is as guilty as Claudius? Why is Hamlet so thoroughly disgusted by her in Act III, Scene iv?
9. Why doesn't Hamlet kill Claudius as he prays (III.iii)? Do you feel any sympathy for Claudius in this scene, or is he presented as a callous murderer?
10. If Hamlet had killed Claudius in Act III and the play had ended there, what would be missing in Hamlet's perceptions of himself and the world? How does his character develop in Acts IV and V? What softens our realization that Hamlet is in various degrees responsible for the deaths of Polonius, Ophelia, Laertes, Rosencrantz, Guildenstern, Claudius, and Gertrude?
11. What purpose does Fortinbras serve in the action? Would anything be lost if he were edited out of the play?
12. Despite its tragic dimensions, *Hamlet* includes humorous scenes and many witty lines delivered by the title character himself. Locate those scenes and lines, and then determine the tone and purpose of the play's humor.

Connections

1. Compare and contrast the humor in *Hamlet* with the humor in Molière's *Tartuffe* (p. 1263). How do you account for the tonal differences in their humor?

2. What kind of a king is Claudius? How does he compare with Creon in Sophocles' *Antigone* (p. 1008)? How are matters of state and the political atmosphere in the world of each play affected by the rules of Claudius and Creon?
3. Here's a long reach but a potentially interesting one: write an essay that considers Gertrude as a wife and mother alongside Nora in Henrik Ibsen's *A Doll's House* (p. 1321). How responsible are they to themselves and to others? Can they be discussed in the same breath, or are they from such different worlds that nothing useful can be said about comparing them? Either way, explain your response.

OTHELLO THE MOOR OF VENICE

Othello has compelled audiences since it was first produced in 1604. Its power is as simple and as complex as the elemental emotions it dramatizes; the play ebbs and flows with the emotional energy derived from the characters' struggles with love and hatred, good and evil, trust and jealousy, appearance and reality. These conflicts are played out on a domestic scale rather than on some metaphysical level. Anyone who has ever been in love will empathize with Othello and Desdemona. They embody a love story gone horribly — tragically — wrong.

Although the plot of *Othello* is filled with Iago's intrigues and a series of opaque mysteries for Othello, it moves swiftly and precisely to its catastrophic ending as the tragedy relentlessly claims its victims. On one level the plot is simple. As the Moorish general of the Venetian army, Othello chooses Cassio to serve as his lieutenant, a selection Iago resents and decides to subvert. To discredit Cassio, Iago poisons Othello's faith in his wife, Desdemona, by falsely insinuating that she and Cassio are having an affair. Through a series of cleverly demonic manipulations, Iago succeeds in convincing Othello of his wife's infidelity and his lieutenant's betrayal. Believing these lies, Othello insists upon taking his revenge.

If the plot of *Othello* is relatively direct and simple in its focus on Iago's manipulation of events, the play's major characters are considerably more complex. As in *Hamlet,* love and jealousy are central in *Othello.* The Moor's virtues of openness and trust cause him to experience betrayal as intensely as he does love. He is distinguished by his nobility, bravery, strength, and deep sense of honor, but he is also vulnerable to the doubts Iago raises owing to his race ("I am black") and marginal status in Venetian society.

Iago, whose motivations are much deeper and more mysterious than his maneuvering for a coveted lieutenancy, personifies a nearly inexplicable evil in the play. Just as Desdemona's nature seems to be all goodness, Iago's is malignant destruction. His profound villainy both horrifies and fascinates us: How can he be what he is? He thrives on ambition, envy, deception, jealousy, and doubt. Although he commands absolutely no respect, he holds our attention because of his cunning duplicity.

The play is finally, however, Othello's story. As we watch him be seduced by Iago's veiled hints and seeming confidences, we see how his trusting nature is inextricably related to his propensity to suspect Desdemona. Iago plays on the complexity and paradox of Othello's character and manipulates those tensions to keep him off balance and blind to the truth of Desdemona's faithfulness. Ultimately, though, Othello must take responsibility for the destruction of his love, a responsibility that is both his tragedy and his redemption.

WILLIAM SHAKESPEARE (1564–1616)

Othello the Moor of Venice 1604

The Names of the Actors
Othello, the Moor
Brabantio, [a Venetian senator,] father to Desdemona
Cassio, an honorable lieutenant [to Othello]
Iago, [Othello's ancient,] a villain
Roderigo, a gulled gentleman
Duke of Venice
Senators [of Venice]
Montano, governor of Cyprus
Lodovico and Gratiano, [kinsmen to Brabantio,] two noble Venetians
Sailors
Clowns
Desdemona, wife to Othello
Emilia, wife to Iago
Bianca, a courtesan
[Messenger, Herald, Officers, Venetian Gentlemen, Musicians, Attendants

SCENE: *Venice and Cyprus*]

ACT I

SCENE I: *A street in Venice.*

Enter Roderigo and Iago.

Roderigo: Tush, never tell me! I take it much unkindly
 That thou, Iago, who hast had my purse
 As if the strings were thine, shouldst know of this.°
Iago: 'Sblood,° but you'll not hear me!
 If ever I did dream of such a matter,
 Abhor me.
Roderigo: Thou told'st me thou didst hold him in thy hate.
Iago: Despise me if I do not. Three great ones of the city,
 In personal suit to make me his lieutenant,

ACT I. SCENE I. 3 *this:* I.e., Desdemona's elopement. 4 *'Sblood:* By God's blood.

Off-capped to him;° and, by the faith of man,
I know my price; I am worth no worse a place.
But he, as loving his own pride and purposes,
Evades them with a bombast circumstance.°
Horribly stuffed with epithets of war;
[And, in conclusion,]
Nonsuits° my mediators; for, "Certes," says he,
"I have already chose my officer."
And what was he?
Forsooth, a great arithmetician,°
One Michael Cassio, a Florentine
(A fellow almost damned in a fair wife°)
That never set a squadron in the field,
Nor the division of a battle knows
More than a spinster; unless the bookish theoric,
Wherein the togèd consuls can propose
As masterly as he. Mere prattle without practice
Is all his soldiership. But he, sir, had th' election;
And I (of whom his eyes had seen the proof
At Rhodes, at Cyprus, and on other grounds
Christian and heathen) must be belee'd and calmed°
By debitor and creditor; this counter-caster,°
He, in good time, must his lieutenant be,
And I — God bless the mark! — his Moorship's ancient.°

Roderigo: By heaven, I rather would have been his hangman.

Iago: Why, there's no remedy; 'tis the curse of service.
Preferment goes by letter and affection,°
And not by old gradation, where each second
Stood heir to th' first. Now, sir, be judge yourself,
Whether I in any just term am affined°
To love the Moor.

Roderigo: I would not follow him then.

Iago: O, sir, content you;
I follow him to serve my turn upon him.
We cannot all be masters, nor all masters
Cannot be truly followed. You shall mark
Many a duteous and knee-crooking knave
That, doting on his own obsequious bondage,
Wears out his time, much like his master's ass,
For naught but provender; and when he's old, cashiered.°
Whip me such honest knaves! Others there are
Who, trimmed° in forms and visages of duty,
Keep yet their hearts attending on themselves;
And, throwing but shows of service on their lords,

10 *him:* I.e., Othello. 13 *a bombast circumstance:* Pompous circumlocutions. 16 *Nonsuits:* Rejects. 19 *arithmetician:* Theoretician. 21 *almost . . . wife:* (An obscure allusion; Cassio is unmarried, but see IV, i, 123). 30 *belee'd and calmed:* Left in the lurch. 31 *counter-caster:* Bookkeeper. 33 *ancient:* Ensign. 36 *affection:* Favoritism. 39 *affined:* Obliged. 48 *cashiered:* Turned off. 50 *trimmed:* Dressed up.

Do well thrive by them, and when they have lined their coats,
Do themselves homage. These fellows have some soul;
And such a one do I profess myself. For, sir,
It is as sure as you are Roderigo,
Were I the Moor, I would not be Iago.
In following him, I follow but myself;
Heaven is my judge, not I for love and duty,
But seeming so, for my peculiar end;
For when my outward action doth demonstrate
The native act and figure of my heart°
In compliment extern,° 'tis not long after
But I will wear my heart upon my sleeve
For daws to peck at; I am not what I am.

Roderigo: What a full fortune does the thick-lips° owe°
If he can carry't thus!

Iago: Call up her father,
Rouse him. Make after him, poison his delight,
Proclaim him in the streets. Incense her kinsmen,
And though he in a fertile climate dwell,
Plague him with flies; though that his joy be joy,
Yet throw such changes of vexation on't
As it may lose some color.

Roderigo: Here is her father's house. I'll call aloud.

Iago: Do, with like timorous° accent and dire yell
As when, by night and negligence, the fire
Is spied in populous cities.

Roderigo: What, ho, Brabantio! Signior Brabantio, ho!

Iago: Awake! What, ho, Brabantio! Thieves! thieves! thieves!
Look to your house, your daughter, and your bags!
Thieves! thieves!

Brabantio at a window.°

Brabantio (above): What is the reason of this terrible summons?
What is the matter there?

Roderigo: Signior, is all your family within?

Iago: Are your doors locked?

Brabantio: Why, wherefore ask you this?

Iago: Zounds, sir, y' are robbed! For shame, put on your gown!
Your heart is burst; you have lost half your soul.
Even now, now, very now, an old black ram
Is tupping your white ewe. Arise, arise!
Awake the snorting° citizens with the bell,
Or else the devil will make a grandsire of you.
Arise, I say!

62 *The . . . heart:* What I really believe and intend. 63 *compliment extern:* Outward appearance. 66 *thick-lips:* (Elizabethans made no clear distinction between Moors and Negroes); *owe:* Own. 75 *timorous:* Terrifying. 81 s.d. *Brabantio at a window* (added from quarto). 90 *snorting:* Snoring.

Brabantio: What, have you lost your wits?
Roderigo: Most reverend signior, do you know my voice?
Brabantio: Not I. What are you?
Roderigo: My name is Roderigo.
Brabantio: The worser welcome!
I have charged thee not to haunt about my doors.
In honest plainness thou hast heard me say
My daughter is not for thee; and now, in madness,
Being full of supper and distemp'ring draughts,
Upon malicious knavery dost thou come
To start my quiet.
Roderigo: Sir, sir, sir —
Brabantio: But thou must needs be sure
My spirit and my place have in them power
To make this bitter to thee.
Roderigo: Patience, good sir.
Brabantio: What tell'st thou me of robbing? This is Venice;
My house is not a grange.°
Roderigo: Most grave Brabantio,
In simple and pure soul I come to you.
Iago: Zounds, sir, you are one of those that will not serve God if the devil bid you. Because we come to do you service, and you think we are ruffians, you'll have your daughter covered with a Barbary horse; you'll have your nephews° neigh to you; you'll have coursers for cousins, and gennets° for germans.
Brabantio: What profane wretch art thou?
Iago: I am one, sir, that comes to tell you your daughter and the Moor are now making the beast with two backs.
Brabantio: Thou art a villain.
Iago: You are — a senator.
Brabantio: This thou shalt answer. I know thee, Roderigo.
Roderigo: Sir, I will answer anything. But I beseech you,
If't be your pleasure and most wise consent,
As partly I find it is, that your fair daughter,
At this odd-even° and dull watch o' th' night,
Transported, with no worse nor better guard
But with a knave of common hire, a gondolier,
To the gross clasps of a lascivious Moor —
If this be known to you, and your allowance,°
We then have done you bold and saucy wrongs;
But if you know not this, my manners tell me
We have your wrong rebuke. Do not believe
That, from the sense° of all civility,
I thus would play and trifle with your reverence.
Your daughter, if you have not given her leave,

107 *grange:* Isolated farmhouse. 113 *nephews:* I.e., grandsons. 114 *gennets for germans:* Spanish horses for near kinsmen. 123 *odd-even:* Between night and morning. 127 *allowance:* Approval. 131 *from the sense:* In violation.

I say again, hath made a gross revolt,
Tying her duty, beauty, wit, and fortunes
In an extravagant and wheeling° stranger
Of here and everywhere. Straight satisfy yourself.
If she be in her chamber, or your house,
Let loose on me the justice of the state
For thus deluding you.

Brabantio: Strike on the tinder, ho!
Give me a taper! Call up all my people!
This accident° is not unlike my dream.
Belief of it oppresses me already.
Light, I say! light! *Exit [above].*

Iago: Farewell, for I must leave you.
It seems not meet, nor wholesome to my place,
To be produced — as, if I stay, I shall —
Against the Moor. For I do know the state,
However this may gall him with some check,°
Cannot with safety cast° him; for he's embarked
With such loud reason to the Cyprus wars,
Which even now stand in act,° that for their souls
Another of his fathom° they have none
To lead their business; in which regard,
Though I do hate him as I do hell-pains,
Yet, for necessity of present life,
I must show out a flag and sign of love,
Which is indeed but sign. That you shall surely find him,
Lead to the Sagittary° the raisèd search;
And there will I be with him. So farewell. *Exit.*

Enter [below] Brabantio in his nightgown,° and Servants with torches.

Brabantio: It is too true an evil. Gone she is;
And what's to come of my despisèd time
Is naught but bitterness. Now, Roderigo,
Where didst thou see her? — O unhappy girl! —
With the Moor, say'st thou? — Who would be a father? —
How didst thou know 'twas she! — O, she deceives me
Past thought! — What said she to you? — Get moe° tapers!
Raise all my kindred! — Are they married, think you?

Roderigo: Truly I think they are.

Brabantio: O heaven! How got she out? O treason of the blood!
Fathers, from hence trust not your daughters' minds
By what you see them act. Is there not charms
By which the property° of youth and maidhood
May be abused? Have you not read, Roderigo,
Of some such thing?

136 *extravagant and wheeling:* Expatriate and roving 142 *accident:* Occurence. 148 *Check:* Reprimand. 149 *cast:* Discharge. 151 *stand in act:* Are going on. 152 *fathom:* Capacity. 158 *Sagittary:* An inn. 159 s.d. *nightgown:* Drèssing gown. 166 *moe:* More. 172 *property:* Nature.

Roderigo: Yes, sir, I have indeed.
Brabantio: Call up my brother. — O, would you had had her! —
Some one way, some another. — Do you know
Where we may apprehend her and the Moor?
Roderigo: I think I can discover him, if you please
To get good guard and go along with me.
Brabantio: I pray you lead on. At every house I'll call;
I may command at most. — Get weapons, ho!
And raise some special officers of night. —
On, good Roderigo; I'll deserve° your pains. *Exeunt.*

SCENE II: *Before the lodgings of Othello.*

Enter Othello, Iago, and Attendants with torches.

Iago: Though in the trade of war I have slain men,
Yet do I hold it very stuff o' th' conscience
To do no contrived murther. I lack iniquity
Sometimes to do me service. Nine or ten times
I had thought t' have yerked° him here under the ribs.
Othello: 'Tis better as it is.
Iago: Nay, but he prated,
And spoke such scurvy and provoking terms
Against your honor
That with the little godliness I have
I did full hard forbear him. But I pray you, sir,
Are you fast married?° Be assured of this,
That the magnifico° is much beloved,
And hath in his effect a voice potential°
As double° as the Duke's. He will divorce you,
Or put upon you what restraint and grievance
The law, with all his might to enforce it on,
Will give him cable.
Othello: Let him do his spite.
My services which I have done the signiory°
Shall out-tongue his complaints. 'Tis yet to know° —
Which, when I know that boasting is an honor,
I shall promulgate — I fetch my life and being
From men of royal siege;° and my demerits
May speak unbonneted to as proud a fortune
As this that I have reached.° For know, Iago,
But that I love the gentle Desdemona,
I would not my unhousèd° free condition

183 *deserve:* Show gratitude for. SCENE II. 5 *yerked:* Stabbed. 11 *fast:* Securely. 12 *magnifico:* Grandee (Brabantio). 13 *potential:* Powerful. 14 *double:* Doubly influential. 18 *signiory:* Venetian government. 19 *yet to know:* Still not generally known. 22 *siege:* Rank; *demerits:* Deserts. 23–24 *May speak . . . reached:* Are equal, I modestly assert, to those of Desdemona's family. 26 *unhousèd:* Unrestrained.

Put into circumscription and confine
For the sea's worth. But look what lights come yond?

Iago: Those are the raisèd father and his friends.
You were best go in.

Othello: Not I; I must be found.
My parts, my title, and my perfect soul°
Shall manifest me rightly. Is it they?

Iago: By Janus, I think no.

Enter Cassio, with torches, Officers.

Othello: The servants of the Duke, and my lieutenant.
The goodness of the night upon you, friends!
What is the news?

Cassio: The Duke does greet you, general;
And he requires your haste-post-haste appearance
Even on the instant.

Othello: What's the matter, think you?

Cassio: Something from Cyprus, as I may divine.
It is a business of some heat. The galleys
Have sent a dozen sequent° messengers
This very night at one another's heels,
And many of the consuls, raised and met,
Are at the Duke's already. You have been hotly called for;
When, being not at your lodging to be found,
The Senate hath sent about three several quests
To search you out.

Othello: 'Tis well I am found by you.
I will but spend a word here in the house,
And go with you. *[Exit]*

Cassio: Ancient, what makes he here?

Iago: Faith, he to-night hath boarded a land carack.°
If it prove lawful prize, he's made for ever.

Cassio: I do not understand.

Iago: He's married.

Cassio: To who?

[Enter Othello.]

Iago: Marry, to — Come, captain, will you go?

Othello: Have with you.

Cassio: Here comes another troop to seek for you.

Enter Brabantio, Roderigo, and others with lights and weapons.

Iago: It is Brabantio. General, be advised.
He comes to bad intent.

Othello: Holla! stand there!

Roderigo: Signior, it is the Moor.

Brabantio: Down with him, thief!

31 *perfect soul:* Stainless conscience. 41 *sequent:* Consecutive. 50 *carack:* Treausre ship.

[They draw on both sides.]

Iago: You, Roderigo! Come, sir, I am for you.
Othello: Keep up° your bright swords, for the dew will rust them.
Good signior, you shall more command with years
Than with your weapons.
Brabantio: O thou foul thief, where hast thou stowed my daughter?
Damned as thou art, thou hast enchanted her!
For I'll refer me to all things of sense,
If she in chains of magic were not bound,
Whether a maid so tender, fair, and happy,
So opposite to marriage that she shunned
The wealthy curlèd darlings of our nation,
Would ever have, t' incur a general mock,
Run from her guardage to the sooty bosom
Of such a thing as thou — to fear, not to delight.
Judge me the world if 'tis not gross in sense°
That thou hast practiced on her with foul charms,
Abused her delicate youth with drugs or minerals
That weaken motion.° I'll have't disputed on;
'Tis probable, and palpable to thinking.
I therefore apprehend and do attach° thee
For an abuser of the world, a practicer
Of arts inhibited and out of warrant.
Lay hold upon him. If he do resist,
Subdue him at his peril.
Othello: Hold your hands,
Both you of my inclining and the rest.
Were it my cue to fight, I should have known it
Without a prompter. Where will you that I go
To answer this your charge?
Brabantio: To prison, till fit time
Of law and course of direct session°
Call thee to answer.
Othello: What if I do obey?
How may the Duke be therewith satisfied,
Whose messengers are here about my side
Upon some present business of the state
To bring me to him?
Officer: 'Tis true, most worthy signior.
The Duke's in council, and your noble self
I am sure is sent for.
Brabantio: How? The Duke in council?
In this time of the night? Bring him away.
Mine's not an idle° cause. The Duke himself,
Or any of my brothers of the state,
Cannot but feel this wrong as 'twere their own;

59 *Keep up:* I.e., sheath. 72 *gross in sense:* Obvious. 75 *motion:* Perception. 77 *attach:* Arrest. 86 *direct session:* Regular trial. 95 *idle:* Trifling.

For if such actions may have passage free,
Bondslaves and pagans shall our statesmen be. *Exeunt.*

Scene III. *The Venetian Senate Chamber.*

Enter Duke and Senators, set at a table, with lights and Attendants.

Duke: There is no composition° in these news
That gives them credit.
1. Senator: Indeed they are disproportioned.
My letters say a hundred and seven galleys.
Duke: And mine a hundred forty.
2. Senator: And mine two hundred.
But though they jump° not on a just account —
As in these cases where the aim° reports
'Tis oft with difference — yet do they all confirm
A Turkish fleet, and bearing up to Cyprus.
Duke: Nay, it is possible enough to judgment.
I do not so secure me° in the error
But the main article° I do approve°
In fearful sense.
Sailor (within): What, ho! what, ho! what, ho!
Officer: A messenger from the galleys.

Enter Sailor.

Duke: Now, what's the business?
Sailor: The Turkish preparation makes for Rhodes.
So was I bid report here to the state
By Signior Angelo.
Duke: How say you by this change?
1. Senator: This cannot be
By no assay° of reason. 'Tis a pageant
To keep us in false gaze.° When we consider
Th' importancy of Cyprus to the Turk,
And let ourselves again but understand
That, as it more concerns the Turk than Rhodes,
So may he with° more facile question bear° it,
For that it stands not in such warlike brace,°
But altogether lacks th' abilities
That Rhodes is dressed in — if we make thought of this,
We must not think the Turk is so unskillful
To leave that latest which concerns him first,
Neglecting an attempt of ease and gain
To wake and wage° a danger profitless.
Duke: Nay, in all confidence, he's not for Rhodes.

Scene III. 1 *composition:* Consistency. 5 *jump:* Agree. 6 *aim:* Conjecture 10 *so secure me:* Take such comfort. 11 *article:* Substance; *approve:* Accept. 18 *assay:* test. 19 *in false gaze:* Looking the wrong way. 23 *with . . . bear:* More easily capture. 24 *brace:* Posture of defense. 30 *wake and wage:* Rouse and risk.

Officer: Here is more news.

Enter a Messenger.

Messenger: The Ottomites, reverend and gracious,
Steering with due course toward the isle of Rhodes,
Have there injointed them with an after fleet.
1. Senator: Ay, so I thought. How many, as you guess?
Messenger: Of thirty sail; and now they do restem°
Their backward course, bearing with frank appearance
Their purposes toward Cyprus. Signior Montano,
Your trusty and most valiant servitor,
With his free duty recommends you thus,
And prays you to believe him.
Duke: 'Tis certain then for Cyprus.
Marcus Luccicos,° is not he in town?
1. Senator: He's now in Florence.
Duke: Write from us to him; post, post-haste dispatch.
1. Senator: Here comes Brabantio and the valiant Moor.

Enter Brabantio, Othello, Cassio, Iago, Roderigo, and Officers.

Duke: Valiant Othello, we must straight employ you
Against the general enemy Ottoman. *[To Brabantio.]*
I did not see you. Welcome, gentle signior.
We lacked your counsel and your help to-night.
Brabantio: So did I yours. Good your grace, pardon me.
Neither my place, nor aught I heard of business,
Hath raised me from my bed; nor doth the general care
Take hold on me; for my particular grief
Is of so floodgate° and o'erbearing nature
That it engluts° and swallows other sorrows,
And it is still itself.
Duke: Why, what's the matter?
Brabantio: My daughter! O, my daughter!
All: Dead?
Brabantio: Ay, to me.
She is abused, stol'n from me, and corrupted
By spells and medicines bought of mountebanks;
For nature so prepost'rously to err,
Being not deficient,° blind, or lame of sense,
Sans witchcraft could not.
Duke: Whoe'er he be that in this foul proceeding
Hath thus beguiled your daughter of herself,
And you of her, the bloody book of law
You shall yourself read in the bitter letter
After your own sense; yea, though our proper° son
Stood in your action.°

37 *restem:* Steer again. 44 *Marcus Luccicos:* (Presumably a Venetian envoy). 56 *floodgate:* Torrential. 57 *engluts:* Devours. 63 *deficient:* Feeble-minded. 69 *our proper:* My own. 70 *Stood in your action:* Were accused by you.

Brabantio: Humbly I thank your grace.
Here is the man — this Moor, whom now, it seems,
Your special mandate for the state affairs
Hath hither brought.
All: We are very sorry for't.
Duke [to Othello]: What, in your own part, can you say to this?
Brabantio: Nothing, but this is so.
Othello: Most potent, grave, and reverend signiors,
My very noble, and approved° good masters,
That I have ta'en away this old man's daughter,
It is most true; true I have married her.
The very head and front of my offending
Hath this extent, no more. Rude° am I in my speech,
And little blessed with the soft phrase of peace;
For since these arms of mine had seven years' pith°
Till now some nine moons wasted, they have used
Their dearest action in the tented field;
And little of this great world can I speak
More than pertains to feats of broil and battle;
And therefore little shall I grace my cause
In speaking for myself. Yet, by your gracious patience,
I will a round° unvarnished tale deliver
Of my whole course of love — what drugs, what charms,
What conjuration, and what mighty magic
(For such proceeding am I charged withal)
I won his daughter.
Brabantio: A maiden never bold;
Of spirit so still and quiet that her motion
Blushed° at herself; and she — in spite of nature,
Of years, of country, credit, everything —
To fall in love with what she feared to look on!
It is a judgment maimed and most imperfect
That will confess perfection so could err
Against all rules of nature, and must be driven
To find out practices° of cunning hell
Why this should be. I therefore vouch° again
That with some mixtures pow'rful o'er the blood,°
Or with some dram, conjured to this effect,
He wrought upon her.
Duke: To vouch this is no proof,
Without more certain and more overt test
Than these thin habits° and poor likelihoods
Of modern seeming° do prefer against him.
1. Senator: But, Othello, speak.

77 *approved:* Tested by experience. 81 *Rude:* Unpolished 83 *pith:* Strength. 90 *round;* Plain. 95–96 *her motion Blushed:* Her own emotions caused her to blush. 102 *practices:* Plots. 103 *vouch:* Assert. 104 *blood:* Passions. 108 *thin habits:* Slight appearances. 109 *modern seeming:* Everyday supposition.

Did you by indirect and forcèd° courses
Subdue and poison this young maid's affections?
Or came it by request, and such fair question°
As soul to soul affordeth?

Othello: I do beseech you,
Send for the lady to the Sagittary
And let her speak of me before her father.
If you do find me foul in her report,
The trust, the office, I do hold of you
Not only take away, but let your sentence
Even fall upon my life.

Duke: Fetch Desdemona hither.

Othello: Ancient, conduct them; you best know the place.

Exit [Iago, with] two or three [Attendants].

And till she come, as truly as to heaven
I do confess the vices of my blood,
So justly to your grave ears I'll present
How I did thrive in this fair lady's love,
And she in mine.

Duke: Say it, Othello.

Othello: Her father loved me, oft invited me;
Still° questioned me the story of my life
From year to year — the battles, sieges, fortunes
That I have passed.
I ran it through, even from my boyish days
To th' very moment that he bade me tell it.
Wherein I spoke of most disastrous chances,
Of moving accidents by flood and field;
Of hairbreadth scapes i' th' imminent deadly breach;
Of being taken by the insolent foe
And sold to slavery; of my redemption thence
And portance° in my travels' history;
Wherein of anters° vast and deserts idle,
Rough quarries, rocks, and hills whose heads touch heaven,
It was my hint° to speak — such was the process;
And of the Cannibals that each other eat,
The Anthropophagi,° and men whose heads
Do grow beneath their shoulders. This to hear
Would Desdemona seriously incline;
But still the house affairs would draw her thence;
Which ever as she could with haste dispatch,
She'ld come again, and with a greedy ear
Devour up my discourse. Which I observing,
Took once a pliant° hour, and found good means
To draw from her a prayer of earnest heart

111 *forcèd:* Violent. 113 *question:* Conversation. 129 *Still:* Continually. 139 *portance:* Behavior. 140 *anters:* Caves 142 *hint:* Occasion. 144 *Anthropophagi:* Man-eaters. 151 *pliant:* Propitious.

That I would all my pilgrimage dilate,°
Whereof by parcels° she had something heard,
But not intentively.° I did consent,
And often did beguile her of her tears
When I did speak of some distressful stroke
That my youth suffered. My story being done,
She gave me for my pains a world of sighs.
She swore, i' faith, 'twas strange, 'twas passing strange;
'Twas pitiful, 'twas wondrous pitiful.
She wished she had not heard it; yet she wished
That heaven had made her such a man. She thanked me;
And bade me, if I had a friend that loved her,
I should but teach him how to tell my story,
And that would woo her. Upon this hint° I spake.
She loved me for the dangers I had passed,
And I loved her that she did pity them.
This only is the witchcraft I have used.
Here comes the lady. Let her witness it.

Enter Desdemona, Iago, Attendants.

Duke: I think this tale would win my daughter too.
Good Brabantio,
Take up this mangled matter at the best.
Men do their broken weapons rather use
Than their bare hands.
Brabantio: I pray you hear her speak.
If she confess that she was half the wooer,
Destruction on my head if my bad blame
Light on the man! Come hither, gentle mistress.
Do you perceive in all this noble company
Where most you owe obedience?
Desdemona: My noble father,
I do perceive here a divided duty.
To you I am bound for life and education;°
My life and education both do learn me
How to respect you: you are the lord of duty;
I am hitherto your daughter. But here's my husband;
And so much duty as my mother showed
To you, preferring you before her father,
So much I challenge° that I may profess
Due to the Moor my lord.
Brabantio: God be with you! I have done.
Please it your grace, on to the state affairs.
I had rather to adopt a child than get° it.
Come hither, Moor.

153 *dilate:* Recount in full. 154 *parcels:* Portions. 155 *intentively:* With full attention. 166 *hint:* Opportunity. 182 *education:* Upbringing. 188 *challenge:* Claim the right. 191 *get:* Beget.

I here do give thee that with all my heart
Which, but thou hast already, with all my heart
I would keep from thee. For your sake,° jewel,
I am glad at soul I have no other child;
For thy escape° would teach me tyranny,
To hang clogs on them. I have done, my lord.

Duke: Let me speak like yourself° and lay a sentence
Which, as a grise° or step, may help these lovers
[Into your favor.]
When remedies are past, the griefs are ended
By seeing the worst, which late on hopes depended.
To mourn a mischief that is past and gone
Is the next way to draw new mischief on.
What cannot be preserved when fortune takes,
Patience her injury a mock'ry makes.
The robbed that smiles steals something from the thief;
He robs himself that spends a bootless grief.

Brabantio: So let the Turk of Cyprus us beguile:
We lose it not so long as we can smile.
He bears the sentence well that nothing bears
But the free comfort which from thence he hears;
But he bears both the sentence and the sorrow
That to pay grief must of poor patience borrow.
These sentences, to sugar, or to gall,
Being strong on both sides, are equivocal.
But words are words. I never yet did hear
That the bruised heart was piercèd through the ear.
Beseech you, now to the affairs of state.

Duke: The Turk with a most mighty preparation makes for Cyprus. Othello, the fortitude° of the place is best known to you; and though we have there a substitute of most allowed° sufficiency, yet opinion,° a more sovereign mistress of effects, throws a more safer voice on you. You must therefore be content to slubber° the gloss of your new fortunes with this more stubborn and boist'rous expedition.

Othello: The tyrant custom, most grave senators,
Hath made the flinty and steel couch of war
My thrice-driven bed of down. I do agnize
A natural and prompt alacrity
I find in hardness;° and do undertake
These present wars against the Ottomites.
Most humbly, therefore, bending to your state,
I crave fit disposition for my wife,
Due reference of place, and exhibition,°
With such accommodation and besort°

195 *For your sake:* Because of you. 197 *escape:* Escapade. 199 *like yourself:* As you should; *sentence:* Maxim. 200 *grise:* Step. 222 *fortitude:* Fortification. 223 *allowed:* Acknowledged; *opinion:* Public opinion. 225 *slubber:* Sully. 229–33 *agnize . . . hardness:* Recognize in myself a natural and easy response to hardship. 235 *exhibition:* Allowance of money. 236 *besort:* Suitable company.

As levels° with her breeding.
Duke: If you please,
Be't at her father's.
Brabantio: I will not have it so.
Othello: Nor I.
Desdemona: Nor I. I would not there reside,
To put my father in impatient thoughts
By being in his eye. Most gracious Duke,
To my unfolding lend your prosperous ear,
And let me find a charter in your voice,
T' assist my simpleness.°
Duke: What would you, Desdemona?
Desdemona: That I did love the Moor to live with him,
My downright violence, and storm of fortunes,
May trumpet to the world. My heart's subdued
Even to the very quality of my lord.
I saw Othello's visage in his mind,
And to his honors and his valiant parts
Did I my soul and fortunes consecrate.
So that, dear lords, if I be left behind,
A moth of peace, and he go to the war,
The rites for which I love him are bereft me,
And I a heavy interim shall support
By his dear absence. Let me go with him.
Othello: Let her have your voice.
Vouch with me, heaven, I therefore beg it not
To please the palate of my appetite,
Not to comply with heat°— the young affects°
In me defunct — and proper satisfaction;
But to be free and bounteous to her mind;
And heaven defend your good souls that you think
I will your serious and great business scant
When she is with me. No, when light-winged toys
Of feathered Cupid seel° with wanton dullness
My speculative and officed instruments,°
That° my disports corrupt and taint my business,
Let housewives make a skillet of my helm,
And all indign° and base adversities
Make head against my estimation!°
Duke: Be it as you shall privately determine,
Either for her stay or going. Th' affair cries haste,
And speed must answer it.
1. Senator: You must away to-night.
Othello: With all my heart.

237 *levels:* Corresponds. 243 *prosperous:* Favorable. 245 *simpleness:* Lack of skill. 262 *heat:* Passions; *young affects:* Tendencies of youth. 268 *seel:* Blind. 269 *My . . . instruments:* My perceptive and responsible faculties. 270 *That:* So that. 272 *indign:* Unworthy. 273 *estimation:* Reputation.

Duke: At nine i' th' morning here we'll meet again.
Othello, leave some officer behind,
And he shall our commission bring to you,
With such things else of quality and respect
As doth import° you.
Othello: So please your grace, my ancient;
A man he is of honesty and trust
To his conveyance I assign my wife,
With what else needful your good grace shall think
To be sent after me.
Duke: Let it be so.
Good night to every one.
[To Brabantio.] And, noble signior,
If virtue no delighted° beauty lack,
Your son-in-law is far more fair than black.
1. Senator: Adieu, brave Moor. Use Desdemona well.
Brabantio: Look to her, Moor, if thou hast eyes to see:
She has deceived her father, and may thee.
Exeunt [Duke, Senators, Officers, &c.].
Othello: My life upon her faith!—Honest Iago,
My Desdemona must I leave to thee.
I prithee let thy wife attend on her,
And bring them after in the best advantage.°
Come, Desdemona. I have but an hour
Of love, of worldly matters and direction,
To spend with thee. We must obey the time.
Exit Moor and Desdemona.
Roderigo: Iago,—
Iago: What say'st thou, noble heart?
Roderigo: What will I do, think'st thou?
Iago: Why, go to bed and sleep.
Roderigo: I will incontinently° drown myself.
Iago: If thou dost, I shall never love thee after. Why, thou silly gentleman!
Roderigo: It is silliness to live when to live is torment; and then have we a prescription to die when death is our physician.
Iago: O villainous! I have looked upon the world for four times seven years; and since I could distinguish betwixt a benefit and an injury, I never found man that knew how to love himself. Ere I would say I would drown myself for the love of a guinea hen, I would change my humanity with a baboon.
Roderigo: What should I do? I confess it is my shame to be so fond, but it is not in my virtue to amend it.
Iago: Virtue? a fig! 'Tis in ourselves that we are thus or thus. Our bodies are our gardens, to which our wills are gardeners; so that if we will plant nettles or sow lettuce, set hyssop and weed up thyme, supply it with one gender° of herbs or distract it with many—either to have it

282 *import:* Concern. 288 *delighted:* Delightful. 296 *in the best advantage:* At the best opportunity. 303 *incontinently:* Forthwith. 317 *gender:* Species.

sterile with idleness or manured with industry — why, the power and corrigible authority° of this lies in our wills. If the balance of our lives had not one scale of reason to poise° another of sensuality, the blood and baseness° of our natures would conduct us to most preposterous conclusions. But we have reason to cool our raging motions,° our carnal stings, our unbitted° lusts; whereof I take this that you call love to be a sect or scion.°

Roderigo: It cannot be.

Iago: It is merely a lust of the blood and a permission of the will. Come, be a man! Drown thyself? Drown cats and blind puppies! I have professed me thy friend, and I confess me knit to thy deserving with cables of perdurable toughness. I could never better stead thee than now. Put money in thy purse. Follow thou the wars; defeat thy favor° with an usurped beard. I say, put money in thy purse. It cannot be that Desdemona should long continue her love to the Moor — put money in thy purse — nor he his to her. It was a violent commencement in her, and thou shalt see an answerable sequestration° — put but money in thy purse. These Moors are changeable in their wills — fill thy purse with money. The food that to him now is as luscious as locusts shall be to him shortly as bitter as coloquintida.° She must change for youth: when she is sated with his body, she will find the error of her choice. [She must have change, she must.] Therefore put money in thy purse. If thou wilt needs damn thyself, do it a more delicate way than drowning. Make° all the money thou canst. If sanctimony and a frail vow betwixt an erring° barbarian and a supersubtle Venetian be not too hard for my wits and all the tribe of hell, thou shalt enjoy her. Therefore make money. A pox of drowning thyself! 'Tis clean out of the way. Seek thou rather to be hanged in compassing thy joy than to be drowned and go without her.

Roderigo: Wilt thou be fast to my hopes, if I depend on the issue?

Iago: Thou art sure of me. Go, make money. I have told thee often, and I retell thee again and again, I hate the Moor. My cause is hearted;° thine hath no less reason. Let us be conjunctive in our revenge against him. If thou canst cuckold him, thou dost thyself a pleasure, me a sport. There are many events in the womb of time, which will be delivered. Traverse,° go, provide thy money! We will have more of this to-morrow. Adieu.

Roderigo: Where shall we meet i' th' morning?

Iago: At my lodging.

Roderigo: I'll be with thee betimes.

Iago: Go to, farewell — Do you hear, Roderigo?

[*Roderigo:* What say you?

Iago: No more of drowning, do you hear?

Roderigo: I am changed.

319 *corrigible authority:* Corrective power. 320 *poise:* Counterbalance. 320–21 *blood and baseness:* Animal instincts. 322 *motions:* Appetites. 323 *unbitted:* Uncontrolled. 324 *sect or scion:* Offshoot, cutting. 330 *defeat thy favor:* Spoil thy appearance. 334 *sequestration:* Estrangement 337 *coloquintida:* A medicine. 340 *Make:* Raise. 341 *erring:* Wandering. 348 *My cause is hearted:* My heart is in it. 352 *Traverse:* Foward march.

Iago: Go to, farewell, Put money enough in your purse.]
Roderigo: I'll sell all my land. *Exit.*
Iago: Thus do I ever make my fool my purse;
For I mine own gained knowledge should profane
If I would time expend with such a snipe°
But for my sport and profit. I hate the Moor;
And it is thought abroad that 'twixt my sheets
H'as done my office. I know not if't be true;
But I, for mere suspicion in that kind,
Will do as if for surety. He holds me well;°
The better shall my purpose work on him.
Cassio's a proper man. Let me see now:
To get his place, and to plume up° my will
In double knavery — How, how? — Let's see: —
After some time, to abuse Othello's ears
That he is too familiar with his wife.
He hath a person and a smooth dispose°
To be suspected — framed to make women false.
The Moor is of a free° and open nature
That thinks men honest that but seem to be so;
And will as tenderly be led by th' nose
As asses are.
I have't! It is engend'red! Hell and night
Must bring this monstrous birth to the world's light. *Exit.*

ACT II

SCENE I: *An open place in Cyprus, near the harbor.*

Enter Montano and two Gentlemen.

Montano: What from the cape can you discern at sea?
1. Gentleman: Nothing at all: it is a high-wrought flood.
I cannot 'twixt the heaven and the main
Descry a sail.
Montano: Methinks the wind hath spoke aloud at land;
A fuller blast ne'er shook our battlements.
If it hath ruffianed so upon the sea,
What ribs of oak, when mountains melt on them,
Can hold the mortise?° What shall we hear of this?
2. Gentleman: A segregation° of the Turkish fleet.
For do but stand upon the foaming shore,
The chidden billow seems to pelt the clouds;
The wind-shaked surge, with high and monstrous mane,

365 *snipe:* Fool. 370 *well:* In high regard. 373 *plume up:* Gratify. 377 *dispose:* Manner. 379 *free:* Frank. ACT II. SCENE 1. 9 *hold the mortise:* Hold their joints together. 10 *segregation:* Scattering.

Seems to cast water on the burning Bear
And quench the Guards° of th' ever-fixèd pole.°
I never did like molestation° view
On the enchafèd flood.

Montano: If that the Turkish fleet
Be not ensheltered and embayed, they are drowned;
It is impossible to bear it out.

Enter a third Gentleman.

3. Gentleman: News, lads! Our wars are done.
The desperate tempest hath so banged the Turks
That their designment halts.° A noble ship of Venice
Hath seen a grievous wrack and sufferance°
On most part of their fleet.

Montano: How? Is this true?

3. Gentleman: The ship is here put in,
A Veronesa;° Michael Cassio,
Lieutenant to the warlike Moor Othello,
Is come on shore; the Moor himself at sea,
And is in full commission here for Cyprus.

Montano: I am glad on't. 'Tis a worthy governor.

3. Gentleman: But this same Cassio, though he speak of comfort
Touching the Turkish loss, yet he looks sadly
And prays the Moor be safe, for they were parted
With foul and violent tempest.

Montano: Pray heaven he be;
For I have served him, and the man commands
Like a full soldier. Let's to the seaside, ho!
As well to see the vessel that's come in
As to throw out our eyes for brave Othello,
Even till we make the main and th' aerial blue
An indistinct regard.°

3 Gentleman: Come, let's do so;
For every minute is expectancy
Of more arrivance.

Enter Cassio.

Cassio: Thanks, you the valiant of this warlike isle,
That so approve the Moor! O, let the heavens
Give him defense against the elements,
For I have lost him on a dangerous sea!

Montano: Is he well shipped?

Cassio: His bark is stoutly timbered, and his pilot
Of very expert and approved allowance;
Therefore my hopes, not surfeited to death,°

15 *Guards:* Stars near the North Star; *pole:* Polestar. 16 *molestation:* Tumult. 22 *designment halts:* Plan is crippled. 23. *sufferance:* Disaster. 26 *Veronesa:* Ship furnished by Verona. 40 *An indistinct regard:* Indistinguishable. 50 *surfeited to death:* Overindulged.

Stand in bold cure.°
(*Within.*) A sail, a sail, a sail! Enter a messenger.

Cassio: What noise?
Messenger: The town is empty; on the brow o' th' sea
Stand ranks of people, and they cry "A sail!"
Cassio: My hopes do shape him for the governor.

A shot.

2. Gentleman: They do discharge their shot of courtesy:
Our friends at least.
Cassio: I pray you, sir, go forth
And give us truth who 'tis that is arrived
2. Gentleman: I shall. *Exit.*
Montano: But, good lieutenant, is your general wived?
Cassio: Most fortunately. He hath achieved a maid
That paragons° description and wild fame;
One that excels the quirks° of blazoning° pens,
And in th' essential vesture of creation
Does tire the ingener.°

Enter Second Gentleman.

How now? Who has put in?
2. Gentleman: 'Tis one Iago, ancient to the general.
Cassio: H'as had most favorable and happy speed:
Tempests themselves, high seas, and howling winds,
The guttered° rocks and congregated sands,
Traitors ensteeped° to clog the guiltless keel,
As having sense of beauty, do omit
Their mortal° natures, letting go safely by
The divine Desdemona.
Montano: What is she?
Cassio: She that I spake of, our great captain's captain,
Left in the conduct of the bold Iago,
Whose footing° here anticipates our thoughts
A se'nnight's° speed. Great Jove, Othello guard,
And swell his sail with thine own pow'rful breath,
That he may bless this bay with his tall ship,
Make love's quick pants in Desdemona's arms,
Give renewed fire to our extincted spirits,
[And bring all Cyprus comfort!]

Enter Desdemona, Iago, Roderigo, and Emilia [with Attendants].

O, behold!

51 *in bold cure:* A good chance of fulfillment. 62 *paragons:* Surpasses. 63 *quirks:* Ingenuities; *blazoning:* Describing. 64–65 *And . . . ingener:* Merely to describe her as God made her exhausts her praiser. 69 *guttered:* Jagged. 70 *ensteeped:* Submerged. 72 *mortal:* Deadly. 76 *footing:* Landing. 77 *se'nnight's:* Week's.

The riches of the ship is come on shore!
You men of Cyprus, let her have your knees.°
Hail to thee, lady! and the grace of heaven,
Before, behind thee, and on every hand,
Enwheel thee round!
Desdemona: I thank you, valiant Cassio.
What tidings can you tell me of my lord?
Cassio: He is not yet arrived; nor know I aught
But that he's well and will be shortly here.
Desdemona: O but I fear! How lost you company?
Cassio: The great contention of the sea and skies
Parted our fellowship.
(Within.) A sail, a sail! *[A shot.]*
But hark. A sail!
2. Gentleman: They give their greeting to the citadel;
This likewise is a friend.
Cassio: See for the news.
[Exit Gentleman.]
Good ancient, you are welcome.
[To Emilia.] Welcome, mistress. —
Let it not gall your patience, good Iago,
That I extend my manners. 'Tis my breeding
That gives me this bold show of courtesy.
[Kisses Emilia.°]
Iago: Sir, would she give you so much of her lips
As of her tongue she oft bestows on me,
You would have enough.
Desdemona: Alas, she has no speech!
Iago: In faith, too much.
I find it still when I have list to sleep.
Marry, before your ladyship, I grant,
She puts her tongue a little in her heart
And chides with thinking.
Emilia: You have little cause to say so.
Iago: Come on, come on! You are pictures out of doors,
Bells in your parlors, wildcats in your kitchens,
Saints in your injuries, devils being offended,
Players in your housewifery,° and housewives° in your beds.
Desdemona: O, fie upon thee, slanderer!
Iago: Nay, it is true, or else I am a Turk:
You rise to play, and go to bed to work.
Emilia: You shall not write my praise.
Iago: No, let me not.
Desdemona: What wouldst thou write of me, if thou shouldst praise me?

84 *knees:* I.e. kneeling. 99 s.d. *Kisses Emilia:* (Kissing was a common Elizabethan form of social courtesy). 112 *housewifery:* Housekeeping; *housewives:* Hussies.

Iago: O gentle lady, do not put me to't,
For I am nothing if not critical.
Desdemona: Come on, assay.° — There's one gone to the harbor?
Iago: Ay, madam.
Desdemona: I am not merry; but I do beguile
The thing I am by seeming otherwise. —
Come, how wouldst thou praise me?
Iago: I am about it; but indeed my invention
Comes from my pate as birdlime° does from frieze° —
It plucks out brains and all. But my Muse labors,
And thus she is delivered:
If she be fair and wise, fairness and wit —
The one's for use, the other useth it.
Desdemona: Well praised! How if she be black° and witty?
Iago: If she be black, and thereto have a wit,
She'll find a white that shall her blackness fit.
Desdemona: Worse and worse!
Emilia: How if fair and foolish?
Iago: She never yet was foolish that was fair,
For even her folly° helped her to an heir.
Desdemona: These are old fond° paradoxes to make fools laugh i' th' alehouse. What miserable praise hast thou for her that's foul° and foolish?
Iago: There's none so foul, and foolish thereunto,
But does foul pranks which fair and wise ones do.
Desdemona: O heavy ignorance! Thou praisest the worst best. But what praise couldst thou bestow on a deserving woman indeed — one that in the authority of her merit did justly put on the vouch° of very malice itself?
Iago: She that was ever fair, and never proud;
Had tongue at will, and yet was never loud;
Never lacked gold, and yet went never gay;
Fled from her wish, and yet said "Now I may";
She that, being ang'red, her revenge being nigh,
Bade her wrong stay, and her displeasure fly;
She that in wisdom never was so frail
To change the cod's head for the salmon's tail;°
She that could think, and ne'er disclose her mind;
See suitors following, and not look behind:
She was a wight (if ever such wight were) —
Desdemona: To do what?
Iago: To suckle fools and chronicle small beer.°
Desdemona: O most lame and impotent conclusion! Do not learn of him,

120 *assay:* Try. 126 *birdlime:* A sticky paste; *frieze:* Rough cloth. 131 *black:* Brunette. 137 *folly:* Wantonness. 138 *fond:* Foolish. 139 *foul:* Ugly. 144 *put on the vouch:* Compel the approval. 153 *To . . . tail:* I.e., to exchange the good for the poor but expensive. 158 *chronicle small beer:* Keep petty household accounts.

Emilia, though he be thy husband. How say you, Cassio? Is he not a most profane and liberal° counsellor?

Cassio: He speaks home,° madam. You may relish him more in the soldier than in the scholar.

Iago [aside]: He takes her by the palm. Ay, well said, whisper! With as little a web as this will I ensnare as great a fly as Cassio. Ay, smile upon her, do! I will gyve thee in thine own courtship.°— You say true; 'tis so, indeed! — If such tricks as these strip you out of your lieutenantry, it had been better you had not kissed your three fingers so oft — which now again you are most apt to play the sir° in. Very good! well kissed! an excellent courtesy! 'Tis so, indeed. Yet again your fingers to your lips? Would they were clyster pipes° for your sake! *(Trumpet within.)* The Moor! I know his trumpet.

Cassio: 'Tis truly so.

Desdemona: Let's meet him and receive him.

Cassio: Lo, where he comes.

Enter Othello and Attendants.

Othello: O my fair warrior!

Desdemona: My dear Othello!

Othello: It gives me wonder great as my content
To see you here before me. O my soul's joy!
If after every tempest come such calms,
May the winds blow till they have wakened death!
And let the laboring bark climb hills of seas
Olympus-high, and duck again as low
As hell 's from heaven! If it were now to die,
'Twere now to be most happy;° for I fear
My soul hath her content so absolute
That not another comfort like to this
Succeeds in unknown fate.

Desdemona: The heavens forbid
But that our loves and comforts should increase
Even as our days do grow.

Othello: Amen to that, sweet powers!
I cannot speak enough of this content;
It stops me here; it is too much of joy.
And this, and this, the greatest discords be

They kiss.

That e'er our hearts shall make!

Iago [aside]: O, you are well tuned now!
But I'll set down° the pegs that make this music,
As honest as I am.

Othello: Come, let us to the castle.

161 *profane and liberal:* Worldly and licentious. 162 *home:* Bluntly. 166 *gyve . . . courtship:* Manacle you by means of your courtly manners. 169 *sir:* Courtly gentleman. 171 *clyster pipes:* Syringes. 184 *happy:* Fortunate. 194 *set down:* Loosen.

News, friends! Our wars are done; the Turks are drowned.
How does my old acquaintance of this isle?—
Honey, you shall be well desired° in Cyrpus;
I have found great love amongst them. O my sweet,
I prattle out of fashion, and I dote
In mine own comforts. I prithee, good Iago,
Go to the bay and disembark my coffers.
Bring thou the master° to the citadel;
He is a good one, and his worthiness
Does challenge° much respect.—Come, Desdemona,
Once more well met at Cyprus.

Exit Othello [with all but Iago and Roderigo].

Iago [to an Attendant, who goes out]: Do thou meet me presently at the harbor. *[To Roderigo.]* Come hither. If thou be'st valiant (as they say base men being in love have then a nobility in their natures more than is native to them), list me. The lieutenant to-night watches on the court of guard.° First, I must tell thee this: Desdemona is directly in love with him.

Roderigo: With him? Why, 'tis not possible.

Iago: Lay thy finger thus,° and let thy soul be instructed. Mark me with what violence she first loved the Moor, but for bragging and telling her fantastical lies; and will she love him still for prating? Let not thy discreet heart think it. Her eye must be fed; and what delight shall she have to look on the devil? When the blood is made dull with the act of sport, there should be, again to inflame it and to give satiety a fresh appetite, loveliness in favor, sympathy in years, manners, and beauties; all which the Moor is defective in. Now for want of these required conveniences,° her delicate tenderness will find itself abused, begin to heave the gorge,° disrelish and abhor the Moor. Very nature will instruct her in it and compel her to some second choice. Now sir, this granted—as it is a most pregnant° and unforced position—who stands so eminent in the degree of this fortune as Cassio does? A knave very voluble; no further conscionable° than in putting on the mere form of civil and humane° seeming for the better compassing of his salt° and most hidden loose affection? Why, none! why, none! A slipper° and subtle knave; a finder-out of occasions; that has an eye can stamp and counterfeit advantages, though true advantage never present itself; a devilish knave! Besides, the knave is handsome, young, and hath all those requisites in him that folly and green minds look after. A pestilent complete knave! and the woman hath found him already.

Roderigo: I cannot believe that in her; she's full of most blessed condtion.°

Iago: Blessed fig's-end! The wine she drinks is made of grapes. If she had been blessed, she would never have loved the Moor. Blessed pudding!

198 *well desired:* Warmly welcomed. 203 *master:* Ship captain. 205 *challenge:* Deserve. 210 *court of guard:* Headquarters. 213 *thus:* I.e., on your lips. 220 *conveniences:* Compatibilities. 221 *heave the gorge:* Be nauseated. 224 *pregnant:* Evident. 226 *conscionable:* Conscientious; *humane:* Polite. 227 *salt:* Lecherous. 228 *slipper:* Slippery. 234 *condition:* Character.

Didst thou not see her paddle with the palm of his hand? Didst not mark that?

Roderigo: Yes, that I did; but that was but courtesy.

Iago: Lechery, by this hand! an index and obscure prologue to the history of lust and foul thoughts. They met so near with their lips that their breaths embraced together. Villainous thoughts, Roderigo! When these mutualities° so marshal the way, hard at hand comes the master and main exercise, th' incorporate° conclusion. Pish! But, sir, be you ruled by me: I have brought you from Venice. Watch you to-night; for the command, I'll lay't upon you. Cassio knows you not. I'll not be far from you: do you find some occasion to anger Cassio, either by speaking too loud, or tainting° his discipline, or from what other course you please which the time shall more favorably minister.

Roderigo: Well.

Iago: Sir, he's rash and very sudden in choler,° and haply with his truncheon may strike at you. Provoke him that he may; for even out of that will I cause these of Cyprus to mutiny; whose qualification° shall come into no true taste° again but by the displanting of Cassio. So shall you have a shorter journey to your desires by the means I shall then have to prefer° them; and the impediment most profitably removed without the which there were no expectation of our prosperity.

Roderigo: I will do this if you can bring it to any opportunity.

Iago: I warrant thee. Meet me by and by at the citadel; I must fetch his necessaries ashore. Farewell.

Roderigo: Adieu. *Exit.*

Iago: That Cassio loves her, I do well believe't;
That she loves him, 'tis apt° and of great credit.
The Moor, howbeit that I endure him not,
Is of a constant, loving, noble nature,
And I dare think he'll prove to Desdemona
A most dear husband. Now I do love her too;
Not out of absolute lust, though peradventure
I stand accountant° for as great a sin,
But partly led to diet° my revenge,
For that I do suspect the lusty Moor
Hath leaped into my seat; the thought whereof
Doth, like a poisonous mineral, gnaw my inwards;
And nothing can or shall content my soul
Till I am evened with him, wife for wife;
Or failing so, yet that I put the Moor
At least into a jealousy so strong
That judgment cannot cure. Which thing to do,
If this poor trash of Venice, whom I trash°
For° his quick hunting, stand the putting on,°

243 *mutualities:* Exchanges. 244 *incorporate:* Carnal 248 *tainting:* Discrediting. 251 *sudden in choler:* Violent in anger. 253 *qualification:* Appeasement. 254 *true taste:* Satisfactory state. 256 *prefer:* Advance. 263 *apt:* Probable. 269 *accountant:* Accountable. 270 *diet:* Feed. 279 *I trash:* I weight down (in order to keep under control). 280 *For:* In order to develop; *stand the putting on:* Responds to my inciting.

I'll have our Michael Cassio on the hip,°
Abuse him to the Moor in the rank garb°
(For I fear Cassio with my nightcap too),
Make the Moor thank me, love me, and reward me
For making him egregiously an ass
And practicing upon° his peace and quiet
Even to madness. 'Tis here, but yet confused:
Knavery's plain face is never seen till used. *Exit.*

SCENE II. *A street in Cyprus.*

Enter Othello's Herald, with a proclamation.

Herald: It is Othello's pleasure, our noble and valiant general, that, upon certain tidings now arrived, importing the mere perdition° of the Turkish fleet, every man put himself into triumph; some to dance, some to make bonfires, each man to what sport and revels his addiction leads him. For, besides these beneficial news, it is the celebration of his nuptial. So much was his pleasure should be proclaimed. All offices° are open, and there is full liberty of feasting from the present hour of five till the bell have told eleven. Heaven bless the isle of Cyprus and our noble general Othello! *Exit.*

SCENE III. *The Cyprian Castle.*

Enter Othello, Desdemona, Cassio, and Attendants.

Othello: Good Michael, look you to the guard to-night.
Let's teach ourselves that honorable stop,
Not to outsport discretion.
Cassio: Iago hath direction what to do;
But not withstanding, with my personal eye
Will I look to't.
Othello: Iago is most honest.
Michael, good night. To-morrow with your earliest
Let me have speech with you.
[To Desdemona.] Come, my dear love.
The purchase made, the fruits are to ensue;
That profit 's yet to come 'tween me and you. —
Good night.
Exit [Othello with Desdemona and Attendants].

Enter Iago.

Cassio: Welcome, Iago. We must to the watch.
Iago: Not this hour, lieutenant; 'tis not yet ten o' th' clock. Our general cast us thus early for the love of his Desdemona; who let us not therefore

281 *on the hip:* At my mercy. 282 *rank garb:* Gross manner. 286 *practicing upon:* Plotting against. SCENE II. 2 *mere perdition:* Complete destruction. 6 *offices:* Kitchens and storerooms. SCENE III. 13 *cast:* Dismissed.

blame. He hath not yet made wanton the night with her, and she is sport for Jove.

Cassio: She's a most exquisite lady.

Iago: And, I'll warrant her, full of game.

Cassio: Indeed, she's a most fresh and delicate creature.

Iago: What an eye she has! Methinks it sounds a parley to provocation.

Cassio: An inviting eye; and yet methinks right modest.

Iago: And when she speaks, is it not an alarum to love?

Cassio: She is indeed perfection.

Iago: Well, happiness to their sheets! Come, lieutenant, I have a stoup° of wine, and here without are a brace of Cyprus gallants that would fain have a measure to the health of black Othello.

Cassio: Not to-night, good Iago. I have very poor and unhappy brains for drinking; I could well wish courtesy would invent some other custom of entertainment.

Iago: O, they are our friends. But one cup! I'll drink for you.

Cassio: I have drunk but one cup to-night, and that was craftily qualified° too; and behold what innovation° it makes here. I am unfortunate in the infirmity and dare not task my weakness with any more.

Iago: What, man! 'Tis a night of revels: the gallants desire it.

Cassio: Where are they?

Iago: Here at the door; I pray you call them in.

Cassio: I'll do't, but it dislikes me. *Exit.*

Iago: If I can fasten but one cup upon him
With that which he hath drunk to-night already,
He'll be as full of quarrel and offense
As my young mistress' dog. Now my sick fool Roderigo,
Whom love hath turned almost the wrong side out,
To Desdemona hath to-night caroused
Potations pottle-deep;° and he's to watch.
Three lads of Cyprus — noble swelling spirits,
That hold their honors in a wary distance,°
The very elements of this warlike isle —
Have I to-night flustered with flowing cups,
And they watch too. Now, 'mongst this flock of drunkards
Am I to put our Cassio in some action
That may offend the isle.

Enter Cassio, Montano, and Gentlemen [; Servants following with wine].

But here they come.
If consequence do but approve my dream,
My boat sails freely, both with wind and stream.

Cassio: 'Fore God, they have given me a rouse already.

Montano: Good faith, a little one; not past a pint, as I am a soldier.

Iago: Some wine, ho!

24 *stoup:* Two-quart tankard. 31 *qualified:* Diluted. 32 *innovation:* Disturbance. 44 *pottle-deep:* Bottoms up. 46 *That . . . distance:* Very sensitive about their honor. 47 *very elements:* True representatives. 54 *rouse:* Bumper.

[Sings.] And let me the canakin clink, clink;
And let me the canakin clink.
A soldier's a man;
A life's but a span,
Why then, let a soldier drink.

Some wine, boys!

Cassio: 'Fore God, an excellent song!

Iago: I learned it in England, where indeed they are most potent in potting. Your Dane, your German, and your swag-bellied Hollander — Drink, ho! — are nothing to your English.

Cassio: Is your Englishman so expert in his drinking?

Iago: Why, he drinks you with facility your Dane dead drunk; he sweats not to overthrow your Almain; he gives your Hollander a vomit ere the next pottle can be filled.

Cassio: To the health of our general!

Montano: I am for it, lieutenant, and I'll do you justice.

Iago: O sweet England!

[Sings.] King Stephen was a worthy peer;
His breeches cost him but a crown;
He held 'em sixpence all too dear,
With that he called the tailor lown.°
He was a wight of high renown,
And thou art but of low degree.
'Tis pride that pulls the country down;
Then take thine auld cloak about thee.

Some wine, ho!

Cassio: 'Fore God, this is a more exquisite song than the other.

Iago: Will you hear't again?

Cassio: No, for I hold him to be unworthy of his place that does those things.° Well, God's above all; and there be souls must be saved, and there be souls must not be saved.

Iago: It's true, good lieutenant.

Cassio: For mine own part — no offense to the general, nor any man of quality — I hope to be saved.

Iago: And so do I too, lieutenant.

Cassio: Ay, but, by your leave, not before me. The lieutenant is to be saved before the ancient. Let's have no more of this; let's to our affairs. — God forgive us our sins! — Gentlemen, let's look to our business. Do not think, gentlemen, I am drunk. This is my ancient; this is my right hand, and this is my left. I am not drunk now. I can stand well enough, and I speak well enough.

All: Excellent well!

Cassio: Why, very well then. You must not think then that I am drunk. *Exit.*

Montano: To th' platform, masters. Come, let's set the watch.

Iago: You see this fellow that is gone before.
He's a soldier fit to stand by Caesar

76 *lown:* Rascal. 84–85 *does . . . things:* I.e., behaves in this fashion.

And give direction; and do but see his vice.
'Tis to his virtue a just equinox,
The one as long as th' other. 'Tis pity of him.
I fear the trust Othello puts him in,
On some odd time of his infirmity,
Will shake this island.

Montano: But is he often thus?

Iago: 'Tis evermore his prologue to his sleep:
He'll watch the horologe a double set
If drink rock not his cradle.

Montano: It were well
The general were put in mind of it.
Perhaps he sees it not, or his good nature
Prizes the virtue that appears in Cassio
And looks not on his evils. Is not this true?

Enter Roderigo.

Iago: [aside to him]: How now, Roderigo?
I pray you after the lieutenant, go! *Exit Roderigo.*

Montano: And 'tis great pity that the noble Moor
Should hazard such a place as his own second
With one of an ingraft infirmity.
It were an honest action to say
So to the Moor.

Iago: Not I, for this fair island!
I do love Cassio well and would do much
To cure him of this evil.
(Within.) Help! help!
But hark! What noise?

Enter Cassio, driving in Roderigo.

Cassio: Zounds, you rogue! you rascal!

Montano: What's the matter, lieutenant?

Cassio: A knave teach me my duty?
I'll beat the knave into a twiggen bottle.

Roderigo: Beat me?

Cassio: Dost thou prate, rogue? *[Strikes him.]*

Montano: Nay, good lieutenant! *[Stays him.]*
I pray you, sir, hold your hand.

Cassio: Let me go, sir,
Or I'll knock you o'er the mazzard.

Montano: Come, come, you're drunk!

Cassio: Drunk?

They fight.

103 *just equinox:* Exact equivalent. 109 *watch . . . set:* Stay awake twice around the clock. 119 *ingraft:* I.e., ingrained. 127 *Twiggen:* Wicker-covered. 130 *mazzard:* Head.

Iago [aside to Roderigo]: Away, I say! Go out and cry a mutiny!

Exit Roderigo.

Nay, good lieutenant. God's will, gentlemen!
Help, ho! — lieutenant — sir — Montano — sir —
Help, masters! — Here's a goodly watch indeed!

A bell rung.

Who's that which rings the bell? Diablo, ho!
The town will rise.° God's will, lieutenant, hold!
You'll be shamed for ever.

Enter Othello and Gentlemen with weapons.

Othello: What is the matter here?
Montano: Zounds, I bleed still. I am hurt to th' death.
He dies!
Othello: Hold for your lives!
Iago: Hold, hold! Lieutenant — sir — Montano — gentlemen!
Have you forgot all sense of place and duty?
Hold! The general speaks to you. Hold, for shame!
Othello: Why, how now, ho? From whence ariseth this?
Are we turned Turks, and to ourselves do that
Which heaven hath forbid the Ottomites?
For Christian shame put by this barbarous brawl!
He that stirs next to carve for° his own rage
Holds his soul light; he dies upon his motion.
Silence that dreadful bell! It frights the isle
From her propriety.° What is the matter, masters?
Honest Iago, that looks dead with grieving,
Speak. Who began this? On thy love, I charge thee.
Iago: I do not know. Friends all, but now, even now,
In quarter,° and in terms like bride and groom
Devesting them for bed; and then, but now —
As if some planet had unwitted men —
Swords out, and tilting one at other's breast
In opposition bloody. I cannot speak
Any beginning to this peevish odds,°
And would in action glorious I had lost
Those legs that brought me to a part of it!
Othello: How comes it, Michael, you are thus forgot?
Cassio: I pray you pardon me; I cannot speak.
Othello: Worthy Montano, you were wont to be civil;
The gravity and stillness of your youth
The world hath noted, and your name is great
In mouths of wisest censure.° What's the matter
That you unlace° your reputation thus
And spend your rich opinion° for the name

137 *rise:* Grow riotous. 149 *carve for:* Indulge. 152 *propriety:* Proper self. 156 *quarter:* Friendliness. 161 *peevish odds:* Childish quarrel. 169 *censure:* Judgment. 170 *unlace:* Undo. 171 *rich opinion:* High reputation.

Of a night-brawler? Give me answer to it.
Montano: Worthy Othello, I am hurt to danger.
Your officer, Iago, can inform you,
While I spare speech, which something now offends° me,
Of all that I do know; nor know I aught
By me that's said or done amiss this night,
Unless self-charity be sometimes a vice,
And to defend ourselves it be a sin
When violence assails us.
Othello: Now, by heaven,
My blood° begins my safer guides to rule,
And passion, having my best judgment collied,°
Assays° to lead the way. If I once stir
Or do but lift this arm, the best of you
Shall sink in my rebuke. Give me to know
How this foul rout began, who set it on;
And he that is approved in° this offense,
Though he had twinned with me, both at a birth,
Shall lose me. What! in a town of war,
Yet wild, the people's hearts brimful of fear,
To manage° private and domestic quarrel?
In night, and on the court and guard of safety?
'Tis monstrous. Iago, who began't?
Montano: If partially affined, or leagued in office,°
Thou dost deliver more or less than truth,
Thou art no soldier.
Iago: Touch me not so near.
I had rather have this tongue cut from my mouth
Than it should do offense to Michael Cassio;
Yet I persuade myself, to speak the truth
Shall nothing wrong him. This it is, general.
Montano and myself being in speech,
There comes a fellow crying out for help,
And Cassio following him with determined sword
To execute° upon him. Sir, this gentleman
Steps in to Cassio and entreats his pause.
Myself the crying fellow did pursue,
Lest by his clamor — as it so fell out —
The town might fall in fright. He, swift of foot,
Outran my purpose; and I returned then rather
For that I heard the clink and fall of swords,
And Cassio high in oath;° which till to-night
I ne'er might say before. When I came back —
For this was brief — I found them close together
At blow and thrust, even as again they were

175 *offends:* Pains. 181 *blood:* Passion. 182 *collied:* Darkened. 183 *Assays:* Tries. 187 *approved in:* proved guilty of. 191 *manage:* Carry on. 194 *partially . . . office:* Prejudiced by comradeship or official relations. 205 *execute:* Work his will. 212 *high in oath:* Cursing.

When you yourself did part them.
More of this matter cannot I report;
But men are men; the best sometimes forget.
Though Cassio did some little wrong to him,
As men in rage strike those that wish them best,
Yet surely Cassio I believe received
From him that fled some strange indignity,
Which patience could not pass.°

Othello: I know, Iago,
Thy honesty and love doth mince this matter,
Making it light to Cassio. Cassio, I love thee;
But never more be officer of mine.

Enter Desdemona, attended.

Look if my gentle love be not raised up!
I'll make thee an example.

Desdemona: What's the matter?

Othello: All's well now, sweeting; come away to bed.
[To Montano.]
Sir, for your hurts, myself will be your surgeon.
Lead him off.

[Montano is led off.]

Iago, look with care about the town
And silence those whom this vile brawl distracted.°
Come, Desdemona; 'tis the soldiers' life
To have their balmy slumbers waked with strife.

Exit [with all but Iago and Cassio].

Iago: What, are you hurt, lieutenant?

Cassio: Ay, past all surgery.

Iago: Marry, God forbid!

Cassio: Reputation, reputation, reputation! O, I have lost my reputation! I have lost the immortal part of myself, and what remains is bestial. My reputation, Iago, my reputation!

Iago: As I am an honest man, I thought you had received some bodily wound. There is more sense in that than in reputation. Reputation is an idle and most false imposition; oft got without merit and lost without deserving. You have lost no reputation at all unless you repute yourself such a loser. What, man! there are ways to recover° the general again. You are but now cast in his mood° — a punishment more in policy than in malice, even so as one would beat his offenseless dog to affright an imperious lion. Sue to him again, and he's yours.

Cassio: I will rather sue to be despised than to deceive so good a commander with so slight, so drunken, and so indiscreet an officer. Drunk! and speak parrot!° and squabble! swagger! swear! and discourse fustian°

224 *pass:* Pass over, ignore. 233 *distracted:* Excited. 246 *recover:* Regain favor with. 247 *cast in his mood:* Dismissed because of his anger. 252 *parrot:* Meaningless phrases; *fustian:* Bombastic nonsense.

with one's own shadow! O thou invisible spirit of wine, if thou hast no name to be known by, let us call thee devil!

Iago: What was he that you followed with your sword? What had he done to you?

Cassio: I know not.

Iago: Is't possible?

Cassio: I remember a mass of things, but nothing distinctly; a quarrel, but nothing wherefore. O God, that men should put an enemy in their mouths to steal away their brains! that we should with joy, pleasance, revel, and applause° transform ourselves into beasts!

Iago: Why, but you are now well enough. How came you thus recovered?

Cassio: It hath pleased the devil drunkenness to give place to the devil wrath. One unperfectness shows me another, to make me frankly despise myself.

Iago: Come, you are too severe a moraler. As the time, the place, and the condition of this country stands, I could heartily wish this had not so befall'n; but since it is as it is, mend it for your own good.

Cassio: I will ask him for my place again: he shall tell me I am a drunkard! Had I as many mouths as Hydra,° such an answer would stop them all. To be now a sensible man, by and by a fool, and presently a beast! O strange! Every inordinate cup is unblest, and the ingredient° is a devil.

Iago: Come, come, good wine is a good familiar creature if it be well used. Exclaim no more against it. And, good lieutenant, I think you think I love you.

Cassio: I have well approved° it, sir. I drunk!

Iago: You or any man living may be drunk at some time, man. I'll tell you what you shall do. Our general's wife is now the general. I may say so in this respect, for that he hath devoted and given up himself to the contemplation, mark, and denotement of her parts and graces. Confess yourself freely to her; importune her help to put you in your place again. She is of so free,° so kind, so apt, so blessed a disposition she holds it a vice in her goodness not to do more than she is requested. This broken joint between you and her husband entreat her to splinter;° and my fortunes against any lay° worth naming, this crack of your love shall grow stronger than it was before.

Cassio: You advise me well.

Iago: I protest, in the sincerity of love and honest kindness.

Cassio: I think it freely; and betimes in the morning will I beseech the virtuous Desdemona to undertake for me. I am desperate of my fortunes if they check me here.

Iago: You are in the right. Good night, lieutenant; I must to the watch.

Cassio: Good night, honest Iago. *Exit Cassio.*

Iago: And what's he then that says I play the villain,
When this advice is free I give and honest,
Probal° to thinking, and indeed the course

262 *applause:* Desire to please. 271 *Hydra:* Monster with many heads. 273 *ingredient:* Contents. 277 *approved:* Proved. 283 *free:* Bounteous. 285 *splinter:* Bind up with splints. 286 *lay:* Wager. 297 *Probal:* Probable.

To win the Moor again? For 'tis most easy
Th' inclining Desdemona to subdue°
In any honest suit; she's framed as fruitful
As the free elements. And then for her
To win the Moor — were't to renounce his baptism,
All seals and symbols of redeemèd sin —
His soul is so enfettered to her love
That she may make, unmake, do what she list,
Even as her appetite shall play the god
With his weak function. How am I then a villain
To counsel Cassio to this parallel° course,
Directly to his good? Divinity° of hell!
When devils will the blackest sins put on,°
They do suggest at first with heavenly shows,
As I do now. For whiles this honest fool
Plies Desdemona to repair his fortunes,
And she for him pleads strongly to the Moor,
I'll pour this pestilence into his ear,
That she repeals him° for her body's lust;
And by how much she strives to do him good,
She shall undo her credit with the Moor.
So will I turn her virtue into pitch,
And out of her own goodness make the net
That shall enmesh them all.

Enter Roderigo.

How, now, Roderigo?

Roderigo: I do follow here in the chase, not like a hound that hunts, but one that fills up the cry.° My money is almost spent; I have been to-night exceedingly well cudgelled; and I think the issue will be — I shall have so much experience for my pains; and so, with no money at all, and a little more wit, return again to Venice.

Iago: How poor are they that have not patience!
What wound did ever heal but by degrees?
Thou know'st we work by wit, and not by witchcraft;
And wit depends on dilatory time.
Does't not go well? Cassio hath beaten thee,
And thou by that small hurt hast cashiered Cassio.°
Though other things grow fair against the sun,
Yet fruits that blossom first will first be ripe.
Content thyself awhile. By the mass, 'tis morning!
Pleasure and action make the hours seem short.
Retire thee; go where thou art billeted.
Away, I say! Thou shalt know more hereafter.
Nay, get thee gone! *Exit Roderigo.*

299 *subdue:* Persuade. 308 *parallel:* Corresponding. 309 *Divinity:* Theology. 310 *put on:* Incite. 316 *repeals him:* Seeks his recall. 323 *cry:* Pack. 332 *cashiered Cassio:* Maneuvered Cassio's discharge.

Two things are to be done:
My wife must move for Cassio to her mistress;
I'll set her on;
Myself the while to draw the Moor apart
And bring him jump° when he may Cassio find
Soliciting his wife. Ay, that's the way!
Dull not device by coldness and delay. *Exit.*

ACT III

SCENE I. *Before the chamber of Othello and Desdemona.*

Enter Cassio, with Musicians and the Clown.

Cassio: Masters, play here, I will content° your pains:
Something that's brief; and bid "Good morrow, general."

[They play]

Clown: Why, masters, ha' your instruments been in Naples,° that they speak i' th' nose thus?
Musician: How, sir, how?
Clown: Are these, I pray you, called wind instruments?
Musician: Ay, marry, are they, sir.
Clown: O, thereby hangs a tail.
Musician: Whereby hangs a tale, sir?
Clown: Marry, sir, by many a wind instrument that I know. But, masters, here's money for you; and the general so likes your music that he desires you, for love's sake, to make no more noise with it.
Musician: Well, sir, we will not.
Clown: If you have any music that may not be heard, to't again: but, as they say, to hear music the general does not greatly care.
Musician: We have none such, sir.
Clown: Then put up your pipes in your bag, for I'll away. Go, vanish into air, away! *Exit Musician [with his fellows].*
Cassio: Dost thou hear, my honest friend?
Clown: No, I hear not your honest friend. I hear you.
Cassio: Prithee keep up thy quillets.° There's a poor piece of gold for thee. If the gentlewoman that attends the general's wife be stirring, tell her there's one Cassio entreats her a little favor of speech. Wilt thou do this?
Clown: She is stirring sir. If she will stir hither, I shall seem to notify unto her.
Cassio: [Do, good my friend.] *Exit Clown.*

Enter Iago.

343 *jump:* At the exact moment. ACT III. SCENE I. 1 *content:* Reward. 3 *Naples:* (Notorious for its association with venereal disease). 21 *quillets:* Quips.

In happy time,° Iago.

Iago: You have not been abed then?

Cassio: Why, no; the day had broke
Before we parted. I have made bold, Iago,
To send in to your wife: my suit to her
Is that she will to virtuous Desdemona
Procure me some access.

Iago: I'll send her to you presently;
And I'll devise a mean to draw the Moor
Out of the way, that your converse and business
May be more free.

Cassio: I humbly thank you for't. *Exit [Iago].*
I never knew
A Florentine° more kind and honest.

Enter Emilia.

Emilia: Good morrow, good lieutenant. I am sorry
For your displeasure: but all will sure be well.
The general and his wife are talking of it,
And she speaks for you stoutly. The Moor replied
That he you hurt is of great fame in Cyprus
And great affinity,° and that in wholesome wisdom
He might not but refuse you; but he protests he loves you,
And needs no other suitor but his likings
[To take the safest occasion° by the front°]
To bring you in again.

Cassio: Yet I beseech you,
If you think fit, or that it may be done,
Give me advantage of some brief discourse
With Desdemona alone.

Emilia: Pray you come in.
I will bestow you where you shall have time
To speak your bosom° freely.

Cassio: I am much bound to you. *Exeunt.*

SCENE II. *The castle.*

Enter Othello, Iago, and Gentlemen.

Othello: These letters give, Iago, to the pilot
And by him do my duties to the Senate.
That done, I will be walking on the works;°
Repair there to me.

Iago: Well, my good lord, I'll do't.

Othello: This fortification, gentlemen, shall we see't?

Gentlemen: We'll wait upon your lordship. *Exeunt.*

27 *In happy time:* Well met. 38 *Florentine:* I.e., even a Florentine (like Cassio; Iago was a Venetian). 44 *affinity:* Family connections. 47 *occasion:* Opportunity; *front:* Forelock. 53 *your bosom:* Your inmost thoughts. SCENE II. 3 *works:* Fortifications.

Scene III. *The castle grounds.*

Enter Desdemona, Cassio, and Emilia.

Desdemona: Be thou assured, good Cassio, I will do
All my abilities in thy behalf.
Emilia: Good madam, do. I warrant it grieves my husband
As if the cause were his.
Desdemona: O, that's an honest fellow. Do not doubt, Cassio,
But I will have my lord and you again
As friendly as you were.
Cassio: Bounteous madam,
Whatever shall become of Michael Cassio,
He's never anything but your true servant.
Desdemona: I know't; I thank you. You do love my lord;
You have known him long; and be you well assured
He shall in strangeness° stand no farther off
Than in a politic distance.°
Cassio: Ay, but, lady,
That policy may either last so long,
Or feed upon such nice and waterish diet,°
Or breed itself so out of circumstance,
That, I being absent, and my place supplied,
My general will forget my love and service.
Desdemona: Do not doubt° that; before Emilia here
I give thee warrant of thy place. Assure thee,
If I do vow a friendship, I'll perform it
To the last article. My lord shall never rest;
I'll watch him tame° and talk him out of patience;
His bed shall seem a school, his board a shrift;°
I'll intermingle everything he does
With Cassio's suit. Therefore be merry, Cassio,
For thy solicitor shall rather die
Than give thy cause away.

Enter Othello and Iago [at a distance].

Emilia: Madam, here comes my lord.
Cassio: Madam, I'll take my leave.
Desdemona: Why, stay, and hear me speak.
Cassio: Madam, not now: I am very ill at ease,
Unfit for mine own purposes.
Desdemona: Well, do your discretion. *Exit Cassio.*
Iago: Ha! I like not that.
Othello: What dost thou say?
Iago: Nothing, my lord; or if — I know not what.
Othello: Was not that Cassio parted from my wife?
Iago: Cassio, my lord? No, sure, I cannot think it,

Scene III. 12 *strangeness:* Aloofness. 13 *Than . . . distance:* Than wise policy requires. 15 *Or . . . diet:* Or be continued for such slight reasons. 19 *doubt:* Fear. 23 *watch him tame:* Keep him awake until he gives in. 24 *shrift:* Confessional.

That he would steal away so guilty-like,
Seeing your coming.

Othello: I do believe 'twas he.

Desdemona: How now, my lord?
I have been talking with a suitor here,
A man that languishes in your displeasure.

Othello: Who is't you mean?

Desdemona: Why, your lieutenant, Cassio. Good my lord,
If I have any grace or power to move you,
His present° reconciliation take;
For if he be not one that truly loves you,
That errs in ignorance, and not in cunning,
I have no judgment in an honest face,
I prithee call him back.

Othello: Went he hence now?

Desdemona: Yes, faith; so humbled
That he hath left part of his grief with me
To suffer with him. Good love, call him back.

Othello: Now now, sweet Desdemon; some other time.

Desdemona: But shall't be shortly?

Othello: The sooner, sweet, for you.

Desdemona: Shall't be to-night at supper?

Othello: No, not to-night.

Desdemona: To-morrow dinner then?

Othello: I shall not dine at home;
I meet the captains at the citadel.

Desdemona: Why then, to-morrow night, or Tuesday morn,
On Tuesday noon or night, or Wednesday morn.
I prithee name the time, but let it not
Exceed three days. I' faith, he's penitent;
And yet his trespass, in our common reason
(Save that, they say, the wars must make examples
Out of their best), is not almost° a fault
T' incur a private check.° When shall he come?
Tell me, Othello. I wonder in my soul
What you could ask me that I should deny
Or stand so mamm'ring on.° What? Michael Cassio,
That came a-wooing with you, and so many a time,
When I have spoke of you dispraisingly,
Hath ta'en your part — to have so much to do
To bring him in? By'r Lady, I could do much —

Othello: Prithee no more. Let him come when he will!
I will deny thee nothing.

Desdemona: Why, this is not a boon;
'Tis as I should entreat you wear your gloves,
Or feed on nourishing dishes, or keep you warm,

47 *present:* Immediate. 66 *not almost:* Hardly. 67 *a private check:* Even a private reprimand.
70 *mamm'ring on:* Hesitating about.

Or sue to you to do a peculiar profit
To your own person. Nay, when I have a suit
Wherein I mean to touch your love indeed,
It shall be full of poise and difficult weight,
And fearful° to be granted.

Othello: I will deny thee nothing!
Whereon I do beseech thee grant me this,
To leave me but a little to myself.

Desdemona: Shall I deny you? No. Farewell, my lord.

Othello: Farewell, my Desdemon: I'll come to thee straight.

Desdemona: Emilia, come. — Be as your fancies teach you;
Whate'er you be, I am obedient. *Exit [with Emilia].*

Othello: Excellent wretch!° Perdition catch my soul
But I do love thee! and when I love thee not,
Chaos is come again.

Iago: My noble lord —

Othello: What dost thou say, Iago?

Iago: Did Michael Cassio, when you wooed my lady,
Know of your love?

Othello: He did, from first to last. Why dost thou ask?

Iago: But for a satisfaction of my thought;
No further harm.

Othello: Why of thy thought, Iago?

Iago: I did not think he had been acquainted with her.

Othello: O, yes, and went between us° very oft.

Iago: Indeed?

Othello: Indeed? Ay, indeed! Discern'st thou aught in that?
Is he not honest?

Iago: Honest, my lord?

Othello: Honest. Ay, honest.

Iago: My lord, for aught I know.

Othello: What dost thou think?

Iago: Think, my lord?

Othello: Think, my lord?
By heaven, he echoes me,
As if there were some monster in his thought
Too hideous to be shown. Thou dost mean something:
I heard thee say even now, thou lik'st not that,
When Cassio left my wife. What didst not like?
And when I told thee he was of my counsel
In my whole course of wooing, thou cried'st "Indeed?"
And didst contract and purse thy brow together,
As if thou then hadst shut up in thy brain
Some horrible conceit.° If thou dost love me,
Show me thy thought

Iago: My lord, you know I love you.

83 *fearful:* Dangerous. 90 *wretch:* (A term of endearment). 100 *went . . . us:* (I.e., as messenger). 115 *conceit:* Fancy.

Othello: I think thou dost;
And, for I know thou'rt full of love and honesty
And weigh'st thy words before thou giv'st them breath,
Therefore these stops of thine fright me the more;
For such things in a false disloyal knave
Are tricks of custom; but in a man that's just
They are close dilations, working from the heart
That passion cannot rule.°
Iago: For Michael Cassio,
I dare be sworn I think that he is honest.
Othello: I think so too.
Iago: Men should be what they seem;
Or those that be not, would they might seem none!°
Othello: Certain, men should be what they seem.
Iago: Why then, I think Cassio's an honest man.
Othello: Nay, yet there's more in this.
I prithee speak to me as to thy thinkings,
As thou dost ruminate, and give thy worst of thoughts
The worst of words.
Iago: Good my lord, pardon me:
Though I am bound to every act of duty,
I am not bound to that all slaves are free to.°
Utter my thoughts? Why, say they are vile and false,
As where's that palace whereinto foul things
Sometimes intrude not? Who has a breast so pure
But some uncleanly apprehensions
Keep leets and law days,° and in Sessions sit
With meditations lawful?
Othello: Thou dost conspire against thy friend, Iago,
If thou but think'st him wronged, and mak'st his ear
A stranger to thy thoughts.
Iago: I do beseech you—
Though I perchance am vicious in my guess
(As I confess it is my nature's plague
To spy into abuses, and oft my jealousy°
Shapes faults that are not), that your wisdom yet
From one that so imperfectly conjects°
Would take no notice, nor build yourself a trouble
Out of his scattering and unsure observance.
It were not for your quiet nor your good,
Nor for my manhood, honesty, and wisdom,
To let you know my thoughts.

123–24 *close dilations . . . rule:* Secret emotions which well up in spite of restraint. 127 *seem none:* I.e., not pretend to be men when they are really monsters. 135 *bound . . . free to:* Bound to tell that which even slaves are allowed to keep to themselves. 140 *leets and law days:* Sittings of the courts. 147 *jealousy:* Suspicion. 149 *conjects:* Conjectures.

Othello: What dost thou mean?
Iago: Good name in man and woman, dear my lord,
Is the immediate° jewel of their souls.
Who steals my purse steals trash; 'tis something, nothing;
'Twas mine, 'tis his, and has been slave to thousands;
But he that filches from me my good name
Robs me of that which not enriches him
And makes me poor indeed.
Othello: By heaven, I'll know thy thoughts!
Iago: You cannot, if my heart were in your hand;
Nor shall not whilst 'tis in my custody.
Othello: Ha!
Iago: O, beware, my lord, of jealousy!
It is the green-eyed monster, which doth mock°
The meat it feeds on. That cuckold lives in bliss
Who, certain of his fate, loves not his wronger;
But O, what damnèd minutes tells he o'er
Who dotes, yet doubts — suspects, yet strongly loves!
Othello: O misery!
Iago: Poor and content is rich, and rich enough;
But riches fineless° is as poor as winter
To him that ever fears he shall be poor.
Good God, the souls of all my tribe defend
From jealousy!
Othello: Why, why is this?
Think'st thou I'ld make a life of jealousy,
To follow still the changes of the moon
With fresh suspicions? No! To be once in doubt
Is once to be resolved. Exchange me for a goat
When I shall turn the business of my soul
To such exsufflicate and blown° surmises,
Matching this inference. 'Tis not to make me jealous
To say my wife is fair, feeds well, loves company,
Is free of speech, sings, plays, and dances;
Where virtue is, these are more virtuous.
Nor from mine own weak merits will I draw
The smallest fear or doubt of her revolt,°
For she had eyes, and chose me. No, Iago;
I'll see before I doubt; when I doubt, prove;
And on the proof there is no more but this —
Away at once with love or jealousy!
Iago: I am glad of this; for now I shall have reason
To show the love and duty that I bear you
With franker spirit. Therefore, as I am bound,

156 *immediate:* Nearest the heart. 166 *mock:* Play with, like a cat with a mouse. 173 *fineless:* Unlimited. 182 *exsufflicate and blown:* Spat out and flyblown. 188 *revolt:* Unfaithfulness.

Receive it from me. I speak not yet of proof.
Look to your wife; observe her well with Cassio;
Wear your eyes thus, not jealous nor secure:°
I would not have your free and noble nature,
Out of self-bounty,° be abused. Look to't.
I know our country disposition well:
In Venice they do let God see the pranks
They dare not show their husbands; their best conscience
Is not to leave't undone, but keep't unknown.

Othello: Dost thou say so?

Iago: She did deceive her father, marrying you;
And when she seemed to shake and fear your looks,
She loved them most.

Othello: And so she did.

Iago: Why, go to then!
She that, so young, could give out such a seeming
To seel° her father's eyes up close as oak°—
He thought 'twas witchcraft — but I am much to blame.
I humbly do beseech you of your pardon
For too much loving you.

Othello: I am bound to thee for ever.

Iago: I see this hath a little dashed your spirits.

Othello: Not a jot, not a jot.

Iago: I' faith, I fear it has.
I hope you will consider what is spoke
Comes from my love. But I do see y' are moved.
I am to pray you not to strain my speech
To grosser issues° nor to larger reach
Than to suspicion.

Othello: I will not.

Iago: Should you do so, my lord,
My speech should fall into such vile success°
As my thoughts aim not at. Cassio 's my worthy friend —
My lord, I see y' are moved.

Othello: No, not much moved:
I do not think but Desdemona 's honest.°

Iago: Long live she so! and long live you to think so!

Othello: And yet, how nature erring from itself —

Iago: Ay, there's the point! as (to be bold with you)
Not to affect many proposèd matches
Of her own clime, complexion, and degree,
Whereto we see in all things nature tends —
Foh! one may smell in such a will most rank,
Foul disproportions, thoughts unnatural —
But pardon me — I do not in position°

198 *secure:* Overconfident. 200 *self-bounty:* Natural goodness. 210 *seel:* Close; *oak:* Oak grain. 219 *To grosser issues:* To mean something more monstrous. 222 *vile success:* Evil outcome. 225 *honest:* Chaste. 234 *position:* Definite assertion.

Distinctly speak of her; though I may fear
Her will, recoiling° to her better judgment,
May fall to match° you with her country forms,
And happily° repent.

Othello: Farewell, farewell!
If more thou dost perceive, let me know more.
Set on thy wife to observe. Leave me, Iago.

Iago: My lord, I take my leave. *[Going.]*

Othello: Why did I marry? This honest creature doubtless
Sees and knows more, much more, than he unfolds.

Iago [returns]: My lord, I would I might entreat your honor
To scan this thing no further: leave it to time.
Although 'tis fit that Cassio have his place,
For sure he fills it up with great ability,
Yet, if you please to hold him off a while,
You shall by that perceive him and his means.
Note if your lady strain his entertainment°
With any strong or vehement importunity;
Much will be seen in that. In the mean time
Let me be thought too busy° in my fears
(As worthy cause I have to fear I am)
And hold her free,° I do beseech your honor.

Othello: Fear not my government.°

Iago: I once more take my leave. *Exit.*

Othello: This fellow 's of exceeding honesty,
And knows all qualities,° with a learned spirit
Of° human dealings. If I do prove her haggard,°
Though that her jesses° were my dear heartstrings,
I'd whistle her off and let her down the wind
To prey at fortune.° Haply, for I am black
And have not those soft parts of conversation°
That chamberers° have, or for I am declined
Into the vale of years — yet that's not much —
She's gone. I am abused, and my relief
Must be to loathe her. O curse of marriage,
That we can call these delicate creatures ours,
And not their appetites! I had rather be a toad
And live upon the vapor of a dungeon
Than keep a corner in the thing I love
For others' uses. Yet 'tis the plague of great ones;°
Prerogatived° are they less than the base.
'Tis destiny unshunnable, like death.

236 *recoiling:* Reverting. 237 *fall to match:* Happen to compare. 238 *happily:* Haply, perhaps. 250 *strain his entertainment:* Urge his recall. 253 *busy:* Meddlesome. 255 *hold her free:* Consider her guiltless. 256 *government:* Self-control. 259 *qualities:* Natures. 259–60 *learned spirit Of:* Mind informed about. 260 *haggard:* A wild hawk. 261 *jesses:* Thongs for controlling a hawk. 262–63 *whistle . . . fortune:* Turn her out and let her take care of herself. 264 *soft . . . conversation:* Ingratiating manners. 265 *chamberers:* Courtiers. 273 *great ones:* Prominent men. 274 *Prerogatived:* Privileged.

Even then this forkèd plague° is fated to us
When we do quicken.° Look where she comes.

Enter Desdemona and Emilia.

If she be false, O, then heaven mocks itself!
I'll not believe't.
Desdemona: How now, my dear Othello?
Your dinner, and the generous° islanders
By you invited, do attend your presence.
Othello: I am to blame.
Desdemona: Why do you speak so faintly?
Are you not well?
Othello: I have a pain upon my forehead, here.
Desdemona: Faith, that's with watching;° 'twill away again.
Let me but bind it hard, within this hour
It will be well.
Othello: Your napkin° is too little;

[He pushes the handkerchief from him, and it falls unnoticed.]

Let it° alone. Come, I'll go in with you.
Desdemona: I am very sorry that you are not well. *Exit [with Othello.]*
Emilia: I am glad I have found this napkin;
This was her first remembrance from the Moor,
My wayward husband hath a hundred times
Wooed me to steal it; but she so loves the token
(For he conjured her she should ever keep it)
That she reserves it evermore about her
To kiss and talk to. I'll have the work ta'en out°
And give't Iago.
What he will do with it heaven knows, not I;
I nothing but to please his fantasy.°

Enter Iago.

Iago: How now? What do you here alone?
Emilia: Do not you chide; I have a thing for you.
Iago: A thing for me? It is a common thing —
Emilia: Ha?
Iago: To have a foolish wife.
Emilia: O, is that all? What will you give me now
For that same handkerchief?
Iago: What handkerchief?
Emilia: What handkerchief!
Why, that the Moor first gave to Desdemona;
That which so often you did bid me steal.
Iago: Hast stol'n it from her?
Emilia: No, faith; she let it drop by negligence,

276 *forkèd plague:* I.e. horns of a cuckold. 277 *do quicken:* Are born. 280 *generous:* Noble. 285 *watching:* Working late. 287 *napkin:* Handkerchief. 288 *it:* I.e., his forehead. 296 *work ta'en out:* Pattern copied. 299 *fantasy:* Whim.

And to th' advantage,° I, being here, took't up.
Look, here it is.

Iago: A good wench! Give it me.

Emilia: What will you do with't, that you have been so earnest
To have me filch it?

Iago: Why, what is that to you?

[Snatches it.]

Emilia: If it be not for some purpose of import,°
Give't me again. Poor lady, she'll run mad
When she shall lack it.

Iago: Be not acknown on't;° I have use for it.
Go, leave me. *Exit Emilia.*
I will in Cassio's lodgings lose this napkin
And let him find it. Trifles light as air
Are to the jealous confirmations strong
As proofs of holy writ. This may do something.
The Moor already changes with my poison:
Dangerous conceits° are in their natures poisons,
Which at the first are scarce found to distaste,
But with a little act upon the blood
Burn like the mines of sulphur.

Enter Othello.

I did say so.
Look where he comes! Not poppy nor mandragora,°
Nor all the drowsy syrups of the world,
Shall ever med'cine thee to that sweet sleep
Which thou owedst yesterday.

Othello: Ha! ha! false to me?

Iago: Why, how now, general? No more of that!

Othello: Avaunt! be gone! Thou hast set me on the rack.
I swear 'tis better to be much abused
Than but to know't a little.

Iago: How now, my lord?

Othello: What sense had I of her stol'n hours of lust?
I saw't not, thought it not, it harmed not me;
I slept the next night well, fed well, was free° and merry;
I found not Cassio's kisses on her lips.
He that is robbed, not wanting° what is stol'n,
Let him not know't, and he's not robbed at all.

Iago: I am sorry to hear this.

Othello: I had been happy if the general camp,
Pioneers° and all, had tasted her sweet body,
So I had nothing known. O, now for ever

312 *to th' advantage:* Opportunely. 316 *import:* Importance. 319 *Be . . . on't:* Do not acknowledge it. 326 *conceits:* Ideas. 330 *mandragora:* A narcotic. 340 *free:* Carefree. 342 *wanting:* Missing. 346 *Pioneers:* Sappers, laborers.

Farewell the tranquil mind! farewell content!
Farewell the plumèd troop, and the big° wars
That make ambition virtue! O, farewell!
Farewell the neighing steed and the shrill trump,
The spirit-stirring drum, th' ear-piercing fife,
The royal banner, and all quality,
Pride, pomp, and circumstance° of glorious war!
And O you mortal engines° whose rude throats
Th' immortal Jove's dread clamors counterfeit,°
Farewell! Othello's occupation 's gone!

Iago: Is't possible, my lord?

Othello: Villain, be sure thou prove my love a whore!
Be sure of it; give me the ocular proof;
Or, by the worth of mine eternal soul,
Thou hadst been better have been born a dog
Than answer my waked wrath!

Iago: Is't come to this?

Othello: Make me to see't; or at the least so prove it
That the probation° bear no hinge nor loop
To hang a doubt on — or woe upon thy life!

Iago: My noble lord —

Othello: If thou dost slander her and torture me,
Never pray more; abandon all remorse;
On horror's head horrors accumulate;
Do deeds to make heaven weep, all earth amazed;
For nothing canst thou to damnation add
Greater than that.

Iago: O grace! O heaven forgive me!
Are you a man? Have you a soul or sense? —
God b' wi' you! take mine office. O wretched fool,
That liv'st to make thine honesty a vice!
O monstrous world! Take note, take note, O world,
To be direct and honest is not safe.
I thank you for this profit;° and from hence
I'll love no friend, sith love breeds such offense.

Othello: Nay, stay. Thou shouldst be honest.

Iago: I should be wise; for honesty 's a fool
And loses that it works for.

Othello: By the world,
I think my wife be honest, and think she is not;
I think that thou art just, and think thou art not.
I'll have some proof. Her name, that was as fresh
As Dian's visage, is now begrimed and black
As mine own face. If there be cords, or knives,

349 *big:* Stately. 354 *circumstance:* Pageantry. 355 *mortal engines:* Deadly artillery. 356 *counterfeit:* Imitate. 365 *probation:* Proof. 379 *profit:* Profitable lesson.

Poison, or fire, or suffocating streams,
I'll not endure it. Would I were satisfied!°

Iago: I see, sir, you are eaten up with passion:
I do repent me that I put it to you.
You would be satisfied?

Othello: Would? Nay, I will.

Iago: And may; but how? how satisfied, my lord?
Would you, the supervisor,° grossly gape on?
Behold her topped?

Othello: Death and damnation! O!

Iago: It were a tedious difficulty, I think,
To bring them to that prospect. Damn them then,
If ever mortal eyes do see them bolster°
More than their own! What then? How then?
What shall I say? Where's satisfaction?
It is impossible you should see this,
Were they as prime° as goats, as hot as monkeys,
As salt° as wolves in pride,° and fools as gross
As ignorance made drunk. But yet, I say,
If imputation and strong circumstances
Which lead directly to the door of truth
Will give you satisfaction, you may have't.

Othello: Give me a living reason she's disloyal.

Iago: I do not like the office.
But sith I am ent'red in this cause so far,
Pricked to't by foolish honesty and love,
I will go on. I lay with Cassio lately,
And being troubled with a raging tooth,
I could not sleep.
There are a kind of men so loose of soul
That in their sleeps will mutter their affairs.
One of this kind is Cassio.
In sleep I heard him say, "Sweet Desdemona,
Let us be wary, let us hide our loves!"
And then, sir, would he gripe and wring my hand,
Cry "O sweet creature!" and then kiss me hard,
As if he plucked up kisses by the roots
That grew upon my lips; then laid his leg
Over my thigh, and sighed, and kissed, and then
Cried "Cursèd fate that gave thee to the Moor!"

Othello: O monstrous! monstrous!

Iago: Nay, this was but his dream.

Othello: But this denoted a foregone conclusion:°
'Tis a shrewd doubt,° though it be but a dream.

390 *satisfied:* Completely informed. 395 *supervisor:* Spectator. 399 *bolster:* Lie together. 403 *prime:* Lustful. 404 *salt:* Lecherous; *pride:* Heat. 428 *foregone conclusion:* Previous experience. 429 *a shrewd doubt:* Cursedly suspicious.

Iago: And this may help to thicken other proofs
That do demonstrate thinly.
Othello: I'll tear her all to pieces!
Iago: Nay, but be wise. Yet we see nothing done;
She may be honest yet. Tell me but this—
Have you not sometimes seen a handkerchief
Spotted with strawberries in your wife's hand?
Othello: I gave her such a one; 'twas my first gift.
Iago: I know not that; but such a handkerchief—
I am sure it was your wife's—did I to-day
See Cassio wipe his beard with.
Othello: If it be that—
Iago: If it be that, or any that was hers,
It speaks against her with the other proofs.
Othello: O, that the slave had forty thousand lives!
One is too poor, too weak for my revenge.
Now do I see 'tis true. Look here, Iago:
All my fond love thus do I blow to heaven.
'Tis gone.
Arise, black vengeance, from the hollow hell!
Yield up, O love, thy crown and hearted throne
To tyrannous hate! Swell, bosom, with thy fraught,°
For 'tis of aspics'° tongues!
Iago: Yet be content.
Othello: O, blood, blood, blood!
Iago: Patience, I say. Your mind perhaps may change.
Othello: Never, Iago. Like to the Pontic sea,°
Whose icy current and compulsive course
Ne'er feels retiring ebb, but keeps due on
To the Propontic and the Hellespont,
Even so my bloody thoughts, with violent pace,
Shall ne'er look back, ne'er ebb to humble love,
Till that a capable° and wide revenge
Swallow them up.
(He kneels.) Now, by yond marble heaven,
In the due reverence of a sacred vow
I here engage my words.
Iago: Do not rise yet.
(Iago kneels.)
Witness, you ever-burning lights above,
You elements that clip° us round about,
Witness that here Iago doth give up
The execution° of his wit,° hands, heart
To wronged Othello's service! Let him command,

449 *fraught:* Burden. 450 *aspics:* Deadly poisonous snakes. 453 *Pontic sea:* Black Sea. 459 *capable:* All-embracing. 464 *clip:* Encompass. 466 *execution:* Activities; *wit:* Mind.

And to obey shall be in me remorse,°
What bloody business ever.

[They rise.]

Othello: I greet thy love,
Not with vain thanks but with acceptance bounteous,
And will upon the instant put thee to't.
Within these three days let me hear thee say
That Cassio's not alive.
Iago: My friend is dead; 'tis done at your request.
But let her live.
Othello: Damn her, lewd minx! O, damn her! damn her!
Come, go with me apart. I will withdraw
To furnish me with some swift means of death
For the fair devil. Now art thou my lieutenant.
Iago: I am your own forever. *Exeunt.*

SCENE IV. *The environs of the castle.*

Enter Desdemona, Emilia, and Clown.

Desdemona: Do you know, sirrah, where Lieutenant Cassio lies?
Clown: I dare not say he lies° anywhere.
Desdemona: Why, man?
Clown: He's a soldier, and for me to say a soldier lies is stabbing.
Desdemona: Go to. Where lodges he?
Clown: To tell you where he lodges is to tell you where I lie.
Desdemona: Can anything be made of this?
Clown: I know not where he lodges; and for me to devise a lodging, and say he lies here or he lies there, were to lie in mine own throat.
Desdemona: Can you enquire him out, and be edified by report?
Clown: I will catechize the world for him; that is, make questions, and by them answer.
Desdemona: Seek him, bid him come hither. Tell him I have moved° my lord on his behalf and hope all will be well.
Clown: To do this is within the compass of man's wit, and therefore I'll attempt the doing of it. *Exit.*
Desdemona: Where should I lose that handkerchief, Emilia?
Emilia: I know not, madam.
Desdemona: Believe me, I had rather have lost my purse
Full of crusadoes;° and but my noble Moor
Is true of mind, and made of no such baseness
As jealous creatures are, it were enough
To put him to ill thinking.
Emilia: Is he not jealous?
Desdemona: Who? he? I think the sun where he was born
Drew all such humors° from him.

468 *remorse:* Pity. SCENE IV. 2 *lies:* Lives, lodges. 13 *moved:* Made proposals. 20 *crusadoes:* Portuguese gold coins. 25 *humors:* Inclinations.

Enter Othello.

Emilia: Look where he comes.
Desdemona: I will not leave him now till Cassio
Be called to him—How is't with you, my lord?
Othello: Well, my good lady. *[Aside.]* O, hardness to dissemble!—
How do you, Desdemona?
Desdemona: Well, my good lord.
Othello: Give me your hand. This hand is moist, my lady.
Desdemona: It yet hath felt no age nor known no sorrow.
Othello: This argues fruitfulness and liberal heart.
Hot, hot, and moist. This hand of yours requires
A sequester° from liberty, fasting and prayer,
Much castigation, exercise devout;
For here's a young and sweating devil here
That commonly rebels. 'Tis a good hand,
A frank one.
Desdemona: You may, indeed, say so;
For 'twas that hand that gave away my heart.
Othello: A liberal hand! The hearts of old gave hands;
But our new heraldry° is hands, not hearts.
Desdemona: I cannot speak of this. Come now, your promise!
Othello: What promise, chuck?
Desdemona: I have sent to bid Cassio come speak with you.
Othello: I have a salt and sorry rheum° offends me.
Lend me thy handkerchief.
Desdemona: Here, my lord.
Othello: That which I gave you.
Desdemona: I have it not about me.
Othello: Not?
Desdemona: No, faith, my lord.
Othello: That's a fault.
That handkerchief
Did an Egyptian° to my mother give.
She was a charmer,° and could almost read
The thoughts of people. She told her, while she kept it,
'Twould make her amiable° and subdue my father
Entirely to her love; but if she lost it
Or made a gift of it, my father's eye
Should hold her loathèd, and his spirits should hunt
After new fancies. She, dying, gave it me,
And bid me, when my fate would have me wive;
To give it her. I did so; and take heed on't;
Make it a darling like your precious eye.
To lose't or give't away were such perdition°
As nothing else could match.

34 *sequester:* Removal. 42 *heraldry:* Heraldic symbolism. 46 *salt . . . rheum:* Distressing head cold. 51 *Egyptian:* Gypsy. 52 *charmer:* Sorceress. 54 *amiable:* Lovable. 62 *perdition:* Disaster.

Desdemona: Is't possible?
Othello: 'Tis true. There's magic in the web of it.
A sibyl that had numb'red in the world
The sun to course two hundred compasses,°
In her prophetic fury sewed the work;
The worms were hallowed that did breed the silk;
And it was dyed in mummy° which the skillful
Conserved of maidens' hearts.
Desdemona: I' faith? Is't true?
Othello: Most veritable. Therefore look to't well.
Desdemona: Then would to God that I had never seen't!
Othello: Ha! Wherefore?
Desdemona: Why do you speak so startingly and rash?
Othello: Is't lost? Is't gone? Speak, is it out o' th' way?
Desdemona: Heaven bless us!
Othello: Say you?
Desdemona: It is not lost. But what an if it were?
Othello: How?
Desdemona: I say it is not lost.
Othello: Fetch't, let me see't!
Desdemona: Why, so I can, sir; but I will not now.
This is a trick to put° me from my suit:
Pray you let Cassio be received again.
Othello: Fetch me the handkerchief! My mind misgives.
Desdemona: Come, come!
You'll never meet a more sufficient man.
Othello: The handkerchief!
[*Desdemona:* I pray talk me of Cassio.
Othello: The handkerchief!]
Desdemona: A man that all his time°
Hath founded his good fortunes on your love,
Shared dangers with you—
Othello: The handkerchief!
Desdemona: I' faith, you are to blame.
Othello: Zounds! *Exit Othello.*
Emilia: Is not this man jealous?
Desdemona: I ne'er saw this before.
Sure there's some wonder in this handkerchief;
I am most unhappy in the loss of it.
Emilia: 'Tis not a year or two shows us a man.
They are all but stomachs, and we all but food;
They eat us hungerly, and when they are full,
They belch us.

Enter Iago and Cassio.

Look you—Cassio and my husband!

66 *compasses:* Annual rounds. 69 *mummy:* A drug made from mummies. 82 *put:* Divert. 88 *all . . . time:* During his whole career.

Iago: There is no other way; 'tis she must do't.
And lo the happiness!° Go and importune her.
Desdemona: How now, good Cassio? What's the news with you?
Cassio: Madam, my former suit. I do beseech you
That by your virtuous means I may again
Exist, and be a member of his love
Whom I with all the office of my heart
Entirely honor. I would not be delayed.
If my offense be of such mortal kind
That neither service past, nor present sorrows,
Nor purposed merit in futurity,
Can ransom me into his love again,
But to know so must be my benefit.
So shall I clothe me in a forced content,
And shut myself up in° some other course,
To fortune's alms.
Desdemona: Alas, thrice-gentle Cassio!
My advocation° is not now in tune.
My lord is not my lord; nor should I know him,
Were he in favor° as in humor altered.
So help me every spirit sanctified
As I have spoken for you all my best
And stood wtihin the blank° of his displeasure
For my free speech! You must a while be patient.
What I can do I will; and more I will
Than for myself I dare. Let that suffice you.
Iago: Is my lord angry?
Emilia: He went hence but now,
And certainly in strange unquietness.
Iago: Can he be angry? I have seen the cannon
When it hath blown his ranks into the air
And, like the devil, from his very arm
Puffed his own brother — and is he angry?
Something of moment then. I will go meet him.
There's matter in't indeed if he be angry.
Desdemona: I prithee do so. *Exit [Iago].*
Something sure of state,°
Either from Venice or some unhatched practice°
Made demonstrable here in Cyprus to him,
Hath puddled° his clear spirit; and in such cases
Men's natures wrangle with inferior things,
Though great ones are their object. 'Tis even so;
For let our finger ache, and it endues°
Our other, healthful members even to a sense

103 *happiness:* Good luck. 116 *shut myself up in:* Confine myself to. 118 *advocation:* Advocacy. 120 *favor:* Appearance. 123 *blank:* Bull's-eye of the target. 135 *state:* Public affairs. 136 *unhatched practice:* Budding plot. 138 *puddled:* Muddied. 141 *endues:* Brings.

Of pain. Nay, we must think men are not gods,
Nor of them look for such observancy
As fits the bridal. Beshrew me much, Emilia,
I was, unhandsome warrior° as I am,
Arraigning his unkindness with my soul;°
But now I find I had suborned the witness,
And he's indicted falsely.

Emilia: Pray heaven it be state matters, as you think,
And no conception nor no jealous toy°
Concerning you.

Desdemona: Alas the day! I never gave him cause.

Emilia: But jealous souls will not be answered so;
They are not ever jealous for the cause,
But jealous for they're jealous. 'Tis a monster
Begot upon itself,° born on itself.

Desdemona: Heaven keep that monster from Othello's mind!

Emilia: Lady, amen.

Desdemona: I will go seek him. Cassio, walk here about:
If I do find him fit, I'll move your suit
And seek to effect it to my uttermost.

Cassio: I humbly thank your ladyship.

Exeunt Desdemona and Emilia.

Enter Bianca.

Bianca: Save you, friend Cassio!

Cassio: What make you from home?
How is't with you, my most fair Bianca?
I' faith, sweet love, I was coming to your house.

Bianca: And I was going to your lodging, Cassio.
What, keep a week away? seven days and nights?
Eightscore eight hours? and lovers' absent hours,
More tedious than the dial° eightscore times?
O weary reck'ning!

Cassio: Pardon me, Bianca:
I have this while with leaden thoughts been pressed;
But I shall in a more continuate° time
Strike off this score of absence. Sweet Bianca,

[Gives her Desdemona's handkerchief.]

Take me this work out.°

Bianca: O Cassio, whence came this?
This is some token from a newer friend.
To the felt absence now I feel a cause.
Is't come to this? Well, well.

Cassio: Go to, woman!

146 *unhandsome warrior:* Inadequate soldier. 147 *Arraigning . . . soul:* Indicting his unkindness before the bar of my soul. 151 *toy:* Fancy. 152 *Begot . . . itself:* Self-engendered. 170 *dial:* Clock. 173 *continuate:* Uninterrupted. 175 *Take . . . out:* Copy this embroidery for me.

Throw your vile guesses in the devil's teeth,
From whence you have them. You are jealous now
That this is from some mistress, some remembrance.
No, by my faith, Bianca.
Bianca: Why, whose is it?
Cassio: I know not, sweet; I found it in my chamber.
I like the work° well; ere it be demanded,
As like enough it will, I'd have it copied.
Take it and do't, and leave me for this time.
Bianca: Leave you? Wherefore?
Cassio: I do attend here on the general
And think it no addition, nor my wish,
To have him see me womaned.
Bianca: Why, I pray you?
Cassio: Not that I love you not.
Bianca: But that you do not love me!
I pray you bring me on the way a little,
And say if I shall see you soon at night.
Cassio: 'Tis but a little way that I can bring you,
For I attend here; but I'll see you soon.
Bianca: 'Tis very good. I must be circumstanced.° *Exeunt.*

ACT IV

SCENE I. *The environs of the castle.*

Enter Othello and Iago.

Iago: Will you think so?
Othello: Think so, Iago?
Iago: What,
To kiss in private?
Othello: An unauthorized kiss.
Iago: Or to be naked with her friend in bed
An hour or more, not meaning any harm?
Othello: Naked in bed, Iago, and not mean harm?
It is hypocrisy against the devil.°
They that mean virtuously, and yet do so,
The devil their virtue tempts, and they tempt heaven.
Iago: So they do nothing, 'tis a venial slip.
But if I give my wife a handkerchief—
Othello: What then?
Iago: Why, then 'tis hers, my lord; and being hers,
She may, I think, bestow't on any man.
Othello: She is protectress of her honor too;
May she give that?

184 *work:* Needlework. 196 *circumstanced:* Governed by circumstances. ACT IV. SCENE I. 6 *hypocrisy . . . devil:* I.e., feigned sin instead of feigned virtue.

Iago: Her honor is an essence that's not seen;
They have it very oft that have it not.
But for the handkerchief —
Othello: By heaven, I would most gladly have forgot it!
Thou said'st — O, it comes o'er my memory
As doth the raven o'er the infected° house,
Boding to all! — he had my handkerchief.
Iago: Ay, what of that?
Othello: That's not so good now.
Iago: What
If I had said I had seen him do you wrong?
Or heard him say — as knaves be such abroad
Who having, by their own importunate suit,
Or voluntary dotage of some mistress,
Convincèd or supplied° them, cannot choose
But they must blab —
Othello: Hath he said anything?
Iago: He hath, my lord; but be you well assured,
No more than he'll unswear.
Othello: What hath he said?
Iago: Faith, that he did — I know not what he did.
Othello: What? what?
Iago: Lie —
Othello: With her?
Iago: With her, on her; what you will.
Othello: Lie with her? lie on her? — We say lie on her when they belie her. — Lie with her! Zounds, that's fulsome. — Handkerchief — confessions — handkerchief! — To confess, and be hanged for his labor — first to be hanged, and then to confess! I tremble at it. Nature would not invest herself in such shadowing passion without some instruction.° It is not words that shakes me thus. — Pish! Noses, ears, and lips? Is't possible? — Confess? — Handkerchief? — O devil!

(Falls in a trance.)

Iago: Work on,
My med'cine, work! Thus credulous fools are caught,
And many worthy and chaste dames even thus,
All guiltless, meet reproach. — What, ho! my lord!
My lord, I say! Othello!
Enter Cassio. How now, Cassio?
Cassio: What's the matter?
Iago: My lord is fall'n into an epilepsy.
This is his second fit; he had one yesterday.
Cassio: Rub him about the temples.

21 *infected:* Plague-stricken. 28 *Convincèd or supplied:* Overcome or gratified. 39–40 *Nature . . . instruction:* My natural faculties would not be so overcome by passion without reason.

Iago: No, forbear.
The lethargy° must have his quiet course.
If not, he foams at mouth,° and by and by
Breaks out to savage madness. Look, he stirs.
Do you withdraw yourself a little while.
He will recover straight. When he is gone,
I would on great occasion speak with you. *[Exit Cassio.]*
How is it, general? Have you not hurt your head?
Othello: Dost thou mock me?
Iago: I mock you? No, by heaven.
Would you would bear your fortune like a man!
Othello: A hornèd man 's° a monster and a beast.
Iago: There's many a beast then in a populous city,
And many a civil monster.
Othello: Did he confess it?
Iago: Good sir, be a man.
Think every bearded fellow that's but yoked
May draw with you. There's millions now alive
That nightly lie in those unproper° beds
Which they dare swear peculiar:° your case is better.
O, 'tis the spite of hell, the fiend's arch-mock,
To lip a wanton in a secure° couch,
And to suppose her chaste! No, let me know;
And knowing what I am, I know what she shall be.
Othello: O, thou art wise! 'Tis certain.
Iago: Stand you awhile apart;
Confine yourself but in a patient list.°
Whilst you were here, o'erwhelmèd with your grief—
A passion most unsuiting such a man—
Cassio came hither. I shifted him away
And laid good 'scuse upon your ecstasy;°
Bade him anon return, and here speak with me;
The which he promised. Do but encave° yourself
And mark the fleers, the gibes, and notable scorns
That dwell in every region of his face;
For I will make him tell the tale anew—
Where, how, how oft, how long ago, and when
He hath, and is again to cope° your wife.
I say, but mark his gesture. Marry, patience!
Or I shall say y'are all in all in spleen,°
And nothing of a man.
Othello: Dost thou hear, Iago?
I will be found most cunning in my patience;
But—dost thou hear?—most bloody.

52 *lethargy:* Coma. 61 *hornèd man:* Cuckold. 67 *unproper:* Not exclusively their own. 68 *peculiar:* Exclusively their own. 70 *secure:* Free from fear of rivalry. 74 *in a patient list:* Within the limits of self-control. 78 *ecstasy:* Trance. 80 *encave:* Conceal. 85 *cope:* Meet. 87 *all in all in spleen:* Wholly overcome by your passion.

Iago: That's not amiss;
But yet keep time in all. Will you withdraw?
[Othello retires.]
Now will I question Cassio of Bianca,
A huswife° that by selling her desires
Buys herself bread and clothes. It is a creature
That dotes on Cassio, as 'tis the strumpet's plague
To beguile many and be beguiled by one.
He, when he hears of her, cannot refrain
From the excess of laughter. Here he comes.

Enter Cassio.

As he shall smile, Othello shall go mad;
And his unbookish° jealousy must conster°
Poor Cassio's smiles, gestures, and light behavior
Quite in the wrong. How do you now, lieutenant?
Cassio: The worser that you give me the addition°
Whose want even kills me.
Iago: Ply Desdemona well, and you are sure on't.
Now, if this suit lay in Bianca's power,
How quickly should you speed!
Cassio: Alas, poor caitiff!°
Othello: Look how he laughs already!
Iago: I never knew a woman love man so.
Cassio: Alas, poor rogue! I think, i' faith, she loves me.
Othello: Now he denies it faintly, and laughs it out.
Iago: Do you hear, Cassio?
Othello: Now he importunes him
To tell it o'er. Go to! Well said, well said!
Iago: She gives out that you shall marry her.
Do you intend it?
Cassio: Ha, ha, ha!
Othello: Do you triumph, Roman? Do you triumph?
Cassio: I marry her? What, a customer?° Prithee bear some charity to my wit; do not think it so unwholesome. Ha, ha, ha!
Othello: So, so, so, so! They laugh that win!
Iago: Faith, the cry goes that you shall marry her.
Cassio: Prithee say true.
Iago: I am a very villain else.
Othello: Have you scored me?° Well.
Cassio: This is the monkey's own giving out. She is persuaded I will marry her out of her own love and flattery, not out of my promise.
Othello: Iago beckons° me; now he begins the story.
Cassio: She was here even now; she haunts me in every place. I was t' other

93 *huswife:* Hussy. 100 *unbookish:* Uninstructed; *conster:* Construe, interpret. 103 *addition:* Title. 107 *caitiff:* Wretch. 118 *customer:* Prostitute. 124 *scored me:* Settled my account (?) 127 *beckons:* Signals.

day talking on the sea bank with certain Venetians, and thither comes the bauble,° and, by this hand, she falls me thus about my neck —

Othello: Crying "O dear Cassio!" as it were. His gesture imports it.

Cassio: So hangs, and lolls, and weeps upon me; so shakes and pulls me! Ha, ha, ha!

Othello: Now he tells how she plucked him to my chamber. O, I see that nose of yours, but not that dog I shall throw it to.

Cassio: Well, I must leave her company.

Enter Bianca.

Iago: Before me! Look where she comes.

Cassio: 'Tis such another fitchew!° marry, a perfumed one. What do you mean by this haunting of me?

Bianca: Let the devil and his dam haunt you! What did you mean by that same handkerchief you gave me even now? I was a fine fool to take it. I must take out the whole work? A likely piece of work that you should find it in your chamber and know not who left it there! This is some minx's token, and I must take out the work? There! Give it your hobby-horse.° Wheresoever you had it, I'll take out no work on't.

Cassio: How now, my sweet Bianca? How now? how now?

Othello: By heaven, that should be my handkerchief!

Bianca: An you'll come to supper to-night, you may; an you will not, come when you are next prepared for. *Exit.*

Iago: After her, after her!

Cassio: Faith, I must; she'll rail in the street else.

Iago: Will you sup there?

Cassio: Yes, I intend so.

Iago: Well, I may chance to see you; for I would very fain speak with you.

Cassio: Prithee come. Will you?

Iago: Go to! say no more. *Exit Cassio.*

Othello [comes forward]: How shall I murder him, Iago?

Iago: Did you perceive how he laughed at his vice?°

Othello: O Iago!

Iago: And did you see the handkerchief?

Othello: Was that mine?

Iago: Yours, by this hand! And to see how he prizes° the foolish woman your wife! She gave it him, and he hath giv'n it his whore.

Othello: I would have him nine years a-killing! — A fine woman! a fair woman! a sweet woman!

Iago: Nay, you must forget that.

Othello: Ay, let her rot, and perish, and be damned to-night; for she shall not live. No, my heart is turned to stone; I strike it, and it hurts my hand. O, the world hath not a sweeter creature! She might lie by an emperor's side and command him tasks.

Iago: Nay, that's not your way.

130 *bauble:* Plaything. 138 *fitchew:* Polecat (slang for whore). 145 *hobby-horse:* Harlot. 158 *vice:* I.e., vicious conduct. 162 *prizes:* Values.

Othello: Hang her! I do but say what she is. So delicate with her needle! an admirable musician! O, she will sing the savageness out of a bear! Of so high and plenteous wit and invention°—

Iago: She's the worse for all this.

Othello: O, a thousand thousand times! And then, of so gentle a condition!°

Iago: Ay, too gentle.

Othello: Nay, that's certain. But yet the pity of it, Iago! O Iago, the pity of it, Iago!

Iago: If you are so fond over her iniquity, give her patent° to offend; for if it touch not you, it comes near nobody.

Othello: I will chop her into messes! Cuckold me!

Iago: O, 'tis foul in her.

Othello: With mine officer!

Iago: That's fouler.

Othello: Get me some poison, Iago, this night. I'll not expostulate with her, lest her body and beauty unprovide° my mind again. This night, Iago!

Iago: Do it not with poison. Strangle her in her bed, even the bed she hath contaminated.

Othello: Good, good! The justice of it pleases. Very good!

Iago: And for Cassio, let me be his undertaker:° you shall hear more by midnight.

Othello: Excellent good!

A trumpet.

What trumpet is that same?

Iago: I warrant something from Venice.

Enter Lodovico, Desdemona, and Attendants.

'Tis Lodovico.

This comes from the Duke; and see, your wife is with him.

Lodovico: God save you, worthy general!

Othelio: With all my heart, sir.

Lodovico: The Duke and senators of Venice greet you.

[Gives him a letter.]

Othello: I kiss the instrument of their pleasures.

[Opens the letter and reads.]

Desdemona: And what's the news, good cousin Lodovico?

Iago: I am very glad to see you, signior.
Welcome to Cyprus.

Lodovico: I thank you. How does Lieutenant Cassio?

Iago: Lives, sir.

Desdemona: Cousin, there's fall'n between him and my lord
An unkind breach; but you shall make all well.

Othello: Are you sure of that?

Desdemona: My lord?

174 *invention:* Imagination. 176 *condition:* Disposition. 180 *patent:* License. 187 *unprovide:* Disarm. 191 *be his undertaker:* Undertake to deal with him.

Lodovico: He did not call; he's busy in the paper.
Is there division 'twixt thy lord and Cassio?
Desdemona: A most unhappy one. I would do much
T' atone° them, for the love I bear to Cassio.
Othello: Fire and brimstone!
Desdemona: My lord?
Othello: Are you wise?
Desdemona: What, is he angry?
Lodovico: May be the letter moved him;
For, as I think, they do command him home,
Deputing Cassio in his government.
Desdemona: By my troth, I am glad on't.
Othello: Indeed?
Desdemona: My lord?
Othello: I am glad to see you mad.°
Desdemona: Why, sweet Othello —
Othello: Devil!

[Strikes her.]

Desdemona: I have not deserved this.
Lodovico: My lord, this would not be believed in Venice,
Though I should swear I saw't. 'Tis very much.
Make her amends; she weeps.
Othello: O devil, devil!
If that the earth could teem° with woman's tears,
Each drop she falls would prove a crocodile.°
Out of my sight!
Desdemona: I will not stay to offend you. *[Going.]*
Lodovico: Truly, an obedient lady.
I do beseech your lordship call her back.
Othello: Mistress!
Desdemona: My lord?
Othello: What would you with her, sir?
Lodovico: Who? I, my lord?
Othello: Ay! You did wish that I would make her turn.
Sir, she can turn, and turn, and yet go on
And turn again; and she can weep, sir, weep;
And she's obedient; as you say, obedient,
Very obedient. — Proceed you in your tears. —
Concerning this, sir — O well-painted passion!° —
I am commanded home. — Get you away;
I'll send for you anon. — Sir, I obey the mandate
And will return to Venice. — Hence, avaunt!
[Exit Desdemona.]

Cassio shall have my place. And, sir, to-night

212 *atone:* Reconcile. 218 *mad:* I.e., waggish. 224 *teem:* Breed. 225 *crocodile:* (Crocodiles were supposed to shed hypocritical tears to lure men to destruction). 237 *passion:* Grief.

I do entreat that we may sup together.
You are welcome, sir, to Cyprus. — Goats and monkeys!
Exit.

Lodovico: Is this the noble Moor whom our full Senate
Call all in all sufficient? Is this the nature
Whom passion could not shake? whose solid virtue
The shot of accident nor dart of chance
Could neither graze nor pierce?

Iago: He is much changed.

Lodovico: Are his wits safe? Is he not light of brain?

Iago: He's that he is; I may not breathe my censure.
What he might be — if what he might he is not —
I would to heaven he were!

Lodovico: What, stike his wife?

Iago: Faith, that was not so well; yet would I knew
That stroke would prove the worst!

Lodovico: Is it his use?°
Or did the letters work upon his blood
And new-create this fault?

Iago: Alas, alas!
It is not honesty in me to speak
What I have seen and known. You shall observe him,
And his own courses will denote him so
That I may save my speech. Do but go after
And mark how he continues.

Lodovico: I am sorry that I am deceived in him. *Exeunt.*

Scene II. *Within the castle.*

Enter Othello and Emilia.

Othello: You have seen nothing then?

Emilia: Nor ever heard, nor ever did suspect.

Othello: Yes, you have seen Cassio and she together.

Emilia: But then I saw no harm, and then I heard
Each syllable that breath made up between them.

Othello: What, did they never whisper?

Emilia: Never, my lord.

Othello: Nor send you out o' th' way?

Emilia: Never.

Othello: To fetch her fan, her gloves, her mask, nor nothing?

Emilia: Never, my lord.

Othello: That's strange.

Emilia: I durst, my lord, to wager she is honest,
Lay down my soul at stake. If you think other,
Remove your thought; it doth abuse your bosom.°
If any wretch have put this in your head,

254 *use:* Custom. Scene II. 14 *abuse . . . bosom:* Deceive your heart.

Let heaven requite it with the serpent's curse!°
For if she be not honest, chaste, and true,
There's no man happy; the purest of their wives
Is foul as slander.

Othello: Bid her come hither. Go. *Exit Emilia.*
She says enough; yet she's a simple bawd
That cannot say as much. This is a subtle whore,
A closet lock and key of villainous secrets;
And yet she'll kneel and pray; I have seen her do't.

Enter Desdemona and Emilia.

Desdemona: My lord, what is your will?
Othello: Pray, chuck, come hither.
Desdemona: What is your pleasure?
Othello: Let me see your eyes.
Look in my face.
Desdemona: What horrible fancy's this?
Othello [to Emilia]: Some of your function, mistress.
Leave procreants° alone and shut the door;
Cough or cry hem if anybody come.
Your mystery, your mystery!° Nay, dispatch!
Exit Emilia.
Desdemona: Upon my knees, what doth your speech import?
I understand a fury in your words,
[But not the words.]
Othello: Why, what art thou?
Desdemona: Your wife, my lord; your true
And loyal wife.
Othello: Come, swear it, damn thyself;
Lest, being like one of heaven,° the devils themselves
Should fear to seize thee. Therefore be double-damned—
Swear thou art honest.
Desdemona: Heaven doth truly know it.
Othello: Heaven truly knows that thou art false as hell.
Desdemona: To whom, my lord? With whom? How am I false?
Othello: Ah, Desdemon! away! away! away!
Desdemona: Alas the heavy day! Why do you weep?
Am I the motive of these tears, my lord?
If haply you my father do suspect
An instrument° of this your calling back,
Lay not your blame on me. If you have lost him,
Why, I have lost him too.
Othello: Had it pleased heaven
To try me with affliction, had they rained
All kinds of sores and shames on my bare head,

16 *serpent's curse:* (cf. Genesis 3:14). 28 *procreants:* Mating couples. 30 *mystery:* Trade, occupation. 36 *being . . . heaven:* Looking like an angel. 38 *honest:* Chaste. 45 *An instrument:* To be the cause.

Steeped me in poverty to the very lips,
Given to captivity me and my utmost hopes,
I should have found in some place of my soul
A drop of patience. But, alas, to make me
A fixèd figure for the time of scorn°
To point his slow unmoving finger at!
Yet could I bear that too; well, very well.
But there where I have garnered up my heart,
Where either I must live or bear no life,
The fountain from the which my current runs
Or else dries up — to be discarded thence,
Or keep it as a cistern for foul toads
To knot and gender in — turn thy complexion there,°
Patience, thou young and rose-lipped cherubin!
Ay, there look grim as hell!

Desdemona: I hope my noble lord esteems me honest.

Othello: O, ay; as summer flies are in the shambles,°
That quicken even with blowing. O thou weed,
Who art so lovely fair, and smell'st so sweet,
That the sense aches at thee, would thou hadst ne'er been born!

Desdemona: Alas, what ignorant sin have I committed?

Othello: Was this fair paper, this most goodly book,
Made to write "whore" upon? What committed?
Committed? O thou public commoner!°
I should make very forges of my cheeks
That would to cinders burn up modesty,
Did I but speak they deeds. What committed?
Heaven stops the nose at it, and the moon winks;°
The bawdy wind, that kisses all it meets,
Is hushed within the hollow mine of earth
And will not hear it. What committed?
Impudent strumpet!

Desdemona: By heaven, you do me wrong!

Othello: Are not you a strumpet?

Desdemona: No, as I am a Christian!
If to preserve this vessel for my lord
From any other foul unlawful touch
Be not to be a strumpet, I am none.

Othello: What, not a whore?

Desdemona: No, as I shall be saved!

Othello: Is't possible?

Desdemona: O, heaven forgive us!

Othello: I cry you mercy° then.
I took you for that cunning whore of Venice
That married with Othello. — *[Calling.]* You, mistress,

54 *time of scorn:* Scornful world. 62 *turn thy complexion there:* Change thy color at that point. 66 *shambles:* Slaughterhouse. 67 *quicken:* Come to life. 73 *commoner:* Harlot. 77 *winks:* Closes her eyes. 88 *cry you mercy:* Beg your pardon.

That have the office opposite to Saint Peter
And keep the gate of hell!

Enter Emilia.

You, you, ay, you!
We have done our course; there's money for your pains:
I pray you turn the key, and keep our counsel. *Exit.*

Emilia: Alas, what does this gentleman conceive?
How do you, madam? How do you, my good lady?
Desdemona: Faith, half asleep.°
Emilia: Good madam, what's the matter with my lord?
Desdemona: With who?
Emilia: Why, with my lord, madam.
Desdemona: Who is thy lord?
Emilia: He that is yours, sweet lady.
Desdemona: I have none. Do not talk to me, Emilia.
I cannot weep; nor answers have I none
But what should go by water. Prithee to-night
Lay on my bed my wedding sheets, remember;
And call thy husband hither.
Emilia: Here's a change indeed! *Exit.*
Desdemona: 'Tis meet I should be used so, very meet.
How have I been behaved, that he might stick
The small'st opinion° on my least misuse?°

Enter Iago and Emilia.

Iago: What is your pleasure, madam? How is't with you?
Desdemona: I cannot tell. Those that do teach young babes
Do it with gentle means and easy tasks:
He might have chid me so; for, in good faith,
I am a child to chiding.
Iago: What is the matter, lady?
Emilia: Alas, Iago, my lord hath so bewhored her,
Thrown such despite and heavy terms upon her
As true hearts cannot bear.
Desdemona: Am I that name, Iago?
Iago: What name, fair lady?
Desdemona: Such as she said my lord did say I was.
Emilia: He called her whore. A beggar in his drink
Could not have laid such terms upon his callet.°
Iago: Why did he so?
Desdemona: I do not know; I am sure I am none such.
Iago: Do not weep, do not weep. Alas the day!
Emilia: Hath she forsook so many noble matches,
Her father and her country, and her friends,
To be called whore? Would it not make one weep?
Desdemona: It is my wretched fortune.

97 *half asleep:* I.e., stunned. 109 *small'st opinion:* Least suspicion; *least misuse:* Slightest misconduct. 121 *callet:* Whore.

Iago: Beshrew him for't!
How comes this trick° upon him?
Desdemona: Nay, heaven doth know.
Emilia: I will be hanged if some eternal villain,
Some busy and insinuating rogue,
Some cogging, cozening° slave, to get some office,
Have not devised this slander. I'll be hanged else.
Iago: Fie, there is no such man! It is impossible.
Desdemona: If any such there be, heaven pardon him!
Emilia: A halter pardon him! and hell gnaw his bones!
Why should he call her whore? Who keeps her company?
What place? what time? what form? what likelihood?
The Moor 's abused by some most villainous knave,
Some base notorious knave, some scurvy fellow.
O heaven, that such companions° thou 'dst unfold,°
And put in every honest hand a whip
To lash the rascals naked through the world
Even from the east to th' west!
Iago: Speak within door.°
Emilia: O, fie upon them! Some such squire he was
That turned your wit the seamy side without
And made you to suspect me with the Moor.
Iago: You are a fool. Go to.
Desdemona: Alas, Iago,
What shall I do to win my lord again?
Good friend, go to him; for, by this light of heaven,
I know not how I lost him. Here I kneel:
If e'er my will did trespass 'gainst his love
Either in discourse° of thought or actual deed,
Or that mine eyes, mine ears, or any sense
Delighted them in any other form,
Or that I do not yet, and ever did,
And ever will (though he do shake me off
To beggarly divorcement) love him dearly,
Comfort forswear° me! Unkindness may do much;
And his unkindness may defeat° my life,
But never taint my love. I cannot say "whore."
It does abhor me now I speak the word;
To do the act that might the addition earn
Not the world's mass of vanity could make me.
Iago: I pray you be content. 'Tis but his humor.
The business of the state does him offense,
[And he does chide with you.]
Desdemona: If 'twere no other —
Iago: 'Tis but so, I warrant.

129 *trick:* Freakish behavior. 132 *cogging, cozening:* Cheating, defrauding. 141 *companions:* Rogues; *unfold:* Expose. 144 *within door:* With restraint. 153 *discourse:* Course. 159 *Comfort forswear:* Happiness forsake. 160 *defeat:* Destroy.

[Trumpets within.]

Hark how these instruments summon you to supper.
The messengers of Venice stay the meat:
Go in, and weep not. All things shall be well.

Exeunt Desdemona and Emilia.

Enter Roderigo.

How now, Roderigo?

Roderigo: I do not find that thou deal'st justly with me.

Iago: What in the contrary?

Roderigo: Every day thou daff'st me with some device,° Iago, and rather, as it seems to me now, keep'st from me all conveniency° than suppliest me with the least advantage of hope. I will indeed no longer endure it; nor am I yet persuaded to put up in peace what already I have foolishly suffered.

Iago: Will you hear me, Roderigo?

Roderigo: Faith, I have heard too much; for your words and performances are no kin together.

Iago: You charge me most unjustly.

Roderigo: With naught but truth. I have wasted myself out of my means. The jewels you have had from me to deliver to Desdemona would half have corrupted a votarist.° You have told me she hath received them, and returned me expectations and comforts of sudden respect° and acquaintance; but I find none.

Iago: Well, go to; very well.

Roderigo: Very well! go to! I cannot go to, man; nor 'tis not very well. By this hand, I say 'tis very scurvy, and begin to find myself fopped° in it.

Iago: Very well.

Roderigo: I tell you 'tis not very well. I will make myself known to Desdemona. If she will return me my jewels, I will give over my suit and repent my unlawful solicitation; if not, assure yourself I will seek satisfaction of you.

Iago: You have said now.

Roderigo: Ay, and said nothing but what I protest intendment of doing.

Iago: Why, now I see there's mettle in thee; and even from this instant do build on thee a better opinion than ever before. Give me thy hand, Roderigo. Thou hast taken against me a most just exception; but yet I protest I have dealt most directly° in thy affair.

Roderigo: It hath not appeared.

Iago: I grant indeed it hath not appeared, and your suspicion is not without wit and judgment. But, Roderigo, if thou hast that in thee indeed which I have greater reason to believe now than ever, I mean purpose, courage, and valor, this night show it. If thou the next night following enjoy

175 *thou . . . device:* You put me off with some trick. 176 *conveniency:* Favorable opportunities. 186 *votarist:* Nun. 187 *sudden respect:* Immediate notice. 197 *fopped:* Duped. 202 *directly:* Straightforwardly.

not Desdemona, take me from this world with treachery and devise engines for° my life.

Roderigo: Well, what is it? Is it within reason and compass?

Iago: Sir, there is especial commission come from Venice to depute Cassio in Othello's place.

Roderigo: Is that true? Why, then Othello and Desdemona return again to Venice.

Iago: O, no; he goes into Mauritania and takes away with him the fair Desdemona, unless his abode be lingered here° by some accident; wherein none can be so determinate° as the removing of Cassio.

Roderigo: How do you mean removing of him?

Iago: Why, by making him uncapable of Othello's place — knocking out his brains.

Roderigo: And that you would have me to do?

Iago: Ay, if you dare do yourself a profit and a right. He sups to-night with a harlotry, and thither will I go to him. He knows not yet of his honorable fortune. If you will watch his going thence, which I will fashion to fall out between twelve and one, you may take him at your pleasure. I will be near to second your attempt, and he shall fall between us. Come, stand not amazed at it, but go along with me. I will show you such a necessity in his death that you shall think yourself bound to put it on him. It is now high supper time, and the night grows to waste. About it!

Roderigo: I will hear further reason for this.

Iago: And you shall be satisfied. *Exeunt.*

Scene III. *Within the castle.*

Enter Othello, Lodovico, Desdemona, Emilia, and Attendants.

Lodovico: I do beseech you, sir, trouble yourself no further.

Othello: O, pardon me; 'twill do me good to walk.

Lodovico: Madam, good night. I humbly thank your ladyship.

Desdemona: Your honor is most welcome.

Othello: Will you walk, sir?
O, Desdemona —

Desdemona: My lord?

Othello: Get you to bed on th' instant; I will be returned forthwith. Dismiss your attendant there. Look't be done.

Desdemona: I will, my lord.

Exit [Othello, with Lodovico and Attendants].

Emilia: How goes it now? He looks gentler than he did.

Desdemona: He says he will return incontinent.°
He hath commanded me to go to bed,
And bade me to dismiss you.

209 *engines for:* Plots against. 216 *abode . . . here:* Stay here be extended. 217 *determinate:* Effective. Scene III. 11 *incontinent:* At once.

Emilia: Dismiss me?
Desdemona: It was his bidding; therefore, good Emilia,
Give me my nightly wearing, and adieu.
We must not now displease him.
Emilia: I would you had never seen him!
Desdemona: So would not I. My love doth so approve him
That even his stubbornness,° his checks,° his frowns —
Prithee unpin me — have grace and favor in them.
Emilia: I have laid those sheets you bade me on the bed.
Desdemona: All's one. Good faith, how foolish are our minds!
If I do die before thee, prithee shroud me
In one of those same sheets.
Emilia: Come, come! You talk.
Desdemona: My mother had a maid called Barbary.
She was in love; and he she loved proved mad°
And did forsake her. She had a song of "Willow";
An old thing 'twas; but it expressed her fortune,
And she died singing it. That song to-night
Will not go from my mind; I have much to do
But to go hang my head all at one side
And sing it like poor Barbary. Prithee dispatch.
Emilia: Shall I go fetch your nightgown?°
Desdemona: No, unpin me here.
This Lodovico is a proper man.
Emilia: A very handsome man.
Desdemona: He speaks well.
Emilia: I know a lady in Venice would have walked barefoot to Palestine for a touch of his nether lip.
Desdemona (sings): "The poor soul sat sighing by a sycamore tree
Sing all a green willow;
Her hand on her bosom, her head on her knee,
Sing willow, willow, willow.
The fresh streams ran by her and murmured her moans;
Sing willow, willow, willow;
Her salt tears fell from her, and soft'ned the stones" —
Lay by these.
"Sing willow, willow, willow" —
Prithee hie thee;° he'll come anon.
"Sing all a green willow must be my garland.
Let nobody blame him; his scorn I approve" —
Nay, that's not next. Hark! who is't that knocks?
Emilia: It's the wind.
Desdemona [sings]: "I call my love false love; but what said he then?
Sing willow, willow, willow:
If I court moe women, you'll couch with moe men."
So get thee gone; good night. Mine eyes do itch.

19 *stubbornness:* Roughness; *checks:* Rebukes. 26 *mad:* Wild, faithless. 33 *nightgown:* Dressing gown. 48 *hie thee:* Hurry.

Doth that bode weeping?
Emilia: 'Tis neither here nor there.
Desdemona: I have heard it said so. O, these men, these men!
Dost thou in conscience think — tell me, Emilia —
That there be women do abuse their husbands
In such gross kind?
Emilia: There be some such, no question.
Desdemona: Wouldst thou do such a deed for all the world?
Emilia: Why, would not you?
Desdemona: No, by this heavenly light!
Emilia: Nor I neither by this heavenly light.
I might do't as well i' th' dark.
Desdemona: Wouldst thou do such a deed for all the world?
Emilia: The world's a huge thing; it is a great price for a small vice.
Desdemona: In troth, I think thou wouldst not.

Emilia: In troth, I think I should; and undo't when I had done it. Marry, I would not do such a thing for a joint-ring,° nor for measures of lawn, nor for gowns, petticoats, nor caps, nor any petty exhibition;° but, for all the whole world — 'Ud's pity! who would not make her husband a cuckold to make him a monarch? I should venture purgatory for't.

Desdemona: Beshrew me if I would do such a wrong
For the whole world.

Emilia: Why, the wrong is but a wrong i' th' world; and having the world for your labor, 'tis a wrong in your own world, and you might quickly make it right.

Desdemona: I do not think there is any such woman.
Emilia: Yes, a dozen; and as many to th' vantage° as
would store° the world they played for.
But I do think it is their husbands' faults
If wives do fall. Say that they slack their duties
And pour our treasures into foreign laps;
Or else break out in peevish° jealousies,
Throwing restraint upon us; or say they strike us,
Or scant our former having° in despite —
Why, we have galls;° and though we have some grace,
Yet have we some revenge. Let husbands know
Their wives have sense like them. They see, and smell,
And have their palates both for sweet and sour,
As husbands have. What is it that they do
When they change us for others? Is it sport?
I think it is. And doth affection breed it?
I think it doth. Is't frailty that thus errs?
It is so too. And have not we affections,
Desires for sport, and frailty, as men have?
Then let them use us well; else let them know,
The ills we do, their ills instruct us so.

70 *joint-ring:* Ring made in separable halves. 71 *exhibition:* Gift. 80 *to th' vantage:* Besides. 81 *store:* Populate. 85 *peevish:* Senseless. 87 *having:* Allowance. 88 *galls:* Spirits to resent.

Desdemona: Good night, good night. God me such usage° send,
Not to pick bad from bad, but by bad mend! *Exeunt.*

ACT V

SCENE I. *A street in Cyprus.*

Enter Iago and Roderigo.

Iago: Here, stand behind this bulk;° straight will he come.
Wear thy good rapier bare, and put it home.
Quick, quick! Fear nothing; I'll be at thy elbow.
It makes us, or it mars us — think on that,
And fix most firm thy resolution.
Roderigo: Be near at hand; I may miscarry in't.
Iago: Here, at thy hand. Be bold, and take thy stand.

[Stands aside.]

Roderigo: I have no great devotion to the deed,
And yet he hath given me satisfying reasons.
'Tis but a man gone. Forth my sword! He dies!
Iago: I have rubbed this young quat° almost to the sense,°
And he grows angry. Now whether he kill Cassio,
Or Cassio him, or each do kill the other,
Every way makes my gain. Live Roderigo,
He calls me to a restitution large
Of gold and jewels that I bobbed° from him
As gifts to Desdemona.
It must not be. If Cassio do remain,
He hath a daily beauty in his life
That makes me ugly; and besides, the Moor
May unfold me to him; there stand I in much peril.
No, he must die. Be't so! I hear him coming.

Enter Cassio.

Roderigo: I know his gait. 'Tis he. Villain, thou diest!

[Makes a pass at Cassio.]

Cassio: That thrust had been mine enemy indeed
But that my coat° is better than thou know'st.
I will make proof of thine.

[Draws, and wounds Roderigo.]

Roderigo: O, I am slain!

[Iago darts from concealment behind Cassio, wounds him in the leg, and exit.]

Cassio: I am maimed for ever. Help, ho! Murder! murder!

100 *usage:* Habits. ACT V. SCENE 1. 1 *bulk:* Projecting shop-front. 11 *quat:* Pimple; *sense:* Quick. 16 *bobbed:* Swindled. 25 *coat:* Undershirt of mail.

[Falls.]
Enter Othello.

Othello: The voice of Cassio. Iago keeps his word.
Roderigo: O, villain that I am!
Othello: It is even so.
Cassio: O, help, ho! light! a surgeon!
Othello: 'Tis he. O brave Iago, honest and just,
That hast such noble sense of thy friend's wrong!
Thou teachest me. Minion,° your dear lies dead,
And your unblest fate hies.° Strumpet, I come.
Forth of my heart those charms, thine eyes, are blotted.
Thy bed, lust-stained, shall with lust's blood be spotted.
Exit Orthello.

Enter Lodovico and Gratiano.

Cassio: What, ho? No watch? No passage?° Murder! murder!
Gratiano: 'Tis some mischance. The cry is very direful.
Cassio: O, help!
Lodovico: Hark!
Roderigo: O wretched villain!
Lodovico: Two or three groan. It is a heavy° night.
These may be counterfeits. Let's think't unsafe
To come in to the cry without more help.
Roderigo: Nobody come? Then shall I bleed to death.
Lodovico: Hark!

Enter Iago, with a light.

Gratiano: Here's one comes in his shirt, with light and weapons.
Iago: Who's there? Whose noise is this that cries on° murder?
Lodovico: We do not know.
Iago: Did not you hear a cry?
Cassio: Here, here! For heaven's sake, help me!
Iago: What's the matter?
Gratiano: This is Othello's ancient, as I take it.
Lodovico: The same indeed, a very valiant fellow.
Iago: What are you here that cry so grievously?
Cassio: Iago? O, I am spoiled, undone by villains!
Give me some help.
Iago: O me, lieutenant! What villains have done this?
Cassio: I think that one of them is hereabout
And cannot make° away.
Iago: O treacherous villains!

[To Lodovico and Gratiano.]

What are you there? Come in, and give some help.
Roderigo: O, help me here!

33 *Minion:* Mistress. 34 *hies:* Hurries on. 37 *passage:* Passersby. 42 *heavy:* Cloudy, dark. 48 *cries on:* Raises the cry of. 58 *make:* Get.

Cassio: That's one of them.
Iago: O murd'rous slave! O villain!

[Stabs Roderigo.]

Roderigo: O damned Iago! O inhuman dog!
Iago: Kill men i' th' dark? — Where be these bloody thieves? —
How silent is this town! — Ho! murder! murder! —
What may you be? Are you of good or evil?
Lodovico: As you shall prove us, praise us.
Iago: Signior Lodovico?
Lodovico: He, sir.
Iago: I cry you mercy. Here's Cassio hurt by villains.
Gratiano: Cassio?
Iago: How is't, brother?
Cassio: My leg is cut in two.
Iago: Marry,° heaven forbid!
Light, gentleman. I'll bind it with my shirt.

Enter Bianca.

Bianca: What is the matter, ho? Who is't that cried?
Iago: Who is't that cried?
Bianca: O my dear Cassio! my sweet Cassio!
O Cassio, Cassio, Cassio!
Iago: O notable strumpet! — Cassio, may you suspect
Who they should be that have thus mangled you?
Cassio: No.
Gratiano: I am sorry to find you thus. I have been to seek you.
Iago: Lend me a garter. So. O for a chair°
To bear him easily hence!
Bianca: Alas, he faints! O Cassio, Cassio, Cassio!
Iago: Gentlemen all, I do suspect this trash
To be a party in this injury. —
Patience a while, good Cassio. — Come, come!
Lend me a light. Know we this face or no?
Alas, my friend and my dear countryman
Roderigo? No. — Yes, sure. — O heaven, Roderigo!
Gratiano: What, of Venice?
Iago: Even he, sir. Did you know him?
Gratiano: Know him? Ay.
Iago: Signior Gratiano? I cry your gentle pardon.
These bloody accidents must excuse my manners
That so neglected you.
Gratiano: I am glad to see you.
Iago: How do you, Cassio? — O, a chair, a chair!
Gratiano: Roderigo?
Iago: He, he, 'tis he!

[A chair brought in.]

72 *Marry:* (From By Mary). 82 *chair:* Litter.

O, that's well said;° the chair.
Some good man bear him carefully from hence.

[To Bianca.]

For you, mistress,
Save you your labor. — He that lies slain here, Cassio,
Was my dear friend. What malice was between you?
Cassio: None in the world; nor do I know the man.
Iago [to Bianca]: What, look you pale? — O, bear him out o' th' air.

[Cassio and Roderigo are borne off.]

Stay you, good gentlemen. — Look you pale, mistress? —
Do you perceive the gastness° of her eye? —
Nay, if you stare, we shall hear more anon.
Behold her well; I pray you look upon her.
Do you see, gentlemen? Nay, guiltiness will speak,
Though tongues were out of use.

Enter Emilia.

Emilia: 'Las, what's the matter? What's the matter, husband?
Iago: Cassio hath here been set on in the dark
By Roderigo, and fellows that are scaped.
He's almost slain, and Roderigo dead.
Emilia: Alas, good gentleman! alas, good Cassio!
Iago: This is the fruits of whoring. Prithee, Emilia,
Go know of Cassio where he supped to-night.

[To Bianca.]

What, do you shake at that?
Bianca: He supped at my house; but I therefore shake not.
Iago: O, did he so? I charge you go with me.
Emilia: Fie, fie upon thee, strumpet!
Bianca: I am no strumpet, but of life as honest°
As you that thus abuse me.
Emilia: As I? Foh! fie upon thee!
Iago: Kind gentlemen, let's go see poor Cassio dressed.

[To Bianca.]

Come, mistress, you must tell's another tale.
Emilia, run you to the citadel
And tell my lord and lady what hath happed.

[Exit Emilia.]

Will you go on afore? *Exeunt [all but Iago.]*
This is the night
That either makes me or fordoes° me quite. *[Exit.]*

SCENE II. *A bedchamber in the castle.*

Desdemona [asleep] in her bed. Enter Othello with a light.

98 *well said:* Well done. 106 *gastness:* Terror. 122 *honest:* Chaste. 129 *fordoes:* Destroys.

Othello: It is the cause, it is the cause,° my soul.
Let me not name it to you, you chaste stars!
It is the cause. Yet I'll not shed her blood,
Nor scar that whiter skin of hers than snow,
And smooth as monumental alabaster.
Yet she must die, else she'll betray more men.
Put out the light, and then put out the light.
If I quench thee, thou flaming minister,°
I can again thy former light restore,
Should I repent me; but once put out thy light,
Thou cunning'st pattern of excelling nature,
I know not where is that Promethean heat°
That can thy light relume.° When I have plucked the rose,
I cannot give it vital growth again;
It needs must wither. I'll smell thee on the tree.

(He kisses her.)

O balmy breath, that dost almost persuade
Justice to break her sword! One more, one more!
Be thus when thou art dead, and I will kill thee,
And love thee after. One more, and that's the last!
So sweet was ne'er so fatal. I must weep,
But they are cruel tears. This sorrow's heavenly;
It strikes where it doth love. She wakes.
Desdemona: Who's there? Othello?
Othello: Ay, Desdemona.
Desdemona: Will you come to bed, my lord?
Othello: Have you prayed to-night, Desdemon?
Desdemona: Ay, my lord.
Othello: If you bethink yourself of any crime°
Unreconciled as yet to heaven and grace,
Solicit for it straight.
Desdemona: Alack, my lord, what may you mean by that?
Othello: Well, do it, and be brief; I will walk by.
I would not kill thy unpreparèd spirit.
No, heaven forfend!° I would not kill thy soul.
Desdemona: Talk you of killing?
Othello: Ay, I do.
Desdemona: Then heaven
Have mercy on me!
Othello: Amen, with all my heart!
Desdemona: If you say so, I hope you will not kill me.
Othello: Hum!
Desdemona: And yet I fear you; for you're fatal then
When your eyes roll so. Why I should fear I know not,
Since guiltiness I know not; but yet I feel I fear.

SCENE II. 1 *cause:* Cause of justice. 8 *minister:* Servant. 12 *Promethean heat:* Divine fire. 13 *relume:* Relight. 26 *crime:* Sin. 32 *forfend:* Forbid.

Othello: Think on thy sins.
Desdemona: They are loves I bear to you.
Othello: Ay, and for that thou diest.
Desdemona: That death 's unnatural that kills for loving.
Alas, why gnaw you so your nether lip?
Some bloody passion shakes your very frame.
These are portents;° but yet I hope, I hope,
They do not point on me.
Othello: Peace and be still!
Desdemona: I will so. What's the matter?
Othello: That handkerchief which I so loved and gave thee
Thou gav'st to Cassio.
Desdemona: No, by my life and soul!
Send for the man and ask him.
Othello: Sweet soul, take heed,
Take heed of perjury; thou art on thy deathbed.
Desdemona: Ay, but not yet to die.
Othello: Yes, presently.°
Therefore confess thee freely of thy sin;
For to deny each article with oath
Cannot remove nor choke the strong conception°
That I do groan withal. Thou art to die.
Desdemona: Then Lord have mercy on me!
Othello: I say amen.
Desdemona: And have you mercy too! I never did
Offend° you in my life; never loved Cassio
But with such general warranty of heaven
As I might love. I never gave him token.
Othello: By heaven, I saw my handkerchief in's hand!
O perjured woman! thou dost stone my heart,°
And mak'st me call what I intend to do
A murder, which I thought a sacrifice.
I saw the handkerchief.
Desdemona: He found it then.
I never gave it him. Send for him hither.
Let him confess a truth.
Othello: He hath confessed.
Desdemona: What, my lord?
Othello: That he hath used thee.
Desdemona: How? Unlawfully?
Othello: Ay.
Desdemona: He will not say so.
Othello: No, his mouth is stopped.
Honest Iago hath ta'en order° for't.
Desdemona: O, my fear interprets. What, is he dead?

45 *portents:* Signs of impending violence. 52 *presently:* At once. 55 *conception:* Belief. 59 *Offend:* Wrong. 63 *stone my heart:* Turn my heart to stone. 72 *ta'en order:* Taken measures.

Othello: Had all his hairs been lives, my great revenge
Had stomach for them all.
Desdemona: Alas, he is betrayed, and I undone!
Othello: Out, strumpet! Weep'st thou for him to my face?
Desdemona: O, banish me, my lord, but kill me not!
Othello: Down, strumpet!
Desdemona: Kill me to-morrow; let me live to-night!
Othello: Nay, if you strive —
Desdemona: But half an hour!
Othello: Being done, there is no pause.
Desdemona: But while I say one prayer!
Othello: It is too late.

(Smothers her.)

[*Desdemona:* O Lord, Lord, Lord!]

Emilia at the door.

Emilia (calls within): My lord, my lord! What, ho! my lord, my lord!
Othello: What noise is this? Not dead? not yet quite dead?
I that am cruel am yet merciful;
I would not have thee linger in thy pain.
So, so.
Emilia (within): What, ho! my lord, my lord!
Othello: Who's there?
Emilia [within]: O, good my lord, I would speak a word with you!
Othello: Yes, 'tis Emilia. — By and by.° — She's dead. —
'Tis like she comes to speak of Cassio's death.
The noise was here. Ha! no more moving?
Still as the grave. — Shall she come in? Were't good! —
I think she stirs again. No. — What's best to do?
If she come in, she'll sure speak to my wife.
My wife! my wife! what wife? I have no wife.
O, insupportable! O heavy hour!
Methinks it should be now a huge eclipse
Of sun and moon, and that th' affrighted globe
Should yawn° at alteration.
Emilia [within]: I do beseech you
That I may speak with you, O good my lord!
Othello: I had forgot thee. O, come in, Emilia.
Soft, by and by. — Let me the curtains draw. —

[Closes the bed-curtains.]

Where art thou?

[Opens the door.]
Enter Emilia.

What's the matter with thee now?
Emilia: O my good lord, yonder's foul murder done!

92 *By and by:* Just a moment (addressed to Emilia). 102 *yawn:* Open, as in an earthquake.

Othello: What? Now?
Emilia: But now, my lord.
Othello: It is the very error° of the moon.
She comes more nearer earth than she was wont
And makes men mad.
Emilia: Cassio, my lord, hath killed a young Venetian
Called Roderigo.
Othello: Roderigo killed?
And Cassio killed?
Emilia: No, Cassio is not killed.
Othello: Not Cassio killed? Then murder 's out of tune,
And sweet revenge grows harsh.
Desdemona: O, falsely, falsely murdered?
Emilia: O Lord! what cry is that?
Othello: That? What?
Emilia: Out and alas! that was my lady's voice.
Help! help, ho! help! O lady, speak again!
Sweet Desdemona! O sweet mistress, speak!
Desdemona: A guiltless death I die.
Emilia: O, who hath done this deed?
Desdemona: Nobody — I myself. Farewell.
Commend° me to my kind lord. O, farewell!

(She dies.)

Othello: Why, how should she be murd'red?
Emilia: Alas, who knows?
Othello: You heard her say herself, it was not I.
Emilia: She said so. I must needs report the truth.
Othello: She's like a liar gone to burning hell!
'Twas I that killed her.
Emilia: O, the more angel she,
And you the blacker devil!
Othello: She turned to folly, and she was a whore.
Emilia: Thou dost belie her, and thou art a devil.
Othello: She was false as water.°
Emilia: Thou art rash as fire to say
That she was false. O, she was heavenly true!
Othello: Cassio did top her. Ask thy husband else.
O, I were damned beneath all depth in hell
But that I did proceed upon just grounds
To this extremity. Thy husband knew it all.
Emilia: My husband?
Othello: Thy husband.
Emilia: That she was false to wedlock?
Othello: Ay, with Cassio. Nay, had she been true,
If heaven would make me such another world

110 *error:* Straying off course. 126 *Commend:* Remember. 135 *water:* (Which is yielding).

Of one entire and perfect chrysolite,°
I'ld not have sold her for it.

Emilia: My husband?

Othello: Ay 'twas he that told me first.
An honest man he is, and hates the slime
That sticks on filthy deeds.

Emilia: My husband?

Othello: What needs this iterance,° woman? I say thy husband.

Emilia: O mistress, villainy hath made mocks with love!
My husband say that she was false?

Othello: He, woman.
I say, thy husband. Dost understand the word?
My friend, thy husband; honest, honest Iago.

Emilia: If he say so, may his pernicious soul
Rot half a grain a day! he lies to th' heart.
She was too fond of her most filthy bargain.

Othello: Ha!

Emilia: Do thy worst.
This deed of thine is no more worthy heaven
Than thou wast worthy her.

Othello: Peace, you were best.

Emilia: Thou hast not half the power to do me harm
As I have to be hurt.° O gull! O dolt!
As ignorant as dirt! thou hast done a deed—
I care not for thy sword; I'll make thee known,
Though I lost twenty lives. Help! help! Ho! help!
The Moor hath killed my mistress! Murder! murder!

Enter Montano, Gratiano, Iago, and others.

Montano: What is the matter? How now, general?

Emilia: O, are you come, Iago? You have done well,
That men must lay their murders on your neck.

Gratiano: What is the matter?

Emilia: Disprove this villain, if thou be'st a man.
He says thou told'st him that his wife was false.
I know thou didst not; thou'rt not such a villain.
Speak, for my heart is full.

Iago: I told him what I thought, and told no more
Than what he found himself was apt and true.

Emilia: But did you ever tell him she was false?

Iago: I did.

Emilia: You told a lie, an odious damnèd lie!
Upon my soul, a lie! a wicked lie!
She false with Cassio? Did you say with Cassio?

Iago: With Cassio, mistress. Go to, charm° your tongue.

Emilia: I will not charm my tongue; I am bound to speak:
My mistress here lies murdered in her bed—

146 *chrysolite:* (Precious topaz). 151 *iterance:* Repetition. 164 *to be hurt:* To endure hurt. 184 *charm:* Cast a spell on.

All: O heavens forfend!
Emilia: And your reports have set the murder on.
Othello: Nay, stare not, masters. It is true indeed.
Gratiano: 'Tis a strange truth.
Montano: O monstrous act!
Emilia: Villainy, villainy, villainy!
I think upon't — I think I smell't! — O villainy!
I thought so then. — I'll kill myself for grief. —
O villainy, villainy!
Iago: What, are you mad? I charge you get you home.
Emilia: Good gentlemen, let me have leave to speak.
'Tis proper I obey him, but not now.
Perchance, Iago, I will ne'er go home.
Othello: O! O! O! *(Falls on the bed.)*
Emilia: Nay, lay thee down and roar!
For thou hast killed the sweetest innocent
That e'er did lift up eye.
Othello: O, she was foul!

[Rises.]

I scarce did know you, uncle. There lies your niece,
Whose breath, indeed, these hands have newly stopped.
I know this act shows° horrible and grim.
Gratiano: Poor Desdemon! I am glad thy father's dead.
Thy match was mortal to him, and pure grief
Shore his old thread in twain. Did he live now,
This sight would make him do a desperate turn;°
Yea, curse his better angel from his side,
And fall to reprobation.°
Othello: 'Tis pitiful; but yet Iago knows
That she with Cassio hath the act of shame
A thousand times committed. Cassio confessed it;
And she did gratify° his amorous works
With that recognizance° and pledge of love
Which I first gave her. I saw it in his hand.
It was a handkerchief, an antique token
My father gave my mother.
Emilia: O God! O heavenly God!
Iago: Zounds, hold your peace!
Emilia: 'Twill out, 'twill out! I peace?
No, I will speak as liberal as the north.°
Let heaven and men and devils, let them all,
All, all, cry shame against me, yet I'll speak.
Iago: Be wise, and get you home.
Emilia: I will not.
[Iago draws and threatens Emilia.]

204 *shows:* Appears. 208 *turn:* Act. 210 *reprobation:* Rejection by God, damnation. 214 *gratify:* Reward. 215 *recognizance:* Token. 221 *liberal as the north:* Unchecked as the north wind blows.

Gratiano: Fie!
Your sword upon a woman?
Emilia: O thou dull Moor, that handkerchief thou speak'st of
I found by fortune, and did give my husband;
For often with a solemn earnestness —
More than indeed belonged to such a trifle —
He begged of me to steal't.
Iago: Villainous whore!
Emilia: She give it Cassio? No, alas, I found it,
And I did give't my husband.
Iago: Filth, thou liest!
Emilia: By heaven, I do not, I do not, gentlemen.
O murd'rous coxcomb! what should such a fool
Do with so good a wife?
Othello: Are there no stones° in heaven
But what serves for the thunder? Precious villain!

The Moor runs at Iago [but is disarmed by Montano].
Iago kills his wife.

Gratiano: The woman falls. Sure he hath killed his wife.
Emilia: Ay, ay. O, lay me by my mistress' side. *Exit Iago.*
Gratiano: He's gone, but his wife's killed.
Montano: 'Tis a notorious° villain. Take you this weapon,
Which I have here recovered from the Moor.
Come, guard the door without. Let him not pass,
But kill him rather. I'll after that same villain,
For 'tis a damnèd slave.

Exit [Montano, with all but Othello and Emilia].

Othello: I am not valiant neither;
But every puny whipster° gets my sword.
But why should honor outlive honesty?
Let it go all.
Emilia: What did thy song bode, lady?
Hark, canst thou hear me? I will play the swan,
And die in music. *[Sings.]* "Willow, willow, willow."
Moor, she was chaste. She loved thee, cruel Moor:
So come my soul to bliss as I speak true.
So speaking as I think, alas, I die.

(She dies.)

Othello: I have another weapon in this chamber;
It is a sword of Spain, the ice brook's° temper.
O, here it is. — Uncle, I must come forth.
Gratiano (within): If thou attempt it, it will cost thee dear.
Thou hast no weapon, and perforce must suffer.

235 *stones:* Bolts like those used for thunderbolts. 240 *notorious:* Notable. 245 *puny whipster:* Top-whipping boy. 254 *ice brook's:* I.e., a Spanish blade, tempered in cold running water.

Othello: Look in upon me then and speak with me,
Or, naked° as I am, I will assault thee.

[Enter Gratiano.]

Gratiano: What is the matter?
Othello: Behold, I have a weapon;
A better never did itself sustain
Upon a soldier's thigh. I have seen the day
That with this little arm and this good sword
I have made my way through more impediments
Than twenty times your stop.° But O vain boast!
Who can control his fate? 'Tis not so now.
Be not afraid, though you do see me weaponed.
Here is my journey's end, here is my butt,°
And very seamark° of my utmost sail:
Do you go back dismayed? 'Tis a lost° fear.
Man but a rush° against Othello's breast,
And he retires. Where should Othello go?
Now, how dost thou look now? O ill-starred wench!
Pale as thy smock! When we shall meet at compt,°
This look of thine will hurl my soul from heaven,
And fiends will snatch at it. Cold, cold, my girl?
Even like thy chastity.
O cursèd, cursèd slave! Whip me, ye devils,
From the possession of this heavenly sight!
Blow me about in winds! roast me in sulphur!
Wash me in steep-down gulfs of liquid fire!
Oh Desdemon! dead Desdemon! dead! Oh! Oh!

Enter Lodovico, Montano, Iago [as prisoner], and Officers; Cassio in a chair.

Lodovico: Where is this rash and most unfortunate man?
Othello: That's he that was Othello. Here I am.
Lodovico: Where is that viper? Bring the villain forth.
Othello: I look down towards his feet°—but that's a fable.
If that thou be'st a devil, I cannot kill thee.

[Wounds Iago.]

Lodovico: Wrench his sword from him.

[Othello is disarmed.]

Iago: I bleed, sir, but not killed.
Othello: I am not sorry neither. I'ld have thee live;
For in my sense, 'tis happiness to die.
Lodovico: O thou Othello that wert once so good,
Fall'n in the practice° of a damnèd slave,
What shall be said to thee?

259 *naked:* Disarmed. 265 *stop:* Power to stop. 268 *butt:* Limit. 269 *seamark:* Beacon, destination. 270 *lost:* Wasted. 271 *Man but a rush:* Wield only a reed. 274 *compt:* Final accounting, Last Judgment. 286 *I . . . feet:* I.e., to see if they are cloven, like the Devil's. 292 *practice:* Plot.

Othello: Why, anything:
An honorable murderer, if you will;
For naught did I in hate, but all in honor.
Lodovico: This wretch hath part confessed his villainy.
Did you and he consent in° Cassio's death?
Othello: Ay.
Cassio: Dear general, I never gave you cause.
Othello: I do believe it, and I ask your pardon.
Will you, I pray, demand that demi-devil
Why he hath thus ensnared my soul and body?
Iago: Demand me nothing. What you know, you know.
From this time forth I never will speak word.
Lodovico: What, not to pray?
Gratiano: Torments will ope your lips.
Othello: Well, thou dost best.
Lodovico: Sir, you shall understand what hath befall'n,
Which, as I think, you know not. Here is a letter
Found in the pocket of the slain Roderigo;
And here another. The one of them imports
The death of Cassio to be undertook
By Roderigo.
Othello: O villain!
Cassio: Most heathenish and most gross!
Lodovico: Now here's another discontented paper
Found in his pocket too; and this, it seems,
Roderigo meant t' have sent this damnèd villain;
But that, belike, Iago in the nick°
Came in and satisfied him.
Othello: O thou pernicious caitiff! —
How came you, Cassio, by that handkerchief
That was my wife's?
Cassio: I found it in my chamber;
And he himself confessed but even now
That there he dropped it for a special purpose
Which wrought to his desire.
Othello: O fool! fool! fool!
Cassio: There is besides in Roderigo's letter,
How he upbraids Iago that he made him
Brave me upon the watch; whereon it came
That I was cast;° and even but now he spake,
After long seeming dead — Iago hurt him,
Iago set him on.
Lodovico: You must forsake this room and go with us.
Your power and your command is taken off,
And Cassio rules in Cyprus. For this slave,
If there be any cunning cruelty
That can torment him much and hold him long,

297 *consent in:* Agree upon. 317 *nick:* Nick of time. 327 *cast:* Dismissed.

It shall be his. You shall close prisoner rest
Till that the nature of your fault be known
To the Venetian state. Come, bring away.

Othello: Soft you! a word or two before you go.
I have done the state some service, and they know't.
No more of that. I pray you, in your letters,
When you shall these unlucky° deeds relate,
Speak of me as I am. Nothing extenuate,
Nor set down aught in malice. Then must you speak
Of one that loved not wisely, but too well;
Of one not easily jealous, but, being wrought,
Perplexed° in the extreme; of one whose hand,
Like the base Judean,° threw a pearl away
Richer than all his tribe; of one whose subdued° eyes,
Albeit unusèd to the melting mood,
Drop tears as fast as the Arabian trees
Their med'cinable gum. Set you down this.
And say besides that in Aleppo once,
Where a malignant and a turbaned Turk
Beat a Venetian and traduced the state,
I took by th' throat the circumcisèd dog
And smote him — thus.

(He stabs himself.)

Lodovico: O bloody period!°

Gratiano: All that's spoke is marred.

Othello: I kissed thee ere I killed thee. No way but this,
Killing myself, to die upon a kiss.

(He [falls upon the bed and] dies.)

Cassio: This did I fear, but thought he had no weapon;
For he was great of heart.

Lodovico [to Iago]: O Spartan dog,
More fell° than anguish, hunger, or the sea!
Look on the tragic loading of this bed.
This is thy work. The object poisons sight;
Let it be hid.° Gratiano, keep the house,
And seize upon° the fortunes of the Moor,
For they succeed on you. To you, lord governor,
Remains the censure° of this hellish villain,
The time, the place, the torture. O, enforce it!
Myself will straight aboard, and to the state
This heavy act with heavy heart relate.

Exeunt.

341 *unlucky:* Fatal. 346 *Perplexed:* Distracted. 347 *Judean:* Judas Iscariot (?) (quarto reads "Indian"). 348 *subdued:* I.e., conquered by grief. 357 *period:* Ending. 362 *fell:* Cruel. 365 *Let it be hid:* I.e., draw the bed curtains. 366 *seize upon:* Take legal possession of. 368 *censure:* Judicial sentence.

Considerations

1. Characterize Othello. In what ways is he presented as having a jealous disposition as well as a noble one? Why is he so vulnerable to Iago's villainy? Are Othello's actions credible?
2. Explain how Iago presents himself to the world. What is beneath the surface of his public identity? Why does he hate Othello so passionately? What makes Iago so effective at manipulating people? What do other characters, besides Othello, think of him?
3. Explain whether you think Othello could have protected himself from Iago's schemes. What could Othello have done differently to avoid the suffering that ends the play? Is Iago to be blamed for everything, or must Othello shoulder some of the blame?
4. Explain why you think Othello's racial background does or doesn't affect events in the play.
5. Describe how the two settings, Venice and Cyprus, reflect different social and psychological environments as well as different behavior among the characters.
6. How does Othello change during the course of the play? Do you feel the same about him from beginning to end? Trace your response to his character as it develops, paying particular attention to Othello's final speech.
7. Consider how women — Desdemona, Emilia, and Bianca — are presented in the play. What characteristics do they have in common? How do they relate to the men in their lives?
8. Despite its grinding emotional impact and bleak ending, *Othello* does have its humorous moments. Locate a scene that includes humor and describe its tone and function in the play.
9. Choose a soliloquy by Iago and write an analysis of it so that you reveal some significant portion of his character.
10. To what extent do chance and coincidence conspire along with Iago to shape events in the play? Do you think Shakespeare merely manipulates incidents to move the plot, or do chance and coincidence have some thematic significance? Explain your answer.
11. Why does Othello insist that he must kill Desdemona immediately in Act V, Scene ii? Do you think this action is an impulse or a decision? How does your answer to this question affect your view of Othello?
12. Shakespeare uses both poetry and prose for his characters' speeches. Locate instances of a change from one to the other and discuss the effect of this change.

Connections

1. How might Desdemona and Ophelia in *Hamlet* be regarded as versions of each other? What qualities and liabilities do they share? Are there differences that clearly distinguish their characters, or are they merely interchangeable?
2. Explain how revenge is central to the plots of *Othello* and *Hamlet.* Drawing upon the consequences of revenge in each play, write an essay about the corrosive effects of revenge on the title characters.
3. Iago is a snake if ever there was one. Compare his villainy with that of Molière's character Tartuffe (p. 1263). How are their strategies for getting what they want similar or different? Consider their aims as well as their methods. Which do you find more villainous? Which more recognizable? Explain why.
4. Compare Iago's manipulation of Othello with Song Liling's manipulation of Gallimard in Henry David Hwang's *M. Butterfly* (p. 1707). Which manipulator do you think betrays his victim more? Explain.

Objections to the Elizabethan Theater by the Mayor of London 1597

The inconueniences that grow by Stage playes abowt the Citie of London.

1. They are a speaciall cause of corrupting their Youth, conteninge nothinge but vnchast matters, lascivious devices, shiftes of Coozenage, & other lewd & vngodly practizes, being so as that they impresse the very qualitie & corruption of manners which they represent, Contrary to the rules & art prescribed for the makinge of Comedies eaven amonge the Heathen, who vsed them seldom & at certen sett tymes, and not all the year longe as our manner is. Whearby such as frequent them, beinge of the base & refuze sort of people or such young gentlemen as haue small regard of credit or conscience, drawe the same into imitacion and not to the avoidinge the like vices which they represent.

2. They are the ordinary places for vagrant persons, Maisterles men, thieves, horse stealers, whoremongers, Coozeners, Conycatchers, contrivers of treason, and other idele and daungerous persons to meet together & to make theire matches to the great displeasure of Almightie God & the hurt & annoyance of her Maiesties people, which cannot be prevented nor discovered by the Gouernours of the Citie for that they are owt of the Citiees iurisdiction.

3. They maintaine idlenes in such persons as haue no vocation & draw apprentices and other seruantes from theire ordinary workes and all sortes of people from the resort vnto sermons and other Christian exercises, to the great hinderance of traides & prophanation of religion established by her highnes within this Realm.

4. In the time of sickness it is fownd by experience, that many hauing sores and yet not hart sicke take occasion hearby to walk abroad & to recreat them-selves by heareinge a play Whearby others are infected, and them selves also many things miscarry.

From Edmund K. Chambers, *The Elizabethan Stage*

Considerations

1. Summarize the mayor's objections to the theater. Do any of his reasons for protesting theatrical productions seem reasonable to you? Why or why not?
2. Are any of these concerns reflected in attitudes about the theater today? Why or why not?
3. How would you defend *Hamlet* or *Othello* against charges that they draw some people into "imitacion and not to the avoidinge the like vices which they represent"?

SAMUEL JOHNSON (1709–1784)

On Shakespeare's Characters 1765

Shakespeare is above all writers, at least above all modern writers, the poet of nature: the poet that holds up to his readers a faithful mirror of manners and life. His characters are not modified by the customs of particular places, unpracticed by the rest of the world; by the peculiarities of studies or professions, which can operate but upon small numbers; or by the accidents of transient fashions or temporary opinions: they are the genuine progeny of common humanity, such as the world will always supply, and observation will always find. His persons act and speak by the influence of those general passions and principles by which all minds are agitated, and the whole system of life is continued in motion. In the writings of other poets a character is too often an individual; in those of Shakespeare it is commonly a species.

From the Preface to Johnson's Edition of Shakespeare.

Considerations

1. Johnson made this famous assessment of Shakespeare's ability to portray "common humanity" in the eighteenth century. As a twentieth-century reader, explain why you agree or disagree with Johnson's view that Shakespeare's characters have universal appeal.
2. Write an essay discussing whether you think it is desirable or necessary for characters to be "a faithful mirror of manners and life." Along the way consider whether you encountered any characters in *Hamlet* or *Othello* that do not provide what you consider to be an accurate mirror of human life.

SIGMUND FREUD (1856–1939)

On Repression in Hamlet 1900

Another of the great creations of tragic poetry, Shakespeare's *Hamlet,* has its roots in the same soil as *Oedipus Rex.* But the changed treatment of the same material reveals the whole difference in the mental life of these two widely separated epochs of civilization: the secular advance of repression in the emotional life of mankind. In the *Oedipus* the child's wishful fantasy that underlies it is brought into the open and realized as it would be in a dream. In *Hamlet* it remains repressed; and — just as in the case of a neurosis — we only learn of its existence from its inhibiting consequences. Strangely enough, the overwhelming effect produced by the more modern tragedy has turned out to be compatible with the fact that people have remained completely in the dark as to the hero's character. The play is built up on Hamlet's hesitations over fulfilling the task of revenge that is assigned to him; but its text offers no reasons or motives for these hesitations and an immense variety of attempts at interpreting them have failed to produce a result. According to the view which was originated by Goethe and is still the prevailing one today, Hamlet represents the type of man whose power of direct action is paralyzed by an excessive development of his intellect. (He is "sicklied o'er with the pale cast of thought.") According to another view, the dramatist has tried to portray a pathologically irresolute character which might be classed as neurasthenic. The plot of the drama shows us, however, that Hamlet is far from being represented as a person incapable of taking any action. We see him doing so on two occasions: first in a sudden outburst of temper, when he runs his sword through the eavesdropper behind the arras, and secondly in a premeditated and even crafty fashion, when, with all the callousness of a Renaissance prince, he sends the two courtiers to the death that had been planned for himself. What is it, then, that inhibits him in fulfilling the task set him by his father's ghost? The answer, once again, is that it is the peculiar nature of the task. Hamlet is able to do anything — except take vengeance on the man who did away with his father and took that father's place with his mother, the man who shows him the repressed wishes of his own childhood realized. Thus the loathing which should drive him on to revenge is replaced in him by self-reproaches, by scruples of conscience, which remind him that he himself is literally no better than the sinner whom he is to punish. Here I have translated into conscious terms what was bound to remain unconscious in Hamlet's mind; and if anyone is inclined to call him a hysteric, I can only accept the fact as one that is implied by my interpretation. The distaste for sexuality expressed by Hamlet in his conversation with Ophelia fits in very well with this: the same distaste which was destined to take possession of the poet's mind more and more during the years that followed, and which reached its extreme expression in *Timon of Athens*. For it can of course only be the poet's own mind which confronts us in Hamlet. I observe in a book on Shakespeare by Georg Brandes (1896) a statement that *Hamlet* was written immediately after the death of Shakespeare's father (in 1601), that is, under the immediate impact of his bereavement and, as we may well assume, while his childhood feelings about his father had been freshly revived. It is known, too, that Shakespeare's own son who died at an early age bore the name of "Hamnet," which is identical with "Hamlet." Just as *Hamlet* deals with the relation of a son to his parents, so *Macbeth* (written at approximately the same period) is concerned with the subject of childlessness. But just as all neurotic symptoms, and, for that matter, dreams, are capable of being "overinterpreted" and indeed need to be, if they are to be fully understood, so all genuinely creative writings are the product of more than a single motive and more than a single impulse in the poet's mind, and are open to more than a single interpretation. In what I have written I have only attempted to interpret the deepest layer of impulses in the mind of the creative writer.

From *The Interpretation of Dreams*

Considerations

1. What reason does Freud offer for Hamlet's inability to avenge his father's death? Explain whether you find Freud's reasoning convincing.
2. Read the section on psychological criticism (p. 1783) in Chapter 32, "Critical Strategies for Reading," and then discuss Freud's assertion that "it can of course only be the poet's mind which confronts us in Hamlet." Explain why you agree or disagree.

3. Write an essay discussing whether you think Freud's approach to *Hamlet* opens up perspectives on the play or narrowly limits them.

JAN KOTT (b. 1914)
On Producing Hamlet

1964

No Dane of flesh and blood has been written about so extensively as Hamlet. Shakespeare's prince is certainly the best known representative of his nation. Innumerable glossaries and commentaries have grown round Hamlet, and he is one of the few literary heroes who live apart from the text, apart from the theater. His name means something even to those who have never seen or read Shakespeare's play. In this respect he is rather like Leonardo's Mona Lisa. We know she is smiling even before we have seen the picture, as it were. It contains not only what Leonardo expressed in it but also everything that has been written about it. Too many people — girls, women, poets, painters — have tried to solve the mystery of that smile. It is not just Mona Lisa that is smiling at us now, but all those who have tried to analyze, or imitate, that smile.

This is also the case with *Hamlet,* or rather — with *Hamlet* in the theater. For we have been separated from the text not only by Hamlet's "independent life" in our culture, but simply by the size of the play. *Hamlet* cannot be performed in its entirety, because the performance would last nearly six hours. One has to select, curtail, and cut. One can perform only one of several *Hamlets* potentially existing in this arch-play. It will always be a poorer *Hamlet* than Shakespeare's *Hamlet* is; but it may also be a *Hamlet* enriched by being of our time. It may, but I would rather say — it must be so.

For *Hamlet* cannot be played simply. This may be the reason why it is so tempting to producers and actors. Many generations have seen their own reflections in this play. The genius of *Hamlet* consists, perhaps, in the fact that the play can serve as a mirror. An ideal *Hamlet* would be one most true to Shakespeare and most modern at the same time. Is this possible? I do not know. But we can only appraise any Shakespearean production by asking how much there is of Shakespeare in it, and how much of us.

What I have in mind is not a forced topicality, a *Hamlet* that would be set in a cellar of young existentialists. *Hamlet* has been performed for that matter in evening dress and in circus tights; in medieval armor and in Renaissance costume. Costumes do not matter. What matters is that through Shakespeare's text we ought to get at our modern experience, anxiety, and sensibility.

There are many subjects in *Hamlet.* There is politics, force opposed to morality; there is discussion of the divergence between theory and practice, of the ultimate purpose of life; there is tragedy of love, as well as family drama; political, eschatological, and metaphysical problems are considered. There is everything you want, including deep psychological analysis, a bloody story, a duel, and general slaughter. One can select at will. But one must know what one selects, and why.

From "*Hamlet* of the Mid-Century" in *Shakespeare Our Contemporary,*
translated by Boleslaw Taborski

Considerations

1. "Many generations have seen their own reflections in this play." Use this statement as a basis for researching productions of *Hamlet.* How have events contemporary to the play's performances influenced the ways it has been presented?
2. Explain why you think it is good or bad for a producer to interpret a play in light of events contemporary to it.
3. If you were to produce *Hamlet* today, what would you emphasize? Consider how you would handle the setting, costuming, casting, and theme.
4. What do you think a reader-response critic would have to say about Kott's comments on producing *Hamlet?* Base your answer on the discussion of reader-response criticism in Chapter 32, "Critical Strategies for Reading," p. 1777.

KAREN S. HENRY (b. 1954)

The Play Within the Play in Hamlet 1989

Imprisoned in a world of spies, Hamlet imagines the theater to be the ultimate watcher — the spy set on spies. Lionel Abel describes the perverted interaction between the characters in Elsinore as projection or dramatization: "What has not been noticed . . . is that there is hardly a scene in the whole work in which some character is not trying to dramatize another" (*Metatheatre* 45). Abel's comment highlights the theatricalization of all experience that is rampant in this play. Hamlet, one of the many directors in the play, turns to the theater to mirror Claudius's crime back to him and thus expose him. The theater, however, becomes more than Hamlet's means of seeing through and exposing corruption; the play within the play exposes Hamlet to Claudius just as it reveals Claudius to Hamlet, setting off a series of events that lead to the inevitable and fatal conflict between these characters.

Hamlet intends his play to reestablish the ground for judgment and decision: "I'll have grounds/ More relative than this. The play's the thing/ Wherein I'll catch the conscience of the King." But Hamlet never lets the play do its work; he never trusts that it can have a strong enough effect. Like the bad actors he warns the players against imitating, he saws the air too much and "in the very torrent, tempest, and whirlwind" of his passion he deforms his play. As he becomes more and more impassioned, his interpretations of the dramatic action usurp it entirely, becoming the central action in the scene. We see Hamlet as the director who cannot step out of the show. His interruptions are a way of manipulating Ophelia, Gertrude, and ultimately Claudius, but they are also nearly out of his control, and so they make him vulnerable to his enemies. He hurts and embarrasses Ophelia and forces a reaction out of Gertrude that merely frustrates him further. With these two, the interruptions remain part of the theatrical scene as the play within the play continues. With Claudius, however, theater breaks into life at Elsinore when the King stops the play within the play.

Before that moment, the *Mousetrap* advances the larger plot by interacting dynamically with it. The play within the play proceeds as Claudius asks questions of Hamlet, giving the Prince an opportunity to twist the knife a bit further with each answer:

King: Have you heard the argument? Is there no offence in't?
Hamlet: No, no, they do but jest, poison in jest; no offence i' the world.
King: What do you call the play?
Hamlet: The Mouse-trap. . . . 'tis a knavish piece of work: but what o' that? Your majesty, and we that have free souls, it touches us not: let the galled jade winch, our withers are unwrung.

(III, ii, 209–211, 213–215)

Hamlet's thinly veiled irony complicates the larger plot. Once Claudius is certain that Hamlet is baiting him, he cannot let the nephew escape.

In his excess, Hamlet subverts his own contrivance. Instead of detaching himself from the action to watch Claudius's response to the mirror image of his crime, Hamlet enters wildly and makes himself conspicuous as the antagonist of the King. Any objective perception of Claudius is therefore marred. Who in the court, except Horatio, would be willing to say that the King suffers from a guilty conscience and not from anger against his mad nephew who seems to threaten him with assassination. By manipulating the play, Hamlet provokes and warns Claudius — the nephew knows the uncle's secret. Hamlet threatens to expose Claudius with the exposition about the poisoning: " 'A poisons him i' the garden for his estate. . . . You shall see anon how the murderer gets the love of Gonzago's wife" (III, ii, 232–234). And Claudius responds by calling for lights, thus stopping Hamlet's game. Hamlet and Horatio interpret Claudius's act as a confession of guilt, but only the theater audience (watchers watching watchers) can confirm this interpretation.

From "The Shattering of Resemblance:
The Mirror in Shakespeare"

Considerations

1. Explain in detail how the play within the play creates the crisis in *Hamlet.*
2. In what sense is Hamlet "one of the many directors in the play"? What other characters also function as directors? How do their actions warrant such a description?
3. In an essay explore the significance of Henry's provocative phrase describing the theater audience as "watchers watching watchers." How might this phrase also be used to describe other scenes in the play? What does it suggest about the nature of Hamlet's world?

HELEN GARDNER (b. 1908)
On Freedom in Hamlet *and* Othello 1955

Othello is like a hero of the ancient world in that he is not a man like us, but a man recognized as extraordinary. He seems born to do great deeds and live in legend. He has the obvious heroic qualities of courage and strength, and no actor can attempt the role who is not physically impressive. He has the heroic capacity for passion. But the thing which most sets him apart is his solitariness. He is a stranger, a man of alien race, without ties of nature or natural duties. His value is not in what the world thinks of him, although the world rates him highly, and does not derive in any way from his station. It is inherent. He is, in a sense, a "self-made man," the product of a certain kind of life which he has chosen to lead. In this he is in sharp contrast to the tragic hero who immediately precedes him. Hamlet is son and prince. He is in the universal situation of man born in time, creature of circumstances and duties which he has not chosen. The human relation which arises from choice is the least important in the play, or rather it is important in its failure. Hamlet the son, Ophelia the daughter, are not free to love. The possibility of freedom is the very thing which is in question in *Hamlet.* The infected will, the dubieties of moral choice, the confusions of speculation are different aspects of our sense of bondage. The gate of death is barred in *Hamlet;* man, who has not chosen to be born, cannot choose to die. The choice of death is forbidden by religion in the first soliloquy; later it is seen as a choice made impossible by our ignorance of what we choose in choosing death, so that the puzzled will cannot be absolute for life or death. At the close the hero finds death at another's hand, and not by choice.

To this vision of man bound *Othello* presents a vision of man free. The past, whose claim upon the present is at the heart of *Hamlet,* is in *Othello* a country which the hero has passed through and left behind, the scene of his "travels' history." The ancestors of royal siege, the father and mother, between whom the handkerchief passed and from whom it came to him, have no claim upon him. His status in Venice is contractual. The Senate are his "very noble and approv'd good masters" because he and they have chosen it should be so. His loyalties are not the tangle of inherited loyalties, but the few and simple loyalites of choice. His duties are not the duties of his station, but the duties of his profession. Othello is free as intensely as Hamlet is unfree, and the relation which fails to establish itself in *Hamlet* is the one relation which counts here, the free relation of love. It is presented in its most extreme, that is in heroic, form, as a relation between individuals, owing nothing to, and indeed triumphing over, circumstances and natural inclination. The universality of the play lies here, in its presentation of man as freely choosing and expressing choice by acts: Desdemona crossing the Senate floor to take her place beside her husband, Othello slaying her and slaying himself, Emilia crying out the truth at the cost of her life. *Othello* is particularly concerned with that deep, instinctive level where we feel ourselves to be free.

From "The Noble Moor" in *Shakespeare Criticism, 1935–1960,*
selected by Ann Ridler

Considerations

1. In what sense does Gardner view Othello as a "self-made man"? How does that make him different from Hamlet, according to Gardner? Explain why you agree or disagree.
2. How does Gardner define freedom? Discuss whether you concur with her judgment that Othello is more free than Hamlet.
3. Write an essay exploring Hamlet's and Othello's relations to the past. To what extent does the past inform the present for each of them?

A. C. BRADLEY (1851–1935)

On Iago's Intellect and Will 1904

In order to see how this tragedy arises let us now look more closely into Iago's inner man. We find here, in the first place . . . very remarkable powers both of intellect and of will. Iago's insight, within certain limits, into human nature; his ingenuity and address in working upon it; his quickness and versatility in dealing with sudden difficulties and unforeseen opportunities, have probably no parallel among dramatic characters. Equally remarkable is his strength of will. . . . It is not merely that he never betrays his true nature; he seems to be master of *all* the motions that might affect his will. In the most dangerous moments of his plot, when the least slip or accident would be fatal, he never shows a trace of nervousness. When Othello takes him by the throat he merely shifts his part with his usual instantaneous adroitness. When he is attacked and wounded at the end he is perfectly unmoved. . . . He is equally unassailable by the temptations of indolence or of sensuality. It is difficult to imagine him inactive; and though he has an obscene mind, and doubtless took his pleasures when and how he chose, he certainly took them by choice and not from weakness, and if pleasure interfered with his purposes the holiest of ascetics would not put it more resolutely by. "What should I do?" Roderigo whimpers to him; "I confess it is my shame to be so fond; but it is not in my virtue to amend it." He answers: "Virtue! a fig! 'tis in ourselves that we are thus and thus." It all depends on our will. Love is "merely a lust of the blood and a permission of the will. Come, be a man. . . . Ere I would say I would drown myself for the love of a guinea-hen, I would change my humanity with a baboon." Forget for a moment that love is for Iago the appetite of a baboon; forget that he is as little assailable by pity as by fear or pleasure; and you will acknowledge that this lordship of the will, which is his practice as well as his doctrine, is great, almost sublime. Indeed, in intellect (always within certain limits) and in will (considered as a mere power, and without regard to its objects) Iago *is* great.

From *Shakespearean Tragedy*

Considerations

1. How does Iago demonstrate his insights into human nature in the play? Does he have the same kind of insight into himself? Explain.
2. How well does the phrase "lordship of the will" describe Iago's behavior for you?
3. Write an essay comparing Iago's intellect and will with those of Hamlet. What important similarities and differences do you find? What do you think Iago would have done in Hamlet's situation?

JANE ADAMSON

On Desdemona's Role in Othello 1980

One of the oddest things about criticism of *Othello* is how little usually gets said about Desdemona. She is often considered as a necessary element in the drama only because she is a necessary element in its plot — the woman with whom Othello just happens to be in love — rather than a major dramatic figure conceived in relation to everyone else. There is a strong tendency in critics of all persuasions to take her as a helpless, hapless victim — like one of those ideal Victorian heroines in whose mouths not even margarine would melt. As Marvin Rosenberg points out [in *The Masks of Othello*], "Desdemona has been in grave danger of being canonized," with the result that the play is made to seem much simpler than it is. . . . As Rosenberg also points out, however, the same result follows from the (not uncommon) alternative view of Desdemona, which sees her not as an innocent victim but as the culpable agent of her fate, or as someone whose "flaws" or "indiscretions" are such that she partly "deserves" what happens because she "brings it upon herself."

It seems to me that Rosenberg is right: neither of these views of Desdemona will do. Not only is she a more interesting and complex character, but she also emerges as a crucial and complex element in the dramatic design. To miss or distort what she — and Emilia and Bianca, the play's other women in love — represent in the world of *Othello* is to miss an essential element in its tragic power. What [F. R.] Leavis, for instance, asserts [in "Diabolic Intellect and the Noble Hero"] but nowhere explains is true: "the tragedy is inherent in the Othello-Desdemona relation."

From Othello *as Tragedy: Some Problems of Judgment and Feeling*

Considerations

1. How might Desdemona be regarded as a "helpless, hapless victim"? What evidence is there in the play to support such a view?
2. Try to make a case for Desdemona as "the culpable agent of her fate."
3. Adamson agrees with Leavis that "the tragedy is inherent in the Othello-Desdemona relation." In an essay explore the possibilities of this provocative suggestion. What is there in these characters' relationship that could lead to their mutual suffering?

27. Neoclassical Drama

The French ***neoclassical drama*** of the seventeenth century developed from the Renaissance revival of classical Greek and Roman literature (*neo-* means new). During the reign of Louis XIV, the absolute monarch known as the Sun King, drama in France grew vigorously, as it had about a half century earlier in Elizabethan England. The arts were part of the elegant luxury that Louis XIV surrounded himself with in his palace at Versailles. Though he was fiercely jealous of power and characterized his relationship to his subjects with the declaration "I am the state," he was also a generous patron of the theater, who encouraged and supported a variety of playwrights. The two most successful tragedians of French neoclassical theater were Pierre Corneille (1606–1684) and Jean Racine (1639–1699), while the unrivaled writer of comedy was Molière (1622–1673).

Molière (whose real name was Jean-Baptiste Poquelin) was the son of a prosperous Paris furniture maker who was also an official upholsterer to the king. The young Poquelin studied the classics, philosophy, and law. With his fine education and family connections, he could have lived a secure, respectable life as a lawyer or as the successor to his father's post, but instead he devoted his entire adult life to drama. The career he chose was neither easy nor highly regarded; the theater was then widely perceived as corruptive and disreputable. Indeed, Molière may have taken his stage name to avoid embarrassing his family. In 1643 he joined a dramatic troupe called The Illustrious Theater, which soon went bankrupt and landed him in debtor's prison for a short while.

Since there was little chance of success in Paris, the troupe toured the provinces for more than a dozen years, during which Molière developed his acting and writing skills. In 1658 the troupe was invited to perform before the court of Louis XIV. Favorably impressed with the performance, the king gave the troupe official recognition and a theater in Paris. This royal favor provided Molière with the opportunity to write, direct, and act for the rest of his life. From among the roughly thirty plays he wrote, the best known and most important comedies, in addition to *Tartuffe* (1669), include *The School for Wives* (1662), *The Misanthrope* (1666), *The Doctor in Spite of Himself* (1666), *The Miser* (1668), and *The Would-Be Gentleman* (1670). Molière's death came only a few hours after he had acted the leading role in his last play, ironically titled *The Imaginary Invalid* (1673).

THEATRICAL CONVENTIONS OF NEOCLASSICAL DRAMA

Like Shakespeare, Molière was both an actor and a playwright; he knew intimately the theater for which he wrote. French neoclassical theater differed from Shakespeare's because Molière's contemporaries placed heavy emphasis on the ***classical unities*** of time, place, and action. Neoclassical scholars and critics, deriving their principles from Renaissance interpretations of Aristotle's *Poetics,* insisted that a play must confine itself to a twenty-four-hour period, restrict its setting to one location, and develop only one line of action, without digressions or elaborate subplots. Unity of action also means that comedy and tragedy must be kept entirely separate; there was to be no mixing of comic scenes with the high seriousness of tragedy and no blending of permanent pain and suffering with laughter. It was assumed that a play had to observe these unities to be a great work of art; plays that violated these standards were often judged badly made or crude.

Molière respects the classical unities in *Tartuffe* with no strain: the consistent action — comic throughout despite its teetering on several dangerous, almost disastrous precipices — occurs within a single day in a setting restricted to a room of Orgon's house. Viewed from a historical perspective, these unities reflect neoclassical ideals of order and restraint, but as critical standards they represent theatrical fashions rather than irrefutable principles. *Hamlet,* to name only one example, ignores all three classical unities. Molière himself dispensed with them when they did not suit his purposes.

Neoclassical theater derived its physical structure from Italian Renaissance stages and eventually developed into the kind of theater familiar to modern playgoers. In contrast to classical Greek or Elizabethan performing areas, the theater in Molière's time was enclosed by a roof that protected an auditorium as elegantly appointed as the aristocrats and well-to-do merchants who attended the performances. The stage was at one end of a long rectangle so that the audience viewed the action either from seats in front of the stage or from galleries along the sides of the auditorium. The ***proscenium arch*** separated the actors from the audience and formed a ***picture-frame stage,*** which, when the curtain that hung from the proscenium arch was drawn, created the effect of looking into a room that had one of its walls removed.

The stage and auditorium were lighted by hundreds of candles in chandeliers. Although the dim lighting could not be focused exclusively on the stage, the audience could see the painted scenery that served as background to the action. The scenes typically portrayed a room, a courtyard, or a street; they were usually neither elaborate nor realistic. No attempt would have been made in a seventeenth-century production of *Tartuffe,* for example, to detail the room in which the action occurs; a painted background and a table for a prop would have sufficed.

Costuming, however, was more elaborate, because actors wore contemporary dress that reflected their characters' social position. Paris became known as the center of fashion during the reign of Louis XIV. Earlier, boys had been used to act women's roles, but women were permitted on stage in neoclassical theater. Thus, both actors and actresses could convincingly re-create in their dress and manners the social milieu of the majority of their affluent audience.

Molière's plays were considerably less physical than those of the Elizabethan stage, in which sword play and brawls might result in more characters being dead than alive by the end of the final scene. Neoclassical comedies relied more on wit and sophisticated manners for their drama. The classical unities influenced the nature of the action onstage by creating a sense of proportion and decorum, while offstage the restraint and moderation of the social environment determined that conflicts would be resolved through reasoned, witty dialogue rather than violence.

SATIRE

Molière's reputation rests on his brilliant satires of the fashions, conventions, and morals of middle- and upper-class society. This kind of satire, known as a ***comedy of manners,*** uses characters that tend to be more types than individualized personalities. These types developed from stock characterizations popular in sixteenth-century Italian ***commedia dell'arte,*** a form of farce that also featured gags and improvisational acting. Young lovers, a shrewd servant, a bumbling fool, a rich tyrannical father, or a convincing hypocrite appear in various forms in Molière's comedies and in the work of many subsequent comic writers. In *Tartuffe,* Orgon and Dorine are more interesting and developed than stock characters, but their origins can be traced to the characterizations of the foolish father and clever, faithful maid that developed in *commedia dell'arte.*

Unlike a romantic comedy, such as Shakespeare's *Twelfth Night,* a comedy of manners plays down complicated plots (usually involving lovers) and emphasizes clever, refined dialogue, whose humor is pointed and whose purpose is reform as well as entertainment. Satire is directed against human follies and any behavior that fails to measure up to the standards of moderate, rational, responsible conduct. In *Tartuffe,* Valère and Mariane correspond to the type of young lovers so familiar in genial romantic comedies, but the predominant tone is critical instead of celebratory. In spite of the many laughs Molière's satire provides, his criticism of human faults represents a serious impulse.

In his preface to *Tartuffe,* Molière makes clear that this satiric comedy is calculated to expose vices that might otherwise be overlooked, tolerated, or even mistakenly revered.

> If the function of comedy is to correct men's vices, I do not see why any should be exempt. Such a condition in our society would be much more dangerous than the thing itself; and we have seen that the theater is admirably suited to provide correction. The most forceful lines of a serious moral statement are usually less powerful than those of satire; and nothing will reform most men better than the depiction of their faults. It is a vigorous blow to vices to expose them to public laughter. Criticism is taken lightly, but men will not tolerate satire. They are quite willing to be mean, but they never like to be ridiculed.

Tartuffe is a satire of religious hypocrisy and the gullibility of those who accept the fraudulent piety of rapacious liars.

Molière found that his audiences of aristocrats and rising middle-class hopefuls offered plenty to satirize; affected ladies, quacks, misers, wicked noblemen, and other eccentrics all merited exposure. If he sometimes made his audiences uncomfortable, it was because they felt the sting of his ridicule. Molière believed his job was to reveal the absurdities of his time and "make respectable people laugh" at those who took themselves too seriously and were therefore ridiculous, dangerous, or both.

TARTUFFE

Although *Tartuffe*'s ending befits a comedy, the play's beginnings on the stage were anything but happy. Molière's first version of the play was presented before Louis XIV at Versailles in 1664. The king liked the play, but the church pressured him to ban it, because it was perceived as a wholesale attack on the clergy. One critic described Molière as "a demon in the flesh . . . who should be burned alive." To defuse this criticism and make clear that he was attacking only false piety, Molière revised the play and changed the title to *The Impostor* in 1667, when it was again produced. His critics, however, descended on the play once more and succeeded in persuading the king to ban it. Not until 1669 was Molière allowed to produce the play as it now exists. Since then *Tartuffe* has been popular with readers and viewers who enjoy seeing self-serving hypocrites exposed and blind zealots restored to sight.

But finally the play is compelling less for the justice meted out to Tartuffe than for his character. He is a first-class villain. Even if the play's ending is not convincing, Tartuffe's evil is because he so thoroughly preys on Orgon and his family. Tartuffe is not content to gain Orgon's and his mother's confidence; he would also appropriate Orgon's wife, daughter, and all his wealth.

But Orgon is also a threat to the family's happiness. He is hopelessly blind to the hypocrite's deceptions. Indeed, were it not for the rest of his family we might be tempted to leave him to Tartuffe's manipulations; he very nearly deserves to be victimized for his stupidity. In contrast to Orgon are Cléante, Dorine, and Elmire, who see through Tartuffe's assumed piety. These characters represent Molière's own values of moderation and deep suspicion of irrational extremes. They see clearly and help Orgon to discover his delusion. We are invited to judge Orgon as well as Tartuffe.

Molière wrote in tightly balanced rhyming couplets that create a concise, light, playful effect. In French these couplets are in iambic hexameter, a form known as ***alexandrines***. The following English translation by Richard Wilbur, however, uses iambic pentameter rhymed couplets, because they capture Molière's elegant language while avoiding the too-obvious rhythms created by six-foot English lines. With pentameter lines Wilbur re-creates the nimble wit of the original French.

MOLIÈRE
[JEAN-BAPTISTE POQUELIN] (1622–1673)
Tartuffe 1669

TRANSLATED BY RICHARD WILBUR

Characters

Madame Pernelle, Orgon's mother
Orgon, Elmire's husband
Elmire, Orgon's wife
Damis, Orgon's son, Elmire's stepson
Mariane, Orgon's daughter, Elmire's stepdaughter, in love with Valère
Valère, in love with Mariane
Cléante, Orgon's brother-in-law
Tartuffe, a hypocrite
Dorine, Mariane's lady's-maid
M. Loyal, a bailiff
A Police Officer
Flipote, Mme Pernelle's maid

The scene throughout: Orgon's house in Paris

ACT I

SCENE I

Madame Pernelle and Flipote, her maid; Elmire, Dorine, Cléante, Mariane, Damis

Madame Pernelle: Come, come, Flipote; it's time I left this place.
Elmire: I can't keep up, you walk at such a pace.

Madame Pernelle: Don't trouble, child; no need to show me out.
It's not your manners I'm concerned about.
Elmire: We merely pay you the respect we owe.
But, Mother, why this hurry? Must you go?
Madame Pernelle: I must. This house appalls me. No one in it
Will pay attention for a single minute.
Children, I take my leave much vexed in spirit.
I offer good advice, but you won't hear it.
You all break in and chatter on and on.
It's like a madhouse with the keeper gone.
Dorine: If . . .
Madame Pernelle: Girl, you talk too much, and I'm afraid
You're far too saucy for a lady's-maid.
You push in everywhere and have your say.
Damis: But . . .
Madame Pernelle: You, boy, grow more foolish every day.
To think my grandson should be such a dunce!
I've said a hundred times, if I've said it once,
That if you keep the course on which you've started,
You'll leave your worthy father broken-hearted.
Mariane: I think . . .
Madame Pernelle: And you, his sister, seems so pure,
So shy, so innocent, and so demure.
But you know what they say about still waters.
I pity parents with secretive daughters.
Elmire: Now, Mother . . .
Madame Pernelle: And as for you, child, let me add
That your behavior is extremely bad,
And a poor example for these children, too.
Their dear, dead mother did far better than you.
You're much too free with money, and I'm distressed
To see you so elaborately dressed.
When it's one's husband that one aims to please,
One has no need of costly fripperies.
Cléante: Oh, Madam, really . . .
Madame Pernelle: You are her brother, Sir,
And I respect and love you; yet if I were
My son, this lady's good and pious spouse,
I wouldn't make you welcome in my house.
You're full of worldly counsels which, I fear,
Aren't suitable for decent folk to hear.
I've spoken bluntly, Sir; but it behooves us
Not to mince words when righteous fervor moves us.
Damis: Your man Tartuffe is full of holy speeches . . .
Madame Pernelle: And practises precisely what he preaches.
He's a fine man, and should be listened to.
I will not hear him mocked by fools like you.
Damis: Good God! Do you expect me to submit
To the tyranny of that carping hypocrite?

Must we forgo all joys and satisfactions
Because that bigot censures all our actions?
Dorine: To hear him talk — and he talks all the time —
There's nothing one can do that's not a crime.
He rails at everything, your dear Tartuffe.
Madame Pernelle: Whatever he reproves deserves reproof.
He's out to save your souls, and all of you
Must love him, as my son would have you do.
Damis: Ah no, Grandmother, I could never take
To such a rascal, even for my father's sake.
That's how I feel, and I shall not dissemble.
His every action makes me seethe and tremble
With helpless anger, and I have no doubt
That he and I will shortly have it out.
Dorine: Surely it is a shame and a disgrace
To see this man usurp the master's place —
To see this beggar who, when first he came,
Had not a shoe or shoestring to his name
So far forget himself that he behaves
As if the house were his, and we his slaves.
Madame Pernelle: Well, mark my words, your souls would fare far better
If you obeyed his precepts to the letter.
Dorine: You see him as a saint. I'm far less awed;
In fact, I see right through him. He's a fraud.
Madame Pernelle: Nonsense!
Dorine: His man Laurent's the same, or worse;
I'd not trust either with a penny purse.
Madame Pernelle: I can't say what his servant's morals may be;
His own great goodness I can guarantee.
You all regard him with distaste and fear
Because he tells you what you're loath to hear,
Condemns your sins, points out your moral flaws,
And humbly strives to further Heaven's cause.
Dorine: If sin is all that bothers him, why is it
He's so upset when folk drop in to visit?
Is Heaven so outraged by a social call
That he must prophesy against us all?
I'll tell you what I think: if you ask me,
He's jealous of my mistress' company.
Madame Pernelle: Rubbish! *(To Elmire.)* He's not alone, child, in complaining
Of all your promiscuous entertaining.
Why, the whole neighborhood's upset, I know,
By all these carriages that come and go,
With crowds of guests parading in and out
And noisy servants loitering about.
In all of this, I'm sure there's nothing vicious;
But why give people cause to be suspicious?
Cléante: They need no cause; they'll talk in any case.

Madam, this world would be a joyless place
If, fearing what malicious tongues might say,
We locked our doors and turned our friends away.
And even if one did so dreary a thing,
D'you think those tongues would cease their chattering?
One can't fight slander; it's a losing battle;
Let us instead ignore their tittle-tattle.
Let's strive to live by conscience' clear decrees,
And let the gossips gossip as they please.

Dorine: If there is talk against us, I know the source:
It's Daphne and her little husband, of course.
Those who have greatest cause for guilt and shame
Are quickest to besmirch a neighbor's name.
When there's a chance for libel, they never miss it;
When something can be made to seem illicit
They're off at once to spread the joyous news,
Adding to fact what fantasies they choose.
By talking up their neighbor's indiscretions
They seek to camouflage their own transgressions,
Hoping that other's innocent affairs
Will lend a hue of innocence to theirs,
Or that their own black guilt will come to seem
Part of a general shady color-scheme.

Madame Pernelle: All that is quite irrelevant. I doubt
That anyone's more virtuous and devout
Than dear Orante; and I'm informed that she
Condemns your mode of life most vehemently.

Dorine: Oh, yes, she's strict, devout, and has no taint
Of worldliness; in short, she seems a saint.
But it was time which taught her that disguise;
She's thus because she can't be otherwise.
So long as her attractions could enthrall,
She flounced and flirted and enjoyed it all,
But now that they're no longer what they were
She quits a world which fast is quitting her,
And wears a veil of virtue to conceal
Her bankrupt beauty and her lost appeal.
That's what becomes of old coquettes today:
Distressed when all their lovers fall away,
They see no recourse but to play the prude,
And so confer a style on solitude.
Thereafter, they're severe with everyone,
Condemning all our actions, pardoning none,
And claiming to be pure, austere, and zealous
When, if the truth were known, they're merely jealous.
And cannot bear to see another know
The pleasures time has forced them to forgo.

Madame Pernelle (initially to Elmire): That sort of talk is what you like to hear;

Therefore you'd have us all keep still, my dear,
While Madam rattles on the livelong day,
Nevertheless, I mean to have my say.
I tell you that you're blest to have Tartuffe
Dwelling, as my son's guest, beneath this roof;
That Heaven has sent him to forestall its wrath
By leading you, once more, to the true path;
That all he reprehends is reprehensible,
And that you'd better heed him, and be sensible.
These visits, balls, and parties in which you revel
Are nothing but inventions of the Devil.
One never hears a word that's edifying:
Nothing but chaff and foolishness and lying,
As well as vicious gossip in which one's neighbor
Is cut to bits with epee, foil, and saber.
People of sense are driven half-insane
At such affairs, where noise and folly reign
And reputations perish thick and fast.
As a wise preacher said on Sunday last,
Parties are Towers of Babylon, because
The guests all babble on with never a pause;
And then he told a story which, I think . . .
(To Cléante.) I heard that laugh, Sir, and I saw that wink!
Go find your silly friends and laugh some more!
Enough; I'm going; don't show me to the door.
I leave this household much dismayed and vexed;
I cannot say when I shall see you next.
(Slapping Flipote.) Wake up, don't stand there gaping into space!
I'll slap some sense into that stupid face.
Move, move, you slut.

Scene II

Cléante, Dorine

Cléante: I think I'll stay behind;
I want no further pieces of her mind.
How that old lady . . .
Dorine: Oh, what wouldn't she say
If she could hear you speak of her that way!
She'd thank you for the *lady,* but I'm sure
She'd find the *old* a little premature.
Cléante: My, what a scene she made, and what a din!
And how this man Tartuffe has taken her in!
Dorine: Yes, but her son is even worse deceived;
His folly must be seen to be believed.
In the late troubles, he played an able part
And served his king with wise and loyal heart,
But he's quite lost his senses since he fell

Beneath Tartuffe's infatuating spell.
He calls him brother, and loves him as his life,
Preferring him to mother, child, or wife.
In him and him alone will he confide;
He's made him his confessor and his guide;
He pets and pampers him with love more tender
Than any pretty mistress could engender,
Gives him the place of honor when they dine,
Delights to see him gorging like a swine,
Stuffs him with dainties till his guts distend,
And when he belches, cries "God bless you, friend!"
In short, he's mad; he worships him; he dotes;
His deeds he marvels at, his words he quotes,
Thinking each act a miracle, each word
Oracular as those that Moses heard.
Tartuffe, much pleased to find so easy a victim,
Has in a hundred ways beguiled and tricked him,
Milked him of money, and with his permission
Established here a sort of Inquisition.
Even Laurent, his lackey, dares to give
Us arrogant advice on how to live;
He sermonizes us in thundering tones
And confiscates our ribbons and colognes.
Last week he tore a kerchief into pieces
Because he found it pressed in a *Life of Jesus:*
He said it was a sin to juxtapose
Unholy vanities and holy prose.

Scene III

Elmire, Damis, Dorine, Mariane, Cléante

Elmire (to Cléante): You did well not to follow; she stood in the door
And said *verbatim* all she'd said before.
I saw my husband coming. I think I'd best
Go upstairs now, and take a little rest.
Cléante: I'll wait and greet him here; then I must go.
I've really only time to say hello.
Damis: Sound him about my sister's wedding, please.
I think Tartuffe's against it, and that he's
Been urging Father to withdraw his blessing.
As you well know, I'd find that most distressing.
Unless my sister and Valère can marry,
My hopes to wed *his* sister will miscarry,
And I'm determined . . .
Dorine: He's coming.

Scene IV

Orgon, Cléante, Dorine

Orgon: Ah, Brother, good-day.
Cléante: Well, welcome back. I'm sorry I can't stay.
How was the country? Blooming, I trust, and green?
Orgon: Excuse me, Brother; just one moment.
(To Dorine.) Dorine . . .
(To Cléante.) To put my mind at rest, I always learn
The household news the moment I return.
(To Dorine.) Has all been well, these two days I've been gone?
How are the family? What's been going on?
Dorine: Your wife, two days ago, had a bad fever,
And a fierce headache which refused to leave her.
Orgon: Ah. And Tartuffe?
Dorine: Tartuffe? Why, he's round and red,
Bursting with health, and excellently fed.
Orgon: Poor fellow!
Dorine: That night, the mistress was unable
To take a single bite at the dinner-table.
Her headache-pains, she said, were simply hellish.
Orgon: Ah. And Tartuffe?
Dorine: He ate his meal with relish,
And zealously devoured in her presence
A leg of mutton and a brace of pheasants.
Orgon: Poor fellow!
Dorine: Well, the pains continued strong,
And so she tossed and tossed the whole night long,
Now icy-cold, now burning like a flame.
We sat beside her bed till morning came.
Orgon: Ah. And Tartuffe?
Dorine: Why, having eaten, he rose
And sought his room, already in a doze,
Got into his warm bed, and snored away
In perfect peace until the break of day.
Orgon: Poor fellow!
Dorine: After much ado, we talked her
Into dispatching someone for the doctor.
He bled her, and the fever quickly fell.
Orgon: Ah. And Tartuffe?
Dorine: He bore it very well.
To keep his cheerfulness at any cost,
And make up for the blood *Madame* had lost,
He drank, at lunch, four beakers full of port.
Orgon: Poor fellow!
Dorine: Both are doing well, in short.
I'll go and tell *Madame* that you've expressed
Keen sympathy and anxious interest.

Scene V

Orgon, Cléante

Cléante: That girl was laughing in your face, and though
I've no wish to offend you, even so
I'm bound to say that she had some excuse.
How can you possibly be such a goose?
Are you so dazed by this man's hocus-pocus
That all the world, save him, is out of focus?
You've given him clothing, shelter, food, and care;
Why must you also . . .

Orgon: Brother, stop right there.
You do not know the man of whom you speak.

Cléante: I grant you that. But my judgment's not so weak
That I can't tell, by his effect on others . . .

Orgon: Ah, when you meet him, you two will be like brothers!
There's been no loftier soul since time began.
He is a man who . . . a man who . . . an excellent man.
To keep his precepts is to be reborn,
And view this dunghill of a world with scorn.
Yes, thanks to him I'm a changed man indeed.
Under his tutelage my soul's been freed
From earthly loves, and every human tie:
My mother, children, brother, and wife could die,
And I'd not feel a single moment's pain.

Cléante: That's a fine sentiment, Brother; most humane.

Orgon: Oh, had you seen Tartuffe as I first knew him,
Your heart, like mine, would have surrendered to him.
He used to come into our church each day
And humbly kneel nearby, and start to pray.
He'd draw the eyes of everybody there
By the deep fervor of his heartfelt prayer;
He'd sigh and weep, and sometimes with a sound
Of rapture he would bend and kiss the ground;
And when I rose to go, he'd run before
To offer me holy-water at the door.
His serving-man, no less devout than he,
Informed me of his master's poverty;
I gave him gifts, but in his humbleness
He'd beg me every time to give him less.
"Oh, that's too much," he'd cry, "too much by twice!
I don't deserve it. The half, Sir, would suffice."
And when I wouldn't take it back, he'd share
Half of it with the poor, right then and there.
At length, Heaven prompted me to take him in
To dwell with us, and free our souls from sin.
He guides our lives, and to protect my honor
Stays by my wife, and keeps an eye upon her;
He tells me whom she sees, and all she does,

And seems more jealous than I ever was!
And how austere he is! Why, he can detect
A mortal sin where you would least suspect;
In smallest trifles, he's extremely strict.
Last week, his conscience was severely pricked
Because, while praying, he had caught a flea
And killed it, so he felt, too wrathfully.

Cléante: Good God, man! Have you lost your common sense —
Or is this all some joke at my expense?
How can you stand there and in all sobriety . . .

Orgon: Brother, your language savors of impiety.
Too much free-thinking's made your faith unsteady,
And as I've warned you many times already,
'Twill get you into trouble before you're through.

Cléante: So I've been told before by dupes like you:
Being blind, you'd have all others blind as well;
The clear-eyed man you call an infidel,
And he who sees through humbug and pretense
Is charged, by you, with want of reverence.
Spare me your warnings, Brother; I have no fear
Of speaking out, for you and Heaven to hear,
Against affected zeal and pious knavery.
There's true and false in piety, as in bravery,
And just as those whose courage shines the most
In battle, are the least inclined to boast,
So those whose hearts are truly pure and lowly
Don't make a flashy show of being holy.
There's a vast difference, so it seems to me,
Between true piety and hypocrisy:
How do you fail to see it, may I ask?
Is not a face quite different from a mask?
Cannot sincerity and cunning art,
Reality and semblance, be told apart?
Are scarecrows just like men, and do you hold
That a false coin is just as good as gold?
Ah, Brother, man's a strangely fashioned creature
Who seldom is content to follow Nature,
But recklessly pursues his inclination
Beyond the narrow bounds of moderation,
And often, by transgressing Reason's laws,
Perverts a lofty aim or noble cause.
A passing observation, but it applies.

Orgon: I see, dear Brother, that you're profoundly wise;
You harbor all the insight of the age.
You are our one clear mind, our only sage,
The era's oracle, its Cato° too,
And all mankind are fools compared to you.

91 *Cato:* (234–149 B.C.) Roman statesman who upheld high morals and the simple life.

Cléante: Brother, I don't pretend to be a sage,
Nor have I all the wisdom of the age.
There's just one insight I would dare to claim:
I know that true and false are not the same;
And just as there is nothing I more revere
Than a soul whose faith is steadfast and sincere,
Nothing that I more cherish and admire
Than honest zeal and true religious fire,
So there is nothing that I find more base
Than specious piety's dishonest face —
Than these bold mountebanks, these histrios
Whose impious mummeries and hollow shows
Exploit our love of Heaven, and make a jest
Of all that men think holiest and best;
These calculating souls who offer prayers
Not to their Maker, but as public wares,
And seek to buy respect and reputation
With lifted eyes and sighs of exaltation;
These charlatans, I say, whose pilgrim souls
Proceed, by way of Heaven, toward earthly goals,
Who weep and pray and swindle and extort,
Who preach the monkish life, but haunt the court,
Who make their zeal the partner of their vice —
Such men are vengeful, sly, and cold as ice,
And when there is an enemy to defame
They cloak their spite in fair religion's name,
Their private spleen and malice being made
To seem a high and virtuous crusade,
Until, to mankind's reverent applause,
They crucify their foe in Heaven's cause.
Such knaves are all too common; yet, for the wise,
True piety isn't hard to recognize,
And, happily, these present times provide us
With bright examples to instruct and guide us.
Consider Ariston and Périandre;
Look at Oronte, Alcidamas, Clitandre;°
Their virtue is acknowledged; who could doubt it?
But you won't hear them beat the drum about it.
They're never ostentatious, never vain,
And their religion's moderate and humane;
It's not their way to criticize and chide:
They think censoriousness a mark of pride,
And therefore, letting others preach and rave,
They show, by deeds, how Christians should behave.
They think no evil of their fellow man,
But judge of him as kindly as they can.

127–128 *Consider . . . Clitandre:* Made-up classical-sounding names; not real people.

They don't intrigue and wangle and conspire;
To lead a good life is their one desire;
The sinner wakes no rancorous hate in them;
It is the sin alone which they condemn;
Nor do they try to show a fiercer zeal
For Heaven's cause than Heaven itself could feel.
These men I honor, these men I advocate
As models for us all to emulate.
Your man is not their sort at all, I fear:
And, while your praise of him is quite sincere,
I think that you've been dreadfully deluded.

Orgon: Now then, dear Brother, is your speech concluded?

Cléante: Why, yes.

Orgon: Your servant, Sir. *(He turns to go.)*

Cléante: No, Brother; wait.
There's one more matter. You agreed of late
That young Valère might have your daughter's hand.

Orgon: I did.

Cléante: And set the date, I understand.

Orgon: Quite so.

Cléante: You've now postponed it; is that true?

Orgon: No doubt.

Cléante: The match no longer pleases you?

Orgon: Who knows?

Cléante: D'you mean to go back on your word?

Orgon: I won't say that.

Cléante: Has anything occurred
Which might entitle you to break your pledge?

Orgon: Perhaps.

Cléante: Why must you hem, and haw, and hedge?
The boy asked me to sound you in this affair . . .

Orgon: It's been a pleasure.

Cléante: But what shall I tell Valère?

Orgon: Whatever you like.

Cléante: But what have you decided?
What are your plans?

Orgon: I plan, Sir, to be guided
By Heaven's will.

Cléante: Come, Brother, don't talk rot.
You've given Valère your word; will you keep it, or not?

Orgon: Good day.

Cléante: This looks like poor Valère's undoing;
I'll go and warn him that there's trouble brewing.

ACT II

Scene I

Orgon, Mariane

Orgon: Mariane.
Mariane: Yes, Father?
Orgon: A word with you; come here.
Mariane: What are you looking for?
Orgon (peering into a small closet): Eavesdroppers, dear.
I'm making sure we shan't be overheard.
Someone in there could catch our every word.
Ah, good, we're safe. Now, Mariane, my child,
You're a sweet girl who's tractable and mild,
Whom I hold dear, and think most highly of.
Mariane: I'm deeply grateful, Father, for your love.
Orgon: That's well said, Daughter; and you can repay me
If, in all things, you'll cheerfully obey me.
Mariane: To please you, Sir, is what delights me best
Orgon: Good, good. Now, what d'you think of Tartuffe, our guest?
Mariane: I, Sir?
Orgon. Yes. Weigh your answer; think it through.
Mariane: Oh, dear. I'll say whatever you wish me to.
Orgon: That's wisely said, my Daughter. Say of him, then,
That he's the very worthiest of men,
And that you're fond of him, and would rejoice
In being his wife, if that should be my choice.
Well?
Mariane: What?
Orgon: What's that?
Mariane: I . . .
Orgon: Well?
Mariane: Forgive me, pray.
Orgon: Did you not hear me?
Mariane: Of *whom,* Sir, must I say
That I am fond of him, and would rejoice
In being his wife, if that should be your choice?
Orgon: Why, of Tartuffe.
Mariane: But, Father, that's false, you know.
Why would you have me say what isn't so?
Orgon: Because I am resolved it shall be true.
That it's my wish should be enough for you.
Mariane: You can't mean, Father . . .
Orgon: Yes, Tartuffe shall be
Allied by marriage to this family,
And he's to be your husband, is that clear?
It's a father's privilege . . .

Scene II

Dorine, Orgon, Mariane

Orgon (to Dorine): What are you doing in here?
Is curiosity so fierce a passion
With you, that you must eavesdrop in this fashion?
Dorine: There's lately been a rumor going about —
Based on some hunch or chance remark, no doubt —
That you mean Mariane to wed Tartuffe.
I've laughed it off, of course, as just a spoof.
Orgon: You find it so incredible?
Dorine: Yes, I do.
I won't accept that story, even from you.
Orgon: Well, you'll believe it when the thing is done.
Dorine: Yes, yes, of course. Go on and have your fun.
Orgon: I've never been more serious in my life.
Dorine: Ha!
Orgon: Daughter, I mean it; you're to be his wife.
Dorine: No, don't believe your father; it's all a hoax.
Orgon: See here, young woman . . .
Dorine: Come, Sir, no more jokes;
You can't fool us.
Orgon: How dare you talk that way?
Dorine: All right, then: we believe you, sad to say.
But how a man like you, who looks so wise
And wears a moustache of such splendid size,
Can be so foolish as to . . .
Orgon: Silence, please!
My girl, you take too many liberties.
I'm master here, as you must not forget.
Dorine: Do let's discuss this calmly; don't be upset.
You can't be serious, Sir, about this plan.
What should that bigot want with Mariane?
Praying and fasting ought to keep him busy.
And then, in terms of wealth and rank, what is he?
Why should a man of property like you
Pick out a beggar son-in-law?
Orgon: That will do.
Speak of his poverty with reverence.
His is a pure and saintly indigence
Which far transcends all worldly pride and pelf.
He lost his fortune, as he says himself,
Because he cared for Heaven alone, and so
Was careless of his interests here below.
I mean to get him out of his present straits
And help him to recover his estates —

Which, in his part of the world, have no small fame.
Poor though he is, he's a gentleman just the same.
Dorine: Yes, so he tells us; and, Sir, it seems to me
Such pride goes very ill with piety.
A man whose spirit spurns this dungy earth
Ought not to brag of lands and noble birth;
Such worldly arrogance will hardly square
With meek devotion and the life of prayer.
. . . But this approach, I see, has drawn a blank;
Let's speak, then, of his person, not his rank.
Doesn't it seem to you a trifle grim
To give a girl like her to a man like him?
When two are so ill-suited, can't you see
What the sad consequence is bound to be?
A young girl's virtue is imperilled, Sir,
When such a marriage is imposed on her;
For if one's bridegroom isn't to one's taste,
It's hardly an inducement to be chaste,
And many a man with horns upon his brow
Has made his wife the thing that she is now.
It's hard to be a faithful wife, in short,
To certain husbands of a certain sort,
And he who gives his daughter to a man she hates
Must answer for her sins at Heaven's gates.
Think, Sir, before you play so risky a role.
Orgon: This servant-girl presumes to save my soul!
Dorine: You would do well to ponder what I've said.
Orgon: Daughter, we'll disregard this dunderhead.
Just trust your father's judgment. Oh, I'm aware
That I once promised you to young Valère;
But now I hear he gambles, which greatly shocks me;
What's more, I've doubts about his orthodoxy.
His visits to church, I note, are very few.
Dorine: Would you have him go at the same hours as you,
And kneel nearby, to be sure of being seen?
Orgon: I can dispense with such remarks, Dorine.
(To Mariane.) Tartuffe, however, is sure of Heaven's blessing,
And that's the only treasure worth possessing.
This match will bring you joys beyond all measure;
Your cup will overflow with every pleasure;
You two will interchange your faithful loves
Like two sweet cherubs, or two turtle-doves.
No harsh word shall be heard, no frown be seen.
And he shall make you happy as a queen.
Dorine: And she'll make him a cuckold, just wait and see.
Orgon: What language!
Dorine: Oh, he's a man of destiny;
He's *made* for horns, and what the stars demand
Your daughter's virtue surely can't withstand.

Orgon: Don't interrupt me further. Why can't you learn
That certain things are none of your concern?
Dorine: It's for your own sake that I interfere.

She repeatedly interrupts Orgon just as he is turning to speak to his daughter.

Orgon: Most kind of you. Now, hold your tongue, d'you hear?
Dorine: If I didn't love you . . .
Orgon: Spare me your affection.
Dorine: I love you, Sir, in spite of your objection.
Orgon: Blast!
Dorine: I can't bear, Sir, for your honor's sake,
To let you make this ludicrous mistake.
Orgon: You mean to go on talking?
Dorine: If I didn't protest
This sinful marriage, my conscience couldn't rest.
Orgon: If you don't hold your tongue, you little shrew . . .
Dorine: What, lost your temper? A pious man like you?
Orgon: Yes! Yes! You talk and talk. I'm maddened by it.
Once and for all, I tell you to be quiet.
Dorine: Well, I'll be quiet. But I'll be thinking hard.
Orgon: Think all you like, but you had better guard
That saucy tongue of yours, or I'll . . .
(Turning back to Mariane.) Now, child,
I've weighed this matter fully.
Dorine (aside): It drives me wild
That I can't speak.

Orgon turns his head, and she is silent.

Orgon: Tartuffe is no young dandy,
But, still, his person . . .
Dorine (aside): Is as sweet as candy.
Orgon: Is such that, even if you shouldn't care
For his other merits . . .

He turns and stands facing Dorine, arms crossed.

Dorine (aside): They'll make a lovely pair.
If I were she, no man would marry me
Against my inclination, and go scot-free.
He'd learn, before the wedding-day was over,
How readily a wife can find a lover.
Orgon (to Dorine): It seems you treat my orders as a joke.
Dorine: Why, what's the matter? 'Twas not to you I spoke.
Orgon: What *were* you doing?
Dorine: Talking to myself, that's all.
Orgon: Ah! *(Aside.)* One more bit of impudence and gall,
And I shall give her a good slap in the face.

He puts himself in position to slap her; Dorine, whenever he glances at her, stands immobile and silent.

Daughter, you shall accept, and with good grace,
The husband I've selected . . . Your wedding-day . . .
(To Dorine.) Why don't you talk to yourself?

Dorine: I've nothing to say.

Orgon: Come, just one word.

Dorine: No thank you, Sir. I pass.

Orgon: Come, speak; I'm waiting.

Dorine: I'd not be such an ass.

Orgon (turning to Mariane): In short, dear Daughter, I mean to be obeyed,
And you must bow to the sound choice I've made.

Dorine (moving away): I'd not wed such a monster, even in jest.

Orgon attempts to slap her, but misses.

Orgon: Daughter, that maid of yours is a thorough pest;
She makes me sinfully annoyed and nettled.
I can't speak further; my nerves are too unsettled.
She's so upset me by her insolent talk,
I'll calm myself by going for a walk.

Scene III

Dorine, Mariane

Dorine (returning): Well, have you lost your tongue, girl? Must I play
Your part, and say the lines you ought to say?
Faced with a fate so hideous and absurd,
Can you not utter one dissenting word?

Mariane: What good would it do? A father's power is great.

Dorine: Resist him now, or it will be too late.

Mariane: But . . .

Dorine: Tell him one cannot love at a father's whim;
That you shall marry for yourself, not him;
That since it's you who are to be the bride,
It's you, not he, who must be satisfied;
And that if his Tartuffe is so sublime,
He's free to marry him at any time.

Mariane: I've bowed so long to Father's strict control,
I couldn't oppose him now, to save my soul.

Dorine: Come, come, Mariane. Do listen to reason, won't you?
Valère has asked your hand. Do you love him, or don't you?

Mariane: Oh, how unjust of you! What can you mean
By asking such a question, dear Dorine?
You know the depth of my affection for him;
I've told you a hundred times how I adore him.

Dorine: I don't believe in everything I hear;
Who knows if your professions were sincere?

Mariane: They were, Dorine, and you do me wrong to doubt it;
Heaven knows that I've been all too frank about it.

Dorine: You love him, then?

Mariane: Oh, more than I can express.

Dorine: And he, I take it, cares for you no less?
Mariane: I think so.
Dorine: And you both, with equal fire,
Burn to be married?
Mariane: That is our one desire.
Dorine: What of Tartuffe, then? What of your father's plan?
Mariane: I'll kill myself, if I'm forced to wed that man.
Dorine: I hadn't thought of that recourse. How splendid!
Just die, and all your troubles will be ended!
A fine solution. Oh, it maddens me
To hear you talk in that self-pitying key.
Mariane: Dorine, how harsh you are! It's most unfair.
You have no sympathy for my despair.
Dorine: I've none at all for people who talk drivel
And, faced with difficulties, whine and snivel.
Mariane: No doubt I'm timid, but it would be wrong . . .
Dorine: True love requires a heart that's firm and strong.
Mariane: I'm strong in my affection for Valère,
But coping with my father is his affair.
Dorine: But if your father's brain has grown so cracked
Over his dear Tartuffe that he can retract
His blessing, though your wedding-day was named,
It's surely not Valère who's to be blamed.
Mariane: If I defied my father, as you suggest,
Would it not seem unmaidenly, at best?
Shall I defend my love at the expense
Of brazenness and disobedience?
Shall I parade my heart's desires, and flaunt . . .
Dorine: No, I ask nothing of you. Clearly you want
To be Madame Tartuffe, and I feel bound
Not to oppose a wish so very sound.
What right have I to criticize the match?
Indeed, my dear, the man's a brilliant catch.
Monsieur Tartuffe! Now, there's a man of weight!
Yes, yes, Monsieur Tartuffe, I'm bound to state,
Is quite a person; that's not to be denied;
'Twill be no little thing to be his bride.
The world already rings with his renown;
He's a great noble — in his native town;
His ears are red, he has a pink complexion,
And all in all, he'll suit you to perfection.
Mariane: Dear God!
Dorine: Oh, how triumphant you will feel
At having caught a husband so ideal!
Mariane: Oh, do stop teasing, and use your cleverness
To get me out of this appalling mess.
Advise me, and I'll do whatever you say.
Dorine: Ah no, a dutiful daughter must obey
Her father, even if he weds her to an ape.

You've a bright future; why struggle to escape?
Tartuffe will take you back where his family lives,
To a small town aswarm with relatives —
Uncles and cousins whom you'll be charmed to meet.
You'll be received at once by the elite,
Calling upon the bailiff's wife, no less —
Even, perhaps, upon the mayoress,
Who'll sit you down in the *best* kitchen chair.
Then, once a year, you'll dance at the village fair
To the drone of bagpipes — two of them, in fact —
And see a puppet-show, or an animal act.
Your husband . . .

Mariane: Oh, you turn my blood to ice!
Stop torturing me, and give me your advice.

Dorine (threatening to go): Your servant, Madam.

Mariane: Dorine, I beg of you . . .

Dorine: No, you deserve it; this marriage must go through.

Mariane: Dorine!

Dorine: No.

Mariane: Not Tartuffe! You know I think him . . .

Dorine: Tartuffe's your cup of tea, and you shall drink him.

Mariane: I've always told you everything, and relied . . .

Dorine: No. You deserve to be tartuffified.

Mariane: Well, since you mock me and refuse to care,
I'll henceforth seek my solace in despair:
Despair shall be my counsellor and friend,
And help me bring my sorrows to an end.

She starts to leave.

Dorine: There now, come back; my anger has subsided.
You do deserve some pity, I've decided.

Mariane: Dorine, if Father makes me undergo
This dreadful martyrdom, I'll die, I know.

Dorine: Don't fret; it won't be difficult to discover
Some plan of action . . . But here's Valère, your lover.

Scene IV

Valère, Mariane, Dorine

Valère: Madam, I've just received some wondrous news
Regarding which I'd like to hear your views.

Mariane: What news?

Valère: You're marrying Tartuffe.

Mariane: I find
That Father does have such a match in mind.

Valère: Your father, Madam . . .

Mariane: . . . has just this minute said
That it's Tartuffe he wishes me to wed.

Valère: Can he be serious?
Mariane: Oh, indeed he can;
He's clearly set his heart upon the plan.
Valère: And what position do you propose to take, Madam?
Mariane: Why — I don't know.
Valère: For heaven's sake —
You don't know?
Mariane: No.
Valère: Well, well!
Mariane: Advise me, do.
Valère: Marry the man. That's my advice to you.
Mariane: That's your advice?
Valère: Yes.
Mariane: Truly?
Valère: Oh, absolutely.
You couldn't choose more wisely, more astutely.
Mariane: Thanks for this counsel; I'll follow it, of course.
Valère: Do, do; I'm sure 'twill cost you no remorse.
Mariane: To give it didn't cause your heart to break.
Valère: I gave it, Madam, only for your sake.
Mariane: And it's for your sake that I take it, Sir.
Dorine (withdrawing to the rear of the stage): Let's see which fool will prove the stubborner.
Valère: So! I am nothing to you, and it was flat
Deception when you . . .
Mariane: Please, enough of that.
You've told me plainly that I should agree
To wed the man my father's chosen for me,
And since you've designed to counsel me so wisely,
I promise, Sir, to do as you advise me.
Valère: Ah, no, 'twas not by me that you were swayed.
No, your decision was already made;
Though now, to save appearances, you protest
That you're betraying me at my behest.
Mariane: Just as you say.
Valère: Quite so. And I now see
That you were never truly in love with me.
Mariane: Alas, you're free to think so if you choose.
Valère: I choose to think so, and here's a bit of news:
You've spurned my hand, but I know where to turn
For kinder treatment, as you shall quickly learn.
Mariane: I'm sure you do. Your noble qualities
Inspire affection . . .
Valère: Forget my qualities, please.
They don't inspire you overmuch, I find.
But there's another lady I have in mind
Whose sweet and generous nature will not scorn
To compensate me for the loss I've borne.

Mariane: I'm no great loss, and I'm sure that you'll transfer
Your heart quite painlessly from me to her.
Valère: I'll do my best to take it in my stride.
The pain I feel at being cast aside
Time and forgetfulness may put an end to.
Or if I can't forget, I shall pretend to.
No self-respecting person is expected
To go on loving once he's been rejected.
Mariane: Now, that's a fine, high-minded sentiment.
Valère: One to which any sane man would assent.
Would you prefer it if I pined away
In hopeless passion till my dying day?
Am I to yield you to a rival's arms
And not console myself with other charms?
Mariane: Go then: console yourself; don't hesitate.
I wish you to; indeed, I cannot wait.
Valère: You wish me to?
Mariane: Yes.
Valère: That's the final straw.
Madam, farewell. Your wish shall be my law.

He starts to leave, and then returns: this repeatedly.

Mariane: Splendid.
Valère (coming back again):
This breach, remember, is of your making;
It's you who've driven me to the step I'm taking.
Mariane: Of course.
Valère (coming back again):
Remember, too, that I am merely
Following your example.
Mariane: I see that clearly.
Valère: Enough. I'll go and do your bidding, then.
Mariane: Good.
Valère (coming back again):
You shall never see my face again.
Mariane: Excellent.
Valère (walking to the door, then turning about):
Yes?
Mariane: What?
Valère: What's that? What did you say?
Mariane: Nothing. You're dreaming.
Valère: Ah. Well, I'm on my way.
Farewell, *Madame.*

He moves slowly away.

Mariane: Farewell.
Dorine (to Mariane): If you ask me,
Both of you are as mad as mad can be.

Do stop this nonsense, now. I've only let you
Squabble so long to see where it would get you.
Whoa there, Monsieur Valère!

She goes and seizes Valère by the arm; he makes a great show of resistance.

Valère: What's this, Dorine?
Dorine: Come here.
Valère: No, no, my heart's too full of spleen.
Don't hold me back; her wish must be obeyed.
Dorine: Stop!
Valère: It's too late now; my decision's made.
Dorine: Oh, pooh!
Mariane (aside): He hates the sight of me, that's plain.
I'll go, and so deliver him from pain.
Dorine (leaving Valère, running after Mariane):
And now *you* run away! Come back.
Mariane: No, no.
Nothing you say will keep me here. Let go!
Valère (aside): She cannot bear my presence, I perceive.
To spare her further torment, I shall leave.
Dorine (leaving Mariane, running after Valère): Again! You'll not escape,
Sir; don't you try it.
Come here, you two. Stop fussing, and be quiet.

She takes Valère by the hand, then Mariane, and draws them together.

Valère (to Dorine): What do you want of me?
Mariane (to Dorine): What is the point of this?
Dorine: We're going to have a little armistice.
(To Valère.) Now weren't you silly to get so overheated?
Valère: Didn't you see how badly I was treated?
Dorine (to Mariane): Aren't you a simpleton, to have lost your head?
Mariane: Didn't you hear the hateful things he said?
Dorine (to Valère): You're both great fools. Her sole desire, Valère,
Is to be yours in marriage. To that I'll swear.
(To Mariane.) He loves you only, and he wants no wife
But you, Mariane. On that I'll stake my life.
Mariane (to Valère): Then why you advised me so, I cannot see.
Valère (to Mariane): On such a question, why ask advice of *me?*
Dorine: Oh, you're impossible. Give me your hands, you two.
(To Valère.) Yours first.
Valère (giving Dorine his hand): But why?
Dorine (to Mariane): And now a hand from you.
Mariane (also giving Dorine her hand):
What are you doing?
Dorine: There: a perfect fit.
You suit each other better than you'll admit.

Valère and Mariane hold hands for some time without looking at each other.

Valère (turning toward Mariane): Ah, come, don't be so haughty. Give a man
A look of kindness, won't you, Mariane?

Mariane turns toward Valère and smiles.

Dorine: I tell you, lovers are completely mad!
Valère (to Mariane): Now come, confess that you were very bad
To hurt my feelings as you did just now.
I have a just complaint, you must allow.
Mariane: *You* must allow that you were most unpleasant . . .
Dorine: Let's table that discussion for the present;
Your father has a plan which must be stopped.
Mariane: Advise us, then: what means must we adopt?
Dorine: We'll use all manner of means, and all at once.
(To Mariane.) Your father's addled; he's acting like a dunce.
Therefore you'd better humor the old fossil.
Pretend to yield to him, be sweet and docile,
And then postpone, as often as necessary,
The day on which you have agreed to marry.
You'll thus gain time, and time will turn the trick.
Sometimes, for instance, you'll be taken sick,
And that will seem good reason for delay;
Or some bad omen will make you change the day —
You'll dream of muddy water, or you'll pass
A dead man's hearse, or break a looking-glass.
If all else fails, no man can marry you
Unless you take his ring and say "I do."
But now, let's separate. If they should find
Us talking here, our plot might be divined.
(To Valère.) Go to your friends, and tell them what's occurred,
And have them urge her father to keep his word.
Meanwhile, we'll stir her brother into action,
And get Elmire, as well, to join our faction.
Good-bye.
Valère (to Mariane):
Though each of us will do his best,
It's your true heart on which my hopes shall rest.
Mariane (to Valère): Regardless of what Father may decide,
None but Valère shall claim me as his bride.
Valère: Oh, how those words content me! Come what will . . .
Dorine: Oh, lovers, lovers! Their tongues are never still.
Be off, now.
Valère (turning to go, then turning back):
One last word . . .
Dorine:
No time to chat:
You leave by this door; and *you* leave by that.

(Dorine pushes them, by the shoulders, toward opposing doors.)

ACT III

Scene I

Damis, Dorine

Damis: May lightning strike me even as I speak,
May all men call me cowardly and weak,
If any fear or scruple holds me back
From settling things, at once, with that great quack!
Dorine: Now, don't give way to violent emotion.
Your father's merely talked about this notion,
And words and deeds are far from being one.
Much that is talked about is left undone.
Damis: No, I must stop that scoundrel's machinations;
I'll go and tell him off; I'm out of patience.
Dorine: Do calm down and be practical. I had rather
My mistress dealt with him — and with your father.
She has some influence with Tartuffe, I've noted.
He hangs upon her words, seems most devoted,
And may, indeed, be smitten by her charm.
Pray Heaven it's true! 'Twould do our cause no harm.
She sent for him, just now, to sound him out
On this affair you're so incensed about;
She'll find out where he stands, and tell him, too,
What dreadful strife and trouble will ensue
If he lends countenance to your father's plan.
I couldn't get in to see him, but his man
Says that he's almost finished with his prayers.
Go, now. I'll catch him when he comes downstairs.
Damis: I want to hear this conference, and I will.
Dorine: No, they must be alone.
Damis: Oh, I'll keep still.
Dorine: Not you. I know your temper. You'd start a brawl,
And shout and stamp your foot and spoil it all.
Go on.
Damis: I won't; I have a perfect right . . .
Dorine: Lord, you're a nuisance! He's coming; get out of sight.

Damis conceals himself in a closet at the rear of the stage.

Scene II

Tartuffe, Dorine

Tartuffe (observing Dorine, and calling to his manservant offstage):
Hang up my hair-shirt, put my scourge in place,
And pray, Laurent, for Heaven's perpetual grace.
I'm going to the prison now, to share
My last few coins with the poor wretches there.

Dorine (aside): Dear God, what affectation! What a fake!
Tartuffe: You wished to see me?
Dorine: Yes . . .
Tartuffe (taking a handkerchief from his pocket):
For mercy's sake,
Please take this handkerchief, before you speak.
Dorine: What?
Tartuffe: Cover that bosom, girl. The flesh is weak,
And unclean thoughts are difficult to control.
Such sights as that can undermine the soul.
Dorine: Your soul, it seems, has very poor defenses,
And flesh makes quite an impact on your senses.
It's strange that you're so easily excited;
My own desires are not so soon ignited,
And if I saw you naked as a beast,
Not all your hide would tempt me in the least.
Tartuffe: Girl, speak more modestly; unless you do,
I shall be forced to take my leave of you.
Dorine: Oh, no, it's I who must be on my way;
I've just one little message to convey.
Madame is coming down, and begs you, Sir,
To wait and have a word or two with her.
Tartuffe: Gladly.
Dorine (aside): That had a softening effect!
I think my guess about him was correct.
Tartuffe: Will she be long?
Dorine: No: that's her step I hear.
Ah, here she is, and I shall disappear.

Scene III

Elmire, Tartuffe

Tartuffe: May Heaven, whose infinite goodness we adore,
Preserve your body and soul forevermore,
And bless your days, and answer thus the plea
Of one who is its humblest votary.
Elmire: I thank you for that pious wish. But please
Do take a chair and let's be more at ease.

They sit down.

Tartuffe: I trust that you are once more well and strong?
Elmire: Oh, yes: the fever didn't last for long.
Tartuffe: My prayers are too unworthy, I am sure,
To have gained from Heaven this most gracious cure;
But lately, Madam, my every supplication
Has had for object your recuperation.
Elmire: You shouldn't have troubled so. I don't deserve it.

Tartuffe: Your health is priceless, Madam, and to preserve it
I'd gladly give my own, in all sincerity.
Elmire: Sir, you outdo us all in Christian charity.
You've been most kind. I count myself your debtor.
Tartuffe: 'Twas nothing, Madam. I long to serve you better.
Elmire: There's a private matter I'm anxious to discuss.
I'm glad there's no one here to hinder us.
Tartuffe: I too am glad; it floods my heart with bliss
To find myself alone with you like this.
For just this chance I've prayed with all my power —
But prayed in vain, until this happy hour.
Elmire: This won't take long, Sir, and I hope you'll be
Entirely frank and unconstrained with me.
Tartuffe: Indeed, there's nothing I had rather do
Than bare my inmost heart and soul to you.
First, let me say that what remarks I've made
About the constant visits you are paid
Were prompted not by any mean emotion,
But rather by a pure and deep devotion,
A fervent zeal . . .
Elmire: No need for explanation.
Your sole concern, I'm sure, was my salvation.
Tartuffe (taking Elmire's hand and pressing her fingertips): Quite so; and such great fervor do I feel . . .
Elmire: Ooh! Please! You're pinching!
Tartuffe: 'Twas from excess of zeal.
I never meant to cause you pain, I swear.
I'd rather . . .

He places his hand on Elmire's knee.

Elmire: What can your hand be doing there?
Tartuffe: Feeling your gown; what soft, fine-woven stuff!
Elmire: Please, I'm extremely ticklish. That's enough.

She draws her chair away; Tartuffe pulls his after her.

Tartuffe (fondling the lace collar of her gown): My, my, what lovely lacework on your dress!
The workmanship's miraculous, no less.
I've not seen anything to equal it.
Elmire: Yes, quite. But let's talk business for a bit.
They say my husband means to break his word
And give his daughter to you, Sir. Had you heard?
Tartuffe: He did once mention it. But I confess
I dream of quite a different happiness.
It's elsewhere, Madam, that my eyes discern
The promise of that bliss for which I yearn.
Elmire: I see: you care for nothing here below.
Tartuffe: Ah, well — my heart's not made of stone, you know.

Elmire: All your desires mount heavenward, I'm sure,
In scorn of all that's earthly and impure.
Tartuffe: A love of heavenly beauty does not preclude
A proper love for earthly pulchritude;
Our senses are quite rightly captivated
By perfect works our Maker has created.
Some glory clings to all that Heaven has made;
In you, all Heaven's marvels are displayed.
On that fair face, such beauties have been lavished,
The eyes are dazzled and the heart is ravished;
How could I look on you, O flawless creature,
And not adore the Author of all Nature,
Feeling a love both passionate and pure
For you, his triumph of self-portraiture?
At first, I trembled lest that love should be
A subtle snare that Hell had laid for me;
I vowed to flee the sight of you, eschewing
A rapture that might prove my soul's undoing;
But soon, fair being, I became aware
That my deep passion could be made to square
With rectitude, and with my bounden duty.
I thereupon surrendered to your beauty.
It is, I know, presumptuous on my part
To bring you this poor offering of my heart,
And it is not my merit, Heaven knows,
But your compassion on which my hopes repose.
You are my peace, my solace, my salvation;
On you depends my bliss — or desolation;
I bide your judgment and, as you think best,
I shall be either miserable or blest.
Elmire: Your declaration is most gallant, Sir,
But don't you think it's out of character?
You'd have done better to restrain your passion
And think before you spoke in such a fashion.
It ill becomes a pious man like you . . .
Tartuffe: I may be pious, but I'm human too:
With your celestial charms before his eyes,
A man has not the power to be wise.
I know such words sound strangely, coming from me,
But I'm no angel, nor was meant to be,
And if you blame my passion, you must needs
Reproach as well the charms on which it feeds.
Your loveliness I had no sooner seen
Than you became my soul's unrivalled queen;
Before your seraph glance, divinely sweet,
My heart's defenses crumbled in defeat,
And nothing fasting, prayer, or tears might do
Could stay my spirit from adoring you.
My eyes, my sighs have told you in the past

What now my lips make bold to say at last,
And if, in your great goodness, you will deign
To look upon your slave, and ease his pain, —
If, in compassion for my soul's distress,
You'll stoop to comfort my unworthiness,
I'll raise to you, in thanks for that sweet manna,
An endless hymn, an infinite hosanna.
With me, of course, there need be no anxiety,
No fear of scandal or of notoriety.
These young court gallants, whom all the ladies fancy,
Are vain in speech, in action rash and chancy;
When they succeed in love, the world soon knows it;
No favor's granted them but they disclose it
And by the looseness of their tongues profane
The very altar where their hearts have lain.
Men of my sort, however, love discreetly,
And one may trust our reticence completely.
My keen concern for my good name insures
The absolute security of yours;
In short, I offer you, my dear Elmire,
Love without scandal, pleasure without fear.

Elmire: I've heard your well-turned speeches to the end.
And what you urge I clearly apprehend.
Aren't you afraid that I may take a notion
To tell my husband of your warm devotion,
And that, supposing he were duly told,
His feelings toward you might grow rather cold?

Tartuffe: I know, dear lady, that your exceeding charity
Will lead your heart to pardon my temerity;
That you'll excuse my violent affection
As human weakness, human imperfection;
And that — O fairest! — you will bear in mind
That I'm but flesh and blood, and am not blind.

Elmire: Some women might do otherwise, perhaps,
But I shall be discreet about your lapse;
I'll tell my husband nothing of what's occurred
If, in return, you'll give your solemn word
To advocate as forcefully as you can
The marriage of Valère and Mariane,
Renouncing all desire to dispossess
Another of his rightful happiness,
And . . .

Scene IV

Damis, Elmire, Tartuffe

Damis (emerging from the closet where he has been hiding):
No! We'll not hush up this vile affair;
I heard it all inside that closet there,

Where Heaven, in order to confound the pride
Of this great rascal, prompted me to hide.
Ah, now I have my long-awaited chance
To punish his deceit and arrogance,
And give my father clear and shocking proof
Of the black character of his dear Tartuffe.

Elmire: Ah no, Damis; I'll be content if he
Will study to deserve my leniency.
I've promised silence — don't make me break my word;
To make a scandal would be too absurd.
Good wives laugh off such trifles, and forget them;
Why should they tell their husbands, and upset them?

Damis: You have your reasons for taking such a course,
And I have reasons, too, of equal force.
To spare him now would be insanely wrong.
I've swallowed my just wrath for far too long
And watched this insolent bigot bringing strife
And bitterness into our family life.
Too long he's meddled in my father's affairs,
Thwarting my marriage-hopes, and poor Valère's.
It's high time that my father was undeceived,
And now I've proof that can't be disbelieved —
Proof that was furnished me by Heaven above.
It's too good not to take advantage of.
This is my chance, and I deserve to lose it
If, for one moment, I hesitate to use it.

Elmire: Damis . . .

Damis: No, I must do what I think right.
Madam, my heart is bursting with delight,
And, say whatever you will, I'll not consent
To lose the sweet revenge on which I'm bent.
I'll settle matters without more ado;
And here, most opportunely, is my cue.

Scene V

Orgon, Tartuffe, Damis, Elmire

Damis: Father, I'm glad you've joined us. Let us advise you
Of some fresh news which doubtless will surprise you.
You've just now been repaid with interest
For all your loving-kindness to our guest.
He's proved his warm and grateful feelings toward you;
It's with a pair of horns he would reward you.
Yes, I surprised him with your wife, and heard
His whole adulterous offer, every word.
She, with her all too gentle disposition,
Would not have told you of his proposition;

But I shall not make terms with brazen lechery,
And feel that not to tell you would be treachery.
Elmire: And I hold that one's husband's peace of mind
Should not be spoilt by tattle of this kind.
One's honor doesn't require it: to be proficient
In keeping men at bay is quite sufficient.
These are my sentiments, and I wish, Damis,
That you had heeded me and held your peace.

Scene VI

Orgon, Damis, Tartuffe

Orgon: Can it be true, this dreadful thing I hear?
Tartuffe: Yes, Brother, I'm a wicked man, I fear:
A wretched sinner, all depraved and twisted,
The greatest villain that has ever existed.
My life's one heap of crimes, which grows each minute;
There's naught but foulness and corruption in it;
And I perceive that Heaven, outraged by me,
Has chosen this occasion to mortify me.
Charge me with any deed you wish to name;
I'll not defend myself, but take the blame.
Believe what you are told, and drive Tartuffe
Like some base criminal from beneath your roof;
Yes, drive me hence, and with a parting curse:
I shan't protest, for I deserve far worse.
Orgon (to Damis): Ah, you deceitful boy, how dare you try
To stain his purity with so foul a lie?
Damis: What! Are you taken in by such a bluff?
Did you not hear . . . ?
Orgon: Enough, you rogue, enough!
Tartuffe: Ah, Brother, let him speak; you're being unjust.
Believe his story; the boy deserves your trust.
Why, after all, should you have faith in me?
How can you know what I might do, or be?
Is it on my good actions that you base
Your favor? Do you trust my pious face?
Ah, no, don't be deceived by hollow shows;
I'm far, alas, from being what men suppose;
Though the world takes me for a man of worth,
I'm truly the most worthless man on earth.
(To Damis.) Yes, my dear son, speak out now: call me the chief
Of sinners, a wretch, a murderer, a thief;
Load me with all the names men most abhor;
I'll not complain; I've earned them all, and more;
I'll kneel here while you pour them on my head
As a just punishment for the life I've led.

Orgon (to Tartuffe): This is too much, dear Brother.
(To Damis.) Have you no heart?
Damis: Are you so hoodwinked by this rascal's art . . . ?
Orgon: Be still, you monster.
(To Tartuffe.) Brother, I pray you, rise.
(To Damis.) Villain!
Damis: But . . .
Orgon: Silence!
Damis: Can't you realize . . . ?
Orgon: Just one word more, and I'll tear you limb from limb.
Tartuffe: In God's name, Brother, don't be harsh with him.
I'd rather far be tortured at the stake
Than see him bear one scratch for my poor sake.
Orgon (to Damis): Ingrate!
Tartuffe: If I must beg you, on bended knee,
To pardon him . . .
Orgon (falling to his knees, addressing Tartuffe):
Such goodness cannot be!
(To Damis.) Now, *there's* true charity!
Damis: What, you . . . ?
Orgon: Villain, be still!
I know your motives; I know you wish him ill:
Yes, all of you — wife, children, servants, all —
Conspire against him and desire his fall,
Employing every shameful trick you can
To alienate me from this saintly man.
Ah, but the more you seek to drive him away,
The more I'll do to keep him. Without delay,
I'll spite this household and confound its pride
By giving him my daughter as his bride.
Damis: You're going to force her to accept his hand?
Orgon: Yes, and this very night, d'you understand?
I shall defy you all, and make it clear
That I'm the one who gives the orders here.
Come, wretch, kneel down and clasp his blessed feet,
And ask his pardon for your black deceit.
Damis: I ask that swindler's pardon? Why, I'd rather . . .
Orgon: So! You insult him, and defy your father!
A stick! A stick! *(To Tartuffe.)* No, no — release me, do.
(To Damis.) Out of my house this minute! Be off with you,
And never dare set foot in it again.
Damis: Well, I shall go, but . . .
Orgon: Well, go quickly, then.
I disinherit you; an empty purse
Is all you'll get from me — except my curse!

Scene VII

Orgon, Tartuffe

Orgon: How he blasphemed your goodness! What a son!
Tartuffe: Forgive him, Lord, as I've already done.
(To Orgon.) You can't know how it hurts when someone tries
To blacken me in my dear Brother's eyes.
Orgon: Ahh!
Tartuffe: The mere thought of such ingratitude
Plunges my soul into so dark a mood . . .
Such horror grips my heart . . . I gasp for breath,
And cannot speak, and feel myself near death.
Orgon: (He runs, in tears, to the door through which he has just driven his son.) You blackguard! Why did I spare you? Why did I not
Break you in little pieces on the spot?
Compose yourself, and don't be hurt, dear friend.
Tartuffe: These scenes, these dreadful quarrels, have got to end.
I've much upset your household, and I perceive
That the best thing will be for me to leave.
Orgon: What are you saying!
Tartuffe: They're all against me here;
They'd have you think me false and insincere.
Orgon: Ah, what of that? Have I ceased believing in you?
Tartuffe: Their adverse talk will certainly continue,
And charges which you now repudiate
You may find credible at a later date.
Orgon: No, Brother, never.
Tartuffe: Brother, a wife can sway
Her husband's mind in many a subtle way.
Orgon: No, no.
Tartuffe: To leave at once is the solution;
Thus only can I end their persecution.
Orgon: No, no, I'll not allow it; you shall remain.
Tartuffe: Ah well; 'twill mean much martyrdom and pain,
But if you wish it . . .
Orgon: Ah!
Tartuffe: Enough; so be it.
But one thing must be settled, as I see it.
For your dear honor, and for our friendship's sake,
There's one precaution I feel bound to take.
I shall avoid your wife, and keep away . . .
Orgon: No, you shall not, whatever they may say.
It pleases me to vex them, and for spite
I'd have them see you with her day and night.
What's more, I'm going to drive them to despair
By making you my only son and heir;
This very day, I'll give to you alone

Clear deed and title to everything I own.
A dear, good friend and son-in-law-to-be
Is more than wife, or child, or kin to me.
Will you accept my offer, dearest son?
Tartuffe: In all things, let the will of Heaven be done.
Orgon: Poor fellow! Come, we'll go draw up the deed.
Then let them burst with disappointed greed!

ACT IV

Scene I

Cléante, Tartuffe

Cléante: Yes, all the town's discussing it, and truly,
Their comments do not flatter you unduly.
I'm glad we've met, Sir, and I'll give my view
Of this sad matter in a word or two.
As for who's guilty, that I shan't discuss;
Let's say it was Damis who caused the fuss;
Assuming, then, that you have been ill-used
By young Damis, and groundlessly accused,
Ought not a Christian to forgive, and ought
He not to stifle every vengeful thought?
Should you stand by and watch a father make
His only son an exile for your sake?
Again I tell you frankly, be advised:
The whole town, high and low, is scandalized;
This quarrel must be mended, and my advice is
Not to push matters to a further crisis.
No, sacrifice your wrath to God above,
And help Damis regain his father's love.
Tartuffe: Alas, for my part I should take great joy
In doing so. I've nothing against the boy.
I pardon all, I harbor no resentment;
To serve him would afford me much contentment.
But Heaven's interest will not have it so:
If he comes back, then I shall have to go.
After his conduct — so extreme, so vicious —
Our further intercourse would look suspicious.
God knows what people would think! Why, they'd describe
My goodness to him as a sort of bribe;
They'd say that out of guilt I made pretense
Of loving-kindness and benevolence —
That, fearing my accuser's tongue, I strove
To buy his silence with a show of love.
Cléante: Your reasoning is badly warped and stretched,
And these excuses, Sir, are most far-fetched.

Why put yourself in charge of Heaven's cause?
Does Heaven need our help to enforce its laws?
Leave vengeance to the Lord, Sir; while we live,
Our duty's not to punish, but forgive;
And what the Lord commands, we should obey
Without regard to what the world may say.
What! Shall the fear of being misunderstood
Prevent our doing what is right and good?
No, no; let's simply do what Heaven ordains,
And let no other thoughts perplex our brains.

Tartuffe: Again, Sir, let me say that I've forgiven
Damis, and thus obeyed the laws of Heaven;
But I am not commanded by the Bible
To live with one who smears my name with libel.

Cléante: Were you commanded, Sir, to indulge the whim
Of poor Orgon, and to encourage him
In suddenly transferring to your name
A large estate to which you have no claim?

Tartuffe: 'Twould never occur to those who know me best
To think I acted from self-interest.
The treasures of this world I quite despise;
Their specious glitter does not charm my eyes;
And if I have resigned myself to taking
The gift which my dear Brother insists on making,
I do so only, as he well understands,
Lest so much wealth fall into wicked hands,
Lest those to whom it might descend in time
Turn it to purposes of sin and crime,
And not, as I shall do, make use of it
For Heaven's glory and mankind's benefit.

Cléante: Forget these trumped-up fears. Your argument
Is one the rightful heir might well resent;
It *is* a moral burden to inherit
Such wealth, but give Damis a chance to bear it.
And would it not be worse to be accused
Of swindling, than to see that wealth misused?
I'm shocked that you allowed Orgon to broach
This matter, and that you feel no self-reproach;
Does true religion teach that lawful heirs
May freely be deprived of what is theirs?
And if the Lord has told you in your heart
That you and young Damis must dwell apart,
Would it not be the decent thing to beat
A generous and honorable retreat,
Rather than let the son of the house be sent,
For your convenience, into banishment?
Sir, if you wish to prove the honesty
Of your intentions . . .

Tartuffe: Sir, it is half-past three.

I've certain pious duties to attend to,
And hope my prompt departure won't offend you.
Cléante (alone): Damn.

Scene II

Elmire, Cléante, Mariane, Dorine

Dorine: Stay, Sir, and help Mariane, for Heaven's sake!
She's suffering so, I fear her heart will break.
Her father's plan to marry her off tonight
Has put the poor child in a desperate plight.
I hear him coming. Let's stand together, now,
And see if we can't change his mind, somehow,
About this match we all deplore and fear.

Scene III

Orgon, Mariane, Dorine, Elmire, Cléante

Orgon: Hah! Glad to find you all assembled here.
(To Mariane.) This contract, child, contains your happiness,
And what it says I think your heart can guess.
Mariane (falling to her knees): Sir, by that Heaven which sees me here distressed,
And by whatever else can move your breast,
Do not employ a father's power, I pray you,
To crush my heart and force it to obey you,
Nor by your harsh commands oppress me so
That I'll begrudge the duty which I owe —
And do not so embitter and enslave me
That I shall hate the very life you gave me.
If my sweet hopes must perish, if you refuse
To give me to the one I've dared to choose,
Spare me at least — I beg you, I implore —
The pain of wedding one whom I abhor;
And do not, by a heartless use of force,
Drive me to contemplate some desperate course.
Orgon (feeling himself touched by her): Be firm, my soul. No human weakness, now.
Mariane: I don't resent your love for him. Allow
Your heart free rein, Sir; give him your property,
And if that's not enough, take mine from me;
He's welcome to my money; take it, do,
But don't, I pray, include my person too.
Spare me, I beg you; and let me end the tale
Of my sad days behind a convent veil.
Orgon: A convent! Hah! When crossed in their amours,
All lovesick girls have the same thought as yours.

Get up! The more you loathe the man, and dread him,
The more ennobling it will be to wed him.
Marry Tartuffe, and mortify your flesh!
Enough; don't start that whimpering afresh.
Dorine: But why . . . ?
Orgon: Be still, there. Speak when you're spoken to.
Not one more bit of impudence out of you.
Cléante: If I may offer a word of counsel here . . .
Orgon: Brother, in counseling you have no peer;
All your advice is forceful, sound, and clever;
I don't propose to follow it, however.
Elmire (to Orgon): I am amazed, and don't know what to say;
Your blindness simply takes my breath away.
You are indeed bewitched, to take no warning
From our account of what occurred this morning.
Orgon: Madam, I know a few plain facts, and one
Is that you're partial to my rascal son;
Hence, when he sought to make Tartuffe the victim
Of a base lie, you dared not contradict him.
Ah, but you underplayed your part, my pet;
You should have looked more angry, more upset.
Elmire: When men make overtures, must we reply
With righteous anger and a battle-cry?
Must we turn back their amorous advances
With sharp reproaches and with fiery glances?
Myself, I find such offers merely amusing,
And make no scenes and fusses in refusing;
My taste is for good-natured rectitude,
And I dislike the savage sort of prude
Who guards her virtue with her teeth and claws,
And tears men's eyes out for the slightest cause:
The Lord preserve me from such honor as that,
Which bites and scratches like an alley-cat!
I've found that a polite and cool rebuff
Discourages a lover quite enough.
Orgon: I know the facts, and I shall not be shaken.
Elmire: I marvel at your power to be mistaken.
Would it, I wonder, carry weight with you
If I could *show* you that our tale was true?
Orgon: Show me?
Elmire: Yes.
Orgon: Rot.
Elmire: Come, what if I found a way
To make you see the facts as plain as day?
Orgon: Nonsense.
Elmire: Do answer me; don't be absurd.
I'm not now asking you to trust our word.
Suppose that from some hiding-place in here

You learned the whole sad truth by eye and ear —
What would you say of your good friend, after that?
Orgon: Why, I'd say . . . nothing. By Jehoshaphat!
It can't be true.
Elmire: You've been too long deceived.
And I'm quite tired of being disbelieved.
Come now: let's put my statements to the test,
And you shall see the truth made manifest.
Orgon: I'll take that challenge. Now do your uttermost.
We'll see how you make good your empty boast.
Elmire (to Dorine): Send him to me.
Dorine: He's crafty; it may be hard
To catch the cunning scoundrel off his guard.
Elmire: No, amorous men are gullible. Their conceit
So blinds them that they're never hard to cheat.
Have him come down. *(To Cléante and Mariane.)* Please leave us, for a bit.

Scene IV

Elmire, Orgon

Elmire: Pull up this table, and get under it.
Orgon: What?
Elmire: It's essential that you be well-hidden.
Orgon: Why there?
Elmire: Oh, Heavens! Just do as you are bidden.
I have my plans; we'll soon see how they fare.
Under the table, now; and once you're there,
Take care that you are neither seen nor heard.
Orgon: Well, I'll indulge you, since I gave my word
To see you through this infantile charade.
Elmire: Once it is over, you'll be glad we played.
(To her husband, who is now under the table.) I'm going to act quite strangely, now, and you
Must not be shocked at anything I do.
Whatever I may say, you must excuse
As part of that deceit I'm forced to use.
I shall employ sweet speeches in the task
Of making that impostor drop his mask;
I'll give encouragement to his bold desires,
And furnish fuel to his amorous fires.
Since it's for your sake, and for his destruction,
That I shall seem to yield to his seduction,
I'll gladly stop whenever you decide
That all your doubts are fully satisfied.
I'll count on you, as soon as you have seen
What sort of man he is, to intervene,

And not expose me to his odious lust
One moment longer than you feel you must.
Remember: you're to save me from my plight
Whenever . . . He's coming! Hush! Keep out of sight!

Scene V

Tartuffe, Elmire, Orgon

Tartuffe: You wish to have a word with me, I'm told.
Elmire: Yes. I've a little secret to unfold.
Before I speak, however, it would be wise
To close that door, and look about for spies.

Tartuffe goes to the door, closes it, and returns.

The very last thing that must happen now
Is a repetition of this morning's row.
I've never been so badly caught off guard.
Oh, how I feared for you! You saw how hard
I tried to make that troublesome Damis
Control his dreadful temper, and hold his peace.
In my confusion, I didn't have the sense
Simply to contradict his evidence;
But as it happened, that was for the best,
And all has worked out in our interest.
This storm has only bettered your position;
My husband doesn't have the least suspicion,
And now, in mockery of those who do,
He bids me be continually with you.
And that is why, quite fearless of reproof,
I now can be alone with my Tartuffe,
And why my heart — perhaps too quick to yield —
Feels free to let its passion be revealed.
Tartuffe: Madam, your words confuse me. Not long ago,
You spoke in quite a different style, you know.
Elmire: Ah, Sir, if that refusal made you smart,
It's little that you know of woman's heart,
Or what that heart is trying to convey
When it resists in such a feeble way!
Always, at first, our modesty prevents
The frank avowal of tender sentiments;
However high the passion which inflames us,
Still, to confess its power somehow shames us.
Thus we reluct, at first, yet in a tone
Which tells you that our heart is overthrown,
That what our lips deny, our pulse confesses,
And that, in time, all noes will turn to yesses.
I fear my words are all too frank and free,
And a poor proof of woman's modesty;

But since I'm started, tell me, if you will —
Would I have tried to make Damis be still,
Would I have listened, calm and unoffended,
Until your lengthy offer of love was ended,
And been so very mild in my reaction,
Had your sweet words not given me satisfaction?
And when I tried to force you to undo
The marriage-plans my husband has in view,
What did my urgent pleading signify
If not that I admired you, and that I
Deplored the thought that someone else might own
Part of a heart I wished for mine alone?

Tartuffe: Madam, no happiness is so complete
As when, from lips we love, come words so sweet;
Their nectar floods my every sense, and drains
In honeyed rivulets through all my veins.
To please you is my joy, my only goal;
Your love is the restorer of my soul;
And yet I must beg leave, now, to confess
Some lingering doubts as to my happiness.
Might this not be a trick? Might not the catch
Be that you wish me to break off the match
With Mariane, and so have feigned to love me?
I shan't quite trust your fond opinion of me
Until the feelings you've expressed so sweetly
Are demonstrated somewhat more concretely,
And you have shown, by certain kind concessions,
That I may put my faith in your professions.

Elmire (She coughs, to warn her husband.): Why be in such a hurry? Must my heart
Exhaust its bounty at the very start?
To make that sweet admission cost me dear,
But you'll not be content, it would appear,
Unless my store of favors is disbursed
To the last farthing, and at the very first.

Tartuffe: The less we merit, the less we dare to hope,
And with our doubts, mere words can never cope.
We trust no promised bliss till we receive it;
Not till a joy is ours can we believe it.
I, who so little merit your esteem,
Can't credit this fulfillment of my dream,
And shan't believe it, Madam, until I savor
Some palpable assurance of your favor.

Elmire: My, how tyrannical your love can be,
And how it flusters and perplexes me!
How furiously you take one's heart in hand,
And make your every wish a fierce command!
Come, must you hound and harry me to death?
Will you not give me time to catch my breath?

Can it be right to press me with such force,
Give me no quarter, show me no remorse,
And take advantage, by your stern insistence,
Of the fond feelings which weaken my resistance?
Tartuffe: Well, if you look with favor upon my love,
Why, then, begrudge me some clear proof thereof?
Elmire: But how can I consent without offense
To Heaven, toward which you feel such reverence?
Tartuffe: If Heaven is all that holds you back, don't worry.
I can remove that hindrance in a hurry.
Nothing of that sort need obstruct our path.
Elmire: Must one not be afraid of Heaven's wrath?
Tartuffe: Madam, forget such fears, and be my pupil,
And I shall teach you how to conquer scruple.
Some joys, it's true, are wrong in Heaven's eyes;
Yet Heaven is not averse to compromise;
There is a science, lately formulated,
Whereby one's conscience may be liberated,
And any wrongful act you care to mention
May be redeemed by purity of intention.
I'll teach you, Madam, the secrets of that science;
Meanwhile, just place on me your full reliance.
Assuage my keen desires, and feel no dread:
The sin, if any, shall be on my head.

Elmire coughs, this time more loudly.

You've a bad cough.
Elmire: Yes, yes. It's bad indeed.
Tartuffe (producing a little paper bag): A bit of licorice may be what you need.
Elmire: No, I've a stubborn cold, it seems. I'm sure it
Will take much more than licorice to cure it.
Tartuffe: How aggravating.
Elmire: Oh, more than I can say.
Tartuffe: If you're still troubled, think of things this way:
No one shall know our joys, save us alone,
And there's no evil till the act is known;
It's scandal, Madam, which makes it an offense,
And it's no sin to sin in confidence.
Elmire (having coughed once more): Well, clearly I must do as you require,
And yield to your importunate desire.
It is apparent, now, that nothing less
Will satisfy you, and so I acquiesce.
To go so far is much against my will;
I'm vexed that it should come to this; but still,
Since you are so determined on it, since you
Will not allow mere language to convince you,
And since you ask for concrete evidence, I
See nothing for it, now, but to comply.

If this is sinful, if I'm wrong to do it,
So much the worse for him who drove me to it.
The fault can surely not be charged to me.

Tartuffe: Madam, the fault is mine, if fault there be,
And . . .

Elmire: Open the door a little, and peek out;
I wouldn't want my husband poking about.

Tartuffe: Why worry about the man? Each day he grows
More gullible; one can lead him by the nose.
To find us here would fill him with delight,
And if he saw the worst, he'd doubt his sight.

Elmire: Nevertheless, do step out for a minute
Into the hall, and see that no one's in it.

SCENE VI

Orgon, Elmire

Orgon (coming out from under the table): That man's a perfect monster, I must admit!
I'm simply stunned. I can't get over it.

Elmire: What, coming out so soon? How premature!
Get back in hiding, and wait until you're sure.
Stay till the end, and be convinced completely;
We mustn't stop till things are proved concretely.

Orgon: Hell never harbored anything so vicious!

Elmire: Tut, don't be hasty. Try to be judicious.
Wait, and be certain that there's no mistake.
No jumping to conclusions, for Heaven's sake!

She places Orgon behind her, as Tartuffe re-enters.

SCENE VII

Tartuffe, Elmire, Orgon

Tartuffe (not seeing Orgon): Madam, all things have worked out to perfection;
I've given the neighboring rooms a full inspection;
No one's about; and now I may at last . . .

Orgon (intercepting him): Hold on, my passionate fellow, not so fast!
I should advise a little more restraint.
Well, so you thought you'd fool me, my dear saint!
How soon you wearied of the saintly life —
Wedding my daughter, and coveting my wife!
I've long suspected you, and had a feeling
That soon I'd catch you at your double-dealing.
Just now, you've given me evidence galore;
It's quite enough; I have no wish for more.

Elmire (to Tartuffe): I'm sorry to have treated you so slyly,
But circumstances forced me to be wily.
Tartuffe: Brother, you can't think . . .
Orgon: No more talk from you;
Just leave this household, without more ado.
Tartuffe: What I intended . . .
Orgon: That seems fairly clear.
Spare me your falsehoods and get out of here.
Tartuffe: No, I'm the master, and you're the one to go!
This house belongs to me, I'll have you know,
And I shall show you that you can't hurt *me*
By this contemptible conspiracy,
That those who cross me know not what they do,
And that I've means to expose and punish you,
Avenge offended Heaven, and make you grieve
That ever you dared order me to leave.

Scene VIII

Elmire, Orgon

Elmire: What was the point of all that angry chatter?
Orgon: Dear God, I'm worried. This is no laughing matter.
Elmire: How so?
Orgon: I fear I understood his drift.
I'm much disturbed about that deed of gift.
Elmire: You gave him . . . ?
Orgon: Yes, it's all been drawn and signed.
But one thing more is weighing on my mind.
Elmire: What's that?
Orgon: I'll tell you; but first let's see if there's
A certain strong-box in his room upstairs.

ACT V

Scene I

Orgon, Cléante

Cléante: Where are you going so fast?
Orgon: God knows!
Cléante: Then wait;
Let's have a conference, and deliberate
On how this situation's to be met.
Orgon: That strong-box has me utterly upset;
This is the worst of many, many shocks.
Cléante: Is there some fearful mystery in that box?

Orgon: My poor friend Argas brought that box to me
With his own hands, in utmost secrecy;
'Twas on the very morning of his flight.
It's full of papers which, if they came to light,
Would ruin him — or such is my impression.
Cléante: Then why did you let it out of your possession?
Orgon: Those papers vexed my conscience, and it seemed best
To ask the counsel of my pious guest.
The cunning scoundrel got me to agree
To leave the strong-box in his custody,
So that, in case of an investigation,
I could employ a slight equivocation,
And swear I didn't have it, and thereby,
At no expense to conscience, tell a lie.
Cléante: It looks to me as if you're out on a limb.
Trusting him with that box, and offering him
That deed of gift, were actions of a kind
Which scarcely indicate a prudent mind.
With two such weapons, he has the upper hand,
And since you're vulnerable, as matters stand,
You erred once more in bringing him to bay.
You should have acted in some subtler way.
Orgon: Just think of it: behind that fervent face,
A heart so wicked, and a soul so base!
I took him in, a hungry beggar, and then . . .
Enough, by God! I'm through with pious men:
Henceforth I'll hate the whole false brotherhood,
And persecute them worse than Satan could.
Cléante: Ah, there you go — extravagant as ever!
Why can you not be rational? You never
Manage to take the middle course, it seems,
But jump, instead, between absurd extremes.
You've recognized your recent grave mistake
In falling victim to a pious fake;
Now, to correct that error, must you embrace
An even greater error in its place,
And judge our worthy neighbors as a whole
By what you've learned of one corrupted soul?
Come, just because one rascal made you swallow
A show of zeal which turned out to be hollow,
Shall you conclude that all men are deceivers,
And that, today, there are no true believers?
Let atheists make that foolish inference;
Learn to distinguish virtue from pretense,
Be cautious in bestowing admiration,
And cultivate a sober moderation.
Don't humor fraud, but also don't asperse
True piety; the latter fault is worse,

And it is best to err, if err one must,
As you have done, upon the side of trust.

Scene II

Damis, Orgon, Cléante

Damis: Father, I hear that scoundrel's uttered threats
Against you; that he pridefully forgets
How, in his need, he was befriended by you,
And means to use your gifts to crucify you.
Orgon: It's true, my boy. I'm too distressed for tears.
Damis: Leave it to me, Sir; let me trim his ears.
Faced with such insolence, we must not waver.
I shall rejoice in doing you the favor
Of cutting short his life, and your distress.
Cléante: What a display of young hotheadedness!
Do learn to moderate your fits of rage.
In this just kingdom, this enlightened age,
One does not settle things by violence.

Scene III

Madame Pernelle, Dorine, Orgon, Mariane, Damis, Cléante, Elmire

Madame Pernelle: I hear strange tales of very strange events.
Orgon: Yes, strange events which these two eyes beheld.
The man's ingratitude is unparalleled.
I save a wretched pauper from starvation,
House him, and treat him like a blood relation,
Shower him every day with my largesse,
Give him my daughter, and all that I possess;
And meanwhile the unconscionable knave
Tries to induce my wife to misbehave;
And not content with such extreme rascality,
Now threatens me with my own liberality,
And aims, by taking base advantage of
The gifts I gave him out of Christian love,
To drive me from my house, a ruined man,
And make me end a pauper, as he began.
Dorine: Poor fellow!
Madame Pernelle: No, my son, I'll never bring
Myself to think him guilty of such a thing.
Orgon: How's that?
Madame Pernelle: The righteous always were maligned.
Orgon: Speak clearly, Mother. Say what's on your mind.
Madame Pernelle: I mean that I can smell a rat, my dear.
You know how everybody hates him, here.
Orgon: That has no bearing on the case at all.

Madame Pernelle: I told you a hundred times, when you were small,
That virtue in this world is hated ever;
Malicious men may die, but malice never.
Orgon: No doubt that's true, but how does it apply?
Madame Pernelle: They've turned you against him by a clever lie.
Orgon: I've told you, I was there and saw it done.
Madame Pernelle: Ah, slanderers will stop at nothing, Son.
Orgon: Mother, I'll lose my temper . . . For the last time,
I tell you I was witness to the crime.
Madame Pernelle: The tongues of spite are busy night and noon,
And to their venom no man is immune.
Orgon: You're talking nonsense. Can't you realize
I saw it; saw it; saw it with my eyes?
Saw, do you understand me? Must I shout it
Into your ears before you'll cease to doubt it?
Madame Pernelle: Appearances can deceive, my son. Dear me,
We cannot always judge by what we see.
Orgon: Drat! Drat!
Madame Pernelle: One often interprets things awry;
Good can seem evil to a suspicious eye.
Orgon: Was I to see his pawing at Elmire
As an act of charity?
Madame Pernelle: Till his guilt is clear,
A man deserves the benefit of the doubt.
You should have waited, to see how things turned out.
Orgon: Great God in Heaven, what more proof did I need?
Was I to sit there, watching, until he'd . . .
You drive me to the brink of impropriety.
Madame Pernelle: No, no, a man of such surpassing piety
Could not do such a thing. You cannot shake me.
I don't believe it, and you shall not make me.
Orgon: You vex me so that, if you weren't my mother,
I'd say to you . . . some dreadful thing or other.
Dorine: It's your turn now, Sir, not to be listened to;
You'd not trust us, and now she won't trust you.
Cléante: My friends, we're wasting time which should be spent
In facing up to our predicament.
I fear that scoundrel's threats weren't made in sport.
Damis: Do you think he'd have the nerve to go to court?
Elmire: I'm sure he won't: they'd find it all too crude
A case of swindling and ingratitude.
Cléante: Don't be too sure. He won't be at a loss
To give his claims a high and righteous gloss;
And clever rogues with far less valid cause
Have trapped their victims in a web of laws.
I say again that to antagonize
A man so strongly armed was most unwise.
Orgon: I know it; but the man's appalling cheek
Outraged me so, I couldn't control my pique.

Cléante: I wish to Heaven that we could devise
Some truce between you, or some compromise.
Elmire: If I had known what cards he held, I'd not
Have roused his anger by my little plot.
Orgon (to Dorine, as M. Loyal enters): What is that fellow looking for? Who is he?
Go talk to him — and tell him that I'm busy.

Scene IV

Monsieur Loyal, Damis, Elmire, Madame Pernelle, Mariane, Cléante, Orgon, Dorine

Monsieur Loyal: Good day, dear sister. Kindly let me see
Your master.
Dorine: He's involved with company,
And cannot be disturbed just now, I fear.
Monsieur Loyal: I hate to intrude; but what has brought me here
Will not disturb your master, in any event.
Indeed, my news will make him most content.
Dorine: Your name?
Monsieur Loyal: Just say that I bring greetings from
Monsieur Tartuffe, on whose behalf I've come.
Dorine (to Orgon): Sir, he's a very gracious man, and bears
A message from Tartuffe, which he declares,
Will make you most content.
Cléante: Upon my word,
I think this man had best be seen, and heard.
Orgon: Perhaps he has some settlement to suggest.
How shall I treat him? What manner would be best?
Cléante: Control your anger, and if he should mention
Some fair adjustment, give him your full attention.
Monsieur Loyal: Good health to you, good Sir. May Heaven confound
Your enemies, and may your joys abound.
Orgon (aside, to Cléante): A gentle salutation: it confirms
My guess that he is here to offer terms.
Monsieur Loyal: I've always held your family most dear;
I served your father, Sir, for many a year.
Orgon: Sir, I must ask your pardon; to my shame,
I cannot now recall your face or name.
Monsieur Loyal: Loyal's my name; I come from Normandy,
And I'm a bailiff, in all modesty.
For forty years, praise God, it's been my boast
To serve with honor in that vital post,
And I am here, Sir, if you will permit
The liberty, to serve you with this writ . . .
Orgon: To — *what?*
Monsieur Loyal: Now, please, Sir, let us have no friction:

It's nothing but an order of eviction.
You are to move your goods and family out
And make way for new occupants, without
Deferment or delay, and give the keys . . .
Orgon: I? Leave this house?
Monsieur Loyal: Why yes, Sir, if you please.
This house, Sir, from the cellar to the roof,
Belongs now to the good Monsieur Tartuffe,
And he is lord and master of your estate
By virtue of a deed of present date,
Drawn in due form, with clearest legal phrasing . . .
Damis: Your insolence is utterly amazing!
Monsieur Loyal: Young man, my business here is not with you,
But with your wise and temperate father, who,
Like every worthy citizen, stands in awe
Of justice, and would never obstruct the law.
Orgon: But . . .
Monsieur Loyal: Not for a million, Sir, would you rebel
Against authority; I know that well.
You'll not make trouble, Sir, or interfere
With the execution of my duties here.
Damis: Someone may execute a smart tattoo
On that black jacket of yours, before you're through.
Monsieur Loyal: Sir, bid your son be silent. I'd much regret
Having to mention such a nasty threat
Of violence, in writing my report.
Dorine (aside): This man Loyal's a most disloyal sort!
Monsieur Loyal: I love all men of upright character,
And when I agreed to serve these papers, Sir,
It was your feelings that I had in mind.
I couldn't bear to see the case assigned
To someone else, who might esteem you less
And so subject you to unpleasantness.
Orgon: What's more unpleasant than telling a man to leave
His house and home?
Monsieur Loyal: You'd like a short reprieve?
If you desire it, Sir, I shall not press you,
But wait until tomorrow to dispossess you.
Splendid. I'll come and spend the night here, then,
Most quietly, with half a score of men.
For form's sake, you might bring me, just before
You go to bed, the keys to the front door.
My men, I promise, will be on their best
Behavior, and will not disturb your rest.
But bright and early, Sir, you must be quick
And move out all your furniture, every stick:
The men I've chosen are both young and strong,
And with their help it shouldn't take you long.
In short, I'll make things pleasant and convenient,

And since I'm being so extremely lenient,
Please show me, Sir, a like consideration,
And give me your entire cooperation.

Orgon (aside): I may be all but bankrupt, but I vow
I'd give a hundred louis, here and now,
Just for the pleasure of landing one good clout
Right on the end of that complacent snout.

Cléante: Careful; don't make things worse.

Damis: My bootsole itches
To give that beggar a good kick in the breeches.

Dorine: Monsieur Loyal, I'd love to hear the whack
Of a stout stick across your fine broad back.

Monsieur Loyal: Take care: a woman too may go to jail if
She uses threatening language to a bailiff.

Cléante: Enough, enough, Sir. This must not go on.
Give me that paper, please, and then begone.

Monsieur Loyal: Well, *au revoir.* God give you all good cheer!

Orgon: May God confound you, and him who sent you here!

Scene V

Orgon, Elmire, Dorine, Cléante, Madame Pernelle, Damis, Mariane

Orgon: Now, Mother, was I right or not? This writ
Should change your notion of Tartuffe a bit.
Do you perceive his villainy at last?

Madame Pernelle: I'm thunderstruck. I'm utterly aghast.

Dorine: Oh, come, be fair. You mustn't take offense
At this new proof of his benevolence.
He's acting out of selfless love, I know.
Material things enslave the soul, and so
He kindly has arranged your liberation
From all that might endanger your salvation.

Orgon: Will you not ever hold your tongue, you dunce?

Cléante: Come, you must take some action, and at once.

Elmire: Go tell the world of the low trick he's tried.
The deed of gift is surely nullified
By such behavior, and public rage will not
Permit the wretch to carry out his plot.

Scene VI

Valère, Elmire, Damis, Orgon, Mariane, Dorine, Cléante, Madame Pernelle

Valère: Sir, though I hate to bring you more bad news,
Such is the danger that I cannot choose.
A friend who is extremely close to me
And knows my interest in your family
Has, for my sake, presumed to violate

The secrecy that's due to things of state,
And sends me word that you are in a plight
From which your one salvation lies in flight.
That scoundrel who's imposed upon you so
Denounced you to the King an hour ago
And, as supporting evidence, displayed
The strong-box of a certain renegade
Whose secret papers, so he testified,
You had disloyally agreed to hide.
I don't know just what charges may be pressed,
But there's a warrant out for your arrest;
Tartuffe has been instructed, furthermore,
To guide the arresting officer to your door.

Cléante: He's clearly done this to facilitate
His seizure of your house and your estate.

Orgon: That man, I must say, is a vicious beast!

Valère: Quick, Sir; you mustn't tarry in the least.
My carriage is outside, to take you hence;
This thousand louis should cover all expense
Let's lose no time, or you shall be undone;
The sole defense, in this case, is to run.
I shall go with you all the way, and place you
In a safe refuge to which they'll never trace you.

Orgon: Alas, dear boy, I wish that I could show you
My gratitude for everything I owe you.
But now is not the time; I pray the Lord
That I may live to give you your reward.
Farewell, my dears; be careful . . .

Cléante: Brother, hurry.
We shall take care of things; you needn't worry.

Scene VII

The Officer, Elmire, Dorine, Tartuffe, Mariane, Cléante, Valère, Madame Pernelle, Damis, Orgon

Tartuffe: Gently, Sir, gently; stay right where you are.
No need for haste; your lodging isn't far.
You're off to prison, by order of the Prince.

Orgon: This is the crowning blow, you wretch; and since
It means my total ruin and defeat,
Your villainy is now at last complete.

Tartuffe: You needn't try to provoke me; it's no use.
Those who serve Heaven must expect abuse.

Cléante: You are indeed most patient, sweet, and blameless.

Dorine: How he exploits the name of Heaven! It's shameless.

Tartuffe: Your taunts and mockeries are all for naught;
To do my duty is my only thought.

Mariane: Your love of duty is most meritorious,
And what you've done is little short of glorious.
Tartuffe: All deeds are glorious, Madam, which obey
The sovereign prince who sent me here today.
Orgon: I rescued you when you were destitute;
Have you forgotten that, you thankless brute?
Tartuffe: No, no, I well remember everything;
But my first duty is to serve my King.
That obligation is so paramount
That other claims, beside it, do not count;
And for it I would sacrifice my wife,
My family, my friend, or my own life.
Elmire: Hypocrite!
Dorine: All that we most revere, he uses
To cloak his plots and camouflage his ruses.
Cléante: If it is true that you are animated
By pure and loyal zeal, as you have stated,
Why was this zeal not roused until you'd sought
To make Orgon a cuckold, and been caught?
Why weren't you moved to give your evidence
Until your outraged host had driven you hence?
I shan't say that the gift of all his treasure
Ought to have damped your zeal in any measure;
But if he is a traitor, as you declare,
How could you condescend to be his heir?
Tartuffe (to the officer): Sir, spare me all this clamor; it's growing shrill.
Please carry out your orders, if you will.
Officer: Yes, I've delayed too long, Sir. Thank you kindly.
You're just the proper person to remind me.
Come, you are off to join the other boarders
In the King's prison, according to his orders.
Tartuffe: Who? I, Sir?
Officer: Yes.
Tartuffe: To prison? This can't be true!
Officer: I owe an explanation, but not to you.
(To Orgon.) Sir, all is well; rest easy, and be grateful
We serve a Prince to whom all sham is hateful,
A Prince who sees into our inmost hearts,
And can't be fooled by any trickster's arts.
His royal soul, though generous and human,
Views all things with discernment and acumen;
His sovereign reason is not lightly swayed,
And all his judgments are discreetly weighed.
He honors righteous men of every kind,
And yet his zeal for virtue is not blind,
Nor does his love of piety numb his wits
And make him tolerant of hypocrites.
'Twas hardly likely that this man could cozen

A King who's foiled such liars by the dozen.
With one keen glance, the King perceived the whole
Perverseness and corruption of his soul,
And thus high Heaven's justice was displayed:
Betraying you, the rogue stood self-betrayed.
The King soon recognized Tartuffe as one
Notorious by another name, who'd done
So many vicious crimes that one could fill
Ten volumes with them, and be writing still.
But to be brief: our sovereign was appalled
By this man's treachery toward you, which he called
The last, worst villainy of a vile career,
And bade me follow the impostor here
To see how gross his impudence could be,
And force him to restore your property.
Your private papers, by the King's command,
I hereby seize and give into your hand.
The King, by royal order, invalidates
The deed which gave this rascal your estates,
And pardons, furthermore, your grave offense
In harboring an exile's documents.
By these decrees, our Prince rewards you for
Your loyal deeds in the late civil war,
And shows how heartfelt is his satisfaction
In recompensing any worthy action,
How much he prizes merit, and how he makes
More of men's virtues than of their mistakes.

Dorine: Heaven be praised!
Madame Pernelle: I breathe again, at last.
Elmire: We're safe.
Mariane: I can't believe the danger's past.
Orgon (to Tartuffe): Well, traitor, now you see . . .
Cléante: Ah, Brother, please,
Let's not descend to such indignities.
Leave the poor wretch to his unhappy fate,
And don't say anything to aggravate
His present woes; but rather hope that he
Will soon embrace an honest piety,
And mend his ways, and by a true repentance
Move our just King to moderate his sentence.
Meanwhile, go kneel before your sovereign's throne
And thank him for the mercies he has shown.
Orgon: Well said: let's go at once and, gladly kneeling,
Express the gratitude which all are feeling.
Then, when that first great duty has been done,
We'll turn with pleasure to a second one,
And give Valère, whose love has proven so true,
The wedded happiness which is his due.

Considerations

1. In what ways is Orgon like his mother, Madame Pernelle?
2. Although Tartuffe does not appear in Acts I and II, he is characterized through the use of exposition. How do Madame Pernelle's and Orgon's views of Tartuffe differ from those of the other characters, especially Cléante and Dorine? Which perspective is more convincing? Explain why.
3. What effect does Tartuffe have on Orgon? Pay particular attention to Orgon's speech claiming he is a "changed man" (I.v.12–21).
4. How does Cléante distinguish between those who are "true and false in piety" (I.v.68–149)?
5. What reasons does Dorine give in II.ii for Mariane not to marry Tartuffe? Are they sound reasons? How are Dorine and Mariane used as character foils?
6. Describe Dorine's sense of humor. How is it appropriate to her station in life as a companion (not merely a maid) to Mariane?
7. What is the effect of Tartuffe's entrance in III.ii? How do you respond to him? Although he is a rogue, he commands interest. Why?
8. How does Tartuffe stay in Orgon's favor in III.vi even though he has been accused of coveting Orgon's wife?
9. In Act IV Tartuffe tells Elmire that "there's no evil till the act is known" (IV.v.118). Explain how this assertion constitutes an example of dramatic irony.
10. In V.i.35, why does Cléante accuse Orgon of being "extravagant as ever"? What is Cléante's advice to Orgon?
11. What is the effect of Madame Pernelle's refusal to believe Orgon when he describes Tartuffe as an "unconscionable knave" (V.iii.8)?
12. What values does Cléante represent? Why is it significant that Molière does not at any time treat him comically, as he does most of the other characters?
13. How do you respond to the use of the deus ex machina at the play's conclusion, when Molière introduces the king's officer to save Orgon and his family from imprisonment and poverty? Can the ending be justified, or is it too obviously a tribute to Molière's patron?
14. Is it accurate to describe the play as an attack on religion? Why or why not?
15. Choose a scene that is particularly comic and describe how you would stage it. Consider the setting, the costumes, the actors' gestures, and the manner in which they deliver their lines.

Connections

1. Explain how Sophocles or Shakespeare might have changed the ending of *Tartuffe* to transform it into a tragedy. What revisions in the plot do you think one or the other would make? Explain your proposed changes.
2. Write an essay exploring religion in *Tartuffe* and *Antigone* (p. 1008).
3. Choose a brief but interesting incident from Glaspell's *Trifles* (p. 931), Henrik Ibsen's *A Doll's House* (p. 1321), or Anton Chekhov's *The Cherry Orchard* (p. 1375) and rewrite it as you think Molière would if he were to subject the moment you choose to his satiric wit.

PERSPECTIVE

MOLIÈRE (1622–1673)
Defense of Tartuffe

1664

Here is a comedy that has excited a good deal of discussion and that has been under attack for a long time; and the persons who are mocked by it have made it plain that they are more powerful in France than all whom my plays have satirized up to this time. Noblemen, ladies of fashion, cuckolds, and doctors all kindly consented to their presentation, which they themselves seemed to enjoy along with everyone else; but hypocrites do not understand banter: they became angry at once, and found it strange that I was bold enough to represent their actions and to care to describe a profession shared by so many good men. This is a crime for which they cannot forgive me, and they have taken up arms against my comedy in a terrible rage. They were careful not to attack it at the point that had wounded them: they are too crafty for that and too clever to reveal their true character. In keeping with their lofty custom, they have used the cause of God to mask their private interests; and *Tartuffe,* they say, is a play that offends piety: it is filled with abominations from beginning to end, and nowhere is there a line that does not deserve to be burned. Every syllable is wicked, the very gestures are criminal, and the slightest glance, turn of the head, or step from right to left conceals mysteries that they are able to explain to my disadvantage. In vain did I submit the play to the criticism of my friends and the scrutiny of the public: all the corrections I could make, the judgment of the king and queen who saw the play, the approval of great princes and ministers of state who honored it with their presence, the opinion of good men who found it worthwhile, all this did not help. They will not let go of their prey, and every day of the week they have pious zealots abusing me in public and damning me out of charity.

I would care very little about all they might say except that their devices make enemies of men whom I respect and gain the support of genuinely good men, whose faith they know and who, because of the warmth of their piety, readily accept the impressions that others present to them. And it is this which forces me to defend myself. Especially to the truly devout do I wish to vindicate my play, and I beg of them with all my heart not to condemn it before seeing it, to rid themselves of preconceptions, and not aid the cause of men dishonored by their actions.

If one takes the trouble to examine my comedy in good faith, he will surely see that my intentions are innocent throughout, and tend in no way to make fun of what men revere; that I have presented the subject with all the precautions that its delicacy imposes; and that I have used all the art and skill that I could to distinguish clearly the character of the hypocrite from that of the truly devout man. For that purpose I used two whole acts to prepare the appearance of my scoundrel. Never is there a moment's doubt about his character; he is known at once from the qualities I have given him; and from one end of the play to the other, he does not say a word, he does not perform an action which does not depict to the audience the character of a wicked man, and which does not bring out in sharp relief the character of the truly good man which I oppose to it.

From the preface to *Tartuffe,* translated by Richard Wilbur.

Considerations

1. How does Molière use in *Tartuffe* "art and skill . . . to distinguish clearly the character of the hypocrite from that of the truly devout man"?
2. Molière urges his audience not to "condemn" his play "before seeing it, [and] to rid themselves of preconceptions." To what extent do you think censors have preconceptions about the works — whether they are plays, novels, films, music, or magazines — they would suppress?
3. Use library sources to investigate the reception of the early productions of *Tartuffe,* and describe the major issues associated with the play. Explain why you find Molière's defense convincing or not.

28. Modern Drama

REALISM

Realism is a literary technique that attempts to create the appearance of life as it is actually experienced. Characters in modern realistic plays (written during and after the last quarter of the nineteenth century) speak dialogue that we might hear in our daily lives. These characters are not larger than life but representative of it; they seem to speak the way we do rather than in highly poetic language, formal declarations, asides, or soliloquies. It is impossible to imagine a heroic figure such as Oedipus inhabiting a comfortably furnished living room and chatting about his wife's household budget the way Torvald Helmer does in Henrik Ibsen's *A Doll's House.* Realism brings into focus commonplace, everyday life rather than the extraordinary kinds of events that make up Sophocles' *Oedipus the King* or Shakespeare's *Hamlet.*

Realistic characters can certainly be heroic, but like Nora Helmer, they find that their strength and courage are tested in the context of events ordinary people might experience. Work, love, marriage, children, and death are often the focus of realistic dramas. These subjects can also constitute much of the material in nonrealistic plays, but modern realistic dramas present such material in the realm of the probable. Conflicts in realistic plays are likely to reflect problems in our own lives. Hence, making ends meet takes precedence over saving a kingdom; middle- and lower-class individuals take center stage as primary characters in main plots rather than being secondary characters in subplots. Thus we can see why the nineteenth-century movement toward realism paralleled the rise of a middle class eagerly seeking representations of its concerns in the theater.

Before the end of the nineteenth century, however, few attempts were made in the theater to present life as it is actually lived. The chorus's role in Sophocles' *Oedipus the King,* the allegorical figures in morality plays, the remarkable mistaken identities in Shakespeare's comedies, or the rhymed couplets spoken in Molière's *Tartuffe* represent theatrical conventions rather than life. Theatergoers have understood and appreciated these conventions for centuries — and still do — but in the nineteenth century social, political, and industrial revolutions helped create an atmosphere in which some playwrights found it necessary to create works that more directly reflected their audiences' lives.

Playwrights such as Henrik Ibsen and Anton Chekhov refused to join the ranks of their romantic contemporaries, who they felt falsely idealized life. The most popular plays immediately preceding the works of these realistic writers consisted primarily of love stories and action-packed plots. Such ***melodramas*** offer audiences thrills and chills as well as happy endings. They typically include a virtuous individual struggling under the tyranny of a wicked oppressor, who is defeated only at the last moment. Suspense is reinforced by a series of pursuits, captures, and escapes that move the plot quickly and deemphasize character or theme. These representations of extreme conflicts enjoyed wide popularity in the nineteenth century — indeed, they still do — because their formula was varied enough to be entertaining yet their outcomes were always comforting to the audience's sense of justice. But from the realists' perspective, melodramas were merely escape fantasies that distorted life by refusing to examine the real world closely and objectively.

Realists attempted to open their audiences' eyes; to their minds, the only genuine comfort was in knowing the truth. Many of their plays concern controversial issues of the day and focus on people who fall prey to indifferent societal institutions. English dramatist John Galsworthy (1867–1933) examined social values in *Strife* (1909) and *Justice* (1910), two plays whose titles broadly suggest the nature of his concerns. British playwright George Bernard Shaw (1856–1950) often used comedy and irony as means of awakening his audiences to contemporary problems: *Arms and the Man* (1894) satirizes romantic attitudes toward war, and *Mrs. Warren's Profession* (1898) indicts a social and economic system that drives a woman to prostitution. Chekhov's plays are populated by characters frustrated by their social situations and their own sensibilities; they are ordinary people who long for happiness but become entangled in everyday circumstances that limit their lives. Ibsen also took a close look at his characters' daily lives. His plays attack societal conventions and challenge popular attitudes toward marriage; he stunned audiences by dramatizing the suffering of a man dying of syphilis.

With these kinds of materials, Ibsen and his contemporaries popularized the ***problem play,*** a drama that represents a social issue in order to awaken the audience to it. These plays usually reject romantic plots in favor of holding up a mirror that reflects not simply what audiences want to see but what the playwright sees in them. Nineteenth-century realistic theater was no refuge from the social, economic, and psychological problems that melodrama ignored or sentimentalized.

NATURALISM

Related to realism is another movement, called ***naturalism.*** Essentially more of a philosophical attitude than a literary technique, naturalism derives its name from the idea that human beings are part of nature and subject to its laws. According to naturalists, heredity and environment shape and control people's lives; their behavior is determined more by instinct than by reason. This deterministic view argues that human beings have no transcendent identity, because there is no soul or spiritual world that ultimately distinguishes humanity from any other form of life. Characters in naturalistic plays are generally portrayed as victims overwhelmed by internal and external forces. Thus literary naturalism tends to include not only the commonplace but the sordid, destructive, and chaotic aspects of life. Naturalism, then, is an extreme form of realism.

The earliest and most articulate voice of naturalism was that of French author Émile Zola (1840–1902), who urged artists to draw their characters from life and present their histories as faithfully as scientists report laboratory findings. Zola's best-known naturalistic play, *Thérèse Raquin* (1873), is a dramatization of an earlier novel involving a woman whose passion causes her to take a lover and plot with him to kill her husband. In his preface to the novel, Zola explains that his purpose is to take "a strong man and unsatisfied woman," "throw them into a violent drama and note scrupulously the sensations and acts of these creatures." The diction of Zola's statement reveals his nearly clinical approach, which becomes even more explicit when Zola likens his method of revealing character to that of an autopsy: "I have simply done on two living bodies the work which surgeons do on corpses."

Although some naturalistic plays have been successfully produced and admired (notably Maxim Gorky's *The Lower Depths* [1902], set in a grim boardinghouse occupied by characters who suffer poverty, crime, betrayal, disease, and suicide), few important dramatists fully subscribed to naturalism's extreme methods and values. Nevertheless, the movement significantly influenced playwrights. Because of its insistence on the necessity of closely observing characters' environment, playwrights placed a new emphasis on detailed settings and natural acting. This verisimilitude became a significant feature of realistic drama.

THEATRICAL CONVENTIONS OF MODERN DRAMA

The picture-frame stage that is often used for realistic plays typically reproduces the setting of a room in some detail. Within the stage, framed by a proscenium arch (from which the curtain hangs), scenery and props are used to create an illusion of reality. Whether the "small bookcase with leather-bound books" described in the opening scene of Ibsen's *A Doll's House* is only painted scenery or an actual case with books, it will probably look real to the audience. Removing the fourth wall of a room so that an audience can look in fosters the illusion that the actions onstage are real events happening before unseen spectators. The texture of Nora's life is communicated by the set as well as by what she says and does. That doesn't happen in a play like Sophocles' *Antigone.* Technical effects can make us believe there is wood burning in a fireplace or snow falling outside a window. Outdoor settings are made similarly realistic by props and painted sets. In Chekhov's *The Cherry Orchard,* for example, the second act opens in a meadow with the faint outline of a city on the horizon.

In addition to lifelike sets, a particular method of acting is used to create a realistic atmosphere. Actors address each other instead of directing formal speeches toward the audience; they act within the setting, not merely before it. At the beginning of the twentieth century Konstantin Stanislavsky (1863–1938), a Russian director, teacher, and actor, developed a system of acting that was an important influence in realistic theater. He trained actors to identify with the inner emotions of the characters they played. They were encouraged to recall from their own lives emotional responses similar to those they were portraying. The goal was to present a role truthfully by first feeling and then projecting the character's situation. Among Stanislavsky's early successes in this method were the plays of Chekhov.

There are, however, degrees of realism on the stage. Tennessee Williams's *The Glass Menagerie* (p. 1462), for example, is a partially realistic portrayal of characters whose fragile lives are founded on illusions. Williams's dialogue rings true, and individual scenes resemble the kind of real-life action we would imagine such vulnerable characters engaging in, but other elements of the play are nonrealistic. For instance, Williams uses Tom as a major character in the play as well as a narrator and a stage manager. Here is part of Williams's stage directions: "The narrator is an undisguised convention of the play. He takes whatever license with dramatic convention as is convenient to his purposes." Although this play can be accurately described as including realistic elements, Williams, like many other contemporary playwrights, does not attempt an absolute fidelity to reality. He uses flashbacks — as does Arthur Miller in *Death of a Salesman* (p. 1508) — to present incidents that occurred before the opening scene because the past impinges so heavily on the present. Most playwrights don't attempt to duplicate reality, since that can now be done so well by motion pictures.

Realism needn't lock a playwright into a futile attempt to make everything appear as it is in life. There is no way to avoid theatrical conventions: actors impersonate characters in a setting that is, after all, a stage. Indeed, even the dialogue in a realistic play is quite different from the pauses, sentence fragments, repetitions, silences, and incoherencies that characterize the way people usually speak. Realistic dialogue may seem like ordinary speech, but it, like Shakespeare's poetic language, is constructed. If we remember that realistic drama represents only the appearance of reality and that what we read on a page or see and hear onstage is the result of careful selecting, editing, and even distortion, then we are more likely to appreciate the playwright's art.

A DOLL'S HOUSE

Henrik Ibsen was born in Skien, Norway, to wealthy parents, who lost their money while he was a young boy. His early experiences with small-town life and genteel poverty sensitized him to the problems that he subsequently dramatized in a number of his plays. At age sixteen he was apprenticed to a druggist; he later thought about studying medicine, but by his early twenties he was earning a living writing and directing plays in various Norwegian cities. By the time of his death he enjoyed an international reputation for his treatment of social issues related to middle-class life.

Ibsen's earliest dramatic works were historical and romantic plays, some in verse. His first truly realistic work was *The Pillars of Society* (1877), whose title ironically hints at the corruption and hypocrisy exposed in it. The realistic social-problem plays for which he is best known followed. These dramas at once fascinated and shocked international audiences. Among his most produced and admired works are *A Doll's House, Ghosts* (1881), *An Enemy of the People* (1882), *The Wild Duck* (1884), and *Hedda Gabler* (1890). The common denominator in many of Ibsen's dramas is his interest in individuals struggling for an authentic identity in the face of tyrannical social conventions. This conflict often results in his characters being divided between a sense of duty to themselves and their responsibility to others.

Ibsen used such external and internal conflicts to propel his plays' action. Like many of his contemporaries who wrote realistic plays, he adopted the form of the well-made play. A dramatic structure popularized in France by Eugène Scribe (1791–1861) and Victorien Sardou (1831–1908), the ***well-made play*** employs conventions including plenty of suspense created by meticulous plotting. Extensive exposition explains past events that ultimately lead to an inevitable climax. Tension is released when a secret that reverses the protagonist's fortunes is revealed. Ibsen, having directed a number of Scribe's plays in Norway, knew their cause-to-effect plot arrangements and used them for his own purposes in his problem plays.

A Doll's House dramatizes the tensions of a nineteenth-century middle-class marriage in which a wife struggles to step beyond the limited identity imposed on her by her husband and society. Although the Helmers' pleasant apartment seems an unlikely setting for the fierce conflicts that develop, the issues raised in the play are unmistakably real. *A Doll's House* affirms the necessity to reject hypocrisy, complacency, cowardice, and stifling conventions if life is to have dignity and meaning.

HENRIK IBSEN (1828–1906)

A Doll's House° 1879

TRANSLATED BY MICHAEL MEYER

Characters

Torvald Helmer, a lawyer
Nora, his wife
Dr. Rank
Mrs. Linde
Nils Krogstad, also a lawyer
The Helmers' three small children
Anne-Marie, their nurse
Helen, the maid
A Porter

SCENE: *The action takes place in the Helmers' apartment.*

ACT I

A comfortably and tastefully, but not expensively furnished room. Backstage right a door leads out to the hall; backstage left, another door to Helmer's study. Between these two doors stands a piano. In the middle of the left-hand wall is a door, with a window downstage of it. Near the window, a round table with armchairs and a small sofa. In the right-hand wall, slightly upstage, is a door; downstage of this, against the same wall, a stove lined with porcelain tiles, with a couple of armchairs and a rocking-chair in front of it. Between the stove and the side door is a small table. Engravings on the wall. A what-not with china and other bric-a-brac; a small bookcase with leather-bound books. A carpet on the floor; a fire in the stove. A winter day.

A bell rings in the hall outside. After a moment, we hear the front door being opened. Nora enters the room, humming contentedly to herself. She is wearing outdoor clothes and carrying a lot of parcels, which she puts down on the table right. She leaves the door to the hall open; through it, we can see a Porter carrying a Christmas tree and a basket. He gives these to the Maid, who has opened the door for them.

Nora: Hide that Christmas tree away, Helen. The children mustn't see it before I've decorated it this evening. *(To the Porter, taking out her purse.)* How much — ?
Porter: A shilling.
Nora: Here's half a crown. No, keep it.

The Porter touches his cap and goes. Nora closes the door. She continues to laugh happily to herself as she removes her coat, etc. She takes from her pocket

A Doll's House: Another translator of Ibsen, Rolf Fjelde, translates the title as *A Doll House* in order to emphasize that the whole household, including Torvald as well as Nora, lives an unreal, doll-like existence.

a bag containing macaroons and eats a couple. Then she tiptoes across and listens at her husband's door.

Nora: Yes, he's here. *(Starts humming again as she goes over to the table, right.)*

Helmer (from his room): Is that my skylark twittering out there?

Nora (opening some of the parcels): It is!

Helmer: Is that my squirrel rustling?

Nora: Yes!

Helmer: When did my squirrel come home?

Nora: Just now. *(Pops the bag of macaroons in her pocket and wipes her mouth.)* Come out here, Torvald, and see what I've bought.

Helmer: You mustn't disturb me! *(Short pause; then he opens the door and looks in, his pen in his hand.)* Bought, did you say? All that? Has my little squanderbird been overspending again?

Nora: Oh, Torvald, surely we can let ourselves go a little this year! It's the first Christmas we don't have to scrape.

Helmer: Well, you know, we can't afford to be extravagant.

Nora: Oh yes, Torvald, we can be a little extravagant now. Can't we? Just a tiny bit? You've got a big salary now, and you're going to make lots and lots of money.

Helmer: Next year, yes. But my new salary doesn't start till April.

Nora: Pooh; we can borrow till then.

Helmer: Nora! *(Goes over to her and takes her playfully by the ear.)* What a little spendthrift you are! Suppose I were to borrow fifty pounds today, and you spent it all over Christmas, and then on New Year's Eve a tile fell off a roof on to my head —

Nora (puts her hand over his mouth): Oh, Torvald! Don't say such dreadful things!

Helmer: Yes, but suppose something like that did happen? What then?

Nora: If anything as frightful as that happened, it wouldn't make much difference whether I was in debt or not.

Helmer: But what about the people I'd borrowed from?

Nora: Them? Who cares about them? They're strangers.

Helmer: Oh, Nora, Nora, how like a woman! No, but seriously, Nora, you know how I feel about this. No debts! Never borrow! A home that is founded on debts can never be a place of freedom and beauty. We two have stuck it out bravely up to now; and we shall continue to do so for the short time we still have to.

Nora (goes over towards the stove): Very well, Torvald. As you say.

Helmer (follows her): Now, now! My little songbird mustn't droop her wings. What's this? Is little squirrel sulking? *(Takes out his purse.)* Nora; guess what I've got here!

Nora (turns quickly): Money!

Helmer: Look. *(Hands her some banknotes.)* I know how these small expenses crop up at Christmas.

Nora (counts them): One — two — three — four. Oh, thank you, Torvald, thank you! I should be able to manage with this.

Helmer: You'll have to.

Nora: Yes, yes, of course I will. But come over here, I want to show you everything I've bought. And so cheaply! Look, here are new clothes for Ivar — and a sword. And a horse and a trumpet for Bob. And a doll and a cradle for Emmy — they're nothing much, but she'll pull them apart in a few days. And some bits of material and handkerchiefs for the maids. Old Anne-Marie ought to have had something better, really.

Helmer: And what's in that parcel?

Nora (cries): No, Torvald, you mustn't see that before this evening!

Helmer: Very well. But now, tell me, you little spendthrift, what do you want for Christmas?

Nora: Me? Oh, pooh, I don't want anything.

Helmer: Oh, yes, you do. Now tell me, what, within reason, would you most like?

Nora: No, I really don't know. Oh, yes — Torvald — !

Helmer: Well?

Nora (plays with his coat-buttons; not looking at him): If you really want to give me something, you could — you could —

Helmer: Come on, out with it.

Nora (quickly): You could give me money, Torvald. Only as much as you feel you can afford; then later I'll buy something with it.

Helmer: But, Nora —

Nora: Oh yes, Torvald dear, please! Please! Then I'll wrap up the notes in pretty gold paper and hang them on the Christmas tree. Wouldn't that be fun?

Helmer: What's the name of that little bird that can never keep any money?

Nora: Yes, yes, squanderbird; I know. But let's do as I say, Torvald; then I'll have time to think about what I need most. Isn't that the best way? Mm?

Helmer (smiles): To be sure it would be, if you could keep what I give you and really buy yourself something with it. But you'll spend it on all sorts of useless things for the house, and then I'll have to put my hand in my pocket again.

Nora: Oh, but Torvald —

Helmer: You can't deny it, Nora dear. *(Puts his arm round her waist.)* The squanderbird's a pretty little creature, but she gets through an awful lot of money. It's incredible what an expensive pet she is for a man to keep.

Nora: For shame! How can you say such a thing? I save every penny I can.

Helmer (laughs): That's quite true. Every penny you can. But you can't.

Nora (hums and smiles, quietly gleeful): Hm. If you only knew how many expenses we larks and squirrels have, Torvald.

Helmer: You're a funny little creature. Just like your father used to be. Always on the look-out for some way to get money, but as soon as you have any it just runs through your fingers, and you never know where it's gone. Well, I suppose I must take you as you are. It's in your blood. Yes, yes, yes, these things are hereditary, Nora.

Nora: Oh, I wish I'd inherited more of Papa's qualities.

Helmer: And I wouldn't wish my darling little songbird to be any different from what she is. By the way, that reminds me. You look awfully — how shall I put it? — awfully guilty today.

Nora: Do I?

Helmer: Yes, you do. Look me in the eyes.

Nora (looks at him): Well?

Helmer (wags his finger): Has my little sweet-tooth been indulging herself in town today, by any chance?

Nora: No, how can you think such a thing?

Helmer: Not a tiny little digression into a pastry shop?

Nora: No, Torvald, I promise —

Helmer: Not just a wee jam tart?

Nora: Certainly not.

Helmer: Not a little nibble at a macaroon?

Nora: No, Torvald — I promise you, honestly —

Helmer: There, there. I was only joking.

Nora (goes over to the table, right): You know I could never act against your wishes.

Helmer: Of course not. And you've given me your word — *(Goes over to her.)* Well, my beloved Nora, you keep your little Christmas secrets to yourself. They'll be revealed this evening, I've no doubt, once the Christmas tree has been lit.

Nora: Have you remembered to invite Dr. Rank?

Helmer: No. But there's no need; he knows he'll be dining with us. Anyway, I'll ask him when he comes this morning. I've ordered some good wine. Oh, Nora, you can't imagine how I'm looking forward to this evening.

Nora: So am I. And, Torvald, how the children will love it!

Helmer: Yes, it's a wonderful thing to know that one's position is assured and that one has an ample income. Don't you agree? It's good to know that, isn't it?

Nora: Yes, it's almost like a miracle.

Helmer: Do you remember last Christmas? For three whole weeks you shut yourself away every evening to make flowers for the Christmas tree, and all those other things you were going to surprise us with. Ugh, it was the most boring time I've ever had in my life.

Nora: I didn't find it boring.

Helmer (smiles): But it all came to nothing in the end, didn't it?

Nora: Oh, are you going to bring that up again? How could I help the cat getting in and tearing everything to bits?

Helmer: No, my poor little Nora, of course you couldn't. You simply wanted to make us happy, and that's all that matters. But it's good that those hard times are past.

Nora: Yes, it's wonderful.

Helmer: I don't have to sit by myself and be bored. And you don't have to tire your pretty eyes and your delicate little hands —

Nora (claps her hands): No, Torvald, that's true, isn't it — I don't have to any longer? Oh, it's really all just like a miracle. *(Takes his arm.)* Now, I'm going to tell you what I thought we might do, Torvald. As soon as Christmas is over — *(A bell rings in the hall.)* Oh, there's the doorbell. *(Tidies up one or two things in the room.)* Someone's coming. What a bore.

Helmer: I'm not at home to any visitors. Remember!

Maid (in the doorway): A lady's called, madam. A stranger.

Nora: Well, ask her to come in.

Maid: And the doctor's here too, sir.

Helmer: Has he gone to my room?
Maid: Yes, sir.

Helmer goes into his room. The Maid shows in Mrs. Linde, who is dressed in traveling clothes, and closes the door.

Mrs. Linde (shyly and a little hesitantly): Good evening, Nora.
Nora (uncertainly): Good evening —
Mrs. Linde: I don't suppose you recognize me.
Nora: No, I'm afraid I — Yes, wait a minute — surely — *(Exclaims.)* Why, Christine! Is it really you?
Mrs. Linde: Yes, it's me.
Nora: Christine! And I didn't recognize you! But how could I — ? *(More quietly.)* How you've changed, Christine!
Mrs. Linde: Yes, I know. It's been nine years — nearly ten —
Nora: Is it so long? Yes, it must be. Oh, these last eight years have been such a happy time for me! So you've come to town? All that way in winter! How brave of you!
Mrs. Linde: I arrived by the steamer this morning.
Nora: Yes, of course — to enjoy yourself over Christmas. Oh, how splendid! We'll have to celebrate! But take off your coat. You're not cold, are you? *(Helps her off with it.)* There! Now let's sit down here by the stove and be comfortable. No, you take the armchair. I'll sit here in the rocking-chair. *(Clasps Mrs. Linde's hands.)* Yes, now you look like your old self. It was just at first that — you've got a little paler, though, Christine. And perhaps a bit thinner.
Mrs. Linde: And older, Nora. Much, much older.
Nora: Yes, perhaps a little older. Just a tiny bit. Not much. *(Checks herself suddenly and says earnestly.)* Oh, but how thoughtless of me to sit here and chatter away like this! Dear, sweet Christine, can you forgive me?
Mrs. Linde: What do you mean, Nora?
Nora (quietly): Poor Christine, you've become a widow.
Mrs. Linde: Yes. Three years ago.
Nora: I know, I know — I read it in the papers. Oh, Christine, I meant to write to you so often, honestly. But I always put it off, and something else always cropped up.
Mrs. Linde: I understand, Nora dear.
Nora: No, Christine, it was beastly of me. Oh, my poor darling, what you've gone through! And he didn't leave you anything?
Mrs. Linde: No.
Nora: No children, either?
Mrs. Linde: No.
Nora: Nothing at all, then?
Mrs. Linde: Not even a feeling of loss or sorrow.
Nora (looks incredulously at her): But, Christine, how is that possible?
Mrs. Linde (smiles sadly and strokes Nora's hair): Oh, these things happen, Nora.
Nora: All alone. How dreadful that must be for you. I've three lovely children. I'm afraid you can't see them now, because they're out with nanny. But you must tell me everything —

Mrs. Linde: No, no, no. I want to hear about you.

Nora: No, you start. I'm not going to be selfish today, I'm just going to think about you. Oh, but there's one thing I *must* tell you. Have you heard of the wonderful luck we've just had?

Mrs. Linde: No. What?

Nora: Would you believe it — my husband's just been made manager of the bank!

Mrs. Linde: Your husband? Oh, how lucky — !

Nora: Yes, isn't it? Being a lawyer is so uncertain, you know, especially if one isn't prepared to touch any case that isn't — well — quite nice. And of course Torvald's been very firm about that — and I'm absolutely with him. Oh, you can imagine how happy we are! He's joining the bank in the New Year, and he'll be getting a big salary, and lots of percentages too. From now on we'll be able to live quite differently — we'll be able to do whatever we want. Oh, Christine, it's such a relief! I feel so happy! Well, I mean, it's lovely to have heaps of money and not to have to worry about anything. Don't you think?

Mrs. Linde: It must be lovely to have enough to cover one's needs, anyway.

Nora: Not just our needs! We're going to have heaps and heaps of money!

Mrs. Linde (smiles): Nora, Nora, haven't you grown up yet? When we were at school you were a terrible little spendthrift.

Nora (laughs quietly): Yes, Torvald still says that. *(Wags her finger.)* But "Nora, Nora" isn't as silly as you think. Oh, we've been in no position for me to waste money. We've both had to work.

Mrs. Linde: You too?

Nora: Yes, little things — fancy work, crocheting, embroidery and so forth. *(Casually.)* And other things too. I suppose you know Torvald left the Ministry when we got married? There were no prospects of promotion in his department, and of course he needed more money. But the first year he overworked himself quite dreadfully. He had to take on all sorts of extra jobs, and worked day and night. But it was too much for him, and he became frightfully ill. The doctors said he'd have to go to a warmer climate.

Mrs. Linde: Yes, you spent a whole year in Italy, didn't you?

Nora: Yes. It wasn't easy for me to get away, you know. I'd just had Ivar. But of course we had to do it. Oh, it was a marvelous trip! And it saved Torvald's life. But it cost an awful lot of money, Christine.

Mrs. Linde: I can imagine.

Nora: Two hundred and fifty pounds. That's a lot of money, you know.

Mrs. Linde: How lucky you had it.

Nora: Well, actually, we got it from my father.

Mrs. Linde: Oh, I see. Didn't he die just about that time?

Nora: Yes, Christine, just about then. Wasn't it dreadful, I couldn't go and look after him. I was expecting little Ivar any day. And then I had my poor Torvald to care for — we really didn't think he'd live. Dear, kind Papa! I never saw him again, Christine. Oh, it's the saddest thing that's happened to me since I got married.

Mrs. Linde: I know you were very fond of him. But you went to Italy — ?

Nora: Yes. Well, we had the money, you see, and the doctors said we mustn't delay. So we went the month after Papa died.

Mrs. Linde: And your husband came back completely cured?

Nora: Fit as a fiddle!

Mrs. Linde: But — the doctor?

Nora: How do you mean?

Mrs. Linde: I thought the maid said that the gentleman who arrived with me was the doctor.

Nora: Oh yes, that's Doctor Rank, but he doesn't come because anyone's ill. He's our best friend, and he looks us up at least once every day. No, Torvald hasn't had a moment's illness since we went away. And the children are fit and healthy and so am I. *(Jumps up and claps her hands.)* Oh God, oh God, Christine, isn't it a wonderful thing to be alive and happy! Oh, but how beastly of me! I'm only talking about myself. *(Sits on a footstool and rests her arms on Mrs. Linde's knee.)* Oh, please don't be angry with me! Tell me, is it really true you didn't love your husband? Why did you marry him, then?

Mrs. Linde: Well, my mother was still alive; and she was helpless and bedridden. And I had my two little brothers to take care of. I didn't feel I could say no.

Nora: Yes, well, perhaps you're right. He was rich then, was he?

Mrs. Linde: Quite comfortably off, I believe. But his business was unsound, you see, Nora. When he died it went bankrupt, and there was nothing left.

Nora: What did you do?

Mrs. Linde: Well, I had to try to make ends meet somehow, so I started a little shop, and a little school, and anything else I could turn my hand to. These last three years have been just one endless slog for me, without a moment's rest. But now it's over, Nora. My poor dear mother doesn't need me any more; she's passed away. And the boys don't need me either; they've got jobs now and can look after themselves.

Nora: How relieved you must feel —

Mrs. Linde: No, Nora. Just unspeakably empty. No one to live for any more. *(Gets up restlessly.)* That's why I couldn't bear to stay out there any longer, cut off from the world. I thought it'd be easier to find some work here that will exercise and occupy my mind. If only I could get a regular job — office work of some kind —

Nora: Oh but, Christine, that's dreadfully exhausting; and you look practically finished already. It'd be much better for you if you could go away somewhere.

Mrs. Linde (goes over to the window): I have no Papa to pay for my holidays, Nora.

Nora (gets up): Oh, please don't be angry with me.

Mrs. Linde: My dear Nora, it's I who should ask you not to be angry. That's the worst thing about this kind of situation — it makes one so bitter. One has no one to work for; and yet one has to be continually sponging for jobs. One has to live; and so one becomes completely egocentric. When you told me about this luck you've just had with Torvald's new job — can you imagine? — I was happy not so much on your account, as on my own.

Nora: How do you mean? Oh, I understand. You mean Torvald might be able to do something for you?

Mrs. Linde: Yes, I was thinking that.

Nora: He will too, Christine. Just you leave it to me. I'll lead up to it so delicately, so delicately; I'll get him in the right mood. Oh, Christine, I do so want to help you.

Mrs. Linde: It's sweet of you to bother so much about me, Nora. Especially since you know so little of the worries and hardships of life.

Nora: I? You say *I* know little of — ?

Mrs. Linde (smiles): Well, good heavens — those bits of fancy work of yours — well, really — ! You're a child, Nora.

Nora (tosses her head and walks across the room): You shouldn't say that so patronizingly.

Mrs. Linde: Oh?

Nora: You're like the rest. You all think I'm incapable of getting down to anything serious —

Mrs. Linde: My dear —

Nora: You think I've never had any worries like the rest of you.

Mrs. Linde: Nora dear, you've just told me about all your difficulties —

Nora: Pooh — that! *(Quietly.)* I haven't told you about the big thing.

Mrs. Linde: What big thing? What do you mean?

Nora: You patronize me, Christine; but you shouldn't. You're proud that you've worked so long and so hard for your mother.

Mrs. Linde: I don't patronize anyone, Nora. But you're right — I am both proud and happy that I was able to make my mother's last months on earth comparatively easy.

Nora: And you're also proud of what you've done for your brothers.

Mrs. Linde: I think I have a right to be.

Nora: I think so too. But let me tell you something, Christine. I too have done something to be proud and happy about.

Mrs. Linde: I don't doubt it. But — how do you mean?

Nora: Speak quietly! Suppose Torvald should hear! He mustn't, at any price — no one must know, Christine — no one but you.

Mrs. Linde: But what is this?

Nora: Come over here. *(Pulls her down on to the sofa beside her.)* Yes, Christine — I too have done something to be happy and proud about. It was I who saved Torvald's life.

Mrs. Linde: Saved his — ? How did you save it?

Nora: I told you about our trip to Italy. Torvald couldn't have lived if he hadn't managed to get down there —

Mrs. Linde: Yes, well — your father provided the money —

Nora (smiles): So Torvald and everyone else thinks. But —

Mrs. Linde: Yes?

Nora: Papa didn't give us a penny. It was I who found the money.

Mrs. Linde: You? All of it?

Nora: Two hundred and fifty pounds. What do you say to that?

Mrs. Linde: But Nora, how could you? Did you win a lottery or something?

Nora (scornfully): Lottery? *(Sniffs.)* What would there be to be proud of in that?

Mrs. Linde: But where did you get it from, then?

Nora (hums and smiles secretively): Hm; tra-la-la-la!

Mrs. Linde: You couldn't have borrowed it.

Nora: Oh? Why not?

Mrs. Linde: Well, a wife can't borrow money without her husband's consent.

Nora (tosses her head): Ah, but when a wife has a little business sense, and knows how to be clever —

Mrs. Linde: But Nora, I simply don't understand —

Nora: You don't have to. No one has said I borrowed the money. I could have got it in some other way. *(Throws herself back on the sofa.)* I could have got it from an admirer. When a girl's as pretty as I am —

Mrs. Linde: Nora, you're crazy!

Nora: You're dying of curiosity now, aren't you, Christine?

Mrs. Linde: Nora dear, you haven't done anything foolish?

Nora (sits up again): Is it foolish to save one's husband's life?

Mrs. Linde: I think it's foolish if without his knowledge you —

Nora: But the whole point was that he mustn't know! Great heavens, don't you see? He hadn't to know how dangerously ill he was. I was the one they told that his life was in danger and that only going to a warm climate could save him. Do you suppose I didn't try to think of other ways of getting him down there? I told him how wonderful it would be for me to go abroad like other young wives; I cried and prayed; I asked him to remember my condition, and said he ought to be nice and tender to me; and then I suggested he might quite easily borrow the money. But then he got almost angry with me, Christine. He said I was frivolous, and that it was his duty as a husband not to pander to my moods and caprices — I think that's what he called them. Well, well, I thought, you've got to be saved somehow. And then I thought of a way —

Mrs. Linde: But didn't your husband find out from your father that the money hadn't come from him?

Nora: No, never. Papa died just then. I'd thought of letting him into the plot and asking him not to tell. But since he was so ill — ! And as things turned out, it didn't become necessary.

Mrs. Linde: And you've never told your husband about this?

Nora: For heaven's sake, no! What an idea! He's frightfully strict about such matters. And besides — he's so proud of being a *man* — it'd be so painful and humiliating for him to know that he owed anything to me. It'd completely wreck our relationship. This life we have built together would no longer exist.

Mrs. Linde: Will you never tell him?

Nora (thoughtfully, half-smiling): Yes — some time, perhaps. Years from now, when I'm no longer pretty. You mustn't laugh! I mean of course, when Torvald no longer loves me as he does now; when it no longer amuses him to see me dance and dress up and play the fool for him. Then it might be useful to have something up my sleeve. *(Breaks off.)* Stupid, stupid, stupid! That time will never come. Well, what do you think of my big secret, Christine? I'm not completely useless, am I? Mind you, all this has caused me a frightful lot of worry. It hasn't been easy for me to meet my obligations punctually. In case you don't know, in the world of business there are things called quarterly installments and interest, and they're a terrible problem to cope with. So I've had to scrape a little here and save a little there as best I can. I haven't been able to save much on the housekeeping money, because Torvald likes to live well; and I couldn't let the children go short of clothes —

I couldn't take anything out of what he gives me for them. The poor little angels!

Mrs. Linde: So you've had to stint yourself, my poor Nora?

Nora: Of course. Well, after all, it was my problem. Whenever Torvald gave me money to buy myself new clothes, I never used more than half of it; and I always bought what was cheapest and plainest. Thank heaven anything suits me, so that Torvald's never noticed. But it made me a bit sad sometimes, because it's lovely to wear pretty clothes. Don't you think?

Mrs. Linde: Indeed it is.

Nora: And then I've found one or two other sources of income. Last winter I managed to get a lot of copying to do. So I shut myself away and wrote every evening, late into the night. Oh, I often got so tired, so tired. But it was great fun, though, sitting there working and earning money. It was almost like being a man.

Mrs. Linde: But how much have you managed to pay off like this?

Nora: Well, I can't say exactly. It's awfully difficult to keep an exact check on these kind of transactions. I only know I've paid everything I've managed to scrape together. Sometimes I really didn't know where to turn. *(Smiles.)* Then I'd sit here and imagine some rich old gentleman had fallen in love with me —

Mrs. Linde: What! What gentleman?

Nora: Silly! And that now he'd died and when they opened his will it said in big letters: "Everything I possess is to be paid forthwith to my beloved Mrs. Nora Helmer in cash."

Mrs. Linde: But, Nora dear, who was this gentleman?

Nora: Great heavens, don't you understand? There wasn't any old gentleman; he was just something I used to dream up as I sat here evening after evening wondering how on earth I could raise some money. But what does it matter? The old bore can stay imaginary as far as I'm concerned, because now I don't have to worry any longer! *(Jumps up.)* Oh, Christine, isn't it wonderful? I don't have to worry any more! No more troubles! I can play all day with the children, I can fill the house with pretty things, just the way Torvald likes. And, Christine, it'll soon be spring, and the air'll be fresh and the skies blue, — and then perhaps we'll be able to take a little trip somewhere. I shall be able to see the sea again. Oh, yes, yes, it's a wonderful thing to be alive and happy!

The bell rings in the hall.

Mrs. Linde (gets up): You've a visitor. Perhaps I'd better go.

Nora: No, stay. It won't be for me. It's someone for Torvald —

Maid (in the doorway): Excuse me, madam, a gentleman's called who says he wants to speak to the master. But I didn't know — seeing as the doctor's with him —

Nora: Who is this gentleman?

Krogstad (in the doorway): It's me, Mrs. Helmer.

Mrs. Linde starts, composes herself, and turns away to the window.

Nora (takes a step toward him and whispers tensely): You? What is it? What do you want to talk to my husband about?

Krogstad: Business — you might call it. I hold a minor post in the bank, and I hear your husband is to become our new chief —

Nora: Oh — then it isn't — ?

Krogstad: Pure business, Mrs. Helmer. Nothing more.

Nora: Well, you'll find him in his study.

Nods indifferently as she closes the hall door behind him. Then she walks across the room and sees to the stove.

Mrs. Linde: Nora, who was that man?

Nora: A lawyer called Krogstad.

Mrs. Linde: It was him, then.

Nora: Do you know that man?

Mrs. Linde: I used to know him — some years ago. He was a solicitor's clerk in our town, for a while.

Nora: Yes, of course, so he was.

Mrs. Linde: How he's changed!

Nora: He was very unhappily married, I believe.

Mrs. Linde: Is he a widower now?

Nora: Yes, with a lot of children. Ah, now it's alight.

She closes the door of the stove and moves the rocking-chair a little to one side.

Mrs. Linde: He does — various things now, I hear?

Nora: Does he? It's quite possible — I really don't know. But don't let's talk about business. It's so boring.

Dr. Rank enters from Helmer's study.

Rank (still in the doorway): No, no, my dear chap, don't see me out. I'll go and have a word with your wife. *(Closes the door and notices Mrs. Linde.)* Oh, I beg your pardon. I seem to be *de trop* here too.

Nora: Not in the least. *(Introduces them.)* Dr. Rank. Mrs. Linde.

Rank: Ah! A name I have often heard in this house. I believe I passed you on the stairs as I came up.

Mrs. Linde: Yes. Stairs tire me; I have to take them slowly.

Rank: Oh, have you hurt yourself?

Mrs. Linde: No, I'm just a little run down.

Rank: Ah, is that all? Then I take it you've come to town to cure yourself by a round of parties?

Mrs. Linde: I have come here to find work.

Rank: Is that an approved remedy for being run down?

Mrs. Linde: One has to live, Doctor.

Rank: Yes, people do seem to regard it as a necessity.

Nora: Oh, really, Dr. Rank. I bet you want to stay alive.

Rank: You bet I do. However miserable I sometimes feel, I still want to go on being tortured for as long as possible. It's the same with all my patients; and with people who are morally sick, too. There's a moral cripple in with Helmer at this very moment —

Mrs. Linde (softly): Oh!

Nora: Whom do you mean?

Rank: Oh, a lawyer fellow called Krogstad — you wouldn't know him. He's crippled all right; morally twisted. But even he started off by announcing, as though it were a matter of enormous importance, that he had to live.

Nora: Oh? What did he want to talk to Torvald about?

Rank: I haven't the faintest idea. All I heard was something about the bank.

Nora: I didn't know that Krog — that this man Krogstad had any connection with the bank.

Rank: Yes, he's got some kind of job down there. *(To Mrs. Linde.)* I wonder if in your part of the world you too have a species of human being that spends its time fussing around trying to smell out moral corruption? And when they find a case they give him some nice, comfortable position so that they can keep a good watch on him. The healthy ones just have to lump it.

Mrs. Linde: But surely it's the sick who need care most?

Rank (shrugs his shoulders): Well, there we have it. It's that attitude that's turning human society into a hospital.

Nora, lost in her own thoughts, laughs half to herself and claps her hands.

Rank: Why are you laughing? Do you really know what society is?

Nora: What do I care about society? I think it's a bore. I was laughing at something else — something frightfully funny. Tell me, Dr. Rank — will everyone who works at the bank come under Torvald now?

Rank: Do you find that particularly funny?

Nora (smiles and hums): Never you mind! Never you mind! *(Walks around the room.)* Yes, I find it very amusing to think that we — I mean, Torvald — has obtained so much influence over so many people. *(Takes the paper bag from her pocket.)* Dr. Rank, would you like a small macaroon?

Rank: Macaroons! I say! I thought they were forbidden here.

Nora: Yes, well, these are some Christine gave me.

Mrs. Linde: What? I — ?

Nora: All right, all right, don't get frightened. You weren't to know Torvald had forbidden them. He's afraid they'll ruin my teeth. But, dash it — for once — ! Don't you agree, Dr. Rank? Here! *(Pops a macaroon into his mouth.)* You too, Christine. And I'll have one too. Just a little one. Two at the most. *(Begins to walk round again.)* Yes, now I feel really, really happy. Now there's just one thing in the world I'd really love to do.

Rank: Oh? And what is that?

Nora: Just something I'd love to say to Torvald.

Rank: Well, why don't you say it?

Nora: No, I daren't. It's too dreadful.

Mrs. Linde: Dreadful?

Rank: Well, then, you'd better not. But you can say it to us. What is it you'd so love to say to Torvald?

Nora: I've the most extraordinary longing to say: "Bloody hell!"

Rank: Are you mad?

Mrs. Linde: My dear Nora — !

Rank: Say it. Here he is.

Nora (hiding the bag of macaroons): Ssh! Ssh!

Helmer, with his overcoat on his arm and his hat in his hand, enters from his study.

Nora (goes to meet him): Well, Torvald dear, did you get rid of him?

Helmer: Yes, he's just gone.

Nora: May I introduce you — ? This is Christine. She's just arrived in town.

Helmer: Christine — ? Forgive me, but I don't think —

Nora: Mrs. Linde, Torvald dear. Christine Linde.

Helmer: Ah. A childhood friend of my wife's, I presume?

Mrs. Linde: Yes, we knew each other in earlier days.

Nora: And imagine, now she's traveled all this way to talk to you.

Helmer: Oh?

Mrs. Linde: Well, I didn't really —

Nora: You see, Christine's frightfully good at office work, and she's mad to come under some really clever man who can teach her even more than she knows already —

Helmer: Very sensible, madam.

Nora: So when she heard you'd become head of the bank — it was in her local paper — she came here as quickly as she could and — Torvald, you will, won't you? Do a little something to help Christine? For my sake?

Helmer: Well, that shouldn't be impossible. You are a widow, I take it, Mrs. Linde?

Mrs. Linde: Yes.

Helmer: And you have experience of office work?

Mrs. Linde: Yes, quite a bit.

Helmer: Well then, it's quite likely I may be able to find some job for you —

Nora (claps her hands): You see, you see!

Helmer: You've come at a lucky moment, Mrs. Linde.

Mrs. Linde: Oh, how can I ever thank you — ?

Helmer: There's absolutely no need. *(Puts on his overcoat.)* But now I'm afraid I must ask you to excuse me —

Rank: Wait. I'll come with you.

He gets his fur coat from the hall and warms it at the stove.

Nora: Don't be long, Torvald dear.

Helmer: I'll only be an hour.

Nora: Are you going too, Christine?

Mrs. Linde (puts on her outdoor clothes): Yes, I must start to look round for a room.

Helmer: Then perhaps we can walk part of the way together.

Nora (helps her): It's such a nuisance we're so cramped here — I'm afraid we can't offer to —

Mrs. Linde: Oh, I wouldn't dream of it. Goodbye, Nora dear, and thanks for everything.

Nora: Au revoir. You'll be coming back this evening, of course. And you too, Dr. Rank. What? If you're well enough? Of course you'll be well enough. Wrap up warmly, though.

They go out, talking, into the hall. Children's voices are heard from the stairs.

Nora: Here they are! Here they are!

She runs out and opens the door. Anne-Marie, the nurse, enters with the children.

Nora: Come in, come in! *(Stoops down and kisses them.)* Oh, my sweet darlings — ! Look at them, Christine! Aren't they beautiful?

Rank: Don't stand here chattering in this draught!

Helmer: Come, Mrs. Linde. This is for mothers only.

Dr. Rank, Helmer, and Mrs. Linde go down the stairs. The nurse brings the children into the room. Nora follows, and closes the door to the hall.

Nora: How well you look! What red cheeks you've got! Like apples and roses! *(The children answer her inaudibly as she talks to them.)* Have you had fun? That's splendid. You gave Emmy and Bob a ride on the sledge? What, both together? I say! What a clever boy you are, Ivar! Oh, let me hold her for a moment, Anne-Marie! My sweet little baby doll! *(Takes the smallest child from the nurse and dances with her.)* Yes, yes, Mummy will dance with Bob too. What? Have you been throwing snowballs? Oh, I wish I'd been there! No, don't — I'll undress them myself, Anne-Marie. No, please let me; it's such fun. Go inside and warm yourself; you look frozen. There's some hot coffee on the stove. *(The nurse goes into the room on the left. Nora takes off the children's outdoor clothes and throws them anywhere while they all chatter simultaneously.)* What? A big dog ran after you? But he didn't bite you? No, dogs don't bite lovely little baby dolls. Leave those parcels alone, Ivar. What's in them? Ah, wouldn't you like to know! No, no; it's nothing nice. Come on, let's play a game. What shall we play? Hide and seek. Yes, let's play hide and seek. Bob shall hide first. You want me to? All right, let me hide first.

Nora and the children play around the room, and in the adjacent room to the left, laughing and shouting. At length Nora hides under the table. The children rush in, look, but cannot find her. Then they hear her half-stifled laughter, run to the table, lift up the cloth, and see her. Great excitement. She crawls out as though to frighten them. Further excitement. Meanwhile, there has been a knock on the door leading from the hall, but no one has noticed it. Now the door is half-opened and Krogstad enters. He waits for a moment; the game continues.

Krogstad: Excuse me, Mrs. Helmer —

Nora (turns with a stifled cry and half jumps up): Oh! What do you want?

Krogstad: I beg your pardon; the front door was ajar. Someone must have forgotten to close it.

Nora (gets up): My husband is not at home, Mr. Krogstad.

Krogstad: I know.

Nora: Well, what do want here, then?

Krogstad: A word with you.

Nora: With — ? *(To the children, quietly.)* Go inside to Anne-Marie. What? No, the strange gentleman won't do anything to hurt Mummy. When he's gone we'll start playing again.

She takes the children into the room on the left and closes the door behind them.

Nora (uneasy, tense): You want to speak to me?

Krogstad: Yes.

Nora: Today? But it's not the first of the month yet.

Krogstad: No, it is Christmas Eve. Whether or not you have a merry Christmas depends on you.

Nora: What do you want? I can't give you anything today —

Krogstad: We won't talk about that for the present. There's something else. You have a moment to spare?

Nora: Oh, yes. Yes, I suppose so; though —

Krogstad: Good. I was sitting in the café down below and I saw your husband cross the street —

Nora: Yes.

Krogstad: With a lady.

Nora: Well?

Krogstad: Might I be so bold as to ask: was not that lady a Mrs. Linde?

Nora: Yes.

Krogstad: Recently arrived in town?

Nora: Yes, today.

Krogstad: She is a good friend of yours, is she not?

Nora: Yes, she is. But I don't see —

Krogstad: I used to know her too once.

Nora: I know.

Krogstad: Oh? You've discovered that. Yes, I thought you would. Well then, may I ask you a straight question: is Mrs. Linde to be employed at the bank?

Nora: How dare you presume to cross-examine me, Mr. Krogstad? You, one of my husband's employees? But since you ask, you shall have an answer. Yes, Mrs. Linde is to be employed by the bank. And I arranged it, Mr. Krogstad. Now you know.

Krogstad: I guessed right, then.

Nora (walks up and down the room): Oh, one has a little influence, you know. Just because one's a woman it doesn't necessarily mean that — When one is in a humble position, Mr. Krogstad, one should think twice before offending someone who — hm —

Krogstad: — who has influence?

Nora: Precisely.

Krogstad (changes his tone): Mrs. Helmer, will you have the kindness to use your influence on my behalf?

Nora: What? What do you mean?

Krogstad: Will you be so good as to see that I keep my humble position at the bank?

Nora: What do you mean? Who is thinking of removing you from your position?

Krogstad: Oh, you don't need to play innocent with me. I realize it can't be very pleasant for your friend to risk bumping into me; and now I also realize whom I have to thank for being hounded out like this.

Nora: But I assure you —

Krogstad: Look, let's not beat about the bush. There's still time, and I'd advise you to use your influence to stop it.

Nora: But, Mr. Krogstad, I have no influence!

Krogstad: Oh? I thought you just said —

Nora: But I didn't mean it like that! I? How on earth could you imagine that I would have any influence over my husband?

Krogstad: Oh, I've known your husband since we were students together. I imagine he has his weaknesses like other married men.

Nora: If you speak impertinently of my husband, I shall show you the door.

Krogstad: You're a bold woman, Mrs. Helmer.

Nora: I'm not afraid of you any longer. Once the New Year is in, I'll soon be rid of you.

Krogstad (more controlled): Now listen to me, Mrs. Helmer. If I'm forced to, I shall fight for my little job at the bank as I would fight for my life.

Nora: So it sounds.

Krogstad: It isn't just the money; that's the last thing I care about. There's something else — well, you might as well know. It's like this, you see. You know of course, as everyone else does, that some years ago I committed an indiscretion.

Nora: I think I did hear something —

Krogstad: It never came into court; but from that day, every opening was barred to me. So I turned my hand to the kind of business you know about. I had to do something; and I don't think I was one of the worst. But now I want to give up all that. My sons are growing up; for their sake, I must try to regain what respectability I can. This job in the bank was the first step on the ladder. And now your husband wants to kick me off that ladder back into the dirt.

Nora: But my dear Mr. Krogstad, it simply isn't in my power to help you.

Krogstad: You say that because you don't want to help me. But I have the means to make you.

Nora: You don't mean you'd tell my husband that I owe you money?

Krogstad: And if I did?

Nora: That'd be a filthy trick! *(Almost in tears.)* This secret that is my pride and my joy — that he should hear about it in such a filthy, beastly way — hear about it from you! It'd involve me in the most dreadful unpleasantness —

Krogstad: Only — unpleasantness?

Nora (vehemently): All right, do it! You'll be the one who'll suffer. It'll show my husband the kind of man you are, and then you'll never keep your job.

Krogstad: I asked you whether it was merely domestic unpleasantness you were afraid of.

Nora: If my husband hears about it, he will of course immediately pay you whatever is owing. And then we shall have nothing more to do with you.

Krogstad (takes a step closer): Listen, Mrs. Helmer. Either you've a bad memory or else you know very little about financial transactions. I had better enlighten you.

Nora: What do you mean?

Krogstad: When your husband was ill, you came to me to borrow two hundred and fifty pounds.

Nora: I didn't know anyone else.

Krogstad: I promised to find that sum for you —

Nora: And you did find it.

Krogstad: I promised to find that sum for you on certain conditions. You were so worried about your husband's illness and so keen to get the money to take him abroad that I don't think you bothered much about the details. So it won't be out of place if I refresh your memory. Well — I promised to get you the money in exchange for an I.O.U., which I drew up.

Nora: Yes, and which I signed.

Krogstad: Exactly. But then I added a few lines naming your father as security for the debt. This paragraph was to be signed by your father.

Nora: Was to be? He did sign it.

Krogstad: I left the date blank for your father to fill in when he signed this paper. You remember, Mrs. Helmer?

Nora: Yes, I think so —

Krogstad: Then I gave you back this I.O.U. for you to post to your father. Is that not correct?

Nora: Yes.

Krogstad: And of course you posted it at once; for within five or six days you brought it along to me with your father's signature on it. Whereupon I handed you the money.

Nora: Yes, well. Haven't I repaid the installments as agreed?

Krogstad: Mm — yes, more or less. But to return to what we were speaking about — that was a difficult time for you just then, wasn't it, Mrs. Helmer?

Nora: Yes, it was.

Krogstad: And your father was very ill, if I am not mistaken.

Nora: He was dying.

Krogstad: He did in fact die shortly afterwards?

Nora: Yes.

Krogstad: Tell me, Mrs. Helmer, do you by any chance remember the date of your father's death? The day of the month, I mean.

Nora: Papa died on the twenty-ninth of September.

Krogstad: Quite correct; I took the trouble to confirm it. And that leaves me with a curious little problem — *(Takes out a paper.)* — which I simply cannot solve.

Nora: Problem? I don't see —

Krogstad: The problem, Mrs. Helmer, is that your father signed this paper three days after his death.

Nora: What? I don't understand —

Krogstad: Your father died on the twenty-ninth of September. But look at this. Here your father has dated his signature the second of October. Isn't that a curious little problem, Mrs. Helmer? *(Nora is silent.)* Can you suggest any explanation? *(She remains silent.)* And there's another curious thing. The words "second of October" and the year are written in a hand which is not your father's, but which I seem to know. Well, there's a simple explanation to that. Your father could have forgotten to write in the date when he signed, and someone else could have added it before the news came of his death. There's nothing criminal about that. It's the signature itself I'm wondering about. It *is* genuine, I suppose, Mrs. Helmer? It was your father who wrote his name here?

Nora (after a short silence, throws back her head and looks defiantly at him): No, it was not. It was I who wrote Papa's name there.

Krogstad: Look, Mrs. Helmer, do you realize this is a dangerous admission?

Nora: Why? You'll get your money.

Krogstad: May I ask you a question? Why didn't you send this paper to your father?

Nora: I couldn't. Papa was very ill. If I'd asked him to sign this, I'd have had to tell him what the money was for. But I couldn't have told him in his condition that my husband's life was in danger. I couldn't have done that!

Krogstad: Then you would have been wiser to have given up your idea of a holiday.

Nora: But I couldn't! It was to save my husband's life. I couldn't put it off.

Krogstad: But didn't it occur to you that you were being dishonest towards me?

Nora: I couldn't bother about that. I didn't care about you. I hated you because of all the beastly difficulties you'd put in my way when you knew how dangerously ill my husband was.

Krogstad: Mrs. Helmer, you evidently don't appreciate exactly what you have done. But I can assure you that it is no bigger nor worse a crime than the one I once committed, and thereby ruined my whole social position.

Nora: You? Do you expect me to believe that you would have taken a risk like that to save your wife's life?

Krogstad: The law does not concern itself with motives.

Nora: Then the law must be very stupid.

Krogstad: Stupid or not, if I show this paper to the police, you will be judged according to it.

Nora: I don't believe that. Hasn't a daughter the right to shield her father from worry and anxiety when he's old and dying? Hasn't a wife the right to save her husband's life? I don't know much about the law, but there must be something somewhere that says that such things are allowed. You ought to know about that, you're meant to be a lawyer, aren't you? You can't be a very good lawyer, Mr. Krogstad.

Krogstad: Possibly not. But business, the kind of business we two have been transacting — I think you'll admit I understand something about that? Good. Do as you please. But I tell you this. If I get thrown into the gutter for a second time, I shall take you with me.

He bows and goes out through the hall.

Nora (stands for a moment in thought, then tosses her head): What nonsense! He's trying to frighten me! I'm not that stupid. *(Busies herself gathering together the children's clothes; then she suddenly stops.)* But — ? No, it's impossible. I did it for love, didn't I?

Children (in the doorway, left): Mummy, the strange gentleman's gone out into the street.

Nora: Yes, yes, I know. But don't talk to anyone about the strange gentleman. You hear? Not even to Daddy.

Children: No, Mummy. Will you play with us again now?

Nora: No, no. Not now.

Children: Oh but, Mummy, you promised!

Nora: I know, but I can't just now. Go back to the nursery. I've a lot to do. Go away, my darlings, go away. *(She pushes them gently into the other room, and closes the door behind them. She sits on the sofa, takes up her embroidery, stitches for a few moments, but soon stops.)* No! *(Throws the embroidery aside, gets up, goes to the door leading to the hall, and calls.)* Helen!

Bring in the Christmas tree! *(She goes to the table on the left and opens the drawer in it; then pauses again.)* No, but it's utterly impossible!

Maid (enters with the tree): Where shall I put it, madam?

Nora: There, in the middle of the room.

Maid: Will you be wanting anything else?

Nora: No, thank you, I have everything I need.

The maid puts down the tree and goes out.

Nora (busy decorating the tree): Now — candles here — and flowers here. That loathsome man! Nonsense, nonsense, there's nothing to be frightened about. The Christmas tree must be beautiful. I'll do everything that you like, Torvald. I'll sing for you, dance for you —

Helmer, with a bundle of papers under his arm, enters.

Nora: Oh — are you back already?

Helmer: Yes. Has anyone been here?

Nora: Here? No.

Helmer: That's strange. I saw Krogstad come out of the front door.

Nora: Did you? Oh yes, that's quite right — Krogstad was here for a few minutes.

Helmer: Nora, I can tell from your face, he's been here and asked you to put in a good word for him.

Nora: Yes.

Helmer: And you were to pretend you were doing it of your own accord? You weren't going to tell me he'd been here? He asked you to do that too, didn't he?

Nora: Yes, Torvald. But —

Helmer: Nora, Nora! And you were ready to enter into such a conspiracy? Talking to a man like that, and making him promises — and then, on top of it all, to tell me an untruth!

Nora: An untruth?

Helmer: Didn't you say no one had been here? *(Wags his finger.)* My little songbird must never do that again. A songbird must have a clean beak to sing with; otherwise she'll start twittering out of tune. *(Puts his arm round her waist.)* Isn't that the way we want things? Yes, of course it is. *(Lets go of her.)* So let's hear no more about that. *(Sits down in front of the stove.)* Ah, how cozy and peaceful it is here. *(Glances for a few moments at his papers.)*

Nora (busy with the tree; after a short silence): Torvald.

Helmer: Yes.

Nora: I'm terribly looking forward to that fancy dress ball at the Stenborgs on Boxing Day.

Helmer: And I'm terribly curious to see what you're going to surprise me with.

Nora: Oh, it's so maddening.

Helmer: What is?

Nora: I can't think of anything to wear. It all seems so stupid and meaningless.

Helmer: So my little Nora's come to that conclusion, has she?

Nora (behind his chair, resting her arms on its back): Are you very busy, Torvald?

Helmer: Oh —

Nora: What are those papers?

Helmer: Just something to do with the bank.

Nora: Already?

Helmer: I persuaded the trustees to give me authority to make certain immediate changes in the staff and organization. I want to have everything straight by the New Year.

Nora: Then that's why this poor man Krogstad —

Helmer: Hm.

Nora (still leaning over his chair, slowly strokes the back of his head): If you hadn't been so busy, I was going to ask you an enormous favour, Torvald.

Helmer: Well, tell me. What was it to be?

Nora: You know I trust your taste more than anyone's. I'm so anxious to look really beautiful at the fancy dress ball. Torvald, couldn't you help me to decide what I shall go as, and what kind of costume I ought to wear?

Helmer: Aha! So little Miss Independent's in trouble and needs a man to rescue her, does she?

Nora: Yes, Torvald. I can't get anywhere without your help.

Helmer: Well, well, I'll give the matter thought. We'll find something.

Nora: Oh, how kind of you! *(Goes back to the tree. Pause.)* How pretty these red flowers look! But, tell me, is it so dreadful, this thing that Krogstad's done?

Helmer: He forged someone else's name. Have you any idea what that means?

Nora: Mightn't he have been forced to do it by some emergency?

Helmer: He probably just didn't think — that's what usually happens. I'm not so heartless as to condemn a man for an isolated action.

Nora: No, Torvald, of course not!

Helmer: Men often succeed in re-establishing themselves if they admit their crime and take their punishment.

Nora: Punishment?

Helmer: But Krogstad didn't do that. He chose to try and trick his way out of it; and that's what has morally destroyed him.

Nora: You think that would — ?

Helmer: Just think how a man with that load on his conscience must always be lying and cheating and dissembling; how he must wear a mask even in the presence of those who are dearest to him, even his own wife and children! Yes, the children. That's the worst danger, Nora.

Nora: Why?

Helmer: Because an atmosphere of lies contaminates and poisons every corner of the home. Every breath that the children draw in such a house contains the germs of evil.

Nora (comes closer behind him): Do you really believe that?

Helmer: Oh, my dear, I've come across it so often in my work at the bar. Nearly all young criminals are the children of mothers who are constitutional liars.

Nora: Why do you say mothers?

Helmer: It's usually the mother; though of course the father can have the same influence. Every lawyer knows that only too well. And yet this fellow Krogstad has been sitting at home all these years poisoning his children with his lies and pretenses. That's why I say that, morally speaking, he is dead. *(Stretches out his hands towards her.)* So my pretty little Nora must promise me not to plead his case. Your hand on it. Come, come, what's this? Give me your hand. There. That's settled, now. I assure you it'd be quite impossible for me to work in the same building as him. I literally feel physically ill in the presence of a man like that.

Nora (draws her hand from his and goes over to the other side of the Christmas tree): How hot it is in here! And I've so much to do.

Helmer (gets up and gathers his papers): Yes, and I must try to get some of this read before dinner. I'll think about your costume too. And I may even have something up my sleeve to hang in gold paper on the Christmas tree. *(Lays his hand on her head.)* My precious little songbird!

He goes into his study and closes the door.

Nora (softly, after a pause): It's nonsense. It must be. It's impossible. It *must* be impossible!

Nurse (in the doorway, left): The children are asking if they can come in to Mummy.

Nora: No, no, no; don't let them in! You stay with them, Anne-Marie.

Nurse: Very good, madam. *(Closes the door.)*

Nora (pale with fear): Corrupt my little children — ! Poison my home! *(Short pause. She throws back her head.)* It isn't true! It *couldn't* be true!

ACT II

The same room. In the corner by the piano the Christmas tree stands, stripped and disheveled, its candles burned to their sockets. Nora's outdoor clothes lie on the sofa. She is alone in the room, walking restlessly to and fro. At length she stops by the sofa and picks up her coat.

Nora (drops the coat again): There's someone coming! *(Goes to the door and listens.)* No, it's no one. Of course — no one'll come today, it's Christmas Day. Nor tomorrow. But perhaps — ! *(Opens the door and looks out.)* No. Nothing in the letter-box. Quite empty. (*Walks across the room.)* Silly, silly. Of course he won't do anything. It couldn't happen. It isn't possible. Why, I've three small children.

The Nurse, carrying a large cardboard box, enters from the room on the left.

Nurse: I found those fancy dress clothes at last, madam.

Nora: Thank you. Put them on the table.

Nurse (does so): They're all rumpled up.

Nora: Oh, I wish I could tear them into a million pieces!

Nurse: Why, madam! They'll be all right. Just a little patience.

Nora: Yes, of course. I'll go and get Mrs. Linde to help me.

Nurse: What, out again? In this dreadful weather? You'll catch a chill, madam.

Nora: Well, that wouldn't be the worst. How are the children?

Nurse: Playing with their Christmas presents, poor little dears. But —

Nora: Are they still asking to see me?

Nurse: They're so used to having their Mummy with them.

Nora: Yes, but, Anne-Marie, from now on I shan't be able to spend so much time with them.

Nurse: Well, children get used to anything in time.

Nora: Do you think so? Do you think they'd forget their mother if she went away from them — for ever?

Nurse: Mercy's sake, madam! For ever!

Nora: Tell me, Anne-Marie — I've so often wondered. How could you bear to give your child away — to strangers?

Nurse: But I had to when I came to nurse my little Miss Nora.

Nora: Do you mean you wanted to?

Nurse: When I had the chance of such a good job? A poor girl what's got into trouble can't afford to pick and choose. That good-for-nothing didn't lift a finger.

Nora: But your daughter must have completely forgotten you.

Nurse: Oh no, indeed she hasn't. She's written to me twice, once when she got confirmed and then again when she got married.

Nora (hugs her): Dear old Anne-Marie, you were a good mother to me.

Nurse: Poor little Miss Nora, you never had any mother but me.

Nora: And if my little ones had no one else, I know you would — no, silly, silly, silly! *(Opens the cardboard box.)* Go back to them, Anne-Marie. Now I must — Tomorrow you'll see how pretty I shall look.

Nurse: Why, there'll be no one at the ball as beautiful as my Miss Nora.

She goes into the room, left.

Nora (begins to unpack the clothes from the box, but soon throws them down again): Oh, if only I dared to go out! If I could be sure no one would come, and nothing would happen while I was away! Stupid, stupid! No one will come. I just mustn't think about it. Brush this muff. Pretty gloves, pretty gloves! Don't think about it, don't think about it! One, two, three, four, five, six — *(Cries.)* Ah — they're coming — !

She begins to run toward the door, but stops uncertainly. Mrs. Linde enters from the hall, where she has been taking off her outdoor clothes.

Nora: Oh, it's you, Christine. There's no one else out there, is there? Oh, I'm so glad you've come.

Mrs. Linde: I hear you were at my room asking for me.

Nora: Yes, I just happened to be passing. I want to ask you to help me with something. Let's sit down here on the sofa. Look at this. There's going to be a fancy dress ball tomorrow night upstairs at Consul Stenborg's, and Torvald wants me to go as a Neapolitan fisher-girl and dance the tarantella. I learned it on Capri.

Mrs. Linde: I say, are you going to give a performance?

Nora: Yes, Torvald says I should. Look, here's the dress. Torvald had it made for me in Italy; but now it's all so torn, I don't know —

Mrs. Linde: Oh, we'll soon put that right; the stitching's just come away. Needle and thread? Ah, here we are.

Nora: You're being awfully sweet.

Mrs. Linde (sews): So you're going to dress up tomorrow, Nora? I must pop over for a moment to see how you look. Oh, but I've completely forgotten to thank you for that nice evening yesterday.

Nora (gets up and walks across the room): Oh, I didn't think it was as nice as usual. You ought to have come to town a little earlier, Christine. . . . Yes, Torvald understands how to make a home look attractive.

Mrs. Linde: I'm sure you do, too. You're not your father's daughter for nothing. But, tell me. Is Dr. Rank always in such low spirits as he was yesterday?

Nora: No, last night it was very noticeable. But he's got a terrible disease; he's got spinal tuberculosis, poor man. His father was a frightful creature who kept mistresses and so on. As a result Dr. Rank has been sickly ever since he was a child — you understand —

Mrs. Linde (puts down her sewing): But, my dear Nora, how on earth did you get to know about such things?

Nora (walks about the room): Oh, don't be silly, Christine — when one has three children, one comes into contact with women who — well, who know about medical matters, and they tell one a thing or two.

Mrs. Linde (sews again; a short silence): Does Dr. Rank visit you every day?

Nora: Yes, every day. He's Torvald's oldest friend, and a good friend to me too. Dr. Rank's almost one of the family.

Mrs. Linde: But, tell me — is he quite sincere? I mean, doesn't he rather say the sort of thing he thinks people want to hear?

Nora: No, quite the contrary. What gave you that idea?

Mrs. Linde: When you introduced me to him yesterday, he said he'd often heard my name mentioned here. But later I noticed your husband had no idea who I was. So how could Dr. Rank — ?

Nora: Yes, that's quite right, Christine. You see, Torvald's so hopelessly in love with me that he wants to have me all to himself — those were his very words. When we were first married, he got quite jealous if I as much as mentioned any of my old friends back home. So naturally, I stopped talking about them. But I often chat with Dr. Rank about that kind of thing. He enjoys it, you see.

Mrs. Linde: Now listen, Nora. In many ways you're still a child; I'm a bit older than you and have a little more experience of the world. There's something I want to say to you. You ought to give up this business with Dr. Rank.

Nora: What business?

Mrs. Linde: Well, everything. Last night you were speaking about this rich admirer of yours who was going to give you money —

Nora: Yes, and who doesn't exist — unfortunately. But what's that got to do with — ?

Mrs. Linde: Is Dr. Rank rich?

Nora: Yes.

Mrs. Linde: And he has no dependents?

Nora: No, no one. But —

Mrs. Linde: And he comes here to see you every day?

Nora: Yes, I've told you.

Mrs. Linde: But how dare a man of his education be so forward?

Nora: What on earth are you talking about?

Mrs. Linde: Oh, stop pretending, Nora. Do you think I haven't guessed who it was who lent you that two hundred pounds?

Nora: Are you out of your mind? How could you imagine such a thing? A friend, someone who comes here every day! Why, that'd be an impossible situation!

Mrs. Linde: Then it really wasn't him?

Nora: No, of course not. I've never for a moment dreamed of — anyway, he hadn't any money to lend then. He didn't come into that till later.

Mrs. Linde: Well, I think that was a lucky thing for you, Nora dear.

Nora: No, I could never have dreamed of asking Dr. Rank — Though I'm sure that if I ever did ask him —

Mrs. Linde: But of course you won't.

Nora: Of course not. I can't imagine that it should ever become necessary. But I'm perfectly sure that if I did speak to Dr. Rank —

Mrs. Linde: Behind your husband's back?

Nora: I've got to get out of this other business; and *that's* been going on behind his back. I've *got* to get out of it.

Mrs. Linde: Yes, well, that's what I told you yesterday. But —

Nora (walking up and down): It's much easier for a man to arrange these things than a woman —

Mrs. Linde: One's own husband, yes.

Nora: Oh, bosh. *(Stops walking.)* When you've completely repaid a debt, you get your I.O.U. back, don't you?

Mrs. Linde: Yes, of course.

Nora: And you can tear it into a thousand pieces and burn the filthy, beastly thing!

Mrs. Linde (looks hard at her, puts down her sewing, and gets up slowly): Nora, you're hiding something from me.

Nora: Can you see that?

Mrs. Linde: Something has happened since yesterday morning. Nora, what is it?

Nora (goes toward her): Christine! *(Listens.)* Ssh! There's Torvald. Would you mind going into the nursery for a few minutes? Torvald can't bear to see sewing around. Anne-Marie'll help you.

Mrs. Linde (gathers some of her things together): Very well. But I shan't leave this house until we've talked this matter out.

She goes into the nursery, left. As she does so, Helmer enters from the hall.

Nora (runs to meet him): Oh, Torvald dear, I've been so longing for you to come back!

Helmer: Was that the dressmaker?

Nora: No, it was Christine. She's helping me mend my costume. I'm going to look rather splendid in that.

Helmer: Yes, that was quite a bright idea of mine, wasn't it?

Nora: Wonderful! But wasn't it nice of me to give in to you?

Helmer (takes her chin in his hand): Nice — to give in to your husband? All right, little silly, I know you didn't mean it like that. But I won't disturb you. I expect you'll be wanting to try it on.

Nora: Are you going to work now?

Helmer: Yes. *(Shows her a bundle of papers.)* Look at these. I've been down to the bank — (*Turns to go into his study.)*

Nora: Torvald.

Helmer (stops): Yes.

Nora: If little squirrel asked you really prettily to grant her a wish —

Helmer: Well?

Nora: Would you grant it to her?

Helmer: First I should naturally have to know what it was.

Nora: Squirrel would do lots of pretty tricks for you if you granted her wish.

Helmer: Out with it, then.

Nora: Your little skylark would sing in every room—

Helmer: My little skylark does that already.

Nora: I'd turn myself into a little fairy and dance for you in the moonlight, Torvald.

Helmer: Nora, it isn't that business you were talking about this morning?

Nora (comes closer): Yes, Torvald—oh, please! I beg of you!

Helmer: Have you really the nerve to bring that up again?

Nora: Yes, Torvald, yes, you must do as I ask! You must let Krogstad keep his place at the bank!

Helmer: My dear Nora, his is the job I'm giving to Mrs. Linde.

Nora: Yes, that's terribly sweet of you. But you can get rid of one of the other clerks instead of Krogstad.

Helmer: Really, you're being incredibly obstinate. Just because you thoughtlessly promised to put in a word for him, you expect me to—

Nora: No, it isn't that, Helmer. It's for your own sake. That man writes for the most beastly newspapers—you said so yourself. He could do you tremendous harm. I'm so dreadfully frightened of him—

Helmer: Oh, I understand. Memories of the past. That's what's frightening you.

Nora: What do you mean?

Helmer: You're thinking of your father, aren't you?

Nora: Yes, yes. Of course. Just think what those dreadful men wrote in the papers about Papa! The most frightful slanders. I really believe it would have lost him his job if the Ministry hadn't sent you down to investigate, and you hadn't been so kind and helpful to him.

Helmer: But my dear little Nora, there's a considerable difference between your father and me. Your father was not a man of unassailable reputation. But I am; and I hope to remain so all my life.

Nora: But no one knows what spiteful people may not dig up. We could be so peaceful and happy now, Torvald—we could be free from every worry—you and I and the children. Oh, please, Torvald, please—!

Helmer: The very fact of your pleading his cause makes it impossible for me to keep him. Everyone at the bank already knows that I intend to dismiss Krogstad. If the rumor got about that the new manager had allowed his wife to persuade him to change his mind—

Nora: Well, what then?

Helmer: Oh, nothing, nothing. As long as my little Miss Obstinate gets her way—Do you expect me to make a laughing-stock of myself before my entire staff—give people the idea that I am open to outside influence? Believe me, I'd soon feel the consequences! Besides—there's something else that makes it impossible for Krogstad to remain in the bank while I am its manager.

Nora: What is that?

Helmer: I might conceivably have allowed myself to ignore his moral obloquies—

Nora: Yes, Torvald, surely?

Helmer: And I hear he's quite efficient at his job. But we—well, we were schoolfriends. It was one of those friendships that one enters into overhastily and so often comes to regret later in life. I might as well confess the truth. We — well, we're on Christian name terms. And the tactless idiot makes no attempt to conceal it when other people are present. On the contrary, he thinks it gives him the right to be familiar with me. He shows off the whole time, with "Torvald this," and "Torvald that." I can tell you, I find it damned annoying. If he stayed, he'd make my position intolerable.

Nora: Torvald, you can't mean this seriously.

Helmer: Oh? And why not?

Nora: But it's so petty.

Helmer: What did you say? Petty? You think *I* am petty?

Nora: No, Torvald dear, of course you're not. That's just why —

Helmer: Don't quibble! You call my motives petty. Then I must be petty too. Petty! I see. Well, I've had enough of this. *(Goes to the door and calls into the hall.)* Helen!

Nora: What are you going to do?

Helmer (searching among his papers): I'm going to settle this matter once and for all. *(The Maid enters.)* Take this letter downstairs at once. Find a messenger and see that he delivers it. Immediately! The address is on the envelope. Here's the money.

Maid: Very good, sir. *(Goes out with the letter.)*

Helmer (putting his papers in order): There now, little Miss Obstinate.

Nora (tensely): Torvald — what was in that letter?

Helmer: Krogstad's dismissal.

Nora: Call her back, Torvald! There's still time. Oh, Torvald, call her back! Do it for my sake — for your own sake — for the children! Do you hear me, Torvald? Please do it! You don't realize what this may do to us all!

Helmer: Too late.

Nora: Yes. Too late.

Helmer: My dear Nora, I forgive you this anxiety. Though it is a bit of an insult to me. Oh, but it is! Isn't it an insult to imply that I should be frightened by the vindictiveness of a depraved hack journalist? But I forgive you, because it so charmingly testifies to the love you bear me. *(Takes her in his arms.)* Which is as it should be, my own dearest Nora. Let what will happen, happen. When the real crisis comes, you will not find me lacking in strength or courage. I am man enough to bear the burden for us both.

Nora (fearfully): What do you mean?

Helmer: The whole burden, I say —

Nora (calmly): I shall never let you do that.

Helmer: Very well. We shall share it, Nora — as man and wife. And that is as it should be. *(Caresses her.)* Are you happy now? There, there, there; don't look at me with those frightened little eyes. You're simply imagining things. You go ahead now and do your tarantella, and get some practice on that tambourine. I'll sit in my study and close the door. Then I won't hear anything, and you can make all the noise you want. *(Turns in the doorway.)* When Dr. Rank comes, tell him where to find me. *(He nods to her, goes into his room with his papers, and closes the door.)*

Nora (desperate with anxiety, stands as though transfixed, and whispers): He said he'd do it. He will do it. He will do it, and nothing'll stop him. No, never that. I'd rather anything. There must be some escape — Some way out — ! *(The bell rings in the hall.)* Dr. Rank — ! Anything but that! Anything, I don't care — !

She passes her hand across her face, composes herself, walks across, and opens the door to the hall. Dr. Rank is standing there, hanging up his fur coat. During the following scene, it begins to grow dark.

Nora: Good evening, Dr. Rank. I recognized your ring. But you mustn't go to Torvald yet. I think he's busy.

Rank: And — you?

Nora (as he enters the room and she closes the door behind him): Oh, you know very well I've always time to talk to you.

Rank: Thank you. I shall avail myself of that privilege as long as I can.

Nora: What do you mean by that? As long as you *can?*

Rank: Yes. Does that frighten you?

Nora: Well, it's rather a curious expression. Is something going to happen?

Rank: Something I've been expecting to happen for a long time. But I didn't think it would happen quite so soon.

Nora (seizes his arm): What is it? Dr. Rank, you must tell me!

Rank (sits down by the stove): I'm on the way out. And there's nothing to be done about it.

Nora (sighs with relief): Oh, it's you — ?

Rank: Who else? No, it's no good lying to oneself. I am the most wretched of all my patients, Mrs. Helmer. These last few days I've been going through the books of this poor body of mine, and I find I am bankrupt. Within a month I may be rotting up there in the churchyard.

Nora: Ugh, what a nasty way to talk!

Rank: The facts aren't exactly nice. But the worst is that there's so much else that's nasty to come first. I've only one more test to make. When that's done I'll have a pretty accurate idea of when the final disintegration is likely to begin. I want to ask you a favour. Helmer's a sensitive chap, and I know how he hates anything ugly. I don't want him to visit me when I'm in hospital —

Nora: Oh but, Dr. Rank —

Rank: I don't want him there. On any pretext. I shan't have him allowed in. As soon as I know the worst, I'll send you my visiting card with a black cross on it, and then you'll know that the final filthy process has begun.

Nora: Really, you're being quite impossible this evening. And I did hope you'd be in a good mood.

Rank: With death on my hands? And all this to atone for someone else's sin? Is there justice in that? And in every single family, in one way or another, the same merciless law of retribution is at work —

Nora (holds her hands to her ears): Nonsense! Cheer up! Laugh!

Rank: Yes, you're right. Laughter's all the damned thing's fit for. My poor innocent spine must pay for the fun my father had as a gay young lieutenant.

Nora (at the table, left): You mean he was too fond of asparagus and *foie gras?*

Rank: Yes, and truffles too.

Nora: Yes, of course, truffles, yes. And oysters too, I suppose?

Rank: Yes, oysters, oysters. Of course.

Nora: And all that port and champagne to wash them down. It's too sad that all those lovely things should affect one's spine.

Rank: Especially a poor spine that never got any pleasure out of them.

Nora: Oh yes, that's the saddest thing of all.

Rank (looks searchingly at her): Hm —

Nora (after a moment): Why did you smile?

Rank: No, it was you who laughed.

Nora: No, it was you who smiled, Dr. Rank!

Rank (gets up): You're a worse little rogue than I thought.

Nora: Oh, I'm full of stupid tricks today.

Rank: So it seems.

Nora (puts both her hands on his shoulders): Dear, dear Dr. Rank, you mustn't die and leave Torvald and me.

Rank: Oh, you'll soon get over it. Once one is gone, one is soon forgotten.

Nora (looks at him anxiously): Do you believe that?

Rank: One finds replacements, and then —

Nora: Who will find a replacement?

Rank: You and Helmer both will, when I am gone. You seem to have made a start already, haven't you? What was this Mrs. Linde doing here yesterday evening?

Nora: Aha! But surely you can't be jealous of poor Christine?

Rank: Indeed I am. She will be my successor in this house. When I have moved on, this lady will —

Nora: Ssh — don't speak so loud! She's in there!

Rank: Today again? You see!

Nora: She's only come to mend my dress. Good heavens, how unreasonable you are! *(Sits on the sofa.)* Be nice now, Dr. Rank. Tomorrow you'll see how beautifully I shall dance; and you must imagine that I'm doing it just for you. And for Torvald of course; obviously. *(Takes some things out of the box.)* Dr. Rank, sit down here and I'll show you something.

Rank (sits): What's this?

Nora: Look here! Look!

Rank: Silk stockings!

Nora: Flesh-colored. Aren't they beautiful? It's very dark in here now, of course, but tomorrow — No, no, no; only the soles. Oh well, I suppose you can look a bit higher if you want to.

Rank: Hm —

Nora: Why are you looking so critical? Don't you think they'll fit me?

Rank: I can't really give you a qualified opinion on that.

Nora (looks at him for a moment): Shame on you! *(Flicks him on the ear with the stockings.)* Take that. *(Puts them back in the box.)*

Rank: What other wonders are to be revealed to me?

Nora: I shan't show you anything else. You're being naughty.

She hums a little and looks among the things in the box.

Rank (after a short silence): When I sit here like this being so intimate with you, I can't think — I cannot imagine what would have become of me if I had never entered this house.

Nora (smiles): Yes, I think you enjoy being with us, don't you?

Rank (more quietly, looking into the middle distance): And now to have to leave it all —

Nora: Nonsense. You're not leaving us.

Rank (as before): And not to be able to leave even the most wretched token of gratitude behind; hardly even a passing sense of loss; only an empty place, to be filled by the next comer.

Nora: Suppose I were to ask you to — ? No —

Rank: To do what?

Nora: To give me proof of your friendship —

Rank: Yes, yes?

Nora: No, I mean — to do me a very great service —

Rank: Would you really for once grant me that happiness?

Nora: But you've no idea what it is.

Rank: Very well, tell me, then.

Nora: No, but, Dr. Rank, I can't. It's far too much — I want your help and advice, and I want you to do something for me.

Rank: The more the better. I've no idea what it can be. But tell me. You do trust me, don't you?

Nora: Oh, yes, more than anyone. You're my best and truest friend. Otherwise I couldn't tell you. Well then, Dr. Rank — there's something you must help me to prevent. You know how much Torvald loves me — he'd never hesitate for an instant to lay down his life for me —

Rank (leans over towards her): Nora — do you think he is the only one — ?

Nora (with a slight start): What do you mean?

Rank: Who would gladly lay down his life for you?

Nora (sadly): Oh, I see.

Rank: I swore to myself I would let you know that before I go. I shall never have a better opportunity. . . . Well, Nora, now you know that. And now you also know that you can trust me as you can trust nobody else.

Nora (rises; calmly and quietly): Let me pass, please.

Rank (makes room for her but remains seated): Nora —

Nora (in the doorway to the hall): Helen, bring the lamp. *(Goes over to the stove.)* Oh, dear Dr. Rank, this was really horrid of you.

Rank (gets up): That I have loved you as deeply as anyone else has? Was that horrid of me?

Nora: No — but that you should go and tell me. That was quite unnecessary —

Rank: What do you mean? Did you know, then — ?

The Maid enters with the lamp, puts it on the table, and goes out.

Rank: Nora — Mrs. Helmer — I am asking you, did you know this?

Nora: Oh, what do I know, what did I know, what didn't I know — I really can't say. How could you be so stupid, Dr. Rank? Everything was so nice.

Rank: Well, at any rate now you know that I am ready to serve you, body and soul. So — please continue.

Nora (looks at him): After this?

Rank: Please tell me what it is.

Nora: I can't possibly tell you now.

Rank: Yes, yes! You mustn't punish me like this. Let me be allowed to do what I can for you.

Nora: You can't do anything for me now. Anyway, I don't need any help. It was only my imagination — you'll see. Yes, really. Honestly. *(Sits in the rocking-chair, looks at him, and smiles.)* Well, upon my word you *are* a fine gentleman, Dr. Rank. Aren't you ashamed of yourself, now that the lamp's been lit?

Rank: Frankly, no. But perhaps I ought to say — *adieu?*

Nora: Of course not. You will naturally continue to visit us as before. You know quite well how Torvald depends on your company.

Rank: Yes, but you?

Nora: Oh, I always think it's enormous fun having you here.

Rank: That was what misled me. You're a riddle to me, you know. I'd often felt you'd just as soon be with me as with Helmer.

Nora: Well, you see, there are some people whom one loves, and others whom it's almost more fun to be with.

Rank: Oh yes, there's some truth in that.

Nora: When I was at home, of course I loved Papa best. But I always used to think it was terribly amusing to go down and talk to the servants; because they never told me what I ought to do; and they were such fun to listen to.

Rank: I see. So I've taken their place?

Nora (jumps up and runs over to him): Oh, dear, sweet Dr. Rank, I didn't meant that at all. But I'm sure you understand — I feel the same about Torvald as I did about Papa.

Maid (enters from the hall): Excuse me, madam. *(Whispers to her and hands her a visiting card.)*

Nora (glances at the card): Oh! *(Puts it quickly in her pocket.)*

Rank: Anything wrong?

Nora: No, no, nothing at all. It's just something that — it's my new dress.

Rank: What? But your costume is lying over there.

Nora: Oh — that, yes — but there's another — I ordered it specially — Torvald mustn't know —

Rank: Ah, so that's your big secret?

Nora: Yes, yes. Go in and talk to him — he's in his study — keep him talking for a bit —

Rank: Don't worry. He won't get away from me. *(Goes into Helmer's study.)*

Nora (to the Maid): Is he waiting in the kitchen?

Maid: Yes, madam, he came up the back way —

Nora: But didn't you tell him I had a visitor?

Maid: Yes, but he wouldn't go.

Nora: Wouldn't go?

Maid: No, madam, not until he'd spoken with you.

Nora: Very well, show him in; but quietly. Helen, you mustn't tell anyone about this. It's a surprise for my husband.

Nora: Very good, madam. I understand. *(Goes.)*

Nora: It's happening. It's happening after all. No, no, no, it can't happen, it mustn't happen.

She walks across and bolts the door of Helmer's study. The Maid opens the door from the hall to admit Krogstad, and closes it behind him. He is wearing an overcoat, heavy boots, and a fur cap.

Nora (goes towards him): Speak quietly. My husband's at home.

Krogstad: Let him hear.

Nora: What do you want from me?

Krogstad: Information.

Nora: Hurry up, then. What is it?

Krogstad: I suppose you know I've been given the sack.

Nora: I couldn't stop it, Mr. Krogstad. I did my best for you, but it didn't help.

Krogstad: Does your husband love you so little? He knows what I can do to you, and yet he dares to —

Nora: Surely you don't imagine I told him?

Krogstad: No. I didn't really think you had. It wouldn't have been like my old friend Torvald Helmer to show that much courage —

Nora: Mr. Krogstad, I'll trouble you to speak respectfully of my husband.

Krogstad: Don't worry, I'll show him all the respect he deserves. But since you're so anxious to keep this matter hushed up, I presume you're better informed than you were yesterday of the gravity of what you've done?

Nora: I've learned more than you could ever teach me.

Krogstad: Yes, a bad lawyer like me —

Nora: What do you want from me?

Krogstad: I just wanted to see how things were with you, Mrs. Helmer. I've been thinking about you all day. Even duns and hack journalists have hearts, you know.

Nora: Show some heart, then. Think of my little children.

Krogstad: Have you and your husband thought of mine? Well, let's forget that. I just wanted to tell you, you don't need to take this business too seriously. I'm not going to take any action, for the present.

Nora: Oh, no — you won't, will you? I knew it.

Krogstad: It can all be settled quite amicably. There's no need for it to become public. We'll keep it among the three of us.

Nora: My husband must never know about this.

Krogstad: How can you stop him? Can you pay the balance of what you owe me?

Nora: Not immediately.

Krogstad: Have you any means of raising the money during the next few days?

Nora: None that I would care to use.

Krogstad: Well, it wouldn't have helped anyway. However much money you offered me now I wouldn't give you back that paper.

Nora: What are you going to do with it?

Krogstad: Just keep it. No one else need ever hear about it. So in case you were thinking of doing anything desperate —

Nora: I am.

Krogstad: Such as running away —

Nora: I am.

Krogstad: Or anything more desperate —

Nora: How did you know?

Krogstad: — just give up the idea.

Nora: How did you know?

Krogstad: Most of us think of that at first. I did. But I hadn't the courage —

Nora (dully): Neither have I.

Krogstad (relieved): It's true, isn't it? You haven't the courage either?

Nora: No. I haven't. I haven't.

Krogstad: It'd be a stupid thing to do anyway. Once the first little domestic explosion is over. . . . I've got a letter in my pocket here addressed to your husband —

Nora: Telling him everything?

Krogstad: As delicately as possible.

Nora (quickly): He must never see that letter. Tear it up. I'll find the money somehow —

Krogstad: I'm sorry, Mrs. Helmer, I thought I'd explained —

Nora: Oh, I don't mean the money I owe you. Let me know how much you want from my husband, and I'll find it for you.

Krogstad: I'm not asking your husband for money.

Nora: What do you want, then?

Krogstad: I'll tell you. I want to get on my feet again, Mrs. Helmer. I want to get to the top. And your husband's going to help me. For eighteen months now my record's been clean. I've been in hard straits all that time; I was content to fight my way back inch by inch. Now I've been chucked back into the mud, and I'm not going to be satisfied with just getting back my job. I'm going to get to the top, I tell you. I'm going to get back into the bank, and it's going to be higher up. Your husband's going to create a new job for me —

Nora: He'll never do that!

Krogstad: Oh, yes he will. I know him. He won't dare to risk a scandal. And once I'm in there with him, you'll see! Within a year I'll be his right-hand man. It'll be Nils Krogstad who'll be running that bank, not Torvald Helmer!

Nora: That will never happen.

Krogstad: Are you thinking of — ?

Nora: Now I *have* the courage.

Krogstad: Oh, you can't frighten me. A pampered little pretty like you —

Nora: You'll see! You'll see!

Krogstad: Under the ice? Down in the cold, black water? And then, in the spring, to float up again, ugly, unrecognizable, hairless — ?

Nora: You can't frighten me.

Krogstad: And you can't frighten me. People don't do such things, Mrs. Helmer. And anyway, what'd be the use? I've got him in my pocket.

Nora: But afterwards? When I'm no longer — ?

Krogstad: Have you forgotten that then your reputation will be in my hands? *(She looks at him speechlessly.)* Well, I've warned you. Don't do anything silly. When Helmer's read my letter, he'll get in touch with me. And remember, it's your husband who's forced me to act like this. And for that I'll never forgive him. Goodbye, Mrs. Helmer. *(He goes out through the hall.)*

Nora (runs to the hall door, opens it a few inches, and listens): He's going. He's not going to give him the letter. Oh, no, no, it couldn't possibly happen. *(Opens the door a little wider.)* What's he doing? Standing outside the front door. He's not going downstairs. Is he changing his mind? Yes, he — !

A letter falls into the letter-box. Krogstad's footsteps die away down the stairs.

Nora (with a stifled cry, runs across the room towards the table by the sofa. A pause): In the letter-box. *(Steals timidly over towards the hall door.)* There it is! Oh, Torvald, Torvald! Now we're lost!
Mrs. Linde (enters from the nursery with Nora's costume): Well, I've done the best I can. Shall we see how it looks — ?
Nora (whispers hoarsely): Christine, come here.
Mrs. Linde (throws the dress on the sofa): What's wrong with you? You look as though you'd seen a ghost!
Nora: Come here. Do you see that letter? There — look — through the glass of the letter-box.
Mrs. Linde: Yes, yes, I see it.
Nora: That letter's from Krogstad —
Mrs. Linde: Nora! It was Krogstad who lent you the money!
Nora: Yes. And now Torvald's going to discover everything.
Mrs. Linde: Oh, believe me, Nora, it'll be best for you both.
Nora: You don't know what's happened. I've committed a forgery —
Mrs. Linde: But, for heaven's sake — !
Nora: Christine, all I want is for you to be my witness.
Mrs. Linde: What do you mean? Witness what?
Nora: If I should go out of my mind — and it might easily happen —
Mrs. Linde: Nora!
Nora: Or if anything else should happen to me — so that I wasn't here any longer —
Mrs. Linde: Nora, Nora, you don't know what you're saying!
Nora: If anyone should try to take the blame, and say it was all his fault — you understand — ?
Mrs. Linde: Yes, yes — but how can you think — ?
Nora: Then you must testify that it isn't true, Christine. I'm not mad — I know exactly what I'm saying — and I'm telling you, no one else knows anything about this. I did it entirely on my own. Remember that.
Mrs. Linde: All right. But I simply don't understand —
Nora: Oh, how could you understand? A — miracle — is about to happen.
Mrs. Linde: Miracle?
Nora: Yes. A miracle. But it's so frightening, Christine. It *mustn't* happen, not for anything in the world.
Mrs. Linde: I'll go over and talk to Krogstad.
Nora: Don't go near him. He'll only do something to hurt you.
Mrs. Linde: Once upon a time he'd have done anything for my sake.
Nora: He?
Mrs. Linde: Where does he live?
Nora: Oh, how should I know — ? Oh, yes, wait a moment — ! *(Feels in her pocket.)* Here's his card. But the letter, the letter — !
Helmer (from his study, knocks on the door): Nora!
Nora (cries in alarm): What is it?
Helmer: Now, now, don't get alarmed. We're not coming in; you've closed the door. Are you trying on your costume?

Nora: Yes, yes — I'm trying on my costume. I'm going to look so pretty for you, Torvald.

Mrs. Linde (who has been reading the card): Why, he lives just around the corner.

Nora: Yes; but it's no use. There's nothing to be done now. The letter's lying there in the box.

Mrs. Linde: And your husband has the key?

Nora: Yes, he always keeps it.

Mrs. Linde: Krogstad must ask him to send the letter back unread. He must find some excuse —

Nora: But Torvald always opens the box at just about this time —

Mrs. Linde: You must stop him. Go in and keep him talking. I'll be back as quickly as I can.

She hurries out through the hall.

Nora (goes over to Helmer's door, opens it and peeps in): Torvald!

Helmer (offstage): Well, may a man enter his own drawing-room again? Come on, Rank, now we'll see what — *(In the doorway.)* But what's this?

Nora: What, Torvald dear?

Helmer: Rank's been preparing me for some great transformation scene.

Rank (in the doorway): So I understood. But I seem to have been mistaken.

Nora: Yes, no one's to be allowed to see me before tomorrow night.

Helmer: But, my dear Nora, you look quite worn out. Have you been practicing too hard?

Nora: No, I haven't practiced at all yet.

Helmer: Well, you must.

Nora: Yes, Torvald, I must, I know. But I can't get anywhere without your help. I've completely forgotten everything.

Helmer: Oh, we'll soon put that to rights.

Nora: Yes, help me, Torvald. Promise me you will? Oh, I'm so nervous. All those people — ! You must forget everything except me this evening. You mustn't think of business — I won't even let you touch a pen. Promise me, Torvald?

Helmer: I promise. This evening I shall think of nothing but you — my poor, helpless little darling. Oh, there's just one thing I must see to — *(Goes towards the hall door.)*

Nora: What do you want out there?

Helmer: I'm only going to see if any letters have come.

Nora: No, Torvald, no!

Helmer: Why, what's the matter?

Nora: Torvald, I beg you. There's nothing there.

Helmer: Well, I'll just make sure.

He moves towards the door. Nora runs to the piano and plays the first bars of the tarantella.

Helmer (at the door, turns): Aha!

Nora: I can't dance tomorrow if I don't practice with you now.

Helmer (goes over to her): Are you really so frightened, Nora dear?

Nora: Yes, terribly frightened. Let me start practicing now, at once — we've still time before dinner. Oh, do sit down and play for me, Torvald dear. Correct me, lead me, the way you always do.

Helmer: Very well, my dear, if you wish it.

He sits down at the piano. Nora seizes the tambourine and a long multi-colored shawl from the cardboard box, wraps the latter hastily around her, then takes a quick leap into the center of the room.

Nora: Play for me! I want to dance!

Helmer plays and Nora dances. Dr. Rank stands behind Helmer at the piano and watches her.

Helmer (as he plays): Slower, slower!

Nora: I can't!

Helmer: Not so violently, Nora.

Nora: I must!

Helmer (stops playing): No, no, this won't do at all.

Nora (laughs and swings her tambourine): Isn't that what I told you?

Rank: Let me play for her.

Helmer (gets up): Yes, would you? Then it'll be easier for me to show her.

Rank sits down at the piano and plays. Nora dances more and more wildly. Helmer has stationed himself by the stove and tries repeatedly to correct her, but she seems not to hear him. Her hair works loose and falls over her shoulders; she ignores it and continues to dance. Mrs. Linde enters.

Mrs. Linde (stands in the doorway as though tongue-tied): Ah — !

Nora (as she dances): Oh, Christine, we're having such fun!

Helmer: But, Nora darling, you're dancing as if your life depended on it.

Nora: It does.

Helmer: Rank, stop it! This is sheer lunacy. Stop it, I say!

Rank ceases playing. Nora suddenly stops dancing.

Helmer (goes over to her): I'd never have believed it. You've forgotten everything I taught you.

Nora (throws away the tambourine): You see!

Helmer: I'll have to show you every step.

Nora: You see how much I need you! You must show me every step of the way. Right to the end of the dance. Promise me you will, Torvald?

Helmer: Never fear. I will.

Nora: You mustn't think about anything but me — today or tomorrow. Don't open any letters — don't even open the letter-box —

Helmer: Aha, you're still worried about that fellow —

Nora: Oh, yes, yes, him too.

Helmer: Nora, I can tell from the way you're behaving, there's a letter from him already lying there.

Nora: I don't know. I think so. But you mustn't read it now. I don't want anything ugly to come between us till it's all over.

Rank (quietly, to Helmer): Better give her her way.

Helmer (puts his arm round her): My child shall have her way. But tomorrow night, when your dance is over —

Nora: Then you will be free.

Maid (appears in the doorway, right): Dinner is served, madam.

Nora: Put out some champagne, Helen.

Maid: Very good, madam. *(Goes.)*

Helmer: I say! What's this, a banquet?

Nora: We'll drink champagne until dawn! *(Calls.)* And, Helen! Put out some macaroons! Lots of macaroons — for once!

Helmer (takes her hands in his): Now, now, now. Don't get so excited. Where's my little songbird, the one I know?

Nora: All right. Go and sit down — and you too, Dr. Rank. I'll be with you in a minute. Christine, you must help me put my hair up.

Rank (quietly, as they go): There's nothing wrong, is there? I mean, she isn't — er — expecting — ?

Helmer: Good heavens no, my dear chap. She just gets scared like a child sometimes — I told you before —

They go out right.

Nora: Well?

Mrs. Linde: He's left town.

Nora: I saw it from your face.

Mrs. Linde: He'll be back tomorrow evening. I left a note for him.

Nora: You needn't have bothered. You can't stop anything now. Anyway, it's wonderful really, in a way — sitting here and waiting for the miracle to happen.

Mrs. Linde: Waiting for what?

Nora: Oh, you wouldn't understand. Go in and join them. I'll be with you in a moment.

Mrs. Linde goes into the dining-room.

Nora (stands for a moment as though collecting herself. Then she looks at her watch): Five o'clock. Seven hours till midnight. Then another twenty-four hours till midnight tomorrow. And then the tarantella will be finished. Twenty-four and seven? Thirty-one hours to live.

Helmer (appears in the doorway, right): What's happened to my little songbird?

Nora (runs to him with her arms wide): Your songbird is here!

ACT III

The same room. The table which was formerly by the sofa has been moved into the center of the room; the chairs surround it as before. The door to the hall stands open. Dance music can be heard from the floor above. Mrs. Linde is seated at the table, absent-mindedly glancing through a book. She is trying to read, but seems unable to keep her mind on it. More than once she turns and listens anxiously towards the front door.

Mrs. Linde (looks at her watch): Not here yet. There's not much time left. Please God he hasn't — ! *(Listens again.)* Ah, here he is. *(Goes out into the hall and cautiously opens the front door. Footsteps can be heard softly ascending the stairs. She whispers.)* Come in. There's no one here.

Krogstad (in the doorway): I found a note from you at my lodgings. What does this mean?

Mrs. Linde: I must speak with you.

Krogstad: Oh? And must our conversation take place in this house?

Mrs. Linde: We couldn't meet at my place; my room has no separate entrance. Come in. We're quite alone. The maid's asleep, and the Helmers are at the dance upstairs.

Krogstad (comes into the room): Well, well! So the Helmers are dancing this evening? Are they indeed?

Mrs. Linde: Yes. why not?

Krogstad: True enough. Why not?

Mrs. Linde: Well, Krogstad. You and I must have a talk together.

Krogstad: Have we two anything further to discuss?

Mrs. Linde: We have a great deal to discuss.

Krogstad: I wasn't aware of it.

Mrs. Linde: That's because you've never really understood me.

Krogstad: Was there anything to understand? It's the old story, isn't it — a woman chucking a man because something better turns up?

Mrs. Linde: Do you really think I'm so utterly heartless? You think it was easy for me to give you up?

Krogstad: Wasn't it?

Mrs. Linde: Oh, Nils, did you really believe that?

Krogstad: Then why did you write to me the way you did?

Mrs. Linde: I had to. Since I had to break with you, I thought it my duty to destroy all the feelings you had for me.

Krogstad (clenches his fists): So that was it. And you did this for money!

Mrs. Linde: You mustn't forget I had a helpless mother to take care of, and two little brothers. We couldn't wait for you, Nils. It would have been so long before you'd had enough to support us.

Krogstad: Maybe. But you had no right to cast me off for someone else.

Mrs. Linde: Perhaps not. I've often asked myself that.

Krogstad (more quietly): When I lost you, it was just as though all solid ground had been swept from under my feet. Look at me. Now I am a shipwrecked man, clinging to a spar.

Mrs. Linde: Help may be near at hand.

Krogstad: It was near. But then you came, and stood between it and me.

Mrs. Linde: I didn't know, Nils. No one told me till today that this job I'd found was yours.

Krogstad: I believe you, since you say so. But now you know, won't you give it up?

Mrs. Linde: No — because it wouldn't help you even if I did.

Krogstad: Wouldn't it? I'd do it all the same.

Mrs. Linde: I've learned to look at things practically. Life and poverty have taught me that.

Krogstad: And life has taught me to distrust fine words.

Mrs. Linde: Then it's taught you a useful lesson. But surely you still believe in actions?

Krogstad: What do you mean?

Mrs. Linde: You said you were like a shipwrecked man clinging to a spar.

Krogstad: I have good reason to say it.

Mrs. Linde: I'm in the same position as you. No one to care about, no one to care for.

Krogstad: You made your own choice.

Mrs. Linde: I had no choice — then.

Krogstad: Well?

Mrs. Linde: Nils, suppose we two shipwrecked souls could join hands?

Krogstad: What are you saying?

Mrs. Linde: Castaways have a better chance of survival together than on their own.

Krogstad: Christine!

Mrs. Linde: Why do you suppose I came to this town?

Krogstad: You mean — you came because of me?

Mrs. Linde: I must work if I'm to find life worth living. I've always worked, for as long as I can remember; it's been the greatest joy of my life — my only joy. But now I'm alone in the world, and I feel so dreadfully lost and empty. There's no joy in working just for oneself. Oh, Nils, give me something — someone — to work for.

Krogstad: I don't believe all that. You're just being hysterical and romantic. You want to find an excuse for self-sacrifice.

Mrs. Linde: Have you ever known me to be hysterical?

Krogstad: You mean you really — ? Is it possible? Tell me — you know all about my past?

Mrs. Linde: Yes.

Krogstad: And you know what people think of me here?

Mrs. Linde: You said just now that with me you might have become a different person.

Krogstad: I know I could have.

Mrs. Linde: Couldn't it still happen?

Krogstad: Christine — do you really mean this? Yes — you do — I see it in your face. Have you really the courage — ?

Mrs. Linde: I need someone to be a mother to; and your children need a mother. And you and I need each other. I believe in you, Nils. I am afraid of nothing — with you.

Krogstad (clasps her hands): Thank you, Christine — thank you! Now I shall make the world believe in me as you do! Oh — but I'd forgotten —

Mrs. Linde (listens): Ssh! The tarantella! Go quickly, go!

Krogstad: Why? What is it?

Mrs. Linde: You hear that dance? As soon as it's finished, they'll be coming down.

Krogstad: All right, I'll go. It's no good, Christine. I'd forgotten — you don't know what I've just done to the Helmers.

Mrs. Linde: Yes, Nils. I know.

Krogstad: And yet you'd still have the courage to — ?

Mrs. Linde: I know what despair can drive a man like you to.

Krogstad: Oh, if only I could undo this!

Mrs. Linde: You can. Your letter is still lying in the box.

Krogstad: Are you sure?

Mrs. Linde: Quite sure. But —

Krogstad (looks searchingly at her): Is that why you're doing this? You want to save your friend at any price? Tell me the truth. Is that the reason?

Mrs. Linde: Nils, a woman who has sold herself once for the sake of others doesn't make the same mistake again.

Krogstad: I shall demand my letter back.

Mrs. Linde: No, no.

Krogstad: Of course I shall. I shall stay here till Helmer comes down. I'll tell him he must give me back my letter — I'll say it was only to do with my dismissal, and that I don't want him to read it —

Mrs. Linde: No, Nils, you mustn't ask for that letter back.

Krogstad: But — tell me — wasn't that the real reason you asked me to come here?

Mrs. Linde: Yes — at first, when I was frightened. But a day has passed since then, and in that time I've seen incredible things happen in this house. Helmer must know the truth. This unhappy secret of Nora's must be revealed. They must come to a full understanding; there must be an end of all these shiftings and evasions.

Krogstad: Very well. If you're prepared to risk it. But one thing I can do — and at once —

Mrs. Linde (listens): Hurry! Go, go! The dance is over. We aren't safe here another moment.

Krogstad: I'll wait for you downstairs.

Mrs. Linde: Yes, do. You can see me home.

Krogstad: I've never been so happy in my life before!

He goes out through the front door. The door leading from the room into the hall remains open.

Mrs. Linde (tidies the room a little and gets her hat and coat): What a change! Oh, what a change! Someone to work for — to live for! A home to bring joy into! I won't let this chance of happiness slip through my fingers. Oh, why don't they come? *(Listens.)* Ah, here they are. I must get my coat on.

She takes her hat and coat. Helmer's and Nora's voices become audible outside. A key is turned in the lock and Helmer leads Nora almost forcibly into the hall. She is dressed in an Italian costume with a large black shawl. He is in evening dress, with a black cloak.

Nora (still in the doorway, resisting him): No, no, no — not in here! I want to go back upstairs. I don't want to leave so early.

Helmer: But my dearest Nora —

Nora: Oh, please, Torvald, please! Just another hour!

Helmer: Not another minute, Nora, my sweet. You know what we agreed. Come along, now. Into the drawing-room. You'll catch cold if you stay out here.

He leads her, despite her efforts to resist him, gently into the room.

Mrs. Linde: Good evening.

Nora: Christine!

Helmer: Oh, hullo, Mrs. Linde. You still here?

Mrs. Linde: Please forgive me. I did so want to see Nora in her costume.

Nora: Have you been sitting here waiting for me?

Mrs. Linde: Yes. I got here too late, I'm afraid. You'd already gone up. And I felt I really couldn't go back home without seeing you.

Helmer (takes off Nora's shawl): Well, take a good look at her. She's worth looking at, don't you think? Isn't she beautiful, Mrs. Linde?

Mrs. Linde: Oh, yes, indeed —

Helmer: Isn't she unbelievably beautiful? Everyone at the party said so. But dreadfully stubborn she is, bless her pretty little heart. What's to be done about that? Would you believe it, I practically had to use force to get her away!

Nora: Oh, Torvald, you're going to regret not letting me stay — just half an hour longer.

Helmer: Hear that, Mrs. Linde? She dances her tarantella — makes a roaring success — and very well deserved — though possibly a trifle too realistic — more so than was aesthetically necessary, strictly speaking. But never mind that. Main thing is — she had a success — roaring success. Was I going to let her stay on after that and spoil the impression? No, thank you. I took my beautiful little Capri signorina — my capricious little Capricienne, what? — under my arm — a swift round of the ballroom, a curtsey to the company, and, as they say in novels, the beautiful apparition disappeared! An exit should always be dramatic, Mrs. Linde. But unfortunately that's just what I can't get Nora to realize. I say, it's hot in here. *(Throws his cloak on a chair and opens the door to his study.)* What's this? It's dark in here. Ah, yes, of course — excuse me. *(Goes in and lights a couple of candles.)*

Nora (whispers swiftly, breathlessly): Well?

Mrs. Linde (quietly): I've spoken to him.

Nora: Yes?

Mrs. Linde: Nora — you must tell your husband everything.

Nora (dully): I knew it.

Mrs. Linde: You've nothing to fear from Krogstad. But you must tell him.

Nora: I shan't tell him anything.

Mrs. Linde: Then the letter will.

Nora: Thank you, Christine. Now I know what I must do. Ssh!

Helmer (returns): Well, Mrs. Linde, finished admiring her?

Mrs. Linde: Yes. Now I must say good night.

Helmer: Oh, already? Does this knitting belong to you?

Mrs. Linde (takes it): Thank you, yes. I nearly forgot it.

Helmer: You knit, then?

Mrs. Linde: Why, yes.

Helmer: Know what? You ought to take up embroidery.

Mrs. Linde: Oh? Why?

Helmer: It's much prettier. Watch me, now. You hold the embroidery in your left hand, like this, and then you take the needle in your right hand and go in and out in a slow, easy movement — like this. I am right, aren't I?

Mrs. Linde: Yes, I'm sure —

Helmer: But knitting, now — that's an ugly business — can't help it. Look — arms all huddled up — great clumsy needles going up and down — makes you look like a damned Chinaman. I say, that really was a magnificent champagne they served us.

Mrs. Linde: Well, good night, Nora. And stop being stubborn. Remember!

Helmer: Quite right, Mrs. Linde!

Mrs. Linde: Good night, Mr. Helmer.

Helmer (accompanies her to the door): Good night, good night! I hope you'll manage to get home all right? I'd gladly — but you haven't far to go, have you? Good night, good night. *(She goes. He closes the door behind her and returns.)* Well, we've got rid of her at last. Dreadful bore that woman is!

Nora: Aren't you very tired, Torvald?

Helmer: No, not in the least.

Nora: Aren't you sleepy?

Helmer: Not a bit. On the contrary, I feel extraordinarily exhilarated. But what about you? Yes, you look very sleepy and tired.

Nora: Yes, I am very tired. Soon I shall sleep.

Helmer: You see, you see! How right I was not to let you stay longer!

Nora: Oh, you're always right, whatever you do.

Helmer (kisses her on the forehead): Now my little songbird's talking just like a real big human being. I say, did you notice how cheerful Rank was this evening?

Nora: Oh? Was he? I didn't have a chance to speak with him.

Helmer: I hardly did. But I haven't seen him in such a jolly mood for ages. *(Looks at her for a moment, then comes closer.)* I say, it's nice to get back to one's home again, and be all alone with you. Upon my word, you're a distractingly beautiful young woman.

Nora: Don't look at me like that, Torvald!

Helmer: What, not look at my most treasured possession? At all this wonderful beauty that's mine, mine alone, all mine.

Nora (goes round to the other side of the table): You mustn't talk to me like that tonight.

Helmer (follows her): You've still the tarantella in your blood, I see. And that makes you even more desirable. Listen! Now the other guests are beginning to go. *(More quietly.)* Nora — soon the whole house will be absolutely quiet.

Nora: Yes, I hope so.

Helmer: Yes, my beloved Nora, of course you do! Do you know — when I'm out with you among other people like we were tonight, do you know why I say so little to you, why I keep so aloof from you, and just throw you an occasional glance? Do you know why I do that? It's because I pretend to myself that you're my secret mistress, my clandestine little sweetheart, and that nobody knows there's anything at all between us.

Nora: Oh, yes, yes, yes — I know you never think of anything but me.

Helmer: And then when we're about to go, and I wrap the shawl round your lovely young shoulders, over this wonderful curve of your neck — then I pretend to myself that you are my young bride, that we've just come from the wedding, that I'm taking you to my house for the first time — that, for the first time, I am alone with you — quite alone with you, as you stand there young and trembling and beautiful. All evening I've had no eyes for anyone but you. When I saw you dance the tarantella, like a huntress, a temptress, my blood grew hot, I couldn't stand it any longer! That was why I seized you and dragged you down here with me —

Nora: Leave me, Torvald! Get away from me! I don't want all this.

Helmer: What? Now, Nora, you're joking with me. Don't want, don't want — ? Aren't I your husband — ?

There is a knock on the front door.

Nora (starts): What was that?

Helmer (goes towards the hall): Who is it?

Rank (outside): It's me. May I come in for a moment?

Helmer (quietly, annoyed): Oh, what does he want now? *(Calls.)* Wait a moment. *(Walks over and opens the door.)* Well! Nice of you not to go by without looking in.

Rank: I thought I heard your voice, so I felt I had to say goodbye. *(His eyes travel swiftly around the room.)* Ah, yes — these dear rooms, how well I know them. What a happy, peaceful home you two have.

Helmer: You seemed to be having a pretty happy time yourself upstairs.

Rank: Indeed I did. Why not? Why shouldn't one make the most of this world? As much as one can, and for as long as one can. The wine was excellent —

Helmer: Especially the champagne.

Rank: You noticed that too? It's almost incredible how much I managed to get down.

Nora: Torvald drank a lot of champagne too, this evening.

Rank: Oh?

Nora: Yes. It always makes him merry afterwards.

Rank: Well, why shouldn't a man have a merry evening after a well-spent day?

Helmer: Well-spent? Oh, I don't know that I can claim that.

Rank (slaps him across the back): I can, though, my dear fellow!

Nora: Yes, of course, Dr. Rank — you've been carrying out a scientific experiment today, haven't you?

Rank: Exactly.

Helmer: Scientific experiment! Those are big words for my little Nora to use!

Nora: And may I congratulate you on the finding?

Rank: You may indeed.

Nora: It was good, then?

Rank: The best possible finding — both for the doctor and the patient. Certainty.

Nora (quickly): Certainty?

Rank: Absolute certainty. So aren't I entitled to have a merry evening after that?

Nora: Yes, Dr. Rank. You were quite right to.

Helmer: I agree. Provided you don't have to regret it tomorrow.

Rank: Well, you never get anything in this life without paying for it.

Nora: Dr. Rank — you like masquerades, don't you?

Rank: Yes, if the disguises are sufficiently amusing.

Nora: Tell me. What shall we two wear at the next masquerade?

Helmer: You little gadabout! Are you thinking about the next one already?

Rank: We two? Yes, I'll tell you. You must go as the Spirit of Happiness —

Helmer: You try to think of a costume that'll convey that.

Rank: Your wife need only appear as her normal, everyday self —

Helmer: Quite right! Well said! But what are you going to be? Have you decided that?

Rank: Yes, my dear friend. I have decided that.

Helmer: Well?

Rank: At the next masquerade, I shall be invisible.

Helmer: Well, that's a funny idea.

Rank: There's a big, black hat — haven't you heard of the invisible hat? Once it's over your head, no one can see you any more.

Helmer (represses a smile): Ah yes, of course.

Rank: But I'm forgetting what I came for. Helmer, give me a cigar. One of your black Havanas.

Helmer: With the greatest pleasure. *(Offers him the box.)*

Rank (takes one and cuts off the tip): Thank you.

Nora (strikes a match): Let me give you a light.

Rank: Thank you. *(She holds out the match for him. He lights his cigar.)* And now — goodbye.

Helmer: Goodbye, my dear chap, goodbye.

Nora: Sleep well, Dr. Rank.

Rank: Thank you for that kind wish.

Nora: Wish me the same.

Rank: You? Very well — since you ask. Sleep well. And thank you for the light. *(He nods to them both and goes.)*

Helmer (quietly): He's been drinking too much.

Nora (abstractedly): Perhaps.

Helmer takes his bunch of keys from his pocket and goes out into the hall.

Nora: Torvald, what do you want out there?

Helmer: I must empty the letter-box. It's absolutely full. There'll be no room for the newspapers in the morning.

Nora: Are you going to work tonight?

Helmer: You know very well I'm not. Hullo, what's this? Someone's been at the lock.

Nora: At the lock — ?

Helmer: Yes, I'm sure of it. Who on earth — ? Surely not one of the maids? Here's a broken hairpin. Nora, it's yours —

Nora (quickly): Then it must have been the children.

Helmer: Well, you'll have to break them of that habit. Hm, hm. Ah, that's done it. *(Takes out the contents of the box and calls into the kitchen.)* Helen! Put out the light on the staircase. *(Comes back into the drawing-room with the letters in his hand and closes the door to the hall.)* Look at this! You see how they've piled up? *(Glances through them.)* What on earth's this?

Nora (at the window): The letter! Oh, no, Torvald, no!

Helmer: Two visiting cards — from Rank.

Nora: From Dr. Rank?

Helmer (looks at them): Peter Rank, M.D. They were on top. He must have dropped them in as he left.

Nora: Has he written anything on them?

Helmer: There's a black cross above his name. Look. Rather gruesome, isn't it? It looks just as though he was announcing his death.

Nora: He is.

Helmer: What? Do you know something? Has he told you anything?

Nora: Yes. When these cards come, it means he's said goodbye to us. He wants to shut himself up in his house and die.

Helmer: Ah, poor fellow. I knew I wouldn't be seeing him for much longer. But so soon — ! And now he's going to slink away and hide like a wounded beast.

Nora: When the time comes, it's best to go silently. Don't you think so, Torvald?

Helmer (walks up and down): He was so much a part of our life. I can't realize that he's gone. His suffering and loneliness seemed to provide a kind of dark background to the happy sunlight of our marriage. Well, perhaps it's best this way. For him, anyway. *(Stops walking.)* And perhaps for us too, Nora. Now we have only each other. *(Embraces her.)* Oh, my beloved wife — I feel as though I could never hold you close enough. Do you know, Nora, often I wish some terrible danger might threaten you, so that I could offer my life and my blood, everything, for your sake.

Nora (tears herself loose and says in a clear, firm voice): Read your letters now, Torvald.

Helmer: No, no. Not tonight. Tonight I want to be with you, my darling wife —

Nora: When your friend is about to die — ?

Helmer: You're right. This news has upset us both. An ugliness has come between us; thoughts of death and dissolution. We must try to forget them. Until then — you go to your room; I shall go to mine.

Nora (throws her arms round his neck): Good night, Torvald! Good night!

Helmer (kisses her on the forehead): Good night, my darling little songbird. Sleep well, Nora. I'll go and read my letters.

He goes into the study with the letters in his hand, and closes the door.

Nora (wild-eyed, fumbles around, seizes Helmer's cloak, throws it round herself and whispers quickly, hoarsely): Never see him again. Never. Never. Never. *(Throws the shawl over her head.)* Never see the children again. Them too. Never. Never. Oh — the icy black water! Oh — that bottomless — that — ! Oh, if only it were all over! Now he's got it — he's reading it. Oh, no, no! Not yet! Goodbye, Torvald! Goodbye, my darlings!

She turns to run into the hall. As she does so, Helmer throws open his door and stands there with an open letter in his hand.

Helmer: Nora!

Nora (shrieks): Ah — !

Helmer: What is this? Do you know what is in this letter?

Nora: Yes, I know. Let me go! Let me go!

Helmer (holds her back): Go? Where?

Nora (tries to tear herself loose): You mustn't try to save me, Torvald!

Helmer (staggers back): Is it true? Is it true, what he writes? Oh, my God! No, no — it's impossible, it can't be true!

Nora: It *is* true. I've loved you more than anything else in the world.

Helmer: Oh, don't try to make silly excuses.

Nora (takes a step towards him): Torvald —

Helmer: Wretched woman! What have you done?

Nora: Let me go! You're not going to suffer for my sake. I won't let you!

Helmer: Stop being theatrical. *(Locks the front door.)* You're going to stay here and explain yourself. Do you understand what you've done? Answer me! Do you understand?

Nora (looks unflinchingly at him and, her expression growing colder, says): Yes. Now I am beginning to understand.

Helmer (walking around the room): Oh, what a dreadful awakening! For eight whole years — she who was my joy and my pride — a hypocrite, a liar — worse, worse — a criminal! Oh, the hideousness of it! Shame on you, shame!

Nora is silent and stares unblinkingly at him.

Helmer (stops in front of her): I ought to have guessed that something of this sort would happen. I should have foreseen it. All your father's recklessness and instability — be quiet! — I repeat, all your father's recklessness and instability he has handed on to you. No religion, no morals, no sense of duty! Oh, how I have been punished for closing my eyes to his faults! I did it for your sake. And now you reward me like this.

Nora: Yes. Like this.

Helmer: Now you have destroyed all my happiness. You have ruined my whole future. Oh, it's too dreadful to contemplate! I am in the power of a man who is completely without scruples. He can do what he likes with me, demand what he pleases, order me to do anything — I dare not disobey him. I am condemned to humiliation and ruin simply for the weakness of a woman.

Nora: When I am gone from this world, you will be free.

Helmer: Oh, don't be melodramatic. Your father was always ready with that kind of remark. How would it help me if you were "gone from this world," as you put it? It wouldn't assist me in the slightest. He can still make all the facts public; and if he does, I may quite easily be suspected of having been an accomplice in your crime. People may think that I was behind it — that it was I who encouraged you! And for all this I have to thank you, you whom I have carried on my hands through all the years of our marriage! Now do you realize what you've done to me?

Nora (coldly calm): Yes.

Helmer: It's so unbelievable I can hardly credit it. But we must try to find some way out. Take off that shawl. Take it off, I say! I must try to buy him off somehow. This thing must be hushed up at any price. As regards our relationship — we must appear to be living together just as before. Only *appear,* of course. You will therefore continue to reside here. That is understood. But the children shall be taken out of your hands. I dare no longer entrust them to you. Oh, to have to say this to the woman I once loved so dearly — and whom I still — ! Well, all that must be finished. Henceforth there can be no question of happiness; we must merely strive to save what shreds and tatters — *(The front door bell rings. Helmer starts.)* What can that be? At this hour? Surely not — ? He wouldn't — ? Hide yourself, Nora. Say you're ill.

Nora does not move. Helmer goes to the door of the room and opens it. The maid is standing half-dressed in the hall.

Maid: A letter for madam.

Helmer: Give it to me. *(Seizes the letter and shuts the door.)* Yes, it's from him. You're not having it. I'll read this myself.

Nora: Read it.

Helmer (by the lamp): I hardly dare to. This may mean the end for us both. No, I must know. *(Tears open the letter hastily; reads a few lines; looks at a piece of paper which is enclosed with it; utters a cry of joy.)* Nora! *(She looks at him questioningly.)* Nora! No — I must read it once more. Yes, yes, it's true! I am saved! Nora, I am saved!

Nora: What about me?

Helmer: You too, of course. We're both saved, you and I. Look! He's returning your I.O.U. He writes that he is sorry for what has happened — a happy accident has changed his life — oh, what does it matter what he writes? We are saved, Nora! No one can harm you now. Oh, Nora, Nora — no, first let me destroy this filthy thing. Let me see — ! *(Glances at the I.O.U.)* No, I don't want to look at it. I shall merely regard the whole business as a dream. *(He tears the I.O.U. and both letters into pieces, throws them into the stove, and watches them burn.)* There. Now they're destroyed. He wrote that ever since Christmas Eve you've been — oh, these must have been three dreadful days for you, Nora.

Nora: Yes. It's been a hard fight.

Helmer: It must have been terrible — seeing no way out except — no, we'll forget the whole sordid business. We'll just be happy and go on telling ourselves over and over again: "It's over! It's over!" Listen to me, Nora. You don't seem to realize. It's over! Why are you looking so pale? Ah, my poor little Nora, I understand. You can't believe that I have forgiven you. But I have, Nora. I swear it to you. I have forgiven you everything. I know that what you did you did for your love of me.

Nora: That is true.

Helmer: You have loved me as a wife should love her husband. It was simply that in your inexperience you chose the wrong means. But do you think I love you any the less because you don't know how to act on your own initiative? No, no. Just lean on me. I shall counsel you. I shall guide you. I would not be a true man if your feminine helplessness did not make you doubly attractive in my eyes. You mustn't mind the hard words I said to you in those first dreadful moments when my whole world seemed to be tumbling about my ears. I have forgiven you, Nora. I swear it to you; I have forgiven you.

Nora: Thank you for your forgiveness.

She goes out through the door, right.

Helmer: No, don't go — *(Looks in.)* What are you doing there?

Nora (offstage): Taking off my fancy dress.

Helmer (by the open door): Yes, do that. Try to calm yourself and get your balance again, my frightened little songbird. Don't be afraid. I have broad wings to shield you. *(Begins to walk around near the door.)* How lovely and peaceful this little home of ours is, Nora. You are safe here; I shall watch over you like a hunted dove which I have snatched unharmed from the claws of the falcon. Your wildly beating little heart shall find peace with me. It will happen, Nora; it will take time, but it will happen, believe me. Tomorrow all this will seem quite different. Soon everything will be as it was before. I shall no longer need to remind you that I have forgiven you;

your own heart will tell you that it is true. Do you really think I could ever bring myself to disown you, or even to reproach you? Ah, Nora, you don't understand what goes on in a husband's heart. There is something indescribably wonderful and satisfying for a husband in knowing that he has forgiven his wife — forgiven her unreservedly, from the bottom of his heart. It means that she has become his property in a double sense; he has, as it were, brought her into the world anew; she is now not only his wife but also his child. From now on that is what you shall be to me, my poor, helpless, bewildered little creature. Never be frightened of anything again, Nora. Just open your heart to me. I shall be both your will and your conscience. What's this? Not in bed? Have you changed?

Nora (in her everyday dress): Yes, Torvald. I've changed.

Helmer: But why now — so late — ?

Nora: I shall not sleep tonight.

Helmer: But, my dear Nora —

Nora (looks at her watch): It isn't that late. Sit down here, Torvald. You and I have a lot to talk about.

She sits down on one side of the table.

Helmer: Nora, what does this mean? You look quite drawn —

Nora: Sit down. It's going to take a long time. I've a lot to say to you.

Helmer (sits down on the other side of the table): You alarm me, Nora. I don't understand you.

Nora: No, that's just it. You don't understand me. And I've never understood you — until this evening. No, don't interrupt me. Just listen to what I have to say. You and I have got to face facts, Torvald.

Helmer: What do you mean by that?

Nora (after a short silence): Doesn't anything strike you about the way we're sitting here?

Helmer: What?

Nora: We've been married for eight years. Does it occur to you that this is the first time that we two, you and I, man and wife, have ever had a serious talk together?

Helmer: Serious? What do you mean, serious?

Nora: In eight whole years — no, longer — ever since we first met — we have never exchanged a serious word on a serious subject.

Helmer: Did you expect me to drag you into all my worries — worries you couldn't possibly have helped me with?

Nora: I'm not talking about worries. I'm simply saying that we have never sat down seriously to try to get to the bottom of anything.

Helmer: But, my dear Nora, what on earth has that got to do with you?

Nora: That's just the point. You have never understood me. A great wrong has been done to me, Torvald. First by Papa, and then by you.

Helmer: What? But we two have loved you more than anyone in the world!

Nora (shakes her head): You have never loved me. You just thought it was fun to be in love with me.

Helmer: Nora, what kind of a way is this to talk?

Nora: It's the truth, Torvald. When I lived with Papa, he used to tell me what he thought about everything, so that I never had any opinions but his. And if I did have any of my own, I kept them quiet, because he wouldn't have liked them. He called me his little doll, and he played with me just the way I played with my dolls. Then I came here to live in your house —

Helmer: What kind of a way is that to describe our marriage?

Nora (undisturbed): I mean, then I passed Papa's hands into yours. You arranged everything the way you wanted it, so that I simply took over your taste in everything — or pretended I did — I don't really know — I think it was a little of both — first one and then the other. Now I look back on it, it's as if I've been living here like a pauper, from hand to mouth. I performed tricks for you, and you gave me food and drink. But that was how you wanted it. You and Papa have done me a great wrong. It's your fault that I have done nothing with my life.

Helmer: Nora, how can you be so unreasonable and ungrateful? Haven't you been happy here?

Nora: No; never. I used to think I was; but I haven't ever been happy.

Helmer: Not — not happy?

Nora: No. I've just had fun. You've always been very kind to me. But our home has never been anything but a playroom. I've been your doll-wife, just as I used to be Papa's doll-child. And the children have been my dolls. I used to think it was fun when you came in and played with me, just as they think it's fun when I go in and play games with them. That's all our marriage has been, Torvald.

Helmer: There may be a little truth in what you say, though you exaggerate and romanticize. But from now on it'll be different. Playtime is over. Now the time has come for education.

Nora: Whose education? Mine or the children's?

Helmer: Both yours and the children's, my dearest Nora.

Nora: Oh, Torvald, you're not the man to educate me into being the right wife for you.

Helmer: How can you say that?

Nora: And what about me? Am I fit to educate the children?

Helmer: Nora!

Nora: Didn't you say yourself a few minutes ago that you dare not leave them in my charge?

Helmer: In a moment of excitement. Surely you don't think I meant it seriously?

Nora: Yes. You were perfectly right. I'm not fitted to educate them. There's something else I must do first. I must educate myself. And you can't help me with that. It's something I must do by myself. That's why I'm leaving you.

Helmer (jumps up): What did you say?

Nora: I must stand on my own feet if I am to find out the truth about myself and about life. So I can't go on living here with you any longer.

Helmer: Nora, Nora!

Nora: I'm leaving you now, at once. Christine will put me up for tonight —

Helmer: You're out of your mind! You can't do this! I forbid you!

Nora: It's no use your trying to forbid me any more. I shall take with me nothing but what is mine. I don't want anything from you, now or ever.

Helmer: What kind of madness is this?

Nora: Tomorrow I shall go home — I mean, to where I was born. It'll be easiest for me to find some kind of a job there.

Helmer: But you're blind! You've no experience of the world —

Nora: I must try to get some, Torvald.

Helmer: But to leave your home, your husband, your children! Have you thought what people will say?

Nora: I can't help that. I only know that I must do this.

Helmer: But this is monstrous! Can you neglect your most sacred duties?

Nora: What do you call my most sacred duties?

Helmer: Do I have to tell you? Your duties towards your husband, and your children.

Nora: I have another duty which is equally sacred.

Helmer: You have not. What on earth could that be?

Nora: My duty towards myself.

Helmer: First and foremost you are a wife and a mother.

Nora: I don't believe that any longer. I believe that I am first and foremost a human being, like you — or anyway, that I must try to become one. I know most people think as you do, Torvald, and I know there's something of the sort to be found in books. But I'm no longer prepared to accept what people say and what's written in books. I must think things out for myself, and try to find my own answer.

Helmer: Do you need to ask where your duty lies in your own home? Haven't you an infallible guide in such matters — your religion?

Nora: Oh, Torvald, I don't really know what religion means.

Helmer: What are you saying?

Nora: I only know what Pastor Hansen told me when I went to confirmation. He explained that religion meant this and that. When I get away from all this and can think things out on my own, that's one of the questions I want to look into. I want to find out whether what Pastor Hansen said was right — or anyway, whether it is right for me.

Helmer: But it's unheard of for so young a woman to behave like this! If religion cannot guide you, let me at least appeal to your conscience. I presume you have some moral feelings left? Or — perhaps you haven't? Well, answer me.

Nora: Oh, Torvald, that isn't an easy question to answer. I simply don't know. I don't know where I am in these matters. I only know that these things mean something quite different to me from what they do to you. I've learned now that certain laws are different from what I'd imagined them to be; but I can't accept that such laws can be right. Has a woman really not the right to spare her dying father pain, or save her husband's life? I can't believe that.

Helmer: You're talking like a child. You don't understand how society works.

Nora: No, I don't. But now I intend to learn. I must try to satisfy myself which is right, society or I.

Helmer: Nora, you're ill; you're feverish. I almost believe you're out of your mind.

Nora: I've never felt so sane and sure in my life.

Helmer: You feel sure that it is right to leave your husband and your children?

Nora: Yes. I do.

Helmer: Then there is only one possible explanation.

Nora: What?

Helmer: That you don't love me any longer.

Nora: No, that's exactly it.

Helmer: Nora! How can you say this to me?

Nora: Oh, Torvald, it hurts me terribly to have to say it, because you've always been so kind to me. But I can't help it. I don't love you any longer.

Helmer (controlling his emotions with difficulty): And you feel quite sure about this too?

Nora: Yes, absolutely sure. That's why I can't go on living here any longer.

Helmer: Can you also explain why I have lost your love?

Nora: Yes, I can. It happened this evening, when the miracle failed to happen. It was then that I realized you weren't the man I'd thought you to be.

Helmer: Explain more clearly. I don't understand you.

Nora: I've waited so patiently, for eight whole years — well, good heavens, I'm not such a fool as to suppose that miracles occur every day. Then this dreadful thing happened to me, and then I *knew:* "Now the miracle will take place!" When Krogstad's letter was lying out there, it never occurred to me for a moment that you would let that man trample over you. I *knew* that you would say to him: "Publish the facts to the world." And when he had done this —

Helmer: Yes, what then? When I'd exposed my wife's name to shame and scandal —

Nora: Then I was certain that you would step forward and take all the blame on yourself, and say: "I am the one who is guilty!"

Helmer: Nora!

Nora: You're thinking I wouldn't have accepted such a sacrifice from you? No, of course I wouldn't! But what would my word have counted for against yours? That was the miracle I was hoping for, and dreading. And it was to prevent it happening that I wanted to end my life.

Helmer: Nora, I would gladly work for you night and day, and endure sorrow and hardship for your sake. But no man can be expected to sacrifice his honor, even for the person he loves.

Nora: Millions of women have done it.

Helmer: Oh, you think and talk like a stupid child.

Nora: That may be. But you neither think nor talk like the man I could share my life with. Once you'd got over your fright — and you weren't frightened of what might threaten me, but only of what threatened you — once the danger was past, then as far as you were concerned it was exactly as though nothing had happened. I was your little songbird just as before — your doll whom henceforth you would take particular care to protect from the world because she was so weak and fragile. *(Gets up.)* Torvald, in that moment I realized that for eight years I had been living here with a complete stranger, and had borne him three children — ! Oh, I can't bear to think of it! I could tear myself to pieces!

Helmer (sadly): I see it, I see it. A gulf has indeed opened between us. Oh, but Nora — couldn't it be bridged?

Nora: As I am now, I am no wife for you.

Helmer: I have the strength to change.

Nora: Perhaps — if your doll is taken from you.

Helmer: But to be parted — to be parted from you! No, no, Nora, I can't conceive of it happening!

Nora (goes into the room, right): All the more necessary that it should happen.

She comes back with her outdoor things and a small traveling-bag, which she puts down on a chair by the table.

Helmer: Nora, Nora, not now! Wait till tomorrow!

Nora (puts on her coat): I can't spend the night in a strange man's house.

Helmer: But can't we live here as brother and sister, then — ?

Nora (fastens her hat): You know quite well it wouldn't last. *(Puts on her shawl.)* Goodbye, Torvald. I don't want to see the children. I know they're in better hands than mine. As I am now, I can be nothing to them.

Helmer: But some time, Nora — some time — ?

Nora: How can I tell? I've no idea what will happen to me.

Helmer: But you are my wife, both as you are and as you will be.

Nora: Listen, Torvald. When a wife leaves her husband's house, as I'm doing now, I'm told that according to the law he is freed of any obligations towards her. In any case, I release you from any such obligations. You mustn't feel bound to me in any way, however small, just as I shall not feel bound to you. We must both be quite free. Here is your ring back. Give me mine.

Helmer: That too?

Nora: That too.

Helmer: Here it is.

Nora: Good. Well, now it's over. I'll leave the keys here. The servants know about everything to do with the house — much better than I do. Tomorrow, when I have left town, Christine will come to pack the things I brought here from home. I'll have them sent on after me.

Helmer: This is the end then! Nora, will you never think of me any more?

Nora: Yes, of course. I shall often think of you and the children and this house.

Helmer: May I write to you, Nora?

Nora: No. never. You mustn't do that.

Helmer: But at least you must let me send you —

Nora: Nothing. Nothing.

Helmer: But if you should need help? —

Nora: I tell you, no. I don't accept things from strangers.

Helmer: Nora — can I never be anything but a stranger to you?

Nora (picks up her bag): Oh, Torvald! Then the miracle of miracles would have to happen.

Helmer: The miracle of miracles?

Nora: You and I would both have to change so much that — oh, Torvald, I don't believe in miracles any longer.

Helmer: But I want to believe in them. Tell me. We should have to change so much that — ?

Nora: That life together between us two could become a marriage. Goodbye.

She goes out through the hall.

Helmer (sinks down on a chair by the door and buries his face in his hands): Nora! Nora! *(Looks round and gets up.)* Empty! She's gone! *(A hope strikes him.)* The miracle of miracles — ?

The street door is slammed shut downstairs.

Considerations

1. Nora lies several times during the play. What kind of lies are they? Do her lies indicate that she is not to be trusted, or are they a sign of something else about her personality?
2. What kind of wife does Helmer want Nora to be? He affectionately calls her names such as "skylark" and "squirrel." What does this reveal about his attitude toward her?
3. Why is Nora "pale with fear" at the end of Act I? What is the significance of the "stripped and disheveled" Christmas tree that opens Act II? What other symbols are used in the play?
4. What is Dr. Rank's purpose in the story?
5. How does the relationship between Krogstad and Mrs. Linde serve to emphasize certain qualities in the Helmers' marriage?
6. Is Krogstad's decision not to expose Nora's secret convincing? Does his shift from villainy to generosity seem adequately motivated?
7. Why does Nora reject Helmer's efforts to smooth things over between them and start again? Do you have any sympathy for Helmer?
8. What is the significance of the play's title?
9. Would you describe the ending as essentially happy or unhappy? Is the play more like a comedy or a tragedy?
10. Ibsen once wrote a different ending for the play to head off producers who might have been tempted to change the final scene to placate the public's sense of morality. In the second conclusion, Helmer forces Nora to look in on their sleeping children. This causes her to realize that she cannot leave her family even though it means sacrificing herself. Ibsen called this version of the ending a "barbaric outrage" and didn't use it. Which ending do you prefer? Why?
11. Ibsen believed that a "dramatist's business is not to answer questions, but only to ask them." What questions are raised in the play? Does Ibsen propose any specific answers?
12. What makes this play a work of realism? Are there any elements that seem not to be realistic?

Connections

1. What does Nora have in common with the protagonist in Godwin's "A Sorrowful Woman" (p. 30)? What significant differences are there between them?
2. Explain how Torvald's attitude toward Nora is similar to the men's attitudes toward women in Glaspell's *Trifles* (p. 931). Write an essay exploring how the assumptions the men make about women in both plays contribute to the plays' conflicts.
3. Write an essay that compares and contrasts Nora's response to the social and legal expectations of her society with Antigone's in Sophocles' play (p. 1008). To what values does each character pledge her allegiance?

PERSPECTIVE

HENRIK IBSEN (1828–1906)

Notes for A Doll's House 1878

There are two kinds of spiritual law, two kinds of conscience, one in man and another, altogether different, in woman. They do not understand each other; but in practical life the woman is judged by man's law, as though she were not a woman but a man.

The wife in the play ends by having no idea of what is right or wrong; natural feeling on the one hand and belief in authority on the other have altogether bewildered her.

A woman cannot be herself in the society of the present day, which is an exclusively masculine society, with laws framed by men and with a judicial system that judges feminine conduct from a masculine point of view.

She has committed forgery, and she is proud of it; for she did it out of love for her husband, to save his life. But this husband with his commonplace principles of honor is on the side of the law and looks at the question from the masculine point of view.

Spiritual conflicts. Oppressed and bewildered by the belief in authority, she loses faith in her moral right and ability to bring up her children. Bitterness. A mother in modern society, like certain insects who go away and die when she has done her duty in the propagation of the race. Love of life, of home, of husband and children and family. Now and then a womanly shaking off of her thoughts. Sudden return of anxiety and terror. She must bear it all alone. The catastrophe approaches, inexorably, inevitably. Despair, conflict, and destruction.

From *From Ibsen's Workshop,* translated by A. G. Chater

Considerations

1. Given the ending of *A Doll's House,* what do you think of Ibsen's early view in his notes that "the wife in the play ends by having no idea of what is right or wrong"? Would you describe Nora as "altogether bewildered"? Why or why not?
2. "A woman cannot be herself in the society of the present day, which is an exclusively masculine society." Why is this statement true of Nora? Explain why you agree or disagree that this observation is accurate today.
3. How does oppressive "authority" loom large for Nora? What kind of authority creates "spiritual conflicts" for her?

THE CHERRY ORCHARD

Anton Chekhov, grandson of a serf and son of an unsuccessful grocer, was born in Taganrog, a small town in southern Russia. He studied medicine at Moscow University and began practicing in 1884. During his medical training, he wrote short stories to support himself and his family (one of them, "The Lady with the Pet Dog," appears on p. 146). Within a few years

Chekhov had published two well-received collections of short stories and decided to give up his medical career to be a writer. He did, however, continue to treat his poor neighbors without charge. His compassion and generosity are also reflected in his ability to create sympathetic, convincing characters in his literary works.

Chekhov's first significant success in the theater was *The Seagull* (1896), which was produced by the Moscow Art Theater under the direction of Konstantin Stanislavsky, a champion of realistic methods of acting. *The Seagull* and Chekhov's three other major plays, *Uncle Vanya* (1899), *The Three Sisters* (1901), and *The Cherry Orchard* (1903), are studies of the changing texture of Russian life at the turn of the century. His characters come from a cross section of society, ranging from valiant but ineffectual aristocrats to noble peasants. The future seems bleak for everyone because there is no energy or direction: civil government is merely officious, intellectuals are too self-absorbed, and the church has retreated to backward-looking tradition.

In contrast to Ibsen's plays, little appears to happen in Chekhov's dramas. They lack the sense of inevitable direction intrinsic to the well-made play. Although Ibsen's characters are typically riddled with uncertainties, they take decisive actions or are forcefully acted upon. But in a Chekhov play changes, if any, are measured in small, seemingly inconsequential actions. He creates a slice of life onstage, in which characters frequently talk around issues or past each other so that direct confrontations — the makings of dramatic moments — are relatively rare. Therefore, we must listen carefully to the characters' small talk if we are to follow their deepest concerns. Chekhov uses this method intentionally to mirror the circumstances of most people's lives. He avoids heroics and extreme actions in favor of daily lives; however, his characters' routine activities are typically puncutated by a pistol shot when conflicts break through the polite, trivial veneer. Chekhov does incorpoate some melodramatic elements in his plays, but they occur offstage and are subordinated to his interest in subtleties of character.

The Cherry Orchard focuses on a Russian family whose life is rudely and inexorably changed by an urban industrial order that threatens to transform a country estate into subdivided building lots. Chekhov does not definitively choose sides in this shift in power from landed aristocrats to a new class of capitalists; he simply presents his characters amid historic circumstances, which seem to offer opportunities for some but to bewilder and frustrate others.

ANTON CHEKHOV (1860–1904)

The Cherry Orchard 1903

TRANSLATED BY CONSTANCE GARNETT

Characters
Madame Ranevsky (Lyubov Andreyevna), the owner of the Cherry Orchard
Anya, her daughter, aged seventeen
Varya, her adopted daughter, aged twenty-four
Gaev (Leonid Andreyevitch), brother of Madame Ranevsky
Lopahin (Yermolay Alexeyevitch), a merchant
Trofimov (Pyotr Sergeyevitch), a student
Semyonov-Pishtchik, a landowner
Charlotta Ivanovna, a governess
Epihodov (Semyon Pantaleyevitch), a clerk
Dunyasha, a maid
Firs, an old valet, aged eighty-seven
Yasha, a young valet
A Wayfarer
The Station Master
A Post Office Clerk
Visitors, Servants

The action takes place on the estate of Madame Ranevsky.

ACT I

A room, which has always been called the nursery. One of the doors leads into Anya's room. Dawn, sun rises during the scene. May, the cherry trees in flower, but it is cold in the garden with the frost of early morning. Windows closed.

Enter Dunyasha with a candle and Lopahin with a book in his hand.

Lopahin: The train's in, thank God. What time is it?
Dunyasha: Nearly two o'clock. *(Puts out the candle.)* It's daylight already.
Lopahin: The train's late! Two hours, at least. *(Yawns and stretches.)* I'm a pretty one; what a fool I've been. Came here on purpose to meet them at the station and dropped alseep. . . . Dozed off as I sat in the chair. It's annoying. . . . You might have waked me.
Dunyasha: I thought you had gone. *(Listens.)* There, I do believe they're coming!
Lopahin (listens): No, what with the luggage and one thing and another. *(A pause.)* Lyubov Andreyevna has been abroad five years; I don't know what she is like now. . . . She's a splendid woman. A good-natured, kind-hearted woman. I remember when I was a lad of fifteen, my poor father — he used to keep a little shop here in the village in those days — gave me a punch in the face with his fist and made my nose bleed. We were in the yard here, I forget what we'd come about — he had had a drop. Lyubov Andreyevna — I can see her now — she was a slim young girl then — took me to wash my face, and then brought me into this very room, into the nursery. "Don't cry, little peasant," says she, "it will be well in time for your wedding day." . . . *(A*

pause.) Little peasant. . . . My father was a peasant, it's true, but here am I in a white waistcoat and brown shoes, like a pig in a bun shop. Yes, I'm a rich man, but for all my money, come to think, a peasant I was, and a peasant I am. *(Turns over the pages of the book.)* I've been reading this book and I can't make head or tail of it. I fell asleep over it. *(A pause.)*

Dunyasha: The dogs have been awake all night, they feel that the mistress is coming.

Lopahin: Why, what's the matter with you, Dunyasha?

Dunyasha: My hands are all of a tremble. I feel as though I should faint.

Lopahin: You're a spoilt soft creature, Dunyasha. And dressed like a lady too, and your hair done up. That's not the thing. One must know one's place.

Enter Epihodov with a nosegay; he wears a pea jacket and highly polished creaking top boots; he drops the nosegay as he comes in.

Epihodov (picking up the nosegay): Here! the gardener's sent this, says you're to put it in the dining room. *(Gives Dunyasha the nosegay.)*

Lopahin: And bring me some kvass.

Dunyasha: I will. *(Goes out.)*

Epihodov: It's chilly this morning, three degrees of frost, though the cherries are all in flower. I can't say much for our climate. *(Sighs.)* I can't. Our climate is not often propitious to the occasion. Yermolay Alexeyevitch, permit me to call your attention to the fact that I purchased myself a pair of boots the day before yesterday, and they creak, I venture to assure you, so that there's no tolerating them. What ought I to grease them with?

Lopahin: Oh, shut up! Don't bother me.

Epihodov: Every day some misfortune befalls me. I don't complain, I'm used to it, and I wear a smiling face.

Dunyasha comes in, hands Lopahin the kvass.

Epihodov: I am going. *(Stumbles against a chair, which falls over.)* There! *(As though triumphant.)* There you see now, excuse the expression, an accident like that among others. . . . It's positively remarkable. *(Goes out.)*

Dunyasha: Do you know, Yermolay Alexeyevitch, I must confess, Epihodov has made me a proposal.

Lopahin: Ah!

Dunyasha: I'm sure I don't know. . . . He's a harmless fellow, but sometimes when he begins talking, there's no making anything of it. It's all very fine and expressive, only there's no understanding it. I've a sort of liking for him too. He loves me to distraction. He's an unfortunate man; every day there's something. They tease him about it — two and twenty misfortunes they call him.

Lopahin (listening): There! I do believe they're coming.

Dunyasha: They are coming! What's the matter with me? . . . I'm cold all over.

Lopahin: They really are coming. Let's go and meet them. Will she know me? It's five years since I saw her.

Dunyasha (in a flutter): I shall drop this very minute. . . . Ah, I shall drop.

There is a sound of two carriages driving up to the house. Lopahin and Dunyasha go out quickly. The stage is left empty. A noise is heard in the adjoining rooms. Firs, who has driven to meet Madame Ranevsky, crosses the stage hurriedly leaning on a stick. He is wearing old-fashioned livery and a high hat. He says something to himself, but not a word can be distinguished. The noise behind the scenes goes on increasing. A voice: "Come, let's go in here." Enter Lyubov Andreyevna, Anya, and Charlotta Ivanovna with a pet dog on a chain, all in traveling dresses. Varya in an outdoor coat with a kerchief over her head, Gaev, Semyonov-Pishtchik, Lopahin, Dunyasha with bag and parasol, servants with other articles. All walk across the room.

Anya: Let's come in here. Do you remember what room this is, mamma?

Lyubov (joyfully, through her tears): The nursery!

Varya: How cold it is, my hands are numb. *(To Lyubov Andreyevna.)* Your rooms, the white room and the lavender one, are just the same as ever, mamma.

Lyubov: My nursery, dear delightful room. . . . I used to sleep here when I was little. . . . *(Cries.)* And here I am, like a little child. . . . *(Kisses her brother and Varya, and then her brother again.)* Varya's just the same as ever, like a nun. And I knew Dunyasha. *(Kisses Dunyasha.)*

Gaev: The train was two hours late. What do you think of that? Is that the way to do things?

Charlotta (to Pishtchik): My dog eats nuts, too.

Pishtchik (wonderingly): Fancy that!

They all go out except Anya and Dunyasha.

Dunyasha: We've been expecting you so long. *(Takes Anya's hat and coat.)*

Anya: I haven't slept for four nights on the journey. I feel dreadfully cold.

Dunyasha: You set out in Lent, there was snow and frost, and now? My darling! *(Laughs and kisses her.) I have* missed you, my precious, my joy. I must tell you . . . I can't put it off a minute. . . .

Anya (wearily): What now?

Dunyasha: Epihodov, the clerk, made me a proposal just after Easter.

Anya: It's always the same thing with you. . . . *(Straightening her hair.)* I've lost all my hairpins. *(She is staggering from exhaustion.)*

Dunyasha: I don't know what to think, really. He does love me, he does love me so!

Anya (looking toward her door, tenderly): My own room, my windows just as though I had never gone away. I'm home! Tomorrow morning I shall get up and run into the garden. . . . Oh, if I could get to sleep! I haven't slept all the journey. I was so anxious and worried.

Dunyasha: Pyotr Sergeyevitch came the day before yesterday.

Anya (joyfully): Petya!

Dunyasha: He's asleep in the bath house, he has settled in there. I'm afraid of being in their way, says he. *(Glancing at her watch.)* I was to have waked him, but Varvara Mihalovna told me not to. Don't you wake him, says she.

Enter Varya with a bunch of keys at her waist.

Varya: Dunyasha, coffee and make haste. . . . Mamma's asking for coffee.

Dunyasha: This very minute. *(Goes out.)*

Varya: Well, thank God, you've come. You're home again. *(Petting her.)* My little darling has come back! My precious beauty has come back again!

Anya: I have had a time of it!

Varya: I can fancy.

Anya: We set off in Holy Week — it was so cold then, and all the way Charlotta would talk and show off her tricks. What did you want to burden me with Charlotta for?

Varya: You couldn't have traveled all alone, darling. At seventeen.

Anya: We got to Paris at last, it was cold there — snow. I speak French shockingly. Mamma lives on the fifth floor, I went up to her and there were a lot of French people, ladies, an old priest with a book. The place smelt of tobacco and so comfortless. I felt sorry, oh! so sorry for mamma all at once. I put my arms round her neck, and hugged her and wouldn't let her go. Mamma was as kind as she could be, and she cried. . . .

Varya (through her tears): Don't speak of it, don't speak of it!

Anya: She had sold her villa at Mentone, she had nothing left, nothing. I hadn't a farthing left either, we only just had enough to get here. And mamma doesn't understand! When we had dinner at the stations, she always ordered the most expensive things and gave the waiters a whole ruble. Charlotta's just the same. Yasha too must have the same as we do; it's simply awful. You know Yasha is mamma's valet now, we brought him here with us.

Varya: Yes, I've seen the young rascal.

Anya: Well, tell me — have you paid the arrears on the mortgage?

Varya: How could we get the money?

Anya: Oh, dear! Oh, dear!

Varya: In August the place will be sold.

Anya: My goodness!

Lopahin (peeps in at the door and moos like a cow): Moo! *(Disappears.)*

Varya (weeping): There, that's what I could do to him. *(Shakes her fist.)*

Anya (embracing Varya, softly): Varya, has he made you an offer? *(Varya shakes her head.)* Why, but he loves you. Why is it you don't come to an understanding? What are you waiting for?

Varya: I believe that there never will be anything between us. He has a lot to do, he has not time for me . . . and takes no notice of me. Bless the man, it makes me miserable to see him. . . . Everyone's talking of our being married, everyone's congratulating me, and all the while there's really nothing in it; it's all like a dream. *(In another tone.)* You have a new brooch like a bee.

Anya (mournfully): Mamma bought it. *(Goes into her own room and in a lighthearted childish tone.)* And you know, in Paris I went up in a balloon!

Varya: My darling's home again! My pretty is home again!

Dunyasha returns with the coffee pot and is making the coffee.

Varya (standing at the door): All day long, darling, as I go about looking after the house, I keep dreaming all the time. If only we could marry you to a rich man, then I should feel more at rest. Then I would go off by myself on a pilgrimage to Kiev, to Moscow . . . and so I would spend my life going from one holy place to another. . . . I would go on and on. . . . What bliss!

Anya: The birds are singing in the garden. What time is it?

Varya: It must be nearly three. It's time you were asleep, darling. *(Going into Anya's room.)* What bliss!

Yasha enters with a rug and a traveling bag.

Yasha (crosses the stage, mincingly): May one come in here, pray?

Dunyasha: I shouldn't have known you, Yasha. How you have changed abroad.

Yasha: H'm! . . . And who are you?

Dunyasha: When you went away, I was that high. *(Shows distance from floor.)* Dunyasha, Fyodor's daughter. . . . You don't remember me!

Yasha: H'm! . . . You're a peach! *(Looks round and embraces her: she shrieks and drops a saucer. Yasha goes out hastily.)*

Varya (in the doorway, in a tone of vexation): What now?

Dunyasha (through her tears): I have broken a saucer.

Varya: Well, that brings good luck.

Anya (coming out of her room): We ought to prepare mamma: Petya is here.

Varya: I told them not to wake him.

Anya (dreamily): It's six years since father died. Then only a month later little brother Grisha was drowned in the river, such a pretty boy he was, only seven. It was more than mamma could bear, so she went away, went away without looking back. *(Shuddering.)* . . . How well I understand her, if only she knew! *(A pause.)* And Petya Trofimov was Grisha's tutor, he may remind her.

Enter Firs: he is wearing a pea jacket and a white waistcoat.

Firs (goes up to the coffee pot, anxiously): The mistress will be served here. *(Puts on white gloves.)* Is the coffee ready? *(Sternly to Dunyasha.)* Girl! Where's the cream?

Dunyasha: Ah, mercy on us! *(Goes out quickly.)*

Firs (fussing round the coffee pot): Ech! you good-for-nothing! *(Muttering to himself.)* Come back from Paris. And the old master used to go to Paris too . . . horses all the way. *(Laughs.)*

Varya: What is it, Firs?

Firs: What is your pleasure? *(Gleefully.)* My lady has come home! I have lived to see her again! Now I can die. *(Weeps with joy.)*

Enter Lyubov Andreyevna, Gaev, and Semyonov-Pishtchik; the latter is in a short-waisted full coat of fine cloth, and full trousers. Gaev, as he comes in, makes a gesture with his arms and his whole body, as though he were playing billiards.

Lyubov: How does it go? Let me remember. Cannon off the red!

Gaev: That's it — in off the white! Why, once, sister, we used to sleep together in this very room, and now I'm fifty-one, strange as it seems.

Lopahin: Yes, time flies.

Gaev: What do you say?

Lopahin: Time, I say, flies.

Gaev: What a smell of patchouli!

Anya: I'm going to bed. Good night, mamma. *(Kisses her mother.)*

Lyubov: My precious darling. *(Kisses her hands.)* Are you glad to be home? I can't believe it.

Anya: Good night, uncle.

Gaev (kissing her face and hands): God bless you! How like you are to your mother! *(To his sister.)* At her age you were just the same, Lyuba.

Anya shakes hands with Lopahin and Pishtchik, then goes out, shutting the door after her.

Lyubov: She's quite worn out.

Pishtchik: Aye, it's a long journey, to be sure.

Varya (to Lopahin and Pishtchik): Well, gentlemen? It's three o'clock and time to say good-bye.

Lyubov (laughs): You're just the same as ever, Varya. *(Draws her to her and kisses her.)* I'll just drink my coffee and then we will all go and rest. *(Firs puts a cushion under her feet.)* Thanks, friend. I am so fond of coffee, I drink it day and night. Thanks, dear old man. *(Kisses Firs.)*

Varya: I'll just see whether all the things have been brought in. *(Goes out.)*

Lyubov: Can it really be me sitting here? *(Laughs.)* I want to dance about and clap my hands. *(Covers her face with her hands.)* And I could drop asleep in a moment! God knows I love my country, I love it tenderly; I couldn't look out of the window in the train, I kept crying so. *(Through her tears.)* But I must drink my coffee, though. Thank you, Firs, thanks, dear old man. I'm so glad to find you still alive.

Firs: The day before yesterday.

Gaev: He's rather deaf.

Lopahin: I have to set off for Harkov directly, at five o'clock. . . . It is annoying! I wanted to have a look at you, and a little talk. . . . You are just as splendid as ever.

Pishtchik (breathing heavily): Handsomer, indeed. . . . Dressed in Parisian style . . . completely bowled me over.

Lopahin: Your brother, Leonid Andreyevitch here, is always saying that I'm a low-born knave, that I'm a money grubber, but I don't care one straw for that. Let him talk. Only I do want you to believe in me as you used to. I do want your wonderful tender eyes to look at me as they used to in the old days. Merciful God! My father was a serf of your father and of your grandfather, but you — you — did so much for me once, that I've forgotten all that; I love you as though you were my kin . . . more than my kin.

Lyubov: I can't sit still, I simply can't. . . . *(Jumps up and walks about in violent agitation.)* This happiness is too much for me. . . . You may laugh at me, I know I'm silly. . . . My own bookcase. *(Kisses the bookcase.)* My little table.

Gaev: Nurse died while you were away.

Lyubov (sits down and drinks coffee): Yes, the Kingdom of Heaven be hers! You wrote me of her death.

Gaev: And Anastasy is dead. Squinting Petruchka has left me and is in service now with the police captain in the town. *(Takes a box of caramels out of his pocket and sucks one.)*

Pishtchik: My daughter, Dashenka, wishes to be remembered to you.

Lopahin: I want to tell you something very pleasant and cheering. *(Glancing at his watch.)* I'm going directly . . . there's no time to say much . . . well, I can say it in a couple of words. I needn't tell you your cherry orchard is to be sold to pay your debts; the twenty-second of August is the date fixed for the sale; but don't you worry, dearest lady, you may sleep in peace, there is a way of saving it. . . . This is what I propose. I beg your attention! Your estate is not twenty miles from the town, the railway runs close by it, and if the cherry orchard and the land along the river bank were cut up into building plots and then let on lease for summer villas, you would make an income of at least twenty-five thousand rubles a year out of it.

Gaev: That's all rot, if you'll excuse me.

Lyubov: I don't quite understand you, Yermolay Alexeyevitch.

Lopahin: You will get a rent of at least twenty-five rubles a year for a three-acre plot from summer visitors, and if you say the word now, I'll bet you what you like there won't be one square foot of ground vacant by the autumn, all the plots will be taken up. I congratulate you; in fact, you are saved. It's a perfect situation with that deep river. Only, of course, it must be cleared — all the old buildings, for example, must be removed, this house too, which is really good for nothing and the old cherry orchard must be cut down.

Lyubov: Cut down? My dear fellow, forgive me, but you don't know what you are talking about. If there is one thing interesting — remarkable indeed — in the whole province, it's just our cherry orchard.

Lopahin: The only thing remarkable about the orchard is that it's a very large one. There's a crop of cherries every alternate year, and then there's nothing to be done with them, no one buys them.

Gaev: This orchard is mentioned in the *Encyclopedia.*

Lopahin (glancing at his watch): If we don't decide on something and don't take some steps, on the twenty-second of August the cherry orchard and the whole estate too will be sold by auction. Make up your minds! There is no other way of saving it, I'll take my oath on that. No, No!

Firs: In old days, forty or fifty years ago, they used to dry the cherries, soak them, pickle them, make jam too, and they used —

Gaev: Be quiet, Firs.

Firs: And they used to send the preserved cherries to Moscow and to Harkov by the wagon load. That brought the money in! And the preserved cherries in those days were soft and juicy, sweet and fragrant. . . . They knew the way to do them then. . . .

Lyubov: And where is the recipe now?

Firs: It's forgotten. Nobody remembers it.

Pishtchik (to Lyubov Andreyevna): What's it like in Paris? Did you eat frogs there?

Lyubov: Oh, I ate crocodiles.

Pishtchik: Fancy that now!

Lopahin: There used to be only the gentlefolks and the peasants in the country, but now there are these summer visitors. All the towns, even the small ones, are surrounded nowadays by these summer villas. And one may say for sure that in another twenty years there'll be many more of these people and that they'll be everywhere. At present the summer visitor only drinks tea in his veranda, but maybe he'll take to working his bit of land too, and then your cherry orchard would become happy, rich, and prosperous. . . .

Gaev (indignant): What rot!

Enter Varya and Yasha.

Varya: There are two telegrams for you, mamma. *(Takes out keys and opens an old-fashioned bookcase with a loud crack.)* Here they are.

Lyubov: From Paris. *(Tears the telegrams, without reading them.)* I have done with Paris.

Gaev: Do you know, Lyuba, how old that bookcase is? Last week I pulled out the bottom drawer and there I found the date branded on it. The bookcase was made just a hundred years ago. What do you say to that? We might have celebrated its jubilee. Though it's an inanimate object, still it is a *book case.*

Pishtchik (amazed): A hundred years! Fancy that now.

Gaev: Yes. . . . It is a thing. . . . *(Feeling the bookcase.)* Dear, honored, bookcase! Hail to thee who for more than a hundred years hast served the pure ideals of good and justice; thy silent call to fruitful labor has never flagged in those hundred years, maintaining *(In tears.)* in the generations of man, courage and faith in a brighter future and fostering in us ideals of good and social consciousness. *(A pause.)*

Lopahin: Yes. . . .

Lyubov: You are just the same as ever, Leonid.

Gaev (a little embarrassed): Cannon off the right into the pocket!

Lopahin (looking at his watch): Well, it's time I was off.

Yasha (handing Lyubov Andreyevna medicine): Perhaps you will take your pills now.

Pishtchik: You shouldn't take medicines, my dear madam . . . they do no harm and no good. Give them here . . . honored lady. *(Takes the pillbox, pours the pills into the hollow of his hand, blows on them, puts them in his mouth, and drinks off some kvass.)* There!

Lyubov (in alarm): Why, you must be out of your mind!

Pishtchik: I have taken all the pills.

Lopahin: What a glutton! *(All laugh.)*

Firs: His honor stayed with us in Easter week, ate a gallon and a half of cucumbers. . . . *(Mutters.)*

Lyubov: What is he saying?

Varya: He has taken to muttering like that for the last three years. We are used to it.

Yasha: His declining years!

Charlotta Ivanovna, a very thin, lanky figure in a white dress with a lorgnette in her belt, walks across the stage.

Lopahin: I beg your pardon, Charlotta Ivanovna, I have not had time to greet you. *(Tries to kiss her hand.)*

Charlotta (pulling away her hand): If I let you kiss my hand, you'll be wanting to kiss my elbow, and then my shoulder.

Lopahin: I've no luck today! *(All laugh.)* Charlotta Ivanovna, show us some tricks!

Lyubov: Charlotta, do show us some tricks!

Charlotta: I don't want to. I'm sleepy. *(Goes out.)*

Lopahin: In three weeks' time we shall meet again. *(Kisses Lyubov Andreyevna's hand.)* Good-bye till then — I must go. *(To Gaev.)* Good-bye. *(Kisses Pishtchik.)* Good-bye. *(Gives his hand to Varya, then to Firs and Yasha.)* I don't want to go. *(To Lyubov Andreyevna.)* If you think over my plan for the villas and make up your mind, then let me know; I will lend you fifty thousand rubles. Think of it seriously.

Varya (angrily): Well, do go, for goodness sake.

Lopahin: I'm going, I'm going. *(Goes out.)*

Gaev: Low-born knave! I beg pardon, though . . . Varya is going to marry him, he's Varya's fiancé.

Varya: Don't talk nonsense, uncle.

Lyubov: Well, Varya, I shall be delighted. He's a good man.

Pishtchik: He is, one must acknowledge, a most worthy man. And my Dashenka . . . says too that . . . she says . . . various things. *(Snores, but at once wakes up.)* But all the same, honored lady, could you oblige me . . . with a loan of two hundred forty rubles . . . to pay the interest on my mortgage tomorrow?

Varya (dismayed): No, no.

Lyubov: I really haven't any money.

Pishtchik: It will turn up. *(Laughs.)* I never lose hope. I thought everything was over, I was a ruined man, and lo and behold—the railway passed through my land and . . . they paid me for it. And something else will turn up again, if not today, then tomorrow . . . Dashenka'll win two hundred thousand . . . she's got a lottery ticket.

Lyubov: Well, we've finished our coffee, we can go to bed.

Firs (brushes Gaev, reprovingly): You have got on the wrong trousers again! What am I to do with you?

Varya (softly): Anya's asleep. *(Softly opens the window.)* Now the sun's risen, it's not a bit cold. Look, mamma, what exquisite trees! My goodness! And the air! The starlings are singing!

Gaev (opens another window): The orchard is all white. You've not forgotten it, Lyuba? That long avenue that runs straight, straight as an arrow, how it shines on a moonlight night. You remember? You've not forgotten?

Lyubov (looking out of the window into the garden): Oh, my childhood, my innocence! It was in this nursery I used to sleep, from here I looked out into the orchard, happiness waked with me every morning and in those days the orchard was just the same, nothing has changed. *(Laughs with delight.)* All, all white! Oh, my orchard! After the dark gloomy autumn, and the cold winter; you are young again, and full of happiness, the heavenly angels have never left you. . . . If I could cast off the burden that weighs on my heart, if I could forget the past!

Gaev: Hm! and the orchard will be sold to pay our debts; it seems strange. . . .

Lyubov: See, our mother walking . . . all in white, down the avenue! *(Laughs with delight.)* It is she!

Gaev: Where?

Varya: Oh, don't, mamma!

Lyubov: There is no one. It was my fancy. On the right there, by the path to the arbor, there is a white tree bending like a woman. . . .

Enter Trofimov wearing a shabby student's uniform and spectacles.

Lyubov: What a ravishing orchard! White masses of blossom, blue sky. . . .

Trofimov: Lyubov Andreyevna! *(She looks round at him.)* I will just pay my respects to you and then leave you at once. *(Kisses her hand warmly.)* I was told to wait until morning, but I hadn't the patience to wait any longer. . . .

Lyubov Andreyevna looks at him in perplexity.

Varya (through her tears): This is Petya Trofimov.

Trofimov: Petya Trofimov, who was your Grisha's tutor. . . . Can I have changed so much?

Lyubov Andreyevna embraces him and weeps quietly.

Gaev (in confusion): There, there, Lyuba.

Varya (crying): I told you, Petya, to wait till tomorrow.

Lyubov: My Grisha . . . my boy . . . Grisha . . . my son!

Varya: We can't help it, mamma, it is God's will.

Trofimov (softly through his tears): There . . . there.

Lyubov (weeping quietly): My boy was lost . . . drowned. Why? Oh, why, dear Petya? *(More quietly.)* Anya is asleep in there, and I'm talking loudly . . . making this noise. . . . But, Petya? Why have you grown so ugly? Why do you look so old?

Trofimov: A peasant woman in the train called me a mangy-looking gentleman.

Lyubov: You were quite a boy then, a pretty little student, and now your hair's thin — and spectacles. Are you really a student still? *(Goes toward the door.)*

Trofimov: I seem likely to be a perpetual student.

Lyubov (kisses her brother, then Varya): Well, go to bed. . . . You are older too, Leonid.

Pishtchik (follows her): I suppose it's time we were asleep. . . . Ugh! my gout. I'm staying the night! Lyubov Andreyevna, my dear soul, if you could . . . tomorrow morning . . . two hundred forty rubles.

Gaev: That's always his story.

Pishtchik: Two hundred forty rubles . . . to pay the interest on my mortgage.

Lyubov: My dear man, I have no money.

Pishtchik: I'll pay it back, my dear . . . a trifling sum.

Lyubov: Oh, well, Leonid will give it you. . . . You give him the money, Leonid.

Gaev: Me give it him! Let him wait till he gets it!

Lyubov: It can't be helped, give it him. He needs it. He'll pay it back.

Lyubov Andreyevna, Trofimov, Pishtchik, and Firs go out. Gaev, Varya, and Yasha remain.

Gaev: Sister hasn't got out of the habit of flinging away her money. *(To Yasha.)* Get away, my good fellow, you smell of the henhouse.

Yasha (with a grin): And you, Leonid Andreyevitch, are just the same as ever.

Gaev: What's that? *(To Varya.)* What did he say?

Varya (to Yasha): Your mother has come from the village; she has been sitting in the servants' room since yesterday, waiting to see you.

Yasha: Oh, bother her!

Varya: For shame!

Yasha: What's the hurry? She might just as well have come tomorrow. *(Goes out.)*

Varya: Mamma's just the same as ever, she hasn't changed a bit. If she had her own way, she'd give away everything.

Gaev: Yes. *(A pause.)* If a great many remedies are suggested for some disease, it means that the disease is incurable. I keep thinking and racking my brains; I have many schemes, a great many, and that really means none. If we could only come in for a legacy from somebody, or marry our Anya to a very rich man, or we might go to Yaroslavl and try our luck with our old aunt, the Countess. She's very, very rich, you know.

Varya (weeps): If God would help us.

Gaev: Don't blubber. Aunt's very rich, but she doesn't like us. First, sister married a lawyer instead of a nobleman. . . .

Anya appears in the doorway.

Gaev: And then her conduct, one can't call it virtuous. She is good, and kind, and nice, and I love her, but, however one allows for extenuating circumstances, there's no denying that she's an immoral woman. One feels it in her slightest gesture.

Varya (in a whisper): Anya's in the doorway.

Gaev: What do you say? *(A pause.)* It's queer, there seems to be something wrong with my right eye. I don't see as well as I did. And on Thursday when I was in the district court . . .

Enter Anya.

Varya: Why aren't you asleep, Anya?

Anya: I can't get to sleep.

Gaev: My pet. *(Kisses Anya's face and hands.)* My child. *(Weeps.)* You are not my niece, you are my angel, you are everything to me. Believe me, believe. . . .

Anya: I believe you, uncle. Everyone loves you and respects you . . . but, uncle dear, you must be silent . . . simply be silent. What were you saying just now about my mother, about your own sister? What made you say that?

Gaev: Yes, yes. . . . *(Puts his hand over his face.)* Really, that was awful! My God, save me! And today I made a speech to the bookcase . . . so stupid! And only when I had finished, I saw how stupid it was.

Varya: It's true, uncle, you ought to keep quiet. Don't talk, that's all.

Anya: If you could keep from talking, it would make things easier for you, too.

Gaev: I won't speak. *(Kisses Anya's and Varya's hands.)* I'll be silent. Only this is about business. On Thursday I was in the district court; well, there was a large party of us there and we began talking of one thing and another, and this and that, and do you know, I believe that it will be possible to raise a loan on an I.O.U. to pay the arrears on the mortgage.

Varya: If the Lord would help us!

Gaev: I'm going on Tuesday; I'll talk of it again. *(To Varya.)* Don't blubber. *(To Anya.)* Your mamma will talk to Lopahin; of course, he won't refuse her. And as soon as you're rested you shall go to Yaroslavl to the Countess, your great-aunt. So we shall all set to work in three directions at once, and the business is done. We shall pay off arrears, I'm convinced of it. *(Puts a caramel in his mouth.)* I swear on my honor, I swear by anything you like, the estate shan't be sold. *(Excitedly.)* By my own happiness, I swear it! Here's my hand on it, call me the basest, vilest of men, if I let it come to an auction! Upon my soul I swear it!

Anya (her equanimity has returned, she is quite happy): How good you are, uncle, and how clever! *(Embraces her uncle.)* I'm at peace now! Quite at peace! I'm happy!

Enter Firs.

Firs (reproachfully): Leonid Andreyevitch, have you no fear of God? When are you going to bed?

Gaev: Directly, directly. You can go, Firs. I'll . . . yes, I will undress myself. Come, children, bye-bye. We'll go into details tomorrow, but now go to bed. *(Kisses Anya and Varya.)* I'm a man of the eighties. They run down that period, but still I can say I have had to suffer not a little for my convictions in my life, it's not for nothing that the peasant loves me. One must know the peasant! One must know how. . . .

Anya: At it again, uncle!

Varya: Uncle dear, you'd better be quiet!

Firs (angrily): Leonid Andreyevitch!

Gaev: I'm coming. I'm coming. Go to bed. Potted the shot — there's a shot for you! A beauty! *(Goes out, Firs hobbling after him.)*

Anya: My mind's at rest now. I don't want to go to Yaroslavl, I don't like my great-aunt, but still my mind's at rest. Thanks to uncle. *(Sits down.)*

Varya: We must go to bed. I'm going. Something unpleasant happened while you were away. In the old servants' quarters there are only the old servants, as you know — Efimyushka, Polya, and Yevstigney — and Karp too. They began letting stray people in to spend the night — I said nothing. But all at once I heard they had been spreading a report that I gave them nothing but pease° pudding to eat. Out of stinginess, you know. . . . And it was all Yevstigney's doing. . . . Very well, I said to myself. . . . If that's how it is, I thought, wait a bit. I sent for Yevstigney. . . . *(Yawns.)* He comes. . . . "How's this, Yevstigney," I said, "you could be such a fool as to? . . ." *(Looking at Anya.)* Anitchka! *(A pause.)* She's asleep. *(Puts her arm around Anya.)* Come to bed . . . come along! *(Leads her.)* My darling has fallen asleep! Come . . . *(They go.)*

Far away beyond the orchard a shepherd plays on a pipe. Trofimov crosses the stage and, seeing Varya and Anya, stands still.

Varya: Sh! asleep, asleep. Come, my own.

Anya (softly, half-asleep): I'm so tired. Still those bells. Uncle . . . dear . . . mamma and uncle. . . .

Varya: Come, my own, come along.

They go into Anya's room.

Trofimov (tenderly): My sunshine! My spring.

ACT II

The open country. An old shrine, long abandoned and fallen out of the perpendicular; near it a well, large stones that have apparently once been tombstones, and an old garden seat. The road to Gaev's house is seen. On one side rise dark poplars; and there the cherry orchard begins. In the distance a row of telegraph poles and far, far away on the horizon there is faintly outlined a great town,

pease: Pea.

only visible in very fine clear weather. It is near sunset. Charlotta, Yasha, and Dunyasha are sitting on the seat. Epihodov is standing near, playing something mournful on a guitar. All sit plunged in thought. Charlotta wears an old forage cap; she has taken a gun from her shoulder and is tightening the buckle on the strap.

Charlotta (musingly): I haven't a real passport of my own, and I don't know how old I am, and I always feel that I'm a young thing. When I was a little girl, my father and mother used to travel about to fairs and give performances — very good ones. And I used to dance *salto-mortale*° and all sorts of things. And when papa and mamma died, a German lady took me and had me educated. And so I grew up and became a governess. But where I came from, and who I am, I don't know. . . . Who my parents were, very likely they weren't married. . . . I don't know. *(Takes a cucumber out of her pocket and eats.)* I know nothing at all. *(A pause.)* One wants to talk and has no one to talk to . . . I have nobody.

Epihodov (plays on the guitar and sings): "What care I for the noisy world! What care I for friends or foes!" How agreeable it is to play on the mandolin!

Dunyasha: That's a guitar, not a mandolin. *(Looks in a hand mirror and powders herself.)*

Epihodov: To a man mad with love, it's a mandolin. *(Sings.)* "Were her heart but aglow with love's mutual flame."

Yasha joins in.

Charlotta: How shockingly these people sing! Foo! Like jackals!

Dunyasha (to Yasha): What happiness, though, to visit foreign lands.

Yasha: Ah, yes! I rather agree with you there. *(Yawns, then lights a cigar.)*

Epihodov: That's comprehensible. In foreign lands everything has long since reached full complexion.

Yasha: That's so, of course.

Epihodov: I'm a cultivated man, I read remarkable books of all sorts, but I can never make out the tendency I am myself precisely inclined for, whether to live or to shoot myself, speaking precisely, but nevertheless I always carry a revolver. Here it is. . . . *(Shows revolver.)*

Charlotta: I've had enough, and now I'm going. *(Puts on the gun.)* Epihodov, you're a very clever fellow, and a very terrible one too, all the women must be wild about you. Br-r-r! *(Goes.)* These clever fellows are all so stupid; there's not a creature for me to speak to. . . . Always alone, alone, nobody belonging to me . . . and who I am, and why I'm on earth, I don't know. *(Walks away slowly.)*

Epihodov: Speaking precisely, not touching upon other subjects, I'm bound to admit about myself, that destiny behaves mercilessly to me, as a storm to a little boat. If, let us suppose, I am mistaken, then why did I wake up this morning, to quote an example, and look round, and there on my chest was a spider of fearful magnitude . . . like this. *(Shows with both hands.)* And then I take up a jug of kvass, to quench my thirst, and in it there is something in the highest degree unseemly of the nature of a cockroach. *(A pause.)*

salto-mortale: A standing somersault.

Have you read Buckle?° *(A pause.)* I am desirous of troubling you, Dunyasha, with a couple of words.

Dunyasha: Well, speak.

Epihodov: I should be desirous to speak with you alone. *(Sighs.)*

Dunyasha (embarrassed): Well — only bring me my mantle first. It's by the cupboard. It's rather damp here.

Epihodov: Certainly. I will fetch it. Now I know what I must do with my revolver. *(Takes guitar and goes off playing on it.)*

Yasha: Two and twenty misfortunes! Between ourselves, he's a fool. *(Yawns.)*

Dunyasha: God grant he doesn't shoot himself! *(A pause.)* I am so nervous, I'm always in a flutter. I was a little girl when I was taken into our lady's house, and now I have quite grown out of peasant ways, and my hands are white, as white as a lady's. I'm such a delicate, sensitive creature. I'm afraid of everything. I'm so frightened. And if you deceive me, Yasha, I don't know what will become of my nerves.

Yasha (kisses her): You're a peach! Of course a girl must never forget herself; what I dislike more than anything is a girl being flighty in her behavior.

Dunyasha: I'm passionately in love with you, Yasha; you are a man of culture — you can give your opinion about anything. *(A pause.)*

Yasha (yawns): Yes, that's so. My opinion is this: if a girl loves anyone, that means that she has no principles. *(A pause.)* It's pleasant smoking a cigar in the open air. *(Listens.)* Someone's coming this way . . . it's the gentlefolk. *(Dunyasha embraces him impulsively.)* Go home, as though you had been to the river to bathe; go by that path, or else they'll meet you and suppose I have made an appointment with you here. That I can't endure.

Dunyasha (coughing softly): The cigar has made my head ache. . . . *(Goes off.)*

Yasha remains sitting near the shrine. Enter Lyubov Andreyevna, Gaev, and Lopahin.

Lopahin: You must make up your mind once and for all — there's no time to lose. It's quite a simple question, you know. Will you consent to letting the land for building or not? One word in answer: Yes or no? Only one word!

Lyubov: Who is smoking such horrible cigars here? *(Sits down.)*

Gaev: Now the railway line has been brought near, it's made things very convenient. *(Sits down.)* Here we have been over and lunched in town. Cannon off the white! I should like to go home and have a game.

Lyubov: You have plenty of time.

Lopahin: Only one word! *(Beseechingly.)* Give me an answer!

Gaev (yawning): What do you say?

Lyubov (looks in her purse): I had quite a lot of money here yesterday, and there's scarcely any left today. My poor Varya feeds us all on milk soup for the sake of economy; the old folks in the kitchen get nothing but pease pudding, while I waste my money in a senseless way. *(Drops purse, scattering gold pieces.)* There, they have all fallen out! *(Annoyed.)*

Yasha: Allow me, I'll soon pick them up. *(Collects the coins.)*

Lyubov: Pray do, Yasha. And what did I go off to the town to lunch for? Your restaurant's a wretched place with its music and the tablecloth smelling of

Buckle: Henry Thomas Buckle (1821–1862), a radical historian who formulated a scientific basis for history emphasizing the interrelationship of climate, food production, population, and wealth.

soap. . . . Why drink so much, Leonid? And eat so much? And talk so much? Today you talked a great deal again in the restaurant, and all so inappropriately. About the era of the seventies, about the decadents. And to whom? Talking to waiters about decadents!

Lopahin: Yes.

Gaev (waving his hand): I'm incorrigible; that's evident. *(Irritably to Yasha.)* Why is it you keep fidgeting about in front of us!

Yasha (laughs): I can't help laughing when I hear your voice.

Gaev (to his sister): Either I or he. . . .

Lyubov: Get along! Go away, Yasha.

Yasha (gives Lyubov Andreyevna her purse): Directly. *(Hardly able to suppress his laughter.)* This minute. . . . *(Goes off.)*

Lopahin: Deriganov, the millionaire, means to buy your estate. They say he is coming to the sale himself.

Lyubov: Where did you hear that?

Lopahin: That's what they say in town.

Gaev: Our aunt in Yaroslavl has promised to send help; but when, and how much she will send, we don't know.

Lopahin: How much will she send? A hundred thousand? Two hundred?

Lyubov: Oh, well! . . . Ten or fifteen thousand, and we must be thankful to get that.

Lopahin: Forgive me, but such reckless people as you are — such queer, unbusinesslike people — I never met in my life. One tells you in plain Russian your estate is going to be sold, and you seem not to understand it.

Lyubov: What are we to do? Tell us what to do.

Lopahin: I do tell you every day. Every day I say the same thing. You absolutley must let the cherry orchard and the land on building leases; and do it at once, as quick as may be — the auction's close upon us! Do understand! Once make up your mind to build villas, and you can raise as much money as you like, and then you are saved.

Lyubov: Villas and summer visitors — forgive me saying so — it's so vulgar.

Gaev: There I perfectly agree with you.

Lopahin: I shall sob, or scream, or fall into a fit. I can't stand it! You drive me mad! *(To Gaev.)* You're an old woman!

Gaev: What do you say?

Lopahin: An old woman! *(Gets up to go.)*

Lyubov (in dismay): No, don't go! Do stay, my dear friend! Perhaps we shall think of something.

Lopahin: What is there to think of?

Lyubov: Don't go, I entreat you! With you here it's more cheerful, anyway. *(A pause.)* I keep expecting something, as though the house were going to fall about our ears.

Gaev (in profound dejection): Potted the white! It fails — a kiss.

Lyubov: We have been great sinners. . . .

Lopahin: You have no sins to repent of.

Gaev (puts a caramel in his mouth): They say I've eaten up my property in caramels. *(Laughs.)*

Lyubov: Oh, my sins! I've always thrown my money away recklessly like a lunatic. I married a man who made nothing but debts. My husband died of champagne — he drank dreadfully. To my misery I loved another man, and immediately — it was my first punishment — the blow fell upon me, here, in the river . . . my boy drowned and I went abroad — went away forever, never to return, not to see that river again . . . I shut my eyes, and fled, distracted, and *he* after me . . . pitilessly, brutally. I bought a villa at Mentone, for *he* fell ill there, and for three years I had no rest day or night. His illness wore me out, my soul was dried up. And last year, when my villa was sold to pay my debts, I went to Paris and there he robbed me of everything and abandoned me for another woman; and I tried to poison myself. . . . So stupid, so shameful! . . . And suddenly I felt a yearning for Russia, for my country, for my little girl. . . . *(Dries her tears.)* Lord, Lord, be merciful! Forgive my sins! Do not chastise me more! *(Takes a telegram out of her pocket.)* I got this today from Paris. He implores forgiveness, entreats me to return. *(Tears up the telegram.)* I fancy there is music somewhere. *(Listens.)*

Gaev: That's our famous Jewish orchestra. You remember, four violins, a flute, and a double bass.

Lyubov: That still in existence? We ought to send for them one evening and give a dance.

Lopahin (listens): I can't hear. . . . *(Hums softly.)* "For money the Germans will turn a Russian into a Frenchman." *(Laughs.)* I did see such a piece at the theater yesterday! It was funny!

Lyubov: And most likely there was nothing funny in it. You shouldn't look at plays, you should look at yourselves a little oftener. How gray your lives are! How much nonsense you talk.

Lopahin: That's true. One may say honestly, we live a fool's life. *(Pause.)* My father was a peasant, an idiot; he knew nothing and taught me nothing, only beat me when he was drunk, and always with his stick. In reality I am just such another blockhead and idiot. I've learnt nothing properly. I write a wretched hand. I write so that I feel ashamed before folks, like a pig.

Lyubov: You ought to get married, my dear fellow.

Lopahin: Yes . . . that's true.

Lyubov: You should marry our Varya, she's a good girl.

Lopahin: Yes.

Lyubov: She's a good-natured girl, she's busy all day long, and what's more, she loves you. And you have liked her for ever so long.

Lopahin: Well? I'm not against it. . . . She's a good girl. *(Pause.)*

Gaev: I've been offered a place in the bank: six thousand rubles a year. Did you know?

Lyubov: You would never do for that! You must stay as you are.

Enter Firs with overcoat.

Firs: Put it on, sir, it's damp.

Gaev (putting it on): You bother me, old fellow.

Firs: You can't go on like this. You went away in the morning without leaving word. *(Looks him over.)*

Lyubov: You look older, Firs!

Firs: What is your pleasure?

Lopahin: You look older, she said.

Firs: I've had a long life. They were arranging my wedding before your papa was born. . . . *(Laughs.)* I was the head footman before the emancipation came.° I wouldn't consent to be set free then; I stayed on with the old master. . . . *(A pause.)* I remember what rejoicings they made and didn't know themselves what they were rejoicing over.

Lopahin: Those were fine old times. There was flogging anyway.

Firs (not hearing): To be sure! The peasants knew their place, and the masters knew theirs; but now they're all at sixes and sevens,° there's no making it out.

Gaev: Hold your tongue, Firs. I must go to town tomorrow. I have been promised an introduction to a general, who might let us have a loan.

Lopahin: You won't bring that off. And you won't pay your arrears, you may rest assured of that.

Lyubov: That's all his nonsense. There is no such general.

Enter Trofimov, Anya, and Varya.

Gaev: Here come our girls.

Anya: That's mamma on the seat.

Lyubov (tenderly): Come here, come along. My darlings! *(Embraces Anya and Varya.)* If you only knew how I love you both. Sit beside me, there, like that. *(All sit down.)*

Lopahin: Our perpetual student is always with the young ladies.

Trofimov: That's not your business.

Lopahin: He'll soon be fifty, and he's still a student.

Trofimov: Drop your idiotic jokes.

Lopahin: Why are you so cross, you queer fish?

Trofimov: Oh, don't persist!

Lopahin (laughs): Allow me to ask you what's your idea of me?

Trofimov: I'll tell you my idea of you, Yermolay Alexeyevitch: you are a rich man, you'll soon be a millionaire. Well, just as in the economy of nature a wild beast is of use, who devours everything that comes in his way, so you too have your use.

All laugh.

Varya: Better tell us something about the planets, Petya.

Lyubov: No, let us go on with the conversation we had yesterday.

Trofimov: What was it about?

Gaev: About pride.

Trofimov: We had a long conversation yesterday, but we came to no conclusion. In pride, in your sense of it, there is something mystical. Perhaps you are right from your point of view; but if one looks at it simply, without subtlety, what sort of pride can there be, what sense is there in it, if man in his physiological formation is very imperfect, if in the immense majority of cases he is coarse, dull-witted, profoundly unhappy? One must give up glorification of self. One should work, and nothing else.

Gaev: One must die in any case.

Trofimov: Who knows? And what does it mean — dying? Perhaps man has a hundred senses, and only the five we know are lost at death, while the other ninety-five remain alive.

before emancipation came: Serfs were freed in 1861.
at sixes and sevens: In disorder.

Lyubov: How clever you are, Petya!
Lopahin (ironically): Fearfully clever!
Trofimov: Humanity progresses, perfecting its powers. Everything that is beyond its ken now will one day become familiar and comprehensible; only we must work, we must with all our powers aid the seeker after truth. Here among us in Russia the workers are few in number as yet. The vast majority of the intellectual people I know seek nothing, do nothing, are not fit as yet for work of any kind. They call themselves intellectual, but they treat their servants as inferiors, behave to the peasants as though they were animals, learn little, read nothing seriously, do practically nothing, only talk about science, and know very little about art. They are all serious people, they all have severe faces, they all talk of weighty matters and air their theories, and yet the vast majority of us — ninety-nine percent — live like savages, at the least thing fly to blows and abuse, eat piggishly, sleep in filth and stuffiness, bugs everywhere, stench and damp and moral impurity. And it's clear all our fine talk is only to divert our attention and other people's. Show me where to find the *crèches*° there's so much talk about, and the reading rooms? They only exist in novels: in real life there are none of them. There is nothing but filth and vulgarity and Asiatic apathy. I fear and dislike very serious faces. I'm afraid of serious conversation. We should do better to be silent.
Lopahin: You know, I get up at five o'clock in the morning, and I work from morning to night; and I've money, my own and other people's, always passing through my hands, and I see what people are made of all round me. One has only to begin to do anything to see how few honest decent people there are. Sometimes when I lie awake at night, I think: "Oh! Lord, thou hast given us immense forests, boundless plains, the widest horizons, and living here we ourselves ought really to be giants."
Lyubov: You ask for giants! They are no good except in storybooks; in real life they frighten us.

Epihodov advances in the background, playing on the guitar.

Lyubov (dreamily): There goes Epihodov.
Anya (dreamily): There goes Epihodov.
Gaev: The sun has set, my friends.
Trofimov: Yes.
Gaev (not loudly but, as it were, declaiming): O nature, divine nature, thou art bright with eternal luster, beautiful and indifferent! Thou, whom we call mother, thou dost unite within thee life and death! Thou dost give life and dost destroy!
Varya (in a tone of supplication): Uncle!
Anya: Uncle, you are at it again!
Trofimov: You'd much better be cannoning off the red!
Gaev: I'll hold my tongue, I will.

All sit plunged in thought. Perfect stillness. The only thing audible is the muttering of Firs. Suddenly there is a sound in the distance, as it were from the sky — the sound of a breaking harp string, mournfully dying away.

crèches: Day nurseries, day-care centers.

Lyubov: What is that?

Lopahin: I don't know. Somewhere far away a bucket fallen and broken in the pits. But somewhere very far away.

Gaev: It might be a bird of some sort — such as a heron.

Trofimov: Or an owl.

Lyubov (shudders): I don't know why, but it's horrid. *(A pause.)*

Firs: It was the same before the calamity — the owl hooted and the samovar hissed all the time.

Gaev: Before what calamity?

Firs: Before the emancipation. *(A pause.)*

Lyubov: Come, my friends, let us be going; evening is falling. *(To Anya.)* There are tears in your eyes. What is it, darling? *(Embraces her.)*

Anya: Nothing, mamma; it's nothing.

Trofimov: There is somebody coming.

The Wayfarer appears in a shabby white forage cap and an overcoat; he is slightly drunk.

Wayfarer: Allow me to inquire, can I get to the station this way?

Gaev: Yes. Go along that road.

Wayfarer: I thank you most feelingly. *(Coughing.)* The weather is superb. *(Declaims.)* My brother, my suffering brother! . . . Come out to the Volga! Whose groan do you hear? . . . *(To Varya.)* Mademoiselle, vouchsafe a hungry Russian thirty kopeks.

Varya utters a shriek of alarm.

Lopahin (angrily): There's a right and a wrong way of doing everything!

Lyubov (hurriedly): Here, take this. *(Looks in her purse.)* I've no silver. No matter — here's gold for you.

Wayfarer: I thank you most feelingly! *(Goes off.)*

Laughter.

Varya (frightened): I'm going home — I'm going. . . . Oh, mamma, the servants have nothing to eat, and you gave him gold!

Lyubov: There's no doing anything with me. I'm so silly! When we get home, I'll give you all I possess. Yermolay Alexeyevitch, you will lend me some more! . . .

Lopahin: I will.

Lyubov: Come, friends, it's time to be going. And Varya, we have made a match of it for you. I congratulate you.

Varya (through her tears): Mamma, that's not a joking matter.

Lopahin: "Ophelia, get thee to a nunnery!"°

Gaev: My hands are trembling; it's a long while since I had a game of billiards.

Lopahin: "Ophelia! Nymph, in thy orisons be all my sins remember'd."°

Lyubov: Come, it will soon be suppertime.

Varya: How he frightened me! My heart's simply throbbing.

"Ophelia . . . nunnery!": In Shakespeare's *Hamlet,* Hamlet's famous line rejecting Ophelia (III.i.136).
"Ophelia . . . remember'd": The end of Hamlet's "To be or not to be" soliloquy (III.i.89–90).

Lopahin: Let me remind you, ladies and gentlemen: on the twenty-second of August the cherry orchard will be sold. Think about that! Think about it!

All go off, except Trofimov and Anya.

Anya (laughing): I'm grateful to the wayfarer! He frightened Varya and we are left alone.

Trofimov: Varya's afraid we shall fall in love with each other, and for days together she won't leave us. With her narrow brain she can't grasp that we are above love. To eliminate the petty and transitory which hinder us from being free and happy — that is the aim and meaning of our life. Forward! We go forward irresistibly toward the bright star that shines yonder in the distance. Forward! Do not lag behind, friends.

Anya (claps her hands): How well you speak! *(A pause.)* It is divine here today.

Trofimov: Yes, it's glorious weather.

Anya: Somehow, Petya, you've made me so that I don't love the cherry orchard as I used to. I used to love it so dearly. I used to think that there was no spot on earth like our garden.

Trofimov: All Russia is our garden. The earth is great and beautiful — there are many beautiful places in it. *(A pause.)* Think only, Anya, your grandfather, and great-grandfather, and all your ancestors were slave owners — the owners of living souls — and from every cherry in the orchard, from every leaf, from every trunk there are human creatures looking at you. Cannot you hear their voices? Oh, it is awful! Your orchard is a fearful thing, and when in the evening or at night one walks about the orchard, the old bark on the trees glimmers dimly in the dusk, and the old cherry trees seem to be dreaming of centuries gone by and tortured by fearful visions. Yes! We are at least two hundred years behind, we have really gained nothing yet, we have no definite attitude to the past, we do nothing but theorize or complain of depression or drink vodka. It is clear that to begin to live in the present, we must first expiate our past; we must break with it; and we can expiate it only by suffering, by extraordinary unceasing labor. Understand that, Anya.

Anya: The house we live in has long ceased to be our own, and I shall leave it, I give you my word.

Trofimov: If you have the house keys, fling them into the well and go away. Be free as the wind.

Anya (in ecstasy): How beautifully you said that!

Trofimov: Believe me, Anya, believe me! I am not thirty yet, I am young, I am still a student, but I have gone through so much already! As soon as winter comes I am hungry, sick, careworn, poor as a beggar, and what ups and downs of fortune have I not known! And my soul was always, every minute, day and night, full of inexplicable forebodings. I have a foreboding of happiness, Anya. I see glimpses of it already.

Anya (pensively): The moon is rising.

Epihodov is heard playing still the same mournful song on the guitar. The moon rises. Somewhere near the poplars Varya is looking for Anya and calling "Anya! where are you?"

Trofimov: Yes, the moon is rising. *(A pause.)* Here is happiness — here it comes! It is coming nearer and nearer; already I can hear its footsteps. And if we never see it — if we may never know it — what does it matter? Others will see it after us.

Varya's voice: Anya! Where are you?

Trofimov: That Varya again! *(Angrily.)* It's revolting!

Anya: Well, let's go down to the river. It's lovely there.

Trofimov: Yes, let's go. *(They go.)*

Varya's voice: Anya! Anya!

ACT III

A drawing room divided by an arch from a larger drawing room. A chandelier burning. The Jewish orchestra, the same that was mentioned in Act II, is heard playing in the anteroom. It is evening. In the larger drawing room they are dancing the grand chain. The voice of Semyonov-Pishtchik: "Promenade à une paire!"° Then enter the drawing room in couples, first Pishtchik and Charlotta Ivanova, then Trofimov and Lyubov Andreyevna, thirdly Anya with the Post Office Clerk, fourthly Varya with the Station Master, and other guests. Varya is quietly weeping and wiping away her tears as she dances. In the last couple is Dunyasha. They move across the drawing room. Pishtchik shouts: "Grand rond, balancez!" and "Les Cavaliers à genou et remerciez vos dames."°

Firs in a swallowtail coat brings in seltzer water on a tray. Pishtchik and Trofimov enter the drawing room.

Pishtchik: I am a full-blooded man; I have already had two strokes. Dancing's hard work for me, but as they say, if you're in the pack, you must bark with the rest. I'm as strong, I may say, as a horse. My parent, who would have his joke — may the Kingdom of Heaven be his! — used to say about our origin that the ancient stock of the Semyonov-Pishtchiks was derived from the very horse that Caligula made a member of the senate.° *(Sits down.)* But I've no money, that's where the mischief is. A hungry dog believes in nothing but meat. *(Snores, but at once wakes up.)* That's like me . . . I can think of nothing but money.

Trofimov: There really is something horsy about your appearance.

Pishtchik: Well . . . a horse is a fine beast . . . a horse can be sold.

There is the sound of billiards being played in an adjoining room. Varya appears in the arch leading to the larger drawing room.

Trofimov (tesing): Madame Lopahin! Madame Lopahin!

Varya (angrily): Mangy-looking gentleman!

Trofimov: Yes, I am a mangy-looking gentleman, and I'm proud of it!

Varya (pondering bitterly): Here we have hired musicians and nothing to pay them! *(Goes out.)*

"Promenade à une paire!": French for "Walk in pairs."

"Grand rond . . . dames": Instructions in the dance: "Large circle, . . . Men, kneel down and thank your ladies."

Caligula . . . senate: Caligula (A.D. 12–41) was a Roman emperor (37–41).

Trofimov (to Pishtchik): If the energy you have wasted during your lifetime in trying to find the money to pay your interest had gone to something else, you might in the end have turned the world upside down.

Pishtchik: Nietzsche,° the philosopher, a very great and celebrated man . . . of enormous intellect . . . says in his works that one can make forged bank notes.

Trofimov: Why, have your read Nietzsche?

Pishtchik: What next . . . Dashenka told me. . . . And now I am in such a position, I might just as well forge bank notes. The day after tomorrow I must pay three hundred ten rubles — one hundred thirty I have procured. *(Feels in his pockets, in alarm.)* The money's gone! I have lost my money! *(Through his tears.)* Where's the money? *(Gleefully.)* Why, here it is behind the lining. . . . It has made me hot all over.

Enter Lyubov Andreyevna and Charlotta Ivanovna.

Lyubov (hums the Lezginka°): Why is Leonid so long? What can he be doing in town? *(To Dunyasha.)* Offer the musicians some tea.

Trofimov: The sale hasn't taken place, most likely.

Lyubov: It's the wrong time to have the orchestra, and the wrong time to give a dance. Well, never mind. *(Sits down and hums softly.)*

Charlotta (gives Pishtchik a pack of cards): Here's a pack of cards. Think of any card you like.

Pishtchik: I've thought of one.

Charlotta: Shuffle the pack now. That's right. Give it here, my dear Mr. Pishtchik. *Ein, zwei, drei°* — now look, it's in your breast pocket.

Pishtchik (taking a card out of his breast pocket): The eight of spades! Perfectly right! *(Wonderingly.)* Fancy that now!

Charlotta (holding pack of cards in her hands, to Trofimov): Tell me quickly which is the top card.

Trofimov: Well, the queen of spades.

Charlotta: It is! *(To Pishtchik.)* Well, which card is uppermost?

Pishtchik: The ace of hearts.

Charlotta: It is! *(Claps her hands, pack of cards disappears.)* Ah! what lovely weather it is today!

A mysterious feminine voice which seems coming out of the floor answers her, "Oh, yes, it's magnificent weather, madam."

Charlotta: You are my perfect ideal.

Voice: And I greatly admire you too, madam.

Station Master (applauding): The lady ventriloquist — bravo!

Pishtchik (wonderingly): Fancy that now! Most enchanting, Charlotta Ivanovna. I'm simply in love with you.

Charlotta: In love? *(Shrugging shoulders.)* What do you know of love, *guter Mensch, aber schlechter Musikant?°*

Trofimov (pats Pishtchik on the shoulder): You dear old horse. . . .

Neitzsche: Friedrich Nietzsche (1844–1900), German philosopher and poet who developed the idea of the Superman, beyond traditional morality.
Lezginka: A popular, lively Russian dance.
Ein, zwei, drei: German for "One, two, three."
gutter Mensch, aber schlechter Musikant: German for "Good man, but poor musician."

Charlotta: Attention, please! Another trick! *(Takes a traveling rug from a chair.)* Here's a very good rug; I want to sell it. *(Shaking it out.)* Doesn't anyone want to buy it?

Pishtchik (wonderingly): Fancy that!

Charlotta: Ein, zwei, drei! (Quickly picks up rug she has dropped; behind the rug stands Anya; she makes a curtsy, runs to her mother, embraces her, and runs back into the larger drawing room amidst general enthusiasm.)

Lyubov (applauds): Bravo! Bravo!

Charlotta: Now again! *Ein, zwei, drei! (Lifts up the rug; behind the rug stands Varya, bowing.)*

Pishtchik (wonderingly): Fancy that now!

Charlotta: That's the end. *(Throws the rug at Pishtchik, makes a curtsy, runs into the larger drawing room.)*

Pishtchik (hurries after her): Mischievous creature! Fancy! *(Goes out.)*

Lyubov: And still Leonid doesn't come. I can't understand what he's doing in the town so long! Why, everything must be over by now. The estate is sold, or the sale has not taken place. Why keep us so long in suspense?

Varya (trying to console her): Uncle's bought it. I feel sure of that.

Trofimov (ironically): Oh, yes!

Varya: Great-aunt sent him an authorization to buy it in her name and transfer the debt. She's doing it for Anya's sake, and I'm sure God will be merciful. Uncle will buy it.

Lyubov: My aunt in Yaroslavl sent fifteen thousand to buy the estate in her name, she doesn't trust us — but that's not enough even to pay the arrears. *(Hides her face in her hands.)* My fate is being sealed today, my fate. . . .

Trofimov (teasing Varya): Madame Lopahin.

Varya (angrily): Perpetual student! Twice already you've been sent down from the university.

Lyubov: Why are you angry, Varya? He's teasing you about Lopahin. Well, what of that? Marry Lopahin if you like, he's a good man, and interesting; if you don't want to, don't! Nobody compels you, darling.

Varya: I must tell you plainly, mamma, I look at the matter seriously; he's a good man, I like him.

Lyubov: Well, marry him. I can't see what you're waiting for.

Varya: Mamma. I can't make him an offer myself. For the last two years, everyone's been talking to me about him. Everyone talks; but he says nothing or else makes a joke. I see what it means. He's growing rich, he's absorbed in business, he has no thoughts for me. If I had money, were it ever so little, if I had only a hundred rubles, I'd throw everything up and go far away. I would go into a nunnery.

Trofimov: What bliss!

Varya (to Trofimov): A student ought to have sense! *(In a soft tone with tears.)* How ugly you've grown, Petya! How old you look! *(To Lyubov Andreyevna, no longer crying.)* But I can't do without work, mamma; I must have something to do every minute.

Enter Yasha.

Yasha (hardly restraining his laughter): Epihodov has broken a billiard cue! *(Goes out.)*

Varya: What is Epihodov doing here? Who gave him leave to play billiards? I can't make these people out. *(Goes out.)*

Lyubov: Don't tease her, Petya. You see she has grief enough without that.

Trofimov: She is so very officious, meddling in what's not her business. All the summer she's given Anya and me no peace. She's afraid of a love affair between us. What's it to do with her? Besides, I have given no grounds for it. Such triviality is not in my line. We are above love!

Lyubov: And I suppose I am beneath love. *(Very uneasily.)* Why is it Leonid's not here? If only I could know whether the estate is sold or not! It seems such an incredible calamity that I really don't know what to think. I am distracted . . . I shall scream in a minute . . . I shall do something stupid. Save me, Petya, tell me something, talk to me!

Trofimov: What does it matter whether the estate is sold today or not? That's all done with long ago. There's no turning back, the path is overgrown. Don't worry yourself, dear Lyubov Andreyevna. You mustn't deceive yourself; for once in your life you must face the truth!

Lyubov: What truth? You see where the truth lies, but I seem to have lost my sight, I see nothing. You settle every great problem so boldly, but tell me, my dear boy, isn't it because you're young — because you haven't yet understood one of your problems through suffering? You look forward boldly, and isn't it that you don't see and don't expect anything dreadful because life is still hidden from your young eyes? You're bolder, more honest, deeper than we are, but think, be just a little magnanimous, have pity on me. I was born here, you know, my father and mother lived here, my grandfather lived here, I love this house. I can't conceive of life without the cherry orchard, and if it really must be sold, then sell me with the orchard. *(Embraces Trofimov, kisses him on the forehead.)* My boy was drowned here. *(Weeps.)* Pity me, my dear kind fellow.

Trofimov: You know I feel for you with all my heart.

Lyubov: But that should have been said differently, so differently. *(Takes out her handkerchief, telegram falls on the floor.)* My heart is so heavy today. It's so noisy here, my soul is quivering at every sound, I'm shuddering all over, but can't go away; I'm afraid to be quiet and alone. Don't be hard on me, Petya . . . I love you as though you were one of ourselves. I would gladly let you marry Anya — I swear I would — only, my dear boy, you must take your degree, you do nothing — you're simply tossed by fate from place to place. That's so strange. It is, isn't it? And you must do something with your beard to make it grow somehow. *(Laughs.)* You look so funny!

Trofimov (picks up the telegram): I've no wish to be a beauty.

Lyubov: That's a telegram from Paris. I get one every day. One yesterday and one today. That savage creature is ill again, he's in trouble again. He begs forgiveness, beseeches me to go, and really I ought to go to Paris to see him. You look shocked, Petya. What am I to do, my dear boy, what am I to do? He is ill, he is alone and unhappy, and who'll look after him, who'll keep him from doing the wrong thing, who'll give him his medicine at the right time? And why hide it or be silent? I love him, that's clear. I love him! I love him! He's a millstone about my neck, I'm going to the bottom with him, but I love that stone and can't live without it. *(Presses Trofimov's hand.)* Don't think ill of me, Petya, don't tell me anything, don't tell me. . . .

Trofimov (through his tears): For God's sake forgive my frankness: why, he robbed you!

Lyubov: No! No! No! You mustn't speak like that. *(Covers her ears.)*

Trofimov: He is a wretch! You're the only person that doesn't know it! He's a worthless creature! A despicable wretch!

Lyubov (getting angry, but speaking with restraint): You're twenty-six or twenty-seven years old, but you're still a schoolboy.

Trofimov: Possibly.

Lyubov: You should be a man at your age! You should understand what love means! And you ought to be in love yourself. You ought to fall in love! *(Angrily.)* Yes, yes, and it's not purity in you, you're simply a prude, a comic fool, a freak.

Trofimov (in horror): The things she's saying!

Lyubov: I am above love! You're not above love, but simply as our Firs here says, "You are a good-for-nothing." At your age not to have a mistress!

Trofimov (in horror): This is awful! The things she is saying! *(Goes rapidly into the larger drawing room clutching his head.)* This is awful! I can't stand it! I'm going. *(Goes off, but at once returns.)* All is over between us! *(Goes off into the anteroom.)*

Lyubov (shouts after him): Petya! Wait a minute! You funny creature! I was joking! Petya! *(There is a sound of somebody running quickly downstairs and suddenly falling with a crash. Anya and Varya scream, but there is a sound of laughter at once.)*

Lyubov: What has happened?

Anya runs in.

Anya (laughing): Petya's fallen downstairs! *(Runs out.)*

Lyubov: What a queer fellow that Petya is!

The Station Master stands in the middle of the larger room and reads The Magdalene, *by Alexey Tolstoy.° They listen to him, but before he has recited many lines strains of a waltz are heard from the anteroom and the reading is broken off. All dance. Trofimov, Anya, Varya, and Lyubov Andreyevna come in from the anteroom.*

Lyubov: Come, Petya — come, pure heart! I beg your pardon. Let's have a dance! *(Dances with Petya.)*

Anya and Varya dance. Firs comes in, puts his stick down near the side door. Yasha also comes into the drawing room and looks on at the dancing.

Yasha: What is it, old man?

Firs: I don't feel well. In old days we used to have generals, barons, and admirals dancing at our balls, and now we send for the post office clerk and the station master and even they're not overanxious to come. I am getting feeble. The old master, the grandfather, used to give sealing wax for all complaints. I have been taking sealing wax for twenty years or more. Perhaps that's what's kept me alive.

Alexey Tolstoy: Alexey Konstantinovich Tolstoy (1817–1875), Russian novelist (*Prince Serebryany,* 1863), dramatist (*The Death of Ivan the Terrible,* 1866), and poet. *The Magdalene* is a poem contemporary with this play in which Christ appears at a society banquet.

Yasha: You bore me, old man! *(Yawns.)* It's time you were done with.
Firs: Ach, you're a good-for-nothing! *(Mutters.)*

Trofimov and Lyubov Andreyevna dance in larger room and then on to the stage.

Lyubov: Merci. I'll sit down a little. *(Sits down.)* I'm tired.

Enter Anya.

Anya (excitedly): There's a man in the kitchen has been saying that the cherry orchard's been sold today.
Lyubov: Sold to whom?
Anya: He didn't say to whom. He's gone away.

She dances with Trofimov, and they go off into the larger room.

Yasha: There was an old man gossiping there, a stranger.
Firs: Leonid Andreyevitch isn't here yet, he hasn't come back. He has his light overcoat on, *demi-saison,*° he'll catch cold for sure. *Ach!* Foolish young things!
Lyubov: I feel as though I should die. Go, Yasha, find out to whom it has been sold.
Yasha: But he went away long ago, the old chap. *(Laughs.)*
Lyubov (with slight vexation): What are you laughing at? What are you pleased at?
Yasha: Epihodov is so funny. He's a silly fellow, two and twenty misfortunes.
Lyubov: Firs, if the estate is sold, where will you go?
Firs: Where you bid me, there I'll go.
Lyubov: Why do you look like that? Are you ill? You ought to be in bed.
Firs: Yes. *(Ironically.)* Me go to bed and who's to wait here? Who's to see to things without me? I'm the only one in all the house.
Yasha (to Lyubov Andreyevna): Lyubov Andreyevna, permit me to make a request of you; if you go back to Paris again, be so kind as to take me with you. It's positively impossible for me to stay here. *(Looking about him; in an undertone.)* There's no need to say it, you see for yourself — an uncivilized country, the people have no morals, and then the dullness! The food in the kitchen's abominable, and then Firs runs after one muttering all sorts of unsuitable words. Take me with you, please do!

Enter Pishtchik.

Pishtchik: Allow me to ask you for a waltz, my dear lady. *(Lyubov Andreyevna goes with him.)* Enchanting lady, I really must borrow of you just one hundred eighty rubles, *(Dances)* only one hundred eighty rubles. *(They pass into the larger room.)*

In the larger drawing room, a figure in a gray top hat and in checked trousers is gesticulating and jumping about. Shouts of "Bravo, Charlotta Ivanovna."

Dunyasha (she has stopped to powder herself): My young lady tells me to dance. There are plenty of gentlemen and too few ladies, but dancing makes me giddy and makes my heart beat. Firs, the post office clerk said something to me just now that quite took my breath away.

demi-saison: French for between-season.

Music becomes more subdued.

Firs: What did he say to you?

Dunyasha: He said I was like a flower.

Yasha (yawns): What ignorance! *(Goes out.)*

Dunyasha: Like a flower. I am a girl of such delicate feelings, I am awfully fond of soft speeches.

Firs: Your head's being turned.

Enter Epihodov.

Epihodov: You have no desire to see me, Dunyasha. I might be an insect. *(Sighs.)* Ah! life!

Dunyasha: What is it you want?

Epihodov: Undoubtedly you may be right. *(Sighs.)* But, of course, if one looks at it from that point of view, if I may so express myself, you have, excuse my plain speaking, reduced me to a complete state of mind. I know my destiny. Every day some misfortune befalls me and I have long ago grown accustomed to it, so that I look upon my fate with a smile. You gave me your word, and though I —

Dunyasha: Let us have a talk later, I entreat you, but now leave me in peace, for I am lost in reverie. *(Plays with her fan.)*

Epihodov: I have a misfortune every day, and if I may venture to express myself, I merely smile at it, I even laugh.

Varya enters from the larger drawing room.

Varya: You still have not gone, Epihodov. What a disrespectful creature you are, really! *(To Dunyasha.)* Go along, Dunyasha! *(To Epihodov.)* First you play billiards and break the cue, then you go wandering about the drawing room like a visitor!

Epihodov: You really cannot, if I may so express myself, call me to account like this.

Varya: I'm not calling you to account, I'm speaking to you. You do nothing but wander from place to place and don't do your work. We keep you as a counting house clerk, but what use you are I can't say.

Epihodov (offended): Whether I work or whether I walk, whether I eat or whether I play billiards, is a matter to be judged by persons of understanding and my elders.

Varya: You dare to tell me that! *(Firing up.)* You dare! You mean to say I've no understanding. Begone from here! This minute!

Epihodov (intimidated): I beg you to express yourself with delicacy.

Varya (beside herself with anger): This moment! get out! away! *(He goes toward the door, she following him.)* Two and twenty misfortunes! Take yourself off! Don't let me set eyes on you! *(Epihodov has gone out, behind the door his voice, "I shall lodge a complaint against you.")* What! You're coming back? *(Snatches up the stick Firs has put down near the door.)* Come! Come! I'll show you! What! you're coming? Then take that! *(She swings the stick, at the very moment that Lopahin comes in.)*

Lopahin: Very much obliged to you!

Varya (angrily and ironically): I beg your pardon!

Lopahin: Not at all! I humbly thank you for your kind reception!

Varya: No need of thanks for it. *(Moves away, then looks round and asks softly.)* I haven't hurt you?

Lopahin: Oh, no! Not at all! There's an immense bump coming up, though!

Voices from larger room: Lopahin has come! Yermolay Alexeyevitch!

Pishtchik: What do I see and hear? *(Kisses Lopahin.)* There's a whiff of cognac about you, my dear soul, and we're making merry here too!

Enter Lyubov Andreyevna.

Lyubov: Is it you, Yermolay Alexeyevitch? Why have you been so long? Where's Leonid?

Lopahin: Leonid Andreyevitch arrived with me. He is coming.

Lyubov (in agitation): Well! Well! Was there a sale? Speak!

Lopahin (embarrassed, afraid of betraying his joy): The sale was over at four o'clock. We missed our train — had to wait till half-past nine. *(Sighing heavily.)* Ugh! I feel a little giddy.

Enter Gaev. In his right hand he has purchases, with his left hand he is wiping away his tears.

Lyubov: Well, Leonid? What news? *(Impatiently, with tears.)* Make haste, for God's sake!

Gaev (makes her no answer, simply waves his hand; to Firs, weeping): Here, take them; there's anchovies, Kertch herrings. I have eaten nothing all day. What I have been through! *(Door into the billiard room is open. There is heard a knocking of balls and the voice of Yasha saying "Eighty-seven." Gaev's expression changes, he leaves off weeping.)* I am fearfully tired. Firs, come and help me change my things. *(Goes to his own room across the larger drawing room.)*

Pishtchik: How about the sale? Tell us, do!

Lyubov: Is the cherry orchard sold?

Lopahin: It is sold.

Lyubov: Who has bought it?

Lopahin: I have bought it. *(A pause. Lyubov is crushed; she would fall down if she were not standing near a chair and table.)*

Varya takes keys from her waistband, flings them on the floor in middle of drawing room, and goes out.

Lopahin: I have bought it! Wait a bit, ladies and gentlemen, pray. My head's a bit muddled, I can't speak. *(Laughs.)* We came to the auction. Deriganov was there already. Leonid Andreyevitch only had fifteen thousand and Deriganov bid thirty thousand, besides the arrears, straight off. I saw how the land lay. I bid against him. I bid forty thousand, he bid forty-five thousand, I said fifty-five, and so he went on, adding five thousands and I adding ten. Well . . . So it ended. I bid ninety, and it was knocked down to me. Now the cherry orchard's mine! Mine! *(Chuckles.)* My God, the cherry orchard's mine! Tell me that I'm drunk, that I'm out of my mind, that it's all a dream. *(Stamps with his feet.)* Don't laugh at me! If my father and my grandfather could rise from their graves and see all that has happened! How their Yermolay, ignorant, beaten Yermolay, who used to run about barefoot in winter, how that very Yermolay has bought the finest estate in the world! I have bought the estate where my father and grandfather were slaves, where they weren't even admitted into the kitchen. I am asleep, I am dreaming! It is all fancy, it is the work of your imagination plunged in the darkness of ignorance. *(Picks up keys, smiling fondly.)* She threw away the keys; she means to show she's not the housewife now. *(Jingles the keys.)* Well, no matter. *(The orchestra is heard tuning up.)* Hey, musicians! Play! I want to hear you. Come, all of you, and look how Yermolay Lopahin will take the ax to the cherry orchard, how the trees will fall to the ground! We will build houses on it and our grandsons and great-grandsons will see a new life springing up there. Music! Play up!

Music begins to play. Lyubov Andreyevna has sunk into a chair and is weeping bitterly.

Lopahin (reproachfully): Why, why didn't you listen to me? My poor friend! Dear lady, there's no turning back now. *(With tears.)* Oh, if all this could be over, oh, if our miserable disjointed life could somehow soon be changed!

Pishtchik (takes him by the arm, in an undertone): She's weeping, let us go and leave her alone. Come. *(Takes him by the arm and leads him into the larger drawing room.)*

Lopahin: What's that? Musicians, play up! All must be as I wish it. *(With irony.)* Here comes the new master, the owner of the cherry orchard! *(Accidentally tips over a little table, almost upsetting the candelabra.)* I can pay for everything! *(Goes out with Pishtchik. No one remains on the stage or in the larger drawing room except Lyubov, who sits huddled up, weeping bitterly. The music plays softly. Anya and Trofimov come in quickly. Anya goes up to her mother and falls on her knees before her. Trofimov stands at the entrance to the larger drawing room.)*

Anya: Mamma! Mamma, you're crying, dear, kind, good mamma! My precious! I love you! I bless you! The cherry orchard is sold, it is gone, that's true, that's true! But don't weep, mamma! Life is still before you, you have still your good, pure heart! Let us go, let us go, darling, away from here! We will make a new garden, more splendid than this one; you will see it, you will understand. And joy, quiet, deep joy, will sink into your soul like the sun at evening! And you will smile, mamma! Come, darling, let us go!

ACT IV

Same as in first act. There are neither curtains on the windows nor pictures on the walls: only a little furniture remains piled up in a corner as if for sale. There is a sense of desolation; near the outer door and in the background of the scene are packed trunks, traveling bags, etc. On the left the door is open, and from here the voices of Varya and Anya are audible. Lopahin is standing waiting. Yasha is holding a tray with glasses full of champagne. In front of the stage Epihodov is tying up a box. In the background behind the scene a hum of talk from the peasants who have come to say good-bye. The voice of Gaev: "Thanks, brothers, thanks!"

Yasha: The peasants have come to say good-bye. In my opinion, Yermolay Alexeyevitch, the peasants are good-natured, but they don't know much about things.

The hum of talk dies away. Enter across front of stage Lyubov Andreyevna and Gaev. She is not weeping, but is pale; her face is quivering — she cannot speak.

Gaev: You gave them your purse, Lyuba. That won't do — that won't do!
Lyubov: I couldn't help it! I couldn't help it!

(Both go out.)

Lopahin (in the doorway, calls after them): You will take a glass at parting? Please do. I didn't think to bring any from the town, and at the station I could only get one bottle. Please take a glass. *(A pause.)* What? You don't care for any? *(Comes away from the door.)* If I'd known, I wouldn't have bought it. Well, and I'm not going to drink it. *(Yasha carefully sets the tray down on a chair.)* You have a glass, Yasha, anyway.
Yasha: Good luck to the travelers, and luck to those that stay behind! *(Drinks.)* This champagne isn't the real thing, I can assure you.
Lopahin: It cost eight rubles the bottle. *(A pause.)* It's devilish cold here.
Yasha: They haven't heated the stove today — it's all the same since we're going. *(Laughs.)*
Lopahin: What are you laughing for?
Yasha: For pleasure.
Lopahin: Though it's October, it's as still and sunny as though it were summer. It's just right for building! *(Looks at his watch; says in doorway.)* Take note, ladies and gentlemen, the train goes in forty-seven minutes; so you ought to start for the station in twenty minutes. You must hurry up!

Trofimov comes in from out of doors wearing a greatcoat.

Trofimov: I think it must be time to start, the horses are ready. The devil only knows what's become of my galoshes; they're lost. *(In the doorway.)* Anya! My galoshes aren't here. I can't find them.
Lopahin: And I'm getting off to Harkov. I am going in the same train with you. I'm spending all the winter at Harkov. I've been wasting all my time gossiping with you and fretting with no work to do. I can't get on without work. I don't know what to do with my hands, they flap about so queerly, as if they didn't belong to me.
Trofimov: Well, we're just going away, and you will take up your profitable labors again.
Lopahin: Do take a glass.
Trofimov: No thanks.
Lopahin: Then you're going to Moscow now?
Trofimov: Yes. I shall see them as far as the town, and tomorrow I shall go on to Moscow.
Lopahin: Yes, I daresay, the professors aren't giving any lectures, they're waiting for your arrival.

Trofimov: That's not your business.

Lopahin: How many years have you been at the university?

Trofimov: Do think of something newer than that — that's stale and flat. *(Hunts for galoshes.)* You know we shall most likely never see each other again, so let me give you one piece of advice at parting: don't wave your arms about — get out of the habit. And another thing, building villas, reckoning up that the summer visitors will in time become independent farmers — reckoning like that, that's not the thing to do either. After all, I am fond of you: you have fine delicate fingers like an artist, you've a fine delicate soul.

Lopahin (embraces him): Good-bye, my dear fellow. Thanks for everything. Let me give you money for the journey, if you need it.

Trofimov: What for? I don't need it.

Lopahin: Why, you haven't got a half-penny.

Trofimov: Yes, I have, thank you. I got some money for a translation. Here it is in my pocket, *(Anxiously.)* but where can my galoshes be!

Varya (from the next room): Take the nasty things! *(Flings a pair of galoshes onto the stage.)*

Trofimov: Why are you so cross, Varya? hm! . . . but those aren't my galoshes.

Lopahin: I sowed three thousand acres with poppies in the spring, and now I have cleared forty thousand profit. And when my poppies were in flower, wasn't it a picture! So here, as I say, I made forty thousand, and I'm offering you a loan because I can afford to. Why turn up your nose? I am a peasant — I speak bluntly.

Trofimov: Your father was a peasant, mine was a chemist — and that proves absolutely nothing whatever. *(Lopahin takes out his pocketbook.)* Stop that — stop that. If you were to offer me two hundred thousand I wouldn't take it. I am an independent man, and everything that all of you, rich and poor alike, prize so highly and hold so dear hasn't the slightest power over me — it's like so much fluff fluttering in the air. I can get on without you. I can pass by you. I am strong and proud. Humanity is advancing towards the highest truth, the highest happiness, which is possible on earth, and I am in the front ranks.

Lopahin: Will you get there?

Trofimov: I shall get there. *(A pause.)* I shall get there, or I shall show others the way to get there.

In the distance is heard the stroke of an ax on a tree.

Lopahin: Good-bye, my dear fellow; it's time to be off. We turn up our noses at one another, but life is passing all the while. When I am working hard without resting, then my mind is more at ease, and it seems to me as though I too know what I exist for; but how many people are in Russia, my dear boy, who exist, one doesn't know what for. Well, it doesn't matter. That's not what keeps things spinning. They tell me Leonid Andreyevitch has taken a situation. He is going to be a clerk at the bank — six thousand rubles a year. Only, of course, he won't stick to it — he's too lazy.

Anya (in the doorway): Mamma begs you not to let them chop down the orchard until she's gone.

Trofimov: Yes, really, you might have the tact. *(Walks out across the front of the stage.)*

Lopahin: I'll see to it! I'll see to it! Stupid fellows! *(Goes out after him.)*

Anya: Has Firs been taken to the hospital?

Yasha: I told them this morning. No doubt they have taken him.

Anya (To Epihodov, who passes across the drawing room): Semyon Pantaleyevitch, inquire, please, if Firs has been taken to the hospital.

Yasha (in a tone of offense): I told Yegor this morning—why ask a dozen times?

Epihodov: Firs is advanced in years. It's my conclusive opinion no treatment would do him good; it's time he was gathered to his fathers. And I can only envy him. *(Puts a trunk down on a cardboard hatbox and crushes it.)* There, now, of course—I knew it would be so.

Yasha (jeeringly): Two and twenty misfortunes!

Varya (through the door): Has Firs been taken to the hospital?

Anya: Yes.

Varya: Why wasn't the note for the doctor taken too?

Anya: Oh, then, we must send it after them. *(Goes out.)*

Varya (from the adjoining room): Where's Yasha? Tell him his mother's come to say good-bye to him.

Yasha (waves his hand): They put me out of all patience! *(Dunyasha has all this time been busy about the luggage. Now, when Yasha is left alone, she goes up to him.)*

Dunyasha: You might just give me one look, Yasha. You're going away. You're leaving me. *(Weeps and throws herself on his neck.)*

Yasha: What are you crying for? *(Drinks the champagne.)* In six days I shall be in Paris again. Tomorrow we shall get into the express train and roll away in a flash. I can scarcely believe it! *Vive la France!* It doesn't suit me here—it's not the life for me; there's no doing anything. I have seen enough of the ignorance here. I have had enough of it. *(Drinks champagne.)* What are you crying for? Behave yourself properly, and then you won't cry.

Dunyasha (powders her face, looking in a pocket mirror): Do send me a letter from Paris. You know how I loved you, Yasha—how I loved you! I am a tender creature, Yasha.

Yasha: Here they are coming!

Busies himself about the trunks, humming softly. Enter Lyubov Andreyevna, Gaev, Anya, and Charlotta Ivanovna.

Gaev: We ought to be off. There's not much time now. *(Looking at Yasha.)* What a smell of herrings!

Lyubov: In ten minutes we must get into the carriage. *(Casts a look about the room.)* Farewell, dear house, dear old home of our fathers! Winters will pass and spring will come, and then you will be no more; they will tear you down! How much those walls have seen! *(Kisses her daughter passionately.)* My treasure, how bright you look! Your eyes are sparkling like diamonds! Are you glad? Very glad?

Anya: Very glad! A new life is beginning, mamma.

Gaev: Yes, really, everything is all right now. Before the cherry orchard was sold, we were all worried and wretched, but afterwards, when once the question was settled conclusively, irrevocably, we all felt calm and even cheerful. I am a bank clerk now — I am a financier — cannon off the red. And you, Lyuba, after all, you are looking better; there's no question of that.

Lyubov: Yes. My nerves are better, that's true. *(Her hat and coat are handed to her.)* I'm sleeping well. Carry out my things, Yasha. It's time. *(To Anya.)* My darling, we shall soon see each other again. I am going to Paris. I can live there on the money your Yaroslavl auntie sent us to buy the estate with — hurrah for auntie! — but that money won't last long.

Anya: You'll come back soon, mamma, won't you? I'll be working up for my examination in the high school, and when I have passed that, I shall set to work and be a help to you. We will read all sorts of things together, mamma, won't we? *(Kisses her mother's hands.)* We will read in the autumn evenings. We'll read lots of books, and a new wonderful world will open out before us. *(Dreamily.)* Mamma, come soon.

Lyubov: I shall come, my precious treasure. *(Embraces her.)*

Enter Lopahin. Charlotta softly hums a song.

Gaev: Charlotta's happy; she's singing!

Charlotta (picks up a bundle like a swaddled baby): Bye, bye, my baby. *(A baby is heard crying; "Ooah! ooah!")* Hush, hush, my pretty boy! *("Ooah! ooah!")* Poor little thing! *(Throws the bundle back.)* You must please find me a situation. I can't go on like this.

Lopahin: We'll find you one, Charlotta Ivanovna. Don't you worry yourself.

Gaev: Everyone's leaving us. Varya's going away. We have become of no use all at once.

Charlotta: There's nowhere for me to be in the town. I must go away. *(Hums.)* What care I . . .

Enter Pishtchik.

Lopahin: The freak of nature.

Pishtchik (gasping): Oh . . . let me get my breath. . . . I'm worn out . . . my most honored . . . Give me some water.

Gaev: Want some money, I suppose? Your humble servant! I'll go out of the way of temptation. *(Goes out.)*

Pishtchik: It's a long while since I have been to see you . . . dearest lady. *(To Lopahin.)* You are here . . . glad to see you . . . a man of immense intellect . . . take . . . here *(Gives Lopahin.)* four hundred rubles. That leaves me owing eight hundred forty.

Lopahin (shrugging his shoulders in amazement): It's like a dream. Where did you get it?

Pishtchik: Wait a bit . . . I'm hot . . . a most extraordinary occurrence! Some Englishmen came along and found in my land some sort of white clay. *(To Lyubov Andreyevna.)* And four hundred for you . . . most lovely . . . wonderful. *(Gives money.)* The rest later. *(Sips water.)* A young man in the train was telling me just now that a great philosopher advises jumping off a housetop. "Jump!" says he; "the whole gist of the problem lies in that." *(Wonderingly.)* Fancy that, now! Water, please!

Lopahin: What Englishmen?

Pishtchik: I have made over to them the rights to dig the clay for twenty-four years . . . and now, excuse me . . . I can't stay . . . I must be trotting on. I'm going to Znoikovo . . . to Kardamanovo. . . . I'm in debt all round. *(Sips.)* . . . To your very good health! . . . I'll come in on Thursday.

Lyubov: We are just off to the town, and tomorrow I start for abroad.

Pishtchik: What! *(In agitation.)* Why to the town? Oh, I see the furniture . . . the boxes. No matter . . . *(Through his tears.)* . . . no matter . . . men of enormous intellect . . . those Englishmen. . . . Never mind . . . be happy. God will succor you . . . no matter . . . everything in this world must have an end. *(Kisses Lyubov Andreyevna's hand.)* If the rumor reaches you that my end has come, think of this . . . old horse, and say: "There once was such a man in the world . . . Semyonov-Pishtchik . . . the Kingdom of Heaven be his!" . . . most extraordinary weather . . . yes. *(Goes out in violent agitation, but at once returns and says in the doorway.)* Dashenka wishes to be remembered to you. *(Goes out.)*

Lyubov: Now we can start. I leave with two cares in my heart. The first is leaving Firs ill. *(Looking at her watch.)* We have still five minutes.

Anya: Mamma, Firs has been taken to the hospital. Yasha sent him off this morning.

Lyubov: My other anxiety is Varya. She is used to getting up early and working; and now, without work, she's like a fish out of water. She is thin and pale, and she's crying, poor dear! *(A pause.)* You are well aware, Yermolay Alexeyevitch, I dreamed of marrying her to you, and everything seemed to show that you would get married. *(Whispers to Anya and motions to Charlotta and both go out.)* She loves you — she suits you. And I don't know — I don't know why it is you seem, as it were, to avoid each other. I can't understand it!

Lopahin: I don't understand it myself, I confess. It's queer somehow, altogether. If there's still time, I'm ready now at once. Let's settle it straight off, and go ahead; but without you, I feel I shan't make her an offer.

Lyubov: That's excellent. Why, a single moment's all that's necessary. I'll call her at once.

Lopahin: And there's champagne all ready too. *(Looking into the glasses.)* Empty! Someone's emptied them already. *(Yasha coughs.)* I call that greedy.

Lyubov (eagerly): Capital! We will go out. Yasha, allez!° I'll call her in. *(At the door.)* Varya, leave all that; come here. Come along! *(Goes out with Yasha.)*

Lopahin (looking at his watch): Yes.

A pause. Behind the door, smothered laughter and whispering, and, at last, enter Varya.

Varya (looking a long while over the things): It is strange, I can't find it anywhere.

Lopahin: What are you looking for?

Varya: I packed it myself, and I can't remember. *(A pause.)*

Lopahin: Where are you going now, Varvara Mihailova?

Varya: I? To the Ragulins. I have arranged to go to them to look after the house — as a housekeeper.

allez: French for "Go."

Lopahin: That's in Yashnovo? It'll be seventy miles away. *(A pause.)* So this is the end of life in this house!

Varya (looking among the things): Where is it? Perhaps I put it in the trunk. Yes, life in this house is over — there will be no more of it.

Lopahin: And I'm just off to Harkov — by this next train. I've a lot of business there. I'm leaving Epihodov here, and I've taken him on.

Varya: Really!

Lopahin: This time last year we had snow already, if you remember; but now it's so fine and sunny. Though it's cold, to be sure — three degrees of frost.

Varya: I haven't looked. *(A pause.)* And besides, our thermometer's broken. *(A pause.)*

Voice at the door from the yard: "Yermolay Alexeyevitch!"

Lopahin (as though he had long been expecting this summons): This minute!

Lopahin goes out quickly. Varya sitting on the floor and laying her head on a bag full of clothes, sobs quietly. The door opens. Lyubov Andreyevna comes in cautiously.

Lyubov: Well? *(A pause.)* We must be going.

Varya (has wiped her eyes and is no longer crying): Yes, mamma, it's time to start. I shall have time to get to the Ragulins today, if only you're not late for the train.

Lyubov (in the doorway): Anya, put your things on.

Enter Anya, then Gaev and Charlotta Ivanovna. Gaev has on a warm coat with a hood. Servants and cabmen come in. Epihodov bustles about the luggage.

Lyubov: Now we can start on our travels.

Anya (joyfully): On our travels!

Gaev: My friends — my dear, my precious friends! Leaving this house forever, can I be silent? Can I refrain from giving utterance at leave-taking to those emotions which now flood all my being?

Anya (supplicatingly): Uncle!

Varya: Uncle, you mustn't!

Gaev (dejectedly): Cannon and into the pocket . . . I'll be quiet. . . .

Enter Trofimov and afterward Lopahin.

Trofimov: Well, ladies and gentlemen, we must start.

Lopahin: Epihodov, my coat!

Lyubov: I'll stay just one minute. It seems as though I have never seen before what the walls, what the ceilings in this house were like, and now I look at them with greediness, with such tender love.

Gaev: I remember when I was six years old sitting in that window on Trinity Day watching my father going to church.

Lyubov: Have all the things been taken?

Lopahin: I think all. *(Putting on overcoat, to Epihodov.)* You, Epihodov, mind you see everything is right.

Epihodov (in a husky voice): Don't you trouble, Yermolay Alexeyevitch.

Lopahin: Why, what's wrong with your voice?

Epihodov: I've just had a drink of water, and I choked over something.

Yasha (contemptuously): The ignorance!

Lyubov: We are going — and not a soul will be left here.

Lopahin: Not till the spring.

Varya (pulls a parasol out of a bundle, as though about to hit someone with it; Lopahin makes a gesture as though alarmed): What is it? I didn't mean anything.

Trofimov: Ladies and gentlemen, let us get into the carriage. It's time. The train will be in directly.

Varya: Petya, here they are, your galoshes, by that box. *(With tears.)* And what dirty old things they are!

Trofimov (putting on his galoshes): Let us go, friends!

Gaev (greatly agitated, afraid of weeping): The train — the station! Double balk,° ah!

Lyubov: Let us go!

Lopahin: Are we all here! *(Locks the side door on left.)* The things are all here. We must lock up. Let us go!

Anya: Good-bye, home! Good-bye to the old life!

Trofimov: Welcome to the new life!

Trofimov goes out with Anya, Varya looks round the room and goes out slowly. Yasha and Charlotta Ivanovna, with her dog, go out.

Lopahin: Till the spring, then! Come, friends, till we meet! *(Goes out.)*

Lyubov Andreyevna and Gaev remain alone. As though they had been waiting for this, they throw themselves on each other's necks, and break into subdued smothered sobbing, afraid of being overheard.

Gaev (in despair): Sister, my sister!

Lyubov: Oh, my orchard! — my sweet, beautiful orchard! My life, my youth, my happiness, good-bye! Good-bye!

Voice of Anya (calling gaily): Mamma!

Voice of Trofimov (gaily, excitedly): Aa — oo!

Lyubov: One last look at the walls, at the windows. My dear mother loved to walk about this room.

Gaev: Sister, sister!

Voice of Anya: Mamma!

Voice of Trofimov: Aa — oo!

Lyubov: We are coming. *(They go out.)*

The stage is empty. There is the sound of the doors being locked up, then of the carriages driving away. There is silence. In the stillness there is the dull stroke of an ax in a tree, clanging with a mournful, lonely sound. Footsteps are heard. Firs appears in the doorway on the right. He is dressed as always — in a pea jacket and white waistcoat, with slippers on his feet. He is ill.

Firs (goes up to the door, and tries the handles): Locked! They have gone . . . *(Sits down on sofa.)* They have forgotten me. . . . Never mind . . . I'll sit here a bit. . . . I'll be bound Leonid Andreyevitch hasn't put his fur coat on and has gone off in his thin overcoat. *(Sighs anxiously.)* I didn't see after

balk: A term in billiards.

him. . . . These young people . . . *(Mutters something that can't be distinguished.)* Life has slipped by as though I hadn't lived. *(Lies down.)* I'll lie down a bit. . . . There's no strength in you, nothing left you — all gone! Ech! I'm good for nothing. *(Lies motionless.)*

A sound is heard that seems to come from the sky, like a breaking harp string, dying away mournfully. All is still again, and there is heard nothing but the strokes of the ax far away in the orchard.

Considerations

1. How well do the characters in the play cope with the details of everyday life? How do their outward conversations and actions suggest their inner lives?
2. Many of the play's characters philosophize about the meaning of life. What conclusions do they reach? What do they want from life? What do they get?
3. Why do you think Chekhov uses a cherry orchard rather than simply uncultivated woods as the center of the play's controversy? How does the cherry orchard reveal aspects of its owners?
4. How is life outside the cherry orchard depicted? How does it differ from life in the family's world?
5. Which characters embody the coming "new order"? Describe how Chekhov uses them as foils to those characters associated with the agrarian values of the "old order"?
6. Discuss Chekhov's use of time in the play. How do particular characters relate to the past, present, and future?
7. Comment on the appropriateness of the play's title.
8. Why do you think the play ends with the sound of the ax? What kinds of social changes are represented by the destruction of the orchard?
9. Explain whether you think the play ends on a hopeful or a pessimistic note. Do you think things are likely to get better or worse?
10. Chekhov objected to solemn, melancholy productions of *The Cherry Orchard.* He insisted that the play is not a "heavy drama" or tragedy "but a comedy, in parts even a farce." In contrast, Konstantin Stanislavsky, the director of the play's first production, believed, "It is definitely not a comedy . . . but a tragedy." What is your own view of the play's depiction of Russian life? Explain why you think it is more like a comedy or a tragedy.

Connections

1. How do the love relationships in Ibsen's *A Doll's House* and *The Cherry Orchard* reflect larger social issues in each play?
2. Compare and contrast the way characters try to insulate themselves from the outside world in *The Cherry Orchard* and in Tennessee Williams's *The Glass Menagerie* (p. 1462).
3. Read the section on Marxist criticism (p. 1787) in Chapter 32, "Critical Strategies for Reading." Write an essay discussing how you think a Marxist critic would approach *The Cherry Orchard.*

PERSPECTIVES

ANTON CHEKHOV (1860–1904)

On What Artists Do Best 1888

In conversation with my literary colleagues I always insist that it is not the artist's business to solve problems that require a specialist's knowledge. It is a bad thing if a writer tackles a subject he does not understand. We have specialists for dealing with special questions: it is their business to judge of the commune, of the future, of capitalism, of the evils of drunkenness, of boots, of the diseases of women. An artist must judge only of what he understands, his field is just as limited as that of any other specialist — I repeat this and insist on it always. That in his sphere there are no questions, but only answers, can be maintained only by those who have never written and have had no experience of thinking in images. An artist observes, selects, guesses, combines — and this in itself presupposes a problem: unless he had set himself a problem from the very first there would be nothing to conjecture and nothing to select. To put it briefly, I will end by using the language of psychiatry: if one denies that creative work involves problems and purposes, one must admit that an artist creates without premeditation or intention, in a state of abberation; therefore, if an author boasted to me of having written a novel without a preconceived design, under a sudden inspiration, I should call him mad.

You are right in demanding that an artist should take an intelligent attitude to his work, but you confuse two things: *solving a problem and stating a problem correctly.* It is only the second that is obligatory for the artist. . . . It is the business of the judge to put the right questions, but the answers must be given by the jury according to their own lights.

From a letter to A. S. Souvorin, October 27, 1888,
in *Letters of Anton Tchekhov to His Family and Friends,*
translated by Constance Garnett

Considerations

1. Explain whether you agree with Chekhov that an artist's "field is just as limited as that of any other specialist." Write an essay on Chekhov's assertion that "it is not the artist's business to solve problems."
2. How does *The Cherry Orchard* reflect Chekhov's insistence that his job is to "put the right questions" rather than to answer them?

DAVID MAMET (b. 1947)

Notes on The Cherry Orchard 1985

When playing poker it is a good idea to determine what cards your opponents might be playing. There are two ways to do this. One involves watching their idiosyncrasies — the way they hold their cards when bluffing as opposed to the way they hold them when they have a strong hand; their unconscious self-revelatory gestures; the way they play with their chips when unsure. This method of gathering information is called looking for "tells."

The other way to gather information is to analyze your opponent's hand according to what he *bets*.

These two methods are analogous — in the theater — to a concern with *characterization,* and a concern with *action;* or, to put it a bit differently: a concern with the *way* a character does something and, on the other hand, the actual *thing that he does*.

I recently worked on an adaptation of *The Cherry Orchard*.

My newfound intimacy with the play led me to look past the quiddities of the characters and examine what it is that they are actually doing. I saw this:

The title is a flag of convenience. Nobody in the play gives a damn about the cherry orchard.

In the first act Lyubov returns. We are informed that her beloved Estate is going to be sold unless someone acts quickly to avert this catastrophe.

She is told this by the rich Lopahin. He then immediately tells her that he has a plan: cut down the cherry orchard, raze the house, and build tract housing for the summer people.

This solution would save (although alter) the estate.

Lopahin keeps reiterating his offer throughout the play. Lyubov will not accept. Lopahin finally buys the estate.

"Well," one might say, "one cannot save one's beloved cherry orchard by cutting it down." That, of course, is true. But, in the text, other alternatives are offered.

Reference is made to the Rich Aunt in Yaroslavl ("Who is so very rich"), and who adores Lyubov's daughter, Anya. A flying mendicant mission is proposed but never materializes. The point here is not that this mission is viewed as a good bet, it isn't, but that, if the action of the protagonist (supposedly Lyubov) were to save the cherry orchard, she would grasp *any* possibility of help.

The more likely hope of salvation is fortuitous marriage. Gaev, Lyubov's brother, in enumerating the alternatives lists: inheriting money, begging from the rich aunt, marrying Anya off to a rich man.

The first is idle wishing, and we've struck off the second, but what about the third alternative?

There's nobody much around for Anya. But what about her stepsister, Varya?

Varya, Lyubov's adopted daughter, is not only nubile, she is *in love.* With whom is she in love? She is in love with Lopahin.

Why, *Hell.* If I wanted to save *my* cherry orchard, and *my* adopted daughter was in love (and we are told that her affections are by no means abhorrent to their recipient) with the richest man in town, what would *I* do? What would *you* do? It's the easy way out, the play ends in a half-hour and everybody gets to go home early.

But Lyubov does *not* press this point, though she makes reference to it in every act. She does *not* press on to a happy marriage between Varya and Lopahin. Nor, curiously, is this match ever mentioned as a solution for the problem of the cherry orchard. The problem of the botched courtship of Varya and Lopahin exists only as one of a number of supposed subplots. (More on this later.)

In the penultimate scene of the play Lyubov, who is leaving the now-sold estate to return to Paris, attempts to tie up loose ends. She exhorts Lopahin to propose to Varya, and he says he will. Left alone, Lopahin loses his nerve and does not propose. Why does Lyubov, on learning this, not press her case? Why did she not do so sooner?

Even now, at the end of the play, if Lyubov *really* cared about the cherry orchard, she could easily *force* Lopahin to propose to Varya, and then get the bright idea that all of them could live on the estate as one happy family. And Lopahin would not refuse her.

But she does not do so. Is this from lack of inventiveness? No. It is from lack of concern. The cherry orchard is not her concern.

What about Lopahin? Why is *he* cutting down the cherry orchard? He has been, from youth, infatuated with Lyubov. She is a goddess to him, her estate is a fairyland to him, and his great desire in the play is to please her. (In fact, if one were to lapse into a psychological overview of the play at this point one might say that the reason Lopahin can't propose to Varya is that he is in love with Lyubov.)

Lopahin buys the estate. For ninety-thousand rubles, which means nothing to him. He then proceeds to cut down the trees, which he knows will upset his goddess, Lyubov; and to raze the manor house. His parents were slaves in that house. Lyubov grew up in the house, he doesn't need the money, why is he cutting down the trees? (Yes, yes, yes; we encounter half-hearted addenda in re: future generations being won back to the land. But it doesn't wash. Why? If Lopahin wanted to build a summer colony he could build it anywhere. He could have built it without Lyubov's land and without her permission. If his objective were the building of summer homes and he were faced with two tracts, one where he had to cut down his idol's home, and one where he did not, which would he pick? Well, he has an infinite number of tracts. He can build anywhere he wants. Why cut down the trees and sadden his beloved idol? Having bought the estate he could easily let it sit, and, should the spirit move him subsequently, build his resort elsewhere.)

What, in effect, is going on here?

Nothing that has to do with trees.

The play is a series of scenes about sexuality, and, particularly, frustrated sexuality.

The play was inspired, most probably, by the scene in *Anna Karenina*° between Kitty's friend, Mlle. Varenka, and her gentleman companion, Mr. Koznyshez. The two of them, lonely, nice people, are brought together through the office of mutual friends. Each should marry, they are a perfect match. In one of the finest scenes in the book we are told that each knew the time had arrived, that it was Now or Never. They go for a walk, Mr. Koznyshez is about to propose when a question about mushrooms comes to his mind, the mood is broken, and so the two nice people are doomed to loneliness.

If this description sounds familiar it should. Chekhov, pregnant of his theme, lifted it shamelessly (and probably unconsciously) from Tolstoy and gave it to Lopahin and Varya.

Anna Karenina: Epic novel by the Russian writer Leo Tolstoy (1828–1910).

Not only do *they* play out the scene, EVERYBODY IN THE PLAY PLAYS OUT THE SAME SCENE.

Anya is in love with Pyotr Trofimov, the tutor of her late brother. Trofimov is in love with *her,* but is too repressed to make the first move. He, in fact, declares that he is above love, while, in a soliloquy, refers to Anya as "My springtime, my dear morning sun."

Epihodov, the estate bookkeeper, is in love with Dunyasha, the chambermaid. He keeps trying to propose, but she thinks him a boor and will not hear him out. *She* is in love with Yasha, Lyubov's footman. Yasha seduces and abandons her as he is in love with himself.

Lyubov herself is in love. She gave her fortune to her paramour and nursed him through three years of his sickness. He deserted her for a younger woman.

Now: *this* is the reason she has returned to the estate. It is purely coincidental that she returns just prior to the auction of the orchard. *Why* is it coincidental? Because, as we have seen, she doesn't come back to *save* it. If she wanted to she could. *Why* does she come back? What is the event that prompts her to return again to Paris? The continual telegrams of her roué lover begging forgiveness.

Why did Lyubov come home? To lick her wounds, to play for time, to figure out a new course for her life.

Now: none of these is a theatrically compelling action. (The last comes closest, but it could be done in seclusion and does not need other characters. As, indeed, *Lyubov* is, essentially a monologue — there's nothing she *wants* from anyone onstage.)

If Lyubov is doing nothing but these solitary, reflective acts, why is she the protagonist of the play? She *isn't.*

The play has no protagonist. It has a couple of squad leaders. The reason it has no protagonist is that it has no through-action. It has one scene repeated by various couples.

To continue: Lyubov's brother is Gaev. He is a perennial bachelor, and is referred to several times in the text as an old lady. What does *he* want? Not much of anything. Yes, he cries at the end when the orchard is cut down. But he appears to be just as happy going to work in the bank and playing caroms as he is lounging around the morning room and playing caroms.

The other odd characters are Firs, the ancient butler, who is happy the mistress has returned, and Semyonov Pishtchik, a poor neighbor, who is always looking on the bright side.

He, Firs, and Gaev are local color. They are all celibate, and seen as somewhat doddering in different degrees. And they are all happy. Because they are not troubled by Sex. They are not involved in the play's one and oft-repeated action: to consummate, clarify, or rectify an unhappy sexual situation.

The cherry orchard and its imminent destruction is nothing other than an effective dramatic device.

The play is not "If you don't pay the mortgage I'll take your cow." It is "Kiss me quick because I'm dying of cancer."

The *obstacle* in the play does not grow out of, and does not even *refer* to the actions of the characters. The play works because it is a compilation of brilliant scenes.

I would guess — judging from its similarity to many of his short stories — that he wrote the scenes between the servant girl Dunyasha and Epihodov first. That perhaps sparked the idea of a scene between Dunyasha and the man *she* loves, Yasha, a footman just returned from Paris. Who did this fine footman return with? The mistress. *Et ensuite.*°

To continue this conceit: what did Chekhov do when he had two hours worth of scenes and thirteen characters running around a country house? He had, as any playwright has, three choices.

He could shelve the material as brilliant sketches; he could *examine* the material and attempt to discern any intrinsically dramatic through-action, and extrapolate the play out of *that*. . . .

To return: Chekhov has thirteen people stuck in a summer house. He has a lot of brilliant scenes. His third alternative is to come up with a pretext which will keep them in the same place and *talking* to each other for a while. This is one of the alternatives and dilemmas of the modern dramatist: "Gosh, this material is *fantastic*. What can I do to just keep the people in the house?"

One can have a piece of jewelry stolen, one can have a murder committed, one can have a snowstorm, one can have the car break down, one can have The Olde Estate due to be sold for debts in three weeks unless someone comes up with a good solution.

I picture Chekhov coming up with this pretext and saying, "Naaaa, they'll never go for it." I picture him watching rehearsals and *wincing* every time Lopahin says (as he says frequently): "Just remember, you have only three (two, one) weeks until the cherry orchard is to be sold." "Fine," he must have thought. "That's real playwriting. One doesn't see Horatio coming out every five minutes and saying, 'Don't forget, Hamlet, your uncle killed your dad and now he's sleeping with your Ma!' "

"Oh no," he must have thought, "I'll never get away with it." But he did, and left us a play we cherish.

Why do we cherish the play? Because it is about the struggle between the Old Values of the Russian Aristocracy and their loosening grasp on power? I think not. For, finally, a play is about — and is *only* about — the actions of its characters. We, as audience, understand a play not in terms of the superficial idiosyncrasies or social *states* of its characters (they, finally, *separate* us from the play), but only in terms of the *action* the characters are trying to accomplish. (Set *Hamlet* in Waukegan and it's still a great play.)

The enduring draw of *The Cherry Orchard* is not that it is set in a dying Czarist Russia or that it has rich folks and poor folks. We are drawn to the play because it speaks to our *subconscious* — which is what a play should do. And we subconsciously perceive and enjoy the reiterated action of this reiterated scene: two people at odds — each trying to fulfill his or her frustrated sexuality.

From an adaptation of *The Cherry Orchard*
by David Mamet

Et ensuite: And so on.

Considerations

1. How convincing do you find Mamet's argument that "Nobody in the play gives a damn about the cherry orchard"?

2. Read the discussion on psychological strategies for approaching literature (p. 1783) and write an essay that agrees or disagrees with Mamet's assertion that what the play is really about is "frustrated sexuality."

PETER BROOK (b. 1925)

On Chekhov's "Hypervital" Characters 1987

In Chekhov's work, each character has its own existence: not one of them resembles another, particularly in *The Cherry Orchard,* which presents a microcosm of the political tendencies of the time. There are those who believe in social transformations, others attached to a disappearing past. None of them can achieve satisfaction or plenitude, and seen from outside, their existences might well appear empty, senseless. But they all burn with intense desires. They are not disillusioned, quite the contrary: in their own ways, they are all searching for a better quality of life, emotionally and socially. Their drama is that society — the outside world — blocks their energy. The complexity of their behavior is not indicated in the words, it emerges from the mosaic construction of an infinite number of details. What is essential is to see that these are not plays about lethargic people. They are hypervital people in a lethargic world, forced to dramatize the minutest happening out of a passionate desire to live. They have not given up.

From *The Shifting Point*

Considerations

1. Choose a character from *The Cherry Orchard* and test Brook's assertion that Chekhov's characters are not "lethargic people" but "hypervital people." How is the "complexity" of the character you discuss revealed in "the mosaic construction of an infinite number of details" associated with the character?
2. Write an essay either supporting or refuting Brook's view that the characters in *The Cherry Orchard* "have not given up."

29. Experimental Trends in Drama

BEYOND REALISM

Realistic drama has remained popular throughout the twentieth century, but from its beginnings it has been continually challenged by nonrealistic modes of theater. By the end of the nineteenth century, playwrights reacting against realism began to develop a variety of new approaches to setting, action, and character. Instead of creating a slice of life onstage, modern experimental playwrights drew on purely theatrical devices, ranging from stark sets and ritualistic actions to symbolic characterizations and audience participation. In general, such devices were designed to jar audiences' expectations and to heighten their awareness that what appeared before them was indeed a theatrical production. A glimpse of some of the nonrealistic movements in drama suggests how the possibilities for affecting audiences have been broadened by experimental theater.

Symbolist drama rejected the realists' assumption that life can be understood objectively and scientifically. The symbolists emphasized a subjective, emotional response to life because they believed that ultimate realities can only be recognized intuitively. Since absolute truth cannot be directly perceived, symbolists such as the Belgian playwright Maurice Maeterlinck (1862–1949) sought to express spiritual truth through settings, characters, and actions that suggest a transcendent reality. Maeterlinck's most famous symbolist play, *Pelléas and Mélisande* (1892), is a story of love and vengeance that includes mysterious forebodings, symbolic objects, and unexplained powerful forces. The elements of the play make no attempt to create the texture of ordinary life.

Other playwrights — such as William Butler Yeats (1865–1939) in Ireland, Paul Claudel (1868–1955) in France, Leonid Andreyev (1871–1919) in Russia, and Federico García Lorca (1898–1936) in Spain — also used some of the techniques associated with symbolist plays, but the movement never enjoyed wide popularity because audiences often found the plays' action too vague and their language too cryptic. Nevertheless, symbolist drama had an important influence on the work of subsequent playwrights, such as Tennessee Williams's *The Glass Menagerie* (p. 1462) and Arthur Miller's *Death of a Salesman* (p. 1508); these dramatists effectively used symbols in plays that contain both realistic and nonrealistic qualities.

Another nonrealistic movement, known as ***expressionism,*** was popular from the end of World War I until the mid-1920s. Expressionist playwrights emphasized the internal lives of their characters and deliberately distorted reality by creating an outward manifestation of an inner state of being. The late plays of Swedish dramatist August Strindberg (1849–1912) anticipate expressionistic techniques. Strindberg's preface to *A Dream Play* (1902) reflects the impact that Freudian psychology would eventually have on the theater.

> The author has tried to imitate the disconnected but seemingly logical form of the dream. Anything may happen; everything is possible and probable. Time and space do not exist. On an insignificant background of reality, imagination designs and embroiders novel patterns: a medley of memories, experiences, free fancies, absurdities, and improvisations.

In such nonrealistic drama the action does not have to proceed chronologically because the playwright dramatizes the emotional life of the characters, which blends the past with the present rather than moving in a fixed linear way. This fluidity of development can be seen in the ***flashbacks*** of Williams's *The Glass Menagerie* and Miller's *Death of a Salesman.*

The ***epic theater*** of Bertolt Brecht is, like symbolism and expressionism, a long way from the realistic elements in Ibsen's *A Doll's House.* Brecht kept a distance between his characters and the audience. This strategy of alienation was designed to alert audiences to important social problems that might be overlooked if an individual's struggles became too emotionally absorbing. Brecht's drama, by casting new light on chronic human problems such as poverty, injustice, and war, was a means to convey hope and evidence that society could be changed for the better. Brecht called his drama "epic" to distinguish it from Aristotle's notion of drama. The episodic structure was designed to prevent the audience from being swept up in the action or losing themselves in an inevitable tragedy. Instead, Brecht wanted the audience to analyze the action and realize that certain consequences weren't inevitable but could be avoided. This distancing, the dramatization of societal issues, and the use of loosely connected scenes sometimes narrated by a kind of stage manager are the hallmarks of "epic" drama.

Epic theater revels in stylized theatricality. The major action in *The Caucasian Chalk Circle,* for example, consists of a play within a play. Brecht's dramas use suggestive rather than detailed settings, and their scenery and props are frequently changed as the audience watches. His actors make clear that they are pretending to be characters. They may speak or sing in verse, address the audience, or comment on issues with other characters who are not participants in the immediate action. In brief, Brecht's theater is keenly conscious of itself.

In contrast to this didactic theater, the ***theater of the absurd*** was a response to the twentieth century's loss of faith in reason, religion, and life itself. These doubts produced an approach to drama that emphasizes chaotic, irrational forces and portrays human beings as more the victims than the makers of their world.

Absurdists such as Samuel Beckett (b. 1906), French dramatist Eugène Ionesco (b. 1912), English playwright Harold Pinter (b. 1930), and American writer Edward Albee (b. 1928) employ a variety of approaches to drama, but they share some assumptions about what subjects are important. Absurdism challenges the belief that life is ordered and meaningful. Instead of positing traditional values that give human beings a sense of purpose in life, absurdists dramatize our inability to comprehend fully our identities and destinies. Unlike heroic characters such as Oedipus or Hamlet, who retain their dignity despite their defeats, the characters in absurdist dramas frequently seem pathetically comic as they drift from one destructive moment to the next. These ***antiheroes*** are often bewildered, ineffectual, deluded, and lost. If they learn anything, it is that the world isolates them in an existence devoid of God and absolute values.

The basic premise of absurdism — that life is meaningless — is often presented in a nonrealistic manner to disrupt our expectations. In a realistic play such as Ibsen's *A Doll's House,* characters act pretty much the way we believe people behave. The motivation of these characters and the plausibility of their actions are comprehensible, but in an absurdist drama we are confronted with characters who appear in a series of disconnected incidents that lead to deeper confusion. What would we make of Nora if Ibsen had her appear in the final act costumed as a doll? This would be not only bizarre but unacceptable in a realistic play. However, it could make dramatic sense in an absurdist adaptation that sought to dramatize Nora's loss of identity and dehumanization as a result of her marriage.

Nora's appearance as a doll would, of course, be laughably inconsistent with what we judge to be real or reasonable. And yet we might find ourselves sympathizing with her situation. Suppose that instead of slamming the door and leaving her husband in the final scene, Nora moved stiffly about the room costumed as a doll while Helmer complacently sipped sherry and read the evening paper. Such an ending would suggest that she had been defeated by the circumstances in her life. Her condition — being nothing more than someone's toy — would be both absurd and pathetic. If we laughed at this scene, we would do so because Nora's situation is grotesquely humorous, a parody of her assumptions, hopes, and expectations. This is the world of ***tragicomedy,*** where laughter and pain coexist and where there is neither the happy resolution that typifies comic plots nor the transformational suffering that brings clarification to the tragic hero. It is the world dramatized, for example, in the opening scene of Harold

Pinter's *The Dumb Waiter* when Ben tells Gus about an item he's read in the paper.

Ben: A man of eighty-seven wanted to cross the road. But there was a lot of traffic, see? He couldn't see how he was going to squeeze through. So he crawled under a lorry [truck].
Gus: He what?
Ben: He crawled under a lorry. A stationary lorry.
Gus: No?
Ben: The lorry started and ran over him.
Gus: Go on!
Ben: That's what it says here.
Gus: Get away.
Ben: It's enough to make you want to puke, isn't it?
Gus: Who advised him to do a thing like that?
Ben: A man of eighty-seven crawling under a lorry!
Gus: It's unbelievable.
Ben: It's down here in black and white.
Gus: Incredible.

As much as Gus finds the story difficult to believe and Ben is sickened by it, it is a fact that the old man was crushed under ridiculous circumstances. His death is unexpected, accidental, incomprehensible, and meaningless — except that what happened to the old man is, from an absurdist's perspective, really no different from what life has in store for all of us one way or the other.

An absurdist playwright may, as Pinter does, employ realistic settings and speech, but he or she goes beyond realistic conventions to challenge the rational assumptions we make about our lives. Pinter insists that "a play is not an essay." Background information, character motivation, action — nothing presented on an absurdist's stage is governed by the conventions of realism. The absurdists typically refuse to create the illusion of reality because there is, finally, no reality to imitate. If conversations in their plays are sometimes fragmented and seemingly inconsequential, the reason is that absurdists dramatize people's combined inability and unwillingness to communicate with one another. Indeed, Samuel Beckett's *Act without Words* contains no dialogue, and in his *Krapp's Last Tape* a single character addresses only his own tape-recorded voice. To some extent we must suspend common sense and logic if we are to appreciate the visions and voices in an absurdist play.

Although many other nonrealistic movements developed in the twentieth century, these four — symbolism, expressionism, epic theater, and the theater of the absurd — embrace the major differences between nonrealistic and realistic drama. The theater continually tests its own possibilities. In the 1960s and 1970s, for example, some acting companies in New York completely collapsed the usual distinctions between audience and actors. The Living Theater went even further by moving into the streets, where the actors and audiences engaged in dramatic political statements aimed at raising the social consciousness of people wherever they were. Some critics argued that this was not really theater but merely an exuberant kind of political rally. However, proponents of these productions — known as ***guerrilla theater*** — argued that protest drama is both politically and artistically valid. In any case, although today's playwrights seem considerably less inclined to take to the streets, there is a tolerance for a wide range of possible relationships between actors and audiences. Audiences (and readers) can expect symbolic characters, expressionistic settings, poetic language, monologues, and extreme actions in productions that also contain realistic elements. In *Route 1 & 9* (1981), a piece created by an experimental theater company called The Wooster Group, for example, audiences found themselves confronted with passages from Thornton Wilder's idealized version of America in *Our Town* that were coupled with a pornographic film and a black vaudeville act. This unlikely combination was used to comment on Wilder's conception of America in which issues of sex and race are largely ignored. Increasingly, experimental theater has cultivated an eclectic approach to drama, using a variety of media, cultures, playwrights, and even languages to enrich an audience's experience. Parts of Robert Wilson's *CIVIL warS* (1984) — a work never staged in its entirety in any one place — were performed in several countries, including France, Italy, and the United States, and drew upon different languages as well as cultures to evoke a wide range of experiences from history, literature, myths, and even dreams. The Album of Contemporary Plays in Chapter 30 attests to the traditions and innovations that contemporary dramatists have incorporated into their dramatic art.

KRAPP'S LAST TAPE

Samuel Beckett was born near Dublin to a middle-class Irish-Protestant family. After graduating from Trinity College, Dublin, in 1927, he studied in Paris, where he met James Joyce and was influenced by Joyce's innovative use of language. There Beckett began his own experiments in poetry and fiction. He returned to Ireland to teach at Trinity College and earned an M.A. in 1931, but he left teaching the following year to travel in Europe. He permanently settled in Paris in the late 1930s. During this period his publications included two volumes of poetry, *Whoroscope* (1930) and *Echo's Bones* (1935), a collection of stories, *More Pricks Than Kicks* (1934), and a novel, *Murphy* (1938).

During World War II, Beckett's work for the French resistance made it necessary for him to flee German-occupied France, but he returned to Paris at the end of the war and began writing the works that would earn him the Nobel Prize for literature in 1969. Writing mostly in French and translating his work into English later, Beckett produced both novels — *Molloy* (1951) *Malone Dies* (1951), *Watt* (1953), *The Unnamable* (1953), and *How It Is*

(1961) — and plays — *Waiting for Godot* (1952), *Endgame* (1957), *Krapp's Last Tape* (1958, first written in English), and *Happy Days* (1961).

These works are populated by characters who live meager, isolated existences that sometimes seem barely human. Yet their aspirations and desires are expressed in simple activities that are attempts to transcend the endless meaningless routines that make up their lives. In an illogical and absurdly comic world stripped of any lasting meaning, these characters appear in minimal settings, having little to say and even less to do.

Waiting for Godot, Beckett's most famous play, brought absurdist principles to popular audiences. Its seemingly pointless dialogue is spoken by two clownish vagabonds while they wait for a mysterious Mr. Godot, who never appears. The play has no clearly identifiable conflict; instead, the action tends to be random and repetitive. Nothing much happens, but there is tension nonetheless among strange characters who hope in an apparently hopeless world.

In *Krapp's Last Tape,* Beckett uses only one character onstage. The play is more than a monologue, however, because the protagonist engages in a kind of conversation with his own tape-recorded voice. Every year on his birthday Krapp has recorded his impressions of that year's events and methodically cataloged and indexed them. Krapp observes his sixty-ninth birthday by listening to portions of a tape he recorded thirty years earlier. Hence, there are two Krapps in the play: an elderly man and his younger self on tape. This device allows Beckett to present Krapp's relation to his past in an intriguing, complex manner; we witness a character thinking aloud with a part of himself he no longer knows. If the older Krapp appears strange to us, we should not overlook the fact that he is even stranger to himself.

SAMUEL BECKETT (1906–1989)

Krapp's Last Tape 1958

A Play in One Act

SCENE: *A late evening in the future.*

Krapp's den. Front center a small table, the two drawers of which open towards audience. Sitting at the table, facing front, i.e. across from the drawers, a wearish old man: Krapp.

Rusty black narrow trousers too short for him. Rusty black sleeveless waistcoat, four capacious pockets. Heavy silver watch and chain. Grimy white shirt open at neck, no collar. Surprising pair of dirty white boots, size ten at least, very narrow and pointed.

White face. Purple nose. Disordered gray hair. Unshaven.

Very near-sighted (but unspectacled). Hard of hearing.

Cracked voice. Distinctive intonation.

Laborious walk.

On the table a tape-recorder with microphone and a number of cardboard boxes containing reels of recorded tapes.

Table and immediately adjacent area in strong white light. Rest of stage in darkness.

Krapp remains a moment motionless, heaves a great sigh, looks at his watch, fumbles in his pockets, takes out an envelope, puts it back, fumbles, takes out a small bunch of keys, raises it to his eyes, chooses a key, gets up and moves to front of table. He stoops, unlocks first drawer, peers into it, feels about inside it, takes out a reel of tape, peers at it, puts it back, locks drawer, unlocks second drawer, peers into it, feels about inside it, takes out a large banana, peers at it, locks drawer, puts keys back in his pocket. He turns, advances to edge of stage, halts, strokes banana, peels it, drops skin at his feet, puts end of banana in his mouth and remains motionless, staring vacuously before him. Finally he bites off the end, turns aside, and begins pacing to and fro at edge of stage, in the light, i.e. not more than four or five paces either way, meditatively eating banana. He treads on skin, slips, nearly falls, recovers himself, stoops and peers at skin and finally pushes it, still stooping, with his foot over the edge of stage into pit. He resumes his pacing, finishes banana, returns to table, sits down, remains a moment motionless, heaves a great sigh, takes keys from his pockets, raises them to his eyes, chooses key, gets up and moves to front of table, unlocks second drawer, takes out a second large banana, peers at it, locks drawer, puts back keys in his pocket, turns, advances to edge of stage, halts, strokes banana, peels it, tosses skin into pit, puts end of banana in his mouth, and remains motionless, staring vacuously before him. Finally he has an idea, puts banana in his waistcoat pocket, the end emerging, and goes with all the speed he can muster backstage into darkness. Ten seconds. Loud pop of cork. Fifteen seconds. He comes back into light carrying an old ledger and sits down at table. He lays ledger on table, wipes his mouth, wipes his hands on the front of his waistcoat, brings them smartly together and rubs them.

Krapp (briskly): Ah! *(He bends over ledger, turns the pages, finds the entry he wants, reads.)* Box . . . thrree . . . spool . . . five. *(He raises his head and stares front. With relish.)* Spool! *(Pause.)* Spooool! *(Happy smile. Pause. He bends over table, starts peering and poking at the boxes.)* Box . . . thrree . . . thrree . . . four . . . two . . . *(with surprise)* nine! good God! . . . seven . . . ah! the little rascal! *(He takes up box, peers at it.)* Box thrree. *(He lays it on table, opens it, and peers at spools inside.)* Spool . . . *(he peers at ledger)* . . . five *(he peers at spools)* . . . five . . . five! . . . ah! the little scoundrel! *(He takes out a spool, peers at it.)* Spool five. *(He lays it on table, closes box three, puts it back with the others, takes up the spool.)* Box thrree, spool five. *(He bends over the machine, looks up. With relish.)* Spooool! *(Happy smile. He bends, loads spool on machine, rubs his hands.)* Ah! *(He peers at ledger, reads entry at foot of page.)* Mother at rest at last . . . Hm . . . The black ball . . . *(He raises his head, stares blankly front. Puzzled.)* Black ball? . . . *(He peers again at ledger, reads.)* The dark nurse . . . *(He raises his head, broods, peers again at ledger, reads.)* Slight improvement in bowel condition . . . Hm . . . Memorable . . . what? *(He peers closer.)* Equinox, memorable equinox. *(He raises his head, stares blankly front. Puzzled.)* Memorable equinox? . . . *(Pause. He shrugs his shoulders, peers again at ledger, reads.)* Farewell to — *(he turns the page)* — love.

He raises his head, broods, bends over machine, switches on, and assumes listening posture; i.e. leaning forward, elbows on table, hand cupping ear towards machine, face front.

Tape (strong voice, rather pompous, clearly Krapp's at a much earlier time): Thirty-nine today, sound as a — *(Settling himself more comfortably he knocks one of the boxes off the table, curses, switches off, sweeps boxes and ledger violently to the ground, winds tape back to beginning, switches on, resumes posture.)* Thirty-nine today, sound as a bell, apart from my old weakness, and intellectually I have now every reason to suspect at the . . . *(hesitates)* . . . crest of the wave — or thereabouts. Celebrated the awful occasion, as in recent years, quietly at the Winehouse. Not a soul. Sat before the fire with closed eyes, separating the grain from the husks. Jotted down a few notes, on the back of an envelope. Good to be back in my den, in my old rags. Have just eaten I regret to say three bananas and only with difficulty refrained from a fourth. Fatal things for a man with my condition. *(Vehemently.)* Cut 'em out! *(Pause.)* The new light above my table is a great improvement. With all this darkness round me I feel less alone. *(Pause.)* In a way. *(Pause.)* I love to get up and move about in it, then back here to . . . *(hesitates)* . . . me. *(Pause.)* Krapp.

Pause.

The grain, now what I wonder do I mean by that, I mean . . . *(hesitates)* . . . I suppose I mean those things worth having when all the dust has — when all *my* dust has settled. I close my eyes and try and imagine them.

Pause. Krapp closes his eyes briefly.

Extraordinary silence this evening, I strain my ears and do not hear a sound. Old Miss McGlome always sings at this hour. But not tonight. Songs of her girlhood, she says. Hard to think of her as a girl. Wonderful woman though. Connaught, I fancy. *(Pause.)* Shall I sing when I am her age, if I ever am? No. *(Pause.)* Did I sing as a boy? No. *(Pause.)* Did I ever sing? No.

Pause.

Just been listening to an old year, passages at random. I did not check in the book, but it must be at least ten or twelve years ago. At that time I think I was still living on and off with Bianca in Kedar Street. Well out of that, Jesus yes! Hopeless business. *(Pause.)* Not much about her, apart from a tribute to her eyes. Very warm. I suddenly saw them again. *(Pause.)* Incomparable! *(Pause.)* Ah well . . . *(Pause.)* These old P.M.s are gruesome, but I often find them — *(Krapp switches off, broods, switches on)* — a help before embarking on a new . . . *(hesitates)* . . . retrospect. Hard to believe I was ever that young whelp. The voice! Jesus! And the aspirations! *(Brief laugh in which Krapp joins.)* And the resolutions! *(Brief laugh in which Krapp joins.)* To drink less, in particular. *(Brief laugh of Krapp alone.)* Statistics. Seventeen hundred hours, out of the preceding eight thousand odd, consumed on licensed premises alone. More than 20%, say 40% of his waking life. *(Pause.)* Plans for a less . . . *(hesitates)* . . . engrossing sexual life. Last illness of his father. Flagging pursuit of happiness. Unattainable laxation. Sneers at what he calls his youth and thanks to God that it's over. *(Pause.)* False ring there. *(Pause.)* Shadows of the opus . . . magnum. Closing with a — *(brief laugh)* — yelp to Providence. *(Prolonged laugh in which Krapp joins.)* What remains of all that misery? A girl in a shabby green coat, on a railway-station platform? No?

Pause.

When I look —

Krapp switches off, broods, looks at his watch, gets up, goes backstage into darkness. Ten seconds. Pop of cork. Ten seconds. Second cork. Ten seconds. Third cork. Ten seconds. Brief burst of quavering song.

Krapp (sings): Now the day is over,
Night is drawing nigh-igh,
Shadows —°

Fit of coughing. He comes back into light, sits down, wipes his mouth, switches on, resumes his listening posture.

Tape: — back on the year that is gone, with what I hope is perhaps a glint of the old eye to come, there is of course the house on the canal where mother lay a-dying, in the late autumn, after her long viduity° *(Krapp gives a start),* and the — *(Krapp switches off, winds back tape a little, bends his ear closer to machine, switches on)* — a — dying, after her long viduity, and the —

Krapp switches off, raises his head, stares blankly before him. His lips move in the syllables of "viduity." No sound. He gets up, goes backstage into darkness, comes back with an enormous dictionary, lays it on table, sits down and looks up the word.

Krapp (reading from dictionary): State — or condition of being — or remaining — a widow — or widower. *(Looks up. Puzzled.)* Being — or remaining? . . . *(Pause. He peers again at dictionary. Reading.)* "Deep weeds of viduity" . . . Also of an animal, especially a bird . . . the vidua or weaver-bird . . . Black plumage of male . . . *(He looks up. With relish.)* The vidua-bird!

Pause. He closes dictionary, switches on, resumes listening posture.

Tape: — bench by the weir from where I could see her window. There I sat, in the biting wind, wishing she were gone. *(Pause.)* Hardly a soul, just a few regulars, nursemaids, infants, old men, dogs. I got to know them quite well — oh by appearance of course I mean! One dark young beauty I recollect particularly, all white and starch, incomparable bosom, with a big black hooded perambulator, most funereal thing. Whenever I looked in her direction she had her eyes on me. And yet when I was bold enough to speak to her — not having been introduced — she threatened to call a policeman. As

Now . . . Shadows: From the hymn "Now the Day Is Over" by Sabine Baring-Gould (1834–1924), author of "Onward, Christian Soldiers."
viduity: Widowhood.

if I had designs on her virtue! *(Laugh. Pause.)* The face she had! The eyes! Like . . . *(hesitates)* . . . chrysolite! *(Pause.)* Ah well . . . *(Pause.)* I was there when — *(Krapp switches off, broods, switches on again)* — the blind went down, one of those dirty brown roller affairs, throwing a ball for a little white dog, as chance would have it. I happened to look up and there it was. All over and done with, at last. I sat on for a few moments with the ball in my hand and the dog yelping and pawing at me. *(Pause.)* Moments. Her moments, my moments. *(Pause.)* The dog's moments. *(Pause.)* In the end I held it out to him and he took it in his mouth, gently, gently. A small, old, black, hard, solid rubber ball. *(Pause.)* I shall feel it, in my hand, until my dying day. *(Pause.)* I might have kept it. *(Pause.)* But I gave it to the dog.

Pause.

Ah well . . .

Pause.

Spiritually a year of profound gloom and indigence until that memorable night in March, at the end of the jetty, in the howling wind, never to be forgotten, when suddenly I saw the whole thing. The vision, at last. This I fancy is what I have chiefly to record this evening, against the day when my work will be done and perhaps no place left in my memory, warm or cold, for the miracle that . . . *(hesitates)* . . . for the fire that set it alight. What I suddenly saw then was this, that the belief I had been going on all my life, namely — *(Krapp switches off impatiently, winds tape forward, switches on again)* — great granite rocks the foam flying up in the light of the lighthouse and the wind-gauge spinning like a propellor, clear to me at last that the dark I have always struggled to keep under is in reality my most — *(Krapp curses, switches off, winds tape forward, switches on again)* — unshatterable association until my dissolution of storm and night with the light of the understanding and the fire — *(Krapp curses louder, switches off, winds tape forward, switches on again)* — my face in her breasts and my hand on her. We lay there without moving. But under us all moved, and moved us, gently, up and down, and from side to side.

Pause.

Past midnight. Never knew such silence. The earth might be uninhabited.

Pause.

Here I end —

Krapp switches off, winds tape back, switches on again.

— upper lake, with the punt, bathed off the bank, then pushed out into the stream and drifted. She lay stretched out on the floorboards with her hands under her head and her eyes closed. Sun blazing down, bit of a breeze, water nice and lively. I noticed a scratch on her thigh and asked her how she came by it. Picking gooseberries, she said. I said again I thought it was hopeless and no good going on, and she agreed, without opening her eyes. *(Pause.)* I asked her to look at me and after a few moments — *(pause)* — after a few moments she did, but the eyes just slits, because of the glare. I bent over her to get them in the shadow and they opened. *(Pause. Low.)* Let me in. *(Pause.)* We drifted in among the flags and stuck. The way they went down, sighing, before the stem! *(Pause.)* I lay down across her with my face in her breasts and my hand on her. We lay there without moving. But under us all moved, and moved us, gently, up and down, and from side to side.

Pause.

Past midnight. Never knew —

Krapp switches off, broods. Finally he fumbles in his pockets, encounters the banana, takes it out, peers at it, puts it back, fumbles, brings out the envelope, fumbles, puts back envelope, looks at his watch, gets up and goes backstage into darkness. Ten seconds. Sound of bottle against glass, then brief siphon. Ten seconds. Bottle against glass alone. Ten seconds. He comes back a little unsteadily into light, goes to front of table, takes out keys, raises them to his eyes, chooses key, unlocks first drawer, peers into it, feels about inside, takes out reel, peers at it, locks drawer, puts keys back in his pocket, goes and sits down, takes reel off machine, lays it on dictionary, loads virgin reel on machine, takes envelope from his pocket, consults back of it, lays it on table, switches on, clears his throat, and begins to record.

Krapp: Just been listening to that stupid bastard I took myself for thirty years ago, hard to believe I was ever as bad as that. Thank God that's all done with anyway. *(Pause.)* The eyes she had! *(Broods, realizes he is recording silence, switches off, broods. Finally.)* Everything there, everything, all the — *(Realizes this is not being recorded, switches on.)* Everything there, everything on this old muckball, all the light and dark and famine and feasting of . . . *(hesitates)* . . . the ages! *(In a shout.)* Yes! *(Pause.)* Let that go! Jesus! Take his mind off his homework! Jesus! *(Pause. Weary.)* Ah well, maybe he was right. *(Pause.)* Maybe he was right. *(Broods. Realizes. Switches off. Consults envelope.)* Pah! *(Crumples it and throws it away. Broods. Switches on.)* Nothing to say, not a squeak. What's a year now? The sour cud and the iron stool. *(Pause.)* Revelled in the word spool. *(With relish.)* Spooool! Happiest moment of the past half million. *(Pause.)* Seventeen copies sold, of which eleven at trade price to free circulating libraries beyond the seas. Getting known. *(Pause.)* One pound six and something, eight I have little doubt. *(Pause.)* Crawled out once or twice, before the summer was cold. Sat shivering in the park, drowned in dreams and burning to be gone. Not a soul. *(Pause.)* Last fancies. *(Vehemently.)* Keep 'em under! *(Pause.)* Scalded the eyes out of me reading *Effie* again, a page a day, with tears again. Effie . . . *(Pause.)* Could have been happy with her, up there on the Baltic, and the pines, and the dunes. *(Pause.)* Could I? *(Pause.)* And she? *(Pause.)* Pah! *(Pause.)* Fanny came in a couple of times. Bony old ghost of a whore. Couldn't do much, but I suppose better than a kick in the crutch. The last time wasn't so bad. How do you manage it, she said, at your age? I told her I'd been saving up for her all my life. *(Pause.)* Went to Vespers once, like when I was in short trousers. *(Pause. Sings.)*

Now the day is over.
Night is drawing nigh-igh,

Shadows — *(coughing, then almost inaudible)* — of the evening
Steal across the sky.

(Gasping.) Went to sleep and fell off the pew. *(Pause.)* Sometimes wondered in the night if a last effort mightn't — *(Pause.)* Ah finish your booze now and get to your bed. Go on with this drivel in the morning. Or leave it at that. *(Pause.)* Leave it at that. *(Pause.)* Lie propped up in the dark — and wander. Be again in the dingle on a Christmas Eve, gathering holly, the red-berried. *(Pause.)* Be again on Croghan on a Sunday morning, in the haze, with the bitch, stop and listen to the bells. *(Pause.)* And so on. *(Pause.)* Be again, be again. *(Pause.)* All that old misery. *(Pause.)* Once wasn't enough for you. *(Pause.)* Lie down across her.

Long pause. He suddenly bends over machine, switches off, wrenches off tape, throws it away, puts on the other, winds it forward to the passage he wants, switches on, listens staring front.

Tape: — gooseberries, she said. I said again I thought it was hopeless and no good going on, and she agreed, without opening her eyes. *(Pause.)* I asked her to look at me and after a few moments — *(pause)* — after a few moments she did, but the eyes just slits, because of the glare. I bent over her to get them in the shadow and they opened. *(Pause. Low.)* Let me in. *(Pause.)* We drifted in among the flags and stuck. The way they went down, sighing, before the stem! *(Pause.)* I lay down across her with my face in her breasts and my hand on her. We lay there without moving. But under us all moved, and moved us, gently, up and down, and from side to side.

Pause. Krapp's lips move. No sound.

Past midnight. Never knew such silence. The earth might be uninhabited.

Pause.

Here I end this reel. Box — *(pause)* — three, spool — *(pause)* — five. *(Pause.)* Perhaps my best years are gone. When there was a chance of happiness. But I wouldn't want them back. Not with the fire in me now. No, I wouldn't want them back.

Krapp motionless staring before him. The tape runs on in silence.

Curtain

Considerations

1. Why do you think the play is set in "a late evening in the future" rather than the present?
2. What does Krapp's physical description reveal about him?
3. Why does Krapp make tape recordings? How does he use them?
4. What is the effect of the many pauses in the play?
5. What are Krapp's attitudes toward his earlier perceptions about life? Compare and contrast the sixty-nine-year-old Krapp with the thirty-nine-year-old on the tape.

6. What career hopes did the younger Krapp have? How do you know whether he was successful?
7. How does Krapp, in retrospect, seem to feel about his life?
8. Although Krapp is obviously not a conventional dramatic hero, is there anything heroic about what he says or does? How do you respond to him?
9. What do you make of the play's title? A student once suggested that if the play were to have a subtitle, Beckett could have used the heading of one of Krapp's ledger entries: "Farewell to love." Explain whether this proposed subtitle reflects the play's major concerns.
10. Do you think the sixty-nine-year-old Krapp changes or develops during the play? In the final scene, how does he act differently from the way he behaved in the opening scene?

Connections

1. Write an essay in which you explore some important similarities or differences between Krapp and Willy Loman in Arthur Miller's *Death of a Salesman* (p. 1508) or the narrator in Robert Frost's "The Road Not Taken" (p. 711).
2. Compare and contrast the use of tape recorders in *Krapp's Last Tape* and David Henry Hwang's *M. Butterfly* (p. 1707). Do you think the tape recorders heighten or lessen the dramatic effects of each play?
3. Discuss this assessment of Chekhov and Beckett by Peter Brook *(The Shifting Point):* "With Chekhov, periods, commas, points of suspension, are all of a fundamental importance, as fundamental as the 'pauses' precisely indicated by Beckett. If one fails to observe them, one loses the rhythm and tensions of the play."

PERSPECTIVE

MARTIN ESSLIN (b. 1918)
On the Theater of the Absurd 1961

Concerned as it is with the ultimate realities of the human condition, the relatively few fundamental problems of life and death, isolation and communication, the Theater of the Absurd, however grotesque, frivolous, and irreverent it may appear, represents a return to the original, religious function of the theater — the confrontation of man with the spheres of myth and religious reality. Like ancient Greek tragedy and the medieval mystery plays and baroque allegories, the Theater of the Absurd is intent on making its audience aware of man's precarious and mysterious position in the universe.

The difference is merely that in ancient Greek tragedy — and comedy — as well as in the medieval mystery play and the baroque *auto sacramental,* the ultimate realities concerned were generally known and universally accepted metaphysical systems, while the Theater of the Absurd expresses the absence of any such generally accepted cosmic system of values. Hence, much more modestly, the Theater of the Absurd makes no pretense at explaining the ways of God to man. It can merely present, in anxiety or with derision, an individual human being's intuition of the ultimate realities as he experiences them; the fruits of one man's descent into the depths of his personality, his dreams, fantasies, and nightmares.

While former attempts at confronting man with the ultimate realities of his condition projected a coherent and generally recognized version of the truth, the Theater of the Absurd merely communicates one poet's most intimate and personal intuition of the human situation, his own *sense of being,* his individual vision of the world. This is the *subject matter* of the Theater of the Absurd, and it determines its *form,* which must, of necessity, represent a convention of the stage basically different from the "realistic" theater of our time.

As the Theater of the Absurd is not concerned with conveying information or presenting the problems or destinies of characters that exist outside the author's inner world, as it does not expound a thesis or debate ideological propositions, it is not concerned with the representation of events, the narration of the fate or the adventures of characters, but instead with the presentation of one individual's basic situation. It is a theater of situation as against a theater of events in sequence, and therefore it uses a language based on patterns of concrete images rather than argument and discursive speech. And since it is trying to present a sense of being, it can neither investigate nor solve problems of conduct or morals.

From *The Theatre of the Absurd*

Considerations

1. What does Esslin see as the essential difference between the theater of the absurd and Greek or medieval theaters in terms of their treatment of "ultimate realities"?
2. To what extent does Esslin's description of the theater of the absurd apply to *Krapp's Last Tape*?
3. Here's one to stretch your imagination: Take Krapp's "situation" and write a summary of how you think Sophocles, Shakespeare, or Ibsen might have developed it into a play. Consider, for example, what the focus of the conflict would be and how the story would end.

THE DUMB WAITER

Harold Pinter, one of Britain's most important contemporary playwrights, was born in East London to working-class parents. After studying briefly at the Royal Academy of Dramatic Art, he acted in a touring repertory company from 1949 to 1957. He wrote his first play, *The Room,* in 1957, the same year he wrote *The Birthday Party* and *The Dumb Waiter* (not produced until 1959). Pinter's first commercial success was *The Caretaker* (1960). He has acted, directed, and written for radio, television, film, and the stage. His numerous plays include *A Slight Ache* (1959), *A Night Out* (1960), *The Dwarfs* (1960), *The Homecoming* (1965), *No Man's Land* (1975), and *Betrayal* (1978). His successes have been marked by many theater, television, and film awards.

Although Pinter's plays seem realistic on the surface, they typically turn out to be mysteriously ambiguous and even bizarre. His characters speak and act naturally — the way Ibsen's or Chekhov's might — but their behavior often seems unmotivated as they express deep emotions in highly charged domestic settings that usually consist of a single room.

For example, in *The Homecoming,* one of Pinter's most highly regarded plays, the action is set in a rundown house in London where an all-male family consisting of Max, the father of Lenny, a pimp, and Joey, a demolition worker by day and boxer by night, live together with Max's brother. These characters continually argue and viciously insult each other. Soon a third brother, Teddy, a philosophy professor in America who had left years before, returns with his wife Ruth for a surprise visit. When Max greets Teddy, he shouts, "Who asked you to bring tarts in here?" Ruth is not only verbally assaulted but also subjected to Lenny's attempts to dominate and seduce her. Finally Ruth is seen lying on the sofa with Joey as her philosophical husband looks on. The family proposes that she stay on at the house after Teddy returns to America; she will earn her keep through prostitution when she is not busy with the family. The play ends with Teddy departing and Ruth remaining behind to service the multiple needs of the family.

Characters in Pinter's plays frequently defy rational explanations; their identities shift, their obscure pasts somehow intrude on the present, and they engage in alternately humorous and terrifying conversations filled with troubled meanings. His plays appear direct and simple, but beneath their realistic texture are subtle designs that disrupt conventional expectations.

In *The Dumb Waiter,* while two men wait in a basement room for instructions from their boss, they engage in what sounds like aimless, disconnected conversation about topics ranging from newspaper items to a broken toilet. Suddenly, a service elevator in the wall, a dumb waiter, clatters down with orders that are as surprising as they are mysteriously menacing.

HAROLD PINTER (b. 1930)

The Dumb Waiter 1957

SCENE: *A basement room. Two beds, flat against the back wall. A serving hatch, closed, between the beds. A door to the kitchen and lavatory, left. A door to a passage, right.*

Ben is lying on a bed, left, reading a paper. Gus is sitting on a bed, right, tying his shoelaces, with difficulty. Both are dressed in shirts, trousers, and braces.

Silence.

Gus ties his laces, rises, yawns, and begins to walk slowly to the door, left. He stops, looks down, and shakes his foot.

Ben lowers his paper and watches him. Gus kneels and unties his shoelace and slowly takes off the shoe. He looks inside it and brings out a flattened matchbox. He shakes it and examines it. Their eyes meet. Ben rattles his paper and reads. Gus puts the matchbox in his pocket and bends down to put on his shoe. He ties his lace, with difficulty. Ben lowers his paper and watches him. Gus walks to the door, left, stops, and shakes the other foot. He kneels, unties his shoelace, and slowly takes off the shoe. He looks inside it and brings out a flattened cigarette packet. He shakes it and examines it. Their eyes meet. Ben rattles his paper and reads. Gus puts the packet in his pocket, bends down, puts on his shoe, and ties the lace.

He wanders off, left.

Ben slams the paper down on the bed and glares after him. He picks up the paper and lies on his back, reading.

Silence.

A lavatory chain is pulled twice, off left, but the lavatory does not flush.

Silence.

Gus re-enters, left, and halts at the door, scratching his head.

Ben slams down the paper.

Ben: Kaw!

He picks up the paper.

What about this? Listen to this!

He refers to the paper.

A man of eighty-seven wanted to cross the road. But there was a lot of traffic, see? He couldn't see how he was going to squeeze through. So he crawled under a lorry.

Gus: He what?

Ben: He crawled under a lorry.° A stationary lorry.

Gus: No?

Ben: The lorry started and ran over him.

Gus: Go on!

Ben: That's what it says here.

Gus: Get away.

Ben: It's enough to make you want to puke, isn't it?

Gus: Who advised him to do a thing like that?

Ben: A man of eighty-seven crawling under a lorry!

Gus: It's unbelievable.

Ben: It's down here in black and white.

Gus: Incredible.

Silence.

Gus shakes his head and exits. Ben lies back and reads.

The lavatory chain is pulled once off left, but the lavatory does not flush.

Ben whistles at an item in the paper.

Gus re-enters.

I want to ask you something.

Ben: What are you doing out there?

Gus: Well, I was just —

lorry: Truck.

Ben: What about the tea?
Gus: I'm just going to make it.
Ben: Well, go on, make it.
Gus: Yes, I will. *(He sits in a chair. Ruminatively.)* He's laid on some very nice crockery this time, I'll say that. It's sort of striped. There's a white stripe.

Ben reads.

It's very nice. I'll say that.

Ben turns the page.

You know, sort of round the cup. Round the rim. All the rest of it's black, you see. Then the saucer's black, except for right in the middle, where the cup goes, where it's white.

Ben reads.

Then the plates are the same, you see. Only they've got a black stripe — the plates — right across the middle. Yes, I'm quite taken with the crockery.
Ben (still reading): What do you want plates for? You're not going to eat.
Gus: I've brought a few biscuits.
Ben: Well, you'd better eat them quick.
Gus: I always bring a few biscuits. Or a pie. You know I can't drink tea without anything to eat.
Ben: Well, make the tea then, will you? Time's getting on.

Gus brings out the flattened cigarette packet and examines it.

Gus: You got any cigarettes? I think I've run out.

He throws the packet high up and leans forward to catch it.

I hope it won't be a long job, this one.

Aiming carefully, he flips the packet under his bed.

Oh, I wanted to ask you something.
Ben (slamming his paper down): Kaw!
Gus: What's that?
Ben: A child of eight killed a cat!
Gus: Get away.
Ben: It's a fact. What about that, eh? A child of eight killing a cat!
Gus: How did he do it?
Ben: It was a girl.
Gus: How did she do it?
Ben: She —

He picks up the paper and studies it.

It doesn't say.
Gus: Why not?
Ben: Wait a minute. It just says — Her brother, aged eleven, viewed the incident from the toolshed.
Gus: Go on!
Ben: That's bloody ridiculous.

Pause.

Gus: I bet he did it.
Ben: Who?
Gus: The brother.
Ben: I think you're right.

Pause.

(Slamming down the paper.) What about that, eh? A kid of eleven killing a cat and blaming it on his little sister of eight! It's enough to —

He breaks off in disgust and seizes the paper. Gus rises.

Gus: What time is he getting in touch?

Ben reads.

What time is he getting in touch?
Ben: What's the matter with you? It could be any time. Any time.
Gus (moves to the foot of Ben's bed): Well, I was going to ask you something.
Ben: What?
Gus: Have you noticed the time that tank takes to fill?
Ben: What tank?
Gus: In the lavatory.
Ben: No. Does it?
Gus: Terrible.
Ben: Well, what about it?
Gus: What do you think's the matter with it?
Ben: Nothing.
Gus: Nothing?
Ben: It's got a deficient ballcock, that's all.
Gus: A deficient what?
Ben: Ballcock.
Gus: No? Really?
Ben: That's what I should say.
Gus: Go on! That didn't occur to me.

Gus wanders to his bed and presses the mattress.

I didn't have a very restful sleep today, did you? It's not much of a bed. I could have done with another blanket too. *(He catches sight of a picture on the wall.)* Hello, what's this? *(Peering at it.)* "The First Eleven."° Cricketers. You seen this, Ben?
Ben (reading): What?
Gus: The first eleven.
Ben: What?
Gus: There's a photo here of the first eleven.
Ben: What first eleven?
Gus (studying the photo): It doesn't say.
Ben: What about that tea?
Gus: They all look a bit old to me.

"The First Eleven": A cricket team.

Gus wanders downstage, looks out front, then all about the room.

I wouldn't like to live in this dump. I wouldn't mind if you had a window, you could see what it looked like outside.

Ben: What do you want a window for?

Gus: Well, I like to have a bit of a view, Ben. It wiles away the time.

He walks about the room.

I mean, you come into a place when it's still dark, you come into a room you've never seen before, you sleep all day, you do your job, and then you go away in the night again.

Pause.

I like to get a look at the scenery. You never get the chance in this job.

Ben: You get your holidays, don't you?

Gus: Only a fortnight.

Ben (lowering the paper): You kill me. Anyone would think you're working every day. How often do we do a job? Once a week? What are you complaining about?

Gus: Yes, but we've got to be on tap though, haven't we? You can't move out of the house in case a call comes.

Ben: You know what your trouble is?

Gus: What?

Ben: You haven't got any interests.

Gus: I've got interests.

Ben: What? Tell me one of your interests.

Pause.

Gus: I've got interests.

Ben: Look at me. What have I got?

Gus: I don't know. What?

Ben: I've got my woodwork. I've got my model boats. Have you ever seen me idle? I'm never idle. I know how to occupy my time, to its best advantage. Then when a call comes, I'm ready.

Gus: Don't you ever get a bit fed up?

Ben: Fed up? What with?

Silence.

Ben reads. Gus feels in the pocket of his jacket, which hangs on the bed.

Gus: You got any cigarettes? I've run out.

The lavatory flushes off left.

There she goes.

Gus sits on his bed.

No, I mean, I say the crockery's good. It is. It's very nice. But that's about all I can say for this place. It's worse than the last one. Remember that last place we were in? Last time, where was it? At least there was a wireless there. No, honest. He doesn't seem to bother much about our comfort these days.

Ben: When are you going to stop jabbering?

Gus: You'd get rheumatism in a place like this, if you stay long.

Ben: We're not staying long. Make the tea, will you? We'll be on the job in a minute.

Gus picks up a small bag by his bed and brings out a packet of tea. He examines it and looks up.

Gus: Eh, I've been meaning to ask you.

Ben: What the hell is it now?

Gus: Why did you stop the car this morning, in the middle of that road?

Ben (lowering the paper): I thought you were asleep.

Gus: I was, but I woke up when you stopped. You did stop, didn't you?

Pause.

In the middle of that road. It was still dark, don't you remember? I looked out. It was all misty. I thought perhaps you wanted to kip,° but you were sitting up dead straight, like you were waiting for something.

Ben: I wasn't waiting for anything.

Gus: I must have fallen asleep again. What was all that about then? Why did you stop?

Ben (picking up the paper): We were too early.

Gus: Early? *(He rises.)* What do you mean? We got the call, didn't we, saying we were to start right away. We did. We shoved out on the dot. So how could we be too early?

Ben (quietly): Who took the call, me or you?

Gus: You.

Ben: We were too early.

Gus: Too early for what?

Pause.

You mean someone had to get out before we got in?

He examines the bedclothes.

I thought these sheets didn't look too bright. I thought they ponged° a bit. I was too tired to notice when I got in this morning. Eh, that's taking a bit of a liberty, isn't it? I don't want to share my bed-sheets. I told you things were going down the drain. I mean, we've always had clean sheets laid on up till now. I've noticed it.

Ben: How do you know those sheets weren't clean?

Gus: What do you mean?

Ben: How do you know they weren't clean? You've spent the whole day in them, haven't you?

Gus: What, you mean it might be my pong? *(He sniffs sheets.)* Yes. *(He sits slowly on bed.)* It could be my pong, I suppose. It's difficult to tell. I don't really know what I pong like, that's the trouble.

kip: Nap.
ponged: Smelled.

Ben (referring to the paper): Kaw!
Gus: Eh, Ben.
Ben: Kaw!
Gus: Ben.
Ben: What?
Gus: What town are we in? I've forgotten.
Ben: I've told you. Birmingham.
Gus: Go on!

He looks with interest about the room.

That's in the Midlands. The second biggest city in Great Britain. I'd never have guessed.

He snaps his fingers.

Eh, it's Friday today, isn't it? It'll be Saturday tomorrow.
Ben: What about it?
Gus (excited): We could go and watch the Villa.°
Ben: They're playing away.
Gus: No, are they? Caarr! What a pity.
Ben: Anyway, there's no time. We've got to get straight back.
Gus: Well, we have done in the past, haven't we? Stayed over and watched a game, haven't we? For a bit of relaxation.
Ben: Things have tightened up, mate. They've tightened up.

Gus chuckles to himself.

Gus: I saw the Villa get beat in a cup tie once. Who was it against now? White shirts. It was one-all at half-time. I'll never forget it. Their opponents won by a penalty. Talk about drama. Yes, it was a disputed penalty. Disputed. They got beat two-one, anyway, because of it. You were there yourself.
Ben: Not me.
Gus: Yes, you were there. Don't you remember that disputed penalty?
Ben: No.
Gus: He went down just inside the area. Then they said he was just acting. I didn't think the other bloke touched him myself. But the referee had the ball on the spot.
Ben: Didn't touch him! What are you talking about? He laid him out flat!
Gus: Not the Villa. The Villa don't play that sort of game.
Ben: Get out of it.

Pause.

Gus: Eh, that must have been here, in Birmingham.
Ben: What must?
Gus: The Villa. That must have been here.
Ben: They were playing away.
Gus: Because you know who the other team was? It was the Spurs. It was Tottenham Hotspur.
Ben: Well, what about it?
Gus: We've never done a job in Tottenham.

Villa: A soccer team.

Ben: How do you know?
Gus: I'd remember Tottenham.

Ben turns on his bed to look at him.

Ben: Don't make me laugh, will you?

Ben turns back and reads. Gus yawns and speaks through his yawn.

Gus: When's he going to get in touch?

Pause.

Yes, I'd like to see another football match. I've always been an ardent football fan. Here, what about coming to see the Spurs tomorrow?
Ben (tonelessly): They're playing away.
Gus: Who are?
Ben: The Spurs.
Gus: Then they might be playing here.
Ben: Don't be silly.
Gus: If they're playing away they might be playing here. They might be playing the Villa.
Ben (tonelessly): But the Villa are playing away.

Pause. An envelope slides under the door, right. Gus sees it. He stands, looking at it.

Gus: Ben.
Ben: Away. They're all playing away.
Gus: Ben, look here.
Ben: What?
Gus: Look.

Ben turns his head and sees the envelope. He stands.

Ben: What's that?
Gus: I don't know.
Ben: Where did it come from?
Gus: Under the door.
Ben: Well, what is it?
Gus: I don't know.

They stare at it.

Ben: Pick it up.
Gus: What do you mean?
Ben: Pick it up!

Gus slowly moves towards it, bends and picks it up.

What is it?
Gus: An envelope.
Ben: Is there anything on it?
Gus: No.
Ben: Is it sealed?
Gus: Yes.

Ben: Open it.
Gus: What?
Ben: Open it!

Gus opens it and looks inside.

What's in it?

Gus empties twelve matches into his hand.

Gus: Matches.
Ben: Matches?
Gus: Yes.
Ben: Show it to me.

Gus passes the envelope. Ben examines it.

Nothing on it. Not a word.
Gus: That's funny, isn't it?
Ben: It came under the door?
Gus: Must have done.
Ben: Well, go on.
Gus: Go on where?
Ben: Open the door and see if you can catch anyone outside.
Gus: Who, me?
Ben: Go on!

Gus stares at him; puts the matches in his pocket, goes to his bed, and brings a revolver from under the pillow. He goes to the door, opens it, looks out, and shuts it.

Gus: No one.

He replaces the revolver.

Ben: What did you see?
Gus: Nothing.
Ben: They must have been pretty quick.

Gus takes the matches from pocket and looks at them.

Gus: Well, they'll come in handy.
Ben: Yes.
Gus: Won't they?
Ben: Yes, you're always running out, aren't you?
Gus: All the time.
Ben: Well, they'll come in handy then.
Gus: Yes.
Ben: Won't they?
Gus: Yes, I could do with them. I could do with them too.
Ben: You could, eh?
Gus: Yes.
Ben: Why?
Gus: We haven't got any.
Ben: Well, you've got some now, haven't you?

Gus: I can light the kettle now.
Ben: Yes, you're always cadging° matches. How many have you got there?
Gus: About a dozen.
Ben: Well, don't lose them. Red too. You don't even need a box.

Gus probes his ear with a match.

(Slapping his hand.) Don't waste them! Go on, go and light it.
Gus: Eh?
Ben: Go and light it.
Gus: Light what?
Ben: The kettle.
Gus: You mean the gas.
Ben: Who does?
Gus: You do.
Ben (his eyes narrowing): What do you mean, I mean the gas?
Gus: Well, that's what you mean, don't you? The gas.
Ben (powerfully): If I say go and light the kettle I mean go and light the kettle.
Gus: How can you light a kettle?
Ben: It's a figure of speech! Light the kettle. It's a figure of speech!
Gus: I've never heard it.
Ben: Light the kettle! It's common usage!
Gus: I think you've got it wrong.
Ben (menacing): What do you mean?
Gus: They say put on the kettle.
Ben (taut): Who says?

They stare at each other, breathing hard.

(Deliberately.) I have never in all my life heard anyone say put on the kettle.
Gus: I bet my mother used to say it.
Ben: Your mother? When did you last see your mother?
Gus: I don't know, about —
Ben: Well, what are you talking about your mother for?

They stare.

Gus, I'm not trying to be unreasonable. I'm just trying to point out something to you.
Gus: Yes, but —
Ben: Who's the senior partner here, me or you?
Gus: You.
Ben: I'm only looking after your interests, Gus. You've got to learn, mate.
Gus: Yes, but I've never heard —
Ben (vehemently): Nobody says light the gas! What does the gas light?
Gus: What does the gas — ?
Ben (grabbing him with two hands by the throat, at arm's length): THE KETTLE, YOU FOOL!

Gus takes the hands from his throat.

cadging: Begging.

Gus: All right, all right.

Pause.

Ben: Well, what are you waiting for?
Gus: I want to see if they light.
Ben: What?
Gus: The matches.

He takes out the flattened box and tries to strike.

No.

He throws the box under the bed.
Ben stares at him.
Gus raises his foot.

Shall I try it on here?

Ben stares. Gus strikes a match on his shoe. It lights.

Here we are.
Ben (wearily): Put on the bloody kettle, for Christ's sake.

Ben goes to his bed, but, realising what he has said, stops and half turns. They look at each other. Gus slowly exits, left. Ben slams his paper down on the bed and sits on it, head in hands.

Gus (entering): It's going.
Ben: What?
Gus: The stove.

Gus goes to his bed and sits.

I wonder who it'll be tonight.

Silence.

Eh, I've been wanting to ask you something.
Ben (putting his legs on the bed): Oh, for Christ's sake.
Gus: No. I was going to ask you something.

He rises and sits on Ben's bed.

Ben: What are you sitting on my bed for?

Gus sits.

What's the matter with you? You're always asking me questions. What's the matter with you?
Gus: Nothing.
Ben: You never used to ask me so many damn questions. What's come over you?
Gus: No, I was just wondering.
Ben: Stop wondering. You've got a job to do. Why don't you just do it and shut up?
Gus: That's what I was wondering about.
Ben: What?

Gus: The job.
Ben: What job?
Gus (tentatively): I thought perhaps you might know something.

Ben looks at him.

I thought perhaps you — I mean — have you got any idea — who it's going to be tonight?
Ben: Who what's going to be?

They look at each other.

Gus (at length): Who it's going to be.

Silence.

Ben: Are you feeling all right?
Gus: Sure.
Ben: Go and make the tea.
Gus: Yes, sure.

Gus exits, left, Ben looks after him. He then takes his revolver from under the pillow and checks it for ammunition. Gus re-enters.

The gas has gone out.
Ben: Well, what about it?
Gus: There's a meter.
Ben: I haven't got any money.
Gus: Nor have I.
Ben: You'll have to wait.
Gus: What for?
Ben: For Wilson.
Gus: He might not come. He might just send a message. He doesn't always come.
Ben: Well, you'll have to do without it, won't you?
Gus: Blimey.
Ben: You'll have a cup of tea afterwards. What's the matter with you?
Gus: I like to have one before.

Ben holds the revolver up to the light and polishes it.

Ben: You'd better get ready anyway.
Gus: Well, I don't know, that's a bit much, you know, for my money.

He picks up a packet of tea from the bed and throws it into the bag.

I hope he's got a shilling, anyway, if he comes. He's entitled to have. After all, it's his place, he could have seen there was enough gas for a cup of tea.
Ben: What do you mean, it's his place?
Gus: Well, isn't it?
Ben: He's probably only rented it. It doesn't have to be his place.
Gus: I know it's his place. I bet the whole house is. He's not even laying on any gas now either.

Gus sits on his bed.

It's his place all right. Look at all the other places. You go to this address, there's a key there, there's a teapot, there's never a soul in sight — *(He pauses.)* Eh, nobody ever hears a thing, have you ever thought of that? We never get any complaints, do we, too much noise or anything like that? You never see a soul, do you? — except the bloke who comes. You ever noticed that? I wonder if the walls are soundproof. *(He touches the wall above his bed.)* Can't tell. All you do is wait, eh? Half the time he doesn't even bother to put in an appearance, Wilson.

Ben: Why should he? He's a busy man.

Gus (thoughtfully): I find him hard to talk to, Wilson. Do you know that, Ben?

Ben: Scrub round it, will you?

Pause.

Gus: There are a number of things I want to ask him. But I can never get round to it, when I see him.

Pause.

I've been thinking about the last one.

Ben: What last one?

Gus: That girl.

Ben grabs the paper, which he reads.

(Rising, looking down at Ben.) How many times have you read that paper?

Ben slams the paper down and rises.

Ben (angrily): What do you mean?

Gus: I was just wondering how many times you'd —

Ben: What are you doing, criticizing me?

Gus: No, I was just —

Ben: You'll get a swipe round your earhole if you don't watch your step.

Gus: Now look here, Ben —

Ben: I'm not looking anywhere! *(He addresses the room.)* How many times have I — ! A bloody liberty!

Gus: I didn't mean that.

Ben: You just get on with it, mate. Get on with it, that's all.

Ben gets back on the bed.

Gus: I was just thinking about that girl, that's all.

Gus sits on his bed.

She wasn't much to look at, I know, but still. It was a mess though, wasn't it? What a mess. Honest, I can't remember a mess like that one. They don't seem to hold together like men, women. A looser texture, like. Didn't she spread, eh? She didn't half spread. Kaw! But I've been meaning to ask you.

Ben sits up and clenches his eyes.

Who clears up after we've gone? I'm curious about that. Who does the clearing up? Maybe they don't clear up. Maybe they just leave them there, eh? What do you think? How many jobs have we done? Blimey, I can't count them. What if they never clear anything up after we've gone.

Ben (pityingly): You mutt. Do you think we're the only branch of this organization? Have a bit of common. They got departments for everything.
Gus: What cleaners and all?
Ben: You birk!°
Gus: No, it was that girl made me start to think —

There is a loud clatter and racket in the bulge of wall between the beds, of something descending. They grab their revolvers, jump up, and face the wall. The noise comes to a stop. Silence. They look at each other. Ben gestures sharply towards the wall. Gus approaches the wall slowly. He bangs it with his revolver. It is hollow. Ben moves to the head of his bed, his revolver cocked. Gus puts his revolver on his bed and pats along the bottom of the center panel. He finds a rim. He lifts the panel. Disclosed is a serving-hatch, a "dumb waiter." A wide box is held by pulleys. Gus peers into the box. He brings out a piece of paper.

Ben: What is it?
Gus: You have a look at it.
Ben: Read it.
Gus (reading): Two braised steak and chips. Two sago puddings. Two teas without sugar.
Ben: Let me see that. *(He takes the paper.)*
Gus (to himself): Two teas without sugar.
Ben: Mmnn.
Gus: What do you think of that?
Ben: Well —

The box goes up. Ben levels his revolver.

Gus: Give us a chance? They're in a hurry, aren't they?

Ben rereads the note. Gus looks over his shoulder.

That's a bit — that's a bit funny, isn't it?
Ben (quickly): No. It's not funny. It probably used to be a café here, that's all. Upstairs. These places change hands very quickly.
Gus: A café?
Ben: Yes.
Gus: What, you mean this was the kitchen, down here?
Ben: Yes, they change hands overnight, these places. Go into liquidation. The people who run it, you know, they don't find it a going concern, they move out.
Gus: You mean the people who ran this place didn't find it a going concern and moved out?
Gus: Sure.
Gus: WELL, WHO'S GOT IT NOW?

Silence.

Ben: What do you mean, who's got it now?
Gus: Who's got it now? If they moved out, who moved in?
Ben: Well, that all depends —

birk: Fool.

The box descends with a clatter and bang. Ben levels his revolver. Gus goes to the box and brings out a piece of paper.

Gus (reading): Soup of the day. Liver and onions. Jam tart.

A pause. Gus looks at Ben. Ben takes the note and reads it. He walks slowly to the hatch. Gus follows. Ben looks into the hatch but not up it. Gus puts his hand on Ben's shoulder. Ben throws it off. Gus puts his finger to his mouth. He leans on the hatch and swiftly looks up it. Ben flings him away in alarm. Ben looks at the note. He throws his revolver on the bed and speaks with decision.

Ben: We'd better send something up.
Gus: Eh?
Ben: We'd better send something up.
Gus: Oh! Yes. Yes. Maybe you're right.

They are both relieved at the decision.

Ben (purposefully): Quick! What have you got in that bag?
Gus: Not much.

Gus goes to the hatch and shouts up it.

Wait a minute!
Ben: Don't do that!

Gus examines the contents of the bag and brings them out, one by one.

Gus: Biscuits. A bar of chocolate. Half a pint of milk.
Ben: That all?
Gus: Packet of tea.
Ben: Good.
Gus: We can't send the tea. That's all the tea we've got.
Ben: Well, there's no gas. You can't do anything with it, can you?
Gus: Maybe they can send us down a bob.°
Ben: What else is there?
Gus (reaching into bag): One Eccles cake.°
Ben: One Eccles cake?
Gus: Yes.
Ben: You never told me you had an Eccles cake.
Gus: Didn't I?
Ben: Why only one? Didn't you bring one for me?
Gus: I didn't think you'd be keen.
Ben: Well, you can't send up one Eccles cake, anyway.
Gus: Why not?
Ben: Fetch one of those plates.
Gus: All right

Gus goes towards the door, left, and stops.

Do you mean I can keep the Eccles cake then?
Ben: Keep it?
Gus: Well, they don't know we've got it, do they?

bob: A shilling for the gas meter.
Eccles cake: A sugared pastry.

Ben: That's not the point.
Gus: Can't I keep it?
Ben: No, you can't. Get the plate.

Gus exits, left. Ben looks in the bag. He brings out a packet of crisps.° *Enter Gus with a plate.*

(Accusingly, holding up the crisps.) Where did these come from?
Gus: What?
Ben: Where did these crisps come from?
Gus: Where did you find them?
Ben (hitting him on the shoulder): You're playing a dirty game, my lad!
Gus: I only eat those with beer!
Ben: Well, where were you going to get the beer?
Gus: I was saving them till I did.
Ben: I'll remember this. Put everything on the plate.

They pile everything on to the plate. The box goes up without the plate.

Wait a minute!

They stand.

Gus: It's gone up.
Ben: It's all your stupid fault, playing about!
Gus: What do we do now?
Ben: We'll have to wait till it comes down.

Ben puts the plate on the bed, puts on his shoulder holster, and starts to put on his tie.

You'd better get ready.

Gus goes to his bed, puts on his tie, and starts to fix his holster.

Gus: Hey, Ben.
Ben: What?
Gus: What's going on here?

Pause.

Ben: What do you mean?
Gus: How can this be a café?
Ben: It used to be a café.
Gus: Have you seen the gas stove?
Ben: What about it?
Gus: It's only got three rings.
Ben: So what?
Gus: Well, you couldn't cook much on three rings, not for a busy place like this.
Ben (irritably): That's why the service is slow!

Ben puts on his waistcoat.

Gus: Yes, but what happens when we're not here? What do they do then? All these menus coming down and nothing going up. It might have been going on like this for years.

crisps: Potato chips.

Ben brushes his jacket.

What happens when we go?

Ben puts on his jacket.

They can't do much business.

The box descends. They turn about. Gus goes to the hatch and brings out a note.

Gus (reading): Macaroni Pastitsio. Ormitha Macarounada.
Ben: What was that?
Gus: Macaroni Pastitsio. Ormitha Macarounada.
Ben: Greek dishes.
Gus: No.
Ben: That's right.
Gus: That's pretty high class.
Ben: Quick before it goes up.

Gus puts the plate in the box.

Gus (calling up the hatch): Three McVitie and Price! One Lyons Red Label! One Smith's Crisps! One Eccles cake! One Fruit and Nut!
Ben: Cadbury's.
Gus (up the hatch): Cadbury's!
Ben (handing the milk): One bottle of milk.
Gus (up the hatch): One bottle of milk! Half a pint! *(He looks at the label.)* Express Dairy! *(He puts the bottle in the box.)*

The box goes up.

Just did it.
Ben: You shouldn't shout like that.
Gus: Why not?
Ben: It isn't done.

Ben goes to his bed.

Well, that should be all right, anyway, for the time being.
Gus: You think so, eh?
Ben: Get dressed, will you? It'll be any minute now.

Gus puts on his waistcoat. Ben lies down and looks up at the ceiling.

Gus: This is some place. No tea and no biscuits.
Ben: Eating makes you lazy, mate. You're getting lazy, you know that? You don't want to get slack on your job.
Gus: Who me?
Ben: Slack, mate, slack.
Gus: Who me? Slack?
Ben: Have you checked your gun? You haven't even checked your gun. It looks disgraceful, anyway. Why don't you ever polish it?

Gus rubs his revolver on the sheet. Ben takes out a pocket mirror and straightens his tie.

Gus: I wonder where the cook is. They must have had a few, to cope with that. Maybe they had a few more gas stoves. Eh! Maybe there's another kitchen along the passage.

Ben: Of course there is! Do you know what it takes to make an Ormitha Macarounada?

Gus: No, what?

Ben: An Ormitha — ! Buck your ideas up,° will you?

Gus: Takes a few cooks, eh?

Gus puts his revolver in its holster.

The sooner we're out of this place the better.

He puts on his jacket.

Why doesn't he get in touch? I feel like I've been here years. *(He takes his revolver out of its holster to check the ammunition.)* We've never let him down though, have we? We've never let him down. I was thinking only the other day, Ben. We're reliable, aren't we?

He puts his revolver back in its holster.

Still, I'll be glad when it's over tonight.

He brushes his jacket.

I hope the bloke's not going to get excited tonight, or anything. I'm feeling a bit off. I've got a splitting headache.

Silence.

The box descends. Ben jumps up.

Gus collects the note.

(Reading.) One Bamboo Shoots, Water Chestnuts and Chicken. One Char Siu and Beansprouts.

Ben: Beansprouts?

Gus: Yes.

Ben: Blimey.

Gus: I wouldn't know where to begin.

He looks back at the box. The packet of tea is inside it. He picks it up.

They've sent back the tea.

Ben (anxious): What'd they do that for?

Gus: Maybe it isn't tea-time.

The box goes up. Silence.

Ben (throwing the tea on the bed, and speaking urgently): Look here. We'd better tell them.

Gus: Tell them what?

Ben: That we can't do it, we haven't got it.

Gus: All right then.

Ben: Lend us your pencil. We'll write a note.

Buck . . . up: Be quiet.

Gus, turning for a pencil, suddenly discovers the speaking-tube, which hangs on the right wall of the hatch facing his bed.

Gus: What's this?
Ben: What?
Gus: This.
Ben (examining it): This? It's a speaking-tube.
Gus: How long has that been there?
Ben: Just the job. We should have used it before, instead of shouting up there.
Gus: Funny I never noticed it before.
Ben: Well, come on.
Gus: What do you do?
Ben: See that? That's a whistle.
Gus: What, this?
Ben: Yes, take it out. Pull it out.

Gus does so.

That's it.
Gus: What do we do now?
Ben: Blow into it.
Gus: Blow?
Ben: It whistles up there if you blow. Then they know you want to speak. Blow.

Gus blows. Silence.

Gus (tube at mouth): I can't hear a thing.
Ben: Now you speak! Speak into it!

Gus looks at Ben, then speaks into the tube.

Gus: The larder's bare!
Ben: Give me that!

He grabs the tube and puts it to his mouth.

(Speaking with great deference.) Good evening. I'm sorry to — bother you, but we just thought we'd better let you know that we haven't got anything left. We sent up all we had. There's no more food down here.

He brings the tube slowly to his ear.

What?

To mouth.

What?

To ear. He listens. To mouth.

No, all we had we sent up.

To ear. He listens. To mouth.

Oh, I'm very sorry to hear that.

To ear. He listens. To Gus.

The Eccles cake was stale.

He listens. To Gus.

The chocolate was melted.

He listens. To Gus.

The milk was sour.
Gus: What about the crisps?
Ben (listening): The biscuits were mouldy.

He glares at Gus. Tube to mouth.

Well, we're very sorry about that.

Tube to ear.

What?

To mouth.

What?

To ear.

Yes. Yes.

To mouth.

Yes certainly. Certainly. Right away.

To ear. The voice has ceased. He hangs up the tube.

(Excitedly.) Did you hear that?
Gus: What?
Ben: You know what he said? Light the kettle! Not put on the kettle! Not light the gas! But light the kettle!
Gus: How can we light the kettle?
Ben: What do you mean?
Gus: There's no gas.
Ben (clapping hand to head): Now what do we do?
Gus: What did he want us to light the kettle for?
Ben: For tea. He wanted a cup of tea.
Gus: He wanted a cup of tea! What about me? I've been wanting a cup of tea all night!
Ben (despairingly): What do we do now?
Gus: What are we supposed to drink?

Ben sits on his bed, staring.

What about us?

Ben sits.

I'm thirsty too. I'm starving. And he wants a cup of tea. That beats the band, that does.

Ben lets his head sink on to his chest.

I could do with a bit of sustenance myself. What about you? You look as if you could do with something too.

Gus sits on his bed.

We send him up all we've got and he's not satisfied. No, honest, it's enough to make the cat laugh. Why did you send him up all that stuff? *(Thoughtfully.)* Why did I send it up?

Pause.

Who knows what he's got upstairs? He's probably got a salad bowl. They must have something up there. They won't get much from down here. You notice they didn't ask for any salads? They've probably got a salad bowl up there. Cold meat, radishes, cucumbers. Watercress. Roll mops.

Pause.

Hardboiled eggs.

Pause.

The lot. They've probably got a crate of beer too. Probably eating my crisps with a pint of beer now. Didn't have anything to say about those crisps, did he? They do all right, don't worry about that. You don't think they're just going to sit there and wait for stuff to come up from down here, do you? That'll get them nowhere.

Pause.

They do all right.

Pause.

And he wants a cup of tea.

Pause.

That's past a joke, in my opinion.

He looks over at Ben, rises, and goes to him.

What's the matter with you? You don't look too bright. I feel like an Alka-Seltzer myself.

Ben sits up.

Ben (in a low voice): Time's getting on.
Gus: I know. I don't like doing a job on an empty stomach.
Ben (wearily): Be quiet a minute. Let me give you your instructions.
Gus: What for? We always do it the same way, don't we?
Ben: Let me give you your instructions.

Gus sighs and sits next to Ben on the bed. The instructions are stated and repeated automatically.

When we get the call, you go over and stand behind the door.
Gus: Stand behind the door.
Ben: If there's a knock on the door you don't answer it.
Gus: If there's a knock on the door I don't answer it.
Ben: But there won't be a knock on the door.

Gus: So I won't answer it.
Ben: When the bloke comes in —
Gus: When the bloke comes in —
Ben: Shut the door behind him.
Gus: Shut the door behind him.
Ben: Without divulging your presence.
Gus: Without divulging my presence.
Ben: He'll see me and come towards me.
Gus: He'll see you and come towards you.
Ben: He won't see you.
Gus (absently): Eh?
Ben: He won't see you.
Gus: He won't see me.
Ben: But he'll see me.
Gus: He'll see you.
Ben: He won't know you're there.
Gus: He won't know you're there.
Ben: He won't know *you're* there.
Gus: He won't know I'm there.
Ben: I take out my gun.
Gus: You take out your gun.
Ben: He stops in his tracks.
Gus: He stops in his tracks.
Ben: If he turns round —
Gus: If he turns round —
Ben: You're there.
Gus: I'm here.

Ben frowns and presses his forehead.

You've missed something out.
Ben: I know. What?
Gus: I haven't taken my gun out, according to you.
Ben: You take your gun out —
Gus: After I've closed the door.
Ben: After you've closed the door.
Gus: You've never missed that out before, you know that?
Ben: When he sees you behind him —
Gus: Me behind him —
Ben: And me in front of him —
Gus: And you in front of him —
Ben: He'll feel uncertain —
Gus: Uneasy.
Ben: He won't know what to do.
Gus: So what will he do?
Ben: He'll look at me and he'll look at you.
Gus: We won't say a word.
Ben: We'll look at him.
Gus: He won't say a word.

Ben: He'll look at us.
Gus: And we'll look at him.
Ben: Nobody says a word.

Pause.

Gus: What do we do if it's a girl?
Ben: We do the same.
Gus: Exactly the same?
Ben: Exactly.

Pause.

Gus: We don't do anything different?
Ben: We do exactly the same.
Gus: Oh.

Gus rises, and shivers.

Excuse me.

He exits through the door on the left. Ben remains sitting on the bed, still. The lavatory chain is pulled once off left, but the lavatory does not flush. Silence.

Gus re-enters and stops inside the door, deep in thought. He looks at Ben, then walks slowly across to his own bed. He is troubled. He stands, thinking. He turns and looks at Ben. He moves a few paces towards him.

(Slowly in a low, tense voice.) Why did he send us matches if he knew there was no gas?

Silence.

Ben stares in front of him. Gus crosses to the left side of Ben, to the foot of his bed, to get to his other ear.

Ben. Why did he send us matches if he knew there was no gas?

Ben looks up.

Why did he do that?
Ben: Who?
Gus: Who sent us those matches?
Ben: What are you talking about?

Gus stares down at him.

Gus (thickly): Who is it upstairs?
Ben (nervously): What's one thing to do with another?
Gus: Who is it, though?
Ben: What's one thing to do with another?

Ben fumbles for his paper on the bed.

Gus: I asked you a question.
Ben: Enough!
Gus (with growing agitation): I asked you before. Who moved in? I asked you. You said the people who had it before moved out. Well, who moved in?

Ben (hunched): Shut up.
Gus: I told you, didn't I?
Ben (standing): Shut up!
Gus (feverishly): I told you before who owned this place, didn't I? I told you.

Ben hits him viciously on the shoulder.

I told you who ran this place, didn't I?

Ben hits him viciously on the shoulder.

(Violently.) Well, what's he playing all these games for? That's what I want to know. What's he doing it for?
Ben: What games?
Gus (passionately, advancing): What's he doing it for? We've been through our tests, haven't we? We got right through our tests, years ago, didn't we? We took them together, don't you remember, didn't we? We've proved ourselves before now, haven't we? We've always done our job. What's he doing all this for? What's the idea? What's he playing these games for?

The box in the shaft comes down behind them. The noise is this time accompanied by a shrill whistle, as it falls. Gus rushes to the hatch and seizes the note.

(Reading.) Scampi!

He crumples the note, picks up the tube, takes out the whistle, blows, and speaks.

WE'VE GOT NOTHING LEFT! NOTHING! DO YOU UNDERSTAND?

Ben seizes the tube and flings Gus away. He follows Gus and slaps him hard, back-handed, across the chest.

Ben: Stop it! You maniac!
Gus: But you heard!
Ben (savagely): That's enough! I'm warning you!

Silence.
Ben hangs the tube. He goes to his bed and lies down. He picks up his paper and reads.
Silence.
The box goes up.
They turn quickly, their eyes meet. Ben turns to his paper.
Slowly Gus goes back to his bed, and sits.
Silence.
The hatch falls back into place.
They turn quickly, their eyes meet. Ben turns back to his paper.
Silence.
Ben throws his paper down.

Ben: Kaw!

He picks up the paper and looks at it.

Listen to this!

Pause.

What about that, eh?

Pause.

Kaw!

Pause.

Have you ever heard such a thing?

Gus (dully): Go on!
Ben: It's true.
Gus: Get away.
Ben: It's down here in black and white.
Gus (very low): Is that a fact?
Ben: Can you imagine it.
Gus: It's unbelievable.
Ben: It's enough to make you want to puke, isn't it?
Gus (almost inaudible): Incredible.

Ben shakes his head. He puts the paper down and rises. He fixes the revolver in his holster.
Gus stands up. He goes towards the door on the left.

Ben: Where are you going?
Gus: I'm going to have a glass of water.

He exits. Ben brushes dust off his clothes and shoes. The whistle in the speaking-tube blows. He goes to it, takes the whistle out, and puts the tube to his ear. He listens. He puts it to his mouth.

Ben: Yes.

To ear. He listens. To mouth.

Straight away. Right.

To ear. He listens. To mouth.

Sure we're ready.

To ear. He listens. To mouth.

Understood. Repeat. He has arrived and will be coming in straight away. The normal method to be employed. Understood.

To ear. He listens. To mouth.

Sure we're ready.

To ear. He listens. To mouth.

Right.

He hangs the tube up.

Gus!

He takes out a comb and combs his hair, adjusts his jacket to diminish the bulge of the revolver. The lavatory flushes off left. Ben goes quickly to the door, left.

Gus!

The door right opens sharply. Ben turns, his revolver levelled at the door.
Gus stumbles in.
He is stripped of his jacket, waistcoat, tie, holster, and revolver.
He stops, body stooping, his arms at his sides.
He raises his head and looks at Ben.
A long silence.
They stare at each other.

Curtain

Considerations

1. At what point do you realize that Ben and Gus are not ordinary workers but hired killers? Why isn't the nature of the "job" made clear at the beginning of the play?
2. How are Ben and Gus different from the typical gangsters that appear in stories about professional killers?
3. Contrast Gus's personality and sensibilities with Ben's. Which character is smarter and more competent? Which do you find more sympathetic?
4. Why has the organization ordered Gus's execution? Are there any foreshadowings to suggest that he will be the next victim?
5. Do you think Ben will shoot Gus in the final scene? Why do you suppose Pinter doesn't dramatize the shooting?
6. Many silences and pauses punctuate the play's dialogue. How do they affect your response to the verbal exchanges between Ben and Gus? How do they help create the tone of the play?
7. Does the comedy seem appropriate to the overall tone of the play? What, for instance, is the purpose of their efforts to fill the orders for exotic foods that come from the dumb waiter?
8. Consider this statement by Pinter: "Communication itself between people is so frightening that rather than do that there is a continual cross-talk, a continual talking about other things rather than what is at the root of their relationship." How does dialogue in *The Dumb Waiter* dramatize Pinter's view of the way people communicate with one another?
9. What is the meaning of the play's title? Is there a pun on "dumb waiter"? Does the dumb waiter carry any symbolic meaning?
10. The surface of this play is realistic. The setting is a furnished basement room and the two lower-class criminals speak as we might expect two impatient hired killers to pass the time while awaiting orders. What is it, then, that makes this an absurdist play?

Connections

1. Compare the endings of *The Dumb Waiter* and *A Doll's House* (p. 1321). What kinds of questions about what happens next does the ending of each play produce? What emotions does each ending create for you?
2. Write an essay comparing the humor in *The Dumb Waiter* and *Krapp's Last Tape* (p. 1432).
3. Compare Pinter's use of violence with the violence in one of the short stories by Flannery O'Connor in this anthology. To get started, read Claire Kahane's "The Function of Violence in O'Connor's Fiction" (p. 358). What important similarities and differences do you find in their treatment of violence?

TWIRLER

Jane Martin is a pseudonym. *Twirler* was originally submitted unsigned to the Fifth Annual Festival of New American Plays sponsored by the Actors Theatre of Louisville, Kentucky. The play won, but its author has chosen to remain anonymous. The author's identity is known only to a handful of administrators at the Actors Theatre of Louisville who handle permissions for productions and reprints of the play.

Although only one character appears in *Twirler,* the monologue is surprisingly moving as she describes how she became a national twirling champion and what it means to her. At first glance this subject matter may not seem very promising for drama, but as April March says, that's the "prejudice of the unknowing." Her poetic voice takes us through trivial details to transcendent meanings.

JANE MARTIN

Twirler

1981

Character:

April March

A young woman stands center stage. She is dressed in a spangled, single-piece swimsuit, the kind that is specially made for baton twirlers. She holds a shining, silver baton in her hand.

April: I started when I was six. Momma sawed off a broom handle, and Uncle Carbo slapped some sort of silver paint, well, gray really, on it and I went down in the basement and twirled. Later on, Momma hit the daily double on horses named Spin Dry and Silver Revolver and she said that was a sign so she gave me lessons at the Dainty Deb Dance studio where the lady, Miss Aurelia, taught some twirling on the side.

I won the Ohio Juniors title when I was six and the Midwest Young Adult Division three years later and then in High School I finished fourth in the nationals. Momma and I wore look-alike Statue of Liberty costumes that she had to send clear to Nebraska to get, and Daddy was there in a T-shirt with my name, April . . . my first name is April and my last name is March. There were four thousand people there, and when they yelled my name, golden balloons fell out of the ceiling. Nobody — not even Charlene Ann Morrison — ever finished fourth at my age.

Oh, I've flown high and known tragedy both. My daddy says it's put spirit in my soul and steel in my heart. My left hand was crushed in a riding accident by a horse named Big Blood Red, and though I came back to twirl, I couldn't do it at the highest level. That was denied me by Big Blood Red who clipped my wings. You mustn't pity me though. Oh, by no means! Being denied showed me the way, showed me the glory that sits inside life where you can't see it.

People think you're a twit if you twirl. It's a prejudice of the unknowing. Twirlers are the niggers of a white University. Yes, they are. One time I was doing fire batons at a night game, and all of a sudden I see this guy walk out of the stands. I was doing triples and he walks right out past the half time marshalls, comes up to me . . . he had this blue bead head band, I can still see it. Walks right up, and when I come front after a back reverse, he spits in my face. That's the only, single time I ever dropped a baton. Dropped 'em both in front of sixty thousand people, and he smiles see, and he says this thing I won't repeat. He called me a bodily part in front of half of Ohio. It was like being raped. It shows that beauty inspires hate and that hating beauty is Satan.

You haven't twirled, have you? I can see that by your hands. Would you like to hold my silver baton? Here, hold it.

You can't imagine what it feels like to have that baton up in the air. I used to twirl with this girl who called it blue-collar zen. The "tons" catch the sun when they're up, and when they go up, you go up too. You can't twirl if you're not *inside* the "ton." When you've got 'em up over twenty feet it's like flying or gliding. Your hands are still down, but your insides spin and rise and leave the ground. Only a twirler knows that, so we're not niggers.

The secret for a twirler is the light. You live or die with the light. It's your fate. The best is a February sky clouded right over in the late afternoon. It's all background then, and what happens is that the "tons" leave tracks, traces, they etch the air, and if you're hot, if your hands have it, you can draw on the sky.

Charlene Ann Morrison . . . God, Charlene Ann! She was inspired by something beyond man. She won the nationals nine years in a row. Unparalleled and unrepeatable. The last two years she had leukemia and at the end you could see through her hands when she twirled. Charlene Ann died with a "ton" thirty feet up, her momma swears on that. I did speed with Charlene at a regional in Fargo and she may be fibben' but she says there was a day when her "tons" erased while they turned. Like the sky was a sheet of rain and the "tons" were car wipers and when she had erased this certain part of the sky, you could see the face of the Lord God Jesus, and his hair was all rhinestones and he was doing this incredible singing like the sound of a piccolo. The people who said Charlene was crazy probably never twirled a day in their life.

Twirling is the physical parallel of revelation. You can't know that. Twirling is the throwing of yourself up to God. It's a pure gift, hidden from Satan because it is wrapped and disguised in the midst of football. It is God throwing, spirit fire, and very few come to it. You have to grow eyes in your heart to understand its message, and when it opens to you, it becomes your path to suffer ridicule, to be crucified by misunderstanding, and to be spit upon. I need my baton now.

There is one twirling no one sees. At the winter solstice we go to a meadow God showed us just outside of Green Bay. The God throwers come there on December twenty-first. There's snow, sometimes deep snow and our clothes fall away and we stand unprotected while acolytes bring the "tons." They are ebony "tons" with razors set all along the shaft. They are three feet long. One by one the twirlers throw, two "tons" each, thirty feet up, and as they fall back, they cut your hands. The razors arch into the air and find God and then fly down to take your blood in a crucifixion, and the red drops draw God on the ground and if you are up with the batons you can look down and see him revealed. Red on white. Red on white. You can't imagine. You can't imagine how wonderful it is!

I started twirling when I was six, but I never really twirled until my hand was crushed by the horse named Big Blood Red. I have seen God's face from thirty feet up in the air and I know him.

Listen. I will leave my silver baton here for you. Lying here as if I forgot it and when the people file out you can wait back and pick it up, it can be yours . . . it can be your burden. It is the eye of the needle. I leave it for you.

The lights fade.

Considerations

1. April is dressed as a typical twirler. What associations or stereotypes do you have about twirlers? What assumptions do you make about them? How does the author use those expectations to heighten your perception of April's character?
2. What do you think is the significance of "Big Blood Red"?
3. How do your feelings about April develop during the course of her monologue?
4. What does twirling mean to April?
5. Why do you think April leaves her baton behind in the final paragraph?

Connections

1. Compare and contrast a Shakespeare monologue from either *Hamlet* (p. 1065) or *Othello* (p. 1166) with the style and content of *Twirler*.
2. Describe the nature of April's revelation in *Twirler* and Miss Turpin's in O'Connor's short story "Revelation" (p. 327).
3. How do April's attitudes toward life's potential meanings compare with those of the speaker in Beckett's *Krapp's Last Tape* (p. 1423)?

30. A Collection of Plays

THE GLASS MENAGERIE

Thomas Lanier Williams, who kept his college nickname, Tennessee, was born in Columbus, Mississippi, the son of a traveling salesman. In 1918 the family moved to St. Louis, Missouri, where his father became the sales manager of a shoe company. Williams's mother, the daughter of an Episcopal clergyman, was withdrawn and genteel in contrast to his aggressive father, who contemptuously called him "Miss Nancy" as a way of mocking his weak physical condition and his literary pursuits. This family atmosphere of repression and anger makes its way into many of Williams's works through characterizations of domineering men and psychologically vulnerable women.

Williams began writing in high school and at the age of seventeen published his first short story in *Weird Tales.* His education at the University of Missouri was interrupted when he had to go to work in a shoe factory. This "living death," as he put it, led to a nervous breakdown, but he eventually resumed his studies at Washington University and finally graduated from the University of Iowa in 1938. During his college years, Williams wrote one-act plays; in 1940 his first full-length play, *Battle of Angels,* opened in Boston, but none of these early plays achieved commercial success. In 1945, however, *The Glass Menagerie* won large, enthusiastic audiences as well as the Drama Critics' Circle Award, which marked the beginning of a series of theatrical triumphs for Williams including *Streetcar Named Desire* (1947), *The Rose Tattoo* (1950), *Cat on a Hot Tin Roof* (1955), *Suddenly Last Summer* (1958), and *The Night of the Iguana* (1961).

The Glass Menagerie reflects Williams's fascination with characters who face lonely struggles in emotionally and financially starved environments. Although Williams's use of colloquial southern speech is realistic, the play also employs nonrealistic techniques, such as shifts in time, projections on screens, music, and lighting effects, to express his characters' thoughts and inner lives. (Williams describes these devices in his production notes to the play; see p. 1760.) As much as these techniques are unconventional, Williams believed that they represented "a more penetrating and vivid expression of things as they are." The lasting popularity of *The Glass Menagerie* indicates that his assessment was correct.

TENNESSEE WILLIAMS (1911–1983)

The Glass Menagerie 1945

Nobody, not even the rain, has such small hands.
—E. E. Cummings

List of Characters

Amanda Wingfield, the mother. A little woman of great but confused vitality clinging frantically to another time and place. Her characterization must be carefully created, not copied from type. She is not paranoiac, but her life is paranoia. There is much to admire in Amanda, and as much to love and pity as there is to laugh at. Certainly she has endurance and a kind of heroism, and though her foolishness makes her unwittingly cruel at times, there is tenderness in her slight person.

Laura Wingfield, her daughter. Amanda, having failed to establish contact with reality, continues to live vitally in her illusions, but Laura's situation is even graver. A childhood illness has left her crippled, one leg slightly shorter than the other, and held in a brace. This defect need not be more than suggested on the stage. Stemming from this, Laura's separation increases till she is like a piece of her own glass collection, too exquisitely fragile to move from the shelf.

Tom Wingfield, her son. And the narrator of the play. A poet with a job in a warehouse. His nature is not remorseless, but to escape from a trap he has to act without pity.

Jim O'Connor, the gentleman caller. A nice, ordinary, young man.

SCENE: *An alley in St. Louis.*
PART I: *Preparation for a Gentleman Caller.*
PART II: *The Gentleman Calls.*
TIME: *Now and the Past.*

SCENE I

The Wingfield apartment is in the rear of the building, one of those vast hivelike conglomerations of cellular living-units that flower as warty growths in overcrowded urban centers of lower middle-class population and are symptomatic of the impulse of this largest and fundamentally enslaved section of American society to avoid fluidity and differentiation and to exist and function as one interfused mass of automatism.

The apartment faces an alley and is entered by a fire-escape, a structure whose name is a touch of accidental poetic truth, for all of these huge buildings are always burning with the slow and implacable fires of human desperation. The fire-escape is included in the set — that is, the landing of it and steps descending from it.

The scene is memory and is therefore nonrealistic. Memory takes a lot of poetic license. It omits some details; others are exaggerated, according to the emotional value of the articles it touches, for memory is seated predominantly in the heart. The interior is therefore rather dim and poetic.

At the rise of the curtain, the audience is faced with the dark, grim rear wall of the Wingfield tenement. This building, which runs parallel to the footlights, is flanked on both sides by dark, narrow alleys which run into murky canyons of tangled clotheslines, garbage cans, and the sinister latticework of neighboring fire-escapes. It is up and down these side alleys that exterior entrances and exits are made, during the play. At the end of Tom's opening commentary, the dark tenement wall slowly reveals (by means of a transparency) the interior of the ground floor Wingfield apartment.

Downstage is the living room, which also serves as a sleeping room for Laura, the sofa unfolding to make her bed. Upstage, center, and divided by a wide arch or second proscenium with transparent faded portieres (or second curtain), is the dining room. In an old-fashioned what-not in the living room are seen scores of transparent glass animals. A blown-up photograph of the father hangs on the wall of the living room, facing the audience, to the left of the archway. It is the face of a very handsome young man in a doughboy's First World War cap. He is gallantly smiling, ineluctably smiling, as if to say, "I will be smiling forever."

The audience hears and sees the opening scene in the dining room through both the transparent fourth wall of the building and the transparent gauze portieres of the dining-room arch. It is during this revealing scene that the fourth wall slowly ascends, out of sight. This transparent exterior wall is not brought down again until the very end of the play, during Tom's final speech.

The narrator is an undisguised convention of the play. He takes whatever license with dramatic convention as is convenient to his purposes.

Tom enters dressed as a merchant sailor from alley, stage left, and strolls across the front of the stage to the fire-escape. There he stops and lights a cigarette. He addresses the audience.

Tom: Yes, I have tricks in my pocket, I have things up my sleeve. But I am the opposite of a stage magician. He gives you illusion that has the appearance of truth. I give you truth in the pleasant disguise of illusion. To begin with, I turn back time. I reverse it to that quaint period, the thirties, when the huge middle class of America was matriculating in a school for the blind. Their eyes had failed them, or they had failed their eyes, and so they were having their fingers pressed forcibly down on the fiery Braille alphabet of a dissolving economy. In Spain there was revolution. Here there was only shouting and confusion. In Spain there was Guernica.° Here there were disturbances of labor, sometimes pretty violent, in otherwise peaceful cities such as Chicago, Cleveland, Saint Louis. . . . This is the social background of the play.

Guernica: A town in northern Spain destroyed by German bombers in 1937 during the Spanish Civil War.

(Music.)

The play is memory. Being a memory play, it is dimly lighted, it is sentimental, it is not realistic. In memory everything seems to happen to music. That explains the fiddle in the wings. I am the narrator of the play, and also a character in it. The other characters are my mother, Amanda, my sister, Laura, and a gentleman caller who appears in the final scenes. He is the most realistic character in the play, being an emissary from a world of reality that we were somehow set apart from. But since I have a poet's weakness for symbols, I am using this character also as a symbol; he is the long delayed but always expected something that we live for. There is a fifth character in the play who doesn't appear except in this larger-than-life photograph over the mantel. This is our father who left us a long time ago. He was a telephone man who fell in love with long distances; he gave up his job with the telephone company and skipped the light fantastic out of town. . . . The last we heard of him was a picture post-card from Mazatlán, on the Pacific coast of Mexico, containing a message of two words — "Hello — Good-bye!" and no address. I think the rest of the play will explain itself. . . .

Amanda's voice becomes audible through the portieres.

(Legend on screen: "Où sont les neiges."°)

He divides the portieres and enters the upstage area.

Amanda and Laura are seated at a drop-leaf table. Eating is indicated by gestures without food or utensils. Amanda faces the audience.

Tom and Laura are seated in profile.

The interior has lit up softly and through the scrim we see Amanda and Laura seated at the table in the upstage area.

Amanda (calling): Tom?

Tom: Yes, Mother.

Amanda: We can't say grace until you come to the table!

Tom: Coming, Mother. *(He bows slightly and withdraws, reappearing a few moments later in his place at the table.)*

Amanda (to her son): Honey, don't *push* with your *fingers.* If you have to push with something, the thing to push with is a crust of bread. And chew — chew! Animals have sections in their stomachs which enable them to digest food without mastication, but human beings are supposed to chew their food before they swallow it down. Eat food leisurely, son, and really enjoy it. A well-cooked meal has lots of delicate flavors that have to be held in the mouth for appreciation. So chew your food and give your salivary glands a chance to function!

Tom deliberately lays his imaginary fork down and pushes his chair back from the table.

Tom: I haven't enjoyed one bite of this dinner because of your constant directions on how to eat it. It's you that makes me rush through meals with your hawklike attention to every bite I take. Sickening — spoils my appetite — all this discussion of animals' secretion — salivary glands — mastication!

Où sont les neiges: Part of a line from a poem by the French medieval writer François Villon; the full line translates, "But where are the snows of Yesteryear?"

Amanda (lightly): Temperament like a Metropolitan star! *(He rises and crosses downstage.)* You're not excused from the table.

Tom: I am getting a cigarette.

Amanda: You smoke too much.

Laura rises.

Laura: I'll bring in the blanc mange.

He remains standing with his cigarette by the portieres during the following.

Amanda (rising): No, sister, no, sister — you be the lady this time and I'll be the darky.

Laura: I'm already up.

Amanda: Resume your seat, little sister — I want you to stay fresh and pretty — for gentlemen callers!

Laura: I'm not expecting any gentlemen callers.

Amanda (crossing out to kitchenette. Airily): Sometimes they come when they are least expected! Why, I remember one Sunday afternoon in Blue Mountain — *(Enters kitchenette.)*

Tom: I know what's coming!

Laura: Yes. But let her tell it.

Tom: Again?

Laura: She loves to tell it.

Amanda returns with bowl of dessert.

Amanda: One Sunday afternoon in Blue Mountain — your mother received — *seventeen!* — gentlemen callers! Why, sometimes there weren't chairs enough to accommodate them all. We had to send the nigger over to bring in folding chairs from the parish house.

Tom (remaining at portieres): How did you entertain those gentlemen callers?

Amanda: I understood the art of conversation!

Tom: I bet you could talk.

Amanda: Girls in those days *knew* how to talk, I can tell you.

Tom: Yes?

(Image: Amanda as a girl on a porch greeting callers.)

Amanda: They knew how to entertain their gentlemen callers. It wasn't enough for a girl to be possessed of a pretty face and a graceful figure — although I wasn't slighted in either respect. She also needed to have a nimble wit and a tongue to meet all occasions.

Tom: What did you talk about?

Amanda: Things of importance going on in the world! Never anything coarse or common or vulgar. *(She addresses Tom as though he were seated in the vacant chair at the table though he remains by portieres. He plays this scene as though he held the book.)* My callers were gentlemen — all! Among my callers were some of the most prominent young planters of the Mississippi Delta — planters and sons of planters!

Tom motions for music and a spot of light on Amanda.
Her eyes lift, her face glows, her voice becomes rich and elegiac.
(Screen legend: "Où sont les neiges.")

There was young Champ Laughlin who later became vice-president of the Delta Planters Bank. Hadley Stevenson who was drowned in Moon Lake and left his widow one hundred and fifty thousand in Government bonds. There were the Cutrere brothers, Wesley and Bates. Bates was one of my bright particular beaux! He got in a quarrel with that wild Wainright boy. They shot it out on the floor of Moon Lake Casino. Bates was shot through the stomach. Died in the ambulance on his way to Memphis. His widow was also well-provided for, came into eight or ten thousand acres, that's all. She married him on the rebound — never loved her — carried my picture on him the night he died! And there was that boy that every girl in the Delta had set her cap for! That beautiful, brilliant young Fitzhugh boy from Green County!

Tom: What did he leave his widow?

Amanda: He never married! Gracious, you talk as though all of my old admirers had turned up their toes to the daisies!

Tom: Isn't this the first you mentioned that still survives?

Amanda: That Fitzhugh boy went North and made a fortune — came to be known as the Wolf of Wall Street! He had the Midas touch, whatever he touched turned to gold! And I could have been Mrs. Duncan J. Fitzhugh, mind you! But — I picked your *father!*

Laura (rising): Mother, let me clear the table.

Amanda: No dear, you go in front and study your typewriter chart. Or practice your shorthand a little. Stay fresh and pretty! — It's almost time for our gentlemen callers to start arriving. *(She flounces girlishly toward the kitchenette.)* How many do you suppose we're going to entertain this afternoon?

Tom throws down the paper and jumps up with a groan.

Laura (alone in the dining room): I don't believe we're going to receive any, Mother.

Amanda (reappearing, airily): What? No one — not one? You must be joking! *(Laura nervously echoes her laugh. She slips in a fugitive manner through the half-open portieres and draws them gently behind her. A shaft of very clear light is thrown on her face against the faded tapestry of the curtains.) (Music: "The Glass Menagerie" under faintly.) (Lightly.)* Not one gentleman caller? It can't be true! There must be a flood, there must have been a tornado!

Laura: It isn't a flood, it's not a tornado, Mother. I'm just not popular like you were in Blue Mountain. . . . *(Tom utters another groan. Laura glances at him with a faint, apologetic smile. Her voice catching a little.)* Mother's afraid I'm going to be an old maid.

(The scene dims out with "Glass Menagerie" music.)

SCENE II

"Laura, Haven't You Ever Liked Some Boy?"

On the dark stage the screen is lighted with the image of blue roses.
Gradually Laura's figure becomes apparent and the screen goes out.

The music subsides.

Laura is seated in the delicate ivory chair at the small clawfoot table.

She wears a dress of soft violet material for a kimono — her hair tied back from her forehead with a ribbon.

She is washing and polishing her collection of glass.

Amanda appears on the fire-escape steps. At the sound of her ascent, Laura catches her breath, thrusts the bowl of ornaments away and seats herself stiffly before the diagram of the typewriter keyboard as though it held her spellbound. Something has happened to Amanda. It is written in her face as she climbs to the landing: a look that is grim and hopeless and a little absurd.

She has on one of those cheap or imitation velvety-looking cloth coats with imitation fur collar. Her hat is five or six years old, one of those dreadful cloche hats that were worn in the late twenties, and she is clasping an enormous black patent-leather pocketbook with nickel clasp and initials. This is her full-dress outfit, the one she usually wears to the D.A.R.°

Before entering she looks through the door.

She purses her lips, opens her eyes wide, rolls them upward, and shakes her head.

Then she slowly lets herself in the door. Seeing her mother's expression Laura touches her lips with a nervous gesture.

Laura: Hello, Mother, I was — *(She makes a nervous gesture toward the chart on the wall. Amanda leans against the shut door and stares at Laura with a martyred look.)*

Amanda: Deception? Deception? *(She slowly removes her hat and gloves, continuing the swift suffering stare. She lets the hat and gloves fall on the floor — a bit of acting.)*

Laura (shakily): How was the D.A.R. meeting? *(Amanda slowly opens her purse and removes a dainty white handkerchief, which she shakes out delicately and delicately touches to her lips and nostrils.)* Didn't you go to the D.A.R. meeting, Mother?

Amanda (faintly, almost inaudibly): — No. — No. *(Then more forcibly.)* I did not have the strength — to go to the D.A.R. In fact, I did not have the courage! I wanted to find a hole in the ground and hide myself in it forever! *(She crosses slowly to the wall and removes the diagram of the typewriter keyboard. She holds it in front of her for a second, staring at it sweetly and sorrowfully — then bites her lips and tears it in two pieces.)*

Laura (faintly): Why did you do that, Mother? *(Amanda repeats the same procedure with the chart of the Gregg Alphabet.°)* Why are you —

Amanda: Why? Why? How old are you, Laura?

Laura: Mother, you know my age.

Amanda: I thought that you were an adult; it seems that I was mistaken. *(She crosses slowly to the sofa and sinks down and stares at Laura.)*

Laura: Please don't stare at me, Mother.

Amanda closes her eyes and lowers her head. Count ten.

D.A.R.: Daughters of the American Revolution; members must document that they have ancestors who served the patriots' cause in the Revolutionary War.
Gregg Alphabet: System of shorthand symbols invented by John Robert Gregg.

Amanda: What are we going to do, what is going to become of us, what is the future?

Count ten.

Laura: Has something happened, Mother? *(Amanda draws a long breath and takes out the handkerchief again. Dabbing process.)* Mother, has — something happened?

Amanda: I'll be all right in a minute. I'm just bewildered — *(count five)* — by life. . . .

Laura: Mother, I wish that you would tell me what's happened.

Amanda: As you know, I was supposed to be inducted into my office at the D.A.R. this afternoon. *(Image: A swarm of typewriters.)* But I stopped off at Rubicam's Business College to speak to your teachers about your having a cold and ask them what progress they thought you were making down there.

Laura: Oh. . . .

Amanda: I went to the typing instructor and introduced myself as your mother. She didn't know who you were. Wingfield, she said. We don't have any such student enrolled at the school! I assured her she did, that you had been going to classes since early in January. "I wonder," she said, "if you could be talking about that terribly shy little girl who dropped out of school after only a few days' attendance?" "No," I said, "Laura, my daughter, has been going to school every day for the past six weeks!" "Excuse me," she said. She took the attendance book out and there was your name, unmistakably printed, and all the dates you were absent until they decided that you had dropped out of school. I still said, "No, there must have been some mistake! There must have been some mix-up in the records!" And she said, "No — I remember her perfectly now. Her hand shook so that she couldn't hit the right keys! The first time we gave a speed-test, she broke down completely — was sick at the stomach and almost had to be carried into the wash-room! After that morning she never showed up any more. We phoned the house but never got any answer" — while I was working at Famous and Barr, I suppose, demonstrating those — Oh! I felt so weak I could barely keep on my feet. I had to sit down while they got me a glass of water! Fifty dollars' tuition, all of our plans — my hopes and ambitions for you — just gone up the spout, just gone up the spout like that. *(Laura draws a long breath and gets awkwardly to her feet. She crosses to the Victrola, and winds it up.)* What are you doing?

Laura: Oh! *(She releases the handle and returns to her seat.)*

Amanda: Laura, where have you been going when you've gone out pretending that you were going to business college?

Laura: I've just been going out walking.

Amanda: That's not true.

Laura: It is. I just went walking.

Amanda: Walking? Walking? In winter? Deliberately courting pneumonia in that light coat? Where did you walk to, Laura?

Laura: It was the lesser of two evils, Mother. *(Image: Winter scene in park.)* I couldn't go back up. I — threw up — on the floor!

Amanda: From half past seven till after five every day you mean to tell me you walked around in the park, because you wanted to make me think that you were still going to Rubicam's Business College?

Laura: It wasn't as bad as it sounds. I went inside places to get warmed up.

Amanda: Inside where?

Laura: I went in the art museum and the bird-houses at the Zoo. I visited the penguins every day! Sometimes I did without lunch and went to the movies. Lately I've been spending most of my afternoons in the Jewel-box, that big glass house where they raise the tropical flowers.

Amanda: You did all this to deceive me, just for the deception? *(Laura looks down.)* Why?

Laura: Mother, when you're disappointed, you get that awful suffering look on your face, like the picture of Jesus' mother in the museum!

Amanda: Hush!

Laura: I couldn't face it.

Pause. A whisper of strings.
(Legend: "The Crust of Humility.")

Amanda (hopelessly fingering the huge pocketbook): So what are we going to do the rest of our lives? Stay home and watch the parades go by? Amuse ourselves with the glass menagerie, darling? Eternally play those worn-out phonograph records your father left as a painful reminder of him? We won't have a business career — we've given that up because it gave us nervous indigestion! *(Laughs wearily.)* What is there left but dependency all our lives? I know so well what becomes of unmarried women who aren't prepared to occupy a position. I've seen such pitiful cases in the South — barely tolerated spinsters living upon the grudging patronage of sister's husband or brother's wife! — stuck away in some little mousetrap of a room — encouraged by one in-law to visit another — little birdlike women without any nest — eating the crust of humility all their life! Is that the future that we've mapped out for ourselves? I swear it's the only alternative I can think of! It isn't a very pleasant alternative, is it? Of course — some girls *do marry. (Laura twists her hands nervously.)* Haven't you ever liked some boy?

Laura: Yes. I liked one once. *(Rises.)* I came across his picture a while ago.

Amanda (with some interest): He gave you his picture?

Laura: No, it's in the year-book.

Amanda (disappointed): Oh — a high-school boy.

(Screen image: Jim as a high-school hero bearing a silver cup.)

Laura: Yes. His name was Jim. *(Laura lifts the heavy annual from the clawfoot table.)* Here he is in *The Pirates of Penzance.*

Amanda (absently): The what?

Laura: The operetta the senior class put on. He had a wonderful voice and we sat across the aisle from each other Mondays, Wednesdays, and Fridays in the Aud. Here he is with the silver cup for debating! See his grin?

Amanda (absently): He must have had a jolly disposition.

Laura: He used to call me — Blue Roses.

(Image: Blue roses.)

Amanda: Why did he call you such a name as that?

Laura: When I had that attack of pleurosis — he asked me what was the matter when I came back. I said pleurosis — he thought that I said Blue Roses! So that's what he always called me after that. Whenever he saw me, he'd holler, "Hello, Blue Roses!" I didn't care for the girl that he went out with. Emily Meisenbach. Emily was the best-dressed girl at Soldan. She never struck me, though, as being sincere. . . . It says in the Personal Section — they're engaged. That's — six years ago! They must be married by now.

Amanda: Girls that aren't cut out for business careers usually wind up married to some nice man. *(Gets up with a spark of revival.)* Sister, that's what you'll do!

Laura utters a startled, doubtful laugh. She reaches quickly for a piece of glass.

Laura: But, Mother —

Amanda: Yes? *(Crossing to photograph.)*

Laura (in a tone of frightened apology): I'm — crippled!

(Image: Screen.)

Amanda: Nonsense! Laura, I've told you never, never to use that word. Why, you're not crippled, you just have a little defect — hardly noticeable, even! When people have some slight disadvantage like that, they cultivate other things to make up for it — develop charm — and vivacity — and — *charm!* That's all you have to do! *(She turns again to the photograph.)* One thing your father had *plenty of* — was *charm!*

Tom motions to the fiddle in the wings.
(The scene fades out with music.)

SCENE III

(Legend on the screen: "After the Fiasco — ")
Tom speaks from the fire-escape landing.

Tom: After the fiasco at Rubicam's Business College, the idea of getting a gentleman caller for Laura began to play a more important part in Mother's calculations. It became an obsession. Like some archetype of the universal unconscious, the image of the gentleman caller haunted our small apartment. . . . *(Image: Young man at door with flowers.)* An evening at home rarely passed without some allusion to this image, this specter, this hope. . . . Even when he wasn't mentioned, his presence hung in Mother's preoccupied look and in my sister's frightened, apologetic manner — hung like a sentence passed upon the Wingfields! Mother was a woman of action as well as words. She began to take logical steps in the planned direction. Late that winter and in the early spring — realizing that extra money would be needed to properly feather the nest and plume the bird — she conducted a vigorous campaign on the telephone, roping in subscribers to one of those magazines for matrons called *The Home-maker's Companion,* the type of journal that features the serialized sublimations of ladies of letters who think in terms of delicate cuplike breasts, slim, tapering waists, rich, creamy thighs, eyes like wood-smoke in autumn, fingers that soothe and caress like strains of music, bodies as powerful as Etruscan sculpture.

(Screen image: Glamor magazine cover.)
Amanda enters with phone on long extension cord. She is spotted in the dim stage.

Amanda: Ida Scott? This is Amanda Wingfield! We *missed* you at the D.A.R. last Monday! I said to myself: She's probably suffering with that sinus condition! How is that sinus condition? Horrors! Heaven have mercy! — You're a Christian martyr, yes, that's what you are, a Christian martyr! Well, I just now happened to notice that your subscription to the *Companion*'s about to expire! Yes, it expires with the next issue, honey! — just when that wonderful new serial by Bessie Mae Hopper is getting off to such an exciting start. Oh, honey, it's something that you can't miss! You remember how *Gone with the Wind* took everybody by storm? You simply couldn't go out if you hadn't read it. All everybody *talked* was Scarlett O'Hara. Well, this is a book that critics already compare to *Gone with the Wind.* It's the *Gone with the Wind* of the post–World War generation! — What? — Burning? — Oh, honey, don't let them burn, go take a look in the oven and I'll hold the wire! Heavens — I think she's hung up!

(Dim out.)

(Legend on screen: "You think I'm in love with Continental Shoemakers?")

Before the stage is lighted, the violent voices of Tom and Amanda are heard. They are quarreling behind the portieres. In front of them stands Laura with clenched hands and panicky expression.

A clear pool of light on her figure throughout this scene.

Tom: What in Christ's name am I —
Amanda (shrilly): Don't you use that —
Tom: Supposed to do!
Amanda: Expression! Not in my —
Tom: Ohhh!
Amanda: Presence! Have you gone out of your senses?
Tom: I have, that's true, *driven* out!
Amanda: What is the matter with you, you — big — big — IDIOT!
Tom: Look — I've got *no thing,* no single thing —
Amanda: Lower your voice!
Tom: In my life here that I can call my OWN! Everything is —
Amanda: Stop that shouting!
Tom: Yesterday you confiscated my books! You had the nerve to —
Amanda: I took that horrible novel back to the library — yes! That hideous book by that insane Mr. Lawrence.° *(Tom laughs wildly.)* I cannot control the output of diseased minds or people who cater to them — *(Tom laughs still more wildly.)* BUT I WON'T ALLOW SUCH FILTH BROUGHT INTO MY HOUSE! No, no, no, no, no!
Tom: House, house! Who pays rent on it, who makes a slave of himself to —
Amanda (fairly screeching): Don't you DARE to —

Mr. Lawrence: D. H. Lawrence (1885–1930), English poet and novelist who advocated sexual freedom.

Tom: No, no, *I* mustn't say things! *I've* got to just —

Amanda: Let me tell you —

Tom: I don't want to hear any more! *(He tears the portieres open. The upstage area is lit with a turgid smoky red glow.)*

Amanda's hair is in metal curlers and she wears a very old bathrobe, much too large for her slight figure, a relic of the faithless Mr. Wingfield.

An upright typewriter and a wild disarray of manuscripts are on the drop-leaf table. The quarrel was probably precipitated by Amanda's interruption of his creative labor. A chair lying overthrown on the floor.

Their gesticulating shadows are cast on the ceiling by the fiery glow.

Amanda: You *will* hear more, you —

Tom: No, I won't hear more, I'm going out!

Amanda: You come right back in —

Tom: Out, out, out! Because I'm —

Amanda: Come back here, Tom Wingfield! I'm not through talking to you!

Tom: Oh, go —

Laura (desperately): Tom!

Amanda: You're going to listen, and no more insolence from you! I'm at the end of my patience! *(He comes back toward her.)*

Tom: What do you think I'm at? Aren't I supposed to have any patience to reach the end of, Mother? I know, I know. It seems unimportant to you, what I'm *doing* — what I *want* to do — having a little *difference* between them! You don't think that —

Amanda: I think you've been doing things that you're ashamed of. That's why you act like this. I don't believe that you go every night to the movies. Nobody goes to the movies night after night. Nobody in their right minds goes to the movies as often as you pretend to. People don't go to the movies at nearly midnight, and movies don't let out at two A.M. Come in stumbling. Muttering to yourself like a maniac! You get three hours' sleep and then go to work. Oh, I can picture the way you're doing down there. Moping, doping, because you're in no condition.

Tom (wildly): No, I'm in no condition!

Amanda: What right have you got to jeopardize your job? Jeopardize the security of us all? How do you think we'd manage if you were —

Tom: Listen! You think I'm crazy *about* the *warehouse! (He bends fiercely toward her slight figure.)* You think I'm in love with the Continental Shoemakers? You think I want to spend fifty-five *years* down there in that — *celotex interior!* with — *fluorescent* — *tubes!* Look! I'd rather somebody picked up a crowbar and battered out my brains — than go back mornings! I *go!* Every time you come in yelling that God damn *"Rise and Shine!" "Rise and Shine!"* I say to myself "How *lucky dead* people are!" But I get up. I *go!* For sixty-five dollars a month I give up all that I dream of doing and being *ever!* And you say self — *self's* all I ever think of. Why, listen, if self is what I thought of, Mother, I'd be where he is — GONE! *(Pointing to father's picture.)* As far as the system of transportation reaches! *(He starts past her. She grabs his arm.)* Don't grab at me, Mother!

Amanda: Where are you going?

Tom: I'm going to the *movies!*

Amanda: I don't believe that lie!

Tom (crouching toward her, overtowering her tiny figure. She backs away, gasping): I'm going to opium dens! Yes, opium dens, dens of vice and criminals' hang-outs, Mother. I've joined the Hogan gang, I'm a hired assassin, I carry a tommy-gun in a violin case! I run a string of cat-houses in the Valley! They call me Killer, Killer Wingfield, I'm leading a double-life, a simple, honest warehouse worker by day, by night a dynamic *czar* of the *underworld, Mother.* I go to gambling casinos, I spin away fortunes on the roulette table! I wear a patch over one eye and a false mustache, sometimes I put on green whiskers. On those occasions they call me — *El Diablo!*° Oh, I could tell you things to make you sleepless! My enemies plan to dynamite this place. They're going to blow us all sky-high some night! I'll be glad, very happy, and so will you! You'll go up, up on a broomstick, over Blue Mountain with seventeen gentlemen callers! You ugly — babbling old — *witch. . . . (He goes through a series of violent, clumsy movements, seizing his overcoat, lunging to the door, pulling it fiercely open. The women watch him, aghast. His arm catches in the sleeve of the coat as he struggles to pull it on. For a moment he is pinioned by the bulky garment. With an outraged groan he tears the coat off again, splitting the shoulders of it, and hurls it across the room. It strikes against the shelf of Laura's glass collection, there is a tinkle of shattering glass. Laura cries out as if wounded.)*

(Music legend: "The Glass Menagerie.")

Laura (shrilly): My glass! — menagerie. . . . *(She covers her face and turns away.)*

But Amanda is still stunned and stupefied by the "ugly witch" so that she barely notices this occurrence. Now she recovers her speech.

Amanda (in an awful voice): I won't speak to you — until you apologize! *(She crosses through portieres and draws them together behind her. Tom is left with Laura. Laura clings weakly to the mantel with her face averted. Tom stares at her stupidly for a moment. Then he crosses to shelf. Drops awkwardly to his knees to collect the fallen glass, glancing at Laura as if he would speak but couldn't.)*

"The Glass Menagerie" steals in as
(The scene dims out.)

SCENE IV

The interior is dark. Faint light in the alley.

A deep-voiced bell in a church is tolling the hour of five as the scene commences.

Tom appears at the top of the alley. After each solemn boom of the bell in the tower, he shakes a little noise-maker or rattle as if to express the tiny spasm of man in contrast to the sustained power and dignity of the Almighty. This and the unsteadiness of his advance make it evident that he has been drinking.

As he climbs the few steps to the fire-escape landing light steals up inside. Laura appears in night-dress, observing Tom's empty bed in the front room.

El Diablo: The devil (Spanish).

Tom fishes in his pockets for the door-key, removing a motley assortment of articles in the search, including a perfect shower of movie-ticket stubs and an empty bottle. At last he finds the key, but just as he is about to insert it, it slips from his fingers. He strikes a match and crouches below the door.

Tom (bitterly): One crack — and it falls through!

Laura opens the door.

Laura: Tom! Tom, what are you doing?
Tom: Looking for a door-key.
Laura: Where have you been all this time?
Tom: I have been to the movies.
Laura: All this time at the movies?
Tom: There was a very long program. There was a Garbo picture and a Mickey Mouse and a travelogue and a newsreel and a preview of coming attractions. And there was an organ solo and a collection for the milk-fund — simultaneously — which ended up in a terrible fight between a fat lady and an usher!
Laura (innocently): Did you have to stay through everything?
Tom: Of course! And, oh, I forgot! There was a big stage show! The headliner on this stage show was Malvolio the Magician. He performed wonderful tricks, many of them, such as pouring water back and forth between pitchers. First it turned to wine and then it turned to beer and then it turned to whiskey. I know it was whiskey it finally turned into because he needed somebody to come up out of the audience to help him, and I came up — both shows! It was Kentucky Straight Bourbon. A very generous fellow, he gave souvenirs. *(He pulls from his back pocket a shimmering rainbow-colored scarf.)* He gave me this. This is his magic scarf. You can have it, Laura. You wave it over a canary cage and you get a bowl of gold-fish. You wave it over the gold-fish bowl and they fly away canaries. . . . But the wonderfullest trick of all was the coffin trick. We nailed him into a coffin and he got out of the coffin without removing one nail. *(He has come inside.)* There is a trick that would come in handy for me — get me out of this 2 by 4 situation! *(Flops onto bed and starts removing shoes.)*
Laura: Tom — Shhh!
Tom: What you shushing me for?
Laura: You'll wake up Mother.
Tom: Goody, goody! Pay 'er back for all those "Rise an' Shines." *(Lies down, groaning.)* You know it don't take much intelligence to get yourself into a nailed-up coffin, Laura. But who in hell ever got himself out of one without removing one nail?

As if in answer, the father's grinning photograph lights up.
(Scene dims out.)

Immediately following: The church bell is heard striking six. At the sixth stroke the alarm clock goes off in Amanda's room, and after a few moments we hear her calling: "Rise and Shine! Rise and Shine! Laura, go tell your brother to rise and shine!"

Tom (sitting up slowly): I'll rise — but I won't shine.

The light increases.

Amanda: Laura, tell your brother his coffee is ready.

Laura slips into front room.

Laura: Tom! it's nearly seven. Don't make Mother nervous. *(He stares at her stupidly. Beseechingly.)* Tom, speak to Mother this morning. Make up with her, apologize, speak to her!

Tom: She won't to me. It's her that started not speaking.

Laura: If you just say you're sorry she'll start speaking.

Tom: Her not speaking — is that such a tragedy?

Laura: Please — please!

Amanda (calling from kitchenette): Laura, are you going to do what I asked you to do, or do I have to get dressed and go out myself?

Laura: Going, going — soon as I get on my coat! *(She pulls on a shapeless felt hat with nervous, jerky movement, pleadingly glancing at Tom. Rushes awkwardly for coat. The coat is one of Amanda's, inaccurately made-over, the sleeves too short for Laura.)* Butter and what else?

Amanda (entering upstage): Just butter. Tell them to charge it.

Laura: Mother, they make such faces when I do that.

Amanda: Sticks and stones may break my bones, but the expression on Mr. Garfinkel's face won't harm us! Tell your brother his coffee is getting cold.

Laura (at door): Do what I asked you, will you, will you, Tom?

He looks sullenly away.

Amanda: Laura, go now or just don't go at all!

Laura (rushing out): Going — going! *(A second later she cries out. Tom springs up and crosses to the door. Amanda rushes anxiously in. Tom opens the door.)*

Tom: Laura?

Laura: I'm all right. I slipped, but I'm all right.

Amanda (peering anxiously after her): If anyone breaks a leg on those fire-escape steps, the landlord ought to be sued for every cent he possesses! *(She shuts door. Remembers she isn't speaking and returns to other room.)*

As Tom enters listlessly for his coffee, she turns her back to him and stands rigidly facing the window on the gloomy gray vault of the areaway. Its light on her face with its aged but childish features is cruelly sharp, satirical as a Daumier° print.

(Music under: "Ave Maria.")

Tom glances sheepishly but sullenly at her averted figure and slumps at the table. The coffee is scalding hot; he sips it and gasps and spits it back in the cup. At his gasp, Amanda catches her breath and half turns. Then catches herself and turns back to window.

Tom blows on his coffee, glancing sidewise at his mother. She clears her throat. Tom clears his. He starts to rise. Sinks back down again, scratches his head, clears his throat again. Amanda coughs. Tom raises his cup in both hands to blow on it, his eyes staring over the rim of it at his mother for several moments.

Daumier: Honoré Daumier (1808–1879), French caricaturist, lithographer, and painter who mercilessly satirized bourgeois society.

Then he slowly sets the cup down and awkwardly and hesitantly rises from the chair.

Tom (hoarsely): Mother. I — I apologize. Mother. *(Amanda draws a quick, shuddering breath. Her face works grotesquely. She breaks into childlike tears.)* I'm sorry for what I said, for everything that I said, I didn't mean it.

Amanda (sobbingly): My devotion has made me a witch and so I make myself hateful to my children!

Tom: No, you *don't.*

Amanda: I worry so much, don't sleep, it makes me nervous!

Tom (gently): I understand that.

Amanda: I've had to put up a solitary battle all these years. But you're my right-hand bower! Don't fall down, don't fail!

Tom (gently): I try, Mother.

Amanda (with great enthusiasm): Try and you will SUCCEED! *(The notion makes her breathless.)* Why, you — you're just *full* of natural endowments! Both of my children — they're *unusual* children! Don't you think I know it? I'm so — *proud!* Happy and — feel I've — so much to be thankful for but — Promise me one thing, son!

Tom: What, Mother?

Amanda: Promise, son, you'll — never be a drunkard!

Tom (turns to her grinning): I will never be a drunkard, Mother.

Amanda: That's what frightened me so, that you'd be drinking! Eat a bowl of Purina!

Tom: Just coffee, Mother.

Amanda: Shredded wheat biscuit?

Tom: No. No, Mother, just coffee.

Amanda: You can't put in a day's work on an empty stomach. You've got ten minutes — don't gulp! Drinking too-hot liquids makes cancer of the stomach. . . . Put cream in.

Tom: No, thank you.

Amanda: To cool it.

Tom: No! No, thank you, I want it black.

Amanda: I know, but it's not good for you. We have to do all that we can to build ourselves up. In these trying times we live in, all that we have to cling to is — each other. . . . That's why it's so important to — Tom, I — I sent out your sister so I could discuss something with you. If you hadn't spoken I would have spoken to you. *(Sits down.)*

Tom (gently): What is it, Mother, that you want to discuss?

Amanda: Laura!

Tom puts his cup down slowly.
(Legend on screen: "Laura.")
(Music: "The Glass Menagerie.")

Tom: — Oh. — Laura . . .

Amanda (touching his sleeve): You know how Laura is. So quiet but — still water runs deep! She notices things and I think she — broods about them. *(Tom looks up.)* A few days ago I came in and she was crying.

Tom: What about?

Amanda: You.

Tom: Me?

Amanda: She has an idea that you're not happy here.

Tom: What gave her that idea?

Amanda: What gives her any idea? However, you do act strangely. I — I'm not criticizing, understand *that!* I know your ambitions do not lie in the warehouse, that like everybody in the whole wide world — you've had to — make sacrifices, but — Tom — Tom — life's not easy, it calls for — Spartan endurance! There's so many things in my heart that I cannot describe to you! I've never told you but I — *loved* your father. . . .

Tom (gently): I know that, Mother.

Amanda: And you — when I see you taking after his ways! Staying out late — and — well, you *had* been drinking the night you were in that — terrifying condition! Laura says that you hate the apartment and that you go out nights to get away from it! Is that true, Tom?

Tom: No. You say there's so much in your heart that you can't describe to me. That's true of me, too. There's so much in my heart that I can't describe to *you!* So let's respect each other's —

Amanda: But, why — *why,* Tom — are you always so *restless?* Where do you go to, nights?

Tom: I — go to the movies.

Amanda: Why do you go to the movies so much, Tom?

Tom: I go to the movies because — I like adventure. Adventure is something I don't have much of at work, so I go to the movies.

Amanda: But, Tom, you go to the movies *entirely too much!*

Tom: I like a lot of adventure.

Amanda looks baffled, then hurt. As the familiar inquisition resumes he becomes hard and impatient again. Amanda slips back into her querulous attitude toward him.

(Image on screen: Sailing vessel with Jolly Roger.)

Amanda: Most young men find adventure in their careers.

Tom: Then most young men are not employed in a warehouse.

Amanda: The world is full of young men employed in warehouses and offices and factories.

Tom: Do all of them find adventure in their careers?

Amanda: They do or they do without it! Not everybody has a craze for adventure.

Tom: Man is by instinct a lover, a hunter, a fighter, and none of those instincts are given much play at the warehouse!

Amanda: Man is by instinct! Don't quote instinct to me! Instinct is something that people have got away from! It belongs to animals! Christian adults don't want it!

Tom: What do Christian adults want, then, Mother?

Amanda: Superior things! Things of the mind and the spirit! Only animals have to satisfy instincts! Surely your aims are somewhat higher than theirs! Than monkeys — pigs —

Tom: I reckon they're not.

Amanda: You're joking. However, that isn't what I wanted to discuss.

Tom (rising): I haven't much time.
Amanda (pushing his shoulders): Sit down.
Tom: You want me to punch in red° at the warehouse, Mother?
Amanda: You have five minutes. I want to talk about Laura.

(Legend: "Plans and provisions.")

Tom: All right! What about Laura?
Amanda: We have to be making plans and provisions for her. She's older than you, two years, and nothing has happened. She just drifts along doing nothing. It frightens me terribly how she just drifts along.
Tom: I guess she's the type that people call home girls.
Amanda: There's no such type, and if there is, it's a pity! That is unless the home is hers, with a husband!
Tom: What?
Amanda: Oh, I can see the handwriting on the wall as plain as I see the nose in front of my face! It's terrifying! More and more you remind me of your father! He was out all hours without explanation — Then *left! Goodbye!* And me with the bag to hold. I saw that letter you got from the Merchant Marine. I know what you're dreaming of. I'm not standing here blindfolded. Very well, then. Then *do* it! But not till there's somebody to take your place.
Tom: What do you mean?
Amanda: I mean that as soon as Laura has got somebody to take care of her, married, a home of her own, independent — why, then you'll be free to go wherever you please, on land, on sea, whichever way the wind blows! But until that time you've got to look out for your sister. I don't say me because I'm old and don't matter! I say for your sister because she's young and dependent. I put her in business college — a dismal failure! Frightened her so it made her sick to her stomach. I took her over to the Young People's League at the church. Another fiasco. She spoke to nobody, nobody spoke to her. Now all she does is fool with those pieces of glass and play those worn-out records. What kind of a life is that for a girl to lead!
Tom: What can I do about it?
Amanda: Overcome selfishness! Self, self, self is all that you ever think of! *(Tom springs up and crosses to get his coat. It is ugly and bulky. He pulls on a cap with earmuffs.)* Where is your muffler? Put your wool muffler on! *(He snatches it angrily from the closet and tosses it around his neck and pulls both ends tight.)* Tom! I haven't said what I had in mind to ask you.
Tom: I'm too late to —
Amanda (catching his arms — very importunately. Then shyly.) Down at the warehouse, aren't there some — nice young men?
Tom: No!
Amanda: There *must* be — *some.*
Tom: Mother —

Gesture.

Amanda: Find out one that's clean-living — doesn't drink and — ask him out for sister!

punch in red: Be late for work.

Tom: What?
Amanda: For *sister!* To *meet!* Get *acquainted!*
Tom (stamping to door): Oh, my *go-osh!*
Amanda: Will you? *(He opens door. Imploringly.)* Will you? *(He starts down.)* Will you? *Will* you, dear?
Tom (calling back): YES!

Amanda closes the door hesitantly and with a troubled but faintly hopeful expression.
(Screen image: Glamour magazine cover.)
Spot Amanda at phone.

Amanda: Ella Cartwright? This is Amanda Wingfield! How are you, honey? How is that kidney condition? *(Count five.) Horrors! (Count five.)* You're a Christian martyr, yes, honey, that's what you are, a Christian martyr! Well, I just happened to notice in my little red book that your subscription to the *Companion* has just run out! I knew that you wouldn't want to miss out on the wonderful serial starting in this new issue. It's by Bessie Mae Hopper, the first thing she's written since *Honeymoon for Three.* Wasn't that a strange and interesting story? Well, this one is even lovelier, I believe. It has a sophisticated society background. It's all about the horsey set on Long Island!

(Fade out.)

SCENE V

(Legend on screen: "Annunciation.") Fade with music.

It is early dusk of a spring evening. Supper has just been finished in the Wingfield apartment. Amanda and Laura in light colored dresses are removing dishes from the table, in the upstage area, which is shadowy, their movements formalized almost as a dance or ritual, their moving forms as pale and silent as moths.

Tom, in white shirt and trousers, rises from the table and crosses toward the fire-escape.

Amanda (as he passes her): Son, will you do me a favor?
Tom: What?
Amanda: Comb your hair! You look so pretty when your hair is combed! *(Tom slouches on sofa with evening paper. Enormous caption "Franco Triumphs.")*° There is only one respect in which I would like you to emulate your father.
Tom: What respect is that?
Amanda: The care he always took of his appearance. He never allowed himself to look untidy. *(He throws down the paper and crosses to fire-escape.)* Where are you going?
Tom: I'm going out to smoke.
Amanda: You smoke too much. A pack a day at fifteen cents a pack. How much would that amount to in a month? Thirty time fifteen is how much, Tom?

"Franco Triumphs": In January 1939 the Republican forces of Francisco Franco (1892–1975) defeated the Loyalists, ending the Spanish Civil War.

Figure it out and you will be astounded at what you could save. Enough to give you a night-school course in accounting at Washington U! Just think what a wonderful thing that would be for you, son!

Tom is unmoved by the thought.

Tom: I'd rather smoke. *(He steps out on landing, letting the screen door slam.)*
Amanda (sharply): I know! That's the tragedy of it. . . . *(Alone, she turns to look at her husband's picture.)*

(Dance music: "All the World Is Waiting for the Sunrise!")

Tom (to the audience): Across the alley from us was the Paradise Dance Hall. On evenings in spring the windows and doors were open and the music came outdoors. Sometimes the lights were turned out except for a large glass sphere that hung from the ceiling. It would turn slowly about and filter the dusk with delicate rainbow colors. Then the orchestra played a waltz or a tango, something that had a slow and sensuous rhythm. Couples would come outside, to the relative privacy of the alley. You could see them kissing behind ash-pits and telephone poles. This was the compensation for lives that passed like mine, without any change or adventure. Adventure and change were imminent in this year. They were waiting around the corner for all these kids. Suspended in the mist over the Berchtesgaden,° caught in the folds of Chamberlain's° umbrella — In Spain there was Guernica! But here there was only hot swing music and liquor, dance halls, bars, and movies, and sex that hung in the gloom like a chandelier and flooded the world with brief, deceptive rainbows. . . . All the world was waiting for bombardments!

Amanda turns from the picture and comes outside.

Amanda (sighing): A fire-escape landing's a poor excuse for a porch. *(She spreads a newspaper on a step and sits down, gracefully and demurely as if she were settling into a swing on a Mississippi veranda.)* What are you looking at?
Tom: The moon.
Amanda: Is there a moon this evening?
Tom: It's rising over Garfinkel's Delicatessen.
Amanda: So it is! A little silver slipper of a moon. Have you made a wish on it yet?
Tom: Um-hum.
Amanda: What did you wish for?
Tom: That's a secret.
Amanda: A secret, huh? Well, I won't tell mine either. I will be just as mysterious as you.
Tom: I bet I can guess what yours is.
Amanda: Is my head so transparent?
Tom: You're not a sphinx.

Berchtesgaden: A resort in the German Alps where Adolf Hitler had a heavily protected villa.
Chamberlain: Neville Chamberlain (1869–1940); British prime minister who sought to avoid war with Hitler through a policy of appeasement.

Amanda: No, I don't have secrets. I'll tell you what I wished for on the moon. Success and happiness for my precious children! I wish for that whenever there's a moon, and when there isn't a moon, I wish for it, too.

Tom: I thought perhaps you wished for a gentleman caller.

Amanda: Why do you say that?

Tom: Don't you remember asking me to fetch one?

Amanda: I remember suggesting that it would be nice for your sister if you brought home some nice young man from the warehouse. I think I've made that suggestion more than once.

Tom: Yes, you have made it repeatedly.

Amanda: Well?

Tom: We are going to have one.

Amanda: What?

Tom: A gentleman caller!

(The Annunciation is celebrated with music.)
Amanda rises.
(Image on screen: Caller with bouquet.)

Amanda: You mean you have asked some nice young man to come over?

Tom: Yep. I've asked him to dinner.

Amanda: You really did?

Tom: I did!

Amanda: You did, and did he — *accept?*

Tom: He did!

Amanda: Well, well — well, well! That's — lovely!

Tom: I thought that you would be pleased.

Amanda: It's definite, then?

Tom: Very definite

Amanda: Soon?

Tom: Very soon.

Amanda: For heaven's sake, stop putting on and tell me some things, will you?

Tom: What things do you want me to tell you?

Amanda: Naturally I would like to know when he's *coming!*

Tom: He's coming tomorrow.

Amanda: Tomorrow?

Tom: Yep. Tomorrow.

Amanda: But, Tom!

Tom: Yes, Mother?

Amanda: Tomorrow gives me no time!

Tom: Time for what?

Amanda: Preparations! Why didn't you phone me at once, as soon as you asked him, the minute that he accepted? Then, don't you see, I could have been getting ready!

Tom: You don't have to make any fuss.

Amanda: Oh, Tom, Tom, Tom, of course I have to make a fuss! I want things nice, not sloppy! Not thrown together. I'll certainly have to do some fast thinking, won't I?

Tom: I don't see why you have to think at all.

Amanda: You just don't know. We can't have a gentleman caller in a pig-sty! All my wedding silver has to be polished, the monogrammed table linen ought to be laundered! The windows have to be washed and fresh curtains put up. And how about clothes? We have to *wear* something, don't we?

Tom: Mother, this boy is no one to make a fuss over!

Amanda: Do you realize he's the first young man we've introduced to your sister? It's terrible, dreadful, disgraceful that poor little sister has never received a single gentleman caller! Tom, come inside! *(She opens the screen door.)*

Tom: What for?

Amanda: I want to ask you some things.

Tom: If you're going to make such a fuss, I'll call it off, I'll tell him not to come.

Amanda: You certainly won't do anything of the kind. Nothing offends people worse than broken engagements. It simply means I'll have to work like a Turk! We won't be brilliant, but we'll pass inspection. Come on inside. *(Tom follows, groaning.)* Sit down.

Tom: Any particular place you would like me to sit?

Amanda: Thank heavens I've got that new sofa! I'm also making payments on a floor lamp I'll have sent out! And put the chintz covers on, they'll brighten things up! Of course I'd hoped to have these walls re-papered. . . . What is the young man's name?

Tom: His name is O'Connor.

Amanda: That, of course, means fish — tomorrow is Friday! I'll have that salmon loaf — with Durkee's dressing! What does he do? He works at the warehouse?

Tom: Of course! How else would I —

Amanda: Tom, he — doesn't drink?

Tom: Why do you ask me that?

Amanda: Your father *did!*

Tom: Don't get started on that!

Amanda: He *does* drink, then?

Tom: Not that I know of!

Amanda: Make sure, be certain! The last thing I want for my daughter's a boy who drinks!

Tom: Aren't you being a little premature? Mr. O'Connor has not yet appeared on the scene!

Amanda: But will tomorrow. To meet your sister, and what do I know about his character? Nothing! Old maids are better off than wives of drunkards!

Tom: Oh, my God!

Amanda: Be still!

Tom (leaning forward to whisper): Lots of fellows meet girls whom they don't marry!

Amanda: Oh, talk sensibly, Tom — and don't be sarcastic! *(She has gotten a hairbrush.)*

Tom: What are you doing?

Amanda: I'm brushing that cow-lick down! What is this young man's position at the warehouse?

Tom (submitting grimly to the brush and the interrogation): This young man's position is that of a shipping clerk, Mother.

Amanda: Sounds to me like a fairly responsible job, the sort of a job *you* would be in if you just had more *get-up*. What is his salary? Have you got any idea?

Tom: I would judge it to be approximately eighty-five dollars a month.

Amanda: Well — not princely, but —

Tom: Twenty more than I make.

Amanda: Yes, how well I know! But for a family man, eighty-five dollars a month is not much more than you can just get by on. . . .

Tom: Yes, but Mr. O'Connor is not a family man.

Amanda: He might be, mightn't he? Some time in the future?

Tom: I see. Plans and provisions.

Amanda: You are the only young man that I know of who ignores the fact that the future becomes the present, the present the past, and the past turns into everlasting regret if you don't plan for it!

Tom: I will think that over and see what I can make of it.

Amanda: Don't be supercilious with your mother! Tell me some more about this — what do you call him?

Tom: James D. O'Connor. The D. is for Delaney.

Amanda: Irish on *both* sides! *Gracious!* And doesn't drink?

Tom: Shall I call him up and ask him right this minute?

Amanda: The only way to find out about those things is to make discreet inquiries at the proper moment. When I was a girl in Blue Mountain and it was suspected that a young man drank, the girl whose attentions he had been receiving, if any girl *was,* would sometimes speak to the minister of his church, or rather her father would if her father was living, and sort of feel him out on the young man's character. That is the way such things are discreetly handled to keep a young woman from making a tragic mistake!

Tom: Then how did you happen to make a tragic mistake?

Amanda: That innocent look of your father's had everyone fooled! He *smiled* — the world was *enchanted!* No girl can do worse than put herself at the mercy of a handsome appearance! I hope that Mr. O'Connor is not too good-looking.

Tom: No, he's not too good-looking. He's covered with freckles and hasn't too much of a nose.

Amanda: He's not right-down homely, though?

Tom: Not right-down homely. Just medium homely, I'd say.

Amanda: Character's what to look for in a man.

Tom: That's what I've always said, Mother.

Amanda: You've never said anything of the kind and I suspect you would never give it a thought.

Tom: Don't be suspicious of me.

Amanda: At least I hope he's the type that's up and coming.

Tom: I think he really goes in for self-improvement.

Amanda: What reason have you to think so?

Tom: He goes to night school.

Amanda (beaming): Splendid! What does he do, I mean study?

Tom: Radio engineering and public speaking!

Amanda: Then he has visions of being advanced in the world! Any young man who studies public speaking is aiming to have an executive job some day!

And radio engineering? A thing for the future! Both of these facts are very illuminating. Those are the sort of things that a mother should know concerning any young man who comes to call on her daughter. Seriously or — not.

Tom: One little warning. He doesn't know about Laura. I didn't let on that we had dark ulterior motives. I just said, why don't you come have dinner with us? He said okay and that was the whole conversation.

Amanda: I bet it was! You're eloquent as an oyster. However, he'll know about Laura when he gets here. When he sees how lovely and sweet and pretty she is, he'll thank his lucky stars he was asked to dinner.

Tom: Mother, you mustn't expect too much of Laura.

Amanda: What do you mean?

Tom: Laura seems all those things to you and me because she's ours and we love her. We don't even notice she's crippled any more.

Amanda: Don't say crippled! You know that I never allow that word to be used!

Tom: But face facts, Mother. She is and — that's not all —

Amanda: What do you mean "not all"?

Tom: Laura is very different from other girls.

Amanda: I think the difference is all to her advantage.

Tom: Not quite all — in the eyes of others — strangers — she's terribly shy and lives in a world of her own and those things make her seem a little peculiar to people outside the house.

Amanda: Don't say peculiar.

Tom: Face the facts. She is.

(The dance-hall music changes to a tango that has a minor and somewhat ominous tone.)

Amanda: In what way is she peculiar — may I ask?

Tom (gently): She lives in a world of her own — a world of — little glass ornaments, Mother. . . . *(Gets up. Amanda remains holding brush, looking at him, troubled.)* She plays old phonograph records and — that's about all — *(He glances at himself in the mirror and crosses to door.)*

Amanda (sharply): Where are you going?

Tom: I'm going to the movies. *(Out screen door.)*

Amanda: Not to the movies, every night to the movies! *(Follows quickly to screen door.)* I don't believe you always go to the movies! *(He is gone. Amanda looks worriedly after him for a moment. Then vitality and optimism return and she turns from the door. Crossing to portieres.)* Laura! Laura! *(Laura answers from kitchenette.)*

Laura: Yes, Mother.

Amanda: Let those dishes go and come in front! *(Laura appears with dish towel. Gaily.)* Laura, come here and make a wish on the moon!

Laura (entering): Moon — moon?

Amanda: A little silver slipper of a moon. Look over your left shoulder, Laura, and make a wish! *(Laura looks faintly puzzled as if called out of sleep. Amanda seizes her shoulders and turns her at angle by the door.)* Now! Now, darling, *wish!*

Laura: What shall I wish for, Mother?

Amanda (her voice trembling and her eyes suddenly filling with tears): Happiness! Good Fortune!

The violin rises and the stage dims out.

SCENE VI

(Image: High school hero.)

Tom: And so the following evening I brought Jim home to dinner. I had known Jim slightly in high school. In high school Jim was a hero. He had tremendous Irish good nature and vitality with the scrubbed and polished look of white chinaware. He seemed to move in a continual spotlight. He was a star in basketball, captain of the debating club, president of the senior class and the glee club and he sang the male lead in the annual light operas. He was always running or bounding, never just walking. He seemed always at the point of defeating the law of gravity. He was shooting with such velocity through his adolescence that you would logically expect him to arrive at nothing short of the White House by the time he was thirty. But Jim apparently ran into more interference after his graduation from Soldan. His speed had definitely slowed. Six years after he left high school he was holding a job that wasn't much better than mine.

(Image: Clerk.)

He was the only one at the warehouse with whom I was on friendly terms. I was valuable to him as someone who could remember his former glory, who had seen him win basketball games and the silver cup in debating. He knew of my secret practice of retiring to a cabinet of the washroom to work on poems when business was slack in the warehouse. He called me Shakespeare. And while the other boys in the warehouse regarded me with suspicious hostility, Jim took a humorous attitude toward me. Gradually his attitude affected the others, their hostility wore off, and they also began to smile at me as people smile at an oddly fashioned dog who trots across their paths at some distance.

I knew that Jim and Laura had known each other at Soldan, and I had heard Laura speak admiringly of his voice. I didn't know if Jim remembered her or not. In high school Laura had been as unobtrusive as Jim had been astonishing. If he did remember Laura, it was not as my sister, for when I asked him to dinner, he grinned and said, "You know, Shakespeare, I never thought of you as having folks!"

He was about to discover that I did. . . .

(Light up stage.)

(Legend on screen: "The Accent of a Coming Foot.")

Friday evening. It is about five o'clock of a late spring evening which comes "scattering poems in the sky."

A delicate lemony light is in the Wingfield apartment.

Amanda has worked like a Turk in preparation for the gentleman caller. The results are astonishing. The new floor lamp with its rose-silk shade is in place, a colored paper lantern conceals the broken light fixture in the ceiling, new bil-

lowing white curtains are at the windows, chintz covers are on chairs and sofa, a pair of new sofa pillows make their initial appearance.

Open boxes and tissue paper are scattered on the floor.

Laura stands in the middle with lifted arms while Amanda crouches before her, adjusting the hem of the new dress, devout and ritualistic. The dress is colored and designed by memory. The arrangement of Laura's hair is changed; it is softer and more becoming. A fragile, unearthly prettiness has come out in Laura: she is like a piece of translucent glass touched by light, given a momentary radiance, not actual, not lasting.

Amanda (impatiently): Why are you trembling?

Laura: Mother, you've made me so nervous!

Amanda: How have I made you nervous?

Laura: By all this fuss! You make it seem so important!

Amanda: I don't understand you, Laura. You couldn't be satisfied with just sitting home, and yet whenever I try to arrange something for you, you seem to resist it. *(She gets up.)* Now take a look at yourself. No, wait! Wait just a moment — I have an idea!

Laura: What is it now?

Amanda produces two powder puffs which she wraps in handkerchiefs and stuffs in Laura's bosom.

Laura: Mother, what are you doing?

Amanda: They call them "Gay Deceivers"!

Laura: I won't wear them!

Amanda: You will!

Laura: Why should I?

Amanda: Because, to be painfully honest, your chest is flat.

Laura: You make it seem like we were setting a trap.

Amanda: All pretty girls are a trap, a pretty trap, and men expect them to be. *(Legend: "A Pretty Trap.")* Now look at yourself, young lady. This is the prettiest you will ever be! I've got to fix myself now! You're going to be surprised by your mother's appearance! *(She crosses through portieres, humming gaily.)*

Laura moves slowly to the long mirror and stares solemnly at herself.

A wind blows the white curtains inward in a slow, graceful motion and with a faint, sorrowful sighing.

Amanda (off stage): It isn't dark enough yet. *(She turns slowly before the mirror with a troubled look).*

(Legend on screen: "This Is My Sister: Celebrate Her with Strings!" Music.)

Amanda (laughing, off): I'm going to show you something. I'm going to make a spectacular appearance!

Laura: What is it, Mother?

Amanda: Possess your soul in patience — you will see! Something I've resurrected from that old trunk! Styles haven't changed so terribly much after all. . . . *(She parts the portieres.)* Now just look at your mother! *(She wears a girlish frock of yellowed voile with a blue silk sash. She carries a bunch of jonquils — the legend of her youth is nearly revived. Feverishly.)* This is the dress in which I led the cotillion. Won the cakewalk twice at Sunset Hill, wore one spring to the Governor's ball in Jackson! See how I sashayed around the ballroom, Laura? *(She raises her skirt and does a mincing step around the room.)* I wore it on Sundays for my gentlemen callers! I had it on the day I met your father — I had malaria fever all that spring. The change of climate from East Tennessee to the Delta — weakened resistance — I had a little temperature all the time — not enough to be serious — just enough to make me restless and giddy! Invitations poured in — parties all over the Delta! — "Stay in bed," said Mother, "you have fever!" — but I just wouldn't. — I took quinine but kept on going, going! — Evenings, dances! — Afternoons, long, long rides! Picnics — lovely! — So lovely, that country in May. — All lacy with dogwood, literally flooded with jonquils! — That was the spring I had the craze for jonquils. Jonquils became an absolute obsession. Mother said, "Honey, there's no more room for jonquils." And still I kept bringing in more jonquils. Whenever, wherever I saw them, I'd say, "Stop! Stop! I see jonquils!" I made the young men help me gather the jonquils! It was a joke, Amanda and her jonquils! Finally there were no more vases to hold them, every available space was filled with jonquils. No vases to hold them? All right, I'll hold them myself! And then I — *(She stops in front of the picture.) (Music.)* met your father! Malaria fever and jonquils and then — this — boy. . . . *(She switches on the rose-colored lamp.)* I hope they get here before it starts to rain. *(She crosses upstage and places the jonquils in bowl on table.)* I gave your brother a little extra change so he and Mr. O'Connor could take the service car home.

Laura (with altered look): What did you say his name was?

Amanda: O'Connor.

Laura: What is his first name?

Amanda: I don't remember. Oh, yes, I do. It was — Jim!

Laura sways slightly and catches hold of a chair.
(Legend on screen: "Not Jim!")

Laura (faintly): Not — Jim!

Amanda: Yes, that was it, it was Jim! I've never known a Jim that wasn't nice!

(Music: Ominous.)

Laura: Are you sure his name is Jim O'Connor?

Amanda: Yes. Why?

Laura: Is he the one that Tom used to know in high school?

Amanda: He didn't say so. I think he just got to know him at the warehouse.

Laura: There was a Jim O'Connor we both knew in high school — *(Then, with effort.)* If that is the one that Tom is bringing to dinner — you'll have to excuse me, I won't come to the table.

Amanda: What sort of nonsense is this?

Laura: You asked me once if I'd ever liked a boy. Don't you remember I showed you this boy's picture?

Amanda: You mean the boy you showed me in the year book?

Laura: Yes, that boy.

Amanda: Laura, Laura, were you in love with that boy?

Laura: I don't know, Mother. All I know is I couldn't sit at the table if it was him!

Amanda: It won't be him! It isn't the least bit likely. But whether it is or not, you will come to the table. You will not be excused.

Laura: I'll have to be, Mother.

Amanda: I don't intend to humor your silliness, Laura. I've had too much from you and your brother, both! So just sit down and compose yourself till they come. Tom has forgotten his key so you'll have to let them in, when they arrive.

Laura (panicky): Oh, Mother — *you* answer the door!

Amanda (lightly): I'll be in the kitchen — busy!

Laura: Oh, Mother, please answer the door, don't make me do it!

Amanda (crossing into kitchenette): I've got to fix the dressing for the salmon. Fuss, fuss — silliness! — over a gentleman caller!

Door swings shut. Laura is left alone

(Legend: "Terror!")

She utters a low moan and turns off the lamp — sits stiffly on the edge of the sofa, knotting her fingers together.

(Legend on screen: "The Opening of a Door!")

Tom and Jim appear on the fire-escape steps and climb to landing. Hearing their approach, Laura rises with a panicky gesture. She retreats to the portieres.

The doorbell. Laura catches her breath and touches her throat. Low drums.

Amanda (calling): Laura, sweetheart! The door!

Laura stares at it without moving.

Jim: I think we just beat the rain.

Tom: Uh-huh. *(He rings again, nervously. Jim whistles and fishes for a cigarette.)*

Amanda (very, very gaily): Laura, that is your brother and Mr. O'Connor! Will you let them in, darling?

Laura crosses toward kitchenette door.

Laura (breathlessly): Mother — you go to the door!

Amanda steps out of kitchenette and stares furiously at Laura. She points imperiously at the door.

Laura: Please, please!

Amanda (in a fierce whisper): What is the matter with you, you silly thing?

Laura (desperately): Please, you answer it, *please!*

Amanda: I told you I wasn't going to humor you, Laura. Why have you chosen this moment to lose your mind?

Laura: Please, please, please, you go!

Amanda: You'll have to go to the door because I can't!

Laura (despairingly): I can't either!

Amanda: Why?

Laura: I'm *sick!*

Amanda: I'm sick, too — of your nonsense! Why can't you and your brother be normal people? Fantastic whims and behavior! *(Tom gives a long ring.)* Preposterous goings on! Can you give me one reason — *(Calls out lyrically.)* COMING! JUST ONE SECOND! — why should you be afraid to open a door? Now you answer it, Laura!

Laura: Oh, oh, oh . . . *(She returns through the portieres. Darts to the Victrola and winds it frantically and turns it on.)*

Amanda: Laura Wingfield, you march right to that door!

Laura: Yes — yes, Mother!

A faraway, scratchy rendition of "Dardanella" softens the air and gives her strength to move through it. She slips to the door and draws it cautiously open. Tom enters with the caller, Jim O'Connor.

Tom: Laura, this is Jim. Jim, this is my sister, Laura.

Jim (stepping inside): I didn't know that Shakespeare had a sister!

Laura (retreating stiff and trembling from the door): How — how do you do?

Jim (heartily extending his hand): Okay!

Laura touches it hesitantly with hers.

Jim: Your hand's *cold,* Laura!

Laura: Yes, well — I've been playing the Victrola. . .

Jim: Must have been playing classical music on it! You ought to play a little hot swing music to warm you up!

Laura: Excuse me — I haven't finished playing the Victrola. . .

She turns awkwardly and hurries into the front room. She pauses a second by the Victrola. Then catches her breath and darts through the portieres like a frightened deer.

Jim (grinning): What was the matter?

Tom: Oh — with Laura? Laura is — terribly shy.

Jim: Shy, huh? It's unusual to meet a shy girl nowadays. I don't believe you ever mentioned you had a sister.

Tom: Well, now you know. I have one. Here is the *Post Dispatch.* You want a piece of it?

Jim: Uh-huh.

Tom: What piece? The comics?

Jim: Sports! *(Glances at it.)* Ole Dizzy Dean is on his bad behavior.

Tom (disinterest): Yeah? *(Lights cigarette and crosses back to fire-escape door.)*

Jim: Where are *you* going?

Tom: I'm going out on the terrace.

Jim (goes after him): You know, Shakespeare — I'm going to sell you a bill of goods!

Tom: What goods?

Jim: A course I'm taking.

Tom: Huh?

Jim: In public speaking! You and me, we're not the warehouse type.

Tom: Thanks — that's good news. But what has public speaking got to do with it?

Jim: It fits you for — executive positions!

Tom: Awww.

Jim: I tell you it's done a helluva lot for me.

(Image: Executive at desk.)

Tom: In what respect?

Jim: In every! Ask yourself what is the difference between you an' me and men in the office down front? Brains? — No! — Ability? — No! Then what? Just one little thing —

Tom: What is that one little thing?

Jim: Primarily it amounts to — social poise! Being able to square up to people and hold your own on any social level!

Amanda (off stage): Tom?

Tom: Yes, Mother?

Amanda: Is that you and Mr. O'Connor.

Tom: Yes, Mother.

Amanda: Well, you just make yourselves comfortable in there.

Tom: Yes, Mother.

Amanda: Ask Mr. O'Connor if he would like to wash his hands.

Jim: Aw — no — no — thank you — I took care of that at the warehouse. Tom —

Tom: Yes?

Jim: Mr. Mendoza was speaking to me about you.

Tom: Favorably?

Jim: What do you think?

Tom: Well —

Jim: You're going to be out of a job if you don't wake up.

Tom: I am waking up —

Jim: You show no signs.

Tom: The signs are interior.

(Image on screen: The sailing vessel with Jolly Roger again.)

Tom: I'm planning to change. *(He leans over the rail speaking with quiet exhilaration. The incandescent marquees and signs of the first-run movie houses light his face from across the alley. He looks like a voyager.)* I'm right at the point of committing myself to a future that doesn't include the warehouse and Mr. Mendoza or even a night-school course in public speaking.

Jim: What are you gassing about?

Tom: I'm tired of the movies.

Jim: Movies!

Tom: Yes, movies! Look at them — *(A wave toward the marvels of Grand Avenue.)* All of those glamorous people — having adventures — hogging it all, gobbling the whole thing up! You know what happens? People go to the *movies* instead of *moving!* Hollywood characters are supposed to have all the adventures for everybody in America, while everybody in America sits in a dark room and watches them have them! Yes, until there's a war. That's when adventure becomes available to the masses! *Everyone's* dish, not only Gable's! Then the people in the dark room come out of the dark room to have some adventures themselves — Goody, goody — It's our turn now, to go to the South Sea Island — to make a safari — to be exotic, far-off — But I'm not patient. I don't want to wait till then. I'm tired of the *movies* and I am *about* to *move!*

Jim (incredulously): Move?

Tom: Yes.
Jim: When?
Tom: Soon!
Jim: Where? Where?

(Theme three: Music seems to answer the question, while Tom thinks it over. He searches among his pockets.)

Tom: I'm starting to boil inside. I know I seem dreamy, but inside — well, I'm boiling! Whenever I pick up a shoe, I shudder a little thinking how short life is and what I am doing! — Whatever that means. I know it doesn't mean shoes — except as something to wear on a traveler's feet! *(Finds paper.)* Look —
Jim: What?
Tom: I'm a member.
Jim (reading): The Union of Merchant Seamen.
Tom: I paid my dues this month, instead of the light bill.
Jim: You will regret it when they turn the lights off.
Tom: I won't be here.
Jim: How about your mother?
Tom: I'm like my father. The bastard son of a bastard! See how he grins? And he's been absent going on sixteen years!
Jim: You're just talking, you drip. How does your mother feel about it?
Tom: Shhh — Here comes Mother! Mother is not acquainted with my plans!
Amanda (enters portieres): Where are you all?
Tom: On the terrace, Mother.

They start inside. She advances to them. Tom is distinctly shocked at her appearance. Even Jim blinks a little. He is making his first contact with girlish Southern vivacity and in spite of the night-school course in public speaking is somewhat thrown off the beam by the unexpected outlay of social charm.

Certain responses are attempted by Jim but are swept aside by Amanda's gay laughter and chatter. Tom is embarrassed but after the first shock Jim reacts very warmly. Grins and chuckles, is altogether won over.

(Image: Amanda as a girl.)

Amanda (coyly smiling, shaking her girlish ringlets): Well, well, well, so this is Mr. O'Connor. Introductions entirely unnecessary. I've heard so much about you from my boy. I finally said to him, Tom — good gracious! — why don't you bring this paragon to supper? I'd like to meet this nice young man at the warehouse! — Instead of just hearing him sing your praises so much! I don't know why my son is so stand-offish — that's not Southern behavior! Let's sit down and — I think we could stand a little more air in here! Tom, leave the door open. I felt a nice fresh breeze a moment ago. Where has it gone? Mmm, so warm already! And not quite summer, even. We're going to burn up when summer really gets started. However, we're having — we're having a very light supper. I think light things are better fo' this time of year. The same as light clothes are. Light clothes an' light food are what warm weather calls fo'. You know our blood gets so thick during th' winter — it takes a while fo' us to *adjust* ou'selves! — when the season changes. . . . It's come so quick this year. I wasn't prepared. All of a sudden — heavens! Already summer! — I ran to the trunk an' pulled out this light dress — Terribly old! Historical almost! But feels so good — so good an' co-ol, y'know. . . .

Tom: Mother —

Amanda: Yes, honey?

Tom: How about — supper?

Amanda: Honey, you go ask Sister if supper is ready! You know that Sister is in full charge of supper! Tell her you hungry boys are waiting for it. *(To Jim.)* Have you met Laura?

Jim: She —

Amanda: Let you in? Oh, good, you've met already! It's rare for a girl as sweet an' pretty as Laura to be domestic! But Laura is, thank heavens, not only pretty but also very domestic. I'm not at all. I never was a bit. I never could make a thing but angel-food cake. Well, in the South we had so many servants. Gone, gone, gone. All vestiges of gracious living! Gone completely! I wasn't prepared for what the future brought me. All of my gentlemen callers were sons of planters and so of course I assumed that I would be married to one and raise my family on a large piece of land with plenty of servants. But man proposes — and woman accepts the proposal! — To vary that old, old saying a little bit — I married no planter! I married a man who worked for the telephone company! — that gallantly smiling gentleman over there! *(Points to the picture.)* A telephone man who — fell in love with long distance! — Now he travels and I don't even know where! — But what am I going on for about my — tribulations! Tell me yours — I hope you don't have any! Tom?

Tom (returning): Yes, Mother?

Amanda: Is supper nearly ready?

Tom: It looks to me like supper is on the table.

Amanda: Let me look — *(She rises prettily and looks through portieres.)* Oh, lovely — But where is Sister?

Tom: Laura is not feeling well and she says that she thinks she'd better not come to the table.

Amanda: What? — Nonsense! — Laura? Oh, Laura!

Laura (off stage, faintly): Yes, Mother.

Amanda: You really must come to the table. We won't be seated until you come to the table! Come in, Mr. O'Connor. You sit over there and I'll — Laura? Laura Wingfield! You're keeping us waiting, honey! We can't say grace until you come to the table!

The back door is pushed weakly open and Laura comes in. She is obviously quite faint, her lips trembling, her eyes wide and staring. She moves unsteadily toward the table.

(Legend: "Terror!")

Outside a summer storm is coming abruptly. The white curtains billow inward at the windows and there is a sorrowful murmur and deep blue dusk.

Laura suddenly stumbles — She catches at a chair with a faint moan.

Tom: Laura!

Amanda: Laura! *(There is a clap of thunder.) (Legend: "Ah!") (Despairingly.)* Why, Laura, you *are* sick, darling! Tom, help your sister into the living room, dear! Sit in the living room, Laura — rest on the sofa. Well! *(To the gentleman caller.)* Standing over the hot stove made her ill! — I told her that it was just too warm this evening, but — *(Tom comes back in. Laura is on the sofa.)* Is Laura all right now?

Tom: Yes.

Amanda: What *is* that? Rain? A nice cool rain has come up! *(She gives the gentleman caller a frightened look.)* I think we may — have grace — now . . . *(Tom looks at her stupidly.)* Tom, honey — you say grace!

Tom: Oh . . . "For these and all thy mercies — " *(They bow their heads, Amanda stealing a nervous glance at Jim. In the living room Laura, stretched on the sofa, clenches her hand to her lips, to hold back a shuddering sob.)* God's Holy Name be praised —

(The scene dims out.)

SCENE VII

A Souvenir

Half an hour later. Dinner is just being finished in the upstage area, which is concealed by the drawn portieres.

As the curtain rises Laura is still huddled upon the sofa, her feet drawn under her, her head resting on a pale blue pillow, her eyes wide and mysteriously watchful. The new floor lamp with its shade of rose-colored silk gives a soft, becoming light to her face, bringing out the fragile, unearthly prettiness which usually escapes attention. There is a steady murmur of rain, but it is slackening and stops soon after the scene begins; the air outside becomes pale and luminous as the moon breaks out.

A moment after the curtain rises, the lights in both rooms flicker and go out.

Jim: Hey, there, Mr. Light Bulb!

Amanda laughs nervously.
(Legend: "Suspension of a Public Service.")

Amanda: Where was Moses when the lights went out? Ha-ha. Do you know the answer to that one, Mr. O'Connor?

Jim: No, Ma'am, what's the answer?

Amanda: In the dark! *(Jim laughs appreciatively.)* Everybody sit still. I'll light the candles. Isn't it lucky we have them on the table? Where's a match? Which of you gentlemen can provide a match?

Jim: Here.

Amanda: Thank you, sir.

Jim: Not at all, Ma'am!

Amanda: I guess the fuse has burnt out. Mr. O'Connor, can you tell a burnt-out fuse? I know I can't and Tom is a total loss when it comes to mechanics. *(Sound: Getting up: Voices recede a little to kitchenette.)* Oh, be careful you don't bump into something. We don't want our gentleman caller to break his neck. Now wouldn't that be a fine howdy-do?

Jim: Ha-ha! Where is the fuse-box?

Amanda: Right here next to the stove. Can you see anything?

Jim: Just a minute.

Amanda: Isn't electricity a mysterious thing? Wasn't it Benjamin Franklin who tied a key to a kite? We live in such a mysterious universe, don't we? Some people say that science clears up all the mysteries for us. In my opinion it only creates more! Have you found it yet?

Jim: No, Ma'am. All these fuses look okay to me.

Amanda: Tom!

Tom: Yes, Mother?

Amanda: That light bill I gave you several days ago. The one I told you we got the notices about?

Tom: Oh. — Yeah.

(Legend: "Ha!")

Amanda: You didn't neglect to pay it by any chance?

Tom: Why, I —

Amanda: Didn't! I might have known it!

Jim: Shakespeare probably wrote a poem on that light bill, Mrs. Wingfield.

Amanda: I might have known better than to trust him with it! There's such a high price for negligence in this world!

Jim: Maybe the poem will win a ten-dollar prize.

Amanda: We'll just have to spend the remainder of the evening in the nineteenth century, before Mr. Edison made the Mazda lamp!

Jim: Candlelight is my favorite kind of light.

Amanda: That shows you're romantic! But that's no excuse for Tom. Well, we got through dinner. Very considerate of them to let us get through dinner before they plunged us into everlasting darkness, wasn't it, Mr. O'Connor?

Jim: Ha-ha!

Amanda: Tom, as a penalty for your carelessness you can help me with the dishes.

Jim: Let me give you a hand.

Amanda: Indeed you will not!

Jim: I ought to be good for something.

Amanda: Good for something? *(Her tone is rhapsodic.) You?* Why, Mr. O'Connor, nobody, *nobody's* given me this much entertainment in years — as you have!

Jim: Aw, now, Mrs. Wingfield!

Amanda: I'm not exaggerating, not one bit! But Sister is all by her lonesome. You go keep her company in the parlor! I'll give you this lovely old candelabrum that used to be on the altar at the church of the Heavenly Rest. It was melted a little out of shape when the church burnt down. Lightning struck it one spring. Gypsy Jones was holding a revival at the time and he intimated that the church was destroyed because the Episcopalians gave card parties.

Jim: Ha-ha.

Amanda: And how about coaxing Sister to drink a little wine? I think it would be good for her! Can you carry both at once?

Jim: Sure. I'm Superman!

Amanda: Now, Thomas, get into this apron!

The door of kitchenette swings closed on Amanda's gay laughter; the flickering light approaches the portieres.

Laura sits up nervously as he enters. Her speech at first is low and breathless from the almost intolerable strain of being alone with a stranger.

(Legend: "I Don't Suppose You Remember Me at All!")

In her first speeches in this scene, before Jim's warmth overcomes her paralyzing shyness, Laura's voice is thin and breathless as though she has run up a steep flight of stairs.

Jim's attitude is gently humorous. In playing this scene it should be stressed that while the incident is apparently unimportant, it is to Laura the climax of her secret life.

Jim: Hello, there, Laura.

Laura (faintly): Hello. *(She clears her throat.)*

Jim: How are you feeling now? Better?

Laura: Yes. Yes, thank you.

Jim: This is for you. A little dandelion wine. *(He extends it toward her with extravagant gallantry.)*

Laura: Thank you.

Jim: Drink it — but don't get drunk! *(He laughs heartily. Laura takes the glass uncertainly; laughs shyly.)* Where shall I set the candles?

Laura: Oh — oh, anywhere . . .

Jim: How about here on the floor? Any objections?

Laura: No.

Jim: I'll spread a newspaper under to catch the drippings. I like to sit on the floor. Mind if I do?

Laura: Oh, no.

Jim: Give me a pillow?

Laura: What?

Jim: A pillow!

Laura: Oh . . . (Hands him one quickly.)

Jim: How about you? Don't you like to sit on the floor?

Laura: Oh — yes.

Jim: Why don't you, then?

Laura: I — will.

Jim: Take a pillow! *(Laura does. Sits on the other side of the candelabrum. Jim crosses his legs and smiles engagingly at her.)* I can't hardly see you sitting way over there.

Laura: I can — see you.

Jim: I know, but that's not fair, I'm in the limelight. *(Laura moves her pillow closer.)* Good! Now I can see you! Comfortable?

Laura: Yes.

Jim: So am I. Comfortable as a cow. Will you have some gum?

Laura: No, thank you.

Jim: I think that I will indulge, with your permission. *(Musingly unwraps it and holds it up.)* Think of the fortune made by the guy that invented the first piece of chewing gum. Amazing, huh? The Wrigley Building is one of the sights of Chicago. — I saw it summer before last when I went up to the Century of Progress. Did you take in the Century of Progress?

Laura: No, I didn't.

Jim: Well, it was quite a wonderful exposition. What impressed me most was the Hall of Science. Gives you an idea of what the future will be in America, even more wonderful than the present time is! *(Pause. Smiling at her.)* Your brother tells me you're shy. Is that right, Laura?

Laura: I — don't know.

Jim: I judge you to be an old-fashioned type of girl. Well, I think that's a pretty good type to be. Hope you don't think I'm being too personal — do you?

Laura (hastily, out of embarrassment): I believe I *will* take a piece of gum, if you — don't mind. *(Clearing her throat.)* Mr. O'Connor, have you — kept up with your singing?

Jim: Singing? Me?

Laura: Yes. I remember what a beautiful voice you had.

Jim: When did you hear me sing?

(Voice offstage in the pause.)

Voice (offstage): O blow, ye winds, heigh-ho,
A-roving I will go!
I'm off to my love
With a boxing glove —
Ten thousand miles away!

Jim: You say you've heard me sing?

Laura: Oh, yes! Yes, very often . . . I — don't suppose you remember me — at all?

Jim (smiling doubtfully): You know I have an idea I've seen you before. I had that idea soon as you opened the door. It seemed almost like I was about to remember your name. But the name that I started to call you — wasn't a name! And so I stopped myself before I said it.

Laura: Wasn't it — Blue Roses?

Jim (springs up, grinning): Blue Roses! My gosh, yes — Blue Roses! That's what I had on my tongue when you opened the door! Isn't it funny what tricks your memory plays? I didn't connect you with the high school somehow or other. But that's where it was; it was high school. I didn't even know you were Shakespeare's sister! Gosh, I'm sorry.

Laura: I didn't expect you to. You — barely knew me!

Jim: But we did have a speaking acquaintance, huh?

Laura: Yes, we — spoke to each other.

Jim: When did you recognize me?

Laura: Oh, right away!

Jim: Soon as I came in the door?

Laura: When I heard your name I thought it was probably you. I knew that Tom used to know you a little in high school. So when you came in the door — Well, then I was — sure.

Jim: Why didn't you *say* something, then?

Laura (breathlessly): I didn't know what to say, I was — too surprised!

Jim: For goodness' sakes! You know, this sure is funny!

Laura: Yes! Yes, isn't it, though . . .

Jim: Didn't we have a class in something together?

Laura: Yes, we did.

Jim: What class was that?
Laura: It was — singing — Chorus!
Jim: Aw!
Laura: I sat across the aisle from you in the Aud.
Jim: Aw.
Laura: Mondays, Wednesdays, and Fridays.
Jim: Now I remember — you always came in late.
Laura: Yes, it was so hard for me, getting upstairs. I had that brace on my leg — it clumped so loud!
Jim: I never heard any clumping.
Laura (wincing in the recollection): To me it sounded like — thunder!
Jim: Well, well, well. I never even noticed.
Laura: And everybody was seated before I came in. I had to walk in front of all those people. My seat was in the back row. I had to go clumping all the way up the aisle with everyone watching!
Jim: You shouldn't have been self-conscious.
Laura: I know, but I was. It was always such a relief when the singing started.
Jim: Aw, yes, I've placed you now! I used to call you Blue Roses. How was it that I got started calling you that?
Laura: I was out of school a little while with pleurosis. When I came back you asked me what was the matter. I said I had pleurosis — you thought I said Blue Roses. That's what you always called me after that!
Jim: I hope you didn't mind.
Laura: Oh, no — I liked it. You see, I wasn't acquainted with many — people. . . .
Jim: As I remember you sort of stuck by yourself.
Laura: I — I — never had much luck at — making friends.
Jim: I don't see why you wouldn't.
Laura: Well, I — started out badly.
Jim: You mean being —
Laura: Yes, it sort of — stood between me —
Jim: You shouldn't have let it!
Laura: I know, but it did, and —
Jim: You were shy with people!
Laura: I tried not to be but never could —
Jim: Overcome it?
Laura: No, I — I never could!
Jim: I guess being shy is something you have to work out of kind of gradually.
Laura (sorrowfully): Yes — I guess it —
Jim: Takes time!
Laura: Yes —
Jim: People are not so dreadful when you know them. That's what you have to remember! And everybody has problems, not just you, but practically everybody has got some problems. You think of yourself as having the only problems, as being the only one who is disappointed. But just look around you and you will see lots of people as disappointed as you are. For instance, I hoped when I was going to high school that I would be further along at this time, six years later, than I am now — You remember that wonderful write-up I had in *The Torch?*

Laura: Yes! *(She rises and crosses to table.)*

Jim: It said I was bound to succeed in anything I went into! *(Laura returns with the annual.)* Holy Jeez! *The Torch! (He accepts it reverently. They smile across it with mutual wonder. Laura crouches beside him and they begin to turn through it. Laura's shyness is dissolving in his warmth.)*

Laura: Here you are in *Pirates of Penzance!*

Jim (wistfully): I sang the baritone lead in that operetta.

Laura (rapidly): So — *beautifully!*

Jim (protesting): Aw —

Laura: Yes, yes — beautifully — beautifully!

Jim: You heard me?

Laura: All three times!

Jim: No!

Laura: Yes!

Jim: All three performances?

Laura (looking down): Yes.

Jim: Why?

Laura: I — wanted to ask you to — autograph my program.

Jim: Why didn't you ask me to?

Laura: You were always surrounded by your own friends so much that I never had a chance to.

Jim: You should have just —

Laura: Well, I — thought you might think I was —

Jim: Thought I might think you was — what?

Laura: Oh —

Jim (with reflective relish): I was beleaguered by females in those days.

Laura: You were terribly popular!

Jim: Yeah —

Laura: You had such a — friendly way —

Jim: I was spoiled in high school.

Laura: Everybody — liked you!

Jim: Including you?

Laura: I — yes, I — I did, too — *(She gently closes the book in her lap.)*

Jim: Well, well, well! — Give me that program, Laura. *(She hands it to him. He signs it with a flourish.)* There you are — better late than never!

Laura: Oh, I — what a — surprise!

Jim: My signature isn't worth very much right now. But some day — maybe — it will increase in value! Being disappointed is one thing and being discouraged is something else. I am disappointed but I'm not discouraged. I'm twenty-three years old. How old are you?

Laura: I'll be twenty-four in June.

Jim: That's not old age.

Laura: No, but —

Jim: You finished high school?

Laura (with difficulty): I didn't go back.

Jim: You mean you dropped out?

Laura: I made bad grades in my final examinations. *(She rises and replaces the book and the program. Her voice strained.)* How is — Emily Meisenbach getting along?

Jim: Oh, that kraut-head!
Laura: Why do you call her that?
Jim: That's what she was.
Laura: You're not still — going with her?
Jim: I never see her.
Laura: It said in the Personal Section that you were — engaged!
Jim: I know, but I wasn't impressed by that — propaganda!
Laura: It wasn't — the truth?
Jim: Only in Emily's optimistic opinion!
Laura: Oh —

(Legend: "What Have You Done since High School?")

Jim lights a cigarette and leans indolently back on his elbows smiling at Laura with a warmth and charm which light her inwardly with altar candles. She remains by the table and turns in her hands a piece of glass to cover her tumult.

Jim (after several reflective puffs on a cigarette): What have you done since high school? *(She seems not to hear him.)* Huh? *(Laura looks up.)* I said what have you done since high school, Laura?
Laura: Nothing much.
Jim: You must have been doing something these six long years.
Laura: Yes.
Jim: Well, then, such as what?
Laura: I took a business course at business college —
Jim: How did that work out?
Laura: Well, not very — well — I had to drop out, it gave me — indigestion —

Jim laughs gently.

Jim: What are you doing now?
Laura: I don't do anything — much. Oh, please don't think I sit around doing nothing! My glass collection takes up a good deal of my time. Glass is something you have to take good care of.
Jim: What did you say — about glass?
Laura: Collection I said — I have one — *(She clears her throat and turns away again, acutely shy.)*
Jim (abruptly): You know what I judge to be the trouble with you? Inferiority complex! Know what that is? That's what they call it when someone low-rates himself! I understand it because I had it, too. Although my case was not so aggravated as yours seems to be. I had it until I took up public speaking, developed my voice, and learned that I had an aptitude for science. Before that time I never thought of myself as being outstanding in any way whatsoever! Now I've never made a regular study of it, but I have a friend who says I can analyze people better than doctors that make a profession of it. I don't claim that to be necessarily true, but I can sure guess a person's psychology, Laura! *(Takes out his gum.)* Excuse me, Laura. I always take it out when the flavor is gone. I'll use this scrap of paper to wrap it in. I know how it is to get it stuck on a shoe. Yep — that's what I judge to be your principal trouble. A lack of confidence in yourself as a person. You don't have the proper amount of faith in yourself. I'm basing that fact on a

number of your remarks and also on certain observations I've made. For instance that clumping you thought was so awful in high school. You say that you even dreaded to walk into class. You see what you did? You dropped out of school, you gave up an education because of a clump, which as far as I know was practically nonexistent! A little physical defect is what you have. Hardly noticeable even! Magnified thousands of times by imagination! You know what my strong advice to you is? Think of yourself as *superior* in some way!

Laura: In what way would I think?

Jim: Why, man alive, Laura! Just look about you a little. What do you see? A world full of common people! All of 'em born and all of 'em going to die! Which of them has one-tenth of your good points! Or mine! Or anyone else's, as far as that goes — Gosh! Everybody excels in some one thing. Some in many! *(Unconsciously glances at himself in the mirror.)* All you've got to do is discover in *what!* Take me, for instance. *(He adjusts his tie at the mirror.)* My interest happened to lie in electrodynamics. I'm taking a course in radio engineering at night school, Laura, on top of a fairly responsible job at the warehouse. I'm taking that course and studying public speaking.

Laura: Ohhhh.

Jim: Because I believe in the future of television! *(Turning back to her.)* I wish to be ready to go up right along with it. Therefore I'm planning to get in on the ground floor. In fact, I've already made the right connections and all that remains is for the industry itself to get under way! Full steam — *(His eyes are starry.) Knowledge* — Zzzzzp! *Money* — Zzzzzzp! — *Power!* That's the cycle democracy is built on! *(His attitude is convincingly dynamic. Laura stares at him, even her shyness eclipsed in her absolute wonder. He suddenly grins.)* I guess you think I think a lot of myself!

Laura: No — o-o-o, I —

Jim: Now how about you? Isn't there something you take more interest in than anything else?

Laura: Well, I do — as I said — have my — glass collection —

A peal of girlish laughter from the kitchen.

Jim: I'm not right sure I know what you're talking about. What kind of glass is it?

Laura: Little articles of it, they're ornaments mostly! Most of them are little animals made out of glass, the tiniest little animals in the world. Mother calls them a glass menagerie! Here's an example of one, if you'd like to see it! This one is one of the oldest. It's nearly thirteen. *(He stretches out his hand.) (Music: "The Glass Menagerie.")* Oh, be careful — if you breathe, it breaks!

Jim: I'd better not take it. I'm pretty clumsy with things.

Laura: Go on, I trust you with him! *(Places it in his palm.)* There now — you're holding him gently! Hold him over the light, he loves the light! You see how the light shines through him?

Jim: It sure does shine!

Laura: I shouldn't be partial, but he is my favorite one.

Jim: What kind of thing is this one supposed to be?

Laura: Haven't you noticed the single horn on his forehead?

Jim: A unicorn, huh?

Laura: Mmm-hmmm!

Jim: Unicorns, aren't they extinct in the modern world?

Laura: I know!

Jim: Poor little fellow, he must feel sort of lonesome.

Laura (smiling): Well, if he does he doesn't complain about it. He stays on a shelf with some horses that don't have horns and all of them seem to get along nicely together.

Jim: How do you know?

Laura (lightly): I haven't heard any arguments among them!

Jim (grinning): No arguments, huh? Well, that's a pretty good sign! Where shall I set him?

Laura: Put him on the table. They all like a change of scenery once in a while!

Jim (stretching): Well, well, well, well — Look how big my shadow is when I stretch!

Laura: Oh, oh, yes — it stretches across the ceiling!

Jim (crossing to door): I think it's stopped raining. *(Opens fire-escape door.)* Where does the music come from?

Laura: From the Paradise Dance Hall across the alley.

Jim: How about cutting the rug a little, Miss Wingfield?

Laura: Oh, I —

Jim: Or is your program filled up? Let me have a look at it. *(Grasps imaginary card.)* Why, every dance is taken! I'll have to scratch some out. *(Waltz music: "La Golondrina.")* Ahhh, a waltz! *(He executes some sweeping turns by himself then holds his arms toward Laura.)*

Laura (breathlessly): I — can't dance!

Jim: There you go, that inferiority stuff!

Laura: I've never danced in my life!

Jim: Come on, try!

Laura: Oh, but I'd step on you!

Jim: I'm not made out of glass.

Laura: How — how — how do we start?

Jim: Just leave it to me. You hold your arms out a little.

Laura: Like this?

Jim: A little bit higher. Right. Now don't tighten up, that's the main thing about it — relax.

Laura (laughing breathlessly): It's hard not to.

Jim: Okay.

Laura: I'm afraid you can't budge me.

Jim: What do you bet I can't? *(He swings her into motion.)*

Laura: Goodness, yes, you can!

Jim: Let yourself go, now, Laura, just let yourself go.

Laura: I'm —

Jim: Come on!

Laura: Trying.

Jim: Not so stiff — Easy does it!

Laura: I know but I'm —

Jim: Loosen th' backbone! There now, that's a lot better.

Laura: Am I?

Jim: Lots, lots better! *(He moves her about the room in a clumsy waltz.)*

Laura: Oh, my!
Jim: Ha-ha!
Laura: Goodness, yes you can!
Jim: Ha-ha-ha! *(They suddenly bump into the table. Jim stops.)* What did we hit on?
Laura: Table.
Jim: Did something fall off it? I think—
Laura: Yes.
Jim: I hope it wasn't the little glass horse with the horn!
Laura: Yes.
Jim: Aw, aw, aw. Is it broken?
Laura: Now it is just like all the other horses.
Jim: It's lost its—
Laura: Horn! It doesn't matter. Maybe it's a blessing in disguise.
Jim: You'll never forgive me. I bet that that was your favorite piece of glass.
Laura: I don't have favorites much. It's no tragedy, Freckles. Glass breaks so easily. No matter how careful you are. The traffic jars the shelves and things fall off them.
Jim: Still I'm awfully sorry that I was the cause.
Laura (smiling): I'll just imagine he had an operation. The horn was removed to make him feel less—freakish! *(They both laugh.)* Now he will feel more at home with the other horses, the ones that don't have horns . . .
Jim: Ha-ha, that's very funny! *(Suddenly serious.)* I'm glad to see that you have a sense of humor. You know—you're—well—very different! Surprisingly different from anyone else I know! *(His voice becomes soft and hesitant with a genuine feeling.)* Do you mind me telling you that? *(Laura is abashed beyond speech.)* You make me feel sort of—I don't know how to put it! I'm usually pretty good at expressing things, but— This is something that I don't know how to say! *(Laura touches her throat and clears it—turns the broken unicorn in her hands.) (Even softer.)* Has anyone ever told you that you were pretty?

Pause: Music.

(Laura looks up slowly, with wonder, and shakes her head.) Well, you are! In a very different way from anyone else. And all the nicer because of the difference, too. *(His voice becomes low and husky. Laura turns away, nearly faint with the novelty of her emotions.)* I wish that you were my sister. I'd teach you to have some confidence in yourself. The different people are not like other people, but being different is nothing to be ashamed of. Because other people are not such wonderful people. They're one hundred times one thousand. You're one times one! They walk all over the earth. You just stay here. They're common as—weeds, but—you—well, you're—*Blue Roses!*

(Image on screen: Blue Roses.)
(Music changes.)

Laura: But blue is wrong for—roses . . .
Jim: It's right for you—You're—pretty!
Laura: In what respect am I pretty?

Jim: In all respects — believe me! Your eyes — your hair — are pretty! Your hands are pretty! *(He catches hold of her hand.)* You think I'm making this up because I'm invited to dinner and have to be nice. Oh, I could do that! I could put on an act for you, Laura, and say lots of things without being very sincere. But this time I am. I'm talking to you sincerely. I happened to notice you had this inferiority complex that keeps you from feeling comfortable with people. Somebody needs to build your confidence up and make you proud instead of shy and turning away and — blushing — Somebody ought to — ought to — *kiss* you, Laura! *(His hand slips slowly up her arm to her shoulder.) (Music swells tumultuously.) (He suddenly turns her about and kisses her on the lips. When he releases her Laura sinks on the sofa with a bright, dazed look. Jim backs away and fishes in his pocket for a cigarette.) (Legend on screen: "Souvenir.")* Stumble-john! *(He lights the cigarette, avoiding her look. There is a peal of girlish laughter from Amanda in the kitchen. Laura slowly raises and opens her hand. It still contains the little broken glass animal. She looks at it with a tender, bewildered expression.)* Stumble-john! I shouldn't have done that — That was way off the beam. You don't smoke, do you? *(She looks up, smiling, not hearing the question. He sits beside her a little gingerly. She looks at him speechlessly — waiting. He coughs decorously and moves a little farther aside as he considers the situation and senses her feelings, dimly, with perturbation. Gently.)* Would you — care for a — mint? *(She doesn't seem to hear him but her look grows brighter even.)* Peppermint — Life Saver? My pocket's a regular drug store — wherever I go . . . *(He pops a mint in his mouth. Then gulps and decides to make a clean breast of it. He speaks slowly and gingerly.)* Laura, you know, if I had a sister like you, I'd do the same thing as Tom. I'd bring out fellows — introduce her to them. The right type of boys of a type to — appreciate her. Only — well — he made a mistake about me. Maybe I've got no call to be saying this. That may not have been the idea in having me over. But what if it was? There's nothing wrong about that. The only trouble is that in my case — I'm not in a situation to — do the right thing. I can't take down your number and say I'll phone. I can't call up next week and — ask for a date. I thought I had better explain the situation in case you misunderstood it and — hurt your feelings. . . . *(Pause. Slowly, very slowly, Laura's look changes, her eyes returning slowly from his to the ornament in her palm.)*

Amanda utters another gay laugh in the kitchen.

Laura (faintly): You — won't — call again?

Jim: No, Laura, I can't. *(He rises from the sofa.)* As I was just explaining, I've — got strings on me, Laura, I've — been going steady! I go out all the time with a girl named Betty. She's a home-girl like you, and Catholic, and Irish, and in a great many ways we — get along fine. I met her last summer on a moonlight boat trip up the river to Alton, on the *Majestic.* Well — right away from the start it was — love! *(Legend: Love!) (Laura sways slightly forward and grips the arm of the sofa. He fails to notice, now enrapt in his own comfortable being.)* Being in love has made a new man of me! *(Leaning stiffly forward, clutching the arm of the sofa, Laura struggles visibly with her storm. But Jim is oblivious, she is a long way off.)* The power of love is really pretty tremendous! Love is something that — changes the whole world,

Laura! *(The storm abates a little and Laura leans back. He notices her again.)* It happened that Betty's aunt took sick, she got a wire and had to go to Centralia. So Tom — when he asked me to dinner — I naturally just accepted the invitation, not knowing that you — that he — that I — *(He stops awkwardly.)* Huh — I'm a stumble-john! *(He flops back on the sofa. The holy candles in the altar of Laura's face have been snuffed out! There is a look of almost infinite desolation. Jim glances at her uneasily.)* I wish that you would — say something. *(She bites her lip which was trembling and then bravely smiles. She opens her hand again on the broken glass ornament. Then she gently takes his hand and raises it level with her own. She carefully places the unicorn in the palm of his hand, then pushes his fingers closed upon it.)* What are you — doing that for? You want me to have him? — Laura? *(She nods.)* What for?

Laura: A — souvenir . . .

She rises unsteadily and crouches beside the Victrola to wind it up.

(Legend on screen: "Things Have a Way of Turning Out So Badly.")

(Or image: "Gentleman caller waving good-bye! — Gaily.")

At this moment Amanda rushes brightly back in the front room. She bears a pitcher of fruit punch in an old-fashioned cut-glass pitcher and a plate of macaroons. The plate has a gold border and poppies painted on it.

Amanda: Well, well, well! Isn't the air delightful after the shower? I've made you children a little liquid refreshment. *(Turns gaily to the gentleman caller.)* Jim, do you know that song about lemonade?

"Lemonade, lemonade
Made in the shade and stirred with a spade —
Good enough for any old maid!"

Jim (uneasily): Ha-ha! No — I never heard it.

Amanda: Why, Laura! You look so serious!

Jim: We were having a serious conversation.

Amanda: Good! Now you're better acquainted!

Jim (uncertainly): Ha-ha! Yes.

Amanda: You modern young people are much more serious-minded than my generation. I was so gay as a girl!

Jim: You haven't changed, Mrs. Wingfield.

Amanda: Tonight I'm rejuvenated! The gaiety of the occasion, Mr. O'Connor! *(She tosses her head with a peal of laughter. Spills lemonade.)* Oooo! I'm baptizing myself!

Jim: Here — let me —

Amanda (setting the pitcher down): There now. I discovered we had some maraschino cherries. I dumped them in, juice and all!

Jim: You shouldn't have gone to that trouble, Mrs. Wingfield.

Amanda: Trouble, trouble? Why it was loads of fun! Didn't you hear me cutting up in the kitchen? I bet your ears were burning! I told Tom how outdone with him I was for keeping you to himself so long a time! He should have brought you over much, much sooner! Well, now that you've found your way, I want you to be a very frequent caller! Not just occasional but all the time. Oh, we're going to have a lot of gay times together! I see them coming!

Mmm, just breathe that air! So fresh, and the moon's so pretty! I'll skip back out — I know where my place is when young folks are having a — serious conversation!

Jim: Oh, don't go out, Mrs. Wingfield. The fact of the matter is I've got to be going.

Amanda: Going, now? You're joking! Why, it's only the shank of the evening, Mr. O'Connor!

Jim: Well, you know how it is.

Amanda: You mean you're a young workingman and have to keep workingmen's hours. We'll let you off early tonight. But only on the condition that next time you stay later. What's the best night for you? Isn't Saturday night the best night for you workingmen?

Jim: I have a couple of time-clocks to punch, Mrs. Wingfield. One at morning, another one at night!

Amanda: My, but you *are* ambitious! You work at night, too?

Jim: No, Ma'am, not work but — Betty! *(He crosses deliberately to pick up his hat. The band at the Paradise Dance Hall goes into a tender waltz.)*

Amanda: Betty? Betty? Who's — Betty! *(There is an ominous cracking sound in the sky.)*

Jim: Oh, just a girl. The girl I go steady with! *(He smiles charmingly. The sky falls.)*

(Legend: "The Sky Falls.")

Amanda (a long-drawn exhalation): Ohhhh . . . Is it a serious romance, Mr. O'Connor?

Jim: We're going to be married the second Sunday in June.

Amanda: Ohhhh — how nice! Tom didn't mention that you were engaged to be married.

Jim: The cat's not out of the bag at the warehouse yet. You know how they are. They call you Romeo and stuff like that. *(He stops at the oval mirror to put on his hat. He carefully shapes the brim and the crown to give a discreetly dashing effect.)* It's been a wonderful evening, Mrs. Wingfield. I guess this is what they mean by Southern hospitality.

Amanda: It really wasn't anything at all.

Jim: I hope it don't seem like I'm rushing off. But I promised Betty I'd pick her up at the Wabash depot, an' by the time I get my jalopy down there her train'll be in. Some women are pretty upset if you keep 'em waiting.

Amanda: Yes, I know — The tyranny of women! *(Extends her hand.)* Goodbye, Mr. O'Connor. I wish you luck — and happiness — and success! All three of them, and so does Laura — Don't you, Laura?

Laura: Yes!

Jim (taking her hand): Good-bye, Laura. I'm certainly going to treasure that souvenir. And don't you forget the good advice I gave you. *(Raises his voice to a cheery shout.)* So long, Shakespeare! Thanks again, ladies — Good night!

He grins and ducks jauntily out.

Still bravely grimacing, Amanda closes the door on the gentleman caller. Then she turns back to the room with a puzzled expression. She and Laura don't dare to face each other. Laura crouches beside the Victrola to wind it.

Amanda (faintly): Things have a way of turning out so badly. I don't believe that I would play the Victrola. Well, well — well — Our gentleman caller was engaged to be married! Tom!

Tom (from back): Yes, Mother?

Amanda: Come in here a minute. I want to tell you something awfully funny.

Tom (enters with macaroon and a glass of the lemonade): Has the gentleman caller gotten away already?

Amanda: The gentleman caller has made an early departure. What a wonderful joke you played on us!

Tom: How do you mean?

Amanda: You didn't mention that he was engaged to be married.

Tom: Jim? Engaged?

Amanda: That's what he just informed us.

Tom: I'll be jiggered! I didn't know about that.

Amanda: That seems very peculiar.

Tom: What's peculiar about it?

Amanda: Didn't you call him your best friend down at the warehouse?

Tom: He is, but how did I know?

Amanda: It seems extremely peculiar that you wouldn't know your best friend was going to be married!

Tom: The warehouse is where I work, not where I know things about people!

Amanda: You don't know things anywhere! You live in a dream; you manufacture illusions! *(He crosses to door.)* Where are you going?

Tom: I'm going to the movies.

Amanda: That's right, now that you've had us make such fools of ourselves. The effort, the preparations, all the expense! The new floor lamp, the rug, the clothes for Laura! All for what? To entertain some other girl's fiancé! Go to the movies, go! Don't think about us, a mother deserted, an unmarried sister who's crippled and has no job! Don't let anything interfere with your selfish pleasure! Just go, go, go — to the movies!

Tom: All right, I will! The more you shout about my selfishness to me the quicker I'll go, and I won't go to the movies!

Amanda: Go, then! Then go to the moon — you selfish dreamer!

Tom smashes his glass on the floor. He plunges out on the fire-escape, slamming the door. Laura screams — cut by door.

Dance-hall music up. Tom goes to the rail and grips it desperately, lifting his face in the chill white moonlight penetrating the narrow abyss of the alley.

(Legend on screen: "And So Good-Bye . . .")

Tom's closing speech is timed with the interior pantomime. The interior scene is played as though viewed through sound-proof glass. Amanda appears to be making a comforting speech to Laura who is huddled upon the sofa. Now that we cannot hear the mother's speech, her silliness is gone and she has dignity and tragic beauty. Laura's dark hair hides her face until at the end of the speech she lifts it to smile at her mother. Amanda's gestures are slow and graceful, almost dancelike, as she comforts the daughter. At the end of her speech she glances a moment at the father's picture — then withdraws through the portieres. At close of Tom's speech, Laura blows out the candles, ending the play.

Tom: I didn't go to the moon, I went much further — for time is the longest distance between two places — Not long after that I was fired for writing a poem on the lid of a shoe-box. I left Saint Louis. I descended the steps of this fire-escape for a last time and followed, from then on, in my father's footsteps, attempting to find in motion what was lost in space — I traveled around a great deal. The cities swept about me like dead leaves, leaves that were brightly colored but torn away from the branches. I would have stopped, but I was pursued by something. It always came upon me unawares, taking me altogether by surprise. Perhaps it was a familiar bit of music. Perhaps it was only a piece of transparent glass — Perhaps I am walking along a street at night, in some strange city, before I have found companions. I pass the lighted window of a shop where perfume is sold. The window is filled with pieces of colored glass, tiny transparent bottles in delicate colors, like bits of a shattered rainbow. Then all at once my sister touches my shoulder. I turn around and look into her eyes. . . . Oh, Laura, Laura, I tried to leave you behind me, but I am more faithful than I intended to be! I reach for a cigarette, I cross the street, I run into the movies or a bar, I buy a drink, I speak to the nearest stranger — anything that can blow your candles out! *(Laura bends over the candles)* — for nowadays the world is lit by lightning! Blow out your candles, Laura — and so good-bye . . .

She blows the candles out.
(The Scene Dissolves.)

Connections

1. Discuss the symbolic significance of the glass menagerie in Williams's play and the cherry orchard in Chekhov's play (p. 1375). How do the objects' symbolic values contribute to the theme of each play?
2. Compare and contrast the nonrealistic techniques that Williams uses with those used by Arthur Miller in *Death of a Salesman* (p. 1508).
3. Write an essay that explores Tom's narrative function in *The Glass Menagerie* with that of the Chorus in Sophocles' *Oedipus the King* (p. 964) and *Antigone* (p. 1008).

DEATH OF A SALESMAN

Arthur Miller was born in New York City to middle-class Jewish parents. His mother was a teacher and his father a clothing manufacturer. In 1938 he graduated from the University of Michigan, where he had begun writing plays. Six years later his first Broadway play, *The Man Who Had All the Luck,* closed after only a few performances, but *All My Sons* (1947) earned the admiration of both critics and audiences. This drama of family life launched his career, and his next play was even more successful. *Death of a Salesman* (1949) won a Pulitzer Prize and established his international reputation so that Miller, along with Tennessee Williams, became one of the most successful American playwrights of the 1940s and 1950s. During this period, his plays included an adaptation of Henrik Ibsen's *Enemy of the People* (1951), *The Crucible* (1953), and *A View from the Bridge* (1955). Among his later works are *The Misfits* (1961, a screenplay), *After the Fall* (1964), *Incident at Vichy* (1964), *The Price* (1968), *The Creation of the World and Other Business* (1972), and *The Archbishop's Ceiling* (1976).

In *Death of a Salesman* Miller's concerns and techniques are similar to those of social realism. His characters' dialogue sounds much like ordinary speech and deals with recognizable family problems ranging from feelings about one another to personal aspirations. Like Ibsen and Chekhov, Miller places his characters in a social context so that their behavior within the family suggests larger implications: the death of this salesman raises issues concerning the significance and value of the American dream of success.

Although such qualities resemble some of the techniques and concerns of realistic drama, Miller also uses other techniques to express Willy Loman's thoughts. In a sense, the play allows the audience to observe what goes on inside the protagonist's head. (At one point Miller was going to title the play *The Inside of His Head.*) When Willy thinks of the past, we see those events reenacted on stage in the midst of present events. This reenactment is achieved through the use of symbolic nonrealistic sets that appear or disappear as the stage lighting changes to reveal Willy's state of mind.

Willy Loman is in many ways an ordinary human being — indeed, painfully so. He is neither brilliant nor heroic, and his life is made up of unfulfilled dreams and self-deceptions. Yet Miller conceived of him as a tragic figure because, as he wrote in "Tragedy and the Common Man" (see p. 1763), "the common man is as apt a subject for tragedy . . . as kings." Willy's circumstances are radically different from those of Oedipus or Hamlet, but Miller manages to create a character whose human dignity evokes tragic feelings for many readers and viewers.

ARTHUR MILLER (b. 1915)

Death of a Salesman 1949

CERTAIN PRIVATE CONVERSATIONS IN TWO ACTS AND A REQUIEM

Cast

Willy Loman	*Happy*
Linda	*Bernard*
Biff	*The Woman*

Charley	*Stanley*
Uncle Ben	*Miss Forsythe*
Howard Wagner	*Letta*
Jenny	

SCENE: *The action takes place in Willy Loman's house and yard and in various places he visits in the New York and Boston of today.*

Throughout the play, in the stage directions, left and right mean stage left and stage right.

ACT I

A melody is heard, played upon a flute. It is small and fine, telling of grass and trees and the horizon. The curtain rises.

Before us is the Salesman's house. We are aware of towering, angular shapes behind it, surrounding it on all sides. Only the blue light of the sky falls upon the house and forestage; the surrounding area shows an angry glow of orange. As more light appears, we see a solid vault of apartment houses around the small, fragile-seeming home. An air of the dream clings to the place, a dream rising out of reality. The kitchen at center seems actual enough, for there is a kitchen table with three chairs, and a refrigerator. But no other fixtures are seen. At the back of the kitchen there is a draped entrance, which leads to the living-room. To the right of the kitchen, on a level raised two feet, is a bedroom furnished only with a brass bedstead and a straight chair. On a shelf over the bed a silver athletic trophy stands. A window opens onto the apartment house at the side.

Behind the kitchen, on a level raised six and a half feet, is the boys' bedroom, at present barely visible. Two beds are dimly seen, and at the back of the room a dormer window. (This bedroom is above the unseen living-room.) At the left a stairway curves up to it from the kitchen.

The entire setting is wholly or, in some places, partially transparent. The roof-line of the house is one-dimensional; under and over it we see the apartment buildings. Before the house lies an apron, curving beyond the forestage into the orchestra. This forward area serves as the back yard as well as the locale of all Willy's imaginings and of his city scenes. Whenever the action is in the present the actors observe the imaginary wall-lines, entering the house only through its door at the left. But in the scenes of the past these boundaries are broken, and characters enter or leave a room by stepping "through" a wall onto the fore-stage.

From the right, Willy Loman, the Salesman, enters, carrying two large sample cases. The flute plays on. He hears but is not aware of it. He is past sixty years of age, dressed quietly. Even as he crosses the stage to the doorway of the house, his exhaustion is apparent. He unlocks the door, comes into the kitchen, and thankfully lets his burden down, feeling the soreness of his palms. A word-sigh escapes his lips — it might be "Oh, boy, oh, boy." He closes the door, then carries his cases out into the living-room, through the draped kitchen doorway.

Linda, his wife, has stirred in her bed at the right. She gets out and puts on a robe, listening. Most often jovial, she has developed an iron repression of her exceptions to Willy's behavior — she more than loves him, she admires him, as though his mercurial nature, his temper, his massive dreams and little cruelties, served her only as sharp reminders of the turbulent longings within him, longings which she shares but lacks the temperament to utter and follow to their end.

Linda (hearing Willy outside the bedroom, calls with some trepidation): Willy!

Willy: It's all right. I came back.

Linda: Why? What happened? *(Slight pause.)* Did something happen, Willy?

Willy: No, nothing happened.

Linda: You didn't smash the car, did you?

Willy (with casual irritation): I said nothing happened. Didn't you hear me?

Linda: Don't you feel well?

Willy: I'm tired to the death. *(The flute has faded away. He sits on the bed beside her, a little numb.)* I couldn't make it. I just couldn't make it, Linda.

Linda (very carefully, delicately): Where were you all day? You look terrible.

Willy: I got as far as a little above Yonkers. I stopped for a cup of coffee. Maybe it was the coffee.

Linda: What?

Willy (after a pause): I suddenly couldn't drive any more. The car kept going off onto the shoulder, y'know?

Linda (helpfully): Oh. Maybe it was the steering again. I don't think Angelo knows the Studebaker.

Willy: No, it's me, it's me. Suddenly I realize I'm goin' sixty miles an hour and I don't remember the last five minutes. I'm — I can't seem to — keep my mind to it.

Linda: Maybe it's your glasses. You never went for your new glasses.

Willy: No, I see everything. I came back ten miles an hour. It took me nearly four hours from Yonkers.

Linda (resigned): Well, you'll just have to take a rest, Willy, you can't continue this way.

Willy: I just got back from Florida.

Linda: But you didn't rest your mind. Your mind is overactive, and the mind is what counts, dear.

Willy: I'll start out in the morning. Maybe I'll feel better in the morning. *(She is taking off his shoes.)* These goddam arch supports are killing me.

Linda: Take an aspirin. Should I get you an aspirin? It'll soothe you.

Willy (with wonder): I was driving along, you understand? And I was fine. I was even observing the scenery. You can imagine, me looking at scenery, on the road every week of my life. But it's so beautiful up there, Linda, the trees are so thick, and the sun is warm. I opened the windshield and just let the warm air bathe over me. And then all of a sudden I'm goin' off the road! I'm tellin' ya, I absolutely forgot I was driving. If I'd've gone the other way over the white line I might've killed somebody. So I went on again — and five minutes later I'm dreamin' again, and I nearly — *(He presses two fingers against his eyes.)* I have such thoughts, I have such strange thoughts.

Linda: Willy, dear. Talk to them again. There's no reason why you can't work in New York.

Willy: They don't need me in New York. I'm the New England man. I'm vital in New England.

Linda: But you're sixty years old. They can't expect you to keep traveling every week.

Willy: I'll have to send a wire to Portland. I'm supposed to see Brown and Morrison tomorrow morning at ten o'clock to show the line. Goddammit, I could sell them! *(He starts putting on his jacket.)*

Linda (taking the jacket from him): Why don't you go down to the place tomorrow and tell Howard you've simply got to work in New York? You're too accommodating, dear.

Willy: If old man Wagner was alive I'd a been in charge of New York now! That man was a prince, he was a masterful man. But that boy of his, that Howard, he don't appreciate. When I went north the first time, the Wagner Company didn't know where New England was!

Linda: Why don't you tell those things to Howard, dear?

Willy (encouraged): I will, I definitely will. Is there any cheese?

Linda: I'll make you a sandwich.

Willy: No, go to sleep. I'll take some milk. I'll be up right away. The boys in?

Linda: They're sleeping. Happy took Biff on a date tonight.

Willy (interested): That so?

Linda: It was so nice to see them shaving together, one behind the other, in the bathroom. And going out together. You notice? The whole house smells of shaving lotion.

Willy: Figure it out. Work a lifetime to pay off a house. You finally own it, and there's nobody to live in it.

Linda: Well, dear, life is a casting off. It's always that way.

Willy: No, no, some people — some people accomplish something. Did Biff say anything after I went this morning?

Linda: You shouldn't have criticized him, Willy, especially after he just got off the train. You mustn't lose your temper with him.

Willy: When the hell did I lose my temper? I simply asked him if he was making any money. Is that a criticism?

Linda: But, dear, how could he make any money?

Willy (worried and angered): There's such an undercurrent in him. He became a moody man. Did he apologize when I left this morning?

Linda: He was crestfallen, Willy. You know how he admires you. I think if he finds himself, then you'll both be happier and not fight any more.

Willy: How can he find himself on a farm? Is that a life? A farmhand? In the beginning, when he was young, I thought, well, a young man, it's good for him to tramp around, take a lot of different jobs. But it's more than ten years now and he has yet to make thirty-five dollars a week!

Linda: He's finding himself, Willy.

Willy: Not finding yourself at the age of thirty-four is a disgrace!

Linda: Shh!

Willy: The trouble is he's lazy, goddammit!

Linda: Willy, please!

Willy: Biff is a lazy bum!

Linda: They're sleeping. Get something to eat. Go on down.

Willy: Why did he come home? I would like to know what brought him home.

Linda: I don't know. I think he's still lost, Willy. I think he's very lost.

Willy: Biff Loman is lost. In the greatest country in the world a young man with such — personal attractiveness, gets lost. And such a hard worker. There's one thing about Biff — he's not lazy.

Linda: Never.

Willy (with pity and resolve): I'll see him in the morning; I'll have a nice talk with him. I'll get him a job selling. He could be big in no time. My God! Remember how they used to follow him around in high school? When he smiled at one of them their faces lit up. When he walked down the street . . . *(He loses himself in reminiscences.)*

Linda (trying to bring him out of it): Willy, dear, I got a new kind of American-type cheese today. It's whipped.

Willy: Why do you get American when I like Swiss?

Linda: I just thought you'd like a change —

Willy: I don't want a change! I want Swiss cheese. Why am I always being contradicted?

Linda (with a covering laugh): I thought it would be a surprise.

Willy: Why don't you open a window in here, for God's sake?

Linda (with infinite patience): They're all open, dear.

Willy: The way they boxed us in here. Bricks and windows, windows and bricks.

Linda: We should've bought the land next door.

Willy: The street is lined with cars. There's not a breath of fresh air in the neighborhood. The grass don't grow any more, you can't raise a carrot in the back yard. They should've had a law against apartment houses. Remember those two beautiful elm trees out there? When I and Biff hung the swing between them?

Linda: Yeah, like being a million miles from the city.

Willy: They should've arrested the builder for cutting those down. They massacred the neighborhood. *(Lost.)* More and more I think of those days, Linda. This time of year it was lilac and wisteria. And then the peonies would come out, and the daffodils. What fragrance in this room!

Linda: Well, after all, people had to move somewhere.

Willy: No, there's more people now.

Linda: I don't think there's more people. I think —

Willy: There's more people! That's what's ruining this country! Population is getting out of control. The competition is maddening! Smell the stink from that apartment house! And another one on the other side . . . How can they whip cheese?

On Willy's last line, Biff and Happy raise themselves up in their beds, listening.

Linda: Go down, try it. And be quiet.

Willy (turning to Linda, guiltily): You're not worried about me, are you, sweetheart?

Biff: What's the matter?

Happy: Listen!

Linda: You've got too much on the ball to worry about.

Willy: You're my foundation and my support, Linda.

Linda: Just try to relax, dear. You make mountains out of molehills.

Willy: I won't fight with him any more. If he wants to go back to Texas, let him go.

Linda: He'll find his way.

Willy: Sure. Certain men just don't get started till later in life. Like Thomas Edison, I think. Or B. F. Goodrich. One of them was deaf. *(He starts for the bedroom doorway.)* I'll put my money on Biff.

Linda: And Willy — if it's warm Sunday we'll drive in the country. And we'll open the windshield, and take lunch.

Willy: No, the windshields don't open on the new cars.

Linda: But you opened it today.

Willy: Me? I didn't. *(He stops.)* Now isn't that peculiar! Isn't that a remarkable — *(He breaks off in amazement and fright as the flute is heard distantly.)*

Linda: What, darling?

Willy: That is the most remarkable thing.

Linda: What, dear?

Willy: I was thinking of the Chevy. *(Slight pause.)* Nineteen twenty-eight . . . when I had that red Chevy — *(Breaks off.)* That funny? I coulda sworn I was driving that Chevy today.

Linda: Well, that's nothing. Something must've reminded you.

Willy: Remarkable. Ts. Remember those days? The way Biff used to simonize that car? The dealer refused to believe there was eighty thousand miles on it. *(He shakes his head.)* Heh! *(To Linda.)* Close your eyes, I'll be right up. *(He walks out of the bedroom.)*

Happy (to Biff): Jesus, maybe he smashed up the car again!

Linda (calling after Willy): Be careful on the stairs, dear! The cheese is on the middle shelf! *(She turns, goes over to the bed, takes his jacket, and goes out of the bedroom.)*

Light has risen on the boys' room. Unseen, Willy is heard talking to himself, "Eighty thousand miles," and a little laugh. Biff gets out of bed, comes downstage a bit, and stands attentively. Biff is two years older than his brother Happy, well built, but in these days bears a worn air and seems less self-assured. He has succeeded less, and his dreams are stronger and less acceptable than Happy's. Happy is tall, powerfully made. Sexuality is like a visible color on him, or a scent that many women have discovered. He, like his brother, is lost, but in a different way, for he has never allowed himself to turn his face toward defeat and is thus more confused and hard-skinned, although seemingly more content.

Happy (getting out of bed): He's going to get his license taken away if he keeps that up. I'm getting nervous about him, y'know, Biff?

Biff: His eyes are going.

Happy: No, I've driven with him. He sees all right. He just doesn't keep his mind on it. I drove into the city with him last week. He stops at a green light and then it turns red and he goes. *(He laughs.)*

Biff: Maybe he's color-blind.

Happy: Pop? Why he's got the finest eye for color in the business. You know that.

Biff (sitting down on his bed): I'm going to sleep.

Happy: You're not still sour on Dad, are you, Biff?

Biff: He's all right, I guess.

Willy (underneath them, in the living-room): Yes, sir, eighty thousand miles — eighty-two thousand!

Biff: You smoking?

Happy (holding out a pack of cigarettes): Want one?

Biff (taking a cigarette): I can never sleep when I smell it.

Willy: What a simonizing job, heh!

Happy (with deep sentiment): Funny, Biff, y'know? Us sleeping in here again? The old beds. *(He pats his bed affectionately.)* All the talk that went across those two beds, huh? Our whole lives.

Biff: Yeah. Lotta dreams and plans.

Happy (with a deep and masculine laugh): About five hundred women would like to know what was said in this room.

They share a soft laugh.

Biff: Remember that big Betsy something — what the hell was her name — over on Bushwick Avenue?

Happy (combing his hair): With the collie dog!

Biff: That's the one. I got you in there, remember?

Happy: Yeah, that was my first time — I think. Boy, there was a pig! *(They laugh, almost crudely.)* You taught me everything I know about women. Don't forget that.

Biff: I bet you forgot how bashful you used to be. Especially with girls.

Happy: Oh, I still am, Biff.

Biff: Oh, go on.

Happy: I just control it, that's all. I think I got less bashful and you got more so. What happened, Biff? Where's the old humor, the old confidence? *(He shakes Biff's knee. Biff gets up and moves restlessly about the room.)* What's the matter?

Biff: Why does Dad mock me all the time?

Happy: He's not mocking you, he —

Biff: Everything I say there's a twist of mockery on his face. I can't get near him.

Happy: He just wants you to make good, that's all. I wanted to talk to you about Dad for a long time, Biff. Something's — happening to him. He — talks to himself.

Biff: I noticed that this morning. But he always mumbled.

Happy: But not so noticeable. It got so embarrassing I sent him to Florida. And you know something? Most of the time he's talking to you.

Biff: What's he say about me?

Happy: I can't make it out.

Biff: What's he say about me?

Happy: I think the fact that you're not settled, that you're still kind of up in the air . . .

Biff: There's one or two other things depressing him, Happy.

Happy: What do you mean?

Biff: Never mind. Just don't lay it all to me.

Happy: But I think if you just got started — I mean — is there any future for you out there?

Biff: I tell ya, Hap, I don't know what the future is. I don't know — what I'm supposed to want.

Happy: What do you mean?

Biff: Well, I spent six or seven years after high school trying to work myself up. Shipping clerk, salesman, business of one kind or another. And it's a measly manner of existence. To get on that subway on the hot mornings in summer. To devote your whole life to keeping stock, or making phone calls, or selling or buying. To suffer fifty weeks of the year for the sake of a two-week vacation, when all you really desire is to be outdoors, with your shirt off. And always to have to get ahead of the next fella. And still — that's how you build a future.

Happy: Well, you really enjoy it on a farm? Are you content out there?

Biff (with rising agitation): Hap, I've had twenty or thirty different kinds of jobs since I left home before the war, and it always turns out the same. I just realized it lately. In Nebraska when I herded cattle, and the Dakotas, and Arizona, and now in Texas. It's why I came home now, I guess, because I realized it. This farm I work on, it's spring there now, see? And they've got about fifteen new colts. There's nothing more inspiring or — beautiful than the sight of a mare and a new colt. And it's cool there now, see? Texas is cool now, and it's spring. And whenever spring comes to where I am, I suddenly get the feeling, my God, I'm not gettin' anywhere! What the hell am I doing, playing around with horses, twenty-eight dollars a week! I'm thirty-four years old, I oughta be makin' my future. That's when I come running home. And now, I get here, and I don't know what to do with myself. *(After a pause.)* I've always made a point of not wasting my life, and everytime I come back here I know that all I've done is to waste my life.

Happy: You're a poet, you know that, Biff? You're a — you're an idealist!

Biff: No, I'm mixed up very bad. Maybe I oughta get married. Maybe I oughta get stuck into something. Maybe that's my trouble. I'm like a boy. I'm not married. I'm not in business, I just — I'm like a boy. Are you content, Hap? You're a success, aren't you? Are you content?

Happy: Hell, no!

Biff: Why? You're making money, aren't you?

Happy (moving about with energy, expressiveness): All I can do now is wait for the merchandise manager to die. And suppose I get to be merchandise manager? He's a good friend of mine, and he just built a terrific estate on Long Island. And he lived there about two months and sold it, and now he's building another one. He can't enjoy it once it's finished. And I know that's just what I would do. I don't know what the hell I'm workin' for. Sometimes I sit in my apartment — all alone. And I think of the rent I'm paying. And it's crazy. But then, it's what I always wanted. My own apartment, a car, and plenty of women. And still, goddammit, I'm lonely.

Biff (with enthusiasm): Listen, why don't you come out West with me?

Happy: You and I, heh?

Biff: Sure, maybe we could buy a ranch. Raise cattle, use our muscles. Men built like we are should be working out in the open.

Happy (avidly): The Loman Brothers, heh?

Biff (with vast affection): Sure, we'd be known all over the counties!

Happy (enthralled): That's what I dream about, Biff. Sometimes I want to just rip my clothes off in the middle of the store and outbox that goddam merchandise manager. I mean I can outbox, outrun, and outlift anybody in that store, and I have to take orders from those common, petty sons-of-bitches till I can't stand it any more.

Biff: I'm tellin' you, kid, if you were with me I'd be happy out there.

Happy (enthused): See, Biff, everybody around me is so false that I'm constantly lowering my ideals . . .

Biff: Baby, together we'd stand up for one another, we'd have someone to trust.

Happy: If I were around you —

Biff: Hap, the trouble is we weren't brought up to grub for money. I don't know how to do it.

Happy: Neither can I!

Biff: Then let's go!

Happy: The only thing is — what can you make out there?

Biff: But look at your friend. Builds an estate and then hasn't the peace of mind to live in it.

Happy: Yeah, but when he walks into the store the waves part in front of him. That's fifty-two thousand dollars a year coming through the revolving door, and I got more in my pinky finger than he's got in his head.

Biff: Yeah, but you just said —

Happy: I gotta show some of those pompous, self-important executives over there that Hap Loman can make the grade. I want to walk into the store the way he walks in. Then I'll go with you, Biff. We'll be together yet, I swear. But take those two we had tonight. Now weren't they gorgeous creatures?

Biff: Yeah, yeah, most gorgeous I've had in years.

Happy: I get that any time I want, Biff. Whenever I feel disgusted. The trouble is, it gets like bowling or something. I just keep knockin' them over and it doesn't mean anything. You still run around a lot?

Biff: Naa. I'd like to find a girl — steady, somebody with substance.

Happy: That's what I long for.

Biff: Go on! You'd never come home.

Happy: I would! Somebody with character, with resistance! Like Mom, y'know? You're gonna call me a bastard when I tell you this. That girl Charlotte I was with tonight is engaged to be married in five weeks. *(He tries on his new hat.)*

Biff: No kiddin'!

Happy: Sure, the guy's in line for the vice-presidency of the store. I don't know what gets into me, maybe I just have an overdeveloped sense of competition or something, but I went and ruined her, and furthermore I can't get rid of her. And he's the third executive I've done that to. Isn't that a crummy characteristic? And to top it all, I go to their weddings! *(Indignantly, but laughing.)* Like I'm not supposed to take bribes. Manufacturers offer me a hundred-dollar bill now and then to throw an order their way. You know how honest

I am, but it's like this girl, see. I hate myself for it. Because I don't want the girl, and, still, I take it and — I love it!

Biff: Let's to to sleep.

Happy: I guess we didn't settle anything, heh?

Biff: I just got one idea that I think I'm going to try.

Happy: What's that?

Biff: Remember Bill Oliver?

Happy: Sure, Oliver is very big now. You want to work for him again?

Biff: No, but when I quit he said something to me. He put his arm on my shoulder, and he said, "Biff, if you ever need anything, come to me."

Happy: I remember that. That sounds good.

Biff: I think I'll go to see him. If I could get ten thousand or even seven or eight thousand dollars I could buy a beautiful ranch.

Happy: I bet he'd back you. 'Cause he thought highly of you, Biff. I mean, they all do. You're well liked, Biff. That's why I say to come back here, and we both have the apartment. And I'm tellin' you, Biff, any babe you want . . .

Biff: No, with a ranch I could do the work I like and still be something. I just wonder though. I wonder if Oliver still thinks I stole that carton of basketballs.

Happy: Oh, he probably forgot that long ago. It's almost ten years. You're too sensitive. Anyway, he didn't really fire you.

Biff: Well, I think he was going to. I think that's why I quit. I was never sure whether he knew or not. I know he thought the world of me, though. I was the only one he'd let lock up the place.

Willy (below): You gonna wash the engine, Biff?

Happy: Shh!

Biff looks at Happy, who is gazing down, listening. Willy is mumbling in the parlor.

Happy: You hear that?

They listen. Willy laughs warmly.

Biff (growing angry): Doesn't he know Mom can hear that?

Willy: Don't get your sweater dirty, Biff!

A look of pain crosses Biff's face.

Happy: Isn't that terrible? Don't leave again, will you? You'll find a job here. You gotta stick around. I don't know what to do about him, it's getting embarrassing.

Willy: What a simonizing job!

Biff: Mom's hearing that!

Willy: No kiddin', Biff, you got a date? Wonderful!

Happy: Go on to sleep. But talk to him in the morning, will you?

Biff (reluctantly getting into bed): With her in the house. Brother!

Happy (getting into bed): I wish you'd have a good talk with him.

The light on their room begins to fade.

Biff (to himself in bed): That selfish, stupid . . .

Happy: Sh . . . Sleep, Biff.

Their light is out. Well before they have finished speaking, Willy's form is dimly seen below in the darkened kitchen. He opens the refrigerator, searches in there, and takes out a bottle of milk. The apartment houses are fading out, and the entire house and surroundings become covered with leaves. Music insinuates itself as the leaves appear.

Willy: Just wanna be careful with those girls, Biff, that's all. Don't make any promises. No promises of any kind. Because a girl, y'know, they always believe what you tell 'em, and you're very young, Biff, you're too young to be talking seriously to girls.

Light rises on the kitchen. Willy, talking, shuts the refrigerator door and comes downstage to the kitchen table. He pours milk into a glass. He is totally immersed in himself, smiling faintly.

Willy: Too young entirely, Biff. You want to watch your schooling first. Then when you're all set, there'll be plenty of girls for a boy like you. *(He smiles broadly at a kitchen chair.)* That so? The girls pay for you? *(He laughs.)* Boy, you must really be makin' a hit.

Willy is gradually addressing — physically — a point offstage, speaking through the wall of the kitchen, and his voice has been rising in volume to that of a normal conversation.

Willy: I been wondering why you polish the car so careful. Ha! Don't leave the hubcaps, boys. Get the chamois to the hubcaps. Happy, use newspaper on the windows, it's the easiest thing. Show him how to do it, Biff! You see, Happy? Pad it up, use it like a pad. That's it, that's it, good work. You're doin' all right, Hap. *(He pauses, then nods in approbation for a few seconds, then looks upward.)* Biff, first thing we gotta do when we get time is clip that big branch over the house. Afraid it's gonna fall in a storm and hit the roof. Tell you what. We get a rope and sling her around, and then we climb up there with a couple of saws and take her down. Soon as you finish the car, boys, I wanna see ya. I got a surprise for you, boys.

Biff (offstage): Whatta ya got, Dad?

Willy: No, you finish first. Never leave a job till you're finished — remember that. *(Looking toward the "big trees.")* Biff, up in Albany I saw a beautiful hammock. I think I'll buy it next trip, and we'll hang it right between those two elms. Wouldn't that be something? Just swingin' there under those branches. Boy, that would be . . .

Young Biff and Young Happy appear from the direction Willy was addressing. Happy carries rags and a pail of water. Biff, wearing a sweater with a block "S," carries a football.

Biff (pointing in the direction of the car offstage): How's that, Pop, professional?

Willy: Terrific. Terrific job, boys. Good work, Biff.

Happy: Where's the surprise, Pop?

Willy: In the back seat of the car.

Happy: Boy! *(He runs off.)*

Biff: What is it, Dad? Tell me, what'd you buy?

Willy (laughing, cuffs him): Never mind, something I want you to have.

Biff (turns and starts off): What is it, Hap?
Happy (offstage): It's a punching bag!
Biff: Oh, Pop!
Willy: It's got Gene Tunney's signature on it!

Happy runs onstage with a punching bag.

Biff: Gee, how'd you know we wanted a punching bag?
Willy: Well, it's the finest thing for the timing.
Happy (lies down on his back and pedals with his feet): I'm losing weight, you notice, Pop?
Willy (to Happy): Jumping rope is good too.
Biff: Did you see the new football I got?
Willy (examining the ball): Where'd you get a new ball?
Biff: The coach told me to practice my passing.
Willy: That so? And he gave you the ball, heh?
Biff: Well, I borrowed it from the locker room. *(He laughs confidentially.)*
Willy (laughing with him at the theft): I want you to return that.
Happy: I told you he wouldn't like it!
Biff (angrily): Well, I'm bringing it back!
Willy (stopping the incipient argument, to Happy): Sure, he's gotta practice with a regulation ball, doesn't he? *(To Biff.)* Coach'll probably congratulate you on your initiative!
Biff: Oh, he keeps congratulating my initiative all the time, Pop.
Willy: That's because he likes you. If somebody else took that ball there'd be an uproar. So what's the report, boys, what's the report?
Biff: Where'd you go this time, Dad? Gee we were lonesome for you.
Willy (pleased, puts an arm around each boy and they come down to the apron): Lonesome, heh?
Biff: Missed you every minute.
Willy: Don't say? Tell you a secret, boys. Don't breathe it to a soul. Someday I'll have my own business, and I'll never have to leave home any more.
Happy: Like Uncle Charley, heh?
Willy: Bigger than Uncle Charley! Because Charley is not — liked. He's liked, but he's not — well liked.
Biff: Where'd you go this time, Dad?
Willy: Well, I got on the road, and I went north to Providence. Met the Mayor.
Biff: The Mayor of Providence!
Willy: He was sitting in the hotel lobby.
Biff: What'd he say?
Willy: He said, "Morning!" And I said, "You got a fine city here, Mayor." And then he had coffee with me. And then I went to Waterbury. Waterbury is a fine city. Big clock city, the famous Waterbury clock. Sold a nice bill there. And then Boston — Boston is the cradle of the Revolution. A fine city. And a couple of other towns in Mass., and on to Portland and Bangor and straight home!
Biff: Gee, I'd love to go with you sometime, Dad.
Willy: Soon as summer comes.
Happy: Promise?
Willy: You and Hap and I, and I'll show you all the towns. America is full of

beautiful towns and fine, upstanding people. And they know me, boys, they know me up and down New England. The finest people. And when I bring you fellas up, there'll be open sesame for all of us, 'cause one thing, boys: I have friends. I can park my car in any street in New England, and the cops protect it like their own. This summer, heh?

Biff and Happy (together): Yeah! You bet!

Willy: We'll take our bathing suits.

Happy: We'll carry your bags, Pop!

Willy: Oh, won't that be something! Me comin' into the Boston stores with you boys carryin' my bags. What a sensation!

Biff is prancing around, practicing passing the ball.

Willy: You nervous, Biff, about the game?

Biff: Not if you're gonna be there.

Willy: What do they say about you in school, now that they made you captain?

Happy: There's a crowd of girls behind him everytime the classes change.

Biff (taking Willy's hand): This Saturday, Pop, this Saturday—just for you, I'm going to break through for a touchdown.

Happy: You're supposed to pass.

Biff: I'm takin' one play for Pop. You watch me, Pop, and when I take off my helmet, that means I'm breakin' out. Then you watch me crash through that line!

Willy (kisses Biff): Oh, wait'll I tell this in Boston!

Bernard enters in knickers. He is younger than Biff, earnest and loyal, a worried boy.

Bernard: Biff, where are you? You're supposed to study with me today.

Willy: Hey, looka Bernard. What're you lookin' so anemic about, Bernard?

Bernard: He's gotta study, Uncle Willy. He's got Regents next week.

Happy (tauntingly, spinning Bernard around): Let's box, Bernard!

Bernard: Biff! *(He gets away from Happy.)* Listen, Biff, I heard Mr. Birnbaum say that if you don't start studyin' math, he's gonna flunk you, and you won't graduate. I heard him!

Willy: You better study with him, Biff. Go ahead now.

Bernard: I heard him!

Biff: Oh, Pop, you didn't see my sneakers! *(He holds up a foot for Willy to look at.)*

Willy: Hey, that's a beautiful job of printing!

Bernard (wiping his glasses): Just because he printed University of Virginia on his sneakers doesn't mean they've got to graduate him, Uncle Willy!

Willy (angrily): What're you talking about? With scholarships to three universities they're gonna flunk him?

Bernard: But I heard Mr. Birnbaum say—

Willy: Don't be a pest, Bernard! *(To his boys.)* What an anemic!

Bernard: Okay, I'm waiting for you in my house, Biff.

Bernard goes off. The Lomans laugh.

Willy: Bernard is not well liked, is he?

Biff: He's liked, but he's not well liked.

Happy: That's right, Pop.

Willy: That's just what I mean. Bernard can get the best marks in school, y'understand, but when he gets out in the business world, y'understand, you are going to be five times ahead of him. That's why I thank Almighty God you're both built like Adonises.° Because the man who makes an appearance in the business world, the man who creates personal interest, is the man who gets ahead. Be liked and you will never want. You take me, for instance. I never have to wait in line to see a buyer. "Willy Loman is here!" That's all they have to know, and I go right through.

Biff: Did you knock them dead, Pop?

Willy: Knocked 'em cold in Providence, slaughtered 'em in Boston.

Happy (on his back, pedaling again): I'm losing weight, you notice, Pop?

Linda enters, as of old, a ribbon in her hair, carrying a basket of washing.

Linda (with youthful energy): Hello, dear!

Willy: Sweetheart!

Linda: How'd the Chevy run?

Willy: Chevrolet, Linda, is the greatest car ever built. *(To the boys.)* Since when do you let your mother carry wash up the stairs?

Biff: Grab hold there, boy!

Happy: Where to, Mom?

Linda: Hang them up on the line. And you better go down to your friends, Biff. The cellar is full of boys. They don't know what to do with themselves.

Biff: Ah, when Pop comes home they can wait!

Willy (laughs appreciatively): You better go down and tell them what to do, Biff.

Biff: I think I'll have them sweep out the furnace room.

Willy: Good work, Biff.

Biff (goes through wall-line of kitchen to doorway at back and calls down): Fellas! Everybody sweep out the furnace room! I'll be right down!

Voices: All right! Okay, Biff.

Biff: George and Sam and Frank, come out back! We're hangin' up the wash! Come on, Hap, on the double! *(He and Happy carry out the basket.)*

Linda: The way they obey him!

Willy: Well, that's training, the training. I'm tellin' you, I was sellin' thousands and thousands, but I had to come home.

Linda: Oh, the whole block'll be at that game. Did you sell anything?

Willy: I did five hundred gross in Providence and seven hundred gross in Boston.

Linda: No! Wait a minute, I've got a pencil. *(She pulls pencil and paper out of her apron pocket.)* That makes your commission . . . Two hundred — my God! Two hundred and twelve dollars!

Willy: Well, I didn't figure it yet, but . . .

Linda: How much did you do?

Willy: Well, I — I did — about a hundred and eighty gross in Providence. Well, no — it came to — roughly two hundred gross on the whole trip.

Linda (without hesitation): Two hundred gross. That's . . . *(She figures.)*

Adonis: In Greek mythology a young man known for his good looks and favored by Aphrodite, goddess of love and beauty.

Willy: The trouble was that three of the stores were half closed for inventory in Boston. Otherwise I woulda broke records.

Linda: Well, it makes seventy dollars and some pennies. That's very good.

Willy: What do we owe?

Linda: Well, on the first there's sixteen dollars on the refrigerator —

Willy: Why sixteen?

Linda: Well, the fan belt broke, so it was a dollar eighty.

Willy: But it's brand new.

Linda: Well, the man said that's the way it is. Till they work themselves in, y'know.

They move through the wall-line into the kitchen.

Willy: I hope we didn't get stuck on that machine.

Linda: They got the biggest ads of any of them!

Willy: I know, it's a fine machine. What else?

Linda: Well, there's nine-sixty for the washing machine. And for the vacuum cleaner there's three and a half due on the fifteenth. Then the roof, you got twenty-one dollars remaining.

Willy: It don't leak, does it?

Linda: No, they did a wonderful job. Then you owe Frank for the carburetor.

Willy: I'm not going to pay that man! That goddam Chevrolet, they ought to prohibit the manufacture of that car!

Linda: Well, you owe him three and a half. And odds and ends, comes to around a hundred and twenty dollars by the fifteenth.

Willy: A hundred and twenty dollars! My God, if business don't pick up I don't know what I'm gonna do!

Linda: Well, next week you'll do better.

Willy: Oh, I'll knock 'em dead next week. I'll go to Hartford. I'm very well liked in Hartford. You know, the trouble is, Linda, people don't seem to take to me.

They move onto the forestage.

Linda: Oh, don't be foolish.

Willy: I know it when I walk in. They seem to laugh at me.

Linda: Why? Why would they laugh at you? Don't talk that way, Willy.

Willy moves to the edge of the stage. Linda goes into the kitchen and starts to darn stockings.

Willy: I don't know the reason for it, but they just pass me by. I'm not noticed.

Linda: But you're doing wonderful, dear. You're making seventy to a hundred dollars a week.

Willy: But I gotta be at it ten, twelve hours a day. Other men — I don't know — they do it easier. I don't know why — I can't stop myself — I talk too much. A man oughta come in with a few words. One thing about Charley. He's a man of few words, and they respect him.

Linda: You don't talk too much, you're just lively.

Willy (smiling): Well, I figure, what the hell, life is short, a couple of jokes. *(To himself.)* I joke too much! *(The smile goes.)*

Linda: Why? You're —

Willy: I'm fat. I'm very — foolish to look at, Linda. I didn't tell you, but Christmas time I happened to be calling on F. H. Stewarts, and a salesman I know, as I was going in to see the buyer I heard him say something about — walrus. And I — I cracked him right across the face. I won't take that. I simply will not take that. But they do laugh at me. I know that.

Linda: Darling . . .

Willy: I gotta overcome it. I know I gotta overcome it. I'm not dressing to advantage, maybe.

Linda: Willy, darling, you're the handsomest man in the world —

Willy: Oh, no, Linda.

Linda: To me you are. *(Slight pause.)* The handsomest.

From the darkness is heard the laughter of a woman. Willy doesn't turn to it, but it continues through Linda's lines.

Linda: And the boys, Willy. Few men are idolized by their children the way you are.

Music is heard as behind a scrim, to the left of the house, The Woman, dimly seen, is dressing.

Willy (with great feeling): You're the best there is, Linda, you're a pal, you know that? On the road — on the road I want to grab you sometimes and just kiss the life outa you.

The laughter is loud now, and he moves into a brightening area at the left, where The Woman has come from behind the scrim and is standing, putting on her hat, looking into a "mirror" and laughing.

Willy: 'Cause I get so lonely — especially when business is bad and there's nobody to talk to. I get the feeling that I'll never sell anything again, that I won't make a living for you, or a business, a business for the boys. *(He talks through The Woman's subsiding laughter; The Woman primps at the "mirror.")* There's so much I want to make for —

The Woman: Me? You didn't make me, Willy. I picked you.

Willy (pleased): You picked me?

The Woman (who is quite proper-looking, Willy's age): I did. I've been sitting at that desk watching all the salesmen go by, day in, day out. But you've got such a sense of humor, and we do have such a good time together, don't we?

Willy: Sure, sure. *(He takes her in his arms.)* Why do you have to go now?

The Woman: It's two o'clock . . .

Willy: No, come on in! *(He pulls her.)*

The Woman: . . . my sisters'll be scandalized. When'll you be back?

Willy: Oh, two weeks about. Will you come up again?

The Woman: Sure thing. You do make me laugh. It's good for me. *(She squeezes his arm, kisses him.)* And I think you're a wonderful man.

Willy: You picked me, heh?

The Woman: Sure. Because you're so sweet. And such a kidder.

Willy: Well, I'll see you next time I'm in Boston.

The Woman: I'll put you right through to the buyers.

Willy (slapping her bottom): Right. Well, bottoms up!

The Woman (slaps him gently and laughs): You just kill me, Willy. (*He suddenly grabs her and kisses her roughly.)* You kill me. And thanks for the stockings. I love a lot of stockings. Well, good night.

Willy: Good night. And keep your pores open!

The Woman: Oh, Willy!

The Woman bursts out laughing, and Linda's laughter blends in. The Woman disappears into the dark. Now the area at the kitchen table brightens. Linda is sitting where she was at the kitchen table, but now is mending a pair of her silk stockings.

Linda: You are, Willy. The handsomest man. You've got no reason to feel that —

Willy (coming out of The Woman's dimming area and going over to Linda): I'll make it all up to you, Linda, I'll —

Linda: There's nothing to make up, dear. You're doing fine, better than —

Willy (noticing her mending): What's that?

Linda: Just mending my stockings. They're so expensive —

Willy (angrily, taking them from her): I won't have you mending stockings in this house! Now throw them out!

Linda puts the stockings in her pocket.

Bernard (entering on the run): Where is he? If he doesn't study!

Willy (moving to the forestage, with great agitation): You'll give him the answers!

Bernard: I do, but I can't on a Regents! That's a state exam! They're liable to arrest me!

Willy: Where is he? I'll whip him, I'll whip him!

Linda: And he'd better give back that football, Willy, it's not nice.

Willy: Biff! Where is he? Why is he taking everything?

Linda: He's too rough with the girls, Willy. All the mothers are afraid of him!

Willy: I'll whip him!

Bernard: He's driving the car without a license!

The Woman's laugh is heard.

Willy: Shut up!

Linda: All the mothers —

Willy: Shut up!

Bernard (backing quietly away and out): Mr. Birnbaum says he's stuck up.

Willy: Get outa here!

Bernard: If he doesn't buckle down he'll flunk math! *(He goes off.)*

Linda: He's right, Willy, you've gotta —

Willy (exploding at her): There's nothing the matter with him! You want him to be a worm like Bernard? He's got spirit, personality . . .

As he speaks, Linda, almost in tears, exits into the living-room. Willy is alone in the kitchen, wilting and staring. The leaves are gone. It is night again, and the apartment houses look down from behind.

Willy: Loaded with it. Loaded! What is he stealing? He's giving it back, isn't he? Why is he stealing? What did I tell him? I never in my life told him anything but decent things.

Happy in pajamas has come down the stairs; Willy suddenly becomes aware of Happy's presence.

Happy: Let's go now, come on.

Willy (sitting down at the kitchen table): Huh! Why did she have to wax the floors herself? Everytime she waxes the floors she keels over. She knows that!

Happy: Shh! Take it easy. What brought you back tonight?

Willy: I got an awful scare. Nearly hit a kid in Yonkers. God! Why didn't I go to Alaska with my brother Ben that time! Ben! That man was a genius, that man was success incarnate! What a mistake! He begged me to go.

Happy: Well, there's no use in —

Willy: You guys! There was a man started with the clothes on his back and ended up with diamond mines!

Happy: Boy, someday I'd like to know how he did it.

Willy: What's the mystery? The man knew what he wanted and went out and got it! Walked into a jungle, and comes out, the age of twenty-one, and he's rich! The world is an oyster, but you don't crack it open on a mattress!

Happy: Pop, I told you I'm gonna retire you for life.

Willy: You'll retire me for life on seventy goddam dollars a week? And your women and your car and your apartment, and you'll retire me for life! Christ's sake, I couldn't get past Yonkers today! Where are you guys, where are you? The woods are burning! I can't drive a car!

Charley has appeared in the doorway. He is a large man, slow of speech, laconic, immovable. In all he says, despite what he says, there is pity, and, now, trepidation. He has a robe over pajamas, slippers on his feet. He enters the kitchen.

Charley: Everything all right?

Happy: Yeah, Charley, everything's . . .

Willy: What's the matter?

Charley: I heard some noise. I thought something happened. Can't we do something about the walls? You sneeze in here, and in my house hats blow off.

Happy: Let's go to bed, Dad. Come on.

Charley signals to Happy to go.

Willy: You go ahead, I'm not tired at the moment.

Happy (to Willy): Take it easy, huh? *(He exits.)*

Willy: What're you doin' up?

Charley (sitting down at the kitchen table opposite Willy): Couldn't sleep good. I had a heartburn.

Willy: Well, you don't know how to eat.

Charley: I eat with my mouth.

Willy: No, you're ignorant. You gotta know about vitamins and things like that.

Charley: Come on, let's shoot. Tire you out a little.

Willy (hesitantly): All right. You got cards?

Charley (taking a deck from his pocket): Yeah, I got them. Someplace. What is it with those vitamins?

Willy (dealing): They build up your bones. Chemistry.

Charley: Yeah, but there's no bones in a heartburn.

Willy: What are you talkin' about? Do you know the first thing about it?
Charley: Don't get insulted.
Willy: Don't talk about something you don't know anything about.

They are playing. Pause.

Charley: What're you doin' home?
Willy: A little trouble with the car.
Charley: Oh. *(Pause.)* I'd like to take a trip to California.
Willy: Don't say.
Charley: You want a job?
Willy: I got a job, I told you that. *(After a slight pause.)* What the hell are you offering me a job for?
Charley: Don't get insulted.
Willy: Don't insult me.
Charley: I don't see no sense in it. You don't have to go on this way.
Willy: I got a good job. *(Slight pause.)* What do you keep comin' in here for?
Charley: You want me to go?
Willy (after a pause, withering): I can't understand it. He's going back to Texas again. What the hell is that?
Charley: Let him go.
Willy: I got nothin' to give him, Charley, I'm clean, I'm clean.
Charley: He won't starve. None a them starve. Forget about him.
Willy: Then what have I got to remember?
Charley: You take it too hard. To hell with it. When a deposit bottle is broken you don't get your nickel back.
Willy: That's easy enough for you to say.
Charley: That ain't easy for me to say.
Willy: Did you see the ceiling I put up in the living-room?
Charley: Yeah, that's a piece of work. To put up a ceiling is a mystery to me. How do you do it?
Willy: What's the difference?
Charley: Well, talk about it.
Willy: You gonna put up a ceiling?
Charley: How could I put up a ceiling?
Willy: Then what the hell are you bothering me for?
Charley: You're insulted again.
Willy: A man who can't handle tools is not a man. You're disgusting.
Charley: Don't call me disgusting, Willy.

Uncle Ben, carrying a valise and an umbrella, enters the forestage from around the right corner of the house. He is a stolid man, in his sixties, with a mustache and an authoritative air. He is utterly certain of his destiny, and there is an aura of far places about him. He enters exactly as Willy speaks.

Willy: I'm getting awfully tired, Ben.

Ben's music is heard. Ben looks around at everything.

Charley: Good, keep playing; you'll sleep better. Did you call me Ben?

Ben looks at his watch.

Willy: That's funny. For a second there you reminded me of my brother Ben.

Ben: I only have a few minutes. *(He strolls, inspecting the place. Willy and Charley continue playing.)*

Charley: You never heard from him again, heh? Since that time?

Willy: Didn't Linda tell you? Couple of weeks ago we got a letter from his wife in Africa. He died.

Charley: That so.

Ben (chuckling): So this is Brooklyn, eh?

Charley: Maybe you're in for some of his money.

Willy: Naa, he had seven sons. There's just one opportunity I had with that man . . .

Ben: I must make a train, William. There are several properties I'm looking at in Alaska.

Willy: Sure, sure! If I'd gone with him to Alaska that time, everything would've been totally different.

Charley: Go on, you'd froze to death up there.

Willy: What're you talking about?

Ben: Opportunity is tremendous in Alaska, William. Surprised you're not up there.

Willy: Sure, tremendous.

Charley: Heh?

Willy: There was the only man I ever met who knew the answers.

Charley: Who?

Ben: How are you all?

Willy (taking a pot, smiling): Fine, fine.

Charley: Pretty sharp tonight.

Ben: Is mother living with you?

Willy: No, she died a long time ago.

Charley: Who?

Ben: That's too bad. Fine specimen of a lady, Mother.

Willy (to Charley): Heh?

Ben: I'd hoped to see the old girl.

Charley: Who died?

Ben: Heard anything from Father, have you?

Willy (unnerved): What do you mean, who died?

Charley (taking a pot): What're you talkin' about?

Ben (looking at his watch): William, it's half-past eight!

Willy (as though to dispel his confusion he angrily stops Charley's hand): That's my build!

Charley: I put the ace —

Willy: If you don't know how to play the game I'm not gonna throw my money away on you!

Charley (rising): It was my ace, for God's sake!

Willy: I'm through, I'm through!

Ben: When did Mother die?

Willy: Long ago. Since the beginning you never knew how to play cards.

Charley (picks up the cards and goes to the door): All right! Next time I'll bring a deck with five aces.

Willy: I don't play that kind of game!

Charley (turning to him): You ought to be ashamed of yourself!

Willy: Yeah?

Charley: Yeah! *(He goes out.)*

Willy (slamming the door after him): Ignoramus!

Ben (as Willy comes toward him through the wall-line of the kitchen): So you're William.

Willy (shaking Ben's hand): Ben! I've been waiting for you so long! What's the answer? How did you do it?

Ben: Oh, there's a story in that.

Linda enters the forestage, as of old, carrying the wash basket.

Linda: Is this Ben?

Ben (gallantly): How do you do, my dear.

Linda: Where've you been all these years? Willy's always wondered why you —

Willy (pulling Ben away from her impatiently): Where is Dad? Didn't you follow him? How did you get started?

Ben: Well, I don't know how much you remember.

Willy: Well, I was just a baby, of course, only three or four years old —

Ben: Three years and eleven months.

Willy: What a memory, Ben!

Ben: I have many enterprises, William, and I have never kept books.

Willy: I remember I was sitting under the wagon in — was it Nebraska?

Ben: It was South Dakota, and I gave you a bunch of wild flowers.

Willy: I remember you walking away down some open road.

Ben (laughing): I was going to find Father in Alaska.

Willy: Where is he?

Ben: At that age I had a very faulty view of geography, William. I discovered after a few days that I was heading due south, so instead of Alaska, I ended up in Africa.

Linda: Africa!

Willy: The Gold Coast!

Ben: Principally diamond mines.

Linda: Diamond mines!

Ben: Yes, my dear. But I've only a few minutes —

Willy: No! Boys! Boys! *(Young Biff and Happy appear.)* Listen to this. This is your Uncle Ben, a great man! Tell my boys, Ben!

Ben: Why, boys, when I was seventeen I walked into the jungle, and when I was twenty-one I walked out. *(He laughs.)* And by God I was rich.

Willy (to the boys): You see what I been talking about? The greatest things can happen!

Ben (glancing at his watch): I have an appointment in Ketchikan Tuesday week.

Willy: No, Ben! Please tell about Dad. I want my boys to hear. I want them to know the kind of stock they spring from. All I remember is a man with a big beard, and I was in Mamma's lap, sitting around a fire, and some kind of high music.

Ben: His flute. He played the flute.

Willy: Sure, the flute, that's right!

New music is heard, a high, rollicking tune.

Ben: Father was a very great and a very wild-hearted man. We would start in Boston, and he'd toss the whole family into the wagon, and then he'd drive the team right across the country; through Ohio, and Indiana, Michigan, Illinois, and all the Western states. And we'd stop in the towns and sell the flutes that he'd made on the way. Great inventor, Father. With one gadget he made more in a week than a man like you could make in a lifetime.

Willy: That's just the way I'm bringing them up, Ben — rugged, well liked, all-around.

Ben: Yeah? *(To Biff.)* Hit that, boy — hard as you can. *(He pounds his stomach.)*

Biff: Oh, no, sir!

Ben (taking boxing stance): Come on, get to me. *(He laughs.)*

Willy: Got to it, Biff! Go ahead, show him!

Biff: Okay! *(He cocks his fists and starts in.)*

Linda (to Willy): Why must he fight, dear?

Ben (sparring with Biff): Good boy! Good boy!

Willy: How's that, Ben, heh?

Happy: Give him the left, Biff!

Linda: Why are you fighting?

Ben: Good boy! *(Suddenly comes in, trips Biff, and stands over him, the point of his umbrella poised over Biff's eye.)*

Linda: Look out, Biff!

Biff: Gee!

Ben (patting Biff's knee): Never fight fair with a stranger, boy. You'll never get out of the jungle that way. *(Taking Linda's hand and bowing):* It was an honor and a pleasure to meet you, Linda.

Linda (withdrawing her hand coldly, frightened): Have a nice — trip.

Ben (to Willy): And good luck with your — what do you do?

Willy: Selling.

Ben: Yes. Well . . . *(He raises his hand in farewell to all.)*

Willy: No, Ben, I don't want you to think . . . *(He takes Ben's arm to show him.)* It's Brooklyn, I know, but we hunt too.

Ben: Really, now.

Willy: Oh, sure, there's snakes and rabbits and — that's why I moved out here. Why, Biff can fell any one of these trees in no time! Boys! Go right over to where they're building the apartment house and get some sand. We're gonna rebuild the entire front stoop now! Watch this, Ben!

Biff: Yes, sir! On the double, Hap!

Happy (as he and Biff run off): I lost weight, Pop, you notice?

Charley enters in knickers, even before the boys are gone.

Charley: Listen, if they steal any more from that building the watchman'll put the cops on them!

Linda (to Willy): Don't let Biff . . .

Ben laughs lustily.

Willy: You shoulda seen the lumber they brought home last week. At least a dozen six-by-tens worth all kinds a money.

Charley: Listen, if that watchman —

Willy: I gave them hell, understand. But I got a couple of fearless characters there.

Charley: Willy, the jails are full of fearless characters.

Ben (clapping Willy on the back, with a laugh at Charley): And the stock exchange, friend!

Willy (joining in Ben's laughter): Where are the rest of your pants?

Charley: My wife bought them.

Willy: Now all you need is a golf club and you can go upstairs and go to sleep. *(To Ben).* Great athlete! Between him and his son Bernard they can't hammer a nail!

Bernard (rushing in): The watchman's chasing Biff!

Willy (angrily): Shut up! He's not stealing anything!

Linda (alarmed, hurrying off left): Where is he? Biff, dear! *(She exits.)*

Willy (moving toward the left, away from Ben): There's nothing wrong. What's the matter with you?

Ben: Nervy boy. Good!

Willy (laughing): Oh, nerves of iron, that Biff!

Charley: Don't know what it is. My New England man comes back and he's bleedin', they murdered him up there.

Willy: It's contacts, Charley, I got important contacts!

Charley (sarcastically): Glad to hear it, Willy. Come in later, we'll shoot a little casino. I'll take some of your Portland money. *(He laughs at Willy and exits.)*

Willy (turning to Ben): Business is bad, it's murderous. But not for me, of course.

Ben: I'll stop by on my way back to Africa.

Willy (longingly): Can't you stay a few days? You're just what I need, Ben, because I—I have a fine position here, but I—well, Dad left when I was such a baby and I never had a chance to talk to him and I still feel—kind of temporary about myself.

Ben: I'll be late for my train.

They are at opposite ends of the stage.

Willy: Ben, my boys—can't we talk? They'd go into the jaws of hell for me, see, but I—

Ben: William, you're being first-rate with your boys. Outstanding, manly chaps!

Willy (hanging on to his words): Oh, Ben, that's good to hear! Because sometimes I'm afraid that I'm not teaching them the right kind of—Ben, how should I teach them?

Ben (giving great weight to each word, and with a certain vicious audacity): William, when I walked into the jungle, I was seventeen. When I walked out I was twenty-one. And, by God, I was rich! *(He goes off into darkness around the right corner of the house.)*

Willy: . . . was rich! That's just the spirit I want to imbue them with! To walk into a jungle! I was right! I was right! I was right!

Ben is gone, but Willy is still speaking to him as Linda, in nightgown and robe, enters the kitchen, glances around for Willy, then goes to the door of the house, looks out, and sees him. Comes down to his left. He looks at her.

Linda: Willy, dear? Willy?

Willy: I was right!

Linda: Did you have some cheese? *(He can't answer.)* It's very late, darling. Come to bed, heh?
Willy (looking straight up): Gotta break your neck to see a star in this yard.
Linda: You coming in?
Willy: Whatever happened to that diamond watch fob? Remember? When Ben came from Africa that time? Didn't he give me a watch fob with a diamond in it?
Linda: You pawned it, dear. Twelve, thirteen years ago. For Biff's radio correspondence course.
Willy: Gee, that was a beautiful thing. I'll take a walk.
Linda: But you're in your slippers.
Willy (starting to go around the house at the left): I was right! I was! *(Half to Linda, as he goes, shaking his head.)* What a man! There was a man worth talking to. I was right!
Linda (calling after Willy): But in your slippers, Willy!

Willy is almost gone when Biff, in his pajamas, comes down the stairs and enters the kitchen.

Biff: What is he doing out there?
Linda: Sh!
Biff: God Almighty, Mom, how long has he been doing this?
Linda: Don't, he'll hear you.
Biff: What the hell is the matter with him?
Linda: It'll pass by morning.
Biff: Shouldn't we do anything?
Linda: Oh, my dear, you should do a lot of things, but there's nothing to do, so go to sleep.

Happy comes down the stair and sits on the steps.

Happy: I never heard him so loud, Mom.
Linda: Well, come around more often; you'll hear him. *(She sits down at the table and mends the lining of Willy's jacket.)*
Biff: Why didn't you ever write me about this, Mom?
Linda: How would I write to you? For over three months you had no address.
Biff: I was on the move. But you know I thought of you all the time. You know that, don't you, pal?
Linda: I know, dear, I know. But he likes to have a letter. Just to know that there's still a possibility for better things.
Biff: He's not like this all the time, is he?
Linda: It's when you come home he's always the worst.
Biff: When I come home?
Linda: When you write you're coming, he's all smiles, and talks about the future, and — he's just wonderful. And then the closer you seem to come, the more shaky he gets, and then, by the time you get here, he's arguing, and he seems angry at you. I think it's just that maybe he can't bring himself to — to open up to you. Why are you so hateful to each other? Why is that?
Biff (evasively): I'm not hateful, Mom.
Linda: But you no sooner come in the door than you're fighting!
Biff: I don't know why. I mean to change. I'm tryin', Mom, you understand?

Linda: Are you home to stay now?

Biff: I don't know. I want to look around, see what's doin'.

Linda: Biff, you can't look around all your life, can you?

Biff: I just can't take hold, Mom. I can't take hold of some kind of a life.

Linda: Biff, a man is not a bird, to come and go with the springtime.

Biff: Your hair . . . *(He touches her hair.)* Your hair got so gray.

Linda: Oh, it's been gray since you were in high school. I just stopped dyeing it, that's all.

Biff: Dye it again, will ya? I don't want my pal looking old. *(He smiles.)*

Linda: You're such a boy! You think you can go away for a year and . . . . You've got to get it into your head now that one day you'll knock on this door and there'll be strange people here —

Biff: What are you talking about? You're not even sixty, Mom.

Linda: But what about your father?

Biff (lamely): Well, I meant him too.

Happy: He admires Pop.

Linda: Biff, dear, if you don't have any feeling for him, then you can't have any feeling for me.

Biff: Sure I can, Mom.

Linda: No. You can't just come to see me, because I love him. *(With a threat, but only a threat, of tears.)* He's the dearest man in the world to me, and I won't have anyone making him feel unwanted and low and blue. You've got to make up your mind now, darling, there's no leeway any more. Either he's your father and you pay him that respect, or else you're not to come here. I know he's not easy to get along with — nobody knows that better than me — but . . .

Willy (from the left, with a laugh): Hey, hey, Biffo!

Biff (starting to go out after Willy): What the hell is the matter with him? *(Happy stops him.)*

Linda: Don't — don't go near him!

Biff: Stop making excuses for him! He always, always wiped the floor with you. Never had an ounce of respect for you.

Happy: He's always had respect for —

Biff: What the hell do you know about it?

Happy (surlily): Just don't call him crazy!

Biff: He's got no character — Charley wouldn't do this. Not in his own house — spewing out that vomit from his mind.

Happy: Charley never had to cope with what he's got to.

Biff: People are worse off than Willy Loman. Believe me, I've seen them!

Linda: Then make Charley your father, Biff. You can't do that, can you? I don't say he's a great man. Willy Loman never made a lot of money. His name was never in the paper. He's not the finest character that ever lived. But he's a human being, and a terrible thing is happening to him. So attention must be paid. He's not to be allowed to fall into his grave like an old dog. Attention, attention must be finally paid to such a person. You called him crazy —

Biff: I didn't mean —

Linda: No, a lot of people think he's lost his — balance. But you don't have to be very smart to know what his trouble is. The man is exhausted.

Happy: Sure!

Linda: A small man can be just as exhausted as a great man. He works for a company thirty-six years this March, opens up unheard-of territories to their trademark, and now in his old age they take his salary away.

Happy (indignantly): I didn't know that, Mom.

Linda: You never asked, my dear! Now that you get your spending money someplace else you don't trouble your mind with him.

Happy: But I gave you money last —

Linda: Christmas time, fifty dollars! To fix the hot water it cost ninety-seven fifty! For five weeks he's been on straight commission, like a beginner, an unknown!

Biff: Those ungrateful bastards!

Linda: Are they any worse than his sons? When he brought them business, when he was young, they were glad to see him. But now his old friends, the old buyers that loved him so and always found some order to hand him in a pinch — they're all dead, retired. He used to be able to make six, seven calls a day in Boston. Now he takes his valises out of the car and puts them back and takes them out again and he's exhausted. Instead of walking he talks now. He drives seven hundred miles, and when he gets there no one knows him any more, no one welcomes him. And what goes through a man's mind, driving seven hundred miles home without having earned a cent? Why shouldn't he talk to himself? Why? When he has to go to Charley and borrow fifty dollars a week and pretend to me that it's his pay? How long can that go on? How long? You see what I'm sitting here and waiting for? And you tell me he has no character? The man who never worked a day but for your benefit? When does he get the medal for that? Is this his reward — to turn around at the age of sixty-three and find his sons, who he loved better than his life, one a philandering bum —

Happy: Mom!

Linda: That's all you are, my baby! *(To Biff.)* And you! What happened to the love you had for him? You were such pals! How you used to talk to him on the phone every night! How lonely he was till he could come home to you!

Biff: All right, Mom. I'll live here in my room, and I'll get a job. I'll keep away from him, that's all.

Linda: No, Biff. You can't stay here and fight all the time.

Biff: He threw me out of this house, remember that.

Linda: Why did he do that? I never knew why.

Biff: Because I know he's a fake and he doesn't like anybody around who knows!

Linda: Why a fake? In what way? What do you mean?

Biff: Just don't lay it all at my feet. It's between me and him — that's all I have to say. I'll chip in from now on. He'll settle for half my pay check. He'll be all right. I'm going to bed. *(He starts for the stairs.)*

Linda: He won't be all right.

Biff (turning on the stairs, furiously): I hate this city and I'll stay here. Now what do you want?

Linda: He's dying, Biff.

Happy turns quickly to her, shocked.

Biff (after a pause): Why is he dying?

Linda: He's been trying to kill himself.

Biff (with great horror): How?

Linda: I live from day to day.

Biff: What're you talking about?

Linda: Remember I wrote you that he smashed up the car again? In February?

Biff: Well?

Linda: The insurance inspector came. He said that they have evidence. That all these accidents in the last year — weren't — weren't — accidents.

Happy: How can they tell that? That's a lie.

Linda: It seems there's a woman . . . *(She takes a breath as):*

{ *Biff (sharply but contained):* What woman?
{ *Linda (simultaneously):* . . . and this woman . . .

Linda: What?

Biff: Nothing. Go ahead.

Linda: What did you say?

Biff: Nothing. I just said what woman?

Happy: What about her?

Linda: Well, it seems she was walking down the road and saw his car. She says that he wasn't driving fast at all, and that he didn't skid. She says he came to that little bridge, and then deliberately smashed into the railing, and it was only the shallowness of the water that saved him.

Biff: Oh, no, he probably just fell asleep again.

Linda: I don't think he fell asleep.

Biff: Why not?

Linda: Last month . . . *(With great difficulty.)* Oh, boys, it's so hard to say a thing like this! He's just a big stupid man to you, but I tell you there's more good in him than in many other people. *(She chokes, wipes her eyes.)* I was looking for a fuse. The lights blew out, and I went down the cellar. And behind the fuse box — it happened to fall out — was a length of rubber pipe — just short.

Happy: No kidding?

Linda: There's a little attachment on the end of it. I knew right away. And sure enough, on the bottom of the water heater there's a new little nipple on the gas pipe.

Happy (angrily): That — jerk.

Biff: Did you have it taken off?

Linda: I'm — I'm ashamed to. How can I mention it to him? Every day I go down and take away that little rubber pipe. But, when he comes home, I put it back where it was. How can I insult him that way? I don't know what to do. I live from day to day, boys. I tell you, I know every thought in his mind. It sounds so old-fashioned and silly, but I tell you he put his whole life into you and you've turned your backs on him. *(She is bent over in chair, weeping, her face in her hands.)* Biff, I swear to God! Biff, his life is in your hands!

Happy (to Biff): How do you like that damned fool!

Biff (kissing her): All right, pal, all right. It's all settled now. I've been remiss. I know that, Mom. But now I'll stay, and I swear to you, I'll apply myself. *(Kneeling in front of her, in a fever of self-reproach.)* It's just — you see, Mom, I don't fit in business. Not that I won't try. I'll try, and I'll make good.

Happy: Sure you will. The trouble with you in business was you never tried to please people.

Biff: I know, I —

Happy: Like when you worked for Harrison's. Bob Harrison said you were tops, and then you go and do some damn fool thing like whistling whole songs in the elevator like a comedian.

Biff (against Happy): So what? I like to whistle sometimes.

Happy: You don't raise a guy to a responsible job who whistles in the elevator!

Linda: Well, don't argue about it now.

Happy: Like when you'd go off and swim in the middle of the day instead of taking the line around.

Biff (his resentment rising): Well, don't you run off? You take off sometimes, don't you? On a nice summer day?

Happy: Yeah, but I cover myself!

Linda: Boys!

Happy: If I'm going to take a fade the boss can call any number where I'm supposed to be and they'll swear to him that I just left. I'll tell you something that I hate to say, Biff, but in the business world some of them think you're crazy.

Biff (angered): Screw the business world!

Happy: All right, screw it! Great, but cover yourself!

Linda: Hap, Hap!

Biff: I don't care what they think! They've laughed at Dad for years, and you know why? Because we don't belong in this nuthouse of a city! We should be mixing cement on some open plain, or — or carpenters. A carpenter is allowed to whistle!

Willy walks in from the entrance of the house, at left.

Willy: Even your grandfather was better than a carpenter. *(Pause. They watch him.)* You never grew up. Bernard does not whistle in the elevator, I assure you.

Biff (as though to laugh Willy out of it): Yeah, but you do, Pop.

Willy: I never in my life whistled in an elevator! And who in the business world thinks I'm crazy?

Biff: I didn't mean it like that, Pop. Now don't make a whole thing out of it, will ya?

Willy: Go back to the West! Be a carpenter, a cowboy, enjoy yourself!

Linda: Willy, he was just saying —

Willy: I heard what he said!

Happy (trying to quiet Willy): Hey, Pop, come on now . . .

Willy (continuing over Happy's line): They laugh at me, heh? Go to Filene's, go to the Hub, go to Slattery's, Boston. Call out the name Willy Loman and see what happens! Big shot!

Biff: All right, Pop.

Willy: Big!

Biff: All right!

Willy: Why do you always insult me?

Biff: I didn't say a word. *(To Linda.)* Did I say a word?

Linda: He didn't say anything, Willy.

Willy (going to the doorway of the living-room): All right, good night, good night.

Linda: Willy, dear, he just decided . . .

Willy (to Biff): If you get tired hanging around tomorrow, paint the ceiling I put up in the living-room.

Biff: I'm leaving early tomorrow.

Happy: He's going to see Bill Oliver, Pop.

Willy (interestedly): Oliver? For what?

Biff (with reserve, but trying, trying): He always said he'd stake me. I'd like to go into business, so maybe I can take him up on it.

Linda: Isn't that wonderful?

Willy: Don't interrupt. What's wonderful about it? There's fifty men in the City of New York who'd stake him. *(To Biff.)* Sporting goods?

Biff: I guess so. I know something about it and —

Willy: He knows something about it! You know sporting goods better than Spalding, for God's sake! How much is he giving you?

Biff: I don't know, I didn't even see him yet, but —

Willy: Then what're you talkin' about?

Biff (getting angry): Well, all I said was I'm gonna see him, that's all!

Willy (turning away): Ah, you're counting your chickens again.

Biff (starting left for the stairs): Oh, Jesus, I'm going to sleep!

Willy (calling after him): Don't curse in this house!

Biff (turning): Since when did you get so clean?

Happy (trying to stop them): Wait a . . .

Willy: Don't use that language to me! I won't have it!

Happy (grabbing Biff, shouts): Wait a minute! I got an idea. I got a feasible idea. Come here, Biff, let's talk this over now, let's talk some sense here. When I was down in Florida last time, I thought of a great idea to sell sporting goods. It just came back to me. You and I, Biff — we have a line, the Loman Line. We train a couple of weeks, and put on a couple of exhibitions, see?

Willy: That's an idea!

Happy: Wait! We form two basketball teams, see? Two water-polo teams. We play each other. It's a million dollars' worth of publicity. Two brothers, see? The Loman Brothers. Displays in the Royal Palms — all the hotels. And banners over the ring and the basketball court: "Loman Brothers." Baby, we could sell sporting goods!

Willy: That is a one-million-dollar idea!

Linda: Marvelous!

Biff: I'm in great shape as far as that's concerned.

Happy: And the beauty of it is, Biff, it wouldn't be like a business. We'd be out playin' ball again . . .

Biff (enthused): Yeah, that's . . .

Willy: Million-dollar . . .

Happy: And you wouldn't get fed up with it, Biff. It'd be the family again. There'd be the old honor, and comradeship, and if you wanted to go off for a swim or somethin' — well, you'd do it! Without some smart cooky gettin' up ahead of you!

Willy: Lick the world! You guys together could absolutely lick the civilized world.

Biff: I'll see Oliver tomorrow. Hap, if we could work that out . . .

Linda: Maybe things are beginning to —

Willy (wildly enthused, to Linda): Stop interrupting! *(To Biff.)* But don't wear sport jacket and slacks when you see Oliver.

Biff: No, I'll —

Willy: A business suit, and talk as little as possible, and don't crack any jokes.

Biff: He did like me. Always liked me.

Linda: He loved you!

Willy (to Linda): Will you stop! *(To Biff.)* Walk in very serious. You are not applying for a boy's job. Money is to pass. Be quiet, fine, and serious. Everybody likes a kidder, but nobody lends him money.

Happy: I'll try to get some myself, Biff. I'm sure I can.

Willy: I see great things for you kids, I think your troubles are over. But remember, start big and you'll end big. Ask for fifteen. How much you gonna ask for?

Biff: Gee, I don't know —

Willy: And don't say "Gee." "Gee" is a boy's word. A man walking in for fifteen thousand dollars does not say "Gee!"

Biff: Ten, I think, would be top though.

Willy: Don't be so modest. You always started too low. Walk in with a big laugh. Don't look worried. Start off with a couple of your good stories to lighten things up. It's not what you say, it's how you say it — because personality always wins the day.

Linda: Oliver always thought the highest of him —

Willy: Will you let me talk?

Biff: Don't yell at her, Pop, will ya?

Willy (angrily): I was talking, wasn't I?

Biff: I don't like you yelling at her all the time, and I'm tellin' you, that's all.

Willy: What're you, takin' over this house?

Linda: Willy —

Willy (turning on her): Don't take his side all the time, goddammit!

Biff (furiously): Stop yelling at her!

Willy (suddenly pulling on his cheek, beaten down, guilt ridden): Give my best to Bill Oliver — he may remember me. *(He exits through the living-room doorway.)*

Linda (her voice subdued): What'd you have to start that for? *(Biff turns away.)* You see how sweet he was as soon as you talked hopefully? *(She goes over to Biff.)* Come up and say good night to him. Don't let him go to bed that way.

Happy: Come on, Biff, let's buck him up.

Linda: Please, dear. Just say good night. It takes so little to make him happy. Come. *(She goes through the living-room doorway, calling upstairs from within the living-room.)* Your pajamas are hanging in the bathroom, Willy!

Happy (looking toward where Linda went out): What a woman! They broke the mold when they made her. You know that, Biff?

Biff: He's off salary. My God, working on commission!

Happy: Well, let's face it: he's no hot-shot selling man. Except that sometimes, you have to admit, he's a sweet personality.

Biff (deciding): Lend me ten bucks, will ya? I want to buy some new ties.

Happy: I'll take you to a place I know. Beautiful stuff. Wear one of my striped shirts tomorrow.

Biff: She got gray. Mom got awful old. Gee, I'm gonna go in to Oliver tomorrow and knock him for a —

Happy: Come on up. Tell that to Dad. Let's give him a whirl. Come on.

Biff (steamed up): You know, with ten thousand bucks, boy!

Happy (as they go into the living-room): That's the talk, Biff, that's the first time I've heard the old confidence out of you! *(From within the living-room, fading off.)* You're gonna live with me, kid, and any babe you want just say the word . . . *(The last lines are hardly heard. They are mounting the stairs to their parents' bedroom.)*

Linda (entering her bedroom and addressing Willy, who is in the bathroom. She is straightening the bed for him): Can you do anything about the shower? It drips.

Willy (from the bathroom): All of a sudden everything falls to pieces! Goddam plumbing, oughta be sued, those people. I hardly finished putting it in and the thing . . . *(His words rumble off.)*

Linda: I'm just wondering if Oliver will remember him. You think he might?

Willy (coming out of the bathroom in his pajamas): Remember him? What's the matter with you, you crazy? If he'd've stayed with Oliver he'd be on top by now! Wait'll Oliver gets a look at him. You don't know the average caliber any more. The average young man today — *(he is getting into bed)* — is got a caliber of zero. Greatest thing in the world for him was to bum around.

Biff and Happy enter the bedroom. Slight pause.

Willy (stops short, looking at Biff): Glad to hear it, boy.

Happy: He wanted to say good night to you, sport.

Willy (to Biff): Yeah. Knock him dead, boy. What'd you want to tell me?

Biff: Just take it easy, Pop. Good night. *(He turns to go.)*

Willy (unable to resist): And if anything falls off the desk while you're talking to him — like a package or something — don't you pick it up. They have office boys for that.

Linda: I'll make a big breakfast —

Willy: Will you let me finish? *(To Biff.)* Tell him you were in the business in the West. Not farm work.

Biff: All right, Dad.

Linda: I think everything —

Willy (going right through her speech): And don't undersell yourself. No less than fifteen thousand dollars.

Biff (unable to bear him): Okay. Good night, Mom. *(He starts moving.)*

Willy: Because you got a greatness in you, Biff, remember that. You got all kinds a greatness . . . *(He lies back, exhausted. Biff walks out.)*

Linda (calling after Biff): Sleep well, darling!

Happy: I'm gonna get married, Mom. I wanted to tell you.

Linda: Go to sleep, dear.

Happy (going): I just wanted to tell you.

Willy: Keep up the good work. *(Happy exits.)* God . . . remember that Ebbets Field game? The championship of the city?

Linda: Just rest. Should I sing to you?

Willy: Yeah. Sing to me. *(Linda hums a soft lullaby.)* When that team came out — he was the tallest, remember?

Linda: Oh, yes. And in gold.

Biff enters the darkened kitchen, takes a cigarette, and leaves the house. He comes downstage into a golden pool of light. He smokes, staring at the night.

Willy: Like a young god. Hercules — something like that. And the sun, the sun all around him. Remember how he waved to me? Right up from the field, with the representatives of three colleges standing by? And the buyers I brought, and the cheers when he came out — Loman, Loman, Loman! God Almighty, he'll be great yet. A star like that, magnificent, can never really fade away!

The light on Willy is fading. The gas heater begins to glow through the kitchen wall, near the stairs, a blue flame beneath red coils.

Linda (timidly): Willy dear, what has he got against you?

Willy: I'm so tired. Don't talk any more.

Biff slowly returns to the kitchen. He stops, stares toward the heater.

Linda: Will you ask Howard to let you work in New York?

Willy: First thing in the morning. Everything'll be all right.

Biff reaches behind the heater and draws out a length of rubber tubing. He is horrified and turns his head toward Willy's room, still dimly lit, from which the strains of Linda's desperate but monotonous humming rise.

Willy (staring through the window into the moonlight): Gee, look at the moon moving between the buildings!

Biff wraps the tubing around his hand and quickly goes up the stairs.

Curtain

ACT II

Music is heard, gay and bright. The curtain rises as the music fades away. Willy, in shirt sleeves, is sitting at the kitchen table, sipping coffee, his hat in his lap. Linda is filling his cup when she can.

Willy: Wonderful coffee. Meal in itself.

Linda: Can I make you some eggs?

Willy: No. Take a breath.

Linda: You look so rested, dear.

Willy: I slept like a dead one. First time in months. Imagine, sleeping till ten on a Tuesday morning. Boys left nice and early, heh?

Linda: They were out of here by eight o'clock.

Willy: Good work!

Linda: It was so thrilling to see them leaving together. I can't get over the shaving lotion in this house!

Willy (smiling): Mmm —

Linda: Biff was very changed this morning. His whole attitude seemed to be hopeful. He couldn't wait to get downtown to see Oliver.
Willy: He's heading for a change. There's no question, there simply are certain men that take longer to get — solidified. How did he dress?
Linda: His blue suit. He's so handsome in that suit. He could be a — anything in that suit!

Willy gets up from the table. Linda holds his jacket for him.

Willy: There's no question, no question at all. Gee, on the way home tonight I'd like to buy some seeds.
Linda (laughing): That'd be wonderful. But not enough sun gets back there. Nothing'll grow any more.
Willy: You wait, kid, before it's all over we're gonna get a little place out in the country, and I'll raise some vegetables, a couple of chickens . . .
Linda: You'll do it yet, dear.

Willy walks out of his jacket. Linda follows him.

Willy: And they'll get married, and come for a weekend. I'd build a little guest house. 'Cause I got so many fine tools, all I'd need would be a little lumber and some peace of mind.
Linda (joyfully): I sewed the lining . . .
Willy: I could build two guest houses, so they'd both come. Did he decide how much he's going to ask Oliver for?
Linda (getting him into the jacket): He didn't mention it, but I imagine ten or fifteen thousand. You going to talk to Howard today?
Willy: Yeah. I'll put it to him straight and simple. He'll just have to take me off the road.
Linda: And Willy, don't forget to ask for a little advance, because we've got the insurance premium. It's the grace period now.
Willy: That's a hundred . . . ?
Linda: A hundred and eight, sixty-eight. Because we're a little short again.
Willy: Why are we short?
Linda: Well, you had the motor job on the car . . .
Willy: That goddam Studebaker!
Linda: And you got one more payment on the refrigerator . . .
Willy: But it just broke again!
Linda: Well, it's old, dear.
Willy: I told you we should've bought a well-advertised machine. Charley bought a General Electric and it's twenty years old and it's still good, that son-of-a-bitch.
Linda: But, Willy —
Willy: Whoever heard of a Hastings refrigerator? Once in my life I would like to own something outright before it's broken! I'm always in a race with the junkyard! I just finished paying for the car and it's on its last legs. The refrigerator consumes belts like a goddam maniac. They time those things. They time them so when you finally paid for them, they're used up.
Linda (buttoning up his jacket as he unbuttons it): All told, about two hundred dollars would carry us, dear. But that includes the last payment on the mortgage. After this payment, Willy, the house belongs to us.

Willy: It's twenty-five years!

Linda: Biff was nine years old when we bought it.

Willy: Well, that's a great thing. To weather a twenty-five year mortgage is —

Linda: It's an accomplishment.

Willy: All the cement, the lumber, the reconstruction I put in this house! There ain't a crack to be found in it any more.

Linda: Well, it served its purpose.

Willy: What purpose? Some stranger'll come along, move in, and that's that. If only Biff would take this house, and raise a family . . . *(He starts to go.)* Good-by, I'm late.

Linda (suddenly remembering): Oh, I forgot! You're supposed to meet them for dinner.

Willy: Me?

Linda: At Frank's Chop House on Forty-eighth near Sixth Avenue.

Willy: Is that so! How about you?

Linda: No, just the three of you. They're gonna blow you to a big meal!

Willy: Don't say! Who thought of that?

Linda: Biff came to me this morning, Willy, and he said, "Tell Dad, we want to blow him to a big meal." Be there six o'clock. You and your two boys are going to have dinner.

Willy: Gee whiz! That's really somethin'. I'm gonna knock Howard for a loop, kid. I'll get an advance, and I'll come home with a New York job. Goddammit, now I'm gonna do it!

Linda: Oh, that's the spirit, Willy!

Willy: I will never get behind a wheel the rest of my life!

Linda: It's changing, Willy, I can feel it changing!

Willy: Beyond a question. G'by, I'm late. *(He starts to go again.)*

Linda (calling after him as she runs to the kitchen table for a handkerchief): You got your glasses?

Willy: (feels for them, then comes back in): Yeah, yeah, got my glasses.

Linda (giving him the handkerchief): And a handkerchief.

Willy: Yeah, handkerchief.

Linda: And your saccharine?

Willy: Yeah, my saccharine.

Linda: Be careful on the subway stairs.

She kisses him, and a silk stocking is seen hanging from her hand. Willy notices it.

Willy: Will you stop mending stockings? At least while I'm in the house. It gets me nervous. I can't tell you. Please.

Linda hides the stocking in her hand as she follows Willy across the forestage in front of the house.

Linda: Remember, Frank's Chop House.

Willy (passing the apron): Maybe beets would grow out there.

Linda (laughing): But you tried so many times.

Willy: Yeah. Well, don't work hard today. *(He disappears around the right corner of the house.)*

Linda: Be careful!

As Willy vanishes, Linda waves to him. Suddenly the phone rings. She runs across the stage and into the kitchen and lifts it.

Linda: Hello? Oh, Biff! I'm so glad you called, I just . . . Yes, sure, I just told him. Yes, he'll be there for dinner at six o'clock, I didn't forget. Listen, I was just dying to tell you. You know that little rubber pipe I told you about? That he connected to the gas heater? I finally decided to go down the cellar this morning and take it away and destroy it. But it's gone! Imagine? He took it away himself, it isn't there! *(She listens.)* When? Oh, then you took it. Oh — nothing, it's just that I'd hoped he'd taken it away himself. Oh, I'm not worried, darling, because this morning he left in such high spirits, it was like the old days! I'm not afraid any more. Did Mr. Oliver see you? . . . Well, you wait there then. And make a nice impression on him, darling. Just don't perspire too much before you see him. And have a nice time with Dad. He may have big news too! . . . That's right, a New York job. And be sweet to him tonight, dear. Be loving to him. Because he's only a little boat looking for a harbor. *(She is trembling with sorrow and joy.)* Oh, that's wonderful, Biff, you'll save his life. Thanks, darling. Just put your arm around him when he comes into the restaurant. Give him a smile. That's the boy . . . Good-by, dear. . . . You got your comb? . . . That's fine. Good-by, Biff dear.

In the middle of her speech, Howard Wagner, thirty-six, wheels on a small typewriter table on which is a wire-recording machine and proceeds to plug it in. This is on the left forestage. Light slowly fades on Linda as it rises on Howard. Howard is intent on threading the machine and only glances over his shoulder as Willy appears.

Willy: Pst! Pst!

Howard: Hello, Willy, come in.

Willy: Like to have a little talk with you, Howard.

Howard: Sorry to keep you waiting. I'll be with you in a minute.

Willy: What's that, Howard?

Howard: Didn't you ever see one of these? Wire recorder.

Willy: Oh. Can we talk a minute?

Howard: Records things. Just got delivery yesterday. Been driving me crazy, the most terrific machine I ever saw in my life. I was up all night with it.

Willy: What do you do with it?

Howard: I bought it for dictation, but you can do anything with it. Listen to this. I had it home last night. Listen to what I picked up. The first one is my daughter. Get this. *(He flicks the switch and "Roll Out the Barrel" is heard being whistled.)* Listen to that kid whistle.

Willy: That is lifelike, isn't it?

Howard: Seven years old. Get that tone.

Willy: Ts, ts. Like to ask a little favor if you . . .

The whistling breaks off, and the voice of Howard's daughter is heard.

His Daughter: "Now you, Daddy."

Howard: She's crazy for me! *(Again the same song is whistled.)* That's me! Ha! *(He winks.)*

Willy: You're very good!

The whistling breaks off again. The machine runs silent for a moment.

Howard: Sh! Get this now, this is my son.

His Son: "The capital of Alabama is Montgomery; the capital of Arizona is Phoenix; the capital of Arkansas is Little Rock; the capital of California is Sacramento . . ." *(and on, and on).*

Howard (holding up five fingers): Five years old, Willy!

Willy: He'll make an announcer some day!

His Son (continuing): "The capital . . ."

Howard: Get that — alphabetical order! *(The machine breaks off suddenly.)* Wait a minute. The maid kicked the plug out.

Willy: It certainly is a —

Howard: Sh, for God's sake!

His Son: "It's nine o'clock, Bulova watch time. So I have to go to sleep."

Willy: That really is —

Howard: Wait a minute! The next is my wife.

They wait.

Howard's Voice: "Go on, say something." *(Pause.)* "Well, you gonna talk?"

His Wife: "I can't think of anything."

Howard's Voice: "Well, talk — it's turning."

His Wife (shyly, beaten): "Hello." *(Silence.)* "Oh, Howard, I can't talk into this . . ."

Howard (snapping the machine off): That was my wife.

Willy: That is a wonderful machine. Can we —

Howard: I tell you, Willy, I'm gonna take my camera, and my bandsaw, and all my hobbies, and out they go. This is the most fascinating relaxation I ever found.

Willy: I think I'll get one myself.

Howard: Sure, they're only a hundred and a half. You can't do without it. Supposing you wanna hear Jack Benny, see? But you can't be at home at that hour. So you tell the maid to turn the radio on when Jack Benny comes on, and this automatically goes on with the radio . . .

Willy: And when you come home you . . .

Howard: You can come home twelve o'clock, one o'clock, any time you like, and you get yourself a Coke and sit yourself down, throw the switch, and there's Jack Benny's program in the middle of the night!

Willy: I'm definitely going to get one. Because lots of time I'm on the road, and I think to myself, what I must be missing on the radio!

Howard: Don't you have a radio in the car?

Willy: Well, yeah, but who ever thinks of turning it on?

Howard: Say, aren't you supposed to be in Boston?

Willy: That's what I want to talk to you about, Howard. You got a minute? *(He draws a chair in from the wing.)*

Howard: What happened? What're you doing here?

Willy: Well . . .

Howard: You didn't crack up again, did you?

Willy: Oh, no. No . . .

Howard: Geez, you had me worried there for a minute. What's the trouble?

Willy: Well, tell you the truth, Howard. I've come to the decision that I'd rather not travel any more.

Howard: Not travel! Well, what'll you do?

Willy: Remember, Christmas time, when you had the party here? You said you'd try to think of some spot for me here in town.

Howard: With us?

Willy: Well, sure.

Howard: Oh, yeah, yeah. I remember. Well, I couldn't think of anything for you, Willy.

Willy: I tell ya, Howard. The kids are all grown up, y'know. I don't need much any more. If I could take home — well, sixty-five dollars a week, I could swing it.

Howard: Yeah, but Willy, see I —

Willy: I tell ya why, Howard. Speaking frankly and between the two of us, y'know — I'm just a little tired.

Howard: Oh, I could understand that, Willy. But you're a road man, Willy, and we do a road business. We've only got a half-dozen salesmen on the floor here.

Willy: God knows, Howard, I never asked a favor of any man. But I was with the firm when your father used to carry you in here in his arms.

Howard: I know that, Willy, but —

Willy: Your father came to me the day you were born and asked me what I thought of the name of Howard, may he rest in peace.

Howard: I appreciate that, Willy, but there just is no spot here for you. If I had a spot I'd slam you right in, but I just don't have a single solitary spot.

He looks for his lighter. Willy has picked it up and gives it to him. Pause.

Willy (with increasing anger): Howard, all I need to set my table is fifty dollars a week.

Howard: But where am I going to put you, kid?

Willy: Look, it isn't a question of whether I can sell merchandise, is it?

Howard: No, but it's a business, kid, and everybody's gotta pull his own weight.

Willy (desperately): Just let me tell you a story, Howard —

Howard: 'Cause you gotta admit, business is business.

Willy (angrily): Business is definitely business, but just listen for a minute. You don't understand this. When I was a boy — eighteen, nineteen — I was already on the road. And there was a question in my mind as to whether selling had a future for me. Because in those days I had a yearning to go to Alaska. See, there were three gold strikes in one month in Alaska, and I felt like going out. Just for the ride, you might say.

Howard (barely interested): Don't say.

Willy: Oh, yeah, my father lived many years in Alaska. He was an adventurous man. We've got quite a little streak of self-reliance in our family. I thought I'd go out with my older brother and try to locate him, and maybe settle in the North with the old man. And I was almost decided to go, when I met a salesman in the Parker House. His name was Dave Singleman. And he was eight-four years old, and he'd drummed merchandise in thirty-one states. And old Dave, he'd go up to his room, y'understand, put on his green velvet slippers — I'll never forget — and pick up his phone and call the buyers, and without ever leaving his room, at the age of eighty-four, he made his living. And when I saw that, I realized that selling was the greatest career a man could want. 'Cause what could be more satisfying than to be able to go, at the age of eighty-four, into twenty or thirty different cities, and pick up a phone, and be remembered and loved and helped by so many different people? Do you know? when he died — and by the way he died the death of a salesman, in his green velvet slippers in the smoker of the New York, New Haven, and Hartford, going into Boston — when he died, hundreds of salesmen and buyers were at his funeral. Things were sad on a lotta trains for months after that. *(He stands up. Howard has not looked at him.)* In those days there was personality in it, Howard. There was respect, and comradeship, and gratitude in it. Today, it's all cut and dried, and there's no chance for bringing friendship to bear — or personality. You see what I mean? They don't know me any more.

Howard (moving away, to the right): That's just the thing, Willy.

Willy: If I had forty dollars a week — that's all I'd need. Forty dollars, Howard.

Howard: Kid, I can't take blood from a stone, I —

Willy (desperation is on him now): Howard, the year Al Smith° was nominated, your father came to me and —

Howard (starting to go off): I've got to see some people, kid.

Willy (stopping him): I'm talking about your father! There were promises made across this desk! You mustn't tell me you've got people to see — I put thirty-four years into this firm, Howard, and now I can't pay my insurance! You can't eat the orange and throw the peel away — a man is not a piece of fruit! *(After a pause.)* Now pay attention. Your father — in 1928 I had a big year. I averaged a hundred and seventy dollars a week in commissions.

Howard (impatiently): Now, Willy, you never averaged —

Willy (banging his hand on the desk): I averaged a hundred and seventy dollars a week in the year of 1928! And your father came to me — or rather, I was in the office here — it was right over this desk — and he put his hand on my shoulder —

Howard (getting up): You'll have to excuse me, Willy, I gotta see some people. Pull yourself together. *(Going out.)* I'll be back in a little while.

On Howard's exit, the light on his chair grows very bright and strange.

Willy: Pull myself together! What the hell did I say to him? My God, I was yelling at him! How could I! *(Willy breaks off, staring at the light, which occupies the chair, animating it. He approaches this chair, standing across the desk from it.)* Frank, Frank, don't you remember what you told me that time? How you put your hand on my shoulder, and Frank . . . *(He leans on the desk and as he speaks the dead man's name he accidentally switches on the recorder, and instantly:)*

Howard's Son: ". . . of New York is Albany. The capital of Ohio is Cincinnati, the capital of Rhode Island is . . . ." *(The recitation continues.)*

Willy (leaping away with fright, shouting): Ha! Howard! Howard! Howard!

Howard (rushing in): What happened?

Al Smith: Democratic candidate for president of the United States in 1928; lost the election to Herbert Hoover.

Willy (pointing at the machine, which continues nasally, childishly, with the capital cities): Shut it off! Shut it off!

Howard (pulling the plug out): Look, Willy . . .

Willy (pressing his hands to his eyes): I gotta get myself some coffee. I'll get some coffee . . .

Willy starts to walk out. Howard stops him.

Howard (rolling up the cord): Willy, look . . .

Willy: I'll go to Boston.

Howard: Willy, you can't go to Boston for us.

Willy: Why can't I go?

Howard: I don't want you to represent us. I've been meaning to tell you for a long time now.

Willy: Howard, are you firing me?

Howard: I think you need a good long rest, Willy.

Willy: Howard —

Howard: And when you feel better, come back, and we'll see if we can work something out.

Willy: But I gotta earn money, Howard. I'm in no position to —

Howard: Where are your sons? Why don't your sons give you a hand?

Willy: They're working on a very big deal.

Howard: This is no time for false pride, Willy. You go to your sons and you tell them that you're tired. You've got two great boys, haven't you?

Willy: Oh, no question, no question, but in the meantime . . .

Howard: Then that's that, heh?

Willy: All right, I'll go to Boston tomorrow.

Howard: No, no.

Willy: I can't throw myself on my sons. I'm not a cripple!

Howard: Look, kid, I'm busy this morning.

Willy (grasping Howard's arm): Howard, you've got to let me go to Boston!

Howard (hard, keeping himself under control): I've got a line of people to see this morning. Sit down, take five minutes, and pull yourself together, and then go home, will ya? I need the office, Willy. *(He starts to go, turns, remembering the recorder, starts to push off the table holding the recorder.)* Oh, yeah. Whenever you can this week, stop by and drop off the samples. You'll feel better, Willy, and then come back and we'll talk. Pull yourself together, kid, there's people outside.

Howard exits, pushing the table off left. Willy stares into space, exhausted. Now the music is heard — Ben's music — first distantly, then closer, closer. As Willy speaks, Ben enters from the right. He carries valise and umbrella.

Willy: Oh, Ben, how did you do it? What is the answer? Did you wind up the Alaska deal already?

Ben: Doesn't take much time if you know what you're doing. Just a short business trip. Boarding ship in an hour. Wanted to say good-by.

Willy: Ben, I've got to talk to you.

Ben (glancing at his watch): Haven't the time, William.

Willy (crossing the apron to Ben): Ben, nothing's working out. I don't know what to do.

Ben: Now, look here, William. I've bought timberland in Alaska and I need a man to look after things for me.

Willy: God, timberland! Me and my boys in those grand outdoors!

Ben: You've a new continent at your doorstep, William. Get out of these cities, they're full of talk and time payments and courts of law. Screw on your fists and you can fight for a fortune up there.

Willy: Yes, yes! Linda, Linda!

Linda enters as of old, with the wash.

Linda: Oh, you're back?

Ben: I haven't much time.

Willy: No, wait! Linda, he's got a proposition for me in Alaska.

Linda: But you've got — *(To Ben.)* He's got a beautiful job here.

Willy: But in Alaska, kid, I could —

Linda: You're doing well enough, Willy!

Ben (to Linda): Enough for what, my dear?

Linda (frightened of Ben and angry at him): Don't say those things to him! Enough to be happy right here, right now. *(To Willy, while Ben laughs.)* Why must everybody conquer the world? You're well liked, and the boys love you, and someday — *(to Ben)* — why, old man Wagner told him just the other day that if he keeps it up he'll be a member of the firm, didn't he, Willy?

Willy: Sure, sure. I am building something with this firm, Ben, and if a man is building something he must be on the right track, mustn't he?

Ben: What are you building? Lay your hand on it. Where is it?

Willy (hesitantly): That's true, Linda, there's nothing.

Linda: Why? *(To Ben.)* There's a man eighty-four years old —

Willy: That's right, Ben, that's right. When I look at that man I say, what is there to worry about?

Ben: Bah!

Willy: It's true, Ben. All he has to do is go into any city, pick up the phone, and he's making his living and you know why?

Ben (picking up his valise): I've got to go.

Willy (holding Ben back): Look at this boy!

Biff, in his high school sweater, enters carrying suitcase. Happy carries Biff's shoulder guards, gold helmet, and football pants.

Willy: Without a penny to his name, three great universities are begging for him, and from there the sky's the limit, because it's not what you do, Ben. It's who you know and the smile on your face! It's contacts, Ben, contacts! The whole wealth of Alaska passes over the lunch table at the Commodore Hotel, and that's the wonder, the wonder of this country, that a man can end with diamonds here on the basis of being liked! *(He turns to Biff.)* And that's why when you get out on that field today it's important. Because thousands of people will be rooting for you and loving you. *(To Ben, who has again begun to leave.)* And Ben! when he walks into a business office his name will sound out like a bell and all the doors will open to him! I've seen it, Ben, I've seen it a thousand times! You can't feel it with your hand like timber, but it's there!

Ben: Good-by, William.

Willy: Ben, am I right? Don't you think I'm right? I value your advice.

Ben: There's a new continent at your doorstep, William. You could walk out rich. Rich! *(He is gone.)*

Willy: We'll do it here, Ben! You hear me? We're gonna do it here!

Young Bernard rushes in. The gay music of the Boys is heard.

Bernard: Oh, gee, I was afraid you left already!

Willy: Why? What time is it?

Bernard: It's half-past one!

Willy: Well, come on, everybody! Ebbets Field next stop! Where's the pennants? *(He rushes through the wall-line of the kitchen and out into the living-room.)*

Linda (to Biff): Did you pack fresh underwear?

Biff (who has been limbering up): I want to go!

Bernard: Biff, I'm carrying your helmet, ain't I?

Happy: I'm carrying the helmet.

Bernard: How am I going to get in the locker room?

Linda: Let him carry the shoulder guards. *(She puts her coat and hat on in the kitchen.)*

Bernard: Can I, Biff? 'Cause I told everybody I'm going to be in the locker room.

Happy: In Ebbets Field it's the clubhouse.

Bernard: I meant the clubhouse. Biff!

Happy: Biff!

Biff (grandly, after a slight pause): Let him carry the shoulder guards.

Happy (as he gives Bernard the shoulder guards): Stay close to us now.

Willy rushes in with the pennants.

Willy (handing them out): Everybody wave when Biff comes out on the field. *(Happy and Bernard run off.)* You set now, boy?

The music has died away.

Biff: Ready to go, Pop. Every muscle is ready.

Willy (at the edge of the apron): You realize what this means?

Biff: That's right, Pop.

Willy (feeling Biff's muscles): You're comin' home this afternoon captain of the All-Scholastic Championship Team of the City of New York.

Biff: I got it, Pop. And remember, pal, when I take off my helmet, that touchdown is for you.

Willy: Let's go! *(He is starting out, with his arm around Biff, when Charley enters, as of old, in knickers.)* I got no room for you, Charley.

Charley: Room? For what?

Willy: In the car.

Charley: You goin' for a ride? I wanted to shoot some casino.

Willy (furiously): Casino! *(Incredulously.)* Don't you realize what today is?

Linda: Oh, he knows, Willy. He's just kidding you.

Willy: That's nothing to kid about!

Charley: No, Linda, what's goin' on?

Linda: He's playing in Ebbets Field.

Charley: Baseball in this weather?

Willy: Don't talk to him. Come on, come on! *(He is pushing them out.)*

Charley: Wait a minute, didn't you hear the news?

Willy: What?

Charley: Don't you listen to the radio? Ebbets Field just blew up.

Willy: You go to hell! *(Charley laughs. Pushing them out.)* Come on, come on! We're late.

Charley (as they go): Knock a homer, Biff, knock a homer!

Willy (the last to leave, turning to Charley): I don't think that was funny, Charley. This is the greatest day of his life.

Charley: Willy, when are you going to grow up?

Willy: Yeah, heh? When this game is over, Charley, you'll be laughing out of the other side of your face. They'll be calling him another Red Grange. Twenty-five thousand a year.

Charley (kidding): Is that so?

Willy: Yeah, that's so.

Charley: Well, then, I'm sorry, Willy. But tell me something.

Willy: What?

Charley: Who is Red Grange?

Willy: Put up your hands. Goddam you, put up your hands!

Charley, chuckling, shakes his head and walks away, around the left corner of the stage. Willy follows him. The music rises to a mocking frenzy.

Willy: Who the hell do you think you are, better than everybody else? You don't know everything, you big, ignorant, stupid . . . Put up your hands!

Light rises, on the right side of the forestage, on a small table in the reception room of Charley's office. Traffic sounds are heard. Bernard, now mature, sits whistling to himself. A pair of tennis rackets and an overnight bag are on the floor beside him.

Willy (offstage): What are you walking away for? Don't walk away! If you're going to say something say it to my face! I know you laugh at me behind my back. You'll laugh out of the other side of your goddam face after this game. Touchdown! Touchdown! Eighty thousand people! Touchdown! Right between the goal posts.

Bernard is a quiet, earnest, but self-assured young man. Willy's voice is coming from right upstage now. Bernard lowers his feet off the table and listens. Jenny, his father's secretary, enters.

Jenny (distressed): Say, Bernard, will you go out in the hall?

Bernard: What is that noise? Who is it?

Jenny: Mr. Loman. He just got off the elevator.

Bernard (getting up): Who's he arguing with?

Jenny: Nobody. There's nobody with him. I can't deal with him any more, and your father gets all upset everytime he comes. I've got a lot of typing to do, and your father's waiting to sign it. Will you see him?

Willy (entering): Touchdown! Touch — *(He sees Jenny.)* Jenny, Jenny, good to see you. How're ya? Workin'? Or still honest?

Jenny: Fine. How've you been feeling?

Willy: Not much any more, Jenny. Ha, ha! *(He is surprised to see the rackets.)*

Bernard: Hello, Uncle Willy.

Willy (almost shocked): Bernard! Well, look who's here! *(He comes quickly, guiltily, to Bernard and warmly shakes his hand.)*

Bernard: How are you? Good to see you.

Willy: What are you doing here?

Bernard: Oh, just stopped by to see Pop. Get off my feet till my train leaves. I'm going to Washington in a few minutes.

Willy: Is he in?

Bernard: Yes, he's in his office with the accountant. Sit down.

Willy (sitting down): What're you going to do in Washington?

Bernard: Oh, just a case I've got there, Willy.

Willy: That so? *(Indicating the rackets.)* You going to play tennis there?

Bernard: I'm staying with a friend who's got a court.

Willy: Don't say. His own tennis court. Must be fine people, I bet.

Bernard: They are, very nice. Dad tells me Biff's in town.

Willy (with a big smile): Yeah, Biff's in. Working on a very big deal, Bernard.

Bernard: What's Biff doing?

Willy: Well, he's been doing very big things in the West. But he decided to establish himself here. Very big. We're having dinner. Did I hear your wife had a boy?

Bernard: That's right. Our second.

Willy: Two boys! What do you know!

Bernard: What kind of a deal has Biff got?

Willy: Well, Bill Oliver — very big sporting-goods man — he wants Biff very badly. Called him in from the West. Long distance, carte blanche, special deliveries. Your friends have their own private tennis court?

Bernard: You still with the old firm, Willy?

Willy (after a pause): I'm — I'm overjoyed to see how you made the grade, Bernard, overjoyed. It's an encouraging thing to see a young man really — really — Looks very good for Biff — very — *(He breaks off, then.)* Bernard — *(He is so full of emotion, he breaks off again.)*

Bernard: What is it, Willy?

Willy (small and alone): What — what's the secret?

Bernard: What secret?

Willy: How — how did you? Why didn't he ever catch on?

Bernard: I wouldn't know that, Willy.

Willy (confidentially, desperately): You were his friend, his boyhood friend. There's something I don't understand about it. His life ended after that Ebbets Field game. From the age of seventeen nothing good ever happened to him.

Bernard: He never trained himself for anything.

Willy: But he did, he did. After high school he took so many correspondence courses. Radio mechanics; television; God knows what, and never made the slightest mark.

Bernard (taking off his glasses): Willy, do you want to talk candidly?

Willy (rising, faces Bernard): I regard you as a very brilliant man, Bernard. I value your advice.

Bernard: Oh, the hell with the advice, Willy. I couldn't advise you. There's just one thing I've always wanted to ask you. When he was supposed to graduate, and the math teacher flunked him —

Willy: Oh, that son-of-a-bitch ruined his life.

Bernard: Yeah, but, Willy, all he had to do was go to summer school and make up that subject.

Willy: That's right, that's right.

Bernard: Did you tell him not to go to summer school?

Willy: Me? I begged him to go. I ordered him to go!

Bernard: Then why wouldn't he go?

Willy: Why? Why! Bernard, that question has been trailing me like a ghost for the last fifteen years. He flunked the subject, and laid down and died like a hammer hit him!

Bernard: Take it easy, kid.

Willy: Let me talk to you — I got nobody to talk to. Bernard, Bernard, was it my fault? Y'see? It keeps going around in my mind, maybe I did something to him. I got nothing to give him.

Bernard: Don't take it so hard.

Willy: Why did he lay down? What is the story there? You were his friend!

Bernard: Willy, I remember, it was June, and our grades came out. And he'd flunked math.

Willy: That son-of-a-bitch!

Bernard: No, it wasn't right then. Biff just got very angry, I remember, and he was ready to enroll in summer school.

Willy (surprised): He was?

Bernard: He wasn't beaten by it at all. But then, Willy, he disappeared from the block for almost a month. And I got the idea that he'd gone up to New England to see you. Did he have a talk with you then?

Willy stares in silence.

Bernard: Willy?

Willy (with a strong edge of resentment in his voice): Yeah, he came to Boston. What about it?

Bernard: Well, just that when he came back — I'll never forget this, it always mystifies me. Because I'd thought so well of Biff, even though he'd always taken advantage of me. I loved him, Willy, y'know? And he came back after that month and took his sneakers — remember those sneakers with "University of Virginia" printed on them? He was so proud of those, wore them every day. And he took them down in the cellar, and burned them up in the furnace. We had a fist fight. It lasted at least half an hour. Just the two of us, punching each other down the cellar, and crying right through it. I've often thought of how strange it was that I knew he'd given up his life. What happened in Boston, Willy?

Willy looks at him as at an intruder.

Bernard: I just bring it up because you asked me.

Willy (angrily): Nothing. What do you mean, "What happened?" What's that got to do with anything?

Bernard: Well, don't get sore.

Willy: What are you trying to do, blame it on me? If a boy lays down is that my fault?

Bernard: Now, Willy, don't get —

Willy: Well, don't — don't talk to me that way! What does that mean, "What happened?"

Charley enters. He is in his vest, and he carries a bottle of bourbon.

Charley: Hey, you're going to miss that train. *(He waves the bottle.)*

Bernard: Yeah, I'm going. *(He takes the bottle.)* Thanks, Pop. *(He picks up his rackets and bag.)* Good-by, Willy, and don't worry about it. You know. "If at first you don't succeed . . ."

Willy: Yes, I believe in that.

Bernard: But sometimes, Willy, it's better for a man just to walk away.

Willy: Walk away?

Bernard: That's right.

Willy: But if you can't walk away?

Bernard (after a slight pause): I guess that's when it's tough. *(Extending his hand.)* Good-by, Willy.

Willy (shaking Bernard's hand): Good-by, boy.

Charley (an arm on Bernard's shoulder): How do you like this kid? Gonna argue a case in front of the Supreme Court.

Bernard (protesting): Pop!

Willy (genuinely shocked, pained, and happy): No! The Supreme Court!

Bernard: I gotta run. 'By, Dad!

Charley: Knock 'em dead, Bernard!

Bernard goes off.

Willy (as Charley takes out his wallet): The Supreme Court! And he didn't even mention it!

Charley (counting out money on the desk): He don't have to — he's gonna do it.

Willy: And you never told him what to do, did you? You never took any interest in him.

Charley: My salvation is that I never took any interest in any thing. There's some money — fifty dollars. I got an accountant inside.

Willy: Charley, look . . . *(With difficulty.)* I got my insurance to pay. If you can manage it — I need a hundred and ten dollars.

Charley doesn't reply for a moment; merely stops moving.

Willy: I'd draw it from my bank but Linda would know, and I . . .

Charley: Sit down, Willy.

Willy (moving toward the chair): I'm keeping an account of everything, remember. I'll pay every penny back. *(He sits.)*

Charley: Now listen to me, Willy.

Willy: I want you to know I appreciate . . .

Charley (sitting down on the table): Willy, what're you doin'? What the hell is goin' on in your head?

Willy: Why? I'm simply . . .

Charley: I offered you a job. You can make fifty dollars a week. And I won't send you on the road.

Willy: I've got a job.

Charley: Without pay? What kind of a job is a job without pay? *(He rises.)* Now, look, kid, enough is enough. I'm no genius but I know when I'm being insulted.

Willy: Insulted!

Charley: Why don't you want to work for me?

Willy: What's the matter with you? I've got a job.

Charley: Then what're you walkin' in here every week for?

Willy (getting up): Well, if you don't want me to walk in here —

Charley: I am offering you a job.

Willy: I don't want your goddam job!

Charley: When the hell are you going to grow up?

Willy (furiously): You big ignoramus, if you say that to me again I'll rap you one! I don't care how big you are! *(He's ready to fight.)*

Pause.

Charley (kindly, going to him): How much do you need, Willy?

Willy: Charley, I'm strapped. I'm strapped. I don't know what to do. I was just fired.

Charley: Howard fired you?

Willy: That snotnose. Imagine that? I named him. I named him Howard.

Charley: Willy, when're you gonna realize that them things don't mean anything? You named him Howard, but you can't sell that. The only thing you got in this world is what you can sell. And the funny thing is that you're a salesman, and you don't know that.

Willy: I've always tried to think otherwise, I guess. I always felt that if a man was impressive, and well liked, that nothing —

Charley: Why must everybody like you? Who liked J. P. Morgan? Was he impressive? In a Turkish bath he'd look like a butcher. But with his pockets on he was very well liked. Now listen, Willy, I know you don't like me, and nobody can say I'm in love with you, but I'll give you a job because — just for the hell of it, put it that way. Now what do you say?

Willy: I — I just can't work for you, Charley.

Charley: What're you, jealous of me?

Willy: I can't work for you, that's all, don't ask me why.

Charley (angered, takes out more bills): You been jealous of me all your life, you damned fool! Here, pay your insurance. *(He puts the money in Willy's hand.)*

Willy: I'm keeping strict accounts.

Charley: I've got some work to do. Take care of yourself. And pay your insurance.

Willy (moving to the right): Funny, y'know? After all the highways, and the trains, and the appointments, and the years, you end up worth more dead than alive.

Charley: Willy, nobody's worth nothin' dead. *(After a slight pause.)* Did you hear what I said?

Willy stands still, dreaming.

Charley: Willy!

Willy: Apologize to Bernard for me when you see him. I didn't mean to argue with him. He's a fine boy. They're all fine boys, and they'll end up big — all of them. Someday they'll all play tennis together. Wish me luck, Charley. He saw Bill Oliver today.

Charley: Good luck.

Willy (on the verge of tears): Charley, you're the only friend I got. Isn't that a remarkable thing? *(He goes out.)*

Charley: Jesus!

Charley stares after him a moment and follows. All light blacks out. Suddenly raucous music is heard, and a red glow rises behind the screen at right. Stanley, a young waiter, appears, carrying a table, followed by Happy, who is carrying two chairs.

Stanley (putting the table down): That's all right, Mr. Loman, I can handle it myself. *(He turns and takes the chairs from Happy and places them at the table.)*

Happy (glancing around): Oh, this is better.

Stanley: Sure, in the front there you're in the middle of all kinds a noise. Whenever you got a party, Mr. Loman, you just tell me and I'll put you back here. Y'know, there's a lotta people they don't like it private, because when they go out they like to see a lotta action around them because they're sick and tired to stay in the house by theirself. But I know you, you ain't from Hackensack. You know what I mean?

Happy (sitting down): So how's it coming, Stanley?

Stanley: Ah, it's a dog's life. I only wish during the war they'd a took me in the Army. I coulda been dead by now.

Happy: My brother's back, Stanley.

Stanley: Oh, he come back, heh? From the Far West.

Happy: Yeah, big cattle man, my brother, so treat him right. And my father's coming too.

Stanley: Oh, your father too!

Happy: You got a couple of nice lobsters?

Stanley: Hundred per cent, big.

Happy: I want them with the claws.

Stanley: Don't worry, I don't give you no mice. *(Happy laughs.)* How about some wine? It'll put a head on the meal.

Happy: No. You remember, Stanley, that recipe I brought you from overseas? With the champagne in it?

Stanley: Oh, yeah, sure. I still got it tacked up yet in the kitchen. But that'll have to cost a buck apiece anyways.

Happy: That's all right.

Stanley: What'd you, hit a number or somethin'?

Happy: No, it's a little celebration. My brother is — I think he pulled off a big deal today. I think we're going into business together.

Stanley: Great! That's the best for you. Because a family business, you know what I mean? — that's the best.

Happy: That's what I think.

Stanley: 'Cause what's the difference? Somebody steals? It's in the family. Know what I mean? *(Sotto voce.)*° Like this bartender here. The boss is goin' crazy what kinda leak he's got in the cash register. You put it in but it don't come out.

Happy (raising his head): Sh!

Stanley: What?

Happy: You notice I wasn't lookin' right or left, was I?

Stanley: No.

Happy: And my eyes are closed.

Stanley: So what's the — ?

Happy: Strudel's comin'.

Stanley (catching on, looks around): Ah, no, there's no —

He breaks off as a furred, lavishly dressed girl enters and sits at the next table. Both follow her with their eyes.

Stanley: Geez, how'd ya know?

Happy: I got radar or something. *(Staring directly at her profile.)* Oooooooo . . . Stanley.

Stanley: I think that's for you, Mr. Loman.

Happy: Look at that mouth. Oh, God. And the binoculars.

Stanley: Geez, you got a life, Mr. Loman.

Happy: Wait on her.

Stanley (going to the girl's table): Would you like a menu, ma'am?

Girl: I'm expecting someone, but I'd like a —

Happy: Why don't you bring her — excuse me, miss, do you mind? I sell champagne, and I'd like you to try my brand. Bring her a champagne, Stanley.

Girl: That's awfully nice of you.

Happy: Don't mention it. It's all company money. *(He laughs.)*

Girl: That's a charming product to be selling, isn't it?

Happy: Oh, gets to be like everything else. Selling is selling, y'know.

Girl: I suppose.

Happy: You don't happen to sell, do you?

Girl: No, I don't sell.

Happy: Would you object to a compliment from a stranger? You ought to be on a magazine cover.

Girl (looking at him a little archly): I have been.

Stanley comes in with a glass of champagne.

Happy: What'd I say before, Stanley? You see? She's a cover girl.

Stanley: Oh, I could see, I could see.

Happy (to the Girl): What magazine?

Girl: Oh, a lot of them. *(She takes the drink.)* Thank you.

Happy: You know what they say in France, don't you? "Champagne is the drink of the complexion" — Hya, Biff!

Biff has entered and sits with Happy.

Sotto voce: Softly, "under the breath" (Italian).

Biff: Hello, kid. Sorry I'm late.

Happy: I just got here. Uh, Miss — ?

Girl: Forsythe.

Happy: Miss Forsythe, this is my brother.

Biff: Is Dad here?

Happy: His name is Biff. You might've heard of him. Great football player.

Girl: Really? What team?

Happy: Are you familiar with football?

Girl: No, I'm afraid I'm not.

Happy: Biff is quarterback with the New York Giants.

Girl: Well, that is nice, isn't it? *(She drinks.)*

Happy: Good health.

Girl: I'm happy to meet you.

Happy: That's my name. Hap. It's really Harold, but at West Point they called me Happy.

Girl (now really impressed): Oh, I see. How do you do? *(She turns her profile.)*

Biff: Isn't Dad coming?

Happy: You want her?

Biff: Oh, I could never make that.

Happy: I remember the time that idea would never come into your head. Where's the old confidence, Biff?

Biff: I just saw Oliver —

Happy: Wait a minute. I've got to see that old confidence again. Do you want her? She's on call.

Biff: Oh, no. *(He turns to look at the Girl.)*

Happy: I'm telling you. Watch this. *(Turning to the Girl.)* Honey? *(She turns to him.)* Are you busy?

Girl: Well, I am . . . but I could make a phone call.

Happy: Do that, will you, honey? And see if you can get a friend. We'll be here for a while. Biff is one of the greatest football players in the country.

Girl (standing up): Well, I'm certainly happy to meet you.

Happy: Come back soon.

Girl: I'll try.

Happy: Don't try, honey, try hard.

The Girl exits. Stanley follows, shaking his head in bewildered admiration.

Happy: Isn't that a shame now? A beautiful girl like that? That's why I can't get married. There's not a good woman in a thousand. New York is loaded with them, kid!

Biff: Hap, look —

Happy: I told you she was on call!

Biff (strangely unnerved): Cut it out, will ya? I want to say something to you.

Happy: Did you see Oliver?

Biff: I saw him all right. Now look, I want to tell Dad a couple of things and I want you to help me.

Happy: What? Is he going to back you?

Biff: Are you crazy? You're out of your goddam head, you know that?

Happy: Why? What happened?

Biff (breathlessly): I did a terrible thing today, Hap. It's been the strangest day I ever went through. I'm all numb, I swear.

Happy: You mean he wouldn't see you?

Biff: Well, I waited six hours for him, see? All day. Kept sending my name in. Even tried to date his secretary so she'd get me to him, but no soap.

Happy: Because you're not showin' the old confidence, Biff. He remembered you, didn't he?

Biff (stopping Happy with a gesture): Finally, about five o'clock, he comes out. Didn't remember who I was or anything. I felt like such an idiot, Hap.

Happy: Did you tell him my Florida idea?

Biff: He walked away. I saw him for one minute. I got so mad I could've torn the walls down! How the hell did I ever get the idea I was a salesman there? I even believed myself that I'd been a salesman for him! And then he gave me one look and — I realized what a ridiculous lie my whole life has been! We've been talking in a dream for fifteen years. I was a shipping clerk.

Happy: What'd you do?

Biff (with great tension and wonder): Well, he left, see. And the secretary went out. I was all alone in the waiting-room. I don't know what came over me, Hap. The next thing I know I'm in his office — paneled walls, everything. I can't explain it. I — Hap, I took his fountain pen.

Happy: Geez, did he catch you?

Biff: I ran out. I ran down all eleven flights. I ran and ran and ran.

Happy: That was an awful dumb — what'd you do that for?

Biff (agonized): I don't know, I just — wanted to take something, I don't know. You gotta help me, Hap, I'm gonna tell Pop.

Happy: You crazy? What for?

Biff: Hap, he's got to understand that I'm not the man somebody lends that kind of money to. He thinks I've been spiting him all these years and it's eating him up.

Happy: That's just it. You tell him something nice.

Biff: I can't.

Happy: Say you got a lunch date with Oliver tomorrow.

Biff: So what do I do tomorrow?

Happy: You leave the house tomorrow and come back at night and say Oliver is thinking it over. And he thinks it over for a couple of weeks, and gradually it fades away and nobody's the worse.

Biff: But it'll go on forever!

Happy: Dad is never so happy as when he's looking forward to something!

Willy enters.

Happy: Hello, scout!

Willy: Gee, I haven't been here in years!

Stanley has followed Willy in and sets a chair for him. Stanley starts off but Happy stops him.

Happy: Stanley!

Stanley stands by, waiting for an order.

Biff (going to Willy with guilt, as to an invalid): Sit down, Pop. You want a drink?

Willy: Sure, I don't mind.

Biff: Let's get a load on.

Willy: You look worried.

Biff: N-no. *(To Stanley.)* Scotch all around. Make it doubles.

Stanley: Doubles, right. (*He goes.)*

Willy: You had a couple already, didn't you?

Biff: Just a couple, yeah.

Willy: Well, what happened, boy? *(Nodding affirmatively, with a smile.)* Everything go all right?

Biff (takes a breath, then reaches out and grasps Willy's hand.) Pal . . . *(He is smiling bravely, and Willy is smiling too.)* I had an experience today.

Happy: Terrific, Pop.

Willy: That so? What happened?

Biff (high, slightly alcoholic, above the earth): I'm going to tell you everything from first to last. It's been a strange day. *(Silence. He looks around, composes himself as best he can, but his breath keeps breaking the rhythm of his voice.)* I had to wait quite a while for him, and —

Willy: Oliver.

Biff: Yeah, Oliver. All day, as a matter of cold fact. And a lot of — instances — facts, Pop, facts about my life came back to me. Who was it, Pop? Who ever said I was a salesman with Oliver?

Willy: Well, you were.

Biff: No, Dad, I was a shipping clerk.

Willy: But you were practically —

Biff (with determination): Dad, I don't know who said it first, but I was never a salesman for Bill Oliver.

Willy: What're you talking about?

Biff: Let's hold on to the facts tonight, Pop. We're not going to get anywhere bullin' around. I was a shipping clerk.

Willy (angrily): All right, now listen to me —

Biff: Why don't you let me finish?

Willy: I'm not interested in stories about the past or any crap of that kind because the woods are burning, boys, you understand? There's a big blaze going on all around. I was fired today.

Biff (shocked): How could you be?

Willy: I was fired, and I'm looking for a little good news to tell your mother, because the woman has waited and the woman has suffered. The gist of it is that I haven't got a story left in my head, Biff. So don't give me a lecture about facts and aspects. I am not interested. Now what've you got to say to me?

Stanley enters with three drinks. They wait until he leaves.

Willy: Did you see Oliver?

Biff: Jesus, Dad!

Willy: You mean you didn't go up there?

Happy: Sure he went up there.

Biff: I did. I — saw him. How could they fire you?

Willy (on the edge of his chair): What kind of a welcome did he give you?
Biff: He won't even let you work on commission?
Willy: I'm out! *(Driving.)* So tell me, he gave you a warm welcome?
Happy: Sure, Pop, sure!
Biff (driven): Well, it was kind of —
Willy: I was wondering if he'd remember you. *(To Happy.)* Imagine, man doesn't see him for ten, twelve years and gives him that kind of a welcome!
Happy: Damn right!
Biff (trying to return to the offensive): Pop, look —
Willy: You know why he remembered you, don't you? Because you impressed him in those days.
Biff: Let's talk quietly and get this down to the facts, huh?
Willy (as though Biff had been interrupting): Well, what happened? It's great news, Biff. Did he take you into his office or'd you talk in the waiting-room?
Biff: Well, he came in, see, and —
Willy (with a big smile): What'd he say? Betcha he threw his arm around you.
Biff: Well, he kinda —
Willy: He's a fine man. *(To Happy.)* Very hard man to see, y'know.
Happy (agreeing): Oh, I know.
Willy (to Biff): Is that where you had the drinks?
Biff: Yeah, he gave me a couple of — no, no!
Happy (cutting in): He told him my Florida idea.
Willy: Don't interrupt. *(To Biff.)* How'd he react to the Florida idea?
Biff: Dad, will you give me a minute to explain?
Willy: I've been waiting for you to explain since I sat down here! What happened? He took you into his office and what?
Biff: Well — I talked. And — and he listened, see.
Willy: Famous for the way he listens, y'know. What was his answer?
Biff: His answer was — *(He breaks off, suddenly angry.)* Dad, you're not letting me tell you what I want to tell you!
Willy (accusing, angered): You didn't see him, did you?
Biff: I did see him!
Willy: What'd you insult him or something? You insulted him, didn't you?
Biff: Listen, will you let me out of it, will you just let me out of it!
Happy: What the hell!
Willy: Tell me what happened!
Biff (to Happy): I can't talk to him!

A single trumpet note jars the ear. The light of green leaves stains the house, which holds the air of night and a dream. Young Bernard enters and knocks on the door of the house.

Young Bernard (frantically): Mrs. Loman, Mrs. Loman!
Happy: Tell him what happened!
Biff (to Happy): Shut up and leave me alone!
Willy: No, no! You had to go and flunk math!
Biff: What math? What're you talking about?
Young Bernard: Mrs. Loman, Mrs. Loman!

Linda appears in the house, as of old.

Willy (wildly): Math, math, math!

Biff: Take it easy, Pop!

Young Bernard: Mrs. Loman!

Willy (furiously): If you hadn't flunked you'd've been set by now!

Biff: Now, look, I'm gonna tell you what happened, and you're going to listen to me.

Young Bernard: Mrs. Loman!

Biff: I waited six hours —

Happy: What the hell are you saying?

Biff: I kept sending in my name but he wouldn't see me. So finally he . . . *(He continues unheard as light fades low on the restaurant.)*

Young Bernard: Biff flunked math!

Linda: No!

Young Bernard: Birnbaum flunked him! They won't graduate him!

Linda: But they have to. He's gotta go to the university. Where is he? Biff! Biff!

Young Bernard: No, he left. He went to Grand Central.

Linda: Grand — You mean he went to Boston!

Young Bernard: Is Uncle Willy in Boston?

Linda: Oh, maybe Willy can talk to the teacher. Oh, the poor, poor boy!

Light on house area snaps out.

Biff (at the table, now audible, holding up a gold fountain pen): . . . so I'm washed up with Oliver, you understand? Are you listening to me?

Willy (at a loss): Yeah, sure. If you hadn't flunked —

Biff: Flunked what? What're you talking about?

Willy: Don't blame everything on me! I didn't flunk math — you did! What pen?

Happy: That was awful dumb, Biff, a pen like that is worth —

Willy (seeing the pen for the first time): You took Oliver's pen?

Biff (weakening): Dad, I just explained it to you.

Willy: You stole Bill Oliver's fountain pen!

Biff: I didn't exactly steal it! That's just what I've been explaining to you!

Happy: He had it in his hand and just then Oliver walked in, so he got nervous and stuck it in his pocket!

Willy: My God, Biff!

Biff: I never intended to do it, Dad!

Operator's Voice: Standish Arms, good evening!

Willy (shouting): I'm not in my room!

Biff (frightened): Dad, what's the matter? *(He and Happy stand up.)*

Operator: Ringing Mr. Loman for you!

Willy: I'm not there, stop it!

Biff (horrified, gets down on one knee before Willy): Dad, I'll make good, I'll make good. *(Willy tries to get to his feet. Biff holds him down.)* Sit down now.

Willy: No, you're no good, you're no good for anything.

Biff: I am, Dad, I'll find something else, you understand? Now don't worry about anything. *(He holds up Willy's face.)* Talk to me, Dad.

Operator: Mr. Loman does not answer. Shall I page him?

Willy (attempting to stand, as though to rush and silence the Operator): No, no, no!

Happy: He'll strike something, Pop.

Willy: No, no . . .

Biff (desperately, standing over Willy): Pop, listen! Listen to me! I'm telling you something good. Oliver talked to his partner about the Florida idea. You listening? He — he talked to his partner, and he came to me . . . I'm going to be all right, you hear? Dad, listen to me, he said it was just a question of the amount!

Willy: Then you . . . got it?

Happy: He's gonna be terrific, Pop!

Willy (trying to stand): Then you got it, haven't you? You got it! You got it!

Biff (agonized, holds Willy down): No, no. Look, Pop. I'm supposed to have lunch with them tomorrow. I'm just telling you this so you'll know that I can still make an impression, Pop. And I'll make good somewhere, but I can't go tomorrow, see?

Willy: Why not? You simply —

Biff: But the pen, Pop!

Willy: You give it to him and tell him it was an oversight!

Happy: Sure, have lunch tomorrow!

Biff: I can't say that —

Willy: You were doing a crossword puzzle and accidentally used his pen!

Biff: Listen, kid, I took those balls years ago, now I walk in with his fountain pen? That clinches it, don't you see? I can't face him like that! I'll try elsewhere.

Page's Voice: Paging Mr. Loman!

Willy: Don't you want to be anything?

Biff: Pop, how can I go back?

Willy: You don't want to be anything, is that what's behind it?

Biff (now angry at Willy for not crediting his sympathy): Don't take it that way! You think it was easy walking into that office after what I'd done to him? A team of horses couldn't have dragged me back to Bill Oliver!

Willy: Then why'd you go?

Biff: Why did I go? Why did I go! Look at you! Look at what's become of you!

Off left, The Woman laughs.

Willy: Biff, you're going to lunch tomorrow, or —

Biff: I can't go. I've got no appointment!

Happy: Biff, for . . . !

Willy: Are you spiting me?

Biff: Don't take it that way! Goddammit!

Willy (strikes Biff and falters away from the table): You rotten little louse! Are you spiting me?

The Woman: Someone's at the door, Willy!

Biff: I'm no good, can't you see what I am?

Happy (separating them): Hey, you're in a restaurant! Now cut it out, both of you! *(The girls enter.)* Hello, girls, sit down.

The Woman laughs, off left.

Miss Forsythe: I guess we might as well. This is Letta.

The Woman: Willy, are you going to wake up?

Biff (ignoring Willy): How're ya, miss, sit down. What do you drink?
Miss Forsythe: Letta might not be able to stay long.
Letta: I gotta get up very early tomorrow. I got jury duty. I'm so excited! Were you fellows ever on a jury?
Biff: No, but I been in front of them! *(The girls laugh.)* This is my father.
Letta: Isn't he cute? Sit down with us, Pop.
Happy: Sit him down, Biff!
Biff (going to him): Come on, slugger, drink us under the table. To hell with it! Come on, sit down, pal.

On Biff's last insistence, Willy is about to sit.

The Woman (now urgently): Willy, are you going to answer the door!

The Woman's call pulls Willy back. He starts right, befuddled.

Biff: Hey, where are you going?
Willy: Open the door.
Biff: The door?
Willy: The washroom . . . the door . . . where's the door?
Biff (leading Willy to the left): Just go straight down.

Willy moves left.

The Woman: Willy, Willy, are you going to get up, get up, get up, get up?

Willy exits left.

Letta: I think it's sweet you bring your daddy along.
Miss Forsythe: Oh, he isn't really your father!
Biff (at left, turning to her resentfully): Miss Forsythe, you've just seen a prince walk by. A fine, troubled prince. A hard-working, unappreciated prince. A pal, you understand? A good companion. Always for his boys.
Letta: That's so sweet.
Happy: Well, girls, what's the program? We're wasting time. Come on, Biff. Gather round. Where would you like to go?
Biff: Why don't you do something for him?
Happy: Me!
Biff: Don't you give a damn for him, Hap?
Happy: What're you talking about? I'm the one who —
Biff: I sense it, you don't give a good goddamn about him. *(He takes the rolled-up hose from his pocket and puts it on the table in front of Happy.)* Look what I found in the cellar, for Christ's sake. How can you bear to let it go on?
Happy: Me? Who goes away? Who runs off and —
Biff: Yeah, but he doesn't mean anything to you. You could help him — I can't! Don't you understand what I'm talking about? He's going to kill himself, don't you know that?
Happy: Don't I know it! Me!
Biff: Hap, help him! Jesus . . . help him . . . Help me, help me, I can't bear to look at his face! *(Ready to weep, he hurries out, up right.)*
Happy (starting after him): Where are you going?
Miss Forsythe: What's he so mad about?

Happy: Come on, girls, we'll catch up with him.
Miss Forsythe (as Happy pushes her out): Say, I don't like that temper of his!
Happy: He's just a little overstrung, he'll be all right!
Willy (off left, as The Woman laughs): Don't answer! Don't answer!
Letta: Don't you want to tell your father —
Happy: No, that's not my father. He's just a guy. Come on, we'll catch Biff, and, honey, we're going to paint this town! Stanley, where's the check! Hey, Stanley!

They exit. Stanley looks toward left.

Stanley (calling to Happy indignantly): Mr. Loman! Mr. Loman!

Stanley picks up a chair and follows them off. Knocking is heard off left. The Woman enters, laughing. Willy follows her. She is in a black slip; he is buttoning his shirt. Raw, sensuous music accompanies their speech.

Willy: Will you stop laughing? Will you stop?
The Woman: Aren't you going to answer the door? He'll wake the whole hotel.
Willy: I'm not expecting anybody.
The Woman: Whyn't you have another drink, honey, and stop being so damn self-centered?
Willy: I'm so lonely.
The Woman: You know you ruined me, Willy? From now on, whenever you come to the office, I'll see that you go right through to the buyers. No waiting at my desk any more, Willy. You ruined me.
Willy: That's nice of you to say that.
The Woman: Gee, you are self-centered! Why so sad? You are the saddest, self-centeredest soul I ever did see-saw. *(She laughs. He kisses her.)* Come on inside, drummer boy. It's silly to be dressing in the middle of the night. *(As knocking is heard.)* Aren't you going to answer the door?
Willy: They're knocking on the wrong door.
The Woman: But I felt the knocking. And he heard us talking in here. Maybe the hotel's on fire!
Willy (his terror rising): It's a mistake.
The Woman: Then tell him to go away!
Willy: There's nobody there.
The Woman: It's getting on my nerves, Willy. There's somebody standing out there and it's getting on my nerves!
Willy (pushing her away from him): All right, stay in the bathroom here, and don't come out. I think there's a law in Massachusetts about it, so don't come out. It may be that new room clerk. He looked very mean. So don't come out. It's a mistake, there's no fire.

The knocking is heard again. He takes a few steps away from her, and she vanishes into the wing. The light follows him, and now he is facing Young Biff, who carries a suitcase. Biff steps toward him. The music is gone.

Biff: Why didn't you answer?
Willy: Biff! What are you doing in Boston?
Biff: Why didn't you answer? I've been knocking for five minutes, I called you on the phone —

Willy: I just heard you. I was in the bathroom and had the door shut. Did anything happen home?

Biff: Dad — I let you down.

Willy: What do you mean?

Biff: Dad . . .

Willy: Biffo, what's this about? *(Putting his arm around Biff.)* Come on, let's go downstairs and get you a malted.

Biff: Dad, I flunked math.

Willy: Not for the term?

Biff: The term. I haven't got enough credits to graduate.

Willy: You mean to say Bernard wouldn't give you the answers?

Biff: He did, he tried, but I only got a sixty-one.

Willy: And they wouldn't give you four points?

Biff: Birnbaum refused absolutely. I begged him, Pop, but he won't give me those points. You gotta talk to him before they close the school. Because if he saw the kind of man you are, and you just talked to him in your way, I'm sure he'd come through for me. The class came right before practice, see, and I didn't go enough. Would you talk to him? He'd like you, Pop. You know the way you could talk.

Willy: You're on. We'll drive right back.

Biff: Oh, Dad, good work! I'm sure he'll change it for you!

Willy: Go downstairs and tell the clerk I'm checkin' out. Go right down.

Biff: Yes, sir! See, the reason he hates me, Pop — one day he was late for class so I got up at the blackboard and imitated him. I crossed my eyes and talked with a lithp.

Willy (laughing): You did? The kids like it?

Biff: They nearly died laughing!

Willy: Yeah: What'd you do?

Biff: The thquare root of thixthy twee is . . . *(Willy bursts out laughing; Biff joins him.)* And in the middle of it he walked in!

Willy laughs and The Woman joins in offstage.

Willy (without hesitation): Hurry downstairs and —

Biff: Somebody in there?

Willy: No, that was next door.

The Woman laughs offstage.

Biff: Somebody got in your bathroom!

Willy: No, it's the next room, there's a party —

The Woman (enters, laughing. She lisps this:) Can I come in? There's something in the bathtub, Willy, and it's moving!

Willy looks at Biff, who is staring open-mouthed and horrified at The Woman.

Willy: Ah — you better go back to your room. They must be finished painting by now. They're painting her room so I let her take a shower here. Go back, go back . . . *(He pushes her.)*

The Woman (resisting): But I've got to get dressed, Willy, I can't —

Willy: Get out of here! Go back, go back . . . *(Suddenly striving for the ordi-*

nary): This is Miss Francis, Biff, she's a buyer. They're painting her room. Go back, Miss Francis, go back . . .

The Woman: But my clothes, I can't go out naked in the hall!

Willy (pushing her offstage): Get outa here! Go back, go back!

Biff slowly sits down on his suitcase as the argument continues offstage.

The Woman: Where's my stockings? You promised me stockings, Willy!

Willy: I have no stockings here!

The Woman: You had two boxes of size nine sheers for me, and I want them!

Willy: Here, for God's sake, will you get outa here!

The Woman (enters holding a box of stockings): I just hope there's nobody in the hall. That's all I hope. *(To Biff.)* Are you football or baseball?

Biff: Football.

The Woman (angry, humiliated): That's me too. G'night. *(She snatches her clothes from Willy, and walks out.)*

Willy (after a pause): Well, better get going. I want to get to the school first thing in the morning. Get my suits out of the closet. I'll get my valise. *(Biff doesn't move.)* What's the matter? *(Biff remains motionless, tears falling.)* She's a buyer. Buys for J. H. Simmons. She lives down the hall — they're painting. You don't imagine — *(He breaks off. After a pause.)* Now listen, pal, she's just a buyer. She sees merchandise in her room and they have to keep it looking just so . . . *(Pause. Assuming command.)* All right, get my suits. *(Biff doesn't move.)* Now stop crying and do as I say. I gave you an order. Biff, I gave you an order! Is that what you do when I give you an order? How dare you cry! *(Putting his arm around Biff.)* Now look, Biff, when you grow up you'll understand about these things. You mustn't — you mustn't overemphasize a thing like this. I'll see Birnbaum first thing in the morning.

Biff: Never mind.

Willy (getting down beside Biff): Never mind! He's going to give you those points. I'll see to it.

Biff: He wouldn't listen to you.

Willy: He certainly will listen to me. You need those points for the U. of Virginia.

Biff: I'm not going there.

Willy: Heh? If I can't get him to change that mark you'll make it up in summer school. You've got all summer to —

Biff (his weeping breaking from him): Dad . . .

Willy (infected by it): Oh, my boy . . .

Biff: Dad . . .

Willy: She's nothing to me, Biff. I was lonely, I was terribly lonely.

Biff: You — you gave her Mama's stockings! *(His tears break through and he rises to go.)*

Willy (grabbing for Biff): I gave you an order!

Biff: Don't touch me, you — liar!

Willy: Apologize for that!

Biff: You fake! You phony little fake! You fake! *(Overcome, he turns quickly and weeping fully goes out with his suitcase. Willy is left on the floor on his knees.)*

Willy: I gave you an order! Biff, come back here or I'll beat you! Come back here! I'll whip you!

Stanley comes quickly in from the right and stands in front of Willy.

Willy (shouts at Stanley): I gave you an order . . .
Stanley: Hey, let's pick it up, pick it up, Mr. Loman. *(He helps Willy to his feet.)* Your boys left with the chippies. They said they'll see you home.

A second waiter watches some distance away.

Willy: But we were supposed to have dinner together.

Music is heard, Willy's theme.

Stanley: Can you make it?
Willy: I'll — sure, I can make it. *(Suddenly concerned about his clothes.)* Do I — I look all right?
Stanley: Sure, you look all right. *(He flicks a speck off Willy's lapel.)*
Willy: Here — here's a dollar.
Stanley: Oh, your son paid me. It's all right.
Willy (putting it in Stanley's hand): No, take it. You're a good boy.
Stanley: Oh, no, you don't have to . . .
Willy: Here — here's some more, I don't need it any more. *(After a slight pause.)* Tell me — is there a seed store in the neighborhood?
Stanley: Seeds? You mean like to plant?

As Willy turns, Stanley slips the money back into his jacket pocket.

Willy: Yes. Carrots, peas . . .
Stanley: Well, there's hardware stores on Sixth Avenue, but it may be too late now.
Willy (anxiously): Oh, I'd better hurry. I've got to get some seeds. *(He starts off to the right.)* I've got to get some seeds, right away. Nothing's planted. I don't have a thing in the ground.

Willy hurries out as the light goes down. Stanley moves over to the right after him, watches him off. The other waiter has been staring at Willy.

Stanley (to the waiter): Well, whatta you looking at?

The waiter picks up the chairs and moves off right. Stanley takes the table and follows him. The light fades on this area. There is a long pause, the sound of the flute coming over. The light gradually rises on the kitchen, which is empty. Happy appears at the door of the house, followed by Biff. Happy is carrying a large bunch of long-stemmed roses. He enters the kitchen, looks around for Linda. Not seeing her, he turns to Biff, who is just outside the house door, and makes a gesture with his hands, indicating "Not here, I guess." He looks into the living-room and freezes. Inside, Linda, unseen, is seated, Willy's coat on her lap. She rises ominously and quietly and moves toward Happy, who backs up into the ktichen, afraid.

Happy: Hey, what're you doing up? *(Linda says nothing but moves toward him implacably.)* Where's Pop? *(He keeps backing to the right, and now Linda is in full view in the doorway to the living-room.)* Is he sleeping?

Linda: Where were you?

Happy (trying to laugh it off): We met two girls, Mom, very fine types. Here, we brought you some flowers. *(Offering them to her.)* Put them in your room, Ma.

She knocks them to the floor at Biff's feet. He has now come inside and closed the door behind him. She stares at Biff, silent.

Happy: Now what'd you do that for? Mom, I want you to have some flowers —

Linda (cutting Happy off, violently to Biff): Don't you care whether he lives or dies?

Happy (going to the stairs): Come upstairs, Biff.

Biff (with a flare of disgust, to Happy): Go away from me! *(To Linda.)* What do you mean, lives or dies? Nobody's dying around here, pal.

Linda: Get out of my sight! Get out of here!

Biff: I wanna see the boss.

Linda: You're not going near him!

Biff: Where is he? *(He moves into the living-room and Linda follows.)*

Linda (shouting after Biff): You invite him for dinner. He looks forward to it all day — *(Biff appears in his parents' bedroom, looks around, and exits.)* — and then you desert him there. There's no stranger you'd do that to!

Happy: Why? He had a swell time with us. Listen, when I — *(Linda comes back into the kitchen)* — desert him I hope I don't outlive the day!

Linda: Get out of here!

Happy: Now look, Mom . . .

Linda: Did you have to go to women tonight? You and your lousy rotten whores!

Biff re-enters the kitchen.

Happy: Mom, all we did was follow Biff around trying to cheer him up! *(To Biff.)* Boy, what a night you gave me!

Linda: Get out of here, both of you, and don't come back! I don't want you tormenting him any more. Go on now, get your things together! *(To Biff.)* You can sleep in his apartment. *(She starts to pick up the flowers and stops herself.)* Pick up this stuff, I'm not your maid any more. Pick it up, you bum, you!

Happy turns his back to her in refusal. Biff slowly moves over and gets down on his knees, picking up the flowers.

Linda: You're a pair of animals! Not one, not another living soul would have had the cruelty to walk out on that man in a restaurant!

Biff (not looking at her): Is that what he said?

Linda: He didn't have to say anything. He was so humiliated he nearly limped when he came in.

Happy: But, Mom, he had a great time with us —

Biff (cutting him off violently): Shut up!

Without another word, Happy goes upstairs.

Linda: You! You didn't even go in to see if he was all right!

Biff (still on the floor in front of Linda, the flowers in his hand; with self-loath-

ing.) No. Didn't. Didn't do a damned thing. How do you like that, heh? Left him babbling in a toilet.

Linda: You louse. You . . .

Biff: Now you hit it on the nose! *(He gets up, throws the flowers in the waste-basket.)* The scum of the earth, and you're looking at him!

Linda: Get out of here!

Biff: I gotta talk to the boss, Mom. Where is he?

Linda: You're not going near him. Get out of this house!

Biff (with absolute assurance, determination): No. We're gonna have an abrupt conversation, him and me.

Linda: You're not talking to him!

Hammering is heard from outside the house, off right. Biff turns toward the noise.

Linda (suddenly pleading): Will you please leave him alone?

Biff: What's he doing out there?

Linda: He's planting the garden!

Biff (quietly): Now? Oh, my God!

Biff moves outside, Linda following. The light dies down on them and comes up on the center of the apron as Willy walks into it. He is carrying a flashlight, a hoe, and handful of seed packets. He raps the top of the hoe sharply to fix it firmly, and then moves to the left, measuring off the distance with his foot. He holds the flashlight to look at the seed packets, reading off the instructions. He is in the blue of night.

Willy: Carrots . . . quarter-inch apart. Rows . . . one-foot rows. *(He measures it off.)* One foot. *(He puts down a package and measures off.)* Beets. *(He puts down another package and measures again.)* Lettuce. *(He reads the package, puts it down.)* One foot — *(He breaks off as Ben appears at the right and moves slowly down to him.)* What a proposition, ts, ts. Terrific, terrific. 'Cause she's suffered, Ben, the woman has suffered. You understand me? A man can't go out the way he came in, Ben, a man has got to add up to something. You can't, you can't — *(Ben moves toward him as though to interrupt.)* You gotta consider, now. Don't answer so quick. Remember, it's a guaranteed twenty-thousand-dollar proposition. Now look, Ben, I want you to go through the ins and outs of this thing with me. I've got nobody to talk to, Ben, and the woman has suffered, you hear me?

Ben (standing still, considering): What's the proposition?

Willy: It's twenty thousand dollars on the barrelhead. Guaranteed, gilt-edged, you understand?

Ben: You don't want to make a fool of yourself. They might not honor the policy.

Willy: How can they dare refuse? Didn't I work like a coolie to meet every premium on the nose? And now they don't pay off? Impossible!

Ben: It's called a cowardly thing, William.

Willy: Why? Does it take more guts to stand here the rest of my life ringing up a zero?

Ben (yielding): That's a point, William. *(He moves, thinking, turns.)* And twenty thousand — that *is* something one can feel with the hand, it is there.

Willy (now assured, with rising power): Oh, Ben, that's the whole beauty of it! I see it like a diamond, shining in the dark, hard and rough, that I can pick up and touch in my hand. Not like — like an appointment! This would not be another damned-fool appointment, Ben, and it changes all the aspects. Because he thinks I'm nothing, see, and so he spites me. But the funeral — *(Straightening up.)* Ben, that funeral will be massive! They'll come from Maine, Massachusetts, Vermont, New Hampshire! All the old-timers with the strange license plates — that boy will be thunder-struck, Ben, because he never realized — I am known! Rhode Island, New York, New Jersey — I am known, Ben, and he'll see it with his eyes once and for all. He'll see what I am, Ben! He's in for a shock, that boy!

Ben (coming to the edge of the garden): He'll call you a coward.

Willy (suddenly fearful): No, that would be terrible.

Ben: Yes. And a damned fool.

Willy: No, no, he mustn't, I won't have that! *(He is broken and desperate.)*

Ben: He'll hate, you, William.

The gay music of the Boys is heard.

Willy: Oh, Ben, how do we get back to all the great times? Used to be so full of light, and comradeship, the sleigh-riding in winter, and the ruddiness on his cheeks. And always some kind of good news coming up, always something nice coming up ahead. And never even let me carry the valises in the house, and simonizing, simonizing that little red car! Why, why can't I give him something and not have him hate me?

Ben: Let me think about it. *(He glances at his watch.)* I still have a little time. Remarkable proposition, but you've got to be sure you're not making a fool of yourself.

Ben drifts off upstage and goes out of sight. Biff comes down from the left.

Willy (suddenly conscious of Biff, turns and looks up at him, then begins picking up the packages of seeds in confusion): Where the hell is that seed? *(Indignantly.)* You can't see nothing out here! They boxed in the whole goddamn neighborhood!

Biff: There are people all around here. Don't you realize that?

Willy: I'm busy. Don't bother me.

Biff (taking the hoe from Willy): I'm saying good-by to you, Pop. *(Willy looks at him, silent, unable to move.)* I'm not coming back any more.

Willy: You're not going to see Oliver tomorrow?

Biff: I've got no appointment, Dad.

Willy: He put his arm around you, and you've got no appointment?

Biff: Pop, get this now, will you? Everytime I've left it's been a fight that sent me out of here. Today I realized something about myself and I tried to explain it to you and I — I think I'm just not smart enough to make any sense out of it for you. To hell with whose fault it is or anything like that. *(He takes Willy's arm.)* Let's just wrap it up, heh? Come on in, we'll tell Mom. *(He gently tries to pull Willy to left.)*

Willy (frozen, immobile, with guilt in his voice): No, I don't want to see her.

Biff: Come on! *(He pulls again, and Willy tries to pull away.)*

Willy (highly nervous): No, no, I don't want to see her.

Biff (tries to look into Willy's face, as if to find the answer there): Why don't you want to see her?

Willy (more harshly now): Don't bother me, will you?

Biff: What do you mean, you don't want to see her? You don't want them calling you yellow, do you? This isn't your fault; it's me, I'm a bum. Now come inside! *(Willy strains to get away.)* Did you hear what I said to you?

Willy pulls away and quickly goes by himself into the house. Biff follows.

Linda (to Willy): Did you plant, dear?

Biff (at the door, to Linda): All right, we had it out. I'm going and I'm not writing any more.

Linda (going to Willy in the kitchen): I think that's the best way, dear. 'Cause there's no use drawing it out, you'll just never get along.

Willy doesn't respond.

Biff: People ask where I am and what I'm doing, you don't know, and you don't care. That way it'll be off your mind and you can start brightening up again. All right? That clears it, doesn't it? *(Willy is silent, and Biff goes to him.)* You gonna wish me luck, scout? *(He extends his hand.)* What do you say?

Linda: Shake his hand, Willy.

Willy (turning to her, seething with hurt): There's no necessity to mention the pen at all, y'know.

Biff (gently): I've got no appointment, Dad.

Willy (erupting fiercely): He put his arm around . . . ?

Biff: Dad, you're never going to see what I am, so what's the use of arguing? If I strike oil I'll send you a check. Meantime forget I'm alive.

Willy (to Linda): Spite, see?

Biff: Shake hands, Dad.

Willy: Not my hand.

Biff: I was hoping not to go this way.

Willy: Well, this is the way you're going. Good-by.

Biff looks at him a moment, then turns sharply and goes to the stairs.

Willy (stops him with): May you rot in hell if you leave this house!

Biff (turning): Exactly what is it that you want from me?

Willy: I want you to know, on the train, in the mountains, in the valleys, wherever you go, that you cut down your life for spite!

Biff: No, no.

Willy: Spite, spite, is the word of your undoing! And when you're down and out, remember what did it. When you're rotting somewhere beside the railroad tracks, remember, and don't you dare blame it on me!

Biff: I'm not blaming it on you!

Willy: I won't take the rap for this, you hear?

Happy comes down the stairs and stands on the bottom step, watching.

Biff: That's just what I'm telling you!

Willy (sinking into a chair at the table, with full accusation): You're trying to put a knife in me — don't think I don't know what you're doing!

Biff: All right, phony! Then let's lay it on the line. *(He whips the rubber tube out of his pocket and puts it on the table.)*

Happy: You crazy —

Linda: Biff! *(She moves to grab the hose, but Biff holds it down with his hand.)*

Biff: Leave it there! Don't move it!

Willy (not looking at it): What is that?

Biff: You know goddam well what that is.

Willy (caged, wanting to escape): I never saw that.

Biff: You saw it. The mice didn't bring it into the cellar! What is this supposed to do, make a hero out of you? This supposed to make me sorry for you?

Willy: Never heard of it.

Biff: There'll be no pity for you, you hear it? No pity!

Willy (to Linda:) You hear the spite!

Biff: No, you're going to hear the truth — what you are and what I am!

Linda: Stop it!

Willy: Spite!

Happy (coming down toward Biff): You cut it now!

Biff (to Happy): The man don't know who we are! The man is gonna know! *(To Willy.)* We never told the truth for ten minutes in this house!

Happy: We always told the truth!

Biff (turning on him): You big blow, are you the assistant buyer? You're one of the two assistants to the assistant, aren't you?

Happy: Well, I'm practically —

Biff: You're practically full of it! We all are! And I'm through with it. *(To Willy.)* Now hear this, Willy, this is me.

Willy: I know you!

Biff: You know why I had no address for three months? I stole a suit in Kansas City and I was in jail. *(To Linda, who is sobbing.)* Stop crying. I'm through with it.

Linda turns away from them, her hands covering her face.

Willy: I suppose that's my fault!

Biff: I stole myself out of every good job since high school!

Willy: And whose fault is that?

Biff: And I never got anywhere because you blew me so full of hot air I could never stand taking orders from anybody! That's whose fault it is!

Willy: I hear that!

Linda: Don't, Biff!

Biff: It's goddam time you heard that! I had to be boss big shot in two weeks, and I'm through with it!

Willy: Then hang yourself! For spite, hang yourself!

Biff: No! Nobody's hanging himself, Willy! I ran down eleven flights with a pen in my hand today. And suddenly I stopped, you hear me? And in the middle of that office building, do you hear this? I stopped in the middle of that building and I saw — the sky. I saw the things that I love in this world. The work and the food and time to sit and smoke. And I looked at the pen and said to myself, what the hell am I grabbing this for? Why am I trying to become what I don't want to be? What am I doing in an office, making a contemptuous, begging fool of myself, when all I want is out there, waiting for me the minute I say I know who I am! Why can't I say that, Willy? *(He tries to make Willy face him, but Willy pulls away and moves to the left.)*

Willy: (with hatred, threateningly): The door of your life is wide open!

Biff: Pop! I'm a dime a dozen, and so are you!

Willy (turning on him now in an uncontrolled outburst): I am not a dime a dozen! I am Willy Loman, and you are Biff Loman!

Biff starts for Willy, but is blocked by Happy. In his fury, Biff seems on the verge of attacking his father.

Biff: I am not a leader of men, Willy, and neither are you. You were never anything but a hard-working drummer who landed in the ash can like all the rest of them! I'm one dollar an hour, Willy! I tried seven states and couldn't raise it. A buck an hour! Do you gather my meaning? I'm not bringing home any prizes any more, and you're going to stop waiting for me to bring them home!

Willy (directly to Biff): You vengeful, spiteful mut!

Biff breaks from Happy. Willy, in fright, starts up the stairs. Biff grabs him.

Biff (at the peak of his fury): Pop, I'm nothing! I'm nothing, Pop. Can't you understand that? There's no spite in it any more. I'm just what I am, that's all.

Biff's fury has spent itself, and he breaks down, sobbing, holding on to Willy, who dumbly fumbles for Biff's face.

Willy (astonished): What're you doing? What're you doing? *(To Linda.)* Why is he crying?

Biff (crying, broken): Will you let me go, for Christ's sake? Will you take that phony dream and burn it before something happens? *(Struggling to contain himself, he pulls away and moves to the stairs.)* I'll go in the morning. Put him — put him to bed. *(Exhausted, Biff moves up the stairs to his room.)*

Willy (after a long pause, astonished, elevated): Isn't that — isn't that remarkable? Biff — he likes me!

Linda: He loves you, Willy!

Happy (deeply moved): Always did, Pop.

Willy: Oh, Biff! *(Staring wildly.)* He cried! Cried to me. *(He is choking with his love, and now cries out his promise.)* That boy — that boy is going to be magnificent!

Ben appears in the light just outside the kitchen.

Ben: Yes, outstanding, with twenty thousand behind him.

Linda (sensing the racing of his mind, fearfully, carefully): Now come to bed, Willy. It's all settled now.

Willy (finding it difficult not to rush out of the house): Yes, we'll sleep. Come on. Go to sleep, Hap.

Ben: And it does take a great kind of a man to crack the jungle.

In accents of dread, Ben's idyllic music starts up.

Happy (his arm around Linda): I'm getting married, Pop, don't forget it. I'm changing everything. I'm gonna run that department before the year is up. You'll see, Mom. *(He kisses her.)*

Ben: The jungle is dark but full of diamonds, Willy.

Willy turns, moves, listening to Ben.

Linda: Be good. You're both good boys, just act that way, that's all.

Happy: 'Night, Pop. *(He goes upstairs.)*

Linda (to Willy): Come, dear.

Ben (with greater force): One must go in to fetch a diamond out.

Willy (to Linda, as he moves slowly along the edge of the kitchen, toward the door): I just want to get settled down, Linda. Let me sit alone for a little.

Linda (almost uttering her fear): I want you upstairs.

Willy (taking her in his arms): In a few minutes, Linda. I couldn't sleep right now. Go on, you look awful tired. *(He kisses her.)*

Ben: Not like an appointment at all. A diamond is rough and hard to the touch.

Willy: Go on now. I'll be right up.

Linda: I think this is the only way, Willy.

Willy: Sure, it's the best thing.

Ben: Best thing!

Willy: The only way. Everything is gonna be — go on, kid, get to bed. You look so tired.

Linda: Come right up.

Willy: Two minutes.

Linda goes into the living-room, then reappears in her bedroom. Willy moves just outside the kitchen door.

Willy: Loves me. *(Wonderingly.)* Always loved me. Isn't that a remarkable thing? Ben, he'll worship me for it!

Ben (with promise): It's dark there, but full of diamonds.

Willy: Can you imagine that magnificence with twenty thousand dollars in his pocket?

Linda (calling from her room): Willy! Come up!

Willy (calling into the kitchen): Yes! Yes. Coming! It's very smart, you realize that, don't you, sweetheart? Even Ben sees it. I gotta go, baby. 'By! 'By! *(Going over to Ben, almost dancing.)* Imagine? When the mail comes he'll be ahead of Bernard again!

Ben: A perfect proposition all around.

Willy: Did you see how he cried to me? Oh, if I could kiss him, Ben!

Ben: Time, William, time!

Willy: Oh, Ben, I always knew one way or another we were gonna make it, Biff and I!

Ben (looking at his watch): The boat. We'll be late. *(He moves slowly off into the darkness.)*

Willy (elegiacally, turning to the house): Now when you kick off, boy, I want a seventy-yard boot, and get right down the field under the ball, and when you hit, hit low and hit hard, because it's important, boy. *(He swings around and faces the audience.)* There's all kinds of important people in the stands, and the first thing you know . . . *(Suddenly realizing he is alone.)* Ben! Ben, where do I . . . ? *(He makes a sudden movement of search.)* Ben, how do I . . . ?

Linda (calling): Willy, you coming up?

Willy (uttering a gasp of fear, whirling about as if to quiet her): Sh! *(He turns around as if to find his way; sounds, faces, voices, seem to be swarming in upon him and he flicks at them, crying.)* Sh! Sh! *(Suddenly music, faint and high, stops him. It rises in intensity, almost to an unbearable scream. He goes up and down on his toes, and rushes off around the house.)* Shhh!

Linda: Willy?

There is no answer. Linda waits. Biff gets up off his bed. He is still in his clothes. Happy sits up. Biff stands listening.

Linda (with real fear): Willy, answer me! Willy!

There is the sound of a car starting and moving away at full speed.

Linda: No!

Biff (rushing down the stairs): Pop!

As the car speeds off, the music crashes down in a frenzy of sound, which becomes the soft pulsation of a single cello string. Biff slowly returns to his bedroom. He and Happy gravely don their jackets. Linda slowly walks out of her room. The music has developed into a dead march. The leaves of day are appearing over everything. Charley and Bernard, somberly dressed, appear and knock on the kitchen door. Biff and Happy slowly descend the stairs to the kitchen as Charley and Bernard enter. All stop a moment when Linda, in clothes of mourning, bearing a little bunch of roses, comes through the draped doorway into the kitchen. She goes to Charley and takes his arm. Now all move toward the audience, through the wall-line of the kitchen. At the limit of the apron, Linda lays down the flowers, kneels, and sits back on her heels. All stare down at the grave.

REQUIEM

Charley: It's getting dark, Linda.

Linda doesn't react. She stares at the grave.

Biff: How about it, Mom? Better get some rest, heh? They'll be closing the gate soon.

Linda makes no move. Pause.

Happy (deeply angered): He had no right to do that. There was no necessity for it. We would've helped him.

Charley (grunting): Hmmm.

Biff: Come along, Mom.

Linda: Why didn't anybody come?

Charley: It was a very nice funeral.

Linda: But where are all the people he knew? Maybe they blame him.

Charley: Naa. It's a rough world, Linda. They wouldn't blame him.

Linda: I can't understand it. At this time especially. First time in thirty-five years we were just about free and clear. He only needed a little salary. He was even finished with the dentist.

Charley: No man only needs a little salary.

Linda: I can't understand it.

Biff: There were a lot of nice days. When he'd come home from a trip; or on Sundays, making the stoop; finishing the cellar; putting on the new porch; when he built the extra bathroom; and put up the garage. You know something, Charley, there's more of him in that front stoop than in all the sales he ever made.

Charley: Yeah. He was a happy man with a batch of cement.

Linda: He was so wonderful with his hands.

Biff: He had the wrong dreams. All, all, wrong.

Happy (almost ready to fight Biff): Don't say that!

Biff: He never knew who he was.

Charley (stopping Happy's movement and reply. To Biff): Nobody dast blame this man. You don't understand: Willy was a salesman. And for a salesman, there is no rock bottom to the life. He don't put a bolt to a nut, he don't tell you the law or give you medicine. He's a man way out there in the blue, riding on a smile and a shoeshine. And when they start not smiling back — that's an earthquake. And then you get yourself a couple of spots on your hat, and you're finished. Nobody dast blame this man. A salesman is got to dream, boy. It comes with the territory.

Biff: Charley, the man didn't know who he was.

Happy (infuriated): Don't say that!

Biff: Why don't you come with me, Happy?

Happy: I'm not licked that easily. I'm staying right in this city, and I'm gonna beat this racket! *(He looks at Biff, his chin set.)* The Loman Brothers!

Biff: I know who I am, kid.

Happy: All right, boy. I'm gonna show you and everybody else that Willy Loman did not die in vain. He had a good dream. It's the only dream you can have — to come out number-one man. He fought it out here, and this is where I'm gonna win it for him.

Biff (with a hopeless glance at Happy, bends toward his mother): Let's go, Mom.

Linda: I'll be with you in a minute. Go on, Charley. *(He hesitates.)* I want to, just for a minute. I never had a chance to say good-by.

Charley moves away, followed by Happy. Biff remains a slight distance up and left of Linda. She sits there, summoning herself. The flute begins, not far away, playing behind her speech.

Linda: Forgive me, dear. I can't cry. I don't know what it is, but I can't cry. I don't understand it. Why did you ever do that? Help me, Willy, I can't cry. It seems to me that you're just on another trip. I keep expecting you. Willy, dear, I can't cry. Why did you do it? I search and search and I search, and I can't understand it, Willy. I made the last payment on the house today. Today, dear. And there'll be nobody home. *(A sob rises in her throat.)* We're free and clear. *(Sobbing more fully, released.)* We're free. *(Biff comes slowly toward her.)* We're free . . . We're free . . .

Biff lifts her to her feet and moves out up right with her in his arms. Linda sobs quietly. Bernard and Charley come together and follow them, followed by Happy. Only the music of the flute is left on the darkening stage as over the house the hard towers of the apartment buildings rise into sharp focus, and

The Curtain Falls

Connections

1. Compare and contrast Willy Loman with Polonius in Shakespeare's *Hamlet* (p. 1065). To what extent is each character wise, foolish, deluded, and hypocritical? Explain why Loman can be seen as a tragic character while Polonius cannot be.
2. Read Delmore Schwartz's poem "The True-Blue American" (p. 843), and compare its treatment of the American dream with the one in *Death of a Salesman*. How do the tones of the two works differ?
3. What similarities do you find between the endings of *Death of a Salesman* and Chekhov's *The Cherry Orchard* (p. 1375)? Are the endings happy? unhappy? or something else?

AN ALBUM OF WORLD LITERATURE

THE STRONG BREED

Born Oluwole Akinwande Soyinka in the western Nigerian town of Akinwande, Wole Soyinka has embodied in his life and art the contradictions and tensions that can often seem inevitable for the European-educated, English-speaking, African writer. "Selective eclecticism," he once said, is "the right of every productive being." Although he has written and published novels and poetry, Soyinka is most renowned as a playwright whose work often focuses on the tragic consequences of a clash between colonial and tribal values. Educated at Leeds University in England, he subsequently began an active career as a playwright as well as a political reformer and social critic. His autobiography *The Man Died* (1973) records his experiences as a political prisoner in Nigeria.

Soyinka's many plays include *The Swamp Dwellers* (1958), *The Invention* (1959), *The Lion and the Jewel* (1959), *A Dance of Forests* (1960), *The Strong Breed* (1963), *Madmen and Specialists* (1970), and *Death and the King's Horseman* (1976). He has also written two novels and three volumes of poetry. In 1986 he was awarded the Nobel Prize for literature.

Like nearly all of Soyinka's writing, *The Strong Breed* is steeped in African tribal culture and tradition, but the play's abiding concern for human suffering and social justice invites all readers to step into the small village in which one "night's work" changes the lives of its inhabitants.

WOLE SOYINKA (Nigerian/b. 1934)

The Strong Breed

1963

Characters
Eman, a stranger
Sunma, Jaguna's daughter
Ifada, an idiot
A Girl
Jaguna
Oroge
Attendant Stalwarts, the villagers from Eman's past —
Old Man, his father
Omae, his betrothed
Tutor
Priest
Attendants, the villagers

The scenes are described briefly, but very often a darkened stage with lit area will not only suffice but is necessary. Except for the one indicated place, there can be no break in the action. A distracting scene-change would be ruinous. A mud house, with space in front of it. Eman, in light buba and trousers, stands at the window, looking out. Inside, Sunma is clearing the table of what looks like a modest clinic, putting the things away in a cupboard. Another rough table in the room is piled with exercise books, two or three worn textbooks, etc. Sunma appears agitated. Outside, just below the window, crouches Ifada. He looks up with a shy smile from time to time, waiting for Eman to notice him.

Sunma (hesitant): You will have to make up your mind soon, Eman. The lorry leaves very shortly.

As Eman does not answer, Sunma continues her work, more nervously. Two villagers, obvious travelers, pass hurriedly in front of the house, the man has a small raffia sack, the woman a cloth-covered basket, the man enters first, turns, and urges the woman who is just emerging to hurry.

Sunma (seeing them, her tone is more intense): Eman, are we going or aren't we? You will leave it till too late.
Eman (quietly): There is still time — if you want to go.
Sunma: If I want to go . . . and you?

Eman makes no reply.

Sunma (bitterly): You don't really want to leave here. You never want to go away — even for a minute.

Ifada continues his antics. Eman eventually pats him on the head and the boy grins happily. Leaps up suddenly and returns with a basket of oranges, which he offers Eman.

Eman: My gift for today's festival enh?

Ifada nods, grinning.

Eman: They look ripe — that's a change.
Sunma (she has gone inside the room. Looks round the door): Did you call me?

Eman: No. *(She goes back.)* And what will you do tonight, Ifada? Will you take part in the dancing? Or perhaps you will mount your own masquerade?

Ifada shakes his head, regretfully.

Eman: You won't? So you haven't any? But you would like to own one.

Ifada nods eagerly.

Eman: Then why don't you make your own?

Ifada stares, puzzled by this idea.

Eman: Sunma will let you have some cloth you know. And bits of wool . . .
Sunma (coming out): Who are you talking to, Eman?
Eman: Ifada. I am trying to persuade him to join the young maskers.
Sunma (losing control): What does he want here? Why is he hanging round us?
Eman (amazed): What . . . ? I said Ifada, Ifada.
Sunma: Just tell him to go away. Let him go and play somewhere else!
Eman: What is this? Hasn't he always played here?
Sunma: I don't want him here. *(Rushes to the window.)* Get away, idiot. Don't bring your foolish face here any more, do you hear? Go on, go away from here . . .
Eman (restraining her): Control yourself, Sunma. What on earth has got into you?

Ifada, hurt and bewildered, backs slowly away.

Sunma: He comes crawling round here like some horrible insect. I never want to lay my eyes on him again.
Eman: I don't understand. It *is* Ifada you know, Ifada! The unfortunate one who runs errands for you and doesn't hurt a soul.
Sunma: I cannot bear the sight of him.
Eman: You can't do what? It can't be two days since he last fetched water for you.
Sunma: What else can he do except that? He is useless. Just because we have been kind to him. . . . Others would have put him in an asylum.
Eman: You are not making sense. He is not a madman, he is just a little more unlucky than other children. *(Looks keenly at her.)* But what is the matter?
Sunma: It's nothing. I only wish we had sent him off to one of those places for creatures like him.
Eman: He is quite happy here. He doesn't bother anyone and he makes himself useful.
Sunma: Useful! Is that one of any use to anybody? Boys of his age are already earning a living but all he can do is hang around and drool at the mouth.
Eman: But he does work. You know he does a lot for you.
Sunma: Does he? And what about the farm you started for him! Does he ever work on it? Or have you forgotten that it was really for Ifada you cleared that brush. Now you have to go and work it yourself. You spend all your time on it and you have no room for anything else.
Eman: That wasn't his fault. I should first have asked him if he was fond of farming.

Sunma: Oh, so he can choose? As if he shouldn't be thankful for being allowed to live.

Eman: Sunma!

Sunma: He does not like farming but he knows how to feast his dumb mouth on the fruits.

Eman: But I want him to. I encourage him.

Sunma: Well keep him. I don't want to see him any more.

Eman (after some moments): But why? You cannot be telling all the truth. What has he done?

Sunma: The sight of him fills me with revulsion.

Eman (goes to her and holds her): What really is it? *(Sunma avoids his eyes.)* It is almost as if you are forcing yourself to hate him. Why?

Sunma: That is not true. Why should I?

Eman: Then what is the secret? You've even played with him before.

Sunma: I have always merely tolerated him. But I cannot any more. Suddenly my disgust won't take him any more. Perhaps . . . perhaps it is the new year. Yes, yes, it must be the new year.

Eman: I don't believe that.

Sunma: It must be. I am a woman, and these things matter. I don't want a misshape near me. Surely for one day in the year, I may demand some wholesomeness.

Eman: I do not understand you.

Sunma is silent.

It was cruel of you. And to Ifada who is so helpless and alone. We are the only friends he has.

Sunma: No, just you. I have told you, with me it has always been only an act of kindness. And now I haven't any pity left for him.

Eman: No. He is not a wholesome being.

He turns back to looking through the window.

Sunma (half-pleading): Ifada can rouse your pity. And yet if anything, I need more kindness from you. Every time my weakness betrays me, you close your mind against me . . . Eman . . . Eman . . .

A Girl comes in view, dragging an effigy by a rope attached to one of its legs. She stands for a while gazing at Eman. Ifada, who has crept back shyly to his accustomed position, becomes somewhat excited when he sees the effigy. The Girl is unsmiling. She possesses, in fact, a kind of inscrutability which does not make her hard but is unsettling.

Girl: Is the teacher in?

Eman (smiling): No.

Girl: Where is he gone?

Eman: I don't really know. Shall I ask?

Girl: Yes, do.

Eman (turning slightly): Sunma, a girl outside wants to know . . .

Sunma turns away, goes into the inside room.

Eman: Oh. *(Returns to the girl, but his slight gaiety is lost.)* There is no one at home who can tell me.
Girl: Why are you not in?
Eman: I don't really know. Maybe I went somewhere.
Girl: All right. I will wait until you get back.

She pulls the effigy to her, sits down.

Eman (slowly regaining his amusement): So you are ready for the new year.
Girl (without turning round): I am not going to the festival.
Eman: Then why have you got that?
Girl: Do you mean my carrier? I am unwell you know. My mother says it will take away my sickness with the old year.
Eman: Won't you share the carrier with your playmates?
Girl: Oh, no. Don't you know I play alone? The other children won't come near me. Their mothers would beat them.
Eman: But I have never seen you here. Why don't you come to the clinic?
Girl: My mother said No.

Gets up, begins to move off.

Eman: You are not going away?
Girl: I must not stay talking to you. If my mother caught me . . .
Eman: All right, tell me what you want before you go.
Girl (stops. For some moments she remains silent): I must have some clothes for my carrier.
Eman: Is that all? You wait a moment.

Sunma comes out as he takes down a buba from the wall. She goes to the window and glares almost with hatred at the Girl. The Girl retreats hastily, still impassive.

By the way, Sunma, do you know who that girl is?
Sunma: I hope you don't really mean to give her that.
Eman: Why not? I hardly ever use it.
Sunma: Just the same don't give it to her. She is not a child. She is as evil as the rest of them.
Eman: What has got into you today?
Sunma: All right, all right. Do what you wish.

She withdraws. Baffled, Eman returns to the window.

Eman: Here . . . will this do? Come and look at it.
Girl: Throw it.
Eman: What is the matter? I am not going to eat you.
Girl: No one lets me come near them.
Eman: But I am not afraid of catching your disease.
Girl: Throw it.

Eman shrugs and tosses the buba. She takes it without a word and slips it on the effigy, completely absorbed in the task. Eman watches for a while, then joins Sunma in the inner room.

Girl (after a long, cool survey of Ifada): You have a head like a spider's egg, and your mouth dribbles like a roof. But there is no one else. Would you like to play?

Ifada nods eagerly, quite excited.

Girl: You will have to get a stick.

Ifada rushes around, finds a big stick, and whirls it aloft, bearing down on the carrier.

Girl: Wait. I don't want you to spoil it. If it gets torn I shall drive you away. Now, let me see how you are going to beat it.

Ifada hits it gently.

Girl: You may hit harder than that. As long as there is something left to hang at the end.

She appraises him up and down.

You are not very tall . . . will you be able to hang it from a tree?

Ifada nods, grinning happily.

Girl: You will hang it up and I will set fire to it. *(Then, with surprising venom.)* But just because you are helping me, don't think it is going to cure you. I am the one who will get well at midnight, do you understand? It is my carrier and it is for me alone. *(She pulls at the rope to make sure that it is well attached to the leg.)* Well don't stand there drooling. Let's go.

She begins to walk off, dragging the effigy in the dust. Ifada remains where he is for some moments, seemingly puzzled. Then his face breaks into a large grin and he leaps after the procession, belaboring the effigy with all his strength. The stage remains empty for some moments. Then the horn of a lorry is sounded and Sunma rushes out. The hooting continues for some time with a rhythmic pattern. Eman comes out.

Eman: I am going to the village . . . I shan't be back before nightfall.

Sunma (blankly): Yes.

Eman (hesitates): Well what do you want me to do?

Sunma: The lorry was hooting just now.

Eman: I didn't hear it.

Sunma: It will leave in a few minutes. And you did promise we could go away.

Eman: I promised nothing. Will you go home by yourself or shall I come back for you?

Sunma: You don't even want me here?

Eman: But you have to go home, haven't you?

Sunma: I had hoped we would watch the new year together — in some other place.

Eman: Why do you continue to distress yourself?

Sunma: Because you will not listen to me. Why do you continue to stay where nobody wants you?

Eman: That is not true.

Sunma: It is. You are wasting your life on people who really want you out of their way.

Eman: You don't know what you are saying.

Sunma: You think they love you? Do you think they care at all for what you — or I — do for them?

Eman: Them? These are your own people. Sometimes you talk as if you were a stranger too.

Sunma: I wonder if I really sprang from here. I know they are evil and I am not. From the oldest to the smallest child, they are nourished in evil and unwholesomeness in which I have no part.

Eman: You knew this when you returned?

Sunma: You reproach me then for trying at all?

Eman: I reproach you with nothing? But you must leave me out of your plans. I can have no part in them.

Sunma (nearly pleading): Once I could have run away. I would have gone and never looked back.

Eman: I cannot listen when you talk like that.

Sunma: I swear to you, I do not mind what happens afterwards. But you must help me tear myself away from here. I can no longer do it by myself. . . . It is only a little thing. And we have worked so hard this past year . . . surely we can go away for a week . . . even a few days would be enough.

Eman: I have told you, Sunma . . .

Sunma (desperately): Two days, Eman. Only two days.

Eman (distressed): But I tell you I have no wish to go.

Sunma (suddenly angry): Are you so afraid then?

Eman: Me? Afraid of what?

Sunma: You think you will not want to come back.

Eman (pitying): You cannot dare me that way.

Sunma: Then why won't you leave here, even for an hour? If you are so sure that your life is settled here, why are you afraid to do this thing for me? What is so wrong that you will not go into the next town for a day or two?

Eman: I don't want to. I do not have to persuade you, or myself about anything. I simply have no desire to go away.

Sunma (his quiet confidence appears to incense her): You are afraid. You accuse me of losing my sense of mission, but you are afraid to put yours to the test.

Eman: You are wrong, Sunma. I have no sense of mission. But I have found peace here and I am content with that.

Sunma: I haven't. For a while I thought that too, but I found there could be no peace in the midst of so much cruelty. Eman, tonight at least, the last night of the old year . . .

Eman: No, Sunma. I find this too distressing; you should go home now.

Sunma: It is the time for making changes in one's life, Eman. Let's breathe in the new year away from here.

Eman: You are hurting yourself.

Sunma: Tonight. Only tonight. We will come back tomorrow, as early as you like. But let us go away for this one night. Don't let another year break on me in this place . . . you don't know how important it is to me, but I will tell you, I will tell you on the way . . . but we must not be here today, Eman, do this one thing for me.

Eman (sadly): I cannot.

Sunma (suddenly calm): I was a fool to think it would be otherwise. The whole village may use you as they will but for me there is nothing. Sometimes I think you believe that doing anything for me makes you unfaithful to some part of your life. If it was a woman then I pity her for what she must have suffered.

Eman winces and hardens slowly. Sunma notices nothing.

Keeping faith with so much is slowly making you inhuman. *(Seeing the change in Eman.)* Eman. Eman. What is it?

As she goes towards him, Eman goes into the house.

Sunma (apprehensive, follows him): What did I say? Eman, forgive me, forgive me please.

Eman remains facing into the slow darkness of the room. Sunma, distressed, cannot decide what to do.

I swear I didn't know. . . . I would not have said it for all the world.

A lorry is heard taking off somewhere nearby. The sound comes up and slowly fades away into the distance. Sunma starts visibly, goes slowly to the window.

Sunma (as the sound dies off, to herself): What happens now?

Eman (joining her at the window): What did you say?

Sunma: Nothing.

Eman: Was that not the lorry going off?

Sunma: It was.

Eman: I am sorry I couldn't help you.

Sunma, about to speak, changes her mind.

Eman: I think you ought to go home now.

Sunma: No, don't send me away. It's the least you can do for me. Let me stay here until all the noise is over.

Eman: But are you not needed at home? You have a part in the festival.

Sunma: I have renounced it; I am Jaguna's eldest daughter only in name.

Eman: Renouncing one's self is not so easy — surely you know that.

Sunma: I don't want to talk about it. Will you at least let us be together tonight?

Eman: But . . .

Sunma: Unless you are afraid my father will accuse you of harboring me.

Eman: All right, we will go out together.

Sunma: Go out? I want us to stay here.

Eman: When there is so much going on outside?

Sunma: Some day you will wish that you went away when I tried to make you.

Eman: Are we going back to that?

Sunma: No. I promise you I will not recall it again. But you must know that it was also for your sake that I tried to get us away.

Eman: For me? How?

Sunma: By yourself you can do nothing here. Have you not noticed how tightly we shut out strangers? Even if you lived here for a lifetime, you would remain a stranger.

Eman: Perhaps that is what I like. There is peace in being a stranger.

Sunma: For a while perhaps. But they would reject you in the end. I tell you it is only I who stand between you and contempt. And because of this you have earned their hatred. I don't know why I say this now, except that somehow, I feel that it no longer matters. It is only I who have stood between you and much humiliation.

Eman: Think carefully before you say any more. I am incapable of feeling indebted to you. This will make no difference at all.

Sunma: I ask for nothing. But you must know it all the same. It is true I hadn't the strength to go by myself. And I must confess this now, if you had come with me, I would have done everything to keep you from returning.

Eman: I know that.

Sunma: You see, I bare myself to you. For days I had thought it over, this was to be a new beginning for us. And I placed my fate wholly in your hands. Now the thought will not leave me, I have a feeling which will not be shaken off, that in some way, you have tonight totally destroyed my life.

Eman: You are depressed, you don't know what you are saying.

Sunma: Don't think I am accusing you. I say all this only because I cannot help it.

Eman: We must not remain shut up here. Let us go and be part of the living.

Sunma: No. Leave them alone.

Eman: Surely you don't want to stay indoors when the whole town is alive with rejoicing.

Sunma: Rejoicing! Is that what it seems to you? No, let us remain here. Whatever happens I must not go out until all this is over.

There is silence. It has grown much darker.

Eman: I shall light the lamp.

Sunma (eager to do something): No, let me do it.

She goes into the inner room. Eman paces the room, stops by a shelf, and toys with the seeds in an "ayo" board, takes down the whole board and places it on a table, playing by himself.

The Girl is now seen coming back, still dragging her "carrier." Ifada brings up the rear as before. As he comes round the corner of the house two men emerge from the shadows. A sack is thrown over Ifada's head, the rope is pulled tight rendering him instantly helpless. The Girl has reached the front of the house before she turns round at the sound of scuffle. She is in time to see Ifada thrown over the shoulders and borne away. Her face betraying no emotion at all, the Girl backs slowly away, turns, and flees, leaving the "carrier" behind. Sunma enters, carrying two kerosene lamps. She hangs one up from the wall.

Eman: One is enough.

Sunma: I want to leave one outside.

She goes out, hangs the lamp from a nail just above the door. As she turns she sees the effigy and gasps. Eman rushes out.

Eman: What is it? Oh, is that what frightened you?
Sunma: I thought . . . I didn't really see it properly.

Eman goes towards the object, stoops to pick it up.

Eman: It must belong to that sick girl.
Sunma: Don't touch it.
Eman: Let's keep it for her.
Sunma: Leave it alone. Don't touch it, Eman.
Eman (shrugs and goes back): You are very nervous.
Sunma: Let's go in.
Eman: Wait. *(He detains her by the door, under the lamp.)* I know there is something more than you've told me. What are you afraid of tonight?
Sunma: I was only scared by that thing. There is nothing else.
Eman: I am not blind, Sunma. It is true I would not run away when you wanted me to, but that doesn't mean I do not feel things. What does tonight really mean that it makes you so helpless?
Sunma: It is only a mood. And your indifference to me . . . let's go in.

Eman moves aside and she enters; he remains there for a moment and then follows. She fiddles with the lamp, looks vaguely round the room, then goes and shuts the door, bolting it. When she turns, it is to meet Eman's eyes, questioning.

Sunma: There is a cold wind coming in.

Eman keeps his gaze on her.

Sunma: It *was* getting cold.

She moves guiltily to the table and stands by the ayo board, rearranging the seeds. Eman remains where he is a few moments, then brings a stool and sits opposite her. She sits down also and they begin to play in silence.

Sunma: What brought you here at all, Eman? And what makes you stay?

There is another silence.

Sunma: I am not trying to share your life. I know you too well by now. But at least we have worked together since you came. Is there nothing at all I deserve to know?
Eman: Let me continue a stranger — especially to you. Those who have much to give fulfill themselves only in total loneliness.
Sunma: Then there is no love in what you do.
Eman: There is. Love comes to me more easily with strangers.
Sunma: That is unnatural.
Eman: Not for me. I know I find consummation only when I have spent myself for a total stranger.
Sunma: It seems unnatural to me. But then I am a woman. I have a woman's longings and weaknesses. And the ties of blood are very strong in me.
Eman (smiling): You think I have cut loose from all these — ties of blood.
Sunma: Sometimes you are so inhuman.
Eman: I don't know what that means. But I am very much my father's son.

They play in silence. Suddenly Eman pauses, listening.

Eman: Did you hear that?

Sunma (quickly): I heard nothing . . . it's your turn.

Eman: Perhaps some of the mummers are coming this way.

Eman, about to play, leaps up suddenly.

Sunma: What is it? Don't you want to play any more?

Eman moves to the door.

Sunma: No. Don't go out, Eman.

Eman: If it's the dancers I want to ask them to stay. At least we won't have to miss everything.

Sunma: No, no. Don't open the door. Let us keep out everyone tonight.

A terrified and disordered figure bursts suddenly round the corner, past the window and begins hammering at the door. It is Ifada. Desperate with terror, he pounds madly at the door, dumb-moaning all the while.

Eman: Isn't that Ifada?

Sunma: They are only fooling about. Don't pay any attention.

Eman (looks round the window): That is Ifada. *(Begins to unbolt the door.)*

Sunma (pulling at his hands): It is only a trick they are playing on you. Don't take any notice, Eman.

Eman: What are you saying? The boy is out of his senses with fear.

Sunma: No, no. Don't interfere, Eman. For God's sake don't interfere.

Eman: Do you know something of this then?

Sunma: You are a stranger here, Eman. Just leave us alone and go your own way. There is nothing you can do.

Eman (he tries to push her out of the way but she clings fiercely to him): Have you gone mad? I tell you the boy must come in.

Sunma: Why won't you listen to me, Eman? I tell you it's none of your business. For your own sake do as I say.

Eman pushes her off, unbolts the door. Ifada rushes in, clasps Eman round the knees, dumb-moaning against his legs.

Eman (manages to rebolt the door): What is it, Ifada? What is the matter?

Shouts and voices are heard coming nearer the house.

Sunma: Before it's too late, let him go. For once, Eman, believe what I tell you. Don't harbor him or you will regret it all your life.

Eman tries to calm Ifada, who becomes more and more abject as the outside voices get nearer.

Eman: What have they done to him? At least tell me that. What is going on, Sunma?

Sunma (with sudden venom): Monster! Could you not take yourself somewhere else?

Eman: Stop talking like that.

Sunma: He could have run into the bush couldn't he? Toad! Why must he follow us with his own disasters!

Voices outside: It's here. . . . Round the back. . . . Spread, spread . . . this way . . . no, head him off . . . use the bush path and head him off . . . get some more lights . . .

Eman listens. Lifts Ifada bodily and carries him into the inner room. Returns at once, shutting the door behind him.

Sunma (slumps into a chair, resigned): You always follow your own way.

Jaguna (comes round the corner followed by Oroge and three men, one bearing a torch): I knew he would come here.

Oroge: I hope our friend won't make trouble.

Jaguna: He had better not. You, recall all the men and tell them to surround the house.

Oroge: But he may not be in the house after all.

Jaguna: I know he is here . . . *(To the men.)* . . . go on, do as I say.

He bangs on the door.

Teacher, open your door . . . you two stay by the door. If I need you I will call you.

Eman opens the door.

Jaguna (speaks as he enters): We know he is here.

Eman: Who?

Jaguna: Don't let us waste time. We are grown men, teacher. You understand me and I understand you. But we must take back the boy.

Eman: This is my house.

Jaguna: Daughter, you'd better tell your friend. I don't think he quite knows our ways. Tell him why he must give up the boy.

Sunma: Father, I . . .

Jaguna: Are you going to tell him or aren't you?

Sunma: Father, I beg you, leave us alone tonight . . .

Jaguna: I thought you might be a hindrance. Go home then if you will not use your sense.

Sunma: But there are other ways . . .

Jaguna (turning to the men): See that she gets home. I no longer trust her. If she gives trouble carry her. And see that the women stay with her until all this is over.

Sunma departs, accompanied by one of the men.

Jaguna: Now, teacher . . .

Oroge (restrains him): You see, Mister Eman, it is like this. Right now, nobody knows that Ifada has taken refuge here. No one except us and our men — and they know how to keep their mouths shut. We don't want to have to burn down the house, you see, but if the word gets around, we would have no choice.

Jaguna: In fact, it may be too late already. A carrier should end up in the bush, not in a house. Anyone who doesn't guard his door when the carrier goes by has himself to blame. A contaminated house should be burnt down.

Oroge: But we are willing to let it pass. Only, you must bring him out quickly.

Eman: All right. But at least you will let me ask you something.

Jaguna: What is there to ask? Don't you understand what we have told you?

Eman: Yes. But why did you pick on a helpless boy? Obviously he is not willing.

Jaguna: What is the man talking about? Ifada is a godsend. Does he have to be willing?

Eman: In my home, we believe that a man should be willing.

Oroge: Mister Eman, I don't think you quite understand. This is not a simple matter at all. I don't know what you do, but here, it is not a cheap task for anybody. No one in his senses would do such a job. Why do you think we give refuge to idiots like him? We don't know where he came from. One morning, he is simply there, just like that. From nowhere at all. You see, there is a purpose in that.

Jaguna: We only waste time.

Oroge: Jaguna, be patient. After all, the man has been with us for some time now and deserves to know. The evil of the old year is no light thing to load on any man's head.

Eman: I know something about that.

Oroge: You do? *(Turns to Jaguna, who snorts impatiently.)* You see I told you so, didn't I? From the moment you came I saw you were one of the knowing ones.

Jaguna: Then let him behave like a man and give back the boy.

Eman: It is you who are not behaving like men.

Jaguna (advances aggressively): That is a quick mouth you have . . .

Oroge: Patience, Jaguna . . . if you want the new year to cushion the land there must be no deeds of anger. What did you mean, my friend?

Eman: It is a simple thing. A village which cannot produce its own carrier contains no men.

Jaguna: Enough. Let there be no more talk or this business will be ruined by some rashness. You . . . come inside. Bring the boy out, he must be in the room there.

Eman: Wait.

The men hesitate.

Jaguna (hitting the nearer one and propelling him forward): Go on. Have you changed masters now that you listen to what he says?

Oroge (sadly): I am sorry you would not understand, Mister Eman. But you ought to know that no carrier may return to the village. If he does, the people will stone him to death. It has happened before. Surely it is too much to ask a man to give up his own soil.

Eman: I know others who have done more.

Ifada is brought out, abjectly dumb-moaning.

Eman: You can see him with your own eyes. Does it really have meaning to use one as unwilling as that?

Oroge (smiling): He shall be willing. Not only willing but actually joyous. I am the one who prepares them all, and I have seen worse. This one escaped before I began to prepare him for the event. But you will see him later tonight, the most joyous creature in the festival. Then perhaps you will understand.

Eman: Then it is only a deceit. Do you believe the spirit of a new year is so easily fooled?

Jaguna: Take him out. *(The men carry out Ifada.)* You see, it is so easy to talk. You say there are no men in this village because they cannot provide a willing carrier. And yet I heard Oroge tell you we only use strangers. There is only one other stranger in the village, but I have not heard him offer himself. *(Spits.)* It is so easy to talk is it not?

He turns his back on him. They go off, taking Ifada with them, limp and silent. The only sign of life is that he strains his neck to keep his eyes on Eman till the very moment that he disappears from sight. Eman remains where they left him, staring after the group.

A blackout lasting no more than a minute. The lights come up slowly, and Ifada is seen returning to the house. He stops at the window and looks in. Seeing no one, he bangs on the sill. Appears surprised that there is no response. He slithers down on his favorite spot, then sees the effigy still lying where the Girl had dropped it in her flight. After some hesitation, he goes towards it, begins to strip it of the clothing. Just then the Girl comes in.

Girl: Hey, leave that alone. You know it's mine.

Ifada pauses, then speeds up his action.

Girl: I said it is mine. Leave it where you found it. *(She rushes at him and begins to struggle for possession of the carrier.)* Thief! Thief! Let it go, it is mine. Let it go. You animal, just because I let you play with it. Idiot! Idiot!

The struggle becomes quite violent. The Girl is hanging to the effigy and Ifada lifts her with it, flinging her all about. The Girl hangs on grimly.

Girl: You are spoiling it . . . why don't you get your own? Thief! Let it go, you thief!

Sunma comes in walking very fast, throwing apprehensive glances over her shoulder. Seeing the two children, she becomes immediately angry. Advances on them.

Sunma: So you've made this place your playground. Get away, you untrained pigs. Get out of here.

Ifada flees at once, the Girl retreats also, retaining possession of the carrier.

Sunma goes to the door. She has her hand on the door when the significance of Ifada's presence strikes her for the first time. She stands rooted to the spot, then turns slowly round.

Sunma: Ifada! What are you doing here?

Ifada is bewildered. Sunma turns suddenly and rushes into the house, flying into the inner room and out again.

Eman! Eman! Eman!

She rushes outside.

Where did he go? Where did they take him?

Ifada distressed, points. Sunma seizes him by the arm, drags him off.

Take me there at once. God help you if we are too late. You loathsome thing, if you have let him suffer . . .

Her voice fades into other shouts, running footsteps, banged tins, bells, dogs, etc., rising in volume.

It is a narrow passageway between two mudhouses. At the far end one man after another is seen running across the entry, the noise dying off gradually.

About halfway down the passage, Eman is crouching against the wall, tense with apprehension. As the noise dies off, he seems to relax, but the alert, hunted look is still in his eyes, which are ringed in a reddish color. The rest of his body has been whitened with a floury substance. He is naked down to the waist, wears a baggy pair of trousers, calf-length, and around both feet are bangles.

Eman: I will simply stay here till dawn. I have done enough.

A window is thrown open and a woman empties some slop from a pail. With a startled cry Eman leaps aside to avoid it and the woman puts out her head.

Woman: Oh, my head. What have I done! Forgive me, neighbor . . . . Eh, it's the carrier! *(Very rapidly she clears her throat and spits on him, flings the pail at him and runs off, shouting)* He's here. The carrier is hiding in the passage. Quickly, I have found the carrier!

The cry is taken up and Eman flees down the passage. Shortly afterwards his pursuers come pouring down the passage in full cry. After the last of them come Jaguna and Oroge.

Oroge: Wait, wait. I cannot go so fast.

Jaguna: We will rest a little then. We can do nothing anyway.

Oroge: If only he had let me prepare him.

Jaguna: They are the ones who break first, these fools who think they were born to carry suffering like a hat. What are we to do now?

Oroge: When they catch him I must prepare him.

Jaguna: He? It will be impossible now. There can be no joy left in that one.

Oroge: Still, it took him by surprise. He was not expecting what he met.

Jaguna: Why then did he refuse to listen? Did he think he was coming to sit down to a feast? He had not even gone through one compound before he bolted. Did he think he was taken round the people to be blessed? A woman, that is all he is.

Oroge: No, no. He took the beating well enough. I think he is the kind who would let himself be beaten from night till dawn and not utter a sound. He would let himself be stoned until he dropped dead.

Jaguna: Then what made him run like a coward?

Oroge: I don't know. I don't really know. It is a night of curses, Jaguna. It is not many unprepared minds will remain unhinged under the load.

Jaguna: We must find him. It is a poor beginning for a year when our own curses remain hovering over our homes because the carrier refused to take them.

They go. The scene changes. Eman is crouching beside some shrubs, torn and bleeding.

Eman: They are even guarding my house . . . as if I would go there, but I need water . . . they could at least grant me that . . . I can be thirsty too . . . *(He pricks his ears.)* . . . there must be a stream nearby . . . *(As he looks round him, his eyes widen at a scene he encounters.)*

An Old Man, short and vigorous looking, is seated on a stool. He also is wearing calf-length baggy trousers, white. On his head, a white cap. An attendant is engaged in rubbing his body with oil. Round his eyes, two white rings have already been marked.

Old Man: Have they prepared the boat?
Attendant: They are making the last sacrifice.
Old Man: Good. Did you send for my son?
Attendant: He's on his way.
Old Man: I have never met the carrying of the boat with such a heavy heart. I hope nothing comes of it.
Attendant: The gods will not desert us on that account.
Old Man: A man should be at his strongest when he takes the boat, my friend. To be weighed down inside and out is not a wise thing. I hope when the moment comes I shall have found my strength.

Enter Eman, a wrapper round his waist and a danski° over it.

Old Man: I meant to wait until after my journey to the river, but my mind is so burdened with my own grief and yours I could not delay it. You know I must have all my strength. But I sit here, feeling it all eaten slowly away by my unspoken grief. It helps to say it out. It even helps to cry sometimes.

He signals to the attendant to leave them.

Come nearer . . . we will never meet again, son. Not on this side of the flesh. What I do not know is whether you will return to take my place.
Eman: I will never come back.
Old Man: Do you know what you are saying? Ours is a strong breed, my son. It is only a strong breed that can take this boat to the river year after year and wax stronger on it. I have taken down each year's evils for over twenty years. I hoped you would follow me.
Eman: My life here died with Omae.
Old Man: Omae died giving birth to your child and you think the world is ended. Eman, my pain did not begin when Omae died. Since you sent her to stay with me, son, I lived with the burden of knowing that this child would die bearing your son.
Eman: Father . . .
Old Man: Don't you know it was the same with you? And me? No woman survives the bearing of the strong ones. Son, it is not the mouth of the boaster that says he belongs to the strong breed. It is the tongue that is red with

danski: A garment.

pain and black with sorrow. Twelve years you were away, my son, and for those twelve years I knew the love of an old man for his daughter and the pain of a man helplessly awaiting his loss.

Eman: I wish I had stayed away. I wish I never came back to meet her.

Old Man: It had to be. But you know now what slowly ate away my strength. I awaited your return with love and fear. Forgive me then if I say that your grief is light. It will pass. This grief may drive you now from home. But you must return.

Eman: You do not understand. It is not grief alone.

Old Man: What is it then? Tell me, I can still learn.

Eman: I was away twelve years. I changed much in that time.

Old Man: I am listening.

Eman: I am unfitted for your work, father. I wish to say no more. But I am totally unfitted for your call.

Old Man: It is only time you need, son. Stay longer and you will answer the urge of your blood.

Eman: That I stayed at all was because of Omae. I did not expect to find her waiting. I would have taken her away, but hard as you claim to be, it would have killed you. And I was a tired man. I needed peace. Because Omae was peace, I stayed. Now nothing holds me here.

Old Man: Other men would rot and die doing this task year after year. It is strong medicine which only we can take. Our blood is strong like no other. Anything you do in life must be less than this, son.

Eman: That is not true, father.

Old Man: I tell you it is true. Your own blood will betray you, son, because you cannot hold it back. If you make it do less than this, it will rush to your head and burst it open. I say what I know, my son.

Eman: There are other tasks in life, father. This one is not for me. There are even greater things you know nothing of.

Old Man: I am very sad. You only go to give to others what rightly belongs to us. You will use your strength among thieves. They are thieves because they take what is ours, they have no claim of blood to it. They will even lack the knowledge to use it wisely. Truth is my companion at this moment, my son. I know everything I say will surely bring the sadness of truth.

Eman: I am going, father.

Old Man: Call my attendant. And be with me in your strength for this last journey. A-ah, did you hear that? It came out without my knowing it; this is indeed my last journey. But I am not afraid.

Eman goes out. A few moments later, the attendant enters.

Attendant: The boat is ready.

Old Man: So am I.

He sits perfectly still for several moments. Drumming begins somewhere in the distance, and the Old Man sways his head almost imperceptibly. Two men come in bearing a miniature boat, containing an indefinable mound. They rush it in and set it briskly down near the Old Man, and stand well back. The Old Man gets up slowly, the attendant watching him keenly. He signs to the men, who lift the boat quickly onto the Old Man's head. As soon as it touches his head, he holds it down with both hands and runs off, the men give him a start, then follow at a trot. As the last man disappears Oroge limps in and comes face to face with Eman — as carrier — who is now seen still standing beside the shrubs, staring into the scene he has just witnessed. Oroge, struck by the look on Eman's face, looks anxiously behind him to see what has engaged Eman's attention. Eman notices him then, and the pair stare at each other. Jaguna enters, sees him and shouts, "Here he is," rushes at Eman, who is whipped back to the immediate and flees, Jaguna in pursuit. Three or four others enter and follow them. Oroge remains where he is, thoughtful.

Jaguna (re-enters): They have closed in on him now, we'll get him this time.
Oroge: It is nearly midnight.
Jaguna: You were standing there looking at him as if he was some strange spirit. Why didn't you shout?
Oroge: You shouted didn't you? Did that catch him?
Jaguna: Don't worry. We have him now. But things have taken a bad turn. It is no longer enough to drive him past every house. There is too much contamination about already.
Oroge (not listening): He saw something. Why may I not know what it was?
Jaguna: What are you talking about?
Oroge: Hm. What is it?
Jaguna: I said there is too much harm done already. The year will demand more from this carrier than we thought.
Oroge: What do you mean?
Jaguna: Do we have to talk with the full mouth?
Oroge: S-sh . . . look!

Jaguna turns just in time to see Sunma fly at him, clawing at his face like a crazed tigress.

Sunma: Murderer! What are you doing to him. Murderer! Murderer!

Jaguna finds himself struggling really hard to keep off his daughter, he succeeds in pushing her off and striking her so hard on the face that she falls to her knees. He moves on her to hit her again.

Oroge (comes between): Think what you are doing, Jaguna, she is your daughter.
Jaguna: My daughter! Does this one look like my daughter? Let me cripple the harlot for life.
Oroge: That is a wicked thought, Jaguna.
Jaguna: Don't come between me and her.
Oroge: Nothing in anger — do you forget what tonight is?
Jaguna: Can you blame me for forgetting?

Draws his hand across his cheek — it is covered with blood.

Oroge: This is an unhappy night for us all. I fear what is to come of it.
Jaguna: Let's go. I cannot restrain myself in this creature's presence. My own daughter . . . and for a stranger . . .

They go off, Ifada, who came in with Sunma and had stood apart, horror-stricken, comes shyly forward. He helps Sunma up. They go off, he holding Sunma bent and sobbing.

Enter Eman — as carrier. He is physically present in the bounds of this next scene, a side of a round thatched hut. A young girl, about fourteen, runs in, stops beside the hut. She looks carefully to see that she is not observed, puts her mouth to a little hole in the wall.

Omae: Eman . . . Eman . . .

Eman — as carrier — responds, as he does throughout the scene, but they are unaware of him.

Eman (from inside): Who is it?
Omae: It is me, Omae.
Eman: How dare you come here!

Two hands appear at the hole and, pushing outwards, create a much larger hole through which Eman puts out his head. It is Eman as a boy, the same age as the girl.

Go away at once. Are you trying to get me into trouble!
Omae: What is the matter?
Eman: You. Go away.
Omae: But I came to see you.
Eman: Are you deaf? I say I don't want to see you. Now go before my tutor catches you.
Omae: All right. Come out.
Eman: Do what!
Omae: Come out.
Eman: You must be mad.
Omae (sits on the ground): All right, if you don't come out I shall simply stay here until your tutor arrives.
Eman (about to explode, thinks better of it and the head disappears. A moment later he emerges from behind the hut): What sort of a devil has got into you?
Omae: None. I just wanted to see you.
Eman (his mimicry is nearly hysterical): "None. I just wanted to see you." Do you think this place is the stream where you can go and molest innocent people?
Omae (coyly): Aren't you glad to see me?
Eman: I am not.
Omae: Why?
Eman: Why? Do you really ask me why? Because you are a woman and a most troublesome woman. Don't you know anything about this at all? We are not meant to see any woman. So go away before more harm is done.
Omae (flirtatious): What is so secret about it anyway? What do they teach you?
Eman: Nothing any woman can understand.
Omae: Ha ha. You think we don't know eh? You've all come to be circumcised.
Eman: Shut up. You don't know anything.
Omae: Just think, all this time you haven't been circumcised, and you dared make eyes at us women.

Eman: Thank you — woman. Now go.

Omae: Do they give you enough to eat?

Eman (testily): No. We are so hungry that when silly girls like you turn up, we eat them.

Omae (feigning tears): Oh, oh, oh, he's abusing me. He's abusing me.

Eman (alarmed): Don't try that here. Go quickly if you are going to cry.

Omae: All right, I won't cry.

Eman: Cry or no cry, go away and leave me alone. What do you think will happen if my tutor turns up now?

Omae: He won't.

Eman (mimicking): "He won't." I suppose you are his wife and he tells you where he goes. In fact this is just the time he comes round to our huts. He could be at the next hut this very moment.

Omae: Ha-ha. You're lying. I left him by the stream, pinching the girls' bottoms. Is that the sort of thing he teaches you?

Eman: Don't say anything against him or I shall beat you. Isn't it you loose girls who tease him, wiggling your bottoms under his nose?

Omae (going tearful again): A-ah, so I am one of the loose girls eh?

Eman: Now don't start accusing me of things I didn't say.

Omae: But you said it. You said it.

Eman: I didn't. Look, Omae, someone will hear you and I'll be in disgrace. Why don't you go before anything happens.

Omae: It's all right. My friends have promised to hold your old rascal tutor till I get back.

Eman: Then go back right now. I have work to do. *(Going in.)*

Omae (runs after and tries to hold him. Eman leaps back, genuinely scared): What is the matter? I was not going to bite you.

Eman: Do you know what you nearly did? You almost touched me!

Omae: Well?

Eman: Well! Isn't it enough that you let me set my eyes on you? Must you now totally pollute me with your touch? Don't you understand anything?

Omae: Oh, that.

Eman (nearly screaming): It is not "oh that." Do you think this is only a joke or a little visit like spending the night with your grandmother? This is an important period of my life. Look, these huts, we built them with our own hands. Every boy builds his own. We learn things, do you understand? And we spend much time just thinking. At least, I do. It is the first time I have had nothing to do except think. Don't you see, I am becoming a man. For the first time, I understand that I have a life to fulfill. Has that thought ever worried you?

Omae: You are frightening me.

Eman: There. That is all you can say. And what use will that be when a man finds himself alone — like that? *(Points to the hut.)* A man must go on his own, go where no one can help him, and test his strength. Because he may find himself one day sitting alone in a wall as round as that. In there, my mind could hold no other thought. I may never have such moments again to myself. Don't dare to come and steal any more of it.

Omae (this time, genuinely tearful): Oh, I know you hate me. You only want to drive me away.

Eman (impatiently): Yes, yes, I know I hate you — but go.

Omae (going, all tears. Wipes her eyes, suddenly all mischief): Eman.

Eman: What now?

Omae: I only want to ask one thing . . . do you promise to tell me?

Eman: Well, what is it?

Omae (gleefully): Does it hurt?

She turns instantly and flees, landing straight into the arms of the returning tutor.

Tutor: Te-he-he . . . what have we here? What little mouse leaps straight into the beak of the wise old owl eh?

Omae struggles to free herself, flies to the opposite side, grimacing with distaste.

Tutor: I suppose you merely came to pick some fruits eh? You did not sneak here to see any of my children.

Omae: Yes, I came to steal your fruits.

Tutor: Te-he-he . . . I thought so. And that dutiful son of mine over there. He saw you and came to chase you off my fruit trees didn't he? Te-he-he . . . I'm sure he did, isn't that so, my young Eman?

Eman: I was talking to her.

Tutor: Indeed you were. Now be good enough to go into your hut until I decide your punishment. *(Eman withdraws.)* Te-he-he . . . now now, my little daughter, you need not be afraid of me.

Omae (spiritedly): I am not.

Tutor: Good. Very good. We ought to be friendly. *(His voice becomes leering.)* Now this is nothing to worry you, my daughter . . . a very small thing indeed. Although of course if I were to let it slip that your young Eman had broken a strong taboo, it might go hard on him, you know. I am sure you would not like that to happen, would you?

Omae: No.

Tutor: Good. You are sensible, my girl. Can you wash clothes?

Omae: Yes.

Tutor: Good. If you will come with me now to my hut, I shall give you some clothes to wash, and then we will forget all about this matter eh? Well, come on.

Omae: I shall wait here. You go and bring the clothes.

Tutor: Eh? What is that? Now now, don't make me angry. You should know better than to talk back at your elders. Come now.

He takes her by the arm, and tries to drag her off.

Omae: No no, I won't come to your hut. Leave me. Leave me alone, you shameless old man.

Tutor: If you don't come I shall disgrace the whole family of Eman, and yours too.

Eman reenters with a small bundle.

Eman: Leave her alone. Let us go, Omae.

Tutor: And where do you think you are going?

Eman: Home.

Tutor: Te-he-he . . . As easy as that eh? You think you can leave here any time you please? Get right back inside that hut!

Eman takes Omae by the arm and begins to walk off.

Tutor: Come back at once.

He goes after him and raises his stick. Eman catches it, wrenches it from him, and throws it away.

Omae (hopping delightedly): Kill him. Beat him to death.

Tutor: Help! Help! He is killing me! Help!

Alarmed, Eman clamps his hand over his mouth.

Eman: Old tutor, I don't mean you any harm, but you mustn't try to harm me either. *(He removes his hand.)*

Tutor: You think you can get away with your crime. My report shall reach the elders before you ever get into town.

Eman: You are afraid of what I will say about you? Don't worry. Only if you try to shame me, then I will speak. I am not going back to the village anyway. Just tell them I have gone, no more. If you say one word more than that I shall hear of it the same day and I shall come back.

Tutor: You are telling me what to do? But don't think to come back next year because I will drive you away. Don't think to come back here even ten years from now. And don't send your children. *(Goes off with threatening gestures.)*

Eman: I won't come back.

Omae: Smoked vulture! But Eman, he says you cannot return next year. What will you do?

Eman: It is a small thing one can do in the big towns.

Omae: I thought you were going to beat him that time. Why didn't you crack his dirty hide?

Eman: Listen carefully, Omae . . . I am going on a journey.

Omae: Come on. Tell me about it on the way.

Eman: No, I go that way. I cannot return to the village.

Omae: Because of that wretched man? Anyway you will first talk to your father.

Eman: Go and see him for me. Tell him I have gone away for some time. I think he will know.

Omae: But, Eman . . .

Eman: I haven't finished. You will go and live with him till I get back. I have spoken to him about you. Look after him!

Omae: But what is this journey? When will you come back?

Eman: I don't know. But this is a good moment to go. Nothing ties me down.

Omae: But, Eman, you want to leave me.

Eman: Don't forget all I said. I don't know how long I will be. Stay in my father's house as long as you remember me. When you become tired of waiting, you must do as you please. You understand? You must do as you please.

Omae: I cannot understand anything, Eman. I don't know where you are going or why. Suppose you never came back! Don't go, Eman. Don't leave me by myself.

Eman: I must go. Now let me see you on your way.

Omae: I shall come with you.

Eman: Come with me! And who will look after you? Me? You will only be in my way, you know that! You will hold me back and I shall desert you in a strange place. Go home and do as I say. Take care of my father and let him take care of you. *(He starts going but Omae clings to him.)*

Omae: But, Eman, stay the night at least. You will only lose your way. Your father, Eman, what will he say? I won't remember what you said . . . come back to the village . . . I cannot return alone, Eman . . . come with me as far as the crossroads.

His face set, Eman strides off and Omae loses balance as he increases his pace. Falling, she quickly wraps her arms around his ankle, but Eman continues unchecked, dragging her along.

Omae: Don't go, Eman . . . Eman, don't leave me, don't leave me . . . don't leave your Omae . . . don't go, Eman . . . don't leave your Omae . . .

Eman — as carrier — makes a nervous move as if he intends to go after the vanished pair. He stops but continues to stare at the point where he last saw them. There is stillness for a while. Then the Girl enters from the same place and remains looking at Eman. Startled, Eman looks apprehensively round him. The Girl goes nearer but keeps beyond arm's length.

Girl: Are you the carrier?

Eman: Yes, I am Eman.

Girl: Why are you hiding?

Eman: I really came for a drink of water . . . er . . . is there anyone in front of the house?

Girl: No.

Eman: But there might be people in the house. Did you hear voices?

Girl: There is no one here.

Eman: Good. Thank you. *(He is about to go, stops suddenly.)* Er . . . would you . . . you will find a cup on the table. Could you bring me the water out here? The water pot is in a corner.

The Girl goes. She enters the house, then, watching Eman carefully, slips out and runs off.

Eman (sitting): Perhaps they have all gone home. It will be good to rest. *(He hears voices and listens hard.)* Too late. *(Moves cautiously nearer the house.)* Quickly, girl, I can hear people coming. Hurry up. *(Looks through the window.)* Where are you? Where is she? *(The truth dawns on him suddenly and he moves off, sadly.)*

Enter Jaguna and Oroge, led by the Girl.

Girl (pointing): He was there.

Jaguna: Ay, he's gone now. He is a sly one is your friend. But it won't save him forever.

Oroge: What was he doing when you saw him?
Girl: He asked me for a drink of water.
Jaguna, *Oroge*: Ah! *(They look at each other.)*
Oroge: We should have thought of that.
Jaguna: He is surely finished now. If only we had thought of it earlier.
Oroge: It is not too late. There is still an hour before midnight.
Jaguna: We must call back all the men. Now we need only wait for him — in the right place.
Oroge: Everyone must be told. We don't want anyone heading him off again.
Jaguna: And it works so well. This is surely the help of the gods themselves, Oroge. Don't you know at once what is on the path to the stream?
Oroge: The sacred trees.
Jaguna: I tell you it is the very hand of the gods. Let us go.

An overgrown part of the village. Eman wanders in, aimlessly, seemingly uncaring of discovery. Beyond him, an area lights up, revealing a group of people clustered round a spot, all the heads are bowed. One figure stands away and separate from them. Even as Eman looks, the group breaks up and the people disperse, coming down and past him. Only three people are left, a man (Eman) whose back is turned, the village Priest, and the isolated one. They stand on opposite sides of the grave, the man on the mound of earth. The Priest walks round to the man's side and lays a hand on his shoulder.

Priest: Come.
Eman: I will. Give me a few moments here alone.
Priest: Be comforted.

They fall silent.

Eman: I was gone twelve years but she waited. She whom I thought had too much of the laughing child in her. Twelve years I was a pilgrim, seeking the vain shrine of secret strength. And all the time, strange knowledge, this silent strength of my child-woman.
Priest: We all saw it. It was a lesson to us; we did not know that such goodness could be found among us.
Eman: Then why? Why the wasted years if she had to perish giving birth to my child? *(They are both silent.)* I do not really know for what great meaning I searched. When I returned, I could not be certain I had found it. Until I reached my home and I found her a full-grown woman, still a child at heart. When I grew to believe it, I thought, this, after all, is what I sought. It was here all the time. And I threw away my new-gained knowledge. I buried the part of me that was formed in strange places. I made a home in my birthplace.
Priest: That was as it should be.
Eman: Any truth of that was killed in the cruelty of her brief happiness.
Priest (looks up and sees the figure standing away from them, the child in his arms. He is totally still): Your faher — he is over there.
Eman: I knew he would come. Has he my son with him?
Priest: Yes.

Eman: He will let no one take the child. Go and comfort him, priest. He loved Omae like a daughter, and you all know how well she looked after him. You see how strong we really are. In his heart of hearts the old man's love really awaited a daughter. Go and comfort him. His grief is more than mine.

The Priest goes. The Old Man has stood well away from the burial group. His face is hard and his gaze unswerving from the grave. The Priest goes to him, pauses, but sees that he can make no dent in the man's grief. Bowed, he goes on his way.

Eman, as carrier, walks towards the graveside, the other Eman having gone. His feet sink into the mound and he breaks slowly on to his knees, scooping up the sand in his hands and pouring it on his head. The scene blacks out slowly.

Enter Jaguna and Oroge.

Oroge: We have only a little time.
Jaguna: He will come. All the wells are guarded. There is only the stream left him. The animal must come to drink.
Oroge: You are sure it will not fail — the trap, I mean.
Jaguna: When Jaguna sets the trap, even elephants pay homage — their trunks downwards and one leg up in the sky. When the carrier steps on the fallen twigs, it is up in the sacred trees with him.
Oroge: I shall breathe again when this long night is over.

They go out.
Enter Eman — as carrier — from the same direction as the last two entered. In front of him is a still figure, the Old Man as he was, carrying the dwarf boat.

Eman (joyfully): Father.

The figure does not turn round.

Eman: It is your son. Eman. *(He moves nearer.)* Don't you want to look at me? It is I, Eman. *(He moves nearer still.)*
Old Man: You are coming too close. Don't you know what I carry on my head?
Eman: But, father, I am your son.
Old Man: Then go back. We cannot give the two of us.
Eman: Tell me first where you are going.
Old Man: Do *you* ask that? Where else but to the river?
Eman (visibly relieved): I only wanted to be sure. My throat is burning. I have been looking for the stream all night.
Old Man: It is the other way.
Eman: But you said . . .
Old Man: I take the longer way, you know how I must do this. It is quicker if you take the other way. Go now.
Eman: No, I will only get lost again. I shall go with you.
Old Man: Go back, my son. Go back.
Eman: Why? Won't you even look at me?
Old Man: Listen to your father. Go back.
Eman: But, father!

He makes to hold him. Instantly the Old Man breaks into a rapid trot. Eman hesitates, then follows, his strength nearly gone.

Eman: Wait, father. I am coming with you . . . wait . . . wait for me, father . . .

There is a sound of twigs breaking, of a sudden trembling in the branches. Then silence.

The front of Eman's house. The effigy is hanging from the sheaves. Enter Sunma. Still supported by Ifada, she stands transfixed as she sees the hanging figure. Ifada appears to go mad, rushes at the object, and tears it down. Sunma, her last bit of will gone, crumbles against the wall. Some distance away from them, partly hidden, stands the Girl, impassively watching. Ifada hugs the effigy to him, stands above Sunma. The Girl remains where she is, observing. Almost at once, the villagers begin to return, subdued and guilty. They walk across the front, skirting the house as widely as they can. No word is exchanged. Jaguna and Oroge eventually appear. Jaguna, who is leading, sees Sunma as soon as he comes in view. He stops at once, retreating slightly.

Oroge (almost whispering): What is it?
Jaguna: The viper.

Oroge looks cautiously at the woman.

Oroge: I don't think she will even see you.
Jaguna: Are you sure? I am in no frame of mind for another meeting with her.
Oroge: Let's go home.
Jaguna: I am sick to the heart of the cowardice I have seen tonight.
Oroge: That is the nature of men.
Jaguna: Then it is a sorry world to live in. We did it for them. It was all for their own common good. What did it benefit me whether the man lived or died? But did you see them? One and all they looked up at the man and words died in their throats.
Oroge: It was no common sight.
Jaguna: Women could not have behaved so shamefully. One by one they crept off like sick dogs. Not one could raise a curse.
Oroge: It was not only him they fled. Do you see how unattended we are?
Jaguna: There are those who will pay for this night's work!
Oroge: Ay, let us go home.

They go off. Sunma, Ifada, and the Girl remain as they are, the light fading slowly on them.

Connections

1. Compare and contrast Eman's role as a scapegoat with that of Oedipus in Sophocles' *Oedipus the King* (p. 964).
2. How does the use of flashbacks provide essential information about the two protagonists in *The Strong Breed* and in Miller's *Death of a Salesman* (p. 1508)?
3. Read the discussion of mythological criticism (p. 1790) in Chapter 32, "Critical Strategies for Reading." Explain what you think a mythological critic would have to say about *The Strong Breed.*

PERSPECTIVE

JAMES GIBB

Ritual Sacrifice in The Strong Breed 1986

The Strong Breed is a serious play of considerable substance, it shows a moment of spiritual growth in a community and provides excellent theater. Eman brings the growth, for when faced by moral choices he rises to the occasion and sacrifices himself for his convictions. He insults the men of the village and ridicules the practice of using a vulnerable and unwilling carrier. He argues that "the spirit of a new year [will not be] fooled" by an unwilling carrier. Challenged to be "a man" himself and discovering that Jaguna has captured Ifada, he offers himself: he becomes a willing sacrifice. In this there are deliberate parallels to the self-sacrifice of Christ and of the Yoruba deity Obatala, and the drama takes on the qualities of a passion play. From the reaction of the villagers it is clear that Eman's sacrificial death has an impact on the community. The final mood indicates that a climax has been reached and passed, those who have been part of it will never be the same again. This new year provides opportunities for a new beginning in Jaguna's village.

From *Wole Soyinka*

Considerations

1. What parallels can you find between the self-sacrifice of Eman and that of Christ?
2. Use the library to learn about the Yoruba deity Obatala. How does this story figure in the action of *The Strong Breed?*
3. Write an essay on the impact of Eman's death on the community.
4. Do you agree with Gibb's interpretation of the ending? Are there "opportunities for a new beginning in Jaguna's village"? Explain why or why not.

AN ALBUM OF CONTEMPORARY PLAYS

TOP GIRLS

Caryl Churchill was born in London in 1938 and grew up in Montreal after her family moved to Canada during World War II. She moved back to England to attend Oxford, completing a B.A. in English literature in 1960. She started to write plays during her college years, and some were produced by student groups. She has been associated with the Royal Court Theatre in London since the early 1970s. Some of her best-known work, much of it socialist and feminist in outlook and satiric in manner, was first produced there. Her plays include *Owners* (1972), *Objections to Sex and Violence* (1975), *Vinegar Tom* (1976), *Traps* (1977), *Light Shining in Buckinghamshire* (1978), *Cloud Nine* (1979), *Top Girls* (1982), *Fen* (1984), and *Serious Money* (1987). Churchill has written for radio and television as well as for the stage. *Top Girls* won an Obie Award in 1982–83 and *Fen* won the Blackburn Prize in 1984.

Top Girls examines the price women have had to pay for succeeding in a world dominated by men. By using women from the past as well as contemporary women, Churchill offers a wide-ranging and complex perspective on the successes and failures women have struggled with in their efforts to make their way in the world.

CARYL CHURCHILL (b. 1938)

Top Girls 1982

Characters

Marlene
Waitress/Kit/Shona
Isabella Bird/Joyce/Mrs. Kidd
Lady Nijo/Win
Dull Gret/Angie
Pope Joan/Louise
Patient Griselda/Nell/Jeanine

Production Note

The seating order for Act I Scene I in the original production at the Royal Court was (from right) Gret, Nijo, Marlene, Joan, Griselda, Isabella.

The Characters

Isabella Bird (1831–1904) — lived in Edinburgh, traveled extensively between the ages of forty and seventy.
Lady Nijo (b. 1258) — Japanese, was an emperor's courtesan and later a Buddhist nun who traveled on foot through Japan.
Dull Gret — is the subject of the Brueghel° painting *Dulle Griet,* in which a woman in an apron and armor leads a crowd of women charging through hell and fighting the devils.
Pope Joan — disguised as a man, is thought to have been pope between 854 and 856.
Patient Griselda — is the obedient wife whose story is told by Chaucer in "The Clerk's Tale" of *The Canterbury Tales.°*

The Layout

A speech usually follows the one immediately before it but:

Brueghel: Pieter Brueghel the Elder (1520?–1569), Flemish painter known for his peasant, biblical, and fantastic subjects.
Chaucer: Geoffrey Chaucer (1340?–1400), English author of the *Canterbury Tales,* stories told by pilgrims on their way to Canterbury Cathedral. In "The Clerk's Tale," the virtuous Griselda is cruelly tested by her husband.

1. When one character starts speaking before the other has finished, the point of interruption is marked / . e.g.,

Isabella: This is the emperor of Japan? / I once met the Emperor of Morocco.
Nijo: In fact he was the ex-emperor.

2. A character sometimes continues speaking right through another's speech. e.g.,

Isabella: When I was forty I thought my life was over. / Oh I was pitiful. I was
Nijo: I didn't say I felt it for twenty years. Not every minute.
Isabella: sent on a cruise for my health and felt even worse. Pains in my bones, pins and needles . . . etc.

3. Sometimes a speech follows on from a speech earlier than the one immediately before it, and continuity is marked. e.g.,*

Griselda: I'd seen him riding by, we all had. And he'd seen me in the fields with the sheep.*
Isabella: I would have been well suited to minding sheep.
Nijo: And Mr. Nugent went riding by.
Isabella: Of course not, Nijo, I mean a healthy life in the open air.
Joan: *He just rode up while you were minding the sheep and asked you to marry him?

where "in the fields with the sheep" is the cue to both "I would have been" and "He just rode up."

ACT I

Scene I

Restaurant. Saturday night. There is a table with a white cloth set for dinner with six places. The lights come up on Marlene and the Waitress.

Marlene: Excellent, yes, table for six. One of them's going to be late but we won't wait. I'd like a bottle of Frascati straight away if you've got one really cold.

The Waitress goes. Isabella Bird arrives.

Here we are. Isabella.

Isabella: Congratulations, my dear.

Marlene: Well, it's a step. It makes for a party. I haven't time for a holiday. I'd like to go somewhere exotic like you but I can't get away. I don't know how you could bear to leave Hawaii. / I'd like to lie

Isabella: I did think of settling.

Marlene: in the sun forever, except of course I can't bear sitting still.

Isabella: I sent for my sister Hennie to come and join me. I said, Hennie we'll live here forever and help the natives. You can buy two sirloins of beef for what a pound of chops cost in Edinburgh. And Hennie wrote back, the dear, that yes, she would come to Hawaii if I wished, but I said she had far better stay where she was. Hennie was suited to life in Tobermory.

Marlene: Poor Hennie.

Isabella: Do you have a sister?
Marlene: Yes in fact.
Isabella: Hennie was happy. She was good. I did miss its face, my own pet. But I couldn't stay in Scotland. I loathed the constant murk.

Lady Nijo arrives.

Marlene (seeing her): Ah! Nijo!

The Waitress enters with the wine.

Nijo: Marlene! *(To Isabella.)* So excited when Marlene told me / you were coming.
Isabella: I'm delighted / to meet you.
Marlene: I think a drink while we wait for the others. I think a drink anyway. What a week.

Marlene seats Nijo. The Waitress pours the wine.

Nijo: It was always the men who used to get so drunk. I'd be one of the maidens, passing the sake.
Isabella: I've had sake. Small hot drink. Quite fortifying after a day in the wet.
Nijo: One night my father proposed three rounds of three cups, which was normal, and then the emperor should have said three rounds of three cups, but he said three rounds of nine cups, so you can imagine. Then the emperor passed his sake cup to my father and said, "Let the wild goose come to me this spring."
Marlene: Let the what?
Nijo: It's a literary allusion to a tenth-century epic, / His Majesty was very cultured.
Isabella: This is the emperor of Japan? / I once met the emperor of Morocco.
Nijo: In fact he was the ex-emperor.
Marlene: But he wasn't old? / Did you, Isabella?
Nijo: Twenty-nine.
Isabella: Oh it's a long story.
Marlene: Twenty-nine's an excellent age.
Nijo: Well I was only fourteen and I knew he meant something but I didn't know what. He sent me an eight-layered gown and I sent it back. So when the time came I did nothing but cry. My thin gowns were badly ripped. But even that morning when he left / — he'd a green
Marlene: Are you saying he raped you?
Nijo: robe with a scarlet lining and very heavily embroidered trousers, I already felt different about him. It made me uneasy. No, of course not, Marlene, I belonged to him, it was what I was brought up for from a baby. I soon found I was sad if he stayed away. It was depressing day after day not knowing when he would come. I never enjoyed taking other women to him.
Isabella: I certainly never saw my father drunk. He was a clergyman. / And I didn't get married till I was fifty.

The Waitress brings the menus.

Nijo: Oh, my father was a very religious man. Just before he died he said to me, "Serve His Majesty, be respectful, if you lose his favor enter holy orders."

Marlene: But he meant stay in a convent, not go wandering round the country.

Nijo: Priests were often vagrants, so why not a nun? You think I shouldn't? / I still did what my father wanted.

Marlene: No no, I think you should. / I think it was wonderful.

Dull Gret arrives.

Isabella: I tried to do what my father wanted.

Marlene: Gret, good. Nijo. Gret / I know Griselda's going to be late, but should we wait for Joan? / Let's get you a drink.

Isabella: Hello, Gret! *(Continues to Nijo.)* I tried to be a clergyman's daughter. Needlework, music, charitable schemes. I had a tumor removed from my spine and spent a great deal of time on the sofa. I studied the metaphysical poets and hymnology. / I thought I enjoyed intellectual pursuits.

Nijo: Ah, you like poetry. I come of a line of eight generations of poets. Father had a poem / in the anthology.

Isabella: My father taught me Latin although I was a girl. / But really I was

Marlene: They didn't have Latin at my school.

Isabella: more suited to manual work. Cooking, washing, mending, riding horses. / Better than reading

Nijo: Oh but I'm sure you're very clever.

Isabella: books, eh Gret? A rough life in the open air.

Nijo: I can't say I enjoyed my rough life. What I enjoyed most was being the emperor's favorite / and wearing thin silk.

Isabella: Did you have any horses, Gret?

Gret: Pig.

Pope Joan arrives.

Marlene: Oh Joan, thank God, we can order. Do you know everyone? We were just talking about learning Latin and being clever girls. Joan way by way of an infant prodigy. Of course you were. What excited you when you were ten?

Joan: Because angels are without matter they are not individuals. Every angel is a species.

Marlene: There you are.

They laugh. They look at the menus.

Isabella: Yes. I forgot all my Latin. But my father was the mainspring of my life and when he died I was so grieved. I'll have the chicken, please, / and the soup.

Nijo: Of course you were grieved. My father was saying his prayers and he dozed off in the sun. So I touched his knee to rouse him. "I wonder what will happen," he said, and then he was dead before he finished the sentence. / If he'd

Marlene: What a shock.

Nijo: died saying his prayers he would have gone straight to heaven. / Waldorf salad.

Joan: Death is the return of all creatures to God.

Nijo: I shouldn't have woken him.

Joan: Damnation only means ignorance of the truth. I was always attracted by the teachings of John the Scot,° though he was inclined to confuse / God and the world.
Isabella: Grief always overwhelmed me at the time.
Marlene: What I fancy is a rare steak. Gret?
Isabella: I am of course a member of the / Church of England.
Marlene: Gret?
Gret: Potatoes.
Marlene: I haven't been to church for years. / I like Christmas carols.
Isabella: Good works matter more than church attendance.
Marlene: Make that two steaks and a lot of potatoes. Rare. But I don't do good works either.
Joan: Canelloni,° please, / and a salad.
Isabella: Well, I tried, but oh dear. Hennie did good works.
Nijo: The first half of my life was all sin and the second / all repentance.*
Marlene: Oh what about starters?
Gret: Soup.
Joan: *And which did you like best?
Marlene: Were your travels just a penance? Avocado vinaigrette. Didn't you / enjoy yourself?
Joan: Nothing to start with for me, thank you.
Nijo: Yes, but I was very unhappy. / It hurt to remember the past.
Marlene: And the wine list.
Nijo: I think that was repentance.
Marlene: Well I wonder.
Nijo: I might have just been homesick.
Marlene: Or angry.
Nijo: Not angry, no, / why angry?
Gret: Can we have some more bread?
Marlene: Don't you get angry? I get angry.
Nijo: But what about?
Marlene: Yes let's have two more Frascati. And some more bread, please.

The Waitress exits.

Isabella: I tried to understand Buddhism when I was in Japan but all this birth and death succeeding each other through eternities just filled me with the most profound melancholy. I do like something more active.
Nijo: You couldn't say I was inactive. I walked every day for twenty years.
Isabella: I don't mean walking. / I mean in the head.
Nijo: I vowed to copy five Mahayana sutras.° / Do you know how long they are?
Marlene: I don't think religious beliefs are something we have in common. Activity yes.

Gret empties the bread basket into her apron.

John the Scot (815?–?877): Irish theologian who worked to combine Greek and Neo-Platonist philosophy with Christian doctrine.
Canelloni: Tube-shaped pasta, usually filled with meat or cheese and baked in a sauce.
Mahayana sutras: Scriptures of a sect of Buddhism found chiefly in China and Japan.

Nijo: My head was active. / My head ached.
Joan: It's no good being active in heresy.
Isabella: What heresy? She's calling the Church of England / a heresy.
Joan: There are some very attractive / heresies.
Nijo: I had never heard of Christianity. Never / heard of it. Barbarians.
Marlene: Well I'm not a Christian. / And I'm not a Buddhist.
Isabella: You have heard of it?
Marlene: We don't all have to believe the same.
Isabella: I knew coming to dinner with a pope we should keep off religion.
Joan: I always enjoy a theological argument. But I won't try to convert you, I'm not a missionary. Anyway I'm a heresy myself.
Isabella: There are some barbaric practices in the east.
Nijo: Barbaric?
Isabella: Among the lower classes.
Nijo: I wouldn't know.
Isabella: Well theology always made my head ache.
Marlene: Oh good, some food.

The Waitress brings the first course, serves it during the following, then exits.

Nijo: How else could I have left the court if I wasn't a nun? When father died I had only His Majesty. So when I fell out of favor I had nothing. Religion is a kind of nothing / and I dedicated what was left of me to nothing.
Isabella: That's what I mean about Buddhism. It doesn't brace.
Marlene: Come on, Nijo, have some wine.
Nijo: Haven't you ever felt like that? You've all felt / like that. Nothing will ever happen again. I am dead already.
Isabella: You thought your life was over but it wasn't.
Joan: You wish it was over.
Gret: Sad.
Marlene: Yes, when I first came to London I sometimes . . . and when I got back from America I did. But only for a few hours. Not twenty years.
Isabella: When I was forty I thought my life was over. / Oh I was pitiful. I was sent
Nijo: I didn't say I felt it for twenty years. Not every minute.
Isabella: on a cruise for my health and I felt even worse. Pains in my bones, pins and needles in my hands, swelling behind the ears, and — oh, stupidity. I shook all over, indefinable terror. And Australia seemed to me a hideous country, the acacias stank like drains. / I
Nijo: You were homesick.

Gret steals a bottle of wine.

Isabella: had a photograph taken for Hennie but I told her I wouldn't send it, my hair had fallen out and my clothes were crooked, I looked completely insane and suicidal.
Nijo: So did I, exactly, dressed as a nun. / I was wearing walking shoes for the first time.
Isabella: I longed to go home, / but home to what? Houses are so perfectly dismal.*
Nijo: I longed to go back ten years.

Marlene: *I thought traveling cheered you both up.
Isabella: Oh it did / of course. It was on
Nijo: I'm not a cheerful person, Marlene. I just laugh a lot.
Isabella: the trip from Australia to the Sandwich Isles, I fell in love with the sea. There were rats in the cabin and ants in the food but suddenly it was like a new world. I woke up every morning happy, knowing there would be nothing to annoy me. No nervousness. No dressing.
Nijo: Don't you like getting dressed? I adored my clothes. / When I was chosen
Marlene: You had prettier colors than Isabella.
Nijo: to give sake to His Majesty's brother, the Emperor Kameyana, on his formal visit, I wore raw silk pleated trousers and a seven-layered gown in shades of red, and two outer garments, / yellow lined with green
Marlene: Yes, all that silk must have been very —

The Waitress enters, clears the first course and exits.

Joan: I dressed as a boy when I left home.*
Nijo: and a light green jacket. Lady Betto had a five-layered gown in shades of green and purple.
Isabella: *You dressed as a boy?
Marlene: Of course, / for safety.
Joan: It was easy, I was only twelve. / Also women weren't allowed in the library. We wanted to study in Athens.
Marlene: You ran away alone?
Joan: No, not alone, I went with my friend. / He was
Nijo: Ah, an elopement.
Joan: sixteen but I thought I knew more science than he did and almost as much philosophy.
Isabella: Well I always traveled as a lady and I repudiated strongly any suggestion in the press that I was other than feminine.
Marlene: I don't wear trousers in the office. / I could but I don't.
Isabella: There was no great danger to a woman of my age and appearance.
Marlene: And you got away with it, Joan?
Joan: I did then.

The Waitress brings in the main course.

Marlene: And nobody noticed anything?
Joan: They noticed I was a very clever boy. / And
Marlene: I couldn't have kept pretending for so long.
Joan: when I shared a bed with my friend, that was ordinary — two poor students in a lodging house. I think I forgot I was pretending.
Isabella: Rocky Mountain Jim, Mr. Nugent, showed me no disrespect. He found it interesting, I think, that I could make scones and also lasso cattle. Indeed he declared his love for me, which was most distressing.
Nijo: What did he say? / We always sent poems first.
Marlene: What did you say?
Isabella: I urged him to give up whiskey, / but he said it was too late.
Marlene: Oh Isabella.
Isabella: He had lived alone in the mountains for many years.
Marlene: But did you — ?

The Waitress goes.

Isabella: Mr. Nugent was a man that any woman might love but none could marry. I came back to England.

Nijo: Did you write him a poem when you left? / Snow on the mountains. My sleeves

Marlene: Did you never see him again?

Isabella: No, never.

Nijo: are wet with tears. In England no tears, no snow.

Isabella: Well, I say never. One morning very early in Switzerland, it was a year later, I had a vision of him as I last saw him / in his trapper's clothes with his

Nijo: A ghost!

Isabella: hair round his face, and that was the day, / I learnt later, he died with a

Nijo: Ah!

Isabella: bullet in his brain. / He just bowed to me and vanished.

Marlene: Oh Isabella.

Nijo: When your lover dies — One of my lovers died. / The priest Ariake.

Joan: My friend died. Have we all got dead lovers?

Marlene: Not me, sorry.

Nijo (to Isabella): I wasn't a nun, I was still at court, but he was a priest, and when he came to me he dedicated his whole life to hell. / He knew that when he died he would fall into one of the three lower realms. And he died, he did die.

Joan (to Marlene): I'd quarreled with him over the teachings of John the Scot, who held that our ignorance of God is the same as his ignorance of himself. He only knows what he creates because he creates everything he knows but he himself is above being — do you follow?

Marlene: No, but go on.

Nijo: I couldn't bear to think / in what shape would he be reborn.*

Joan: St. Augustine° maintained that the Neo-Platonic° Ideas are indivisible

Isabella: *Buddhism is really most uncomfortable.

Joan: from God, but I agreed with John that the created world is essences derived from Ideas which derived from God. As Denys the Areopagite° said — the pseudo-Denys — first we give God a name, then deny it, / then reconcile the contradiction

Nijo: In what shape would he return?

Joan: by looking beyond / those terms —

Marlene: Sorry, what? Denys said what?

Joan: Well we disagreed about it, we quarreled. And next day he was ill, / I was so annoyed with him

Nijo: Misery in this life and worse in the next, all because of me.

St. Augustine (354–430): Early Christian philosopher and Church father.

Neo-Platonic: Pertaining to a third-century school of thought which held that everything in the world comes from a single, unitary souce.

Denys the Areopagite: Third-century patron saint of France, popularly identified with Dionysius the Areopagite.

Joan: all the time I was nursing him I kept going over the arguments in my mind. Matter is not a means of knowing the essence. The source of the species is the Idea. But then I realized he'd never understand my arguments again, and that night he died. John the Scot held that the individual disintegrates / and there is no personal immortality.

Isabella: I wouldn't have you think I was in love with Jim Nugent. It was yearning to save him that I felt.

Marlene (to Joan): So what did you do?

Joan: First I decided to stay a man. I was used to it. And I wanted to devote my life to learning. Do you know why I went to Rome? Italian men didn't have beards.

Isabella: The loves of my life were Hennie, my own pet, and my dear husband the doctor, who nursed Hennie in her last illness. I knew it would be terrible when Hennie died but I didn't know how terrible. I felt half of myself had gone. How could I go on my travels without that sweet soul waiting at home for my letters? It was Doctor Bishop's devotion to her in her last illness that made me decide to marry him. He and Hennie had the same sweet character. I had not.

Nijo: I thought His Majesty had sweet character because when he found out about Ariake he was so kind. But really it was because he no longer cared for me. One night he even sent me out to a man who had been pursuing me. / He lay awake on the other side of the screens and listened.

Isabella: I did wish marriage had seemed more of a step. I tried very hard to cope with the ordinary drudgery of life. I was ill again with carbuncles on the spine and nervous prostration. I ordered a tricycle, that was my idea of adventure then. And John himself fell ill, with erysipelas and anemia. I began to love him with my whole heart but it was too late. He was a skeleton with transparent white hands. I wheeled him on various seafronts in a bathchair. And he faded and left me. There was nothing in my life. The doctors said I had gout / and my heart was much affected.

Nijo: There was nothing in my life, nothing, without the emperor's favor. The empress had always been my enemy, Marlene, she said I had no right to wear three-layered gowns. / But I was the adopted daughter of my grandfather the prime minister. I had been publicly granted permission to wear thin silk.

Joan: There was nothing in my life except my studies. I was obsessed with pursuit of the truth. I taught at the Greek School in Rome, which St. Augustine had made famous. I was poor, I worked hard, I spoke apparently brilliantly, I was still very young, I was a stranger, suddenly I was quite famous, I was everyone's favorite. Huge crowds came to hear me. The day after they made me cardinal I fell ill and lay two weeks without speaking, full of terror and regret. / But then I got up determined to

Marlene: Yes, success is very . . .

Joan: go on. I was seized again / with a desperate longing for the absolute.

Isabella: Yes, yes, to go on. I sat in Tobermory among Hennie's flowers and sewed a complete outfit in Jaeger flannel. / I was fifty-six years old.

Nijo: Out of favor but I didn't die. I left on foot, nobody saw me go. For the next twenty years I walked through Japan.

Gret: Walking is good.

Meanwhile, the Waitress enters, pours lots of wine, then shows Marlene the empty bottle.

Joan: Pope Leo° died and I was chosen. All right then. I would be pope. I would know God. I would know everything.

Isabella: I determined to leave my grief behind and set off for Tibet.

Marlene: Magnificent all of you. We need some more wine, please, two bottles I think, Griselda isn't even here yet, and I want to drink a toast to you all.

The Waitress exits.

Isabella: To yourself surely, / we're here to celebrate your success.

Nijo: Yes, Marlene.

Joan: Yes, what is it exactly, Marlene?

Marlene: Well it's not pope but it is managing director.*

Joan: And you find work for people.

Marlene: Yes, an employment agency.

Nijo: *Over all the women you work with. And the men.

Isabella: And very well deserved too. I'm sure it's just the beginning of something extraordinary.

Marlene: Well it's worth a party.

Isabella: To Marlene.*

Marlene: And all of us.

Joan: *Marlene.

Nijo: Marlene.

Gret: Marlene.

Marlene: We've all come a long way. To our courage and the way we changed our lives and our extraordinary achievements.

They laugh and drink a toast.

Isabella: Such adventures. We were crossing a mountain pass at seven thousand feet, the cook was all to pieces, the muleteers suffered fever and snow blindness. But even though my spine was agony I managed very well.*

Marlene: Wonderful.

Nijo: *Once I was ill for four months lying alone at an inn. Nobody to offer a horse to Buddha. I had to live for myself, and I did live.

Isabella: Of course you did. It was far worse returning to Tobermory. I always felt dull when I was stationary. / That's why I could never stay anywhere.

Nijo: Yes, that's it exactly. New sights. The shrine by the beach, the moon shining on the sea. The goddess had vowed to save all living things. / She would even save the fishes. I was full of hope.

Joan: I had thought the pope would know everything. I thought God would speak to me directly. But of course he knew I was a woman.

Marlene: But nobody else even suspected?

The Waitress brings more wine and then exits.

Joan: In the end I did take a lover again.*

Isabella: In the Vatican?

Pope Leo: Leo IV (800?–854), pope from 847 to 854 and a saint.

Gret: *Keep you warm.

Nijo: *Ah, lover.

Marlene: *Good for you.

Joan: He was one of my chamberlains. There are such a lot of servants when you're pope. The food's very good. And I realized I did know the truth. Because whatever the pope says, that's true.

Nijo: What was he like, the chamberlain?*

Gret: Big cock.

Isabella: Oh, Gret.

Marlene: *Did he fancy you when he thought you were a fella?

Nijo: What was he like?

Joan: He could keep a secret.

Marlene: So you did know everything.

Joan: Yes, I enjoyed being pope. I consecrated bishops and let people kiss my feet. I received the king of England when he came to submit to the church. Unfortunately there were earthquakes, and some village reported it had rained blood, and in France there was a plague of giant grasshoppers, but I don't think that can have been my fault, do you?* *(Laughter.)* The grasshoppers fell on the English Channel / and were washed up on shore

Nijo: I once went to sea. It was very lonely. I realized it made very little difference where I went.

Joan: and their bodies rotted and poisoned the air and everyone in those parts died. *(Laughter.)*

Isabella: *Such superstition! I was nearly murdered in China by a howling mob. They thought the barbarians ate babies and put them under railway sleepers to make the tracks steady, and ground up their eyes to make the lenses of cameras. / So they were shouting,

Marlene: And you had a camera!

Isabella: "Child-eater, child-eater." Some people tried to sell girl babies to Europeans for cameras or stew! *(Laughter.)*

Marlene: So apart from the grasshoppers it was a great success.

Joan: Yes, if it hadn't been for the baby I expect I'd have lived to an old age like Theodora of Alexandria, who lived as a monk. She was accused by a girl / who fell in love with her of being the father of her child and—

Nijo: But tell us what happened to your baby. I had some babies.

Marlene: Didn't you think of getting rid of it?

Joan: Wouldn't that be a worse sin than having it? / But a pope with a child was about as bad as possible.

Marlene: I don't know, you're the pope.

Joan: But I wouldn't have known how to get rid of it.

Marlene: Other popes had children, surely.

Joan: They didn't give birth to them.

Nijo: Well you were a woman.

Joan: Exactly and I shouldn't have been a woman. Women, children, and lunatics can't be pope.

Marlene: So the only thing to do / was to get rid of it somehow.

Nijo: You had to have it adopted secretly.

Joan: But I didn't know what was happening. I thought I was getting fatter, but then I was eating more and sitting about, the life of a pope is quite luxurious. I don't think I'd spoken to a woman since I was twelve. The chamberlain was the one who realized.

Marlene: And by then it was too late.

Joan: Oh I didn't want to pay attention. It was easier to do nothing.

Nijo: But you had to plan for having it. You had to say you were ill and go away.

Joan: That's what I should have done I suppose.

Marlene: Did you want them to find out?

Nijo: I too was often in embarrassing situations, there's no need for a scandal. My first child was His Majesty's, which unfortunately died, but my second was Akebono's. I was seventeen. He was in love with me when I was thirteen, he was very upset when I had to go to the emperor, it was very romantic, a lot of poems. Now His Majesty hadn't been near me for two months so he thought I was four months pregnant when I was really six, so when I reached the ninth month / I announced I was seriously ill,

Joan: I never knew what month it was.

Nijo: and Akebono announced he had gone on a religious retreat. He held me round the waist and lifted me up as the baby was born. He cut the cord with a short sword, wrapped the baby in white and took it away. It was only a girl but I was sorry to lose it. Then I told the emperor that the baby had miscarried because of my illness, and there you are. The danger was past.

Joan: But, Nijo, I wasn't used to having a woman's body.

Isabella: So what happened?

Joan: I didn't know of course that it was near the time. It was Rogation Day, there was always a procession. I was on the horse dressed in my robes and a cross was carried in front of me, and all the cardinals were following, and all the clergy of Rome, and a huge crowd of people. / We set off from St. Peter's to go

Marlene: Total pope.

Gret pours the wine and steals the bottle.

Joan: to St. John's. I had felt a slight pain earlier, I thought it was something I'd eaten, and then it came back, and came back more often. I thought when this is over I'll go to bed. There were still long gaps when I felt perfectly all right and I didn't want to attract attention to myself and spoil the ceremony. Then I suddenly realized what it must be. I had to last out till I could get home and hide. Then something changed, my breath started to catch, I couldn't plan things properly any more. We were in a little street that goes between St. Clement's and the Colosseum, and I just had to get off the horse and sit down for a minute. Great waves of pressure were going through my body, I heard sounds like a cow lowing, they came out of my mouth. Far away I heard people screaming, "The pope is ill, the pope is dying." And the baby just slid out onto the road.*

Marlene: The cardinals / won't have known where to put themselves.

Nijo: Oh dear, Joan, what a thing to do! In the street!

Isabella: *How embarrassing.

Gret: In a field, yah. *(They are laughing.)*

Joan: One of the cardinals said, "The Antichrist!" and fell over in a faint. *(They all laugh.)*

Marlene: So what did they do? They weren't best pleased.

Joan: They took me by the feet and dragged me out of town and stoned me to death. *(They stop laughing.)*

Marlene: Joan, how horrible.

Joan: I don't really remember.

Nijo: And the child died too?

Joan: Oh yes, I think so, yes.

The Waitress enters to clear the plates. Pause. They start talking very quietly.

Isabella (to Joan): I never had any children. I was very fond of horses.

Nijo (to Marlene): I saw my daughter once. She was three years old. She wore a plum-red / small sleeved gown. Akebono's wife

Isabella: Birdie was my favorite. A little Indian bay mare I rode in the Rocky Mountains.

Nijo: had taken the child because her own died. Everyone thought I was just a visitor. She was being brought up carefully so she could be sent to the palace like I was.

Gret steals her empty plate.

Isabella: Legs of iron and always cheerful, and such a pretty face. If a stranger led her she reared up like a bronco.

Nijo: I never saw my third child after he was born, the son of Ariake the priest. Ariake held him on his lap the day he was born and talked to him as if he could understand, and cried. My fourth child was Ariake's too. Ariake died before he was born. I didn't want to see anyone, I stayed alone in the hills. It was a boy again, my third son. But oddly enough I felt nothing for him.

Marlene: How many children did you have, Gret?

Gret: Ten.

Isabella: Whenever I came back to England I felt I had so much to atone for. Hennie and John were so good. I did no good in my life. I spent years in self-gratification. So I hurled myself into committees, I nursed the people of Tobermory in the epidemic of influenza, I lectured the Young Women's Christian Association on Thrift. I talked and talked explaining how the East was corrupt and vicious. My travels must do good to someone beside myself. I wore myself out with good causes.

Marlene (pause): Oh God, why are we all so miserable?

Joan (pause): The procession never went down that street again.

Marlene: They rerouted it specially?

Joan: Yes they had to go all round to avoid it. And they introduced a pierced chair.

Marlene: A pierced chair?

Joan: Yes, a chair made out of solid marble with a hole in the seat / and it was

Marlene: You're not serious.

Joan: in the Chapel of the Savior, and after he was elected the pope had to sit in it.

Marlene: And someone looked up his skirts? / Not really!

Isabella. What an extraordinary thing.

Joan: Two of the clergy / made sure he was a man.

Nijo: On their hands and knees!
Marlene: A pierced chair!
Gret: Balls!

Griselda arrives unnoticed.

Nijo: Why couldn't he just pull up his robe?
Joan: He had to sit there and look dignified.
Marlene: You could have made all your chamberlains sit in it.*
Gret: Big one. Small one.
Nijo: Very useful chair at court.
Isabella: *Or the laird of Tobermory in his kilt.

They are quite drunk. They get the giggles. Marlene notices Griselda and gets up to welcome her. The others go on talking and laughing. Gret crosses to Joan, and Isabella and pours them wine from her stolen bottles. The Waitress gives out the menus.

Marlene: Griselda! / There you are. Do you want to eat?
Griselda: I'm sorry I'm so late. No, no, don't bother.
Marlene: Of course it's no bother. / Have you eaten?
Griselda: No really, I'm not hungry.
Marlene: Well have some pudding.
Griselda: I never eat pudding.
Marlene: Griselda, I hope you're not anorexic. We're having pudding, I am, and getting nice and fat.
Griselda: Oh if everyone is. I don't mind.
Marlene: Now who do you know? This is Joan who was pope in the ninth century, and Isabella Bird, the Victorian traveler, and Lady Nijo from Japan, emperor's concubine and Buddhist nun, thirteenth century, nearer your own time, and Gret who was painted by Brueghel. Griselda's in Boccaccio° and Petrarch° and Chaucer because of her extraordinary marriage. I'd like profiteroles because they're disgusting.
Joan: Zabaglione, please.
Isabella: Apple pie / and cream.
Nijo: What's this?
Marlene: Zabaglione, it's Italian, it's what Joan's having, / it's delicious.
Nijo: A Roman Catholic / dessert? Yes please.
Marlene: Gret?
Gret: Cake.
Griselda: Just cheese and biscuits, thank you.

The Waitress exits.

Marlene: Yes, Griselda's life is like a fairy story, except it starts with marrying the prince.
Griselda: He's only a marquis, Marlene.

Boccaccio: Giovanni Boccaccio (1313–1375), Italian author of the *Decameron,* in which the story of patient Griselda was first written.
Petrarch (1304–1374): Italian poet and friend of Boccaccio whose Latin translation of the story of Griselda was Chaucer's source for the tale.

Marlene: Well everyone for miles around is his liege and he's absolute lord of life and death and you were the poor but beautiful peasant girl and he whisked you off. / Near enough a prince.

Nijo: How old were you?

Griselda: Fifteen.

Nijo: I was brought up in court circles and it was still a shock. Had you ever seen him before?

Griselda: I'd seen him riding by, we all had. And he'd seen me in the fields with the sheep.*

Isabella: I would have been well suited to minding sheep.

Nijo: And Mr. Nugent riding by.

Isabella: Of course not, Nijo, I mean a healthy life in the open air.

Joan: *He just rode up while you were minding the sheep and asked you to marry him?

Griselda: No, no, it was on the wedding day. I was waiting outside the door to see the procession. Everyone wanted him to get married so there'd be an heir to look after us when he died, / and at last he

Marlene: I don't think Walter wanted to get married. It is Walter? Yes.

Griselda: announced a day for the wedding but nobody knew who the bride was, we thought it must be a foreign princess, we were longing to see her. Then the carriage stopped outside our cottage and we couldn't see the bride anywhere. And he came and spoke to my father.

Nijo: And your father told you to serve the prince.

Griselda: My father could hardly speak. The marquis said it wasn't an order, I could say no, but if I said yes I must always obey him in everything.

Marlene: That's when you should have suspected.

Griselda: But of course a wife must obey her husband. / And of course I must obey the marquis.*

Isabella: I swore to obey dear John, of course, but it didn't seem to arise. Naturally I wouldn't have wanted to go abroad while I was married.

Marlene: *Then why bother to mention it at all? He'd got a thing about it, that's why.

Griselda: I'd rather obey the marquis than a boy from the village.

Marlene: Yes, that's a point.

Joan: I never obeyed anyone. They all obeyed me.

Nijo: And what did you wear? He didn't make you get married in your own clothes? That would be perverse.*

Marlene: Oh, you wait.

Griselda: *He had ladies with him who undressed me and they had a white silk dress and jewels for my hair.

Marlene: And at first he seemed perfectly normal?

Griselda: Marlene, you're always so critical of him. / Of course he was normal, he was very kind.

Marlene: But, Griselda, come on, he took your baby.

Griselda: Walter found it hard to believe I loved him. He couldn't believe I would always obey him. He had to prove it.

Marlene: I don't think Walter likes women.

Griselda: I'm sure he loved me, Marlene, all the time.

Marlene: He just had a funny way / of showing it.

Griselda: It was hard for him too.
Joan: How do you mean he took away your baby?
Nijo: Was it a boy?
Griselda: No, the first one was a girl.
Nijo: Even so it's hard when they take it away. Did you see it at all?
Griselda: Oh yes, she was six weeks old.
Nijo: Much better to do it straight away.
Isabella: But why did your husband take the child?
Griselda: He said all the people hated me because I was just one of them. And now I had a child they were restless. So he had to get rid of the child to keep them quiet. But he said he wouldn't snatch her, I had to agree and obey and give her up. So when I was feeding her a man came in and took her away. I thought he was going to kill her even before he was out of the room.
Marlene: But you let him take her? You didn't struggle?
Griselda: I asked him to give her back so I could kiss her. And I asked him to bury her where no animals could dig her up. / It was Walter's child to do what he
Isabella: Oh, my dear.
Griselda: liked with.*
Marlene: Walter was bonkers.
Gret: Bastard.
Isabella: *But surely, murder.
Griselda: I had promised.
Marlene: I can't stand this. I'm going for a pee.

Marlene goes out. The Waitress brings the dessert, serves it during the following, then exits.

Nijo: No, I understand. Of course you had to, he was your life. And were you in favor after that?
Griselda: Oh yes, we were very happy together. We never spoke about what had happened.
Isabella: I can see you were doing what you thought was your duty. But didn't it make you ill?
Griselda: No, I was very well, thank you.
Nijo: And you had another child?
Griselda: Not for four years, but then I did, yes, a boy.
Nijo: Ah a boy. / So it all ended happily.
Griselda: Yes he was pleased. I kept my son till he was two years old. A peasant's grandson. It made the people angry. Walter explained.
Isabella: But surely he wouldn't kill his children / just because —
Griselda: Oh it wasn't true. Walter would never give in to the people. He wanted to see if I loved him enough.
Joan: He killed his children / to see if you loved him enough?
Nijo: Was it easier the second time or harder?
Griselda: It was always easy because I always knew I would do what he said. *(Pause. They start to eat.)*
Isabella: I hope you didn't have any more children.
Griselda: Oh no, no more. It was twelve years till he tested me again.

Isabella: So whatever did he do this time? / My poor John, I never loved him enough, and he would never have dreamt . . .

Griselda: He sent me away. He said the people wanted him to marry someone else who'd give him an heir and he'd got special permission from the pope. So I said I'd go home to my father. I came with nothing / so I went with nothing. I took

Nijo: Better to leave if your master doesn't want you.

Griselda: off my clothes. He let me keep a slip so he wouldn't be shamed. And I walked home barefoot. My father came out in tears. Everyone was crying except me.

Nijo: At least your father wasn't dead. / I had nobody.

Isabella: Well it can be a relief to come home. I loved to see Hennie's sweet face again.

Griselda: Oh yes, I was perfectly content. And quite soon he sent for me again.

Joan: I don't think I would have gone.

Griselda: But he told me to come. I had to obey him. He wanted me to help prepare his wedding. He was getting married to a young girl from France / and nobody except me knew how to arrange things the way he liked them.

Nijo: It's always hard taking him another woman.

Marlene comes back.

Joan: I didn't live a woman's life. I don't understand it.

Griselda: The girl was sixteen and far more beautiful than me. I could see why he loved her. / She had her younger brother with her as a page.

The Waitress enters.

Marlene: Oh God, I can't bear it. I want some coffee. Six coffees. Six brandies. / Double brandies. Straightaway.

The Waitress exits.

Griselda: They all went into the feast I'd prepared. And he stayed behind and put his arms round me and kissed me. / I felt half asleep with the shock.

Nijo: Oh, like a dream.

Marlene: And he said. "This is your daughter and your son."

Griselda: Yes.

Joan: What?

Nijo: Oh. Oh I see. You got them back.

Isabella: I did think it was remarkably barbaric to kill them but you learn not to say anything. / So he had them brought up secretly I suppose.

Marlene: Walter's a monster. Weren't you angry? What did you do?

Griselda: Well I fainted. Then I cried and kissed the children. / Everyone was making a fuss of me.

Nijo: But did you feel anything for them?

Griselda: What?

Nijo: Did you feel anything for the children?

Griselda: Of course, I loved them.

Joan: So you forgave him and lived with him?

Griselda: He suffered so much all those years.

Isabella: Hennie had the same sweet nature.

Nijo: So they dressed you again?
Griselda: Cloth of gold.
Joan: I can't forgive anything.
Marlene: You really are exceptional, Griselda.
Nijo: Nobody gave me back my children. *(She cries.)*

The Waitress brings the brandies and then exits. During the following, Joan goes to Nijo.

Isabella: I can never be like Hennie. I was always so busy in England, a kind of business I detested. The very presence of people exhausted my emotional reserves. I could not be like Hennie however I tried. I tried and was as ill as could be. The doctor suggested a steel net to support my head, the weight of my own head was too much for my diseased spine. It is dangerous to put oneself in depressing circumstances. Why should I do it?
Joan (to Nijo): Don't cry.
Nijo: My father and the emperor both died in the autumn. So much pain.
Joan: Yes, but don't cry.
Nijo: They wouldn't let me into the palace when he was dying. I hid in the room with his coffin, then I couldn't find where I'd left my shoes, I ran after the funeral procession in bare feet, I couldn't keep up. When I got there it was over, a few wisps of smoke in the sky, that's all that was left of him. What I want to know is, if I'd still been at court, would I have been allowed to wear full mourning?
Marlene: I'm sure you would.
Nijo: Why do you say that? You don't know anything about it. Would I have been allowed to wear full mourning?
Isabella: How can people live in this dim pale island and wear our hideous clothes? I cannot and will not live the life of a lady.
Nijo: I'll tell you something that made me angry. I was eighteen, at the Full Moon Ceremony. They make a special rice gruel and stir it with their sticks, and then they beat their women across the loins so they'll have sons and not daughters. So the emperor beat us all / very hard as
Marlene: What a sod.

The Waitress enters with the coffees.

Nijo: usual — that's not it, Marlene, that's normal, what made us angry he told his attendants they could beat us too. Well they had a wonderful time. / So Lady Genki and I made a plan, and the ladies
Marlene: I'd like another brandy, please. Better make it six.

The Waitress exits.

Nijo: all hid in his rooms, and Lady Mashimizu stood guard with a stick at the door, and when His Majesty came in Genki seized him and I beat him till he cried out and promised he would never order anyone to hit us again. Afterwards there was a terrible fuss. The nobles were horrified. "We wouldn't even dream of stepping on Your Majesty's shadow." And I had hit him with a stick. Yes, I hit him with a stick.

The Waitress brings the brandy bottle and tops up the glasses. Joan crosses in front of the table and back to her place while drunkenly reciting:

Joan: Suave, mari magno turantibus aequora ventis,
e terra magnum alterius spectare laborem;
non quia vexari quemquamst iucunda voluptas,
sed quibus ipse malis careas quia cernere suave est.
Suave etiam belli certamina magna tueri
per campos instructa tua sine parte pericli.
Sed nil dulcius est, bene quam munita tenere
edita doctrina sapientum templa serena, /
despicere unde queas alios passimque videre
errare atque viam palantis quaerere vitae,

Griselda: I do think — I do wonder — it would have been nicer if Walter hadn't had to.

Isabella: Why should I? Why should I?

Marlene: Of course not.

Nijo: I hit him with a stick.

Joan: certare ingenio, contendere nobilitate,
noctes atque dies niti praestante labore
ad summas emergere opes rerumque potiri.
O miseras hominum mentis, / o pectora caeca!*°

Isabella.: O miseras!

Nijo: *Pectora caeca!

Joan: qualibus in tenebris vitae quantisque periclis
degitur hoc aevi quodcumquest! / none videre
nil aliud sibi naturam latrare, nisi utqui
corpore seiunctus dolor absit, mente fruatur° . . . *(She subsides.)*

Gret: We come to hell through a big mouth. Hell's black and red. / It's

Marlene (to Joan): Shut up, pet.

Griselda: Hush, please.

Isabella: Listen, she's been to hell.

Gret: like the village where I come from. There's a river and a bridge and houses. There's places on fire like when the soldiers come. There's a big devil sat on a roof with a big hole in his arse and he's scooping stuff out of it with a big ladle and it's falling down on us, and it's money, so a lot of the women stop and get some. But most of us is fighting the devils. There's lots of little devils, our size, and we get them down all right and give them a beating.

Suave, . . . o pectora caeca!: Joan's speech is from the Second Book of *On the Nature of Things* by Titus Lucretius Carus (97?–54 B.C.), the Latin poet and philosopher. The following translation of the passage is by Cyril Bailey: Sweet it is, when on the great sea the winds are buffeting the waters, to gaze from the land on another's great struggles; not because it is pleasure or joy that any one should be distressed, but because it is sweet to perceive from what misfortune you yourself are free. Sweet is it too, to behold great contests of war in full array over the plains, when you have no part in the danger. But nothing is more gladdening than to dwell in the calm high places, firmly embattled on the heights by the teaching of the wise, whence you can look down on others, and see them wandering hither and thither, going astray as they seek the way of life, in strife matching their wits or rival claims of birth, struggling night and day by surpassing effort to rise up to the height of power and gain possession of the world. Ah! miserable minds of men, blind hearts!
qualibus . . . fruatur: In what darkness of life, in what great dangers ye spend this little span of years! to think that ye should not see that nature cries aloud for nothing else but that pain may be kept far sundered from the body, and that, withdrawn from care and fear, she may enjoy in mind the sense of pleasure!

There's lots of funny creatures round your feet, you don't like to look, like rats and lizards, and nasty things, a bum with a face, and fish with legs, and faces on things that don't have faces on. But they don't hurt, you just keep going. Well we'd had worse, you see, we'd had the Spanish. We'd all had family killed. My big son die on a wheel. Birds eat him. My baby, a soldier run her through with a sword. I'd had enough, I was mad, I hate the bastards. I come out of my front door that morning and shout till my neighbors come out and I said, "Come on, we're going where the evil come from and pay the bastards out." And they all come out just as they was / from baking or

Nijo: All the ladies come.

Gret: washing in their aprons, and we push down the street and the ground opens up and we go through a big mouth into a street just like ours but in hell. I've got a sword in my hand from somewhere and I fill a basket with gold cups they drink out of down there. You just keep running on and fighting, / you didn't stop for nothing. Oh we give them devils such a beating.*

Nijo: Take that, take that.

Joan: *Something something something mortisque timores
tum vacuum pectus° — damn.
Quod si ridicula —
something something on and on and on
and something splendorem purpureai.

Isabella: I thought I would have a last jaunt up the west river in China. Why not? But the doctors were so very grave I just went to Morocco. The sea was so wild I had to be landed by ship's crane in a coal bucket. / My horse was a terror to me, a powerful black charger.

Gret: Coal bucket good.

Joan: nos in luce timemus
something
terrorem°

Nijo is laughing and crying. Joan gets up and is sick. Griselda looks after her.

Griselda: Can I have some water, please?

The Waitress exits.

Isabella: So off I went to visit the Berber sheikhs in full blue trousers and great brass spurs. I was the only European woman ever to have seen the emperor of Morocco. I was

Something . . . pectus: Fragments from Lucretius meaning "the dread of death leaves your heart empty."

Quod . . . purpureai. . . . nos in luce . . . terrorem: Fragments from the following passage by Lucretius: But if we see that these thoughts are mere mirth and mockery, and in very truth the fears of men and the cares that dog them fear not the clash of arms nor the weapons of war, but pass boldly among kings and lords of the world, nor dread the glitter that comes from gold nor the bright sheen of the purple robe, can you doubt that all such power belongs to reason alone, above all when the whole of life is but a struggle in darkness? For even as children tremble and fear everything in blinding darkness, so we sometimes dread in the light things that are no whit more to be feared than what children shudder at in the dark.

The Waitress brings the water

seventy years old. What lengths to go to for a last chance of joy. I knew my return of vigor was only temporary, but how marvelous while it lasted.

Scene II

"Top Girls" Employment Agency. Monday morning. The lights come up on Marlene and Jeanine.

Marlene: Right, Jeanine, you are Jeanine aren't you? Let's have a look. O's and A's.° / No A's, all those

Jeanine: Six O's.

Marlene: O's you probably could have got an A. / Speeds, not brilliant, not too bad.

Jeanine: I wanted to go to work.

Marlene: Well, Jeanine, what's your present job like?

Jeanine: I'm a secretary.

Marlene: Secretary or typist?

Jeanine: I did start as a typist but the last six months I've been a secretary.

Marlene: To?

Jeanine: To three of them, really, they share me. There's Mr. Ashford, he's the office manager, and Mr. Philby / is sales, and —

Marlene: Quite a small place?

Jeanine: A bit small.

Marlene: Friendly?

Jeanine: Oh it's friendly enough.

Marlene: Prospects?

Jeanine: I don't think so, that's the trouble. Miss Lewis is secretary to the managing director and she's been there forever, and Mrs. Bradford / is —

Marlene: So you want a job with better prospects?

Jeanine: I want a change.

Marlene: So you'll take anything comparable?

Jeanine: No, I do want prospects. I want more money.

Marlene: You're getting — ?

Jeanine: Hundred.

Marlene: It's not bad you know. You're what? Twenty?

Jeanine: I'm saving to get married.

Marlene: Does that mean you don't want a long-term job, Jeanine?

Jeanine: I might do.

Marlene: Because where do the prospects come in? No kids for a bit?

Jeanine: Oh no, not kids, not yet.

Marlene: So you won't tell them you're getting married?

Jeanine: Had I better not?

Marlene: It would probably help.

O's and A's: O-level and A-level examinations in the British education system. An O-level is a public examination for secondary-school students testing basic knowledge in various subjects; it is required before advancement to more specialized courses of study. A-level exams require advanced knowledge in a subject and are taken at the end of secondary school, usually two years after O-levels.

Jeanine: I'm not wearing a ring. We thought we wouldn't spend on a ring.
Marlene: Saves taking it off.
Jeanine: I wouldn't take it off.
Marlene: There's no need to mention it when you go for an interview. / Now, Jeanine, do you have a feel
Jeanine: But what if they ask?
Marlene: for any particular kind of company?
Jeanine: I thought advertising.
Marlene: People often do think advertising. I have got a few vacancies but I think they're looking for something glossier.
Jeanine: You mean how I dress? / I can
Marlene: I mean experience.
Jeanine: dress different. I dress like this on purpose for where I am now.
Marlene: I have a marketing department here of a knitwear manufacturer. / Marketing is near enough
Jeanine: Knitwear?
Marlene: advertising. Secretary to the marketing manager, he's thirty-five, married, I've sent him a girl before and she was happy, left to have a baby, you won't want to mention marriage there. He's very fair I think, good at his job, you won't have to nurse him along. Hundred and ten, so that's better than you're doing now.
Jeanine: I don't know.
Marlene: I've a fairly small concern here, father and two sons, you'd have more say potentially, secretarial and reception duties, only a hundred but the job's going to grow with the concern and then you'll be in at the top with new girls coming in underneath you.
Jeanine: What is it they do?
Marlene: Lampshades. / This would be my first choice for you.
Jeanine: Just lampshades?
Marlene: There's plenty of different kinds of lampshade. So we'll send you there, shall we, and the knitwear second choice. Are you free to go for an interview any day they call you?
Jeanine: I'd like to travel.
Marlene: We don't have any foreign clients. You'd have to go elsewhere.
Jeanine: Yes I know. I don't really . . . I just mean . . .
Marlene: Does your fiancé want to travel?
Jeanine: I'd like a job where I was here in London and with him and everything but now and then — I expect it's silly. Are there jobs like that?
Marlene: There's personal assistant to a top executive in a multinational. If that's the idea you need to be planning ahead. Is that where you want to be in ten years?
Jeanine: I might not be alive in ten years.
Marlene: Yes but you will be. You'll have children.
Jeanine: I can't think about ten years.
Marlene: You haven't got the speeds anyway. So I'll send you to these two shall I? You haven't been to any other agency? Just so we don't get crossed wires. Now, Jeanine, I want you to get one of these jobs, all right? If I send you that means I'm putting myself on the line for you. Your presentation's OK, you look fine, just be confident and go in there convinced that this is the

best job for you and you're the best person for the job. If you don't believe it they won't believe it.

Jeanine: Do you believe it?

Marlene: I think you could make me believe it if you put your mind to it.

Jeanine: Yes, all right.

SCENE III

Joyce's backyard. Sunday afternoon. The house with a back door is upstage. Downstage is a shelter made of junk, made by children. The lights come up on two girls, Angie and Kit, who are squashed together in the shelter. Angie is sixteen, Kit is twelve. They cannot be seen from the house.

Joyce (off, calling from the house): Angie. Angie, are you out there?

Silence. They keep still and wait. When nothing else happens they relax.

Angie: Wish she was dead.

Kit: Wanna watch *The Exterminator?*

Angie: You're sitting on my leg.

Kit: There's nothing on telly. We can have an ice cream. Angie?

Angie: Shall I tell you something?

Kit: Do you wanna watch *The Exterminator?*

Angie: It's X, innit?

Kit: I can get into Xs.

Angie: Shall I tell you something?

Kit: We'll go to something else. We'll go to Ipswich. What's on the Odeon?

Angie: She won't let me, will she?

Kit: Don't tell her.

Angie: I've no money.

Kit: I'll pay.

Angie: She'll moan though, won't she?

Kit: I'll ask her for you if you like.

Angie: I've no money, I don't want you to pay.

Kit: I'll ask her.

Angie: She don't like you.

Kit: I still got three pounds birthday money. Did she say she don't like me? I'll go by myself then.

Angie: Your mum don't let you. I got to take you.

Kit: She won't know.

Angie: You'd be scared who'd sit next to you.

Kit: No I wouldn't. She does like me anyway. Tell me then.

Angie: Tell you what?

Kit: It's you she doesn't like.

Angie: Well I don't like her so tough shit.

Joyce (off): Angie. Angie. Angie. I know you're out there. I'm not coming out after you. You come in here.

Silence. Nothing happens.

Angie: Last night when I was in bed. I been thinking yesterday could I make things move. You know, make things move by thinking about them without touching then. Last night I was in bed and suddenly a picture fell down off the wall.

Kit: What picture?

Angie: My gran, that picture. Not the poster. The photograph in the frame.

Kit: Had you done something to make it fall down?

Angie: I must have done.

Kit: But were you thinking about it?

Angie: Not about it, but about something.

Kit: I don't think that's very good.

Angie: You know the kitten?

Kit: Which one?

Angie: There only is one. The dead one.

Kit: What about it?

Angie: I heard it last night.

Kit: Where?

Angie: Out here. In the dark. What if I left you here in the dark all night?

Kit: You couldn't. I'd go home.

Angie: You couldn't.

Kit: I'd / go home.

Angie: No you couldn't, not if I said.

Kit: I could.

Angie: Then you wouldn't see anything. You'd just be ignorant.

Kit: I can see in the daytime.

Angie: No you can't. You can't hear it in the daytime.

Kit: I don't want to hear it.

Angie: You're scared that's all.

Kit: I'm not scared of anything.

Angie: You're scared of blood.

Kit: It's not the same kitten anyway. You just heard an old cat, / you just heard some old cat.

Angie: You don't know what I heard. Or what I saw. You don't know nothing because you're a baby.

Kit: You're sitting on me.

Angie: Mind my hair / you silly cunt.

Kit: Stupid fucking cow, I hate you.

Angie: I don't care if you do.

Kit: You're horrible.

Angie: I'm going to kill my mother and you're going to watch.

Kit: I'm not playing.

Angie: You're scared of blood.

Kit puts her hand under dress, brings it out with blood on her finger.

Kit: There, see, I got my own blood, so.

Angie takes Kit's hand and licks her finger.

Angie: Now I'm a cannibal. I might turn into a vampire now.

Kit: That picture wasn't nailed up right.

Angie: You'll have to do that when I get mine.

Kit: I don't have to.

Angie: You're scared.

Kit: I'll do it, I might do it. I don't have to just because you say. I'll be sick on you.

Angie: I don't care if you are sick on me, I don't mind sick. I don't mind blood. If I don't get away from here I'm going to die.

Kit: I'm going home.

Angie: You can't go through the house. She'll see you.

Kit: I won't tell her.

Angie: Oh great, fine.

Kit: I'll say I was by myself. I'll tell her you're at my house and I'm going there to get you.

Angie: She knows I'm here, stupid.

Kit: Then why can't I go through the house?

Angie: Because I said not.

Kit: My mum don't like you anyway.

Angie: I don't want her to like me. She's a slag.°

Kit: She is not.

Angie: She does it with everyone.

Kit: She does not.

Angie: You don't even know what it is.

Kit: Yes I do.

Angie: Tell me then.

Kit: We get it all at school, cleverclogs. It's on television. You haven't done it.

Angie: How do you know?

Kit: Because I know you haven't.

Angie: You know wrong then because I have.

Kit: Who with?

Angie: I'm not telling you / who with.

Kit: You haven't anyway.

Angie: How do you know?

Kit: Who with?

Angie: I'm not telling you.

Kit: You said you told me everything.

Angie: I was lying wasn't I?

Kit: Who with? You can't tell me who with because / you never —

Angie: Sh.

Joyce has come out of the house. She stops halfway across the yard and listens. They listen.

Joyce: You there, Angie? Kit? You there, Kitty? Want a cup of tea? I've got some chocolate biscuits. Come on now I'll put the kettle on. Want a choccy biccy, Angie? *(They all listen and wait.)* Fucking rotten little cunt. You can stay there and die. I'll lock the door.

They all wait. Joyce goes back to the house. Angie and Kit sit in silence for a while.

slag: A promiscuous woman.

Kit: When there's a war, where's the safest place?
Angie: Nowhere.
Kit: New Zealand is, my mum said. Your skin's burned right off. Shall we go to New Zealand?
Angie: I'm not staying here.
Kit: Shall we go to New Zealand?
Angie: You're not old enough.
Kit: You're not old enough.
Angie: I'm old enough to get married.
Kit: You don't want to get married.
Angie: No but I'm old enough.
Kit: I'd find out where they were going to drop it and stand right in the place.
Angie: You couldn't find out.
Kit: Better than walking round with your skin dragging on the ground. Eugh. / Would you like walking round with your skin dragging on the ground?
Angie: You couldn't find out, stupid, it's a secret.
Kit: Where are you going?
Angie: I'm not telling you.
Kit: Why?
Angie: It's a secret.
Kit: But you tell me all your secrets.
Angie: Not the true secrets.
Kit: Yes you do.
Angie: No I don't.
Kit: I want to go somewhere away from the war.
Angie: Just forget the war.
Kit: I can't.
Angie: You have to. It's so boring.
Kit: I'll remember it at night.
Angie: I'm going to do something else anyway.
Kit: What? Angie, come on. Angie.
Angie: It's a true secret.
Kit: It can't be worse than the kitten. And killing your mother. And the war.
Angie: Well I'm not telling you so you can die for all I care.
Kit: My mother says there's something wrong with you playing with someone my age. She says why haven't you got friends your own age. People your own age know there's something funny about you. She says you're a bad influence. She says she's going to speak to your mother.

Angie twists Kit's arm till she cries out.

Angie: Say you're a liar.
Kit: She said it not me.
Angie: Say you eat shit.
Kit: You can't make me.

Angie lets go.

Angie: I don't care anyway. I'm leaving.
Kit: Go on then.
Angie: You'll all wake up one morning and find I've gone.

Kit: Good.
Angie: I'm not telling you when.
Kit: Go on then.
Angie: I'm sorry I hurt you.
Kit: I'm tired.
Angie: Do you like me?
Kit: I don't know.
Angie: You do like me.
Kit: I'm going home. *(She gets up.)*
Angie: No you're not.
Kit: I'm tired.
Angie: She'll see you.
Kit: She'll give me a chocolate biscuit.
Angie: Kitty.
Kit: Tell me where you're going.
Angie: Sit down.
Kit (sitting down again): Go on then.
Angie: Swear?
Kit: Swear.
Angie: I'm going to London. To see my aunt.
Kit: And what?
Angie: That's it.
Kit: I see my aunt all the time.
Angie: I don't see my aunt.
Kit: What's so special?
Angie: It is special. She's special.
Kit: Why?
Angie: She is.
Kit: Why?
Angie: She is.
Kit: Why?
Angie: My mother hates her.
Kit: Why?
Angie: Because she does.
Kit: Perhaps she's not very nice.
Angie: She is nice.
Kit: How do you know?
Angie: Because I know her.
Kit: You said you never see her.
Angie: I saw her last year. You saw her.
Kit: Did I?
Angie: Never mind.
Kit: I remember her. That aunt. What's so special?
Angie: She gets people jobs.
Kit: What's so special?
Angie: I think I'm my aunt's child. I think my mother's really my aunt.
Kit: Why?
Angie: Because she goes to America, now shut up.
Kit: I've been to London.

Angie: Now give us a cuddle and shut up because I'm sick.
Kit: You're sitting on my arm.

They curl up in each other's arms. Silence. Joyce comes out of the house and comes up to them quietly.

Joyce: Come on.
Kit: Oh hello.
Joyce: Time you went home.
Kit: We want to go to the Odeon.
Joyce: What time?
Kit: Don't know.
Joyce: What's on?
Kit: Don't know.
Joyce: Don't know much do you?
Kit: That all right then?
Joyce: Angie's got to clean her room first.
Angie: No I don't.
Joyce: Yes you do, it's a pigsty.
Angie: Well I'm not.
Joyce: Then you're not going. I don't care.
Angie: Well I am going.
Joyce: You've no money, have you?
Angie: Kit's paying anyway.
Joyce: No she's not.
Kit: I'll help you with your room.
Joyce: That's nice.
Angie: No you won't. You wait here.
Kit: Hurry then.
Angie: I'm not hurrying. You just wait. *(Goes slowly into the house. Silence.)*
Joyce: I don't know. *(Silence.)* How's school then?
Kit: All right.
Joyce: What are you now? Third year?
Kit: Second year.
Joyce: Your mum says you're good at English. *(Silence.)* Maybe Angie should've stayed on.
Kit: She didn't like it.
Joyce: I didn't like it. And look at me. If your face fits at school it's going to fit other places too. It wouldn't make no difference to Angie. She's not going to get a job when jobs are hard to get. I'd be sorry for anyone in charge of her. She'd better get married. I don't know who'd have her, mind. She's one of those girls might never leave home. What do you want to be when you grow up, Kit?
Kit: Physicist.
Joyce: What?
Kit: Nuclear physicist.
Joyce: Whatever for?
Kit: I could, I'm clever.
Joyce: I know you're clever, pet. *(Silence.)* I'll make a cup of tea. *(Silence.)* Looks like it's going to rain. *(Silence.)* Don't you have friends your own age?

Kit: Yes.
Joyce: Well then.
Kit: I'm old for my age.
Joyce: And Angie's simple is she? She's not simple.
Kit: I love Angie.
Joyce: She's clever in her own way.
Kit: You can't stop me.
Joyce: I don't want to.
Kit: You can't, so.
Joyce: Don't be cheeky, Kitty. She's always kind to little children.
Kit: She's coming so you better leave me alone.

Angie comes out. She has changed into an old best dress, slightly small for her.

Joyce: What you put that on for? Have you done your room? You can't clean your room in that.
Angie: I looked in the cupboard and it was there.
Joyce: Of course it was there, it's meant to be there. Is that why it was a surprise, finding something in the right place? I should think she's surprised, wouldn't you, Kit, to find something in her room in the right place?
Angie: I decided to wear it.
Joyce: Not today, why? To clean your room? You're not going to the pictures till you've done your room. You can put your dress on after if you like.

Angie picks up a brick.

Have you done your room? You're not getting out of it, you know.
Kit: Angie, let's go.
Joyce: She's not going till she's done her room.
Kit: It's starting to rain.
Joyce: Come on, come on then. Hurry and do your room, Angie, and then you can go to the cinema with Kit. Oh it's wet, come on. We'll look up the time in the paper. Does your mother know, Kit, it's going to be a late night for you, isn't it? Hurry up, Angie. You'll spoil your dress. You make me sick.

Joyce and Kit run into the house. Angie stays where she is. There is the sound of rain. Kit comes out of the house.

Kit (shouting): Angie. Angie, come on, you'll get wet. *(She comes back to Angie.)*
Angie: I put on this dress to kill my mother.
Kit: I suppose you thought you'd do it with a brick.
Angie: You can kill people with a brick. *(She puts the brick down.)*
Kit: Well you didn't, so.

ACT II

Scene I

"Top Girls" Employment Agency. Monday morning. There are three desks in the main office and a separate small interviewing area. The lights come up in the main office on Win and Nell, who have just arrived for work.

Nell: Coffee coffee coffee coffee / coffee.
Win: The roses were smashing. / Mermaid.
Nell: Ohhh.
Win: Iceberg. He taught me all their names.

Nell has some coffee now.

Nell: Ah. Now then.
Win: He has one of the finest rose gardens in West Sussex. He exhibits.
Nell: He what?
Win: His wife was visiting her mother. It was like living together.
Nell: Crafty, you never said.
Win: He rang me Saturday morning.
Nell: Lucky you were free.
Win: That's what I told him.
Nell: Did you hell.
Win: Have you ever seen a really beautiful rose garden?
Nell: I don't like flowers. / I like swimming pools.
Win: Marilyn. Esther's Baby. They're all called after birds.
Nell: Our friend's late. Celebrating all weekend I bet you.
Win: I'd call a rose Elvis. Or John Conteh.
Nell: Is Howard in yet?
Win: If he is he'll be bleeping us with a problem.
Nell: Howard can just hang on to himself.
Win: Howard's really cut up.
Nell: Howard thinks because he's a fella the job was his as of right. Our Marlene's got far more balls than Howard and that's that.
Win: Poor little bugger.
Nell: He'll live.
Win: He'll move on.
Nell: I wouldn't mind a change of air myself.
Win: Serious?
Nell: I've never been a staying-put lady. Pastures new.
Win: So who's the pirate?
Nell: There's nothing definite.
Win: Inquiries?
Nell: There's always inquiries. I'd think I'd got bad breath if there stopped being inquiries. Most of them can't afford me. Or you.
Win: I'm all right for the time being. Unless I go to Australia.
Nell: There's not a lot of room upward.
Win: Marlene's filled it up.
Nell: Good luck to her. Unless there's some prospects moneywise.
Win: You can but ask.
Nell: Can always but ask.
Win: So what have we got? I've got a Mr. Holden I saw last week.
Nell: Any use?
Win: Pushy. Bit of a cowboy.
Nell: Goodlooker?
Win: Good dresser.
Nell: High flyer?

Win: That's his general idea certainly but I'm not sure he's got it up there.

Nell: Prestel wants six flyers and I've only seen two and a half.

Win: He's making a bomb on the road but he thinks it's time for an office. I sent him to IBM but he didn't get it.

Nell: Prestel's on the road.

Win: He's not overbright.

Nell: Can he handle an office?

Win: Provided his secretary can punctuate he should go far.

Nell: Bear Prestel in mind then, I might put my head round the door. I've got that poor little nerd I should never have said I could help. Tender heart me.

Win: Tender like old boots. How old?

Nell: Yes well forty-five.

Win: Say no more.

Nell: He knows his place, he's not after calling himself a manager, he's just a poor little bod wants a better commission and a bit of sunshine.

Win: Don't we all.

Nell: He's just got to relocate. He's got a bungalow in Dymchurch.

Win: And his wife says.

Nell: The lady wife wouldn't care to relocate. She's going through the change.

Win: It's his funeral, don't waste your time.

Nell: I don't waste a lot.

Win: Good weekend you?

Nell: You could say.

Win: Which one?

Nell: One Friday, one Saturday.

Win: Aye — aye.

Nell: Sunday night I watched telly.

Win: Which of them do you like best really?

Nell: Sunday was best, I like the Ovaltine.

Win: Holden, Barker, Gardner, Duke.

Nell: I've a lady here thinks she can sell.

Win: Taking her on?

Nell: She's had some jobs.

Win: Services?

Nell: No, quite heavy stuff, electric.

Win: Tough bird like us.

Nell: We could do with a few more here.

Win: There's nothing going here.

Nell: No but I always want the tough ones when I see them. Hang on to them.

Win: I think we're plenty.

Nell: Derek asked me to marry him again.

Win: He doesn't know when he's beaten.

Nell: I told him I'm not going to play house, not even in Ascot.

Win: Mind you, you could play house.

Nell: If I chose to play house I would play house ace.

Win: You could marry him and go on working.

Nell: I could go on working and not marry him.

Marlene arrives.

Marlene: Morning ladies.

Win and Nell cheer and whistle.

Mind my head.

Nell: Coffee coffee coffee.

Win: We're tactfully not mentioning you're late.

Marlene: Fucking tube.

Win: We've heard that one.

Nell: We've used that one.

Win: It's the top executive doesn't come in as early as the poor working girl.

Marlene: Pass the sugar and shut your face, pet.

Win: Well I'm delighted.

Nell: Howard's looking sick.

Win: Howard is sick. He's got ulcers and heart. He told me.

Nell: He'll have to stop then, won't he?

Win: Stop what?

Nell: Smoking, drinking, shouting. Working.

Win: Well, working.

Nell: We're just looking through the day.

Marlene: I'm doing some of Pam's ladies. They've been piling up while she's away.

Nell: Half a dozen little girls and an arts graduate who can't type.

Win: I spent the whole weekend at his place in Sussex.

Nell: She fancies his rose garden.

Win: I had to lie down in the back of the car so the neighbors wouldn't see me go in.

Nell: You're kidding.

Win: It was funny.

Nell: Fuck that for a joke.

Win: It was funny.

Marlene: Anyway they'd see you in the garden.

Win: The garden has extremely high walls.

Nell: I think I'll tell the wife.

Win: Like hell.

Nell: She might leave him and you could have the rose garden.

Win: The minute it's not a secret I'm out on my ear.

Nell: Don't know why you bother.

Win: Bit of fun.

Nell: I think it's time you went to Australia.

Win: I think it's pushy Mr. Holden time.

Nell: If you've any really pretty bastards, Marlene, I want some for Prestel.

Marlene: I might have one this afternoon. This morning it's all Pam's secretarial.

Nell: Not long now and you'll be upstairs watching over us all.

Marlene: Do you feel bad about it?

Nell: I don't like coming second.

Marlene: Who does?

Win: We'd rather it was you than Howard. We're glad for you, aren't we, Nell?

Nell: Oh yes. Aces.

Louise enters the interviewing area. The lights crossfade to Win and Louise in the interviewing area. Nell exits.

Win: Now, Louise, hello, I have your details here. You've been very loyal to the one job I see.

Louise: Yes I have.

Win: Twenty-one years is a long time in one place.

Louise: I feel it is. I feel it's time to move on.

Win: And you are what age now?

Louise: I'm in my early forties.

Win: Exactly?

Louise: Forty-six.

Win: It's not necessarily a handicap, well it is of course we have to face that, but it's not necessarily a disabling handicap, experience does count for something.

Louise: I hope so.

Win: Now between ourselves is there any trouble, any reason why you're leaving that wouldn't appear on the form?

Louise: Nothing like that.

Win: Like what?

Louise: Nothing at all.

Win: No long-term understandings come to a sudden end, making for an insupportable atmosphere?

Louise: I've always completely avoided anything like that at all.

Win: No personality clashes with your immediate superiors or inferiors?

Louise: I've always taken care to get on very well with everyone.

Win: I only ask because it can affect the reference and it also affects your motivation, I want to be quite clear why you're moving on. So I take it the job itself no longer satisfies you. Is it the money?

Louise: It's partly the money. It's not so much the money.

Win: Nine thousand is very respectable. Have you dependents?

Louise: No, no dependents. My mother died.

Win: So why are you making a change?

Louise: Other people make changes.

Win: But why are you, now, after spending most of your life in the one place?

Louise: There you are, I've lived for that company, I've given my life really you could say because I haven't had a great deal of social life, I've worked in the evenings. I haven't had office entanglements for the very reason you just mentioned and if you are committed to your work you don't move in many other circles. I had management status from the age of twenty-seven and you'll appreciate what that means. I've built up a department. And there it is, it works extremely well, and I feel I'm stuck there. I've spent twenty years in middle management. I've seen young men who I trained go on, in my own company or elsewhere, to higher things. Nobody notices me, I don't expect it, I don't attract attention by making mistakes, everybody takes it for granted that my work is perfect. They will notice me when I go, they will be sorry I think to lose me, they will offer me more money of course, I will refuse. They will see when I've gone what I was doing for them.

Win: If they offer you more money you won't stay?

Louise: No I won't.

Win: Are you the only woman?

Louise: Apart from the girls of course, yes. There was one, she was my assistant, it was the only time I took on a young woman assistant. I always had my doubts. I don't care greatly for working with women, I think I pass as a man at work. But I did take on this young woman, her qualifications were excellent, and she did well, she got a department of her own, and left the company for a competitor where she's now on the board and good luck to her. She has a different style, she's a new kind of attractive well-dressed — I don't mean I don't dress properly. But there is a kind of woman who is thirty now who grew up in a different climate. They are not so careful. They take themselves for granted. I have had to justify my existence every minute, and I have done so, I have proved — well.

Win: Let's face it, vacancies are ones where you'll be in competition with younger men. And there are companies that will value your experience enough that you'll be in with a chance. There are also fields that are easier for a woman, there is a cosmetic company here where your experience might be relevant. It's eight and a half, I don't know if that appeals.

Louise: I've proved I can earn money. It's more important to get away. I feel it's now or never. I sometimes / think —

Win: You shouldn't talk too much at an interview.

Louise: I don't. I don't normally talk about myself. I know very well how to handle myself in an office situation. I only talk to you because it seems to me this is different, it's your job to understand me, surely. You asked the questions.

Win: I think I understand you sufficiently.

Louise: Well good, that's good.

Win: Do you drink?

Louise: Certainly not. I'm not a teetotaler, I think that's very suspect, it's seen as being an alcoholic if you're teetotal. What do you mean? I don't drink. Why?

Win: I drink.

Louise: I don't.

Win: Good for you.

The lights crossfade to the main office with Marlene sitting at her desk. Win and Louise exit. Angie arrives in the main office.

Angie: Hello.

Marlene: Have you an appointment?

Angie: It's me. I've come.

Marlene: What? It's not Angie?

Angie: It was hard to find this place. I got lost.

Marlene: How did you get past the receptionist? The girl on the desk, didn't she try to stop you?

Angie: What desk?

Marlene: Never mind.

Angie: I just walked in. I was looking for you.

Marlene: Well you found me.

Angie: Yes.

Marlene: So where's your mum? Are you up in town for the day?

Angie: Not really.

Marlene: Sit down. Do you feel all right?

Angie: Yes thank you.

Marlene: So where's Joyce?

Angie: She's at home.

Marlene: Did you come up on a school trip then?

Angie: I've left school.

Marlene: Did you come up with a friend?

Angie: No. There's just me.

Marlene: You came up by yourself, that's fun. What have you been doing? Shopping? Tower of London?

Angie: No, I just come here. I come to you.

Marlene: That's very nice of you to think of paying your aunty a visit. There's not many nieces make that the first port of call. Would you like a cup of coffee?

Angie: No thank you.

Marlene: Tea, orange?

Angie: No thank you.

Marlene: Do you feel all right?

Angie: Yes thank you.

Marlene: Are you tired from the journey?

Angie: Yes, I'm tired from the journey.

Marlene: You sit there for a bit then. How's Joyce?

Angie: She's all right.

Marlene: Same as ever.

Angie: Oh yes.

Marlene: Unfortunately you've picked a day when I'm rather busy, if there's ever a day when I'm not, or I'd take you out to lunch and we'd go to Madame Tussaud's.° We could go shopping. What time do you have to be back? Have you got a day return?

Angie: No.

Marlene: So what train are you going back on?

Angie: I came on the bus.

Marlene: So what bus are you going back on? Are you staying the night?

Angie: Yes.

Marlene: Who are you staying with? Do you want me to put you up for the night, is that it?

Angie: Yes please.

Marlene: I haven't got a spare bed.

Angie: I can sleep on the floor.

Marlene: You can sleep on the sofa.

Angie: Yes please.

Marlene: I do think Joyce might have phoned me. It's like her.

Madame Tussaud's: A museum containing wax models of famous people.

Angie: This is where you work is it?
Marlene: It's where I have been working the last two years but I'm going to move into another office.
Angie: It's lovely.
Marlene: My new office is nicer than this. There's just the one big desk in it for me.
Angie: Can I see it?
Marlene: Not now, no, there's someone else in it now. But he's leaving at the end of next week and I'm going to do his job.
Angie: Is that good?
Marlene: Yes, it's very good.
Angie: Are you going to be in charge?
Marlene: Yes I am.
Angie: I knew you would be.
Marlene: How did you know?
Angie: I knew you'd be in charge of everything.
Marlene: Not quite everything.
Angie: You will be.
Marlene: Well we'll see.
Angie: Can I see it next week then?
Marlene: Will you still be here next week?
Angie: Yes.
Marlene: Don't you have to go home?
Angie: No.
Marlene: Why not?
Angie: It's all right.
Marlene: Is it all right?
Angie: Yes, don't worry about it.
Marlene: Does Joyce know where you are?
Angie: Yes of course she does.
Marlene: Well does she?
Angie: Don't worry about it.
Marlene: How long are you planning to stay with me then?
Angie: You know when you came to see us last year?
Marlene: Yes, that was nice wasn't it?
Angie: That was the best day of my whole life.
Marlene: So how long are you planning to stay?
Angie: Don't you want me?
Marlene: Yes yes, I just wondered.
Angie: I won't stay if you don't want me.
Marlene: No, of course you can stay.
Angie: I'll sleep on the floor. I won't be any bother.
Marlene: Don't get upset.
Angie: I'm not, I'm not. Don't worry about it.

Mrs. Kidd comes in.

Mrs. Kidd: Excuse me.
Marlene: Yes.
Mrs. Kidd: Excuse me.

Marlene: Can I help you?

Mrs. Kidd: Excuse me bursting in on you like this but I have to talk to you.

Marlene: I am engaged at the moment. / If you could go to reception —

Mrs. Kidd: I'm Rosemary Kidd, Howard's wife, you don't recognize me but we did meet, I remember you of course / but you wouldn't —

Marlene: Yes of course, Mrs. Kidd, I'm sorry, we did meet. Howard's about somewhere I expect, have you looked in his office?

Mrs. Kidd: Howard's not about, no. I'm afraid it's you I've come to see if I could have a minute or two.

Marlene: I do have an appointment in five minutes.

Mrs. Kidd: This won't take five minutes. I'm very sorry. It is a matter of some urgency.

Marlene: Well of course. What can I do for you?

Mrs. Kidd: I just wanted a chat, an informal chat. It's not something I can simply — I'm sorry if I'm interrupting your work. I know office work isn't like housework / which is all interruptions.

Marlene: No no, this is my niece. Angie. Mrs. Kidd.

Mrs. Kidd: Very pleased to meet you.

Angie: Very well thank you.

Mrs. Kidd: Howard's not in today.

Marlene: Isn't he?

Mrs. Kidd: He's feeling poorly.

Marlene: I didn't know. I'm sorry to hear that.

Mrs. Kidd: The fact is he's in a state of shock. About what's happened.

Marlene: What has happened?

Mrs. Kidd: You should know if anyone. I'm referring to you been appointed managing director instead of Howard. He hasn't been at all well all weekend. He hasn't slept for three nights. I haven't slept.

Marlene: I'm sorry to hear that, Mrs. Kidd. Has he thought of sleeping pills?

Mrs. Kidd: It's very hard when someone has worked all these years.

Marlene: Business life is full of little setbacks. I'm sure Howard knows that. He'll bounce back in a day or two. We all bounce back.

Mrs. Kidd: If you could see him you'd know what I'm talking about. What's it going to do to him working for a woman? I think if it was a man he'd get over it as something normal.

Marlene: I think he's going to have to get over it.

Mrs. Kidd: It's me that bears the brunt. I'm not the one that's been promoted. I put him first every inch of the way. And now what do I get? You women this, you women that. It's not my fault. You're going to have to be very careful how you handle him. He's very hurt.

Marlene: Naturally I'll be tactful and pleasant to him, you don't start pushing someone around. I'll consult him over any decisions affecting his department. But that's no different, Mrs. Kidd, from any of my other colleagues.

Mrs. Kidd: I think it is different, because he's a man.

Marlene: I'm not quite sure why you came to see me.

Mrs. Kidd: I had to do something.

Marlene: Well you've done it, you've seen me. I think that's probably all we've time for. I'm sorry he's been taking it out on you. He really is a shit, Howard.

Mrs. Kidd: But he's got a family to support. He's got three children. It's only fair.

Marlene: Are you suggesting I give up the job to him then?

Mrs. Kidd: It had crossed my mind if you were unavailable after all for some reason, he would be the natural second choice I think, don't you? I'm not asking.

Marlene: Good.

Mrs. Kidd: You mustn't tell him I came. He's very proud.

Marlene: If he doesn't like what's happening here he can go and work somewhere else.

Mrs. Kidd: Is that a threat?

Marlene: I'm sorry but I do have some work to do.

Mrs. Kidd: It's not that easy, a man of Howard's age. You don't care. I thought he was going too far but he's right. You're one of these ballbreakers, / that's what you

Marlene: I'm sorry but I do have some work to do.

Mrs. Kidd: are. You'll end up miserable and lonely. You're not natural.

Marlene: Could you please piss off?

Mrs. Kidd: I thought if I saw you at least I'd be doing something. *(She goes.)*

Marlene: I've got to go and do some work now. Will you come back later?

Angie: I think you were wonderful.

Marlene: I've got to go and do some work now.

Angie: You told her to piss off.

Marlene: Will you come back later?

Angie: Can't I stay here?

Marlene: Don't you want to go sightseeing?

Angie: I'd rather stay here.

Marlene: You can stay here I suppose, if it's not boring.

Angie: It's where I most want to be in the world.

Marlene: I'll see you later then.

Marlene goes. Shona and Nell enter the interviewing area. Angie sits at Win's desk. The lights crossfade to Nell and Shona in the interviewing area.

Nell: Is this right? You are Shona?

Shona: Yeh.

Nell: It says here you're twenty-nine.

Shona: Yeh.

Nell: Too many late nights, me. So you've been where you are for four years, Shona, you're earning six basic and three commission. So what's the problem?

Shona: No problem.

Nell: Why do you want a change?

Shona: Just a change.

Nell: Change of product, change of area?

Shona: Both.

Nell: But you're happy on the road?

Shona: I like driving.

Nell: You're not after management status?

Shona: I would like management status.

Nell: You'd be interested in titular management status but not come off the road?

Shona: I want to be on the road, yeh.

Nell: So how many calls have you been making a day?

Shona: Six.

Nell: And what proportion of those are successful?

Shona: Six.

Nell: That's hard to believe.

Shona: Four.

Nell: You find it easy to get the initial interest do you?

Shona: Oh yeh, I get plenty of initial interest.

Nell: And what about closing?

Shona: I close, don't I?

Nell: Because that's what an employer is going to have doubts about with a lady as I needn't tell you, whether she's got the guts to push through to a closing situation. They think we're too nice. They think we listen to the buyer's doubts. They think we consider his needs and his feelings.

Shona: I never consider people's feelings.

Nell: I was selling for six years, I can sell anything, I've sold in three continents, and I'm jolly as they come but I'm not very nice.

Shona: I'm not very nice.

Nell: What sort of time do you have on the road with the other reps? Get on all right? Handle the chat?

Shona: I get on. Keep myself to myself.

Nell: Fairly much of a loner are you?

Shona: Sometimes.

Nell: So what field are you interested in?

Shona: Computers.

Nell: That's a top field as you know and you'll be up against some very slick fellas there, there's some very pretty boys in computers, it's an American-style field.

Shona: That's why I want to do it.

Nell: Video systems appeal? That's a high-flying situation.

Shona: Video systems appeal OK.

Nell: Because Prestel have half a dozen vacancies I'm looking to fill at the moment. We're talking in the area of ten to fifteen thousand here and upwards.

Shona: Sounds OK.

Nell: I've half a mind to go for it myself. But it's good money here if you've got the top clients. Could you fancy it do you think?

Shona: Work here?

Nell: I'm not in a position to offer, there's nothing officially going just now, but we're always on the lookout. There's not that many of us. We could keep in touch.

Shona: I like driving.

Nell: So the Prestel appeals?

Shona: Yeh.

Nell: What about ties?

Shona: No ties.

Nell: So relocation wouldn't be a problem?
Shona: No problem.
Nell: So just fill me in a bit more could you about what you've been doing.
Shona: What I've been doing. It's all down there.
Nell: The bare facts are down here but I've got to present you to an employer.
Shona: I'm twenty-nine years old.
Nell: So it says here.
Shona: We look young. Youngness runs in the family in our family.
Nell: So just describe your present job for me.
Shona: My present job at present. I have a car. I have a Porsche. I go up the M1 a lot. Burn up the M1 a lot. Straight up the M1 in the fast lane to where the clients are, Staffordshire, Yorkshire, I do a lot in Yorkshire. I'm selling electric things. Like dishwashers, washing machines, stainless steel tubs are a feature and the reliability of the program. After-sales service, we offer a very good after-sales service, spare parts, plenty of spare parts. And fridges, I sell a lot of fridges specially in the summer. People want to buy fridges in the summer because of the heat melting the butter and you get fed up standing the milk in a basin of cold water with a cloth over, stand to reason people don't want to do that in this day and age. So I sell a lot of them. Big ones with big freezers. Big freezers. And I stay in hotels at night when I'm away from home. On my expense account. I stay in various hotels. They know me, the ones I go to. I check in, have a bath, have a shower. Then I go down to the bar, have a gin and tonic, have a chat. Then I go into the dining room and have dinner. I usually have fillet steak and mushrooms, I like mushrooms. I like smoked salmon very much. I like having a salad on the side. Green salad. I don't like tomatoes.
Nell: Christ what a waste of time.
Shona: Beg your pardon?
Nell: Not a word of this is true, is it?
Shona: How do you mean?
Nell: You just filled in the form with a pack of lies.
Shona: Not exactly.
Nell: How old are you?
Shona: Twenty-nine.
Nell: Nineteen?
Shona: Twenty-one.
Nell: And what jobs have you done? Have you done any?
Shona: I could though, I bet you.

The lights crossfade to the main office with Angie sitting as before. Win comes in to the main office. Shona and Nell exit.

Win: Who's sitting in my chair?
Angie: What? Sorry.
Win: Who's been eating my porridge?
Angie: What?
Win: It's all right, I saw Marlene. Angie, isn't it? I'm Win. And I'm not going out for lunch because I'm knackered. I'm going to set me down here and have a yogurt. Do you like yogurt?
Angie: No.

Win: That's good because I've only got one. Are you hungry?
Angie: No.
Win: There's a café on the corner.
Angie: No thank you. Do you work here?
Win: How did you guess?
Angie: Because you look as if you might work here and you're sitting at the desk. Have you always worked here?
Win: No I was headhunted. That means I was working for another outfit like this and this lot came and offered me more money. I broke my contract, there was a hell of a stink. There's not many top ladies about. Your aunty's a smashing bird.
Angie: Yes I know.
Win: Fan are you? Fan of your aunty's?
Angie: Do you think I could work here?
Win: Not at the moment.
Angie: How do I start?
Win: What can you do?
Angie: I don't know. Nothing.
Win: Type?
Angie: Not very well. The letters jump up when I do capitals. I was going to do a CSE° in commerce but I didn't.
Win: What have you got?
Angie: What?
Win: CSE's, O's.
Angie: Nothing, none of that. Did you do all that?
Win: Oh yes, all that, and a science degree funnily enough. I started out doing medical research but there's no money in it. I thought I'd go abroad. Did you know they sell Coca-Cola in Russia and Pepsi-Cola in China? You don't have to be qualified as much as you might think. Men are awful bullshitters, they like to make out jobs are harder than they are. Any job I ever did I started doing it better than the rest of the crowd and they didn't like it. So I'd get unpopular and I'd have a drink to cheer myself up. I lived with a fella and supported him for four years, he couldn't get work. After that I went to California. I like the sunshine. Americans know how to live. This country's too slow. Then I went to Mexico, still in sales, but it's no country for a single lady. I came home, went bonkers for a bit, thought I was five different people, got over that all right, the psychiatrist said I was perfectly sane and highly intelligent. Got married in a moment of weakness and he's inside now, he's been inside four years, and I've not been to see him too much this last year. I like this better than sales, I'm not really that aggressive. I started thinking sales was a good job if you want to meet people, but you're meeting people that don't want to meet you. It's no good if you like being liked. Here your clients want to meet you because you're the one doing them some good. They hope.

Angie has fallen asleep. Nell comes in.

CSE: Certificate of Secondary Education.

Nell: You're talking to yourself, sunshine.
Win: So what's new?
Nell: Who is this?
Win: Marlene's little niece.
Nell: What's she got, brother, sister? She never talks about her family.
Win: I was telling her my life story.
Nell: Violins?
Win: No, success story.
Nell: You've heard Howard's had a heart attack?
Win: No, when?
Nell: I heard just now. He hadn't come in, he was at home, he's gone to hospital. He's not dead. His wife was here, she rushed off in a cab.
Win: Too much butter, too much smoke. We must send him some flowers.

Marlene comes in.

You've heard about Howard?
Marlene: Poor sod.
Nell: Lucky he didn't get the job if that's what his health's like.
Marlene: Is she asleep?
Win: She wants to work here.
Marlene: Packer in Tesco more like.
Win: She's a nice kid. Isn't she?
Marlene: She's a bit thick. She's a bit funny.
Win: She thinks you're wonderful.
Marlene: She's not going to make it.

Scene II

Joyce's kitchen. Sunday evening, a year earlier. The lights come up on Joyce, Angie, and Marlene. Marlene is taking presents out of a bright carrier bag. Angie has already opened a box of chocolates.

Marlene: Just a few little things. / I've
Joyce: There's no need.
Marlene: no memory for birthdays have I, and Christmas seems to slip by. So I think I owe Angie a few presents.
Joyce: What do you say?
Angie: Thank you very much. Thank you very much, Aunty Marlene. *(She opens a present. It is the dress from Act One, new.)* Oh look, Mum, isn't it lovely?
Marlene: I don't know if it's the right size. She's grown up since I saw her. / I knew she was always
Angie: Isn't it lovely?
Marlene: tall for her age.
Joyce: She's a big lump.
Marlene: Hold it up, Angie, let's see.
Angie: I'll put it on, shall I?
Marlene: Yes, try it on.
Joyce: Go on to your room then, we don't want / a strip show thank you.

Angie: Of course I'm going to my room, what do you think. Look, Mum, here's something for you. Open it, go on. What is it? Can I open it for you?
Joyce: Yes, you open it, pet.
Angie: Don't you want to open it yourself? / Go on.
Joyce: I don't mind, you can do it.
Angie: It's something hard. It's — what is it? A bottle. Drink is it? No, it's what? Perfume, look. What a lot. Open it, look, let's smell it. Oh it's strong. It's lovely. Put it on me. How do you do it? Put it on me.
Joyce: You're too young.
Angie: I can play wearing it like dressing up.
Joyce: And you're too old for that. Here, give it here, I'll do it, you'll tip the whole bottle over yourself / and we'll have you smelling all summer.
Angie: Put it on you. Do I smell? Put it on Aunty too. Put it on Aunty too. Let's all smell.
Marlene: I didn't know what you'd like.
Joyce: There's no danger I'd have it already, / that's one thing.
Angie: Now we all smell the same.
Marlene: It's a bit of nonsense.
Joyce: It's very kind of you, Marlene, you shouldn't.
Angie: Now I'll put on the dress and then we'll see. *(Angie goes.)*
Joyce: You've caught me on the hop with the place in the mess. / If you'd let me
Marlene: That doesn't matter.
Joyce: know you was coming I'd have got something in to eat. We had our dinner dinnertime. We're just going to have a cup of tea. You could have an egg.
Marlene: No, I'm not hungry. Tea's fine.
Joyce: I don't expect you take sugar.
Marlene: Why not?
Joyce: You take care of yourself.
Marlene: How do you mean you didn't know I was coming?
Joyce: You could have written. I know we're not on the phone but we're not completely in the dark ages, / we do have a postman.
Marlene: But you asked me to come.
Joyce: How did I ask you to come?
Marlene: Angie said when she phoned up.
Joyce: Angie phoned up, did she.
Marlene: Was it just Angie's idea?
Joyce: What did she say?
Marlene: She said you wanted me to come and see you. / It was a couple of
Joyce: Ha.
Marlene: weeks ago. How was I to know that's a ridiculous idea? My diary's always full a couple of weeks ahead so we fixed it for this weekend. I was meant to get here earlier but I was held up. She gave me messages from you.
Joyce: Didn't you wonder why I didn't phone you myself?
Marlene: She said you didn't like using the phone. You're shy on the phone and can't use it. I don't know what you're like, do I?

Joyce: Are there people who can't use the phone?
Marlene: I expect so.
Joyce: I haven't met any.
Marlene: Why should I think she was lying?
Joyce: Because she's like what she's like.
Marlene: How do I know / what she's like?
Joyce: It's not my fault you don't know what she's like. You never come and see her.
Marlene: Well I have now / and you don't seem over the moon.*
Joyce: Good. *Well I'd have got a cake if she'd told me. *(Pause.)*
Marlene: I did wonder why you wanted to see me.
Joyce: I didn't want to see you.
Marlene: Yes, I know. Shall I go?
Joyce: I don't mind seeing you.
Marlene: Great, I feel really welcome.
Joyce: You can come and see Angie any time you like, I'm not stopping you. / You
Marlene: Ta ever so.
Joyce: know where we are. You're the one went away, not me. I'm right here where I was. And will be a few years yet I shouldn't wonder.
Marlene: All right. All right.

Joyce gives Marlene a cup of tea.

Joyce: Tea.
Marlene: Sugar?

Joyce passes Marlene the sugar.

It's very quiet down here.
Joyce: I expect you'd notice it.
Marlene: The air smells different too.
Joyce: That's the scent.
Marlene: No, I mean walking down the lane.
Joyce: What sort of air you get in London then?

Angie comes in, wearing the dress. It fits.

Marlene: Oh, very pretty. / You do look pretty, Angie.
Joyce: That fits all right.
Marlene: Do you like the color?
Angie: Beautiful. Beautiful.
Joyce: You better take it off, / you'll get it dirty.
Angie: I want to wear it. I want to wear it.
Marlene: It is for wearing after all. You can't just hang it up and look at it.
Angie: I love it.
Joyce: Well if you must you must.
Angie: If someone asks me what's my favorite color I'll tell them it's this. Thank you very much, Aunty Marlene.
Marlene: You didn't tell your mum you asked me down.
Angie: I wanted it to be a surprise.
Joyce: I'll give you a surprise / one of these days.

Angie: I thought you'd like to see her. She hasn't been here since I was nine. People do see their aunts.
Marlene: Is it that long? Doesn't time fly.
Angie: I wanted to.
Joyce: I'm not cross.
Angie: Are you glad?
Joyce: I smell nicer anyhow, don't I?

Kit comes in without saying anything, as if she lived there.

Marlene: I think it was a good idea, Angie, about time. We are sisters after all. It's a pity to let that go.
Joyce: This is Kitty, / who lives up the road. This is Angie's Aunty Marlene.
Kit: What's that?
Angie: It's a present. Do you like it?
Kit: It's all right. / Are you coming out?*
Marlene: Hello, Kitty.
Angie: *No.
Kit: What's that smell?
Angie: It's a present.
Kit: It's horrible. Come on.*
Marlene: Have a chocolate.
Angie: *No, I'm busy.
Kit: Coming out later?
Angie: No.
Kit (to Marlene): Hello. *(Kit goes without a chocolate.)*
Joyce: She's a little girl Angie sometimes plays with because she's the only child lives really close. She's like a little sister to her really. Angie's good with little children.
Marlene: Do you want to work with children, Angie? / Be a teacher or a nursery nurse?
Joyce: I don't think she's ever thought of it.
Marlene: What do you want to do?
Joyce: She hasn't an idea in her head what she wants to do. / Lucky to get anything.
Marlene: Angie?
Joyce: She's not clever like you. *(Pause.)*
Marlene: I'm not clever, just pushy.
Joyce: True enough.

Marlene takes a bottle of whiskey out of the bag.

I don't drink spirits.
Angie: You do at Christmas.
Joyce: It's not Christmas, is it?
Angie: It's better than Christmas.
Marlene: Glasses?
Joyce: Just a small one then.
Marlene: Do you want some, Angie?

Angie: I can't, can I?
Joyce: Taste it if you want. You won't like it.

Angie tastes it.

Angie: Mmm.
Marlene: We got drunk together the night your grandfather died.
Joyce: We did not get drunk.
Marlene: I got drunk. You were just overcome with grief.
Joyce: I still keep up the grave with flowers.
Marlene: Do you really?
Joyce: Why wouldn't I?
Marlene: Have you seen Mother?
Joyce: Of course I've seen Mother.
Marlene: I mean lately.
Joyce: Of course I've seen her lately, I go every Thursday.
Marlene (to Angie): Do you remember your grandfather?
Angie: He got me out of the bath one night in a towel.
Marlene: Did he? I don't think he ever gave me a bath. Did he give you a bath, Joyce? He probably got soft in his old age. Did you like him?
Angie: Yes of course.
Marlene: Why?
Angie: What?
Marlene: So what's the news? How's Mrs. Paisley? Still going crazily? / And Dorothy. What happened to Dorothy?*
Angie: Who's Mrs. Paisley?
Joyce: *She went to Canada.
Marlene: Did she? What to do?
Joyce: I don't know. She just went to Canada.
Marlene: Well / good for her.
Angie: Mr. Connolly killed his wife.
Marlene: What, Connolly at Whitegates?
Angie: They found her body in the garden. / Under the cabbages.
Marlene: He was always so proper.
Joyce: Stuck up git, Connolly. Best lawyer money could buy but he couldn't get out of it. She was carrying on with Matthew.
Marlene: How old's Matthew then?
Joyce: Twenty-one. / He's got a motorbike.
Marlene: I think he's about six.
Angie: How can he be six? He's six years older than me. / If he was six I'd be nothing, I'd be just born this minute.
Joyce: Your aunty knows that, she's just being silly. She means it's so long since she's been here she's forgotten about Matthew.
Angie: You were here for my birthday when I was nine. I had a pink cake. Kit was only five then, she was four, she hadn't started school yet. She could read already when she went to school. You remember my birthday? / You remember me?
Marlene: Yes, I remember the cake.
Angie: You remember me?
Marlene: Yes, I remember you.

Angie: And Mum and Dad was there, and Kit was.
Marlene: Yes, how is your dad? Where is he tonight? Up the pub?
Joyce: No, he's not here.
Marlene: I can see he's not here.
Joyce: He moved out.
Marlene: What? When did he? / Just recently?*
Angie: Didn't you know that? You don't know much.
Joyce: *No, it must be three years ago. Don't be rude, Angie.
Angie: I'm not, am I, Aunty? What else don't you know?
Joyce: You was in America or somewhere. You sent a postcard.
Angie: I've got that in my room. It's the Grand Canyon. Do you want to see it? Shall I get it? I can get it for you.
Marlene: Yes, all right.

Angie goes.

Joyce: You could be married with twins for all I know. You must have affairs and break up and I don't need to know about any of that so I don't see what the fuss is about.
Marlene: What fuss?

Angie comes back with the postcard.

Angie: "Driving across the states for a new job in L.A. It's a long way but the car goes very fast. It's very hot. Wish you were here. Love from Aunty Marlene."
Joyce: Did you make a lot of money?
Marlene: I spent a lot.
Angie: I want to go to America. Will you take me?
Joyce: She's not going to America, she's been to America, stupid.
Angie: She might go again, stupid. It's not something you do once. People who go keep going all the time, back and forth on jets. They go on Concorde and Laker and get jet lag. Will you take me?
Marlene: I'm not planning a trip.
Angie: Will you let me know?
Joyce: Angie, / you're getting silly.
Angie: I want to be American.
Joyce: It's time you were in bed.
Angie: No it's not. / I don't have to go to bed at all tonight.
Joyce: School in the morning.
Angie: I'll wake up.
Joyce: Come on now, you know how you get.
Angie: How do I get? / I don't get anyhow.*
Joyce: Angie. *Are you staying the night?
Marlene: Yes, if that's all right. / I'll see you in the morning.
Angie: You can have my bed. I'll sleep on the sofa.
Joyce: You will not, you'll sleep in your bed. / Think
Angie: Mum.
Joyce: I can't see through that? I can just see you going to sleep / with us talking.
Angie: I would, I would go to sleep, I'd love that.
Joyce: I'm going to get cross, Angie.
Angie: I want to show her something.

Joyce: Then bed.
Angie: It's a secret.
Joyce: Then I expect it's in your room so off you go. Give us a shout when you're ready for bed and your aunty'll be up and see you.
Angie: Will you?
Marlene: Yes of course.

Angie goes. Silence.

It's cold tonight.
Joyce: Will you be all right on the sofa? You can / have my bed.
Marlene: The sofa's fine.
Joyce: Yes the forecast said rain tonight but it's held off.
Marlene: I was going to walk down to the estuary but I've left it a bit late. Is it just the same?
Joyce: They cut down the hedges a few years back. Is that since you were here?
Marlene: But it's not changed down the end, all the mud? And the reeds? We used to pick them up when they were bigger than us. Are there still lapwings?
Joyce: You get strangers walking there on a Sunday. I expect they're looking at the mud and the lapwings, yes.
Marlene: You could have left.
Joyce: Who says I wanted to leave?
Marlene: Stop getting at me then, you're really boring.
Joyce: How could I have left?
Marlene: Did you want to?
Joyce: I said how, / how could I?
Marlene: If you'd wanted to you'd have done it.
Joyce: Christ.
Marlene: Are we getting drunk?
Joyce: Do you want something to eat?
Marlene: No, I'm getting drunk.
Joyce: Funny time to visit, Sunday evening.
Marlene: I came this morning. I spent the day —
Angie (off): Aunty! Aunty Marlene!
Marlene: I'd better go.
Joyce: Go on then.
Marlene: All right.
Angie (off): Aunty! Can you hear me? I'm ready.

Marlene goes. Joyce goes on sitting, clears up, sits again. Marlene comes back.

Joyce: So what's the secret?
Marlene: It's a secret.
Joyce: I know what it is anyway.
Marlene: I bet you don't. You always said that.
Joyce: It's her exercise book.
Marlene: Yes, but you don't know what's in it.
Joyce: It's some game, some secret society she has with Kit.
Marlene: You don't know the password. You don't know the code.
Joyce: You're really in it, aren't you. Can you do the handshake?

Marlene: She didn't mention a handshake.

Joyce: I thought they'd have a special handshake. She spends hours writing that but she's useless at school. She copies things out of books about black magic, and politicians out of the paper. It's a bit childish.

Marlene: I think it's a plot to take over the world.

Joyce: She's been in the remedial class the last two years.

Marlene: I came up this morning and spent the day in Ipswich. I went to see Mother.

Joyce: Did she recognize you?

Marlene: Are you trying to be funny?

Joyce: No, she does wander.

Marlene: She wasn't wandering at all, she was very lucid thank you.

Joyce: You were very lucky then.

Marlene: Fucking awful life she's had.

Joyce: Don't tell me.

Marlene: Fucking waste.

Joyce: Don't talk to me.

Marlene: Why shouldn't I talk? Why shouldn't I talk to you? / Isn't she my mother too?

Joyce: Look, you've left, you've gone away, / we can do without you.

Marlene: I left home, so what, I left home. People do leave home / it is normal.

Joyce: We understand that, we can do without you.

Marlene: We weren't happy. Were you happy?

Joyce: Don't come back.

Marlene: So it's your mother is it, your child, you never wanted me round, / you were jealous

Joyce: Here we go.

Marlene: of me because I was the little one and I was clever.

Joyce: I'm not clever enough for all this psychology / if that's what it is.

Marlene: Why can't I visit my own family / without

Joyce: Aah.

Marlene: all this?

Joyce: Just don't go on about Mum's life when you haven't been to see her for how many years. / I go

Marlene: It's up to me.

Joyce: and see her every week.

Marlene: Then don't go and see her every week.

Joyce: Somebody has to.

Marlene: No they don't. / Why do they?

Joyce: How would I feel if I didn't go?

Marlene: A lot better.

Joyce: I hope you feel better.

Marlene: It's up to me.

Joyce: You couldn't get out of here fast enough. *(Pause.)*

Marlene: Of course I couldn't get out of here fast enough. What was I going to do? Marry a dairyman who'd come home pissed? / Don't you fuckin this

Joyce: Christ.

Marlene: fucking that fucking bitch fucking tell me what to fucking do fucking.

Joyce: I don't know how you could leave your own child.

Marlene: You were quick enough to take her.
Joyce: What does that mean?
Marlene: You were quick enough to take her.
Joyce: Or what? Have her put in a home? Have some stranger / take her would you rather?
Marlene: You couldn't have one so you took mine.
Joyce: I didn't know that then.
Marlene: Like hell, / married three years.
Joyce: I didn't know that. Plenty of people / take that long.
Marlene: Well it turned out lucky for you, didn't it?
Joyce: Turned out all right for you by the look of you. You'd be getting a few less thousand a year.
Marlene: Not necessarily.
Joyce: You'd be stuck here / like you said.
Marlene: I could have taken her with me.
Joyce: You didn't want to take her with you. It's no good coming back now, Marlene, / and saying —
Marlene: I know a managing director who's got two children, she breast-feeds in the boardroom, she pays a hundred pounds a week on domestic help alone and she can afford that because she's an extremely high-powered lady earning a great deal of money.
Joyce: So what's that got to do with you at the age of seventeen?
Marlene: Just because you were married and had somewhere to live —
Joyce: You could have lived at home. / Or live
Marlene: Don't be stupid.
Joyce: with me and Frank. / You
Marlene: You never suggested.
Joyce: said you weren't keeping it. You shouldn't have had it / if you wasn't
Marlene: Here we go.
Joyce: going to keep it. You was the most stupid, / for someone so clever you was the most stupid, get yourself pregnant, not go to the doctor, not tell.
Marlene: You wanted it, you said you were glad, I remember the day, you said I'm glad you never got rid of it, I'll look after it, you said that down by the river. So what are you saying, sunshine, you don't want her?
Joyce: Course I'm not saying that.
Marlene: Because I'll take her, / wake her up and pack now.
Joyce: You wouldn't know how to begin to look after her.
Marlene: Don't you want her?
Joyce: Course I do, she's my child.
Marlene: Then what are you going on about / why did I have her?
Joyce: You said I got her off you / when you didn't —
Marlene: I said you were lucky / the way it —
Joyce: Have a child now if you want one. You're not old.
Marlene: I might do.
Joyce: Good. *(Pause.)*
Marlene: I've been on the pill so long / I'm probably sterile.
Joyce: Listen when Angie was six months I did get pregnant and I lost it because I was so tired looking after your fucking baby / because she cried so
Marlene: You never told me.

Joyce: much — yes I did tell you — / and the doctor
Marlene: Well I forgot.
Joyce: said if I'd sat down all day with my feet up I'd've kept it / and that's the only chance I ever had because after that —
Marlene: I've had two abortions, are you interested? Shall I tell you about them? Well I won't, it's boring, it wasn't a problem. I don't like messy talk about blood / and what a bad time we all had. I
Joyce: If I hadn't had your baby. The doctor said.
Marlene: don't want a baby. I don't want to talk about gynecology.
Joyce: Then stop trying to get Angie off of me.
Marlene: I come down here after six years. All night you've been saying I don't come often enough. If I don't come for another six years she'll be twenty-one, will that be OK?
Joyce: That'll be fine, yes, six years would suit me fine. *(Pause.)*
Marlene: I was afraid of this. I only came because I thought you wanted . . . I just want . . . *(She cries.)*
Joyce: Don't grizzle, Marlene, for God's sake. Marly? Come on, pet. Love you really. Fucking stop it, will you? *(She goes to Marlene.)*
Marlene: No, let me cry. I like it. *(They laugh, Marlene begins to stop crying.)* I knew I'd cry if I wasn't careful.
Joyce: Everyone's always crying in this house. Nobody takes notice.
Marlene: You've been wonderful looking after Angie.
Joyce: Don't get carried away.
Marlene: I can't write letters but I do think of you.
Joyce: You're getting drunk. I'm going to make some tea.
Marlene: Love you.

Joyce goes to make tea.

Joyce: I can see why you'd want to leave. It's a dump here.
Marlene: So what's this about you and Frank?
Joyce: He was always carrying on, wasn't he. And if I wanted to go out in the evening he'd go mad, even if it was nothing, a class, I was going to go to an evening class. So he had this girlfriend, only twenty-two poor cow, and I said go on, off you go, hoppit. I don't think he even likes her.
Marlene: So what about money?
Joyce: I've always said I don't want your money.
Marlene: No, does he send you money?
Joyce: I've got four different cleaning jobs. Adds up. There's not a lot round here.
Marlene: Does Angie miss him?
Joyce: She doesn't say.
Marlene: Does she see him?
Joyce: He was never that fond of her to be honest.
Marlene: He tried to kiss me once. When you were engaged.
Joyce: Did you fancy him?
Marlene: No, he looked like a fish.
Joyce: He was lovely then.
Marlene: Ugh.
Joyce: Well I fancied him. For about three years.

Marlene: Have you got someone else?

Joyce: There's not a lot round here. Mind you, the minute you're on your own, you'd be amazed how your friends' husbands drop by. I'd sooner do without.

Marlene: I don't see why you couldn't take my money.

Joyce: I do, so don't bother about it.

Marlene: Only got to ask.

Joyce: So what about you? Good job?

Marlene: Good for a laugh. / Got back

Joyce: Good for more than a laugh I should think.

Marlene: from the US of A a bit wiped out and slotted into this speedy employment agency and still there.

Joyce: You can always find yourself work then?

Marlene: That's right.

Joyce: And men?

Marlene: Oh there's always men.

Joyce: No one special?

Marlene: There's fellas who like to be seen with a high-flying lady. Shows they've got something really good in their pants. But they can't take the day to day. They're waiting for me to turn into the little woman. Or maybe I'm just horrible of course.

Joyce: Who needs them.

Marlene: Who needs them. Well I do. But I need adventures more. So on on into the sunset. I think the eighties are going to be stupendous.

Joyce: Who for?

Marlene: For me. / I think I'm going up up up.

Joyce: Oh for you. Yes, I'm sure they will.

Marlene: And for the country, come to that. Get the economy back on its feet and whoosh. She's a tough lady, Maggie. I'd give her a job. / She just needs to hang

Joyce: You voted for them, did you?

Marlene: in there. This country needs to stop whining. / Monetarism is not

Joyce: Drink your tea and shut up, pet.

Marlene: stupid. It takes time, determination. No more slop. / And

Joyce: Well I think they're filthy bastards.

Marlene: who's got to drive it on? First woman prime minister. Terrifico. Aces. Right on. / You must admit. Certainly gets my vote.

Joyce: What good's first woman if it's her? I suppose you'd have liked Hitler if he was a woman. Ms. Hitler. Got a lot done, Hitlerina. / Great adventures.

Marlene: Bosses still walking on the workers' faces? Still dadda's little parrot? Haven't you learned to think for yourself? I believe in the individual. Look at me.

Joyce: I am looking at you.

Marlene: Come on, Joyce, we're not going to quarrel over politics.

Joyce: We are though.

Marlene: Forget I mentioned it. Not a word about the slimy unions will cross my lips. *(Pause.)*

Joyce: You say Mother had a wasted life.

Marlene: Yes I do. Married to that bastard.
Joyce: What sort of life did he have? /
Marlene: Violent life?
Joyce: Working in the fields like an animal. / Why
Marlene: Come off it.
Joyce: wouldn't he want a drink? You want a drink. He couldn't afford whiskey.
Marlene: I don't want to talk about him.
Joyce: You started, I was talking about her. She had a rotten life because she had nothing. She went hungry.
Marlene: She was hungry because he drank the money. / He used to hit her.
Joyce: It's not all down to him / Their
Marlene: She didn't hit him.
Joyce: lives were rubbish. They were treated like rubbish. He's dead and she'll die soon and what sort of life / did they have?
Marlene: I saw him one night. I came down.
Joyce: Do you think I didn't? / They
Marlene: I still have dreams.
Joyce: didn't get to America and drive across it in a fast car. / Bad nights, they had bad days.
Marlene: America, America, you're jealous. / I had to get out, I knew when I
Joyce: Jealous?
Marlene: was thirteen, out of their house, out of them, never let that happen to me, / never let him, make my own way, out.
Joyce: Jealous of what you've done, you'd be ashamed of me if I came to your office, your smart friends, wouldn't you, I'm ashamed of you, think of nothing but yourself, you've got on, nothing's changed for most people, / has it?
Marlene: I hate the working class / which is what
Joyce: Yes you do.
Marlene: you're going to go on about now, it doesn't exist any more, it means lazy and stupid. / I don't
Joyce: Come on, now we're getting it.
Marlene: like the way they talk. I don't like beer guts and football vomit and saucy tits / and brothers and sisters —
Joyce: I spit when I see a Rolls-Royce, scratch it with my ring / Mercedes it was.
Marlene: Oh very mature —
Joyce: I hate the cows I work for / and their dirty dishes with blanquette of fucking veau.°
Marlene: and I will not be pulled down to their level by a flying picket and I won't be sent to Siberia / or a loony bin just because I'm original. And I support
Joyce: No, you'll be on a yacht, you'll be head of Coca-Cola and you wait, the eighties is going to be stupendous all right because we'll get you lot off our backs —
Marlene: Reagan even if he is a lousy movie star because the reds are swarming up his map and I want to be free in a free world —
Joyce: What? / What?

blanquette of . . . veau: Veal Stew.

Marlene: I know what I mean / by that — not shut up here.

Joyce: So don't be round here when it happens because if someone's kicking you I'll just laugh. *(Silence.)*

Marlene: I don't mean anything personal. I don't believe in class. Anyone can do anything if they've got what it takes.

Joyce: And if they haven't?

Marlene: If they're stupid or lazy or frightened, I'm not going to help them get a job, why should I?

Joyce: What about Angie?

Marlene: What about Angie?

Joyce: She's stupid, lazy, and frightened, so what about her?

Marlene: You run her down too much. She'll be all right.

Joyce: I don't expect so, no. I expect her children will say what a wasted life she had. If she has children. Because nothing's changed and it won't with them in.

Marlene: Them, them. / Us and them?

Joyce: And you're one of them.

Marlene: And you're us, wonderful us, and Angie's us / and Mum and Dad's us.

Joyce: Yes, that's right, and you're them.

Marlene: Come on, Joyce, what a night. You've got what it takes.

Joyce: I know I have.

Marlene: I didn't really mean all that.

Joyce: I did.

Marlene: But we're friends anyway.

Joyce: I don't think so, no.

Marlene: Well it's lovely to be out in the country. I really must make the effort to come more often. I want to go to sleep. I want to go to sleep.

Joyce gets blankets for the sofa.

Joyce: Goodnight then. I hope you'll be warm enough.

Marlene: Goodnight. Joyce —

Joyce: No, pet. Sorry.

Joyce goes. Marlene sits wrapped in a blanket and has another drink. Angie comes in.

Angie: Mum?

Marlene: Angie? What's the matter?

Angie: Mum?

Marlene: No, she's gone to bed. It's Aunty Marlene.

Angie: Frightening.

Marlene: Did you have a bad dream? What happened in it? Well you're awake now, aren't you, pet?

Angie: Frightening.

Connections

1. Discuss the purpose and meaning of the use of the past in Caryl Churchill's *Top Girls* and in Tennessee Williams's *The Glass Menagerie* (p. 1462).

2. Compare and contrast the image of men in *Top Girls* with that in David Henry Hwang's *M. Butterfly* (p. 1707).
3. Write an essay on success and failure as explored in *Top Girls* and in Arthur Miller's *Death of a Salesman* (p. 1508).

FENCES

August Wilson, who, as a young poet "wanted to be Dylan Thomas," has become in the past five years a major force in the American theater. He has projected a sequence of ten plays that will chronicle the black experience in the United States in each decade of the twentieth century. *Ma Rainey's Black Bottom,* the first of these to be completed, premiered at the Yale Repertory Theatre in 1984, went to Broadway shortly thereafter, and eventually won the New York Drama Critics' Circle Award. The plays that have so far followed are *Fences* (1985), *Joe Turner's Come and Gone* (1986), and *The Piano Lesson* (1987).

Born in Pittsburgh, Pennsylvania, Wilson grew up in the Hill, a black neighborhood to which his mother had come from North Carolina. His white father never lived with the family. Wilson quit school at sixteen and worked in a variety of menial jobs, meanwhile submitting poetry to a number of local publications. He didn't begin to find his writing voice, however, until he moved to Minneapolis–St. Paul, where he founded the Black Horizons Theatre Company in 1968 and later started the Playwrights Center. He supported himself during part of this time by writing skits for the Science Museum of Minnesota.

Fences offers a complex look at the internal and external pressures on a black tenement family living in Pittsburgh during the 1950s.

AUGUST WILSON (b. 1945)

Fences 1985

Characters

Troy Maxson
Jim Bono, Troy's friend
Rose, Troy's wife
Lyons, Troy's oldest son by previous marriage
Gabriel, Troy's brother
Cory, Troy and Rose's son
Raynell, Troy's daughter

SETTING: *The setting is the yard which fronts the only entrance to the Maxson household, an ancient two-story brick house set back off a small alley in a big-city neighborhood. The entrance to the house is gained by two or three steps leading to a wooden porch badly in need of paint.*

A relatively recent addition to the house and running its full width, the porch lacks congruence. It is a sturdy porch with a flat roof. One or two chairs of dubious value sit at one end where the kitchen window opens onto the porch. An old-fashioned icebox stands silent guard at the opposite end.

The yard is a small dirt yard, partially fenced, except for the last scene, with a wooden sawhorse, a pile of lumber, and other fence-building equipment set off to the side. Opposite is a tree from which hangs a ball made of rags. A baseball bat leans against the tree. Two oil drums serve as garbage receptacles and sit near the house at right to complete the setting.

THE PLAY: *Near the turn of the century, the destitute of Europe sprang on the city with tenacious claws and an honest and solid dream. The city devoured them. They swelled its belly until it burst into a thousand furnaces and sewing machines, a thousand butcher shops and bakers' ovens, a thousand churches and hospitals and funeral parlors and money-lenders. The city grew. It nourished itself and offered each man a partnership limited only by his talent, his guile, and his willingness and capacity for hard work. For the immigrants of Europe, a dream dared and won true.*

The descendants of African slaves were offered no such welcome or participation. They came from places called the Carolinas and the Virginias, Georgia, Alabama, Mississippi, and Tennessee. They came strong, eager, searching. The city rejected them and they fled and settled along the riverbanks and under bridges in shallow, ramshackle houses made of sticks and tarpaper. They collected rags and wood. They sold the use of their muscles and their bodies. They cleaned houses and washed clothes, they shined shoes, and in quiet desperation and vengeful pride, they stole, and lived in pursuit of their own dream. That they could breathe free, finally, and stand to meet life with the force of dignity and whatever eloquence the heart could call upon.

By 1957, the hard-won victories of the European immigrants had solidified the industrial might of America. War had been confronted and won with new energies that used loyalty and patriotism as its fuel. Life was rich, full, and flourishing. The Milwaukee Braves won the World Series, and the hot winds of change that would make the sixties a turbulent, racing, dangerous, and provocative decade had not yet begun to blow full.

ACT I

SCENE I

It is 1957. Troy and Bono enter the yard, engaged in conversation. Troy is fifty-three years old, a large man with thick, heavy hands; it is this largeness that he strives to fill out and make an accommodation with. Together with his blackness, his largeness informs his sensibilities and the choices he has made in his life.

Of the two men, Bono is obviously the follower. His commitment to their friendship of thirty-odd years is rooted in his admiration of Troy's honesty, capacity for hard work, and his strength, which Bono seeks to emulate.

It is Friday night, payday, and the one night of the week the two men engage in a ritual of talk and drink. Troy is usually the most talkative and at times he can be crude and almost vulgar, though he is capable of rising to profound heights of expression. The men carry lunch buckets and wear or carry burlap aprons and are dressed in clothes suitable to their jobs as garbage collectors.

Bono: Troy, you ought to stop that lying!

Troy: I ain't lying! The nigger had a watermelon this big. *(He indicates with his hands.)* Talking about . . . "What watermelon, Mr. Rand?" I liked to fell out! "What watermelon, Mr. Rand?" . . . And it sitting there big as life.

Bono: What did Mr. Rand say?

Troy: Ain't said nothing. Figure if the nigger too dumb to know he carrying a watermelon, he wasn't gonna get much sense out of him. Trying to hide that great big old watermelon under his coat. Afraid to let the white man see him carry it home.

Bono: I'm like you . . . I ain't got no time for them kind of people.

Troy: Now what he look like getting mad cause he see the man from the union talking to Mr. Rand?

Bono: He come to me talking about . . . "Maxson gonna get us fired." I told him to get away from me with that. He walked away from me calling you a troublemaker. What Mr. Rand say?

Troy: Ain't said nothing. He told me to go down the Commissioner's office next Friday. They called me down there to see them.

Bono: Well, as long as you got your complaint filed, they can't fire you. That's what one of them white fellows tell me.

Troy: I ain't worried about them firing me. They gonna fire me cause I asked a question? That's all I did. I went to Mr. Rand and asked him, "Why? Why you got the white mens driving and the colored lifting?" Told him, "what's the matter, don't I count? You think only white fellows got sense enough to drive a truck. That ain't no paper job! Hell, anybody can drive a truck. How come you got all whites driving and the colored lifting?" He told me "take it to the union." Well, hell, that's what I done! Now they wanna come up with this pack of lies.

Bono: I told Brownie if the man come and ask him any questions . . . just tell the truth! It ain't nothing but something they done trumped up on you cause you filed a complaint on them.

Troy: Brownie don't understand nothing. All I want them to do is change the job description. Give everybody a chance to drive the truck. Brownie can't see that. He ain't got that much sense.

Bono: How you figure he be making out with that gal be up at Taylors' all the time . . . that Alberta gal?

Troy: Same as you and me. Getting just as much as we is. Which is to say nothing.

Bono: It is, huh? I figure you doing a little better than me . . . and I ain't saying what I'm doing.

Troy: Aw, nigger, look here . . . I know you. If you had got anywhere near that gal, twenty minutes later you be looking to tell somebody. And the first one you gonna tell . . . that you gonna want to brag to . . . is me.

Bono: I ain't saying that. I see where you be eyeing her.

Troy: I eye all the women. I don't miss nothing. Don't never let nobody tell you Troy Maxson don't eye the women.

Bono: You been doing more than eyeing her. You done bought her a drink or two.

Troy: Hell yeah, I bought her a drink! What that mean? I bought you one, too. What that mean cause I buy her a drink? I'm just being polite.

Bono: It's all right to buy her one drink. That's what you call being polite. But when you wanna be buying two or three . . . that's what you call eyeing her.

Troy: Look here, as long as you known me . . . you ever known me to chase after women?

Bono: Hell yeah! Long as I done known you. You forgetting I knew you when.

Troy: Naw, I'm talking about since I been married to Rose?

Bono: Oh, not since you been married to Rose. Now, that's the truth, there. I can say that.

Troy: All right then! Case closed.

Bono: I see you be walking up around Alberta's house. You supposed to be at Taylors' and you be walking up around there.

Troy: What you watching where I'm walking for? I ain't watching after you.

Bono: I seen you walking around there more than once.

Troy: Hell, you liable to see me walking anywhere! That don't mean nothing cause you see me walking around there.

Bono: Where she come from anyway? She just kinda showed up one day.

Troy: Tallahassee. You can look at her and tell she one of them Florida gals. They got some big healthy women down there. Grow them right up out the ground. Got a little bit of Indian in her. Most of them niggers down in Florida got some Indian in them.

Bono: I don't know about that Indian part. But she damn sure big and healthy. Woman wear some big stockings. Got them great big old legs and hips as wide as the Mississippi River.

Troy: Legs don't mean nothing. You don't do nothing but push them out of the way. But them hips cushion the ride!

Bono: Troy, you ain't got no sense.

Troy: It's the truth! Like you riding on Goodyears!

Rose enters from the house. She is ten years younger than Troy, her devotion to him stems from her recognition of the possibilities of her life without him: a succession of abusive men and their babies, a life of partying and running the streets, the Church, or aloneness with its attendant pain and frustration. She recognizes Troy's spirit as a fine and illuminating one and she either ignores or forgives his faults, only some of which she recognizes. Though she doesn't drink, her presence is an integral part of the Friday night rituals. She alternates between the porch and the kitchen, where supper preparations are under way.

Rose: What you all out here getting into?

Troy: What you worried about what we getting into for? This is men talk, woman.

Rose: What I care what you all talking about? Bono, you gonna stay for supper?

Bono: No, I thank you, Rose. But Lucille say she cooking up a pot of pigfeet.

Troy: Pigfeet! Hell, I'm going home with you! Might even stay the night if you got some pigfeet. You got something in there to top them pigfeet, Rose?

Rose: I'm cooking up some chicken. I got some chicken and collard greens.

Troy: Well, go on back in the house and let me and Bono finish what we was talking about. This is men talk. I got some talk for you later. You know what kind of talk I mean. You go on and powder it up.

Rose: Troy Maxson, don't you start that now!

Troy (puts his arm around her): Aw, woman . . . come here. Look here, Bono . . . when I met this woman . . . I got out that place, say, "Hitch up my pony, saddle up my mare . . . there's a woman out there for me somewhere. I looked here. Looked there. Saw Rose and latched on to her." I latched on to her and told her — I'm gonna tell you the truth — I told her, "Baby, I don't wanna marry, I just wanna be your man." Rose told me . . . tell him what you told me, Rose.

Rose: I told him if he wasn't the marrying kind, then move out the way so the marrying kind could find me.

Troy: That's what she told me. "Nigger, you in my way. You blocking the view! Move out the way so I can find me a husband." I thought it over two or three days. Come back —

Rose: Ain't no two or three days nothing. You was back the same night.

Troy: Come back, told her . . . "Okay, baby . . . but I'm gonna buy me a banty rooster and put him out there in the backyard . . . and when he see a stranger come, he'll flap his wings and crow . . ." Look here, Bono, I could watch the front door by myself . . . it was that back door I was worried about.

Rose: Troy, you ought not talk like that. Troy ain't doing nothing but telling a lie.

Troy: Only thing is . . . when we first got married . . . forget the rooster . . . we ain't had no yard!

Bono: I hear you tell it. Me and Lucille was staying down there on Logan Street. Had two rooms with the outhouse in the back. I ain't mind the outhouse none. But when that goddamn wind blow through there in the winter . . . that's what I'm talking about! To this day I wonder why in the hell I ever stayed down there for six long years. But see, I didn't know I could do no better. I thought only white folks had inside toilets and things.

Rose: There's a lot of people don't know they can do no better than they doing now. That's just something you got to learn. A lot of folks still shop at Bella's.

Troy: Ain't nothing wrong with shopping at Bella's. She got fresh food.

Rose: I ain't said nothing about if she got fresh food. I'm talking about what she charge. She charge ten cents more than the A&P.

Troy: The A&P ain't never done nothing for me. I spends my money where I'm treated right. I go down to Bella, say, "I need a loaf of bread, I'll pay you Friday." She give it to me. What sense that make when I got money to go and spend it somewhere else and ignore the person who done right by me? That ain't in the Bible.

Rose: We ain't talking about what's in the Bible. What sense it make to shop there when she overcharge?

Troy: You shop where you want to. I'll do my shopping where the people been good to me.

Rose: Well, I don't think it's right for her to overcharge. That's all I was saying.

Bono: Look here . . . I got to get on. Lucille going be raising all kind of hell.

Troy: Where you going, nigger? We ain't finished this pint. Come here, finish this pint.

Bono: Well, hell, I am . . . if you ever turn the bottle loose.

Troy (hands him the bottle): The only thing I say about the A&P is I'm glad Cory got that job down there. Help him take care of his school clothes and things. Gabe done moved out and things getting tight around here. He got that job. . . . He can start to look out for himself.

Rose: Cory done went and got recruited by a college football team.

Troy: I told that boy about that football stuff. The white man ain't gonna let him get nowhere with that football. I told him when he first come to me with it. Now you come telling me he done went and got more tied up in it. He ought to go and get recruited in how to fix cars or something where he can make a living.

Rose: He ain't talking about making no living playing football. It's just something the boys in school do. They gonna send a recruiter by to talk to you. He'll tell you he ain't talking about making no living playing football. It's a honor to be recruited.

Troy: It ain't gonna get him nowhere. Bono'll tell you that.

Bono: If he be like you in the sports . . . he's gonna be all right. Ain't but two men ever played baseball as good as you. That's Babe Ruth° and Josh Gibson.° Them's the only two men ever hit more home runs than you.

Troy: What it ever get me? Ain't got a pot to piss in or a window to throw it out of.

Rose: Times have changed since you was playing baseball, Troy. That was before the war. Times have changed a lot since then.

Troy: How in hell they done changed?

Rose: They got lots of colored boys playing ball now. Baseball and football.

Bono: You right about that, Rose. Times have changed, Troy. You just come along too early.

Troy: There ought not never have been no time called too early! Now you take that fellow . . . what's that fellow they had playing right field for the Yankees back then? You know who I'm talking about, Bono. Used to play right field for the Yankees.

Rose: Selkirk?

Troy: Selkirk! That's it! Man batting .269, understand? .269. What kind of sense that make? I was hitting .432 with thirty-seven home runs! Man batting .269 and playing right field for the Yankees! I saw Josh Gibson's daughter yesterday. She walking around with raggedy shoes on her feet. Now I bet you Selkirk's daughter ain't walking around with raggedy shoes on her feet! I bet you that!

Rose: They got a lot of colored baseball players now. Jackie Robinson° was the first. Folks had to wait for Jackie Robinson.

Troy: I done seen a hundred niggers play baseball better than Jackie Robinson. Hell, I know some teams Jackie Robinson couldn't even make! What you talking about Jackie Robinson. Jackie Robinson wasn't nobody. I'm talking about if you could play ball then they ought to have let you play. Don't care

Babe Ruth (1895–1948): One of the greatest American baseball players.
Josh Gibson (1911–1947): Powerful baseball player known in the 1930s as the Babe Ruth of the Negro leagues.
Jackie Robinson (1919–1972): The first black baseball player in the major leagues (1947).

what color you were. Come telling me I come along too early. If you could play . . . then they ought to have let you play.

Troy takes a long drink from the bottle.

Rose: You gonna drink yourself to death. You don't need to be drinking like that.

Troy: Death ain't nothing. I done seen him. Done wrassled with him. You can't tell me nothing about death. Death ain't nothing but a fastball on the outside corner. And you know what I'll do to that! Lookee here, Bono . . . am I lying? You get one of them fastballs, about waist high, over the outside corner of the plate where you can get the meat of the bat on it . . . and good god! You can kiss it goodbye. Now, am I lying?

Bono: Naw, you telling the truth there. I seen you do it.

Troy: If I'm lying . . . that 450 feet worth of lying! *(Pause.)* That's all death is to me. A fastball on the outside corner.

Rose: I don't know why you want to get on talking about death.

Troy: Ain't nothing wrong with talking about death. That's part of life. Everybody gonna die. You gonna die, I'm gonna die. Bono's gonna die. Hell, we all gonna die.

Rose: But you ain't got to talk about it. I don't like to talk about it.

Troy: You the one brought it up. Me and Bono was talking about baseball . . . you tell me I'm gonna drink myself to death. Ain't that right, Bono? You know I don't drink this but one night out of the week. That's Friday night. I'm gonna drink just enough to where I can handle it. Then I cuts it loose. I leave it alone. So don't you worry about me drinking myself to death. 'Cause I ain't worried about Death. I done seen him. I done wrestled with him.

Look here, Bono . . . I looked up one day and Death was marching straight at me. Like Soldiers on Parade! The Army of Death was marching straight at me. The middle of July, 1941. It got real cold just like it be winter. It seem like Death himself reached out and touched me on the shoulder. He touch me just like I touch you. I got cold as ice and Death standing there grinning at me.

Rose: Troy, why don't you hush that talk.

Troy: I say . . . what you want, Mr. Death? You be wanting me? You done brought your army to be getting me? I looked him dead in the eye. I wasn't fearing nothing. I was ready to tangle. Just like I'm ready to tangle now. The Bible say be ever vigilant. That's why I don't get but so drunk. I got to keep watch.

Rose: Troy was right down there in Mercy Hospital. You remember he had pneumonia? Laying there with a fever talking plumb out of his head.

Troy: Death standing there staring at me . . . carrying that sickle in his hand. Finally he say, "You want bound over for another year?" See, just like that . . . "You want bound over for another year?" I told him, "Bound over hell! Let's settle this now!"

It seem like he kinda fell back when I said that, and all the cold went out of me. I reached down and grabbed that sickle and threw it just as far as I could throw it . . . and me and him commenced to wrestling.

We wrestled for three days and three nights. I can't say where I found the strength from. Every time it seemed like he was gonna get the best of me, I'd reach way down deep inside myself and find the strength to do him one better.

Rose: Every time Troy tell that story he find different ways to tell it. Different things to make up about it.

Troy: I ain't making up nothing. I'm telling you the facts of what happened. I wrestled with Death for three days and three nights and I'm standing here to tell you about it. *(Pause.)* All right. At the end of the third night we done weakened each other to where we can't hardly move. Death stood up, throwed on his robe . . . had him a white robe with a hood on it. He throwed on that robe and went off to look for his sickle. Say, "I'll be back." Just like that. "I'll be back." I told him, say, "Yeah, but . . . you gonna have to find me!" I wasn't no fool. I wan't going looking for him. Death ain't nothing to play with. And I know he's gonna get me. I know I got to join his army . . . his camp followers. But as long as I keep my strength and see him coming . . . as long as I keep up my vigilance . . . he's gonna have to fight to get me. I ain't going easy.

Bono: Well, look here, since you got to keep up your vigilance . . . let me have the bottle.

Troy: Aw hell, I shouldn't have told you that part. I should have left out that part.

Rose: Troy be talking that stuff and half the time don't even know what he be talking about.

Troy: Bono know me better than that.

Bono: That's right. I know you. I know you got some Uncle Remus° in your blood. You got more stories than the devil got sinners.

Troy: Aw hell, I done seen him too! Done talked with the devil.

Rose: Troy, don't nobody wanna be hearing all that stuff.

Lyons enters the yard from the street. Thirty-four years old, Troy's son by a previous marriage, he sports a neatly trimmed goatee, sport coat, white shirt, tieless and buttoned at the collar. Though he fancies himself a musician, he is more caught up in the rituals and "idea" of being a musician than in the actual practice of the music. He has come to borrow money from Troy, and while he knows he will be successful, he is uncertain as to what extent his lifestyle will be held up to scrutiny and ridicule.

Lyons: Hey, Pop.

Troy: What you come "Hey, Popping" me for?

Lyons: How you doing, Rose? *(He kisses her.)* Mr. Bono. How you doing?

Bono: Hey, Lyons . . . how you been?

Troy: He must have been doing all right. I ain't seen him around here last week.

Rose: Troy, leave your boy alone. He come by to see you and you wanna start all that nonsense.

Troy: I ain't bothering Lyons. *(Offers him the bottle.)* Here . . . get you a drink. We got an understanding. I know why he come by to see me and he know I know.

Uncle Remus: Black storyteller who recounts traditional black tales in the book by Joel Chandler Harris.

Lyons: Come on, Pop . . . I just stopped by to say hi . . . see how you was doing.

Troy: You ain't stopped by yesterday.

Rose: You gonna stay for supper, Lyons? I got some chicken cooking in the oven.

Lyons: No, Rose . . . thanks. I was just in the neighborhood and thought I'd stop by for a minute.

Troy: You was in the neighborhood all right, nigger. You telling the truth there. You was in the neighborhood cause it's my payday.

Lyons: Well, hell, since you mentioned it . . . let me have ten dollars.

Troy: I'll be damned! I'll die and go to hell and play blackjack with the devil before I give you ten dollars.

Bono: That's what I wanna know about . . . that devil you done seen.

Lyons: What . . . Pop done seen the devil? You too much, Pops.

Troy: Yeah, I done seen him. Talked to him too!

Rose: You ain't seen no devil. I done told you that man ain't had nothing to do with the devil. Anything you can't understand, you want to call it the devil.

Troy: Look here, Bono . . . I went down to see Hertzberger about some furniture. Got three rooms for two-ninety-eight. That what it say on the radio. "Three rooms . . . two-ninety-eight." Even made up a little song about it. Go down there . . . man tell me I can't get no credit. I'm working every day and can't get no credit. What to do? I got an empty house with some raggedy furniture in it. Cory ain't got no bed. He's sleeping on a pile of rags on the floor. Working every day and can't get no credit. Come back here — Rose'll tell you — madder than hell. Sit down . . . try to figure what I'm gonna do. Come a knock on the door. Ain't been living here but three days. Who know I'm here? Open the door . . . devil standing there bigger than life. White fellow . . . white fellow . . . got on good clothes and everything. Standing there with a clipboard in his hand. I ain't had to say nothing. First words come out of his mouth was . . . "I understand you need some furniture and can't get no credit." I liked to fell over. He say, "I'll give you all the credit you want, but you got to pay the interest on it." I told him, "Give me three rooms worth and charge whatever you want." Next day a truck pulled up here and two men unloaded them three rooms. Man what drove the truck give me a book. Say send ten dollars, first of every month to the address in the book and everything will be all right. Say if I miss a payment the devil was coming back and it'll be hell to pay. That was fifteen years ago. To this day . . . the first of the month I send my ten dollars, Rose'll tell you.

Rose: Troy lying.

Troy: I ain't never seen that man since. Now you tell me who else that could have been but the devil? I ain't sold my soul or nothing like that, you understand. Naw, I wouldn't have truck with the devil about nothing like that. I got my furniture and pays my ten dollars the first of the month just like clockwork.

Bono: How long you say you been paying this ten dollars a month?

Troy: Fifteen years!

Bono: Hell, ain't you finished paying for it yet? How much the man done charged you?

Troy: Ah hell, I done paid for it. I done paid for it ten times over! The fact is I'm scared to stop paying it.

Rose: Troy lying. We got that furniture from Mr. Glickman. He ain't paying no ten dollars a month to nobody.

Troy: Aw hell, woman. Bono know I ain't that big a fool.

Lyons: I was just getting ready to say . . . I know where there's a bridge for sale.

Troy: Look here, I'll tell you this . . . it don't matter to me if he was the devil. It don't matter if the devil give credit. Somebody has got to give it.

Rose: It ought to matter. You going around talking about having truck with the devil . . . God's the one you gonna have to answer to. He's the one gonna be at the Judgment.

Lyons: Yeah, well, look here, Pop . . . let me have that ten dollars. I'll give it back to you. Bonnie got a job working at the hospital.

Troy: What I tell you, Bono? The only time I see this nigger is when he wants something. That's the only time I see him.

Lyons: Come on, Pop, Mr. Bono don't want to hear all that. Let me have the ten dollars. I told you Bonnie working.

Troy: What that mean to me? "Bonnie working." I don't care if she working. Go ask her for the ten dollars if she working. Talking about "Bonnie working." Why ain't you working?

Lyons: Aw, Pop, you know I can't find no decent job. Where am I gonna get a job at? You know I can't get no job.

Troy: I told you I know some people down there. I can get you on the rubbish if you want to work. I told you that the last time you came by here asking me for something.

Lyons: Naw, Pop . . . thanks. That ain't for me. I don't wanna be carrying nobody's rubbish. I don't wanna be punching nobody's time clock.

Troy: What's the matter, you too good to carry people's rubbish? Where you think that ten dollars you talking about come from? I'm just supposed to haul people's rubbish and give my money to you cause you too lazy to work. You too lazy to work and wanna know why you ain't got what I got.

Rose: What hospital Bonnie working at? Mercy?

Lyons: She's down at Passavant working in the laundry.

Troy: I ain't got nothing as it is. I give you that ten dollars and I got to eat beans the rest of the week. Naw . . . you ain't getting no ten dollars here.

Lyons: You ain't got to be eating no beans. I don't know why you wanna say that.

Troy: I ain't got no extra money. Gabe done moved over to Miss Pearl's paying her the rent and things done got tight around here. I can't afford to be giving you every payday.

Lyons: I ain't asked you to give me nothing. I asked you to loan me ten dollars. I know you got ten dollars.

Troy: Yeah, I got it. You know why I got it? Cause I don't throw my money away out there in the streets. You living the fast life . . . wanna be a musician . . . running around in them clubs and things . . . then, you learn to take care of yourself. You ain't gonna find me going and asking nobody for nothing. I done spent too many years without.

Lyons: You and me is two different people, Pop.

Troy: I done learned my mistake and learned to do what's right by it. You still trying to get something for nothing. Life don't owe you nothing. You owe it to yourself. Ask Bono. He'll tell you I'm right.

Lyons: You got your way of dealing with the world . . . I got mine. The only thing that matters to me is the music.

Troy: Yeah, I can see that! It don't matter how you gonna eat . . . where your next dollar is coming from. You telling the truth there.

Lyons: I know I got to eat. But I got to live too. I need something that gonna help me to get out of the bed in the morning. Make me feel like I belong in the world. I don't bother nobody. I just stay with the music cause that's the only way I can find to live in the world. Otherwise there ain't no telling what I might do. Now I don't come criticizing you and how you live. I just come by to ask you for ten dollars. I don't wanna hear all that about how I live.

Troy: Boy, your mamma did a hell of a job raising you.

Lyons: You can't change me, Pop. I'm thirty-four years old. If you wanted to change me, you should have been there when I was growing up. I come by to see you . . . ask for ten dollars and you want to talk about how I was raised. You don't know nothing about how I was raised.

Rose: Let the boy have ten dollars, Troy.

Troy (to Lyons): What the hell you looking at me for? I ain't got no ten dollars. You know what I do with my money. *(To Rose.)* Give him ten dollars if you want him to have it.

Rose: I will. Just as soon as you turn it loose.

Troy (handing Rose the money): There it is. Seventy-six dollars and forty-two cents. You see this, Bono? Now, I ain't gonna get but six of that back.

Rose: You ought to stop telling that lie. Here, Lyons. *(She hands him the money.)*

Lyons: Thanks, Rose. Look . . . I got to run . . . I'll see you later.

Troy: Wait a minute. You gonna say, "thanks, Rose" and ain't gonna look to see where she got that ten dollars from? See how they do me, Bono?

Lyons: I know she got it from you, Pop. Thanks. I'll give it back to you.

Troy: There he go telling another lie. Time I see that ten dollars . . . he'll be owing me thirty more.

Lyons: See you, Mr. Bono.

Bono: Take care, Lyons!

Lyons: Thanks, Pop. I'll see you again.

Lyons exits the yard.

Troy: I don't know why he don't go and get him a decent job and take care of that woman he got.

Bono: He'll be all right, Troy. The boy is still young.

Troy: The *boy* is thirty-four years old.

Rose: Let's not get off into all that.

Bono: Look here . . . I got to be going. I got to be getting on. Lucille gonna be waiting.

Troy (puts his arm around Rose): See this woman, Bono? I love this woman. I love this woman so much it hurts. I love her so much . . . I done run out of ways of loving her. So I got to go back to basics. Don't you come by my house Monday morning talking about time to go to work . . . 'cause I'm still gonna be stroking!

Rose: Troy! Stop it now!

Bono: I ain't paying him no mind, Rose. That ain't nothing but gin-talk. Go on, Troy. I'll see you Monday.

Troy: Don't you come by my house, nigger! I done told you what I'm gonna be doing.

The lights go down to black.

Scene II

The lights come up on Rose hanging up clothes. She hums and sings softly to herself. It is the following morning.

Rose (sings): Jesus, be a fence all around me every day
Jesus, I want you to protect me as I travel on my way.
Jesus, be a fence all around me every day.

Troy enters from the house.

Jesus, I want you to protect me
As I travel on my way.

(To Troy.) 'Morning, You ready for breakfast? I can fix it soon as I finish hanging up these clothes?

Troy: I got the coffee on. That'll be all right. I'll just drink some of that this morning.

Rose: That 651 hit yesterday. That's the second time this month. Miss Pearl hit for a dollar . . . seem like those that need the least always get lucky. Poor folks can't get nothing.

Troy: Them numbers don't know nobody. I don't know why you fool with them. You and Lyons both.

Rose: It's something to do.

Troy: You ain't doing nothing but throwing your money away.

Rose: Troy, you know I don't play foolishly. I just play a nickel here and a nickel there.

Troy: That's two nickels you done thrown away.

Rose: Now I hit sometimes . . . that makes up for it. It always comes in handy when I do hit. I don't hear you complaining then.

Troy: I ain't complaining now. I just say it's foolish. Trying to guess out of six hundred ways which way the number gonna come. If I had all the money niggers, these Negroes, throw away on numbers for one week — just one week — I'd be a rich man.

Rose: Well, you wishing and calling it foolish ain't gonna stop folks from playing numbers. That's one thing for sure. Besides . . . some good things come from playing numbers. Look where Pope done bought him that restaurant off of numbers.

Troy: I can't stand niggers like that. Man ain't had two dimes to rub together. He walking around with his shoes all run over bumming money for cigarettes. All right. Got lucky there and hit the numbers . . .

Rose: Troy, I know all about it.

Troy: Had good sense, I'll say that for him. He ain't throwed his money away. I seen niggers hit the numbers and go through two thousand dollars in four days. Man bought him that restaurant down there . . . fixed it up real nice . . . and then didn't want nobody to come in it! A Negro go in there and can't get no kind of service. I seen a white fellow come in there and order a bowl of stew. Pope picked all the meat out the pot for him. Man ain't had nothing but a bowl of meat! Negro come behind him and ain't got nothing but the potatoes and carrots. Talking about what numbers do for people, you picked a wrong example. Ain't done nothing but make a worser fool out of him than he was before.

Rose: Troy, you ought to stop worrying about what happened at work yesterday.

Troy: I ain't worried. Just told me to be down there at the Commissioner's office on Friday. Everybody think they gonna fire me. I ain't worried about them firing me. You ain't got to worry about that. *(Pause.)* Where's Cory? Cory in the house? *(Calls.)* Cory?

Rose: He gone out.

Troy: Out, huh? He gone out 'cause he know I want him to help me with this fence. I know how he is. That boy scared of work.

Gabriel enters. He comes halfway down the alley and, hearing Troy's voice, stops.

Troy (continues): He ain't done a lick of work in his life.

Rose: He had to go to football practice. Coach wanted them to get in a little extra practice before the season start.

Troy: I got his practice . . . running out of here before he get his chores done.

Rose: Troy, what is wrong with you this morning? Don't nothing set right with you. Go on back in there and go to bed . . . get up on the other side.

Troy: Why something got to be wrong with me? I ain't said nothing wrong with me.

Rose: You got something to say about everything. First it's the numbers . . . then it's the way the man runs his restaurant . . . then you done got on Cory. What's it gonna be next? Take a look up there and see if the weather suits you . . . or is it gonna be how you gonna put up the fence with the clothes hanging in the yard.

Troy: You hit the nail on the head then.

Rose: I know you like I know the back of my hand. Go on in there and get you some coffee . . . see if that straighten you up. 'Cause you ain't right this morning.

Troy starts into the house and sees Gabriel. Gabriel starts singing. Troy's brother, he is seven years younger than Troy. Injured in World War II, he has a metal plate in his head. He carries an old trumpet tied around his waist and believes with every fiber of his being that he is the Archangel Gabriel.° He carries a chipped basket with an assortment of discarded fruits and vegetables he has picked up in the strip district and which he attempts to sell.

Archangel Gabriel: Considered one of God's primary messengers in the Old and New Testaments.

Gabriel (singing): Yes, ma'am, I got plums
You ask me how I sell them
Oh ten cents apiece
Three for a quarter
Come and buy now
'Cause I'm here today
And tomorrow I'll be gone

Gabriel enters.

Hey, Rose!

Rose: How you doing, Gabe?

Gabriel: There's Troy . . . Hey, Troy!

Troy: Hey, Gabe.

Exit into kitchen.

Rose (to Gabriel): What you got there?

Gabriel: You know what I got, Rose. I got fruits and vegetables.

Rose (looking in basket): Where's all these plums you talking about?

Gabriel: I ain't got no plums today, Rose. I was just singing that. Have some tomorrow. Put me in a big order for plums. Have enough plums tomorrow for St. Peter and everybody.

Troy reenters from kitchen, crosses to steps.

(To Rose.) Troy's mad at me.

Troy: I ain't mad at you. What I got to be mad at you about? You ain't done nothing to me.

Gabriel: I just moved over to Miss Pearl's to keep out from in your way. I ain't mean no harm by it.

Troy: Who said anything about that? I ain't said anything about that.

Gabriel: You ain't mad at me, is you?

Troy: Naw . . . I ain't mad at you, Gabe. If I was mad at you I'd tell you about it.

Gabriel: Got me two rooms. In the basement. Got my own door too. Wanna see my key? *(He holds up a key.)* That's my own key! Ain't nobody else got a key like that. That's my key! My two rooms!

Troy: Well, that's good, Gabe. You got your own key . . . that's good.

Rose: You hungry, Gabe? I was just fixing to cook Troy his breakfast.

Gabriel: I'll take some biscuits. You got some biscuits? Did you know when I was in heaven . . . every morning me and St. Peter° would sit down by the gate and eat some big fat biscuits? Oh, yeah! We had us a good time. We'd sit there and eat us them biscuits and then St. Peter would go off to sleep and tell me to wake him up when it's time to open the gates for the judgment.

Rose: Well, come on . . . I'll make up a batch of biscuits.

Rose exits into the house.

Gabriel: Troy . . . St. Peter got your name in the book. I seen it. It say . . . Troy

St. Peter: One of Jesus's disciples, believed to be the keeper of the gates to Heaven.

Maxson. I say . . . I know him! He got the same name like what I got. That's my brother!

Troy: How many times you gonna tell me that, Gabe?

Gabriel: Ain't got my name in the book. Don't have to have my name. I done died and went to heaven. He got your name though. One morning St. Peter was looking at his book . . . marking it up for the judgment . . . and he let me see your name. Got it in there under M. Got Rose's name . . . I ain't seen it like I seen yours . . . but I know it's in there. He got a great big book. Got everybody's name what was ever been born. That's what he told me. But I seen your name. Seen it with my own eyes.

Troy: Go on in the house there. Rose going to fix you something to eat.

Gabriel: Oh, I ain't hungry. I done had breakfast with Aunt Jemimah. She come by and cooked me up a whole mess of flapjacks. Remember how we used to eat them flapjacks?

Troy: Go on in the house and get you something to eat now.

Gabriel: I got to sell my plums. I done sold some tomatoes. Got me two quarters. Wanna see? *(He shows Troy his quarters.)* I'm gonna save them and buy me a new horn so St. Peter can hear me when it's time to open the gates. *(Gabriel stops suddenly. Listens.)* Hear that? That's the hellhounds. I got to chase them out of here. Go on get out of here! Get out!

Gabriel exits singing.

Better get ready for the judgment
Better get ready for the judgment
My Lord is coming down

Rose enters from the house

Troy: He's gone off somewhere.

Gabriel (offstage): Better get ready for the judgment
Better get ready for the judgment morning
Better get ready for the judgment
My God is coming down

Rose: He ain't eating right. Miss Pearl say she can't get him to eat nothing.

Troy: What you want me to do about it, Rose? I done did everything I can for the man. I can't make him get well. Man got half his head blown away . . . what you expect?

Rose: Seem like something ought to be done to help him.

Troy: Man don't bother nobody. He just mixed up from that metal plate he got in his head. Ain't no sense for him to go back into the hospital.

Rose: Least he be eating right. They can help him take care of himself.

Troy: Don't nobody wanna be locked up, Rose. What you wanna lock him up for? Man go over there and fight the war . . . messin' around with them Japs, get half his head blown off . . . and they give him a lousy three thousand dollars. And I had to swoop down on that.

Rose: Is you fixing to go into that again?

Troy: That's the only way I got a roof over my head . . . cause of that metal plate.

Rose: Ain't no sense you blaming yourself for nothing. Gabe wasn't in no condition to manage that money. You done what was right by him. Can't nobody say you ain't done what was right by him. Look how long you took care of him . . . . till he wanted to have his own place and moved over there with Miss Pearl.

Troy: That ain't what I'm saying, woman! I'm just stating the facts. If my brother didn't have that metal plate in his head . . . . I wouldn't have a pot to piss in or a window to throw it out of. And I'm fifty-three years old. Now see if you can understand that!

Troy gets up from the porch and starts to exit the yard.

Rose: Where you going off to? You been running out of here every Saturday for weeks. I thought you was gonna work on this fence?

Troy: I'm gonna walk down to Taylors'. Listen to the ball game. I'll be back in a bit. I'll work on it when I get back.

He exits the yard. The lights go to black.

Scene III

The lights come up on the yard. It is four hours later. Rose is taking down the clothes from the line. Cory enters carrying his football equipment.

Rose: Your daddy like to had a fit with you running out of here this morning without doing your chores.

Cory: I told you I had to go to practice.

Rose: He say you were supposed to help him with this fence.

Cory: He been saying that the last four or five Saturdays, and then he don't never do nothing, but go down to Taylors. Did you tell him about the recruiter?

Rose: Yeah, I told him.

Cory: What he say?

Rose: He ain't said nothing too much. You get in there and get started on your chores before he gets back. Go on and scrub down them steps before he gets back here hollering and carrying on.

Cory: I'm hungry. What you got to eat, Mama?

Rose: Go on and get started on your chores. I got some meat loaf in there. Go on and make you a sandwich . . . and don't leave no mess in there.

Cory exits into the house. Rose continues to take down the clothes. Troy enters the yard and sneaks up and grabs her from behind.

Troy! Go on, now. You liked to scared me to death. What was the score of the game? Lucille had me on the phone and I couldn't keep up with it.

Troy: What I care about the game? Come here, woman. *(He tries to kiss her.)*

Rose: I thought you went down Taylors' to listen to the game. Go on, Troy! You supposed to be putting up this fence.

Troy (attempting to kiss her again): I'll put it up when I finish with what is at hand.

Rose: Go on, Troy. I ain't studying you.

Troy (chasing after her): I'm studying you . . . fixing to do my homework!

Rose: Troy, you better leave me alone.

Troy: Where's Cory? That boy brought his butt home yet?
Rose: He's in the house doing his chores.
Troy (calling): Cory! Get your butt out here, boy!

Rose exits into the house with the laundry. Troy goes over to the pile of wood, picks up a board, and starts sawing. Cory enters from the house.

Troy: You just now coming in here from leaving this morning?
Cory: Yeah, I had to go to football practice.
Troy: Yeah, what?
Cory: Yessir.
Troy: I ain't but two seconds off you noway. The garbage sitting in there overflowing . . . you ain't done none of your chores . . . and you come in here talking about "Yeah."
Cory: I was just getting ready to do my chores now, Pop . . .
Troy: Your first chore is to help me with this fence on Saturday. Everything else come after that. Now get that saw and cut them boards.

Cory takes the saw and begins cutting the boards. Troy continues working. There is a long pause.

Cory: Hey, Pop . . . why don't you buy a TV?
Troy: What I want with a TV? What I want one of them for?
Cory: Everybody got one. Earl, Ba Bra . . . Jesse!
Troy: I ain't asked you who had one. I say what I want with one?
Cory: So you can watch it. They got lots of things on TV. Baseball games and everything. We could watch the World Series.
Troy: Yeah . . . and how much this TV cost?
Cory: I don't know. They got them on sale for around two hundred dollars.
Troy: Two hundred dollars, huh?
Cory: That ain't that much, Pop.
Troy: Naw, it's just two hundred dollars. See that roof you got over your head at night? Let me tell you something about that roof. It's been over ten years since that roof was last tarred. See now . . . the snow come this winter and sit up there on that roof like it is . . . and it's gonna seep inside. It's just gonna be a little bit . . . ain't gonna hardly notice it. Then the next thing you know, it's gonna be leaking all over the house. Then the wood rot from all that water and you gonna need a whole new roof. Now, how much you think it cost to get that roof tarred?
Cory: I don't know.
Troy: Two hundred and sixty-four dollars . . . cash money. While you thinking about a TV, I got to be thinking about the roof . . . and whatever else go wrong here. Now if you had two hundred dollars, what would you do . . . fix the roof or buy a TV?
Cory: I'd buy a TV. Then when the roof started to leak . . . when it needed fixing . . . I'd fix it.
Troy: Where you gonna get the money from? You done spent it for a TV. You gonna sit up and watch the water run all over your brand new TV.
Cory: Aw, Pop. You got money. I know you do.
Troy: Where I got it at, huh?
Cory: You got it in the bank.

Troy: You wanna see my bankbook? You wanna see that seventy-three dollars and twenty-two cents I got sitting up in there.

Cory: You ain't got to pay for it all at one time. You can put a down payment on it and carry it on home with you.

Troy: Not me. I ain't gonna owe nobody nothing if I can help it. Miss a payment and they come and snatch it right out your house. Then what you got? Now, soon as I get two hundred dollars clear, then I'll buy a TV. Right now, as soon as I get two hundred and sixty-four dollars, I'm gonna have this roof tarred.

Cory: Aw . . . Pop!

Troy: You go on and get you two hundred dollars and buy one if ya want it. I got better things to do with my money.

Cory: I can't get no two hundred dollars. I ain't never seen two hundred dollars.

Troy: I'll tell you what . . . you get you a hundred dollars and I'll put the other hundred with it.

Cory: All right, I'm gonna show you.

Troy: You gonna show me how you can cut them boards right now.

Cory begins to cut the boards. There is a long pause.

Cory: The Pirates won today. That makes five in a row.

Troy: I ain't thinking about the Pirates. Got an all-white team. Got that boy . . . that Puerto Rican boy . . . Clemente. Don't even half-play him. That boy could be something if they give him a chance. Play him one day and sit him on the bench the next.

Cory: He gets a lot of chances to play.

Troy: I'm talking about playing regular. Playing every day so you can get your timing. That's what I'm talking about.

Cory: They got some white guys on the team that don't play every day. You can't play everybody at the same time.

Troy: If they got a white fellow sitting on the bench . . . you can bet your last dollar he can't play! The colored guy got to be twice as good before he get on the team. That's why I don't want you to get all tied up in them sports. Man on the team and what it get him? They got colored on the team and don't use them. Same as not having them. All them teams the same.

Cory: The Braves got Hank Aaron and Wes Covington. Hank Aaron hit two home runs today. That makes forty-three.

Troy: Hank Aaron ain't nobody. That what you supposed to do. That's how you supposed to play the game. Ain't nothing to it. It's just a matter of timing . . . getting the right follow-through. Hell, I can hit forty-three home runs right now!

Cory: Not off no major-league pitching, you couldn't.

Troy: We had better pitching in the Negro leagues. I hit seven home runs off of Satchel Paige.° You can't get no better than that!

Cory: Sandy Koufax. He's leading the league in strikeouts.

Troy: I ain't thinking of no Sandy Koufax.

Satchel Paige (1906?–1982): Legendary black pitcher in the Negro leagues.

Cory: You got Warren Spahn and Lew Burdette. I bet you couldn't hit no home runs off of Warren Spahn.

Troy: I'm through with it now. You go on and cut them boards. *(Pause.)* Your mama tell me you done got recruited by a college football team? Is that right?

Cory: Yeah. Coach Zellman say the recruiter gonna be coming by to talk to you. Get you to sign the permission papers.

Troy: I thought you supposed to be working down there at the A&P. Ain't you suppose to be working down there after school?

Cory: Mr. Stawicki say he gonna hold my job for me until after the football season. Say starting next week I can work weekends.

Troy: I thought we had an understanding about this football stuff? You suppose to keep up with your chores and hold that job down at the A&P. Ain't been around here all day on a Saturday. Ain't none of your chores done . . . and now you telling me you done quit your job.

Cory: I'm going to be working weekends.

Troy: You damn right you are! And ain't no need for nobody coming around here to talk to me about signing nothing.

Cory: Hey, Pop . . . you can't do that. He's coming all the way from North Carolina.

Troy: I don't care where he coming from. The white man ain't gonna let you get nowhere with that football noway. You go on and get your book-learning so you can work yourself up in that A&P or learn how to fix cars or build houses or something, get you a trade. That way you have something can't nobody take away from you. You go on and learn how to put your hands to some good use. Besides hauling people's garbage.

Cory: I get good grades, Pop. That's why the recruiter wants to talk with you. You got to keep up your grades to get recruited. This way I'll be going to college. I'll get a chance . . .

Troy: First you gonna get your butt down there to the A&P and get your job back.

Cory: Mr. Stawicki done already hired somebody else 'cause I told him I was playing football.

Troy: You a bigger fool than I thought . . . to let somebody take away your job so you can play some football. Where you gonna get your money to take out your girlfriend and whatnot? What kind of foolishness is that to let somebody take away your job?

Cory: I'm still gonna be working weekends.

Troy: Naw . . . naw. You getting your butt out of here and finding you another job.

Cory: Come on, Pop! I got to practice. I can't work after school and play football too. The team needs me. That's what Coach Zellman say . . .

Troy: I don't care what nobody else say. I'm the boss . . . you understand? I'm the boss around here. I do the only saying what counts.

Cory: Come on, Pop!

Troy: I asked you . . . did you understand?

Cory: Yeah . . .

Troy: What?!

Cory: Yessir.

Troy: You go on down there to that A&P and see if you can get your job back. If you can't do both . . . then you quit the football team. You've got to take the crookeds with the straights.

Cory: Yessir. *(Pause.)* Can I ask you a question?

Troy: What the hell you wanna ask me? Mr. Stawicki the one you got the questions for.

Cory: How come you ain't never liked me?

Troy: Liked you? Who the hell say I got to like you? What law is there say I got to like you? Wanna stand up in my face and ask a damn fool-ass question like that. Talking about liking somebody. Come here, boy, when I talk to you.

Cory comes over to where Troy is working. He stands slouched over and Troy shoves him on his shoulder.

Straighten up, goddammit! I asked you a question . . . what law is there say I got to like you?

Cory: None.

Troy: Well, all right then! Don't you eat every day? *(Pause.)* Answer me when I talk to you! Don't you eat every day?

Cory: Yeah.

Troy: Nigger, as long as you in my house, you put that sir on the end of it when you talk to me!

Cory: Yes . . . sir.

Troy: You eat every day.

Cory: Yessir!

Troy: Got a roof over your head.

Cory: Yessir!

Troy: Got clothes on your back.

Cory: Yessir.

Troy: Why you think that is?

Cory: Cause of you.

Troy: Ah, hell I know it's cause of me . . . but why do you think that is?

Cory (hesitant): Cause you like me.

Troy: Like you? I go out of here every morning . . . bust my butt . . . putting up with them crackers° every day . . . cause I like you? You are the biggest fool I ever saw. *(Pause.)* It's my job. It's my responsibility! You understand that? A man got to take care of his family. You live in my house . . . sleep you behind on my bedclothes . . . fill you belly up with my food . . . cause you my son. You my flesh and blood. Not cause I like you! Cause it's my duty to take care of you. I owe a responsibility to you! Let's get this straight right here . . . before it go along any further . . . I ain't got to like you. Mr. Rand don't give me my money come payday cause he likes me. He give me cause he owe me. I done give you everything I had to give you. I gave you your life! Me and your mama worked that out between us. And liking your black ass wasn't part of the bargain. Don't you try and go through life wor-

crackers: White people, often used to refer disparagingly to poor whites.

rying about if somebody like you or not. You best be making sure they doing right by you. You understand what I'm saying, boy?

Cory: Yessir.

Troy: Then get the hell out of my face, and get on down to that A&P.

Rose has been standing behind the screen door for much of the scene. She enters as Cory exits.

Rose: Why don't you let the boy go ahead and play football, Troy? Ain't no harm in that. He's just trying to be like you with the sports.

Troy: I don't want him to be like me! I want him to move as far away from my life as he can get. You the only decent thing that ever happened to me. I wish him that. But I don't wish him a thing else from my life. I decided seventeen years ago that boy wasn't getting involved in no sports. Not after what they did to me in the sports.

Rose: Troy, why don't you admit you was too old to play in the major leagues? For once . . . . why don't you admit that?

Troy: What do you mean too old? Don't come telling me I was too old. I just wasn't the right color. Hell, I'm fifty-three years old and can do better than Selkirk's .269 right now!

Rose: How's was you gonna play ball when you were over forty? Sometimes I can't get no sense out of you.

Troy: I got good sense, woman. I got sense enough not to let my boy get hurt over playing no sports. You been mothering that boy too much. Worried about if people like him.

Rose: Everything that boy do . . . he do for you. He wants you to say "Good job, son." That's all.

Troy: Rose, I ain't got time for that. He's alive. He's healthy. He's got to make his own way. I made mine. Ain't nobody gonna hold his hand when he get out there in that world.

Rose: Times have changed from when you was young, Troy. People change. The world's changing around you and you can't even see it.

Troy (slow, methodical): Woman . . . I do the best I can do. I come in here every Friday. I carry a sack of potatoes and a bucket of lard. You all line up at the door with your hands out. I give you the lint from my pockets. I give you my sweat and my blood. I ain't got no tears. I done spent them. We go upstairs in that room at night . . . and I fall down on you and try to blast a hole into forever. I get up Monday morning . . . find my lunch on the table. I go out. Make my way. Find my strength to carry me through to the next Friday. *(Pause.)* That's all I got, Rose. That's all I got to give. I can't give nothing else.

Troy exits into the house. The lights go down to black.

Scene IV

It is Friday. Two weeks later. Cory starts out of the house with his football equipment. The phone rings.

Cory (calling): I got it! *(He answers the phone and stands in the screen door talking.)* Hello? Hey, Jesse. Naw . . . I was just getting ready to leave now.

Rose (calling): Cory!

Cory: I told you, man, them spikes is all tore up. You can use them if you want, but they ain't no good. Earl got some spikes.

Rose (calling): Cory!

Cory (calling to Rose): Mam? I'm talking to Jesse. *(Into phone.)* When she say that? *(Pause.)* Aw, you lying, man. I'm gonna tell her you said that.

Rose (calling): Cory, don't you go nowhere!

Cory: I got to go to the game, Ma! *(Into the phone.)* Yeah, hey, look, I'll talk to you later. Yeah, I'll meet you over Earl's house. Later. Bye, Ma.

Cory exits the house and starts out the yard.

Rose: Cory, where you going off to? You got that stuff all pulled out and thrown all over your room.

Cory (in the yard): I was looking for my spikes. Jesse wanted to borrow my spikes.

Rose: Get up there and get that cleaned up before your daddy get back in here.

Cory: I got to go to the game! I'll clean it up *when I get back.*

Cory exits.

Rose: That's all he need to do is see that room all messed up.

Rose exits into the house. Troy and Bono enter the yard. Troy is dressed in clothes other than his work clothes.

Bono: He told him the same thing he told you. Take it to the union.

Troy: Brownie ain't got that much sense. Man wasn't thinking about nothing. He wait until I confront them on it . . . then he wanna come crying seniority. *(Calls.)* Hey, Rose!

Bono: I wish I could have seen Mr. Rand's face when he told you.

Troy: He couldn't get it out of his mouth! Liked to bit his tongue! When they called me down there to the Commissioner's office . . . he thought they was gonna fire me. Like everybody else.

Bono: I didn't think they was gonna fire you. I thought they was gonna put you on the warning paper.

Troy: Hey, Rose! *(To Bono.)* Yeah, Mr. Rand like to bit his tongue.

Troy breaks the seal on the bottle, takes a drink, and hands it to Bono.

Bono: I see you run right down to Taylors' and told that Alberta gal.

Troy (calling): Hey Rose! *(To Bono.)* I told everybody. Hey, Rose! I went down there to cash my check.

Rose (entering from the house): Hush all that hollering, man! I know you out here. What they say down there at the Commissioner's office?

Troy: You supposed to come when I call you, woman. Bono'll tell you that. *(To Bono.)* Don't Lucille come when you call her?

Rose: Man, hush your mouth. I ain't no dog . . . talk about "come when you call me."

Troy (puts his arm around Rose): You hear this, Bono? I had me an old dog used to get uppity like that. You say, "C'mere, Blue!" . . . and he just lay there and look at you. End up getting a stick and chasing him away trying to make him come.

Rose: I ain't studying you and your dog. I remember you used to sing that old song.

Troy (he sings): Hear it ring! Hear it ring! I had a dog his name was Blue.

Rose: Don't nobody wanna hear you sing that old song.

Troy (sings): You know Blue was mighty true.

Rose: Used to have Cory running around here singing that song.

Bono: Hell, I remember that song myself.

Troy (sings): You know Blue was a good old dog.
Blue treed a possum in a hollow log.
That was my daddy's song. My daddy made up that song.

Rose: I don't care who made it up. Don't nobody wanna hear you sing it.

Troy (makes a song like calling a dog): Come here, woman.

Rose: You come in here carrying on, I reckon they ain't fired you. What they say down there at the Commissioner's office?

Troy: Look here, Rose . . . Mr. Rand called me into his office today when I got back from talking to them people down there . . . it come from up top . . . he called me in and told me they was making me a driver.

Rose: Troy, you kidding!

Troy: No I ain't. Ask Bono.

Rose: Well, that's great, Troy. Now you don't have to hassle them people no more.

Lyons enters from the street.

Troy: Aw hell, I wasn't looking to see you today. I thought you was in jail. Got it all over the front page of the *Courier* about them raiding Sefus's place . . . where you be hanging out with all them thugs.

Lyons: Hey, Pop . . . that ain't got nothing to do with me. I don't go down there gambling. I go down there to sit in with the band. I ain't got nothing to do with the gambling part. They got some good music down there.

Troy: They got some rogues . . . is what they got.

Lyons: How you been, Mr. Bono? Hi, Rose.

Bono: I see where you playing down at the Crawford Grill tonight.

Rose: How come you ain't brought Bonnie like I told you? You should have brought Bonnie with you, she ain't been over in a month of Sundays.

Lyons: I was just in the neighborhood . . . thought I'd stop by.

Troy: Here he come . . .

Bono: Your daddy got a promotion on the rubbish. He's gonna be the first colored driver. Ain't got to do nothing but sit up there and read the paper like them white fellows.

Lyons: Hey, Pop . . . if you knew how to read you'd be all right.

Bono: Naw . . . naw . . . you mean if the nigger knew how to *drive* he'd be all right. Been fighting with them people about driving and ain't even got a license. Mr. Rand know you ain't got no driver's license?

Troy: Driving ain't nothing. All you do is point the truck where you want it to go. Driving ain't nothing.

Bono: Do Mr. Rand know you ain't got no driver's license? That's what I'm talking about. I ain't asked if driving was easy. I asked if Mr. Rand know you ain't got no driver's license.

Troy: He ain't got to know. The man ain't got to know my business. Time he find out, I have two or three driver's licenses.

Lyons (going into his pocket): Say, look here, Pop . . .

Troy: I knew it was coming. Didn't I tell you, Bono? I know what kind of "Look here, Pop" that was. The nigger fixing to ask me for some money. It's Friday night. It's my payday. All them rogues down there on the avenue . . . the ones that ain't in jail . . . and Lyons is hopping in his shoes to get down there with them.

Lyons: See, Pop . . . if you give somebody else a chance to talk sometimes, you'd see that I was fixing to pay you back your ten dollars like I told you. Here . . . I told you I'd pay you when Bonnie got paid.

Troy: Naw . . . you go ahead and keep that ten dollars. Put it in the bank. The next time you feel like you wanna come by here and ask me for something . . . you go on down there and get that.

Lyons: Here's your ten dollars, Pop. I told you I don't want you to give me nothing. I just wanted to borrow ten dollars.

Troy: Naw . . . you go on and keep that for the next time you want to ask me.

Lyons: Come on, Pop . . . here go your ten dollars.

Rose: Why don't you go on and let the boy pay you back, Troy?

Lyons: Here you go, Rose. If you don't take it I'm gonna have to hear about it for the next six months. *(He hands her the money.)*

Rose: You can hand yours over here too, Troy.

Troy: You see this, Bono. You see how they do me.

Bono: Yeah, Lucille do me the same way.

Gabriel is heard singing offstage. He enters.

Gabriel: Better get ready for the Judgment! Better get ready for . . . Hey! . . . Hey! . . . There's Troy's boy!

Lyons: How are you doing, Uncle Gabe?

Gabriel: Lyons . . . The King of the Jungle! Rose . . . hey, Rose. Got a flower for you. *(He takes a rose from his pocket.)* Picked it myself. That's the same rose like you is!

Rose: That's right nice of you, Gabe.

Lyons: What you been doing, Uncle Gabe?

Gabriel: Oh, I been chasing hellhounds and waiting on the time to tell St. Peter to open the gates.

Lyons: You been chasing hellhounds, huh? Well . . . you doing the right thing, Uncle Gabe. Somebody got to chase them.

Gabriel: Oh, yeah . . . I know it. The devil's strong. The devil ain't no pushover. Hellhounds snipping at everybody's heels. But I got my trumpet waiting on the judgment time.

Lyons: Waiting on the Battle of Armageddon, huh?

Gabriel: Ain't gonna be too much of a battle when God get to waving that Judgment sword. But the people's gonna have a hell of a time trying to get into heaven if them gates ain't open.

Lyons (putting his arm around Gabriel): You hear this, Pop. Uncle Gabe, you all right!

Gabriel (laughing with Lyons): Lyons! King of the Jungle.

Rose: You gonna stay for supper, Gabe? Want me to fix you a plate?

Gabriel: I'll take a sandwich, Rose. Don't want no plate. Just wanna eat with my hands. I'll take a sandwich.

Rose: How about you, Lyons? You staying? Got some short ribs cooking.

Lyons: Naw, I won't eat nothing till after we finished playing. *(Pause.)* You ought to come down and listen to me play, Pop.

Troy: I don't like that Chinese music. All that noise.

Rose: Go on in the house and wash up, Gabe . . . I'll fix you a sandwich.

Gabriel (to Lyons, as he exits): Troy's mad at me.

Lyons: What you mad at Uncle Gabe for, Pop?

Rose: He thinks Troy's mad at him cause he moved over to Miss Pearl's.

Troy: I ain't mad at the man. He can live where he want to live at.

Lyons: What he move over there for? Miss Pearl don't like nobody.

Rose: She don't mind him none. She treats him real nice. She just don't allow all that singing.

Troy: She don't mind that rent he be paying . . . that's what she don't mind.

Rose: Troy, I ain't going through that with you no more. He's over there cause he want to have his own place. He can come and go as he please.

Troy: Hell, he could come and go as he please here. I wasn't stopping him. I ain't put no rules on him.

Rose: It ain't the same thing, Troy. And you know it.

Gabriel comes to the door.

Now, that's the last I wanna hear about that. I don't wanna hear nothing else about Gabe and Miss Pearl. And next week . . .

Gabriel: I'm ready for my sandwich, Rose.

Rose: And next week . . . when that recruiter come from that school . . . I want you to sign that paper and go on and let Cory play football. Then that'll be the last I have to hear about that.

Troy (to Rose as she exits into the house): I ain't thinking about Cory nothing.

Lyons: What . . . Cory got recruited? What school he going to?

Troy: That boy walking around here smelling his piss . . . thinking he's grown. Thinking he's gonna do what he want, irrespective of what I say. Look here, Bono . . . I left the Commissioner's office and went down to the A&P . . . that boy ain't working down there. He lying to me. Telling me he got his job back . . . telling me he working weekends . . . telling me he working after school . . . Mr. Stawicki tell me he ain't working down there at all!

Lyons: Cory just growing up. He's just busting at the seams trying to fill out your shoes.

Troy: I don't care what he's doing. When he get to the point where he wanna disobey me . . . then it's time for him to move on. Bono'll tell you that. I bet he ain't never disobeyed his daddy without paying the consequences.

Bono: I ain't never had a chance. My daddy came on through . . . but I ain't never knew him to see him . . . or what he had on his mind or where he went. Just moving on through. Searching out the New Land. That's what the old folks used to call it. See a fellow moving around from place to place . . . woman to woman . . . called it searching out the New Land. I can't say if he ever found it. I come along, didn't want no kids. Didn't know if I was gonna be in one place long enough to fix on them right as their daddy. I figured I was going searching too. As it turned out I been hooked up with

Lucille near about as long as your daddy been with Rose. Going on sixteen years.

Troy: Sometimes I wish I hadn't known my daddy. He ain't cared nothing about no kids. A kid to him wasn't nothing. All he wanted was for you to learn how to walk so he could start you to working. When it come time for eating . . . he ate first. If there was anything left over, that's what you got. Man would sit down and eat two chickens and give you the wing.

Lyons: You ought to stop that, Pop. Everybody feed their kids. No matter how hard times is . . . everybody care about their kids. Make sure they have something to eat.

Troy: The only thing my daddy cared about was getting them bales of cotton in to Mr. Lubin. That's the only thing that mattered to him. Sometimes I used to wonder why he was living. Wonder why the devil hadn't come and got him. "Get them bales of cotton in to Mr. Lubin" and find out he owe him money . . .

Lyons: He should have just went on and left when he saw he couldn't get nowhere. That's what I would have done.

Troy: How he gonna leave with eleven kids? And where he gonna go? He ain't knew how to do nothing but farm. No, he was trapped and I think he knew it. But I'll say this for him . . . he felt a responsibility toward us. Maybe he ain't treated us the way I felt he should have . . . but without that responsibility he could have walked off and left us . . . made his own way.

Bono: A lot of them did. Back in those days what you talking about . . . they walk out their front door and just take on down one road or another and keep on walking.

Lyons: There you go! That's what I'm talking about.

Bono: Just keep on walking till you come to something else. Ain't you never heard of nobody having the walking blues? Well, that's what you call it when you just take off like that.

Troy: My daddy ain't had them walking blues! What you talking about? He stayed right there with his family. But he was just as evil as he could be. My mama couldn't stand him. Couldn't stand that evilness. She run off when I was about eight. She sneaked off one night after he had gone to sleep. Told me she was coming back for me. I ain't never seen her no more. All his women run off and left him. He wasn't good for nobody.

When my turn come to head out, I was fourteen and got to sniffing around Joe Canewell's daughter. Had us an old mule we called Greyboy. My daddy sent me out to do some plowing and I tied up Greyboy and went to fooling around with Joe Canewell's daughter. We done found us a nice little spot, got real cozy with each other. She about thirteen and we done figured we was grown anyway . . . so we down there enjoying ourselves . . . ain't thinking about nothing. We didn't know Greyboy had got loose and wandered back to the house and my daddy was looking for me. We down there by the creek enjoying ourselves when my daddy come up on us. Surprised us. He had them leather straps off the mule and commenced to whupping me like there was no tomorrow. I jumped up, mad and embarrassed. I was scared of my daddy. When he commenced to whupping on me . . . quite naturally I run to get out of the way. *(Pause.)* Now I thought he was mad cause I ain't done my work. But I see where he was chasing me off so he could have the gal for himself. When I see what the matter of it was, I lost all fear of my daddy. Right there is where I become a man . . . at fourteen years of age. *(Pause.)* Now it was my turn to run him off. I picked up them same reins that he had used on me. I picked up them reins and commenced to whupping on him. The gal jumped up and run off . . . and when my daddy turned to face me, I could see why the devil had never come to get him . . . cause he was the devil himself. I don't know what happened. When I woke up, I was laying right there by the creek, and Blue . . . this old dog we had . . . was licking my face. I thought I was blind. I couldn't see nothing. Both my eyes were swollen shut. I laid there and cried. I didn't know what I was gonna do. The only thing I knew was the time had come for me to leave my daddy's house. And right there the world suddenly got big. And it was a long time before I could cut it down to where I could handle it.

Part of that cutting down was when I got to the place where I could feel him kicking in my blood and knew that the only thing that separated us was the matter of a few years.

Gabriel enters from the house with a sandwich.

Lyons: What you got there, Uncle Gabe?

Gabriel: Got me a ham sandwich. Rose gave me a ham sandwich.

Troy: I don't know what happened to him. I done lost touch with everybody except Gabriel. But I hope he's dead. I hope he found some peace.

Lyons: That's a heavy story, Pop. I didn't know you left home when you was fourteen.

Troy: And didn't know nothing. The only part of the world I knew was the forty-two acres of Mr. Lubin's land. That's all I knew about life.

Lyons: Fourteen's kinda young to be out on your own. *(Phone rings.)* I don't even think I was ready to be out on my own at fourteen. I don't know what I would have done.

Troy: I got up from the creek and walked on down to Mobile. I was through with farming. Figured I could do better in the city. So I walked the two hundred miles to Mobile.

Lyons: Wait a minute . . . you ain't walked no two hundred miles, Pop. Ain't nobody gonna walk no two hundred miles. You talking about some walking there.

Bono: That's the only way you got anywhere back in them days.

Lyons: Shhh. Damn if I wouldn't have hitched a ride with somebody!

Troy: Who you gonna hitch it with? They ain't had no cars and things like they got now. We talking about 1918.

Rose (entering): What you all out here getting into?

Troy (to Rose): I'm telling Lyons how good he got it. He don't know nothing about this I'm talking.

Rose: Lyons, that was Bonnie on the phone. She say you supposed to pick her up.

Lyons: Yeah, okay, Rose.

Troy: I walked on down to Mobile and hitched up with some of them fellows that was heading this way. Got up here and found out . . . not only couldn't you get a job . . . you couldn't find no place to live. I thought I was in freedom. Shhh. Colored folks living down there on the riverbanks in whatever kind of shelter they could find for themselves. Right down there under the Brady Street Bridge. Living in shacks made of sticks and tarpaper. Messed around there and went from bad to worse. Started stealing. First it was food. Then I figured, hell, if I steal money I can buy me some food. Buy me some shoes too! One thing led to another. Met your mama. I was young and anxious to be a man. Met your mama and had you. What I do that for? Now I got to worry about feeding you and her. Got to steal three times as much. Went out one day looking for somebody to rob . . . that's what I was, a robber. I'll tell you the truth. I'm ashamed of it today. But it's the truth. Went to rob this fellow . . . pulled out my knife . . . and he pulled out a gun. Shot me in the chest. I felt just like somebody had taken a hot branding iron and laid it on me. When he shot me I jumped at him with my knife. They told me I killed him and they put me in the penitentiary and locked me up for fifteen years. That's where I met Bono. That's where I learned how to play baseball. Got out that place and your mama had taken you and went on to make life without me. Fifteen years was a long time for her to wait. But that fifteen years cured me of that robbing stuff. Rose'll tell you. She asked me when I met her if I had gotten all that foolishness out of my system. And I told her, "Baby, it's you and baseball all what count with me." You hear me, Bono? I meant it too. She say, "Which one comes first?" I told her, "Baby, ain't no doubt it's baseball . . . but you stick and get old with me and we'll both outlive this baseball." Am I right, Rose? And it's true.

Rose: Man, hush your mouth. You ain't said no such thing. Talking about, "Baby, you know you'll always be number one with me." That's what you was talking.

Troy: You hear that, Bono. That's why I love her.

Bono: Rose'll keep you straight. You get off the track, she'll straighten you up.

Rose: Lyons, you better get on up and get Bonnie. She waiting on you.

Lyons (gets up to go): Hey, Pop, why don't you come on down to the Grill and hear me play?

Troy: I ain't going down there. I'm too old to be sitting around in them clubs.

Bono: You got to be good to play down at the Grill.

Lyons: Come on, Pop . . .

Troy: I got to get up in the morning.

Lyons: You ain't got to stay long.

Troy: Naw, I'm gonna get my supper and go on to bed.

Lyons: Well, I got to go. I'll see you again.

Troy: Don't you come around my house on my payday.

Rose: Pick up the phone and let somebody know you coming. And bring Bonnie with you. You know I'm always glad to see her.

Lyons: Yeah, I'll do that, Rose. You take care now. See you, Pop. See you, Mr. Bono. See you, Uncle Gabe.

Gabriel: Lyons! King of the Jungle!

Lyons exits.

Troy: Is supper ready, woman? Me and you got some business to take care of. I'm gonna tear it up too.

Rose: Troy, I done told you now!

Troy (puts his arm around Bono): Aw hell, woman . . . this is Bono. Bono like family. I done known this nigger since . . . how long I done know you?

Bono: It's been a long time.

Troy: I done know this nigger since Skippy was a pup. Me and him done been through some times.

Bono: You sure right about that.

Troy: Hell, I done know him longer than I known you. And we still standing shoulder to shoulder. Hey, look here, Bono . . . a man can't ask for no more than that. *(Drinks to him.)* I love you, nigger.

Bono: Hell, I love you too . . . I got to get home see my woman. You got yours in hand. I got to go get mine.

Bono starts to exit as Cory enters the yard, dressed in his football uniform. He gives Troy a hard, uncompromising look.

Cory: What you do that for, Pop?

He throws his helmet down in the direction of Troy.

Rose: What's the matter? Cory . . . what's the matter?

Cory: Papa done went up to the school and told Coach Zellman I can't play football no more. Wouldn't even let me play the game. Told him to tell the recruiter not to come.

Rose: Troy . . .

Troy: What you Troying me for. Yeah, I did it. And the boy know why I did it.

Cory: Why you wanna do that to me? That was the one chance I had.

Rose: Ain't nothing wrong with Cory playing football, Troy.

Troy: The boy lied to me. I told the nigger if he wanna play football . . . to keep up his chores and hold down that job at the A&P. That was the conditions. Stopped down there to see Mr. Stawicki . . .

Cory: I can't work after school during the football season, Pop! I tried to tell you that Mr. Stawicki's holding my job for me. You don't never want to listen to nobody. And then you wanna go and do this to me!

Troy: I ain't done nothing to you. You done it to yourself.

Cory: Just cause you didn't have a chance! You just scared I'm gonna be better than you, that's all.

Troy: Come here.

Rose: Troy . . .

Cory reluctantly crosses over to Troy.

Troy: All right! See. You done made a mistake.

Cory: I didn't even do nothing!

Troy: I'm gonna tell you what your mistake was. See . . . you swung at the ball and didn't hit it. That's strike one. See, you in the batter's box now. You swung and you missed. That's strike one. Don't you strike out!

Lights fade to black.

ACT II

Scene I

The following morning. Cory is at the tree hitting the ball with the bat. He tries to mimic Troy, but his swing is awkward, less sure. Rose enters from the house.

Rose: Cory, I want you to help me with this cupboard.

Cory: I ain't quitting the team. I don't care what Poppa say.

Rose: I'll talk to him when he gets back. He had to go see about your Uncle Gabe. The police done arrested him. Say he was disturbing the peace. He'll be back directly. Come on in here and help me clean out the top of this cupboard.

Cory exits into the house. Rose see Troy and Bono coming down the alley.

Troy . . . what they say down there?

Troy: Ain't said nothing. I give them fifty dollars and they let him go. I'll talk to you about it. Where's Cory?

Rose: He's in there helping me clean out these cupboards.

Troy: Tell him to get his butt out here.

Troy and Bono go over to the pile of wood. Bono picks up the saw and begins sawing.

Troy (to Bono): All they want is the money. That makes six or seven times I done went down there and got him. See me coming they stick out their *hands.*

Bono: Yeah. I know what you mean. That's all they care about . . . that money. They don't care about what's right. *(Pause.)* Nigger, why you got to go and get some hard wood? You ain't doing nothing but building a little old fence. Get you some soft pine wood. That's all you need.

Troy: I know what I'm doing. This is outside wood. You put pine wood inside the house. Pine wood is inside wood. This here is outside wood. Now you tell me where the fence is gonna be?

Bono: You don't need this wood. You can put it up with pine wood and it'll stand as long as you gonna be here looking at it.

Troy: How you know how long I'm gonna be here, nigger? Hell, I might just live forever. Live longer than old man Horsely.

Bono: That's what Magee used to say.

Troy: Magee's a damn fool. Now you tell me who you ever heard of gonna pull their own teeth with a pair of rusty pliers.

Bono: The old folks . . . my granddaddy used to pull his teeth with pliers. They ain't had no dentists for the colored folks back then.

Troy: Get clean pliers! You understand? Clean pliers! Sterilize them! Besides we ain't living back then. All Magee had to do was walk over to Doc Goldblum's.

Bono: I see where you and that Tallahassee gal . . . that Alberta . . . I see where you all done got tight.

Troy: What you mean "got tight"?

Bono: I see where you be laughing and joking with her all the time.

Troy: I laughs and jokes with all of them, Bono. You know me.
Bono: That ain't the kind of laughing and joking I'm talking about.

Cory enters from the house.

Cory: How you doing, Mr. Bono?
Troy: Cory? Get that saw from Bono and cut some wood. He talking about the wood's too hard to cut. Stand back there, Jim, and let that young boy show you how it's done.
Bono: He's sure welcome to it.

Cory takes the saw and begins to cut the wood.

Whew-e-e! Look at that. Big old strong boy. Look like Joe Louis.° Hell, must be getting old the way I'm watching that boy whip through that wood.
Cory: I don't see why Mama want a fence around the yard noways.
Troy: Damn if I know either. What the hell she keeping out with it? She ain't got nothing nobody want.
Bono: Some people build fences to keep people out . . . and other people build fences to keep people in. Rose wants to hold on to you all. She loves you.
Troy: Hell, nigger, I don't need nobody to tell me my wife loves me. Cory . . . go on in the house and see if you can find that other saw.
Cory: Where's it at?
Troy: I said find it! Look for it till you find it!

Cory exits into the house.

What's that supposed to mean? Wanna keep us in?
Bono: Troy . . . I done known you seem like damn near my whole life. You and Rose both. I done know both of you all for a long time. I remember when you met Rose. When you was hitting them baseball out the park. A lot of them old gals was after you then. You had the pick of the litter. When you picked Rose, I was happy for you. That was the first time I knew you had any sense. I said . . . My man Troy knows what he's doing . . . I'm gonna follow this nigger . . . he might take me somewhere. I been following you too. I done learned a whole heap of things about life watching you. I done learned how to tell where the shit lies. How to tell it from the alfalfa. You done learned me a lot of things. You showed me how to not make the same mistakes . . . to take life as it comes along and keep putting one foot in front of the other. *(Pause.)* Rose a good woman, Troy.
Troy: Hell, nigger, I know she a good woman. I been married to her for eighteen years. What you got on your mind, Bono?
Bono: I just say she a good woman. Just like I say anything. I ain't got to have nothing on my mind.
Troy: You just gonna say she a good woman and leave it hanging out there like that? Why you telling me she a good woman?
Bono: She loves you, Troy. Rose loves you.
Troy: You saying I don't measure up. That's what you trying to say. I don't measure up cause I'm seeing this other gal. I know what you trying to say.

Joe Louis (1914–1981): Black American boxer who held the world heavyweight championship.

Bono: I know what Rose means to you, Troy. I'm just trying to say I don't want to see you mess up.

Troy: Yeah, I appreciate that, Bono. If you was messing around on Lucille I'd be telling you the same thing.

Bono: Well, that's all I got to say. I just say that because I love you both.

Troy: Hell, you know me . . . I wasn't out there looking for nothing. You can't find a better woman than Rose. I know that. But seems like this woman just stuck onto me where I can't shake her loose. I done wrestled with it, tried to throw her off me . . . but she just stuck on tighter. Now she's stuck on for good.

Bono: You's in control . . . that's what you tell me all the time. You responsible for what you do.

Troy: I ain't ducking the responsibility of it. As long as it sets right in my heart . . . then I'm okay. Cause that's all I listen to. It'll tell me right from wrong every time. And I ain't talking about doing Rose no bad turn. I love Rose. She done carried me a long ways and I love and respect her for that.

Bono: I know you do. That's why I don't want to see you hurt her. But what you gonna do when she find out? What you got then? If you try and juggle both of them . . . sooner or later you gonna drop one of them. That's common sense.

Troy: Yeah, I hear what you saying, Bono. I been trying to figure a way to work it out.

Bono: Work it out right, Troy. I don't want to be getting all up between you and Rose's business . . . but work it so it come out right.

Troy: Ah hell, I get all up between you and Lucille's business. When you gonna get that woman that refrigerator she been wanting? Don't tell me you ain't got no money now. I know who your banker is. Mellon don't need that money bad as Lucille want that refrigerator. I'll tell you that.

Bono: Tell you what I'll do . . . when you finish building this fence for Rose . . . I'll buy Lucille that refrigerator.

Troy: You done stuck your foot in your mouth now!

Troy grabs up a board and begins to saw. Bono starts to walk out the yard.

Hey, nigger . . . where you going?

Bono: I'm going home. I know you don't expect me to help you now. I'm protecting my money. I wanna see you put that fence up by yourself. That's what I want to see. You'll be here another six months without me.

Troy: Nigger, you ain't right.

Bono: When it comes to my money . . . I'm right as fireworks on the Fourth of July.

Troy: All right, we gonna see now. You better get out your bankbook.

Bono exits, and Troy continues to work. Rose enters from the house.

Rose: What they say down there? What's happening with Gabe?

Troy: I went down there and got him out. Cost me fifty dollars. Say he was disturbing the peace. Judge set up a hearing for him in three weeks. Say to show cause why he shouldn't be recommitted.

Rose: What was he doing that cause them to arrest him?

Troy: Some kids was teasing him and he run them off home. Say he was howling and carrying on. Some folks seen him and called the police. That's all it was.

Rose: Well, what's you say? What'd you tell the judge?

Troy: Told him I'd look after him. It didn't make no sense to recommit the man. He stuck out his big greasy palm and told me to give him fifty dollars and take him on home.

Rose: Where's he at now? Where'd he go off to?

Troy: He's gone about his business. He don't need nobody to hold his hand.

Rose: Well, I don't know. Seem like that would be the best place for him if they did put him into the hospital. I know what you're gonna say. But that's what I think would be best.

Troy: The man done had his life ruined fighting for what? And they wanna take and lock him up. Let him be free. He don't bother nobody.

Rose: Well, everybody got their own way of looking at it I guess. Come on and get your lunch. I got a bowl of lima beans and some cornbread in the oven. Come and get something to eat. Ain't no sense you fretting over Gabe.

Rose turns to go into the house.

Troy: Rose . . . got something to tell you.

Rose: Well, come on . . . wait till I get this food on the table.

Troy: Rose!

She stops and turns around.

I don't know how to say this. *(Pause.)* I can't explain it none. It just sort of grows on you till it gets out of hand. It starts out like a little bush . . . and the next thing you know it's a whole forest.

Rose: Troy . . . what is you talking about?

Troy: I'm talking, woman, let me talk. I'm trying to find a way to tell you . . . I'm gonna be a daddy. I'm gonna be somebody's daddy.

Rose: Troy . . . you're not telling me this? You're gonna be . . . what?

Troy: Rose . . . now . . . see . . .

Rose: You telling me you gonna be somebody's daddy? You telling your *wife* this?

Gabriel enters from the street. He carries a rose in his hand.

Gabriel: Hey, Troy! Hey, Rose!

Rose: I have to wait eighteen years to hear something like this.

Gabriel: Hey, Rose . . . I got a flower for you. *(He hands it to her.)* That's a rose. Same rose like you is.

Rose: Thanks, Gabe.

Gabriel: Troy, you ain't mad at me is you? Them bad mens come and put me away. You ain't mad at me is you?

Troy: Naw, Gabe, I ain't mad at you.

Rose: Eighteen years and you wanna come with this.

Gabriel (takes a quarter out of his pocket): See what I got? Got a brand new quarter.

Troy: Rose . . . it's just . . .

Rose: Ain't nothing you can say, Troy. Ain't no way of explaining that.

Gabriel: Fellow that give me this quarter had a whole mess of them. I'm gonna keep this quarter till it stop shining.

Rose: Gabe, go on in the house there. I got some watermelon in the Frigidaire. Go on and get you a piece.

Gabriel: Say, Rose . . . you know I was chasing hellhounds and them bad mens come and get me and take me away. Troy helped me. He come down there and told them they better let me go before he beat them up. Yeah, he did!

Rose: You go on and get you a piece of watermelon, Gabe. Them bad mens is gone now.

Gabriel: Okay, Rose . . . gonna get me some watermelon. The kind with the stripes on it.

Gabriel exits into the house.

Rose: Why, Troy? Why? After all these years to come dragging this in to me now. It don't make no sense at your age. I could have expected this ten or fifteen years ago, but not now.

Troy: Age ain't got nothing to do with it, Rose.

Rose: I done tried to be everything a wife should be. Everything a wife could be. Been married eighteen years and I got to live to see the day you tell me you been seeing another woman and done fathered a child by her. And you know I ain't never wanted no half nothing in my family. My whole family is half. Everybody got different fathers and mothers . . . my two sisters and my brother. Can't hardly tell who's who. Can't never sit down and talk about Papa and Mama. It's your papa and your mama and my papa and my mama . . .

Troy: Rose . . . stop it now.

Rose: I ain't never wanted that for none of my children. And now you wanna drag your behind in here and tell me something like this.

Troy: You ought to know. It's time for you to know.

Rose: Well, I don't want to know, goddamn it!

Troy: I can't just make it go away. It's done now. I can't wish the circumstance of the thing away.

Rose: And you don't want to either. Maybe you want to wish me and my boy away. Maybe that's what you want? Well, you can't wish us away. I've got eighteen years of my life invested in you. You ought to have stayed upstairs in my bed where you belong.

Troy: Rose . . . now listen to me . . . we can get a handle on this thing. We can talk this out . . . come to an understanding.

Rose: All of a sudden it's "we." Where was "we" at when you was down there rolling around with some godforsaken woman? "We" should have come to an understanding before you started making a damn fool of yourself. You're a day late and a dollar short when it comes to an understanding with me.

Troy: It's just . . . She gives me a different idea . . . a different understanding about myself. I can step out of this house and get away from the pressures and problems . . . be a different man. I ain't got to wonder how I'm gonna pay the bills or get the roof fixed. I can just be a part of myself that I ain't never been.

Rose: What I want to know . . . is do you plan to continue seeing her. That's all you can say to me.

Troy: I can sit up in her house and laugh. Do you understand what I'm saying. I can laugh out loud . . . and it feels good. It reaches all the way down to the bottom of my shoes. *(Pause.)* Rose, I can't give that up.

Rose: Maybe you ought to go on and stay down there with her . . . if she's a better woman than me.

Troy: It ain't about nobody being a better woman or nothing. Rose, you ain't the blame. A man couldn't ask for no woman to be a better wife than you've been. I'm responsible for it. I done locked myself into a pattern trying to take care of you all that I forgot about myself.

Rose: What the hell was I there for? That was my job, not somebody else's.

Troy: Rose, I done tried all my life to live decent . . . to live a clean . . . hard . . . useful life. I tried to be a good husband to you. In every way I knew how. Maybe I come into the world backwards, I don't know. But . . . you born with two strikes on you before you come to the plate. You got to guard it closely . . . always looking for the curve ball on the inside corner. You can't afford to let none get past you. You can't afford a call strike. If you going down . . . you going down swinging. Everything lined up against you. What you gonna do. I fooled them, Rose. I bunted. When I found you and Cory and a halfway decent job . . . I was safe. Couldn't nothing touch me. I wasn't gonna strike out no more. I wasn't going back to the penitentiary. I wasn't gonna lay in the streets with a bottle of wine. I was safe. I had me a family. A job. I wasn't gonna get that last strike. I was on first looking for one of them boys to knock me in. To get me home.

Rose: You should have stayed in my bed, Troy.

Troy: Then when I saw that gal . . . she firmed up my backbone. And I got to thinking that if I tried . . . I just might be able to steal second. Do you understand after eighteen years I wanted to steal second.

Rose: You should have held me tight. You should have grabbed me and held on.

Troy: I stood on first base for eighteen years and I thought . . . well, goddamn it . . . go on for it!

Rose: We're not talking about baseball! We're talking about you going off to lay in bed with another woman . . . and then bring it home to me. That's what we're talking about. We ain't talking about no baseball.

Troy: Rose, you're not listening to me. I'm trying the best I can to explain it to you. It's not easy for me to admit that I been standing in the same place for eighteen years.

Rose: I been standing with you! I been right here with you, Troy. I got a life too. I gave eighteen years of my life to stand in the same spot with you. Don't you think I ever wanted other things? Don't you think I had dreams and hopes? What about my life? What about me. Don't you think it ever crossed my mind to want to know other men? That I wanted to lay up somewhere and forget about my responsibilities? That I wanted someone to make me laugh so I could feel good? You not the only one who's got wants and needs. But I held on to you, Troy. I took all my feelings, my wants and needs, my dreams . . . and I buried them inside you. I planted a seed and watched and prayed over it. I planted myself inside you and waited to bloom.

And it didn't take me no eighteen years to find out the soil was hard and rocky and it wasn't never gonna bloom.

But I held on to you, Troy. I held you tighter. You was my husband. I owed you everything I had. Every part of me I could find to give you. And upstairs in that room . . . with the darkness falling in on me . . . I gave everything I had to try and erase the doubt that you wasn't the finest man in the world. And wherever you was going . . . I wanted to be there with you. Cause you was my husband. Cause that's the only way I was gonna survive as your wife. You always talking about what you give . . . and what you don't have to give. But you take too. You take . . . and don't even know nobody's giving!

Rose turns to exit into the house; Troy grabs her arm.

Troy: You say I take and don't give!
Rose: Troy! You're hurting me!
Troy: You say I take and don't give!
Rose: Troy . . . you're hurting my arm! Let go!
Troy: I done give you everything I got. Don't you tell that lie on me.
Rose: Troy!
Troy: Don't you tell that lie on me!

Cory enters from the house.

Cory: Mama!
Rose: Troy. You're hurting me.
Troy: Don't you tell me about no taking and giving.

Cory comes up behind Troy and grabs him. Troy, surprised, is thrown off balance just as Cory throws a glancing blow that catches him on the chest and knocks him down. Troy is stunned, as is Cory.

Rose: Troy. Troy. No!

Troy gets to his feet and starts at Cory.

Troy . . . no. Please! Troy!

Rose pulls on Troy to hold him back. Troy stops himself.

Troy (to Cory): All right. That's strike two. You stay away from around me, boy. Don't you strike out. You living with a full count. Don't you strike out.

Troy exits out the yard as the lights go down.

Scene II

It is six months later, early afternoon. Troy enters from the house and starts to exit the yard. Rose enters from the house.

Rose: Troy, I want to talk to you.
Troy: All of a sudden, after all this time, you want to talk to me, huh? You ain't wanted to talk to me for months. You ain't wanted to talk to me last night. You ain't wanted no part of me then. What you wanna talk to me about now?

Rose: Tomorrow's Friday.

Troy: I know what day tomorrow is. You think I don't know tomorrow's Friday? My whole life I ain't done nothing but look to see Friday coming and you got to tell me it's Friday.

Rose: I want to know if you're coming home.

Troy: I always come home, Rose. You know that. There ain't never been a night I ain't come home.

Rose: That ain't what I mean . . . and you know it. I want to know if you're coming straight home after work.

Troy: I figure I'd cash my check . . . hang out at Taylors' with the boys . . . maybe play a game of checkers . . .

Rose: Troy, I can't live like this. I won't live like this. You livin' on borrowed time with me. It's been going on six months now you ain't been coming home.

Troy: I be here every night. Every night of the year. That's 365 days.

Rose: I want you to come home tomorrow after work.

Troy: Rose . . . I don't mess up my pay. You know that now. I take my pay and I give it to you. I don't have no money but what you give me back. I just want to have a little time to myself . . . a little time to enjoy life.

Rose: What about me? When's my time to enjoy life?

Troy: I don't know what to tell you, Rose. I'm doing the best I can.

Rose: You ain't been home from work but time enough to change your clothes and run out . . . and you wanna call that the best you can do?

Troy: I'm going over to the hospital to see Alberta. She went into the hospital this afternoon. Look like she might have the baby early. I won't be gone long.

Rose: Well, you ought to know. They went over to Miss Pearl's and got Gabe today. She said you told them to go ahead and lock him up.

Troy: I ain't said no such thing. Whoever told you that is telling a lie. Pearl ain't doing nothing but telling a big fat lie.

Rose: She ain't had to tell me. I read it on the papers.

Troy: I ain't told them nothing of the kind.

Rose: I saw it right there on the papers.

Troy: What it say, huh?

Rose: It said you told them to take him.

Troy: Then they screwed that up, just the way they screw up everything. I ain't worried about what they got on the paper.

Rose: Say the government send part of his check to the hospital and the other part to you.

Troy: I ain't got nothing to do with that if that's the way it works. I ain't made up the rules about how it work.

Rose: You did Gabe just like you did Cory. You wouldn't sign the paper for Cory . . . but you signed for Gabe. You signed that paper.

The telephone is heard ringing inside the house.

Troy: I told you I ain't signed nothing, woman! The only thing I signed was the release form. Hell, I can't read, I don't know what they had on that paper! I ain't signed nothing about sending Gabe away.

Rose: I said send him to the hospital . . . you said let him be free . . . now you done went down there and signed him to the hospital for half his money. You went back on yourself, Troy. You gonna have to answer for that.

Troy: See now . . . you been over there talking to Miss Pearl. She done got mad cause she ain't getting Gabe's rent money. That's all it is. She's liable to say anything.

Rose: Troy, I seen where you signed the paper.

Troy: You ain't seen nothing I signed. What she doing got papers on my brother anyway? Miss Pearl telling a big fat lie. And I'm gonna tell her about it too! You ain't seen nothing I signed. Say . . . you ain't seen nothing I signed.

Rose exits into the house to answer the telephone. Presently she returns.

Rose: Troy . . . that was the hospital. Alberta had the baby.

Troy: What she have? What is it?

Rose: It's a girl.

Troy: I better get on down to the hospital to see her.

Rose: Troy . . .

Troy: Rose . . . I got to go see her now. That's only right . . . what's the matter . . . the baby's all right, ain't it?

Rose: Alberta died having the baby.

Troy: Died . . . you say she's dead? Alberta's dead?

Rose: They said they done all they could. They couldn't do nothing for her.

Troy: The baby? How's the baby?

Rose: They say it's healthy. I wonder who's gonna bury her.

Troy: She had family, Rose. She wasn't living in the world by herself.

Rose: I know she wasn't living in the world by herself.

Troy: Next thing you gonna want to know if she had any insurance.

Rose: Troy, you ain't got to talk like that.

Troy: That's the first thing that jumped out your mouth. "Who's gonna bury her?" Like I'm fixing to take on that task for myself.

Rose: I am your wife. Don't push me away.

Troy: I ain't pushing nobody away. Just give me some space. That's all. Just give me some room to breathe.

Rose exits into the house. Troy walks about the yard.

Troy (with a quiet rage that threatens to consume him): All right . . . Mr. Death. See now . . . I'm gonna tell you what I'm gonna do. I'm gonna take and build me a fence around this yard. See? I'm gonna build me a fence around what belongs to me. And then I want you to stay on the other side. See? You stay over there until you're ready for me. Then you come on. Bring your army. Bring your sickle. Bring your wrestling clothes. I ain't gonna fall down on my vigilance this time. You ain't gonna sneak up on me no more. When you ready for me . . . when the top of your list say Troy Maxson . . . that's when you come around here. You come up and knock on the front door. Ain't nobody else got nothing to do with this. This is between you and me. Man to man. You stay on the other side of that fence until you ready for me. Then you come up and knock on the front door. Anytime you want. I'll be ready for you.

The lights go down to black.

Scene III

The lights come up on the porch. It is late evening three days later. Rose sits listening to the ball game waiting for Troy. The final out of the game is made and Rose switches off the radio. Troy enters the yard carrying an infant wrapped in blankets. He stands back from the house and calls.

Rose enters and stands on the porch. There is a long, awkward silence, the weight of which grows heavier with each passing second.

Troy: Rose . . . I'm standing here with my daughter in my arms. She ain't but a wee bittie little old thing. She don't know nothing about grownups' business. She innocent . . . and she ain't got no mama.

Rose: What you telling me for, Troy?

She turns and exits into the house.

Troy: Well . . . I guess we'll just sit out here on the porch.

He sits down on the porch. There is an awkward indelicateness about the way he handles the baby. His largeness engulfs and seems to swallow it. He speaks loud enough for Rose to hear.

A man's got to do what's right for him. I ain't sorry for nothing I done. It felt right in my heart. *(To the baby.)* What you smiling at? Your daddy's a big man. Got these great big old hands. But sometimes he's scared. And right now your daddy's scared cause we sitting out here and ain't got no home. Oh, I been homeless before. I ain't had no little baby with me. But I been homeless. You just be out on the road by your lonesome and you see one of them trains coming and you just kinda go like this . . .

He sings as a lullaby.

Please, Mr. Engineer let a man ride the line
Please, Mr. Engineer let a man ride the line
I ain't got no ticket please let me ride the blinds

Rose enters from the house. Troy, hearing her steps behind him, stands and faces her.

She's my daughter, Rose. My own flesh and blood. I can't deny her no more than I can deny them boys. *(Pause.)* You and them boys is my family. You and them and this child is all I got in the world. So I guess what I'm saying is . . . I'd appreciate it if you'd help me take care of her.

Rose: Okay, Troy . . . you're right. I'll take care of your baby for you . . . cause . . . like you say . . . she's innocent . . . and you can't visit the sins of the father upon the child. A motherless child has got a hard time. *(She takes the baby from him.)* From right now . . . this child got a mother. But you a womanless man.

Rose turns and exits into the house with the baby. Lights go down to black.

Scene IV

It is two months later. Lyons enters from the street. He knocks on the door and calls.

Lyons: Hey, Rose! *(Pause.)* Rose!

Rose (from inside the house): Stop that yelling. You gonna wake up Raynell. I just got her to sleep.

Lyons: I just stopped by to pay Papa this twenty dollars I owe him. Where's Papa at?

Rose: He should be here in a minute. I'm getting ready to go down to the church. Sit down and wait on him.

Lyons: I got to go pick up Bonnie over her mother's house.

Rose: Well, sit it down there on the table. He'll get it.

Lyons (enters the house and sets the money on the table): Tell Papa I said thanks. I'll see you again.

Rose: All right, Lyons. We'll see you.

Lyons starts to exit as Cory enters.

Cory: Hey, Lyons.

Lyons: What's happening, Cory? Say man, I'm sorry I missed your graduation. You know I had a gig and couldn't get away. Otherwise, I would have been there, man. So what you doing?

Cory: I'm trying to find a job.

Lyons: Yeah I know how that go, man. It's rough out here. Jobs are scarce.

Cory: Yeah, I know.

Lyons: Look here, I got to run. Talk to Papa . . . he know some people. He'll be able to help get you a job. Talk to him . . . see what he say.

Cory: Yeah . . . all right, Lyons.

Lyons: You take care. I'll talk to you soon. We'll find some time to talk.

Lyons exits the yard. Cory wanders over to the tree, picks up the bat, and assumes a batting stance. He studies an imaginary pitcher and swings. Dissatisfied with the result, he tries again. Troy enters. They eye each other for a beat. Cory puts the bat down and exits the yard. Troy starts into the house as Rose exits with Raynell. She is carrying a cake.

Troy: I'm coming in and everybody's going out.

Rose: I'm taking this cake down to the church for the bake sale. Lyons was by to see you. He stopped by to pay you your twenty dollars. It's laying in there on the table.

Troy (going into his pocket): Well . . . here go this money.

Rose: Put it in there on the table, Troy. I'll get it.

Troy: What time you coming back?

Rose: Ain't no use in you studying me. It don't matter what time I come back.

Troy: I just asked you a question, woman. What's the matter . . . can't I ask you a question?

Rose: Troy, I don't want to go into it. Your dinner's in there on the stove. All you got to do is heat it up. And don't you be eating the rest of them cakes in there. I'm coming back for them. We having a bake sale at the church tomorrow.

Rose exits the yard. Troy sits down on the steps, takes a pint bottle from his pocket, opens it, and drinks. He begins to sing.

Troy: Hear it ring! Hear it ring!
Had an old dog his name was Blue
You know Blue was mighty true
You know Blue as a good old dog
Blue trees a possum in a hollow log
You know from that he was a good old dog

Bono enters the yard.

Bono: Hey, Troy.

Troy: Hey, what's happening, Bono?

Bono: I just thought I'd stop by to see you.

Troy: What you stop by and see me for? You ain't stopped by in a month of Sundays. Hell, I must owe you money or something.

Bono: Since you got your promotion I can't keep up with you. Used to see you every day. Now I don't even know what route you working.

Troy: They keep switching me around. Got me out in Greentree now . . . hauling white folks' garbage.

Bono: Greentree, huh? You lucky, at least you ain't got to be lifting them barrels. Damn if they ain't getting heavier. I'm gonna put in my two years and call it quits.

Troy: I'm thinking about retiring myself.

Bono: You got it easy. You can *drive* for another five years.

Troy: It ain't the same, Bono. It ain't like working the back of the truck. Ain't got nobody to talk to . . . feel like you working by yourself. Naw, I'm thinking about retiring. How's Lucille?

Bono: She all right. Her arthritis get to acting up on her sometime. Saw Rose on my way in. She going down to the church, huh?

Troy: Yeah, she took up going down there. All them preachers looking for somebody to fatten their pockets. *(Pause.)* Got some gin here.

Bono: Naw, thanks. I just stopped by to say hello.

Troy: Hell, nigger . . . you can take a drink. I ain't never known you to say no to a drink. You ain't got to work tomorrow.

Bono: I just stopped by. I'm fixing to go over to Skinner's. We got us a domino game going over his house every Friday.

Troy: Nigger, you can't play no dominoes. I used to whup you four games out of five.

Bono: Well, that learned me. I'm getting better.

Troy: Yeah? Well, that's all right.

Bono: Look here . . . I got to be getting on. Stop by sometime, huh?

Troy: Yeah, I'll do that, Bono. Lucille told Rose you bought her a new refrigerator.

Bono: Yeah, Rose told Lucille you had finally built your fence . . . so I figured we'd call it even.

Troy: I knew you would.
Bono: Yeah . . . okay. I'll be talking to you.
Troy: Yeah, take care, Bono. Good to see you. I'm gonna stop over.
Bono: Yeah. Okay, Troy.

Bono exits. Troy drinks from the bottle.

Troy: Old Blue died and I dig his grave
Let him down with a golden chain
Every night when I hear old Blue bark
I know Blue treed a possum in Noah's Ark.
Hear it ring! Hear it ring!

Cory enters the yard. They eye each other for a beat. Troy is sitting in the middle of the steps. Cory walks over.

Cory: I got to get by.
Troy: Say what? What's you say?
Cory: You in my way. I got to get by.
Troy: You got to get by where? This is my house. Bought and paid for. In full. Took me fifteen years. And if you wanna go in my house and I'm sitting on the steps . . . you say excuse me. Like your mama taught you.
Cory: Come on, Pop . . . I got to get by.

Cory starts to maneuver his way past Troy. Troy grabs his leg and shoves him back.

Troy: You just gonna walk over top of me?
Cory: I live here too!
Troy (advancing toward him): You just gonna walk over top of me in my own house?
Cory: I ain't scared of you.
Troy: I ain't asked if you was sacred of me. I asked you if you was fixing to walk over top of me in my own house? That's the question. You ain't gonna say excuse me? You just gonna walk over top of me?
Cory: If you wanna put it like that.
Troy: How else am I gonna put it?
Cory: I was walking by you to go into the house cause you sitting on the steps drunk, singing to yourself. You can put it like that.
Troy: Without saying excuse me???

Cory doesn't respond.

I asked you a question. Without saying excuse me???
Cory: I ain't got to say excuse me to you. You don't count around here no more.
Troy: Oh, I see . . . I don't count around here no more. You ain't got to say excuse me to your daddy. All of a sudden you done got so grown that your daddy don't count around here no more . . . Around here in his own house and yard that he done paid for with the sweat of his brow. You done got so grown to where you gonna take over. You gonna take over my house. Is that right? You gonna wear my pants. You gonna go in there and stretch out on my bed. You ain't got to say excuse me cause I don't count around here no more. Is that right?

Cory: That's right. You always talking this dumb stuff. Now, why don't you just get out my way?

Troy: I guess you got someplace to sleep and something to put in your belly. You got that, huh? You got that? That's what you need. You got that, huh?

Cory: You don't know what I got. You ain't got to worry about what I got.

Troy: You right! You one hundred percent right! I done spent the last seventeen years worrying about what you got. Now it's your turn, see? I'll tell you what to do. You grown . . . we done established that. You a man. Now, let's see you act like one. Turn your behind around and walk out this yard. And when you get out there in the alley . . . you can forget about this house. See? Cause this is my house. You go on and be a man and get your own house. You can forget about this. Cause this is mine. You go on and get yours cause I'm through with doing for you.

Cory: You talking about what you did for me . . . what'd you ever give me?

Troy: Them feet and bones! That pumping heart, nigger! I give you more than anybody else is ever gonna give you.

Cory: You ain't never gave me nothing! You ain't never done nothing but hold me back. Afraid I was gonna be better than you. All you ever did was try and make me scared of you. I used to tremble every time you called my name. Every time I heard your footsteps in the house. Wondering all the time . . . what's Papa gonna say if I do this? . . . What's he gonna say if I do that? . . . What's Papa gonna say if I turn on the radio? And Mama, too . . . she tries . . . but she's scared of you.

Troy: You leave your mama out of this. She ain't got nothing to do with this.

Cory: I don't know how she stand you . . . after what you did to her.

Troy: I told you to leave your mama out of this!

He advances toward Cory.

Cory: What you gonna do . . . give me a whupping? You can't whup me no more. You're too old. You just an old man.

Troy (shoves him on his shoulder): Nigger! That's what you are. You just another nigger on the street to me!

Cory: You crazy! You know that?

Troy: Go on now! You got the devil in you. Get on away from me!

Cory: You just a crazy old man . . . talking about I got the devil in me.

Troy: Yeah, I'm crazy! If you don't get on the other side of that yard . . . I'm gonna show you how crazy I am! Go on . . . get the hell out of my yard.

Cory: It ain't your yard. You took Uncle Gabe's money he got from the army to buy this house and then you put him out.

Troy (advances on Cory): Get your black ass out of my yard!

Troy's advance backs Cory up against the tree. Cory grabs up the bat.

Cory: I ain't going nowhere! Come on . . . put me out! I ain't scared of you.

Troy: That's my bat!

Cory: Come on!

Troy: Put my bat down!

Cory: Come on, put me out.

Cory swings at Troy, who backs across the yard.

What's the matter? You so bad . . . put me out!

Troy advances toward Cory.

Cory (backing up): Come on! Come on!
Troy: You're gonna have to use it! You wanna draw that bat back on me . . . you're gonna have to use it.
Cory: Come on! . . . Come on!

Cory swings the bat at Troy a second time. He misses. Troy continues to advance toward him.

Troy: You're gonna have to kill me! You wanna draw that bat back on me. You're gonna have to kill me.

Cory, backed up against the tree, can go no farther. Troy taunts him. He sticks out his head and offers him a target.

Come on! Come on!

Cory is unable to swing the bat. Troy grabs it.

Troy: Then I'll show you.

Cory and Troy struggle over the bat. The struggle is fierce and fully engaged. Troy ultimately is the stronger and takes the bat from Cory and stands over him ready to swing. He stops himself.

Go on and get away from around my house.

Cory, stung by his defeat, picks himself up, walks slowly out of the yard and up the alley.

Cory: Tell Mama I'll be back for my things.
Troy: They'll be on the other side of that fence.

Cory exits.

Troy: I can't taste nothing. Helluljah! I can't taste nothing no more. *(Troy assumes a batting posture and begins to taunt Death, the fastball on the outside corner.)* Come on! It's between you and me now! Come on! Anytime you want! Come on! I be ready for you . . . but I ain't gonna be easy.

The lights go down on the scene.

Scene V

The time is 1965. The lights come up in the yard. It is the morning of Troy's funeral. A funeral plaque with a light hangs beside the door. There is a small garden plot off to the side. There is noise and activity in the house as Rose, Gabriel, and Bono have gathered. The door opens and Raynell, seven years old, enters dressed in a flannel nightgown. She crosses to the garden and pokes around with a stick. Rose calls from the house.

Rose: Raynell!
Raynell: Mam?

Rose: What you doing out there?
Raynell: Nothing.

Rose comes to the door.

Rose: Girl, get in here and get dressed. What you doing?
Raynell: Seeing if my garden growed.
Rose: I told you it ain't gonna grow overnight. You got to wait.
Raynell: It don't look like it never gonna grow. Dag!
Rose: I told you a watched pot never boils. Get in here and get dressed.
Raynell: This ain't even no pot, Mama.
Rose: You just have to give it a chance. It'll grow. Now you come on and do what I told you. We got to be getting ready. This ain't no morning to be playing around. You hear me?
Raynell: Yes, mam.

Rose exits into the house. Raynell continues to poke at her garden with a stick. Cory enters. He is dressed in a Marine corporal's uniform, and carries a duffel bag. His posture is that of a military man, and his speech has a clipped sternness.

Cory (to Raynell): Hi. *(Pause.)* I bet your name is Raynell.
Raynell: Uh huh.
Cory: Is your mama home?

Raynell runs up on the porch and calls through the screen door.

Raynell: Mama . . . there's some man out here. Mama?

Rose comes to the door.

Rose: Cory? Lord have mercy! Look here, you all!

Rose and Cory embrace in a tearful reunion as Bono and Lyons enter from the house dressed in funeral clothes.

Bono: Aw, looka here . . .
Rose: Done got all grown up!
Cory: Don't cry, Mama. What you crying about?
Rose: I'm just so glad you made it.
Cory: Hey Lyons. How you doing, Mr. Bono.

Lyons goes to embrace Cory.

Lyons: Look at you, man. Look at you. Don't he look good, Rose. Got them Corporal stripes.
Rose: What took you so long?
Cory: You know how the Marines are, Mama. They got to get all their paperwork straight before they let you do anything.
Rose: Well, I'm sure glad you made it. They let Lyons come. Your Uncle Gabe's still in the hospital. They don't know if they gonna let him out or not. I just talked to them a little while ago.
Lyons: A Corporal in the United States Marines.
Bono: Your daddy knew you had it in you. He used to tell me all the time.
Lyons: Don't he look good, Mr. Bono?

Bono: Yeah, he remind me of Troy when I first met him. *(Pause.)* Say, Rose, Lucille's down at the church with the choir. I'm gonna go down and get the pallbearers lined up. I'll be back to get you all.

Rose: Thanks, Jim.

Cory: See you, Mr. Bono.

Lyons (with his arm around Raynell): Cory . . . look at Raynell. Ain't she precious? She gonna break a whole lot of hearts.

Rose: Raynell, come and say hello to your brother. This is your brother, Cory. You remember Cory.

Raynell: No, Mam.

Cory: She don't remember me, Mama.

Rose: Well, we talk about you. She heard us talk about you. *(To Raynell.)* This is your brother, Cory. Come on and say hello.

Raynell: Hi.

Cory: Hi. So you're Raynell. Mama told me a lot about you.

Rose: You all come on into the house and let me fix you some breakfast. Keep up your strength.

Cory: I ain't hungry, Mama.

Lyons: You can fix me something, Rose. I'll be in there in a minute.

Rose: Cory, you sure you don't want nothing? I know they ain't feeding you right.

Cory: No, Mama . . . thanks. I don't feel like eating. I'll get something later.

Rose: Raynell . . . get on upstairs and get that dress on like I told you.

Rose and Raynell exit into the house.

Lyons: So . . . I hear you thinking about getting married.

Cory: Yeah, I done found the right one, Lyons. It's about time.

Lyons: Me and Bonnie been split up about four years now. About the time Papa retired. I guess she just got tired of all them changes I was putting her through. *(Pause.)* I always knew you was gonna make something out yourself. Your head was always in the right direction. So . . . you gonna stay in . . . make it a career . . . put in your twenty years?

Cory: I don't know. I got six already, I think that's enough.

Lyons: Stick with Uncle Sam and retire early. Ain't nothing out here. I guess Rose told you what happened with me. They got me down the workhouse. I thought I was being slick cashing other people's checks.

Cory: How much time you doing?

Lyons: They give me three years. I got that beat now. I ain't got but nine more months. It ain't so bad. You learn to deal with it like anything else. You got to take the crookeds with the straights. That's what Papa used to say. He used to say that when he struck out. I seen him strike out three times in a row . . . and the next time up he hit the ball over the grandstand. Right out there in Homestead Field. He wasn't satisfied hitting in the seats . . . he want to hit it over everything! After the game he had two hundred people standing around waiting to shake his hand. You got to take the crookeds with the straights. Yeah, Papa was something else.

Cory: You still playing?

Lyons: Cory . . . you know I'm gonna do that. There's some fellows down there we got us a band . . . we gonna try and stay together when we get out . . .

but yeah, I'm still playing. It still helps me to get out of bed in the morning. As long as it do that I'm gonna be right there playing and trying to make some sense out of it.

Rose (calling): Lyons, I got these eggs in the pan.

Lyons: Let me go on and get these eggs, man. Get ready to go bury Papa. *(Pause.)* How you doing? You doing all right?

Cory nods. Lyons touches him on the shoulder and they share a moment of silent grief. Lyons exits into the house. Cory wanders about the yard. Raynell enters.

Raynell: Hi.

Cory: Hi.

Raynell: Did you used to sleep in my room?

Cory: Yeah . . . that used to be my room.

Raynell: That's what Papa call it. "Cory's room." It got your football in the closet.

Rose comes to the door.

Rose: Raynell, get in there and get them good shoes on.

Raynell: Mama, can't I wear these? Them other one hurt my feet.

Rose: Well, they just gonna have to hurt your feet for a while. You ain't said they hurt your feet when you went down to the store and got them.

Raynell: They didn't hurt then. My feet done got bigger.

Rose: Don't you give me no backtalk now. You get in there and get them shoes on.

Raynell exits into the house.

Ain't too much changed. He still got that piece of rag tied to that tree. He was out here swinging that bat. I was just ready to go back in the house. He swung that bat and then he just fell over. Seem like he swung it and stood there with this grin on his face . . . and then he just fell over. They carried him on down to the hospital, but I knew there wasn't no need . . . why don't you come on in the house?

Cory: Mama . . . I got something to tell you. I don't know how to tell you this . . . but I've got to tell you . . . I'm not going to Papa's funeral.

Rose: Boy, hush your mouth. That's your daddy you talking about. I don't want hear that kind of talk this morning. I done raised you to come to this? You standing there all healthy and grown talking about you ain't going to your daddy's funeral?

Cory: Mama . . . listen . . .

Rose: I don't want to hear it, Cory. You just get that thought out of your head.

Cory: I can't drag Papa with me everywhere I go. I've got to say no to him. One time in my life I've got to say no.

Rose: Don't nobody have to listen to nothing like that. I know you and your daddy ain't seen eye to eye, but I ain't got to listen to that kind of talk this morning. Whatever was between you and your daddy . . . the time has come to put it aside. Just take it and set it over there on the shelf and forget about it. Disrespecting your daddy ain't gonna make you a man, Cory. You got to find a way to come to that on your own. Not going to your daddy's funeral ain't gonna make you a man.

Cory: The whole time I was growing up . . . living in his house . . . Papa was like a shadow that followed you everywhere. It weighed on you and sunk into your flesh. It would wrap around you and lay there until you couldn't tell which one was you anymore. That shadow digging in your flesh. Trying to crawl in. Trying to live through you. Everywhere I looked, Troy Maxson was staring back at me . . . hiding under the bed . . . in the closet. I'm just saying I've got to find a way to get rid of that shadow, Mama.

Rose: You just like him. You got him in you good.

Cory: Don't tell me that, Mama.

Rose: You Troy Maxson all over again.

Cory: I don't want to be Troy Maxson. I want to be me.

Rose: You can't be nobody but who you are, Cory. That shadow wasn't nothing but you growing into yourself. You either got to grow into it or cut it down to fit you. But that's all you got to make life with. That's all you got to measure yourself against that world out there. Your daddy wanted you to be everything he wasn't . . . and at the same time he tried to make you into everything he was. I don't know if he was right or wrong . . . but I do know he meant to do more good than he meant to do harm. He wasn't always right. Sometimes when he touched he bruised. And sometimes when he took me in his arms he cut.

When I first met your daddy I thought . . . Here is a man I can lay down with and make a baby. That's the first thing I thought when I seen him. I was thirty years old and had done seen my share of men. But when he walked up to me and said, "I can dance a waltz that'll make you dizzy," I thought, Rose Lee, here is a man that you can open yourself up to and be filled to bursting. Here is a man that can fill all them empty spaces you been tipping around the edges of. One of them empty spaces was being somebody's mother.

I married your daddy and settled down to cooking his supper and keeping clean sheets on the bed. When your daddy walked through the house he was so big he filled it up. That was my first mistake. Not to make him leave some room for me. For my part in the matter. But at that time I wanted that. I wanted a house that I could sing in. And that's what your daddy gave me. I didn't know to keep up his strength I had to give up little pieces of mine. I did that. I took on his life as mine and mixed up the pieces so that you couldn't hardly tell which was which anymore. It was my choice. It was my life and I didn't have to live it like that. But that's what life offered me in the way of being a woman and I took it. I grabbed hold of it with both hands.

By the time Raynell came into the house, me and your daddy had done lost touch with one another. I didn't want to make my blessing off of nobody's misfortune . . . but I took on to Raynell like she was all them babies I had wanted and never had.

The phone rings.

Like I'd been blessed to relive a part of my life. And if the Lord see fit to keep up my strength . . . I'm gonna do her just like your daddy did you . . . I'm gonna give her the best of what's in me.

Raynell (entering, still with her old shoes): Mama . . . Reverend Tollivier on the phone.

Rose exits into the house.

Raynell: Hi.
Cory: Hi.
Raynell: You in the Army or the Marines?
Cory: Marines.
Raynell: Papa said it was the Army. Did you know Blue?
Cory: Blue? Who's Blue?
Raynell: Papa's dog what he sing about all the time.
Cory (singing): Hear it ring! Hear it ring!
I had a dog his name was Blue
You know Blue was mighty true
You know Blue was a good old dog
Blue treed a possum in a hollow log
You know from that he was a good old dog.
Hear it ring! Hear it ring!

Raynell joins in singing.

Cory and Raynell: Blue treed a possum out on a limb
Blue looked at me and I looked at him
Grabbed that possum and put him in a sack
Blue stayed there till I came back
Old Blue's feets was big and round
Never allowed a possum to touch the ground.

Old Blue died and I dug his grave
I dug his grave with a silver spade
Let him down with a golden chain
And every night I call his name
Go on Blue, you good dog you
Go on Blue, you good dog you
Raynell: Blue laid down and died like a man
Blue laid down and died . . .
Both: Blue laid down and died like a man
Now he's treeing possums in the Promised Land
I'm gonna tell you this to let you know
Blue's gone where the good dogs go
When I hear old Blue bark
When I hear old Blue bark
Blue treed a possum in Noah's Ark
Blue treed a possum in Noah's Ark.

Rose comes to the screen door.

Rose: Cory, we gonna be ready to go in a minute.
Cory (to Raynell): You go on in the house and change them shoes like Mama told you so we can go to Papa's funeral.

Raynell: Okay, I'll be back.

Raynell exits into the house. Cory gets up and crosses over to the tree. Rose stands in the screen door watching him. Gabriel enters from the alley.

Gabriel (calling): Hey, Rose!
Rose: Gabe?
Gabriel: I'm here, Rose. Hey Rose, I'm here!

Rose enters from the house.

Rose: Lord . . . Look here, Lyons!
Lyons: See, I told you, Rose . . . I told you they'd let him come.
Cory: How you doing, Uncle Gabe?
Lyons: How you doing, Uncle Gabe?
Gabriel: Hey, Rose. It's time. It's time to tell St. Peter to open the gates. Troy, you ready? You ready, Troy. I'm gonna tell St. Peter to open the gates. You get ready now.

Gabriel, with great fanfare, braces himself to blow. The trumpet is without a mouthpiece. He puts the end of it into his mouth and blows with great force, like a man who has been waiting some twenty-odd years for this single moment. No sound comes out of the trumpet. He braces himself and blows again with the same result. A third time he blows. There is a weight of impossible description that falls away and leaves him bare and exposed to a frightful realization. It is a trauma that a sane and normal mind would be unable to withstand. He begins to dance. A slow, strange dance, eerie and life-giving. A dance of atavistic signature and ritual. Lyons attempts to embrace him. Gabriel pushes Lyons away. He begins to howl in what is an attempt at song, or perhaps a song turning back into itself in an attempt at speech. He finishes his dance and the gates of heaven stand open as wide as God's closet.

That's the way that go!

Connections

1. Compare and contrast Troy Maxson with Willy Loman in Miller's *Death of a Salesman* (p. 1508). How do these protagonists relate to their sons?
2. How might the narrator's experiences in Ralph Ellison's short story "Battle Royal" (p. 179) be used to shed light on Troy's conflicts in *Fences*?
3. Consider how the titles for Soyinka's *The Strong Breed* (p. 1577) and Wilson's *Fences* might be used interchangeably.

M. BUTTERFLY

David Henry Hwang is the son of immigrant Chinese-American parents. Educated at Stanford University, he had his first play, *FOB,* produced there in his senior year and subsequently staged at the New York Shakespeare Festival's Public Theater; it won an Obie Award in 1981. His other plays include *The Dance and the Railroad* (1981), *Family Devotions* (1981), and two one-act plays, *The House of Sleeping Beauties* (1983), and *The Sound of a Voice* (1983), all of which were produced at the Public Theater. *Broken Promises* (1983) is a collection of four of his plays.

M. Butterfly premiered in 1988 and quickly claimed several major prizes: the Outer Critics Circle Award for best Broadway play, the Drama Desk Award for best new play, the John Gassner Award for best American play, and the Tony Award for best play of the year. Hwang is already regarded as one of the most interesting and talented young playwrights in the United States, and *M. Butterfly,* based on a fascinating story of espionage and astonishing sexual misidentification, dazzles both audiences and readers with its remarkable eroticism, insights, and beauty.

DAVID HENRY HWANG (b. 1957)

M. Butterfly 1988

The Characters

Rene Gallimard
Song Liling
Marc/Man No. 2/Consul Sharpless
Renee/Woman at Party/Pinup Girl
Comrade Chin/Suzuki/Shu-Fang
Helga
Toulon/Man No. 1/Judge
Dancers

Time and Place

The action of the play takes place in a Paris prison in the present, and, in recall, during the decade 1960–1970 in Beijing, and from 1966 to the present in Paris.

Playwright's Notes

A former French diplomat and a Chinese opera singer have been sentenced to six years in jail for spying for China after a two-day trial that traced a story of clandestine love and mistaken sexual identity. . . .

Mr. Bouriscot was accused of passing information to China after he fell in love with Mr. Shi, whom he believed for twenty years to be a woman.

—*The New York Times,* May 11, 1986

This play was suggested by international newspaper accounts of a recent espionage trial. For purposes of dramatization, names have been changed, characters created, and incidents devised or altered, and this play does not purport to be a factual record of real events or real people.

I could escape this feeling
With my China girl . . .

—*David Bowie & Iggy Pop*

ACT I

SCENE I

M. Gallimard's prison cell. Paris. 1988.

Lights fade up to reveal Rene Gallimard, sixty-five, in a prison cell. He wears a comfortable bathrobe, and looks old and tired. The sparsely furnished cell contains a wooden crate, upon which sits a hot plate with a kettle, and a portable tape recorder. Gallimard sits on the crate staring at the recorder, a sad smile on his face.

Upstage Song, who appears as a beautiful woman in traditional Chinese garb, dances a traditional piece from the Peking Opera, surrounded by the percussive clatter of Chinese music.

Then, slowly, lights and sound cross-fade; the Chinese opera music dissolves into a Western opera, the "Love Duet" from Puccini's Madame Butterfly. *Song continues dancing, now to the Western accompaniment. Though her movements are the same, the difference in music now gives them a balletic quality.*

Gallimard rises, and turns upstage towards the figure of Song, who dances without acknowledging him.

Gallimard: Butterfly, Butterfly . . .

He forces himself to turn away, as the image of Song fades out, and talks to us.

Gallimard: The limits of my cell are as such: four-and-a-half meters by five. There's one window against the far wall; a door, very strong, to protect me from autograph hounds. I'm responsible for the tape recorder, the hot plate, and this charming coffee table.

When I want to eat, I'm marched off to the dining room — hot, steaming slop appears on my plate. When I want to sleep, the light bulb turns itself off — the work of fairies. It's an enchanted space I occupy. The French — we know how to run a prison.

But, to be honest, I'm not treated like an ordinary prisoner. Why? Because I'm a celebrity. You see, I make people laugh.

I never dreamed this day would arrive. I've never been considered witty or clever. In fact, as a young boy, in an informal poll among my grammar school classmates, I was voted "least likely to be invited to a party." It's a title I managed to hold on to for many years. Despite some stiff competition.

But now, how the tables turn! Look at me: the life of every social function in Paris. Paris? Why be modest: My fame has spread to Amsterdam, London, New York. Listen to them! In the world's smartest parlors. I'm the one who lifts their spirits!

With a flourish, Gallimard directs our attention to another part of the stage.

SCENE II

A party. 1988.

Lights go up on a chic-looking parlor, where a well-dressed trio, two men and one woman, make conversation. Gallimard also remains lit; he observes them from his cell.

Woman: And what of Gallimard?

Man 1: Gallimard?

Man 2: Gallimard!

Gallimard (to us): You see? They're all determined to say my name, as if it were some new dance.

Woman: He still claims not to believe the truth.

Man 1: What? Still? Even since the trial?

Woman: Yes. Isn't it mad?

Man 2 (laughing): He says . . . it was dark . . . and she was very modest!

The trio break into laughter.

Man 1: So — what? He never touched her with his hands?

Man 2: Perhaps he did, and simply misidentified the equipment. A compelling case for sex education in the schools.

Woman: To protect the National Security — the Church can't argue with that.

Man 1: That's impossible! How could he not know?

Man 2: Simple ignorance.

Man 1: For twenty years?

Man 2: Time flies when you're being stupid.

Woman: Well, I thought the French were ladies' men.

Man 2: It seems Monsieur Gallimard was overly anxious to live up to his national reputation.

Woman: Well, he's not very good-looking.

Man 1: No, he's not.

Man 2: Certainly not.

Woman: Actually, I feel sorry for him.

Man 2: A toast! To Monsieur Gallimard!

Woman: Yes! To Gallimard!

Man 1: To Gallimard!

Man 2: Vive la différence!

They toast, laughing. Lights down on them.

Scene III

M. Gallimard's cell.

Gallimard (smiling): You see? They toast me. I've become a patron saint of the socially inept. Can they really be so foolish? Men like that — they should be scratching at my door, begging to learn my secrets! For I, Rene Gallimard, you see, I have known, and been loved by . . . the Perfect Woman.

Alone in this cell, I sit night after night, watching our story play through my head, always searching for a new ending, one which redeems my honor, where she returns at last to my arms. And I imagine you — my ideal audience — who come to understand and even, perhaps just a little, to envy me.

He turns on his tape recorder. Over the house speakers, we hear the opening phrases of Madame Butterfly.

Gallimard: In order for you to understand what I did and why, I must introduce you to my favorite opera: *Madame Butterfly.* By Giacomo Puccini. First produced at La Scala, Milan, in 1904, it is now beloved throughout the Western world.

As Gallimard describes the opera, the tape segues in and out to sections he may be describing.

Gallimard: And why not? Its heroine, Cio-Cio-San, also known as Butterfly, is a feminine ideal, beautiful and brave. And its hero, the man for whom she gives up everything, is — *(He pulls out a naval officer's cap from under his crate, pops it on his head, and struts about)* — not very good-looking, not too bright, and pretty much a wimp: Benjamin Franklin Pinkerton of the U.S. Navy. As the curtain rises, he's just closed on two great bargains: one on a house, the other on a woman — call it a package deal.

Pinkerton purchased the rights to Butterfly for one hundred yen — in modern currency, equivalent to about . . . sixty-six cents. So, he's feeling pretty pleased with himself as Sharpless, the American consul, arrives to witness the marriage.

Marc, wearing an official cap to designate Sharpless, enters and plays the character.

Sharpless/Marc: Pinkerton!

Pinkerton/Gallimard: Sharpless! How's it hangin'? It's a great day, just great. Between my house, my wife, and the rickshaw ride in from town, I've saved nineteen cents just this morning.

Sharpless: Wonderful. I can see the inscription on your tombstone already: "I saved a dollar, here I lie." *(He looks around.)* Nice house.

Pinkerton: It's artistic. Artistic, don't you think? Like the way the shoji screens slide open to reveal the wet bar and disco mirror ball? Classy, huh? Great for impressing the chicks.

Sharpless: "Chicks"? Pinkerton, you're going to be a married man!

Pinkerton: Well, sort of.

Sharpless: What do you mean?

Pinkerton: This country — Sharpless, it is okay. You got all these geisha girls running around —

Sharpless: I know! I live here!

Pinkerton: Then, you know the marriage laws, right? I split for one month, it's annulled!

Sharpless: Leave it to you to read the fine print. Who's the lucky girl?

Pinkerton: Cio-Cio-San. Her friends call her Butterfly. Sharpless, she eats out of my hand!

Sharpless: She's probably very hungry.

Pinkerton: Not like American girls. It's true what they say about Oriental girls. They want to be treated bad!

Sharpless: Oh, please!

Pinkerton: It's true!

Sharpless: Are you serious about this girl?

Pinkerton: I'm marrying her, aren't I?

Sharpless: Yes — with generous trade-in terms.

Pinkerton: When I leave, she'll know what it's like to have loved a real man. And I'll even buy her a few nylons.

Sharpless: You aren't planning to take her with you?

Pinkerton: Huh? Where?

Sharpless: Home!

Pinkerton: You mean, America? Are you crazy? Can you see her trying to buy rice in St. Louis?

Sharpless: So, you're not serious.

Pause

Pinkerton/Gallimard (as Pinkerton): Consul, I am a sailor in port. *(as Gallimard.)* They then proceed to sing the famous duet, "The Whole World Over."

The duet plays on the speakers. Gallimard, as Pinkerton, lip-syncs his lines from the opera.

Gallimard: To give a rough translation: "The whole world over, the Yankee travels, casting his anchor wherever he wants. Life's not worth living unless he can win the hearts of the fairest maidens, then hotfoot it off the premises ASAP." *(He turns towards Marc.)* In the preceding scene, I played Pinkerton, the womanizing cad, and my friend Marc from school . . . *(Marc bows grandly for our benefit.)* played Sharpless, the sensitive soul of reason. In life, however, our positions were usually — no, always — reversed.

Scene IV

École Nationale.° Aix-en-Provence. 1947.

Gallimard: No, Marc, I think I'd rather stay home.

Marc: Are you crazy?! We are going to Dad's condo in Marseilles! You know what happened last time?

Gallimard: Of course I do.

Marc: Of course you don't! You never know. . . . They stripped, Rene!

Gallimard: Who stripped?

Marc: The girls!

Gallimard: Girls? Who said anything about girls?

Marc: Rene, we're a buncha university guys goin' up to the woods. What are we gonna do — talk philosophy?

Gallimard: What girls? Where do you get them?

Marc: Who cares? The point is, they come. On trucks. Packed in like sardines. The back flips open, babes hop out, we're ready to roll.

Gallimard: You mean, they just — ?

Marc: Before you know it, every last one of them — they're stripped and splashing around my pool. There's no moon out, they can't see what's going on, their boobs are flapping, right? You close your eyes, reach out — it's grab bag, get it? Doesn't matter whose ass is between whose legs, whose teeth

École Nationale: National School.

are sinking into who. You're just in there, going at it, eyes closed, on and on for as long as you can stand. *(Pause.)* Some fun, huh?

Gallimard: What happens in the morning?

Marc: In the morning, you're ready to talk some philosophy. *(Beat.)* So how 'bout it?

Gallimard: Marc, I can't . . . I'm afraid they'll say no — the girls. So I never ask.

Marc: You don't have to ask! That's the beauty — don't you see? They don't have to say yes. It's perfect for a guy like you, really.

Gallimard: You go ahead . . . I may come later.

Marc: Hey, Rene — it doesn't matter that you're clumsy and got zits — they're not looking!

Gallimard: Thank you very much.

Marc: Wimp.

Marc walks over to the other side of the stage, and starts waving and smiling at women in the audience.

Gallimard (to us): We now return to my version of *Madame Butterfly* and the events leading to my recent conviction for treason.

Gallimard notices Marc making lewd gestures.

Gallimard: Marc, what are you doing?

Marc: Huh? *(Sotto voce.)* Rene, there're a lotta great babes out there. They're probably lookin' at me and thinking, "What a dangerous guy."

Gallimard: Yes — how could they help but be impressed by your cool sophistication?

Gallimard pops the Sharpless cap on Marc's head, and points him offstage. Marc exits, leering.

Scene V

M. Gallimard's cell.

Gallimard: Next, Butterfly makes her entrance. We learn her age — fifteen . . . but very mature for her years.

Lights come up on the area where we saw Song dancing at the top of the play. She appears there again, now dressed as Madame Butterfly, moving to the "Love Duet." Gallimard turns upstage slightly to watch, transfixed.

Gallimard: But as she glides past him, beautiful, laughing softly behind her fan, don't we who are men sigh with hope? We, who are not handsome, nor brave, nor powerful, yet somehow believe, like Pinkerton, that we deserve a Butterfly. She arrives with all her possessions in the folds of her sleeves, lays them all out, for her man to do with as he pleases. Even her life itself — she bows her head as she whispers that she's not even worth the hundred yen he paid for her. He's already given too much, when we know he's really had to give nothing at all.

Music and lights on Song out. Gallimard sits at his crate.

Gallimard: In real life, women who put their total worth at less than sixty-six cents are quite hard to find. The closest we come is in the pages of these magazines. *(He reaches into his crate, pulls out a stack of girlie magazines, and begins flipping through them.)* Quite a necessity in prison. For three or four dollars, you get seven or eight women.

I first discovered these magazines at my uncle's house. One day, as a boy of twelve. The first time I saw them in his closet . . . all lined up — my body shook. Not with lust — no, with power. Here were women — a shelf-ful — who would do exactly as I wanted.

The "Love Duet" creeps in over the speakers. Special comes up, revealing, not Song this time, but a pinup girl in a sexy negligee, her back to us. Gallimard turns upstage and looks at her.

Girl: I know you're watching me.
Gallimard: My throat . . . it's dry.
Girl: I leave my blinds open every night before I go to bed.
Gallimard: I can't move.
Girl: I leave my blinds open and the lights on.
Gallimard: I'm shaking. My skin is hot, but my penis is soft. Why?
Girl: I stand in front of the window.
Gallimard: What is she going to do?
Girl: I toss my hair, and I let my lips part . . . barely.
Gallimard: I shouldn't be seeing this. It's so dirty. I'm so bad.
Girl: Then, slowly, I lift off my nightdress.
Gallimard: Oh, god. I can't believe it. I can't —
Girl: I toss it to the ground.
Gallimard: Now, she's going to walk away. She's going to —
Girl: I stand there, in the light, displaying myself.
Gallimard: No. She's — why is she naked?
Girl: To you.
Gallimard: In front of a window? This is wrong. No —
Girl: Without shame.
Gallimard: No, she must . . . like it.
Girl: I like it.
Gallimard: She . . . she wants me to see.
Girl: I want you to see.
Gallimard: I can't believe it! She's getting excited!
Girl: I can't see you. You can do whatever you want.
Gallimard: I can't do a thing. Why?
Girl: What would you like me to do . . . next?

Lights go down on her. Music off. Silence, as Gallimard puts away his magazines. Then he resumes talking to us.

Gallimard: Act Two begins with Butterfly staring at the ocean. Pinkerton's been called back to the U.S., and he's given his wife a detailed schedule of his plans. In the column marked "return date," he's written "when the robins nest." This failed to ignite her suspicions. Now, three years have passed without a peep from him. Which brings a response from her faithful servant, Suzuki.

Comrade Chin enters, playing Suzuki.

Suzuki: Girl, he's a loser. What'd he ever give you? Nineteen cents and those ugly Day-Glo stockings? Look, it's finished! Kaput! Done! And you should be glad! I mean, the guy was a woofer! He tried before, you know — before he met you, he went down to geisha central and plunked down his spare change in front of the usual candidates — everyone else gagged! These are hungry prostitutes, and they were not interested, get the picture? Now, stop slathering when an American ship sails in, and let's make some bucks — I mean, yen! We are broke!

Now, what about Yamadori? Hey, hey — don't look away — the man is a prince — figuratively, and, what's even better, literally. He's rich, he's handsome, he says he'll die if you don't marry him — and he's even willing to overlook the little fact that you've been deflowered all over the place by a foreign devil. What do you mean, "But he's Japanese?" What do you think you are? You think you've been touched by the whitey god? He was a sailor with dirty hands!

Suzuki stalks offstage.

Gallimard: She's also visited by Consul Sharpless, sent by Pinkerton on a minor errand.

Marc enters, as Sharpless.

Sharpless: I hate this job.

Gallimard: This Pinkerton — he doesn't show up personally to tell his wife he's abandoning her. No, he sends a government diplomat . . . at taxpayers' expense.

Sharpless: Butterfly? Butterfly? I have some bad — I'm going to be ill. Butterfly, I came to tell you —

Gallimard: Butterfly says she knows he'll return and if he doesn't she'll kill herself rather than go back to her own people. *(Beat.)* This causes a lull in the conversation.

Sharpless: Let's put it this way . . .

Gallimard: Butterfly runs into the next room, and returns holding —

Sound cue: a baby crying. Sharpless, "seeing" this, backs away.

Sharpless: Well, good. Happy to see things going so well. I suppose I'll be going now. Ta ta. Ciao. *(He turns away. Sound cue out.)* I hate this job. *(He exits.)*

Gallimard: At that moment, Butterfly spots in the harbor an American ship — the *Abramo Lincoln!*

Music cue: "The Flower Duet." Song, still dressed as Butterfly, changes into a wedding kimono, moving to the music.

Gallimard: This is the moment that redeems her years of waiting. With Suzuki's help, they cover the room with flowers —

Chin, as Suzuki, trudges onstage and drops a lone flower without much enthusiasm.

Gallimard: — and she changes into her wedding dress to prepare for Pinkerton's arrival.

Suzuki helps Butterfly change. Helga enters, and helps Gallimard change into a tuxedo.

Gallimard: I married a woman older than myself — Helga.
Helga: My father was ambassador to Australia. I grew up among criminals and kangaroos.
Gallimard: Hearing that brought me to the altar —

Helga exits.

Gallimard: — where I took a vow renouncing love. No fantasy woman would ever want me, so, yes, I would settle for a quick leap up the career ladder. Passion, I banish, and in its place — practicality!

But my vows had long since lost their charm by the time we arrived in China. The sad truth is that all men want a beautiful woman, and the uglier the man, the greater the want.

Suzuki makes final adjustments of Butterfly's costume, as does Gallimard of his tuxedo.

Gallimard: I married late, at age thirty-one. I was faithful to my marriage for eight years. Until the day when, as a junior-level diplomat in puritanical Peking, in a parlor at the German ambassador's house, during the "Reign of a Hundred Flowers,"° I first saw her . . . singing the death scene from *Madame Butterfly.*

Suzuki runs offstage.

Scene VI

German ambassador's house. Beijing. 1960.

The upstage special area now becomes a stage. Several chairs face upstage, representing seating for some twenty guests in the parlor. A few "diplomats" — Renee, Marc, Toulon — in formal dress enter and take seats.

Gallimard also sits down, but turns towards us and continues to talk. Orchestral accompaniment on the tape is now replaced by a simple piano. Song picks up the death scene from the point where Butterfly uncovers the hara-kiri knife.

Gallimard: The ending is pitiful. Pinkerton, in an act of great courage, stays home and sends his American wife to pick up Butterfly's child. The truth, long deferred, has come up to her door.

Song, playing Butterfly, sings the lines from the opera in her own voice — which, though not classical, should be decent.

Song: "Con onor muore/ chi non puo serbar/ vita con onore."
Gallimard (simultaneously): "Death with honor/ Is better than life/ Life with dishonor."

"Reign of a Hundred Flowers": A brief period in 1957 when freedom of expression was allowed in China.

The stage is illuminated; we are now completely within an elegant diplomat's residence. Song proceeds to play out an abbreviated death scene. Everyone in the room applauds. Song, shyly, takes her bows. Others in the room rush to congratulate her. Gallimard remains with us.

Gallimard: They say in opera the voice is everything. That's probably why I'd never before enjoyed opera. Here . . . here was a Butterfly with little or no voice — but she had the grace, the delicacy . . . I believed this girl. I believed her suffering. I wanted to take her in my arms — so delicate, even I could protect her, take her home, pamper her until she smiled.

Over the course of the preceding speech, Song has broken from the upstage crowd and moved directly upstage of Gallimard.

Song: Excuse me. Monsieur . . . ?

Gallimard turns upstage, shocked.

Gallimard: Oh! Gallimard. Mademoiselle . . . ? A beautiful . . .
Song: Song Liling.
Gallimard: A beautiful performance.
Song: Oh, please.
Gallimard: I usually —
Song: You make me blush. I'm no opera singer at all.
Gallimard: I usually don't like *Butterfly.*
Song: I can't blame you in the least.
Gallimard: I mean, the story —
Song: Ridiculous.
Gallimard: I like the story, but . . . what?
Song: Oh, you like it?
Gallimard: I . . . what I mean is, I've always seen it played by huge women in so much bad makeup.
Song: Bad makeup is not unique to the West.
Gallimard: But, who can believe them?
Song: And you believe me?
Gallimard: Absolutely. You were utterly convincing. It's the first time —
Song: Convincing? As a Japanese woman? The Japanese used hundreds of our people for medical experiments during the war, you know. But I gather such an irony is lost on you.
Gallimard: No! I was about to say, it's the first time I've seen the beauty of the story.
Song: Really?
Gallimard: Of her death. It's a . . . a pure sacrifice. He's unworthy, but what can she do? She loves him . . . so much. It's a very beautiful story.
Song: Well, yes, to a Westerner.
Gallimard: Excuse me?
Song: It's one of your favorite fantasies, isn't it? The submissive Oriental woman and the cruel white man.
Gallimard: Well, I didn't quite mean . . .
Song: Consider it this way: what would you say if a blonde homecoming queen fell in love with a short Japanese businessman? He treats her cruelly, then

goes home for three years, during which time she prays to his picture and turns down marriage from a young Kennedy. Then, when she learns he has remarried, she kills herself. Now, I believe you would consider this girl to be a deranged idiot, correct? But because it's an Oriental who kills herself for a Westerner — ah! — you find it beautiful.

Silence.

Gallimard: Yes . . . well . . . I see your point . . .
Song: I will never do Butterfly again, Monsieur Gallimard. If you wish to see some real theater, come to the Peking Opera sometime. Expand your mind.

Song walks offstage. Other guests exit with her.

Gallimard (to us): So much for protecting her in my big Western arms.

Scene VII

M. Gallimard's apartment. Beijing. 1960.
Gallimard changes from his tux into a casual suit. Helga enters.

Gallimard: The Chinese are an incredibly arrogant people.
Helga: They warned us about that in Paris, remember?
Gallimard: Even Parisians consider them arrogant. That's a switch.
Helga: What is it that Madame Su says? "We are a very old civilization." I never know if she's talking about her country or herself.
Gallimard: I walk around here, all I hear every day, everywhere is how *old* this culture is. The fact that "old" may be synonymous with "senile" doesn't occur to them.
Helga: You're not going to change them. "East is east, west is west, and . . ." whatever that guy said.
Gallimard: It's just that — silly. I met . . . at Ambassador Koening's tonight — you should've been there.
Helga: Koening? Oh god, no. Did he enchant you all again with the history of Bavaria?
Gallimard: No. I met, I suppose, the Chinese equivalent of a diva. She's a singer in the Chinese opera.
Helga: They have an opera, too? Do they sing in Chinese? Or maybe — in Italian?
Gallimard: Tonight, she did sing in Italian.
Helga: How'd she manage that?
Gallimard: She must've been educated in the West before the Revolution. Her French is very good also. Anyway, she sang the death scene from *Madame Butterfly.*
Helga: Madame Butterfly! Then I should have come. *(She begins humming, floating around the room as if dragging long kimono sleeves.)* Did she have a nice costume? I think it's a classic piece of music.
Gallimard: That's what *I* thought, too. Don't let her hear you say that.
Helga: What's wrong?
Gallimard: Evidently the Chinese hate it.
Helga: She hated it, but she performed it anyway? Is she perverse?

Gallimard: They hate it because the white man gets the girl. Sour grapes if you ask me.

Helga: Politics again? Why can't they just hear it as a piece of beautiful music? So, what's in their opera?

Gallimard: I don't know. But, whatever it is, I'm sure it must be *old.*

Helga exits.

Scene VIII

Chinese opera house and the streets of Beijing. 1960.

The sound of gongs clanging fills the stage.

Gallimard: My wife's innocent question kept ringing in my ears. I asked around, but no one knew anything about the Chinese opera. It took four weeks, but my curiosity overcame my cowardice. This Chinese diva — this unwilling Butterfly — what did she do to make her so proud?

The room was hot, and full of smoke. Wrinkled faces, old women, teeth missing — a man with a growth on his neck, like a human toad. All smiling, pipes falling from their mouths, cracking nuts between their teeth, a live chicken pecking at my foot — all looking, screaming, gawking . . . at her.

The upstage area is suddenly hit with a harsh white light. It has become the stage for the Chinese opera performance. Two dancers enter, along with Song. Gallimard stands apart, watching. Song glides gracefully amidst the two dancers. Drums suddenly slam to a halt. Song strikes a pose, looking straight at Gallimard. Dancers exit. Light change. Pause, then Song walks right off the stage and straight up to Gallimard.

Song: Yes. You. White man. I'm looking straight at you.

Gallimard: Me?

Song: You see any other white men? It was too easy to spot you. How often does a man in my audience come in a tie?

Song starts to remove her costume. Underneath, she wears simple baggy clothes. They are now backstage. The show is over.

Song: So, you are an adventurous imperialist?

Gallimard: I . . . thought it would further my education.

Song: It took you four weeks. Why?

Gallimard: I've been busy.

Song: Well, education has always been undervalued in the West, hasn't it?

Gallimard (laughing): I don't think that's true.

Song: No, you wouldn't. You're a Westerner. How can you objectively judge your own values?

Gallimard: I think it's possible to achieve some distance.

Song: Do you? *(Pause.)* It stinks in here. Let's go.

Gallimard: These are the smells of your loyal fans.

Song: I love them for being my fans, I hate the smell they leave behind. I too can distance myself from my people. *(She looks around, then whispers in his ear.)* "Art for the masses" is a shitty excuse to keep artists poor. *(She pops a cigarette in her mouth.)* Be a gentleman, will you? And light my cigarette.

Gallimard fumbles for a match.

Gallimard: I don't . . . smoke.

Song (lighting her own): Your loss. Had you lit my cigarette, I might have blown a puff of smoke right between your eyes. Come.

They start to walk about the stage. It is a summer night on the Beijing streets. Sounds of the city play on the house speakers.

Song: How I wish there were even a tiny café to sit in. With cappuccinos, and men in tuxedos and bad expatriate jazz.

Gallimard: If my history serves me correctly, you weren't even allowed into the clubs in Shanghai before the Revolution.

Song: Your history serves you poorly, Monsieur Gallimard. True, there were signs reading "No dogs and Chinamen." But a woman, especially a delicate Oriental woman — we always go where we please. Could you imagine it otherwise? Clubs in China filled with pasty, big-thighed white women, while thousands of slender lotus blossoms wait just outside the door? Never. The clubs would be empty. *(Beat.)* We have always held a certain fascination for you Caucasian men, have we not?

Gallimard: But . . . that fascination is imperialist, or so you tell me.

Song: Do you believe everything I tell you? Yes. It is always imperialist. But sometimes . . . sometimes, it is also mutual. Oh — this is my flat.

Gallimard: I didn't even —

Song: Thank you. Come another time and we will further expand your mind.

Song exits. Gallimard continues roaming the streets as he speaks to us.

Gallimard: What was that? What did she mean, "Sometimes . . . it is mutual"? Women do not flirt with me. And I normally can't talk to them. But tonight, I held up my end of the conversation.

Scene IX

Gallimard's bedroom. Beijing. 1960.
Helga enters.

Helga: You didn't tell me you'd be home late.

Gallimard: I didn't intend to. Something came up.

Helga: Oh? Like what?

Gallimard: I went to the . . . to the Dutch ambassador's home.

Helga: Again?

Gallimard: There was a reception for a visiting scholar. He's writing a six-volume treatise on the Chinese revolution. We all gathered that meant he'd have to live here long enough to actually write six volumes, and we all expressed our deepest sympathies.

Helga: Well, I had a good night too. I went with the ladies to a martial arts demonstration. Some of those men — when they break those thick boards — *(she mimes fanning herself.)* whoo-whoo!

Helga exits. Lights dim.

Gallimard: I lied to my wife. Why? I've never had any reason to lie before. But what reason did I have tonight? I didn't do anything wrong. That night, I had a dream. Other people, I've been told, have dreams when angels appear. Or dragons, or Sophia Loren in a towel. In my dream, Marc from school appeared.

Marc enters, in a nightshirt and cap.

Marc: Rene! You met a girl!

Gallimard and Marc stumble down the Beijing streets. Night sounds over the speakers.

Gallimard: It's not that amazing, thank you.
Marc: No! It's so monumental, I heard about it halfway around the world in my sleep!
Gallimard: I've met girls before, you know.
Marc: Name one. I've come across time and space to congratulate you. *(He hands Gallimard a bottle of wine.)*
Gallimard: Marc, this is expensive.
Marc: On those rare occasions when you become a formless spirit, why not steal the best?

Marc pops open the bottle, begins to share it with Gallimard.

Gallimard: You embarrass me. She . . . there's no reason to think she likes me.
Marc: "Sometimes, it is mutual"?
Gallimard: Oh.
Marc: "Mutual"? "Mutual"? What does that mean?
Gallimard: You heard?
Marc: It means the money is in the bank, you only have to write the check!
Gallimard: I am a married man!
Marc: And an excellent one too. I cheated after . . . six months. Then again and again, until now — three hundred girls in twelve years.
Gallimard: I don't think we should hold that up as a model.
Marc: Of course not! My life — it is disgusting! Phooey! Phooey! But, you — you are the model husband.
Gallimard: Anyway, it's impossible. I'm a foreigner.
Marc: Ah, yes. She cannot love you, it is taboo, but something deep inside her heart . . . she cannot help herself . . . she must surrender to you. It is her destiny.
Gallimard: How do you imagine all this?
Marc: The same way you do. It's an old story. It's in our blood. They fear us, Rene. Their women fear us. And their men — their men hate us. And, you know something? They are all correct.

They spot a light in a window.

Marc: There! There, Rene!
Gallimard: It's her window.
Marc: Late at night — it burns. The light — it burns for you.
Gallimard: I won't look. It's not respectful.
Marc: We don't have to be respectful. We're foreign devils.

Enter Song, in a sheer robe, her face completely swathed in black cloth. The "One Fine Day" aria creeps in over the speakers. With her back to us, Song mimes attending to her toilette. Her robe comes loose, revealing her white shoulders.

Marc: All your life you've waited for a beautiful girl who would lay down for you. All your life you've smiled like a saint when it's happened to every other man you know. And you see them in magazines and you see them in movies. And you wonder, what's wrong with me? Will anyone beautiful ever want me? As the years pass, your hair thins and you struggle to hold on to even your hopes. Stop struggling, Rene. The wait is over. *(He exits.)*

Gallimard: Marc? Marc?

At that moment, Song, her back still towards us, drops her robe. A second of her naked back, then a sound cue: a phone ringing, very loud. Blackout, followed in the next beat by a special up on the bedroom area, where a phone now sits. Gallimard stumbles across the stage and picks up the phone. Sound cue out. Over the course of his conversation, area lights fill in the vicinity of his bed. It is the following morning.

Gallimard: Yes? Hello?

Song (offstage): Is it very early?

Gallimard: Why, yes.

Song (offstage): How early?

Gallimard: It's . . . it's 5:30. Why are you — ?

Song (offstage): But it's light outside. Already.

Gallimard: It is. The sun must be in confusion today.

Over the course of Song's next speech, her upstage special comes up again. She sits in a chair, legs crossed, in a robe, telephone to her ear.

Song: I waited until I saw the sun. That was as much discipline as I could manage for one night. Do you forgive me?

Gallimard: Of course . . . for what?

Song: Then I'll ask you quickly. Are you really interested in the opera?

Gallimard: Why, yes. Yes I am.

Song: Then come again next Thursday. I am playing *The Drunken Beauty.* May I count on you?

Gallimard: Yes. You may.

Song: Perfect. Well, I must be getting to bed. I'm exhausted. It's been a very long night for me.

Song hangs up; special on her goes off. Gallimard begins to dress for work.

Scene X

Song Liling's apartment. Beijing. 1960.

Gallimard: I returned to the opera that next week, and the week after that . . . she keeps our meetings so short — perhaps fifteen, twenty minutes at most. So I am left each week with a thirst which is intensified. In this way, fifteen weeks have gone by. I am starting to doubt the words of my friend Marc.

But no, not really. In my heart, I know she has . . . an interest in me. I suspect this is her way. She is outwardly bold and outspoken, yet her heart is shy and afraid. It is the Oriental in her at war with her Western education.

Song (offstage): I will be out in an instant. Ask the servant for anything you want.

Gallimard: Tonight, I have finally been invited to enter her apartment. Though the idea is almost beyond belief, I believe she is afraid of me.

Gallimard looks around the room. He picks up a picture in a frame, studies it. Without his noticing, Song enters, dressed elegantly in a black gown from the twenties. She stands in the doorway looking like Anna May Wong.°

Song: That is my father.

Gallimard (surprised): Mademoiselle Song . . .

She glides up to him, snatches away the picture.

Song: It is very good that he did not live to see the Revolution. They would, no doubt, have made him kneel on broken glass. Not that he didn't deserve such a punishment. But he is my father. I would've hated to see it happen.

Gallimard: I'm very honored that you've allowed me to visit your home.

Song curtseys.

Song: Thank you. Oh! Haven't you been poured any tea?

Gallimard: I'm really not —

Song (to her offstage servant): Shu-Fang! Cha! Kwai-lah! *(to Gallimard.)* I'm sorry. You want everything to be perfect —

Gallimard: Please.

Song: — and before the evening even begins —

Gallimard: I'm really not thirsty.

Song: — it's ruined.

Gallimard (sharply): Mademoiselle Song!

Song sits down.

Song: I'm sorry.

Gallimard: What are you apologizing for now?

Pause; Song starts to giggle.

Song: I don't know!

Gallimard laughs.

Gallimard: Exactly my point.

Song: Oh, I am silly. Light-headed. I promise not to apologize for anything else tonight, do you hear me?

Gallimard: That's a good girl.

Shu-Fang, a servant girl, comes out with a tea tray and starts to pour.

Song (to Shu-Fang): No! I'll pour myself for the gentleman!

Anna May Wong (1905–1961): Chinese-American actress known for her exotic beauty but most often cast as a villainess.

Shu-Fang, staring at Gallimard, exits.

Gallimard: You have a beautiful home.
Song: No, I . . . I don't even know why I invited you up.
Gallimard: Well, I'm glad you did.

Song looks around the room.

Song: There is an element of danger to your presence.
Gallimard: Oh?
Song: You must know.
Gallimard: It doesn't concern me. We both know why I'm here.
Song: It doesn't concern me either. No . . . well perhaps . . .
Gallimard: What?
Song: Perhaps I am slightly afraid of scandal.
Gallimard: What are we doing?
Song: I'm entertaining you. In my parlor.
Gallimard: In France, that would hardly—
Song: France. France is a country living in the modern era. Perhaps even ahead of it. China is a nation whose soul is firmly rooted two thousand years in the past. What I do, even pouring the tea for you now . . . it has . . . implications. The walls and windows say so. Even my own heart, strapped inside this Western dress . . . even it says things—things I don't care to hear.

Song hands Gallimard a cup of tea. Gallimard puts his hand over both the teacup and Song's hand.

Gallimard: This is a beautiful dress.
Song: Don't.
Gallimard: What?
Song: I don't even know if it looks right on me.
Gallimard: Believe me—
Song: You are from France. You see so many beautiful women.
Gallimard: France? Since when are the European women—?
Song: Oh! What am I trying to do, anyway?!

Song runs to the door, composes herself, then turns towards Gallimard.

Song: Monsieur Gallimard, perhaps you should go.
Gallimard: But . . . why?
Song: There's something wrong about this.
Gallimard: I don't see what.
Song: I feel . . . I am not myself.
Gallimard: No. You're nervous.
Song: Please. Hard as I try to be modern, to speak like a man, to hold a Western woman's strong face up to my own . . . in the end, I fail. A small, frightened heart beats too quickly and gives me away. Monsieur Gallimard, I'm a Chinese girl. I've never . . . never invited a man up to my flat before. The forwardness of my actions makes my skin burn.
Gallimard: What are you afraid of? Certainly not me, I hope.
Song: I'm a modest girl.
Gallimard: I know. And very beautiful. *(He touches her hair.)*
Song: Please—go now. The next time you see me, I shall again be myself.

Gallimard: I like you the way you are right now.
Song: You are a cad.
Gallimard: What do you expect? I'm a foreign devil.

Gallimard walks downstage. Song exits.

Gallimard (to us): Did you hear the way she talked about Western women? Much differently than the first night. She does — she feels inferior to them — and to me.

SCENE XI

The French embassy. Beijing. 1960.
Gallimard moves towards a desk.

Gallimard: I determined to try an experiment. In *Madame Butterfly,* Cio-Cio-San fears that the Western man who catches a butterfly will pierce its heart with a needle, then leave it to perish. I began to wonder: had I, too, caught a butterfly who would writhe on a needle?

Marc enters, dressed as a bureaucrat, holding a stack of papers. As Gallimard speaks, Marc hands papers to him. He peruses, then signs, stamps, or rejects them.

Gallimard: Over the next five weeks, I worked like a dynamo. I stopped going to the opera, I didn't phone or write her. I knew this little flower was waiting for me to call, and, as I wickedly refused to do so, I felt for the first time that rush of power — the absolute power of a man.

Marc continues acting as the bureaucrat, but he now speaks as himself.

Marc: Rene! It's me.
Gallimard: Marc — I hear your voice everywhere now. Even in the midst of work.
Marc: That's because I'm watching you — all the time.
Gallimard: You were always the most popular guy in school.
Marc: Well, there's no guarantee of failure in life like happiness in high school. Somehow I knew I'd end up in the suburbs working for Renault and you'd be in the Orient picking exotic women off the trees. And they say there's no justice.
Gallimard: That's why you were my friend?
Marc: I gave you a little of my life, so that now you can give me some of yours. *(Pause.)* Remember Isabelle?
Gallimard: Of course I remember! She was my first experience.
Marc: We all wanted to ball her. But she only wanted me.
Gallimard: I had her.
Marc: Right. You balled her.
Gallimard: You were the only one who ever believed me.
Marc: Well, there's a good reason for that. *(Beat.)* C'mon. You must've guessed.
Gallimard: You told me to wait in the bushes by the cafeteria that night. The next thing I knew, she was on me. Dress up in the air.
Marc: She never wore underwear.

Gallimard: My arms were pinned to the dirt.

Marc: She loved the superior position. A girl ahead of her time.

Gallimard: I looked up, and there was this woman . . . bouncing up and down on my loins.

Marc: Screaming, right?

Gallimard: Screaming, and breaking off the branches all around me, and pounding my butt up and down into the dirt.

Marc: Huffing and puffing like a locomotive.

Gallimard: And in the middle of all this, the leaves were getting into my mouth, my legs were losing circulation, I thought, "God. So this is *it?*"

Marc: You thought that?

Gallimard: Well, I was worried about my legs falling off.

Marc: You didn't have a good time?

Gallimard: No, that's not what I — I had a great time!

Marc: You're sure?

Gallimard: Yeah. Really.

Marc: 'Cuz I wanted you to have a good time.

Gallimard: I did.

Pause.

Marc: Shit. *(Pause.)* When all is said and done, she was kind of a lousy lay, wasn't she? I mean, there was a lot of energy there, but you never knew what she was doing with it. Like when she yelled "I'm coming!" — hell, it was so loud, you wanted to go, "Look, it's not that big a deal."

Gallimard: I got scared. I thought she meant someone was actually coming. *(Pause.)* But, Marc?

Marc: What?

Gallimard: Thanks.

Marc: Oh, don't mention it.

Gallimard: It was my first experience.

Marc: Yeah. You got her.

Gallimard: I got her.

Marc: Wait! Look at that letter again!

Gallimard picks up one of the papers he's been stamping, and rereads it.

Gallimard (to us): After six weeks, they began to arrive. The letters.

Upstage special on Song, as Madame Butterfly. The scene is underscored by the "Love Duet."

Song: Did we fight? I do not know. Is the opera no longer of interest to you? Please come — my audiences miss the white devil in their midst.

Gallimard looks up from the letter, towards us.

Gallimard (to us): A concession, but much too dignified. *(Beat; he discards the letter.)* I skipped the opera again that week to complete a position paper on trade.

The bureaucrat hands him another letter.

Song: Six weeks have passed since last we met. Is this your practice — to leave friends in the lurch? Sometimes I hate you, sometimes I hate myself, but always I miss you.

Gallimard (to us): Better, but I don't like the way she calls me "friend." When a woman calls a man her "friend," she's calling him a eunuch or a homosexual. *(Beat; he discards the letter.)* I was absent from the opera for the seventh week, feeling a sudden urge to clean out my files.

Bureaucrat hands him another letter.

Song: Your rudeness is beyond belief. I don't deserve this cruelty. Don't bother to call. I'll have you turned away at the door.

Gallimard (to us): I didn't. *(He discards the letter; bureaucrat hands him another.)* And then finally, the letter that concluded my experiment.

Song: I am out of words. I can hide behind dignity no longer. What do you want? I have already given you my shame.

Gallimard gives the letter back to Marc, slowly. Special on Song fades out.

Gallimard (to us): Reading it, I became suddenly ashamed. Yes, my experiment had been a success. She was turning on my needle. But the victory seemed hollow.

Marc: Hollow?! Are you crazy?

Gallimard: Nothing, Marc. Please go away.

Marc (exiting, with papers): Haven't I taught you anything?

Gallimard: "I have already given you my shame." I had to attend a reception that evening. On the way, I felt sick. If there is a God, surely he would punish me now. I had finally gained power over a beautiful woman, only to abuse it cruelly. There must be justice in the world. I had the strange feeling that the ax would fall this very evening.

Scene XII

Ambassador Toulon's residence. Beijing. 1960.

Sound cue: party noises. Light change. We are now in a spacious residence. Toulon, the French ambassador, enters and taps Gallimard on the shoulder.

Toulon: Gallimard? Can I have a word? Over here.

Gallimard (to us): Manuel Toulon. French ambassador to China. He likes to think of us all as his children. Rather like God.

Toulon: Look, Gallimard, there's not much to say. I've liked you. From the day you walked in. You were no leader, but you were tidy and efficient.

Gallimard: Thank you, sir.

Toulon: Don't jump the gun. Okay, our needs in China are changing. It's embarrassing that we lost Indochina. Someone just wasn't on the ball there. I don't mean you personally, of course.

Gallimard: Thank you, sir.

Toulon: We're going to be doing a lot more information-gathering in the future. The nature of our work here is changing. Some people are just going to have to go. It's nothing personal.

Gallimard: Oh.

Toulon: Want to know a secret? Vice-Consul LeBon is being transferred.
Gallimard (to us): My immediate superior!
Toulon: And most of his department.
Gallimard (to us): Just as I feared! God has seen my evil heart—
Toulon: But not you.
Gallimard (to us): —and he's taking her away just as . . . *(To Toulon.)* Excuse me, sir?
Toulon: Scare you? I think I did. Cheer up, Gallimard. I want you to replace LeBon as vice-consul.
Gallimard: You—? Yes, well, thank you, sir.
Toulon: Anytime.
Gallimard: I . . . accept with great humility.
Toulon: Humility won't be part of the job. You're going to coordinate the revamped intelligence division. Want to know a secret? A year ago, you would've been out. But the past few months, I don't know how it happened, you've become this new aggressive confident . . . thing. And they also tell me you get along with the Chinese. So I think you're a lucky man, Gallimard. Congratulations.

They shake hands. Toulon exits. Party noises out. Gallimard stumbles across a darkened stage.

Gallimard: Vice-consul? Impossible! As I stumbled out of the party, I saw it written across the sky: There is no God. Or, no—say that there is a God. But that God . . . understands. Of course! God who creates Eve to serve Adam, who blesses Solomon with his harem but ties Jezebel to a burning bed°—that God is a man. And he understands! At age thirty-nine, I was suddenly initiated into the way of the world.

Scene XIII

Song Liling's apartment. Beijing. 1960.
Song enters, in a sheer dressing gown.

Song: Are you crazy?
Gallimard: Mademoiselle Song—
Song: To come here—at this hour? After . . . after eight weeks?
Gallimard: It's the most amazing—
Song: You bang on my door? Scare my servants, scandalize the neighbors?
Gallimard: I've been promoted. To vice-consul.

Pause.

Song: And what is that supposed to mean to me?
Gallimard: Are you my Butterfly?
Song: What are you saying?
Gallimard: I've come tonight for an answer: are you my Butterfly?
Song: Don't you know already?
Gallimard: I want you to say it.

God who creates Eve . . . burning bed: Eve, Adam, Solomon, and Jezebel are biblical characters. See Gen. 2:18–25; I Kings 11:1–8; and II Kings 9:11–37.

Song: I don't want to say it.
Gallimard: So, that is your answer?
Song: You know how I feel about —
Gallimard: I do remember one thing.
Song: What?
Gallimard: In the letter I received today.
Song: Don't.
Gallimard: "I have already given you my shame."
Song: It's enough that I even wrote it.
Gallimard: Well, then —
Song: I shouldn't have it splashed across my face.
Gallimard: — if that's all true —
Song: Stop!
Gallimard: Then what is one more short answer?
Song: I don't want to!
Gallimard: Are you my Butterfly? *(Silence; he crosses the room and begins to touch her hair.)* I want from you honesty. There should be nothing false between us. No false pride.

Pause.

Song: Yes, I am. I am your Butterfly.
Gallimard: Then let me be honest with you. It is because of you that I was promoted tonight. You have changed my life forever. My little Butterfly, there should be no more secrets: I love you.

He starts to kiss her roughly. She resists slightly.

Song: No . . . no . . . gently . . . please, I've never . . .
Gallimard: No?
Song: I've tried to appear experienced, but . . . the truth is . . . no.
Gallimard: Are you cold?
Song: Yes. Cold.
Gallimard: Then we will go very, very slowly.

He starts to caress her; her gown begins to open.

Song: No . . . let me . . . keep my clothes . . .
Gallimard: But . . .
Song: Please . . . it all frightens me. I'm a modest Chinese girl.
Gallimard: My poor little treasure.
Song: I am your treasure. Though inexperienced, I am not . . . ignorant. They teach us things, our mothers, about pleasing a man.
Gallimard: Yes?
Song: I'll do my best to make you happy. Turn off the lights.

Gallimard gets up and heads for a lamp. Song, propped up on one elbow, tosses her hair back and smiles.

Song: Monsieur Gallimard?
Gallimard: Yes, Butterfly?
Song: *"Vieni, vieni!"*
Gallimard: "Come, darling."

Song: "Ah! Dolce notte!"
Gallimard: "Beautiful night."
Song: "Tutto estatico d'amor ride il ciel!"
Gallimard: "All ecstatic with love, the heavens are filled with laughter."

He turns off the lamp. Blackout.

ACT II

Scene I

M. Gallimard's cell. Paris. 1988.

Lights up on Gallimard. He sits in his cell, reading from a leaflet.

Gallimard: This, from a contemporary critic's commentary on *Madame Butterfly:* "Pinkerton suffers from . . . being an obnoxious bounder whom every man in the audience itches to kick." Bully for us men in the audience! Then, in the same note: "Butterfly is the most irresistibly appealing of Puccini's 'Little Women.' Watching the succession of her humiliations is like watching a child under torture." *(He tosses the pamphlet over his shoulder.)* I suggest that, while we men may all want to kick Pinkerton, very few of us would pass up the opportunity to *be* Pinkerton.

Gallimard moves out of his cell.

Scene II

Gallimard and Butterfly's flat. Beijing. 1960.

We are in a simple but well-decorated parlor. Gallimard moves to sit on a sofa, while Song, dressed in a chong sam,° enters and curls up at his feet.

Gallimard (to us): We secured a flat on the outskirts of Peking. Butterfly, as I was calling her now, decorated our "home" with Western furniture and Chinese antiques. And there, on a few stolen afternoons or evenings each week, Butterfly commenced her education.
Song: The Chinese men — they keep us down.
Gallimard: Even in the "New Society"?
Song: In the "New Society," we are all kept ignorant equally. That's one of the exciting things about loving a Western man. I know you are not threatened by a woman's education.
Gallimard: I'm no saint, Butterfly.
Song: But you come from a progressive society.
Gallimard: We're not always reminding each other how "old" we are, if that's what you mean.
Song: Exactly. We Chinese — once, I suppose, it is true, we ruled the world. But so what? How much more exciting to be part of the society ruling the world today. Tell me — what's happening in Vietnam?
Gallimard: Oh, Butterfly — you want me to bring my work home?

chong sam: A tight-fitting dress with side slits in the skirt.

Song: I want to know what you know. To be impressed by my man. It's not the particulars so much as the fact that you're making decisions which change the shape of the world.

Gallimard: Not the world. At best, a small corner.

Toulon enters, and sits at a desk upstage.

Scene III

French embassy. Beijing. 1961.

Gallimard moves downstage, to Toulon's desk. Song remains upstage, watching.

Toulon: And a more troublesome corner is hard to imagine.

Gallimard: So, the Americans plan to begin bombing?

Toulon: This is very secret, Gallimard: yes. The Americans don't have an embassy here. They're asking us to be their eyes and ears. Say Jack Kennedy signed an order to bomb North Vietnam, Laos. How would the Chinese react?

Gallimard: I think the Chinese will squawk—

Toulon: Uh-huh.

Gallimard: —but, in their hearts, they don't even like Ho Chi Minh.°

Pause.

Toulon: What a bunch of jerks. Vietnam was *our* colony. Not only didn't the Americans help us fight to keep them, but now, seven years later, they've come back to grab the territory for themselves. It's very irritating.

Gallimard: With all due respect, sir, why should the Americans have won our war for us back in fifty-four if we didn't have the will to win it ourselves?

Toulon: You're kidding, aren't you?

Pause.

Gallimard: The Orientals simply want to be associated with whoever shows the most strength and power. You live with the Chinese, sir. Do you think they like Communism?

Toulon: I live in China. Not with the Chinese.

Gallimard: Well, I—

Toulon: You live with the Chinese.

Gallimard: Excuse me?

Toulon: I can't keep a secret.

Gallimard: What are you saying?

Toulon: Only that I'm not immune to gossip. So, you're keeping a native mistress? Don't answer. It's none of my business. *(Pause.)* I'm sure she must be gorgeous.

Gallimard: Well . . .

Toulon: I'm impressed. You had the stamina to go out into the streets and hunt one down. Some of us have to be content with the wives of the expatriate community.

Ho Chi Minh (1890–1969): President of North Vietnam (1945–1969).

Gallimard: I do feel . . . fortunate.

Toulon: So, Gallimard, you've got the inside knowledge — what *do* the Chinese think?

Gallimard: Deep down, they miss the old days. You know, cappuccinos, men in tuxedos —

Toulon: So what do we tell the Americans about Vietnam?

Gallimard: Tell them there's a natural affinity between the West and the Orient.

Toulon: And that you speak from experience?

Gallimard: The Orientals are people too. They want the good things we can give them. If the Americans demonstrate the will to win, the Vietnamese will welcome them into a mutually beneficial union.

Toulon: I don't see how the Vietnamese can stand up to American firepower.

Gallimard: Orientals will always submit to a greater force.

Toulon: I'll note your opinions in my report. The Americans always love to hear how "welcome" they'll be. *(He starts to exit.)*

Gallimard: Sir?

Toulon: Mmmm?

Gallimard: This . . . rumor you've heard.

Toulon: Uh-huh?

Gallimard: How . . . widespread do you think it is?

Toulon: It's only widespread within this embassy. Where nobody talks because everybody is guilty. We were worried about you, Gallimard. We thought you were the only one here without a secret. Now you go and find a lotus blossom . . . and top us all. *(He exits.)*

Gallimard (to us): Toulon knows! And he approves! I was learning the benefits of being a man. We form our own clubs, sit behind thick doors, smoke — and celebrate the fact that we're still boys. *(He starts to move downstage, towards Song.)* So, over the —

Suddenly Comrade Chin enters. Gallimard backs away.

Gallimard (to Song): No! Why does she have to come in?

Song: Rene, be sensible. How can they understand the story without her? Now, don't embarrass yourself.

Gallimard moves down center.

Gallimard (to us): Now, you will see why my story is so amusing to so many people. Why they snicker at parties in disbelief. Please — try to understand it from my point of view. We are all prisoners of our time and place. *(He exits.)*

Scene IV

Gallimard and Butterfly's flat. Beijing. 1961.

Song (to us): 1961. The flat Monsieur Gallimard rented for us. An evening after he has gone.

Chin: Okay, see if you can find out when the Americans plan to start bombing Vietnam. If you can find out what cities, even better.

Song: I'll do my best, but I don't want to arouse his suspicions.

Chin: Yeah, sure, of course. So, what else?

Song: The Americans will increase troops in Vietnam to 170,000 soldiers with 120,000 militia and 11,000 American advisors.

Chin (writing): Wait, wait, 120,000 militia and —

Song: — 11,000 American —

Chin: — American advisors. *(Beat.)* How do you remember so much?

Song: I'm an actor.

Chin: Yeah. *(Beat.)* Is that how come you dress like that?

Song: Like what, Miss Chin?

Chin: Like that dress! You're wearing a dress. And every time I come here, you're wearing a dress. Is that because you're an actor? Or what?

Song: It's a . . . disguise, Miss Chin.

Chin: Actors, I think they're all weirdos. My mother tells me actors are like gamblers or prostitutes or —

Song: It helps me in my assignment.

Pause.

Chin: You're not gathering information in any way that violates Communist Party principles, are you?

Song: Why would I do that?

Chin: Just checking. Remember: when working for the Great Proletarian State, you represent our Chairman Mao in every position you take.

Song: I'll try to imagine the Chairman taking my positions.

Chin: We all think of him this way. Good-bye, comrade. *(She starts to exit.)* Comrade?

Song: Yes?

Chin: Don't forget: there is no homosexuality in China!

Song: Yes, I've heard.

Chin: Just checking. *(She exits.)*

Song (to us): What passes for a woman in modern China.

Gallimard sticks his head out from the wings.

Gallimard: Is she gone?

Song: Yes, Rene. Please continue in your own fashion.

Scene V

Beijing. 1961–1963.

Gallimard moves to the couch where Song still sits. He lies down in her lap, and she strokes his forehead.

Gallimard (to us): And so, over the years 1961, '62, '63, we settled into our routine, Butterfly and I. She would always have prepared a light snack and then, ever so delicately, and only if I agreed, she would start to pleasure me. With her hands, her mouth . . . too many ways to explain, and too sad, given my present situation. But mostly we would talk. About my life. Perhaps there is nothing more rare than to find a woman who passionately listens.

Song remains upstage, listening, as Helga enters and plays a scene downstage with Gallimard.

Helga: Rene, I visited Dr. Bolleart this morning.

Gallimard: Why? Are you ill?

Helga: No, no. You see, I wanted to ask him . . . that question we've been discussing.

Gallimard: And I told you, it's only a matter of time. Why did you bring a doctor into this? We just have to keep trying — like a crapshoot, actually.

Helga: I went, I'm sorry. But listen: he says there's nothing wrong with me.

Gallimard: You see? Now, will you stop — ?

Helga: Rene, he says he'd like you to go in and take some tests.

Gallimard: Why? So he can find there's nothing wrong with both of us?

Helga: Rene, I don't ask for much. One trip! One visit! And then, whatever you want to do about it — you decide.

Gallimard: You're assuming he'll find something defective!

Helga: No! Of course not! Whatever he finds — if he finds nothing, we decide what to do about nothing! But go!

Gallimard: If he finds nothing, we keep trying. Just like we do now.

Helga: But at least we'll know! *(Pause.)* I'm sorry. *(She starts to exit.)*

Gallimard: Do you really want me to see Dr. Bolleart?

Helga: Only if you want a child, Rene. We have to face the fact that time is running out. Only if you want a child. *(She exits.)*

Gallimard (to Song): I'm a modern man, Butterfly. And yet, I don't want to go. It's the same old voodoo. I feel like God himself is laughing at me if I can't produce a child.

Song: You men of the West — you're obsessed by your odd desire for equality. Your wife can't give you a child, and *you're* going to the doctor?

Gallimard: Well, you see, she's already gone.

Song: And because this incompetent can't find the defect, you now have to subject yourself to him? It's unnatural.

Gallimard: Well, what is the "natural" solution?

Song: In Imperial China, when a man found that one wife was inadequate, he turned to another — to give him his son.

Gallimard: What do you — ? I can't . . . marry you, yet.

Song: Please. I'm not asking you to be my husband. But I am already your wife.

Gallimard: Do you want to . . . have my child?

Song: I thought you'd never ask.

Gallimard: But, your career . . . your —

Song: Phooey on my career! That's your Western mind, twisting itself into strange shapes again. Of course I love my career. But what would I love most of all? To feel something inside me — day and night — something I know is yours. *(Pause.)* Promise me . . . you won't go to this doctor. Who is this Western quack to set himself as judge over the man I love? I know who is a man, and who is not. *(She exits.)*

Gallimard (to us): Dr. Bolleart? Of course I didn't go. What man would?

SCENE VI

Beijing. 1963

Party noises over the house speakers. Renee enters, wearing a revealing gown.

Gallimard: 1963. A party at the Austrian embassy. None of us could remember the Austrian ambassador's name, which seemed somehow appropriate. *(To Renee.)* So, I tell the Americans, Diem° must go. The U.S. wants to be respected by the Vietnamese, and yet they're propping up this nobody seminarian as her president. A man whose claim to fame is his sister-in-law imposing fanatic "moral order" campaigns? Oriental women — when they're good, they're very good, but when they're bad, they're Christians.

Renee: Yeah.

Gallimard: And what do you do?

Renee: I'm a student. My father exports a lot of useless stuff to the Third World.

Gallimard: How useless?

Renee: You know. Squirt guns, confectioner's sugar, Hula Hoops . . .

Gallimard: I'm sure they appreciate the sugar.

Renee: I'm here for two years to study Chinese.

Gallimard: Two years!

Renee: That's what everybody says.

Gallimard: When did you arrive?

Renee: Three weeks ago.

Gallimard: And?

Renee: I like it. It's primitive, but . . . well, this is the place to learn Chinese, so here I am.

Gallimard: Why Chinese?

Renee: I think it'll be important someday.

Gallimard: You do?

Renee: Don't ask me when, but . . . that's what I think.

Gallimard: Well, I agree with you. One hundred percent. That's very farsighted.

Renee: Yeah. Well of course, my father thinks I'm a complete weirdo.

Gallimard: He'll thank you someday.

Renee: Like when the Chinese start buying Hula Hoops?

Gallimard: There're a billion bellies out there.

Renee: And if they end up taking over the world — well, then I'll be lucky to know Chinese too, right?

Pause.

Gallimard: At this point, I don't see how the Chinese can possibly take —

Renee: You know what I *don't* like about China?

Gallimard: Excuse me? No — what?

Renee: Nothing to do at night.

Gallimard: You come to parties at embassies like everyone else.

Renee: Yeah, but they get out at ten. And then what?

Gallimard: I'm afraid the Chinese idea of a dance hall is a dirt floor and a man with a flute.

Renee: Are you married?

Gallimard: Yes. Why?

Renee: You wanna . . . fool around?

Pause.

Diem: Ngo Dinh Diem (1901–1963), president of South Vietnam (1955–1963), assassinated in a coup d'etat supported by the United States.

Gallimard: Sure.

Renee: I'll wait for you outside. What's your name?

Gallimard: Gallimard. Rene.

Renee: Weird. I'm Renee too. *(She exits.)*

Gallimard (to us): And so, I embarked on my first extra-extramarital affair. Renee was picture perfect. With a body like those girls in the magazines. If I put a tissue paper over my eyes, I wouldn't have been able to tell the difference. And it was exciting to be with someone who wasn't afraid to be seen completely naked. But is it possible for a woman to be *too* uninhibited, *too* willing, so as to seem almost too . . . masculine?

Chuck Berry° blares from the house speakers, then comes down in volume as Renee enters, toweling her hair.

Renee: You have a nice weenie.

Gallimard: What?

Renee: Penis. You have a nice penis.

Gallimard: Oh. Well, thank you. That's very . . .

Renee: What — can't take a compliment?

Gallimard: No, it's very . . . reassuring.

Renee: But most girls don't come out and say it, huh?

Gallimard: And also . . . what did you call it?

Renee: Oh. Most girls don't call it a "weenie," huh?

Gallimard: It sounds very —

Renee: Small, I know.

Gallimard: I was going to say, "young."

Renee: Yeah. Young, small, same thing. Most guys are pretty, uh, sensitive about that. Like, you know, I had a boyfriend back home in Denmark. I got mad at him once and called him a little weeniehead. He got so mad! He said at least I should call him a great big weeniehead.

Gallimard: I suppose I just say "penis."

Renee: Yeah. That's pretty clinical. There's "cock," but that sounds like a chicken. And "prick" is painful, and "dick" is like you're talking about someone who's not in the room.

Gallimard: Yes. It's a . . . bigger problem than I imagined.

Renee: I — I think maybe it's because I really don't know what to do with them — that's why I call them "weenies."

Gallimard: Well, you did quite well with . . . mine.

Renee: Thanks, but I mean, really *do* with them. Like, okay, have you ever looked at one? I mean, really?

Gallimard: No, I suppose when it's part of you, you sort of take it for granted.

Renee: I guess. But, like, it just hangs there. This little . . . flap of flesh. And there's so much fuss that we make about it. Like, I think the reason we fight wars is because we wear clothes. Because no one knows — between the men, I mean — who has the biggest . . . weenie. So, if I'm a guy with a small one, I'm going to build a really big building or take over a really big piece of land or write a really long book so the other men don't know, right? But, see, it never really works, that's the problem. I mean, you con-

Chuck Berry: Influential American rock 'n' roll musician whose first recording came out in 1955.

quer the country, or whatever, but you're still wearing clothes, so there's no way to prove absolutely whose is bigger or smaller. And that's what we call a civilized society. The whole world run by a bunch of men with pricks the size of pins. *(She exits.)*

Gallimard (to us): This was simply not acceptable.

A high-pitched chime rings through the air. Song, dressed as Butterfly, appears in the upstage special. She is obviously distressed. Her body swoons as she attempts to clip the stems of flowers she's arranging in a vase.

Gallimard: But I kept up our affair, wildly, for several months. Why? I believe because of Butterfly. She knew the secret I was trying to hide. But, unlike a Western woman, she didn't confront me, threaten, even pout. I remembered the words of Puccini's *Butterfly:*

Song: "Noi siamo gente avvezza/ alle piccole cose/ umili e silenziose."

Gallimard: "I come from a people/ Who are accustomed to little/ Humble and silent." I saw Pinkerton and Butterfly, and what she would say if he were unfaithful . . . nothing. She would cry, alone, into those wildly soft sleeves, once full of possessions, now empty to collect her tears. It was her tears and her silence that excited me, every time I visited Renee.

Toulon (offstage): Gallimard!

Toulon enters. Gallimard turns towards him. During the next section, Song, up center, begins to dance with the flowers. It is a drunken, reckless dance, where she breaks small pieces off the stems.

Toulon: They're killing him.

Gallimard: Who? I'm sorry? What?

Toulon: Bother you to come over at this late hour?

Gallimard: No . . . of course not.

Toulon: Not after you hear my secret. Champagne?

Gallimard: Um . . . thank you.

Toulon: You're surprised. There's something that you've wanted, Gallimard. No, not a promotion. Next time. Something in the world. You're not aware of this, but there's an informal gossip circle among intelligence agents. And some of ours heard from some of the Americans —

Gallimard: Yes?

Toulon: That the U.S. will allow the Vietnamese generals to stage a coup . . . and assassinate President Diem.

The chime rings again. Toulon freezes. Gallimard turns upstage and looks at Butterfly, who slowly and deliberately clips a flower off its stem. Gallimard turns back towards Toulon.

Gallimard: I think . . . that's a very wise move!

Toulon unfreezes.

Toulon: It's what you've been advocating. A toast?

Gallimard: Sure. I consider this a vindication.

Toulon: Not exactly. "To the test. Let's hope you pass."

They drink. The chime rings again. Toulon freezes. Gallimard turns upstage, and Song clips another flower.

Gallimard (to Toulon): The test?

Toulon (unfreezing): It's a test of everything you've been saying. I personally think the generals probably will stop the Communists. And you'll be a hero. But if anything goes wrong, then your opinions won't be worth a pig's ear. I'm sure that won't happen. But sometimes it's easier when they don't listen to you.

Gallimard: They're your opinions too, aren't they?

Toulon: Personally, yes.

Gallimard: So we agree.

Toulon: But my opinions aren't on that report. Yours are. Cheers.

Toulon turns away from Gallimard and raises his glass. At that instant Song picks up the vase and hurls it to the ground. It shatters. Song sinks down amidst the shards of the vase, in a calm, childlike trance. She sings softly, as if reciting a child's nursery rhyme.

Song (repeat as necessary): "The whole world over, the white man travels, setting anchor, wherever he likes. Life's not worth living, unless he finds, the finest maidens, of every land . . ."

Gallimard turns downstage towards us. Song continues singing.

Gallimard: I shook as I left his house. That coward! That worm! To put the burden for his decisions on my shoulders!

I started for Renee's. But no, that was all I needed. A schoolgirl who would question the role of the penis in modern society. What I wanted was revenge. A vessel to contain my humiliation. Though I hadn't seen her in several weeks, I headed for Butterfly's.

Gallimard enters Song's apartment.

Song: Oh! Rene . . . I was dreaming!

Gallimard: You've been drinking?

Song: If I can't sleep, then yes, I drink. But then, it gives me these dreams which — Rene, it's been almost three weeks since you visited me last.

Gallimard: I know. There's been a lot going on in the world.

Song: Fortunately I am drunk. So I can speak freely. It's not the world, it's you and me. And an old problem. Even the softest skin becomes like leather to a man who's touched it too often. I confess I don't know how to stop it. I don't know how to become another woman.

Gallimard: I have a request.

Song: Is this a solution? Or are you ready to give up the flat?

Gallimard: It may be a solution. But I'm sure you won't like it.

Song: Oh well, that's very important. "Like it?" Do you think I "like" lying here alone, waiting, always waiting for your return? Please — don't worry about what I may not "like."

Gallimard: I want to see you . . . naked.

Silence.

Song: I thought you understood my modesty. So you want me to — what — strip? Like a big cowboy girl? Shiny pasties on my breasts? Shall I fling my kimono over my head and yell "ya-hoo" in the process? I thought you respected my shame!

Gallimard: I believe you gave me your shame many years ago.

Song: Yes — and it is just like a white devil to use it against me. I can't believe it. I thought myself so repulsed by the passive Oriental and the cruel white man. Now I see — we are always most revolted by the things hidden within us.

Gallimard: I just mean —

Song: Yes?

Gallimard: — that it will remove the only barrier left between us.

Song: No, Rene. Don't couch your request in sweet words. Be yourself — a cad — and know that my love is enough, that I submit — submit to the worst you can give me. *(Pause.)* Well, come. Strip me. Whatever happens, know that you have willed it. Our love, in your hands. I'm helpless before my man.

Gallimard starts to cross the room.

Gallimard: Did I not undress her because I knew, somewhere deep down, what I would find? Perhaps. Happiness is so rare that our mind can turn somersaults to protect it.

At the time, I only knew that I was seeing Pinkerton stalking towards his Butterfly, ready to reward her love with his lecherous hands. The image sickened me, pulled me to my knees, so I was crawling towards her like a worm. By the time I reached her, Pinkerton . . . had vanished from my heart. To be replaced by something new, something unnatural, that flew in the face of all I'd learned in the world — something very close to love.

He grabs her around the waist; she strokes his hair.

Gallimard: Butterfly, forgive me.

Song: Rene . . .

Gallimard: For everything. From the start.

Song: I'm . . .

Gallimard: I want to —

Song: I'm pregnant. *(Beat.)* I'm pregnant. *(Beat.)* I'm pregnant.

Beat.

Gallimard: I want to marry you!

Scene VII

Gallimard and Butterfly's flat. Beijing. 1963.

Downstage, Song paces as Comrade Chin reads from her notepad. Upstage, Gallimard is still kneeling. He remains on his knees throughout the scene, watching it.

Song: I need a baby.

Chin (from pad): He's been spotted going to a dorm.

Song: I need a baby.

Chin: At the Foreign Language Institute.
Song: I need a baby.
Chin: The room of a Danish girl. . . . What do you mean, you need a baby?!
Song: Tell Comrade Kang — last night, the entire mission, it could've ended.
Chin: What do you mean?
Song: Tell Kang — he told me to strip.
Chin: Strip?!
Song: Write!
Chin: I tell you, I don't understand nothing about this case anymore. Nothing.
Song: He told me to strip, and I took a chance. Oh, we Chinese, we know how to gamble.
Chin (writing): ". . . told him to strip."
Song: My palms were wet, I had to make a split-second decision.
Chin: Hey! Can you slow down?!

Pause.

Song: You write faster, I'm the artist here. Suddenly, it hit me — "All he wants is for her to submit. Once a woman submits, a man is always ready to become 'generous.' "
Chin: You're just gonna end up with rough notes.
Song: And it worked! He gave in! Now, if I can just present him with a baby. A Chinese baby with blond hair — he'll be mine for life!
Chin: Kang will never agree! The trading of babies has to be a counterrevolutionary act!
Song: Sometimes, a counterrevolutionary act is necessary to counter a counterrevolutionary act.

Pause.

Chin: Wait.
Song: I need one . . . in seven months. Make sure it's a boy.
Chin: This doesn't sound like something the Chairman would do. Maybe you'd better talk to Comrade Kang yourself.
Song: Good. I will.

Chin gets up to leave.

Song: Miss Chin? Why, in the Peking Opera, are women's roles played by men?
Chin: I don't know. Maybe, a reactionary remnant of male —
Song: No. *(Beat.)* Because only a man knows how a woman is supposed to act.

Chin exits. Song turns upstage, towards Gallimard.

Gallimard (calling after Chin): Good riddance! *(To Song.)* I could forget all that betrayal in an instant, you know. If you'd just come back and become Butterfly again.
Song: Fat chance. You're here in prison, rotting in a cell. And I'm on a plane, winging my way back to China. Your President pardoned me of our treason, you know.
Gallimard: Yes, I read about that.
Song: Must make you feel . . . lower than shit.
Gallimard: But don't you, even a little bit, wish you were here with me?

Song: I'm an artist, Rene. You were my greatest . . . acting challenge. *(She laughs.)* It doesn't matter how rotten I answer, does it? You still adore me. That's why I love you, Rene. *(She points to us.)* So — you were telling your audience about the night I announced I was pregnant.

Gallimard puts his arms around Song's waist. He and Song are in the positions they were in at the end of Scene VI.

Scene VIII

Same.

Gallimard: I'll divorce my wife. We'll live together here, and then later in France.
Song: I feel so . . . ashamed.
Gallimard: Why?
Song: I had begun to lose faith. And now, you shame me with your generosity.
Gallimard: Generosity? No, I'm proposing for very selfish reasons.
Song: Your apologies only make me feel more ashamed. My outburst a moment ago!
Gallimard: Your outburst? What about my request?!
Song: You've been very patient dealing with my . . . eccentricities. A Western man, used to women freer with their bodies —
Gallimard: It was sick! Don't make excuses for me.
Song: I have to. You don't seem willing to make them for yourself.

Pause.

Gallimard: You're crazy.
Song: I'm happy. Which often looks like crazy.
Gallimard: Then make me crazy. Marry me.

Pause.

Song: No.
Gallimard: What?
Song: Do I sound silly, a slave, if I say I'm not worthy?
Gallimard: Yes. In fact you do. No one has loved me like you.
Song: Thank you. And no one ever will. I'll see to that.
Gallimard: So what is the problem?
Song: Rene, we Chinese are realists. We understand rice, gold, and guns. You are a diplomat. Your career is skyrocketing. Now, what would happen if you divorced your wife to marry a Communist Chinese actress?
Gallimard: That's not being realistic. That's defeating yourself before you begin.
Song: We conserve our strength for the battles we can win.
Gallimard: That sounds like a fortune cookie!
Song: Where do you think fortune cookies come from!
Gallimard: I don't care.
Song: You do. So do I. And we should. That is why I say I'm not worthy. I'm worthy to love and even to be loved by you. But I am not worthy to end the career of one of the West's most promising diplomats.
Gallimard: It's not that great a career! I made it sound like more than it is!

Song: Modesty will get you nowhere. Flatter yourself, and you flatter me. I'm flattered to decline your offer. *(She exits.)*

Gallimard (to us): Butterfly and I argued all night. And, in the end, I left, knowing I would never be her husband. She went away for several months — to the countryside, like a small animal. Until the night I received her call.

A baby's cry from offstage. Song enters, carrying a child.

Song: He looks like you.

Gallimard: Oh! *(Beat; he approaches the baby.)* Well, babies are never very attractive at birth.

Song: Stop!

Gallimard: I'm sure he'll grow more beautiful with age. More like his mother.

Song: *"Chi vide mai/ a bimbo del Giappon . . ."*

Gallimard: "What baby, I wonder, was ever born in Japan" — or China, for that matter —

Song: *". . . occhi azzurrini?"*

Gallimard: "With azure eyes" — they're actually sort of brown, wouldn't you say?

Song: *"E il labbro."*

Gallimard: "And such lips!" *(He kisses Song.)* And such lips.

Song: *"E i ricciolini d'oro schietto?"*

Gallimard: "And such a head of golden" — if slightly patchy — "curls?"

Song: I'm going to call him "Peepee."

Gallimard: Darling, could you repeat that because I'm sure a rickshaw just flew by overhead.

Song: You heard me.

Gallimard: "Song Peepee"? May I suggest Michael, or Stephan, or Adolph?

Song: You may, but I won't listen.

Gallimard: You can't be serious. Can you imagine the time this child will have in school?

Song: In the West, yes.

Gallimard: It's worse than naming him Ping Pong or Long Dong or —

Song: But he's never going to live in the West, is he?

Pause.

Gallimard: That wasn't my choice.

Song: It is mine. And this is my promise to you: I will raise him, he will be our child, but he will never burden you outside of China.

Gallimard: Why do you make these promises? I want to be burdened! I want a scandal to cover the papers!

Song (to us): Prophetic.

Gallimard: I'm serious.

Song: So am I. His name is as I registered it. And he will never live in the West.

Song exits with the child.

Gallimard (to us): Is it possible that her stubbornness only made me want her more. That drawing back at the moment of my capitulation was the most brilliant strategy she could have chosen. It is possible. But it is also possible that by this point she could have said, could have done . . . anything, and I would have adored her still.

Scene IX

Beijing. 1966.

A driving rhythm of Chinese percussion fills the stage.

Gallimard: And then, China began to change. Mao became very old, and his cult became very strong. And, like many old men, he entered his second childhood. So he handed over the reins of state to those with minds like his own. And children ruled the Middle Kingdom° with complete caprice. The doctrine of the Cultural Revolution° implied continuous anarchy. Contact between Chinese and foreigners became impossible. Our flat was confiscated. Her fame and my money now counted against us.

Two dancers in Mao suits and red-starred caps enter, and begin crudely mimicking revolutionary violence, in an agitprop fashion.

Gallimard: And somehow the American war went wrong too. Four hundred thousand dollars were being spent for every Viet Cong° killed; so General Westmoreland's° remark that the Oriental does not value life the way Americans do was oddly accurate. Why weren't the Vietnamese people giving in? Why were they content instead to die and die and die again?

Toulon enters. Percussion and dancers continue upstage.

Toulon: Congratulations, Gallimard.

Gallimard: Excuse me, sir?

Toulon: Not a promotion. That was last time. You're going home.

Gallimard: What?

Toulon: Don't say I didn't warn you.

Gallimard: I'm being transferred . . . because I was wrong about the American war?

Toulon: Of course not. We don't care about the Americans. We care about your mind. The quality of your analysis. In general, everything you've predicted here in the Orient . . . just hasn't happened.

Gallimard: I think that's premature.

Toulon: Don't force me to be blunt. Okay, you said China was ready to open to Western trade. The only thing they're trading out there are Western heads. And, yes, you said the Americans would succeed in Indochina. You were kidding, right?

Gallimard: I think the end is in sight.

Toulon: Don't be pathetic. And don't take this personally. You were wrong. It's not your fault.

Gallimard: But I'm going home.

Middle Kingdom: The royal domain of China during its feudal period.
Cultural Revolution: The reactionary campaign of 1965–1967 against opponents of the ideas of China's leader, Mao Tse-tung.
Viet Cong: Member of the Vietnamese Communist movement, against which U.S. forces were fighting.
General Westmoreland: William Westmoreland (b. 1914), commander of American troops in Vietnam from 1964 to 1968.

Toulon: Right. Could I have the number of your mistress? *(Beat.)* Joke! Joke! Eat a croissant for me.

Toulon exits. Song, wearing a Mao suit, is dragged in from the wings as part of the upstage dance. They "beat" her, then lampoon the acrobatics of the Chinese opera, as she is made to kneel onstage.

Gallimard (simultaneously): I don't care to recall how Butterfly and I said our hurried farewell. Perhaps it was better to end our affair before it killed her.

Gallimard exits. Percussion rises in volume. The lampooning becomes faster, more frenetic. At its height, Comrade Chin walks across the stage with a banner reading: "The Actor Renounces His Decadent Profession!" She reaches the kneeling Song. At the moment Chin touches Song's chin, percussion stops with a thud. Dancers strike poses.

Chin: Actor-oppressor, for years you have lived above the common people and looked down on their labor. While the farmer ate millet—
Song: I ate pastries from France and sweetmeats from silver trays.
Chin: And how did you come to live in such an exalted position?
Song: I was a plaything for the imperialists!
Chin: What did you do?
Song: I shamed China by allowing myself to be corrupted by a foreigner . . .
Chin: What does this mean? The People demand a full confession!
Song: I engaged in the lowest perversions with China's enemies!
Chin: What perversions? Be more clear!
Song: I let him put it up my ass!

Dancers look over, disgusted.

Chin: Aaaa-ya! How can you use such sickening language?!
Song: My language . . . is only as foul as the crimes I committed . . .
Chin: Yeah. That's better. So—what do you want to do . . . now?
Song: I want to serve the people

Percussion starts up, with Chinese strings.

Chin: What?
Song: I want to serve the people!

Dancers regain their revolutionary smiles, and begin a dance of victory.

Chin: What?!
Song: I want to serve the people!!

Dancers unveil a banner: "The Actor Is Re-Habilitated!" Song remains kneeling before Chin, as the dancers bounce around them, then exit. Music out.

Scene X

A commune. Hunan Province. 1970

Chin: How you planning to do that?
Song: I've already worked four years in the fields of Hunan, Comrade Chin.
Chin: So? Farmers work all their lives. Let me see your hands.

Song holds them out for her inspection.

Chin: Goddamn! Still so smooth! How long does it take to turn you actors into good anythings? Hunh. You've just spent too many years in luxury to be any good to the Revolution.

Song: I served the Revolution.

Chin: Serve the Revolution? Bullshit! You wore dresses! Don't tell me — I was there. I saw you! You and your white vice-consul! Stuck up there in your flat, living off the People's Treasury! Yeah, I knew what was going on! You two . . . homos! Homos! Homos! *(Pause; she composes herself.)* Ah! Well . . . you will serve the people, all right. But not with the Revolution's money. This time, you use your own money.

Song: I have no money.

Chin: Shut up! And you won't stink up China anymore with your pervert stuff. You'll pollute the place where pollution begins — the West.

Song: What do you mean?

Chin: Shut up! You're going to France. Without a cent in your pocket. You find your consul's house, you make him pay your expenses —

Song: No.

Chin: And you give us weekly reports! Useful information!

Song: That's crazy. It's been four years.

Chin: Either that, or back to rehabilitation center!

Song: Comrade Chin, he's not going to support me! Not in France! He's a white man! I was just his plaything —

Chin: Oh yuck! Again with the sickening language? Where's my stick?

Song: You don't understand the mind of a man.

Pause.

Chin: Oh no? No I don't? Then how come I'm married, huh? How come I got a man? Five, six years ago, you always tell me those kind of things, I felt very bad. But not now! Because what does the Chairman say? He tells us *I'm* now the smart one, you're now the nincompoop! *You're* the blockhead, the hare-brain, the nitwit! You think you're so smart? You understand "The Mind of a Man"? Good! Then *you* go to France and be a pervert for Chairman Mao!

Chin and Song exit in opposite directions.

Scene XI

Paris. 1968–1970.
Gallimard enters.

Gallimard: And what was waiting for me back in Paris? Well, better Chinese food than I'd eaten in China. Friends and relatives. A little accounting, regular schedule, keeping track of traffic violations in the suburbs. . . . And the indignity of students shouting the slogans of Chairman Mao at me — in French.

Helga: Rene? Rene? *(She enters, soaking wet.)* I've had a . . . problem. *(She sneezes.)*

Gallimard: You're wet.

Helga: Yes, I . . . coming back from the grocer's. A group of students, waving red flags, they—

Gallimard fetches a towel.

Helga: —they ran by, I was caught up along with them. Before I knew what was happening—

Gallimard gives her the towel.

Helga: Thank you. The police started firing water cannons at us. I tried to shout, to tell them I was the wife of a diplomat, but—you know how it is . . . *(Pause.)* Needless to say, I lost the groceries. Rene, what's happening to France?

Gallimard: What's—? Well, nothing, really.

Helga: Nothing?! The storefronts are in flames, there's glass in the streets, buildings are toppling—and I'm wet!

Gallimard: Nothing! . . . that I care to think about.

Helga: And is that why you stay in this room?

Gallimard: Yes, in fact.

Helga: With the incense burning? You know something? I hate incense. It smells so sickly sweet.

Gallimard: Well, I hate the French. Who just smell—period!

Helga: And the Chinese were better?

Gallimard: Please—don't start.

Helga: When we left, this exact same thing, the riots—

Gallimard: No, no . . .

Helga: Students screaming slogans, smashing down doors—

Gallimard: Helga—

Helga: It was all going on in China, too. Don't you remember?!

Gallimard: Helga! Please! *(Pause.)* You have never understood China, have you? You walk in here with these ridiculous ideas, that the West is falling apart, that China was spitting in our faces. You come in, dripping of the streets, and you leave water all over my floor. *(He grabs Helga's towel, begins mopping up the floor.)*

Helga: But it's the truth!

Gallimard: Helga, I want a divorce.

Pause; Gallimard continues mopping the floor.

Helga: I take it back. China is . . . beautiful. Incense, I like incense.

Gallimard: I've had a mistress.

Helga: So?

Gallimard: For eight years.

Helga: I knew you would. I knew you would the day I married you. And now what? You want to marry her?

Gallimard: I can't. She's in China.

Helga: I see. You know that no one else is ever going to marry me, right?

Gallimard: I'm sorry.

Helga: And you want to leave. For someone who's not here, is that right?

Gallimard: That's right.

Helga: You can't live with her, but still you don't want to live with me.
Gallimard: That's right.

Pause.

Helga: Shit. How terrible that I can figure that out. *(Pause.)* I never thought I'd say it. But, in China, I was happy. I knew, in my own way, I knew that you were not everything you pretended to be. But the pretense — going on your arm to the embassy ball, visiting your office and the guards saying, "Good morning, good morning, Madame Gallimard" — the pretense . . . was very good indeed. *(Pause.)* I hope everyone is mean to you for the rest of your life. *(She exits.)*
Gallimard (to us): Prophetic.

Marc enters with two drinks.

Gallimard (to Marc): In China, I was different from all other men.
Marc: Sure. You were white. Here's your drink.
Gallimard: I felt . . . touched.
Marc: In the head? Rene, I don't want to hear about the Oriental love goddess. Okay? One night — can we just drink and throw up without a lot of conversation?
Gallimard: You still don't believe me, do you?
Marc: Sure I do. She was the most beautiful, et cetera, et cetera, blasé, blasé.

Pause.

Gallimard: My life in the West has been such a disappointment.
Marc: Life in the West is like that. You'll get used to it. Look, you're driving me away. I'm leaving. Happy, now? *(He exits, then returns.)* Look, I have a date tomorrow night. You wanna come? I can fix you up with —
Gallimard: Of course. I would love to come.

Pause.

Marc: Uh — on second thought, no. You'd better get ahold of yourself first.

He exits; Gallimard nurses his drink.

Gallimard (to us): This is the ultimate cruelty, isn't it? That I can talk and talk and to anyone listening, it's only air — too rich a diet to be swallowed by a mundane world. Why can't anyone understand? That in China, I once loved, and was loved by, very simply, the Perfect Woman.

Song enters, dressed as Butterfly in wedding dress.

Gallimard (to Song): Not again. My imagination is hell. Am I asleep this time? Or did I drink too much?
Song: Rene!
Gallimard: God, it's too painful! That you speak?
Song: What are you talking about? Rene — touch me.
Gallimard: Why?
Song: I'm real. Take my hand.

Gallimard: Why? So you can disappear again and leave me clutching at the air? For the entertainment of my neighbors who — ?

Song touches Gallimard.

Song: Rene?

Gallimard takes Song's hand. Silence.

Gallimard: Butterfly? I never doubted you'd return.

Song: You hadn't . . . forgotten — ?

Gallimard: Yes, actually, I've forgotten everything. My mind, you see — there wasn't enough room in this hard head — not for the world *and* for you. No, there was only room for one. *(Beat.)* Come, look. See? Your bed has been waiting, with the Klimt° poster you like, and — see? The *xiang lu*° you gave me?

Song: I . . . I don't know what to say.

Gallimard: There's nothing to say. Not at the end of a long trip. Can I make you some tea?

Song: But where's your wife?

Gallimard: She's by my side. She's by my side at last.

Gallimard reaches to embrace Song. Song sidesteps, dodging him.

Gallimard: Why?!

Song (to us): So I did return to Rene in Paris. Where I found —

Gallimard: Why do you run away? Can't we show them how we embraced that evening?

Song: Please. I'm talking.

Gallimard: You have to do what I say! I'm conjuring you up in *my* mind!

Song: Rene, I've never done what you've said. Why should it be any different in your mind? Now split — the story moves on, and I must change.

Gallimard: I welcomed you into my home! I didn't have to, you know! I could've left you penniless on the streets of Paris! But I took you in!

Song: Thank you.

Gallimard: So . . . please . . . don't change.

Song: You know I have to. You know I will. And anyway, what difference does it make? No matter what your eyes tell you, you can't ignore the truth. You already know too much.

Gallimard exits. Song turns to us.

Song: The change I'm going to make requires about five minutes. So I thought you might want to take this opportunity to stretch your legs, enjoy a drink, or listen to the musicians. I'll be here, when you return, right where you left me.

Song goes to a mirror in front of which is a wash basin of water. She starts to remove her makeup as stagelights go to half and houselights come up.

Klimt: Gustav Klimt (1863–1918), painter of the Austrian Secession style.
xiang lu: Incense burner.

ACT III

Scene I

A courthouse in Paris. 1986.

As he promised, Song has completed the bulk of his transformation onstage by the time the houselights go down and the stagelights come up full. As he speaks to us, he removes his wig and kimono, leaving them on the floor. Underneath, he wears a well-cut suit.

Song: So I'd done my job better than I had a right to expect. Well, give him some credit, too. He's right — I was in a fix when I arrived in Paris. I walked from the airport into town, then I located, by blind groping, the Chinatown district. Let me make one thing clear: whatever else may be said about the Chinese, they are stingy! I slept in doorways three days until I could find a tailor who would make me this kimono on credit. As it turns out, maybe I didn't even need it. Maybe he would've been happy to see me in a simple shift and mascara. But . . . better safe than sorry.

That was 1970, when I arrived in Paris. For the next fifteen years, yes, I lived a very comfy life. Some relief, believe me, after four years on a fucking commune in Nowheresville, China. Rene supported the boy and me, and I did some demonstrations around the country as part of my "cultural exchange" cover. And then there was the spying.

Song moves upstage, to a chair. Toulon enters as a judge, wearing the appropriate wig and robes. He sits near Song. It's 1986, and Song is testifying in a courtroom.

Song: Not much at first. Rene had lost all his high-level contacts. Comrade Chin wasn't very interested in parking-ticket statistics. But finally, at my urging, Rene got a job as a courier, handling sensitive documents. He'd photograph them for me, and I'd pass them on to the Chinese embassy.

Judge: Did he understand the extent of his activity?

Song: He didn't ask. He knew that I needed those documents, and that was enough.

Judge: But he must've known he was passing classified information.

Song: I can't say.

Judge: He never asked what you were going to do with them?

Song: Nope.

Pause.

Judge: There is one thing that the court — indeed, that all of France — would like to know.

Song: Fire away.

Judge: Did Monsieur Gallimard know you were a man?

Song: Well, he never saw me completely naked. Ever.

Judge: But surely, he must've . . . how can I put this?

Song: Put it however you like. I'm not shy. He must've felt around?

Judge: Mmmmm.

Song: Not really. I did all the work. He just laid back. Of course we did enjoy more . . . complete union, and I suppose he *might* have wondered why I was always on my stomach, but. . . . But what you're thinking is, "Of course a wrist must've brushed . . . a hand hit . . . over twenty years!" Yeah. Well, Your Honor, it was my job to make him think I was a woman. And chew on this: it wasn't all that hard. See, my mother was a prostitute along the Bundt before the Revolution. And, uh, I think it's fair to say she learned a few things about Western men. So I borrowed her knowledge. In service to my country.

Judge: Would you care to enlighten the court with this secret knowledge? I'm sure we're all very curious.

Song: I'm sure you are. *(Pause.)* Okay, Rule One is: Men always believe what they want to hear. So a girl can tell the most obnoxious lies and the guys will believe them every time — "This is my first time" — "That's the biggest I've ever seen" — or *both,* which, if you really think about it, is not possible in a single lifetime. You've maybe heard those phrases a few times in your own life, yes, Your Honor?

Judge: It's not my life, Monsieur Song, which is on trial today.

Song: Okay, okay, just trying to lighten up the proceedings. Tough room.

Judge: Go on.

Song: Rule Two: As soon as a Western man comes into contact with the East — he's already confused. The West has sort of an international rape mentality towards the East. Do you know rape mentality?

Judge: Give us your definition, please.

Song: Basically, "Her mouth says no, but her eyes say yes."

The West thinks of itself as masculine — big guns, big industry, big money — so the East is feminine — weak, delicate, poor . . . but good at art, and full of inscrutable wisdom — the feminine mystique.

Her mouth says no, but her eyes say yes. The West believes the East, deep down, *wants* to be dominated — because a woman can't think for herself.

Judge: What does this have to do with my question?

Song: You expect Oriental countries to submit to your guns, and you expect Oriental women to be submissive to your men. That's why you say they make the best wives.

Judge: But why would that make it possible for you to fool Monsieur Gallimard? Please — get to the point.

Song: One, because when he finally met his fantasy woman, he wanted more than anything to believe that she was, in fact, a woman. And second, I am an Oriental. And being an Oriental, I could never be completely a man.

Pause.

Judge: Your armchair political theory is tenuous, Monsieur Song.

Song: You think so? That's why you'll lose in all your dealings with the East.

Judge: Just answer my question: did he know you were a man?

Pause.

Song: You know, Your Honor, I never asked.

Scene II

Same.

Music from the "Death Scene" from Butterfly blares over the house speakers. It is the loudest thing we've heard in this play.

Gallimard enters, crawling towards Song's wig and kimono.

Gallimard: Butterfly? Butterfly?

Song remains a man, in the witness box, delivering a testimony we do not hear.

Gallimard (to us): In my moment of greatest shame, here, in this courtroom — with that . . . person up there, telling the world. . . . What strikes me especially is how shallow he is, how glib and obsequious . . . completely . . . without substance! The type that prowls around discos with a gold medallion stinking of garlic. So little like my Butterfly.

Yet even in this moment my mind remains agile, flip-flopping like a man on a trampoline. Even now, my picture dissolves, and I see that . . . witness . . . talking to me.

Song suddenly stands straight up in his witness box, and looks at Gallimard.

Song: Yes. You. White man.

Song steps out of the witness box, and moves downstage towards Gallimard. Light change.

Gallimard (to Song): Who? Me?
Song: Do you see any other white men?
Gallimard: Yes. There're white men all around. This is a French courtroom.
Song: So you are an adventurous imperialist. Tell me, why did it take you so long? To come back to this place?
Gallimard: What place?
Song: This theater in China. Where we met many years ago.
Gallimard (to us): And once again, against my will, I am transported.

Chinese opera music comes up on the speakers. Song begins to do opera moves, as he did the night they met.

Song: Do you remember? The night you gave your heart?
Gallimard: It was a long time ago.
Song: Not long enough. A night that turned your world upside down.
Gallimard: Perhaps.
Song: Oh, be honest with me. What's another bit of flattery when you've already given me twenty years' worth? It's a wonder my head hasn't swollen to the size of China.
Gallimard: Who's to say it hasn't?
Song: Who's to say? And what's the shame? In pride? You think I could've pulled this off if I wasn't already full of pride when we met? No, not just pride. Arrogance. It takes arrogance, really — to believe you can will, with your eyes and your lips, the destiny of another. *(He dances.)* C'mon. Admit it. You still want me. Even in slacks and a button-down collar.
Gallimard: I don't see what the point of —

Song: You don't? Well maybe, Rene, just maybe — I want you.

Gallimard: You do?

Song: Then again, maybe I'm just playing with you. How can you tell? *(Reprising his feminine character, he sidles up to Gallimard.)* "How I wish there were even a small café to sit in. With men in tuxedos, and cappuccinos, and bad expatriate jazz." Now you want to kiss me, don't you?

Gallimard (pulling away): What makes you — ?

Song: — so sure? See? I take the words from your mouth. Then I wait for you to come and retrieve them. *(He reclines on the floor.)*

Gallimard: Why?! Why do you treat me so cruelly?

Song: Perhaps I *was* treating you cruelly. But now — I'm being nice. Come here, my little one.

Gallimard: I'm not your little one!

Song: My mistake. It's I who am *your* little one, right?

Gallimard: Yes, I —

Song: So come get your little one. If you like, I may even let you strip me.

Gallimard: I mean, you were! Before . . . but not like this!

Song: I was? Then perhaps I still am. If you look hard enough. *(He starts to remove his clothes.)*

Gallimard: What — what are you doing?

Song: Helping you to see through my act.

Gallimard: Stop that! I don't want to! I don't —

Song: Oh, but you asked me to strip, remember?

Gallimard: What? That was years ago! And I took it back!

Song: No. You postponed it. Postponed the inevitable. Today, the inevitable has come calling.

From the speakers, cacophony: Butterfly mixed in with Chinese gongs.

Gallimard: No! Stop! I don't want to see!

Song: Then look away.

Gallimard: You're only in my mind! All this is in my mind! I order you! To stop!

Song: To what? To strip? That's just what I'm —

Gallimard: No! Stop! I want you — !

Song: You want me?

Gallimard: To stop!

Song: You know something, Rene? Your mouth says no, but your eyes say yes. Turn them away. I dare you.

Gallimard: I don't have to! Every night, you say you're going to strip, but then I beg you and you stop!

Song: I guess tonight is different.

Gallimard: Why? Why should that be?

Song: Maybe I've become frustrated. Maybe I'm saying "Look at me, you fool!" Or maybe I'm just feeling . . . sexy. *(He is down to his briefs.)*

Gallimard: Please. This is unnecessary. I know what you are.

Song: You do? What am I?

Gallimard: A — a man.

Song: You don't really believe that.

Gallimard: Yes I do! I knew all the time somewhere that my happiness was temporary, my love a deception. But my mind kept the knowledge at bay. To make the wait bearable.

Song: Monsieur Gallimard — the wait is over.

Song drops his briefs. He is naked. Sound cue out. Slowly, we and Song come to the realization that what we had thought to be Gallimard's sobbing is actually his laughter.

Gallimard: Oh god! What an idiot! Of course!

Song: Rene — what?

Gallimard: Look at you! You're a man! *(He bursts into laughter again.)*

Song: I fail to see what's so funny!

Gallimard: "You fail to see — !" I mean, you never did have much of a sense of humor, did you? I just think it's ridiculously funny that I've wasted so much time on just a man!

Song: Wait. I'm not "just a man."

Gallimard: No? Isn't that what you've been trying to convince me of?

Song: Yes, but what I mean —

Gallimard: And now, I finally believe you, and you tell me it's not true? I think you must have some kind of identity problem.

Song: Will you listen to me?

Gallimard: Why?! I've been listening to you for twenty years. Don't I deserve a vacation?

Song: I'm not just any man!

Gallimard: Then, what exactly are you?

Song: Rene, how can you ask — ? Okay, what about this?

He picks up Butterfly's robes, starts to dance around. No music.

Gallimard: Yes, that's very nice. I have to admit.

Song holds out his arm to Gallimard.

Song: It's the same skin you've worshipped for years. Touch it.

Gallimard: Yes, it does feel the same.

Song: Now — close your eyes.

Song covers Gallimard's eyes with one hand. With the other, Song draws Gallimard's hand up to his face. Gallimard, like a blind man, lets his hands run over Song's face.

Gallimard: This skin, I remember. The curve of her face, the softness of her cheek, her hair against the back of my hand . . .

Song: I'm your Butterfly. Under the robes, beneath everything, it was always me. Now, open your eyes and admit it — you adore me. *(He removes his hand from Gallimard's eyes.)*

Gallimard: You, who knew every inch of my desires — how could you, of all people, have made such a mistake?

Song: What?

Gallimard: You showed me your true self. When all I loved was the lie. A perfect lie, which you let fall to the ground — and now, it's old and soiled.

Song: So — you never really loved me? Only when I was playing a part?

Gallimard: I'm a man who loved a woman created by a man. Everything else — simply falls short.

Pause.

Song: What am I supposed to do now?
Gallimard: You were a fine spy, Monsieur Song, with an even finer accomplice. But now I believe you should go. Get out of my life!
Song: Go where? Rene, you can't live without me. Not after twenty years.
Gallimard: I certainly can't live with you — not after twenty years of betrayal.
Song: Don't be stubborn! Where will you go?
Gallimard: I have a date . . . with my Butterfly.
Song: So, throw away your pride. And come . . .
Gallimard: Get away from me! Tonight, I've finally learned to tell fantasy from reality. And, knowing the difference, I choose fantasy.
Song: I'm your fantasy!
Gallimard: You? You're as real as hamburger. Now get out! I have a date with my Butterfly and I don't want your body polluting the room! *(He tosses Song's suit at him.)* Look at these — you dress like a pimp.
Song: Hey! These are Armani slacks and — ! *(He puts on his briefs and slacks.)* Let's just say . . . I'm disappointed in you, Rene. In the crush of your adoration, I thought you'd become something more. More like . . . a woman.

But no. Men. You're like the rest of them. It's all in the way we dress, and make up our faces, and bat our eyelashes. You really have so little imagination!
Gallimard: You, Monsieur Song? Accuse me of too little imagination? You, if anyone, should know — I am pure imagination. And in imagination I will remain. Now get out!

Gallimard bodily removes Song from the stage, taking his kimono.

Song: Rene! I'll never put on those robes again! You'll be sorry!
Gallimard (to Song): I'm already sorry! *(Looking at the kimono in his hands.)* Exactly as sorry . . . as a Butterfly.

Scene III

M. Gallimard's prison cell. Paris. 1988.

Gallimard: I've played out the events of my life night after night, always searching for a new ending to my story, one where I leave this cell and return forever to my Butterfly's arms.

Tonight I realize my search is over. That I've looked all along in the wrong place. And now, to you, I will prove that my love was not in vain — by returning to the world of fantasy where I first met her.

He picks up the kimono; dancers enter.

Gallimard: There is a vision of the Orient that I have. Of slender women in chong sams and kimonos who die for the love of unworthy foreign devils. Who are born and raised to be the perfect women. Who take whatever punishment we give them, and bounce back, strengthened by love, unconditionally. It is a vision that has become my life.

Dancers bring the washbasin to him and help him make up his face.

Gallimard: In public, I have continued to deny that Song Liling is a man. This brings me headlines, and is a source of great embarrassment to my French colleagues, who can now be sent into a coughing fit by the mere mention of Chinese food. But alone, in my cell, I have long since faced the truth.

And the truth demands a sacrifice. For mistakes made over the course of a lifetime. My mistakes were simple and absolute — the man I loved was a cad, a bounder. He deserved nothing but a kick in the behind, and instead I gave him . . . all my love.

Yes — love. Why not admit it all? That was my undoing, wasn't it? Love warped my judgment, blinded my eyes, rearranged the very lines on my face . . . until I could look in the mirror and see nothing but . . . a woman.

Dancers help him put on the Butterfly wig.

Gallimard: I have a vision. Of the Orient. That, deep within its almond eyes, there are still women. Women willing to sacrifice themselves for the love of a man. Even a man whose love is completely without worth.

Dancers assist Gallimard in donning the kimono. They hand him a knife.

Gallimard: Death with honor is better than life . . . life with dishonor. *(He sets himself center stage, in a seppuku position.)* The love of a Butterfly can withstand many things — unfaithfulness, loss, even abandonment. But how can it face the one sin that implies all others? The devastating knowledge that, underneath it all, the object of her love was nothing more, nothing less than . . . a man. *(He sets the tip of the knife against his body.)* It is 1988. And I have found her at last. In a prison on the outskirts of Paris. My name is Rene Gallimard — also known as Madame Butterfly.

Gallimard turns upstage and plunges the knife into his body, as music from the "Love Duet" blares over the speakers. He collapses into the arms of the dancers, who lay him reverently on the floor. The image holds for several beats. Then a tight special up on Song, who stands as a man, staring at the dead Gallimard. He smokes a cigarette; the smoke filters up through the lights. Two words leave his lips.

Song: Butterfly? Butterfly?

Smoke rises as lights fade slowly to black.

Connections

1. At first glance Rene Gallimard and Sophocles' Oedipus in *Oedipus the King* (p. 964) are very different kinds of characters, but how might their situations — particularly their discoveries about themselves — be compared? What significant similarities do you find in these two characters? Explain whether you think Gallimard can be seen as a tragic character.
2. Compare the function of Puccini's *Madame Butterfly* in *M. Butterfly* with that of the play within the play in Shakespeare's *Hamlet* (p. 1065). How are these inter-

nal dramatic actions used to comment on the events of each larger play? How is role playing relevant to the theme of each play?

3. Write an essay comparing Gallimard's illusions with those of Amanda in Tennessee Williams's *The Glass Menagerie* (p. 1462).
4. Compare and contrast the way women are represented in *M. Butterfly* and Caryl Churchill's *Top Girls* (p. 1603).

31. Perspectives on Drama

Among the selections in this chapter are commentaries that focus on individual plays as well as drama in general. Included are the opening scene from Susan Glaspell's short story version of *Trifles,* Tennessee Williams's production notes to *The Glass Menagerie,* Arthur Miller on tragedy in the twentieth century, Eric Bentley on drama as literature and performance, a student essay on *Death of a Salesman,* and interviews with Caryl Churchill, August Wilson, and David Henry Hwang. These and several other miscellaneous items should stimulate responses to both particular plays and broad issues associated with dramatic literature and performances.

OWEN DAVIS (1874–1956)
On Formulaic Melodrama 1914

The plays that we produced were written largely by rule. In fact the actual writing of one of these sensational melodramas I had reduced to a formula, about as follows:

Title (at least fifty per cent of success)
Plot: Brief story of the play.
Cast: Leading Man, very (even painfully) virtuous.
Leading Woman, in love with him.
Comedy Man, always faithful friend of *Hero.*
Soubrette, very worthy person (poor but honest) and always in love with *Comedian.*
Heavy Man, a villain, not for any special reason, but, like "Topsy," "born bad."
Heavy Woman, — here I had a wider choice, his lady being allowed to fasten her affections upon either *Hero* or *Villain* (sometimes both) but never happily.

Father (or *Mother*), to provide sentiment.

Fill in as desired with character parts.

Act I — Start the trouble.

Act II — Here things look bad. The lady having left home, is quite at the mercy of *Villain*.

Act III — The lady is saved by the help of the Stage Carpenter. (The big scenic and mechanical effects were always in Act III.)

Act IV — The lovers are united and the villains are punished.

I suppose that I have been responsible for as many executions as the Queen in "Alice in Wonderland." I am honest enough to admit my cold-blooded attitude; but apply this chart to many plays of authors who consider their work inspired, and see if it fits.

These plays depended very greatly upon scenic effect, sensational dramatic title, and enormously melodramatic pictorial display on the bill boards. I think we touched upon every theme known to man, and every location. We limited ourselves, however, to American subjects. We always had a clear and dominant love interest, which we crossed with an element of danger, usually furnished by a rather impossible villain or adventuress. The themes of some of these plays were absolutely legitimate and the stories in many cases, with different dressing, would have done for a Broadway theater of the present day. But we had to, or fancied we had to, have such an overabundance of climactic material that our plays resulted in an undigested mass of unprepared situations. Where one carefully prepared and well-developed episode would really have been of far greater dramatic value, we made a rule of dividing our plays into no less than fifteen scenes, the end of each being a moment of perilous suspense or terrifying danger. This gave the playwright rather less than seven minutes to instruct his audience, to prepare his climaxes, to plant the seed for the next scene, and to *reach* his climaxes, which of course was absurdly impossible and resulted, I feel sure, in a form of entertainment which was only too ready to yield to the encroachment of the cheap vaudeville and moving pictures.

From "Why I Quit Writing Melodrama," *American Magazine*

Considerations

1. Davis was a popular writer of melodrama at the turn of the century who went on to win a Pulitzer Prize for *Icebound* in 1923. What are his major objections to melodrama?
2. The formula Davis describes is still used in some contemporary films and television shows. Discuss an example or two and explain why you think they remain popular.
3. Choose any play in this text and discuss why its plot does not fit the melodramatic formula.

SUSAN GLASPELL (1882–1948)

From the Short Story Version of Trifles 1917

When Martha Hale opened the storm-door and got a cut of the north wind, she ran back for her big woolen scarf. As she hurriedly wound that round her head her eye made a scandalized sweep of her kitchen. It was no ordinary thing that called her away — it was probably farther from ordinary than anything that had ever happened in Dickson County. But what her eye took in was that her kitchen was in no shape for leaving: her bread all ready for mixing, half the flour sifted and half unsifted.

She hated to see things half done; but she had been at that when the team from town stopped to get Mr. Hale, and then the sheriff came running in to say his wife wished Mrs. Hale would come too — adding, with a grin, that he guessed she was getting scarey and wanted another woman along. So she had dropped everything right where it was.

"Martha!" now came her husband's impatient voice. "Don't keep folks waiting out here in the cold."

She again opened the storm-door, and this time joined the three men and the one woman waiting for her in the big two-seated buggy.

After she had the robes tucked around her she took another look at the woman who sat beside her on the back seat. She had met Mrs. Peters the year before at the county fair, and the thing she remembered about her was that she didn't seem like a sheriff's wife. She was small and thin and didn't have a strong voice. Mrs. Gorman, sheriff's wife before Gorman went out and Peters came in, had a voice that somehow seemed to be backing up the law with every word. But if Mrs. Peters didn't look like a sheriff's wife, Peters made it up in looking like a sheriff. He was to a dot the kind of man who could get himself elected sheriff — a heavy man with a big voice, who was particularly genial with the law-abiding, as if to make it plain that he knew the difference between criminals and noncriminals. And right there it came into Mrs. Hale's mind, with a stab, that this man who was so pleasant and lively with all of them was going to the Wrights' now as a sheriff.

"The country's not very pleasant this time of year," Mrs. Peters at last ventured, as if she felt they ought to be talking as well as the men.

Mrs. Hale scarcely finished her reply, for they had gone up a little hill and could see the Wright place now, and seeing it did not make her feel like talking. It looked very lonesome this cold March morning. It had always been a lonesome-looking place. It was down in a hollow, and the poplar trees around it were lonesome-looking trees. The men were looking at it and talking about what had happened. The county attorney was bending to one side of the buggy, and kept looking steadily at the place as they drew up to it.

"I'm glad you came with me," Mrs. Peters said nervously, as the two women were about to follow the men in through the kitchen door.

Even after she had her foot on the door-step, her hand on the knob, Martha Hale had a moment of feeling she could not cross that threshold. And the reason it seemed she couldn't cross it now was simply because she hadn't crossed it before. Time and time again it had been in her mind, "I ought to go over and see Minnie Foster" — she still thought of her as Minnie Foster, though for twenty years she had been Mrs. Wright. And then there was always something to do and Minnie Foster would go from her mind. But *now* she could come.

The men went over to the stove. The women stood close together by the door. Young Henderson, the county attorney, turned around and said, "Come up to the fire, ladies."

Mrs. Peters took a step forward, then stopped. "I'm not — cold," she said.

And so the two women stood by the door, at first not even so much as looking around the kitchen.

The men talked for a minute about what a good thing it was the sheriff had sent his deputy out that morning to make a fire for them, and then Sheriff Peters stepped back from the stove, unbuttoned his outer coat, and leaned his hands on the kitchen table in a way that seemed to mark the beginning of official business. "Now, Mr. Hale," he said in a sort of semiofficial voice, "before we move things about, you tell Mr. Henderson just what it was you saw when you came here yesterday morning."

The county attorney was looking around the kitchen.

"By the way," he said, "has anything been moved?" He turned to the sheriff. "Are things just as you left them yesterday?"

Peters looked from cupboard to sink; from that to a small worn rocker a little to one side of the kitchen table.

"It's just the same."

"Somebody should have been left here yesterday," said the county attorney.

"Oh — yesterday," returned the sheriff, with a little gesture as of yesterday having been more than he could bear to think of. "When I had to send Frank to Morris Center for that man who went crazy — let me tell you, I had my hands full *yesterday*. I knew you could get back from Omaha by to-day, George, and as long as I went over everything here myself —"

"Well, Mr. Hale," said the county attorney, in a way of letting what was past and gone go, "tell just what happened when you came here yesterday morning."

Mrs. Hale, still leaning against the door, had that sinking feeling of the mother whose child is about to speak a piece. Lewis often wandered along and got things mixed up in a story. She hoped he would tell this straight and plain, and not say unnecessary things that would just make things harder for Minnie Foster. He didn't begin at once, and she noticed that he looked queer — as if standing in that kitchen and having to tell what he had seen there yesterday morning made him almost sick.

"Yes, Mr. Hale?" the county attorney reminded.

"Harry and I had started to town with a load of potatoes," Mrs. Hale's husband began.

Harry was Mrs. Hale's oldest boy. He wasn't with them now, for the very good reason that those potatoes never got to town yesterday and he was taking them this morning, so he hadn't been home when the sheriff stopped to say he wanted Mr. Hale to come over to the Wright place and tell the county attorney his story there, where he could point it all out. With all Mrs. Hale's other emotions came the fear that maybe Harry wasn't dressed warm enough — they hadn't any of them realized how that north wind did bite.

"We come along this road," Hale was going on, with a motion of his hand to the road over which they had just come, "and as we got in sight of the house

I says to Harry, 'I'm goin' to see if I can't get John Wright to take a telephone.' You see," he explained to Henderson, "unless I can get somebody to go in with me they won't come out this branch road except for a price *I* can't pay. I'd spoke to Wright about it once before; but he put me off, saying folks talked too much anyway, and all he asked was peace and quiet — guess you know about how much he talked himself. But I thought maybe if I went to the house and talked about it before his wife, and said all the women-folks liked the telephones, and that in this lonesome stretch of road it would be a good thing — well, I said to Harry that that was what I was going to say — though I said at the same time that I didn't know as what his wife wanted made much difference to John —"

Now, there he was! — saying things he didn't need to say. Mrs. Hale tried to catch her husband's eye, but fortunately the county attorney interrupted with:

"Let's talk about that a little later, Mr. Hale. I do want to talk about that, but I'm anxious now to get along to just what happened when you got here."

From "A Jury of Her Peers"

Considerations

1. In this opening scene from the story, how is the setting established differently from the way it is in the play (p. 931)?
2. What kind of information is provided in the opening paragraphs of the story that is missing from the play's initial scene? What is emphasized early in the story but not in the play?
3. Which version brings us into more intimate contact with the characters? How is that achieved?
4. Does the short story title, "A Jury of Her Peers," suggest any shift in emphasis from the play's title, *Trifles?*
5. Explain why you prefer one version over another.

TENNESSEE WILLIAMS (1911–1983)

Production Notes to The Glass Menagerie 1945

Being a "memory play," *The Glass Menagerie* can be presented with unusual freedom of convention. Because of its considerably delicate or tenuous material, atmospheric touches and subtleties of direction play a particularly important part. Expressionism and all other unconventional techniques in drama have only one valid aim, and that is a closer approach to truth. When a play employs unconventional techniques, it is not, or certainly shouldn't be, trying to escape its responsibility of dealing with reality, or interpreting experience, but is actually or should be attempting to find a closer approach, a more penetrating and vivid expression of things as they are. The straight realistic play with its genuine Frigidaire and authentic ice cubes, its characters that speak exactly as its audience speaks, corresponds to the academic landscape and has the same virtue of a photographic likeness. Everyone should know nowadays the unimportance of the photographic in art: that truth, life, or reality is an organic thing which the poetic imagination can represent or suggest, in essence, only through transformation, through changing into other forms than those which were merely present in appearance.

These remarks are not meant as a preface only to this particular play. They have to do with a conception of a new, plastic theater which must take the place of the exhausted theater of realistic conventions if the theater is to resume vitality as a part of our culture.

The Screen Device. There is *only one important difference between the original and acting version of the play* and that is the *omission* in the latter of the device which I tentatively included in my *original* script. This device was the use of a screen on which were projected magic-lantern slides bearing images or titles. I do not regret the omission of this device from the present Broadway production. The extraordinary power of Miss Taylor's° performance made it suitable to have the utmost simplicity in the physical production. But I think it may be interesting to some readers to see how this device was conceived. So I am putting it into the published manuscript. These images and legends, projected from behind, were cast on a section of wall between the front-room and dining-room areas, which should be indistinguishable from the rest when not in use.

The purpose of this will probably be apparent. It is to give accent to certain values in each scene. Each scene contains a particular point (or several) which is structurally the most important. In an episodic play, such as this, the basic structure or narrative line may be obscured from the audience; the effect may seem fragmentary rather than architectural. This may not be the fault of the play so much as a lack of attention in the audience. The legend or image upon the screen will strengthen the effect of what is merely allusion in the writing and allow the primary point to be made more simply and lightly than if the entire responsibility were on the spoken lines. Aside from this structural value, I think the screen will have a definite emotional appeal, less definable but just as important. An imaginative producer or director may invent many other uses for this device than those indicated in the present script. In fact the possibilities of the device seem much larger to me than the instance of this play can possibly utilize.

The Music. Another extra-literary accent in this play is provided by the use of music. A single recurring tune, "The Glass Menagerie," is used to give emotional emphasis to suitable passages. This tune is like circus music, not when you are on the grounds or in the immediate vicinity of the parade, but when you are at some distance and very likely thinking of something else. It seems under those circumstances to continue almost interminably and it weaves in and out of your preoccupied consciousness; then it is the lightest, most delicate music in the world and perhaps the saddest. It expresses the surface vivacity of life with the underlying strain of immutable and inexpressible sorrow. When you look at a piece of delicately spun glass you think of two things: how beautiful it is and how easily it can be broken. Both of those ideas should be woven into the recurring tune, which dips in and out of the play as if it were carried on a wind

Miss Taylor's: Laurette Taylor (1884–1946) played the role of Amanda in the original Broadway production.

that changes. It serves as a thread of connection and allusion between the narrator with his separate point in time and space and the subject of his story. Between each episode it returns as reference to the emotion, nostalgia, which is the first condition of the play. It is primarily Laura's music and therefore comes out most clearly when the play focuses upon her and the lovely fragility of glass which is her image.

The Lighting. The lighting in the play is not realistic. In keeping with the atmosphere of memory, the stage is dim. Shafts of light are focused on selected areas or actors, sometimes in contradistinction to what is the apparent center. For instance, in the quarrel scene between Tom and Amanda, in which Laura has no active part, the clearest pool of light is on her figure. This is also true of the supper scene, when her silent figure on the sofa should remain the visual center. The light upon Laura should be distinct from the others, having a peculiar pristine clarity such as light used in early religious portraits of female saints or madonnas. A certain correspondence to light in religious paintings, such as El Greco's,° where the figures are radiant in atmosphere that is relatively dusky, could be effectively used throughout the play. (It will also permit a more effective use of the screen.) A free, imaginative use of light can be of enormous value in giving a mobile, plastic quality to plays of a more or less static nature.

El Greco (1541–1614): Greek painter who worked primarily in Spain and is known for the unearthly lighting in his large canvases.

Considerations

1. What was your response to the screen device as you read the play? Do you think the device would enhance a production of the play or prove to be a distraction?
2. How does Williams's description of music and lighting serve as a summary of the play's tone? Does this tone come through in your reading of the play or is it dependent upon the music and lighting? Explain your answer.
3. Explain whether you agree with Williams's assertion that "theater of realistic conventions" is "exhausted."

TENNESSEE WILLIAMS (1911–1983)

On Theme

1948

For a writer who is not intentionally obscure, and never, in his opinion, obscure at all, I do get asked a hell of a lot of questions which I can't answer. I have never been able to say what was the theme of my play and I don't think I've ever been conscious of writing with a theme in mind. I am always surprised when, after a play has opened, I read in the papers what the play is about. . . . I am thankful for these highly condensed and stimulating analyses, but it would never have occurred to me that that was the story I was trying to tell. Usually when asked about a theme, I look vague and say, "It is a play about life. . . ."

From *Where I Live: Selected Essays,*
edited by Christine R. Day

Considerations

1. Williams's disclaimer invites the inevitable question: What is the theme of *The Glass Menagerie*? Write an essay that answers this question.
2. Discuss whether you think it is likely (or possible) to write a play without "a theme in mind."
3. How do Williams's comments on theme compare with Thomas McCormack's in "On the Problem of Teaching Theme" (p. 226)?

ARTHUR MILLER (b. 1915)
Tragedy and the Common Man 1949

In this age few tragedies are written. It has often been held that the lack is due to a paucity of heroes among us, or else that modern man has had the blood drawn out of his organs of belief by the skepticism of science, and the heroic attack on life cannot feed on an attitude of reserve and circumspection. For one reason or another, we are often held to be below tragedy — or tragedy above us. The inevitable conclusion is, of course, that the tragic mode is archaic, fit only for the very highly placed, the kings or the kingly, and where this admission is not made in so many words it is most often implied.

I believe that the common man is as apt a subject for tragedy in its highest sense as kings were. On the face of it this ought to be obvious in the light of modern psychiatry, which bases its analysis upon classic formulations, such as the Oedipus and Orestes complexes, for instance, which were enacted by royal beings, but which apply to everyone in similar emotional situations.

More simply, when the question of tragedy in art is not at issue, we never hesitate to attribute to the well-placed and the exalted the very same mental processes as the lowly. And finally, if the exaltation of tragic action were truly a property of the high-bred character alone, it is inconceivable that the mass of mankind should cherish tragedy above all other forms, let alone be capable of understanding it.

As a general rule, to which there may be exceptions unknown to me, I think the tragic feeling is evoked in us when we are in the presence of a character who is ready to lay down his life, if need be, to secure one thing — his sense of personal dignity. From Orestes to Hamlet, Medea to Macbeth, the underlying struggle is that of the individual attempting to gain his "rightful" position in his society.

Sometimes he is one who has been displaced from it, sometimes one who seeks to attain it for the first time, but the fateful wound from which the inevitable events spiral is the wound of indignity, and its dominant force is indignation. Tragedy, then, is the consequence of a man's total compulsion to evaluate himself justly.

In the sense of having been initiated by the hero himself, the tale always reveals what has been called his "tragic flaw," a failing that is not peculiar to grand or elevated characters. Nor is it necessarily a weakness. The flaw, or crack in the character, is really nothing — and need be nothing — but his inherent unwillingness to remain passive in the face of what he conceives to be a challenge to his dignity, his image of his rightful status. Only the passive, only those who accept their lot without active retaliation, are "flawless." Most of us are in that category.

But there are among us today, as there always have been, those who act against the scheme of things that degrades them, and in the process of action, everything we have accepted out of fear or insensitivity or ignorance is shaken before us and examined, and from this total onslaught by an individual against the seemingly stable cosmos surrounding us — from this total examination of the "unchangeable" environment — comes the terror and the fear that is classically associated with tragedy.

More important, from this total questioning of what has been previously unquestioned, we learn. And such a process is not beyond the common man. In revolutions around the world, these past thirty years, he has demonstrated again and again this inner dynamic of all tragedy.

Insistence upon the rank of the tragic hero, or the so-called nobility of his character, is really but a clinging to the outward forms of tragedy. If rank or nobility of character was indispensable, then it would follow that the problems of those with rank were the particular problems of tragedy. But surely the right of one monarch to capture the domain from another no longer raises our passions, nor are our concepts of justice what they were to the mind of an Elizabethan king.

The quality in such plays that does shake us, however, derives from the underlying fear of being displaced, the disaster inherent in being torn away from our chosen image of what and who we are in this world. Among us today this fear is as strong, and perhaps stronger, than it ever was. In fact, it is the common man who knows this fear best.

Now, if it is true that tragedy is the consequence of a man's total compulsion to evaluate himself justly, his destruction in the attempt posits a wrong or an evil in his environment. And this is precisely the morality of tragedy and its lesson. The discovery of the moral law, which is what the enlightenment of tragedy consists of, is not the discovery of some abstract or metaphysical quantity.

The tragic right is a condition of life, a condition in which the human personality is able to flower and realize itself. The wrong is the condition which suppresses man, perverts the flowing out of his love and creative instinct. Tragedy enlightens — and it must, in that it points the heroic finger at the enemy of man's freedom. The thrust for freedom is the quality in tragedy which exalts. The revolutionary questioning of the stable environment is what terrifies. In no way is the common man debarred from such thoughts or such actions.

Seen in this light, our lack of tragedy may be partially accounted for by the turn which modern literature has taken toward the purely psychiatric view of life, or the purely sociological. If all our miseries, our indignities, are born and bred within our minds, then all action, let alone the heroic action, is obviously impossible.

And if society alone is responsible for the cramping of our lives, then the protagonist must needs be so pure and faultless as to force us to deny his validity as a character. From neither of these views can tragedy derive, simply because neither represents a balanced concept of life. Above all else, tragedy requires the finest appreciation by the writer of cause and effect.

No tragedy can therefore come about when its author fears to question absolutely everything, when he regards any institution, habit, or custom as being either everlasting, immutable, or inevitable. In the tragic view the need of man to wholly realize himself is the only fixed star, and whatever it is that hedges his nature and lowers it is ripe for attack and examination. Which is not to say that tragedy must preach revolution.

The Greeks could probe the very heavenly origin of their ways and return to confirm the rightness of laws. And Job could face God in anger, demanding his right, and end in submission. But for a moment everything is in suspension, nothing is accepted, and in this stretching and tearing apart of the cosmos, in the very action of so doing, the character gains "size," the tragic stature which is spuriously attached to the royal or the high born in our minds. The commonest of men may take on that stature to the extent of his willingness to throw all he has into the contest, the battle to secure his rightful place in his world.

There is a misconception of tragedy with which I have been struck in review after review, and in many conversations with writers and readers alike. It is the idea that tragedy is of necessity allied to pessimism. Even the dictionary says nothing more about the word than that it means a story with a sad or unhappy ending. This impression is so firmly fixed that I almost hesitate to claim that in truth tragedy implies more optimism in its author than does comedy, and that its final result ought to be the reinforcement of the onlooker's brightest opinions of the human animal.

For, if it is true to say that in essence the tragic hero is intent upon claiming his whole due as a personality, and if this struggle must be total and without reservation, then it automatically demonstrates the indestructible will of man to achieve his humanity.

The possibility of victory must be there in tragedy. Where pathos rules, where pathos is finally derived, a character has fought a battle he could not possibly have won. The pathetic is achieved when the protagonist is, by virtue of his witlessness, his insensitivity, or the very air he gives off, incapable of grappling with a much superior force.

Pathos truly is the mode for the pessimist. But tragedy requires a nicer balance between what is possible and what is impossible. And it is curious, although edifying, that the plays we revere, century after century, are the tragedies. In them, and in them alone, lies the belief — optimistic, if you will — in the perfectibility of man.

It is time, I think, that we who are without kings, took up this bright thread of our history and followed it to the only place it can possibly lead in our time — the heart and spirit of the average man.

From *Theater Essays of Arthur Miller*

Considerations

1. According to Miller, why is there a "lack" of tragedy in modern literature? Why do psychological and sociological accounts of human behavior limit the possibilities for tragedy?
2. Why is the "common man" a suitable subject for tragedy? How does Miller's view of tragedy compare with Aristotle's (p. 1045)?
3. What distinction does Miller make between tragedy and pathos? Which term best characterizes Willy Loman in *Death of a Salesman?* Explain why.

ARTHUR MILLER (b. 1915)

On Biff and Willy Loman 1950

A serious theme is entertaining to the extent that it is not trifled with, not cleverly angled, but met in head-on collision. [The audience] will not consent to suffer while the creators stand by with tongue in cheek. They have a way of knowing. Nobody can blame them.

And there have been certain disappointments, one above all. I am sorry the self-realization of the older son, Biff, is not a weightier counterbalance to Willy's disaster in the audience's mind.

And certain things are more clearly known, or so it seems now. We want to give of ourselves, and yet all we train for is to take, as though nothing less will keep the world at a safe distance. Every day we contradict our will to create, which is to give. The end of man is not security, but without security we are without the elementary condition of humaneness.

To me the tragedy of Willy Loman is that he gave his life, or sold it, in order to justify the waste of it. It is the tragedy of a man who did believe that he alone was not meeting the qualifications laid down for mankind by those clean-shaven frontiersmen who inhabit the peaks of broadcasting and advertising offices. From those forests of canned goods high up near the sky, he heard the thundering command to succeed as it ricocheted down the newspaper-lined canyons of his city, heard not a human voice, but a wind of a voice to which no human can reply in kind, except to stare into the mirror at a failure.

From the *New York Times,* February 5, 1950

Considerations

1. Discuss what you think Miller has in mind when he refers to Biff's "self-realization."
2. According to Miller, what influences Willy to make him feel like a failure?
3. How is Miller's description of "the tragedy of Willy Loman" dramatized in the play?

ERIC BENTLEY (b. 1916)

On Drama as Literature and Performance 1964

Is a play complete without performance? The question has been answered with equal vehemence in both the affirmative and the negative. The choice goes by temperamental preference: "literary" persons believe in the unaided script; "theatrical" persons believe in performance. Both are right. A good play leads a double existence, and is a complete "personality" in both its lives. When a theatrical person says a play has been misinterpreted in performance, he is certainly implying that a play is *there* and has its integrity before the interpreters touch it. As for literary persons, their concession that a play does have another life as well as that of the book is to be found, if nowhere else, in their dismissal of bits they don't like as "merely theatrical." In other words, their position really is not that the theatrical dimension doesn't exist but that they wish it didn't.

Each group is trying to make a virtue of its own *déformation professionnelle.*° Theatrical people have their limitations as interpreters of literature. Literary people have theirs as interpreters of theater. If we can avoid the blindnesses of both parties, the only real problem lies in understanding the *difference* between script-alone and script-as-performed, for any given passage may have a different import in the two different contexts. Finally, one is not forced into any choice between literature and theater, and to know *Hamlet,* or any great play, should be to know it from stage and study, both. A fine performance will never fail to throw light on at least an aspect of the play, while even the best reading in the study will fall far short of embracing all its aspects.

The question whether one should prefer to read or to see a play is best answered pragmatically. If one can read well to oneself, one will hardly prefer to go and see a mediocre performance. But, for anyone capable of relishing theater — and that includes more people than know it — even though the written script has its own completeness, there is no pleasure to top that of seeing a dramatic masterpiece masterfully performed. What is added means so much in such an immediate, sensuous way. If plot, characterization, and dialogue give body to the theme, and transform thought into wisdom, and a view into a vision, adequate performance helps them to do so in various ways but above all by adding that final and conclusive concretion, the living actor.

From "Enactment" in *The Life of the Drama*

déformation professionnelle: Professional bias.

Considerations

1. How does Bentley resolve the competing claims of "literary" and "theatrical" people who argue over whether a play can be "complete without performance"?
2. Explain why you prefer to read or see a play. If you do both, which do you prefer first — the reading or the performance? Why?

JOHN WAGNER (b. 1967)

A Student Essay on Death of a Salesman 1986

THEY USED TO TELL ME I WAS BUILDING A DREAM

In the requiem to *Death of a Salesman* Charley says that a salesman is "a man out there in the blue, riding on a smile and a shoeshine." Through Charley's short speech Arthur Miller drives home his reason for making Willy Loman a salesman, and not a lawyer, a teacher, or a writer. A person in sales builds a life on the intangible, the unreal. He or she markets a personal attractiveness that comes from confidence, the ability to make a buyer believe the catchy slogans even though they are rarely the truth. Sales is a business built on bombast, on bull. (Wear these stockings, madam, and the men will follow you all around town!) If products sold according to their worth, there would be no need for salespeople. A person in sales does not sell a product so much as an idea, a persona, an image.

When Willy Loman decided to become a salesman, the career held promise, like a brightly colored orange hanging from a tree. He pictured himself growing old like Dave Singleman, the eighty-year-old salesman who made his living phoning buyers from his hotel room. Instead, with age Willy's personal attractiveness has grown as stale as his jokes and as weak as his smile, thin and empty as the guarantee on a broken refrigerator. Now that the shine has become dull and there is no color, no flavor left to the man, Willy shouts, "You can't eat the orange and throw the peel away!" But isn't that the sensible thing to do? What good is the peel, once the fruit is gone? Willy has made the comparison himself — he has as little to offer as a withered orange peel, as a cracked and faded shell with no life left to protect.

No one forces Willy to declare himself worthless. No one drives him off the road. No one told him what to do with his life. His brother Ben invited him to go to Alaska and Africa, where the rewards are concrete, but Willy believed in the life he was building as a young man and he believes in it right up to the end. When Ben comes back to ask "What are you building? Lay your hand on it. Where is it?" Willy insists that what he is building cannot be felt with the hand, but that it is there all the same.

Willy never loses sight of the future he has bargained for. Hopefully he borrows his last dollars to make his insurance payments, trading in the last of his credibility on a gamble. He happily sells his life for a possible twenty thousand dollars, for a dream. And when the salesman dies, he leaves no railroad, no tower to the sun. Once has has made his last sale, nothing remains.

Considerations

1. Wagner asserts that "a person in sales does not sell a product so much as an idea, a persona, an image." Discuss this idea along with Miller's comment in his introduction to the play that "when asked what Willy was selling, what was in his bags, I could only reply, 'Himself.' "
2. Does Wagner seem sympathetic to Willy? Are you? Specifically, what is unheroic about Willy's behavior? What, if anything, do you find heroic about him?

3. How is Willy's dream representative of the American dream of success? Do you think his story is relevant only to American culture?

KATHLEEN BETSKO, RACHEL KOENIG, AND EMILY MANN

An Interview with Caryl Churchill 1987

Interviewer: In Laurie Stone's *Village Voice* interview [March 1, 1983], you talked about women becoming Coca-Cola executives and you said, "Well, that's not what I mean by feminism." What exactly do you mean by feminism?

Churchill: When I was in the States in '79 I talked to some women who were saying how well things were going for women in America now with far more top executives being women, and I was struck by the difference between that and the feminism I was used to in England, which is far more closely connected with socialism. And that was one of the ideas behind writing *Top Girls,* that achieving things isn't necessarily good, it matters *what* you achieve.

Thatcher had just become prime minister; there was talk about whether it was an advance to have a woman prime minister if it was someone with policies like hers: She may be a woman but she isn't a sister, she may be a sister but she isn't a comrade. And, in fact, things have got much worse for women under Thatcher. So that's the context of that remark. I do find it hard to conceive of a right-wing feminism. Of course, socialism and feminism aren't synonymous, but I feel strongly about both and wouldn't be interested in a form of one that didn't include the other.

Interviewer: Do you think it's odd, given the fact that there is at best indifference, at worst hostility, to political plays in America, that your works are so popular here?

Churchill: Is it true that on the whole plays here tend to be more family-centered, personal, individual-centered?

Interviewer: Yes, more psychological.

Churchill: Whereas I've been quite heavily exposed to a tradition of looking at the larger context of groups of people. It doesn't mean you don't look at families or individuals within that, but you are also looking at bigger things. Like with the kind of work Joint Stock Theatre Group has done, where you go and research a subject and where you have a lot of characters, even if played by only a few people. It tends to open things out.

Interviewer: The critics do ask, "Where are the American plays with the larger social issues?" Unfortunately, when one comes along our own critics usually turn thumbs down if the politics are overt. An overt political position is considered poor craft or preaching. . . .

Tell me the ways in which *Top Girls* has been misunderstood.

Churchill: What I was intending to do was make it first look as though it was celebrating the achievements of women and then — by showing the main character, Marlene, being successful in a very competitive, destructive, capitalist way — ask, what kind of achievement is that? The idea was that it would start out looking like a feminist play and turn into a socialist one, as well. And I think on the whole it's mostly been understood like that. A lot of people have latched on to Marlene leaving her child, which interestingly was something that came very late. Originally the idea was just that Marlene was "writing off" her niece, Angie, because she'd never make it; I didn't yet have the plot idea that Angie was actually Marlene's own child. Of course women are pressured to make choices between working and having children in a way that men aren't, so it *is* relevant, but it isn't the main point of it.

There's another thing that I've recently discovered with other productions of *Top Girls*. In Greece, for example, where fewer women go out to work, the attitude from some men seeing it was, apparently, that the women in the play who'd gone out to work weren't very nice, weren't happy, and they abandoned their children. They felt the play was obviously saying women *shouldn't* go out to work — they took it to mean what they were wanting to say about women themselves, which is depressing. Highly depressing. [Laughter.] Another example of its being open to misunderstanding was a production in Cologne, Germany, where the women characters were played as miserable and quarrelsome and competitive at the dinner, and the women in the office were neurotic and incapable. The waitress slunk about in a catsuit like a bunnygirl and Win changed her clothes on stage in the office. It just turned into a complete travesty of what it was supposed to be. So that's the sort of moment when you think you'd rather write novels, because the productions can't be changed.

From *Interviews with Contemporary Women Playwrights*

Considerations

1. Consider Churchill's comment that "one of the ideas behind writing *Top Girls* [is] that achieving things isn't necessarily good, it matters *what* you achieve." Discuss how the play dramatizes this point.
2. Discuss whether you think August Wilson's *Fences* (p. 1657) is a "political" play or one that is more "family-centered, personal, [and] individual-centered"? How does *Fences* compare with *Top Girls* on these matters?
3. Compare *Top Girls* and Henry David Hwang's *M. Butterfly* (p. 1707) in terms of the "larger social issues" Churchill mentions. Does either play take an "overt political position"? Explain.
4. Read the discussion on reader-response criticism in Chapter 32, p. 1792. How do you think a reader-response critic would make sense of the misreadings of *Top Girls* that Churchill describes?

DAVID SAVRAN (b. 1950)

An Interview with August Wilson 1987

Savran: In reading *Fences,* I came to view Troy more and more critically as the play progressed, sharing Rose's point of view. We see that Troy has been crippled by his father. That's being replayed in Troy's relationship with Cory. Do you think there'a a way out of that cycle?

Wilson: Surely. First of all, we're all like our parents. The things we are taught early in life, how to respond to the world, our sense of morality — everything, we get from them. Now you can take that legacy and do with it anything you want to do. It's in your hands. Cory is Troy's son. How can he be Troy's son without sharing Troy's values? I was trying to get at why Troy made the choices he made, how they have influenced his values, and how he attempts to pass those along to his son. Each generation gives the succeeding generation what they think they need. One question in the play is "Are the tools we are given sufficient to compete in a world that is different from the one our parents knew?" I think they are — it's just that we have to do different things with the tools. That's all Troy has to give. Troy's flaw is that he does not recognize that the world was changing. That's because he spent fifteen years in a penitentiary.

As African-Americans, we should demand to participate in society as Africans. That's the way out of the vicious cycle of poverty and neglect that exists in 1987 in America, where you have a huge percentage of blacks living in the equivalent of South African townships, in housing projects. No one is inviting these people to participate in society. Look at the poverty levels — $8,500 for a family of four, if you have $8,501 you're not counted. Those statistics would go up enormously if we had an honest assessment of the cost of living in America. I don't know how anybody can support a family of four on $8,500. What I'm saying is that 85 or 90 percent of blacks in America are living in abject poverty and, for the most part, are crowded into what amount to concentration camps. The situation for blacks in America is worse than it was forty years ago. Some sociologists will tell you about the tremendous progress we've made. They didn't put me out when I walked in the door. And you can always point to someone who works on Wall Street, or is a doctor. But they don't count in the larger scheme of things.

Savran: Do you have any idea how these political changes could take place?

Wilson: I'm not sure. I know that blacks must be allowed their cultural differences. I think the process of assimilation to white American society was a big mistake. We don't want to be like you. Blacks living in housing projects are isolated from the society, for the most part — living as they choose, as Africans. Only they don't realize the value in what they're doing because they have accepted their victimization. They've marked themselves as victims. Once they recognize that, they can begin to move through society in a different manner, from a stronger position, and claim what is theirs.

Savran: A project of yours is to point up what happens when oppression is internalized.

Wilson: Yes, transfer of aggression to the wrong target. I think it's interesting that the two roads open to blacks for "full participation" are entertainment and sports. *Ma Rainey* and *Fences,* and I didn't plan it that way. I don't think that they're the correct roads. I think Troy's right. Now with the benefit of historical perspective, I can say that the athletic scholarship was actually a way of exploiting. Now you've got two million kids who think they're going to play in the NBA. In the sixties the universities made a lot of money off of athletics. You had kids playing for free who, by and large, were not getting educated, were taking courses in basketweaving. Some of them could barely read.

Savran: Troy may be right about that issue, but it seems that he has passed on certain destructive traits in spite of himself. Take the hostility between father and son.

Wilson: I think every generation says to the previous generation: you're in my way, I've got to get by. The father-son conflict is actually a normal generational conflict that happens all the time.

Savran: So it's a healthy and a good thing?

Wilson: Oh, sure. Troy is seeing this boy walk around, smelling his piss. Two men cannot live in the same household. Troy would have been tremendously disappointed if Cory had not challenged him. Troy knows that this boy has to go out and do battle with that world: "So I had best prepare him because I know that's a harsh, cruel place out there. But that's going to be easy compared to what he's getting here. Ain't nobody gonna whip your ass like I'm gonna whip it." He has a tremendous love for the kid. But he's not going to say, "I love you," he's going to demonstrate it. He's carrying garbage for seventeen years just for the kid. The only world Troy knows is the one that he made. Cory's going to go on to find another one, he's going to arrive at the same place as Troy. I think one of the most important lines in the play is when Troy is talking about his father: "I got to the place where I could feel him kicking in my blood and knew that the only thing that separated us was the matter of a few years."

Hopefully, Cory will do things a bit differently with his son. For Troy, sports was not the way to go, the white man wouldn't let him get away with that. "Get you a job, with your hands, something that nobody can take away from you." The idea of school — he doesn't know what that is. That's for white folks. Very few blacks had paperwork jobs. But if you knew how to fix cars, you could always make some money. That's what Troy wants for Cory. There aren't many people who ever jumped up in Troy's face. So he's proud of the kid at the same time that he expresses a hurt that all men feel. You got to cut your kid loose at some point. There's that sense of loss and separation. You find out how Troy left his father's house and you see how Cory leaves his house. I suspect with Cory it will repeat with some differences and maybe, after five or six generations, they'll find a different way to do it.

Savran: Where Cory ends up is very ambiguous, as a marine in 1965.

Wilson: Yes. For the average black kid on the street, that was an alternative. You went into the army because you could learn how to do something. I can remember my parents talking about the son of some friends: "He's in the navy. He *did* something" — as opposed to standing on the street corner, shooting drugs, drinking wine, and robbing stores. Lyons says to Cory, "I always knew you were going to make something out of yourself." It really wounds me. He's a corporal in the marines. For blacks, that is a sense of accomplishment. Therein lies one of the tragedies of blacks in America. Cory says, "I don't know. I put in six years. That's enough." Anyone who goes into the army and makes a career out of it is a loser. They sit there and are nurtured by the army and they don't have to confront life. Then they get out of the army and find there's nothing to do. They didn't learn any skills. And if they did, they can't find a job. Four months later, they're shooting dope. In the sixties a whole bunch of blacks went over, fought, and died in the Vietnam War. The survivors came back to the same street corners and found out nothing had changed. They still couldn't get a job.

At the end of *Fences* every person, with the exception of Raynell, is institutionalized. Rose is in a church. Lyons is in a penitentiary. Gabriel's in a mental hospital, and Cory's in the marines. The only free person is the girl, Troy's daughter, the hope for the future. That was conscious on my part because in '57 that's what I saw. Blacks have relied on institutions which are really foreign — except for the black church, which has been our saving grace. I have some problems with it but I recognize it as a central social organization and sometimes an economic organization for the black community. I would like to see blacks develop their own institutions that respond to their needs.

From *In Their Own Voices*

Considerations

1. Wilson describes Troy's "flaw" as an inability to "recognize that the world was changing." Discuss how completely this assessment describes Troy.
2. Write an essay discussing how Wilson uses the hostility between father and son in *Fences* as a means of treating larger social issues for blacks in America.
3. Read the section on historical criticism (p. 1785) in Chapter 32, "Critical Strategies for Reading." Discuss how useful and accurate you think *Fences* is in depicting black life in America for the past several decades.

RICHARD BERNSTEIN (b. 1944)
The News Source for M. Butterfly 1986

FRANCE JAILS TWO IN ODD CASE OF ESPIONAGE

Paris, May 10. A former French diplomat and a Chinese opera singer have been sentenced to six years in jail for spying for China after a two-day trial that traced a story of clandestine love and mistaken sexual identity.

A member of the French counterespionage service said at the trial, which ended Tuesday, that the operation to collect information on France was carried out by a Chinese Communist Party intelligence unit that no longer exists.

The Chinese government has denied any involvement in the case.

The case has been the talk of Paris lately, not so much because of the charge of spying itself as because of the circumstances. The case centered on a love affair between a young French diplomat, Bernard Boursicot, now forty-one years old, who was stationed in Peking two decades ago, and a popular Chinese opera singer, Shi Peipu, forty-six.

Mr. Boursicot was accused of passing information to China after he fell in love with Mr. Shi, whom he believed for twenty years to be a woman.

Testimony in the trial indicated that the affair began in 1964 when Mr. Boursicot, then twenty years old, was posted at the French Embassy in Peking as an accountant. There he met Mr. Shi, a celebrated singer at the Peking Opera, where female roles have, according to tradition, often been played by men.

Mr. Shi was a well-known cultural figure in Peking and one of the few individuals allowed by the Chinese authorities to have contacts with foreigners.

According to testimony, Mr. Shi told Mr. Boursicot at a reception in the French Embassy in Peking that he was actually a woman.

A love affair between the two ensued to the point where, after several months, Mr. Shi told Mr. Boursicot that he was pregnant; later he announced to the apparently credulous Mr. Boursicot that he had had a son, Shi Dudu, that the diplomat had fathered.

Asked by the trial judge how he could have been so completely taken in, Mr. Boursicot said: "I was shattered to learn that he is a man, but my conviction remains unshakable that for me at that time he was really a woman and was the first love of my life. And then, there was the child that I saw, Shi Dudu. He looked like me."

Further explaining his sexual misidentification of Mr. Shi, Mr. Boursicot said their meetings had been hasty affairs that always took place in the dark.

"He was very shy," Mr. Boursicot said. "I thought it was a Chinese custom."

Mr. Boursicot's espionage activities began in 1969, when he returned to Peking after a three-year absence. By then, China was at the height of the Cultural Revolution, and it was virtually impossible for foreigners to have personal relations with Chinese citizens.

Mr. Boursicot testified that a member of the Chinese secret service, whom he said he knew only as "Kang," approached him and said he could continue to see Mr. Shi if he provided intelligence information from the French Embassy. Mr. Boursicot apparently believed that if he refused to comply, Mr. Shi would be persecuted.

Mr. Boursicot was accused of having turned over some 150 documents to Shi Peipu, who passed them on to "Kang." Mr. Boursicot said at the trial that the materials were generally not sensitive and were publicly available.

Later, from 1977 to 1979, Mr. Boursicot was posted at the French Embassy in Ulan Bator in Mongolia, where one of his duties was to make a weekly trip to Peking with the diplomatic pouch. He said he made photocopies of the documents in the diplomatic pouch and turned them over to Mr. Shi.

The case was uncovered in 1983 when Mr. Shi, accompanied by his putative son, Shi Dudu, was allowed to leave China. He lived in Paris with Mr. Boursicot, who said he continued to believe that Mr. Shi was a woman.

The arrival of a Chinese citizen in the home of a former French diplomat attracted the attention of the French counterespionage service. When the French police questioned Mr. Boursicot about his relations with Mr. Shi, he disclosed his spying activities.

From the *New York Times,* May 11, 1986

Considerations

1. What details of the news story does Hwang use? Which does he ignore?
2. Explain whether your knowledge of its source has any effect on your understanding or enjoyment of *M. Butterfly.*
3. Write a response to this explanation of the relationship: Mr. Shi "was very shy," Mr. Boursicot said. "I thought it was a Chinese custom."

DAVID SAVRAN (b. 1950)
An Interview with David Henry Hwang 1988

Savran: You strongly historicize the personal story [in *M. Butterfly*], comparing various imperialist ventures, like Vietnam, with Bouriscot's sexual imperialism.

Hwang: What I was trying to do in *Butterfly* — I didn't really know this except in retrospect — was to link imperialism, racism, and sexism. It necessitates a certain historical perspective.

Savran: And a look at the mythologies created to justify them.

Hwang: Particularly Puccini's *Madame Butterfly.*

Savran: So the play is really focused on two systems of domination, the cultural and the sexual.

Hwang: Cultural superiority is essentially economic. Whatever country dominates the world economically determines what culture is, for a while. There's a lag, because the country gets to determine the culture even after somebody else takes over economically. It still has the mystique of being the old culture, whether it's Britain or the United States. Probably the next world power is going to be Japan. You can't deal with cultural mystique unless you deal with political mystique, political power.

Savran: I was interested in how you handled the fact that Bouriscot's mistress, Shi Peipu, is really a man. That makes for the reversal at the end, the fact that Shi turns out to be Pinkerton.

Hwang: That's the axis on which the play turns. Insofar as this is possible, I would like to seduce the audience during the first act into believing that Shi is a woman. We're so conditioned to think in certain ways about Oriental women and the relationship of the West to the East, that I think it would be fun to get into the audience's head in the first act, in a very reactionary way, and then blow it out later. I don't know to what degree that's possible because anyone who goes to see this play, especially if it runs any length of time, will probably know what it's about. But I still think it can work on some level.

Savran: So you want Shi played by a man?

Hwang: Definitely. You have to create the illusion for the audience, you have to trick them. It's dirty pool if you give them a woman and say, this is a woman, and later, when he appears as a man, you give them a man. You have to play by the rules. If you're saying that Bouriscot was seduced by a man, then you have to seduce the audience with a man. *Butterfly* runs the risk of indulging the sin it condemns, like violent movies that are supposedly antiviolence. If you cast a woman in that role, you'd condemn the oppression of women by oppressing a woman in a very attractive way on the stage. If you oppress a woman who actually is a man, it's much more interesting.

From *In Their Own Voices*

Considerations

1. Why does Hwang think it is essential that Shi/Song be played by a man? Discuss whether you agree or disagree with his assessment of who should play the role.

2. Consider your response to Song as you read the play. How does knowing that Song is actually a man rather than a woman affect your response to him and to Gallimard?
3. Write an essay that discusses the ways in which Hwang weaves his concerns about imperialism, racism, and sexism into the play.

32. Critical Strategies for Reading

Maybe this has happened to you: The assignment is to write an analysis of some aspect of a work, let's say Nathaniel Hawthorne's *The Scarlet Letter,* that interests you and takes into account critical sources that comment on and interpret the work. You cheerfully begin research in the library but quickly find yourself bewildered by several seemingly unrelated articles. The first traces the thematic significance of images of light and darkness in the novel; the second makes a case for Hester Prynne as a liberated woman; the third argues that Arthur Dimmesdale's guilt is a projection of Hawthorne's own emotions; and the fourth analyzes the introduction, "The Custom House," as an attack on bourgeois values. These disparate treatments may seem random and capricious — a confirmation of your worst suspicions that interpretations of literature are hit-or-miss excursions into areas that you know little about or didn't know even existed. But if you understand that the articles are written from different perspectives — formalist, feminist, psychological, and Marxist — and that the purpose of each is to enhance your understanding of the novel by discussing a particular element of it, then you can see that their varying strategies represent potentially interesting ways of opening up the text that might otherwise never have occurred to you. There are many ways to approach a text, and a useful first step is to develop a sense of direction, an understanding of how a perspective — your own or a critic's — shapes a discussion of a text.

This chapter offers an introduction to critical approaches to literature by outlining a variety of strategies for reading fiction, poetry, or drama. These strategies include approaches that have long been practiced by readers who have used, for example, the insights gleaned from biography and history to illuminate literary works as well as more recent approaches, such as those used by feminist, reader-response, and deconstructionist critics. Each of these perspectives is sensitive to point of view, symbol, tone, irony, and other literary elements that you have been studying, but each also casts those elements in a special light. The formalist approach emphasizes how the elements within a work achieve their effects, whereas biographical and psychological approaches lead outward from the work to consider the author's life and other writings. Even broader approaches, such as historical and sociological perspectives, connect the work to historic, social, and economic forces. Mythological interpretations represent the broadest approach, because they discuss the cultural and universal responses readers have to a work.

Any given strategy raises its own types of questions and issues while seeking particular kinds of evidence to support itself. An awareness of the assumptions and methods that inform an approach can help you to understand better the validity and value of a given critic's strategy for making sense of a work. More important, such an understanding can widen and deepen the responses of your own reading.

The following overview is neither exhaustive in the types of critical approaches covered nor complete in its presentation of the complexities inherent in them, but it should help you to develop an appreciation of the intriguing possibilities that attend literary interpretation. The emphasis in this chapter is on ways of thinking about literature rather than on daunting lists of terms, names, and movements. Although a working knowledge of critical schools may be valuable and necessary for a fully informed use of a given critical approach, the aim here is more modest and practical. This chapter is no substitute for the shelves of literary criticism that can be found in your library, but it does suggest how readers using different perspectives organize their responses to texts.

The summaries of critical approaches that follow are descriptive, not evaluative. Each approach has its advantages and limitations, but those matters are best left to further study. Like literary artists, critics have their personal values, tastes, and styles. The appropriateness of a specific critical approach will depend, at least in part, on the nature of the literary work under discussion as well as on your own sensibilities and experience. However, any approach, if it is to enhance understanding, requires sensitivity, tact, and an awareness of the various literary elements of the text, including, of course, its use of language.

Successful critical approaches avoid eccentric decodings that reveal so-called hidden meanings which are not only hidden but totally absent from the text. For a parody of this sort of critical excess, see "A Reading of 'Stopping by Woods on a Snowy Evening'" (p. 738), in which Herbert R. Coursen, Jr., has some fun with a Robert Frost poem and Santa Claus while making a serious point about the dangers of overly ingenious readings. Literary criticism attempts, like any valid hypothesis, to account for phenomena — the text — without distorting or misrepresenting what it describes.

FORMALIST STRATEGIES

Formalist critics focus on the formal elements of a work — its language, structure, and tone. A formalist reads literature as an independent work of art rather than as a reflection of the author's state of mind or as a representation of a moment in history. Historic influences on a work, an author's intentions, or anything else outside the work are generally not treated by formalists (this is particularly true of the most famous modern formalists, known as the *New Critics,* who dominated American criticism from the 1940s through the 1960s). Instead, formalists offer intense examinations of the relationship between form and meaning within a work, emphasizing the subtle complexity of how a work is arranged. This kind of close reading pays special attention to what are often described as *intrinsic* matters in a literary work, such as diction, irony, paradox, metaphor, and symbol, as well as larger elements, such as plot, characterization, and narrative technique. Formalists examine how these elements work together to give a coherent shape to a work while contributing to its meaning. The answers to the questions formalists raise about how the shape and effect of a work are related come from the work itself. Other kinds of information that go beyond the text — biography, history, politics, economics, and so on — are typically regarded by formalists as *extrinsic* matters, which are considerably less important than what goes on within the autonomous text.

Poetry especially lends itself to close readings, because a poem's relative brevity allows for detailed analyses of nearly all its words and how they achieve their effects. For a student's formalist reading of how a pervasive sense of death is worked into a poem, see "A Reading of Dickinson's 'There's a certain Slant of light' " (p. 1825).

Formalist strategies are also useful for analyzing drama and fiction. In his well-known essay "The World of *Hamlet,*" Maynard Mack explores Hamlet's character and predicament by paying close attention to the words and images that Shakespeare uses to build a world in which appearances mask reality and mystery is embedded in scene after scene. Mack points to recurring terms, such as *apparition, seems, assume,* and *put on,* as well as repeated images of acting, clothing, disease, and painting, to indicate the treacherous surface world Hamlet must penetrate to get to the truth. This pattern of deception provides an organizing principle around which Mack offers a reading of the entire play:

> Hamlet's problem, in its crudest form, is simply the problem of the avenger: he must carry out the injunction of the ghost and kill the king. But this problem . . . is presented in terms of a certain kind of world. The ghost's injunction to act becomes so inextricably bound up for Hamlet with the character of the world in which the action must be taken — its mysteriousness, its baffling appearances, its deep consciousness of infection, frailty, and loss — that he cannot come to terms with either without coming to terms with both.

Although Mack places *Hamlet* in the tradition of revenge tragedy, his reading of the play emphasizes Shakespeare's arrangement of language rather than literary history as a means of providing an interpretation that accounts for various elements of the play. Mack's formalist strategy explores how diction reveals meaning and how repeated words and images evoke and reinforce important thematic significances.

For an example of a work in which the shape of the plot serves as the major organizing principle, let's examine Kate Chopin's "The Story of an Hour" (p. 12), a two-page short story that takes only a few minutes to read. With the story fresh in your mind, consider how you might approach it from a formalist perspective. A first reading probably results in surprise at the story's ending: a grieving wife "afflicted with a heart trouble" suddenly dies of a heart attack, not because she's learned that her kind and loving husband has been killed in a terrible train accident but because she discovers that he is very much alive. Clearly, we are faced with an ironic situation since there is such a powerful incongruity between what is expected to happen and what actually happens. A likely formalist strategy for analyzing this story would be to raise questions about the ironic ending. Is this merely a trick ending, or is it a carefully wrought culmination of other elements in the story so that in addition to creating surprise the ending snaps the story shut on an interesting and challenging theme? Formalists value such complexities over simple surprise effects.

A second, closer reading indicates that Chopin's third-person narrator presents the story in a manner similar to Josephine's gentle attempts to break the news about Brently Mallard's death. The story is told in "veiled hints that [reveal] in half concealing." But unlike Josephine, who tries to protect her sister's fragile heart from stress, the narrator seeks to reveal Mrs. Mallard's complex heart. A formalist would look back over the story for signs of the ending in the imagery. Although Mrs. Mallard grieves immediately and unreservedly when she hears about the train disaster, she soon begins to feel a different emotion as she looks out the window at "the tops of trees . . . all aquiver with the new spring life." This symbolic evocation of renewal and rebirth — along with "the delicious breath of rain," the sounds of life in the street, and the birds singing — causes her to feel, in spite of her own efforts to repress her thoughts and emotions, "free, free, free!" She feels alive with a sense of possibility, with a "clear and exalted perception" that she "would live for herself" instead of for and through her husband.

It is ironic that this ecstatic "self-assertion" is interpreted by Josephine as grief, but the crowning irony for this "goddess of Victory" is the doctors' assumption that she dies of joy rather than of the shock of having to abandon her newly discovered self once she realizes her husband is still alive. In the course of an hour, Mrs. Mallard's life is irretrievably changed: her husband's assumed accidental death frees her, but the fact that he lives and all the expectations imposed on her by his continued life kill her. She does, indeed, die of a broken heart, but only Chopin's readers know the real ironic meaning of that explanation.

Although this brief discussion of some of the formal elements of Chopin's story does not describe all there is to say about how they produce an effect and create meaning, it does suggest the kinds of questions, issues, and evidence that a formalist strategy might raise in providing a close reading of the text itself.

BIOGRAPHICAL STRATEGIES

A knowledge of an author's life can help readers understand his or her work more fully. Events in a work might follow actual events in a writer's life just as characters might be based on people known by the author. Ernest Hemingway's "Soldier's Home" (p. 121) is a story about the difficulties of a World War I veteran named Krebs returning to his small hometown in Oklahoma, where he cannot adjust to the pious assumptions of his family and neighbors. He refuses to accept their innocent blindness to the horrors he has witnessed during the war. They have no sense of the brutality of modern life; instead they insist he resume his life as if nothing has happened. There is plenty of biographical evidence to indicate that Krebs's unwillingness to lie about his war experiences reflects Hemingway's own responses upon his return to Oak Park, Illinois, in 1919. Krebs, like Hemingway, finds he has to leave the sentimentality, repressiveness, and smug complacency that threaten to render his experiences unreal: "the world they were in was not the world he was in."

An awareness of Hemingway's own war experiences and subsequent disillusionment with his hometown can be readily developed through available biographies, letters, and other works he wrote. Consider, for example, this passage from *By Force of Will: The Life and Art of Ernest Hemingway,* in which Scott Donaldson describes Hemingway's response to World War I:

> In poems, as in *[A Farewell to Arms],* Hemingway expressed his distaste for the first war. The men who had to fight the war did not die well:
>
> Soldiers pitch and cough and twitch —
> All the world roars red and black;
> Soldiers smother in a ditch,
> Choking through the whole attack.
>
> And what did they die for? They were "sucked in" by empty words and phrases —
>
> King and country,
> Christ Almighty,
> And the rest,

> Patriotism,
> Democracy,
> Honor —
>
> which spelled death. The bitterness of these outbursts derived from the distinction Hemingway drew between the men on the line and those who started the wars that others had to fight.

This kind of information can help to deepen our understanding of just how empathetically Krebs is presented in the story. Relevant facts about Hemingway's life will not make "Soldier's Home" a better written story than it is, but such information can make clearer the source of Hemingway's convictions and how his own experiences inform his major concerns as a storyteller.

Some formalist critics — some New Critics, for example — argue that interpretation should be based exclusively on internal evidence rather than on any biographical information outside the work. They argue that it is not possible to determine an author's intention and that the work must stand by itself. Although this is a useful caveat for keeping the work in focus, a reader who finds biography relevant would argue that biography can at the very least serve as a control on interpretation. A reader who, for example, finds Krebs at fault for not subscribing to the values of his hometown would be misreading the story, given both its tone and the biographical information available about the author. Although the narrator never *tells* the reader that Krebs is right or wrong for leaving town, the story's tone sides with his view of things. If, however, someone were to argue otherwise, insisting that the tone is not decisive and that Krebs's position is problematic, a reader familiar with Hemingway's own reactions could refute that argument with a powerful confirmation of Krebs's instincts to withdraw. Hence, many readers find biography useful for interpretation.

However, it is also worth noting that biographical information can complicate a work. Chopin's "Story of an Hour" presents a repressed wife's momentary discovery of what freedom from her husband might mean to her. She awakens to a new sense of herself when she learns of her husband's death, only to collapse of a heart attack when she sees that he is alive. Readers might be tempted to interpret this story as Chopin's fictionalized commentary about her own marriage, because her husband died twelve years before she wrote the story and seven years before she began writing fiction seriously. Biographers seem to agree, however, that Chopin's marriage was evidently satisfying to her and that she was not oppressed by her husband and did not feel oppressed.

Moreover, consider this diary entry from only one month after Chopin wrote the story (quoted by Per Seyersted in *Kate Chopin: A Critical Biography*):

> If it were possible for my husband and my mother to come back to earth, I feel that I would unhesitatingly give up everything that has come into

my life since they left it and join my existence again with theirs. To do that, I would have to forget the past ten years of my growth — my real growth. But I would take back a little wisdom with me; it would be the spirit of perfect acquiescence.

This passage raises provocative questions instead of resolving them. How does that "spirit of perfect acquiescence" relate to Mrs. Mallard's insistence that she "would live for herself"? Why would Chopin be willing to "forget the past ten years of . . . growth" given her protagonist's desire for "self-assertion"? Although these and other questions raised by the diary entry cannot be answered here, this kind of biographical perspective certainly adds to the possibilities of interpretation.

Sometimes biographical information does not change our understanding so much as it enriches our appreciation of a work. It matters, for instance, that much of John Milton's poetry, so rich in visual imagery, was written after he became blind; and it is just as significant — to shift to a musical example — that a number of Ludwig van Beethoven's greatest works, including the Ninth Symphony, were composed after he succumbed to total deafness.

PSYCHOLOGICAL STRATEGIES

Given the enormous influence that Sigmund Freud's psychoanalytic theories have had on twentieth-century interpretations of human behavior, it is nearly inevitable that most people have some familiarity with his ideas concerning dreams, unconscious desires, and sexual repression, as well as his terms for different aspects of the psyche — the id, ego, and superego. Psychological approaches to literature draw upon Freud's theories and other psychoanalytic theories to understand more fully the text, the writer, and the reader. Critics use such approaches to explore the motivations of characters and the symbolic meanings of events, while biographers speculate about a writer's own motivations — conscious or unconscious — in a literary work. Psychological approaches are also used to describe and analyze the reader's personal responses to a text.

Although it is not feasible to explain psychoanalytic terms and concepts in so brief a space as this, it is possible to suggest the nature of a psychological approach. It is a strategy based heavily on the idea of the existence of a human unconscious — those impulses, desires, and feelings about which a person is unaware but which influence emotions and behavior.

Central to a number of psychoanalytic critical readings is Freud's concept of what he called the ***Oedipus complex,*** a term derived from Sophocles's tragedy *Oedipus the King* (p. 964). This complex is predicated on a boy's unconscious rivalry with his father for his mother's love and his desire to eliminate his father in order to take his father's place with his mother. In

The Interpretation of Dreams, Freud explains why *Oedipus the King* "moves a modern audience no less than it did the contemporary Greek one." What unites their powerful attraction to the play is an unconscious response:

> There must be something which makes a voice within us ready to recognize the compelling force of destiny in the *Oedipus*. . . . His destiny moves us only because it might have been ours — because the oracle laid the same curse upon us before our birth as upon him. It is the fate of all of us, perhaps, to direct our first sexual impulse towards our mother and our first hatred and our first murderous wish against our father. Our dreams convince us that this is so. King Oedipus, who slew his father Laius and married his mother Jocasta, merely shows us the fulfillment of our own childhood wishes . . . and we shrink back from him with the whole force of the repression by which those wishes have since that time been held down within us.

In this passage Freud interprets the unconscious motives of Sophocles in writing the play, Oedipus in acting within it, and the audience in responding to it.

A further application of the Oedipus complex can be observed in a classic interpretation of *Hamlet* by Ernest Jones, who used this concept to explain why Hamlet delays in avenging his father's death. This reading has been tightly summarized by Norman Holland, a recent psychoanalytic critic, in *The Shakespearean Imagination.* Holland shapes the issues into four major components:

> One, people over the centuries have been unable to say why Hamlet delays in killing the man who murdered his father and married his mother. Two, psychoanalytic experience shows that every child wants to do just exactly that. Three, Hamlet delays because he cannot punish Claudius for doing what he himself wished to do as a child and, unconsciously, still wishes to do: he would be punishing himself. Four, the fact that this wish is unconscious explains why people could not explain Hamlet's delay.

Although the Oedipus complex is, of course, not relevant to all psychological interpretations of literature, interpretations involving this complex do offer a useful example of how psychoanalytic critics tend to approach a text. (For Freud's discussion of *Hamlet,* see p. 1251.)

The situation in which Mrs. Mallard finds herself in Chopin's "The Story of an Hour" is not related to an Oedipal complex, but it is clear that news of her husband's death has released powerful unconscious desires for freedom that she had previously suppressed. As she grieved, "something" was "coming to her and she was waiting for it, fearfully." What comes to her is what she senses about the life outside her window; that's the stimulus, but the true source of what was to "possess her," which she strove to "beat . . . back with her [conscious] will" is her desperate desire for the autonomy and fulfillment she had been unable to admit did not exist in her marriage. A psychological approach to her story amounts to a case study in the destructive nature of self-repression. Moreover, the story might reflect Chopin's own views of her marriage — despite her conscious statements about her loving husband. And what about the reader's response? How might a psychological approach account for different responses in female and male readers to Mrs. Mallard's death? One needn't be versed in psychoanalytic terms to entertain this question.

HISTORICAL STRATEGIES

Historians sometimes use literature as a window onto the past, because literature frequently provides the nuances of an historic period that cannot be readily perceived through other sources. The characters in Harriet Beecher Stowe's *Uncle Tom's Cabin* (1852) display, for example, a complex set of white attitudes toward blacks in mid-nineteenth-century America that is absent from more traditional historic documents, such as census statistics or state laws. Another way of approaching the relationship between literature and history, however, is to use history as a means of understanding a literary work more clearly. The plot pattern of pursuit, escape, and capture in nineteenth-century slave narratives had a significant influence on Stowe's plotting of action in *Uncle Tom's Cabin.* This relationship demonstrates that the writing contemporary to an author is an important element of the history that helps to shape a work.

Literary historians shift the emphasis from the period to the work. Hence a literary historian might also examine mid-nineteenth-century abolitionist attitudes toward blacks to determine whether Stowe's novel is representative of those views or significantly to the right or left of them. Such a study might even indicate how closely the book reflects racial attitudes of twentieth-century readers. A work of literature may transcend time to the extent that it addresses the concerns of readers over a span of decades or centuries, but it remains for the literary historian a part of the past in which it was composed, a past that can reveal more fully a work's language, ideas, and purposes.

Literary historians move beyond both the facts of an author's personal life and the text itself to the social and intellectual currents in which the author composed the work. They place the work in the context of its time (as do many critical biographers, who write "life and times" studies), and sometimes they make connections with other literary works that may have influenced the author. The basic strategy of literary historians is to illuminate the historic background in order to shed light on some aspect of the work itself.

In Hemingway's "Soldier's Home" we learn that Krebs had been at Belleau Wood, Soissons, the Champagne, St. Mihiel, and the Argonne. Although nothing is said of these battles in the story, they were among the most bloody battles of the war; the wholesale butchery and staggering casualties incurred by both sides make credible the way Krebs's unstated but lingering memories have turned him into a psychological prisoner of war. Knowing something about the ferocity of those battles helps us account for Krebs's response in the story. Moreover, we can more fully appreciate Hemingway's refusal to have Krebs lie about the realities of war for the folks back home if we are aware of the numerous poems, stories, and plays published during World War I that presented war as a glorious, manly, transcendent sacrifice for God and country. Juxtaposing those works with "Soldier's Home" brings the differences into sharp focus.

Similarly, a reading of William Blake's poem "London" (p. 551) is less complete if we do not know of the horrific social conditions — the poverty, disease, exploitation, and hypocrisy — that characterized the city Blake laments in the late eighteenth century.

One last example: The repression expressed in the lines on Mrs. Mallard's face is more distinctly seen if Chopin's "The Story of an Hour" is placed in the context of "the women's question" as it continued to develop in the 1890s. Mrs. Mallard's impulse toward "self-assertion" runs parallel with a growing women's movement away from the role of long-suffering housewife. This desire was widely regarded by traditionalists as a form of dangerous selfishness that was considered as unnatural as it was immoral. It is no wonder that Chopin raises the question of whether Mrs. Mallard's sense of freedom owing to her husband's death isn't a selfish, "monstrous joy." Mrs. Mallard, however, dismisses this question as "trivial" in the face of her new perception of life, a dismissal that Chopin endorses by way of the story's ironic ending. The larger social context of this story would have been more apparent to Chopin's readers in 1894 than it is to readers in the 1990s. That is why an historical reconstruction of the limitations placed on married women helps to explain the pressures, tensions, and momentary — only momentary — release that Mrs. Mallard experiences.

Since the 1960s a development in historical approaches to literature known as ***New Historicism*** has emphasized the interaction between the historic context of a work and a modern reader's understanding and interpretation of the work. In contrast to many traditional literary historians, however, new historicists attempt to describe the culture of a period by reading many different kinds of texts that traditional historians might have previously left for sociologists and anthropologists. New Historicists attempt to read a period in all its dimensions, including political, economic, social, and aesthetic concerns. These considerations could be used to explain the pressures that destroy Mrs. Mallard. A New Historicist might examine not only the story and the public attitudes toward women contemporary to "The Story of an Hour" but also documents such as suffragette tracts and medical diagnoses in order to explore how the same forces — expectations about how women are supposed to feel, think, and behave — shape different kinds of texts and how these texts influence each other. A New Historicist might, for example, examine medical records for evidence of "nervousness" and "hysteria" as common diagnoses for women who led lives regarded as too independent by their contemporaries.

Without an awareness of just how selfish and self-destructive Mrs. Mallard's impulses would have been in the eyes of her contemporaries, twentieth-century readers might miss the pervasive pressures embedded not only in her marriage but in the social fabric surrounding her. Her death is made more understandable by such an awareness. The doctors who diagnose her as suffering from "the joy that kills" are not merely insensitive or stupid; they represent a contrasting set of assumptions and values that are as historic and real as Mrs. Mallard's yearnings.

New Historicist criticism acknowledges more fully than traditional historical approaches the competing nature of readings of the past and thereby tends to offer new emphases and perspectives. New Historicism reminds us that there is not only one historic context for "The Story of an Hour." Those doctors reveal additional dimensions of late-nineteenth-century social attitudes that warrant our attention, whether we agree with them or not. By emphasizing that historical perceptions are governed, at least in part, by our own concerns and preoccupations, New Historicists sensitize us to the fact that the history on which we choose to focus is colored by being reconstructed from our own present moment. This reconstructed history affects our reading of texts.

SOCIOLOGICAL STRATEGIES, INCLUDING MARXIST AND FEMINIST STRATEGIES

Sociological approaches examine social groups, relationships, and values as they are manifested in literature. These approaches necessarily overlap historical analyses, but sociological approaches to a work emphasize more specifically the nature and effect of the social forces that shape power relationships between groups or classes of people. Such readings treat literature as either a document reflecting social conditions or a product of those conditions. The former view brings into focus the social milieu; the latter emphasizes the work. A sociological reading of Arthur Miller's *Death of a Salesman* (p. 1508) might, for instance, discuss how the characters' efforts to succeed reflect an increasingly competitive twentieth-century urban sensibility in America. Or it might emphasize how the "American Dream" of success shapes Willy Loman's aspirations and behavior. Clearly, there are numerous ways to talk about the societal aspects of a work. Two sociological strategies that have been especially influential are Marxist and feminist approaches.

Marxist Criticism

Marxist readings developed from the heightened interest in radical reform during the 1930s, when many critics looked to literature as a means of furthering proletarian social and economic goals, based largely on the writings of Karl Marx. ***Marxist critics*** focus on the ideological content of a work — its explicit and implicit assumptions and values about matters such as culture, race, class, and power. Marxist studies typically aim at not only revealing and clarifying ideological issues but also correcting social injustices. Some Marxist critics have used literature to describe the competing socioeconomic interests that too often advance capitalist money and power rather than socialist morality and justice. They argue that criticism, like literature, is essentially political because it either challenges or supports economic oppression. Even if criticism attempts to ignore class conflicts, it is politicized, according to Marxists, because it supports the status quo.

It is not surprising that Marxist critics pay more attention to the content and themes of literature than to its form. A Marxist critic would more likely be concerned with the exploitive economic forces that cause Willy Loman to feel trapped in Miller's *Death of a Salesman* than with the playwright's use of nonrealistic dramatic techniques to reveal Loman's inner thoughts. Similarly, a Marxist reading of Chopin's "A Story of an Hour" might draw on the evidence made available in a book published only a few years after the story by Charlotte Perkins Gilman titled *Women and Economics: A Study of the Economic Relation between Men and Women as a Factor in Social Evolution* (1898). An examination of this study could help explain how some of the "repression" Mrs. Mallard experiences was generated by the socioeconomic structure contemporary to her and how Chopin challenges the validity of that structure by having Mrs. Mallard resist it with her very life. A Marxist reading would see the protagonist's conflict as not only an individual issue but part of a larger class struggle.

Feminist Criticism

Feminist critics would also be interested in Gilman's study of *Women and Economics,* because they seek to correct or supplement what they regard as a predominantly male-dominated critical perspective with a feminine consciousness. Like other forms of sociological criticism, feminist criticism places literature in a social context, and, like those of Marxist criticism, its analyses often have sociopolitical purposes, purposes that might explain, for example, how images of women in literature reflect the patriarchal social forces that have impeded women's efforts to achieve full equality with men.

Feminists have analyzed literature by both men and women in an effort to understand literary representations of women as well as the writers and cultures that create them. Related to concerns about how gender affects the way men and women write about each other is an interest in whether women use language differently from the way men do. Consequently, feminist critics' approach to literature is characterized by the use of a broad range of disciplines, including history, sociology, psychology, and linguistics, to provide a perspective sensitive to feminist issues.

A feminist approach to Chopin's "The Story of an Hour" might explore the psychological stress created by the expectations that marriage imposes on Mrs. Mallard, expectations that literally and figuratively break her heart. Given that her husband is kind and loving, the issue is not her being married to Brently but her being married at all. Chopin presents marriage as an institution that creates in both men and women the assumed "right to impose a private will upon a fellow-creature." That "right," however, is seen, especially from a feminist perspective, as primarily imposed on women by men. A feminist critic might note, for instance, that the protagonist is introduced as "Mrs. Mallard" (we learn that her first name is Louise only later); she is defined by her marital status and her husband's name, a name whose origin from the Old French is related to the word *masle,* which means "male." The appropriateness of her name points up the fact that her emotions and the cause of her death are interpreted in male terms by the doctors. The value of a feminist perspective on this work can be readily discerned if a reader imagines Mrs. Mallard's story being told from the point of view of one of the doctors who diagnoses the cause of her death as a weak heart rather than as a fierce struggle.

Restructuring the Literary Canon

Another development related to feminist criticism is the reassessment of works by women previously neglected by male-oriented criticism. Feminist critics have rediscovered many women writers who were left out of the standard literary traditions posited by earlier histories or collections of literature. This reassessment has resulted in a restructuring of the literary ***canon,*** those works generally regarded as significant and worthy of serious study.

During the past twenty years many more women writers have been read alongside the male writers who traditionally dominated literary history. Hence, a reader of Henry James and Stephen Crane is now just as likely to encounter Kate Chopin in a literature anthology. Until fairly recently Chopin was mostly regarded as a minor "local colorist" of Louisiana life. In the 1960s, however, the feminist movement helped to establish her present reputation as a significant voice in American literature owing to the feminist concerns so compellingly articulated by her female characters. This kind of enlargement of the canon is also reflected in another reform movement of the 1960s. The civil rights movement sensitized literary critics to the political, moral, and aesthetic necessity of rediscovering black literature. Moreover, on a broader scale the canon is being revised and enlarged to include the writings of non-Western and Third World writers, a development that reflects the changing values and concerns of the past quarter century.

MYTHOLOGICAL STRATEGIES

Mythological approaches to literature attempt to identify what in a work creates deep universal responses in readers. Whereas psychological critics interpret the symbolic meanings of characters and actions in order to understand more fully the unconscious dimensions of an author's mind, a character's motivation, or a reader's response, mythological critics (also frequently referred to as archetypal critics) interpret the hopes, fears, and expectations of entire cultures.

In this context myth is not to be understood simply as referring to stories about imaginary gods who perform astonishing feats in the causes of love, jealousy, or hatred. Nor are myths to be judged as merely erroneous, primitive accounts of how nature runs its course and humanity its affairs. Instead, literary critics use myths as a strategy for understanding how human beings try to account for their lives symbolically. Myths can be a window onto a culture's deepest perceptions about itself, because myths attempt to explain what otherwise seems unexplainable: a people's origin, purpose, and destiny.

All human beings have a need to make sense of their lives, whether they are concerned about their natural surroundings, the seasons, sexuality, birth, death, or the very meaning of existence. Myths help people organize their experiences; these systems of belief (less formally held than religious or political tenets but no less important) embody a culture's assumptions and values. What is important to the mythological critic is not the validity or truth of those assumptions and values; what matters is that they reveal common human concerns.

It is not surprising that although the details of mythic stories vary enormously, the essential patterns are often similar, because these myths attempt to explain universal experiences. There are, for example, numerous myths that redeem humanity from permanent death through a hero's resurrection and rebirth. The resurrection of Jesus for Christians symbolizes the ultimate defeat of death and coincides with the rebirth of nature's fertility in spring. Features of this rebirth parallel the Greek myths of Adonis and Hyacinth, who die but are subsequently transformed into living flowers; there are also similarities that connect these stories to the reincarnation of the Indian Buddha or the rebirth of the Egyptian Osiris. To be sure, important differences exist among these stories, but each reflects a basic human need to limit the power of death and to hope for eternal life.

Mythological critics look for underlying, recurrent patterns in literature that reveal universal meanings and basic human experiences for readers regardless of when or where they live. The characters, images, and themes that symbolically embody these meanings and experiences are called ***archetypes.*** This term designates universal symbols, which evoke deep and perhaps unconscious responses in a reader because archetypes bring with them the heft of our hopes and fears since the beginning of human time. Surely one of the most powerfully compelling archetypes is the death/rebirth theme that relates the human life cycle to the cycle of the seasons. Many others could be cited and would be exhausted only after all human concerns were catalogued, but a few examples can suggest some of the range of plots, images, and characters addressed.

Among the most common literary archetypes are stories of quests, initiations, scapegoats, meditative withdrawals, descents to the underworld, and heavenly ascents. These stories are often filled with archetypal images: bodies of water that may symbolize the unconscious or eternity or baptismal rebirth; rising suns, suggesting reawakening and enlightenment; setting suns, pointing toward death; colors such as green, evocative of growth and fertility, or black, indicating chaos, evil, and death. Along the way are earth mothers, fatal women, wise old men, desert places, and paradisal gardens. No doubt your own reading has introduced you to any number of archetypal plots, images, and characters.

Mythological critics attempt to explain how archetypes are embodied in literary works. Employing various disciplines, these critics articulate the power a literary work has over us. Some critics are deeply grounded in classical literature, whereas others are more conversant with philology, anthropology, psychology, or cultural history. Whatever their emphases, however, mythological critics examine the elements of a work in order to make larger connections that explain the work's lasting appeal.

A mythological reading of Sophocles' *Oedipus the King,* for example, might focus on the relationship between Oedipus's role as a scapegoat and the plague and drought that threaten to destroy Thebes. The city is saved and the fertility of its fields restored only after the corruption is located in Oedipus. His subsequent atonement symbolically provides a kind of rebirth for the city. Thus, the plot recapitulates ancient rites in which the well-being of a king was directly linked to the welfare of his people. If a leader were sick or corrupt, he had to be replaced in order to guarantee the health of the community.

A similar pattern can be seen in the rottenness that Shakespeare exposes in Hamlet's Denmark. *Hamlet* reveals an archetypal pattern similar to that of *Oedipus the King:* not until the hero sorts out the corruption in his world and in himself can vitality and health be restored in his world. Hamlet avenges his father's death and becomes a scapegoat in the process. When he fully accepts his responsibility to set things right, he is swept away along with the tide of intrigue and corruption that has polluted life in Denmark. The new order — established by Fortinbras at the play's end — is achieved precisely because Hamlet is willing and finally able to sacrifice himself in a necessary purgation of the diseased state.

These kinds of archetypal patterns exist potentially in any literary period. Consider how in Chopin's "The Story of an Hour" Mrs. Mallard's life parallels the end of winter and the earth's renewal in spring. When she feels a surge of new life after grieving over her husband's death, her own sensibilities are closely aligned with the "new spring life" that is "all aquiver" outside her window. Although she initially tries to resist that renewal by "beat[ing] it back with her will," she cannot control the life force that surges within her and all around her. When she finally gives herself to the energy and life she experiences, she feels triumphant — like a "goddess of Victory." But this victory is short-lived when she learns that her husband is still alive and with him all the obligations that made her marriage feel like a wasteland. Her death is an ironic version of a rebirth ritual. The coming of spring is an ironic contrast to her own discovery that she can no longer live a repressed, circumscribed life with her husband. Death turns out to be preferable to the living death that her marriage means to her. Although spring will go on, this "goddess of Victory" is defeated by a devastating social contract. The old, corrupt order continues, and that for Chopin is a cruel irony that mythological critics would see as an unnatural disruption of the nature of things.

READER-RESPONSE STRATEGIES

Reader-response criticism, as its name implies, focuses its attention on the reader rather than the work itself. This approach to literature describes what goes on in the reader's mind during the process of reading a text. In a sense, all critical approaches (especially psychological and mythological criticism) concern themselves with a reader's response to literature, but there is a stronger emphasis in reader-response criticism on the reader's active construction of the text. Although many critical theories inform reader-response criticism, all ***reader-response critics*** aim to describe the reader's experience of a work: in effect we get a reading of the reader, who comes to the work with certain expectations and assumptions, which are either met or not met. Hence the consciousness of the reader — produced by reading the work — is the subject matter of reader-response critics. Just as writing is a creative act, reading is, since it also produces a text.

Reader-response critics do not assume that a literary work is a finished product with fixed formal properties, as, for example, formalist critics do. Instead, the literary work is seen as an evolving creation of the reader's as he or she processes characters, plots, images, and other elements while reading. Some reader-response critics argue that this act of creative reading is, to a degree, controlled by the text, but it can produce many interpretations of the same text by different readers. There is no single definitive reading of a work, because the crucial assumption is that readers create rather than discover meanings in texts. Readers who have gone back to works they had read earlier in their lives often find that a later reading yields very different responses from them. What earlier seemed unimportant is now crucial; what at first seemed central is now barely worth noting. The reason, put simply, is that two different people have read the same text.

Reader-response critics are not after the "correct" reading of the text or what the author presumably intended; instead they are interested in the reader's experience with the text.

These experiences change with readers; although the text remains the same, the readers do not. Social and cultural values influence readings, so that, for example, an avowed Marxist would be likely to come away from Miller's *Death of a Salesman* with a very different view of American capitalism than that of, say, a successful sales representative, who might attribute Willy Loman's fall more to his character than to the American economic system. Moreover, readers from different time periods respond differently to texts. An Elizabethan — concerned perhaps with the stability of monarchical rule — might respond differently to Hamlet's problems than would a twentieth-century reader well versed in psychology and concepts of what Freud called the Oedipus complex. This is not to say that anything goes, that Miller's play can be read as an amoral defense of cheating and rapacious business practices or that *Hamlet* is about the dangers of living away from home. The text does, after all, establish some limits that allow us to reject certain readings as erroneous. But reader-response critics do reject formalist approaches that describe a literary work as a self-contained object, the meaning of which can be determined without reference to any extrinsic matters, such as the social and cultural values assumed by either the author or the reader.

Reader-response criticism calls attention to how we read and what influences our readings. It does not attempt to define what a literary work means on the page but rather what it does to an informed reader, a reader who understands the language and conventions used in a given work. Reader-response criticism is not a rationale for mistaken or bizarre readings of works but an exploration of the possibilities for a plurality of readings shaped by the readers' experience with the text. This kind of strategy can help us understand how our responses are shaped by both the text and ourselves.

Chopin's "The Story of an Hour" illustrates how reader-response critical strategies read the reader. Chopin doesn't say that Mrs. Mallard's marriage is repressive; instead, that troubling fact dawns on the reader at the same time that the recognition forces its way into Mrs. Mallard's consciousness. Her surprise is also the reader's, because although she remains in the midst of intense grief, she is on the threshold of a startling discovery about the new possibilities life offers. How the reader responds to that discovery, however, is not entirely controlled by Chopin. One reader, perhaps someone who has recently lost a spouse, might find Mrs. Mallard's "joy" indeed "monstrous" and selfish. Certainly that's how Mrs. Mallard's doctors — the seemingly authoritative diagnosticians in the story — would very likely read her. But for other readers — especially late-twentieth-century readers steeped in feminist values — Mrs. Mallard's feelings require no justification. Such readers might find Chopin's ending to the story more ironic than she seems to have intended, because Mrs. Mallard's death could be read as Chopin's inability to envision a protagonist who has the strength of her convictions. In contrast, a reader in 1894 might have seen the ending as Mrs. Mallard's only escape from the repressive marriage her husband's assumed death suddenly allowed her to see. A late-twentieth-century reader probably would argue that it was the marriage that should have died rather than Mrs. Mallard, that she had other alternatives, not just obligations (as the doctors would have insisted), to consider.

By imagining different readers we can imagine a variety of responses to the story that are influenced by the readers' own impressions, memories, or experiences with marriage. Such imagining suggests the ways in which reader-response criticism opens up texts to a number of interpretations. As one final example, consider how readers' responses to "The Story of an Hour" would be affected if it were printed in two different magazines, read in the context of either *Ms.* or *Good Housekeeping*. What assumptions and beliefs would each magazine's readership be likely to bring to the story? How do you think the respective experiences and values of each magazine's readers would influence their readings?

DECONSTRUCTIONIST STRATEGIES

Deconstructionist critics insist that literary works do not yield fixed, single meanings. They argue that there can be no absolute knowledge about anything because language can never say what we intend it to mean. Anything we write conveys meanings we did not intend, so the deconstructionist argument goes. Language is not a precise instrument but a power whose meanings are caught in an endless web of possibilities that cannot be untangled. Accordingly, any idea or statement that insists on being understood separately can ultimately be "deconstructed" to reveal its relations and connections to contradictory and opposite meanings.

Unlike other forms of criticism, deconstructionism seeks to destabilize meanings instead of establishing them. In contrast to formalists such as the New Critics, who closely examine a work in order to call attention to how its various components interact to establish a unified whole, deconstructionists try to show how a close examination of the language in a text inevitably reveals conflicting, contradictory impulses that "deconstruct" or break down its apparent unity.

Although deconstructionists and New Critics both examine the language of a text closely, deconstructionists focus on the gaps and ambiguities that reveal a text's instability and indeterminacy, whereas New Critics look for patterns that explain how the text's fixed meaning is structured. Deconstructionists painstakingly examine the competing meanings within the text rather than attempting to resolve them into a unified whole.

The questions deconstructionists ask are aimed at discovering and describing how a variety of possible readings are generated by the elements of a text. In contrast to a New Critic's concerns about the ultimate meaning of a work, a deconstructionist is primarily interested in how the use of language — diction, tone, metaphor, symbol, and so on — yields only provisional, not definitive, meanings. Deconstructionists look for ways to question and extend the meanings of a text. A deconstructionist might find, for example, the ironic ending of Chopin's "The Story of an Hour" less tidy and conclusive than would a New Critic, who might attribute Mrs. Mallard's death to her sense of lost personal freedom. A deconstructionist might use the story's ending to suggest that the narrative shares the doctor's inability to imagine a life for Mrs. Mallard apart from her husband.

As difficult as it is controversial, deconstructionism is not easily summarized or paraphrased. For an example of deconstructionism in practice and how it differs from New Criticism, see Andrew P. Debicki's "New Criticism and Deconstructionism: Two Attitudes in Teaching Poetry" in Perspectives (p. 1803).

SELECTED BIBLIOGRAPHY

Formalist Strategies

Brooks, Cleanth. *The Well Wrought Urn: Studies in the Structure of Poetry.* New York: Reynal and Hitchcock, 1947.

Crane, Ronald Salmon. *The Languages of Criticism and the Structure of Poetry.* Toronto: University of Toronto Press, 1953.

Eliot, Thomas Stearns. *The Sacred Wood: Essays in Poetry and Criticism.* London: Methuen, 1920.

Lemon, Lee T., and Marion J. Reis, eds. *Russian Formalist Criticism: Four Essays.* Lincoln: University of Nebraska Press, 1965.

Ransom, John Crowe. *The New Criticism.* Norfolk, CT: New Directions, 1941.

Wellek, Rene, and Austin Warren. *Theory of Literature.* New York: Harcourt, Brace and World, 1949.

Biographical and Psychological Strategies

Bleich, David. *Subjective Criticism.* Baltimore: Johns Hopkins University Press, 1978.

Bloom, Harold. *The Anxiety of Influence.* New York: Oxford University Press, 1975.

Crews, Frederick. *The Sins of the Fathers: Hawthorne's Psychological Themes.* New York: Oxford University Press, 1966.

Felman, Shoshana, ed. *Literature and Psychoanalysis: The Question of Reading: Otherwise.* Baltimore: Johns Hopkins University Press, 1981.

Freud, Sigmund. *The Standard Edition of the Complete Psychological Works.* 24 vols. 1940–1968. London: Hogarth Press and the Institute of Psychoanalysis, 1953.

Holland, Norman. *The Dynamics of Literary Response.* New York: Oxford University Press, 1968.

Jones, Ernest. *Hamlet and Oedipus.* New York: Doubleday, 1949.

Lesser, Simon O. *Fiction and the Unconscious.* Chicago: University of Chicago Press, 1957.

Skura, Meredith Anne. *The Literary Use of the Psychoanalytic Process.* New Haven: Yale University Press, 1981.

Historical and New Historicist Strategies

Dollimore, Jonathan. *Radical Tragedy: Religion, Ideology and Power in the Drama of Shakespeare and His Contemporaries.* Brighton, Eng.: Harvester Press, 1984.

Geertz, Clifford. *The Interpretation of Cultures: Selected Essays.* New York: Basic Books, 1973.

Greenblatt, Stephen. *Renaissance Self-Fashioning: From More to Shakespeare.* Chicago: University of Chicago Press, 1980.

Lindenberger, Herbert. *Historical Drama: The Relation of Literature and Reality.* Chicago: University of Chicago Press, 1975.

McGann, Jerome. *The Beauty of Inflections: Literary Investigations in Historical Method and Theory.* Oxford: Clarendon Press, 1985.

Tennenhouse, Leonard. *Power on Display: The Politics of Shakespeare's Genres.* New York: Methuen, 1986.

White, Hayden. *Tropics of Discourse: Essays in Cultural Criticism.* Baltimore, Johns Hopkins University Press, 1978.

Sociological Strategies (Including Marxist and Feminist Strategies)

Adorno, Theodor. *Prisms: Cultural Criticism and Society.* 1955. London: Neville Spearman, 1967.

Beauvoir, Simone de. *The Second Sex.* Trans. H. M. Parshley. New York: Knopf, 1972. Trans. of *Le deuxième sexe.* Paris: Gallimard, 1949.

Benjamin, Walter. *Illuminations.* New York: Harcourt, Brace and World, 1968.

Eagleton, Terry. *Criticism and Ideology: A Study in Marxist Literary Theory.* London: New Left Books, 1976.

Fetterley, Judith. *The Resisting Reader: A Feminist Approach to American Fiction.* Bloomington: Indiana University Press, 1978.

Gilbert, Sandra M., and Susan Gubar. *The Madwoman in the Attic: The Woman Writer and the Nineteenth-Century Literary Imagination.* New Haven: Yale University Press, 1979.

Irigaray, Luce. *This Sex Which Is Not One.* Ithaca: Cornell University Press, 1985. Trans. of *Ce sexe qui n'en est pas un.* Paris. Editions de Minuit, 1977.

Jameson, Fredric. *The Political Unconscious: Studies in the Ideology of Form.* Ithaca: Cornell University Press, 1979.

Kolodny, Annette. "Some Notes on Defining a 'Feminist Literary Criticism.'" *Critical Inquiry* 2 (1975): 75–92.

Lukacs, Georg. *Realism in Our Time: Literature and the Class Struggle.* 1957. New York: Harper and Row, 1964.

Marx, Karl, and Fredrich Engels. *Marx and Engels on Literature and Art.* St. Louis: Telos Press, 1973.

Millet, Kate. *Sexual Politics.* New York: Avon Books, 1970.

Showalter, Elaine. *A Literature of Their Own: British Women Novelists from Brontë to Lessing.* Princeton: Princeton University Press, 1977.

Smith, Barbara. *Toward a Black Feminist Criticism.* New York: Out and Out Books, 1977.

Trotsky, Leon. *Literature and the Revolution.* 1924. Ann Arbor: University of Michigan Press, 1960.

Williams, Raymond. *Culture and Society, 1780–1950.* London: Chatto and Windus, 1958.

Mythological Strategies

Bodkin, Maud. *Archetypal Patterns in Poetry.* London: Oxford University Press, 1934.

Frye, Northrop. *Anatomy of Criticism: Four Essays.* Princeton: Princeton University Press,1957.

Jung, Carl Gustav. *Complete Works.* Eds. Herbert Read, Michael Fordham, and Gerhard Adler. 17 vols. New York: Pantheon, 1953–.

Reader-Response Strategies

Booth, Wayne, C. *The Rhetoric of Fiction.* 2nd ed. Chicago: University of Chicago Press, 1983.

Eco, Umberto. *The Role of the Reader: Explorations in the Semiotics of Texts.* Bloomington: Indiana University Press, 1979.

Escarpit, Robert. *Sociology of Literature.* Painesville, Ohio: Lake Erie College Press, 1965.

Fish, Stanley. *Is There a Text in This Class? The Authority of Interpretive Communities.* Cambridge: Harvard University Press, 1980.

Holland, Norman N. *5 Readers Reading.* New Haven: Yale University Press, 1975.

Iser, Wolfgang. *The Implied Reader: Patterns of Communication in Prose Fiction from Bunyan to Beckett.* Baltimore: Johns Hopkins University Press, 1974.

Jauss, Hans Robert. "Literary History as a Challenge to Literary Theory." *Toward an Aesthetics of Reception.* Trans. Timothy Bahti. Minneapolis: University of Minnesota Press, 1982. pp. 3–46.

Rosenblatt, Louise. *Literature as Exploration.* 1938. New York: Modern Language Association, 1983.

Suleiman, Susan, and Inge Crosman, eds. *The Reader in the Text: Essays on Audience and Interpretation.* Princeton: Princeton University Press, 1980.

Tompkins, Jane P., ed. *Reader-Response Criticism: From Formalism to Post-Structuralism.* Baltimore: Johns Hopkins University Press, 1980.

Deconstructionist and Other Poststructuralist Strategies

Culler, Jonathan. *On Deconstruction: Theory and Criticism after Structuralism.* Ithaca: Cornell University Press, 1982.

de Man, Paul. *Blindness and Insight.* New York: Oxford University Press, 1971.

Derrida, Jacques. *Of Grammatology.* 1967. Baltimore: Johns Hopkins University Press, 1976.

———. *Writing and Difference.* 1967. Chicago: University of Chicago Press, 1978.

Foucault, Michel. *The Order of Things: An Archaeology of the Human Sciences.* 1966. London: Tavistock, 1970.

———. *Language, Counter-Memory, Practice.* Ithaca: Cornell University Press, 1977.

Gasche, Rodolphe. "Deconstruction as Criticism." *Glyph* 6 (1979): 177–216.

Hartman, Geoffrey H. *Criticism in the Wilderness.* New Haven: Yale University Press, 1980.

Johnson, Barbara. *The Critical Difference: Essays in the Contemporary Rhetoric of Reading.* Baltimore: Johns Hopkins University Press, 1980.

Said, Edward W. *The World, the Text, and the Critic.* Cambridge: Harvard University Press, 1983.

Smith, Barbara Hernstein. *On the Margins of Discourse: The Relation of Literature to Language.* Chicago: University of Chicago Press, 1979.

PERSPECTIVES ON CRITICAL READING

SUSAN SONTAG (b. 1933)

Against Interpretation — 1964

Like the fumes of the automobile and of heavy industry which befoul the urban atmosphere, the effusion of interpretations of art today poisons our sensibilities. In a culture whose already classical dilemma is the hypertrophy of the intellect at the expense of energy and sensual capability, interpretation is the revenge of the intellect upon art.

Even more. It is the revenge of the intellect upon the world. To interpret is to impoverish, to deplete the world — in order to set up a shadow world of "meanings." It is to turn *the* world into *this* world. ("This world"! As if there were any other.)

The world, our world, is depleted, impoverished enough. Away with all duplicates of it, until we again experience more immediately what we have. . . .

In most modern instances, interpretation amounts to the philistine refusal to leave the work of art alone. Real art has the capacity to make us nervous. By reducing the work of art to its content and then interpreting *that,* one tames the work of art. Interpretation makes art manageable, conformable.

This philistinism of interpretation is more rife in literature than in any other art. For decades now, literary critics have understood it to be their task to translate the elements of the poem or play or novel or story into something else.

From *Against Interpretation*

Considerations

1. What are Sontag's objections to "interpretation"? Explain whether you agree or disagree with them.
2. In what sense does interpretation make art "manageable" and "conformable"?
3. In an essay explore what you take to be both the dangers of interpretation and its contributions to your understanding of literature.

JUDITH FETTERLEY (b. 1938)

A Feminist Reading of "A Rose for Emily" 1978

"A Rose for Emily" is a story not of a conflict between the South and the North or between the old order and the new; it is a story of the patriarchy North and South, new and old, and of the sexual conflict within it. As Faulkner himself has implied, it is a story of a woman victimized and betrayed by the system of sexual politics, who nevertheless has discovered, within the structures that victimize her, sources of power for herself. . . . "A Rose for Emily" is the story of how to murder your gentleman caller and get away with it. Faulkner's story is an analysis of how men's attitudes toward women turn back upon themselves; it is a demonstration of the thesis that it is impossible to oppress without in turn being oppressed, it is impossible to kill without creating the conditions for your own murder. "A Rose for Emily" is the story of a *lady* and of her revenge for that grotesque identity. . . .

Not only is "A Rose for Emily" a supreme analysis of what men do to women by making them ladies; it is also an exposure of how this act in turn defines and recoils upon men. This is the significance of the dynamic that Faulkner establishes between Emily and Jefferson. And it is equally the point of the dynamic implied between the tableau of Emily and her father and the tableau which greets the men who break down the door of that room in the region above the stairs. When the would-be "suitors" finally get into her father's house, they discover the consequences of his oppression of her, for the violence contained in the rotted corpse of Homer Barron is the mirror image of the violence represented in the tableau, the back-flung front door flung back with a vengeance. Having been consumed by her father, Emily in turn feeds off Homer Barron, becoming, after his death, suspiciously fat. Or, to put it another way, it is as if, after her father's death, she has reversed his act of incorporating her by incorporating and becoming him, metamorphosed from the slender figure in white to the obese figure in black whose hair is "a vigorous iron-gray, like the hair of an active man." She has taken into herself the violence in him which thwarted her and has reenacted it upon Homer Barron.

That final encounter, however, is not simply an image of the reciprocity of violence. Its power of definition also derives from its grotesqueness, which makes finally explicit the grotesqueness that has been latent in the description of Emily throughout the story: "Her skeleton was small and spare: perhaps that was why what would have been merely plumpness in another was obesity in her. She looked bloated, like a body long submerged in motionless water, and of that pallid hue. Her eyes, lost in the fatty ridges of her face, looked like two small pieces of coal pressed into a lump of dough." The impact of this description depends on the contrast it establishes between Emily's reality as a fat, bloated figure in black and the conventional image of a lady — expectations that are fostered in the town by its emblematic memory of Emily as a slender figure in white and in us by the narrator's tone of romantic invocation and by the passage itself. Were she not expected to look so different, were her skeleton not small and spare, Emily would not be so grotesque. Thus, the focus is on the grotesqueness that results when stereotypes are imposed upon reality. And the implication of this focus is that the real grotesque is the stereotype itself. If Emily is both lady and grotesque, then the syllogism must be completed thus: the idea of a lady is grotesque. So Emily is metaphor and mirror for the town of Jefferson; and when, at the end, the town folk finally discover who and what she is, they have in fact encountered who and what they are.

From *The Resisting Reader: A Feminist Approach to American Fiction*

Considerations

1. Discuss Fetterley's claim that Emily Grierson is a victim of a "system of sexual politics." What details of the story support this view?
2. What are the consequences of Emily's oppression by her father? How are the men in the story affected by it?
3. Write an essay that supports or refutes Fetterley's argument that "A Rose for Emily" is an implicitly feminist story about "the patriarchy North and South."

STANLEY FISH (b. 1938)

On What Makes an Interpretation Acceptable 1980

. . . After all, while "The Tyger" is obviously open to more than one interpretation, it is not open to an infinite number of interpretations. There may be disagreements as to whether the tiger is good or evil, or whether the speaker is Blake or a persona, and so on, but no one is suggesting that the poem is an allegory of the digestive processes or that it predicts the second World War, and its limited plurality is simply a testimony to the capacity of a great work of art to generate multiple readings. The point is one that Wayne Booth makes when he asks, "Are we *right* to rule out at least some readings?" and then answers his own question with a resounding yes. It would be my answer too; but the real question is what gives us the right so to be right. A pluralist is committed to saying that there is something in the text which rules out some readings and allows others (even though no one reading can ever capture the text's "inexhaustible richness and complexity"). His best evidence is that in practice "we all in fact" do reject unacceptable readings and that more often than not we agree on the readings that are not rejected. . . . Booth concludes that there are justified limits to what we can legitimately do with a text, for "surely we could not go on disputing at all if a core of agreement did not exist." Again, I agree, but if, as I have argued, the text is always a function of interpretation, then the text cannot be the location of the core of agreement by means of which we reject interpretations. We seem to be at an impasse: on the one hand there would seem to be no basis for labeling an interpretation unacceptable, but on the other we do it all the time.

This, however, is an impasse only if one assumes that the activity of interpretation is itself unconstrained; but in fact the shape of that activity is determined by the literary institution which at any one time will authorize only a finite number of interpretative strategies. Thus, while there is no core of agreement *in* the text, there is a core of agreement (although one subject to change) concerning the ways of *producing* the text. Nowhere is this set of acceptable ways written down, but it is a part of everyone's knowledge of what it means to be operating within the literary institution as it is now constituted. A student of mine recently demonstrated this knowledge when, with an air of giving away a trade secret, she confided that she could go into any classroom, no matter what the subject of the course, and win approval for running one of a number of well-defined interpretive routines: she could view the assigned text as an instance of the tension between nature and culture; she could look in the text for evidence of large mythological oppositions; she could argue that the true subject of the text was its own composition, or that in the guise of fashioning a narrative the speaker was fragmenting and displacing his own anxieties and fears. She could not . . . argue that the text was a prophetic message inspired by the ghost of her Aunt Tilly.

My student's understanding of what she could and could not get away with, of the unwritten rules of the literary game, is shared by everyone who plays that game, by those who write and judge articles for publication in learned journals, by those who read and listen to papers at professional meetings, by those who seek and award tenure in innumerable departments of English and comparative literature, by the armies of graduate students for whom knowledge of the rules is the real mark of professional initiation. This does not mean that these rules and the practices they authorize are either monolithic or stable. Within the literary community there are subcommunities. . . . In a classroom whose authority figures include David Bleich and Norman Holland, a student might very well relate a text to her memories of a favorite aunt, while in other classrooms, dominated by the spirit of [Cleanth] Brooks and [Robert Penn] Warren, any such activity would immediately be dismissed as nonliterary, as something that isn't done.

The point is that while there is always a category of things that are not done (it is simply the reverse or flip side of the category of things that *are* done), the membership in that category is continually changing. It changes laterally as one moves from subcommunity to subcommunity, and it changes through time when once interdicted interpretive strategies are admitted into the ranks of the acceptable. Twenty years ago one of the things that literary critics didn't do was talk about the reader, at least in a way that made his experience the focus of the critical act. The prohibition on such talk was largely the result of [W. K.] Wimsatt's and [Monroe] Beardsley's famous essay "The Affective Fallacy," which argued that the variability of readers renders any investigation of their responses ad-hoc and relativistic: "The poem itself," the authors complained, "as an object of specifically critical judgment, tends to disappear." So influential was this essay that it was possible for a reviewer to dismiss a book merely by finding in it evidence that the affective fallacy had been committed. The use of a juridical terminology is not accidental; this was in a very real sense a *legal* finding of activity in violation of understood and institutionalized decorums. Today, however, the affective fallacy, no longer a fallacy but a methodology, is committed all the time, and its practitioners have behind them the full and authorizing weight of a fully articulated institutional apparatus. The "reader in literature" is regularly the subject of forums and workshops at the convention of the Modern Language Association; there is a reader newsletter which reports on the multitudinous labors of a reader industry; any list of currently active schools of literary criticism includes the school of "reader response," and two major university presses have published collections of essays designed both to display the variety of reader-centered criticism (the emergence of factions within a once interdicted activity is a sure sign of its having achieved the status of an orthodoxy) and to detail its history. None of this of course means that a reader-centered criticism is now invulnerable to challenge or attack, merely that it is now recognized as a competing literary strategy that cannot be dismissed simply by being named. It is acceptable not because everyone accepts it but because those who do not are now obliged to argue against it.

From *Is There a Text in This Class?*

Considerations

1. Why *can't* William Blake's "The Tyger" (see p. 635) be read as "an allegory of the digestive processes"? What principle does Fish use to rule out such a reading?
2. What kinds of strategies for reading have you encountered in your classroom experiences? Which have you found to be the most useful? Explain why.
3. Write an essay that describes what you "could and could not get away with" in the literature courses you have taken in high school and college.

ANNETTE KOLODNY (b. 1941)

On the Commitments of Feminist Criticism 1980

If feminist criticism calls anything into question, it must be that dog-eared myth of intellectual neutrality. For what I take to be the underlying spirit or message of any consciously ideologically premised criticism — that is, that ideas are important *because* they determine the ways we live, or want to live, in the world — is vitiated by confining those ideas to the study, the classroom, or the pages of our books. To write chapters decrying the sexual stereotyping of women in our literaure, while closing our eyes to the sexual harassment of our women students and colleagues; to display Katharine Hepburn and Rosalind Russell in our courses on "The Image of the Independent Career Women in Film," while managing not to notice the paucity of female administrators on our own campus; to study the women who helped make universal enfranchisement a political reality, while keeping silent about our activist colleagues who are denied promotion or tenure; to include segments on "Women in the Labor Movement" in our American studies or women's studies courses, while remaining willfully ignorant of the department secretary fired for efforts to organize a clerical workers' union; to glory in the delusions of "merit," "privilege," and "status" which accompany campus life in order to insulate ourselves from the millions of women who labor in poverty — all this is not merely hypocritical; it destroys both the spirit and the meaning of what we are about.

From "Dancing through the Minefield: Some Observations on the Theory, Practice, and Politics of a Feminist Literary Criticism," *Feminist Studies,* 6, 1980

Considerations

1. Why does Kolodny reject "intellectual neutrality" as a "myth"? Explain whether you agree or disagree with her point of view.
2. Kolodny argues that feminist criticism can be used as an instrument for social reform. Discuss the possibility and desirability of her position. Do you think other kinds of criticism can and should be used to create social change?

ANDREW P. DEBICKI (b. 1934)
New Criticism and Deconstructionism: Two Attitudes in Teaching Poetry 1985

[Let's] look at the ways in which a New Critic and a deconstructivist might handle a poem. My first example, untitled, is a work by Pedro Salinas, which I first analyzed many years ago and which I have recently taught to a group of students influenced by deconstruction:

Sand: sleeping on the beach today
and tomorrow caressed
in the bosom of the sea:
the sun's today, water's prize tomorrow.

Softly you yield
to the hand that presses you
and go away with the first
courting wind that appears.
Pure and fickle sand,
changing and clear beloved,
I wanted you for my own,
and held you against my chest and soul.
But you escaped with the waves, the wind, the sun,
and I remained without a beloved,
my face turned to the wind which robbed her,
and my eyes to the far-off sea in which she had
green loves in a green shelter.

My original study of this poem, written very much in the New Critical tradition, focused on the unusual personification of sand and beloved and on the metaphorical pattern that it engendered. In the first part of the work, the physical elusiveness of sand (which slips through one's hand, flies with the wind, moves from shore to sea) evokes a coquettish woman, yielding to her lover and then escaping, running off with a personified wind, moving from one being to another. Watching these images, the reader gradually forgets that the poem is metaphorically describing sand and becomes taken up by the unusual correspondences with the figure of a flirting woman. When in the last part of the poem the speaker laments his loss, the reader is drawn into his lament for a fickle lover who has abandoned him.

Continuing a traditional analysis of this poem, we would conclude that its unusual personification/metaphor takes us beyond a literal level and leads us to a wider vision. The true subject of this poem is not sand, nor is it a flirt who tricks a man. The comparison between sand and woman, however, has made us feel the elusiveness of both, as well as the effect that this elusiveness has had on the speaker, who is left sadly contemplating it at the end of the poem. The poem has used its main image to embody a general vision of fleetingness and its effects.

My analysis, as developed thus far, is representative of a New Critical study. It focuses on the text and its central image, it describes a tension produced within the text, and it suggests a way in which this tension is resolved so as to move the poem beyond its literal level. In keeping with the tenets of traditional analytic criticism, it shows how the poem conveys a meaning that is far richer than its plot or any possible conceptual message. But while it is careful not to reduce the poem to a simple idea or to an equivalent of its prose summary, it does attempt to work all of its elements into a single interpretation which would satisfy every reader . . . : it makes all of the poem's meanings reside in its verbal structures, and it suggests that those meanings can be discovered and combined into a single cohesive vision as we systematically analyze those structures.

By attempting to find a pattern that will incorporate and resolve the poem's tensions, however, this reading leaves some loose ends, which I noticed even in my New Critical perspective — and which I found difficult to explain. To see the poem as the discovery of the theme of fleetingness by an insightful speaker, we have to ignore the fanciful nature of the comparison, the whimsical attitude to reality that it suggests, and the excessively serious lament of the speaker, which is difficult to take at face value — he laments the loss of *sand* with the excessive emotion of a romantic lover! The last lines, with their evocation of the beloved/sand in an archetypal kingdom of the sea, ring a bit hollow. Once we notice all of this, we see the speaker as being somehow unreliable in his strong response to the situation. He tries too hard to equate the loss of sand with the loss of love, he paints himself as too much of a romantic, and he loses our assent when we realize that his rather cliché declarations are not very fitting. Once we become aware of the speaker's limitations, our perspective about the poem changes: we come to see its "meaning" as centered, not on the theme of fleetingness as such, but on a portrayal of the speaker's exaggerated efforts to embody this theme in the image of sand.

For the traditional New Critic, this would pose a dilemma. The reading of the poem as a serious embodiment of the theme of evanescence is undercut by an awareness of the speaker's unreliability. One can account for the conflict between readings, to some extent, by speaking of the poem's use of irony and by seeing a tension between the theme of evanescence and the speaker's excessive concern with an imaginary beloved (which blinds him to the larger issues presented by the poem). That still leaves unresolved, however, the poem's final meaning and effect. In class discussions, in fact, a debate between those students who asserted that the importance of the poem lay in its engendering the theme of fleetingness and those who noted the absurdity of the speaker often ended in an agreement that this was a "problem poem" which never resolved or integrated its "stresses" and its double vision. . . .

The deconstructive critic, however, would not be disturbed by a lack of resolution in the meanings of the poem and would use the conflict between interpretations as the starting point for further study. Noting that the view of evanescence produced by the poem's central metaphor is undercut by the speaker's unreliability, the deconstructive critic would explore the play of signification that the undercutting engenders. Calling into question the attempt to neatly define evanescence, on the one hand, and the speaker's excessive romanticism on the other, the poem would represent, for this critic, a creative confrontation of irresoluble visions. The image of the sand as woman, as well as the portrayal of the speaker, would represent a sort of "seam" in the text, an area of indeterminacy that would open the way to further readings. This image lets us see the speaker as a sentimental poet, attempting unsuccessfully to define evanescence by means of a novel metaphor but getting trapped in the theme of lost love, which he himself has engendered; it makes us think of the inadequacy of language, of the ways in which metaphorical expression and the clichés of a love lament can undercut each other.

Once we adopt such a deconstructivist perspective, we will find in the text details that will carry forward our reading. The speaker's statement that he held "her" against his "chest and his soul" underlines the conflict in his perspective: it juggles a literal perspective (he rubs sand against himself) and a metaphorical one (he reaches for his beloved), but it cannot fully combine them — "soul" is ludicrously inappropriate in reference to the former. The reader, noting the inappropriateness, has to pay attention to the inadequacy of language as used here. All in all, by engendering a conflict between various levels and perspectives, the poem makes us feel the incompleteness of any one reading, the way in which each one is a "misreading" (not because it is wrong, but because it is incomplete), and the creative lack of closure in the poem. By not being subject to closure, in fact, this text becomes all the more exciting: its view of the possibilities and limitations of metaphor, language, and perspective seems more valuable than any static portrayal of "evanescence."

The analyses I have offered of this poem exemplify the different classroom approaches that would be taken by a stereotypical New Critic, on the one hand, and a deconstructive critic on the other. Imbued with the desire to come to an overview of the literary work, the former will attempt to resolve its tensions (and probably remain unsatisfied with the poem). Skeptical of such a possibility and of the very existence of a definable "work," the latter will focus on the tensions that can be found in the text as vehicles for multiple readings. Given his or her attitude to the text, the deconstructive critic will not worry about going beyond its "limits" (which really do not exist). This will allow, of course, for more speculative readings; it will also lead to a discussion of ways in which the text can be extended and "cured" in successive readings, to the fact that it reflects on the process of its own creation, and to ways in which it will relate to other texts.

From *Writing and Reading DIFFERENTLY: Deconstruction and the Teaching of Composition and Literature,* *edited by G. Douglas Atkins and Michael L. Johnson*

Considerations

1. Explain how the New Critical and deconstructionist approaches to the Salinas poem differ. What kinds of questions are raised by each? What elements of the poem are focused on in each approach?
2. Write an essay explaining which reading of the poem you find more interesting. In your opening paragraph define what you mean by "interesting."
3. Choose one of the critical strategies for reading discussed in this chapter and discuss Salinas's poem from that perspective.

BROOK THOMAS
A New Historical Approach to Keats's "Ode on a Grecian Urn" 1987

The traditional reception of the poem invites a discussion of its implied aesthetic. The poem's aesthetic is, however, intricately linked to its attitude to the past. The urn is, after all, Keats's "sylvan historian." To ask what sort of history a piece of art presents to us is, of course, to raise one of the central questions of historical criticism. It also opens up a variety of directions to take in historicizing the teaching of literature. . . .

To ask what history the urn relates to the reader easily leads to a discussion of how much our sense of the past depends upon art and the consequences of that dependency. These are important questions, because even if our students have little knowledge of the past or even interest in it, they do have an attitude toward it. A poem like Keats's "Ode" can help them reflect upon what that attitude is and on how it has been produced.

Such a discussion also offers a way to raise what critics have traditionally seen as the poem's central conflict: that between the temporal world of man and the atemporal world of art. The urn records two different visions of the past, both at odds with what we normally associate with historical accounts. On the one hand, it preserves a beauty that resists the destructive force of time. On the other, it records a quotidian scene populated by nameless people rather than the account of "famous" personages and "important" events our students often associate with traditional histories. Art, Keats seems to suggest, both keeps alive a sense of beauty in a world of change *and* gives us a sense of the felt life of the past. But in its search for a realm in which truth and beauty coexist, art risks freezing the "real" world and becoming a "cold pastoral," cut off from the very felt life it records. In dramatizing this conflict Keats's "Ode" allows students to see both art's power to keep the past alive and its tendency to distort it.

Chances are, however, that not all students share Keats's sense of the relationship between art and history. Rather than demonstrate their lack of "aesthetic appreciation," this difference can open up another direction to pursue in discussing the poem. To acknowledge a difference between our present attitude and the one embodied by Keats's poem is to call into question the conditions that have contributed to the changed attitude. Thus, if the first approach to the poem aims at having students reflect generally upon the influence art has on our attitude toward the past, this approach demands that we look at the specific historical conditions that help shape our general attitude toward both art and the past. In the case of the "Ode," this can lead to a discussion of the economic and political conditions of early nineteenth-century England that helped shape Keats's image of ancient Greece. On the one hand, there was England's self-image as the inheritor of ancient Greece's republican institutions and, on the other, a nostalgia for a harmonious pastoral world in contrast to the present state of industrialized, fragmented British society. Thus, the two versions of the past offered by Keats's sylvan historian — the aesthetic one in which harmony and beauty are preserved and the democratic one in which the life of everyday people is recorded — are related to specific historical conditions at the time Keats wrote. The challenge for our students — and for us — would be to speculate on how our attitudes towards art and history are shaped by our historical moment — how that moment is different from and similar to Keats's.

A third way to teach the poem historically is to concentrate on the urn itself as a historical as well as aesthetic object. "Where," we might ask our students, "would Keats have seen such an urn?" Most likely someone will respond, "A museum." If so, we are ready to discuss the phenomenon of the rise of the art museum in eighteenth- and nineteenth-century Europe, how cultural artifacts from the past were removed from their social setting and placed in museums to be contemplated as art. Seemingly taking us away from Keats's poem, such a discussion might be the best way to help our students understand Keats's aesthetic, for they will clearly see that in Keats's poem an urn that once had a practical social function now sparks aesthetic contemplation about the nature of truth, beauty, and the past. If we ask why the urn takes on this purely aesthetic function in a society that was increasingly practical, our students might start to glimpse how our modern notion of art has been defined in response to the social order.

To consider the urn a historical as well as an aesthetic object is also to raise political questions. For how, we might ask, did a Grecian urn (or the Elgin marbles, if we were to teach another Keats poem) end up in England in the first place? Such a question moves us from Keats's image of ancient Greece to a consideration of Greece in the early nineteenth century, and to how a number of Englishmen who sympathized with its struggle for liberation at the same time pillaged its cultural treasures and set them on display in London to advertise Britain's "advanced" cultural state. Thus, a very simple historical question about Keats's urn can force us to consider the political consequences of our cultural heritage. As Walter Benjamin warned, the cultural treasures that we so love have an origin we should not contemplate without horror: "They owe their existence not only to the efforts of the great minds and talents who have created them, but also to the anonymous toil of their contemporaries. There is no document of civilization which is not at the same time a document of barbarism" ("Theses on the Philosophy of History" in *Illuminations,* 256).

If we consider the task of historical scholarship to re-create the conditions of the past so that we can recover the author's original intention, the questions I have asked about Keats's "Ode" are not valid ones to ask. Clearly my questions are not primarily directed at recovering that intention. Instead, I am treating Keats's poem as social text, one that in telling us about the society that produced it also tells us about the society we inhabit today. This approach is not to say that we should completely abandon the effort to recover Keats's intention, but that, as in the case of formalist criticism, we need to go beyond the traditional historical scholar's efforts. We need to try both to reconstruct the author's intention — for instance, what Keats thought about art and history — and to read against the grain of his intention.

From "The Historical Necessities for — and Difficulties with — New Historical Analysis in Introductory Literature Courses," *College English,* September 1987

Considerations

1. Summarize the three historical approaches to "Ode on a Grecian Urn" (p. 698) Thomas describes. Which do you consider the most interesting? Explain why.
2. Write an essay that explores Thomas's claim that "a very simple historical question about the urn can force us to consider the political consequences of our cultural heritage."
3. Choose another poem from this anthology and treat it as a "social text." What kinds of questions can you ask about it that suggest the poem's historical significances?

WRITING ABOUT LITERATURE

33. Reading and Writing

THE PURPOSE AND VALUE OF WRITING ABOUT LITERATURE

Introductory literature courses typically include three components: reading, discussion, and writing. Students usually find the readings a pleasure, the class discussions a revelation, and the writing assignments — at least initially — a little intimidating. Writing an analysis of Melville's use of walls in "Bartleby, the Scrivener," for example, may seem considerably more daunting than making a case for animal rights or analyzing a campus newspaper editorial that calls for grade reforms. Like Bartleby, you might want to respond with "I would prefer not to." Literary topics are not, however, all that different from the kinds of papers assigned in English composition courses; many of the same skills are required for both. Regardless of the type of paper, you must develop a thesis and support it with evidence in language that is clear and persuasive.

Whether the subject matter is a marketing survey, a political issue, or a literary work, writing is a method of communicating information and perceptions. Writing teaches. But before writing becomes an instrument for informing the reader, it serves as a means of learning for the writer. An essay is a process of discovery as well as a record of what has been discovered. One of the chief benefits of writing is that we frequently realize what we want to say only after trying out ideas on a page and seeing our thoughts take shape in language.

More specifically, writing about a literary work encourages us to be better readers, because it requires a close examination of the elements of a short story, poem, or play. To determine how plot, character, setting, point of view, style, tone, irony, or any number of other literary elements function in a work, we must study them in relation to one another as well as separately. Speed-reading won't do. To read a text accurately and validly — neither ignoring nor distorting significant details — we must return to the work repeatedly to test our responses and interpretations. By paying attention to details and being sensitive to the author's use of language, we develop a clearer understanding of how the work conveys its effects and meanings.

Nevertheless, students sometimes ask why it is necessary or desirable to write about a literary work. Why not allow stories, poems, and plays to speak for themselves? Isn't it presumptuous to interpret Hemingway, Dickinson, or Shakespeare? These writers do, of course, speak for themselves, but they do so indirectly. Literary criticism does not seek to replace the text by explaining it but to enhance our readings of works by calling attention to elements that we might have overlooked or only vaguely sensed.

Another misunderstanding about the purpose of literary criticism is that it crankily restricts itself to finding faults in a work. Critical essays are sometimes mistakenly equated with newspaper and magazine reviews of recently published works. Reviews typically include summaries and evaluations to inform readers about a work's nature and quality, but critical essays assume that readers are already familiar with a work. Although a critical essay may point out limitations and flaws, most criticism — and certainly the kind of essay usually written in an introductory literature course — is designed to explain, analyze, and reveal the complexities of a work. Such sensitive consideration increases our appreciation of the writer's achievement and significantly adds to our enjoyment of a short story, poem, or play. In short, the purpose and value of writing about literature are that doing so leads to greater understanding and pleasure.

READING THE WORK CLOSELY

Know the piece of literature you are writing about before you begin your essay. Think about how the work makes you feel and how it is put together. The more familiar you are with how the various elements of the text convey effects and meanings, the more confident you will be explaining whatever perspective on it you ultimately choose. Do not insist that everything make sense on a first reading. Relax and enjoy yourself; you can be attentive and still allow the author's words to work their magic on you. With subsequent readings, however, go more slowly and analytically as you try to establish relations between characters, actions, images, or whatever else seems important. Ask yourself why you respond as you do. Think as you read, and notice how the parts of a work contribute to its overall nature. Whether the work is a short story, poem, or play, you will read relevant portions of it over and over, and you will very likely find more to discuss in each review if the work is rich.

It's best to avoid reading other critical discussions of a work before you are thoroughly familiar with it. There are several good reasons for following this advice. By reading interpretations before you know a work, you deny yourself the pleasure of discovery. That is a bit like starting with the last chapter in a mystery novel. But perhaps even more important than protecting the surprise and delight that a work might offer is that a premature reading of a critical discussion will probably short-circuit your own responses. You will see the work through the critic's eyes and have to struggle with someone else's perceptions and ideas before you can develop your own.

Reading criticism can be useful, but not until you have thought through your own impressions of the text. A guide should not be permitted to become a tyrant. This does not mean, however, that you should avoid background information about a work, for example, that Joyce Carol Oates's story "The Lady with the Pet Dog" was based on a similar story by Anton Chekhov. Knowing something about the author as well as historic and literary contexts can help to create expectations that enhance your reading.

TAKING NOTES

As you read, get in the habit of making marginal notations in your textbook. If you are working with a library book, use notecards and write down page or line numbers so that you can easily return to annotated passages. Use these cards to record reactions, raise questions, and make comments. They will freshen your memory and allow you to keep track of what goes on in the text.

Taking notes will preserve your initial reactions to the work. Many times first impressions are the best. Your response to a peculiar character in a story, a striking phrase in a poem, or a subtle bit of stage business in a play might lead to larger perceptions. The student paper on John Updike's "A & P" (p. 407), for example, began with the student writing "how come?" next to the story's title in her textbook. She thought it strange that the title didn't refer to a character or the story's conflict. That response eventually led her to examine the significance of the setting, which became the central idea of her paper.

You should take detailed notes only after you've read through the work. If you write too many notes during the first reading, you're likely to disrupt your response. Moreover, until you have a sense of the entire work, it will be difficult to determine how connections can be made among its various elements. In addition to recording your first impressions and noting significant passages, characters, actions, and so on, you should consult the Questions for Responsive Reading (fiction p. 362; poetry, p. 742; and drama, p. 954). These questions can assist you in getting inside a work as well as organizing your notes.

Inevitably, you will take more notes than you finally use in the paper. Note taking is a form of thinking aloud, but because your ideas are on paper you don't have to worry about forgetting them. As you develop a better sense of a potential topic, your notes will become more focused and detailed.

CHOOSING A TOPIC

If your instructor assigns a topic or offers a choice from among an approved list of topics, some of your work is already completed. Instead of being asked to come up with a topic about *Antigone,* you may be assigned a three-page essay that specifically discusses "Antigone's Decision to Defy Creon." You also have the assurance that a specified topic will be manageable within the suggested number of pages. Unless you ask your instructor for permission to write on a different or related topic, be certain to address yourself to the assignment. An essay that does not discuss Antigone's decision but instead describes her relationship with her sister would be missing the point. Notice too that there is room even in an assigned topic to develop your own approach. One question that immediately comes to mind is whether Antigone is justified in defying Creon's authority. Assigned topics do not relieve you of thinking about an aspect of a work, but they do focus your thinking.

At some point during the course, you may have to begin an essay from scratch. You might, for example, be asked to write about a short story that somehow impressed you or that seemed particularly well written or filled with insights. Before you start considering a topic, you should have a sense of how long the paper will be, because the assigned length can help to determine the extent to which you should develop your topic. Ideally, the paper's length should be based on how much space you deem necessary to present your discussion clearly and convincingly, but if you have any doubts and no specific guidelines have been indicated, ask. The question is important; a topic that might be appropriate for a three-page paper could be too narrow for ten pages. Three pages would probably be adequate for a discussion of why Emily murders Homer in Faulkner's "A Rose for Emily." Conversely, it would be futile to try to summarize Faulkner's use of the South in his fiction in even ten pages; this would have to be narrowed to something like "Images of the South in 'A Rose for Emily.'" Be sure that the topic you choose can be adequately covered in the assigned number of pages.

Once you have a firm sense of how much you are expected to write, you can begin to decide on your topic. If you are to choose what work to write about, select one that genuinely interests you. Too often students pick a story, poem, or play because it is mercifully short or seems simple. Such works can certainly be the subjects of fine essays, but simplicity should not be the major reason for selecting them. Choose a work that has moved you so that you have something to say about it. The student who wrote about "A & P" was initially attracted to the story's title because she had once worked in a similar store. After reading the story, she became fascinated with its setting because Updike's descriptions seemed so accurate. Her paper then grew out of her curiosity about the setting's purpose. When a writer is engaged in a topic, the paper has a better chance of being interesting to a reader.

After you have settled on a particular work, your notes and annotations of the text should prove useful for generating a topic. The paper on "The A & P as a State of Mind" developed naturally from the notes (p. 1830) that the student jotted down about the setting and antagonist. If you think with a pen in your hand, you are likely to find when you review your notes that your thoughts have clustered into one or more topics. Perhaps there are patterns of imagery that seem to make a point about life. There may be scenes that are ironically paired or secondary characters who reveal certain qualities about the protagonist. Your notes and annotations on such aspects can lead you to a particular effect or impression. Having chuckled your way through Mark Twain's "The Story of the Bad Little Boy," you may discover that your notations about the story's humor point to a serious satire of society's values.

DEVELOPING A THESIS

When you are satisfied that you have something interesting to say about a work and that your notes have led you to a focused topic, you can formulate a ***thesis,*** the central idea of the paper. Whereas the topic indicates what the paper focuses on (the setting in "A & P"), the thesis explains what you have to say about the topic (because the intolerant setting of "A & P" is the antagonist in the story, it is crucial to our understanding of Sammy's decision to quit his job). The thesis should be a complete sentence (though sometimes it may require more than one sentence) that establishes your topic in clear, unambiguous language. The thesis may be revised as you get further into the topic and discover what you want to say about it, but once the thesis is firmly established it will serve as a guide for you and your reader, because all the information and observations in your essay should be related to the thesis.

One student on an initial reading of Andrew Marvell's "To His Coy Mistress" (p. 534) saw that the male speaker of the poem urges a woman to love now before time runs out for them. This reading gave him the impression that the poem is a simple celebration of the pleasures of the flesh, but on subsequent readings he underlined or noted these images: "Time's wingèd chariot hurrying near"; "Deserts of vast eternity"; "marble vault"; "worms"; "dust"; "ashes"; and these two lines: "The grave's a fine and private place, / But none, I think, do there embrace."

By listing these images associated with time and death, he established an inventory that could be separated from the rest of his notes on point of view, character, sounds, and other subjects. Inventorying notes allows patterns to emerge that you might have only vaguely perceived otherwise. Once these images are grouped, they call attention to something darker and more complex in Marvell's poem than a first impression might suggest.

These images may create a different feeling about the poem, but they still don't explain very much. One simple way to generate a thesis about a literary work is to ask the question "why?" Why do these images appear in the poem? Why does Hamlet hesitate to avenge his father's death? Why does Hemingway choose the Midwest as the setting of "Soldier's Home"? Your responses to these kinds of questions can lead to a thesis.

Writers sometimes use free writing to help themselves explore possible answers to such questions. It can be an effective way of generating ideas. Free writing is exactly that: the technique calls for nonstop writing without concern for mechanics or editing of any kind. Free writing for ten minutes or so on a question will result in fragments and repetitions, but it can also produce some ideas. Here's an example of a student's response to the question about the images in "To His Coy Mistress":

> He wants her to make love. Love poem. There's little time. Her crime. He exaggerates. Sincere? Sly? What's he want? She says nothing--he says it all. What about deserts, ashes, graves, and worms? Some love poem. Sounds like an old Vincent Price movie. Full of sweetness but death creeps in. Death--hurry hurry! Tear pleasures. What passion! Where's death in this? How can a love poem be so ghoulish? She does nothing. Maybe frightened? Convinced? Why death? Love and death--time--death.

This free writing contains several ideas; it begins by alluding to the poem's plot and speaker, but the central idea seems to be death. This emphasis led the student to four potential thesis statements for his essay about the poem:

1. "To His Coy Mistress" is a difficult poem.
2. Death in "To His Coy Mistress."
3. There are many images of death in "To His Coy Mistress."
4. On the surface, "To His Coy Mistress" is a celebration of the pleasures of the flesh, but this witty seduction is tempered by a chilling recognition of the reality of death.

The first statement is too vague to be useful. In what sense is the poem difficult? A more precise phrasing, indicating the nature of the difficulty, is needed. The second statement is a topic rather than a thesis. Because it is not a sentence, it does not express a complete idea about how the poem treats death. Although this could be an appropriate title, it is inadequate as a thesis statement. The third statement, like the first one, identifies the topic, but even though it is a sentence, it is not a complete idea that tells us anything significant beyond the fact it states. After these preliminary attempts to develop a thesis, the student remembered his first impression of the poem and incorporated it into his thesis statement. The fourth thesis is a useful approach to the poem because it limits the topic and indicates how it will be treated in the paper: the writer will begin with an initial impression of the poem and then go on to qualify it. An effective thesis, like this one, makes a clear statement about a manageable topic and provides a firm sense of direction for the paper.

Most writing assignments in a literature course require you to persuade readers that your thesis is reasonable and supported with evidence. Papers that report information without comment or evaluation are simply summaries. A plot summary of Shakespeare's *Othello,* for example, would have no thesis, but a paper that discussed how Iago manipulates coincidences for his own villainous purposes would argue a thesis. Similarly, a paper that merely pointed out the death images in "To His Coy Mistress" would not contain a thesis, but a paper that attempted to make a case for the death imagery as a grim reminder of how vulnerable flesh is would involve persuasion. In developing a thesis, remember that you are expected not merely to present information but to argue a point.

ORGANIZING A PAPER

After you have chosen a manageable topic and developed a thesis, a central idea about it, you can begin to organize your paper. Your thesis, even if it is still somewhat tentative, should help you decide what information will need to be included and provide you with a sense of direction.

Consider again the sample thesis in the preceding section:

> On the surface, "To His Coy Mistress" is a celebration of the pleasures of the flesh, but this witty seduction is tempered by a chilling recognition of the reality of death.

This thesis indicates that the paper can be divided into two parts: the pleasures of the flesh and the reality of death. It also indicates an order: Because the central point is to show that the poem is more than a simple celebration, the pleasures of the flesh should be discussed first so that another, more complex, reading of the poem can follow. If the paper began with the reality of death, its point would be anticlimactic.

Having established such a broad and informal outline, you can draw upon your underlinings, margin notations, and notecards for the subheadings and evidence required to explain the major sections of your paper. This next level of detail would look like the following:

1. Pleasures of the flesh
   Part of the traditional tone of love poetry
2. Recognition of death
   Ironic treatment of love
      Diction
      Images
      Figures of speech
      Symbols
      Tone

This list was initially a jumble of terms, but the student arranged the items so that each of the two major sections leads to a discussion of tone. (The student also found it necessary to drop some biographical information from his notes because it was irrelevant to the thesis.) The list indicates that the first part of the paper will establish the traditional tone of love poetry that celebrates the pleasures of the flesh, while the second part will present a more detailed discussion about the ironic recognition of death. The emphasis is on the latter because that is the point to be argued in the paper. Hence, the thesis has helped to organize the parts of the paper, establish an order, and indicate the paper's proper proportions.

The next step is to fill in the subheadings with information from your notes. Many experienced writers find that making lists of information to be included under each subheading is an efficient way to develop paragraphs. For a longer paper (perhaps a research paper), you should be able to develop a paragraph or more on each subheading. On the other hand, a shorter paper may require that you combine several subheadings in a paragraph. You may also discover that while an informal list is adequate for a brief paper, a ten-page assignment could require a more detailed outline. Use the method that is most productive for you. Whatever the length of the essay, your presentation must be in a coherent and logical order that allows your reader to follow the argument and evaluate the evidence. The quality of your reading can be demonstrated only by the quality of your writing.

WRITING A DRAFT

The time for sharpening pencils, arranging your desk, and doing almost anything else instead of writing has ended. The first draft will appear on the page only if you stop avoiding the inevitable and sit, stand up, or lie down to write. It makes no difference how you write, just so you do. Now that you have developed a topic into a tentative thesis, you can assemble your notes and begin to flesh out whatever outline you have made.

Be flexible. Your outline should smoothly conduct you from one point to the next, but do not permit it to railroad you. If a relevant and important idea occurs to you now, work it into the draft. By using the first draft as a means of thinking about what you want to say, you will very likely discover more than your notes originally suggested. Plenty of good writers don't use outlines at all but discover ordering principles as they write. Do not attempt to compose a perfectly correct draft the first time around. Grammar, punctuation, and spelling can wait until you revise. Concentrate on what you are saying. Good writing most often occurs when you are in hot pursuit of an idea rather than in a nervous search for errors.

To make revising easier, leave wide margins and extra space between lines so that you can easily add words, sentences, and corrections. Write on only one side of the paper. Your pages will be easier to keep track of that way, and, if you have to clip a paragraph to place it elsewhere, you will not lose any writing on the other side.

If you are working on a word processor, you can take advantage of its capacity to make additions and deletions as well as move entire paragraphs by making just a few simple keyboard commands. Some software programs can also check spelling and certain grammatical elements in your writing. It's worth remembering, however, that though a clean copy fresh off a printer may look terrific, it will read only as well as the thinking and writing that have gone into it. Many writers prudently store their data on disks and print their pages each time they finish a draft to avoid loosing any material because of power failures or other problems. These printouts are also easier to read than the screen when you work on revisions.

Once you have a first draft on paper, you can delete material that is unrelated to your thesis and add material necessary to illustrate your points and make your paper convincing. The student who wrote "The A & P as a State of Mind" wisely dropped a paragraph that questioned whether Sammy displays chauvinistic attitudes toward women. Although this is an interesting issue, it has nothing to do with the thesis, which explains how the setting influences Sammy's decision to quit his job. Instead of including that paragraph, she added one that described Lengel's crabbed response to the girls so that she could lead up to the A & P "policy" he enforces.

Remember that your initial draft is only that. You should go through the paper many times — and then again — working to substantiate and clarify your ideas. You may even end up with several entire versions of the paper. Rewrite. The sentences within each paragraph should be related to a single topic. Transitions should connect one paragraph to the next so that there are no abrupt or confusing shifts. Awkward or wordy phrasing or unclear sentences and paragraphs should be mercilessly poked and prodded into shape.

Writing the Introduction and Conclusion

After you have clearly and adequately developed the body of your paper, pay particular attention to the introductory and concluding paragraphs. It's probably best to write the introduction — at least the final version of it — last, after you know precisely what you are introducing. Because this paragraph is crucial for generating interest in the topic, it should engage the reader and provide a sense of what the paper is about. There is no formula for writing effective introductory paragraphs, because each writing situation is different — depending on the audience, topic, and approach — but if you pay attention to the introductions of the essays you read, you will notice a variety of possibilities. The introductory paragraph to "The A & P as a State of Mind," for example, is a straightforward explanation of why the story's setting is important for understanding Updike's treatment of the antagonist. The rest of the paper then offers evidence to support this point.

Concluding paragraphs demand equal attention because they leave the reader with a final impression. The conclusion should provide a sense of closure instead of starting a new topic or ending abruptly. In the final paragraph about the significance of the setting in "A & P," the student brings together the reasons Sammy quit his job by referring to his refusal to accept Lengel's store policies. At the same time she makes this point, she also explains the significance of Sammy ringing up the "No Sale" mentioned in her introductory paragraph. Thus, we are brought back to where we began, but we now have a greater understanding of why Sammy quits his job. Of course, the body of your paper is the most important part of your presentation, but do remember that first and last impressions have a powerful impact on readers.

Using Quotations

Quotations can be a valuable means of marshaling evidence to illustrate and support your ideas. A judicious use of quoted material will make your points clearer and more convincing. Here are some guidelines that should help you use quotations effectively.

1. Brief quotations (four lines or fewer of prose or three lines or fewer of poetry) should be carefully introduced and integrated into the text of your paper with quotation marks around them.

> According to the narrator, Bertha "had a reputation for strictness." He tells us that she always "wore dark clothes, dressed her hair simply, and expected contrition and obedience from her pupils."

For brief poetry quotations, use a slash to indicate a division between lines.

> The concluding lines of Blake's "The Tyger" pose a disturbing question: "What immortal hand or eye / Dare frame thy fearful symmetry?"

Lengthy quotations should be separated from the text of your paper. More than three lines of poetry should be double spaced and centered on the page. More than four lines of prose should be double spaced and indented ten spaces from the left margin, with the right margin the same as for the text. Do *not* use quotation marks for the passage; the indentation indicates that the passage is a quotation. Lengthy quotations should not be used in place of your own writing. Use them only if they are absolutely necessary.

2. If any words are added to a quotation, use brackets to distinguish your addition from the original source.

> "He [Young Goodman Brown] is portrayed as self-righteous and disillusioned."

Any words inside quotation marks and not in brackets must be precisely those of the author. Brackets can also be used to change the grammatical structure of a quotation so that it fits into your sentence.

> Smith argues that Chekhov "present[s] the narrator in an ambivalent light."

If you drop any words from the source, use ellipses to indicate the omission.

> "Early to bed . . . makes a man healthy, wealthy, and wise."

Use ellipses following a period to indicate an omission at the end of a sentence.

> "Early to bed and early to rise makes a man healthy. . . ."

Use a single line of spaced periods to indicate the omission of a line or more of poetry or more than one paragraph of prose.

> Nothing would sleep in that cellar, dank as a ditch,
> Bulbs broke out of boxes hunting for chinks in the dark,
> . . . .
> Nothing would give up life:
> Even the dirt kept breathing a small breath.

3. You will be able to punctuate quoted material accurately and confidently if you observe these conventions.

Place commas and periods inside quotation marks.

> "Even the dirt," Roethke insists, "kept breathing a small breath."

Even though a comma does not appear after "dirt" in the original quotation, it is placed inside the quotation mark. The exception to this rule occurs when a parenthetical reference to a source follows the quotation.

> "Even the dirt," Roethke insists, "kept breathing a small breath" (11).

Punctuation marks other than commas or periods go outside the quotation marks unless they are part of the material quoted.

> What does Roethke mean when he writes that "the dirt kept breathing a small breath"?

> Yeats asked, "How can we know the dancer from the dance?"

REVISING AND EDITING

Put some distance — a day or so if you can — between yourself and each draft of your paper. The phrase that seemed just right on Wednesday may be revealed as all wrong on Friday. You'll have a better chance of detecting lumbering sentences and thin paragraphs if you plan ahead and give yourself the time to read your paper from a fresh perspective. Through the process of revision, you can transform a competent paper into an excellent one.

Begin by asking yourself if your approach to the topic requires any rethinking. Is the argument carefully thought out and logically presented? Are there any gaps in the presentation? How well is the paper organized? Do the paragraphs lead into one another? Does the body of the paper deliver what the thesis promises? Is the interpretation sound? Are any relevant and important elements of the work ignored or distorted to advance the thesis? Are the points supported with evidence? These large questions should be addressed before you focus on more detailed matters. If you uncover serious problems as a result of considering these questions, you'll probably have quite a lot of rewriting to do, but at least you will have the opportunity to correct the problems — even if doing so takes several drafts.

A useful technique for spotting awkward or unclear moments in the paper is to read it aloud. You might also try having a friend read it aloud to you. If your handwriting is legible, your friend's reading — perhaps accompanied by hesitations and puzzled expressions — could alert you to passages that need reworking. Having identified problems, you can readily correct them on a word processor or on the draft provided you've skipped lines and used wide margins. The final draft you hand in should be neat and carefully proofread for any inadvertent errors.

The following checklist offers questions to ask about your paper as you revise and edit it. Most of these questions will be familiar to you; however, if you need help with any of them, ask your instructor or review the appropriate section in a composition handbook.

Revision Checklist

1. Is the topic manageable? Is it too narrow or too broad?
2. Is the thesis clear? Is it based on a careful reading of the work?
3. Is the paper logically organized? Does it have a firm sense of direction?
4. Should any material be deleted? Do any important points require further illustration or evidence?
5. Does the opening paragraph introduce the topic in an interesting manner?
6. Are the paragraphs developed, unified, and coherent? Are any too short or long?
7. Are there transitions linking the paragraphs?

8. Does the concluding paragraph provide a sense of closure?
9. Is the tone appropriate? Is it unduly flippant or pretentious?
10. Is the title engaging and suggestive?
11. Are the sentences clear, concise, and complete?
12. Are simple, complex, and compound sentences used for variety?
13. Have technical terms been used correctly? Are you certain of the meanings of all the words in the paper? Are they spelled correctly?
14. Have you documented any information borrowed from books, articles, or other sources? Have you quoted too much instead of summarizing or paraphrasing secondary material?
15. Have you used a standard format for citing sources (see p. 1847)?
16. Have you followed your instructor's guidelines for the manuscript format of the final draft?
17. Have you carefully proofread the final draft?

When you proofread your final draft, you may find a few typographical errors that must be corrected but do not warrant retyping an entire page. Provided there are not more than a handful of such errors throughout the page, they can be corrected as shown in the following passage. This example condenses a short paper's worth of errors; no single passage should be this shabby in your essay.

> To add a letter or word, use a caret on the line where the addition
> is
> ^needed. To delete a word draw a single line through ~~through~~ it.
> Run-on words are separated by a vertical/line, and inadvertent
> spaces are closed like t his. Transposed letters are indicated
> this wya. New paragraphs are noted with the sign ¶ in front of
> where the next paragraph is to begin. ¶ Unless you . . .

These sorts of errors can be minimized by using correction fluids or tapes while you type. If you use a word processor, you can eliminate such errors completely by simply entering corrections as you proofread on the screen.

MANUSCRIPT FORM

The novelist and poet Peter De Vries once observed in his characteristically humorous way that he very much enjoyed writing but that he couldn't bear the "paper work." Behind this playful pun is a half-serious impatience with the mechanics of it all. You may feel some of that too, but this is not the time to allow a thoughtful, carefully revised paper to trip over minor details that can be easily accommodated. The final draft you hand in to your instructor should not only read well but look neat. If your instructor does not provide specific instructions concerning the format for the paper, follow these guidelines.

1. Papers (particularly long ones) should be typed on $8\frac{1}{2} \times 11$-inch paper in double space. Avoid transparent paper such as onionskin; it is difficult to read and write comments on. The ribbon should be dark and the letters on the machine clear. If you compose on a word processor with a dot-matrix printer, be certain that the dots are close enough together to be legible. And don't forget to separate your pages and remove the strips of holes on each side of the pages if your printer uses a continuous paper feed. If your instructor accepts handwritten papers, write legibly in ink on only one side of a wide-lined page.

2. Use a one-inch margin at the top, bottom, and sides of each page. Unless you are instructed to include a separate title page, type your name, instructor's name, course number and section, and date on separate lines one inch below the upper-left corner of the first page. Double space between these lines and then center the title two spaces below the date. Do not underline or put quotation marks around your paper's title, but do use quotation marks around the titles of poems, short stories, or other brief works, and underline the titles of books and plays (for instance, Racial Stereotypes in "Battle Royal" and <u>Fences</u>). Begin the text of your paper four spaces below the title. If you have used secondary sources, center the heading "Notes" or "Works Cited" one inch from the top of a separate page and then double space between it and the entries.

3. Number each page consecutively, beginning with page 2, a half inch from the top of the page in the upper-right corner.

4. Gather the pages with a paper clip rather than staples, folders, or some other device. That will make it easier for your instructor to handle the paper.

TYPES OF WRITING ASSIGNMENTS

The types of papers most frequently assigned in literature classes are explication, analysis, and comparison and contrast. Most writing about literature involves some combination of these skills. This section includes a sample explication, an analysis, and a comparison and contrast paper. (For a sample research paper that demonstrates a variety of strategies for documenting outside sources, see p. 1853.)

Explication

The purpose of this approach to a literary work is to make the implicit explicit. *Explication* is a detailed explanation of a passage of poetry or prose. Because explication is an intensive examination of a text line by line, it is mostly used to interpret a short poem in its entirety or a brief passage from a long poem, short story, or play. Explication can be used in any kind of paper when you want to be specific about how a writer achieves a certain effect. An explication pays careful attention to language: the connotations of words, allusions, figurative language, irony, symbol, rhythm, sound, and so on. These elements are examined in relation to one another and to the overall effect and meaning of the work.

The simplest way to organize an explication is to move through the passage line by line, explaining whatever seems significant. It is wise to avoid, however, an assembly-line approach that begins each sentence with "In line one. . . ." Instead, organize your paper in whatever way best serves your thesis. You might find that the right place to start is with the final lines, working your way back to the beginning of the poem or passage. The following sample explication on Dickinson's "There's a certain Slant of light" does just that. The student's opening paragraph refers to the final line of the poem in order to present her thesis. She explains that though the poem begins with an image of light, it is not a bright or cheery poem but one concerned with "the look of Death." Since the last line prompted her thesis, that is where she begins the explication.

You might also find it useful to structure a paper by discussing various elements of literature, so that you have a paragraph on connotative words followed by one on figurative language and so on. However your paper is organized, keep in mind that the aim of an explication is not simply to summarize the passage but to comment on the effects and meanings produced by the author's use of language in it. An effective explication (the Latin word *explicare* means "to unfold") displays a text to reveal how it works and what it signifies. Although writing an explication requires some patience and sensitivity, it is an excellent method for coming to understand and appreciate the elements and qualities that constitute literary art.

The sample paper by Elizabeth Needham is the result of an assignment calling for an explication of about 750 words on any poem by Emily Dickinson. Needham selected "There's a certain Slant of light."

EMILY DICKINSON (1830–1886)
There's a certain Slant of light c. 1861

There's a certain Slant of light,
Winter Afternoons —
That oppresses, like the Heft
Of Cathedral Tunes —

Heavenly Hurt, it gives us —
We can find no scar,
But internal difference,
Where the Meanings, are —

(Text continues on page 1829.)

Elizabeth Needham

Professor Grey

English 109-2

October 26, 1989

A Reading of Dickinson's

"There's a certain Slant of light"

Because Emily Dickinson did not provide titles for her poetry, editors follow the customary practice of using the first line of a poem as its title. However, a more appropriate title for "There's a certain Slant of light," one that suggests what the speaker in the poem is most concerned about, can be drawn from the poem's last line, which ends with "the look of Death." Although the first line begins with an image of light, nothing bright, carefree, or cheerful appears in the poem. Instead, the predominant mood and images are darkened by a sense of despair resulting from the speaker's awareness of death.

In the first stanza, the "certain Slant of light" is associated with "Winter Afternoons," a phrase that connotes the end of a day, a season, and even life itself. Such light is hardly warm or comforting. Not a ray or beam, this slanting light suggests something unusual or distorted and creates in the speaker a certain slant on life that is consistent with the cold, dark mood that winter afternoons can produce. Like the speaker, most of us have seen and felt this sort of light: it "oppresses" and pervades our sense of things when we encounter it. Dickinson uses the senses of hearing and touch as well as sight to describe the overwhelming oppressiveness that the speaker experiences. The light is trans-

2

formed into sound by a simile that tells us it is "like the Heft / Of Cathedral Tunes." Moreover, the "Heft" of that sound--the slow, solemn measures of tolling church bells and organ music--weighs heavily on our spirits. Through the use of shifting imagery, Dickinson evokes a kind of spiritual numbness that we keenly feel and perceive through our senses.

By associating the winter light with "Cathedral Tunes," Dickinson lets us know that the speaker is concerned about more than the weather. Whatever it is that "oppresses" is related by connotation to faith, mortality, and God. The second and third stanzas offer several suggestions about this connection. The pain caused by the light is a "Heavenly Hurt." This "imperial affliction / Sent us of the Air" apparently comes from God above, and yet it seems to be part of the very nature of life. The oppressiveness we feel is in the air, and it can neither be specifically identified at this point in the poem nor be eliminated, for "None may teach it--Any." All we can know is that existence itself seems depressing under the weight of this "Seal [of] Despair." The impression left by this "Seal" is stamped within the mind or soul rather than externally. "We can find no scar," but once experienced this oppressiveness challenges our faith in life and its "Meanings."

The final stanza does not explain what those "Meanings" are, but it does make clear that the speaker is acutely aware of death. As the winter daylight fades, Dickinson projects the speaker's anxiety onto the surrounding landscape and shadows, which will soon be engulfed by the darkness that follows this light: "The Landscape listens-- / Shadows--hold their breath."

This image firmly aligns the winter light in the first stanza with darkness. Paradoxically, the light in this poem illuminates the nature of darkness. Tension is released when the light is completely gone, but what remains is the despair that the "imperial affliction" has imprinted on the speaker's sensibilities, for it is "like the Distance / On the look of Death." There can be no relief from what that "certain Slant of light" has revealed, because what has been experienced is permanent--like the fixed stare in the eyes of someone who is dead.

The speaker's awareness of death is conveyed in a thoughtful, hushed tone. The lines are filled with fluid _l_ and smooth _s_ sounds that are appropriate for the quiet, meditative voice in the poem. The voice sounds tentative and uncertain--perhaps a little frightened. This seems to be reflected in the slightly irregular meter of the lines. The stanzas are trochaic with the second and fourth lines of each stanza having five syllables, but no stanza is identical because each works a slight variation on the first stanza's seven syllables in the first and third lines. The rhymes also combine exact patterns with variations. The first and third lines of each stanza are not exact rhymes, but the second and fourth lines are exact so that the paired words are more closely related: _Afternoons_, _Tunes_; _scar_, _are_; _Despair_, _Air_; and _breath_, _Death_. There is a pattern to the poem, but it is unobtrusively woven into the speaker's voice in much the same way that "the look of Death" is subtly present in the images and language of the poem.

None may teach it — Any —
'Tis the Seal Despair —
An imperial affliction
Sent us of the Air —

When it comes, the Landscape listens —
Shadows — hold their breath —
When it goes, 'tis like the Distance
On the look of Death —

This essay comments on every line of the poem and provides a coherent reading that relates each line to the speaker's intense awareness of death. Although the essay discusses each stanza in the order that it appears, the introductory paragraph provides a brief overview explaining how the poem's images contribute to its total meaning. In addition, the student does not hesitate to discuss a line out of sequence when it can be usefully connected to another phrase. This is especially apparent in the third paragraph, in her discussion of stanzas 2 and 3. The final paragraph describes some of the formal elements of the poem. It might be argued that this discussion could have been integrated into the previous paragraphs rather than placed at the end, but the student does make a connection in her concluding sentence between the pattern of language and its meaning.

Several other matters are worth noticing. The student works quotations into her own sentences to support her points. She quotes exactly as the words appear in the poem, even Dickinson's irregular use of capital letters. When something is added to a quotation to clarify it, it is enclosed in brackets so that the essayist's words will not be mistaken for the poet's: "Seal [of] Despair." A slash is used to separate line divisions as in "imperial affliction/Sent us of the Air." And, finally, because the essay focuses on a short poem, it is not necessary to include line numbers, though they would be required in a study of a longer work.

Analysis

The preceding sample essay shows how an explication examines in detail the important elements in a work and relates them to the whole. An analysis, however, usually examines only a single element — such as plot, character, point of view, symbol, tone, or irony — and relates it to the entire work. An analytic topic separates the work into parts and focuses on a specific one; you might consider "Point of View in 'A Rose for Emily,'" "Patterns of Rhythm in Browning's 'My Last Duchess,'" or "The Significance of Fortinbras in *Hamlet*." The specific element must be related to the work as a whole or it will appear irrelevant. It is not enough to point out that there are many death images in Marvell's "To His Coy Mistress"; the images must somehow be connected to the poem's overall effect.

Whether an analytic paper is just a few pages or many, it cannot attempt to discuss everything about the work it is considering. Only those elements

(Text continues on page 1832.)

Sue Bernstein

Professor Facchinetti

English 102-12

April 1, 1989

The A & P as a State of Mind

The setting of John Updike's "A & P" is crucial to our understanding of Sammy's decision to quit his job. Although Sammy is the central character in the story and we learn that he is a principled, good-natured nineteen-year-old with a sense of humor, Updike seems to invest as much effort in describing the setting as he does in Sammy. The setting is the antagonist and plays a role that is as important as Sammy's. The title, after all, is not "Youthful Rebellion" or "Sammy Quits" but "A & P." Even though Sammy knows that his quitting will make life more difficult for him, he instinctively insists upon rejecting what the A & P comes to represent in the story. When he rings up a "No Sale" and "saunter[s]" out of the store, he leaves behind not only a job but the rigid state of mind associated with the A & P.

Sammy's descriptions of the A & P present a setting that is ugly, monotonous, and rigidly regulated. The fluorescent light is as blandly cool as the "checkerboard green-and-cream rubber-tile floor." We can see the uniformity Sammy describes because we have all been in chain stores. The "usual traffic" moves in one direction (except for the swimsuited girls, who move against it), and everything is neatly ordered and categorized in tidy aisles. The dehumanizing routine of this environment is suggested by Sammy's offhanded references to the typical shoppers as "sheep," "houseslaves," and "pigs." They seem to pace through the store in a stupor; as Sammy tells us, not even dynamite could move them.

The A & P is appropriately located "right in the middle" of a proper, conservative, traditional New England town north of Boston. This location, coupled with the fact that the town is only five miles from Salem, the site of the famous seventeenth-century witch trials, suggests a narrow, intolerant social atmosphere in which there is no room for stepping beyond the boundaries of what is regarded as normal and proper. The importance of this setting can be appreciated even more if we imagine the action taking place in, say, a mellow suburb of southern California. In this prim New England setting, the girls in their bathing suits are bound to offend somebody's sense of propriety.

As soon as Lengel sees the girls, the inevitable conflict begins. He embodies the dull conformity represented by the A & P. As "manager," he is both the guardian and enforcer of "policy." When he gives the girls "that sad Sunday-school-superintendent stare," we know we are in the presence of the A & P's version of a dreary bureaucrat who "doesn't miss that much." He is as unsympathetic and unpleasant as the woman "with rouge on her cheeks and no eyebrows" who pounces on Sammy for ringing up her "HiHo crackers" twice. Like the "electric eye" in the doorway, her vigilant eyes allow nothing to escape their notice. For Sammy the logical extension of Lengel's "policy" is the half-serious notion that one day the A & P might be known as the "Great

3

Alexandrov and Petrooshki Tea Company." Sammy's connection between what he regards as mindless "policy" and Soviet oppression is obviously an exaggeration, but the reader is invited to entertain the similarities anyway.

The reason Sammy quits his job has less to do with defending the girls than with his own sense of what it means to be a decent human being. His decision is not an easy one. He doesn't want to make trouble or disappoint his parents, and he knows his independence and self-reliance (the other side of New England tradition) will make life more complex for him. In spite of his own hesitations, he finds himself blurting out "Fiddle-de-doo" to Lengel's policies and in doing so knows that his grandmother "would have been pleased." Sammy's "No Sale" rejects the crabbed perspective on life that Lengel represents as manager of the A & P. This gesture is more than just negative, however, for as he punches in that last entry on the cash register, "the machine whirs 'pee-pul.'" His decision to quit his job at the A & P is an expression of his refusal to regard policies as more important than people.

that are relevant to the topic can be treated. This kind of focusing makes the topic manageable; this is why most papers that you write will probably be some form of analysis. Explications are useful for a short passage, but a line-by-line commentary on a story, play, or long poem simply isn't practical. Because analysis allows you to consider the central effect or meaning of an entire work by studying a single important element, it is a useful and common approach to longer works.

Sue Bernstein's paper analyzes the setting in John Updike's "A & P" (the entire story appears on p. 407). The assignment simply asked for an essay of approximately 750 words on a short story written in the twentieth century. The approach was left to the student.

The idea for this essay began with Bernstein asking herself why Updike used "A & P" as the title. The initial answer to the question was that "the setting is important in this story." This answer was the rough beginning of a tentative thesis. What still had to be explained, though, was how the setting is important. To determine the significance of the setting, Bernstein jotted down some notes based on her underlinings and marginal notations.

A & P
"usual traffic"
lights and tile
"electric eye"
shoppers like "sheep," "houseslaves," "pigs"
"Alexandrov and Petrooshki" — Russia

New England Town
typical: bank, church, etc.
traditional
conservative
proper
near Salem — witch trials
puritanical
intolerant

Lengel
"manager"
"doesn't miss that much" (like lady shopper)
Sunday school
"It's our policy"
spokesman for A & P values

From these notes Bernstein saw that Lengel serves as the voice of the A & P. He is, in a sense, a personification of the intolerant atmosphere of the setting. This insight led to another version of her thesis statement: "The setting of 'A & P' is the antagonist of the story." That explained at least some of the setting's importance. By seeing Lengel as a spokesman for "A & P" policies, she could view him as a voice that articulates the morally smug atmosphere created by the setting. Finally, she considered why it is significant that the setting is the antagonist, and this generated her last thesis: "Because the intolerant setting of 'A & P' is the antagonist in the story, it is crucial to our understanding of Sammy's decision to quit his job." This thesis sentence does not appear precisely in these words in the essay, but it is the backbone of the introductory paragraph.

The remaining paragraphs consist of details that describe the A & P in the second paragraph, the New England town in the third, Lengel in the fourth, and Sammy's reasons for quitting in the concluding paragraph. Paragraphs 2, 3, and 4 are largely based on Bernstein's notes, which she used as an outline once her thesis was established. The essay is sharply focused, well organized, and generally well written. In addition, it suggests a number of useful guidelines for analytic papers.

1. Only those points related to the thesis are included. In another type of paper the role of the girls in the bathing suits, for example, might have been considerably more prominent.
2. The analysis keeps the setting in focus while at the same time indicating how it is significant in the major incident in the story—Sammy's quitting.
3. The title is a useful lead into the paper; it provides a sense of what the topic is. In addition, the title is drawn from a sentence (the final one of the first paragraph) that clearly explains its meaning.
4. The introductory paragraph is direct and clearly indicates the paper will argue that the setting serves as the antagonist of the story.
5. Brief quotations are deftly incorporated into the text of the paper to illustrate points. We are told what we need to know about the story as evidence is provided to support ideas. There is no unnecessary plot summary. Because "A & P" is only a few pages in length and is an assigned topic, page numbers are not included after quoted phrases. If the story were longer, page numbers would be helpful for the reader.
6. The paragraphs are well developed, unified, and coherent. They flow naturally from one to another. Notice, for example, the smooth transition worked into the final sentence of the third paragraph and the first sentence of the fourth paragraph.
7. Bernstein makes excellent use of her careful reading and notes by finding revealing connections among the details she has observed. The store's "electric eye," for instance, is related to the woman's and Lengel's watchfulness.
8. As events are described, the present tense is used. This avoids awkward tense shifts and lends an immediacy to the discussion.
9. The concluding paragraph establishes the significance of why the setting should be seen as the antagonist and provides a sense of closure by referring again to Sammy's "No Sale," which has been mentioned at the end of the first paragraph.
10. In short, Bernstein has demonstrated that she has read the work closely, has understood the relation of the setting to the major action, and has argued her thesis convincingly by using evidence from the story.

Comparison and Contrast

Another essay assignment in literature courses often combined with analytic topics is the type that requires you to write about similarities and differences between or within works. You might be asked to discuss "How Sounds Express Meanings in May Swenson's 'A Nosty Fright' and Lewis Carroll's 'Jabberwocky,'" or "Sammy's and Stokesie's Attitudes about Conformity in Updike's 'A & P.'" A *comparison* of either topic would emphasize their similarities, while a *contrast* would stress their differences. It is possible, of course, to include both perspectives in a paper if you find significant likenesses and differences. A comparison of Andrew Marvell's "To His Coy Mistress" and Richard Wilbur's "A Late Aubade" would, for example, yield similarities, because each poem describes a man urging his lover to make the most of their precious time together; however, important differences also exist in the tone and theme of each poem that would constitute a contrast. (You should, incidentally, be aware that the term *comparison* is sometimes used inclusively to refer to both similarities and differences. If you are assigned a comparison of two works, be sure that you understand what your instructor's expectations are; you may be required to include both approaches in the essay.)

When you choose your own topic, the paper will be more successful — more manageable — if you write on works that can be meaningfully related to each other. Although Robert Herrick's "To the Virgins, to Make Much of Time" and Shakespeare's *Hamlet* both have something to do with hesitation, the likelihood of anyone making a connection between the two that reveals something interesting and important is remote — though perhaps not impossible if the topic were conceived imaginatively and tactfully. That is not to say that comparisons of works from different genres should be avoided, but the relation between them should be strong, as would a treatment of black identity in Carl M. Holman's "Mr. Z" and August Wilson's *Fences.* Choose a topic that encourages you to ask significant questions about each work; the purpose of a comparison or contrast is to understand the works more clearly for having examined them together. Despite the obvious differences between Henrik Ibsen's *A Doll's House* and Gail Godwin's "A Sorrowful Woman," the two are closely related if we ask why the wife in each work withdraws from her family.

Choose works to compare or contrast that intersect with each other in some significant way. They may, for example, be written by the same author, in the same genre, or about the same subject. Perhaps you can compare their use of some technique, such as irony or point of view. Regardless of the specific topic, be sure to have a thesis that allows you to organize your paper around a central idea that argues a point about the two works. If you merely draw up a list of similarities or differences without a thesis in mind, your paper will be little more than a series of observations with no apparent purpose. Keep in the foreground of your thinking what the comparison or contrast reveals about the works.

There is no single way to organize comparative papers since each topic is likely to have its own particular issues to resolve, but it is useful to be aware of two basic patterns that can be helpful with a comparison, a contrast, or a combination of both. One method that can be effective for relatively short papers consists of dividing the paper in half, first discussing one work and then the other. Here, for example, is a partial informal outline for a discussion of Sophocles' *Oedipus the King* and Shakespeare's *Hamlet;* the topic is a comparison and contrast: "Oedipus and Hamlet as Tragic Figures."

1. Oedipus
   a. The nature of the conflict
   b. Strengths and stature
   c. Weaknesses and mistakes
   d. What is learned
2. Hamlet
   a. The nature of the conflict
   b. Strengths and stature
   c. Weaknesses and mistakes
   d. What is learned

This organizational strategy can be effective provided that the second part of the paper combines the discussion of Hamlet with references to Oedipus so that the thesis is made clear and the paper unified without being repetitive. If the two characters were treated entirely separately, then the discussion would be merely parallel rather than integrated. In a lengthy paper, this organization probably would not work well because a reader would have difficulty remembering the points made in the first half as he or she reads on.

Thus for a longer paper it is usually better to create a more integrated structure that discusses both works as you take up each item in your outline. Here is the second basic pattern using the elements in partial outline just cited.

1. The nature of the conflict
   a. Oedipus
   b. Hamlet
2. Strengths and stature
   a. Oedipus
   b. Hamlet
3. Weaknesses and mistakes
   a. Oedipus
   b. Hamlet
4. What is learned
   a. Oedipus
   b. Hamlet

This pattern allows you to discuss any number of topics without requiring that your reader recall what you first said about the conflict Oedipus confronts before you discuss Hamlet's conflicts fifteen pages later. However you structure your comparison or contrast paper, make certain that a reader can follow its elements and keep track of its thesis.

The following paper is in response to an assignment that required a comparison and contrast — about 750 words — of two assigned plays. The student chose to write an analysis of how the protagonists in each play evoke different responses in readers to similar situations.

Timothy Matthews

Professor Jackson

English 105-4

March 12, 1990

The Protagonists in A Doll's House and Top Girls:

A Possibility and a Warning

Though more than one hundred years separate the publication of Henrik Ibsen's A Doll's House (1879) and Caryl Churchill's Top Girls (1982), both authors raise similar questions about their respective protagonists' efforts to achieve self-fulfilling lives in a male-dominated world. Each play implicitly answers the question of whether or not the central character's behavior is warranted in order to shape a life for herself. In A Doll's House Ibsen makes a strong case for the necessity of Nora's decision to leave her husband and children in order to "find out the truth" about herself, but in Top Girls Churchill complicates matters by having Marlene mistakenly abandon much of her own humanity even as she searches for it.

Nora has apparently always tried to please the men in her life--notably her father and her husband, Torvald--by accommodating herself to their expectations about her. Unfortunately, her devotion and eagerness to defer to their wishes have turned her into a "little doll," controlled first by her father's raising of her as a "doll-child" and then by her husband's treatment of her as a "doll-wife." Torvald's self-centeredness and self-righteousness blind him to Nora's real virtues. She sacrifices everything to borrow money for a year's trip to Italy to save her husband's life. Though she commits forgery to borrow the money necessary to make the trip, her actions reveal her authentic strength and love. Torvald, however, sees her as merely a childish "little spendthrift" and "little squanderbird" whose frivolity ultimately betrays her deceitfulness and recklessness in breaking the law.

Torvald's obsession with his own status and respectability renders his moralistic response to Nora's risks and sacrifices intolerable to her. Once Nora sees and understands her husband's superficiality and selfishness--that Torvald was frightened only by what might threaten him--she realizes she no longer loves this "complete stranger," and so she decides to leave him and the children in order to "think things out" (1369). When she slams the door on her family, she sets off on a perilous attempt to become a complete human being rather than a mere doll. Ibsen invites us to ponder not only the risks she takes but also the necessity and desirability of her actions.

Like Nora, Churchill's Marlene finds herself in a male-dominated world, but Marlene rejects the patriarchal assumptions of that world much earlier in her life than Nora does. Churchill provides a long foreground in Scene I of the first act by presenting a group of women ranging from Joan, who posed as a man to become pope, to Lady Nijo, who was a thirteenth-century Japanese courtesan. These women discuss their varied troubled relationships with men in different times and cultures to reveal that all of them suffered injustices perpetrated by male assumptions, values, and actions. These women also demonstrate resilience and the ability to adapt to their circumstances so that they become the "top girls" of their time. Marlene's toast establishes the connection we are to make between her and these earlier women: "We've all come a long way. To our courage and the way we changed our lives and our extraordinary achievements" (1612).

Churchill, however, is less congratulatory than Marlene. For though the rest of the play explores many of the issues that self-determined women must face in our own times--economic exploitation, job discrimination, upward mobility, and so on--Churchill makes clear that women can be as ruthless and selfish in their efforts to climb to the top as men. When Ibsen has Nora close the door on her husband and children, we know that her decision is as painful as it is necessary, but when we learn of Marlene's abandonment of Angie and her cold assessment of her daughter as one of those who is "not going to make it" (1644), we are reminded more of Torvald's insensitivity than of Nora's absolute need to become human. Marlene is a tough-minded, enthusiastic supporter of the conservatism associated with Thatcher and Reagan because she believes that they too have no tolerance for the "stupid or lazy or frightened" (1656). Her personal life and political values reveal that she pledges her allegiance only to the survival of the fittest. Rather than rejecting the rapaciousness and exploitation of the male world she's worked her way into she simply wants to make sure that she's in a position of power. As her sister Joyce points out, Marlene thinks of nothing but herself, and as Angie inadvertently sums up in the final lines, Marlene is "frightening."

Through Nora, Ibsen presents a woman trapped by convention, values, and laws that dehumanize her until she breaks free of the "great wrong" (1367) perpetrated upon her by patriarchal authority. By the final scene of <u>A Doll's House</u>, we know Nora must leave

4

regardless of the consequences, because she has already paid too high a price by giving up her humanity and allowing herself to be wholly defined by her father and husband. In contrast, Churchill creates in Marlene a woman who is successful in a man's world but who abandons her family and the ability to love for false values, material success, and a selfish individuality. Nora represents the possibility of a new future for women, whereas Churchill, writing from the perspective of the 1980s and having witnessed some of that future, offers a warning of what women risk becoming if they merely change places with the callous, competitive, dominant men who preceded them. If Nora's situation at the end of the play is an uncertain and unpredictable future, Marlene's position is a frightening warning.

Although these two plays are fairly lengthy, Timothy Matthews's brief analysis of them is satisfying because he specifically focuses his thesis on the question of whether or not the protagonists' behavior is justified. After introducing the topic in the first paragraph, he takes up *A Doll's House* and then *Top Girls* in a pattern similar to the first outline suggested for "Oedipus and Hamlet as Tragic Figures." Notice how Matthews works in subsequent references to *A Doll's House* as he discusses *Top Girls* so that his treatment is integrated and we are reminded of why he is comparing and contrasting the two works. His final paragraph sums up his points without being repetitive and reiterates the thesis with which he began.

34. The Literary Research Paper

A close reading of a primary source such as a short story, poem, or play can give insights into a work's themes and effects, but sometimes you will want to know more. A published commentary by a critic who knows the work well and is familiar with the author's life and times can provide insights that otherwise may not be available. Such comments and interpretations — known as *secondary sources* — are, of course, not a substitute for the work itself, but they often can take you into a work further than if you made the journey by yourself.

After imagination, good sense, and energy, perhaps the next most important quality for writing a research paper is the ability to organize material. A research paper on a literary topic requires a writer to take account of quite a lot at once: the text, ideas, sources, and documentation techniques all make demands on one's efforts to present a topic clearly and convincingly.

The following list should give you a sense of what goes into creating a research paper. Although some steps on the list can be folded into one another, they offer an overview of the work that will involve you.

1. Choosing a topic
2. Finding sources
3. Evaluating sources
4. Taking notes
5. Developing a thesis
6. Organizing an outline
7. Writing drafts
8. Revising
9. Documenting sources
10. Preparing the final draft and proofreading

Even if you have never written a research paper, you most likely have already had experience choosing a topic, developing a thesis, organizing an outline, and writing a draft that you then revised, proofread, and handed in. Those skills represent six of the ten items on the list. This chapter briefly reviews some of these steps and focuses on the remaining tasks, unique to research paper assignments.

CHOOSING A TOPIC

Chapter 33 discussed the importance of reading a work closely and taking careful notes as a means of generating topics for writing about literature. If you know a work well and record your understanding of it in notes, you'll have impressions and ideas to choose from for potential topics. You may find it useful to review the information on pages 1812–1813 before reading the advice about putting together a research paper in this chapter.

The student author of the sample research paper "How the Narrator Cultivates a Rose for Emily" (p. 1853) was asked to write a five-page paper that demonstrated some familiarity with published critical perspectives on a Faulkner story of his choice. Before looking into critical discussions of the story, he read "A Rose for Emily" several times, taking notes and making comments in the margin of his textbook on each reading.

What prompted his choice of "A Rose for Emily" was a class discussion in which many of his classmates found the story's title inappropriate or misleading, because they could not understand how and why the story constituted a tribute to Emily given that she murdered a man and slept with his dead body over many years. The gruesome surprise ending revealing Emily as a murderer and necrophiliac hardly seemed to warrant a rose and a tribute for the central character. Why did Faulkner use such a title? Only after having thoroughly examined the story did the student go to the library to see what professional critics had to say about this question.

FINDING SOURCES

Whether your college library is large or small, its reference librarians can usually help you locate secondary sources about a particular work or author. Unless you choose a very recently published story, poem, or play about which little or nothing has been written, you should be able to find commentaries about a literary work efficiently and quickly. Here are some useful reference sources that can help you to establish both an overview of a potential topic and a list of relevant books and articles.

Annotated List of References

Altick, Richard, and Andrew Wright. *Selective Bibliography for the Study of English and American Literature.* 6th ed. New York: Macmillan, 1979. Especially designed for students, a very selective guide to research material on English and American writers.

Bryer, Jackson, ed. *Sixteen Modern American Authors: A Survey of Research and Criticism.* New York: Norton, 1973. Extensive bibliographic essays on Sherwood Anderson, Willa Cather, Hart Crane, Theodore Dreiser, T. S. Eliot, William Faulkner, F. Scott Fitzgerald, Robert Frost, Ernest Hemingway, Eugene O'Neill, Ezra Pound, Edwin Arlington Robinson, John Steinbeck, Wallace Stevens, William Carlos Williams, and Thomas Wolfe.

Corse, Larry B., and Sandra B. Corse. *Articles on American and British Literature: An Index to Selected Periodicals, 1950–1977.* Athens, OH: Swallow Press, 1981. Specifically designed for students using small college libraries.

Eddleman, Floyd E., ed. *American Drama Criticism: Interpretations, 1890–1977.* 2nd ed. Hamden, CT: Shoe String Press, 1979.

Holman, C. Hugh, and William Harmon. *A Handbook to Literature.* 5th ed. New York: Macmillan, 1986. A thorough dictionary of literary terms that also provides brief, clear overviews of literary movements such as Romanticism.

Kuntz, Joseph M., and Nancy C. Martinez. *Poetry Explication: A Checklist of Interpretation since 1925 of British and American Poems Past and Present.* Boston: Hall, 1980.

MLA International Bibliography of Books and Articles on Modern Language and Literature. New York: MLA, 1921–. Compiled annually; a major source for articles and books.

The New Cambridge Bibliography of English Literature. 5 vols. Cambridge, Eng.: Cambridge University Press, 1967–77. An important source on the literature from A.D. 600 to 1950.

The Oxford History of English Literature. 12 vols. Oxford, Eng.: Oxford University Press, 1945–, in progress. The most comprehensive literary history.

The Penguin Companion to World Literature. 4 vols. New York: McGraw-Hill, 1969–71. Covers classical, Oriental, African, European, English, and American literature.

Preminger, Alex, ed. *Princeton Encyclopedia of Poetry and Poetics.* Princeton, NJ: Princeton University Press, 1975. Includes entries on technical terms and poetic movements.

Rees, Robert, and Earl N. Harbert. *Fifteen American Authors before 1900: Bibliographic Essays on Research and Criticism.* Madison: University of Wisconsin Press, 1971. Among the writers covered are Stephen Crane and Emily Dickinson.

Schweik, Robert C., and Dieter Riesner. *Reference Sources in English and American Literature: An Annotated Bibliography.* New York: Norton, 1977. Includes biographical, historical, critical, and bibliographic sources.

Spiller, Robert E., et al. *Literary History of the United States.* 4th ed. 2 vols. New York: Macmillan, 1974. Coverage of literary movements and individual writers from colonial times to the 1960s.

Walker, Warren S. *Twentieth-Century Short Story Explication.* 3rd ed. Hamden, CT: Shoe String Press, 1977. A bibliography of criticism on short stories written since 1800.

These sources are available in the reference sections of most college libraries; ask a reference librarian to help you locate them.

Computer Searches

Researchers can locate materials in a variety of sources, including card catalogues, specialized encyclopedias, bibliographies, and indexes to periodicals. Many libraries now also provide computer searches that are linked to a data base of the libraries' holdings. This can be an efficient way to establish a bibliography on a specific topic. If your library has such a service, consult a reference librarian about how to use it and to determine if it is feasible for your topic. You may discover that the library charges a fee for such services. If a computer service is impractical, you can still collect the same information from printed sources.

EVALUATING SOURCES AND TAKING NOTES

Evaluate your sources for their reliability and the quality of their evidence. Check to see if an article or book has been superseded by later studies; try to use up-to-date sources. A popular magazine article will probably not be as authoritative as an article in a scholarly journal. Sources that are well documented with primary and secondary materials usually indicate that the author has done his or her homework. Books printed by university presses and established trade presses are preferable to books privately printed. But there are always exceptions. If you are uncertain about how to assess a book, try to find out something about the author. Are there any other books listed in the card catalogue that indicate the author's expertise? What do book reviews say about the work? Three valuable indexes to book reviews of literary studies are *Book Review Digest, Book Review Index,* and *Index to Book Reviews in the Humanities.* Your reference librarian can show you how to use these important tools for evaluating books. Reviews can be a quick means to get a broad perspective on writers and their works because reviewers often survey previous approaches to the topic under discussion.

As you prepare a list of reliable sources relevant to your topic, record the necessary bibliographic information so that it will be available when you make up the list of works cited for your paper. (See the illustration of a sample bibliography card.) For a book include the author, complete title, place of publication, publisher, and date. For an article include author, complete title, name of periodical, volume number, date of issue, and page numbers.

Once you have assembled a tentative bibliography, you will need to take notes on your readings. If you are not using a word processor, use 3×5, 4×6, or 5×8-inch cards for note taking. They are easy to manipulate and can be readily sorted later on when you establish subheadings for your paper. Be sure to keep track of where the information comes from by writing the author's name and page number on each notecard. If you use more than one work by the same author include a brief title as well as the author's name. (See the illustration of the sample notecard.)

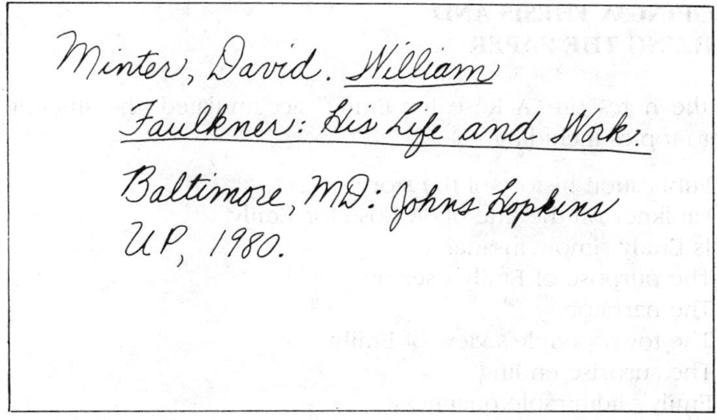
Minter, David. William Faulkner: His Life and Work. Baltimore, MD: Johns Hopkins UP, 1980.

Sample Bibliography Card for a Book

The sample notecard records the source of information (the complete publishing information is on the bibliography card) and provides a heading that will allow easy sorting later on. Notice that the information is summarized rather than quoted in large chunks. The student also includes a short note asking himself if this will be relevant to the topic — the meaning of the title of "A Rose for Emily." (As it turned out, this was not directly related to the topic, so it was dropped.)

Notecards can combine quotations, paraphrases, and summaries; you can also use them to cite your own ideas and give them headings so that you don't lose track of them. As you take notes try to record only points relevant to your topic. Although the sample card on Scribner's rejection of "A Rose for Emily" wasn't used in the paper, it might have been. At least that fact was an interesting possibility, even if it wasn't, finally, worth developing.

On the publication of "A Rose for Emily" Minter 116

Minter describes "A Rose" as "one of Faulkner's finest short stories" yet it was rejected at Scribner's when Faulkner submitted it.

[Can I work this in?]

Sample Notecard

DEVELOPING A THESIS AND ORGANIZING THE PAPER

As the notes on "A Rose for Emily" accumulated, the student sorted them into topics including

1. Publication history of the story
2. Faulkner on the title of "A Rose for Emily"
3. Is Emily simply insane?
4. The purpose of Emily's servant
5. The narrator
6. The townspeople's view of Emily
7. The surprise ending
8. Emily's admirable qualities
9. Homer's character

The student quickly saw that items 1, 4, and 9 were not directly related to his topic concerning the significance of the story's title. The remaining numbers (2, 3, 5, 6, 7, 8) are the topics taken up in the paper. The student had begun his reading of secondary sources with a tentative thesis that stemmed from his question about the appropriateness of the title. That "why" shaped itself into the expectation that he would have a thesis something like this: "The title justifies Emily's murder of Homer because . . ."

The assumption was that he would find information that indicated some specific reason. But the more he read the more he discovered that it was possible only to speak about how the narrator prevents the reader from making a premature judgment about Emily rather than justifying her actions. Hence, he wisely changed his tentative thesis to this final thesis: "The narrator describes incidents and withholds information in such a way as to cause the reader to sympathize with Emily before her crime is revealed." This thesis helped the student explain why the title is accurate and useful rather than misleading.

Because the assignment was relatively brief, the student did not write up a formal outline but instead organized his stacks of usable notecards and proceeded to write the first draft from them.

REVISING

After writing your first draft, you should review the advice and revision checklist on pp. 1822–1823 so that you can read your paper with an objective eye. Two days after writing his next-to-last draft, the writer of "How the Narrator Cultivates a Rose for Emily" realized that he had allotted too much space for critical discussions of the narrator that were not directly related to his approach. He wanted to demonstrate a familiarity with these studies, but it was not essential that he summarize or discuss them. He corrected this by consolidating parenthetical references: "Though a number of studies discuss the story's narrator (see, for example, Kempton; Sullivan; and Watkins)." His earlier draft had included summaries of these studies that were tangential to his argument. The point is that he saw this himself after he took some time to approach the paper from a fresh perspective.

DOCUMENTING SOURCES

You must acknowledge the use of a source when you (1) quote someone's exact words, (2) summarize or borrow someone's opinions or ideas, or (3) use information and facts that are not considered to be common knowledge. The purpose of this documentation is to acknowledge your sources, to demonstrate that you are familiar with what others have thought about the topic, and to provide your reader access to the same sources. If your paper is not adequately documented, it will be vulnerable to a charge of *plagiarism* — the presentation of someone else's work as your own. Conscious plagiarism is easy to avoid; honesty takes care of that for most people. However, there is a more problematic form of plagiarism that is often inadvertent. Whether inadequate documentation is conscious or not, plagiarism is a serious matter and must be avoided. Papers can be evaluated only by what is on the page, not by their writers' intentions.

Let's look more closely at what constitutes plagiarism. Consider the following passage quoted from John Gassner's introduction to *Four Great Plays by Henrik Ibsen* (New York: Bantam, 1959), p. viii:

> Today it seems incredible that *A Doll's House* should have created the furor it did. In exploding Victorian ideals of feminine dependency the play seemed revolutionary in 1879. When its heroine Nora left her home in search of self-development it seemed as if the sanctity of marriage had been flouted by a playwright treading the stage with cloven-feet.

Now read this plagiarized version:

> *A Doll's House* created a furor in 1879 by blowing up Victorian ideals about a woman's place in the world. Nora's search for self-fulfillment outside her home appeared to be an attack on the sanctity of marriage by a cloven-footed playwright.

Though the writer has shortened the passage and made some changes in the wording, this paragraph is basically the same as Gassner's. Indeed, several of his phrases are lifted almost intact. Even if a parenthetical reference had been included at the end of the passage and the source included in "Works Cited," the language of this passage would still be plagiarism because it is presented as the writer's own. Both language and ideas must be acknowledged.

Here is an adequately documented version of the passage:

> John Gassner has observed how difficult it is for today's readers to comprehend the intense reaction against *A Doll's House* in 1879. When Victorian audiences watched Nora walk out of her stifling marriage, they assumed that Ibsen was expressing a devilish contempt for the "sanctity of marriage" (viii).

This passage makes absolutely clear that the observation is Gassner's, and it is written in the student's own language with the exception of one quoted phrase. Had Gassner not been named in the passage, the parenthetical reference would have included his name: (Gassner viii).

Some mention should be made of the notion of common knowledge before we turn to the standard format for documenting sources. Observations and facts that are widely known and routinely included in many of your sources do not require documentation. It is not necessary to cite a source for the fact that Alfred, Lord Tennyson, was born in 1809 or that Ernest Hemingway loved to fish and hunt. Sometimes it will be difficult for you to determine what common knowledge is for a topic that you know little about. If you are in doubt, the best strategy is to supply a reference.

There are two basic ways to document sources. Traditionally, sources have been cited in footnotes at the bottom of each page or in endnotes grouped together at the end of the paper. Here is how a portion of the sample paper would look if footnotes were used instead of parenthetical documentation:

> As Heller points out, before we learn of Emily's bizarre behavior we see her as a sympathetic--if antiquated--figure in a town whose life and concerns have passed her by; hence, "we are disposed to see Emily as victimized."[1]
>
> [1]Terry Heller, "The Telltale Hair: A Critical Study of William Faulkner's 'A Rose for Emily,'" <u>Arizona Quarterly</u> 28 (1972): 306.

Unlike endnotes, which are double spaced throughout under the title of "Notes" on separate pages at the end of the paper, footnotes appear four spaces below the text. They are single spaced with double spaces between notes.

No doubt you will have encountered these documentation methods in your reading. A different style is recommended, however, in the third edition of the Modern Language Association's *MLA Handbook for Writers of Research Papers* (1988). The new style employs parenthetical references within the text of the paper; these are keyed to an alphabetical list of works cited at the end of the paper. This method is designed to be less distracting for the reader. Unless you are instructed to follow the footnote or endnote style for documentation, use the new parenthetical method explained in the next section.

The List of Works Cited

Items in the list of works cited are arranged alphabetically according to the author's last name and indented five spaces after the first line. This allows the reader to locate quickly the complete bibliographic information for the author's name cited within the parenthetical reference in the text. The following are common entries for literature papers and should be used as models. If some of your sources are of a different nature, consult Joseph Gibaldi and Walter S. Achtert, *MLA Handbook for Writers of Research Papers,* 3rd ed. (New York: MLA, 1988); many of the bibliographic possibilities you are likely to need are included in this source.

A Book by One Author

Hendrickson, Robert. The Literary Life and Other Curiosities. New York: Viking, 1981.

Notice that the author's name is in reverse order. This information, along with the full title, place of publication, publisher, and date should be taken from the title and copyright pages of the book. The title is underlined to indicate italics and is also followed by a period. If the city of publication is well known, it is unnecessary to include the state. Use the publication date on the title page; if none appears there use the copyright date (after ©) on the back of the title page.

A Book by Two Authors

Horton, Rod W., and Herbert W. Edwards. Backgrounds of American Literary Thought. 3rd ed. Englewood Cliffs: Prentice, 1974.

Only the first author's name is given in reverse order. The edition number appears after the title.

A Book with More than Three Authors

Abrams, M. H., et al., eds. The Norton Anthology of English Literature. 5th ed. 2 vols. New York: Norton, 1986. Vol. 1.

The abbreviation *et al.* means "and others." It is used to avoid having to list all fourteen editors of this first volume of a two-volume work.

A Work in a Collection by the Same Author

O'Connor, Flannery. "Greenleaf." The Complete Stories. By O'Connor. New York: Farrar, 1971. 311-34.

Page numbers are given because the reference is to only a single story in the collection.

A Work in a Collection by Different Writers

Frost, Robert. "Design." The Bedford Introduction to Literature. Ed. Michael Meyer. 2nd ed. New York: Bedford-St. Martin's, 1990. 725.

The hyphenated publisher's name indicates a publisher's imprint: Bedford Books of St. Martin's Press.

A Translated Book

Grass, Günter. The Tin Drum. Trans. Ralph Manheim. New York: Vintage-Random, 1962.

An Introduction, Preface, Foreword, or Afterword

Johnson, Thomas H. Introduction. Final Harvest: Emily Dickinson's Poems. By Emily Dickinson. Boston: Little, 1961. vii-xiv.

This cites the introduction by Johnson. Notice that a colon is used between the book's main title and subtitle. To cite a poem in this book use this method:

Dickinson, Emily. "A Tooth upon Our Peace." Final Harvest: Emily Dickinson's Poems. Ed. Thomas H. Johnson. Boston: Little, 1961. 110.

An Encyclopedia

"Wordsworth, William." The New Encyclopaedia Britannica. 1984 ed.

Because this encyclopedia is organized alphabetically, no page number or other information is given, only the edition number (if available) and date.

An Article in a Magazine

Morrow, Lance. "Scribble, Scribble, Eh, Mr. Toad?" Time 24 Feb. 1986: 84.

The citation for an unsigned article would begin with the title and be alphabetized by the first word of the title other than "a," "an," or "the."

An Article in a Scholarly Journal with Continuous Pagination beyond a Single Issue

Mahar, William J. "Black English in Early Blackface Minstrelsy: A New Interpretation of the Sources of Minstrel Show Dialect." American Quarterly 37 (1985): 260-85.

Because this journal uses continuous pagination instead of separate pagination for each issue, it is not necessary to include the month, season, or number of the issue. Only one of the quarterly issues will have pages numbered 260–85. If you are not certain whether a journal's pages are numbered continuously throughout a volume, supply the month, season, or issue number, as in the next entry.

An Article in a Scholarly Journal with Separate Pagination for Each Issue

Updike, John. "The Cultural Situation of the American Writer." American Studies International 15 (Spring 1977): 19-28.

By noting the spring issue, the entry saves a reader looking through each issue of the 1977 volume for the correct article on pages 19–28.

An Article in a Newpaper

Ziegler, Philip. "The Lure of Gossip, the Rules of History." New York Times 23 Feb. 1986: sec. 7: 1+.

This citation indicates that the article appears on page 1 of section 7 and continues onto another page.

A Lecture

Stern, Milton. "Melville's View of Law." English 270 class lecture. University of Connecticut, Storrs, 12 Mar. 1988.

Parenthetical References

A list of works cited is not an adequate indication of how you have used sources in your paper. You must also provide the precise location of quotations and other information by using parenthetical references within the text of the paper. You do this by citing the author's name (or the source's title if the work is anonymous) and the page number.

> Philipps points out that "Nabokov was misunderstood by early reviewers of his work" (28).

or

> Nabokov's first critics misinterpreted his stories (Philipps 28).

Either way a reader will find the complete bibliographic entry in the list of works cited under Philipps's name and know that the information cited in the paper appears on page 28. Notice that the end punctuation comes after the parentheses.

If you have listed more than one work by the same author, you would add a brief title to the parenthetical reference to distinguish between them. You could also include the full title in your text.

> Nabokov's first critics misinterpreted his stories (Philipps "Early Reviews" 28).

or

> Philipps points out in "Early Reviews of Nabokov's Fiction" that his early work was misinterpreted by reviewers (28).

There can be many variations on what is included in a parenthetical reference, depending on the nature of the entry in the list of works cited. But the general principle is simple enough: provide enough parenthetical information for a reader to find the work in "Works Cited." Examine the sample research paper for more examples of works cited and strategies for including parenthetical references. If you are puzzled by a given situation, ask your reference librarian to show you the *MLA Handbook*.

SAMPLE STUDENT RESEARCH PAPER

The following research paper by Tony Groulx follows the format described in the *MLA Handbook for Writers of Research Papers* (1988). This format is discussed in the preceding section on Documentation and in Chapter 33, in the section "Manuscript Form" (pp. 1823–1824). Though the sample paper is short, it illustrates many of the techniques and strategies useful for writing an essay that includes secondary sources. (Faulkner's "A Rose for Emily" is reprinted on p. 47.)

Tony Groulx

Professor Hugo

English 109-3

December 3, 1989

How the Narrator Cultivates a Rose for Emily

William Faulkner's "A Rose for Emily" is an absorbing mystery story whose chilling ending contains a gruesome surprise. When we discover, along with the narrator and townspeople, what was left of Homer Barron's body, we may be surprised or not, depending upon how carefully we have been reading the story and keeping track of details such as Emily Grierson's purchase of rat poison and Homer's disappearance. Probably most readers anticipate finding Homer's body at the end of the story, because Faulkner carefully prepares the groundwork for the discovery as the townspeople force their way into that mysterious upstairs room where a "thin, acrid pall as of the tomb seemed to lie everywhere" (53). But very few readers, if any, are prepared for the story's final paragraph, when we realize that the strand of "iron-gray hair" (the last three words of the story) on the second pillow indicates that Emily has slept with Homer since she murdered him. This last paragraph produces the real horror in the story and an extraordinary revelation about Emily's character.

The final paragraph seems like the right place to begin a discussion of this story because the surprise ending not only creates a powerful emotional effect in us but also raises an important question about what we are to think of Emily. Is this isolated, eccentric woman simply mad? All the circumstantial evidence indicates that she is a murderer and necrophiliac, and yet Faulkner titles the story "A Rose for Emily," as if she is due some kind of tribute. The title somehow qualifies the gasp of horror that the story leads up to in the final paragraph. Why would anyone offer this woman a "rose"? What's behind the title?

Faulkner was once directly asked the meaning of the title and replied:

> Oh it's simply the poor woman had had no life at all. Her father had kept her more or less locked up and then she had a lover who was about to quit her, she had to murder him. It was just "A Rose for Emily"--that's all. (Gwynn and Blotner 87-88)

This reply explains some of Emily's motivation for murdering Homer but it doesn't actually address the purpose and meaning of the title. If Emily killed Homer out of a kind of emotional necessity--out of a fear of abandonment--how does that explain the fact that the title seems to suggest that the story is a way of paying respect to Emily? The question remains.

Whatever respect the story creates for Emily cannot be the result of her actions. Surely there can be no convincing excuse made for murder and necrophilia; there is nothing to praise about what she does. Instead, the tribute comes in the form of how her story is told rather than what we are told about her. To do this Faulkner uses a narrator who tells Emily's story in such a way as to maximize our sympathy for her. The grim information about Emily's "iron-gray hair" on the pillow is withheld until the very end not only to produce a surprise but to permit the reader to develop a sympathetic understanding of her before we are shocked and disgusted by her necrophilia.

Significantly, the narrator begins the story with Emily's death rather than Homer's. Though a number of studies discuss the story's narrator (see, for example, Kempton; Sullivan; and Watkins), Terry Heller's is one of the most comprehensive in its focus on the narrator's effects on the readers' response to Emily. As Heller points out, before we learn of Emily's bizarre behavior we see her as a sympathetic--if antiquated--figure in a town whose life and concerns have passed her by; hence, "we are disposed to see Emily as victimized" (306). Her refusal to pay her taxes is an index to her isolation and eccentricity, but this incident also suggests a degree of dignity and power lacking in the town officials who fail to collect her taxes. Her encounters with the officials of Jefferson--whether in the form of the sneaking aldermen who try to cover up the smell around her house or the druggist who unsuccessfully tries to get her to conform to the law when she buys arsenic--place her in an admirable light, because her willfulness is based upon her personal strength. Moreover, it is relatively easy to side with Emily when the townspeople are described as taking pleasure in her being reduced to poverty as a result of her father's death, because "now she too would know the old thrill and the old despair of a penny more or less" (49). The narrator's account of their pettiness, jealousy, and inability to make sense of Emily causes the reader to sympathize with Emily's eccentricities before we must judge her murderous behavior. We admire her for taking life on her own terms, and the narrator makes sure this response is in place prior to our realization that she also takes life.

We don't really know much about Emily because the narrator arranges the details of her life so that it's difficult to know what she's been up to. We learn, for example, about the smell around the house before she buys the poison and Homer disappears, so that the cause and effect relationship among these events is obscured. The narrator's chronology of events is a bit slippery (for a detailed reconstruction of the chronology see McGlynn and Nebecker's revision of McGlynn's work), but the effect is to suspend judgment of Emily. By the time we realize what she has done we are already inclined to see her as outside community values almost out of necessity. That's not to say that the murdering of Homer is justified by the narrator, but it is to say that her life maintains its private--though no longer secret--dignity. Despite the final revelation, Emily remains "dear, inescapable, impervious, tranquil, and perverse" (52).

The narrator's "rose" to Emily is his recognition that Emily is all these things--including "perverse." She evokes "a sort of respectful affection for a fallen monument" (47). She is, to be sure, "fallen," but she is also somehow central--a "monument"--to the life of the community. Faulkner does not offer a definitive reading of Emily but he does have the narrator pay tribute to her by attempting to provide a complex set of contexts for her actions--contexts that include a repressive father, resistance to a changing South and impinging North, the passage of time and its influence on the present, and relations between men and women as well as relations between generations. Robert Crosman points out that the "narrator is himself a 'reader' of Emily's story, trying to put together from fragments a complete picture, trying to find the meaning of her life in its impact upon an audience, the citizens of Jefferson, of which he is a member" (212). The narrator refuses to dismiss Emily as simply mad or to treat her life as merely a grotesque, sensational horror story. Instead, his narrative method brings us into her life before we too hastily reject her, and in doing so it offers us a complex imaginative treatment of fierce determination and strength coupled with illusions and shocking eccentricities. The narrator's rose for Emily is paying her the tribute of placing that "long strand of iron-gray hair" in the context of her entire life.

Works Cited

Crosman, Robert. "How Readers Make Meaning." College Literature 9 (1982): 207-15.

Faulkner, William. "A Rose for Emily." The Bedford Introduction to Literature. Ed. Michael Meyer. 2nd ed. New York: Bedford-St. Martin's, 1990. 47-53.

Gwynn, Frederick, and Joseph Blotner, eds. Faulkner in the University: Class Conferences at the University of Virginia, 1957-58. Charlottesville: U of Virginia P, 1959.

Heller, Terry. "The Telltale Hair: A Critical Study of William Faulkner's 'A Rose for Emily.'" Arizona Quarterly 28 (1972): 310-18.

Kempton, K. P. The Short Story. Cambridge: Harvard UP, 1954. 104-06.

McGlynn, Paul D. "The Chronology of 'A Rose for Emily.'" Studies in Short Fiction 6 (1969): 461-62.

Nebecker, Helen E. "Chronology Revised." Studies in Short Fiction 8 (1971): 471-73.

Sullivan, Ruth. "The Narrator in 'A Rose for Emily.'" The Journal of Narrative Technique 1 (1971): 159-78.

Watkins, F. C. "The Structure of 'A Rose for Emily.'" Modern Language Notes 69 (1954): 508-10.

Acknowledgments *(continued from p. iv)*

Louise Erdrich. "Fleur" from *Tracks* by Louise Erdrich. Copyright © 1988 by Louise Erdrich. Reprinted by permission of Henry Holt and Company, Inc.

William Faulkner. "A Rose for Emily," copyright 1930 and renewed 1958 by William Faulkner and "Barn Burning" copyright © 1939 and renewed 1967 by Estelle Faulkner and Jill Faulkner Summers. Reprinted from *The Collected Stories of William Faulkner* by permission of Random House, Inc. "On the Demands of Writing Short Stories" and "On 'A Rose for Emily' " from *Faulkner in the University* by Gwynn and Blotner. Reprinted by permission of the University Press of Virginia.

Judith Fetterley. "A Feminist Reading of 'The Birthmark' " from *The Resisting Reader: A Feminist Approach to American Fiction.* Copyright © 1978. Reprinted by permission of Indiana University Press.

F. Scott Fitzgerald. "On the Continuity of a Writer's Works" from "One Hundred False Starts" in *Afternoon of an Author.* Reprinted from the *Saturday Evening Post.* Copyright 1933, the Curtis Publishing Company. Reprinted by permission.

Gabriel García Márquez. "A Very Old Man With Enormous Wings" from *Leaf Storm and Other Stories* by Gabriel García Márquez (English Translation). Reprinted by permission of Harper & Row, Publishers, Inc.

Gail Godwin. "A Sorrowful Woman," copyright © 1971 by Gail Godwin, first appeared in *Esquire* Magazine. Reprinted by permission of John Hawkins & Associates, Inc.

Liliana Hecker. "The Stolen Party" Copyright © 1982 by Liliana Hecker. Translation Copyright © 1985 by Alberto Manguel. Reprinted from *Other Fires: Short Fiction by Latin American Women,* edited by Alberto Manguel, by permission of Clarkson N. Potter Publishers, published by Crown Publishers, a Division of Random House, Inc.

Ernest Hemingway. "Soldier's Home." Reprinted with permission of Charles Scribner's Sons, an imprint of Macmillan Publishing Company from *In Our Time* by Ernest Hemingway. Copyright 1925 Charles Scribner's Sons; copyright renewed 1953 by Ernest Hemingway.

James Joyce. "Araby" from *Dubliners* by James Joyce. Copyright 1916 by B. W. Huebsch, Inc. Definitive Text Copyright © 1967 by The Estate of James Joyce. All rights reserved. Reprinted by permission of Viking Penguin, a division of Penguin Books USA, Inc.

Franz Kafka. "A Hunger Artist" from *The Penal Colony* by Franz Kafka, translated by Willa and Edwin Muir. Copyright © 1948 and renewed 1976 by Schocken Books Inc. Reprinted by permission of the publisher.

Claire Kahane. "The Function of Violence in O'Connor's Fiction" from "Flannery O'Connor's Rage of Vision," Reprinted with permission from *American Literature* 46:1 (March 1974), pp. 54–67. Copyright 1974 by Duke University Press.

Jamaica Kincaid. "Girl" from *At the Bottom of the River* by Jamaica Kincaid. Copyright © 1978, 1979, 1981, 1982, 1983 by Jamaica Kincaid. Reprinted by permission of Farrar, Straus and Giroux, Inc.

D. H. Lawrence. "The Horse Dealer's Daughter" from *The Complete Short Stories of D. H. Lawrence,* Vol. III, by D. H. Lawrence. Copyright 1933 by the Estate of D. H. Lawrence, renewed © 1961 by Angelo Ravagli and C. Montague Weekley, Executors of the Estate of Frieda Lawrence Ravagli. Reprinted by permission of Viking Penguin a division of Penguin Books USA, Inc.

Ursula K. Le Guin. "On Conflict in Fiction" from *Dancing at the Edge of the World.* Copyright © 1989 by Ursula K. Le Guin. Reprinted by permission of Grove Weidenfeld.

Thomas McCormack. "On the Problem of Teaching Theme" from *The Fiction Editor, the Novel, and the Novelist* by Thomas McCormack. Copyright © 1988 by Daniel and Jessie McCormack, St. Martin's Press, Inc., New York.

Dorothy T. McFarland. "A Formalist Reading of 'Revelation,' " From *Flannery O'Connor* by Dorothy T. McFarland. Copyright © 1976 by the Frederick Ungar Publishing Company. Reprinted by permission of the publisher.

Katherine Mansfield. "Miss Brill" from *The Short Stories of Katherine Mansfield.* Copyright 1922 by Alfred A. Knopf, Inc. and renewed 1950 by John Middleton Murry. Reprinted by permission of the publisher. "On the Style of 'Miss Brill' " from *The Letters of Katherine Mansfield,* edited by John Middleton Murry. Reprinted by permission of Alfred A. Knopf, Inc.

Mordecai Marcus. "What Is an Initiation Story?" from *The Journal of Aesthetics and Art Criticism* 19:2, pp. 222–223. Reprinted by permission.

Yukio Mishima. "Patriotism" from *Death in Midsummer.* Copyright © 1966 by New Directions Publishing Corporation. Reprinted by permission of New Directions Publishing Corporation.

Alice Munro. "How I Met My Husband," copyright © 1974 by Alice Munro. From *Something I've Been Meaning to Tell You.* All rights reserved. Published in Canada by McGraw-Hill Ryerson. Reprinted by permission of Virginia Barber Literary Agency.

Kay Mussell. "A Defense of Formula Fiction" from *Fantasy and Reconciliation: Contemporary Formulas of Women's Romance Fiction* (Greenwood Press, Inc., Westport, CT, 1984, pp. 184–187). Copyright © 1984 by Kay Mussell. Used by permission of the publisher.

Vladimir Nabokov. "Good Readers and Good Writers" from *Lectures on Literature* by Vladimir Nabokov. Copyright © 1980 by the Estate of Vladimir Nabokov. Reprinted by permission of Harcourt Brace Jovanovich, Inc.

R. K. Narayan. "Trail of the Green Blazer," *Malgudi Days* by R. K. Narayan. Copyright © 1978 by R. K. Narayan. All rights reserved. Reprinted by permission of Viking Penguin, a division of Penguin Books USA, Inc.

Joyce Carol Oates. "The Lady with the Pet Dog" reprinted from *Marriages and Infidelities* by Joyce Carol Oates. Copyright © 1968, 1969, 1970, 1971, 1972 by Joyce Carol Oates. Reprinted by permission of Vanguard Press, a Division of Random House, Inc.

Tim O'Brien. "How to Tell a True War Story," published in *Esquire,* October 1987. Copyright © 1987 by Tim O'Brien. Reprinted by permission of International Creative Management.

Flannery O'Connor. "Good Country People" from *A Good Man Is Hard to Find and Other Stories.* Copyright © 1955 by Flannery O'Connor; renewed 1983 by Regina O'Connor. "A Good Man Is Hard to Find," copyright 1953 by Flannery O'Connor; renewed 1981 by Regina O'Connor. Reprinted from *A Good Man Is Hard to Find and Other Stories* by Flannery O'Connor. Both stories reprinted by permission of Harcourt Brace Jovanovich, Inc. "Greenleaf," "Everything That Rises Must Converge," and "Revelation" from *The Complete Stories* by Flannery O'Connor. Copyright © 1961, 1964, 1965 by the Estate of Mary Flannery O'Connor. Reprinted by permission of Farrar, Straus and Giroux, Inc. "On Faith" from "Letter to 'A' " in *The Habit of Being* by Flannery O'Connor. Copyright © 1979 by Regina O'Connor. Reprinted by permission of Farrar, Straus and Giroux, Inc. "On the Materials of Fiction," "On the Use of Exaggeration and Distortion," and "On Theme and Symbol" from "The Nature and Aim of Fiction" in *Mystery and Manners* by Flannery O'Connor. Copyright © 1957, 1961, 1963, 1964, 1966, 1967, 1969 by the Estate of Mary Flannery O'Connor. Reprinted by permission of Farrar, Straus and Giroux, Inc.

Tillie Olsen. "I Stand Here Ironing" excerpted from the book *Tell Me a Riddle* by Tillie Olsen. Copyright © 1956 by Tillie Olsen. Reprinted by permission of Delacorte Press/Seymour Lawrence, a division of Bantam, Doubleday, Dell Publishing Group, Inc.

Grace Paley. "A Conversation With My Father" from *Enormous Changes at the Last Minute* by Grace Paley. Copyright © 1972, 1974 by Grace Paley. Reprinted by permission of Farrar, Straus and Giroux, Inc.

Katherine Anne Porter. "The Grave" from *The Leaning Tower and Other Stories,* copyright 1944 and renewed 1972 by Katherine Anne Porter, reprinted by permission of Harcourt Brace Jovanovich, Inc.

Kent Thompson. "A Short Short Story: 'Unreeling.' " Copyright © 1989 by The New York Times Company. Reprinted by permission.

John Updike. "A & P," copyright © 1962 by John Updike. Reprinted from *Pigeon Feathers and Other Stories* by John Updike, by permission of Alfred A. Knopf, Inc. "Fiction's Subtlety" from "The Importance of Fiction" in *Esquire,* August 1985. Reprinted by permission of the author.

Karen Van Der Zee. "A Secret Sorrow." Copyright © 1981 by Karen Van Der Zee. All rights reserved. Reproduction with the permission of the Publisher, Harlequin Enterprises Ltd., 225 Duncan Mill Road, Don Mills, Ontario, Canada M3B, 3K9.

Gore Vidal. "The Popularity of the Tarzan Books," excerpt from "Tarzan Revisited," *Esquire,* December 1963. Copyright © 1963 by Gore Vidal. Reprinted by permission of the William Morris Agency, Inc. on behalf of the author.

Hyatt H. Waggoner. "Hawthorne's Style" from *Nathaniel Hawthorne* by Hyatt H. Waggoner. University of Minnesota Pamphlets on American Writers #23. © copyright by the University of Minnesota. Reprinted by permission of the publisher. Reprinted by permission of the University of Minnesota Press.

Fay Weldon. "IND AFF" Copyright © Fay Weldon 1988. First published in *The Observer* magazine, 7th August 1988, reprinted by permission of the author and Anthony Sheil Associates, 43 Doughty Street, London WC1N 2LF.

Eudora Welty. "Livvie" from *The Wide Net and Other Stories,* copyright 1942, 1970 by Eudora Welty. Reprinted by permission of Harcourt Brace Jovanovich, Inc. "Eudora Welty on the Plots of 'The Bride Comes to Yellow Sky' and 'Miss Brill,'" excerpts from "The Reading and Writing of Short Stories" by Eudora Welty in *The Atlantic Monthly* 183 (February–March 1949). "Place in Fiction," *South Atlantic Quarterly.* Reprinted by permission of Russell & Volkening as agents for the author. Copyright © 1956 by Eudora Welty. Renewed 1984 by Eudora Welty.

POETRY

Katharyn Machan Aal. "Hazel Tells LaVerne" from *Light Year '85.* Reprinted by permission of the author.

Leonard Adame. "Black and White" reprinted by permission of the author.

Anna Akhmatova. "Apparition" from *The Complete Poems of Anna Akhmatova,* translated by Judith Hemschemeyer (Zephyr Press, 1989). Copyright © 1989 by Judith Hemschemeyer. Used with permission.

Claribel Alegria. "I Am Mirror" from *Sobrevivo.* Reprinted by permission of the author.

Muhammad al-Maghut. "Tourist" from *Modern Arabic Poetry* edited by Jayyusi. Copyright © 1987 by Columbia University Press. Reprinted by permission.

A. R. Ammons. "Coward" is reprinted from *Diversifications: Poems by A. R. Ammons,* copyright © 1975 by A. R. Ammons. "Winter Saint" is reprinted from *Collected Poems 1951–1971* by A. R. Ammons, copyright © 1972 by A. R. Ammons. Both poems reprinted by permission of W. W. Norton & Company, Inc.

Maya Angelou. "Africa" from *Oh Pray My Wings Are Gonna Fit Me Well* by Maya Angelou. Copyright © 1975 by Maya Angelou. Reprinted by permission of Random House, Inc.

Richard Armour. "Going to Extremes" from *Light Armour.* Reprinted by permission of Kathleen S. Armour.

John Ashbery. "Crazy Weather" from *Selected Poems* by John Ashbery. Copyright © 1983 by John Ashberry. All Rights Reserved. Reprinted by permission of Viking Penguin, a division of Penguin Books USA, Inc.

Margaret Atwood. "you fit into me" by Margaret Atwood from *Power Politics* (Toronto: House of Anansi Press, 1971). Reprinted by permission of the author. "Dreams of the Animals" from *Procedures for Underground* in *Selected Poems 1965–1975.* Copyright © 1976 by Margaret Atwood. Reprinted by permission of Houghton Mifflin Company. "Spelling" reprinted by permission of Margaret Atwood.

W. H. Auden. "As I Walked Out One Evening," "The Unknown Citizen," "Musée des Beaux Arts," and "Lay Your Sleeping Head, My Love" copyright 1940 and renewed 1968 by W. H. Auden. Reprinted from *W. H. Auden: Collected Poems,* edited by Edward Mendelson, by permission of Random House, Inc.

Regina Barreca. "Nighttime Fires" in *The Minnesota Review,* Fall, 1986, reprinted by permission of the author.

Matsuo Bashō. "Under cherry trees," translated by Peter Beilenson, from *Japanese Haiku,* Series I, © 1955–1956, Peter Beilenson editor. Reprinted by permission of Peter Pauper Press, Inc.

Charles Baudelaire, "To the Reader" from *Imitations* translated by Robert Lowell. Copyright © 1958, 1959, 1960, 1961 by Robert Lowell. Reprinted by permission of Farrar, Straus and Giroux, Inc.

Edmund Clerihew Bentley. "John Stuart Mill" reprinted from *The Complete Clerihews of E. Clerihew Bentley* (1981) by permission of Oxford University Press.

John Berryman. "#14" from *The Dream Songs* by John Berryman. Copyright © 1959, 1962, 1963, 1964, 1965, 1966, 1967, 1968, 1969 by John Berryman. Reprinted by permission of Farrar, Straus and Giroux, Inc.

Elizabeth Bishop. "The Fish," "Five Flights Up," "Sestina," and "One Art" from *The Complete Poems, 1927–1979* by Elizabeth Bishop. Copyright © 1979, 1983 by Alice Helen Methfessel. Reprinted by permission of Farrar, Straus and Giroux, Inc.

Harold Bloom. "On 'Bright Star'" from *The Visionary Company* by Harold Bloom. Copyright © 1971 by Harold Bloom.

Robert Bly. "Snowfall in the Afternoon" reprinted from *Silence in the Snowy Fields,* Wesleyan University Press, 1962. Copyright © 1960 by Robert Bly; reprinted with his permission.

Louise Bogan. "Dark Summer" from *The Blue Estuaries* by Louise Bogan. Copyright © 1929, 1957, 1968 by Louise Bogan. "The Dragonfly" from *The Blue Estuaries* by Louise Bogan. Copyright © 1963 by Louise Bogan. Reprinted by permission of Farrar, Straus and Giroux, Inc.

Anne Bradstreet. "Before the Birth of One of Her Children" and "The Author to Her Book" reprinted by permission of the publisher from *The Works of Anne Bradstreet,* edited by Janine Hansley, Foreword by Adrienne Rich, Cambridge Massachusetts: Harvard University Press. Copyright © 1967 by the President and Fellows of Harvard College. All rights reserved.

Gwendolyn Brooks. "We Real Cool," "The Mother," and "The Bean Eaters" from *The World of Gwendolyn Brooks* (Harper & Row). Reprinted by permission of the author.

Michael Cadnum. "Cat Spy," copyright © by Michael Cadnum. First appeared in *Light Year '86.* Reprinted by permission of the author.

Tracy Chapman. "Fast Car" © 1988 SBK APRIL MUSIC INC. and PURPLE RABBIT MUSIC. All Rights Controlled and Administered by SBK APRIL MUSIC INC. All Rights Reserved. International Copyright Secured. Used by Permission.

Helen Chasin. "The Word *Plum*" from *Coming Close and Other Poems* by Helen Chasin. Copyright © 1968 by Yale University. Reprinted by permission of Yale University Press.

Amy Clampitt. "Nothing Stays Put." Reprinted by permission; © 1989 Amy Clampitt. Originally in *The New Yorker.*

Lucille Clifton. "For deLawd" from *Good Times* by Lucille Clifton. Copyright © 1969 by Lucille Clifton. Reprinted by permission of Random House, Inc.

Leonard Cohen. "Suzanne" by Leonard Cohen. Copyright © 1966 by Leonard Cohen. Used by permission of Leonard Cohen, 146 W. 75th St., New York, NY 10023.

Edmund Conti. "Pragmatist" from *Light Year '86.* Reprinted by permission of the author.

Herbert R. Coursen, Jr. "A Reading of 'Stopping by Woods on a Snowy Evening'" from "The Ghost of Christmas Past: 'Stopping By Woods on a Snowy Evening,'" *College English* 24 (December 1962). Copyright © 1962 by the National Council of Teachers of English. Reprinted by permission.

Adelaide Crapsey. "Triad" from *Verse* by Adelaide Crapsey. Copyright 1922 by Algernon S. Crapsey and renewed 1950 by the Adelaide Crapsey Foundation. Reprinted by permission of Alfred A. Knopf, Inc.

Robert Creeley. "Fathers" from *Memory Gardens.* Copyright © 1986 by Robert Creeley. Reprinted by permission of New Directions Publishing Corporation.

Sally Croft. "Home-Baked Bread" from *Light Year '86.* Reprinted by permission of the author.

Countee Cullen. "For a Lady I Know" and "Saturday's Child" reprinted by permission of GRM Associates, Inc., agents for the Estate of Ida M. Cullen, from the book *On These I Stand* by Countee Cullen. Copyright 1925 by Harper and Brothers; copyright renewed 1953 by Ida M. Cullen.

E. E. Cummings. "l(a" and "anyone lived in a pretty how town" reprinted form *Complete Poems, 1913–1962,* by E. E. Cummings, by permission of Liveright Publishing Corporation. Copyright © 1923, 1925, 1931, 1935, 1938, 1939, 1940. 1944, 1945, 1946, 1947, 1948, 1949, 1950, 1951, 1952, 1953, 1954, 1955, 1956, 1957, 1958, 1959, 1960, 1961, 1962 by the Trustees for the E. E. Cummings Trust. Copyright © 1961, 1963, 1968 by Marion Morehouse Cummings. "she being Brand," and "next to of course god america" are reprinted from *IS 5* by E. E. Cummings. Copyright © 1985 by the E. E. Cummings Trust. Copyright 1926 by Horace Liveright, copyright © 1954 by E. E. Cummings, copyright © 1985 by George James Firmage. Reprinted by permission of Liveright Publishing Corporation. "Buffalo Bill 's" and "in Just-" are reprinted from *Tulips & Chimneys* by E. E. Cummings. Copyright 1923, 1925 and renewed 1951, 1953 by E. E. Cummings. Copyright © 1973, 1976 by the Trustees for the

E. E. Cummings Trust, copyright © 1973, 1976 by George James Firmage. Reprinted by permission of Liveright Publishing Corporation. "On the Artist's Responsibility" reprinted by permission of the publishers from *i: six nonlectures* by E. E. Cummings. Cambridge, Mass.: Harvard University Press. Copyright 1953 by E. E. Cummings. Copyright © 1981 by the E. E. Cummings Trust.

Andrew P. Debicki. "New Criticism and Deconstructionism: Two Attitudes in Teaching Poetry" in *Writing and Reading Differently: Deconstruction and the Teaching of Composition and Literature,* edited by G. Douglas Atkins and Michael L. Johnson. Copyright © 1985 by The University Press of Kansas. Reprinted by permission of the University Press of Kansas.

Peter De Vries. "To His Importunate Mistress," copyright © 1986 by Peter De Vries. This poem first appeared in *The New Yorker.* Reprinted by permission of Watkins/Loomis Agency Inc.

James Dickey. "Cherrylog Road," copyright © 1963 by James Dickey. Reprinted from *Collected Poems.* "Cherrylog Road" first appeared in *The New Yorker.* Reprinted by permission of Wesleyan University Press.

Emily Dickinson. "A narrow Fellow in the grass," "The Brain Is Wider than the Sky," "Because I could not stop for Death," "I heard a Fly buzz—when I died," "I Know that He exists," "It dropped so low—in my Regard," "Much Madness is divinest Sense," "Success is counted sweetest," "Wild Nights—Wild Nights!" "A Bird came down the Walk," "Lightly stepped a yellow star," "Portraits are to daily faces," "The thought beneath so slight a film," "Presentiment—is that long Shadow—on the lawn," "If I shouldn't be alive," "If I can stop one Heart from breaking," "To make a prairie it takes a clover and one bee," "There's a certain Slant of light," and "Faith is a fine invention" reprinted by permission of the publishers and Trustees of Amherst College from *The Poems of Emily Dickinson,* edited by Thomas H. Johnson. Cambridge, Mass.: The Belknap Press of Harvard University Press. Copyright 1951, © 1955, 1979, 1983 by the President and Fellows of Harvard College. Also from *The Complete Poems of Emily Dickinson,* edited by Thomas H. Johnson. Copyright 1914, 1942 by Martha Dickinson Bianchi. Copyright © renewed 1960 by Mary L. Hampson. Reprinted by permission of Little, Brown and Company.

H. D. (Hilda Doolittle). "Garden II" (Heat) and "Leda" from *H. D.: Collected Poems 1912–1944.* Copyright © 1982 by the Estate of Hilda Doolittle. Reprinted by permission of New Directions Publishing Corporation.

Rita Dove. "Parsley" reprinted from *Museum* by permission of Carnegie-Mellon University Press. © 1983 by Rita Dove.

Bernard Duyfhuizen. " 'To His Coy Mistress': On How a Female Might Respond" from "Textual Harassment of Marvell's Coy Mistress the Institutionalization of Masculine Criticism," *College English,* April 1988. Copyright 1988 by the National Council of Teachers of English. Reprinted with permission.

Richard Eberhart. "The Groundhog" from *Collected Poems 1930–1976* by Richard Eberhart. Copyright © 1960, 1976 by Richard Eberhart. Reprinted by permission of Oxford University Press, Inc.

T. S. Eliot. "Journey of the Magi" and "The Love Song of J. Alfred Prufrock" from *Collected Poems 1909–1962* by T. S. Eliot, copyright 1936 by Harcourt Brace Jovanovich, Inc. Copyright © 1963, 1964 by T. S. Eliot. Reprinted by permission of Harcourt Brace Jovanovich, Inc. and Faber and Faber Ltd.

Ruth Fainlight. "Flower Feet." Reprinted by permission. © 1989 by Ruth Fainlight. Originally published in *The New Yorker.*

Blanche Farley. "The Lover Not Taken" from *Light Year '85.* Reprinted by permission of the author.

Kenneth Fearing. "AD" from *New and Collected Poems* (Indiana University Press, 1956). Reprinted by permission of the Estate of Kenneth Fearing.

Lawrence Ferlinghetti. "Constantly risking absurdity" from *A Coney Island of the Mind.* Copyright © 1958 by Lawrence Ferlinghetti. Reprinted by permission of New Directions Publishing Corporation.

Carolyn Forché. "The Colonel" from *The Country Between Us.* Copyright © 1980 by Carolyn Forché. Reprinted by permission of Harper & Row Publishers, Inc.

Robert Francis. "Catch" and "Pitcher," copyright © 1950, 1953 by Robert Francis. Reprinted from *The Orb Weaver* by permission of Wesleyan University Press. "Excellence" and "Glass" reprinted from *Robert Francis: Collected Poems, 1936–1976* (Amherst: University of Massachusetts Press, 1976), copyright © 1941, 1949, 1972 by Robert Francis. "On 'Hard Poetry' " reprinted from *The Satirical Rogue on Poetry,* by Robert Francis (Amherst: University of Massachusetts Press, 1968), copyright © 1968 by Robert Francis.

Robert Frost. "The Road Not Taken," "The Pasture," "Mending Wall," "Home Burial," "After Apple-Picking," "Birches," "Out, Out—" "Fire and Ice," "Dust of Snow," "Stopping by Woods on a Snowy Evening," "The Need of Being Versed in Country Things," "Once by the Pacific," "Desert Places," "Design," "Neither out Far Nor in Deep," "Provide Provide," "The Silken Tent," "Departmental," "Acquainted with the Night," and "The Gift Outright" from *The Poetry of Robert Frost,* edited by Edward Connery Lathem. Copyright © 1969 by Holt, Rinehart and Winston. Copyright © 1962 by Robert Frost. Copyright © 1975 by Lesley Frost Ballantine. Reprinted by permission of Henry Holt and Company. "In White" from *The Dimensions of Robert Frost* by Reginald L. Cook. Copyright © 1958 by Reginald L. Cook. Reprinted by permission of Henry Holt and Company. "On the Way to Read a Poem" from "Poetry and School" by Robert Frost in *The Atlantic Monthly,* June 1951. Reprinted by permission of Alfred C. Edwards. "On the Living Part of a Poem" reprinted by permission of New York University Press from *A Swinger of Birches: A Portrait of Robert Frost* by Sidney Cox. Copyright © 1957 by New York University Press, Inc. "Frost on the Figure a Poem Makes" from *Selected Prose of Robert Frost* edited by Hyde Cox and Edward Connery Lathem. Copyright 1939, © 1967 by Holt, Rinehart and Winston, Inc. Reprinted by arrangement with Henry Holt and Company, Inc.

Alice Fulton. "On the Validity of Free Verse" from *Ecstatic Occasions, Expedient Forms,* David Lehman, ed. Reprinted by permission of the author.

Jonathan Galassi. "Our Wives" from *Morning Run.* Copyright © 1988 by Jonathan Galassi. Reprinted by permission of the author.

Federico García Lorca. "Somnabule Ballad" from *The Selected Poems of Federico García Lorca.* Copyright 1955 by New Directions Publishing Corporation. Translated by Stephen Spender and J. L. Gili. Reprinted by permission of New Directions Publishing Corporation.

Allen Ginsberg. "A Supermarket in California," copyright © 1955 by Allen Ginsberg, and "America," copyright © 1956, 1959 by Allen Ginsberg from *Collected Poems 1947–1980.* Reprinted by permission of Harper & Row, Publishers, Inc.

Nikki Giovanni. "Poetry" from *The Women and the Men.* Copyright © 1970, 1975 by Nikki Giovanni. "Nikki-Rossa" from *Black Feeling, Black Talk, Black Judgement* by Nikki Giovanni. Copyright © 1968–1970 by Nikki Giovanni. Reprinted by permission of William Morrow & Company.

Judy Grahn. "She Who Bears It" from *The Work of the Common Woman.* Reprinted by permission of The Crossing Press.

Robert Graves. "Down Wanton Down" from *Collected Poems 1975* by Robert Graves. Reprinted by permission of Oxford University Press, Inc. and A. P. Watt Ltd. on behalf of the Executors of the Estate of Robert Graves.

Donald J. Greiner, "An Analysis of 'After Apple-Picking' " from "The Indispensable Robert Frost" in *Critical Essays on Robert Frost,* edited by Philip L. Gerber (1982). Reprinted by permission of Twayne Publishers (a division of G. K. Hall & Co., Boston.)

Donald Hall. "My Son, My Executioner" from *The Alligator Bride,* copyright © by Donald Hall. Reprinted by permission of the author. "To a Waterfowl" from *The Town of Hill* by Donald Hall. Copyright © 1975 by Donald Hall. Reprinted by permission of David R. Godine, Publisher, Boston.

Michael S. Harper. "The Militance of a Photograph in the Passbook of a Bantu Under Detention" from *Healing Song for the Inner Ear,* copyright 1985 by Michael S. Harper. Reprinted by permission of the University of Illinois Press.

William Hathaway. "Oh, Oh" from *Light Year '86.* This poem was originally published in the *Cincinnati Poetry Review.* Reprinted by permission of the author.

Robert Hayden. "Those Winter Sundays" is reprinted from *Angle of Ascent, New and Selected Poems,* by Robert Hayden, by permission of Liveright Publishing Corporation. Copyright © 1975, 1972, 1970, 1966 by Robert Hayden.

Seamus Heaney. "Digging" and "Mid-Term Break" from *Poems, 1965–1975* by Seamus Heaney. Copyright © 1966, 1969, 1972, 1975, 1980 by Seamus Heaney. Reprinted by permission of Farrar, Straus and Giroux, Inc.

Anthony Hecht. "The Dover Bitch" from *The Hard Hours.* Copyright © 1967 by Anthony E. Hecht. Reprinted with the permission of the author.

Conrad Hilberry. "Tongue," reprinted from *The Moon Seen as a Slice of Pineapple* by Conrad Hilberry, © 1984 by Conrad Hilberry. Reprinted by permission of the University of Georgia Press. "The Frying Pan" first appeared in *Field* 19 (Fall 1978). Reprinted by permission of Oberlin College.

Edward Hirsch. "Fast Break" from *Wild Gratitude* by Edward Hirsch. Copyright © 1985 by Edward Hirsch. Reprinted by permission of Alfred A. Knopf, Inc.

M. Carl Holman. "Mr. Z." Reprinted by permission of Mariella A. Holman.

A. E. Housman. "Is my team ploughing," "Terence, this is stupid stuff," "Eight O'Clock," "To an Athlete Dying Young," "When I was one-and-twenty," and "Loveliest of trees, the cherry now" from "A Shropshire Lad"—Authorized Edition—from *The Collected Poems of A. E. Housman.* Copyright © 1965 by Holt, Rinehart and Winston, Inc. Reprinted by permission of Henry Holt and Company.

Langston Hughes. "Harlem (A Dream Deferred)," copyright 1951 by Langston Hughes. Reprinted from *The Panther and the Lash: Poems of Our Times* by Langston Hughes by permission of Alfred A. Knopf, Inc. "Ballad of the Landlord" from *Montage of a Dream Deferred.* Copyright 1951 by Langston Hughes. Copyright renewed 1979 by George Houston Bass. Reprinted by permission of Harold Ober Associates Incorporated.

Ted Hughes. "The Thought-Fox" from *Selected Poems* by Ted Hughes. Copyright © 1957 by Ted Hughes. Reprinted by permission of Harper & Row, Publishers, Inc.

Paul Humphrey. "Blow" from *Light Year '86.* Reprinted by permission of the author.

Randall Jarrell. "The Death of the Ball Turrett Gunner" from *The Complete Poems* by Randall Jarrell. Copyright 1945, copyright renewed © 1972 by Mrs. Randall Jarrell. Reprinted by permission of Farrar, Straus and Giroux, Inc. "The Woman At the Washington Zoo" from *The Woman at the Washington Zoo.* Copyright © 1960 Randall Jarrell. Reprinted with the permission of Atheneum Publishers, an imprint of Macmillan Publishing Company.

Donald Justice. "Order in the Streets" from *Looser Weepers.* Reprinted by permission of the author.

John Keats. Excerpts from *The Letters of John Keats,* Hyder E. Rollins, ed. "On the Truth of the Imagination," "On Unobtrusive Poetry," "On the Vale of Soul-Making," and "Keats's Poetic Principles" © 1958 by the President and Fellows of Harvard College; © 1986 by Herschel C. Baker.

X. J. Kennedy. "In a Prominent Bar in Secaucus One Day" from *Cross Ties,* © 1985 by X. J. Kennedy. Reprinted by permission of the University of Georgia Press.

Jane Kenyon. "Thinking of Madame Bovary" from *The Boat of Quiet Hours.* Copyright © 1986 by Jane Kenyon. Reprinted by permission of Graywolf Press. This poem first appeared in *The New Yorker.*

Galway Kinnell. "Blackberry Eating" and "After Making Love" from *Mortal Acts, Mortal Words* by Galway Kinnell. Copyright © 1980 by Galway Kinnell. Reprinted by permission of Houghton Mifflin Company. Excerpt from "For Robert Frost" from *Flower Herding on Mt. Monadnock* by Galway Kinnell. Copyright © 1964 by Galway Kinnell. Reprinted by permission of Houghton Mifflin Company. "The Female and Male Principles of Poetry," from "Being with Reality: An Interview with Galway Kinnell," *Columbia Magazine of Poetry and Prose,* 14 (1989). Reprinted by permission of Galway Kinnell.

Etheridge Knight. "Eastern Guard Tower" from *Poems from Prison* by Etheridge Knight. Copyright © 1968 by Etheridge Knight (Broadside Press). "A Watts Mother Mourns While Boiling Beans" from *Belly Song and Other Poems* by Etheridge Knight. Copyright © 1973. (Broadside Press).

Ted Kooser. "Selecting a Reader" reprinted from *Sure Signs: New and Selected Poems* by Ted Kooser by permission of the University of Pittsburgh Press. © 1980 by Ted Kooser.

Maxine Kumin. "Woodchucks" from *Our Ground Time Here Will Be Brief* by Maxine Kumin. Copyright © 1971 by Maxine Kumin. Reprinted by permission of Viking Penguin Inc.

Philip Larkin. "A Study of Reading Habits" from *The Whitsun Weddings* by Philip Larkin. Reprinted by permission of Faber and Faber Ltd. "Church Going" and "Toads" from *The Less Deceived* by Philip Larkin, published by the Marvell Press. Reprinted by permission.

Richmond Lattimore. "The Crabs" from *Poems from Three Decades* (Scribner's). Reprinted by permission of Mrs. Richmond Lattimore.

D. H. Lawrence. "Snake" from *The Complete Poems of D. H. Lawrence.* Collected and edited by Vivian de Sola Pinto and F. Warren Roberts. Copyright © 1964, 1971 by Angelo Ravagli and C. M. Weekley, Executors of the Estate of Frieda Lawrence Ravagli. Reprinted by permission of Viking Penguin, a division of Penguin Books USA, Inc.

David Lenson. "On the Contemporary Use of Rhyme" from *The Chronicle of Higher Education,* February 24, 1988. Reprinted by permission of the author.

Denise Levertov. "O Taste and See" and "The Ache of Marriage" from *Poems; 1960–1967.* Copyright © 1964 by Denise Levertov Goodman. "Gathered at the River" from *Oblique Prayers.* Copyright © 1984 by Denise Levertov. All of these reprinted by permission of New Directions Publishing Corporation. "On 'Gathered at the River' " from " 'Gathered at the River': Background and Form" in *Singular Voices: American Poetry Today,* edited by Stephen Berg. Reprinted by permission of Denise Levertov.

Li Ho. "A Beautiful Girl Combs Her Hair" from *Four T'ang Poets: Field Translation Series #4.* Copyright © Oberlin College Press, 1980. Reprinted by permission.

Audre Lorde. "Hanging Fire" is reprinted from *The Black Unicorn: Poems of Audre Lorde,* copyright © 1978 by Audre Lorde. Reprinted by permission of W. W. Norton & Company, Inc. Permission to use "Poems Are Not Luxuries" is granted by Audre Lorde.

Robert Lowell. "Skunk Hour" from *Life Studies* by Robert Lowell. Copyright © 1956, 1959 by Robert Lowell. Renewal copyright © 1987 by Harriet Lowell. Reprinted by permission of Farrar, Straus and Giroux, Inc. "Mr. Edwards and the Spider" from *Lord Weary's Castle,* copyright 1946, 1974 by Robert Lowell. Reprinted by permission of Harcourt, Brace Jovanovich, Inc.

David McCord. "Epitaph on a Waiter" from *Odds without Ends.* Reprinted by permission of the author.

Michael McFee. "In Medias Res" from *Light Year '86.* Reprinted by permission of the author.

Claude McKay. "America" from *Selected Poems of Claude McKay.* Copyright © 1981 and reprinted with the permission of Twayne Publishers, a division of G. K. Hall & Co., Boston.

Archibald MacLeish. "Ars Poetica" and "You, Andrew Marvell" from *New and Collected Poems 1917–1976* by Archibald MacLeish. Copyright © 1985 by Archibald MacLeish. Reprinted by permission of Houghton Mifflin Company.

Elaine Magarrell. "The Joy of Cooking" from *Sometime the Cow Kick Your Head, Light Year 88/89.* Reprinted by permission of the author.

Peter Meinke. "ABC of Aerobics," © 1987 Peter Meinke from *Night Watch on the Chesapeake,* by permission of University of Pittsburgh Press.

James Merrill. "Topics," #1: "Casual Wear." Reprinted with permission of Atheneum Publishers, an imprint of Macmillan Publishing Company, from *Late Settings* by James Merrill. Copyright © 1985 by James Merrill.

Edna St. Vincent Millay. "Never May the Fruit Be Plucked" by Edna St. Vincent Millay. From *Collected Poems,* Harper & Row. Copyright 1923, 1951 by Edna St. Vincent Millay and Norma Millay Ellis. "I too beneath your moon, almighty Sex" and Sonnet XLII of *Fatal Interview* by Edna St. Vincent Millay. From *Collected Sonnets,* Revised and Expanded Edition, Harper & Row, 1988. Copyright © 1931, 1939, 1958, 1967 by Edna St. Vincent Millay and Norma Millay Ellis. All poems reprinted by permission of Elizabeth Barnett, Literary Executor.

Czeslaw Milosz. "A Poor Christian Looks at the Ghetto" copyright © 1965 by Czeslaw Milosz. From *Postwar Polish Poetry* by Czeslaw Milosz. Used by permission of Doubleday, a division of Bantam, Doubleday, Dell Publishing Group, Inc.

Felix Mnthali. "The Stranglehold of English Lit." from *The Penguin Book of Modern African Poetry,* Third Edition, edited by Gerald Moore and Ulli Beier.

Janice Townley Moore. "To a Wasp" from *Light Year '85.* Reprinted by permission of the author.

Marianne Moore. "Poetry" from *Collected Poems* by Marianne Moore. Copyright 1935 by Marinane Moore, renewed 1963 by Marianne Moore and T. S. Eliot. Reprinted with permission of Macmillan Publishing Company.

Robert Morgan. "Mountain Graveyard" reprinted in *Truck* by permission of the author. "On the Shape of a Poem" (*Epoch* Fall/Winter, 1983) reprinted by permission of the author.

Ogden Nash. "Very Like a Whale" from *Verses from 1929 On* by Ogden Nash. Copyright 1934 by Ogden Nash. First appeared in the *Saturday Evening Post.* Reprinted by permission of Little, Brown and Company.

Howard Nemerov. "Life Cycle of Common Man" from *The Collected Poems of Howard Nemerov* (University of Chicago Press, 1977). Reprinted by permission of the author.

Pablo Neruda. "Sweetness, Always" from *Extravagaria* by Pablo Neruda, translated by Alastair Reid. English translation copyright © 1969, 1970, 1972, 1974 by Alastair Reid. Reprinted by permission of Farrar, Straus and Giroux, Inc.

John Frederick Nims. "Love Poem" from *The Iron Pastoral.* Copyright © 1947 by John Frederick Nims. New York: William Sloane Associates.

Frank O'Hara. "Ave Maria" from *The Collected Poems of Frank O'Hara.*

Sharon Olds. "Sex Without Love" Copyright © 1984 by Sharon Olds. "The Elder Sister" Copyright © 1983 by Sharon Olds. Both poems from *The Dead and the Living* by Sharon Olds. Reprinted by permission of Alfred A. Knopf, Inc.

Mary Oliver. "The Black Snake" from *Twelve Moons: Poems* by Mary Oliver. Copyright © 1979 by Mary Oliver. Reprinted by permission of Little, Brown and Company.

Simon J. Ortiz. "When It Was Taking Place" from *From Sand Creek.*

Wilfred Owen. "Anthem for Doomed Youth" and "Dulce et Decorum Est" from *Collected Poems,* edited by C. Day Lewis. Copyright © 1963 by Chatto & Windus, Ltd. Reprinted by permission of New Directions Publishing Corporation.

Dorothy Parker. "One Perfect Rose," *The Portable Dorothy Parker* by Dorothy Parker. Copyright 1926, renewed 1954 by Dorothy Parker. All rights reserved. Reprinted by permission of Viking Penguin, a division of Penguin Books USA, Inc.

Linda Pastan. "Marks" is reprinted from *The Five Stages of Grief: Poems by Linda Pastan,* copyright © 1978 by Linda Pastan. Reprinted by permission of W. W. Norton & Company, Inc.

Andrea Paterson, "Because I Could Not Dump" from *The Brand-X Anthology of Poetry,* edited by William Zaranka (Apple Wood Books). Reprinted by permission.

Octavio Paz. "The Street" from *Early Poems 1935–1955.* Reprinted by permission of Indiana University Press.

Laurence Perrine. "The limerick's never averse" from *Light Year '86.* Reprinted by permission of the author.

Robert Phillips. "Running on Empty," © Robert Phillips, 1978. *Running on Empty: The Poems of Robert Phillips,* © copyright 1981 Robert Phillips, renewed 1986. Reprinted by permission of Weiser & Weiser.

Marge Piercy. "The Secretary Chant" and "A Work of Artifice" Copyright © 1969 by Marge Piercy. Reprinted from *Circles on the Water* by Marge Piercy, by permission of Alfred A. Knopf, Inc.

Sylvia Plath. "Daddy," "Elm," and "Mirror," copyright © 1963 by Ted Hughes. "Metaphors," copyright © 1960 by Ted Hughes. "Morning Song," copyright © 1961 by Ted Hughes. All poems from *The Collected Poems of Sylvia Plath,* edited by Ted Hughes. Reprinted by permission of Harper & Row, Publishers, Inc. "On 'Headline Poetry' " from "Context," *London Magazine,* February, 1962. Reprinted by permission.

Ezra Pound. "In a Station of the Metro," "River-Merchant's Wife," and "Portrait d'une Femme" from *Personae.* Copyright 1926 by Ezra Pound. "On Free Verse" from *The Literary Essays of Ezra Pound.* Copyright 1935 by Ezra Pound. Reprinted by permission of New Directions Publishing Corporation.

Paul Ramsey. "On Industrialism" from *Light Year '85.* Reprinted by permission of the author.

Dudley Randall. "The Ballad of Birmingham from *Poem Counter Poem* by Danner and Randall (Broadside Press).

John Crowe Ransom. "Bells for John Whiteside's Daughter," copyright 1924 and renewed 1952 by John Crowe Ransom. Reprinted from *Selected Poems,* Third Edition, Revised and Enlarged, by John Crowe Ransom by permission of Alfred A. Knopf, Inc.

Henry Reed. "Naming of Parts" from *A Map of Verona.* Reprinted by permission of the Estate of Henry Reed.

John Repp. "Cursing the Hole in the Screen, Wondering at the Romance Some Find in Summer." Reprinted by permission of the author.

Adrienne Rich. "Diving into the Wreck," "Rape," and "Living in Sin" are reprinted from *The Fact of a Doorframe: Poems Selected and New, 1950–1984* by Adrienne Rich. Copyright © 1984 by Adrienne Rich. Copyright © 1975, 1978 by W. W. Norton & Company, Inc., copyright © 1981 by Adrienne Rich. Reprinted by permission of W. W. Norton & Company, Inc.

Ranier Maria Rilke. "The Panther" from *The Selected Poetry of Ranier Maria Rilke* edited and translated by Stephen Mitchell. Copyright © 1982 by Stephen Mitchell. Reprinted by permission of Random House, Inc.

Alberto Ríos. "Seniors" from *Five Indiscretions.* Reprinted by permission of the author.

Edwin Arlington Robinson. "Mr. Flood's Party" from *Collected Poems.* Copyright 1921 by Edwin Arlington Robinson, renewed 1949 by Ruth Nivison. "New England" from *Collected Poems.* Copyright 1925 by Edwin Arlington Robinson, renewed 1953 by Ruth Nivison and Barbara R. Holt. Reprinted with permission of Macmillan Publishing Company.

Theodore Roethke. "I Knew a Woman," copyright 1954 by Theodore Roethke. "The Waking," copyright 1953 by Theodore Roethke. "Root Cellar," copyright 1943 by Modern Poetry Association, Inc. "My Papa's Waltz," copyright 1942 by Hearst Magazine, Inc. All from *The Collected Poems of Theodore Roethke.* Reprinted by permission of Doubleday, a division of Bantam, Doubleday, Dell Publishing Group, Inc.

Pedro Salinas. "Presagios" from *The Complete Poems of Pedro Salinas* Reprinted by permission of Mercedes Casanovas, Barcelona.

Sappho. "With his venom . . ." from *Sappho: A New Translation,* translated/edited by Mary Barnard © 1958, 1984 by Mary Barnard. Reprinted by permission of the University of California Press.

Delmore Schwartz. "The True Blue American" from *Selected Poems: Summer Knowledge.* Copyright © 1959 by Delmore Schwartz. Reprinted by permission of New Directions Publishing Corporation.

John R. Searle. "Figuring Out Metaphors" from *Expression and Meaning.* Reprinted by permission of Cambridge University Press.

Anne Sexton. "The Kiss" from *Love Poems* by Anne Sexton. Copyright © 1967, 1968, 1969 by Anne Sexton. "Lobster" from *45 Mercy Street* by Anne Sexton. Copyright © 1976 by Linda Gray Sexton and Loring Conant, Jr. Reprinted by permission of Houghton Mifflin Company.

Leslie Marmon Silko. "Deer Song" from *Storyteller* by Leslie Marmon Silko. Reprinted by permission of Seaver Books, New York, NY 1981.

David R. Slavitt. "Titanic" reprinted by permission of Louisiana State University Press from *Big Nose* by David R. Slavitt. Copyright © 1980, 1981, and 1983 by David R. Slavitt.

Ernest Slyman. "Lightning Bugs" from *Sometime the Cow Kick Your Head, Light Year 88/89.* Reprinted by permission of the author.

Stevie Smith. "How Cruel is the Story of Eve" from Stevie Smith, *Collected Poems of Stevie Smith.* Copyright © 1972 by Stevie Smith. Reprinted by permission of New Directions Publishing Corporation.

W. D. Snodgrass. "April Inventory," copyright © 1957 by W. D. Snodgrass. Reprinted from *Heart's Needle* by W. D. Snodgrass by permission of Alfred A. Knopf, Inc. "Lobsters in the Window" copyright © 1967 by W. D. Snodgrass. Reprinted from *W. D. Snodgrass: Selected Poems 1957–1987.* Copyright © 1987 by W. D. Snodgrass. Reprinted by permission of Soho Press, Inc.

Gary Snyder. "Hitch Haiku" from *The Back Country.* Copyright © 1967 by Gary Snyder. Reprinted by permission of New Directions Publishing Corporation. "Hay for the Horses" from *Riprap and Cold Mountain Poems* copyright © Gary Snyder 1965. Reprinted by permission of the author.

Cathy Song. "The White Porch" from *Picture Bride.* Copyright © 1983 by Cathy Song. Foreword Copyright © 1983 by Yale University. Reprinted by permission of Yale University Press.

William Stafford. "A Way of Writing" from *Field* 2 (Spring 1970). Reprinted by permission of *Field.* "Traveling through the Dark" from *Stories That Could Be True* by William Stafford. Copyright © 1960 by William Stafford. Reprinted by permission of Harper & Row Publishers, Inc.

George Starbuck. "Japanese Fish" from *Light Year '86.* Reprinted by permission of the author.

Wallace Stevens. "Sunday Morning," "Thirteen Ways of Looking at a Blackbird," "The Emperor of Ice-Cream," and "Disillusionment of Ten O'Clock," copyright 1923 and renewed 1951 by Wallace Stevens. Reprinted from *The Collected Poems of Wallace Stevens* by permission of Alfred A. Knopf, Inc.

Jack Stillinger, "On 'The Eve of St. Agnes'" from "The Hoodwinking of Madeline: Skepticism in the Eve of St. Agnes," *Studies in Philology*, 58, (1961). Copyright © 1961 by University of North Carolina Press. Reprinted by permission.

Mark Strand. "Pot Roast" from *Selected Poems*. Copyright © 1980 Mark Strand. Reprinted with the permission of Atheneum Publishers, an imprint of Macmillan Publishing Company.

May Swenson. "The Secret in the Cat" by May Swenson is reprinted by permission of the author, copyright © 1964 by May Swenson in *Harper's* Magazine. "A Nosty Fright" by May Swenson is reprinted by permission of the author, copyright © 1983 by May Swenson; first appeared in *Light Year '84*.

Shinkichi Takahashi. "Explosion" from *The Penguin Book of Zen Poetry*, edited and translated by Lucien Stryk and Takashi Ikemoto. Reprinted by permission of Lucien Stryk.

Dylan Thomas. "Do not go gentle into that good night," "Fern Hill," and "The Hand That Signed the Paper" from *Poems of Dylan Thomas*. Copyright 1939 by New Directions Publishing Corporation, 1945 by the Trustees for the Copyrights of Dylan Thomas, 1952 by Dylan Thomas. Reprinted by permission of New Directions Publishing Corporation. "On the Words in Poetry" from *Early Prose Writings*. Copyright © 1964 by New Directions Publishing Corporation. Reprinted by permission of New Directions Publishing Corporation.

Jean Toomer. "Reapers" is reprinted from *Cane* by Jean Toomer, copyright 1923 by Boni & Liveright. Copyright renewed 1951 by Jean Toomer. Reprinted by permission of Liveright Publishing Corporation.

Lionel Trilling. "On Frost as a Terrifying Poet" from *Partisan Review*, Volume 26, Summer 1959. Reprinted by permission of Diana Trilling.

John Updike. "Player Piano," copyright © 1954, 1957, 1982 by John Updike. Reprinted from *The Carpentered Hen and Other Tame Creatures* by John Updike. "Dog's Death" Copyright © 1969 by John Updike. Reprinted from *Midpoint and Other Poems* by John Updike. Both poems reprinted by permission of Alfred A. Knopf, Inc.

Robert Wallace. "The Double Play" © 1961 by Robert Wallace from *Views of a Ferris Wheel*. Reprinted by permission of the author.

Richard Wilbur. "Sleepless at Crown Point" from *The Mind Reader and Other Poems*. Copyright © 1973 by Richard Wilbur. "Love Calls Us to the Things of This World" from *Things of This World*, copyright 1956, 1984 by Richard Wilbur. "A Simile for Her Smile" and "The Death of a Toad" from *Ceremony and Other Poems*, copyright 1950, 1978 by Richard Wilbur. "A Late Aubade," copyright © 1968 by Richard Wilbur from *Walking to Sleep*. "Praise in Summer" from *The Beautiful Changes* by Richard Wilbur, copyright © 1947 and renewed 1975 by Richard Wilbur. The poems reprinted by permission of Harcourt Brace Jovanovich, Inc.

William Carlos Williams. "The Red Wheelbarrow," "Spring and All," "Poem," and "This Is Just to Say" from *Collected Earlier Poems*. Copyright 1938 by New Directions Publishing Corporation. "The Dance" from *Collected Later Poems*. Copyright 1944 by William Carlos Williams. Reprinted by permission of New Directions Publishing Corporation.

James Wright. "Lying in a Hammock at William Duffy's Farm in Pine Island, Minnesota," copyright © 1961 by James Wright. Reprinted from *The Branch Will Not Break* by permission of Wesleyan University Press.

William Butler Yeats. "Crazy Jane Talks with the Bishop" reprinted with permission of Macmillan Publishing Company from *Collected Poems* by W. B. Yeats. Copyright 1933 by Macmillan Publishing Company, renewed 1961 by Bertha Georgie Yeats. "Leda and the Swan" and "Sailing to Byzantium," reprinted with permission of Macmillan Publishing Company from *Collected Poems* by W. B. Yeats. Copyright 1928 by Macmillan Publishing Company, renewed 1956 by Georgie Yeats. "The Second Coming" reprinted with permission of Macmillan Publishing Company from *Collected Poems* by W. B. Yeats. Copyright 1924 by Macmillan Publishing Company, renewed 1952 by Bertha Georgie Yeats. "Adam's Curse," "That the Night Come," and "The Lake Isle of Innisfree" from *Collected Poems of W. B. Yeats* (New York: Macmillan, 1956).

DRAMA

Jane Adamson. "On Desdemona's Role in *Othello*" from *Othello as Tragedy: Some Problems of Judgment and Feeling*. Reprinted by permission of Cambridge University Press.

Jean Anouilh. From *Antigone*, translated by Lewis Galantière. Copyright 1946 by Random House Inc. and renewed 1974 by Lewis Galantière. Reprinted by permission of Random House Inc.

Aristotle. Reprinted from *Aristotle's Poetics*, translated by James Hutton, by permission of W. W. Norton & Company, Inc. Copyright © 1982 by W. W. Norton & Company, Inc.

Samuel Beckett. *Krapp's Last Tape*. Copyright © 1957 by Samuel Beckett. Copyright © 1958, 1959, 1960, 1986 by Grove Press, Inc.

Eric Bentley. Excerpted from *Life of the Drama*. Copyright © 1964 Eric Bentley. Reprinted with the permission of Antheneum Publishers, an imprint of Macmillan Publishing Company.

Richard Bernstein. "The News Source for *M. Butterfly*," from "France Jails 2 in Odd Case of Espionage" by Richard Bernstein, May 11, 1986. Copyright © 1950/86 by The New York Times Company. Reprinted by permission.

Kathleen Betsko, Rachel Koenig, and Emily Mann, "Interview with Caryl Churchill" from *Interviews with Contemporary Women Playwrights*, copyright © 1987 by Kathleen Betsko, Rachel Koenig and Emily Mann. Reprinted by permission of William Morrow & Co.

Peter Brook. "On Chekhov's 'Hypervital' Characters" from *The Shifting Point* by Peter Brook. Copyright © 1987 by Peter Brook. Reprinted by permission of Harper and Row Publishers, Inc.

Cagney & Lacey excerpt. "You Call This Plainclothes?" reprinted with permission of Orion TV Productions. Written by Barbara Avedon and Barbara Corday. Adapted by Barney Rosenzweig.

Caryl Churchill. *Top Girls* by Caryl Churchill. First published by Methuen London. Copyright © 1982, 1984 by Caryl Churchill. Reprinted by kind courtesy of Methuen Drama.

Martin Esslin. From *The Theatre of the Absurd*. Copyright © 1961 by Martin Esslin. Reprinted by permission of Doubleday, a division of Bantam, Doubleday, Dell Publishing Group, Inc.

Helen Gardner. "On Freedom in *Hamlet* and *Othello*" From "The Noble Moor" by Helen Gardner, by permission of the British Academy. *Proceedings of the British Academy*, Volume XLI, 1955.

James Gibb. "Ritual Sacrifice in *The Strong Breed*" from *Wole Soyinka*, Grove Press, 1986.

Susan Glaspell. *Trifles* by Susan Glaspell Copyright, 1951 by Walter H. Baker Company. Text Revised, Prompt Book Added and New Material. For all production rights on use of *Trifles*, contact Baker's Plays, Boston, MA 02111. Excerpt from "A Jury of Her Peers" by Susan Glaspell reprinted by permission of the Estate of Susan Glaspell.

Karen S. Henry. "The Play Within the Play in *Hamlet*" from *The Shattering of Resemblance: The Mirror in Shakespeare*, Dissertation. Tufts University, Copyright © 1989 by Karen S. Henry. Reprinted by permission.

David Henry Hwang. From *M. Butterfly* by David Henry Hwang. Copyright © 1986 by David Henry Hwang. Reprinted by arrangement with New American Library, a Division of Penguin Books USA, Inc.

Henrik Ibsen. *A Doll's House*, Michael Meyer, translator, from *Ghosts and Three Other Plays* (1966). Copyright © 1966 by Michael Meyer. Reprinted by permission of Harold Ober Associates Incorporated. This play is fully protected, in whole, in part or in any form under the copyright laws of the United States of America, the British Empire including the Dominion of Canada, and all other countries of the Copyright Union, and is subject to royalty. All rights including motion picture, radio, television, recitation, public reading, are strictly reserved. For professional rights and amateur rights, all inquiries should be addressed to the author's agent, Robert A. Freedman Dramatic Agency, Inc., 1501 Broadway, New York, N.Y. 10036.

Jan Kott. "On Producing *Hamlet*" excerpt from "Hamlet of the Mid-Century" from *Shakespeare Our Contemporary* by Jan Kott, translated by Boleslaw Taborski. Copyright © 1964 by Panstwowe Wydawnictiwo Naukowe. Reprinted by permission of the publisher and Doubleday, a division of Bantam, Doubleday, Dell Publishing Group.

David Mamet. "Notes on *The Cherry Orchard*" from *The Cherry Orchard* by Anton Chekhov, adapted by David Mamet. Copyright © 1985 by David Mamet. Reprinted by permission of Grove Weidenfeld.

Jane Martin. *Twirler.* Copyright © 1980 by Alexander Speer as Trustee. All rights reserved. *CAUTION:* Professionals and amateurs are hereby warned that *Twirler,* being fully protected under the Copyright Laws of the United States of America, the British Commonwealth, including the Dominion of Canada, and all other countries of the International Copyright Union and the Universal Copyright Convention, is subject to royalty. All rights, including professional, amateur, motion picture, recitation, lecturing, public reading, radio and television broadcasting, and the rights of translation into foreign languages, are strictly reserved. Particular emphasis is laid on the question of readings, permission for which must be secured from the author's agents in writing. All inquiries concerning rights should be addressed to the author's representatives, Samuel French, Inc., 45 West 25th Street, New York, N.Y. 10010.

Arthur Miller. *Death of a Salesman* copyright 1949, renewed © 1977 by Arthur Miller. Reprinted by permission of Viking Penguin Inc. This play in its printed form is designed for the reading public only. All dramatic rights in it are fully protected by copyright, and no public or private performance — professional or amateur — may be given without the written permission of the author and the payment of royalty. As the courts have also ruled that the public reading of a play constitutes a public performance, no such reading may be given except under the conditions stated above. Communication should be addressed to the author's representative, International Creative Management Inc., 40 West 57th Street, New York, N.Y. 10019. "Tragedy and the Common Man" by Arthur Miller. Reprinted by permission of International Creative Management Inc. Copyright 1949, 1976 by Arthur Miller reprinted by permission of Viking Penguin, a division of Penguin Books USA, Inc. "On Biff and Willy Loman," from *The New York Times,* February 5, 1950. Copyright © 1950/86 by The New York Times Company. Reprinted by permission.

Molière. *Tartuffe,* translated and copyright © 1961, 1962, 1963 by Richard Wilbur is reprinted by permission of Harcourt Brace Jovanovich, Inc. *CAUTION:* Professionals and amateurs are hereby warned that this translation, being fully protected under the copyright laws of the United States, the British Commonwealth, including the Dominion of Canada, and all other countries which are signatories to the Universal Copyright Convention and the International Copyright Union, is subject to royalty. All rights, including professional, amateur, motion picture, recitation, lecturing, public reading, radio broadcasting, and television are strictly reserved. Particular emphasis is laid on the question of readings, permission for which must be secured from the author's agent in writing. Inquiries on professional rights (except for amateur rights) should be addressed to Curtis Brown Ltd., 10 Aster Place, New York, NY 10003. Inquiries on translation rights should be addressed to Harcourt Brace Jovanovich, Inc., Copyrights and Permissions Department, Orlando, Florida 32887. "Molière's Defense of Tartuffe." The Preface and Three Petitions are from Molière's *Tartuffe,* translated by Haskell M. Block. Copyright © 1958 Appleton Century Crofts, Inc. Reprinted by permission of Appleton Century Crofts.

Harold Pinter. *The Dumb Waiter* by Harold Pinter. Copyright © 1960 by Harold Pinter. Reprinted by permission of Grove Weidenfeld.

Muriel Rukeyser. "Myth" from *Breaking Open* by Muriel Rukeyser. Reprinted by permission of International Creative Management, Inc. Copyright © 1973 by Muriel Rukeyser.

Maurice Sagoff. "A Humorous Distillation of *Antigone*" from *Shrinklits: Seventy of the World's Towering Classics Cut Down to Size.* © 1970, 1980 by Maurice Sagoff. Reprinted by permission of Workman Publishing Company, Inc. All rights reserved.

Carl Sautter. "On the Principles of Screenwriting" from *How to Sell Your Screenplay: The Real Rules of Film and Television* (New Chapter Press, New York). Copyright © 1988, Carl Sautter.

David Savran. "Interview with David Henry Hwang" and "Interview with August Wilson" from *In Their Own Voices* by David Savran. Reprinted by permission of Theatre Communications Group.

William Shakespeare. Text and Notes of *Othello* by William Shakespeare, edited by Gerald Eades Bentley (Penguin Books, Revised Edition, 1970), copyright © Penguin Books Inc., 1958, 1970, pp. 26–154. Reprinted by permission of Penguin Books Ltd. Introduction and footnotes to accompany *Hamlet* from *An Introduction to Shakespeare* edited by Hardin Craig and David Bevington. Copyright © 1975, 1973 by Scott, Foresman and Company. Reprinted by permission.

Sophocles. *Antigone* and *Oedipus the King* from *Sophocles: The Three Theban Plays,* translated by Robert Fagles with notes by Bernard Knox. Copyright © 1977, 1979, 1982 by Robert Fagles. Annotations copyright © 1982 by Bernard Knox. Reprinted by permission of Viking Penguin Inc. These plays in their printed form are designed for the reading public only. All dramatic rights in them are fully protected by copyrights and no public or private performances — professional or amateur — and no public readings for profit may be given without the written permission of the author and the payment of a royalty. Anyone disregarding the author's rights renders himself liable to prosecution. Communications should be addressed to the author's representative, Georges Borchardt, Inc., 136 East 57th Street, New York, N.Y. 10022. "Another Translation of a Scene from *Oedipus the King*" reprinted from *Oedipus the King,* translated by J. T. Sheppard, by permission of Cambridge University Press. Copyright 1920 by Cambridge University Press.

Wole Soyinka. *The Strong Breed* from *Wole Soyinka: Collected Plays 1* (1973) pp. 115–146 © Oxford University Press 1964. Reprinted by permission of Oxford University Press.

Tennessee Williams. *The Glass Menagerie* from *The Glass Menagerie* by Tennessee Williams. Copyright 1945 by Tennessee Williams and Edwina D. Williams and renewed 1973 by Tennessee Williams. Reprinted by permission of Random House, Inc. "On Theme" by Tennessee Williams from *Where I Live.* Copyright © 1978 by Tennessee Williams. Reprinted by permission of New Directions Publishing Corporation.

August Wilson. From *Fences* by August Wilson. Copyright © 1986 by August Wilson. Reprinted by arrangement with New American Library, a Division of Penguin Books USA, Inc., New York, New York.

LITERARY THEORY

Judith Fetterley. "A Feminist Reading of 'A Rose for Emily' " from *The Resisting Reader: A Feminist Approach to American Fiction* by Judith Fetterley. Copyright © 1978. Reprinted by permission of the Indiana University Press.

Stanley Fish. Excerpt from "What Makes an Interpretation Acceptable" reprinted by permission of the publisher from *Is There a Text in This Class? The Authority of Interpretative Communities* by Stanley Fish, Cambridge Massachusetts: Harvard University Press, Copyright © 1980 by the President and Fellows of Harvard College. All rights reserved.

Annette Kolodny. "On the Commitments of Feminist Criticism" from *Dancing Through the Minefield: Some Observations on the Theory, Practice and Politics of a Feminist Literary Criticism. Feminist Studies* 6, 1980. Reprinted by permission of the author.

Susan Sontag. "Against Interpretation" from *Against Interpretation* by Susan Sontag. Copyright © 1964 by Susan Sontag. Reprinted by permission of Farrar, Straus and Giroux, Inc.

Brook Thomas. "A New Historical Approach to Keats' 'Ode on a Grecian Urn' " from "The Historical Necessities for — and Difficulties with — New Historical Analysis in Introductory Literature Courses," *College English,* September 1987. Copyright © 1987 by the National Council of Teachers of English. Reprinted with permission.

Index of First Lines

Index of Authors and Titles

Index of Terms